MATCH OF THE DAY

BBC SPORT

FOOTBALL YEARBOOK

2005/2006

BBC

First published 2005

Data collation by Warner Leach Ltd

ISBN 0 954 98190 1

Published by Interact Publishing Limited
Lordship Farm, Cottered, Herts SG9 9QL

Editor: Terry Pratt

Data interpretation: Tony Warner, Stephen Hall

Data management: Peter Watts, John Haines

Design: John Paul Warner

Programming: Jonathan Proud

Printed and bound in Great Britain by Bath Press Ltd

Cover photographs by Action Images plc.

By arrangement with the BBC

DELVING FOR HEROES

At the headline level, football is all about heroes. Chelsea, Liverpool and the stubborn Baggies filled our back pages with heroic and historic feats.

Dig a little deeper and the unsung heroes emerge, blinking and a little surprised to find themselves at or near the top of our charts: Everton's **Alan Stubbs**, Pompey's **Steve Stone, Claude Makelele.**

And there's the perennial **Dennis Bergkamp**. Last season, **Thierry Henry** and **Robert Pires** hogged the headlines with 58 goals between them. The Dutch master had scored just five but, when he was on the pitch, Arsenal scored every 42 minutes.

'Attacking Power' is the label we've stuck on this measure of making goals happen. It's not always easy to spot how they do it but goals just seem to accumulate around certain players when they are on the pitch. Last season, **Bergkamp's** Attacking Power of 42 was four better than **Henry's**.

This season, **Bergkamp's** beaten his old record by a whole nine minutes – Arsenal score every 33 minutes when he's playing. And yet, he's no longer the best in the Premiership!

Finding out who's taken his crown is part of the fun of **the Match of the Day Football Yearbook**.

Another part is comparing the stars and clubs across different leagues. The book boils down their performances to an essence that allows the comparison to be made and we sort the best into charts of the most effective teams and players in Britain and Europe. However, these Round-up Charts are just our headlines, intended to provoke you to delve into the stories that lie behind and around them.

As always, we aim to provide you with all the ammunition you need for a tough new season of endless debate and speculation, plus a stimulating record of the thrilling and remarkable season just ended.

As always, I'm indebted to Tony Warner, Steve Hall, John Haines, Peter Watts, John-Paul Warner and Jonathan Proud for all their hard work and deep knowledge. Thanks too to Action Images PLC for the many pictures.

Terry Pratt

8

He's worth 15 points a season to us

What's Nigel Martyn worth to Everton? Four examples of players whose performance charts speak volumes

Martyn: earned a Champions League spot

12

English Leagues

Chelsea are off the scale in midfield and defence but there are relegated forwards who can give them lessons in Strike Rate

Mourinho: won it without a top striker

BANK OF SCOTLAND

230

Scottish Leagues

The Old Firm save the final twist to the last two minutes of the season - the chart that every Rangers fan will want on their wall

"The biggest spine-tingler"

BECKHAM
23

270

Spanish League

Primera Liga is full of stunning forwards – but look who's top of its Strike Rate charts!?

Beckham: played with La Liga's chart-topping scorer

312

Italian League

Jonathan Zebina changes clubs but there's no change for Serie A's forwards – they still can't get past him!

Zebina: teaching the Italians about defending

PHILIPS

354

Dutch League

Robben arrived and sent shock waves through Premiership defences. Run the rule over Holland - Europe's top exporter of raw talent

PSV's Park: ravaged Milan's defence

Carragher
Zambrotta
Gerrard
Makelele
van Bommel
Mintal
Makaay

329

German League

Playing midfield for a team just outside the Bundesliga relegation zone… why did Marek Mintal get into so many World XIs?

Nuremberg's Mintal; a dark horse

430

French League

The next Vieira? Ghana's Michael Essien leads Lyon's masterful midfield to their dominance of le Championnat

Mahamadou Diarra, Mikael Essien and Honorato Nilmar celebrate winning their fourth league trophy

THE CLUBS

10

96

FA Cup

Rooney and Ruud strike the woodwork but Lehmann makes the decisive touch as The Gunners and United bring glamour back to the cup

Ljungberg heads van Nistelrooy's strike against the bar

474

The Champions League

Defiant! Stevie G defies the 'boring draw' pundits, the 'it's all over now' merchants, and 'the Italian defence' theorists – all in six glorious minutes!

Gerrard reflects on an astonishing comeback

494

Uefa Cup

Abramovich's 'B team' ensure that Chelsea don't steal all the glory. CSKA bring Russia her first-ever European trophy

CSKA storm Sporting in Lisbon

498

Best in Europe Charts

Arsenal lose one of their European crowns to French side Lyon

Wenger no longer manager of the most cosmopolitan team in Europe

CHARTING PERFORMANCE

Goalkeepers

He's worth 15 points a season to us

Nigel Martyn is arguably worth all of that to Everton. We'll never know where they would have finished the season with a less able keeper, but the facts stack up to telling effect, and suggest that the Champions League place would have been a pipe dream.
Here's a quick guide to our Goalkeeper charts: -

Goals Conceded in the League
The team conceded **26** League Goals while Martyn was guarding the Everton net.

Goals Conceded in all competitions
Add cups to the league games he played and he conceded **28** goals in all competitions.

KEY GOALKEEPER

Nigel Martyn	
Goals Conceded in the League Number of League goals conceded while the player was on the pitch	26
Goals Conceded in all competitions Total number of goals conceded while the player was on the pitch	28
League minutes played Number of minutes played in league matches	2834
Clean Sheets In games when player was on pitch for at least 70 minutesmins	13
Goals to Shots Ratio The average number of shots on target per each League goal conceded	8
Defensive Rating Ave mins between League goals conceded while on the pitch	109

Clean Sheets
In the league, Everton recorded **13** Clean Sheets in games where Martyn played for at least 70 minutes and the game finished without a goal being scored against him.

Defensive Rating
His Defensive Rating of **109** is determined by dividing the number of minutes he played by the number of League goals the team conceded. In Martyn's case it is 2834 minutes divided by 26. We use this rating to compare keepers in our Round-up Tables.
In the few league games he didn't play, Everton conceded a goal every 29 minutes!

Goals to Shots Ratio
In the Premiership, we record each keeper's Goals to Shots Ratio by dividing the number of Shots on Target he faced by the number of goals conceded. It's a good indicator of whether a keeper is out-performing his defence. Martyn's Ratio of **8** Shots per goal is the second-best in the division and in any of the last two seasons he would have topped the Premiership table comfortably – not this time though!
His Ratio compares with a Premiership average of 5 shots per goal, so by this measure alone it could be argued that Martyn was worth 15 league goals to his club.

Midfielders

He's a box-to-box player

George Boateng's season was disrupted by injury just before Xmas with Boro riding high at fifth in the Premiership table and top of Group E in the Uefa Cup. When he returned they were dumped out of Europe and lying ninth. Here's our guide to his Midfielders chart: -

Goals in the League
Boateng scored his first goal for the club this season and finished with **3**, all scored in the league, with none added in the cups or in Europe.

Assists
In the Premiership, we keep a tally of every Assist, where the player has made the final telling pass or header to set up a colleague for a goal. Boateng made **2** Assists.

Defensive Rating
Midfielders have defensive duties and Boateng particularly. His Rating is determined by dividing the number of minutes he played by the number of goals the team conceded during that time. It equals **94**, which means Boro are conceding less than a goal a game when Boateng is protecting the defence. It's the 11th best Defensive Rating among Midfielders in our Premiership Round-up table.

KEY PLAYERS - MIDFIELDERS

George Boateng	
Goals in the League	3
Goals in all competitions	3
Assists League goals scored by a team mate where the player delivered the final pass	2
Defensive Rating Average number of mins between League goals conceded while on the pitch	94
Contribution to Attacking Power Average number of minutes between League team goals while on pitch	59
Scoring Difference Defensive Rating minus Contribution to Attacking Power	35

888.com

Contribution to Attacking Power
Boateng's Power is **59**, which means the team scores a goal on average every 59 minutes when he plays. The lower it is the more regularly they score.

Scoring Difference
This measure is the personal goal difference for a player. It is found by taking away their Attacking Power from their Defensive Rating. In Boateng's case it's 94 minus 59, which delivers a Scoring Difference of **+35**. A positive figure means the team are more likely to score than concede when he is on the pitch. A negative figure means the team are move likely to let goals in than score. Boro's top five midfield players vary hugely from Boateng at +35 right down to Doriva at -28. It shows why Boateng plays when he's fit and why we use it to compare our midfield players.

Goalscorers

It only takes a second to score a goal

Dean Ashton was parachuted into Norwich's bid for Premiership survival from Championship Crewe and his goals nearly kept the Canaries in the top flight. He features on both the Crewe and the Norwich pages and tops the Goalscorers chart for both clubs. This is his Norwich chart: -

Goals in the League

Ashton didn't play in any cup games for Norwich so his **7** League Goals total isn't added to in Goals All.

KEY PLAYERS - GOALSCORERS

Dean Ashton	
Goals in the League	7
Goals in all competitions	7
Assists League goals scored by a team mate where the player delivered the final pass	3
Contribution to Attacking Power Average number of minutes between League team goals while on pitch	61
Player Strike Rate Average number of minutes between League goals scored by player	**203**
Club Strike Rate Average minutes between League goals scored by club	81

SHTA
36
HONDA

Assists

As well as scoring his own goals, he laid on **3** for club colleagues.

Contribution to Attacking Power

Norwich were struggling for goals with just **19** from 22 matches when Ashton arrived. He improved their scoring rate with 23 coming from the final 16 games. This shows in his Attacking Power, which doesn't measure individual goals but how often the team scores when a certain player is playing. Ashton's is calculated by dividing his 1418 minutes on the pitch by the 23 goals Norwich scored and averages a goal every **61** minutes.

Club Strike Rate

Ashton's influence shows when compared to the Club's Strike Rate. Over the whole league season, the club only averaged a goal every **81** minutes.

Player Strike Rate

This measures Ashton's individual Strike Rate. It shows how regularly he scored for Norwich - a goal every **203** minutes on average. This can be compared with the rest of the goalscorers in the Premiership (or any other league) even though most will have played more matches than Ashton.

He tops Norwich's Goalscorers chart because he has the best Strike Rate. Leon McKenzie has also scored 7 league goals but only averaged one every 345 minutes. Damian Francis (third in the Norwich chart) is a Midfielder but any player who has a good enough Strike Rate can appear in the Goalscorers chart.

Defenders

It's about his positional play

New Zealander Ryan Nelsen joined from Washington's DC United and was an ever present for Blackburn over their last 18 games. He had an impressive effect on their defence as you can see from his chart: -

Goals Conceded in the League

The team let in **9** goals in Nelsen's 15 league games. This increased to **13** when you include the four FA Cup ties he played in.

League minutes played

He played **1350** minutes just in the league matches.

Clean Sheets

We only measure Clean Sheets in league games where the player has influenced the game for at least 70 minutes. These we call **Counting Games**. There were **9** league games when Nelsen helped the defence to completely shut out the attack, including a headline-grabbing performance against van Nistelrooy. You have to have played at least 12 Counting Games to qualify for a club's Key Defenders chart, so Nelsen is in with 15. However you need 17+ Counting Games to get into the Divisional Round-up chart, so Nelsen misses out there.

Defensive Rating

This shows how regularly the team concede a league goal when this player is on the pitch. While Nelsen was playing, Blackburn conceded a league goal only once every 150 minutes so his Defensive Rating is **150**. It's calculated by dividing the minutes played by the league goals conceded. This Rating is used to rank Defenders.

KEY PLAYERS - DEFENDERS

Ryan Nelsen	
Goals Conceded in the League Number of League goals conceded while the player was on the pitch	9
Goals Conceded in all competitions Total number of goals conceded while the player was on the pitch	13
League minutes played Number of minutes played in league matches	1350
Clean Sheets In games when player was on pitch for at least 70 minutes	9
Defensive Rating **Average number of mins between League goals conceded while on the pitch**	**150**
Club Defensive Rating Average number of mins between League goals conceded by the club this season	80

HSA

Club Defensive Rating

This is a quick way to compare whether a player is improving the defence or not. It shows the average amount of time between league goals conceded by the club. And over the season Blackburn conceded 43 league goals at an average of one every **80** minutes.

This is the seventh tightest defence in the Premiership, but the figure shows that Nelsen strengthened the defence immensely. Three of his Blackburn colleagues had Defensive Ratings in the 70s.

Squad Appearances

It's not an 11-a-side game anymore

Increasingly managers rotate their team, to rest players, try out different combinations or formations or reverse a poor run. The Squad Appearances table shows at a glance how a player is used.

Squares

A dark green square ■ shows the player was in the starting XI and finished the game. A light green square ■ shows he was on the bench but didn't get subbed on. A blank square shows they didn't make it to the bench.

Arrows

A dark green arrow « shows the player started the game but was subbed off or sent off. A light green arrow » shows they started on the bench but were subbed on.

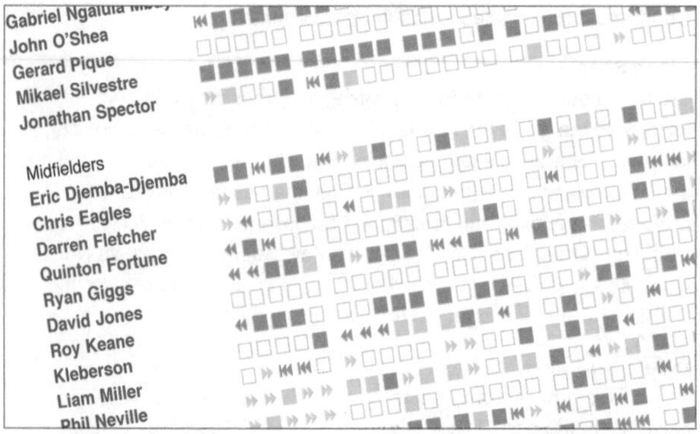

John O'Shea
Gerard Pique
Mikael Silvestre
Jonathan Spector
Midfielders
Eric Djemba-Djemba
Chris Eagles
Darren Fletcher
Quinton Fortune
Ryan Giggs
David Jones
Roy Keane
Kleberson
Liam Miller
Phil Neville

Counting Games

A player earns a Counting Game when they play for more than 70 minutes in a match. Managers often take a view around the 70-minute mark. If the result's a foregone conclusion, they may as well rest players or if they are under pressure, it's time to sacrifice a player to change things around. A dark green arrow with a small line before it |« means they were subbed off *after* 70 minutes and it counts as a Counting Game. A light green arrow with a small line after it means they were subbed on in the first 20 minutes and played a full 70 minutes after that – also a Counting Game.

Competition Key

A quick guide to the Competition, Venue and Result is shown at the top of the Squad Appearances Chart. **H**, **A** or **N** in Venue refer to **H**ome, **A**way or **N**eutral. The result is **W**, **L** or **D** and shown in the appropriate colour. The Competitions are: **L** = League; **F** = FA Cup; **C** = Champions League; **E** = Uefa Cup; **W** = the League Cup in the English or Scottish divisions; **O** = Other, e.g. a play-off match.

Finally the numbers along the top refer to the game number and can be checked against the Results chart for more details.

There's more information of how squads are used in the Premiership round up pages.

Team of the Season

Selecting the most effective 4-4-2

The club XI

Each club has a team of the season generated by our computer. This ensures that all our own in-built favouritism and subjectivity is factored out. The computer selects first from players who have played at least 12 Counting Games **CG**.

TEAM OF THE SEASON
CECH
CG 35 DR 242
FERREIRA
CG 29 DR 261
CARVALHO
CG 21 DR 152
TERRY
CG 36 DR 249
GALLAS
CG 26 DR 245
ROBBEN
CG 13 SD +177
MAKELELE
CG 36 SD +183
LAMPARD
CG 38 SD +180
DUFF
CG 27 SD +172
GUDJOHNSEN
CG 22 AP 47
DROGBA
CG 12 SR 163

Defence

If there is a choice of keeper, it chooses the one with the best (highest) Defensive Rating **DR**. It then selects the best four Defensive Ratings among the club's Defenders. They will be the defence that concedes goals least regularly.

Midfield

It selects the four Midfielders with the highest Scoring Difference **SD**. Positive figures mean the side scores more often than it concedes when they play. A Midfielder who has seen his side concede a goal a game while he was on the pitch has a Defensive Rating of **90**. If they also scored two goals a game while he played, he will have an Attacking Power of **45**. Take the 45 away from the 90 and his Scoring Difference is **+45**. In relegated teams, it's common to find midfields full of minus figures.

Attack
In most divisions, the computer selects the two best Strike Rates among the club's forwards. In the Premiership, we give it a little more leeway, if the club plays with a withdrawn forward or an advanced midfield player, we ask for the second forward to be judged on Attacking Power.

Very rarely, it finds a team that has chopped and changed so much that it can't select a full 4-4-2 who have all played sufficient games. Then we reduce the Counting Games criteria below 12.

Divisional Teams of the Season
The most effective players in each division are sorted into a top 20 chart of Goalkeepers, Defenders, Midfielders and Goalscorers. We raise the inclusion barrier to 17 or more Counting Games. The most effective 4-4-2 across a division is selected the same way as the clubs, with one difference: no team is allowed to have more than one of its players in each position. So the most even Chelsea can put into this XI is 4 players.

Goal Attempts

He's got to hit the target from there

Shots For
We record Goals Attempts in Premier League matches. The Goal Attempts For details the featured side's attacking prowess. Shots On Target are split into Home and Away totals and the overall figure is also shown as an average per league game. We do the same with Shots Off Target and run both together for the team's complete shots record. Newcastle have hit **305** shots at home and **180** away, giving them the third highest shots total in the division at **485**.

Two other stats come out of this information. The number of shots on target a side requires to score a goal. In Newcastle's case shots didn't often translate into goals with an average of **5.4** shots on target required to score each goal. In terms of Accuracy, Newcastle managed to hit **52.6%** of their total shots On Target

GOAL ATTEMPTS

FOR Goal attempts recorded in League games	HOME	AWAY	TOTAL	AVE	AGAINST Goal attempts recorded in League games	HOME	AWAY	TOTAL	AVE
shots on target	163	92	255	6.7	shots on target	88	133	221	5.8
shots off target	142	88	230	6.1	shots off target	81	92	173	4.6
TOTAL	305	180	485	12.8	TOTAL	169	225	394	10.4
Ratio of goals to shots Average number of shots on target per League goal scored				5.4	Ratio of goals to shots Average number of shots on target per League goal scored				3.9
Accuracy rating Average percentage of total goal attempts which were on target				52.6	Accuracy rating Average percentage of total goal attempts which were on target				56.1

Shots Against
This is the defensive side of Goal Attempts, showing how many times opposing teams had a shot at the Newcastle goal. The Ratio of Goals to Shots is a reflection on the goalkeeping while the Accuracy rating gives a feel for how much pressure Newcastle put the opposing forwards under.

Disciplinary Records

The refs go out looking for him

BOOKINGS

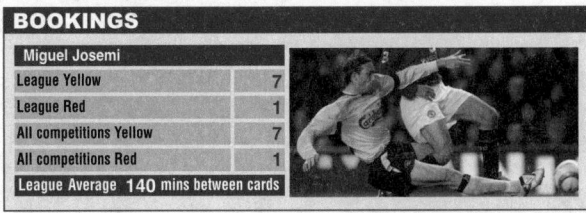

Miguel Josemi	
League Yellow	7
League Red	1
All competitions Yellow	7
All competitions Red	1
League Average 140 mins between cards	

Disciplinary records are shown for teams in most of the divisions. Miguel Josemi tops the Liverpool chart with **7** league yellows and **1** league red card. He didn't gain any cards in his cup games.

The chart position is determined by how regularly the player gets a card of any colour in a league game. Josemi's eight cards came in 1121 minutes of league action. He averages a card every **140** minutes. Nunez is second in the Liverpool chart. He has received fewer cards than Garcia has but Nunez enjoys a worse average, so appears higher in the chart than Garcia.

Top Point Earners

Players who are winners

Average points
Portsmouth's Steve Stone made a difference in the games he played. He heads Pompey's Top Points Earners Chart with an average of **1.37** points in the games he influenced for at least 70 minutes.

Club Average Points
Stone played 19 Counting Games, or half a league season. The club as a whole averaged **1.03** points per game over the whole season.

TOP POINT EARNERS

Steve Stone	
Counting Games League games when player was on pitch for at least 70 minutes	19
Average points Average League points taken in Counting games	1.37
Club Average points Average points taken in League games	1.03

Most Missed Players
Stone may have topped Pompey's chart but he barely got into the top 100 in the division as a whole. Yet, if we compare his average with the club's average, we can see that in the other 19 games; Pompey must have little more than half a point a game. In the divisional Round-up tables we chart the most badly missed players, comparing the player's individual average with the club's average and in this table, Stone comes fourth.

THE PREMIERSHIP ROUND-UP

Chelsea tore apart the Premiership records book and wrote whole new chapters about defending. Some, it is hard to imagine, will ever be erased. They recorded the fewest goals ever conceded in a Premiership season, 15; they enjoyed the most clean sheets, 25; and achieved the most victories, 29. They notched 11 1-0 victories and totalled the most points ever claimed by a team in the Premiership.

Surprisingly, they did it all without a top-class goalscorer. Chelsea's players have claimed all the significant places in the individual Divisional Round-up tables, with the exception of Goalscorers where Gudjohnsen only just crept into the top ten.

Perhaps a special mention for Petr Cech, who played behind the best defence in Europe but if you think it had it easy, take a look at the Goalkeeping charts.

At the other end of the table, Southampton somehow managed to finish bottom despite having two strikers in the top 12 of the Goalscorers chart.

CLUB STRIKE FORCE

Reyes and Edu celebrate

Goals scored in the League	87
Goals scored in all competitions	117
Shots on target (SoT) Shots on target hit by the team recorded in League games	299

1 Arsenal

Club Strike Rate (CSR) Average number of minutes between League goals scored by club	39

	CLUB	LGE	ALL	SoT	CSR
1	Arsenal	87	117	299	**39**
2	Chelsea	72	108	300	**48**
3	Man Utd	58	100	331	**59**
4	Middlesbrough	53	74	250	**65**
5	Fulham	52	70	182	**66**
6	Liverpool	52	82	237	**66**
7	Bolton	49	59	264	**70**
8	Man City	47	55	214	**73**
9	Newcastle	47	85	255	**73**
10	Tottenham	47	71	247	**73**
11	Aston Villa	45	50	204	**76**
12	Everton	45	56	185	**76**
13	Southampton	45	63	194	**76**
14	Portsmouth	43	50	195	**80**
15	Charlton	42	53	169	**81**
16	Norwich	42	44	188	**81**
17	Crystal Palace	41	46	178	**83**
18	Birmingham	40	46	177	**86**
19	West Brom	36	41	187	**95**
20	Blackburn	32	45	212	**107**
	TOTAL:	LEAGUE: 975		AL COMPS: 1315	

CLUB DEFENCES

1 Chelsea

Club Defensive Rate (CDR) Average number of minutes between League goals conceded by club	228

	CLUB	LGE	ALL	CS	SoT	CDR
1	Chelsea	15	34	25	145	**228**
2	Man Utd	26	44	19	151	**132**
3	Arsenal	36	51	16	138	**95**
4	Man City	39	43	11	179	**88**
5	Liverpool	41	56	7	161	**83**
6	Tottenham	41	50	13	196	**83**
7	Blackburn	43	53	15	216	**80**
8	Bolton	44	50	8	209	**78**
9	Birmingham	46	50	9	192	**74**
10	Everton	46	54	13	262	**74**
11	Middlesbrough	46	62	11	232	**74**
12	Aston Villa	52	59	11	236	**66**
13	Newcastle	57	74	6	221	**60**
14	Charlton	58	65	12	278	**59**
15	Portsmouth	59	65	5	261	**58**
16	Fulham	60	70	8	226	**57**
17	West Brom	61	67	7	243	**56**
18	Crystal Palace	62	68	10	306	**55**
19	Southampton	66	82	7	277	**52**
20	Norwich	77	80	6	339	**44**

Chelsea's Terry determined

Goals conceded in the League	15
Goals conceded in all competitions	34
Clean Sheets (CS) Number of league games where no goals were conceded	25
Shots on Target Against (SoT) Shots on Target conceded by team in League games	145

PLAYER NATIONALITIES

Overseas country with the most player appearances in the Premiership - France

In the squad	857	Percentage of League action	7.45
Appearances in League games	751	Caps for France this season	49
Most appearances	Distin	Percentage of time on pitch	99.5

	COUNTRY	PLAYERS	IN SQUAD	LGE APP	% LGE ACT	CAPS	MOST APP	APP
1	England	249	5013	4177	**41.44**	141	Jamie Carragher	100
2	France	45	857	751	**7.45**	49	Sylvain Distin	99.5
3	Rep of Ireland	28	612	548	**5.68**	113	Shay Given	94.7
4	Holland	19	485	402	**4.03**	23	J-F Hasselbaink	94.6
5	Wales	15	360	301	**3.11**	61	Gary Speed	97.6
6	Scotland	18	364	309	**2.79**	26	David Weir	88.7
7	Australia	8	216	214	**2.32**		Lucas Neill	92.1
8	Spain	14	296	249	**2.23**	6	Javier Luis Garcia	68.4
9	N Ireland	10	257	214	**2.22**	32	Maik Taylor	100
10	Denmark	13	300	225	**2.19**	43	Thomas Sorensen	93.4
11	Sweden	10	254	229	**2.18**	38	Olof Mellberg	77.6
12	Portugal	9	196	186	**1.83**	35	Paulo Ferreira	76.3
13	Finland	9	199	146	**1.46**		Sami Hyypia	81.3
14	United States	10	191	141	**1.46**		Brad Friedel	100
15	Nigeria	7	141	128	**1.27**		Ayegbeni Yakubu	71.9
16	Germany	5	149	127	**1.26**	16	Moritz Volz	81.1
17	Senegal	9	160	132	**1.26**	25	Papa Bouba Diop	73.5
18	Iceland	3	108	107	**1.16**		Jussi Jaaskelainen	94.6
19	Czech Republic	7	137	120	**1.13**	19	Petr Cech	92.1
20	Norway	4	104	93	**1.03**		Claus Lundekvam	88.2

CLUB MAKE-UP – HOME AND OVERSEAS PLAYERS

1 Arsenal

Overseas players in the squad	22	Home country players	5
Percent of overseas players	81.5	Percent of League action	86.3
Most appearances	Toure	Appearance percentage	91.6

	CLUB	OVERSEAS	HOME	% OVERSEAS	% LGE ACT	MOST APP	APP %
1	Arsenal	22	5	81.5	**86.3**	Habib Kolo Toure	91.6
2	Liverpool	21	11	65.6	**70.1**	John Arne Riise	87
3	Bolton	16	9	64	**68**	Bruno N'Gotty	95.2
4	Chelsea	20	10	66.7	**65.1**	Claude Makelele	94.7
5	Fulham	14	13	51.9	**62.5**	Edwin Van der Sar	86
6	Middlesbrough	13	19	40.6	**57.6**	J-F Hasselbaink	94.6
7	Portsmouth	17	13	56.7	**57.4**	Dejan Stefanovic	84.2
8	Aston Villa	11	13	45.8	**48**	Thomas Sorensen	93.4
9	Blackburn	15	18	45.5	**47.9**	Brad Friedel	100
10	Charlton	9	14	39.1	**39**	Hermann Hreidarsson	86.5
11	Southampton	14	23	37.8	**38.7**	Claus Lundekvam	88.2
12	Tottenham	15	21	41.7	**37**	Erik Edman	69.6
13	Man City	12	17	41.4	**35.4**	Sylvain Distin	99.5
14	Man Utd	13	15	46.4	**34.4**	Mikael Silvestre	86.2
15	Crystal Palace	10	18	35.7	**31.5**	Gabor Kiraly	84.2
16	West Brom	9	20	31	**27.1**	Zoltan Gera	79.6
17	Everton	6	20	23.1	**26.2**	Alessandro Pistone	80
18	Birmingham	13	17	43.3	**25.6**	Maik Taylor	100
19	Newcastle	8	22	26.7	**22.6**	Laurent Robert	55.7
20	Norwich	5	22	18.5	**14.5**	Mattias Jonson	43.4

CLUB STARTING FORMATIONS

1 Tottenham	
Most used starting formation	4-4-2
Number of different formations used	3
How often the club used its most frequently used formation	83.3%

	CLUB	Formation	Number	Used %
1	Tottenham	4-4-2	3	**83.3**
2	Southampton	4-4-2	3	**82.6**
3	Middlesbrough	4-4-2	5	**81.3**
4	Arsenal	4-4-2	3	**78.9**
5	Birmingham	4-4-2	4	**76.2**
6	West Brom	4-4-2	7	**73.2**
7	Blackburn	4-4-2	3	**71.7**
8	Newcastle	4-4-2	7	**70.2**
9	Man City	4-4-2	5	**68.3**
10	Aston Villa	4-4-2	6	**65.9**
11	Crystal Palace	4-5-1	5	**54.8**
12	Norwich	4-4-2	8	**48.8**
13	Charlton	4-5-1	4	**46.5**
14	Portsmouth	4-4-2	8	**45.5**
15	Man United	4-4-2	9	**43.3**
16	Everton	4-1-4-1	7	**40.9**
17	Liverpool	4-4-2	10	**40.4**
18	Fulham	4-4-2	9	**38.3**
19	Bolton	4-1-4-1	9	**34.1**
20	Chelsea	4-3-2-1	9	**23.7**

We are recording the most commonly quoted formations for each Premier team at the start of each game.

The most commonly used formation in the Premiership is 4-4-2, which is used as the starting formation in 54% of matches.

It is followed by 4-5-1 and 4-1-4-1, both used in 11% of matches.

In all 17 different formations were recorded with Liverpool's Benitez using the most variations although Mourinho was the most flexible

Average number of different formations used by Premiership clubs	6.2

FINAL LEAGUE TABLE

	HOME						AWAY					TOTAL			
	P	W	D	L	F	A	W	D	L	F	A	F	A	DIF	PTS
Chelsea	38	14	5	0	35	6	15	3	1	37	9	72	15	57	95
Arsenal	38	13	5	1	54	19	12	3	4	33	17	87	36	51	83
Man Utd	38	12	6	1	31	12	10	5	4	27	14	58	26	32	77
Everton	38	12	2	5	24	15	6	5	8	21	31	45	46	-1	61
Liverpool	38	12	4	3	31	15	5	3	11	21	26	52	41	11	58
Bolton	38	9	5	5	25	18	7	5	7	24	26	49	44	5	58
Middlesbrough	38	9	6	4	29	19	5	7	7	24	27	53	46	7	55
Man City	38	8	6	5	24	14	5	7	7	23	25	47	39	8	52
Tottenham	38	9	5	5	36	22	5	5	9	11	19	47	41	6	52
Aston Villa	38	8	6	5	26	17	4	5	10	19	35	45	52	-7	47
Charlton	38	8	4	7	29	29	4	6	9	13	29	42	58	-16	46
Birmingham	38	8	6	5	24	15	3	6	10	16	31	40	46	-6	45
Fulham	38	8	4	7	29	26	4	4	11	23	34	52	60	-8	44
Newcastle	38	7	7	5	25	25	3	7	9	22	32	47	57	-10	44
Blackburn	38	5	8	6	21	22	4	7	8	11	21	32	43	-11	42
Portsmouth	38	8	4	7	30	26	2	5	12	13	33	43	59	-16	39
West Brom	38	5	8	6	17	24	1	8	10	19	37	36	61	-25	34
Crystal Palace	38	6	5	8	21	19	1	7	11	20	43	41	62	-21	33
Norwich	38	7	5	7	29	32	0	7	12	13	45	42	77	-35	33
Southampton	38	5	9	5	30	30	1	5	13	15	36	45	66	-21	32

CLUB GOAL ATTEMPTS FOR

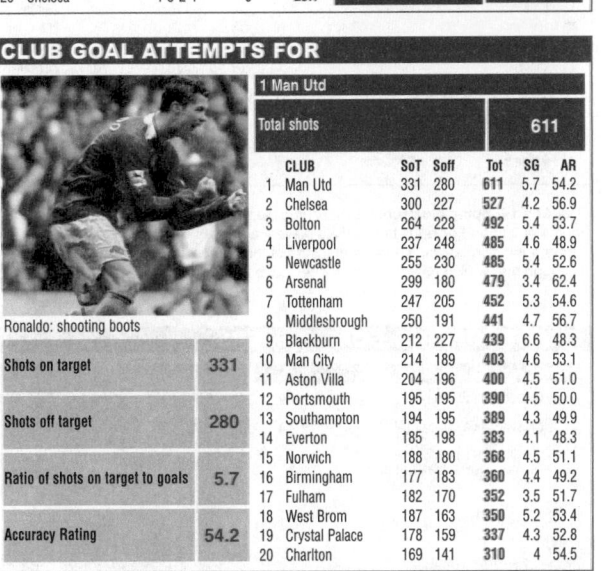

Ronaldo: shooting boots

1 Man Utd	
Total shots	611
Shots on target	331
Shots off target	280
Ratio of shots on target to goals	5.7
Accuracy Rating	54.2

	CLUB	SoT	Soff	Tot	SG	AR
1	Man Utd	331	280	**611**	5.7	54.2
2	Chelsea	300	227	**527**	4.2	56.9
3	Bolton	264	228	**492**	5.4	53.7
4	Liverpool	237	248	**485**	4.6	48.9
5	Newcastle	255	230	**485**	5.4	52.6
6	Arsenal	299	180	**479**	3.4	62.4
7	Tottenham	247	205	**452**	5.3	54.6
8	Middlesbrough	250	191	**441**	4.7	56.7
9	Blackburn	212	227	**439**	6.6	48.3
10	Man City	214	189	**403**	4.6	53.1
11	Aston Villa	204	196	**400**	4.5	51.0
12	Portsmouth	195	195	**390**	4.5	50.0
13	Southampton	194	195	**389**	4.3	49.9
14	Everton	185	198	**383**	4.1	48.3
15	Norwich	188	180	**368**	4.5	51.1
16	Birmingham	177	183	**360**	4.4	49.2
17	Fulham	182	170	**352**	3.5	51.7
18	West Brom	187	163	**350**	5.2	53.4
19	Crystal Palace	178	159	**337**	4.3	52.8
20	Charlton	169	141	**310**	4	54.5

CLUB GOAL ATTEMPTS AGAINST

1 Birmingham	
Total shots against	322

	CLUB	SoT	Soff	Tot	SG	AR
1	Birmingham	192	130	**322**	4.2	59.6
2	Liverpool	161	164	**325**	3.9	49.5
3	Arsenal	138	193	**331**	3.8	41.7
4	Chelsea	145	205	**350**	9.7	41.4
5	Tottenham	196	168	**364**	4.8	53.8
6	Man City	179	186	**365**	4.6	49
7	Man Utd	151	215	**366**	5.8	41.3
8	Bolton	209	158	**367**	4.8	56.9
9	Blackburn	216	157	**373**	5	57.9
10	Newcastle	221	173	**394**	3.9	56.1
11	Fulham	226	188	**414**	3.8	54.6
12	Middlesbrough	232	196	**428**	5	54.2
13	Aston Villa	236	197	**433**	4.5	54.5
14	Charlton	278	157	**435**	4.8	63.9
15	Portsmouth	261	180	**441**	4.4	59.2
16	Everton	262	181	**443**	5.7	59.1
17	West Brom	243	214	**457**	4	53.2
18	Crystal Palace	306	166	**472**	4.9	64.8
19	Southampton	277	198	**475**	4.2	58.3
20	Norwich	339	203	**542**	4.4	62.5

Cunningham defiant for Blues

Shots on target against	192
Shots off target against	130
Ratio of shots on target to goals	4.2
Accuracy Rating	59.6

STADIUM CAPACITY AND HOME CROWDS

	TEAM	CAPACITY	AVE	HIGH	LOW
1	Man Utd	68190	99.53	67989	67704
2	Portsmouth	20210	99.24	20210	19520
3	Tottenham	36214	99.06	36105	35105
4	Newcastle	52326	99.04	52326	50000
5	Chelsea	42449	98.64	42328	40864
6	Arsenal	38500	98.63	38164	37010
7	Charlton	27116	97.37	27104	24263
8	Birmingham	30016	95.82	29382	27177
9	Southampton	32251	94.91	32066	27343
10	Man City	48000	94.15	47221	42453
11	Liverpool	45362	93.88	44224	35064
12	Norwich	26034	93.53	25522	23549
13	West Brom	28003	93.18	27751	23849
14	Crystal Palace	26309	91.63	26193	20705
15	Middlesbrough	35100	91.2	34836	29603
16	Everton	40569	90.79	40552	32406
17	Bolton	28723	90.54	27880	23692
18	Fulham	22000	90.17	21940	16180
19	Aston Villa	43275	86.32	42593	31312
20	Blackburn	31367	71.14	29271	18006

Key: Average. The percentage of each stadium filled in League games over the season (AVE), the stadium capacity and the highest and lowest crowds recorded.

AWAY ATTENDANCE

	TEAM	AVE	HIGH	LOW
1	Liverpool	97.82	67857	20205
2	Man Utd	97.44	52320	20190
3	Arsenal	96.08	67862	20170
4	Everton	95.73	67803	20125
5	Chelsea	95.45	67832	20210
6	Newcastle	95.26	67845	19003
7	Norwich	94.74	67812	20015
8	Man City	94.69	67863	20101
9	Tottenham	94.57	67962	20121
10	Aston Villa	93.4	67859	17624
11	West Brom	93.02	67827	16180
12	Crystal Palace	91.97	67814	18006
13	Birmingham	91.65	67838	18706
14	Southampton	91.61	67921	19237
15	Portsmouth	91.54	67989	20502
16	Blackburn	91.53	67939	19103
17	Middlesbrough	91.08	67988	17759
18	Bolton	90.74	67867	17541
19	Fulham	90.42	67959	18991
20	Charlton	90.03	67704	18290

Key: Average. How close each club has come to filling grounds in its away league matches (AVE) and the highest and lowest crowds recorded.

CHART-TOPPING MIDFIELDERS

1 Claude Makelele - Chelsea	
Goals scored in the League	1
Assists in league games	2
Defensive Rating Av number of mins between League goals conceded while on the pitch	231
Contribution to Attacking Power Average number of minutes between League team goals while on pitch	48
Scoring Difference Defensive Rating minus Contribution to Attacking Power	183

	PLAYER	CLUB	GOALS	ASS	DEF R	POWER	SCORE DIFF
1	Makelele	Chelsea	1	2	231	48	**183 mins**
2	Lampard	Chelsea	13	18	227	47	**180 mins**
3	Duff	Chelsea	6	7	218	46	**172 mins**
4	Giggs	Man Utd	6	9	137	48	**89 mins**
5	Keane	Man Utd	1	2	137	54	**83 mins**
6	Scholes	Man Utd	9	4	118	57	**61 mins**
7	Ronaldo	Man Utd	5	4	127	69	**58 mins**
8	Vieira	Arsenal	6	6	100	47	**53 mins**
9	Fabregas	Arsenal	1	6	92	39	**53 mins**
10	Pires	Arsenal	14	3	93	42	**51 mins**
11	Barton	Man City	1	4	104	68	**36 mins**
12	Boateng	Middlesbrough	3	2	94	59	**35 mins**
13	Ljungberg	Arsenal	10	9	77	43	**34 mins**
14	Stellios	Bolton	7	5	98	71	**27 mins**
15	Carrick	Tottenham	0	5	85	58	**27 mins**
16	Riise	Liverpool	6	6	88	63	**25 mins**
17	Hamann	Liverpool	0	6	84	60	**24 mins**
18	Xabi Alonso	Liverpool	2	3	79	55	**24 mins**
19	S Wright-Phillips	Man City	10	6	88	71	**17 mins**
20	Downing	Middlesbrough	5	11	77	61	**16 mins**

The Divisional Round-up charts combine the records of chart-topping keepers, defenders, midfield players and forwards, from every club in the division.. The one above is for **the Chart-topping Midfielders**. The players are ranked by their Scoring Difference although other attributes are shown for you to compare.

CHART-TOPPING GOALSCORERS

1 Thierry Henry - Arsenal	
Goals scored in the League (GL)	25
Goals scored in all competitions (ALL)	30
Contribution to Attacking Power Average number of minutes between League team goals while on pitch	37
Player Strike Rate (S Rate) Average number of minutes between League goals scored by player	113
Club Strike Rate (CSR) Average minutes between League goals scored by club	39

	PLAYER	CLUB	GOALS: LGE	ALL	POWER	CSR	S RATE
1	Henry	Arsenal	25	30	37	39	**113 mins**
2	Crouch	Southampton	12	16	62	76	**157 mins**
3	Johnson	Crystal Palace	21	22	85	83	**158 mins**
4	Pires	Arsenal	14	17	42	39	**165 mins**
5	Yakubu	Portsmouth	13	17	72	80	**189 mins**
6	Defoe	Tottenham	13	22	78	73	**194 mins**
7	Rooney	Man Utd	11	17	47	59	**198 mins**
8	Keane	Tottenham	11	17	70	73	**200 mins**
9	Baros	Liverpool	9	13	59	66	**206 mins**
10	Gudjohnsen	Chelsea	12	16	47	48	**208 mins**
11	Ljungberg	Arsenal	10	14	42	39	**209 mins**
12	Cole	Fulham	12	13	75	66	**209 mins**
13	Phillips	Southampton	10	13	72	76	**209 mins**
14	Reyes	Arsenal	9	12	34	39	**224 mins**
15	Diouf	Bolton	9	9	70	70	**227 mins**
16	Bergkamp	Arsenal	8	8	33	39	**240 mins**
17	Cahill	Everton	11	12	81	76	**245 mins**
18	Hasselbaink	Middlesbrough	13	16	63	65	**249 mins**
19	Fowler	Man City	10	11	67	73	**252 mins**
20	Bellamy	Newcastle	7	10	59	73	**255 mins**

The Chart-topping Goalscorers measures the players by Strike Rate. They are most likely to be Forwards but Midfield players and even Defenders do come through the club tables. It is not a measure of the number of League goals scored - although that is also noted - but how often on average they have scored.

CHART-TOPPING DEFENDERS

1 Paulo Ferreira - Chelsea	
Goals Conceded in the League The number of League goals conceded while he was on the pitch	10
Goals Conceded in all competitions The number of goals conceded while he was on the pitch in all competitions	20
Clean Sheets In games when he played at least 70 mins	21
Defensive Rating Average number of minutes between League goals conceded while on pitch	261
Club Defensive Rating Average mins between League goals conceded by the club this season	228

	PLAYER	CLUB	CON: LGE	ALL	CS	CDR	DEF RATE
1	Ferreira	Chelsea	10	20	21	228	**261 mins**
2	Terry	Chelsea	13	30	25	228	**249 mins**
3	Gallas	Chelsea	10	26	19	228	**245 mins**
4	Carvalho	Chelsea	13	30	12	228	**152 mins**
5	Todd	Blackburn	16	22	14	80	**143 mins**
6	Heinze	Man Utd	16	27	14	132	**143 mins**
7	Ferdinand	Man Utd	20	29	17	132	**140 mins**
8	Brown	Man Utd	12	20	9	132	**137 mins**
9	Silvestre	Man Utd	23	35	16	132	**128 mins**
10	G Neville	Man Utd	18	30	8	132	**105 mins**
11	Stubbs	Everton	24	32	9	74	**102 mins**
12	Lauren	Arsenal	29	38	15	95	**101 mins**
13	Toure	Arsenal	31	43	15	95	**101 mins**
14	Gardner	Bolton	29	35	8	78	**92 mins**
15	Ben Haim	Bolton	19	25	6	78	**92 mins**
16	Thatcher	Man City	17	21	4	88	**91 mins**
17	Cole	Arsenal	35	42	14	95	**90 mins**
18	Jordan	Man City	18	19	6	88	**90 mins**
19	Edman	Tottenham	27	29	9	83	**88 mins**
20	Distin	Man City	39	42	11	88	**87 mins**

The Chart-topping Defenders are resolved by their Defensive Rating, how often their team concedes a goal while they are playing. All these rightly favour players at the best performing clubs because good players win matches. However, good players in lower-table clubs will chart where they have lifted the team's performance.

CHART-TOPPING GOALKEEPERS

1 Petr Cech - Chelsea	
Goals conceded in the League	13
Goals conceded in all comps (ALL)	29
Counting Games (CG) League games when he played at least 70 minutes	35
Clean Sheets (CS) In games when he played at least 70 mins	24
Goals to Shots Ratio (GSR) The average number of shots on target per each League goal conceded	9.9
Defensive Rating Average number of minutes between League goals conceded while on pitch	242

	PLAYER	CLUB	CG	CON: LGE	ALL	CS	GSR	DEF RATE
1	Cech	Chelsea	35	13	29	24	9.9	**242 mins**
2	Carroll	Man Utd	26	16	21	15	6.5	**146 mins**
3	Martyn	Everton	32	26	28	13	8	**109 mins**
4	Lehmann	Arsenal	28	27	37	11	3.7	**93 mins**
5	James	Man City	38	39	40	11	4.6	**88 mins**
6	Dudek	Liverpool	24	25	37	5	4.3	**86 mins**
7	Jaaskelainen	Bolton	36	40	42	8	4.9	**81 mins**
8	Friedel	Blackburn	38	43	50	15	5	**80 mins**
9	Robinson	Tottenham	36	40	46	12	4.5	**80 mins**
10	Sorensen	Aston Villa	36	43	50	11	4.8	**74 mins**
11	Taylor, Maik	Birmingham	38	46	50	9	4.2	**74 mins**
12	Schwarzer	Middlesbrough	31	39	51	9	5.2	**72 mins**
13	Hislop	Portsmouth	17	23	23	3	5.5	**67 mins**
14	Given	Newcastle	36	52	67	6	4	**62 mins**
15	Kiely	Charlton	36	53	60	12	4.9	**61 mins**
16	Kiraly	Crystal Palace	32	49	52	10	5	**59 mins**
17	Van der Sar	Fulham	34	51	58	7	3.7	**58 mins**
18	Hoult	West Brom	36	60	61	6	4	**53 mins**
19	Niemi	Southampton	27	48	52	5	3.8	**51 mins**
20	Green	Norwich	38	75	78	6	4.5	**45 mins**

The Chart-topping Goalkeepers are positioned by their Defensive Rating. We also show Clean Sheets where the team has not conceded and the Keeper has played all or most (at least 70 minutes) of the game. Only the top keeper for each team is included in this chart.

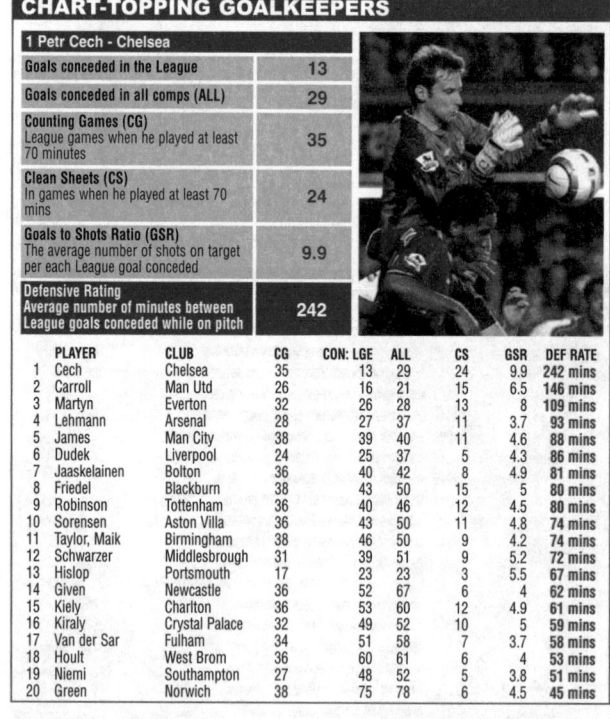

GOALS

	PLAYER	TEAM	LGE	SR
1	Henry	Arsenal	**25**	113
2	Johnson	Crystal Palace	**21**	158
3	Pires	Arsenal	**14**	165
4	Yakubu	Portsmouth	**13**	189
5	Defoe	Tottenham	**13**	194
6	Hasselbaink	Middlesboro	**13**	249
7	Lampard	Chelsea	**13**	262
8	Crouch	Southampton	**12**	157
9	Gudjohnsen	Chelsea	**12**	208
10	Cole	Fulham	**12**	209
11	Rooney	Man Utd	**11**	198
12	Keane	Tottenham	**11**	200
13	Cahill	Everton	**11**	245
14	Ljungberg	Arsenal	**10**	209
15	Phillips	Southampton	**10**	209
16	Fowler	Man City	**10**	252
17	Heskey	Birmingham	**10**	290
18	Wright-Phillips S	Man City	**10**	300
19	Baros	Liverpool	**9**	206
20	Reyes	Arsenal	**9**	224
21	Diouf	Bolton	**9**	227
22	Dickov	Blackburn	**9**	262
23	Scholes	Man Utd	**9**	290
24	Bergkamp	Arsenal	**8**	240
25	Luis Garcia	Liverpool	**8**	292

GOALS – MIDFIELDERS

	PLAYER	TEAM	LGE	SR
1	Pires	Arsenal	**14**	165
2	Lampard	Chelsea	**13**	262
3	Cahill	Everton	**11**	245
4	Ljungberg	Arsenal	**10**	209
5	Wright-Phillips, S	Man City	**10**	300
6	Scholes	Man Utd	**9**	290
7	Boa Morte	Fulham	**8**	325
8	Solano	Aston Villa	**8**	349
9	Stellios	Bolton	**7**	337
10	Gerrard	Liverpool	**7**	353
11	Barry	Aston Villa	**7**	405
12	Francis	Norwich	**7**	409
13	Duff	Chelsea	**6**	399
14	Giggs	Man Utd	**6**	387
15	Vieira	Arsenal	**6**	466
16	Riise	Liverpool	**6**	496
17	Hendrie	Aston Villa	**5**	404

GOALS – DEFENDERS

	PLAYER	TEAM	LGE	SR
1	Jaidi	Bolton	**5**	368
2	El Karkouri	Charlton	**5**	500
3	Queudrue	Middlesbrough	**5**	548
4	Mellberg	Aston Villa	**3**	885
5	De Zeeuw	Portsmouth	**3**	919
6	Clement	West Brom	**3**	1034
7	Granville	Crystal Palace	**3**	1038

TEAM OF THE SEASON

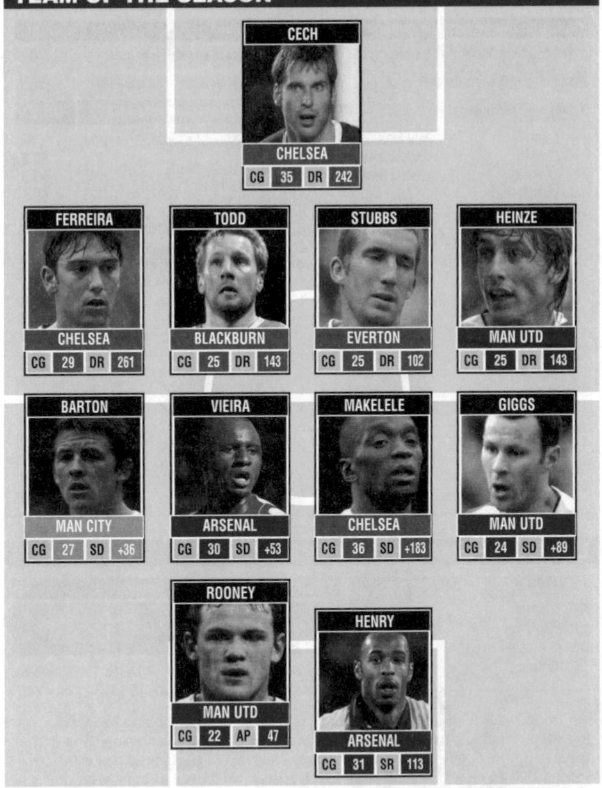
CECH
CHELSEA
CG 35 DR 242
FERREIRA
CHELSEA
CG 29 DR 261
TODD
BLACKBURN
CG 25 DR 143
STUBBS
EVERTON
CG 25 DR 102
HEINZE
MAN UTD
CG 25 DR 143
BARTON
MAN CITY
CG 27 SD +36
VIEIRA
ARSENAL
CG 30 SD +53
MAKELELE
CHELSEA
CG 36 SD +183
GIGGS
MAN UTD
CG 24 SD +89
ROONEY
MAN UTD
CG 22 AP 47
HENRY
ARSENAL
CG 31 SR 113

The Premiership Team of the Season shows a 4-4-2 of the best players in the Premiership based upon the selection criteria used for the chart-toppers. The players selected are taken from the lists for each club except that to get into a Divisional Team of the Season you must have played at least 17 Counting Games in the league (roughly half the league season) and not 12 as is the case in the club lists. The other restriction is that we are only allowing one player from each club in each position. So the maximum number of players one club can have in the divisional team is four.

- **The Divisional team's goalkeeper** is the player with the highest *Defensive Rating*
- **The Divisional team's defenders** are also tested by *Defensive Rating*, i.e. the average number of minutes between league goals conceded while on the pitch.
- **The Divisional team's midfield** are selected on their *Scoring Difference*, i.e.their *Defensive Rating* minus their *Contribution to Attacking Power* (average number of minutes between league goals scored while on the pitch. It takes no account of Assists.
- **The Divisional team strikeforce** is made up of the striker with the highest *Strike Rate* (his average number of minutes between league goals scored while on the pitch) together with the striker with the highest *Contribution to Attacking Power*.

ASSISTS

	PLAYER	TEAM	LGE ASSISTS
1	Frank Lampard	Chelsea	**18**
2	Thierry Henry	Arsenal	**16**
3	Dennis Bergkamp	Arsenal	**12**
4	Luis Boa Morte	Fulham	**11**
5	Stewart Downing	Middlesbrough	**11**
6	Jose Reyes	Arsenal	**10**
7	Fredrik Ljungberg	Arsenal	**9**
8	Arjen Robben	Chelsea	**9**
9	Ryan Giggs	Man Utd	**9**
10	Eidur Gudjohnsen	Chelsea	**8**
11	Damien Duff	Chelsea	**7**
12	Steed Malbranque	Fulham	**7**
13	J-F Hasselbaink	Middlesbrough	**7**
14	Darren Huckerby	Norwich	**7**
15	Patrick Vieira	Arsenal	**6**
16	Nolberto Solano	Aston Villa	**6**
17	Gary Speed	Bolton	**6**
18	Danny Murphy	Charlton	**6**
19	Thomas Gravesen	Everton	**6**
20	John Arne Riise	Liverpool	**6**
21	S Wright-Phillips	Man City	**6**
22	Peter Crouch	Southampton	**6**
23	Frederic Kanoute	Tottenham	**6**
24	Emile Heskey	Birmingham	**5**
25	Stellios	Bolton	**5**

SHARE OF GOALS

	PLAYER	TEAM	% LGE GOALS
1	Johnson	Crystal Palace	**51.22**
2	Yakubu	Portsmouth	**30.23**
3	Henry	Arsenal	**28.74**
4	Dickov	Blackburn	**28.13**
5	Defoe	Tottenham	**27.66**
6	Crouch	Southampton	**26.67**
7	Heskey	Birmingham	**25.00**
8	Hasselbaink	Middlesbrough	**24.53**
9	Cahill	Everton	**24.44**
10	Keane	Tottenham	**23.40**
11	Cole	Fulham	**23.08**
12	Phillips	Southampton	**22.22**
13	Fowler	Man City	**21.28**
14	Wright-Phillips, S	Man City	**21.28**
15	Rooney	Man Utd	**18.97**
16	Diouf	Bolton	**18.37**
17	Lampard	Chelsea	**18.06**
18	Solano	Aston Villa	**17.78**
19	Baros	Liverpool	**17.31**
20	Gudjohnsen	Chelsea	**16.67**
21	McKenzie	Norwich	**16.67**
22	Francis	Norwich	**16.67**
23	Gera	West Brom	**16.67**
24	Davies	Bolton	**16.33**
25	Pires	Arsenal	**16.09**

PREMIERSHIP CHART-TOPPING POINT EARNERS

Fly Emirates

1 William Gallas - Chelsea

Counting Games Played at least 70mins.	26
Total Points Taken in Counting Games	68
Average Taken in Counting Games	2.62

	PLAYER	TEAM	GAMES	POINTS	AVE
1	Gallas	Chelsea	26	68	**2.62**
2	Makelele	Chelsea	36	91	**2.53**
3	Cech	Chelsea	35	88	**2.51**
4	Reyes	Arsenal	18	43	**2.39**
5	Fabregas	Arsenal	22	52	**2.36**
6	Lauren	Arsenal	32	75	**2.34**
7	Gudjohnsen	Chelsea	22	51	**2.32**
8	Rooney	Man Utd	22	51	**2.32**
9	Carroll	Man Utd	26	60	**2.31**
10	Lehmann	Arsenal	28	63	**2.25**
11	Giggs	Man Utd	24	54	**2.25**
12	Brown	Man Utd	17	37	**2.18**
13	Gravesen	Everton	20	39	**1.95**
14	Bent	Everton	26	49	**1.88**
15	Stellios	Bolton	19	35	**1.84**
16	Diouf	Bolton	19	35	**1.84**
17	Martyn	Everton	31	57	**1.84**
18	Baros	Liverpool	19	34	**1.79**
19	Stubbs	Everton	25	44	**1.76**
20	Kishishev	Charlton	18	31	**1.72**

For the Top Point Earners we have applied the same rule of only allowing one player per position for each club, the same as the Team of the Season. The most one club can have in the top 20 is four players, one keeper, one defender, one midfielder and a forward.

PREMIERSHIP MOST MISSED PLAYERS

	PLAYER	TEAM	AVERAGE	CLUB	DIFF
1	Kishishev	Charlton	1.72	1.21	**0.51**
2	Albrechtsen	West Brom	1.39	0.89	**0.50**
3	Wallwork	West Brom	1.26	0.89	**0.37**
4	Stone	Portsmouth	1.37	1.03	**0.34**
5	Gravesen	Everton	1.95	1.61	**0.34**
6	Hendrie	Aston Villa	1.56	1.24	**0.32**
7	Stellios	Bolton	1.84	1.53	**0.31**
8	Diouf	Bolton	1.84	1.53	**0.31**
9	Barton	Man City	1.67	1.37	**0.30**
10	Johansson	Blackburn	1.41	1.11	**0.30**
11	Rooney	Man Utd	2.32	2.03	**0.29**
14	Carroll	Man Utd	2.31	2.03	**0.28**
15	Le Saux	Southampton	1.11	0.84	**0.27**
17	Bartlett	Charlton	1.48	1.21	**0.27**
18	Bentley	Norwich	1.14	0.87	**0.27**
19	Bent	Everton	1.88	1.61	**0.27**
20	Baros	Liverpool	1.79	1.53	**0.26**

The Most Missed Players we have applied the same rule of only allowing one player per position for each club, the same as the Team of the Season. The most one club can have in the top 20 is four players, one keeper, one defender, one midfielder and a forward.

all:sports

1 Radostin Kishishev - Charlton

Average points	1.72
Club average	1.21
Difference	0.51

MANAGERS - SUBSTITUTIONS USED

Club with the highest percentage of subs used - Chelsea | **Jose Mourinho**

Matches where no subs were used	0	Matches where one sub was used	0
Matches where two subs were used	2	Matches where three subs were used	36
Total subs used in season	112	Percentage of possible subs used	98.2

	CLUB	MAIN MANAGER	0 SUBS	1 SUB	2 SUBS	3 SUBS	TOTAL	%
1	Chelsea	Jose Mourinho	0	0	2	36	112	98.2
2	Liverpool	Rafael Benitez	0	1	5	32	107	93.9
3	Birmingham	Steve Bruce	0	2	7	29	103	90.4
4	Everton	David Moyes	0	1	10	27	102	89.5
5	Bolton	Sam Allardyce	0	2	9	27	101	88.6
6	Tottenham	Martin Jol	0	3	11	24	97	85.1
7	Portsmouth	Velimir Zajec	0	1	17	20	95	83.3
8	Charlton	Alan Curbishley	2	3	8	25	94	82.5
9	Norwich	Nigel Worthington	1	2	14	21	93	81.6
10	Aston Villa	David O'Leary	1	4	12	21	91	79.8
11	Crystal Palace	Iain Dowie	1	5	10	22	91	79.8
12	Man Utd	Sir Alex Ferguson	1	5	12	20	89	78.1
13	West Brom	Bryan Robson	0	5	15	18	89	78.1
14	Arsenal	Arsene Wenger	1	7	10	20	87	76.3
15	Newcastle	Graeme Souness	1	7	12	18	85	74.6
16	Blackburn	Mark Hughes	0	5	20	13	84	73.7
17	Middlesbrough	Steve McClaren	0	5	20	13	84	73.7
18	Southampton	Harry Redknapp	3	5	17	13	78	68.4
19	Fulham	Chris Coleman	3	10	18	7	67	58.8
20	Man City	Kevin Keegan	5	8	16	9	67	58.8

MANAGERS - SUBSTITUTION TIMES

Club making earliest substitutions - Chelsea | **Jose Mourinho**

Substitutes made during first half	2	Substitutes made between 46 and 69 minutes (mainly tactical)	49
Substitutes made between 70-85 mins	47		
Substitutes made after 86 mins	14	Total subs used in season	112

	CLUB	MANAGER	0-45 MINS	46-69	70-85	86+	TOTAL
1	Chelsea	Jose Mourinho	2	49	47	14	112
2	Aston Villa	David O'Leary	5	43	32	11	91
3	Newcastle	Graeme Souness	2	41	34	8	85
4	Bolton	Sam Allardyce	3	40	38	20	101
5	Norwich	Nigel Worthington	5	39	36	13	93
6	Blackburn	Mark Hughes	9	38	31	6	84
7	Southampton	Harry Redknapp	7	38	27	6	78
8	Liverpool	Rafael Benitez	10	37	47	13	107
9	Everton	David Moyes	4	36	42	20	102
10	Portsmouth	Velimir Zajec	10	36	42	7	95
11	Charlton	Alan Curbishley	4	34	49	7	94
12	Crystal Palace	Iain Dowie	3	34	35	19	91
13	Man Utd	Sir Alex Ferguson	6	33	44	6	89
14	Birmingham	Steve Bruce	9	32	46	16	103
15	Middlesbrough	Steve McClaren	10	32	28	14	84
16	Tottenham	Martin Jol	5	32	47	13	97
17	West Brom	Bryan Robson	8	32	39	10	89
18	Arsenal	Arsene Wenger	2	29	49	7	87
19	Fulham	Chris Coleman	3	29	26	9	67
20	Man City	Kevin Keegan	2	20	36	9	67

LEAGUE PENALTY TAKERS

Johnson nets against Norwich

Penalties scored	11
Penalties saved	2
Penalties missed	0
League total	13
Percentage scored	84.6
% of all League penalties taken	16.0

1 Andy Johnson - Crystal Palace

Penalties Taken Total number of penalties taken in the league	13

PLAYER	CLUB	TOTAL	Sc	Sa	Mi	%Scored
Johnson	Crystal Palace	13	11	2	0	84.6
Okocha	Bolton	4	4	0	0	100
Yakubu	Portsmouth	4	4	0	0	100
Barry	Aston Villa	3	3	0	0	100
Lampard	Chelsea	3	3	0	0	100
van Nistelrooy	Man Utd	3	3	0	0	100
Shearer	Newcastle	3	3	0	0	100
Dickov	Blackburn	3	2	1	0	66.7
Baros	Liverpool	3	2	1	0	66.7
Fowler	Man City	3	2	1	0	66.7
Earnshaw	West Brom	3	2	0	1	66.7
Angel	Aston Villa	3	0	3	0	0
Diouf	Bolton	2	2	0	0	100
Gravesen	Everton	2	2	0	0	100
Anelka	Man City	2	2	0	0	100
Huckerby	Norwich	2	2	0	0	100
Unsworth	Portsmouth	2	2	0	0	100
Savage	Bham/Bburn	2	1	1	0	50
Cole	Fulham	2	1	0	1	50
Others (19)		19	16	2	1	84.2
TOTALS		81	67	11	3	82.7

CLUB - LEAGUE SQUAD USAGE

1 Everton

Players used Total number of players used by the club in the league	22

CLUB	Players used	% by 11	% by 16	Avge
Everton	22	71.9	92.7	23.6
Aston Villa	22	69.7	91.0	23.1
Charlton	22	68.4	90.6	23.3
Man City	25	71.1	88.7	19.4
Bolton	25	70.3	92.3	20.8
Fulham	25	70.1	89.3	19.4
Arsenal	25	68.7	86.9	20.2
Norwich	25	68.1	87.1	20.4
Man Utd	26	65.1	84.2	19.5
Portsmouth	26	62.6	81.7	19.7
West Brom	27	68.4	87.4	18.8
Middlesbrough	27	68.3	86.1	18.6
Crystal Palace	27	67.0	86.4	18.9
Birmingham	27	65.3	81.4	19.3
Newcastle	27	60.8	80.9	18.6
Liverpool	29	62.7	76.8	18.1
Chelsea	30	67.4	86.4	17.7
Tottenham	31	64.3	82.9	16.6
Blackburn	31	63.3	81.5	16.2
Southampton	34	62.9	77.8	14.6
TOTAL	533			

Moyes: tight knit squad

% of games played by leading 11 players	71.9
% of games played by leading 16 players	92.7
Average number of appearances per player	23.6

LEADING APPEARANCES

DEFENDERS

	PLAYER	GAMES	TIME
=1	Jamie Carragher	38	3420 mins
=1	Craig Fleming	38	3420 mins
=1	Ledley King	38	3420 mins
4	Sylvain Distin	38	3402 mins
5	Bruno N'Gotty	37	3255 mins
=6	Matthew Upson	36	3240 mins
=6	Luke Young	36	3240 mins
=6	John Terry	36	3240 mins
=6	Gareth Southgate	36	3240 mins
10	Tony Hibbert	36	3184 mins
11	Fitz Hall	36	3169 mins
12	Kenny Cunningham	36	3164 mins
=13	Ashley Cole	35	3150 mins
=13	Lucas Neill	36	3150 mins
15	Zatyiah Knight	35	3136 mins
16	Habib Kolo Toure	35	3134 mins
17	Richard Dunne	35	3123 mins
18	Danny Granville	35	3113 mins

MIDFIELDERS

	PLAYER	GAMES	TIME
1	Gary Speed	38	3337 mins
2	Danny Murphy	38	3241 mins
3	Kevin Kilbane	38	3215 mins
4	Wayne Routledge	38	3142 mins
5	Damien Johnson	36	3104 mins
6	Brett Emerton	37	3087 mins
7	Boudewijn Zenden	36	3055 mins
8	Lee Carsley	36	3029 mins
9	Rory Delap	37	3027 mins
10	Michael Hughes	36	3014 mins
11	Shaun Wright-Phillips	34	2998 mins
12	John Arne Riise	37	2975 mins
13	Damian Francis	32	2864 mins
14	Antoine Sibierski	35	2857 mins
15	Jonathan Greening	34	2849 mins
16	Gareth Barry	34	2836 mins
17	Ray Parlour	33	2801 mins
18	Nolberto Solano	36	2794 mins

FORWARDS

	PLAYER	GAMES	TIME
1	Andrew Johnson	37	3327 mins
2	Jimmy-Floyd Hasselbaink	36	3234 mins
3	Darren Huckerby	37	3186 mins
4	Emile Heskey	34	2903 mins
5	Kevin Davies	35	2838 mins
6	Thierry Henry	32	2826 mins
7	Juan Pablo Angel	35	2717 mins
8	Marcus Bent	37	2659 mins
9	Jermain Defoe	35	2525 mins
10	Robbie Fowler	32	2515 mins
11	Andrew Cole	31	2502 mins
12	Eidur Gudjohnsen	37	2494 mins
13	Ayegbeni Yakubu	30	2458 mins
14	Leon McKenzie	37	2413 mins
15	Paul Dickov	29	2354 mins
16	Javier Luis Garcia	29	2339 mins
17	Alan Shearer	28	2261 mins
18	Tomasz Radzinski	35	2209 mins

FIRST SCORERS

SCORED FIRST

CLUB	MATCHES	WON	DRAWN	LOST
Arsenal	30	23	6	1
Chelsea	28	27	1	0
Man Utd	23	19	3	1
Newcastle	23	10	11	2
Bolton	22	15	4	2
Man City	20	12	7	1
Everton	18	16	1	1
Middlesbrough	18	13	4	1
Aston Villa	17	10	6	1
Liverpool	17	13	4	0
Tottenham	17	13	3	1
Charlton	16	12	3	1
Birmingham	15	10	4	1
Crystal Palace	14	7	5	2
Blackburn	13	9	2	2
Fulham	13	9	3	1
Portsmouth	13	8	2	3
West Brom	13	6	5	2
Norwich	10	4	4	2
Southampton	10	4	2	4

CONCEDED FIRST

CLUB	MATCHES	WON	DRAWN	LOST
Chelsea	6	2	3	1
Arsenal	7	2	1	4
Man Utd	9	3	2	4
Newcastle	12	0	0	12
Man City	14	1	2	11
Bolton	15	1	5	9
Tottenham	17	1	3	13
Aston Villa	18	2	2	14
Charlton	18	0	3	15
Everton	18	2	4	12
Middlesbrough	18	1	7	10
Blackburn	19	0	7	12
Birmingham	20	1	5	14
Liverpool	20	4	2	14
Crystal Palace	21	0	4	17
West Brom	22	0	8	14
Southampton	23	2	7	14
Fulham	24	3	4	17
Portsmouth	24	2	6	16
Norwich	25	3	5	17

CLUB DISCIPLINARY RECORDS

Thompson: walks after Riley red

League Yellow	78
League Red	6
League Total	84
All Competitions Yellow	93
All Competitions Red	6
TOTAL	99

1 Blackburn

Cards Average in League
Average number of minutes between a card being shown of either colour: **41**

	CLUB	LEAGUE		TOTAL		AVE
1	Blackburn	78 Y	6 R	93 Y	6 R	41
2	Birmingham	64	3	67	3	51
3	Fulham	59	7	72	8	52
4	Newcastle	59	5	87	7	53
5	Crystal Palace	59	3	68	4	55
6	Bolton	57	2	70	3	58
7	Everton	56	3	64	4	58
8	Aston Villa	56	2	57	2	59
9	Man Utd	52	5	81	5	60
10	Tottenham	56	1	69	1	60
11	Middlesbrough	54	2	70	3	61
12	Portsmouth	54	2	65	3	61
13	Chelsea	53	0	86	2	65
14	Arsenal	47	1	80	5	71
15	West Brom	43	5	51	5	71
16	Man City	44	3	45	3	73
17	Southampton	45	2	52	2	73
18	Liverpool	43	2	76	3	76
19	Charlton	38	3	41	3	83
20	Norwich	35	2	36	2	92

PLAYER DISCIPLINARY RECORD

1 Tugay - Blackburn

Cards Average in League
Average number of minutes between a card being shown of either colour: **140**

	PLAYER		LEAGUE		TOTAL		AVE
1	Tugay	Blackburn	8Y	1R	8Y	1R	140
2	Josemi	Liverpool	7	1	7	1	140
3	Nafti	Birmingham	4	0	4	0	151
4	Amoruso	Blackburn	2	1	2	1	151
5	Redknapp	Tottenham	5	0	5	0	152
6	Naysmith	Everton	2	1	4	1	155
7	Arteta	Everton	5	0	5	0	161
8	Taylor	Newcastle	5	1	6	1	168
9	Dunn	Birmingham	4	0	4	0	179
10	van Persie	Arsenal	4	1	5	1	181
11	Prutton	Southampton	8	1	10	1	187
12	Faye	Portsmouth	7	1	7	1	191
13	McCann	Southampton	3	0	3	0	195
14	Hendrie	Aston Villa	9	1	9	1	202
15	Izzet	Birmingham	3	1	3	1	204
16	Brown	Tottenham	8	0	9	0	214
17	Parlour	Middlesboro	12	1	14	1	215
18	Helveg	Norwich	6	0	6	0	223
19	Lakis	Crystal Pal'	2	1	2	1	228
20	Diop	Fulham	9	2	10	2	228

(Playing a minimum of 500 minutes in the League)

Hughes consoles Tugay

League Yellow	8
League Red	1
League Total	9
All Competitions Yellow	8
All Competitions Red	1
TOTAL	9

REFEREES - PENALTIES

1 Phil Dowd

Penalties Average
Average number of minutes between penalties awarded: **236**

	REF	Home	Away	Total	Avge
1	P Dowd	6	2	8	236 mins
2	R Styles	4	4	8	259 mins
3	H M Webb	3	3	6	345 mins
4	B Knight	3	3	6	240 mins
5	C J Foy	2	3	5	306 mins
6	S G Bennett	2	3	5	468 mins
7	S W Dunn	3	2	5	414 mins
8	G Poll	3	1	4	675 mins
9	M L Dean	2	2	4	270 mins
10	U D Rennie	3	1	4	338 mins
11	M Clattenburg	0	4	4	360 mins
12	M A Riley	3	1	4	608 mins
13	A P D'Urso	3	0	3	330 mins
14	D J Gallagher	2	1	3	630 mins
15	M D Messias	3	0	3	330 mins
16	A G Wiley	1	1	2	945 mins
17	M R Halsey	0	2	2	990 mins
18	P Walton	1	1	2	720 mins
19	N S Barry	2	0	2	900 mins
20	M Atkinson	1	0	1	270 mins
	TOTAL			81	

Phil Dowd: most penalties

Games	21
Penalties awarded to home side	6
Penalties awarded to away side	2
Total	8

REFEREES - CARDS

Matt Messias: card in hand

Games	11
Yellow	44
Yellow/Red	0
Straight reds	0

1 Matt Messias

Cards Average
Average number of cards per match of either colour: **4.00**

	REF	Games	Y	Y/R	R	AVE
1	M D Messias	11	44	0	0	4.00
2	S G Bennett	26	98	4	1	3.96
3	A P D'Urso	11	36	2	1	3.55
4	P Crossley	2	7	0	0	3.50
5	P Dowd	21	66	1	6	3.48
6	G Poll	30	97	2	2	3.37
7	M Clattenburg	16	50	2	1	3.31
8	H M Webb	23	72	0	2	3.22
9	R Styles	22	63	2	5	3.18
10	M A Riley	27	79	3	3	3.15
11	M L Dean	12	31	2	2	2.92
12	P Walton	16	45	0	1	2.88
13	A G Wiley	21	50	4	0	2.57
14	D J Gallagher	21	51	0	3	2.57
15	M R Halsey	22	48	0	2	2.27
16	S W Dunn	23	50	0	1	2.22
17	B Knight	16	31	0	4	2.19
18	U D Rennie	15	31	1	0	2.13
19	N S Barry	20	38	0	2	2.00
20	R J Beeby	1	2	0	0	2.00
21	C J Foy	17	31	0	1	1.88
22	A Marriner	4	7	0	0	1.75
23	M Atkinson	3	5	0	0	1.67
	TOTAL	380	1032	23	37	2.87

CLUB - LEAGUE PENALTIES AWARDED

Johnson earned his penalties

Awarded at home	8
Awarded away	5
Number scored	11
Number saved	2
Number missed	0
% of League penalties awarded	16.0
Number of takers	1

1 Crystal Palace

Penalties Awarded
Total number of penalties awarded to the club in the league: **13**

	CLUB	H	A	Total	Sc	Sa	M	%	No
1	Crystal Palace	8	5	13	11	2	0	16.0	1
2	Aston Villa	0	6	6	3	3	0	7.4	2
3	Bolton	2	4	6	6	0	0	7.4	2
4	Chelsea	4	2	6	5	1	0	7.4	4
5	Man City	4	2	6	5	1	0	7.4	3
6	Portsmouth	6	0	6	6	0	0	7.4	2
7	Arsenal	3	1	4	3	0	1	4.9	4
8	Blackburn	2	2	4	2	2	0	4.9	3
9	Liverpool	3	1	4	3	1	0	4.9	2
10	Man Utd	2	2	4	3	1	0	4.9	2
11	Birmingham	3	0	3	3	0	0	3.7	3
12	Fulham	1	2	3	2	0	1	3.7	2
13	Newcastle	2	1	3	3	0	0	3.7	1
14	Norwich	3	0	3	3	0	0	3.7	2
15	Southampton	1	2	3	3	0	0	3.7	3
16	West Brom	1	2	3	2	0	1	3.7	1
17	Everton	0	2	2	2	0	0	2.5	1
18	Middlesbrough	1	0	1	1	0	0	1.2	1
19	Tottenham	1	0	1	1	0	0	1.2	1
20	Charlton	0	0	0	0	0	0	0	0
	TOTALS	47	34	81	67	11	3		40

CLUB - LEAGUE PENALTIES CONCEDED

1 Fulham

Penalties Conceded
Total number of penalties conceded by the club in the league: **9**

	CLUB	H	A	Total	Sc	Sa	M	%
1	Fulham	4	5	9	5	3	1	11.1
2	Newcastle	6	2	8	8	0	0	9.9
3	Birmingham	2	5	7	7	0	0	8.6
4	Charlton	3	3	6	4	2	0	7.4
5	Crystal Palace	3	3	6	5	1	0	7.4
6	Southampton	1	5	6	5	0	1	7.4
7	Tottenham	4	2	6	6	0	0	7.4
8	Aston Villa	0	5	5	4	0	1	6.2
9	Man City	3	2	5	4	1	0	6.2
10	Arsenal	1	2	3	3	0	0	3.7
11	Blackburn	1	2	3	3	0	0	3.7
12	Middlesbrough	2	1	3	2	1	0	3.7
13	Norwich	1	2	3	3	0	0	3.7
14	West Brom	1	2	3	2	1	0	3.7
15	Chelsea	0	2	2	1	1	0	2.5
16	Man Utd	1	1	2	2	0	0	2.5
17	Bolton	0	1	1	1	0	0	1.2
18	Everton	0	1	1	1	0	0	1.2
19	Liverpool	0	1	1	1	0	0	1.2
20	Portsmouth	1	0	1	0	1	0	1.2
	TOTALS	34	47	81	67	11	3	

Fulham: penalty pain

Conceded at home	4
Conceded away	5
League Total	9
Number scored	5
Number missed	3
% of League penalties conceded	11.1

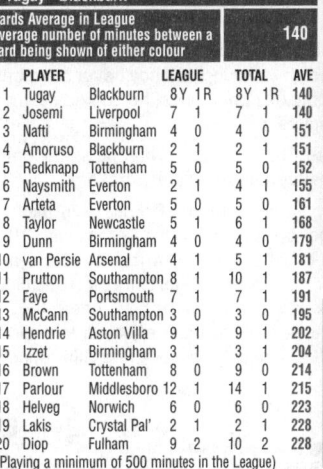

CHELSEA

In defence and midfield, Mourinho's astonishing team are off the scale, while **Arjen Robben** has added an attacking potency never seen before in the Premiership. In his 18 league appearances, he scored seven and created nine Assists for colleagues.

His Attacking Power (how often Chelsea score when he's playing) is a goal every 32 minutes - one better than Arsenal's Bergkamp.

Frank Lampard scored the most goals of any Premiership midfielder with 19 in total and topped the division's table for Assists with 18. Yet neither Robben nor Lampard could dislodge **Claude Makelele** at the top of the Midfielders Chart. His Scoring Difference of 183 minutes (comparing how often goals are scored with how often they are conceded when he played) made him the most effective midfielder in the division. For comparison, last season's best Scoring Difference was 111. And as for the defence...

NICKNAME: THE BLUES

KEY: Won Drawn Lost

1	prem	**Man Utd**	H	W	1-0	Gudjohnsen 15
2	prem	**Birmingham**	A	W	1-0	Cole, J 68
3	prem	**Crystal Palace**	A	W	2-0	Drogba 28; Tiago 73
4	prem	**Southampton**	H	W	2-1	Beattie 34 og; Lampard 41 pen
5	prem	**Aston Villa**	A	D	0-0	
6	cl gh	**Paris SG**	A	W	3-0	Terry 29; Drogba 45,76
7	prem	**Tottenham**	H	D	0-0	
8	prem	**Middlesbrough**	A	W	1-0	Drogba 81
9	cl gh	**Porto**	H	W	3-1	Smertin 7; Drogba 50; Terry 70
10	prem	**Liverpool**	H	W	1-0	Cole, J 64
11	prem	**Man City**	A	L	0-1	
12	cl gh	**CSKA Moscow**	H	W	2-0	Terry 9; Gudjohnsen 45
13	prem	**Blackburn**	H	W	4-0	Gudjohnsen 37,38,51 pen; Duff 74
14	ccr3	**West Ham**	H	W	1-0	Kezman 57
15	prem	**West Brom**	A	W	4-1	Gallas 45; Gudjohnsen 51; Duff 59; Lampard 81
16	cl gh	**CSKA Moscow**	A	W	1-0	Robben 24
17	prem	**Everton**	H	W	1-0	Robben 72
18	ccr4	**Newcastle**	A	W	2-0	Gudjohnsen 100; Robben 112
19	prem	**Fulham**	A	W	4-1	Lampard 33; Robben 59; Gallas 73; Tiago 81
20	prem	**Bolton**	H	D	2-2	Duff 1; Tiago 48
21	cl gh	**Paris SG**	H	D	0-0	
22	prem	**Charlton**	A	W	4-0	Duff 4; Terry 47,50; Gudjohnsen 59
23	ccqf	**Fulham**	A	W	2-1	Duff 55; Lampard 88
24	prem	**Newcastle**	H	W	4-0	Lampard 63; Drogba 69; Robben 89; Kezman 90 pen
25	cl gh	**Porto**	A	L	1-2	Duff 33
26	prem	**Arsenal**	A	D	2-2	Terry 17; Gudjohnsen 46
27	prem	**Norwich**	H	W	4-0	Duff 10; Lampard 34; Robben 44; Drogba 83
28	prem	**Aston Villa**	H	W	1-0	Duff 30
29	prem	**Portsmouth**	A	W	2-0	Robben 79; Cole 90
30	prem	**Liverpool**	A	W	1-0	Cole 80
31	prem	**Middlesbrough**	H	W	2-0	Drogba 15,17
32	facr3	**Scunthorpe**	H	W	3-1	Kezman 26; Crosby 58 og; Gudjohnsen 86
33	ccsfl1	**Man Utd**	H	D	0-0	
34	prem	**Tottenham**	A	W	2-0	Lampard 39 pen,90
35	prem	**Portsmouth**	H	W	3-0	Drogba 15,39; Robben 21
36	ccsfl2	**Man Utd**	A	W	2-1	Lampard 29; Duff 85
37	facr4	**Birmingham**	H	W	2-0	Huth 6; Terry 80
38	prem	**Blackburn**	A	W	1-0	Robben 5
39	prem	**Man City**	H	D	0-0	
40	prem	**Everton**	A	W	1-0	Gudjohnsen 70
41	facr5	**Newcastle**	A	L	0-1	
42	clr2l1	**Barcelona**	A	L	1-2	Belletti 33 og
43	cccf	**Liverpool**	N	W	3-2	Gerrard 79 og; Drogba 107; Kezman 112
44	prem	**Norwich**	A	W	3-1	Cole 22; Kezman 71; Carvalho 79
45	clr2l2	**Barcelona**	H	W	4-2	Gudjohnsen 8; Lampard 17; Duff 19; Terry 76
46	prem	**West Brom**	H	W	1-0	Drogba 26
47	prem	**Crystal Palace**	H	W	4-1	Lampard 29; Cole 54; Kezman 78,90
48	prem	**Southampton**	A	W	3-1	Lampard 22; Gudjohnsen 39,83
49	clqfl1	**Bayern Munich**	H	W	4-2	Cole 4; Lampard 59,70; Drogba 81
50	prem	**Birmingham**	H	D	1-1	Drogba 82
51	clqfl2	**Bayern Munich**	A	L	2-3	Lampard 30; Drogba 80
52	prem	**Arsenal**	H	D	0-0	
53	prem	**Fulham**	H	W	3-1	Cole 17; Lampard 64; Gudjohnsen 87
54	clsfl1	**Liverpool**	H	D	0-0	
55	prem	**Bolton**	A	W	2-0	Lampard 60,76
56	clsfl2	**Liverpool**	A	L	0-1	
57	prem	**Charlton**	H	W	1-0	Makelele 90
58	prem	**Man Utd**	A	W	3-1	Tiago 17; Gudjohnsen 61; Cole 82
59	prem	**Newcastle**	A	D	1-1	Lampard 35 pen

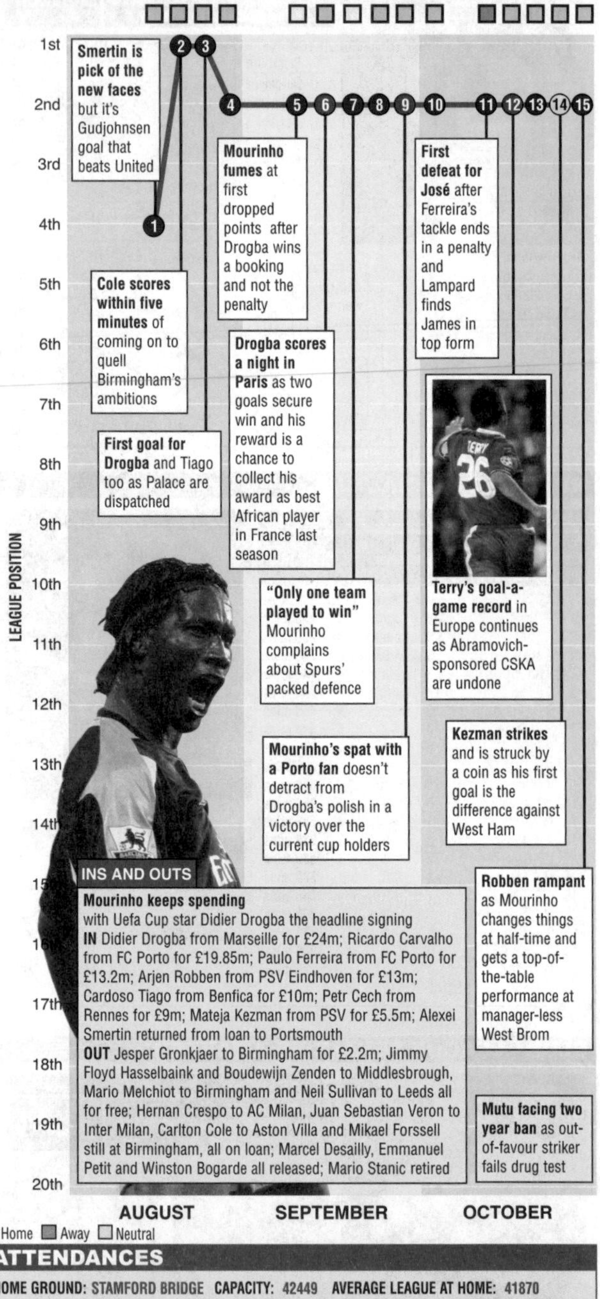

LEAGUE POSITION
1st
2nd
3rd
4th
5th
6th
7th
8th
9th
10th
11th
12th
13th
14th
15th
16th
17th
18th
19th
20th
Smertin is pick of the new faces but it's Gudjohnsen goal that beats United
Cole scores within five minutes of coming on to quell Birmingham's ambitions
First goal for Drogba and Tiago too as Palace are dispatched
Mourinho fumes at first dropped points after Drogba wins a booking and not the penalty
Drogba scores a night in Paris as two goals secure win and his reward is a chance to collect his award as best African player in France last season
"Only one team played to win" Mourinho complains about Spurs' packed defence
Mourinho's spat with a Porto fan doesn't detract from Drogba's polish in a victory over the current cup holders
First defeat for José after Ferreira's tackle ends in a penalty and Lampard finds James in top form
Terry's goal-a-game record in Europe continues as Abramovich-sponsored CSKA are undone
Kezman strikes and is struck by a coin as his first goal is the difference against West Ham
Robben rampant as Mourinho changes things at half-time and gets a top-of-the-table performance at manager-less West Brom
Mutu facing two year ban as out-of-favour striker fails drug test
AUGUST
SEPTEMBER
OCTOBER
Home Away Neutral

INS AND OUTS

Mourinho keeps spending with Uefa Cup star Didier Drogba the headline signing
IN Didier Drogba from Marseille for £24m; Ricardo Carvalho from FC Porto for £19.85m; Paulo Ferreira from FC Porto for £13.2m; Arjen Robben from PSV Eindhoven for £13m; Cardoso Tiago from Benfica for £10m; Petr Cech from Rennes for £9m; Mateja Kezman from PSV for £5.5m; Alexei Smertin returned from loan to Portsmouth
OUT Jesper Gronkjaer to Birmingham for £2.2m; Jimmy Floyd Hasselbaink and Boudewijn Zenden to Middlesbrough, Mario Melchiot to Birmingham and Neil Sullivan to Leeds all for free; Hernan Crespo to AC Milan, Juan Sebastian Veron to Inter Milan, Carlton Cole to Aston Villa and Mikael Forssell still at Birmingham, all on loan; Marcel Desailly, Emmanuel Petit and Winston Bogarde all released; Mario Stanic retired

ATTENDANCES

HOME GROUND: STAMFORD BRIDGE **CAPACITY:** 42449 **AVERAGE LEAGUE AT HOME:** 41870

43	Liverpool	78000	20	Bolton	42203	45	Barcelona	41515	12	CSKA Mos	33945
42	Barcelona	78000	39	Man City	42093	33	Man Utd	41492	8	Middlesboro	32341
58	Man Utd	67832	53	Fulham	42081	31	Middlesboro	40982	48	Southampton	31949
36	Man Utd	67000	27	Norwich	42071	4	Southampton	40864	2	Birmingham	28559
51	Bay Munich	59000	57	Charlton	42065	54	Liverpool	40479	16	CSKA Mos	28000
59	Newcastle	52326	50	Birmingham	42031	37	Birmingham	40379	55	Bolton	27653
41	Newcastle	45740	10	Liverpool	42028	40	Everton	40270	15	West Brom	27399
11	Man City	45047	17	Everton	41965	49	Bay Munich	40253	22	Charlton	26355
6	Paris SG	45000	28	Aston Villa	41950	32	Scunthorpe	40019	3	Crystal Palace	24953
30	Liverpool	43886	1	Man Utd	41813	21	Paris SG	39626	44	Norwich	24506
56	Liverpool	42529	14	West Ham	41774	9	Porto	39237	38	Blackburn	23414
25	Porto	42409	46	West Brom	41713	26	Arsenal	38153	19	Fulham	21877
24	Newcastle	42328	47	Crystal Palace	41667	18	Newcastle	38055	29	Portsmouth	20210
35	Portsmouth	42267	52	Arsenal	41621	5	Aston Villa	36691	23	Fulham	14531
7	Tottenham	42246	13	Blackburn	41546	34	Tottenham	36105			

José ends 50-year wait in style

Final Position: **1st**

KEY: ● League ● Champions Lge ● UEFA Cup ● FA Cup ○ League Cup ● Other

16 17 18 19 20 21 22 23 24 25 26 27 28 29 30 31 32 33 34 35 36 37 38 39 40 41 42 43 44 45 46 47 48 49 50 51 52 53 54 55 56 57 58 59

Group winners with two games to go as wingers cut loose in Moscow with Robben scoring his first goal

Drogba returns as sub against PSG but misses a late one-on-one and the match ends goalless

Duff delight reveals determination to win that extends to the Carling Cup as Fulham succumb

November Player of the Month Robben scores after Lampard opens the floodgates and Manager of the Month Mourinho goes eight points clear

Porto perform as Champions to impress their old manager and hand out a rare defeat to his new charges

Cech caught napping by Henry's cheek at freekick but Terry and Gudjohnsen ensure the game of the season ends all square

Duff delivers with his sixth opening goal in nine games and it's enough to beat dogged Villa

Super sub Cole nets again to do a personal double over Liverpool

Robben serves it up on a plate for Drogba as Pompey are three down in 38 minutes and Fergie admits it's all over

Cech banks record for not conceding a Premiership goal. His penalty save at Blackburn makes it 781 minutes without a goal against

Four trophy dream unravels at St James' as second XI are reduced to ten by Bridge injury and then nine as Cudicini sees red

Rijkaard accused of getting Frisky at halftime and Drogba sending off turns a goal lead into a full-time defeat at Barca

Mourinho banished after 'hushing' gesture causes uproar but Drogba and Kezman goals claim the Carling Cup in extra time

Terry's all gold header knocks out Barcelona after three-goal start is overturned by Ronaldinho but captain has final word

Drogba bags points but misses a hat-trick of simple chances against the Baggies

Lampard screamer and howler puts Palace behind and brings them level, before Cole and Kezman win it

Mourinho speculation dominates the tie even in his absence but fabulous Frank Lampard scores a brace to blast Bayern and silence Uefa

Lampard slots goal 100 for the season as neighbours Fulham make a fight of it but go pointless

Cech keeps Liverpool out as Lampard blazes over the best chance of the first leg

Champions after 50 seasons in the club's Centenary Year as Lampard brace settles it at Bolton in April

No-one knows if it crossed the line but it denies Mourinho his place in history as Liverpool's disputed goal wins semi-final

Lampard's 19th goal of the season deprives Newcastle of a scalp and stretches the points record to 95

Terry tops players' poll to become the first defender to win PFA award for 12 years

Mutu ban too lenient claims Kenyon as seven months are imposed

INS AND OUTS

IN Jiri Jarosik from CSKA Moscow undisclosed
OUT Celestine Babayaro to Newcastle undisclosed

Average League position over the season: 1.3

MONTH BY MONTH POINTS TALLY

AUGUST	12	100%
SEPTEMBER	5	56%
OCTOBER	9	75%
NOVEMBER	10	83%
DECEMBER	13	87%
JANUARY	12	100%
FEBRUARY	7	78%
MARCH	9	100%
APRIL	11	73%
MAY	7	78%

NOVEMBER DECEMBER JANUARY FEBRUARY MARCH APRIL MAY

GOAL ATTEMPTS

FOR — Goal attempts recorded in League games

	HOME	AWAY	TOTAL	AVE
shots on target	155	145	300	7.9
shots off target	125	102	227	6
TOTAL	280	247	527	13.9

Ratio of goals to shots — Average number of shots on target per League goal scored: **4.2**

Accuracy rating — Average percentage of total goal attempts which were on target: **56.9**

AGAINST — Goal attempts recorded in League games

	HOME	AWAY	TOTAL	AVE
shots on target	60	85	145	3.8
shots off target	60	145	205	5.4
TOTAL	120	230	350	9.2

Ratio of goals to shots — Average number of shots on target per League goal scored: **9.7**

Accuracy rating — Average percentage of total goal attempts which were on target: **41.4**

GOALS

Frank Lampard

League	13
FA Cup	0
League Cup	2
Europe	4
Other	0
TOTAL	19

League Average 262 mins between goals

	PLAYER	LGE	FAC	LC	Euro	TOT	AVE
1	Lampard	13	0	2	4	19	262
2	Gudjohnsen	12	1	1	2	16	208
3	Drogba	10	0	1	5	16	163
4	Duff	6	0	2	2	10	399
5	Cole	8	0	0	1	9	204
6	Robben	7	0	1	1	9	179
7	Terry	3	1	0	4	8	1080
8	Kezman	4	1	2	0	7	189
9	Tiago	4	0	0	0	4	493
10	Gallas	2	0	0	0	2	1223
11	Carvalho	1	0	0	0	1	1970
12	Makelele	1	0	0	0	1	3238
13	Huth	0	1	0	0	1	
14	Smertin	0	0	0	1	1	
	Other	1	1	1	1	4	
	TOTAL	72	5	10	21	108	

SQUAD APPEARANCES

Match 1 2 3 4 5 6 7 8 9 10 11 12 13 14 15 16 17 18 19 20 21 22 23 24 25 26 27 28 29 30 31 32 33 34 35 36 37 38 39 40 41 42 43 44 45 46 47 48 49 50 51 52 53 54 55 56 57 58 59

Venue H A A H A A H A H H A H H H A A H A A H H A A H A A H H A A H H H A H A H A H A A A N A H H H A H H A H H H A A H A A

Competition L L L L L C L L C L L C L W L C L W L L C L W L C L L L L L L F W L L W F L L L F C W L C L L L C L C L L C L C L L L

Result W W W W D W D W W W L W W W W W W W W D D W W W L D W W W W W W D W W W W W D W L L W W W W W W W D L D W D W L W W D

Goalkeepers

Petr Cech

Carlo Cudicini

Lenny Pidgeley

Defenders

Celestine Babayaro

Wayne Bridge

Ricardo Carvalho

Paulo Ferreira

William Gallas

Robert Huth

Glen Johnson

Nuno Morais

John Terry

Steven Watt

Midfielders

Joe Cole

Damien Duff

Geremi Nitjap

Anthony Grant

Jiri Jarosik

Frank Lampard

Claude Makelele

Scott Parker

Arjen Robben

Alexei Smertin

Cardoso Tiago

Forwards

Didier Drogba

Mikael Forssell

Eidur Gudjohnsen

Mateja Kezman

Adrian Mutu

Filipe Oliveira

KEY: On all match · On bench · Subbed or sent off (Counting game) · Subbed or sent off (playing less than 70 mins) · Subbed on from bench (Counting Game) · Subbed on (playing less than 70 mins) · Subbed on and then subbed or sent off (Counting Game) · Subbed on and then subbed or sent off (playing less than 70 mins) · Not in 16

KEY PLAYERS - GOALSCORERS

Didier Drogba

Goals in the League	10
Goals in all competitions	16
Assists League goals scored by a team mate where the player delivered the final pass	5
Contribution to Attacking Power Average number of minutes between League team goals while on pitch	56
Player Strike Rate Average number of minutes between League goals scored by player	163
Club Strike Rate Average minutes between League goals scored by club	48

Fly Emirates

	PLAYER	GOALS LGE	GOALS ALL	ASSISTS	POWER	S RATE
1	Didier Drogba	10	16	5	56	163 mins
2	Arjen Robben	7	9	9	32	179 mins
3	Eidur Gudjohnsen	12	16	8	47	208 mins
4	Frank Lampard	13	19	18	47	262 mins
5	Damien Duff	6	10	7	46	399 mins

KEY PLAYERS - MIDFIELDERS

Claude Makelele

Goals in the League	1
Goals in all competitions	1
Assists League goals scored by a team mate where the player delivered the final pass	2
Defensive Rating Average number of mins between League goals conceded while on the pitch	231
Contribution to Attacking Power Average number of minutes between League team goals while on pitch	48
Scoring Difference Defensive Rating minus Contribution to Attacking Power	183

Fly Emirates

	PLAYER	GOALS LGE	GOALS ALL	ASSISTS	DEF RATE	POWER	SC DIFF
1	Claude Makelele	1	1	2	231	48	183 mins
2	Frank Lampard	13	19	18	227	47	180 mins
3	Arjen Robben	7	9	9	209	32	177 mins
4	Damien Duff	6	10	7	218	46	172 mins
5	Cardoso Tiago	4	4	3	179	56	123 mins

PLAYER APPEARANCES

	AGE (on 01/07/05)	IN NAMED 16	APPEARANCES	COUNTING GAMES	MINUTES ON PITCH	APPEARANCES	MINUTES ON PITCH	THIS SEASON	HOME COUNTRY
Goalkeepers									
Petr Cech	23	37	35	35	3150	48	4350	7	Czech Republic (2)
Carlo Cudicini	31	33	3	3	261	11	1011	-	Italy
Lenny Pidgeley	20	6	1	0	9	1	9	-	England
Defenders									
Celestine Babayaro	26	4	4	3	282	5	372	-	Nigeria
Wayne Bridge	24	19	15	11	1149	25	2079	3	England (6)
Ricardo Carvalho	27	29	25	21	1970	39	3260	6	Portugal (9)
Paulo Ferreira	26	29	29	29	2610	42	3679	8	Portugal (9)
William Gallas	27	32	28	26	2445	46	4041	9	France (4)
Robert Huth	20	15	10	5	541	15	767	5	Germany (19)
Glen Johnson	20	20	17	11	1158	29	2073	-	England
Nuno Morais	21	2	2	0	7	4	98	-	Portugal
John Terry	24	36	36	36	3240	53	4830	8	England (6)
Steven Watt	20	1	1	0	1	2	91	-	Scotland
Midfielders									
Joe Cole	23	30	28	11	1629	46	2812	5	England (6)
Damien Duff	26	30	30	27	2396	48	3607	9	Rep of Ireland (15)
Geremi Nitjap	26	14	13	5	592	20	897	-	Cameroon
Anthony Grant	18	2	1	0	1	1	1	-	England
Jiri Jarosik	27	15	14	2	443	20	711	5	Czech Republic (2)
Frank Lampard	27	38	38	38	3412	58	4922	9	England (6)
Claude Makelele	32	36	36	36	3238	50	4528	1	France (4)
Scott Parker	24	7	4	1	128	11	631	-	England
Arjen Robben	21	18	18	13	1255	29	1825	2	Holland (5)
Alexei Smertin	30	19	16	5	778	25	1467	-	Russia
Cardoso Tiago	24	34	34	13	1970	51	2918	6	Portugal (9)
Forwards									
Didier Drogba	27	26	26	12	1625	41	2705	2	Ivory Coast (44)
Mikael Forssell	24	2	1	0	24	2	26	-	Finland
Eidur Gudjohnsen	26	38	37	22	2494	57	3638	-	Iceland
Mateja Kezman	26	31	25	2	754	41	1630	5	Serbia & Mont (46)
Adrian Mutu	26	3	2	0	51	2	51	-	Romania
Filipe Oliveira	21	1	1	0	7	1	7	-	Portugal

KEY: LEAGUE ALL COMPS CAPS (MAY FIFA RANKING)

TEAM OF THE SEASON

CECH
CG 35 DR 242
FERREIRA
CG 29 DR 261
CARVALHO
CG 21 DR 152
TERRY
CG 36 DR 249
GALLAS
CG 26 DR 245
ROBBEN
CG 13 SD +177
MAKELELE
CG 36 SD +183
LAMPARD
CG 38 SD +180
DUFF
CG 27 SD +172
GUDJOHNSEN
CG 22 AP 47
DROGBA
CG 12 SR 163

KEY: DR = Defensive Rating, SD = Scoring Difference AP = Attacking Power SR = Strike Rate, CG=Counting games – League games playing at least 70 minutes

TOP POINT EARNERS

Arjen Robben

Counting Games League games when player was on pitch for at least 70 minutes	13
Average points Average League points taken in Counting games	2.69
Club Average points Average points taken in League games	2.50

	PLAYER	GAMES	PTS
1	Arjen Robben	13	2.69
2	William Gallas	26	2.62
3	Paulo Ferreira	29	2.55
4	Cardoso Tiago	13	2.54
5	Claude Makelele	36	2.53
6	John Terry	36	2.53
7	Damien Duff	27	2.52
8	Petr Cech	35	2.51
9	Frank Lampard	38	2.50
10	Didier Drogba	12	2.50

KEY PLAYERS - DEFENDERS

Paulo Ferreira

Goals Conceded in the League Number of League goals conceded while the player was on the pitch	10
Goals Conceded in all competitions Total number of goals conceded while player was on the pitch	20
League minutes played Number of minutes played in league matches	2610
Clean Sheets In games when player was on pitch for at least 70 minutes	21
Defensive Rating Average number of mins between League goals conceded while on the pitch	261
Club Defensive Rating Average number of mins between League goals conceded by the club this season	228

Fly Emirates

	PLAYER	CON LGE	CON ALL	MINS	C SHEETS	DEF RATE
1	Paulo Ferreira	10	20	2610	21	261 mins
2	John Terry	13	30	3240	25	249 mins
3	William Gallas	10	26	2445	19	245 mins
4	Ricardo Carvalho	13	30	1970	12	152 mins

KEY GOALKEEPER

Petr Cech

Goals Conceded in the League Number of League goals conceded while the player was on the pitch	13
Goals Conceded in all competitions Total number of goals conceded while the player was on the pitch	29
League minutes played Number of minutes played in league matches	3150
Clean Sheets In games when player was on pitch for at least 70 minutes	24
Goals to Shots Ratio The average number of shots on target per each League goal conceded	9.9
Defensive Rating Ave mins between League goals conceded while on the pitch	242

BOOKINGS

Arjen Robben

League Yellow	5
League Red	0
All competitions Yellow	5
All competitions Red	0

League Average **251** mins between cards

	PLAYER	LEAGUE Y	LEAGUE R	TOTAL Y	TOTAL R	AVE
1	Robben	5	0	5	0	251
2	Kezman	3	0	8	0	251
3	Cole	5	0	7	0	325
4	Smertin	2	0	4	0	389
5	Terry	7	0	7	0	462
6	Tiago	4	0	7	0	492
7	Makelele	6	0	8	0	539
8	Lampard	6	0	8	0	568
9	Johnson	2	0	5	0	579
10	Geremi	1	0	2	0	592
11	Drogba	2	0	7	1	812
12	Carvalho	2	0	5	0	985
13	Ferreira	2	0	3	0	1305
14	Duff	1	0	2	0	2396
15	Gallas	1	0	3	0	2445
	Other	1	0	2	0	
	TOTAL	50	0	83	1	

ARSENAL

Thierry Henry scored five less individual league goals than last year, but served up 16 Assists to his colleagues – the second best record in the division.

Arsenal scored 15 more goals than Chelsea and were less reliant on Henry, who hit 29% of the club's league goals (41% last year). Henry has the best Strike Rate in the Premiership with a goal every 113 minutes – over 40 minutes better than his nearest rival.

Arsenal are most likely to score when **Dennis Bergkamp** is on the pitch. The club average a goal every 33 minutes when the Dutch maestro plays.

Philipe Senderos is the pick of the youngsters coming through. He knocked **Ashley Cole** out of the club's most effective four defenders. Senderos' 12 games generated a Defensive Rating of 182 minutes – that's better than one goal every two games.

NICKNAME: THE GUNNERS KEY: Won / Drawn / Lost

1	fash	**Man Utd**	N	W	3-1	Gilberto Silva 49; Reyes 59; Silvestre 79 og
2	prem	**Everton**	A	W	4-1	Bergkamp 23; Reyes 39; Ljungberg 54; Pires 82
3	prem	**Middlesbrough**	H	W	5-3	Henry 25,90; Bergkamp 54; Pires 65; Reyes 65
4	prem	**Blackburn**	H	W	3-0	Henry 50; Gilberto Silva 58; Reyes 79
5	prem	**Norwich**	A	W	4-1	Reyes 22; Henry 36; Pires 40; Bergkamp 90
6	prem	**Fulham**	A	W	3-0	Ljungberg 62; Knight 65 og; Reyes 71
7	cl ge	**PSV Eindhoven**	H	W	1-0	Alex 42 og
8	prem	**Bolton**	H	D	2-2	Henry 31; Pires 66
9	prem	**Man City**	A	W	1-0	Cole 14
10	cl ge	**Rosenborg BK**	A	D	1-1	Ljungberg 6
11	prem	**Charlton**	H	W	4-0	Ljungberg 33; Henry 48,69; Reyes 70
12	prem	**Aston Villa**	H	W	3-1	Pires 19 pen,72; Henry 45
13	cl ge	**Panathinaikos**	A	D	2-2	Ljungberg 18; Henry 74
14	prem	**Man Utd**	A	L	0-2	
15	ccr3	**Man City**	A	W	2-1	van Persie 78; Karabassiyoon 90
16	prem	**Southampton**	H	D	2-2	Henry 67; van Persie 90
17	cl ge	**Panathinaikos**	H	D	1-1	Henry 16 pen
18	prem	**Crystal Palace**	A	D	1-1	Henry 63
19	ccr4	**Everton**	H	W	3-1	Owusu-Abeyie 25; Lupoli 52,85
20	prem	**Tottenham**	A	W	5-4	Henry 45; Lauren 55 pen; Vieira 60; Ljungberg 69; Pires 81
21	prem	**West Brom**	H	D	1-1	Pires 54
22	cl ge	**PSV Eindhoven**	A	D	1-1	Henry 31
23	prem	**Liverpool**	A	L	1-2	Vieira 57
24	ccqf	**Man Utd**	A	L	0-1	
25	prem	**Birmingham**	H	W	3-0	Pires 33; Henry 80,86
26	cl ge	**Rosenborg BK**	H	W	5-1	Reyes 3; Henry 24; Fabregas 29; Pires 41 pen; van Persie 84
27	prem	**Chelsea**	H	D	2-2	Henry 2,29
28	prem	**Portsmouth**	A	W	1-0	Campbell 75
29	prem	**Fulham**	H	W	2-0	Henry 12; Pires 71
30	prem	**Newcastle**	A	W	1-0	Vieira 45
31	prem	**Charlton**	A	W	3-1	Ljungberg 35,48; van Persie 67
32	prem	**Man City**	H	D	1-1	Ljungberg 75
33	facr3	**Stoke**	H	W	2-1	Reyes 50; van Persie 70
34	prem	**Bolton**	A	L	0-1	
35	prem	**Newcastle**	H	W	1-0	Bergkamp 19
36	facr4	**Wolverhampton**	H	W	2-0	Vieira 53 pen; Ljungberg 82
37	prem	**Man Utd**	H	L	2-4	Vieira 8; Bergkamp 36
38	prem	**Aston Villa**	A	W	3-1	Ljungberg 10; Henry 14; Cole 28
39	prem	**Crystal Palace**	H	W	5-1	Bergkamp 32; Reyes 35; Henry 39,77; Vieira 54
40	facr5	**Sheff Utd**	H	D	1-1	Pires 78
41	clr2l1	**Bayern Munich**	A	L	1-3	Toure 88
42	prem	**Southampton**	A	D	1-1	Ljungberg 45
43	facr5r	**Sheff Utd**	A	W	0-0*	(*aet, won 4-2 on penalties)
44	prem	**Portsmouth**	H	W	3-0	Henry 39,53,85
45	clr2l2	**Bayern Munich**	H	W	1-0	Henry 66
46	facqf	**Bolton**	A	W	1-0	Ljungberg 3
47	prem	**Blackburn**	A	W	1-0	van Persie 43
48	prem	**Norwich**	H	W	4-1	Henry 19,22,66; Ljungberg 50
49	prem	**Middlesbrough**	A	W	1-0	Pires 73
50	facsf	**Blackburn**	N	W	3-0	Pires 42; van Persie 86,90
51	prem	**Chelsea**	A	D	0-0	
52	prem	**Tottenham**	H	W	1-0	Reyes 22
53	prem	**West Brom**	A	W	2-0	van Persie 66; Edu 90
54	prem	**Liverpool**	H	W	3-1	Pires 25; Reyes 29; Fabregas 90
55	prem	**Everton**	H	W	7-0	van Persie 8; Pires 11,50; Vieira 37; Edu 69 pen; Bergkamp 77; Flamini 85
56	prem	**Birmingham**	A	L	1-2	Bergkamp 88
57	facf	**Man Utd**	N	W	0-0*	(*aet, won 5-4 on penalties)

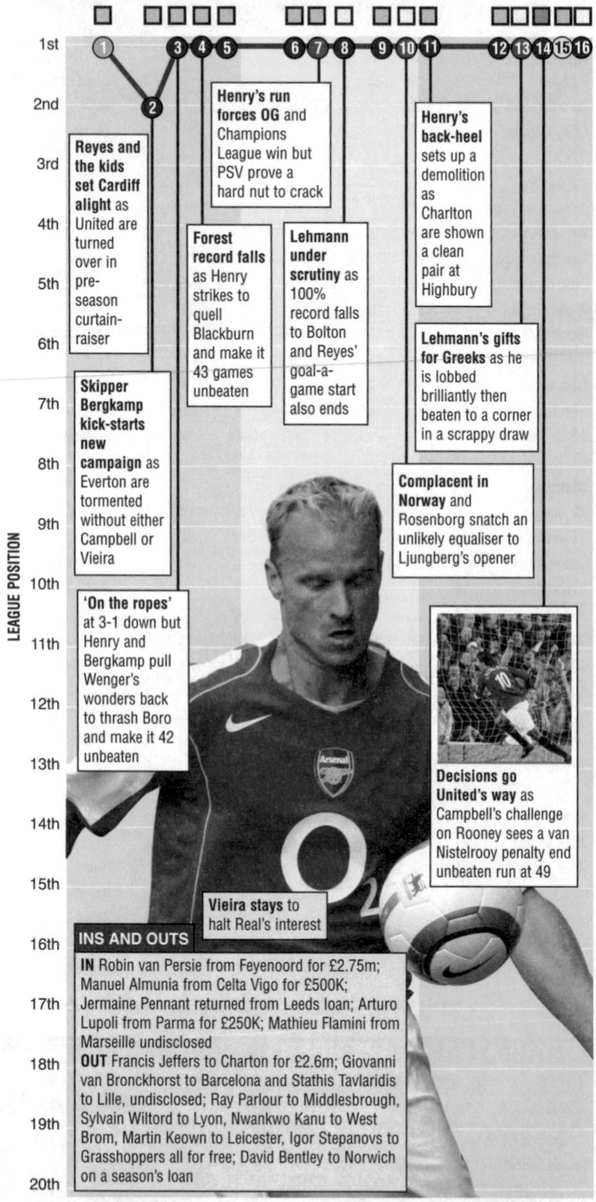

1st
2nd
3rd
4th
5th
6th
7th
8th
9th
10th
11th
12th
13th
14th
15th
16th
17th
18th
19th
20th
LEAGUE POSITION
1 2 3 4 5 6 7 8 9 10 11 12 13 14 15 16
Reyes and the kids set Cardiff alight as United are turned over in pre-season curtain-raiser
Skipper Bergkamp kick-starts new campaign as Everton are tormented without either Campbell or Vieira
'On the ropes' at 3-1 down but Henry and Bergkamp pull Wenger's wonders back to thrash Boro and make it 42 unbeaten
Forest record falls as Henry strikes to quell Blackburn and make it 43 games unbeaten
Henry's run forces OG and Champions League win but PSV prove a hard nut to crack
Lehmann under scrutiny as 100% record falls to Bolton and Reyes' goal-a-game start also ends
Complacent in Norway and Rosenborg snatch an unlikely equaliser to Ljungberg's opener
Henry's back-heel sets up a demolition as Charlton are shown a clean pair at Highbury
Lehmann's gifts for Greeks as he is lobbed brilliantly then beaten to a corner in a scrappy draw
Decisions go United's way as Campbell's challenge on Rooney sees a van Nistelrooy penalty end unbeaten run at 49
Vieira stays to halt Real's interest

INS AND OUTS

IN Robin van Persie from Feyenoord for £2.75m; Manuel Almunia from Celta Vigo for £500K; Jermaine Pennant returned from Leeds loan; Arturo Lupoli from Parma for £250K; Mathieu Flamini from Marseille undisclosed

OUT Francis Jeffers to Charton for £2.6m; Giovanni van Bronckhorst to Barcelona and Stathis Tavlaridis to Lille, undisclosed; Ray Parlour to Middlesbrough, Sylvain Wiltord to Lyon, Nwankwo Kanu to West Brom, Martin Keown to Leicester, Igor Stepanovs to Grasshoppers all for free; David Bentley to Norwich on a season's loan

AUGUST SEPTEMBER OCTOBER

Home / Away / Neutral

ATTENDANCES

HOME GROUND: HIGHBURY CAPACITY: 38500 AVERAGE LEAGUE AT HOME: 37972

57	Man Utd	71876	35	Newcastle	38137	8	Bolton	37010	34	Bolton	27514
14	Man Utd	67862	12	Aston Villa	38137	40	Sheff Utd	36891	53	West Brom	27351
24	Man Utd	67103	21	West Brom	38109	33	Stoke	36579	31	Charlton	26711
1	Man Utd	63317	11	Charlton	38103	20	Tottenham	36095	18	Crystal Palace	26193
41	Bay Munich	59000	32	Man City	38086	2	Everton	35521	5	Norwich	23944
30	Newcastle	52320	44	Portsmouth	38079	45	Bay Munich	35463	46	Bolton	23523
50	Blackburn	52077	55	Everton	38073	26	Rosenborg	35421	47	Blackburn	22992
9	Man City	47015	48	Norwich	38066	17	Panathinaikos	35137	15	Man City	21708
23	Liverpool	43730	25	Birmingham	38064	22	PSV Eindhov	35000	6	Fulham	21681
38	Aston Villa	42593	39	Crystal Palace	38056	7	PSV Eindhov	34068	10	Rosenborg	21000
51	Chelsea	41621	29	Fulham	38047	49	Middlesboro	33874	28	Portsmouth	20170
37	Man Utd	38164	54	Liverpool	38000	42	Southampton	31815	13	Panathinaikos	12000
27	Chelsea	38153	4	Blackburn	37496	56	Birmingham	29302			
52	Tottenham	38147	3	Middlesboro	37415	19	Everton	27791			
16	Southampton	38141	36	Wolves	37153	43	Sheff Utd	27595			

Youngsters show character to claim cup

Final Position: 2nd

KEY: ● League ● Champions Lge ● UEFA Cup ● FA Cup ○ League Cup ● Other

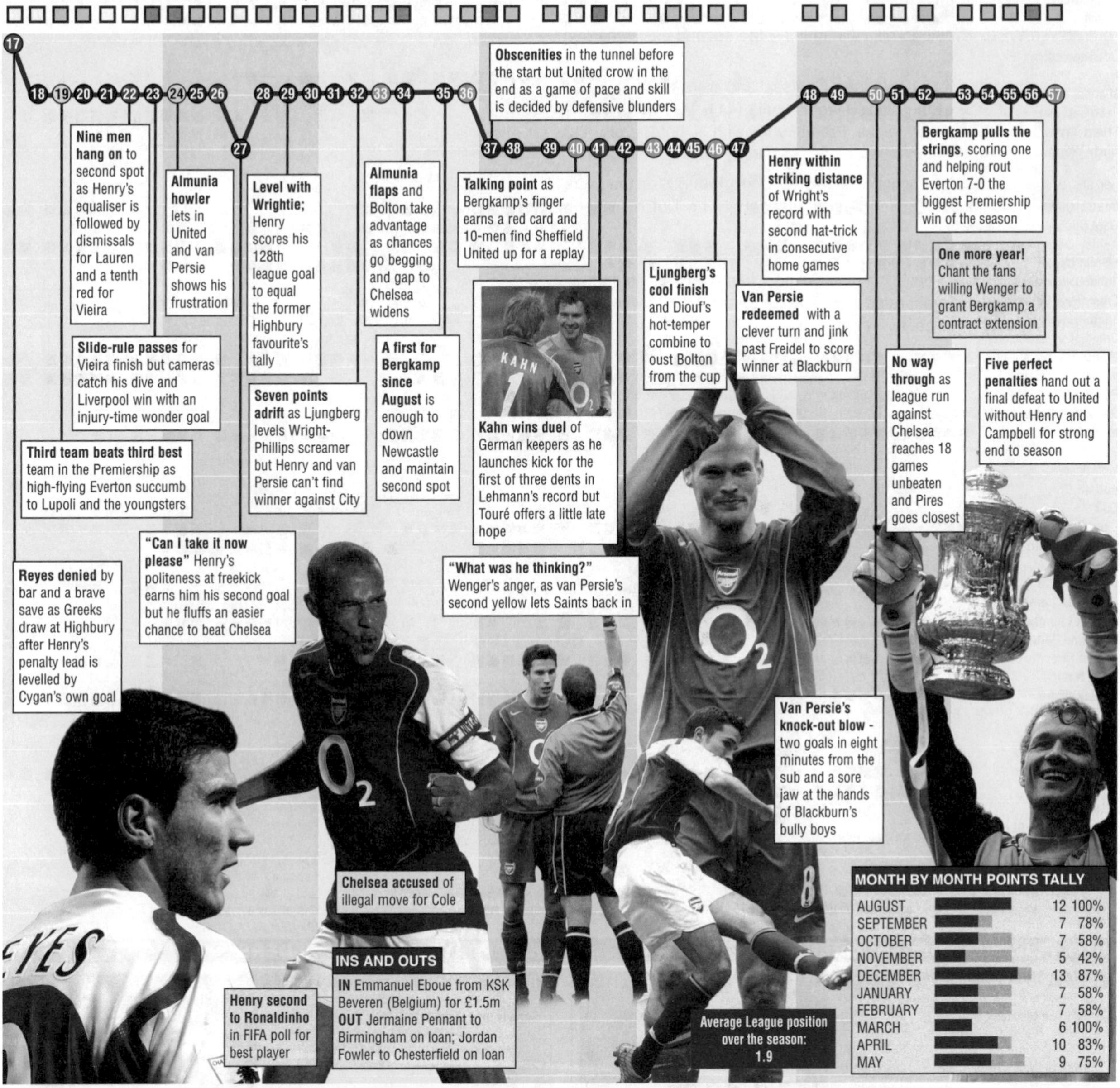
17 18 19 20 21 22 23 24 25 26 27 28 29 30 31 32 33 34 35 36 37 38 39 40 41 42 43 44 45 46 47 48 49 50 51 52 53 54 55 56 57
Reyes denied by bar and a brave save as Greeks draw at Highbury after Henry's penalty lead is levelled by Cygan's own goal
Third team beats third best team in the Premiership as high-flying Everton succumb to Lupoli and the youngsters
Slide-rule passes for Vieira finish but cameras catch his dive and Liverpool win with an injury-time wonder goal
Nine men hang on to second spot as Henry's equaliser is followed by dismissals for Lauren and a tenth red for Vieira
Almunia howler lets in United and van Persie shows his frustration
"Can I take it now please" Henry's politeness at freekick earns him his second goal but he fluffs an easier chance to beat Chelsea
Level with Wrightie; Henry scores his 128th league goal to equal the former Highbury favourite's tally
Seven points adrift as Ljungberg levels Wright-Phillips screamer but Henry and van Persie can't find winner against City
Chelsea accused of illegal move for Cole
Almunia flaps and Bolton take advantage as chances go begging and gap to Chelsea widens
A first for Bergkamp since August is enough to down Newcastle and maintain second spot
Obscenities in the tunnel before the start but United crow in the end as a game of pace and skill is decided by defensive blunders
Talking point as Bergkamp's finger earns a red card and 10-men find Sheffield United up for a replay
KAHN
Kahn wins duel of German keepers as he launches kick for the first of three dents in Lehmann's record but Touré offers a little late hope
"What was he thinking?" Wenger's anger, as van Persie's second yellow lets Saints back in
Ljungberg's cool finish and Diouf's hot-temper combine to oust Bolton from the cup
Van Persie redeemed with a clever turn and jink past Freidel to score winner at Blackburn
Henry within striking distance of Wright's record with second hat-trick in consecutive home games
Van Persie's knock-out blow - two goals in eight minutes from the sub and a sore jaw at the hands of Blackburn's bully boys
No way through as league run against Chelsea reaches 18 games unbeaten and Pires goes closest
Bergkamp pulls the strings, scoring one and helping rout Everton 7-0 the biggest Premiership win of the season
One more year! Chant the fans willing Wenger to grant Bergkamp a contract extension
Five perfect penalties hand out a final defeat to United without Henry and Campbell for strong end to season
Henry second to Ronaldinho in FIFA poll for best player
Average League position over the season: 1.9
NOVEMBER DECEMBER JANUARY FEBRUARY MARCH APRIL MAY

INS AND OUTS

IN Emmanuel Eboue from KSK Beveren (Belgium) for £1.5m
OUT Jermaine Pennant to Birmingham on loan; Jordan Fowler to Chesterfield on loan

MONTH BY MONTH POINTS TALLY

Month	Points	%
AUGUST	12	100%
SEPTEMBER	7	78%
OCTOBER	7	58%
NOVEMBER	5	42%
DECEMBER	13	87%
JANUARY	7	58%
FEBRUARY	7	58%
MARCH	6	100%
APRIL	10	83%
MAY	9	75%

GOAL ATTEMPTS

FOR — Goal attempts recorded in League games

	HOME	AWAY	TOTAL	AVE
shots on target	163	136	299	7.9
shots off target	93	87	180	4.7
TOTAL	256	223	479	12.6

Ratio of goals to shots Average number of shots on target per League goal scored: **3.4**

Accuracy rating Average percentage of total goal attempts which were on target: **62.4**

AGAINST — Goal attempts recorded in League games

	HOME	AWAY	TOTAL	AVE
shots on target	55	83	138	3.6
shots off target	57	136	193	5.1
TOTAL	112	219	331	8.7

Ratio of goals to shots Average number of shots on target per League goal scored: **3.8**

Accuracy rating Average percentage of total goal attempts which were on target: **41.7**

GOALS

Thierry Henry

League	25
FA Cup	0
League Cup	0
Europe	5
Other	0
TOTAL	30

League Average 113 mins between goals

	PLAYER	LGE	FAC	LC	Euro	TOT	AVE
1	Henry	25	0	0	5	**30**	113
2	Pires	14	2	0	1	**17**	165
3	Ljungberg	10	2	0	2	**14**	209
4	Reyes	9	1	0	1	**12**	224
5	van Persie	4	3	1	1	**9**	227
6	Bergkamp	8	0	0	0	**8**	240
7	Vieira	6	1	0	0	**7**	466
8	Cole	2	0	0	0	**2**	1575
9	Edu	2	0	0	0	**2**	297
10	Gilberto Silva	1	0	0	0	**2**	1124
11	Fabregas	1	0	0	1	**2**	2118
12	Campbell	1	0	0	0	**1**	1419
13	Flamini	1	0	0	0	**1**	960
14	Lauren	1	0	0	0	**1**	2939
	Other	2	0	3	2	8	
	TOTAL	**87**	**9**	**5**	**13**	**117**	

SQUAD APPEARANCES

Match	1	2	3	4	5	6	7	8	9	10	11	12	13	14	15	16	17	18	19	20	21	22	23	24	25	26	27	28	29	30
Venue	N	A	H	H	A	A	H	H	A	A	H	H	A	A	A	H	H	A	H	A	H	A	A	A	H	H	H	A	H	A
Competition	O	L	L	L	L	L	C	L	L	C	L	L	C	L	W	L	C	L	W	L	L	C	L	W	L	C	L	L	L	L
Result	W	W	W	W	W	W	W	D	W	D	W	W	D	L	W	D	D	D	W	W	D	D	L	L	W	W	D	W	W	W

Match	31	32	33	34	35	36	37	38	39	40	41	42	43	44	45	46	47	48	49	50	51	52	53	54	55	56	57
Venue	A	H	H	A	H	H	H	A	H	H	A	A	A	H	H	A	A	H	A	N	A	H	A	H	H	A	N
Competition	L	L	F	L	L	F	L	L	L	F	C	L	F	L	C	F	L	L	L	F	L	L	L	L	L	L	F
Result	W	D	W	L	W	W	L	W	W	D	L	D	W	W	W	W	W	W	W	W	D	W	W	W	W	L	W

Goalkeepers
Manuel Almunia
Michael Jordan
Jens Lehmann
Stuart Taylor
Chris Wright

Defenders
Sol Campbell
Gael Clichy
Ashley Cole
Pascal Cygan
Johan Djourou
Emmanuel Eboue
Justin Hoyte
Daniel Karbassiyoon
Etame Mayer Lauren
Philippe Senderos
Frankie Simek
Sebastian Svard
Habib Kolo Toure

Midfielders
Patrick Cregg
Edu
Cesc Fabregas
Mathieu Flamini
Jordan Fowler
Gilberto Silva
Sebastian Larsson
Fredrik Ljungberg
Jermaine Pennant
Robert Pires
Ryan Smith
Patrick Vieira

Forwards
Jeremie Aliadiere
Dennis Bergkamp
Thierry Henry
Arturo Lupoli
Quincy Owusu-Abeyie
Jose Antonio Reyes
Robin van Persie

KEY: On all match · On bench · Subbed or sent off (Counting game) · Subbed or sent off (playing less than 70 mins) · Subbed on from bench (Counting Game) · Subbed on (playing less than 70 mins) · Subbed on and then subbed or sent off (Counting Game) · Subbed on and then subbed or sent off (playing less than 70 mins) · Not in 16

KEY PLAYERS - GOALSCORERS

Thierry Henry

Goals in the League	25
Goals in all competitions	30
Assists League goals scored by a team mate where the player delivered the final pass	16
Contribution to Attacking Power Average number of minutes between League team goals while on the pitch	37
Player Strike Rate Average number of minutes between League goals scored by player	113
Club Strike Rate Average minutes between League goals scored by club	39

	PLAYER	GOALS LGE	GOALS ALL	ASSISTS	POWER	S RATE
1	Thierry Henry	25	30	16	37	113 mins
2	Robert Pires	14	17	3	42	165 mins
3	Fredrik Ljungberg	10	14	9	43	209 mins
4	Jose Antonio Reyes	9	12	10	34	224 mins
5	Dennis Bergkamp	8	8	12	33	240 mins

KEY PLAYERS - MIDFIELDERS

Patrick Vieira

Goals in the League	6
Goals in all competitions	7
Assists League goals scored by a team mate where the player delivered the final pass	6
Defensive Rating Average number of mins between League goals conceded while on the pitch	100
Contribution to Attacking Power Average number of minutes between League team goals while on the pitch	47
Scoring Difference Defensive Rating minus Contribution to Attacking Power	53

	PLAYER	GOALS LGE	GOALS ALL	ASSISTS	DEF RATE	POWER	SC DIFF
1	Patrick Vieira	6	7	6	100	47	53 mins
2	Cesc Fabregas	1	2	6	92	39	53 mins
3	Robert Pires	14	17	3	93	42	51 mins
4	Fredrik Ljungberg	10	14	9	77	43	34 mins

PLAYER APPEARANCES

	AGE (on 01/07/05)	IN NAMED 16	APPEARANCES	COUNTING GAMES	MINUTES ON PITCH	APPEARANCES	MINUTES ON PITCH	THIS SEASON	HOME COUNTRY
Goalkeepers									
Manuel Almunia	28	34	10	10	900	16	1470	-	Spain
Michael Jordan	19	0	0	0	0	0	0	-	England
Jens Lehmann	35	38	28	28	2520	41	3720	6	Germany (19)
Stuart Taylor	24	4	0	0	0	0	0	-	England
Chris Wright	19	0	0	0	0	0	0	-	England
Defenders									
Sol Campbell	30	20	16	16	1419	21	1869	2	England (6)
Gael Clichy	19	18	15	7	780	24	1463	-	France
Ashley Cole	24	35	35	35	3150	47	4192	9	England (6)
Pascal Cygan	31	22	15	14	1283	23	1948	-	France
Johan Djourou	18	0	0	0	0	3	182	-	Switzerland
Emmanuel Eboue	22	7	1	0	16	4	266	2	Ivory Coast (44)
Justin Hoyte	20	15	5	4	372	12	785	-	England
Daniel Karbassiyoon	20	0	0	0	0	3	109	-	United States
Etame Mayer Lauren	28	34	33	32	2939	45	4054	-	Cameroon
Philippe Senderos	20	24	13	12	1089	23	2049	-	Switzerland
Frankie Simek	20	0	0	0	0	0	0	-	United States
Sebastian Svard	22	0	0	0	0	1	4	-	Denmark
Habib Kolo Toure	24	36	35	35	3134	50	4455	-	Ivory Coast
Midfielders									
Patrick Cregg	19	0	0	0	0	2	21	-	Rep of Ireland
Edu	27	13	12	4	593	18	902	8	Brazil (1)
Cesc Fabregas	18	36	33	22	2118	46	3092	-	Spain
Mathieu Flamini	21	23	21	8	960	32	1829	-	France
Jordan Fowler	20	0	0	0	0	0	0	-	England
Gilberto Silva	28	13	13	11	1124	17	1514	5	Brazil (1)
Sebastian Larsson	20	2	0	0	0	3	187	-	Sweden
Fredrik Ljungberg	28	27	27	21	2086	39	3079	7	Sweden (13)
Jermaine Pennant	22	9	7	1	210	12	658	-	England
Robert Pires	31	33	33	22	2316	47	3361	5	France (4)
Ryan Smith	18	0	0	0	0	3	102	-	England
Patrick Vieira	29	32	32	30	2794	44	3922	8	France (4)
Forwards									
Jeremie Aliadiere	22	6	4	0	41	7	58	-	France
Dennis Bergkamp	36	29	29	20	1920	38	2572	-	Holland
Thierry Henry	27	32	32	31	2826	42	3681	8	France (4)
Arturo Lupoli	18	0	0	0	0	4	281	-	Italy
Q Owusu-Abeyie	19	4	1	1	73	7	349	-	Holland
Jose Antonio Reyes	21	30	30	18	2013	45	3214	6	Spain (8)
Robin van Persie	21	31	25	4	906	40	1572	1	Holland (5)

KEY: LEAGUE ALL COMPS CAPS (MAY FIFA RANKING)

TEAM OF THE SEASON

LEHMANN
CG 28 DR 93
LAUREN
CG 32 DR 101
SENDEROS
CG 12 DR 182
CAMPBELL
CG 16 DR 101
TOURE
CG 35 DR 101
LJUNGBERG
CG 21 SD +34
FABREGAS
CG 22 SD +53
VIEIRA
CG 30 SD +53
PIRES
CG 22 SD +51
BERGKAMP
CG 20 AP 33
HENRY
CG 31 SR 113

KEY: DR = Defensive Rating, SD = Scoring Difference AP = Attacking Power SR = Strike Rate, CG=Counting games – League games playing at least 70 minutes

TOP POINT EARNERS

Jose Antonio Reyes

Counting Games League games when player was on pitch for at least 70 minutes	18
Average points Average League points taken in Counting games	2.39
Club Average points Average points taken in League games	2.18

	PLAYER	GAMES	PTS
1	Jose Antonio Reyes	18	2.39
2	Cesc Fabregas	22	2.36
3	Etame Mayer Lauren	32	2.34
4	Jens Lehmann	28	2.25
5	Philippe Senderos	12	2.25
6	Habib Kolo Toure	35	2.20
7	Thierry Henry	31	2.16
8	Dennis Bergkamp	20	2.15
9	Ashley Cole	35	2.11
10	Pascal Cygan	14	2.07

KEY PLAYERS - DEFENDERS

Philippe Senderos

Goals Conceded in the League Number of League goals conceded while the player was on the pitch	6
Goals Conceded in all competitions Total number of goals conceded while the player was on the pitch	11
League minutes played Number of minutes played in league matches	1089
Clean Sheets In games when player was on pitch for at least 70 minutes	7
Defensive Rating Average number of mins between League goals conceded while on the pitch	182
Club Defensive Rating Average number of mins between League goals conceded by the club this season	95

	PLAYER	CON LGE	CON ALL	MINS	C SHEETS	DEF RATE
1	Philippe Senderos	6	11	1089	7	182 mins
2	Etame Mayer Lauren	29	38	2939	15	101 mins
3	Habib Kolo Toure	31	43	3134	15	101 mins
4	Sol Campbell	14	19	1419	8	101 mins
5	Ashley Cole	35	42	3150	14	90 mins

KEY GOALKEEPER

Jens Lehmann

Goals Conceded in the League Number of League goals conceded while the player was on the pitch	27
Goals Conceded in all competitions Total number of goals conceded while the player was on the pitch	37
League minutes played Number of minutes played in league matches	2520
Clean Sheets In games when player was on pitch for at least 70 minutes	11
Goals to Shots Ratio Average number of shots on target per each League goal conceded	3.7
Defensive Rating Ave mins between League goals conceded while on the pitch	93

BOOKINGS

Robin van Persie

League Yellow	4
League Red	1
All competitions Yellow	5
All competitions Red	1

League Average **181** mins between cards

	PLAYER	LEAGUE 4Y	LEAGUE 1R	TOTAL 5Y	TOTAL 1R	AVE
1	van Persie	4	1	5	1	181
2	Vieira	9	0	13	1	310
3	Clichy	2	0	3	0	390
4	Cole	7	0	10	0	450
5	Fabregas	4	0	8	0	529
6	Edu	1	0	2	0	593
7	Cygan	2	0	2	0	641
8	Reyes	3	0	7	1	671
9	Lauren	4	0	10	1	734
10	Flamini	1	0	3	0	960
11	Ljungberg	2	0	3	0	1043
12	Senderos	1	0	2	0	1089
13	Pires	2	0	3	0	1158
14	Henry	2	0	3	0	1413
15	Campbell	1	0	1	0	1419
	Other	2	0	5	1	
	TOTAL	47	1	80	5	

MANCHESTER UNITED

Frustration for United fans as they saw their side average over 16 shots a game – far more than Chelsea and Arsenal – but score from less than one in ten of them. Arsenal's conversion rate was nearly twice that.

Wayne Rooney was a positive, scoring 17 goals. His 11 in the league came at the Premier's seventh best Strike Rate of one every 198 minutes, up from his 271 at Everton. **Ruud van Nistelrooy's** season was disrupted but he still managed 16 goals in total.

Ryan Giggs had nine Assists and finishes fourth in the divisional Midfielders chart. **Darren Fletcher** ran him close, he was the United player most likely to turn performances into points with a Chelsea-standard average of 2.38 points each time he played at least 70 minutes.

Roy Carroll's Defensive Rating of 146 was the second best in the Premiership, while **Tim Howard's** was 108.

NICKNAME: RED DEVILS

KEY: Won Drawn Lost

1	fash	**Arsenal**	N	L	1-3	Smith 55
2	clql1	**Din Bucharest**	A	W	2-1	Giggs 38; Alistar 71 og
3	prem	**Chelsea**	A	L	0-1	
4	prem	**Norwich**	H	W	2-1	Bellion 33; Smith 50
5	clql2	**Din Bucharest**	H	W	3-0	Smith 47,50; Bellion 70
6	prem	**Blackburn**	A	D	1-1	Smith 90
7	prem	**Everton**	H	D	0-0	
8	prem	**Bolton**	A	D	2-2	Heinze 44; Smith 90
9	cl gd	**Lyon**	A	D	2-2	van Nistelrooy 56,61
10	prem	**Liverpool**	H	W	2-1	Silvestre 20,66
11	prem	**Tottenham**	H	W	1-0	van Nistelrooy 42 pen
12	cl gd	**Fenerbahce**	H	W	6-2	Giggs 7; Rooney 17,28,54; van Nistelrooy 78; Bellion 81
13	prem	**Middlesbrough**	H	D	1-1	Smith 81
14	prem	**Birmingham**	A	D	0-0	
15	cl gd	**Sparta Prague**	A	D	0-0	
16	prem	**Arsenal**	H	W	2-0	van Nistelrooy 73 pen; Rooney 90
17	ccr3	**Crewe**	A	W	3-0	Smith 10; Miller 57; Foster 59 og
18	prem	**Portsmouth**	A	L	0-2	
19	cl gd	**Sparta Prague**	H	W	4-1	van Nistelrooy 14,25 pen,60,90
20	prem	**Man City**	H	D	0-0	
21	ccr4	**Crystal Palace**	H	W	2-0	Saha 22; Richardson 39
22	prem	**Newcastle**	A	W	3-1	Rooney 7,90; van Nistelrooy 74
23	prem	**Charlton**	H	W	2-0	Giggs 41; Scholes 50
24	cl gd	**Lyon**	H	W	2-1	Neville, G 19; van Nistelrooy 53
25	prem	**West Brom**	A	W	3-0	Scholes 53,82; van Nistelrooy 72
26	ccqf	**Arsenal**	H	W	1-0	Bellion 1
27	prem	**Southampton**	H	W	3-0	Scholes 53; Rooney 58; Ronaldo 87
28	cl gd	**Fenerbahce**	A	L	0-3	
29	prem	**Fulham**	A	D	1-1	Smith 33
30	prem	**Crystal Palace**	H	W	5-2	Scholes 22,49; Smith 35; Boyce 47 og; O'Shea 90
31	prem	**Bolton**	H	W	2-0	Giggs 10; Scholes 89
32	prem	**Aston Villa**	A	W	1-0	Giggs 41
33	prem	**Middlesbrough**	A	W	2-0	Fletcher 9; Giggs 79
34	prem	**Tottenham**	H	D	0-0	
35	facr3	**Exeter**	H	D	0-0	
36	ccsfl1	**Chelsea**	A	D	0-0	
37	prem	**Liverpool**	A	W	1-0	Rooney 21
38	facr3r	**Exeter**	A	W	2-0	Ronaldo 9; Rooney 87
39	prem	**Aston Villa**	H	W	3-1	Ronaldo 8; Saha 69; Scholes 70
40	ccsfl2	**Chelsea**	H	L	1-2	Giggs 67
41	facr4	**Middlesbrough**	H	W	3-0	O'Shea 10; Rooney 67,82
42	prem	**Arsenal**	A	W	4-2	Giggs 18; Ronaldo 54,58; O'Shea 89
43	prem	**Birmingham**	H	W	2-0	Keane 55; Rooney 78
44	prem	**Man City**	A	W	2-0	Rooney 68; Dunne 75 og
45	facr5	**Everton**	A	W	2-0	Fortune 23; Ronaldo 58
46	clr2l1	**AC Milan**	H	L	0-1	
47	prem	**Portsmouth**	H	W	2-1	Rooney 8,81
48	prem	**Crystal Palace**	A	D	0-0	
49	clr2l2	**AC Milan**	A	L	0-1	
50	facqf	**Southampton**	A	W	4-0	Keane 2; Ronaldo 45; Scholes 48,87
51	prem	**Fulham**	H	W	1-0	Ronaldo 21
52	prem	**Blackburn**	H	D	0-0	
53	prem	**Norwich**	A	L	0-2	
54	facsf	**Newcastle**	N	W	4-1	van Nistelrooy 19,58; Scholes 45; Ronaldo 76
55	prem	**Everton**	A	L	0-1	
56	prem	**Newcastle**	H	W	2-1	Rooney 57; Brown 74
57	prem	**Charlton**	A	W	4-0	Scholes 34; Fletcher 44; Smith 62; Rooney 67
58	prem	**West Brom**	H	D	1-1	Giggs 21
59	prem	**Chelsea**	H	L	1-3	van Nistelrooy 8
60	prem	**Southampton**	A	W	2-1	Fletcher 19; van Nistelrooy 63
61	facf	**Arsenal**	N	L	0-0*	(*aet, lost 5-4 on penalties)

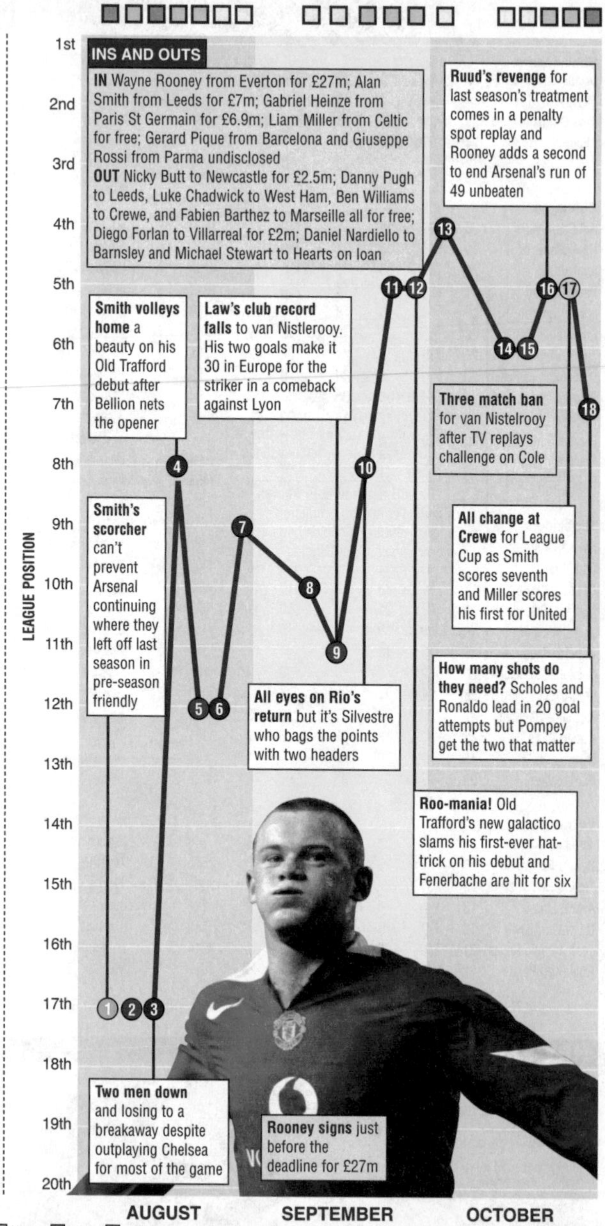

1st
2nd
3rd
4th
5th
6th
7th
8th
9th
10th
11th
12th
13th
14th
15th
16th
17th
18th
19th
20th
LEAGUE POSITION
INS AND OUTS
IN Wayne Rooney from Everton for £27m; Alan Smith from Leeds for £7m; Gabriel Heinze from Paris St Germain for £6.9m; Liam Miller from Celtic for free; Gerard Pique from Barcelona and Giuseppe Rossi from Parma undisclosed
OUT Nicky Butt to Newcastle for £2.5m; Danny Pugh to Leeds, Luke Chadwick to West Ham, Ben Williams to Crewe, and Fabien Barthez to Marseille all for free; Diego Forlan to Villarreal for £2m; Daniel Nardiello to Barnsley and Michael Stewart to Hearts on loan
Ruud's revenge for last season's treatment comes in a penalty spot replay and Rooney adds a second to end Arsenal's run of 49 unbeaten
Smith volleys home a beauty on his Old Trafford debut after Bellion nets the opener
Law's club record falls to van Nistlerooy. His two goals make it 30 in Europe for the striker in a comeback against Lyon
Three match ban for van Nistelrooy after TV replays challenge on Cole
All change at Crewe for League Cup as Smith scores seventh and Miller scores his first for United
Smith's scorcher can't prevent Arsenal continuing where they left off last season in pre-season friendly
All eyes on Rio's return but it's Silvestre who bags the points with two headers
How many shots do they need? Scholes and Ronaldo lead in 20 goal attempts but Pompey get the two that matter
Roo-mania! Old Trafford's new galactico slams his first-ever hat-trick on his debut and Fenerbache are hit for six
Two men down and losing to a breakaway despite outplaying Chelsea for most of the game
Rooney signs just before the deadline for £27m
AUGUST
SEPTEMBER
OCTOBER

Home Away Neutral

ATTENDANCES

HOME GROUND: OLD TRAFFORD CAPACITY: 68190 AVERAGE LEAGUE AT HOME: 67870

49	AC Milan	79000	59	Chelsea	67832	2	Din Bucharest	58000	50	Southampton	30971
61	Arsenal	71876	58	West Brom	67827	22	Newcastle	52320	14	Birmingham	29221
54	Newcastle	69280	30	Crystal Palace	67814	21	Crystal Palace	48891	8	Bolton	27766
47	Portsmouth	67989	4	Norwich	67812	44	Man City	47111	25	West Brom	27709
13	Middlesbroro	67988	7	Everton	67803	37	Liverpool	44183	57	Charlton	26789
34	Tottenham	67962	23	Charlton	67704	32	Aston Villa	42593	6	Blackburn	26155
51	Fulham	67959	35	Exeter	67551	3	Chelsea	41813	48	Crystal Palace	26021
52	Blackburn	67939	41	Middlesboro	67251	36	Chelsea	41492	53	Norwich	25522
27	Southampton	67921	46	AC Milan	67162	45	Everton	38664	29	Fulham	21940
31	Bolton	67867	12	Fenerbahce	67128	42	Arsenal	38164	15	Sp Prague	21507
20	Man City	67863	26	Arsenal	67103	55	Everton	37160	18	Portsmouth	20190
16	Arsenal	67862	40	Chelsea	67000	11	Tottenham	36103	17	Crewe	10103
39	Aston Villa	67859	19	Sp Prague	66706	9	Lyon	35000	38	Exeter	9033
10	Liverpool	67857	24	Lyon	66398	28	Fenerbahce	35000			
56	Newcastle	67845	1	Arsenal	63317	33	Middlesboro	34199			
43	Birmingham	67838	5	Din Bucharest	61041	60	Southampton	32066			

No finish: Cup travesty sums up season

Final Position: 3rd

KEY: League, Champions Lge, UEFA Cup, FA Cup, League Cup, Other

Clinical! Van Nistelrooy hits all four against Prague for club record 35 goals in 36 European matches

Three directors voted off by Glazer's shares

19 20 21 22

Saha's skill is rewarded by first goal since April to set up a quarter-final tie with Arsenal

23

The 'Old Firm' return to form as first Giggs then super Scholes strike to subdue Charlton

24

One thousand up for Fergie and Neville celebrates with a rare goal while van Nistelrooy scores to inflict first defeat this season for Lyon

25

"He will reach double figures now" Ferguson's prediction looks good as Scholes bags a brace against the Baggies

26 27 28 29 30

Second string second best as Ferguson uses final group game as a learning ground

Scholes makes it six from five as Palace defence is shattered despite Rooney's penalty miss

31

Giggs acrobatics gains first goal and Scholes weighs in with yet another but Rooney's raised hand writes headlines

32 33 34 35 36

Carroll lets it off his chest and a metre over the line but ref waves play on so it's goalless against Spurs

Reserves look also-rans against non-league Exeter who subject Fergie to an unwanted replay

37

Third consecutive win at Anfield despite Brown's red card as Dudek fails to hold Rooney's drive

38 39 40

"Two of my best goals" Rooney sums up the glorious chip and stunning volley that knock-out Boro

41

Game-of-the-season candidate as Ronaldo hits two and Arsenal are out-gunned despite Silvestre's red card in Gunners' first home defeat for nearly two years

42 43

Keane's 50th goal comes at last in his 460th appearance as Ronaldo presents chance with a back-heel on his 20th birthday

44 45 46

Chelsea reject does the damage for AC after Carroll spills a shot and Crespo pounces for away win

47

Van's back from injury, and Howard from bench exile but Rooney's the difference with two goals

Done to a Crespo as Milan striker repeats the score-line from Old Trafford with another goal in the second leg

48 49

Scholes sinks Saints without trace after Keane and Ronaldo put them two-down at the break

50 51

Ronaldo special gains win but 23 shots don't add to early lead and Fulham hit the woodwork at the end

Red mist descends on Gary Neville - off for kicking ball into the crowd – and Scholes as Everton gain first win for ten years

52 53

Rooney posts a warning, and Keane posts another but this time Blackburn survive 23 shot barrage

Van Nistelrooy's savours cup as his first goals since November sink Newcastle

54 55 56

Goal of the season!? Rooney's sensational curving volley rockets into the net and Brown's winner is his first Premier goal

Rooney award as PFA's Young Player of the year

57 58

Guard of honour for Chelsea who go on to beat United's Premiership points record

Twelve corners, 27 shots but only one goal leaves Ferguson embarrassed and Baggies get a point

59

Van Nistelrooy extends his record against Saints to seven goals in nine games to send them down

Glazer succeeds in share bid

60 61

Rooney and Ronaldo reign as Arsenal barely get a kick at Cardiff yet still end up with the Cup

INS AND OUTS

OUT Eric Djemba-Djemba to Aston Villa for £1.85m; Bojan Djorjic to Rangers for free; Chris Eagles to Watford on loan; Kieran Richardson to West Brom on loan

MONTH BY MONTH POINTS TALLY

Month	Points	%
AUGUST	5	42%
SEPTEMBER	7	78%
OCTOBER	5	42%
NOVEMBER	10	83%
DECEMBER	13	87%
JANUARY	10	83%
FEBRUARY	12	100%
MARCH	4	67%
APRIL	4	33%
MAY	7	58%

Average League position over the season: 4.7

NOVEMBER DECEMBER JANUARY FEBRUARY MARCH APRIL MAY

GOAL ATTEMPTS

FOR Goal attempts recorded in League games

	HOME	AWAY	TOTAL	AVE
shots on target	191	140	331	8.7
shots off target	162	118	280	7.4
TOTAL	**353**	**258**	**611**	**16.1**

Ratio of goals to shots Average number of shots on target per League goal scored: **5.7**

Accuracy rating Average percentage of total goal attempts which were on target: **54.2**

AGAINST Goal attempts recorded in League games

	HOME	AWAY	TOTAL	AVE
shots on target	66	85	151	4
shots off target	75	140	215	5.7
TOTAL	**141**	**225**	**366**	**9.6**

Ratio of goals to shots Average number of shots on target per League goal scored: **5.8**

Accuracy rating Average percentage of total goal attempts which were on target: **41.3**

GOALS

Wayne Rooney

League	11
FA Cup	3
League Cup	0
Europe	3
Other	0
TOTAL	17

League Average 198 mins between goals

	PLAYER	LGE	FAC	LC	Euro	TOT	AVE
1	Rooney	11	3	0	3	17	198
2	van Nistelrooy	6	2	0	8	16	227
3	Scholes	9	3	0	0	12	290
4	Smith	7	0	1	2	11	292
5	Giggs	6	0	1	2	9	387
6	Ronaldo	5	4	0	0	9	484
7	Bellion	1	0	1	2	4	215
8	Fletcher	3	0	0	0	3	457
9	O'Shea	2	1	0	0	3	745
10	Silvestre	2	0	0	0	2	1475
11	Saha	1	0	1	0	2	672
12	Keane	1	1	0	0	2	2610
13	Heinze	1	0	0	0	1	2286
14	Brown	1	0	0	0	1	1642
15	Richardson	0	0	1	0	1	
	Other	2	1	2	2	7	
	TOTAL	**58**	**15**	**7**	**19**	**100**	

SQUAD APPEARANCES

Match	1 2 3 4 5	6 7 8 9 10	11 12 13 14 15	16 17 18 19 20	21 22 23 24 25	26 27 28 29 30	31 32 33 34 35	36 37 38 39 40	41 42 43 44 45	46 47 48 49 50	51 52 53 54 55	56 57 58 59 60	61
Venue	N A A H H	A H A A H	A H H A A	H A A H H	H A H H A	H H A A H	H A A H H	A A A H H	H A H A A	H H A A A	H H A N A	H A H H A	N
Competition	O C L L C	L L L C L	L C L L C	L W L C L	W L L C L	W L C L L	L L L L F	W L F L W	F L L L F	C L L C F	L L L F L	L L L L L	F
Result	L W L W W	D D D D W	W W D D D	W W L W D	W W W W W	W W L D W	W W W D D	D W W W L	W W W W W	L W D L W	W D L W L	W W D L W	L

Goalkeepers
Roy Carroll
Tim Howard
Lopez Ricardo

Defenders
Wes Brown
Rio Ferdinand
Gabriel Ivan Heinze
Paul McShane
Gary Neville
Gabriel Ngalula Mbuyi
John O'Shea
Gerard Pique
Mikael Silvestre
Jonathan Spector

Midfielders
Eric Djemba-Djemba
Chris Eagles
Darren Fletcher
Quinton Fortune
Ryan Giggs
David Jones
Roy Keane
Kleberson
Liam Miller
Phil Neville
Keiron Richardson
Christiano Ronaldo
Paul Scholes

Forwards
David Bellion
Sylvain Ebanks-Blake
Diego Forlan
Wayne Rooney
Giuseppe Rossi
Louis Saha
Alan Smith
Ruud van Nistelrooy

KEY: On all match; On bench; Subbed or sent off (Counting game); Subbed or sent off (playing less than 70 mins); Subbed on from bench (Counting Game); Subbed on (playing less than 70 mins); Subbed on and then subbed or sent off (Counting Game); Subbed on and then subbed or sent off (playing less than 70 mins); Not in 16

KEY PLAYERS - GOALSCORERS

Wayne Rooney

Goals in the League	11
Goals in all competitions	17
Assists League goals scored by a team mate where the player delivered the final pass	5
Contribution to Attacking Power Average number of minutes between League team goals while on pitch	47
Player Strike Rate Average number of minutes between League goals scored by player	198
Club Strike Rate Average minutes between League goals scored by club	59

	PLAYER	GOALS LGE	GOALS ALL	ASSISTS	POWER	S RATE
1	Wayne Rooney	11	17	5	47	198 mins
2	Ruud van Nistelrooy	6	16	1	71	227 mins
3	Paul Scholes	9	12	4	56	290 mins
4	Alan Smith	7	11	5	61	292 mins
5	Ryan Giggs	6	9	9	48	387 mins

KEY PLAYERS - MIDFIELDERS

Ryan Giggs

Goals in the League	6
Goals in all competitions	9
Assists League goals scored by a team mate where the player delivered the final pass	9
Defensive Rating Average number of mins between League goals conceded while on the pitch	137
Contribution to Attacking Power Average number of minutes between League team goals while on pitch	48
Scoring Difference Defensive Rating minus Contribution to Attacking Power	89

	PLAYER	GOALS LGE	GOALS ALL	ASSISTS	DEF RATE	POWER	SC DIFF
1	Ryan Giggs	6	9	9	137	48	89 mins
2	Darren Fletcher	3	3	2	137	49	88 mins
3	Roy Keane	1	2	2	137	54	83 mins
4	Paul Scholes	9	12	4	118	57	61 mins
5	Christiano Ronaldo	5	9	4	127	69	58 mins

PLAYER APPEARANCES

	AGE (on 01/07/05)	IN NAMED 16	APPEARANCES	COUNTING GAMES	MINUTES ON PITCH	APPEARANCES	MINUTES ON PITCH	THIS SEASON	HOME COUNTRY
Goalkeepers									
Roy Carroll	27	36	26	26	2340	34	3090	8	N Ireland (114)
Tim Howard	26	31	12	12	1080	27	2430	-	United States
Lopez Ricardo	33	9	0	0	0	0	0	-	Spain
Defenders									
Wes Brown	25	26	21	17	1642	37	3033	1	England (6)
Rio Ferdinand	26	31	31	31	2790	42	3810	5	England (6)
Gabriel Ivan Heinze	27	26	26	25	2286	39	3403	8	Argentina (3)
Paul McShane	19	0	0	0	0	0	0	-	Rep of Ireland
Gary Neville	30	24	22	21	1888	35	2966	9	England (6)
Gabriel Mbuyi	23	0	0	0	0	0	0	-	Belgium
John O'Shea	24	30	23	13	1490	37	2636	8	Rep of Ireland (15)
Gerard Pique	18	0	0	0	0	3	142	-	Spain
Mikael Silvestre	27	35	35	32	2949	50	4093	2	France (4)
Jonathan Spector	19	5	3	2	171	8	394	-	United States
Midfielders									
Eric Djemba-Djemba	24	8	5	3	281	17	1320	4	Cameroon (26)
Chris Eagles	19	1	0	0	0	7	287	-	England
Darren Fletcher	21	21	18	13	1370	30	2087	4	Scotland (85)
Quinton Fortune	28	22	17	9	1042	33	2208	-	South Africa
Ryan Giggs	31	32	32	24	2321	44	3075	3	Wales (74)
David Jones	20	0	0	0	0	2	102	-	England
Roy Keane	33	32	31	28	2610	43	3648	6	Rep of Ireland (15)
Kleberson	26	12	8	0	413	14	861	4	Brazil (1)
Liam Miller	24	15	8	2	268	19	894	6	Rep of Ireland (15)
Phil Neville	28	30	19	9	1072	34	1959	1	England (6)
Keiron Richardson	20	2	2	0	24	9	484	-	England
Christiano Ronaldo	20	35	33	24	2422	50	3708	8	Portugal (9)
Paul Scholes	30	33	33	27	2606	49	3900	-	England
Forwards									
David Bellion	22	16	10	1	215	18	847	-	France
Sylvain Ebanks-Blake	19	0	0	0	0	1	6	-	England
Diego Forlan	26	1	1	0	18	3	60	4	Uruguay (16)
Wayne Rooney	19	29	29	22	2181	43	3388	6	England (6)
Giuseppe Rossi	18	0	0	0	0	2	17	-	Italy
Louis Saha	26	16	14	5	672	22	1102	3	France (4)
Alan Smith	24	33	31	19	2042	42	2516	6	England (6)
Ruud van Nistelrooy	29	17	17	15	1362	27	2189	4	Holland (5)

KEY: LEAGUE ALL COMPS CAPS (MAY FIFA RANKING)

TEAM OF THE SEASON

CARROLL
CG 26 DR 146
BROWN
CG 17 DR 137
FERDINAND
CG 31 DR 140
O'SHEA
CG 13 DR 166
HEINZE
CG 25 DR 143
RONALDO
CG 24 SD +58
FLETCHER
CG 13 SD +88
KEANE
CG 28 SD +83
GIGGS
CG 24 SD +89
SCHOLES
CG 27 AP 56
ROONEY
CG 22 SR 198

KEY: DR = Defensive Rating, SD = Scoring Difference AP = Attacking Power SR = Strike Rate, CG=Counting games – League games playing at least 70 minutes

TOP POINT EARNERS

Darren Fletcher

Counting Games League games when player was on pitch for at least 70 minutes	13
Average points Average League points taken in Counting games	2.38
Club Average points Average points taken in League games	2.03

	PLAYER	GAMES	PTS
1	Darren Fletcher	13	2.38
2	Wayne Rooney	22	2.32
3	Roy Carroll	26	2.31
4	Ryan Giggs	24	2.25
5	Wes Brown	17	2.18
6	Gabriel Ivan Heinze	25	2.16
7	John O'Shea	13	2.15
8	Roy Keane	28	2.11
9	Rio Ferdinand	31	2.10
10	Ruud van Nistelrooy	15	2.07

KEY PLAYERS - DEFENDERS

John O'Shea

Goals Conceded in the League Number of League goals conceded while the player was on the pitch	9
Goals Conceded in all competitions Total number of goals conceded while the player was on the pitch	18
League minutes played Number of minutes played in league matches	1490
Clean Sheets In games when player was on pitch for at least 70 minutes	6
Defensive Rating Average number of mins between League goals conceded while on the pitch	166
Club Defensive Rating Average number of mins between League goals conceded by the club this season	132

	PLAYER	CON LGE	CON ALL	MINS	C SHEETS	DEF RATE
1	John O'Shea	9	18	1490	6	166 mins
2	Gabriel Ivan Heinze	16	27	2286	14	143 mins
3	Rio Ferdinand	20	29	2790	17	140 mins
4	Wes Brown	12	20	1642	9	137 mins
5	Mikael Silvestre	23	35	2949	16	128 mins

KEY GOALKEEPER

Roy Carroll

Goals Conceded in the League Number of League goals conceded while the player was on the pitch	16
Goals Conceded in all competitions Total number of goals conceded while the player was on the pitch	21
League minutes played Number of minutes played in league matches	2340
Clean Sheets In games when player was on pitch for at least 70 minutes	15
Goals to Shots Ratio The average number of shots on target per each League goal conceded	6.5
Defensive Rating Ave mins between League goals conceded while on the pitch	146

BOOKINGS

Roy Keane

League Yellow	9
League Red	0
All competitions Yellow	12
All competitions Red	0

League Average 290 mins between cards

	PLAYER	LEAGUE		TOTAL		AVE
1	Keane	9 Y	0 R	12 Y	0 R	290
2	Rooney	7	0	7	0	311
3	Neville, P	3	0	4	0	357
4	Smith	4	1	6	1	408
5	Brown	3	1	5	1	410
6	Scholes	5	1	8	1	434
7	Heinze	4	0	9	0	571
8	Neville, G	2	1	3	1	629
9	Giggs	3	0	3	0	773
10	Ronaldo	3	0	5	0	807
11	Ferdinand	3	0	3	0	930
12	Silvestre	2	1	4	1	983
13	Fortune	1	0	3	0	1042
14	van Nistelrooy	1	0	1	0	1362
15	O'Shea	1	0	1	0	1490
	Other	0	0	0	0	
	TOTAL	51	5	74	5	

EVERTON

Tim Cahill's goals were crucial in gaining the fourth Champions League spot and made him Everton's best Goalscorer with a Strike Rate of a goal every 245 minutes on average – the fourth highest midfielder in the Premiership. He also earned 11 cards including one red for celebrating a goal by removing his shirt.

Nigel Martyn saw nearly 60% of the opponent's shots arrive on target and saved eight on average for every goal he conceded - the second best record in the Premiership.

Alan Stubbs was Everton's meanest defender by a long way and gets into our Premiership Team of the Season. His Defensive Rating was a league goal conceded on average for every 102 minutes played. The next best averaged 78 minutes. **Thomas Gravesen** was the fifth most-missed player in the Premiership. The team averaged 1.95 points in the 20 games he played and 1.22 without him

NICKNAME: THE TOFFEES KEY: Won Drawn Lost

1	prem	**Arsenal**	H	L	1-4	Carsley 64
2	prem	**Crystal Palace**	A	W	3-1	Gravesen 19 pen,62; Bent, M 82
3	prem	**West Brom**	H	W	2-1	Osman 2,70
4	prem	**Man Utd**	A	D	0-0	
5	prem	**Man City**	A	W	1-0	Cahill 60
6	prem	**Middlesbrough**	H	W	1-0	Bent, M 47
7	ccr2	**Bristol City**	A	W	4-3*	Ferguson 30 pen; Chadwick 45 (*on penalties)
8	prem	**Portsmouth**	A	W	1-0	Cahill 80
9	prem	**Tottenham**	H	L	0-1	
10	prem	**Southampton**	H	W	1-0	Osman 88
11	prem	**Norwich**	A	W	3-2	Kilbane 10; Bent 40; Ferguson 73
12	ccr3	**Preston**	H	W	2-0	Carsley 52; Bent 90
13	prem	**Aston Villa**	H	D	1-1	Bent 33
14	prem	**Chelsea**	A	L	0-1	
15	ccr4	**Arsenal**	A	L	1-3	Gravesen 7
16	prem	**Birmingham**	A	W	1-0	Gravesen 69 pen
17	prem	**Fulham**	H	W	1-0	Ferguson 67
18	prem	**Newcastle**	A	D	1-1	Carsley 56
19	prem	**Bolton**	H	W	3-2	Ferguson 45; Gravesen 75; Jaidi 85 og
20	prem	**Liverpool**	H	W	1-0	Carsley 68
21	prem	**Blackburn**	A	D	0-0	
22	prem	**Man City**	H	W	2-1	Cahill 22; Bent 63
23	prem	**Charlton**	A	L	0-2	
24	prem	**Tottenham**	A	L	2-5	Cahill 40; McFadden 87
25	prem	**Portsmouth**	H	W	2-1	Stubbs 29; Osman 90
26	facr3	**Plymouth**	A	W	3-1	Osman 16; McFadden 18; Chadwick 84
27	prem	**Middlesbrough**	A	D	1-1	Cahill 76
28	prem	**Charlton**	H	L	0-1	
29	facr4	**Sunderland**	H	W	3-0	McFadden 9; Beattie 27; Cahill 80
30	prem	**Norwich**	H	W	1-0	Doherty 78 og
31	prem	**Southampton**	A	D	2-2	Beattie 4; Bent 90
32	prem	**Chelsea**	H	L	0-1	
33	facr5	**Man Utd**	H	L	0-2	
34	prem	**Aston Villa**	A	W	3-1	Osman 17,67; Cahill 48
35	prem	**Blackburn**	H	L	0-1	
36	prem	**Liverpool**	A	L	1-2	Cahill 82
37	prem	**West Brom**	A	L	0-1	
38	prem	**Crystal Palace**	H	W	4-0	Arteta 7; Cahill 48,54; Vaughan 87
39	prem	**Man Utd**	H	W	1-0	Ferguson 55
40	prem	**Birmingham**	H	D	1-1	Ferguson 86
41	prem	**Fulham**	A	L	0-2	
42	prem	**Newcastle**	H	W	2-0	Weir 43; Cahill 59
43	prem	**Arsenal**	A	L	0-7	
44	prem	**Bolton**	A	L	2-3	Cahill 9; Carsley 63

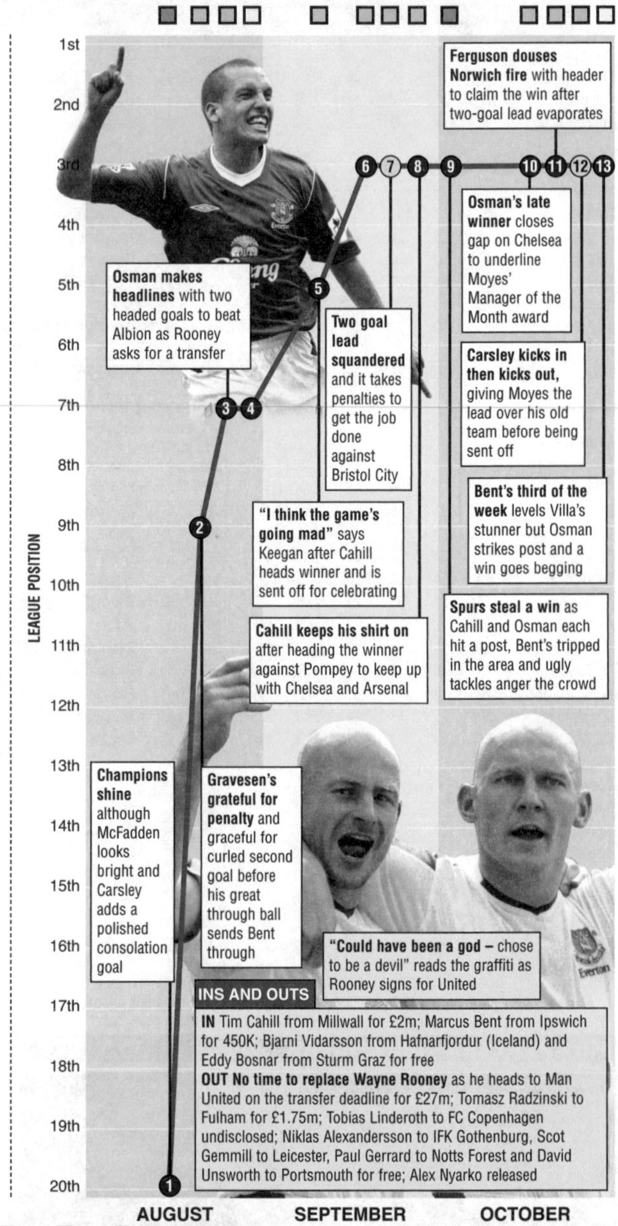
1st
2nd
3rd
4th
5th
6th
7th
8th
9th
10th
11th
12th
13th
14th
15th
16th
17th
18th
19th
20th
LEAGUE POSITION
Ferguson douses Norwich fire with header to claim the win after two-goal lead evaporates
Osman's late winner closes gap on Chelsea to underline Moyes' Manager of the Month award
Osman makes headlines with two headed goals to beat Albion as Rooney asks for a transfer
Two goal lead squandered and it takes penalties to get the job done against Bristol City
Carsley kicks in then kicks out, giving Moyes the lead over his old team before being sent off
Bent's third of the week levels Villa's stunner but Osman strikes post and a win goes begging
"I think the game's going mad" says Keegan after Cahill heads winner and is sent off for celebrating
Spurs steal a win as Cahill and Osman each hit a post, Bent's tripped in the area and ugly tackles anger the crowd
Cahill keeps his shirt on after heading the winner against Pompey to keep up with Chelsea and Arsenal
Champions shine although McFadden looks bright and Carsley adds a polished consolation goal
Gravesen's grateful for penalty and graceful for curled second goal before his great through ball sends Bent through
"Could have been a god – chose to be a devil" reads the graffiti as Rooney signs for United
INS AND OUTS
IN Tim Cahill from Millwall for £2m; Marcus Bent from Ipswich for 450K; Bjarni Vidarsson from Hafnarfjordur (Iceland) and Eddy Bosnar from Sturm Graz for free
OUT No time to replace Wayne Rooney as he heads to Man United on the transfer deadline for £27m; Tomasz Radzinski to Fulham for £1.75m; Tobias Linderoth to FC Copenhagen undisclosed; Niklas Alexandersson to IFK Gothenburg, Scot Gemmill to Leicester, Paul Gerrard to Notts Forest and David Unsworth to Portsmouth for free; Alex Nyarko released
AUGUST
SEPTEMBER
OCTOBER

Home Away Neutral

ATTENDANCES

HOME GROUND: GOODISON PARK **CAPACITY:** 40569 **AVERAGE LEAGUE AT HOME:** 36834

4	Man Utd	67803	9	Tottenham	38264	25	Portsmouth	35480	15	Arsenal	27791
18	Newcastle	51247	43	Arsenal	38073	10	Southampton	35256	44	Bolton	27701
5	Man City	47006	13	Aston Villa	37816	17	Fulham	34763	23	Charlton	27001
36	Liverpool	44224	30	Norwich	37485	3	West Brom	34510	37	West Brom	26805
14	Chelsea	41965	39	Man Utd	37160	6	Middlesboro	34078	21	Blackburn	25191
20	Liverpool	40552	40	Birmingham	36828	12	Preston	33922	11	Norwich	23871
22	Man City	40530	38	Crystal Palace	36519	29	Sunderland	33186	2	Crystal Palace	23666
42	Newcastle	40438	24	Tottenham	36102	35	Blackburn	32406	41	Fulham	21881
32	Chelsea	40270	28	Charlton	36041	27	Middlesboro	31794	8	Portsmouth	20125
34	Aston Villa	40248	19	Bolton	35929	31	Southampton	31509	26	Plymouth	20112
33	Man Utd	38664	1	Arsenal	35521	16	Birmingham	28388	7	Bristol City	15264

No Rooney! No Gravesen! No problem!

Final Position: **4th**

KEY: ● League ● Champions Lge ● UEFA Cup ● FA Cup ○ League Cup ○ Other

Story of two goal-line clearances as Izzet handballs for penalty while Hibbert heads clear

Chances at Chelsea as Cahill goes close and Stubbs heads wide in a narrow defeat at Stamford Bridge

Arsenal youngsters fight-back to give a lesson in exuberance at Highbury

Closing the gap as Ferguson comes on to breach Fulham defence and both leaders slip up

Carsley bends it in but Bent can't do likewise with open-goal chance to claim all three points at St James'

Up to second as Carsley secures first win over old rivals for ten games - does it get any better than this?

'Big Duncan' is back in the team and in the goals with a trademark header as fighting spirit gains win over Bolton

Bent heads in his first since October for the winner but suffers a bad tackle from Man City sub

'Big Duncan' is off for elbow and Martyn off injured so Charlton take advantage

Stubbs' first since 2002 and Osman's last kick of the game gains a victory half a minute beyond stoppage time

Destroyed by Spurs without Stubbs or Martyn the defence collapses and Cahill and McFadden goals are poor consolation

Rooney's return spoilt by coin-throwing and United's imperious form although Bent misses chance to upset the holders

Beattie's first and McFadden's third in six, show gulf in class over Premier hopefuls Sunderland

Beattie's mad charge ends in red card after just eight minutes against the league leaders who eventually make the pressure tell

Bent devastates Saints with a stunning last-second finish to claim a draw after Beattie volleys home early goal

Arteta injury disrupts formation but Blackburn have more fight and snatch points on the break

Cahill carves Villa apart and Osman hits two in record 180th meeting between two top-flight clubs

Martyn smarting after misjudgement of speculator for Liverpool's second and Cahill cracker too late to gain a point against ten men

Gap down to one point ahead of Liverpool as West Brom continue their escape act

Vaughan snatches Rooney's crown as youngest Everton and youngest Premier scorer at 16 years 269 days

Ten years on Ferguson falls to 'Big Dunc' again as Scot's diving header clinches first win for a decade over Man United

Ferguson embraces supporters after clinching a late point against Birmingham after Beattie fails in first start since February

Buried by Bergkamp – a dismal Highbury record of ten straight defeats continues with this 7-0 rout

Acrobatic Cahill catches Bolton out with an overhead kick and catches a slap from N'Gotty before the Lancastrians win a best-of-five thriller

Weir douses Newcastle's fire with first goal of the season and Cahill adds a second - his 11th of the season

Champions League spot confirmed as Liverpool go down at Highbury

Real deal too big a lure for Gravesen

INS AND OUTS

Beattie plumps for Everton

IN James Beattie from Southampton for £6m; Mikel Arteta from Real Sociedad on loan; Guillaume Plessis from Lens for free

OUT Thomas Gravesen to Real Madrid for £2.5m; Kevin Campbell to West Brom for free

Average League position over the season: 4.3

MONTH BY MONTH POINTS TALLY

Month	Points	%
AUGUST	7	58%
SEPTEMBER	9	100%
OCTOBER	7	58%
NOVEMBER	7	58%
DECEMBER	10	67%
JANUARY	4	33%
FEBRUARY	7	58%
MARCH	0	0%
APRIL	7	47%
MAY	3	33%

NOVEMBER DECEMBER JANUARY FEBRUARY MARCH APRIL MAY

GOAL ATTEMPTS

FOR Goal attempts recorded in League games

	HOME	AWAY	TOTAL	AVE
shots on target	104	81	185	4.9
shots off target	116	82	198	5.2
TOTAL	220	163	383	10.1

Ratio of goals to shots — Average number of shots on target per League goal scored: 4.1

Accuracy rating — Average percentage of total goal attempts which were on target: 48.3

AGAINST Goal attempts recorded in League games

	HOME	AWAY	TOTAL	AVE
shots on target	120	142	262	6.9
shots off target	100	81	181	4.8
TOTAL	220	223	443	11.7

Ratio of goals to shots — Average number of shots on target per League goal scored: 5.7

Accuracy rating — Average percentage of total goal attempts which were on target: 59.1

GOALS

Tim Cahill

League	11
FA Cup	1
League Cup	0
Europe	0
Other	0
TOTAL	12

League Average 245 mins between goals

	PLAYER	LGE	FAC	LC	Euro	TOT	AVE
1	Cahill	11	1	0	0	12	245
2	Bent	6	0	1	0	7	443
3	Osman	6	1	0	0	7	360
4	Ferguson	5	0	1	0	6	244
5	Carsley	4	0	1	0	5	757
6	Gravesen	4	0	1	0	5	453
7	McFadden	1	2	0	0	3	768
8	Beattie	1	1	0	0	2	567
14	Chadwick	0	1	1	0	2	0
9	Arteta	1	0	0	0	1	808
10	Weir	1	0	0	0	1	3033
11	Stubbs	1	0	0	0	1	2439
12	Vaughan	1	0	0	0	1	28
13	Kilbane	1	0	0	0	1	3215
	Other	2	0	0	0	2	
	TOTAL	45	6	5	0	56	

SQUAD APPEARANCES

Match	1	2	3	4	5	6	7	8	9	10	11	12	13	14	15	16	17	18	19	20	21	22
Venue	H	A	H	A	A	H	A	A	H	H	A	H	H	A	A	A	H	A	H	H	A	H
Competition	L	L	L	L	L	L	W	L	L	L	L	W	L	L	W	L	L	L	L	L	L	L
Result	L	W	W	D	W	W	W	W	L	W	W	W	D	L	L	W	W	D	W	W	D	W

Match	23	24	25	26	27	28	29	30	31	32	33	34	35	36	37	38	39	40	41	42	43	44
Venue	A	A	H	A	A	H	H	H	A	H	H	A	H	A	A	H	H	H	A	H	A	A
Competition	L	L	L	F	L	L	F	L	L	L	F	L	L	L	L	L	L	L	L	L	L	L
Result	L	L	W	W	D	L	W	W	D	L	L	W	L	L	L	W	W	D	L	W	L	L

Goalkeepers
- Nigel Martyn
- Iain Turner
- Richard Wright

Defenders
- Daniel Fox
- Anthony Gerrard
- Tony Hibbert
- Gary Naysmith
- Alessandro Pistone
- Alan Stubbs
- David Weir
- Joseph Yobo

Midfielders
- Mikel Arteta
- Tim Cahill
- Lee Carsley
- Thomas Gravesen
- Kevin Kilbane
- Leon Osman
- Guillaume Plessis
- Steve Watson

Forwards
- James Beattie
- Marcus Bent
- Kevin Campbell
- Nick Chadwick
- Duncan Ferguson
- James McFadden
- James Vaughan

KEY: On all match | On bench | Subbed or sent off (Counting game) | Subbed or sent off (playing less than 70 mins) | Subbed on from bench (Counting Game) | Subbed on (playing less than 70 mins) | Subbed on and then subbed or sent off (Counting Game) | Subbed on and then subbed or sent off (playing less than 70 mins) | Not in 16

KEY PLAYERS - GOALSCORERS

Tim Cahill	
Goals in the League	11
Goals in all competitions	12
Assists League goals scored by a team mate where the player delivered the final pass	5
Contribution to Attacking Power Average number of minutes between League team goals while on pitch	81
Player Strike Rate Average number of minutes between League goals scored by player	245
Club Strike Rate Average minutes between League goals scored by club	76

	PLAYER	GOALS LGE	GOALS ALL	ASSISTS	POWER	S RATE
1	Tim Cahill	11	12	5	82	245 mins
2	Leon Osman	6	7	2	77	360 mins
3	Marcus Bent	6	7	3	69	443 mins
4	Thomas Gravesen	4	5	6	67	453 mins
5	Lee Carsley	4	5	2	78	757 mins

KEY PLAYERS - MIDFIELDERS

Leon Osman	
Goals in the League	6
Goals in all competitions	7
Assists League goals scored by a team mate where the player delivered the final pass	2
Defensive Rating Average number of mins between League goals conceded while on the pitch	90
Contribution to Attacking Power Average number of minutes between League team goals while on pitch	77
Scoring Difference Defensive Rating minus Contribution to Attacking Power	13

	PLAYER	GOALS LGE	GOALS ALL	ASSISTS	DEF RATE	POWER	SC DIFF
1	Leon Osman	6	7	2	90	77	13 mins
2	Thomas Gravesen	4	5	6	79	67	12 mins
3	Tim Cahill	11	12	5	93	82	11 mins
4	Lee Carsley	4	5	2	70	78	-8 mins
5	Kevin Kilbane	1	1	3	73	82	-9 mins

PLAYER APPEARANCES

	AGE (on 01/07/05)	IN NAMED 16	APPEARANCES	COUNTING GAMES	MINUTES ON PITCH	APPEARANCES	MINUTES ON PITCH	THIS SEASON	HOME COUNTRY
Goalkeepers									
Nigel Martyn	38	33	32	31	2834	33	2924	-	England
Iain Turner	21	5	0	0	0	0	0	-	Scotland
Richard Wright	27	38	7	6	586	12	1066	-	England
Defenders									
Daniel Fox	19	1	0	0	0	0	0	-	England
Anthony Gerrard	19	1	0	0	0	0	0	-	England
Tony Hibbert	24	36	36	35	3184	40	3574	-	England
Gary Naysmith	26	18	11	5	466	15	804	5	Scotland (85)
Alessandro Pistone	29	36	33	30	2737	39	3160	-	Italy
Alan Stubbs	33	33	31	25	2439	36	2893	-	England
David Weir	35	36	34	33	3033	37	3172	1	Scotland (85)
Joseph Yobo	24	33	27	18	1772	33	2342	-	Nigeria
Midfielders									
Mikel Arteta	23	12	12	8	808	13	887	-	Spain
Tim Cahill	25	33	33	27	2698	38	3019	-	Australia
Lee Carsley	31	36	36	32	3029	41	3491	-	Rep of Ireland
Thomas Gravesen	29	21	21	20	1811	23	1913	7	Denmark (19)
Kevin Kilbane	28	38	38	34	3215	43	3651	9	Rep of Ireland (15)
Leon Osman	24	29	29	21	2158	35	2579	-	England
Guillaume Plessis	20	6	0	0	0	0	0	-	France
Steve Watson	31	28	25	10	1192	28	1472	-	England
Forwards									
James Beattie	27	11	11	4	567	13	713	-	England
Marcus Bent	27	37	37	26	2659	42	2858	-	England
Kevin Campbell	35	10	6	2	307	7	348	-	England
Nick Chadwick	22	4	1	0	1	5	181	-	England
Duncan Ferguson	33	35	35	5	1220	37	1387	-	Scotland
James McFadden	22	34	23	6	768	29	1302	4	Scotland (85)
James Vaughan	16	4	2	0	28	2	28	-	England

KEY: LEAGUE ALL COMPS CAPS (MAY FIFA RANKING)

TEAM OF THE SEASON

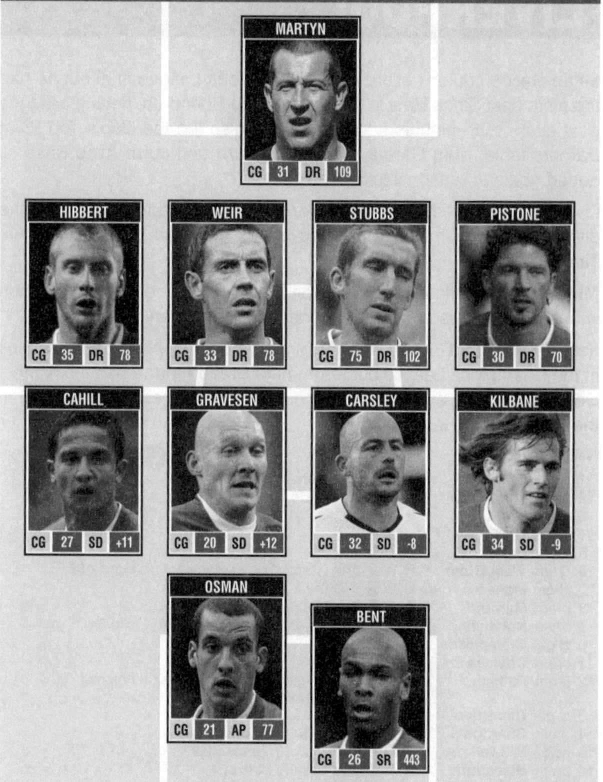

MARTYN
CG 31 DR 109
HIBBERT
CG 35 DR 78
WEIR
CG 33 DR 78
STUBBS
CG 75 DR 102
PISTONE
CG 30 DR 70
CAHILL
CG 27 SD +11
GRAVESEN
CG 20 SD +12
CARSLEY
CG 32 SD -8
KILBANE
CG 34 SD -9
OSMAN
CG 21 AP 77
BENT
CG 26 SR 443

KEY: DR = Defensive Rating, SD = Scoring Difference AP = Attacking Power SR = Strike Rate, CG=Counting games – League games playing at least 70 minutes

TOP POINT EARNERS

Thomas Gravesen

Counting Games League games when player was on pitch for at least 70 minutes	20
Average points Average League points taken in Counting games	1.95
Club Average points Average points taken in League games	1.61

	PLAYER	GAMES	PTS
1	Thomas Gravesen	20	1.95
2	Marcus Bent	26	1.88
3	Nigel Martyn	31	1.84
4	Alan Stubbs	25	1.76
5	Tony Hibbert	35	1.74
6	Lee Carsley	32	1.72
7	Tim Cahill	27	1.67
8	Kevin Kilbane	34	1.59
9	Alessandro Pistone	30	1.50
10	David Weir	33	1.48

KEY PLAYERS - DEFENDERS

Alan Stubbs

Goals Conceded in the League Number of League goals conceded while the player was on the pitch	24
Goals Conceded in all competitions Total number of goals conceded while the player was on the pitch	32
League minutes played Number of minutes played in league matches	2439
Clean Sheets In games when player was on pitch for at least 70 minutes	9
Defensive Rating Average number of mins between League goals conceded while on the pitch	102
Club Defensive Rating Average number of mins between League goals conceded by the club this season	74

	PLAYER	CON LGE	CON ALL	MINS	C SHEETS	DEF RATE
1	Alan Stubbs	24	32	2439	9	102 mins
2	David Weir	39	39	3033	12	78 mins
3	Tony Hibbert	41	48	3184	13	78 mins
4	Alessandro Pistone	39	43	2737	10	70 mins
5	Joseph Yobo	35	43	1772	3	51 mins

KEY GOALKEEPER

Nigel Martyn

Goals Conceded in the League Number of League goals conceded while the player was on the pitch	26
Goals Conceded in all competitions Total number of goals conceded while the player was on the pitch	28
League minutes played Number of minutes played in league matches	2834
Clean Sheets In games when player was on pitch for at least 70 minutesmins	13
Goals to Shots Ratio The average number of shots on target per each League goal conceded	8
Defensive Rating Ave mins between League goals conceded while on the pitch	109

BOOKINGS

Gary Naysmith

League Yellow	2
League Red	1
All competitions Yellow	4
All competitions Red	1
League Average	155 mins between cards

	PLAYER	LEAGUE		TOTAL		AVE
1	Naysmith	2Y	1R	4Y	1R	155
2	Arteta	5	0	5	0	161
3	Cahill	10	1	10	1	245
4	Beattie	1	1	2	1	283
5	Hibbert	9	0	9	0	353
6	Ferguson	2	1	3	1	406
7	Carsley	7	0	7	1	432
8	Gravesen	3	0	3	0	603
9	Osman	3	0	3	0	719
10	McFadden	1	0	2	0	768
11	Weir	3	0	4	0	1011
12	Kilbane	3	0	4	0	1071
13	Watson	1	0	1	0	1192
14	Bent	2	0	2	0	1329
15	Pistone	2	0	2	0	1368
	Other	1	0	2	0	
	TOTAL	56	3	64	4	

LIVERPOOL

Milan Baros couldn't score in the Champions League final but he had the ninth best Strike Rate in the Premiership Round-up, netting a league goal every 206 minutes on average. He also led the club's Top Point Earners table. **Luis Garcia**, **Steven Gerrard** and **John Arne Riise** all added goals at reasonable Strike Rates.

Liverpool averaged 12.8 shots per game – the third highest in the division – but their Accuracy rating shows they had less than half On Target.

Miguel Josemi had the joint worst disciplinary record in the division with seven yellows and a red, averaging a card every 140 minutes.

Jamie Carragher rightly won the praise for his inspired performances in the Champions League but team-mate **Steve Finnan** had the highest Defensive Rating at the club – although it only earned him 23rd spot in the Premiership Round-up.

NICKNAME: THE REDS KEY: Won Drawn Lost

1	clql1	**Grazer AK**	A	W	2-0	Gerrard 23,79
2	prem	**Tottenham**	A	D	1-1	Cisse 38
3	prem	**Man City**	H	W	2-1	Baros 48; Gerrard 75
4	clql2	**Grazer AK**	H	L	0-1	
5	prem	**Bolton**	A	L	0-1	
6	prem	**West Brom**	H	W	3-0	Gerrard 16; Finnan 42; Luis Garcia 60
7	cl ga	**Monaco**	H	W	2-0	Cisse 22; Baros 84
8	prem	**Man Utd**	A	L	1-2	O'Shea 54 og
9	prem	**Norwich**	H	W	3-0	Baros 23; Luis Garcia 26; Cisse 64
10	cl ga	**Olympiakos**	A	L	0-1	
11	prem	**Chelsea**	A	L	0-1	
12	prem	**Fulham**	A	W	4-2	Knight 50 og; Baros 71; Xabi Alonso 79; Biscan 90
13	cl ga	**Deportivo**	H	D	0-0	
14	prem	**Charlton**	H	W	2-0	Riise 52; Luis Garcia 74
15	ccr3	**Millwall**	A	W	3-0	Diao 18; Baros 70,90
16	prem	**Blackburn**	A	D	2-2	Riise 7; Baros 54
17	cl ga	**Deportivo**	A	W	1-0	Andrade 14 og
18	prem	**Birmingham**	H	L	0-1	
19	ccr4	**Middlesbrough**	H	W	2-0	Mellor 83,89
20	prem	**Crystal Palace**	H	W	3-2	Baros 23 pen,45,90 pen
21	prem	**Middlesbrough**	A	L	0-2	
22	cl ga	**Monaco**	A	L	0-1	
23	prem	**Arsenal**	H	W	2-1	Xabi Alonso 41; Mellor 90
24	ccqf	**Tottenham**	A	W	1-1*	Sinama-Pongolle 117 pen (*aet, won 4-3 on penalties)
25	prem	**Aston Villa**	A	D	1-1	Kewell 16
26	cl ga	**Olympiakos**	H	W	3-1	Sinama-Pongolle 47; Mellor 80; Gerrard 86
27	prem	**Everton**	A	L	0-1	
28	prem	**Portsmouth**	H	D	1-1	Gerrard 70
29	prem	**Newcastle**	H	W	3-1	Bramble 36 og; Mellor 39; Baros 61
30	prem	**West Brom**	A	W	5-0	Riise 17,82; Sinama-Pongolle 51; Gerrard 55; Luis Garcia 89
31	prem	**Southampton**	H	W	1-0	Sinama-Pongolle 44
32	prem	**Chelsea**	H	L	0-1	
33	prem	**Norwich**	A	W	2-1	Luis Garcia 58; Riise 63
34	ccsfl1	**Watford**	H	W	1-0	Gerrard 56
35	prem	**Man Utd**	H	L	0-1	
36	facr3	**Burnley**	A	L	0-1	
37	prem	**Southampton**	A	L	0-2	
38	ccsfl2	**Watford**	A	W	1-0	Gerrard 77
39	prem	**Charlton**	A	W	2-1	Morientes 61; Riise 79
40	prem	**Fulham**	H	W	3-1	Morientes 9; Hyypia 63; Baros 77
41	prem	**Birmingham**	A	L	0-2	
42	clr2l1	**B Leverkusen**	H	W	3-1	Luis Garcia 15; Riise 35; Hamann 90
43	cccf	**Chelsea**	H	L	2-3	Riise 1; Nunez 113
44	prem	**Newcastle**	A	L	0-1	
45	clr2l2	**B Leverkusen**	A	W	3-1	Luis Garcia 28,32; Baros 67
46	prem	**Blackburn**	H	D	0-0	
47	prem	**Everton**	H	W	2-1	Gerrard 27; Luis Garcia 32
48	prem	**Bolton**	H	W	1-0	Biscan 86
49	clqfl1	**Juventus**	H	W	2-1	Hyypia 10; Luis Garcia 25
50	prem	**Man City**	A	L	0-1	
51	clqfl2	**Juventus**	A	D	0-0	
52	prem	**Tottenham**	H	D	2-2	Luis Garcia 44; Hyypia 63
53	prem	**Portsmouth**	A	W	2-1	Morientes 4; Luis Garcia 45
54	prem	**Crystal Palace**	A	L	0-1	
55	clsfl1	**Chelsea**	A	D	0-0	
56	prem	**Middlesbrough**	H	D	1-1	Gerrard 52
57	ecsfl2	**Chelsea**	H	W	1-0	Luis Garcia 4
58	prem	**Arsenal**	A	L	1-3	Gerrard 51
59	prem	**Aston Villa**	H	W	2-1	Cisse 20 pen,27
60	clfin	**AC Milan**	A	W	3-3*	Gerrard 54; Smicer 56; Xabi Alonso 60 (*aet, won 3-2 on penalties)

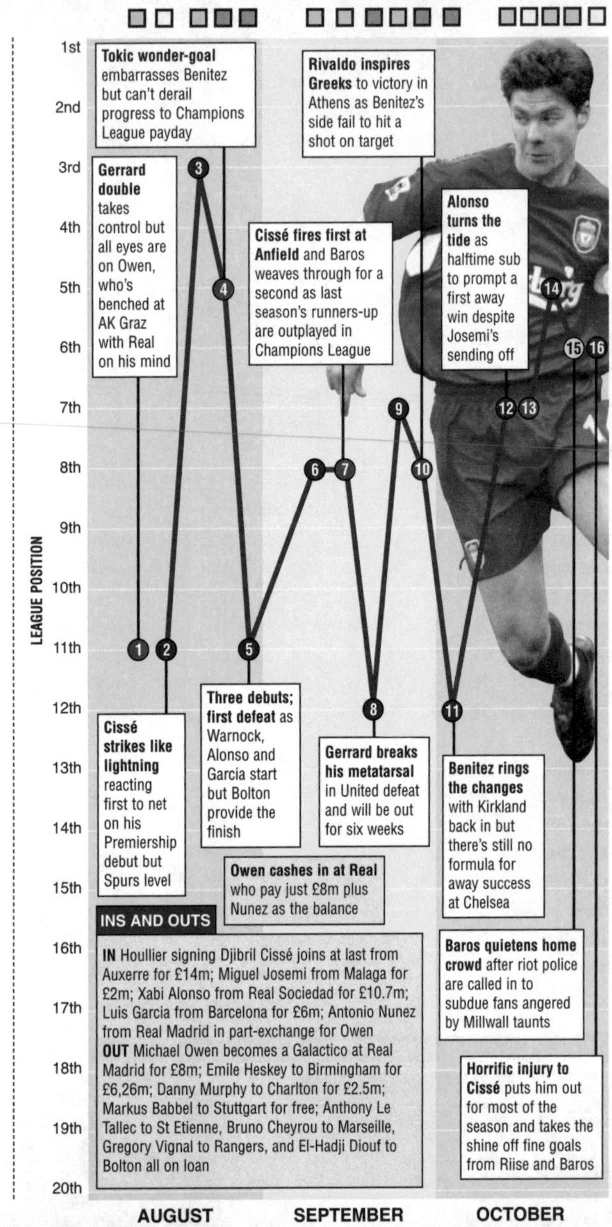

1st
2nd
3rd
4th
5th
6th
7th
8th
9th
10th
11th
12th
13th
14th
15th
16th
17th
18th
19th
20th
LEAGUE POSITION
Tokic wonder-goal embarrasses Benitez but can't derail progress to Champions League payday
Gerrard double takes control but all eyes are on Owen, who's benched at AK Graz with Real on his mind
Rivaldo inspires Greeks to victory in Athens as Benitez's side fail to hit a shot on target
Cissé fires first at Anfield and Baros weaves through for a second as last season's runners-up are outplayed in Champions League
Alonso turns the tide as halftime sub to prompt a first away win despite Josemi's sending off
Cissé strikes like lightning reacting first to net on his Premiership debut but Spurs level
Three debuts; first defeat as Warnock, Alonso and Garcia start but Bolton provide the finish
Gerrard breaks his metatarsal in United defeat and will be out for six weeks
Benitez rings the changes with Kirkland back in but there's still no formula for away success at Chelsea
Owen cashes in at Real who pay just £8m plus Nunez as the balance
INS AND OUTS
IN Houllier signing Djibril Cissé joins at last from Auxerre for £14m; Miguel Josemi from Malaga for £2m; Xabi Alonso from Real Sociedad for £10.7m; Luis Garcia from Barcelona for £6m; Antonio Nunez from Real Madrid in part-exchange for Owen
OUT Michael Owen becomes a Galactico at Real Madrid for £8m; Emile Heskey to Birmingham for £6,26m; Danny Murphy to Charlton for £2.5m; Markus Babbel to Stuttgart for free; Anthony Le Tallec to St Etienne, Bruno Cheyrou to Marseille, Gregory Vignal to Rangers, and El-Hadji Diouf to Bolton all on loan
Baros quietens home crowd after riot police are called in to subdue fans angered by Millwall taunts
Horrific injury to Cissé puts him out for most of the season and takes the shine off fine goals from Riise and Baros
AUGUST
SEPTEMBER
OCTOBER

Home Away Neutral

ATTENDANCES

HOME GROUND: ANFIELD CAPACITY: 45362 AVERAGE LEAGUE AT HOME: 42586

43	Chelsea	78000	56	Middlesboro	43250	27	Everton	40552	19	Middlesboro	28176
8	Man Utd	67857	9	Norwich	43152	55	Chelsea	40479	5	Bolton	27880
60	AC Milan	65000	4	Grazer AK	42950	13	Deportivo	40236	30	West Brom	27533
44	Newcastle	52323	6	West Brom	42947	58	Arsenal	38000	39	Charlton	27102
51	Juventus	50000	20	Crystal Palace	42862	46	Blackburn	37763	16	Blackburn	26314
50	Man City	47203	3	Man City	42831	24	Tottenham	36100	54	Crystal Palace	26043
47	Everton	44224	18	Birmingham	42669	34	Watford	35739	33	Norwich	24503
35	Man Utd	44183	25	Aston Villa	42593	2	Tottenham	35105	45	B Leverkusen	23000
52	Tottenham	44029	57	Chelsea	42529	28	Portsmouth	35064	12	Fulham	21884
32	Chelsea	43886	31	Southampton	42382	21	Middlesboro	34751	53	Portsmouth	20205
29	Newcastle	43856	26	Olympiakos	42045	7	Monaco	33517	38	Watford	19797
48	Bolton	43755	11	Chelsea	42028	10	Olympiakos	33000	36	Burnley	19033
23	Arsenal	43730	14	Charlton	41625	37	Southampton	32017	15	Millwall	17655
40	Fulham	43534	49	Juventus	41216	17	Deportivo	32000	1	Grazer AK	15000
59	Aston Villa	43406	42	B Leverkusen	40942	41	Birmingham	29318	22	Monaco	15000

Second on Merseyside, first in Europe

Final Position: **5th**

KEY: ● League ● Champions Lge ● UEFA Cup ● FA Cup ○ League Cup ● Other

"In front of the Kop, in the last minute..." Mellor describes his wonder-goal - his first in the Premiership - which beats Arsenal

Mellor magic ousts holders from the cup on night when youngsters do academy proud

Deadly in the box as Baros is bought down three times and scores a hat-trick, including two penalties

Cool Sinama strikes from the spot twice, once to equalise and again to settle it on penalties

Sinama's fourth in December is enough to sink Saints

Riise routs Baggies with volleyed opener and a net-bulging fourth in a fine five-goal win

Everton go second with first derby win at Goodison for seven years as Benitez changes fail to make impact

Gerrard lashes home again to lift Anfield spirits before Dudek's injury time flap gifts a point to Pompey

Captain fantastic! Gerrard fires in the clincher to ensure progress from the group stage

Gerrard creates a gap over Watford in the north end of the Carling Cup semies

Alonso's broken ankle, a clear handball not given as a penalty and a late deflected goal among the hard-luck stories as Chelsea win but are second best

Morientes signs and starts against United who hang onto a narrow win after Dudek slip

Gerrard strides forward to fire Benitez into the Carling final in his first season in charge

Garcia's perfect start is followed by Riise's power and Hamann's last minute finish only for Dudek's fumble to be the final word

First for Morientes as striker pounces to level against Charlton before Riise hits a well-worked winner

Made in Spain as Garcia's delightful cross is powered home by Morientes for first Anfield goal

Gerrard's bizarre own goal gets Mourinho banished from the touchline and Chelsea back in the game that they win in extra time

Garcia grabs the headlines with two goals fashioned by Gerrard to ensure an easy route into the last eight

The Toffee's wobble starts here? A Gerrard first against Everton and Garcia follow-up to a Morientes speculator earn win despite Baros' misses and red mist

Hyypia and Garcia volleys shock Juvé in first competitive reunion since Heysel but Cannavaro header makes Italians slight favourites

Injured duo return to glory in Turin as Alonso anchors midfield and Cissé comes on to help secure an all-English semi-final against Chelsea

Benitez wins chess game in midfield to keep Chelsea goalless at the Bridge

Carragher the hero as the blue waves are snuffed out with barely a shot on goal and the Kop celebrates a place in the Champions League final

Eleventh away defeat gifts fourth place to Everton as Arsenal secure second spot at Highbury

Cissé shows what Anfield has missed with two goals to make a bid for Final spot

Six minutes that rocked Europe! Gerrard leads a miraculous comeback from 3-0 down and Dudek makes the saves that secure the Champions League trophy

"Our best performance" says Benitez after return to Spain ends in win over Deportivo

'Crazy Horse' tributes after Emlyn Hughes dies aged 57

INS AND OUTS

Moriententes completes the Real deal
IN Fernando Morientes from Real Madrid for £6.3m; Mauricio Pellegrino from Valencia for free; Scott Carson from Leeds for £750K; Anthony Le Tallec from St Etienne loan return
OUT Salif Diao to Birmingham on loan; Stefane Henchoz to Celtic for free

Average League position over the season: 6.2

MONTH BY MONTH POINTS TALLY

AUGUST	4	44%
SEPTEMBER	6	67%
OCTOBER	7	58%
NOVEMBER	6	50%
DECEMBER	11	61%
JANUARY	3	25%
FEBRUARY	6	67%
MARCH	4	44%
APRIL	8	44%
MAY	3	50%

NOVEMBER DECEMBER JANUARY FEBRUARY MARCH APRIL MAY

GOAL ATTEMPTS

FOR – Goal attempts recorded in League games

	HOME	AWAY	TOTAL	AVE
shots on target	133	104	237	6.2
shots off target	136	112	248	6.5
TOTAL	269	216	485	12.8

Ratio of goals to shots – Average number of shots on target per League goal scored: 4.6

Accuracy rating – Average percentage of total goal attempts which were on target: 48.9

AGAINST – Goal attempts recorded in League games

	HOME	AWAY	TOTAL	AVE
shots on target	65	96	161	4.2
shots off target	60	104	164	4.3
TOTAL	125	200	325	8.6

Ratio of goals to shots – Average number of shots on target per League goal scored: 3.9

Accuracy rating – Average percentage of total goal attempts which were on target: 49.5

GOALS

1 Milan Baros

League	9
FA Cup	0
League Cup	2
Europe	2
Other	0
TOTAL	13

League Average 206 mins between goals

	PLAYER	LGE	FAC	LC	Euro	TOT	AVE
1	Baros	9	0	2	2	13	206
2	Luis Garcia	8	0	0	5	13	292
3	Gerrard	7	0	2	4	13	353
4	Riise	6	0	1	1	8	496
5	Cisse	4	0	0	1	5	233
6	Mellor	2	0	2	1	5	239
7	Sinama-Pongolle	2	0	1	1	4	330
8	Morientes	3	0	0	0	3	338
9	Xabi Alonso	2	0	0	1	3	904
10	Hyypia	2	0	0	1	3	1390
11	Biscan	2	0	0	0	2	367
12	Finnan	1	0	0	0	1	2545
13	Kewell	1	0	0	0	1	1403
15	Smicer	0	0	0	1	1	
	Other	3	0	2	2	6	
	TOTAL	52	0	10	20	82	

SQUAD APPEARANCES

Match	1 2 3 4 5	6 7 8 9 10	11 12 13 14 15	16 17 18 19 20	21 22 23 24 25	26 27 28 29 30	31 32 33 34 35	36 37 38 39 40	41 42 43 44 45	46 47 48 49 50	51 52 53 54 55	56 57 58 59 60
Venue	A A H H A	H H A H A	A A H H A	A A H H H	A A H A A	H A H H A	H H A H H	A A A A H	A H N A A	H H H H A	A H A A A	H H A H N
Competition	C L L C L	L C L L C	L L C L W	L C L W L	L C L W L	C L L L L	L L L W L	F L W L L	L C W L C	L L L C L	C L L L C	L C L L C
Result	W D W L L	W W L W L	L W D W W	D W L W W	L L W W D	W L D W W	W L W W L	L L W W W	L W L L W	D W W W L	D D W L D	D W L W W

Goalkeepers
Scott Carson
Jerzy Dudek
Paul Harrison
Chris Kirkland
Patrice Luzi

Defenders
Jamie Carragher
Steve Finnan
Stephane Henchoz
Sami Hyypia
Miguel Josemi
Jon Otsemobor
Mauricio Pellegrino
David Raven
Djimi Traore
Stephen Warnock
Zak Whitbread

Midfielders
Igor Biscan
Salif Diao
Steven Gerrard
Dietmar Hamann
Anthony Le Tallec
Antonio Nunez
Ritchie Partridge
Darren Potter
John Arne Riise
Vladimir Smicer
Mark Smyth
John Welsh
Xabi Alonso

Forwards
Milan Baros
Djibril Cisse
Robbie Foy
Harry Kewell
Javier Luis Garcia
Neil Mellor
Fernando Morientes
Michael Owen
Florent Sinama-Pongolle

KEY: On all match / On bench / Subbed or sent off (Counting game) / Subbed or sent off (playing less than 70 mins) / Subbed on from bench (Counting Game) / Subbed on (playing less than 70 mins) / Subbed on and then subbed or sent off (Counting Game) / Subbed on and then subbed or sent off (playing less than 70 mins) / Not in 16

KEY PLAYERS - GOALSCORERS

Milan Baros

Goals in the League	9
Goals in all competitions	13
Assists League goals scored by a team mate where the player delivered the final pass	2
Contribution to Attacking Power Average number of minutes between League team goals while on pitch	59
Player Strike Rate Average number of minutes between League goals scored by player	206
Club Strike Rate Average minutes between League goals scored by club	66

	PLAYER	GOALS LGE	GOALS ALL	ASSISTS	POWER	S RATE
1	Milan Baros	9	13	2	59	206 mins
2	Javier Luis Garcia	8	13	3	61	292 mins
3	Steven Gerrard	7	13	4	80	353 mins
4	John Arne Riise	6	8	6	63	496 mins
5	Xabi Alonso	2	3	3	55	904 mins

KEY PLAYERS - MIDFIELDERS

John Arne Riise

Goals in the League	6
Goals in all competitions	8
Assists League goals scored by a team mate where the player delivered the final pass	6
Defensive Rating Average number of mins between League goals conceded while on the pitch	88
Contribution to Attacking Power Average number of minutes between League team goals while on pitch	63
Scoring Difference Defensive Rating minus Contribution to Attacking Power	25

	PLAYER	GOALS LGE	GOALS ALL	ASSISTS	DEF RATE	POWER	SC DIFF
1	John Arne Riise	6	8	6	88	63	25 mins
2	Xabi Alonso	2	3	3	79	55	24 mins
3	Dietmar Hamann	0	1	6	84	60	24 mins
4	Steven Gerrard	7	13	4	85	80	5 mins

PLAYER APPEARANCES

	AGE (on 01/07/05)	IN NAMED 16	APPEARANCES	COUNTING GAMES	MINUTES ON PITCH	APPEARANCES	MINUTES ON PITCH	THIS SEASON	HOME COUNTRY
Goalkeepers									
Scott Carson	19	15	4	4	360	5	450	-	England
Jerzy Dudek	32	38	24	24	2160	41	3780	-	Poland
Paul Harrison	20	9	0	0	0	0	0	-	England
Chris Kirkland	24	13	10	10	900	14	1260	-	England
Patrice Luzi	24	1	0	0	0	0	0	-	France
Defenders									
Jamie Carragher	27	38	38	38	3420	56	5079	7	England (6)
Steve Finnan	29	34	33	27	2545	52	4014	8	Rep of Ireland (15)
Stephane Henchoz	30	1	0	0	0	4	390	7	Switzerland (45)
Sami Hyypia	31	38	32	30	2779	49	4369	-	Finland
Miguel Josemi	25	16	15	12	1121	23	1709	-	Spain
Jon Otsemobor	22	0	0	0	0	0	0	-	England
Mauricio Pellegrino	33	15	12	9	911	13	1001	-	Argentina
David Raven	20	2	1	0	24	3	234	-	England
Djimi Traore	25	30	26	18	1775	42	3119	-	France
Stephen Warnock	23	25	19	7	805	30	1409	-	England
Zak Whitbread	21	0	0	0	0	4	390	-	United States
Midfielders									
Biscan	27	24	19	5	734	35	2008	-	Croatia
Salif Diao	28	17	8	3	417	14	807	3	Senegal (33)Igor
Steven Gerrard	25	30	30	25	2473	43	3690	6	England (6)
Dietmar Hamann	31	31	30	19	2024	43	3044	-	Germany
Anthony Le Tallec	20	4	4	2	220	7	312	-	France
Antonio Nunez	26	18	18	8	906	27	1413	-	Spain
Ritchie Partridge	24	0	0	0	0	2	32	-	Rep of Ireland
Darren Potter	20	2	2	0	55	10	547	-	England
John Arne Riise	24	38	37	29	2975	57	4647	-	Norway
Vladimir Smicer	32	10	10	1	331	16	511	-	Czech Republic
Mark Smyth	20	0	0	0	0	1	51	-	England
John Welsh	21	4	3	2	175	7	355	-	England
Xabi Alonso	23	24	24	18	1807	32	2468	-	Spain
Forwards									
Milan Baros	23	26	26	19	1853	45	3131	7	Czech Republic (2)
Djibril Cisse	23	16	16	7	932	25	1368	5	France (4)
Robbie Foy	19	0	0	0	0	0	0	-	Scotland
Harry Kewell	26	18	18	14	1403	31	2050	-	Australia
Javier Luis Garcia	27	29	29	24	2339	44	3550	-	Spain
Neil Mellor	22	11	9	3	477	16	853	-	England
Fernando Morientes	29	13	13	11	1014	15	1177	-	Spain
Michael Owen	25	0	0	0	0	0	0	9	England (6)
F Sinama-Pongolle	20	18	15	4	659	25	1143	-	France

KEY: LEAGUE   ALL COMPS   CAPS (FIFA RANKING)

TEAM OF THE SEASON

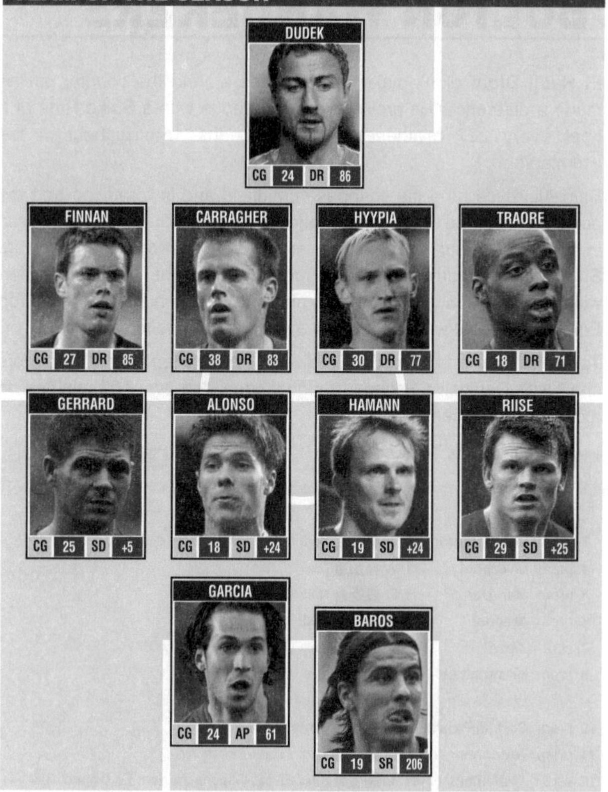

DUDEK
CG 24 DR 86
FINNAN
CG 27 DR 85
CARRAGHER
CG 38 DR 83
HYYPIA
CG 30 DR 77
TRAORE
CG 18 DR 71
GERRARD
CG 25 SD +5
ALONSO
CG 18 SD +24
HAMANN
CG 19 SD +24
RIISE
CG 29 SD +25
GARCIA
CG 24 AP 61
BAROS
CG 19 SR 206

KEY: DR = Defensive Rating, SD = Scoring Difference AP = Attacking Power SR = Strike Rate, CG=Counting games – League games playing at least 70 minutes

TOP POINT EARNERS

1 Milan Baros	
Counting Games League games when player was on pitch for at least 70 minutes	19
Average points Average League points taken in Counting games	1.79
Club Average points Average points taken in League games	1.53

	PLAYER	GAMES	PTS
1	Milan Baros	19	1.79
2	Steve Finnan	27	1.67
3	John Arne Riise	29	1.59
4	Javier Luis Garcia	24	1.58
5	Jerzy Dudek	24	1.58
6	Sami Hyypia	30	1.57
7	Jamie Carragher	38	1.53
8	Dietmar Hamann	19	1.53
9	Djimi Traore	18	1.44
10	Xabi Alonso	18	1.44

KEY PLAYERS - DEFENDERS

Steve Finnan	
Goals Conceded in the League Number of League goals conceded while the player was on the pitch	30
Goals Conceded in all competitions Total number of goals conceded while player was on the pitch	41
League minutes played Number of minutes played in league matches	2545
Clean Sheets In games when player was on pitch for at least 70 minutes	6
Defensive Rating Average number of mins between League goals conceded while on the pitch	85
Club Defensive Rating Average number of mins between League goals conceded by the club this season	83

Carlsberg

	PLAYER	CON LGE	CON ALL	MINS	C SHEETS	DEF RATE
1	Steve Finnan	30	41	2545	6	85 mins
2	Jamie Carragher	41	53	3420	7	83 mins
3	Sami Hyypia	36	50	2779	5	77 mins
4	Djimi Traore	25	33	1775	3	71 mins
5	Miguel Josemi	18	20	1121	1	62 mins

KEY GOALKEEPER

Jerzy Dudek	
Goals Conceded in the League Number of League goals conceded while the player was on the pitch	25
Goals Conceded in all competitions Total number of goals conceded while player was on the pitch	37
League minutes played Number of minutes played in league matches	2160
Clean Sheets In games when player was on pitch for at least 70 minutes	5
Goals to Shots Ratio The average number of shots on target per each League goal conceded	4.3
Defensive Rating Ave mins between League goals conceded while on the pitch	86

BOOKINGS

Miguel Josemi	
League Yellow	7
League Red	1
All competitions Yellow	7
All competitions Red	1
League Average **140** mins between cards	

	PLAYER	LEAGUE		TOTAL		AVE
		7Y	1R	7Y	1R	140
1	Josemi					
2	Hamann	6	0	11	0	337
3	Nunez	2	0	2	1	453
4	Luis Garcia	5	0	5	0	467
5	Baros	2	1	7	1	617
6	Sinama-Pongolle	1	0	1	0	659
7	Warnock	1	0	3	0	805
8	Gerrard	3	0	6	0	824
9	Finnan	3	0	5	0	848
10	Carragher	4	0	8	0	855
11	Pellegrino	1	0	1	0	911
12	Morientes	1	0	1	0	1014
13	Hyypia	2	0	4	0	1389
14	Traore	1	0	3	0	1775
15	Xabi Alonso	1	0	3	0	1807
	Other	1	0	5	0	
	TOTAL	41	2	72	3	

BOLTON WANDERERS

El Hadji Diouf didn't make many friends around the country but he made a difference. He provided a cutting edge with a Strike Rate of a goal every 227 minutes on average - the 15th highest in the Premiership.

Sam Allardyce rang the changes in midfield and in formation and the goals were shared around with **Stelios Giannakopoulos** scoring seven in the league and **Kevin Nolan** and **Jay-Jay Okocha** weighing in. Stelios added four Assists to his record, topped the Midfielders chart with the best Scoring Difference, and shared the honours in the Top Point Earners list with Diouf. They averaged 1.84 points a game.

Tal Ben Haim and **Ricardo Gardner** were joint top of the Defenders chart with Defensive Ratings of a goal conceded every 92 minutes on average – less than one a game.

NICKNAME: THE TROTTERS

KEY: Won Drawn Lost

1	prem	**Charlton**	H	W	4-1	Okocha 11,59; Pedersen 30,72
2	prem	**Fulham**	A	L	0-2	
3	prem	**Southampton**	A	W	2-1	Pedersen 7; Okocha 27 pen
4	prem	**Liverpool**	H	W	1-0	Davies 38
5	prem	**Man Utd**	H	D	2-2	Nolan 52; Ferdinand 90
6	prem	**Arsenal**	A	D	2-2	Jaidi 63; Pedersen 85
7	ccr2	**Yeovil**	A	W	2-0	Julio Cesar 80; Pedersen 87
8	prem	**Birmingham**	H	D	1-1	Jaidi 16
9	prem	**West Brom**	A	L	1-2	Giannakopoulos 73
10	prem	**Crystal Palace**	H	W	1-0	Davies 45
11	prem	**Tottenham**	A	W	2-1	Jaidi 11; Pedersen 75
12	ccr3	**Tottenham**	H	L	3-4	King 27 og; Okocha 75 pen; Ferdinand 105
13	prem	**Newcastle**	H	W	2-1	Diouf 52; Davies 70
14	prem	**Middlesbrough**	A	D	1-1	Pedersen 72
15	prem	**Aston Villa**	H	L	1-2	Diouf 21
16	prem	**Chelsea**	A	D	2-2	Davies 52; Jaidi 87
17	prem	**Portsmouth**	H	L	0-1	
18	prem	**Everton**	A	L	2-3	Davies 16,59
19	prem	**Norwich**	A	L	2-3	Okocha 19 pen; Hierro 23
20	prem	**Man City**	H	L	0-1	
21	prem	**Man Utd**	A	L	0-2	
22	prem	**Blackburn**	H	L	0-1	
23	prem	**West Brom**	H	D	1-1	Diouf 85
24	prem	**Birmingham**	A	W	2-1	Diouf 17; Nolan 90
25	facr3	**Ipswich**	A	W	3-1	Giannakopoulos 60; Pedersen 65,68
26	prem	**Arsenal**	H	W	1-0	Giannakopoulos 41
27	prem	**Blackburn**	A	W	1-0	Diouf 77 pen
28	facr4	**Oldham**	A	W	1-0	Vaz Te 9
29	prem	**Tottenham**	H	W	3-1	Diouf 49 pen; Ben Haim 86; Davies 87
30	prem	**Crystal Palace**	A	W	1-0	Nolan 31
31	prem	**Middlesbrough**	H	D	0-0	
32	facr5	**Fulham**	H	W	1-0	Davies 12
33	prem	**Newcastle**	A	L	1-2	Giannakopoulos 41
34	prem	**Man City**	A	W	1-0	Diouf 45
35	facqf	**Arsenal**	H	L	0-1	
36	prem	**Norwich**	H	W	1-0	Giannakopoulos 42
37	prem	**Liverpool**	A	L	0-1	
38	prem	**Fulham**	H	W	3-1	Okocha 13 pen; Nolan 33; Giannakopoulos 54
39	prem	**Charlton**	A	W	2-1	Okocha 7 pen; Diouf 58
40	prem	**Southampton**	H	D	1-1	Giannakopoulos 25
41	prem	**Aston Villa**	A	D	1-1	Speed 54
42	prem	**Chelsea**	H	L	0-2	
43	prem	**Portsmouth**	A	D	1-1	Diouf 11
44	prem	**Everton**	H	W	3-2	Jaidi 53; Davies 61; Giannakopoulos 66

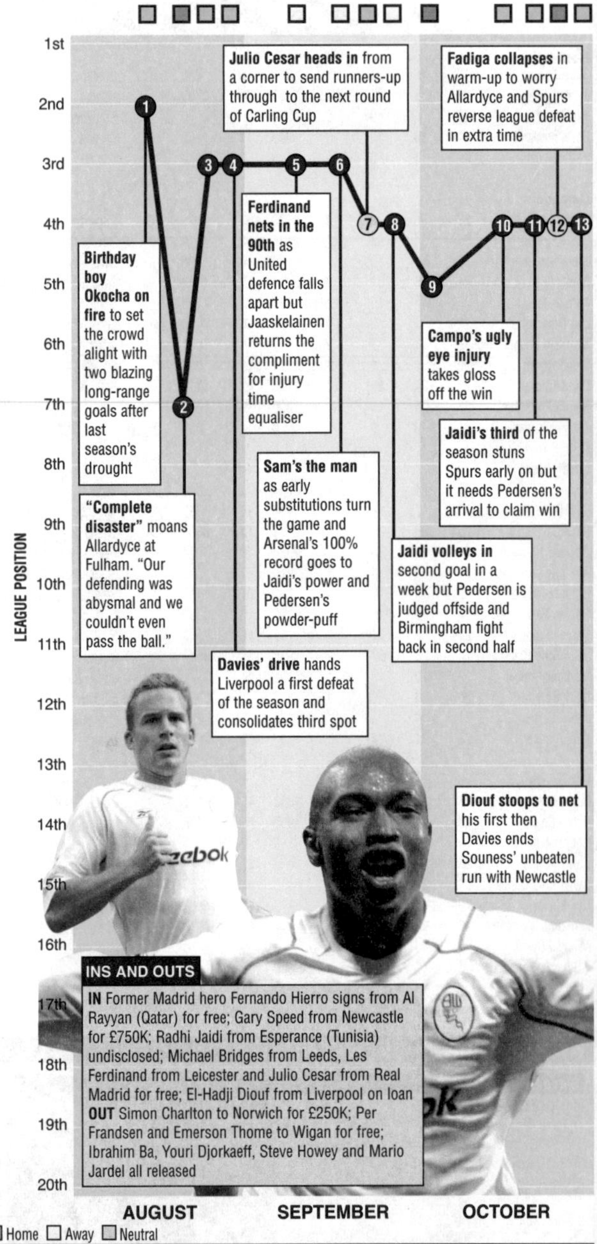
1st
2nd
3rd
4th
5th
6th
7th
8th
9th
10th
11th
12th
13th
14th
15th
16th
17th
18th
19th
20th
LEAGUE POSITION
Birthday boy Okocha on fire to set the crowd alight with two blazing long-range goals after last season's drought
"Complete disaster" moans Allardyce at Fulham. "Our defending was abysmal and we couldn't even pass the ball."
Julio Cesar heads in from a corner to send runners-up through to the next round of Carling Cup
Ferdinand nets in the 90th as United defence falls apart but Jaaskelainen returns the compliment for injury time equaliser
Sam's the man as early substitutions turn the game and Arsenal's 100% record goes to Jaidi's power and Pedersen's powder-puff
Davies' drive hands Liverpool a first defeat of the season and consolidates third spot
Fadiga collapses in warm-up to worry Allardyce and Spurs reverse league defeat in extra time
Campo's ugly eye injury takes gloss off the win
Jaidi's third of the season stuns Spurs early on but it needs Pedersen's arrival to claim win
Jaidi volleys in second goal in a week but Pedersen is judged offside and Birmingham fight back in second half
Diouf stoops to net his first then Davies ends Souness' unbeaten run with Newcastle
AUGUST
SEPTEMBER
OCTOBER
Home Away Neutral

INS AND OUTS

IN Former Madrid hero Fernando Hierro signs from Al Rayyan (Qatar) for free; Gary Speed from Newcastle for £750K; Radhi Jaidi from Esperance (Tunisia) undisclosed; Michael Bridges from Leeds, Les Ferdinand from Leicester and Julio Cesar from Real Madrid for free; El-Hadji Diouf from Liverpool on loan **OUT** Simon Charlton to Norwich for £250K; Per Frandsen and Emerson Thome to Wigan for free; Ibrahim Ba, Youri Djorkaeff, Steve Howey and Mario Jardel all released

ATTENDANCES

HOME GROUND: REEBOK STADIUM CAPACITY: 28723 AVERAGE LEAGUE AT HOME: 26005

21	Man Utd	67867	4	Liverpool	27880	10	Crystal Palace	25501	19	Norwich	23549
33	Newcastle	50000	5	Man Utd	27766	38	Fulham	25493	35	Arsenal	23523
37	Liverpool	43755	44	Everton	27701	23	West Brom	25205	30	Crystal Palace	23163
34	Man City	43050	42	Chelsea	27653	40	Southampton	25125	43	Portsmouth	20188
16	Chelsea	42203	26	Arsenal	27514	36	Norwich	25081	25	Ipswich	20080
6	Arsenal	37010	20	Man City	27274	17	Portsmouth	25008	27	Blackburn	20056
41	Aston Villa	36053	13	Newcastle	27196	29	Tottenham	24780	12	Tottenham	18037
11	Tottenham	36025	24	Birmingham	27177	31	Middlesboro	24322	2	Fulham	17541
18	Everton	35929	22	Blackburn	27038	1	Charlton	24100	32	Fulham	16151
3	Southampton	30713	39	Charlton	26708	9	West Brom	23849	28	Oldham	12029
14	Middlesboro	29656	15	Aston Villa	25779	8	Birmingham	23692	7	Yeovil	8047

Midfield goals secure Sam's Uefa prize

Final Position **6th**

KEY: ● League ● Champions Lge ● UEFA Cup ● FA Cup ○ League Cup ● Other

Super sub Pedersen scores but Boro equalise in time added for Diouf's time-wasting after Jaasekelainen is sent off
Sam switches to plan B as Chelsea strike after 36 seconds but Jaidi goal clinches a third 2-2 draw against the big three
Diouf strikes early and hits a post but Villa hit-back late with goal to win at Reebok
Spitting Diouf dominates the headlines as Pompey battle to a tight win
Back four are "amateurish" claims Allardyce as two headed goals gift Norwich a rare win
A point at last but a penalty is turned down and Okocha hits the bar before Diouf equalises
Okocha finds his shooting boots and Diouf and Nolan pick up the rebounds from shell-shocked Birmingham
Three goals in eight minutes downs Ipswich as Pedersen's power gives Championship leaders a blast of Premiership quality
Vaz Te heads into next round of cup but Hunt ends up in hospital
Ben Haim nets first goal and Davies scores first for nine games as Spurs are left with ten men and penalty complaints
Nolan flick over line correctly given by linesman but Palace are wasteful in front of goal
Crowd votes to stay away on a bitter day with only Davies' winner for warmth
Out of the Hunt as bizarre ricochet dislocates fullback's shoulder and Newcastle also damage European hopes
Up to sixth with Diouf tap-in securing first win at Man City in the top flight since 1956
Diouf elbow ends cup run after just eight minutes at one down to Arsenal and it's a battle from then on
Stelios picks his spot to beat Green while Candela and midfield hero Hierro pepper his goal from range
Early pressure comes to nothing and a late header wins vital points for Liverpool in battle for fifth spot
Nolan makes sure against Fulham, heading in the second and setting up Stelios for third goal against ten men
Diouf marks return after only four minutes on as sub with winning goal to take fifth spot
Jussi's just fantastic as a whole range of saves limits Villa to an Heirro own goal, while Speed nets at last to draw
Dominant against new Champs but chances go missing and Chelsea battle through to victory and celebrate championship
Ten men battle back from a goal behind against Everton after N'Gotty's dismissal to claim all three points
Diouf defies boo-boys at Portsmouth to send Wanderers on first-ever European travels
NOVEMBER
DECEMBER
JANUARY
FEBRUARY
MARCH
APRIL
MAY

INS AND OUTS

IN Vincent Candela from AS Roma undisclosed
OUT Les Ferdinand to Reading for free

Average League position over the season: 6.5

MONTH BY MONTH POINTS TALLY

Month	Points	%
AUGUST	9	75%
SEPTEMBER	3	33%
OCTOBER	9	75%
NOVEMBER	2	17%
DECEMBER	0	0%
JANUARY	10	83%
FEBRUARY	7	58%
MARCH	6	100%
APRIL	8	44%
MAY	4	67%

GOAL ATTEMPTS

FOR Goal attempts recorded in League games

	HOME	AWAY	TOTAL	AVE
shots on target	180	84	264	6.9
shots off target	135	93	228	6
TOTAL	315	177	492	12.9

Ratio of goals to shots — Average number of shots on target per League goal scored: **5.4**

Accuracy rating — Average percentage of total goal attempts which were on target: **53.7**

AGAINST Goal attempts recorded in League games

	HOME	AWAY	TOTAL	AVE
shots on target	81	128	209	5.5
shots off target	74	84	158	4.2
TOTAL	155	212	367	9.7

Ratio of goals to shots — Average number of shots on target per League goal scored: **4.8**

Accuracy rating — Average percentage of total goal attempts which were on target: **56.9**

GOALS

El Hadji Diouf

League	9
FA Cup	0
League Cup	0
Europe	0
Other	0
TOTAL	9

League Average 227 mins between goals

	PLAYER	LGE	FAC	LC	Euro	TOT	AVE
1	Diouf	9	0	0	0	9	227
2	Davies	8	1	0	0	9	355
3	Pedersen	6	2	1	0	9	227
4	Giannakopoulos	7	1	0	0	8	337
5	Okocha	6	0	1	0	7	402
6	Jaidi	5	0	0	0	5	368
7	Nolan	4	0	0	0	4	624
8	Ferdinand	1	0	1	0	2	258
9	Ben Haim	1	0	0	0	1	1753
10	Vaz Te	0	1	0	0	1	
11	Speed	1	0	0	0	1	3337
12	Julio Cesar	0	0	1	0	1	
13	Hierro	1	0	0	0	1	1431
	Other	0	0	1	0	1	
	TOTAL	49	5	5	0	59	

SQUAD APPEARANCES

Match	1	2	3	4	5	6	7	8	9	10	11	12	13	14	15	16	17	18	19	20	21	22
Venue	H	A	A	H	H	A	A	H	A	H	A	H	H	A	H	A	H	A	A	H	A	H
Competition	L	L	L	L	L	L	W	L	L	L	L	W	L	L	L	L	L	L	L	L	L	L
Result	W	L	W	W	D	D	W	D	L	W	W	L	W	D	L	D	L	L	L	L	L	L

Match	23	24	25	26	27	28	29	30	31	32	33	34	35	36	37	38	39	40	41	42	43	44
Venue	H	A	A	H	A	A	H	A	H	H	A	A	H	H	A	H	A	H	A	H	A	H
Competition	L	L	F	L	L	F	L	L	L	F	L	L	F	L	L	L	L	L	L	L	L	L
Result	D	W	W	W	W	W	W	W	D	W	L	W	L	W	L	W	W	D	D	L	D	W

Goalkeepers
Jussi Jaaskelainen
Andy Oakes
Kevin Poole

Defenders
Anthony Barness
Tal Ben Haim
Vincent Candela
Ricardo Gardner
Nicky Hunt
Radhi Jaidi
Julio Cesar
Blessing Kaku
Florent Laville
Bruno N'Gotty
Jason Talbot

Midfielders
Ivan Campo
Stelios Giannakopoulos
Fernando Hierro
Kevin Nolan
Joey O'Brien
Augustine Okocha
Gary Speed

Forwards
Kevin Davies
El Hadji Diouf
Khalilou Fadiga
Les Ferdinand
Henrik Pedersen
Ricky Shakes
Ricardo Vaz Te

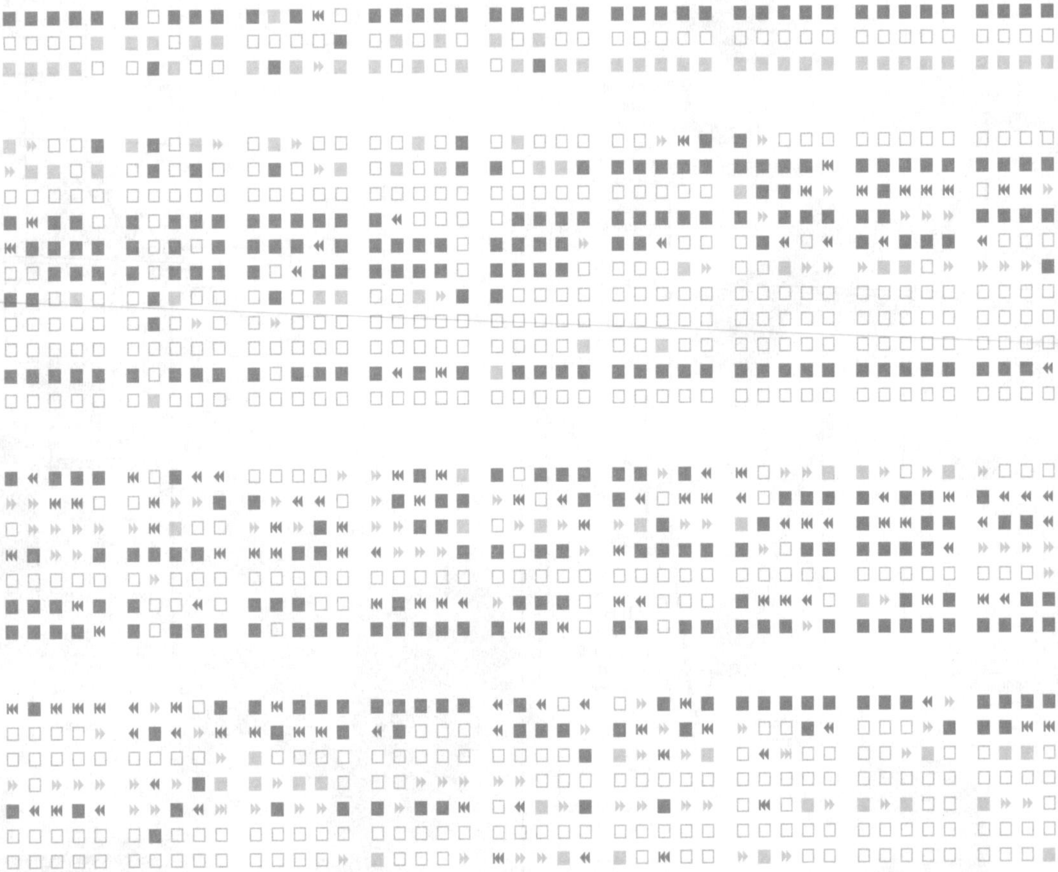

KEY: On all match / On bench / Subbed or sent off (Counting game) / Subbed or sent off (playing less than 70 mins) / Subbed on from bench (Counting Game) / Subbed on (playing less than 70 mins) / Subbed on and then subbed or sent off (Counting Game) / Subbed on and then subbed or sent off (playing less than 70 mins) / Not in 16

KEY PLAYERS - GOALSCORERS

El Hadji Diouf

Goals in the League	9
Goals in all competitions	9
Assists League goals scored by a team mate where the player delivered the final pass	4
Contribution to Attacking Power Average number of minutes between League team goals while on pitch	70
Player Strike Rate Average number of minutes between League goals scored by player	227
Club Strike Rate Average minutes between League goals scored by club	70

	PLAYER	GOALS LGE	GOALS ALL	ASSISTS	POWER	S RATE
1	El Hadji Diouf	9	9	4	70	227 mins
2	Stelios Giannakopoulos	7	8	5	71	337 mins
3	Kevin Davies	8	9	1	72	355 mins
4	Radhi Jaidi	5	5	1	65	368 mins
5	Augustine Okocha	6	7	2	65	402 mins

KEY PLAYERS - MIDFIELDERS

Stelios Giannakopoulos

Goals in the League	7
Goals in all competitions	8
Assists League goals scored by a team mate where the player delivered the final pass	5
Defensive Rating Average number of mins between League goals conceded while he was on the pitch	98
Contribution to Attacking Power Average number of minutes between League team goals while on pitch	71
Scoring Difference Defensive Rating minus Contribution to Attacking Power	27

	PLAYER	GOALS LGE	GOALS ALL	ASSISTS	DEF RATE	POWER	SC DIFF
1	Stelios Giannakopoulos	7	8	5	98	71	27 mins
2	Kevin Nolan	4	4	2	83	73	10 mins
3	Ivan Campo	0	0	0	75	66	9 mins
4	Fernando Hierro	1	1	1	68	60	8 mins
5	Gary Speed	1	1	6	78	73	5 mins

PLAYER APPEARANCES

	AGE (on 01/07/05)	IN NAMED 16	APPEARANCES	COUNTING GAMES	MINUTES ON PITCH	APPEARANCES	MINUTES ON PITCH	THIS SEASON	HOME COUNTRY
Goalkeepers									
Jussi Jaaskelainen	30	36	36	36	3236	40	3596	-	Iceland
Andy Oakes	28	9	1	1	90	1	90	-	England
Kevin Poole	41	31	2	1	93	4	303	-	England
Defenders									
Anthony Barness	33	13	8	5	480	11	611	-	England
Tal Ben Haim	23	29	21	19	1753	27	2313	-	Israel
Vincent Candela	31	11	10	9	774	12	887	-	France
Ricardo Gardner	26	33	33	29	2678	38	3097	-	Jamaica
Nicky Hunt	21	29	29	25	2407	34	2745	-	England
Radhi Jaidi	29	31	27	19	1840	28	1863	-	Tunisia
Julio Cesar	29	10	5	4	361	7	571	10	Brazil (1)
Blessing Kaku	27	1	1	0	26	3	145	-	Nigeria
Florent Laville	31	0	0	0	0	0	0	-	France
Bruno N'Gotty	34	38	37	35	3255	41	3615	-	France
Jason Talbot	19	0	0	0	0	0	0	-	England
Midfielders									
Ivan Campo	31	30	27	16	1715	29	1815	-	Spain
Stelios Giannakop.	30	34	34	19	2358	38	2658	-	Greece
Fernando Hierro	37	34	29	12	1431	35	1940	-	Spain
Kevin Nolan	23	36	36	25	2497	42	2888	-	England
Joey O'Brien	19	1	1	0	9	2	12	-	Rep of Ireland
Augustine Okocha	31	32	31	24	2413	33	2617	-	Nigeria
Gary Speed	35	38	38	37	3337	40	3517	5	Wales (74)
Forwards									
Kevin Davies	28	35	35	29	2838	41	3240	-	England
El Hadji Diouf	24	27	27	19	2043	32	2330	3	Senegal (33)
Khalilou Fadiga	30	11	5	1	125	8	364	-	Senegal
Les Ferdinand	38	16	12	1	258	14	360	-	England
Henrik Pedersen	30	32	27	10	1361	33	1762	3	Denmark (19)
Ricky Shakes	20	0	0	0	0	1	90	-	England
Ricardo Vaz Te	18	11	7	0	193	9	331	-	Portugal
	KEY:LEAGUE					ALL COMPS		CAPS	(MAY FIFA RANKING)

TEAM OF THE SEASON

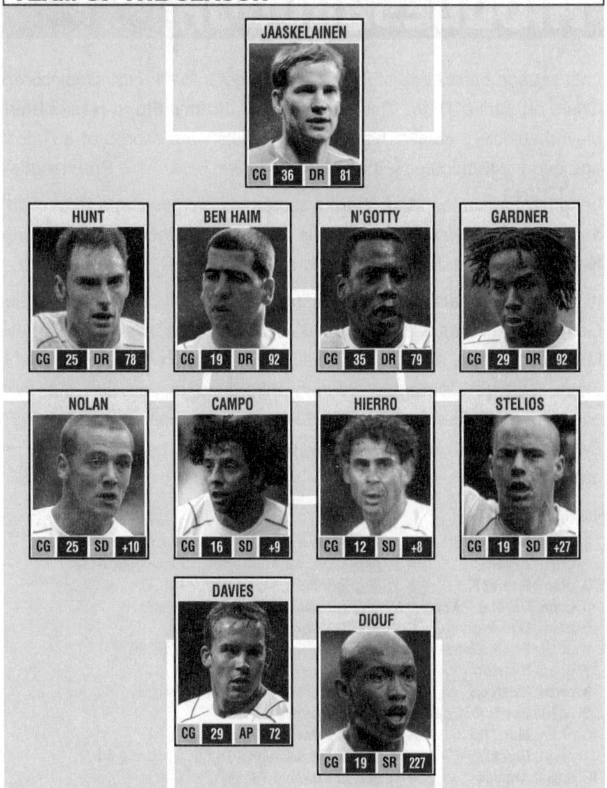

JAASKELAINEN
CG 36 DR 81
HUNT
CG 25 DR 78
BEN HAIM
CG 19 DR 92
N'GOTTY
CG 35 DR 79
GARDNER
CG 29 DR 92
NOLAN
CG 25 SD +10
CAMPO
CG 16 SD +9
HIERRO
CG 12 SD +8
STELIOS
CG 19 SD +27
DAVIES
CG 29 AP 72
DIOUF
CG 19 SR 227

KEY: DR = Defensive Rating, SD = Scoring Difference AP = Attacking Power SR = Strike Rate, CG=Counting games – League games playing at least 70 minutes

TOP POINT EARNERS

Stelios Giannakopoulos

Counting Games League games when player was on pitch for at least 70 minutes	19
Average points Average League points taken in Counting games	1.84
Club Average points Average points taken in League games	1.53

	PLAYER	GAMES	PTS
1	Stelios Giannakopoulos	19	1.84
2	El Hadji Diouf	19	1.84
3	Kevin Nolan	25	1.80
4	Ricardo Gardner	29	1.72
5	Nicky Hunt	25	1.68
6	Ivan Campo	16	1.63
7	Tal Ben Haim	19	1.63
8	Jussi Jaaskelainen	36	1.58
9	Augustine Okocha	24	1.58
10	Bruno N'Gotty	35	1.57

KEY PLAYERS - DEFENDERS

Ricardo Gardner

Goals Conceded in the League Number of League goals conceded while the player was on the pitch	29
Goals Conceded in all competitions Total number of goals conceded while the player was on the pitch	35
League minutes played Number of minutes played in league matches	2678
Clean Sheets In games when player was on pitch for at least 70 minutes	8
Defensive Rating Average number of mins between League goals conceded while on the pitch	92
Club Defensive Rating Average number of mins between League goals conceded by the club this season	78

Reebok

	PLAYER	CON LGE	CON ALL	MINS	C SHEETS	DEF RATE
1	Ricardo Gardner	29	35	2678	8	92 mins
2	Tal Ben Haim	19	25	1753	6	92 mins
3	Bruno N'Gotty	41	43	3255	8	79 mins
4	Nicky Hunt	31	36	2407	5	78 mins
5	Radhi Jaidi	28	28	1840	2	66 mins

KEY GOALKEEPER

Jussi Jaaskelainen

Goals Conceded in the League Number of League goals conceded while the player was on the pitch	40
Goals Conceded in all competitions Total number of goals conceded while the player was on the pitch	42
League minutes played Number of minutes played in league matches	3236
Clean Sheets In games when player was on pitch for at least 70 minutes	8
Goals to Shots Ratio The average number of shots on target per each League goal conceded	4.9
Defensive Rating Ave mins between League goals conceded while on the pitch	81

BOOKINGS

Vincent Candela

League Yellow	3
League Red	0
All competitions Yellow	3
All competitions Red	0
League Average 258 mins between cards	

	PLAYER	LEAGUE 3Y	LEAGUE 0R	TOTAL 3Y	TOTAL 0R	AVE
1	Candela	3	0	3	0	258
2	Diouf	7	0	7	1	291
3	Ben Haim	5	0	7	0	350
4	Campo	4	0	4	0	428
5	Giannakopoulos	5	0	6	0	471
6	Hierro	3	0	4	0	477
7	Hunt	5	0	7	0	481
8	Nolan	5	0	8	0	499
9	Davies	5	0	6	0	567
10	N'Gotty	4	1	4	1	651
11	Gardner	3	0	3	0	892
12	Jaidi	2	0	3	0	920
13	Okocha	2	0	2	0	1206
14	Jaaskelainen	1	1	1	1	1618
15	Speed	1	0	2	0	3337
	Other	0	0	0	0	
	TOTAL	55	2	67	3	

MIDDLESBROUGH

Last season barely one of Boro's strikers got into the club Goalscorers' Chart on Strike Rate. This season only **Jimmy Floyd-Hasselbaink** played sufficient games, his 13 league goals were scored at a Rate of one every 249 minutes – the 18th best Strike Rate in the Premiership.

Long term absentee **Mark Viduka** scored his five goals at a Rate of 219 and **Joseph-Desire Job** four goals at 252 but neither they nor **Szilard Nemeth** played sufficient games to make the chart.

It leaves **Stewart Downing** filling the second spot in the club Goalscorers chart with five goals. He was also runners-up in the Midfielders chart, and his 11 Assists put him fourth in the Premiership table. **George Boateng's** Scoring Difference makes him the most effective Midfielder by some distance and he heads the Top Point Earners chart with **Stuart Parnaby**, both averaging nearly 1.7 points per game.

NICKNAME: BORO

KEY: Won / Drawn / Lost

1	prem	**Newcastle**	H	D	2-2	Downing 73; Hasselbaink 90
2	prem	**Arsenal**	A	L	3-5	Job 43; Hasselbaink 50; Queudrue 53
3	prem	**Fulham**	A	W	2-0	Viduka 54; Nemeth 79
4	prem	**Crystal Palace**	H	W	2-1	Popovic 61 og; Hasselbaink 78
5	prem	**Birmingham**	H	W	2-1	Viduka 27,48
6	uc1rl1	**Banik Ostrava**	H	W	3-0	Hasselbaink 57; Viduka 63,80
7	prem	**Everton**	A	L	0-1	
8	prem	**Chelsea**	H	L	0-1	
9	uc1rl2	**Banik Ostrava**	A	D	1-1	Morrison 90
10	prem	**Man Utd**	A	D	1-1	Downing 33
11	prem	**Blackburn**	A	W	4-0	Hasselbaink 46,57,90; Boateng 50
12	ucgpe	**Aigaleo**	A	W	1-0	Downing 78
13	prem	**Portsmouth**	H	D	1-1	Downing 74
14	ccr3	**Coventry**	H	W	3-0	Nemeth 4; Morrison 25; Graham 70
15	prem	**Charlton**	A	W	2-1	El Karkouri 21 og; Zenden 58
16	ucgpe	**Lazio**	H	W	2-0	Zenden 16,71
17	prem	**Bolton**	H	D	1-1	Boateng 90
18	ccr4	**Liverpool**	A	L	0-2	
19	prem	**West Brom**	A	W	2-1	Purse 32 og; Zenden 52
20	prem	**Liverpool**	H	W	2-0	Riggott 36; Zenden 62
21	ucgpe	**Villarreal**	A	L	0-2	
22	prem	**Tottenham**	A	L	0-2	
23	prem	**Man City**	H	W	3-2	Viduka 9,54; Hasselbaink 65
24	prem	**Southampton**	A	D	2-2	Higginbotham 89 og; Downing 90
25	ucgpe	**Partizan**	H	W	3-0	Nemeth 10; Job 22; Morrison 90
26	prem	**Aston Villa**	H	W	3-0	Hasselbaink 20; Job 68; Reiziger 88
27	prem	**Birmingham**	A	L	0-2	
28	prem	**Norwich**	H	W	2-0	Job 52,54
29	prem	**Man Utd**	H	L	0-2	
30	prem	**Chelsea**	A	L	0-2	
31	facr3	**Notts County**	A	W	2-1	Doriva 54; Job 76
32	prem	**Everton**	H	D	1-1	Zenden 26
33	prem	**Norwich**	A	D	4-4	Hasselbaink 34,78; Queudrue 49,55
34	facr4	**Man Utd**	A	L	0-3	
35	prem	**Portsmouth**	A	L	1-2	Christie 35
36	prem	**Blackburn**	H	W	1-0	Queudrue 35
37	prem	**Bolton**	A	D	0-0	
38	uc3rl1	**Grazer AK**	A	D	2-2	Zenden 52; Hasselbaink 66
39	uc3rl2	**Grazer AK**	H	W	2-1	Morrison 19; Hasselbaink 61
40	prem	**Charlton**	H	D	2-2	Riggott 74; Graham 86
41	prem	**Aston Villa**	A	L	0-2	
42	uc4rl1	**Sp Lisbon**	H	L	2-3	Job 79; Riggott 86
43	uc4rl2	**Sp Lisbon**	A	L	0-1	
44	prem	**Southampton**	H	L	1-3	Hasselbaink 41
45	prem	**Crystal Palace**	A	W	1-0	Queudrue 35
46	prem	**Arsenal**	H	L	0-1	
47	prem	**Fulham**	H	D	1-1	Zenden 90 pen
48	prem	**West Brom**	H	W	4-0	Nemeth 27,37; Hasselbaink 33; Downing 90
49	prem	**Newcastle**	A	D	0-0	
50	prem	**Liverpool**	A	D	1-1	Nemeth 4
51	prem	**Tottenham**	H	W	1-0	Boateng 11
52	prem	**Man City**	A	D	1-1	Hasselbaink 23

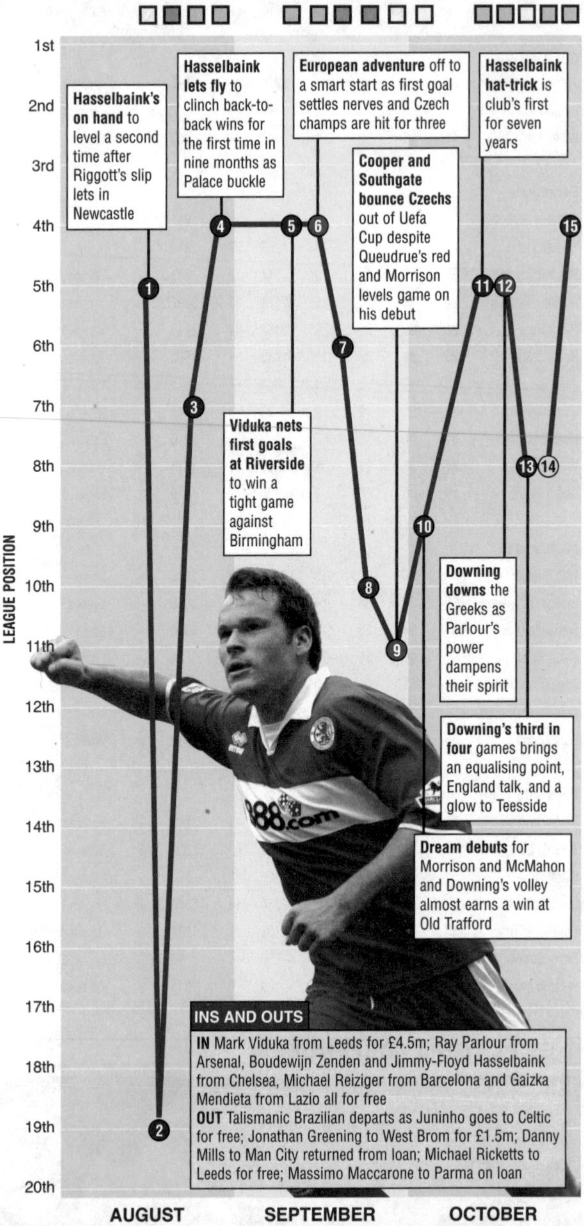

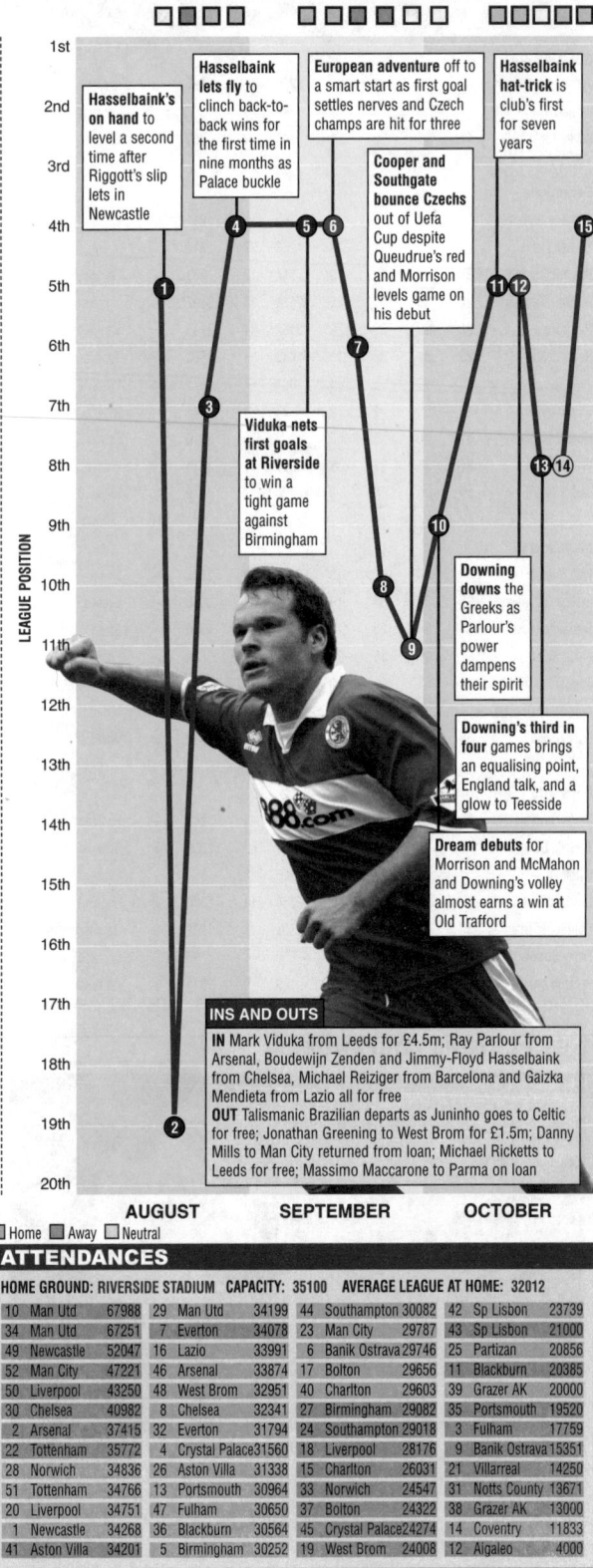

1st
2nd
3rd
4th
5th
6th
7th
8th
9th
10th
11th
12th
13th
14th
15th
16th
17th
18th
19th
20th
LEAGUE POSITION
Hasselbaink's on hand to level a second time after Riggott's slip lets in Newcastle
Hasselbaink lets fly to clinch back-to-back wins for the first time in nine months as Palace buckle
European adventure off to a smart start as first goal settles nerves and Czech champs are hit for three
Hasselbaink hat-trick is club's first for seven years
Cooper and Southgate bounce Czechs out of Uefa Cup despite Queudrue's red and Morrison levels game on his debut
Viduka nets first goals at Riverside to win a tight game against Birmingham
Downing downs the Greeks as Parlour's power dampens their spirit
Downing's third in four games brings an equalising point, England talk, and a glow to Teesside
Dream debuts for Morrison and McMahon and Downing's volley almost earns a win at Old Trafford
888.com
AUGUST
SEPTEMBER
OCTOBER

INS AND OUTS

IN Mark Viduka from Leeds for £4.5m; Ray Parlour from Arsenal, Boudewijn Zenden and Jimmy-Floyd Hasselbaink from Chelsea, Michael Reiziger from Barcelona and Gaizka Mendieta from Lazio all for free

OUT Talismanic Brazilian departs as Juninho goes to Celtic for free; Jonathan Greening to West Brom for £1.5m; Danny Mills to Man City returned from loan; Michael Ricketts to Leeds for free; Massimo Maccarone to Parma on loan

Home / Away / Neutral

ATTENDANCES

HOME GROUND: RIVERSIDE STADIUM **CAPACITY:** 35100 **AVERAGE LEAGUE AT HOME:** 32012

10	Man Utd	67988	29	Man Utd	34199	44	Southampton	30082	42	Sp Lisbon	23739
34	Man Utd	67251	7	Everton	34078	23	Man City	29787	43	Sp Lisbon	21000
49	Newcastle	52047	16	Lazio	33991	6	Banik Ostrava	29746	25	Partizan	20856
52	Man City	47221	46	Arsenal	33874	17	Bolton	29656	11	Blackburn	20385
50	Liverpool	43250	48	West Brom	32951	40	Charlton	29603	39	Grazer AK	20000
30	Chelsea	40982	8	Chelsea	32341	27	Birmingham	29082	35	Portsmouth	19520
2	Arsenal	37415	32	Everton	31794	24	Southampton	29018	3	Fulham	17759
22	Tottenham	35772	4	Crystal Palace	31560	18	Liverpool	28176	9	Banik Ostrava	15351
28	Norwich	34836	26	Aston Villa	31338	15	Charlton	26031	21	Villarreal	14250
51	Tottenham	34766	13	Portsmouth	30964	33	Norwich	24547	31	Notts County	13671
20	Liverpool	34751	47	Fulham	30650	37	Bolton	24322	38	Grazer AK	13000
1	Newcastle	34268	36	Blackburn	30564	45	Crystal Palace	24274	14	Coventry	11833
41	Aston Villa	34201	5	Birmingham	30252	19	West Brom	24008	12	Aigaleo	4000

Teesside gets a taste for Euro nights

Final Position: **7th**

KEY: ● League ● Champions Lge ● UEFA Cup ● FA Cup ○ League Cup ● Other

Schwarzer's sensational save denies fellow Aussie Kewell and McMahon earns plaudits in defeat of Liverpool

Lone striker Job unemployed as Villarreal give McClaren a lesson in European football

Queudrue sent off - his sixth dismissal in four seasons – to let Spurs in

Zenden strikes twice to dismiss outplayed 'favourites' Lazio and go top of the group

Key players out as Viduka and Riggott fail fitness tests and United are more determined

Strikers back in the goals as Viduka ends 12 game drought with two and Hasselbaink scores after nine blanks

Destroyer Downing ruins Redknapp's big day scoring in the 90th minute to snatch a draw from nowhere

Job done as the Cameroon international scores two neat goals and comes close to a hat-trick against Norwich

Three goal lead blown away in last ten minutes as Norwich fight back from Hasselbaink brace and Queudrue double

Notts County ahead for nearly an hour before Doriva levels and Job finishes them off

Zenden chance to level at Old Trafford is brilliantly saved, then Rooney strikes to end cup hopes

Schwarzer stands out against Bolton with a great double save to secure a point

Wings clipped as injuries to Downing and scorer Morrison take the shine off reaching the last 16 in Uefa as Hasselbaink despatches Graz

Graz steal a draw but lose best player Kollmann to a red while Zenden and Hasselbaink hit away goals

Southgate gees-up team-mates after a poor showing against his old club threatens Euro-spot

Job far from done as sub starts the long haul back from three down at home with a spectacular overhead kick but Sporting hold the advantage

Injuries add up to exit as makeshift side make chances in Lisbon but fail to turn them into goals

Euro hangover turns into a league headache with a drop to ninth as Crouch heads Saints to first away win

Queudrue ends wait with winner against Palace after four straight defeats and Viduka comeback lasts just 12 minutes

Southgate sublime after Nemeth nets at Anfield and only a stunning strike from Gerrard finds a way through

'First penalty for 13 months' earns a point as triple-Dutch incident sees van der Sar foul Hasselbaink for Zenden to score

Robson returns and so does European prospects as Nemeth helps hit Baggies for four and Jones is inspired at the other end

Jones secure in goalless draw as point at Newcastle makes both teams happy

Average League position over the season: 6.3

Uefa six-pointer snatched by Nemeth who hits the bar and sets up Boateng to strike the winner against Spurs

Schwarzer secures Europe on merit saving an unlikely penalty two minutes into injury time to deny Fowler and Man City

INS AND OUTS

OUT Massimo Maccarone loan change from Parma to Siena; Andy Davies to QPR on loan; Mark Wilson to Livingston on loan

MONTH BY MONTH POINTS TALLY

Month	Points	%
AUGUST	7	58%
SEPTEMBER	3	33%
OCTOBER	8	67%
NOVEMBER	7	58%
DECEMBER	10	67%
JANUARY	2	17%
FEBRUARY	5	42%
MARCH	0	0%
APRIL	9	50%
MAY	4	67%

NOVEMBER DECEMBER JANUARY FEBRUARY MARCH APRIL MAY

GOAL ATTEMPTS

FOR – Goal attempts recorded in League games

	HOME	AWAY	TOTAL	AVE
shots on target	145	105	250	6.6
shots off target	113	78	191	5
TOTAL	258	183	441	11.6

Ratio of goals to shots Average number of shots on target per League goal scored: **4.7**

Accuracy rating Average percentage of total goal attempts which were on target: **56.7**

AGAINST – Goal attempts recorded in League games

	HOME	AWAY	TOTAL	AVE
shots on target	93	139	232	6.1
shots off target	91	105	196	5.2
TOTAL	184	244	428	11.3

Ratio of goals to shots Average number of shots on target per League goal scored: **5**

Accuracy rating Average percentage of total goal attempts which were on target: **54.2**

GOALS

Jimmy-Floyd Hasselbaink

League	13
FA Cup	0
League Cup	0
Europe	3
Other	0
TOTAL	16

League Average **249** mins between goals

	PLAYER	LGE	FAC	LC	Euro	TOT	AVE
1	Hasselbaink	13	0	0	3	16	249
2	Zenden	5	0	0	3	8	611
3	Viduka	5	0	0	2	7	219
4	Job	4	1	0	2	7	252
5	Downing	5	0	0	1	6	540
6	Nemeth	4	0	1	1	6	425
7	Queudrue	5	0	0	0	5	548
8	Morrison	0	0	1	3	4	0
9	Boateng	3	0	0	0	3	749
10	Riggott	2	0	0	1	3	889
11	Graham	1	0	1	0	2	194
12	Reiziger	1	0	0	0	1	1317
13	Christie	1	0	0	0	1	133
14	Doriva	0	1	0	0	1	0
	Other	4	0	0	0	4	
	TOTAL	53	2	3	16	74	

SQUAD APPEARANCES

Match	1	2	3	4	5	6	7	8	9	10	11	12	13	14	15	16	17	18	19	20	21	22	23	24	25	26	27	28	29	30	31	32	33	34	35	36	37	38	39	40	41	42	43	44	45	46	47	48	49	50	51	52
Venue	H	A	A	H	H	H	A	H	A	A	A	A	H	H	A	H	H	A	A	H	A	A	H	A	H	H	A	H	H	A	A	H	A	A	A	H	A	A	H	H	A	H	A	H	A	H	H	H	A	A	H	A
Competition	L	L	L	L	L	E	L	L	E	L	L	E	L	W	L	E	L	W	L	L	E	L	L	L	E	L	L	L	L	L	F	L	L	F	L	L	L	E	E	L	L	E	E	L	L	L	L	L	L	L	L	L
Result	D	L	W	W	W	W	L	L	D	D	W	W	D	W	W	W	D	L	W	W	L	L	W	D	W	W	L	W	L	L	W	D	D	L	L	W	D	D	W	D	L	L	L	L	W	L	D	W	D	D	W	D

Goalkeepers
Bradley Jones
David Knight
Carlo Nash
Mark Schwarzer

Defenders
Matthew Bates
Colin Cooper
Andrew Davies
Ugo Ehiogu
Anthony McMahon
Stuart Parnaby
Franck Queudrue
Michael Reiziger
Chris Riggott
Gareth Southgate
Andrew Taylor
David Wheater

Midfielders
George Boateng
Doriva
Stewart Downing
Adam Johnson
Jason Kennedy
Gaizka Mendieta
James Morrison
Ray Parlour
Mark Wilson
Boudewijn Zenden

Forwards
Malcolm Christie
Danny Graham
Jimmy-Floyd Hasselbaink
Joseph-Desire Job
Massimo Maccarone
Szilard Nemeth
Mark Viduka

KEY: On all match | On bench | Subbed or sent off (Counting game) | Subbed or sent off (playing less than 70 mins) | Subbed on from bench (Counting Game) | Subbed on (playing less than 70 mins) | Subbed on and then subbed or sent off (Counting Game) | Subbed on and then subbed or sent off (playing less than 70 mins) | Not in 16

KEY PLAYERS - GOALSCORERS

Jimmy-Floyd Hasselbaink

Goals in the League	13
Goals in all competitions	16
Assists League goals scored by a team mate where the player delivered the final pass	7
Contribution to Attacking Power Average number of minutes between League team goals while on pitch	63
Player Strike Rate Average number of minutes between League goals scored by player	249
Club Strike Rate Average minutes between League goals scored by club	65

	PLAYER	GOALS LGE	GOALS ALL	ASSISTS	POWER	S RATE
1	Jimmy-Floyd Hasselbaink	13	16	7	63	249 mins
2	Stewart Downing	5	6	11	61	540 mins
3	Franck Queudrue	5	5	4	74	548 mins
4	Boudewijn Zenden	5	8	1	61	611 mins
5	George Boateng	3	3	2	59	749 mins

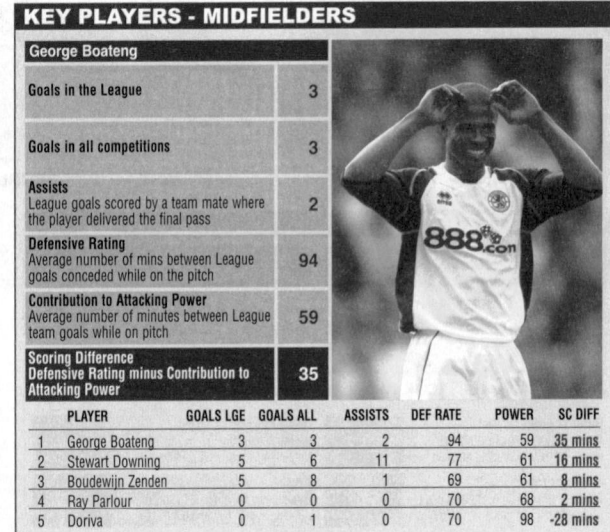

KEY PLAYERS - MIDFIELDERS

George Boateng

Goals in the League	3
Goals in all competitions	3
Assists League goals scored by a team mate where the player delivered the final pass	2
Defensive Rating Average number of mins between League goals conceded while on the pitch	94
Contribution to Attacking Power Average number of minutes between League team goals while on pitch	59
Scoring Difference Defensive Rating minus Contribution to Attacking Power	35

888.com

	PLAYER	GOALS LGE	GOALS ALL	ASSISTS	DEF RATE	POWER	SC DIFF
1	George Boateng	3	3	2	94	59	35 mins
2	Stewart Downing	5	6	11	77	61	16 mins
3	Boudewijn Zenden	5	8	1	69	61	8 mins
4	Ray Parlour	0	0	0	70	68	2 mins
5	Doriva	0	1	0	70	98	-28 mins

PLAYER APPEARANCES

	AGE (on 01/07/05)	IN NAMED 16	APPEARANCES	COUNTING GAMES	MINUTES ON PITCH	APPEARANCES	MINUTES ON PITCH	THIS SEASON	HOME COUNTRY
Goalkeepers									
Bradley Jones	23	7	5	5	450	5	450	-	United States
David Knight	18	8	0	0	0	0	0	-	England
Carlo Nash	31	29	2	2	180	4	360	-	England
Mark Schwarzer	32	31	31	31	2790	43	3870	-	Australia
Defenders									
Matthew Bates	18	4	2	0	2	2	2	-	England
Colin Cooper	38	30	15	10	1042	21	1570	-	England
Andrew Davies	20	9	3	2	234	5	414	-	England
Ugo Ehiogu	32	13	10	7	707	12	887	-	England
Anthony McMahon	19	22	13	11	1073	19	1430	-	England
Stuart Parnaby	22	19	19	12	1324	24	1729	-	England
Franck Queudrue	26	31	31	30	2740	43	3788	-	France
Michael Reiziger	32	21	18	14	1317	25	1831	-	Holland
Chris Riggott	24	21	21	19	1778	32	2768	-	England
Gareth Southgate	34	36	36	36	3240	47	4230	-	England
Andrew Taylor	18	1	0	0	0	0	0	-	England
David Wheater	18	4	0	0	0	1	1	-	England
Midfielders									
George Boateng	29	25	25	25	2247	29	2607	-	Holland
Doriva	33	35	26	13	1477	38	2411	-	Brazil
Stewart Downing	20	36	35	28	2701	48	3751	1	England (6)
Adam Johnson	17	1	0	0	0	1	11	-	England
Jason Kennedy	18	2	1	0	5	1	5	-	England
Gaizka Mendieta	31	7	7	5	516	8	561	-	Spain
James Morrison	19	20	14	4	530	23	1132	-	England
Ray Parlour	32	33	33	30	2801	41	3494	-	England
Mark Wilson	26	0	0	0	0	1	90	-	England
Boudewijn Zenden	28	36	36	31	3055	49	4119	1	Holland (5)
Forwards									
Malcolm Christie	26	2	2	0	133	3	141	-	England
Danny Graham	19	13	11	0	194	17	378	-	England
J-Floyd Hasselbaink	33	36	36	36	3234	45	3912	-	Holland
Joseph-Desire Job	27	27	23	6	1006	33	1606	5	Cameroon (26)
Massimo Maccarone	25	1	0	0	0	0	0	-	Italy
Szilard Nemeth	26	32	31	9	1698	40	2370	-	Hungary
Mark Viduka	29	16	16	11	1095	21	1479	-	Australia

KEY: LEAGUE ALL COMPS CAPS (MAY FIFA RANKING)

TEAM OF THE SEASON

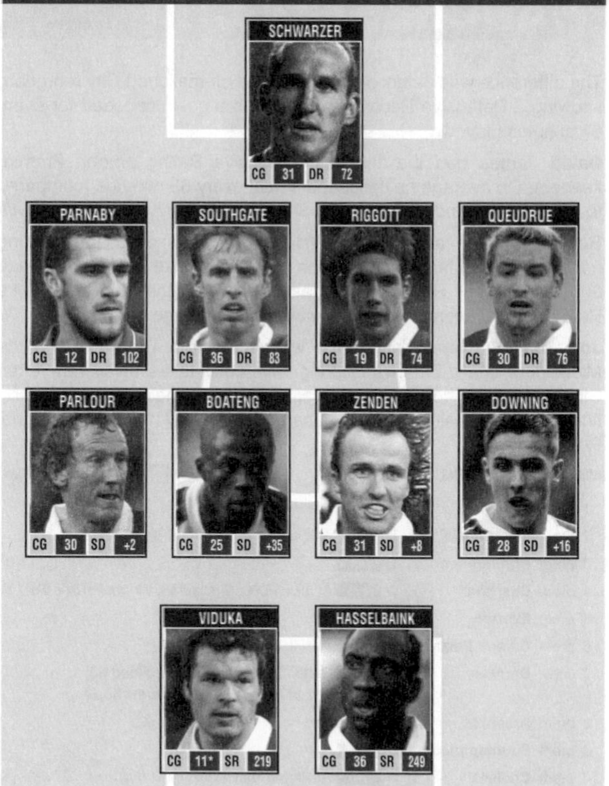
SCHWARZER
CG 31 DR 72
PARNABY
CG 12 DR 102
SOUTHGATE
CG 36 DR 83
RIGGOTT
CG 19 DR 74
QUEUDRUE
CG 30 DR 76
PARLOUR
CG 30 SD +2
BOATENG
CG 25 SD +35
ZENDEN
CG 31 SD +8
DOWNING
CG 28 SD +16
VIDUKA
CG 11* SR 219
HASSELBAINK
CG 36 SR 249

KEY: DR = Defensive Rating, SD = Scoring Difference SR = Strike Rate, CG=Counting games – League games playing at least 70 minutes *No other striker played 12 CG

TOP POINT EARNERS

George Boateng

Counting Games League games when player was on pitch for at least 70 minutes	25
Average points Average League points taken in Counting games	1.68
Club Average points Average points taken in League games	1.45

	PLAYER	GAMES	PTS
1	George Boateng	25	1.68
2	Stuart Parnaby	12	1.67
3	Mark Schwarzer	31	1.55
4	Gareth Southgate	36	1.50
5	Stewart Downing	28	1.50
6	Ray Parlour	30	1.50
7	Chris Riggott	19	1.42
8	Jimmy-Floyd Hasselbaink	36	1.42
9	Boudewijn Zenden	31	1.42
10	Franck Queudrue	30	1.40

KEY PLAYERS - DEFENDERS

Stuart Parnaby

Goals Conceded in the League Number of League goals conceded while the player was on the pitch	13
Goals Conceded in all competitions Total number of goals conceded while player was on the pitch	18
League minutes played Number of minutes played in league matches	1324
Clean Sheets In games when player was on pitch for at least 70 minutes	5
Defensive Rating Average number of mins between League goals conceded while on the pitch	102
Club Defensive Rating Average number of mins between League goals conceded by the club this season	74

	PLAYER	CON LGE	CON ALL	MINS	C SHEETS	DEF RATE
1	Stuart Parnaby	13	18	1324	5	102 mins
2	Gareth Southgate	39	50	3240	11	83 mins
3	Franck Queudrue	36	50	2740	9	76 mins
4	Chris Riggott	24	34	1778	5	74 mins
5	Michael Reiziger	25	31	1317	4	53 mins

KEY GOALKEEPER

Mark Schwarzer

Goals Conceded in the League Number of League goals conceded while the player was on the pitch	39
Goals Conceded in all competitions Total number of goals conceded while player was on the pitch	51
League minutes played Number of minutes played in league matches	2790
Clean Sheets In games when player was on pitch for at least 70 minutes	9
Goals to Shots Ratio The average number of shots on target per each League goal conceded	5.2
Defensive Rating Ave mins between League goals conceded while on the pitch	72

BOOKINGS

Ray Parlour

League Yellow	12
League Red	1
All competitions Yellow	14
All competitions Red	1
League Average **215** mins between cards	

	PLAYER	LEAGUE Y	LEAGUE R	TOTAL Y	TOTAL R	AVE
1	Parlour	12	1	14	1	215
2	Boateng	8	0	8	0	280
3	Doriva	4	0	6	0	369
4	Zenden	8	0	9	0	381
5	Queudrue	6	1	9	2	391
6	Mendieta	1	0	1	0	516
7	Morrison	1	0	2	0	530
8	McMahon	2	0	3	0	536
9	Riggott	3	0	4	0	592
10	Ehiogu	1	0	1	0	707
11	Southgate	4	0	6	0	810
12	Hasselbaink	2	0	3	0	1617
13	Nemeth	1	0	1	0	1698
14	Downing	1	0	1	0	2701
	Other	0	0	2	0	
	TOTAL	54	2	70	3	

MANCHESTER CITY

The difference was defence with four of the oft-maligned City rearguard showing a Defensive Record of better than a goal conceded for every 87 minutes played.

David James had the fifth best Defensive Rating among Premier keepers. On average he conceded a goal every 88 minutes (compared to 70 last year) and had 11 Clean Sheets.

Robbie Fowler and **Shaun Wright-Phillips** shared the scoring honours with ten league goals each scoring at Strike Rates of 252 and 300 respectively. However, **Nicolas Anelka** had the best club Strike Rate at a goal scored every 216 minutes on average.

Joey Barton pipped last year's winner **Claudio Reyna** to top the Midfielders chart. Barton's Scoring Difference takes away how often City score from how often they concede when he's playing and he finished with a positive of 36 minutes. It places him 11th in the Divisional Round-up chart.

NICKNAME: BLUES/CITIZENS

KEY: Won / Drawn / Lost

1	prem	**Fulham**	H	D	1-1	Fowler 28
2	prem	**Liverpool**	A	L	1-2	Anelka 45
3	prem	**Birmingham**	A	L	0-1	
4	prem	**Charlton**	H	W	4-0	Anelka 13,60; Sinclair 34; Wright-Phillips 78
5	prem	**Everton**	H	L	0-1	
6	prem	**Crystal Palace**	A	W	2-1	Anelka 55,64 pen
7	ccr2	**Barnsley**	H	W	7-1	Barton 21; Macken 28,45; Flood 33; Wright-Phillips, S 36; Sibierski 56,84
8	prem	**Arsenal**	H	L	0-1	
9	prem	**Southampton**	A	D	0-0	
10	prem	**Chelsea**	H	W	1-0	Anelka 11 pen
11	prem	**Newcastle**	A	L	3-4	Wright-Phillips, S 64,77; Fowler 67 pen
12	ccr3	**Arsenal**	H	L	1-2	Fowler 90
13	prem	**Norwich**	H	D	1-1	Flood 11
14	prem	**Man Utd**	A	D	0-0	
15	prem	**Blackburn**	H	D	1-1	Sibierski 45
16	prem	**Portsmouth**	A	W	3-1	Wright-Phillips, S 6; Sibierski 79; Bosvelt 87
17	prem	**Aston Villa**	H	W	2-0	Macken 29; Wright-Phillips, S 38
18	prem	**Middlesbrough**	A	L	2-3	Fowler 39; Wright-Phillips, B 80
19	prem	**Tottenham**	H	L	0-1	
20	prem	**Bolton**	A	W	1-0	Barton 52
21	prem	**Everton**	A	L	1-2	Fowler 42
22	prem	**West Brom**	H	D	1-1	Anelka 32
23	prem	**Southampton**	H	W	2-1	Bosvelt 19; Wright-Phillips, S 40
24	prem	**Arsenal**	A	D	1-1	Wright-Phillips, S 31
25	facr3	**Oldham**	A	L	0-1	
26	prem	**Crystal Palace**	H	W	3-1	Wright-Phillips, S 12,90; Fowler 15
27	prem	**West Brom**	A	L	0-2	
28	prem	**Newcastle**	H	D	1-1	Fowler 49 pen
29	prem	**Chelsea**	A	D	0-0	
30	prem	**Man Utd**	H	L	0-2	
31	prem	**Norwich**	A	W	3-2	Sibierski 25; Fowler 37,90
32	prem	**Bolton**	H	L	0-1	
33	prem	**Tottenham**	A	L	1-2	Reyna 44
34	prem	**Charlton**	A	D	2-2	Hreidarsson 4 og; Fowler 38
35	prem	**Liverpool**	H	W	1-0	Musampa 90
36	prem	**Fulham**	A	D	1-1	Reyna 20
37	prem	**Birmingham**	H	W	3-0	Taylor, Maik 55 og; Dunne 80; Sibierski 86 pen
38	prem	**Blackburn**	A	D	0-0	
39	prem	**Portsmouth**	H	W	2-0	Distin 4; Fowler 16
40	prem	**Aston Villa**	A	W	2-1	Wright-Phillips, S 5; Musampa 12
41	prem	**Middlesbrough**	H	D	1-1	Musampa 46

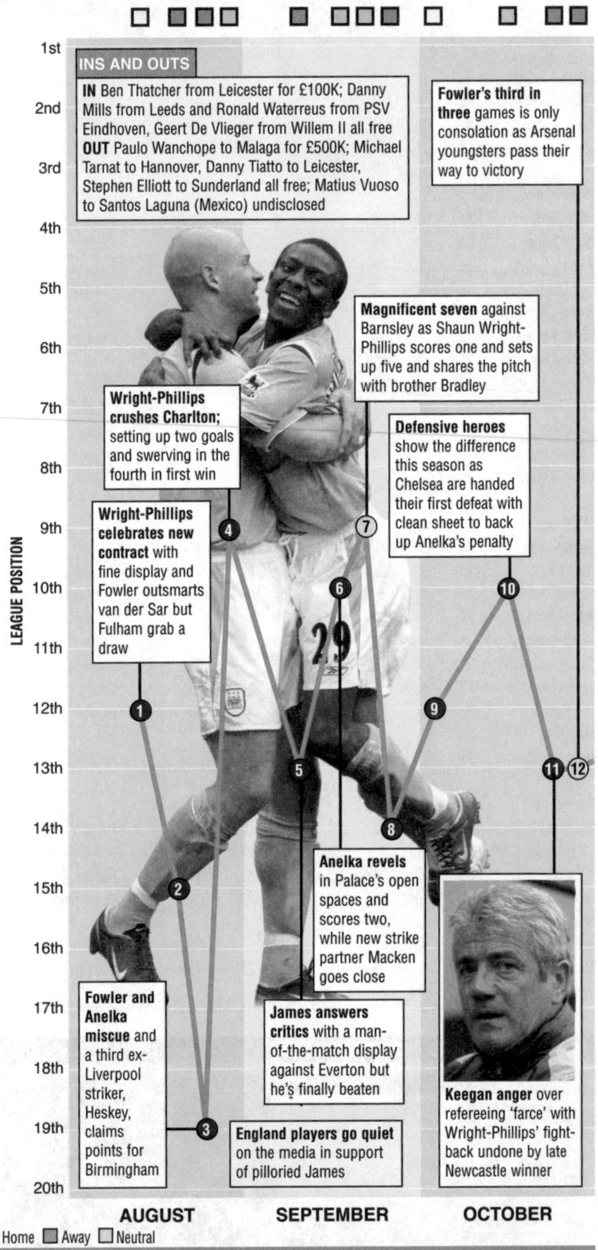

1st
2nd
3rd
4th
5th
6th
7th
8th
9th
10th
11th
12th
13th
14th
15th
16th
17th
18th
19th
20th
LEAGUE POSITION
INS AND OUTS
IN Ben Thatcher from Leicester for £100K; Danny Mills from Leeds and Ronald Waterreus from PSV Eindhoven, Geert De Vlieger from Willem II all free OUT Paulo Wanchope to Malaga for £500K; Michael Tarnat to Hannover, Danny Tiatto to Leicester, Stephen Elliott to Sunderland all free; Matius Vuoso to Santos Laguna (Mexico) undisclosed
Fowler's third in three games is only consolation as Arsenal youngsters pass their way to victory
Magnificent seven against Barnsley as Shaun Wright-Phillips scores one and sets up five and shares the pitch with brother Bradley
Wright-Phillips crushes Charlton; setting up two goals and swerving in the fourth in first win
Defensive heroes show the difference this season as Chelsea are handed their first defeat with clean sheet to back up Anelka's penalty
Wright-Phillips celebrates new contract with fine display and Fowler outsmarts van der Sar but Fulham grab a draw
Anelka revels in Palace's open spaces and scores two, while new strike partner Macken goes close
Fowler and Anelka miscue and a third ex-Liverpool striker, Heskey, claims points for Birmingham
James answers critics with a man-of-the-match display against Everton but he's finally beaten
England players go quiet on the media in support of pilloried James
Keegan anger over refereeing 'farce' with Wright-Phillips' fight-back undone by late Newcastle winner
AUGUST
SEPTEMBER
OCTOBER

Home / Away / Neutral

ATTENDANCES

HOME GROUND: CITY OF MANCHESTER STM **CAPACITY:** 48000 **AVERAGE LEAGUE AT HOME:** 45192

14	Man Utd	67863	15	Blackburn	45504	29	Chelsea	42093	6	Crystal Palace	25002
11	Newcastle	52316	10	Chelsea	45047	21	Everton	40530	38	Blackburn	24646
41	Middlesboro	47221	17	Aston Villa	44530	40	Aston Villa	39645	31	Norwich	24302
35	Liverpool	47203	1	Fulham	44026	24	Arsenal	38086	36	Fulham	21796
22	West Brom	47177	26	Crystal Palace	44010	33	Tottenham	35681	12	Arsenal	21708
30	Man Utd	47111	4	Charlton	43593	18	Middlesboro	29787	16	Portsmouth	20101
8	Arsenal	47015	32	Bolton	43050	9	Southampton	28605	7	Barnsley	19578
5	Everton	47006	23	Southampton	42895	3	Birmingham	28551	25	Oldham	13171
39	Portsmouth	46454	2	Liverpool	42831	20	Bolton	27274			
19	Tottenham	45805	13	Norwich	42803	34	Charlton	26436			
28	Newcastle	45752	37	Birmingham	42453	27	West Brom	25348			

Pearce's unbeatable case for permanence

Final Position: **8th**

KEY: ● League ● Champions Lge ● UEFA Cup ● FA Cup ○ League Cup ● Other

Dunne and Distin defiant as United are kept at bay and a rare point gained at Old Trafford

Mills red card is the turning point as Keegan reject Dickov scores from resulting penalty to earn Blackburn a point

Supreme temperament as Wright-Phillips forgets Spain to floor Pompey and win high praise from Keegan

England players outraged as Wright-Phillips is subject to racial abuse

Xmas party scuffle with cigar ends in £60,000 fine for Barton

Brother Bradley Wright-Phillips scores on debut after Fowler shows goal instincts but Boro hang onto the points

Anelka left out of starting XI after comments about playing for a bigger club and Spurs take control

Dunne like a kipper as ball bobbles off the defender's ankle past James to give chanceless Albion a point

Wright-Phillips jinks through the rain to unleash a shot into the corner and make sure of the points against Saints

A rare point at Highbury as Wright-Phillips unleashes a cracker to give his dad mixed emotions

A double dose of Wright-Phillips can't find a way past Oldham who survive 19 attempts on goal

Fowler finds his touch to score one and set up one of Shaun Wright-Phillips' two goals

Fowler's spot on for the sixth of his season to level and claim a point against Newcastle

'Save of the season' from James to take four points from Chelsea in the League

Dunne scoring twice in the wrong net for United while McManaman and Fowler miss sitters

"There's only one Jamie Oliver!" Delia's halftime rant inspires City fans and Fowler's winner – his 151st goal in the Premiership

Masumpa miss gives Bolton first top-division away win over Blues since 1956 and smashes Keegan's promise of 16 more months

Keegan calls it a day to pre-empt board's plans for a summer replacement.

Pearce steps in as 'caretaker'

Barton elbowed off the ball as Spurs score the winner but no excuses from Pearce in his first game in charge

Enough chances to win three games as Macken misses a hat-trick of one-on-ones and Charlton snatch a last-minute equaliser

Musampa's first goal gains Pearce's first win as the dreadlocked midfielder strikes home Croft's 90th minute cross

Shaun Wright-Phillips returns to action after seven weeks out

Pearce's claim for permanence gains credibility as Fowler header puts the skids under Birmingham

Into European reckoning as Distin's looping header is first of the season and Fowler free-kick makes sure

Manager of the month award for April goes to modest Pearce

Wright-Phillips slaloms through Villa to score and Musampa adds a second to be just one win away from Europe

Europe decided on a spot kick as Fowler faces Schwarzer with Uefa qualification as the prize and the Boro keeper saves

Pearce wins a contract to manage City for the next two years

Average League position over the season: 11.1

INS AND OUTS

Anelka ends sparring with move
IN Kiki Musampa from Atletico Madrid on loan
OUT Nicolas Anelka to Fenerbahce for £7m; Christian Negouai to Coventry on loan; Ronald Waterreus to Rangers for £100K; Kevin Stuhr-Ellegaard to Blackpool on loan

MONTH BY MONTH POINTS TALLY

Month	Points	%
AUGUST	4	33%
SEPTEMBER	3	33%
OCTOBER	4	44%
NOVEMBER	9	60%
DECEMBER	4	27%
JANUARY	7	58%
FEBRUARY	5	42%
MARCH	0	0%
APRIL	12	67%
MAY	4	67%

NOVEMBER DECEMBER JANUARY FEBRUARY MARCH APRIL MAY

GOAL ATTEMPTS

FOR – Goal attempts recorded in League games

	HOME	AWAY	TOTAL	AVE
shots on target	110	104	214	5.6
shots off target	102	87	189	5
TOTAL	212	191	403	10.6

Ratio of goals to shots Average number of shots on target per League goal scored: 4.6

Accuracy rating Average percentage of total goal attempts which were on target: 53.1

AGAINST – Goal attempts recorded in League games

	HOME	AWAY	TOTAL	AVE
shots on target	53	126	179	4.7
shots off target	82	104	186	4.9
TOTAL	135	230	365	9.6

Ratio of goals to shots Average number of shots on target per League goal scored: 4.6

Accuracy rating Average percentage of total goal attempts which were on target: 49

GOALS

Robbie Fowler

League	10
FA Cup	0
League Cup	1
Europe	0
Other	0
TOTAL	11

League Average 300 mins between goals

	PLAYER	LGE	FAC	LC	Euro	TOT	AVE
1	Fowler	10	0	1	0	11	252
2	S Wright-Phillips	10	0	1	0	11	300
3	Anelka	7	0	0	0	7	216
4	Sibierski	4	0	2	0	6	714
5	Musampa	3	0	0	0	3	414
6	Macken	1	0	2	0	3	1368
7	Reyna	2	0	0	0	2	732
8	Bosvelt	2	0	0	0	2	1214
9	Barton	1	0	1	0	2	2502
10	Flood	1	0	1	0	2	381
11	Distin	1	0	0	0	1	3402
12	B Wright-Phillips	1	0	0	0	1	198
13	Sinclair	1	0	0	0	1	194
14	Dunne	1	0	0	0	1	3123
	Other	2	0	0	0	2	
	TOTAL	47	0	8	0	55	

SQUAD APPEARANCES

Match	1	2	3	4	5	6	7	8	9	10	11	12	13	14	15	16	17	18	19	20	21	22	23	24	25	26	27	28	29	30	31	32	33	34	35	36	37	38	39	40	41
Venue	H	A	A	H	H	A	H	H	A	H	A	H	H	A	H	A	H	A	H	A	A	H	H	A	A	H	A	H	A	H	A	H	A	A	H	A	H	A	H	A	H
Competition	L	L	L	L	L	L	W	L	L	L	L	W	L	L	L	L	L	L	L	L	L	L	L	L	F	L	L	L	L	L	L	L	L	L	L	L	L	L	L	L	L
Result	D	L	L	W	L	W	W	L	D	W	L	L	D	D	D	W	W	L	L	W	L	D	W	D	L	W	L	D	D	L	W	L	L	D	W	D	W	D	W	W	D

Goalkeepers
David James
Kevin Stuhr-Ellegaard
Ronald Waterreus
Nicky Weaver

Defenders
Mikkel Bischoff
Sylvain Distin
Richard Dunne
Stephen Jordan
Patrick McCarthy
Danny Mills
Nedum Onuoha
David Sommeil
Sun Jihai
Ben Thatcher

Midfielders
Joey Barton
Paul Bosvelt
Jonathan D'Laryea
Willo Flood
Steve McManaman
Kiki Musampa
Claudio Reyna
Antoine Sibierski
Trevor Sinclair
Shaun Wright-Phillips

Forwards
Nicolas Anelka
Lee Croft
Robbie Fowler
Jonathan Macken
Christian Negouai
Bradley Wright-Phillips

KEY: On all match / On bench / Subbed or sent off (Counting game) / Subbed or sent off (playing less than 70 mins) / Subbed on from bench (Counting Game) / Subbed on (playing less than 70 mins) / Subbed on and then subbed or sent off (Counting Game) / Subbed on and then subbed or sent off (playing less than 70 mins) / Not in 16

KEY PLAYERS - GOALSCORERS

Nicolas Anelka

Goals in the League	7
Goals in all competitions	7
Assists League goals scored by a team mate where the player delivered the final pass	2
Contribution to Attacking Power Average number of minutes between League team goals while on pitch	88
Player Strike Rate Average number of minutes between League goals scored by player	216
Club Strike Rate Average minutes between League goals scored by club	73

	PLAYER	GOALS LGE	GOALS ALL	ASSISTS	POWER	S RATE
1	Nicolas Anelka	7	7	2	88	216 mins
2	Robbie Fowler	10	11	4	67	252 mins
3	Shaun Wright-Phillips	10	11	6	71	300 mins
4	Kiki Musampa	3	3	1	73	414 mins
5	Antoine Sibierski	4	6	1	73	714 mins

KEY PLAYERS - MIDFIELDERS

Joey Barton

Goals in the League	1
Goals in all competitions	2
Assists League goals scored by a team mate where the player delivered the final pass	4
Defensive Rating Average number of mins between League goals conceded while on the pitch	104
Contribution to Attacking Power Average number of minutes between League team goals while on pitch	68
Scoring Difference Defensive Rating minus Contribution to Attacking Power	36

	PLAYER	GOALS LGE	GOALS ALL	ASSISTS	DEF RATE	POWER	SC DIFF
1	Joey Barton	1	2	4	104	68	36 mins
2	Claudio Reyna	2	2	1	98	70	28 mins
3	Kiki Musampa	3	3	1	96	73	23 mins
4	Shaun Wright-Phillips	10	11	6	88	71	17 mins
5	Antoine Sibierski	4	6	1	82	73	9 mins

PLAYER APPEARANCES

	AGE (on 01/07/05)	IN NAMED 16	APPEARANCES	COUNTING GAMES	MINUTES ON PITCH	APPEARANCES	MINUTES ON PITCH	THIS SEASON	HOME COUNTRY
Goalkeepers									
David James	34	38	38	38	3420	39	3510	8	England (6)
Kevin Stuhr-Ellegaard	22	3	0	0	0	0	0	-	Denmark
Ronald Waterreus	34	21	0	0	0	2	180	-	Holland
Nicky Weaver	26	14	1	0	3	1	3	-	England
Defenders									
Mikkel Bischoff	23	2	0	0	0	0	0	-	Denmark
Sylvain Distin	27	38	38	38	3402	41	3627	-	France
Richard Dunne	25	35	35	34	3123	36	3213	4	Rep of Ireland (15)
Stephen Jordan	23	26	19	17	1620	21	1671	-	England
Patrick McCarthy	22	2	0	0	0	0	0	-	Rep of Ireland
Danny Mills	28	36	32	29	2608	35	2878	-	England
Nedum Onuoha	18	27	17	10	1069	18	1159	-	England
David Sommeil	30	11	1	1	90	2	135	-	France
Sun Jihai	27	9	6	3	333	7	423	-	China PR
Ben Thatcher	29	20	18	17	1544	21	1771	-	England
Midfielders									
Joey Barton	22	32	31	27	2502	33	2682	-	England
Paul Bosvelt	35	31	28	27	2428	30	2608	-	Holland
Jonathan D'Laryea	19	0	0	0	0	1	78	-	England
Willo Flood	20	21	9	2	381	12	584	-	Rep of Ireland
Steve McManaman	33	19	13	5	643	14	665	-	England
Kiki Musampa	27	14	14	14	1242	14	1242	-	Holland
Claudio Reyna	31	17	17	16	1463	17	1463	-	United States
Antoine Sibierski	30	35	35	30	2857	38	3104	-	France
Trevor Sinclair	32	4	4	2	194	5	262	-	England
Shaun Wright-Phillips	23	34	34	33	2998	37	3268	7	England (6)
Forwards									
Nicolas Anelka	26	19	19	15	1509	19	1509	-	France
Lee Croft	20	8	7	0	83	7	83	-	England
Robbie Fowler	30	35	32	25	2515	33	2605	-	England
Jonathan Macken	27	28	23	13	1368	25	1503	-	England
Christian Negouai	27	3	1	0	4	2	18	-	France
Bradley Wright-Phillips	20	26	13	0	198	16	323	-	England

KEY: LEAGUE — ALL COMPS — CAPS (MAY FIFA RANKING)

TEAM OF THE SEASON

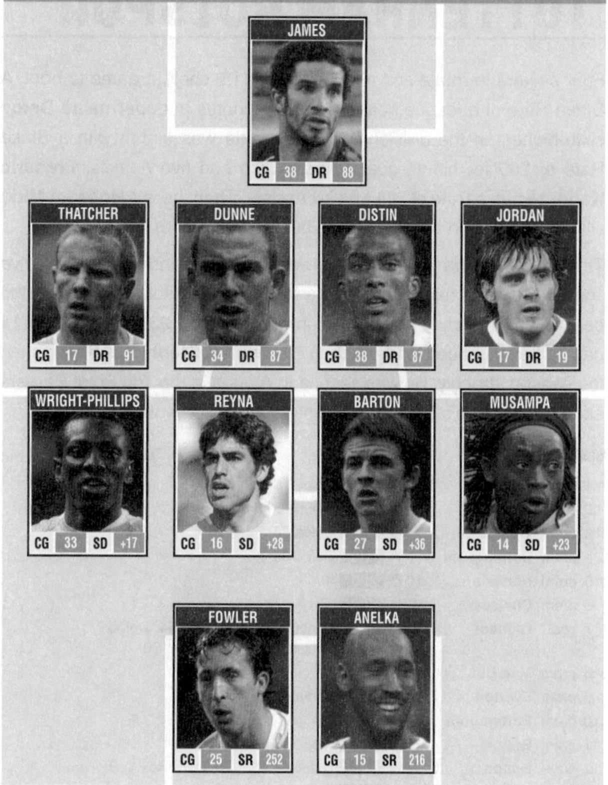
JAMES
CG 38 DR 88
THATCHER
CG 17 DR 91
DUNNE
CG 34 DR 87
DISTIN
CG 38 DR 87
JORDAN
CG 17 DR 19
WRIGHT-PHILLIPS
CG 33 SD +17
REYNA
CG 16 SD +28
BARTON
CG 27 SD +36
MUSAMPA
CG 14 SD +23
FOWLER
CG 25 SR 252
ANELKA
CG 15 SR 216

KEY: DR = Defensive Rating, SD = Scoring Difference SR = Strike Rate, CG=Counting games – League games playing at least 70 minutes

TOP POINT EARNERS

Joey Barton

Counting Games League games when player was on pitch for at least 70 minutes	27
Average points Average League points taken in Counting games	1.67
Club Average points Average points taken in League games	1.37

	PLAYER	GAMES	PTS
1	Joey Barton	27	1.67
2	Kiki Musampa	14	1.50
3	Jonathan Macken	13	1.46
4	Claudio Reyna	16	1.44
5	Antoine Sibierski	30	1.43
6	Shaun Wright-Phillips	33	1.42
7	Stephen Jordan	17	1.41
8	Ben Thatcher	17	1.41
9	Richard Dunne	34	1.38
10	David James	38	1.37

KEY PLAYERS - DEFENDERS

Ben Thatcher

Goals Conceded in the League Number of League goals conceded while the player was on the pitch	17
Goals Conceded in all competitions Total number of goals conceded while the player was on the pitch	21
League minutes played Number of minutes played in league matches	1544
Clean Sheets In games when player was on pitch for at least 70 minutes	4
Defensive Rating Average number of mins between League goals conceded while on the pitch	91
Club Defensive Rating Average number of mins between League goals conceded by the club this season	88

Thomas Cook

	PLAYER	CON LGE	CON ALL	MINS	C SHEETS	DEF RATE
1	Ben Thatcher	17	21	1544	4	91 mins
2	Stephen Jordan	18	19	1620	6	90 mins
3	Sylvain Distin	39	42	3402	11	87 mins
4	Richard Dunne	36	37	3123	11	87 mins
5	Danny Mills	33	37	2608	7	79 mins

KEY GOALKEEPER

David James

Goals Conceded in the League Number of League goals conceded while the player was on the pitch	39
Goals Conceded in all competitions Total number of goals conceded while the player was on the pitch	40
League minutes played Number of minutes played in league matches	3420
Clean Sheets In games when player was on pitch for at least 70 minutes	11
Goals to Shots Ratio The average number of shots on target per each League goal conceded	4.6
Defensive Rating Ave mins between League goals conceded while on the pitch	88

BOOKINGS

Joey Barton

League Yellow	9
League Red	0
All competitions Yellow	9
All competitions Red	0

League Average 278 mins between cards

	PLAYER	LEAGUE		TOTAL		AVE
1	Barton	9 Y	0 R	9 Y	0 R	278
2	Jordan	5	0	5	0	324
3	Dunne	7	1	7	1	390
4	Mills	5	1	5	1	434
5	Bosvelt	5	0	5	0	485
6	McManaman	1	0	1	0	643
7	Thatcher	2	0	2	0	772
8	Fowler	3	0	3	0	838
9	Sibierski	3	0	3	0	952
10	Distin	3	0	3	0	1134
	Other	0	0	0	0	
	TOTAL	43	2	43	2	

TOTTENHAM HOTSPUR

Four strikers to rotate and an average of 11.9 shots a game to boot. A Strike Rate of a league goal every 194 minutes puts **Jermaine Defoe** sixth-highest in the division. **Robbie Keane** was eighth with a Strike Rate of 200 for his 11 goals. Keane also had five Assists. **Frederic Kanouté** has a Rate of 284 and six Assists. Then there's **Hossam Mido** with three goals in only four starts but the best Strike Rate at 191.

Timothee Atouba alternated between midfield and defence. We've scored him as a midfielder and he tops the club table and is also the best at accumulating points, a high average of 1.93 points in the 14 games he influenced for more than 70 minutes. **Stephen Kelly** finished the season strongly. He was second to Atouba in the Top Point Earners and tops the club's Defensive Rating table by some way.

NICKNAME: SPURS KEY: Won Drawn Lost

1	prem	Liverpool	H	D	1-1	Defoe 70
2	prem	Newcastle	A	W	1-0	Atouba 51
3	prem	West Brom	A	D	1-1	Defoe 34
4	prem	Birmingham	H	W	1-0	Defoe 35
5	prem	Norwich	H	D	0-0	
6	prem	Chelsea	A	D	0-0	
7	ccr2	Oldham	A	W	6-0	Kanoute 37,90; Keane 64; Defoe 71; Bunjevcevic 87; Gardner 90
8	prem	Man Utd	H	L	0-1	
9	prem	Everton	A	W	1-0	Pamarot 53
10	prem	Portsmouth	A	L	0-1	
11	prem	Bolton	H	L	1-2	Keane 41
12	ccr3	Bolton	A	W	4-3	Defoe 44,103; Bunjevcevic 84; Brown 95
13	prem	Fulham	A	L	0-2	
14	prem	Charlton	H	L	2-3	Keane 69 pen; Defoe 79
15	ccr4	Burnley	A	W	3-0	Keane 31,52; Defoe 58
16	prem	Arsenal	H	L	4-5	Naybet 37; Defoe 61; King 74; Kanoute 88
17	prem	Aston Villa	A	L	0-1	
18	prem	Middlesbrough	H	W	2-0	Defoe 49; Kanoute 76
19	ccqf	Liverpool	H	L	1-1*	Defoe 108 (*aet, lost 4-3 on penalties)
20	prem	Blackburn	A	W	1-0	Keane 56
21	prem	Man City	A	W	1-0	Kanoute 57
22	prem	Southampton	H	W	5-1	Defoe 8,27,61; Kanoute 44; Keane 88
23	prem	Norwich	A	W	2-0	Keane 73; Brown 77
24	prem	Crystal Palace	H	D	1-1	Defoe 54
25	prem	Everton	H	W	5-2	Marney 16,80; Ziegler 27; Mendes 59; Keane 68
26	prem	Man Utd	A	D	0-0	
27	facr3	Brighton	H	W	2-1	King 40; Keane 83
28	prem	Chelsea	H	L	0-2	
29	prem	Crystal Palace	A	L	0-3	
30	facr4	West Brom	A	D	1-1	Defoe 31 pen
31	prem	Bolton	A	L	1-3	Defoe 66
32	prem	Portsmouth	H	W	3-1	Mido 34,57; Keane 83
33	facr4r	West Brom	H	W	3-1	Keane 44 pen; Defoe 50,55
34	facr5	Nottm Forest	H	D	1-1	Defoe 45
35	prem	Fulham	H	W	2-0	Kanoute 78; Keane 90
36	facr5r	Nottm Forest	A	W	3-0	Pamarot 60; Keane 72; Mido 90
37	prem	Southampton	A	L	0-1	
38	facqf	Newcastle	A	L	0-1	
39	prem	Charlton	A	L	0-2	
40	prem	Man City	H	W	2-1	Defoe 16; Keane 84
41	prem	Birmingham	A	D	1-1	Kelly 59
42	prem	Newcastle	H	W	1-0	Defoe 42
43	prem	Liverpool	A	D	2-2	Edman 12; Keane 55
44	prem	West Brom	H	D	1-1	Keane 52
45	prem	Arsenal	A	L	0-1	
46	prem	Aston Villa	H	W	5-1	Kanoute 6,27; King 19; Reid 67; Kelly 90
47	prem	Middlesbrough	A	L	0-1	
48	prem	Blackburn	H	D	0-0	

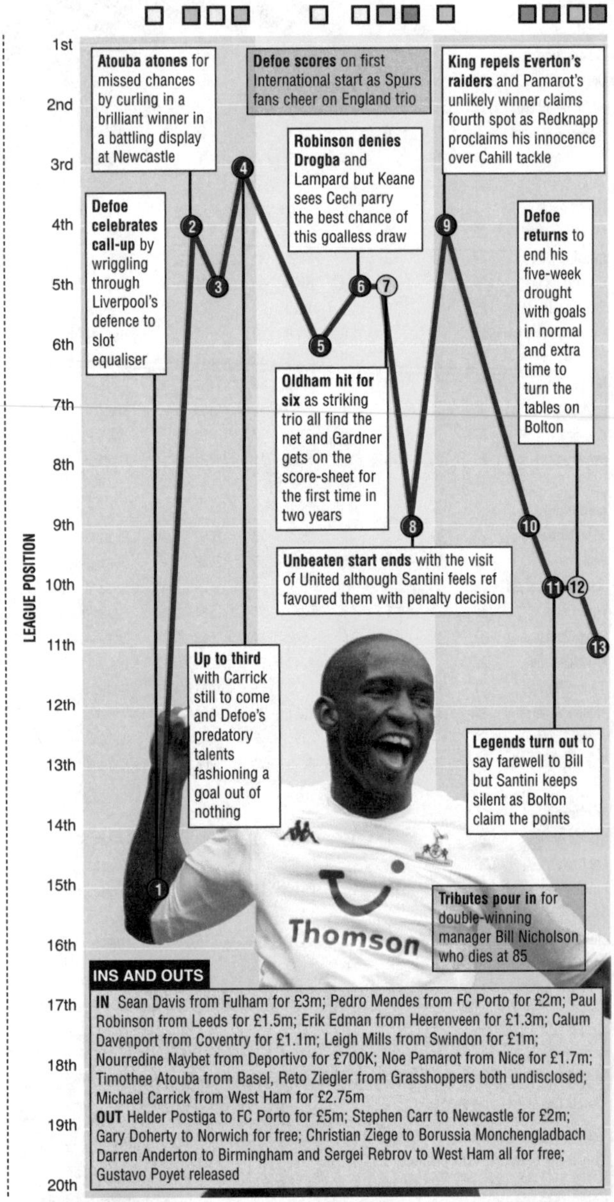
1st
2nd
3rd
4th
5th
6th
7th
8th
9th
10th
11th
12th
13th
14th
15th
16th
17th
18th
19th
20th
LEAGUE POSITION
Atouba atones for missed chances by curling in a brilliant winner in a battling display at Newcastle
Defoe scores on first International start as Spurs fans cheer on England trio
King repels Everton's raiders and Pamarot's unlikely winner claims fourth spot as Redknapp proclaims his innocence over Cahill tackle
Robinson denies Drogba and Lampard but Keane sees Cech parry the best chance of this goalless draw
Defoe celebrates call-up by wriggling through Liverpool's defence to slot equaliser
Defoe returns to end his five-week drought with goals in normal and extra time to turn the tables on Bolton
Oldham hit for six as striking trio all find the net and Gardner gets on the score-sheet for the first time in two years
Unbeaten start ends with the visit of United although Santini feels ref favoured them with penalty decision
Up to third with Carrick still to come and Defoe's predatory talents fashioning a goal out of nothing
Legends turn out to say farewell to Bill but Santini keeps silent as Bolton claim the points
Tributes pour in for double-winning manager Bill Nicholson who dies at 85
Thomson
AUGUST
SEPTEMBER
OCTOBER
Home Away Neutral

INS AND OUTS

IN Sean Davis from Fulham for £3m; Pedro Mendes from FC Porto for £2m; Paul Robinson from Leeds for £1.5m; Erik Edman from Heerenveen for £1.3m; Calum Davenport from Coventry for £1.1m; Leigh Mills from Swindon for £1m; Nourredine Naybet from Deportivo for £700K; Noe Pamarot from Nice for £1.7m; Timothee Atouba from Basel, Reto Ziegler from Grasshoppers both undisclosed; Michael Carrick from West Ham for £2.75m

OUT Helder Postiga to FC Porto for £5m; Stephen Carr to Newcastle for £2m; Gary Doherty to Norwich for free; Christian Ziege to Borussia Monchengladbach Darren Anderton to Birmingham and Sergei Rebrov to West Ham all for free; Gustavo Poyet released

ATTENDANCES

HOME GROUND: WHITE HART LANE CAPACITY: 36214 AVERAGE LEAGUE AT HOME: 35872

26	Man Utd	67962	19	Liverpool	36100	18	Middlesboro	35772	3	West Brom	27191
2	Newcastle	52185	24	Crystal Palace	36100	17	Aston Villa	35702	39	Charlton	26870
38	Newcastle	51307	16	Arsenal	36095	40	Man City	35681	31	Bolton	24780
21	Man City	45805	5	Norwich	36095	34	Nottm Forest	35640	23	Norwich	24508
43	Liverpool	44029	27	Brighton	36094	14	Charlton	35423	29	Crystal Palace	23723
6	Chelsea	42246	46	Aston Villa	36078	4	Birmingham	35290	30	West Brom	22441
9	Everton	38264	22	Southampton	36054	1	Liverpool	35105	20	Blackburn	22182
45	Arsenal	38147	11	Bolton	36025	47	Middlesboro	34766	13	Fulham	21317
32	Portsmouth	36105	44	West Brom	35885	37	Southampton	31903	10	Portsmouth	20121
28	Chelsea	36105	42	Newcastle	35885	41	Birmingham	29304	12	Bolton	18037
8	Man Utd	36103	35	Fulham	35885	36	Nottm Forest	28062	15	Burnley	10639
25	Everton	36102	48	Blackburn	35797	33	West Brom	27860	7	Oldham	8548

Manager style changes but results don't

Final Position: **9th**

KEY: ● League ● Champions Lge ● UEFA Cup ● FA Cup ○ League Cup ● Other

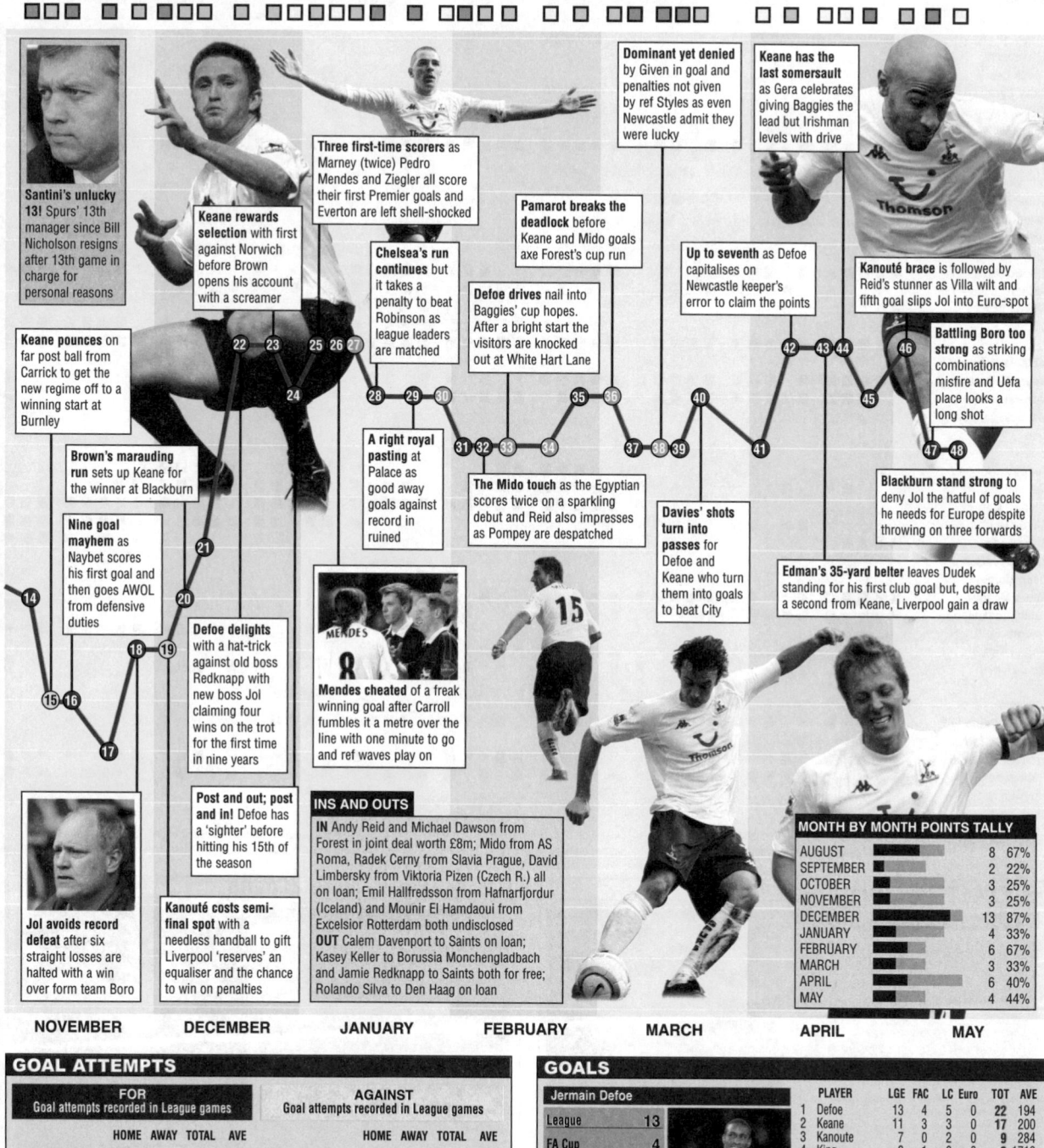

Santini's unlucky 13! Spurs' 13th manager since Bill Nicholson resigns after 13th game in charge for personal reasons

Keane pounces on far post ball from Carrick to get the new regime off to a winning start at Burnley

Brown's marauding run sets up Keane for the winner at Blackburn

Nine goal mayhem as Naybet scores his first goal and then goes AWOL from defensive duties

Jol avoids record defeat after six straight losses are halted with a win over form team Boro

Kanouté costs semi-final spot with a needless handball to gift Liverpool 'reserves' an equaliser and the chance to win on penalties

Defoe delights with a hat-trick against old boss Redknapp with new boss Jol claiming four wins on the trot for the first time in nine years

Post and out; post and in! Defoe has a 'sighter' before hitting his 15th of the season

Keane rewards selection with first against Norwich before Brown opens his account with a screamer

Three first-time scorers as Marney (twice) Pedro Mendes and Ziegler all score their first Premier goals and Everton are left shell-shocked

Chelsea's run continues but it takes a penalty to beat Robinson as league leaders are matched

A right royal pasting at Palace as good away goals against record in ruined

Mendes cheated of a freak winning goal after Carroll fumbles it a metre over the line with one minute to go and ref waves play on

Pamarot breaks the deadlock before Keane and Mido goals axe Forest's cup run

Defoe drives nail into Baggies' cup hopes. After a bright start the visitors are knocked out at White Hart Lane

The Mido touch as the Egyptian scores twice on a sparkling debut and Reid also impresses as Pompey are despatched

Dominant yet denied by Given in goal and penalties not given by ref Styles as even Newcastle admit they were lucky

Davies' shots turn into passes for Defoe and Keane who turn them into goals to beat City

Up to seventh as Defoe capitalises on Newcastle keeper's error to claim the points

Keane has the last somersault as Gera celebrates giving Baggies the lead but Irishman levels with drive

Edman's 35-yard belter leaves Dudek standing for his first club goal but, despite a second from Keane, Liverpool gain a draw

Kanouté brace is followed by Reid's stunner as Villa wilt and fifth goal slips Jol into Euro-spot

Battling Boro too strong as striking combinations misfire and Uefa place looks a long shot

Blackburn stand strong to deny Jol the hatful of goals he needs for Europe despite throwing on three forwards

INS AND OUTS

IN Andy Reid and Michael Dawson from Forest in joint deal worth £8m; Mido from AS Roma, Radek Cerny from Slavia Prague, David Limbersky from Viktoria Pizen (Czech R.) all on loan; Emil Hallfredsson from Hafnarfjordur (Iceland) and Mounir El Hamdaoui from Excelsior Rotterdam both undisclosed
OUT Calem Davenport to Saints on loan; Kasey Keller to Borussia Monchengladbach and Jamie Redknapp to Saints both for free; Rolando Silva to Den Haag on loan

MONTH BY MONTH POINTS TALLY

AUGUST	8	67%
SEPTEMBER	2	22%
OCTOBER	3	25%
NOVEMBER	3	25%
DECEMBER	13	87%
JANUARY	4	33%
FEBRUARY	6	67%
MARCH	3	33%
APRIL	6	40%
MAY	4	44%

NOVEMBER DECEMBER JANUARY FEBRUARY MARCH APRIL MAY

GOAL ATTEMPTS

FOR – Goal attempts recorded in League games

	HOME	AWAY	TOTAL	AVE
shots on target	153	94	247	6.5
shots off target	115	90	205	5.4
TOTAL	268	184	452	11.9

Ratio of goals to shots – Average number of shots on target per League goal scored: **5.3**

Accuracy rating – Average percentage of total goal attempts which were on target: **54.6**

AGAINST – Goal attempts recorded in League games

	HOME	AWAY	TOTAL	AVE
shots on target	80	116	196	5.2
shots off target	74	94	168	4.4
TOTAL	154	210	364	9.6

Ratio of goals to shots – Average number of shots on target per League goal scored: **4.8**

Accuracy rating – Average percentage of total goal attempts which were on target: **53.8**

GOALS

Jermain Defoe

League	13
FA Cup	4
League Cup	5
Europe	0
Other	0
TOTAL	22

League Average **194** mins between goals

	PLAYER	LGE	FAC	LC	Euro	TOT	AVE
1	Defoe	13	4	5	0	**22**	194
2	Keane	11	3	3	0	**17**	200
3	Kanoute	7	0	2	0	**9**	284
4	King	2	1	0	0	**3**	1710
5	Mido	2	1	0	0	**3**	191
6	Marney	2	0	0	0	**2**	151
7	Kelly	2	0	0	0	**2**	642
8	Pamarot	1	1	0	0	**2**	1948
9	Bunjevcevic	0	0	2	0	**2**	
10	Brown	1	0	1	0	**2**	1712
11	Reid	1	0	0	0	**1**	1072
12	Naybet	1	0	0	0	**1**	2322
13	Ziegler	1	0	0	0	**1**	1094
14	Atouba	1	0	0	0	**1**	1389
15	Mendes	1	0	0	0	**1**	1947
	Other	1	0	1	0	2	
	TOTAL	**47**	**10**	**14**	**0**	**71**	

SQUAD APPEARANCES

Match	1	2	3	4	5	6	7	8	9	10	11	12	13	14	15	16	17	18	19	20	21	22	23	24
Venue	H	A	A	H	H	A	A	H	A	A	H	A	A	H	A	H	A	H	H	A	A	H	A	H
Competition	L	L	L	L	L	L	W	L	L	L	L	W	L	L	W	L	L	L	W	L	L	L	L	L
Result	D	W	D	W	D	D	W	L	W	L	L	W	L	L	W	L	L	W	L	W	W	W	W	D

Match	25	26	27	28	29	30	31	32	33	34	35	36	37	38	39	40	41	42	43	44	45	46	47	48
Venue	H	A	H	H	A	A	A	H	H	H	H	A	A	A	A	H	A	H	A	H	A	H	A	H
Competition	L	L	F	L	L	F	L	L	F	F	L	F	L	F	L	L	L	L	L	L	L	L	L	L
Result	W	D	W	L	L	D	L	W	W	D	W	W	L	L	L	W	D	W	D	D	L	W	L	D

Goalkeepers
- Radek Cerny
- Nicky Eyre
- Marton Fulop
- Kasey Keller
- Paul Robinson

Defenders
- Goran Bunjevcevic
- Calum Davenport
- Michael Dawson
- Gary Doherty
- Erik Edman
- Anthony Gardner
- Philip Ifil
- Stephen Kelly
- Ledley King
- Mbulelo Mabizela
- Noureddine Naybet
- Noe Pamarot
- Mauricio Taricco

Midfielders
- Timothee Atouba
- Michael Brown
- Michael Carrick
- Simon Davies
- Sean Davis
- Johnnie Jackson
- Dean Marney
- Pedro Mendes
- Jamie Redknapp
- Andrew Reid
- Rohan Ricketts
- Reto Ziegler

Forwards
- Jermain Defoe
- Rolando Silva
- Frederic Kanoute
- Robbie Keane
- Hossam Mido
- Mark Yeates

KEY: On all match; On bench; Subbed or sent off (Counting game); Subbed or sent off (playing less than 70 mins); Subbed on from bench (Counting Game); Subbed on (playing less than 70 mins); Subbed on and then subbed or sent off (Counting Game); Subbed on and then subbed or sent off (playing less than 70 mins); Not in 16

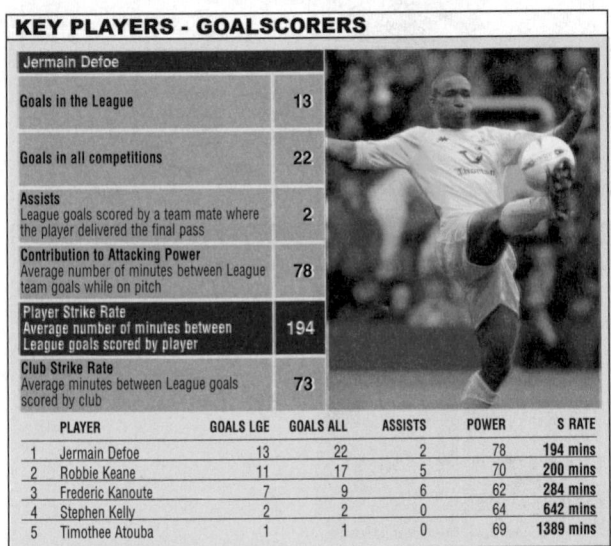

KEY PLAYERS - GOALSCORERS

Jermain Defoe

Goals in the League	13
Goals in all competitions	22
Assists League goals scored by a team mate where the player delivered the final pass	2
Contribution to Attacking Power Average number of minutes between League team goals while on pitch	78
Player Strike Rate Average number of minutes between League goals scored by player	194
Club Strike Rate Average minutes between League goals scored by club	73

	PLAYER	GOALS LGE	GOALS ALL	ASSISTS	POWER	S RATE
1	Jermain Defoe	13	22	2	78	194 mins
2	Robbie Keane	11	17	5	70	200 mins
3	Frederic Kanoute	7	9	6	62	284 mins
4	Stephen Kelly	2	2	0	64	642 mins
5	Timothee Atouba	1	1	0	69	1389 mins

KEY PLAYERS - MIDFIELDERS

Timothee Atouba

Goals in the League	1
Goals in all competitions	1
Assists League goals scored by a team mate where the player delivered the final pass	0
Defensive Rating Average number of mins between League goals conceded while on the pitch	116
Contribution to Attacking Power Average number of minutes between League team goals while on pitch	69
Scoring Difference Defensive Rating minus Contribution to Attacking Power	47

	PLAYER	GOALS LGE	GOALS ALL	ASSISTS	DEF RATE	POWER	SC DIFF
1	Timothee Atouba	1	1	0	116	69	47 mins
2	Michael Carrick	0	0	5	85	58	27 mins
3	Michael Brown	1	2	2	86	71	15 mins
4	Pedro Mendes	1	1	1	89	89	0 mins
5	Simon Davies	0	0	4	77	77	0 mins

PLAYER APPEARANCES

	AGE (on 01/07/05)	IN NAMED 16	APPEARANCES	COUNTING GAMES	MINUTES ON PITCH	APPEARANCES	MINUTES ON PITCH	THIS SEASON	HOME COUNTRY
Goalkeepers									
Radek Cerny	31	14	3	2	206	3	206	-	Czech Republic
Nicky Eyre	19	1	0	0	0	0	0	-	England
Marton Fulop	22	13	0	0	0	0	0	-	Hungary
Kasey Keller	35	12	0	0	0	2	210	-	United States
Paul Robinson	25	36	36	35	3214	44	3964	9	England (6)
Defenders									
Goran Bunjevcevic	32	10	3	2	187	5	397	-	Serbia & Montenegro
Calum Davenport	22	5	1	0	8	1	8	-	England
Michael Dawson	21	5	5	5	450	5	450	-	England
Gary Doherty	25	1	1	0	21	1	21	9	Rep of Ireland (15)
Erik Edman	26	29	28	24	2380	31	2569	5	Sweden (13)
Anthony Gardner	24	24	17	8	835	24	1408	-	England
Philip Ifil	18	4	2	2	180	3	194	-	England
Stephen Kelly	21	18	17	13	1284	23	1806	-	Rep of Ireland
Ledley King	24	38	38	38	3420	47	4290	7	England (6)
Mbulelo Mabizela	24	2	1	0	66	2	156	-	South Africa
Noureddine Naybet	35	28	27	26	2322	31	2709	-	Morocco
Noe Pamarot	26	26	23	22	1948	28	2433	-	France
Mauricio Taricco	32	1	0	0	0	0	0	-	Argentina
Midfielders									
Timothee Atouba	23	19	18	14	1389	24	1923	5	Cameroon (26)
Michael Brown	28	29	24	17	1712	34	2596	-	England
Michael Carrick	23	29	29	26	2374	38	3078	-	England
Simon Davies	25	21	21	16	1627	29	2192	5	Wales (74)
Sean Davis	25	16	15	10	1027	16	1117	-	England
Johnnie Jackson	22	8	8	3	274	9	364	-	England
Dean Marney	21	9	5	3	301	8	346	-	England
Pedro Mendes	26	24	24	19	1947	30	2347	-	Portugal
Jamie Redknapp	32	19	14	7	762	15	822	-	England
Andrew Reid	22	13	13	11	1072	13	1072	7	Rep of Ireland (15)
Rohan Ricketts	22	6	6	3	373	8	457	-	England
Reto Ziegler	19	27	23	7	1094	31	1849	-	Switzerland
Forwards									
Jermain Defoe	22	35	35	26	2525	44	3248	8	England
Rolando Silva	21	4	0	0	0	0	0	-	Cape Verde
Frederic Kanoute	27	32	32	20	1991	41	2697	-	Mali
Robbie Keane	24	36	35	21	2196	45	2761	8	Rep of Ireland (15)
Hossam Mido	22	10	9	1	381	11	423	-	Egypt
Mark Yeates	20	4	2	0	32	3	45	-	Rep of Ireland

KEY: LEAGUE ALL COMPS CAPS (MAY FIFA RANKING)

TEAM OF THE SEASON

ROBINSON
CG 35 DR 80
KELLY
CG 13 DR 99
NAYBET
CG 26 DR 86
KING
CG 38 DR 83
EDMAN
CG 24 DR 88
BROWN
CG 17 SD +15
MENDES
CG 19 SD 0
CARRICK
CG 26 SD +27
ATOUBA
CG 14 SD +47
KEANE
CG 21 SR 200
DEFOE
CG 26 SR 194

KEY: DR = Defensive Rating, SD = Scoring Difference SR = Strike Rate, CG=Counting games – League games playing at least 70 minutes

TOP POINT EARNERS

Timothee Atouba	
Counting Games League games when player was on pitch for at least 70 minutes	14
Average points Average League points taken in Counting games	1.93
Club Average points Average points taken in League games	1.37

	PLAYER	GAMES	PTS
1	Timothee Atouba	14	1.93
2	Stephen Kelly	13	1.69
3	Michael Brown	17	1.53
4	Michael Carrick	26	1.50
5	Noureddine Naybet	26	1.42
6	Frederic Kanoute	20	1.40
7	Jermain Defoe	26	1.38
8	Simon Davies	16	1.38
9	Ledley King	38	1.37
10	Paul Robinson	35	1.37

KEY PLAYERS - DEFENDERS

Stephen Kelly	
Goals Conceded in the League Number of League goals conceded while the player was on the pitch	13
Goals Conceded in all competitions Total number of goals conceded while the player was on the pitch	17
League minutes played Number of minutes played in league matches	1284
Clean Sheets In games when player was on pitch for at least 70 minutes	4
Defensive Rating Average number of mins between League goals conceded while on the pitch	99
Club Defensive Rating Average number of mins between League goals conceded by the club this season	83

Thomson

	PLAYER	CON LGE	CON ALL	MINS	C SHEETS	DEF RATE
1	Stephen Kelly	13	17	1284	4	99 mins
2	Erik Edman	27	29	2380	9	88 mins
3	Noureddine Naybet	27	32	2322	11	86 mins
4	Ledley King	41	50	3420	13	83 mins
5	Noe Pamarot	25	30	1948	8	78 mins

KEY GOALKEEPER

Dermott

Paul Robinson	
Goals Conceded in the League Number of League goals conceded while the player was on the pitch	40
Goals Conceded in all competitions Total number of goals conceded while the player was on the pitch	46
League minutes played Number of minutes played in league matches	3214
Clean Sheets In games when player was on pitch for at least 70 minutes	12
Goals to Shots Ratio The average number of shots on target per each League goal conceded	4.5
Defensive Rating Ave mins between League goals conceded while on the pitch	80

BOOKINGS

Jamie Redknapp	
League Yellow	5
League Red	0
All competitions Yellow	5
All competitions Red	0

League Average **152** mins between cards

	PLAYER	LEAGUE Y	LEAGUE R	TOTAL Y	TOTAL R	AVE
1	Redknapp	5	0	5	0	152
2	Brown	8	0	9	0	214
3	Davis	4	0	4	0	256
4	Pamarot	4	0	6	0	487
5	Kanoute	3	1	3	1	497
6	Defoe	5	0	6	0	505
7	Reid	2	0	2	0	536
8	Naybet	4	0	5	0	580
9	Mendes	3	0	3	0	649
10	Edman	3	0	4	0	793
11	Ziegler	1	0	2	0	1094
12	Kelly	1	0	1	0	1284
13	Atouba	1	0	3	0	1389
14	King	2	0	2	0	1710
15	Carrick	1	0	2	0	2374
	Other	0	0	3	0	
	TOTAL	47	1	60	1	

ASTON VILLA

That **Nolberto Solano** has Villa's best Strike Rate, sums up the club's problem. Solano scores on average every 349 minutes, the 12th highest Premier midfield player, but he eclipses all of O'Leary's main strikers. **Juan Pablo Angel** is 42nd in the Premiership with a Strike Rate of 388 and Vassell and Cole barely chart.

Lee Hendrie's goals were a feature of the first third of the season and he tops the Midfielders Table with the best Scoring Difference, determined by how often goals are conceded and scored when he was playing. **Tomas Hitzlsperger** heads Villa's Top Point Earners chart, which lists the players with the best points average, showing why he has been a fans' favourite.

Olof Mellberg is the stand-out defender, though he and **Thomas Sorensen** benefited from missing the Spurs' match.

NICKNAME: THE VILLANS — **KEY:** Won / Drawn / Lost

1	prem	**Southampton**	H	W	2-0	Vassell 12; Cole, C 34
2	prem	**West Brom**	A	D	1-1	Mellberg 4
3	prem	**Charlton**	A	L	0-3	
4	prem	**Newcastle**	H	W	4-2	Mellberg 4; Cole, C 53; Barry 71; Angel 82
5	prem	**Chelsea**	H	D	0-0	
6	prem	**Norwich**	A	D	0-0	
7	ccr2	**QPR**	H	W	3-1	Vassell 29; Angel 38; Solano 78
8	prem	**Crystal Palace**	H	D	1-1	Hendrie 36
9	prem	**Blackburn**	A	D	2-2	Angel 25; Mellberg 80
10	prem	**Arsenal**	A	L	1-3	Hendrie 3
11	prem	**Fulham**	H	W	2-0	Solano 29; Hendrie 75
12	ccr3	**Burnley**	A	L	1-3	Angel 81
13	prem	**Everton**	A	D	1-1	Hendrie 26
14	prem	**Portsmouth**	H	W	3-0	Whittingham 18; Angel 25; Solano 40
15	prem	**Bolton**	A	W	2-1	McCann 41; Hitzlsperger 89
16	prem	**Tottenham**	H	W	1-0	Solano 57
17	prem	**Man City**	A	L	0-2	
18	prem	**Liverpool**	H	D	1-1	Solano 44
19	prem	**Birmingham**	H	L	1-2	Barry 90
20	prem	**Middlesbrough**	A	L	0-3	
21	prem	**Chelsea**	A	L	0-1	
22	prem	**Man Utd**	H	L	0-1	
23	prem	**Blackburn**	H	W	1-0	Solano 88
24	prem	**Crystal Palace**	A	L	0-2	
25	facr3	**Sheff Utd**	A	L	1-3	Barry 47
26	prem	**Norwich**	H	W	3-0	Ridgewell 9; Hendrie 27; Solano 76
27	prem	**Man Utd**	A	L	1-3	Barry 53
28	prem	**Fulham**	A	D	1-1	Angel 55
29	prem	**Arsenal**	H	L	1-3	Angel 74
30	prem	**Portsmouth**	A	W	2-1	De Zeeuw 17 og; Hitzlsperger 73
31	prem	**Everton**	H	L	1-3	Solano 46
32	prem	**Middlesbrough**	H	W	2-0	Laursen 64; Moore, L 79
33	prem	**Birmingham**	A	L	0-2	
34	prem	**Newcastle**	A	W	3-0	Angel 5; Barry 73 pen,80 pen
35	prem	**West Brom**	H	D	1-1	Vassell 26
36	prem	**Southampton**	A	W	3-2	Cole 55; Solano 70; Davis 72
37	prem	**Charlton**	H	D	0-0	
38	prem	**Bolton**	H	D	1-1	Hierro 26 og
39	prem	**Tottenham**	A	L	1-5	Barry 45 pen
40	prem	**Man City**	H	L	1-2	Angel 61
41	prem	**Liverpool**	A	L	1-2	Barry 67

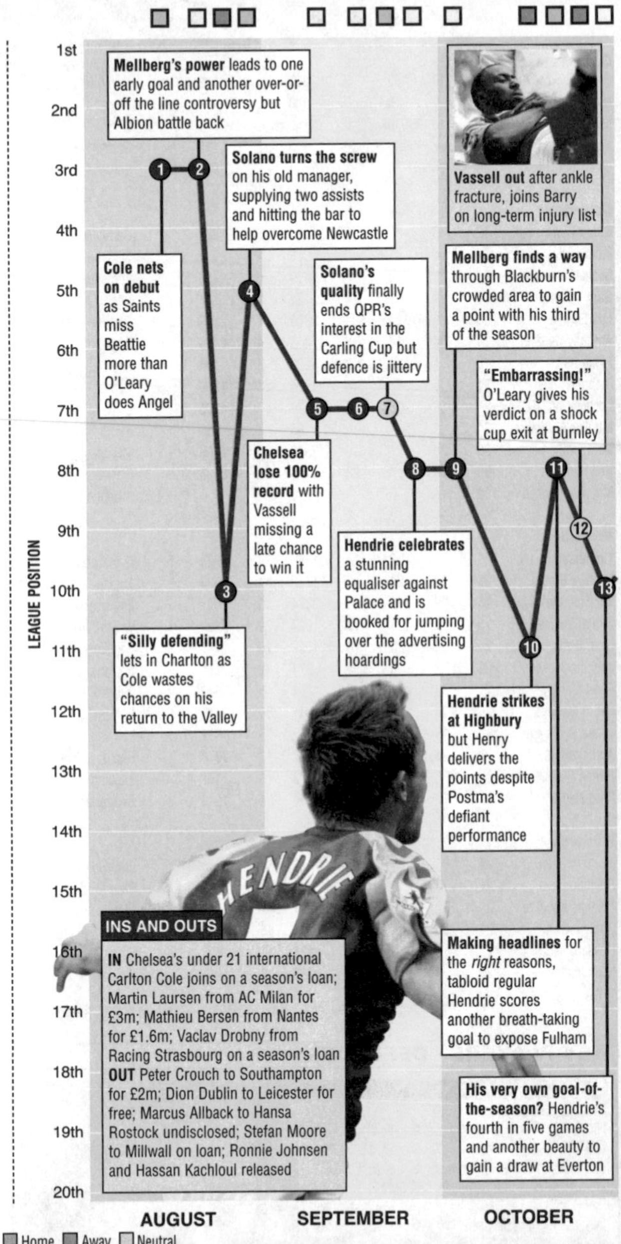
1st
2nd
3rd
4th
5th
6th
7th
8th
9th
10th
11th
12th
13th
14th
15th
16th
17th
18th
19th
20th
LEAGUE POSITION
Mellberg's power leads to one early goal and another over-or-off the line controversy but Albion battle back
Solano turns the screw on his old manager, supplying two assists and hitting the bar to help overcome Newcastle
Vassell out after ankle fracture, joins Barry on long-term injury list
Cole nets on debut as Saints miss Beattie more than O'Leary does Angel
Solano's quality finally ends QPR's interest in the Carling Cup but defence is jittery
Mellberg finds a way through Blackburn's crowded area to gain a point with his third of the season
"Embarrassing!" O'Leary gives his verdict on a shock cup exit at Burnley
Chelsea lose 100% record with Vassell missing a late chance to win it
Hendrie celebrates a stunning equaliser against Palace and is booked for jumping over the advertising hoardings
"Silly defending" lets in Charlton as Cole wastes chances on his return to the Valley
Hendrie strikes at Highbury but Henry delivers the points despite Postma's defiant performance
INS AND OUTS
IN Chelsea's under 21 international Carlton Cole joins on a season's loan; Martin Laursen from AC Milan for £3m; Mathieu Bersen from Nantes for £1.6m; Vaclav Drobny from Racing Strasbourg on a season's loan **OUT** Peter Crouch to Southampton for £2m; Dion Dublin to Leicester for free; Marcus Allback to Hansa Rostock undisclosed; Stefan Moore to Millwall on loan; Ronnie Johnsen and Hassan Kachloul released
Making headlines for the *right* reasons, tabloid regular Hendrie scores another breath-taking goal to expose Fulham
His very own goal-of-the-season? Hendrie's fourth in five games and another beauty to gain a draw at Everton
AUGUST
SEPTEMBER
OCTOBER
Home
Away
Neutral

ATTENDANCES

HOME GROUND: VILLA PARK   CAPACITY: 43275   AVERAGE LEAGUE AT HOME: 37354

27	Man Utd	67859	35	West Brom	39402	11	Fulham	34460	15	Bolton	25779
34	Newcastle	52306	26	Norwich	38172	23	Blackburn	34265	24	Crystal Palace	24140
17	Man City	44530	10	Arsenal	38137	32	M'brough	34201	6	Norwich	23805
41	Liverpool	43406	13	Everton	37816	14	Portsmouth	32633	9	Blackburn	20502
18	Liverpool	42593	5	Chelsea	36691	36	Southampton	31926	30	Portsmouth	20160
29	Arsenal	42593	1	Southampton	36690	20	M'brough	31338	28	Fulham	17624
22	Man Utd	42593	4	Newcastle	36305	37	Charlton	31312	25	Sheff Utd	14003
21	Chelsea	41950	39	Tottenham	36078	33	Birmingham	29382	12	Burnley	11184
19	Birmingham	41329	38	Bolton	36053	7	QPR	26975			
31	Everton	40248	16	Tottenham	35702	2	West Brom	26601			
40	Man City	39645	8	Crystal Palace	34843	3	Charlton	26190			

Still a strike force short of Europe

Final Position: **10th**

KEY: ● League ● Champions Lge ● UEFA Cup ● FA Cup ○ League Cup ○ Other

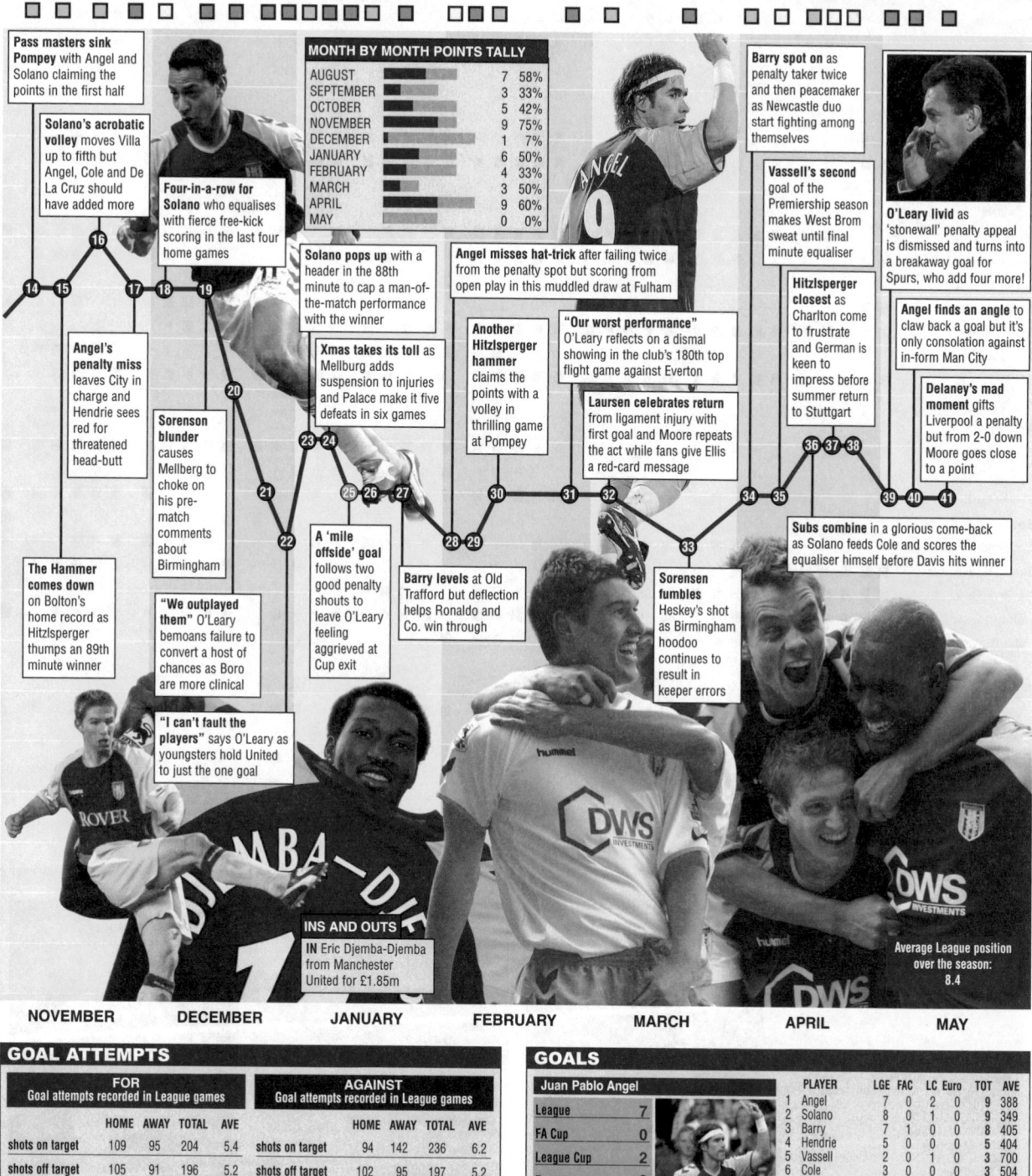

Pass masters sink Pompey with Angel and Solano claiming the points in the first half
Solano's acrobatic volley moves Villa up to fifth but Angel, Cole and De La Cruz should have added more
Four-in-a-row for Solano who equalises with fierce free-kick scoring in the last four home games
Angel's penalty miss leaves City in charge and Hendrie sees red for threatened head-butt
The Hammer comes down on Bolton's home record as Hitzlsperger thumps an 89th minute winner
Sorenson blunder causes Mellberg to choke on his pre-match comments about Birmingham
"We outplayed them" O'Leary bemoans failure to convert a host of chances as Boro are more clinical
"I can't fault the players" says O'Leary as youngsters hold United to just the one goal
Solano pops up with a header in the 88th minute to cap a man-of-the-match performance with the winner
Xmas takes its toll as Mellburg adds suspension to injuries and Palace make it five defeats in six games
A 'mile offside' goal follows two good penalty shouts to leave O'Leary feeling aggrieved at Cup exit
Angel misses hat-trick after failing twice from the penalty spot but scoring from open play in this muddled draw at Fulham
Another Hitzlsperger hammer claims the points with a volley in thrilling game at Pompey
Barry levels at Old Trafford but deflection helps Ronaldo and Co. win through
"Our worst performance" O'Leary reflects on a dismal showing in the club's 180th top flight game against Everton
Laursen celebrates return from ligament injury with first goal and Moore repeats the act while fans give Ellis a red-card message
Sorensen fumbles Heskey's shot as Birmingham hoodoo continues to result in keeper errors
Barry spot on as penalty taker twice and then peacemaker as Newcastle duo start fighting among themselves
Vassell's second goal of the Premiership season makes West Brom sweat until final minute equaliser
Hitzlsperger closest as Charlton come to frustrate and German is keen to impress before summer return to Stuttgart
O'Leary livid as 'stonewall' penalty appeal is dismissed and turns into a breakaway goal for Spurs, who add four more!
Angel finds an angle to claw back a goal but it's only consolation against in-form Man City
Delaney's mad moment gifts Liverpool a penalty but from 2-0 down Moore goes close to a point
Subs combine in a glorious come-back as Solano feeds Cole and scores the equaliser himself before Davis hits winner
14 15 16 17 18 19 20 21 22 23 24 25 26 27 28 29 30 31 32 33 34 35 36 37 38 39 40 41
ANGEL 9
hummel
DWS INVESTMENTS
ROVER
DJEMBA-DJEMBA
INS AND OUTS
IN Eric Djemba-Djemba from Manchester United for £1.85m
Average League position over the season: 8.4

MONTH BY MONTH POINTS TALLY

AUGUST	7	58%
SEPTEMBER	3	33%
OCTOBER	5	42%
NOVEMBER	9	75%
DECEMBER	1	7%
JANUARY	6	50%
FEBRUARY	4	33%
MARCH	3	50%
APRIL	9	60%
MAY	0	0%

NOVEMBER DECEMBER JANUARY FEBRUARY MARCH APRIL MAY

GOAL ATTEMPTS

FOR
Goal attempts recorded in League games

	HOME	AWAY	TOTAL	AVE
shots on target	109	95	204	5.4
shots off target	105	91	196	5.2
TOTAL	214	186	400	10.5

Ratio of goals to shots Average number of shots on target per League goal scored	4.5
Accuracy rating Average percentage of total goal attempts which were on target	51

AGAINST
Goal attempts recorded in League games

	HOME	AWAY	TOTAL	AVE
shots on target	94	142	236	6.2
shots off target	102	95	197	5.2
TOTAL	196	237	433	11.4

Ratio of goals to shots Average number of shots on target per League goal scored	4.5
Accuracy rating Average percentage of total goal attempts which were on target	54.5

GOALS

Juan Pablo Angel

League	7
FA Cup	0
League Cup	2
Europe	0
Other	0
TOTAL	9

League Average
388
mins between goals

	PLAYER	LGE	FAC	LC	Euro	TOT	AVE
1	Angel	7	0	2	0	9	388
2	Solano	8	0	1	0	9	349
3	Barry	7	1	0	0	8	405
4	Hendrie	5	0	0	0	5	404
5	Vassell	2	0	1	0	3	700
6	Cole	3	0	0	0	3	504
7	Mellberg	3	0	0	0	3	885
8	Hitzlsperger	2	0	0	0	2	807
9	McCann	1	0	0	0	1	1763
10	Laursen	1	0	0	0	1	1035
11	Ridgewell	1	0	0	0	1	1130
12	Moore, L	1	0	0	0	1	849
13	Davis	1	0	0	0	1	1899
14	Whittingham	1	0	0	0	1	573
	Other	2	0	0	0	2	
	TOTAL	45	1	4	0	50	

SQUAD APPEARANCES

Match	1	2	3	4	5	6	7	8	9	10	11	12	13	14	15	16	17	18	19	20	21	22	23	24	25	26	27	28	29	30	31	32	33	34	35	36	37	38	39	40	41
Venue	H	A	A	H	H	A	H	H	A	A	H	A	A	H	A	H	A	H	H	A	A	H	H	A	A	H	A	A	H	A	H	H	A	A	H	A	H	H	A	H	A
Competition	L	L	L	L	L	L	W	L	L	L	L	W	L	L	L	L	L	L	L	L	L	L	L	L	F	L	L	L	L	L	L	L	L	L	L	L	L	L	L	L	L
Result	W	D	L	W	D	D	W	D	D	L	W	L	D	W	W	W	L	D	L	L	L	L	W	L	L	W	L	D	L	W	L	W	L	W	D	W	D	D	L	L	L

Goalkeepers
Wayne Henderson
Stefan Postma
Thomas Sorensen

Defenders
Ulises De La Cruz
Mark Delaney
Vaclav Drobny
Martin Laursen
Olof Mellberg
Liam Ridgewell
Jlloyd Samuel

Midfielders
Gareth Barry
Mathieu Berson
Steven Davis
Eric Djemba-Djemba
Lee Hendrie
Tomas Hitzlsperger
Gavin McCann
Nolberto Solano
Peter Whittingham

Forwards
Juan Pablo Angel
Carlton Cole
Luke Moore
Stefan Moore
Darius Vassell

KEY: On all match | On bench | Subbed or sent off (Counting game) | Subbed or sent off (playing less than 70 mins) | Subbed on from bench (Counting Game) | Subbed on (playing less than 70 mins) | Subbed on and then subbed or sent off (Counting Game) | Subbed on and then subbed or sent off (playing less than 70 mins) | Not in 16

KEY PLAYERS - GOALSCORERS

Nolberto Solano

Goals in the League	8
Goals in all competitions	9
Assists League goals scored by a team mate where the player delivered the final pass	6
Contribution to Attacking Power Average number of minutes between League team goals while on the pitch	75
Player Strike Rate Average number of minutes between League goals scored by player	349
Club Strike Rate Average minutes between League goals scored by club	76

	PLAYER	GOALS LGE	GOALS ALL	ASSISTS	POWER	S RATE
1	Nolberto Solano	8	9	6	76	349 mins
2	Juan Pablo Angel	7	9	4	75	388 mins
3	Lee Hendrie	5	5	3	67	404 mins
4	Gareth Barry	7	8	1	81	405 mins
5	Darius Vassell	2	3	2	77	700 mins

KEY PLAYERS - MIDFIELDERS

Lee Hendrie

Goals in the League	5
Goals in all competitions	5
Assists League goals scored by a team mate where the player delivered the final pass	3
Defensive Rating Average number of mins between League goals conceded while on the pitch	70
Contribution to Attacking Power Average number of minutes between League team goals while on pitch	67
Scoring Difference Defensive Rating minus Contribution to Attacking Power	3

	PLAYER	GOALS LGE	GOALS ALL	ASSISTS	DEF RATE	POWER	SC DIFF
1	Lee Hendrie	5	5	3	70	67	3 mins
2	Tomas Hitzlsperger	2	2	2	67	65	2 mins
3	Gavin McCann	1	1	1	77	77	0 mins
4	Nolberto Solano	8	9	6	67	76	-9 mins
5	Gareth Barry	7	8	1	60	81	-21 mins

PLAYER APPEARANCES

	AGE (on 01/07/05)	IN NAMED 16	APPEARANCES	COUNTING GAMES	MINUTES ON PITCH	APPEARANCES	MINUTES ON PITCH	THIS SEASON	HOME COUNTRY
Goalkeepers									
Wayne Henderson	21	2	0	0	0	0	0	-	Rep of Ireland
Stefan Postma	28	37	3	2	225	3	225	-	Holland
Thomas Sorensen	29	37	36	35	3195	39	3465	6	Denmark (19)
Defenders									
Ulises De La Cruz	30	37	34	31	2834	35	2924	-	Ecuador
Mark Delaney	29	31	30	27	2542	32	2722	7	Wales (74)
Vaclav Drobny	24	2	0	0	0	0	0	-	Czech Republic
Martin Laursen	27	16	12	11	1035	12	1035	2	Denmark (19)
Olof Mellberg	27	30	30	29	2655	33	2925	8	Sweden (13)
Liam Ridgewell	20	25	15	11	1130	17	1310	-	England
Jlloyd Samuel	24	35	35	32	3009	38	3249	-	England
Midfielders									
Gareth Barry	24	34	34	31	2836	36	3009	-	England
Mathieu Berson	25	21	11	5	629	13	676	-	France
Steven Davis	20	32	28	19	1899	29	1923	4	N Ireland (114)
Eric Djemba-Djemba	24	9	6	2	357	6	357	4	Cameroon (26)
Lee Hendrie	28	30	29	18	2022	32	2275	-	England
Tomas Hitzlsperger	23	30	28	13	1613	30	1660	4	Germany (19)
Gavin McCann	27	21	20	19	1763	23	1993	-	England
Nolberto Solano	30	37	36	29	2794	39	3021	-	Peru
Peter Whittingham	20	20	13	4	573	15	753	-	England
Forwards									
Juan Pablo Angel	29	35	35	27	2717	38	2987	-	Colombia
Carlton Cole	21	30	27	11	1511	30	1709	-	England
Luke Moore	19	32	25	3	849	27	881	-	England
Stefan Moore	21	4	1	0	4	1	4	-	England
Darius Vassell	25	21	21	12	1399	22	1458	3	England (6)

KEY: LEAGUE ALL COMPS CAPS (MAY FIFA RANKING)

TEAM OF THE SEASON

SORENSEN
CG 35 DR 74
DE LA CRUZ
CG 31 DR 67
MELLBERG
CG 29 DR 72
DELANEY
CG 27 DR 65
SAMUEL
CG 32 DR 65
SOLANO
CG 29 SD -9
HENDRIE
CG 18 SD +3
McCANN
CG 19 SD 0
HITZLSPERGER
CG 13 SD +2
VASSELL
CG 12 AP 77
ANGEL
CG 27 SR 388

KEY: DR = Defensive Rating, SD = Scoring Difference AP = Attacking Power SR = Strike Rate, CG=Counting games – League games playing at least 70 minutes

TOP POINT EARNERS

Tomas Hitzlsperger	
Counting Games League games when player was on pitch for at least 70 minutes	13
Average points **Average League points taken in Counting games**	1.62
Club Average points Average points taken in League games	1.24

	PLAYER	GAMES	PTS
1	Tomas Hitzlsperger	13	1.62
2	Lee Hendrie	18	1.56
3	Jlloyd Samuel	32	1.44
4	Gavin McCann	19	1.42
5	Thomas Sorensen	35	1.34
6	Mark Delaney	27	1.33
7	Olof Mellberg	29	1.31
8	Juan Pablo Angel	27	1.30
9	Nolberto Solano	29	1.21
10	Darius Vassell	12	1.17

KEY PLAYERS - DEFENDERS

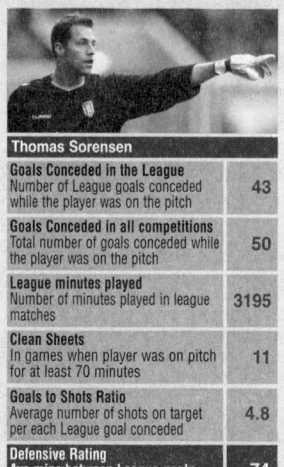

Olof Mellberg	
Goals Conceded in the League Number of League goals conceded while the player was on the pitch	37
Goals Conceded in all competitions Total number of goals conceded while the player was on the pitch	44
League minutes played Number of minutes played in league matches	2655
Clean Sheets In games when player was on pitch for at least 70 minutes	9
Defensive Rating **Average number of mins between League goals conceded while on the pitch**	72
Club Defensive Rating Average number of mins between League goals conceded by the club this season	66

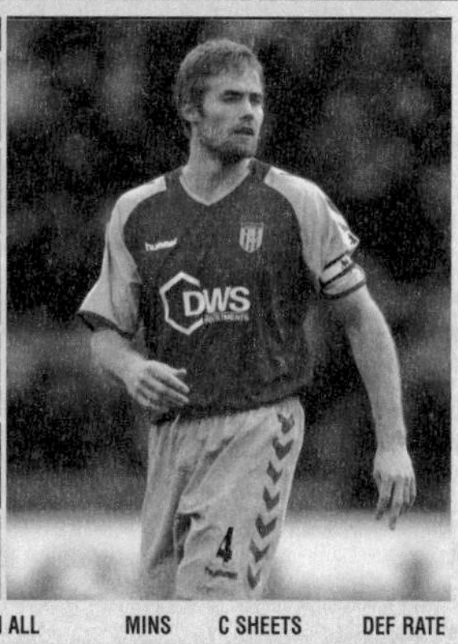

	PLAYER	CON LGE	CON ALL	MINS	C SHEETS	DEF RATE
1	Olof Mellberg	37	44	2655	9	72 mins
2	Ulises De La Cruz	42	43	2834	8	67 mins
3	Mark Delaney	39	45	2542	9	65 mins
4	Jlloyd Samuel	46	51	3009	11	65 mins

KEY GOALKEEPER

Thomas Sorensen	
Goals Conceded in the League Number of League goals conceded while the player was on the pitch	43
Goals Conceded in all competitions Total number of goals conceded while the player was on the pitch	50
League minutes played Number of minutes played in league matches	3195
Clean Sheets In games when player was on pitch for at least 70 minutes	11
Goals to Shots Ratio Average number of shots on target per each League goal conceded	4.8
Defensive Rating **Ave mins between League goals conceded while on the pitch**	74

BOOKINGS

Lee Hendrie	
League Yellow	9
League Red	1
All competitions Yellow	9
All competitions Red	1
League Average **202** mins between cards	

	PLAYER	LEAGUE Y	LEAGUE R	TOTAL Y	TOTAL R	AVE
1	Hendrie	9 Y	1 R	9 Y	1 R	202
2	Ridgewell	3	1	3	1	282
3	Berson	2	0	3	0	314
4	Laursen	3	0	3	0	345
5	Mellberg	6	0	6	0	442
6	Solano	6	0	6	0	465
7	Samuel	6	0	6	0	501
8	Whittingham	1	0	1	0	573
9	McCann	3	0	3	0	587
10	Delaney	3	0	3	0	847
11	Moore, L	1	0	1	0	849
12	Davis	2	0	2	0	949
13	De La Cruz	2	0	2	0	1417
14	Barry	2	0	2	0	1418
15	Cole	1	0	1	0	1511
	Other	3	0	3	0	
	TOTAL	53	2	54	2	

CHARLTON ATHLETIC

Taken over the season Charlton's average league position was ninth but the usual slump saw the points dry up in the months after January, dropping to 11th.

Talal El Karkouri was the second-highest scorer among the Premier defenders with five. He combined some spectacular shooting with the club's best Defensive Rating of a goal conceded every 69 minutes on average.

Charlton's Total Shots averaged just 8.2 per game, the lowest in the Premiership. Not surprisingly main forward **Shaun Bartlett's** Strike Rate of a goal every 340 minutes was only the 33rd best in the Divisional Round-up table.

Radostin Kishishev tops the Divisional Round-up chart for Most Missed Player in the Premiership over his 18 games. He averages 1.72 points a game. **Jerome Thomas** had an even higher points average but didn't play enough games to get into the divisional chart. He headed the club's Top Point Earners and Midfielders charts.

NICKNAME: THE ADDICKS

KEY: Won Drawn Lost

1	prem	**Bolton**	A	L	1-4	Lisbie 67
2	prem	**Portsmouth**	H	W	2-1	Euell 23; Unsworth 87 og
3	prem	**Aston Villa**	H	W	3-0	Jeffers 29,34; Young 58
4	prem	**Man City**	A	L	0-4	
5	prem	**Southampton**	H	D	0-0	
6	prem	**Birmingham**	A	D	1-1	Young 49
7	ccr2	**Grimsby**	A	W	2-0	Murphy 8; Jeffers 79
8	prem	**Blackburn**	H	W	1-0	El Karkouri 49
9	prem	**Arsenal**	A	L	0-4	
10	prem	**Newcastle**	H	D	1-1	O'Brien 51 og
11	prem	**Liverpool**	A	L	0-2	
12	ccr3	**Crystal Palace**	H	L	1-2	Hreidarsson 5
13	prem	**Middlesbrough**	H	L	1-2	Johansson 46
14	prem	**Tottenham**	A	W	3-2	Bartlett 17,39; Thomas 50
15	prem	**Norwich**	H	W	4-0	Johansson 15,21; Konchesky 75; Euell 88
16	prem	**Man Utd**	A	L	0-2	
17	prem	**Chelsea**	H	L	0-4	
18	prem	**Crystal Palace**	A	W	1-0	Rommedahl 90
19	prem	**West Brom**	A	W	1-0	Holland 30
20	prem	**Fulham**	H	W	2-1	Thomas 27; El Karkouri 66
21	prem	**Southampton**	A	D	0-0	
22	prem	**Everton**	H	W	2-0	El Karkouri 82; Hreidarsson 85
23	prem	**Arsenal**	H	L	1-3	El Karkouri 45
24	prem	**Blackburn**	A	L	0-1	
25	facr3	**Rochdale**	H	W	4-1	Hughes 19,56; Fortune 44; Murphy 64
26	prem	**Birmingham**	H	W	3-1	El Karkouri 9; Bartlett 67; Murphy 75
27	prem	**Everton**	A	W	1-0	Holland 45
28	facr4	**Yeovil**	H	W	3-2	Hughes 37; Jeffers 51; Bartlett 57
29	prem	**Liverpool**	H	L	1-2	Bartlett 20
30	prem	**Newcastle**	A	D	1-1	Rommedahl 53
31	facr5	**Leicester**	H	L	1-2	Bartlett 45
32	prem	**Middlesbrough**	A	D	2-2	Holland 14; Bartlett 80
33	prem	**Fulham**	A	D	0-0	
34	prem	**Tottenham**	H	W	2-0	Thomas 4; Murphy 85
35	prem	**West Brom**	H	L	1-4	Johansson 24
36	prem	**Man City**	H	D	2-2	Bartlett 10; Perry 90
37	prem	**Portsmouth**	A	L	2-4	Fortune 22; Murphy 45
38	prem	**Bolton**	H	L	1-2	Jeffers 29
39	prem	**Aston Villa**	A	D	0-0	
40	prem	**Norwich**	A	L	0-1	
41	prem	**Man Utd**	H	L	0-4	
42	prem	**Chelsea**	A	L	0-1	
43	prem	**Crystal Palace**	H	D	2-2	Hughes 30; Fortune 82

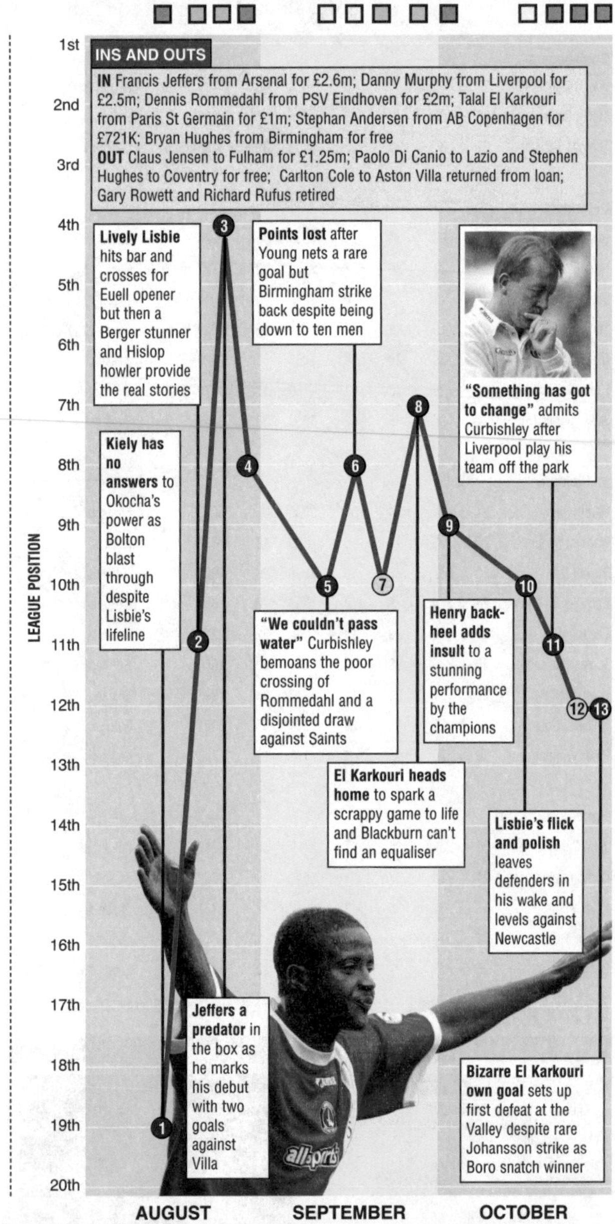
INS AND OUTS
IN Francis Jeffers from Arsenal for £2.6m; Danny Murphy from Liverpool for £2.5m; Dennis Rommedahl from PSV Eindhoven for £2m; Talal El Karkouri from Paris St Germain for £1m; Stephan Andersen from AB Copenhagen for £721K; Bryan Hughes from Birmingham for free
OUT Claus Jensen to Fulham for £1.25m; Paolo Di Canio to Lazio and Stephen Hughes to Coventry for free; Carlton Cole to Aston Villa returned from loan; Gary Rowett and Richard Rufus retired
1st
2nd
3rd
4th
5th
6th
7th
8th
9th
10th
11th
12th
13th
14th
15th
16th
17th
18th
19th
20th
LEAGUE POSITION
Lively Lisbie hits bar and crosses for Euell opener but then a Berger stunner and Hislop howler provide the real stories
Points lost after Young nets a rare goal but Birmingham strike back despite being down to ten men
"Something has got to change" admits Curbishley after Liverpool play his team off the park
Kiely has no answers to Okocha's power as Bolton blast through despite Lisbie's lifeline
"We couldn't pass water" Curbishley bemoans the poor crossing of Rommedahl and a disjointed draw against Saints
Henry back-heel adds insult to a stunning performance by the champions
El Karkouri heads home to spark a scrappy game to life and Blackburn can't find an equaliser
Lisbie's flick and polish leaves defenders in his wake and levels against Newcastle
Jeffers a predator in the box as he marks his debut with two goals against Villa
Bizarre El Karkouri own goal sets up first defeat at the Valley despite rare Johansson strike as Boro snatch winner
1
2
3
4
5
6
7
8
9
10
11
12
13
AUGUST
SEPTEMBER
OCTOBER

Home Away Neutral

ATTENDANCES

HOME GROUND: THE VALLEY **CAPACITY:** 27116 **AVERAGE LEAGUE AT HOME:** 26402

16	Man Utd	67704	6	Birmingham	27400	10	Newcastle	26553	1	Bolton	24100
30	Newcastle	51114	35	West Brom	27104	36	Man City	26436	31	Leicester	23719
4	Man City	43593	29	Liverpool	27102	17	Chelsea	26355	28	Yeovil	22873
42	Chelsea	42065	15	Norwich	27057	8	Blackburn	26193	18	Crystal Palace	20705
11	Liverpool	41625	22	Everton	27001	3	Aston Villa	26190	37	Portsmouth	20108
9	Arsenal	38103	34	Tottenham	26870	26	Birmingham	26111	24	Blackburn	19819
27	Everton	36041	43	Crystal Palace	26870	20	Fulham	26108	12	Crystal Palace	19030
14	Tottenham	35423	41	Man Utd	26789	13	Middlesboro	26031	33	Fulham	18290
39	Aston Villa	31312	23	Arsenal	26711	40	Norwich	25459	25	Rochdale	13955
21	Southampton	31195	38	Bolton	26708	2	Portsmouth	25204	7	Grimsby	5735
32	Middlesboro	29603	19	West Brom	26697	5	Southampton	24263			

Curbishley confounded by spring wilt

Final Position: 11th

KEY: ● League ● Champions Lge ● UEFA Cup ● FA Cup ○ League Cup ● Other

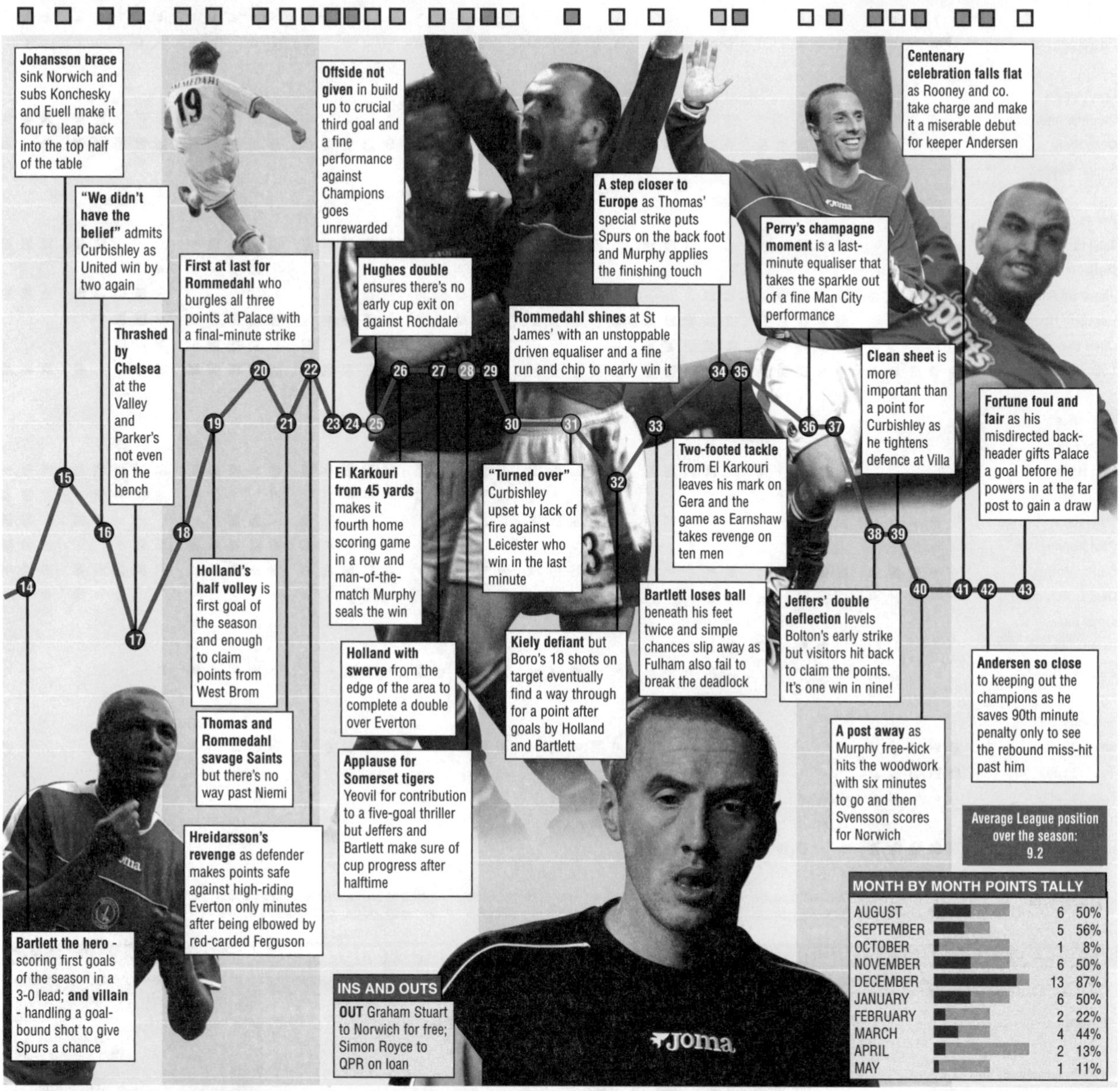
Johansson brace sink Norwich and subs Konchesky and Euell make it four to leap back into the top half of the table
Bartlett the hero - scoring first goals of the season in a 3-0 lead; **and villain** - handling a goal-bound shot to give Spurs a chance
"We didn't have the belief" admits Curbishley as United win by two again
Thrashed by Chelsea at the Valley and Parker's not even on the bench
First at last for Rommedahl who burgles all three points at Palace with a final-minute strike
Holland's half volley is first goal of the season and enough to claim points from West Brom
Thomas and Rommedahl savage Saints but there's no way past Niemi
Hreidarsson's revenge as defender makes points safe against high-riding Everton only minutes after being elbowed by red-carded Ferguson
Offside not given in build up to crucial third goal and a fine performance against Champions goes unrewarded
Hughes double ensures there's no early cup exit on against Rochdale
El Karkouri from 45 yards makes it fourth home scoring game in a row and man-of-the-match Murphy seals the win
Holland with swerve from the edge of the area to complete a double over Everton
Applause for Somerset tigers Yeovil for contribution to a five-goal thriller but Jeffers and Bartlett make sure of cup progress after halftime
Rommedahl shines at St James' with an unstoppable driven equaliser and a fine run and chip to nearly win it
"Turned over" Curbishley upset by lack of fire against Leicester who win in the last minute
Kiely defiant but Boro's 18 shots on target eventually find a way through for a point after goals by Holland and Bartlett
A step closer to Europe as Thomas' special strike puts Spurs on the back foot and Murphy applies the finishing touch
Two-footed tackle from El Karkouri leaves his mark on Gera and the game as Earnshaw takes revenge on ten men
Bartlett loses ball beneath his feet twice and simple chances slip away as Fulham also fail to break the deadlock
Perry's champagne moment is a last-minute equaliser that takes the sparkle out of a fine Man City performance
Jeffers' double deflection levels Bolton's early strike but visitors hit back to claim the points. It's one win in nine!
Clean sheet is more important than a point for Curbishley as he tightens defence at Villa
A post away as Murphy free-kick hits the woodwork with six minutes to go and then Svensson scores for Norwich
Centenary celebration falls flat as Rooney and co. take charge and make it a miserable debut for keeper Andersen
Fortune foul and fair as his misdirected back-header gifts Palace a goal before he powers in at the far post to gain a draw
Andersen so close to keeping out the champions as he saves 90th minute penalty only to see the rebound miss-hit past him
14 15 16 17 18 19 20 21 22 23 24 25 26 27 28 29 30 31 32 33 34 35 36 37 38 39 40 41 42 43
NOVEMBER
DECEMBER
JANUARY
FEBRUARY
MARCH
APRIL
MAY

Average League position over the season: 9.2

MONTH BY MONTH POINTS TALLY

AUGUST	6	50%
SEPTEMBER	5	56%
OCTOBER	1	8%
NOVEMBER	6	50%
DECEMBER	13	87%
JANUARY	6	50%
FEBRUARY	2	22%
MARCH	4	44%
APRIL	2	13%
MAY	1	11%

INS AND OUTS

OUT Graham Stuart to Norwich for free; Simon Royce to QPR on loan

GOAL ATTEMPTS

FOR — Goal attempts recorded in League games

	HOME	AWAY	TOTAL	AVE
shots on target	105	64	169	4.4
shots off target	67	74	141	3.7
TOTAL	172	138	310	8.2

Ratio of goals to shots — Average number of shots on target per League goal scored: **4**

Accuracy rating — Average percentage of total goal attempts which were on target: **54.5**

AGAINST — Goal attempts recorded in League games

	HOME	AWAY	TOTAL	AVE
shots on target	126	152	278	7.3
shots off target	93	64	157	4.1
TOTAL	219	216	435	11.4

Ratio of goals to shots — Average number of shots on target per League goal scored: **4.8**

Accuracy rating — Average percentage of total goal attempts which were on target: **63.9**

GOALS

Shaun Bartlett

League	6
FA Cup	2
League Cup	0
Europe	0
Other	0
TOTAL	8

League Average **340** mins between goals

	PLAYER	LGE	FAC	LC	Euro	TOT	AVE
1	Bartlett	6	2	0	0	8	340
2	Murphy	3	1	1	0	5	1080
3	Jeffers	3	1	1	0	5	289
4	El Karkouri	5	0	0	0	5	500
5	Hughes	1	3	0	0	4	964
6	Johansson	4	0	0	0	4	363
7	Thomas	3	0	0	0	3	568
8	Holland	3	0	0	0	3	897
9	Fortune	2	1	0	0	3	1293
10	Young	2	0	0	0	2	1620
11	Rommedahl	2	0	0	0	2	829
12	Euell	2	0	0	0	2	475
13	Hreidarsson	1	0	1	0	2	2959
14	Perry	1	0	0	0	1	1504
15	Konchesky	1	0	0	0	1	1557
	Other	3	0	0	0	3	
	TOTAL	42	8	3	0	53	

SQUAD APPEARANCES

Match	1	2	3	4	5	6	7	8	9	10	11	12	13	14	15	16	17	18	19	20	21	22	23	24	25	26	27	28	29	30	31	32	33	34	35	36	37	38	39	40	41	42	43
Venue	A	H	H	A	H	A	A	H	A	H	A	H	H	A	H	A	H	A	A	H	A	H	H	A	H	H	A	H	H	A	H	A	A	H	H	H	A	H	A	A	H	A	H
Competition	L	L	L	L	L	L	W	L	L	L	L	W	L	L	L	L	L	L	L	L	L	L	L	L	F	L	L	F	L	L	F	L	L	L	L	L	L	L	L	L	L	L	L
Result	L	W	W	L	D	D	W	W	L	D	L	L	L	W	W	L	L	W	W	W	D	W	L	L	W	W	W	W	L	D	L	D	D	W	L	D	L	L	D	L	L	L	D

Goalkeepers
Stephen Andersen
Dean Kiely
Simon Royce

Defenders
Talal El Karkouri
Mark Fish
Jonathan Fortune
Hermann Hreidarsson
Chris Perry
Luke Young

Midfielders
Barry Fuller
Matt Holland
Bryan Hughes
Radostin Kishishev
Paul Konchesky
Danny Murphy
Dennis Rommedahl
Lloyd Sam
Graham Stuart
Jerome Thomas

Forwards
Shaun Bartlett
Jason Euell
Francis Jeffers
Jonatan Johansson
Kevin Lisbie

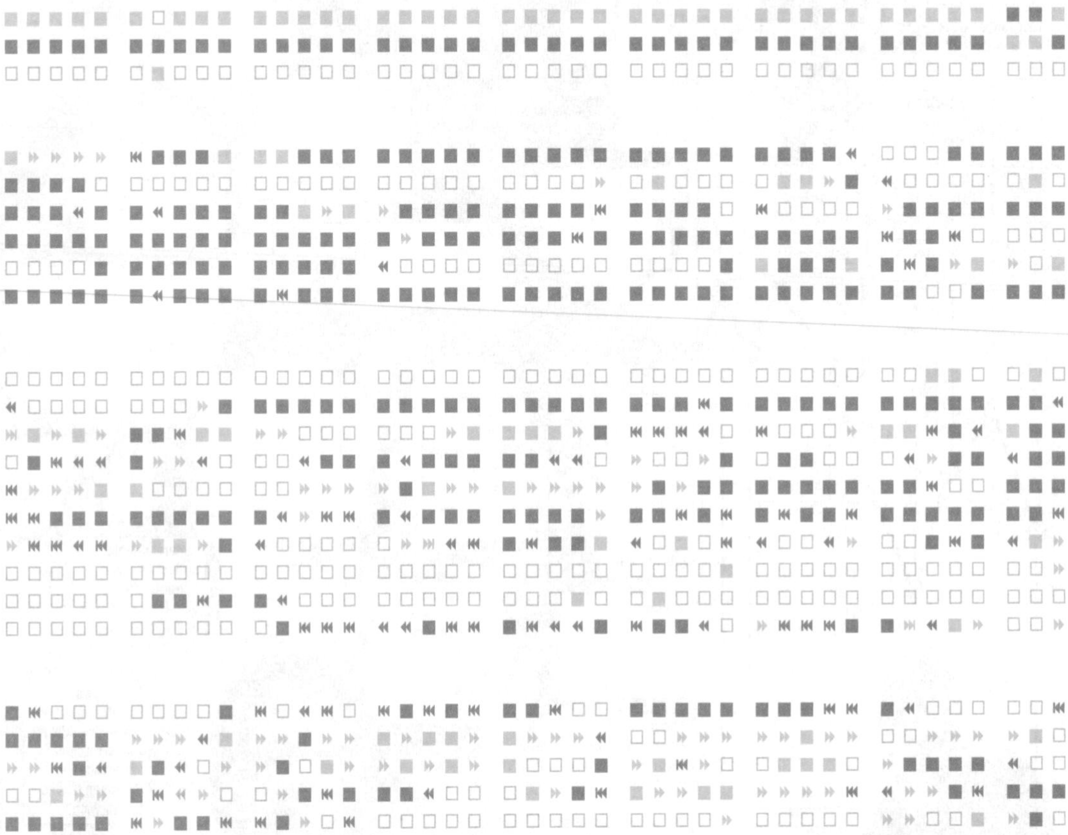

KEY: On all match — On bench — Subbed or sent off (Counting game) — Subbed or sent off (playing less than 70 mins) — Subbed on from bench (Counting Game) — Subbed on (playing less than 70 mins) — Subbed on and then subbed or sent off (Counting Game) — Subbed on and then subbed or sent off (playing less than 70 mins) — Not in 16

KEY PLAYERS - GOALSCORERS

Shaun Bartlett

Goals in the League	6
Goals in all competitions	8
Assists League goals scored by a team mate where the player delivered the final pass	3
Contribution to Attacking Power Average number of minutes between League team goals while on pitch	72
Player Strike Rate Average number of minutes between League goals scored by player	340
Club Strike Rate Average minutes between League goals scored by club	81

	PLAYER	GOALS LGE	GOALS ALL	ASSISTS	POWER	S RATE
1	Shaun Bartlett	6	8	3	72	340 mins
2	Jonatan Johansson	4	4	1	90	363 mins
3	Talal El Karkouri	5	5	0	83	500 mins
4	Jerome Thomas	3	3	2	66	568 mins
5	Dennis Rommedahl	2	2	0	103	829 mins

KEY PLAYERS - MIDFIELDERS

Jerome Thomas

Goals in the League	3
Goals in all competitions	3
Assists League goals scored by a team mate where the player delivered the final pass	2
Defensive Rating Average number of mins between League goals conceded while on the pitch	61
Contribution to Attacking Power Average number of minutes between League team goals while on pitch	66
Scoring Difference Defensive Rating minus Contribution to Attacking Power	-5

	PLAYER	GOALS LGE	GOALS ALL	ASSISTS	DEF RATE	POWER	SC DIFF
1	Jerome Thomas	3	3	2	61	66	-5 mins
2	Matt Holland	3	3	1	63	82	-19 mins
3	Radostin Kishishev	0	0	1	63	85	-22 mins
4	Paul Konchesky	1	1	2	47	71	-24 mins
5	Danny Murphy	3	5	6	62	88	-26 mins

PLAYER APPEARANCES

	AGE (on 01/07/05)	IN NAMED 16	APPEARANCES	COUNTING GAMES	MINUTES ON PITCH	APPEARANCES	MINUTES ON PITCH	THIS SEASON	HOME COUNTRY
Goalkeepers									
Stephen Andersen	23	38	2	2	180	2	180	1	Denmark (19)
Dean Kiely	34	38	36	36	3240	41	3690	-	Rep of Ireland
Simon Royce	33	0	0	0	0	0	0	-	England
Defenders									
Talal El Karkouri	29	35	32	27	2501	36	2861	-	Morocco
Mark Fish	31	11	7	5	510	8	527	-	South Africa
Jonathan Fortune	24	33	31	27	2586	36	2964	-	England
Hermann Hreidarsson	30	34	34	33	2959	39	3409	-	Iceland
Chris Perry	32	22	19	16	1504	21	1684	-	England
Luke Young	25	36	36	36	3240	41	3633	-	England
Midfielders									
Barry Fuller	20	3	0	0	0	0	0	-	England
Matt Holland	31	32	32	29	2690	36	3050	2	Rep of Ireland
Bryan Hughes	29	28	17	9	964	22	1309	-	Wales
Radostin Kishishev	30	31	31	18	2198	32	2243	-	Bulgaria
Paul Konchesky	24	32	28	15	1557	31	1674	-	England
Danny Murphy	28	38	38	36	3241	43	3614	-	England
Dennis Rommedahl	26	28	26	14	1657	27	1702	7	Denmark (19)
Lloyd Sam	20	2	1	0	15	1	15	-	England
Graham Stuart	34	6	4	4	343	6	500	-	England
Jerome Thomas	22	25	24	15	1703	28	2018	-	England
Forwards									
Shaun Bartlett	32	25	25	23	2041	27	2221	-	South Africa
Jason Euell	28	33	26	6	950	31	1073	-	England
Francis Jeffers	24	29	20	6	867	24	1213	-	England
Jonatan Johansson	29	31	26	13	1453	31	1657	-	Finland
Kevin Lisbie	26	18	17	12	1134	19	1246	-	Jamaica

KEY: LEAGUE   ALL COMPS   CAPS (MAY FIFA RANKING)

TEAM OF THE SEASON

KIELY
CG 36 DR 61
FORTUNE
CG 31 DR 60
EL KARKOURI
CG 32 DR 69
PERRY
CG 19 DR 65
HREIDARSSON
CG 34 DR 64
THOMAS
CG 15 SD +5
HOLLAND
CG 29 SD -19
KISHISHEV
CG 18 SD -22
KONCHESKY
CG 15 SD -24
MURPHY
CG 36 AP 88
BARTLETT
CG 23 SR 340

KEY: DR = Defensive Rating, SD = Scoring Difference AP = Attacking Power SR = Strike Rate, CG=Counting games – League games playing at least 70 minutes

TOP POINT EARNERS

Jerome Thomas

Counting Games League games when player was on pitch for at least 70 minutes	15
Average points Average League points taken in Counting games	1.87
Club Average points Average points taken in League games	1.21

	PLAYER	GAMES	PTS
1	Jerome Thomas	15	1.87
2	Radostin Kishishev	18	1.72
3	Shaun Bartlett	23	1.48
4	Dennis Rommedahl	14	1.43
5	Talal El Karkouri	27	1.37
6	Hermann Hreidarsson	33	1.36
7	Dean Kiely	36	1.28
8	Danny Murphy	36	1.28
9	Luke Young	36	1.25
10	Kevin Lisbie	12	1.25

KEY PLAYERS - DEFENDERS

Talal El Karkouri

Goals Conceded in the League Number of League goals conceded while the player was on the pitch	36
Goals Conceded in all competitions Total number of goals conceded while the player was on the pitch	41
League minutes played Number of minutes played in league matches	2501
Clean Sheets In games when player was on pitch for at least 70 minutes	10
Defensive Rating Average number of mins between League goals conceded while on the pitch	69
Club Defensive Rating Average number of mins between League goals conceded by the club this season	59

all:sports
15

	PLAYER	CON LGE	CON ALL	MINS	C SHEETS	DEF RATE
1	Talal El Karkouri	36	41	2501	10	69 mins
2	Chris Perry	23	25	1504	5	65 mins
3	Hermann Hreidarsson	46	53	2959	12	64 mins
4	Jonathan Fortune	43	49	2586	9	60 mins
5	Luke Young	56	63	3240	11	58 mins

KEY GOALKEEPER

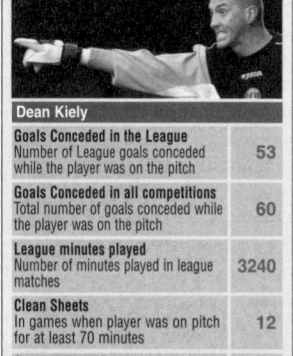

Dean Kiely

Goals Conceded in the League Number of League goals conceded while the player was on the pitch	53
Goals Conceded in all competitions Total number of goals conceded while the player was on the pitch	60
League minutes played Number of minutes played in league matches	3240
Clean Sheets In games when player was on pitch for at least 70 minutes	12
Goals to Shots Ratio The average number of shots on target per each League goal conceded	4.9
Defensive Rating Ave mins between League goals conceded while on the pitch	61

BOOKINGS

Chris Perry

League Yellow	3
League Red	1
All competitions Yellow	3
All competitions Red	1

League Average 376 mins between cards

	PLAYER	LEAGUE Y	LEAGUE R	TOTAL Y	TOTAL R	AVE
1	Perry	3Y	1R	3Y	1R	376
2	El Karkouri	5	1	5	1	416
3	Jeffers	2	0	2	0	433
4	Konchesky	3	0	3	0	519
5	Kishishev	4	0	4	0	549
6	Hreidarsson	4	0	5	0	739
7	Murphy	4	0	4	0	810
8	Young	4	0	4	0	810
9	Thomas	2	0	3	0	851
10	Euell	1	0	1	0	950
11	Hughes	1	0	2	0	964
12	Rommedahl	1	0	1	0	1657
13	Bartlett	0	1	0	1	2041
14	Fortune	1	0	1	0	2586
	Other	0	0	0	0	
	TOTAL	35	3	38	3	

BIRMINGHAM CITY

Robbie Savage tops Birmingham's Midfielders Table. His Scoring Difference is the only one showing a positive when comparing how often goals were scored and conceded when he was on the pitch.

The transferred player is also runner-up in the Goalscorers chart scoring a goal every 403 minutes on average. He is second only to **Emile Heskey** who is 24th in the Premiership with a Strike Rate of a goal every 290-minutes. The club missed Forssell, whose 155 Strike Rate was in the top five in the division last year. Neither Blake, Pandiani or Morrison played sufficient games to chart.

Maik Taylor played every minute but his Ratio of 4.2 shots on target saved for every goal conceded is way down on his record of 5.8 last season. **Mehdi Nafti** made his 10 appearances count and finishes with one of the worst three averages in Bookings – a card every 151 minutes.

NICKNAME: THE BLUES

KEY: Won / Drawn / Lost

1	prem	**Portsmouth**	A	D	1-1	Savage 10
2	prem	**Chelsea**	H	L	0-1	
3	prem	**Man City**	H	W	1-0	Heskey 8
4	prem	**Tottenham**	A	L	0-1	
5	prem	**Middlesbrough**	A	L	1-2	Heskey 42
6	prem	**Charlton**	H	D	1-1	Yorke 68
7	ccr2	**Lincoln**	H	W	3-1	Gronkjaer 64; Morrison 77; Savage 80 pen
8	prem	**Bolton**	A	D	1-1	Izzet 49
9	prem	**Newcastle**	H	D	2-2	Yorke 23; Upson 57
10	prem	**Man Utd**	H	D	0-0	
11	prem	**Southampton**	A	D	0-0	
12	ccr3	**Fulham**	H	L	0-1	
13	prem	**Crystal Palace**	H	L	0-1	
14	prem	**Liverpool**	A	W	1-0	Anderton 77
15	prem	**Everton**	H	L	0-1	
16	prem	**Blackburn**	A	D	3-3	Anderton 17; Savage 38; Dunn 45
17	prem	**Norwich**	H	D	1-1	Morrison 9
18	prem	**Arsenal**	A	L	0-3	
19	prem	**Aston Villa**	A	W	2-1	Morrison 9; Dunn 18
20	prem	**West Brom**	H	W	4-0	Savage 4 pen; Morrison 23; Heskey 30; Anderton 80
21	prem	**Middlesbrough**	H	W	2-0	Morrison 10; Heskey 45
22	prem	**Fulham**	A	W	3-2	Heskey 25; Carter 41; Savage 53
23	prem	**Newcastle**	A	L	1-2	Heskey 64
24	prem	**Bolton**	H	L	1-2	Upson 66
25	facr3	**Leeds**	H	W	3-0	Heskey 11; Carter 21,65
26	prem	**Charlton**	A	L	1-3	Melchiot 55
27	prem	**Fulham**	H	L	1-2	Volz 51 og
28	facr4	**Chelsea**	A	L	0-2	
29	prem	**Southampton**	H	W	2-1	Pandiani 12; Blake 41 pen
30	prem	**Man Utd**	A	L	0-2	
31	prem	**Liverpool**	H	W	2-0	Pandiani 38 pen; Gray 45
32	prem	**Crystal Palace**	A	L	0-2	
33	prem	**West Brom**	A	L	0-2	
34	prem	**Aston Villa**	H	W	2-0	Heskey 52; Gray 89
35	prem	**Tottenham**	H	D	1-1	Carter 66
36	prem	**Chelsea**	A	D	1-1	Pandiani 65
37	prem	**Portsmouth**	H	D	0-0	
38	prem	**Man City**	A	L	0-3	
39	prem	**Everton**	A	D	1-1	Heskey 5
40	prem	**Blackburn**	H	W	2-1	Blake 61; Heskey 80
41	prem	**Norwich**	A	L	0-1	
42	prem	**Arsenal**	H	W	2-1	Pandiani 80; Heskey 90

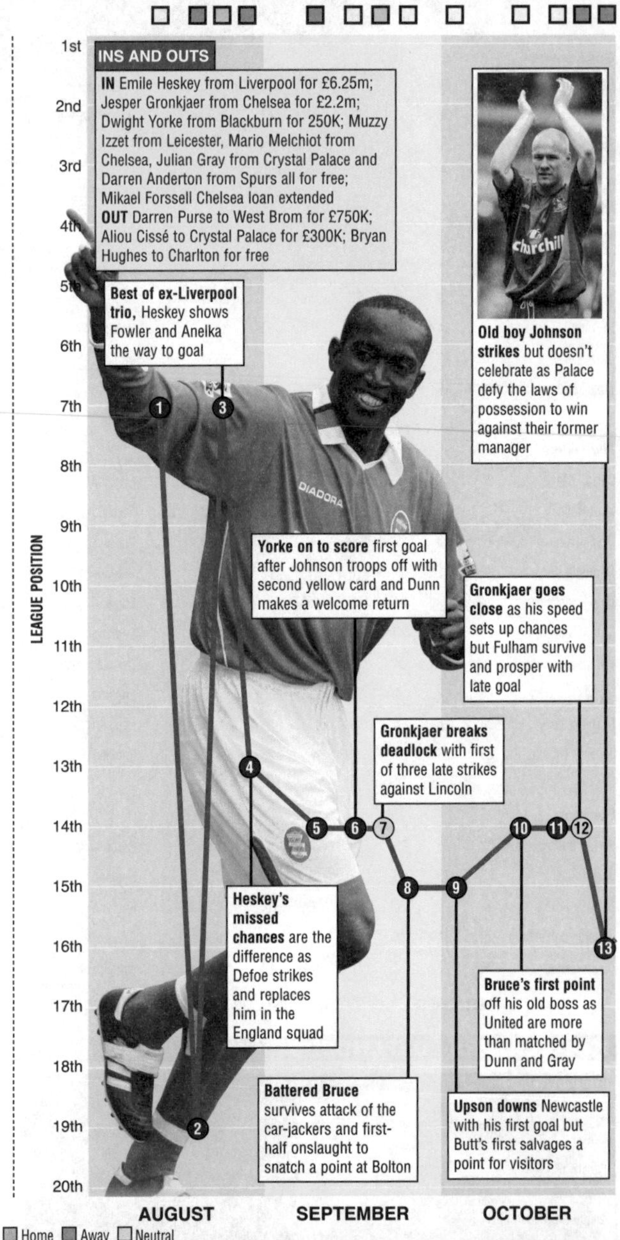

1st
2nd
3rd
4th
5th
6th
7th
8th
9th
10th
11th
12th
13th
14th
15th
16th
17th
18th
19th
20th
LEAGUE POSITION
INS AND OUTS
IN Emile Heskey from Liverpool for £6.25m; Jesper Gronkjaer from Chelsea for £2.2m; Dwight Yorke from Blackburn for 250K; Muzzy Izzet from Leicester, Mario Melchiot from Chelsea, Julian Gray from Crystal Palace and Darren Anderton from Spurs all for free; Mikael Forssell Chelsea loan extended
OUT Darren Purse to West Brom for £750K; Aliou Cissé to Crystal Palace for £300K; Bryan Hughes to Charlton for free
Best of ex-Liverpool trio, Heskey shows Fowler and Anelka the way to goal
Old boy Johnson strikes but doesn't celebrate as Palace defy the laws of possession to win against their former manager
Yorke on to score first goal after Johnson troops off with second yellow card and Dunn makes a welcome return
Gronkjaer goes close as his speed sets up chances but Fulham survive and prosper with late goal
Gronkjaer breaks deadlock with first of three late strikes against Lincoln
Heskey's missed chances are the difference as Defoe strikes and replaces him in the England squad
Bruce's first point off his old boss as United are more than matched by Dunn and Gray
Battered Bruce survives attack of the car-jackers and first-half onslaught to snatch a point at Bolton
Upson downs Newcastle with his first goal but Butt's first salvages a point for visitors
AUGUST
SEPTEMBER
OCTOBER
Home Away Neutral

ATTENDANCES

HOME GROUND: ST ANDREWS CAPACITY: 30016 AVERAGE LEAGUE AT HOME: 28759

30	Man Utd	67838	34	Aston Villa	29382	29	Southampton	28797	33	West Brom	25749
23	Newcastle	52222	31	Liverpool	29318	40	Blackburn	28621	41	Norwich	25477
14	Liverpool	42669	35	Tottenham	29304	2	Chelsea	28559	25	Leeds	25159
38	Man City	42453	42	Arsenal	29302	3	Man City	28551	8	Bolton	23692
36	Chelsea	42031	10	Man Utd	29221	27	Fulham	28512	32	Crystal Palace	23376
19	Aston Villa	41329	17	Norwich	29120	15	Everton	28388	16	Blackburn	20290
28	Chelsea	40379	21	Middlesboro	29082	11	Southampton	27568	1	Portsmouth	20021
18	Arsenal	38064	9	Newcastle	29021	6	Charlton	27400	22	Fulham	18706
39	Everton	36828	13	Crystal Palace	28916	24	Bolton	27177	7	Lincoln	14500
4	Tottenham	35290	37	Portsmouth	28883	12	Fulham	26371			
5	Middlesboro	30252	20	West Brom	28880	26	Charlton	26111			

Mid-table security despite key injuries

Final Position: 12th

KEY: ● League ● Champions Lge ● UEFA Cup ● FA Cup ○ League Cup ● Other

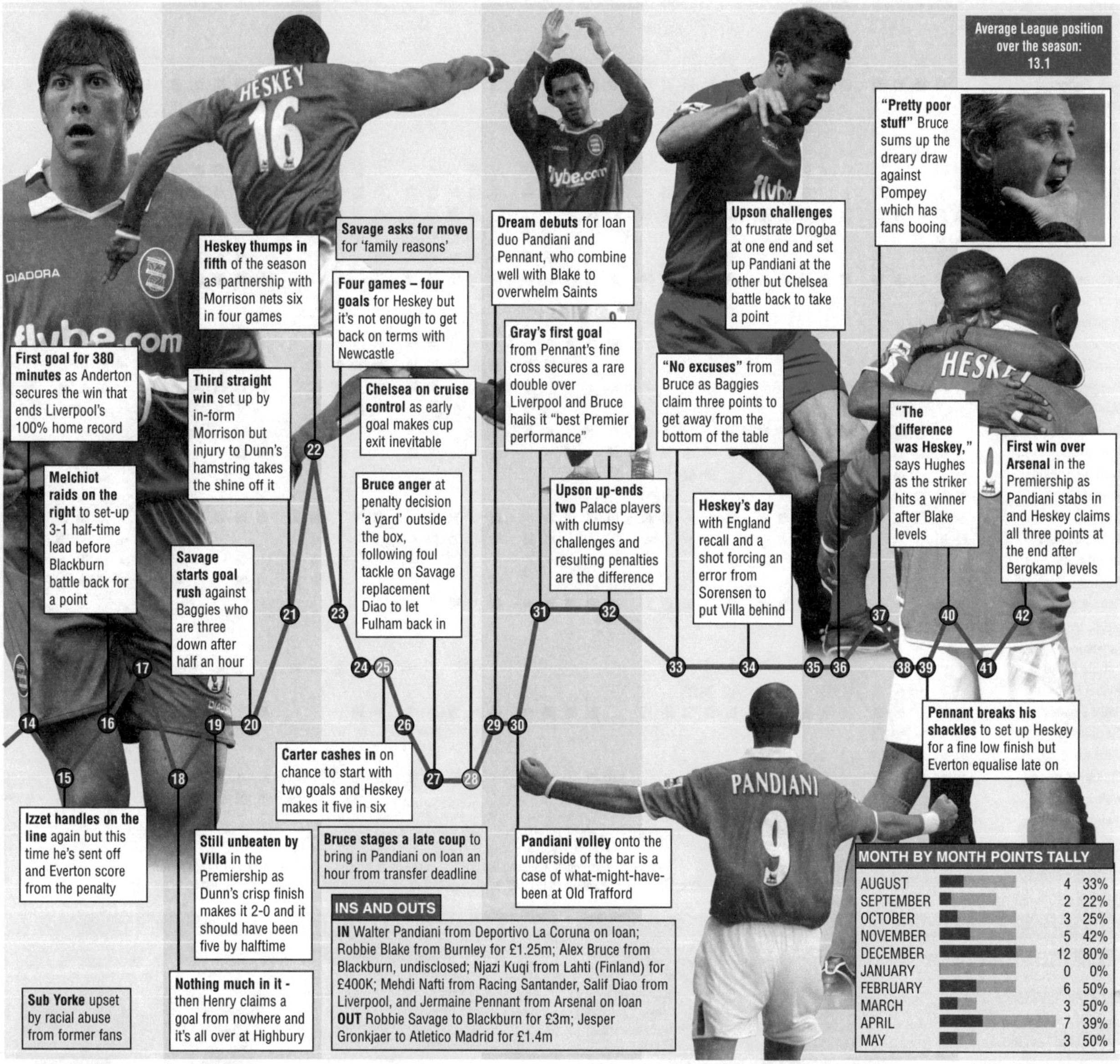
Average League position over the season: 13.1
"Pretty poor stuff" Bruce sums up the dreary draw against Pompey which has fans booing
First goal for 380 minutes as Anderton secures the win that ends Liverpool's 100% home record
Melchiot raids on the right to set-up 3-1 half-time lead before Blackburn battle back for a point
Izzet handles on the line again but this time he's sent off and Everton score from the penalty
Sub Yorke upset by racial abuse from former fans
Heskey thumps in fifth of the season as partnership with Morrison nets six in four games
Third straight win set up by in-form Morrison but injury to Dunn's hamstring takes the shine off it
Savage starts goal rush against Baggies who are three down after half an hour
Still unbeaten by Villa in the Premiership as Dunn's crisp finish makes it 2-0 and it should have been five by halftime
Nothing much in it - then Henry claims a goal from nowhere and it's all over at Highbury
Savage asks for move for 'family reasons'
Four games – four goals for Heskey but it's not enough to get back on terms with Newcastle
Chelsea on cruise control as early goal makes cup exit inevitable
Bruce anger at penalty decision 'a yard' outside the box, following foul tackle on Savage replacement Diao to let Fulham back in
Carter cashes in on chance to start with two goals and Heskey makes it five in six
Bruce stages a late coup to bring in Pandiani on loan an hour from transfer deadline
Dream debuts for loan duo Pandiani and Pennant, who combine well with Blake to overwhelm Saints
Gray's first goal from Pennant's fine cross secures a rare double over Liverpool and Bruce hails it "best Premier performance"
Upson up-ends two Palace players with clumsy challenges and resulting penalties are the difference
Pandiani volley onto the underside of the bar is a case of what-might-have-been at Old Trafford
Upson challenges to frustrate Drogba at one end and set up Pandiani at the other but Chelsea battle back to take a point
"No excuses" from Bruce as Baggies claim three points to get away from the bottom of the table
Heskey's day with England recall and a shot forcing an error from Sorensen to put Villa behind
"The difference was Heskey," says Hughes as the striker hits a winner after Blake levels
First win over Arsenal in the Premiership as Pandiani stabs in and Heskey claims all three points at the end after Bergkamp levels
Pennant breaks his shackles to set up Heskey for a fine low finish but Everton equalise late on
NOVEMBER
DECEMBER
JANUARY
FEBRUARY
MARCH
APRIL
MAY

INS AND OUTS

IN Walter Pandiani from Deportivo La Coruna on loan; Robbie Blake from Burnley for £1.25m; Alex Bruce from Blackburn, undisclosed; Njazi Kuqi from Lahti (Finland) for £400K; Mehdi Nafti from Racing Santander, Salif Diao from Liverpool, and Jermaine Pennant from Arsenal on loan **OUT** Robbie Savage to Blackburn for £3m; Jesper Gronkjaer to Atletico Madrid for £1.4m

MONTH BY MONTH POINTS TALLY

AUGUST	4	33%
SEPTEMBER	2	22%
OCTOBER	3	25%
NOVEMBER	5	42%
DECEMBER	12	80%
JANUARY	0	0%
FEBRUARY	6	50%
MARCH	3	50%
APRIL	7	39%
MAY	3	50%

GOAL ATTEMPTS

FOR Goal attempts recorded in League games

	HOME	AWAY	TOTAL	AVE
shots on target	107	70	177	4.7
shots off target	95	88	183	4.8
TOTAL	202	158	360	9.5

Ratio of goals to shots — Average number of shots on target per League goal scored: **4.4**

Accuracy rating — Average percentage of total goal attempts which were on target: **49.2**

AGAINST Goal attempts recorded in League games

	HOME	AWAY	TOTAL	AVE
shots on target	75	117	192	5.1
shots off target	60	70	130	3.4
TOTAL	135	187	322	8.5

Ratio of goals to shots — Average number of shots on target per League goal scored: **4.2**

Accuracy rating — Average percentage of total goal attempts which were on target: **59.6**

GOALS

Emile Heskey

League	10
FA Cup	1
League Cup	0
Europe	0
Other	0
TOTAL	11

League Average 290 mins between goals

	PLAYER	LGE	FAC	LC	Euro	TOT	AVE
1	Heskey	10	1	0	0	11	290
2	Savage	4	0	1	0	5	403
3	Morrison	4	0	1	0	5	309
4	Pandiani	4	0	0	0	4	258
5	Carter	2	2	0	0	4	520
6	Anderton	3	0	0	0	3	291
7	Upson	2	0	0	0	2	1620
8	Gray	2	0	0	0	2	946
9	Blake	2	0	0	0	2	171
10	Yorke	2	0	0	0	2	263
11	Dunn	2	0	0	0	2	359
12	Gronkjaer	0	0	1	0	1	
13	Izzet	1	0	0	0	1	817
14	Melchiot	1	0	0	0	1	2839
	Other	1	0	0	0	1	
	TOTAL	40	3	3	0	46	

SQUAD APPEARANCES

Match	1	2	3	4	5	6	7	8	9	10	11	12	13	14	15	16	17	18	19	20	21	22	23	24	25	26	27	28	29	30	31	32	33	34	35	36	37	38	39	40	41	42
Venue	A	H	H	A	A	H	H	A	H	H	A	H	H	A	H	A	H	A	A	H	H	A	A	H	H	A	H	A	H	A	H	A	A	H	H	A	H	A	A	H	A	H
Competition	L	L	L	L	L	L	W	L	L	L	L	W	L	L	L	L	L	L	L	L	L	L	L	L	F	L	L	F	L	L	L	L	L	L	L	L	L	L	L	L	L	L
Result	D	L	W	L	L	D	W	D	D	D	D	L	L	W	L	D	D	L	W	W	W	W	L	L	W	L	L	L	W	L	W	L	L	W	D	D	D	L	D	W	L	W

Goalkeepers
Ian Bennett
Maik Taylor
Nico Vaesen

Defenders
Jamie Clapham
Kenny Cunningham
Mario Melchiot
Martin Taylor
Olivier Tebily
Matthew Upson

Midfielders
Darren Anderton
Darren Carter
Stephen Clemence
Salif Diao
David Dunn
Julian Gray
Jesper Gronkjaer
Mustafa Izzet
Damien Johnson
Stan Lazaridis
Mehdi Nafti
Jermaine Pennant
Robbie Savage

Forwards
Robbie Blake
Mikael Forssell
Emile Heskey
Stern John
Njazi Kuqi
Clinton Morrison
Walter Pandiani
Dwight Yorke

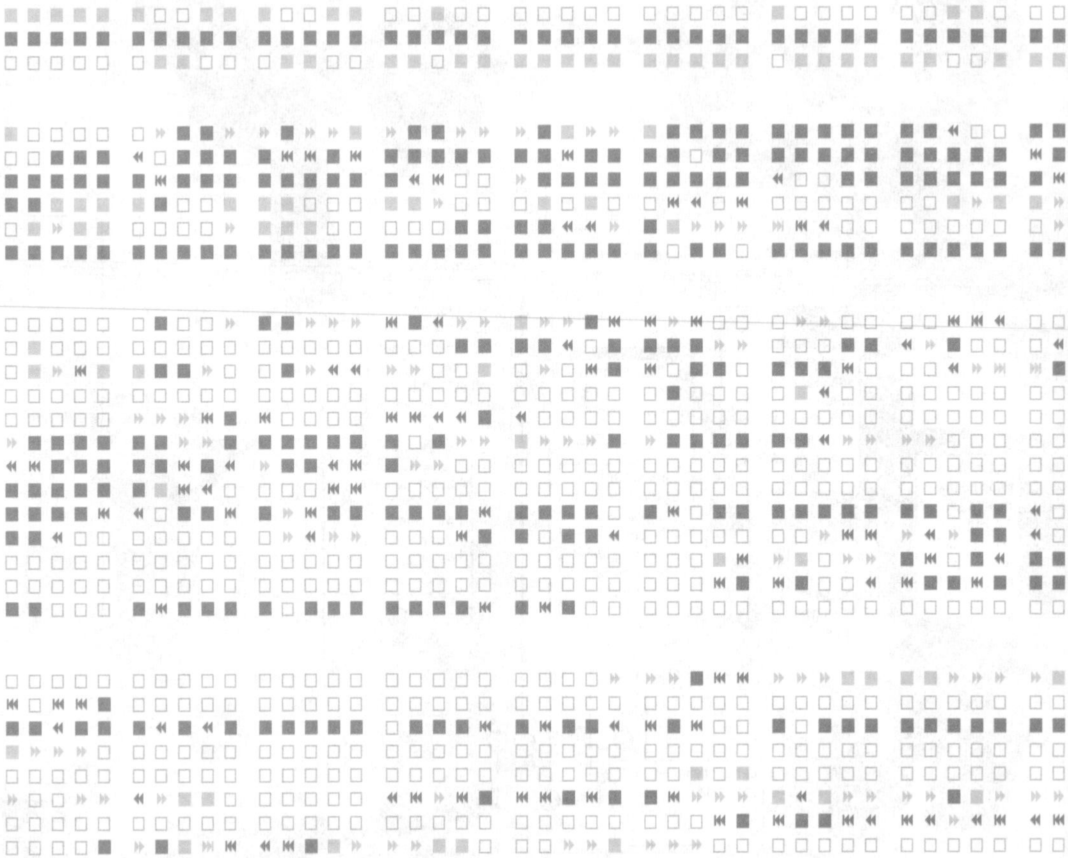

KEY: On all match | On bench | Subbed or sent off (Counting game) | Subbed or sent off (playing less than 70 mins) | Subbed on from bench (Counting Game) | Subbed on (playing less than 70 mins) | Subbed on and then subbed or sent off (Counting Game) | Subbed on and then subbed or sent off (playing less than 70 mins) | Not in 16

KEY PLAYERS - GOALSCORERS

Emile Heskey

Goals in the League	10
Goals in all competitions	11
Assists League goals scored by team-mates where he delivered the final pass	5
Contribution to Attacking Power Average number of minutes between League team goals while on pitch	87
Player Strike Rate Average number of minutes between League goals scored by player	290
Club Strike Rate Average minutes between League goals scored by club	86

	PLAYER	GOALS LGE	GOALS ALL	ASSISTS	POWER	S RATE
1	Emile Heskey	10	11	5	87	290 mins
2	Robbie Savage	4	5	2	73	403 mins
3	Julian Gray	2	2	0	118	946 mins
4	Matthew Upson	2	2	1	83	1620 mins
5	Mario Melchiot	1	1	2	101	2839 mins

KEY PLAYERS - MIDFIELDERS

Robbie Savage

Goals in the League	4
Goals in all competitions	5
Assists League goals scored by team-mates where he delivered the final pass	2
Defensive Rating Average number of mins between League goals conceded while on the pitch	85
Contribution to Attacking Power Average number of minutes between League team goals while on pitch	73
Scoring Difference Defensive Rating minus Contribution to Attacking Power	12

	PLAYER	GOALS LGE	GOALS ALL	ASSISTS	DEF RATE	POWER	SC DIFF
1	Robbie Savage	4	5	2	85	73	12 mins
2	Damien Johnson	0	0	1	78	86	-8 mins
3	Stephen Clemence	0	0	0	81	100	-19 mins
4	Julian Gray	2	2	0	65	118	-53 mins

PLAYER APPEARANCES

	AGE (on 01/07/05)	IN NAMED 16	APPEARANCES	COUNTING GAMES	MINUTES ON PITCH	APPEARANCES	MINUTES ON PITCH	THIS SEASON	HOME COUNTRY
Goalkeepers									
Ian Bennett	33	15	0	0	0	0	0	-	England
Maik Taylor	33	38	38	38	3420	42	3780	8	N Ireland (114)
Nico Vaesen	35	23	0	0	0	0	0	-	Belgium
Defenders									
Jamie Clapham	29	31	27	17	1678	31	1920	-	England
Kenny Cunningham	34	36	36	35	3164	38	3336	9	Rep of Ireland (15)
Mario Melchiot	28	34	34	31	2839	38	3192	4	Holland (5)
Martin Taylor	25	20	7	4	358	9	472	-	England
Olivier Tebily	29	21	15	7	765	17	845	-	Ivory Coast
Matthew Upson	26	36	36	36	3240	40	3600	2	England (6)
Midfielders									
Darren Anderton	33	21	20	7	872	24	1203	-	England
Darren Carter	21	16	15	9	1040	17	1220	-	England
Stephen Clemence	27	26	22	12	1298	26	1658	-	England
Salif Diao	28	3	2	1	157	2	157	3	Senegal (33)
David Dunn	25	11	11	6	717	12	724	-	England
Julian Gray	25	32	31	17	1891	35	2251	-	England
Jesper Gronkjaer	27	16	16	10	1141	18	1321	6	Denmark (19)
Mustafa Izzet	30	10	10	8	817	10	817	-	Turkey
Damien Johnson	26	36	36	34	3104	37	3112	6	N Ireland (114)
Stan Lazaridis	32	20	20	11	1344	22	1401	-	Australia
Mehdi Nafti	26	12	10	6	606	10	606	-	France
Jermaine Pennant	22	12	12	11	1011	12	1011	-	England
Robbie Savage	30	18	18	18	1611	19	1690	4	Wales (74)
Forwards									
Robbie Blake	29	16	11	2	342	13	456	-	England
Mikael Forssell	24	4	4	4	328	4	328	-	Finland
Emile Heskey	27	34	34	32	2903	38	3197	2	England (6)
Stern John	28	4	3	0	64	3	64	-	Trinidad & Tobago
Njazi Kuqi	22	1	0	0	0	0	0	-	Finland
Clinton Morrison	26	31	26	9	1237	29	1369	7	Rep of Ireland (15)
Walter Pandiani	29	14	14	9	1033	14	1033	-	Uruguay
Dwight Yorke	33	17	13	4	526	16	703	-	Trinidad & Tobago

KEY: LEAGUE — ALL COMPS — CAPS (MAY FIFA RANKING)

TEAM OF THE SEASON

TAYLOR
CG 38 DR 74
MELCHIOT
CG 31 DR 75
CUNNINGHAM
CG 35 DR 72
UPSON
CG 36 DR 77
CLAPHAM
CG 17 DR 70
JOHNSON
CG 34 SD -8
SAVAGE
CG 18 SD +12
CLEMENCE
CG 12 SD -19
GRAY
CG 17 SD -53
PANDIANI
CG 9* SR 258
HESKEY
CG 32 SR 290

KEY: DR = Defensive Rating, SD = Scoring Difference SR = Strike Rate, CG=Counting games – League games playing at least 70 minutes *No other striker played 12 CG

TOP POINT EARNERS

Stephen Clemence

Counting Games League games when player was on pitch for at least 70 minutes	12
Average points Average League points taken in Counting games	1.33
Club Average points Average points taken in League games	1.18

	PLAYER	GAMES	PTS
1	Stephen Clemence	12	1.33
2	Robbie Savage	18	1.28
3	Matthew Upson	36	1.25
4	Jamie Clapham	17	1.24
5	Kenny Cunningham	35	1.23
6	Damien Johnson	34	1.21
7	Maik Taylor	38	1.18
8	Emile Heskey	32	1.16
9	Mario Melchiot	31	1.03
10	Julian Gray	17	0.94

KEY PLAYERS - DEFENDERS

Matthew Upson

Goals Conceded in the League Number of League goals conceded while the player was on the pitch	42
Goals Conceded in all competitions Total number of goals conceded while the player was on the pitch	46
League minutes played Number of minutes played in league matches	3240
Clean Sheets In games when he played at least70 mins	9
Defensive Rating Average number of mins between League goals conceded while on the pitch	77
Club Defensive Rating Average number of mins between League goals conceded by the club this season	74

flybe.com

	PLAYER	CON LGE	CON ALL	MINS	C SHEETS	DEF RATE
1	Matthew Upson	42	46	3240	9	77 mins
2	Mario Melchiot	38	41	2839	6	75 mins
3	Kenny Cunningham	44	45	3164	9	72 mins
4	Jamie Clapham	24	28	1678	3	70 mins

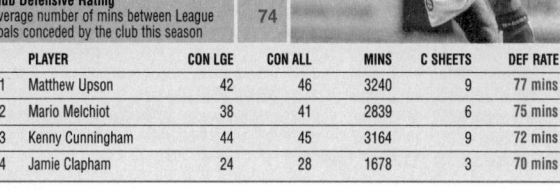

KEY GOALKEEPER

Maik Taylor

Goals Conceded in the League Number of League goals conceded while the player was on the pitch	46
Goals Conceded in all competitions Total number of goals conceded while the player was on the pitch	50
League minutes played Number of minutes played in league matches	3420
Clean Sheets In games when he played at least 70 mins	9
Goals to Shots Ratio The average number of shots on target per each League goal conceded	4.2
Defensive Rating Ave mins between League goals conceded while on the pitch	74

BOOKINGS

Mehdi Nafti

League Yellow	4
League Red	0
All competitions Yellow	4
All competitions Red	0

League Average **151** mins between cards

	PLAYER	LEAGUE Y	LEAGUE R	TOTAL Y	TOTAL R	AVE
1	Nafti	4	0	4	0	151
2	Dunn	4	0	4	0	179
3	Izzet	3	1	3	1	204
4	Savage	6	0	6	0	268
5	Johnson	9	2	9	2	282
6	Morrison	4	0	4	0	309
7	Pennant	3	0	3	0	337
8	Tebily	2	0	2	0	382
9	Clemence	3	0	3	0	432
10	Heskey	6	0	6	0	483
11	Pandiani	2	0	2	0	516
12	Yorke	1	0	1	0	526
13	Upson	5	0	7	0	648
14	Anderton	1	0	2	0	872
15	Melchiot	3	0	3	0	946
	Other	6	0	6	0	
	TOTAL	62	3	65	3	

FULHAM

Fulham didn't have as many Shots On Target as other sides, but they made them count. Their ratio of 3.5 shots for every goal scored was only bettered by Arsenal.

Andy Cole's 12 goals in the league came at a Strike Rate of one every 209 minutes on average, the 12th highest in the division and better than his Blackburn Strike Rate of 238 last season.

Brian McBride scored six at a Strike Rate of 255. **Luis Boa Morte** hit eight at 325 but his ten Assists was the fifth best record in the division.

Steed Malbranque's stop-start season brought six goals and he headed the Top Point Earners chart with an average of 1.42 points, in the games he started - good enough for Europe!

Papa Bouba Diop won 11 cards at an average of one every 228 minutes.

NICKNAME: THE COTTAGERS

KEY: Won, Drawn, Lost

1	prem	**Man City**	A	D	1-1	John 56
2	prem	**Bolton**	H	W	2-0	Cole 5,82
3	prem	**Middlesbrough**	H	L	0-2	
4	prem	**Portsmouth**	A	L	3-4	Cole 39; Boa Morte 41; Bocanegra 75
5	prem	**Arsenal**	H	L	0-3	
6	prem	**West Brom**	A	D	1-1	Cole 72
7	ccr2	**Boston**	A	W	4-1	Radzinski 9,70; Malbranque 28; McBride 34
8	prem	**Southampton**	H	W	1-0	Radzinski 24
9	prem	**Crystal Palace**	A	L	0-2	
10	prem	**Liverpool**	H	L	2-4	Boa Morte 24,30
11	prem	**Aston Villa**	A	L	0-2	
12	ccr3	**Birmingham**	A	W	1-0	Pembridge 76
13	prem	**Tottenham**	H	W	2-0	Boa Morte 33; Cole 61
14	prem	**Newcastle**	A	W	4-1	John 28; Malbranque 65,70 pen; Boa Morte 76
15	ccr4	**Nottm Forest**	A	W	4-2	Radzinski 86,93; McBride 101; Cole 119
16	prem	**Chelsea**	H	L	1-4	Diop 57
17	prem	**Everton**	A	L	0-1	
18	prem	**Blackburn**	H	L	0-2	
19	ccqf	**Chelsea**	H	L	1-2	McBride 74
20	prem	**Norwich**	A	W	1-0	Cole 7
21	prem	**Man Utd**	H	D	1-1	Diop 87
22	prem	**Charlton**	A	L	1-2	Radzinski 82
23	prem	**Arsenal**	A	L	0-2	
24	prem	**Birmingham**	H	L	2-3	Legwinski 34; Radzinski 90
25	prem	**Crystal Palace**	H	W	3-1	Cole 4,60; Radzinski 73
26	prem	**Southampton**	A	D	3-3	Diop 20; Malbranque 43; Radzinski 50
27	facr3	**Watford**	A	D	1-1	Knight 17
28	prem	**West Brom**	H	W	1-0	Diop 90
29	facr3r	**Watford**	H	W	2-0	Volz 13; Radzinski 65
30	prem	**Birmingham**	A	W	2-1	Cole 78 pen; Diop 83
31	facr4	**Derby**	A	D	1-1	John 71
32	prem	**Aston Villa**	H	D	1-1	Clark 90
33	prem	**Liverpool**	A	L	1-3	Cole 16
34	facr4r	**Derby**	H	W	4-2	Diop 45 pen; Boa Morte 50; John 94; Jensen 105
35	facr5	**Bolton**	A	L	0-1	
36	prem	**Tottenham**	A	L	0-2	
37	prem	**Charlton**	H	D	0-0	
38	prem	**Man Utd**	A	L	0-1	
39	prem	**Portsmouth**	H	W	3-1	Cole 63; McBride 81; Boa Morte 90
40	prem	**Bolton**	A	L	1-3	Boa Morte 47
41	prem	**Man City**	H	D	1-1	Boa Morte 76
42	prem	**Middlesbrough**	A	D	1-1	McBride 82
43	prem	**Chelsea**	A	L	1-3	John 41
44	prem	**Everton**	H	W	2-0	John 15; McBride 39
45	prem	**Newcastle**	H	L	1-3	Radzinski 86
46	prem	**Blackburn**	A	W	3-1	Malbranque 20,77; McBride 53
47	prem	**Norwich**	H	W	6-0	McBride 10,86; Diop 35; Knight 54; Malbranque 72; Cole 90

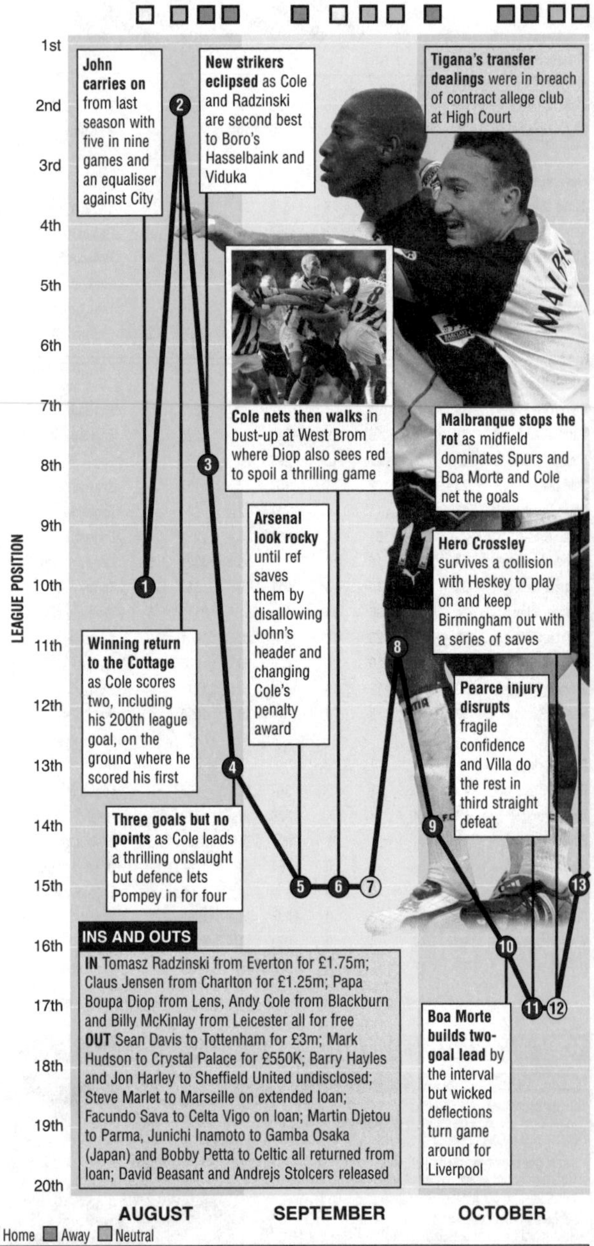
1st
2nd
3rd
4th
5th
6th
7th
8th
9th
10th
11th
12th
13th
14th
15th
16th
17th
18th
19th
20th
LEAGUE POSITION
John carries on from last season with five in nine games and an equaliser against City
New strikers eclipsed as Cole and Radzinski are second best to Boro's Hasselbaink and Viduka
Tigana's transfer dealings were in breach of contract allege club at High Court
Cole nets then walks in bust-up at West Brom where Diop also sees red to spoil a thrilling game
Malbranque stops the rot as midfield dominates Spurs and Boa Morte and Cole net the goals
Arsenal look rocky until ref saves them by disallowing John's header and changing Cole's penalty award
Hero Crossley survives a collision with Heskey to play on and keep Birmingham out with a series of saves
Winning return to the Cottage as Cole scores two, including his 200th league goal, on the ground where he scored his first
Pearce injury disrupts fragile confidence and Villa do the rest in third straight defeat
Three goals but no points as Cole leads a thrilling onslaught but defence lets Pompey in for four
INS AND OUTS
IN Tomasz Radzinski from Everton for £1.75m; Claus Jensen from Charlton for £1.25m; Papa Boupa Diop from Lens, Andy Cole from Blackburn and Billy McKinlay from Leicester all for free
OUT Sean Davis to Tottenham for £3m; Mark Hudson to Crystal Palace for £550K; Barry Hayles and Jon Harley to Sheffield United undisclosed; Steve Marlet to Marseille on extended loan; Facundo Sava to Celta Vigo on loan; Martin Djetou to Parma, Junichi Inamoto to Gamba Osaka (Japan) and Bobby Petta to Celtic all returned from loan; David Beasant and Andrejs Stolcers released
Boa Morte builds two-goal lead by the interval but wicked deflections turn game around for Liverpool
AUGUST
SEPTEMBER
OCTOBER
Home
Away
Neutral

ATTENDANCES

HOME GROUND: CRAVEN COTTAGE CAPACITY: 22000 AVERAGE LEAGUE AT HOME: 19838

38	Man Utd	67959	12	Birmingham	26371	41	Man City	21796	3	Middlesboro	17759
14	Newcastle	51118	22	Charlton	26108	5	Arsenal	21681	32	Aston Villa	17624
1	Man City	44026	40	Bolton	25493	13	Tottenham	21317	2	Bolton	17541
33	Liverpool	43534	6	West Brom	24128	39	Portsmouth	20502	28	West Brom	16180
43	Chelsea	42081	20	Norwich	23755	4	Portsmouth	19728	35	Bolton	16151
23	Arsenal	38047	31	Derby	22040	8	Southampton	19237	34	Derby	15528
36	Tottenham	35885	21	Man Utd	21940	18	Blackburn	19103	27	Watford	14896
17	Everton	34763	47	Norwich	21927	45	Newcastle	19003	19	Chelsea	14531
11	Aston Villa	34460	10	Liverpool	21884	46	Blackburn	18991	29	Watford	11306
42	Middlesboro	30650	44	Everton	21881	24	Birmingham	18706	15	Nottm Forest	9252
30	Birmingham	28512	16	Chelsea	21877	25	Crystal Palace	18680	7	Boston	5373
26	Southampton	27343	9	Crystal Palace	21825	37	Charlton	18290			

On target; surviving with final flourish

Final Position: **13th**

KEY: League, Champions Lge, UEFA Cup, FA Cup, League Cup, Other

Crossley's 'finest game' and the surprise of the weekend as Newcastle are hit for four before they can reply
Bouba Diop's first goal is a stunning volleyed equaliser but it only spurs Robben to better efforts for Chelsea
"We got out what we put in – nothing" Coleman fumes after Knight sees red and Blackburn gain first away win
Only one win in nine and revival comes too late against Birmingham despite Legwinski's first of the season
McBride dents Chelsea resilience with well worked equaliser before Lampard earns rivals a semi-final place
Cole goal ends run of four defeats as Coleman's outspoken comments get the desired response
Bouba Diop lets fly and his 88th minute thunderbolt dents United's championship chances
Tigana wins case for payment in full
Cole brace so nearly a hat-trick as Palace are beaten to move six points clear of the relegation places
Knight's height nets first goal in six years but woodwork saves Watford three times and they claim a draw
Unbeaten in five as Volz scores first for club and Radzinksi settles it to exit Watford
Bouba Diop opens up a seven point gap from the relegation battle with a last-gasp winner against West Brom
Game of three penalties leaves van der Sar the hero with two saves and a draw as Clark levels in injury time after earlier Cole penalty miss
Cole's diving header levels it at Anfield but defence can't hold out against quality crosses
Sub Jensen nets first goal in extra time to settle tie after battling Derby are reduced to ten men
Stubborn defence for 78 minutes ends when Spurs' striking subs net one apiece
Radzinski leads the assault on Bolton's goal but the home side hang on for cup win
Malbranque returns but attack still falters as Cole looks isolated and Charlton miss the better chances
Boa Morte shreds Pompey with a run to set up Cole and the final goal in a late win that lifts relegation fears
The woodwork saves United as Clark strikes it and Bocanegra follow-up finds Howard while Radzinski misses a chance for a point with his final kick
McBride's leap sets up Boa Morte for a point after comedy of errors gifts Man City the lead
Coleman fury as van der Sar is judged to have clattered Hasselbaink in the box and resulting penalty levels McBride's second league goal
Safe! Coleman sticks with John and McBride who both score to down Everton and ensure survival despite Bouba-Diop red
Hit for six! Norwich come seeking salvation and leave with a thorough hiding led by McBride and including Knight's first league goal
Malbranque's double delight with two goals in a classy performance to battle back against Blackburn in ten-a-side game after Rosenior's dismissal
14 15 16 17 18 19 20 21 22 23 24 25 26 27 28 29 30 31 32 33 34 35 36 37 38 39 40 41 42 43 44 45 46 47
NOVEMBER DECEMBER JANUARY FEBRUARY MARCH APRIL MAY

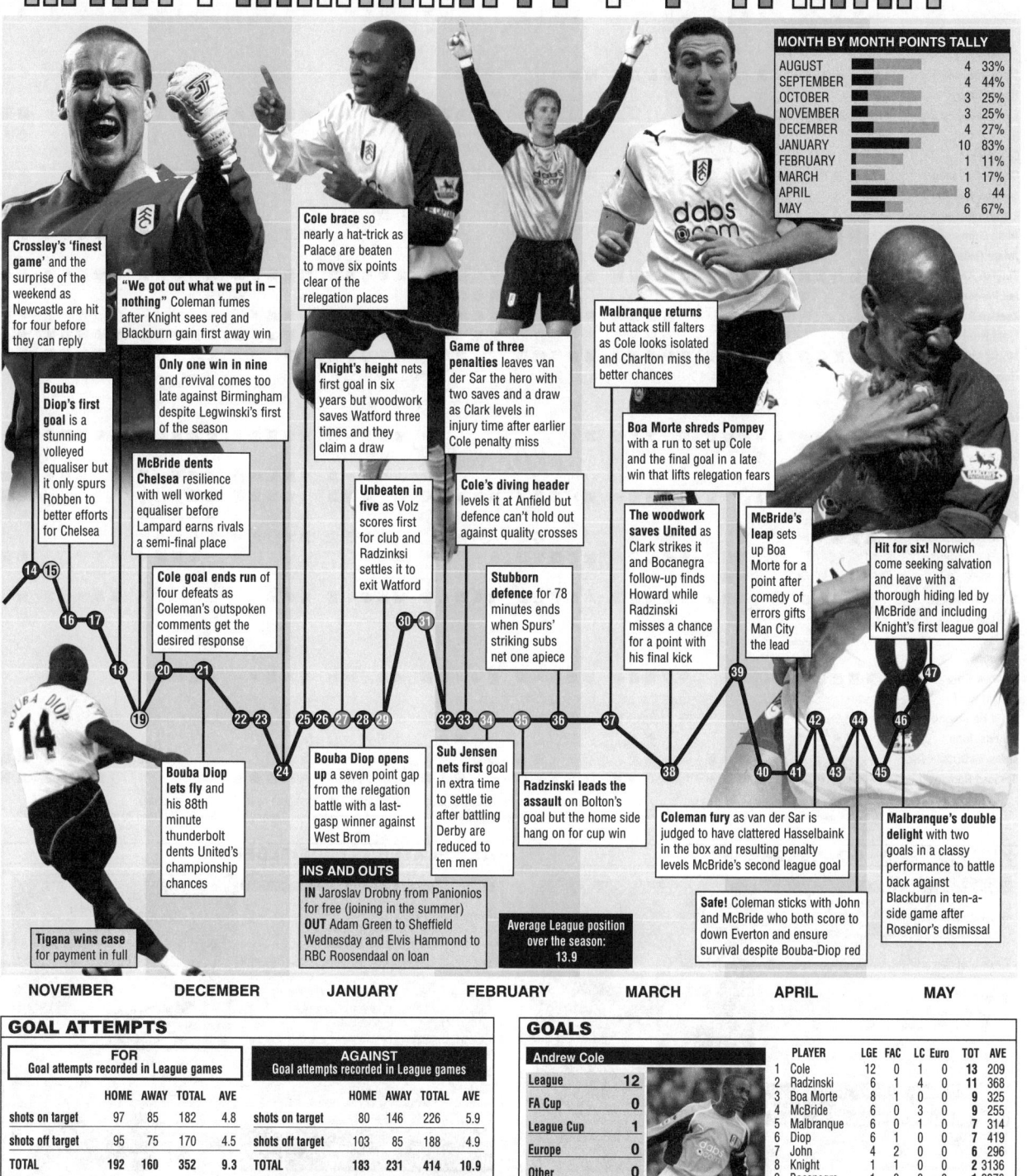

MONTH BY MONTH POINTS TALLY

AUGUST	4	33%
SEPTEMBER	4	44%
OCTOBER	3	25%
NOVEMBER	3	25%
DECEMBER	4	27%
JANUARY	10	83%
FEBRUARY	1	11%
MARCH	1	17%
APRIL	8	44
MAY	6	67%

INS AND OUTS

IN Jaroslav Drobny from Panionios for free (joining in the summer)
OUT Adam Green to Sheffield Wednesday and Elvis Hammond to RBC Roosendaal on loan

Average League position over the season: 13.9

GOAL ATTEMPTS

FOR – Goal attempts recorded in League games

	HOME	AWAY	TOTAL	AVE
shots on target	97	85	182	4.8
shots off target	95	75	170	4.5
TOTAL	**192**	**160**	**352**	**9.3**

Ratio of goals to shots Average number of shots on target per League goal scored	3.5
Accuracy rating Average percentage of total goal attempts which were on target	51.7

AGAINST – Goal attempts recorded in League games

	HOME	AWAY	TOTAL	AVE
shots on target	80	146	226	5.9
shots off target	103	85	188	4.9
TOTAL	**183**	**231**	**414**	**10.9**

Ratio of goals to shots Average number of shots on target per League goal scored	3.8
Accuracy rating Average percentage of total goal attempts which were on target	54.6

GOALS

Andrew Cole

League	12
FA Cup	0
League Cup	1
Europe	0
Other	0
TOTAL	13

League Average 209 mins between goals

	PLAYER	LGE	FAC	LC	Euro	TOT	AVE
1	Cole	12	0	1	0	**13**	209
2	Radzinski	6	1	4	0	**11**	368
3	Boa Morte	8	1	0	0	**9**	325
4	McBride	6	0	3	0	**9**	255
5	Malbranque	6	0	1	0	**7**	314
6	Diop	6	1	0	0	**7**	419
7	John	4	2	0	0	**6**	296
8	Knight	1	1	0	0	**2**	3136
9	Bocanegra	1	0	0	0	**1**	2376
10	Clark	1	0	0	0	**1**	1421
11	Legwinski	1	0	0	0	**1**	1127
12	Pembridge	0	0	1	0	**1**	
13	Volz	0	1	0	0	**1**	
14	Jensen	0	1	0	0	**1**	
	Other	0	0	0	0	0	
	TOTAL	**52**	**8**	**10**	**0**	**70**	

SQUAD APPEARANCES

Match	1	2	3	4	5	6	7	8	9	10	11	12	13	14	15	16	17	18	19	20	21	22	23	24
Venue	A	H	H	A	H	A	A	H	A	H	A	A	H	A	A	H	A	H	H	A	H	A	A	H
Competition	L	L	L	L	L	L	W	L	L	L	L	W	L	L	W	L	L	L	W	L	L	L	L	L
Result	D	W	L	L	L	D	W	W	L	L	L	W	W	W	W	L	L	L	L	W	D	L	L	L

Match	25	26	27	28	29	30	31	32	33	34	35	36	37	38	39	40	41	42	43	44	45	46	47
Venue	H	A	A	H	H	A	A	H	A	H	A	A	H	A	H	A	H	A	A	H	H	A	H
Competition	L	L	F	L	F	L	F	L	L	F	F	L	L	L	L	L	L	L	L	L	L	L	L
Result	W	D	D	W	W	W	D	D	L	W	L	L	D	L	W	L	D	D	L	W	L	W	W

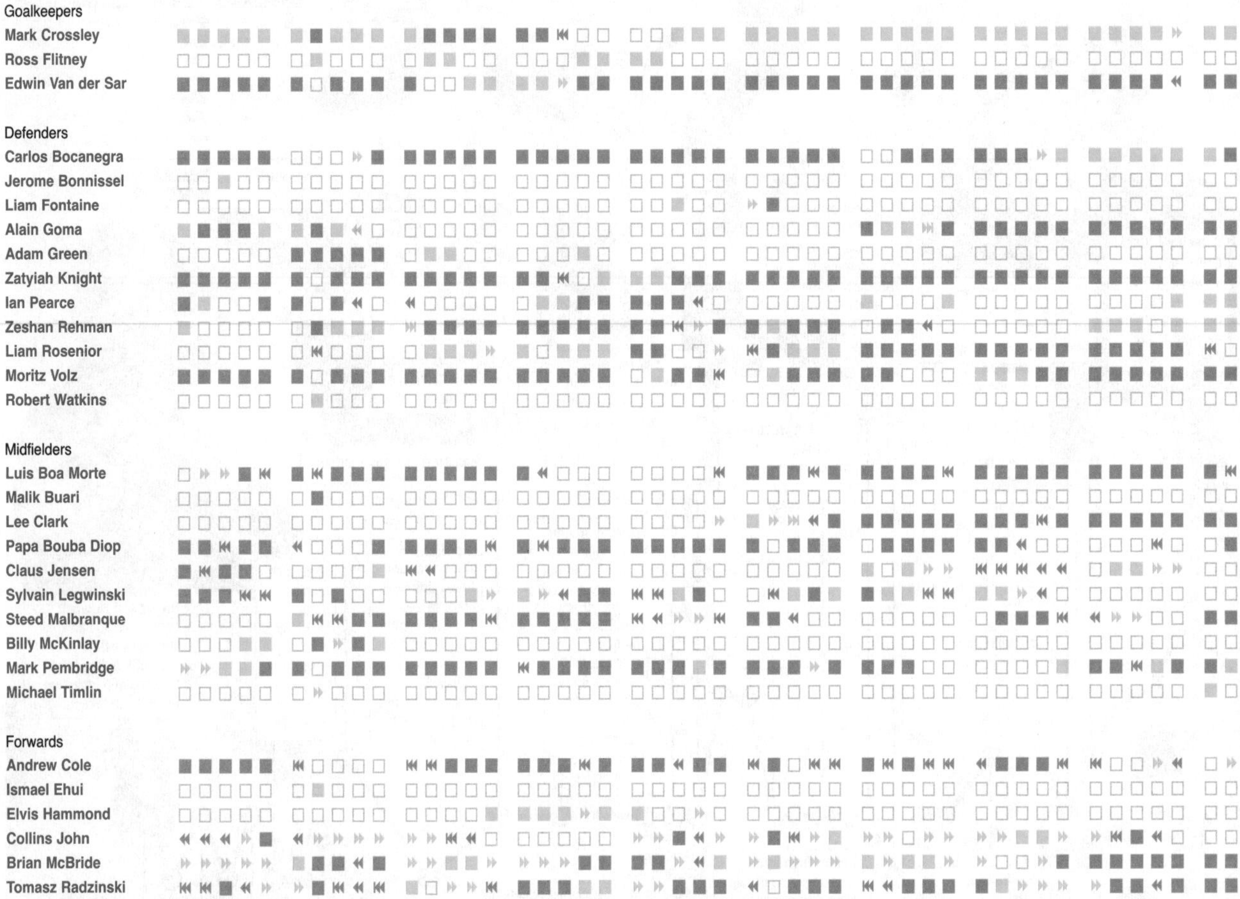

Goalkeepers
Mark Crossley
Ross Flitney
Edwin Van der Sar
Defenders
Carlos Bocanegra
Jerome Bonnissel
Liam Fontaine
Alain Goma
Adam Green
Zatyiah Knight
Ian Pearce
Zeshan Rehman
Liam Rosenior
Moritz Volz
Robert Watkins
Midfielders
Luis Boa Morte
Malik Buari
Lee Clark
Papa Bouba Diop
Claus Jensen
Sylvain Legwinski
Steed Malbranque
Billy McKinlay
Mark Pembridge
Michael Timlin
Forwards
Andrew Cole
Ismael Ehui
Elvis Hammond
Collins John
Brian McBride
Tomasz Radzinski

KEY: On all match | Subbed or sent off (Counting game) | Subbed on from bench (Counting Game) | Subbed on and then subbed or sent off (Counting Game) | Not in 16
On bench | Subbed or sent off (playing less than 70 mins) | Subbed on (playing less than 70 mins) | Subbed on and then subbed or sent off (playing less than 70 mins)

KEY PLAYERS - GOALSCORERS

Andrew Cole

Goals in the League	12
Goals in all competitions	13
Assists League goals scored by a team mate where the player delivered the final pass	3
Contribution to Attacking Power Average number of minutes between League team goals while on pitch	75
Player Strike Rate Average number of minutes between League goals scored by player	209
Club Strike Rate Average minutes between League goals scored by club	66

	PLAYER	GOALS LGE	GOALS ALL	ASSISTS	POWER	S RATE
1	Andrew Cole	12	13	3	75	209 mins
2	Brian McBride	6	9	3	52	255 mins
3	Steed Malbranque	6	7	7	59	314 mins
4	Luis Boa Morte	8	9	11	58	325 mins
5	Tomasz Radzinski	6	11	4	51	368 mins

KEY PLAYERS - MIDFIELDERS

Lee Clark

Goals in the League	1
Goals in all competitions	1
Assists League goals scored by a team mate where the player delivered the final pass	2
Defensive Rating Average number of mins between League goals conceded while he was on the pitch	68
Contribution to Attacking Power Average number of minutes between League team goals while on pitch	62
Scoring Difference Defensive Rating minus Contribution to Attacking Power	6

	PLAYER	GOALS LGE	GOALS ALL	ASSISTS	DEF RATE	POWER	SC DIFF
1	Lee Clark	1	1	2	68	62	6 mins
2	Steed Malbranque	6	7	7	61	59	2 mins
3	Luis Boa Morte	8	9	11	55	59	-4 mins
4	Papa Bouba Diop	6	7	0	58	64	-6 mins
5	Mark Pembridge	0	1	6	58	73	-15 mins

PLAYER APPEARANCES

	AGE (on 01/07/05)	IN NAMED 16	APPEARANCES	COUNTING GAMES	MINUTES ON PITCH	APPEARANCES	MINUTES ON PITCH	THIS SEASON	HOME COUNTRY
Goalkeepers									
Mark Crossley	36	35	6	5	478	9	778	5	Wales (74)
Ross Flitney	21	4	0	0	0	0	0	-	England
Edwin Van der Sar	34	37	34	32	2942	40	3512	9	Holland (5)
Defenders									
Carlos Bocanegra	26	35	28	26	2376	35	3066	-	United States
Jerome Bonnissel	32	1	0	0	0	0	0	-	France
Liam Fontaine	19	2	1	0	1	2	91	-	England
Alain Goma	32	22	16	15	1403	20	1748	-	France
Adam Green	21	5	4	4	360	5	450	-	England
Zatyiah Knight	25	38	35	35	3136	42	3826	-	England
Ian Pearce	31	17	11	8	780	12	870	-	England
Zeshan Rehman	21	27	17	16	1466	23	1991	-	England
Liam Rosenior	20	24	17	16	1434	23	1915	-	England
Moritz Volz	22	35	31	31	2775	36	3255	1	Germany (19)
Robert Watkins	19	0	0	0	0	0	0	-	England
Midfielders									
Luis Boa Morte	27	31	31	28	2602	39	3341	7	Portugal (9)
Malik Buari	21	0	0	0	0	1	90	-	Ghana
Lee Clark	32	18	17	16	1421	22	1791	-	England
Papa Bouba Diop	27	29	29	27	2513	35	3072	4	Senegal (33)
Claus Jensen	28	16	12	7	786	15	891	4	Denmark (19)
Sylvain Legwinski	31	24	15	11	1127	22	1652	-	France
Steed Malbranque	25	27	26	19	1885	31	2354	-	France
Billy McKinlay	36	5	2	1	96	3	186	-	Scotland
Mark Pembridge	34	34	28	26	2332	34	2840	5	Wales (74)
Michael Timlin	20	1	0	0	0	1	10	-	England
Forwards									
Andrew Cole	33	31	31	25	2502	39	3189	-	England
Ismael Ehui	18	0	0	0	0	0	0	-	France
Elvis Hammond	24	6	1	0	34	2	52	-	Ghana
Collins John	19	30	27	6	1184	34	1400	2	Holland (5)
Brian McBride	33	36	31	13	1532	37	1787	-	United States
Tomasz Radzinski	31	38	35	19	2209	41	2787	-	Canada

KEY: LEAGUE ALL COMPS CAPS (MAY FIFA RANKING)

TEAM OF THE SEASON

VAN DER SAR
CG 32 DR 58
VOLZ
CG 31 DR 58
REHMAN
CG 16 DR 59
KNIGHT
CG 35 DR 56
GOMA
CG 15 DR 61
MALBRANQUE
CG 19 SD +2
CLARK
CG 16 SD +6
BOUBA DIOP
CG 27 SD -6
BOA MORTE
CG 28 SD -4
RADZINSKI
CG 19 AP 51
COLE
CG 25 SR 209

KEY: DR = Defensive Rating, SD = Scoring Difference AP = Attacking Power SR = Strike Rate, CG=Counting games – League games playing at least 70 minutes

TOP POINT EARNERS

Steed Malbranque

Counting Games League games when player was on pitch for at least 70 minutes	19
Average points Average League points taken in Counting games	1.42
Club Average points Average points taken in League games	1.16

	PLAYER	GAMES	PTS
1	Steed Malbranque	19	**1.42**
2	Brian McBride	13	**1.38**
3	Lee Clark	16	**1.38**
4	Moritz Volz	31	**1.32**
5	Zeshan Rehman	16	**1.31**
6	Luis Boa Morte	28	**1.29**
7	Alain Goma	15	**1.20**
8	Papa Bouba Diop	27	**1.19**
9	Edwin Van der Sar	32	**1.19**
10	Mark Pembridge	26	**1.15**

KEY PLAYERS - DEFENDERS

Alain Goma

Goals Conceded in the League Number of League goals conceded while the player was on the pitch	23
Goals Conceded in all competitions Total number of goals conceded while the player was on the pitch	27
League minutes played Number of minutes played in league matches	1403
Clean Sheets In games when player was on pitch for at least 70 minutes	4
Defensive Rating Average number of mins between League goals conceded while on the pitch	61
Club Defensive Rating Average number of mins between League goals conceded by the club this season	57

dabs
com

	PLAYER	CON LGE	CON ALL	MINS	C SHEETS	DEF RATE
1	Alain Goma	23	27	1403	4	**61 mins**
2	Zeshan Rehman	25	31	1466	3	**59 mins**
3	Moritz Volz	48	53	2775	7	**58 mins**
4	Zatyiah Knight	56	63	3136	7	**56 mins**
5	Liam Rosenior	26	32	1434	2	**55 mins**

KEY GOALKEEPER

dabs
com

Edwin Van der Sar

Goals Conceded in the League Number of League goals conceded while the player was on the pitch	51
Goals Conceded in all competitions Number of goals conceded while he was on the pitch in all competitions	58
League minutes played Number of minutes played in league matches	2942
Clean Sheets In games when player was on pitch for at least 70 minutes	7
Goals to Shots Ratio The average number of shots on target per each League goal conceded	3.7
Defensive Rating Ave mins between League goals conceded while on the pitch	58

BOOKINGS

Papa Bouba Diop

League Yellow	9
League Red	2
All competitions Yellow	10
All competitions Red	2

League Average 228 mins between cards

	PLAYER	LEAGUE		TOTAL		AVE
1	Diop	9 Y	2 R	10 Y	2 R	**228**
2	Rosenior	3	1	5	2	**358**
3	Rehman	4	0	6	0	**366**
4	Boa Morte	7	0	7	0	**371**
5	Legwinski	3	0	3	0	**375**
6	Cole	4	1	7	1	**500**
7	Knight	5	1	5	1	**522**
8	Volz	5	0	6	0	**555**
9	John	2	0	3	0	**592**
10	Bocanegra	4	0	6	0	**594**
11	Goma	2	0	2	0	**701**
12	Clark	2	0	2	0	**710**
13	Van der Sar	4	0	4	0	**735**
14	Pearce	0	1	0	1	**780**
15	Jensen	0	1	0	1	**786**
	Other	3	0	3	0	
	TOTAL	**57**	**7**	**69**	**8**	

NEWCASTLE UNITED

Newcastle are geared to attack, averaging 12.8 shots a game, the third highest in the Premiership, and better than Arsenal. A good percentage of those shots are on target but not enough fly into the net.

Craig Bellamy tops the club Goalscorers chart for the highest Strike Rate. He scored a goal on average every 255 minutes – the 20th best record in the division. **Alan Shearer** saved his major scoring feats for Europe and his return of seven league goals at a Strike Rate of one every 323 minutes is his worst performance.

Laurent Robert, **Kieron Dyer** and **Lee Bowyer** all courted controversy but were in the top four in the Midfielders chart, Robert with five Assists.

A settled defence would help and could be built on **Jean-Alain Boumsong** and **Titus Bramble**, who emerge with far better Defensive Ratings than their colleagues.

NICKNAME: THE MAGPIES

KEY: Won / Drawn / Lost

1	prem	**Middlesbrough**	A	D	2-2	Bellamy 14; Shearer 83 pen
2	prem	**Tottenham**	H	L	0-1	
3	prem	**Norwich**	H	D	2-2	Bellamy 40; Hughes 50
4	prem	**Aston Villa**	A	L	2-4	Kluivert 28; O'Brien 36
5	prem	**Blackburn**	H	W	3-0	Flitcroft 9 og; Shearer 16; O'Brien 83
6	uc1rl1	**Bnei Sachnin**	H	W	2-0	Kluivert 4,42
7	prem	**Southampton**	A	W	2-1	Prutton 45 og; Carr 57
8	prem	**West Brom**	H	W	3-1	Kluivert 70; Milner 78; Shearer 86
9	uc1rl2	**Bnei Sachnin**	A	W	5-1	Kluivert 9,42; Shearer 38,52 pen,90
10	prem	**Birmingham**	A	D	2-2	Jenas 3; Butt 67
11	prem	**Charlton**	A	D	1-1	Bellamy 39
12	ucgpd	**Panionios**	A	W	1-0	Shearer 87 pen
13	prem	**Man City**	H	W	4-3	Robert 49; Shearer 58 pen; Elliott 69; Bellamy 89
14	ccr3	**Norwich**	H	W	2-1	Jenas 2; Ameobi 42 pen
15	prem	**Bolton**	A	L	1-2	Ambrose 55
16	ucgpd	**Dinamo Tbilisi**	H	W	2-0	Shearer 38; Bellamy 56
17	prem	**Fulham**	H	L	1-4	Bellamy 78
18	ccr4	**Chelsea**	H	L	0-2	
19	prem	**Man Utd**	H	L	1-3	Shearer 71
20	prem	**Crystal Palace**	A	W	2-0	Kluivert 79; Bellamy 88
21	ucgpd	**Sochaux**	A	W	4-0	Bowyer 29; Ameobi 46; Bellamy 75; Robert 90
22	prem	**Everton**	H	D	1-1	Bellamy 5
23	prem	**Chelsea**	A	L	0-4	
24	prem	**Portsmouth**	H	D	1-1	Bowyer 3
25	ucgpd	**Sp Lisbon**	H	D	1-1	Bellamy 5
26	prem	**Liverpool**	A	L	1-3	Kluivert 32
27	prem	**Blackburn**	A	D	2-2	Dyer 6; Robert 34
28	prem	**Arsenal**	H	L	0-1	
29	prem	**Birmingham**	H	W	2-1	Ameobi 6; Bowyer 44
30	prem	**West Brom**	A	D	0-0	
31	facr3	**Yeading**	A	W	2-0	Bowyer 51; Ameobi 61
32	prem	**Southampton**	H	W	2-1	Shearer 9 pen; Bramble 38
33	prem	**Arsenal**	A	L	0-1	
34	facr4	**Coventry**	H	W	3-1	Shearer 37; Ameobi 42; Babayaro 52
35	prem	**Man City**	A	D	1-1	Shearer 9
36	prem	**Charlton**	H	D	1-1	Dyer 52
37	uc3rl1	**Heerenveen**	A	W	2-1	Shearer 69; Bowyer 82
38	facr5	**Chelsea**	H	W	1-0	Kluivert 4
39	uc3rl2	**Heerenveen**	H	W	2-1	Breuer 10 og; Shearer 25
40	prem	**Bolton**	H	W	2-1	Bowyer 35; Dyer 69
41	prem	**Liverpool**	H	W	1-0	Robert 70
42	uc4rl1	**Olympiakos**	A	W	3-1	Shearer 13 pen; Robert 34; Kluivert 69
43	facqf	**Tottenham**	H	W	1-0	Kluivert 5
44	uc4rl2	**Olympiakos**	H	W	4-0	Dyer 18; Shearer 45,69; Bowyer 54
45	prem	**Portsmouth**	A	D	1-1	Dyer 43
46	prem	**Aston Villa**	H	L	0-3	
47	ucqfl1	**Sp Lisbon**	H	W	1-0	Shearer 37
48	prem	**Tottenham**	A	L	0-1	
49	ucqfl2	**Sp Lisbon**	A	L	1-4	Dyer 20
50	facsf	**Man Utd**	N	L	1-4	Ameobi 59
51	prem	**Norwich**	A	L	1-2	Kluivert 90
52	prem	**Man Utd**	A	L	1-2	Ambrose 27
53	prem	**Middlesbrough**	H	D	0-0	
54	prem	**Crystal Palace**	H	D	0-0	
55	prem	**Fulham**	A	W	3-1	Ambrose 18; Kluivert 62; Ameobi 75
56	prem	**Everton**	A	L	0-2	
57	prem	**Chelsea**	H	D	1-1	Geremi 33 og

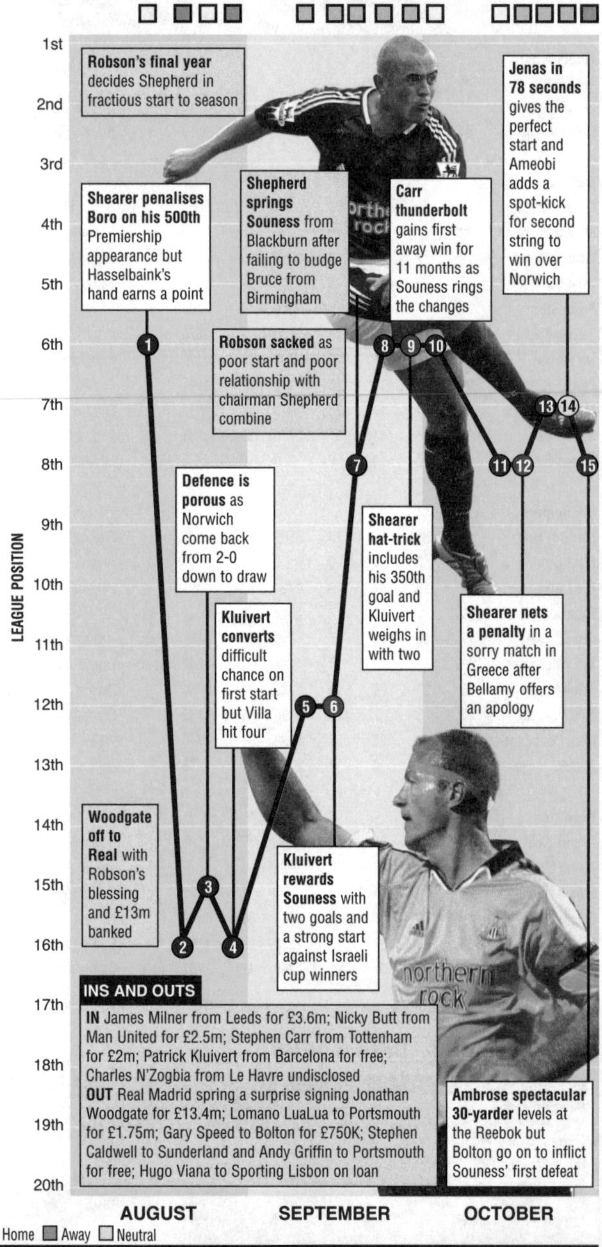

1st
2nd
3rd
4th
5th
6th
7th
8th
9th
10th
11th
12th
13th
14th
15th
16th
17th
18th
19th
20th
LEAGUE POSITION
Robson's final year decides Shepherd in fractious start to season
Shearer penalises Boro on his 500th Premiership appearance but Hasselbaink's hand earns a point
Shepherd springs Souness from Blackburn after failing to budge Bruce from Birmingham
Carr thunderbolt gains first away win for 11 months as Souness rings the changes
Jenas in 78 seconds gives the perfect start and Ameobi adds a spot-kick for second string to win over Norwich
Robson sacked as poor start and poor relationship with chairman Shepherd combine
Defence is porous as Norwich come back from 2-0 down to draw
Shearer hat-trick includes his 350th goal and Kluivert weighs in with two
Kluivert converts difficult chance on first start but Villa hit four
Shearer nets a penalty in a sorry match in Greece after Bellamy offers an apology
Woodgate off to Real with Robson's blessing and £13m banked
Kluivert rewards Souness with two goals and a strong start against Israeli cup winners
INS AND OUTS
IN James Milner from Leeds for £3.6m; Nicky Butt from Man United for £2.5m; Stephen Carr from Tottenham for £2m; Patrick Kluivert from Barcelona for free; Charles N'Zogbia from Le Havre undisclosed
OUT Real Madrid spring a surprise signing Jonathan Woodgate for £13.4m; Lomano LuaLua to Portsmouth for £1.75m; Gary Speed to Bolton for £750K; Stephen Caldwell to Sunderland and Andy Griffin to Portsmouth for free; Hugo Viana to Sporting Lisbon on loan
Ambrose spectacular 30-yarder levels at the Reebok but Bolton go on to inflict Souness' first defeat
AUGUST
SEPTEMBER
OCTOBER
Home
Away
Neutral

ATTENDANCES

HOME GROUND: ST JAMES' PARK CAPACITY: 52326 AVERAGE LEAGUE AT HOME: 51821

50	Man Utd	69280	24	Portsmouth	51480	33	Arsenal	38137	11	Charlton	26553
52	Man Utd	67845	43	Tottenham	51307	18	Chelsea	38055	39	Heerenveen	26000
57	Chelsea	52326	32	Southampton	51266	47	Sp Lisbon	36753	51	Norwich	25503
41	Liverpool	52323	22	Everton	51247	4	Aston Villa	36305	30	West Brom	25259
28	Arsenal	52320	17	Fulham	51118	48	Tottenham	35885	20	Crystal Palace	22937
19	Man Utd	52320	36	Charlton	51114	1	Middlesboro	34268	45	Portsmouth	20165
13	Man City	52316	40	Bolton	50000	42	Olympiakos	33000	37	Heerenveen	19500
8	West Brom	52308	35	Man City	45752	44	Olympiakos	32163	55	Fulham	19003
46	Aston Villa	52306	38	Chelsea	45740	7	Southampton	30709	21	Sochaux	15173
29	Birmingham	52222	49	Sp Lisbon	45000	6	Bnei Sachnin	30221	31	Yeading	10824
2	Tottenham	52185	34	Coventry	44044	27	Blackburn	29271	12	Panionios	8000
54	Crystal Palace	52123	26	Liverpool	43856	10	Birmingham	29021	9	Bnei Sachnin	1200
53	Middlesboro	52047	23	Chelsea	42328	25	Sp Lisbon	28017			
5	Blackburn	52015	14	Norwich	42153	16	Din Tbilisi	27218			
3	Norwich	51574	56	Everton	40438	15	Bolton	27196			

Shambolic start to embarrassing finish

Final Position: 14th

KEY: ● League ● Champions Lge ● UEFA Cup ● FA Cup ○ League Cup ● Other

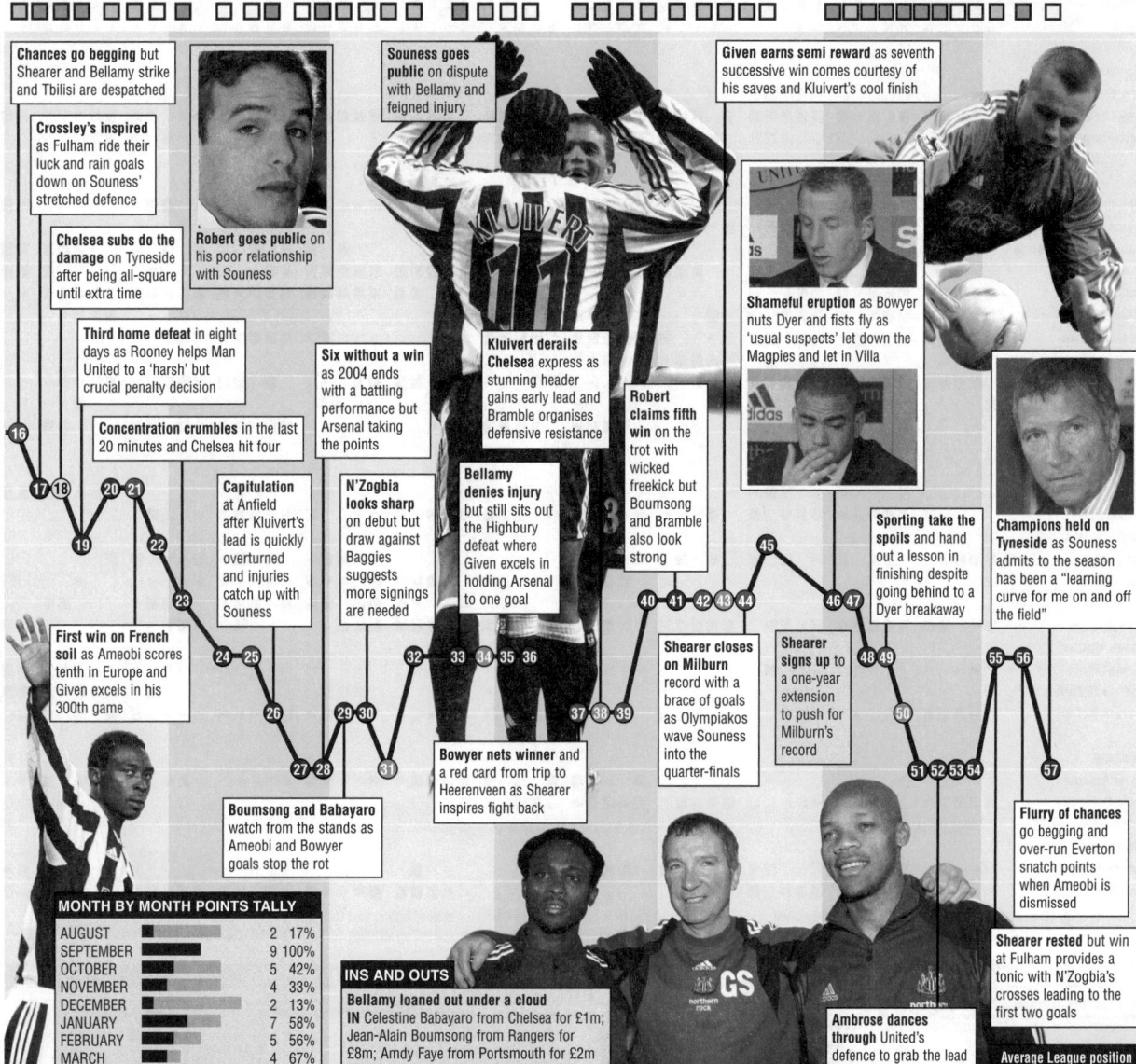

Chances go begging but Shearer and Bellamy strike and Tbilisi are despatched

Crossley's inspired as Fulham ride their luck and rain goals down on Souness' stretched defence

Chelsea subs do the damage on Tyneside after being all-square until extra time

Third home defeat in eight days as Rooney helps Man United to a 'harsh' but crucial penalty decision

First win on French soil as Ameobi scores tenth in Europe and Given excels in his 300th game

Concentration crumbles in the last 20 minutes and Chelsea hit four

Robert goes public on his poor relationship with Souness

Capitulation at Anfield after Kluivert's lead is quickly overturned and injuries catch up with Souness

Six without a win as 2004 ends with a battling performance but Arsenal taking the points

Boumsong and Babayaro watch from the stands as Ameobi and Bowyer goals stop the rot

N'Zogbia looks sharp on debut but draw against Baggies suggests more signings are needed

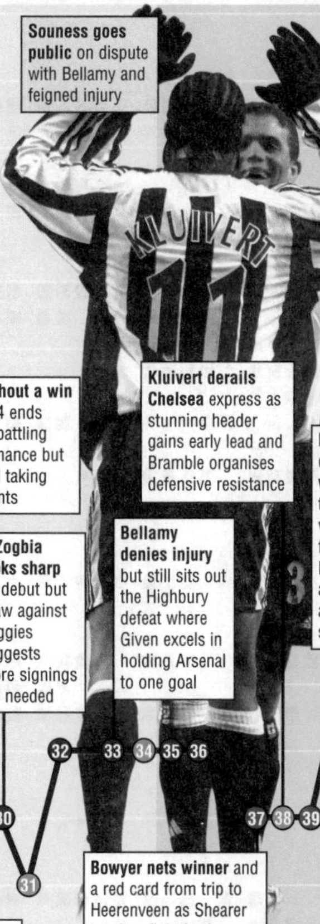

Souness goes public on dispute with Bellamy and feigned injury

Bellamy denies injury but still sits out the Highbury defeat where Given excels in holding Arsenal to one goal

Kluivert derails Chelsea express as stunning header gains early lead and Bramble organises defensive resistance

Bowyer nets winner and a red card from trip to Heerenveen as Shearer inspires fight back

Robert claims fifth win on the trot with wicked freekick but Boumsong and Bramble also look strong

Given earns semi reward as seventh successive win comes courtesy of his saves and Kluivert's cool finish

Shearer closes on Milburn record with a brace of goals as Olympiakos wave Souness into the quarter-finals

Shearer signs up to a one-year extension to push for Milburn's record

Shameful eruption as Bowyer nuts Dyer and fists fly as 'usual suspects' let down the Magpies and let in Villa

Sporting take the spoils and hand out a lesson in finishing despite going behind to a Dyer breakaway

Ambrose dances through United's defence to grab the lead but Rooney's super strike breaks resistance

Flurry of chances go begging and over-run Everton snatch points when Ameobi is dismissed

Shearer rested but win at Fulham provides a tonic with N'Zogbia's crosses leading to the first two goals

Champions held on Tyneside as Souness admits to the season has been a "learning curve for me on and off the field"

MONTH BY MONTH POINTS TALLY

AUGUST	2	17%
SEPTEMBER	9	100%
OCTOBER	5	42%
NOVEMBER	4	33%
DECEMBER	2	13%
JANUARY	7	58%
FEBRUARY	5	56%
MARCH	4	67%
APRIL	2	11%
MAY	4	44%

INS AND OUTS

Bellamy loaned out under a cloud
IN Celestine Babayaro from Chelsea for £1m; Jean-Alain Boumsong from Rangers for £8m; Amdy Faye from Portsmouth for £2m
OUT Craig Bellamy to Celtic on loan; Olivier Bernard to Southampton for £400K

Average League position over the season: 11.4

NOVEMBER DECEMBER JANUARY FEBRUARY MARCH APRIL MAY

GOAL ATTEMPTS

FOR – Goal attempts recorded in League games

	HOME	AWAY	TOTAL	AVE
shots on target	163	92	255	6.7
shots off target	142	88	230	6.1
TOTAL	305	180	485	12.8

Ratio of goals to shots – Average number of shots on target per League goal scored: **5.4**

Accuracy rating – Average percentage of total goal attempts which were on target: **52.6**

AGAINST – Goal attempts recorded in League games

	HOME	AWAY	TOTAL	AVE
shots on target	88	133	221	5.8
shots off target	81	92	173	4.6
TOTAL	169	225	394	10.4

Ratio of goals to shots – Average number of shots on target per League goal scored: **3.9**

Accuracy rating – Average percentage of total goal attempts which were on target: **56.1**

GOALS

Alan Shearer

League	7
FA Cup	1
League Cup	0
Europe	11
Other	0
TOTAL	19

League Average **323** mins between goals

	PLAYER	LGE	FAC	LC	Euro	TOT	AVE
1	Shearer	7	1	0	11	19	323
2	Kluivert	6	2	0	5	13	215
3	Bellamy	7	0	0	3	10	255
4	Ameobi	2	3	1	1	7	841
5	Bowyer	3	1	0	3	7	724
6	Dyer	4	0	0	2	6	440
7	Robert	3	0	0	2	5	635
8	Ambrose	3	0	0	0	3	247
9	O'Brien	2	0	0	0	2	974
10	Jenas	1	0	1	0	2	2539
11	Milner	1	0	0	0	1	1265
12	Bramble	1	0	0	0	1	1651
13	Hughes	1	0	0	0	1	1678
14	Butt	1	0	0	0	1	1423
15	Carr	1	0	0	0	1	2131
	Other	4	1	0	1	6	
	TOTAL	47	8	2	28	85	

SQUAD APPEARANCES

Match	1	2	3	4	5	6	7	8	9	10	11	12	13	14	15	16	17	18	19	20
Venue	A	H	H	A	H	H	A	H	A	A	A	A	H	H	A	H	H	H	H	A
Competition	L	L	L	L	L	E	L	L	E	L	L	E	L	W	L	C	L	W	L	L
Result	D	L	D	L	W	W	W	W	W	D	D	W	W	W	L	W	L	L	L	W

Match	21	22	23	24	25	26	27	28	29	30	31	32	33	34	35	36	37	38	39	40
Venue	A	H	A	H	H	A	A	H	H	A	A	H	A	H	A	H	A	H	H	H
Competition	E	L	L	L	E	L	L	L	L	L	F	L	L	F	L	L	E	F	E	L
Result	W	D	L	D	D	L	D	L	W	D	W	W	L	W	D	D	W	W	W	W

Match	41	42	43	44	45	46	47	48	49	50	51	52	53	54	55	56	57
Venue	H	A	H	H	A	H	H	A	A	N	A	A	H	H	A	A	H
Competition	L	E	F	E	L	L	E	L	E	F	L	L	L	L	L	L	L
Result	W	W	W	W	D	L	W	L	L	L	L	L	D	D	W	L	D

Goalkeepers
Tony Caig
Shay Given
Steve Harper

Defenders
Celestine Babayaro
Olivier Bernard
Jean-Alain Boumsong
Titus Bramble
Stephen Carr
Robbie Elliott
Aaron Hughes
Ronny Johnsen
Andy O'Brien
Peter Ramage
Steven Taylor

Midfielders
Darren Ambrose
Lee Bowyer
Martin Brittain
Nicky Butt
Kieron Dyer
Amdy Faye
Jermaine Jenas
James McClen
James Milner
Charles N'Zogbia
Laurent Robert

Forwards
Shola Ameobi
Craig Bellamy
Michael Chopra
Lewis Guy
Patrick Kluivert
Alan Shearer

KEY: On all match | On bench | Subbed or sent off (Counting game) | Subbed or sent off (playing less than 70 mins) | Subbed on from bench (Counting Game) | Subbed on (playing less than 70 mins) | Subbed on and then subbed or sent off (Counting Game) | Subbed on and then subbed or sent off (playing less than 70 mins) | Not in 16

KEY PLAYERS - GOALSCORERS

Craig Bellamy

Goals in the League	7
Goals in all competitions	10
Assists League goals scored by a team mate where the player delivered the final pass	4
Contribution to Attacking Power Average number of minutes between League team goals while on pitch	59
Player Strike Rate Average number of minutes between League goals scored by player	255
Club Strike Rate Average minutes between League goals scored by club	73

	PLAYER	GOALS LGE	GOALS ALL	ASSISTS	POWER	S RATE
1	Craig Bellamy	7	10	4	59	255 mins
2	Alan Shearer	7	19	0	68	323 mins
3	Kieron Dyer	4	6	0	73	440 mins
4	Laurent Robert	3	5	5	66	635 mins
5	Lee Bowyer	3	7	3	70	724 mins

KEY PLAYERS - MIDFIELDERS

Laurent Robert

Goals in the League	3
Goals in all competitions	5
Assists League goals scored by a team mate where the player delivered the final pass	5
Defensive Rating Average number of mins between League goals conceded while he was on the pitch	58
Contribution to Attacking Power Average number of minutes between League team goals while on pitch	66
Scoring Difference Defensive Rating minus Contribution to Attacking Power	-8

	PLAYER	GOALS LGE	GOALS ALL	ASSISTS	DEF RATE	POWER	SC DIFF
1	Laurent Robert	3	5	5	58	66	-8 mins
2	Kieron Dyer	4	6	0	63	73	-10 mins
3	Jermaine Jenas	1	2	3	58	71	-13 mins
4	Lee Bowyer	3	7	3	57	70	-13 mins
5	Nicky Butt	1	1	0	43	62	-19 mins

PLAYER APPEARANCES

	AGE (on 01/07/05)	IN NAMED 16	APPEARANCES	COUNTING GAMES	MINUTES ON PITCH	APPEARANCES	MINUTES ON PITCH	THIS SEASON	HOME COUNTRY
Goalkeepers									
Tony Caig	31	3	0	0	0	0	0	-	England
Shay Given	29	36	36	36	3240	52	4620	8	Rep of Ireland (15)
Steve Harper	31	37	2	2	180	7	540	-	England
Defenders									
Celestine Babayaro	26	7	7	7	625	13	1081	-	Nigeria
Olivier Bernard	25	21	21	17	1673	29	2406	-	France
Jean-Alain Boumsong	25	14	14	13	1237	18	1597	8	France (4)
Titus Bramble	23	21	19	18	1651	32	2653	-	England
Stephen Carr	28	26	26	22	2131	39	3277	6	Rep of Ireland (15)
Robbie Elliott	31	21	17	13	1327	22	1755	-	England
Aaron Hughes	25	29	22	17	1678	36	2644	8	N Ireland (114)
Ronny Johnsen	36	4	3	2	235	5	445	-	Norway
Andy O'Brien	26	30	23	21	1947	38	3092	7	Rep of Ireland (15)
Peter Ramage	21	8	4	2	261	5	285	-	England
Steven Taylor	19	15	13	10	1012	22	1555	-	England
Midfielders									
Darren Ambrose	21	21	12	6	742	18	1119	-	England
Lee Bowyer	28	27	27	24	2171	39	3047	-	England
Martin Brittain	20	6	0	0	0	0	0	-	England
Nicky Butt	30	20	18	15	1423	26	2012	4	England (6)
Kieron Dyer	26	23	23	18	1758	34	2448	6	England (6)
Amdy Faye	28	9	9	7	704	17	1363	3	Senegal (33)
Jermaine Jenas	22	31	31	27	2539	48	3911	5	England (6)
James McClen	26	1	0	0	0	0	0	-	England
James Milner	19	31	25	10	1265	41	1941	-	England
Charles N'Zogbia	19	15	14	8	808	19	1020	-	France
Laurent Robert	30	38	31	17	1904	47	3055	-	France
Forwards									
Shola Ameobi	23	33	31	12	1681	45	2612	-	England
Craig Bellamy	25	21	21	19	1782	29	2452	8	Wales (74)
Michael Chopra	21	1	1	0	15	1	15	-	England
Lewis Guy	19	0	0	0	0	1	12	-	England
Patrick Kluivert	29	29	25	9	1290	37	2211	-	Holland
Alan Shearer	35	28	28	23	2261	42	3479	-	England

KEY: LEAGUE ALL COMPS CAPS (MAY FIFA RANKING)

TEAM OF THE SEASON

GIVEN
CG 36 DR 62
CARR
CG 22 DR 67
BOUMSONG
CG 13 DR 77
BRAMBLE
CG 18 DR 72
HUGHES
CG 17 DR 58
DYER
CG 18 SD -10
BOWYER
CG 24 SD -13
JENAS
CG 27 SD -13
ROBERT
CG 17 SD -8
BELLAMY
CG 19 SR 255
SHEARER
CG 23 SR 323

KEY: DR = Defensive Rating, SD = Scoring Difference SR = Strike Rate, CG=Counting games – League games playing at least 70 minutes

TOP POINT EARNERS

Kieron Dyer

Counting Games League games when player was on pitch for at least 70 minutes	18
Average points Average League points taken in Counting games	1.39
Club Average points Average points taken in League games	1.16

	PLAYER	GAMES	PTS
1	Kieron Dyer	18	1.39
2	Lee Bowyer	24	1.33
3	Titus Bramble	18	1.33
4	Craig Bellamy	19	1.26
5	Laurent Robert	17	1.24
6	Olivier Bernard	17	1.24
7	Jean-Alain Boumsong	13	1.23
8	Stephen Carr	22	1.23
9	Robbie Elliott	13	1.23
10	Alan Shearer	23	1.22

KEY PLAYERS - DEFENDERS

Jean-Alain Boumsong

Goals Conceded in the League Number of League goals conceded while the player was on the pitch	16
Goals Conceded in all competitions Total number of goals conceded while the player was on the pitch	20
League minutes played Number of minutes played in league matches	1237
Clean Sheets In games when player was on pitch for at least 70 minutes	3
Defensive Rating Average number of mins between League goals conceded while on the pitch	77
Club Defensive Rating Average number of mins between League goals conceded by the club this season	60

	PLAYER	CON LGE	CON ALL	MINS	C SHEETS	DEF RATE
1	Jean-Alain Boumsong	16	20	1237	3	77 mins
2	Titus Bramble	23	32	1651	3	72 mins
3	Stephen Carr	32	45	2131	4	67 mins
4	Aaron Hughes	29	34	1678	4	58 mins
5	Olivier Bernard	29	34	1673	2	58 mins

KEY GOALKEEPER

Shay Given

Goals Conceded in the League Number of League goals conceded while the player was on the pitch	52
Goals Conceded in all competitions Total number of goals conceded while the player was on the pitch	67
League minutes played Number of minutes played in league matches	3240
Clean Sheets In games when player was on pitch for at least 70 minutes	6
Goals to Shots Ratio The average number of shots on target per each League goal conceded	4
Defensive Rating Ave mins between League goals conceded while on the pitch	62

BOOKINGS

Steven Taylor

League Yellow	5
League Red	1
All competitions Yellow	6
All competitions Red	1

League Average 168 mins between cards

	PLAYER	LEAGUE Y	LEAGUE R	TOTAL Y	TOTAL R	AVE
1	Taylor	5	1	6	1	168
2	Faye	3	0	3	0	234
3	Elliott	5	0	5	0	265
4	Bowyer	6	2	14	3	271
5	N'Zogbia	2	0	2	0	404
6	Bernard	4	0	6	0	418
7	Ameobi	3	1	6	1	420
8	Carr	5	0	7	0	426
9	Kluivert	3	0	3	0	430
10	Butt	3	0	4	1	474
11	Robert	4	0	5	0	476
12	Babayaro	1	0	1	0	625
13	Jenas	4	0	5	0	634
14	O'Brien	3	0	5	0	649
15	Ambrose	1	0	2	0	742
	Other	5	1	11	1	
	TOTAL	57	5	85	7	

BLACKBURN ROVERS

Ryan Nelsen and **Morten Gamst Pedersen** have been great additions. Nelsen's Defensive Rating of 150 is second only to Chelsea players this season. Sadly, he didn't play enough games to get into our Divisional Round-up chart.

Andy Todd does get into the Premier Team of the Season on his Defensive Rating of a goal conceded every 143 minutes.

Pedersen tops the Midfielders chart on Scoring Difference by a country mile. It compares how often goals are scored to how often conceded while he is on the pitch and he is the only Blackburn player with a positive score.

John Stead sees his impressive Strike Rate (180 minutes last season) slump to 893 this. **Paul Dickov's** Strike Rate of 262 was lower than his previous 229 for relegated Leicester.

The club's ratio of one goal scored for every 6.6 Shots On Target is the worst in the Premiership.

NICKNAME: ROVERS

KEY: Won Drawn Lost

1	prem	**West Brom**	H	D	1-1	Short 70
2	prem	**Southampton**	A	L	2-3	Ferguson 50; Dickov 68
3	prem	**Arsenal**	A	L	0-3	
4	prem	**Man Utd**	H	D	1-1	Dickov 17
5	prem	**Newcastle**	A	L	0-3	
6	prem	**Portsmouth**	H	W	1-0	Jansen 75
7	ccr2	**Bournemouth**	H	L	3-3*	Emerton 8; Pedersen 90; Gallagher 91 (*lost 7-6 on penalties)
8	prem	**Charlton**	A	L	0-1	
9	prem	**Aston Villa**	H	D	2-2	Ferguson 30; Emerton 63
10	prem	**Middlesbrough**	H	L	0-4	
11	prem	**Chelsea**	A	L	0-4	
12	prem	**Liverpool**	H	D	2-2	Bothroyd 16; Emerton 45
13	prem	**Norwich**	A	D	1-1	Dickov 86
14	prem	**Man City**	A	D	1-1	Dickov 78 pen
15	prem	**Birmingham**	H	D	3-3	Jansen 4; Reid 57; Gallagher 63
16	prem	**Fulham**	A	W	2-0	Gallagher 10; Dickov 77 pen
17	prem	**Tottenham**	H	L	0-1	
18	prem	**Crystal Palace**	A	D	0-0	
19	prem	**Everton**	H	D	0-0	
20	prem	**Newcastle**	H	D	2-2	Dickov 26; Todd 54
21	prem	**Bolton**	A	W	1-0	Dickov 6
22	prem	**Aston Villa**	A	L	0-1	
23	prem	**Charlton**	H	W	1-0	Emerton 41
24	facr3	**Cardiff**	A	D	1-1	Pedersen 5
25	prem	**Portsmouth**	A	W	1-0	Pedersen 55
26	facr3r	**Cardiff**	H	W	3-2	Thompson 9,32; Pedersen 47
27	prem	**Bolton**	H	L	0-1	
28	facr4	**Colchester**	H	W	3-0	Watson 21 og; Johnson 27; Matteo 51
29	prem	**Chelsea**	H	L	0-1	
30	prem	**Middlesbrough**	A	L	0-1	
31	prem	**Norwich**	H	W	3-0	Pedersen 17; Dickov 39,62
32	facr5	**Burnley**	A	D	0-0	
33	facr5r	**Burnley**	H	W	2-1	Tugay 31; Pedersen 86
34	prem	**Everton**	A	W	1-0	Stead 71
35	facqf	**Leicester**	H	W	1-0	Dickov 83 pen
36	prem	**Liverpool**	A	D	0-0	
37	prem	**Arsenal**	H	L	0-1	
38	prem	**Man Utd**	A	D	0-0	
39	prem	**Southampton**	H	W	3-0	Pedersen 11; Jakobsson 48 og; Reid 55
40	facsf	**Arsenal**	N	L	0-3	
41	prem	**Crystal Palace**	H	W	1-0	Pedersen 45
42	prem	**Man City**	H	D	0-0	
43	prem	**West Brom**	A	D	1-1	Emerton 64
44	prem	**Birmingham**	A	L	1-2	Stead 13
45	prem	**Fulham**	H	L	1-3	Neill 6
46	prem	**Tottenham**	A	D	0-0	

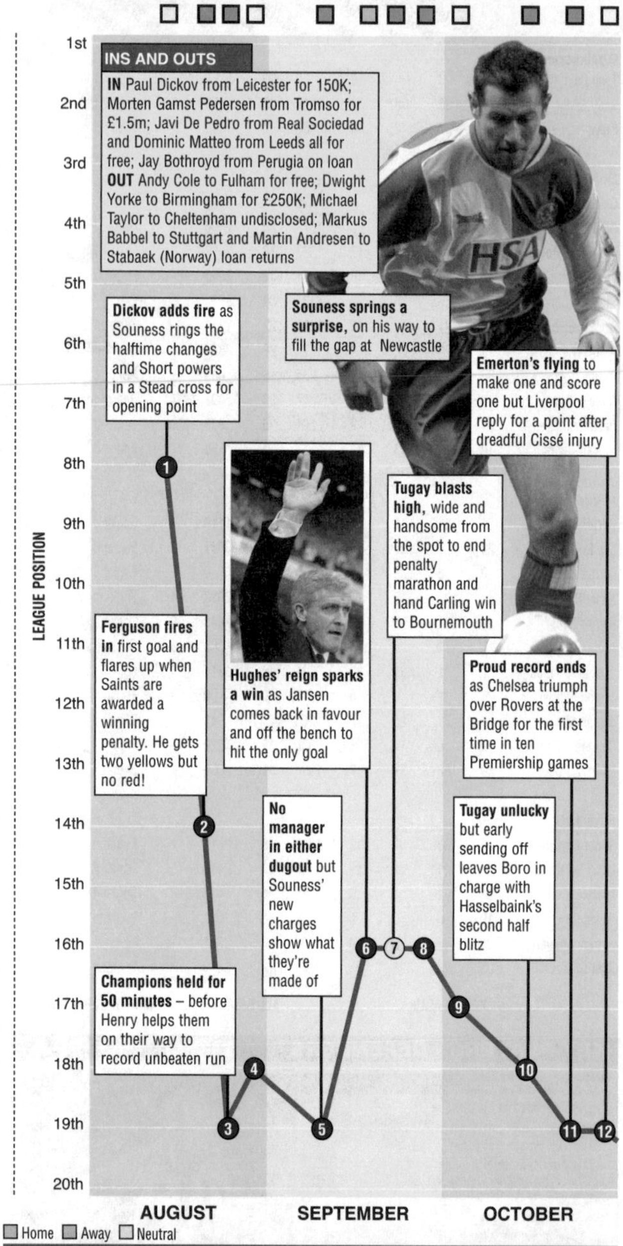

1st
2nd
3rd
4th
5th
6th
7th
8th
9th
10th
11th
12th
13th
14th
15th
16th
17th
18th
19th
20th
LEAGUE POSITION
INS AND OUTS
IN Paul Dickov from Leicester for 150K; Morten Gamst Pedersen from Tromso for £1.5m; Javi De Pedro from Real Sociedad and Dominic Matteo from Leeds all for free; Jay Bothroyd from Perugia on loan
OUT Andy Cole to Fulham for free; Dwight Yorke to Birmingham for £250K; Michael Taylor to Cheltenham undisclosed; Markus Babbel to Stuttgart and Martin Andresen to Stabaek (Norway) loan returns
Dickov adds fire as Souness rings the halftime changes and Short powers in a Stead cross for opening point
Souness springs a surprise, on his way to fill the gap at Newcastle
Emerton's flying to make one and score one but Liverpool reply for a point after dreadful Cissé injury
Tugay blasts high, wide and handsome from the spot to end penalty marathon and hand Carling win to Bournemouth
Ferguson fires in first goal and flares up when Saints are awarded a winning penalty. He gets two yellows but no red!
Hughes' reign sparks a win as Jansen comes back in favour and off the bench to hit the only goal
Proud record ends as Chelsea triumph over Rovers at the Bridge for the first time in ten Premiership games
No manager in either dugout but Souness' new charges show what they're made of
Tugay unlucky but early sending off leaves Boro in charge with Hasselbaink's second half blitz
Champions held for 50 minutes – before Henry helps them on their way to record unbeaten run
1
2
3
4
5
6
7
8
9
10
11
12
AUGUST
SEPTEMBER
OCTOBER
Home
Away
Neutral

ATTENDANCES

HOME GROUND: EWOOD PARK **CAPACITY:** 31367 **AVERAGE LEAGUE AT HOME:** 22315

38	Man Utd	67939	33	Burnley	28691	29	Chelsea	23414	27	Bolton	20056
40	Arsenal	52077	44	Birmingham	28621	37	Arsenal	22992	25	Portsmouth	19904
5	Newcastle	52015	2	Southampton	27492	17	Tottenham	22182	23	Charlton	19819
14	Man City	45504	21	Bolton	27038	35	Leicester	22113	16	Fulham	19103
11	Chelsea	41546	12	Liverpool	26314	18	Crystal Palace	22010	45	Fulham	18991
36	Liverpool	37763	8	Charlton	26193	32	Burnley	21468	41	Crystal Palace	18006
3	Arsenal	37496	4	Man Utd	26155	31	Norwich	20923	24	Cardiff	14145
46	Tottenham	35797	19	Everton	25191	39	Southampton	20726	28	Colchester	10634
22	Aston Villa	34265	43	West Brom	25154	6	Portsmouth	20647	26	Cardiff	9140
34	Everton	32406	42	Man City	24646	9	Aston Villa	20502	7	Bournemouth	7226
30	Middlesboro	30564	13	Norwich	23834	10	Middlesboro	20385			
20	Newcastle	29271	1	West Brom	23475	15	Birmingham	20290			

Hughes' side is dogged but lacks spark

Final Position: **15th**

KEY: ● League ● Champions Lge ● UEFA Cup ● FA Cup ○ League Cup ● Other

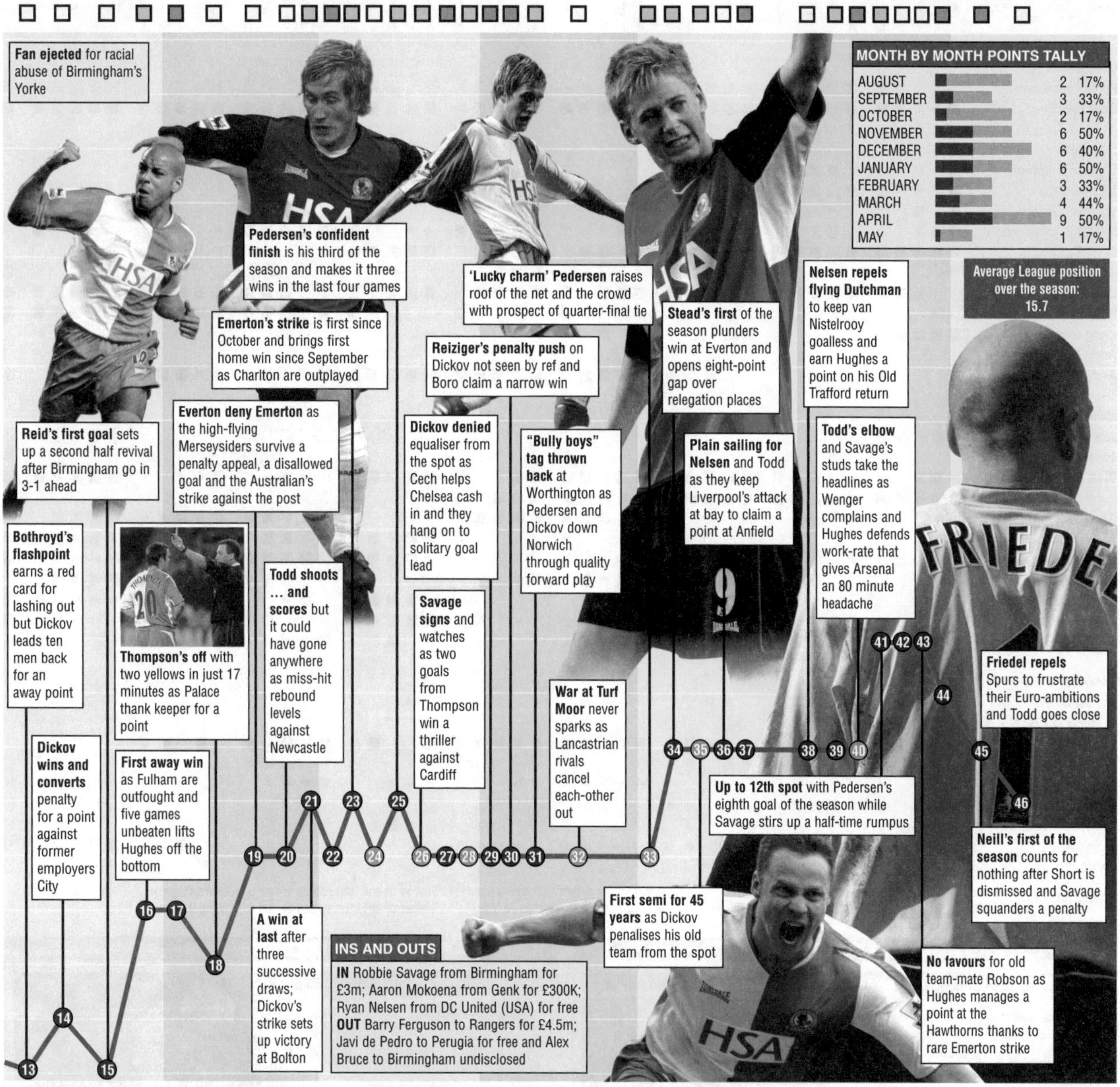
Fan ejected for racial abuse of Birmingham's Yorke
Reid's first goal sets up a second half revival after Birmingham go in 3-1 ahead
Bothroyd's flashpoint earns a red card for lashing out but Dickov leads ten men back for an away point
Dickov wins and converts penalty for a point against former employers City
Thompson's off with two yellows in just 17 minutes as Palace thank keeper for a point
First away win as Fulham are outfought and five games unbeaten lifts Hughes off the bottom
Everton deny Emerton as the high-flying Merseysiders survive a penalty appeal, a disallowed goal and the Australian's strike against the post
Emerton's strike is first since October and brings first home win since September as Charlton are outplayed
Pedersen's confident finish is his third of the season and makes it three wins in the last four games
Todd shoots ... and scores but it could have gone anywhere as miss-hit rebound levels against Newcastle
A win at last after three successive draws; Dickov's strike sets up victory at Bolton
Dickov denied equaliser from the spot as Cech helps Chelsea cash in and they hang on to solitary goal lead
Savage signs and watches as two goals from Thompson win a thriller against Cardiff
Reiziger's penalty push on Dickov not seen by ref and Boro claim a narrow win
'Lucky charm' Pedersen raises roof of the net and the crowd with prospect of quarter-final tie
"Bully boys" tag thrown back at Worthington as Pedersen and Dickov down Norwich through quality forward play
War at Turf Moor never sparks as Lancastrian rivals cancel each-other out
Stead's first of the season plunders win at Everton and opens eight-point gap over relegation places
Plain sailing for Nelsen and Todd as they keep Liverpool's attack at bay to claim a point at Anfield
First semi for 45 years as Dickov penalises his old team from the spot
Up to 12th spot with Pedersen's eighth goal of the season while Savage stirs up a half-time rumpus
Nelsen repels flying Dutchman to keep van Nistelrooy goalless and earn Hughes a point on his Old Trafford return
Todd's elbow and Savage's studs take the headlines as Wenger complains and Hughes defends work-rate that gives Arsenal an 80 minute headache
Friedel repels Spurs to frustrate their Euro-ambitions and Todd goes close
Neill's first of the season counts for nothing after Short is dismissed and Savage squanders a penalty
No favours for old team-mate Robson as Hughes manages a point at the Hawthorns thanks to rare Emerton strike
FRIEDEL
NOVEMBER
DECEMBER
JANUARY
FEBRUARY
MARCH
APRIL
MAY

INS AND OUTS

IN Robbie Savage from Birmingham for £3m; Aaron Mokoena from Genk for £300K; Ryan Nelsen from DC United (USA) for free
OUT Barry Ferguson to Rangers for £4.5m; Javi de Pedro to Perugia for free and Alex Bruce to Birmingham undisclosed

MONTH BY MONTH POINTS TALLY

AUGUST	2	17%
SEPTEMBER	3	33%
OCTOBER	2	17%
NOVEMBER	6	50%
DECEMBER	6	40%
JANUARY	6	50%
FEBRUARY	3	33%
MARCH	4	44%
APRIL	9	50%
MAY	1	17%

Average League position over the season: 15.7

GOAL ATTEMPTS

FOR – Goal attempts recorded in League games

	HOME	AWAY	TOTAL	AVE
shots on target	125	87	212	5.6
shots off target	122	105	227	6
TOTAL	247	192	439	11.6

Ratio of goals to shots – Average number of shots on target per League goal scored: **6.6**

Accuracy rating – Average percentage of total goal attempts which were on target: **48.3**

AGAINST – Goal attempts recorded in League games

	HOME	AWAY	TOTAL	AVE
shots on target	104	112	216	5.7
shots off target	70	87	157	4.1
TOTAL	174	199	373	9.8

Ratio of goals to shots – Average number of shots on target per League goal scored: **5**

Accuracy rating – Average percentage of total goal attempts which were on target: **57.9**

GOALS

Paul Dickov

League	9
FA Cup	1
League Cup	0
Europe	0
Other	0
TOTAL	10

League Average: 262 mins between goals

	PLAYER	LGE	FAC	LC	Euro	TOT	AVE
1	Dickov	9	1	0	0	10	262
2	Pedersen	4	3	1	0	8	385
3	Emerton	4	0	1	0	5	772
4	Gallagher	2	0	1	0	3	265
5	Thompson	0	2	0	0	2	
6	Jansen	2	0	0	0	2	151
7	Reid	2	0	0	0	2	980
8	Stead	2	0	0	0	2	893
9	Ferguson	2	0	0	0	2	945
10	Bothroyd	1	0	0	0	1	488
11	Todd	1	0	0	0	1	2294
12	Short	1	0	0	0	1	1051
13	Johnson	0	1	0	0	1	
14	Matteo	0	1	0	0	1	
15	Neill	1	0	0	0	1	3150
	Other	1	2	0	0	3	
	TOTAL	32	10	3	0	45	

SQUAD APPEARANCES

Match	1	2	3	4	5	6	7	8	9	10	11	12	13	14	15	16	17	18	19	20	21	22	23	24	25	26	27	28	29	30	31	32	33	34	35	36	37	38	39	40	41	42	43	44	45	46
Venue	H	A	A	H	A	H	H	A	H	H	A	H	A	A	H	A	H	A	H	H	A	A	H	A	A	H	H	H	H	A	H	A	H	A	H	A	H	A	H	N	H	H	A	A	H	A
Competition	L	L	L	L	L	L	W	L	L	L	L	L	L	L	L	L	L	L	L	L	L	L	L	F	L	F	L	F	L	L	L	F	F	L	F	L	L	L	L	F	L	L	L	L	L	L
Result	D	L	L	D	L	W	L	L	D	L	L	D	D	D	D	W	L	D	D	D	W	L	W	D	W	W	L	W	L	L	W	D	W	W	W	D	L	D	W	L	W	D	D	L	L	D

Goalkeepers
Peter Enckelman
Brad Friedel

Defenders
Lorenzo Amoruso
Michael Gray
Vratislav Gresko
Nils-Eric Johansson
Dominic Matteo
James McEveley
Lucas Neill
Ryan Nelsen
Craig Short
Andy Taylor
Andy Todd

Midfielders
Javi Francisco De Pedro
Jonathan Douglas
Brett Emerton
Barry Ferguson
Garry Flitcroft
Aaron Mokoena
Morten Gamst Pedersen
Steven Reid
Robbie Savage
David Thompson
Kerimoglu Tugay

Forwards
Jay Bothroyd
Matthew Derbyshire
Paul Dickov
Youri Djorkaeff
Paul Gallagher
Matthew Jansen
Jemal Johnson
John Stead
Dwight Yorke

KEY: On all match · On bench · Subbed or sent off (Counting game) · Subbed or sent off (playing less than 70 mins) · Subbed on from bench (Counting Game) · Subbed on (playing less than 70 mins) · Subbed on and then subbed or sent off (Counting Game) · Subbed on and then subbed or sent off (playing less than 70 mins) · Not in 16

KEY PLAYERS - GOALSCORERS

Paul Dickov

Goals in the League	9
Goals in all competitions	10
Assists League goals scored by a team mate where the player delivered the final pass	2
Contribution to Attacking Power Average number of minutes between League team goals while on pitch	87
Player Strike Rate Average number of minutes between League goals scored by player	262
Club Strike Rate Average minutes between League goals scored by club	107

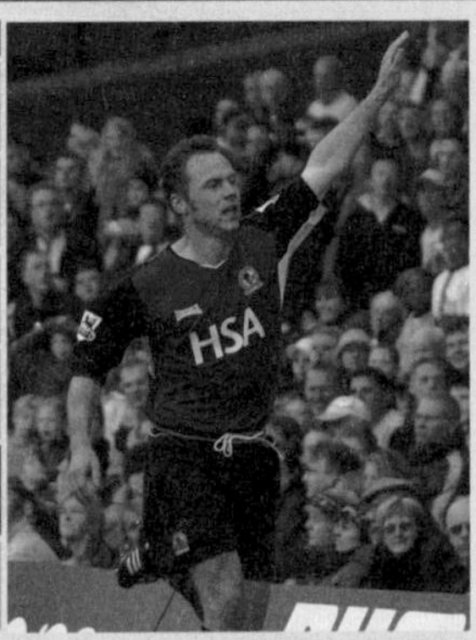

	PLAYER	GOALS LGE	GOALS ALL	ASSISTS	POWER	S RATE
1	Paul Dickov	9	10	2	87	262 mins
2	Morten Gamst Pedersen	4	8	2	118	385 mins
3	Brett Emerton	4	5	4	103	772 mins
4	John Stead	2	2	1	148	893 mins
5	Barry Ferguson	2	2	1	95	945 mins

KEY PLAYERS - MIDFIELDERS

Morten Gamst Pedersen

Goals in the League	4
Goals in all competitions	8
Assists League goals scored by a team mate where the player delivered the final pass	2
Defensive Rating Average number of mins between League goals conceded while on the pitch	140
Contribution to Attacking Power Average number of minutes between League team goals while on pitch	118
Scoring Difference Defensive Rating minus Contribution to Attacking Power	22

	PLAYER	GOALS LGE	GOALS ALL	ASSISTS	DEF RATE	POWER	SC DIFF
1	Morten Gamst Pedersen	4	8	2	140	118	22 mins
2	Steven Reid	2	2	4	85	103	-18 mins
3	Brett Emerton	4	5	4	77	103	-26 mins
4	Barry Ferguson	2	2	1	63	95	-32 mins
5	Garry Flitcroft	0	0	0	90	131	-41 mins

PLAYER APPEARANCES

	AGE (on 01/07/05)	IN NAMED 16	APPEARANCES	COUNTING GAMES	MINUTES ON PITCH	APPEARANCES	MINUTES ON PITCH	THIS SEASON	HOME COUNTRY
Goalkeepers									
Peter Enckelman	28	37	0	0	0	1	120	-	Finland
Brad Friedel	34	38	38	38	3420	45	4050	-	United States
Defenders									
Lorenzo Amoruso	34	10	6	4	453	7	573	-	Italy
Michael Gray	30	10	9	9	801	9	801	-	England
Vratislav Gresko	27	3	3	1	137	4	221	-	Slovakia
Nils-Eric Johansson	25	29	22	17	1711	28	2222	-	Sweden
Dominic Matteo	31	30	28	24	2237	32	2589	-	Scotland
James McEveley	19	9	5	5	450	5	450	-	England
Lucas Neill	27	36	36	34	3150	44	3900	-	Australia
Ryan Nelsen	27	15	15	15	1350	20	1749	-	New Zealand
Craig Short	37	16	14	11	1051	14	1051	-	England
Andy Taylor	19	1	0	0	0	0	0	-	England
Andy Todd	30	27	26	25	2294	32	2834	-	England
Midfielders									
Javi De Pedro	31	4	2	0	59	3	115	-	Spain
Jonathan Douglas	23	3	1	0	45	2	165	-	Rep of Ireland
Brett Emerton	26	37	37	34	3087	44	3611	-	Australia
Barry Ferguson	27	21	21	21	1890	22	1932	5	Scotland (85)
Garry Flitcroft	32	27	19	14	1442	23	1717	-	England
Aaron Mokoena	24	16	16	11	1282	22	1707	-	South Africa
M Gamst Pedersen	23	28	19	16	1539	27	2213	-	Norway
Steven Reid	24	29	28	20	1960	34	2205	1	Rep of Ireland (15)
Robbie Savage	30	9	9	7	724	13	977	4	Wales (74)
David Thompson	27	26	24	9	1179	30	1610	-	England
Kerimoglu Tugay	34	29	21	10	1265	26	1687	-	Turkey
Forwards									
Jay Bothroyd	23	12	11	2	488	13	568	-	England
Matthew Derbyshire	19	1	1	0	9	1	9	-	England
Paul Dickov	32	29	29	24	2354	35	2875	-	England
Youri Djorkaeff	37	5	3	2	199	3	199	-	France
Paul Gallagher	20	20	16	3	530	21	796	-	England
Matthew Jansen	27	8	7	1	301	8	421	-	England
Jemal Johnson	20	6	3	0	90	6	199	-	United States
John Stead	22	32	29	14	1785	34	1966	-	England
Dwight Yorke	33	4	4	1	190	4	190	-	Trinidad & Tobago

KEY: LEAGUE   ALL COMPS   CAPS (MAY FIFA RANKING)

TEAM OF THE SEASON

FRIEDEL
CG 38 DR 80
NEILL
CG 34 DR 77
NELSEN
CG 15 DR 150
TODD
CG 25 DR 143
MATTEO
CG 24 DR 77
EMERTON
CG 34 SD -26
FERGUSON
CG 21 SD -32
REID
CG 20 SD -18
PEDERSEN
CG 16 SD +22
STEAD
CG 14 AP 148
DICKOV
CG 24 SR 262

KEY: DR = Defensive Rating, SD = Scoring Difference AP = Attacking Power SR = Strike Rate, CG=Counting games – League games playing at least 70 minutes * = Played less than 12 counting games

TOP POINT EARNERS

Nils-Eric Johansson

Counting Games League games when player was on pitch for at least 70 minutes	17
Average points Average League points taken in Counting games	1.41
Club Average points Average points taken in League games	1.11

	PLAYER	GAMES	PTS
1	Nils-Eric Johansson	17	1.41
2	Andy Todd	25	1.40
3	Ryan Nelsen	15	1.33
4	Morten Gamst Pedersen	16	1.31
5	Paul Dickov	24	1.25
6	Steven Reid	20	1.25
7	Garry Flitcroft	14	1.21
8	Brad Friedel	38	1.11
9	John Stead	14	1.07
10	Barry Ferguson	21	1.05

KEY PLAYERS - DEFENDERS

Ryan Nelsen

Goals Conceded in the League Number of League goals conceded while the player was on the pitch	9
Goals Conceded in all competitions Total number of goals conceded while the player was on the pitch	13
League minutes played Number of minutes played in league matches	1350
Clean Sheets In games when player was on pitch for at least 70 minutes	9
Defensive Rating Average number of mins between League goals conceded while on the pitch	150
Club Defensive Rating Average number of mins between League goals conceded by the club this season	80

	PLAYER	CON LGE	CON ALL	MINS	C SHEETS	DEF RATE
1	Ryan Nelsen	9	13	1350	9	150 mins
2	Andy Todd	16	22	2294	14	143 mins
3	Lucas Neill	41	51	3150	13	77 mins
4	Dominic Matteo	29	33	2237	9	77 mins
5	Nils-Eric Johansson	23	28	1711	7	74 mins

KEY GOALKEEPER

Brad Friedel

Goals Conceded in the League Number of League goals conceded while the player was on the pitch	43
Goals Conceded in all competitions Total number of goals conceded while the player was on the pitch	50
League minutes played Number of minutes played in league matches	3420
Clean Sheets In games when player was on pitch for at least 70 minutes	15
Goals to Shots Ratio The average number of shots on target per each League goal conceded	5
Defensive Rating Ave mins between League goals conceded while on the pitch	80

BOOKINGS

Kerimoglu Tugay

League Yellow	8
League Red	1
All competitions Yellow	8
All competitions Red	1
League Average	140 mins between cards

	PLAYER	LEAGUE Y	LEAGUE R	TOTAL Y	TOTAL R	AVE
1	Tugay	8	1	8	1	140
2	Amoruso	2	1	2	1	151
3	Thompson	4	1	5	1	235
4	Savage	3	0	5	0	241
5	Mokoena	5	0	7	0	256
6	Stead	6	0	6	0	297
7	Ferguson	5	1	5	1	315
8	Matteo	7	0	8	0	319
9	Dickov	7	0	9	0	336
10	Neill	9	0	12	0	350
11	Flitcroft	4	0	5	0	360
12	Bothroyd	0	1	0	1	488
13	Short	1	1	1	1	525
14	Todd	4	0	6	0	573
15	Reid	3	0	3	0	653
	Other	9	0	10	0	
	TOTAL	77	6	92	6	

PORTSMOUTH

Released keeper **Shaka Hislop** has every right to feel hard done by. His Defensive Rating of a goal conceded every 67 minutes is better than all but one of his defensive colleagues. The Goals to Shots Ratio says a lot about whether a keeper is outperforming his defence and Hislop's reads 5.5 shots saved for every goal conceded. On this measure he is one of the top four keepers in the Premiership.

Yakubu Ayegbeni had the fifth highest Strike Rate in the Premiership with his 13 league goals coming at a Rate of one every 189 minutes on average.

Steve Stone outperformed his midfield colleagues in terms of Scoring Difference - the only player with a positive result - showing that Pompey are more likely to score than concede when he's playing. Stone also headed the Top Point Earners chart, averaging 1.37 points a game making him the fourth most badly-missed player in the division.

NICKNAME: POMPEY KEY: Won Drawn Lost

1	prem	**Birmingham**	H	D	1-1	Unsworth 16 pen
2	prem	**Charlton**	A	L	1-2	Berger 53
3	prem	**Fulham**	H	W	4-3	Berkovic 19; Yakubu 22 pen,28,72
4	prem	**Crystal Palace**	H	W	3-1	Fuller 3; Berger 47; Popovic 85 og
5	prem	**Blackburn**	A	L	0-1	
6	ccr2	**Tranmere**	A	W	1-0	Kamara 65
7	prem	**Everton**	H	L	0-1	
8	prem	**Norwich**	A	D	2-2	Yakubu 37; Berger 65
9	prem	**Tottenham**	H	W	1-0	Yakubu 63
10	prem	**Middlesbrough**	A	D	1-1	Kamara 5
11	ccr3	**Leeds**	H	W	2-1	Kamara 14; Berkovic 32 pen
12	prem	**Man Utd**	H	W	2-0	Unsworth 53 pen; Yakubu 72
13	prem	**Aston Villa**	A	L	0-3	
14	ccr4	**Cardiff**	A	W	2-0	Yakubu 47,55 pen
15	prem	**Southampton**	A	L	1-2	Jakobsson 12 og
16	prem	**Man City**	H	L	1-3	O'Neil 8
17	prem	**Bolton**	A	W	1-0	De Zeeuw 45
18	ccqf	**Watford**	A	L	0-3	
19	prem	**West Brom**	H	W	3-2	Purse 35 og; De Zeeuw 85; LuaLua 89
20	prem	**Newcastle**	A	D	1-1	Stone 30
21	prem	**Liverpool**	A	D	1-1	LuaLua 90
22	prem	**Arsenal**	H	L	0-1	
23	prem	**Crystal Palace**	A	W	1-0	Primus 69
24	prem	**Chelsea**	H	L	0-2	
25	prem	**Norwich**	H	D	1-1	Yakubu 61 pen
26	prem	**Everton**	A	L	1-2	Yakubu 31
27	facr3	**Gillingham**	H	W	1-0	Yakubu 49
28	prem	**Blackburn**	H	L	0-1	
29	prem	**Chelsea**	A	L	0-3	
30	facr4	**Southampton**	A	L	1-2	Yakubu 56 pen
31	prem	**Middlesbrough**	H	W	2-1	Taylor 40; Yakubu 58
32	prem	**Tottenham**	A	L	1-3	Kamara 28
33	prem	**Aston Villa**	H	L	1-2	Yakubu 24 pen
34	prem	**Man Utd**	A	L	1-2	O'Neil 47
35	prem	**Arsenal**	A	L	0-3	
36	prem	**Newcastle**	H	D	1-1	Stone 45
37	prem	**Fulham**	A	L	1-3	LuaLua 32
38	prem	**Charlton**	H	W	4-2	Yakubu 3; Stone 20; Kamara 83; LuaLua 90
39	prem	**Birmingham**	A	D	0-0	
40	prem	**Liverpool**	H	L	1-2	Kamara 34
41	prem	**Southampton**	H	W	4-1	Yakubu 4 pen; De Zeeuw 17; LuaLua 22,27
42	prem	**Man City**	A	L	0-2	
43	prem	**Bolton**	H	D	1-1	Yakubu 72
44	prem	**West Brom**	A	L	0-2	

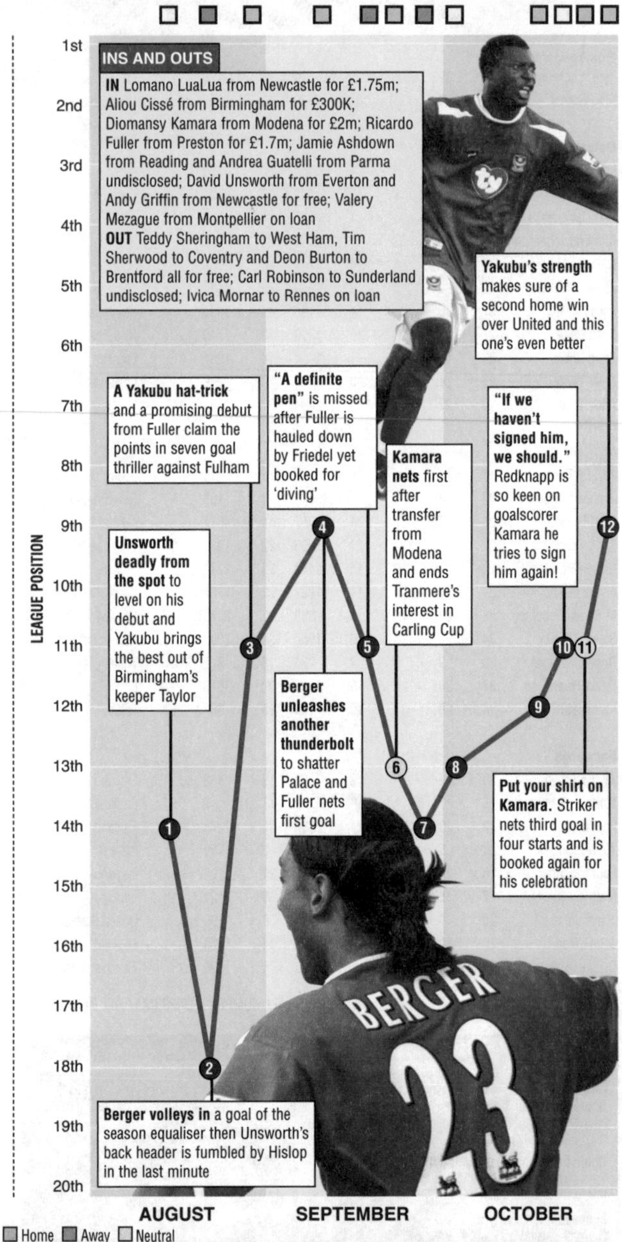

1st
2nd
3rd
4th
5th
6th
7th
8th
9th
10th
11th
12th
13th
14th
15th
16th
17th
18th
19th
20th
LEAGUE POSITION
INS AND OUTS
IN Lomano LuaLua from Newcastle for £1.75m; Aliou Cissé from Birmingham for £300K; Diomansy Kamara from Modena for £2m; Ricardo Fuller from Preston for £1.7m; Jamie Ashdown from Reading and Andrea Guatelli from Parma undisclosed; David Unsworth from Everton and Andy Griffin from Newcastle for free; Valery Mezague from Montpellier on loan
OUT Teddy Sheringham to West Ham, Tim Sherwood to Coventry and Deon Burton to Brentford all for free; Carl Robinson to Sunderland undisclosed; Ivica Mornar to Rennes on loan
Yakubu's strength makes sure of a second home win over United and this one's even better
A Yakubu hat-trick and a promising debut from Fuller claim the points in seven goal thriller against Fulham
"A definite pen" is missed after Fuller is hauled down by Friedel yet booked for 'diving'
Kamara nets first after transfer from Modena and ends Tranmere's interest in Carling Cup
"If we haven't signed him, we should." Redknapp is so keen on goalscorer Kamara he tries to sign him again!
Unsworth deadly from the spot to level on his debut and Yakubu brings the best out of Birmingham's keeper Taylor
Berger unleashes another thunderbolt to shatter Palace and Fuller nets first goal
Put your shirt on Kamara. Striker nets third goal in four starts and is booked again for his celebration
Berger volleys in a goal of the season equaliser then Unsworth's back header is fumbled by Hislop in the last minute
BERGER 23
1 2 3 4 5 6 7 8 9 10 11 12
AUGUST
SEPTEMBER
OCTOBER
Home Away Neutral

ATTENDANCES

HOME GROUND: FRATTON PARK **CAPACITY:** 20210 **AVERAGE LEAGUE AT HOME:** 20055

34	Man Utd	67989	30	Southampton	29453	12	Man Utd	20190	4	Crystal Palace	20019
20	Newcastle	51480	39	Birmingham	28883	43	Bolton	20188	25	Norwich	20015
42	Man City	46454	44	West Brom	27751	22	Arsenal	20170	41	Southampton	20000
29	Chelsea	42267	23	Crystal Palace	25238	36	Newcastle	20165	28	Blackburn	19904
35	Arsenal	38079	2	Charlton	25204	33	Aston Villa	20160	3	Fulham	19728
32	Tottenham	36105	17	Bolton	25008	7	Everton	20125	31	Middlesboro	19520
26	Everton	35480	8	Norwich	23853	9	Tottenham	20121	18	Watford	18877
21	Liverpool	35064	5	Blackburn	20647	19	West Brom	20110	11	Leeds	15215
13	Aston Villa	32633	37	Fulham	20502	38	Charlton	20108	27	Gillingham	14252
10	Middlesboro	30964	24	Chelsea	20210	16	Man City	20101	14	Cardiff	13555
15	Southampton	30921	40	Liverpool	20205	1	Birmingham	20021	6	Tranmere	6966

Perrin in to deliver blow to Redknapp

Final Position: 16th

KEY: ● League ● Champions Lge ● UEFA Cup ● FA Cup ○ League Cup ● Other

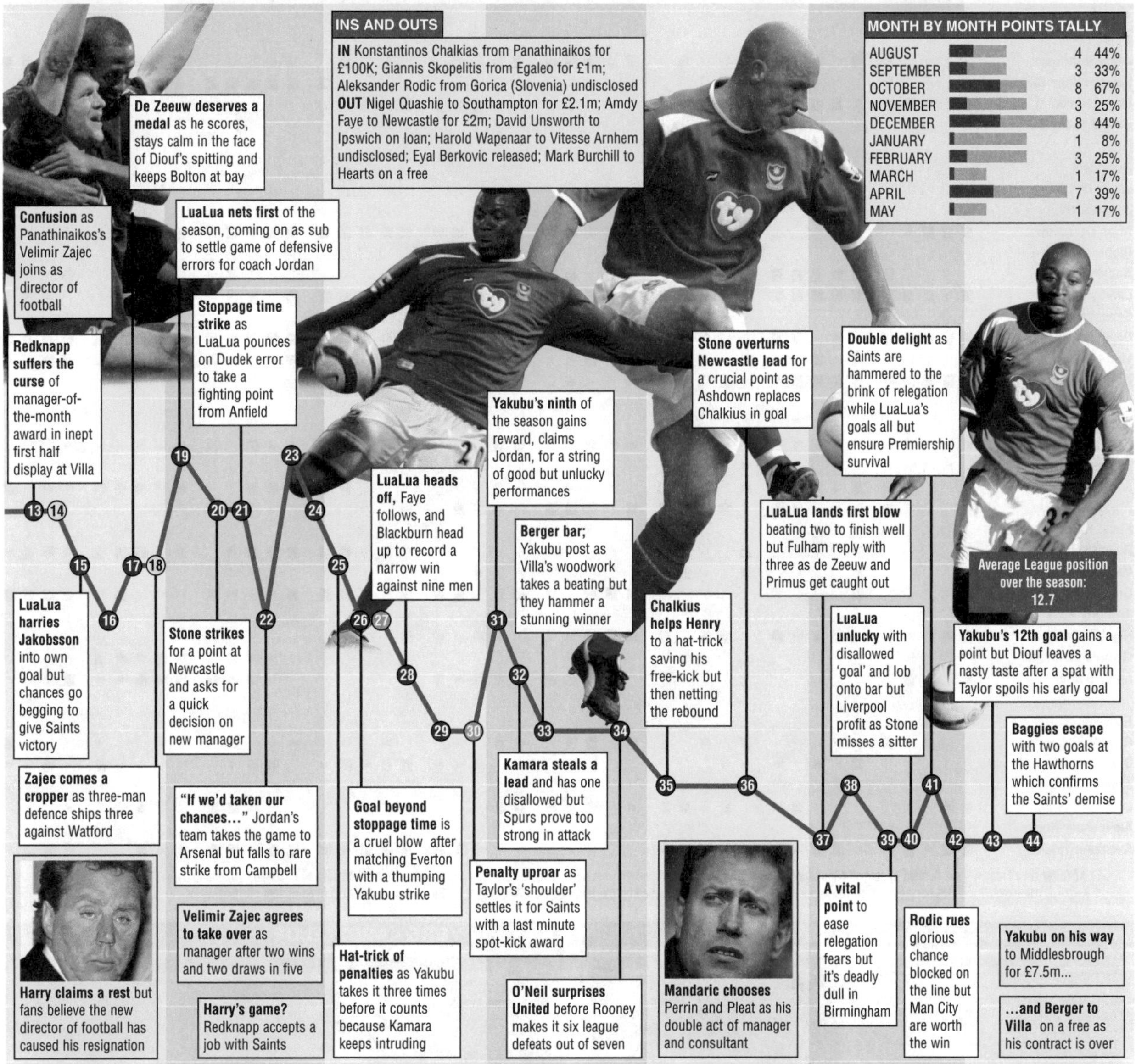
13
14
15
16
17
18
19
20
21
22
23
24
25
26
27
28
29
30
31
32
33
34
35
36
37
38
39
40
41
42
43
44

INS AND OUTS

IN Konstantinos Chalkias from Panathinaikos for £100K; Giannis Skopelitis from Egaleo for £1m; Aleksander Rodic from Gorica (Slovenia) undisclosed **OUT** Nigel Quashie to Southampton for £2.1m; Amdy Faye to Newcastle for £2m; David Unsworth to Ipswich on loan; Harold Wapenaar to Vitesse Arnhem undisclosed; Eyal Berkovic released; Mark Burchill to Hearts on a free

MONTH BY MONTH POINTS TALLY

Month	Points	%
AUGUST	4	44%
SEPTEMBER	3	33%
OCTOBER	8	67%
NOVEMBER	3	25%
DECEMBER	8	44%
JANUARY	1	8%
FEBRUARY	3	25%
MARCH	1	17%
APRIL	7	39%
MAY	1	17%

Redknapp suffers the curse of manager-of-the-month award in inept first half display at Villa

Confusion as Panathinaikos's Velimir Zajec joins as director of football

De Zeeuw deserves a medal as he scores, stays calm in the face of Diouf's spitting and keeps Bolton at bay

LuaLua harries Jakobsson into own goal but chances go begging to give Saints victory

Zajec comes a cropper as three-man defence ships three against Watford

Harry claims a rest but fans believe the new director of football has caused his resignation

LuaLua nets first of the season, coming on as sub to settle game of defensive errors for coach Jordan

Stoppage time strike as LuaLua pounces on Dudek error to take a fighting point from Anfield

Stone strikes for a point at Newcastle and asks for a quick decision on new manager

"If we'd taken our chances..." Jordan's team takes the game to Arsenal but falls to rare strike from Campbell

Velimir Zajec agrees to take over as manager after two wins and two draws in five

Harry's game? Redknapp accepts a job with Saints

LuaLua heads off, Faye follows, and Blackburn head up to record a narrow win against nine men

Goal beyond stoppage time is a cruel blow after matching Everton with a thumping Yakubu strike

Hat-trick of penalties as Yakubu takes it three times before it counts because Kamara keeps intruding

Yakubu's ninth of the season gains reward, claims Jordan, for a string of good but unlucky performances

Penalty uproar as Taylor's 'shoulder' settles it for Saints with a last minute spot-kick award

Berger bar; Yakubu post as Villa's woodwork takes a beating but they hammer a stunning winner

Kamara steals a lead and has one disallowed but Spurs prove too strong in attack

O'Neil surprises United before Rooney makes it six league defeats out of seven

Chalkius helps Henry to a hat-trick saving his free-kick but then netting the rebound

Stone overturns Newcastle lead for a crucial point as Ashdown replaces Chalkius in goal

Mandaric chooses Perrin and Pleat as his double act of manager and consultant

LuaLua lands first blow beating two to finish well but Fulham reply with three as de Zeeuw and Primus get caught out

LuaLua unlucky with disallowed 'goal' and lob onto bar but Liverpool profit as Stone misses a sitter

A vital point to ease relegation fears but it's deadly dull in Birmingham

Double delight as Saints are hammered to the brink of relegation while LuaLua's goals all but ensure Premiership survival

Rodic rues glorious chance blocked on the line but Man City are worth the win

Yakubu's 12th goal gains a point but Diouf leaves a nasty taste after a spat with Taylor spoils his early goal

Baggies escape with two goals at the Hawthorns which confirms the Saints' demise

Yakubu on his way to Middlesbrough for £7.5m...

...and Berger to Villa on a free as his contract is over

Average League position over the season: 12.7

NOVEMBER DECEMBER JANUARY FEBRUARY MARCH APRIL MAY

GOAL ATTEMPTS

FOR — Goal attempts recorded in League games

	HOME	AWAY	TOTAL	AVE
shots on target	123	72	195	5.1
shots off target	118	77	195	5.1
TOTAL	241	149	390	10.3

Ratio of goals to shots Average number of shots on target per League goal scored: 4.5

Accuracy rating Average percentage of total goal attempts which were on target: 50

AGAINST — Goal attempts recorded in League games

	HOME	AWAY	TOTAL	AVE
shots on target	120	141	261	6.9
shots off target	108	72	180	4.7
TOTAL	228	213	441	11.6

Ratio of goals to shots Average number of shots on target per League goal scored: 4.4

Accuracy rating Average percentage of total goal attempts which were on target: 59.2

GOALS

Ayegbeni Yakubu

League	13
FA Cup	2
League Cup	2
Europe	0
Other	0
TOTAL	17

League Average: 189 mins between goals

	PLAYER	LGE	FAC	LC	Euro	TOT	AVE
1	Yakubu	13	2	2	0	17	189
2	LuaLua	6	0	0	0	6	289
3	Kamara	4	0	2	0	6	343
4	Berger	3	0	0	0	3	832
5	Stone	3	0	0	0	3	624
6	De Zeeuw	3	0	0	0	3	919
7	Berkovic	1	0	1	0	2	444
8	Unsworth	2	0	0	0	2	596
9	O'Neil	2	0	0	0	2	945
10	Fuller	1	0	0	0	1	1481
11	Taylor	1	0	0	0	1	2156
12	Primus	1	0	0	0	1	2870
	Other	3	0	0	0	3	
	TOTAL	43	2	5	0	50	

SQUAD APPEARANCES

Match	1	2	3	4	5	6	7	8	9	10	11	12	13	14	15	16	17	18	19	20	21	22	23	24	25	26	27	28	29	30	31	32	33	34	35	36	37	38	39	40	41	42	43	44
Venue	H	A	H	H	A	A	H	A	H	A	H	H	A	A	A	H	A	A	H	A	A	H	A	H	H	A	H	H	A	A	H	A	H	A	A	H	A	H	A	H	H	A	H	A
Competition	L	L	L	L	L	W	L	L	L	L	W	L	L	W	L	L	L	W	L	L	L	L	L	L	L	L	F	L	L	F	L	L	L	L	L	L	L	L	L	L	L	L	L	L
Result	D	L	W	W	L	W	L	D	W	D	W	W	L	W	L	L	W	L	W	D	D	L	W	L	D	L	W	L	L	L	W	L	L	L	L	D	L	W	D	L	W	L	D	L

Goalkeepers
Jamie Ashdown
Konstantinos Chalkias
Shaka Hislop
Harald Wapenaar

Defenders
Lewis Buxton
John Curtis
Arjan De Zeeuw
Richard Duffy
Andrew Griffin
Linvoy Primus
Sebastien Schemmel
Dejan Stefanovic
Matthew Taylor
David Unsworth

Midfielders
Patrik Berger
Eyal Berkovic
Aliou Cisse
Amdy Faye
Kevin Harper
Richard Hughes
Valery Mezague
Gary O'Neil
Anthony Pulis
Nigel Quashie
Giannis Skopelitis
Steve Stone

Forwards
Ricardo Fuller
Diomansy Mehdi Kamara
James Keene
Lomana LuaLua
Aleksandar Rodic
Ayegbeni Yakubu

KEY: On all match · On bench · Subbed or sent off (Counting game) · Subbed or sent off (playing less than 70 mins) · Subbed on from bench (Counting Game) · Subbed on (playing less than 70 mins) · Subbed on and then subbed or sent off (Counting Game) · Subbed on and then subbed or sent off (playing less than 70 mins) · Not in 16

KEY PLAYERS - GOALSCORERS

Ayegbeni Yakubu

Goals in the League	13
Goals in all competitions	17
Assists League goals scored by team-mates where he delivered the final pass	3
Contribution to Attacking Power Average number of minutes between League team goals while on pitch	72
Player Strike Rate Average number of minutes between League goals scored by player	189
Club Strike Rate Average minutes between League goals scored by club	80

	PLAYER	GOALS LGE	GOALS ALL	ASSISTS	POWER	S RATE
1	Ayegbeni Yakubu	13	17	3	72	189 mins
2	Lomana LuaLua	6	6	4	72	289 mins
3	David Unsworth	2	2	3	70	596 mins
4	Steve Stone	3	3	4	62	624 mins
5	Patrik Berger	3	3	5	69	832 mins

KEY PLAYERS - MIDFIELDERS

Steve Stone

Goals in the League	3
Goals in all competitions	3
Assists League goals scored by team-mates where he delivered the final pass	4
Defensive Rating Average number of mins between League goals conceded while on the pitch	67
Contribution to Attacking Power Average number of minutes between League team goals while on pitch	62
Scoring Difference Defensive Rating minus Contribution to Attacking Power	5

	PLAYER	GOALS LGE	GOALS ALL	ASSISTS	DEF RATE	POWER	SC DIFF
1	Steve Stone	3	3	4	67	62	5 mins
2	Patrik Berger	3	3	5	62	69	-7 mins
3	Nigel Quashie	0	0	0	65	77	-12 mins
4	Amdy Faye	0	0	0	69	102	-33 mins
5	Gary O'Neil	2	2	2	53	111	-58 mins

PLAYER APPEARANCES

	AGE (on 01/07/05)	IN NAMED 16	APPEARANCES	COUNTING GAMES	MINUTES ON PITCH	APPEARANCES	MINUTES ON PITCH	THIS SEASON	HOME COUNTRY
Goalkeepers									
Jamie Ashdown	24	36	16	16	1440	21	1890	-	England
K Chalkias	31	9	5	5	450	6	540	-	Greece
Shaka Hislop	36	29	17	17	1530	17	1530	-	Trinidad & Tobago
Harald Wapenaar	35	2	0	0	0	0	0	-	Holland
Defenders									
Lewis Buxton	21	0	0	0	0	0	0	-	Wales
John Curtis	26	3	1	0	21	1	21	-	England
Arjan De Zeeuw	35	33	32	30	2756	37	3206	-	Holland
Richard Duffy	19	1	0	0	0	0	0	-	Wales
Andrew Griffin	26	24	22	17	1611	27	1985	-	England
Linvoy Primus	31	37	35	29	2870	40	3233	-	England
Sebastien Schemmel	30	1	0	0	0	0	0	-	France
Dejan Stefanovic	30	33	32	32	2880	36	3151	-	Serbia & Montenegro
Matthew Taylor	23	36	32	22	2156	37	2606	-	England
David Unsworth	31	17	15	12	1191	19	1506	-	England
Midfielders									
Patrik Berger	31	33	32	26	2496	37	2877	-	Czech Republic
Eyal Berkovic	33	16	11	2	444	13	545	-	Israel
Aliou Cisse	29	30	20	11	1162	25	1522	-	Senegal
Amdy Faye	28	20	20	17	1528	21	1606	3	Senegal (33)
Kevin Harper	29	1	0	0	0	1	45	-	England
Richard Hughes	26	19	16	11	1144	20	1426	3	Scotland (85)
Valery Mezague	21	17	11	1	373	14	643	-	Cameroon
Gary O'Neil	22	27	24	20	1890	28	2216	-	England
Anthony Pulis	20	0	0	0	0	1	1	-	England
Nigel Quashie	26	20	19	19	1691	21	1812	-	England
Giannis Skopelitis	27	14	13	7	800	13	800	-	Greece
Steve Stone	33	24	23	19	1873	25	1996	-	England
Forwards									
Ricardo Fuller	25	34	31	9	1481	37	1854	-	Jamaica
Diomansy Kamara	24	26	25	9	1373	29	1693	-	France
James Keene	19	2	2	1	111	2	111	-	England
Lomana LuaLua	24	26	25	16	1732	26	1822	-	Congo DR
Aleksandar Rodic	25	8	4	0	120	4	120	-	Slovenia
Ayegbeni Yakubu	22	30	30	25	2458	35	2746	-	Nigeria

KEY: LEAGUE ALL COMPS CAPS (MAY FIFA RANKING)

TEAM OF THE SEASON

HISLOP
CG 17 DR 67
GRIFFIN
CG 17 DR 85
DE ZEEUW
CG 32 DR 55
STEFANOVIC
CG 32 DR 54
PRIMUS
CG 29 DR 62
STONE
CG 19 SD +5
QUASHIE
CG 19 SD -12
FAYE
CG 17 SD -33
BERGER
CG 26 SD -17
LUALUA
CG 16 AP 72
YAKUBU
CG 25 SR 189

KEY: DR = Defensive Rating, SD = Scoring Difference AP = Attacking Power SR = Strike Rate, CG=Counting games – League games playing at least 70 minutes

TOP POINT EARNERS

Steve Stone

Counting Games League games when player was on pitch for at least 70 minutes	19
Average points Average League points taken in Counting games	1.37
Club Average points Average points taken in League games	1.03

	PLAYER	GAMES	PTS
1	Steve Stone	19	1.37
2	Nigel Quashie	19	1.32
3	Andrew Griffin	17	1.24
4	David Unsworth	12	1.17
5	Patrik Berger	26	1.15
6	Shaka Hislop	17	1.12
7	Ayegbeni Yakubu	25	1.08
8	Jamie Ashdown	16	1.06
9	Arjan De Zeeuw	30	1.03
10	Linvoy Primus	29	1.03

KEY PLAYERS - DEFENDERS

Andrew Griffin

Goals Conceded in the League Number of League goals conceded while the player was on the pitch	19
Goals Conceded in all competitions Total number of goals conceded while the player was on the pitch	22
League minutes played Number of minutes played in league matches	1611
Clean Sheets In games when he played at least70 mins	4
Defensive Rating Average number of mins between League goals conceded while on the pitch	85
Club Defensive Rating Average number of mins between League goals conceded by the club this season	58

	PLAYER	CON LGE	CON ALL	MINS	C SHEETS	DEF RATE
1	Andrew Griffin	19	22	1611	4	85 mins
2	Linvoy Primus	46	52	2870	5	62 mins
3	Arjan De Zeeuw	50	56	2756	4	55 mins
4	Dejan Stefanovic	53	55	2880	3	54 mins
5	David Unsworth	23	24	1191	2	52 mins

KEY GOALKEEPER

Shaka Hislop

Goals Conceded in the League Number of League goals conceded while the player was on the pitch	23
Goals Conceded in all competitions Total number of goals conceded while the player was on the pitch	23
League minutes played Number of minutes played in league matches	1530
Clean Sheets In games when he played at least 70 mins	3
Goals to Shots Ratio The average number of shots on target per each League goal conceded	5.5
Defensive Rating Ave mins between League goals conceded while on the pitch	67

BOOKINGS

Amdy Faye

League Yellow	7
League Red	1
All competitions Yellow	7
All competitions Red	1
League Average **191** mins between cards	

	PLAYER	LEAGUE		TOTAL		AVE
1	Faye	7 Y	1 R	7 Y	1 R	191
2	Griffin	7	0	8	0	230
3	Hughes	4	0	5	0	286
4	Unsworth	4	0	5	0	297
5	Fuller	4	0	4	0	370
6	Skopelitis	2	0	2	0	400
7	Kamara	3	0	6	1	457
8	Taylor	4	0	4	0	539
9	O'Neil	3	0	3	0	630
10	Stefanovic	4	0	5	0	720
11	Quashie	2	0	2	0	845
12	LuaLua	1	1	1	1	866
13	De Zeeuw	3	0	4	0	918
14	Cisse	1	0	2	0	1162
15	Yakubu	2	0	2	0	1229
	Other	3	0	4	0	
	TOTAL	54	2	64	3	

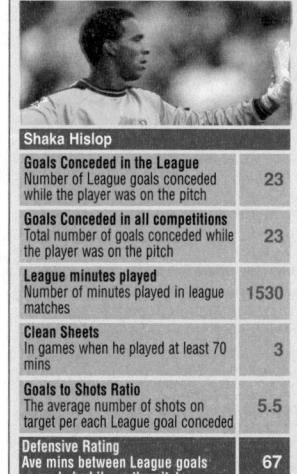

WEST BROMWICH ALBION

Robert Earnshaw tops the club's Goalscorers chart with 11 league goals scored at a Strike Rate of one every 157 minutes. He didn't play enough Counting Games to make our divisional chart but his Strike Rate would have been in the best three in the Premiership.

Ronnie Wallwork played around half the season but tops the Baggie's Midfielders chart. His Scoring Difference measures how often the club concedes goals compared to how often it scores them when he is playing and he's the only player not in minus figures.

Mid-season recruit **Kevin Campbell** brought spirit to the club and finished with the best points record. They averaged 1.46 points per game when he influenced events for at least 70 minutes. **Geoff Horsfield** had a similar effect at the end of the season averaging 1.43 points against the club's season average of .89 per game.

NICKNAME: BAGGIES KEY: Won Drawn Lost

1	prem	**Blackburn**	A	D	1-1	Clement 33
2	prem	**Aston Villa**	H	D	1-1	Clement 38
3	prem	**Tottenham**	H	D	1-1	Gera 3
4	prem	**Everton**	A	L	1-2	Dobie 7
5	prem	**Liverpool**	A	L	0-3	
6	prem	**Fulham**	H	D	1-1	Kanu 88
7	ccr2	**Colchester**	A	L	1-2	Horsfield 50
8	prem	**Newcastle**	A	L	1-3	Horsfield 87
9	prem	**Bolton**	H	W	2-1	Kanu 56; Gera 65
10	prem	**Norwich**	H	D	0-0	
11	prem	**Crystal Palace**	A	L	0-3	
12	prem	**Chelsea**	H	L	1-4	Gera 56
13	prem	**Southampton**	A	D	2-2	Earnshaw 29,37
14	prem	**Middlesbrough**	H	L	1-2	Earnshaw 37
15	prem	**Arsenal**	A	D	1-1	Earnshaw 79
16	prem	**Man Utd**	H	L	0-3	
17	prem	**Portsmouth**	A	L	2-3	Stefanovic 14 og; Earnshaw 45
18	prem	**Charlton**	H	L	0-1	
19	prem	**Birmingham**	A	L	0-4	
20	prem	**Liverpool**	H	L	0-5	
21	prem	**Man City**	A	D	1-1	Dunne 85 og
22	prem	**Bolton**	A	D	1-1	Gera 13
23	prem	**Newcastle**	H	D	0-0	
24	facr3	**Preston**	A	W	2-0	Earnshaw 76,83
25	prem	**Fulham**	A	L	0-1	
26	prem	**Man City**	H	W	2-0	Campbell 5; Wallwork 81
27	facr4	**Tottenham**	H	D	1-1	Earnshaw 17
28	prem	**Crystal Palace**	H	D	2-2	Campbell 82; Earnshaw 90
29	prem	**Norwich**	A	L	2-3	Earnshaw 41; Richardson 49
30	facr4r	**Tottenham**	A	L	1-3	Kanu 12
31	prem	**Southampton**	H	D	0-0	
32	prem	**Birmingham**	H	W	2-0	Clement 53; Campbell 64
33	prem	**Chelsea**	A	L	0-1	
34	prem	**Charlton**	A	W	4-1	Horsfield 9; Earnshaw 73,84,90 pen
35	prem	**Everton**	H	W	1-0	Gera 63
36	prem	**Aston Villa**	A	D	1-1	Robinson 89
37	prem	**Tottenham**	A	D	1-1	Gera 24
38	prem	**Middlesbrough**	A	L	0-4	
39	prem	**Blackburn**	H	D	1-1	Richardson 32
40	prem	**Arsenal**	H	L	0-2	
41	prem	**Man Utd**	A	D	1-1	Earnshaw 63 pen
42	prem	**Portsmouth**	H	W	2-0	Horsfield 58; Richardson 75

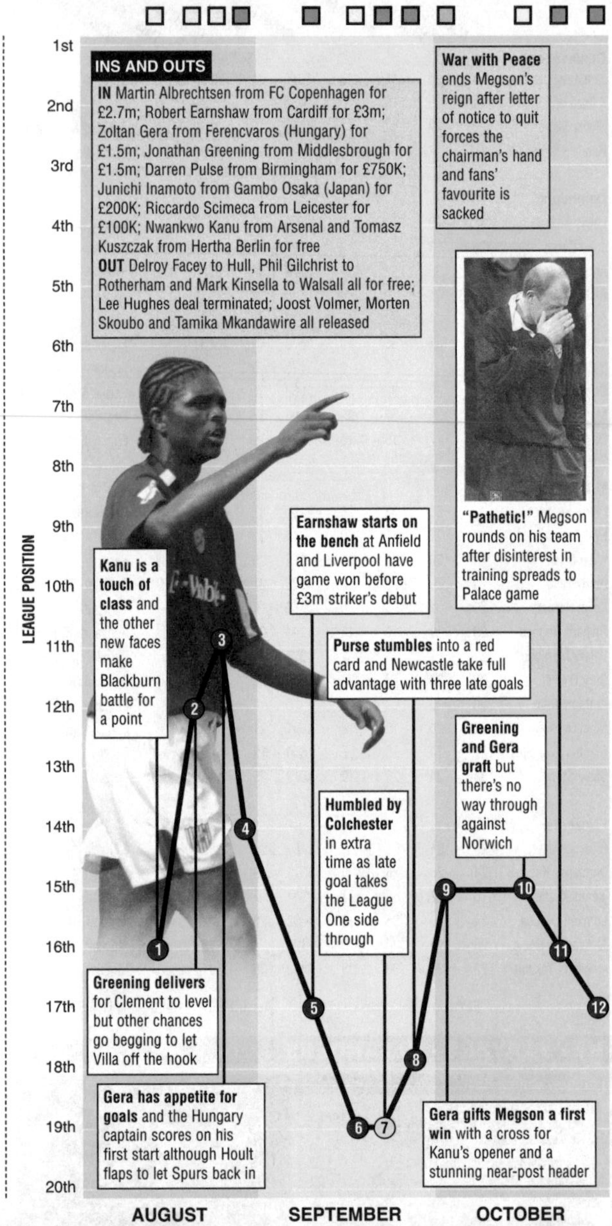

1st
2nd
3rd
4th
5th
6th
7th
8th
9th
10th
11th
12th
13th
14th
15th
16th
17th
18th
19th
20th
LEAGUE POSITION
INS AND OUTS
IN Martin Albrechtsen from FC Copenhagen for £2.7m; Robert Earnshaw from Cardiff for £3m; Zoltan Gera from Ferencvaros (Hungary) for £1.5m; Jonathan Greening from Middlesbrough for £1.5m; Darren Pulse from Birmingham for £750K; Junichi Inamoto from Gambo Osaka (Japan) for £200K; Riccardo Scimeca from Leicester for £100K; Nwankwo Kanu from Arsenal and Tomasz Kuszczak from Hertha Berlin for free
OUT Delroy Facey to Hull, Phil Gilchrist to Rotherham and Mark Kinsella to Walsall all for free; Lee Hughes deal terminated; Joost Volmer, Morten Skoubo and Tamika Mkandawire all released
War with Peace ends Megson's reign after letter of notice to quit forces the chairman's hand and fans' favourite is sacked
Kanu is a touch of class and the other new faces make Blackburn battle for a point
Earnshaw starts on the bench at Anfield and Liverpool have game won before £3m striker's debut
"Pathetic!" Megson rounds on his team after disinterest in training spreads to Palace game
Purse stumbles into a red card and Newcastle take full advantage with three late goals
Greening and Gera graft but there's no way through against Norwich
Humbled by Colchester in extra time as late goal takes the League One side through
Greening delivers for Clement to level but other chances go begging to let Villa off the hook
Gera has appetite for goals and the Hungary captain scores on his first start although Hoult flaps to let Spurs back in
Gera gifts Megson a first win with a cross for Kanu's opener and a stunning near-post header
AUGUST
SEPTEMBER
OCTOBER
Home Away Neutral

ATTENDANCES

HOME GROUND: THE HAWTHORNS CAPACITY: 28003 AVERAGE LEAGUE AT HOME: 26091

41	Man Utd	67827	19	Birmingham	28880	2	Aston Villa	26601	14	Middlesboro	24008
8	Newcastle	52308	30	Tottenham	27860	10	Norwich	26257	9	Bolton	23849
21	Man City	47177	42	Portsmouth	27751	31	Southampton	25865	1	Blackburn	23475
5	Liverpool	42947	16	Man Utd	27709	32	Birmingham	25749	11	Crystal Palace	22922
33	Chelsea	41713	20	Liverpool	27533	26	Man City	25348	27	Tottenham	22441
36	Aston Villa	39402	12	Chelsea	27399	23	Newcastle	25259	17	Portsmouth	20110
15	Arsenal	38109	40	Arsenal	27351	22	Bolton	25205	25	Fulham	16180
37	Tottenham	35885	3	Tottenham	27191	39	Blackburn	25154	24	Preston	13005
4	Everton	34510	34	Charlton	27104	28	Crystal Palace	25092	7	Colchester	4591
38	Middlesboro	32951	35	Everton	26805	29	Norwich	24292			
13	Southampton	31057	18	Charlton	26697	6	Fulham	24128			

Robson rewrites relegation rulebook

Final Position: **17th**

KEY: ● League ● Champions Lge ● UEFA Cup ● FA Cup ○ League Cup ● Other

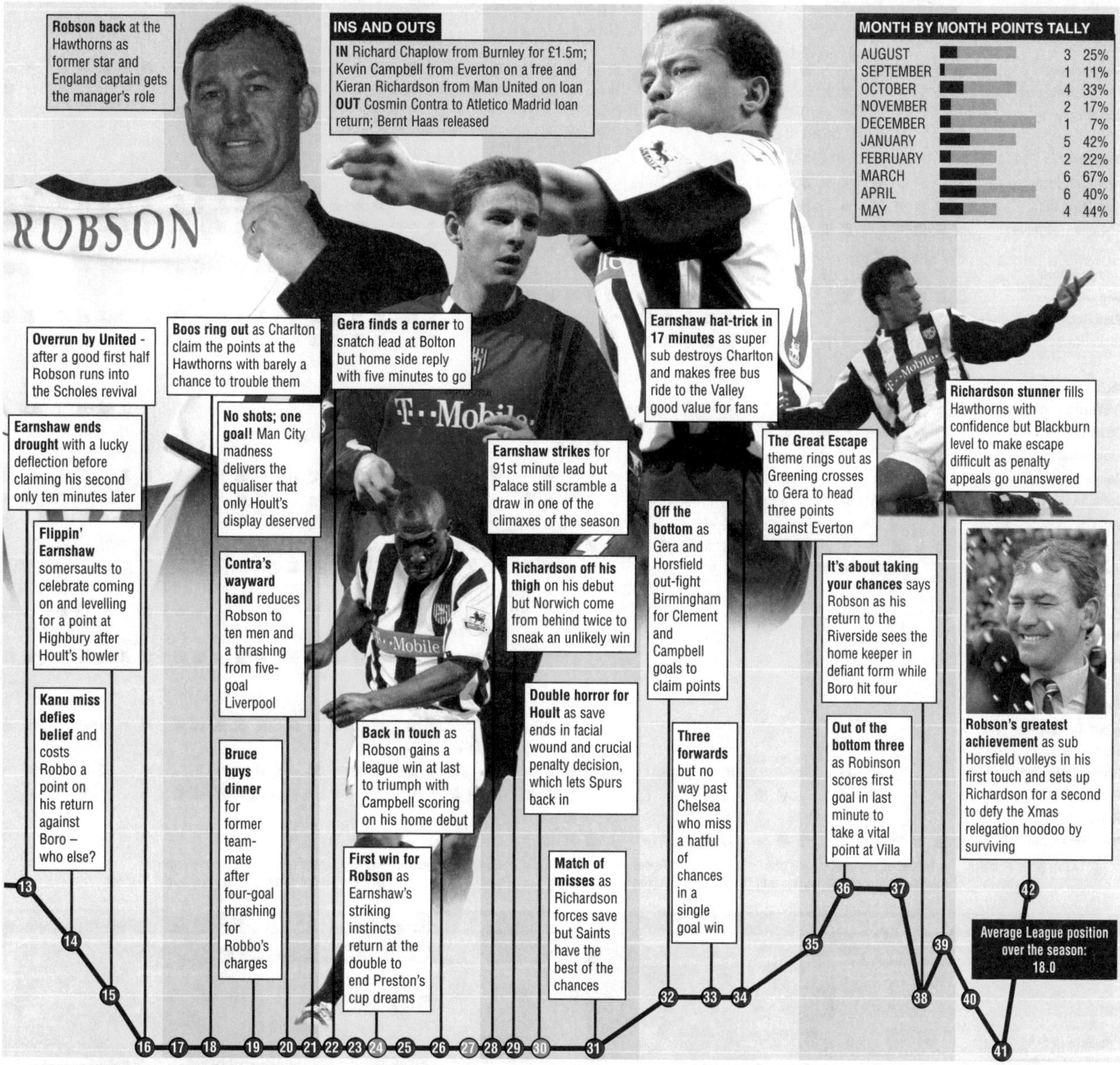

Robson back at the Hawthorns as former star and England captain gets the manager's role

INS AND OUTS

IN Richard Chaplow from Burnley for £1.5m; Kevin Campbell from Everton on a free and Kieran Richardson from Man United on loan
OUT Cosmin Contra to Atletico Madrid loan return; Bernt Haas released

MONTH BY MONTH POINTS TALLY

Month	Points	%
AUGUST	3	25%
SEPTEMBER	1	11%
OCTOBER	4	33%
NOVEMBER	2	17%
DECEMBER	1	7%
JANUARY	5	42%
FEBRUARY	2	22%
MARCH	6	67%
APRIL	6	40%
MAY	4	44%

Overrun by United - after a good first half Robson runs into the Scholes revival

Kanu miss defies belief and costs Robbo a point on his return against Boro – who else?

Flippin' Earnshaw somersaults to celebrate coming on and levelling for a point at Highbury after Hoult's howler

Earnshaw ends drought with a lucky deflection before claiming his second only ten minutes later

Boos ring out as Charlton claim the points at the Hawthorns with barely a chance to trouble them

Bruce buys dinner for former team-mate after four-goal thrashing for Robbo's charges

No shots; one goal! Man City madness delivers the equaliser that only Hoult's display deserved

Contra's wayward hand reduces Robson to ten men and a thrashing from five-goal Liverpool

Gera finds a corner to snatch lead at Bolton but home side reply with five minutes to go

First win for Robson as Earnshaw's striking instincts return at the double to end Preston's cup dreams

Back in touch as Robson gains a league win at last to triumph with Campbell scoring on his home debut

Earnshaw strikes for 91st minute lead but Palace still scramble a draw in one of the climaxes of the season

Richardson off his thigh on his debut but Norwich come from behind twice to sneak an unlikely win

Double horror for Hoult as save ends in facial wound and crucial penalty decision, which lets Spurs back in

Match of misses as Richardson forces save but Saints have the best of the chances

Off the bottom as Gera and Horsfield out-fight Birmingham for Clement and Campbell goals to claim points

Three forwards but no way past Chelsea who miss a hatful of chances in a single goal win

Earnshaw hat-trick in 17 minutes as super sub destroys Charlton and makes free bus ride to the Valley good value for fans

The Great Escape theme rings out as Greening crosses to Gera to head three points against Everton

Out of the bottom three as Robinson scores first goal in last minute to take a vital point at Villa

It's about taking your chances says Robson as his return to the Riverside sees the home keeper in defiant form while Boro hit four

Richardson stunner fills Hawthorns with confidence but Blackburn level to make escape difficult as penalty appeals go unanswered

Robson's greatest achievement as sub Horsfield volleys in his first touch and sets up Richardson for a second to defy the Xmas relegation hoodoo by surviving

Average League position over the season: 18.0

NOVEMBER DECEMBER JANUARY FEBRUARY MARCH APRIL MAY

GOAL ATTEMPTS

FOR – Goal attempts recorded in League games

	HOME	AWAY	TOTAL	AVE
shots on target	87	100	187	4.9
shots off target	88	75	163	4.3
TOTAL	175	175	350	9.2

Ratio of goals to shots – Average number of shots on target per League goal scored: **5.2**

Accuracy rating – Average percentage of total goal attempts which were on target: **53.4**

AGAINST – Goal attempts recorded in League games

	HOME	AWAY	TOTAL	AVE
shots on target	99	144	243	6.4
shots off target	114	100	214	5.6
TOTAL	213	244	457	12

Ratio of goals to shots – Average number of shots on target per League goal scored: **4**

Accuracy rating – Average percentage of total goal attempts which were on target: **53.2**

GOALS

Robert Earnshaw

League	11
FA Cup	3
League Cup	0
Europe	0
Other	0
TOTAL	14

League Average **157** mins between goals

	PLAYER	LGE	FAC	LC	Euro	TOT	AVE
1	Earnshaw	11	3	0	0	14	157
2	Gera	6	0	0	0	6	454
3	Horsfield	3	0	1	0	4	540
4	Clement	3	0	0	0	3	1034
5	Richardson	3	0	0	0	3	295
6	Campbell	3	0	0	0	3	435
7	Kanu	2	1	0	0	3	964
8	Wallwork	1	0	0	0	1	1726
9	Dobie	1	0	0	0	1	187
10	Robinson	1	0	0	0	1	2491
	Other	2	0	0	0	2	
	TOTAL	36	4	1	0	41	

SQUAD APPEARANCES

Match	1	2	3	4	5	6	7	8	9	10	11	12	13	14	15	16	17	18	19	20	21	22	23	24	25	26	27	28	29	30	31	32	33	34	35	36	37	38	39	40	41	42
Venue	A	H	H	A	A	H	A	A	H	H	A	H	A	H	A	H	A	H	A	H	A	A	H	A	A	H	H	H	A	A	H	H	A	A	H	A	A	A	H	H	A	H
Competition	L	L	L	L	L	L	W	L	L	L	L	L	L	L	L	L	L	L	L	L	L	L	L	F	L	L	F	L	L	F	L	L	L	L	L	L	L	L	L	L	L	L
Result	D	D	D	L	L	D	L	L	W	D	L	L	D	L	D	L	L	L	L	L	D	D	D	W	L	W	D	D	L	L	D	W	L	W	W	D	D	L	D	L	D	W

Goalkeepers
- Russell Hoult
- Tomasz Kuszczak
- Joe Murphy

Defenders
- Martin Albrechtsen
- Neil Clement
- Thomas Gaardsoe
- Bernt Haas
- Darren Moore
- Darren Purse
- Paul Robinson
- Riccardo Scimeca

Midfielders
- Richard Chaplow
- Cosmin Contra
- Lloyd Dyer
- Zoltan Gera
- Jonathan Greening
- Junichi Inamoto
- Andy Johnson
- Jason Koumas
- James O'Connor
- Keiron Richardson
- Artim Sakiri
- Ronnie Wallwork

Forwards
- Kevin Campbell
- Scott Dobie
- Robert Earnshaw
- Geoff Horsfield
- Robert Hulse
- Nwankwo Kanu

KEY: On all match | On bench | Subbed or sent off (Counting game) | Subbed or sent off (playing less than 70 mins) | Subbed on from bench (Counting Game) | Subbed on (playing less than 70 mins) | Subbed on and then subbed or sent off (Counting Game) | Subbed on and then subbed or sent off (playing less than 70 mins) | Not in 16

KEY PLAYERS - GOALSCORERS

Robert Earnshaw

Goals in the League	11
Goals in all competitions	14
Assists League goals scored by a team mate where the player delivered the final pass	1
Contribution to Attacking Power Average number of minutes between League team goals while on pitch	86
Player Strike Rate Average number of minutes between League goals scored by player	157
Club Strike Rate Average minutes between League goals scored by club	95

	PLAYER	GOALS LGE	GOALS ALL	ASSISTS	POWER	S RATE
1	Robert Earnshaw	11	14	1	86	157 mins
2	Kevin Campbell	3	3	1	72	435 mins
3	Zoltan Gera	6	6	3	85	454 mins
4	Geoff Horsfield	3	4	4	77	540 mins
5	Nwankwo Kanu	2	3	0	113	964 mins

KEY PLAYERS - MIDFIELDERS

Ronnie Wallwork

Goals in the League	1
Goals in all competitions	1
Assists League goals scored by a team mate where the player delivered the final pass	0
Defensive Rating Average number of mins between League goals conceded while on the pitch	82
Contribution to Attacking Power Average number of minutes between League team goals while on pitch	82
Scoring Difference Defensive Rating minus Contribution to Attacking Power	0

	PLAYER	GOALS LGE	GOALS ALL	ASSISTS	DEF RATE	POWER	SC DIFF
1	Ronnie Wallwork	1	1	0	82	82	0 mins
2	Zoltan Gera	6	6	3	57	85	-28 mins
3	Jonathan Greening	0	0	8	56	95	-39 mins
4	Andy Johnson	0	0	1	53	116	-63 mins

PLAYER APPEARANCES

	AGE (on 01/07/05)	IN NAMED 16	APPEARANCES	COUNTING GAMES	MINUTES ON PITCH	APPEARANCES	MINUTES ON PITCH	THIS SEASON	HOME COUNTRY
Goalkeepers									
Russell Hoult	32	36	36	35	3171	39	3392	-	England
Tomasz Kuszczak	23	36	3	3	249	5	418	-	Poland
Joe Murphy	24	2	0	0	0	0	0	-	Rep of Ireland
Defenders									
Martin Albrechtsen	25	28	24	18	1774	28	2164	-	Denmark
Neil Clement	26	35	35	34	3101	38	3371	-	England
Thomas Gaardsoe	25	34	29	22	2140	31	2350	1	Denmark (19)
Bernt Haas	27	12	10	6	754	10	754	5	Switzerland (45)
Darren Moore	31	25	16	10	991	17	1111	-	England
Darren Purse	28	23	22	21	1953	24	2133	-	England
Paul Robinson	26	31	30	26	2491	33	2761	9	England (6)
Riccardo Scimeca	30	36	33	26	2476	36	2754	-	England
Midfielders									
Richard Chaplow	20	7	4	2	247	4	247	-	England
Cosmin Contra	29	10	5	2	294	6	367	-	Romania
Lloyd Dyer	22	7	4	0	83	5	203	-	England
Zoltan Gera	26	38	38	28	2721	42	3054	-	Hungary
Jonathan Greening	26	34	34	30	2849	37	3068	-	England
Junichi Inamoto	25	5	3	0	120	3	120	-	Japan
Andy Johnson	31	22	22	19	1848	23	1938	2	Wales (74)
Jason Koumas	25	16	10	4	531	13	759	7	Wales (74)
James O'Connor	25	4	0	0	0	2	69	-	Rep of Ireland
Keiron Richardson	20	12	12	9	886	12	886	-	England
Artim Sakiri	31	3	3	2	178	3	178	-	Macedonia
Ronnie Wallwork	27	20	20	19	1726	23	1996	-	England
Forwards									
Kevin Campbell	35	16	16	13	1304	18	1407	-	England
Scott Dobie	26	6	5	1	187	6	284	-	England
Robert Earnshaw	24	34	31	14	1723	34	1919	7	Wales (74)
Geoff Horsfield	31	34	29	14	1620	32	1770	-	England
Robert Hulse	25	8	5	0	90	7	185	-	England
Nwankwo Kanu	28	34	28	19	1927	30	2066	-	Nigeria

KEY: LEAGUE ALL COMPS CAPS (MAY FIFA RANKING)

TEAM OF THE SEASON

HOULT
CG 35 DR 53
ALBRECHTSEN
CG 18 DR 84
CLEMENT
CG 34 DR 55
GAARDSOE
CG 22 DR 52
ROBINSON
CG 26 DR 64
GERA
CG 28 SD -28
WALLWORK
CG 19 SD 0
JOHNSON
CG 19 SD -63
GREENING
CG 30 SD -39
CAMPBELL
CG 13 AP 72
EARNSHAW
CG 14 SR 157

KEY: DR = Defensive Rating, SD = Scoring Difference AP = Attacking Power SR = Strike Rate, CG=Counting games – League games playing at least 70 minutes

TOP POINT EARNERS

Kevin Campbell

Counting Games League games when player was on pitch for at least 70 minutes	13
Average points Average League points taken in Counting games	1.46
Club Average points Average points taken in League games	0.89

	PLAYER	GAMES	PTS
1	Kevin Campbell	13	1.46
2	Geoff Horsfield	14	1.43
3	Martin Albrechtsen	18	1.39
4	Ronnie Wallwork	19	1.26
5	Paul Robinson	26	1.08
6	Zoltan Gera	28	1.07
7	Thomas Gaardsoe	22	1.00
8	Neil Clement	34	0.88
9	Jonathan Greening	30	0.87
10	Russell Hoult	35	0.83

KEY PLAYERS - DEFENDERS

Martin Albrechtsen

Goals Conceded in the League Number of League goals conceded while the player was on the pitch	21
Goals Conceded in all competitions Total number of goals conceded while player was on the pitch	27
League minutes played Number of minutes played in league matches	1774
Clean Sheets In games when player was on pitch for at least 70 minutes	7
Defensive Rating Average number of mins between League goals conceded while on the pitch	84
Club Defensive Rating Average number of mins between League goals conceded by the club this season	56

	PLAYER	CON LGE	CON ALL	MINS	C SHEETS	DEF RATE
1	Martin Albrechtsen	21	27	1774	7	84 mins
2	Paul Robinson	39	43	2491	6	64 mins
3	Neil Clement	56	60	3101	6	55 mins
4	Thomas Gaardsoe	41	46	2140	5	52 mins
5	Darren Purse	38	39	1953	2	51 mins

KEY GOALKEEPER

Russell Hoult

Goals Conceded in the League Number of League goals conceded while the player was on the pitch	60
Goals Conceded in all competitions Total number of goals conceded while the player was on the pitch	61
League minutes played Number of minutes played in league matches	3171
Clean Sheets In games when player was on pitch for at least 70 minutes	6
Goals to Shots Ratio The average number of shots on target per each League goal conceded	4
Defensive Rating Ave mins between League goals conceded while on the pitch	53

BOOKINGS

Darren Moore

League Yellow	3
League Red	0
All competitions Yellow	3
All competitions Red	0
League Average 330 mins between cards	

	PLAYER	LEAGUE Y	LEAGUE R	TOTAL Y	TOTAL R	AVE
1	Moore	3	0	3	0	330
2	Purse	4	1	4	1	390
3	Robinson	6	0	6	0	415
4	Richardson	2	0	2	0	443
5	Koumas	1	0	2	0	531
6	Greening	4	1	5	1	569
7	Johnson	3	0	3	0	616
8	Gera	4	0	4	0	680
9	Gaardsoe	2	1	3	1	713
10	Haas	1	0	1	0	754
11	Clement	3	1	3	1	775
12	Horsfield	2	0	2	0	810
13	Scimeca	3	0	4	0	825
14	Kanu	2	0	2	0	963
15	Wallwork	1	0	2	0	1726
	Other	2	0	4	0	
	TOTAL	43	4	50	4	

CRYSTAL PALACE

Andrew Johnson left his mark with an astonishing 11 penalties scored during the season, out of 13 awarded. His 21 league goals came at a third-highest Premiership Strike Rate of a goal every 158 minutes on average and won him England caps. He hit 51% of Palace's league goals. No other club was so reliant on one player.

He was on his own up front with very few goals coming from midfield, where young **Ben Watson** topped the Midfielders table without scoring. **Wayne Routledge** only added one goal but showed his potential with nine Assists.

Palace's opponents hit a surprising 65% of shots On Target. It meant **Gabor Kiraly** had plenty to deal with and his Goals to Shots Ratio of five saved for every goal conceded is fifth highest in the Premier list.

Palace gates rose nearly 7,000 to watch Dowie's battlers fight against relegation.

NICKNAME: THE EAGLES

KEY: Won Drawn Lost

1	prem	**Norwich**	A	D	1-1	Johnson 73
2	prem	**Everton**	H	L	1-3	Hudson 9
3	prem	**Chelsea**	H	L	0-2	
4	prem	**Middlesbrough**	A	L	1-2	Johnson 52 pen
5	prem	**Portsmouth**	A	L	1-3	Granville 43
6	prem	**Man City**	H	L	1-2	Johnson 77 pen
7	ccr2	**Hartlepool**	H	W	2-1	Freedman 80; Soares 110
8	prem	**Aston Villa**	A	D	1-1	Johnson 6
9	prem	**Fulham**	H	W	2-0	Johnson 53; Riihilahti 69
10	prem	**Bolton**	A	L	0-1	
11	prem	**West Brom**	H	W	3-0	Hall 5; Johnson 12 pen,50
12	ccr3	**Charlton**	A	W	2-1	Freedman 41; Torghelle 54
13	prem	**Birmingham**	A	W	1-0	Johnson 41
14	prem	**Arsenal**	H	D	1-1	Riihilahti 65
15	ccr4	**Man Utd**	A	L	0-2	
16	prem	**Liverpool**	A	L	2-3	Kolkka 44; Hughes 52
17	prem	**Newcastle**	H	L	0-2	
18	prem	**Southampton**	A	D	2-2	Johnson 48; Routledge 54
19	prem	**Charlton**	H	L	0-1	
20	prem	**Blackburn**	H	D	0-0	
21	prem	**Man Utd**	A	L	2-5	Granville 27; Kolkka 46
22	prem	**Portsmouth**	H	L	0-1	
23	prem	**Tottenham**	A	D	1-1	Johnson 79
24	prem	**Fulham**	A	L	1-3	Johnson 35
25	prem	**Aston Villa**	H	W	2-0	Johnson 33,66 pen
26	facr3	**Sunderland**	A	L	1-2	Collins og 41
27	prem	**Man City**	A	L	1-3	Powell, D 32
28	prem	**Tottenham**	H	W	3-0	Leigertwood 66; Granville 70; Johnson 77 pen
29	prem	**West Brom**	A	D	2-2	Johnson 47; Riihilahti 90
30	prem	**Bolton**	H	L	0-1	
31	prem	**Arsenal**	A	L	1-5	Johnson 63 pen
32	prem	**Birmingham**	H	W	2-0	Johnson 41 pen,68 pen
33	prem	**Man Utd**	H	D	0-0	
34	prem	**Chelsea**	A	L	1-4	Riihilahti 42
35	prem	**Middlesbrough**	H	L	0-1	
36	prem	**Everton**	A	L	0-4	
37	prem	**Norwich**	H	D	3-3	Kolkka 5; Hughes 73; Johnson 83 pen
38	prem	**Blackburn**	A	L	0-1	
39	prem	**Liverpool**	H	W	1-0	Johnson 34
40	prem	**Newcastle**	A	D	0-0	
41	prem	**Southampton**	H	D	2-2	Hall 34; Ventola 72
42	prem	**Charlton**	A	D	2-2	Freedman 58; Johnson 71 pen

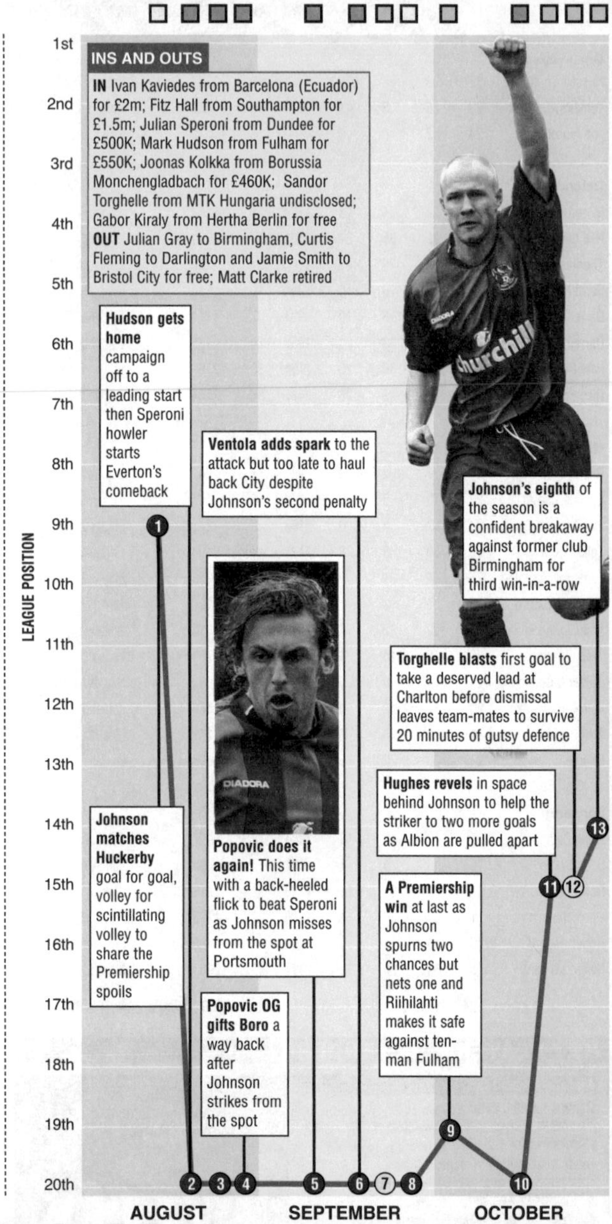
1st
2nd
3rd
4th
5th
6th
7th
8th
9th
10th
11th
12th
13th
14th
15th
16th
17th
18th
19th
20th
LEAGUE POSITION
INS AND OUTS
IN Ivan Kaviedes from Barcelona (Ecuador) for £2m; Fitz Hall from Southampton for £1.5m; Julian Speroni from Dundee for £500K; Mark Hudson from Fulham for £550K; Joonas Kolkka from Borussia Monchengladbach for £460K; Sandor Torghelle from MTK Hungaria undisclosed; Gabor Kiraly from Hertha Berlin for free
OUT Julian Gray to Birmingham, Curtis Fleming to Darlington and Jamie Smith to Bristol City for free; Matt Clarke retired
Hudson gets home campaign off to a leading start then Speroni howler starts Everton's comeback
Ventola adds spark to the attack but too late to haul back City despite Johnson's second penalty
Johnson's eighth of the season is a confident breakaway against former club Birmingham for third win-in-a-row
Torghelle blasts first goal to take a deserved lead at Charlton before dismissal leaves team-mates to survive 20 minutes of gutsy defence
Hughes revels in space behind Johnson to help the striker to two more goals as Albion are pulled apart
Johnson matches Huckerby goal for goal, volley for scintillating volley to share the Premiership spoils
Popovic does it again! This time with a back-heeled flick to beat Speroni as Johnson misses from the spot at Portsmouth
A Premiership win at last as Johnson spurns two chances but nets one and Riihilahti makes it safe against ten-man Fulham
Popovic OG gifts Boro a way back after Johnson strikes from the spot
1
2
3
4
5
6
7
8
9
10
11
12
13
AUGUST
SEPTEMBER
OCTOBER

Home Away Neutral

ATTENDANCES

HOME GROUND: SELHURST PARK **CAPACITY:** 26309 **AVERAGE LEAGUE AT HOME:** 24105

21	Man Utd	67814	4	Middlesboro	31560	6	Man City	25002	20	Blackburn	22010
40	Newcastle	52123	13	Birmingham	28916	3	Chelsea	24953	9	Fulham	21825
15	Man Utd	48891	42	Charlton	26870	35	Middlesboro	24274	19	Charlton	20705
27	Man City	44010	14	Arsenal	26193	25	Aston Villa	24140	5	Portsmouth	20019
16	Liverpool	42862	41	Southampton	26066	28	Tottenham	23723	12	Charlton	19030
34	Chelsea	41667	39	Liverpool	26043	1	Norwich	23717	24	Fulham	18680
31	Arsenal	38056	33	Man Utd	26021	2	Everton	23666	38	Blackburn	18006
36	Everton	36519	37	Norwich	25754	32	Birmingham	23376	26	Sunderland	17536
23	Tottenham	36100	10	Bolton	25501	30	Bolton	23163	7	Hartlepool	4233
8	Aston Villa	34843	22	Portsmouth	25238	17	Newcastle	22937			
18	Southampton	31833	29	West Brom	25092	11	West Brom	22922			

Johnson's goals so nearly save Dowie

Final Position: 18th

KEY: League, Champions Lge, UEFA Cup, FA Cup, League Cup, Other

Average League position over the season: 17.4

INS AND OUTS

OUT Ivan Kaviedes released; Cedric Berthelin to Mons undisclosed

MONTH BY MONTH POINTS TALLY

AUGUST	1	8%
SEPTEMBER	1	11%
OCTOBER	9	75%
NOVEMBER	2	17%
DECEMBER	2	13%
JANUARY	6	50%
FEBRUARY	4	33%
MARCH	1	17%
APRIL	5	28%
MAY	2	33%

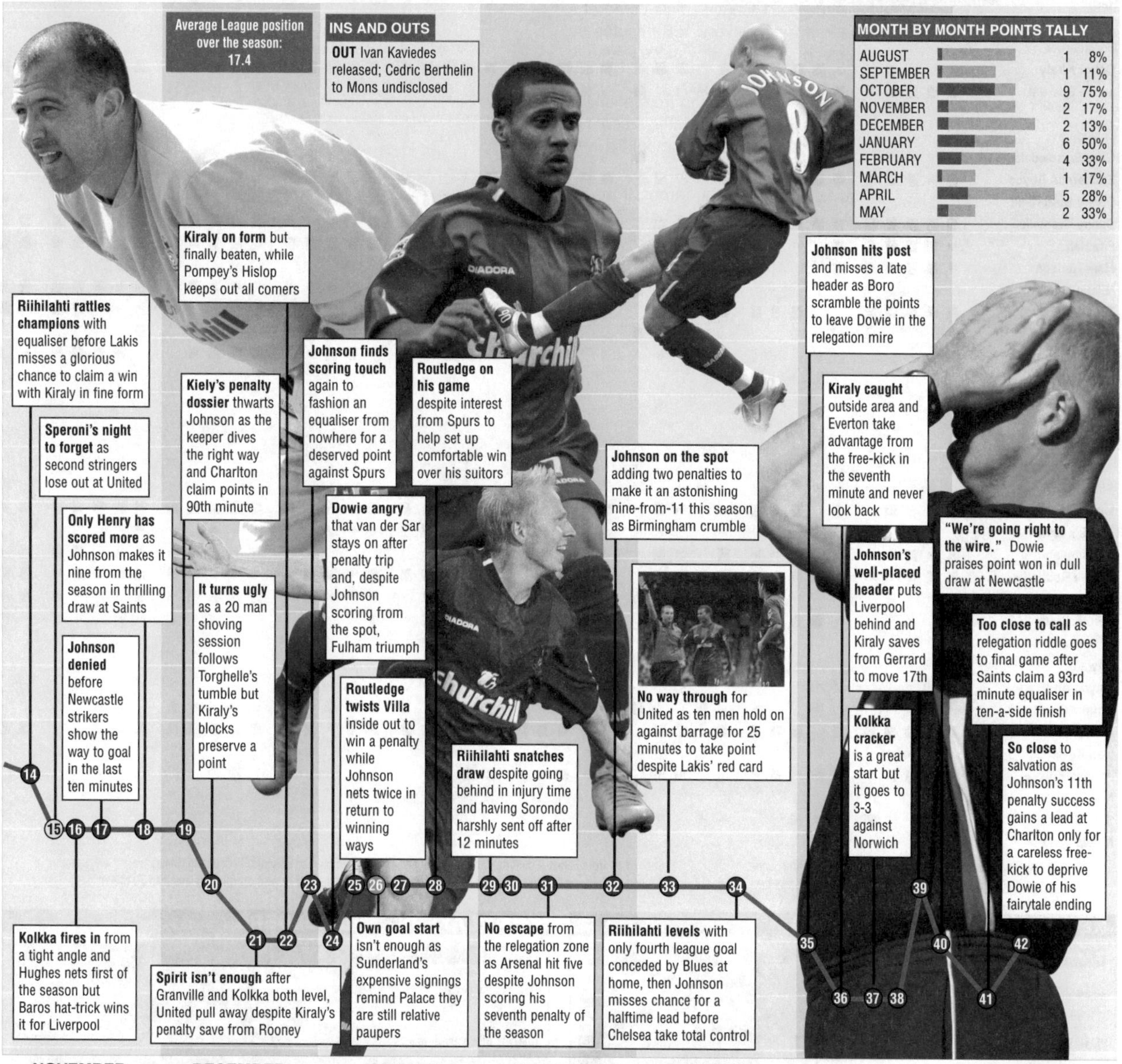

Riihilahti rattles champions with equaliser before Lakis misses a glorious chance to claim a win with Kiraly in fine form
Speroni's night to forget as second stringers lose out at United
Only Henry has scored more as Johnson makes it nine from the season in thrilling draw at Saints
Johnson denied before Newcastle strikers show the way to goal in the last ten minutes
Kolkka fires in from a tight angle and Hughes nets first of the season but Baros hat-trick wins it for Liverpool
Kiraly on form but finally beaten, while Pompey's Hislop keeps out all comers
Kiely's penalty dossier thwarts Johnson as the keeper dives the right way and Charlton claim points in 90th minute
It turns ugly as a 20 man shoving session follows Torghelle's tumble but Kiraly's blocks preserve a point
Spirit isn't enough after Granville and Kolkka both level, United pull away despite Kiraly's penalty save from Rooney
Johnson finds scoring touch again to fashion an equaliser from nowhere for a deserved point against Spurs
Routledge on his game despite interest from Spurs to help set up comfortable win over his suitors
Dowie angry that van der Sar stays on after penalty trip and, despite Johnson scoring from the spot, Fulham triumph
Routledge twists Villa inside out to win a penalty while Johnson nets twice in return to winning ways
Own goal start isn't enough as Sunderland's expensive signings remind Palace they are still relative paupers
Riihilahti snatches draw despite going behind in injury time and having Sorondo harshly sent off after 12 minutes
No escape from the relegation zone as Arsenal hit five despite Johnson scoring his seventh penalty of the season
Johnson on the spot adding two penalties to make it an astonishing nine-from-11 this season as Birmingham crumble
No way through for United as ten men hold on against barrage for 25 minutes to take point despite Lakis' red card
Riihilahti levels with only fourth league goal conceded by Blues at home, then Johnson misses chance for a halftime lead before Chelsea take total control
Johnson hits post and misses a late header as Boro scramble the points to leave Dowie in the relegation mire
Kiraly caught outside area and Everton take advantage from the free-kick in the seventh minute and never look back
Johnson's well-placed header puts Liverpool behind and Kiraly saves from Gerrard to move 17th
Kolkka cracker is a great start but it goes to 3-3 against Norwich
"We're going right to the wire." Dowie praises point won in dull draw at Newcastle
Too close to call as relegation riddle goes to final game after Saints claim a 93rd minute equaliser in ten-a-side finish
So close to salvation as Johnson's 11th penalty success gains a lead at Charlton only for a careless free-kick to deprive Dowie of his fairytale ending
14 15 16 17 18 19 20 21 22 23 24 25 26 27 28 29 30 31 32 33 34 35 36 37 38 39 40 41 42
NOVEMBER
DECEMBER
JANUARY
FEBRUARY
MARCH
APRIL
MAY

GOAL ATTEMPTS

FOR – Goal attempts recorded in League games

	HOME	AWAY	TOTAL	AVE
shots on target	106	72	178	4.7
shots off target	95	64	159	4.2
TOTAL	201	136	337	8.9

Ratio of goals to shots – Average number of shots on target per League goal scored: **4.3**

Accuracy rating – Average percentage of total goal attempts which were on target: **52.8**

AGAINST – Goal attempts recorded in League games

	HOME	AWAY	TOTAL	AVE
shots on target	136	170	306	8.1
shots off target	94	72	166	4.4
TOTAL	230	242	472	12.4

Ratio of goals to shots – Average number of shots on target per League goal scored: **4.9**

Accuracy rating – Average percentage of total goal attempts which were on target: **64.8**

GOALS

Andrew Johnson

League	21
FA Cup	1
League Cup	0
Europe	0
Other	0
TOTAL	22

League Average **158** mins between goals

	PLAYER	LGE	FAC	LC	Euro	TOT	AVE
1	Johnson	21	1	0	0	22	158
2	Riihilahti	4	0	0	0	4	557
3	Kolkka	3	0	0	0	3	566
4	Freedman	1	0	2	0	3	894
5	Granville	3	0	0	0	3	1038
6	Hughes	2	0	0	0	2	1507
7	Hall	2	0	0	0	2	1585
8	Powell	1	0	0	0	1	438
9	Routledge	1	0	0	0	1	3142
10	Leigertwood	1	0	0	0	1	1566
11	Hudson	1	0	0	0	1	630
12	Ventola	1	0	0	0	1	79
13	Soares	0	0	1	0	1	
14	Torghelle	0	0	1	0	1	
	Other	0	0	0	0	0	
	TOTAL	41	1	4	0	46	

SQUAD APPEARANCES

Match	1	2	3	4	5	6	7	8	9	10	11	12	13	14	15	16	17	18	19	20	21	22	23	24	25	26	27	28	29	30	31	32	33	34	35	36	37	38	39	40	41	42
Venue	A	H	H	A	A	H	H	A	H	A	H	A	A	H	A	A	H	A	H	H	A	H	A	A	H	A	A	H	A	H	A	H	H	A	H	A	H	A	H	A	H	A
Competition	L	L	L	L	L	L	W	L	L	L	L	W	L	L	W	L	L	L	L	L	L	L	L	L	L	F	L	L	L	L	L	L	L	L	L	L	L	L	L	L	L	L
Result	D	L	L	L	L	L	W	D	W	L	W	W	W	D	L	L	L	D	L	D	L	L	D	L	W	L	L	W	D	L	L	W	D	L	L	L	D	L	W	D	D	D

Goalkeepers
Gabor Kiraly
Julian Speroni

Defenders
Gary Borrowdale
Emmerson Boyce
Danny Butterfield
Danny Granville
Fitz Hall
Mark Hudson
Mikele Leigertwood
Tony Popovic
Darren Powell
Gonzalo Sorondo
Sam Togwell

Midfielders
Thomas Black
Anthony Danze
Shaun Derry
Michael Hughes
Vassilis Lakis
Aki Riihilahti
Wayne Routledge
Tom Soares
Ben Watson

Forwards
Wayne Andrews
Dougie Freedman
Andrew Johnson
Ivan Kaviedes
Joonas Kolkka
Neil Shipperley
Sandor Torghelle
Nicola Ventola

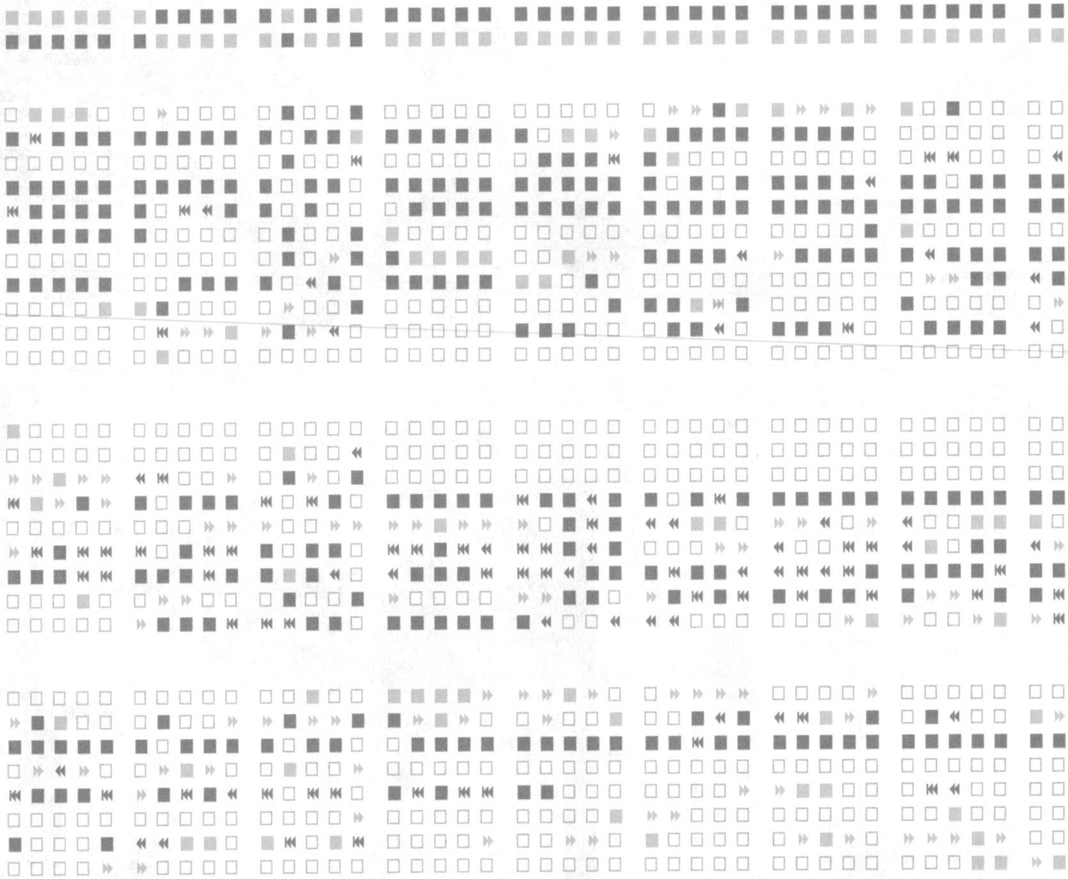

KEY: On all match; On bench; Subbed or sent off (Counting game); Subbed or sent off (playing less than 70 mins); Subbed on from bench (Counting Game); Subbed on (playing less than 70 mins); Subbed on and then subbed or sent off (Counting Game); Subbed on and then subbed or sent off (playing less than 70 mins); Not in 16

KEY PLAYERS - GOALSCORERS

Andrew Johnson

Goals in the League	21
Goals in all competitions	22
Assists League goals scored by a team mate where the player delivered the final pass	2
Contribution to Attacking Power Average number of minutes between League team goals while on pitch	85
Player Strike Rate Average number of minutes between League goals scored by player	158
Club Strike Rate Average minutes between League goals scored by club	83

churchill

	PLAYER	GOALS LGE	GOALS ALL	ASSISTS	POWER	S RATE
1	Andrew Johnson	21	22	2	85	158 mins
2	Aki Riihilahti	4	4	4	89	557 mins
3	Joonas Kolkka	3	3	2	77	566 mins
4	Danny Granville	3	3	0	81	1038 mins
5	Michael Hughes	2	2	3	81	1507 mins

KEY PLAYERS - MIDFIELDERS

Ben Watson

Goals in the League	0
Goals in all competitions	0
Assists League goals scored by a team mate where the player delivered the final pass	0
Defensive Rating Average number of mins between League goals conceded while on the pitch	61
Contribution to Attacking Power Average number of minutes between League team goals while on pitch	70
Scoring Difference Defensive Rating minus Contribution to Attacking Power	-9

churchill

	PLAYER	GOALS LGE	GOALS ALL	ASSISTS	DEF RATE	POWER	SC DIFF
1	Ben Watson	0	0	0	61	70	-9 mins
2	Michael Hughes	2	2	3	62	81	-19 mins
3	Wayne Routledge	1	1	9	57	81	-24 mins
4	Aki Riihilahti	4	4	4	62	89	-27 mins
5	Tom Soares	0	1	3	50	82	-32 mins

PLAYER APPEARANCES

	AGE (on 01/07/05)	IN NAMED 16	APPEARANCES	COUNTING GAMES	MINUTES ON PITCH	APPEARANCES	MINUTES ON PITCH	THIS SEASON	HOME COUNTRY
Goalkeepers									
Gabor Kiraly	29	38	32	32	2880	34	3090	-	Hungary
Julian Speroni	26	38	6	6	540	8	720	-	Argentina
Defenders									
Gary Borrowdale	19	14	7	2	278	10	491	-	England
Emmerson Boyce	25	29	27	26	2342	28	2462	-	England
Danny Butterfield	25	8	7	6	545	10	801	-	England
Danny Granville	30	35	35	34	3113	37	3323	-	England
Fitz Hall	24	36	36	35	3169	37	3259	-	England
Mark Hudson	23	9	7	7	630	9	810	-	England
Mikele Leigertwood	22	25	20	14	1566	23	1836	-	England
Tony Popovic	32	25	23	19	1842	23	1842	-	Australia
Darren Powell	29	9	6	5	438	10	755	-	England
Gonzalo Sorondo	25	21	20	13	1356	22	1533	-	Uruguay
Sam Togwell	20	0	0	0	0	0	0	-	England
Midfielders									
Thomas Black	28	1	0	0	0	0	0	-	England
Anthony Danze	21	0	0	0	0	1	45	-	Australia
Shaun Derry	27	8	7	0	119	10	374	-	England
Michael Hughes	33	37	36	31	3014	37	3104	2	N Ireland (114)
Vassilis Lakis	28	24	18	3	684	20	790	-	Greece
Aki Riihilahti	28	33	32	22	2227	32	2227	-	Finland
Wayne Routledge	20	38	38	32	3142	40	3352	-	England
Tom Soares	18	23	22	16	1553	26	1807	-	England
Ben Watson	19	23	21	12	1396	24	1654	-	England
Forwards									
Wayne Andrews	27	15	9	0	131	9	131	-	England
Dougie Freedman	30	25	20	7	894	23	1194	-	Scotland
Andrew Johnson	24	37	37	37	3327	38	3417	1	England (6)
Ivan Kaviedes	27	5	4	0	104	6	186	-	Ecuador
Joonas Kolkka	30	25	23	18	1698	24	1818	-	Finland
Neil Shipperley	30	3	1	0	14	3	53	-	England
Sandor Torghelle	23	18	12	2	404	15	602	-	Hungary
Nicola Ventola	27	6	3	0	79	3	79	-	Italy

KEY: LEAGUE ALL COMPS CAPS (MAY FIFA RANKING)

TEAM OF THE SEASON

KIRALY
CG 32 DR 59
HALL
CG 35 DR 55
SORONDO
CG 13 DR 62
POPOVIC
CG 19 DR 66
GRANVILLE
CG 34 DR 56
ROUTLEDGE
CG 32 SD -24
RIIHIAHTI
CG 22 SD -27
HUGHES
CG 31 SD -19
WATSON
CG 12 SD -9
KOLKKA
CG 18 AP 77
JOHNSON
CG 37 SR 158

KEY: DR = Defensive Rating, SD = Scoring Difference AP = Attacking Power SR = Strike Rate, CG=Counting games – League games playing at least 70 minutes

TOP POINT EARNERS

Ben Watson

Counting Games League games when player was on pitch for at least 70 minutes	12
Average points Average League points taken in Counting games	1.17
Club Average points Average points taken in League games	0.87

	PLAYER	GAMES	PTS
1	Ben Watson	12	1.17
2	Mikele Leigertwood	14	1.00
3	Gabor Kiraly	32	1.00
4	Gonzalo Sorondo	13	1.00
5	Michael Hughes	31	0.97
6	Wayne Routledge	32	0.94
7	Danny Granville	34	0.94
8	Tom Soares	16	0.94
9	Aki Riihilahti	22	0.91
10	Andrew Johnson	37	0.89

KEY PLAYERS - DEFENDERS

Tony Popovic

Goals Conceded in the League Number of League goals conceded while the player was on the pitch	28
Goals Conceded in all competitions Total number of goals conceded while the player was on the pitch	28
League minutes played Number of minutes played in league matches	1842
Clean Sheets In games when player was on pitch for at least 70 minutes	5
Defensive Rating Average number of mins between League goals conceded while on the pitch	66
Club Defensive Rating Average number of mins between League goals conceded by the club this season	55

churchill

	PLAYER	CON LGE	CON ALL	MINS	C SHEETS	DEF RATE
1	Tony Popovic	28	28	1842	5	66 mins
2	Gonzalo Sorondo	22	24	1356	5	62 mins
3	Danny Granville	56	59	3113	10	56 mins
4	Fitz Hall	58	60	3169	9	55 mins
5	Emmerson Boyce	43	44	2342	7	54 mins

KEY GOALKEEPER

Gabor Kiraly

Goals Conceded in the League Number of League goals conceded while the player was on the pitch	49
Goals Conceded in all competitions Total number of goals conceded while the player was on the pitch	52
League minutes played Number of minutes played in league matches	2880
Clean Sheets In games when player was on pitch for at least 70 minutes	10
Goals to Shots Ratio The average number of shots on target per each League goal conceded	5
Defensive Rating Ave mins between League goals conceded while on the pitch	59

BOOKINGS

Vassilis Lakis

League Yellow	2
League Red	1
All competitions Yellow	2
All competitions Red	1
League Average	228 mins between cards

	PLAYER	LEAGUE 2Y	LEAGUE 1R	TOTAL 2Y	TOTAL 1R	AVE
1	Lakis	2	1	2	1	228
2	Sorondo	3	2	5	2	271
3	Butterfield	2	0	2	0	272
4	Hughes	9	0	10	0	334
5	Soares	4	0	4	0	388
6	Granville	7	0	7	0	444
7	Popovic	4	0	4	0	460
8	Watson	3	0	3	0	465
9	Leigertwood	3	0	4	0	522
10	Hudson	1	0	2	0	630
11	Riihilahti	3	0	3	0	742
12	Johnson	4	0	5	0	831
13	Kiraly	3	0	3	0	960
14	Hall	3	0	3	0	1056
15	Boyce	2	0	2	0	1171
	Other	2	0	3	0	
	TOTAL	55	3	62	3	

NORWICH CITY

Dean Ashton looks a Premiership striker and led the fight to stave off relegation with seven league goals in 16 games. His Strike Rate of a goal every 203 minutes would have been in the Division's top 10 had he played enough games to qualify him. Ashton also had the best Attacking Power figure at the club, meaning Norwich were most likely to score when he was playing.

Darren Huckerby spent much of the season bolstering midfield and finished with six league goals, scored at a Rate of 531, but he did add seven Assists.

Thomas Helveg was the pick of some poor Scoring Differences in midfield and led the Top Point Earners' chart, averaging 1.31 points per game. He also topped the Bookings table with his six yellows coming at an average of a card every 223 minutes, although Norwich had the lowest cards in the Premiership.

NICKNAME: THE CANARIES

KEY: Won Drawn Lost

1	prem	**Crystal Palace**	H	D	1-1	Huckerby 16
2	prem	**Man Utd**	A	L	1-2	McVeigh 75
3	prem	**Newcastle**	A	D	2-2	Bentley 52; Doherty 74
4	prem	**Arsenal**	H	L	1-4	Huckerby 50 pen
5	prem	**Tottenham**	A	D	0-0	
6	prem	**Aston Villa**	H	D	0-0	
7	ccr2	**Bristol Rovers**	H	W	1-0	Safri 45
8	prem	**Liverpool**	A	L	0-3	
9	prem	**Portsmouth**	H	D	2-2	Huckerby 63; Charlton 67
10	prem	**West Brom**	A	D	0-0	
11	prem	**Everton**	H	L	2-3	McKenzie 48; Francis 57
12	ccr3	**Newcastle**	A	L	1-2	Huckerby 56 pen
13	prem	**Man City**	A	D	1-1	Francis 46
14	prem	**Blackburn**	H	D	1-1	Svensson 56
15	prem	**Charlton**	A	L	0-4	
16	prem	**Southampton**	H	W	2-1	Francis 28,52
17	prem	**Birmingham**	A	D	1-1	Huckerby 64
18	prem	**Fulham**	H	L	0-1	
19	prem	**Bolton**	H	W	3-2	Svensson 19,84; Huckerby 69 pen
20	prem	**Chelsea**	A	L	0-4	
21	prem	**Tottenham**	H	L	0-2	
22	prem	**Middlesbrough**	A	L	0-2	
23	prem	**Portsmouth**	A	D	1-1	Francis 9
24	prem	**Liverpool**	H	L	1-2	Jarvis 88
25	facr3	**West Ham**	A	L	0-1	
26	prem	**Aston Villa**	A	L	0-3	
27	prem	**Middlesbrough**	H	D	4-4	Francis 18; Ashton 80; McKenzie 90; Drury 90
28	prem	**Everton**	A	L	0-1	
29	prem	**West Brom**	H	W	3-2	Fleming 45; Doherty 62; Francis 85
30	prem	**Blackburn**	A	L	0-3	
31	prem	**Man City**	H	L	2-3	Ashton 12; McKenzie 15
32	prem	**Chelsea**	H	L	1-3	McKenzie 64
33	prem	**Bolton**	A	L	0-1	
34	prem	**Arsenal**	A	L	1-4	Huckerby 30
35	prem	**Man Utd**	H	W	2-0	Ashton 55; McKenzie 66
36	prem	**Crystal Palace**	A	D	3-3	Ashton 22,46; McKenzie 53
37	prem	**Newcastle**	H	W	2-1	Safri 68; Ashton 90
38	prem	**Charlton**	H	W	1-0	Svensson 88
39	prem	**Southampton**	A	L	3-4	Bentley 3; Higginbotham 31 og; McKenzie 45
40	prem	**Birmingham**	H	W	1-0	Ashton 45 pen
41	prem	**Fulham**	A	L	0-6	

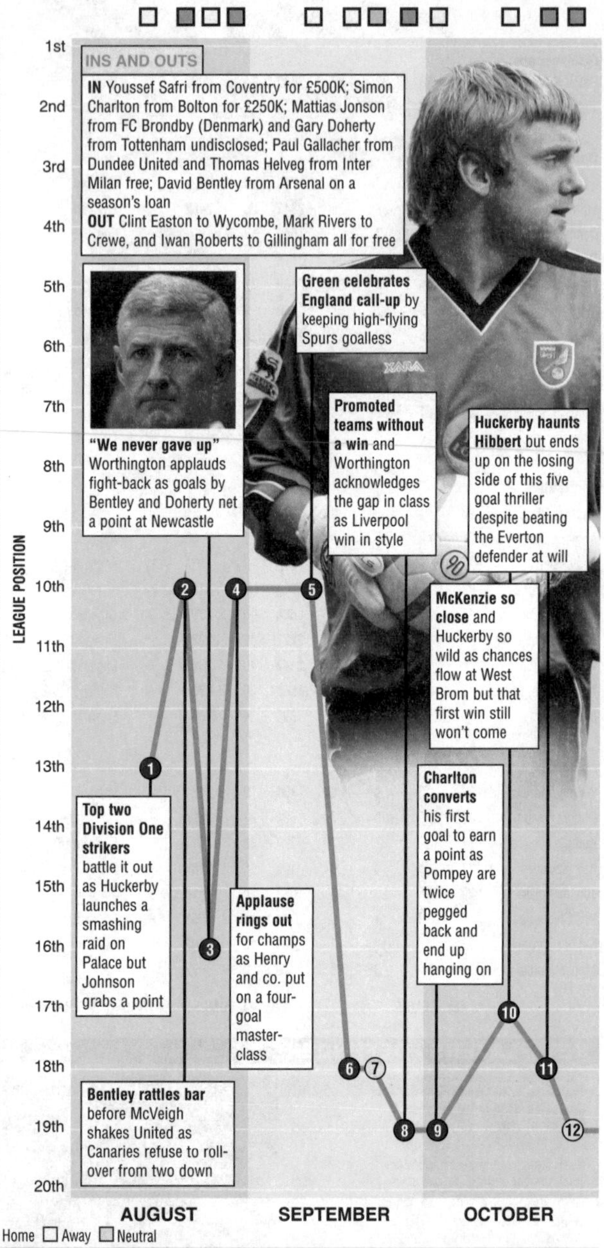
1st
2nd
3rd
4th
5th
6th
7th
8th
9th
10th
11th
12th
13th
14th
15th
16th
17th
18th
19th
20th
LEAGUE POSITION
INS AND OUTS
IN Youssef Safri from Coventry for £500K; Simon Charlton from Bolton for £250K; Mattias Jonson from FC Brondby (Denmark) and Gary Doherty from Tottenham undisclosed; Paul Gallacher from Dundee United and Thomas Helveg from Inter Milan free; David Bentley from Arsenal on a season's loan
OUT Clint Easton to Wycombe, Mark Rivers to Crewe, and Iwan Roberts to Gillingham all for free
"We never gave up" Worthington applauds fight-back as goals by Bentley and Doherty net a point at Newcastle
Green celebrates England call-up by keeping high-flying Spurs goalless
Promoted teams without a win and Worthington acknowledges the gap in class as Liverpool win in style
Huckerby haunts Hibbert but ends up on the losing side of this five goal thriller despite beating the Everton defender at will
McKenzie so close and Huckerby so wild as chances flow at West Brom but that first win still won't come
Charlton converts his first goal to earn a point as Pompey are twice pegged back and end up hanging on
Top two Division One strikers battle it out as Huckerby launches a smashing raid on Palace but Johnson grabs a point
Applause rings out for champs as Henry and co. put on a four-goal master-class
Bentley rattles bar before McVeigh shakes United as Canaries refuse to roll-over from two down
AUGUST
SEPTEMBER
OCTOBER
Home
Away
Neutral

ATTENDANCES

HOME GROUND: CARROW ROAD **CAPACITY:** 26034 **AVERAGE LEAGUE AT HOME:** 24350

2	Man Utd	67812	39	Southampton	31944	21	Tottenham	24508	1	Crystal Palace	23717
3	Newcastle	51574	17	Birmingham	29120	32	Chelsea	24506	16	Southampton	23706
8	Liverpool	43152	15	Charlton	27057	24	Liverpool	24503	19	Bolton	23549
13	Man City	42803	10	West Brom	26257	31	Man City	24302	25	West Ham	23389
12	Newcastle	42153	36	Crystal Palace	25754	29	West Brom	24292	41	Fulham	21927
20	Chelsea	42071	35	Man Utd	25522	4	Arsenal	23944	30	Blackburn	20923
26	Aston Villa	38172	37	Newcastle	25503	11	Everton	23871	23	Portsmouth	20015
34	Arsenal	38066	40	Birmingham	25477	9	Portsmouth	23853	7	Brist Rovers	18658
28	Everton	37485	38	Charlton	25459	14	Blackburn	23834			
5	Tottenham	36095	33	Bolton	25081	6	Aston Villa	23805			
22	Middlesboro	34836	27	Middlesboro	24547	18	Fulham	23755			

Ashton adds spicy end to Delia's season

Final Position: **19th**

KEY: ● League ● Champions Lge ● UEFA Cup ● FA Cup ○ League Cup ● Other

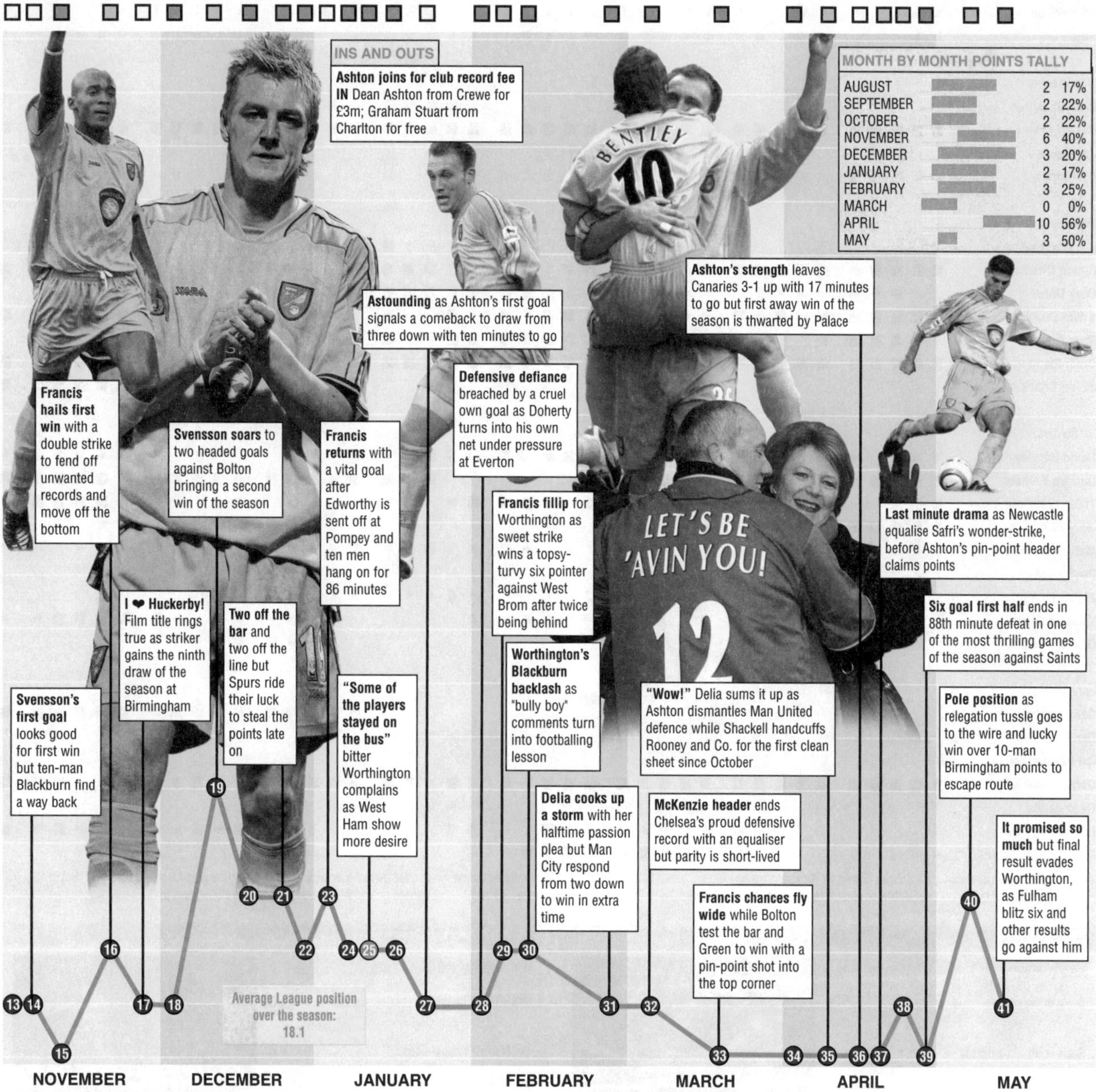

INS AND OUTS
Ashton joins for club record fee IN Dean Ashton from Crewe for £3m; Graham Stuart from Charlton for free
Francis hails first win with a double strike to fend off unwanted records and move off the bottom
Svensson soars to two headed goals against Bolton bringing a second win of the season
Francis returns with a vital goal after Edworthy is sent off at Pompey and ten men hang on for 86 minutes
Astounding as Ashton's first goal signals a comeback to draw from three down with ten minutes to go
Defensive defiance breached by a cruel own goal as Doherty turns into his own net under pressure at Everton
Ashton's strength leaves Canaries 3-1 up with 17 minutes to go but first away win of the season is thwarted by Palace
Last minute drama as Newcastle equalise Safri's wonder-strike, before Ashton's pin-point header claims points
Francis fillip for Worthington as sweet strike wins a topsy-turvy six pointer against West Brom after twice being behind
LET'S BE 'AVIN YOU!
12
I ❤ Huckerby! Film title rings true as striker gains the ninth draw of the season at Birmingham
Two off the bar and two off the line but Spurs ride their luck to steal the points late on
Six goal first half ends in 88th minute defeat in one of the most thrilling games of the season against Saints
Svensson's first goal looks good for first win but ten-man Blackburn find a way back
"Some of the players stayed on the bus" bitter Worthington complains as West Ham show more desire
Worthington's Blackburn backlash as "bully boy" comments turn into footballing lesson
"Wow!" Delia sums it up as Ashton dismantles Man United defence while Shackell handcuffs Rooney and Co. for the first clean sheet since October
Pole position as relegation tussle goes to the wire and lucky win over 10-man Birmingham points to escape route
Delia cooks up a storm with her halftime passion plea but Man City respond from two down to win in extra time
McKenzie header ends Chelsea's proud defensive record with an equaliser but parity is short-lived
It promised so much but final result evades Worthington, as Fulham blitz six and other results go against him
Francis chances fly wide while Bolton test the bar and Green to win with a pin-point shot into the top corner
Average League position over the season: 18.1
13 14 15 16 17 18 19 20 21 22 23 24 25 26 27 28 29 30 31 32 33 34 35 36 37 38 39 40 41
NOVEMBER
DECEMBER
JANUARY
FEBRUARY
MARCH
APRIL
MAY

MONTH BY MONTH POINTS TALLY

AUGUST	2	17%
SEPTEMBER	2	22%
OCTOBER	2	22%
NOVEMBER	6	40%
DECEMBER	3	20%
JANUARY	2	17%
FEBRUARY	3	25%
MARCH	0	0%
APRIL	10	56%
MAY	3	50%

GOAL ATTEMPTS

FOR
Goal attempts recorded in League games

	HOME	AWAY	TOTAL	AVE
shots on target	118	70	188	4.9
shots off target	100	80	180	4.7
TOTAL	218	150	368	9.7

Ratio of goals to shots Average number of shots on target per League goal scored	4.5
Accuracy rating Average percentage of total goal attempts which were on target	51.1

AGAINST
Goal attempts recorded in League games

	HOME	AWAY	TOTAL	AVE
shots on target	168	171	339	8.9
shots off target	133	70	203	5.3
TOTAL	301	241	542	14.3

Ratio of goals to shots Average number of shots on target per League goal scored	4.4
Accuracy rating Average percentage of total goal attempts which were on target	62.5

GOALS

Damien Francis

League	7
FA Cup	0
League Cup	0
Europe	0
Other	0
TOTAL	7

League Average
409
mins between goals

	PLAYER	LGE	FAC	LC	Euro	TOT	AVE
1	Francis	7	0	0	0	7	409
2	Ashton	7	0	0	0	7	203
3	McKenzie	7	0	0	0	7	345
4	Huckerby	6	0	1	0	7	531
5	Svensson	4	0	0	0	4	234
6	Bentley	2	0	0	0	2	998
7	Doherty	2	0	0	0	2	750
8	Safri	1	0	1	0	2	1081
9	McVeigh	1	0	0	0	1	510
10	Jarvis	1	0	0	0	1	116
11	Fleming	1	0	0	0	1	3420
12	Drury	1	0	0	0	1	2816
13	Charlton	1	0	0	0	1	1878
	Other	1	0	0	0	1	
	TOTAL	42	0	2	0	44	

SQUAD APPEARANCES

Match	1	2	3	4	5	6	7	8	9	10	11	12	13	14	15	16	17	18	19	20	21	22	23	24	25	26	27	28	29	30	31	32	33	34	35	36	37	38	39	40	41
Venue	H	A	A	H	A	H	H	A	H	A	H	A	A	H	A	H	A	H	H	A	H	A	A	H	A	A	H	A	H	A	H	H	A	A	H	A	H	H	A	H	A
Competition	L	L	L	L	L	L	W	L	L	L	L	W	L	L	L	L	L	L	L	L	L	L	L	L	F	L	L	L	L	L	L	L	L	L	L	L	L	L	L	L	L
Result	D	L	D	L	D	D	W	L	D	D	L	L	D	D	L	W	D	L	W	L	L	L	D	L	L	L	D	L	W	L	L	L	L	L	W	D	W	W	L	W	L

Goalkeepers
- Paul Gallacher
- Robert Green
- Joe Lewis
- Darren Ward

Defenders
- Jim Brennan
- Simon Charlton
- Gary Doherty
- Adam Drury
- Marc Edworthy
- Craig Fleming
- Jason Shackell

Midfielders
- David Bentley
- Damian Francis
- Thomas Helveg
- Gary Holt
- Mattias Jonson
- Paul McVeigh
- Phillip Mulryne
- Youssef Safri
- Graham Stuart

Forwards
- Dean Ashton
- Danny Crow
- Ian Henderson
- Darren Huckerby
- Ryan Jarvis
- Leon McKenzie
- Mathias Svensson

KEY: On all match | On bench | Subbed or sent off (Counting game) | Subbed or sent off (playing less than 70 mins) | Subbed on from bench (Counting Game) | Subbed on (playing less than 70 mins) | Subbed on and then subbed or sent off (Counting Game) | Subbed on and then subbed or sent off (playing less than 70 mins) | Not in 16

KEY PLAYERS - GOALSCORERS

Dean Ashton

HONDA

Goals in the League	7
Goals in all competitions	7
Assists League goals scored by a team mate where the player delivered the final pass	3
Contribution to Attacking Power Average number of minutes between League team goals while on pitch	61
Player Strike Rate Average number of minutes between League goals scored by player	203
Club Strike Rate Average minutes between League goals scored by club	81

	PLAYER	GOALS LGE	GOALS ALL	ASSISTS	POWER	S RATE
1	Dean Ashton	7	7	3	61	203 mins
2	Leon McKenzie	7	7	4	75	345 mins
3	Damian Francis	7	7	1	77	409 mins
4	Darren Huckerby	6	7	7	83	531 mins
5	Gary Doherty	2	2	0	93	750 mins

KEY PLAYERS - MIDFIELDERS

Thomas Helveg

Goals in the League	0
Goals in all competitions	0
Assists League goals scored by a team mate where the player delivered the final pass	2
Defensive Rating Average number of mins between League goals conceded while he was on the pitch	52
Contribution to Attacking Power Average number of minutes between League team goals while on pitch	71
Scoring Difference Defensive Rating minus Contribution to Attacking Power	-19

	PLAYER	GOALS LGE	GOALS ALL	ASSISTS	DEF RATE	POWER	SC DIFF
1	Thomas Helveg	0	0	2	52	71	-19 mins
2	David Bentley	2	2	4	57	87	-30 mins
3	Damian Francis	7	7	1	44	77	-33 mins
4	Gary Holt	0	0	1	43	87	-44 mins

PLAYER APPEARANCES

	AGE (on 01/07/05)	IN NAMED 16	APPEARANCES	COUNTING GAMES	MINUTES ON PITCH	APPEARANCES	MINUTES ON PITCH	THIS SEASON	HOME COUNTRY
Goalkeepers									
Paul Gallacher	25	9	0	0	0	0	0	1	Scotland (85)
Robert Green	25	38	38	37	3392	41	3662	-	England
Joe Lewis	17	2	0	0	0	0	0	-	England
Darren Ward	31	27	1	0	28	1	28	-	England
Defenders									
Jim Brennan	28	11	10	4	604	11	694	-	Canada
Simon Charlton	33	28	24	20	1878	26	2058	-	England
Gary Doherty	25	26	20	16	1500	23	1723	9	Rep of Ireland (15)
Adam Drury	26	36	33	31	2816	35	2970	-	England
Marc Edworthy	32	30	28	26	2344	31	2532	-	England
Craig Fleming	33	38	38	38	3420	41	3690	-	England
Jason Shackell	21	18	11	11	990	12	1080	-	England
Midfielders									
David Bentley	20	26	26	21	1996	28	2053	-	England
Damian Francis	26	32	32	32	2864	35	3134	-	England
Thomas Helveg	34	29	20	13	1340	23	1512	6	Denmark (19)
Gary Holt	32	28	27	18	1918	29	2053	4	Scotland (85)
Mattias Jonson	31	33	28	10	1484	30	1658	5	Sweden (13)
Paul McVeigh	27	23	17	1	510	18	591	4	N Ireland (114)
Phillip Mulryne	27	12	10	3	636	11	678	2	N Ireland (114)
Youssef Safri	28	24	18	9	1081	20	1208	-	Morocco
Graham Stuart	34	8	8	4	543	8	543	-	England
Forwards									
Dean Ashton	21	16	16	16	1418	16	1418	-	England
Danny Crow	19	4	3	0	43	4	49	-	England
Ian Henderson	20	4	3	0	56	4	86	-	England
Darren Huckerby	29	37	37	34	3186	40	3456	-	England
Ryan Jarvis	18	8	4	1	116	5	150	-	England
Leon McKenzie	27	37	37	23	2413	37	2413	-	England
Mathias Svensson	30	24	22	7	935	24	1042	-	Sweden

KEY:LEAGUE ALL COMPS CAPS (MAY FIFA RANKING)

TEAM OF THE SEASON

GREEN
CG 37 DR 45
DRURY
CG 31 DR 44
CHARLTON
CG 20 DR 48
DOHERTY
CG 16 DR 44
FLEMING
CG 38 DR 44
BENTLEY
CG 21 SD -30
FRANCIS
CG 32 SD -33
HELVEG
CG 13 SD -19
HOLT
CG 18 SD -44
MCKENZIE
CG 23 AP 75
ASHTON
CG 16 SR 203

KEY: DR = Defensive Rating, SD = Scoring Difference AP = Attacking Power SR = Strike Rate, CG=Counting games – League games playing at least 70 minutes

TOP POINT EARNERS

Thomas Helveg

Counting Games League games when player was on pitch for at least 70 minutes	13
Average points Average League points taken in Counting games	1.31
Club Average points Average points taken in League games	0.87

	PLAYER	GAMES	PTS
1	Thomas Helveg	13	1.31
2	David Bentley	21	1.14
3	Dean Ashton	16	1.06
4	Leon McKenzie	23	1.00
5	Damian Francis	32	0.91
6	Robert Green	37	0.89
7	Craig Fleming	38	0.87
8	Adam Drury	31	0.81
9	Simon Charlton	20	0.80
10	Darren Huckerby	34	0.79

KEY PLAYERS - DEFENDERS

Simon Charlton

Goals Conceded in the League Number of League goals conceded while the player was on the pitch	39
Goals Conceded in all competitions Total number of goals conceded while the player was on the pitch	40
League minutes played Number of minutes played in league matches	1878
Clean Sheets In games when player was on pitch for at least 70 minutes	3
Defensive Rating Average number of mins between League goals conceded while on the pitch	48
Club Defensive Rating Average number of mins between League goals conceded by the club this season	44

Lotus Car
16

	PLAYER	CON LGE	CON ALL	MINS	C SHEETS	DEF RATE
1	Simon Charlton	39	40	1878	3	48 mins
2	Gary Doherty	34	37	1500	2	44 mins
3	Adam Drury	64	66	2816	6	44 mins
4	Craig Fleming	77	80	3420	6	44 mins
5	Marc Edworthy	55	58	2344	3	43 mins

KEY GOALKEEPER

Robert Green

Goals Conceded in the League Number of League goals conceded while the player was on the pitch	75
Goals Conceded in all competitions Total number of goals conceded while the player was on the pitch	78
League minutes played Number of minutes played in league matches	3392
Clean Sheets In games when player was on pitch for at least 70 minutes	6
Goals to Shots Ratio The average number of shots on target per each League goal conceded	4.5
Defensive Rating Ave mins between League goals conceded while on the pitch	45

BOOKINGS

Thomas Helveg

League Yellow	6
League Red	0
All competitions Yellow	6
All competitions Red	0
League Average **223** mins between cards	

	PLAYER	LEAGUE		TOTAL		AVE
		Y	R	Y	R	
1	Helveg	6	0	6	0	223
2	Jonson	4	1	4	1	296
3	Bentley	6	0	6	0	332
4	Safri	3	0	3	0	360
5	Stuart	1	0	1	0	543
6	McKenzie	4	0	4	0	603
7	Svensson	1	0	1	0	935
8	Francis	3	0	3	0	954
9	Shackell	1	0	1	0	990
10	Edworthy	1	1	1	1	1172
11	Drury	2	0	2	0	1408
12	Fleming	2	0	2	0	1710
13	Charlton	1	0	1	0	1878
	Other	0	0	1	0	
	TOTAL	35	2	36	2	

SOUTHAMPTON

Peter Crouch is the owner of the second-best Strike Rate in the Premiership. His 12 league goals have come at an average of one every 157 minutes.

And, unusually for a team at the foot of the table, the striker lying second in Saints' Goalscoring chart also has a good Strike Rate. **Kevin Phillips'** ten league goals came at a rate of 209. **Henri Camara's** end of season cameo was only 818 minutes but led to five goals with a league Strike Rate of 273.

Jamie Redknapp has the best Scoring Difference in midfield but at -14, the team is still more likely to concede goals than score them when he's playing. **David Prutton** finished the season returning from a ban and his eight league yellows and one red came at an average of a card every 187 minutes.

NICKNAME: THE SAINTS

KEY: Won Drawn Lost

1	prem	**Aston Villa**	A	L	0-2	
2	prem	**Blackburn**	H	W	3-2	Phillips 32; Svensson, A 74; Beattie 90 pen
3	prem	**Bolton**	H	L	1-2	Crouch 85
4	prem	**Chelsea**	A	L	1-2	Beattie 1
5	prem	**Charlton**	A	D	0-0	
6	prem	**Newcastle**	H	L	1-2	Svensson, A 53
7	ccr2	**Northampton**	A	W	3-0	Phillips 32; Prutton 35; McCann 65
8	prem	**Fulham**	A	L	0-1	
9	prem	**Man City**	H	D	0-0	
10	prem	**Everton**	A	L	0-1	
11	prem	**Birmingham**	H	D	0-0	
12	ccr3	**Colchester**	H	W	3-2	Blackstock 50,54,80
13	prem	**Arsenal**	A	D	2-2	Delap 80,85
14	prem	**West Brom**	H	D	2-2	Svensson, A 28; Robinson 87 og
15	ccr4	**Watford**	A	L	2-5	Blackstock 84; Ormerod 88
16	prem	**Portsmouth**	H	W	2-1	Blackstock 18; Phillips 71
17	prem	**Norwich**	A	L	1-2	Beattie 24
18	prem	**Crystal Palace**	H	D	2-2	Phillips 50; Jakobsson 76
19	prem	**Man Utd**	A	L	0-3	
20	prem	**Middlesbrough**	H	D	2-2	Phillips 45; Crouch 64
21	prem	**Tottenham**	A	L	1-5	Crouch 47
22	prem	**Charlton**	H	D	0-0	
23	prem	**Liverpool**	A	L	0-1	
24	prem	**Man City**	A	L	1-2	Phillips 90 pen
25	prem	**Fulham**	H	D	3-3	Phillips 21,29; Rosenior 70 og
26	facr3	**Northampton**	A	W	3-1	Phillips 29; Crouch 41; Redknapp 53
27	prem	**Newcastle**	A	L	1-2	Crouch 42
28	prem	**Liverpool**	H	W	2-0	Prutton 5; Crouch 22
29	facr4	**Portsmouth**	H	W	2-1	Oakley 54; Crouch 90 pen
30	prem	**Birmingham**	A	L	1-2	Camara 52
31	prem	**Everton**	H	D	2-2	Crouch 36; Camara 54
32	facr5	**Brentford**	H	D	2-2	Camara 4,36
33	prem	**West Brom**	A	D	0-0	
34	prem	**Arsenal**	H	D	1-1	Crouch 67
35	facr5r	**Brentford**	A	W	3-1	Crouch 11,90; Phillips 66
36	prem	**Tottenham**	H	W	1-0	Quashie 51
37	facqf	**Man Utd**	H	L	0-4	
38	prem	**Middlesbrough**	A	W	3-1	Jakobsson 14; Crouch 60,67
39	prem	**Chelsea**	H	L	1-3	Phillips 69
40	prem	**Blackburn**	A	L	0-3	
41	prem	**Aston Villa**	H	L	2-3	Phillips 4; Crouch 13
42	prem	**Bolton**	A	D	1-1	Phillips 69
43	prem	**Portsmouth**	A	L	1-4	Camara 20
44	prem	**Norwich**	H	W	4-3	Oakley 7; Crouch 20; Le Saux 39; Camara 88
45	prem	**Crystal Palace**	A	D	2-2	Crouch 37 pen; Higginbotham 90
46	prem	**Man Utd**	H	L	1-2	O'Shea 10 og

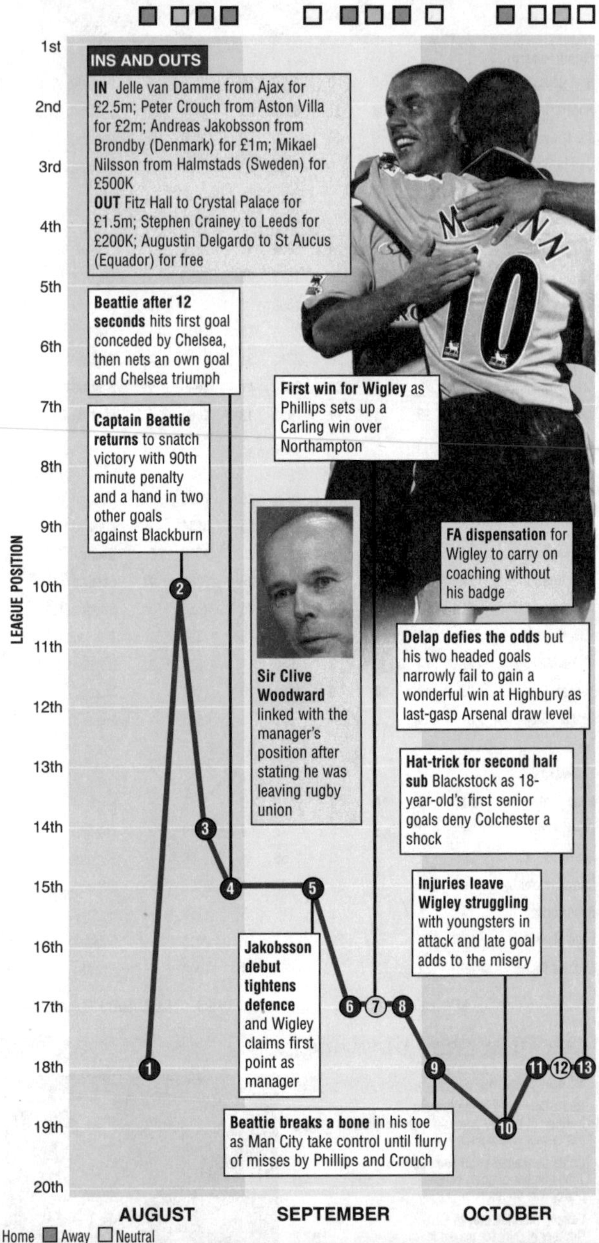

1st
2nd
3rd
4th
5th
6th
7th
8th
9th
10th
11th
12th
13th
14th
15th
16th
17th
18th
19th
20th
LEAGUE POSITION
INS AND OUTS
IN Jelle van Damme from Ajax for £2.5m; Peter Crouch from Aston Villa for £2m; Andreas Jakobsson from Brondby (Denmark) for £1m; Mikael Nilsson from Halmstads (Sweden) for £500K
OUT Fitz Hall to Crystal Palace for £1.5m; Stephen Crainey to Leeds for £200K; Augustin Delgardo to St Aucus (Equador) for free
Beattie after 12 seconds hits first goal conceded by Chelsea, then nets an own goal and Chelsea triumph
Captain Beattie returns to snatch victory with 90th minute penalty and a hand in two other goals against Blackburn
First win for Wigley as Phillips sets up a Carling win over Northampton
Sir Clive Woodward linked with the manager's position after stating he was leaving rugby union
FA dispensation for Wigley to carry on coaching without his badge
Delap defies the odds but his two headed goals narrowly fail to gain a wonderful win at Highbury as last-gasp Arsenal draw level
Hat-trick for second half sub Blackstock as 18-year-old's first senior goals deny Colchester a shock
Injuries leave Wigley struggling with youngsters in attack and late goal adds to the misery
Jakobsson debut tightens defence and Wigley claims first point as manager
Beattie breaks a bone in his toe as Man City take control until flurry of misses by Phillips and Crouch
1
2
3
4
5
6
7
8
9
10
11
12
13
AUGUST
SEPTEMBER
OCTOBER
Home Away Neutral

ATTENDANCES

HOME GROUND: ST MARY'S STADIUM **CAPACITY:** 32251 **AVERAGE LEAGUE AT HOME:** 30609

19	Man Utd	67921	44	Norwich	31944	38	Middlesboro	30082	5	Charlton	24263
27	Newcastle	51266	41	Aston Villa	31926	29	Portsmouth	29453	17	Norwich	23706
24	Man City	42895	36	Tottenham	31903	20	Middlesboro	29018	40	Blackburn	20726
23	Liverpool	42382	18	Crystal Palace	31833	30	Birmingham	28797	12	Colchester	20588
4	Chelsea	40864	34	Arsenal	31815	9	Man City	28605	43	Portsmouth	20000
13	Arsenal	38141	31	Everton	31509	11	Birmingham	27568	8	Fulham	19237
1	Aston Villa	36690	22	Charlton	31195	2	Blackburn	27492	15	Watford	13008
21	Tottenham	36054	14	West Brom	31057	25	Fulham	27343	35	Brentford	11720
10	Everton	35256	37	Man Utd	30971	45	Crystal Palace	26066	26	Northampton	7183
46	Man Utd	32066	16	Portsmouth	30921	33	West Brom	25865	7	Northampton	6343
28	Liverpool	32017	3	Bolton	30713	42	Bolton	25125			
39	Chelsea	31949	6	Newcastle	30709	32	Brentford	24741			

Lowe point reached after 27 years!

Final Position: **20th**

KEY: ● League ● Champions Lge ● UEFA Cup ● FA Cup ○ League Cup ● Other

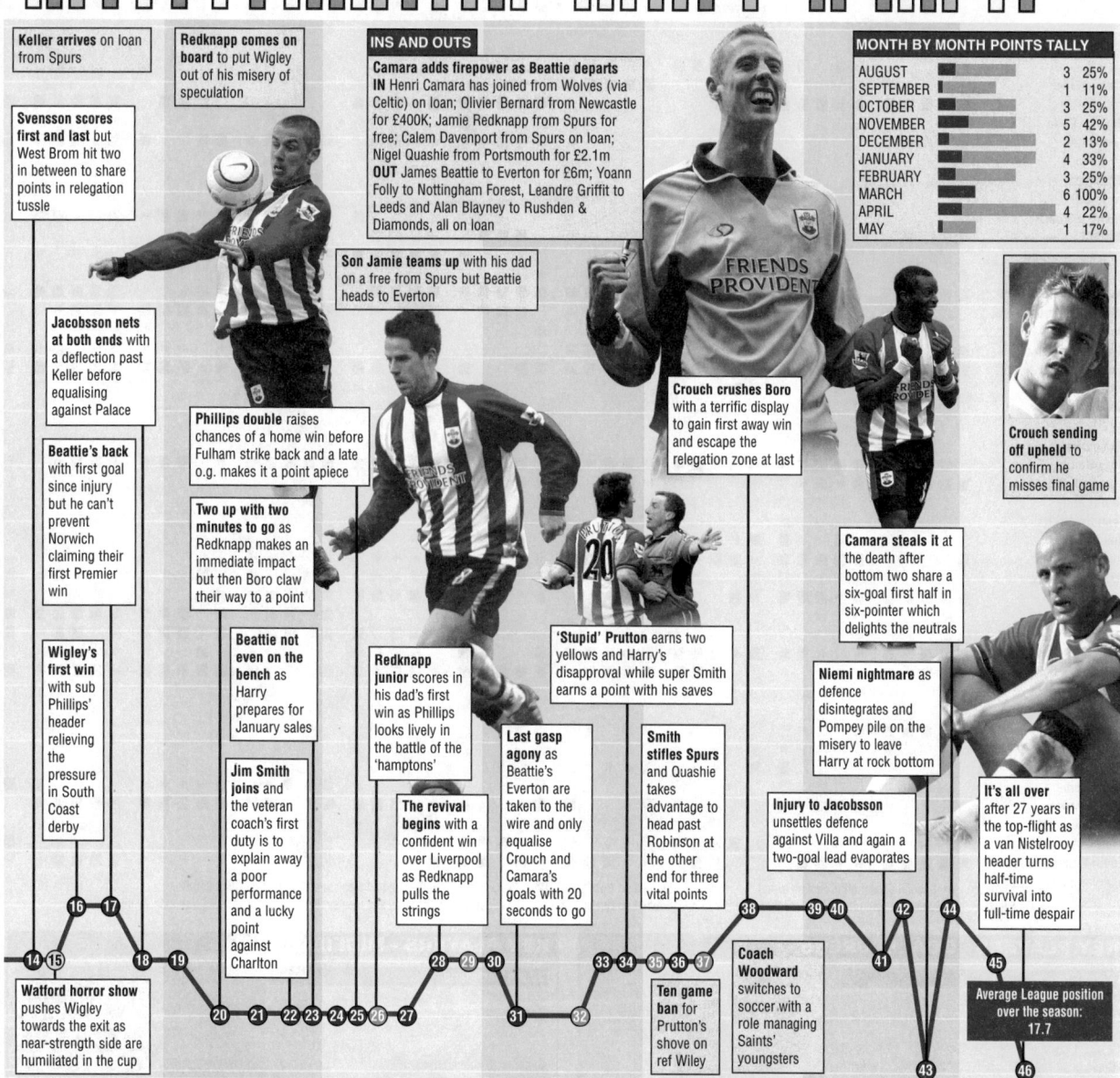

Keller arrives on loan from Spurs

Svensson scores first and last but West Brom hit two in between to share points in relegation tussle

Redknapp comes on board to put Wigley out of his misery of speculation

Jacobsson nets at both ends with a deflection past Keller before equalising against Palace

Beattie's back with first goal since injury but he can't prevent Norwich claiming their first Premier win

Wigley's first win with sub Phillips' header relieving the pressure in South Coast derby

Watford horror show pushes Wigley towards the exit as near-strength side are humiliated in the cup

Phillips double raises chances of a home win before Fulham strike back and a late o.g. makes it a point apiece

Two up with two minutes to go as Redknapp makes an immediate impact but then Boro claw their way to a point

Beattie not even on the bench as Harry prepares for January sales

Jim Smith joins and the veteran coach's first duty is to explain away a poor performance and a lucky point against Charlton

INS AND OUTS

Camara adds firepower as Beattie departs
IN Henri Camara has joined from Wolves (via Celtic) on loan; Olivier Bernard from Newcastle for £400K; Jamie Redknapp from Spurs for free; Calem Davenport from Spurs on loan; Nigel Quashie from Portsmouth for £2.1m
OUT James Beattie to Everton for £6m; Yoann Folly to Nottingham Forest, Leandre Griffit to Leeds and Alan Blayney to Rushden & Diamonds, all on loan

Son Jamie teams up with his dad on a free from Spurs but Beattie heads to Everton

Redknapp junior scores in his dad's first win as Phillips looks lively in the battle of the 'hamptons'

The revival begins with a confident win over Liverpool as Redknapp pulls the strings

Last gasp agony as Beattie's Everton are taken to the wire and only equalise Crouch and Camara's goals with 20 seconds to go

'Stupid' Prutton earns two yellows and Harry's disapproval while super Smith earns a point with his saves

Smith stifles Spurs and Quashie takes advantage to head past Robinson at the other end for three vital points

Ten game ban for Prutton's shove on ref Wiley

Crouch crushes Boro with a terrific display to gain first away win and escape the relegation zone at last

Coach Woodward switches to soccer with a role managing Saints' youngsters

Injury to Jacobsson unsettles defence against Villa and again a two-goal lead evaporates

Camara steals it at the death after bottom two share a six-goal first half in six-pointer which delights the neutrals

Niemi nightmare as defence disintegrates and Pompey pile on the misery to leave Harry at rock bottom

MONTH BY MONTH POINTS TALLY

AUGUST	3	25%
SEPTEMBER	1	11%
OCTOBER	3	25%
NOVEMBER	5	42%
DECEMBER	2	13%
JANUARY	4	33%
FEBRUARY	3	25%
MARCH	6	100%
APRIL	4	22%
MAY	1	17%

Crouch sending off upheld to confirm he misses final game

It's all over after 27 years in the top-flight as a van Nistelrooy header turns half-time survival into full-time despair

Average League position over the season: 17.7

NOVEMBER DECEMBER JANUARY FEBRUARY MARCH APRIL MAY

GOAL ATTEMPTS

FOR
Goal attempts recorded in League games

	HOME	AWAY	TOTAL	AVE
shots on target	110	84	194	5.1
shots off target	116	79	195	5.1
TOTAL	226	163	389	10.2

Ratio of goals to shots
Average number of shots on target per League goal scored: **4.3**

Accuracy rating
Average percentage of total goal attempts which were on target: **49.9**

AGAINST
Goal attempts recorded in League games

	HOME	AWAY	TOTAL	AVE
shots on target	121	156	277	7.3
shots off target	114	84	198	5.2
TOTAL	235	240	475	12.5

Ratio of goals to shots
Average number of shots on target per League goal scored: **4.2**

Accuracy rating
Average percentage of total goal attempts which were on target: **58.3**

GOALS

Peter Crouch

League	12
FA Cup	4
League Cup	0
Europe	0
Other	0
TOTAL	16

League Average
157
mins between goals

	PLAYER	LGE	FAC	LC	Euro	TOT	AVE
1	Crouch	12	4	0	0	16	157
2	Phillips	10	2	1	0	13	209
3	Camara	3	2	0	0	5	273
4	Blackstock	1	0	4	0	5	680
5	Beattie	3	0	0	0	3	269
6	Svensson, A	3	0	0	0	3	658
7	Delap	2	0	0	0	2	1514
8	Jakobsson	2	0	0	0	2	1016
9	Prutton	1	0	1	0	2	1690
10	Oakley	1	1	0	0	2	417
11	Quashie	1	0	0	0	1	1170
12	Higginbotham	1	0	0	0	1	1808
13	Le Saux	1	0	0	0	1	1926
14	McCann	0	0	1	0	1	
15	Redknapp	0	1	0	0	1	
	Other	4	0	1	0	5	
	TOTAL	45	10	8	0	63	

SQUAD APPEARANCES

Match	1	2	3	4	5	6	7	8	9	10	11	12	13	14	15	16	17	18	19	20	21	22	23
Venue	A	H	H	A	A	H	A	A	H	A	H	H	A	H	A	H	A	H	A	H	A	H	A
Competition	L	L	L	L	L	L	W	L	L	L	L	W	L	L	W	L	L	L	L	L	L	L	L
Result	L	W	L	L	D	L	W	L	D	L	D	W	D	D	L	W	L	D	L	D	L	D	L

Match	24	25	26	27	28	29	30	31	32	33	34	35	36	37	38	39	40	41	42	43	44	45	46
Venue	A	H	A	A	H	H	A	H	H	A	H	A	H	H	A	H	A	H	A	A	H	A	H
Competition	L	L	F	L	L	F	L	L	F	L	L	F	L	F	L	L	L	L	L	L	L	L	L
Result	L	D	W	L	W	W	L	D	D	D	D	W	W	L	W	L	L	L	D	L	W	D	L

Goalkeepers
Alan Blayney
Kasey Keller
Antti Niemi
Michael Poke
Paul Smith

Defenders
Chris Baird
Olivier Bernard
Martin Cranie
Calum Davenport
Jason Dodd
Danny Higginbotham
Andreas Jakobsson
Darren Kenton
Graeme Le Saux
Claus Lundekvam
Jelle van Damme
Alledine Yahia

Midfielders
Rory Delap
Fabrice Fernandes
Yoann Folly
Leandre Griffit
Neil McCann
Mikael Nilsson
Matthew Oakley
David Prutton
Nigel Quashie
Jamie Redknapp
Anders Svensson
Paul Telfer

Forwards
James Beattie
Leon Best
Dextor Blackstock
Henri Camara
Peter Crouch
Kenwyne Jones
Brett Ormerod
Kevin Phillips

KEY: On all match — On bench — Subbed or sent off (Counting game) — Subbed or sent off (playing less than 70 mins) — Subbed on from bench (Counting Game) — Subbed on (playing less than 70 mins) — Subbed on and then subbed or sent off (Counting Game) — Subbed on and then subbed or sent off (playing less than 70 mins) — Not in 16

KEY PLAYERS - GOALSCORERS

Peter Crouch

Goals in the League	12
Goals in all competitions	16
Assists League goals scored by a team mate where the player delivered the final pass	6
Contribution to Attacking Power Average number of minutes between League team goals while on pitch	62
Player Strike Rate Average number of minutes between League goals scored by player	157
Club Strike Rate Average minutes between League goals scored by club	76

	PLAYER	GOALS LGE	GOALS ALL	ASSISTS	POWER	S RATE
1	Peter Crouch	12	16	6	62	157 mins
2	Kevin Phillips	10	13	1	72	209 mins
3	Anders Svensson	3	3	0	76	658 mins
4	Andreas Jakobsson	2	2	0	92	1016 mins
5	Nigel Quashie	1	1	2	62	1170 mins

KEY PLAYERS - MIDFIELDERS

Jamie Redknapp

Goals in the League	0
Goals in all competitions	1
Assists League goals scored by a team mate where the player delivered the final pass	2
Defensive Rating Average number of mins between League goals conceded while on the pitch	46
Contribution to Attacking Power Average number of minutes between League team goals while on pitch	60
Scoring Difference Defensive Rating minus Contribution to Attacking Power	-14

	PLAYER	GOALS LGE	GOALS ALL	ASSISTS	DEF RATE	POWER	SC DIFF
1	Jamie Redknapp	0	1	2	46	60	-14 mins
2	Nigel Quashie	1	1	2	47	62	-15 mins
3	Anders Svensson	3	3	0	58	76	-18 mins
4	Paul Telfer	0	0	2	44	64	-20 mins
5	Rory Delap	2	2	4	56	78	-22 mins

PLAYER APPEARANCES

	AGE (on 01/07/05)	IN NAMED 16	APPEARANCES	COUNTING GAMES	MINUTES ON PITCH	APPEARANCES	MINUTES ON PITCH	THIS SEASON	HOME COUNTRY
Goalkeepers									
Alan Blayney	23	13	1	1	90	2	180	-	N Ireland
Kasey Keller	35	4	4	4	360	4	360	-	United States
Antti Niemi	33	28	28	27	2435	32	2795	-	Finland
Michael Poke	19	4	0	0	0	0	0	-	England
Paul Smith	25	27	6	6	535	9	805	-	England
Defenders									
Chris Baird	23	1	0	0	0	0	0	4	N Ireland (114)
Olivier Bernard	25	13	13	12	1104	16	1325	-	France
Martin Cranie	18	7	3	3	270	6	381	-	England
Calum Davenport	22	15	7	5	501	12	906	-	England
Jason Dodd	34	8	5	3	367	5	367	-	England
Danny Higginbotham	26	34	21	20	1808	26	2258	-	England
Andreas Jakobsson	32	30	27	20	2031	33	2499	-	Sweden
Darren Kenton	26	12	9	9	792	11	945	-	England
Graeme Le Saux	36	25	25	19	1926	26	1993	-	England
Claus Lundekvam	32	34	34	33	3015	41	3600	-	Norway
Jelle van Damme	21	8	6	3	391	9	598	-	Belgium
Alledine Yahia	23	1	0	0	0	0	0	-	France
Midfielders									
Rory Delap	29	37	37	31	3027	43	3567	-	Rep of Ireland
Fabrice Fernandes	25	19	16	10	1105	18	1182	-	France
Yoann Folly	20	5	3	0	129	4	158	-	France
Leandre Griffit	21	4	2	0	34	3	79	-	France
Neil McCann	30	11	11	4	585	17	874	1	Scotland (85)
Mikael Nilsson	27	17	16	10	1075	21	1453	7	Sweden (13)
Matthew Oakley	27	10	7	2	417	12	794	-	England
David Prutton	23	23	23	18	1690	28	2127	-	England
Nigel Quashie	26	13	13	13	1170	13	1170	-	England
Jamie Redknapp	32	16	16	16	1428	17	1483	-	England
Anders Svensson	28	33	29	19	1973	33	2317	6	Sweden (13)
Paul Telfer	33	33	30	26	2441	36	2936	-	Scotland
Forwards									
James Beattie	27	12	11	8	808	11	808	-	England
Leon Best	18	6	3	0	79	5	148	-	England
Dextor Blackstock	19	9	9	5	680	11	752	-	England
Henri Camara	28	14	12	7	818	15	1000	4	Senegal (33)
Peter Crouch	24	32	28	18	1879	34	2416	-	England
Kenwyne Jones	21	2	2	0	47	3	74	-	Trinidad & Tobago
Brett Ormerod	28	16	9	3	442	12	625	-	England
Kevin Phillips	31	32	30	20	2091	36	2488	-	England

KEY: LEAGUE — ALL COMPS — CAPS (MAY FIFA RANKING)

TEAM OF THE SEASON

NIEMI
CG 27 DR 51
BERNARD
CG 12 DR 50
JAKOBSSON
CG 20 DR 55
LUNDEKVAAM
CG 33 DR 53
LE SAUX
CG 19 DR 52
TELFER
CG 26 SD -20
REDKNAPP
CG 16 SD -14
QUASHIE
CG 13 SD -16
SVENSSON
CG 19 SD -18
PHILLIPS
CG 20 SR 209
CROUCH
CG 18 SR 157

KEY: DR = Defensive Rating, SD = Scoring Difference SR = Strike Rate, CG=Counting games – League games playing at least 70 minutes

TOP POINT EARNERS

Graeme Le Saux

Counting Games League games when player was on pitch for at least 70 minutes	19
Average points Average League points taken in Counting games	1.11
Club Average points Average points taken in League games	0.84

	PLAYER	GAMES	PTS
1	Graeme Le Saux	19	1.11
2	Olivier Bernard	12	1.08
3	Nigel Quashie	13	1.08
4	Peter Crouch	18	1.06
5	Jamie Redknapp	16	1.06
6	Anders Svensson	19	0.95
7	Danny Higginbotham	20	0.90
8	Paul Telfer	26	0.85
9	Claus Lundekvam	33	0.85
10	Rory Delap	31	0.81

KEY PLAYERS - DEFENDERS

Andreas Jakobsson

Goals Conceded in the League Number of League goals conceded while the player was on the pitch	37
Goals Conceded in all competitions Total number of goals conceded while player was on the pitch	49
League minutes played Number of minutes played in league matches	2031
Clean Sheets In games when player was on pitch for at least 70 minutes	5
Defensive Rating Average number of mins between League goals conceded while on the pitch	55
Club Defensive Rating Average number of mins between League goals conceded by the club this season	52

FRIENDS PROVIDENT

	PLAYER	CON LGE	CON ALL	MINS	C SHEETS	DEF RATE
1	Andreas Jakobsson	37	49	2031	5	55 mins
2	Claus Lundekvam	57	70	3015	7	53 mins
3	Graeme Le Saux	37	39	1926	3	52 mins
4	Olivier Bernard	22	28	1104	2	50 mins
5	Danny Higginbotham	40	52	1808	3	45 mins

KEY GOALKEEPER

Antti Niemi

Goals Conceded in the League Number of League goals conceded while the player was on the pitch	48
Goals Conceded in all competitions Total number of goals conceded while player was on the pitch	52
League minutes played Number of minutes played in league matches	2435
Clean Sheets In games when player was on pitch for at least 70 minutes	5
Goals to Shots Ratio The average number of shots on target per each League goal conceded	3.8
Defensive Rating Ave mins between League goals conceded while on the pitch	51

BOOKINGS

David Prutton

League Yellow	8
League Red	1
All competitions Yellow	10
All competitions Red	1

League Average **187** mins between cards

	PLAYER	LEAGUE Y	LEAGUE R	TOTAL Y	TOTAL R	AVE
1	Prutton	8 Y	1 R	10 Y	1 R	187
2	McCann	3	0	3	0	195
3	Kenton	3	0	3	0	264
4	Redknapp	5	0	5	0	285
5	Bernard	3	0	3	0	368
6	Camara	2	0	2	0	409
7	Delap	5	0	6	0	605
8	Blackstock	1	0	1	0	680
9	Phillips	3	0	3	0	697
10	Lundekvam	4	0	4	0	753
11	Crouch	1	1	2	1	939
12	Le Saux	2	0	3	0	963
13	Quashie	1	0	1	0	1170
14	Telfer	2	0	3	0	1220
15	Jakobsson	1	0	1	0	2031
	Other	0	0	0	0	
	TOTAL	44	2	50	2	

THE AXA FA CUP

1ST ROUND

Aldershot (0) 4 **Canvey I** (0) 0
Dixon 46,79 — 2,600
McLean 65,90

Alfreton (0) 1 **Macclesfield** (0) 1
Sale 90 — Whitaker 86
2,251

Barnet (0) 1 **Bath City** (0) 2
Hatch 48 — Partridge 65,90
2,147

Billericay (0) 0 **Stevenage** (0) 1
1,804 — Hanlon 72

Blackpool (1) 3 **Tamworth** (0) 0
Wellens 9,76 — 4,796
Parker 46

Boston (0) 5 **Hornchurch** (1) 2
Thompson 48 — Castle 4
McManus 49,67 — Everett 78
Noble 81 — 2,437
Ellender 89

Bradford (0) 0 **Rushden & D** (0) 1
4,171 — Robinson 87

Bristol City (0) 1 **Brentford** (1) 1
Lita 89 — Salako 7
10,000

Bristol Rovers (0) 1 **Carlisle** (0) 1
Walker 77 — McGill 79
5,658

Bury (4) 5 **Vauxhall Motors** (0) 2
Mattis 8,26 — McDermott 61
Porter 19 — O'Donnell 73
Challinor 39 — 2,566
Nugent 74

Cambridge City (0) 2 **Leigh RMI** (1) 1
Sadler 58 — Simms 14
Stevenson 90 — 930

Cheltenham (0) 1 **Swansea** (1) 3
Spencer 71 — O'Leary 19
4,551 — Trundle 46
Connor 90

Darlington (1) 3 **Yeovil** (0) 3
Armstrong 19,73 — Miles 46
Keltie 86 — Tarachulski 55,90
3,698

Exeter (1) 1 **Grimsby** (0) 0
Gaia 6 — 3,378

Forest Green (0) 1 **Bournemouth** (1) 1
Louis 56 — Fletcher 24
1,837

Halifax (1) 3 **Cambridge** (1) 1
Foster 6 — Tudor 35
Midgley 69 — 2,368
Ross 84

Hartlepool (3) 3 **Lincoln** (0) 0
Williams 23 — 4,533
Robson 27
Porter 43

Hayes (0) 0 **Wrexham** (3) 4
1,751 — Holt 17
Lawrence 30
Sam 37
Llewellyn 82

Hinckley (1) 2 **Torquay** (0) 0
Lavery 38 — 2,129
Cartwright 79

Histon (1) 2 **Shrewsbury** (0) 0
Cambridge 4 — 1,538
Liban 90

Hull City (1) 3 **Morecambe** (1) 2
Green 30 — Bentley 12
Keane 66 — Twiss 60
Walters 86 — 10,129

Leyton Orient (2) 3 **Dag & Red** (0) 1
Lockwood 11 — Moore 83 pen
Hunt 37 — 4,155
Carlisle 58

Mansfield (1) 1 **Colchester** (1) 1
Baptiste 28 — Halford 25
3,202

MK Dons (0) 1 **Lancaster** (0) 0
Small 48 — 2,065

Northampton (1) 1 **Barnsley** (0) 0
McGleish 5 — 4,876

Notts County (1) 2 **Woking** (0) 0
Baudet 35 pen — 4,700
Gordon 90

Peterborough (1) 2 **Tranmere** (1) 1
Kennedy 10 — Taylor 42
Woodhouse 89 — 2,940

Port Vale (0) 3 **Kidderminster** (1) 1
Paynter 53,65 — Hatswell 4
Reid 59 — 4,141

Rochdale (1) 2 **Oxford** (1) 1
Holt 36,90 — Bradbury 20
2,333

Scunthorpe (1) 2 **Chesterfield** (0) 0
Hayes 13 — 4,869
Baraclough 76

Slough (1) 2 **Walsall** (1) 1
Hodges 24 — Wrack 32
Harris 73 — 2,023

Southend (0) 0 **Luton** (3) 3
6,683 — Howard 12,15
Brkovic 33

Southport (0) 1 **Hereford** (1) 3
Fearns 75 — Mills 26
2,045 — Stansfield 58
Purdie 63

Stafford (0) 0 **Chester** (1) 2
2,492 — Belle 32
Rapley 71

Stockport (3) 3 **Huddersfield** (0) 1
Williams, A 8 — Abbott 90
Feeney 19,45 — 3,479

Swindon (1) 4 **Sheff Wed** (0) 1
Howard 43 — Whelan 63
Jenkins 48 — 6,160
Duke 83
Roberts 86

Thurrock (0) 0 **Oldham** (0) 1
1,156 — Killen 48 pen

Tiverton (0) 1 **Doncaster** (2) 3
Winter 90 pen — McIndoe 18
1,618 — Fenton 26
Blundell 84

Wycombe (0) 1 **Coalville** (0) 0
Johnson 71 — 2,816

Yeading (2) 2 **Halesowen** (1) 1
Haywood 5 og — Cowley 9
Campbell 45 pen — 524

1ST ROUND REPLAYS

Bournemouth (1) 3 **Forest Green** (0) 1
Connell 10 — Lyttle 88
Spicer 70 — 5,489
Rodrigues 90

Brentford (1) 1 **Bristol City** (0) 1
Frampton 44 — Heffernan 77
3,706

Carlisle (0) 1 **Bristol Rovers** (0) 0
Vieira 109 — 4,813

Colchester (2) 4 **Mansfield** (0) 1
Garcia 10 — Neil 87
Curtis 14 og — 2,492
Fagan 67 pen
Williams 90 pen

Macclesfield (0) 2 **Alfreton** (0) 0
Parkin 54 — 1,783
Sheron 78

Yeovil (0) 1 **Darlington** (0) 0
Way 56 — 5,365

2ND ROUND

Blackpool (0) 1 **Port Vale** (0) 0
Taylor 76 — 4,669

Bournemouth (0) 2 **Carlisle** (0) 1
Holmes 48 — Farrell 89
Connell 64 — 5,815

Cambridge City (0) 0 **Wimbledon** (1) 1
2,000 — Smart 6

Exeter (1) 2 **Doncaster** (0) 1
Flack 25 — Blundell 86
Moxey 49 — 4,797

Halifax (0) 1 **Chester** (1) 3
Ross 66 — Branch 41,50 pen
4,497 — Rapley 74

Hartlepool (2) 5 **Aldershot** (1) 1
Westwood 13,30 — Sills 36
Boyd 63,68 — 4,556
Tinkler 75

Hereford (1) 2 **Boston** (1) 3
Mkandawire 9 — Lee 30
Stanley 89 — Kirk 71,78
3,601

Hinckley (0) 0 **Brentford** (0) 0
2,661

Histon (0) 1 **Yeovil** (0) 3
Kennedy 71 — Jevons 52 pen
2,564 — Johnson 57
Odubade 90

Hull City (3) 4 **Macclesfield** (0) 0
France 28 — 9,831
Facey 35,46
Elliott 39

Northampton (1) 1 **Bury** (0) 0
McGleish 23 — 4,415

Oldham (2) 4 **Leyton Orient** (0) 0
Killen 26,39,65 — 4,657
Croft 85

Peterborough (2) 2 **Bath City** (0) 0
Willock 36,41 — 4,187

Rushden & D (0) 2 **Colchester** (3) 5
Broughton 82 — Halford 4,47,90
Gray 86 — Fagan 25,35
3,077

Scunthorpe (1) 2 **Wrexham** (0) 0
Ridley 14 — 5,698
Sparrow 54

Slough (1) 1 **Yeading** (1) 3
Harris 3 pen — Campbell 27,52
2,418 — Haule 62

Stevenage (0) 0 **Rochdale** (0) 2
2,700 — Holt 70,90

Stockport (0) 0 **Swansea** (0) 0
2,680

Swindon (1) 1 **Notts County** (0) 1
O'Hanlon 19 — Oakes 90
5,768

Wycombe (0) 0 **Luton** (1) 3
4,767 — Howard 20,80
Nicholls 70

2ND ROUND REPLAYS

Brentford (0) 2 **Hinckley** (0) 1
Rhodes 52 pen — Lavery 57
Talbot 59 — 4,002

Notts County (1) 2 **Swindon** (0) 0
Gordon 31,47 — 3,770

Swansea (0) 2 **Stockport** (0) 1
Connor 47 — Griffin 72
Goodfellow 88 — 5,572

3RD ROUND

Arsenal (0) 2 **Stoke** (1) 1
Reyes 50 — Thomas 45
van Persie 70 — 36,579

Birmingham (2) 3 **Leeds** (0) 0
Heskey 11 — 25,159
Carter 21,65

Bournemouth (1) 2 **Chester** (0) 1
Maher 33 — Ellison 69
Elliott 56 — 7,653

Burnley (0) 1 **Liverpool** (0) 0
Traore 51 og — 19,033

Turfed out of the cup at Turf Moor after an own goal by Liverpool's Traoré and a sending off for Nunez give Burnley a prize scalp

Cardiff (1) 1 **Blackburn** (1) 1
Lee 35 — Pedersen 5
14,145

Charlton (2) 4 **Rochdale** (0) 1
Hughes 19,56 — Holt 51
Fortune 44 — 13,955
Murphy 64

Chelsea (1) 3 **Scunthorpe** (1) 1
Kezman 26 — Hayes 8
Crosby 58 og — 40,019
Gudjohnsen 86

HAYES
9
23

Hayes highlights holes in the best Premier defence with an early strike and although Chelsea come back to leads Scunthorpe have enough chances to force a draw

Coventry (2) 3 **Crewe** (0) 0
McSheffrey 25,69 — 7,629
John 45

Derby (0) 2 **Wigan** (1) 1
Idiakez 71 — Mahon 30
Junior 79 — 14,457

Hartlepool (0) 0 **Boston** (0) 0
5,342

Hull City (0) 0 **Colchester** (2) 2
14,027
Williams 27
Fagan 29

Ipswich (0) 1 **Bolton** (0) 3
Miller 70
Giannakopoulos 60
Pedersen 65,68
20,080

Leicester (1) 2 **Blackpool** (1) 2
Edwards, R 15 og
Williams 82
Clarke 32
Southern 77
16,750

Luton (0) 0 **Brentford** (0) 2
6,861
Hargreaves 71
Tabb 89

Man Utd (0) 0 **Exeter** (0) 0
67,551

F.A. CUP
3rd ROUND
MANCHESTER UNITED
versus
EXETER CITY
OLD TRAFFORD
MANCHESTER

Exeter still dreaming as the Conference League side earn a draw at Old Trafford to go into the hat for the fourth round

Northampton (1) 1 **Southampton** (2) 3
Williamson 30
7,183
Phillips 29
Crouch 41
Redknapp 53

Notts County (1) 1 **Middlesbro** (0) 2
Scully 2
13,671
Doriva 54
Job 76

Nearly an hour in the lead for struggling Notts County as Boro's European pedigree is given a thorough test at Meadow Lane

Oldham (1) 1 **Man City** (0) 0
Vernon 14
13,171

Plymouth (1) 1 **Everton** (2) 3
Gudjonsson 34
20,112
Osman 16
McFadden 18, Chadwick 84

Portsmouth (0) 1 **Gillingham** (0) 0
Yakubu 49
14,252

Preston (0) 0 **West Brom** (0) 2
13,005
Earnshaw 76,83

QPR (0) 0 **Nottm Forest** (2) 3
11,140
Reid 24
Commons 25
Folly 82

Reading (0) 1 **Swansea** (1) 1
Ingimarsson 88
13,642
Connor 32

Rotherham (0) 0 **Yeovil** (0) 3
5,397
Jevons 61 pen
Way 87
Stolcers 90

Sheff Utd (0) 3 **Aston Villa** (0) 1
Cullip 55
Liddell 82,83
Barry 47
14,003

Blades fall behind to Barry early in the second half before Cullip levels to reflect the balance of play. Liddell's brace include a suspicion of offside and a mistake from Sorensen but sum up United's superiority

Sunderland (1) 2 **Crystal P** (1) 1
Welsh 44
Stewart 60 pen
Johnson 41
17,536

Tottenham (1) 2 **Brighton** (0) 1
King 40
Keane 83
Carpenter 48
36,094

Watford (1) 1 **Fulham** (1) 1
Helguson 42 pen
14,896
Knight 17

West Ham (0) 1 **Norwich** (0) 0
Harewood 81
23,389

Wimbledon (0) 0 **Peterborough** (1) 2
4,407
Logan 45
Arber 57

Wolves (2) 2 **Millwall** (0) 0
Seol 1
Cort 11
12,566

Yeading (0) 0 **Newcastle** (0) 2
10,824
Bowyer 51
Ameobi 61

3RD ROUND REPLAYS

Blackburn (2) 3 **Cardiff** (1) 2
Thompson 9,32
Pedersen 47
9,140
McAnuff 24
Collins 54

Blackpool (0) 0 **Leicester** (1) 1
6,938
Gudjonsson 16

Boston (0) 0 **Hartlepool** (0) 1
3,653
Boyd 72

Exeter (0) 0 **Man Utd** (1) 2
9,033
Ronaldo 9
Rooney 87

Fulham (1) 2 **Watford** (0) 0
Volz 13
Radzinski 65
11,306

Swansea (0) 0 **Reading** (0) 1
7,354
Forster 95
After Extra Time

4TH ROUND

Arsenal (0) 2 **Wolves** (0) 0
Vieira 53 pen
Ljungberg 82
37,153

Blackburn (2) 3 **Colchester** (0) 0
Watson 21 og
Johnson 27
Matteo 51
10,634

Davison connects with pure air as a back-pass bobble from Colchester colleague Watson sets Blackburn on their way and gives the media a new goalkeeping fall-guy

Brentford (0) 0 **Hartlepool** (0) 0
8,967

Burnley (1) 2 **Bournemouth** (0) 0
Moore 17,90
9,944

Charlton (1) 3 **Yeovil** (1) 2
Hughes 37
Jeffers 51
Bartlett 57
Terry 44
Davies 66
22,873

Chelsea (1) 2 **Birmingham** (0) 0
Huth 6
Terry 80
40,379

Derby (0) 1 **Fulham** (0) 1
Tudgay 56
22,040
John 71

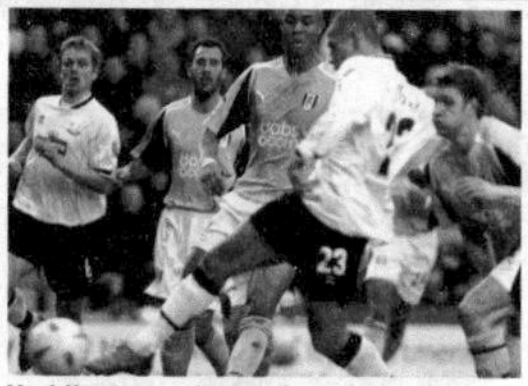

Huddlestone wins praise of manager Burley as Derby have the best of their tie with Fulham. Tudgay's half volley gives the Midlanders the lead before Fulham sub John levels

Everton (2) 3 **Sunderland** (0) 0
McFadden 9
Beattie 27
Cahill 80
33,186

McFadden takes his chance on a rare start for Everton, Beattie scores the first goal for his new club and Cahill adds a third as Sunderland are given a dose of Premiership quality

Man Utd (1) 3 **Middlesbro** (0) 0
O'Shea 10
Rooney 67,82
67,251

Rooney's a handful and destroys Boro with two of the 'best goals' he's ever scored – a chip and a volley

Newcastle (2) 3 **Coventry** (1) 1
Shearer 37
Ameobi 42
Babayaro 52
Adebola 45
44,044

Nottm Forest (1) 1 **Peterborough** (0) 0
King 10
16,774

Oldham (0) 0 **Bolton** (1) 1
12,029
Vaz Te 9

Reading (1) 1 **Leicester** (1) 2
Forster 10
14,825
Williams 32
Scowcroft 90

Southampton (0) 2 **Portsmouth** (0) 1
Oakley 54
Crouch 90 pen
Yakubu 56 pen
29,453

Cruel for Pompey when a controversial 90th minute penalty against fullback Taylor is converted by Crouch to give returning manager Redknapp local bragging rights

West Brom (1) 1 **Tottenham** (1) 1
Earnshaw 17
22,441
Defoe 31 pen

West Ham (1) 1 **Sheff Utd** (0) 1
Harewood 39
19,444
Jagielka 57

4TH ROUND REPLAYS

Fulham (1) 4 **Derby** (1) 2
Diop 45 pen
Boa Morte 50
John 94
Jensen 105
Rasiak 4
Peschisolido 86
15,528
After Extra Time

Hartlepool (0) 0 **Brentford** (0) 1
7,580
Rankin 48

Sheff Utd (1) 1 **West Ham** (0) 1
Liddell 8
15,067
Sheringham 63 pen
Sheff Utd win 3-1 on penalties

Tottenham (1) 3 **West Brom** (1) 1
Keane 44 pen
Defoe 50,55
Kanu 12
27,860

5TH ROUND

Arsenal	(0) **1**	**Sheff Utd**	(0) **1**
Pires 78			Gray 90 pen
36,891			

Bolton	(1) **1**	**Fulham**	(0) **0**
Davies 12			16,151

Burnley	(0) **0**	**Blackburn**	(0) **0**
			21,468

Charlton	(1) **1**	**Leicester**	(1) **2**
Bartlett 45			Dabizas 38
23,719			Dublin 90

Charlton choke again as league form fails to translate to the cup and Leicester's experienced pair of Dabizas and Dublin send the Championship side into the next round

Everton	(0) **0**	**Man Utd**	(1) **2**
38,664			Fortune 23
			Ronaldo 58

Newcastle	(1) **1**	**Chelsea**	(0) **0**
Kluivert 4			45,740

Kluivert shows his class guiding his header into the top corner of Chelsea's net as Mourinho's half-time substitutions misfire after Bridge is injured and Cudicini sent off

Southampton	(2) **2**	**Brentford**	(1) **2**
Camara 4,36			Rankin 40
24,741			Sodje 58

Sodje has Harry swearing with a headed equaliser for League One Brentford which sends Saints into a replay despite their two goal start in the first half

Tottenham	(1) **1**	**Nottm Forest**	(0) **1**
Defoe 45			Taylor 56
			35,640

Commons senses his moment to impress and tears into Spurs who struggle after taking the lead through a tame Defoe free-kick and are forced into a replay after Taylor equalises for Forest

5TH ROUND REPLAYS

Blackburn	(1) **2**	**Burnley**	(1) **1**
Tugay 31			Hyde 42
Pedersen 86			28,691

Brentford	(1) **1**	**Southampton**	(1) **3**
Hutchinson 4			Crouch 11,90
11,720			Phillips 66

Nottm Forest	(0) **0**	**Tottenham**	(0) **3**
28,062			Pamarot 60
			Keane 72
			Mido 90

Sheff Utd	(0) **0**	**Arsenal**	(0) **0**
			27,595

Arsenal win 4-2 on penalties

QUARTER-FINALS

Blackburn	(0) **1**	**Leicester**	(0) **0**
Dickov 83 pen			22,113

Dickov ignores taunts of his former club's supporters to fire his 83rd minute spot-kick home after Pedersen is sent sprawling by Kenton's tackle.It's a poor reward for Dublin who marshals Leicester's defence well to frustrate the Premiership team

Bolton	(0) **0**	**Arsenal**	(1) **1**
23,523			Ljungberg 3

Diouf damages his cause and damns Bolton to playing against Arsenal with ten men for 81 minutes. The Senegalese forward swings an arm at Lehmann to see red after Ljungberg's early strike and although Bolton battle hard there's no way past the Champions' young defence

Newcastle	(1) **1**	**Tottenham**	(0) **0**
Kluivert 5			51,307

Outplayed by Spurs but into the next round as Kluivert's early goal and Given's outstanding double save combine to help Newcastle progress

Southampton	(0) **0**	**Man Utd**	(2) **4**
30,971			Keane 2
			Ronaldo 45
			Scholes 48,87

Smith's the star for Saints but his saves only prevent Man United from turning a comfortable win into a complete rout. Keane beats the young keeper in the second minute before goals from Ronaldo and two from Scholes leave Redknapp to concentrate on relegation priorities

SEMI-FINALS

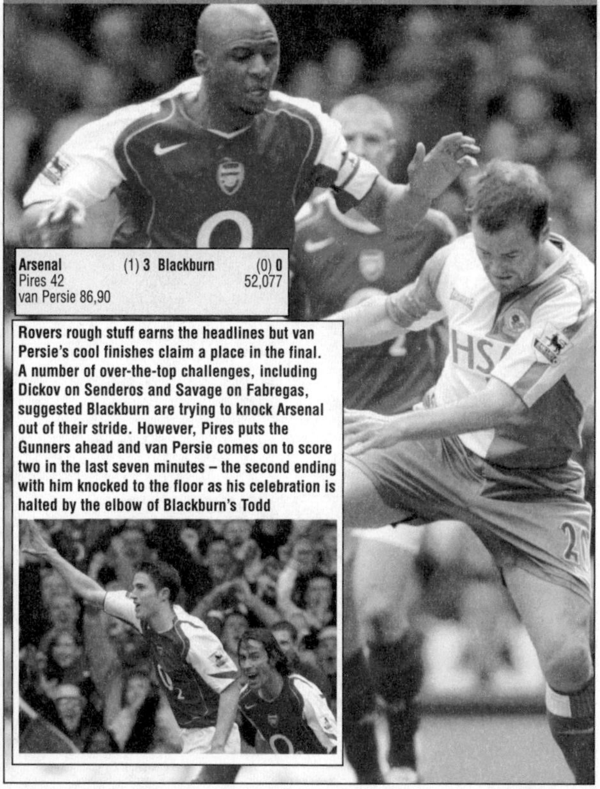

Arsenal (1) **3** **Blackburn** (0) **0**
Pires 42 52,077
van Persie 86,90

Rovers rough stuff earns the headlines but van Persie's cool finishes claim a place in the final. A number of over-the-top challenges, including Dickov on Senderos and Savage on Fabregas, suggested Blackburn are trying to knock Arsenal out of their stride. However, Pires puts the Gunners ahead and van Persie comes on to score two in the last seven minutes – the second ending with him knocked to the floor as his celebration is halted by the elbow of Blackburn's Todd

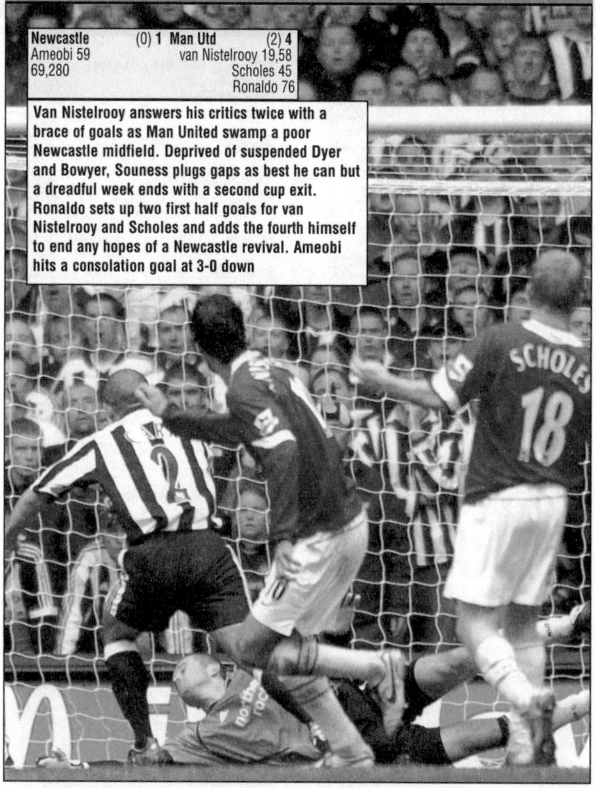
SCHOLES
18

Newcastle (0) **1** **Man Utd** (2) **4**
Ameobi 59 van Nistelrooy 19,58
69,280 Scholes 45
Ronaldo 76

Van Nistelrooy answers his critics twice with a brace of goals as Man United swamp a poor Newcastle midfield. Deprived of suspended Dyer and Bowyer, Souness plugs gaps as best he can but a dreadful week ends with a second cup exit. Ronaldo sets up two first half goals for van Nistelrooy and Scholes and adds the fourth himself to end any hopes of a Newcastle revival. Ameobi hits a consolation goal at 3-0 down

FINAL

Arsenal (0) **0** **Man Utd** (0) **0**
71,876
Arsenal win 5-4 on penalties

United pay the penalty for two open-goal misses, two strikes onto the woodwork and giving Lehmann a chance to grab Scholes' penalty and the headlines.
Ronaldo and Rooney open up Arsenal down the flanks, while Keane and the defence restrict them to one strike on goal, but Arsenal's youngsters show character to hang on.
And when it comes to the first-ever FA Cup to be decided by penalties they are faultless - despite losing Reyes to a second yellow card in the final second. Vieira takes the winning penalty to claim victory over United with the last kick of the top-flight domestic season

THE CARLING FOOTBALL LEAGUE CUP

1ST ROUND

Boston (1) 4 **Luton** (0) 3
Pitt 23 — Lee 52 og
Lee 57 — Nicholls 77 pen
Thompson 90,94 — Showunmi 90
2,631

Bradford (1) 1 **Notts County** (0) 2
Windass 6 pen — Richardson 64
3,517 — Ullathorne 105

Brighton (1) 1 **Bristol Rovers** (2) 2
Butters 11 — Thorpe 25
4,217 — Walker 30

Bury (2) 2 **Burnley** (2) 3
Mattis 12 — Mattis 17 og
Challinor 18 — Blake 33 pen,52
3,648

Colchester (1) 2 **Cheltenham** (0) 1
Fagan 12 — Devaney 70
Johnson 61 — 2,144

Coventry (0) 4 **Torquay** (0) 1
Hughes 51 — Osei-Kuffour 74
Suffo 63,66, Morrell 82 — 6,180

Crewe (4) 4 **Blackpool** (0) 1
Jones, S 3,44 — Taylor 75
Rivers 9, Ashton 12 — 2,994

Darlington (0) 0 **Barnsley** (1) 2
2,789 — Shuker 14, Reid 75 pen

Doncaster (1) 3 **Port Vale** (1) 1
Fortune-West 36 — Smith, D 25
Doolan 53, McIndoe 56 — 3,943

Gillingham (0) 1 **Northampton** (2) 2
Sidibe 56 — Sabin 32
3,108 — McGleish 41

Grimsby (1) 1 **Wigan** (0) 0
Parkinson 17 — 3,005

Hartlepool (0) 2 **Macclesfield** (0) 1
Boyd 79 — Parkin 48
Sweeney 87 — 2,883

Hull City (1) 2 **Wrexham** (2) 2
Keane 22 — Sam 14
France 66 — Ferguson 35
6,079
Wrexham win 3-1 on penalties

Ipswich (0) 2 **Brentford** (0) 0
Miller, T 73 — 10,190
Westlake 90

Kidderminster (1) 1 **Cardiff** (1) 1
Brown 32 — Earnshaw 28
1,897
Cardiff win 5-4 on penalties

Leeds (1) 1 **Huddersfield** (0) 0
Pugh 23 — 30,115

Leyton Orient (1) 1 **Bournemouth** (1) 3
Steele 12 — Browning 33
1,705 — Cummings 64
Hayter 71

Lincoln (0) 3 **Derby** (1) 1
Taylor-Fletcher 79 pen — Idiakez 28
Yeo 80, McCombe 90 — 4,982

Mansfield (0) 0 **Preston** (3) 4
3,208 — Cresswell 3
Alexander 9
Daley 31, Lynch 84

Nottm Forest (1) 2 **Scunthorpe** (0) 0
Taylor 36 — 7,344
King 78

Oldham (0) 2 **Stoke** (1) 1
Eyres, D 72 — Asaba 25
Eyre, J 76 pen — 2,861

Oxford (0) 0 **Reading** (0) 2
5,919 — Goater 62
Hughes 77

Peterborough (0) 0 **MK Dons** (0) 3
2,886 — McLeod 63
Smart 80, Kamara 90

QPR (1) 3 **Swansea** (0) 0
Cureton 39 — 4,882
Rowlands 77
Gallen 90

Rochdale (2) 2 **Wolves** (1) 4
Holt 4 — Ince 42
Tait 26 — Clarke 53
3,292 — Miller 60
Andrews 78

Rotherham (1) 2 **Chesterfield** (1) 1
Proctor 33 — Allott 15
Barker, R 83 — 3,845

Rushden & D (0) 0 **Swindon** (0) 1
1,672 — Hewlett 90

Sheff Utd (1) 4 **Stockport** (1) 1
Morgan 36 — Harley 2 og
Cutler 108 og — 5,399
Tonge 112
Lester 116

Sheff Wed (1) 1 **Walsall** (0) 0
Peacock 20 — 8,959

Sunderland (1) 3 **Chester** (0) 0
Hessey 41 og — 11,450
Kyle 55, Caldwell 69

Tranmere (0) 2 **Shrewsbury** (0) 1
Zola 49 — Rodgers 67
McAteer 80 — 4,489

Watford (0) 1 **Cambridge** (0) 0
Ferrell 82 — 6,558

West Ham (1) 2 **Southend** (0) 0
Harewood 11,90 — 16,910

Wycombe (0) 0 **Bristol City** (0) 1
1,778 — Lita 70

Yeovil (1) 3 **Plymouth** (2) 2
Johnson 28,69,102 — Crawford 30
6,217 — Wotton 42 pen

2ND ROUND

Aston Villa (2) 3 **QPR** (0) 1
Vassell 29 — McLeod 48
Angel 38 — 26,975
Solano 78

Birmingham (0) 3 **Lincoln** (0) 1
Gronkjaer 64 — Yeo 84 pen
Morrison 77 — 14,500
Savage 80 pen

Blackburn (1) 3 **Bournemouth** (1) 3
Emerton 8 — O'Connor 13
Pedersen 90 — Broadhurst 82
Gallagher 91 — Spicer 115
7,226
Bournemouth win 7-6 on penalties

Boston (0) 1 **Fulham** (3) 4
Beevers 56 — Radzinski 9,70
5,373 — Malbranque 28
McBride 34

Bristol City (0) 2 **Everton** (2) 2
Stubbs 50 og — Ferguson 30 pen
Lita 53 — Chadwick 45
15,264
Everton win 4-3 on penalties

Burnley (0) 1 **Wolves** (1) 1
Blake 50 — Seol 45
5,013
Burnley win 4-2 on penalties

Colchester (1) 2 **West Brom** (0) 1
Fagan 29 — Horsfield 50
May 118 — 4,591

Coventry (1) 1 **Sheff Wed** (0) 0
Doyle 36 — 8,362

Crewe (1) 3 **Sunderland** (1) 3
Jones, S 19 — Brown 37,83
Ashton 64 — Elliott 103
Foster 119 — 3,804
Crewe win 4-2 on penalties

Crystal P (0) 2 **Hartlepool** (0) 1
Freedman 80 — Williams, E 70
Soares 110 — 4,233

Doncaster (1) 2 **Ipswich** (0) 0
Ravenhill 6 — 6,020
McSporran 46

Grimsby (0) 0 **Charlton** (1) 2
5,735 — Murphy 8, Jeffers 79

Leeds (1) 1 **Swindon** (0) 0
Ricketts 9 — 18,476

Leicester (0) 2 **Preston** (1) 3
Gudjonsson 68 pen — Cresswell 34,90 pen,113
Blake 75 — 6,751

Man City (5) 7 **Barnsley** (0) 1
Barton 21 — Conlon 47
Macken 28,45 — 19,578
Flood 33
Wright-Phillips, S 36
Sibierski 56,84

MK Dons (0) 1 **Cardiff** (3) 4
McLeod 85 — Thorne 14,21
2,266 — Bullock 19, Anthony 72

Northampton (0) 0 **Southampton** (2) 3
6,343 — Phillips 32
Prutton 35
McCann 65

Norwich (1) 1 **Bristol Rovers** (0) 0
Safri 45 — 18,658

Nottm Forest (1) 2 **Rotherham** (1) 1
Taylor 17,94 — Sedgwick 9
11,168

Oldham (0) 0 **Tottenham** (1) 6
8,548 — Kanoute 37,90
Keane 64, Defoe 71
Bunjevcevic 87, Gardner 90

Reading (0) 0 **Watford** (1) 3
8,429 — Cox 14 pen
Bouazza 90
Ingimarsson 90 og

Tranmere (0) 0 **Portsmouth** (0) 1
6,966 — Kamara 65

West Ham (1) 3 **Notts County** (1) 2
Zamora 1,54 — Wilson 13
Rebrov 62 — Richardson 57
11,111

Zamora (pictured celebrating with Harewood) strikes twice for West Ham but Rebrov scores the winner

Wrexham (2) 2 **Sheff Utd** (1) 3
Morgan 6 — Gray 21,69
Llewellyn 45 — Jagielka, P 54
3,423

Yeovil (0) 0 **Bolton** (0) 2
8,047 — Julio Cesar 80
Pedersen 87

3RD ROUND

Birmingham (0) 0 **Fulham** (0) 1
26,371 — Pembridge 76

Bolton (1) 3 **Tottenham** (1) 4
King 27 og — Defoe 44,103
Okocha 75 pen — Bunjevcevic 84
Ferdinand 105 — Brown 95
18,037

Bournemouth (1) 3 **Cardiff** (1) 3
Hayter 8,90 — Lee 24
Stock 118 — Bullock 49
5,598 — Jerome 108
Cardiff win 5-4 on penalties

Burnley (1) 3 **Aston Villa** (0) 1
Branch 9 — Angel 81
Camara 65 — 11,184
Valois 86

Charlton (1) 1 **Crystal P** (1) 2
Hreidarsson 5 — Freedman 41
19,030 — Torghelle 54

Chelsea (0) 1 **West Ham** (0) 0
Kezman 57 — 41,774

Crewe (0) 0 **Man Utd** (1) 3
10,103 — Smith 10
Miller 57
Foster 59 og

Doncaster (0) 0 **Nottm Forest** (1) 2
9,261 — King 33, Perch 63

Everton (0) 2 **Preston** (0) 0
Carsley 52 — 33,922
Bent 90

Man City (0) 1 **Arsenal** (0) 2
Fowler 90 — van Persie 78
21,708 — Karabassiyoon 90

Middlesbro (2) 3 **Coventry** (0) 0
Nemeth 4 — 11,833
Morrison 25
Graham 70

Millwall (0) 0 **Liverpool** (1) 3
17,655 — Diao 18
Baros 70,90

Newcastle (2) 2 **Norwich** (0) 1
Jenas 2 — Huckerby 56 pen
Ameobi 42 pen — 42,153

Portsmouth (2) 2 **Leeds** (1) 1
Kamara 14 — Deane 40
Berkovic 32 pen — 15,215

Sheff Utd (0) 0 **Watford** (0) 0
7,689
Watford win 4-2 on penalties

Southampton (0) 3 **Colchester** (1) 2
Blackstock 50,54,80 — Danns 7
20,588 — Halford 64

4TH ROUND

Arsenal (1) 3 **Everton** (1) 1
Owusu-Abeyie 25 — Gravesen 7
Lupoli 52,85 — 27,791

Burnley (0) 0 **Tottenham** (1) 3
10,639 — Keane 31,52
Defoe 58

Cardiff (0) 0 **Portsmouth** (0) 2
13,555 — Yakubu 47,55 pen

Liverpool (0) 2 **Middlesbro** (0) 0
Mellor 83,89 — 28,176

Man Utd (2) 2 **Crystal P** (0) 0
Saha 22 — 48,891
Richardson 39

Newcastle (0) 0 **Chelsea** (0) 2
38,055 — Gudjohnsen 100
Robben 112

Nottm Forest (0) 2 **Fulham** (0) 4
King 71 — Radzinski 86,93
Reid 104 — McBride 101
9,252 — Cole 119

Watford (1) 5 **Southampton** (0) 2
Dyer 39 — Blackstock 84
Chambers, J 52,62 — Ormerod 88
Helguson 66 — 13,008
Bouazza 84

Dyer scores the first goal for Watford to open the floodgates against hapless Saints

QUARTER-FINALS

Fulham	(0) 1	Chelsea	(0) 2
McBride 74			Duff 55
14,531			Lampard 88

Chelsea battle on four fronts reaching the semi-finals despite six changes from the league side. A Duff deflection earns the lead with McBride replying for Fulham before a tame Lampard shot eludes van der Sar

Watford	(1) 3	Portsmouth	(0) 0
Helguson 24,57			18,877
Dyer 61			

Helguson take two as Watford's striker scores twice for the Herts side to despatch a second South Coast Premiership team in the Carling Cup

Man Utd	(1) 1	Arsenal	(0) 0
Bellion 1			67,103

Bellion (shown under a sea of congratulating team-mates) bobbles a first minute shot through the hands of Arsenal's Manuel Almunia to put Man United Reserves in front against Arsenal's kids. It is enough.

Tottenham	(0) 1	Liverpool	(0) 1
Defoe 108			Sinama-Pongolle 117 pen
			36,100

A weakened Liverpool side still musters the resolve to hang in against Spurs and equalise Defoe's extra-time goal through Sinama Pongolle before winning on penalties, putting both managers (pictured) through it

SEMI-FINALS

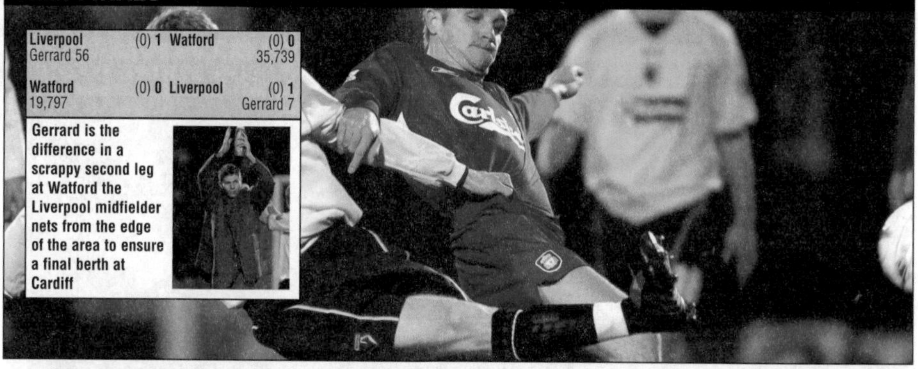

Liverpool	(0) 1	Watford	(0) 0
Gerrard 56			35,739
Watford	(0) 0	Liverpool	(0) 1
19,797			Gerrard 7

Gerrard is the difference in a scrappy second leg at Watford the Liverpool midfielder nets from the edge of the area to ensure a final berth at Cardiff

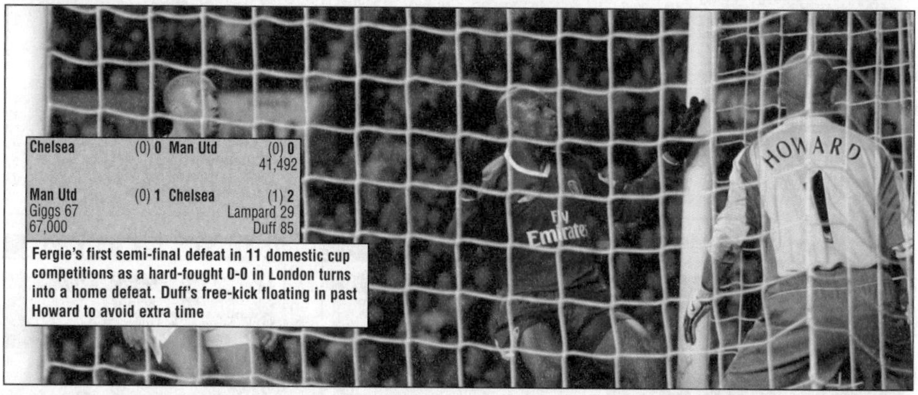
HOWARD

Chelsea	(0) 0	Man Utd	(0) 0
			41,492
Man Utd	(0) 1	Chelsea	(1) 2
Giggs 67			Lampard 29
67,000			Duff 85

Fergie's first semi-final defeat in 11 domestic cup competitions as a hard-fought 0-0 in London turns into a home defeat. Duff's free-kick floating in past Howard to avoid extra time

FINAL

CARLING CUP

Liverpool	(1) 2	Chelsea	(0) 3
Riise 1			Gerrard 79 og
Nunez 113			Drogba 107
78,000			Kezman 112

Gerrard nets for Chelsea but into his own Liverpool net as he provides an unlikely route back for the Blues with 11 minutes remaining. This takes the game to extra time after Riise's goal in the first minute.
In extra time new recruits Drogba and Kezman mark their first season in the Premiership with cup final goals in Cardiff and Chelsea look comfortable despite a consolation strike from Nunez.
Mourinho still managers to get in the limelight with a hushing gesture which angers Liverpool fans but Chelsea are well worth their first silverware of the season.

CHAMPIONSHIP ROUND-UP

FINAL LEAGUE TABLE

	HOME						AWAY					TOTAL			
	P	W	D	L	F	A	W	D	L	F	A	F	A	DIF	PTS
Sunderland	46	16	4	3	45	21	13	3	7	31	20	76	41	35	94
Wigan	46	13	5	5	42	15	12	7	4	37	20	79	35	44	87
Ipswich	46	17	3	3	53	26	7	10	6	32	30	85	56	29	85
Derby	46	10	7	6	38	30	12	3	8	33	30	71	60	11	76
Preston	46	14	7	2	44	22	7	5	11	23	36	67	58	9	75
West Ham	46	12	5	6	36	24	9	5	9	30	32	66	56	10	73
Reading	46	13	7	3	33	15	6	6	11	18	29	51	44	7	70
Sheff Utd	46	9	7	7	28	23	9	6	8	29	33	57	56	1	67
Wolverhampton	46	9	11	3	40	26	6	10	7	32	33	72	59	13	66
Millwall	46	12	5	6	33	22	6	7	10	18	23	51	45	6	66
QPR	46	10	7	6	32	26	7	4	12	22	32	54	58	-4	62
Stoke	46	11	2	10	22	18	6	8	9	14	20	36	38	-2	61
Burnley	46	10	7	6	26	19	5	8	10	12	20	38	39	-1	60
Leeds	46	7	10	6	28	26	7	8	8	21	26	49	52	-3	60
Leicester	46	8	8	7	24	20	4	13	6	25	26	49	46	3	57
Cardiff	46	10	4	9	24	19	3	11	9	24	32	48	51	-3	54
Plymouth	46	9	8	6	31	23	5	3	15	21	41	52	64	-12	53
Watford	46	5	10	8	25	25	7	6	10	27	34	52	59	-7	52
Coventry	46	8	7	8	32	28	5	6	12	29	45	61	73	-12	52
Brighton	46	7	7	9	24	29	6	5	12	16	36	40	65	-25	51
Crewe	46	6	8	9	37	38	6	6	11	29	48	66	86	-20	50
Gillingham	46	10	6	7	22	23	2	8	13	23	43	45	66	-21	50
Nottm Forest	46	7	10	6	26	28	2	7	14	16	38	42	66	-24	44
Rotherham	46	2	7	14	17	34	3	7	13	18	35	35	69	-34	29

CLUB STRIKE FORCE

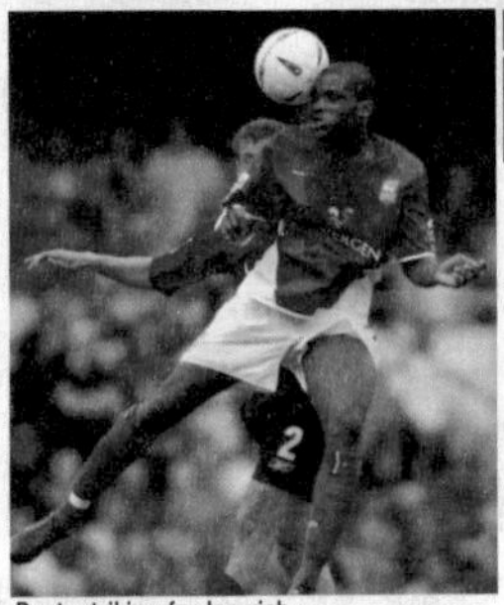

Bent; striking for Ipswich

Goals scored in the League	85
Goals scored in all competitions	90
Shots on target (SoT) Shots on target hit by the team recorded in League games	367

1 Ipswich

Club Strike Rate (CSR) Average number of minutes between League goals scored by club	49

	CLUB	LGE	ALL	SoT	CSR
1	Ipswich	85	90	367	49
2	Wigan	79	80	337	52
3	Sunderland	76	84	304	54
4	Derby	71	77	310	58
5	Wolverhampton	72	79	272	58
6	Preston	67	76	270	62
7	Crewe	66	73	207	63
8	West Ham	66	79	244	63
9	Coventry	61	70	249	68
10	Sheff Utd	57	70	300	73
11	QPR	54	58	212	77
12	Plymouth	52	55	282	80
13	Watford	52	65	230	80
14	Millwall	51	53	203	81
15	Reading	51	56	218	81
16	Leeds	49	52	253	84
17	Leicester	49	58	285	84
18	Cardiff	48	59	246	86
19	Gillingham	45	46	215	92
20	Nottm Forest	42	55	223	99
21	Brighton	40	42	184	104
22	Burnley	38	49	170	109
23	Stoke	36	38	210	115
24	Rotherham	35	38	196	118

CLUB DISCIPLINARY RECORDS

Powell; adds to Forest's card total

League Yellow	88
League Red	8
League Total	96
All Competitions Yellow	103
All Competitions Red	8
TOTAL ALL COMPETITIONS	111

1 Nottm Forest

Cards Average in League Average number of minutes between a card being shown of either colour	43

	CLUB	LEAGUE		TOTAL		AVE
1	Nottm Forest	88Y	8R	103 Y	8R	43
2	Leeds	87	7	89	7	44
3	Millwall	85	8	91	8	45
4	Leicester	81	8	93	8	47
5	Stoke	80	6	86	7	48
6	Burnley	74	4	84	4	53
7	QPR	72	5	74	5	54
8	Sunderland	73	2	80	2	55
9	Gillingham	69	4	69	4	57
10	West Ham	67	6	81	6	57
11	Preston	67	4	80	6	58
12	Rotherham	69	1	78	1	59
13	Brighton	64	5	68	5	60
14	Coventry	59	3	62	3	67
15	Plymouth	59	3	62	3	67
16	Watford	58	2	62	2	69
17	Derby	56	3	64	3	70
18	Sheff Utd	52	5	61	6	73
19	Wolverhampton	55	2	58	2	73
20	Ipswich	54	1	58	1	75
21	Cardiff	50	4	63	6	77
22	Wigan	48	1	52	1	84
23	Reading	41	0	47	1	101
24	Crewe	25	1	26	1	159

CLUB DEFENCES

1 Wigan

Club Defensive Rate (CDR) Average number of minutes between League goals conceded by club	118

	CLUB	LGE	ALL	CS	SoT	CDR
1	Wigan	35	38	20	184	118
2	Stoke	38	42	20	239	109
3	Burnley	39	48	19	231	106
4	Sunderland	41	48	18	206	101
5	Reading	44	50	19	244	94
6	Millwall	45	54	15	196	92
7	Leicester	46	54	15	242	90
8	Cardiff	51	62	12	207	81
9	Leeds	52	57	11	250	80
10	Ipswich	56	65	11	269	74
11	Sheff Utd	56	63	14	221	74
12	West Ham	56	63	14	189	74
13	Preston	58	65	12	230	71
14	QPR	58	64	15	195	71
15	Watford	59	66	14	283	70
16	Wolverhampton	59	64	7	225	70
17	Derby	60	71	14	257	69
18	Plymouth	64	70	13	193	65
19	Brighton	65	69	11	285	64
20	Gillingham	66	69	8	323	63
21	Nottm Forest	66	75	12	305	63
22	Rotherham	69	75	8	330	60
23	Coventry	73	80	6	298	57
24	Crewe	86	96	4	385	48

Eaden; clearing for Wigan

Goals conceded in the League	35
Goals conceded in all competitions	38
Clean Sheets (CS) Number of league games where no goals were conceded	20
Shots on Target Against (SoT) Shots on Target conceded by team in League games	184

STADIUM CAPACITY AND HOME CROWDS

	TEAM	CAPACITY	AVE	HIGH	LOW
1	Brighton	7053	91.11	6848	5996
2	Wolverhampton	29400	90.54	28516	24336
3	QPR	18500	86.79	18363	13559
4	Ipswich	30300	84.66	30003	21246
5	Plymouth	20922	78.48	20555	13308
6	Nottm Forest	30602	77	28887	19209
7	West Ham	35647	76.87	33482	22031
8	Derby	33597	75.06	31237	22096
9	Leicester	32500	74.27	30231	21249
10	Gillingham	11582	73.63	10810	6089
11	Crewe	10066	73.54	9269	5409
12	Leeds	40204	72.65	34496	24585
13	Reading	24200	70.95	23203	11404
14	Coventry	23627	67.87	22728	11966
15	Watford	22100	65.25	19673	11084
16	Cardiff	20000	64.88	17006	10007
17	Rotherham	9707	64.61	9050	3804
18	Sheff Utd	30936	63.34	22959	16079
19	Preston	22225	62.49	20221	10339
20	Sunderland	48300	59.67	47350	22267
21	Millwall	20146	58.72	19025	8835
22	Stoke	28218	58.39	23029	12785
23	Burnley	22546	55.29	17789	7200
24	Wigan	25000	46.25	20745	7547

Key: Average. The percentage of each stadium filled in League games over the season (AVE), the stadium capacity and the highest and lowest crowds recorded.

AWAY ATTENDANCE

	TEAM	AVE	HIGH	LOW
1	Leeds	84.18	43253	6716
2	West Ham	79.41	34115	6819
3	Nottm Forest	75.43	32270	6704
4	Sunderland	74.89	33482	6026
5	Wigan	74.01	28286	6306
6	Derby	73.68	30459	6587
7	Ipswich	73.41	31723	5504
8	Wolverhampton	72.88	29773	6693
9	QPR	71.39	31365	5387
10	Sheff Utd	71.19	28936	6418
11	Stoke	70.28	47350	5925
12	Plymouth	68.71	34496	5088
13	Preston	68.7	31237	5996
14	Reading	68.49	34237	3804
15	Leicester	68.49	34815	6089
16	Coventry	68.08	29424	5742
17	Burnley	67.54	27490	6109
18	Brighton	67.53	29514	6549
19	Cardiff	67.14	32788	5093
20	Rotherham	65.96	30900	6076
21	Millwall	65.92	28221	5062
22	Crewe	65.55	32303	4498
23	Watford	65.11	25060	5438
24	Gillingham	64.36	27995	4367

Key: Average. How close each club has come to filling grounds in its away league matches (AVE) and the highest and lowest crowds recorded.

CHART-TOPPING MIDFIELDERS

JJB

1 McCulloch - Wigan	
Goals scored in the League	14
Defensive Rating Av number of mins between League goals conceded while on the pitch	120
Contribution to Attacking Power Average number of minutes between League team goals while on pitch	48
Scoring Difference Defensive Rating minus Contribution to Attacking Power	72

	PLAYER	CLUB	GOALS	DEF RATE	POWER	S DIFF
1	McCulloch	Wigan	14	120	48	72
2	Mahon	Wigan	7	119	53	66
3	Bullard	Wigan	3	119	54	65
4	Robinson	Sunderland	4	107	51	56
5	Whitehead	Sunderland	5	105	56	49
6	Teale	Wigan	3	96	49	47
7	Arca	Sunderland	9	95	53	42
8	Whitley	Sunderland	0	95	57	38
9	Sedgwick	Preston	3	84	48	36
10	Sweeney	Millwall	2	110	75	35
11	O'Connor	Burnley	2	133	104	29
12	Magilton	Ipswich	3	73	45	28
13	Westlake	Ipswich	7	76	48	28
14	Miller	Ipswich	13	75	48	27
15	Cameron	Wolverhampton	3	80	54	26

CHART-TOPPING GOALSCORERS

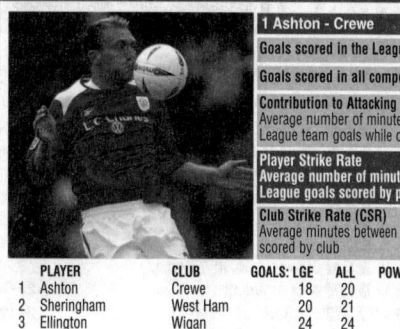

1 Ashton - Crewe	
Goals scored in the League (GL)	18
Goals scored in all competitions (GA)	20
Contribution to Attacking Power (AP) Average number of minutes between League team goals while on pitch	47
Player Strike Rate Average number of minutes between League goals scored by player	111
Club Strike Rate (CSR) Average minutes between League goals scored by club	63

	PLAYER	CLUB	GOALS: LGE	ALL	POWER	CSR	S RATE
1	Ashton	Crewe	18	20	47	63	111
2	Sheringham	West Ham	20	21	55	63	122
3	Ellington	Wigan	24	24	51	52	156
4	Kitson	Reading	19	19	74	81	168
5	Elliott	Sunderland	15	16	46	54	174
6	Kuqi	Ipswich	19	20	48	49	178
7	Furlong	QPR	19	19	69	77	182
8	Webber	Watford	12	12	70	80	182
9	Miller	Wolverhampton	19	20	59	58	187
10	Rasiak	Derby	16	17	58	58	190
12	Stewart	Sunderland	16	17	61	54	195
13	Bent	Ipswich	20	20	47	49	197
14	John	Coventry	11	12	65	68	202
15	Hayles	Millwall	12	12	67	81	203

CHART-TOPPING DEFENDERS

Britannia

1 Duberry - Stoke	
Goals Conceded in the League The number of League goals conceded while he was on the pitch	17
Goals Conceded in all competitions The number of goals conceded while he was on the pitch in all competitions	17
Clean Sheets In games when he played at least 70 mins	11
Defensive Rating Average number of minutes between League goals conceded while on pitch	132
Club Defensive Rating Average mins between League goals conceded by the club this season	109

	PLAYER	CLUB	CON: LGE	ALL	CS	CDR	DEF RATE
1	Duberry	Stoke	17	17	11	109	132
2	Cahill	Burnley	20	25	12	106	121
3	Eaden	Wigan	25	26	15	118	120
4	Jackson	Wigan	26	26	15	118	119
5	Breckin	Wigan	32	35	18	118	118
6	Duff	Burnley	27	36	15	106	117
7	Phillips	Millwall	20	22	9	92	113
8	Baines	Wigan	32	33	17	118	113
9	Halls	Stoke	16	19	8	109	111
10	Hill	Stoke	25	27	15	109	109
11	Sinclair	Burnley	29	34	15	106	107
12	McCartney	Sunderland	30	34	15	101	107
13	McGreal	Burnley	33	36	16	106	105
14	Camara	Burnley	39	48	18	106	104
15	Heath	Leicester	16	20	5	90	103

CHART-TOPPING GOALKEEPERS

1 Filan - Wigan	
Goals conceded in the League (CL)	35
Goals conceded in all comps (CA)	37
Counting Games League games when he played at least 70 minutes	46
Clean Sheets In games when he played at least 70 mins	20
Goals to Shots Ratio (GSR) The average number of shots on target per each League goal conceded	5.3
Defensive Rating Average number of minutes between League goals conceded while on pitch	118

	PLAYER	CLUB	CG	CON: LGE	ALL	CS	GSR	DEF RATE
1	Filan	Wigan	46	35	37	20	5.3	118
2	Simonsen	Stoke	29	23	27	14	6.5	116
3	Jensen	Burnley	26	21	27	11	7.2	114
4	Stack	Millwall	26	23	32	9	4.7	98
5	de Goey	Stoke	15	15	15	6	6.7	98
6	Coyne	Burnley	19	18	21	8	4.7	96
7	Alexander	Cardiff	17	16	20	5	4.8	96
8	Myhre	Sunderland	29	28	35	11	5	95
9	Hahnemann	Reading	46	44	50	19	5.5	94
10	Marshall	Millwall	22	22	22	6	4.3	86
11	Lonergan	Preston	22	25	29	6	4.6	81
12	Sullivan	Leeds	46	52	57	11	4.8	80
13	Walker	Leicester	22	25	28	5	4.2	79
14	Brown	Gillingham	17	20	22	6	5.6	77
15	Kuipers	Brighton	30	36	40	9	5.2	75

PLAYER DISCIPLINARY RECORD

DUNNE
27

4 Dunne - Millwall	
Cards Average mins between cards	162
League Yellow	6
League Red	2
TOTAL	8

	PLAYER		LY	LR	TOT	AVE
1	Powell	Nottm Forest	6	1	7	120
2	Thornton	Sunderland	5	0	5	120
3	Davies	QPR	4	1	5	153
4	Dunne	Millwall	6	2	8	162
5	Tiatto	Leicester	13	0	13	168
6	McCarthy	Leicester	6	0	6	170
7	Brevett	West Ham	4	1	5	172
8	Wise	Millwall	9	0	9	175
9	Johnson,L	Gillingham	3	0	3	183
10	Hulse	Leeds	6	0	6	189
11	Impey	Nottm Forest	7	1	8	192
12	Ricketts	Leeds	4	0	4	194
13	Derry	Leeds	2	1	3	203
14	Sinclair	Burnley	14	1	15	206
15	Serioux	Millwall	3	1	4	216
16	Hjelde	Nottm Forest	4	1	5	216
17	Vincent	Derby	5	1	6	221
18	Sherwood	Coventry	4	0	4	222
19	Gregan	Leeds	14	0	14	222
20	Carey	Coventry	8	1	9	223
21	Robinson	Cardiff	3	0	3	228
22	Lee	Cardiff	9	1	10	231
23	Dawson	Nottm Forest	5	0	5	234
24	Harris	Nottm Forest	2	0	2	235

TEAM OF THE SEASON

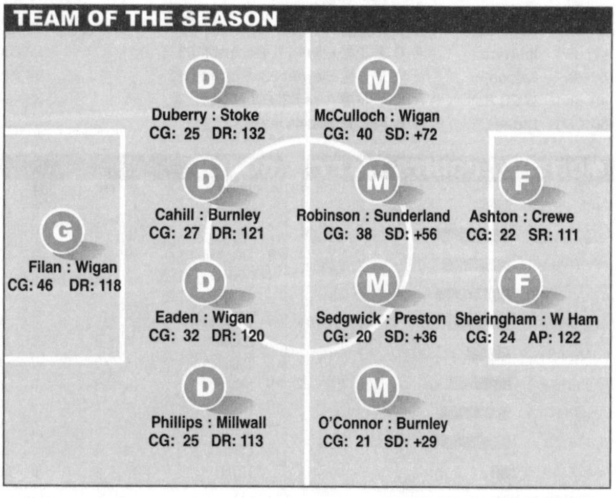
D
Duberry : Stoke
CG: 25 DR: 132
M
McCulloch : Wigan
CG: 40 SD: +72
G
Filan : Wigan
CG: 46 DR: 118
D
Cahill : Burnley
CG: 27 DR: 121
M
Robinson : Sunderland
CG: 38 SD: +56
F
Ashton : Crewe
CG: 22 SR: 111
D
Eaden : Wigan
CG: 32 DR: 120
M
Sedgwick : Preston
CG: 20 SD: +36
F
Sheringham : W Ham
CG: 24 AP: 122
D
Phillips : Millwall
CG: 25 DR: 113
M
O'Connor : Burnley
CG: 21 SD: +29

COCA-COLA CHAMPIONSHIP CHAMPIONS

SUNDERLAND

Final Position: **1st**

NICKNAME: MACKEMS/BLACKCATS   KEY: ☐ Won ☐ Drawn ☐ Lost

							Attendance
1	div1	Coventry	A	L	0-2		16,460
2	div1	Crewe	H	W	3-1	Robinson 12; Stewart 67; Elliott 90	22,341
3	div1	QPR	H	D	2-2	Stewart 33; Caldwell 90	26,063
4	div1	Plymouth	A	L	1-2	Stewart 71	16,874
5	ccr1	Chester	H	W	3-0	Hessey 41 og; Kyle 55; Caldwell 69	11,450
6	div1	Wigan	H	D	1-1	Elliott 82	26,330
7	div1	Reading	A	L	0-1		15,792
8	div1	Gillingham	A	W	4-0	Stewart 4,20,68; Elliott 17	8,775
9	div1	Nottm Forest	H	W	2-0	Arca 4; Wright 11	23,540
10	div1	Preston	H	W	3-1	Elliott 27,52; Carter 45	24,264
11	ccr2	Crewe	A	L	3-3*	Brown 37,83; Elliott 103 (*aet, lost 4-2 on penalties)	3,804
12	div1	Leeds	A	W	1-0	Robinson 65	28,926
13	div1	Sheff Utd	A	L	0-1		17,908
14	div1	Derby	H	D	0-0		29,881
15	div1	Millwall	H	W	1-0	Muscat 72 og	23,839
16	div1	Watford	A	D	1-1	Elliott 22	13,198
17	div1	Rotherham	A	W	1-0	Whitehead 61	6,026
18	div1	Brighton	H	W	2-0	Arca 64; Lawrence 82 pen	25,532
19	div1	Wolverhampton	H	W	3-1	Lawrence 57,80; Elliott 68	23,925
20	div1	Millwall	A	L	0-2		10,513
21	div1	Leicester	A	W	1-0	Caldwell 69	25,897
22	div1	Ipswich	H	W	2-0	Elliott 60; Brown 75	31,723
23	div1	Stoke	A	W	1-0	Bridges 83	16,980
24	div1	West Ham	H	L	0-2		29,510
25	div1	Cardiff	A	W	2-0	Whitehead 67; Lawrence 77	12,528
26	div1	Burnley	H	W	2-1	Arca 35; Lawrence 52	27,102
27	div1	Leeds	H	L	2-3	Lawrence 43 pen; Arca 90	43,253
28	div1	Nottm Forest	A	W	2-1	Elliott 49; Stewart 90	27,457
29	div1	Preston	A	L	2-3	Elliott 72; Thornton 81	16,940
30	div1	Gillingham	H	D	1-1	Brown 19	27,147
31	facr3	Crystal Palace	H	W	2-1	Welsh 44; Stewart 60 pen	17,536
32	div1	Derby	A	W	2-0	Elliott 51; Whitehead 66	22,995
33	div1	Sheff Utd	H	W	1-0	Stewart 44	27,337
34	facr4	Everton	A	L	0-3		33,186
35	div1	Wolverhampton	A	D	1-1	Elliott 12	26,968
36	div1	Watford	H	W	4-2	Stewart 18,33 pen,51; Brown 73	24,948
37	div1	Brighton	A	L	1-2	Arca 80	6,647
38	div1	Rotherham	H	W	4-1	Whitehead 13; Thornton 36,73; Breen 49	22,267
39	div1	Cardiff	H	W	2-1	Breen 4; Stewart 42	32,788
40	div1	Burnley	A	W	2-0	Lawrence 26; Stewart 89	12,103
41	div1	Crewe	A	W	1-0	Elliott 58	7,949
42	div1	Plymouth	H	W	5-1	Whitehead 31; Arca 40; Stewart 45 pen; Caldwell 75; Thornton 90	25,258
43	div1	Coventry	H	W	1-0	Brown 76	29,424
44	div1	QPR	A	W	3-1	Welsh 46; Brown 63; Arca 75	18,198
45	div1	Wigan	A	W	1-0	Stewart 3	20,745
46	div1	Reading	H	L	1-2	Arca 52	34,237
47	div1	Ipswich	A	D	2-2	Elliott 71; Robinson 83	29,230
48	div1	Leicester	H	W	2-1	Stewart 23; Caldwell 60	34,815
49	div1	West Ham	A	W	2-1	Arca 52; Elliott 68	33,482
50	div1	Stoke	H	W	1-0	Robinson 57	47,350

KEY PLAYERS - GOALSCORERS

Stephen Elliott

Goals in the League	15
Goals in all competitions	16
Contribution to Attacking Power Average number of minutes between League team goals while on pitch	46
Player Strike Rate Average number of minutes between League goals scored by player	174
Club Strike Rate Average number of minutes between League goals scored by club	54

	PLAYER	GOALS LGE	GOALS ALL	POWER	S RATE
1	Stephen Elliott	15	16	46	174 mins
2	Marcus Stewart	16	17	61	195 mins
3	Liam Lawrence	7	7	62	275 mins
4	Julio Arca	9	9	53	371 mins
5	Dean Whitehead	5	5	55	690 mins

KEY PLAYERS - MIDFIELDERS

Carl Robinson

Goals in the League	4
Goals in all competitions	4
Defensive Rating Average number of mins between League goals conceded while on the pitch	107
Contribution to Attacking Power Average number of minutes between League team goals while on pitch	51
Scoring Difference Defensive Rating minus Contribution to Attacking Power	56

	PLAYER	GOALS LGE	GOALS ALL	DEF RATE	ATT POWER	SCORE DIFF
1	Carl Robinson	4	4	107	51	56 mins
2	Dean Whitehead	5	5	105	56	49 mins
3	Julio Arca	9	9	95	53	42 mins
4	Jeff Whitley	0	0	95	57	38 mins
5	Liam Lawrence	7	7	92	62	30 mins

KEY PLAYERS - DEFENDERS

George McCartney

Goals Conceded in League	30
Goals Conceded in all competitions	34
Clean Sheets In games when player was on pitch for at least 70 minutes	15
Defensive Rating Ave number of mins between League goals conceded while on the pitch	107
Club Defensive Rating Average number of mins between League goals conceded by the club this season	101

	PLAYER	CON LGE	CON ALL	CLN SHEETS	DEF RATE
1	George McCartney	30	34	15	107 mins
2	Stephen Caldwell	35	39	16	102 mins
3	Stephen Wright	35	39	15	99 mins
4	Gary Breen	37	37	14	94 mins

MONTHLY POINTS TALLY

AUGUST	5	28%
SEPTEMBER	12	80%
OCTOBER	11	73%
NOVEMBER	12	80%
DECEMBER	9	60%
JANUARY	7	58%
FEBRUARY	10	67%
MARCH	12	100%
APRIL	13	72%
MAY	3	100%

GOALS

	PLAYER	LGE	FAC	LC	Oth	TOT
1	Stewart	16	1	0	0	17
2	Elliott	15	0	1	0	16
3	Arca	9	0	0	0	9
4	Lawrence	7	0	0	0	7
5	Brown	5	0	2	0	7
6	Whitehead	5	0	0	0	5
7	Caldwell	4	0	1	0	5
8	Thornton	4	0	0	0	4
9	Robinson	4	0	0	0	4
10	Welsh	1	1	0	0	2
11	Breen	2	0	0	0	2
	Other	4	0	2	0	6
	TOTAL	76	2	6	0	84

KEY GOALKEEPER

Thomas Myhre

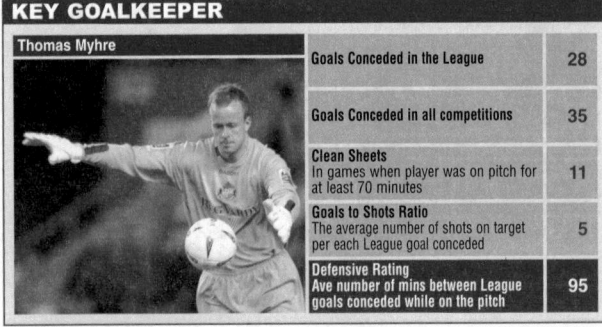

Goals Conceded in the League	28
Goals Conceded in all competitions	35
Clean Sheets In games when player was on pitch for at least 70 minutes	11
Goals to Shots Ratio The average number of shots on target per each League goal conceded	5
Defensive Rating Ave number of mins between League goals conceded while on the pitch	95

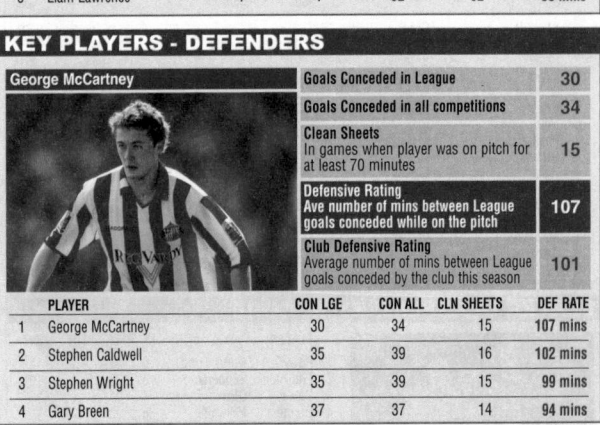

DISCIPLINARY RECORDS

	PLAYER	YELLOW	RED	AVE
1	Thornton	5	0	120
2	Kyle	2	0	243
3	Whitley	9	0	284
4	Brown	5	0	314
5	Wright	10	0	346
6	Robinson	9	0	390
7	Arca	7	0	477
8	Breen	5	1	578
9	Lawrence	3	0	641
10	Whitehead	5	0	689
11	Carter	1	0	714
12	Caldwell	4	1	715
13	McCartney	4	0	799
	Other	3	0	
	TOTAL	72	2	

TOP POINT EARNERS

	PLAYER	GAMES	AV PTS
1	Stephen Elliott	24	2.42
2	Liam Lawrence	16	2.19
3	Julio Arca	34	2.18
4	Thomas Myhre	29	2.17
5	Gary Breen	38	2.16
6	Stephen Caldwell	39	2.15
7	Marcus Stewart	29	2.14
8	Stephen Wright	38	2.13
9	Carl Robinson	38	2.13
10	Jeff Whitley	22	2.09
	CLUB AVERAGE:		2.04

LEAGUE APPEARANCES GOALS AND BOOKINGS

	AGE (on 01/07/05)	IN NAMED 16	APPEARANCES	COUNTING GAMES	MINUTES ON PITCH	LEAGUE GOALS		
Goalkeepers								
Ben Alnwick	18	30	3	3	270	0	1	0
Trevor Carson	17	3	0	0	0	0	0	0
Michael Ingham	24	8	2	1	135	0	0	0
Euan McLean	19	1	1	1	90	0	0	0
Thomas Myhre	31	38	30	29	2655	0	0	0
Mart Poom	33	12	11	11	990	0	0	0
Defenders								
Gary Breen	31	40	40	38	3473	2	5	1
Stephen Caldwell	24	41	41	39	3575	4	4	1
Ben Clark	22	2	2	1	87	0	0	0
Danny Collins	24	23	14	6	646	0	0	0
Neil Collins	21	18	11	8	779	0	0	0
Mark Lynch	23	21	11	3	445	0	0	0
George McCartney	24	36	36	35	3198	0	4	0
Darren Williams	28	2	1	1	90	0	0	0
Stephen Wright	25	39	39	38	3460	1	10	0
Midfielders								
Julio Arca	24	40	40	34	3342	9	7	0
Darren Carter	21	14	10	8	714	1	1	0
Liam Lawrence	23	34	32	16	1923	7	3	0
Grant Leadbitter	19	1	0	0	0	0	0	0
John Oster	26	10	9	3	458	0	0	0
Carl Robinson	28	40	40	38	3515	4	9	0
Sean Thornton	22	23	16	2	603	4	5	0
Andrew Welsh	21	11	7	2	290	1	0	0
Dean Whitehead	23	43	42	36	3449	5	5	0
Jeff Whitley	26	36	35	22	2556	0	9	0
Forwards								
Michael Bridges	26	25	19	3	658	1	0	0
Chris Brown	20	38	37	9	1574	5	5	0
Brian Deane	37	6	4	0	52	0	0	0
Stephen Elliott	21	43	42	24	2606	15	1	0
Simon Johnson	22	5	5	0	119	0	0	0
Kevin Kyle	24	6	6	5	486	0	2	0
Matthew Piper	23	3	2	0	78	0	0	0
Marcus Stewart	32	44	43	29	3123	16	2	0
Neil Teggart	20	0	0	0	0	0	0	0

TEAM OF THE SEASON

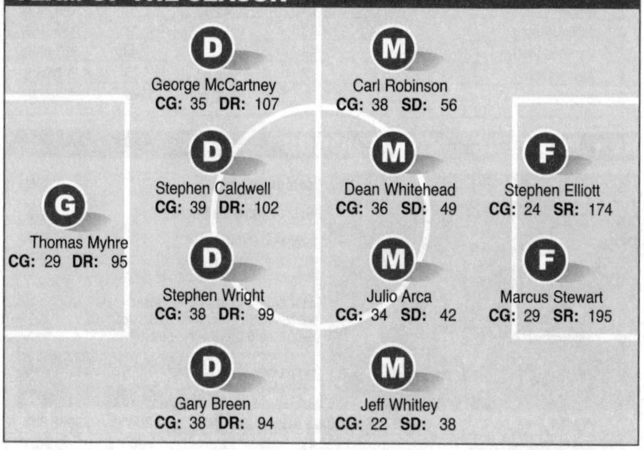

D
George McCartney
CG: 35 DR: 107
M
Carl Robinson
CG: 38 SD: 56
D
Stephen Caldwell
CG: 39 DR: 102
M
Dean Whitehead
CG: 36 SD: 49
F
Stephen Elliott
CG: 24 SR: 174
G
Thomas Myhre
CG: 29 DR: 95
D
Stephen Wright
CG: 38 DR: 99
M
Julio Arca
CG: 34 SD: 42
F
Marcus Stewart
CG: 29 SR: 195
D
Gary Breen
CG: 38 DR: 94
M
Jeff Whitley
CG: 22 SD: 38

SQUAD APPEARANCES

Match	1	2	3	4	5	6	7	8	9	10	11	12	13	14	15	16	17	18	19	20	21	22	23	24	25
Venue	A	H	H	A	H	H	A	A	H	H	A	A	A	H	H	A	A	H	H	A	A	H	A	H	A
Competition	L	L	L	L	W	L	L	L	L	L	W	L	L	L	L	L	L	L	L	L	L	L	L	L	L
Result	L	W	D	L	W	D	L	W	W	W	L	W	L	D	W	D	W	W	W	L	W	W	W	L	W

Match	26	27	28	29	30	31	32	33	34	35	36	37	38	39	40	41	42	43	44	45	46	47	48	49	50
Venue	H	H	A	A	H	H	A	H	A	A	H	A	H	H	A	A	H	H	A	A	H	A	H	A	H
Competition	L	L	L	L	L	F	L	L	F	L	L	L	L	L	L	L	L	L	L	L	L	L	L	L	L
Result	W	L	W	L	D	W	W	W	L	D	W	L	W	W	W	W	W	W	W	W	L	D	W	W	W

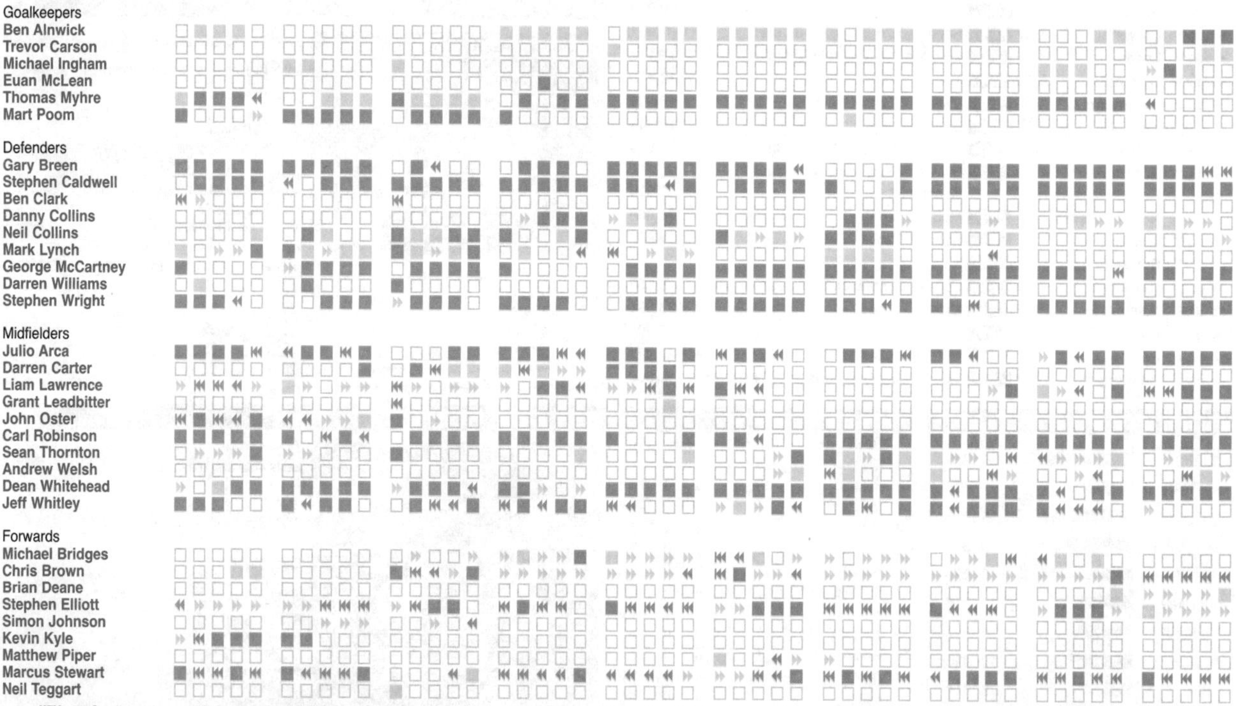

Goalkeepers
Ben Alnwick
Trevor Carson
Michael Ingham
Euan McLean
Thomas Myhre
Mart Poom
Defenders
Gary Breen
Stephen Caldwell
Ben Clark
Danny Collins
Neil Collins
Mark Lynch
George McCartney
Darren Williams
Stephen Wright
Midfielders
Julio Arca
Darren Carter
Liam Lawrence
Grant Leadbitter
John Oster
Carl Robinson
Sean Thornton
Andrew Welsh
Dean Whitehead
Jeff Whitley
Forwards
Michael Bridges
Chris Brown
Brian Deane
Stephen Elliott
Simon Johnson
Kevin Kyle
Matthew Piper
Marcus Stewart
Neil Teggart

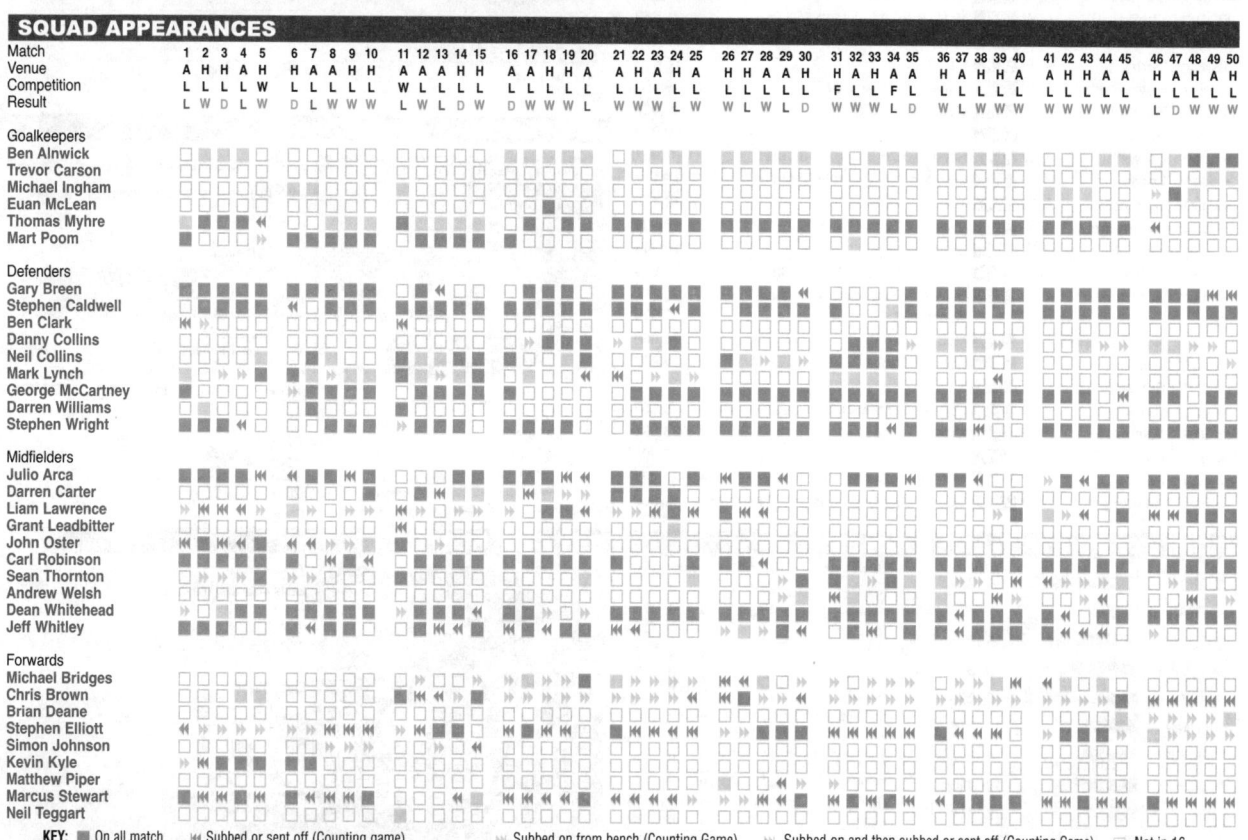

KEY: On all match | On bench | Subbed or sent off (Counting game) | Subbed or sent off (playing less than 70 minutes) | Subbed on from bench (Counting Game) | Subbed on (playing less than 70 minutes) | Subbed on and then subbed or sent off (Counting Game) | Subbed on and then subbed or sent off (playing less than 70 minutes) | Not in 16

WIGAN ATHLETIC

Final Position: **2nd**

NICKNAME: THE LATICS

KEY: ☐Won ☐Drawn ☐Lost

							Attendance
1	div1	Nottm Forest	H	D	1-1	McCulloch 38	12,035
2	div1	Millwall	A	W	2-0	McCulloch 51; Roberts, J 75	10,660
3	div1	West Ham	A	W	3-1	Ellington 5,58; Roberts, J 45	23,271
4	div1	Brighton	H	W	3-0	Ellington 45,49; Frandsen 77	8,681
5	ccr1	Grimsby	A	L	0-1		3,005
6	div1	Sunderland	A	D	1-1	Roberts, J 18	26,330
7	div1	Cardiff	H	W	2-1	Ellington 16 pen; Roberts, J 36	9,004
8	div1	Wolverhampton	A	D	3-3	Jackson 23; Ellington 28; Roberts, J 75 pen	26,790
9	div1	Burnley	H	D	0-0		9,746
10	div1	Sheff Utd	H	W	4-0	Ellington 29,35; Roberts, J 33,90	10,682
11	div1	Derby	A	D	1-1	McCulloch 19	26,113
12	div1	Watford	A	D	0-0		11,161
13	div1	Rotherham	H	W	2-0	Roberts, J 11; Mahon 63	7,937
14	div1	Plymouth	A	W	2-1	Roberts, J 54,69	14,443
15	div1	Crewe	H	W	4-1	McCulloch 18; Ellington 25,48; Bullard 84	7,547
16	div1	Coventry	H	W	4-1	Mahon 15; Graham 53; Ellington 63; Flynn 90	9,632
17	div1	Leeds	A	W	2-0	Mahon 46; Bullard 52	27,432
18	div1	Stoke	A	W	1-0	McCulloch 87	15,882
19	div1	Plymouth	H	L	0-2		10,294
20	div1	QPR	A	L	0-1		15,804
21	div1	Leicester	H	D	0-0		10,924
22	div1	Reading	A	D	1-1	Mahon 26	22,114
23	div1	Preston	H	W	5-0	McCulloch 27; Mahon 52; Ellington 56,72; Roberts 79 pen	10,565
24	div1	Gillingham	H	W	2-0	Ellington 17; McCulloch 88	8,451
25	div1	Ipswich	A	L	1-2	Baines 57	28,286
26	div1	Derby	H	L	1-2	Roberts 27	12,420
27	div1	Burnley	A	L	0-1		16,485
28	div1	Sheff Utd	A	W	2-0	McCulloch 7; Ellington 73	21,869
29	div1	Wolverhampton	H	W	2-0	Ellington 17,26 pen	10,135
30	facr3	Derby	A	L	1-2	Mahon 30	14,457
31	div1	Rotherham	A	W	2-0	Teale 69; Roberts 90	9,050
32	div1	Watford	H	D	2-2	McCulloch 25,52	9,008
33	div1	Stoke	H	L	0-1		9,938
34	div1	Crewe	A	W	3-1	Roberts 3,76; Ellington 68 pen	7,981
35	div1	Leeds	H	W	3-0	Ellington 10; Roberts 56; Mahon 75	17,177
36	div1	Coventry	A	W	2-1	Teale 9; Ellington 68	12,130
37	div1	Gillingham	A	L	1-2	Ellington 55	7,209
38	div1	Ipswich	H	W	1-0	Ellington 43 pen	16,744
39	div1	Millwall	H	W	2-0	Ellington 58 pen; Roberts 82	9,614
40	div1	Brighton	A	W	4-2	Bullard 2; McCulloch 4; Teale 17; Roberts 34	6,306
41	div1	Nottm Forest	A	D	1-1	McCulloch 46	24,008
42	div1	West Ham	H	L	1-2	Roberts 51	12,993
43	div1	Sunderland	H	L	0-1		20,745
44	div1	Cardiff	A	W	2-0	Roberts 51; Mahon 86	16,858
45	div1	Leicester	A	W	2-0	Ormerod 25,59	23,894
46	div1	QPR	H	D	0-0		12,007
47	div1	Preston	A	D	1-1	McCulloch 24	20,221
48	div1	Reading	H	W	3-1	McCulloch 18; Roberts 21; Ellington 85	19,662

KEY PLAYERS - GOALSCORERS

Nathan Ellington

Goals in the League	24
Goals in all competitions	24
Contribution to Attacking Power Average number of minutes between League team goals while on pitch	51
Player Strike Rate Average number of minutes between League goals scored by player	156
Club Strike Rate Average number of minutes between League goals scored by club	52

	PLAYER	GOALS LGE	GOALS ALL	POWER	S RATE
1	Nathan Ellington	24	24	51	156 mins
2	Jason Roberts	19	19	52	205 mins
3	Lee McCulloch	14	14	48	257 mins
4	Alan Mahon	7	8	53	272 mins
5	Gary Teale	3	3	49	834 mins

KEY PLAYERS - MIDFIELDERS

Lee McCulloch

Goals in the League	14
Goals in all competitions	14
Defensive Rating Average number of mins between League goals conceded while on the pitch	120
Contribution to Attacking Power Average number of minutes between League team goals while on pitch	48
Scoring Difference Defensive Rating minus Contribution to Attacking Power	72

	PLAYER	GOALS LGE	GOALS ALL	DEF RATE	ATT POWER	SCORE DIFF
1	Lee McCulloch	14	14	120	48	72 mins
2	Alan Mahon	7	8	119	53	66 mins
3	Jimmy Bullard	3	3	119	54	65 mins
4	Gary Teale	3	3	96	49	47 mins

KEY PLAYERS - DEFENDERS

Nicky Eaden

Goals Conceded in League	25
Goals Conceded in all competitions	26
Clean Sheets In games when player was on pitch for at least 70 minutes	15
Defensive Rating Ave number of mins between League goals conceded while on the pitch	120
Club Defensive Rating Average number of mins between League goals conceded by the club this season	118

	PLAYER	CON LGE	CON ALL	CLN SHEETS	DEF RATE
1	Nicky Eaden	25	26	15	120 mins
2	Matt Jackson	26	26	15	119 mins
3	Ian Breckin	32	35	18	118 mins
4	Leighton Baines	32	33	17	113 mins
5	David Wright	20	22	6	93 mins

MONTHLY POINTS TALLY

AUGUST	14	78%
SEPTEMBER	7	47%
OCTOBER	15	100%
NOVEMBER	5	33%
DECEMBER	6	40%
JANUARY	10	83%
FEBRUARY	9	60%
MARCH	10	83%
APRIL	8	44%
MAY	3	100%

GOALS

	PLAYER	LGE	FAC	LC	Oth	TOT
1	Ellington	24	0	0	0	24
2	Roberts	19	0	0	0	19
3	McCulloch	14	0	0	0	14
4	Mahon	7	1	0	0	8
5	Teale	3	0	0	0	3
6	Bullard	3	0	0	0	3
7	Ormerod	2	0	0	0	2
8	Frandsen	1	0	0	0	1
9	Jackson	1	0	0	0	1
10	Graham	1	0	0	0	1
11	Flynn	1	0	0	0	1
	Other	3	0	0	0	3
	TOTAL	79	1	0	0	80

KEY GOALKEEPER

John Filan

Goals Conceded in the League	35
Goals Conceded in all competitions	37
Clean Sheets In games when player was on pitch for at least 70 minutes	20
Goals to Shots Ratio The average number of shots on target per each League goal conceded	5.3
Defensive Rating Ave number of mins between League goals conceded while on the pitch	118

DISCIPLINARY RECORDS

	PLAYER	YELLOW	RED	AVE
1	Kavanagh	3	0	322
2	Roberts	9	0	433
3	McCulloch	7	1	448
4	Jarrett	1	0	480
5	Bullard	5	0	808
6	Breckin	4	0	943
7	Mahon	2	0	952
8	Thome	1	0	1001
9	Eaden	3	0	1003
10	Filan	4	0	1035
11	Baines	3	0	1205
12	Graham	1	0	1325
13	Jackson	2	0	1547
	Other	2	0	
	TOTAL	47	1	

TOP POINT EARNERS

	PLAYER	GAMES	AV PTS
1	Lee McCulloch	40	2.05
2	Nathan Ellington	41	1.98
3	David Wright	18	1.94
4	Ian Breckin	42	1.90
5	Leighton Baines	40	1.90
6	John Filan	46	1.89
7	Gary Teale	24	1.88
8	Jason Roberts	43	1.88
9	Jimmy Bullard	45	1.87
10	Matt Jackson	34	1.85
	CLUB AVERAGE:		1.89

TEAM OF THE SEASON

D
Nicky Eaden
CG: 32 DR: 120
M
Lee McCulloch
CG: 40 SD: 72
D
Matt Jackson
CG: 34 DR: 119
M
Alan Mahon
CG: 19 SD: 66
F
Nathan Ellington
CG: 41 SR: 156
G
John Filan
CG: 46 DR: 118
D
Ian Breckin
CG: 42 DR: 118
M
Jimmy Bullard
CG: 45 SD: 65
F
Jason Roberts
CG: 43 SR: 205
D
Leighton Baines
CG: 40 DR: 113
M
Gary Teale
CG: 24 SD: 47

LEAGUE APPEARANCES GOALS AND BOOKINGS

	AGE (on 01/07/05)	IN NAMED 16	APPEARANCES	COUNTING GAMES	MINUTES ON PITCH	LEAGUE GOALS	Yellow	Red
Goalkeepers								
John Filan	35	46	46	46	4140	0	4	0
James Salisbury	21	2	0	0	0	0	0	0
Gary Walsh	37	44	0	0	0	0	0	0
Defenders								
Leighton Baines	20	42	41	40	3616	1	3	0
Ian Breckin	29	45	42	42	3772	0	4	0
Nicky Eaden	33	42	39	32	3011	0	3	0
Matt Jackson	33	42	36	34	3094	1	2	0
Steven McMillan	29	20	8	5	544	0	0	0
Paul Mitchell	23	5	1	0	5	0	0	0
Emerson Thome	33	22	15	11	1001	0	1	0
David Wright	25	42	31	18	1861	0	1	0
Midfielders								
Jimmy Bullard	26	46	46	45	4040	3	5	0
Tony Dinning	30	1	0	0	0	0	0	0
Michael Flynn	24	20	13	0	267	1	1	0
Per Frandsen	35	9	9	8	786	1	0	0
Jason Jarrett	25	15	14	3	480	0	1	0
Andreas Johansson	27	6	1	0	16	0	0	0
Graham Kavanagh	31	11	11	10	968	0	3	0
Alan Mahon	27	39	27	19	1904	7	2	0
Lee McCulloch	27	42	42	40	3591	14	7	1
Gary Teale	26	40	37	24	2501	3	1	0
Greg Traynor	20	0	0	0	0	0	0	0
Gareth Whalley	31	18	8	5	540	0	0	0
Forwards								
Nathan Ellington	24	45	45	41	3744	24	0	0
David Graham	26	41	30	11	1325	1	1	0
Brett Ormerod	28	6	6	3	342	2	0	0
Jason Roberts	27	44	44	43	3898	19	9	0
Neil Roberts	27	1	1	1	90	0	0	0

SQUAD APPEARANCES

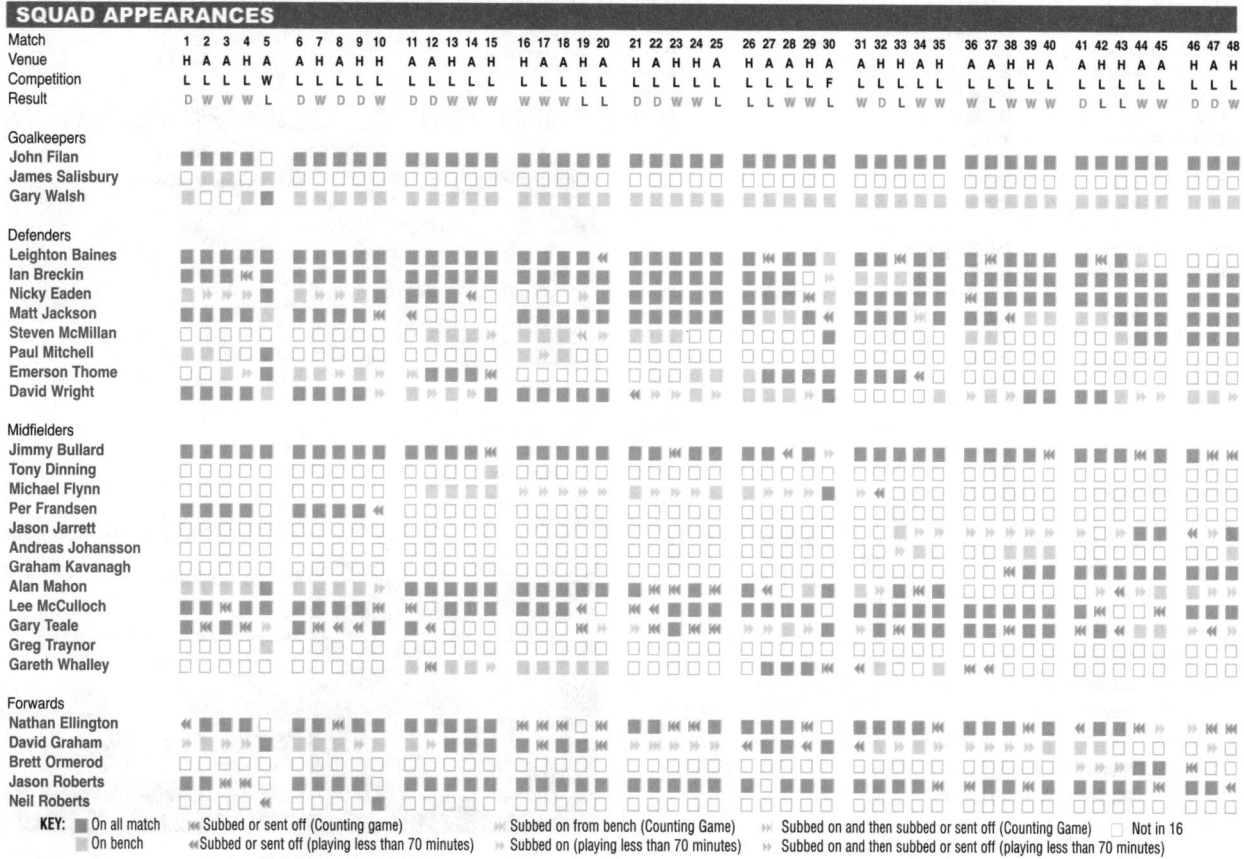

Match	1	2	3	4	5	6	7	8	9	10	11	12	13	14	15	16	17	18	19	20	21	22	23	24	25
Venue	H	A	A	H	A	A	H	A	H	H	A	A	H	A	H	H	A	A	H	A	H	A	H	H	A
Competition	L	L	L	L	W	L	L	L	L	L	L	L	L	L	L	L	L	L	L	L	L	L	L	L	L
Result	D	W	W	W	L	D	W	D	D	W	D	D	W	W	W	W	W	W	L	L	D	D	W	W	L

Match	26	27	28	29	30	31	32	33	34	35	36	37	38	39	40	41	42	43	44	45	46	47	48
Venue	H	A	A	H	A	A	H	H	A	H	A	A	H	H	A	A	H	H	A	A	H	A	H
Competition	L	L	L	L	F	L	L	L	L	L	L	L	L	L	L	L	L	L	L	L	L	L	L
Result	L	L	W	W	L	W	D	L	W	W	W	L	W	W	W	D	L	L	W	W	D	D	W

Goalkeepers
John Filan
James Salisbury
Gary Walsh

Defenders
Leighton Baines
Ian Breckin
Nicky Eaden
Matt Jackson
Steven McMillan
Paul Mitchell
Emerson Thome
David Wright

Midfielders
Jimmy Bullard
Tony Dinning
Michael Flynn
Per Frandsen
Jason Jarrett
Andreas Johansson
Graham Kavanagh
Alan Mahon
Lee McCulloch
Gary Teale
Greg Traynor
Gareth Whalley

Forwards
Nathan Ellington
David Graham
Brett Ormerod
Jason Roberts
Neil Roberts

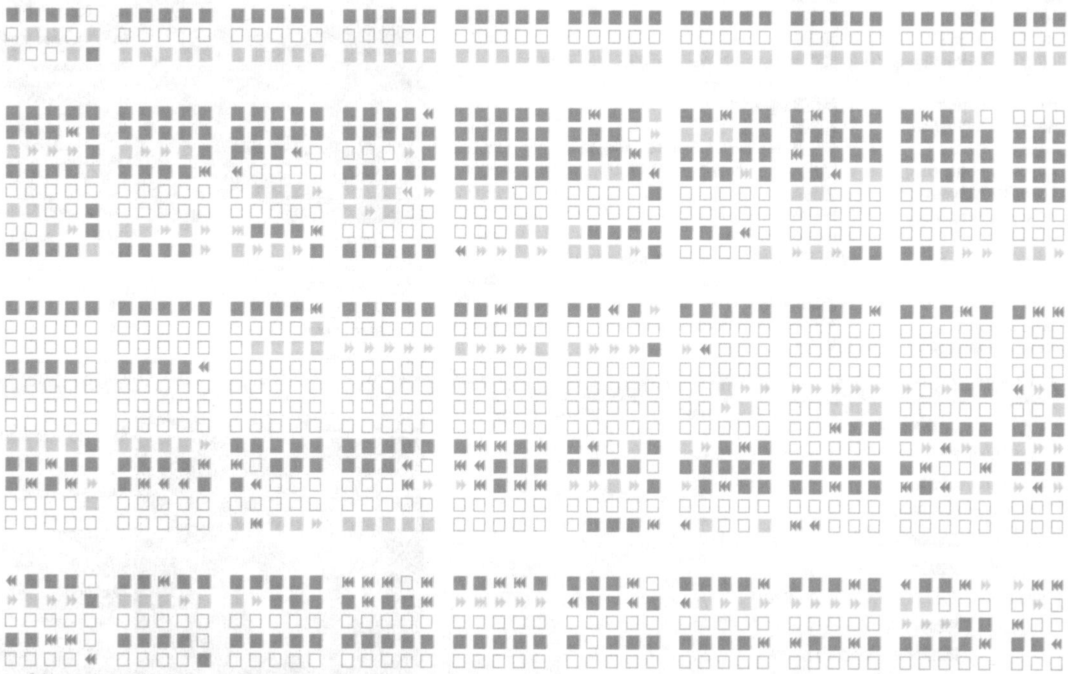

KEY: On all match | On bench | Subbed or sent off (Counting game) | Subbed or sent off (playing less than 70 minutes) | Subbed on from bench (Counting Game) | Subbed on (playing less than 70 minutes) | Subbed on and then subbed or sent off (Counting Game) | Subbed on and then subbed or sent off (playing less than 70 minutes) | Not in 16

IPSWICH TOWN

Final Position: **3rd**

NICKNAME: TRACTOR BOYS

KEY: ☐ Won ☐ Drawn ☐ Lost

							Attendance
1	div1	Gillingham	H	W	2-1	Naylor 35; Bowditch 46	23,130
2	div1	Nottm Forest	A	D	1-1	Bent 54	21,125
3	div1	Derby	A	L	2-3	Miller, T 41 pen; Bowditch 43	22,234
4	div1	Cardiff	H	W	3-1	Bent 21; Miller, T 67; Westlake 86	21,828
5	ccr1	Brentford	H	W	2-0	Miller, T 73; Westlake 90	10,190
6	div1	Rotherham	A	W	2-0	Kuqi 43,47	5,504
7	div1	Wolverhampton	H	W	2-1	Bent 28; Miller, T 50 pen	24,590
8	div1	Millwall	H	W	2-0	Bent 83; Counago 90	21,246
9	div1	Stoke	A	L	2-3	De Vos 41; Westlake 62	23,029
10	div1	West Ham	A	D	1-1	Counago 57	28,812
11	ccr2	Doncaster	A	L	0-2		6,020
12	div1	Plymouth	H	W	3-2	De Vos 24; Kuqi 82,85	23,270
13	div1	Reading	H	D	1-1	Kuqi 10	23,167
14	div1	Coventry	A	W	2-1	Bowditch 70; Mills 87 og	12,608
15	div1	Burnley	H	D	1-1	Richards 90	23,183
16	div1	Leicester	A	D	2-2	Westlake 2; Heath 89 og	22,497
17	div1	Watford	A	D	2-2	Westlake 50; Bent 63	15,894
18	div1	Preston	H	W	3-0	Kuqi 44; Miller 45; Bent 72	23,745
19	div1	Sheff Utd	H	W	5-1	Miller 22 pen; Kuqi 23,68; Naylor 62; Westlake 77	22,977
20	div1	Burnley	A	W	2-0	Bent 15,65	11,969
21	div1	Leeds	H	W	1-0	Bent 51	29,955
22	div1	Sunderland	A	L	0-2		31,723
23	div1	Brighton	H	W	1-0	Kuqi 22	26,269
24	div1	Crewe	A	D	2-2	Naylor 55; Bent 59	7,236
25	div1	QPR	A	W	4-2	De Vos 25; Bent 58; Currie 72; Kuqi 77	18,231
26	div1	Wigan	H	W	2-1	Naylor 66; Bent 89	28,286
27	div1	Millwall	A	L	1-3	Kuqi 62	14,532
28	div1	Stoke	H	W	1-0	Kuqi 34	26,217
29	div1	West Ham	H	L	0-2		30,003
30	div1	Plymouth	A	W	2-1	Currie 67 pen,85	17,923
31	facr3	Bolton	H	L	1-3	Miller 70	20,080
32	div1	Coventry	H	W	3-2	Bent 45,59; Kuqi 77	23,670
33	div1	Reading	A	D	1-1	Bent 90	23,203
34	div1	Sheff Utd	A	W	2-0	Unsworth 20; Kuqi 61	20,680
35	div1	Leicester	H	W	2-1	Kuqi 2; de Vries 24 og	27,392
36	div1	Preston	A	D	1-1	Miller 69	14,418
37	div1	Watford	H	L	1-2	Miller 87 pen	23,993
38	div1	QPR	H	L	0-2		29,008
39	div1	Wigan	A	L	0-1		16,744
40	div1	Nottm Forest	H	W	6-0	Naylor 27; Westlake 35; Miller 50,64 pen; Kuqi 67; Bent 71	25,765
41	div1	Cardiff	A	W	1-0	Miller 62 pen	11,768
42	div1	Gillingham	A	D	0-0		9,311
43	div1	Derby	H	W	3-2	Magilton 24; Bent 46; Miller 71	28,796
44	div1	Rotherham	H	W	4-3	Westlake 6; Bent 25,57; Magilton 60	26,017
45	div1	Wolverhampton	A	L	0-2		25,882
46	div1	Sunderland	H	D	2-2	Naylor 66; Bent 89	29,230
47	div1	Leeds	A	D	1-1	Kuqi 11	29,607
48	div1	Crewe	H	W	5-1	Kuqi 6; Magilton 12; Miller 51,81; Counago 82	28,244
49	div1	Brighton	A	D	1-1	Kuqi 4	6,848
50	d1po1	West Ham	A	D	2-2	Walker 45 og; Kuqi 74	33,723
51	d1po2	West Ham	H	L	0-2		

MONTHLY POINTS TALLY

AUGUST	13	72%
SEPTEMBER	8	53%
OCTOBER	9	60%
NOVEMBER	12	80%
DECEMBER	10	67%
JANUARY	7	58%
FEBRUARY	7	47%
MARCH	7	58%
APRIL	11	61%
MAY	1	33%

GOALS

	PLAYER	LGE	FAC	LC	Oth	TOT
1	Bent	20	0	0	0	20
2	Kuqi	19	0	0	1	20
3	Miller	13	1	1	0	15
4	Westlake	7	0	1	0	8
5	Naylor	6	0	0	0	6
6	De Vos	3	0	0	0	3
7	Currie	3	0	0	0	3
8	Magilton	3	0	0	0	3
9	Bowditch	3	0	0	0	3
10	Counago	3	0	0	0	3
11	Richards	1	0	0	0	1
	Other	4	0	0	1	5
	TOTAL	85	1	2	2	90

KEY PLAYERS - GOALSCORERS

Shefki Kuqi

POWERGEN

Goals in the League	19
Goals in all competitions	20
Contribution to Attacking Power Average number of minutes between League team goals while on pitch	48
Player Strike Rate Average number of minutes between League goals scored by player	178
Club Strike Rate Average number of minutes between League goals scored by club	49

	PLAYER	GOALS LGE	GOALS ALL	POWER	S RATE
1	Shefki Kuqi	19	20	48	178 mins
2	Darren Bent	20	20	47	197 mins
3	Tommy Miller	13	15	48	300 mins
4	Ian Westlake	7	8	48	532 mins
5	Darren Currie	3	3	48	572 mins

KEY PLAYERS - MIDFIELDERS

Ian Westlake

POWERGEN

Goals in the League	7
Goals in all competitions	8
Defensive Rating Average number of mins between League goals conceded while on the pitch	76
Contribution to Attacking Power Average number of minutes between League team goals while on pitch	48
Scoring Difference Defensive Rating minus Contribution to Attacking Power	28

	PLAYER	GOALS LGE	GOALS ALL	DEF RATE	ATT POWER	SCORE DIFF
1	Ian Westlake	7	8	76	48	28 mins
2	Jim Magilton	3	3	73	45	28 mins
3	Darren Currie	3	3	75	48	27 mins
4	Tommy Miller	13	15	75	48	27 mins
5	Kevin Horlock	0	0	67	55	12 mins

KEY PLAYERS - DEFENDERS

Richard Naylor

Goals Conceded in League	55
Goals Conceded in all competitions	61
Clean Sheets In games when player was on pitch for at least 70 minutes	11
Defensive Rating Ave number of mins between League goals conceded while on the pitch	74
Club Defensive Rating Average number of mins between League goals conceded by the club this season	74

	PLAYER	CON LGE	CON ALL	CLN SHEETS	DEF RATE
1	Richard Naylor	55	61	11	74 mins
2	Jason De Vos	54	63	11	74 mins
3	Drissa Diallo	28	32	6	74 mins
4	David Unsworth	19	19	4	74 mins
5	Fabian Wilnis	48	55	11	73 mins

KEY GOALKEEPER

Kelvin Davis

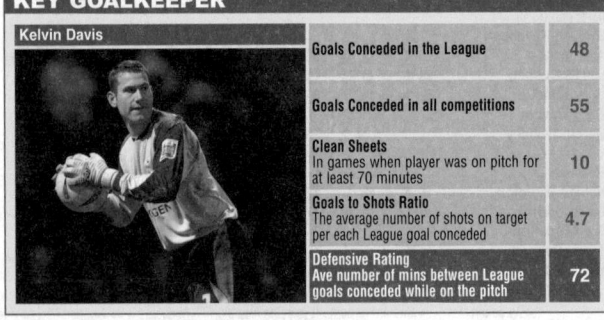

Goals Conceded in the League	48
Goals Conceded in all competitions	55
Clean Sheets In games when player was on pitch for at least 70 minutes	10
Goals to Shots Ratio The average number of shots on target per each League goal conceded	4.7
Defensive Rating Ave number of mins between League goals conceded while on the pitch	72

DISCIPLINARY RECORDS

	PLAYER	YELLOW	RED	AVE
1	Counago	2	0	323
2	Unsworth	3	0	470
3	Horlock	6	0	493
4	Diallo	4	0	519
5	Kuqi	5	0	677
6	Bowditch	1	0	684
7	Wilnis	4	1	696
8	Magilton	4	0	725
9	De Vos	5	0	796
10	Naylor	5	0	819
11	Westlake	4	0	931
12	Miller	3	0	1299
13	Richards	1	0	1511
	Other	1	0	
	TOTAL	48	1	

TOP POINT EARNERS

	PLAYER	GAMES	AV PTS
1	Jim Magilton	29	2.07
2	Shefki Kuqi	34	2.00
3	Darren Currie	15	2.00
4	Drissa Diallo	21	2.00
5	Darren Bent	43	1.95
6	Ian Westlake	39	1.90
7	Fabian Wilnis	38	1.89
8	Kelvin Davis	38	1.87
9	Jason De Vos	44	1.86
10	Richard Naylor	45	1.82
	CLUB AVERAGE:		1.85

TEAM OF THE SEASON

D
Jason De Vos
CG: 44 DR: 74
M
Jim Magilton
CG: 29 SD: 28
D
Drissa Diallo
CG: 21 DR: 74
M
Ian Westlake
CG: 39 SD: 28
F
Shefki Kuqi
CG: 34 SR: 178
G
Kelvin Davis
CG: 38 DR: 72
D
Richard Naylor
CG: 45 DR: 74
M
Darren Currie
CG: 15 SD: 27
F
Darren Bent
CG: 43 SR: 197
D
David Unsworth
CG: 15 DR: 74
M
Tommy Miller
CG: 42 SD: 27

LEAGUE APPEARANCES GOALS AND BOOKINGS

	AGE (on 01/07/05)	IN NAMED 16	APPEARANCES	COUNTING GAMES	MINUTES ON PITCH	LEAGUE GOALS	Yellow	Red
Goalkeepers								
Kelvin Davis	28	40	39	38	3464	0	0	0
Lewis Price	20	39	8	7	676	0	0	0
Shane Supple	18	12	0	0	0	0	0	0
Defenders								
Scott Barron	19	6	0	0	0	0	0	0
Aidan Collins	18	9	0	0	0	0	0	0
Jason De Vos	31	45	45	44	3983	3	5	0
Drissa Diallo	32	26	26	21	2079	0	4	0
Daniel Karbassiyoon	20	12	5	2	243	0	1	0
Richard Naylor	28	46	46	45	4097	6	5	0
Matthew Richards	20	39	24	11	1511	1	1	0
Jerome Sobers	19	2	0	0	0	0	0	0
David Unsworth	31	16	16	15	1412	1	3	0
Fabian Wilnis	34	43	41	38	3484	0	4	1
Midfielders								
Dean Bowditch	19	36	21	2	684	3	1	0
Darren Currie	30	24	24	15	1715	3	0	0
Tony Dinning	30	10	7	2	293	0	1	0
Owen Garvan	17	1	0	0	0	0	0	0
Kevin Horlock	32	45	41	29	2962	0	6	0
Jimmy Juan	22	1	0	0	0	0	0	0
Jim Magilton	36	41	39	29	2900	3	4	0
Tommy Miller	26	45	45	42	3898	13	3	0
Scott Mitchell	19	7	0	0	0	0	0	0
Antonio Murray	20	1	0	0	0	0	0	0
James Scowcroft	31	13	9	2	376	0	4	0
Ian Westlake	21	45	45	39	3725	7	4	0
Forwards								
Darren Bent	21	45	45	43	3932	20	1	0
Pablo Counago	25	42	19	2	646	3	2	0
Darryl Knights	17	1	1	0	11	0	0	0
Shefki Kuqi	28	43	43	34	3385	19	5	0

SQUAD APPEARANCES

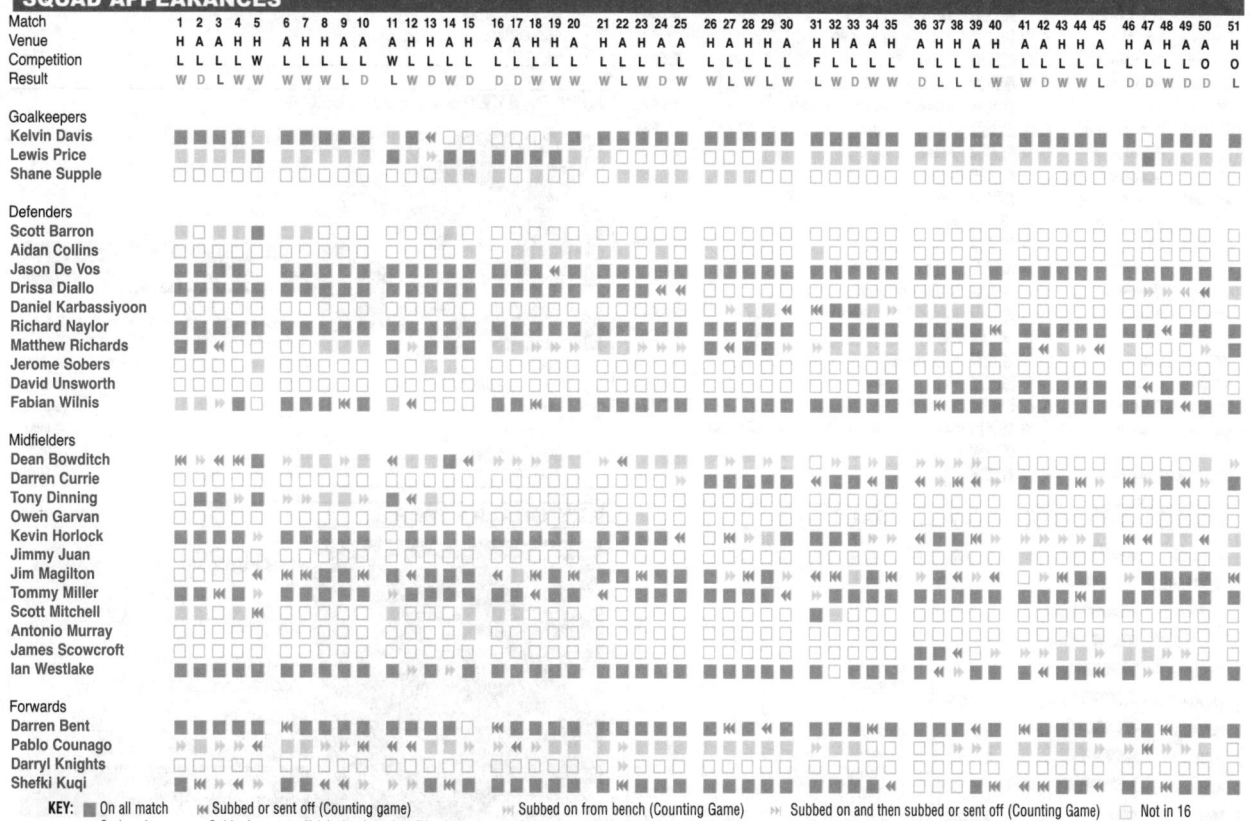

Match	1	2	3	4	5	6	7	8	9	10	11	12	13	14	15	16	17	18	19	20	21	22	23	24	25	26	27	28	29	30	31	32	33	34	35	36	37	38	39	40	41	42	43	44	45	46	47	48	49	50	51
Venue	H	A	A	H	H	A	H	H	A	A	A	H	H	A	H	A	A	H	H	A	H	A	H	A	A	H	A	H	H	A	H	H	A	A	H	A	H	H	A	H	A	A	H	H	A	H	A	H	A	A	H
Competition	L	L	L	L	W	L	L	L	L	L	W	L	L	L	L	L	L	L	L	L	L	L	L	L	L	L	L	L	L	L	F	L	L	L	L	L	L	L	L	L	L	L	L	L	L	L	L	L	L	O	O
Result	W	D	L	W	W	W	W	W	L	D	L	W	D	W	D	D	D	W	W	W	W	L	W	D	W	W	L	W	L	W	L	W	D	W	W	D	L	L	L	W	W	D	W	W	L	D	D	W	D	D	L

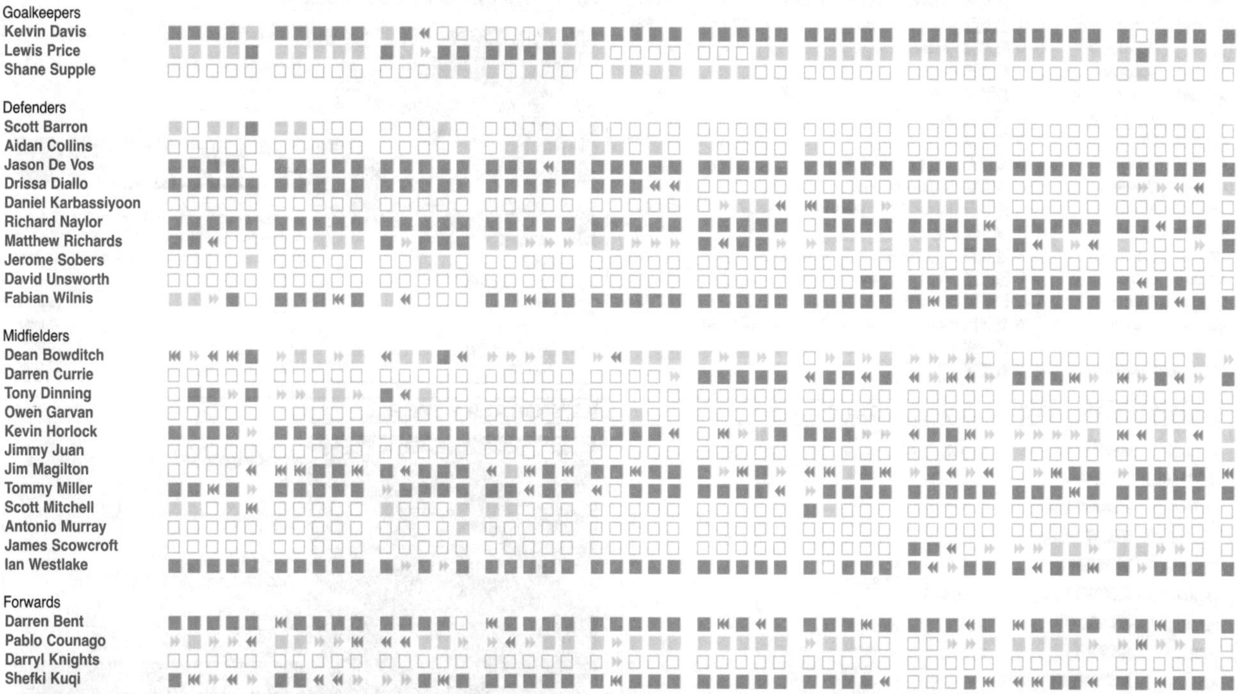
Goalkeepers
Kelvin Davis
Lewis Price
Shane Supple
Defenders
Scott Barron
Aidan Collins
Jason De Vos
Drissa Diallo
Daniel Karbassiyoon
Richard Naylor
Matthew Richards
Jerome Sobers
David Unsworth
Fabian Wilnis
Midfielders
Dean Bowditch
Darren Currie
Tony Dinning
Owen Garvan
Kevin Horlock
Jimmy Juan
Jim Magilton
Tommy Miller
Scott Mitchell
Antonio Murray
James Scowcroft
Ian Westlake
Forwards
Darren Bent
Pablo Counago
Darryl Knights
Shefki Kuqi

KEY: On all match · On bench · Subbed or sent off (Counting game) · Subbed or sent off (playing less than 70 minutes) · Subbed on from bench (Counting Game) · Subbed on (playing less than 70 minutes) · Subbed on and then subbed or sent off (Counting Game) · Subbed on and then subbed or sent off (playing less than 70 minutes) · Not in 16

DERBY COUNTY

Final Position: **4th**

NICKNAME: THE RAMS

KEY: ☐Won ☐Drawn ☐Lost

							Attendance
1	div1	Leeds	A	L	0-1		30,459
2	div1	Leicester	H	L	1-2	Tudgay 69	26,650
3	div1	Ipswich	H	W	3-2	Reich 36,65; Idiakez 58	22,234
4	div1	QPR	A	W	2-0	Smith 8; Tudgay 17	15,295
5	ccr1	Lincoln	A	L	1-3	Idiakez 28	4,982
6	div1	Crewe	H	L	2-4	Tudgay 16; Idiakez 46	24,436
7	div1	Stoke	A	L	0-1		18,673
8	div1	Reading	H	W	2-1	Smith 70; Tudgay 83	22,096
9	div1	Cardiff	A	W	2-0	Reich 34; Taylor 49	12,008
10	div1	Millwall	A	L	1-3	Reich 49	9,132
11	div1	Wigan	H	D	1-1	Smith 17	26,113
12	div1	West Ham	H	D	1-1	Johnson 6	23,112
13	div1	Sunderland	A	D	0-0		29,881
14	div1	Watford	H	D	2-2	Smith 39; Rasiak 85	23,253
15	div1	Wolverhampton	A	L	0-2		26,465
16	div1	Burnley	A	W	2-0	Tudgay 57; Reich 63	13,703
17	div1	Rotherham	H	W	3-2	Rasiak 39; Peschisolido 58; Vincent 66	25,096
18	div1	Brighton	H	W	3-0	Smith 9; Rasiak 49,80	22,480
19	div1	Watford	A	D	2-2	Taylor 58; Peschisolido 73	16,689
20	div1	Gillingham	A	W	2-0	Rasiak 42; Taylor 90	8,015
21	div1	Sheff Utd	H	L	0-1		25,725
22	div1	Preston	A	L	0-3		12,702
23	div1	Coventry	H	D	2-2	Rasiak 88; Peschisolido 90	22,648
24	div1	Nottm Forest	H	W	3-0	Smith 4; Rasiak 75,89	30,793
25	div1	Plymouth	A	W	2-0	Coughlan 9 og; Peschisolido 62	15,335
26	div1	Wigan	A	W	2-1	Rasiak 64; Smith 82	12,420
27	div1	Millwall	H	L	0-3		27,725
28	div1	Cardiff	H	L	0-1		22,800
29	div1	Reading	A	W	1-0	Smith 45	15,491
30	facr3	Wigan	H	W	2-1	Idiakez 71; Junior 79	14,457
31	div1	Sunderland	H	L	0-2		22,995
32	div1	West Ham	A	W	2-1	Rasiak 10,63	30,347
33	div1	Leeds	H	W	2-0	Smith 64; Bolder 90	25,648
34	facr4	Fulham	H	D	1-1	Tudgay 56	22,040
35	div1	Brighton	A	W	3-2	Bisgaard 13; Tudgay 43,72	6,587
36	facr4r	Fulham	A	L	2-4	Rasiak 4; Peschisolido 86	15,528
37	div1	Rotherham	A	W	3-1	Rasiak 32; Tudgay 47; Idiakez 77 pen	7,937
38	div1	Burnley	H	D	1-1	Peschisolido 70	23,701
39	div1	Nottm Forest	A	D	2-2	Rasiak 12,78	26,160
40	div1	Wolverhampton	H	D	3-3	Idiakez 9,77 pen; Reich 90	24,109
41	div1	Plymouth	H	W	1-0	Idiakez 24	27,581
42	div1	QPR	H	D	0-0		24,486
43	div1	Ipswich	A	L	2-3	Tudgay 7; Idiakez 85	28,796
44	div1	Crewe	A	W	2-1	Rasiak 16; Smith 74	8,026
45	div1	Stoke	H	W	3-1	Rasiak 8; Bisgaard 44; Idiakez 79	27,640
46	div1	Sheff Utd	A	W	1-0	Bisgaard 74	20,794
47	div1	Gillingham	H	W	2-0	Bisgaard 33; Peschisolido 72	27,481
48	div1	Leicester	A	L	0-1		25,762
49	div1	Coventry	A	L	2-6	Bolder 51; Peschisolido 63	22,728
50	div1	Preston	H	W	3-1	Idiakez 45; Smith 49; Peschisolido 90	31,237
51	d1po1	Preston	A	L	0-2		20,315
52	d1po2	Preston	H	D	0-0		31,310

KEY PLAYERS - GOALSCORERS

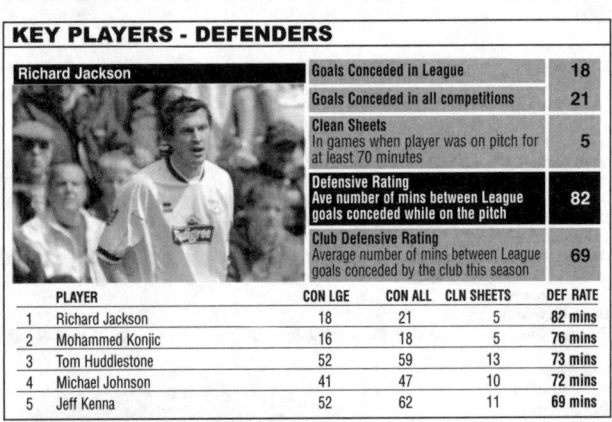

Grzegorz Rasiak

Pedigree

Goals in the League	16
Goals in all competitions	17
Contribution to Attacking Power Average number of minutes between League team goals while on pitch	58
Player Strike Rate Average number of minutes between League goals scored by player	190
Club Strike Rate Average number of minutes between League goals scored by club	58

	PLAYER	GOALS LGE	GOALS ALL	POWER	S RATE
1	Grzegorz Rasiak	16	17	58	190 mins
2	Marcus Tudgay	9	10	46	212 mins
3	Tommy Smith	11	11	63	312 mins
4	Marco Reich	6	6	62	361 mins
5	Inigo Idiakez	9	11	56	394 mins

KEY PLAYERS - MIDFIELDERS

Marco Reich

Goals in the League	6
Goals in all competitions	6
Defensive Rating Average number of mins between League goals conceded while on the pitch	77
Contribution to Attacking Power Average number of minutes between League team goals while on pitch	62
Scoring Difference Defensive Rating minus Contribution to Attacking Power	15

	PLAYER	GOALS LGE	GOALS ALL	DEF RATE	ATT POWER	SCORE DIFF
1	Marco Reich	6	6	77	62	15 mins
2	Adam Bolder	2	2	71	59	12 mins
3	Morten Bisgaard	4	4	67	57	10 mins
4	Inigo Idiakez	9	11	64	56	8 mins
5	Ian Taylor	3	3	71	64	7 mins

KEY PLAYERS - DEFENDERS

Richard Jackson

Pedigree

Goals Conceded in League	18
Goals Conceded in all competitions	21
Clean Sheets In games when player was on pitch for at least 70 minutes	5
Defensive Rating Ave number of mins between League goals conceded while on the pitch	82
Club Defensive Rating Average number of mins between League goals conceded by the club this season	69

	PLAYER	CON LGE	CON ALL	CLN SHEETS	DEF RATE
1	Richard Jackson	18	21	5	82 mins
2	Mohammed Konjic	16	18	5	76 mins
3	Tom Huddlestone	52	59	13	73 mins
4	Michael Johnson	41	47	10	72 mins
5	Jeff Kenna	52	62	11	69 mins

MONTHLY POINTS TALLY

AUGUST	6	33%
SEPTEMBER	8	53%
OCTOBER	8	53%
NOVEMBER	7	47%
DECEMBER	10	67%
JANUARY	9	60%
FEBRUARY	8	67%
MARCH	5	56%
APRIL	12	57%
MAY	3	100%

GOALS

	PLAYER	LGE	FAC	LC	Oth	TOT
1	Rasiak	16	1	0	0	17
2	Smith	11	0	0	0	11
3	Idiakez	9	1	1	0	11
4	Tudgay	9	1	0	0	10
5	Peschisolido	8	1	0	0	9
6	Reich	6	0	0	0	6
7	Bisgaard	4	0	0	0	4
8	Taylor	3	0	0	0	3
9	Bolder	2	0	0	0	2
10	Johnson	1	0	0	0	1
11	Vincent	1	0	0	0	1
	Other	1	1	0	0	2
	TOTAL	71	5	1	0	77

KEY GOALKEEPER

Lee Camp

Goals Conceded in the League	58
Goals Conceded in all competitions	69
Clean Sheets In games when player was on pitch for at least 70 minutes	13
Goals to Shots Ratio The average number of shots on target per each League goal conceded	4.4
Defensive Rating Ave number of mins between League goals conceded while on the pitch	69

DISCIPLINARY RECORDS

	PLAYER	YELLOW	RED	AVE
1	Vincent	5	1	221
2	Konjic	4	0	302
3	Idiakez	9	0	393
4	Bolder	5	0	469
5	Junior	1	0	470
6	Johnson	6	0	493
7	Huddlestone	6	0	636
8	Peschisolido	2	0	730
9	Taylor	2	1	807
10	Kenna	4	0	890
11	Bisgaard	3	0	909
12	Rasiak	3	0	1014
13	Reich	2	0	1083
	Other	3	1	
	TOTAL	55	3	

TOP POINT EARNERS

	PLAYER	GAMES	AV PTS
1	Marco Reich	16	2.06
2	Marcus Tudgay	14	1.93
3	Tom Huddlestone	40	1.78
4	Grzegorz Rasiak	33	1.76
5	Richard Jackson	16	1.75
6	Michael Johnson	31	1.74
7	Morten Bisgaard	30	1.73
8	Adam Bolder	22	1.73
9	Mohammed Konjic	13	1.69
10	Chris Makin	13	1.69
	CLUB AVERAGE:		1.65

LEAGUE APPEARANCES GOALS AND BOOKINGS

	AGE (on 01/07/05)	IN NAMED 16	APPEARANCES	COUNTING GAMES	MINUTES ON PITCH	LEAGUE GOALS	Yellow	Red
Goalkeepers								
Lee Camp	20	45	45	44	3976	0	1	1
Lee Grant	22	38	2	2	163	0	0	0
Kevin Miller	36	8	0	0	0	0	0	0
Liam Richardson	19	1	0	0	0	0	0	0
Defenders								
Nathan Doyle	18	5	3	3	270	0	1	0
Tom Huddlestone	18	46	45	40	3817	0	6	0
Richard Jackson	25	21	19	16	1484	0	0	0
Michael Johnson	32	36	36	31	2962	1	6	0
Blessing Kaku	27	4	4	1	208	0	0	0
Jeff Kenna	34	42	40	39	3563	0	4	0
Mohammed Konjic	35	17	16	13	1211	0	4	0
Chris Makin	38	13	13	13	1170	0	0	0
Pablo Mills	21	37	22	14	1503	0	0	0
Jason Talbot	19	3	2	2	166	0	0	0
Chris Turner	18	0	0	0	0	0	0	0
Jamie Vincent	30	17	15	15	1331	1	5	1
Midfielders								
Morten Bisgaard	31	36	36	30	2727	4	3	0
Paul Boertien	26	4	0	0	0	0	0	0
Adam Bolder	24	42	36	22	2348	2	5	0
Lee Holmes	18	10	3	0	88	0	0	0
Inigo Idiakez	31	41	41	39	3543	9	9	0
Marco Reich	27	40	37	16	2166	6	2	0
Ian Taylor	37	41	39	22	2422	3	2	1
Forwards								
Junior	28	31	18	2	470	0	1	0
Paul Peschisolido	34	43	32	10	1461	8	2	0
Grzegorz Rasiak	26	35	35	33	3042	16	3	0
Tommy Smith	25	42	42	36	3427	11	2	0
Marcus Tudgay	22	38	34	14	1904	9	0	0

TEAM OF THE SEASON

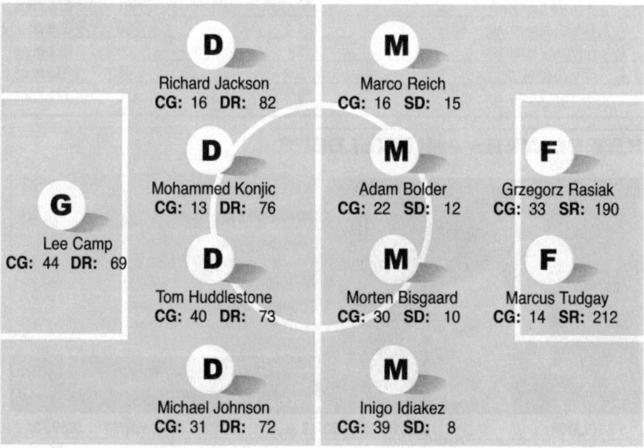
D
Richard Jackson
CG: 16 DR: 82
M
Marco Reich
CG: 16 SD: 15
D
Mohammed Konjic
CG: 13 DR: 76
M
Adam Bolder
CG: 22 SD: 12
F
Grzegorz Rasiak
CG: 33 SR: 190
G
Lee Camp
CG: 44 DR: 69
D
Tom Huddlestone
CG: 40 DR: 73
M
Morten Bisgaard
CG: 30 SD: 10
F
Marcus Tudgay
CG: 14 SR: 212
D
Michael Johnson
CG: 31 DR: 72
M
Inigo Idiakez
CG: 39 SD: 8

SQUAD APPEARANCES

Match	1	2	3	4	5	6	7	8	9	10	11	12	13	14	15	16	17	18	19	20	21	22	23	24	25	26	27	28	29	30	31	32	33	34	35	36	37	38	39	40	41	42	43	44	45	46	47	48	49	50	51	52
Venue	A	H	H	A	A	H	A	H	A	A	H	H	A	H	A	A	H	H	A	A	H	A	H	H	A	A	H	H	A	H	H	A	H	H	A	A	A	H	A	H	H	H	A	A	H	A	H	A	A	H	A	H
Competition	L	L	L	L	W	L	L	L	L	L	L	L	L	L	L	L	L	L	L	L	L	L	L	L	L	L	L	L	L	F	L	L	L	F	L	F	L	L	L	L	L	L	L	L	L	L	L	L	L	L	O	O
Result	L	L	W	W	L	L	L	W	W	L	D	D	D	D	L	W	W	W	D	W	L	L	D	W	W	W	L	L	W	W	L	W	W	D	W	L	W	D	D	D	W	D	L	W	W	W	W	L	L	W	L	D

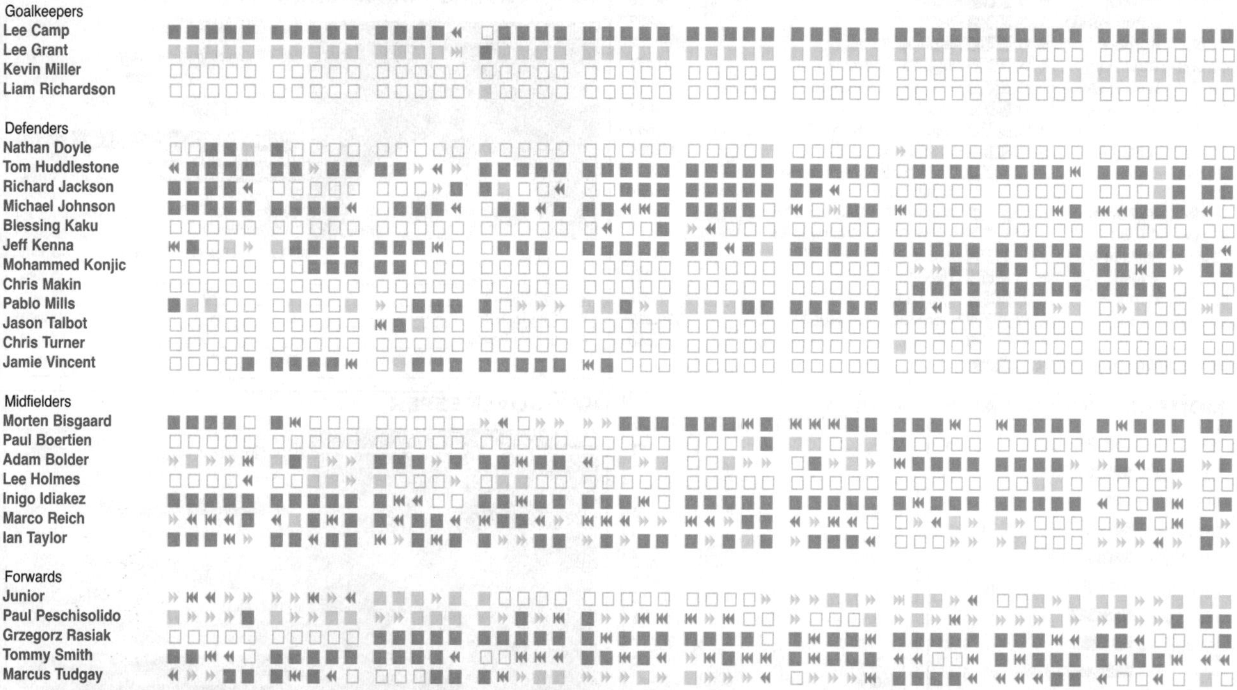
Goalkeepers
Lee Camp
Lee Grant
Kevin Miller
Liam Richardson
Defenders
Nathan Doyle
Tom Huddlestone
Richard Jackson
Michael Johnson
Blessing Kaku
Jeff Kenna
Mohammed Konjic
Chris Makin
Pablo Mills
Jason Talbot
Chris Turner
Jamie Vincent
Midfielders
Morten Bisgaard
Paul Boertien
Adam Bolder
Lee Holmes
Inigo Idiakez
Marco Reich
Ian Taylor
Forwards
Junior
Paul Peschisolido
Grzegorz Rasiak
Tommy Smith
Marcus Tudgay

KEY: On all match | On bench | Subbed or sent off (Counting game) | Subbed or sent off (playing less than 70 minutes) | Subbed on from bench (Counting Game) | Subbed on (playing less than 70 minutes) | Subbed on and then subbed or sent off (Counting Game) | Subbed on and then subbed or sent off (playing less than 70 minutes) | Not in 16

PRESTON NORTH END

Final Position: **5th**

NICKNAME: THE LILYWHITES

KEY: Won / Drawn / Lost

	Comp	Opponent	Venue	Res	Score	Scorers	Attendance
1	div1	Watford	H	W	2-1	Cresswell 34; Healy 77 pen	12,208
2	div1	Wolverhampton	A	D	2-2	Lucketti 4; Healy 15	26,115
3	div1	Gillingham	A	L	1-2	Fuller 34	7,073
4	div1	Sheff Utd	H	L	0-1		12,084
5	div1	Brighton	A	L	0-1		5,996
6	div1	Rotherham	H	W	2-0	Etuhu 15,45	11,439
7	div1	Stoke	H	W	3-0	Cresswell 27,79; Healy 80	12,759
8	div1	Reading	A	L	1-3	Healy 45	11,857
9	div1	Sunderland	A	L	1-3	Alexander 39 pen	24,264
10	ccr1	Mansfield	A	W	4-0	Cresswell 3; Alexander 9; Daley 31; Lynch 84	3,208
11	div1	Crewe	H	W	1-0	Davidson 40	11,823
12	div1	Plymouth	H	D	1-1	Cresswell 66	11,445
13	div1	Leicester	A	D	1-1	Lonergan 39	21,249
14	ccr2	Leicester	A	W	3-2	Cresswell 34,90 pen,113	6,751
15	div1	Leeds	A	L	0-1		30,458
16	div1	QPR	H	W	2-1	Healy 11; Cresswell 78 pen	10,548
17	div1	Nottm Forest	H	W	3-2	McKenna 11; Lucketti 36; Etuhu 57	12,439
18	ccr3	Everton	A	L	0-2		33,922
19	div1	Ipswich	A	L	0-3		23,745
20	div1	Coventry	A	D	1-1	Lewis 68	12,478
21	div1	Leeds	H	L	2-4	Cresswell 54,83	18,531
22	div1	Millwall	H	D	1-1	Lewis 15	10,339
23	div1	Cardiff	A	W	1-0	Mawene 14	10,950
24	div1	Derby	H	W	3-0	Alexander 13,43 pen; Cresswell 88	12,702
25	div1	Wigan	A	L	0-5		10,565
26	div1	Burnley	A	L	0-2		15,318
27	div1	West Ham	H	W	2-1	Lewis 9; O'Neill 45	13,451
28	div1	Stoke	A	D	0-0		20,350
29	div1	Reading	H	W	3-0	Agyemang 17; Hughes 26 og; Lewis 67	12,795
30	div1	Sunderland	H	W	3-2	Cresswell 13,30,43	16,940
31	div1	Crewe	A	W	2-1	Sedgwick 9; O'Neil 59	8,667
32	facr3	West Brom	H	L	0-2		13,005
33	div1	Leicester	H	D	1-1	McKenna 64	12,677
34	div1	Plymouth	A	W	2-0	Sedgwick 29; Agyemang 34	13,663
35	div1	Coventry	H	W	3-2	Alexander 22 pen; Cresswell 23; Lucketti 48	13,691
36	div1	QPR	A	W	2-1	Nugent 67; Lucketti 75	15,620
37	div1	Ipswich	H	D	1-1	Nugent 36	14,418
38	div1	Nottm Forest	A	L	0-2		19,209
39	div1	Burnley	H	W	1-0	Alexander 82 pen	18,202
40	div1	West Ham	A	W	2-1	Nugent 17; Agyemang 81	26,442
41	div1	Wolverhampton	H	D	2-2	Cresswell 3; Alexander 53 pen	16,296
42	div1	Sheff Utd	A	D	1-1	Cresswell 48	18,647
43	div1	Watford	A	W	2-0	Nugent 60; McKenna 71	19,649
44	div1	Gillingham	H	D	1-1	Brown 28 og	15,054
45	div1	Brighton	H	W	3-0	Alexander 31 pen; Cresswell 45; Nugent 51	14,234
46	div1	Rotherham	A	W	2-1	Sedgwick 51; Mawene 62	6,312
47	div1	Cardiff	H	W	3-0	Nugent 67,79; Cresswell 85	15,141
48	div1	Millwall	A	L	1-2	Nugent 58	11,417
49	div1	Wigan	H	D	1-1	O'Neil 42	20,221
50	div1	Derby	A	L	1-3	Agyemang 69	31,237
51	d1po1	Derby	H	W	2-0	Nugent 38; Cresswell 89	20,315
52	d1po2	Derby	A	D	0-0		31,310
53	d1pof	West Ham	N	L	0-1		70,275

KEY PLAYERS - GOALSCORERS

Richard Cresswell

Goals in the League	16
Goals in all competitions	21
Contribution to Attacking Power Average number of minutes between League team goals while on pitch	61
Player Strike Rate Average number of minutes between League goals scored by player	254
Club Strike Rate Average number of minutes between League goals scored by club	62

	PLAYER	GOALS LGE	GOALS ALL	POWER	S RATE
1	Richard Cresswell	16	21	61	254 mins
2	Patrick Agyemang	4	4	58	339 mins
3	Graham Alexander	7	8	60	521 mins
4	Chris Sedgwick	3	3	48	645 mins
5	Dickson Etuhu	3	3	70	721 mins

KEY PLAYERS - MIDFIELDERS

Chris Sedgwick

Goals in the League	3
Goals in all competitions	3
Defensive Rating Average number of mins between League goals conceded while on the pitch	84
Contribution to Attacking Power Average number of minutes between League team goals while on pitch	48
Scoring Difference Defensive Rating minus Contribution to Attacking Power	36

	PLAYER	GOALS LGE	GOALS ALL	DEF RATE	ATT POWER	SCORE DIFF
1	Chris Sedgwick	3	3	84	48	36 mins
2	Paul McKenna	3	3	82	60	22 mins
3	Brian O'Neil	2	2	79	60	19 mins
4	Eddie Lewis	4	4	77	59	18 mins
5	Dickson Etuhu	3	3	55	70	-15 mins

KEY PLAYERS - DEFENDERS

Callum Davidson

Goals Conceded in League	14
Goals Conceded in all competitions	16
Clean Sheets In games when player was on pitch for at least 70 minutes	4
Defensive Rating Ave number of mins between League goals conceded while on the pitch	95
Club Defensive Rating Average number of mins between League goals conceded by the club this season	71

	PLAYER	CON LGE	CON ALL	CLN SHEETS	DEF RATE
1	Callum Davidson	14	16	4	95 mins
2	Youl Mawene	53	60	12	76 mins
3	Chris Lucketti	52	57	10	70 mins
4	Graham Alexander	53	58	11	69 mins
5	Claude Davis	30	32	4	62 mins

MONTHLY POINTS TALLY

AUGUST	7	39%
SEPTEMBER	7	47%
OCTOBER	7	47%
NOVEMBER	8	53%
DECEMBER	7	47%
JANUARY	10	83%
FEBRUARY	10	67%
MARCH	8	67%
APRIL	11	61%
MAY	0	0%

GOALS

	PLAYER	LGE	FAC	LC	Oth	TOT
1	Cresswell	16	0	4	1	21
2	Nugent	8	0	0	1	9
3	Alexander	7	0	1	0	8
4	Healy	5	0	0	0	5
5	Agyemang	4	0	0	0	4
6	Lewis	4	0	0	0	4
7	Lucketti	4	0	0	0	4
8	Sedgwick	3	0	0	0	3
9	McKenna	3	0	0	0	3
10	Etuhu	3	0	0	0	3
11	Mawene	2	0	0	0	2
	Other	8	0	2	0	10
	TOTAL	67	0	7	2	76

KEY GOALKEEPER

Andrew Lonergan

Goals Conceded in the League	25
Goals Conceded in all competitions	29
Clean Sheets In games when player was on pitch for at least 70 minutes	6
Goals to Shots Ratio The average number of shots on target per each League goal conceded	4.6
Defensive Rating Ave number of mins between League goals conceded while on the pitch	81

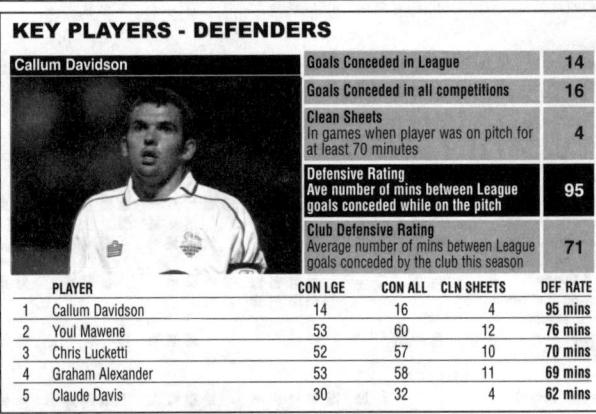

DISCIPLINARY RECORDS

	PLAYER	YELLOW	RED	AVE
1	Davis	7	0	**265**
2	Sedgwick	6	0	**322**
3	Lewis	9	1	**332**
4	McKenna	8	0	**411**
5	Davidson	3	0	**445**
6	Cresswell	8	0	**508**
7	O'Neil	5	1	**593**
8	Broomes	1	0	**723**
9	Alexander	5	0	**730**
10	Mawene	5	0	**801**
11	Healy	1	0	**941**
12	Hill	1	0	**1046**
13	Lucketti	3	0	**1215**
	Other	1	1	
	TOTAL	63	3	

TOP POINT EARNERS

	PLAYER	GAMES	AV PTS
1	Chris Sedgwick	20	**2.10**
2	Patrick Agyemang	13	**1.92**
3	Callum Davidson	13	**1.85**
4	Brian O'Neil	38	**1.79**
5	Eddie Lewis	35	**1.77**
6	Youl Mawene	43	**1.74**
7	Chris Lucketti	40	**1.73**
8	Andrew Lonergan	22	**1.73**
9	Paul McKenna	36	**1.67**
10	Richard Cresswell	45	**1.67**
	CLUB AVERAGE:		**1.63**

LEAGUE APPEARANCES GOALS AND BOOKINGS

	AGE (on 01/07/05)	IN NAMED 16	APPEARANCES	COUNTING GAMES	MINUTES ON PITCH	LEAGUE GOALS	Yellow	Red
Goalkeepers								
Chris Day	29	6	6	6	540	0	0	0
Jonathan Gould	36	8	4	4	360	0	0	0
Andrew Lonergan	21	23	23	22	2018	1	0	0
Carlo Nash	31	7	7	7	630	0	0	0
Gavin Ward	35	43	7	6	584	0	0	0
Defenders								
Graham Alexander	33	43	42	41	3650	7	5	0
Marlon Broomes	27	15	11	6	723	0	1	0
John Curtis	26	12	12	11	1027	0	0	0
Callum Davidson	29	24	19	13	1336	1	3	0
Claude Davis	26	38	32	18	1860	0	7	0
Matthew Hill	24	17	14	11	1046	0	1	0
Robert Kozluk	27	2	1	0	29	0	0	0
Chris Lucketti	33	42	41	40	3645	4	3	0
Youl Mawene	25	46	46	43	4008	2	5	0
Tyrone Mears	22	5	4	1	123	0	1	0
Midfielders								
Omar Daley	24	25	14	1	278	0	0	0
Dickson Etuhu	23	37	35	21	2162	3	0	1
Yoann Folly	20	4	2	0	28	0	0	0
Eddie Lewis	31	40	40	35	3321	4	9	1
Alan McCormack	21	8	3	0	33	0	0	0
Paul McKenna	27	40	39	36	3295	3	8	0
Brian O'Neil	32	46	43	38	3558	2	5	1
Chris Sedgwick	25	24	24	20	1936	3	6	0
Eric Skora	23	11	9	2	447	0	0	0
Forwards								
Patrick Agyemang	24	27	27	13	1354	4	1	0
Richard Cresswell	27	46	46	45	4071	16	8	0
Ricardo Fuller	25	2	2	1	132	1	0	0
David Healy	25	11	11	10	941	5	1	0
Mark Jackson	19	3	2	0	31	0	0	0
Simon Lynch	23	15	9	1	254	0	0	1
Guylain Ndumbu-Nsungu	22	7	6	1	290	0	1	0
David Nugent	20	18	18	11	1168	8	0	0
Joe O'Neill	22	6	2	0	11	0	0	0
Filipe Oliveira	21	6	5	1	146	0	1	0
Andrew Smith	24	23	14	1	379	0	1	0

TEAM OF THE SEASON

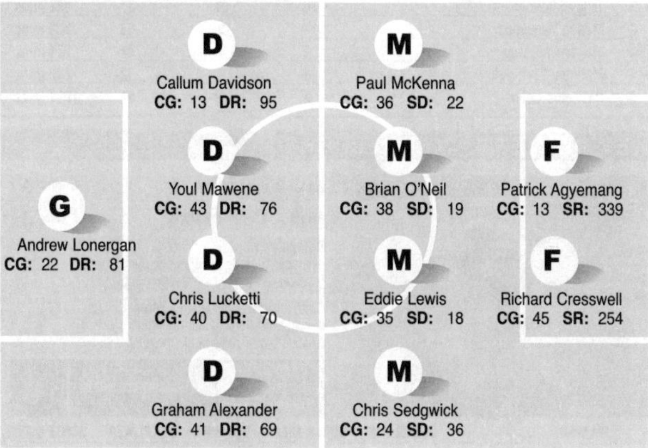

G
Andrew Lonergan
CG: 22 DR: 81
D
Callum Davidson
CG: 13 DR: 95
D
Youl Mawene
CG: 43 DR: 76
D
Chris Lucketti
CG: 40 DR: 70
D
Graham Alexander
CG: 41 DR: 69
M
Paul McKenna
CG: 36 SD: 22
M
Brian O'Neil
CG: 38 SD: 19
M
Eddie Lewis
CG: 35 SD: 18
M
Chris Sedgwick
CG: 24 SD: 36
F
Patrick Agyemang
CG: 13 SR: 339
F
Richard Cresswell
CG: 45 SR: 254

SQUAD APPEARANCES

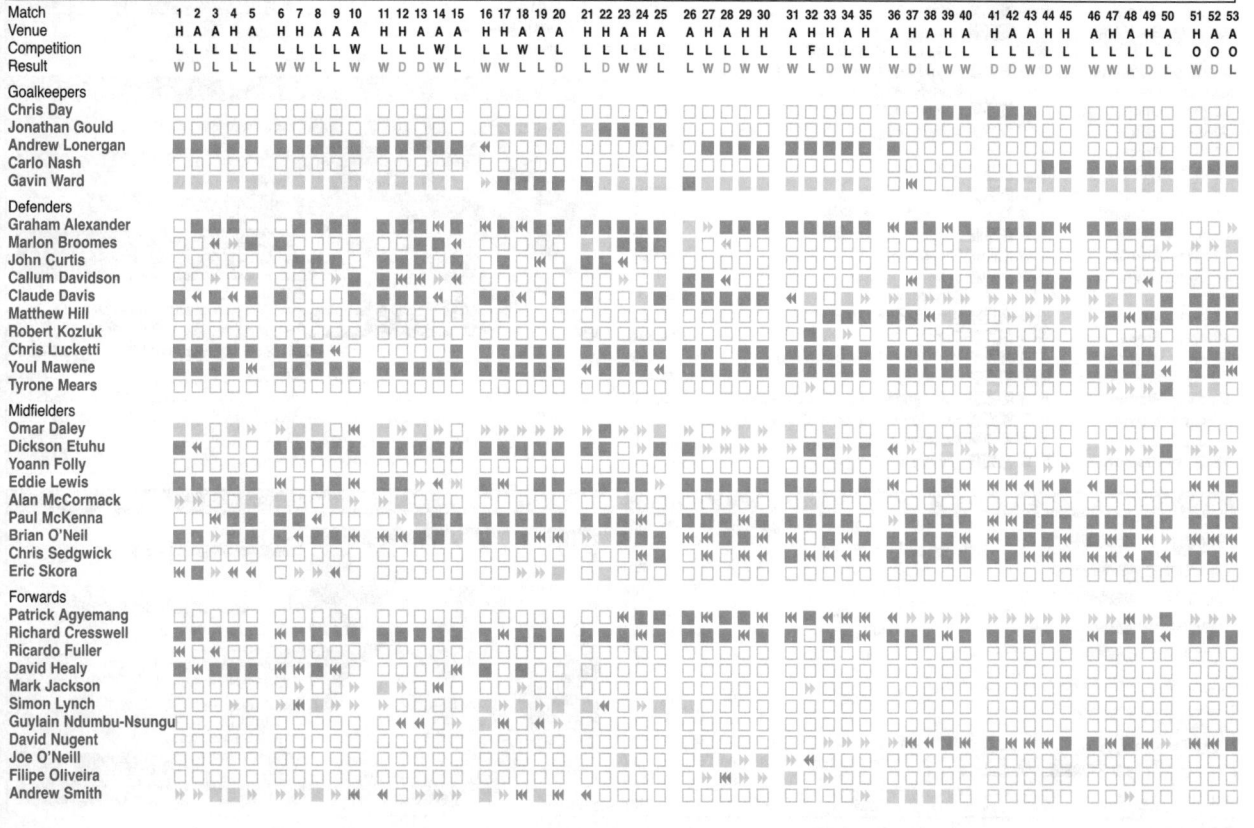

Match	1	2	3	4	5	6	7	8	9	10	11	12	13	14	15	16	17	18	19	20	21	22	23	24	25	26	27
Venue	H	A	A	H	A	H	H	A	A	A	H	H	A	A	A	H	H	A	A	A	H	H	A	H	A	A	H
Competition	L	L	L	L	L	L	L	L	L	W	L	L	L	W	L	L	L	W	L	L	L	L	L	L	L	L	L
Result	W	D	L	L	L	W	W	L	L	W	W	D	D	W	L	W	W	L	L	D	L	D	W	W	L	L	W

Match	28	29	30	31	32	33	34	35	36	37	38	39	40	41	42	43	44	45	46	47	48	49	50	51	52	53
Venue	A	H	H	A	H	H	A	H	A	H	A	H	A	H	A	A	H	H	A	H	A	H	A	H	A	A
Competition	L	L	L	L	F	L	L	L	L	L	L	L	L	L	L	L	L	L	L	L	L	L	L	O	O	O
Result	D	W	W	W	L	D	W	W	W	D	L	W	W	D	D	W	D	W	W	W	L	D	L	W	D	L

Goalkeepers
Chris Day
Jonathan Gould
Andrew Lonergan
Carlo Nash
Gavin Ward

Defenders
Graham Alexander
Marlon Broomes
John Curtis
Callum Davidson
Claude Davis
Matthew Hill
Robert Kozluk
Chris Lucketti
Youl Mawene
Tyrone Mears

Midfielders
Omar Daley
Dickson Etuhu
Yoann Folly
Eddie Lewis
Alan McCormack
Paul McKenna
Brian O'Neil
Chris Sedgwick
Eric Skora

Forwards
Patrick Agyemang
Richard Cresswell
Ricardo Fuller
David Healy
Mark Jackson
Simon Lynch
Guylain Ndumbu-Nsungu
David Nugent
Joe O'Neill
Filipe Oliveira
Andrew Smith

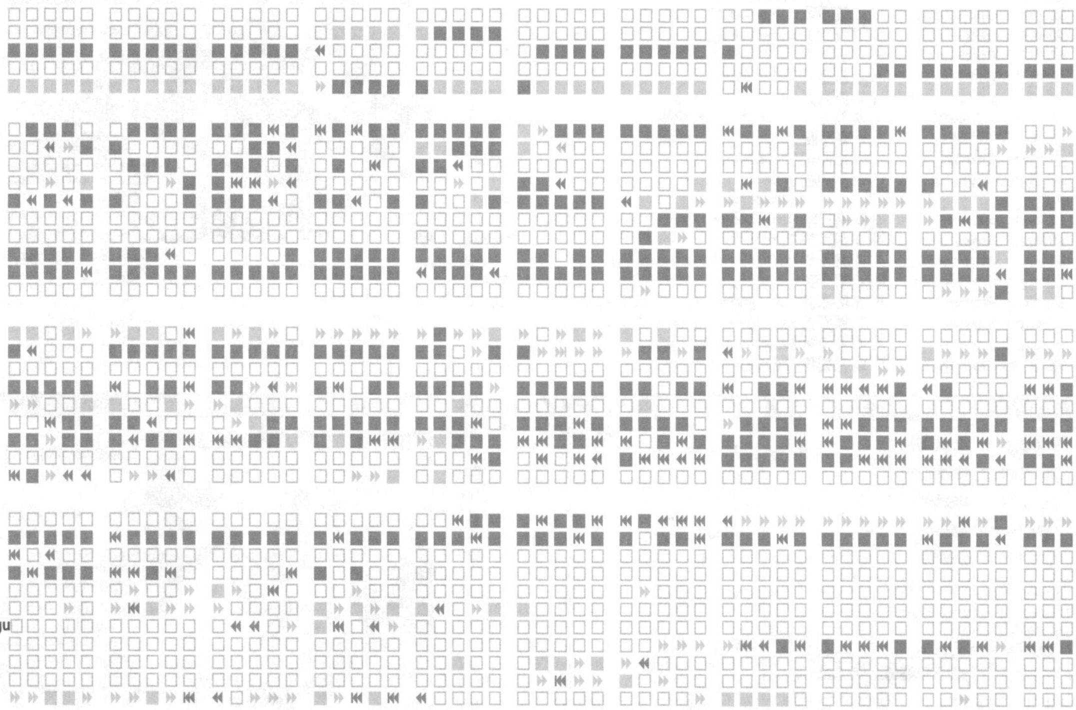

WEST HAM UNITED

PROMOTED VIA THE PLAY-OFFS Final Position: **6th**

NICKNAME: THE HAMMERS KEY: Won Drawn Lost

							Attendance
1	div1	Leicester	A	D	0-0		30,231
2	div1	Reading	H	W	1-0	Sheringham 81	26,242
3	div1	Wigan	H	L	1-3	Zamora 69	23,271
4	div1	Crewe	A	W	3-2	Sheringham 16,22; Brevett 30	7,857
5	ccr1	Southend	H	W	2-0	Harewood 11,90	16,910
6	div1	Burnley	H	W	1-0	Nowland 62	22,119
7	div1	Coventry	A	L	1-2	Sheringham 42	17,404
8	div1	Sheff Utd	A	W	2-1	Harewood 9; Sheringham 85	21,058
9	div1	Rotherham	H	W	1-0	Etherington 69	26,233
10	div1	Ipswich	H	D	1-1	Mackay 11	28,812
11	ccr2	Notts County	H	W	3-2	Zamora 1,54; Rebrov 62	11,111
12	div1	Nottm Forest	A	L	1-2	Harewood 58	25,615
13	div1	Derby	A	D	1-1	Etherington 11	23,112
14	div1	Wolverhampton	H	W	1-0	Sheringham 75	29,585
15	div1	QPR	A	L	0-1		18,363
16	div1	Stoke	H	W	2-0	Harewood 31; Sheringham 59	29,808
17	div1	Gillingham	H	W	3-1	Zamora 18; Harewood 25; Mullins 39	25,247
18	ccr3	Chelsea	A	L	0-1		41,774
19	div1	Plymouth	A	D	1-1	Lomas 43	20,220
20	div1	Cardiff	A	L	1-4	Harewood 69 pen	14,222
21	div1	QPR	H	W	2-1	Harewood 36 pen,84	31,365
22	div1	Brighton	H	L	0-1		29,514
23	div1	Millwall	A	L	0-1		19,025
24	div1	Watford	H	W	3-2	Reo-Coker 28; Powell, D 30; Rebrov 58	24,541
25	div1	Sunderland	A	W	2-0	Harewood 59; Sheringham 90	29,510
26	div1	Leeds	H	D	1-1	Chadwick 50	30,684
27	div1	Preston	A	L	1-2	Reo-Coker 50	13,451
28	div1	Nottm Forest	H	W	3-2	Etherington 17; Sheringham 39,82	32,270
29	div1	Rotherham	A	D	2-2	Sheringham 71 pen; Harewood 76 pen	7,769
30	div1	Ipswich	A	W	2-0	Harewood 1; Etherington 90	30,003
31	div1	Sheff Utd	H	L	0-2		27,424
32	facr3	Norwich	H	W	1-0	Harewood 81	23,389
33	div1	Wolverhampton	A	L	2-4	Zamora 36,57	28,411
34	div1	Derby	H	L	1-2	Fletcher 26	30,347
35	facr4	Sheff Utd	H	D	1-1	Harewood 39	19,444
36	div1	Cardiff	H	W	1-0	Fletcher 89	23,716
37	facr4r	Sheff Utd	A	L	1-1*	Sheringham 63 pen (*aet, lost 3-1 on penalties)	15,067
38	div1	Plymouth	H	W	5-0	Harewood 10 pen; Worrell 23 og; Mackay 40; Sheringham 76,84 pen	25,490
39	div1	Gillingham	A	W	1-0	Harewood 13	9,510
40	div1	Leeds	A	L	1-2	Williams 68	34,115
41	div1	Preston	H	L	1-2	Zamora 87	26,442
42	div1	Reading	A	L	1-3	Sheringham 82	22,268
43	div1	Crewe	H	D	1-1	Sheringham 76	26,593
44	div1	Leicester	H	D	2-2	Sheringham 28,62	22,031
45	div1	Wigan	A	W	2-1	Sheringham 55; Harewood 67	12,993
46	div1	Burnley	A	W	1-0	Sheringham 83	12,209
47	div1	Coventry	H	W	3-0	Shaw 76 og; Sheringham 89 pen; Zamora 90	26,839
48	div1	Millwall	H	D	1-1	Harewood 35	28,221
49	div1	Stoke	A	W	1-0	Zamora 78	14,534
50	div1	Brighton	A	D	2-2	Reo-Coker 8; Harewood 55	6,819
51	div1	Sunderland	H	L	1-2	Harewood 43	33,482
52	div1	Watford	A	W	2-1	Ferdinand 42; Harewood 70 pen	19,673
53	d1po1	Ipswich	H	D	2-2	Harewood 7; Zamora 13	33,723
54	d1po2	Ipswich	A	W	2-0	Zamora 61,72	30,010
55	d1pof	Preston	N	W	1-0	Zamora 57	70,275

KEY PLAYERS - GOALSCORERS

Teddy Sheringham

Goals in the League	20
Goals in all competitions	21
Contribution to Attacking Power Average number of minutes between League team goals while on pitch	55
Player Strike Rate Average number of minutes between League goals scored by player	122
Club Strike Rate Average number of minutes between League goals scored by club	63

	PLAYER	GOALS LGE	GOALS ALL	POWER	S RATE
1	Teddy Sheringham	20	21	55	122 mins
2	Marlon Harewood	17	22	68	229 mins
3	Malcolm Mackay	2	2	55	751 mins
4	Matthew Etherington	4	4	62	760 mins
5	Nigel Reo-Coker	3	3	61	1060 mins

KEY PLAYERS - MIDFIELDERS

Nigel Reo-Coker

Goals in the League	3
Goals in all competitions	3
Defensive Rating Average number of mins between League goals conceded while on the pitch	84
Contribution to Attacking Power Average number of minutes between League team goals while on pitch	61
Scoring Difference Defensive Rating minus Contribution to Attacking Power	23

	PLAYER	GOALS LGE	GOALS ALL	DEF RATE	ATT POWER	SCORE DIFF
1	Nigel Reo-Coker	3	3	84	61	23 mins
2	Matthew Etherington	4	4	76	62	14 mins
3	Carl Fletcher	2	2	75	69	6 mins
4	Luke Chadwick	1	1	66	64	2 mins
5	Steve Lomas	1	1	62	64	-2 mins

KEY PLAYERS - DEFENDERS

Anton Ferdinand

Goals Conceded in League	28
Goals Conceded in all competitions	33
Clean Sheets In games when player was on pitch for at least 70 minutes	8
Defensive Rating Ave number of mins between League goals conceded while on the pitch	79
Club Defensive Rating Average number of mins between League goals conceded by the club this season	74

	PLAYER	CON LGE	CON ALL	CLN SHEETS	DEF RATE
1	Anton Ferdinand	28	33	8	79 mins
2	Tomas Repka	49	56	13	76 mins
3	Chris Powell	43	47	10	74 mins
4	Hayden Mullins	40	46	9	69 mins
5	Malcolm Mackay	22	26	6	68 mins

MONTHLY POINTS TALLY

AUGUST	10	56%
SEPTEMBER	8	53%
OCTOBER	10	67%
NOVEMBER	6	40%
DECEMBER	8	53%
JANUARY	3	25%
FEBRUARY	9	75%
MARCH	2	17%
APRIL	14	67%
MAY	3	100%

GOALS

	PLAYER	LGE	FAC	LC	Oth	TOT
1	Sheringham	20	1	0	0	21
2	Harewood	17	2	2	1	22
3	Zamora	7	0	2	4	13
4	Etherington	4	0	0	0	4
5	Reo-Coker	3	0	0	0	3
6	Fletcher	2	0	0	0	2
7	Mackay	2	0	0	0	2
8	Williams	1	0	0	0	1
9	Rebrov	1	0	1	0	2
10	Chadwick	1	0	0	0	1
11	Ferdinand	1	0	0	0	1
	Other	7	0	0	0	7
	TOTAL	66	3	5	5	79

KEY GOALKEEPER

Stephen Bywater

Goals Conceded in the League	43
Goals Conceded in all competitions	45
Clean Sheets In games when player was on pitch for at least 70 minutes	11
Goals to Shots Ratio The average number of shots on target per each League goal conceded	3.6
Defensive Rating Ave number of mins between League goals conceded while on the pitch	75

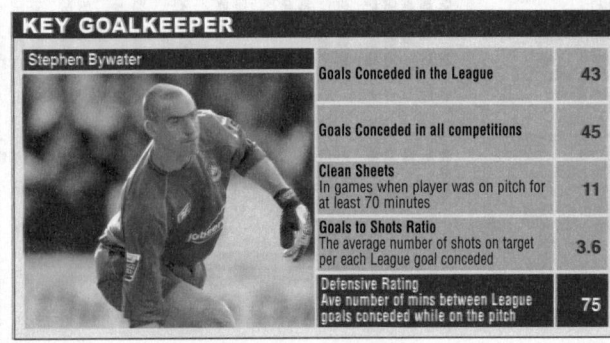

DISCIPLINARY RECORDS

	PLAYER	YELLOW	RED	AVE
1	Brevett	4	1	172
2	Williams	2	0	281
3	Ward	3	0	301
4	Reo-Coker	10	0	318
5	Rebrov	3	0	356
6	Harewood	9	1	389
7	Zamora	4	0	390
8	Fletcher	6	0	399
9	Noble	2	0	471
10	Repka	6	1	531
11	Mullins	4	1	554
12	Lomas	2	1	575
13	Walker	1	0	900
	Other	7	0	
	TOTAL	63	5	

TOP POINT EARNERS

	PLAYER	GAMES	AV PTS
1	Luke Chadwick	12	1.92
2	Teddy Sheringham	24	1.79
3	Nigel Reo-Coker	33	1.79
4	Anton Ferdinand	23	1.78
5	Tomas Repka	41	1.66
6	Marlon Harewood	43	1.63
7	Stephen Bywater	36	1.56
8	Malcolm Mackay	17	1.53
9	Hayden Mullins	29	1.52
10	Chris Powell	35	1.51
	CLUB AVERAGE:		1.59

LEAGUE APPEARANCES GOALS AND BOOKINGS

	AGE (on 01/07/05)	IN NAMED 16	APPEARANCES	COUNTING GAMES	MINUTES ON PITCH	LEAGUE GOALS	Yellow	Red
Goalkeepers								
Robert Burch	21	6	0	0	0	0	0	0
Stephen Bywater	24	46	36	36	3240	0	1	0
James Walker	32	40	10	10	900	0	1	0
Defenders								
Darren Blewitt	-	0	0	0	0	0	0	0
Rufus Brevett	35	20	10	10	862	1	4	1
Chris Cohen	18	15	11	1	218	0	0	1
Christian Dailly	31	3	3	2	181	0	1	0
Calum Davenport	22	10	10	10	900	0	0	0
Anton Ferdinand	20	36	29	23	2199	1	1	0
Malcolm Mackay	33	18	18	17	1501	2	1	0
Trent McClenahan	20	6	2	0	37	0	0	0
Andy Melville	36	8	3	2	240	0	0	0
Hayden Mullins	26	42	37	29	2771	1	4	1
Darren Powell	29	5	5	5	439	1	1	0
Chris Powell	35	38	36	35	3166	0	1	0
Tomas Repka	31	42	42	41	3720	0	6	1
Mauricio Taricco	32	1	1	0	26	0	0	0
Elliott Ward	20	2	0	0	0	0	0	0
Midfielders								
Luke Chadwick	24	37	32	12	1857	1	2	0
Matthew Etherington	23	41	39	30	3041	4	0	0
Carl Fletcher	25	36	32	25	2398	2	6	0
Don Hutchison	34	6	5	2	219	0	2	0
Steve Lomas	31	24	23	17	1726	1	2	1
Jobi McAnuff	23	1	1	0	18	0	0	0
Shaun Newton	29	11	11	11	958	0	0	0
Mark Noble	18	15	13	10	943	0	2	0
Nigel Reo-Coker	21	42	39	33	3181	3	10	0
Gavin Williams	24	12	10	6	563	1	2	0
Forwards								
Richard Garcia	23	1	1	0	7	0	0	0
Marlon Harewood	25	45	45	43	3897	17	9	1
Adam Nowland	24	8	4	2	268	1	0	0
Sergei Rebrov	31	34	26	7	1069	1	3	0
Teddy Sheringham	39	33	33	24	2438	20	1	0
Bobby Zamora	24	39	34	10	1560	7	4	0

TEAM OF THE SEASON

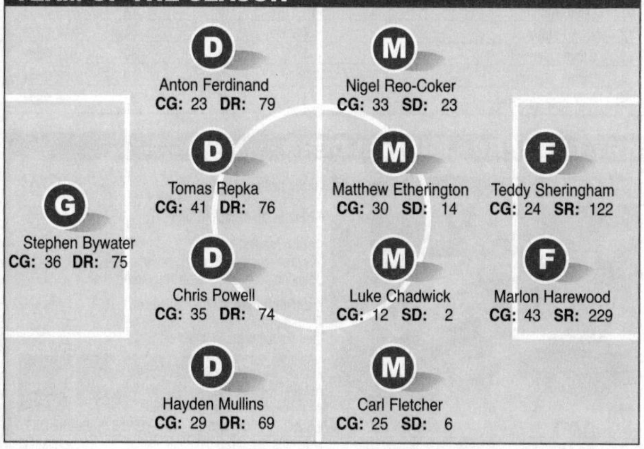
D
Anton Ferdinand
CG: 23 DR: 79
M
Nigel Reo-Coker
CG: 33 SD: 23
D
Tomas Repka
CG: 41 DR: 76
M
Matthew Etherington
CG: 30 SD: 14
F
Teddy Sheringham
CG: 24 SR: 122
G
Stephen Bywater
CG: 36 DR: 75
D
Chris Powell
CG: 35 DR: 74
M
Luke Chadwick
CG: 12 SD: 2
F
Marlon Harewood
CG: 43 SR: 229
D
Hayden Mullins
CG: 29 DR: 69
M
Carl Fletcher
CG: 25 SD: 6

SQUAD APPEARANCES

Match	1	2	3	4	5	6	7	8	9	10	11	12	13	14	15	16	17	18	19	20	21	22	23	24	25	26	27	28
Venue	A	H	H	A	H	H	A	A	H	H	H	A	A	H	A	H	H	A	A	A	H	H	A	H	A	H	A	H
Competition	L	L	L	L	W	L	L	L	L	L	W	L	L	L	L	L	L	W	L	L	L	L	L	L	L	L	L	L
Result	D	W	L	W	W	W	L	W	W	D	W	L	D	W	L	W	W	L	D	L	W	L	L	W	W	D	L	W

Match	29	30	31	32	33	34	35	36	37	38	39	40	41	42	43	44	45	46	47	48	49	50	51	52	53	54	55
Venue	A	A	H	H	A	H	H	H	A	H	A	A	H	A	H	H	A	A	H	H	A	A	H	A	H	A	H
Competition	L	L	L	F	L	L	F	L	F	L	L	L	L	L	L	L	L	L	L	L	L	L	L	L	O	O	O
Result	D	W	L	W	L	L	D	W	L	W	W	L	L	L	D	D	W	W	W	D	W	D	L	W	D	W	W

Goalkeepers
Robert Burch
Stephen Bywater
James Walker

Defenders
Darren Blewitt
Rufus Brevett
Chris Cohen
Christian Dailly
Calum Davenport
Anton Ferdinand
Malcolm Mackay
Trent McClenahan
Andy Melville
Hayden Mullins
Chris Powell
Darren Powell
Tomas Repka
Mauricio Taricco
Elliott Ward

Midfielders
Luke Chadwick
Matthew Etherington
Carl Fletcher
Don Hutchison
Steve Lomas
Jobi McAnuff
Shaun Newton
Mark Noble
Nigel Reo-Coker
Gavin Williams

Forwards
Richard Garcia
Marlon Harewood
Adam Nowland
Sergei Rebrov
Teddy Sheringham
Bobby Zamora

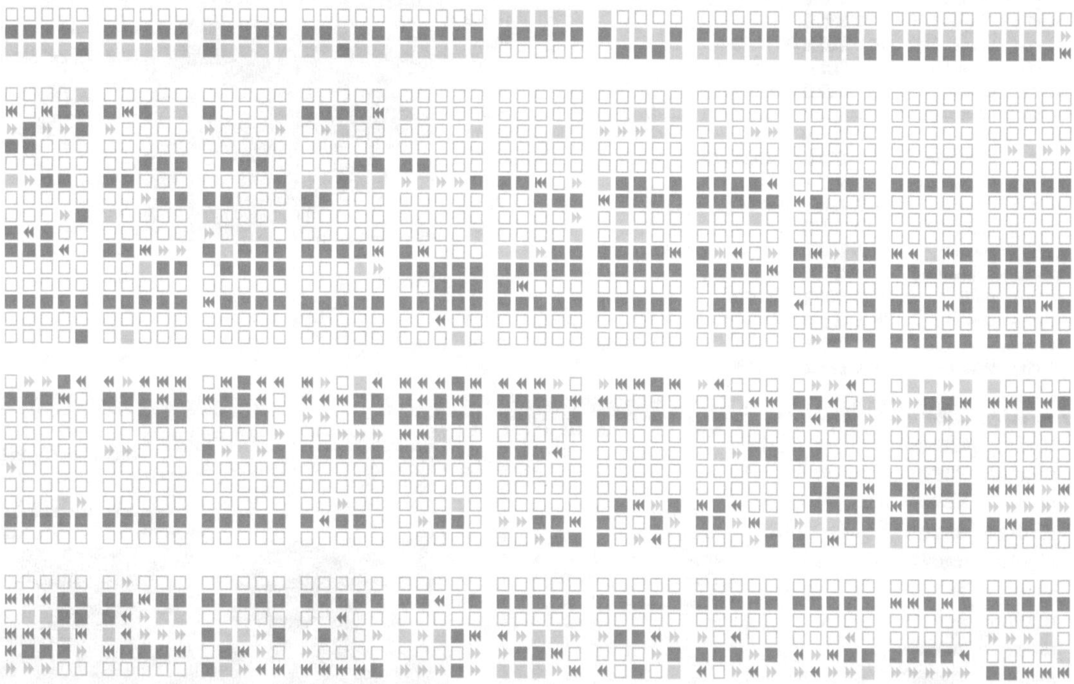

KEY: On all match | Subbed or sent off (Counting game) | Subbed on from bench (Counting Game) | Subbed on and then subbed or sent off (Counting Game) | Not in 16
On bench | Subbed or sent off (playing less than 70 minutes) | Subbed on (playing less than 70 minutes) | Subbed on and then subbed or sent off (playing less than 70 minutes)

READING

Final Position: **7th**

NICKNAME: THE ROYALS

KEY: ☐ Won ☐ Drawn ☐ Lost

							Attendance
1	div1	Brighton	H	W	3-2	Kitson 2; Harper 41; Forster 59	15,641
2	div1	West Ham	A	L	0-1		26,242
3	div1	Sheff Utd	A	W	1-0	Harper 41	22,429
4	div1	Rotherham	H	W	1-0	Kitson 45 pen	11,404
5	ccr1	Oxford	A	W	2-0	Goater 62; Hughes 77	5,919
6	div1	Millwall	A	L	0-1		12,098
7	div1	Sunderland	H	W	1-0	Forster 2	15,792
8	div1	Derby	A	L	1-2	Shorey 88	22,096
9	div1	Preston	H	W	3-1	Kitson 11; Forster 34,85	11,857
10	div1	Gillingham	H	W	3-1	Kitson 1,16 pen,28 pen	13,867
11	ccr2	Watford	H	L	0-3		8,429
12	div1	Watford	A	W	1-0	Hughes 65	13,389
13	div1	Ipswich	A	D	1-1	Kitson 26	23,167
14	div1	Burnley	H	D	0-0		15,400
15	div1	Stoke	A	W	1-0	Shorey 41	15,574
16	div1	Leeds	H	D	1-1	Owusu 45	22,230
17	div1	Crewe	H	W	4-0	Sidwell 21; Kitson 25; Owusu 45; Ingimarsson 47	13,630
18	div1	Coventry	A	L	2-3	Owusu 11; Kitson 71	13,663
19	div1	Plymouth	A	D	2-2	Coughlan 51 og; Kitson 90	14,336
20	div1	Stoke	H	W	1-0	Kitson 23	14,831
21	div1	Cardiff	H	W	2-1	Morgan 13; Kitson 39	16,107
22	div1	Nottm Forest	A	L	0-1		21,138
23	div1	Wigan	H	D	1-1	Owusu 42	22,114
24	div1	Wolverhampton	A	L	1-4	Morgan 47	25,572
25	div1	Leicester	A	W	2-0	Sidwell 68; Ingimarsson 82	24,068
26	div1	QPR	H	W	1-0	Shorey 64	20,272
27	div1	Watford	H	W	3-0	Sonko 3; Sidwell 76; Owusu 88	18,757
28	div1	Preston	A	L	0-3		12,795
29	div1	Gillingham	A	D	0-0		8,570
30	div1	Derby	H	L	0-1		15,491
31	facr3	Swansea	H	D	1-1	Ingimarsson 88	13,642
32	div1	Burnley	A	D	0-0		11,392
33	facr3r	Swansea	A	W	1-0	Forster 95	7,354
34	div1	Ipswich	H	D	1-1	Ingimarsson 90	23,203
35	facr4	Leicester	H	L	1-2	Forster 10	14,825
36	div1	Plymouth	H	D	0-0		19,783
37	div1	Leeds	A	L	1-3	Owusu 89	30,034
38	div1	Coventry	H	L	1-2	Ferdinand 8	15,904
39	div1	Crewe	A	D	1-1	Kitson 70	5,703
40	div1	Leicester	H	D	0-0		14,651
41	div1	QPR	A	D	0-0		16,971
42	div1	West Ham	H	W	3-1	Kitson 13,27,57	22,268
43	div1	Rotherham	A	L	0-1		3,804
44	div1	Brighton	A	W	1-0	Forster 64	6,108
45	div1	Sheff Utd	H	D	0-0		18,899
46	div1	Millwall	H	W	2-1	Kitson 73; Forster 83	14,379
47	div1	Sunderland	A	W	2-1	Kitson 76,81 pen	34,237
48	div1	Nottm Forest	H	W	1-0	Harper 74	17,905
49	div1	Cardiff	A	L	0-2		14,821
50	div1	Wolverhampton	H	L	1-2	Forster 8	20,495
51	div1	Wigan	A	L	1-3	Sidwell 90	19,662

KEY PLAYERS - GOALSCORERS

David Kitson

estcoast

Goals in the League	19
Goals in all competitions	19
Contribution to Attacking Power Average number of minutes between League team goals while on pitch	74
Player Strike Rate Average number of minutes between League goals scored by player	168
Club Strike Rate Average number of minutes between League goals scored by club	81

	PLAYER	GOALS LGE	GOALS ALL	POWER	S RATE
1	David Kitson	19	19	74	168 mins
2	Nick Forster	7	9	87	348 mins
3	Steven Sidwell	4	4	80	977 mins
4	James Harper	3	3	79	1162 mins
5	Ivar Ingimarsson	3	4	82	1288 mins

KEY PLAYERS - MIDFIELDERS

Paul Brooker

Goals in the League	0
Goals in all competitions	0
Defensive Rating Average number of mins between League goals conceded while on the pitch	108
Contribution to Attacking Power Average number of minutes between League team goals while on pitch	78
Scoring Difference Defensive Rating minus Contribution to Attacking Power	30

	PLAYER	GOALS LGE	GOALS ALL	DEF RATE	ATT POWER	SCORE DIFF
1	Paul Brooker	0	0	108	78	30 mins
2	Andrew Hughes	1	2	105	88	17 mins
3	Steven Sidwell	4	4	91	80	11 mins
4	Glen Little	0	0	89	83	6 mins
5	James Harper	3	3	83	79	4 mins

KEY PLAYERS - DEFENDERS

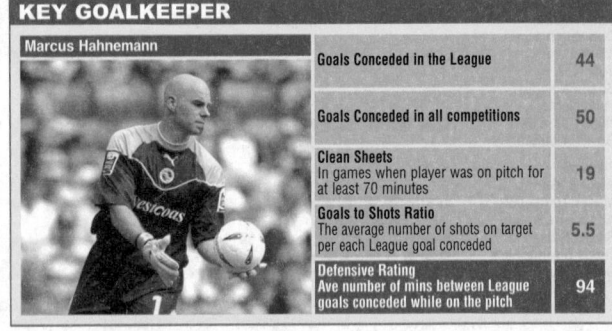

Nicky Shorey

Westcoast

Goals Conceded in League	39
Goals Conceded in all competitions	42
Clean Sheets In games when player was on pitch for at least 70 minutes	19
Defensive Rating Ave number of mins between League goals conceded while on the pitch	102
Club Defensive Rating Average number of mins between League goals conceded by the club this season	94

	PLAYER	CON LGE	CON ALL	CLN SHEETS	DEF RATE
1	Nicky Shorey	39	42	19	102 mins
2	Graeme Murty	37	42	15	97 mins
3	Ivar Ingimarsson	41	47	18	94 mins
4	Ibrahima Sonko	35	38	15	92 mins

MONTHLY POINTS TALLY

AUGUST	12	67%
SEPTEMBER	10	67%
OCTOBER	8	53%
NOVEMBER	8	53%
DECEMBER	9	60%
JANUARY	3	25%
FEBRUARY	3	20%
MARCH	7	58%
APRIL	10	56%
MAY	0	0%

GOALS

	PLAYER	LGE	FAC	LC	Oth	TOT
1	Kitson	19	0	0	0	19
2	Forster	7	2	0	0	9
3	Owusu	6	0	0	0	6
4	Ingimarsson	3	1	0	0	4
5	Sidwell	4	0	0	0	4
6	Harper	3	0	0	0	3
7	Shorey	3	0	0	0	3
8	Morgan	2	0	0	0	2
9	Hughes	1	0	1	0	2
10	Ferdinand	1	0	0	0	1
11	Sonko	1	0	0	0	1
	Other	1	0	1	0	2
	TOTAL	51	3	2	0	56

KEY GOALKEEPER

Marcus Hahnemann

Goals Conceded in the League	44
Goals Conceded in all competitions	50
Clean Sheets In games when player was on pitch for at least 70 minutes	19
Goals to Shots Ratio The average number of shots on target per each League goal conceded	5.5
Defensive Rating Ave number of mins between League goals conceded while on the pitch	94

DISCIPLINARY RECORDS

	PLAYER	YELLOW	RED	AVE
1	Sidwell	11	0	355
2	Ferdinand	1	0	458
3	Williams	2	0	467
4	Newman	2	0	492
5	Little	4	0	623
6	Owusu	2	0	684
7	Kitson	4	0	796
8	Harper	4	0	871
9	Sonko	2	0	1604
10	Hughes	2	0	1725
11	Murty	2	0	1796
12	Shorey	2	0	1980
13	Forster	1	0	2436
	Other	1	0	
	TOTAL	40	0	

TOP POINT EARNERS

	PLAYER	GAMES	AV PTS
1	Paul Brooker	16	2.06
2	David Kitson	34	1.74
3	Nicky Shorey	44	1.59
4	James Harper	37	1.54
5	Marcus Hahnemann	46	1.52
6	Ivar Ingimarsson	42	1.52
7	Steven Sidwell	43	1.51
8	Andrew Hughes	38	1.47
9	Graeme Murty	39	1.46
10	Nick Forster	25	1.44
	CLUB AVERAGE:		1.52

LEAGUE APPEARANCES GOALS AND BOOKINGS

	AGE (on 01/07/05)	IN NAMED 16	APPEARANCES	COUNTING GAMES	MINUTES ON PITCH	LEAGUE GOALS	Yellow	Red
Goalkeepers								
Marcus Hahnemann	33	46	46	46	4140	0	0	0
Jamie Young	20	46	0	0	0	0	0	0
Defenders								
Ivar Ingimarsson	27	46	44	42	3864	3	1	0
Martin Keown	38	11	5	3	314	0	1	0
Graeme Murty	30	41	41	39	3593	0	2	0
Nicky Shorey	24	44	44	44	3960	3	2	0
Ibrahima Sonko	24	45	39	35	3209	1	2	0
Adrian Williams	33	11	11	10	934	0	2	0
Midfielders								
Paul Brooker	29	42	31	16	1938	0	0	0
James Harper	24	46	41	37	3485	3	4	0
Andrew Hughes	27	44	41	38	3450	1	2	0
Glen Little	29	35	35	25	2493	0	4	0
Ricky Newman	34	44	17	9	984	0	2	0
Steven Sidwell	22	44	44	43	3906	4	11	0
Forwards								
Booby Convey	22	32	18	4	645	0	0	0
Les Ferdinand	38	12	12	2	458	1	1	0
Nick Forster	31	31	30	25	2436	7	1	0
Shaun Goater	35	17	9	1	192	0	0	0
David Kitson	25	37	37	34	3187	19	4	0
Dean Morgan	21	29	18	8	984	2	0	0
Lloyd Owusu	28	28	25	11	1368	6	2	0
Basir Savage	23	5	0	0	0	0	0	0

TEAM OF THE SEASON

G — Marcus Hahnemann — CG: 46 DR: 94

D — Nicky Shorey — CG: 44 DR: 102

D — Graeme Murty — CG: 39 DR: 97

D — Ivar Ingimarsson — CG: 42 DR: 94

D — Ibrahima Sonko — CG: 35 DR: 92

M — Paul Brooker — CG: 16 SD: 30

M — Andrew Hughes — CG: 38 SD: 17

M — Steven Sidwell — CG: 43 SD: 11

M — Glen Little — CG: 25 SD: 6

F — David Kitson — CG: 34 SR: 168

F — Nick Forster — CG: 25 SR: 348

SQUAD APPEARANCES

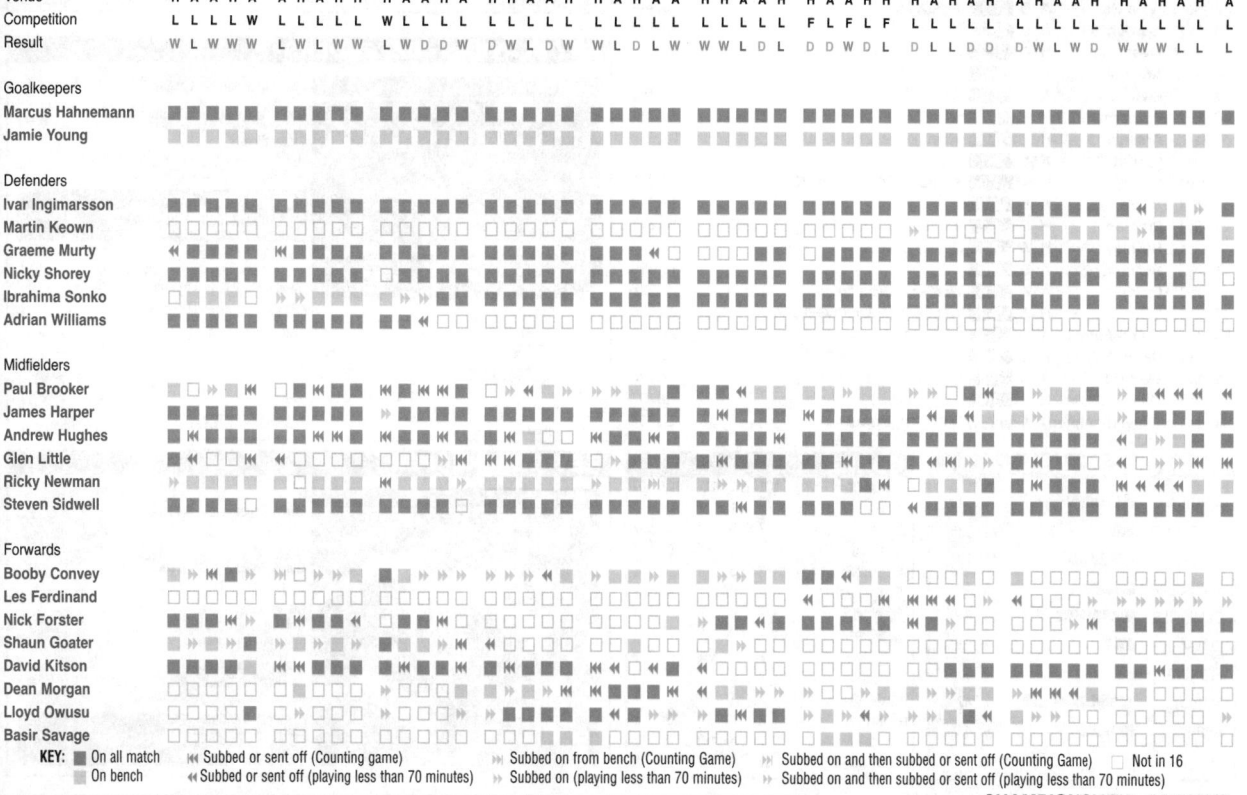

Match	1	2	3	4	5	6	7	8	9	10	11	12	13	14	15	16	17	18	19	20	21	22	23	24	25
Venue	H	A	A	H	A	A	H	A	H	H	H	A	A	H	A	H	H	A	A	H	H	A	H	A	A
Competition	L	L	L	L	W	L	L	L	L	L	W	L	L	L	L	L	L	L	L	L	L	L	L	L	L
Result	W	L	W	W	W	L	W	L	W	W	L	W	D	D	W	D	W	L	D	W	W	L	D	L	W

Match	26	27	28	29	30	31	32	33	34	35	36	37	38	39	40	41	42	43	44	45	46	47	48	49	50	51
Venue	H	H	A	A	H	H	A	A	H	H	H	A	H	A	H	A	H	A	A	H	H	A	H	A	H	A
Competition	L	L	L	L	L	F	L	F	L	F	L	L	L	L	L	L	L	L	L	L	L	L	L	L	L	L
Result	W	W	L	D	L	D	D	W	D	L	D	L	L	D	D	D	W	L	W	D	W	W	W	L	L	L

Goalkeepers

Marcus Hahnemann

Jamie Young

Defenders

Ivar Ingimarsson

Martin Keown

Graeme Murty

Nicky Shorey

Ibrahima Sonko

Adrian Williams

Midfielders

Paul Brooker

James Harper

Andrew Hughes

Glen Little

Ricky Newman

Steven Sidwell

Forwards

Booby Convey

Les Ferdinand

Nick Forster

Shaun Goater

David Kitson

Dean Morgan

Lloyd Owusu

Basir Savage

KEY: On all match · On bench · Subbed or sent off (Counting game) · Subbed or sent off (playing less than 70 minutes) · Subbed on from bench (Counting Game) · Subbed on (playing less than 70 minutes) · Subbed on and then subbed or sent off (Counting Game) · Subbed on and then subbed or sent off (playing less than 70 minutes) · Not in 16

SHEFFIELD UNITED

Final Position: **8th**

NICKNAME: THE BLADES | KEY: ☐Won ☐Drawn ☐Lost

						Attendance
1	div1	**Burnley**	A D	1-1	Gray 52	16,956
2	div1	**Stoke**	H D	0-0		19,723
3	div1	**Reading**	H L	0-1		22,429
4	div1	**Preston**	A W	1-0	Gray 4	12,084
5	ccR1	**Stockport**	H W	4-1	Morgan 36; Cutler 108 og; Tonge 112; Lester 116	5,399
6	div1	**Leeds**	H W	2-0	Ward 50; Harley 64	22,959
7	div1	**QPR**	A W	1-0	Gray 17	13,805
8	div1	**West Ham**	H L	1-2	Quinn 65	21,058
9	div1	**Leicester**	A L	2-3	Morgan 75; Forte 84	23,422
10	div1	**Wigan**	A L	0-4		10,682
11	ccr2	**Wrexham**	A W	3-2	Gray 21,69; Jagielka, P 54	3,423
12	div1	**Coventry**	H D	1-1	Black 30	16,337
13	div1	**Sunderland**	H W	1-0	Shaw 67	17,908
14	div1	**Brighton**	A D	1-1	Shaw 62	6,418
15	div1	**Gillingham**	A W	3-1	Shaw 9,59; Tonge 71	6,964
16	div1	**Nottm Forest**	H D	1-1	Liddell 26	19,445
17	div1	**Plymouth**	H W	2-1	Bromby 78; Gray 85	18,893
18	ccr3	**Watford**	H L	0-0*	(*aet, lost 4-2 on penalties)	7,689
19	div1	**Crewe**	A W	3-2	Harley 5; Gray 10; Cadamarteri 12	7,131
20	div1	**Ipswich**	A L	1-5	Bromby 45	22,977
21	div1	**Gillingham**	H D	0-0		16,598
22	div1	**Watford**	H D	1-1	Quinn 30	18,454
23	div1	**Derby**	A W	1-0	Quinn 61	25,725
24	div1	**Wolverhampton**	H D	3-3	Bromby 28; Thirlwell 53; Shaw 72	18,946
25	div1	**Millwall**	A W	2-1	Liddell 77; Geary 84	11,207
26	div1	**Rotherham**	A D	2-2	Tonge 45; Shaw 47	8,195
27	div1	**Cardiff**	H W	2-1	Liddell 69; Gray 79	18,240
28	div1	**Coventry**	A W	2-1	Morgan 33; Gray 40	21,146
29	div1	**Leicester**	H W	2-0	Gray 52; Quinn 65	22,100
30	div1	**Wigan**	H L	0-2		21,869
31	div1	**West Ham**	A W	2-0	Repka 40 og; Bromby 60	27,424
32	facr3	**Aston Villa**	H W	3-1	Cullip 55; Liddell 82,83	14,003
33	div1	**Brighton**	H L	1-2	Mayo 59 og	21,482
34	div1	**Sunderland**	A L	0-1		27,337
35	facr4	**West Ham**	A D	1-1	Jagielka 57	19,444
36	div1	**Ipswich**	H L	0-2		20,680
37	facr4r	**West Ham**	H W	3-1*	Liddell 8 (*on penalties)	15,067
38	facr5	**Arsenal**	A D	1-1	Gray 90 pen	36,891
39	div1	**Plymouth**	A L	0-3		13,953
40	div1	**Rotherham**	H W	1-0	Shaw 51	18,431
41	facr5r	**Arsenal**	H L	0-0*	(*aet, lost 4-2 on penalties)	27,595
42	div1	**Cardiff**	A L	0-1		12,250
43	div1	**Crewe**	H W	4-0	Kabba 14,66; Gray 39,75	16,079
44	div1	**Stoke**	A L	0-2		17,019
45	div1	**Preston**	H D	1-1	Bromby 31	18,647
46	div1	**Burnley**	H W	2-1	Quinn 29; Gray 49	19,374
47	div1	**Reading**	A D	0-0		18,899
48	div1	**Leeds**	A W	4-0	Webber 2; Montgomery 30; Gray 47,74	28,936
49	div1	**QPR**	H W	3-2	Webber 43,53; Gray 90 pen	20,426
50	div1	**Nottm Forest**	A D	1-1	Quinn 71	21,903
51	div1	**Derby**	H L	0-1		20,794
52	div1	**Watford**	A D	0-0		17,138
53	div1	**Millwall**	H L	0-1		19,797
54	div1	**Wolverhampton**	A L	2-4	Quinn 13; Gray 37	27,454

KEY PLAYERS - GOALSCORERS

Paul Shaw

Goals in the League	7
Goals in all competitions	7
Contribution to Attacking Power Average number of minutes between League team goals while on pitch	62
Player Strike Rate Average number of minutes between League goals scored by player	196
Club Strike Rate Average number of minutes between League goals scored by club	73

	PLAYER	GOALS LGE	GOALS ALL	POWER	S RATE
1	Paul Shaw	7	7	62	196 mins
2	Andy Gray	15	18	74	235 mins
3	Alan Quinn	7	7	65	471 mins
4	Andy Liddell	3	6	59	785 mins
5	Leigh Bromby	5	5	72	828 mins

KEY PLAYERS - MIDFIELDERS

Andy Liddell

Goals in the League	3
Goals in all competitions	6
Defensive Rating Average number of mins between League goals conceded while on the pitch	79
Contribution to Attacking Power Average number of minutes between League team goals while on pitch	59
Scoring Difference Defensive Rating minus Contribution to Attacking Power	20

	PLAYER	GOALS LGE	GOALS ALL	DEF RATE	ATT POWER	SCORE DIFF
1	Andy Liddell	3	6	79	59	20 mins
2	Michael Tonge	2	3	90	74	16 mins
3	Alan Quinn	7	7	78	65	13 mins
4	Paul Thirlwell	1	1	66	70	-4 mins
5	Nick Montgomery	1	1	52	83	-31 mins

KEY PLAYERS - DEFENDERS

Derek Geary

Goals Conceded in League	18
Goals Conceded in all competitions	20
Clean Sheets In games when player was on pitch for at least 70 minutes	4
Defensive Rating Ave number of mins between League goals conceded while on the pitch	77
Club Defensive Rating Average number of mins between League goals conceded by the club this season	74

	PLAYER	CON LGE	CON ALL	CLN SHEETS	DEF RATE
1	Derek Geary	18	20	4	77 mins
2	Jon Harley	51	58	14	77 mins
3	Leigh Bromby	56	63	14	74 mins
4	Chris Morgan	47	51	12	74 mins
5	Philip Jagielka	56	63	13	73 mins

MONTHLY POINTS TALLY

AUGUST	11	61%
SEPTEMBER	4	27%
OCTOBER	11	73%
NOVEMBER	6	40%
DECEMBER	13	87%
JANUARY	3	25%
FEBRUARY	3	33%
MARCH	7	47%
APRIL	9	43%
MAY	0	0%

GOALS

	PLAYER	LGE	FAC	LC	Oth	TOT
1	Gray	15	1	2	0	18
2	Shaw	7	0	0	0	7
3	Quinn	7	0	0	0	7
4	Liddell	3	3	0	0	6
5	Bromby	5	0	0	0	5
6	Webber	3	0	0	0	3
7	Morgan	2	0	1	0	3
8	Tonge	2	0	1	0	3
9	Kabba	2	0	0	0	2
10	Jagielka	0	1	1	0	2
11	Harley	2	0	0	0	2
	Other	9	1	2	0	12
	TOTAL	57	6	7	0	70

KEY GOALKEEPER

Patrick Kenny

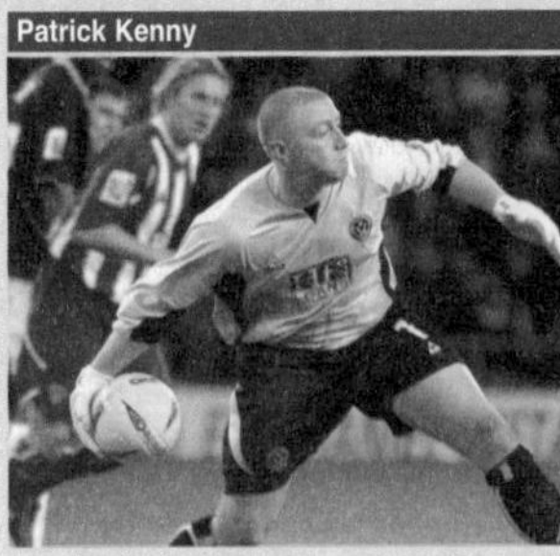

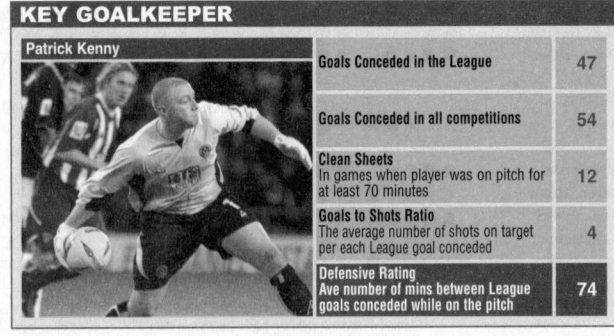

Goals Conceded in the League	47
Goals Conceded in all competitions	54
Clean Sheets In games when player was on pitch for at least 70 minutes	12
Goals to Shots Ratio The average number of shots on target per each League goal conceded	4
Defensive Rating Ave number of mins between League goals conceded while on the pitch	74

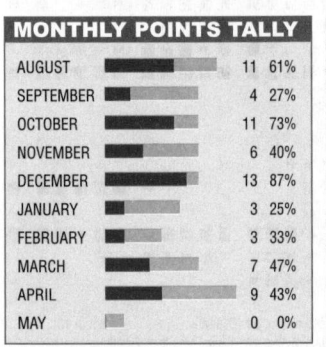

DISCIPLINARY RECORDS

	PLAYER	YELLOW	RED	AVE
1	Kabba	2	0	279
2	Quinn	8	1	366
3	Morgan	8	1	388
4	Geary	3	0	463
5	Cullip	2	0	478
6	Harley	8	0	493
7	Ward	1	0	527
8	Thirlwell	4	0	557
9	Tonge	5	0	559
10	Montgomery	2	0	708
11	Bromby	4	0	1035
12	Cadamarteri	1	0	1269
13	Kenny	1	1	1746
	Other	1	2	
	TOTAL	50	5	

TOP POINT EARNERS

	PLAYER	GAMES	AV PTS
1	Paul Shaw	14	1.79
2	Andy Liddell	23	1.65
3	Michael Tonge	30	1.63
4	Alan Quinn	34	1.59
5	Paul Thirlwell	24	1.58
6	Jon Harley	44	1.50
7	Chris Morgan	38	1.50
8	Leigh Bromby	46	1.46
9	Philip Jagielka	45	1.42
10	Andy Gray	37	1.41
	CLUB AVERAGE:		1.46

TEAM OF THE SEASON

D
Jon Harley
CG: 44 DR: 77
M
Andy Liddell
CG: 23 SD: 20
D
Leigh Bromby
CG: 46 DR: 74
M
Michael Tonge
CG: 30 SD: 16
F
Paul Shaw
CG: 14 SR: 196
G
Patrick Kenny
CG: 38 DR: 74
D
Chris Morgan
CG: 38 DR: 74
M
Alan Quinn
CG: 34 SD: 13
F
Andy Gray
CG: 37 SR: 235
D
Derek Geary
CG: 13 DR: 77
M
Paul Thirlwell
CG: 24 SD: -4

LEAGUE APPEARANCES GOALS AND BOOKINGS

	AGE (on 01/07/05)	IN NAMED 16	APPEARANCES	COUNTING GAMES	MINUTES ON PITCH	LEAGUE GOALS	Yellow	Red
Goalkeepers								
Philip Barnes	26	18	1	1	90	0	0	0
Ian Bennett	33	5	5	5	450	0	0	0
Patrick Kenny	26	40	40	38	3493	0	1	1
Defenders								
Leigh Bromby	25	46	46	46	4140	5	4	0
Danny Cullip	28	12	11	11	957	0	2	0
Simon Francis	20	11	6	1	169	0	0	0
Emanuele Gabrieli	24	3	1	0	14	0	0	0
Derek Geary	25	29	19	13	1391	1	3	0
Jon Harley	25	45	44	44	3951	2	8	0
Philip Jagielka	22	46	46	45	4064	0	0	1
Robert Kozluk	27	9	9	8	783	0	0	0
Chris Morgan	27	41	41	38	3495	2	8	1
Alan Wright	33	23	14	8	977	0	0	0
Midfielders								
Thomas Black	28	4	4	1	256	1	0	0
Kevan Hurst	19	3	1	0	1	0	0	0
Andy Liddell	32	37	33	23	2355	3	0	0
Stuart McCall	41	6	0	0	0	0	0	0
Nick Montgomery	24	41	25	14	1417	1	2	0
Alan Quinn	26	44	43	34	3296	7	8	1
Ian Ross	19	4	0	0	0	0	0	0
Paul Thirlwell	26	43	30	24	2231	1	4	0
Michael Tonge	22	34	34	30	2799	2	5	0
Forwards								
Luke Beckett	28	9	5	0	121	0	0	0
Danny Cadamarteri	25	21	21	11	1269	1	1	0
Jonathan Forte	18	32	22	0	476	1	0	0
Andy Gray	27	43	43	37	3519	15	1	1
Barry Hayles	33	5	4	0	254	0	0	0
Tommy Johnson	34	10	5	0	113	0	1	0
Steve Kabba	24	12	11	5	558	2	2	0
Jack Lester	29	12	12	0	217	0	1	0
Billy Sharp	19	5	2	0	11	0	0	0
Paul Shaw	31	25	21	14	1372	7	0	0
Ashley Ward	34	10	10	4	527	1	1	0
Danny Webber	23	7	7	6	537	3	0	0

SQUAD APPEARANCES

Match	1	2	3	4	5	6	7	8	9	10	11	12	13	14	15	16	17	18	19	20	21	22	23	24	25	26	27
Venue	A	H	H	A	H	H	A	H	A	A	A	H	H	A	A	H	H	H	A	A	H	H	A	H	A	A	H
Competition	L	L	L	L	W	L	L	L	L	L	W	L	L	L	L	L	L	W	L	L	L	L	L	L	L	L	L
Result	D	D	L	W	W	W	W	L	L	L	W	D	W	D	W	D	W	L	W	L	D	D	W	D	W	D	W

Match	28	29	30	31	32	33	34	35	36	37	38	39	40	41	42	43	44	45	46	47	48	49	50	51	52	53	54
Venue	A	H	H	A	H	H	A	A	H	H	A	A	H	H	A	H	A	H	H	A	A	H	A	H	A	H	A
Competition	L	L	L	L	F	L	L	F	L	F	F	L	L	F	L	L	L	L	L	L	L	L	L	L	L	L	L
Result	W	W	L	W	W	L	L	D	L	W	D	L	W	L	L	W	L	D	W	D	W	W	D	L	D	L	L

Goalkeepers
Philip Barnes
Ian Bennett
Patrick Kenny

Defenders
Leigh Bromby
Danny Cullip
Simon Francis
Emanuele Gabrieli
Derek Geary
Jon Harley
Philip Jagielka
Robert Kozluk
Chris Morgan
Alan Wright

Midfielders
Thomas Black
Kevan Hurst
Andy Liddell
Stuart McCall
Nick Montgomery
Alan Quinn
Ian Ross
Paul Thirlwell
Michael Tonge

Forwards
Luke Beckett
Danny Cadamarteri
Jonathan Forte
Andy Gray
Barry Hayles
Tommy Johnson
Steve Kabba
Jack Lester
Billy Sharp
Paul Shaw
Ashley Ward
Danny Webber

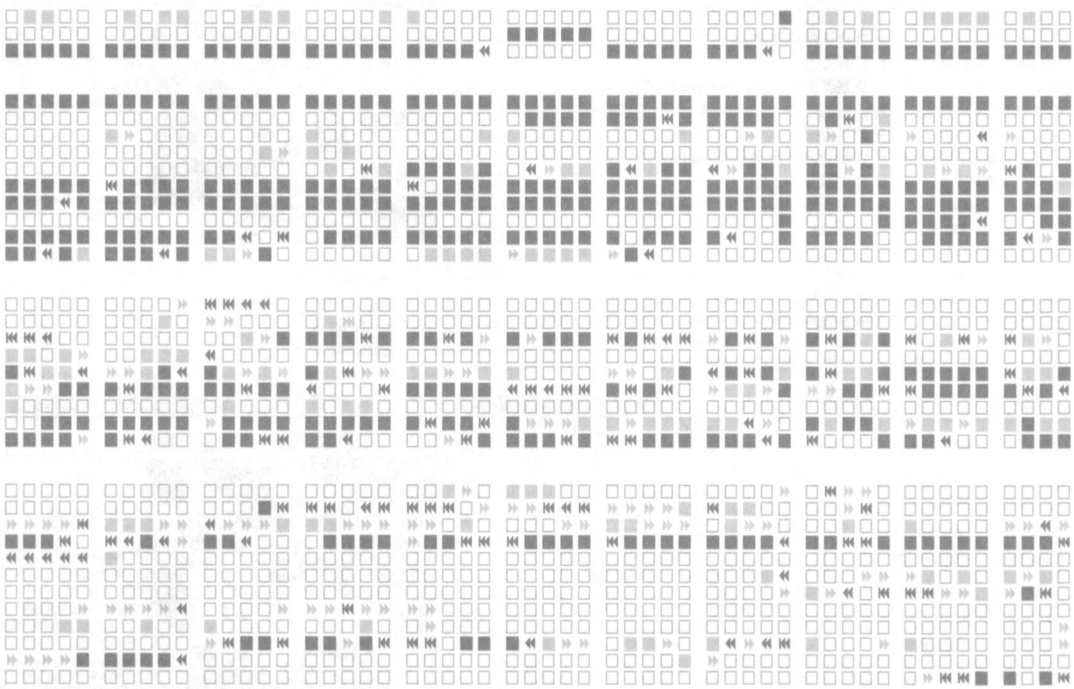

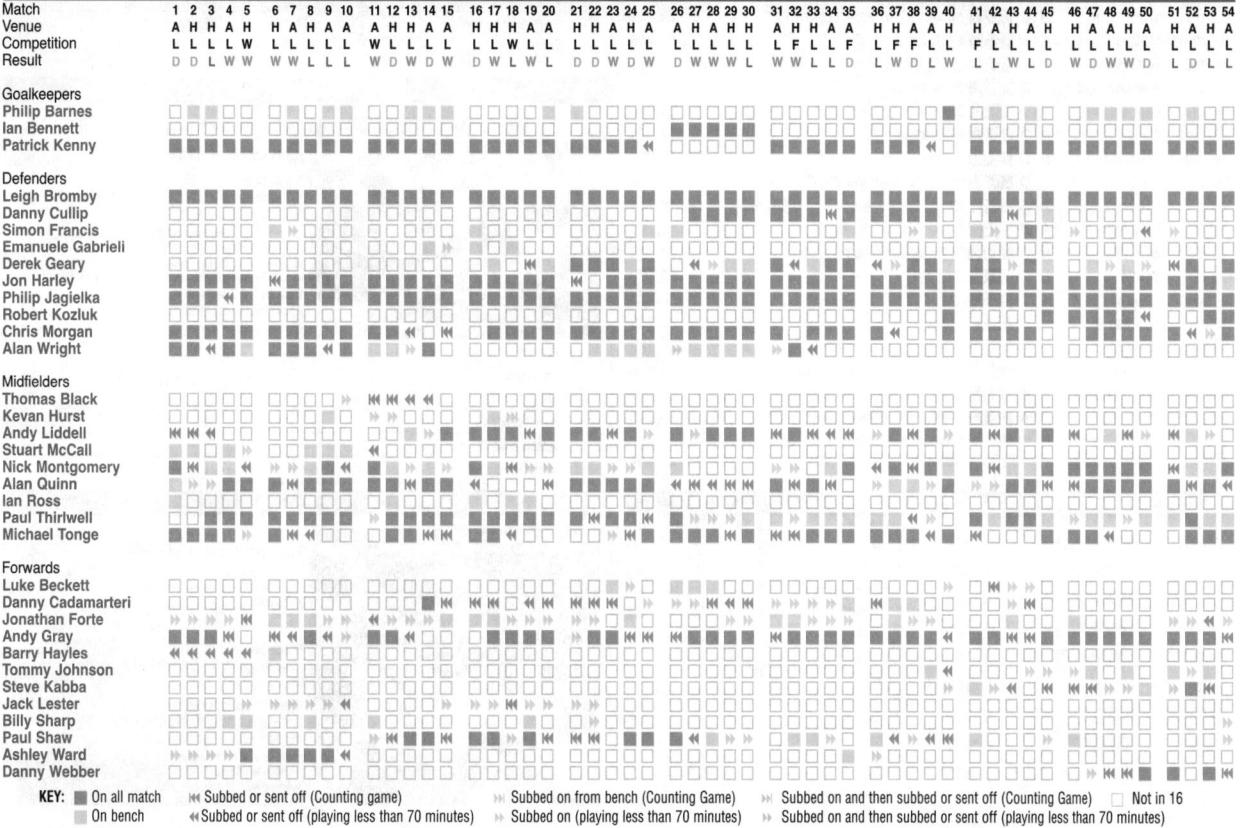

KEY: On all match | On bench | Subbed or sent off (Counting game) | Subbed or sent off (playing less than 70 minutes) | Subbed on from bench (Counting Game) | Subbed on (playing less than 70 minutes) | Subbed on and then subbed or sent off (Counting Game) | Subbed on and then subbed or sent off (playing less than 70 minutes) | Not in 16

WOLVERHAMPTON WANDERERS

Final Position: **9th**

NICKNAME: WOLVES

KEY: Won Drawn Lost

							Attendance
1	div1	Stoke	A	L	1-2	Miller 87 pen	17,066
2	div1	Preston	H	D	2-2	Clarke 76; Miller 79	26,115
3	div1	Leeds	H	D	0-0		28,397
4	div1	Burnley	A	D	1-1	Newton 15	13,869
5	ccr1	Rochdale	A	W	4-2	Ince 42; Clarke 53; Miller 60; Andrews 78	3,292
6	div1	Leicester	H	D	1-1	Miller 52	27,550
7	div1	Ipswich	A	L	1-2	Olofinjana 54	24,590
8	div1	Wigan	H	D	3-3	Miller 15,65; Cameron 90	26,790
9	div1	Brighton	A	W	1-0	Miller 22	6,804
10	div1	Plymouth	A	W	2-1	Cort 77 pen; Sturridge 85	18,635
11	ccr2	Burnley	A	L	1-1*	Seol 45 (*aet, lost 4-2 on penalties)	5,013
12	div1	Cardiff	H	L	2-3	Cort 12; Ince 85	27,896
13	div1	West Ham	A	L	0-1		29,585
14	div1	Nottm Forest	A	L	0-1		21,865
15	div1	Derby	H	W	2-0	Cooper 19 pen,50	26,465
16	div1	QPR	H	W	2-1	Cort 22,70	27,070
17	div1	Gillingham	A	L	0-1		9,112
18	div1	Sunderland	A	L	1-3	Miller 18	23,925
19	div1	Nottm Forest	H	W	2-1	Cooper 19 pen; Bischoff 43	27,605
20	div1	Rotherham	A	W	2-1	Cooper 69; Cort 79	6,693
21	div1	Coventry	H	L	0-1		26,291
22	div1	Sheff Utd	A	D	3-3	Olofinjana 7; Cort 50; Lescott 87	18,946
23	div1	Reading	H	W	4-1	Cameron 31; Olofinjana 45; Clarke 77,90	25,572
24	div1	Millwall	H	L	1-2	Cooper 57 pen	24,748
25	div1	Watford	A	D	1-1	Olofinjana 35	14,605
26	div1	Crewe	H	D	1-1	Cort 90	25,340
27	div1	Cardiff	A	D	1-1	Miller 75	16,699
28	div1	Brighton	H	D	1-1	Miller 33	28,516
29	div1	Plymouth	H	D	1-1	Seol 24	27,564
30	div1	Wigan	A	L	0-2		10,135
31	facr3	Millwall	H	W	2-0	Seol 1; Cort 11	12,566
32	div1	West Ham	H	W	4-2	Miller 29,54; Ince 72; Cort 75	28,411
33	div1	Millwall	A	W	2-1	Olofinjana 37; Seol 90	13,145
34	facr4	Arsenal	A	L	0-2		37,153
35	div1	Sunderland	H	D	1-1	Seol 13	26,968
36	div1	Gillingham	H	D	2-2	Miller 60; Clarke 90	24,949
37	div1	QPR	A	D	1-1	Cort 85	15,029
38	div1	Watford	H	D	0-0		25,060
39	div1	Derby	A	D	3-3	Miller 12; Lescott 72; Cort 90	24,109
40	div1	Crewe	A	W	4-1	Cort 13,45; Miller 35 pen,60	8,212
41	div1	Preston	A	D	2-2	Craddock 10; Seol 73	16,296
42	div1	Burnley	H	W	2-0	Miller 38; Ince 60	24,336
43	div1	Stoke	H	D	1-1	Cort 90	28,103
44	div1	Leeds	A	D	1-1	Cort 40	29,773
45	div1	Leicester	A	D	1-1	Lescott 88	22,950
46	div1	Ipswich	H	W	2-0	Cameron 5; Cort 22	25,882
47	div1	Coventry	A	D	2-2	Clarke 15; Naylor 79	19,412
48	div1	Rotherham	H	W	2-0	Miller 55,90	25,177
49	div1	Reading	A	W	2-1	Clarke 53; Ricketts 84	20,495
50	div1	Sheff Utd	H	W	4-2	Lescott 12; Clarke 23; Cooper 50; Miller 60	27,454

MONTHLY POINTS TALLY

AUGUST	4	22%
SEPTEMBER	7	58%
OCTOBER	6	40%
NOVEMBER	7	47%
DECEMBER	7	39%
JANUARY	7	58%
FEBRUARY	4	33%
MARCH	9	60%
APRIL	12	67%
MAY	3	100%

GOALS

	PLAYER	LGE	FAC	LC	Oth	TOT
1	Miller	19	0	1	0	20
2	Cort	15	1	0	0	16
3	Clarke	7	0	1	0	8
4	Cooper	6	0	0	0	6
5	Seol	4	1	1	0	6
6	Olofinjana	5	0	0	0	5
7	Lescott	4	0	0	0	4
8	Ince	3	0	1	0	4
9	Cameron	3	0	0	0	3
10	Ricketts	1	0	0	0	1
11	Bischoff	1	0	0	0	1
	Other	4	0	1	0	5
	TOTAL	72	2	5	0	79

KEY PLAYERS - GOALSCORERS

Kenny Miller

Goals in the League	19
Goals in all competitions	20
Contribution to Attacking Power Average number of minutes between League team goals while on pitch	59
Player Strike Rate The total number of minutes he was on the pitch for every League goal scored	187
Club Strike Rate Average number of minutes between League goals scored by club	58

	PLAYER	GOALS LGE	GOALS ALL	POWER	S RATE
1	Kenny Miller	19	20	59	187 mins
2	Carl Cort	15	16	54	205 mins
3	Kevin Cooper	6	6	51	264 mins
4	Ki-Hyeun Seol	4	6	55	620 mins
5	Seyi Olofinjana	5	5	59	694 mins

KEY PLAYERS - MIDFIELDERS

Kevin Cooper

Goals in the League	6
Goals in all competitions	6
Defensive Rating Average number of mins between League goals conceded while on the pitch	79
Contribution to Attacking Power Average number of minutes between League team goals while on pitch	51
Scoring Difference Defensive Rating minus Contribution to Attacking Power	28

	PLAYER	GOALS LGE	GOALS ALL	DEF RATE	ATT POWER	SCORE DIFF
1	Kevin Cooper	6	6	79	51	28 mins
2	Colin Cameron	3	3	80	54	26 mins
3	Paul Ince	3	4	73	58	15 mins
4	Keith Andrews	0	1	68	61	7 mins
5	Seyi Olofinjana	5	5	64	59	5 mins

KEY PLAYERS - DEFENDERS

Lee Naylor

Goals Conceded in League	42
Goals Conceded in all competitions	45
Clean Sheets In League games when he played at least 70 mins	6
Defensive Rating Ave number of mins between League goals conceded while on the pitch	74
Club Defensive Rating Average number of mins between League goals conceded by the club this season	70

	PLAYER	CON LGE	CON ALL	CLN SHEETS	DEF RATE
1	Lee Naylor	42	45	6	74 mins
2	Rob Edwards	18	20	4	73 mins
3	Jody Craddock	51	56	7	71 mins
4	Joleon Lescott	52	54	5	71 mins
5	Mark Clyde	25	28	2	60 mins

KEY GOALKEEPER

Michael Oakes

Goals Conceded in the League	42
Goals Conceded in all competitions	47
Clean Sheets In games when he played at least 70 mins	5
Goals to Shots Ratio The average number of shots on target per each League goal conceded	3.8
Defensive Rating Ave number of mins between League goals conceded while on the pitch	75

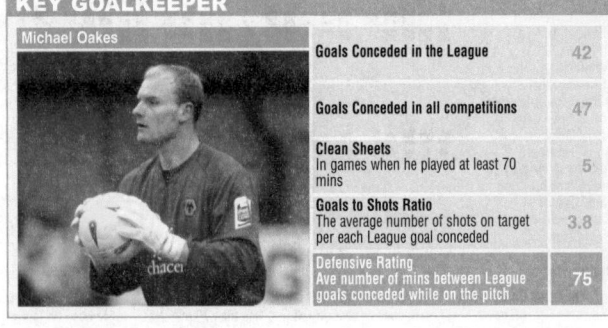

DISCIPLINARY RECORDS

	PLAYER	YELLOW	RED	AVE
1	Ince	7	0	322
2	Miller	9	1	355
3	Clyde	4	0	373
4	Clarke	3	0	435
5	Edwards	2	0	658
6	Olofinjana	5	0	693
7	Lescott	5	0	738
8	Naylor	4	0	772
9	Cameron	3	0	795
10	Craddock	4	0	908
11	Seol	2	0	1240
12	Cooper	0	1	1585
13	Newton	1	0	1870
	Other	3	0	
	TOTAL	52	2	

TOP POINT EARNERS

	PLAYER	GAMES	AV PTS
1	Ki-Hyeun Seol	23	1.65
2	Lee Naylor	33	1.58
3	Colin Cameron	22	1.50
4	Michael Oakes	35	1.49
5	Joleon Lescott	41	1.49
6	Seyi Olofinjana	34	1.47
7	Mark Kennedy	24	1.46
8	Paul Ince	24	1.46
9	Kenny Miller	37	1.46
10	Rob Edwards	13	1.46
	CLUB AVERAGE:		1.43

LEAGUE APPEARANCES GOALS AND BOOKINGS

	AGE (on 01/07/05)	IN NAMED 16	APPEARANCES	COUNTING GAMES	MINUTES ON PITCH	LEAGUE GOALS	Yellow	Red
Goalkeepers								
Carl Ikeme	19	5	0	0	0	0	0	0
Paul Jones	38	21	10	10	900	0	0	0
Matt Murray	24	17	1	1	90	0	0	0
Michael Oakes	31	46	35	35	3150	0	1	0
Defenders								
Mikkel Bischoff	23	15	11	8	812	1	0	0
Joachim Bjorklund	34	11	3	0	167	0	0	0
Mark Clyde	22	20	18	15	1492	0	4	0
Jody Craddock	29	45	42	40	3632	1	4	0
Rob Edwards	22	18	17	13	1316	0	2	0
Joleon Lescott	22	41	41	41	3690	4	5	0
Keith Lowe	19	15	11	7	865	0	0	0
Lee Naylor	25	43	38	33	3091	1	4	0
Midfielders								
Keith Andrews	24	34	20	13	1228	0	0	0
Colin Cameron	32	41	37	22	2387	3	3	0
Sammy Clingan	21	2	0	0	0	0	0	0
Kevin Cooper	30	40	30	12	1585	6	0	1
Lewis Gobern	20	0	0	0	0	0	0	0
Paul Ince	37	31	28	24	2259	3	7	0
Mark Kennedy	29	31	30	24	2324	0	1	0
Shaun Newton	29	30	24	19	1870	1	1	0
Seyi Olofinjana	25	46	42	34	3469	5	5	0
Rohan Ricketts	22	9	7	2	333	1	1	0
Forwards								
Leon Clarke	20	38	28	11	1305	7	3	0
Christopher Cornes	18	3	0	0	0	0	0	0
Carl Cort	27	37	37	33	3076	15	1	0
Kenny Miller	25	45	44	37	3554	19	9	1
Gary Mulligan	20	2	1	0	9	0	0	0
Ki-Hyeun Seol	26	38	37	23	2480	4	2	0
Dean Sturridge	31	12	11	1	431	1	2	0

TEAM OF THE SEASON

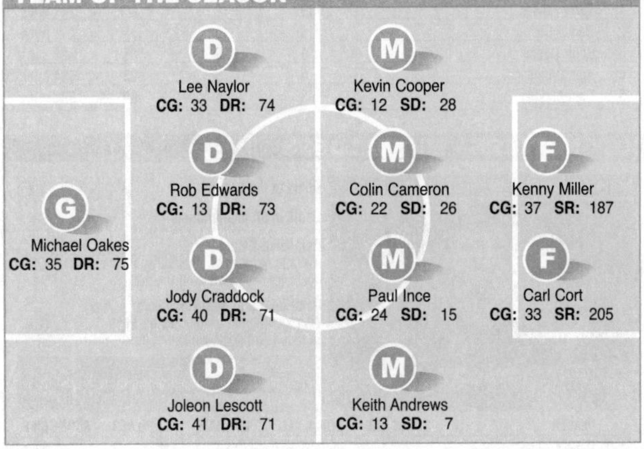

D
Lee Naylor
CG: 33 DR: 74
M
Kevin Cooper
CG: 12 SD: 28
D
Rob Edwards
CG: 13 DR: 73
M
Colin Cameron
CG: 22 SD: 26
F
Kenny Miller
CG: 37 SR: 187
G
Michael Oakes
CG: 35 DR: 75
D
Jody Craddock
CG: 40 DR: 71
M
Paul Ince
CG: 24 SD: 15
F
Carl Cort
CG: 33 SR: 205
D
Joleon Lescott
CG: 41 DR: 71
M
Keith Andrews
CG: 13 SD: 7

SQUAD APPEARANCES

Match	1	2	3	4	5	6	7	8	9	10	11	12	13	14	15	16	17	18	19	20	21	22	23	24	25
Venue	A	H	H	A	A	H	A	H	A	A	A	H	A	A	H	H	A	A	H	A	H	A	H	H	A
Competition	L	L	L	L	W	L	L	L	L	L	W	L	L	L	L	L	L	L	L	L	L	L	L	L	L
Result	L	D	D	D	W	D	L	D	W	W	L	L	L	L	W	W	L	L	W	W	L	D	W	L	D

Match	26	27	28	29	30	31	32	33	34	35	36	37	38	39	40	41	42	43	44	45	46	47	48	49	50
Venue	H	A	H	H	A	H	H	A	A	H	H	A	H	A	A	A	H	H	A	A	H	A	H	A	H
Competition	L	L	L	L	L	F	L	L	F	L	L	L	L	L	L	L	L	L	L	L	L	L	L	L	L
Result	D	D	D	D	L	W	W	W	L	D	D	D	D	D	W	D	W	D	D	D	W	D	W	W	W

Goalkeepers
Carl Ikeme
Paul Jones
Matt Murray
Michael Oakes

Defenders
Mikkel Bischoff
Joachim Bjorklund
Mark Clyde
Jody Craddock
Rob Edwards
Joleon Lescott
Keith Lowe
Lee Naylor

Midfielders
Keith Andrews
Colin Cameron
Sammy Clingan
Kevin Cooper
Lewis Gobern
Paul Ince
Mark Kennedy
Shaun Newton
Seyi Olofinjana
Rohan Ricketts

Forwards
Leon Clarke
Christopher Cornes
Carl Cort
Kenny Miller
Gary Mulligan
Ki-Hyeun Seol
Dean Sturridge

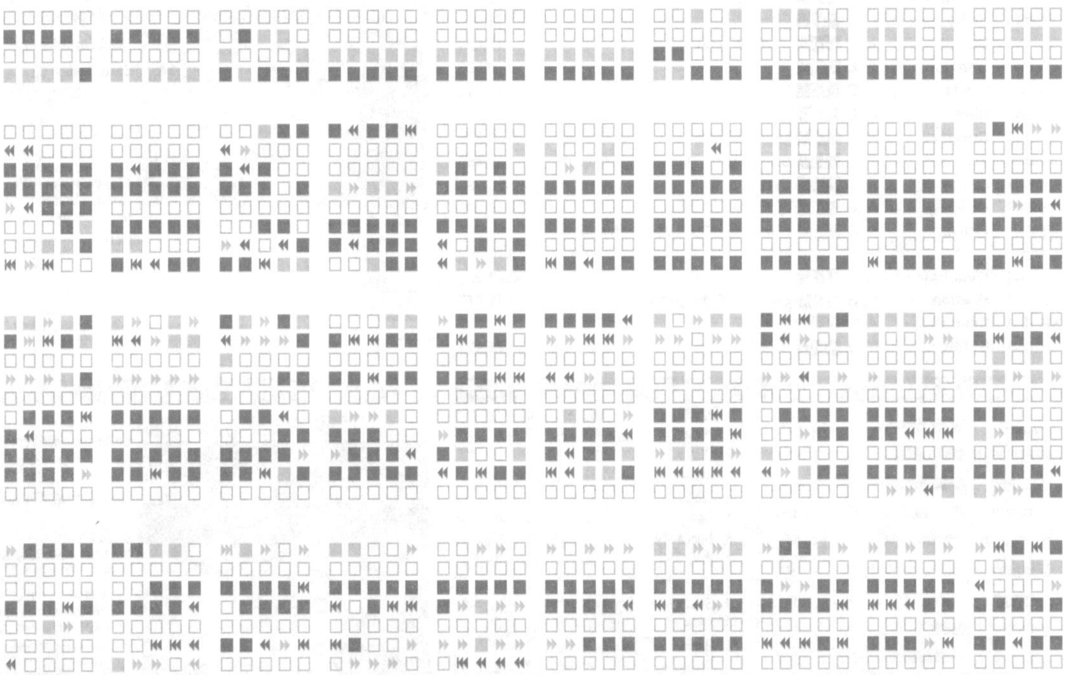

KEY: On all match · On bench · Subbed or sent off (Counting game) · Subbed or sent off (playing less than 70 minutes) · Subbed on from bench (Counting Game) · Subbed on (playing less than 70 minutes) · Subbed on and then subbed or sent off (Counting Game) · Subbed on and then subbed or sent off (playing less than 70 minutes) · Not in 16

MILLWALL

Final Position: **10th**

NICKNAME: THE LIONS

KEY: Won Drawn Lost

							Attendance
1	div1	Plymouth	A	D	0-0		16,063
2	div1	Wigan	H	L	0-2		10,660
3	div1	Leicester	H	W	2-0	Morris 37; Dichio 76	11,754
4	div1	Coventry	A	W	1-0	Dichio 80	13,910
5	div1	Reading	H	W	1-0	Dichio 79	12,098
6	div1	Ipswich	A	L	0-2		21,246
7	uc1rl1	Ferencvaros	H	D	1-1	Wise 66	15,000
8	div1	Watford	H	L	0-2		10,865
9	div1	Derby	H	W	3-1	Wise 2; Serioux 48; Ifill 90	9,132
10	div1	Rotherham	A	D	1-1	Hearn 77	5,062
11	uc1rl2	Ferencvaros	A	L	1-3	Wise 45	15,229
12	div1	Nottm Forest	H	W	1-0	Livermore 45	11,233
13	div1	Sunderland	A	L	0-1		23,839
14	div1	Gillingham	H	W	2-1	Hayles 33; Dunne 44	10,722
15	div1	Cardiff	H	D	2-2	Tessem 47; Harris 74	10,476
16	ccr3	Liverpool	H	L	0-3		17,655
17	div1	Stoke	A	L	0-1		14,625
18	div1	QPR	A	D	1-1	Hayles 51	16,685
19	div1	Sunderland	H	W	2-0	Wise 33 pen; Livermore 45	10,513
20	div1	Preston	A	D	1-1	Hayles 87	10,339
21	div1	West Ham	H	W	1-0	Dichio 78	19,025
22	div1	Burnley	A	L	0-1		11,471
23	div1	Crewe	A	L	1-2	Ifill 71	5,409
24	div1	Sheff Utd	H	L	1-2	Phillips 58	11,207
25	div1	Wolverhampton	A	W	2-1	Dobie 9; Dichio 72	24,748
26	div1	Brighton	H	W	2-0	Dobie 21; Ifill 78	12,196
27	div1	Leeds	A	D	1-1	Morris 86 pen	26,265
28	div1	Ipswich	H	W	3-1	Hayles 45; Dichio 52; Dobie 79	14,532
29	div1	Derby	A	W	3-0	Hayles 18,51,58	27,725
30	div1	Watford	A	L	0-1		13,158
31	div1	Rotherham	H	L	1-2	Dunne 16	11,725
32	facr3	Wolverhampton	A	L	0-2		12,566
33	div1	Nottm Forest	A	W	2-1	Hayles 11; Dunne 37	25,949
34	div1	Wolverhampton	H	L	1-2	Wise 77 pen	13,145
35	div1	QPR	H	D	0-0		15,603
36	div1	Gillingham	A	D	0-0		9,127
37	div1	Stoke	H	L	0-1		11,036
38	div1	Cardiff	A	W	1-0	Dichio 20 pen	11,424
39	div1	Brighton	A	L	0-1		6,608
40	div1	Leeds	H	D	1-1	Robinson 17	11,510
41	div1	Wigan	A	L	0-2		9,614
42	div1	Coventry	H	D	1-1	Morris 69 pen	8,835
43	div1	Plymouth	H	W	3-0	Sweeney 15; Hayles 56; Dichio 63	11,465
44	div1	Leicester	A	L	1-3	Dichio 68	22,338
45	div1	Reading	A	L	1-2	Dichio 39	14,379
46	div1	Crewe	H	W	4-3	Hayles 26; Elliott 49; Morris 50; May 85 pen	10,767
47	div1	West Ham	A	D	1-1	Hayles 12	28,221
48	div1	Preston	H	W	2-1	Sweeney 9; Hayles 76	11,417
49	div1	Sheff Utd	A	W	1-0	Morris 5	19,797
50	div1	Burnley	H	D	0-0		12,171

MONTHLY POINTS TALLY

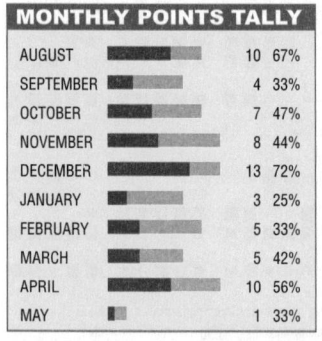

AUGUST	10	67%
SEPTEMBER	4	33%
OCTOBER	7	47%
NOVEMBER	8	44%
DECEMBER	13	72%
JANUARY	3	25%
FEBRUARY	5	33%
MARCH	5	42%
APRIL	10	56%
MAY	1	33%

GOALS

	PLAYER	LGE	FAC	LC	Oth	TOT
1	Hayles	12	0	0	0	12
2	Dichio	10	0	0	0	10
3	Morris	5	0	0	0	5
4	Wise	3	0	0	2	5
5	Dobie	3	0	0	0	3
6	Dunne	3	0	0	0	3
7	Ifill	3	0	0	0	3
8	Livermore	2	0	0	0	2
9	Sweeney	2	0	0	0	2
10	Phillips	1	0	0	0	1
11	Harris	1	0	0	0	1
	Other	6	0	0	0	6
	TOTAL	51	0	0	2	53

KEY PLAYERS - GOALSCORERS

Barry Hayles

Goals in the League	12
Goals in all competitions	12
Contribution to Attacking Power Average number of minutes between League team goals while on pitch	67
Player Strike Rate Average number of minutes between League goals scored by player	203
Club Strike Rate Average number of minutes between League goals scored by club	81

	PLAYER	GOALS LGE	GOALS ALL	POWER	S RATE
1	Barry Hayles	12	12	67	203 mins
2	Danny Dichio	10	10	73	250 mins
3	Scott Dobie	3	3	85	426 mins
4	Alan Dunne	3	3	93	434 mins
5	Dennis Wise	3	5	63	527 mins

KEY PLAYERS - MIDFIELDERS

Dennis Wise

Goals in the League	3
Goals in all competitions	5
Defensive Rating Average number of mins between League goals conceded while on the pitch	113
Contribution to Attacking Power Average number of minutes between League team goals while on pitch	63
Scoring Difference Defensive Rating minus Contribution to Attacking Power	50

	PLAYER	GOALS LGE	GOALS ALL	DEF RATE	ATT POWER	SCORE DIFF
1	Dennis Wise	3	5	113	63	50 mins
2	Peter Sweeney	2	2	110	75	35 mins
3	David Livermore	2	2	97	74	23 mins
4	Josh Simpson	0	0	98	81	17 mins
5	Jody Morris	5	5	96	85	11 mins

KEY PLAYERS - DEFENDERS

Marcus Phillips

Goals Conceded in League	20
Goals Conceded in all competitions	22
Clean Sheets In games when player was on pitch for at least 70 minutes	9
Defensive Rating Ave number of mins between League goals conceded while on the pitch	113
Club Defensive Rating Average number of mins between League goals conceded by the club this season	92

	PLAYER	CON LGE	CON ALL	CLN SHEETS	DEF RATE
1	Marcus Phillips	20	22	9	113 mins
2	Kevin Muscat	23	30	8	95 mins
3	Darren Ward	41	48	14	93 mins
4	Matt Lawrence	43	52	12	86 mins

KEY GOALKEEPER

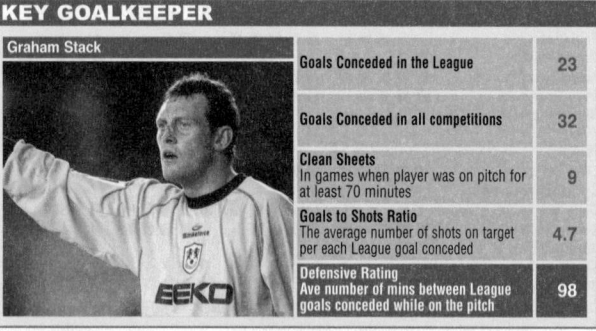

Graham Stack

Goals Conceded in the League	23
Goals Conceded in all competitions	32
Clean Sheets In games when player was on pitch for at least 70 minutes	9
Goals to Shots Ratio The average number of shots on target per each League goal conceded	4.7
Defensive Rating Ave number of mins between League goals conceded while on the pitch	98

DISCIPLINARY RECORDS

	PLAYER	YELLOW	RED	AVE
1	Dunne	6	2	162
2	Wise	9	0	175
3	Serioux	3	1	216
4	Muscat	8	1	242
5	Harris	2	0	261
6	Robinson, P	2	0	270
7	Dichio	7	2	277
8	Hayles	7	0	348
9	Phillips	5	1	375
10	Livermore	7	1	461
11	Ifill	2	0	497
12	Elliott	5	0	588
13	Morris	4	0	740
	Other	13	0	
	TOTAL	80	8	

TOP POINT EARNERS

	PLAYER	GAMES	AV PTS
1	Josh Simpson	15	2.00
2	Dennis Wise	14	1.79
3	Marvin Elliott	29	1.69
4	Barry Hayles	23	1.65
5	Danny Dichio	26	1.62
6	Scott Dobie	13	1.62
7	David Livermore	41	1.59
8	Marcus Phillips	25	1.56
9	Peter Sweeney	18	1.50
10	Jody Morris	30	1.47
	CLUB AVERAGE:		1.47

LEAGUE APPEARANCES GOALS AND BOOKINGS

	AGE (on 01/07/05)	IN NAMED 16	APPEARANCES	COUNTING GAMES	MINUTES ON PITCH	LEAGUE GOALS	Yellow	Red
Goalkeepers								
Andy Marshall	30	43	22	21	1893	0	2	0
Terry Masterson	19	1	0	0	0	0	0	0
Graham Stack	23	36	26	24	2247	0	0	0
Defenders								
Tony Craig	20	11	10	9	820	0	1	0
Matt Lawrence	31	45	44	39	3679	0	3	0
Kevin Muscat	31	26	26	24	2178	0	8	1
Marcus Phillips	22	28	25	25	2250	1	5	1
Paul Robinson	23	14	6	6	540	0	2	0
Adrian Serioux	26	30	19	5	864	0	3	1
Darren Ward	26	43	43	42	3819	0	2	0
Midfielders								
Barry Cogan	19	10	7	2	254	0	1	0
Alan Dunne	22	26	19	13	1302	3	6	2
Marvin Elliott	20	46	41	29	2944	1	5	0
Andrew Impey	33	5	5	0	107	0	0	0
David Livermore	25	42	41	41	3690	2	7	1
Jody Morris	26	38	37	30	2962	5	4	0
Trevor Robinson	20	3	3	1	178	0	0	0
Josh Simpson	22	39	30	15	1955	0	1	0
Peter Sweeney	20	28	24	18	1871	2	2	0
Jo Tessem	33	12	12	8	929	1	1	0
Curt Weston	18	11	3	1	155	0	0	0
Dennis Wise	38	31	25	14	1582	3	9	0
Forwards								
Kevin Braniff	22	2	1	1	76	0	0	0
Danny Dichio	30	32	32	26	2495	10	7	2
Scott Dobie	26	16	16	13	1279	3	1	0
Neil Harris	27	15	12	3	523	1	2	0
Barry Hayles	33	32	32	23	2439	12	7	0
Joe Healy	18	3	2	0	41	0	0	0
Paul Ifill	25	18	18	7	995	3	2	0
Ben May	21	11	7	1	298	0	2	0
Mark McCammon	26	15	8	1	359	0	1	0
Stefan Moore	21	7	6	1	278	0	0	0
Bob Peeters	31	8	3	0	62	0	0	0
Mark Quigley	19	9	8	2	340	0	1	0

TEAM OF THE SEASON

G
Graham Stack
CG: 24 DR: 98
D
Marcus Phillips
CG: 25 DR: 113
D
Kevin Muscat
CG: 24 DR: 95
D
Darren Ward
CG: 42 DR: 93
D
Matt Lawrence
CG: 39 DR: 86
M
Dennis Wise
CG: 14 SD: 50
M
Peter Sweeney
CG: 18 SD: 35
M
David Livermore
CG: 41 SD: 23
M
Josh Simpson
CG: 15 SD: 17
F
Danny Dichio
CG: 26 SR: 250
F
Barry Hayles
CG: 23 SR: 203

SQUAD APPEARANCES

Match	1	2	3	4	5	6	7	8	9	10	11	12	13	14	15	16	17	18	19	20	21	22	23	24	25	26	27	28	29	30	31	32	33	34	35	36	37	38	39	40	41	42	43	44	45	46	47	48	49	50
Venue	A	H	H	A	H	A	H	H	H	A	A	H	A	H	H	H	A	A	H	A	H	A	A	H	A	H	A	H	A	A	H	A	A	H	H	A	H	A	A	H	A	H	H	A	A	H	A	H	A	H
Competition	L	L	L	L	L	L	E	L	L	L	E	L	L	L	L	W	L	L	L	L	L	L	L	L	L	L	L	L	L	L	L	F	L	L	L	L	L	L	L	L	L	L	L	L	L	L	L	L	L	L
Result	D	L	W	W	W	L	D	L	W	D	L	W	L	W	D	L	L	D	W	D	W	L	L	L	W	W	D	W	W	L	L	L	W	L	D	D	L	W	L	D	L	D	W	L	L	W	D	W	W	D

Goalkeepers
Andy Marshall
Terry Masterson
Graham Stack

Defenders
Tony Craig
Matt Lawrence
Kevin Muscat
Marcus Phillips
Paul Robinson
Adrian Serioux
Darren Ward

Midfielders
Barry Cogan
Alan Dunne
Marvin Elliott
Andrew Impey
David Livermore
Jody Morris
Trevor Robinson
Josh Simpson
Peter Sweeney
Jo Tessem
Curt Weston
Dennis Wise

Forwards
Kevin Braniff
Danny Dichio
Scott Dobie
Neil Harris
Barry Hayles
Joe Healy
Paul Ifill
Ben May
Mark McCammon
Stefan Moore
Bob Peeters
Mark Quigley

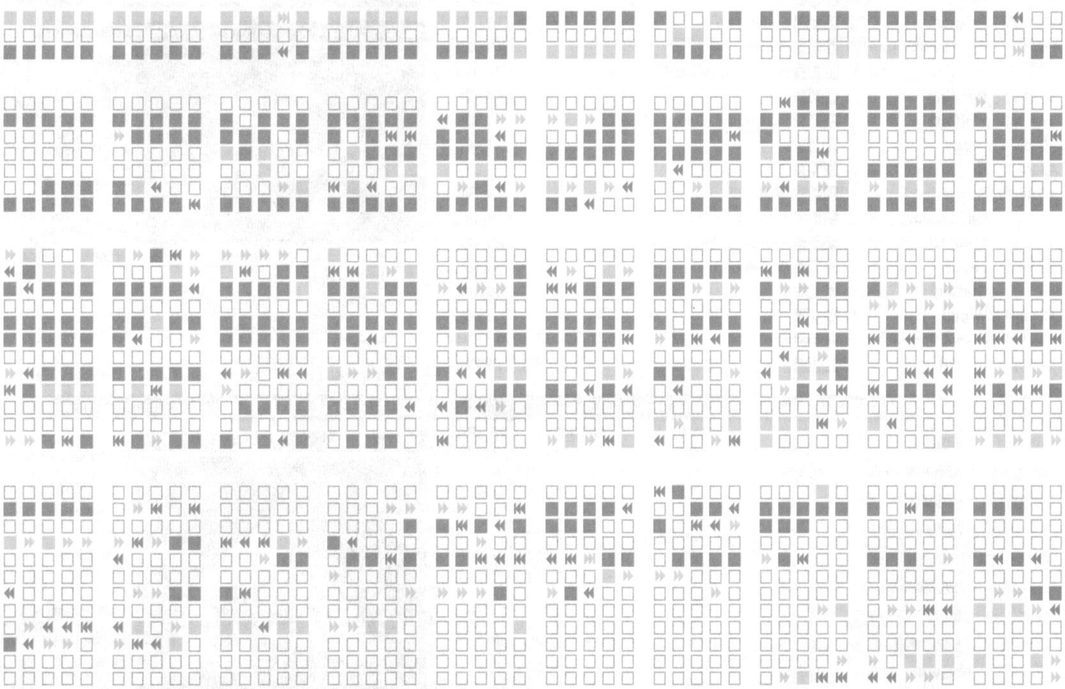

KEY: On all match | On bench | Subbed or sent off (Counting game) | Subbed or sent off (playing less than 70 minutes) | Subbed on from bench (Counting Game) | Subbed on (playing less than 70 minutes) | Subbed on and then subbed or sent off (Counting Game) | Subbed on and then subbed or sent off (playing less than 70 minutes) | Not in 16

QUEENS PARK RANGERS

Final Position: **11th**

NICKNAME: RANGERS

KEY: Won / Drawn / Lost

							Attendance
1	div1	Rotherham	H	D	1-1	Ainsworth 5	14,547
2	div1	Watford	A	L	0-3		14,737
3	div1	Sunderland	A	D	2-2	Furlong 12; Rowlands 71	26,063
4	div1	Derby	H	L	0-2		15,295
5	ccr1	Swansea	H	W	3-0	Cureton 39; Rowlands 77; Gallen 90	4,882
6	div1	Gillingham	A	W	1-0	Bean 29	7,391
7	div1	Sheff Utd	H	L	0-1		13,805
8	div1	Plymouth	H	W	3-2	Furlong 29,72; Gallen 89	15,425
9	div1	Crewe	A	W	2-0	Furlong 22; Santos 68	5,682
10	div1	Brighton	A	W	3-2	Gallen 16; Furlong 74; Rose 90	6,612
11	ccr2	Aston Villa	A	L	1-3	McLeod 48	26,975
12	div1	Leicester	H	W	3-2	Cook 58; Furlong 70,90	15,535
13	div1	Coventry	H	W	4-1	Cureton 32,41,74; Furlong 90	14,680
14	div1	Stoke	A	W	1-0	Gallen 69	16,877
15	div1	West Ham	H	W	1-0	Rose 22	18,363
16	div1	Preston	A	L	1-2	Santos 8	10,548
17	div1	Wolverhampton	A	L	1-2	Gallen 90	27,070
18	div1	Burnley	H	W	3-0	Gallen 13 pen; Santos 16; Furlong 24	15,638
19	div1	Millwall	H	D	1-1	Furlong 87	16,685
20	div1	West Ham	A	L	1-2	McLeod 72	31,365
21	div1	Wigan	H	W	1-0	Furlong 86	15,804
22	div1	Leeds	A	L	1-6	Ainsworth 2	29,739
23	div1	Cardiff	H	W	1-0	Shittu 23	15,146
24	div1	Nottm Forest	A	L	1-2	Santos 49	26,099
25	div1	Ipswich	H	L	2-4	Furlong 27,30	18,231
26	div1	Reading	A	L	0-1		20,272
27	div1	Plymouth	A	L	1-2	Furlong 53	19,535
28	div1	Crewe	H	L	1-2	Shittu 81	15,770
29	div1	Brighton	H	D	0-0		15,898
30	div1	Leicester	A	L	0-1		23,754
31	facr3	Nottm Forest	H	L	0-3		11,140
32	div1	Stoke	H	W	1-0	Cook 18	13,559
33	div1	Coventry	A	W	2-1	Cureton 13; Furlong 90	16,595
34	div1	Millwall	A	D	0-0		15,603
35	div1	Preston	H	L	1-2	Furlong 26	15,620
36	div1	Wolverhampton	H	D	1-1	Gallen 11	15,029
37	div1	Ipswich	A	W	2-0	Furlong 4; Shittu 75	29,008
38	div1	Reading	H	D	0-0		16,971
39	div1	Watford	H	W	3-1	Furlong 34; Gallen 45,58	16,638
40	div1	Derby	A	D	0-0		24,486
41	div1	Rotherham	A	W	1-0	Rowlands 53	5,387
42	div1	Sunderland	H	L	1-3	Shittu 22	18,198
43	div1	Gillingham	H	D	1-1	Furlong 54	16,431
44	div1	Sheff Utd	A	L	2-3	Rowlands 26; Gallen 66	20,426
45	div1	Leeds	H	D	1-1	Gallen 85	18,182
46	div1	Burnley	A	L	0-2		10,396
47	div1	Wigan	A	D	0-0		12,007
48	div1	Nottm Forest	H	W	2-1	Curtis 45 og; Bircham 51	17,834
49	div1	Cardiff	A	L	0-1		15,722

KEY PLAYERS - GOALSCORERS

Paul Furlong

Binatone

Goals in the League	19
Goals in all competitions	19
Contribution to Attacking Power Average number of minutes between League team goals while on pitch	69
Player Strike Rate Average number of minutes between League goals scored by player	182
Club Strike Rate Average number of minutes between League goals scored by club	77

	PLAYER	GOALS LGE	GOALS ALL	POWER	S RATE
1	Paul Furlong	19	19	69	182 mins
2	Kevin Gallen	10	11	76	405 mins
3	Jamie Cureton	4	5	81	449 mins
4	Danny Shittu	4	4	80	746 mins
5	Georges Santos	4	4	76	862 mins

KEY PLAYERS - MIDFIELDERS

Martin Rowlands

Goals in the League	3
Goals in all competitions	4
Defensive Rating Average number of mins between League goals conceded while on the pitch	84
Contribution to Attacking Power Average number of minutes between League team goals while on pitch	74
Scoring Difference Defensive Rating minus Contribution to Attacking Power	10

	PLAYER	GOALS LGE	GOALS ALL	DEF RATE	ATT POWER	SCORE DIFF
1	Martin Rowlands	3	4	84	74	10 mins
2	Marc Bircham	1	1	66	66	0 mins
3	Lee Cook	2	2	79	81	-2 mins
4	Georges Santos	4	4	73	77	-4 mins

KEY PLAYERS - DEFENDERS

Matthew Rose

Goals Conceded in League	23
Goals Conceded in all competitions	23
Clean Sheets In games when player was on pitch for at least 70 minutes	8
Defensive Rating Ave number of mins between League goals conceded while on the pitch	89
Club Defensive Rating Average number of mins between League goals conceded by the club this season	71

	PLAYER	CON LGE	CON ALL	CLN SHEETS	DEF RATE
1	Matthew Rose	23	23	8	89 mins
2	Danny Shittu	40	46	12	75 mins
3	Marcus Bignot	52	55	13	71 mins
4	Gino Padula	45	46	6	55 mins

MONTHLY POINTS TALLY

AUGUST	5	28%
SEPTEMBER	15	100%
OCTOBER	9	60%
NOVEMBER	7	47%
DECEMBER	0	0%
JANUARY	7	58%
FEBRUARY	5	42%
MARCH	8	67%
APRIL	6	29%
MAY	0	0%

GOALS

	PLAYER	LGE	FAC	LC	Oth	TOT
1	Furlong	19	0	0	0	19
2	Gallen	10	0	1	0	11
3	Cureton	4	0	1	0	5
4	Santos	4	0	0	0	4
5	Rowlands	3	0	1	0	4
6	Shittu	4	0	0	0	4
7	Rose	2	0	0	0	2
8	McLeod	1	0	1	0	2
9	Cook	2	0	0	0	2
10	Ainsworth	2	0	0	0	2
11	Bean	1	0	0	0	1
	Other	2	0	0	0	2
	TOTAL	54	0	4	0	58

KEY GOALKEEPER

Simon Royce

Goals Conceded in the League	12
Goals Conceded in all competitions	12
Clean Sheets In games when player was on pitch for at least 70 minutes	6
Goals to Shots Ratio The average number of shots on target per each League goal conceded	4.3
Defensive Rating Ave number of mins between League goals conceded while on the pitch	98

DISCIPLINARY RECORDS

	PLAYER	YELLOW	RED	AVE
1	Davies	4	1	153
2	Santos	12	1	265
3	Miller	2	1	273
4	Bircham	9	0	314
5	Furlong	7	1	433
6	Rowlands	6	0	433
7	Bignot	8	0	459
8	Edghill	2	0	613
9	Cook	5	0	632
10	McLeod	1	0	646
11	Ainsworth	2	0	653
12	Padula	3	0	829
13	Cureton	1	1	898
	Other	6	0	
	TOTAL	68	5	

TOP POINT EARNERS

	PLAYER	CG	AV PTS
1	Jamie Cureton	17	1.82
2	Matthew Rose	20	1.75
3	Lee Cook	30	1.63
4	Paul Furlong	38	1.58
5	Simon Royce	13	1.54
6	Marc Bircham	30	1.50
7	Martin Rowlands	26	1.50
8	Georges Santos	36	1.47
9	Kevin Gallen	45	1.36
10	Marcus Bignot	41	1.34
	CLUB AVERAGE:		1.35

TEAM OF THE SEASON

D
Matthew Rose
CG: 20 DR: 89
M
Martin Rowlands
CG: 26 SD: 10
D
Danny Shittu
CG: 33 DR: 75
M
Marc Bircham
CG: 30 SD: 0
F
Paul Furlong
CG: 38 SR: 182
G
Simon Royce
CG: 13 DR: 98
D
Gino Padula
CG: 20 DR: 55
M
Lee Cook
CG: 30 SD: -2
F
Kevin Gallen
CG: 45 SR: 405
D
Marcus Bignot
CG: 41 DR: 71
M
Georges Santos
CG: 36 SD: -4

LEAGUE APPEARANCES GOALS AND BOOKINGS

	AGE (on 01/07/05)	IN NAMED 16	APPEARANCES	COUNTING GAMES	MINUTES ON PITCH	LEAGUE GOALS	Yellow	Red
Goalkeepers								
Jake Cole	19	18	0	0	0	0	0	0
Chris Day	29	40	30	30	2700	0	0	0
Generoso Rossi	26	8	3	3	270	0	1	0
Simon Royce	33	13	13	13	1170	0	0	0
Defenders								
Marcus Bignot	30	44	43	41	3674	0	8	0
Serge Branco	24	16	7	1	262	0	0	0
Andrew Davies	20	9	9	8	765	0	4	1
Richard Edghill	30	32	20	11	1227	0	2	0
Terrell Forbes	23	3	3	1	153	0	0	0
Arthur Gnohere	26	6	3	3	270	0	0	0
Patrick Kanyuka	-	4	1	1	90	0	1	0
Gino Padula	28	41	33	27	2489	0	3	0
Matthew Rose	29	31	28	20	2057	2	1	0
Danny Shittu	24	35	34	33	2982	4	1	0
Frankie Simek	20	6	5	5	430	0	1	0
Midfielders								
Gareth Ainsworth	32	24	23	11	1306	2	2	0
Stefan Bailey	17	3	2	1	124	0	1	0
Marcus Bean	20	30	20	11	1260	1	0	0
Marc Bircham	27	36	35	30	2834	1	9	0
Aaron Brown	25	1	1	0	23	0	0	0
Lee Cook	22	42	42	30	3161	2	5	0
Scott Donnelly	17	3	2	0	31	0	0	0
Richard Johnson	31	9	6	5	489	0	0	0
Kevin McLeod	24	28	24	2	646	1	1	0
Adam Miller	23	20	14	8	820	0	2	1
Martin Rowlands	26	35	35	26	2598	3	6	0
Georges Santos	34	43	43	36	3448	4	12	1
Forwards								
Shabazz Baidoo	25	6	4	0	95	0	0	0
Leon Best	18	5	5	1	211	0	0	0
Jamie Cureton	29	37	30	17	1796	4	1	1
Paul Furlong	36	40	40	38	3464	19	7	1
Kevin Gallen	29	45	45	45	4048	10	4	0
Dean Sturridge	31	2	2	0	52	0	0	0
Tony Thorpe	31	13	10	3	405	0	0	0
Luke Townsend	18	2	2	0	81	0	0	0

SQUAD APPEARANCES

Match	1	2	3	4	5	6	7	8	9	10	11	12	13	14	15	16	17	18	19	20	21	22	23	24	25
Venue	H	A	A	H	H	A	H	H	A	A	A	H	H	A	H	A	A	H	H	A	H	A	H	A	H
Competition	L	L	L	L	W	L	L	L	L	L	W	L	L	L	L	L	L	L	L	L	L	L	L	L	L
Result	D	L	D	L	W	W	L	W	W	W	L	W	W	W	W	L	L	W	D	L	W	L	W	L	L

Match	26	27	28	29	30	31	32	33	34	35	36	37	38	39	40	41	42	43	44	45	46	47	48	49
Venue	A	A	H	H	A	H	H	A	A	H	H	A	H	H	A	A	H	H	A	H	A	A	H	A
Competition	L	L	L	L	L	F	L	L	L	L	L	L	L	L	L	L	L	L	L	L	L	L	L	L
Result	L	L	L	D	L	L	W	W	D	L	D	W	D	W	D	W	L	D	L	D	L	D	W	L

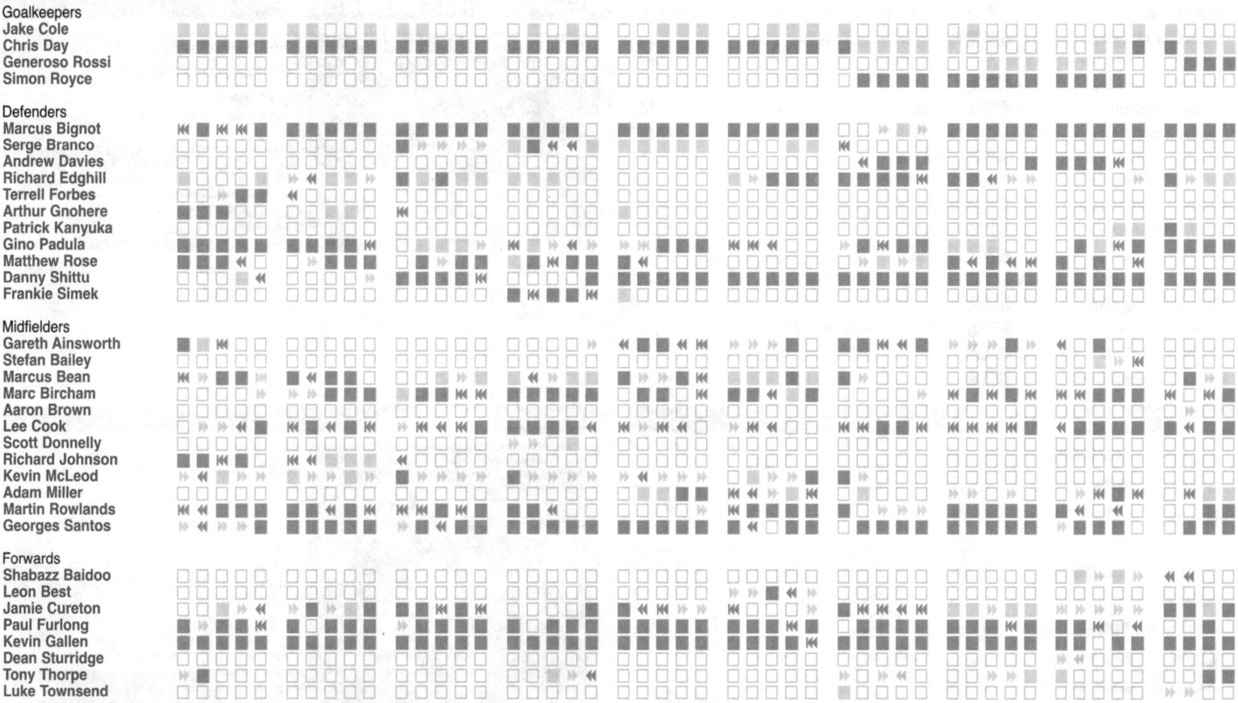
Goalkeepers
Jake Cole
Chris Day
Generoso Rossi
Simon Royce
Defenders
Marcus Bignot
Serge Branco
Andrew Davies
Richard Edghill
Terrell Forbes
Arthur Gnohere
Patrick Kanyuka
Gino Padula
Matthew Rose
Danny Shittu
Frankie Simek
Midfielders
Gareth Ainsworth
Stefan Bailey
Marcus Bean
Marc Bircham
Aaron Brown
Lee Cook
Scott Donnelly
Richard Johnson
Kevin McLeod
Adam Miller
Martin Rowlands
Georges Santos
Forwards
Shabazz Baidoo
Leon Best
Jamie Cureton
Paul Furlong
Kevin Gallen
Dean Sturridge
Tony Thorpe
Luke Townsend

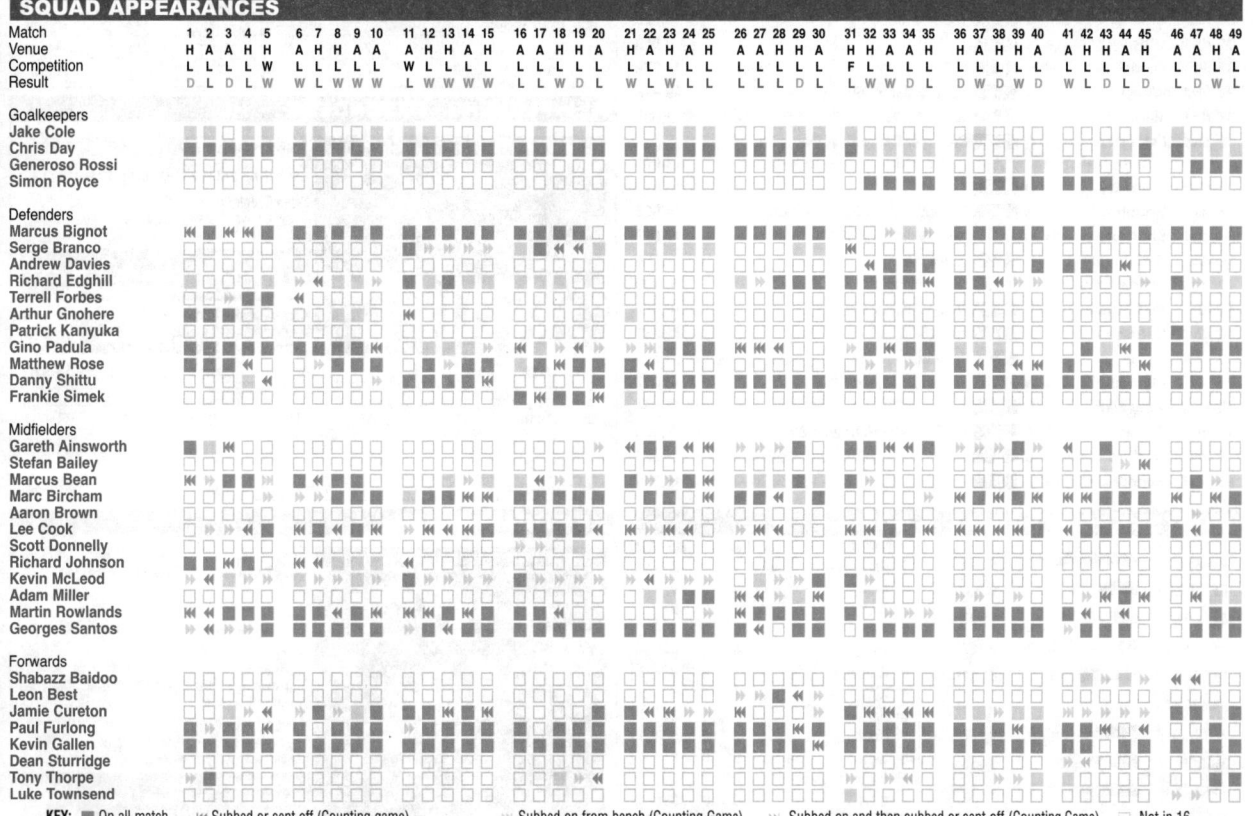

KEY: On all match; On bench; Subbed or sent off (Counting game); Subbed or sent off (playing less than 70 minutes); Subbed on from bench (Counting Game); Subbed on (playing less than 70 minutes); Subbed on and then subbed or sent off (Counting Game); Subbed on and then subbed or sent off (playing less than 70 minutes); Not in 16

STOKE CITY

Final Position: **12th**

NICKNAME: THE POTTERS

KEY: Won Drawn Lost

							Attendance
1	div1	Wolverhampton	H	W	2-1	Russell 55; Clarke, Clive 70 pen	17,066
2	div1	Sheff Utd	A	D	0-0		19,723
3	div1	Rotherham	A	D	1-1	Akinbiyi 85	5,925
4	div1	Gillingham	H	W	2-0	Noel-Williams 42; Akinbiyi 72	13,234
5	ccr1	Oldham	A	L	1-2	Asaba 25	2,861
6	div1	Cardiff	A	W	1-0	Noel-Williams 37	12,929
7	div1	Derby	H	W	1-0	Hall 90	18,673
8	div1	Preston	A	L	0-3		12,759
9	div1	Ipswich	H	W	3-2	Thomas 45,75; Akinbiyi 85	23,029
10	div1	Nottm Forest	H	D	0-0		21,115
11	div1	Burnley	A	D	2-2	Akinbiyi 34,50	12,981
12	div1	Leeds	A	D	0-0		25,759
13	div1	QPR	H	L	0-1		16,877
14	div1	Reading	H	L	0-1		15,574
15	div1	West Ham	A	L	0-2		29,808
16	div1	Leicester	A	D	1-1	Asaba 37	22,882
17	div1	Millwall	H	W	1-0	Greenacre 86	14,625
18	div1	Wigan	H	L	0-1		15,882
19	div1	Reading	A	L	0-1		14,831
20	div1	Crewe	H	W	1-0	Noel-Williams 64	17,640
21	div1	Plymouth	A	D	0-0		15,264
22	div1	Sunderland	H	L	0-1		16,980
23	div1	Watford	A	W	1-0	Noel-Williams 24	12,169
24	div1	Coventry	H	W	1-0	Akinbiyi 21	15,744
25	div1	Brighton	A	W	1-0	Akinbiyi 85	6,028
26	div1	Preston	H	D	0-0		20,350
27	div1	Ipswich	A	L	0-1		26,217
28	div1	Nottm Forest	A	L	0-1		22,051
29	div1	Burnley	H	L	0-1		15,689
30	facr3	Arsenal	A	L	1-2	Thomas 45	36,579
31	div1	QPR	A	L	0-1		13,559
32	div1	Leeds	H	L	0-1		18,372
33	div1	Wigan	A	W	1-0	Noel-Williams 39	9,938
34	div1	Millwall	A	W	1-0	Jones 15	11,036
35	div1	Leicester	H	W	3-2	Brammer 24; Noel-Williams 34; Taggart 59	14,076
36	div1	Coventry	A	D	0-0		13,871
37	div1	Brighton	H	W	2-0	Noel-Williams 39 pen,44 pen	14,908
38	div1	Sheff Utd	H	W	2-0	Noel-Williams 57,59	17,019
39	div1	Gillingham	A	L	1-2	Jones 54	7,766
40	div1	Wolverhampton	A	D	1-1	Noel-Williams 41	28,103
41	div1	Rotherham	H	L	1-2	Noel-Williams 83	16,552
42	div1	Cardiff	H	L	1-3	Hill 40	12,785
43	div1	Derby	A	L	1-3	Taggart 7	27,640
44	div1	Plymouth	H	W	2-0	Jones 28; Russell 41	13,017
45	div1	West Ham	H	L	0-1		14,534
46	div1	Crewe	A	W	2-0	Neal 79; Noel-Williams 89	9,166
47	div1	Watford	H	L	0-1		15,229
48	div1	Sunderland	A	L	0-1		47,350

MONTHLY POINTS TALLY

AUGUST	14	78%
SEPTEMBER	6	40%
OCTOBER	4	27%
NOVEMBER	4	27%
DECEMBER	10	67%
JANUARY	0	0%
FEBRUARY	10	83%
MARCH	7	58%
APRIL	6	29%
MAY	0	0%

GOALS

	PLAYER	LGE	FAC	LC	Oth	TOT
1	Noel-Williams	13	0	0	0	13
2	Akinbiyi	7	0	0	0	7
3	Thomas	2	1	0	0	3
4	Jones	3	0	0	0	3
5	Taggart	2	0	0	0	2
6	Russell	2	0	0	0	2
7	Asaba	1	0	1	0	2
8	Hill	1	0	0	0	1
9	Greenacre	1	0	0	0	1
10	Neal	1	0	0	0	1
11	Clarke, Clive	1	0	0	0	1
	Other	2	0	0	0	2
	TOTAL	36	1	1	0	38

KEY PLAYERS - GOALSCORERS

Gifton Noel-Williams

Goals in the League	13
Goals in all competitions	13
Contribution to Attacking Power Average number of minutes between League team goals while on pitch	102
Player Strike Rate Average number of minutes between League goals scored by player	269
Club Strike Rate Average number of minutes between League goals scored by club	115

	PLAYER	GOALS LGE	GOALS ALL	POWER	S RATE
1	Gifton Noel-Williams	13	13	102	269 mins
2	Ade Akinbiyi	7	7	143	369 mins
3	Gerry Taggart	2	2	91	1368 mins
4	Carl Asaba	1	2	153	1531 mins
5	Wayne Thomas	2	3	124	1553 mins

KEY PLAYERS - MIDFIELDERS

Clive Clarke

Goals in the League	1
Goals in all competitions	1
Defensive Rating Average number of mins between League goals conceded while on the pitch	119
Contribution to Attacking Power Average number of minutes between League team goals while on pitch	119
Scoring Difference Defensive Rating minus Contribution to Attacking Power	0

	PLAYER	GOALS LGE	GOALS ALL	DEF RATE	ATT POWER	SCORE DIFF
1	Clive Clarke	1	1	119	119	0 mins
2	Chris Greenacre	1	1	121	121	0 mins
3	David Brammer	1	1	113	117	-4 mins
4	Darel Russell	2	2	106	115	-9 mins
5	Karl Henry	0	0	87	123	-36 mins

KEY PLAYERS - DEFENDERS

Michael Duberry

Goals Conceded in League	17
Goals Conceded in all competitions	17
Clean Sheets In games when player was on pitch for at least 70 minutes	11
Defensive Rating Ave number of mins between League goals conceded while on the pitch	132
Club Defensive Rating Average number of mins between League goals conceded by the club this season	109

	PLAYER	CON LGE	CON ALL	CLN SHEETS	DEF RATE
1	Michael Duberry	17	17	11	132 mins
2	John Halls	16	19	8	111 mins
3	Clinton Hill	25	27	15	109 mins
4	Marcus Hall	16	20	8	99 mins
5	Gerry Taggart	28	30	13	98 mins

KEY GOALKEEPER

Steve Simonsen

Goals Conceded in the League	23
Goals Conceded in all competitions	27
Clean Sheets In games when player was on pitch for at least 70 minutes	14
Goals to Shots Ratio The average number of shots on target per each League goal conceded	6.5
Defensive Rating Ave number of mins between League goals conceded while on the pitch	116

DISCIPLINARY RECORDS

	PLAYER	YELLOW	RED	AVE
1	Taggart	9	1	273
2	Halls	5	1	295
3	Buxton	4	0	326
4	Hill	7	1	341
5	Asaba	4	0	382
6	Clarke, Clive	7	1	445
7	Duberry	4	1	450
8	Henry	3	0	492
9	Akinbiyi	5	0	517
10	Brammer	7	0	518
11	Russell	7	0	575
12	Harper	1	0	681
13	Thomas	4	0	776
	Other	9	1	
	TOTAL	76	6	

TOP POINT EARNERS

	PLAYER	GAMES	AV PTS
1	Marcus Hall	16	1.56
2	John Halls	19	1.53
3	Gifton Noel-Williams	35	1.49
4	Gerry Taggart	30	1.43
5	Karl Henry	12	1.42
6	David Brammer	39	1.41
7	Clinton Hill	29	1.38
8	Chris Greenacre	16	1.38
9	Clive Clarke	38	1.34
10	Ed de Goey	15	1.33
	CLUB AVERAGE:		1.33

TEAM OF THE SEASON

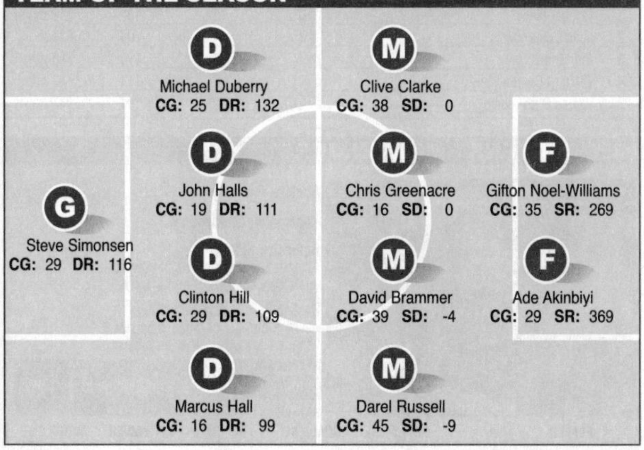
D
Michael Duberry
CG: 25 DR: 132
D
John Halls
CG: 19 DR: 111
D
Clinton Hill
CG: 29 DR: 109
D
Marcus Hall
CG: 16 DR: 99
G
Steve Simonsen
CG: 29 DR: 116
M
Clive Clarke
CG: 38 SD: 0
M
Chris Greenacre
CG: 16 SD: 0
M
David Brammer
CG: 39 SD: -4
M
Darel Russell
CG: 45 SD: -9
F
Gifton Noel-Williams
CG: 35 SR: 269
F
Ade Akinbiyi
CG: 29 SR: 369

LEAGUE APPEARANCES GOALS AND BOOKINGS

	AGE (on 01/07/05)	IN NAMED 16	APPEARANCES	COUNTING GAMES	MINUTES ON PITCH	LEAGUE GOALS	Yellow	Red
Goalkeepers								
Ed de Goey	38	43	17	15	1473	0	0	0
Ben Foster	22	3	0	0	0	0	0	0
Steve Simonsen	26	46	31	29	2667	0	2	0
Defenders								
Chris Barker	25	4	4	3	338	0	0	0
Lewis Buxton	21	21	16	14	1307	0	4	0
Carl Dickinson	18	4	1	0	1	0	0	0
Michael Duberry	29	26	25	25	2250	0	4	1
Marcus Hall	29	22	20	16	1578	1	2	0
John Halls	23	22	22	19	1773	0	5	1
Clinton Hill	26	39	32	29	2732	1	7	1
Gareth Owen	22	4	2	0	28	0	0	0
Gerry Taggart	34	31	31	30	2736	2	9	1
Wayne Thomas	26	35	35	34	3105	2	4	0
Andy Wilkinson	20	1	1	0	9	0	0	0
Midfielders								
David Brammer	30	43	43	39	3630	1	7	0
Chris Clark	21	5	3	1	93	0	0	0
Clive Clarke	25	41	41	38	3562	1	7	1
Jay Denny	19	5	0	0	0	0	0	0
John Eustace	25	9	7	1	193	0	2	0
Chris Greenacre	27	41	32	16	1695	1	2	0
Thordur Gudjonsson	31	5	2	0	22	0	0	0
Steve Guppy	36	6	4	0	86	0	0	0
Kevin Harper	29	9	9	7	681	0	1	0
Karl Henry	22	44	34	12	1477	0	3	0
Jason Jarrett	25	2	2	1	153	0	0	0
Lewis Neal	23	36	23	4	935	1	0	0
Darel Russell	24	45	45	45	4025	2	7	0
Forwards								
Ade Akinbiyi	30	29	29	29	2585	7	5	0
Carl Asaba	32	33	33	14	1531	1	4	0
Tryggvi Gudmundsson	30	1	0	0	0	0	0	0
Kenwyne Jones	21	13	13	10	997	3	1	0
Gifton Noel-Williams	25	46	46	35	3496	13	2	1
Jermaine Palmer	18	4	1	0	2	0	0	0
Martin Paterson	18	4	3	0	70	0	0	0
Michael Ricketts	26	13	11	0	208	0	2	0

SQUAD APPEARANCES

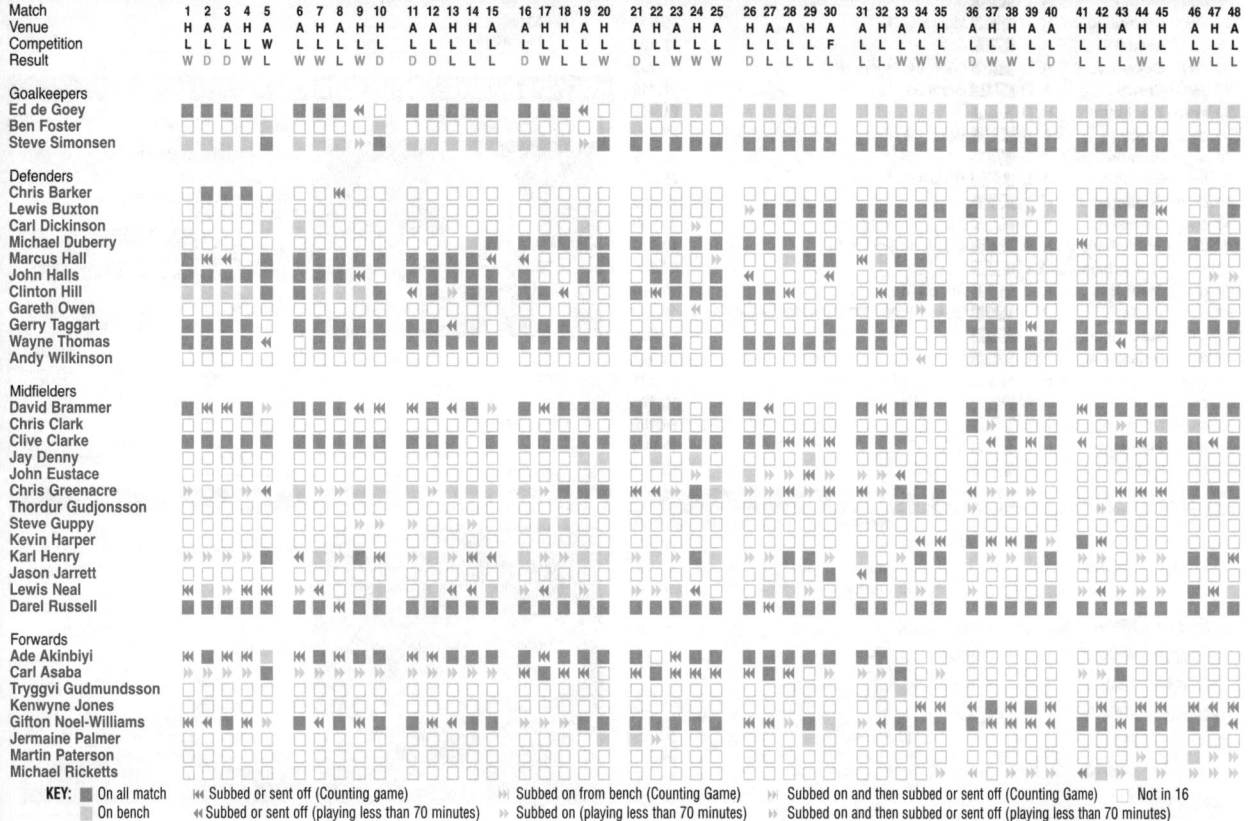

Match	1	2	3	4	5	6	7	8	9	10	11	12	13	14	15	16	17	18	19	20	21	22	23	24	25	26	27	28	29	30	31	32	33	34	35	36	37	38	39	40	41	42	43	44	45	46	47	48
Venue	H	A	A	H	A	A	H	A	H	H	A	A	H	H	A	A	H	H	A	H	A	H	A	H	A	H	A	A	H	A	A	H	A	A	H	A	H	H	A	A	H	H	A	H	H	A	H	A
Competition	L	L	L	L	W	L	L	L	L	L	L	L	L	L	L	L	L	L	L	L	L	L	L	L	L	L	L	L	L	F	L	L	L	L	L	L	L	L	L	L	L	L	L	L	L	L	L	L
Result	W	D	D	W	L	W	W	L	W	D	D	D	L	L	L	D	W	L	L	W	D	L	W	W	W	D	L	L	L	L	L	L	W	W	W	D	W	W	L	D	L	L	L	W	L	W	L	L

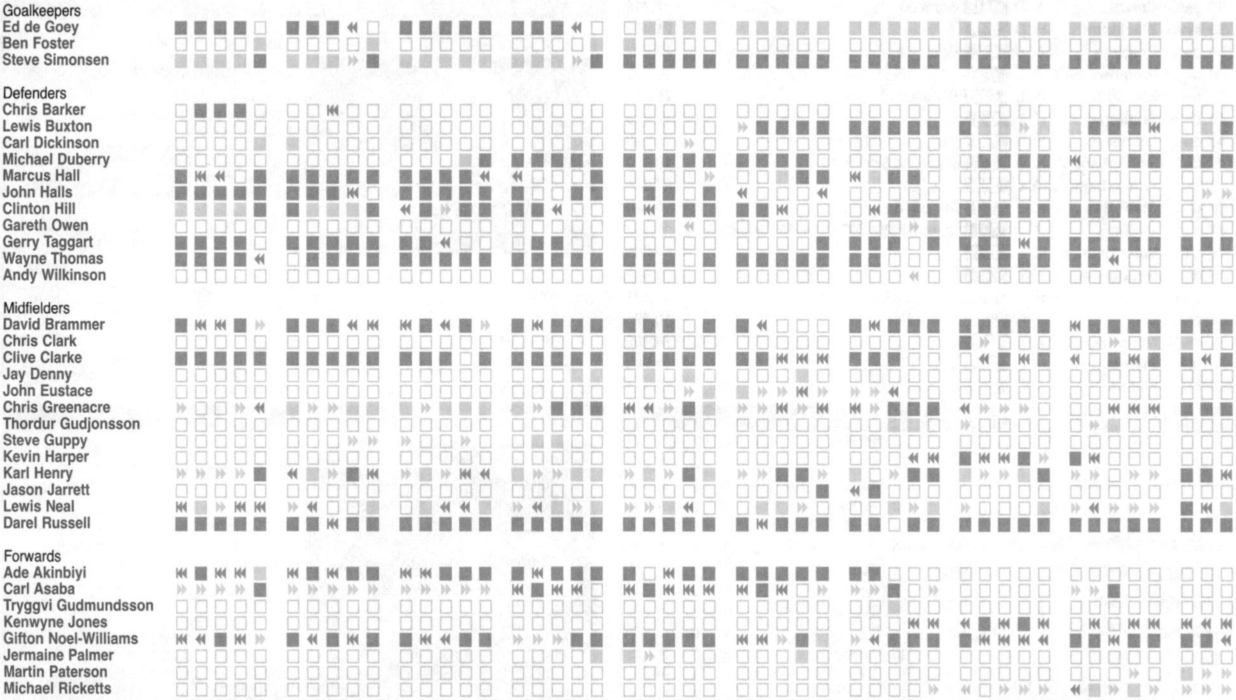
Goalkeepers
Ed de Goey
Ben Foster
Steve Simonsen
Defenders
Chris Barker
Lewis Buxton
Carl Dickinson
Michael Duberry
Marcus Hall
John Halls
Clinton Hill
Gareth Owen
Gerry Taggart
Wayne Thomas
Andy Wilkinson
Midfielders
David Brammer
Chris Clark
Clive Clarke
Jay Denny
John Eustace
Chris Greenacre
Thordur Gudjonsson
Steve Guppy
Kevin Harper
Karl Henry
Jason Jarrett
Lewis Neal
Darel Russell
Forwards
Ade Akinbiyi
Carl Asaba
Tryggvi Gudmundsson
Kenwyne Jones
Gifton Noel-Williams
Jermaine Palmer
Martin Paterson
Michael Ricketts

KEY: ■ On all match | ■ On bench | ⏮ Subbed or sent off (Counting game) | « Subbed or sent off (playing less than 70 minutes) | ⏭ Subbed on from bench (Counting Game) | » Subbed on (playing less than 70 minutes) | Subbed on and then subbed or sent off (Counting Game) | Subbed on and then subbed or sent off (playing less than 70 minutes) | □ Not in 16

BURNLEY

Final Position: **13th**

NICKNAME: THE CLARETS   KEY: Won Drawn Lost

							Attendance
1	div1	Sheff Utd	H	D	1-1	Hyde 16	16,956
2	div1	Rotherham	A	D	0-0		6,243
3	div1	Watford	A	W	1-0	Moore, I 64	12,048
4	div1	Wolverhampton	H	D	1-1	Blake 24	13,869
5	ccR1	Bury	A	W	3-2	Mattis 17 og; Blake 33 pen,52	3,648
6	div1	West Ham	A	L	0-1		22,119
7	div1	Gillingham	H	L	1-2	Moore, I 87	11,574
8	div1	Crewe	H	W	3-0	McGreal 12; Blake 42; Chaplow 49	11,274
9	div1	Wigan	A	D	0-0		9,746
10	div1	Leicester	A	D	0-0		22,495
11	ccR2	Wolverhampton	H	W	4-2*	Blake 50 (*on penalties)	5,013
12	div1	Stoke	H	D	2-2	Moore, I 3; Blake 19 pen	12,981
13	div1	Cardiff	H	W	1-0	Chaplow 88	7,200
14	div1	Reading	A	D	0-0		15,400
15	div1	Ipswich	A	D	1-1	Blake 19	23,183
16	div1	Coventry	H	D	2-2	Blake 65 pen; Branch 73	10,919
17	div1	Derby	H	L	0-2		13,703
18	ccR3	Aston Villa	H	W	3-1	Branch 9; Camara 65; Valois 86	11,184
19	div1	QPR	A	L	0-3		15,638
20	div1	Leeds	A	W	2-1	Roche 10; Duffy 31	27,490
21	div1	Ipswich	H	L	0-2		11,969
22	ccR4	Tottenham	H	L	0-3		10,639
23	div1	Nottm Forest	H	W	1-0	Blake 6	11,622
24	div1	Brighton	A	W	1-0	Blake 70	6,109
25	div1	Millwall	H	W	1-0	Blake 61 pen	11,471
26	div1	Plymouth	A	L	0-1		13,308
27	div1	Preston	H	W	2-0	Blake 45,85	15,318
28	div1	Sunderland	A	L	1-2	Branch 36	27,102
29	div1	Wigan	H	W	1-0	Branch 24	16,485
30	div1	Stoke	A	W	1-0	Cahill 79	15,689
31	div1	Reading	H	D	0-0		11,392
32	facr3	Liverpool	H	W	1-0	Traore 51 og	19,033
33	div1	Cardiff	A	L	0-2		11,562
34	facr4	Bournemouth	H	W	2-0	Moore 17,90	9,944
35	div1	Leeds	H	L	0-1		17,789
36	div1	Coventry	A	W	2-0	Oster 64; Moore 69	13,236
37	div1	Crewe	A	D	1-1	Grant 53	7,718
38	facr5	Blackburn	H	D	0-0		21,468
39	div1	Derby	A	D	1-1	Valois 34	23,701
40	div1	Preston	A	L	0-1		18,202
41	facr5r	Blackburn	A	L	1-2	Hyde 42	28,691
42	div1	Sunderland	H	L	0-2		12,103
43	div1	Leicester	H	D	0-0		10,933
44	div1	Rotherham	H	W	2-1	Grant 11; Sinclair 14	10,539
45	div1	Wolverhampton	A	L	0-2		24,336
46	div1	Sheff Utd	A	L	1-2	Akinbiyi 84	19,374
47	div1	Watford	H	W	3-1	Bowditch 20; O'Connor 43; Valois 90	11,507
48	div1	West Ham	H	L	0-1		12,209
49	div1	Gillingham	A	L	0-1		9,447
50	div1	Brighton	H	D	1-1	Akinbiyi 23	11,611
51	div1	QPR	H	W	2-0	Akinbiyi 43,81	10,396
52	div1	Nottm Forest	A	L	0-1		24,165
53	div1	Plymouth	H	W	2-0	Valois 87 pen; O'Connor 90	12,893
54	div1	Millwall	A	D	0-0		12,171

MONTHLY POINTS TALLY

AUGUST	6	33%
SEPTEMBER	9	60%
OCTOBER	3	20%
NOVEMBER	12	80%
DECEMBER	6	50%
JANUARY	4	44%
FEBRUARY	5	33%
MARCH	4	27%
APRIL	10	48%
MAY	1	33%

GOALS

	PLAYER	LGE	FAC	LC	Oth	TOT
1	Blake	10	0	3	0	13
2	Moore	4	2	0	0	6
3	Akinbiyi	4	0	0	0	4
4	Branch	3	0	1	0	4
5	Valois	3	0	1	0	4
6	O'Connor	2	0	0	0	2
7	Hyde	1	1	0	0	2
8	Chaplow	2	0	0	0	2
9	Grant	2	0	0	0	2
10	Bowditch	1	0	0	0	1
11	Duffy	1	0	0	0	1
	Other	5	1	2	0	8
	TOTAL	38	4	7	0	49

KEY PLAYERS - GOALSCORERS

Robbie Blake

Goals in the League	10
Goals in all competitions	13
Contribution to Attacking Power Average number of minutes between League team goals while on pitch	102
Player Strike Rate Average number of minutes between League goals scored by player	216
Club Strike Rate Average number of minutes between League goals scored by club	109

	PLAYER	GOALS LGE	GOALS ALL	POWER	S RATE
1	Robbie Blake	10	13	102	216 mins
2	Jean Louis Valois	3	4	104	522 mins
3	Ian Moore	4	6	116	698 mins
4	Richard Chaplow	2	2	114	741 mins
5	James O'Connor	2	2	104	933 mins

KEY PLAYERS - MIDFIELDERS

James O'Connor

Goals in the League	2
Goals in all competitions	2
Defensive Rating Average number of mins between League goals conceded while on the pitch	133
Contribution to Attacking Power Average number of minutes between League team goals while on pitch	104
Scoring Difference Defensive Rating minus Contribution to Attacking Power	29

	PLAYER	GOALS LGE	GOALS ALL	DEF RATE	ATT POWER	SCORE DIFF
1	James O'Connor	2	2	133	104	29 mins
2	Richard Chaplow	2	2	135	114	21 mins
3	Tony Grant	2	2	120	116	4 mins
4	Micah Hyde	1	2	89	100	-11 mins
5	Graham Branch	3	4	109	121	-12 mins

KEY PLAYERS - DEFENDERS

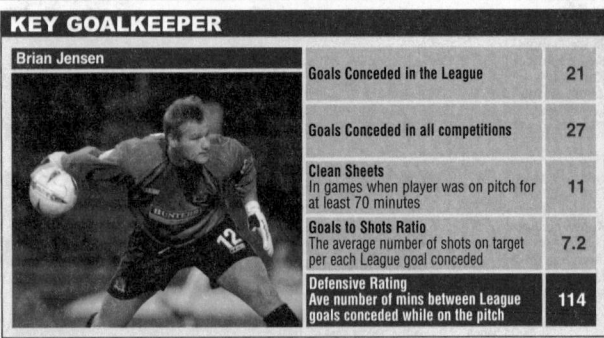

Gary Cahill

Goals Conceded in League	20
Goals Conceded in all competitions	25
Clean Sheets In games when player was on pitch for at least 70 minutes	12
Defensive Rating Ave number of mins between League goals conceded while on the pitch	121
Club Defensive Rating Average number of mins between League goals conceded by the club this season	106

	PLAYER	CON LGE	CON ALL	CLN SHEETS	DEF RATE
1	Gary Cahill	20	25	12	121 mins
2	Mike Duff	27	36	15	117 mins
3	Frank Sinclair	29	34	15	107 mins
4	John McGreal	33	36	16	105 mins
5	Lee Roche	16	20	7	105 mins

KEY GOALKEEPER

Brian Jensen

Goals Conceded in the League	21
Goals Conceded in all competitions	27
Clean Sheets In games when player was on pitch for at least 70 minutes	11
Goals to Shots Ratio The average number of shots on target per each League goal conceded	7.2
Defensive Rating Ave number of mins between League goals conceded while on the pitch	114

DISCIPLINARY RECORDS

	PLAYER	YELLOW	RED	AVE
1	Sinclair	14	1	206
2	Roche	6	0	280
3	Duff	10	1	287
4	Whittingham	2	0	294
5	McGreal	8	1	385
6	Akinbiyi	1	1	406
7	Cahill	4	0	607
8	O'Connor	3	0	622
9	Hyde	5	0	661
10	Bowditch	1	0	720
11	Valois	2	0	783
12	Branch	4	0	844
13	Camara	4	0	1012
	Other	7	0	
	TOTAL	71	4	

TOP POINT EARNERS

	PLAYER	GAMES	AV PTS
1	James O'Connor	21	1.57
2	Brian Jensen	26	1.54
3	Lee Roche	15	1.53
4	Tony Grant	35	1.51
5	Gary Cahill	27	1.41
6	Robbie Blake	24	1.38
7	Frank Sinclair	34	1.35
8	John McGreal	38	1.32
9	Mohammed Camara	45	1.31
10	Ian Moore	30	1.30
	CLUB AVERAGE:		1.30

LEAGUE APPEARANCES GOALS AND BOOKINGS

	AGE (on 01/07/05)	IN NAMED 16	APPEARANCES	COUNTING GAMES	MINUTES ON PITCH	LEAGUE GOALS	Yellow	Red
Goalkeepers								
Danny Coyne	26	36	20	19	1736	0	0	0
Brian Jensen	30	46	27	26	2404	0	0	0
Defenders								
Gary Cahill	19	28	27	27	2429	1	4	0
Mohammed Camara	30	45	45	45	4050	0	4	0
Mike Duff	27	42	41	34	3167	0	10	1
Richard Duffy	19	11	7	3	375	1	3	0
John McGreal	33	39	39	38	3467	1	8	1
Lee Roche	24	40	30	15	1681	1	6	0
Paul Scott	20	15	0	0	0	0	0	0
Frank Sinclair	33	36	36	34	3098	1	14	1
Ryan Townsend	19	9	0	0	0	0	0	0
Midfielders								
Dean Bowditch	19	11	10	7	720	1	1	0
Graham Branch	33	43	43	36	3379	3	4	0
Richard Chaplow	20	21	21	16	1481	2	1	0
Tony Grant	30	43	42	35	3239	2	3	0
Micah Hyde	30	38	38	36	3308	1	5	0
James O'Connor	25	21	21	21	1866	2	3	0
Matthew O'Neill	21	26	2	0	6	0	0	0
John Oster	26	17	15	10	1049	1	0	0
Joel Pilkington	20	32	1	0	1	0	0	0
Amadou Sanokho	-	17	3	1	99	0	0	0
Jean Louis Valois	31	33	30	12	1566	3	2	0
Peter Whittingham	20	7	7	7	589	0	2	0
Mark Yates	35	8	0	0	0	0	0	0
Forwards								
Ade Akinbiyi	30	10	10	9	813	4	1	1
Robbie Blake	29	25	24	24	2159	10	1	0
Cayne Hanley	-	2	0	0	0	0	0	0
Ian Moore	28	35	35	30	2792	4	2	0

TEAM OF THE SEASON

G – Brian Jensen, CG: 26 DR: 114

D – Gary Cahill, CG: 27 DR: 121

D – Mike Duff, CG: 34 DR: 117

D – Frank Sinclair, CG: 34 DR: 107

D – John McGreal, CG: 38 DR: 105

M – James O'Connor, CG: 21 SD: 29

M – Richard Chaplow, CG: 16 SD: 21

M – Tony Grant, CG: 35 SD: 4

M – Micah Hyde, CG: 36 SD: -11

F – Robbie Blake, CG: 24 SR: 216

F – Ian Moore, CG: 30 SR: 698

SQUAD APPEARANCES

Match	1	2	3	4	5	6	7	8	9	10	11	12	13	14	15	16	17	18	19	20	21	22	23	24	25	26	27	28	29	30	31	32	33	34	35	36	37	38	39	40	41	42	43	44	45	46	47	48	49	50	51	52	53	54
Venue	H	A	A	H	A	A	H	H	A	A	H	H	H	A	A	H	H	H	A	A	H	H	H	A	H	A	H	A	H	A	H	H	A	H	H	A	A	H	A	A	A	H	H	H	A	A	H	H	A	H	H	A	H	A
Competition	L	L	L	L	W	L	L	L	L	L	W	L	L	L	L	L	L	W	L	L	L	W	L	L	L	L	L	L	L	L	L	F	L	F	L	L	L	F	L	L	F	L	L	L	L	L	L	L	L	L	L	L	L	L
Result	D	D	W	D	W	L	L	W	D	D	W	D	W	D	D	D	L	W	L	W	L	L	W	W	W	L	W	L	W	W	D	W	L	W	L	W	D	D	D	L	L	L	D	W	L	L	W	L	L	D	W	L	W	D

Goalkeepers: Danny Coyne, Brian Jensen

Defenders: Gary Cahill, Mohammed Camara, Mike Duff, Richard Duffy, John McGreal, Lee Roche, Paul Scott, Frank Sinclair, Ryan Townsend

Midfielders: Dean Bowditch, Graham Branch, Richard Chaplow, Tony Grant, Micah Hyde, James O'Connor, Matthew O'Neill, John Oster, Joel Pilkington, Amadou Sanokho, Jean Louis Valois, Peter Whittingham, Mark Yates

Forwards: Ade Akinbiyi, Robbie Blake, Cayne Hanley, Ian Moore

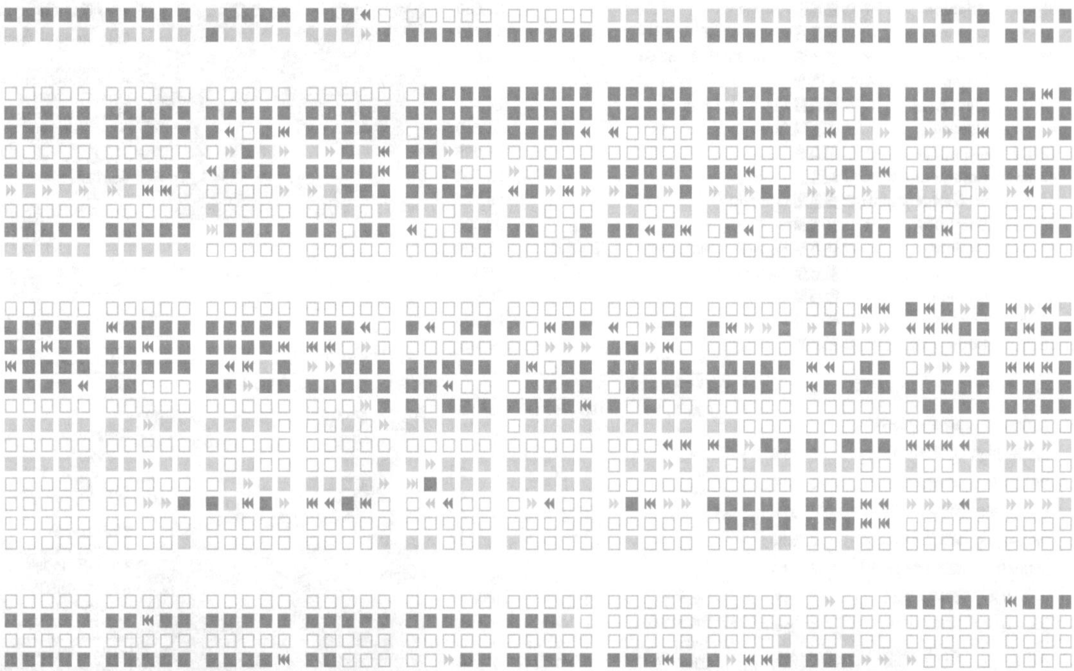

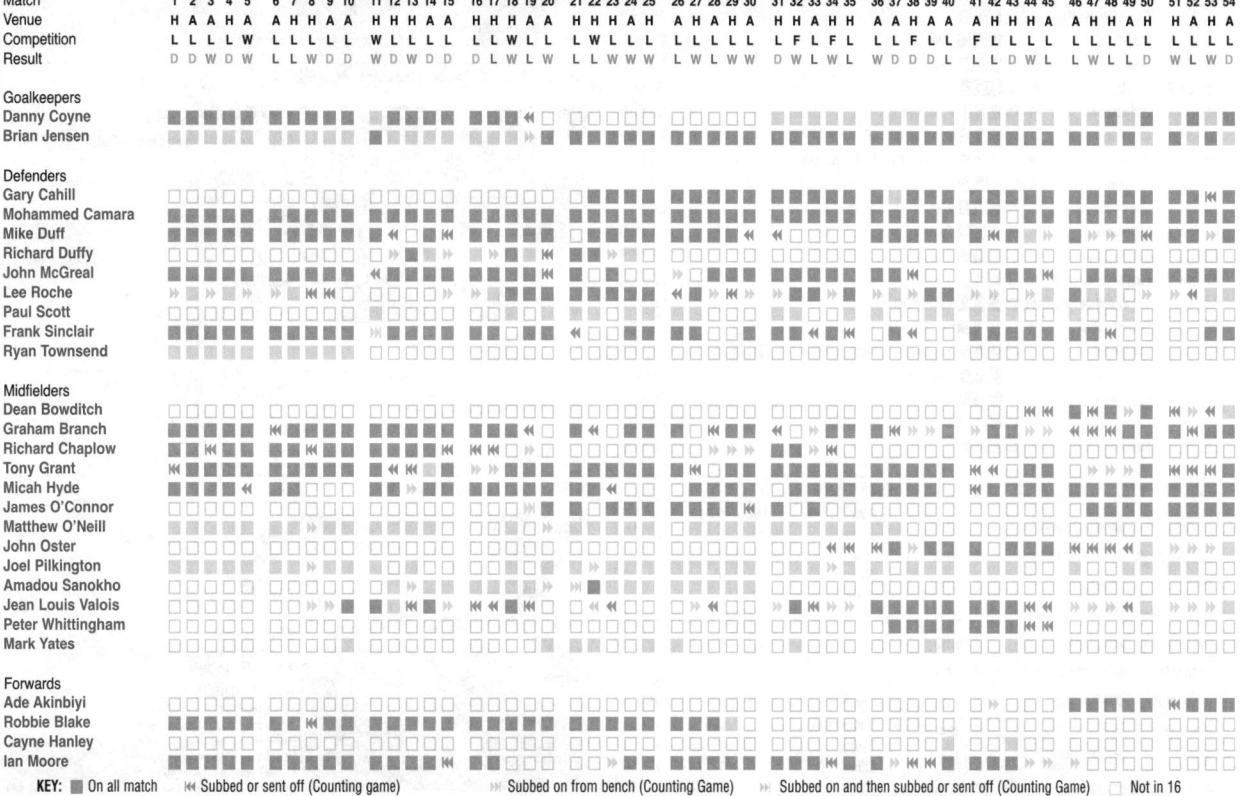

KEY: On all match · On bench · Subbed or sent off (Counting game) · Subbed or sent off (playing less than 70 minutes) · Subbed on from bench (Counting Game) · Subbed on (playing less than 70 minutes) · Subbed on and then subbed or sent off (Counting Game) · Subbed on and then subbed or sent off (playing less than 70 minutes) · Not in 16

LEEDS UNITED

Final Position: **14th**

NICKNAME: UNITED KEY: ☐Won ☐Drawn ☐Lost

							Attendance
1	div1	Derby	H	W	1-0	Richardson 72	30,459
2	div1	Gillingham	A	L	1-2	Pugh 80	10,739
3	div1	Wolverhampton	A	D	0-0		28,397
4	div1	Nottm Forest	H	D	1-1	Guppy 25	31,808
5	ccr1	Huddersfield	H	W	1-0	Pugh 23	30,115
6	div1	Sheff Utd	A	L	0-2		22,959
7	div1	Coventry	H	W	3-0	Carlisle 40; Joachim 71; Pugh 90	26,725
8	div1	Plymouth	A	W	1-0	Keith 43 og	20,555
9	div1	Crewe	A	D	2-2	Pugh 53,89	9,095
10	ccr2	Swindon	H	W	1-0	Ricketts 9	18,476
11	div1	Sunderland	H	L	0-1		28,926
12	div1	Stoke	H	D	0-0		25,759
13	div1	Cardiff	A	D	0-0		17,006
14	div1	Preston	H	W	1-0	Pugh 78	30,458
15	div1	Reading	A	D	1-1	Walton 1	22,230
16	div1	Brighton	A	L	0-1		6,716
17	ccr3	Portsmouth	A	L	1-2	Deane 40	15,215
18	div1	Wigan	H	L	0-2		27,432
19	div1	Burnley	H	L	1-2	Wright 1	27,490
20	div1	Preston	A	W	4-2	Deane 13; Healy 15,44; Walton 72	18,531
21	div1	Ipswich	A	L	0-1		29,955
22	div1	QPR	H	W	6-1	Healy 9; Deane 13,42,44,72; Wright 23	29,739
23	div1	Watford	H	D	2-2	Wright 21; Carlisle 86	24,585
24	div1	Rotherham	A	L	0-1		8,860
25	div1	Leicester	H	L	0-2		27,384
26	div1	West Ham	A	D	1-1	Healy 90 pen	30,684
27	div1	Millwall	H	D	1-1	Oster 43	26,265
28	div1	Sunderland	A	W	3-2	Lennon 30; Deane 61; Joachim 85	43,253
29	div1	Plymouth	H	W	2-1	Gilbert 46 og; Healy 90	34,496
30	div1	Crewe	H	L	0-2		32,303
31	div1	Coventry	A	W	2-1	Blake 28; Healy 65	19,084
32	facr3	Birmingham	A	L	0-3		25,159
33	div1	Cardiff	H	D	1-1	Walton 14	29,548
34	div1	Stoke	A	W	1-0	Thomas 72 og	18,372
35	div1	Derby	A	L	0-2		25,648
36	div1	Brighton	H	D	1-1	Carlisle 43	27,033
37	div1	Burnley	A	W	1-0	Einarsson 66	17,789
38	div1	Reading	H	W	3-1	Healy 36; Hulse 56,63	30,034
39	div1	Wigan	A	L	0-3		17,177
40	div1	West Ham	H	W	2-1	Hulse 51; Derry 86	34,115
41	div1	Millwall	A	D	1-1	Hulse 78	11,510
42	div1	Gillingham	H	D	1-1	Hulse 81	27,995
43	div1	Nottm Forest	A	D	0-0		25,101
44	div1	Wolverhampton	H	D	1-1	Derry 50	29,773
45	div1	Sheff Utd	H	L	0-4		28,936
46	div1	Watford	A	W	2-1	Hulse 28; Carlisle 67	16,306
47	div1	QPR	A	D	1-1	Johnson, Se 24	18,182
48	div1	Ipswich	H	D	1-1	Spring 12	29,607
49	div1	Leicester	A	L	0-2		26,593
50	div1	Rotherham	H	D	0-0		30,900

MONTHLY POINTS TALLY

AUGUST	5	33%
SEPTEMBER	8	53%
OCTOBER	5	33%
NOVEMBER	7	39%
DECEMBER	8	53%
JANUARY	8	44%
FEBRUARY	9	75%
MARCH	3	33%
APRIL	6	40%
MAY	1	17%

GOALS

	PLAYER	LGE	FAC	LC	Oth	TOT
1	Deane	6	0	1	0	7
2	Healy	7	0	0	0	7
3	Hulse	6	0	0	0	6
4	Pugh	5	0	1	0	6
5	Carlisle	4	0	0	0	4
6	Wright	3	0	0	0	3
7	Walton	3	0	0	0	3
8	Derry	2	0	0	0	2
9	Joachim	2	0	0	0	2
10	Johnson, Se	1	0	0	0	1
11	Spring	1	0	0	0	1
	Other	9	0	1	0	10
	TOTAL	49	0	3	0	52

KEY PLAYERS - GOALSCORERS

Robert Hulse

Goals in the League	6
Goals in all competitions	6
Contribution to Attacking Power Average number of minutes between League team goals while on pitch	94
Player Strike Rate Average number of minutes between League goals scored by player	190
Club Strike Rate Average number of minutes between League goals scored by club	84

	PLAYER	GOALS LGE	GOALS ALL	POWER	S RATE
1	Robert Hulse	6	6	94	190 mins
2	David Healy	7	7	70	333 mins
3	Brian Deane	6	7	76	334 mins
4	Danny Pugh	5	6	81	600 mins
5	Simon Walton	3	3	75	653 mins

KEY PLAYERS - MIDFIELDERS

Jermaine Wright

Goals in the League	3
Goals in all competitions	3
Defensive Rating Average number of mins between League goals conceded while on the pitch	90
Contribution to Attacking Power Average number of minutes between League team goals while on pitch	80
Scoring Difference Defensive Rating minus Contribution to Attacking Power	10

	PLAYER	GOALS LGE	GOALS ALL	DEF RATE	ATT POWER	SCORE DIFF
1	Jermaine Wright	3	3	90	80	10 mins
2	Simon Walton	3	3	75	75	0 mins
3	Aaron Lennon	1	1	85	85	0 mins
4	Danny Pugh	5	6	79	81	-2 mins
5	Sean Gregan	0	0	76	84	-8 mins

KEY PLAYERS - DEFENDERS

Clarke Carlisle

Goals Conceded in League	31
Goals Conceded in all competitions	33
Clean Sheets In games when player was on pitch for at least 70 minutes	8
Defensive Rating Ave number of mins between League goals conceded while on the pitch	85
Club Defensive Rating Average number of mins between League goals conceded by the club this season	80

	PLAYER	CON LGE	CON ALL	CLN SHEETS	DEF RATE
1	Clarke Carlisle	31	33	8	85 mins
2	Gary Kelly	46	51	11	83 mins
3	Frazer Richardson	31	36	6	80 mins
4	Paul Butler	44	44	10	79 mins
5	Matthew Kilgallon	32	35	4	73 mins

KEY GOALKEEPER

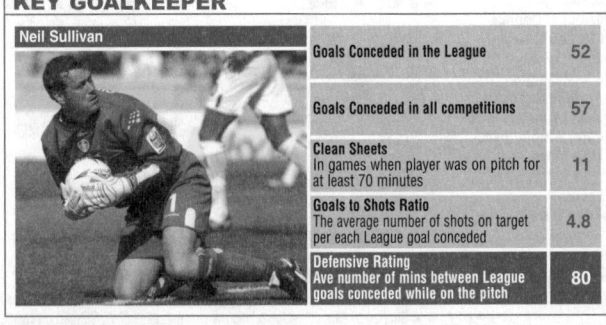

Neil Sullivan

Goals Conceded in the League	52
Goals Conceded in all competitions	57
Clean Sheets In games when player was on pitch for at least 70 minutes	11
Goals to Shots Ratio The average number of shots on target per each League goal conceded	4.8
Defensive Rating Ave number of mins between League goals conceded while on the pitch	80

DISCIPLINARY RECORDS

	PLAYER	YELLOW	RED	AVE
1	Hulse	6	0	189
2	Ricketts	4	0	194
3	Derry	2	1	203
4	Gregan	14	0	222
5	Walton	6	0	326
6	Carlisle	7	1	328
7	Butler	7	2	388
8	Kilgallon	4	1	466
9	Healy	5	0	466
10	Pugh	6	0	499
11	Deane	4	0	500
12	Einarsson	1	0	529
13	Kelly	5	0	764
	Other	8	1	
	TOTAL	79	6	

TOP POINT EARNERS

	PLAYER	GAMES	AV PTS
1	Aaron Lennon	15	1.60
2	Clarke Carlisle	28	1.43
3	Jermaine Wright	31	1.42
4	Brian Deane	18	1.39
5	David Healy	26	1.35
6	Danny Pugh	32	1.34
7	Gary Kelly	42	1.31
8	Paul Butler	39	1.31
9	Neil Sullivan	46	1.30
10	Simon Walton	20	1.30
	CLUB AVERAGE:		1.30

LEAGUE APPEARANCES GOALS AND BOOKINGS

	AGE (on 01/07/05)	IN NAMED 16	APPEARANCES	COUNTING GAMES	MINUTES ON PITCH	LEAGUE GOALS	Yellow	Red
Goalkeepers								
Scott Carson	19	29	0	0	0	0	0	0
Neil Sullivan	35	46	46	46	4140	0	2	0
Defenders								
Paul Butler	32	40	39	39	3493	0	7	2
Clarke Carlisle	25	40	35	28	2629	4	7	1
Stephen Crainey	24	11	9	9	810	0	0	0
Michael Duberry	29	10	4	4	356	0	3	1
Michael Gray	30	10	10	8	844	0	0	1
Gary Kelly	31	43	43	42	3824	0	5	0
Matthew Kilgallon	21	33	26	26	2330	0	4	1
Lucas Radebe	36	4	3	0	48	0	0	0
Frazer Richardson	22	41	38	24	2487	1	1	0
Midfielders								
Shaun Derry	27	7	7	7	611	2	2	1
Gylfi Einarsson	26	14	8	4	529	1	1	0
Sean Gregan	31	35	35	34	3112	0	14	0
Leandre Griffit	21	3	1	0	26	0	0	0
Steve Guppy	36	4	3	1	97	1	0	0
Seth Johnson	26	11	6	4	372	1	1	0
Aaron Lennon	18	32	27	15	1694	1	1	0
Jamie McMaster	22	8	7	0	70	0	1	0
John Oster	26	8	8	7	662	1	0	0
Danny Pugh	22	39	38	32	2998	5	6	0
Matthew Spring	25	27	13	4	468	1	0	0
Simon Walton	17	34	30	20	1960	3	6	0
Jermaine Wright	29	39	35	31	2892	3	3	0
Forwards								
Nathan Blake	33	2	2	2	168	1	1	0
Brian Deane	37	32	31	18	2001	6	4	0
David Healy	25	28	28	26	2332	7	5	0
Robert Hulse	25	13	13	13	1138	6	6	0
Julian Joachim	30	29	27	7	1139	2	1	0
Simon Johnson	22	2	2	1	99	0	1	0
Marlon King	25	9	9	2	375	0	0	0
Ian Moore	28	6	6	4	462	0	0	0
Brett Ormerod	28	6	6	6	524	0	0	0
Michael Ricketts	26	28	21	3	778	0	4	0

TEAM OF THE SEASON

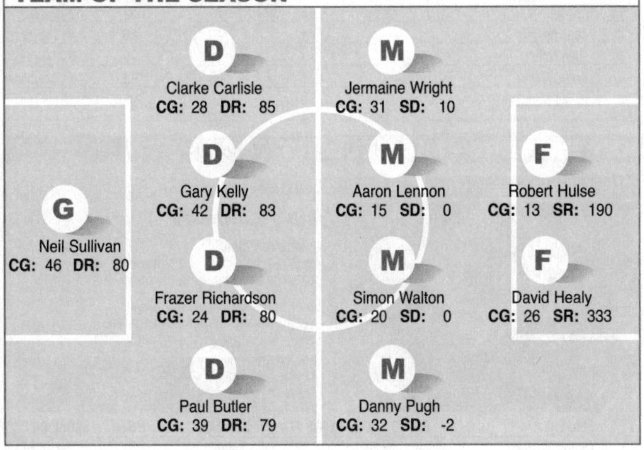
D
Clarke Carlisle
CG: 28 DR: 85
M
Jermaine Wright
CG: 31 SD: 10
D
Gary Kelly
CG: 42 DR: 83
M
Aaron Lennon
CG: 15 SD: 0
F
Robert Hulse
CG: 13 SR: 190
G
Neil Sullivan
CG: 46 DR: 80
D
Frazer Richardson
CG: 24 DR: 80
M
Simon Walton
CG: 20 SD: 0
F
David Healy
CG: 26 SR: 333
D
Paul Butler
CG: 39 DR: 79
M
Danny Pugh
CG: 32 SD: -2

SQUAD APPEARANCES

Match	1	2	3	4	5	6	7	8	9	10	11	12	13	14	15	16	17	18	19	20	21	22	23	24	25	26	27	28	29	30	31	32	33	34	35	36	37	38	39	40	41	42	43	44	45	46	47	48	49	50
Venue	H	A	A	H	H	A	H	A	A	H	H	H	A	H	A	A	A	H	H	A	A	H	H	A	H	A	H	A	H	H	A	A	H	A	A	H	A	H	A	H	A	H	A	H	H	A	A	H	A	H
Competition	L	L	L	L	W	L	L	L	L	W	L	L	L	L	L	L	W	L	L	L	L	L	L	L	L	L	L	L	L	L	L	F	L	L	L	L	L	L	L	L	L	L	L	L	L	L	L	L	L	L
Result	W	L	D	D	W	L	W	W	D	W	L	D	D	W	D	L	L	L	L	W	L	W	D	L	L	D	D	W	W	L	W	L	D	W	L	D	W	W	L	W	D	D	D	D	L	W	D	D	L	D

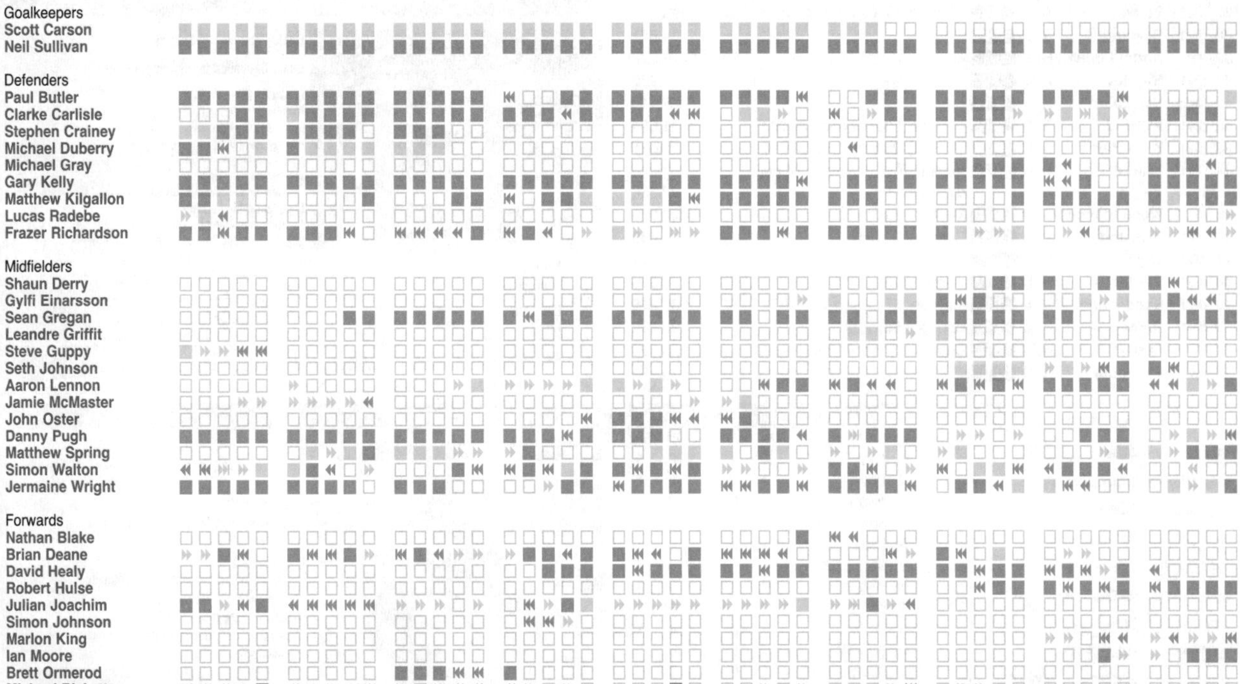
Goalkeepers
Scott Carson
Neil Sullivan
Defenders
Paul Butler
Clarke Carlisle
Stephen Crainey
Michael Duberry
Michael Gray
Gary Kelly
Matthew Kilgallon
Lucas Radebe
Frazer Richardson
Midfielders
Shaun Derry
Gylfi Einarsson
Sean Gregan
Leandre Griffit
Steve Guppy
Seth Johnson
Aaron Lennon
Jamie McMaster
John Oster
Danny Pugh
Matthew Spring
Simon Walton
Jermaine Wright
Forwards
Nathan Blake
Brian Deane
David Healy
Robert Hulse
Julian Joachim
Simon Johnson
Marlon King
Ian Moore
Brett Ormerod
Michael Ricketts

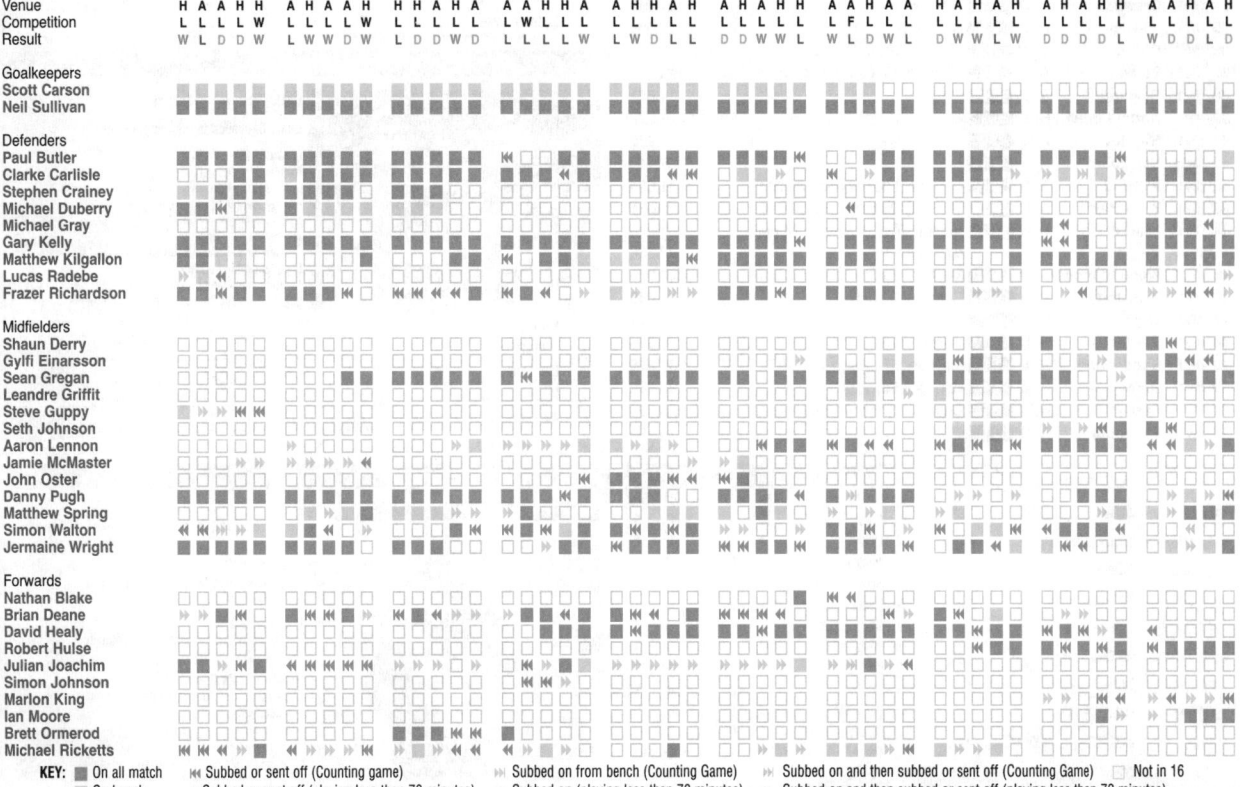

KEY: On all match · On bench · Subbed or sent off (Counting game) · Subbed or sent off (playing less than 70 minutes) · Subbed on from bench (Counting Game) · Subbed on (playing less than 70 minutes) · Subbed on and then subbed or sent off (Counting Game) · Subbed on and then subbed or sent off (playing less than 70 minutes) · Not in 16

LEICESTER CITY

Final Position: **15th**

NICKNAME: THE FOXES

KEY: ☐ Won ☐ Drawn ☐ Lost

							Attendance
1	div1	West Ham	H	D	0-0		30,231
2	div1	Derby	A	W	2-1	Nalis 41; Benjamin 76	26,650
3	div1	Millwall	A	L	0-2		11,754
4	div1	Watford	H	L	0-1		22,478
5	div1	Wolverhampton	A	D	1-1	Scowcroft 4	27,550
6	div1	Brighton	H	L	0-1		22,263
7	div1	Rotherham	A	W	2-0	Nalis 44; Dublin 59	6,272
8	div1	Sheff Utd	H	W	3-2	Scowcroft 8; Dabizas 29; Wilcox 52	23,422
9	div1	Burnley	H	D	0-0		22,495
10	div1	QPR	A	L	2-3	Scowcroft 29; Connolly 45	15,535
11	div1	Gillingham	A	W	2-0	Heath 49; Dublin 71	6,089
12	div1	Preston	H	D	1-1	Benjamin 4	21,249
13	ccr2	Preston	H	L	2-3	Gudjonsson 68 pen; Blake 75	6,751
14	div1	Coventry	A	D	1-1	Dublin 70	18,054
15	div1	Ipswich	H	D	2-2	Connolly 34; Heath 60	22,497
16	div1	Stoke	H	D	1-1	Halls 21 og	22,882
17	div1	Cardiff	A	D	0-0		13,759
18	div1	Crewe	A	D	2-2	Nalis 45; Gudjonsson 53	6,849
19	div1	Coventry	H	W	3-0	Nalis 26; Tiatto 45; Heath 72	22,479
20	div1	Sunderland	H	L	0-1		25,897
21	div1	Wigan	A	D	0-0		10,924
22	div1	Plymouth	H	W	2-1	Scowcroft 49; Dublin 52	23,799
23	div1	Leeds	A	W	2-0	Nalis 48; Kelly 78 og	27,384
24	div1	Reading	H	L	0-2		24,068
25	div1	Nottm Forest	A	D	1-1	Connolly 90	21,415
26	div1	Rotherham	H	L	0-1		27,014
27	div1	Sheff Utd	A	L	0-2		22,100
28	div1	QPR	H	W	1-0	Connolly 9 pen	23,754
29	facr3	Blackpool	H	D	2-2	Edwards, R 15 og; Williams 82	16,750
30	div1	Preston	A	D	1-1	Connolly 25	12,677
31	facr3r	Blackpool	A	W	1-0	Gudjonsson 16	6,938
32	div1	Gillingham	H	W	2-0	Connolly 19; Heath 29	23,457
33	facr4	Reading	A	W	2-1	Williams 32; Scowcroft 90	14,825
34	div1	Crewe	H	D	1-1	Gillespie 58	27,011
35	div1	Ipswich	A	L	1-2	Stewart 82	27,392
36	facr5	Charlton	A	W	2-1	Dabizas 38; Dublin 90	23,719
37	div1	Stoke	A	L	2-3	Williams 15; Gudjonsson 86	14,076
38	div1	Reading	A	D	0-0		14,651
39	div1	Nottm Forest	H	L	0-1		27,277
40	div1	Burnley	A	D	0-0		10,933
41	facqf	Blackburn	A	L	0-1		22,113
42	div1	Watford	A	D	2-2	Connolly 56; Hughes 72	11,084
43	div1	West Ham	A	D	2-2	Connolly 25 pen; Gillespie 44	22,031
44	div1	Millwall	H	W	3-1	Stearman 15; Connolly 74 pen; de Vries 83	22,338
45	div1	Wolverhampton	H	D	1-1	Maybury 73	22,950
46	div1	Brighton	A	D	1-1	Connolly 34 pen	6,638
47	div1	Wigan	H	L	0-2		23,894
48	div1	Cardiff	H	D	1-1	Connolly 33	21,336
49	div1	Sunderland	A	L	1-2	Maybury 5	34,815
50	div1	Derby	H	W	1-0	Connolly 50	25,762
51	div1	Leeds	H	W	2-0	Dublin 6; Connolly 39	26,593
52	div1	Plymouth	A	D	0-0		19,199

MONTHLY POINTS TALLY

AUGUST	5	28%
SEPTEMBER	10	67%
OCTOBER	5	33%
NOVEMBER	8	53%
DECEMBER	4	27%
JANUARY	7	78%
FEBRUARY	2	17%
MARCH	3	25%
APRIL	9	43%
MAY	4	67%

GOALS

	PLAYER	LGE	FAC	LC	Oth	TOT
1	Connolly	13	0	0	0	13
2	Dublin	5	1	0	0	6
3	Nalis	5	0	0	0	5
4	Scowcroft	4	1	0	0	5
5	Heath	4	0	0	0	4
6	Gudjonsson	2	1	1	0	4
7	Williams	1	2	0	0	3
8	Dabizas	1	1	0	0	2
9	Maybury	2	0	0	0	2
10	Benjamin	2	0	0	0	2
11	Gillespie	2	0	0	0	2
	Other	8	1	1	0	10
	TOTAL	49	7	2	0	58

KEY PLAYERS - GOALSCORERS

David Connolly

Goals in the League	13
Goals in all competitions	13
Contribution to Attacking Power Average number of minutes between League team goals while on pitch	82
Player Strike Rate Average number of minutes between League goals scored by player	290
Club Strike Rate Average number of minutes between League goals scored by club	84

	PLAYER	GOALS LGE	GOALS ALL	POWER	S RATE
1	David Connolly	13	13	82	290 mins
2	Matt Heath	4	4	86	411 mins
3	Lilian Nalis	5	5	79	572 mins
4	Dion Dublin	5	6	73	576 mins
5	James Scowcroft	4	5	85	661 mins

KEY PLAYERS - MIDFIELDERS

Danny Tiatto

Goals in the League	1
Goals in all competitions	1
Defensive Rating Average number of mins between League goals conceded while on the pitch	99
Contribution to Attacking Power Average number of minutes between League team goals while on pitch	78
Scoring Difference Defensive Rating minus Contribution to Attacking Power	21

	PLAYER	GOALS LGE	GOALS ALL	DEF RATE	ATT POWER	SCORE DIFF
1	Danny Tiatto	1	1	99	78	21 mins
2	Lilian Nalis	5	5	95	79	16 mins
3	Jordan Stewart	1	1	103	90	13 mins
4	Gareth Williams	1	3	85	76	9 mins
5	Keith Gillespie	2	2	86	78	8 mins

KEY PLAYERS - DEFENDERS

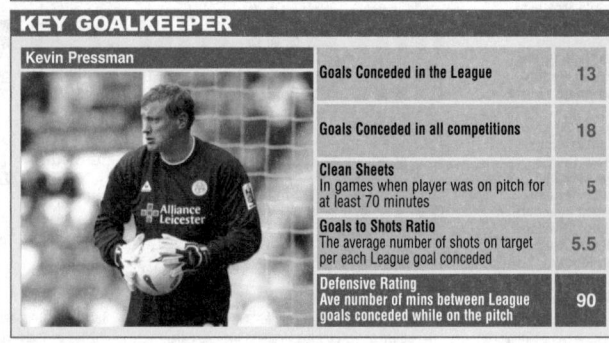

Matt Heath

Goals Conceded in League	16
Goals Conceded in all competitions	20
Clean Sheets In games when player was on pitch for at least 70 minutes	5
Defensive Rating Ave number of mins between League goals conceded while on the pitch	103
Club Defensive Rating Average number of mins between League goals conceded by the club this season	90

	PLAYER	CON LGE	CON ALL	CLN SHEETS	DEF RATE
1	Matt Heath	16	20	5	103 mins
2	Chris Makin	20	24	8	93 mins
3	Nikos Dabizas	34	40	11	86 mins
4	Alan Maybury	18	22	5	84 mins
5	Martin Keown	17	18	4	82 mins

KEY GOALKEEPER

Kevin Pressman

Goals Conceded in the League	13
Goals Conceded in all competitions	18
Clean Sheets In games when player was on pitch for at least 70 minutes	5
Goals to Shots Ratio The average number of shots on target per each League goal conceded	5.5
Defensive Rating Ave number of mins between League goals conceded while on the pitch	90

DISCIPLINARY RECORDS

	PLAYER	YELLOW	RED	AVE
1	Tiatto	13	0	168
2	McCarthy	6	0	170
3	Gudjonsson	9	0	259
4	Hughes	3	1	277
5	Maybury	5	0	301
6	Dabizas	7	2	324
7	Dublin	6	1	411
8	Keown	3	0	462
9	Connolly	7	1	471
10	Wilcox	1	0	843
11	de Vries	1	0	871
12	Scowcroft	3	0	881
13	Gillespie	1	1	900
	Other	6	2	
	TOTAL	71	8	

TOP POINT EARNERS

	PLAYER	GAMES	AV PTS
1	Lilian Nalis	28	1.61
2	Gareth Williams	21	1.52
3	Chris Makin	20	1.50
4	Kevin Pressman	13	1.46
5	Jordan Stewart	31	1.42
6	Martin Keown	14	1.36
7	James Scowcroft	29	1.31
8	Dion Dublin	31	1.29
9	Nikos Dabizas	32	1.28
10	David Connolly	42	1.26
	CLUB AVERAGE:		1.24

LEAGUE APPEARANCES GOALS AND BOOKINGS

	AGE (on 01/07/05)	IN NAMED 16	APPEARANCES	COUNTING GAMES	MINUTES ON PITCH	LEAGUE GOALS	Yellow	Red
Goalkeepers								
Lars Hirschfeld	26	14	1	1	90	0	0	0
Kevin Pressman	37	17	13	13	1170	0	0	0
Stuart Taylor	24	10	10	10	900	0	0	0
Ian Walker	33	24	22	22	1980	0	0	0
Defenders								
Peter Canero	24	8	6	6	534	0	0	0
Nikos Dabizas	31	38	33	32	2917	1	7	2
Matt Elliott	36	5	2	1	142	0	0	0
Matt Heath	24	29	22	17	1642	4	1	0
Darren Kenton	26	11	10	8	800	0	0	0
Martin Keown	38	20	18	14	1386	0	3	0
Chris Makin	38	26	21	20	1858	0	0	1
Alan Maybury	26	17	17	17	1508	2	5	0
Patrick McCarthy	22	13	12	11	1024	0	6	0
Alan Sheehan	18	1	1	1	90	0	1	0
Richard Stearman	17	16	8	2	319	1	4	0
Midfielders								
Scot Gemmill	34	30	17	9	931	0	0	0
Keith Gillespie	30	32	30	15	1801	2	1	1
Johannes Gudjonsson	25	37	35	22	2335	2	9	0
Kevin Harper	29	2	2	1	138	0	0	0
Stephen Hughes	22	16	16	11	1108	1	3	1
Lilian Nalis	33	43	39	28	2860	5	3	0
Chris O'Grady	19	1	0	0	0	0	0	0
James Scowcroft	31	31	31	29	2644	4	3	0
Jordan Stewart	23	36	35	31	2884	1	2	1
Danny Tiatto	25	31	30	22	2186	1	13	0
Jason Wilcox	33	15	14	7	843	1	1	0
Gareth Williams	23	35	33	21	2294	1	0	0
Forwards								
Trevor Benjamin	26	17	10	2	386	2	2	0
Nathan Blake	33	20	14	2	421	0	2	0
David Connolly	28	44	44	42	3772	13	7	1
Mark de Vries	29	16	16	7	871	1	1	0
Dion Dublin	36	40	37	31	2881	5	6	1
Stefan Moore	21	11	7	1	243	0	1	0
Lee Morris	25	10	9	0	219	0	0	0
Tommy Wright	20	14	7	0	125	0	0	0

TEAM OF THE SEASON

G
Kevin Pressman
CG: 13 DR: 90
D
Alan Maybury
CG: 17 DR: 84
D
Matt Heath
CG: 17 DR: 103
D
Nikos Dabizas
CG: 32 DR: 86
D
Chris Makin
CG: 20 DR: 93
M
Danny Tiatto
CG: 22 SD: 21
M
Lilian Nalis
CG: 28 SD: 16
M
Jordan Stewart
CG: 31 SD: 13
M
Gareth Williams
CG: 21 SD: 9
F
David Connolly
CG: 42 SR: 290
F
Dion Dublin
CG: 31 SR: 576

SQUAD APPEARANCES

Match	1	2	3	4	5	6	7	8	9	10	11	12	13	14	15	16	17	18	19	20	21	22	23	24	25	26
Venue	H	A	A	H	A	H	A	H	H	A	A	H	H	A	H	H	A	A	H	H	A	H	A	H	A	H
Competition	L	L	L	L	L	L	L	L	L	L	L	L	W	L	L	L	L	L	L	L	L	L	L	L	L	L
Result	D	W	L	L	D	L	W	W	D	L	W	D	L	D	D	D	D	D	W	L	D	W	W	L	D	L

Match	27	28	29	30	31	32	33	34	35	36	37	38	39	40	41	42	43	44	45	46	47	48	49	50	51	52
Venue	A	H	H	A	A	H	A	H	A	A	A	A	H	A	A	A	A	H	H	A	H	H	A	H	H	A
Competition	L	L	F	L	F	L	F	L	L	F	L	L	L	L	F	L	L	L	L	L	L	L	L	L	L	L
Result	L	W	D	D	W	W	W	D	L	W	L	D	L	D	L	D	D	W	D	D	L	D	L	W	W	D

Goalkeepers
Lars Hirschfeld
Kevin Pressman
Stuart Taylor
Ian Walker

Defenders
Peter Canero
Nikos Dabizas
Matt Elliott
Matt Heath
Darren Kenton
Martin Keown
Chris Makin
Alan Maybury
Patrick McCarthy
Alan Sheehan
Richard Stearman

Midfielders
Scot Gemmill
Keith Gillespie
Johannes Gudjonsson
Kevin Harper
Stephen Hughes
Lilian Nalis
Chris O'Grady
James Scowcroft
Jordan Stewart
Danny Tiatto
Jason Wilcox
Gareth Williams

Forwards
Trevor Benjamin
Nathan Blake
David Connolly
Mark de Vries
Dion Dublin
Stefan Moore
Lee Morris
Tommy Wright

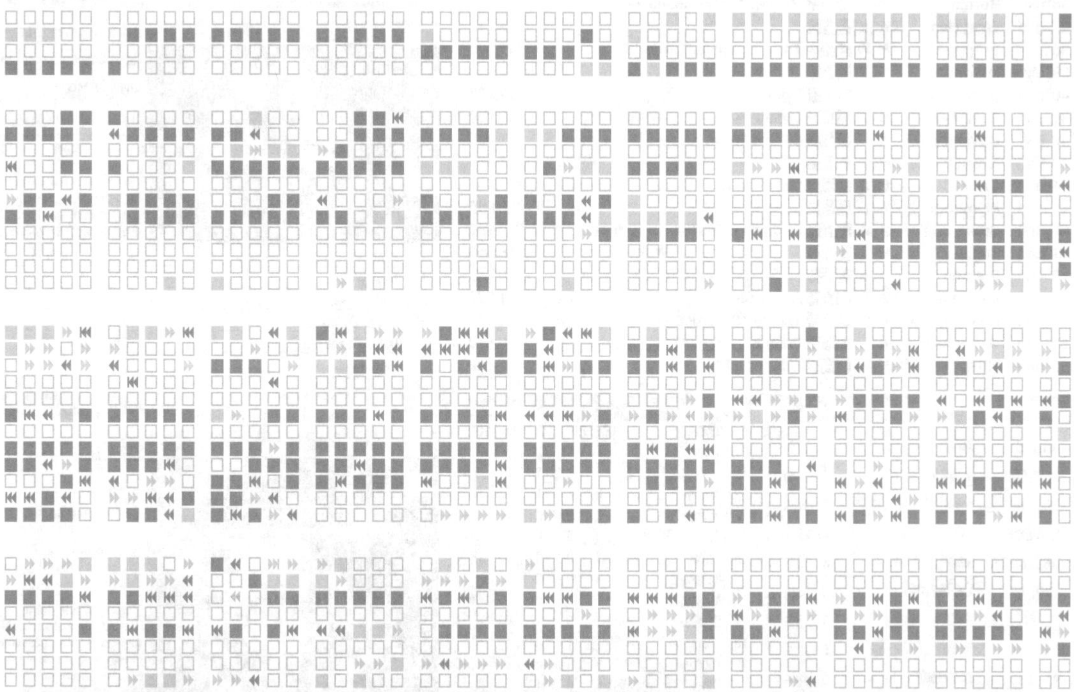

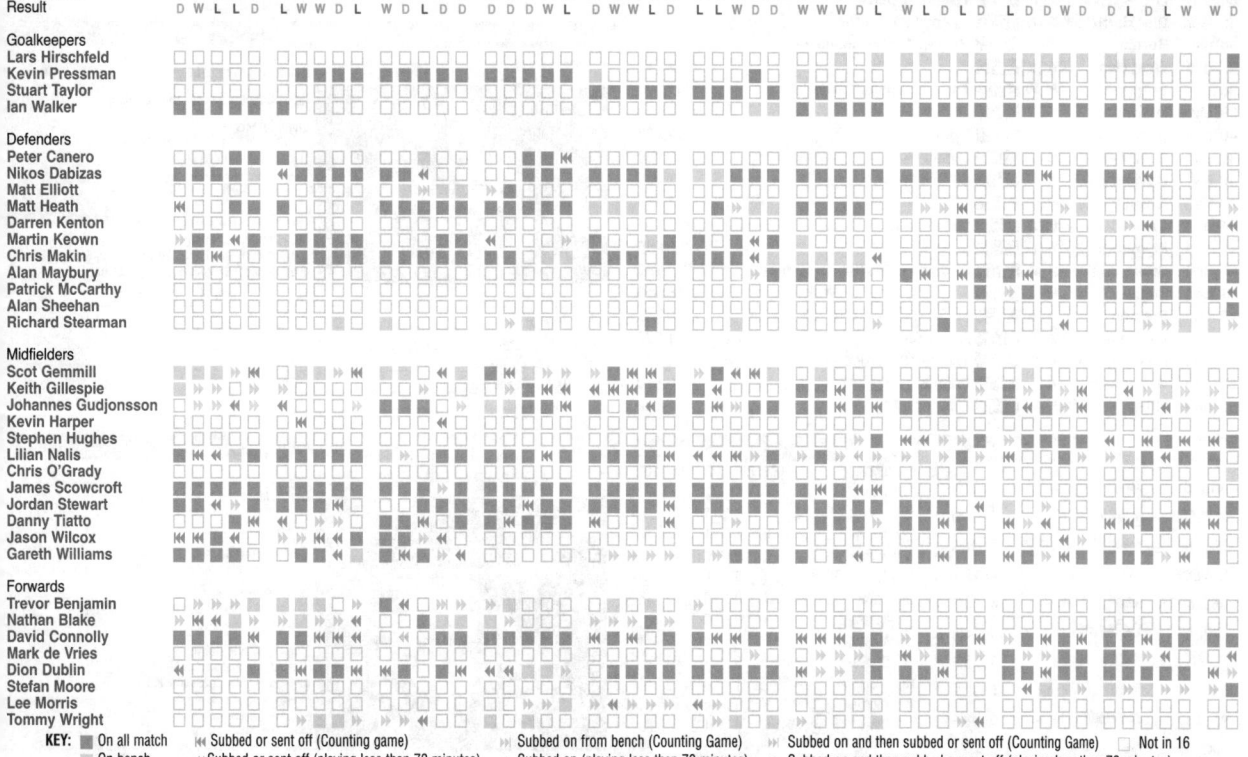

KEY: On all match | On bench | Subbed or sent off (Counting game) | Subbed or sent off (playing less than 70 minutes) | Subbed on from bench (Counting Game) | Subbed on (playing less than 70 minutes) | Subbed on and then subbed or sent off (Counting Game) | Subbed on and then subbed or sent off (playing less than 70 minutes) | Not in 16

CARDIFF CITY

Final Position: **16th**

NICKNAME: THE BLUEBIRDS KEY: ☐ Won ☐ Drawn ☐ Lost

							Attendance
1	div1	Crewe	A	D	2-2	Robinson 44; Lee 59	7,339
2	div1	Coventry	H	W	2-1	Earnshaw 54; Bullock 61	14,031
3	div1	Plymouth	H	L	0-1		12,697
4	div1	Ipswich	A	L	1-3	Lee 55	21,828
5	ccr1	Kidderminster	A	W	1-1*	Earnshaw 28 (*aet won 5-4 on penalties)	1,897
6	div1	Stoke	H	L	0-1		12,929
7	div1	Wigan	A	L	1-2	Lee 66 pen	9,004
8	div1	Nottm Forest	A	D	0-0		21,607
9	div1	Watford	H	L	0-3		10,606
10	div1	Derby	H	L	0-2		12,008
11	ccr2	MK Dons	A	W	4-1	Thorne 14,21; Bullock 19; Anthony 72	2,266
12	div1	Wolverhampton	A	W	3-2	Parry 11; Thorne 48; Kavanagh 59	27,896
13	div1	Burnley	A	L	0-1		7,200
14	div1	Leeds	H	D	0-0		17,006
15	div1	Rotherham	H	W	2-0	Thorne 56,75	11,004
16	div1	Brighton	A	D	1-1	Bullock 81	6,112
17	div1	Millwall	A	D	2-2	O'Neil 40; Lee 68	10,476
18	ccr3	Bournemouth	A	W	3-3*	Lee 24; Bullock 49; Jerome 108 (*aet won 5-4 on penalties)	5,598
19	div1	Leicester	H	D	0-0		13,759
20	div1	West Ham	H	W	4-1	Lee 3; Ledley 16; Parry 54; McAnuff 77	14,222
21	div1	Rotherham	A	D	2-2	Ledley 70; Parry 74	5,093
22	ccr4	Portsmouth	H	L	0-2		13,555
23	div1	Reading	A	L	1-2	Jerome 87	16,107
24	div1	Preston	H	L	0-1		10,950
25	div1	QPR	A	L	0-1		15,146
26	div1	Gillingham	H	W	3-1	Jerome 13; Thorne 41 pen,55	10,623
27	div1	Sunderland	H	L	0-2		12,528
28	div1	Sheff Utd	A	L	1-2	Harris 41	18,240
29	div1	Wolverhampton	H	D	1-1	Jerome 17	16,699
30	div1	Watford	A	D	0-0		13,409
31	div1	Derby	A	W	1-0	Thorne 27	22,800
32	div1	Nottm Forest	H	W	3-0	Thorne 55 pen,86; Kavanagh 90	13,545
33	facr3	Blackburn	H	D	1-1	Lee 35	14,145
34	div1	Leeds	A	D	1-1	Thorne 52 pen	29,548
35	facr3r	Blackburn	A	L	2-3	McAnuff 24; Collins 54	9,140
36	div1	Burnley	H	W	2-0	Langley 13; Kavanagh 74	11,562
37	div1	West Ham	A	L	0-1		23,716
38	div1	Brighton	H	W	2-0	Thorne 16 pen; Collins 19	11,435
39	div1	Millwall	H	L	0-1		11,424
40	div1	Sunderland	A	L	1-2	Vidmar 85	32,788
41	div1	Sheff Utd	H	W	1-0	Ledley 75	12,250
42	div1	Coventry	A	D	1-1	Bullock 19	17,059
43	div1	Ipswich	H	L	0-1		11,768
44	div1	Crewe	H	D	1-1	Gabbidon 21	10,007
45	div1	Plymouth	A	D	1-1	Langley 22	18,045
46	div1	Stoke	A	W	3-1	Jerome 26,58; Thorne 60 pen	12,785
47	div1	Wigan	H	L	0-2		16,858
48	div1	Preston	A	L	0-3		15,141
49	div1	Leicester	A	D	1-1	Ardley 58	21,336
50	div1	Reading	H	W	2-0	Thorne 12; Jerome 30	14,821
51	div1	Gillingham	A	D	1-1	Parry 85	10,810
52	div1	QPR	H	W	1-0	McAnuff 27	15,722

MONTHLY POINTS TALLY

AUGUST	4	22%
SEPTEMBER	4	27%
OCTOBER	7	47%
NOVEMBER	4	27%
DECEMBER	5	33%
JANUARY	10	83%
FEBRUARY	3	25%
MARCH	5	42%
APRIL	9	43%
MAY	3	100%

GOALS

	PLAYER	LGE	FAC	LC	Oth	TOT
1	Thorne	12	0	2	0	14
2	Lee	5	1	1	0	7
3	Jerome	6	0	1	0	7
4	Bullock	3	0	2	0	5
5	Parry	4	0	0	0	4
6	Ledley	3	0	0	0	3
7	Kavanagh	3	0	0	0	3
8	McAnuff	2	1	0	0	3
9	Earnshaw	1	0	1	0	2
10	Collins	1	1	0	0	2
11	Langley	2	0	0	0	2
	Other	6	0	1	0	7
	TOTAL	48	3	8	0	59

KEY PLAYERS - GOALSCORERS

Peter Thorne

Goals in the League	12
Goals in all competitions	14
Contribution to Attacking Power Average number of minutes between League team goals while on pitch	81
Player Strike Rate Average number of minutes between League goals scored by player	204
Club Strike Rate Average number of minutes between League goals scored by club	86

	PLAYER	GOALS LGE	GOALS ALL	POWER	S RATE
1	Peter Thorne	12	14	81	204 mins
2	Cameron Jerome	6	7	85	283 mins
3	Alan Lee	5	7	82	462 mins
4	Joe Ledley	3	3	77	613 mins
5	Graham Kavanagh	3	3	79	813 mins

KEY PLAYERS - MIDFIELDERS

Richard Langley

Goals in the League	2
Goals in all competitions	2
Defensive Rating Average number of mins between League goals conceded while on the pitch	85
Contribution to Attacking Power Average number of minutes between League team goals while on pitch	78
Scoring Difference Defensive Rating minus Contribution to Attacking Power	7

	PLAYER	GOALS LGE	GOALS ALL	DEF RATE	ATT POWER	SCORE DIFF
1	Richard Langley	2	2	85	78	7 mins
2	Jobi McAnuff	2	3	94	89	5 mins
3	Graham Kavanagh	3	3	74	79	-5 mins
4	Joe Ledley	3	3	71	77	-6 mins
5	Willie Boland	0	0	69	104	-35 mins

KEY PLAYERS - DEFENDERS

Rhys Weston

Goals Conceded in League	20
Goals Conceded in all competitions	26
Clean Sheets In games when player was on pitch for at least 70 minutes	7
Defensive Rating Ave number of mins between League goals conceded while on the pitch	94
Club Defensive Rating Average number of mins between League goals conceded by the club this season	81

	PLAYER	CON LGE	CON ALL	CLN SHEETS	DEF RATE
1	Rhys Weston	20	26	7	94 mins
2	Chris Barker	39	49	11	88 mins
3	James Collins	33	44	8	85 mins
4	Daniel Gabbidon	48	55	12	84 mins
5	Darren Williams	20	20	4	83 mins

KEY GOALKEEPER

Neil Alexander

Goals Conceded in the League	16
Goals Conceded in all competitions	20
Clean Sheets In games when player was on pitch for at least 70 minutes	5
Goals to Shots Ratio The average number of shots on target per each League goal conceded	4.8
Defensive Rating Ave number of mins between League goals conceded while on the pitch	96

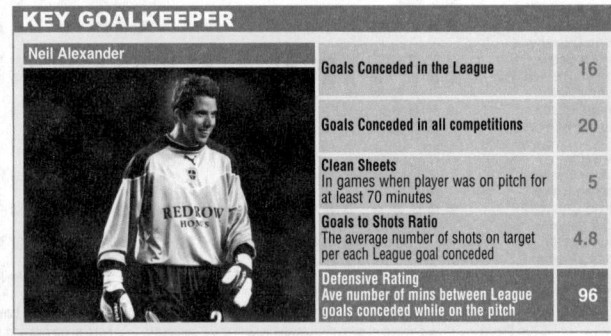

DISCIPLINARY RECORDS

	PLAYER	YELLOW	RED	AVE
1	Robinson	3	0	228
2	Lee	9	1	231
3	Kavanagh	5	2	348
4	Langley	4	0	529
5	Inamoto	2	0	531
6	Jerome	3	0	566
7	Collins	3	1	705
8	Vidmar	3	0	711
9	Page	1	0	765
10	McAnuff	4	0	912
11	Weston	2	0	942
12	Barker	3	0	1139
13	Parry	1	0	1192
	Other	6	0	
	TOTAL	49	4	

TOP POINT EARNERS

	PLAYER	GAMES	AV PTS
1	Richard Langley	22	1.55
2	Cameron Jerome	16	1.50
3	Neil Alexander	17	1.35
4	Peter Thorne	25	1.32
5	Chris Barker	38	1.29
6	Jobi McAnuff	39	1.26
7	James Collins	31	1.26
8	Willie Boland	14	1.21
9	Rhys Weston	20	1.20
10	Daniel Gabbidon	45	1.20
	CLUB AVERAGE:		1.17

TEAM OF THE SEASON

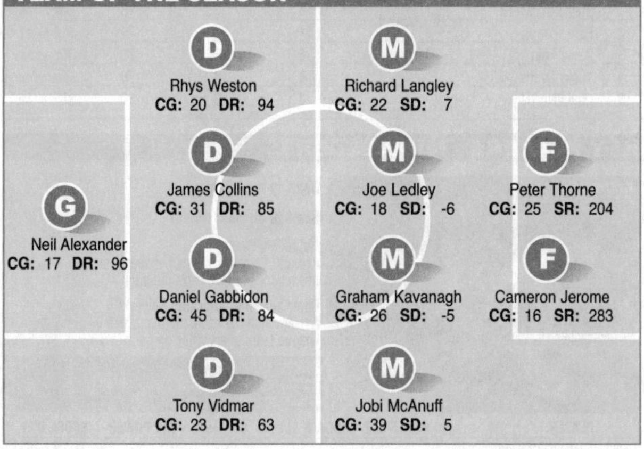
G
Neil Alexander
CG: 17 DR: 96
D
Rhys Weston
CG: 20 DR: 94
D
James Collins
CG: 31 DR: 85
D
Daniel Gabbidon
CG: 45 DR: 84
D
Tony Vidmar
CG: 23 DR: 63
M
Richard Langley
CG: 22 SD: 7
M
Joe Ledley
CG: 18 SD: -6
M
Graham Kavanagh
CG: 26 SD: -5
M
Jobi McAnuff
CG: 39 SD: 5
F
Peter Thorne
CG: 25 SR: 204
F
Cameron Jerome
CG: 16 SR: 283

LEAGUE APPEARANCES GOALS AND BOOKINGS

	AGE (on 01/07/05)	IN NAMED 16	APPEARANCES	COUNTING GAMES	MINUTES ON PITCH	LEAGUE GOALS	Yellow	Red
Goalkeepers								
Neil Alexander	27	40	17	17	1530	0	0	0
Martyn Margetson	33	17	4	4	342	0	0	0
Tony Warner	31	35	26	25	2268	0	0	0
Defenders								
Byron Anthony	20	2	0	0	0	0	0	0
Chris Barker	25	39	39	38	3419	0	3	0
James Collins	21	44	34	31	2820	1	3	1
Gary Croft	31	3	1	0	4	0	0	0
Daniel Gabbidon	25	45	45	45	4040	1	3	0
Robert Page	30	10	9	8	765	0	1	0
Tony Vidmar	35	43	28	23	2133	1	3	0
Rhys Weston	24	30	25	20	1885	0	2	0
Darren Williams	28	28	20	18	1658	0	1	0
Midfielders								
Neal Ardley	32	8	8	8	719	1	0	0
Willie Boland	29	25	20	14	1457	0	1	0
Lee Bullock	24	40	21	9	957	3	0	0
Nicky Fish	20	0	0	0	0	0	0	0
Junichi Inamoto	25	14	14	10	1062	0	2	0
Graham Kavanagh	31	28	28	26	2438	3	5	2
Toni Koskela	22	4	2	0	40	0	0	0
Richard Langley	25	28	25	22	2119	2	4	0
Joe Ledley	18	29	28	18	1840	3	1	0
Jobi McAnuff	23	43	43	39	3651	2	4	0
Gary O'Neil	22	9	9	8	731	1	0	0
John Robinson	33	11	8	8	686	1	3	0
Forwards								
Michael Boulding	29	5	5	1	156	0	0	0
Andy Campbell	26	13	12	4	530	0	0	0
Robert Earnshaw	24	4	4	4	324	1	0	0
Stuart Fleetwood	19	8	6	0	95	0	0	0
Neil Harris	27	3	3	1	125	1	1	0
Cameron Jerome	18	30	29	16	1700	6	3	0
Alan Lee	26	38	38	20	2310	5	9	1
Paul Parry	24	28	24	10	1192	4	1	0
Danny Thomas	20	1	1	0	9	0	0	0
Peter Thorne	32	31	31	25	2453	12	0	0

SQUAD APPEARANCES

Match	Venue	Competition	Result
1	A	L	D
2	H	L	W
3	H	L	L
4	A	L	L
5	A	W	W
6	H	L	L
7	A	L	L
8	A	L	D
9	H	L	L
10	H	L	L
11	A	W	W
12	A	L	W
13	A	L	L
14	H	L	D
15	H	L	W
16	A	L	D
17	A	L	D
18	A	W	W
19	H	L	D
20	H	L	W
21	A	L	D
22	H	W	L
23	A	L	L
24	H	L	L
25	A	L	L
26	H	L	W
27	H	L	L
28	A	L	L
29	H	L	D
30	A	L	D
31	A	L	W
32	H	L	W
33	H	F	D
34	A	L	D
35	A	F	L
36	H	L	W
37	A	L	L
38	H	L	W
39	H	L	L
40	A	L	L
41	H	L	W
42	A	L	D
43	H	L	L
44	H	L	D
45	A	L	D
46	A	L	W
47	H	L	L
48	A	L	L
49	A	L	D
50	H	L	W
51	A	L	D
52	H	L	W

Goalkeepers
Neil Alexander
Martyn Margetson
Tony Warner

Defenders
Byron Anthony
Chris Barker
James Collins
Gary Croft
Daniel Gabbidon
Robert Page
Tony Vidmar
Rhys Weston
Darren Williams

Midfielders
Neal Ardley
Willie Boland
Lee Bullock
Nicky Fish
Junichi Inamoto
Graham Kavanagh
Toni Koskela
Richard Langley
Joe Ledley
Jobi McAnuff
Gary O'Neil
John Robinson

Forwards
Michael Boulding
Andy Campbell
Robert Earnshaw
Stuart Fleetwood
Neil Harris
Cameron Jerome
Alan Lee
Paul Parry
Danny Thomas
Peter Thorne

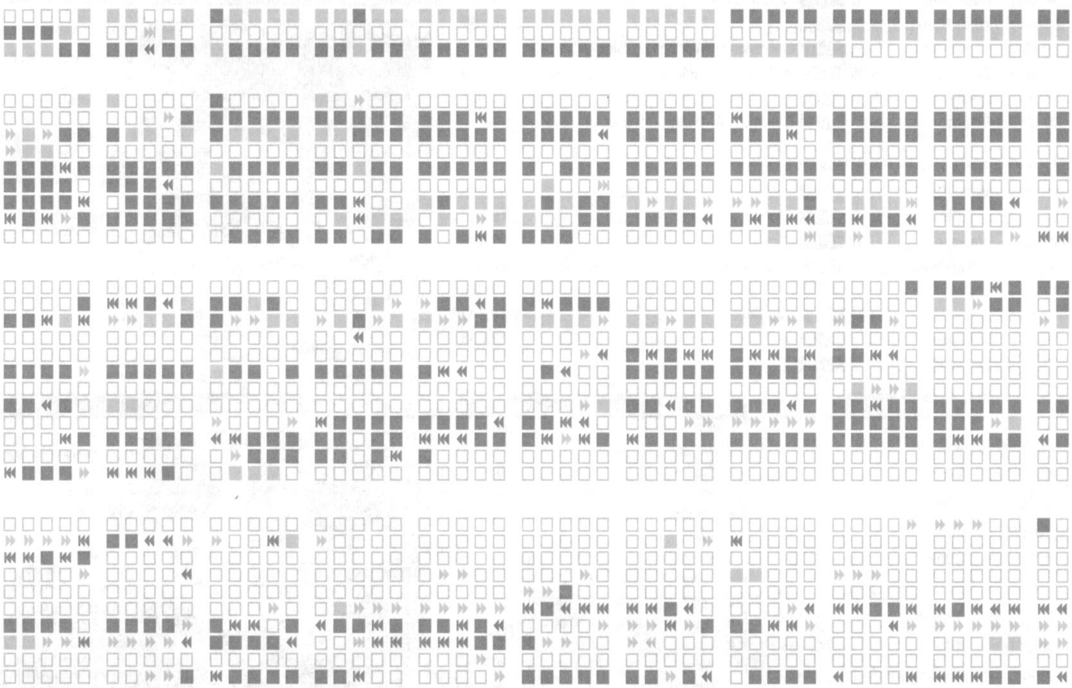

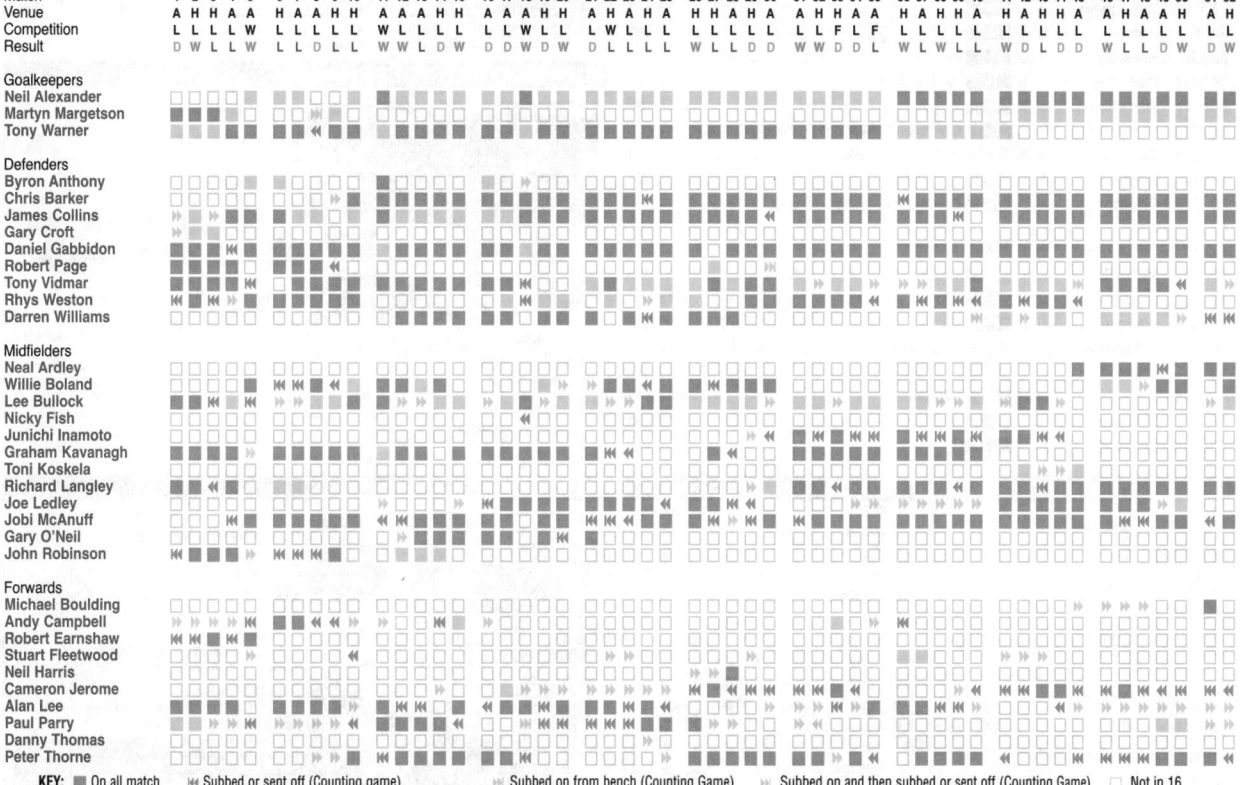

KEY: On all match / On bench / Subbed or sent off (Counting game) / Subbed or sent off (playing less than 70 minutes) / Subbed on from bench (Counting Game) / Subbed on (playing less than 70 minutes) / Subbed on and then subbed or sent off (Counting Game) / Subbed on and then subbed or sent off (playing less than 70 minutes) / Not in 16

PLYMOUTH ARGYLE

Final Position: **17th**

NICKNAME: THE PILGRIMS   KEY: Won Drawn Lost

							Attendance
1	div1	Millwall	H	D	0-0		16,063
2	div1	Brighton	A	W	2-0	Cullip 11 og; Wotton 45 pen	6,387
3	div1	Cardiff	A	W	1-0	Vidmar 24 og	12,697
4	div1	Sunderland	H	W	2-1	Wotton 1; Crawford 40	16,874
5	ccr1	Yeovil	A	L	2-3	Crawford 30; Wotton 42 pen	6,217
6	div1	Watford	A	L	1-3	Evans 18	13,104
7	div1	Nottm Forest	H	W	3-2	Norris 26; Coughlan 40; Worrell 90 pen	17,538
8	div1	QPR	A	L	2-3	Friio 7; Keith 90	15,425
9	div1	Leeds	H	L	0-1		20,555
10	div1	Wolverhampton	H	L	1-2	Friio 62	18,635
11	div1	Ipswich	A	L	2-3	Adams 12; Crawford 13	23,270
12	div1	Preston	A	D	1-1	Doumbe 19	11,445
13	div1	Gillingham	H	W	2-1	Friio 90,90	13,665
14	div1	Wigan	H	L	1-2	Crawford 78	14,443
15	div1	Rotherham	A	W	1-0	Doumbe 65	5,088
16	div1	Sheff Utd	A	L	1-2	Friio 87	18,893
17	div1	West Ham	H	D	1-1	Wotton 76	20,220
18	div1	Reading	H	D	2-2	Ingimarsson 18 og; Crawford 41	14,336
19	div1	Wigan	A	W	2-0	Wotton 40; Crawford 69	10,294
20	div1	Coventry	A	L	1-2	Evans 48	15,314
21	div1	Stoke	H	D	0-0		15,264
22	div1	Leicester	A	L	1-2	Capaldi 9	23,799
23	div1	Burnley	H	W	1-0	Wotton 90 pen	13,308
24	div1	Crewe	A	L	0-3		6,823
25	div1	Derby	H	L	0-2		15,335
26	div1	QPR	H	W	2-1	Wotton 13; Evans 49	19,535
27	div1	Leeds	A	L	1-2	Crawford 90	34,496
28	div1	Wolverhampton	A	D	1-1	Friio 58	27,564
29	div1	Ipswich	H	L	1-2	Evans 87	17,923
30	facr3	Everton	H	L	1-3	Gudjonsson 34	20,112
31	div1	Gillingham	A	L	0-1		8,451
32	div1	Preston	H	L	0-2		13,663
33	div1	Reading	A	D	0-0		19,783
34	div1	Rotherham	H	D	1-1	Wotton 51 pen	14,798
35	div1	West Ham	A	L	0-5		25,490
36	div1	Sheff Utd	H	W	3-0	Coughlan 3; Wotton 47; Blackstock 88	13,953
37	div1	Crewe	H	W	3-0	Wotton 25; Blackstock 68; Taylor 90	14,918
38	div1	Derby	A	L	0-1		27,581
39	div1	Brighton	H	W	5-1	Chadwick 8; Wotton 13 pen,21; Norris 36; Taylor 88	15,606
40	div1	Sunderland	A	L	1-5	Taylor 88	25,258
41	div1	Millwall	A	L	0-3		11,465
42	div1	Cardiff	H	D	1-1	Aljofree 60	18,045
43	div1	Watford	H	W	1-0	Buzsaky 10	15,333
44	div1	Nottm Forest	A	W	3-0	Blackstock 3,59; Norris 23	28,887
45	div1	Stoke	A	L	0-2		13,017
46	div1	Coventry	H	D	1-1	Capaldi 90	18,443
47	div1	Burnley	A	L	0-2		12,893
48	div1	Leicester	H	D	0-0		19,199

MONTHLY POINTS TALLY

AUGUST	13	72%
SEPTEMBER	1	7%
OCTOBER	7	47%
NOVEMBER	5	33%
DECEMBER	6	40%
JANUARY	1	8%
FEBRUARY	8	53%
MARCH	3	25%
APRIL	8	44%
MAY	1	33%

GOALS

	PLAYER	LGE	FAC	LC	Oth	TOT
1	Wotton	11	0	1	0	12
2	Crawford	6	0	1	0	7
3	Friio	6	0	0	0	6
4	Blackstock	4	0	0	0	4
5	Evans	4	0	0	0	4
6	Norris	3	0	0	0	3
7	Taylor	3	0	0	0	3
8	Coughlan	2	0	0	0	2
9	Doumbe	2	0	0	0	2
10	Capaldi	2	0	0	0	2
11	Worrell	1	0	0	0	1
	Other	8	1	0	0	9
	TOTAL	52	1	2	0	55

KEY PLAYERS - GOALSCORERS

Stevie Crawford

Goals in the League	6
Goals in all competitions	7
Contribution to Attacking Power Average number of minutes between League team goals while on pitch	75
Player Strike Rate Average number of minutes between League goals scored by player	300
Club Strike Rate Average number of minutes between League goals scored by club	80

	PLAYER	GOALS LGE	GOALS ALL	POWER	S RATE
1	Stevie Crawford	6	7	75	300 mins
2	Paul Wotton	11	12	74	312 mins
3	David Friio	6	6	79	355 mins
4	Micky Evans	4	4	76	709 mins
5	David Norris	3	3	80	965 mins

KEY PLAYERS - MIDFIELDERS

Anthony Capaldi

Goals in the League	2
Goals in all competitions	2
Defensive Rating Average number of mins between League goals conceded while on the pitch	67
Contribution to Attacking Power Average number of minutes between League team goals while on pitch	75
Scoring Difference Defensive Rating minus Contribution to Attacking Power	-8

	PLAYER	GOALS LGE	GOALS ALL	DEF RATE	ATT POWER	SCORE DIFF
1	Anthony Capaldi	2	2	67	75	-8 mins
2	David Norris	3	3	67	80	-13 mins
3	Steve Adams	1	1	71	93	-22 mins
4	David Friio	6	6	56	79	-23 mins
5	Akos Buzsaky	1	1	71	101	-30 mins

KEY PLAYERS - DEFENDERS

Paul Wotton

Goals Conceded in League	50
Goals Conceded in all competitions	56
Clean Sheets In games when player was on pitch for at least 70 minutes	12
Defensive Rating Ave number of mins between League goals conceded while on the pitch	69
Club Defensive Rating Average number of mins between League goals conceded by the club this season	65

	PLAYER	CON LGE	CON ALL	CLN SHEETS	DEF RATE
1	Paul Wotton	50	56	12	69 mins
2	Peter Gilbert	48	54	11	68 mins
3	David Worrell	40	43	10	66 mins
4	Graham Coughlan	58	63	13	65 mins
5	Mathias Doumbe	37	41	5	61 mins

KEY GOALKEEPER

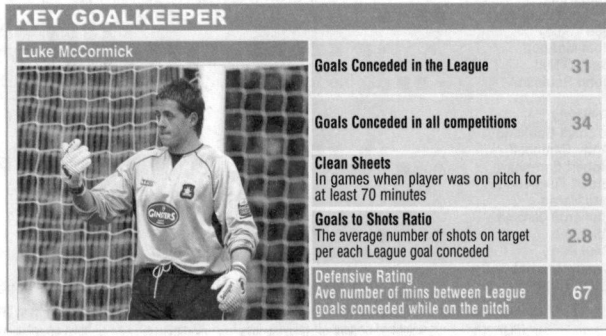

Luke McCormick

Goals Conceded in the League	31
Goals Conceded in all competitions	34
Clean Sheets In games when player was on pitch for at least 70 minutes	9
Goals to Shots Ratio The average number of shots on target per each League goal conceded	2.8
Defensive Rating Ave number of mins between League goals conceded while on the pitch	67

DISCIPLINARY RECORDS

	PLAYER	YELLOW	RED	AVE
1	Makel	3	0	401
2	Connolly	3	1	427
3	Wotton	7	0	489
4	Capaldi	4	0	521
5	Gudjonsson	2	0	529
6	Friio	4	0	532
7	Doumbe	3	1	562
8	Evans	5	0	567
9	Keith, M	1	0	592
10	Buzsaky	2	0	607
11	Coughlan	5	1	632
12	Worrell	4	0	656
13	Gilbert	4	0	818
	Other	12	0	
	TOTAL	59	3	

TOP POINT EARNERS

	PLAYER	GAMES	AV PTS
1	Anthony Capaldi	20	1.50
2	Luke McCormick	23	1.43
3	Steve Adams	14	1.43
4	Akos Buzsaky	13	1.31
5	David Worrell	30	1.20
6	Paul Wotton	38	1.18
7	Stevie Crawford	17	1.18
8	Peter Gilbert	35	1.17
9	Graham Coughlan	42	1.17
10	David Norris	30	1.13
	CLUB AVERAGE:		1.15

TEAM OF THE SEASON

G
Luke McCormick
CG: 23 DR: 67
D
Paul Wotton
CG: 38 DR: 69
D
Peter Gilbert
CG: 35 DR: 68
D
David Worrell
CG: 30 DR: 66
D
Graham Coughlan
CG: 42 DR: 65
M
Anthony Capaldi
CG: 20 SD: -8
M
David Norris
CG: 30 SD: -13
M
David Friio
CG: 22 SD: -23
M
Steve Adams
CG: 14 SD: -22
F
Micky Evans
CG: 26 SR: 709
F
Stevie Crawford
CG: 17 SR: 437

LEAGUE APPEARANCES GOALS AND BOOKINGS

	AGE (on 01/07/05)	IN NAMED 16	APPEARANCES	COUNTING GAMES	MINUTES ON PITCH	LEAGUE GOALS	Yellow	Red
Goalkeepers								
Romain Larrieu	28	27	23	23	2070	0	1	0
Luke McCormick	21	23	23	23	2070	0	2	0
Defenders								
Hasney Aljofree	26	18	12	11	1058	1	1	0
Paul Connolly	21	22	19	19	1710	0	3	1
Graham Coughlan	30	43	43	42	3797	2	5	1
Jason Dodd	34	4	4	4	360	0	0	0
Mathias Doumbe	25	40	26	25	2249	2	3	1
Peter Gilbert	21	42	38	35	3272	0	4	0
David Worrell	27	32	30	30	2627	1	4	0
Paul Wotton	27	45	40	38	3428	11	7	0
Midfielders								
Steve Adams	24	33	20	14	1481	1	1	0
Akos Buzsaky	23	15	15	13	1214	1	2	0
Anthony Capaldi	23	35	35	20	2086	2	4	0
Ryan Dickson	18	4	3	2	175	0	0	0
David Friio	32	28	28	22	2128	6	4	0
Bjarni Gudjonsson	26	18	15	10	1059	0	2	0
Lee Hodges	31	29	19	11	1092	0	1	0
Keith Lasley	25	45	24	10	1195	0	1	0
Lee Makel	32	19	19	11	1204	0	3	0
David Norris	24	38	35	30	2896	3	3	0
Luke Summerfield	26	2	1	0	14	0	0	0
Forwards								
Dextor Blackstock	19	14	14	9	898	4	1	0
Nick Chadwick	22	15	15	10	1032	1	1	0
Stevie Crawford	31	26	26	17	1801	6	0	0
Micky Evans	32	46	42	26	2837	4	5	0
Marino Keith	30	23	16	5	592	1	1	0
Nathan Lowndes	28	8	4	0	100	0	0	0
Steven Milne	25	18	12	0	198	0	0	0
Blair Sturrock	23	2	0	0	0	0	0	0
Scott Taylor	29	20	16	8	808	3	0	0
Stewart Yetton	19	2	1	0	8	0	0	0

SQUAD APPEARANCES

Match	1	2	3	4	5	6	7	8	9	10	11	12	13	14	15	16	17	18	19	20	21	22	23	24	25	26	27	28	29	30	31	32	33	34	35	36	37	38	39	40	41	42	43	44	45	46	47	48
Venue	H	A	A	H	A	A	H	A	H	H	A	A	H	H	A	A	H	H	A	A	H	A	H	A	H	H	A	A	H	H	A	H	A	H	A	H	H	A	H	A	A	H	H	A	A	H	A	H
Competition	L	L	L	L	W	L	L	L	L	L	L	L	L	L	L	L	L	L	L	L	L	L	L	L	L	L	L	L	L	F	L	L	L	L	L	L	L	L	L	L	L	L	L	L	L	L	L	L
Result	D	W	W	W	L	L	W	L	L	L	L	D	W	L	W	L	D	D	W	L	D	L	W	L	L	W	L	D	L	L	L	L	D	D	L	W	W	L	W	L	L	D	W	W	L	D	L	D

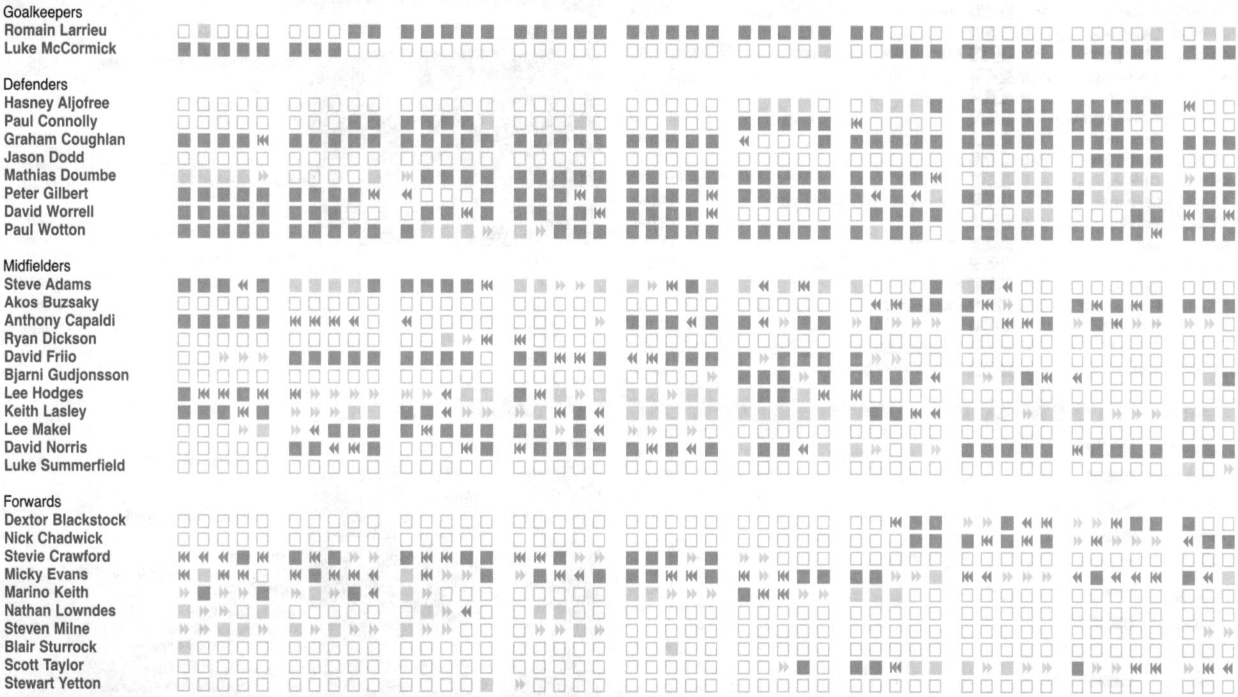

Goalkeepers
Romain Larrieu
Luke McCormick
Defenders
Hasney Aljofree
Paul Connolly
Graham Coughlan
Jason Dodd
Mathias Doumbe
Peter Gilbert
David Worrell
Paul Wotton
Midfielders
Steve Adams
Akos Buzsaky
Anthony Capaldi
Ryan Dickson
David Friio
Bjarni Gudjonsson
Lee Hodges
Keith Lasley
Lee Makel
David Norris
Luke Summerfield
Forwards
Dextor Blackstock
Nick Chadwick
Stevie Crawford
Micky Evans
Marino Keith
Nathan Lowndes
Steven Milne
Blair Sturrock
Scott Taylor
Stewart Yetton

KEY: On all match · On bench · Subbed or sent off (Counting game) · Subbed or sent off (playing less than 70 minutes) · Subbed on from bench (Counting Game) · Subbed on (playing less than 70 minutes) · Subbed on and then subbed or sent off (Counting Game) · Subbed on and then subbed or sent off (playing less than 70 minutes) · Not in 16

WATFORD

Final Position: **18th**

NICKNAME: THE HORNETS — KEY: ☐Won ☐Drawn ☐Lost

							Attendance
1	div1	Preston	A	L	1-2	Devlin 47	12,208
2	div1	QPR	H	W	3-0	Webber 12,59; Dyer 45	14,737
3	div1	Burnley	H	L	0-1		12,048
4	div1	Leicester	A	W	1-0	Webber 90	22,478
5	ccr1	Cambridge	H	W	1-0	Ferrell 82	6,558
6	div1	Plymouth	H	W	3-1	Ardley 33; Webber 46,58	13,104
7	div1	Brighton	H	D	1-1	Webber 53	14,148
8	div1	Cardiff	A	W	3-0	Webber 11,86; Ardley 45	10,606
9	div1	Millwall	A	W	2-0	Webber 65; Helguson 76	10,865
10	ccr2	Reading	A	W	3-0	Cox 14 pen; Bouazza 90; Ingimarsson 90 og	8,429
11	div1	Reading	H	L	0-1		13,389
12	div1	Wigan	H	D	0-0		11,161
13	div1	Crewe	A	L	0-3		6,382
14	div1	Derby	A	D	2-2	Helguson 7,14	23,253
15	div1	Sunderland	H	D	1-1	Ardley 9	13,198
16	div1	Ipswich	H	D	2-2	Helguson 67; Bouazza 73	15,894
17	ccr3	Sheff Utd	A	W	0-0*	(*aet, won 4-2 on penalties)	7,689
18	div1	Nottm Forest	A	W	2-1	Helguson 20,27	24,473
19	div1	Gillingham	A	D	0-0		7,009
20	div1	Derby	H	D	2-2	Helguson 41; Gunnarsson 82	16,689
21	ccr4	Southampton	H	W	5-2	Dyer 39; Chambers, J 52,62; Helguson 66; Bouazza 84	13,008
22	div1	Sheff Utd	A	D	1-1	Gunnarsson 65	18,454
23	div1	Rotherham	H	D	0-0		17,780
24	div1	Leeds	A	D	2-2	Dyer 9,71	24,585
25	div1	West Ham	A	L	2-3	Gunnarsson 5; Dyer 21	24,541
26	ccqf	Portsmouth	H	W	3-0	Helguson 24,57; Dyer 61	18,877
27	div1	Stoke	H	L	0-1		12,169
28	div1	Wolverhampton	H	D	1-1	Helguson 4	14,605
29	div1	Coventry	A	L	0-1		14,193
30	div1	Reading	A	L	0-3		18,757
31	div1	Cardiff	H	D	0-0		13,409
32	div1	Millwall	H	W	1-0	Helguson 75	13,158
33	div1	Brighton	A	L	1-2	Helguson 11	6,335
34	facr3	Fulham	H	D	1-1	Helguson 42 pen	14,896
35	ccsfl1	Liverpool	A	L	0-1		35,739
36	div1	Crewe	H	W	3-1	Helguson 9,29; DeMerit 46	11,223
37	facr3r	Fulham	A	L	0-2		11,306
38	div1	Wigan	A	D	2-2	Dyer 13; Webber 27	9,008
39	ccsfl2	Liverpool	H	L	0-1		19,797
40	div1	Gillingham	H	W	2-0	Ashby 23 og; Eagles 90	15,188
41	div1	Sunderland	A	L	2-4	Dyer 76,90	24,948
42	div1	Ipswich	A	W	2-1	DeMerit 45; Dyer 81	23,993
43	div1	Wolverhampton	A	D	0-0		25,060
44	div1	Coventry	H	L	2-3	Dyer 32; Webber 84	13,794
45	div1	Nottm Forest	H	L	0-2		12,118
46	div1	QPR	A	L	1-3	Ardley 80	16,638
47	div1	Leicester	H	D	2-2	DeMerit 40; Webber 44 pen	11,084
48	div1	Preston	H	L	0-2		19,649
49	div1	Burnley	A	L	1-3	Blizzard 77	11,507
50	div1	Plymouth	A	L	0-1		15,333
51	div1	Leeds	H	L	1-2	Helguson 41	16,306
52	div1	Rotherham	A	W	1-0	Helguson 32	5,438
53	div1	Sheff Utd	H	D	0-0		17,138
54	div1	Stoke	A	W	1-0	Helguson 51	15,229
55	div1	West Ham	H	L	1-2	Helguson 89 pen	19,673

MONTHLY POINTS TALLY

AUGUST	9	60%
SEPTEMBER	8	53%
OCTOBER	6	40%
NOVEMBER	5	28%
DECEMBER	2	13%
JANUARY	7	58%
FEBRUARY	7	58%
MARCH	1	7%
APRIL	7	39%
MAY	0	0%

GOALS

	PLAYER	LGE	FAC	LC	Oth	TOT
1	Helguson	16	1	3	0	20
2	Webber	12	0	0	0	12
3	Dyer	9	0	2	0	11
4	Ardley	4	0	0	0	4
5	Gunnarsson	3	0	0	0	3
6	DeMerit	3	0	0	0	3
7	Bouazza	1	0	2	0	3
8	Chambers, J	0	0	2	0	2
9	Blizzard	1	0	0	0	1
10	Ferrell	0	0	1	0	1
11	Eagles	1	0	0	0	1
	Other	2	0	2	0	4
	TOTAL	52	1	12	0	65

KEY PLAYERS - GOALSCORERS

Danny Webber

Goals in the League	12
Goals in all competitions	12
Contribution to Attacking Power Average number of minutes between League team goals while on pitch	70
Player Strike Rate Average number of minutes between League goals scored by player	182
Club Strike Rate Average number of minutes between League goals scored by club	80

	PLAYER	GOALS LGE	GOALS ALL	POWER	S RATE
1	Danny Webber	12	12	70	182 mins
2	Bruce Dyer	9	11	73	204 mins
3	Heidar Helguson	16	20	89	206 mins
4	Neal Ardley	4	4	65	619 mins
5	Jay DeMerit	3	3	74	643 mins

KEY PLAYERS - MIDFIELDERS

Paul Devlin

Goals in the League	1
Goals in all competitions	1
Defensive Rating Average number of mins between League goals conceded while on the pitch	100
Contribution to Attacking Power Average number of minutes between League team goals while on pitch	77
Scoring Difference Defensive Rating minus Contribution to Attacking Power	23

	PLAYER	GOALS LGE	GOALS ALL	DEF RATE	ATT POWER	SCORE DIFF
1	Paul Devlin	1	1	100	77	23 mins
2	Neal Ardley	4	4	71	65	6 mins
3	Gavin Mahon	0	0	77	82	-5 mins
4	Brynjar Gunnarsson	3	3	79	90	-11 mins
5	Ashley Young	0	0	67	84	-17 mins

KEY PLAYERS - DEFENDERS

Sean Dyche

Goals Conceded in League	23
Goals Conceded in all competitions	25
Clean Sheets In games when player was on pitch for at least 70 minutes	7
Defensive Rating Ave number of mins between League goals conceded while on the pitch	87
Club Defensive Rating Average number of mins between League goals conceded by the club this season	70

	PLAYER	CON LGE	CON ALL	CLN SHEETS	DEF RATE
1	Sean Dyche	23	25	7	87 mins
2	Paul Mayo	13	13	5	85 mins
3	Lloyd Doyley	30	32	10	74 mins
4	Neil Cox	47	53	12	71 mins
5	Jermaine Darlington	32	39	6	67 mins

KEY GOALKEEPER

Richard Lee

Goals Conceded in the League	43
Goals Conceded in all competitions	45
Clean Sheets In games when player was on pitch for at least 70 minutes	8
Goals to Shots Ratio The average number of shots on target per each League goal conceded	5.1
Defensive Rating Ave number of mins between League goals conceded while on the pitch	68

DISCIPLINARY RECORDS

	PLAYER	YELLOW	RED	AVE
1	Jackson	4	0	285
2	Helguson	9	0	366
3	Mayo	3	0	368
4	DeMerit	4	1	386
5	Gunnarsson	6	1	426
6	Chambers, J	8	0	441
7	Blizzard	2	0	493
8	Mahon	7	0	529
9	Smith, J	1	0	547
10	Young	3	0	559
11	Eagles	1	0	833
12	Cox	4	0	833
13	Devlin	1	0	1302
	Other	4	0	
	TOTAL	57	2	

TOP POINT EARNERS

	PLAYER	GAMES	AV PTS
1	Paul Devlin	13	1.62
2	Paul Mayo	12	1.50
3	Neal Ardley	25	1.40
4	Lloyd Doyley	22	1.36
5	Sean Dyche	21	1.33
6	Danny Webber	22	1.32
7	Heidar Helguson	36	1.19
8	Neil Cox	36	1.17
9	Gavin Mahon	41	1.17
10	Ashley Young	12	1.17
	CLUB AVERAGE:		1.13

TEAM OF THE SEASON

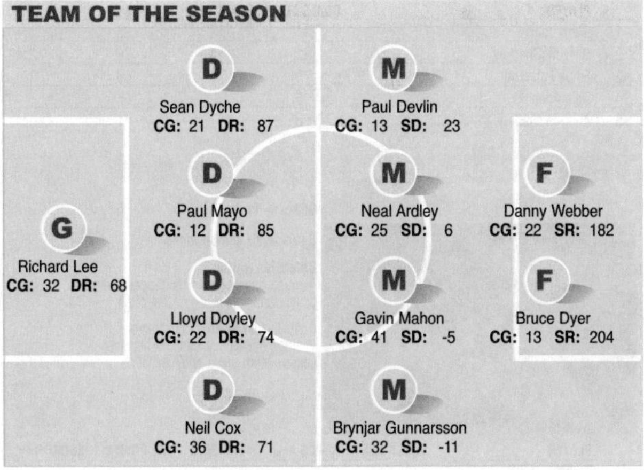

D
Sean Dyche
CG: 21 DR: 87
M
Paul Devlin
CG: 13 SD: 23
D
Paul Mayo
CG: 12 DR: 85
M
Neal Ardley
CG: 25 SD: 6
F
Danny Webber
CG: 22 SR: 182
G
Richard Lee
CG: 32 DR: 68
D
Lloyd Doyley
CG: 22 DR: 74
M
Gavin Mahon
CG: 41 SD: -5
F
Bruce Dyer
CG: 13 SR: 204
D
Neil Cox
CG: 36 DR: 71
M
Brynjar Gunnarsson
CG: 32 SD: -11

LEAGUE APPEARANCES GOALS AND BOOKINGS

	AGE (on 01/07/05)	IN NAMED 16	APPEARANCES	COUNTING GAMES	MINUTES ON PITCH	LEAGUE GOALS	Yellow	Red
Goalkeepers								
Alec Chamberlain	41	45	5	4	422	0	0	0
Paul Jones	38	9	9	9	810	0	0	0
Reece Kirk	17	4	0	0	0	0	0	0
Richard Lee	22	33	33	32	2908	0	1	0
Defenders								
James Chambers	24	40	40	39	3532	0	8	0
Neil Cox	33	40	39	36	3334	0	4	0
Danny Cullip	28	4	4	4	360	0	0	0
Jermaine Darlington	31	32	26	23	2159	0	1	0
Jay DeMerit	25	31	24	21	1930	3	4	1
Lloyd Doyley	22	37	29	22	2207	0	0	0
Sean Dyche	34	25	23	21	1990	0	1	0
Marcus Gayle	34	4	3	0	42	0	0	0
Adrian Mariappa	18	1	0	0	0	0	0	0
Paul Mayo	23	14	13	12	1104	0	3	0
Junior Osborne	17	2	1	0	13	0	0	0
Jack Smith	21	12	7	5	547	0	1	0
Midfielders								
Neal Ardley	32	33	30	25	2476	4	0	0
Alhassan Bangura	-	2	2	1	151	0	0	0
Dominic Blizzard	21	29	16	9	987	1	2	0
Paul Devlin	33	17	17	13	1302	1	1	0
Chris Eagles	19	14	13	8	833	1	1	0
Andy Ferrell	21	0	0	0	0	0	0	0
Brynjar Gunnarsson	29	37	37	32	2986	3	6	1
Jamie Hand	21	0	0	0	0	0	0	0
Johnnie Jackson	22	15	15	11	1141	0	4	0
Gavin Mahon	28	43	43	41	3709	0	7	0
Anthony McNamee	21	16	14	1	345	0	1	0
Ashley Young	19	37	34	12	1677	0	3	0
Forwards								
Hameur Bouazza	20	38	28	8	1030	1	0	0
Bruce Dyer	30	45	36	13	1832	9	1	0
Scott P Fitzgerald	25	8	7	0	116	0	0	0
Joel Grant	-	1	0	0	0	0	0	0
Heidar Helguson	27	39	39	36	3302	16	9	0
Danny Webber	23	29	28	22	2186	12	0	0

SQUAD APPEARANCES

Match	1	2	3	4	5	6	7	8	9	10	11	12	13	14	15	16	17	18	19	20	21	22	23	24	25	26	27	28	29	30
Venue	A	H	H	A	H	H	H	A	A	A	H	H	A	A	H	H	A	A	A	H	H	A	H	A	A	H	H	H	A	A
Competition	L	L	L	L	W	L	L	L	L	W	L	L	L	L	L	L	W	L	L	L	W	L	L	L	L	W	L	L	L	L
Result	L	W	L	W	W	W	D	W	W	W	L	D	L	D	D	D	W	W	D	D	W	D	D	D	L	W	L	D	L	L

Match	31	32	33	34	35	36	37	38	39	40	41	42	43	44	45	46	47	48	49	50	51	52	53	54	55
Venue	H	H	A	H	A	H	A	A	H	H	A	A	A	H	H	A	H	H	A	A	H	A	H	A	H
Competition	L	L	L	F	W	L	F	L	W	L	L	L	L	L	L	L	L	L	L	L	L	L	L	L	L
Result	D	W	L	D	L	W	L	D	L	W	L	W	D	L	L	L	D	L	L	L	L	W	D	W	L

Goalkeepers
Alec Chamberlain
Paul Jones
Reece Kirk
Richard Lee

Defenders
James Chambers
Neil Cox
Danny Cullip
Jermaine Darlington
Jay DeMerit
Lloyd Doyley
Sean Dyche
Marcus Gayle
Adrian Mariappa
Paul Mayo
Junior Osborne
Jack Smith

Midfielders
Neal Ardley
Alhassan Bangura
Dominic Blizzard
Paul Devlin
Chris Eagles
Andy Ferrell
Brynjar Gunnarsson
Jamie Hand
Johnnie Jackson
Gavin Mahon
Anthony McNamee
Ashley Young

Forwards
Hameur Bouazza
Bruce Dyer
Scott P Fitzgerald
Joel Grant
Heidar Helguson
Danny Webber

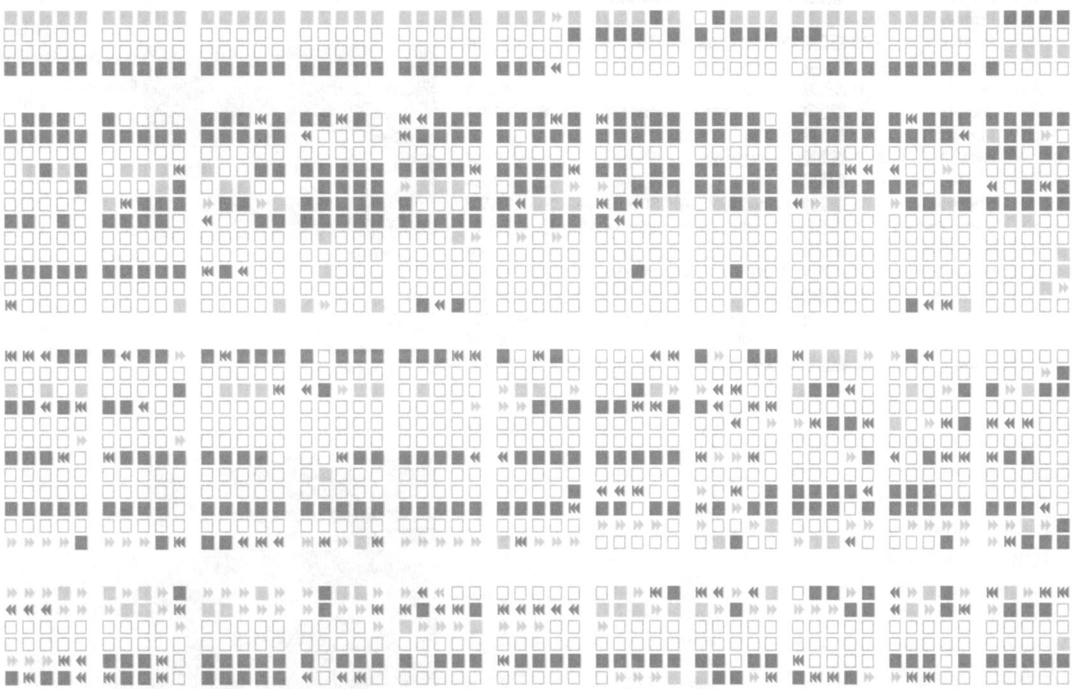

KEY: On all match | Subbed or sent off (Counting game) | Subbed on from bench (Counting Game) | Subbed on and then subbed or sent off (Counting Game) | Not in 16
On bench | Subbed or sent off (playing less than 70 minutes) | Subbed on (playing less than 70 minutes) | Subbed on and then subbed or sent off (playing less than 70 minutes)

COVENTRY CITY

Final Position: **19th**

NICKNAME: THE SKY BLUES

KEY: Won, Drawn, Lost

							Attendance
1	div1	Sunderland	H	W	2-0	Suffo 83 pen; Johnson 90	16,460
2	div1	Cardiff	A	L	1-2	Barrett 29	14,031
3	div1	Brighton	A	D	1-1	Hughes 69	6,368
4	div1	Millwall	H	L	0-1		13,910
5	ccr1	Torquay	H	W	4-1	Hughes 51; Suffo 63,66; Morrell 82	6,180
6	div1	Nottm Forest	A	W	4-1	Morrell 41,52; Johnson 59; Hughes 70	23,041
7	div1	West Ham	H	W	2-1	Doyle 25; Morrell 76	17,404
8	div1	Leeds	A	L	0-3		26,725
9	div1	Gillingham	H	D	2-2	Morrell 31; John 49 pen	11,966
10	div1	Rotherham	H	D	0-0		13,834
11	ccr2	Sheff Wed	H	W	1-0	Doyle 36	8,362
12	div1	Sheff Utd	A	D	1-1	Morrell 15	16,337
13	div1	QPR	A	L	1-4	Barrett 49	14,680
14	div1	Ipswich	H	L	1-2	Suffo 77	12,608
15	div1	Leicester	H	D	1-1	Makin 80 og	18,054
16	div1	Burnley	A	D	2-2	Johnson 62; Barrett 70	10,919
17	div1	Wigan	A	L	1-4	Johnson 32	9,63r
18	ccr3	Middlesbrough	A	L	0-3		11,833
19	div1	Reading	H	W	3-2	John 14 pen; Morrell 51; Johnson 66	13,663
20	div1	Preston	H	D	1-1	Suffo 49 pen	12,478
21	div1	Leicester	A	L	0-3		22,479
22	div1	Plymouth	H	W	2-1	Hughes 9; Barrett 15	15,314
23	div1	Wolverhampton	A	W	1-0	McSheffrey 61	26,291
24	div1	Crewe	H	L	0-1		12,823
25	div1	Derby	A	D	2-2	Hughes 22; Adebola 80	22,648
26	div1	Stoke	A	L	0-1		15,744
27	div1	Watford	H	W	1-0	McSheffrey 45	14,193
28	div1	Sheff Utd	H	L	1-2	John 19	21,146
29	div1	Gillingham	A	L	1-3	Adebola 37	8,734
30	div1	Rotherham	A	W	2-1	John 58; Williams 75	5,742
31	div1	Leeds	H	L	1-2	McSheffrey 82	19,084
32	facr3	Crewe	H	W	3-0	McSheffrey 25,69; John 45	7,629
33	div1	Ipswich	A	L	2-3	John 12; McSheffrey 61 pen	23,670
34	div1	QPR	H	L	1-2	Williams 59	16,595
35	facr4	Newcastle	A	L	1-3	Adebola 45	44,044
36	div1	Preston	A	L	2-3	Jorgensen 14; McSheffrey 72	13,691
37	div1	Burnley	H	L	0-2		13,236
38	div1	Reading	A	W	2-1	McSheffrey 63; John 72	15,904
39	div1	Wigan	H	L	1-2	McSheffrey 22 pen	12,130
40	div1	Stoke	H	D	0-0		13,871
41	div1	Watford	A	W	3-2	Benjamin 14; Jorgensen 54; Doyle 78	13,794
42	div1	Cardiff	H	D	1-1	John 16	17,059
43	div1	Millwall	A	D	1-1	Jorgensen 89	8,835
44	div1	Sunderland	A	L	0-1		29,424
45	div1	Brighton	H	W	2-1	McSheffrey 47 pen; Staunton 84	18,606
46	div1	Nottm Forest	H	W	2-0	McSheffrey 24 pen; Adebola 41	22,221
47	div1	West Ham	A	L	0-3		26,839
48	div1	Wolverhampton	H	D	2-2	McSheffrey 19 pen; John 90	19,412
49	div1	Plymouth	A	D	1-1	John 45	18,443
50	div1	Derby	H	W	6-2	McSheffrey 20,29 pen; Adebola 37; John 40,55; Whing 68	22,728
51	div1	Crewe	A	L	1-2	Adebola 23	9,269

MONTHLY POINTS TALLY

AUGUST	10	56%
SEPTEMBER	3	20%
OCTOBER	5	33%
NOVEMBER	7	47%
DECEMBER	4	27%
JANUARY	3	25%
FEBRUARY	4	27%
MARCH	5	42%
APRIL	11	61%
MAY	0	0%

GOALS

	PLAYER	LGE	FAC	LC	Oth	TOT
1	McSheffrey	12	2	0	0	14
2	John	11	1	0	0	12
3	Morrell	6	0	1	0	7
4	Adebola	5	1	0	0	6
5	Suffo	3	0	2	0	5
6	Johnson	5	0	0	0	5
7	Hughes	4	0	1	0	5
8	Barrett	4	0	0	0	4
9	Doyle	2	0	1	0	3
10	Jorgensen	3	0	0	0	3
11	Williams	2	0	0	0	2
	Other	4	0	0	0	4
	TOTAL	61	4	5	0	70

KEY PLAYERS - GOALSCORERS

Stern John

Goals in the League	11
Goals in all competitions	12
Contribution to Attacking Power Average number of minutes between League team goals while on pitch	65
Player Strike Rate Average number of minutes between League goals scored by player	202
Club Strike Rate Average number of minutes between League goals scored by club	68

	PLAYER	GOALS LGE	GOALS ALL	POWER	S RATE
1	Stern John	11	12	65	202 mins
2	Gary McSheffrey	12	14	75	231 mins
3	Eddie Johnson	5	5	66	318 mins
4	Dele Adebola	5	6	66	320 mins
5	Andy Morrell	6	7	71	358 mins

KEY PLAYERS - MIDFIELDERS

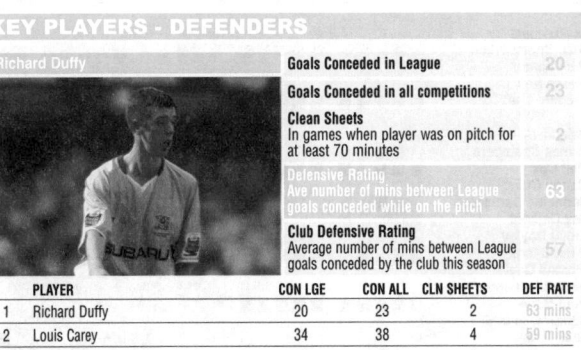

Stephen Hughes

Goals in the League	4
Goals in all competitions	5
Defensive Rating Average number of mins between League goals conceded while on the pitch	59
Contribution to Attacking Power Average number of minutes between League team goals while on pitch	66
Scoring Difference Defensive Rating minus Contribution to Attacking Power	-7

	PLAYER	GOALS LGE	GOALS ALL	DEF RATE	ATT POWER	SCORE DIFF
1	Stephen Hughes	4	5	59	66	-7 mins
2	Michael Doyle	2	3	56	67	-11 mins
3	Gary McSheffrey	12	14	62	75	-13 mins
4	Andy Morrell	6	7	58	72	-14 mins

KEY PLAYERS - DEFENDERS

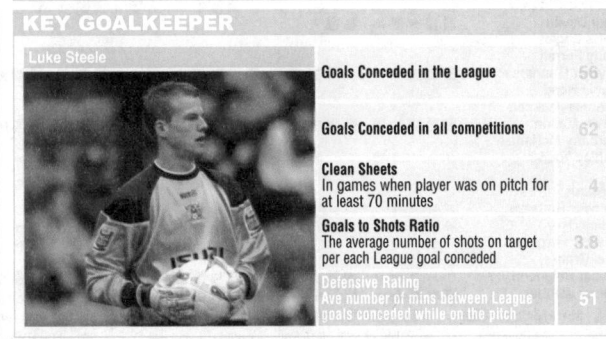

Richard Duffy

Goals Conceded in League	20
Goals Conceded in all competitions	23
Clean Sheets In games when player was on pitch for at least 70 minutes	2
Defensive Rating Ave number of mins between League goals conceded while on the pitch	63
Club Defensive Rating Average number of mins between League goals conceded by the club this season	57

	PLAYER	CON LGE	CON ALL	CLN SHEETS	DEF RATE
1	Richard Duffy	20	23	2	63 mins
2	Louis Carey	34	38	4	59 mins
3	Steve Staunton	49	49	4	58 mins
4	Richard Shaw	49	53	4	54 mins
5	Adrian Williams	35	38	2	53 mins

KEY GOALKEEPER

Luke Steele

Goals Conceded in the League	56
Goals Conceded in all competitions	62
Clean Sheets In games when player was on pitch for at least 70 minutes	4
Goals to Shots Ratio The average number of shots on target per each League goal conceded	3.8
Defensive Rating Ave number of mins between League goals conceded while on the pitch	51

DISCIPLINARY RECORDS

	PLAYER	YELLOW	RED	AVE
1	Sherwood	4	0	222
2	Carey	8	1	223
3	Davenport	2	0	270
4	Duffy	3	0	417
5	Doyle	9	0	431
6	McSheffrey	6	0	461
7	Whing	2	0	489
8	Bennett	0	1	491
9	Jorgensen	2	0	532
10	Osbourne	1	0	551
11	Suffo	1	0	558
12	Wood	1	0	586
13	Benjamin	1	0	618
	Other	15	1	
	TOTAL	55	3	

TOP POINT EARNERS

	PLAYER	GAMES	AV PTS
1	Richard Duffy	14	1.43
2	Eddie Johnson	15	1.33
3	Dele Adebola	15	1.20
4	Richard Shaw	28	1.14
5	Louis Carey	22	1.14
6	Stephen Hughes	35	1.14
7	Gary McSheffrey	29	1.14
8	Michael Doyle	43	1.12
9	Steve Staunton	29	1.07
10	Luke Steele	32	1.03
	CLUB AVERAGE:		1.13

LEAGUE APPEARANCES GOALS AND BOOKINGS

	AGE (on 01/07/05)	IN NAMED 16	APPEARANCES	COUNTING GAMES	MINUTES ON PITCH	LEAGUE GOALS	YELLOW	RED
Goalkeepers								
Ian Bennett	33	6	6	5	491	0	0	1
Scott Shearer	24	32	8	8	720	0	0	0
Luke Steele	20	36	32	32	2880	0	1	0
Defenders								
Louis Carey	28	23	23	22	2008	0	8	1
Calum Davenport	22	6	6	6	540	0	2	0
Eric Deloumeaux	32	7	2	0	56	0	1	0
Richard Duffy	19	14	14	14	1252	0	3	0
Marcus Hall	29	10	10	10	900	0	1	0
Florent Laville	31	10	6	4	421	0	2	0
Dean Leacock	21	13	13	11	1084	0	1	0
Matthew Mills	18	4	4	4	351	0	1	0
Robert Page	30	9	9	9	810	0	1	0
Richard Shaw	36	36	33	28	2667	0	2	0
Steve Staunton	36	43	35	29	2828	1	1	1
Andrew Whing	20	29	16	9	979	1	2	0
Adrian Williams	33	21	21	20	1859	2	1	0
Midfielders								
Graham Barrett	23	29	24	9	1205	4	0	0
Michael Doyle	23	44	44	43	3883	2	9	0
Lloyd Dyer	22	6	6	4	469	0	0	0
Stuart Giddings	19	17	12	9	944	0	0	0
Bjarni Gudjonsson	26	11	10	3	417	0	0	0
Stephen Hughes	28	40	40	35	3310	4	3	0
Claus Jorgensen	29	20	17	9	1064	3	2	0
Gary McSheffrey	23	37	37	29	2769	12	6	0
Andy Morrell	30	38	34	21	2146	6	2	0
Isaac Osbourne	19	14	9	6	551	0	1	0
Rohan Ricketts	22	6	6	4	409	0	0	0
Tim Sherwood	36	14	11	10	891	0	4	0
Neil Wood	22	14	13	3	586	0	1	0
Forwards								
Dele Adebola	30	28	25	15	1598	5	0	0
Trevor Benjamin	26	14	12	6	618	1	1	0
Shaun Goater	35	7	6	2	342	0	0	0
Stern John	28	31	30	21	2223	11	1	0
Eddie Johnson	20	30	26	15	1589	5	1	0
Patrick Kenge Suffo	27	21	21	1	558	3	1	0

TEAM OF THE SEASON

D
Louis Carey
CG: 22 DR: 59
D
Richard Duffy
CG: 14 DR: 63
D
Steve Staunton
CG: 29 DR: 58
D
Richard Shaw
CG: 28 DR: 54
G
Luke Steele
CG: 32 DR: 51
M
Stephen Hughes
CG: 35 SD: -7
M
Michael Doyle
CG: 43 SD: -11
M
Gary McSheffrey
CG: 29 SD: -13
M
Andy Morrell
CG: 21 SD: -14
F
Stern John
CG: 21 SR: 202
F
Eddie Johnson
CG: 15 SR: 318

SQUAD APPEARANCES

Match	1	2	3	4	5	6	7	8	9	10	11	12	13	14	15	16	17	18	19	20	21	22	23	24	25
Venue	H	A	A	H	H	A	H	A	H	H	H	A	A	H	H	A	A	A	H	H	A	H	A	H	A
Competition	L	L	L	L	W	L	L	L	L	L	W	L	L	L	L	L	L	W	L	L	L	L	L	L	L
Result	W	L	D	L	W	W	W	L	D	D	W	D	L	L	D	D	L	L	W	D	L	W	W	L	D

Match	26	27	28	29	30	31	32	33	34	35	36	37	38	39	40	41	42	43	44	45	46	47	48	49	50	51
Venue	A	H	H	A	A	H	H	A	H	A	A	H	A	H	H	A	H	A	A	H	H	A	H	A	H	A
Competition	L	L	L	L	L	L	F	L	L	F	L	L	L	L	L	L	L	L	L	L	L	L	L	L	L	L
Result	L	W	L	L	W	L	W	L	L	L	L	L	W	L	D	W	D	D	L	W	W	L	D	D	W	L

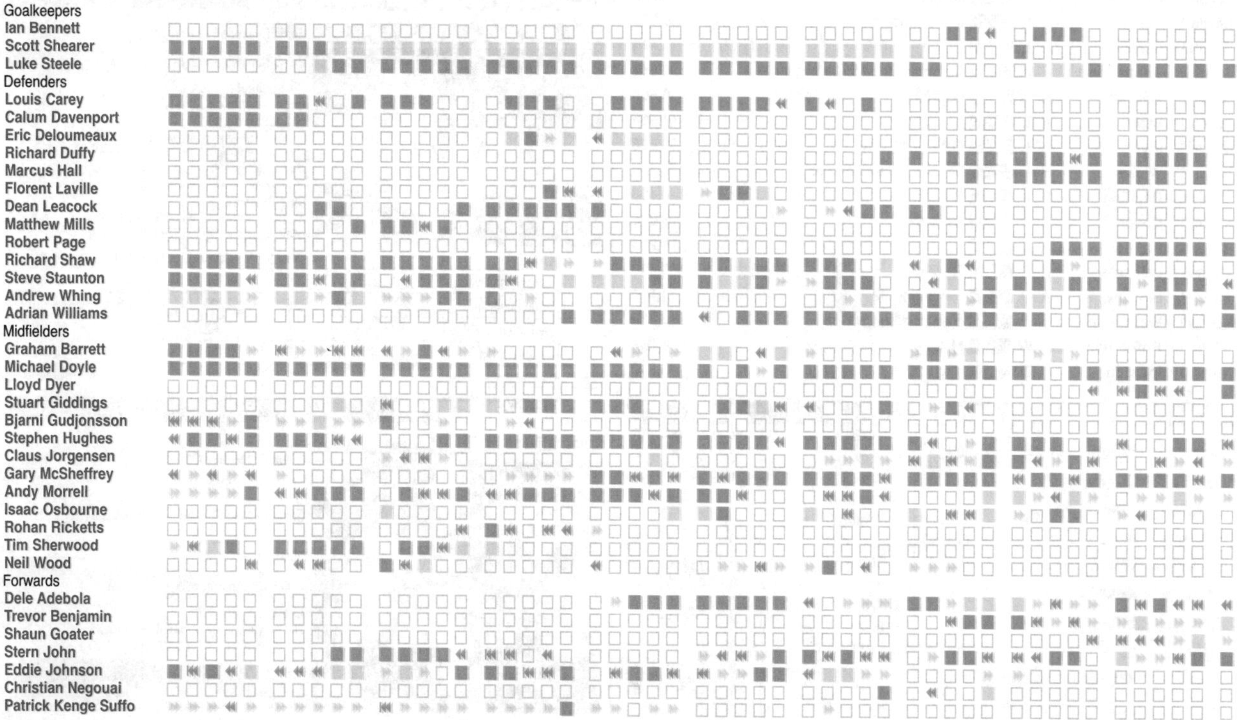

Goalkeepers
Ian Bennett
Scott Shearer
Luke Steele
Defenders
Louis Carey
Calum Davenport
Eric Deloumeaux
Richard Duffy
Marcus Hall
Florent Laville
Dean Leacock
Matthew Mills
Robert Page
Richard Shaw
Steve Staunton
Andrew Whing
Adrian Williams
Midfielders
Graham Barrett
Michael Doyle
Lloyd Dyer
Stuart Giddings
Bjarni Gudjonsson
Stephen Hughes
Claus Jorgensen
Gary McSheffrey
Andy Morrell
Isaac Osbourne
Rohan Ricketts
Tim Sherwood
Neil Wood
Forwards
Dele Adebola
Trevor Benjamin
Shaun Goater
Stern John
Eddie Johnson
Christian Negouai
Patrick Kenge Suffo

BRIGHTON & HOVE ALBION

Final Position: **20th**

NICKNAME: THE SEAGULLS

KEY: □ Won □ Drawn □ Lost

							Attendance
1	div1	Reading	A	L	2-3	Molango 1; Robinson 63	15,641
2	div1	Plymouth	H	L	0-2		6,387
3	div1	Coventry	H	D	1-1	Virgo 89	6,368
4	div1	Wigan	A	L	0-3		8,681
5	ccr1	Bristol Rovers	H	L	1-2	Butters 11	4,217
6	div1	Preston	H	W	1-0	Broomes 30 pen	5,996
7	div1	Leicester	A	W	1-0	Virgo 41	22,263
8	div1	Watford	A	D	1-1	Virgo 85	14,148
9	div1	Wolverhampton	H	L	0-1		6,804
10	div1	QPR	H	L	2-3	Hinshelwood 23; Currie 44	6,612
11	div1	Gillingham	A	W	1-0	Knight 79 pen	8,365
12	div1	Nottm Forest	A	W	1-0	Virgo 25	20,109
13	div1	Sheff Utd	H	D	1-1	Currie 22	6,418
14	div1	Crewe	A	L	1-3	Jarrett 79	6,811
15	div1	Cardiff	H	D	1-1	Knight 10	6,112
16	div1	Leeds	H	W	1-0	Carlisle 58 og	6,716
17	div1	Sunderland	A	L	0-2		25,532
18	div1	Derby	A	L	0-3		22,480
19	div1	Crewe	H	L	1-3	Reid 85	6,163
20	div1	West Ham	A	W	1-0	Butters 68	29,514
21	div1	Burnley	H	L	0-1		6,109
22	div1	Ipswich	A	L	0-1		26,269
23	div1	Rotherham	H	W	1-0	Harding 82	6,076
24	div1	Millwall	A	L	0-2		12,196
25	div1	Stoke	H	L	0-1		6,028
26	div1	Gillingham	H	W	2-1	Carpenter 79; Virgo 88	6,420
27	div1	Wolverhampton	A	D	1-1	Hart 4	28,516
28	div1	QPR	A	D	0-0		15,898
29	div1	Watford	H	W	2-1	Mayo 15; Knight 69	6,335
30	facr3	Tottenham	A	L	1-2	Carpenter 48	36,094
31	div1	Sheff Utd	A	W	2-1	Carpenter 45; Knight 90	21,482
32	div1	Nottm Forest	H	D	0-0		6,704
33	div1	Leeds	A	D	1-1	Butters 81	27,033
34	div1	Derby	H	L	2-3	McCammon 14,60	6,587
35	div1	Cardiff	A	L	0-2		11,435
36	div1	Sunderland	H	W	2-1	Carpenter 26; McCammon 43	6,647
37	div1	Millwall	H	W	1-0	Hart 90	6,608
38	div1	Stoke	A	L	0-2		14,908
39	div1	Plymouth	A	L	1-5	Oatway 11	15,606
40	div1	Wigan	H	L	2-4	Virgo 36; Hammond 83	6,306
41	div1	Reading	H	L	0-1		6,108
42	div1	Coventry	A	L	1-2	Virgo 62	18,606
43	div1	Preston	A	L	0-3		14,234
44	div1	Leicester	H	D	1-1	Reid 80	6,638
45	div1	Burnley	A	D	1-1	Hammond 52	11,611
46	div1	West Ham	H	D	2-2	Hammond 54,90	6,819
47	div1	Rotherham	A	W	1-0	McLaren 19 og	6,549
48	div1	Ipswich	H	D	1-1	Virgo 10	6,848

MONTHLY POINTS TALLY

AUGUST	7	39%
SEPTEMBER	7	47%
OCTOBER	5	33%
NOVEMBER	3	20%
DECEMBER	7	47%
JANUARY	9	60%
FEBRUARY	6	50%
MARCH	0	0%
APRIL	6	33%
MAY	1	33%

GOALS

	PLAYER	LGE	FAC	LC	Oth	TOT
1	Virgo	8	0	0	0	8
2	Carpenter	3	1	0	0	4
3	Hammond	4	0	0	0	4
4	Knight	4	0	0	0	4
5	McCammon	3	0	0	0	3
6	Butters	2	0	1	0	3
7	Reid	2	0	0	0	2
8	Hart	2	0	0	0	2
9	Currie	2	0	0	0	2
10	Hinshelwood	1	0	0	0	1
11	Molango	1	0	0	0	1
	Other	8	0	0	0	8
	TOTAL	40	1	1	0	42

KEY PLAYERS - GOALSCORERS

Adam Virgo

Goals in the League	8
Goals in all competitions	8
Contribution to Attacking Power Average number of minutes between League team goals while on pitch	94
Player Strike Rate Average number of minutes between League goals scored by player	391
Club Strike Rate Average number of minutes between League goals scored by club	104

	PLAYER	GOALS LGE	GOALS ALL	POWER	S RATE
1	Adam Virgo	8	8	94	391 mins
2	Dean Hammond	4	4	101	453 mins
3	Leon Knight	4	4	112	762 mins
4	Gary Hart	2	2	82	775 mins
5	Richard Carpenter	3	4	105	872 mins

KEY PLAYERS - MIDFIELDERS

Gary Hart

SKINT

Goals in the League	2
Goals in all competitions	2
Defensive Rating Average number of mins between League goals conceded while on the pitch	65
Contribution to Attacking Power Average number of minutes between League team goals while on pitch	82
Scoring Difference Defensive Rating minus Contribution to Attacking Power	-17

	PLAYER	GOALS LGE	GOALS ALL	DEF RATE	ATT POWER	SCORE DIFF
1	Gary Hart	2	2	65	82	-17 mins
2	Dean Hammond	4	4	70	101	-31 mins
3	Richard Carpenter	3	4	73	105	-32 mins
4	Charlie Oatway	1	1	65	105	-40 mins
5	Alexis Nicolas	0	0	59	102	-43 mins

KEY PLAYERS - DEFENDERS

Adam Hinshelwood

Goals Conceded in League	50
Goals Conceded in all competitions	54
Clean Sheets In games when player was on pitch for at least 70 minutes	10
Defensive Rating Ave number of mins between League goals conceded while on the pitch	66
Club Defensive Rating Average number of mins between League goals conceded by the club this season	64

	PLAYER	CON LGE	CON ALL	CLN SHEETS	DEF RATE
1	Adam Hinshelwood	50	54	10	66 mins
2	Danny Cullip	25	27	6	65 mins
3	Guy Butters	58	62	9	63 mins
4	Daniel Harding	56	60	10	62 mins
5	Kerry Mayo	33	35	3	58 mins

KEY GOALKEEPER

Michel Kuipers

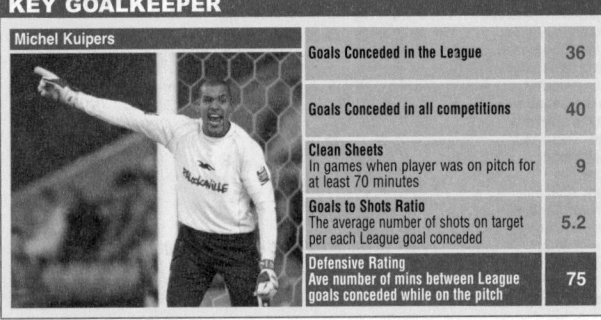

Goals Conceded in the League	36
Goals Conceded in all competitions	40
Clean Sheets In games when player was on pitch for at least 70 minutes	9
Goals to Shots Ratio The average number of shots on target per each League goal conceded	5.2
Defensive Rating Ave number of mins between League goals conceded while on the pitch	75

DISCIPLINARY RECORDS

	PLAYER	YELLOW	RED	AVE
1	Cullip	6	0	270
2	Virgo	9	2	284
3	Knight	9	0	338
4	El-Abd	3	0	363
5	Oatway	5	1	453
6	Jones	1	0	559
7	McCammon	2	0	584
8	Currie	3	0	618
9	Harding	5	0	697
10	Hart	1	1	774
11	Kuipers	3	0	898
12	Hammond	2	0	905
13	Mayo	2	0	961
	Other	10	1	
	TOTAL	61	5	

TOP POINT EARNERS

	PLAYER	GAMES	AV PTS
1	Dean Hammond	15	1.53
2	Richard Carpenter	28	1.36
3	Adam Hinshelwood	35	1.26
4	Leon Knight	31	1.26
5	Gary Hart	12	1.25
6	Michel Kuipers	30	1.23
7	Adam Virgo	34	1.12
8	Paul Reid	28	1.11
9	Danny Cullip	18	1.11
10	Guy Butters	40	1.10
	CLUB AVERAGE:		1.11

TEAM OF THE SEASON

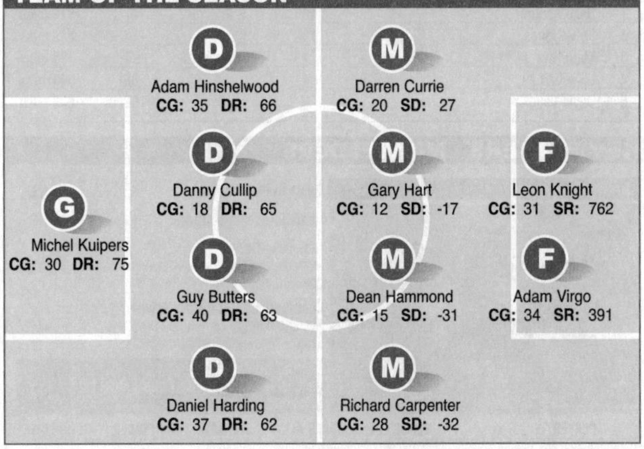
D
Adam Hinshelwood
CG: 35 DR: 66
M
Darren Currie
CG: 20 SD: 27
D
Danny Cullip
CG: 18 DR: 65
M
Gary Hart
CG: 12 SD: -17
F
Leon Knight
CG: 31 SR: 762
G
Michel Kuipers
CG: 30 DR: 75
D
Guy Butters
CG: 40 DR: 63
M
Dean Hammond
CG: 15 SD: -31
F
Adam Virgo
CG: 34 SR: 391
D
Daniel Harding
CG: 37 DR: 62
M
Richard Carpenter
CG: 28 SD: -32

LEAGUE APPEARANCES GOALS AND BOOKINGS

	AGE (on 01/07/05)	IN NAMED 16	APPEARANCES	COUNTING GAMES	MINUTES ON PITCH	LEAGUE GOALS	Yellow	Red
Goalkeepers								
Alan Blayney	23	7	7	7	630	0	0	0
Michel Kuipers	31	30	30	30	2694	0	3	0
Chris May	19	31	1	0	6	0	0	0
Ben Roberts	30	4	0	0	0	0	0	0
Rami Shaaban	30	13	6	6	540	0	0	0
David Yelldell	23	6	3	3	270	0	0	0
Defenders								
Guy Butters	35	41	41	40	3664	2	3	0
Danny Cullip	28	18	18	18	1620	0	6	0
Joe Dolan	25	5	3	1	213	0	1	0
Adam El-Abd	20	24	16	8	1091	0	3	0
Gary Elphick	19	1	0	0	0	0	0	0
Daniel Harding	21	43	43	37	3488	1	5	0
Adam Hinshelwood	21	39	38	35	3295	1	2	0
Joel Lynch	17	1	0	0	0	0	0	0
Kerry Mayo	27	41	27	18	1922	1	2	0
Paul Reid	26	36	34	28	2798	2	2	0
Paul Watson	30	13	4	0	136	0	0	0
Midfielders								
Richard Carpenter	32	34	32	28	2616	3	1	1
Dean Cox	-	1	0	0	0	0	0	0
Darren Currie	30	22	22	20	1854	2	3	0
Dean Hammond	22	38	30	15	1810	4	2	0
Gary Hart	28	31	26	12	1549	2	1	1
Albert Jarrett	20	17	12	0	382	1	1	0
Nathan Jones	32	26	19	1	559	0	1	0
Alexis Nicolas	22	39	33	23	2347	0	2	0
Charlie Oatway	31	37	34	26	2720	1	5	1
John Piercy	25	2	2	0	94	0	0	0
Forwards								
Steve Claridge	39	5	5	5	449	0	0	0
Leon Knight	22	40	39	31	3047	4	9	0
Mark McCammon	26	18	18	9	1168	3	2	0
Chris McPhee	22	17	16	3	666	0	0	0
Maheta Molango	22	8	5	4	308	1	1	0
Jake Robinson	18	12	10	1	317	1	0	0
Adam Virgo	22	36	36	34	3129	8	9	2

SQUAD APPEARANCES

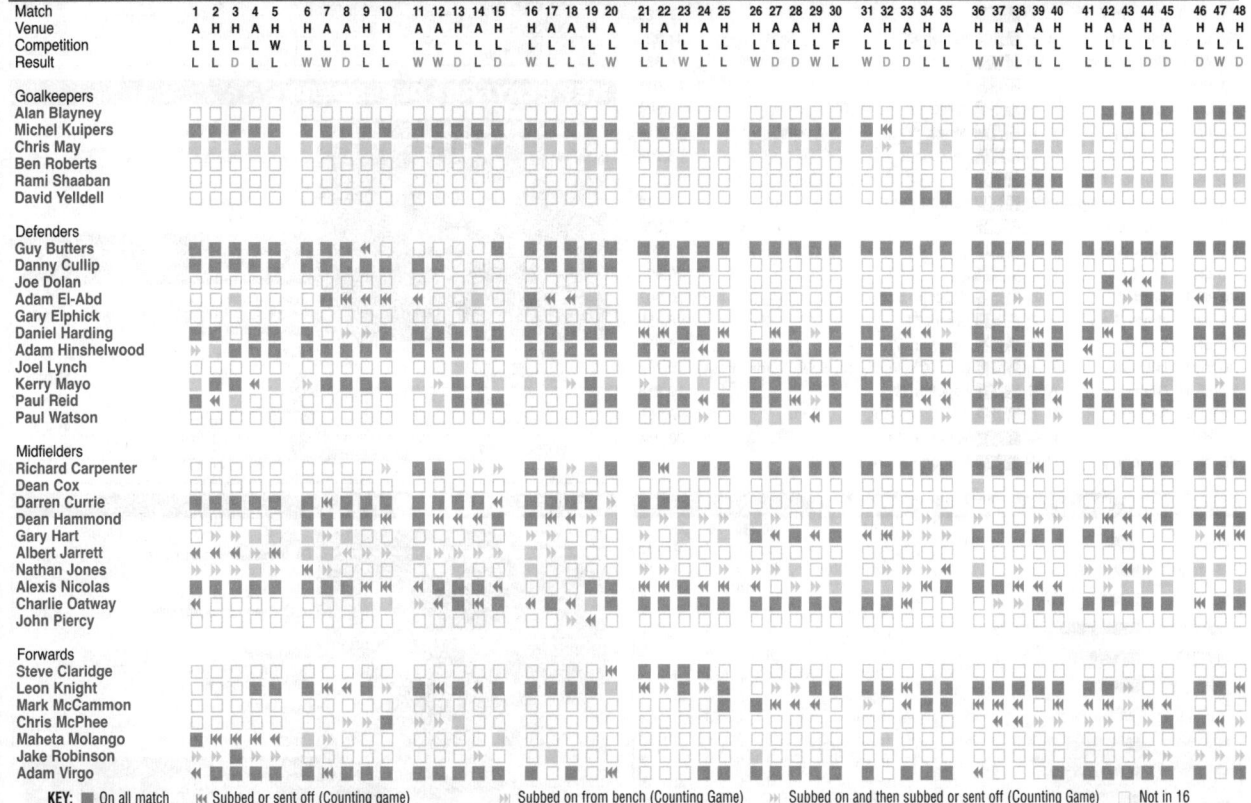

Match	1	2	3	4	5	6	7	8	9	10	11	12	13	14	15	16	17	18	19	20	21	22	23	24	25	26	27	28	29	30	31	32	33	34	35	36	37	38	39	40	41	42	43	44	45	46	47	48
Venue	A	H	H	A	H	H	A	A	H	H	A	A	H	A	H	H	A	A	H	A	H	A	H	A	H	H	A	A	H	A	A	H	A	H	A	H	H	A	A	H	H	A	A	H	A	H	A	H
Competition	L	L	L	L	W	L	L	L	L	L	L	L	L	L	L	L	L	L	L	L	L	L	L	L	L	L	L	L	L	F	L	L	L	L	L	L	L	L	L	L	L	L	L	L	L	L	L	L
Result	L	L	D	L	L	W	W	D	L	L	W	W	D	L	D	W	L	L	L	W	L	L	W	L	L	W	D	D	W	L	W	D	D	L	L	W	W	L	L	L	L	L	L	D	D	D	W	D

Goalkeepers
Alan Blayney
Michel Kuipers
Chris May
Ben Roberts
Rami Shaaban
David Yelldell

Defenders
Guy Butters
Danny Cullip
Joe Dolan
Adam El-Abd
Gary Elphick
Daniel Harding
Adam Hinshelwood
Joel Lynch
Kerry Mayo
Paul Reid
Paul Watson

Midfielders
Richard Carpenter
Dean Cox
Darren Currie
Dean Hammond
Gary Hart
Albert Jarrett
Nathan Jones
Alexis Nicolas
Charlie Oatway
John Piercy

Forwards
Steve Claridge
Leon Knight
Mark McCammon
Chris McPhee
Maheta Molango
Jake Robinson
Adam Virgo

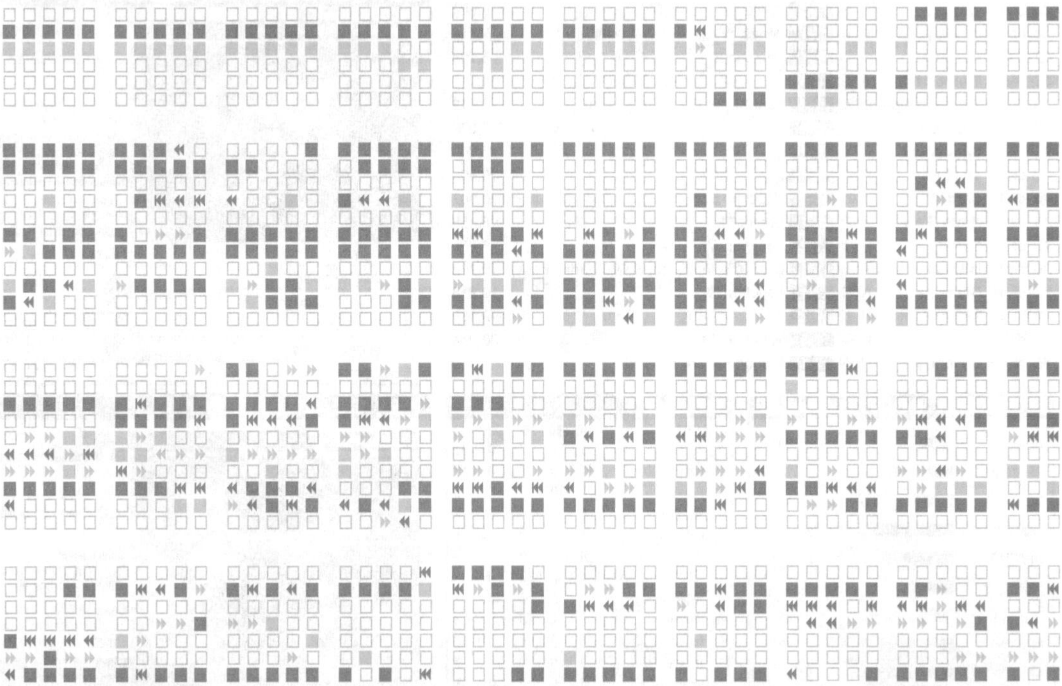

KEY: On all match | On bench | Subbed or sent off (Counting game) | Subbed or sent off (playing less than 70 minutes) | Subbed on from bench (Counting Game) | Subbed on (playing less than 70 minutes) | Subbed on and then subbed or sent off (Counting Game) | Subbed on and then subbed or sent off (playing less than 70 minutes) | Not in 16

CREWE ALEXANDRA

Final Position: **21st**

NICKNAME: THE RAILWAYMEN   KEY: ☐Won ☐Drawn ☐Lost

							Attendance
1	div1	Cardiff	H	D	2-2	Ashton 5 pen; Higdon 85	7,339
2	div1	Sunderland	A	L	1-3	Rivers 43	22,341
3	div1	Nottm Forest	A	D	2-2	Rivers 21,44	24,201
4	div1	West Ham	H	L	2-3	Ashton 31,82	7,857
5	ccr1	Blackpool	H	W	4-1	Jones, S 3,44; Rivers 9; Ashton 12	2,994
6	div1	Derby	A	W	4-2	Jones, S 5,83; Vaughan 12; Ashton 74	24,436
7	div1	Burnley	A	L	0-3		11,274
8	div1	QPR	H	L	0-2		5,682
9	div1	Leeds	H	D	2-2	Ashton 48 pen; Jones, S 83	9,095
10	ccr2	Sunderland	H	W	3-3*	Jones, S 19; Ashton 64; Foster 119 (*aet, won 4-2 on penalties)	3,804
11	div1	Preston	A	L	0-1		11,823
12	div1	Rotherham	A	W	3-2	Ashton 19 pen,71; Lunt 61	4,498
13	div1	Watford	H	W	3-0	Jones, S 20; Sorvel 23,38	6,382
14	div1	Brighton	H	W	3-1	Lunt 9; White 34; Higdon 69	6,811
15	div1	Wigan	A	L	1-4	Jones, S 56	7,547
16	div1	Reading	A	L	0-4		13,630
17	ccR3	Man Utd	H	L	0-3		10,103
18	div1	Sheff Utd	H	L	2-3	Foster 24; Thirlwell 90 og	7,131
19	div1	Leicester	H	D	2-2	Rivers 49; Otsemobor 61	6,849
20	div1	Brighton	A	W	3-1	Ashton 40,59; Rivers 50	6,163
21	div1	Stoke	A	L	0-1		17,640
22	div1	Gillingham	H	W	4-1	Vaughan 35; Ashton 71,80; Jones, S 89	6,128
23	div1	Coventry	A	W	1-0	Ashton 26 pen	12,823
24	div1	Millwall	H	W	2-1	Ashton 1; Varney 76	5,409
25	div1	Ipswich	H	D	2-2	Ashton 24,27	7,236
26	div1	Plymouth	H	W	3-0	Lunt 42; Ashton 57; Doumbe 80 og	6,823
27	div1	Wolverhampton	A	D	1-1	Ashton 38	25,340
28	div1	QPR	A	W	2-1	Walker 39; Rivers 45	15,770
29	div1	Leeds	A	W	2-0	Ashton 16; Rivers 54	32,303
30	div1	Preston	H	L	1-2	Walker 81	8,667
31	facr3	Coventry	A	L	0-3		7,629
32	div1	Watford	A	L	1-3	Varney 68	11,223
33	div1	Rotherham	H	D	1-1	White 79	6,382
34	div1	Leicester	A	D	1-1	White 36	27,011
35	div1	Wigan	H	L	1-3	White 45	7,981
36	div1	Burnley	H	D	1-1	Jones, S 18	7,718
37	div1	Reading	H	D	1-1	Varney 12	5,703
38	div1	Plymouth	A	L	0-3		14,918
39	div1	Wolverhampton	H	L	1-4	Lunt 11 pen	8,212
40	div1	Sheff Utd	A	L	0-4		16,079
41	div1	Sunderland	H	L	0-1		7,949
42	div1	West Ham	A	D	1-1	Jones, S 90	26,593
43	div1	Cardiff	A	D	1-1	Vaughan 57	10,007
44	div1	Nottm Forest	H	D	1-1	Sorvel 71	8,458
45	div1	Derby	H	L	1-2	Vaughan 90	8,026
46	div1	Millwall	A	L	3-4	Lunt 62 pen; Jones, S 68; Varney 81	10,767
47	div1	Gillingham	A	D	1-1	Vaughan 73	10,315
48	div1	Stoke	H	L	0-2		9,166
49	div1	Ipswich	A	L	1-5	Vaughan 90	28,244
50	div1	Coventry	H	W	2-1	Higdon 54; Jones, S 72	9,269

MONTHLY POINTS TALLY

AUGUST	5	33%
SEPTEMBER	4	27%
OCTOBER	6	40%
NOVEMBER	13	72%
DECEMBER	8	67%
JANUARY	4	33%
FEBRUARY	3	20%
MARCH	2	13%
APRIL	2	11%
MAY	3	100%

GOALS

	PLAYER	LGE	FAC	LC	Oth	TOT
1	Ashton	18	0	2	0	20
2	Jones, S	10	0	3	0	13
3	Rivers	7	0	1	0	8
4	Vaughan	6	0	0	0	6
5	Lunt	5	0	0	0	5
6	Varney	4	0	0	0	4
7	White	4	0	0	0	4
8	Higdon	3	0	0	0	3
9	Sorvel	3	0	0	0	3
10	Foster	1	0	1	0	2
11	Walker	2	0	0	0	2
	Other	3	0	0	0	3
	TOTAL	66	0	7	0	73

KEY PLAYERS - GOALSCORERS

Dean Ashton

Goals in the League	18
Goals in all competitions	20
Contribution to Attacking Power Average number of minutes between League team goals while on pitch	47
Player Strike Rate Average number of minutes between League goals scored by player	111
Club Strike Rate Average number of minutes between League goals scored by club	63

	PLAYER	GOALS LGE	GOALS ALL	POWER	S RATE
1	Dean Ashton	18	20	47	111 mins
2	Steve Jones	10	13	54	220 mins
3	Mark Rivers	7	8	71	315 mins
4	Luke Varney	4	4	88	398 mins
5	David Vaughan	6	6	62	643 mins

KEY PLAYERS - MIDFIELDERS

Justin Cochrane

Goals in the League	0
Goals in all competitions	0
Defensive Rating Average number of mins between League goals conceded while on the pitch	49
Contribution to Attacking Power Average number of minutes between League team goals while on pitch	48
Scoring Difference Defensive Rating minus Contribution to Attacking Power	1

	PLAYER	GOALS LGE	GOALS ALL	DEF RATE	ATT POWER	SCORE DIFF
1	Justin Cochrane	0	0	49	48	1 mins
2	Kenny Lunt	5	5	48	63	-15 mins
3	David Vaughan	6	6	47	62	-15 mins
4	Neil Sorvel	3	3	48	64	-16 mins
5	Lee Bell	0	0	57	119	-62 mins

KEY PLAYERS - DEFENDERS

Jon Otsemobor

Goals Conceded in League	20
Goals Conceded in all competitions	23
Clean Sheets In games when player was on pitch for at least 70 minutes	3
Defensive Rating Ave number of mins between League goals conceded while on the pitch	63
Club Defensive Rating Average number of mins between League goals conceded by the club this season	48

	PLAYER	CON LGE	CON ALL	CLN SHEETS	DEF RATE
1	Jon Otsemobor	20	23	3	63 mins
2	Colin Murdock	24	24	0	54 mins
3	Steve Foster	55	65	4	54 mins
4	Chris McCready	33	34	1	51 mins
5	Anthony Tonkin	60	64	2	49 mins

KEY GOALKEEPER

Clayton Ince

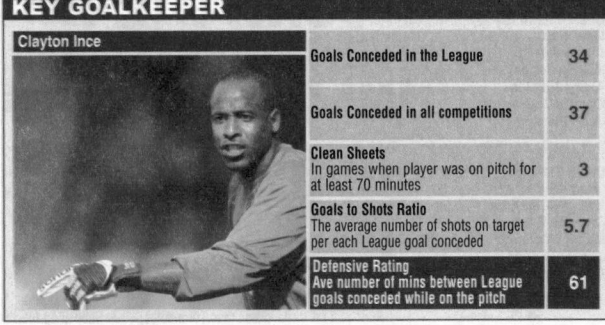

Goals Conceded in the League	34
Goals Conceded in all competitions	37
Clean Sheets In games when player was on pitch for at least 70 minutes	3
Goals to Shots Ratio The average number of shots on target per each League goal conceded	5.7
Defensive Rating Ave number of mins between League goals conceded while on the pitch	61

DISCIPLINARY RECORDS

	PLAYER	YELLOW	RED	AVE
1	Jones, B	4	0	416
2	Cochrane	3	0	658
3	Varney	2	0	795
4	Moses	2	0	860
5	Foster	2	1	985
6	Lunt	4	0	1032
7	Murdock	1	0	1301
8	Bell	1	0	1431
9	Walker	1	0	1529
10	McCready	1	0	1697
11	Jones, S	1	0	2195
12	Rivers	1	0	2208
13	Tonkin	1	0	2962
	Other	1	0	
	TOTAL	25	1	

TOP POINT EARNERS

	PLAYER	GAMES	AV PTS
1	Jon Otsemobor	14	1.86
2	Dean Ashton	22	1.64
3	Justin Cochrane	20	1.60
4	Clayton Ince	23	1.39
5	Billy Jones	18	1.33
6	Steve Foster	32	1.22
7	Mark Rivers	21	1.19
8	Steve Jones	20	1.15
9	Adrian Moses	19	1.11
10	Kenny Lunt	46	1.09
	CLUB AVERAGE:		1.09

TEAM OF THE SEASON

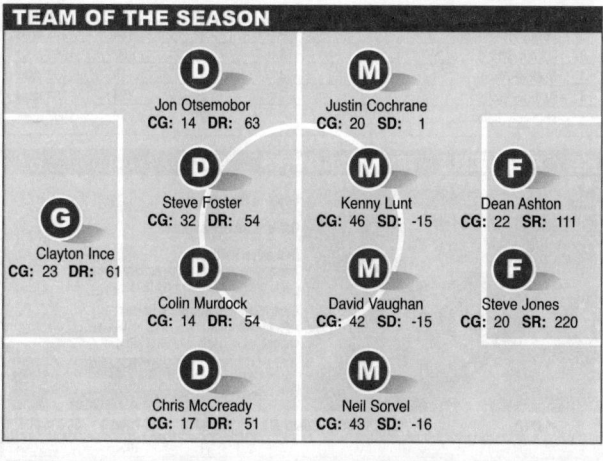

G – Clayton Ince CG: 23 DR: 61

D – Jon Otsemobor CG: 14 DR: 63
D – Steve Foster CG: 32 DR: 54
D – Colin Murdock CG: 14 DR: 54
D – Chris McCready CG: 17 DR: 51

M – Justin Cochrane CG: 20 SD: 1
M – Kenny Lunt CG: 46 SD: -15
M – David Vaughan CG: 42 SD: -15
M – Neil Sorvel CG: 43 SD: -16

F – Dean Ashton CG: 22 SR: 111
F – Steve Jones CG: 20 SR: 220

LEAGUE APPEARANCES GOALS AND BOOKINGS

	AGE (on 01/07/05)	IN NAMED 16	APPEARANCES	COUNTING GAMES	MINUTES ON PITCH	LEAGUE GOALS	Yellow	Red
Goalkeepers								
Clayton Ince	32	38	23	23	2070	0	0	0
Stuart Tomlinson	21	6	0	0	0	0	0	0
Ben Williams	22	43	23	23	2070	0	0	0
Karl Wills	17	5	0	0	0	0	0	0
Defenders								
Paul Bignot	19	10	5	3	310	0	0	0
Steve Foster	24	34	34	32	2955	1	2	1
Billy Jones	18	21	20	18	1664	0	4	0
Robert Lloyd	18	2	0	0	0	0	0	0
Chris McCready	24	25	20	17	1697	0	1	0
Adrian Moses	30	22	21	19	1720	0	2	0
Darren Moss	24	8	6	6	537	0	0	0
Colin Murdock	30	16	16	14	1301	0	1	0
Jon Otsemobor	22	14	14	14	1260	1	0	0
Mark Roberts	21	10	6	3	295	0	0	0
Anthony Tonkin	25	36	35	32	2962	0	1	0
Richard Walker	24	37	23	15	1529	2	1	0
Midfielders								
Lee Bell	21	26	17	15	1431	0	1	0
Keith Briggs	23	3	3	2	219	0	0	0
Justin Cochrane	23	38	29	20	1974	0	3	0
Michael Higdon	21	26	20	1	435	3	0	0
Kenny Lunt	25	46	46	46	4130	5	4	0
Ben Rix	21	3	0	0	0	0	0	0
Gary Roberts	18	6	2	2	168	0	0	0
James Robinson	22	2	0	0	0	0	0	0
Neil Sorvel	32	46	46	43	3982	3	1	0
David Vaughan	22	44	44	42	3860	6	0	0
Forwards								
Dean Ashton	21	24	24	22	1989	18	0	0
Steve Jones	28	42	37	20	2195	10	1	0
Matthew Platt	21	1	1	0	15	0	0	0
Mark Rivers	29	42	34	21	2208	7	1	0
Luke Varney	22	32	25	16	1591	4	2	0
Andy White	23	28	22	7	928	4	0	0

SQUAD APPEARANCES

Match	1	2	3	4	5	6	7	8	9	10	11	12	13	14	15	16	17	18	19	20	21	22	23	24	25
Venue	H	A	A	H	H	A	A	H	H	H	A	A	H	H	A	A	H	H	H	A	A	H	A	H	H
Competition	L	L	L	L	W	L	L	L	L	W	L	L	L	L	L	L	W	L	L	L	L	L	L	L	L
Result	D	L	D	L	W	W	L	L	D	W	L	W	W	W	L	L	L	L	D	W	L	W	W	W	D

Match	26	27	28	29	30	31	32	33	34	35	36	37	38	39	40	41	42	43	44	45	46	47	48	49	50
Venue	H	A	A	A	H	A	A	H	A	H	H	H	A	H	A	H	A	A	H	H	A	A	H	A	H
Competition	L	L	L	L	L	F	L	L	L	L	L	L	L	L	L	L	L	L	L	L	L	L	L	L	L
Result	W	D	W	W	L	L	L	D	D	L	D	D	L	L	L	L	D	D	D	L	L	D	L	L	W

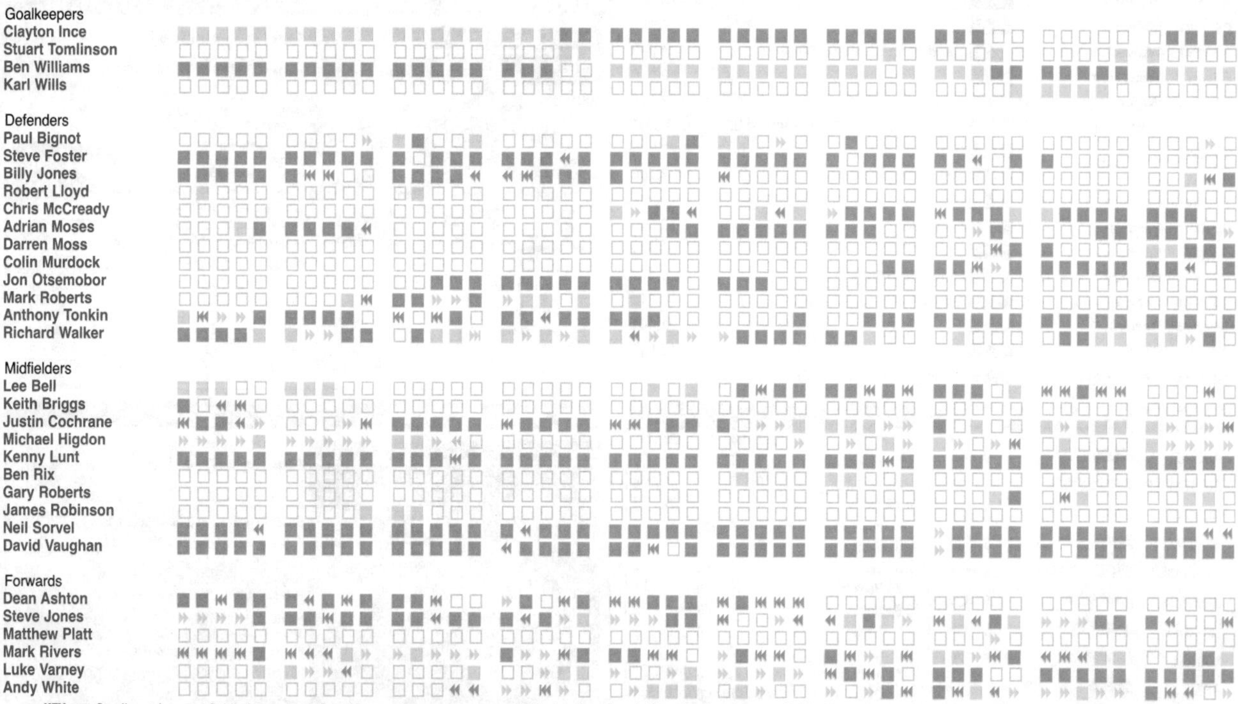
Goalkeepers
Clayton Ince
Stuart Tomlinson
Ben Williams
Karl Wills
Defenders
Paul Bignot
Steve Foster
Billy Jones
Robert Lloyd
Chris McCready
Adrian Moses
Darren Moss
Colin Murdock
Jon Otsemobor
Mark Roberts
Anthony Tonkin
Richard Walker
Midfielders
Lee Bell
Keith Briggs
Justin Cochrane
Michael Higdon
Kenny Lunt
Ben Rix
Gary Roberts
James Robinson
Neil Sorvel
David Vaughan
Forwards
Dean Ashton
Steve Jones
Matthew Platt
Mark Rivers
Luke Varney
Andy White

KEY: On all match · On bench · Subbed or sent off (Counting game) · Subbed or sent off (playing less than 70 minutes) · Subbed on from bench (Counting Game) · Subbed on (playing less than 70 minutes) · Subbed on and then subbed or sent off (Counting Game) · Subbed on and then subbed or sent off (playing less than 70 minutes) · Not in 16

GILLINGHAM

Final Position: **22nd**

NICKNAME: THE GILLS

KEY: Won, Drawn, Lost

							Attendance
1	div1	Ipswich	A	L	1-2	Smith 24	23,130
2	div1	Leeds	H	W	2-1	Byfield 4; Roberts 45	10,739
3	div1	Preston	H	W	2-1	Byfield 16; Roberts 78	7,073
4	div1	Stoke	A	L	0-2		13,234
5	ccr1	Northampton	H	L	1-2	Sidibe 56	3,108
6	div1	QPR	H	L	0-1		7,391
7	div1	Burnley	A	W	2-1	Roberts 5; Byfield 69	11,574
8	div1	Sunderland	H	L	0-4		8,775
9	div1	Coventry	A	D	2-2	Agyemang 65,76	11,966
10	div1	Reading	A	L	1-3	Byfield 55	13,867
11	div1	Brighton	H	L	0-1		8,365
12	div1	Leicester	H	L	0-2		6,089
13	div1	Plymouth	A	L	1-2	Henderson 47	13,665
14	div1	Sheff Utd	H	L	1-3	Bromby 74 og	6,964
15	div1	Millwall	A	L	1-2	Nowland 47	10,722
16	div1	West Ham	A	L	1-3	Byfield 45	25,247
17	div1	Wolverhampton	H	W	1-0	Jarvis 18	9,112
18	div1	Watford	H	D	0-0		7,009
19	div1	Sheff Utd	A	D	0-0		16,598
20	div1	Derby	H	L	0-2		8,015
21	div1	Crewe	A	L	1-4	Henderson 73	6,128
22	div1	Nottm Forest	H	W	2-1	Henderson 76 pen; Johnson, T 82	8,784
23	div1	Cardiff	A	L	1-3	Johnson, T 33	10,623
24	div1	Wigan	A	L	0-2		8,451
25	div1	Rotherham	H	W	3-1	Hope 70; Jarvis 80; Vernazza 90 og	8,576
26	div1	Brighton	A	L	1-2	Crofts 34	6,420
27	div1	Coventry	H	W	3-1	Byfield 15; Cox 48,49	8,734
28	div1	Reading	H	D	0-0		8,570
29	div1	Sunderland	A	D	1-1	Henderson 15	27,147
30	facr3	Portsmouth	A	L	0-1		14,252
31	div1	Plymouth	H	W	1-0	Crofts 61	8,451
32	div1	Leicester	A	L	0-2		23,457
33	div1	Watford	A	L	0-2		15,188
34	div1	Millwall	H	D	0-0		9,127
35	div1	Wolverhampton	A	D	2-2	Henderson 55; Flynn 90	24,949
36	div1	West Ham	H	L	0-1		9,510
37	div1	Wigan	H	W	2-1	Henderson 53,65	7,209
38	div1	Rotherham	A	W	3-1	Flynn 26; Sidibe 72; Henderson 82	4,367
39	div1	Leeds	A	D	1-1	Hope 43	27,995
40	div1	Stoke	H	W	2-1	McEveley 2; Smith 70	7,766
41	div1	Ipswich	H	D	0-0		9,311
42	div1	Preston	A	D	1-1	Smith 90	15,054
43	div1	QPR	A	D	1-1	Flynn 17	16,431
44	div1	Burnley	H	W	1-0	Henderson 56	9,447
45	div1	Crewe	H	D	1-1	Southall 80	10,315
46	div1	Derby	A	L	0-2		27,481
47	div1	Cardiff	H	D	1-1	Jarvis 72	10,810
48	div1	Nottm Forest	A	D	2-2	Melville 61 og; Sidibe 77	24,800

KEY PLAYERS - GOALSCORERS

Darius Henderson

Goals in the League	9
Goals in all competitions	9
Contribution to Attacking Power Average number of minutes between League team goals while on pitch	104
Player Strike Rate Average number of minutes between League goals scored by player	255
Club Strike Rate Average number of minutes between League goals scored by club	92

	PLAYER	GOALS LGE	GOALS ALL	POWER	S RATE
1	Darius Henderson	9	9	104	255 mins
2	Darren Byfield	6	6	92	401 mins
3	Michael Flynn	3	3	109	437 mins
4	Andrew Crofts	2	2	124	994 mins
5	Mamady Sidibe	2	3	70	1062 mins

KEY PLAYERS - MIDFIELDERS

Michael Flynn

Goals in the League	3
Goals in all competitions	3
Defensive Rating Average number of mins between League goals conceded while on the pitch	94
Contribution to Attacking Power Average number of minutes between League team goals while on pitch	109
Scoring Difference Defensive Rating minus Contribution to Attacking Power	-15

	PLAYER	GOALS LGE	GOALS ALL	DEF RATE	ATT POWER	SCORE DIFF
1	Michael Flynn	3	3	94	109	-15 mins
2	Nicky Southall	1	1	67	86	-19 mins
3	Paul Smith	3	3	63	89	-26 mins
4	Daniel Spiller	0	0	45	90	-45 mins
5	Andrew Crofts	2	2	71	124	-53 mins

KEY PLAYERS - DEFENDERS

Richard Rose

Goals Conceded in League	21
Goals Conceded in all competitions	24
Clean Sheets In games when player was on pitch for at least 70 minutes	5
Defensive Rating Ave number of mins between League goals conceded while on the pitch	70
Club Defensive Rating Average number of mins between League goals conceded by the club this season	63

	PLAYER	CON LGE	CON ALL	CLN SHEETS	DEF RATE
1	Richard Rose	21	24	5	70 mins
2	Barry Ashby	28	30	2	69 mins
3	Nayron Nosworthy	49	49	7	66 mins
4	Ian Cox	41	44	5	65 mins
5	Chris Hope	51	52	6	59 mins

MONTHLY POINTS TALLY

AUGUST	9	50%
SEPTEMBER	1	7%
OCTOBER	3	20%
NOVEMBER	5	33%
DECEMBER	6	40%
JANUARY	5	42%
FEBRUARY	5	33%
MARCH	8	67%
APRIL	7	39%
MAY	1	33%

GOALS

	PLAYER	LGE	FAC	LC	Oth	TOT
1	Henderson	9	0	0	0	9
2	Byfield	6	0	0	0	6
3	Smith	3	0	0	0	3
4	Sidibe	2	0	1	0	3
5	Flynn	3	0	0	0	3
6	Jarvis	3	0	0	0	3
7	Roberts	3	0	0	0	3
8	Crofts	2	0	0	0	2
9	Hope	2	0	0	0	2
10	Cox	2	0	0	0	2
11	Johnson	2	0	0	0	2
	Other	8	0	0	0	8
	TOTAL	45	0	1	0	46

KEY GOALKEEPER

Jason Brown

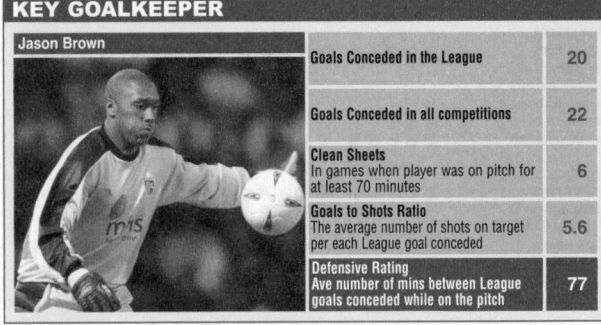

Goals Conceded in the League	20
Goals Conceded in all competitions	22
Clean Sheets In games when player was on pitch for at least 70 minutes	6
Goals to Shots Ratio The average number of shots on target per each League goal conceded	5.6
Defensive Rating Ave number of mins between League goals conceded while on the pitch	77

DISCIPLINARY RECORDS

	PLAYER	YELLOW	RED	AVE
1	Johnson, L	3	0	183
2	Hills	6	1	236
3	Roberts	4	0	249
4	Henderson	7	1	286
5	Hessenthaler	4	0	293
6	McEveley	3	0	299
7	Douglas	3	0	300
8	Cox	6	1	379
9	Byfield	5	0	481
10	Southall	4	1	552
11	Nosworthy	5	0	643
12	Ashby	3	0	645
13	Flynn	2	0	656
	Other	9	0	
	TOTAL	64	4	

TOP POINT EARNERS

	PLAYER	GAMES	AV PTS
1	Michael Flynn	12	1.50
2	Mamady Sidibe	19	1.42
3	Barry Ashby	21	1.29
4	Andrew Crofts	20	1.20
5	Richard Rose	16	1.19
6	John Hills	17	1.18
7	Nicky Southall	29	1.14
8	Paul Smith	40	1.13
9	Chris Hope	33	1.12
10	Steve Banks	26	1.12
	CLUB AVERAGE:		1.09

LEAGUE APPEARANCES GOALS AND BOOKINGS

	AGE (on 01/07/05)	IN NAMED 16	APPEARANCES	COUNTING GAMES	MINUTES ON PITCH	LEAGUE GOALS	Yellow	Red
Goalkeepers								
Steve Banks	33	42	26	26	2328	0	0	0
Bertrand Bossu	24	14	1	0	12	0	0	0
Jason Brown	23	33	17	17	1530	0	1	0
Paul Gallacher	25	3	3	3	270	0	0	0
Defenders								
Barry Ashby	34	24	22	21	1936	0	3	0
Dean Beckwith	21	9	1	0	8	0	0	0
Ian Cox	34	37	31	30	2655	2	6	1
John Hills	27	33	23	17	1655	0	6	1
Chris Hope	32	37	37	33	3018	2	2	0
James McEveley	19	10	10	10	899	1	3	0
Nayron Nosworthy	24	37	37	35	3217	0	5	0
Richard Rose	22	22	18	16	1480	0	0	0
Midfielders								
Andrew Crofts	21	36	26	20	1988	2	2	0
Jonathan Douglas	23	10	10	10	900	0	3	0
Michael Flynn	24	16	16	12	1312	3	2	0
Andy Hessenthaler	39	21	17	11	1175	0	4	0
Leon Johnson	24	20	8	5	550	0	3	0
Dean Marney	21	4	3	3	251	0	1	0
David Perpetuini	26	5	3	3	260	0	0	0
Alan Pouton	28	16	12	6	691	0	1	0
John Robinson	33	5	5	2	288	0	0	0
Mark Saunders	34	3	3	2	184	0	0	0
Paul Smith	33	41	41	40	3645	3	1	0
Nicky Southall	33	33	33	29	2762	1	4	1
Daniel Spiller	24	24	22	18	1709	0	1	0
Forwards								
Patrick Agyemang	24	15	13	5	740	2	0	0
Matt Bodkin	18	6	2	0	35	0	0	0
Darren Byfield	28	39	38	20	2406	6	5	0
Darius Henderson	23	33	32	22	2295	9	7	1
Matthew Jarvis	19	37	30	9	1464	3	0	0
Tommy Johnson	34	8	8	2	315	2	2	0
Adam Nowland	24	3	3	3	270	1	2	0
Iwan Roberts	37	22	20	8	996	3	4	0
Mamady Sidibe	25	37	35	19	2124	2	1	0

TEAM OF THE SEASON

D
Richard Rose
CG: 16 DR: 70
M
Nicky Southall
CG: 29 SD: -19
D
Barry Ashby
CG: 21 DR: 69
M
Paul Smith
CG: 40 SD: -26
F
Darren Byfield
CG: 20 SR: 401
G
Jason Brown
CG: 17 DR: 77
D
Nayron Nosworthy
CG: 35 DR: 66
M
Daniel Spiller
CG: 18 SD: -45
F
Darius Henderson
CG: 22 SR: 255
D
Ian Cox
CG: 30 DR: 65
M
Michael Flynn
CG: 12 SD: -15

SQUAD APPEARANCES

Match	1	2	3	4	5	6	7	8	9	10	11	12	13	14	15	16	17	18	19	20	21	22	23	24	25	26	27	28	29	30	31	32	33	34	35	36	37	38	39	40	41	42	43	44	45	46	47	48
Venue	A	H	H	A	H	H	A	H	A	A	H	H	A	H	A	A	H	H	A	H	A	H	A	A	H	A	H	H	A	A	H	A	A	H	A	H	H	A	A	H	H	A	A	H	H	A	H	A
Competition	L	L	L	L	W	L	L	L	L	L	L	L	L	L	L	L	L	L	L	L	L	L	L	L	L	L	L	L	L	F	L	L	L	L	L	L	L	L	L	L	L	L	L	L	L	L	L	L
Result	L	W	W	L	L	L	W	L	D	L	L	L	L	L	L	L	W	D	D	L	L	W	L	L	W	L	W	D	D	L	W	L	L	D	D	L	W	W	D	W	D	D	D	W	D	L	D	D

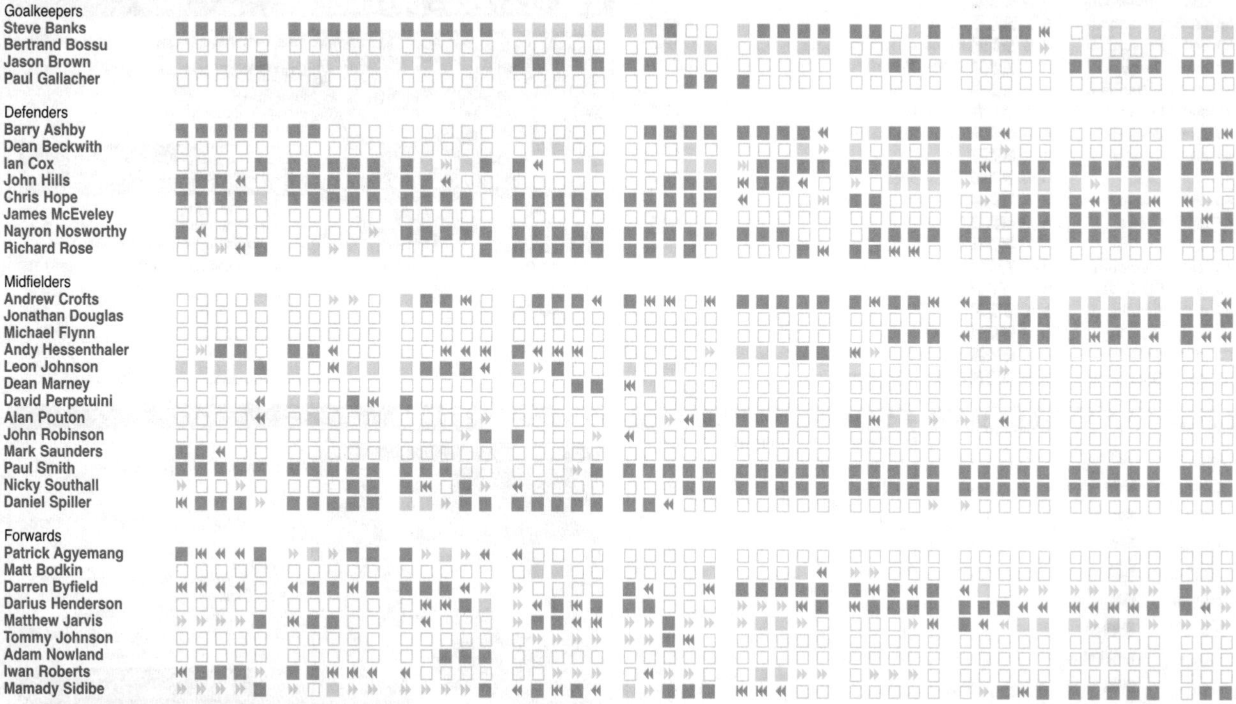

Goalkeepers
Steve Banks
Bertrand Bossu
Jason Brown
Paul Gallacher
Defenders
Barry Ashby
Dean Beckwith
Ian Cox
John Hills
Chris Hope
James McEveley
Nayron Nosworthy
Richard Rose
Midfielders
Andrew Crofts
Jonathan Douglas
Michael Flynn
Andy Hessenthaler
Leon Johnson
Dean Marney
David Perpetuini
Alan Pouton
John Robinson
Mark Saunders
Paul Smith
Nicky Southall
Daniel Spiller
Forwards
Patrick Agyemang
Matt Bodkin
Darren Byfield
Darius Henderson
Matthew Jarvis
Tommy Johnson
Adam Nowland
Iwan Roberts
Mamady Sidibe

KEY: On all match · On bench · Subbed or sent off (Counting game) · Subbed or sent off (playing less than 70 minutes) · Subbed on from bench (Counting Game) · Subbed on (playing less than 70 minutes) · Subbed on and then subbed or sent off (Counting Game) · Subbed on and then subbed or sent off (playing less than 70 minutes) · Not in 16

NOTTINGHAM FOREST

Final Position: **23rd**

NICKNAME: THE REDS

KEY: Won Drawn Lost

No	Comp	Opponent	H/A	Res	Score	Scorers	Attendance
1	div1	Wigan	A	D	1-1	Taylor 55	12,035
2	div1	Ipswich	H	D	1-1	Evans 25	21,125
3	div1	Crewe	H	D	2-2	Taylor 39; King 71	24,201
4	div1	Leeds	A	D	1-1	Reid 78 pen	31,808
5	ccR1	Scunthorpe	H	W	2-0	Taylor 36; King 78	7,344
6	div1	Coventry	H	L	1-4	Johnson 74	23,041
7	div1	Plymouth	A	L	2-3	Jess 44,80	17,538
8	div1	Cardiff	H	D	0-0		21,607
9	div1	Sunderland	A	L	0-2		23,540
10	div1	Stoke	A	D	0-0		21,115
11	ccR2	Rotherham	H	W	2-1	Taylor 17,94	11,168
12	div1	West Ham	H	W	2-1	Evans 84; King 90	25,615
13	div1	Brighton	H	L	0-1		20,109
14	div1	Millwall	A	L	0-1		11,233
15	div1	Wolverhampton	H	W	1-0	Reid 42	21,865
16	div1	Sheff Utd	A	D	1-1	Johnson 84	19,445
17	div1	Preston	A	L	2-3	King 78,80	12,439
18	ccR3	Doncaster	A	W	2-0	King 33; Perch 63	9,261
19	div1	Watford	H	L	1-2	Reid 45	24,473
20	div1	Rotherham	H	D	2-2	Johnson 52; King 63 pen	21,619
21	div1	Wolverhampton	A	L	1-2	Johnson 25	27,605
22	ccR4	Fulham	H	L	2-4	King 71; Reid 104	9,252
23	div1	Burnley	A	L	0-1		11,622
24	div1	Reading	H	W	1-0	Taylor 26	21,138
25	div1	Gillingham	A	L	1-2	Taylor 14	8,784
26	div1	QPR	H	W	2-1	Reid 15; Lester 58	26,099
27	div1	Derby	A	L	0-3		30,793
28	div1	Leicester	H	D	1-1	Dawson 57	21,415
29	div1	West Ham	A	L	2-3	Johnson 65,68	32,270
30	div1	Sunderland	H	L	1-2	Reid 55	27,457
31	div1	Stoke	H	W	1-0	Bopp 68	22,051
32	div1	Cardiff	A	L	0-3		13,545
33	facr3	QPR	A	W	3-0	Reid 24; Commons 25; Folly 82	11,140
34	div1	Millwall	H	L	1-2	Commons 87	25,949
35	div1	Brighton	A	D	0-0		6,704
36	facr4	Peterborough	H	W	1-0	King 10	16,774
37	div1	Rotherham	A	D	0-0		8,448
38	facr5	Tottenham	A	D	1-1	Taylor 56	35,640
39	div1	Preston	H	W	2-0	Evans 77; Commons 82	19,209
40	div1	Derby	H	D	2-2	Evans 36 pen; Taylor 69	26,160
41	facr5r	Tottenham	H	L	0-3		28,062
42	div1	Leicester	A	W	1-0	Taylor 41	27,277
43	div1	Watford	A	W	2-0	Commons 45,79	12,118
44	div1	Ipswich	A	L	0-6		25,765
45	div1	Leeds	H	D	0-0		25,101
46	div1	Wigan	H	D	1-1	Taylor 85	24,008
47	div1	Crewe	A	D	1-1	Dobie 37	8,458
48	div1	Coventry	A	L	0-2		22,221
49	div1	Plymouth	H	L	0-3		28,887
50	div1	Sheff Utd	H	D	1-1	Commons 47	21,903
51	div1	Reading	A	L	0-1		17,905
52	div1	Burnley	H	W	1-0	Commons 70	24,165
53	div1	QPR	A	L	1-2	Bopp 77	17,834
54	div1	Gillingham	H	D	2-2	Morgan 29; Bopp 85	24,800

KEY PLAYERS - GOALSCORERS

Kristian Commons

CapitalOne

Goals in the League	6
Goals in all competitions	7
Contribution to Attacking Power Average number of minutes between League team goals while on pitch	89
Player Strike Rate Average number of minutes between League goals scored by player	326
Club Strike Rate Average number of minutes between League goals scored by club	99

	PLAYER	GOALS LGE	GOALS ALL	POWER	S RATE
1	Kristian Commons	6	7	89	326 mins
2	Marlon King	5	9	87	349 mins
3	David Johnson	6	6	84	366 mins
4	Gareth Taylor	7	11	110	426 mins
5	Andrew Reid	5	7	101	443 mins

KEY PLAYERS - MIDFIELDERS

Kristian Commons

CapitalOne

Goals in the League	6
Goals in all competitions	7
Defensive Rating Average number of mins between League goals conceded while on the pitch	70
Contribution to Attacking Power Average number of minutes between League team goals while on pitch	89
Scoring Difference Defensive Rating minus Contribution to Attacking Power	-19

	PLAYER	GOALS LGE	GOALS ALL	DEF RATE	ATT POWER	SCORE DIFF
1	Kristian Commons	6	7	70	89	-19 mins
2	Paul Evans	4	4	62	97	-35 mins
3	Andrew Reid	5	7	62	101	-39 mins
4	Andrew Impey	0	0	55	140	-85 mins

KEY PLAYERS - DEFENDERS

James Perch

CapitalOne

Goals Conceded in League	20
Goals Conceded in all competitions	27
Clean Sheets In games when player was on pitch for at least 70 minutes	4
Defensive Rating Ave number of mins between League goals conceded while on the pitch	78
Club Defensive Rating Average number of mins between League goals conceded by the club this season	63

	PLAYER	CON LGE	CON ALL	CLN SHEETS	DEF RATE
1	James Perch	20	27	4	78 mins
2	John Thompson	18	24	3	72 mins
3	Chris Doig	28	33	8	66 mins
4	Alan Rogers	41	47	7	65 mins
5	Wes Morgan	60	69	12	64 mins

MONTHLY POINTS TALLY

Month	Points	%
AUGUST	4	22%
SEPTEMBER	5	33%
OCTOBER	4	27%
NOVEMBER	4	27%
DECEMBER	4	27%
JANUARY	4	33%
FEBRUARY	5	56%
MARCH	8	53%
APRIL	5	24%
MAY	1	33%

GOALS

	PLAYER	LGE	FAC	LC	Oth	TOT
1	Taylor	7	1	3	0	11
2	King	5	1	3	0	9
3	Commons	6	1	0	0	7
4	Reid	5	1	1	0	7
5	Johnson	6	0	0	0	6
6	Evans	4	0	0	0	4
7	Bopp	3	0	0	0	3
8	Jess	2	0	0	0	2
9	Perch	0	0	1	0	1
10	Dawson	1	0	0	0	1
11	Folly	0	1	0	0	1
	Other	3	0	0	0	3
	TOTAL	42	5	8	0	55

KEY GOALKEEPER

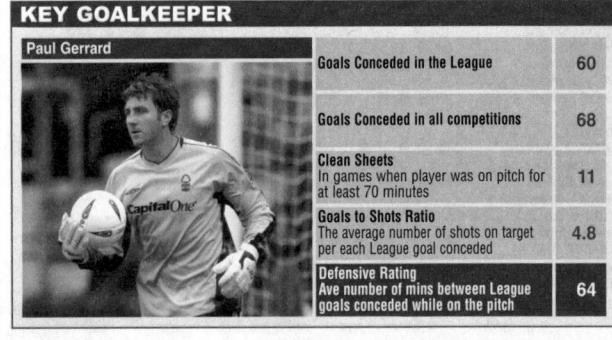

Paul Gerrard

CapitalOne

Goals Conceded in the League	60
Goals Conceded in all competitions	68
Clean Sheets In games when player was on pitch for at least 70 minutes	11
Goals to Shots Ratio The average number of shots on target per each League goal conceded	4.8
Defensive Rating Ave number of mins between League goals conceded while on the pitch	64

DISCIPLINARY RECORDS

	PLAYER	YELLOW	RED	AVE
1	Powell	6	1	120
2	Impey	7	1	192
3	Hjelde	4	1	216
4	Dawson	5	0	234
5	Harris	2	0	235
6	Reid	8	1	246
7	Thompson	5	0	260
8	Derry	2	0	315
9	Evans	9	0	344
10	Louis-Jean	5	0	372
11	Taylor	6	2	372
12	Commons	5	0	391
13	Robertson	2	1	402
	Other	21	1	
	TOTAL	87	8	

TOP POINT EARNERS

	PLAYER	GAMES	AV PTS
1	Andy Melville	13	1.23
2	Gareth Taylor	32	1.16
3	Jon Olav Hjelde	12	1.08
4	James Perch	15	1.07
5	Kristian Commons	17	1.06
6	Chris Doig	20	1.05
7	John Thompson	13	1.00
8	Wes Morgan	42	0.98
9	Alan Rogers	27	0.96
10	Paul Gerrard	43	0.93
	CLUB AVERAGE:		0.96

LEAGUE APPEARANCES GOALS AND BOOKINGS

	AGE (on 01/07/05)	IN NAMED 16	APPEARANCES	COUNTING GAMES	MINUTES ON PITCH	LEAGUE GOALS	Yellow	Red
Goalkeepers								
Colin Doyle	19	25	3	2	199	0	0	0
Paul Gerrard	32	43	43	43	3851	0	6	1
Barry Roche	23	21	1	1	90	0	0	0
Defenders								
John Curtis	26	11	11	10	910	0	0	0
Michael Dawson	21	14	14	13	1173	1	5	0
Chris Doig	24	30	21	20	1840	0	1	0
Jon Olav Hjelde	32	20	14	12	1084	0	4	1
Matthieu Louis-Jean	29	25	25	20	1861	0	5	0
Andy Melville	36	13	13	13	1150	0	0	0
Wes Morgan	21	43	43	42	3825	1	4	0
James Perch	19	28	22	15	1554	0	1	0
Gregor Robertson	21	32	20	9	1208	0	2	1
Alan Rogers	28	34	33	27	2662	0	4	0
John Thompson	24	25	20	13	1301	0	5	0
Des Walker	39	1	1	0	16	0	0	0
Midfielders								
Eugen Bopp	21	23	18	4	710	3	0	0
Kristian Commons	21	37	30	17	1955	6	5	0
Shaun Derry	27	7	7	7	630	0	2	0
Paul Evans	30	39	39	30	3099	4	9	0
Yoann Folly	20	2	1	0	35	0	0	0
David Friio	32	5	5	3	378	0	0	0
Ross Gardner	19	23	14	7	848	0	2	0
Andrew Impey	33	22	20	14	1537	0	7	1
Eoin Jess	34	21	20	10	1281	2	1	0
Darryl Powell	28	12	11	8	844	0	6	1
Andrew Reid	22	25	25	24	2215	5	8	1
Forwards								
Scott Dobie	26	12	12	8	929	1	1	0
Neil Harris	27	18	13	2	471	0	2	0
Kevin James	25	10	7	1	217	0	0	0
David Johnson	28	32	31	22	2196	6	1	0
Marlon King	25	30	26	17	1747	5	0	0
Jack Lester	29	3	3	2	229	1	1	0
Adam Nowland	24	6	5	3	316	0	0	0
Gareth Taylor	32	36	36	32	2980	7	6	2
Craig Westcarr	20	1	1	0	7	0	0	0

TEAM OF THE SEASON

Position	Player	Stats
G	Paul Gerrard	CG: 43 DR: 64
D	James Perch	CG: 15 DR: 78
D	John Thompson	CG: 13 DR: 72
D	Chris Doig	CG: 20 DR: 66
D	Alan Rogers	CG: 27 DR: 65
M	Kristian Commons	CG: 17 SD: -19
M	Paul Evans	CG: 30 SD: -35
M	Andrew Reid	CG: 24 SD: -39
M	Andrew Impey	CG: 14 SD: -85
F	Marlon King	CG: 17 SR: 349
F	David Johnson	CG: 22 SR: 366

SQUAD APPEARANCES

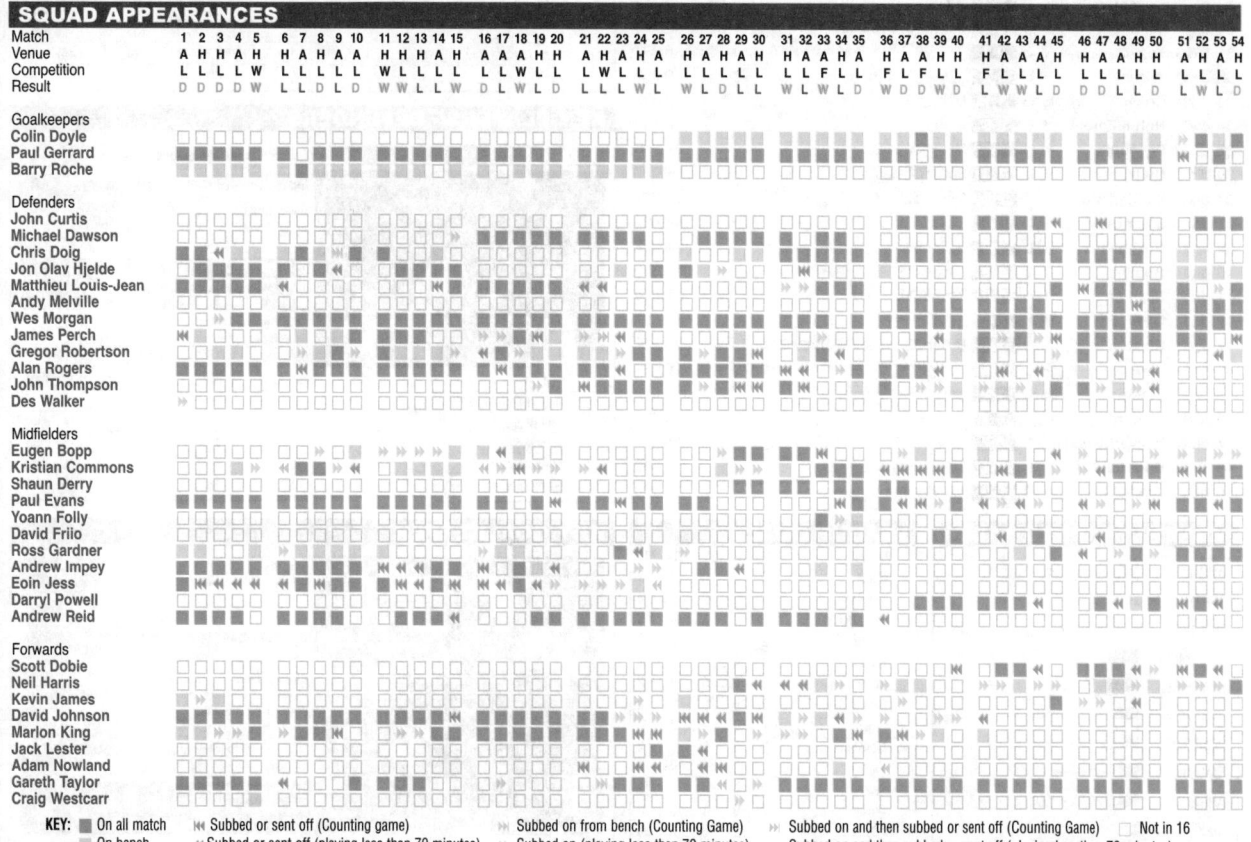

Match	1	2	3	4	5	6	7	8	9	10	11	12	13	14	15	16	17	18	19	20	21	22	23	24	25	26	27	28	29	30	31	32	33	34	35	36	37	38	39	40	41	42	43	44	45	46	47	48	49	50	51	52	53	54
Venue	A	H	H	A	H	H	A	H	A	A	H	H	H	A	H	A	A	A	H	H	A	H	A	H	A	H	A	H	A	H	H	A	A	H	A	H	A	A	H	H	H	A	A	A	H	H	A	A	H	H	A	H	A	H
Competition	L	L	L	L	W	L	L	L	L	L	W	L	L	L	L	L	L	W	L	L	L	W	L	L	L	L	L	L	L	L	L	L	F	L	L	F	L	F	L	L	F	L	L	L	L	L	L	L	L	L	L	L	L	L
Result	D	D	D	D	W	L	L	D	L	D	W	W	L	L	W	D	L	W	L	D	L	L	L	W	L	W	L	D	L	L	W	L	W	L	D	W	D	D	W	D	L	W	W	L	D	D	D	L	L	D	L	W	L	D

Goalkeepers
Colin Doyle
Paul Gerrard
Barry Roche

Defenders
John Curtis
Michael Dawson
Chris Doig
Jon Olav Hjelde
Matthieu Louis-Jean
Andy Melville
Wes Morgan
James Perch
Gregor Robertson
Alan Rogers
John Thompson
Des Walker

Midfielders
Eugen Bopp
Kristian Commons
Shaun Derry
Paul Evans
Yoann Folly
David Friio
Ross Gardner
Andrew Impey
Eoin Jess
Darryl Powell
Andrew Reid

Forwards
Scott Dobie
Neil Harris
Kevin James
David Johnson
Marlon King
Jack Lester
Adam Nowland
Gareth Taylor
Craig Westcarr

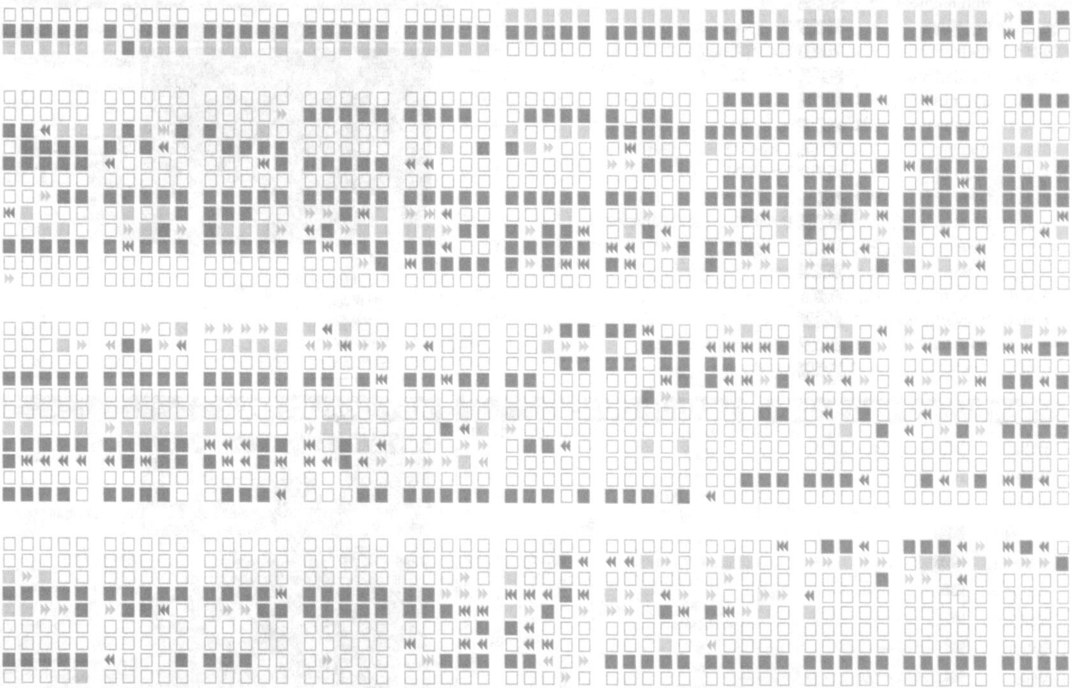

KEY: On all match · On bench · Subbed or sent off (Counting game) · Subbed or sent off (playing less than 70 minutes) · Subbed on from bench (Counting Game) · Subbed on (playing less than 70 minutes) · Subbed on and then subbed or sent off (Counting Game) · Subbed on and then subbed or sent off (playing less than 70 minutes) · Not in 16

ROTHERHAM UNITED

Final Position: **24th**

NICKNAME: THE MERRY MILLERS   KEY: ☐ Won ☐ Drawn ☐ Lost

							Attendance
1	div1	QPR	A	D	1-1	Shaw 15	14,547
2	div1	Burnley	H	D	0-0		6,243
3	div1	Stoke	H	D	1-1	Shaw 56	5,925
4	div1	Reading	A	L	0-1		11,404
5	ccr1	Chesterfield	H	W	2-1	Proctor 33; Barker, R 83	3,845
6	div1	Ipswich	H	L	0-2		5,504
7	div1	Preston	A	L	0-2		11,439
8	div1	Leicester	H	L	0-2		6,272
9	div1	West Ham	A	L	0-1		26,233
10	div1	Coventry	A	D	0-0		13,834
11	ccr2	Nottm Forest	A	L	1-2	Sedgwick 9	11,168
12	div1	Millwall	H	D	1-1	Sedgwick 87	5,062
13	div1	Crewe	H	L	2-3	Burchill 17; Barker, S 87	4,498
14	div1	Wigan	A	L	0-2		7,937
15	div1	Cardiff	A	L	0-2		11,004
16	div1	Plymouth	H	L	0-1		5,088
17	div1	Sunderland	H	L	0-1		6,026
18	div1	Derby	A	L	2-3	Swailes 8; Scott 34	25,096
19	div1	Nottm Forest	A	D	2-2	Sedgwick 19; Junior 27	21,619
20	div1	Cardiff	H	D	2-2	McLaren 76; Proctor 80	5,093
21	div1	Wolverhampton	H	L	1-2	McIntosh 36	6,693
22	div1	Watford	A	D	0-0		17,780
23	div1	Leeds	H	W	1-0	McIntosh 76	8,860
24	div1	Brighton	A	L	0-1		6,076
25	div1	Sheff Utd	H	D	2-2	Swailes 54; McIntosh 71	8,195
26	div1	Gillingham	A	L	1-3	Hoskins 89	8,576
27	div1	Leicester	A	W	1-0	Barker, S 37	27,014
28	div1	West Ham	H	D	2-2	Butler 13; McIntosh 37	7,769
29	div1	Coventry	H	L	1-2	Junior 39	5,742
30	div1	Millwall	A	W	2-1	Butler 43; Scott 69	11,725
31	facr3	Yeovil	H	L	0-3		5,397
32	div1	Wigan	H	L	0-2		9,050
33	div1	Crewe	A	D	1-1	Mullin 33	6,382
34	div1	Nottm Forest	H	D	0-0		8,448
35	div1	Plymouth	A	D	1-1	Monkhouse 26	14,798
36	div1	Derby	H	L	1-3	Butler 24 pen	7,937
37	div1	Sunderland	A	L	1-4	Monkhouse 77	22,267
38	div1	Sheff Utd	A	L	0-1		18,431
39	div1	Gillingham	H	L	1-3	Butler 56	4,367
40	div1	Burnley	A	L	1-2	Gilchrist 4	10,539
41	div1	Reading	H	W	1-0	Warne 90	3,804
42	div1	QPR	H	L	0-1		5,387
43	div1	Stoke	A	W	2-1	Butler 23; Noel-Williams 90 og	16,552
44	div1	Ipswich	A	L	3-4	Thorpe 26; Butler 67; McIntosh 79	26,017
45	div1	Preston	H	L	1-2	Hoskins 23	6,312
46	div1	Watford	H	L	0-1		5,438
47	div1	Wolverhampton	A	L	0-2		25,177
48	div1	Brighton	H	L	0-1		6,549
49	div1	Leeds	A	D	0-0		30,900

KEY PLAYERS - GOALSCORERS

Martin Butler

Goals in the League	6
Goals in all competitions	6
Contribution to Attacking Power Average number of minutes between League team goals while on pitch	95
Player Strike Rate Average number of minutes between League goals scored by player	303
Club Strike Rate Average number of minutes between League goals scored by club	118

	PLAYER	GOALS LGE	GOALS ALL	POWER	S RATE
1	Martin Butler	6	6	95	303 mins
2	Martin McIntosh	5	5	86	400 mins
3	Rob Scott	2	2	74	823 mins
4	Chris Sedgwick	2	3	168	840 mins
5	Shaun Barker	2	2	126	1330 mins

KEY PLAYERS - MIDFIELDERS

Jamal Campbell-Ryce

Goals in the League	0
Goals in all competitions	0
Defensive Rating Average number of mins between League goals conceded while on the pitch	55
Contribution to Attacking Power Average number of minutes between League team goals while on pitch	97
Scoring Difference Defensive Rating minus Contribution to Attacking Power	-42

	PLAYER	GOALS LGE	GOALS ALL	DEF RATE	ATT POWER	SCORE DIFF
1	Jamal Campbell-Ryce	0	0	55	97	-42 mins
2	Paul McLaren	1	1	59	102	-43 mins
3	Paolo Vernazza	0	0	43	106	-63 mins
4	John Mullin	1	1	67	134	-67 mins
5	Chris Sedgwick	2	3	62	168	-106 mins

KEY PLAYERS - DEFENDERS

Scott Minto

Goals Conceded in League	16
Goals Conceded in all competitions	18
Clean Sheets In games when player was on pitch for at least 70 minutes	3
Defensive Rating Ave number of mins between League goals conceded while on the pitch	74
Club Defensive Rating Average number of mins between League goals conceded by the club this season	60

	PLAYER	CON LGE	CON ALL	CLN SHEETS	DEF RATE
1	Scott Minto	16	18	3	74 mins
2	Phil Gilchrist	30	35	3	64 mins
3	Robbie Stockdale	38	41	4	62 mins
4	Martin McIntosh	33	36	5	61 mins
5	Shaun Barker	45	46	6	59 mins

MONTHLY POINTS TALLY

AUGUST	3	17%
SEPTEMBER	2	13%
OCTOBER	0	0%
NOVEMBER	6	40%
DECEMBER	5	33%
JANUARY	4	33%
FEBRUARY	2	13%
MARCH	3	25%
APRIL	3	17%
MAY	1	33%

LEAGUE GOALS

	PLAYER	LGE	FAC	LC	Oth	TOT
1	Butler	6	0	0	0	6
2	McIntosh	5	0	0	0	5
3	Sedgwick	2	0	1	0	3
4	Junior	2	0	0	0	2
5	Hoskins	2	0	0	0	2
6	Scott	2	0	0	0	2
7	Barker, S	2	0	0	0	2
8	Proctor	1	0	1	0	2
9	Monkhouse	2	0	0	0	2
10	Shaw	2	0	0	0	2
11	Swailes	2	0	0	0	2
	Other	7	0	1	0	8
	TOTAL	35	0	3	0	38

KEY GOALKEEPER

Mike Pollitt

Goals Conceded in the League	67
Goals Conceded in all competitions	73
Clean Sheets In games when player was on pitch for at least 70 minutes	8
Goals to Shots Ratio The average number of shots on target per each League goal conceded	4.8
Defensive Rating Ave number of mins between League goals conceded while on the pitch	60

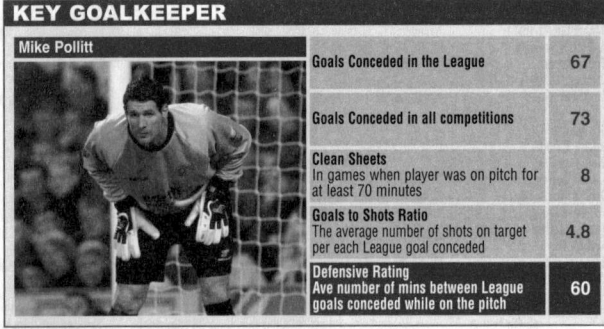

DISCIPLINARY RECORDS

	PLAYER	YELLOW	RED	AVE
1	Monkhouse	4	0	258
2	Junior	2	1	336
3	Campbell-Ryce	6	0	340
4	Swailes	8	0	403
5	Keane	2	0	405
6	Sedgwick	4	0	420
7	Barker	6	0	443
8	Butler	4	0	454
9	Scott	3	0	548
10	McLaren	5	0	550
11	Stockdale	4	0	592
12	Garner	2	0	652
13	McIntosh	3	0	666
	Other	16	0	
	TOTAL	69	1	

TOP POINT EARNERS

	PLAYER	GAMES	AV PTS
1	Jamal Campbell-Ryce	22	0.95
2	Martin Butler	20	0.85
3	Mike Proctor	12	0.83
4	Martin McIntosh	22	0.82
5	Rob Scott	15	0.80
6	Paul McLaren	30	0.77
7	Chris Swailes	35	0.69
8	Paul Hurst	38	0.66
9	Mike Pollitt	45	0.64
10	Shaun Barker	28	0.57
	CLUB AVERAGE:		0.63

LEAGUE APPEARANCES GOALS AND BOOKINGS

	AGE (on 01/07/05)	IN NAMED 16	APPEARANCES	COUNTING GAMES	MINUTES ON PITCH	LEAGUE GOALS	Yellow	Red
Goalkeepers								
Gary Montgomery	22	46	1	1	90	0	0	0
Mike Pollitt	33	46	45	45	4050	0	1	0
Defenders								
Shaun Barker	22	34	33	28	2659	2	6	0
Phil Gilchrist	31	32	24	20	1912	1	0	0
Paul Hurst	30	44	39	38	3428	0	5	0
Martin McIntosh	34	24	23	22	2000	5	3	0
Scott Minto	33	26	14	12	1187	0	0	0
Rob Scott	31	38	24	15	1646	2	3	0
Robbie Stockdale	25	27	27	26	2368	0	4	0
Chris Swailes	34	37	37	35	3230	2	8	0
Midfielders								
Jamal Campbell-Ryce	22	24	24	22	2041	0	6	0
Sam Duncum	-	2	2	1	97	0	0	0
Darren Garner	33	23	18	11	1305	0	2	0
Leandre Griffit	21	3	2	0	61	0	0	0
Michael Keane	22	10	10	8	810	0	2	0
Paul McLaren	28	35	33	30	2751	1	5	0
Andy Monkhouse	24	16	14	11	1035	2	4	0
John Mullin	29	35	31	23	2277	1	3	0
Chris Sedgwick	25	20	20	18	1680	2	4	0
Paolo Vernazza	25	42	27	14	1583	0	2	0
Forwards								
Richard Barker	30	19	17	14	1400	0	2	0
Mark Burchill	24	3	3	2	208	1	0	0
Martin Butler	30	21	21	20	1819	6	4	0
William Hoskins	18	26	22	4	773	2	1	0
Junior	28	12	12	11	1010	2	2	1
Marc Newsham	18	8	4	0	60	0	0	0
Mike Proctor	24	34	28	12	1554	1	2	0
Paul Shaw	31	9	9	8	782	2	0	0
Tony Thorpe	31	5	5	5	447	1	0	0
Paul Warne	32	32	24	11	1249	1	0	0

TEAM OF THE SEASON

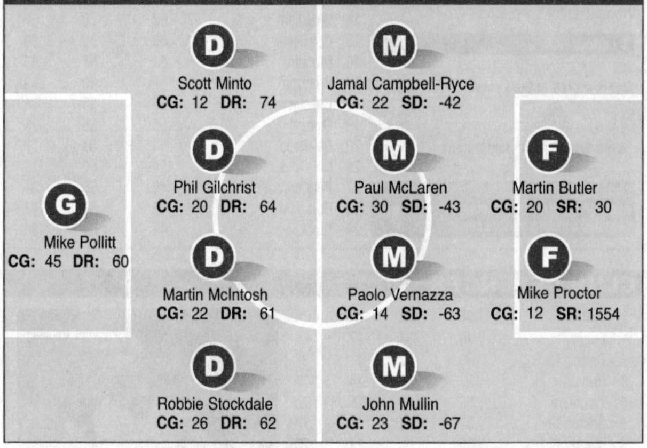

D
Scott Minto
CG: 12 DR: 74
D
Phil Gilchrist
CG: 20 DR: 64
D
Martin McIntosh
CG: 22 DR: 61
D
Robbie Stockdale
CG: 26 DR: 62
G
Mike Pollitt
CG: 45 DR: 60
M
Jamal Campbell-Ryce
CG: 22 SD: -42
M
Paul McLaren
CG: 30 SD: -43
M
Paolo Vernazza
CG: 14 SD: -63
M
John Mullin
CG: 23 SD: -67
F
Martin Butler
CG: 20 SR: 30
F
Mike Proctor
CG: 12 SR: 1554

SQUAD APPEARANCES

Match	1	2	3	4	5	6	7	8	9	10	11	12	13	14	15	16	17	18	19	20	21	22	23	24	25	26	27	28	29	30	31	32	33	34	35	36	37	38	39	40	41	42	43	44	45	46	47	48	49
Venue	A	H	H	A	H	H	A	H	A	A	A	H	H	A	A	H	H	A	A	H	H	A	H	A	H	A	A	H	H	A	H	H	A	H	A	H	A	A	H	A	H	H	A	A	H	H	A	H	A
Competition	L	L	L	L	W	L	L	L	L	L	W	L	L	L	L	L	L	L	L	L	L	L	L	L	L	L	L	L	L	L	F	L	L	L	L	L	L	L	L	L	L	L	L	L	L	L	L	L	L
Result	D	D	D	L	W	L	L	L	L	D	L	D	L	L	L	L	L	L	D	D	L	D	W	L	D	L	W	D	L	W	L	L	D	D	D	L	L	L	L	L	W	L	W	L	L	L	L	L	D

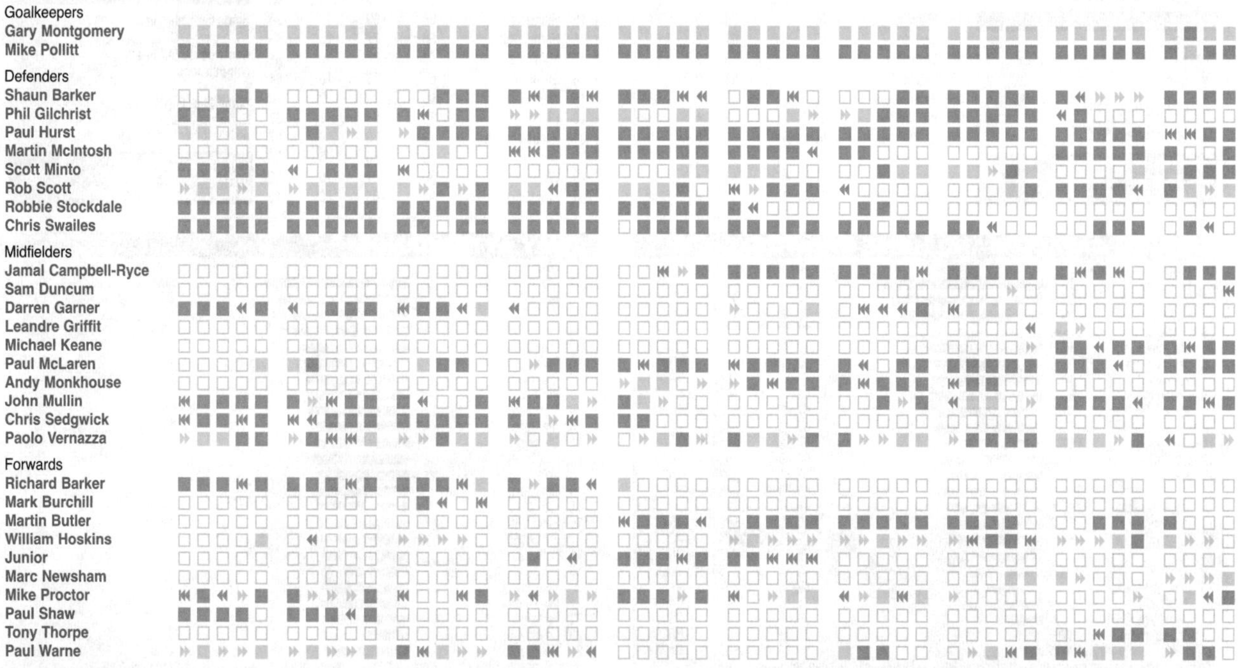

Goalkeepers
Gary Montgomery
Mike Pollitt
Defenders
Shaun Barker
Phil Gilchrist
Paul Hurst
Martin McIntosh
Scott Minto
Rob Scott
Robbie Stockdale
Chris Swailes
Midfielders
Jamal Campbell-Ryce
Sam Duncum
Darren Garner
Leandre Griffit
Michael Keane
Paul McLaren
Andy Monkhouse
John Mullin
Chris Sedgwick
Paolo Vernazza
Forwards
Richard Barker
Mark Burchill
Martin Butler
William Hoskins
Junior
Marc Newsham
Mike Proctor
Paul Shaw
Tony Thorpe
Paul Warne

KEY: ■ On all match | ■ On bench | ⏮ Subbed or sent off (Counting game) | « Subbed or sent off (playing less than 70 minutes) | ⏭ Subbed on from bench (Counting Game) | » Subbed on (playing less than 70 minutes) | ⏭ Subbed on and then subbed or sent off (Counting Game) | » Subbed on and then subbed or sent off (playing less than 70 minutes) | □ Not in 16

LEAGUE ONE ROUND-UP

FINAL LEAGUE TABLE

		HOME					AWAY					TOTAL			
	P	W	D	L	F	A	W	D	L	F	A	F	A	DIF	PTS
Luton	46	17	4	2	46	16	12	7	4	41	32	87	48	39	98
Hull City	46	16	5	2	42	17	10	3	10	38	36	80	53	27	86
Tranmere	46	14	5	4	43	23	8	8	7	30	32	73	55	18	79
Brentford	46	15	4	4	34	22	7	5	11	23	38	57	60	-3	75
Sheff Wed	46	10	6	7	34	28	9	9	5	43	31	77	59	18	72
Hartlepool	46	15	3	5	51	30	6	5	12	25	36	76	66	10	71
Bristol City	46	9	8	6	42	25	9	8	6	32	32	74	57	17	70
Bournemouth	46	9	7	7	40	30	11	3	9	37	34	77	64	13	70
Huddersfield	46	12	6	5	42	28	8	4	11	32	37	74	65	9	70
Doncaster	46	10	11	2	35	20	6	7	10	30	40	65	60	5	66
Bradford	46	9	6	8	40	35	8	8	7	24	27	64	62	2	65
Swindon	46	12	5	6	40	30	5	7	11	26	38	66	68	-2	63
Barnsley	46	7	11	5	38	31	7	8	8	31	33	69	64	5	61
Walsall	46	11	7	5	40	28	5	5	13	25	41	65	69	-4	60
Colchester	46	8	6	9	27	23	6	11	6	33	27	60	50	10	59
Blackpool	46	8	7	8	28	30	7	5	11	26	29	54	59	-5	57
Chesterfield	46	9	8	6	32	28	5	7	11	23	34	55	62	-7	57
Port Vale	46	13	2	8	33	23	4	3	16	16	36	49	59	-10	56
Oldham	46	10	5	8	42	34	4	5	14	18	39	60	73	-13	52
MK Dons	46	8	10	5	33	28	4	5	14	21	40	54	68	-14	51
Torquay	46	8	5	10	27	36	4	10	9	28	43	55	79	-24	51
Wrexham	46	6	8	9	26	37	7	6	10	36	43	62	80	-18	43
Peterborough	46	5	6	12	27	35	4	6	13	22	38	49	73	-24	39
Stockport	46	3	4	16	26	46	3	4	16	23	52	49	98	-49	26

CLUB STRIKE FORCE

travel
extras

Howard; Luton's top scorer

1 Luton - 48

Goals scored in the League	87
Goals scored in all competions	96
Club Strike Rate (CSR) Average number of minutes between League goals scored	48

	CLUB	LGE	ALL	CSR
1	Luton	87	96	48
2	Hull City	80	89	52
3	Bournemouth	77	94	54
4	Hartlepool	76	92	54
5	Sheff Wed	77	86	54
6	Bristol City	74	79	56
7	Huddersfield	74	75	56
8	Tranmere	73	78	57
9	Barnsley	69	72	60
10	Swindon	66	72	63
11	Doncaster	65	74	64
12	Walsall	65	66	64
13	Bradford	64	65	65
14	Wrexham	62	70	67
15	Colchester	60	78	69
16	Oldham	60	68	69
17	Brentford	57	68	73
18	Chesterfield	55	56	75
19	Torquay	55	56	75
20	Blackpool	54	61	77
21	MK Dons	54	60	77
22	Peterborough	49	55	84
23	Port Vale	49	53	84
24	Stockport	49	54	84

CLUB DISCIPLINARY RECORDS

Windass; 13 cards for Bradford

1 Bradford

League Yellow	90
League Red	4
All Competitions Yellow	95
All Competitions Red	4
Cards Average in League Average number of minutes between a card being shown	44

	CLUB	LEAGUE		TOTAL		AVE
1	Bradford	90Y	4R	95Y	4R	44
2	Bristol City	83	2	90	2	49
3	Barnsley	77	6	81	6	50
4	Brentford	78	5	98	5	50
5	Oldham	78	1	83	1	52
6	Chesterfield	72	6	73	6	53
7	Huddersfield	72	6	73	6	53
8	Port Vale	70	5	71	5	55
9	Tranmere	71	4	78	5	55
10	Doncaster	69	4	72	4	57
11	MK Dons	71	1	80	2	58
12	Stockport	70	1	78	1	58
13	Torquay	70	2	71	2	58
14	Luton	65	4	75	4	60
15	Blackpool	65	3	70	3	61
16	Swindon	63	5	67	6	61
17	Wrexham	66	2	73	2	61
18	Colchester	58	3	67	3	68
19	Peterborough	59	2	66	3	68
20	Walsall	58	3	60	4	68
21	Sheff Wed	50	5	53	6	75
22	Hartlepool	50	1	57	3	81
23	Hull City	46	4	51	4	83
24	Bournemouth	36	3	41	3	106

CLUB DEFENCES

	CLUB	LGE	ALL	CS	CDR
1	Luton	48	54	17	86
2	Colchester	50	62	11	83
3	Hull City	53	59	14	78
4	Tranmere	55	61	15	75
5	Bristol City	57	61	15	73
6	Blackpool	59	66	11	70
7	Port Vale	59	64	11	70
8	Sheff Wed	59	67	14	70
9	Brentford	60	73	18	69
10	Doncaster	60	66	13	69
11	Bradford	62	65	11	67
12	Chesterfield	62	66	11	67
13	Barnsley	64	72	12	65
14	Bournemouth	64	77	12	65
15	Huddersfield	65	69	10	64
16	Hartlepool	66	77	10	63
17	MK Dons	68	74	9	61
18	Swindon	68	73	10	61
19	Walsall	69	72	9	60
20	Oldham	73	81	6	57
21	Peterborough	73	78	9	57
22	Torquay	79	85	8	52
23	Wrexham	80	87	6	52
24	Stockport	98	105	6	42

travel
extras

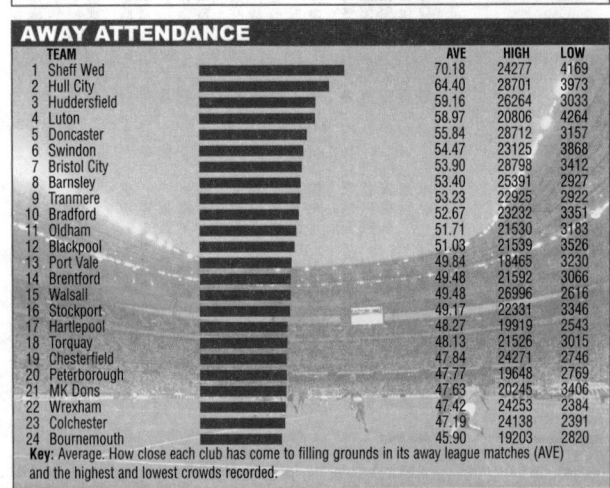

Foley; heading Luton's defensive table

1 Luton

Goals conceded in the League	48
Goals conceded in all competitions	54
Clean Sheets (CS) Number of league games where no goals were conceded	17
Club Defensive Rate (CDR) Average number of minutes between League goals conceded	86

STADIUM CAPACITY AND HOME CROWDS

	TEAM	CAPACITY	AVE	HIGH	LOW
1	Luton	9975	79.61	9500	6603
2	Bournemouth	9600	74.21	9058	5390
3	Hull City	25504	70.68	24277	14317
4	Hartlepool	7629	68.16	6520	4206
5	Blackpool	9000	67.02	8774	4179
6	Doncaster	10550	65.27	10131	5209
7	Torquay	6000	58.52	5347	2384
8	Chesterfield	8504	58.34	7831	3715
9	Sheff Wed	39859	57.95	28798	18465
10	Colchester	6200	57.00	4834	2616
11	Tranmere	16587	54.52	12684	7613
12	MK Dons	9000	54.40	7620	3015
13	Walsall	11300	53.81	8225	4966
14	Bristol City	21479	53.03	14852	8267
15	Huddersfield	24500	48.61	17292	9194
16	Brentford	12763	47.65	9604	4643
17	Oldham	13624	47.43	9645	4291
18	Stockport	11000	45.45	7473	3850
19	Barnsley	23009	42.50	19659	7466
20	Swindon	15728	37.10	8275	4484
21	Bradford	25136	35.16	15417	6409
22	Wrexham	15500	30.65	7833	2391
23	Peterborough	15314	28.35	7662	3048
24	Port Vale	23000	21.62	8671	3496

Key: Average. The percentage of each stadium filled in League games over the season (AVE), the stadium capacity and the highest and lowest crowds recorded.

AWAY ATTENDANCE

	TEAM	AVE	HIGH	LOW
1	Sheff Wed	70.18	24277	4169
2	Hull City	64.40	28701	3973
3	Huddersfield	59.16	26264	3033
4	Luton	58.97	20806	4264
5	Doncaster	55.84	28712	3157
6	Swindon	54.47	23125	3868
7	Bristol City	53.90	28798	3412
8	Barnsley	53.40	25391	2927
9	Tranmere	53.23	22925	2922
10	Bradford	52.67	23232	3351
11	Oldham	51.71	21530	3183
12	Blackpool	51.03	21539	3526
13	Port Vale	49.84	18465	3230
14	Brentford	49.48	21592	3066
15	Walsall	49.48	26996	2616
16	Stockport	49.17	22331	3346
17	Hartlepool	48.27	19919	2543
18	Torquay	48.13	21526	3015
19	Chesterfield	47.84	24271	2746
20	Peterborough	47.77	19648	2769
21	MK Dons	47.63	20245	3406
22	Wrexham	47.42	24253	2384
23	Colchester	47.19	24138	2391
24	Bournemouth	45.90	19203	2820

Key: Average. How close each club has come to filling grounds in its away league matches (AVE) and the highest and lowest crowds recorded.

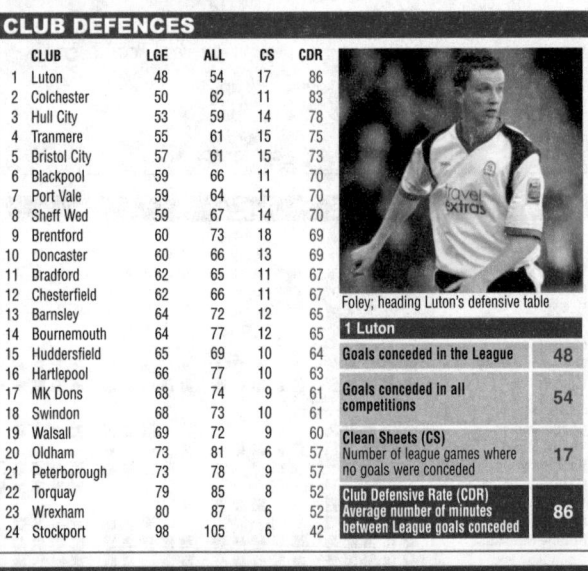

CHART-TOPPING MIDFIELDERS

1 Ross - Hartlepool	
Goals scored in the League	0
Defensive Rating Av number of mins between League goals conceded while on the pitch	104
Contribution to Attacking Power Average number of minutes between League team goals while on pitch	50
Scoring Difference Defensive Rating minus Contribution to Attacking Power	54

	PLAYER	CLUB	GOALS	DEF RATE	POWER	S DIFF
1	Ross	Hartlepool	0	104	50	54
2	Brkovic	Luton	15	100	49	51
3	Robinson	Luton	4	90	46	44
4	Underwood	Luton	5	86	44	42
5	France	Hull City	2	87	50	37
6	Green	Hull City	8	84	51	33
7	Nicholls	Luton	12	83	50	33
8	Ashbee	Hull City	1	81	51	30
9	Talbot	Brentford	1	101	73	28
10	McAteer	Tranmere	4	81	54	27
11	Danns	Colchester	11	96	70	26
12	Murray	Bristol City	8	77	52	25
13	Doherty	Bristol City	1	71	50	21
14	Wilkshire	Bristol City	9	75	55	20
15	Whelan	Sheff Wed	2	70	50	20

CHART-TOPPING GOALSCORERS

BONUS
ELECTRICAL

1 Elliot - Hull City	
Goals scored in the League (GL)	27
Goals scored in all competitions (GA)	28
Contribution to Attacking Power (AP) Average number of minutes between League team goals while on pitch	46
Player Strike Rate Average number of minutes between League goals scored by player	114
Club Strike Rate (CSR) Average minutes between League goals scored by club	52

	PLAYER	CLUB	GOALS: LGE	ALL	POWER	CSR	S RATE
1	Elliott	Hull City	27	28	46	52	114
2	Ugarte	Wrexham	16	16	55	67	124
3	Windass	Bradford	27	28	64	65	128
4	Abbott	Huddersfield	26	27	50	56	128
5	Fryatt	Walsall	15	15	60	64	144
6	Lita	Bristol City	24	27	56	56	153
7	Parkin	Swindon	23	23	62	63	160
8	Hayter	Bournemouth	19	22	51	54	171
9	Brooker	Bristol City	16	16	58	56	171
10	Matthews	Port Vale	11	11	67	84	171
11	MacLean	Sheff Wed	18	19	48	54	173
12	Boyd	Hartlepool	22	28	54	54	175
13	Taylor	Blackpool	12	14	74	77	179
14	Feeney	Stockport	15	17	72	84	179
15	Akinfenwa	Torquay	14	14	70	75	190

CHART-TOPPING DEFENDERS

1 Lee - Sheff Wed	
Goals Conceded in the League The number of League goals conceded while he was on the pitch	18
Goals Conceded in all competitions The number of goals conceded while he was on the pitch in all competitions	22
Clean Sheets In games when he played at least 70 mins	7
Defensive Rating Average number of minutes between League goals conceded while on pitch	97
Club Defensive Rating Average mins between League goals conceded by the club this season	70

	PLAYER	CLUB	CON: LGE	ALL	CS	CDR	DEF RATE
1	Lee	Sheff Wed	18	22	7	70	97
2	Pensee-Bilong	MK Dons	17	17	3	61	94
3	Walsh	Port Vale	21	22	7	70	93
4	Stockley	Colchester	34	45	10	83	89
5	Baldwin	Colchester	35	46	9	83	89
6	Foley	Luton	37	39	13	86	89
7	Davies	Luton	45	51	16	86	88
8	Halford	Colchester	45	55	11	83	87
9	Coid	Blackpool	34	41	9	70	86
10	"Edwards, R"	Blackpool	26	33	8	70	83
11	Davis	Luton	48	52	15	86	83
12	Coyne	Luton	42	48	14	86	83
13	Taylor	Tranmere	46	52	15	75	83
14	Delaney	Hull City	47	53	13	78	82
15	Clarke	Blackpool	42	45	10	70	81

CHART-TOPPING GOALKEEPERS

1 Beresford - Luton	
Counting Games League games when he played at least 70 minutes	38
Goals Conceded in the League The number of League goals conceded while he was on the pitch	35
Goals Conceded in all competitions The number of goals conceded while he was on the pitch in all competitions	41
Clean Sheets In games when he played at least 70 mins	15
Defensive Rating Average number of minutes between League goals conceded while on pitch	96

	PLAYER	CLUB	CG	CONC LGE	CONC ALL	CS	DEF RATE
1	Beresford	Luton	37	35	41	15	96
2	Goodlad	Port Vale	20	19	19	7	92
3	Davison	Colchester	33	33	41	8	90
4	Lucas	Sheff Wed	32	35	43	13	83
5	Achterberg	Tranmere	38	42	48	14	82
6	Myhill	Hull City	45	51	55	14	79
7	Baker	MK Dons	20	23	23	4	78
8	Phillips	Bristol City	46	57	61	15	73
9	Warrington	Doncaster	34	42	48	11	73
10	Jones, L	Blackpool	29	37	41	7	71
11	Turnbull	Barnsley	23	29	30	7	70
12	Konstantopoulos	Hartlepool	25	32	40	7	70
13	Nelson	Brentford	43	56	69	17	69
14	Henderson	Bradford	40	53	56	10	68
15	Moss, N	Bournemouth	46	64	77	12	65

PLAYER DISCIPLINARY RECORD

1 Mair - Stockport	
Cards Average mins between cards	132
League Yellow	7
League Red	0
TOTAL	7

	PLAYER		LY	LR	TOT	AVE
1	Mair	Stockport	7	0	7	132
2	Myers	Brentford	2	1	3	155
3	Priet	Doncaster	3	0	3	160
4	Lawrence	Brentford	5	0	5	161
5	Robinson, P	Torquay	6	0	6	180
6	Ravenhill	Doncaster	9	1	10	181
7	Armstrong	Wrexham	9	1	10	181
8	Doherty	Bristol City	12	0	12	183
9	Armstrong	Port Vale	3	0	3	187
10	Fagan	Colchester	11	1	12	190
11	Fowler	Huddersfield	4	1	5	192
12	Bruce	Oldham	4	0	4	195
13	Johnson	Oldham	5	1	6	195
14	McClenahan	MK Dons	3	0	3	213
15	McLeod	MK Dons	15	1	16	215
16	Eyre, J	Oldham	7	0	7	221
17	Sodje, E	Huddersfield	8	2	10	225
18	Branston	Sheff Wed	3	1	4	227
19	Sonner	Port Vale	5	0	5	228
20	Brown	Bristol City	5	0	5	229
21	Roper	Walsall	7	2	9	230
22	Price	Hull City	4	0	4	237
23	Gosling	Torquay	2	0	2	237
24	Edwards, P	Blackpool	8	0	8	241

TEAM OF THE SEASON

G
Beresford : Luton
CG: 37 DR: 96
D
Lee : Sheff Wed
CG: 17 DR: 97
D
Pensee-Bilong : MK Dons
CG: 17 DR: 94
D
Walsh : Port Vale
CG: 21 DR: 93
D
Stockley : Colchester
CG: 33 DR: 89
M
Ross : Hartlepool
CG: 19 SD: +54
M
Brkovic : Luton
CG: 37 SD: +51
M
France : Hull City
CG: 19 SD: +37
M
Talbot : Brentford
CG: 27 SD: +28
F
Elliot : Hull City
CG: 33 SR: 114
F
Ugarte : Wrexham
CG: 15 SR: 124

COCA-COLA LEAGUE ONE CHAMPIONS

LUTON TOWN

Final Position: **1st**

NICKNAME: THE HATTERS

KEY: ☐ Won ☐ Drawn ☐ Lost

							Attendance
1	lge1	Oldham	H	W	2-1	Howard 19; Underwood 65	6,634
2	lge1	Swindon	A	W	3-2	Nicholls 24 pen; Fallon 37 og; Howard 51	6,286
3	lge1	Barnsley	A	W	4-3	Howard 4; Vine 44; Brkovic 45; Robinson 66	10,057
4	lge1	Torquay	H	W	1-0	Howard 36	6,664
5	lge1	Blackpool	A	W	3-1	Howard 58; Brkovic 59,90	5,793
6	lge1	Bournemouth	H	W	1-0	Nicholls 81	7,404
7	lge1	Sheff Wed	A	D	0-0		20,806
8	ccr1	Boston	A	L	3-4	Lee 52 og; Nicholls 77 pen; Showunmi 90	2,631
9	lge1	Chesterfield	H	W	1-0	Vine 49	7,532
10	lge1	Stockport	A	W	3-1	Robinson 33; Vine 35; Brkovic 54	5,128
11	lge1	Peterborough	H	W	2-1	Vine 31; Underwood 57	7,694
12	lge1	Tranmere	A	D	1-1	Coyne 76	10,884
13	lge1	Hartlepool	H	W	3-0	Howard 36; Brkovic 51; McSheffrey 84	7,865
14	lge1	Huddersfield	H	L	1-2	Underwood 57	8,192
15	lge1	Walsall	A	L	0-2		5,963
16	lge1	Hull City	A	L	0-3		18,575
17	lge1	Bradford	H	W	4-0	Brkovic 14,69; Howard 33; Underwood 37	7,975
18	lge1	Wrexham	H	W	5-1	Robinson 13; Davis 17; O'Leary 22; Howard 44; Brkovic 62	7,144
19	facr1	Southend	A	W	3-0	Howard 12,15; Brkovic 33	6,683
20	lge1	MK Dons	A	W	4-1	Vine 8; Howard 45,66,83	7,620
21	lge1	Doncaster	H	D	1-1	Nicholls 60	8,142
22	facr2	Wycombe	A	W	3-0	Howard 20,80; Nicholls 70	4,767
23	lge1	Brentford	A	L	0-2		6,393
24	lge1	Port Vale	H	W	1-0	Brkovic 84	6,974
25	lge1	Bristol City	A	W	2-1	Coyne 34; Showunmi 90	13,414
26	lge1	Chesterfield	A	W	1-0	Showunmi 87	7,158
27	lge1	Colchester	H	D	2-2	Vine 37,48	8,806
28	lge1	Sheff Wed	H	D	1-1	Howard 47	9,500
29	lge1	Peterborough	A	D	2-2	Nicholls 54; Howard 85	7,662
30	facr3	Brentford	H	L	0-2		6,861
31	lge1	Stockport	H	W	3-0	Coyne 29; Howard 54; Nicholls 74 pen	6,603
32	lge1	Colchester	A	D	0-0		4,309
33	lge1	Tranmere	H	D	1-1	Nicholls 54 pen	8,594
34	lge1	Huddersfield	A	D	1-1	Brkovic 34	12,611
35	lge1	Hull City	H	W	1-0	Brkovic 89	9,500
36	lge1	Hartlepool	A	W	3-2	Coyne 21; Showunmi 58; Foley 64	5,542
37	lge1	Bradford	A	W	1-0	Vine 10	8,702
38	lge1	Walsall	H	W	1-0	Nicholls 88 pen	7,236
39	lge1	Port Vale	A	L	1-3	Foley 6	5,353
40	lge1	Bristol City	H	W	5-0	Brkovic 10,79; Nicholls 26 pen; Davis 45; Holmes 61	8,330
41	lge1	Swindon	H	W	3-1	Nicholls 13 pen; Brkovic 27; Holmes 84	8,173
42	lge1	Oldham	A	D	2-2	Underwood 6; Howard 90	5,809
43	lge1	Barnsley	H	L	1-3	Showunmi 67	7,548
44	lge1	Torquay	A	W	4-1	Nicholls 23; Holmes 32; Howard 51; Vine 71	4,264
45	lge1	Blackpool	H	W	1-0	Howard 15	7,816
46	lge1	Bournemouth	A	W	1-0	Showunmi 84	9,058
47	lge1	MK Dons	H	W	1-0	Chorley 31 og	9,000
48	lge1	Wrexham	A	W	2-1	Davies 52; Coyne 59	6,614
49	lge1	Brentford	H	W	4-2	Brkovic 5; Nicholls 84 pen; Showunmi 90; Robinson 90	9,313
50	lge1	Doncaster	A	D	3-3	Perrett 32; Howard 36; Nicholls 63	8,928

MONTHLY POINTS TALLY

AUGUST	18	100%
SEPTEMBER	10	83%
OCTOBER	7	39%
NOVEMBER	7	78%
DECEMBER	10	67%
JANUARY	7	47%
FEBRUARY	13	72%
MARCH	10	67%
APRIL	15	100%
MAY	1	33%

KEY PLAYERS - GOALSCORERS

Steven Howard

Goals in the League	18	Player Strike Rate Average number of minutes between League goals scored by player	195
Contribution to Attacking Power Average number of minutes between League team goals while on pitch	45	Club Strike Rate Average number of minutes between League goals scored by club	48

	PLAYER	LGE GOALS	GOALS ALL	POWER	STRIKE RATE
1	Steven Howard	18	22	45	**195 mins**
2	Ahmet Brkovic	15	16	49	**227 mins**
3	Kevin Nicholls	12	14	50	**327 mins**
4	Rowan Vine	9	9	44	**391 mins**
5	Steve Robinson	4	4	46	**627 mins**

KEY PLAYERS - MIDFIELDERS

Ahmet Brkovic

Goals in the League	15	Contribution to Attacking Power Average number of minutes between League team goals while on pitch	49
Defensive Rating Average number of mins between League goals conceded while on the pitch	100	Scoring Difference Defensive Rating minus Contribution to Attacking Power	51

	PLAYER	LGE GOALS	GOALS ALL	DEF RATE	POWER	SCORE DIFF
1	Ahmet Brkovic	15	16	100	49	**51 mins**
2	Steve Robinson	4	4	90	46	**44 mins**
3	Paul Underwood	5	5	86	44	**42 mins**
4	Kevin Nicholls	12	14	83	50	**33 mins**

KEY PLAYERS - DEFENDERS

Kevin Foley

Goals Conceded Number of League goals conceded while the player was on the pitch	37	Clean Sheets In games when player was on pitch for at least 70 minutes	13
Defensive Rating Ave number of mins between League goals conceded while on the pitch	89	Club Defensive Rating Average number of mins between League goals conceded by the club this season	86

	PLAYER	CON LGE	CON ALL	CLEAN SHEETS	DEF RATE
1	Kevin Foley	37	39	13	**89 mins**
2	Curtis Davies	45	51	16	**88 mins**
3	Sol Davis	48	52	15	**83 mins**
4	Chris Coyne	42	48	14	**83 mins**

KEY GOALKEEPER

Marlon Beresford

Goals Conceded in the League	35	Counting Games Games when player was on pitch for at least 70 minutes	37
Defensive Rating Ave number of mins between League goals conceded while on the pitch	96	Clean Sheets In Games when player was on pitch for at least 70 minutes	15

LEAGUE GOALS

Steven Howard

Minutes on the pitch	3510	League average (mins between goals)	195
Goals in the League	18		

	PLAYER	MINS	GOALS	AVE
1	Howard	3510	**18**	195
2	Brkovic	3412	**15**	227
3	Nicholls	3919	**12**	327
4	Vine	3517	**9**	391
5	Showunmi	975	**6**	163
6	Coyne	3500	**5**	700
7	Underwood	3196	**5**	639
8	Robinson	2508	**4**	627
9	Holmes	1227	**3**	409
10	Davis	3980	**2**	1990
11	Foley	3292	**2**	1646
12	Perrett	801	**1**	801
	Other		5	
	TOTAL		87	

DISCIPLINARY RECORDS

	PLAYER	YELLOW	RED	AVE
1	Perrett	2	1	267
2	Howard	12	1	270
3	Robinson	6	0	418
4	Brkovic	7	0	487
5	Nicholls	7	1	489
6	Davis	8	0	497
7	Holmes	2	0	613
8	Davies	6	0	660
9	Coyne	4	1	700
10	Vine	5	0	703
11	O'Leary	1	0	950
12	Underwood	2	0	1598
13	Foley	2	0	1646
	Other	0	0	
	TOTAL	64	4	

TOP POINT EARNERS

	PLAYER	GAMES	AV PTS
1	Ahmet Brkovic	37	2.27
2	Marlon Beresford	37	2.27
3	Kevin Foley	36	2.19
4	Paul Underwood	36	2.19
5	Steve Robinson	26	2.15
6	Kevin Nicholls	43	2.14
7	Curtis Davies	44	2.14
8	Sol Davis	43	2.14
9	Steven Howard	39	2.10
10	Chris Coyne	39	2.08
	CLUB AVERAGE:		2.13

TEAM OF THE SEASON

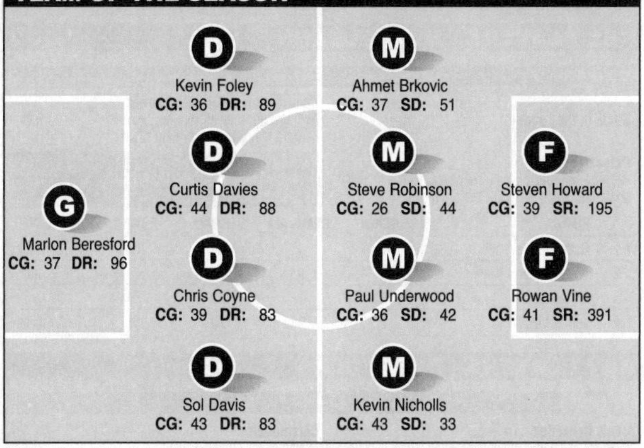

G
Marlon Beresford
CG: 37 DR: 96
D
Kevin Foley
CG: 36 DR: 89
D
Curtis Davies
CG: 44 DR: 88
D
Chris Coyne
CG: 39 DR: 83
D
Sol Davis
CG: 43 DR: 83
M
Ahmet Brkovic
CG: 37 SD: 51
M
Steve Robinson
CG: 26 SD: 44
M
Paul Underwood
CG: 36 SD: 42
M
Kevin Nicholls
CG: 43 SD: 33
F
Steven Howard
CG: 39 SR: 195
F
Rowan Vine
CG: 41 SR: 391

LEAGUE APPEARANCES GOALS AND BOOKINGS

	AGE (on 01/07/05)	IN NAMED 16	APPEARANCES	COUNTING GAMES	MINUTES ON PITCH	LEAGUE GOALS	Yellow	Red
Goalkeepers								
Rob Beckwith	20	6	0	0	0	0	0	0
Marlon Beresford	35	38	38	37	3344	0	0	0
Dean Brill	18	1	0	0	0	0	0	0
Simon Royce	33	2	2	2	180	0	0	0
Dino Seremet	24	45	7	7	616	0	0	0
Defenders								
Leon Barnett	19	6	0	0	0	0	0	0
David Bayliss	29	4	0	0	0	0	0	0
Chris Coyne	26	41	40	39	3500	5	4	1
Curtis Davies	20	44	44	44	3960	1	6	0
Sol Davis	25	45	45	43	3980	2	8	0
Kevin Foley	20	40	39	36	3292	2	2	0
Ian Hillier	25	2	0	0	0	0	0	0
Allan Neilson	32	14	9	5	562	0	0	0
Russell Perrett	32	26	12	8	801	1	2	1
Midfielders								
Ahmet Brkovic	30	42	42	37	3412	15	7	0
Peter Holmes	24	28	19	11	1227	3	2	0
Keith Keane	18	31	17	11	1077	0	0	0
Michael Leary	22	23	8	0	159	0	1	0
Lee Mansell	22	5	1	0	15	0	0	0
Gary McSheffrey	23	5	5	1	190	1	0	0
Kevin Nicholls	26	44	44	43	3919	12	7	1
Stephen O'Leary	19	20	17	8	950	1	1	0
Steve Robinson	30	32	31	26	2508	4	6	0
Paul Underwood	31	37	37	36	3196	5	2	0
Forwards								
Calvin Andrew	18	12	8	1	234	0	0	0
Matthew Blinkhorn	20	7	2	0	20	0	0	0
Warren Feeney	24	6	6	1	210	0	0	0
Steven Howard	29	40	40	39	3510	18	12	1
Enoch Showunmi	22	45	35	6	975	6	0	0
Rowan Vine	22	45	45	41	3517	9	5	0

SQUAD APPEARANCES

Match	1	2	3	4	5	6	7	8	9	10	11	12	13	14	15	16	17	18	19	20	21	22	23	24	25
Venue	H	A	A	H	A	H	A	A	H	A	H	A	H	H	A	A	H	H	A	A	H	A	A	H	A
Competition	L	L	L	L	L	L	L	W	L	L	L	L	L	L	L	L	L	L	F	L	L	F	L	L	L
Result	W	W	W	W	W	W	D	L	W	W	W	D	W	L	L	L	W	W	W	W	D	W	L	W	W

Match	26	27	28	29	30	31	32	33	34	35	36	37	38	39	40	41	42	43	44	45	46	47	48	49	50
Venue	A	H	H	A	H	H	A	H	A	H	A	A	H	A	H	H	A	H	A	H	A	H	A	H	A
Competition	L	L	L	L	F	L	L	L	L	L	L	L	L	L	L	L	L	L	L	L	L	L	L	L	L
Result	W	D	D	D	L	W	D	D	D	W	W	W	W	L	W	W	D	L	W	W	W	W	W	W	D

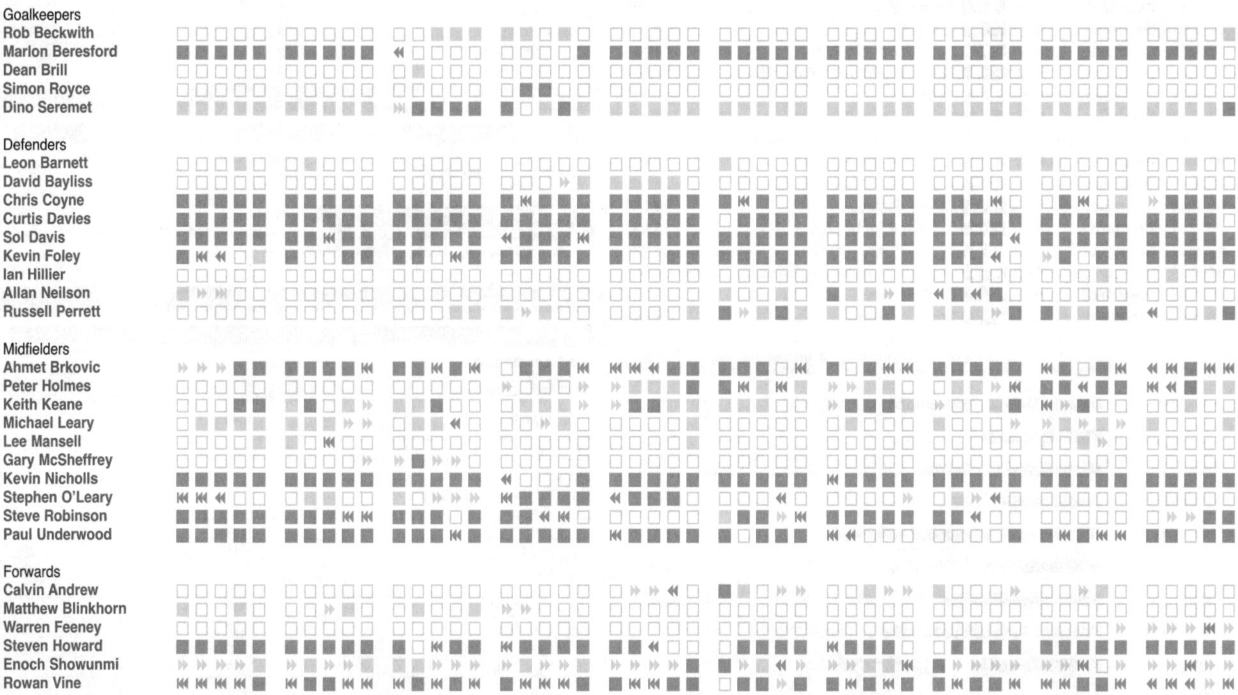

Goalkeepers
Rob Beckwith
Marlon Beresford
Dean Brill
Simon Royce
Dino Seremet
Defenders
Leon Barnett
David Bayliss
Chris Coyne
Curtis Davies
Sol Davis
Kevin Foley
Ian Hillier
Allan Neilson
Russell Perrett
Midfielders
Ahmet Brkovic
Peter Holmes
Keith Keane
Michael Leary
Lee Mansell
Gary McSheffrey
Kevin Nicholls
Stephen O'Leary
Steve Robinson
Paul Underwood
Forwards
Calvin Andrew
Matthew Blinkhorn
Warren Feeney
Steven Howard
Enoch Showunmi
Rowan Vine

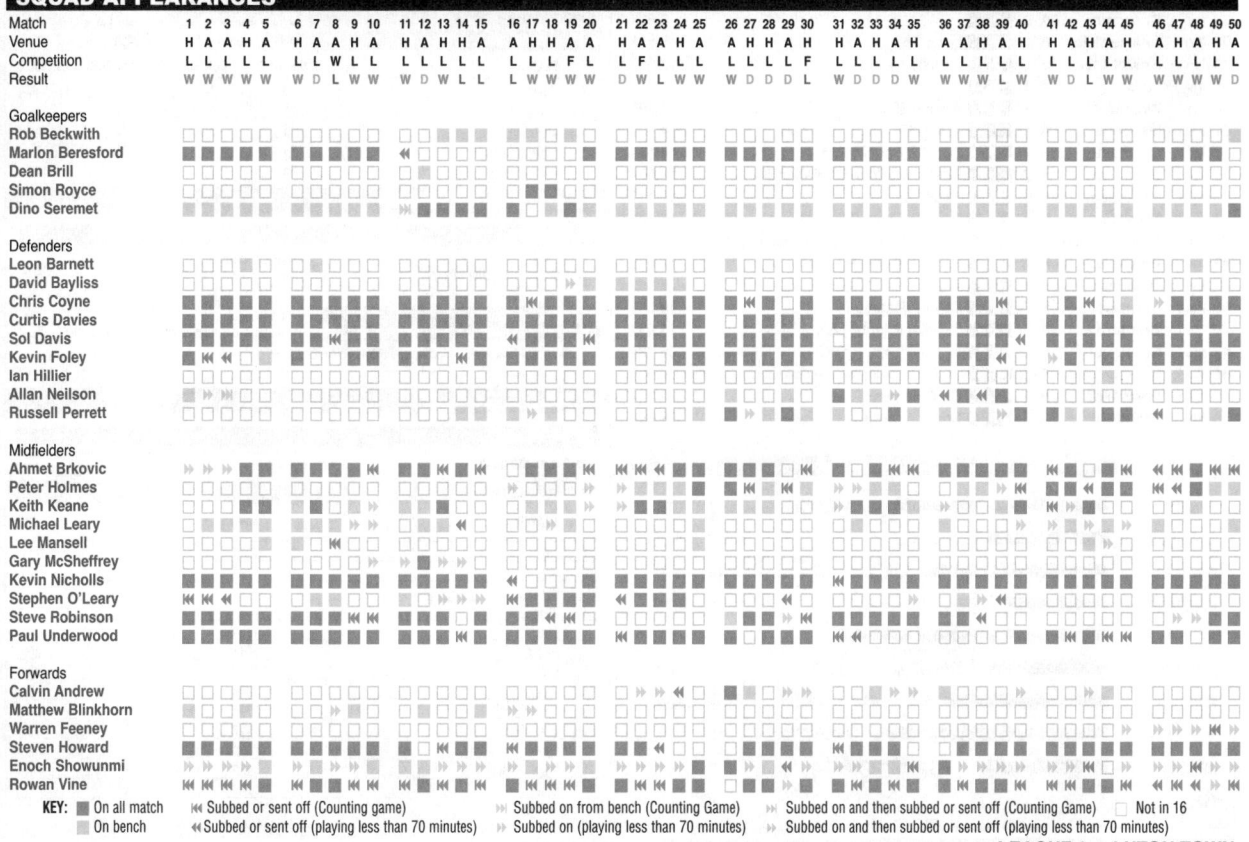

KEY: On all match | On bench | Subbed or sent off (Counting game) | Subbed or sent off (playing less than 70 minutes) | Subbed on from bench (Counting Game) | Subbed on (playing less than 70 minutes) | Subbed on and then subbed or sent off (Counting Game) | Subbed on and then subbed or sent off (playing less than 70 minutes) | Not in 16

HULL CITY

Final Position: **2nd**

NICKNAME: THE TIGERS

KEY: ☐ Won ☐ Drawn ☐ Lost

								Attendance
1	lge1	Bournemouth	H	W	1-0	Green 3 pen		17,569
2	lge1	Torquay	A	W	3-0	Green 9; Elliott 19,57		3,973
3	lge1	Port Vale	A	L	2-3	Barmby 14; Elliott 90		6,736
4	lge1	Oldham	H	W	2-0	Allsopp 27; Green 45		16,916
5	ccR1	Wrexham	H	L	2-2*	Keane 22; France 66 (*aet, lost 3-1 on penalties)		6,079
6	lge1	Barnsley	A	W	2-1	Elliott 58; Keane 88		13,175
7	lge1	Bradford	H	L	0-1			16,865
8	lge1	Huddersfield	A	L	0-4			13,542
9	lge1	Blackpool	H	W	2-1	Green 14; Elliott 57		15,568
10	lge1	Peterborough	A	W	3-2	Elliott 22,65; Cort 53		5,745
11	lge1	Stockport	H	D	0-0			16,182
12	lge1	Hartlepool	A	L	0-2			5,768
13	lge1	Chesterfield	H	W	1-0	Green 64		15,500
14	lge1	Bristol City	A	L	1-3	Facey 54		12,011
15	lge1	MK Dons	H	W	3-2	Green 1,90; Keane 88		14,317
16	lge1	Luton	H	W	3-0	Elliott 11,33; Facey 22		18,575
17	lge1	Wrexham	A	D	2-2	Cort 36; Facey 55		5,601
18	lge1	Walsall	H	W	3-1	Barmby 1; Elliott 34; Lewis 39		16,010
19	facr1	Morecambe	H	W	3-2	Green 30; Keane 66; Walters 86		10,129
20	lge1	Swindon	A	L	2-4	Walters 36; Elliott 90		6,348
21	lge1	Brentford	H	W	2-0	Elliott 32,82		15,710
22	facr2	Macclesfield	H	W	4-0	France 28; Facey 35,46; Elliott 39		9,831
23	lge1	Sheff Wed	A	W	4-2	Keane 14 pen; Barmby 22,43; Allsopp 83		28,701
24	lge1	Colchester	A	W	2-1	France 11; Elliott 50		4,046
25	lge1	Tranmere	H	W	6-1	Ashbee 34; Elliott 54,68,75 pen; Barmby 56; Allsopp 88		20,064
26	lge1	Blackpool	A	W	2-0	Elliott 60,85		8,774
27	lge1	Doncaster	H	W	2-1	Allsopp 21; Elliott 86		24,117
28	lge1	Huddersfield	H	W	2-1	Elliott 42; Wilbraham 49		22,291
29	lge1	Stockport	A	W	3-1	Wilbraham 10; Price 61; Allsopp 65		6,670
30	facr3	Colchester	H	L	0-2			14,027
31	lge1	Peterborough	H	D	2-2	Barmby 46; Green 60		16,149
32	lge1	Doncaster	A	L	0-1			9,633
33	lge1	Chesterfield	A	D	1-1	Lewis 74		5,517
34	lge1	Bristol City	H	D	1-1	Barmby 59		17,637
35	lge1	Luton	A	L	0-1			9,500
36	lge1	Wrexham	H	W	2-1	Allsopp 35,58		15,995
37	lge1	MK Dons	A	D	1-1	Facey 86		4,407
38	lge1	Colchester	H	W	2-0	Cort 16; Barmby 33		16,484
39	lge1	Tranmere	A	W	3-1	Ellison 43; Price 63; Fagan 69		12,684
40	lge1	Hartlepool	H	W	1-0	Elliott 14		17,112
41	lge1	Torquay	H	W	2-0	Fagan 61 pen; Elliott 73 pen		17,147
42	lge1	Bournemouth	A	W	4-0	France 26; Elliott 31,58; Delaney 64		8,895
43	lge1	Port Vale	H	D	2-2	Cort 33; Fagan 90 pen		17,678
44	lge1	Oldham	A	L	0-1			8,562
45	lge1	Barnsley	H	W	2-1	Cort 4; Fagan 69		19,341
46	lge1	Bradford	A	W	2-0	Elliott 4; Barmby 68		13,631
47	lge1	Swindon	H	D	0-0			23,125
48	lge1	Walsall	A	L	0-3			7,958
49	lge1	Sheff Wed	H	L	1-2	Elliott 60 pen		24,277
50	lge1	Brentford	A	L	1-2	Cort 1		9,604

MONTHLY POINTS TALLY

AUGUST	12	67%
SEPTEMBER	7	58%
OCTOBER	10	56%
NOVEMBER	6	67%
DECEMBER	15	100%
JANUARY	7	58%
FEBRUARY	9	50%
MARCH	13	72%
APRIL	7	47%
MAY	0	0%

KEY PLAYERS - GOALSCORERS

Stuart Elliott

Goals in the League	27	**Player Strike Rate** Average number of minutes between League goals scored by player	114
Contribution to Attacking Power Average number of minutes between League team goals while on pitch	46	**Club Strike Rate** Average number of minutes between League goals scored by club	52

	PLAYER	LGE GOALS	GOALS ALL	POWER	STRIKE RATE
1	Stuart Elliott	27	28	46	114 mins
2	Stuart Green	8	9	51	274 mins
3	Nick Barmby	9	9	52	324 mins
4	Leon Cort	6	6	51	648 mins
5	Ryan France	2	4	50	1048 mins

KEY PLAYERS - MIDFIELDERS

Ryan France

Goals in the League	2	**Contribution to Attacking Power** Average number of minutes between League team goals while on pitch	50
Defensive Rating Average number of mins between League goals conceded while on the pitch	87	**Scoring Difference** Defensive Rating minus Contribution to Attacking Power	37

	PLAYER	LGE GOALS	GOALS ALL	DEF RATE	POWER	SCORE DIFF
1	Ryan France	2	4	87	50	37 mins
2	Stuart Green	8	9	84	51	33 mins
3	Ian Ashbee	1	1	81	51	30 mins
4	Junior Lewis	2	2	70	58	12 mins

KEY PLAYERS - DEFENDERS

Roland Edge

Goals Conceded Number of League goals conceded while the player was on the pitch	10	**Clean Sheets** In games when player was on pitch for at least 70 minutes	4
Defensive Rating Ave number of mins between League goals conceded while on the pitch	115	**Club Defensive Rating** Average number of mins between League goals conceded while on the pitch	78

	PLAYER	CON LGE	CON ALL	CLEAN SHEETS	DEF RATE
1	Roland Edge	10	12	4	115 mins
2	Damien Delaney	47	53	13	82 mins
3	Leon Cort	49	55	13	79 mins
4	Andrew Dawson	39	43	10	74 mins
5	Marc Joseph	35	39	5	63 mins

KEY GOALKEEPER

Boaz Myhill

Goals Conceded in the League	51	**Counting Games** Games when player was on pitch for at least 70 minutes	45
Defensive Rating Ave number of mins between League goals conceded while on the pitch	79	**Clean Sheets** In games when player was on pitch for at least 70 minutes	14

LEAGUE GOALS

Stuart Elliott

Minutes on the pitch	3086	League average (mins between goals)	114
Goals in the League	27		

	PLAYER	MINS	GOALS	AVE
1	Elliott	3086	27	114
2	Green	2194	8	274
3	Barmby	2912	9	324
4	Allsopp	1318	7	188
5	Cort	3890	6	648
6	Facey	1158	4	290
7	Keane	1150	3	383
8	Fagan	944	4	236
9	France	2095	2	1048
10	Wilbraham	917	2	459
11	Lewis	2852	2	1426
12	Price	950	2	475
	Other		4	
	TOTAL		80	

DISCIPLINARY RECORDS

	PLAYER	YELLOW	RED	AVE
1	Price	4	0	237
2	Ashbee	11	2	267
3	Keane	3	0	383
4	Barmby	5	1	485
5	Ellison	2	0	520
6	Edge	2	0	576
7	Dawson	5	0	579
8	Walters	1	0	643
9	Elliott	4	0	771
10	Wilbraham	0	1	917
11	Stockdale	1	0	1037
12	Green	2	0	1097
13	Delaney	2	0	1935
	Other	3	0	
	TOTAL	45	4	

TOP POINT EARNERS

	PLAYER	GAMES	AV PTS
1	Elliott	33	2.15
2	France	19	2.11
3	Green	22	2.05
4	Ashbee	37	1.95
5	Joseph	21	1.95
6	Barmby	30	1.93
7	Edge	12	1.92
8	Myhill	45	1.91
9	Delaney	43	1.91
10	Dawson	31	1.90
	CLUB AVERAGE:		1.87

LEAGUE APPEARANCES GOALS AND BOOKINGS

	AGE (on 01/07/05)	IN NAMED 16	APPEARANCES	COUNTING GAMES	MINUTES ON PITCH	LEAGUE GOALS	Yellow	Red
Goalkeepers								
Stuart Brock	28	5	0	0	0	0	0	0
Matt Duke	27	39	2	1	102	0	0	0
Boaz Myhill	22	45	45	45	4038	0	2	0
Defenders								
Stevland Angus	24	2	2	1	111	0	1	0
Leon Cort	25	45	44	43	3890	6	0	0
Andrew Dawson	26	36	34	31	2899	0	5	0
Damien Delaney	23	43	43	43	3870	1	2	0
Roland Edge	26	22	14	12	1152	0	2	0
Richard Hinds	24	12	6	3	437	0	0	0
Marc Joseph	28	30	29	21	2207	0	1	0
Robbie Stockdale	25	15	14	10	1037	0	1	0
Alton Thelwell	24	3	3	0	141	0	0	0
Scott Wiseman	19	3	3	2	181	0	0	0
Midfielders								
Ian Ashbee	28	40	40	37	3479	1	11	2
Ryan France	24	35	31	19	2095	2	0	0
Russell Fry	19	1	1	0	31	0	0	0
Stuart Green	24	33	29	22	2194	8	2	0
Andy Hessenthaler	39	17	10	5	613	0	0	0
Michael Keane	22	24	20	10	1150	3	3	0
Junior Lewis	31	46	39	29	2852	2	0	0
Jason Price	28	33	27	5	950	2	4	0
Forwards								
Daniel Allsopp	26	31	28	7	1318	7	0	0
Nick Barmby	31	39	39	30	2912	9	5	1
Ben Burgess	23	2	2	0	38	0	0	0
Stuart Elliott	26	36	36	33	3086	27	4	0
Kevin Ellison	26	17	16	11	1040	1	2	0
Delroy Facey	25	22	21	8	1158	4	0	0
Craig Fagan	22	12	12	9	944	4	0	0
Jonathan Walters	21	23	21	1	643	1	1	0
Aaron Wilbraham	25	25	19	5	917	2	0	1

TEAM OF THE SEASON

D
Roland Edge
CG: 12 DR: 115
M
Ryan France
CG: 19 SD: 37
D
Damien Delaney
CG: 43 DR: 82
M
Stuart Green
CG: 22 SD: 33
F
Stuart Elliott
CG: 33 SR: 114
G
Boaz Myhill
CG: 45 DR: 79
D
Leon Cort
CG: 43 DR: 79
M
Ian Ashbee
CG: 37 SD: 30
F
Nick Barmby
CG: 30 SR: 324
D
Andrew Dawson
CG: 31 DR: 74
M
Junior Lewis
CG: 29 SD: 12

SQUAD APPEARANCES

Match	1	2	3	4	5	6	7	8	9	10	11	12	13	14	15	16	17	18	19	20	21	22	23	24	25
Venue	H	A	A	H	H	A	H	A	H	A	H	A	H	A	H	H	A	H	H	A	H	H	A	A	H
Competition	L	L	L	L	W	L	L	L	L	L	L	L	L	L	L	L	L	L	F	L	L	F	L	L	L
Result	W	W	L	W	L	W	L	L	W	W	D	L	W	L	W	W	D	W	W	L	W	W	W	W	W

Match	26	27	28	29	30	31	32	33	34	35	36	37	38	39	40	41	42	43	44	45	46	47	48	49	50
Venue	A	H	H	A	H	H	A	A	H	A	H	A	H	A	H	H	A	H	A	H	A	H	A	H	A
Competition	L	L	L	L	F	L	L	L	L	L	L	L	L	L	L	L	L	L	L	L	L	L	L	L	L
Result	W	W	W	W	L	D	L	D	D	L	W	D	W	W	W	W	W	D	L	W	W	D	L	L	L

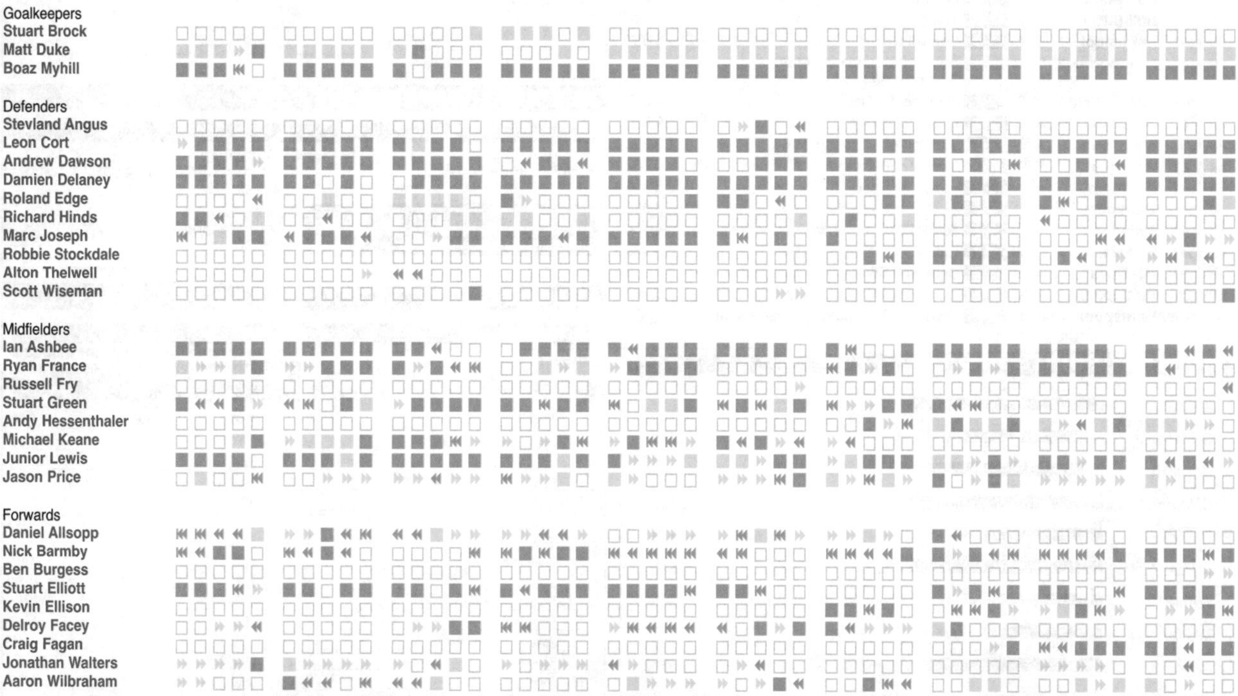

Goalkeepers
Stuart Brock
Matt Duke
Boaz Myhill
Defenders
Stevland Angus
Leon Cort
Andrew Dawson
Damien Delaney
Roland Edge
Richard Hinds
Marc Joseph
Robbie Stockdale
Alton Thelwell
Scott Wiseman
Midfielders
Ian Ashbee
Ryan France
Russell Fry
Stuart Green
Andy Hessenthaler
Michael Keane
Junior Lewis
Jason Price
Forwards
Daniel Allsopp
Nick Barmby
Ben Burgess
Stuart Elliott
Kevin Ellison
Delroy Facey
Craig Fagan
Jonathan Walters
Aaron Wilbraham

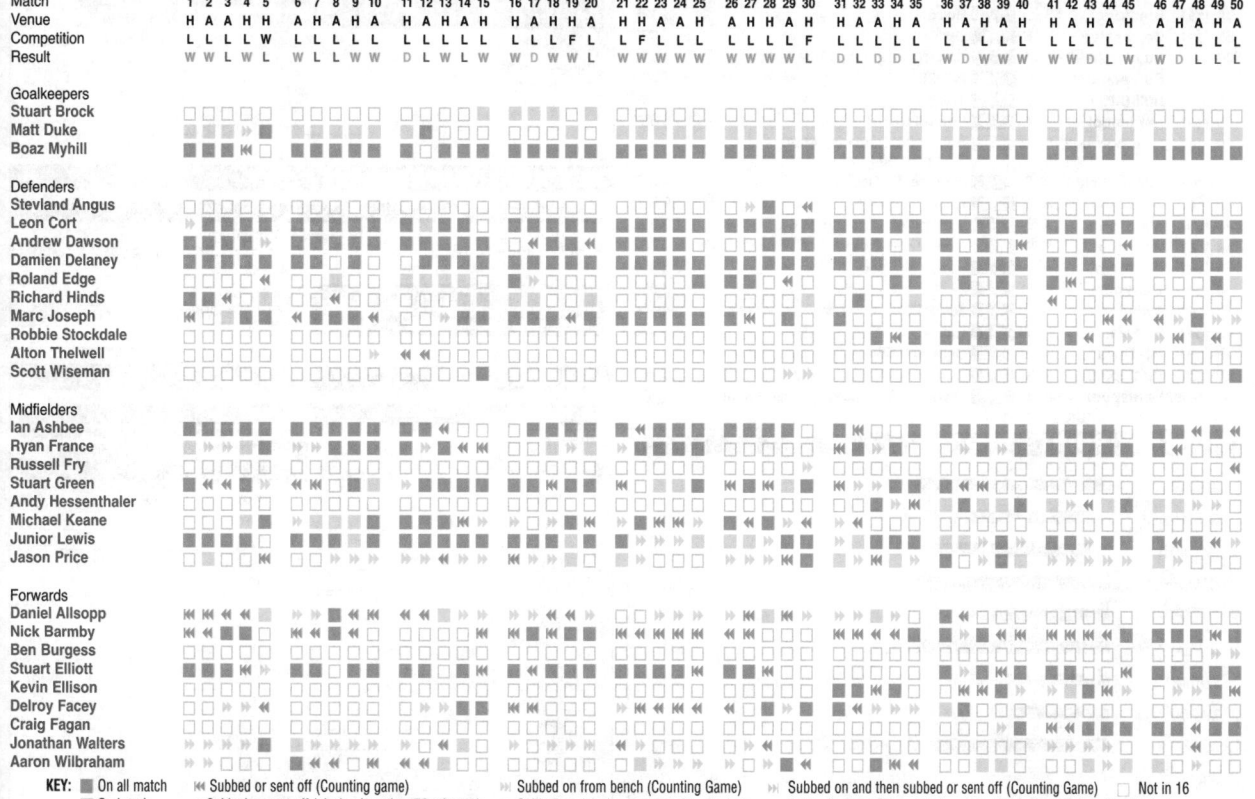

KEY: On all match · On bench · Subbed or sent off (Counting game) · Subbed or sent off (playing less than 70 minutes) · Subbed on from bench (Counting Game) · Subbed on (playing less than 70 minutes) · Subbed on and then subbed or sent off (Counting Game) · Subbed on and then subbed or sent off (playing less than 70 minutes) · Not in 16

TRANMERE ROVERS

Final Position: **3rd**

NICKNAME: ROVERS

KEY: ☐Won ☐Drawn ☐Lost

							Attendance
1	lge1	Peterborough	A	L	0-1		5,390
2	lge1	Hartlepool	H	W	2-1	Taylor 27 pen; Dagnall 68	8,128
3	lge1	Chesterfield	H	W	1-0	Dadi 42	8,287
4	lge1	Doncaster	A	D	0-0		6,040
5	ccr1	Shrewsbury	H	W	2-1	Zola 49; McAteer 80	4,489
6	lge1	Sheff Wed	H	W	4-2	Zola 12; Jackson, Mi 18; Taylor 30 pen; Hume 64	9,506
7	lge1	Stockport	A	D	1-1	Jackson, Mi 54	5,502
8	lge1	Barnsley	A	D	0-0		8,615
9	lge1	Oldham	H	W	2-0	Dadi 65; Hume 73	8,437
10	lge1	Wrexham	H	D	1-1	Roberts 59	9,826
11	ccr2	Portsmouth	H	L	0-1		6,966
12	lge1	Torquay	A	W	2-1	Hume 2,87	2,922
13	lge1	Luton	H	D	1-1	Taylor 32	10,884
14	lge1	Bradford	H	L	4-5	Taylor 45 pen; Hume 66,87; Beresford 82	8,901
15	lge1	Huddersfield	A	W	3-1	Whitmore 15,61; Dagnall 65	10,324
16	lge1	Colchester	A	W	2-1	Dagnall 29; Zola 81	3,420
17	lge1	Brentford	H	W	1-0	Sharps 53	8,740
18	lge1	Swindon	H	W	2-1	Hall 34,74	8,419
19	lge1	Bristol City	A	L	0-4		11,098
20	facr1	Peterborough	A	L	1-2	Taylor 42	2,940
21	lge1	Blackpool	A	W	1-0	Goodison 38	6,490
22	lge1	MK Dons	H	W	2-0	Hall 53; Whitmore 84	8,402
23	lge1	Port Vale	A	L	1-3	Jackson 73	4,027
24	lge1	Bournemouth	H	W	2-0	Hume 45; Hall 89	8,557
25	lge1	Hull City	A	L	1-6	Dadi 55	20,064
26	lge1	Barnsley	H	D	1-1	Hume 73	11,519
27	lge1	Walsall	A	W	2-0	McAteer 57; Taylor 81	7,217
28	lge1	Oldham	A	D	2-2	Taylor 37 pen; Hume 52	6,876
29	lge1	Torquay	H	W	4-1	Dadi 8; McAteer 66; Jones 77; Hall 90	8,792
30	lge1	Bristol City	H	L	0-1		8,183
31	lge1	Wrexham	A	W	5-1	Dagnall 21; Hume 42; Roberts 49; Whitmore 79; Hall 81	6,221
32	lge1	Walsall	H	W	2-1	Hume 8; Dagnall 50	8,651
33	lge1	Luton	A	D	1-1	Dadi 5	8,594
34	lge1	Bradford	A	D	1-1	Hume 1	8,129
35	lge1	Colchester	H	D	1-1	Dadi 8	8,098
36	lge1	Huddersfield	H	W	3-0	Dadi 16; Hume 24; Roberts 90	7,613
37	lge1	Bournemouth	A	D	1-1	Hall 22	7,305
38	lge1	Hull City	H	L	1-3	Taylor 7	12,684
39	lge1	Hartlepool	A	W	1-0	Dagnall 53	4,887
40	lge1	Peterborough	H	W	5-0	Hall 16,80; Hume 29; McAteer 45; Whitmore 60	8,401
41	lge1	Chesterfield	A	D	2-2	Jackson 72; Dadi 86	4,293
42	lge1	Doncaster	H	L	2-4	Dadi 11; Hall 44	9,730
43	lge1	Sheff Wed	A	W	2-1	Jackson 42; Howarth, R 60	22,925
44	lge1	Stockport	H	W	1-0	McAteer 66	8,757
45	lge1	Brentford	A	L	0-1		6,005
46	lge1	Blackpool	H	D	0-0		8,568
47	lge1	Swindon	A	L	1-2	Taylor 20	4,484
48	lge1	Port Vale	H	W	1-0	Hall 40	8,940
49	lge1	MK Dons	A	L	1-2	Beresford 65	7,359
50	d2po1	Hartlepool	A	L	0-2		6,604
51	d2po2	Hartlepool	H	L	2-0*	Taylor 70; Beresford 87 (lost 5-6 on pens)	13,356

MONTHLY POINTS TALLY

AUGUST	11	61%
SEPTEMBER	8	67%
OCTOBER	10	67%
NOVEMBER	9	75%
DECEMBER	7	47%
JANUARY	11	61%
FEBRUARY	6	50%
MARCH	7	47%
APRIL	10	56%
MAY	0	0%

KEY PLAYERS - GOALSCORERS

Iain Hume

Goals in the League	14	Player Strike Rate Average number of minutes between League goals scored by player	242
Contribution to Attacking Power Average number of minutes between League team goals while on pitch	55	Club Strike Rate Average number of minutes between League goals scored by club	57

	PLAYER	LGE GOALS	GOALS ALL	POWER	STRIKE RATE
1	Iain Hume	14	14	55	242 mins
2	Paul Hall	11	11	60	329 mins
3	Ryan Taylor	8	10	55	477 mins
4	Jason McAteer	4	5	54	672 mins
5	Michael Jackson	5	5	56	741 mins

KEY PLAYERS - MIDFIELDERS

Jason McAteer

Goals in the League	4	Contribution to Attacking Power Average number of minutes between League team goals while on pitch	54
Defensive Rating Average number of mins between League goals conceded while on the pitch	81	Scoring Difference Defensive Rating minus Contribution to Attacking Power	27

	PLAYER	LGE GOALS	GOALS ALL	DEF RATE	POWER	SCORE DIFF
1	Jason McAteer	4	5	81	54	27 mins
2	Mark Rankine	0	0	74	59	15 mins
3	Paul Hall	11	11	71	60	11 mins
4	Danny Harrison	0	0	66	59	7 mins

KEY PLAYERS - DEFENDERS

Ryan Taylor

Goals Conceded Number of League goals conceded while the player was on the pitch	46	Clean Sheets In games when player was on pitch for at least 70 minutes	15
Defensive Rating Ave number of mins between League goals conceded while on the pitch	83	Club Defensive Rating Average number of mins between League goals conceded by the club this season	75

	PLAYER	CON LGE	CON ALL	CLEAN SHEETS	DEF RATE
1	Ryan Taylor	46	52	15	83 mins
2	Gareth Roberts	45	51	13	80 mins
3	Ian Sharps	51	57	15	77 mins
4	Michael Jackson	49	54	13	76 mins
5	Ian Goodison	49	54	11	73 mins

KEY GOALKEEPER

John Achterberg

Goals Conceded in the League	42	Counting Games Games when player was on pitch for at least 70 minutes	38
Defensive Rating Ave number of mins between League goals conceded while on the pitch	82	Clean Sheets In Games when player was on pitch for at least 70 minutes	14

LEAGUE GOALS

Iain Hume

Minutes on the pitch	3383	League average (mins between goals)	242
Goals in the League	14		

	PLAYER	MINS	GOALS	AVE
1	Hume	3383	14	242
2	Hall	3623	11	329
3	Dadi	1467	9	163
4	Taylor	3817	8	477
5	Dagnall	1098	6	183
6	Jackson	3704	5	741
7	Whitmore	1650	5	330
8	McAteer	2689	4	672
9	Roberts	3591	3	1197
10	Beresford	947	2	474
11	Zola	671	2	336
12	Sharps	3945	1	3945
13	Jones	462	1	462
	Other		2	
	TOTAL		73	

DISCIPLINARY RECORDS

	PLAYER	YELLOW	RED	AVE
1	Dadi	5	1	244
2	Dagnall	3	1	274
3	Hume	9	0	375
4	McAteer	7	0	384
5	Sharps	9	0	438
6	Linwood	1	0	460
7	Jones	1	0	462
8	Taylor	7	0	545
9	Harrison	3	0	574
10	Jackson	5	1	617
11	Rankine	5	0	708
12	Roberts	4	1	718
13	Hall	4	0	905
	Other	6	0	
	TOTAL	69	4	

TOP POINT EARNERS

	PLAYER	GAMES	AV PTS
1	Roberts	40	1.85
2	Harrison	12	1.83
3	Taylor	42	1.83
4	Goodison	36	1.81
5	McAteer	29	1.79
6	Hume	37	1.78
7	Sharps	44	1.73
8	Jackson	40	1.73
9	Achterberg	38	1.71
10	Hall	38	1.63
	CLUB AVERAGE:		1.72

LEAGUE APPEARANCES GOALS AND BOOKINGS

	AGE (on 01/07/05)	IN NAMED 16	APPEARANCES	COUNTING GAMES	MINUTES ON PITCH	LEAGUE GOALS	Yellow	Red
Goalkeepers								
John Achterberg	34	39	39	38	3439	0	3	0
Russell Howarth	23	45	8	7	656	0	0	0
Philip Palethorpe	18	3	0	0	0	0	0	0
Defenders								
Ian Goodison	32	44	44	36	3574	1	3	0
Michael Jackson	31	43	43	40	3704	5	5	1
Paul Linwood	21	22	10	4	460	0	1	0
Tyrone Loran	24	3	2	0	54	0	0	0
Gareth Roberts	27	40	40	40	3591	3	4	1
Ian Sharps	24	44	44	44	3945	1	9	0
Ryan Taylor	20	43	43	42	3817	8	7	0
Carl Tremarco	19	3	3	2	209	0	0	0
Midfielders								
David Beresford	28	33	19	6	947	2	0	0
Paul Hall	33	46	46	38	3623	11	4	0
Danny Harrison	22	41	32	12	1723	0	3	0
Stephen Jennings	20	21	11	3	447	0	0	0
Gary Jones	30	15	10	3	462	1	1	0
Jason McAteer	34	34	34	29	2689	4	7	0
Mark Rankine	35	41	41	38	3544	0	5	0
Theodore Whitmore	32	42	33	11	1650	5	0	0
Forwards								
Paul Brown	-	5	4	0	110	0	1	0
Eugene Dadi	31	40	31	7	1467	9	5	1
Chris Dagnall	20	28	23	7	1098	6	3	1
Simon Haworth	28	3	3	2	180	0	1	0
Iain Hume	21	43	42	37	3383	14	9	0
Calvin Zola	20	15	15	3	671	2	0	0

TEAM OF THE SEASON

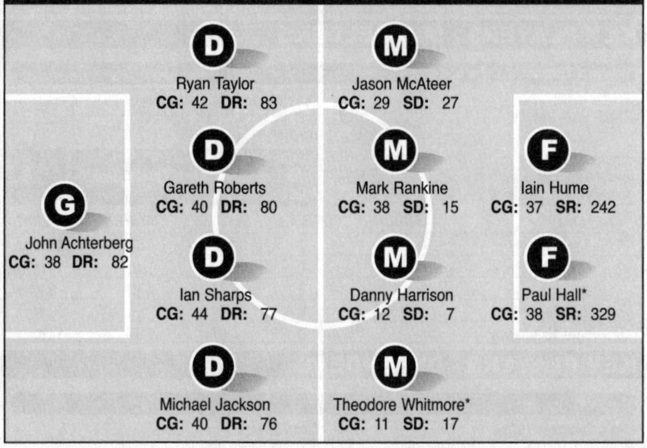
D
Ryan Taylor
CG: 42 DR: 83
M
Jason McAteer
CG: 29 SD: 27
D
Gareth Roberts
CG: 40 DR: 80
M
Mark Rankine
CG: 38 SD: 15
F
Iain Hume
CG: 37 SR: 242
G
John Achterberg
CG: 38 DR: 82
D
Ian Sharps
CG: 44 DR: 77
M
Danny Harrison
CG: 12 SD: 7
F
Paul Hall*
CG: 38 SR: 329
D
Michael Jackson
CG: 40 DR: 76
M
Theodore Whitmore*
CG: 11 SD: 17

SQUAD APPEARANCES

Match	1	2	3	4	5	6	7	8	9	10	11	12	13	14	15	16	17	18	19	20	21	22	23	24	25
Venue	A	H	H	A	H	H	A	A	H	H	H	A	H	H	A	A	H	H	A	A	A	H	A	H	A
Competition	L	L	L	L	W	L	L	L	L	L	W	L	L	L	L	L	L	L	L	F	L	L	L	L	L
Result	L	W	W	D	W	W	D	D	W	D	L	W	D	L	W	W	W	W	L	L	W	W	L	W	L

Match	26	27	28	29	30	31	32	33	34	35	36	37	38	39	40	41	42	43	44	45	46	47	48	49	50	51
Venue	H	A	A	H	H	A	H	A	A	H	H	A	H	A	H	A	H	A	H	A	H	A	H	A	A	H
Competition	L	L	L	L	L	L	L	L	L	L	L	L	L	L	L	L	L	L	L	L	L	L	L	L	O	O
Result	D	W	D	W	L	W	W	D	D	D	W	D	L	W	W	D	L	W	W	L	D	L	W	L	L	L

Goalkeepers
John Achterberg
Russell Howarth
Philip Palethorpe

Defenders
Ian Goodison
Michael Jackson
Paul Linwood
Tyrone Loran
Gareth Roberts
Ian Sharps
Ryan Taylor
Carl Tremarco

Midfielders
David Beresford
Paul Hall
Danny Harrison
Stephen Jennings
Gary Jones
Jason McAteer
Mark Rankine
Theodore Whitmore

Forwards
Paul Brown
Eugene Dadi
Chris Dagnall
Simon Haworth
Iain Hume
Calvin Zola

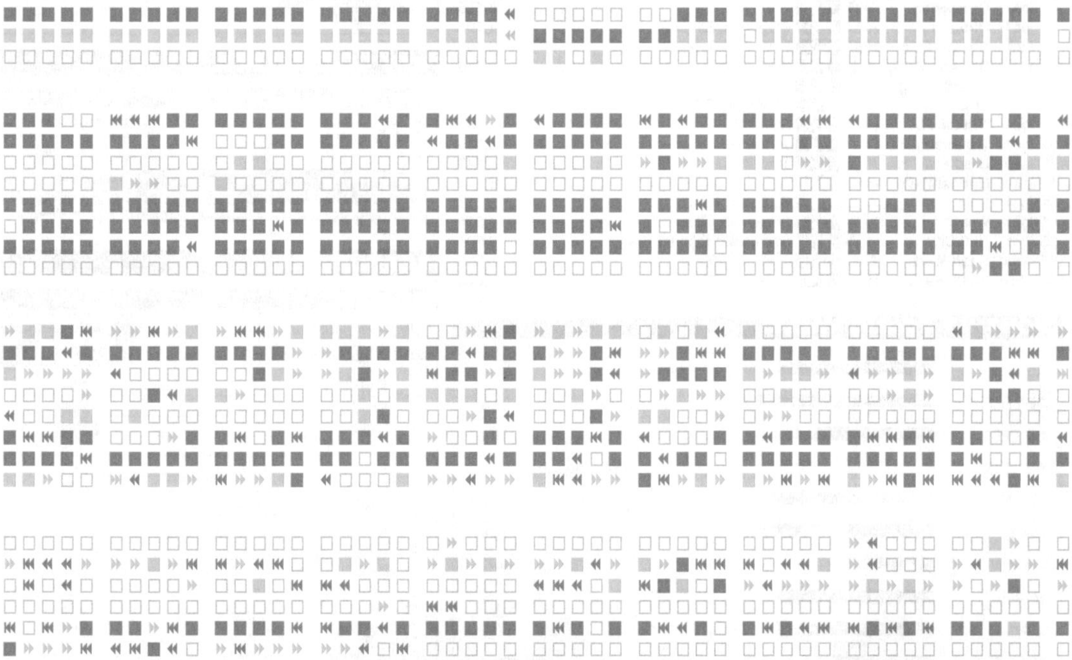

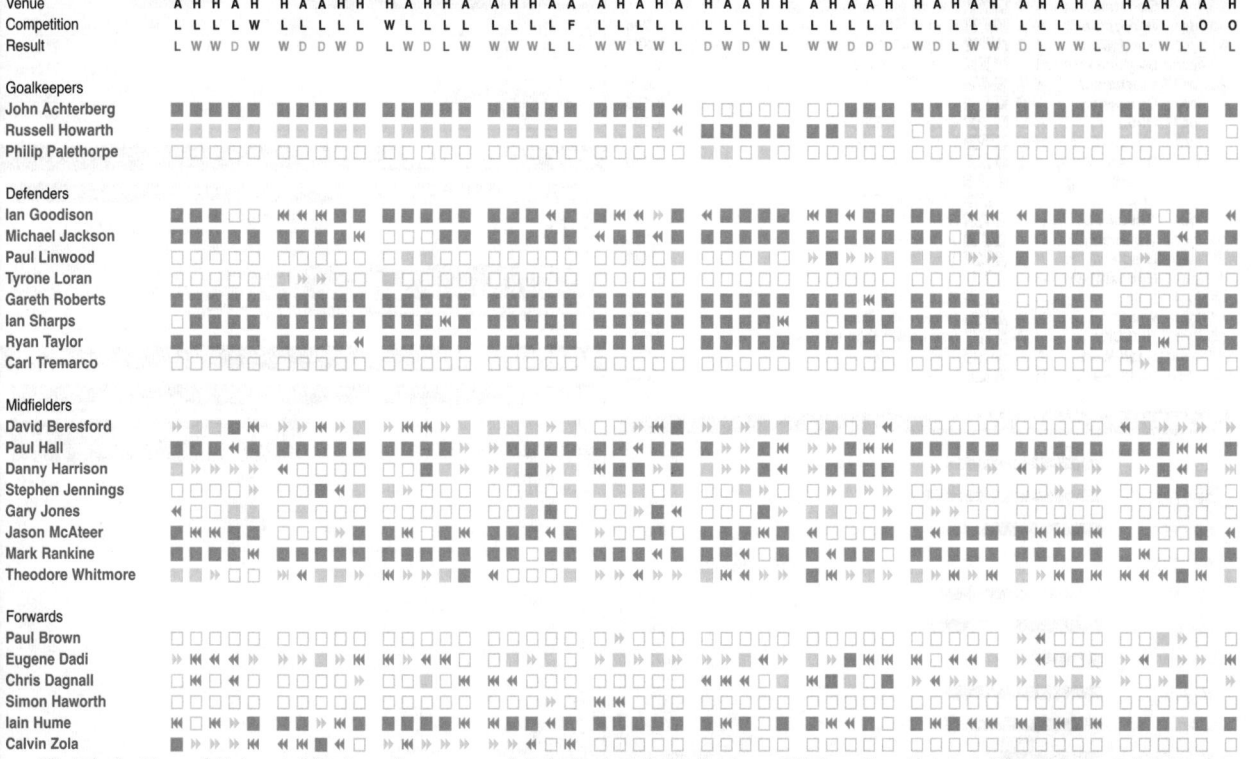

KEY: On all match / On bench / Subbed or sent off (Counting game) / Subbed or sent off (playing less than 70 minutes) / Subbed on from bench (Counting Game) / Subbed on (playing less than 70 minutes) / Subbed on and then subbed or sent off (Counting Game) / Subbed on and then subbed or sent off (playing less than 70 minutes) / Not in 16

BRENTFORD

Final Position: **4th**

NICKNAME: THE BEES

KEY: Won Drawn Lost

						Attendance
1	lge1	Chesterfield	A L	1-3	Rhodes 70	4,651
2	lge1	Doncaster	H W	4-3	Rankin 35; Hargreaves 53; Burton 54; Tabb 63	5,621
3	lge1	Wrexham	H W	1-0	O'Connor 85	5,091
4	lge1	Peterborough	A L	0-3		4,868
5	ccR1	Ipswich	A L	0-2		10,190
6	lge1	Stockport	H W	3-0	Dobson 4; Salako 16; Burton 30	4,643
7	lge1	Bristol City	A L	1-4	O'Connor 61	10,296
8	lge1	Bournemouth	H W	2-1	Talbot 32; Rankin 47	5,682
9	lge1	Torquay	A D	2-2	Hargreaves 69; Sodje 77	3,458
10	lge1	Port Vale	H W	1-0	Salako 25 pen	5,442
11	lge1	Walsall	A W	1-0	Salako 30 pen	5,302
12	lge1	Oldham	H W	2-0	Rankin 45; Burton 47	5,818
13	lge1	Barnsley	A D	0-0		8,453
14	lge1	MK Dons	A D	0-0		5,924
15	lge1	Hartlepool	H W	2-1	Rankin 35; Burton 90	4,797
16	lge1	Blackpool	H L	0-3		6,722
17	lge1	Tranmere	A L	0-1		8,740
18	lge1	Huddersfield	A D	1-1	Sodje 62	10,810
19	facr1	Bristol City	A D	1-1	Salako 7	10,000
20	lge1	Bradford	H L	1-2	Rhodes 90	5,909
21	facr1r	Bristol City	H W	4-3*	Frampton 44 (*on penalties)	3,706
22	lge1	Hull City	A L	0-2		15,710
23	facr2	Hinckley	A D	0-0		2,661
24	lge1	Luton	H W	2-0	Burton 41; May 62	6,393
25	lge1	Sheff Wed	A W	2-1	Rhodes 81; Burton 82	21,592
26	facr2r	Hinckley	H W	2-1	Rhodes 52 pen; Talbot 59	4,002
27	lge1	Colchester	H W	1-0	Salako 45	5,634
28	lge1	Torquay	H L	1-3	Sodje 26	6,419
29	lge1	Swindon	A L	0-3		6,875
30	lge1	Bournemouth	A L	2-3	Rankin 50,65	8,072
31	lge1	Walsall	H W	1-0	Broad 25 og	5,084
32	facr3	Luton	A W	2-0	Hargreaves 71; Tabb 89	6,861
33	lge1	Port Vale	A W	1-0	Hutchinson 29	4,230
34	lge1	Swindon	H W	2-1	Burton 44; Hunt 81	5,857
35	lge1	Barnsley	H D	1-1	Sodje 59	4,835
36	facr4	Hartlepool	H D	0-0		8,967
37	lge1	MK Dons	H W	1-0	Hunt 78 pen	5,077
38	facr4r	Hartlepool	A W	1-0	Rankin 48	7,580
39	facr5	Southampton	A D	2-2	Rankin 40; Sodje 58	24,741
40	lge1	Hartlepool	A L	1-3	Rankin 50	4,206
41	lge1	Sheff Wed	H D	3-3	Burton 43; Peters 82; Hunt 90	8,323
42	facr5r	Southampton	H L	1-3	Hutchinson 4	11,720
43	lge1	Colchester	A W	1-0	Tabb 58	3,066
44	lge1	Doncaster	A D	0-0		5,525
45	lge1	Oldham	A W	2-0	Fitzgerald, SP 54,63	4,291
46	lge1	Chesterfield	H D	2-2	Burton 68; Tabb 77	6,097
47	lge1	Blackpool	A L	1-2	Pratley 84	5,478
48	lge1	Peterborough	H D	0-0		6,341
49	lge1	Stockport	A W	2-1	Fitzgerald, SP 57; Sodje 86	4,408
50	lge1	Bristol City	H W	1-0	Sodje 12	6,780
51	lge1	Tranmere	H W	1-0	Turner 69	6,005
52	lge1	Bradford	A L	1-4	Tabb 79	6,743
53	lge1	Huddersfield	H L	0-1		7,703
54	lge1	Luton	A L	2-4	Sodje 21; Burton 26	9,313
55	lge1	Wrexham	A W	2-1	Rankin 68; Fitzgerald, SP 90	4,374
56	lge1	Hull City	H W	2-1	Sobers 43; Tabb 86	9,604
57	d2po1	Sheff Wed	A L	0-1		28,625
58	d2po2	Sheff Wed	H L	1-2	Frampton 87	10,823

MONTHLY POINTS TALLY

AUGUST	9	50%
SEPTEMBER	10	83%
OCTOBER	8	44%
NOVEMBER	1	11%
DECEMBER	9	60%
JANUARY	10	67%
FEBRUARY	4	44%
MARCH	9	50%
APRIL	9	50%
MAY	6	100%

KEY PLAYERS - GOALSCORERS

Deon Burton

Goals in the League	10	Player Strike Rate Average number of minutes between League goals scored by player	318
Contribution to Attacking Power Average number of minutes between League team goals while on pitch	72	Club Strike Rate Average number of minutes between League goals scored by club	73

	PLAYER	LGE GOALS	GOALS ALL	POWER	STRIKE RATE
1	Deon Burton	10	10	72	318 mins
2	Isaiah Rankin	8	10	78	391 mins
3	Sam Sodje	7	8	79	488 mins
4	Jay Tabb	5	6	67	566 mins
5	John Salako	4	5	67	654 mins

KEY PLAYERS - MIDFIELDERS

Stewart Talbot

Goals in the League	1	Contribution to Attacking Power Average number of minutes between League team goals while on pitch	73
Defensive Rating Average number of mins between League goals conceded while on the pitch	101	Scoring Difference Defensive Rating minus Contribution to Attacking Power	28

	PLAYER	LGE GOALS	GOALS ALL	DEF RATE	POWER	SCORE DIFF
1	Stewart Talbot	1	2	101	73	28 mins
2	Eddie Hutchinson	1	2	72	61	11 mins
3	Jay Tabb	5	6	76	67	9 mins
4	John Salako	4	5	59	67	-8 mins
5	Chris Hargreaves	2	3	62	76	-14 mins

KEY PLAYERS - DEFENDERS

Kevin O'Connor

Goals Conceded (GC) Number of League goals conceded while the player was on the pitch	41	Clean Sheets In games when player was on pitch for at least 70 minutes	13
Defensive Rating Ave number of mins between League goals conceded while on the pitch	72	Club Defensive Rating Average number of mins between League goals conceded while on the pitch	69

	PLAYED	CON LGE	CON ALL	CLEAN SHEETS	DEF RATE
1	Kevin O'Connor	41	48	13	72 mins
2	Sam Sodje	48	59	15	71 mins
3	Andrew Frampton	42	53	13	70 mins
4	Michael Turner	58	68	18	68 mins

KEY GOALKEEPER

Stuart Nelson

Goals Conceded in the League	56	Counting Games Games when player was on pitch for at least 70 minutes	43
Defensive Rating Ave number of mins between League goals conceded while on the pitch	69	Clean Sheets In games when player was on pitch for at least 70 minutes	17

LEAGUE GOALS

Deon Burton

Minutes on the pitch	3180	League average (mins between goals)	318
Goals in the League	10		

	PLAYER	MINS	GOALS	AVE
1	Burton	3180	10	318
2	Rankin	3130	8	391
3	Sodje	3415	7	488
4	Tabb	2830	5	566
5	Fitzgerald, SP	654	4	164
6	Salako	2614	4	654
7	Rhodes	736	3	245
8	Hunt	1207	3	402
9	O'Connor	2957	2	1479
10	Hargreaves	2430	2	1215
11	Turner	3935	1	3935
12	Hutchinson	1288	1	1288
13	Sobers	90	1	90
	Other		6	
	TOTAL		57	

DISCIPLINARY RECORDS

	PLAYER	YELLOW	RED	AVE
1	Myers	2	1	155
2	Lawrence	5	0	161
3	Pratley	4	0	264
4	Hargreaves	9	0	270
5	May	2	0	288
6	Fitzgerald, SP	2	0	327
7	Burton	6	2	397
8	Talbot	7	0	417
9	Sodje	8	0	426
10	Hutchinson	3	0	429
11	Frampton	6	0	486
12	Fitzgerald, SB	2	0	505
13	Rankin	6	0	521
	Other	15	1	
	TOTAL	77	4	

TOP POINT EARNERS

	PLAYER	GAMES	AV PTS
1	Talbot	27	2.11
2	Tabb	25	1.92
3	Burton	34	1.76
4	Frampton	29	1.72
5	Sodje	36	1.69
6	Hutchinson	14	1.64
7	Turner	43	1.60
8	O'Connor	31	1.58
9	Nelson	43	1.58
10	Salako	24	1.58
	CLUB AVERAGE:		1.63

LEAGUE APPEARANCES GOALS AND BOOKINGS

	AGE (on 01/07/05)	IN NAMED 16	APPEARANCES	COUNTING GAMES	MINUTES ON PITCH	LEAGUE GOALS	Yellow	Red
Goalkeepers								
Ademola Bankole	35	17	3	3	270	0	0	0
Alan Julian	29	27	0	0	0	0	0	0
Stuart Nelson	23	45	43	43	3870	0	0	0
Defenders								
Michael Dobson	24	19	18	11	1178	1	1	0
Scott B Fitzgerald	35	17	12	11	1010	0	2	0
Andrew Frampton	25	35	35	29	2919	0	6	0
Marcus Gayle	34	6	6	2	358	0	0	0
George Moleski	17	2	1	0	35	0	0	0
Andy Myers	31	30	10	2	466	0	2	1
Kevin O'Connor	23	38	37	31	2957	2	2	0
Karleigh Osborne	17	2	1	1	90	0	0	0
Jamie Palmer	19	2	0	0	0	0	0	0
Jerome Sobers	19	1	1	1	90	1	0	0
Sam Sodje	24	40	40	36	3415	7	8	0
Matt Somner	22	3	2	0	53	0	0	1
Michael Turner	21	45	45	43	3935	1	4	1
Midfielders								
Darius Charles	17	1	1	1	90	0	0	0
Chris Hargreaves	33	31	30	24	2430	2	9	0
Stephen Hunt	23	21	19	10	1207	3	2	0
Eddie Hutchinson	23	15	15	14	1288	1	3	0
Charlie Ide	-	1	1	0	1	0	0	0
Jamie Lawrence	35	18	14	7	807	0	5	0
Darren Pratley	20	15	14	10	1058	1	4	0
Alex Rhodes	23	23	22	3	736	3	1	0
John Salako	36	39	35	24	2614	4	0	0
Jay Smith	23	6	2	0	21	0	0	0
Jay Tabb	23	40	40	25	2830	5	5	0
Stewart Talbot	32	38	37	27	2923	1	7	0
Ryan Watts	-	1	1	0	13	0	0	0
Forwards								
Deon Burton	28	40	40	34	3180	10	6	2
Steve Claridge	39	5	4	2	230	0	0	0
Scott P Fitzgerald	25	13	12	5	654	4	2	0
Matt Harrold	21	24	19	4	590	0	0	0
Ben May	21	12	10	5	576	1	2	0
Richard Pacquette	22	1	1	1	90	0	0	0
Ryan Peters	17	12	9	0	231	1	1	0
Isaiah Rankin	27	42	41	33	3130	8	6	0

TEAM OF THE SEASON

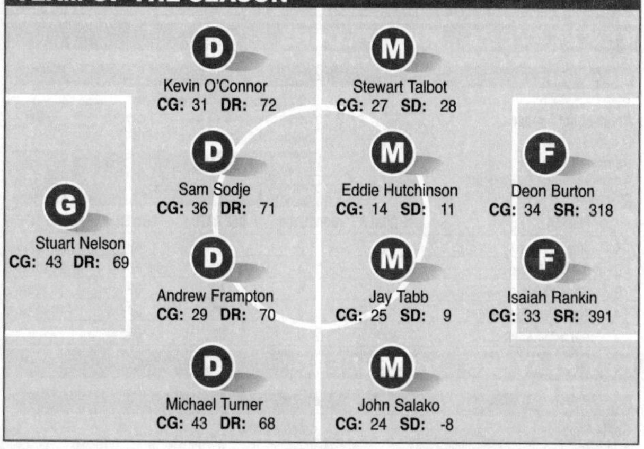

D
Kevin O'Connor
CG: 31 DR: 72
M
Stewart Talbot
CG: 27 SD: 28
D
Sam Sodje
CG: 36 DR: 71
M
Eddie Hutchinson
CG: 14 SD: 11
F
Deon Burton
CG: 34 SR: 318
G
Stuart Nelson
CG: 43 DR: 69
D
Andrew Frampton
CG: 29 DR: 70
M
Jay Tabb
CG: 25 SD: 9
F
Isaiah Rankin
CG: 33 SR: 391
D
Michael Turner
CG: 43 DR: 68
M
John Salako
CG: 24 SD: -8

SQUAD APPEARANCES

Match	Venue	Competition	Result
1	A	L	L
2	H	L	W
3	H	L	W
4	A	L	L
5	A	W	L
6	H	L	W
7	A	L	L
8	H	L	W
9	A	L	D
10	H	L	W
11	A	L	W
12	H	L	W
13	A	L	D
14	A	L	D
15	H	L	W
16	H	L	L
17	A	L	L
18	A	L	D
19	A	F	D
20	H	L	L
21	H	F	W
22	A	L	L
23	A	F	D
24	H	L	W
25	A	L	W
26	H	F	W
27	H	L	W
28	H	L	L
29	A	L	L
30	A	L	L
31	H	L	W
32	A	F	W
33	A	L	W
34	H	L	W
35	H	L	D
36	H	F	D
37	H	L	W
38	A	F	W
39	A	F	D
40	A	L	L
41	H	L	D
42	H	F	L
43	A	L	W
44	A	L	D
45	A	L	W
46	H	L	D
47	A	L	L
48	H	L	D
49	A	L	W
50	H	L	W
51	H	L	W
52	A	L	L
53	H	L	L
54	A	L	L
55	A	L	W
56	H	L	W
57	A	O	L
58	H	O	L

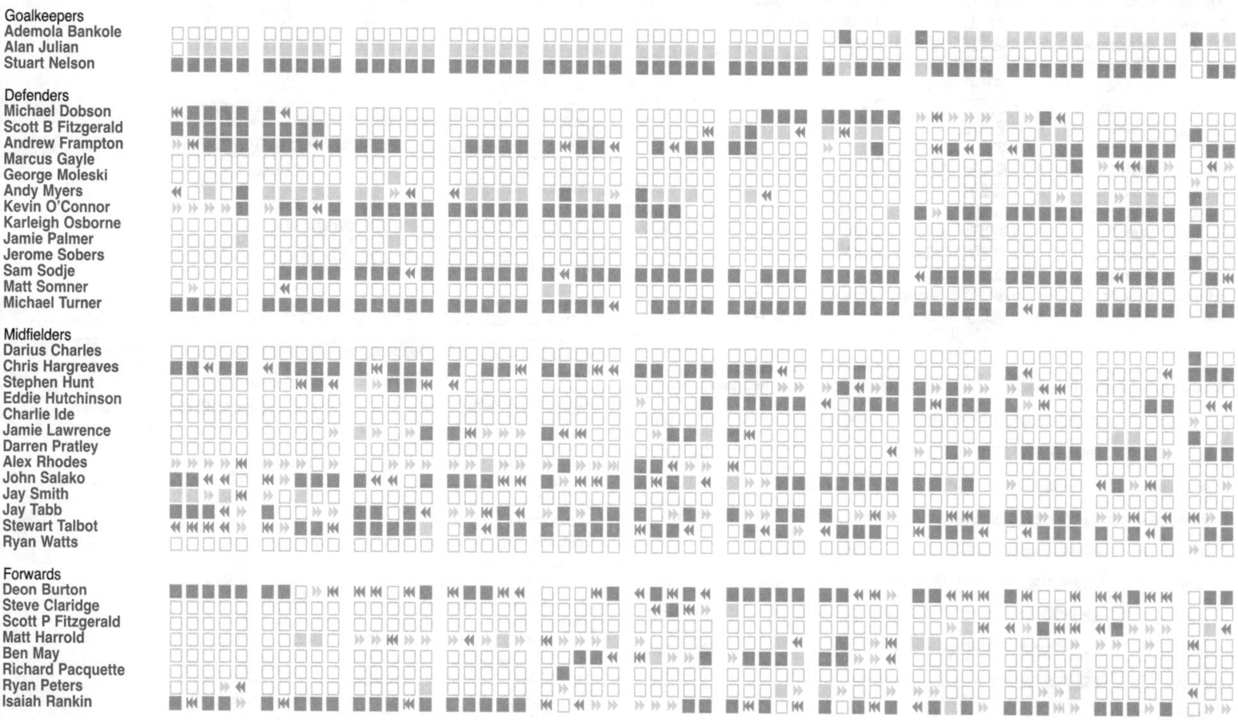

Goalkeepers
Ademola Bankole
Alan Julian
Stuart Nelson
Defenders
Michael Dobson
Scott B Fitzgerald
Andrew Frampton
Marcus Gayle
George Moleski
Andy Myers
Kevin O'Connor
Karleigh Osborne
Jamie Palmer
Jerome Sobers
Sam Sodje
Matt Somner
Michael Turner
Midfielders
Darius Charles
Chris Hargreaves
Stephen Hunt
Eddie Hutchinson
Charlie Ide
Jamie Lawrence
Darren Pratley
Alex Rhodes
John Salako
Jay Smith
Jay Tabb
Stewart Talbot
Ryan Watts
Forwards
Deon Burton
Steve Claridge
Scott P Fitzgerald
Matt Harrold
Ben May
Richard Pacquette
Ryan Peters
Isaiah Rankin

SHEFFIELD WEDNESDAY

PROMOTED VIA PLAY-OFFS Final Position: **5th**

NICKNAME: THE OWLS

KEY: Won / Drawn / Lost

							Attendance
1	lge1	**Colchester**	H	L	0-3		24,138
2	lge1	**Blackpool**	A	W	2-1	Bullen 44; McMahon 80	6,713
3	lge1	**Torquay**	A	W	4-2	MacLean 8 pen; Lee 51; Peacock 74; Heckingbottom 80	5,005
4	lge1	**Huddersfield**	H	W	1-0	MacLean 21	26,264
5	ccr1	**Walsall**	H	W	1-0	Peacock 20	8,959
6	lge1	**Tranmere**	A	L	2-4	MacLean 27; Ndumbu-Nsungu 45	9,506
7	lge1	**Oldham**	H	D	1-1	Brunt 70	21,530
8	lge1	**Luton**	H	D	0-0		20,806
9	lge1	**Walsall**	A	D	1-1	Whelan 16	6,403
10	lge1	**Bournemouth**	H	L	0-1		19,203
11	ccr2	**Coventry**	A	L	0-1		8,362
12	lge1	**Wrexham**	A	W	3-0	MacLean 25; Brunt 55; Proudlock 62	5,688
13	lge1	**MK Dons**	H	D	1-1	McGovern 65	20,245
14	lge1	**Barnsley**	H	W	1-0	Proudlock 24	25,391
15	lge1	**Peterborough**	A	D	1-1	Bullen 85	5,875
16	lge1	**Bradford**	A	L	1-3	Bullen 73	13,717
17	lge1	**Swindon**	A	L	2-3	Bullen 4; MacLean 63	6,972
18	lge1	**Chesterfield**	H	D	2-2	Proudlock 9; MacLean 15 pen	24,271
19	lge1	**Stockport**	A	W	3-0	Proudlock 40; McGovern 50; McMahon 88	7,222
20	facr1	**Swindon**	A	L	1-4	Whelan 63	6,160
21	lge1	**Hartlepool**	H	W	2-0	MacLean 59; Hamshaw 85	19,919
22	lge1	**Bristol City**	A	W	4-1	Proudlock 15,63; Brunt 61; Collins 84	14,852
23	lge1	**Hull City**	H	L	2-4	O'Brien 9; McGovern 81	28,701
24	lge1	**Brentford**	H	L	1-2	MacLean 22 pen	21,592
25	lge1	**Doncaster**	A	W	4-0	MacLean 9,59,76; Jones 22	10,131
26	lge1	**Walsall**	H	W	3-2	Jones 30; Wright 65 og; MacLean 73 pen	26,996
27	lge1	**Port Vale**	A	W	2-0	Jones 27; McGovern 43	8,671
28	lge1	**Luton**	A	D	1-1	Jones 45	9,500
29	lge1	**Wrexham**	H	W	4-0	MacLean 49 pen; Jones 55,59; Heckingbottom 84	24,253
30	lge1	**Swindon**	H	W	2-0	O'Brien 40; Jones 69	20,804
31	lge1	**Bournemouth**	A	D	1-1	Heckingbottom 90	8,847
32	lge1	**Port Vale**	H	W	1-0	MacLean 15	18,465
33	lge1	**MK Dons**	A	D	2-2	Quinn 11; Chorley 62 og	7,325
34	lge1	**Barnsley**	A	D	0-0		19,659
35	lge1	**Bradford**	H	L	1-2	MacLean 71	23,232
36	lge1	**Chesterfield**	A	W	3-1	MacLean 15,55; Peacock 78	7,831
37	lge1	**Peterborough**	H	W	2-1	MacLean 36 pen; Heckingbottom 52	19,648
38	lge1	**Brentford**	A	D	3-3	Peacock 4,41; Bullen 49	8,323
39	lge1	**Doncaster**	H	W	2-0	Bullen 45; Talbot 78	28,712
40	lge1	**Blackpool**	H	W	3-2	Rocastle 27; Talbot 84,90	21,539
41	lge1	**Colchester**	A	D	1-1	McGovern 63	4,169
42	lge1	**Torquay**	H	D	2-2	Bullen 54; Barrett 60	21,526
43	lge1	**Huddersfield**	A	L	0-1		17,292
44	lge1	**Tranmere**	H	L	1-2	Brunt 31 pen	22,925
45	lge1	**Oldham**	A	D	1-1	Whelan 54	9,645
46	lge1	**Hartlepool**	A	L	0-3		6,429
47	lge1	**Stockport**	H	D	0-0		22,331
48	lge1	**Hull City**	A	W	2-1	Talbot 19; Quinn 90	24,277
49	lge1	**Bristol City**	H	L	2-3	McGovern 52; Wood 61	28,798
50	d2po1	**Brentford**	H	W	1-0	McGovern 12	28,625
51	d2po2	**Brentford**	A	W	2-1	Peacock 27; Brunt 53	10,823
52	d2pof	**Hartlepool**	A	W	4-2	McGovern 45; MacLean 82 pen; Whelan 94; Talbot 120	59,808

MONTHLY POINTS TALLY

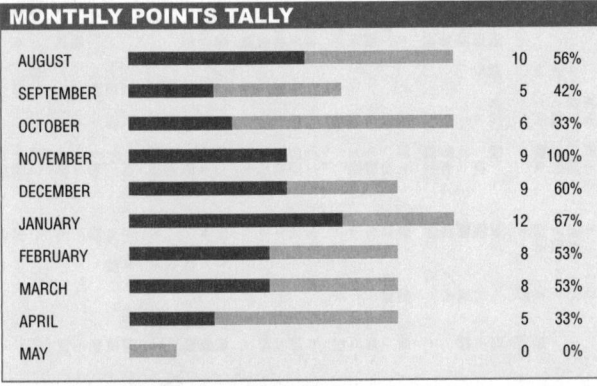

AUGUST	10	56%
SEPTEMBER	5	42%
OCTOBER	6	33%
NOVEMBER	9	100%
DECEMBER	9	60%
JANUARY	12	67%
FEBRUARY	8	53%
MARCH	8	53%
APRIL	5	33%
MAY	0	0%

KEY PLAYERS - GOALSCORERS

Steven MacLean

Goals in the League	18	Player Strike Rate Average number of minutes between League goals scored by player	173
Contribution to Attacking Power Average number of minutes between League team goals while on pitch	48	Club Strike Rate Average number of minutes between League goals scored by club	54

	PLAYER	LGE GOALS	GOALS ALL	POWER	STRIKE RATE
1	Steven MacLean	18	19	48	173 mins
2	Lee Peacock	4	6	52	449 mins
3	Lee Bullen	7	7	53	591 mins
4	Joey O'Brien	2	2	48	634 mins
5	Chris Brunt	4	5	51	648 mins

KEY PLAYERS - MIDFIELDERS

Joey O'Brien

Goals in the League	2	Contribution to Attacking Power Average number of minutes between League team goals while on pitch	49
Defensive Rating Average number of mins between League goals conceded while on the pitch	75	Scoring Difference Defensive Rating minus Contribution to Attacking Power	26

	PLAYER	LGE GOALS	GOALS ALL	DEF RATE	POWER	SCORE DIFF
1	Joey O'Brien	2	2	75	49	26 mins
2	Glenn Whelan	2	4	70	50	20 mins
3	Chris Brunt	4	5	70	52	18 mins
4	John-Paul McGovern	6	8	70	54	16 mins
5	Chris Marsden	0	0	61	64	-3 mins

KEY PLAYERS - DEFENDERS

Graeme Lee

Goals Conceded Number of League goals conceded while the player was on the pitch	18	Clean Sheets In games when player was on pitch for at least 70 minutes	7
Defensive Rating Ave number of mins between League goals conceded while on the pitch	97	Club Defensive Rating Average number of mins between League goals conceded while on the pitch	70

	PLAYER	CON LGE	CON ALL	CLEAN SHEETS	DEF RATE
1	Graeme Lee	18	22	7	97 mins
2	Richard Wood	39	46	10	75 mins
3	Lee Bullen	59	63	14	70 mins
4	Paul Heckingbottom	50	53	12	66 mins
5	Patrick Collins	36	41	7	64 mins

KEY GOALKEEPER

David Lucas

Goals Conceded in the League	35	Counting Games Games when player was on pitch for at least 70 minutes	32
Defensive Rating Ave number of mins between League goals conceded while on the pitch	83	Clean Sheets In games when player was on pitch for at least 70 minutes	13

LEAGUE GOALS

Steven MacLean

Minutes on the pitch	3117	League average (mins between goals)	173
Goals in the League	18		

	PLAYER	MINS	GOALS	AVE
1	MacLean	3117	18	173
2	Jones	588	7	84
3	Bullen	4135	7	591
4	McGovern	3994	6	666
5	Proudlock	944	6	157
6	Heckingbottom	3309	4	827
7	Talbot	502	4	126
8	Peacock	1797	4	449
9	Brunt	2591	4	648
10	O'Brien	1268	2	634
11	McMahon	1146	2	573
12	Whelan	3205	2	1603
13	Quinn	785	2	393
	Other		9	
	TOTAL		77	

DISCIPLINARY RECORDS

	PLAYER	YELLOW	RED	AVE
1	Branston	3	1	227
2	Quinn	3	0	261
3	Heckingbottom	7	0	472
4	Whelan	5	1	534
5	McMahon	2	0	573
6	Collins	4	0	576
7	Jones	1	0	588
8	O'Brien	2	0	634
9	Brunt	4	0	647
10	Bullen	6	0	689
11	Gallacher	0	1	709
12	Rocastle	1	0	793
13	Hamshaw	1	0	918
	Other	10	0	
	TOTAL	49	3	

TOP POINT EARNERS

	PLAYER	GAMES	AV PTS
1	Graeme Lee	17	2.24
2	David Lucas	32	1.88
3	Chris Brunt	24	1.79
4	Steven MacLean	34	1.74
5	Lee Peacock	16	1.69
6	John-Paul McGovern	44	1.64
7	Joey O'Brien	14	1.64
8	Lee Bullen	46	1.57
9	Glenn Whelan	36	1.56
10	Paul Heckingbottom	36	1.56
	CLUB AVERAGE:		

LEAGUE APPEARANCES GOALS AND BOOKINGS

	AGE (on 01/07/05)	IN NAMED 16	APPEARANCES	COUNTING GAMES	MINUTES ON PITCH	LEAGUE GOALS	Yellow	Red
Goalkeepers								
Chris Adamson	26	12	2	2	173	0	0	0
Paul Gallacher	25	9	8	8	709	0	0	1
David Lucas	27	34	34	32	2910	0	1	0
Robert Poulter	19	16	0	0	0	0	0	0
Ola Tidman	26	16	4	3	337	0	0	0
Defenders								
Hasney Aljofree	26	2	2	2	180	0	1	0
Zigor Aranalde	32	5	2	1	99	0	0	1
Guy Branston	26	13	11	10	911	0	3	1
Alex Bruce	20	7	6	4	440	0	0	1
Lee Bullen	34	46	46	46	4135	7	6	0
Patrick Collins	20	38	28	25	2304	1	4	0
Adam Green	21	3	3	2	230	0	0	0
Paul Heckingbottom	27	39	38	36	3309	4	7	0
Graeme Lee	27	25	22	17	1745	1	0	0
Richard Wood	20	39	34	32	2936	1	3	0
Midfielders								
Steve Adams	24	10	9	8	721	0	0	0
Craig Armstrong	30	6	0	0	0	0	0	0
Graham Barrett	23	7	6	1	354	1	0	0
Chris Brunt	20	45	42	24	2591	4	4	0
Ross Greenwood	19	13	2	0	12	0	0	0
Matthew Hamshaw	23	29	20	8	918	1	1	0
Chris Marsden	36	16	15	15	1350	0	1	0
John-Paul McGovern	24	46	46	44	3994	6	0	0
Lewis McMahon	20	18	15	10	1146	2	2	0
Joey O'Brien	19	15	15	14	1268	2	2	0
Craig Rocastle	23	14	11	9	793	1	1	0
Paul Smith	29	8	8	5	538	0	0	0
Glenn Whelan	21	37	36	36	3205	2	5	1
Forwards								
Kenwyne Jones	21	7	7	7	588	7	1	0
Steven MacLean	22	36	36	34	3117	18	3	0
Guylain Ndumbu-Nsungu	22	16	11	2	320	1	0	0
Lee Peacock	28	29	29	16	1797	4	1	0
Adam Proudlock	24	15	14	9	944	6	1	0
James Quinn	30	17	15	7	785	2	3	0
Jon Shaw	21	8	3	0	71	0	0	0
Andrew Talbot	-	30	21	2	502	4	0	0

TEAM OF THE SEASON

D
Graeme Lee
CG: 17 DR: 97
M
Joey O'Brien
CG: 14 SD: 26
D
Richard Wood
CG: 32 DR: 75
M
Glenn Whelan
CG: 36 SD: 20
F
Steven MacLean
CG: 34 SR: 173
G
David Lucas
CG: 32 DR: 83
D
Lee Bullen
CG: 46 DR: 70
M
Chris Brunt
CG: 24 SD: 18
F
Lee Peacock
CG: 16 SR: 449
D
Paul Heckingbottom
CG: 36 DR: 66
M
John-Paul McGovern
CG: 44 SD: 16

SQUAD APPEARANCES

Match	1	2	3	4	5	6	7	8	9	10	11	12	13	14	15	16	17	18	19	20	21	22	23	24	25	26
Venue	H	A	A	H	H	A	H	H	A	H	A	A	H	H	A	A	A	H	A	A	H	A	H	H	A	H
Competition	L	L	L	L	W	L	L	L	L	L	W	L	L	L	L	L	L	L	L	F	L	L	L	L	L	L
Result	L	W	W	W	W	L	D	D	D	L	L	W	D	W	D	L	L	D	W	L	W	W	L	L	W	W

Match	27	28	29	30	31	32	33	34	35	36	37	38	39	40	41	42	43	44	45	46	47	48	49	50	51	52
Venue	A	A	H	H	A	H	A	A	H	A	H	A	H	H	A	H	A	H	A	A	H	A	H	H	A	A
Competition	L	L	L	L	L	L	L	L	L	L	L	L	L	L	L	L	L	L	L	L	L	L	L	O	O	O
Result	W	D	W	W	D	W	D	D	L	W	W	D	W	W	D	D	L	L	D	L	D	W	L	W	W	W

Goalkeepers
Chris Adamson
Paul Gallacher
David Lucas
Robert Poulter
Ola Tidman

Defenders
Hasney Aljofree
Zigor Aranalde
Guy Branston
Alex Bruce
Lee Bullen
Patrick Collins
Adam Green
Paul Heckingbottom
Graeme Lee
Richard Wood

Midfielders
Steve Adams
Craig Armstrong
Graham Barrett
Chris Brunt
Ross Greenwood
Matthew Hamshaw
Chris Marsden
John-Paul McGovern
Lewis McMahon
Joey O'Brien
Craig Rocastle
Paul Smith
Glenn Whelan

Forwards
Kenwyne Jones
Steven MacLean
Guylain Ndumbu-Nsungu
Lee Peacock
Adam Proudlock
James Quinn
Jon Shaw
Andrew Talbot

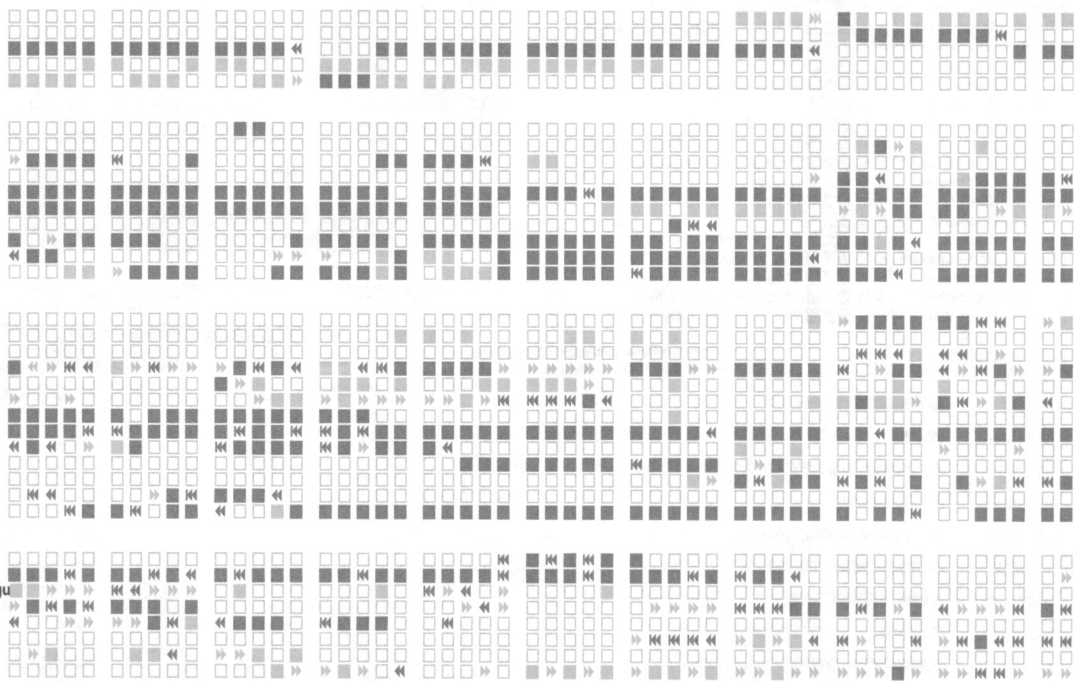

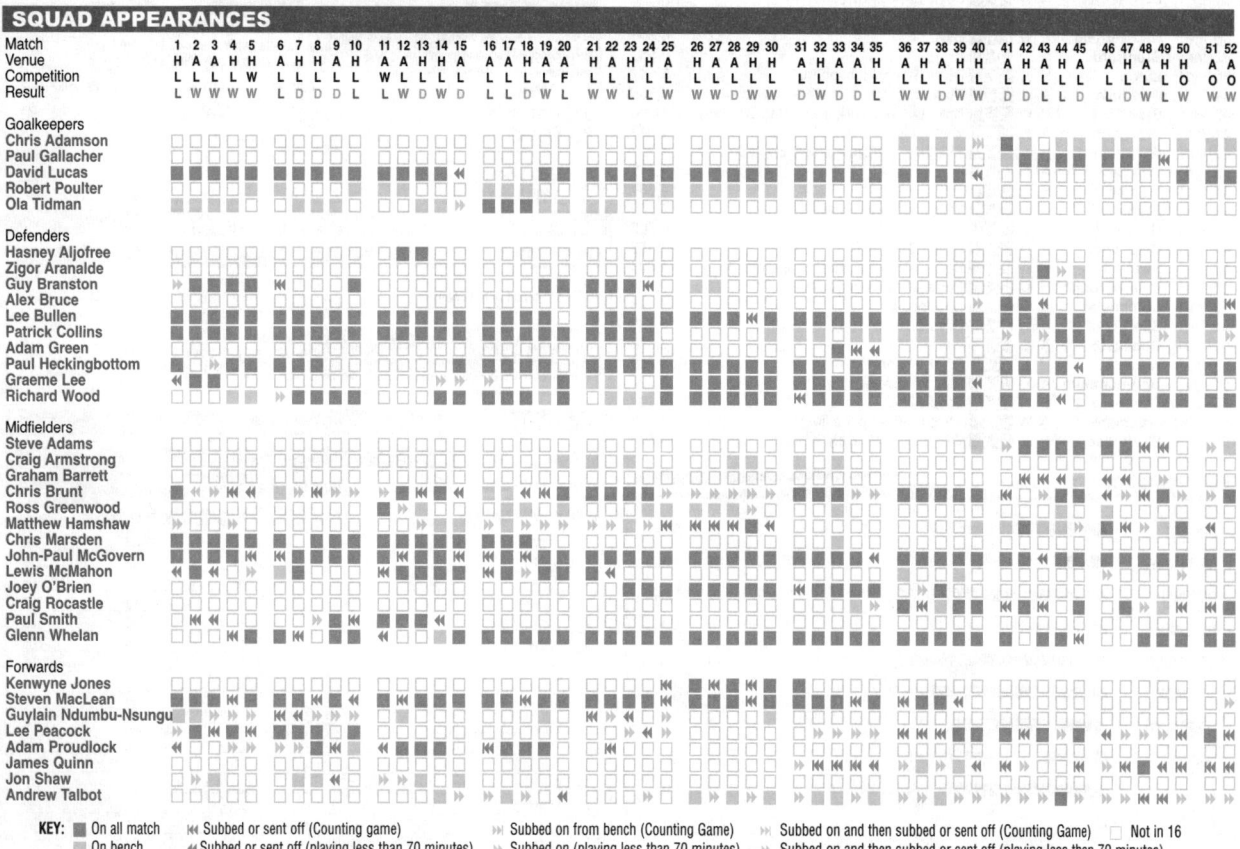

KEY: ■ On all match ■ On bench ⏮ Subbed or sent off (Counting game) « Subbed or sent off (playing less than 70 minutes) ⏭ Subbed on from bench (Counting Game) » Subbed on (playing less than 70 minutes) ⏭ Subbed on and then subbed or sent off (Counting Game) » Subbed on and then subbed or sent off (playing less than 70 minutes) □ Not in 16

HARTLEPOOL

Final Position: **6th**

NICKNAME: THE POOL

KEY: Won / Drawn / Lost

							Attendance
1	lge1	Bradford	H	W	2-1	Boyd 75 pen; Robertson 81	6,032
2	lge1	Tranmere	A	L	1-2	Robertson 23	8,128
3	lge1	Huddersfield	A	W	2-0	Betsy 68; Tinkler 70	9,968
4	lge1	Blackpool	H	D	1-1	Williams, E 24	5,144
5	ccr1	Macclesfield	H	W	2-1	Boyd 79; Sweeney 87	2,883
6	lge1	Swindon	A	L	0-3		5,365
7	lge1	Colchester	H	W	2-1	Williams, E 38; Boyd 70	4,371
8	lge1	Barnsley	H	D	1-1	Boyd 77	5,119
9	lge1	Oldham	A	L	2-3	Westwood 78; Griffin 90 og	5,805
10	lge1	Torquay	H	W	4-1	Porter 6; Sweeney 64; Tinkler 73; Humphreys 83	4,485
11	ccr2	Crystal Palace	A	L	1-2	Williams, E 70	4,233
12	lge1	MK Dons	A	L	2-4	Boyd 20,87	3,685
13	lge1	Hull City	H	W	2-0	Porter 8; Boyd 50	5,768
14	lge1	Luton	A	L	0-3		7,865
15	lge1	Chesterfield	H	W	3-2	Sweeney 3,8,83	4,617
16	lge1	Brentford	A	L	1-2	Robson 31	4,797
17	lge1	Peterborough	A	L	0-3		3,841
18	lge1	Port Vale	H	W	1-0	Williams, E 24	4,755
19	lge1	Doncaster	H	W	2-1	Porter 78,89	5,495
20	facr1	Lincoln	H	W	3-0	Williams 23; Robson 27; Porter 43	4,533
21	lge1	Sheff Wed	A	L	0-2		19,919
22	lge1	Bournemouth	H	W	3-2	Westwood 23; Nelson 88; Appleby 90	4,376
23	facr2	Aldershot	H	W	5-1	Westwood 13,30; Boyd 63,68; Tinkler 75	4,556
24	lge1	Walsall	A	L	1-2	Boyd 33	5,522
25	lge1	Stockport	H	W	3-1	Westwood 28,51; Porter 55	4,572
26	lge1	Wrexham	A	W	5-1	Humphreys 8; Sweeney 18,72; Porter 35; Boyd 37	3,582
27	lge1	Oldham	H	W	2-1	Boyd 7 pen,23 pen	6,520
28	lge1	Bristol City	A	D	0-0		13,034
29	lge1	Barnsley	A	D	0-0		9,595
30	lge1	MK Dons	H	W	5-0	Sweeney 21; Boyd 49,57; Porter 80 pen; Appleby 90	5,060
31	facr3	Boston	H	D	0-0		5,342
32	lge1	Torquay	A	W	2-1	Porter 68; Sweeney 71	2,543
33	facr3r	Boston	A	W	1-0	Boyd 72	3,653
34	lge1	Bristol City	H	W	2-1	Boyd 16 pen; Sweeney 71	5,399
35	facr4	Brentford	A	D	0-0		8,967
36	lge1	Chesterfield	A	W	1-0	Boyd 55	4,606
37	facr4r	Brentford	H	L	0-1		7,580
38	lge1	Luton	H	L	2-3	Davis 62 og; Robson 90	5,542
39	lge1	Port Vale	A	W	1-0	Porter 2	4,366
40	lge1	Brentford	H	W	3-1	Boyd 54 pen; Williams, E 74; Sweeney 87	4,206
41	lge1	Stockport	A	L	0-1		4,548
42	lge1	Wrexham	H	L	4-6	Strachan 4; Porter 31,84; Boyd 62	4,707
43	lge1	Hull City	A	L	0-1		17,112
44	lge1	Tranmere	H	L	0-1		4,887
45	lge1	Bradford	A	W	2-1	Williams, E 42; Porter 73	7,509
46	lge1	Huddersfield	H	L	0-1		6,205
47	lge1	Blackpool	A	D	2-2	Boyd 27,28	6,853
48	lge1	Swindon	H	W	3-0	Porter 31; Butler 49; Humphreys 83	4,936
49	lge1	Peterborough	H	D	2-2	Porter 22; Sweeney 36	4,579
50	lge1	Colchester	A	D	1-1	Sweeney 54	3,148
51	lge1	Sheff Wed	H	W	3-0	Boyd 2,18,58	6,429
52	lge1	Doncaster	A	L	0-2		7,024
53	lge1	Walsall	H	L	1-3	Boyd 77 pen	6,389
54	lge1	Bournemouth	A	D	2-2	Daly 20; Sweeney 65	8,620
55	d2po1	Tranmere	H	W	2-0	Boyd 32,68	6,604
56	d2po2	Tranmere	A	W	0-2*	(*won 6-5 on penalties)	13,356
57	d2pof	Sheff Wed	H	L	2-4	Williams, E 47; Daly 71	59,808

MONTHLY POINTS TALLY

AUGUST	10	56%
SEPTEMBER	4	33%
OCTOBER	9	50%
NOVEMBER	6	67%
DECEMBER	10	67%
JANUARY	10	83%
FEBRUARY	9	60%
MARCH	4	22%
APRIL	8	44%
MAY	1	33%

KEY PLAYERS - GOALSCORERS

Adam Boyd

Goals in the League	22	Player Strike Rate Average number of minutes between League goals scored by player	175
Contribution to Attacking Power Average number of minutes between League team goals while on pitch	54	Club Strike Rate Average number of minutes between League goals scored by club	54

	PLAYER	LGE GOALS	GOALS ALL	POWER	STRIKE RATE
1	Adam Boyd	22	28	54	175 mins
2	Joel Porter	14	15	47	205 mins
3	Anthony Sweeney	13	14	54	303 mins
4	Eifion Williams	5	7	61	565 mins
5	Hugh Robertson	2	2	51	765 mins

KEY PLAYERS - MIDFIELDERS

Jack Ross

Goals in the League	0	Contribution to Attacking Power Average number of minutes between League team goals while on pitch	50
Defensive Rating Average number of mins between League goals conceded while on the pitch	104	Scoring Difference Defensive Rating minus Contribution to Attacking Power	54

	PLAYER	LGE GOALS	GOALS ALL	DEF RATE	POWER	SCORE DIFF
1	Jack Ross	0	0	104	50	54 mins
2	Richie Humphreys	3	3	63	54	9 mins
3	Anthony Sweeney	13	14	62	54	8 mins
4	Mark Tinkler	2	3	61	53	8 mins
5	Gavin Strachan	1	1	55	50	5 mins

KEY PLAYERS - DEFENDERS

Hugh Robertson

Goals Conceded Number of League goals conceded while the player was on the pitch	16	Clean Sheets In games when player was on pitch for at least 70 minutes	5
Defensive Rating Ave number of mins between League goals conceded while on the pitch	17	Club Defensive Rating Average number of mins between League goals conceded by the club this season	96

	PLAYER	CON LGE	CON ALL	CLEAN SHEETS	DEF RATE
1	Hugh Robertson	16	17	5	96 mins
2	Ben Clark	26	28	5	71 mins
3	Chris Westwood	48	56	8	67 mins
4	Michael Nelson	61	71	9	61 mins
5	Matty Robson	39	48	4	52 mins

KEY GOALKEEPER

Demitrios Konstantopoulos

Goals Conceded in the League	32	Counting Games Games when player was on pitch for at least 70 minutes	25
Defensive Rating Ave number of mins between League goals conceded while on the pitch	70	Clean Sheets In Games when player was on pitch for at least 70 minutes	7

LEAGUE GOALS

Adam Boyd

Minutes on the pitch	3855	League average (mins between goals)	175
Goals in the League	22		

	PLAYER	MINS	GOALS	AVE
1	Boyd	3855	22	175
2	Porter	2876	14	205
3	Sweeney	3937	13	303
4	Williams, E	2827	5	565
5	Westwood	3231	4	808
6	Humphreys	4094	3	1365
7	Robertson	1530	2	765
8	Robson	2034	2	1017
9	Tinkler	2612	2	1306
10	Appleby	317	2	159
11	Nelson	3714	1	3714
12	Daly	452	1	452
13	Strachan	1752	1	1752
	Other		4	
	TOTAL		76	

DISCIPLINARY RECORDS

	PLAYER	YELLOW	RED	AVE
1	Craddock	2	0	338
2	Tinkler	6	0	435
3	Nelson	7	0	530
4	Clark	3	0	614
5	Sweeney	4	1	787
6	Westwood	4	0	807
7	Barron	1	0	896
8	Ross	2	0	932
9	Williams, E	3	0	942
10	Provett	2	0	945
11	Robson	2	0	1017
12	Boyd	3	0	1285
13	Porter	2	0	1438
	Other	2	0	
	TOTAL	43	1	

TOP POINT EARNERS

	PLAYER	GAMES	AV PTS
1	Ross	19	2.05
2	Robertson	16	2.00
3	Konstantopoulos	25	1.84
4	Tinkler	27	1.78
5	Porter	29	1.76
6	Clark	18	1.67
7	Westwood	35	1.60
8	Strachan	17	1.59
9	Humphreys	45	1.58
10	Sweeney	44	1.55
	CLUB AVERAGE:		1.54

TEAM OF THE SEASON

D
Hugh Robertson
CG: 16 DR: 96
M
Jack Ross
CG: 19 SD: 54
D
Ben Clark
CG: 18 DR: 71
M
Richie Humphreys
CG: 45 SD: 9
F
Adam Boyd
CG: 41 SR: 175
G
Konstantopoulos
CG: 25 DR: 70
D
Chris Westwood
CG: 35 DR: 67
M
Anthony Sweeney
CG: 44 SD: 8
F
Joel Porter
CG: 29 SR: 205
D
Michael Nelson
CG: 40 DR: 61
M
Mark Tinkler
CG: 27 SD: 8

LEAGUE APPEARANCES GOALS AND BOOKINGS

	AGE (on 01/07/05)	IN NAMED 16	APPEARANCES	COUNTING GAMES	MINUTES ON PITCH	LEAGUE GOALS		
Goalkeepers								
Konstantopoulos	26	46	25	25	2250	0	0	0
Jim Provett	22	46	21	21	1890	0	2	0
Defenders								
Michael Barron	30	18	13	8	896	0	1	0
John Brackstone	20	15	9	7	685	0	0	0
Ben Clark	22	26	25	18	1844	0	3	0
Darren Craddock	20	20	9	7	677	0	2	0
Steve Howey	33	3	1	0	43	0	0	0
Graham Low	18	1	0	0	0	0	0	0
Michael Nelson	23	43	43	40	3714	1	7	0
Hugh Robertson	30	21	20	16	1530	2	1	0
Matty Robson	20	29	27	21	2034	2	2	0
Chris Westwood	28	39	37	35	3231	4	4	0
Neil Wilkinson	19	4	3	0	139	0	0	0
Midfielders								
Thomas Butler	24	9	9	3	465	1	0	0
Darrell Clarke	27	3	1	1	90	0	0	0
Lewis Gobern	20	1	1	1	69	0	0	0
Richie Humphreys	27	46	46	45	4094	3	0	0
Steven Istead	19	31	17	0	210	0	3	0
Michael Maidens	18	1	1	0	3	0	0	0
Alan Pouton	28	5	5	4	415	0	2	0
Jack Ross	29	24	24	19	1865	0	2	0
Gavin Strachan	26	46	29	17	1752	1	1	0
Anthony Sweeney	21	44	44	44	3937	13	4	1
Mark Tinkler	30	34	33	27	2612	2	6	0
Steve Turnbull	18	5	2	0	57	0	0	0
Martin Woods	19	6	6	1	261	0	1	0
Forwards								
Andrew Appleby	19	20	15	0	317	2	0	0
Kevin Betsy	27	6	6	3	341	1	1	0
Adam Boyd	23	45	45	41	3855	22	3	0
James Brown	-	1	0	0	0	0	0	0
Jon Daly	22	15	12	3	452	1	0	0
David Foley	17	4	2	1	94	0	0	0
Joel Porter	26	41	39	29	2876	14	2	0
Eifion Williams	29	38	38	26	2827	5	3	0

SQUAD APPEARANCES

Match	Venue	Competition	Result
1	H	L	W
2	A	L	L
3	A	L	W
4	H	L	D
5	H	W	W
6	A	L	L
7	H	L	W
8	H	L	D
9	A	L	L
10	H	L	W
11	A	W	L
12	A	L	L
13	H	L	W
14	A	L	L
15	H	L	W
16	A	L	L
17	A	L	L
18	H	L	W
19	H	L	W
20	H	F	W
21	A	L	L
22	H	L	W
23	H	F	W
24	A	L	L
25	H	L	W
26	A	L	W
27	H	L	W
28	A	L	D
29	A	L	D
30	H	L	W
31	H	F	D
32	A	L	W
33	A	F	W
34	H	L	W
35	A	F	D
36	A	L	W
37	H	F	L
38	H	L	L
39	A	L	W
40	H	L	W
41	A	L	L
42	H	L	L
43	A	L	L
44	H	L	L
45	A	L	W
46	H	L	L
47	A	L	D
48	H	L	W
49	H	L	D
50	A	L	D
51	H	L	W
52	A	L	L
53	H	L	L
54	A	L	D
55	H	O	W
56	A	O	W
57	H	O	L

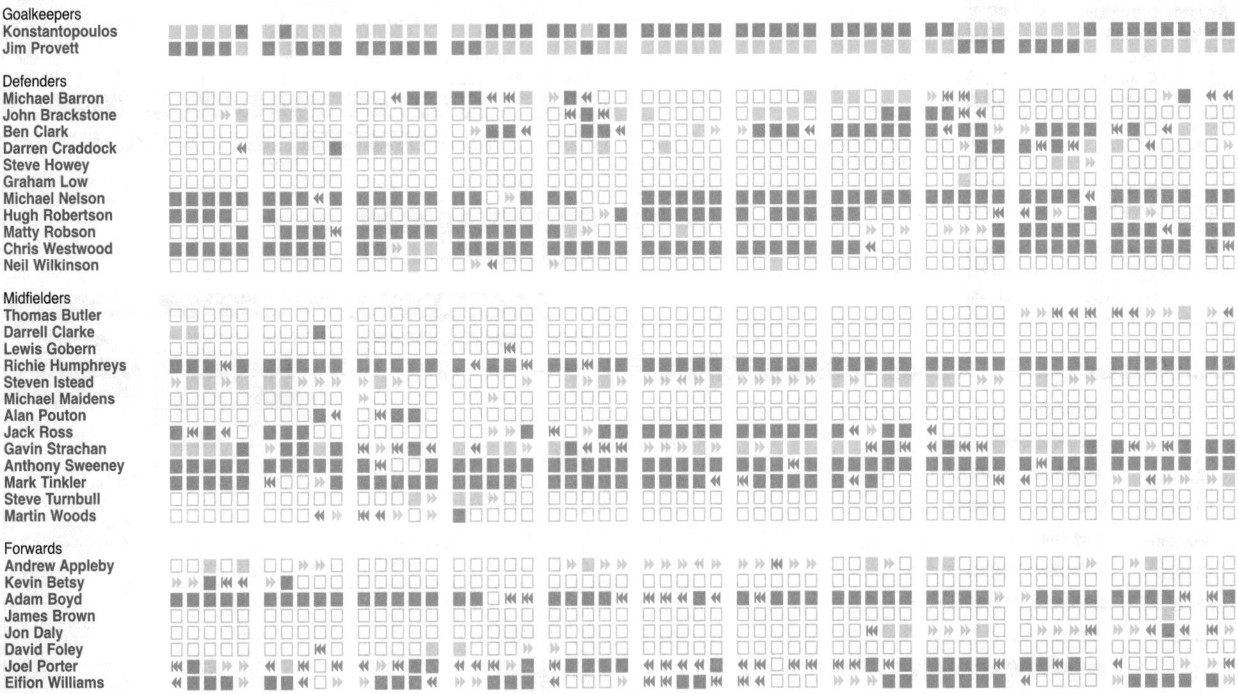
Goalkeepers
Konstantopoulos
Jim Provett
Defenders
Michael Barron
John Brackstone
Ben Clark
Darren Craddock
Steve Howey
Graham Low
Michael Nelson
Hugh Robertson
Matty Robson
Chris Westwood
Neil Wilkinson
Midfielders
Thomas Butler
Darrell Clarke
Lewis Gobern
Richie Humphreys
Steven Istead
Michael Maidens
Alan Pouton
Jack Ross
Gavin Strachan
Anthony Sweeney
Mark Tinkler
Steve Turnbull
Martin Woods
Forwards
Andrew Appleby
Kevin Betsy
Adam Boyd
James Brown
Jon Daly
David Foley
Joel Porter
Eifion Williams

KEY: On all match · On bench · Subbed or sent off (Counting game) · Subbed or sent off (playing less than 70 minutes) · Subbed on from bench (Counting Game) · Subbed on (playing less than 70 minutes) · Subbed on and then subbed or sent off (Counting Game) · Subbed on and then subbed or sent off (playing less than 70 minutes) · Not in 16

BRISTOL CITY

Final Position: **7th**

NICKNAME: THE ROBINS

KEY: ☐Won ☐Drawn ☐Lost

						Attendance
1 lge1	**Torquay**	H D	1-1	Lita 59		14,275
2 lge1	**Barnsley**	A L	1-2	Lita 88		10,435
3 lge1	**Bournemouth**	A D	2-2	Lita 77; Smith 90		6,918
4 lge1	**Swindon**	H L	1-2	Doherty 45		13,389
5 ccR1	**Wycombe**	A W	1-0	Lita 70		1,778
6 lge1	**Port Vale**	A L	0-3			5,377
7 lge1	**Brentford**	H W	4-1	Wilkshire 25,69; Murray 48,73		10,296
8 lge1	**Peterborough**	A W	1-0	Lita 72		4,227
9 lge1	**Stockport**	H W	5-0	Tinnion 11; Roberts 24; Lita 31,80; Heffernan 79		10,811
10 lge1	**Bradford**	A L	1-4	Murray 88		7,235
11 ccR2	**Everton**	H L	3-4*	Stubbs 50 og; Lita 53 (*on penalties)		15,264
12 lge1	**Huddersfield**	H D	3-3	Murray 9; Lita 82 pen; Mirfin 90 og		10,783
13 lge1	**Chesterfield**	A D	2-2	Murray 47; Coles 54		4,854
14 lge1	**Hull City**	H W	3-1	Brooker 38; Wilkshire 58; Butler 85		12,011
15 lge1	**Oldham**	A D	0-0			5,090
16 lge1	**Walsall**	A W	2-1	Lita 64,90		7,105
17 lge1	**Colchester**	H D	0-0			11,678
18 lge1	**MK Dons**	H W	4-1	Lita 4,25; Brooker 29; Wilkshire 63		10,717
19 lge1	**Tranmere**	H W	4-0	Brooker 19,57; Wilkshire 41,90 pen		11,098
20 facr1	**Brentford**	H D	1-1	Lita 89		10,000
21 lge1	**Wrexham**	A W	3-1	Bell 36 pen; Murray 44; Brooker 52		7,833
22 facr1r	**Brentford**	A L	3-4*	Heffernan 77 (*on penalties)		3,706
23 lge1	**Sheff Wed**	H L	1-4	Murray 56		14,852
24 lge1	**Doncaster**	A D	1-1	Brooker 45		5,608
25 lge1	**Blackpool**	A D	1-1	Wilkshire 21		5,220
26 lge1	**Luton**	H L	1-2	Lita 66		13,414
27 lge1	**Stockport**	A W	2-1	Butler 5; Heffernan 55		5,071
28 lge1	**Hartlepool**	H D	0-0			13,034
29 lge1	**Peterborough**	H W	2-0	Brooker 30; Heffernan 34		10,873
30 lge1	**Huddersfield**	A D	2-2	Lita 71; Clarke, N 90 og		11,151
31 lge1	**Tranmere**	A W	1-0	Lita 10		8,183
32 lge1	**Bradford**	H D	0-0			11,605
33 lge1	**Hartlepool**	A L	1-2	Brooker 26		5,399
34 lge1	**Chesterfield**	H L	2-3	Brooker 67; Smith 70		10,103
35 lge1	**Hull City**	A D	1-1	Lita 76		17,637
36 lge1	**Walsall**	H L	0-1			10,820
37 lge1	**Colchester**	A W	2-0	Brooker 51; Lita 71		3,412
38 lge1	**Oldham**	H W	5-1	Lita 8,23; Wilkshire 45; Brooker 52; Branston 87 og		9,007
39 lge1	**Blackpool**	H D	1-1	Brooker 21		10,977
40 lge1	**Luton**	A L	0-5			8,330
41 lge1	**Barnsley**	H D	0-0			9,321
42 lge1	**Torquay**	A W	4-0	Lita 9,12,21; Heffernan 54		4,299
43 lge1	**Port Vale**	H W	2-0	Lita 14; Heffernan 68		10,284
44 lge1	**Bournemouth**	H L	0-2			12,008
45 lge1	**Brentford**	A L	0-1			6,780
46 lge1	**Swindon**	A D	0-0			6,977
47 lge1	**Wrexham**	H W	1-0	Murray 66		8,267
48 lge1	**MK Dons**	A W	2-1	Lita 45,70		5,656
49 lge1	**Doncaster**	H D	2-2	Brooker 62,90		12,375
50 lge1	**Sheff Wed**	A W	3-2	Brooker 25,45; Wilkshire 81 pen		28,798

MONTHLY POINTS TALLY

AUGUST	5	28%
SEPTEMBER	7	58%
OCTOBER	9	60%
NOVEMBER	9	75%
DECEMBER	6	40%
JANUARY	8	44%
FEBRUARY	8	53%
MARCH	4	44%
APRIL	11	52%
MAY	3	100%

KEY PLAYERS - GOALSCORERS

Leroy Lita

Goals in the League	24	Player Strike Rate Average number of minutes between League goals scored by player	153
Contribution to Attacking Power Average number of minutes between League team goals while on pitch	56	Club Strike Rate Average number of minutes between League goals scored by club	56

	PLAYER	LGE GOALS	GOALS ALL	POWER	STRIKE RATE
1	Leroy Lita	24	27	56	153 mins
2	Stephen Brooker	16	16	58	171 mins
3	Luke Wilkshire	9	9	55	316 mins
4	Scott Murray	8	8	52	357 mins
5	Anthony Butler	2	2	49	932 mins

KEY PLAYERS - MIDFIELDERS

Scott Murray

Goals in the League	8	Contribution to Attacking Power Average number of minutes between League team goals while on pitch	52
Defensive Rating Average number of mins between League goals conceded while on the pitch	77	Scoring Difference Defensive Rating minus Contribution to Attacking Power	25

	PLAYER	LGE GOALS	GOALS ALL	DEF RATE	POWER	SCORE DIFF
1	Scott Murray	8	8	77	52	25 mins
2	Tommy Doherty	1	1	71	50	21 mins
3	Luke Wilkshire	9	9	75	55	20 mins
4	Bradley Orr	0	0	80	83	-3 mins

KEY PLAYERS - DEFENDERS

Louis Carey

Goals Conceded Number of League goals conceded while the player was on the pitch	16	Clean Sheets In games when player was on pitch for at least 70 minutes	4
Defensive Rating Ave number of mins between League goals conceded while on the pitch	77	Club Defensive Rating Average number of mins between League goals conceded by the club this season	73

	PLAYER	CON LGE	CON ALL	CLEAN SHEETS	DEF RATE
1	Louis Carey	16	16	4	77 mins
2	Danny Coles	44	47	12	75 mins
3	Anthony Butler	25	29	6	75 mins
4	Clayton Fortune	24	25	5	74 mins
5	Mick Bell	33	34	8	70 mins

KEY GOALKEEPER

Steve Phillips

Goals Conceded in the League	57	Counting Games Games when player was on pitch for at least 70 minutes	46
Defensive Rating Ave number of mins between League goals conceded while on the pitch	73	Clean Sheets In Games when player was on pitch for at least 70 minutes	15

LEAGUE GOALS

Leroy Lita

Minutes on the pitch	3675	League average (mins between goals)	153
Goals in the League	24		

	PLAYER	MINS	GOALS	AVE
1	Lita	3675	24	153
2	Brooker	2743	16	171
3	Wilkshire	2840	9	316
4	Murray	2855	8	357
5	Heffernan	1238	5	248
6	Butler	1863	2	932
7	Smith	3032	2	1516
8	Roberts	479	1	479
9	Tinnion	1366	1	1366
10	Doherty	2197	1	2197
11	Bell	2310	1	2310
12	Coles	3282	1	3282
	Other		3	
	TOTAL		74	

DISCIPLINARY RECORDS

	PLAYER	YELLOW	RED	AVE
1	Doherty	12	0	183
2	Brown	5	0	229
3	Butler	7	0	266
4	Tinnion	5	0	273
5	Coles	11	1	273
6	Orr	6	0	371
7	Brooker	7	0	391
8	Dinning	3	0	421
9	Smith	6	1	433
10	Roberts	1	0	479
11	Fortune	2	0	891
12	Wilkshire	3	0	946
13	Murray	3	0	951
	Other	9	0	
	TOTAL	80	2	

TOP POINT EARNERS

	PLAYER	GAMES	AV PTS
1	Luke Wilkshire	28	1.93
2	Danny Coles	35	1.77
3	Anthony Butler	19	1.74
4	Louis Carey	13	1.69
5	Mick Bell	24	1.67
6	Stephen Brooker	28	1.64
7	Scott Murray	28	1.61
8	Steve Phillips	46	1.52
9	Tommy Doherty	23	1.48
10	Matthew Hill	22	1.45
	CLUB AVERAGE:		1.52

LEAGUE APPEARANCES GOALS AND BOOKINGS

	AGE (on 01/07/05)	IN NAMED 16	APPEARANCES	COUNTING GAMES	MINUTES ON PITCH	LEAGUE GOALS	Yellow	Red
Goalkeepers								
Jonathan Gould	36	1	0	0	0	0	0	0
Steve Phillips	27	46	46	46	4140	0	3	0
Defenders								
Kevin Amankwaah	23	9	5	1	159	0	0	0
Mick Bell	33	35	31	24	2310	1	1	0
Anthony Butler	32	22	22	19	1863	2	7	0
Louis Carey	28	14	14	13	1228	0	1	0
Danny Coles	23	40	38	35	3282	1	11	1
Clayton Fortune	22	38	30	15	1783	0	2	0
Scott Goldbourne	17	11	9	7	634	0	0	0
Ryan Harley	20	4	2	0	69	0	0	0
Matthew Hill	24	23	23	22	2037	0	1	0
Craig Ireland	29	5	5	5	450	0	2	0
Cole Skuse	19	10	7	4	433	0	1	0
Jamie Smith	30	40	39	30	3032	2	6	1
Craig Woodman	22	7	3	3	254	0	0	0
Midfielders								
Joe Anyinsah	20	13	7	1	228	0	0	0
Scott Brown	20	24	19	8	1146	0	5	0
Tony Dinning	30	20	19	11	1263	0	3	0
Tommy Doherty	26	31	29	23	2197	1	12	0
Marc Goodfellow	23	8	5	1	188	0	0	0
Joe Keith	26	4	3	2	227	0	0	0
Scott Murray	31	42	42	28	2855	8	3	0
Bradley Orr	22	44	37	19	2228	0	6	0
Brian Tinnion	37	27	22	11	1366	1	5	0
Luke Wilkshire	23	39	37	28	2840	9	3	0
Danny Wring	18	1	1	0	4	0	0	0
Forwards								
Stephen Brooker	24	33	33	28	2743	16	7	0
David Cotterill	17	15	12	6	648	0	0	0
Stephen Gillespie	21	22	8	0	207	0	0	0
Paul Heffernan	23	42	27	8	1238	5	1	0
Leroy Lita	20	44	44	39	3675	24	2	0
Lee Miller	22	13	7	1	247	0	0	0
Christian Roberts	25	9	8	4	479	1	1	0

TEAM OF THE SEASON

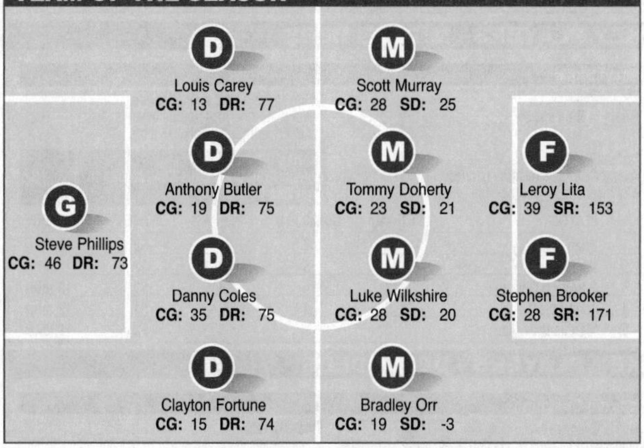
D
Louis Carey
CG: 13 DR: 77
M
Scott Murray
CG: 28 SD: 25
D
Anthony Butler
CG: 19 DR: 75
M
Tommy Doherty
CG: 23 SD: 21
F
Leroy Lita
CG: 39 SR: 153
G
Steve Phillips
CG: 46 DR: 73
D
Danny Coles
CG: 35 DR: 75
M
Luke Wilkshire
CG: 28 SD: 20
F
Stephen Brooker
CG: 28 SR: 171
D
Clayton Fortune
CG: 15 DR: 74
M
Bradley Orr
CG: 19 SD: -3

SQUAD APPEARANCES

Match	1	2	3	4	5	6	7	8	9	10	11	12	13	14	15	16	17	18	19	20	21	22	23	24	25	26	27	28	29	30	31	32	33	34	35	36	37	38	39	40	41	42	43	44	45	46	47	48	49	50
Venue	H	A	A	H	A	A	H	A	H	A	H	H	A	H	A	A	H	H	H	H	A	A	H	A	A	H	A	H	H	A	A	H	A	H	A	H	A	H	H	A	H	A	H	H	A	A	H	A	H	A
Competition	L	L	L	L	W	L	L	L	L	L	W	L	L	L	L	L	L	L	L	F	L	F	L	L	L	L	L	L	L	L	L	L	L	L	L	L	L	L	L	L	L	L	L	L	L	L	L	L	L	L
Result	D	L	D	L	W	L	W	W	W	L	L	D	D	W	D	W	D	W	W	D	W	L	L	D	D	L	W	D	W	D	W	D	L	L	D	L	W	W	D	L	D	W	W	L	L	D	W	W	D	W

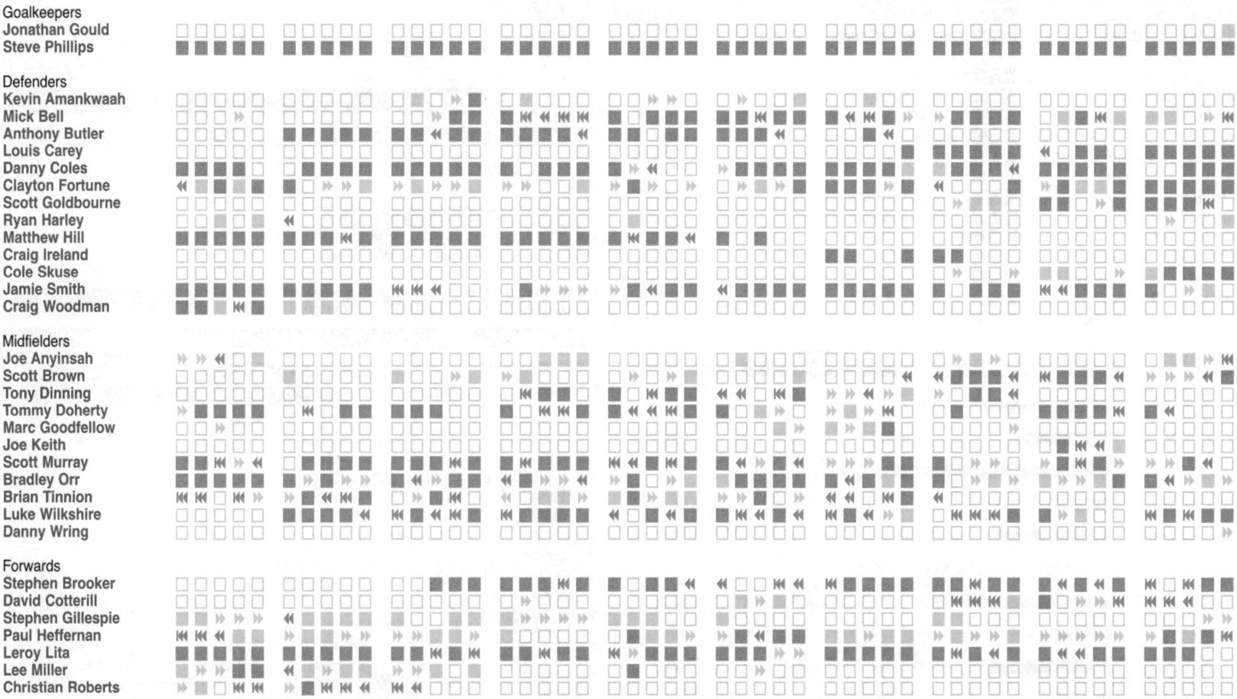
Goalkeepers
Jonathan Gould
Steve Phillips
Defenders
Kevin Amankwaah
Mick Bell
Anthony Butler
Louis Carey
Danny Coles
Clayton Fortune
Scott Goldbourne
Ryan Harley
Matthew Hill
Craig Ireland
Cole Skuse
Jamie Smith
Craig Woodman
Midfielders
Joe Anyinsah
Scott Brown
Tony Dinning
Tommy Doherty
Marc Goodfellow
Joe Keith
Scott Murray
Bradley Orr
Brian Tinnion
Luke Wilkshire
Danny Wring
Forwards
Stephen Brooker
David Cotterill
Stephen Gillespie
Paul Heffernan
Leroy Lita
Lee Miller
Christian Roberts

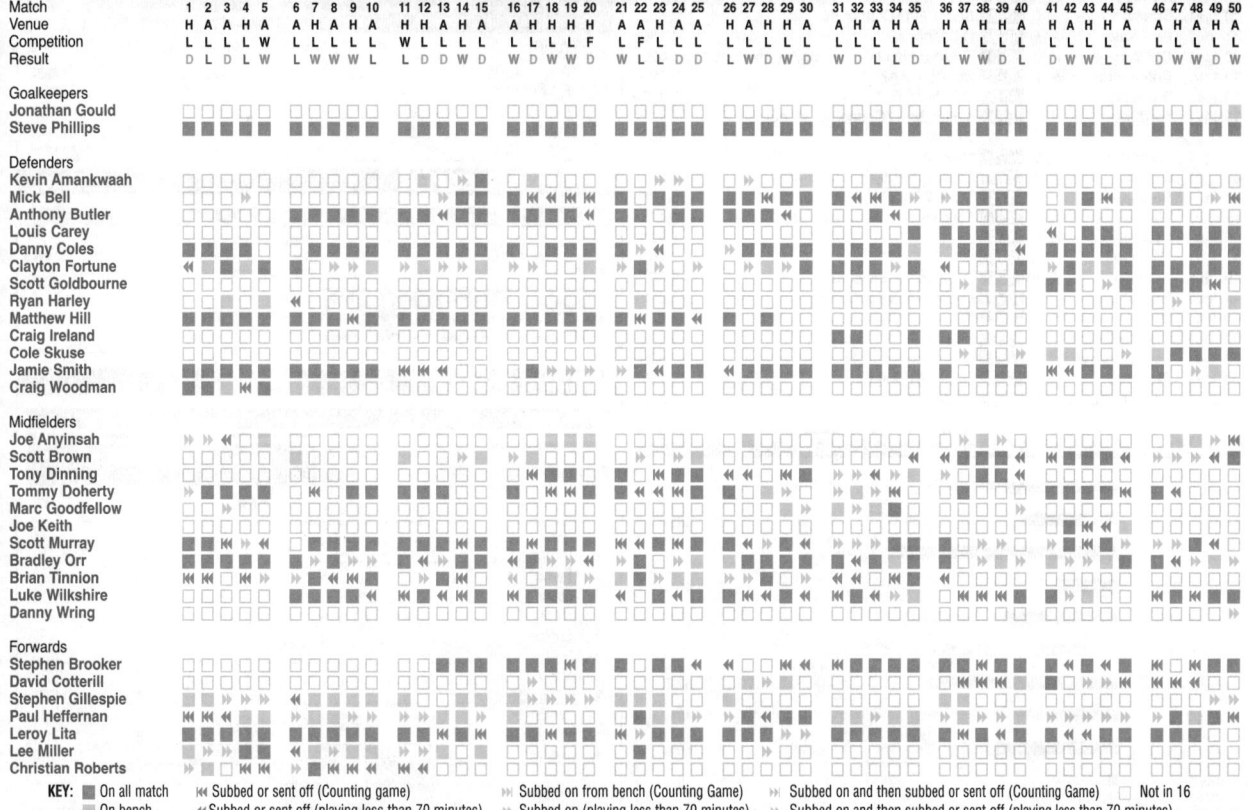

KEY: ■ On all match | ⏮ Subbed or sent off (Counting game) | ⏭ Subbed on from bench (Counting Game) | Subbed on and then subbed or sent off (Counting Game) | □ Not in 16
On bench | « Subbed or sent off (playing less than 70 minutes) | » Subbed on (playing less than 70 minutes) | Subbed on and then subbed or sent off (playing less than 70 minutes)

BOURNEMOUTH

Final Position: **8th**

NICKNAME: THE CHERRIES

KEY: Won / Drawn / Lost

							Attendance
1	lge1	**Hull City**	A	L	0-1		17,569
2	lge1	**Walsall**	H	D	2-2	Hayter 72; Elliott 74	6,485
3	lge1	**Bristol City**	H	D	2-2	Fletcher 38; Hayter 88	6,918
4	lge1	**MK Dons**	A	W	3-1	Hayter 21,76; Fletcher 90	3,230
5	ccR1	**Leyton Orient**	A	W	3-1	Browning 33; Cummings 64; Hayter 71	1,705
6	lge1	**Wrexham**	H	W	1-0	Connell 28	5,774
7	lge1	**Luton**	A	L	0-1		7,404
8	lge1	**Brentford**	A	L	1-2	Holmes 50	5,682
9	lge1	**Colchester**	H	L	1-3	Stockley 74 og	5,944
10	lge1	**Sheff Wed**	A	W	1-0	Spicer 41	19,203
11	ccr2	**Blackburn**	A	W	7-6*	O'Connor 13; Broadhurst 82; Spicer 115 (*on penalties)	7,226
12	lge1	**Doncaster**	H	W	5-0	Rodrigues 3; Hayter 5,70; Howe 19; O'Connor 25	6,588
13	lge1	**Blackpool**	A	D	3-3	Hayter 12; Rodrigues 28,64	5,525
14	lge1	**Stockport**	H	W	2-1	Stock 22; Hayter 45	6,925
15	lge1	**Port Vale**	H	W	4-0	Spicer 9; Stock 39,45; Cummings 46	6,119
16	lge1	**Torquay**	A	W	2-1	Fletcher 57; O'Connor 62	3,055
17	lge1	**Oldham**	A	W	2-1	Hayter 59,76	5,335
18	ccr3	**Cardiff**	H	L	4-5*	Hayter 8,90; Stock 118 (*on penalties)	5,598
19	lge1	**Barnsley**	H	L	1-3	Elliott 52	7,709
20	lge1	**Peterborough**	A	W	1-0	Hayter 4	4,004
21	facr1	**Forest Green**	A	D	1-1	Fletcher 24	1,837
22	lge1	**Chesterfield**	H	D	0-0		6,565
23	facr1r	**Forest Green**	H	W	3-1	Connell 10; Spicer 70; Rodrigues 90	5,489
24	lge1	**Hartlepool**	A	L	2-3	Holmes 34; Stock 45	4,376
25	facr2	**Carlisle**	H	W	2-1	Holmes 48; Connell 64	5,815
26	lge1	**Bradford**	H	W	2-0	Broadhurst 12; Connell 18	5,578
27	lge1	**Tranmere**	A	L	0-2		8,557
28	lge1	**Swindon**	H	W	2-1	O'Connor 51; Maher 77	7,110
29	lge1	**Huddersfield**	H	D	2-2	Spicer 17,51	8,448
30	lge1	**Brentford**	H	W	3-2	Fletcher 5,35,58	8,072
31	lge1	**Doncaster**	A	D	1-1	Spicer 44	6,016
32	facr3	**Chester**	H	W	2-1	Maher 33; Elliott 56	7,653
33	lge1	**Sheff Wed**	H	D	1-1	O'Connor 11	8,847
34	lge1	**Huddersfield**	A	L	2-3	Hayter 45,62	9,754
35	facr4	**Burnley**	A	L	0-2		9,944
36	lge1	**Stockport**	A	D	2-2	Spicer 6; O'Connor 83	3,850
37	lge1	**Port Vale**	A	L	1-2	O'Connor 13	4,186
38	lge1	**Oldham**	H	W	4-0	Fletcher 28; O'Connor 60,90; Hayter 81	6,622
39	lge1	**Colchester**	A	L	1-3	Cummings 47	2,820
40	lge1	**Barnsley**	A	W	1-0	O'Connor, G 77	8,153
41	lge1	**Torquay**	H	W	3-0	Maher 29; O'Connor, G 48 pen; Fletcher 84	5,887
42	lge1	**Tranmere**	H	D	1-1	Mills 43	7,305
43	lge1	**Swindon**	A	W	3-0	Elliott 1; Hayter 56; Mills 74	8,275
44	lge1	**Blackpool**	H	L	2-3	Stock 7; Hayter 90 pen	5,390
45	lge1	**Walsall**	A	W	2-1	Fletcher 40; O'Connor, G 53	5,126
46	lge1	**Hull City**	H	L	0-4		8,895
47	lge1	**MK Dons**	H	L	0-1		7,064
48	lge1	**Wrexham**	A	W	2-1	Purches 58; Elliott 67	3,801
49	lge1	**Bristol City**	A	W	2-0	O'Connor, G 60,77 pen	12,008
50	lge1	**Luton**	H	L	0-1		9,058
51	lge1	**Chesterfield**	A	W	3-2	Fletcher 47,90; Stock 63	4,009
52	lge1	**Peterborough**	H	L	0-1		7,929
53	lge1	**Bradford**	A	L	2-4	Hayter 61; Mills 63	10,263
54	lge1	**Hartlepool**	H	D	2-2	Hayter 12,31	8,620

MONTHLY POINTS TALLY

AUGUST	8	44%
SEPTEMBER	6	50%
OCTOBER	13	72%
NOVEMBER	4	44%
DECEMBER	7	58%
JANUARY	5	42%
FEBRUARY	11	52%
MARCH	6	40%
APRIL	9	50%
MAY	1	33%

KEY PLAYERS - GOALSCORERS

James Hayter

Goals in the League	19	Player Strike Rate Average number of minutes between League goals scored by player	171
Contribution to Attacking Power Average number of minutes between League team goals while on pitch	51	Club Strike Rate Average number of minutes between League goals scored by club	54

	PLAYER	LGE GOALS	GOALS ALL	POWER	STRIKE RATE
1	James Hayter	19	22	51	171 mins
2	Garreth O'Connor	13	14	53	259 mins
3	Steve Fletcher	9	10	54	303 mins
4	Matthew Mills	3	3	54	360 mins
5	Brian Stock	6	7	52	555 mins

KEY PLAYERS - MIDFIELDERS

Brian Stock

Goals in the League	6	Contribution to Attacking Power Average number of minutes between League team goals while on pitch	52
Defensive Rating Average number of mins between League goals conceded while on the pitch	68	Scoring Difference Defensive Rating minus Contribution to Attacking Power	16

	PLAYER	LGE GOALS	GOALS ALL	DEF RATE	POWER	SCORE DIFF
1	Brian Stock	6	7	68	52	16 mins
2	Wade Elliott	4	5	68	52	16 mins
3	Garreth O'Connor	13	14	66	53	13 mins
4	John Spicer	6	8	63	51	12 mins
5	Marcus Browning	0	1	60	72	-12 mins

KEY PLAYERS - DEFENDERS

Warren Cummings

Goals Conceded Number of League goals conceded while the player was on the pitch	35	Clean Sheets In games when player was on pitch for at least 70 minutes	9
Defensive Rating Ave number of mins between League goals conceded while on the pitch	76	Club Defensive Rating Average number of mins between League goals conceded by the club this season	65

	PLAYER	CON LGE	CON ALL	CLEAN SHEETS	DEF RATE
1	Warren Cummings	35	43	9	76 mins
2	Eddie Howe	43	50	8	67 mins
3	Karl Broadhurst	39	52	7	65 mins
4	Neil Young	34	41	4	60 mins
5	Matthew Mills	18	18	3	60 mins

KEY GOALKEEPER

Neil Moss

Goals Conceded in the League	64	Counting Games Games when player was on pitch for at least 70 minutes	46
Defensive Rating Ave number of mins between League goals conceded while on the pitch	65	Clean Sheets In Games when player was on pitch for at least 70 minutes	12

LEAGUE GOALS

James Hayter

Minutes on the pitch	3247	League average (mins between goals)	171
Goals in the League	19		

	PLAYER	MINS	GOALS	AVE
1	Hayter	3247	19	171
2	O'Connor, G	3373	13	259
3	Fletcher	2727	9	303
4	Spicer	3477	6	580
5	Stock	3328	6	555
6	Elliott	3785	4	946
7	Mills	1080	3	360
8	Maher	2633	2	1317
9	Cummings	2663	2	1332
10	Connell	897	2	449
11	Rodrigues	832	2	416
12	Holmes	791	2	396
	Other		7	
	TOTAL		77	

DISCIPLINARY RECORDS

	PLAYER	YELLOW	RED	AVE
1	Young	4	2	342
2	Mills	2	0	540
3	Browning	3	0	620
4	Stock	5	0	665
5	Howe	4	0	720
6	Rodrigues	1	0	832
7	Maher	2	1	877
8	Connell	1	0	897
9	O'Connor, G	3	0	1124
10	Spicer	3	0	1159
11	Elliott	3	0	1261
12	Cummings	2	0	1331
13	Fletcher	2	0	1363
	Other	0	0	
	TOTAL	35	3	

TOP POINT EARNERS

	PLAYER	GAMES	AV PTS
1	Brian Stock	34	1.74
2	Neil Young	19	1.68
3	Garreth O'Connor	38	1.63
4	Wade Elliott	42	1.60
5	John Spicer	39	1.59
6	Matthew Mills	12	1.58
7	James Hayter	36	1.58
8	Karl Broadhurst	28	1.57
9	Warren Cummings	29	1.55
10	Eddie Howe	31	1.55
	CLUB AVERAGE:		1.52

LEAGUE APPEARANCES GOALS AND BOOKINGS

	AGE (on 01/07/05)	IN NAMED 16	APPEARANCES	COUNTING GAMES	MINUTES ON PITCH	LEAGUE GOALS	Yellow	Red
Goalkeepers								
Neil Moss	30	47	46	46	4140	0	0	0
Gareth Stewart	25	44	0	0	0	0	0	0
Defenders								
Karl Broadhurst	25	29	29	28	2548	1	0	0
Martin Cranie	18	3	3	2	193	0	0	0
Warren Cummings	24	30	30	29	2663	2	2	0
Adam Green	21	5	3	3	237	0	1	0
Eddie Howe	27	36	35	31	2883	1	4	0
Shaun Maher	27	43	36	28	2633	2	2	1
Matthew Mills	18	12	12	12	1080	3	2	0
James O'Connor	20	6	6	6	540	0	0	0
Frankie Simek	20	8	8	7	669	0	0	0
Neil Young	31	33	30	19	2055	0	4	2
Midfielders								
Diogo Andrade	19	3	0	0	0	0	0	0
Marcus Browning	34	42	40	17	1860	0	3	0
James Coutts	18	16	1	0	15	0	0	0
Wade Elliott	26	43	43	42	3785	4	3	0
Carl Fletcher	25	6	6	6	540	2	0	0
Garreth O'Connor	26	41	40	38	3373	13	3	0
Stephen Purches	25	19	14	9	903	1	0	0
James Rowe	18	4	2	0	31	0	0	0
John Spicer	21	39	39	39	3477	6	3	0
Brian Stock	23	41	41	34	3328	6	5	0
Forwards								
Alan Connell	22	44	34	5	897	2	1	0
Steve Fletcher	33	36	36	28	2727	9	2	0
James Hayter	26	39	39	36	3247	19	0	0
Derek Holmes	26	32	23	4	791	2	0	0
Ryan Moss	–	1	1	0	1	0	0	0
Brett Pitman	–	1	0	0	0	0	0	0
Dani Rodrigues	25	33	23	8	832	2	1	0

TEAM OF THE SEASON

D
Warren Cummings
CG: 29 DR: 76
M
Wade Elliott
CG: 42 SD: 16
D
Eddie Howe
CG: 31 DR: 67
M
Brian Stock
CG: 34 SD: 16
F
James Hayter
CG: 36 SR: 171
G
Neil Moss
CG: 46 DR: 65
D
Karl Broadhurst
CG: 28 DR: 65
M
Garreth O'Connor
CG: 38 SD: 13
F
Steve Fletcher
CG: 28 SR: 303
D
Matthew Mills
CG: 12 DR: 60
M
John Spicer
CG: 39 SD: 12

SQUAD APPEARANCES

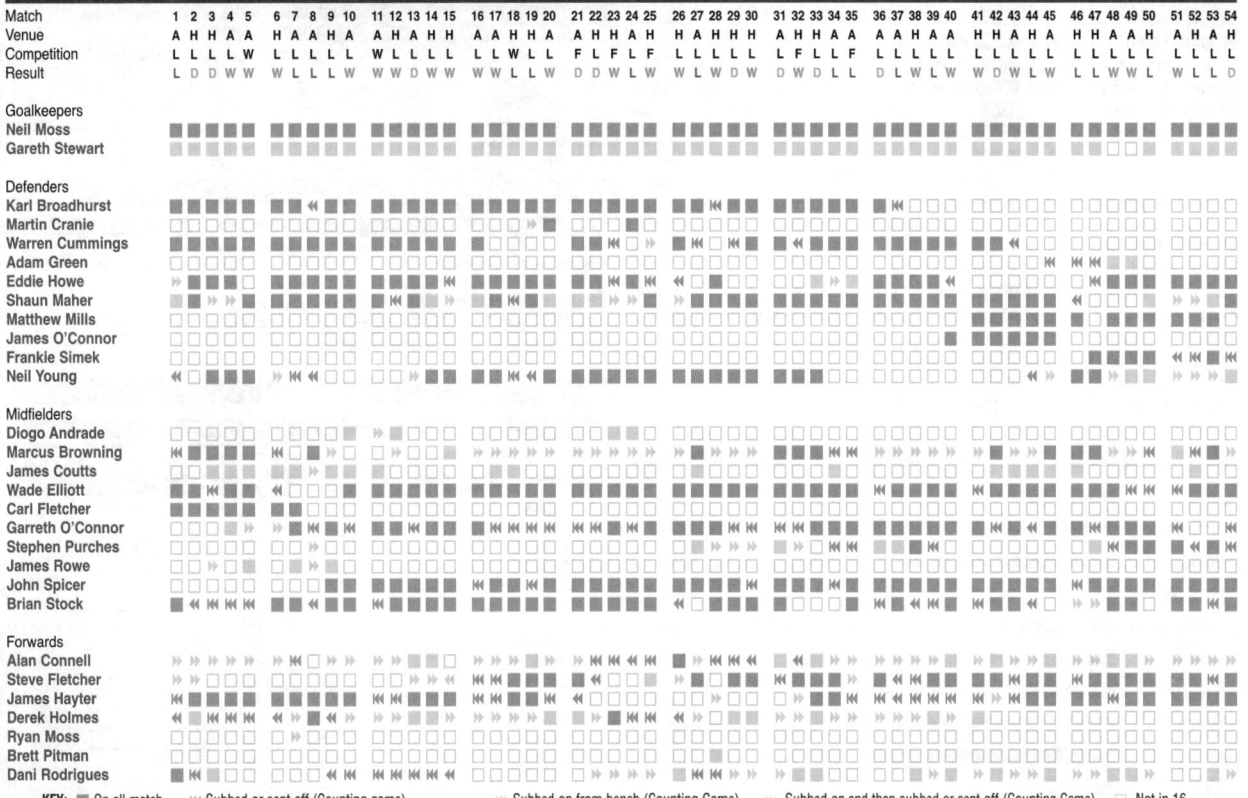

Match	1	2	3	4	5	6	7	8	9	10	11	12	13	14	15	16	17	18	19	20	21	22	23	24	25	26	27
Venue	A	H	H	A	A	H	A	A	H	A	A	H	A	H	H	A	A	H	H	A	A	H	H	A	H	H	A
Competition	L	L	L	L	W	L	L	L	L	L	W	L	L	L	L	L	L	W	L	L	F	L	F	L	F	L	L
Result	L	D	D	W	W	W	L	L	L	W	W	W	D	W	W	W	W	L	L	W	D	D	W	L	W	W	L

Match	28	29	30	31	32	33	34	35	36	37	38	39	40	41	42	43	44	45	46	47	48	49	50	51	52	53	54
Venue	H	H	H	A	H	H	A	A	A	A	H	A	A	H	H	A	H	A	H	H	A	A	H	A	H	A	H
Competition	L	L	L	L	F	L	L	F	L	L	L	L	L	L	L	L	L	L	L	L	L	L	L	L	L	L	L
Result	W	D	W	D	W	D	L	L	D	L	W	L	W	W	D	W	L	W	L	L	W	W	L	W	L	L	D

Goalkeepers
Neil Moss
Gareth Stewart

Defenders
Karl Broadhurst
Martin Cranie
Warren Cummings
Adam Green
Eddie Howe
Shaun Maher
Matthew Mills
James O'Connor
Frankie Simek
Neil Young

Midfielders
Diogo Andrade
Marcus Browning
James Coutts
Wade Elliott
Carl Fletcher
Garreth O'Connor
Stephen Purches
James Rowe
John Spicer
Brian Stock

Forwards
Alan Connell
Steve Fletcher
James Hayter
Derek Holmes
Ryan Moss
Brett Pitman
Dani Rodrigues

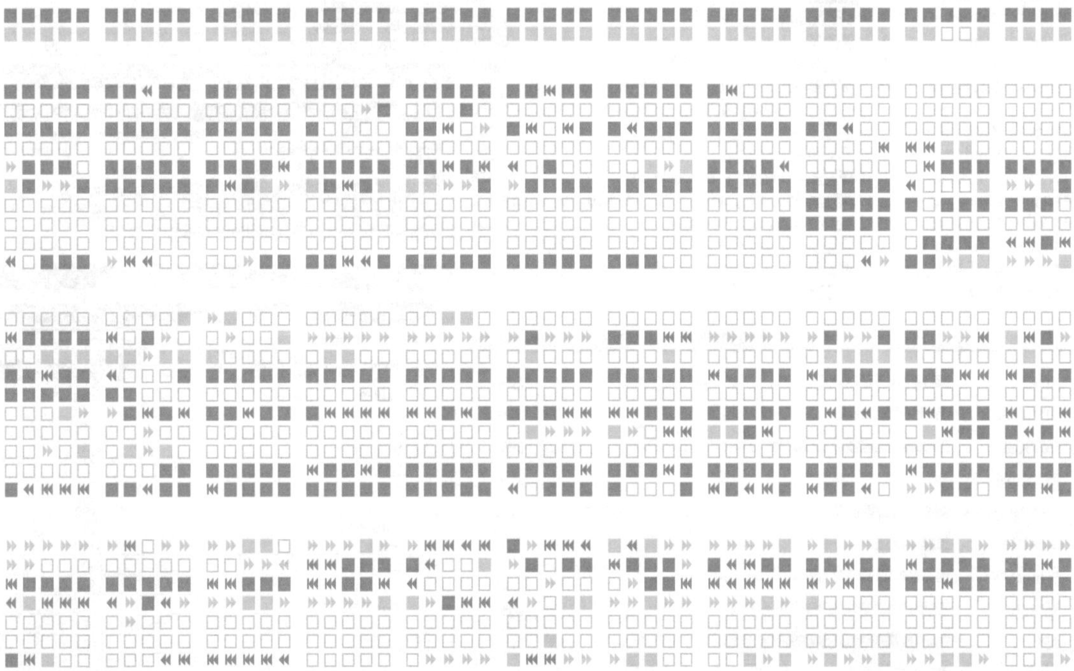

KEY: On all match · On bench · Subbed or sent off (Counting game) · Subbed or sent off (playing less than 70 minutes) · Subbed on from bench (Counting Game) · Subbed on (playing less than 70 minutes) · Subbed on and then subbed or sent off (Counting Game) · Subbed on and then subbed or sent off (playing less than 70 minutes) · Not in 16

HUDDERSFIELD TOWN

Final Position: **9th**

NICKNAME: THE TERRIERS

KEY: Won / Drawn / Lost

						Score	Scorers	Attendance
1	lge1	Stockport	A	W	3-2	Carss 45; Booth 87; Abbott 90	7,473
2	lge1	Chesterfield	H	D	0-0		11,942
3	lge1	Hartlepool	H	L	0-2		9,968
4	lge1	Sheff Wed	A	L	0-1		26,264
5	ccr1	Leeds	A	L	0-1		30,115
6	lge1	Peterborough	H	W	2-1	McAliskey 16; Worthington 48	9,531
7	lge1	Doncaster	A	L	1-2	Worthington 83	7,068
8	lge1	Hull City	H	W	4-0	Abbott 7; Edwards 19; Brandon 74; Booth 87	13,542
9	lge1	Port Vale	A	W	3-0	Abbott 62,67,75	6,298
10	lge1	Barnsley	H	L	0-2		14,794
11	lge1	Bristol City	A	D	3-3	Schofield 28; Abbott 35; Brandon 60	10,783
12	lge1	Walsall	H	W	3-1	Abbott 29,68; Junior Mendes 30	11,324
13	lge1	Torquay	A	L	1-2	Junior Mendes 39	3,033
14	lge1	Luton	A	W	2-1	Junior Mendes 14,36	8,192
15	lge1	Tranmere	H	L	1-3	Abbott 33	10,324
16	lge1	MK Dons	H	W	3-1	Abbott 33,45 pen; Junior Mendes 45	10,709
17	lge1	Blackpool	A	D	1-1	Booth 15	7,676
18	lge1	Brentford	H	D	1-1	Abbott 71	10,810
19	facr1	Stockport	A	L	1-3	Abbott 90	3,479
20	lge1	Colchester	A	D	0-0		3,972
21	lge1	Wrexham	H	L	1-2	Schofield 41	11,127
22	lge1	Swindon	A	W	2-1	Abbott 19; Brandon 34	4,828
23	lge1	Oldham	A	L	1-2	Abbott 7	8,389
24	lge1	Bradford	H	L	0-1		17,281
25	lge1	Port Vale	H	W	2-1	Schofield 4; Abbott 8	12,243
26	lge1	Bournemouth	A	D	2-2	McAliskey 38; Mirfin 60	8,448
27	lge1	Hull City	A	L	1-2	Brandon 40	22,291
28	lge1	Bristol City	H	D	2-2	Orr 18 og; Abbott 58	11,151
29	lge1	Torquay	H	D	1-1	Sodje, E 24	9,194
30	lge1	Barnsley	A	L	2-4	Abbott 55 pen; Booth 70	11,725
31	lge1	Bournemouth	H	W	3-2	Abbott 8 pen; Beckett 35,45	9,754
32	lge1	Walsall	A	L	3-4	Booth 7; Beckett 11,33	5,727
33	lge1	Luton	H	D	1-1	Beckett 90	12,611
34	lge1	MK Dons	A	L	1-2	Booth 30	4,793
35	lge1	Blackpool	H	W	1-0	Beckett 2	10,614
36	lge1	Tranmere	A	L	0-3		7,613
37	lge1	Oldham	H	W	2-1	Abbott 4,29	11,161
38	lge1	Bradford	A	L	0-2		15,417
39	lge1	Chesterfield	A	L	1-2	Mirfin 79	4,827
40	lge1	Stockport	H	W	5-3	Booth 4; Abbott 51; Mirfin 82; Ahmed 83; Dolan 90 og	11,180
41	lge1	Hartlepool	A	W	1-0	Booth 42	6,205
42	lge1	Sheff Wed	H	W	1-0	Worthington 7	17,292
43	lge1	Peterborough	A	W	2-1	Brandon 21; Schofield 84	3,976
44	lge1	Doncaster	H	W	3-1	Abbott 1; Booth 43; Brandon 56	12,972
45	lge1	Colchester	H	D	2-2	Abbott 20; Schofield 62	10,831
46	lge1	Brentford	A	W	1-0	Abbott 26	7,703
47	lge1	Swindon	H	W	4-0	Abbott 62,80; Booth 79; Edwards 85	13,559
48	lge1	Wrexham	A	W	1-0	Mirfin 43	7,151

MONTHLY POINTS TALLY

AUGUST	7	39%
SEPTEMBER	7	58%
OCTOBER	10	56%
NOVEMBER	2	22%
DECEMBER	7	47%
JANUARY	5	28%
FEBRUARY	7	47%
MARCH	9	60%
APRIL	13	87%
MAY	3	100%

KEY PLAYERS - GOALSCORERS

Pawel Abbott

Goals in the League	26	Player Strike Rate Average number of minutes between League goals scored by player	128
Contribution to Attacking Power Average number of minutes between League team goals while on pitch	50	Club Strike Rate Average number of minutes between League goals scored by club	56

	PLAYER	LGE GOALS	GOALS ALL	POWER	STRIKE RATE
1	Pawel Abbott	26	27	50	128 mins
2	Andy Booth	10	10	50	214 mins
3	Junior Mendes	5	5	48	262 mins
4	Danny Schofield	5	5	65	393 mins
5	Chris Brandon	6	6	54	619 mins

KEY PLAYERS - MIDFIELDERS

Adnan Ahmed

Goals in the League	1	Contribution to Attacking Power Average number of minutes between League team goals while on pitch	57
Defensive Rating Average number of mins between League goals conceded while on the pitch	72	Scoring Difference Defensive Rating minus Contribution to Attacking Power	15

	PLAYER	LGE GOALS	GOALS ALL	DEF RATE	POWER	SCORE DIFF
1	Adnan Ahmed	1	1	72	57	15 mins
2	Chris Brandon	6	6	65	54	11 mins
3	Andy Holdsworth	0	0	70	63	7 mins
4	John Worthington	3	3	61	61	0 mins
5	Danny Schofield	5	5	63	65	-2 mins

KEY PLAYERS - DEFENDERS

David Mirfin

Goals Conceded Number of League goals conceded while the player was on the pitch	41	Clean Sheets In games when player was on pitch for at least 70 minutes	10
Defensive Rating Ave number of mins between League goals conceded while on the pitch	77	Club Defensive Rating Average number of mins between League goals conceded while on the pitch	64

	PLAYER	CON LGE	CON ALL	CLEAN SHEETS	DEF RATE
1	David Mirfin	41	45	10	77 mins
2	Rob Edwards	26	27	5	72 mins
3	Nathan Clarke	52	56	4	61 mins
4	Efetobore Sodje	39	40	3	58 mins
5	Steve Yates	25	28	4	51 mins

KEY GOALKEEPER

Paul Rachubka

Goals Conceded in the League	43	Counting Games games when player was on pitch for at least 70 minutes	30
Defensive Rating Ave number of mins between League goals conceded while on the pitch	63	Clean Sheets In games when player was on pitch for at least 70 minutes	7

LEAGUE GOALS

Pawel Abbott

Minutes on the pitch	3318	League average (mins between goals)	128
Goals in the League	26		

	PLAYER	MINS	GOALS	AVE
1	Abbott	3318	26	128
2	Booth	2141	10	214
3	Beckett	626	6	104
4	Brandon	3715	6	619
5	Schofield	1963	5	393
6	Junior Mendes	1308	5	262
7	Mirfin	3177	4	794
8	Worthington	3500	3	1167
9	Edwards	1860	2	930
10	McAliskey	695	2	348
11	Ahmed	1374	1	1374
12	Carss	2083	1	2083
	Other		3	
	TOTAL		74	

DISCIPLINARY RECORDS

	PLAYER	YELLOW	RED	AVE
1	Fowler	4	1	192
2	Sodje, E	8	2	225
3	Clarke, T	2	1	327
4	Ahmed	4	0	343
5	Worthington	10	0	350
6	Clarke, N	7	1	395
7	Brandon	7	1	464
8	Carss	4	0	520
9	Abbott	6	0	553
10	Beckett	1	0	626
11	Yates	2	0	643
12	Schofield	3	0	654
13	Booth	3	0	713
	Other	9	0	
	TOTAL	70	6	

TOP POINT EARNERS

	PLAYER	GAMES	AV PTS
1	Ahmed	15	1.93
2	Mirfin	32	1.84
3	Booth	22	1.82
4	Yates	12	1.75
5	Edwards	19	1.68
6	Holdsworth	34	1.62
7	Gray	12	1.58
8	Rachubka	30	1.53
9	Abbott	34	1.53
10	Brandon	40	1.48
	CLUB AVERAGE:		1.52

TEAM OF THE SEASON

D
David Mirfin
CG: 32 DR: 77
M
Adnan Ahmed
CG: 15 SD: 15
D
Rob Edwards
CG: 19 DR: 72
M
Chris Brandon
CG: 40 SD: 11
F
Pawel Abbott
CG: 34 SR: 128
G
Paul Rachubka
CG: 30 DR: 63
D
Nathan Clarke
CG: 33 DR: 61
M
Andy Holdsworth
CG: 34 SD: 7
F
Andy Booth
CG: 22 SR: 214
D
Efetobore Sodje
CG: 24 DR: 58
M
John Worthington
CG: 39 SD: 0

LEAGUE APPEARANCES GOALS AND BOOKINGS

	AGE (on 01/07/05)	IN NAMED 16	APPEARANCES	COUNTING GAMES	MINUTES ON PITCH	LEAGUE GOALS	Yellow	Red
Goalkeepers								
Ian Gray	30	12	12	12	1073	0	0	0
Paul Rachubka	24	30	30	30	2700	0	1	0
Phil Senior	22	46	5	4	367	0	0	0
Defenders								
Daniel Adams	29	6	5	5	426	0	1	0
Nathan Clarke	21	40	37	33	3167	0	7	1
Tom Clarke	17	13	12	10	982	0	2	1
Rob Edwards	35	24	24	19	1860	2	2	0
Anthony Lloyd	21	17	11	8	849	0	0	0
John McCombe	20	11	5	4	425	0	1	0
David Mirfin	20	42	41	32	3177	4	2	0
Efetobore Sodje	32	31	28	24	2251	1	8	2
Steve Yates	35	20	17	12	1287	0	2	0
Midfielders								
Adnan Ahmed	21	23	18	15	1374	1	4	0
Chris Brandon	29	44	44	40	3715	6	7	1
Nathaniel Brown	24	31	17	9	863	0	0	0
Anthony Carss	29	27	27	22	2083	1	4	0
Michael Collins	19	8	8	4	556	0	0	0
Lee Fowler	22	34	20	7	964	0	4	1
Andy Holdsworth	21	40	40	34	3274	0	4	0
Danny Schofield	25	39	33	16	1963	5	3	0
Akpo Sodje	25	11	7	0	150	0	0	0
John Worthington	22	39	39	39	3500	3	10	0
Forwards								
Pawel Abbott	23	44	44	34	3318	26	6	0
Luke Beckett	28	7	7	7	626	6	1	0
Andy Booth	31	29	29	22	2141	10	3	0
Delroy Facey	25	4	4	4	349	0	0	0
Junior Mendes	28	38	25	13	1308	5	0	0
John McAliskey	20	26	18	7	695	2	0	0

SQUAD APPEARANCES

Match	1	2	3	4	5	6	7	8	9	10	11	12	13	14	15	16	17	18	19	20	21	22	23	24	25	26	27	28	29	30	31	32	33	34	35	36	37	38	39	40	41	42	43	44	45	46	47	48
Venue	A	H	H	A	A	H	A	H	A	H	A	H	A	A	H	H	A	H	A	A	H	A	A	H	H	A	A	H	H	A	H	A	H	A	H	A	H	A	A	H	H	A	H	H	H	A	H	A
Competition	L	L	L	L	W	L	L	L	L	L	L	L	L	L	L	L	L	L	F	L	L	L	L	L	L	L	L	L	L	L	L	L	L	L	L	L	L	L	L	L	L	L	L	L	L	L	L	L
Result	W	D	L	L	L	W	L	W	W	L	D	W	L	W	L	W	D	D	L	D	L	W	L	L	W	D	L	D	D	L	W	L	D	L	W	L	W	L	L	W	W	W	W	W	D	W	W	W

Goalkeepers
Ian Gray
Paul Rachubka
Phil Senior

Defenders
Daniel Adams
Nathan Clarke
Tom Clarke
Rob Edwards
Anthony Lloyd
John McCombe
David Mirfin
Efetobore Sodje
Steve Yates

Midfielders
Adnan Ahmed
Chris Brandon
Nathaniel Brown
Anthony Carss
Michael Collins
Lee Fowler
Andy Holdsworth
Danny Schofield
John Worthington

Forwards
Pawel Abbott
Luke Beckett
Andy Booth
Delroy Facey
Junior Mendes
John McAliskey

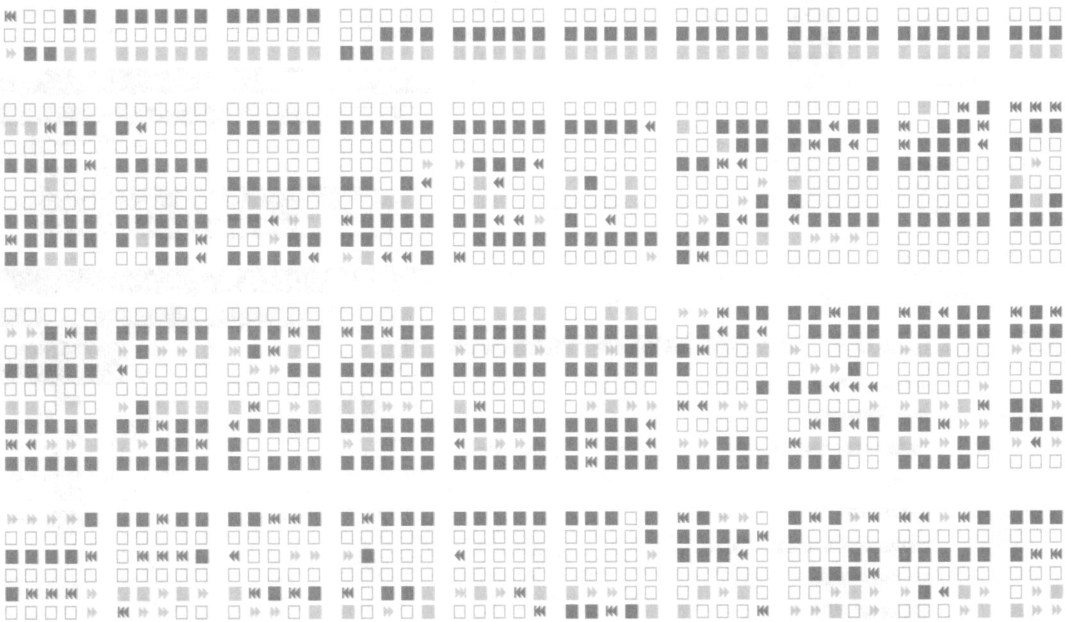

KEY: On all match | On bench | Subbed or sent off (Counting game) | Subbed or sent off (playing less than 70 minutes) | Subbed on from bench (Counting Game) | Subbed on (playing less than 70 minutes) | Subbed on and then subbed or sent off (Counting Game) | Subbed on and then subbed or sent off (playing less than 70 minutes) | Not in 16

DONCASTER ROVERS

Final Position: **10th**

NICKNAME: ROVERS

KEY: □Won □Drawn □Lost

							Attendance
1	lge1	**Blackpool**	H	W	2-0	Ryan 8; Fortune-West 81	7,082
2	lge1	**Brentford**	A	L	3-4	McIndoe 4,45 pen; Green 84	5,621
3	lge1	**Bradford**	A	L	0-2		10,444
4	lge1	**Tranmere**	H	D	0-0		6,040
5	ccR1	**Port Vale**	H	W	3-1	Fortune-West 36; Doolan 53; McIndoe 56	3,943
6	lge1	**Colchester**	A	L	1-4	Doolan 45	3,803
7	lge1	**Huddersfield**	H	W	2-1	Fortune-West 28; Green 56	7,068
8	lge1	**Walsall**	H	W	3-1	Fenton 20; McIndoe 50; Blundell 88	6,146
9	lge1	**MK Dons**	A	W	1-0	Albrighton 66	4,334
10	lge1	**Oldham**	H	D	1-1	McIndoe 45 pen	6,774
11	ccr2	**Ipswich**	H	W	2-0	Ravenhill 6; McSporran 46	6,020
12	lge1	**Bournemouth**	A	L	0-5		6,588
13	lge1	**Wrexham**	H	D	0-0		7,567
14	lge1	**Port Vale**	A	L	0-2		5,314
15	lge1	**Torquay**	H	D	2-2	McIndoe 18,27	5,529
16	lge1	**Barnsley**	A	W	3-1	Reid 45 og; Blundell 57; Vaughan 59 og	12,478
17	lge1	**Chesterfield**	A	D	0-0		6,219
18	ccR3	**Nottm Forest**	H	L	0-2		9,261
19	lge1	**Peterborough**	H	W	2-1	McIndoe 4; Green 87	6,039
20	lge1	**Hartlepool**	A	L	1-2	Roberts 30	5,495
21	facr1	**Tiverton**	A	W	3-1	McIndoe 18; Fenton 26; Blundell 84	1,618
22	lge1	**Stockport**	H	W	3-1	Blundell 9,67; Ryan 65	6,697
23	lge1	**Luton**	A	D	1-1	Roberts 82	8,142
24	facr2	**Exeter**	A	L	1-2	Blundell 86	4,797
25	lge1	**Bristol City**	H	D	1-1	Roberts 34	5,608
26	lge1	**Swindon**	A	D	1-1	Blundell 39	5,452
27	lge1	**Sheff Wed**	H	L	0-4		10,131
28	lge1	**MK Dons**	H	W	3-0	Edds 8 og; Johnson 60,62	6,153
29	lge1	**Hull City**	A	L	1-2	Mulligan 45	24,117
30	lge1	**Walsall**	A	D	1-1	Bennett 11 og	6,021
31	lge1	**Bournemouth**	H	D	1-1	Green 69	6,016
32	lge1	**Port Vale**	H	W	2-0	Ryan 45; Green 90	5,209
33	lge1	**Oldham**	A	W	2-1	Blundell 1; McSporran 81	7,401
34	lge1	**Hull City**	H	W	1-0	McIndoe 59	9,633
35	lge1	**Wrexham**	A	D	0-0		6,115
36	lge1	**Torquay**	A	L	1-2	Johnson, Si 87	3,157
37	lge1	**Chesterfield**	H	L	0-1		6,765
38	lge1	**Peterborough**	A	W	2-0	Roberts 55; Foster 81	4,983
39	lge1	**Barnsley**	H	W	4-0	Blundell 16,31; Doolan 69; Green 84	7,286
40	lge1	**Swindon**	H	D	1-1	Roberts 30	7,696
41	lge1	**Sheff Wed**	A	L	0-2		28,712
42	lge1	**Brentford**	H	D	0-0		5,525
43	lge1	**Blackpool**	A	D	1-1	Ryan 40	6,548
44	lge1	**Bradford**	H	D	1-1	Bower 22 og	6,688
45	lge1	**Tranmere**	A	W	4-2	McIndoe 3; Blundell 5; Ravenhill 52; Roberts 81	9,730
46	lge1	**Colchester**	H	D	1-1	Guy 76	6,774
47	lge1	**Huddersfield**	A	L	1-3	Fortune-West 15	12,972
48	lge1	**Stockport**	A	W	4-2	Ravenhill 2; Green 72; McIndoe 82; Brown 87	4,508
49	lge1	**Hartlepool**	H	W	2-0	Ravenhill 59; Fortune-West 90	7,024
50	lge1	**Bristol City**	A	D	2-2	Fortune-West 34,88	12,375
51	lge1	**Luton**	H	D	3-3	Guy 1,65; Robinson 51 og	8,928

MONTHLY POINTS TALLY

AUGUST	7	39%
SEPTEMBER	7	58%
OCTOBER	9	50%
NOVEMBER	4	44%
DECEMBER	5	33%
JANUARY	12	67%
FEBRUARY	7	47%
MARCH	6	40%
APRIL	8	53%
MAY	1	33%

KEY PLAYERS - GOALSCORERS

Leo Fortune-West

Goals in the League	6	Player Strike Rate Average number of minutes between League goals scored by player	236
Contribution to Attacking Power Average number of minutes between League team goals while on pitch	58	Club Strike Rate Average number of minutes between League goals scored by club	64

	PLAYER	LGE GOALS	GOALS ALL	POWER	STRIKE RATE
1	Leo Fortune-West	6	7	58	236 mins
2	Greg Blundell	9	11	60	330 mins
3	Michael McIndoe	10	12	62	385 mins
4	Neil Roberts	6	6	65	438 mins
5	Paul Green	7	7	62	483 mins

KEY PLAYERS - MIDFIELDERS

Paul Green

Goals in the League	7	Contribution to Attacking Power Average number of minutes between League team goals while on pitch	63
Defensive Rating Average number of mins between League goals conceded while on the pitch	75	Scoring Difference Defensive Rating minus Contribution to Attacking Power	12

	PLAYER	LGE GOALS	GOALS ALL	DEF RATE	POWER	SCORE DIFF
1	Paul Green	7	7	75	63	12 mins
2	Jermaine McSporran	1	2	88	79	9 mins
3	Michael McIndoe	10	12	68	62	6 mins
4	John Doolan	2	3	67	63	4 mins
5	James Coppinger	0	0	68	66	2 mins

KEY PLAYERS - DEFENDERS

Dave Mulligan

Goals Conceded Number of League goals conceded while the player was on the pitch	32	Clean Sheets In games when player was on pitch for at least 70 minutes	10
Defensive Rating Ave number of mins between League goals conceded while on the pitch	76	Club Defensive Rating Average number of mins between League goals conceded while on the pitch	69

	PLAYED	CON LGE	CON ALL	CLEAN SHEETS	DEF RATE
1	Dave Mulligan	32	32	10	76 mins
2	Tim Ryan	46	52	11	74 mins
3	Mark Albrighton	19	19	5	73 mins
4	Stephen Foster	43	44	11	70 mins
5	Nicky Fenton	53	59	9	63 mins

KEY GOALKEEPER

Andy Warrington

Goals Conceded in the League	42	Counting Games Games when player was on pitch for at least 70 minutes	34
Defensive Rating Ave number of mins between League goals conceded while on the pitch	73	Clean Sheets In games when player was on pitch for at least 70 minutes	11

LEAGUE GOALS

Michael McIndoe

Minutes on the pitch	3851	League average (mins between goals)	385
Goals in the League	10		

	PLAYER	MINS	GOALS	AVE
1	McIndoe	3851	10	385
2	Blundell	2969	9	330
3	Green	3384	7	483
4	Fortune-West	1415	6	236
5	Roberts	2629	6	438
6	Ryan	3401	4	850
7	Ravenhill	1815	3	605
8	Guy	460	3	153
9	Doolan	2825	2	1413
10	Johnson, Si	648	1	648
11	McSporran	1493	1	1493
12	Foster	3025	1	3025
	Other		12	
	TOTAL		65	

DISCIPLINARY RECORDS

	PLAYER	YELLOW	RED	AVE
1	Priet	3	0	160
2	Ravenhill	9	1	181
3	Albrighton	5	0	277
4	Fortune-West	5	0	283
5	Ryan	12	0	283
6	Doolan	8	1	313
7	Morley	2	0	405
8	Fenton	6	0	556
9	Mulligan	4	0	608
10	McSporran	1	1	746
11	McIndoe	4	0	962
12	Foster	3	0	1008
13	Green	2	0	1692
	Other	2	0	
	TOTAL	66	3	

TOP POINT EARNERS

	PLAYER	GAMES	AV PTS
1	McSporran	13	1.77
2	Blundell	31	1.58
3	Roberts	28	1.54
4	Foster	33	1.52
5	Ryan	37	1.51
6	McIndoe	42	1.48
7	Ravenhill	15	1.47
8	Fenton	37	1.46
9	Coppinger	22	1.45
10	Fortune-West	16	1.44
	CLUB AVERAGE:		1.43

LEAGUE APPEARANCES GOALS AND BOOKINGS

	AGE (on 01/07/05)	IN NAMED 16	APPEARANCES	COUNTING GAMES	MINUTES ON PITCH	LEAGUE GOALS	Yellow	Red
Goalkeepers								
Lee Cockerham	-	3	0	0	0	0	0	0
Ross Flitney	21	6	0	0	0	0	0	0
Michael Ingham	24	3	1	1	90	0	0	0
Stuart Jones	27	27	4	3	271	0	0	0
Iain Turner	21	8	8	8	720	0	0	0
Andy Warrington	29	45	34	34	3059	0	0	0
Defenders								
Mark Albrighton	29	27	17	15	1389	1	5	0
Nicky Fenton	25	43	38	37	3336	1	6	0
Stephen Foster	30	34	34	33	3025	1	3	0
Simon Marples	29	12	12	11	1050	0	0	0
David Morley	27	17	9	9	810	0	2	0
Dave Mulligan	23	36	31	26	2434	1	4	0
Jamie Price	23	8	6	4	426	0	0	0
Nicolas Priet	22	11	7	5	482	0	3	0
Tim Ryan	30	39	39	37	3401	4	12	0
Midfielders								
Chris Beech	30	5	2	2	179	0	0	0
James Coppinger	24	34	31	22	2237	0	1	0
John Doolan	31	42	38	30	2825	2	8	1
Paul Green	22	44	42	37	3384	7	2	0
Michael McIndoe	25	44	44	42	3851	10	4	0
Jermaine McSporran	28	28	26	13	1493	1	1	1
Ricky Ravenhill	24	41	35	15	1815	3	9	1
Francis Tierney	29	1	0	0	0	0	0	0
Mark Wilson	26	4	3	1	122	0	0	0
Forwards								
Chris Beardsley	21	5	4	1	100	0	0	0
Greg Blundell	29	42	41	31	2969	9	1	0
Adam Brown	16	4	3	0	116	1	0	0
Andy Campbell	26	3	3	1	111	0	0	0
Leo Fortune-West	34	26	24	16	1415	6	5	0
Lewis Guy	19	9	9	3	460	3	0	0
Guy Ipoua	29	11	9	0	165	0	1	0
Ben Jackson	19	1	1	0	21	0	0	0
Simon Johnson	22	11	11	6	648	1	0	0
Jon Maloney	20	5	2	1	120	0	0	0
Craig Nelthorpe	-	1	1	0	35	0	0	0
Adriano Rigoglioso	26	25	12	1	285	0	2	1
Neil Roberts	27	31	31	28	2629	6	0	0

TEAM OF THE SEASON

D
Dave Mulligan
CG: 26 DR: 76
M
Paul Green
CG: 37 SD: 12
D
Tim Ryan
CG: 37 DR: 74
M
Jermaine McSporran
CG: 13 SD: 9
F
Leo Fortune-West
CG: 16 SR: 236
G
Andy Warrington
CG: 34 DR: 73
D
Mark Albrighton
CG: 15 DR: 73
M
Michael McIndoe
CG: 42 SD: 6
F
Greg Blundell
CG: 31 SR: 330
D
Stephen Foster
CG: 33 DR: 70
M
John Doolan
CG: 30 SD: 4

SQUAD APPEARANCES

Match	1	2	3	4	5	6	7	8	9	10	11	12	13	14	15	16	17	18	19	20	21	22	23	24	25
Venue	H	A	A	H	H	A	H	H	A	H	H	A	H	A	H	A	A	H	H	A	A	H	A	A	H
Competition	L	L	L	L	W	L	L	L	L	L	W	L	L	L	L	L	L	W	L	L	F	L	L	F	L
Result	W	L	L	D	W	L	W	W	W	D	W	L	D	L	D	W	D	L	W	L	W	W	D	L	D

Match	26	27	28	29	30	31	32	33	34	35	36	37	38	39	40	41	42	43	44	45	46	47	48	49	50	51
Venue	A	H	H	A	A	H	H	A	H	A	A	H	A	H	H	A	H	A	H	A	H	A	A	H	A	H
Competition	L	L	L	L	L	L	L	L	L	L	L	L	L	L	L	L	L	L	L	L	L	L	L	L	L	L
Result	D	L	W	L	D	D	W	W	W	D	L	L	W	W	D	L	D	D	D	W	D	L	W	W	D	D

Goalkeepers
Lee Cockerham
Ross Flitney
Michael Ingham
Stuart Jones
Iain Turner
Andy Warrington
Defenders
Mark Albrighton
Nicky Fenton
Stephen Foster
Simon Marples
David Morley
Dave Mulligan
Jamie Price
Nicolas Priet
Tim Ryan
Midfielders
Chris Beech
James Coppinger
John Doolan
Paul Green
Michael McIndoe
Jermaine McSporran
Ricky Ravenhill
Francis Tierney
Mark Wilson
Forwards
Chris Beardsley
Greg Blundell
Adam Brown
Andy Campbell
Leo Fortune-West
Lewis Guy
Guy Ipoua
Ben Jackson
Simon Johnson
Jon Maloney
Craig Nelthorpe
Adriano Rigoglioso
Neil Roberts

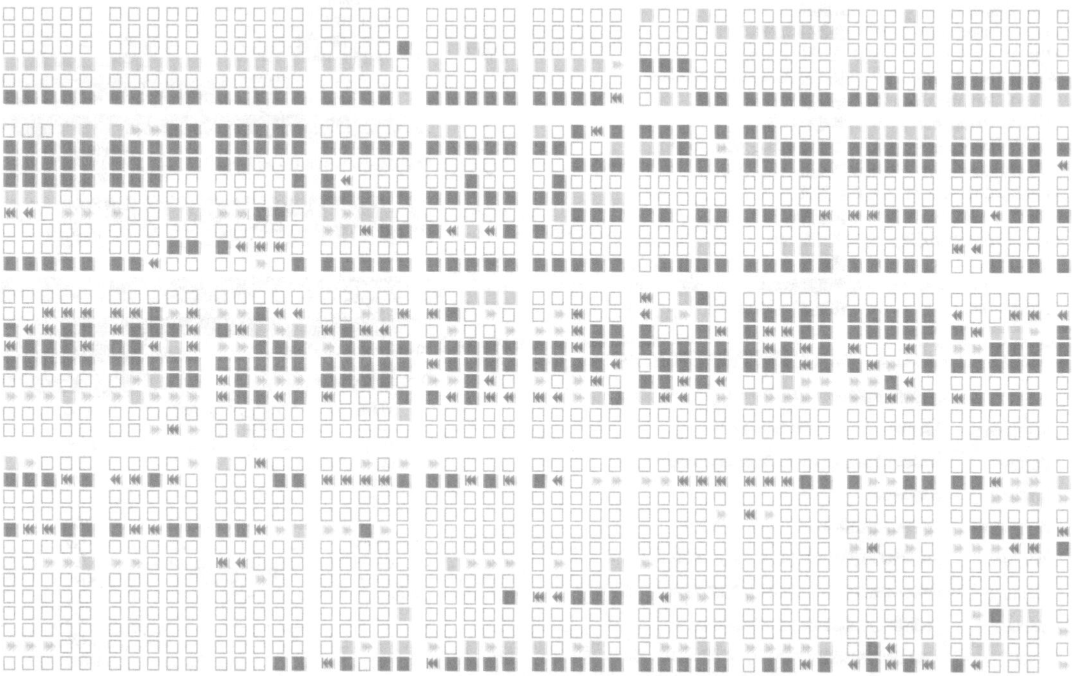

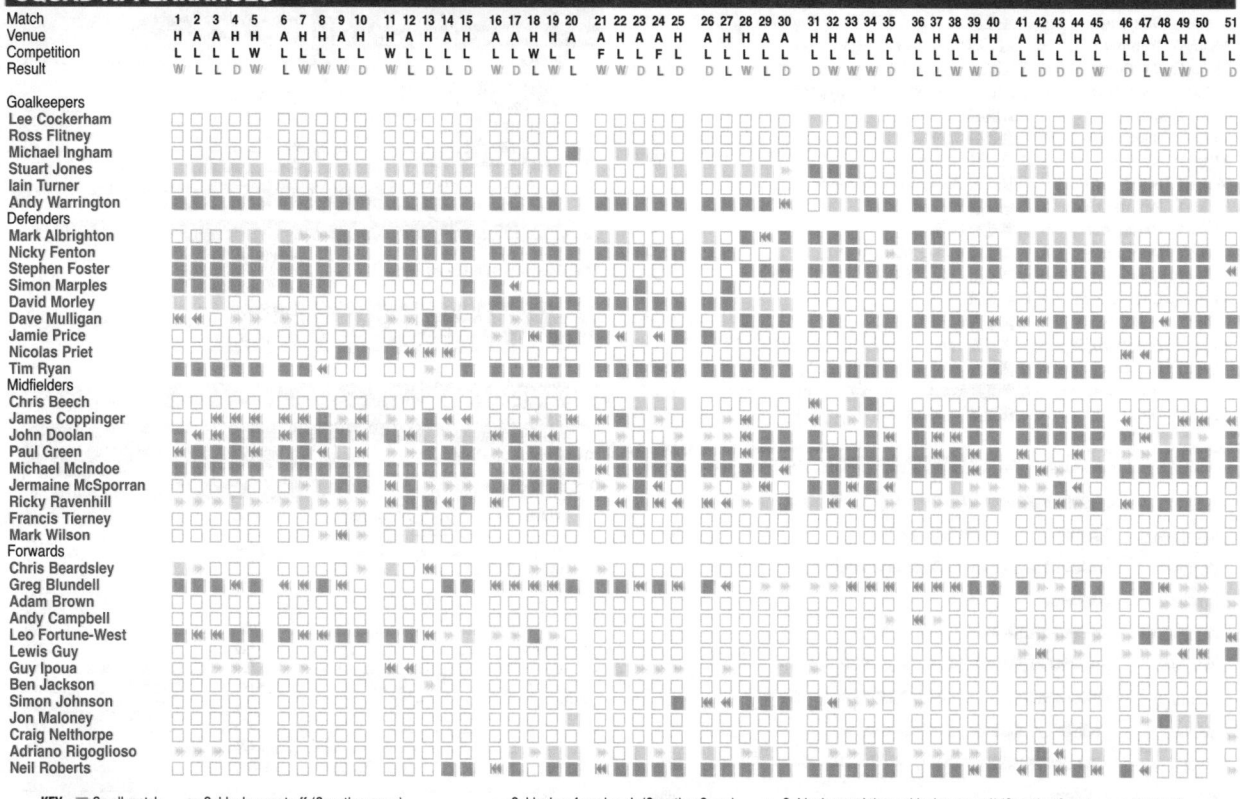

KEY: On all match · On bench · Subbed or sent off (Counting game) · Subbed or sent off (playing less than 70 minutes) · Subbed on from bench (Counting Game) · Subbed on (playing less than 70 minutes) · Subbed on and then subbed or sent off (Counting Game) · Subbed on and then subbed or sent off (playing less than 70 minutes) · Not in 16

BRADFORD

Final Position: **11th**

NICKNAME: THE BANTAMS

KEY: ☐Won ☐Drawn ☐Lost

							Attendance
1	lge1	**Hartlepool**	A	L	1-2	Windass 54	6,032
2	lge1	**Peterborough**	H	D	2-2	Windass 9; Wetherall 84	6,929
3	lge1	**Doncaster**	H	W	2-0	Bower 8; Crooks 45	10,444
4	lge1	**Stockport**	A	W	1-0	Windass 76	5,338
5	ccR1	**Notts County**	H	L	1-2	Windass 6 pen	3,517
6	lge1	**Chesterfield**	H	L	2-3	Windass 41,54	7,590
7	lge1	**Hull City**	A	W	1-0	Holloway 77	16,865
8	lge1	**Port Vale**	H	L	0-2		7,043
9	lge1	**Wrexham**	A	L	0-1		3,712
10	lge1	**Bristol City**	H	W	4-1	Schumacher 30; Roberts, N 38; Wetherall 61; Adebola 80	7,235
11	lge1	**Swindon**	A	L	0-1		5,189
12	lge1	**Barnsley**	H	W	1-0	Windass 63 pen	8,715
13	lge1	**MK Dons**	A	W	2-1	Kearney 55; Adebola 90	4,532
14	lge1	**Tranmere**	A	W	5-4	Schumacher 33; Summerbee 53; Windass 70; Muirhead 81; Wetherall 90	8,901
15	lge1	**Blackpool**	H	W	2-1	Adebola 36; Summerbee 89	7,622
16	lge1	**Sheff Wed**	H	W	3-1	Symes 59,78; Windass 62	13,717
17	lge1	**Luton**	A	L	0-4		7,975
18	lge1	**Colchester**	H	D	2-2	Windass 23,81	7,851
19	facr1	**Rushden & D**	H	L	0-1		4,171
20	lge1	**Brentford**	A	W	2-1	Abbey 2; Forrest 78	5,909
21	lge1	**Oldham**	H	L	1-3	Windass 27	8,647
22	lge1	**Bournemouth**	A	L	0-2		5,578
23	lge1	**Walsall**	H	D	1-1	Wetherall 83	6,732
24	lge1	**Huddersfield**	A	W	1-0	Morrison 42	17,281
25	lge1	**Wrexham**	H	D	1-1	Schumacher 54	10,268
26	lge1	**Torquay**	A	D	0-0		4,119
27	lge1	**Port Vale**	A	W	1-0	Forrest 61	5,001
28	lge1	**Swindon**	H	L	1-2	Windass 56	8,239
29	lge1	**Bristol City**	A	D	0-0		11,605
30	lge1	**Torquay**	H	D	2-2	Cooke 33; Windass 36	8,209
31	lge1	**Barnsley**	A	D	2-2	Windass 27,32 pen	8,729
32	lge1	**Tranmere**	H	D	1-1	Windass 77	8,129
33	lge1	**MK Dons**	H	L	1-4	Windass 50	6,409
34	lge1	**Sheff Wed**	A	W	2-1	Summerbee 6; Morrison 90	23,232
35	lge1	**Luton**	H	L	0-1		8,702
36	lge1	**Blackpool**	A	L	1-2	Cooke 54	4,805
37	lge1	**Walsall**	A	D	1-1	Schumacher 20	4,966
38	lge1	**Huddersfield**	H	W	2-0	Cooke 44; Windass 54	15,417
39	lge1	**Peterborough**	A	D	2-2	Windass 64,73	3,472
40	lge1	**Hartlepool**	H	L	1-2	Bower 60	7,509
41	lge1	**Doncaster**	A	D	1-1	Bridge-Wilkinson 10	6,688
42	lge1	**Stockport**	H	W	3-1	Cooke 2; Schumacher 5; Windass 64	7,263
43	lge1	**Chesterfield**	A	D	0-0		4,663
44	lge1	**Hull City**	H	L	0-2		13,631
45	lge1	**Brentford**	H	W	4-1	Windass 6,37; Bridge-Wilkinson 23,45	6,743
46	lge1	**Colchester**	A	D	0-0		3,351
47	lge1	**Bournemouth**	H	W	4-2	Windass 19,75,90; Schumacher 38	10,263
48	lge1	**Oldham**	A	L	1-2	Windass 10	9,381

MONTHLY POINTS TALLY

AUGUST	10	56%
SEPTEMBER	3	25%
OCTOBER	15	83%
NOVEMBER	4	44%
DECEMBER	6	40%
JANUARY	6	40%
FEBRUARY	5	28%
MARCH	8	53%
APRIL	8	53%
MAY	0	0%

KEY PLAYERS - GOALSCORERS

Dean Windass

Goals in the League	27	Player Strike Rate Average number of minutes between League goals scored by player	128
Contribution to Attacking Power Average number of minutes between League team goals while on pitch	64	**Club Strike Rate** Average number of minutes between League goals scored by club	65

	PLAYER	LGE GOALS	GOALS ALL	POWER	STRIKE RATE
1	Dean Windass	27	28	64	128 mins
2	Marc Bridge-Wilkinson	3	3	57	360 mins
3	Andrew Cooke	4	4	60	411 mins
4	Steve Schumacher	6	6	63	633 mins
5	Owen Morrison	2	2	57	747 mins

KEY PLAYERS - MIDFIELDERS

Marc Bridge-Wilkinson

Goals in the League	3	**Contribution to Attacking Power** Average number of minutes between League team goals while on pitch	57
Defensive Rating Average number of mins between League goals conceded while on the pitch	77	Scoring Difference Defensive Rating minus Contribution to Attacking Power	20

	PLAYER	LGE GOALS	GOALS ALL	DEF RATE	POWER	SCORE DIFF
1	Marc Bridge-Wilkinson	3	3	77	57	20 mins
2	Nicky Summerbee	3	3	82	63	19 mins
3	Owen Morrison	2	2	68	57	11 mins
4	Steve Schumacher	6	6	72	63	9 mins
5	Thomas Kearney	1	1	54	52	2 mins

KEY PLAYERS - DEFENDERS

Darren Holloway

Goals Conceded Number of League goals conceded while the player was on the pitch	37	**Clean Sheets** In games when player was on pitch for at least 70 minutes	10
Defensive Rating Ave number of mins between League goals conceded while on the pitch	77	**Club Defensive Rating** Average number of mins between League goals conceded while on the pitch	67

	PLAYER	CON LGE	CON ALL	CLEAN SHEETS	DEF RATE
1	Darren Holloway	37	40	10	77 mins
2	Mark Bower	62	65	11	67 mins
3	David Wetherall	61	62	11	66 mins
4	Lewis Emanuel	42	45	5	59 mins
5	Peter Atherton	23	23	1	52 mins

KEY GOALKEEPER

Paul Henderson

Goals Conceded in the League	53	**Counting Games** Games when player was on pitch for at least 70 minutes	40
Defensive Rating Ave number of mins between League goals conceded while on the pitch	68	**Clean Sheets** In games when player was on pitch for at least 70 minutes	10

LEAGUE GOALS

Dean Windass

Minutes on the pitch	3444	League average (mins between goals)	128
Goals in the League	27		

	PLAYER	MINS	GOALS	AVE
1	Windass	3444	27	128
2	Schumacher	3795	6	633
3	Cooke	1642	4	411
4	Wetherall	4050	4	1013
5	Bridge-Wilkinson	1080	3	360
6	Adebola	1150	3	383
7	Summerbee	2709	3	903
8	Bower	4140	2	2070
9	Forrest	670	2	335
10	Symes	508	2	254
11	Morrison	1493	2	747
12	Abbey	440	1	440
	Other		5	
	TOTAL		64	

DISCIPLINARY RECORDS

	PLAYER	YELLOW	RED	AVE
1	Bridge-Wilkinson	4	0	270
2	Tierney	4	0	278
3	Crooks	8	1	283
4	Kearney	4	0	284
5	Morrison	5	0	298
6	Windass	10	1	313
7	Adebola	3	0	383
8	Cooke	4	0	410
9	Emanuel	6	0	413
10	Schumacher	9	0	421
11	Holloway	6	0	477
12	Symes	1	0	508
13	Muirhead	5	0	508
	Other	18	1	
	TOTAL	87	3	

TOP POINT EARNERS

	PLAYER	GAMES	AV PTS
1	Thomas Kearney	12	1.83
2	Darren Holloway	31	1.68
3	Nicky Summerbee	27	1.67
4	Ben Muirhead	21	1.57
5	Steve Schumacher	42	1.45
6	Paul Henderson	40	1.43
7	David Wetherall	45	1.42
8	Marc Bridge-Wilkinson	12	1.42
9	Dean Windass	37	1.41
10	Mark Bower	46	1.41
	CLUB AVERAGE:		1.41

TEAM OF THE SEASON

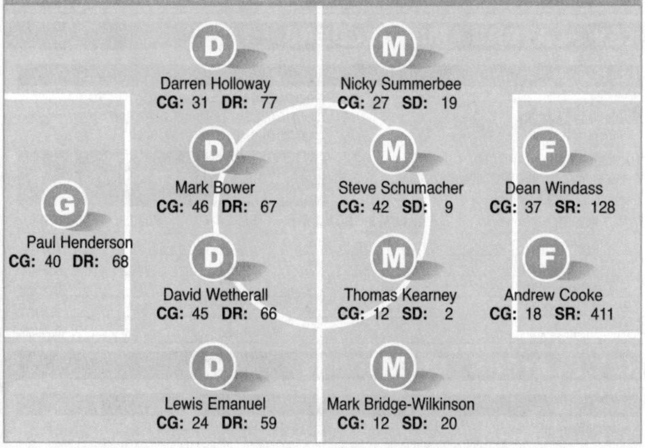

G
Paul Henderson
CG: 40 DR: 68
D
Darren Holloway
CG: 31 DR: 77
D
Mark Bower
CG: 46 DR: 67
D
David Wetherall
CG: 45 DR: 66
D
Lewis Emanuel
CG: 24 DR: 59
M
Nicky Summerbee
CG: 27 SD: 19
M
Steve Schumacher
CG: 42 SD: 9
M
Thomas Kearney
CG: 12 SD: 2
M
Mark Bridge-Wilkinson
CG: 12 SD: 20
F
Dean Windass
CG: 37 SR: 128
F
Andrew Cooke
CG: 18 SR: 411

LEAGUE APPEARANCES, GOALS AND BOOKINGS

	AGE (on 01/07/05)	IN NAMED 16	APPEARANCES	COUNTING GAMES	MINUTES ON PITCH	LEAGUE GOALS	Yellow	Red
Goalkeepers								
Paul Henderson	29	44	40	40	3600	0	0	0
Donovan Ricketts	28	38	4	4	360	0	0	0
Ross Turnbull	20	3	2	2	180	0	0	0
Defenders								
Peter Atherton	35	23	16	12	1202	0	1	0
Craig Bentham	20	15	2	0	32	0	1	0
Mark Bower	25	46	46	46	4140	2	4	0
Lewis Emanuel	21	40	36	24	2483	0	6	0
Jason Gavin	25	21	3	0	96	0	0	0
Darren Holloway	27	33	33	31	2863	1	6	0
Wayne Jacobs	36	14	14	11	1054	0	1	0
Luke Richardson	18	1	0	0	0	0	0	0
John Swift	20	19	5	2	219	0	0	0
David Wetherall	34	45	45	45	4050	4	7	0
Midfielders								
Craig Armstrong	30	11	7	4	398	0	2	0
Marc Bridge-Wilkinson	26	12	12	12	1080	3	4	0
Joe Colbeck	18	0	0	0	0	0	0	0
Lee Crooks	27	35	32	25	2553	1	8	1
Liam Flynn	20	1	0	0	0	0	0	0
Thomas Kearney	23	15	13	12	1136	1	4	0
Owen Morrison	23	25	22	15	1493	2	5	0
Ben Muirhead	22	43	40	21	2542	1	5	0
Thomas Penford	20	9	3	0	63	0	0	0
Steve Schumacher	21	43	43	42	3795	6	9	0
Nicky Summerbee	33	34	33	27	2709	3	4	1
Paul Tierney	22	18	16	9	1113	0	4	0
Forwards								
Zema Abbey	28	6	6	5	440	1	0	1
Dele Adebola	30	15	15	11	1150	3	3	0
Andrew Cooke	31	20	20	18	1642	4	4	0
Danny Forrest	20	29	20	4	670	2	1	0
Neil Roberts	27	3	3	3	260	1	0	0
Kevin Sanasy	20	6	3	0	84	0	0	0
Michael Symes	21	28	12	4	508	2	1	0
Dean Windass	36	41	41	37	3444	27	10	1

SQUAD APPEARANCES

Match	1	2	3	4	5	6	7	8	9	10	11	12	13	14	15	16	17	18	19	20	21	22	23	24	25	26	27	28	29	30	31	32	33	34	35	36	37	38	39	40	41	42	43	44	45	46	47	48
Venue	A	H	H	A	H	H	A	H	A	H	A	H	A	A	H	H	A	H	H	A	H	A	H	A	H	A	A	H	A	H	A	H	H	A	H	A	A	H	A	H	A	H	A	H	H	A	H	A
Competition	L	L	L	L	W	L	L	L	L	L	L	L	L	L	L	L	L	L	F	L	L	L	L	L	L	L	L	L	L	L	L	L	L	L	L	L	L	L	L	L	L	L	L	L	L	L	L	L
Result	L	D	W	W	L	L	W	L	L	W	L	W	W	W	W	W	L	D	L	W	L	L	D	W	D	D	W	L	D	D	D	D	L	W	L	L	D	W	D	L	D	W	D	L	W	D	W	L

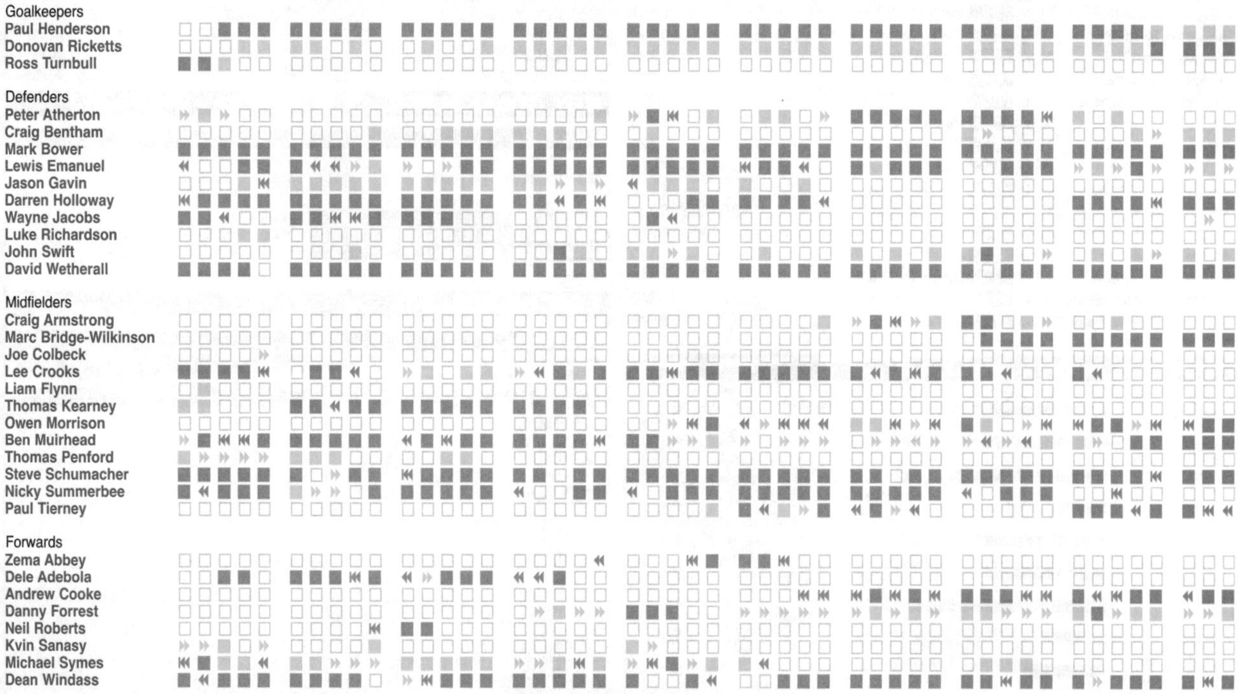

Goalkeepers
Paul Henderson
Donovan Ricketts
Ross Turnbull
Defenders
Peter Atherton
Craig Bentham
Mark Bower
Lewis Emanuel
Jason Gavin
Darren Holloway
Wayne Jacobs
Luke Richardson
John Swift
David Wetherall
Midfielders
Craig Armstrong
Marc Bridge-Wilkinson
Joe Colbeck
Lee Crooks
Liam Flynn
Thomas Kearney
Owen Morrison
Ben Muirhead
Thomas Penford
Steve Schumacher
Nicky Summerbee
Paul Tierney
Forwards
Zema Abbey
Dele Adebola
Andrew Cooke
Danny Forrest
Neil Roberts
Kvin Sanasy
Michael Symes
Dean Windass

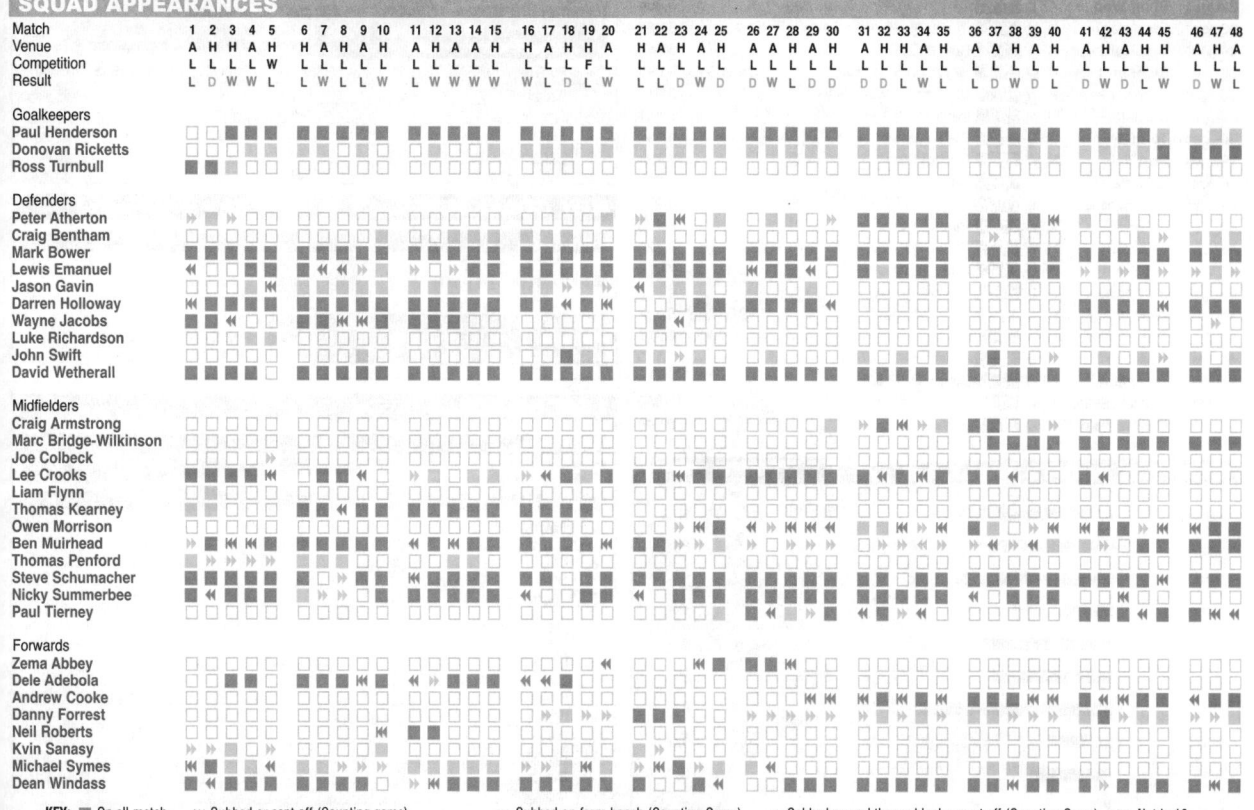

KEY: On all match | On bench | Subbed or sent off (Counting game) | Subbed or sent off (playing less than 70 minutes) | Subbed on from bench (Counting Game) | Subbed on (playing less than 70 minutes) | Subbed on and then subbed or sent off (Counting Game) | Subbed on and then subbed or sent off (playing less than 70 minutes) | Not in 16

SWINDON TOWN

Final Position: **12th**

NICKNAME: THE ROBINS   KEY: ☐Won ☐Drawn ☐Lost

								Attendance
1	lge1	Wrexham	A	L	1-2	Caton 90		5,099
2	lge1	Luton	H	L	2-3	Parkin 45; Reeves 65		6,286
3	lge1	MK Dons	H	W	2-1	Parkin 23; Howard 63		5,060
4	lge1	Bristol City	A	W	2-1	Henderson 23,60		13,389
5	ccR1	Rushden & D	A	W	1-0	Hewlett 90		1,672
6	lge1	Hartlepool	H	W	3-0	Henderson 17; Parkin 37; Nelson 40 og		5,365
7	lge1	Walsall	A	L	2-3	Howard 5; Henderson 25		5,951
8	lge1	Colchester	A	W	1-0	Parkin 7		3,868
9	lge1	Peterborough	H	L	0-1			5,777
10	lge1	Blackpool	A	D	1-1	Henderson 69		5,229
11	ccR2	Leeds	A	L	0-1			18,476
12	lge1	Bradford	H	W	1-0	Igoe 87		5,189
13	lge1	Stockport	A	D	3-3	Fallon 13,66; McMaster 45		4,394
14	lge1	Oldham	H	W	1-0	Roberts 14		5,522
15	lge1	Port Vale	A	L	0-1			3,872
16	lge1	Barnsley	A	D	2-2	Igoe 28; Roberts 82		8,837
17	lge1	Sheff Wed	H	W	3-2	Howard 78; Parkin 86; Fallon 88		6,972
18	lge1	Torquay	H	D	3-3	Parkin 27; Igoe 32; Howard 36		6,724
19	lge1	Tranmere	A	L	1-2	Duke 69		8,419
20	facr1	Sheff Wed	H	W	4-1	Howard 43; Jenkins 48; Duke 83; Roberts 86		6,160
21	lge1	Hull City	H	W	4-2	Parkin 22,87; O'Hanlon 74; Roberts 90		6,348
22	lge1	Chesterfield	A	L	0-1			4,244
23	facr2	Notts County	H	D	1-1	O'Hanlon 19		5,768
24	lge1	Huddersfield	H	L	1-2	Smith, G 89		4,828
25	lge1	Doncaster	H	D	1-1	Parkin 72		5,452
26	facr2r	Notts County	A	L	0-2			3,770
27	lge1	Bournemouth	A	L	1-2	O'Hanlon 60		7,110
28	lge1	Peterborough	A	W	2-0	Igoe 54; Parkin 85		4,212
29	lge1	Brentford	H	W	3-0	Hewlett 42; Howard 67; Parkin 76		6,875
30	lge1	Colchester	H	L	0-3			6,468
31	lge1	Bradford	A	W	2-1	Smith, G 46,47		8,239
32	lge1	Sheff Wed	A	L	0-2			20,804
33	lge1	Blackpool	H	D	2-2	Parkin 36,45		5,526
34	lge1	Brentford	A	L	1-2	Smith, G 20		5,857
35	lge1	Stockport	H	W	3-0	Heywood 61; O'Hanlon 63; Smith, G 64		5,090
36	lge1	Oldham	A	W	2-1	Parkin 60; Smith, G 69		5,810
37	lge1	Barnsley	H	W	2-1	Parkin 13,76		5,511
38	lge1	Torquay	A	D	2-2	Parkin 38,58		4,190
39	lge1	Port Vale	H	W	1-0	Proctor 25		4,724
40	lge1	Doncaster	A	D	1-1	Holmes 5		7,696
41	lge1	Bournemouth	H	L	0-3			8,275
42	lge1	Luton	A	L	1-3	Proctor 34		8,173
43	lge1	Wrexham	H	W	4-2	Parkin 40,76,90 pen; Smith, G 80		5,123
44	lge1	MK Dons	A	D	1-1	Smith, G 43		7,019
45	lge1	Hartlepool	A	L	0-3			4,936
46	lge1	Walsall	H	L	1-2	Parkin 84 pen		5,592
47	lge1	Bristol City	H	D	0-0			6,977
48	lge1	Hull City	A	D	0-0			23,125
49	lge1	Tranmere	H	W	2-1	Smith, G 57,59		4,484
50	lge1	Huddersfield	A	L	0-4			13,559
51	lge1	Chesterfield	H	D	1-1	Parkin 13		6,044

MONTHLY POINTS TALLY

AUGUST	9	50%
SEPTEMBER	7	58%
OCTOBER	9	50%
NOVEMBER	3	33%
DECEMBER	7	47%
JANUARY	7	39%
FEBRUARY	11	73%
MARCH	4	33%
APRIL	5	28%
MAY	1	33%

KEY PLAYERS - GOALSCORERS

Sam Parkin

Goals in the League	23	**Player Strike Rate** Average number of minutes between League goals scored by player	160
Contribution to Attacking Power Average number of minutes between League team goals while on pitch	63	**Club Strike Rate** Average number of minutes between League goals scored by club	63

	PLAYER	LGE GOALS	GOALS ALL	POWER	STRIKE RATE
1	Sam Parkin	23	23	63	160 mins
2	Grant Smith	10	10	70	216 mins
3	Christian Roberts	3	4	68	499 mins
4	Brian Howard	5	6	59	504 mins
5	Sam Igoe	4	4	66	919 mins

KEY PLAYERS - MIDFIELDERS

Lee Holmes

Goals in the League	1	**Contribution to Attacking Power** Average number of minutes between League team goals while on pitch	53
Defensive Rating Average number of mins between League goals conceded while on the pitch	64	**Scoring Difference** Defensive Rating minus Contribution to Attacking Power	11

	PLAYER	LGE GOALS	GOALS ALL	DEF RATE	POWER	SCORE DIFF
1	Lee Holmes	1	1	64	53	11 mins
2	Brian Howard	5	6	63	59	4 mins
3	Matt Hewlett	1	2	67	64	3 mins
4	Sam Igoe	4	4	62	66	-4 mins
5	Grant Smith	10	10	62	70	-8 mins

KEY PLAYERS - DEFENDERS

David Duke

Goals Conceded Number of League goals conceded while the player was on the pitch	54	**Clean Sheets** In games when player was on pitch for at least 70 minutes	8
Defensive Rating Ave number of mins between League goals conceded while on the pitch	65	**Club Defensive Rating** Average number of mins between League goals conceded by the club this season	61

	PLAYER	CON LGE	CON ALL	CLEAN SHEETS	DEF RATE
1	David Duke	54	59	8	65 mins
2	Jerel Ifil	42	45	8	65 mins
3	Sean O'Hanlon	56	61	9	63 mins
4	Stephen Jenkins	36	38	6	63 mins
5	Matthew Heywood	49	53	4	53 mins

KEY GOALKEEPER

Rhys Evans

Goals Conceded in the League	64	**Counting Games** Games when player was on pitch for at least 70 minutes	44
Defensive Rating Ave number of mins between League goals conceded while on the pitch	62	**Clean Sheets** In Games when player was on pitch for at least 70 minutes	10

LEAGUE GOALS

Sam Parkin

Minutes on the pitch	3680	League average (mins between goals)	160
Goals in the League	23		

	PLAYER	MINS	GOALS	AVE
1	Parkin	3680	23	160
2	Smith, G	2162	10	216
3	Howard	2519	5	504
4	Henderson	513	5	103
5	Roberts	1496	3	499
6	O'Hanlon	3516	3	1172
7	Igoe	3674	4	919
8	Fallon	1354	3	451
9	Proctor	297	2	149
10	Duke	3526	1	3526
11	Hewlett	2557	1	2557
12	McMaster	205	1	205
	Other		5	
	TOTAL		66	

DISCIPLINARY RECORDS

	PLAYER	YELLOW	RED	AVE
1	Gurney	2	0	247
2	Henderson	2	0	256
3	Ifil	8	2	272
4	Reeves	2	0	305
5	Smith, G	6	0	360
6	Howard	6	0	419
7	Roberts	3	0	498
8	Robinson	2	0	503
9	Duke	4	2	587
10	Mitchell	1	0	630
11	Hewlett	4	0	639
12	Heywood	4	0	648
13	Garrard	1	0	722
	Other	14	1	
	TOTAL	59	5	

TOP POINT EARNERS

	PLAYER	GAMES	AV PTS
1	Lee Holmes	13	1.85
2	Jerel Ifil	29	1.59
3	Matt Hewlett	25	1.56
4	Christian Roberts	14	1.50
5	David Duke	36	1.47
6	Grant Smith	22	1.41
7	Brian Howard	27	1.37
8	Sam Parkin	41	1.37
9	Sam Igoe	39	1.36
10	Stephen Jenkins	25	1.36
	CLUB AVERAGE:		1.37

LEAGUE APPEARANCES GOALS AND BOOKINGS

	AGE (on 01/07/05)	IN NAMED 16	APPEARANCES	COUNTING GAMES	MINUTES ON PITCH	LEAGUE GOALS	Yellow	Red
Goalkeepers								
Steve Book	36	46	2	2	163	0	0	0
Rhys Evans	23	46	45	44	3977	0	1	0
Defenders								
David Duke	26	44	44	36	3526	1	4	2
Luke Garrard	20	17	9	8	722	0	1	0
Andy Gurney	31	6	6	5	495	0	2	0
Matthew Heywood	25	36	32	28	2593	1	4	0
Jerel Ifil	23	39	34	29	2728	0	8	2
Stephen Jenkins	32	26	26	25	2278	0	3	0
Kyle Lapham	19	2	1	1	90	0	0	0
Paul Mitchell	23	7	7	7	630	0	1	0
Andrew Nicholas	21	20	16	8	860	0	0	0
Sean O'Hanlon	22	40	40	39	3516	3	3	0
Alan Reeves	37	22	8	6	610	1	2	0
Adrian Viveash	35	1	0	0	0	0	0	0
Midfielders								
Matt Hewlett	29	32	31	25	2557	1	4	0
Lee Holmes	18	15	15	13	1216	1	0	0
Brian Howard	22	41	35	27	2519	5	6	0
Sam Igoe	29	43	43	39	3674	4	4	0
Jamie McMaster	22	4	4	2	205	1	0	0
Stefani Miglioranzi	27	23	21	13	1311	0	0	0
Michael Pook	19	10	5	3	297	0	0	0
Steve Robinson	29	29	18	8	1007	0	2	0
Grant Smith	25	37	30	22	2162	10	6	0
Ben Wells	17	4	1	0	45	0	0	0
Forwards								
Andy Caton	17	12	8	0	178	1	0	0
Rory Fallon	23	40	31	10	1354	3	1	0
Darius Henderson	23	6	6	6	513	5	2	0
Ashan Holgate	-	3	2	0	45	0	0	0
Lloyd Opara	21	1	0	0	0	0	0	0
Sam Parkin	24	41	41	41	3680	23	2	1
Mike Proctor	24	4	4	2	297	2	1	0
Christian Roberts	25	21	21	14	1496	3	3	0
Jamie Slabber	20	12	9	4	448	0	2	0
Mark Yeates	20	6	4	1	235	0	1	0

TEAM OF THE SEASON

D
David Duke
CG: 36 DR: 65
D
Jerel Ifil
CG: 29 DR: 65
D
Stephen Jenkins
CG: 25 DR: 63
D
Sean O'Hanlon
CG: 39 DR: 63
G
Rhys Evans
CG: 44 DR: 62
M
Lee Holmes
CG: 13 SD: 11
M
Brian Howard
CG: 27 SD: 4
M
Matt Hewlett
CG: 25 SD: 3
M
Sam Igoe
CG: 39 SD: -4
F
Sam Parkin
CG: 41 SR: 160
F
Christian Roberts
CG: 14 SR: 499

SQUAD APPEARANCES

Match	1	2	3	4	5	6	7	8	9	10	11	12	13	14	15	16	17
Venue	A	H	H	A	A	H	A	A	H	A	A	H	A	H	A	A	H
Competition	L	L	L	L	W	L	L	L	L	L	W	L	L	L	L	L	L
Result	L	L	W	W	W	W	L	W	L	D	L	W	D	W	L	D	W

Match	18	19	20	21	22	23	24	25	26	27	28	29	30	31	32	33	34
Venue	H	A	H	H	A	H	H	H	A	A	A	H	H	A	A	H	A
Competition	L	L	F	L	L	F	L	L	F	L	L	L	L	L	L	L	L
Result	D	L	W	W	L	D	L	D	L	L	W	W	L	W	L	D	L

Match	35	36	37	38	39	40	41	42	43	44	45	46	47	48	49	50	51
Venue	H	A	H	A	H	A	H	A	H	A	A	H	H	A	H	A	H
Competition	L	L	L	L	L	L	L	L	L	L	L	L	L	L	L	L	L
Result	W	W	W	D	W	D	L	L	W	D	L	L	D	D	W	L	D

Goalkeepers
Steve Book
Rhys Evans

Defenders
David Duke
Luke Garrard
Andy Gurney
Matthew Heywood
Jerel Ifil
Stephen Jenkins
Kyle Lapham
Paul Mitchell
Andrew Nicholas
Sean O'Hanlon
Alan Reeves
Adrian Viveash

Midfielders
Matt Hewlett
Lee Holmes
Brian Howard
Sam Igoe
Jamie McMaster
Stefani Miglioranzi
Michael Pook
Steve Robinson
Grant Smith
Ben Wells

Forwards
Andy Caton
Rory Fallon
Darius Henderson
Ashan Holgate
Lloyd Opara
Sam Parkin
Mike Proctor
Christian Roberts
Jamie Slabber
Mark Yeates

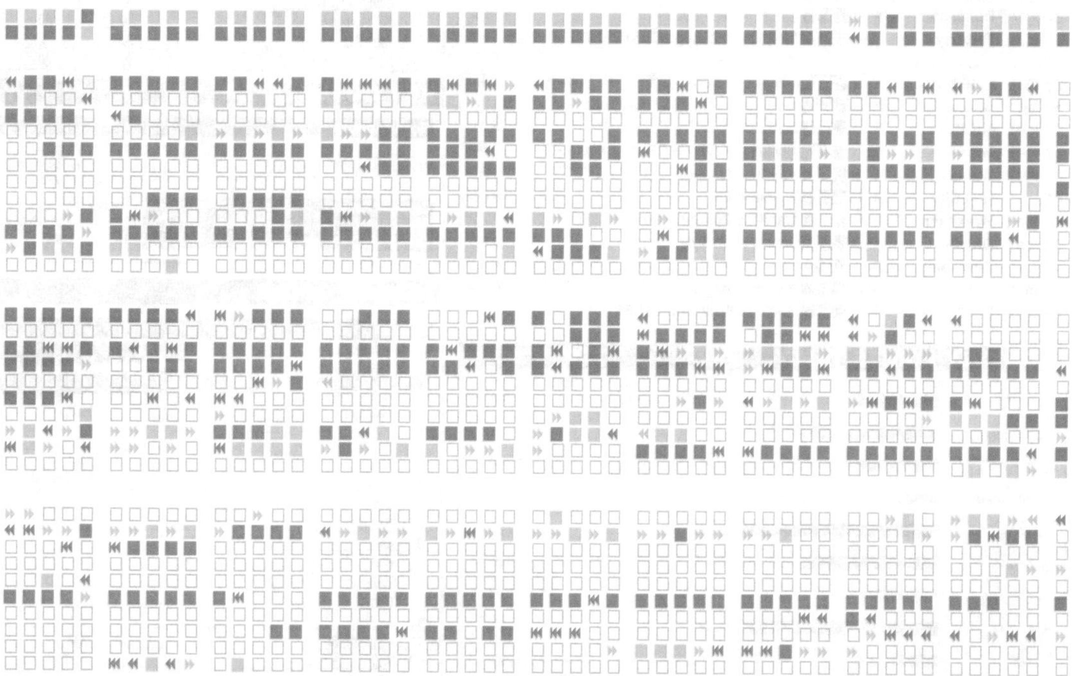

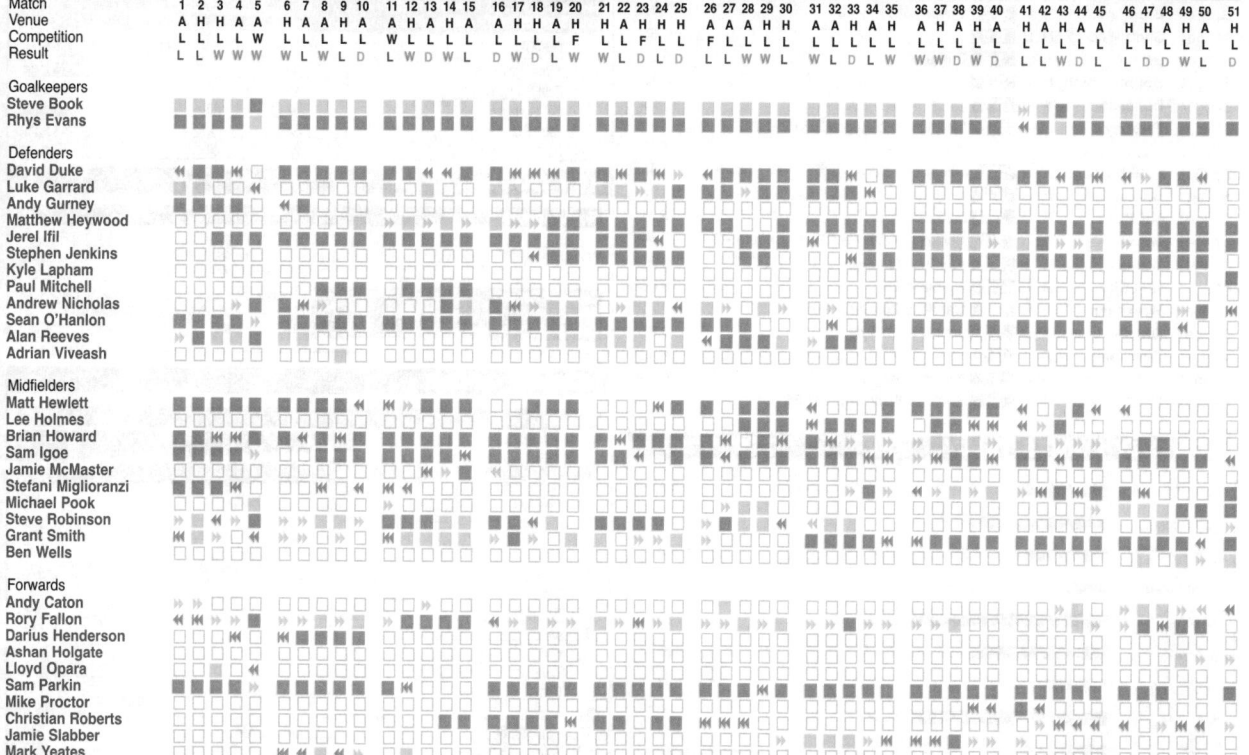

KEY: On all match / On bench; Subbed or sent off (Counting game) / Subbed or sent off (playing less than 70 minutes); Subbed on from bench (Counting Game) / Subbed on (playing less than 70 minutes); Subbed on and then subbed or sent off (Counting Game) / Subbed on and then subbed or sent off (playing less than 70 minutes); Not in 16

BARNSLEY

Final Position: **13th**

NICKNAME: THE TYKES

KEY: Won / Drawn / Lost

							Attendance
1	lge1	MK Dons	A	D	1-1	Reid 22	4,720
2	lge1	Bristol City	H	W	2-1	Shuker 68,76	10,435
3	lge1	Luton	H	L	3-4	Boulding 2,90; McPhail 72	10,057
4	lge1	Walsall	A	D	2-2	Vaughan 16; Conlon 49	6,059
5	ccR1	Darlington	A	W	2-0	Shuker 14; Reid 75 pen	2,789
6	lge1	Hull City	H	L	1-2	Conlon 12	13,175
7	lge1	Wrexham	A	L	1-2	Nardiello 62	4,223
8	lge1	Hartlepool	A	D	1-1	Chopra 38	5,119
9	lge1	Tranmere	H	D	0-0		8,615
10	lge1	Huddersfield	A	W	2-0	Conlon 10; Mirfin 21 og	14,794
11	ccR2	Man City	A	L	1-7	Conlon 47	19,578
12	lge1	Chesterfield	H	W	1-0	Kay 87	9,792
13	lge1	Bradford	A	L	0-1		8,715
14	lge1	Brentford	H	D	0-0		8,453
15	lge1	Sheff Wed	A	L	0-1		25,391
16	lge1	Doncaster	H	L	1-3	Chopra 71	12,478
17	lge1	Swindon	H	D	2-2	Chopra 41; Reid 66	8,837
18	lge1	Bournemouth	A	W	3-1	Conlon 20 pen,36; Chopra 69	7,709
19	lge1	Port Vale	H	L	1-2	Conlon 44 pen	8,642
20	facr1	Northampton	A	L	0-1		4,876
21	lge1	Oldham	A	L	2-3	Boulding 11; Chopra 55	5,593
22	lge1	Blackpool	H	W	1-0	Burns 75	9,084
23	lge1	Colchester	A	W	2-0	Kay 34,54	2,927
24	lge1	Torquay	A	W	1-0	Boulding 45	2,983
25	lge1	Peterborough	H	W	4-0	Chopra 14,57,77; Shuker 51	8,536
26	lge1	Tranmere	A	D	1-1	Kay 90	11,519
27	lge1	Stockport	H	D	3-3	Vaughan 14,47; Shuker 43	10,236
28	lge1	Hartlepool	H	D	0-0		9,595
29	lge1	Chesterfield	A	D	2-2	Boulding 38,45	5,985
30	lge1	Huddersfield	H	W	4-2	Chopra 9,24,87 pen; Boulding 38	11,725
31	lge1	Stockport	A	D	2-2	Boulding 31; Vaughan 63	5,326
32	lge1	Brentford	A	D	1-1	Boulding 34	4,835
33	lge1	Bradford	H	D	2-2	Chopra 54; Kay 88	8,729
34	lge1	Sheff Wed	H	D	0-0		19,659
35	lge1	Swindon	A	L	1-2	Burns 30	5,511
36	lge1	Bournemouth	H	L	0-1		8,153
37	lge1	Doncaster	A	L	0-4		7,286
38	lge1	Torquay	H	W	4-1	McPhail 24; Chopra 27; Reid 29; Boulding 64	7,466
39	lge1	Peterborough	A	W	3-1	Chopra 67 pen; Nardiello 89; Shuker 90	3,485
40	lge1	Bristol City	A	D	0-0		9,321
41	lge1	MK Dons	H	D	1-1	Nardiello 45	8,111
42	lge1	Luton	A	W	3-1	Shuker 33; Davies 37 og; Chopra 42	7,548
43	lge1	Walsall	H	W	3-2	Kay 37; Nardiello 48; Chopra 80	8,358
44	lge1	Hull City	A	L	1-2	Nardiello 64	19,341
45	lge1	Wrexham	H	D	2-2	Nardiello 26; Chopra 72	7,753
46	lge1	Oldham	H	D	2-2	Johnson, Si 6,79	8,856
47	lge1	Port Vale	A	L	0-5		4,324
48	lge1	Colchester	H	D	1-1	Nardiello 41	8,162
49	lge1	Blackpool	A	W	2-0	Shuker 38; Williams, R 85	7,571

MONTHLY POINTS TALLY

AUGUST	5	28%
SEPTEMBER	8	67%
OCTOBER	5	28%
NOVEMBER	3	33%
DECEMBER	11	73%
JANUARY	8	44%
FEBRUARY	4	27%
MARCH	11	73%
APRIL	3	20%
MAY	3	100%

KEY PLAYERS - GOALSCORERS

Michael Chopra

Goals in the League	17	Player Strike Rate Average number of minutes between League goals scored by player	197
Contribution to Attacking Power Average number of minutes between League team goals while on pitch	58	Club Strike Rate Average number of minutes between League goals scored by club	60

	PLAYER	LGE GOALS	GOALS ALL	POWER	STRIKE RATE
1	Michael Chopra	17	17	58	197 mins
2	Michael Boulding	10	10	55	199 mins
3	Barry Conlon	6	7	72	267 mins
4	Chris Shuker	7	8	60	473 mins
5	Tony Vaughan	4	4	61	525 mins

KEY PLAYERS - MIDFIELDERS

Stephen McPhail

Goals in the League	2	Contribution to Attacking Power Average number of minutes between League team goals while on pitch	59
Defensive Rating Average number of mins between League goals conceded while on the pitch	69	Scoring Difference Defensive Rating minus Contribution to Attacking Power	10

	PLAYER	LGE GOALS	GOALS ALL	DEF RATE	POWER	SCORE DIFF
1	Stephen McPhail	2	2	69	59	10 mins
2	Antony Kay	6	6	65	58	7 mins
3	Jacob Burns	2	2	66	60	6 mins
4	Chris Shuker	7	8	65	60	5 mins
5	Nicky Wroe	0	0	65	64	1 mins

KEY PLAYERS - DEFENDERS

Tommy Williams

Goals Conceded Number of League goals conceded while the player was on the pitch	46	Clean Sheets In games when player was on pitch for at least 70 minutes	11
Defensive Rating Ave number of mins between League goals conceded while on the pitch	75	Club Defensive Rating Average number of mins between League goals conceded by the club this season	65

	PLAYER	CON LGE	CON ALL	CLEAN SHEETS	DEF RATE
1	Tommy Williams	46	54	11	75 mins
2	Paul Reid	49	50	10	68 mins
3	Bobby Hassell	52	60	9	65 mins
4	Tony Vaughan	33	33	7	64 mins
5	Matthew Carbon	28	29	2	57 mins

KEY GOALKEEPER

Ross Turnbull

Goals Conceded in the League	29	Counting Games Games when player was on pitch for at least 70 minutes	23
Defensive Rating Ave number of mins between League goals conceded while on the pitch	70	Clean Sheets In Games when player was on pitch for at least 70 minutes	7

LEAGUE GOALS

Michael Chopra

Minutes on the pitch	3341	League average (mins between goals)	197
Goals in the League	17		

	PLAYER	MINS	GOALS	AVE
1	Chopra	3341	17	197
2	Boulding	1985	10	199
3	Shuker	3310	7	473
4	Conlon	1601	6	267
5	Nardiello	1175	7	168
6	Kay	3256	6	543
7	Reid	3331	3	1110
8	Vaughan	2100	4	525
9	Burns	2901	2	1451
10	McPhail	2960	2	1480
11	Johnson, Si	836	2	418
12	Williams, R	1210	1	1210
	Other		2	
	TOTAL		69	

DISCIPLINARY RECORDS

	PLAYER	YELLOW	RED	AVE
1	Nardiello	4	0	293
2	Chopra	10	1	303
3	Burns	8	1	322
4	Vaughan	4	2	350
5	Kay	9	0	361
6	Shuker	7	1	413
7	Hassell	7	0	484
8	McPhail	6	0	493
9	Austin	2	0	495
10	Conlon	3	0	533
11	Williams, T	5	0	687
12	Carbon	2	0	802
13	Flinders	1	0	990
	Other	9	1	
	TOTAL	77	6	

TOP POINT EARNERS

	PLAYER	GAMES	AV PTS
1	McPhail	32	1.53
2	Tonge	14	1.50
3	Kay	34	1.44
4	Chopra	37	1.43
5	Hassell	37	1.43
6	Wroe	24	1.42
7	Williams, R	12	1.42
8	Reid	34	1.38
9	Vaughan	21	1.38
10	Williams, T	38	1.37
	CLUB AVERAGE:		1.33

TEAM OF THE SEASON

D
Tommy Williams
CG: 38 DR: 75
M
Stephen McPhail
CG: 32 SD: 10
D
Paul Reid
CG: 34 DR: 68
M
Antony Kay
CG: 34 SD: 7
F
Michael Chopra
CG: 37 SR: 197
G
Nick Colgan
CG: 12 DR: 62
D
Bobby Hassell
CG: 37 DR: 65
M
Jacob Burns
CG: 32 SD: 6
F
Michael Boulding
CG: 22 SR: 199
D
Tony Vaughan
CG: 21 DR: 64
M
Chris Shuker
CG: 33 SD: 5

LEAGUE APPEARANCES GOALS AND BOOKINGS

	AGE (on 01/07/05)	IN NAMED 16	APPEARANCES	COUNTING GAMES	MINUTES ON PITCH	LEAGUE GOALS	Yellow	Red
Goalkeepers								
Nick Colgan	31	28	13	12	1120	0	1	0
Scott Flinders	18	18	11	11	990	0	1	0
David Scarsella	22	23	0	0	0	0	0	0
Ross Turnbull	20	23	23	22	2030	0	0	1
Defenders								
Robert Atkinson	18	5	1	0	6	0	0	0
Neil Austin	22	31	15	9	991	0	2	0
Matthew Carbon	30	28	26	14	1605	0	2	0
Bobby Hassell	25	42	40	37	3394	0	7	0
Ryan Laight	19	3	0	0	0	0	0	0
Paul Reid	23	42	41	34	3331	3	3	0
Tony Vaughan	29	29	26	21	2100	4	4	2
Robbie Williams	21	21	17	12	1210	1	1	0
Tommy Williams	24	39	39	38	3438	0	5	0
Midfielders								
Tom Baker	20	10	3	0	41	0	0	0
Jacob Burns	27	36	34	32	2901	2	8	1
Simon Heslop	18	1	0	0	0	0	0	0
Antony Kay	22	39	39	34	3256	6	9	0
Stephen McPhail	25	37	36	32	2960	2	6	0
Chris Shuker	23	45	45	33	3310	7	7	1
Dale Tonge	20	19	14	14	1189	0	1	0
Nicky Wroe	19	40	30	24	2355	0	2	0
Forwards								
Michael Boulding	29	34	29	22	1985	10	1	0
Michael Chopra	21	39	39	37	3341	17	10	1
Barry Conlon	26	26	24	17	1601	6	3	0
Nathan Jarman	18	9	6	1	130	0	0	0
Simon Johnson	22	11	11	9	836	2	0	0
Nathan Joynes	19	2	1	0	20	0	0	0
Daniel Nardiello	22	36	28	11	1175	7	4	0
Fola Onibuje	20	6	3	0	17	0	0	0
Mark Stallard	30	14	5	0	41	0	0	0

SQUAD APPEARANCES

Match	1	2	3	4	5	6	7	8	9	10	11	12	13	14	15	16	17	18	19	20	21	22	23	24	25	26	27	28	29	30	31	32	33	34	35	36	37	38	39	40	41	42	43	44	45	46	47	48	49
Venue	A	H	H	A	A	H	A	A	H	A	A	H	A	H	A	H	H	A	H	A	A	H	A	A	H	A	H	H	A	H	A	A	H	H	A	H	A	H	A	A	H	A	H	A	H	H	A	H	A
Competition	L	L	L	L	W	L	L	L	L	L	W	L	L	L	L	L	L	L	L	F	L	L	L	L	L	L	L	L	L	L	L	L	L	L	L	L	L	L	L	L	L	L	L	L	L	L	L	L	L
Result	D	W	L	D	W	L	L	D	D	W	L	W	L	D	L	L	D	W	L	L	L	W	W	W	W	D	D	D	D	W	D	D	D	D	L	L	L	W	W	D	D	W	W	L	D	D	L	D	W

Goalkeepers
Nick Colgan
Scott Flinders
David Scarsella
Ross Turnbull

Defenders
Robert Atkinson
Neil Austin
Matthew Carbon
Bobby Hassell
Ryan Laight
Paul Reid
Tony Vaughan
Robbie Williams
Tommy Williams

Midfielders
Tom Baker
Jacob Burns
Simon Heslop
Antony Kay
Stephen McPhail
Chris Shuker
Dale Tonge
Nicky Wroe

Forwards
Michael Boulding
Michael Chopra
Barry Conlon
Nathan Jarman
Simon Johnson
Nathan Joynes
Daniel Nardiello
Fola Onibuje
Mark Stallard

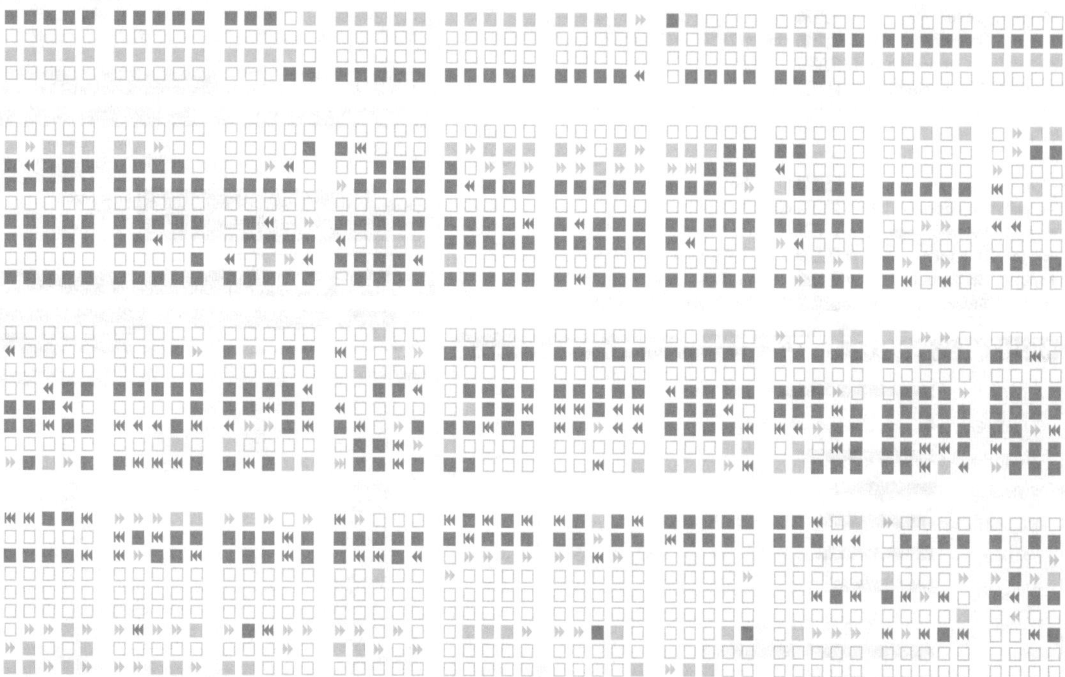

KEY: On all match; On bench; Subbed or sent off (Counting game); Subbed or sent off (playing less than 70 minutes); Subbed on from bench (Counting Game); Subbed on (playing less than 70 minutes); Subbed on and then subbed or sent off (Counting Game); Subbed on and then subbed or sent off (playing less than 70 minutes); Not in 16

WALSALL

Final Position: **14th**

NICKNAME: THE SADDLERS

KEY: ☐Won ☐Drawn ☐Lost

							Attendance
1	lge1	Port Vale	H	W	3-2	Fryatt 12 pen; Williams 82; Taylor 86	8,225
2	lge1	Bournemouth	A	D	2-2	Taylor, D 37; Taylor, K 51	6,485
3	lge1	Oldham	A	L	3-5	Fryatt 29,78 pen; Taylor, D 34	5,654
4	lge1	Barnsley	H	D	2-2	Fryatt 36; Wrack 90	6,059
5	ccR1	Sheff Wed	A	L	0-1		8,959
6	lge1	Torquay	A	D	0-0		3,791
7	lge1	Swindon	H	W	3-2	Leitao 28,34; Birch 87	5,951
8	lge1	Doncaster	A	L	1-3	Fryatt 73	6,146
9	lge1	Sheff Wed	H	D	1-1	Standing 39	6,403
10	lge1	Chesterfield	A	L	0-1		4,755
11	lge1	Brentford	H	L	0-1		5,302
12	lge1	Huddersfield	A	L	1-3	Clarke, N 73 og	11,324
13	lge1	Colchester	H	W	2-1	Bennett 73; Emblen 84	5,203
14	lge1	Wrexham	A	D	1-1	Bennett 74	3,803
15	lge1	Luton	H	W	2-0	Merson 7; Fryatt 72	5,963
16	lge1	Bristol City	H	L	1-2	Fryatt 49 pen	7,105
17	lge1	MK Dons	A	D	1-1	Wrack 13	4,247
18	lge1	Hull City	A	L	1-3	Standing 49	16,010
19	facr1	Slough	A	L	1-2	Wrack 32	2,023
20	lge1	Peterborough	H	W	2-1	Wrack 62; Birch 68	5,465
21	lge1	Stockport	A	W	1-0	Wrack 14	4,448
22	lge1	Hartlepool	H	W	2-1	Fryatt 51; Leitao 69	5,522
23	lge1	Bradford	A	D	1-1	Robinson 61	6,732
24	lge1	Blackpool	H	W	3-2	Leitao 45; Robinson 55,70	5,476
25	lge1	Sheff Wed	A	L	2-3	Robinson 42; McShane 81	26,996
26	lge1	Tranmere	H	L	0-2		7,217
27	lge1	Doncaster	H	D	1-1	Standing 21	6,021
28	lge1	Brentford	A	L	0-1		5,084
29	lge1	Chesterfield	H	W	3-0	Wrack 14; Leitao 26; Fryatt 90	5,177
30	lge1	Tranmere	A	L	1-2	Leitao 62	8,651
31	lge1	Colchester	A	L	0-5		2,616
32	lge1	Huddersfield	H	W	4-3	Merson 16; Fryatt 45,50 pen,74	5,727
33	lge1	Wrexham	H	D	2-2	Wrack 20; Leitao 42	5,659
34	lge1	Bristol City	A	W	1-0	Surman 75	10,820
35	lge1	MK Dons	H	D	0-0		5,888
36	lge1	Luton	A	L	0-1		7,236
37	lge1	Bradford	H	D	1-1	Emblen 72	4,966
38	lge1	Blackpool	A	L	0-2		6,844
39	lge1	Bournemouth	H	L	1-2	Fryatt 1	5,126
40	lge1	Port Vale	A	L	0-2		5,085
41	lge1	Oldham	H	L	0-1		6,794
42	lge1	Barnsley	A	L	2-3	Joachim 51; Leitao 53	8,358
43	lge1	Torquay	H	D	1-1	Fryatt 80	5,694
44	lge1	Swindon	A	W	2-1	Joachim 44; Wright 90	5,592
45	lge1	Peterborough	A	W	2-0	Standing 64; Wrack 76	3,841
46	lge1	Hull City	H	W	3-0	Joachim 34,53,68	7,958
47	lge1	Hartlepool	A	W	3-1	Robson 10 og; Joachim 14; Surman 42	6,389
48	lge1	Stockport	H	W	3-0	Fryatt 86; Taylor, K 89; Wright 90	6,971

MONTHLY POINTS TALLY

AUGUST	9	50%
SEPTEMBER	1	8%
OCTOBER	8	44%
NOVEMBER	6	67%
DECEMBER	7	47%
JANUARY	7	39%
FEBRUARY	6	40%
MARCH	0	0%
APRIL	13	87%
MAY	3	100%

KEY PLAYERS - GOALSCORERS

Matty Fryatt

Goals in the League	15	Player Strike Rate Average number of minutes between League goals scored by player	144
Contribution to Attacking Power Average number of minutes between League team goals while on pitch	60	Club Strike Rate Average number of minutes between League goals scored by club	64

	PLAYER	LGE GOALS	GOALS ALL	POWER	STRIKE RATE
1	Matty Fryatt	15	15	60	144 mins
2	Jorge Leitao	8	8	64	373 mins
3	Darren Wrack	7	8	61	545 mins
4	Michael Standing	4	4	62	587 mins
5	Julian Bennett	2	2	66	1358 mins

KEY PLAYERS - MIDFIELDERS

Michael Standing

Goals in the League	4	Contribution to Attacking Power Average number of minutes between League team goals while on pitch	62
Defensive Rating Average number of mins between League goals conceded while on the pitch	81	Scoring Difference Defensive Rating minus Contribution to Attacking Power	19

	PLAYER	LGE GOALS	GOALS ALL	DEF RATE	POWER	SCORE DIFF
1	Michael Standing	4	4	81	62	19 mins
2	Darren Wrack	7	8	60	61	-1 mins
3	Mark Kinsella	0	0	50	57	-7 mins
4	Simon Osborn	0	0	62	70	-8 mins

KEY PLAYERS - DEFENDERS

Ian Roper

Goals Conceded Number of League goals conceded while the player was on the pitch	29	Clean Sheets In games when player was on pitch for at least 70 minutes	4
Defensive Rating Ave number of mins between League goals conceded while on the pitch	71	Club Defensive Rating Average number of mins between League goals conceded by the club this season	60

	PLAYER	CON LGE	CON ALL	CLEAN SHEETS	DEF RATE
1	Ian Roper	29	29	4	71 mins
2	Mark Wright	48	50	8	66 mins
3	Zigor Aranalde	43	46	5	59 mins
4	Neil Emblen	57	59	6	53 mins
5	Julian Bennett	52	54	4	52 mins

KEY GOALKEEPER

Joe Murphy

Goals Conceded in the League	34	Counting Games Games when player was on pitch for at least 70 minutes	24
Defensive Rating Ave number of mins between League goals conceded while on the pitch	65	Clean Sheets In Games when player was on pitch for at least 70 minutes	5

LEAGUE GOALS

Matty Fryatt

Minutes on the pitch	2164	League average (mins between goals)	144
Goals in the League	15		

	PLAYER	MINS	GOALS	AVE
1	Fryatt	2164	15	144
2	Leitao	2984	8	373
3	Wrack	3816	7	545
4	Joachim	643	6	107
5	Robinson	535	4	134
6	Standing	2348	4	587
7	Taylor, K	927	3	309
8	Birch	881	2	441
9	Bennett	2715	2	1358
10	Taylor, D	1110	2	555
11	Wright	3189	2	1595
12	Surman	885	2	443
13	Emblen	3047	2	1524
	Other		6	
	TOTAL		65	

DISCIPLINARY RECORDS

	PLAYER	YELLOW	RED	AVE
1	Roper	7	2	230
2	Bazeley	2	0	280
3	Perpetuini	2	0	315
4	Aranalde	6	0	424
5	Birch	2	0	440
6	Bennett	6	0	452
7	Broad	1	0	525
8	Robinson	1	0	535
9	Osborn	5	0	561
10	Emblen	5	0	609
11	Gerrard	1	0	720
12	Pead	1	0	720
13	Kinsella	2	0	855
	Other	15	1	
	TOTAL	56	3	

TOP POINT EARNERS

	PLAYER	GAMES	AV PTS
1	Mark Kinsella	17	1.65
2	Michael Standing	22	1.64
3	Joe Murphy	24	1.42
4	Mark Wright	35	1.40
5	Darren Wrack	42	1.38
6	Zigor Aranalde	28	1.32
7	Ian Roper	20	1.25
8	Simon Osborn	28	1.25
9	Neil Emblen	32	1.22
10	Paul Merson	30	1.20
	CLUB AVERAGE:		

TEAM OF THE SEASON

G — Joe Murphy — CG: 24 DR: 65

D — Ian Roper — CG: 20 DR: 71

D — Mark Wright — CG: 35 DR: 66

D — Zigor Aranalde — CG: 28 DR: 59

D — Neil Emblen — CG: 32 DR: 53

M — Michael Standing — CG: 22 SD: 19

M — Darren Wrack — CG: 42 SD: -1

M — Mark Kinsella — CG: 17 SD: -7

M — Simon Osborn — CG: 28 SD: -8

F — Matty Fryatt — CG: 18 SR: 144

F — Jorge Leitao — CG: 28 SR: 373

LEAGUE APPEARANCES GOALS AND BOOKINGS

	AGE (on 01/07/05)	IN NAMED 16	APPEARANCES	COUNTING GAMES	MINUTES ON PITCH	LEAGUE GOALS		
Goalkeepers								
Dean Coleman	19	11	2	1	135	0	0	0
Richard McKinney	26	10	3	3	270	0	0	0
Joe Murphy	24	31	25	24	2193	0	1	1
Andy Oakes	28	9	9	9	810	0	0	0
Mark Paston	28	28	9	8	732	0	0	0
Defenders								
Zigor Aranalde	32	30	30	28	2544	0	6	0
Darren Bazeley	32	8	7	5	560	0	2	0
Julian Bennett	20	36	31	30	2715	2	6	0
Jonathan Bewers	22	1	1	1	90	0	0	0
Mark Bradley	-	1	1	0	56	0	0	0
Kofi Dakinah	25	1	1	0	34	0	0	0
Scott Dann	18	4	1	0	1	0	0	0
Neil Emblen	34	40	36	32	3047	2	5	0
Anthony Gerrard	19	8	8	8	720	0	1	0
Paul McShane	19	4	4	2	288	1	2	0
Ian Roper	28	34	26	20	2071	0	7	2
Mark Wright	23	38	37	35	3189	2	1	0
Midfielders								
Joe Broad	22	29	10	3	525	0	1	0
John Harkness		1	1	1	77	0	0	0
Mark Kinsella	32	29	22	17	1710	0	2	0
Paul Merson	37	38	36	30	2894	2	3	0
Simon Osborn	33	43	38	28	2809	0	5	0
Craig Pead	23	8	8	8	720	0	1	0
David Perpetuini	26	7	7	7	630	0	2	0
Michael Standing	24	37	32	22	2348	4	2	0
Andrew Surman	18	16	14	7	885	2	1	0
Daryl Taylor	20	28	18	9	1110	2	0	0
Kris Taylor	21	20	13	8	927	3	1	0
Darren Wrack	29	44	43	42	3816	7	1	0
Forwards								
Taiwo Atieno	19	6	3	0	73	0	0	0
Gary Birch	23	18	13	6	881	2	2	0
Matty Fryatt	19	39	36	18	2164	15	2	0
Moreira Herivelto	29	3	1	0	15	0	0	0
Julian Joachim	30	8	8	7	643	6	0	0
Jorge Leitao	31	44	42	28	2984	8	3	0
Marvin Robinson	25	11	10	4	535	4	1	0
Leroy Williams	18	11	7	1	220	1	0	0

SQUAD APPEARANCES

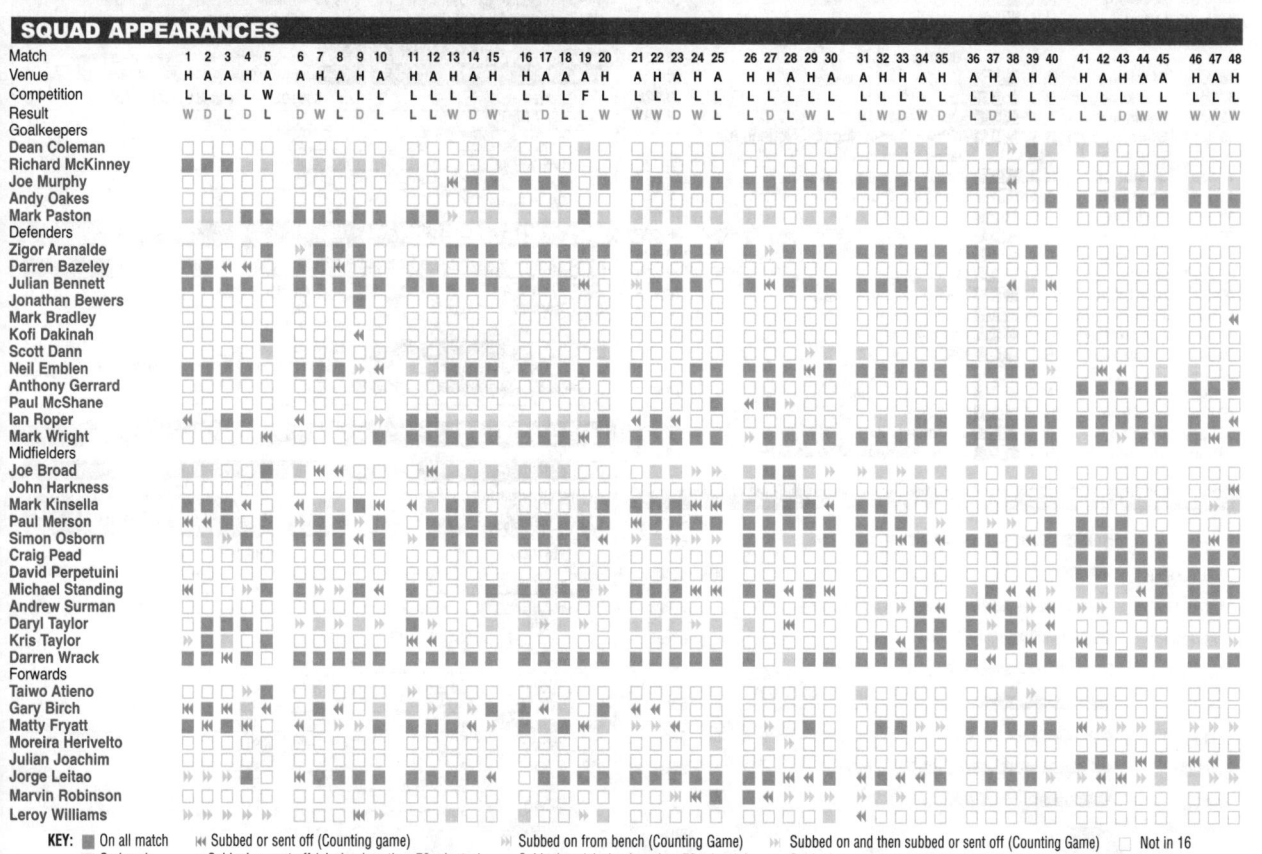

Match	1	2	3	4	5	6	7	8	9	10	11	12	13	14	15	16	17	18	19	20	21	22	23	24
Venue	H	A	A	H	A	A	H	A	H	A	H	A	H	A	H	H	A	A	A	H	A	H	A	H
Competition	L	L	L	L	W	L	L	L	L	L	L	L	L	L	L	L	L	L	F	L	L	L	L	L
Result	W	D	L	D	L	D	W	L	D	L	L	L	W	D	W	L	D	L	L	W	W	W	D	W

Match	25	26	27	28	29	30	31	32	33	34	35	36	37	38	39	40	41	42	43	44	45	46	47	48
Venue	A	H	H	A	H	A	A	H	H	A	H	A	H	A	H	A	H	A	H	A	A	H	A	H
Competition	L	L	L	L	L	L	L	L	L	L	L	L	L	L	L	L	L	L	L	L	L	L	L	L
Result	L	L	D	L	W	L	L	W	D	W	D	L	D	L	L	L	L	L	D	W	W	W	W	W

Goalkeepers
Dean Coleman
Richard McKinney
Joe Murphy
Andy Oakes
Mark Paston
Defenders
Zigor Aranalde
Darren Bazeley
Julian Bennett
Jonathan Bewers
Mark Bradley
Kofi Dakinah
Scott Dann
Neil Emblen
Anthony Gerrard
Paul McShane
Ian Roper
Mark Wright
Midfielders
Joe Broad
John Harkness
Mark Kinsella
Paul Merson
Simon Osborn
Craig Pead
David Perpetuini
Michael Standing
Andrew Surman
Daryl Taylor
Kris Taylor
Darren Wrack
Forwards
Taiwo Atieno
Gary Birch
Matty Fryatt
Moreira Herivelto
Julian Joachim
Jorge Leitao
Marvin Robinson
Leroy Williams

KEY: On all match · On bench · Subbed or sent off (Counting game) · Subbed or sent off (playing less than 70 minutes) · Subbed on from bench (Counting Game) · Subbed on (playing less than 70 minutes) · Subbed on and then subbed or sent off (Counting Game) · Subbed on and then subbed or sent off (playing less than 70 minutes) · Not in 16

COLCHESTER UNITED

Final Position: **15th**

NICKNAME: THE U'S

KEY: Won Drawn Lost

							Attendance
1	lge1	Sheff Wed	A	W	3-0	Fagan 85; Stockley 89; Keith, J 90	24,138
2	lge1	Stockport	H	W	3-2	Watson 19; Andrews 30; Fagan 41	3,346
3	lge1	Peterborough	H	W	2-1	Andrews 58 pen; Ireland 64 og	3,754
4	lge1	Chesterfield	A	L	1-2	Johnson 44	4,028
5	ccr1	Cheltenham	H	W	2-1	Fagan 12; Johnson 61	2,144
6	lge1	Doncaster	H	W	4-1	Fagan 16; Johnson 22; Halford 27; Keith, J 70	3,803
7	lge1	Hartlepool	A	L	1-2	Keith, J 90	4,371
8	lge1	Swindon	H	L	0-1		3,868
9	lge1	Bournemouth	A	W	3-1	Fagan 10; Williams 24; May 79	5,944
10	lge1	MK Dons	H	L	0-1		3,460
11	ccR2	West Brom	H	W	2-1	Fagan 29; May 118	4,591
12	lge1	Oldham	A	D	1-1	Halford 56	5,166
13	lge1	Port Vale	H	W	2-1	Danns 10,19	3,230
14	lge1	Walsall	A	L	1-2	Garcia 71	5,203
15	lge1	Blackpool	A	D	1-1	Watson 80	6,464
16	lge1	Wrexham	H	L	1-2	Danns 49	2,866
17	lge1	Tranmere	H	L	1-2	Halford 83	3,420
18	ccR3	Southampton	A	L	2-3	Danns 7; Halford 64	20,588
19	lge1	Bristol City	A	D	0-0		11,678
20	lge1	Bradford	A	D	2-2	Johnson, G 8,39	7,851
21	facr1	Mansfield	A	D	1-1	Halford 25	3,202
22	lge1	Huddersfield	H	D	0-0		3,972
23	facr1r	Mansfield	H	W	4-1	Garcia 10; Curtis 14 og; Fagan 67 pen; Williams 90 pen	2,492
24	lge1	Torquay	A	W	3-1	Fagan 67,72; Garcia 78	2,984
25	facr2	Rushden & D	A	W	5-2	Halford 4,47,90; Fagan 25,35	3,077
26	lge1	Barnsley	H	L	0-2		2,927
27	lge1	Hull City	H	L	1-2	Williams 73	4,046
28	lge1	Brentford	A	L	0-1		5,634
29	lge1	Luton	A	D	2-2	Garcia 34; Halford 62	8,806
30	lge1	Swindon	A	W	3-0	Johnson, G 31; Danns 38; Garcia 47	6,468
31	lge1	Oldham	H	D	0-0		3,873
32	facr3	Hull City	A	W	2-0	Williams 27; Fagan 29	14,027
33	lge1	MK Dons	A	L	0-2		3,833
34	lge1	Luton	H	D	0-0		4,309
35	lge1	Walsall	H	W	5-0	Fagan 18 pen,22; Johnson, G 34; Williams 44; Hunt 90	2,616
36	facr4	Blackburn	A	L	0-3		10,634
37	lge1	Blackpool	H	L	0-1		3,526
38	lge1	Tranmere	A	D	1-1	Keith, J 65	8,098
39	lge1	Bournemouth	H	W	3-1	Johnson, G 54; Ndumbu-Nsungu 82; Danns 83	2,820
40	lge1	Bristol City	H	L	0-2		3,412
41	lge1	Wrexham	A	D	2-2	Danns 60; Brown 71	2,391
42	lge1	Hull City	A	L	0-2		16,484
43	lge1	Brentford	H	L	0-1		3,066
44	lge1	Port Vale	A	D	0-0		3,496
45	lge1	Stockport	A	W	2-1	Danns 30 pen,90	4,004
46	lge1	Sheff Wed	H	D	1-1	Heckingbottom 48 og	4,169
47	lge1	Peterborough	A	W	3-0	Goodfellow 45; Danns 70; Keith, M 83 pen	4,084
48	lge1	Chesterfield	H	W	1-0	Keith, M 75	3,471
49	lge1	Doncaster	A	D	1-1	Keith, M 14	6,774
50	lge1	Hartlepool	H	D	1-1	Johnson, G 39	3,148
51	lge1	Huddersfield	A	D	2-2	Danns 19; Chilvers 90	10,831
52	lge1	Bradford	H	D	0-0		3,351
53	lge1	Barnsley	A	D	1-1	Johnson, G 88	8,162
54	lge1	Torquay	H	W	2-1	Danns 42; Keith, M 90	4,834

MONTHLY POINTS TALLY

AUGUST	12	67%
SEPTEMBER	4	33%
OCTOBER	5	28%
NOVEMBER	5	56%
DECEMBER	1	8%
JANUARY	8	53%
FEBRUARY	5	28%
MARCH	11	61%
APRIL	5	33%
MAY	3	100%

KEY PLAYERS - GOALSCORERS

Neil Danns

Goals in the League	11	Player Strike Rate Average number of minutes between League goals scored by player	254
Contribution to Attacking Power Average number of minutes between League team goals while on pitch	70	Club Strike Rate Average number of minutes between League goals scored by club	69

	PLAYER	LGE GOALS	GOALS ALL	POWER	STRIKE RATE
1	Neil Danns	11	12	70	254 mins
2	Craig Fagan	8	14	63	285 mins
3	Richard Garcia	4	5	92	415 mins
4	Gavin Johnson	7	7	72	433 mins
5	Joe Keith	4	4	66	614 mins

KEY PLAYERS - MIDFIELDERS

Neil Danns

Goals in the League	11	Contribution to Attacking Power Average number of minutes between League team goals while on pitch	70
Defensive Rating Average number of mins between League goals conceded while on the pitch	96	Scoring Difference Defensive Rating minus Contribution to Attacking Power	26

	PLAYER	LGE GOALS	GOALS ALL	DEF RATE	POWER	SCORE DIFF
1	Neil Danns	11	12	96	70	26 mins
2	Kevin Watson	2	2	84	68	16 mins
3	Gavin Johnson	7	7	84	72	12 mins
4	Joe Keith	4	4	74	66	8 mins

KEY PLAYERS - DEFENDERS

Pat Baldwin

Goals Conceded Number of League goals conceded while the player was on the pitch	35	Clean Sheets In games when player was on pitch for at least 70 minutes	9
Defensive Rating Ave number of mins between League goals conceded while on the pitch	89	Club Defensive Rating Average number of mins between League goals conceded by the club this season	83

	PLAYER	CON LGE	CON ALL	CLEAN SHEETS	DEF RATE
1	Pat Baldwin	35	46	9	89 mins
2	Sam Stockley	34	45	10	89 mins
3	Greg Halford	45	55	11	87 mins
4	Stephen Hunt	17	25	3	86 mins
5	Wayne Brown	43	53	9	80 mins

KEY GOALKEEPER

Aidan Davison

Goals Conceded in the League	33	Counting Games Games when player was on pitch for at least 70 minutes	33
Defensive Rating Ave number of mins between League goals conceded while on the pitch	90	Clean Sheets In Games when player was on pitch for at least 70 minutes	8

LEAGUE GOALS

Craig Fagan

Minutes on the pitch	2281	League average (mins between goals)	285
Goals in the League	8		

	PLAYER	MINS	GOALS	AVE
1	Fagan	2281	8	285
2	Danns	2794	11	254
3	Halford	3902	4	976
4	Johnson, G	3032	7	433
5	Garcia	1660	4	415
6	Williams	1253	3	418
7	Keith, M	1056	4	264
8	Keith, J	2457	4	614
9	Watson	3947	2	1974
10	Andrews	344	2	172
11	May	523	1	523
12	Chilvers	3513	1	3513
	Other		9	
	TOTAL		60	

DISCIPLINARY RECORDS

	PLAYER	YELLOW	RED	AVE
1	Fagan	11	1	190
2	Danns	11	0	254
3	Chilvers	7	1	439
4	Stockley	5	0	606
5	Hunt	1	1	731
6	Halford	5	0	780
7	Keith, J	3	0	819
8	Garcia	2	0	830
9	Brown	4	0	859
10	Johnson, G	3	0	1010
11	Baldwin	2	0	1549
12	Watson	2	0	1973
13	Davison	1	0	2970
	Other	0	0	
	TOTAL	57	3	

TOP POINT EARNERS

	PLAYER	GAMES	AV PTS
1	Aidan Davison	33	1.42
2	Sam Stockley	33	1.39
3	Gavin Johnson	33	1.36
4	Greg Halford	43	1.35
5	Neil Danns	31	1.35
6	Kevin Watson	44	1.34
7	John White	14	1.29
8	Pat Baldwin	34	1.24
9	Craig Fagan	25	1.24
10	Joe Keith	25	1.24
	CLUB AVERAGE:		1.28

LEAGUE APPEARANCES GOALS AND BOOKINGS

	AGE (on 01/07/05)	IN NAMED 16	APPEARANCES	COUNTING GAMES	MINUTES ON PITCH	LEAGUE GOALS	Yellow	Red
Goalkeepers								
Mark Cousins	2006	8	0	0	0	0	0	0
Aidan Davison	37	36	33	33	2970	0	1	0
Dean Gerken	20	46	13	13	1170	0	0	0
Andy Marriott	34	2	0	0	0	0	0	0
Defenders								
Pat Baldwin	22	43	38	34	3099	0	2	0
Ben Bowditch	21	12	5	0	50	0	0	0
Wayne Brown	27	43	40	37	3436	1	4	0
Liam Chilvers	23	41	41	37	3513	1	7	1
George Elokobi	19	9	0	0	0	0	0	0
Greg Halford	20	46	44	43	3902	4	5	0
Stephen Hunt	20	29	20	16	1462	1	1	1
Garry Richards	19	1	0	0	0	0	0	0
Sam Stockley	27	37	37	33	3033	1	5	0
John White	18	36	20	14	1399	0	0	0
Midfielders								
Bobby Bowry	34	15	11	6	598	0	0	0
Neil Danns	22	32	32	31	2794	11	11	0
Marc Goodfellow	23	6	5	4	319	1	0	0
Kemal Izzet	24	7	4	3	277	0	0	0
Gavin Johnson	34	39	37	33	3032	7	3	0
Craig Johnston	19	1	0	0	0	0	0	0
Joe Keith	26	36	31	25	2457	4	3	0
Robbie King	-	3	0	0	0	0	0	0
Kevin Watson	31	44	44	44	3947	2	2	0
Forwards								
Wayne Andrews	27	5	5	4	344	2	0	0
Jamie Cade	21	15	9	3	417	0	0	0
Craig Fagan	22	26	26	25	2281	8	11	1
Richard Garcia	23	27	24	16	1660	4	2	0
Jamie Guy	-	8	2	0	12	0	0	0
Ryan Jarvis	18	6	6	2	249	0	0	0
Marino Keith	30	12	12	11	1056	4	0	0
Ben May	21	14	14	3	523	1	0	0
Guylain Ndumbu-Nsungu	22	12	8	1	219	1	1	0
Gareth Williams	22	39	29	10	1253	3	0	0

TEAM OF THE SEASON

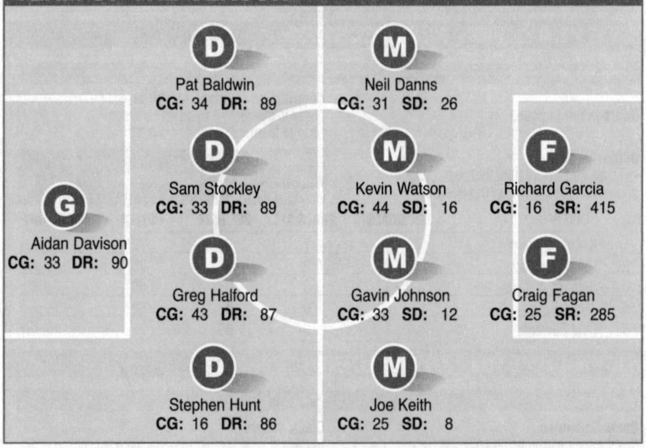

D
Pat Baldwin
CG: 34 DR: 89
M
Neil Danns
CG: 31 SD: 26
D
Sam Stockley
CG: 33 DR: 89
M
Kevin Watson
CG: 44 SD: 16
F
Richard Garcia
CG: 16 SR: 415
G
Aidan Davison
CG: 33 DR: 90
D
Greg Halford
CG: 43 DR: 87
M
Gavin Johnson
CG: 33 SD: 12
F
Craig Fagan
CG: 25 SR: 285
D
Stephen Hunt
CG: 16 DR: 86
M
Joe Keith
CG: 25 SD: 8

SQUAD APPEARANCES

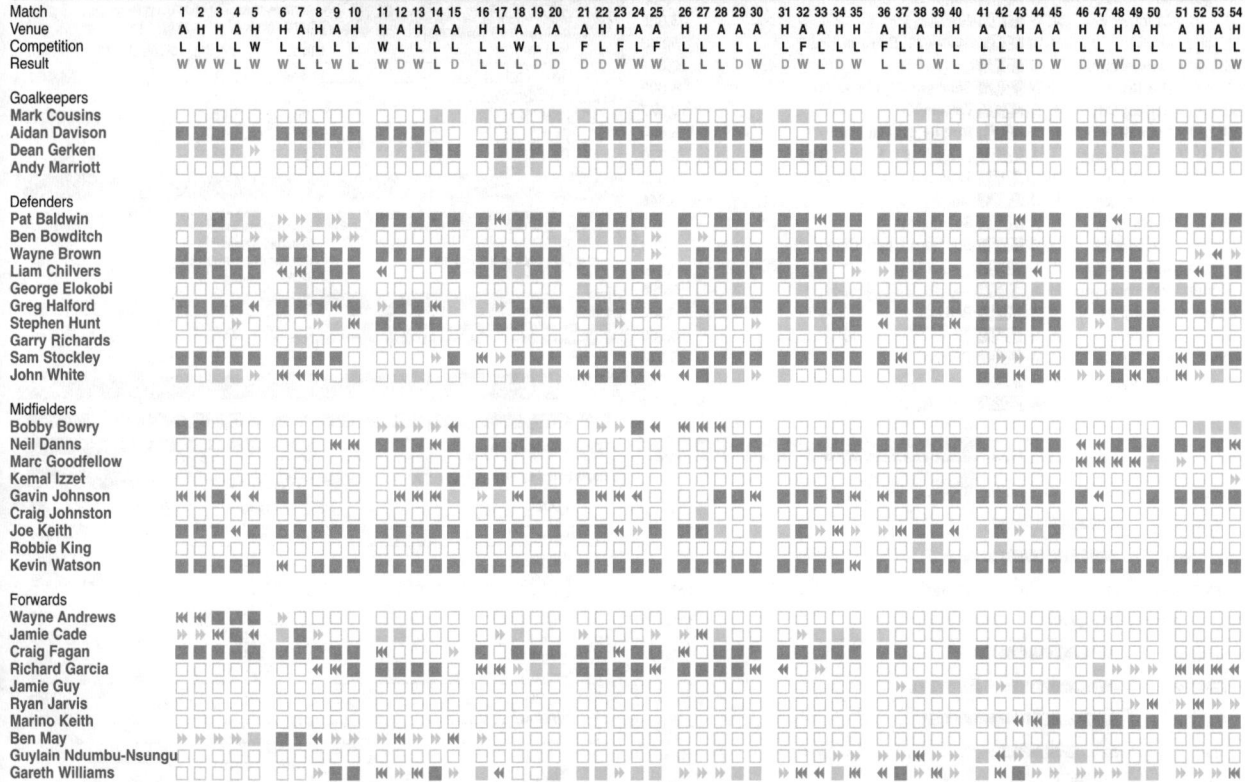

Match	1	2	3	4	5	6	7	8	9	10	11	12	13	14	15	16	17	18	19	20	21	22	23	24	25	26	27	28	29	30	31	32	33	34	35	36	37	38	39	40	41	42	43	44	45	46	47	48	49	50	51	52	53	54
Venue	A	H	H	A	H	H	A	H	A	H	H	A	H	A	A	H	H	A	A	A	A	H	H	A	A	H	H	A	A	A	H	A	A	H	H	A	H	A	H	H	A	A	H	A	A	H	A	H	A	H	A	H	A	H
Competition	L	L	L	L	W	L	L	L	L	L	W	L	L	L	L	L	L	W	L	L	F	L	F	L	F	L	L	L	L	L	L	F	L	L	L	F	L	L	L	L	L	L	L	L	L	L	L	L	L	L	L	L	L	L
Result	W	W	W	L	W	W	L	L	W	L	W	D	W	L	D	L	L	L	D	D	D	D	W	W	W	L	L	L	D	W	D	W	L	D	W	L	L	D	W	L	D	L	L	D	W	D	W	W	D	D	D	D	D	W

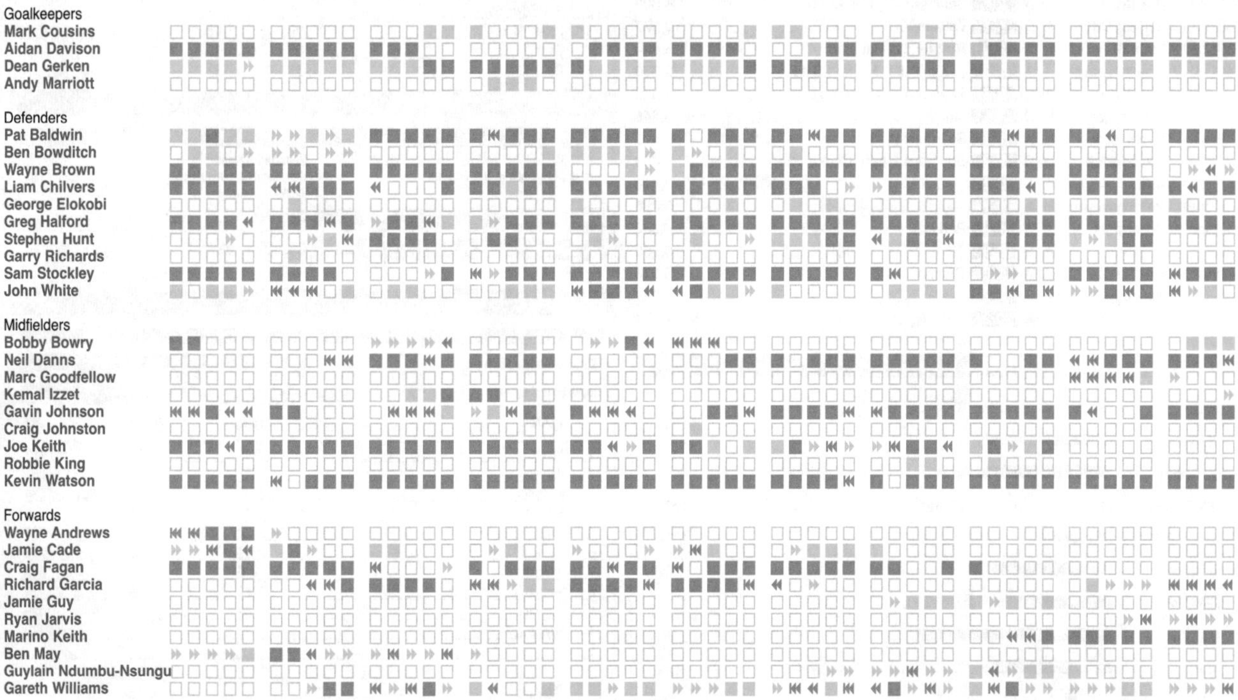

Goalkeepers
Mark Cousins
Aidan Davison
Dean Gerken
Andy Marriott
Defenders
Pat Baldwin
Ben Bowditch
Wayne Brown
Liam Chilvers
George Elokobi
Greg Halford
Stephen Hunt
Garry Richards
Sam Stockley
John White
Midfielders
Bobby Bowry
Neil Danns
Marc Goodfellow
Kemal Izzet
Gavin Johnson
Craig Johnston
Joe Keith
Robbie King
Kevin Watson
Forwards
Wayne Andrews
Jamie Cade
Craig Fagan
Richard Garcia
Jamie Guy
Ryan Jarvis
Marino Keith
Ben May
Guylain Ndumbu-Nsungu
Gareth Williams

KEY: On all match | Subbed or sent off (Counting game) | Subbed on from bench (Counting Game) | Subbed on and then subbed or sent off (Counting Game) | Not in 16
On bench | Subbed or sent off (playing less than 70 minutes) | Subbed on (playing less than 70 minutes) | Subbed on and then subbed or sent off (playing less than 70 minutes)

BLACKPOOL

Final Position: **16th**

NICKNAME: THE SEASIDERS

KEY: Won Drawn Lost

							Attendance
1	lge1	Doncaster	A	L	0-2		7,082
2	lge1	Sheff Wed	H	L	1-2	Edwards 74	6,713
3	lge1	Stockport	H	L	0-4		6,334
4	lge1	Hartlepool	A	D	1-1	Taylor 72	5,144
5	ccr1	Crewe	A	L	1-4	Taylor 75	2,994
6	lge1	Luton	H	L	1-3	Taylor 4	5,793
7	lge1	Peterborough	A	D	0-0		4,142
8	lge1	Hull City	A	L	1-2	Taylor 37	15,568
9	lge1	Swindon	H	D	1-1	Taylor 33	5,229
10	lge1	Port Vale	A	W	3-0	Taylor 6; Vernon 27,47	5,347
11	lge1	Bournemouth	H	D	3-3	Clarke 2; Vernon 10; Edwards, P 42	5,525
12	lge1	Oldham	A	W	2-1	Murphy 43; Wellens 68	7,125
13	lge1	Colchester	H	D	1-1	Murphy 10	6,464
14	lge1	Bradford	A	L	1-2	Taylor 76 pen	7,622
15	lge1	Brentford	A	W	3-0	Murphy 14,53; Taylor 79	6,722
16	lge1	Huddersfield	H	D	1-1	Murphy 51	7,676
17	lge1	Chesterfield	A	L	0-1		4,978
18	lge1	Wrexham	H	W	2-1	Clarke 46; Taylor 66 pen	5,054
19	facr1	Tamworth	H	W	3-0	Wellens 9,76; Parker 46	4,796
20	lge1	Tranmere	H	L	0-1		6,490
21	lge1	Barnsley	A	L	0-1		9,084
22	facr2	Port Vale	H	W	1-0	Taylor 76	4,669
23	lge1	Torquay	H	W	4-0	Taylor 20; Parker 67,86,90	4,179
24	lge1	Bristol City	H	D	1-1	Taylor 45 pen	5,220
25	lge1	Walsall	A	L	2-3	Taylor 32; Parker 57	5,476
26	lge1	Hull City	H	L	0-2		8,774
27	lge1	MK Dons	A	L	1-3	Taylor 81 pen	4,943
28	lge1	Wrexham	A	W	2-1	Murphy 64,77	5,601
29	lge1	Port Vale	H	L	0-2		5,115
30	facr3	Leicester	A	D	2-2	Clarke 32; Southern 77	16,750
31	lge1	Swindon	A	D	2-2	Parker 18; Clarke 90	5,526
32	facr3r	Leicester	H	L	0-1		6,938
33	lge1	MK Dons	H	W	1-0	Edwards, P 8	5,798
34	lge1	Colchester	A	W	1-0	Grayson 75	3,526
35	lge1	Oldham	H	W	2-0	Clarke 72; Edwards, P 86	5,563
36	lge1	Huddersfield	A	L	0-1		10,614
37	lge1	Bradford	H	W	2-1	Southern 48; Parker 90	4,805
38	lge1	Bristol City	A	D	1-1	Wellens 60	10,977
39	lge1	Walsall	H	W	2-0	Murphy 57; Southern 70	6,844
40	lge1	Bournemouth	A	W	3-2	Parker 1,51; Maher 26 og	5,390
41	lge1	Sheff Wed	A	L	2-3	Southern 47; Wellens 90	21,539
42	lge1	Doncaster	H	D	1-1	Murphy 53	6,548
43	lge1	Brentford	H	W	2-1	Southern 7,15	5,478
44	lge1	Hartlepool	H	D	2-2	Southern 3 pen; Clarke 82	6,853
45	lge1	Luton	A	L	0-1		7,816
46	lge1	Peterborough	H	L	0-1		5,090
47	lge1	Stockport	A	W	1-0	Parker 6	4,302
48	lge1	Tranmere	A	D	0-0		8,568
49	lge1	Chesterfield	H	W	1-0	Grayson 18	5,613
50	lge1	Torquay	A	L	0-2		5,347
51	lge1	Barnsley	H	L	0-2		7,571

MONTHLY POINTS TALLY

AUGUST	2	11%
SEPTEMBER	4	44%
OCTOBER	9	50%
NOVEMBER	3	25%
DECEMBER	4	27%
JANUARY	7	58%
FEBRUARY	10	67%
MARCH	11	61%
APRIL	7	39%
MAY	0	0%

KEY PLAYERS - GOALSCORERS

Scott Taylor

Goals in the League	12	Player Strike Rate Average number of minutes between League goals scored by player	179
Contribution to Attacking Power Average number of minutes between League team goals while on pitch	74	**Club Strike Rate** Average number of minutes between League goals scored by club	77

	PLAYER	LGE GOALS	GOALS ALL	POWER	STRIKE RATE
1	Scott Taylor	12	14	74	179 mins
2	Keigan Parker	9	10	71	262 mins
3	John Murphy	9	9	91	294 mins
4	Keith Southern	6	7	77	386 mins
5	Paul Edwards	3	3	77	643 mins

KEY PLAYERS - MIDFIELDERS

Keith Southern

Goals in the League	6	**Contribution to Attacking Power** Average number of minutes between League team goals while on pitch	77
Defensive Rating Average number of mins between League goals conceded while on the pitch	80	Scoring Difference Defensive Rating minus Contribution to Attacking Power	3

	PLAYER	LGE GOALS	GOALS ALL	DEF RATE	POWER	SCORE DIFF
1	Keith Southern	6	7	80	77	3 mins
2	Simon Grayson	2	2	77	75	2 mins
3	Richard Wellens	3	5	67	69	-2 mins
4	Jamie Burns	0	0	66	69	-3 mins
5	Paul Edwards	3	3	69	77	-8 mins

KEY PLAYERS - DEFENDERS

Danny Coid

Goals Conceded Number of League goals conceded while the player was on the pitch	34	**Clean Sheets** In games when player was on pitch for at least 70 minutes	9
Defensive Rating Ave number of mins between League goals conceded while on the pitch	86	**Club Defensive Rating** Average number of mins between League goals conceded while on the pitch	70

	PLAYER	CON LGE	CON ALL	CLEAN SHEETS	DEF RATE
1	Danny Coid	34	41	9	86 mins
2	Rob Edwards	26	33	8	83 mins
3	Peter Clarke	42	45	10	81 mins
4	Gareth Evans	25	25	5	78 mins
5	Robert Clare	25	32	4	68 mins

KEY GOALKEEPER

Bradley Jones

Goals Conceded in the League	11	**Counting Games** Games when player was on pitch for at least 70 minutes	12
Defensive Rating Ave number of mins between League goals conceded while on the pitch	98	**Clean Sheets** In games when player was on pitch for at least 70 minutes	4

LEAGUE GOALS

Scott Taylor

Minutes on the pitch	2149	League average (mins between goals)	179
Goals in the League	12		

	PLAYER	MINS	GOALS	AVE
1	Taylor	2149	12	179
2	Parker	2357	9	262
3	Murphy	2648	9	294
4	Southern	2315	6	386
5	Clarke	3420	5	684
6	Wellens	2329	3	776
7	Edwards, P	1929	3	643
8	Vernon	341	3	114
9	Grayson	2852	2	1426
10	Edwards, R	2170	1	2170
	Other		1	
	TOTAL		54	

DISCIPLINARY RECORDS

	PLAYER	YELLOW	RED	AVE
1	Edwards, P	8	0	241
2	Evans	7	0	278
3	Parker	8	0	294
4	Wellens	4	2	388
5	Southern	5	0	463
6	McGregor	6	1	464
7	Donnelly	1	0	473
8	Butler	1	0	545
9	Coid	5	0	585
10	Taylor	3	0	716
11	Edwards, R	3	0	723
12	Richardson	2	0	851
13	Clarke	4	0	855
	Other	8	0	
	TOTAL	65	3	

TOP POINT EARNERS

	PLAYER	GAMES	AV PTS
1	Evans	21	1.57
2	Southern	25	1.52
3	Parker	24	1.50
4	Coid	32	1.50
5	Burns	13	1.46
6	Clarke	38	1.45
7	Edwards, P	18	1.44
8	Jones	12	1.42
9	Grayson	31	1.29
10	Jones, L	29	1.28
	CLUB AVERAGE:		1.24

TEAM OF THE SEASON

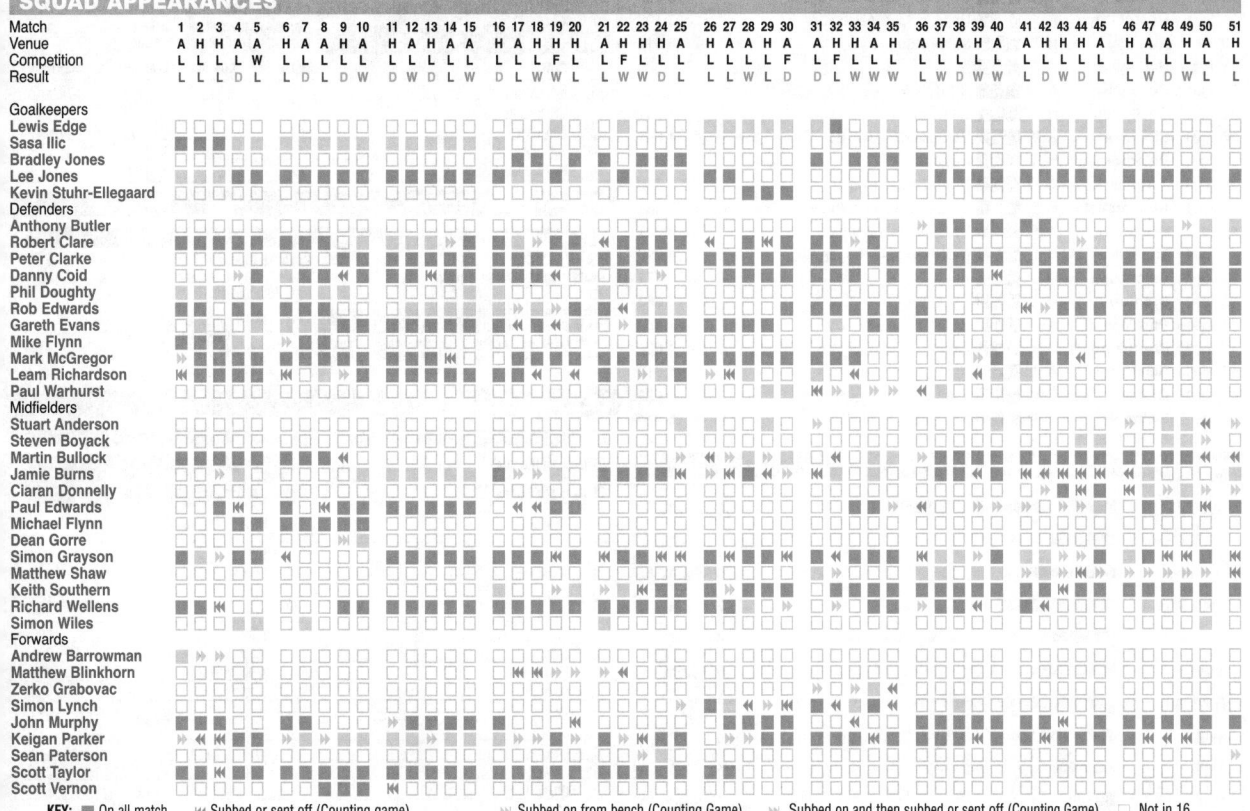

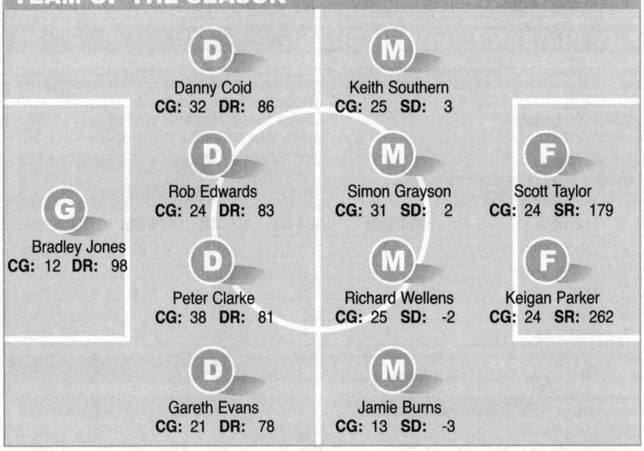
D
Danny Coid
CG: 32 DR: 86
M
Keith Southern
CG: 25 SD: 3
D
Rob Edwards
CG: 24 DR: 83
M
Simon Grayson
CG: 31 SD: 2
F
Scott Taylor
CG: 24 SR: 179
G
Bradley Jones
CG: 12 DR: 98
D
Peter Clarke
CG: 38 DR: 81
M
Richard Wellens
CG: 25 SD: -2
F
Keigan Parker
CG: 24 SR: 262
D
Gareth Evans
CG: 21 DR: 78
M
Jamie Burns
CG: 13 SD: -3

LEAGUE APPEARANCES CLUBS AND BOOKINGS

	AGE (on 01/07/05)	IN NAMED 16	APPEARANCES	COUNTING GAMES	MINUTES ON PITCH	LEAGUE GOALS	Yellow	Red
Goalkeepers								
Lewis Edge	18	18	0	0	0	0	0	0
Sasa Ilic	32	15	3	3	270	0	0	0
Bradley Jones	23	12	12	12	1080	0	0	0
Lee Jones	34	40	29	29	2610	0	1	0
Kevin Stuhr-Ellegaard	22	3	2	2	180	0	0	0
Defenders								
Anthony Butler	32	12	8	6	545	0	1	0
Robert Clare	22	32	23	17	1708	0	1	0
Peter Clarke	23	38	38	38	3420	5	4	0
Danny Coid	23	37	35	32	2926	0	5	0
Phil Doughty	18	10	0	0	0	0	0	0
Rob Edwards	32	35	26	24	2170	1	3	0
Gareth Evans	24	27	22	21	1950	0	7	0
Mike Flynn	36	7	6	5	480	0	0	0
Mark McGregor	28	38	38	35	3250	0	6	1
Leam Richardson	25	30	23	15	1702	0	2	0
Paul Warhurst	35	7	4	1	170	0	0	0
Midfielders								
Stuart Anderson	19	10	4	0	84	0	0	0
Steven Boyack	28	5	1	0	22	0	0	0
Martin Bullock	30	31	28	20	2096	0	1	0
Jamie Burns	21	33	23	13	1591	0	1	0
Ciaran Donnelly	21	10	8	3	473	0	1	0
Paul Edwards	25	29	28	18	1929	3	8	0
Michael Flynn	24	6	6	6	540	0	0	0
Dean Gorre	34	2	1	1	74	0	0	0
Simon Grayson	35	42	36	31	2852	2	3	0
Matthew Shaw	21	17	10	2	272	0	0	0
Keith Southern	21	29	27	25	2315	6	5	0
Richard Wellens	25	30	28	25	2329	3	4	2
Simon Wiles	20	4	0	0	0	0	0	0
Forwards								
Andrew Barrowman	20	3	2	0	40	0	0	0
Matthew Blinkhorn	20	4	4	2	180	0	0	0
Zerko Grabovac	22	4	3	0	110	0	0	0
Simon Lynch	23	10	7	3	429	0	0	0
John Murphy	28	31	31	29	2648	9	1	0
Keigan Parker	23	43	35	24	2357	9	8	0
Sean Paterson	-	3	2	0	18	0	0	0
Scott Taylor	29	24	24	24	2149	12	3	0
Scott Vernon	21	4	4	4	341	3	0	0

SQUAD APPEARANCES

Match	1	2	3	4	5	6	7	8	9	10	11	12	13	14	15	16	17	18	19	20	21	22	23	24	25
Venue	A	H	H	A	A	H	A	A	H	A	H	A	H	A	A	H	A	H	H	H	A	H	H	H	A
Competition	L	L	L	L	W	L	L	L	L	L	L	L	L	L	L	L	L	L	F	L	L	F	L	L	L
Result	L	L	L	D	L	L	D	L	D	W	D	W	D	L	W	D	L	W	W	L	L	W	W	D	L

Match	26	27	28	29	30	31	32	33	34	35	36	37	38	39	40	41	42	43	44	45	46	47	48	49	50	51
Venue	H	A	A	H	A	A	H	H	A	H	A	H	A	H	A	A	H	H	H	A	H	A	A	H	A	H
Competition	L	L	L	L	F	L	F	L	L	L	L	L	L	L	L	L	L	L	L	L	L	L	L	L	L	L
Result	L	L	W	L	D	D	L	W	W	W	L	W	D	W	W	L	D	W	D	L	L	W	D	W	L	L

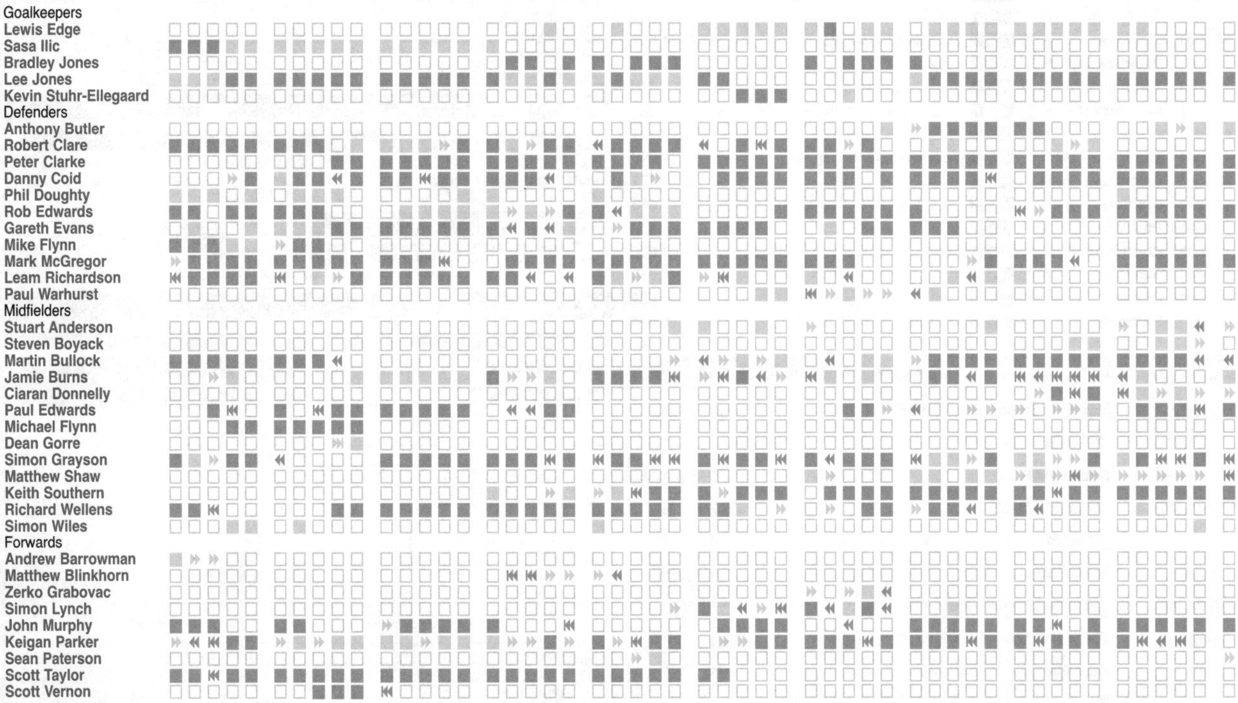
Goalkeepers
Lewis Edge
Sasa Ilic
Bradley Jones
Lee Jones
Kevin Stuhr-Ellegaard
Defenders
Anthony Butler
Robert Clare
Peter Clarke
Danny Coid
Phil Doughty
Rob Edwards
Gareth Evans
Mike Flynn
Mark McGregor
Leam Richardson
Paul Warhurst
Midfielders
Stuart Anderson
Steven Boyack
Martin Bullock
Jamie Burns
Ciaran Donnelly
Paul Edwards
Michael Flynn
Dean Gorre
Simon Grayson
Matthew Shaw
Keith Southern
Richard Wellens
Simon Wiles
Forwards
Andrew Barrowman
Matthew Blinkhorn
Zerko Grabovac
Simon Lynch
John Murphy
Keigan Parker
Sean Paterson
Scott Taylor
Scott Vernon

KEY: On all match | On bench | Subbed or sent off (Counting game) | Subbed or sent off (playing less than 70 minutes) | Subbed on from bench (Counting Game) | Subbed on (playing less than 70 minutes) | Subbed on and then subbed or sent off (Counting Game) | Subbed on and then subbed or sent off (playing less than 70 minutes) | Not in 16

CHESTERFIELD

Final Position: **17th**

NICKNAME: THE SPIREITES

KEY: □Won □Drawn □Lost

							Attendance
1	lge1	Brentford	H	W	3-1	Allison 17; Folan 64; N'Toya 90	4,651
2	lge1	Huddersfield	A	D	0-0		11,942
3	lge1	Tranmere	A	L	0-1		8,287
4	lge1	Colchester	H	W	2-1	N'Toya 9,55	4,028
5	ccR1	Rotherham	A	L	1-2	Allott 15	3,845
6	lge1	Bradford	A	W	3-2	Nicholson 78 pen; Folan 79,88	7,590
7	lge1	Port Vale	H	W	1-0	N'Toya 53	5,150
8	lge1	MK Dons	H	D	2-2	N'Toya 31; Downes 48	4,537
9	lge1	Luton	A	L	0-1		7,532
10	lge1	Walsall	H	W	1-0	Hudson 21	4,755
11	lge1	Barnsley	A	L	0-1		9,792
12	lge1	Bristol City	H	D	2-2	Nicholson 33 pen; Bailey 88	4,854
13	lge1	Hull City	A	L	0-1		15,500
14	lge1	Hartlepool	A	L	2-3	Nicholson 25 pen; Stallard 50	4,617
15	lge1	Stockport	H	W	4-0	Clingan 16; N'Toya 21; Blatherwick 51; Allott 84	4,567
16	lge1	Doncaster	H	D	0-0		6,219
17	lge1	Sheff Wed	A	D	2-2	Blatherwick 13; Clingan 55	24,271
18	lge1	Blackpool	H	W	1-0	Folan 90	4,978
19	facr1	Scunthorpe	A	L	0-2		4,869
20	lge1	Bournemouth	A	D	0-0		6,565
21	lge1	Swindon	H	W	1-0	Allison 63	4,244
22	lge1	Oldham	A	L	1-4	Folan 76	5,207
23	lge1	Peterborough	A	W	2-1	Downes 24; Evatt 54	3,865
24	lge1	Torquay	H	D	1-1	Allison 73	4,133
25	lge1	Luton	H	L	0-1		7,158
26	lge1	Wrexham	A	L	1-3	Stallard 44	4,273
27	lge1	MK Dons	A	D	1-1	Evatt 84	4,214
28	lge1	Barnsley	H	D	2-2	Folan 50; Nicholson 88	5,985
29	lge1	Walsall	A	L	0-3		5,177
30	lge1	Wrexham	H	L	2-4	Evatt 40; Nicholson 75 pen	3,966
31	lge1	Bristol City	A	W	3-2	Hudson 1,87; Allison 14	10,103
32	lge1	Hull City	H	D	1-1	Myhill 82 og	5,517
33	lge1	Hartlepool	H	L	0-1		4,606
34	lge1	Doncaster	A	W	1-0	N'Toya 87	6,765
35	lge1	Sheff Wed	H	L	1-3	De Bolla 90	7,831
36	lge1	Stockport	A	W	2-1	De Bolla 51; Allott 81	4,201
37	lge1	Peterborough	H	L	1-3	Davies 24	3,715
38	lge1	Torquay	A	D	2-2	Niven 31; Hudson 50	2,746
39	lge1	Huddersfield	H	W	2-1	Nicholson 53 pen,78 pen	4,827
40	lge1	Brentford	A	D	2-2	De Bolla 38; Allison 66	6,097
41	lge1	Tranmere	H	D	2-2	Blatherwick 45; Logan 90	4,293
42	lge1	Colchester	A	L	0-1		3,471
43	lge1	Bradford	H	D	0-0		4,663
44	lge1	Port Vale	A	L	0-1		4,489
45	lge1	Bournemouth	H	L	2-3	Allison 17; Blatherwick 76	4,009
46	lge1	Blackpool	A	L	0-1		5,613
47	lge1	Oldham	H	W	1-0	Evatt 69	5,421
48	lge1	Swindon	A	D	1-1	N'Toya 21	6,044

MONTHLY POINTS TALLY

AUGUST	13	72%
SEPTEMBER	4	33%
OCTOBER	6	33%
NOVEMBER	7	78%
DECEMBER	4	27%
JANUARY	5	33%
FEBRUARY	7	39%
MARCH	6	40%
APRIL	4	27%
MAY	1	33%

KEY PLAYERS - GOALSCORERS

Tcham N'Toya

Goals in the League	8	Player Strike Rate Average number of minutes between League goals scored by player	233
Contribution to Attacking Power Average number of minutes between League team goals while on pitch	77	Club Strike Rate Average number of minutes between League goals scored by club	75

	PLAYER	LGE GOALS	GOALS ALL	POWER	STRIKE RATE
1	Tcham N'Toya	8	8	77	233 mins
2	Caleb Folan	6	6	66	279 mins
3	Wayne Allison	6	6	71	395 mins
4	Shane Nicholson	7	7	75	540 mins
5	Sammy Clingan	2	2	75	675 mins

KEY PLAYERS - MIDFIELDERS

Jamal Campbell-Ryce

Goals in the League	0	Contribution to Attacking Power Average number of minutes between League team goals while on pitch	60
Defensive Rating Average number of mins between League goals conceded while on the pitch	100	Scoring Difference Defensive Rating minus Contribution to Attacking Power	40

	PLAYER	LGE GOALS	GOALS ALL	DEF RATE	POWER	SCORE DIFF
1	Jamal Campbell-Ryce	0	0	100	60	40 mins
2	Sammy Clingan	2	2	71	75	-4 mins
3	Derek Niven	1	1	68	74	-6 mins
4	Mark Allott	2	3	66	73	-7 mins
5	Mark Hudson	4	4	63	84	-21 mins

KEY PLAYERS - DEFENDERS

Mark Innes

Goals Conceded Number of League goals conceded while the player was on the pitch	21	Clean Sheets In games when player was on pitch for at least 70 minutes	3
Defensive Rating Ave number of mins between League goals conceded while on the pitch	70	Club Defensive Rating Average number of mins between League goals conceded while on the pitch	67

	PLAYER	CON LGE	CON ALL	CLEAN SHEETS	DEF RATE
1	Mark Innes	21	23	3	70 mins
2	Steven Blatherwick	42	44	9	69 mins
3	Alex Bailey	59	63	11	68 mins
4	Ian Evatt	54	58	10	68 mins
5	Shane Nicholson	57	61	10	66 mins

KEY GOALKEEPER

Carl Muggleton

Goals Conceded in the League	53	Counting Games Games when player was on pitch for at least 70 minutes	38
Defensive Rating Ave number of mins between League goals conceded while on the pitch	65	Clean Sheets In games when player was on pitch for at least 70 minutes	9

LEAGUE GOALS

Tcham N'Toya

Minutes on the pitch	1863	League average (mins between goals)	233
Goals in the League	8		

	PLAYER	MINS	GOALS	AVE
1	N'Toya	1863	8	233
2	Nicholson	3781	7	540
3	Folan	1674	6	279
4	Allison	2368	6	395
5	Hudson	2759	4	690
6	Evatt	3689	4	922
7	Blatherwick	2899	4	725
8	De Bolla	1313	3	438
9	Allott	4040	2	2020
10	Clingan	1350	2	675
11	Downes	638	2	319
12	Stallard	589	2	295
	Other		5	
	TOTAL		55	

DISCIPLINARY RECORDS

	PLAYER	YELLOW	RED	AVE
1	Stallard	2	0	294
2	Niven	9	1	310
3	Davies	3	0	328
4	Nicholson	9	1	378
5	Campbell-Ryce	3	0	400
6	Folan	3	1	418
7	Allott	9	0	448
8	Evatt	8	0	461
9	N'Toya	4	0	465
10	Blatherwick	5	1	483
11	McMaster	1	0	486
12	Fulop	1	0	630
13	Downes	1	0	638
	Other	11	1	
	TOTAL	69	5	

TOP POINT EARNERS

	PLAYER	GAMES	AV PTS
1	Innes	12	1.92
2	N'Toya	14	1.86
3	O'Hare	14	1.71
4	Campbell-Ryce	12	1.58
5	Niven	32	1.34
6	Allison	24	1.33
7	Evatt	41	1.27
8	Allott	45	1.27
9	Muggleton	38	1.26
10	Bailey	44	1.20
	CLUB AVERAGE:		1.24

LEAGUE APPEARANCES GOALS AND BOOKINGS

	AGE (on 01/07/05)	IN NAMED 16	APPEARANCES	COUNTING GAMES	MINUTES ON PITCH	LEAGUE GOALS	Yellow	Red
Goalkeepers								
Marton Fulop	22	7	7	7	630	0	1	0
Carl Muggleton	36	39	38	38	3420	0	0	0
Andy Richmond	22	37	0	0	0	0	0	0
Glyn Thompson	24	2	1	1	90	0	0	0
Defenders								
Alex Bailey	21	45	45	44	4010	1	3	0
Steven Blatherwick	31	35	35	31	2899	4	5	1
Kevin Dawson	24	8	1	1	90	0	0	0
Aaron Downes	20	21	9	5	638	2	1	0
Ian Evatt	23	41	41	41	3689	4	8	0
Mark Innes	26	27	21	12	1469	0	0	1
Shane Nicholson	35	44	43	42	3781	7	9	1
Alan O'Hare	22	41	21	14	1362	0	0	0
Midfielders								
Mark Allott	27	45	45	45	4040	2	9	0
Jamal Campbell-Ryce	22	14	14	12	1200	0	3	0
Sammy Clingan	21	15	15	15	1350	2	2	0
Gareth Davies	22	34	19	9	986	1	3	0
Jordan Fowler	20	7	6	2	281	0	3	1
Michael Fox	19	2	1	0	4	0	0	0
Mark Hudson	24	36	34	30	2759	4	1	0
Carlos Logan	-	11	9	4	563	1	0	0
Jamie McMaster	22	8	8	3	486	0	1	0
Derek Niven	21	38	38	32	3107	1	9	1
Forwards								
Wayne Allison	36	39	38	24	2368	6	3	0
Mark De Bolla	22	33	28	10	1313	3	1	0
Caleb Folan	19	32	32	13	1674	6	3	1
Tcham N'Toya	21	43	38	14	1863	8	4	0
Adam Smith	19	20	16	4	734	0	1	0
Mark Stallard	30	12	9	6	589	2	2	0

TEAM OF THE SEASON

G
Carl Muggleton
CG: 38 DR: 65
D
Steven Blatherwick
CG: 31 DR: 69
D
Alex Bailey
CG: 44 DR: 68
D
Ian Evatt
CG: 41 DR: 68
D
Shane Nicholson
CG: 42 DR: 66
M
Jamal Campbell-Ryce
CG: 12 SD: 40
M
Sammy Clingan
CG: 15 SD: -4
M
Derek Niven
CG: 32 SD: -6
M
Mark Allott
CG: 45 SD: -7
F
Tcham N'Toya
CG: 14 SR: 233
F
Caleb Folan
CG: 13 SR: 279

SQUAD APPEARANCES

Match	1	2	3	4	5	6	7	8	9	10	11	12	13	14	15	16	17	18	19	20	21	22	23	24	25	26	27	28	29	30	31	32	33	34	35	36	37	38	39	40	41	42	43	44	45	46	47	48
Venue	H	A	A	H	A	A	H	H	A	H	A	H	A	A	H	H	A	H	A	A	H	A	A	H	H	A	A	H	A	H	A	H	H	A	H	A	H	A	H	A	H	A	H	A	H	A	H	A
Competition	L	L	L	L	W	L	L	L	L	L	L	L	L	L	L	L	L	L	F	L	L	L	L	L	L	L	L	L	L	L	L	L	L	L	L	L	L	L	L	L	L	L	L	L	L	L	L	L
Result	W	D	L	W	L	W	W	D	L	W	L	D	L	L	W	D	D	W	L	D	W	L	W	D	L	L	D	D	L	L	W	D	L	W	L	W	L	D	W	D	D	L	D	L	L	L	W	D

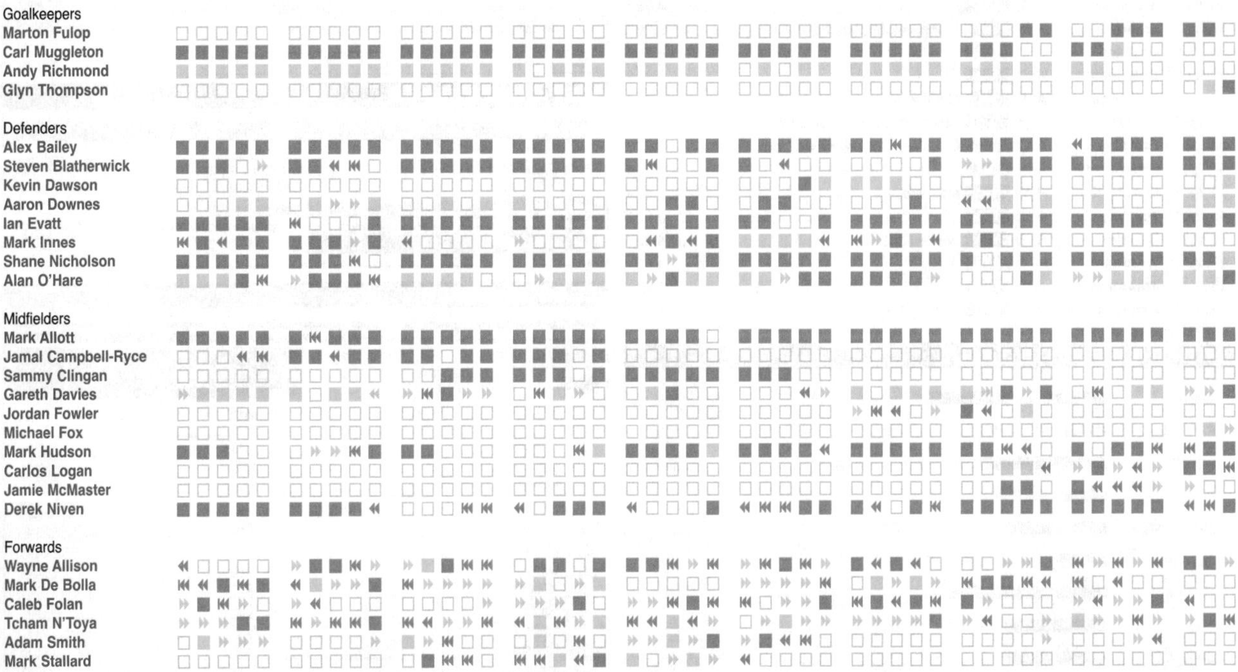

Goalkeepers
Marton Fulop
Carl Muggleton
Andy Richmond
Glyn Thompson
Defenders
Alex Bailey
Steven Blatherwick
Kevin Dawson
Aaron Downes
Ian Evatt
Mark Innes
Shane Nicholson
Alan O'Hare
Midfielders
Mark Allott
Jamal Campbell-Ryce
Sammy Clingan
Gareth Davies
Jordan Fowler
Michael Fox
Mark Hudson
Carlos Logan
Jamie McMaster
Derek Niven
Forwards
Wayne Allison
Mark De Bolla
Caleb Folan
Tcham N'Toya
Adam Smith
Mark Stallard

KEY: On all match / On bench | Subbed or sent off (Counting game) / Subbed or sent off (playing less than 70 minutes) | Subbed on from bench (Counting Game) / Subbed on (playing less than 70 minutes) | Subbed on and then subbed or sent off (Counting Game) / Subbed on and then subbed or sent off (playing less than 70 minutes) | Not in 16

PORT VALE

Final Position: **18th**

NICKNAME: THE VALIANTS

KEY: Won Drawn Lost

							Attendance
1	lge1	**Walsall**	A	L	2-3	Paynter 61; Matthews 90	8,225
2	lge1	**MK Dons**	H	W	3-2	Brooker 43; Armstrong 46,64	4,602
3	lge1	**Hull City**	H	W	3-2	Collins 26; Brooker 51,90	6,736
4	lge1	**Wrexham**	A	D	1-1	Brooker 64	5,005
5	ccR1	**Doncaster**	A	L	1-3	Smith, D 25	3,943
6	lge1	**Bristol City**	H	W	3-0	James 37; Brooker 45; Armstrong 66	5,377
7	lge1	**Chesterfield**	A	L	0-1		5,150
8	lge1	**Bradford**	A	W	2-0	Paynter 40; Smith, J 49	7,043
9	lge1	**Huddersfield**	H	L	0-3		6,298
10	lge1	**Brentford**	A	L	0-1		5,442
11	lge1	**Blackpool**	H	L	0-3		5,347
12	lge1	**Colchester**	A	L	1-2	Matthews 84	3,230
13	lge1	**Doncaster**	H	W	2-0	Paynter 15; Matthews 29	5,314
14	lge1	**Bournemouth**	A	L	0-4		6,119
15	lge1	**Swindon**	H	W	1-0	Birchall 76	3,872
16	lge1	**Stockport**	H	D	0-0		5,025
17	lge1	**Hartlepool**	A	L	0-1		4,755
18	lge1	**Barnsley**	A	W	2-1	Paynter 65; Williams, R 69 og	8,642
19	facr1	**Kidderminster**	H	W	3-1	Paynter 53,65; Reid 59	4,141
20	lge1	**Torquay**	H	L	1-2	Cummins 50	4,763
21	lge1	**Peterborough**	A	L	0-4		3,785
22	facr2	**Blackpool**	A	L	0-1		4,669
23	lge1	**Tranmere**	H	W	3-1	Birchall 9,52; Paynter 17	4,027
24	lge1	**Luton**	A	L	0-1		6,974
25	lge1	**Oldham**	H	W	3-1	Paynter 36; Birchall 62; Matthews 79 pen	4,849
26	lge1	**Huddersfield**	A	L	1-2	Eldershaw 38	12,243
27	lge1	**Sheff Wed**	H	L	0-2		8,671
28	lge1	**Bradford**	H	L	0-1		5,001
29	lge1	**Blackpool**	A	W	2-0	Matthews 72,78 pen	5,115
30	lge1	**Doncaster**	A	L	0-2		5,209
31	lge1	**Brentford**	H	L	0-1		4,230
32	lge1	**Sheff Wed**	A	L	0-1		18,465
33	lge1	**Bournemouth**	H	W	2-1	Paynter 17; Birchall 34	4,186
34	lge1	**Stockport**	A	W	2-1	Lowndes 22; Paynter 52	4,587
35	lge1	**Hartlepool**	H	L	0-1		4,366
36	lge1	**Swindon**	A	L	0-1		4,724
37	lge1	**Luton**	H	W	3-1	Hibbert 42,59; Matthews 81	5,353
38	lge1	**Oldham**	A	L	0-3		5,799
39	lge1	**Colchester**	H	D	0-0		3,496
40	lge1	**MK Dons**	A	D	1-1	Matthews 69	4,676
41	lge1	**Walsall**	H	W	2-0	Cummins 51; Matthews 57	5,085
42	lge1	**Hull City**	A	D	2-2	Matthews 13; Delaney 67 og	17,678
43	lge1	**Bristol City**	A	L	0-2		10,284
44	lge1	**Chesterfield**	H	W	1-0	Matthews 49	4,489
45	lge1	**Torquay**	A	L	0-1		3,592
46	lge1	**Barnsley**	H	W	5-0	Birchall 16; Paynter 41,50; Dinning 57,70	4,324
47	lge1	**Wrexham**	H	L	0-2		4,151
48	lge1	**Tranmere**	A	L	0-1		8,940
49	lge1	**Peterborough**	H	W	1-0	Dinning 63	4,815

MONTHLY POINTS TALLY

AUGUST	10	56%
SEPTEMBER	3	25%
OCTOBER	7	39%
NOVEMBER	3	33%
DECEMBER	6	40%
JANUARY	3	20%
FEBRUARY	9	60%
MARCH	6	40%
APRIL	6	33%
MAY	3	100%

KEY PLAYERS - GOALSCORERS

Lee Matthews

Goals in the League	11	Player Strike Rate Average number of minutes between League goals scored by player	171
Contribution to Attacking Power Average number of minutes between League team goals while on pitch	67	Club Strike Rate Average number of minutes between League goals scored by club	84

	PLAYER	LGE GOALS	GOALS ALL	POWER	STRIKE RATE
1	Lee Matthews	11	11	67	**171 mins**
2	William Paynter	10	12	96	**384 mins**
3	Christopher Birchall	6	6	81	**446 mins**
4	Michael Cummins	2	2	75	**1688 mins**
5	Craig James	1	1	71	**2141 mins**

KEY PLAYERS - MIDFIELDERS

Danny Sonner

Goals in the League	0	Contribution to Attacking Power Average number of minutes between League team goals while on pitch	76
Defensive Rating Average number of mins between League goals conceded while on the pitch	104	Scoring Difference Defensive Rating minus Contribution to Attacking Power	28

	PLAYER	LGE GOALS	GOALS ALL	DEF RATE	POWER	SCORE DIFF
1	Danny Sonner	0	0	104	76	**28 mins**
2	Michael Cummins	2	2	65	75	**-10 mins**
3	Christopher Birchall	6	6	70	81	**-11 mins**
4	Robin Hulbert	0	0	75	93	**-18 mins**
5	Levi Reid	0	1	55	92	**-37 mins**

KEY PLAYERS - DEFENDERS

George Abbey

Goals Conceded Number of League goals conceded while the player was on the pitch	13	Clean Sheets In games when player was on pitch for at least 70 minutes	4
Defensive Rating Ave number of mins between League goals conceded while on the pitch	109	Club Defensive Rating Average number of mins between League goals conceded by the club this season	70

	PLAYER	CON LGE	CON ALL	CLEAN SHEETS	DEF RATE
1	George Abbey	13	13	4	**109 mins**
2	Michael Walsh	21	22	7	**93 mins**
3	George Pilkington	50	55	10	**73 mins**
4	Sam Collins	41	45	8	**72 mins**
5	Steve Rowland	22	23	2	**72 mins**

KEY GOALKEEPER

Mark Goodlad

Goals Conceded in the League	19	Counting Games Games when player was on pitch for at least 70 minutes	19
Defensive Rating Ave number of mins between League goals conceded while on the pitch	92	Clean Sheets In Games when player was on pitch for at least 70 minutes	7

LEAGUE GOALS

William Paynter

Minutes on the pitch	3843	League average (mins between goals)	384
Goals in the League	10		

	PLAYER	MINS	GOALS	AVE
1	Paynter	3843	**10**	384
2	Matthews	1885	**11**	171
3	Birchall	2678	**6**	446
4	Brooker	787	**5**	157
5	Dinning	585	**3**	195
6	Armstrong	562	**3**	187
7	Cummins	3375	**2**	1688
8	Hibbert	251	**2**	126
9	Lowndes	555	**1**	555
10	Smith, J	2147	**1**	2147
11	Eldershaw	536	**1**	536
12	James	2141	**1**	2141
	Other		4	
	TOTAL		**49**	

DISCIPLINARY RECORDS

	PLAYER	YELLOW	RED	AVE
1	Armstrong	3	0	**187**
2	Sonner	5	0	**228**
3	Hulbert	8	0	**244**
4	James	8	0	**267**
5	Walsh	7	0	**280**
6	Dinning	2	0	**292**
7	Reid	3	1	**457**
8	Cummins	6	1	**482**
9	Rowland	3	0	**525**
10	Paynter	6	1	**549**
11	Lowndes	1	0	**555**
12	Collins	5	0	**593**
13	Abbey	2	0	**705**
	Other	11	2	
	TOTAL	**70**	**5**	

TOP POINT EARNERS

	PLAYER	GAMES	AV PTS
1	Danny Sonner	12	**1.50**
2	Lee Matthews	17	**1.47**
3	Mark Goodlad	19	**1.42**
4	Michael Cummins	35	**1.34**
5	George Abbey	15	**1.33**
6	Steve Rowland	16	**1.31**
7	Michael Walsh	21	**1.29**
8	Christopher Birchall	28	**1.29**
9	George Pilkington	40	**1.23**
10	Robin Hulbert	22	**1.18**
	CLUB AVERAGE:		**1.22**

TEAM OF THE SEASON

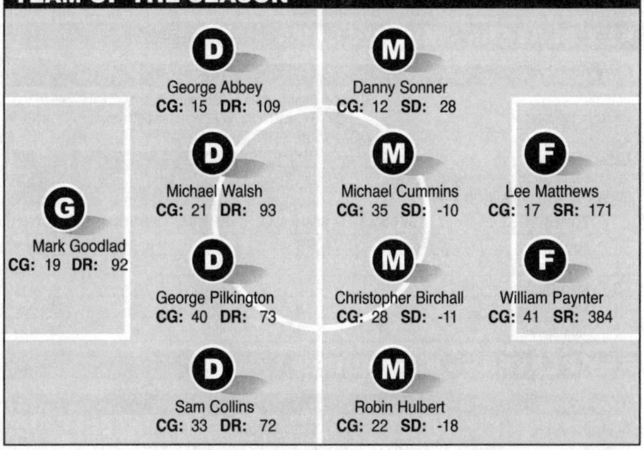
D
George Abbey
CG: 15 DR: 109
M
Danny Sonner
CG: 12 SD: 28
G
Mark Goodlad
CG: 19 DR: 92
D
Michael Walsh
CG: 21 DR: 93
M
Michael Cummins
CG: 35 SD: -10
F
Lee Matthews
CG: 17 SR: 171
D
George Pilkington
CG: 40 DR: 73
M
Christopher Birchall
CG: 28 SD: -11
F
William Paynter
CG: 41 SR: 384
D
Sam Collins
CG: 33 DR: 72
M
Robin Hulbert
CG: 22 SD: -18

LEAGUE APPEARANCES GOALS AND BOOKINGS

	AGE (on 01/07/05)	IN NAMED 16	APPEARANCES	COUNTING GAMES	MINUTES ON PITCH	LEAGUE GOALS	Yellow	Red
Goalkeepers								
Joe Anyon	18	23	0	0	0	0	0	0
Jonathan Brain	22	42	27	26	2390	0	1	0
Mark Goodlad	25	27	20	19	1750	0	0	0
Defenders								
George Abbey	26	20	18	15	1411	0	2	0
Ryan Brown	20	30	20	12	1341	0	0	0
Sam Collins	28	33	33	33	2965	1	5	0
Christian Hanson	23	11	6	3	310	0	0	0
Mark Innes	26	7	5	2	230	0	0	0
Craig James	22	32	30	21	2141	1	8	0
Andreas Lipa	34	4	2	0	12	0	0	0
Tyrone Loran	24	6	6	6	540	0	0	0
James O'Connor	20	13	13	12	1114	0	0	0
George Pilkington	23	43	43	40	3646	0	2	1
Simon Robinson	20	3	0	0	0	0	0	0
Steve Rowland	27	30	24	16	1577	0	3	0
Dean Smith	34	22	13	9	995	0	0	1
Michael Walsh	27	24	23	21	1960	0	7	0
Midfielders								
Christopher Birchall	21	38	33	28	2678	6	3	0
Michael Cummins	27	39	39	35	3375	2	6	1
Tony Dinning	30	7	7	6	585	3	2	0
Marc Goodfellow	23	5	5	4	372	0	0	0
Daniel Holmes	18	1	0	0	0	0	0	0
Robin Hulbert	25	24	24	22	1959	0	8	0
Daryl McMahon	22	6	5	0	93	0	0	0
Andy Porter	36	4	2	1	133	0	0	0
Levi Reid	22	37	30	17	1830	0	3	1
Jeff Smith	25	40	34	19	2147	1	2	0
Danny Sonner	33	13	13	12	1143	0	5	0
Tommy Widdrington	33	6	6	2	267	0	0	0
Forwards								
Ian Armstrong	23	14	9	5	562	3	3	0
Stephen Brooker	24	9	9	9	787	5	1	0
Simon Eldershaw	21	23	13	5	536	1	0	0
Dave Hibbert	19	10	9	1	251	2	0	0
Nathan Lowndes	28	14	12	4	555	1	1	0
Lee Matthews	26	31	31	17	1885	11	2	0
William Paynter	20	45	45	41	3843	10	6	1

SQUAD APPEARANCES

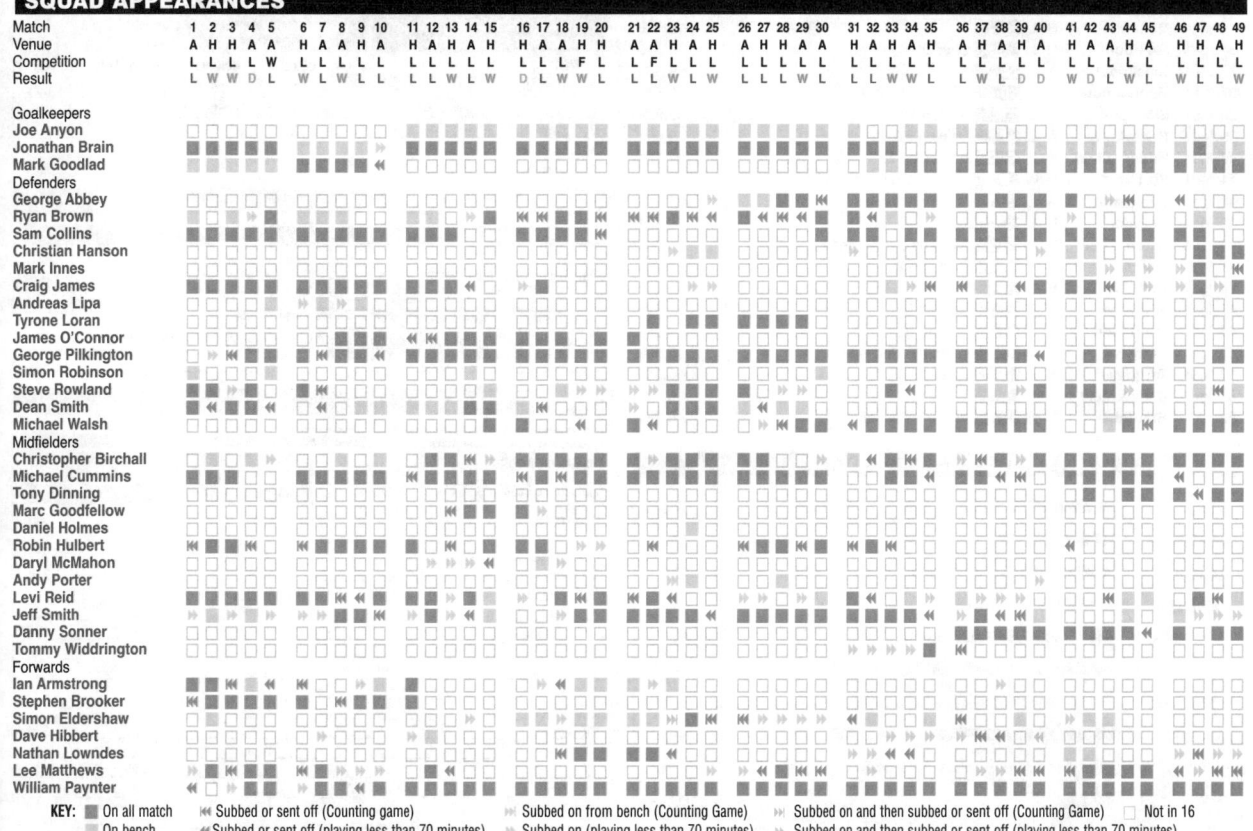

Match	1	2	3	4	5	6	7	8	9	10	11	12	13	14	15	16	17	18	19	20	21	22	23	24	25	26	27	28	29	30	31	32	33	34	35	36	37	38	39	40	41	42	43	44	45	46	47	48	49
Venue	A	H	H	A	A	H	A	A	H	A	H	A	H	A	H	H	A	A	H	H	A	A	H	A	H	A	H	H	A	A	H	A	H	A	H	A	H	A	H	A	H	A	A	H	A	H	H	A	H
Competition	L	L	L	L	W	L	L	L	L	L	L	L	L	L	L	L	L	L	F	L	L	F	L	L	L	L	L	L	L	L	L	L	L	L	L	L	L	L	L	L	L	L	L	L	L	L	L	L	L
Result	L	W	W	D	L	W	L	W	L	L	L	L	W	L	W	D	L	W	W	L	L	L	W	L	W	L	L	L	W	L	L	L	W	W	L	L	W	L	D	D	W	D	L	W	L	W	L	L	W

Goalkeepers
Joe Anyon
Jonathan Brain
Mark Goodlad
Defenders
George Abbey
Ryan Brown
Sam Collins
Christian Hanson
Mark Innes
Craig James
Andreas Lipa
Tyrone Loran
James O'Connor
George Pilkington
Simon Robinson
Steve Rowland
Dean Smith
Michael Walsh
Midfielders
Christopher Birchall
Michael Cummins
Tony Dinning
Marc Goodfellow
Daniel Holmes
Robin Hulbert
Daryl McMahon
Andy Porter
Levi Reid
Jeff Smith
Danny Sonner
Tommy Widdrington
Forwards
Ian Armstrong
Stephen Brooker
Simon Eldershaw
Dave Hibbert
Nathan Lowndes
Lee Matthews
William Paynter

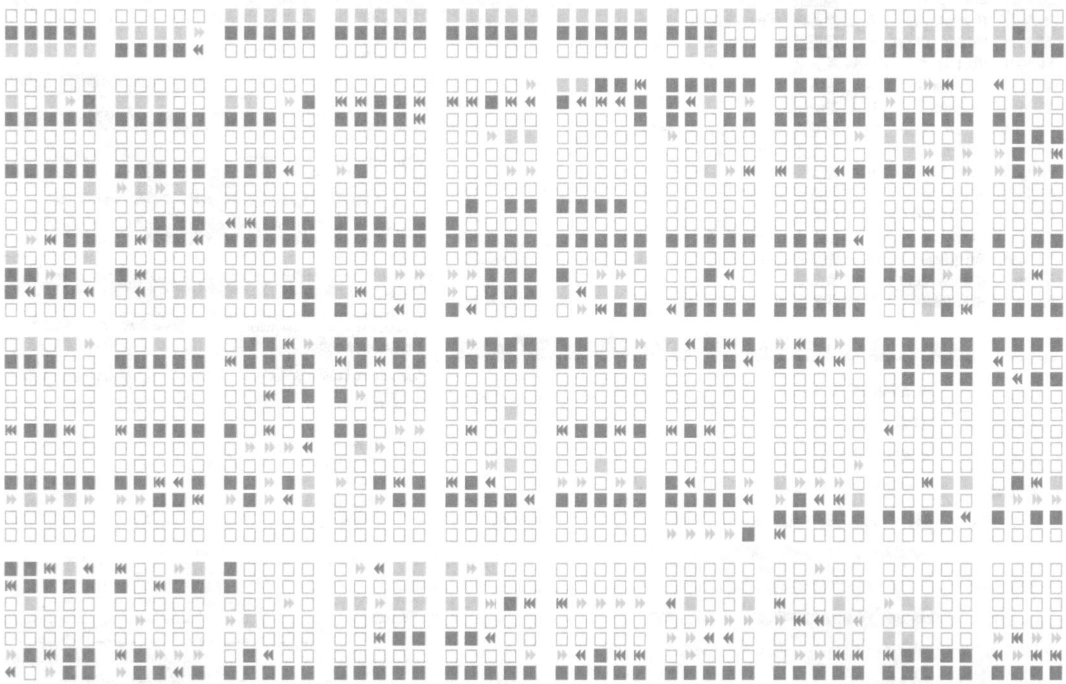

KEY: On all match — On bench — Subbed or sent off (Counting game) — Subbed or sent off (playing less than 70 minutes) — Subbed on from bench (Counting Game) — Subbed on (playing less than 70 minutes) — Subbed on and then subbed or sent off (Counting Game) — Subbed on and then subbed or sent off (playing less than 70 minutes) — Not in 16

OLDHAM ATHLETIC

Final Position: **19th**

NICKNAME: THE LATICS

KEY: Won / Drawn / Lost

							Attendance
1	lge1	Luton	A	L	1-2	Haining 10	6,634
2	lge1	Wrexham	H	L	2-3	Boshell 71; Jack 79	6,143
3	lge1	Walsall	H	W	5-3	Eyres, D 42,45; Holden 50; Jack 54; Griffin 90	5,654
4	lge1	Hull City	A	L	0-2		16,916
5	ccR1	Stoke	H	W	2-1	Eyres, D 72; Eyre, J 76 pen	2,861
6	lge1	MK Dons	H	W	3-0	Johnson 39; Killen 43; Arber 61	5,066
7	lge1	Sheff Wed	A	D	1-1	Johnson 75	21,530
8	lge1	Hartlepool	H	W	3-2	Eyre, J 43; Betsy 60; Johnson 82	5,805
9	lge1	Tranmere	A	L	0-2		8,437
10	lge1	Doncaster	A	D	1-1	Johnson 39	6,774
11	ccr2	Tottenham	H	L	0-6		8,548
12	lge1	Colchester	H	D	1-1	Eyres, D 22	5,166
13	lge1	Brentford	A	L	0-2		5,818
14	lge1	Blackpool	H	L	1-2	Haining 39	7,125
15	lge1	Swindon	A	L	0-1		5,522
16	lge1	Bristol City	H	D	0-0		5,090
17	lge1	Bournemouth	H	L	1-2	Vernon 3 pen	5,335
18	lge1	Stockport	A	W	2-1	Wilbraham 13,39	6,146
19	lge1	Torquay	A	L	0-2		3,183
20	facr1	Thurrock	A	W	1-0	Killen 48 pen	1,156
21	lge1	Barnsley	H	W	3-2	Killen 17,90; Vernon 90	5,593
22	lge1	Bradford	A	W	3-1	Kilkenny 12,82; Killen 63	8,647
23	facr2	Leyton Orient	H	W	4-0	Killen 26,39,65; Croft 85	4,657
24	lge1	Chesterfield	H	W	4-1	Killen 3,19 pen; Betsy 55; Kilkenny 62	5,207
25	lge1	Huddersfield	H	W	2-1	Haining 4; Betsy 38	8,389
26	lge1	Port Vale	A	L	1-3	Vernon 34	4,849
27	lge1	Hartlepool	A	L	1-2	Holden 64	6,520
28	lge1	Peterborough	H	W	2-1	Vernon 46; Kilkenny 54	5,618
29	lge1	Tranmere	H	D	2-2	Griffin 39; Vernon 71	6,876
30	lge1	Colchester	A	D	0-0		3,873
31	facr3	Man City	H	W	1-0	Vernon 14	13,171
32	lge1	Doncaster	H	L	1-2	Vernon 87	7,401
33	lge1	Peterborough	A	W	2-1	Betsy 7,63	4,047
34	facr4	Bolton	H	L	0-1		12,029
35	lge1	Swindon	H	L	1-2	Cooper 14	5,810
36	lge1	Blackpool	A	L	0-2		5,563
37	lge1	Bournemouth	A	L	0-4		6,622
38	lge1	Stockport	H	L	1-2	Vernon 70	5,924
39	lge1	Bristol City	A	L	1-5	Haining 57	9,007
40	lge1	Huddersfield	A	L	1-2	Branston 75	11,161
41	lge1	Port Vale	H	W	3-0	Haining 27; Cooper 52,54	5,799
42	lge1	Wrexham	A	L	0-1		4,170
43	lge1	Brentford	H	L	0-2		4,291
44	lge1	Luton	H	D	2-2	Kilkenny 39; Beckett 48	5,809
45	lge1	Walsall	A	W	1-0	Beckett 72	6,794
46	lge1	Hull City	H	W	1-0	Killen 71	8,562
47	lge1	MK Dons	A	D	1-1	Beckett 5	5,426
48	lge1	Sheff Wed	H	D	1-1	Beckett 28	9,645
49	lge1	Barnsley	A	D	2-2	Killen 37; Beckett 66	8,856
50	lge1	Torquay	H	L	1-2	Eyres, D 25	8,941
51	lge1	Chesterfield	A	L	0-1		5,421
52	lge1	Bradford	H	W	2-1	Killen 3; Beckett 22	9,381

MONTHLY POINTS TALLY

AUGUST	7	39%
SEPTEMBER	5	42%
OCTOBER	4	22%
NOVEMBER	6	67%
DECEMBER	9	60%
JANUARY	5	42%
FEBRUARY	0	0%
MARCH	10	56%
APRIL	3	20%
MAY	3	100%

KEY PLAYERS - GOALSCORERS

Christopher Killen

Goals in the League	9	Player Strike Rate Average number of minutes between League goals scored by player	231
Contribution to Attacking Power Average number of minutes between League team goals while on pitch	54	Club Strike Rate Average number of minutes between League goals scored by club	69

	PLAYER	LGE GOALS	GOALS ALL	POWER	STRIKE RATE
1	Christopher Killen	9	13	54	231 mins
2	Jermaine Johnson	4	4	73	294 mins
3	Neil Kilkenny	5	5	59	434 mins
4	Will Haining	5	5	64	592 mins
5	Kevin Betsy	5	5	79	623 mins

KEY PLAYERS - MIDFIELDERS

Neil Kilkenny

Goals in the League	5	Contribution to Attacking Power Average number of minutes between League team goals while on pitch	59
Defensive Rating Average number of mins between League goals conceded while on the pitch	60	Scoring Difference Defensive Rating minus Contribution to Attacking Power	1

	PLAYER	LGE GOALS	GOALS ALL	DEF RATE	POWER	SCORE DIFF
1	Neil Kilkenny	5	5	60	59	1 mins
2	David Eyres	4	5	59	60	-1 mins
3	Mark Hughes	0	0	55	63	-8 mins
4	Mark Bonner	0	0	52	65	-13 mins
5	John Eyre	1	2	46	81	-35 mins

KEY PLAYERS - DEFENDERS

Dean Holden

Goals Conceded Number of League goals conceded while the player was on the pitch	55	Clean Sheets In games when player was on pitch for at least 70 minutes	5
Defensive Rating Ave number of mins between League goals conceded while on the pitch	62	Club Defensive Rating Average number of mins between League goals conceded while on the pitch	57

	PLAYER	CON LGE	CON ALL	CLEAN SHEETS	DEF RATE
1	Dean Holden	55	62	5	62 mins
2	Will Haining	51	59	5	58 mins
3	Daniel Hall	32	33	2	55 mins
4	Mark Arber	24	31	1	52 mins
5	Adam Griffin	58	66	3	50 mins

KEY GOALKEEPER

Leslie Pogliacomi

Goals Conceded in the League	58	Counting Games Games when player was on pitch for at least 70 minutes	37
Defensive Rating Ave number of mins between League goals conceded while on the pitch	56	Clean Sheets In games when player was on pitch for at least 70 minutes	4

LEAGUE GOALS

Christopher Killen

Minutes on the pitch	2075	League average (mins between goals)	231
Goals in the League	9		

	PLAYER	MINS	GOALS	AVE
1	Killen	2075	9	231
2	Vernon	1245	7	178
3	Beckett	794	6	132
4	Betsy	3116	5	623
5	Kilkenny	2170	5	434
6	Eyres, D	3446	4	862
7	Haining	2958	5	592
8	Johnson	1175	4	294
9	Cooper	433	3	144
10	Jack	539	2	270
11	Holden	3399	2	1700
12	Griffin	2894	2	1447
	Other		6	
	TOTAL		60	

DISCIPLINARY RECORDS

	PLAYER	YELLOW	RED	AVE
1	Bruce	4	0	195
2	Johnson	5	1	195
3	Eyre, J	7	0	221
4	Appleby	4	0	246
5	Tierney	3	0	263
6	Hughes	8	0	275
7	Arber	4	0	312
8	Kilkenny	6	0	361
9	Hall, D	4	0	441
10	Boshell	2	0	444
11	Stam	2	0	462
12	Holden	7	0	485
13	Killen	4	0	518
	Other	18	0	
	TOTAL	78	1	

TOP POINT EARNERS

	PLAYER	GAMES	AV PTS
1	Killen	22	1.45
2	Kilkenny	24	1.38
3	Eyres, D	37	1.32
4	Holden	37	1.30
5	Hall, D	19	1.26
6	Hughes	22	1.18
7	Griffin	30	1.17
8	Pogliacomi	36	1.14
9	Haining	32	1.13
10	Johnson	12	1.08
	CLUB AVERAGE:		1.13

TEAM OF THE SEASON

D
Dean Holden
CG: 37 DR: 62
M
Neil Kilkenny
CG: 24 SD: 1
D
Will Haining
CG: 32 DR: 58
M
David Eyres
CG: 37 SD: -1
F
Luke Beckett
CG: 9 SR: 193
G
Leslie Pogliacomi
CG: 36 DR: 56
D
Daniel Hall
CG: 19 DR: 55
M
Mark Hughes
CG: 22 SD: -8
F
Christopher Killen
CG: 22 SR: 231
D
Adam Griffin
CG: 30 DR: 50
M
Mark Bonner
CG: 14 SD: -13

LEAGUE APPEARANCES GOALS AND BOOKINGS

	AGE (on 01/07/05)	IN NAMED 16	APPEARANCES	COUNTING GAMES	MINUTES ON PITCH	LEAGUE GOALS	Yellow card	Red card
Goalkeepers								
Bertrand Bossu	24	2	0	0	0	0	0	0
Craig Mawson	26	13	4	4	347	0	0	0
Steve Mildenhall	27	20	6	6	540	0	0	0
Leslie Pogliacomi	29	44	37	36	3253	0	2	0
Defenders								
Mark Arber	27	17	14	14	1249	1	4	0
David Beharall	26	17	3	2	211	0	0	0
Guy Branston	26	10	7	6	585	1	1	0
Alex Bruce	20	13	12	8	780	0	4	0
Adam Griffin	20	37	35	30	2894	2	1	0
Will Haining	22	35	35	32	2958	5	3	0
Daniel Hall	21	25	21	19	1765	0	4	0
Dean Holden	25	40	40	37	3399	2	7	0
Kevin Lomax	18	12	9	7	680	0	0	0
Gareth Owen	22	9	9	8	746	0	1	0
Stefan Stam	28	15	13	10	925	0	2	0
Marc Tierney	19	17	11	8	789	0	3	0
Midfielders								
Matthew Appleby	29	24	17	9	986	0	4	0
Mark Bonner	31	29	19	14	1363	0	1	0
Danny Boshell	24	19	16	8	888	1	2	0
John Eyre	30	27	24	15	1547	1	7	0
David Eyres	41	44	42	37	3446	4	3	0
Mark Hughes	21	27	27	22	2204	0	8	0
Neil Kilkenny	19	27	27	24	2170	5	6	0
David Lee	25	8	7	5	491	0	0	0
Amadou Sanokho	-	4	1	0	10	0	0	0
Ashley Winn	19	3	2	0	11	0	0	0
Forwards								
Matty Barlow	18	15	9	1	214	0	0	0
Luke Beckett	28	9	9	9	794	6	1	0
Kevin Betsy	27	37	36	34	3116	5	5	0
Kenny Cooper	20	9	7	3	433	3	0	0
Lee Croft	20	12	12	8	941	0	0	0
Delroy Facey	25	6	6	1	135	0	0	0
Christopher Hall	18	9	6	1	198	0	0	0
Rodney Jack	32	10	10	5	539	2	0	0
Jermaine Johnson	25	23	19	12	1175	4	5	1
Christopher Killen	23	26	26	22	2075	9	4	0
Scott Vernon	21	26	22	11	1245	7	0	0
Aaron Wilbraham	25	4	4	2	296	2	0	0

SQUAD APPEARANCES

Match	1	2	3	4	5	6	7	8	9	10	11	12	13	14	15	16	17	18	19	20	21	22	23	24	25	26
Venue	A	H	H	A	H	H	A	H	A	A	H	H	A	H	A	H	H	A	A	A	H	A	H	H	H	A
Competition	L	L	L	L	W	L	L	L	L	L	W	L	L	L	L	L	L	L	L	F	L	L	F	L	L	L
Result	L	L	W	L	W	W	D	W	L	D	L	D	L	L	L	D	L	W	L	W	W	W	W	W	W	L

Match	27	28	29	30	31	32	33	34	35	36	37	38	39	40	41	42	43	44	45	46	47	48	49	50	51	52
Venue	A	H	H	A	H	H	A	H	H	A	A	H	A	A	H	A	H	H	A	H	A	H	A	H	A	H
Competition	L	L	L	L	F	L	L	F	L	L	L	L	L	L	L	L	L	L	L	L	L	L	L	L	L	L
Result	L	W	D	D	W	L	W	L	L	L	L	L	L	L	W	L	L	D	W	W	D	D	D	L	L	W

Goalkeepers
Bertrand Bossu
Craig Mawson
Steve Mildenhall
Leslie Pogliacomi
Defenders
Mark Arber
David Beharall
Guy Branston
Alex Bruce
Adam Griffin
Will Haining
Daniel Hall
Dean Holden
Kevin Lomax
Gareth Owen
Stefan Stam
Marc Tierney
Midfielders
Matthew Appleby
Mark Bonner
Danny Boshell
John Eyre
David Eyres
Mark Hughes
Neil Kilkenny
David Lee
Amadou Sanokho
Ashley Winn
Forwards
Matty Barlow
Luke Beckett
Kevin Betsy
Kenny Cooper
Lee Croft
Delroy Facey
Christopher Hall
Rodney Jack
Jermaine Johnson
Christopher Killen
Scott Vernon
Aaron Wilbraham

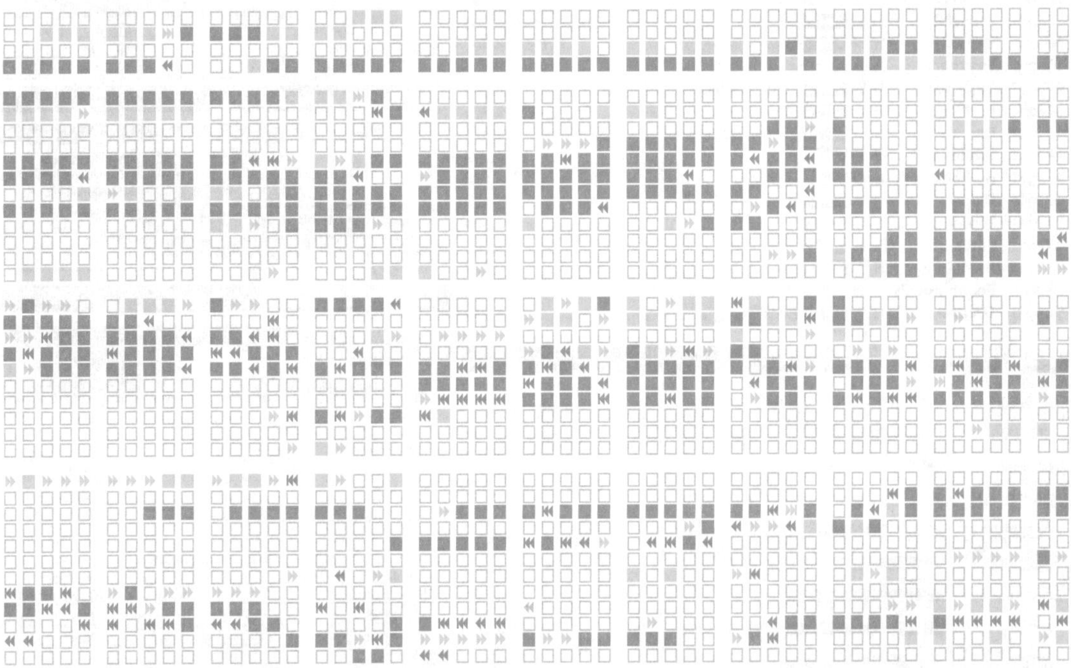

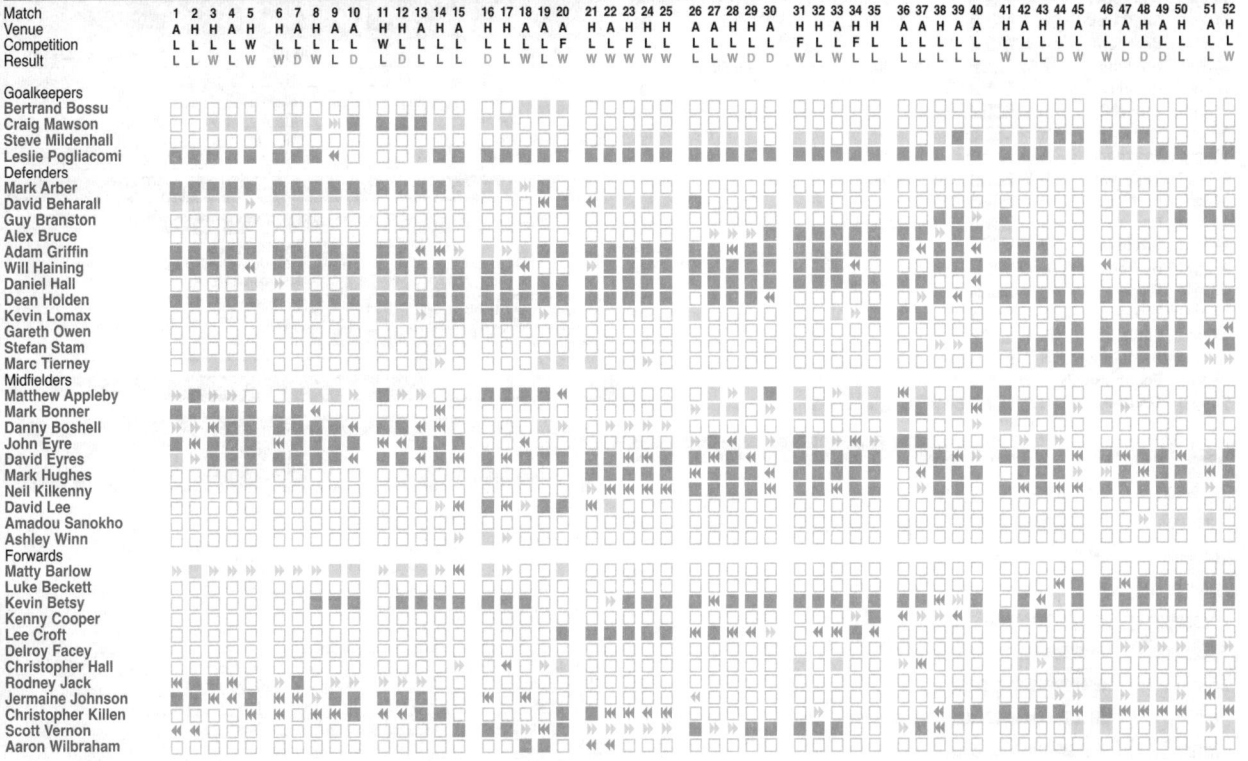

KEY: On all match · On bench · Subbed or sent off (Counting game) · Subbed or sent off (playing less than 70 minutes) · Subbed on from bench (Counting Game) · Subbed on (playing less than 70 minutes) · Subbed on and then subbed or sent off (Counting Game) · Subbed on and then subbed or sent off (playing less than 70 minutes) · Not in 16

MK DONS

Final Position: **20th**

NICKNAME: THE DONS/WOMBLES

KEY: Won, Drawn, Lost

							Attendance
1	lge1	Barnsley	H	D	1-1	McLeod 76	4,720
2	lge1	Port Vale	A	L	2-3	Harding 19,75	4,602
3	lge1	Swindon	A	L	1-2	Smart 42	5,060
4	lge1	Bournemouth	H	L	1-3	Smart 49 pen	3,230
5	ccR1	Peterborough	A	W	3-0	McLeod 63; Smart 80; Kamara 90	2,886
6	lge1	Oldham	A	L	0-3		5,066
7	lge1	Torquay	H	W	1-0	Puncheon 45	3,015
8	lge1	Chesterfield	A	D	2-2	McLeod 64; Small 88	4,537
9	lge1	Doncaster	H	L	0-1		4,334
10	lge1	Colchester	A	W	1-0	McLeod 45	3,460
11	ccR2	Cardiff	H	L	1-4	McLeod 85	2,266
12	lge1	Hartlepool	H	W	4-2	McLeod 31,57; Small 46; Smith 50 pen	3,685
13	lge1	Sheff Wed	A	D	1-1	McLeod 89	20,245
14	lge1	Bradford	H	L	1-2	McLeod 20	4,532
15	lge1	Brentford	H	D	0-0		5,924
16	lge1	Hull City	A	L	2-3	McLeod 33; Chorley 76	14,317
17	lge1	Huddersfield	A	L	1-3	Chorley 86 pen	10,709
18	lge1	Walsall	H	D	1-1	Kamara 36	4,247
19	lge1	Bristol City	A	L	1-4	Small 52	10,717
20	facr1	Lancaster	H	W	1-0	Small 48	2,065
21	lge1	Luton	H	L	1-4	Small 45	7,620
22	lge1	Tranmere	A	L	0-2		8,402
23	facr2	Cambridge City	A	W	1-0	Smart 6	2,000
24	lge1	Peterborough	H	D	1-1	Small 53	3,913
25	lge1	Wrexham	H	W	3-0	Rizzo 7; Small 50,84	3,601
26	lge1	Stockport	A	L	1-3	Tapp 77	3,902
27	lge1	Doncaster	A	L	0-3		6,153
28	lge1	Blackpool	H	W	3-1	McLeod 41; Palmer 73; Smart 82	4,943
29	lge1	Chesterfield	H	D	1-1	Smart 5 pen	4,214
30	lge1	Hartlepool	A	L	0-5		5,060
31	facr3	Peterborough	H	L	0-2		4,407
32	lge1	Colchester	H	W	2-0	Harding 2; Small 18	3,833
33	lge1	Blackpool	A	L	0-1		5,798
34	lge1	Sheff Wed	H	D	2-2	Platt 58; McLeod 85	7,325
35	lge1	Brentford	A	L	0-1		5,077
36	lge1	Bradford	A	W	4-1	Small 32; McLeod 44,57; Harding 55	6,409
37	lge1	Huddersfield	H	W	2-1	McLeod 33; Platt 90	4,793
38	lge1	Walsall	A	D	0-0		5,888
39	lge1	Hull City	H	D	1-1	Lewington 50	4,407
40	lge1	Wrexham	A	D	0-0		3,406
41	lge1	Stockport	H	W	2-1	Lewington 34; Edds 59	4,146
42	lge1	Port Vale	H	D	1-1	Platt 72	4,676
43	lge1	Barnsley	A	D	1-1	Pensee-Bilong 55	8,111
44	lge1	Swindon	H	D	1-1	Small 14	7,019
45	lge1	Bournemouth	A	W	1-0	Edds 73	7,064
46	lge1	Oldham	H	D	1-1	Edds 84	5,426
47	lge1	Torquay	A	L	0-1		3,509
48	lge1	Luton	A	L	0-1		9,000
49	lge1	Bristol City	H	L	1-2	McLeod 8	5,656
50	lge1	Peterborough	A	W	3-0	Rizzo 9; McLeod 22,85	3,742
51	lge1	Tranmere	H	W	2-1	Edds 6,84	7,359

MONTHLY POINTS TALLY

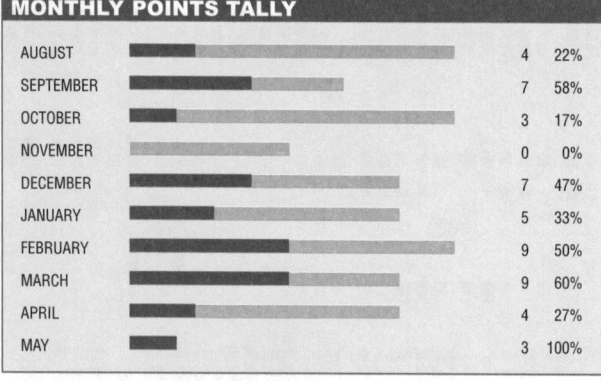

AUGUST	4	22%
SEPTEMBER	7	58%
OCTOBER	3	17%
NOVEMBER	0	0%
DECEMBER	7	47%
JANUARY	5	33%
FEBRUARY	9	50%
MARCH	9	60%
APRIL	4	27%
MAY	3	100%

KEY PLAYERS - GOALSCORERS

Izale McLeod

Goals in the League	16	Player Strike Rate Average number of minutes between League goals scored by player	215
Contribution to Attacking Power Average number of minutes between League team goals while on pitch	73	Club Strike Rate Average number of minutes between League goals scored by club	77

	PLAYER	LGE GOALS	GOALS ALL	POWER	STRIKE RATE
1	Izale McLeod	16	18	73	215 mins
2	Allan Smart	4	6	86	325 mins
3	Wade Small	10	11	71	353 mins
4	Ben Harding	4	4	77	462 mins
5	Clive Platt	3	3	75	600 mins

KEY PLAYERS - MIDFIELDERS

Ben Harding

Goals in the League	4	Contribution to Attacking Power Average number of minutes between League team goals while on pitch	77
Defensive Rating Average number of mins between League goals conceded while on the pitch	92	Scoring Difference Defensive Rating minus Contribution to Attacking Power	15

	PLAYER	LGE GOALS	GOALS ALL	DEF RATE	POWER	SCORE DIFF
1	Ben Harding	4	4	92	77	15 mins
2	Wade Small	10	11	62	71	-9 mins
3	Gary Smith	1	1	55	65	-10 mins
4	Steve Palmer	1	1	50	73	-23 mins
5	Malvin Kamara	1	2	46	97	-51 mins

KEY PLAYERS - DEFENDERS

Michel Pensee-Bilong

Goals Conceded Number of League goals conceded while the player was on the pitch	17	Clean Sheets In games when player was on pitch for at least 70 minutes	3
Defensive Rating Ave number of mins between League goals conceded while on the pitch	94	Club Defensive Rating Average number of mins between League goals conceded while on the pitch	61

	PLAYER	CON LGE	CON ALL	CLEAN SHEETS	DEF RATE
1	Michel Pensee-Bilong	17	17	3	94 mins
2	Shola Oyedele	22	25	3	75 mins
3	Dean Lewington	57	63	9	67 mins
4	Ben Chorley	59	65	9	62 mins
5	Paul Mitchell	19	21	2	60 mins

KEY GOALKEEPER

Matthew Baker

Goals Conceded in the League	23	Counting Games In games when player was on pitch for at least 70 minutes	20
Defensive Rating Ave number of mins between League goals conceded while on the pitch	78	Clean Sheets In games when player was on pitch for at least 70 minutes	4

LEAGUE GOALS

Izale McLeod

Minutes on the pitch	3443	League average (mins between goals)	215
Goals in the League	16		

	PLAYER	MINS	GOALS	AVE
1	McLeod	3443	16	215
2	Small	3528	10	353
3	Edds	3315	5	663
4	Harding	1846	4	462
5	Smart	1298	4	325
6	Platt	1800	3	600
7	Chorley	3679	2	1840
8	Lewington	3840	2	1920
9	Rizzo	1127	2	564
10	Pensee-Bilong	1597	1	1597
11	Tapp	561	1	561
12	Smith	1695	1	1695
	Other		3	
	TOTAL		54	

DISCIPLINARY RECORDS

	PLAYER	YELLOW	RED	AVE
1	McClenahan	3	0	213
2	McLeod	15	1	215
3	Mitchell	4	0	285
4	Chorley	9	0	408
5	Lewington	9	0	426
6	Herve	3	0	431
7	Smart	3	0	432
8	Puncheon	2	0	510
9	Tapp	1	0	561
10	Rizzo	2	0	563
11	Kamara	2	0	773
12	Pensee-Bilong	2	0	798
13	Edds	4	0	828
	Other	12	0	
	TOTAL	71	1	

TOP POINT EARNERS

	PLAYER	GAMES	AV PTS
1	Clive Platt	20	1.45
2	Matthew Baker	20	1.45
3	Paul Mitchell	12	1.42
4	Shola Oyedele	17	1.35
5	Ben Harding	19	1.21
6	Dean Lewington	42	1.21
7	Michel Pensee-Bilong	17	1.18
8	Ben Chorley	41	1.17
9	Gareth Edds	36	1.14
10	Wade Small	36	1.14
	CLUB AVERAGE:		1.11

LEAGUE APPEARANCES GOALS AND BOOKINGS

	AGE (on 01/07/05)	IN NAMED 16	APPEARANCES	COUNTING GAMES	MINUTES ON PITCH	LEAGUE GOALS	Yellow cards	Red cards
Goalkeepers								
Matthew Baker	25	23	20	20	1800	0	0	0
Scott Bevan	25	12	7	7	630	0	0	0
David Martin	19	29	15	15	1350	0	0	0
Paul Rachubka	24	4	4	4	360	0	0	0
Defenders								
Ben Chorley	22	41	41	41	3679	2	9	0
Leon Crooks	19	26	17	10	1194	0	0	0
Gareth Edds	24	43	39	36	3315	5	4	0
Nathan Koo-Boothe	19	1	1	0	45	0	0	0
Dean Lewington	21	43	43	42	3840	2	9	0
Trent McClenahan	20	8	8	7	641	0	3	0
Paul Mitchell	23	13	13	12	1141	0	4	0
Harry Ntimban-Zeh	31	17	11	11	986	0	1	0
Shola Oyedele	20	34	25	17	1653	0	1	0
Michel Pensee-Bilong	32	18	18	17	1597	1	2	0
Mark Williams	34	18	13	11	998	0	1	0
Midfielders								
Anthony Danze	21	2	2	1	145	0	0	0
Ben Harding	20	26	26	19	1846	4	2	0
Laurent Herve	29	34	20	13	1294	0	3	0
Richard Johnson	31	2	2	2	180	0	0	0
Malvin Kamara	21	30	25	13	1547	1	2	0
Steve Palmer	37	46	32	26	2496	1	0	0
Jason Puncheon	19	28	25	7	1021	1	2	0
Nicky Rizzo	26	24	18	11	1127	2	2	0
Wade Small	21	44	44	36	3528	10	4	0
Gary Smith	21	27	23	17	1695	1	2	0
Alex Tapp	23	13	12	3	561	1	1	0
Forwards								
Julien Hornuss	19	9	3	0	31	0	0	0
Jamie Mackie	19	7	3	0	74	0	0	0
Serge Makofo	18	1	1	0	25	0	0	0
Izale McLeod	20	43	43	38	3443	16	15	1
Richard Pacquette	22	6	5	1	135	0	0	0
Clive Platt	27	20	20	20	1800	3	1	0
Allan Smart	31	32	18	13	1298	4	3	0
Craig Westcarr	20	5	4	0	49	0	0	0

TEAM OF THE SEASON

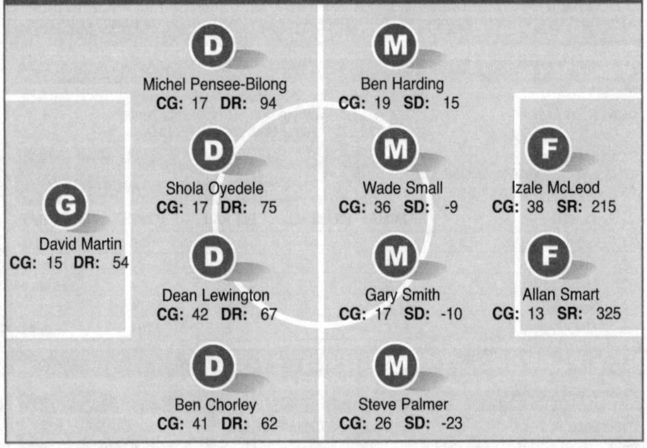
G
David Martin
CG: 15 DR: 54
D
Michel Pensee-Bilong
CG: 17 DR: 94
D
Shola Oyedele
CG: 17 DR: 75
D
Dean Lewington
CG: 42 DR: 67
D
Ben Chorley
CG: 41 DR: 62
M
Ben Harding
CG: 19 SD: 15
M
Wade Small
CG: 36 SD: -9
M
Gary Smith
CG: 17 SD: -10
M
Steve Palmer
CG: 26 SD: -23
F
Izale McLeod
CG: 38 SR: 215
F
Allan Smart
CG: 13 SR: 325

SQUAD APPEARANCES

Match	1	2	3	4	5	6	7	8	9	10	11	12	13	14	15	16	17	18	19	20	21	22	23	24	25	26	27	28	29	30	31	32	33	34	35	36	37	38	39	40	41	42	43	44	45	46	47	48	49	50	51
Venue	H	A	A	H	A	A	H	A	H	A	H	H	A	H	H	A	A	H	A	H	H	A	A	H	H	A	A	H	H	A	H	H	A	H	A	A	H	A	H	A	H	H	A	H	A	H	A	A	H	A	H
Competition	L	L	L	L	W	L	L	L	L	L	W	L	L	L	L	L	L	L	L	F	L	L	F	L	L	L	L	L	L	L	F	L	L	L	L	L	L	L	L	L	L	L	L	L	L	L	L	L	L	L	L
Result	D	L	L	L	W	L	W	D	L	W	L	W	D	L	D	L	L	D	L	W	L	L	W	D	W	L	L	W	D	L	L	W	L	D	L	W	W	D	D	D	W	D	D	D	W	D	L	L	L	W	W

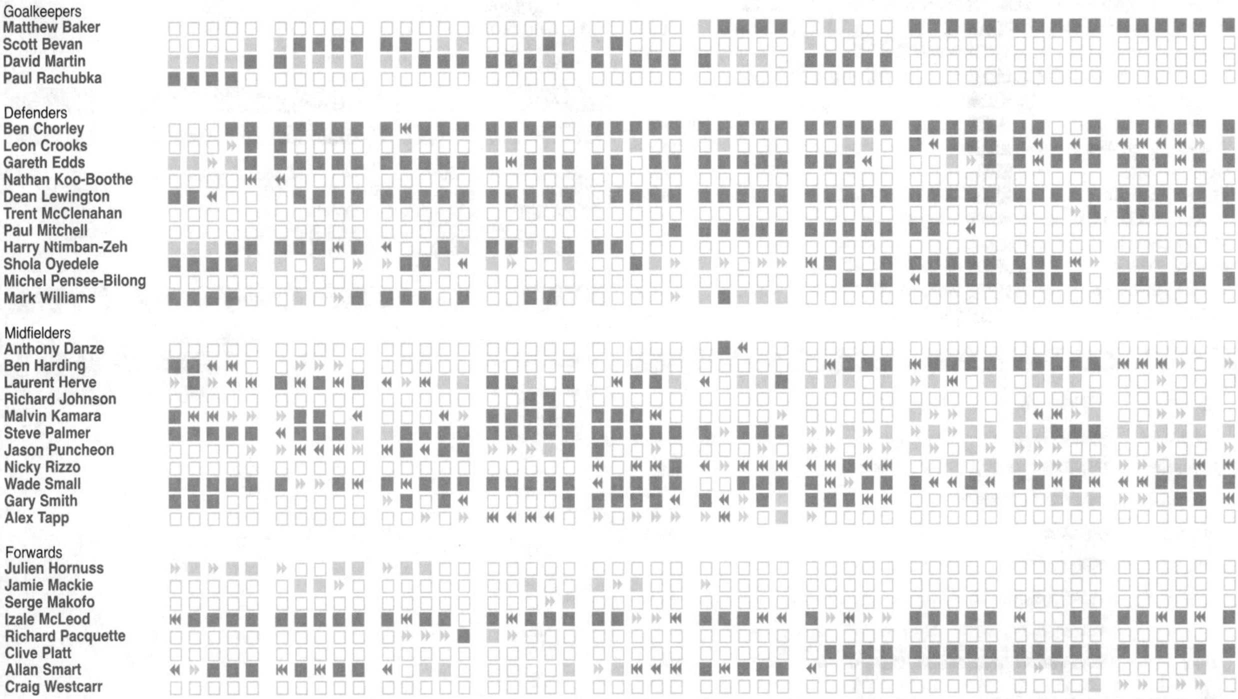
Goalkeepers
Matthew Baker
Scott Bevan
David Martin
Paul Rachubka
Defenders
Ben Chorley
Leon Crooks
Gareth Edds
Nathan Koo-Boothe
Dean Lewington
Trent McClenahan
Paul Mitchell
Harry Ntimban-Zeh
Shola Oyedele
Michel Pensee-Bilong
Mark Williams
Midfielders
Anthony Danze
Ben Harding
Laurent Herve
Richard Johnson
Malvin Kamara
Steve Palmer
Jason Puncheon
Nicky Rizzo
Wade Small
Gary Smith
Alex Tapp
Forwards
Julien Hornuss
Jamie Mackie
Serge Makofo
Izale McLeod
Richard Pacquette
Clive Platt
Allan Smart
Craig Westcarr

KEY: On all match | On bench | Subbed or sent off (Counting game) | Subbed or sent off (playing less than 70 minutes) | Subbed on from bench (Counting Game) | Subbed on (playing less than 70 minutes) | Subbed on and then subbed or sent off (Counting Game) | Subbed on and then subbed or sent off (playing less than 70 minutes) | Not in 16

TORQUAY

Final Position: **21st**

NICKNAME: THE GULLS

KEY: ☐ Won ☐ Drawn ☐ Lost

							Attendance
1	lge1	Bristol City	A	D	1-1	Woods 72 pen	14,275
2	lge1	Hull City	H	L	0-3		3,973
3	lge1	Sheff Wed	H	L	2-4	Osei-Kuffour 44; Gritton 60	5,005
4	lge1	Luton	A	L	0-1		6,664
5	ccR1	Coventry	A	L	1-4	Osei-Kuffour 74	6,180
6	lge1	Walsall	H	D	0-0		3,791
7	lge1	MK Dons	A	L	0-1		3,015
8	lge1	Stockport	A	W	2-0	Gritton 30,58	4,372
9	lge1	Brentford	H	D	2-2	Wardley 38,48	3,458
10	lge1	Hartlepool	A	L	1-4	Gritton 10	4,485
11	lge1	Tranmere	H	L	1-2	Russell 55	2,922
12	lge1	Peterborough	A	D	1-1	Russell 34	3,828
13	lge1	Huddersfield	H	W	2-1	Hill 49; Osei-Kuffour 84	3,033
14	lge1	Doncaster	A	D	2-2	Akinfenwa 9; Osei-Kuffour 90	5,529
15	lge1	Bournemouth	H	L	1-2	Hill 54	3,055
16	lge1	Swindon	A	D	3-3	Constantine 16; Akinfenwa 66,84	6,724
17	lge1	Oldham	H	W	2-0	Constantine 9; Gritton 71	3,183
18	facr1	Hinckley	A	L	0-2		2,129
19	lge1	Port Vale	A	W	2-1	Hill 42; Constantine 65	4,763
20	lge1	Wrexham	H	W	1-0	Bedeau 26	2,384
21	lge1	Colchester	H	L	1-3	Gritton 74 pen	2,984
22	lge1	Blackpool	A	L	0-4		4,179
23	lge1	Barnsley	H	L	0-1		2,983
24	lge1	Chesterfield	A	D	1-1	Gosling 48	4,133
25	lge1	Brentford	A	W	3-1	Constantine 55,70,83	6,419
26	lge1	Bradford	H	D	0-0		4,119
27	lge1	Stockport	H	L	1-2	Hill 45	3,456
28	lge1	Tranmere	A	L	1-4	Akinfenwa 21	8,792
29	lge1	Huddersfield	A	D	1-1	Hill 56	9,194
30	lge1	Hartlepool	H	L	1-2	Osei-Kuffour 13	2,543
31	lge1	Bradford	A	D	2-2	Bedeau 40; Akinfenwa 42	8,209
32	lge1	Doncaster	H	W	2-1	Constantine 7; Akinfenwa 19	3,157
33	lge1	Wrexham	A	D	1-1	Osei-Kuffour 20	3,608
34	lge1	Peterborough	H	W	2-1	Akinfenwa 24,75	2,769
35	lge1	Swindon	H	D	2-2	Constantine 25; Osei-Kuffour 63	4,190
36	lge1	Bournemouth	A	L	0-3		5,887
37	lge1	Barnsley	A	L	1-4	Phillips 88	7,466
38	lge1	Chesterfield	H	D	2-2	Akinfenwa 20; Phillips 88	2,746
39	lge1	Hull City	A	L	0-2		17,147
40	lge1	Bristol City	H	L	0-4		4,299
41	lge1	Sheff Wed	A	D	2-2	Akinfenwa 25; Woods 49	21,526
42	lge1	Luton	H	L	1-4	Akinfenwa 6	4,264
43	lge1	Walsall	A	D	1-1	Akinfenwa 59	5,694
44	lge1	MK Dons	H	W	1-0	Abbey 82	3,509
45	lge1	Port Vale	H	W	1-0	Constantine 90 pen	3,592
46	lge1	Oldham	A	W	2-1	Hockley 41; Akinfenwa 49	8,941
47	lge1	Blackpool	H	W	2-0	Akinfenwa 16; Russell 54	5,347
48	lge1	Colchester	A	L	1-2	Woodman 90	4,834

MONTHLY POINTS TALLY

AUGUST	2	11%
SEPTEMBER	4	33%
OCTOBER	6	40%
NOVEMBER	9	75%
DECEMBER	5	33%
JANUARY	2	13%
FEBRUARY	8	44%
MARCH	2	13%
APRIL	13	87%
MAY	0	0%

KEY PLAYERS - GOALSCORERS

Adebayo Akinfenwa

Goals in the League	14	Player Strike Rate Average number of minutes between League goals scored by player	190
Contribution to Attacking Power Average number of minutes between League team goals while on pitch	70	Club Strike Rate Average number of minutes between League goals scored by club	75

	PLAYER	LGE GOALS	GOALS ALL	POWER	STRIKE RATE
1	Adebayo Akinfenwa	14	14	70	190 mins
2	Leon Constantine	9	9	68	237 mins
3	Jo Osei-Kuffour	6	7	78	404 mins
4	Kevin Hill	5	5	73	664 mins
5	Martin Phillips	2	2	76	844 mins

KEY PLAYERS - MIDFIELDERS

Anthony Bedeau

Goals in the League	2	Contribution to Attacking Power Average number of minutes between League team goals while on pitch	65
Defensive Rating Average number of mins between League goals conceded while on the pitch	53	Scoring Difference Defensive Rating minus Contribution to Attacking Power	-12

	PLAYER	LGE GOALS	GOALS ALL	DEF RATE	POWER	SCORE DIFF
1	Anthony Bedeau	2	2	53	65	-12 mins
2	Alex Russell	3	3	54	72	-18 mins
3	Martin Phillips	2	2	53	77	-24 mins
4	Kevin Hill	5	5	49	74	-25 mins
5	Matt Hockley	1	1	60	104	-44 mins

KEY PLAYERS - DEFENDERS

Stephen Woods

Goals Conceded Number of League goals conceded while the player was on the pitch	57	Clean Sheets In games when player was on pitch for at least 70 minutes	7
Defensive Rating Ave number of mins between League goals conceded while on the pitch	57	Club Defensive Rating Average number of mins between League goals conceded while on the pitch	52

	PLAYER	CON LGE	CON ALL	CLEAN SHEETS	DEF RATE
1	Stephen Woods	57	61	7	57 mins
2	Craig Taylor	54	56	7	57 mins
3	Craig Woodman	32	32	4	56 mins
4	Paul Robinson	20	20	1	54 mins
5	Brian McGlinchey	56	62	4	49 mins

KEY GOALKEEPER

Olafur Gottskalksson

Goals Conceded in the League	23	Counting Games In games when player was on pitch for at least 70 minutes	15
Defensive Rating Ave number of mins between League goals conceded while on the pitch	59	Clean Sheets In games when player was on pitch for at least 70 minutes	2

LEAGUE GOALS

Adebayo Akinfenwa

Minutes on the pitch	2662	League average (mins between goals)	190
Goals in the League	14		

	PLAYER	MINS	GOALS	AVE
1	Akinfenwa	2662	14	190
2	Constantine	2136	9	237
3	Osei-Kuffour	2421	6	404
4	Gritton	1257	6	210
5	Hill	3319	5	664
6	Russell	3251	3	1084
7	Wardley	508	2	254
8	Woods	3233	2	1617
9	Phillips	1688	2	844
10	Bedeau	2868	2	1434
11	Abbey	245	1	245
13	Gosling	475	1	475
	Other		2	
	TOTAL		55	

DISCIPLINARY RECORDS

	PLAYER	YELLOW	RED	AVE
1	Robinson, P	6	0	180
2	Gosling	2	0	237
3	Hockley	6	0	310
4	Hill	10	0	331
5	Taylor	7	2	340
6	Garner	2	0	358
7	Bedeau	7	0	409
8	McGlinchey	6	0	459
9	Meirelles	1	0	507
10	Woodman	3	0	594
11	Canoville	4	0	634
12	Russell	5	0	650
13	Woods	4	0	808
	Other	5	0	
	TOTAL	68	2	

TOP POINT EARNERS

	PLAYER	GAMES	AV PTS
1	Phillips	13	1.69
2	Constantine	22	1.68
3	Taylor	33	1.33
4	Hockley	16	1.31
5	Russell	35	1.29
6	Woodman	19	1.21
7	Robinson, P	12	1.17
8	Bedeau	30	1.17
9	Hill	36	1.08
10	Woods	36	1.08
	CLUB AVERAGE:		1.11

TEAM OF THE SEASON

D
Craig Taylor
CG: 33 DR: 57
M
Anthony Bedeau
CG: 30 SD: -12
D
Stephen Woods
CG: 36 DR: 57
M
Alex Russell
CG: 35 SD: -18
F
Adebayo Akinfenwa
CG: 25 SR: 190
G
Olafur Gottskalksson
CG: 15 DR: 59
D
Craig Woodman
CG: 19 DR: 56
M
Martin Phillips
CG: 13 SD: -24
F
Leon Constantine
CG: 22 SR: 237
D
Paul Robinson
CG: 12 DR: 54
M
Kevin Hill
CG: 36 SD: -25

LEAGUE APPEARANCES GOALS AND BOOKINGS

	AGE (on 01/07/05)	IN NAMED 16	APPEARANCES	COUNTING GAMES	MINUTES ON PITCH	LEAGUE GOALS	Yellow	Red
Goalkeepers								
Philip Barnes	26	5	5	5	450	0	0	0
Bertrand Bossu	24	2	2	2	180	0	0	0
Kevin Dearden	35	14	5	5	450	0	0	0
Olafur Gottskalksson	37	17	15	15	1350	0	0	0
Paul Jarvie	23	10	1	1	90	0	0	0
Andy Marriott	34	11	11	11	990	0	0	0
Arjan Van Heusden	32	11	7	7	630	0	0	0
Defenders								
Lee Canoville	24	36	31	27	2539	0	4	0
Brian McGlinchey	27	34	33	30	2756	0	6	0
Gareth Owen	22	10	4	2	216	0	1	0
Paul Robinson	23	12	12	12	1080	0	6	0
Craig Taylor	31	36	36	33	3060	0	7	2
Matthew Villis	21	39	22	12	1286	0	0	0
Craig Woodman	22	25	22	19	1784	1	3	0
Stephen Woods	28	36	36	36	3233	2	4	0
Midfielders								
Anthony Bedeau	26	37	35	30	2868	2	7	0
Stuart Boardley	20	17	6	2	217	0	0	0
Aaron Brown	25	5	5	3	367	0	1	0
Jason Fowler	30	14	12	3	524	0	0	0
Darren Garner	33	9	9	7	716	0	2	0
Jamie Gosling	29	8	7	3	475	1	2	0
Kevin Hill	29	39	39	36	3319	5	10	0
Matt Hockley	23	41	34	16	1865	1	6	0
Osvaldo Lopes	25	1	1	1	77	0	0	0
Bruno Meirelles	23	11	9	4	507	0	1	0
Martin Phillips	29	43	29	13	1688	2	1	0
Anthony Pulis	20	8	3	1	111	0	0	0
Alex Russell	32	38	38	35	3251	3	5	0
Nick Skinner	19	9	0	0	0	0	0	0
Stuart Wardley	30	7	7	5	508	2	0	0
Forwards								
Zema Abbey	28	10	6	1	245	1	0	0
Adebayo Akinfenwa	23	40	37	25	2662	14	2	0
Leon Constantine	27	27	27	22	2136	9	1	0
Martin Gritton	27	20	18	11	1257	6	1	0
Stuart Noble	21	3	3	1	150	0	0	0
Jo Osei-Kuffour	23	40	34	21	2421	6	0	0
Owen Story	20	5	2	0	22	0	0	0
Kevin Wills	24	1	0	0	0	0	0	0

SQUAD APPEARANCES

Match	1	2	3	4	5	6	7	8	9	10	11	12	13	14	15	16	17	18	19	20	21	22	23	24	25	26	27	28	29	30	31	32	33	34	35	36	37	38	39	40	41	42	43	44	45	46	47	48
Venue	A	H	H	A	A	H	A	A	H	A	H	A	H	A	H	A	H	A	A	H	H	A	H	A	A	H	H	A	A	H	A	H	A	H	H	A	A	H	A	H	A	H	A	H	H	A	H	A
Competition	L	L	L	L	W	L	L	L	L	L	L	L	L	L	L	L	L	F	L	L	L	L	L	L	L	L	L	L	L	L	L	L	L	L	L	L	L	L	L	L	L	L	L	L	L	L	L	L
Result	D	L	L	L	L	D	L	W	D	L	L	D	W	D	L	D	W	L	W	W	L	L	L	D	W	D	L	L	D	L	D	W	D	W	D	L	L	D	L	L	D	L	D	W	W	W	W	L

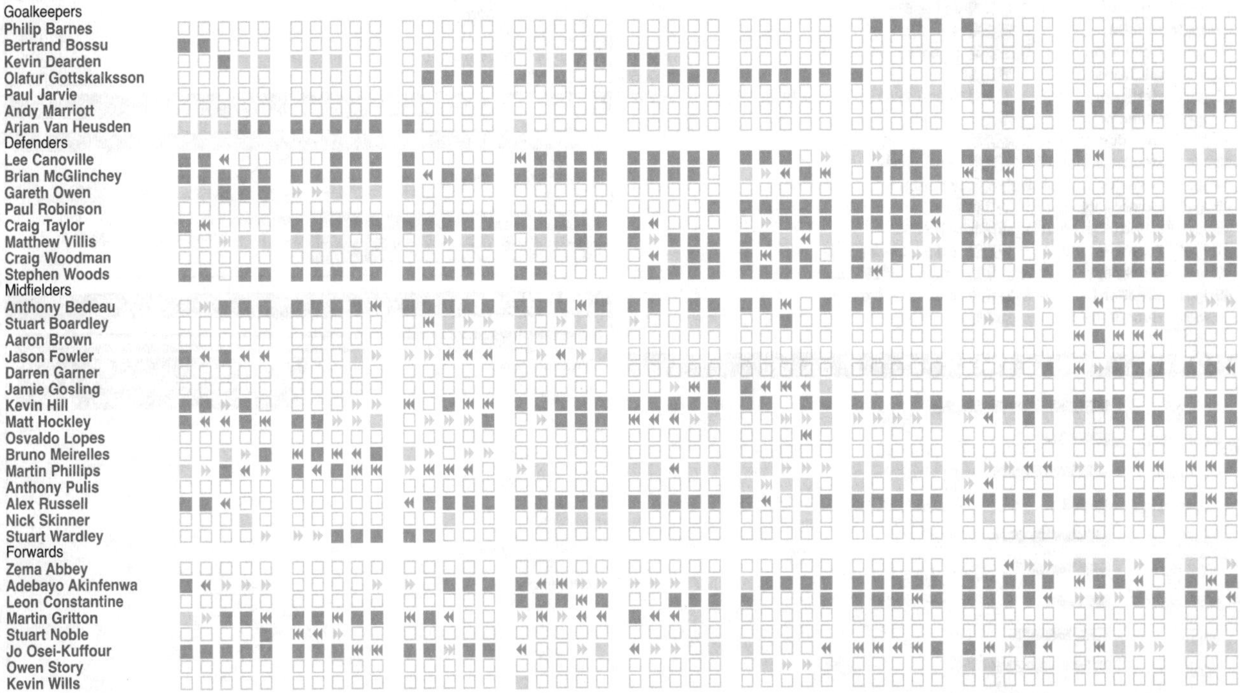
Goalkeepers
Philip Barnes
Bertrand Bossu
Kevin Dearden
Olafur Gottskalksson
Paul Jarvie
Andy Marriott
Arjan Van Heusden
Defenders
Lee Canoville
Brian McGlinchey
Gareth Owen
Paul Robinson
Craig Taylor
Matthew Villis
Craig Woodman
Stephen Woods
Midfielders
Anthony Bedeau
Stuart Boardley
Aaron Brown
Jason Fowler
Darren Garner
Jamie Gosling
Kevin Hill
Matt Hockley
Osvaldo Lopes
Bruno Meirelles
Martin Phillips
Anthony Pulis
Alex Russell
Nick Skinner
Stuart Wardley
Forwards
Zema Abbey
Adebayo Akinfenwa
Leon Constantine
Martin Gritton
Stuart Noble
Jo Osei-Kuffour
Owen Story
Kevin Wills

KEY: On all match / On bench / Subbed or sent off (Counting game) / Subbed or sent off (playing less than 70 minutes) / Subbed on from bench (Counting Game) / Subbed on (playing less than 70 minutes) / Subbed on and then subbed or sent off (Counting Game) / Subbed on and then subbed or sent off (playing less than 70 minutes) / Not in 16

WREXHAM *Deducted 10pts

Final Position: **22nd**

NICKNAME: THE ROBINS

KEY: ☐ Won ☐ Drawn ☐ Lost

							Attendance
1	lge1	Swindon	H	W	2-1	Lawrence 24; Armstrong 73 pen	5,099
2	lge1	Oldham	A	W	3-2	Sam 2,24,62	6,143
3	lge1	Brentford	A	L	0-1		5,091
4	lge1	Port Vale	H	D	1-1	Holt 72	5,005
5	ccR1	Hull City	A	W	2-2*	Sam 14; Ferguson 35 (*aet, won 3-1 on penalties)	6,079
6	lge1	Bournemouth	A	L	0-1		5,774
7	lge1	Barnsley	H	W	2-1	Armstrong 45; Roberts 61	4,223
8	lge1	Bradford	H	W	1-0	Lawrence 2	3,712
9	lge1	Tranmere	A	D	1-1	Armstrong 38	9,826
10	ccR2	Sheff Utd	H	L	2-3	Morgan 6; Llewellyn 45	3,423
11	lge1	Sheff Wed	H	L	0-3		5,688
12	lge1	Doncaster	A	D	0-0		7,567
13	lge1	Walsall	H	D	1-1	Lawrence 16	3,803
14	lge1	Colchester	A	W	2-1	Roberts 59; Llewellyn 90	2,866
15	lge1	Peterborough	H	D	1-1	Lawrence 87	3,009
16	lge1	Hull City	H	D	2-2	Llewellyn 13; Ferguson 29	5,601
17	lge1	Luton	A	L	1-5	Sam 73	7,144
18	lge1	Blackpool	A	L	1-2	Holt 23	5,054
19	facr1	Hayes	A	W	4-0	Holt 17; Lawrence 30; Sam 37; Llewellyn 82	1,751
20	lge1	Bristol City	H	L	1-3	Armstrong 77	7,833
21	lge1	Torquay	A	L	0-1		2,384
22	lge1	Huddersfield	A	W	2-1	Holt 9; Armstrong 50 pen	11,127
23	facr2	Scunthorpe	A	L	0-2		5,698
24	lge1	Stockport	H	W	2-1	Holt 45; Sam 61	3,984
25	lge1	MK Dons	A	L	0-3		3,601
26	lge1	Hartlepool	H	L	1-5	Ugarte 25	3,582
27	lge1	Bradford	A	D	1-1	Armstrong 90 pen	10,268
28	lge1	Chesterfield	H	W	3-1	Roberts 14; Jones, Ma 36; Llewellyn 61	4,273
29	lge1	Blackpool	H	L	1-2	Llewellyn 18	5,601
30	lge1	Sheff Wed	A	L	0-4		24,253
31	lge1	Peterborough	A	D	2-2	Ugarte 45; Branston 79 og	3,048
32	lge1	Tranmere	H	L	1-5	Armstrong 67	6,221
33	lge1	Chesterfield	A	W	4-2	Ugarte 45,45,59,64	3,966
34	lge1	Doncaster	H	D	0-0		6,115
35	lge1	Walsall	A	D	2-2	Ferguson 12; Llewellyn 22	5,659
36	lge1	Torquay	H	D	1-1	Ugarte 87	3,608
37	lge1	Hull City	A	L	1-2	Sam 75	15,995
38	lge1	Colchester	H	D	2-2	Jones, Ma 50; Sam 80	2,391
39	lge1	MK Dons	H	D	0-0		3,406
40	lge1	Hartlepool	A	W	6-4	Ugarte 11,21,35 pen,68,89; Jones, Ma 86	4,707
41	lge1	Oldham	H	W	1-0	Sam 90	4,170
42	lge1	Swindon	A	L	2-4	Ugarte 16; Sam 32	5,123
43	lge1	Bournemouth	H	L	1-2	Armstrong 69	3,801
44	lge1	Barnsley	A	D	2-2	Ferguson 58; Llewellyn 64	7,753
45	lge1	Bristol City	A	L	0-1		8,267
46	lge1	Luton	H	L	1-2	Holt 31	6,614
47	lge1	Port Vale	A	W	2-0	Holt 21; Llewellyn 42	4,151
48	lge1	Stockport	A	W	4-1	Ugarte 5,11,29; Edwards 14	5,480
49	lge1	Brentford	H	L	1-2	Hutchinson 6 og	4,374
50	lge1	Huddersfield	H	L	0-1		7,151

MONTHLY POINTS TALLY

AUGUST	10	56%
SEPTEMBER	4	44%
OCTOBER	7	47%
NOVEMBER	3	20%
DECEMBER	7	47%
JANUARY	5	28%
FEBRUARY	4	27%
MARCH	6	67%
APRIL	7	39%
MAY	0	0%

KEY PLAYERS - GOALSCORERS

Juan Ugarte

Goals in the League	16	Player Strike Rate Average number of minutes between League goals scored by player	124
Contribution to Attacking Power Average number of minutes between League team goals while on pitch	55	Club Strike Rate Average number of minutes between League goals scored by club	67

	PLAYER	LGE GOALS	GOALS ALL	POWER	STRIKE RATE
1	Juan Ugarte	16	16	55	124 mins
2	Hector Sam	9	11	73	204 mins
3	Chris Armstrong	8	8	78	226 mins
4	Mark Jones	3	3	65	499 mins
5	Chris Llewellyn	7	9	67	548 mins

KEY PLAYERS - MIDFIELDERS

Danny Williams

Goals in the League	0	Contribution to Attacking Power Average number of minutes between League team goals while on pitch	69
Defensive Rating Average number of mins between League goals conceded while on the pitch	77	Scoring Difference Defensive Rating minus Contribution to Attacking Power	8

	PLAYER	LGE GOALS	GOALS ALL	DEF RATE	POWER	SCORE DIFF
1	Danny Williams	0	0	77	69	8 mins
2	Matt Crowell	0	0	47	50	-3 mins
3	Carlos Edwards	1	1	51	55	-4 mins
4	Mark Jones	3	3	55	65	-10 mins
5	Darren Ferguson	3	4	56	68	-12 mins

KEY PLAYERS - DEFENDERS

Craig Morgan

Goals Conceded Number of League goals conceded while the player was on the pitch	35	Clean Sheets In games when player was on pitch for at least 70 minutes	4
Defensive Rating Ave number of mins between League goals conceded while on the pitch	54	Club Defensive Rating Average number of mins between League goals conceded while on the pitch	52

	PLAYER	CON LGE	CON ALL	CLEAN SHEETS	DEF RATE
1	Craig Morgan	35	39	4	54 mins
2	Dennis Lawrence	73	75	6	52 mins
3	Andy Holt	79	86	5	50 mins
4	Shaun Pejic	57	64	2	48 mins
5	Stephen Roberts	65	67	4	47 mins

KEY GOALKEEPER

Ben Foster

Goals Conceded in the League	26	Counting Games Games when player was on pitch for at least 70 minutes	17
Defensive Rating Ave number of mins between League goals conceded while on the pitch	59	Clean Sheets In games when player was on pitch for at least 70 minutes	4

LEAGUE GOALS

Juan Ugarte

Minutes on the pitch	1984	League average (mins between goals)	124
Goals in the League	16		

	PLAYER	MINS	GOALS	AVE
1	Ugarte	1984	16	124
2	Sam	1833	9	204
3	Llewellyn	3835	7	548
4	Armstrong	1810	8	226
5	Holt	3949	6	658
6	Lawrence	3811	4	953
7	Ferguson	3489	3	1163
8	Jones, Ma	1497	3	499
9	Roberts	3044	3	1015
10	Edwards	1584	1	1584
	Other		2	
	TOTAL		62	

DISCIPLINARY RECORDS

	PLAYER	YELLOW	RED	AVE
1	Armstrong	9	1	181
2	Williams	6	0	308
3	Crowell	6	0	326
4	Carey	2	0	396
5	Llewellyn	9	0	426
6	Ferguson	8	0	436
7	Jones, Ma	3	0	499
8	Morgan	3	0	634
9	Ugarte	3	0	661
10	Roberts	4	0	761
11	Sam	1	1	916
12	Pejic	3	0	919
13	Holt	4	0	987
	Other	5	0	
	TOTAL	66	2	

TOP POINT EARNERS

	PLAYER	GAMES	AV PTS
1	Williams	20	1.40
2	Smith	14	1.36
3	Dibble	14	1.29
4	Sam	14	1.29
5	Ugarte	18	1.28
6	Llewellyn	41	1.27
7	Ferguson	38	1.24
8	Jones, Ma	14	1.21
9	Lawrence	41	1.20
10	Edwards	18	1.17
	CLUB AVERAGE:		0.93

LEAGUE APPEARANCES GOALS AND BOOKINGS

	AGE (on 01/07/05)	IN NAMED 16	APPEARANCES	COUNTING GAMES	MINUTES ON PITCH	LEAGUE GOALS	Yellow	Red
Goalkeepers								
Matthew Baker	25	21	13	11	1036	0	0	0
Andy Dibble	40	18	15	14	1304	0	1	0
Daniel Evans	19	10	0	0	0	0	0	0
Ben Foster	22	17	17	17	1530	0	0	0
Ryan Harrison	18	10	0	0	0	0	0	0
Michael Jones	-	9	1	0	45	0	0	0
Xavi Valero	32	3	3	2	225	0	0	0
Defenders								
Brian Carey	37	10	10	9	793	0	2	0
Andy Holt	27	45	45	43	3949	6	4	0
Dennis Lawrence	31	45	44	41	3811	4	2	0
Craig Morgan	20	32	26	18	1904	0	3	0
Shaun Pejic	22	45	34	29	2757	0	3	0
Stephen Roberts	25	35	35	33	3044	3	4	0
Simon Spender	19	26	13	9	863	0	0	0
Midfielders								
Dean Bennett	27	22	14	8	811	0	0	0
Matt Crowell	20	33	28	20	1958	0	6	0
Matt Done	16	4	0	0	0	0	0	0
Carlos Edwards	26	18	18	18	1584	1	0	0
Darren Ferguson	33	40	40	38	3489	3	8	0
Scott Green	35	15	12	4	561	0	0	0
Mark Jones	21	35	26	14	1497	3	3	0
Levi Mackin	19	16	10	4	439	0	0	0
Matthew Shaw	21	1	1	0	1	0	0	0
Alex Smith	29	35	24	14	1487	0	1	0
Jim Whitley	30	16	16	12	1121	0	1	0
Danny Williams	25	22	21	20	1853	0	6	0
Forwards								
Chris Armstrong	34	35	33	16	1810	8	9	1
Chris Llewellyn	25	45	45	41	3835	7	9	0
Hector Sam	27	43	38	14	1833	9	1	1
Juan Ugarte	24	30	30	18	1984	16	3	0

TEAM OF THE SEASON

D
Craig Morgan
CG: 18 DR: 54
M
Danny Williams
CG: 20 SD: 8
D
Dennis Lawrence
CG: 41 DR: 52
M
Matt Crowell
CG: 20 SD: -3
F
Juan Ugarte
CG: 18 SR: 124
G
Ben Foster
CG: 17 DR: 59
D
Andy Holt
CG: 43 DR: 50
M
Carlos Edwards
CG: 18 SD: -4
F
Hector Sam
CG: 14 SR: 204
D
Shaun Pejic
CG: 29 DR: 48
M
Mark Jones
CG: 14 SD: -10

SQUAD APPEARANCES

Match	1	2	3	4	5	6	7	8	9	10	11	12	13	14	15	16	17	18	19	20	21	22	23	24	25
Venue	H	A	A	H	A	A	H	H	A	H	H	A	H	A	H	H	A	A	A	H	A	A	A	H	A
Competition	L	L	L	L	W	L	L	L	L	W	L	L	L	L	L	L	L	L	F	L	L	L	F	L	L
Result	W	W	L	D	W	L	W	W	D	L	L	D	D	W	D	D	L	L	W	L	L	W	L	W	L

Match	26	27	28	29	30	31	32	33	34	35	36	37	38	39	40	41	42	43	44	45	46	47	48	49	50
Venue	H	A	H	H	A	A	H	A	H	A	H	A	H	H	A	H	A	H	A	A	H	A	A	H	H
Competition	L	L	L	L	L	L	L	L	L	L	L	L	L	L	L	L	L	L	L	L	L	L	L	L	L
Result	L	D	W	L	L	D	L	W	D	D	D	L	D	D	W	W	L	L	D	L	L	W	W	L	L

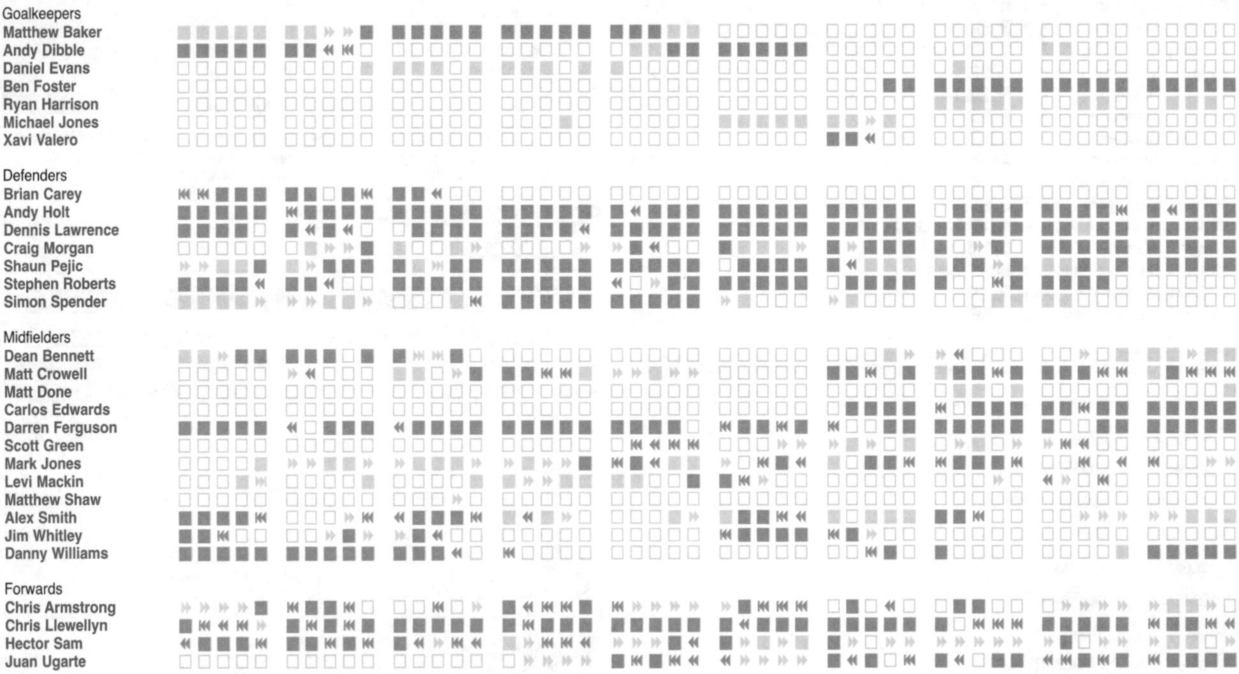
Goalkeepers
Matthew Baker
Andy Dibble
Daniel Evans
Ben Foster
Ryan Harrison
Michael Jones
Xavi Valero
Defenders
Brian Carey
Andy Holt
Dennis Lawrence
Craig Morgan
Shaun Pejic
Stephen Roberts
Simon Spender
Midfielders
Dean Bennett
Matt Crowell
Matt Done
Carlos Edwards
Darren Ferguson
Scott Green
Mark Jones
Levi Mackin
Matthew Shaw
Alex Smith
Jim Whitley
Danny Williams
Forwards
Chris Armstrong
Chris Llewellyn
Hector Sam
Juan Ugarte

KEY: On all match; On bench; Subbed or sent off (Counting game); Subbed or sent off (playing less than 70 minutes); Subbed on from bench (Counting Game); Subbed on (playing less than 70 minutes); Subbed on and then subbed or sent off (Counting Game); Subbed on and then subbed or sent off (playing less than 70 minutes); Not in 16

PETERBOROUGH UNITED

Final Position: **23th**

NICKNAME: THE POSH

KEY: ☐Won ☐Drawn ☐Lost

							Attendance
1	lge1	**Tranmere**	H	W	1-0	Burton 80	5,390
2	lge1	**Bradford**	A	D	2-2	Platt 20; Kennedy 56	6,929
3	lge1	**Colchester**	A	L	1-2	Farrell 10	3,754
4	lge1	**Brentford**	H	W	3-0	Platt 20; Legg 46; Clarke 53	4,868
5	ccR1	**MK Dons**	H	L	0-3		2,886
6	lge1	**Huddersfield**	A	L	1-2	Woodhouse 45 pen	9,531
7	lge1	**Blackpool**	H	D	0-0		4,142
8	lge1	**Bristol City**	H	L	0-1		4,227
9	lge1	**Swindon**	A	W	1-0	Jenkins 34	5,777
10	lge1	**Hull City**	H	L	2-3	Willock 2; Clarke 90	5,745
11	lge1	**Luton**	A	L	1-2	Woodhouse 48	7,694
12	lge1	**Torquay**	H	D	1-1	Clarke 42	3,828
13	lge1	**Stockport**	A	L	0-1		4,119
14	lge1	**Sheff Wed**	H	D	1-1	Platt 21	5,875
15	lge1	**Hartlepool**	H	W	3-0	Kennedy 15; Willock 18; Legg 55	3,841
16	lge1	**Wrexham**	A	D	1-1	Willock 69	3,009
17	lge1	**Doncaster**	A	L	1-2	Platt 27	6,039
18	lge1	**Bournemouth**	H	L	0-1		4,004
19	facr1	**Tranmere**	H	W	2-1	Kennedy 10; Woodhouse 89	2,940
20	lge1	**Walsall**	A	L	1-2	Purser 11	5,465
21	lge1	**Port Vale**	H	W	4-0	Purser 36; Farrell 62; Boucaud 69; Woodhouse 83 pen	3,785
22	facr2	**Bath City**	H	W	2-0	Willock 36,41	4,187
23	lge1	**MK Dons**	A	D	1-1	Constantine 26	3,913
24	lge1	**Chesterfield**	H	L	1-2	Woodhouse 76	3,865
25	lge1	**Barnsley**	A	L	0-4		8,536
26	lge1	**Swindon**	H	L	0-2		4,212
27	lge1	**Oldham**	A	L	1-2	Logan 48	5,618
28	lge1	**Bristol City**	A	L	0-2		10,873
29	lge1	**Luton**	H	D	2-2	Willock 73,82	7,662
30	facr3	**MK Dons**	A	W	2-0	Logan 45; Arber 57	4,407
31	lge1	**Wrexham**	H	D	2-2	Willock 2; Branston 12	3,048
32	lge1	**Hull City**	A	D	2-2	Thomson 26; Willock 90	16,149
33	lge1	**Oldham**	H	L	1-2	Legg 20	4,047
34	facr4	**Nottm Forest**	A	L	0-1		16,774
35	lge1	**Stockport**	H	W	2-1	Willock 24; Logan 60	3,719
36	lge1	**Torquay**	A	L	1-2	Willock 64	2,769
37	lge1	**Doncaster**	H	L	0-2		4,983
38	lge1	**Sheff Wed**	A	L	1-2	Purser 21	19,648
39	lge1	**Chesterfield**	A	W	3-1	Logan 12; Purser 14,62	3,715
40	lge1	**Barnsley**	H	L	1-3	Legg 73	3,485
41	lge1	**Bradford**	H	D	2-2	Thomson 28; Legg 31	3,472
42	lge1	**Tranmere**	A	L	0-5		8,401
43	lge1	**Colchester**	H	L	0-3		4,084
44	lge1	**Brentford**	A	D	0-0		6,341
45	lge1	**Huddersfield**	H	L	1-2	Purser 45	3,976
46	lge1	**Hartlepool**	A	D	2-2	Logan 49; Willock 56	4,579
47	lge1	**Blackpool**	A	W	1-0	Willock 42	5,090
48	lge1	**Walsall**	H	L	0-2		3,841
49	lge1	**Bournemouth**	A	W	1-0	Willock 17	7,929
50	lge1	**MK Dons**	H	L	0-3		3,742
51	lge1	**Port Vale**	A	L	0-1		4,815

MONTHLY POINTS TALLY

AUGUST	8	44%
SEPTEMBER	3	25%
OCTOBER	6	33%
NOVEMBER	3	33%
DECEMBER	1	7%
JANUARY	3	20%
FEBRUARY	6	40%
MARCH	2	13%
APRIL	7	39%
MAY	0	0%

KEY PLAYERS - GOALSCORERS

Callum Willock

Goals in the League	12	Player Strike Rate Average number of minutes between League goals scored by player	192
Contribution to Attacking Power Average number of minutes between League team goals while on pitch	72	Club Strike Rate Average number of minutes between League goals scored by club	84

	PLAYER	LGE GOALS	GOALS ALL	POWER	STRIKE RATE
1	Callum Willock	12	14	72	192 mins
2	Clive Platt	4	4	93	372 mins
3	Andy Legg	5	5	75	633 mins
4	Curtis Woodhouse	4	5	91	724 mins
5	Dave Farrell	2	2	74	1001 mins

KEY PLAYERS - MIDFIELDERS

Dave Farrell

Goals in the League	2	Contribution to Attacking Power Average number of minutes between League team goals while on pitch	74
Defensive Rating Average number of mins between League goals conceded while on the pitch	65	Scoring Difference Defensive Rating minus Contribution to Attacking Power	-9

	PLAYER	LGE GOALS	GOALS ALL	DEF RATE	POWER	SCORE DIFF
1	Dave Farrell	2	2	65	74	-9 mins
2	Andy Legg	5	5	57	75	-18 mins
3	Stephen Thomson	2	2	54	80	-26 mins
4	Curtis Woodhouse	4	5	58	91	-33 mins

KEY PLAYERS - DEFENDERS

Sagi Burton

Goals Conceded Number of League goals conceded while the player was on the pitch	19	Clean Sheets In games when player was on pitch for at least 70 minutes	3
Defensive Rating Ave number of mins between League goals conceded while on the pitch	72	Club Defensive Rating Average number of mins between League goals conceded while on the pitch	57

	PLAYER	CON LGE	CON ALL	CLEAN SHEETS	DEF RATE
1	Sagi Burton	19	21	3	72 mins
2	Simon Rea	18	21	3	65 mins
3	Adam Newton	42	43	5	59 mins
4	Craig Ireland	36	39	5	55 mins
5	Sean St Ledger-Hall	58	60	4	51 mins

KEY GOALKEEPER

Mark Tyler

Goals Conceded in the League	73	Counting Games Games when player was on pitch for at least 70 minutes	46
Defensive Rating Ave number of mins between League goals conceded while on the pitch	57	Clean Sheets In games when player was on pitch for at least 70 minutes	9

LEAGUE GOALS

Callum Willock

Minutes on the pitch	2306	League average (mins between goals)	192
Goals in the League	12		

	PLAYER	MINS	GOALS	AVE
1	Willock	2306	12	192
2	Purser	1438	6	240
3	Logan	1453	4	363
4	Woodhouse	2896	4	724
5	Legg	3164	5	633
6	Platt	1488	4	372
7	Kennedy	1204	2	602
8	Clarke, A	1474	3	491
9	Thomson	2548	2	1274
10	Farrell	2002	2	1001
11	Branston	331	1	331
12	Constantine	495	1	495
	Other		3	
	TOTAL		49	

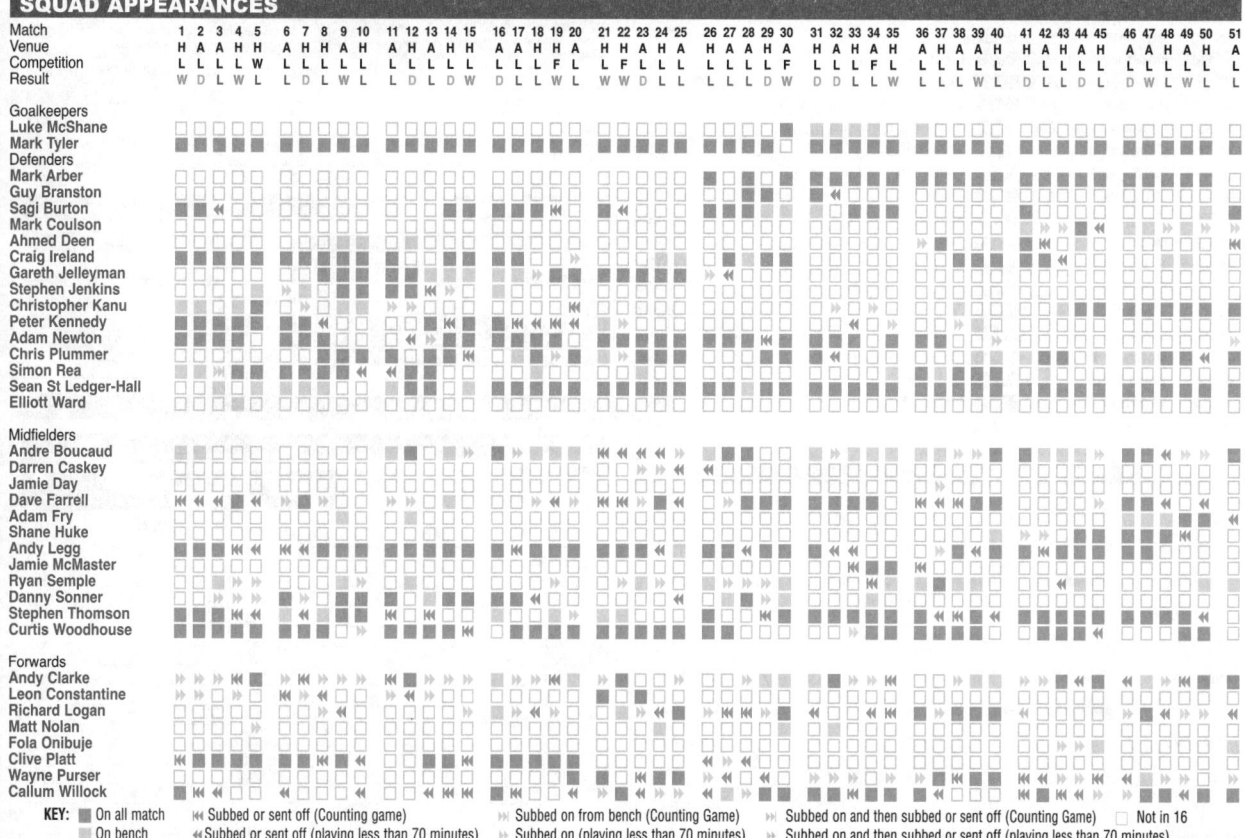

DISCIPLINARY RECORDS

	PLAYER	YELLOW	RED	AVE
1	Jenkins	2	0	242
2	Huke	2	0	273
3	Woodhouse	10	0	289
4	Plummer	4	1	359
5	Rea	3	0	390
6	Ireland	5	0	396
7	Kanu	2	0	444
8	Burton	3	0	454
9	Farrell	4	0	500
10	Newton	4	0	621
11	Boucaud	2	0	639
12	Clarke, A	2	0	737
13	Legg	3	1	791
	Other	10	0	
	TOTAL	56	2	

TOP POINT EARNERS

	PLAYER	GAMES	AV PTS
1	Farrell	16	1.25
2	Thomson	26	1.08
3	Platt	15	1.07
4	Burton	15	1.07
5	Ireland	21	1.00
6	Willock	19	1.00
7	Rea	12	0.92
8	Newton	26	0.88
9	Legg	32	0.88
10	Woodhouse	31	0.87
	CLUB AVERAGE:		0.85

TEAM OF THE SEASON

G — Mark Tyler, CG: 46 DR: 57

D — Sagi Burton, CG: 15 DR: 72
D — Simon Rea, CG: 12 DR: 65
D — Adam Newton, CG: 26 DR: 59
D — Craig Ireland, CG: 21 DR: 55

M — Dave Farrell, CG: 16 SD: -9
M — Andy Legg, CG: 32 SD: -18
M — Stephen Thomson, CG: 26 SD: -26
M — Curtis Woodhouse, CG: 31 SD: -33

F — Callum Willock, CG: 19 SR: 192
F — Clive Platt, CG: 15 SR: 372

LEAGUE APPEARANCES GOALS AND BOOKINGS

	AGE (on 01/07/05)	IN NAMED 16	APPEARANCES	COUNTING GAMES	MINUTES ON PITCH	LEAGUE GOALS	Yellow cards	Red cards
Goalkeepers								
Luke McShane	19	4	0	0	0	0	0	0
Mark Tyler	28	46	46	46	4140	0	0	0
Defenders								
Mark Arber	27	21	21	21	1890	0	1	0
Guy Branston	26	4	4	3	331	1	0	0
Sagi Burton	27	19	16	15	1364	1	3	0
Mark Coulson	19	11	7	1	305	0	0	0
Ahmed Deen	20	10	5	3	330	0	0	0
Craig Ireland	29	28	23	21	1980	0	5	0
Gareth Jelleyman	24	18	13	10	1032	0	0	0
Stephen Jenkins	32	9	7	5	485	1	2	0
Christopher Kanu	25	20	13	8	889	0	2	0
Peter Kennedy	31	19	17	11	1204	2	1	0
Adam Newton	24	30	30	26	2484	0	4	0
Chris Plummer	28	29	21	19	1799	0	4	1
Simon Rea	28	21	14	12	1170	0	3	0
Sean St Ledger-Hall	20	40	33	33	2970	0	3	0
Elliott Ward	20	1	0	0	0	0	0	0
Midfielders								
Andre Boucaud	20	37	22	10	1279	1	2	0
Darren Caskey	30	4	4	0	206	0	1	0
Jamie Day	20	1	1	0	27	0	0	0
Dave Farrell	33	32	31	16	2002	2	4	0
Adam Fry	20	8	3	2	246	0	1	0
Shane Huke	19	9	8	6	547	0	2	0
Andy Legg	38	40	39	32	3164	5	3	1
Jamie McMaster	22	3	3	3	251	0	0	0
Ryan Semple	20	20	8	1	240	0	0	0
Danny Sonner	33	17	15	9	988	0	1	0
Stephen Thomson	27	35	31	26	2548	2	2	0
Curtis Woodhouse	25	34	34	31	2896	4	10	0
Forwards								
Andy Clarke	37	40	33	10	1474	3	2	0
Leon Constantine	27	11	11	3	495	1	0	0
Richard Logan	23	27	26	9	1453	4	1	0
Matt Nolan	23	2	0	0	0	0	0	0
Fola Onibuje	20	4	2	0	49	0	1	0
Clive Platt	27	19	19	15	1488	4	0	0
Wayne Purser	25	27	26	11	1438	6	0	0
Callum Willock	23	36	35	19	2306	12	1	0

SQUAD APPEARANCES

Match	1	2	3	4	5	6	7	8	9	10	11	12	13	14	15	16	17	18	19	20	21	22	23	24	25	26	27	28	29	30	31	32	33	34	35	36	37	38	39	40	41	42	43	44	45	46	47	48	49	50	51
Venue	H	A	A	H	H	A	H	H	A	H	A	H	A	H	H	A	A	H	H	A	H	H	A	H	A	H	A	A	H	A	H	A	H	A	H	A	H	A	A	H	H	A	H	A	H	A	A	H	A	H	A
Competition	L	L	L	L	W	L	L	L	L	L	L	L	L	L	L	L	L	L	F	L	L	F	L	L	L	L	L	L	L	F	L	L	L	F	L	L	L	L	L	L	L	L	L	L	L	L	L	L	L	L	L
Result	W	D	L	W	L	L	D	L	W	L	L	D	L	D	W	D	L	L	W	L	W	W	D	L	L	L	L	L	D	W	D	D	L	L	W	L	L	L	W	L	D	L	L	D	L	D	W	L	W	L	L

Goalkeepers
Luke McShane
Mark Tyler
Defenders
Mark Arber
Guy Branston
Sagi Burton
Mark Coulson
Ahmed Deen
Craig Ireland
Gareth Jelleyman
Stephen Jenkins
Christopher Kanu
Peter Kennedy
Adam Newton
Chris Plummer
Simon Rea
Sean St Ledger-Hall
Elliott Ward

Midfielders
Andre Boucaud
Darren Caskey
Jamie Day
Dave Farrell
Adam Fry
Shane Huke
Andy Legg
Jamie McMaster
Ryan Semple
Danny Sonner
Stephen Thomson
Curtis Woodhouse

Forwards
Andy Clarke
Leon Constantine
Richard Logan
Matt Nolan
Fola Onibuje
Clive Platt
Wayne Purser
Callum Willock

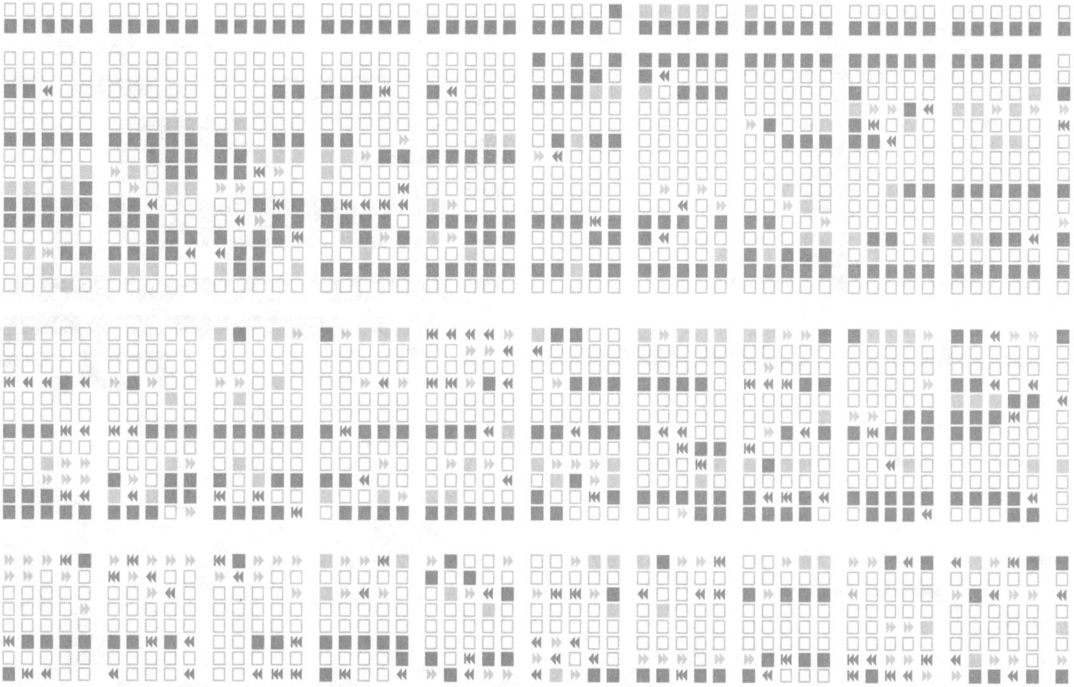

KEY: On all match; On bench; Subbed or sent off (Counting game); Subbed or sent off (playing less than 70 minutes); Subbed on from bench (Counting Game); Subbed on (playing less than 70 minutes); Subbed on and then subbed or sent off (Counting Game); Subbed on and then subbed or sent off (playing less than 70 minutes); Not in 16

STOCKPORT COUNTY

Final Position: **24th**

NICKNAME: COUNTY

KEY: Won / Drawn / Lost

							Attendance
1	lge1	**Huddersfield**	H	L	2-3	Beckett 57; Feeney 68	7,473
2	lge1	**Colchester**	A	L	2-3	Cartwright 66; Beckett 79	3,346
3	lge1	**Blackpool**	A	W	4-0	Jackman 10; Feeney 31; Beckett 50,64	6,334
4	lge1	**Bradford**	H	L	0-1		5,338
5	ccr1	**Sheff Utd**	A	L	1-4	Harley 2 og	5,399
6	lge1	**Brentford**	A	L	0-3		4,643
7	lge1	**Tranmere**	H	D	1-1	Feeney 81	5,502
8	lge1	**Torquay**	H	L	0-2		4,372
9	lge1	**Bristol City**	A	L	0-5		10,811
10	lge1	**Luton**	H	L	1-3	Lambert 80	5,128
11	lge1	**Hull City**	A	D	0-0		16,182
12	lge1	**Swindon**	H	D	3-3	Beckett 72,80; Barlow 83	4,394
13	lge1	**Bournemouth**	A	L	1-2	Feeney 85	6,925
14	lge1	**Peterborough**	H	W	1-0	Beckett 64	4,119
15	lge1	**Chesterfield**	A	L	0-4		4,567
16	lge1	**Port Vale**	A	D	0-0		5,025
17	lge1	**Oldham**	H	L	1-2	Bridge-Wilkinson 43	6,146
18	lge1	**Sheff Wed**	H	L	0-3		7,222
19	facr1	**Huddersfield**	H	W	3-1	Williams, A 8; Feeney 19,45	3,479
20	lge1	**Doncaster**	A	L	1-3	Feeney 50	6,697
21	lge1	**Walsall**	H	L	0-1		4,448
22	facr2	**Swansea**	H	D	0-0		2,680
23	lge1	**Wrexham**	A	L	1-2	Bridge-Wilkinson 17	3,984
24	lge1	**Hartlepool**	A	L	1-3	Daly 26	4,572
25	facr2r	**Swansea**	A	L	1-2	Griffin 72	5,572
26	lge1	**MK Dons**	H	W	3-1	Daly 1,41; Williams, A 87	3,902
27	lge1	**Bristol City**	H	L	1-2	Feeney 19	5,071
28	lge1	**Barnsley**	A	D	3-3	Feeney 60; Barlow 73; Lambert 81	10,236
29	lge1	**Torquay**	A	W	2-1	Lambert 47,89 pen	3,456
30	lge1	**Hull City**	H	L	1-3	Adams 24	6,670
31	lge1	**Luton**	A	L	0-3		6,603
32	lge1	**Barnsley**	H	D	2-2	Briggs 5; Feeney 90 pen	5,326
33	lge1	**Swindon**	A	L	0-3		5,090
34	lge1	**Bournemouth**	H	D	2-2	Armstrong 26; Dolan 78	3,850
35	lge1	**Peterborough**	A	L	1-2	Jackman 49	3,719
36	lge1	**Port Vale**	H	L	1-2	Le Fondre 88	4,587
37	lge1	**Oldham**	A	W	2-1	Hurst 37; Feeney 60	5,924
38	lge1	**Chesterfield**	H	L	1-2	Feeney 45	4,201
39	lge1	**Hartlepool**	H	W	1-0	Feeney 19	4,548
40	lge1	**MK Dons**	A	L	1-2	Briggs 74	4,146
41	lge1	**Colchester**	H	L	1-2	Feeney 4	4,004
42	lge1	**Huddersfield**	A	L	3-5	Feeney 2,57 pen,65	11,180
43	lge1	**Bradford**	A	L	1-3	Le Fondre 40	7,263
44	lge1	**Brentford**	H	L	1-2	Le Fondre 80 pen	4,408
45	lge1	**Tranmere**	A	L	0-1		8,757
46	lge1	**Blackpool**	H	L	0-1		4,302
47	lge1	**Doncaster**	H	L	2-4	Allen 28; Le Fondre 45	4,508
48	lge1	**Sheff Wed**	A	D	0-0		22,331
49	lge1	**Wrexham**	H	L	1-4	Barlow 27	5,480
50	lge1	**Walsall**	A	L	0-3		6,971

MONTHLY POINTS TALLY

AUGUST	4	22%
SEPTEMBER	1	8%
OCTOBER	5	28%
NOVEMBER	0	0%
DECEMBER	4	27%
JANUARY	4	27%
FEBRUARY	7	39%
MARCH	0	0%
APRIL	1	6%
MAY	0	0%

KEY PLAYERS - GOALSCORERS

Warren Feeney

Goals in the League	15	Player Strike Rate Average number of minutes between League goals scored by player	179
Contribution to Attacking Power Average number of minutes between League team goals while on pitch	72	Club Strike Rate Average number of minutes between League goals scored by club	84

	PLAYER	LGE GOALS	GOALS ALL	POWER	STRIKE RATE
1	Warren Feeney	15	17	72	179 mins
2	Luke Beckett	7	7	84	193 mins
3	Rickie Lambert	4	4	82	592 mins
4	Keith Briggs	2	2	96	628 mins
5	Marc Bridge-Wilkinson	2	2	82	782 mins

KEY PLAYERS - MIDFIELDERS

Mark Robertson

Goals in the League	0	Contribution to Attacking Power Average number of minutes between League team goals while on pitch	74
Defensive Rating Average number of mins between League goals conceded while on the pitch	51	Scoring Difference Defensive Rating minus Contribution to Attacking Power	-23

	PLAYER	LGE GOALS	GOALS ALL	DEF RATE	POWER	SCORE DIFF
1	Mark Robertson	0	0	51	74	-23 mins
2	Rickie Lambert	4	4	44	82	-38 mins
3	Marc Bridge-Wilkinson	2	2	42	82	-40 mins
4	Kevan Hurst	1	1	45	87	-42 mins
5	Damien Allen	1	1	36	83	-47 mins

KEY PLAYERS - DEFENDERS

Keith Briggs

Goals Conceded Number of League goals conceded while the player was on the pitch	26	Clean Sheets In games when player was on pitch for at least 70 minutes	2
Defensive Rating Ave number of mins between League goals conceded while on the pitch	48	Club Defensive Rating Average number of mins between League goals conceded while on the pitch	42

	PLAYER	CON LGE	CON ALL	CLEAN SHEETS	DEF RATE
1	Keith Briggs	26	26	2	48 mins
2	Daniel Griffin	31	34	3	44 mins
3	Daniel Adams	55	60	4	44 mins
4	John Hardiker	51	58	3	44 mins
5	Ashley Williams	95	102	6	42 mins

KEY GOALKEEPER

James Spencer

Goals Conceded in the League	50	Counting Games Games when player was on pitch for at least 70 minutes	24
Defensive Rating Ave number of mins between League goals conceded while on the pitch	43	Clean Sheets In games when player was on pitch for at least 70 minutes	3

LEAGUE GOALS

Warren Feeney

Minutes on the pitch	2686	League average (mins between goals)	179
Goals in the League	15		

	PLAYER	MINS	GOALS	AVE
1	Feeney	2686	15	179
2	Beckett	1350	7	193
3	Le Fondre	1154	4	289
4	Lambert	2368	4	592
5	Daly	911	3	304
6	Barlow	1261	3	420
7	Jackman	2185	2	1093
8	Briggs	1255	2	628
9	Bridge-Wilkinson	1564	2	782
10	Armstrong	757	1	757
11	Cartwright	1595	1	1595
12	Williams, A	3946	1	3946
	Other		4	
	TOTAL		49	

DISCIPLINARY RECORDS

	PLAYER	YELLOW	RED	AVE
1	Mair	7	0	132
2	Briggs	5	0	251
3	Goodwin	10	0	279
4	Hardiker	6	1	317
5	Adams	7	0	343
6	Geary	3	0	373
7	Horwood	2	0	417
8	Barlow	3	0	420
9	Lambert	5	0	473
10	Robertson	3	0	495
11	Le Fondre	2	0	577
12	Griffin	2	0	675
13	Williams, A	5	0	789
	Other	9	0	
	TOTAL	69	1	

TOP POINT EARNERS

	PLAYER	GAMES	AV PTS
1	Griffin	14	0.93
2	Robertson	14	0.79
3	Hardiker	22	0.77
4	Feeney	30	0.77
5	Lambert	25	0.72
6	Cutler	22	0.68
7	Geary	12	0.67
8	Briggs	12	0.67
9	Beckett	15	0.67
10	Bridge-Wilkinson	15	0.67
	CLUB AVERAGE:		0.57

TEAM OF THE SEASON

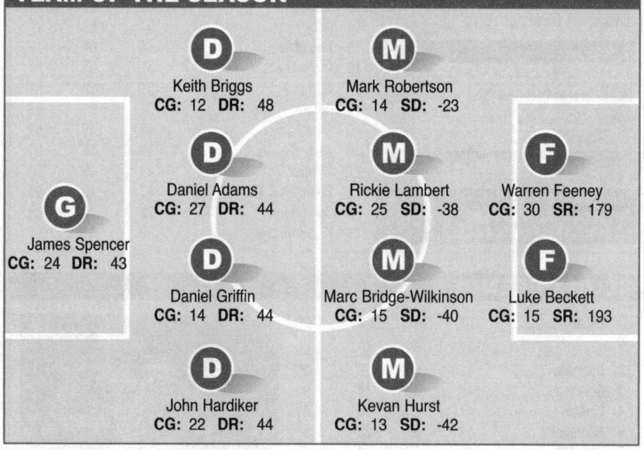
D
Keith Briggs
CG: 12 DR: 48
M
Mark Robertson
CG: 14 SD: -23
D
Daniel Adams
CG: 27 DR: 44
M
Rickie Lambert
CG: 25 SD: -38
F
Warren Feeney
CG: 30 SR: 179
G
James Spencer
CG: 24 DR: 43
D
Daniel Griffin
CG: 14 DR: 44
M
Marc Bridge-Wilkinson
CG: 15 SD: -40
F
Luke Beckett
CG: 15 SR: 193
D
John Hardiker
CG: 22 DR: 44
M
Kevan Hurst
CG: 13 SD: -42

LEAGUE APPEARANCES GOALS AND BOOKINGS

	AGE (on 01/07/05)	IN NAMED 16	APPEARANCES	COUNTING GAMES	MINUTES ON PITCH	LEAGUE GOALS	Yellow	Red
Goalkeepers								
Neil Cutler	28	42	22	22	1980	0	2	0
Sam McEwen	18	1	0	0	0	0	0	0
James Spencer	20	35	24	24	2160	0	0	0
Defenders								
Daniel Adams	29	28	27	27	2404	1	7	0
Keith Briggs	23	16	16	12	1255	2	5	0
Liam Brownhill	18	1	0	0	0	0	0	0
Ludovic Dje	26	4	3	1	157	0	0	0
Joe Dolan	25	11	11	11	990	1	0	0
Derek Geary	25	14	13	12	1120	0	3	0
James Goodwin	23	42	36	30	2798	0	10	0
Daniel Griffin	27	17	16	14	1351	0	2	0
John Hardiker	23	35	29	22	2223	0	6	1
Evan Horwood	19	10	10	9	835	0	2	0
Danny Jackman	22	44	33	22	2185	2	2	0
Jamie Kay	-	1	0	0	0	0	0	0
Lee Mair	24	20	14	8	926	0	7	0
Michael Raynes	17	22	19	15	1370	0	0	0
Ashley Williams	20	45	44	44	3946	1	5	0
Midfielders								
Damien Allen	18	26	21	12	1335	1	1	0
Marc Bridge-Wilkinson	26	29	22	15	1564	2	1	0
Lee Cartwright	32	22	19	17	1595	1	0	0
Jordan Hadfield	18	2	1	0	53	0	0	0
Kevan Hurst	19	14	14	13	1213	1	0	0
Rickie Lambert	23	30	29	25	2368	4	5	0
Owen Morrison	23	2	1	0	29	0	0	0
Mark Robertson	28	21	20	14	1486	0	3	0
Harpal Singh	23	6	6	4	424	0	1	0
Ezekeil Tomlinson	-	9	5	1	226	0	0	0
Andrew Welsh	21	15	13	3	614	0	0	0
Forwards								
Chris Armstrong	20	11	11	9	757	1	0	0
Mathew Bailey	19	5	1	0	2	0	0	0
Stuart Barlow	36	43	31	7	1261	3	3	0
Luke Beckett	28	15	15	15	1350	7	0	0
Jon Daly	22	18	14	9	911	3	1	0
Warren Feeney	24	31	31	30	2686	15	2	0
Adam Le Fondre	18	24	20	10	1154	4	2	0
Marvin Robinson	25	5	3	2	215	0	0	0
Andrew Smith	24	1	1	1	90	0	0	0
Chris Williams	20	15	9	5	456	0	0	0

SQUAD APPEARANCES

Match	1	2	3	4	5	6	7	8	9	10	11	12	13	14	15	16	17	18	19	20	21	22	23	24	25
Venue	H	A	A	H	A	A	H	H	A	H	A	H	A	H	A	A	H	H	H	A	H	H	A	A	A
Competition	L	L	L	L	W	L	L	L	L	L	L	L	L	L	L	L	L	L	F	L	L	F	L	L	F
Result	L	L	W	L	L	L	D	L	L	L	D	D	L	W	L	D	L	L	W	L	L	D	L	L	L

Match	26	27	28	29	30	31	32	33	34	35	36	37	38	39	40	41	42	43	44	45	46	47	48	49	50
Venue	H	H	A	A	H	A	H	A	H	A	H	A	H	H	A	H	A	A	H	A	H	H	A	H	A
Competition	L	L	L	L	L	L	L	L	L	L	L	L	L	L	L	L	L	L	L	L	L	L	L	L	L
Result	W	L	D	W	L	L	D	L	D	L	L	W	L	W	L	L	L	L	L	L	L	L	D	L	L

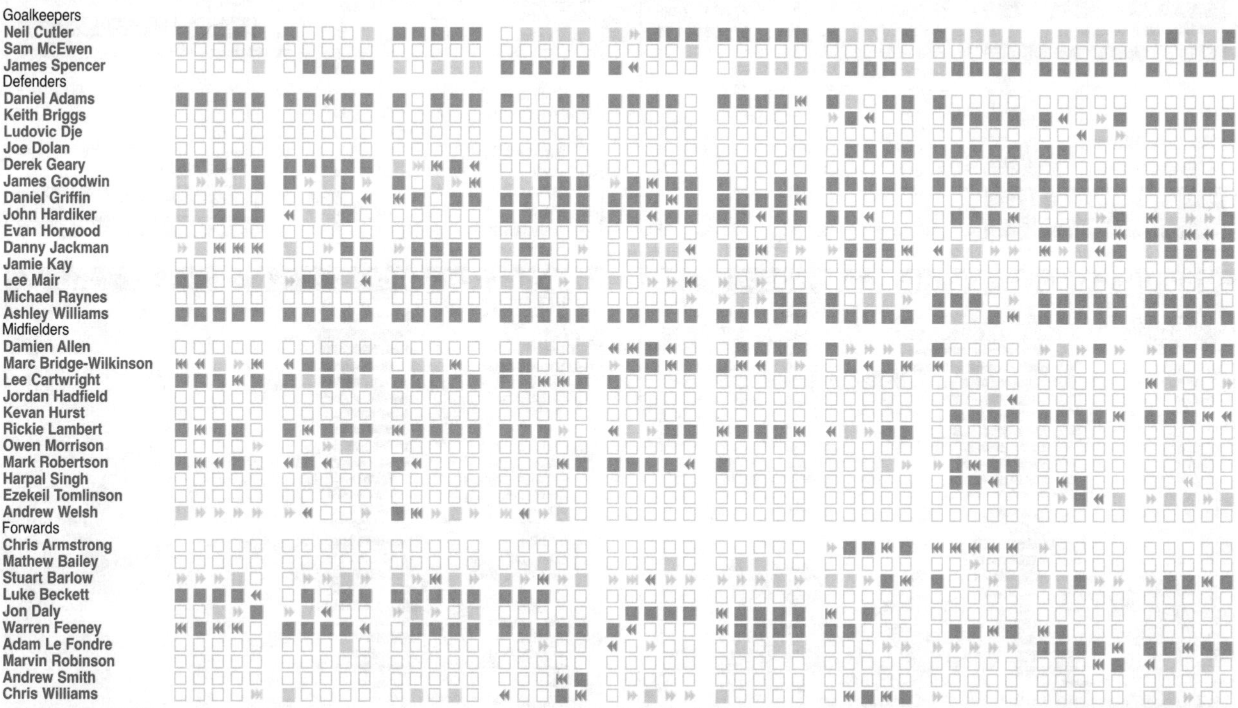
Goalkeepers
Neil Cutler
Sam McEwen
James Spencer
Defenders
Daniel Adams
Keith Briggs
Ludovic Dje
Joe Dolan
Derek Geary
James Goodwin
Daniel Griffin
John Hardiker
Evan Horwood
Danny Jackman
Jamie Kay
Lee Mair
Michael Raynes
Ashley Williams
Midfielders
Damien Allen
Marc Bridge-Wilkinson
Lee Cartwright
Jordan Hadfield
Kevan Hurst
Rickie Lambert
Owen Morrison
Mark Robertson
Harpal Singh
Ezekeil Tomlinson
Andrew Welsh
Forwards
Chris Armstrong
Mathew Bailey
Stuart Barlow
Luke Beckett
Jon Daly
Warren Feeney
Adam Le Fondre
Marvin Robinson
Andrew Smith
Chris Williams

KEY: On all match | On bench | Subbed or sent off (Counting game) | Subbed or sent off (playing less than 70 minutes) | Subbed on from bench (Counting Game) | Subbed on (playing less than 70 minutes) | Subbed on and then subbed or sent off (Counting Game) | Subbed on and then subbed or sent off (playing less than 70 minutes) | Not in 16

LEAGUE TWO ROUND-UP

FINAL LEAGUE TABLE

		HOME					AWAY					TOTAL			
	P	W	D	L	F	A	W	D	L	F	A	F	A	DIF	PTS
Yeovil	46	16	4	3	57	28	9	4	10	33	35	90	63	27	83
Scunthorpe	46	16	5	2	43	16	6	9	8	26	26	69	42	27	80
Swansea	46	15	5	3	36	16	9	3	11	26	27	62	43	19	80
Southend	46	13	5	5	31	14	9	7	7	34	32	65	46	19	78
Macclesfield	46	15	3	5	39	24	7	6	10	21	25	60	49	11	75
Lincoln	46	11	8	4	37	22	9	4	10	27	25	64	47	17	72
Northampton	46	11	9	3	35	20	9	3	11	27	31	62	51	11	72
Darlington	46	13	4	6	33	21	7	8	8	24	28	57	49	8	72
Rochdale	46	11	8	4	34	21	5	10	8	20	27	54	48	6	66
Wycombe	46	8	7	8	28	26	9	7	7	30	26	58	52	6	65
Leyton Orient	46	10	8	5	40	30	6	7	10	25	37	65	67	-2	63
Mansfield	46	9	8	6	29	24	6	7	10	27	32	56	56	0	60
Cheltenham	46	10	5	8	27	23	6	7	10	24	31	51	54	-3	60
Bristol Rovers	46	10	12	1	39	22	3	9	11	21	35	60	57	3	59
Oxford	46	11	4	8	29	24	5	7	11	21	39	50	63	-13	59
Boston	46	11	8	4	39	24	3	8	12	23	34	62	58	4	58
Bury	46	8	9	6	26	18	6	7	10	28	36	54	54	0	58
Grimsby	46	8	10	5	28	19	6	6	11	23	33	51	52	-1	58
Notts County	46	6	7	10	21	27	7	6	10	25	35	46	62	-16	52
Chester	46	7	8	8	25	33	5	8	10	18	36	43	69	-26	52
Shrewsbury	46	9	7	7	34	18	2	9	12	14	35	48	53	-5	49
Rushden & D	46	8	6	9	29	29	2	8	13	13	34	42	63	-21	44
Cambridge	46	7	6	10	22	27	1	10	12	17	35	39	62	-23	40
Kidderminster	46	6	6	11	21	39	4	2	17	18	46	39	85	-46	38

CLUB STRIKE FORCE

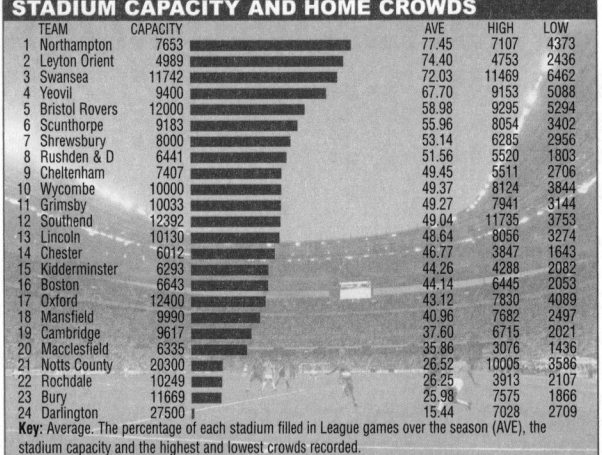

Jevons; top scorer for Yeovil

1 Yeovil

Goals scored in the League	90
Goals scored in all competions	105
Club Strike Rate (CSR) Average number of minutes between League goals scored	46

	CLUB	LGE	ALL	CSR
1	Yeovil	90	105	46
2	Scunthorpe	69	74	60
3	Leyton Orient	65	69	64
4	Southend	65	68	64
5	Lincoln	64	70	65
6	Boston	62	75	67
7	Northampton	62	67	67
8	Swansea	62	68	67
9	Bristol Rovers	60	63	69
10	Macclesfield	60	65	69
11	Wycombe	58	59	71
12	Darlington	57	60	73
13	Mansfield	56	58	74
14	Bury	54	61	77
15	Rochdale	54	61	77
16	Cheltenham	51	53	81
17	Grimsby	51	52	81
18	Oxford	50	51	83
19	Shrewsbury	48	49	86
20	Notts County	46	56	90
21	Chester	43	49	96
22	Rushden & D	42	45	99
23	Cambridge	39	40	106
24	Kidderminster	39	41	106

CLUB DISCIPLINARY RECORDS

Over 100 cards for Chester

1 Chester

League Yellow	104
League Red	10
All Competitions Yellow	110
All Competitions Red	10
Cards Average in League Average number of minutes between a card being shown	36

	CLUB	LEAGUE		TOTAL		AVE
1	Chester	104Y	10R	110Y	10R	36
2	Boston	101	2	107	2	40
3	Oxford	88	5	89	5	45
4	Rochdale	82	9	85	9	45
5	Swansea	84	6	96	6	46
6	Kidderminster	71	9	73	9	52
7	Northampton	73	4	78	4	54
8	Leyton Orient	70	5	74	5	55
9	Shrewsbury	67	8	70	8	55
10	Notts County	65	4	74	4	60
11	Cambridge	63	3	65	3	63
12	Darlington	63	2	70	3	64
13	Southend	60	3	67	3	66
14	Lincoln	59	2	67	2	68
15	Rushden & D	56	5	59	5	68
16	Scunthorpe	58	3	59	3	68
17	Bury	56	4	60	4	69
18	Grimsby	57	2	62	3	70
19	Bristol Rovers	49	8	58	9	73
20	Mansfield	51	4	53	6	75
21	Wycombe	51	2	54	2	78
22	Macclesfield	48	2	56	2	83
23	Yeovil	47	2	58	2	84
24	Cheltenham	46	2	50	2	86

CLUB DEFENCES

	CLUB	LGE	ALL	CS	CDR
1	Scunthorpe	42	47	19	99
2	Swansea	43	50	19	96
3	Southend	46	51	16	90
4	Lincoln	47	57	19	88
5	Rochdale	48	57	20	86
6	Darlington	49	55	15	84
7	Macclesfield	49	58	14	84
8	Northampton	51	59	15	81
9	Grimsby	52	55	13	80
10	Wycombe	52	56	9	80
11	Shrewsbury	53	57	15	78
12	Bury	54	60	11	77
13	Cheltenham	54	59	14	77
14	Mansfield	56	65	15	74
15	Bristol Rovers	57	61	15	73
16	Boston	58	70	11	71
17	Cambridge	62	66	11	67
18	Notts County	62	69	14	67
19	Oxford	63	67	9	66
20	Rushden & D	63	69	15	66
21	Yeovil	65	76	8	64
22	Leyton Orient	67	75	8	62
23	Chester	69	75	10	60
24	Kidderminster	85	89	8	49

Crosby; leading Scunthorpe's defence

1 Scunthorpe

Goals conceded in the League	42
Goals conceded in all competitions	47
Clean Sheets (CS) Number of league games where no goals were conceded	19
Club Defensive Rate (CDR) Average number of minutes between League goals conceded	99

STADIUM CAPACITY AND HOME CROWDS

	TEAM	CAPACITY	AVE	HIGH	LOW
1	Northampton	7653	77.45	7107	4373
2	Leyton Orient	4989	74.40	4753	2436
3	Swansea	11742	72.03	11469	6462
4	Yeovil	9400	67.70	9153	5088
5	Bristol Rovers	12000	58.98	9295	5294
6	Scunthorpe	9183	55.96	8054	3402
7	Shrewsbury	8000	53.14	6285	2956
8	Rushden & D	6441	51.56	5520	1803
9	Cheltenham	7407	49.45	5511	2706
10	Wycombe	10000	49.37	8124	3844
11	Grimsby	10033	49.27	7941	3144
12	Southend	12392	49.04	11735	3753
13	Lincoln	10130	48.64	8056	3274
14	Chester	6012	46.77	3847	1643
15	Kidderminster	6293	44.26	4288	2082
16	Boston	6643	44.14	6445	2053
17	Oxford	12400	43.12	7830	4089
18	Mansfield	9990	40.96	7682	2497
19	Cambridge	9617	37.60	6715	2021
20	Macclesfield	6335	35.86	3076	1436
21	Notts County	20300	26.52	10005	3586
22	Rochdale	10249	26.25	3913	2107
23	Bury	11669	25.98	7575	1866
24	Darlington	27500	15.44	7028	2709

Key: Average. The percentage of each stadium filled in League games over the season (AVE), the stadium capacity and the highest and lowest crowds recorded.

AWAY ATTENDANCE

	TEAM	AVE	HIGH	LOW
1	Scunthorpe	52.60	8224	2167
2	Yeovil	52.16	11735	2402
3	Lincoln	50.69	8855	1633
4	Bristol Rovers	50.66	9153	2082
5	Oxford	49.74	10602	2007
6	Swansea	49.51	7575	2164
7	Grimsby	49.09	8056	2128
8	Southend	48.89	10190	2218
9	Notts County	48.83	8225	2229
10	Northampton	48.60	9578	2073
11	Mansfield	48.09	10005	2456
12	Shrewsbury	48.08	11469	2233
13	Boston	47.09	10162	2001
14	Cambridge	47.03	8664	1436
15	Leyton Orient	46.83	9189	2192
16	Darlington	46.36	7824	1872
17	Chester	46.03	8989	2698
18	Bury	45.8	8705	1803
19	Wycombe	45.70	7421	1866
20	Macclesfield	45.66	9809	2290
21	Rochdale	44.92	7656	2337
22	Kidderminster	44.72	7020	2001
23	Rushden & D	44.72	7410	2334
24	Cheltenham	42.11	7320	1643

Key: Average. How close each club has come to filling grounds in its away league matches (AVE) and the highest and lowest crowds recorded.

CHART-TOPPING MIDFIELDERS

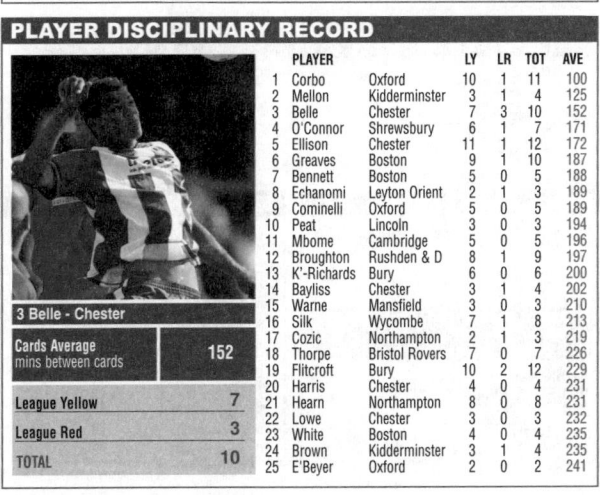

3 Beagrie - Scunthorpe	
Goals scored in the League	2
Defensive Rating Av number of mins between League goals conceded while on the pitch	115
Contribution to Attacking Power Average number of minutes between League team goals while on pitch	56
Scoring Difference Defensive Rating minus Contribution to Attacking Power	59

	PLAYER	CLUB	GOALS	DEF RATE	POWER	S DIFF
1	Ashton	Shrewsbury	0	139	67	72
2	Forbes	Swansea	7	129	69	60
3	Beagrie	Scunthorpe	2	115	56	59
4	Sandwith	Lincoln	2	105	58	47
5	Kell	Scunthorpe	5	108	61	47
6	Baraclough	Scunthorpe	3	105	60	45
7	Gower	Southend	6	106	65	41
8	Rowson	Northampton	2	99	59	40
9	Martinez	Swansea	0	112	72	40
10	O'Leary	Swansea	1	118	78	40
11	Clarke	Rochdale	1	107	68	39
12	Taylor	Scunthorpe	6	88	49	39
13	Cooksey	Rochdale	5	103	70	33
14	Bentley	Southend	5	98	67	31
15	Gain	Lincoln	0	91	63	28

CHART-TOPPING GOALSCORERS

1 Kirk - Boston	
Goals scored in the League (GL)	19
Goals scored in all competitions (GA)	21
Contribution to Attacking Power (AP) Average number of minutes between League team goals while on pitch	69
Player Strike Rate Average number of minutes between League goals scored by player	113
Club Strike Rate (CSR) Average minutes between League goals scored by club	67

	PLAYER	CLUB	GOALS: LGE	ALL	POWER	CSR	S RATE
1	Kirk	Boston	19	21	69	67	113
2	Jevons	Yeovil	27	29	48	46	136
3	Eastwood	Southend	19	21	61	64	141
4	Tyson	Wycombe	22	22	70	71	158
5	Yeo	Lincoln	21	23	58	65	159
6	Trundle	Swansea	22	23	65	67	166
7	Parkin	Macclesfield	22	24	64	69	171
8	Walker	Bristol Rovers	10	12	62	69	176
9	Agogo	Bristol Rovers	19	19	65	69	178
10	Wijnhard	Darlington	14	14	65	73	191
11	Holt	Rochdale	17	23	73	77	203
12	Nugent	Bury	11	12	72	77	205
13	Steele	Leyton Orient	16	17	60	64	205
14	Hayes	Scunthorpe	17	19	57	60	208
15	Tarachulski	Yeovil	11	13	46	46	218

CHART-TOPPING DEFENDERS

2 Swailes - Bury	
Goals Conceded in the League The number of League goals conceded while he was on the pitch	15
Goals Conceded in all competitions The number of goals conceded while he was on the pitch in all competitions	18
Clean Sheets In games when he played at least 70 mins	6
Defensive Rating Average number of minutes between League goals conceded while on pitch	117
Club Defensive Rating Average mins between League goals conceded by the club this season	77

	PLAYER	CLUB	CON: LGE	ALL	CS	CDR	DEF RATE
1	Gurney	Swansea	18	21	11	96	120
2	Swailes	Bury	15	18	6	77	117
3	Monk	Swansea	26	33	15	96	113
4	Valentine	Darlington	26	30	12	84	112
5	Goodall	Rochdale	23	28	14	86	111
6	Crosby	Scunthorpe	36	41	18	99	106
7	Stanton	Scunthorpe	16	18	7	99	105
8	Futcher	Lincoln	30	39	16	88	104
9	Morley	Macclesfield	17	19	7	84	101
10	Buxton	Mansfield	26	31	14	74	101
11	Ridley	Scunthorpe	39	44	18	99	99
12	Morgan	Lincoln	36	42	17	88	98
13	Walton	Shrewsbury	18	21	8	78	98
14	Woodthorpe	Bury	26	29	8	77	97
15	Wilson	Southend	37	40	15	90	97

CHART-TOPPING GOALKEEPERS

1 Gilks - Rochdale	
Counting Games League games when he played at least 70 minutes	31
Goals Conceded in the League The number of League goals conceded while he was on the pitch	26
Goals Conceded in all competitions The number of goals conceded while he was on the pitch in all competitions	31
Clean Sheets In games when he played at least 70 mins	15
Defensive Rating Average number of minutes between League goals conceded while on pitch	107

	PLAYER	CLUB	CG	CONC LGE	CONC ALL	CS	DEF RATE
1	Gilks	Rochdale	31	26	31	15	107
2	Musselwhite	Scunthorpe	46	42	47	19	99
3	Gueret	Swansea	44	40	47	19	99
4	Fettis	Macclesfield	27	26	29	10	96
5	Flahavan	Southend	25	25	25	9	94
6	Miller	Bristol Rovers	28	27	31	11	93
7	Griemink	Southend	19	18	23	7	92
8	Marriott	Lincoln	45	46	56	19	88
9	Russell, S	Darlington	46	49	55	15	84
10	Harper	Northampton	36	40	45	12	81
11	Williams	Grimsby	46	52	55	13	80
12	Talia	Wycombe	45	50	54	9	80
13	Pilkington	Mansfield	42	48	57	15	79
14	Turley	Rushden & D	22	25	31	8	79
15	Garner	Bury	27	31	34	6	78

PLAYER DISCIPLINARY RECORD

3 Belle - Chester	
Cards Average mins between cards	152
League Yellow	7
League Red	3
TOTAL	10

	PLAYER		LY	LR	TOT	AVE
1	Corbo	Oxford	10	1	11	100
2	Mellon	Kidderminster	3	1	4	125
3	Belle	Chester	7	3	10	152
4	O'Connor	Shrewsbury	6	1	7	171
5	Ellison	Chester	11	1	12	172
6	Greaves	Boston	9	1	10	187
7	Bennett	Boston	5	0	5	188
8	Echanomi	Leyton Orient	2	1	3	189
9	Cominelli	Oxford	5	0	5	189
10	Peat	Lincoln	3	0	3	194
11	Mbome	Cambridge	5	0	5	196
12	Broughton	Rushden & D	8	1	9	197
13	K'-Richards	Bury	6	0	6	200
14	Bayliss	Chester	3	1	4	202
15	Warne	Mansfield	3	0	3	210
16	Silk	Wycombe	7	1	8	213
17	Cozic	Northampton	2	1	3	219
18	Thorpe	Bristol Rovers	7	0	7	226
19	Flitcroft	Bury	10	2	12	229
20	Harris	Chester	4	0	4	231
21	Hearn	Northampton	8	0	8	231
22	Lowe	Chester	3	0	3	232
23	White	Boston	4	0	4	235
24	Brown	Kidderminster	3	1	4	235
25	E'Beyer	Oxford	2	0	2	241

TEAM OF THE SEASON

G
Gilks : Rochdale
CG: 31 DR: 107

D
Gurney : Swansea
CG: 22 DR: 120

D
Swailes : Bury
CG: 19 DR: 117

D
Valentine : Darlington
CG: 30 DR: 112

D
Goodall : Rochdale
CG: 27 DR: 111

M
Ashton : Shrewsbury
CG: 19 SD: + 72

M
Forbes : Swansea
CG: 25 SD: + 60

M
Beagrie : Scunthorpe
CG: 33 SD: + 59

M
Sandwith : Lincoln
CG: 32 SD: + 47

F
Kirk : Boston
CG: 25 SR: 113

F
Jevons : Yeovil
CG: 36 SR: 136

YEOVIL

Final Position: **1st**

NICKNAME: THE GLOVERS

KEY: Won / Drawn / Lost

No	Comp	Opponent	H/A	Res	Score	Scorers	Attendance
1	lge2	**Bury**	A	L	1-3	Caceres 39	3,171
2	lge2	**Darlington**	H	D	1-1	Jevons 6	5,116
3	lge2	**Boston**	H	W	2-0	Jevons 49; Tarachulski 65	5,178
4	lge2	**Notts County**	A	W	2-1	Terry 68; Jevons 81	5,024
5	ccr1	**Plymouth**	H	W	3-2	Johnson 28,69,102	6,217
6	lge2	**Rushden & D**	H	W	3-1	Johnson 18; Tarachulski 44; Jevons 45	5,088
7	lge2	**Mansfield**	A	L	1-4	Skiverton 24	3,826
8	lge2	**Swansea**	H	W	1-0	Williams 85 pen	5,826
9	lge2	**Cheltenham**	A	D	1-1	Way 29	3,966
10	lge2	**Oxford**	H	W	6-1	Stolcers 38,49; Jevons 59,69,79; Gall 75	5,467
11	ccr2	**Bolton**	H	L	0-2		8,047
12	lge2	**Shrewsbury**	A	W	2-1	Johnson 69; Tarachulski 72	4,196
13	lge2	**Northampton**	H	D	1-1	Jevons 14	5,944
14	lge2	**Rochdale**	A	L	1-2	Jevons 48	2,402
15	lge2	**Macclesfield**	H	L	1-2	Way 51	5,313
16	lge2	**Bristol Rovers**	A	D	2-2	Terry 27; Williams 57	9,295
17	lge2	**Scunthorpe**	A	L	0-1		4,470
18	lge2	**Chester**	H	W	4-1	Jevons 25 pen,66 pen,90; Caceres 56	5,741
19	lge2	**Wycombe**	A	W	1-0	Tarachulski 84	5,453
20	facr1	**Darlington**	A	D	3-3	Miles 46; Tarachulski 55,90	3,698
21	lge2	**Southend**	H	W	3-1	Jevons 43; Guyett 83; Tarachulski 85	5,839
22	facr1r	**Darlington**	H	W	1-0	Way 56	5,365
23	lge2	**Lincoln**	A	L	1-3	Skiverton 81	4,714
24	facr2	**Histon**	A	W	3-1	Jevons 52 pen; Johnson 57; Odubade 90	2,564
25	lge2	**Kidderminster**	H	W	2-1	Lindegaard 38; Tarachulski 83	5,639
26	lge2	**Grimsby**	H	W	2-1	Johnson 43; Tarachulski 47	5,733
27	lge2	**Leyton Orient**	A	W	3-2	Tarachulski 26; Terry 45; Davies 77	3,867
28	lge2	**Cheltenham**	H	W	4-1	Gall 30; Jevons 44; Davies 80; Terry 86	7,320
29	lge2	**Cambridge**	A	W	5-3	Jevons 55 pen,81 pen; Way 56; Johnson 69; Stolcers 90	3,828
30	lge2	**Swansea**	A	W	2-0	Stolcers 78; Jevons 90	11,225
31	lge2	**Shrewsbury**	H	W	4-2	Way 34; Terry 78; Caceres 84; Gall 89	7,250
32	facr3	**Rotherham**	A	W	3-0	Jevons 61 pen; Way 87; Stolcers 90	5,397
33	lge2	**Oxford**	A	L	1-2	Guyett 82	6,778
34	lge2	**Cambridge**	H	W	2-1	Terry 46; Jevons 86 pen	6,204
35	lge2	**Rochdale**	H	D	2-2	Tarachulski 54; Johnson 85 pen	5,180
36	facr4	**Charlton**	A	L	2-3	Terry 44; Davies 66	22,873
37	lge2	**Macclesfield**	A	L	1-3	Whitaker 90 og	2,471
38	lge2	**Bristol Rovers**	H	W	4-2	Jevons 26,53 pen,64; Tarachulski 72	9,153
39	lge2	**Chester**	A	W	2-0	Davies 12; Jevons 32 pen	3,072
40	lge2	**Scunthorpe**	H	W	4-3	Tarachulski 16; Johnson 47; Fallon 82; Davies 86	7,598
41	lge2	**Grimsby**	A	L	1-2	Davies 11	4,414
42	lge2	**Northampton**	A	D	1-1	Davies 31	5,630
43	lge2	**Leyton Orient**	H	W	1-0	Jevons 9 pen	6,545
44	lge2	**Darlington**	A	L	1-2	Way 81	4,121
45	lge2	**Bury**	H	L	0-1		6,269
46	lge2	**Boston**	A	W	2-1	Skiverton 10,82	3,069
47	lge2	**Notts County**	H	L	1-3	Jevons 86 pen	7,221
48	lge2	**Rushden & D**	A	L	0-2		3,726
49	lge2	**Mansfield**	H	W	5-2	Davies 5; Way 53,81; Rose 71; Jevons 72	6,471
50	lge2	**Kidderminster**	A	D	1-1	Davies 61	4,014
51	lge2	**Wycombe**	H	D	1-1	Johnson 25	7,421
52	lge2	**Southend**	A	W	1-0	Jevons 83	11,735
53	lge2	**Lincoln**	H	W	3-0	Sodje, E 45,78; Jevons 54 pen	8,855

TEAM OF THE SEASON

G – Chris Weale – CG: 37 DR: 62

D – Liam Fontaine – CG: 13 DR: 89

D – Michael Rose – CG: 31 DR: 65

D – Terry Skiverton – CG: 36 DR: 62

D – Colin Miles – CG: 13 DR: 57

M – Aaron Davies – CG: 15 SD: 25

M – Andrejs Stolcers – CG: 19 SD: 21

M – Lee Johnson – CG: 44 SD: 19

M – Paul Terry – CG: 34 SD: 18

F – Phil Jevons – CG: 36 SR: 136

F – Bartozs Tarachulski – CG: 19 SR: 218

KEY PLAYER APPEARANCES

	PLAYER	POS	AGE	APP	MINS ON	GOALS	CARDS(Y/R)	
1	Darren Way	MID	25	45	4026	7	4	0
2	Lee Johnson	MID	24	44	3937	7	4	0
3	Phil Jevons	ATT	25	46	3669	27	4	0
4	Chris Weale	GK	23	38	3337	0	1	0
5	Terry Skiverton	DEF	30	38	3294	4	5	0
6	Paul Terry	MID	26	39	3141	6	3	0
7	Michael Rose	DEF	22	40	3118	1	2	0
8	Kevin Gall	ATT	23	43	2609	3	0	0
9	Bartozs Tarachulski	ATT	30	41	2396	11	7	0
10	Andrejs Stolcers	MID	30	36	2108	4	2	0
11	Andrew Lindegaard	MID	24	29	1800	1	4	0
12	Aaron Davies	MID	21	23	1606	8	0	0
13	Colin Miles	DEF	26	21	1425	0	3	1
14	Scott Guyett	DEF	29	19	1331	2	2	0
15	Liam Fontaine	DEF	19	15	1248	0	0	0
16	Gavin Williams	MID	24	13	1035	2	1	1
17	Roy O'Brien	DEF	30	13	964	0	0	0
18	Kevin Amankwaah	DEF	23	14	853	0	2	0

KEY PLAYERS - GOALSCORERS

Phil Jevons

Goals in the League	27
Contribution to Attacking Power Average number of minutes between League team goals while on pitch	48
Player Strike Rate Average number of minutes between League goals scored by player	136
Club Strike Rate Average number of minutes between League goals scored by club	46

	PLAYER	LGE GOALS	POWER	STRIKE RATE
1	Phil Jevons	27	48	136 mins
2	Aaron Davies	8	37	201 mins
3	Bartozs Tarachulski	11	46	218 mins
4	Paul Terry	6	49	524 mins
5	Andrejs Stolcers	4	45	527 mins

KEY PLAYERS - MIDFIELDERS

Aaron Davies

Goals in the League	8
Defensive Rating Average number of mins between League goals conceded while on the pitch	62
Contribution to Attacking Power Average number of minutes between League team goals while on pitch	37
Scoring Difference Defensive Rating minus Contribution to Attacking Power	25

	PLAYER	LGE GOALS	DEF RATE	POWER	SCORE DIFF
1	Aaron Davies	8	62	37	25 mins
2	Andrejs Stolcers	4	66	45	21 mins
3	Lee Johnson	7	66	47	19 mins
4	Darren Way	7	63	45	18 mins
5	Paul Terry	6	67	49	18 mins

KEY PLAYERS - DEFENDERS

Liam Fontaine

Goals Conceded while on the pitch	14
Defensive Rating Ave number of mins between League goals conceded while on the pitch	89
Clean Sheets In games when player was on pitch for at least 70 minutes	2
Club Defensive Rating Average number of mins between League goals conceded by the club this season.	64

	PLAYER	CON LGE	CLN SHEETS	DEF RATE
1	Liam Fontaine	14	2	89 mins
2	Michael Rose	48	5	65 mins
3	Terry Skiverton	53	6	62 mins
4	Colin Miles	25	2	57 mins
5	Scott Guyett	24	3	55 mins

KEY GOALKEEPER

Chris Weale

Goals Conceded in the League	54
Defensive Rating Ave number of mins between League goals conceded while on the pitch.	62
Counting Games Games when player was on pitch for at least 70 minutes	37
Clean Sheets In Games when player was on pitch for at least 70 minutes	6

TOP POINT EARNERS

	PLAYER	GAMES	AV PTS
1	Bartozs Tarachulski	19	2.32
2	Colin Miles	13	2.23
3	Kevin Gall	23	2.00
4	Chris Weale	37	1.92
5	Michael Rose	31	1.90
6	Andrejs Stolcers	19	1.89
7	Liam Fontaine	13	1.85
8	Terry Skiverton	36	1.83
9	Phil Jevons	36	1.83
10	Scott Guyett	12	1.83
	CLUB AVERAGE:		1.80

SCUNTHORPE UNITED

Final Position: **2nd**

NICKNAME: THE IRON

KEY: ☐Won ☐Drawn ☐Lost

	Comp	Opponent	H/A	Res	Score	Scorers	Attendance
1	lge2	Rochdale	H	W	3-1	Taylor 68; Hayes 75; Sparrow 90	4,409
2	lge2	Cheltenham	A	W	2-0	Kell 10; Keogh 88	3,647
3	lge2	Oxford	A	D	1-1	Hayes 38	4,920
4	lge2	Lincoln	H	W	3-2	Kell 6; Butler 58,90	5,215
5	ccr1	Nottm Forest	A	L	0-2		7,344
6	lge2	Macclesfield	A	D	2-2	Sparrow 29; Hayes 51	2,321
7	lge2	Northampton	H	W	2-0	Keogh 43; Crosby 73 pen	4,201
8	lge2	Darlington	A	D	0-0		3,983
9	lge2	Chester	H	L	1-2	Butler 76	4,203
10	lge2	Bury	A	W	1-0	Rankine 89	2,846
11	lge2	Mansfield	H	D	1-1	Baraclough 3	4,563
12	lge2	Boston	A	L	1-2	Hayes 42	3,640
13	lge2	Wycombe	H	W	2-0	Hayes 27; Crosby 39 pen	4,373
14	lge2	Kidderminster	A	L	2-3	Torpey 18; Hayes 58	2,167
15	lge2	Southend	H	W	3-2	Torpey 35; Hayes 44; Crosby 72	3,402
16	lge2	Yeovil	H	W	1-0	Butler 78	4,470
17	lge2	Leyton Orient	A	D	1-1	Torpey 52	4,359
18	lge2	Grimsby	H	W	2-0	Hayes 16,69	8,054
19	facr1	Chesterfield	H	W	2-0	Hayes 13; Baraclough 76	4,869
20	lge2	Bristol Rovers	A	W	3-0	Hayes 18,53; Torpey 20	7,039
21	lge2	Shrewsbury	H	W	3-1	Beagrie 32 pen; Hayes 71; Taylor 76	4,418
22	facr2	Wrexham	H	W	2-0	Ridley 14; Sparrow 54	5,698
23	lge2	Cambridge	A	W	2-1	Torpey 88; Taylor 90	2,666
24	lge2	Swansea	H	W	1-0	Torpey 1	5,075
25	lge2	Rushden & D	A	W	3-1	Butler 31,49; Torpey 90	3,198
26	lge2	Chester	A	D	1-1	Torpey 3	3,216
27	lge2	Notts County	H	D	0-0		6,399
28	lge2	Darlington	H	L	0-1		5,131
29	lge2	Mansfield	A	L	0-1		5,315
30	facr3	Chelsea	A	L	1-3	Hayes 8	40,019
31	lge2	Bury	H	W	3-2	Butler 6; Torpey 64,87	5,365
32	lge2	Notts County	A	L	0-2		6,429
33	lge2	Boston	H	D	1-1	Butler 60	5,056
34	lge2	Kidderminster	H	W	2-1	Baraclough 20; Hayes 78	5,023
35	lge2	Southend	A	D	0-0		8,224
36	lge2	Wycombe	A	L	1-2	Sparrow 87	4,089
37	lge2	Leyton Orient	H	W	1-0	Keogh 68	5,162
38	lge2	Yeovil	A	L	3-4	Hayes 36,90; Butler 45	7,598
39	lge2	Swansea	A	L	1-2	Butler 33	7,249
40	lge2	Rushden & D	H	W	1-0	Beagrie 90	4,932
41	lge2	Cheltenham	H	W	4-1	Sparrow 44,55; Kell 85; Byrne 90	4,659
42	lge2	Rochdale	A	D	0-0		3,605
43	lge2	Oxford	H	D	1-1	Baraclough 90	5,977
44	lge2	Lincoln	A	L	0-2		6,729
45	lge2	Macclesfield	H	D	0-0		5,536
46	lge2	Northampton	A	W	2-1	Hayes 14; Kell 21	6,523
47	lge2	Cambridge	H	W	4-0	Kell 34; Crosby 63; Taylor 81,83	5,642
48	lge2	Grimsby	A	D	0-0		7,941
49	lge2	Bristol Rovers	H	W	4-0	Torpey 8,14; Hayes 46; Taylor 69	6,925
50	lge2	Shrewsbury	A	D	0-0		6,285

TEAM OF THE SEASON

G — Paul Musselwhite CG: 46 DR: 99

D — Andrew Crosby CG: 41 DR: 106
D — Nathan Stanton CG: 17 DR: 105
D — Lee Ridley CG: 42 DR: 99
D — Clifford Byrne CG: 21 DR: 96

M — Peter Beagrie CG: 33 SD: 59
M — Richard Kell CG: 34 SD: 47
M — Ian Baraclough CG: 43 SD: 45
M — Cleveland Taylor CG: 17 SD: 39

F — Paul Hayes CG: 37 SR: 208
F — Steve Torpey CG: 33 SR: 250

KEY PLAYER APPEARANCES

	PLAYER	POS	AGE	APP	MINS ON	GOALS	CARDS(Y/R)	
1	Paul Musselwhite	GK	36	46	4140	0	2	0
2	Ian Baraclough	MID	34	45	3992	3	6	0
3	Lee Ridley	DEF	22	44	3843	0	5	0
4	Andrew Crosby	DEF	32	44	3809	4	7	0
5	Paul Hayes	ATT	21	46	3528	17	3	0
6	Richard Kell	MID	25	43	3452	5	7	0
7	Andy Butler	DEF	21	37	3144	10	2	1
8	Peter Beagrie	MID	39	36	3102	2	6	0
9	Steve Torpey	ATT	34	34	3005	12	4	1
10	Matthew Sparrow	MID	21	44	3004	5	4	0
11	Clifford Byrne	DEF	23	29	2199	1	2	0
12	Cleveland Taylor	MID	21	44	2117	6	4	0
13	Nathan Stanton	DEF	24	21	1681	0	0	0
14	Andrew Keogh	ATT	19	25	1111	3	2	0
15	Stevland Angus	DEF	24	9	738	0	0	1
16	Richard Hinds	DEF	24	7	551	0	0	0
17	Kevin Sharp	DEF	30	6	383	0	2	0
18	Michael Rankine	ATT	2006	21	335	1	1	0

KEY PLAYERS - GOALSCORERS

Paul Hayes

Goals in the League	17
Contribution to Attacking Power Average number of minutes between League team goals while on pitch	57
Player Strike Rate Average number of minutes between League goals scored by player	208
Club Strike Rate Average number of minutes between League goals scored by club	60

	PLAYER	LGE GOALS	POWER	STRIKE RATE
1	Paul Hayes	17	57	208 mins
2	Steve Torpey	12	58	250 mins
3	Andy Butler	10	54	314 mins
4	Cleveland Taylor	6	49	353 mins
5	Matthew Sparrow	5	75	601 mins

KEY PLAYERS - MIDFIELDERS

Peter Beagrie

Goals in the League	2
Defensive Rating Average number of mins between League goals conceded while on the pitch	115
Contribution to Attacking Power Average number of minutes between League team goals while on pitch	56
Scoring Difference Defensive Rating minus Contribution to Attacking Power	59

	PLAYER	LGE GOALS	DEF RATE	POWER	SCORE DIFF
1	Peter Beagrie	2	115	56	59 mins
2	Richard Kell	5	108	61	47 mins
3	Ian Baraclough	3	105	60	45 mins
4	Cleveland Taylor	6	88	49	39 mins
5	Matthew Sparrow	5	88	75	13 mins

KEY PLAYERS - DEFENDERS

Andrew Crosby

Goals Conceded while on the pitch	36
Defensive Rating Ave number of mins between League goals conceded while on the pitch	106
Clean Sheets In games when player was on pitch for at least 70 minutes	18
Club Defensive Rating Average number of mins between League goals conceded by the club this season.	99

	PLAYER	CON LGE	CLN SHEETS	DEF RATE
1	Andrew Crosby	36	18	106 mins
2	Nathan Stanton	16	7	105 mins
3	Lee Ridley	39	18	99 mins
4	Clifford Byrne	23	10	96 mins
5	Andy Butler	33	14	95 mins

KEY GOALKEEPER

Paul Musselwhite

Goals Conceded in the League	42
Defensive Rating Ave number of mins between League goals conceded while on the pitch.	99
Counting Games Games when player was on pitch for at least 70 minutes	46
Clean Sheets In Games when player was on pitch for at least 70 minutes	19

TOP POINT EARNERS

	PLAYER	GAMES	AV PTS
1	Peter Beagrie	33	2.00
2	Andrew Crosby	41	1.93
3	Richard Kell	34	1.91
4	Paul Hayes	37	1.89
5	Andy Butler	34	1.88
6	Steve Torpey	33	1.85
7	Lee Ridley	42	1.81
8	Clifford Byrne	21	1.81
9	Ian Baraclough	43	1.79
10	Nathan Stanton	17	1.76
	CLUB AVERAGE:		1.74

SWANSEA

Final Position: **3rd**

NICKNAME: THE SWANS

KEY: Won / Drawn / Lost

							Attendance
1	lge2	Northampton	H	L	0-2		9,578
2	lge2	Rochdale	A	W	2-0	Nugent 21; Robinson 61	2,514
3	lge2	Macclesfield	A	L	0-1		2,164
4	lge2	Cheltenham	H	D	1-1	Trundle 76	6,874
5	ccr1	QPR	A	L	0-3		4,882
6	lge2	Cambridge	A	W	1-0	Trundle 22	2,949
7	lge2	Lincoln	H	W	1-0	Iriekpen 3	6,948
8	lge2	Yeovil	A	L	0-1		5,826
9	lge2	Kidderminster	H	W	3-0	Connor 16,87; Trundle 53	6,462
10	lge2	Wycombe	A	W	1-0	Robinson 14	5,247
11	lge2	Rushden & D	H	W	1-0	Nugent 36	7,410
12	lge2	Chester	A	D	1-1	Trundle 55 pen	3,847
13	lge2	Mansfield	H	W	1-0	Forbes 89	8,868
14	lge2	Southend	A	L	2-4	Connor 11; Forbes 82	4,940
15	lge2	Leyton Orient	H	W	1-0	Forbes 44	8,485
16	lge2	Grimsby	A	D	1-1	Trundle 70 pen	4,618
17	lge2	Bristol Rovers	H	W	1-0	Trundle 88 pen	8,778
18	facr1	Cheltenham	A	W	3-1	O'Leary 19; Trundle 46; Connor 90	4,551
19	lge2	Darlington	H	W	2-1	Trundle 55; Robinson 59	7,824
20	lge2	Shrewsbury	A	L	0-2		5,055
21	lge2	Bury	H	L	1-3	Nugent 2	6,971
22	facr2	Stockport	A	D	0-0		2,680
23	lge2	Oxford	A	W	1-0	Goodfellow 61	4,767
24	lge2	Scunthorpe	A	L	0-1		5,075
25	facr2r	Stockport	H	W	2-1	Connor 47; Goodfellow 88	5,572
26	lge2	Notts County	H	W	4-0	Trundle 42,71,90 pen; Connor 76	6,609
27	lge2	Kidderminster	A	W	5-1	Connor 1; Iriekpen 9; Robinson 89 pen,90; Goodfellow 90	4,288
28	lge2	Boston	H	W	3-1	Trundle 4; Forbes 21; Goodfellow 27	10,162
29	lge2	Yeovil	H	L	0-2		11,225
30	lge2	Rushden & D	A	W	2-0	Connor 4; Robinson 22	3,382
31	facr3	Reading	A	D	1-1	Connor 32	13,642
32	lge2	Wycombe	H	D	2-2	Connor 51; Trundle 59 pen	6,793
33	facr3r	Reading	H	L	0-1		7,354
34	lge2	Boston	A	W	3-2	Trundle 52,90 pen; Robinson 62	2,545
35	lge2	Chester	H	W	3-0	Trundle 42,61; Connor 50	8,989
36	lge2	Southend	H	D	1-1	Trundle 55	10,190
37	lge2	Mansfield	A	L	0-1		3,829
38	lge2	Leyton Orient	A	L	1-3	Thorpe 81	4,050
39	lge2	Grimsby	H	D	0-0		7,760
40	lge2	Darlington	A	L	1-2	Forbes 37	2,709
41	lge2	Scunthorpe	H	W	2-1	Trundle 25,60 pen	7,249
42	lge2	Notts County	A	L	0-1		4,644
43	lge2	Rochdale	H	D	2-2	Gurney 46; Holt 52 og	6,804
44	lge2	Northampton	A	D	2-2	Connor 30; Trundle 70	5,799
45	lge2	Macclesfield	H	W	2-0	Thorpe 25; Connor 32	9,809
46	lge2	Cheltenham	A	W	2-1	Thorpe 3; Britton 82	4,669
47	lge2	Cambridge	H	W	3-0	Robinson 66; Trundle 83,88	8,664
48	lge2	Lincoln	A	L	0-1		5,207
49	lge2	Oxford	H	W	1-0	O'Leary 44	10,602
50	lge2	Bristol Rovers	A	L	0-2		7,433
51	lge2	Shrewsbury	H	W	1-0	Forbes 8	11,469
52	lge2	Bury	A	W	1-0	Forbes 1	7,575

TEAM OF THE SEASON

G — Willy Gueret, CG: 44 DR: 99

D — Andy Gurney, CG: 22 DR: 120

D — Gary Monk, CG: 31 DR: 113

D — Kevin Austin, CG: 40 DR: 95

D — Ezomo Iriekpen, CG: 26 DR: 95

M — Adrian Forbes, CG: 25 SD: 60

M — Roberto Martinez, CG: 32 SD: 40

M — Kristian O'Leary, CG: 31 SD: 40

M — Andy Robinson, CG: 25 SD: 26

F — Lee Trundle, CG: 40 SR: 166

F — Paul Connor, CG: 23 SR: 273

KEY PLAYER APPEARANCES

	PLAYER	POS	AGE	APP	MINS ON	GOALS	CARDS(Y	/R)
1	Willy Gueret	GK	31	44	3960	0	4	0
2	Samuel Ricketts	DEF	23	42	3779	0	6	0
3	Kevin Austin	DEF	32	42	3690	0	7	0
4	Lee Trundle	ATT	28	42	3647	22	4	0
5	Roberto Martinez	MID	31	37	3033	0	9	0
6	Gary Monk	DEF	26	34	2950	0	5	3
7	Adrian Forbes	MID	26	40	2843	7	8	0
8	Kristian O'Leary	MID	27	32	2820	1	5	0
9	Paul Connor	ATT	26	40	2731	10	8	0
10	Andy Robinson	MID	21	37	2587	8	5	2
11	Ezomo Iriekpen	DEF	23	29	2479	2	3	0
12	Andy Gurney	DEF	31	28	2167	1	5	1
13	Leon Britton	MID	22	30	1735	1	1	0
14	Alan Tate	DEF	22	23	1670	0	6	0
15	Lee Thorpe	ATT	29	15	856	3	2	0
16	Kevin Nugent	ATT	36	19	806	3	3	0
17	Ijah Anderson	DEF	29	13	714	0	1	0
18	Kevin McLeod	MID	24	11	666	0	0	0

KEY PLAYERS - GOALSCORERS

Lee Trundle

Goals in the League	22	Player Strike Rate: Average number of minutes between League goals scored by player	166
Contribution to Attacking Power: Average number of minutes between League team goals while on pitch	65	Club Strike Rate: Average number of minutes between League goals scored by club	67

	PLAYER	LGE GOALS	POWER	STRIKE RATE
1	Lee Trundle	22	65	166 mins
2	Paul Connor	10	65	273 mins
3	Andy Robinson	8	70	323 mins
4	Adrian Forbes	7	69	406 mins
5	Ezomo Iriekpen	2	56	1240 mins

KEY PLAYERS - MIDFIELDERS

Adrian Forbes

Goals in the League	7	Contribution to Attacking Power: Average number of minutes between League team goals while on pitch	69
Defensive Rating: Average number of mins between League goals conceded while on the pitch	129	Scoring Difference: Defensive Rating minus Contribution to Attacking Power	60

	PLAYER	LGE GOALS	DEF RATE	POWER	SCORE DIFF
1	Adrian Forbes	7	129	69	60 mins
2	Kristian O'Leary	1	118	78	40 mins
3	Roberto Martinez	0	112	72	40 mins
4	Andy Robinson	8	96	70	26 mins
5	Leon Britton	1	96	79	17 mins

KEY PLAYERS - DEFENDERS

Andy Gurney

Goals Conceded while on the pitch	18	Clean Sheets: In games when player was on pitch for at least 70 minutes	11
Defensive Rating: Ave number of mins between League goals conceded while on the pitch	120	Club Defensive Rating: Average number of mins between League goals conceded by the club this season.	96

	PLAYER	CON LGE	CLN SHEETS	DEF RATE
1	Andy Gurney	18	11	120 mins
2	Gary Monk	26	15	113 mins
3	Kevin Austin	39	17	95 mins
4	Ezomo Iriekpen	26	9	95 mins
5	Samuel Ricketts	40	18	94 mins

KEY GOALKEEPER

Willy Gueret

Goals Conceded in the League	40
Defensive Rating: Ave number of mins between League goals conceded while on the pitch.	99
Counting Games: Games when player was on pitch for at least 70 minutes	44
Clean Sheets: In Games when player was on pitch for at least 70 minutes	19

TOP POINT EARNERS

	PLAYER	GAMES	AV PTS
1	Adrian Forbes	25	2.36
2	Gary Monk	31	2.00
3	Andy Gurney	22	1.95
4	Paul Connor	23	1.91
5	Kristian O'Leary	31	1.90
6	Roberto Martinez	32	1.88
7	Ezomo Iriekpen	26	1.77
8	Willy Gueret	44	1.75
9	Lee Trundle	40	1.75
10	Kevin Austin	40	1.75
	CLUB AVERAGE:		1.74

SOUTHEND UNITED

PROMOTED VIA PLAY OFFS Final Position: **4th**

NICKNAME: THE SHRIMPERS

KEY: ☐ Won ☐ Drawn ☐ Lost

							Attendance
1	lge2	**Cheltenham**	H	L	0-2		5,332
2	lge2	**Lincoln**	A	D	1-1	Gray 34 pen	3,991
3	lge2	**Rochdale**	A	L	0-2		2,218
4	lge2	**Cambridge**	H	D	0-0		3,941
5	ccr1	**West Ham**	A	L	0-2		16,910
6	lge2	**Bristol Rovers**	A	L	1-2	Barrett 71	9,287
7	lge2	**Macclesfield**	H	W	2-1	Barrett 42,55	3,753
8	lge2	**Rushden & D**	A	W	4-1	Dudfield 19,54 pen; Bramble 70; Barrett 90	2,804
9	lge2	**Wycombe**	H	L	1-2	Bentley 42	4,771
10	lge2	**Notts County**	A	W	2-1	Barrett 28,55	4,487
11	lge2	**Kidderminster**	H	W	1-0	Gower 27	4,087
12	lge2	**Darlington**	A	L	0-4		3,901
13	lge2	**Boston**	H	W	2-1	Gower 15; Gray 22	5,688
14	lge2	**Swansea**	H	W	4-2	Eastwood 1,58,87; Prior 42	4,940
15	lge2	**Scunthorpe**	A	L	2-3	Eastwood 30; Corbett 63	3,402
16	lge2	**Shrewsbury**	A	D	1-1	Gray 59	3,719
17	lge2	**Northampton**	H	W	2-1	Gower 27; Gray 76	5,696
18	lge2	**Oxford**	H	W	4-0	Gower 47; Eastwood 75; Barrett 81; Dudfield 90 pen	5,608
19	facr1	**Luton**	H	L	0-3		6,683
20	lge2	**Yeovil**	A	L	1-3	Barrett 62	5,839
21	lge2	**Grimsby**	H	D	1-1	Eastwood 60	5,192
22	lge2	**Leyton Orient**	A	D	2-2	Eastwood 28; Gray 35	3,852
23	lge2	**Bury**	A	W	1-0	Gray 27 pen	2,522
24	lge2	**Chester**	H	W	1-0	Dudfield 88	4,837
25	lge2	**Wycombe**	A	W	1-0	Eastwood 17	5,669
26	lge2	**Mansfield**	H	L	0-1		7,082
27	lge2	**Rushden & D**	H	W	3-0	Maher 17; Edwards 59; Bentley 90	5,930
28	lge2	**Kidderminster**	A	W	3-1	Eastwood 10,84; Nicolau 82	2,755
29	lge2	**Boston**	A	L	0-2		2,389
30	lge2	**Notts County**	H	D	0-0		5,304
31	lge2	**Mansfield**	A	D	1-1	Gower 59	3,894
32	lge2	**Darlington**	H	W	2-0	Bentley 77; Eastwood 90	7,358
33	lge2	**Swansea**	A	D	1-1	Gray 59	10,190
34	lge2	**Scunthorpe**	H	D	0-0		8,224
35	lge2	**Northampton**	A	W	2-1	Barrett 72,90	6,602
36	lge2	**Shrewsbury**	H	W	1-0	Eastwood 78	4,219
37	lge2	**Bury**	H	W	1-0	Eastwood 42	5,553
38	lge2	**Chester**	A	D	2-2	Gower 38; Eastwood 85	2,396
39	lge2	**Lincoln**	H	D	1-1	Eastwood 90 pen	5,824
40	lge2	**Cheltenham**	A	W	3-0	Gray 16,45; Eastwood 66	3,689
41	lge2	**Rochdale**	H	W	3-0	Eastwood 44; Bentley 55; Gray 60	7,656
42	lge2	**Cambridge**	A	W	2-0	Prior 23; Barrett 45	6,715
43	lge2	**Bristol Rovers**	H	W	2-0	Bentley 26; Gray 26 pen	7,858
44	lge2	**Leyton Orient**	H	L	0-1		9,189
45	lge2	**Macclesfield**	A	W	2-1	McCormack 31,90	2,768
46	lge2	**Oxford**	A	L	1-2	Eastwood 60	5,916
47	lge2	**Yeovil**	H	L	0-1		11,735
48	lge2	**Grimsby**	A	D	1-1	Eastwood 70	6,259
49	d3po1	**Northampton**	A	D	0-0		6,601
50	d3po2	**Northampton**	H	W	1-0	Eastwood 49 pen	9,152

TEAM OF THE SEASON

- **G** Darryl Flahavan — CG: 25 DR: 94
- **D** Che Wilson — CG: 40 DR: 97
- **D** Spencer Prior — CG: 39 DR: 95
- **D** Adam Barrett — CG: 42 DR: 91
- **D** Nicky Nicolau — CG: 12 DR: 88
- **M** Mark Gower — CG: 29 SD: 41
- **M** Mark Bentley — CG: 34 SD: 31
- **M** Carl Pettefer — CG: 44 SD: 27
- **M** Kevin Maher — CG: 42 SD: 26
- **F** Freddy Eastwood — CG: 31 SR: 141
- **F** Wayne Gray — CG: 29 SR: 273

KEY PLAYER APPEARANCES

	PLAYER	POS	AGE	APP	MINS ON	GOALS	CARDS(Y/R)	
1	Carl Pettefer	MID	24	46	3993	0	4	0
2	Adam Barrett	DEF	25	43	3822	11	1	0
3	Kevin Maher	MID	28	42	3772	1	11	1
4	Spencer Prior	DEF	34	41	3601	2	6	0
5	Che Wilson	DEF	26	40	3600	0	5	0
6	Mark Bentley	MID	27	39	3151	5	9	0
7	Wayne Gray	ATT	24	44	3005	11	4	1
8	Freddy Eastwood	ATT	22	33	2686	19	0	0
9	Mark Gower	MID	26	38	2645	6	1	0
10	Duncan Jupp	DEF	30	31	2608	0	3	0
11	Lewis Hunt	DEF	22	31	2435	0	3	0
12	Darryl Flahavan	GK	26	28	2356	0	0	1
13	Bart Griemink	GK	33	19	1649	0	0	0
14	Lawrie Dudfield	ATT	25	36	1608	4	3	0
15	Nicky Nicolau	DEF	21	22	1314	1	3	0
16	Tesfaye Bramble	ATT	24	20	982	1	2	0
17	Andrew Edwards	DEF	33	12	797	1	1	0
18	Alan McCormack	MID	21	7	438	2	2	0

KEY PLAYERS - GOALSCORERS

Fredy Eastwood

Goals in the League	19
Contribution to Attacking Power Average number of minutes between League team goals while on pitch	61
Player Strike Rate Average number of minutes between League goals scored by player	141
Club Strike Rate Average number of minutes between League goals scored by club	64

	PLAYER	LGE GOALS	POWER	STRIKE RATE
1	Freddy Eastwood	19	61	141 mins
2	Wayne Gray	11	66	273 mins
3	Adam Barrett	11	59	347 mins
4	Lawrie Dudfield	4	67	402 mins
5	Mark Gower	6	65	441 mins

KEY PLAYERS - MIDFIELDERS

Mark Gower

Goals in the League	6
Defensive Rating Average number of mins between League goals conceded while on the pitch	106
Contribution to Attacking Power Average number of minutes between League team goals while on pitch	65
Scoring Difference Defensive Rating minus Contribution to Attacking Power	41

	PLAYER	LGE GOALS	DEF RATE	POWER	SCORE DIFF
1	Mark Gower	6	106	65	41 mins
2	Mark Bentley	5	98	67	31 mins
3	Carl Pettefer	0	89	62	27 mins
4	Kevin Maher	1	92	66	26 mins

KEY PLAYERS - DEFENDERS

Che Wilson

Goals Conceded while on the pitch	37
Defensive Rating Ave number of mins between League goals conceded while on the pitch	97
Clean Sheets In games when player was on pitch for at least 70 minutes	15
Club Defensive Rating Average number of mins between League goals conceded by the club this season.	90

	PLAYER	CON LGE	CLN SHEETS	DEF RATE
1	Che Wilson	37	15	97 mins
2	Spencer Prior	38	14	95 mins
3	Adam Barrett	42	15	91 mins
4	Nicky Nicolau	15	4	88 mins
5	Lewis Hunt	28	9	87 mins

KEY GOALKEEPER

Darryl Flahavan

Goals Conceded in the League	25
Defensive Rating Ave number of mins between League goals conceded while on the pitch.	94
Counting Games Games when player was on pitch for at least 70 minutes	25
Clean Sheets In Games when player was on pitch for at least 70 minutes	9

TOP POINT EARNERS

	PLAYER	GAMES	AV PTS
1	Lawrie Dudfield	14	2.14
2	Che Wilson	40	1.90
3	Spencer Prior	39	1.85
4	Adam Barrett	42	1.81
5	Fredy Eastwood	31	1.74
6	Darryl Flahavan	25	1.72
7	Mark Bentley	34	1.71
8	Carl Pettefer	44	1.70
9	Lewis Hunt	26	1.69
10	Kevin Maher	42	1.69
	CLUB AVERAGE:		1.70

MACCLESFIELD

Final Position: **5th**

NICKNAME: THE SILKMEN

KEY: ☐Won ☐Drawn ☐Lost

						Attendance
1	lge2	**Leyton Orient**	A W	3-1	Tipton 40; Parkin 74,82	4,540
2	lge2	**Shrewsbury**	H W	2-1	Parkin 18; Barras 28	2,641
3	lge2	**Swansea**	H W	1-0	Parkin 17	2,164
4	lge2	**Boston**	A D	1-1	Parkin 79	2,736
5	ccr1	**Hartlepool**	A L	1-2	Parkin 48	2,883
6	lge2	**Scunthorpe**	H D	2-2	Harsley 45; Tipton 71 pen	2,321
7	lge2	**Southend**	A L	1-2	Whitaker 51	3,753
8	lge2	**Chester**	A L	0-1		2,913
9	lge2	**Grimsby**	H W	3-1	Harsley 67; Miles 71; Potter 83	2,128
10	lge2	**Kidderminster**	A L	0-1		2,290
11	lge2	**Darlington**	H W	1-0	Bailey 47	1,872
12	lge2	**Bury**	A L	1-2	Tipton 9	2,859
13	lge2	**Notts County**	H L	1-2	Parkin 17	2,456
14	lge2	**Yeovil**	A W	2-1	Skiverton 24 og; Parkin 86	5,313
15	lge2	**Cambridge**	H D	1-1	Tipton 49	1,436
16	lge2	**Oxford**	H W	1-0	Sheron 50	2,007
17	lge2	**Rochdale**	A L	0-3		2,704
18	lge2	**Mansfield**	A W	1-0	Sheron 41	3,816
19	facr1	**Alfreton**	A D	1-1	Whitaker 86	2,251
20	lge2	**Cheltenham**	H L	0-2		1,796
21	facr1r	**Alfreton**	H W	2-0	Parkin 54; Sheron 78	1,783
22	lge2	**Rushden & D**	A W	2-0	Potter 44; Parkin 89	2,643
23	facr2	**Hull City**	A L	0-4		9,831
24	lge2	**Lincoln**	H W	2-1	Parkin 82,89	1,633
25	lge2	**Bristol Rovers**	A D	0-0		6,504
26	lge2	**Northampton**	H L	1-3	Potter 64	2,073
27	lge2	**Grimsby**	A D	0-0		5,108
28	lge2	**Wycombe**	H W	2-1	Whitaker 6; Navarro 90	1,908
29	lge2	**Chester**	H L	1-2	Sheron 19	3,076
30	lge2	**Darlington**	A L	1-3	Parkin 42	3,677
31	lge2	**Kidderminster**	H W	2-0	Tipton 18; Parkin 54	2,001
32	lge2	**Wycombe**	A D	1-1	Parkin 36	4,105
33	lge2	**Notts County**	A W	5-0	Swailes 26; Parkin 38,57,90 pen; Welch 83	3,586
34	lge2	**Bury**	H W	2-1	Welch 48; Parkin 89	2,513
35	lge2	**Yeovil**	H W	3-1	Tipton 38; Potter 46,83	2,471
36	lge2	**Cambridge**	A W	1-0	Potter 80	2,926
37	lge2	**Rochdale**	H W	3-0	Tipton 8,12,90	3,031
38	lge2	**Bristol Rovers**	H W	2-1	Parkin 45,62	2,114
39	lge2	**Northampton**	A L	0-1		5,804
40	lge2	**Shrewsbury**	A W	1-0	Miles 81	4,262
41	lge2	**Leyton Orient**	H W	3-1	Parkin 33; Tipton 53 pen; Harsley 74	2,234
42	lge2	**Swansea**	A L	0-2		9,809
43	lge2	**Boston**	H D	1-1	Bailey 84	2,501
44	lge2	**Scunthorpe**	A D	0-0		5,536
45	lge2	**Oxford**	A D	1-1	Miles 87	4,273
46	lge2	**Lincoln**	A L	0-2		5,289
47	lge2	**Southend**	H L	1-2	Morley 28	2,768
48	lge2	**Mansfield**	H W	3-1	Parkin 6; Tipton 58; Morley 62	2,456
49	lge2	**Cheltenham**	A L	0-3		3,622
50	lge2	**Rushden & D**	H W	1-0	Parkin 60	2,658
51	d3po1	**Lincoln**	A L	0-1		7,032
52	d3po2	**Lincoln**	H D	1-1	Harsley 76	5,223

TEAM OF THE SEASON

G
Alan Fettis
CG: 27 DR: 96
D
Danny Swailes
CG: 16 DR: 104
D
David Morley
CG: 19 DR: 101
D
Graham Potter
CG: 39 DR: 91
D
Matthew Carragher
CG: 23 DR: 82
M
Kevin McIntyre
CG: 21 SD: 25
M
Paul Harsley
CG: 43 SD: 22
M
Danny Whitaker
CG: 23 SD: 10
M
Mark Bailey
CG: 17 SD: 8
F
Jonathan Parkin
CG: 42 SR: 171
F
Matthew Tipton
CG: 40 SR: 334

KEY PLAYER APPEARANCES

	PLAYER	POS	AGE	APP	MINS ON	GOALS	CARDS(Y/R)	
1	Paul Harsley	MID	27	46	3949	3	2	0
2	Jonathan Parkin	ATT	23	42	3765	22	8	1
3	Matthew Tipton	ATT	25	44	3679	11	6	0
4	Graham Potter	DEF	30	41	3556	6	1	1
5	Michael Welch	DEF	23	31	2673	2	3	0
6	Alan Fettis	GK	34	28	2495	0	0	0
7	Danny Whitaker	MID	24	36	2395	2	1	0
8	Matthew Carragher	DEF	29	31	2368	0	2	0
9	Anthony Barras	DEF	34	24	2030	1	3	0
10	Kevin McIntyre	MID	27	23	1886	0	3	0
11	Tommy Widdrington	MID	33	23	1728	0	2	0
12	David Morley	DEF	27	19	1710	2	4	0
13	Mark Bailey	MID	28	21	1703	2	3	0
14	Steve Wilson	GK	31	19	1645	0	0	0
15	John Miles	ATT	23	30	1551	3	2	0
16	Danny Swailes	DEF	26	17	1458	1	2	0
17	Mike Sheron	ATT	33	26	1371	3	0	0
18	Neil MacKenzie	MID	29	18	1202	0	1	0

KEY PLAYERS - GOALSCORERS

Jonathan Parkin

Goals in the League	22
Contribution to Attacking Power Average number of minutes between League team goals while on pitch	64
Player Strike Rate Average number of minutes between League goals scored by player	171
Club Strike Rate Average number of minutes between League goals scored by club	69

	PLAYER	LGE GOALS	POWER	STRIKE RATE
1	Jonathan Parkin	22	64	171 mins
2	Matthew Tipton	11	69	334 mins
3	John Miles	3	77	517 mins
4	Graham Potter	6	67	593 mins
5	Mark Bailey	2	77	852 mins

KEY PLAYERS - MIDFIELDERS

Kevin McIntyre

Goals in the League	0
Defensive Rating Average number of mins between League goals conceded while on the pitch	86
Contribution to Attacking Power Average number of minutes between League team goals while on pitch	61
Scoring Difference Defensive Rating minus Contribution to Attacking Power	25

	PLAYER	LGE GOALS	DEF RATE	POWER	SCORE DIFF
1	Kevin McIntyre	0	86	61	25 mins
2	Paul Harsley	3	88	66	22 mins
3	Danny Whitaker	2	80	70	10 mins
4	Mark Bailey	2	85	77	8 mins
5	Tommy Widdrington	0	79	79	0 mins

KEY PLAYERS - DEFENDERS

Danny Swailes

Goals Conceded while on the pitch	14
Defensive Rating Ave number of mins between League goals conceded while on the pitch	104
Clean Sheets In games when player was on pitch for at least 70 minutes	6
Club Defensive Rating Average number of mins between League goals conceded by the club this season.	84

	PLAYER	CON LGE	CLN SHEETS	DEF RATE
1	Danny Swailes	14	6	104 mins
2	David Morley	17	7	101 mins
3	Graham Potter	39	12	91 mins
4	Matthew Carragher	29	8	82 mins
5	Michael Welch	34	9	79 mins

KEY GOALKEEPER

Alan Fettis

Goals Conceded in the League	26
Defensive Rating Ave number of mins between League goals conceded while on the pitch.	96
Counting Games Games when player was on pitch for at least 70 minutes	27
Clean Sheets In Games when player was on pitch for at least 70 minutes	10

TOP POINT EARNERS

	PLAYER	GAMES	AV PTS
1	Alan Fettis	27	2.04
2	Danny Swailes	16	2.00
3	Matthew Carragher	23	1.83
4	Tommy Widdrington	15	1.80
5	David Morley	19	1.79
6	Kevin McIntyre	21	1.76
7	Jonathan Parkin	42	1.71
8	Danny Whitaker	23	1.70
9	Graham Potter	39	1.69
10	Paul Harsley	43	1.67
	CLUB AVERAGE:		1.63

LINCOLN CITY

Final Position: **6th**

NICKNAME: THE RED IMPS

KEY: Won / Drawn / Lost

							Attendance
1	lge2	Shrewsbury	A	W	1-0	Taylor-Fletcher 52	4,843
2	lge2	Southend	H	D	1-1	Taylor-Fletcher 9	3,991
3	lge2	Rushden & D	H	L	1-3	Taylor-Fletcher 55	4,127
4	lge2	Scunthorpe	A	L	2-3	Taylor-Fletcher 76 pen; Futcher 90	5,215
5	ccr1	Derby	H	W	3-1	Taylor-Fletcher 79 pen; Yeo 80; McCombe 90	4,982
6	lge2	Notts County	H	L	1-2	Pearson 90	5,173
7	lge2	Swansea	A	L	0-1		6,948
8	lge2	Bury	A	W	1-0	Bloomer 45	3,188
9	lge2	Boston	H	D	2-2	McCombe 33; Green 59	7,142
10	lge2	Bristol Rovers	A	D	0-0		7,004
11	ccr2	Birmingham	A	L	1-3	Yeo 84 pen	14,500
12	lge2	Chester	H	D	1-1	Green 27	3,985
13	lge2	Mansfield	A	D	2-2	Mcauley 15; Yeo 45	5,349
14	lge2	Kidderminster	H	W	3-0	Yeo 43; Sandwith 58; Taylor-Fletcher 74	3,605
15	lge2	Oxford	A	W	1-0	Green 45	4,089
16	lge2	Rochdale	H	D	1-1	Bloomer 50	3,274
17	lge2	Leyton Orient	H	L	3-4	Mcauley 3,48; Yeo 14	4,246
18	lge2	Cambridge	A	W	1-0	Green 73	3,604
19	lge2	Northampton	H	W	3-2	Yeo 54,57; Richardson 90	4,808
20	facr1	Hartlepool	A	L	0-3		4,533
21	lge2	Darlington	A	W	3-0	Yeo 36; Richardson 45; Butcher 70	4,035
22	lge2	Yeovil	H	W	3-1	Richardson 30,78; Taylor-Fletcher 45	4,714
23	lge2	Macclesfield	A	L	1-2	McCombe 90	1,633
24	lge2	Cheltenham	H	D	0-0		4,097
25	lge2	Wycombe	A	L	0-1		4,277
26	lge2	Grimsby	H	D	0-0		8,056
27	lge2	Bury	H	W	1-0	Westcarr 24	3,962
28	lge2	Chester	A	W	1-0	Yeo 90	2,839
29	lge2	Kidderminster	A	L	1-2	Green 7	2,283
30	lge2	Bristol Rovers	H	D	1-1	Green 62	3,929
31	lge2	Grimsby	A	W	4-2	Yeo 13,27,60; Toner 71	7,091
32	lge2	Mansfield	H	W	2-0	Toner 54; Yeo 82	5,511
33	lge2	Oxford	H	W	3-0	Yeo 31 pen,90; Taylor-Fletcher 57	4,535
34	lge2	Rochdale	A	L	1-3	Yeo 24 pen	2,847
35	lge2	Boston	A	W	2-0	Hanlon 36; Yeo 70	6,445
36	lge2	Cambridge	H	W	2-1	Yeo 17; Taylor-Fletcher 26	4,672
37	lge2	Leyton Orient	A	D	1-1	Yeo 3	2,436
38	lge2	Cheltenham	A	L	0-1		3,187
39	lge2	Wycombe	H	L	2-3	Sandwith 63; Yeo 68 pen	4,250
40	lge2	Southend	A	D	1-1	Futcher 87	5,824
41	lge2	Shrewsbury	H	W	2-0	Green 4; Yeo 17	4,255
42	lge2	Rushden & D	A	W	4-1	Yeo 20; Futcher 75; McCombe 79; Taylor-Fletcher 83	4,213
43	lge2	Scunthorpe	H	W	2-0	Yeo 1; Taylor-Fletcher 78	6,729
44	lge2	Notts County	A	L	0-1		7,103
45	lge2	Swansea	H	W	1-0	Monk 90 og	5,207
46	lge2	Macclesfield	H	W	2-0	Butcher 33; Green 68	5,289
47	lge2	Northampton	A	L	0-1		6,435
48	lge2	Darlington	H	D	0-0		7,753
49	lge2	Yeovil	A	L	0-3		8,855
50	d3po1	Macclesfield	H	W	1-0	Mcauley 11	7,032
51	d3po2	Macclesfield	A	D	1-1	Mcauley 15	5,223

TEAM OF THE SEASON

G Alan Marriott CG: 45 DR: 88

D Ben Futcher CG: 34 DR: 104

D Paul Morgan CG: 39 DR: 98

D Jamie McCombe CG: 34 DR: 90

D Gareth Mcauley CG: 30 DR: 85

M Kevin Sandwith CG: 32 SD: 47

M Peter Gain CG: 34 SD: 28

M Richard Butcher CG: 46 SD: 23

M Francis Green CG: 22 SD: 19

F Simon Yeo CG: 35 SR: 159

F Gary Taylor-Fletcher CG: 34 SR: 310

KEY PLAYER APPEARANCES

	PLAYER	POS	AGE	APP	MINS ON	GOALS	CARDS(Y/R)	
1	Richard Butcher	MID	24	46	4140	2	5	0
2	Alan Marriott	GK	26	45	4050	0	0	0
3	Paul Morgan	DEF	26	39	3510	0	7	0
4	Simon Yeo	ATT	31	44	3343	21	6	0
5	Jamie McCombe	DEF	22	41	3339	3	1	0
6	Peter Gain	MID	28	40	3285	0	7	0
7	Ben Futcher	DEF	24	35	3119	3	5	1
8	Gary Taylor-Fletcher	ATT	24	38	3098	10	4	0
9	Kevin Sandwith	MID	27	37	3039	2	1	0
10	Gareth Mcauley	DEF	25	37	2886	3	3	0
11	Matthew Bloomer	DEF	26	37	2702	2	0	0
12	Francis Green	MID	25	37	2474	8	6	0
13	Ciaran Toner	MID	24	15	874	2	0	0
14	Martin Carruthers	ATT	32	11	670	0	1	0
15	Marcus Richardson	ATT	27	14	649	4	0	1
16	Derek Asamoah	ATT	24	10	589	0	0	0
17	Nathan Peat	MID	22	10	583	0	3	0
18	Richie Hanlon	MID	27	12	554	1	1	0

KEY PLAYERS - GOALSCORERS

Simon Yeo

Goals in the League: **21**

Contribution to Attacking Power — Average number of minutes between League team goals while on pitch: **58**

Player Strike Rate — Average number of minutes between League goals scored by player: **159**

Club Strike Rate — Average number of minutes between League goals scored by club: **65**

	PLAYER	LGE GOALS	POWER	STRIKE RATE
1	Simon Yeo	21	58	159 mins
2	Francis Green	8	69	309 mins
3	Gary Taylor-Fletcher	10	58	310 mins
4	Gareth Mcauley	3	55	962 mins
5	Ben Futcher	3	74	1040 mins

KEY PLAYERS - MIDFIELDERS

Kevin Sandwith

Goals in the League: **2**

Defensive Rating — Average number of mins between League goals conceded while on the pitch: **105**

Contribution to Attacking Power — Average number of minutes between League team goals while on pitch: **58**

Scoring Difference — Defensive Rating minus Contribution to Attacking Power: **47**

	PLAYER	LGE GOALS	DEF RATE	POWER	SCORE DIFF
1	Kevin Sandwith	2	105	58	47 mins
2	Peter Gain	0	91	63	28 mins
3	Richard Butcher	2	88	65	23 mins
4	Francis Green	8	88	69	19 mins

KEY PLAYERS - DEFENDERS

Ben Futcher

Goals Conceded while on the pitch: **30**

Defensive Rating — Ave number of mins between League goals conceded while on the pitch: **104**

Clean Sheets — In games when player was on pitch for at least 70 minutes: **16**

Club Defensive Rating — Average number of mins between League goals conceded by the club this season: **88**

	PLAYER	CON LGE	CLN SHEETS	DEF RATE
1	Ben Futcher	30	16	104 mins
2	Paul Morgan	36	17	98 mins
3	Jamie McCombe	37	15	90 mins
4	Gareth Mcauley	34	12	85 mins
5	Matthew Bloomer	36	12	75 mins

KEY GOALKEEPER

Alan Marriott

Goals Conceded in the League: **46**

Defensive Rating — Ave number of mins between League goals conceded while on the pitch: **88**

Counting Games — Games when player was on pitch for at least 70 minutes: **45**

Clean Sheets — In Games when player was on pitch for at least 70 minutes: **19**

TOP POINT EARNERS

	PLAYER	GAMES	AV PTS
1	Kevin Sandwith	32	1.91
2	Francis Green	22	1.82
3	Jamie McCombe	34	1.68
4	Gareth Mcauley	30	1.67
5	Simon Yeo	35	1.63
6	Paul Morgan	39	1.59
7	Alan Marriott	45	1.58
8	Richard Butcher	46	1.57
9	Matthew Bloomer	29	1.55
10	Ben Futcher	34	1.53
	CLUB AVERAGE:		1.57

NORTHAMPTON TOWN

Final Position: **7th**

NICKNAME: THE COBBLERS

KEY: Won / Drawn / Lost

							Attendance
1	lge2	Swansea	A	W	2-0	McGleish 3; Ricketts 82 og	9,578
2	lge2	Rushden & D	H	W	1-0	Sabin 75	7,107
3	lge2	Wycombe	H	D	1-1	Richards 46	6,049
4	lge2	Shrewsbury	A	L	0-2		3,980
5	ccr1	Gillingham	A	W	2-1	Sabin 32; McGleish 41	3,108
6	lge2	Leyton Orient	H	D	2-2	Richards 37; McGleish 65	5,577
7	lge2	Scunthorpe	A	L	0-2		4,201
8	lge2	Mansfield	A	L	1-4	Sabin 37	5,173
9	lge2	Notts County	H	D	0-0		5,471
10	lge2	Darlington	A	D	1-1	Morison 53	4,028
11	ccr2	Southampton	H	L	0-3		6,343
12	lge2	Bristol Rovers	H	W	2-1	McGleish 4,23	5,645
13	lge2	Yeovil	A	D	1-1	Sabin 79	5,944
14	lge2	Grimsby	H	L	0-1		5,805
15	lge2	Cambridge	A	W	1-0	Sabin 41	4,118
16	lge2	Oxford	H	W	1-0	McGleish 83	5,455
17	lge2	Rochdale	H	W	5-1	Burgess 9 og; Smith 21 pen,28; Edwards 63 og; Low 90	5,342
18	lge2	Southend	A	L	1-2	Sabin 87	5,696
19	lge2	Lincoln	A	L	2-3	Sabin 6; McGleish 38	4,808
20	facr1	Barnsley	H	W	1-0	McGleish 5	4,876
21	lge2	Chester	H	D	1-1	Smith 7	5,625
22	lge2	Kidderminster	A	W	2-0	McGleish 16; Alsop 76	2,701
23	facr2	Bury	H	W	1-0	McGleish 23	4,415
24	lge2	Cheltenham	H	D	1-1	McGleish 64	4,373
25	lge2	Boston	H	W	2-1	Smith 72; McGleish 86	5,245
26	lge2	Macclesfield	A	W	3-1	Low 50,86; Hearn 78	2,073
27	lge2	Bury	H	W	2-0	Rowson 40; Low 73	6,041
28	lge2	Mansfield	H	W	2-1	Benjamin 53; Smith 77	6,122
29	lge2	Bristol Rovers	A	L	1-3	Sabin 81	6,961
30	facr3	Southampton	H	L	1-3	Williamson 30	7,183
31	lge2	Grimsby	A	W	2-1	McGleish 49; Benjamin 55	3,774
32	lge2	Darlington	H	D	1-1	Galbraith 87	5,762
33	lge2	Bury	A	L	0-2		2,687
34	lge2	Cambridge	H	D	2-2	Rowson 3; McGleish 82	6,615
35	lge2	Oxford	A	W	2-1	Sabin 64; McGleish 70	7,032
36	lge2	Notts County	A	D	0-0		4,645
37	lge2	Southend	H	L	1-2	Smith 7	6,602
38	lge2	Boston	A	W	1-0	Smith 73	2,749
39	lge2	Yeovil	H	D	1-1	Crow 88	5,630
40	lge2	Macclesfield	H	W	1-0	Crow 2	5,804
41	lge2	Rochdale	A	L	0-1		2,107
42	lge2	Rushden & D	A	L	2-3	Smith 45; Kirk 52	5,520
43	lge2	Swansea	H	D	2-2	Smith 35; Kirk 40	5,799
44	lge2	Wycombe	A	W	1-0	McGleish 44	7,417
45	lge2	Shrewsbury	H	W	2-0	Smith 16; Westwood 38	6,514
46	lge2	Leyton Orient	A	L	2-3	Kirk 68; Westwood 75	3,585
47	lge2	Scunthorpe	H	L	1-2	Kirk 4	6,523
48	lge2	Cheltenham	A	L	0-1		3,689
49	lge2	Lincoln	H	W	1-0	Low 69	6,435
50	lge2	Chester	A	W	2-0	Kirk 22,47	3,455
51	lge2	Kidderminster	H	W	3-0	Kirk 68; Low 85,87	6,786
52	d3po1	Southend	H	D	0-0		6,601
53	d3po2	Southend	A	L	0-1		9,152

TEAM OF THE SEASON

D
Tommy Jaszczun
CG: 19 DR: 92
M
David Rowson
CG: 33 SD: 40
G
Lee Harper
CG: 36 DR: 81
D
Fred Murray
CG: 36 DR: 86
M
Lee Williamson
CG: 30 SD: 28
F
Scott McGleish
CG: 41 SR: 288
D
Christopher Willmott
CG: 44 DR: 82
M
Charlie Hearn
CG: 18 SD: 26
F
Eric Sabin
CG: 25 SR: 319
D
Pedj Bojic
CG: 23 DR: 81
M
Joshua Low
CG: 33 SD: 19

KEY PLAYER APPEARANCES

	PLAYER	POS	AGE	APP	MINS ON	GOALS	CARDS(Y	/R)
1	Christopher Willmott	DEF	27	45	4010	0	8	0
2	Scott McGleish	ATT	31	44	3741	13	5	0
3	Fred Murray	DEF	23	38	3366	0	5	1
4	Lee Harper	GK	33	36	3240	0	0	0
5	David Rowson	MID	28	37	3153	2	4	0
6	Joshua Low	MID	26	34	2929	7	2	0
7	Lee Williamson	MID	23	37	2785	0	9	0
8	Martin Smith	MID	30	33	2685	10	2	0
9	Eric Sabin	ATT	30	40	2550	8	3	0
10	Pedj Bojic	DEF	21	35	2426	0	3	0
11	Tommy Jaszczun	DEF	27	31	2024	0	3	0
12	Luke Chambers	DEF	19	27	1880	0	4	0
13	Charlie Hearn	MID	21	24	1850	1	8	0
14	Ashley Westwood	DEF	28	19	1535	2	3	0
15	David Galbraith	MID	21	25	933	1	1	0
16	Paul Rachubka	GK	24	10	900	0	1	0
17	Marc Richards	ATT	22	12	664	2	0	0
18	Andy Kirk	ATT	26	8	661	7	2	0

KEY PLAYERS - GOALSCORERS

Martin Smith

Goals in the League	10
Contribution to Attacking Power Average number of minutes between League team goals while on pitch	67
Player Strike Rate Average number of minutes between League goals scored by player	269
Club Strike Rate Average number of minutes between League goals scored by club	67

	PLAYER	LGE GOALS	POWER	STRIKE RATE
1	Martin Smith	10	67	269 mins
2	Scott McGleish	13	63	288 mins
3	Eric Sabin	8	68	319 mins
4	Joshua Low	7	60	418 mins
5	Ashley Westwood	2	61	768 mins

KEY PLAYERS - MIDFIELDERS

David Rowson

Goals in the League	2
Defensive Rating Average number of mins between League goals conceded while on the pitch	99
Contribution to Attacking Power Average number of minutes between League team goals while on pitch	59
Scoring Difference Defensive Rating minus Contribution to Attacking Power	40

	PLAYER	LGE GOALS	DEF RATE	POWER	SCORE DIFF
1	David Rowson	2	99	59	40 mins
2	Lee Williamson	0	99	71	28 mins
3	Charlie Hearn	1	97	71	26 mins
4	Joshua Low	7	79	60	19 mins
5	Martin Smith	10	75	67	8 mins

KEY PLAYERS - DEFENDERS

Tommy Jaszczun

Goals Conceded while on the pitch	22
Defensive Rating Ave number of mins between League goals conceded while on the pitch	92
Clean Sheets In games when player was on pitch for at least 70 minutes	6
Club Defensive Rating Average number of mins between League goals conceded by the club this season.	81

	PLAYER	CON LGE	CLN SHEETS	DEF RATE
1	Tommy Jaszczun	22	6	92 mins
2	Fred Murray	39	14	86 mins
3	Christopher Willmott	49	15	82 mins
4	Pedj Bojic	30	5	81 mins
5	Luke Chambers	25	6	75 mins

KEY GOALKEEPER

Lee Harper

Goals Conceded in the League	40
Defensive Rating Ave number of mins between League goals conceded while on the pitch.	81
Counting Games Games when player was on pitch for at least 70 minutes	36
Clean Sheets In Games when player was on pitch for at least 70 minutes	12

TOP POINT EARNERS

	PLAYER	GAMES	AV PTS
1	David Rowson	33	1.85
2	Fred Murray	36	1.67
3	Joshua Low	33	1.64
4	Tommy Jaszczun	19	1.63
5	Pedj Bojic	23	1.61
6	Scott McGleish	41	1.61
7	Lee Harper	36	1.58
8	Christopher Willmott	44	1.57
9	Charlie Hearn	18	1.56
10	Lee Williamson	30	1.50
	CLUB AVERAGE:		1.57

DARLINGTON

Final Position: **8th**

NICKNAME: THE QUAKERS

KEY: Won / Drawn / Lost

	Comp	Opponent			Score	Scorers	Attendance
1	lge2	Grimsby	H	W	1-0	Clark, I 83	4,807
2	lge2	Yeovil	A	D	1-1	Clarke, M 53	5,116
3	lge2	Kidderminster	A	L	0-1		2,303
4	lge2	Bristol Rovers	H	L	0-1		3,661
5	ccr1	Barnsley	H	L	0-2		2,789
6	lge2	Chester	A	W	3-0	Wainwright 16; Kendrick 25; Clarke, M 64	2,392
7	lge2	Cambridge	H	D	1-1	Valentine 76	3,350
8	lge2	Scunthorpe	H	D	0-0		3,983
9	lge2	Rochdale	A	D	1-1	Hignett 87	2,616
10	lge2	Northampton	H	D	1-1	Hignett 23	4,028
11	lge2	Macclesfield	A	L	0-1		1,872
12	lge2	Southend	H	W	4-0	Armstrong 15,40,52; Wijnhard 24	3,901
13	lge2	Oxford	A	W	2-1	Wijnhard 51; Clark, I 74	5,881
14	lge2	Bury	H	L	1-2	Wijnhard 89	4,642
15	lge2	Notts County	A	D	1-1	Armstrong 69	3,620
16	lge2	Wycombe	H	W	1-0	Wijnhard 35 pen	4,292
17	lge2	Rushden & D	A	W	2-1	Hignett 21,82	3,036
18	facr1	Yeovil	H	D	3-3	Armstrong 19,73; Keltie 86	3,698
19	lge2	Swansea	A	L	1-2	Liddle 26	7,824
20	lge2	Lincoln	H	L	0-3		4,035
21	facr1r	Yeovil	A	L	0-1		5,365
22	lge2	Cheltenham	A	W	2-0	Gill 40 og; Armstrong 57	3,578
23	lge2	Mansfield	H	W	2-1	Wijnhard 63; Hignett 74	3,686
24	lge2	Leyton Orient	H	W	3-0	White 5 og; Wijnhard 59; Armstrong 74	3,702
25	lge2	Boston	A	L	1-3	Hignett 57 pen	2,428
26	lge2	Rochdale	H	L	0-3		7,028
27	lge2	Shrewsbury	A	L	0-4		3,915
28	lge2	Scunthorpe	A	W	1-0	Armstrong 60	5,131
29	lge2	Macclesfield	H	W	3-1	Wijnhard 26; Maddison 40; Armstrong 81	3,677
30	lge2	Oxford	H	D	1-1	Gregorio 8	3,735
31	lge2	Northampton	A	D	1-1	Gregorio 7	5,762
32	lge2	Shrewsbury	H	W	3-0	Wainwright 28; Hignett 67,74	3,934
33	lge2	Southend	A	L	0-2		7,358
34	lge2	Bury	A	W	1-0	Petta 29	2,971
35	lge2	Notts County	H	L	1-2	McGurk 21	4,213
36	lge2	Wycombe	A	D	1-1	Wijnhard 34	4,326
37	lge2	Swansea	H	W	2-1	Clarke, M 34; Wainwright 84	2,709
38	lge2	Leyton Orient	A	L	0-1		3,430
39	lge2	Boston	H	W	1-0	McGurk 69	3,219
40	lge2	Yeovil	H	W	2-1	Wijnhard 13; Armstrong 61	4,121
41	lge2	Grimsby	A	W	1-0	St Juste 11	4,578
42	lge2	Kidderminster	H	L	0-2		6,972
43	lge2	Bristol Rovers	A	D	3-3	Russell, C 1; Hignett 50 pen; St Juste 63	5,918
44	lge2	Chester	H	W	1-0	Wijnhard 76 pen	3,778
45	lge2	Cambridge	A	L	1-3	Wijnhard 9	3,116
46	lge2	Mansfield	A	D	1-1	Wijnhard 66	3,569
47	lge2	Rushden & D	H	W	2-0	Wijnhard 49 pen,54 pen	4,579
48	lge2	Lincoln	A	D	0-0		7,753
49	lge2	Cheltenham	H	W	3-1	Dickman 43; Wainwright 89; Sodje, A 90	5,575

TEAM OF THE SEASON

G — Sam Russell CG: 46 DR: 84

D — Ryan Valentine CG: 30 DR: 112

D — Joe Kendrick CG: 16 DR: 97

D — Craig Liddle CG: 19 DR: 90

D — Matthew Clarke CG: 39 DR: 80

M — Adolfo Gregorio CG: 12 SD: 22

M — Neil Maddison CG: 17 SD: 17

M — Craig Hignett CG: 13 SD: 14

M — Brian Close CG: 34 SD: 10

F — Clyde Wijnhard CG: 29 SR: 191

F — Alun Armstrong CG: 27 SR: 287

KEY PLAYER APPEARANCES

	PLAYER	POS	AGE	APP	MINS ON	GOALS	CARDS(Y/R)	
1	Sam Russell	GK	22	46	4140	0	5	0
2	Matthew Clarke	DEF	24	43	3746	3	9	0
3	Brian Close	MID	23	38	3263	0	9	1
4	Ryan Valentine	DEF	22	36	2899	1	0	0
5	Clyde Wijnhard	ATT	31	31	2676	14	5	1
6	Alun Armstrong	ATT	30	32	2586	9	4	0
7	Neil Wainwright	MID	27	38	2520	4	5	0
8	Curtis Fleming	DEF	36	27	2182	0	1	0
9	Joe Kendrick	DEF	22	31	1837	1	3	0
10	Neil Maddison	MID	35	24	1717	1	1	0
11	Craig Liddle	DEF	33	20	1707	0	4	0
12	Craig Russell	ATT	31	28	1637	1	1	0
13	Adolfo Gregorio	MID	22	24	1557	2	3	0
14	Adrian Webster	MID	24	22	1446	0	2	0
15	Craig Hignett	MID	35	19	1403	9	0	0
16	Ian Clark	MID	30	24	1334	2	0	0
17	Clark Keltie	MID	21	21	1054	0	1	0
18	Mark Convery	ATT	24	23	1024	0	1	0

KEY PLAYERS - GOALSCORERS

Craig Hignett

Goals in the League	9	Player Strike Rate — Average number of minutes between League goals scored by player	156
Contribution to Attacking Power — Average number of minutes between League team goals while on pitch	56	Club Strike Rate — Average number of minutes between League goals scored by club	73

	PLAYER	LGE GOALS	POWER	STRIKE RATE
1	Craig Hignett	9	56	156 mins
2	Clyde Wijnhard	14	65	191 mins
3	Alun Armstrong	9	69	287 mins
4	Neil Wainwright	4	76	630 mins
5	Adolfo Gregorio	2	65	779 mins

KEY PLAYERS - MIDFIELDERS

Adolfo Gregorio

Goals in the League	2	Contribution to Attacking Power — Average number of minutes between League team goals while on pitch	65
Defensive Rating — Average number of mins between League goals conceded while on the pitch	87	Scoring Difference — Defensive Rating minus Contribution to Attacking Power	22

	PLAYER	LGE GOALS	DEF RATE	POWER	SCORE DIFF
1	Adolfo Gregorio	2	87	65	22 mins
2	Neil Maddison	1	78	61	17 mins
3	Craig Hignett	9	70	56	14 mins
4	Brian Close	0	88	78	10 mins
5	Neil Wainwright	4	81	76	5 mins

KEY PLAYERS - DEFENDERS

Ryan Valentine

Goals Conceded while on the pitch	26	Clean Sheets — In games when player was on pitch for at least 70 minutes	12
Defensive Rating — Ave number of mins between League goals conceded while on the pitch	112	Club Defensive Rating — Average number of mins between League goals conceded by the club this season.	84

	PLAYER	CON LGE	CLN SHEETS	DEF RATE
1	Ryan Valentine	26	12	112 mins
2	Joe Kendrick	19	6	97 mins
3	Craig Liddle	19	5	90 mins
4	Matthew Clarke	47	11	80 mins
5	Curtis Fleming	28	6	78 mins

KEY GOALKEEPER

Sam Russell

Goals Conceded in the League	49
Defensive Rating — Ave number of mins between League goals conceded while on the pitch.	84
Counting Games — Games when player was on pitch for at least 70 minutes	46
Clean Sheets — In Games when player was on pitch for at least 70 minutes	15

TOP POINT EARNERS

	PLAYER	GAMES	AV PTS
1	Joe Kendrick	16	1.94
2	Ryan Valentine	30	1.80
3	Clyde Wijnhard	29	1.72
4	Adolfo Gregorio	12	1.67
5	Brian Close	34	1.65
6	Adrian Webster	13	1.62
7	Sam Russell	46	1.57
8	Alun Armstrong	27	1.56
9	Craig Hignett	13	1.54
10	Neil Maddison	17	1.47
	CLUB AVERAGE:		1.57

ROCHDALE

Final Position: **9th**

NICKNAME: THE DALE

KEY: Won / Drawn / Lost

	Comp	Opponent	H/A	Res	Score	Scorers	Attendance
1	lge2	Scunthorpe	A	L	1-3	Bertos 45 pen	4,409
2	lge2	Swansea	H	L	0-2		2,514
3	lge2	Southend	H	W	2-0	Jones 3,60 pen	2,218
4	lge2	Wycombe	A	W	3-0	Holt 70; McGivern 90; Jones 90 pen	4,440
5	ccr1	Wolverhampton	H	L	2-4	Holt 4; Tait 26	3,292
6	lge2	Bury	H	L	0-3		3,913
7	lge2	Leyton Orient	A	L	1-2	Holt 70	3,243
8	lge2	Grimsby	A	W	1-0	Holt 80	4,795
9	lge2	Darlington	H	D	1-1	Holt 30	2,616
10	lge2	Mansfield	A	L	0-1		4,266
11	lge2	Notts County	H	L	0-3		2,370
12	lge2	Rushden & D	A	D	0-0		2,619
13	lge2	Yeovil	H	W	2-1	Holt 68; Jones 82	2,402
14	lge2	Cheltenham	H	L	1-2	Jones 88 pen	2,778
15	lge2	Lincoln	A	D	1-1	Clarke 86	3,274
16	lge2	Northampton	A	L	1-5	Griffiths 77	5,342
17	lge2	Macclesfield	H	W	3-0	Holt 42; Cooksey 55; Jones 67	2,704
18	lge2	Cambridge	H	W	2-1	Holt 31,83	2,353
19	facr1	Oxford	H	W	2-1	Holt 36,90	2,333
20	lge2	Oxford	A	W	1-0	Tardif 90 og	4,204
21	lge2	Boston	H	W	2-0	Bertos 62; Cooksey 84	2,474
22	facr2	Stevenage	A	W	2-0	Holt 70,90	2,700
23	lge2	Shrewsbury	A	W	2-0	Tait 53; Holt 66	3,677
24	lge2	Kidderminster	A	L	1-2	Holt 36	2,337
25	lge2	Bristol Rovers	H	D	0-0		2,623
26	lge2	Darlington	A	W	3-0	Atieno 18; Holt 62,78	7,028
27	lge2	Chester	H	D	2-2	Bertos 58; Atieno 64	3,724
28	lge2	Notts County	A	D	0-0		5,258
29	facr3	Charlton	A	L	1-4	Holt 51	13,955
30	lge2	Mansfield	H	D	1-1	Tait 4	2,576
31	lge2	Chester	A	D	0-0		2,985
32	lge2	Yeovil	A	D	2-2	Goodall 8; Bertos 77	5,180
33	lge2	Rushden & D	H	W	2-0	Cooksey 56; Holt 82	2,664
34	lge2	Cheltenham	A	L	0-2		2,951
35	lge2	Lincoln	H	W	3-1	Holt 7; Heald 59; Goodall 74	2,847
36	lge2	Macclesfield	A	L	0-3		3,031
37	lge2	Kidderminster	H	D	1-1	Lambert 40	2,385
38	lge2	Grimsby	H	W	2-0	Lambert 27; Jones 90	2,312
39	lge2	Bristol Rovers	A	D	0-0		5,464
40	lge2	Northampton	H	W	1-0	Lambert 56	2,107
41	lge2	Swansea	A	D	2-2	Holt 31; Lambert 90	6,804
42	lge2	Scunthorpe	H	D	0-0		3,605
43	lge2	Southend	A	L	0-3		7,656
44	lge2	Wycombe	H	D	1-1	Jones 16 pen	2,707
45	lge2	Bury	A	D	0-0		4,606
46	lge2	Leyton Orient	H	W	2-0	Richards 47,59	2,255
47	lge2	Shrewsbury	H	D	1-1	Lambert 40	3,142
48	lge2	Cambridge	A	D	0-0		3,738
49	lge2	Oxford	H	W	5-1	Heald 3; Cooksey 11; Holt 14,69; Lambert 25	2,579
50	lge2	Boston	A	D	1-1	Cooksey 50	2,528

TEAM OF THE SEASON

G: Mathew Gilks — CG: 31 DR: 107

D: Alan Goodall — CG: 27 DR: 111

D: Gareth Griffiths — CG: 37 DR: 93

D: Wayne Evans — CG: 39 DR: 87

D: Scott Warner — CG: 18 DR: 85

M: Jamie Clarke — CG: 32 SD: 39

M: Ernie Cooksey — CG: 21 SD: 33

M: Rickie Lambert — CG: 14 SD: 19

M: Gary Jones — CG: 38 SD: 16

F: Grant Holt — CG: 37 SR: 203

F: Paul Tait — CG: 25 SR: 1157

KEY PLAYER APPEARANCES

	PLAYER	POS	AGE	APP	MINS ON	GOALS	CARDS(Y/R)	
1	Wayne Evans	DEF	33	40	3570	0	0	2
2	Gary Jones	MID	36	39	3457	8	6	0
3	Grant Holt	ATT	24	40	3443	17	14	0
4	Gareth Griffiths	DEF	35	38	3335	1	9	1
5	Leo Bertos	MID	23	42	3073	4	6	1
6	Jamie Clarke	MID	22	41	3005	1	0	0
7	Tony Gallimore	DEF	33	34	2834	0	4	0
8	Mathew Gilks	GK	23	31	2784	0	0	0
9	Alan Goodall	DEF	23	34	2564	2	9	0
10	Greg Heald	DEF	33	29	2476	2	3	0
11	Ernie Cooksey	MID	25	34	2369	5	5	2
12	Paul Tait	ATT	30	36	2314	2	7	1
13	Scott Warner	DEF	21	28	1960	0	3	0
14	Daryl Burgess	DEF	34	21	1479	0	3	2
15	Neil Edwards	GK	34	16	1440	0	0	0
16	Rickie Lambert	MID	23	15	1314	6	1	0
17	Taiwo Atieno	ATT	19	13	584	2	1	0
18	Neil Brisco	MID	27	11	573	0	2	0

KEY PLAYERS - GOALSCORERS

Grant Holt

Goals in the League	17	Player Strike Rate – Average number of minutes between League goals scored by player	203
Contribution to Attacking Power – Average number of minutes between League team goals while on pitch	73	Club Strike Rate – Average number of minutes between League goals scored by club	77

	PLAYER	LGE GOALS	POWER	STRIKE RATE
1	Grant Holt	17	73	203 mins
2	Rickie Lambert	6	82	219 mins
3	Gary Jones	8	76	432 mins
4	Ernie Cooksey	5	70	474 mins
5	Leo Bertos	4	77	768 mins

KEY PLAYERS - MIDFIELDERS

Jamie Clarke

Goals in the League	1	Contribution to Attacking Power – Average number of minutes between League team goals while on pitch	68
Defensive Rating – Average number of mins between League goals conceded while on the pitch	107	Scoring Difference – Defensive Rating minus Contribution to Attacking Power	39

	PLAYER	LGE GOALS	DEF RATE	POWER	SCORE DIFF
1	Jamie Clarke	1	107	68	39 mins
2	Ernie Cooksey	5	103	70	33 mins
3	Rickie Lambert	6	101	82	19 mins
4	Gary Jones	8	93	77	16 mins
5	Leo Bertos	4	90	77	13 mins

KEY PLAYERS - DEFENDERS

Alan Goodall

Goals Conceded while on the pitch	23	Clean Sheets – In games when player was on pitch for at least 70 minutes	14
Defensive Rating – Ave number of mins between League goals conceded while on the pitch	111	Club Defensive Rating – Average number of mins between League goals conceded by the club this season.	86

	PLAYER	CON LGE	CLN SHEETS		DEF RATE
1	Alan Goodall	23	28	14	111 mins
2	Gareth Griffiths	36	37	17	93 mins
3	Wayne Evans	41	50	17	87 mins
4	Scott Warner	23	23	8	85 mins
5	Greg Heald	30	38	12	83 mins

KEY GOALKEEPER

Mathew Gilks

Goals Conceded in the League	26
Defensive Rating – Ave number of mins between League goals conceded while on the pitch.	107
Counting Games – Games when player was on pitch for at least 70 minutes	31
Clean Sheets – In Games when player was on pitch for at least 70 minutes	15

TOP POINT EARNERS

	PLAYER	GAMES	AV PTS
1	Paul Tait	25	1.60
2	Jamie Clarke	32	1.59
3	Ernie Cooksey	21	1.57
4	Mathew Gilks	31	1.55
5	Gareth Griffiths	37	1.54
6	Grant Holt	37	1.54
7	Gary Jones	38	1.50
8	Alan Goodall	27	1.48
9	Tony Gallimore	31	1.48
10	Daryl Burgess	15	1.47
	CLUB AVERAGE:		1.43

WYCOMBE WANDERERS

Final Position: **10th**

NICKNAME: THE CHAIRBOYS

KEY: ☐ Won ☐ Drawn ☐ Lost

	Comp	Opponent	H/A	Res	Score	Scorers	Attendance
1	lge2	Cambridge	H	W	2-1	Tyson 55,81	4,726
2	lge2	Chester	A	W	2-0	Williamson 23; Senda 84	2,881
3	lge2	Northampton	A	D	1-1	Stonebridge 42	6,049
4	lge2	Rochdale	H	L	0-3		4,440
5	ccr1	Bristol City	H	L	0-1		1,778
6	lge2	Kidderminster	A	W	2-0	Tyson 21; Ahmed 90	2,444
7	lge2	Grimsby	H	W	2-0	Birchill 43,51	4,320
8	lge2	Oxford	H	D	1-1	Tyson 45 pen	6,348
9	lge2	Southend	A	W	2-1	Tyson 60; Senda 82	4,771
10	lge2	Swansea	H	L	0-1		5,247
11	lge2	Cheltenham	A	D	1-1	Ryan 74	3,663
12	lge2	Shrewsbury	H	D	1-1	Senda 74	4,634
13	lge2	Scunthorpe	A	L	0-2		4,373
14	lge2	Boston	A	L	0-2		2,635
15	lge2	Rushden & D	H	D	1-1	Birchill 14	3,844
16	lge2	Mansfield	H	D	1-1	Birchill 60	4,215
17	lge2	Darlington	A	L	0-1		4,292
18	lge2	Yeovil	H	L	0-1		5,453
19	facr1	Coalville	H	W	1-0	Johnson 71	2,816
20	lge2	Leyton Orient	A	W	2-1	Tyson 49; Johnson 67	4,047
21	lge2	Bristol Rovers	H	W	1-0	Tyson 54 pen	4,999
22	facr2	Luton	H	L	0-3		4,767
23	lge2	Bury	A	D	2-2	Tyson 61,79	1,866
24	lge2	Notts County	A	W	1-0	Stonebridge 42	6,529
25	lge2	Lincoln	H	W	1-0	Ryan 89	4,277
26	lge2	Southend	H	L	0-1		5,669
27	lge2	Macclesfield	A	L	1-2	Johnson 90	1,908
28	lge2	Oxford	A	L	1-2	Senda 90 pen	7,195
29	lge2	Cheltenham	H	D	1-1	Tyson 70	4,394
30	lge2	Swansea	A	D	2-2	Johnson 77; Guppy 83	6,793
31	lge2	Macclesfield	H	D	1-1	Johnson 55	4,105
32	lge2	Shrewsbury	A	W	1-0	Tyson 29 pen	3,884
33	lge2	Boston	H	L	1-2	Dixon 39 pen	4,091
34	lge2	Rushden & D	A	W	2-1	Bloomfield 74; Tyson 90	3,490
35	lge2	Scunthorpe	H	W	2-1	Claridge 13; Tyson 43	4,089
36	lge2	Darlington	H	D	1-1	Claridge 36	4,326
37	lge2	Mansfield	A	W	4-1	Claridge 59 pen,90; Stonebridge 59; Uhlenbeek 87	2,497
38	lge2	Notts County	H	L	1-2	Stonebridge 14	4,199
39	lge2	Lincoln	A	W	3-2	Tyson 12,30,40	4,250
40	lge2	Chester	H	W	4-2	Tyson 43,52; Uhlenbeek 57; Johnson 59	8,124
41	lge2	Cambridge	A	L	1-2	Uhlenbeek 18	4,649
42	lge2	Northampton	H	L	0-1		7,417
43	lge2	Rochdale	A	D	1-1	Tyson 47	2,707
44	lge2	Kidderminster	H	W	3-0	Tyson 25,36,67	4,608
45	lge2	Grimsby	A	D	0-0		3,452
46	lge2	Bury	H	L	1-2	Johnson 10	4,703
47	lge2	Yeovil	A	D	1-1	Easton 23	7,421
48	lge2	Leyton Orient	H	W	3-2	Bloomfield 2; Williamson 23; Uhlenbeek 30	5,333
49	lge2	Bristol Rovers	A	L	0-1		7,358

TEAM OF THE SEASON

G
Frank Talia
CG: 44 DR: 80
D
Gary Silk
CG: 18 DR: 90
D
Mike Williamson
CG: 32 DR: 85
D
Tony Craig
CG: 14 DR: 84
D
Roger Johnson
CG: 39 DR: 77
M
Matt Bloomfield
CG: 15 SD: 24
M
Clint Easton
CG: 26 SD: 18
M
Joe Burnell
CG: 19 SD: 15
M
Keith Ryan
CG: 31 SD: 15
F
Nathan Tyson
CG: 35 SR: 158
F
Steve Claridge
CG: 14 SR: 343

KEY PLAYER APPEARANCES

	PLAYER	POS	AGE	APP	MINS ON	GOALS	CARDS(Y)	CARDS(R)
1	Frank Talia	GK	32	45	4005	0	3	0
2	Danny Senda	MID	24	44	3828	4	5	0
3	Roger Johnson	DEF	22	42	3614	6	2	1
4	Nathan Tyson	ATT	23	42	3470	22	4	0
5	Gus Uhlenbeek	DEF	34	42	3234	4	8	0
6	Keith Ryan	MID	35	38	2995	2	3	0
7	Mike Williamson	DEF	21	37	2989	2	4	0
8	Ian Stonebridge	ATT	23	38	2859	4	1	0
9	Clint Easton	MID	27	33	2508	1	2	0
10	Stuart Nethercott	DEF	32	29	2327	0	2	0
11	Joe Burnell	MID	24	24	1908	0	0	0
12	Gary Silk	DEF	20	22	1709	0	7	1
13	Matt Bloomfield	MID	21	26	1671	2	2	0
14	Steve Claridge	ATT	39	19	1373	4	0	0
15	Tony Craig	DEF	20	14	1260	0	2	0
16	Steve Guppy	MID	36	14	1005	1	0	0
17	Adam Birchill	ATT	20	12	985	4	0	0
18	Craig Faulconbridge	ATT	27	8	565	0	0	0

KEY PLAYERS - GOALSCORERS

Nathan Tyson

Goals in the League	22
Contribution to Attacking Power Average number of minutes between League team goals while on pitch	70
Player Strike Rate Average number of minutes between League goals scored by player	158
Club Strike Rate Average number of minutes between League goals scored by club	71

	PLAYER	LGE GOALS	POWER	STRIKE RATE
1	Nathan Tyson	22	70	158 mins
2	Steve Claridge	4	65	343 mins
3	Roger Johnson	6	72	602 mins
4	Ian Stonebridge	4	66	715 mins
5	Gus Uhlenbeek	4	66	809 mins

KEY PLAYERS - MIDFIELDERS

Matt Bloomfield

Goals in the League	2
Defensive Rating Average number of mins between League goals conceded while on the pitch	80
Contribution to Attacking Power Average number of minutes between League team goals while on pitch	56
Scoring Difference Defensive Rating minus Contribution to Attacking Power	24

	PLAYER	LGE GOALS	DEF RATE	POWER	SCORE DIFF
1	Matt Bloomfield	2	80	56	24 mins
2	Clint Easton	1	78	60	18 mins
3	Keith Ryan	2	79	64	15 mins
4	Joe Burnell	0	83	68	15 mins
5	Danny Senda	4	80	71	9 mins

KEY PLAYERS - DEFENDERS

Gary Silk

Goals Conceded while on the pitch	19
Defensive Rating Ave number of mins between League goals conceded while on the pitch	90
Clean Sheets In games when player was on pitch for at least 70 minutes	5
Club Defensive Rating Average number of mins between League goals conceded by the club this season.	80

	PLAYER	CON LGE	CLN SHEETS	DEF RATE
1	Gary Silk	19	5	90 mins
2	Mike Williamson	35	9	85 mins
3	Tony Craig	15	3	84 mins
4	Roger Johnson	47	7	77 mins
5	Gus Uhlenbeek	43	7	75 mins

KEY GOALKEEPER

Frank Talia

Goals Conceded in the League	50
Defensive Rating Ave number of mins between League goals conceded while on the pitch.	80
Counting Games Games when player was on pitch for at least 70 minutes	44
Clean Sheets In Games when player was on pitch for at least 70 minutes	9

TOP POINT EARNERS

	PLAYER	GAMES	AV PTS
1	Keith Ryan	31	1.74
2	Clint Easton	26	1.62
3	Ian Stonebridge	29	1.59
4	Gus Uhlenbeek	31	1.58
5	Stuart Nethercott	24	1.54
6	Matt Bloomfield	15	1.53
7	Gary Silk	18	1.50
8	Steve Claridge	14	1.50
9	Nathan Tyson	35	1.49
10	Frank Talia	44	1.48
	CLUB AVERAGE:		1.41

LEYTON ORIENT

Final Position: **11th**

NICKNAME: THE O'S

KEY: ☐ Won ☐ Drawn ☐ Lost

							Attendance
1	lge2	Macclesfield	H	L	1-3	Purser 83	4,540
2	lge2	Cambridge	A	D	1-1	Scott 41	4,114
3	lge2	Cheltenham	A	W	2-1	Steele 35; Ibehre 68	3,346
4	lge2	Oxford	H	D	0-0		3,426
5	ccr1	Bournemouth	H	L	1-3	Steele 12	1,705
6	lge2	Northampton	A	D	2-2	Carlisle 6,62	5,577
7	lge2	Rochdale	H	W	2-1	Steele 26; Newey 77	3,243
8	lge2	Kidderminster	A	W	2-1	Alexander 20; Lockwood 69 pen	2,367
9	lge2	Bristol Rovers	H	W	4-2	Simpson 34; Steele 63; Carlisle 65; Alexander 70	3,972
10	lge2	Grimsby	A	L	0-2		5,082
11	lge2	Boston	H	D	0-0		4,753
12	lge2	Notts County	A	W	2-1	Steele 20; Alexander 71	5,141
13	lge2	Bury	H	D	1-1	Steele 9	3,398
14	lge2	Shrewsbury	H	W	4-1	Steele 17,85; Scott 19,25	3,718
15	lge2	Swansea	A	L	0-1		8,485
16	lge2	Lincoln	A	W	4-3	Steele 11,78,89; Ibehre 37	4,246
17	lge2	Scunthorpe	H	D	1-1	Scott 51	4,359
18	lge2	Chester	A	D	1-1	Steele 38	3,125
19	facr1	Dag & Red	H	W	3-1	Lockwood 11; Hunt 37; Carlisle 58	4,155
20	lge2	Wycombe	H	L	1-2	Carlisle 29	4,047
21	lge2	Mansfield	A	W	1-0	Scott 51	3,803
22	facr2	Oldham	A	L	0-4		4,657
23	lge2	Southend	H	D	2-2	Lockwood 15 pen; Scott 59	3,852
24	lge2	Darlington	A	L	0-3		3,702
25	lge2	Yeovil	H	L	2-3	Echanomi 67; Chillingworth 74	3,867
26	lge2	Bristol Rovers	A	D	1-1	Lockwood 6 pen	8,414
27	lge2	Rushden & D	H	D	2-2	Echanomi 88; Chillingworth 90	3,777
28	lge2	Kidderminster	H	W	2-1	Scott 74,84	3,573
29	lge2	Boston	A	D	2-2	McMahon 32,90	3,183
30	lge2	Bury	A	D	0-0		2,192
31	lge2	Grimsby	H	L	1-2	Echanomi 81	3,816
32	lge2	Rushden & D	A	L	0-2		3,288
33	lge2	Notts County	H	W	2-0	Youngs 56; Barnard, D 85	3,440
34	lge2	Shrewsbury	A	L	1-4	Echanomi 90	3,496
35	lge2	Swansea	H	W	3-1	Scott 15; McMahon 34; Lockwood 52 pen	4,050
36	lge2	Scunthorpe	A	L	0-1		5,162
37	lge2	Lincoln	H	D	1-1	Mackie 83	2,436
38	lge2	Darlington	H	W	1-0	Steele 26	3,430
39	lge2	Yeovil	A	L	0-1		6,545
40	lge2	Cambridge	H	D	1-1	Lockwood 72	3,759
41	lge2	Macclesfield	A	L	1-3	Steele 50	2,234
42	lge2	Cheltenham	H	L	2-3	Alexander 50; Mackie 84	3,261
43	lge2	Oxford	A	D	2-2	Steele 1; Simpson 72	5,320
44	lge2	Northampton	H	W	3-2	Mackie 16; Steele 63,90	3,585
45	lge2	Rochdale	A	L	0-2		2,255
46	lge2	Southend	A	W	1-0	Mackie 22	9,189
47	lge2	Chester	H	W	2-0	Echanomi 14; Lockwood 31 pen	3,192
48	lge2	Wycombe	A	L	2-3	Alexander 48,49	5,333
49	lge2	Mansfield	H	W	2-1	Alexander 26,33	3,882

TEAM OF THE SEASON

G — Lee Harrison, CG: 34 DR: 70

D — Donny Barnard, CG: 19 DR: 70
D — Alan White, CG: 26 DR: 67
D — Justin Miller, CG: 42 DR: 64
D — Gabriel Zakauni, CG: 29 DR: 62

M — Daryl McMahon, CG: 18 SD: 0
M — Michael Simpson, CG: 45 SD: -2
M — Wayne Carlisle, CG: 15 SD: -5
M — David Hunt, CG: 21 SD: -2

F — Lee Steele, CG: 35 SR: 205
F — Gary Alexander, CG: 22 SR: 274

KEY PLAYER APPEARANCES

	PLAYER	POS	AGE	APP	MINS ON	GOALS	CARDS(Y/R)	
1	Michael Simpson	MID	31	45	4050	2	8	0
2	Justin Miller	DEF	24	43	3817	0	2	0
3	Matthew Lockwood	DEF	28	43	3620	6	3	0
4	Lee Steele	ATT	31	39	3278	16	2	0
5	Lee Harrison	GK	33	34	3060	0	2	0
6	Andy Scott	MID	32	39	2995	9	5	0
7	Gabriel Zakauni	DEF	19	33	2803	0	4	0
8	Alan White	DEF	29	26	2340	0	5	1
9	John Mackie	DEF	29	27	2320	4	7	0
10	Gary Alexander	ATT	25	28	2193	8	4	1
11	Donny Barnard	DEF	21	33	2019	1	7	0
12	David Hunt	MID	22	27	1988	0	6	1
13	Wayne Carlisle	MID	25	28	1961	4	1	0
14	Daryl McMahon	MID	22	24	1867	3	5	0
15	Glenn Morris	GK	21	12	1080	0	0	0
16	Jabo Ibehre	ATT	22	19	1074	2	0	0
17	Brian Saah	MID	18	12	801	0	0	0
18	Daniel Chillingworth	ATT	23	8	689	2	0	0

KEY PLAYERS - GOALSCORERS

Lee Steele

Goals in the League	16
Contribution to Attacking Power — Average number of minutes between League team goals while on pitch	60
Player Strike Rate — Average number of minutes between League goals scored by player	205
Club Strike Rate — Average number of minutes between League goals scored by club	64

	PLAYER	LGE GOALS	POWER	STRIKE RATE
1	Lee Steele	16	60	205 mins
2	Gary Alexander	8	59	274 mins
3	Andy Scott	9	67	333 mins
4	Wayne Carlisle	4	73	490 mins
5	John Mackie	4	68	580 mins

KEY PLAYERS - MIDFIELDERS

Daryl McMahon

Goals in the League	3
Defensive Rating — Average number of mins between League goals conceded while on the pitch	62
Contribution to Attacking Power — Average number of minutes between League team goals while on pitch	62
Scoring Difference — Defensive Rating minus Contribution to Attacking Power	0

	PLAYER	LGE GOALS	DEF RATE	POWER	SCORE DIFF
1	Daryl McMahon	3	62	62	0 mins
2	David Hunt	0	62	64	-2 mins
3	Michael Simpson	2	62	64	-2 mins
4	Wayne Carlisle	4	68	73	-5 mins
5	Andy Scott	9	61	67	-6 mins

KEY PLAYERS - DEFENDERS

Donny Barnard

Goals Conceded while on the pitch	29
Defensive Rating — Ave number of mins between League goals conceded while on the pitch	70
Clean Sheets — In games when player was on pitch for at least 70 minutes	6
Club Defensive Rating — Average number of mins between League goals conceded by the club this season.	62

	PLAYER	CON LGE	CLN SHEETS	DEF RATE
1	Donny Barnard	29	6	70 mins
2	Alan White	35	5	67 mins
3	Justin Miller	60	7	64 mins
4	Gabriel Zakauni	45	4	62 mins
5	Matthew Lockwood	60	7	60 mins

KEY GOALKEEPER

Lee Harrison

Goals Conceded in the League	44
Defensive Rating — Ave number of mins between League goals conceded while on the pitch.	70
Counting Games — Games when player was on pitch for at least 70 minutes	34
Clean Sheets — In Games when player was on pitch for at least 70 minutes	7

TOP POINT EARNERS

	PLAYER	GAMES	AV PTS
1	Donny Barnard	19	1.63
2	Wayne Carlisle	15	1.60
3	Gary Alexander	22	1.59
4	Daryl McMahon	18	1.50
5	Matthew Lockwood	37	1.49
6	Andy Scott	29	1.48
7	Lee Harrison	34	1.47
8	Gabriel Zakauni	29	1.45
9	Alan White	26	1.42
10	Michael Simpson	45	1.38
	CLUB AVERAGE:		1.37

BRISTOL ROVERS

Final Position: **12th**

NICKNAME: THE PIRATES

KEY: Won Drawn Lost

							Attendance
1	lge2	**Mansfield**	A	W	2-0	Agogo 31,52	5,709
2	lge2	**Bury**	H	D	2-2	Forrester 43 pen; Anderson, J 50	8,705
3	lge2	**Notts County**	H	W	2-1	Edwards 62; Agogo 81	8,225
4	lge2	**Darlington**	A	W	1-0	Agogo 77	3,661
5	ccr1	**Brighton**	A	W	2-1	Thorpe 25; Walker 30	4,217
6	lge2	**Southend**	H	W	2-1	Thorpe 13; Hunt 86	9,287
7	lge2	**Rushden & D**	A	D	0-0		3,367
8	lge2	**Shrewsbury**	H	D	0-0		8,381
9	lge2	**Leyton Orient**	A	L	2-4	Forrester 28; Trollope 53	3,972
10	lge2	**Lincoln**	H	D	0-0		7,004
11	ccr2	**Norwich**	A	L	0-1		18,658
12	lge2	**Northampton**	A	L	1-2	Savage 81	5,645
13	lge2	**Oxford**	H	W	2-0	Agogo 44,82	8,049
14	lge2	**Cambridge**	A	L	0-1		2,748
15	lge2	**Grimsby**	A	D	0-0		4,691
16	lge2	**Yeovil**	H	D	2-2	Hunt 64; Agogo 86	9,295
17	lge2	**Kidderminster**	H	W	2-0	Agogo 21,74	7,020
18	lge2	**Boston**	A	D	2-2	Forrester 88; Agogo 90	2,723
19	lge2	**Swansea**	A	L	0-1		8,778
20	facr1	**Carlisle**	H	D	1-1	Walker 77	5,658
21	lge2	**Scunthorpe**	H	L	0-3		7,039
22	facr1r	**Carlisle**	A	L	0-1		4,813
23	lge2	**Wycombe**	A	L	0-1		4,999
24	lge2	**Chester**	H	W	4-1	Disley 3; Forrester 45 pen; Thorpe 71; Trollope 74	5,524
25	lge2	**Macclesfield**	H	D	0-0		6,504
26	lge2	**Rochdale**	A	D	0-0		2,623
27	lge2	**Leyton Orient**	H	D	1-1	Forrester 51 pen	8,414
28	lge2	**Cheltenham**	A	D	1-1	Forrester 4	5,511
29	lge2	**Shrewsbury**	A	L	0-2		5,043
30	lge2	**Northampton**	H	W	3-1	Hunt 39; Edwards 51; Agogo 90	6,961
31	lge2	**Cambridge**	H	D	1-1	Agogo 25 pen	6,510
32	lge2	**Lincoln**	A	D	1-1	Agogo 67	3,929
33	lge2	**Cheltenham**	H	D	1-1	Thorpe 45	6,954
34	lge2	**Oxford**	A	L	2-3	Agogo 46; Walker 90	7,830
35	lge2	**Grimsby**	H	W	3-0	Hunt 27; Williams 38; Walker 45	6,134
36	lge2	**Yeovil**	A	L	2-4	Disley 17; Walker 88	9,153
37	lge2	**Boston**	H	D	1-1	Agogo 74	5,563
38	lge2	**Kidderminster**	A	D	1-1	Agogo 53	2,082
39	lge2	**Macclesfield**	A	L	1-2	Elliott 55	2,114
40	lge2	**Rochdale**	H	D	0-0		5,464
41	lge2	**Bury**	A	D	1-1	Disley 30	2,132
42	lge2	**Mansfield**	H	D	4-4	Williams 21; Walker 45 pen; Agogo 82 pen; Forrester 88	5,294
43	lge2	**Notts County**	A	W	2-1	Baudet 44 og; Walker 53	4,258
44	lge2	**Darlington**	H	D	3-3	Walker 45,71; Elliott 69	5,918
45	lge2	**Southend**	A	L	0-2		7,858
46	lge2	**Rushden & D**	H	W	3-0	Walker 22; Disley 59; Shearer 83 og	5,740
47	lge2	**Chester**	A	D	2-2	Williams 23; Agogo 30	2,475
48	lge2	**Swansea**	H	W	2-0	Walker 14; Agogo 26	7,433
49	lge2	**Scunthorpe**	A	L	0-4		6,925
50	lge2	**Wycombe**	H	W	1-0	Walker 12	7,358

TEAM OF THE SEASON

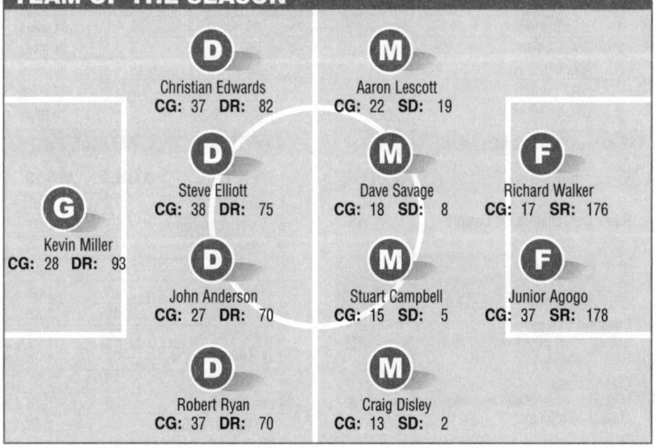

D
Christian Edwards
CG: 37 DR: 82
M
Aaron Lescott
CG: 22 SD: 19
G
Kevin Miller
CG: 28 DR: 93
D
Steve Elliott
CG: 38 DR: 75
M
Dave Savage
CG: 18 SD: 8
F
Richard Walker
CG: 17 SR: 176
D
John Anderson
CG: 27 DR: 70
M
Stuart Campbell
CG: 15 SD: 5
F
Junior Agogo
CG: 37 SR: 178
D
Robert Ryan
CG: 37 DR: 70
M
Craig Disley
CG: 13 SD: 2

KEY PLAYER APPEARANCES

	PLAYER	POS	AGE	APP	MINS ON	GOALS	CARDS(Y/R)	
1	James Hunt	MID	28	41	3577	4	5	2
2	Christian Edwards	DEF	29	42	3533	2	6	0
3	Steve Elliott	DEF	26	41	3516	2	2	1
4	Robert Ryan	DEF	28	40	3419	0	5	1
5	Junior Agogo	ATT	25	43	3386	19	2	1
6	Craig Hinton	DEF	27	38	2957	0	3	0
7	Kevin Miller	GK	36	28	2520	0	0	0
8	John Anderson	DEF	32	34	2516	1	2	1
9	Paul Trollope	MID	33	30	2195	2	3	0
10	Aaron Lescott	MID	26	26	2147	0	2	0
11	Stuart Campbell	MID	27	25	1796	0	3	0
12	Richard Walker	ATT	27	27	1762	10	1	0
13	Jamie Forrester	ATT	30	35	1738	7	1	0
14	Dave Savage	MID	31	27	1733	1	3	1
15	Ryan Clarke	GK	23	18	1620	0	0	0
16	Lee Thorpe	ATT	29	25	1587	3	7	0
17	Craig Disley	MID	23	28	1556	4	2	1
18	Alistair Gibb	MID	29	23	1480	0	1	0

KEY PLAYERS - GOALSCORERS

Richard Walker

Goals in the League	10	Player Strike Rate Average number of minutes between League goals scored by player	176
Contribution to Attacking Power Average number of minutes between League team goals while on pitch	62	Club Strike Rate Average number of minutes between League goals scored by club	69

	PLAYER	LGE GOALS	POWER	STRIKE RATE
1	Richard Walker	10	62	176 mins
2	Junior Agogo	19	65	178 mins
3	Jamie Forrester	7	75	248 mins
4	Craig Disley	4	56	389 mins
5	Lee Thorpe	3	72	529 mins

KEY PLAYERS - MIDFIELDERS

Aaron Lescott

Goals in the League	0	Contribution to Attacking Power Average number of minutes between League team goals while on pitch	61
Defensive Rating Average number of mins between League goals conceded while on the pitch	80	Scoring Difference Defensive Rating minus Contribution to Attacking Power	19

	PLAYER	LGE GOALS	DEF RATE	POWER	SCORE DIFF
1	Aaron Lescott	0	80	61	19 mins
2	Dave Savage	1	83	75	8 mins
3	Stuart Campbell	0	72	67	5 mins
4	Craig Disley	4	58	56	2 mins
5	James Hunt	4	69	67	2 mins

KEY PLAYERS - DEFENDERS

Christian Edwards

Goals Conceded while on the pitch	43	Clean Sheets In games when player was on pitch for at least 70 minutes	14
Defensive Rating Ave number of mins between League goals conceded while on the pitch	82	Club Defensive Rating Average number of mins between League goals conceded by the club this season.	73

	PLAYER	CON LGE	CLN SHEETS	DEF RATE
1	Christian Edwards	43	14	82 mins
2	Steve Elliott	47	13	75 mins
3	John Anderson	36	10	70 mins
4	Robert Ryan	49	12	70 mins
5	Craig Hinton	45	7	66 mins

KEY GOALKEEPER

Kevin Miller

Goals Conceded in the League	27
Defensive Rating Ave number of mins between League goals conceded while on the pitch.	93
Counting Games Games when player was on pitch for at least 70 minutes	28
Clean Sheets In Games when player was on pitch for at least 70 minutes	11

TOP POINT EARNERS

	PLAYER	GAMES	AV PTS
1	Alistair Gibb	13	1.77
2	Christian Edwards	37	1.43
3	John Anderson	27	1.41
4	Aaron Lescott	22	1.41
5	Ryan Clarke	18	1.39
6	Craig Disley	13	1.38
7	Robert Ryan	37	1.35
8	Richard Walker	17	1.35
9	Junior Agogo	37	1.35
10	Paul Trollope	21	1.33
	CLUB AVERAGE:		1.28

MANSFIELD TOWN

Final Position: **13th**

NICKNAME: THE STAGS

KEY: ☐Won ☐Drawn ☐Lost

						Attendance
1	lge2	Bristol Rovers	H L	0-2		5,709
2	lge2	Oxford	A L	0-1		5,029
3	lge2	Chester	A W	3-0	Asamoah 46; Buxton 62; Larkin 78	2,648
4	lge2	Kidderminster	H W	2-1	Larkin 16,48	3,859
5	lge2	Grimsby	A L	0-2		5,693
6	lge2	Yeovil	H W	4-1	Asamoah 8; Artell 67; Larkin 67; Corden 71	3,826
7	lge2	Northampton	H W	4-1	Asamoah 12; Corden 44,86; Larkin 55	5,173
8	lge2	Cambridge	A D	2-2	Larkin 44; MacKenzie 63	3,549
9	lge2	Rochdale	H W	1-0	Larkin 85	4,266
10	ccr1	Preston	H L	0-4		3,208
11	lge2	Scunthorpe	A D	1-1	Artell 70	4,563
12	lge2	Lincoln	H D	2-2	Murray 45; Baptiste 51	5,349
13	lge2	Swansea	A L	0-1		8,868
14	lge2	Notts County	H W	3-1	Day 25; Woodman 45; Larkin 69	7,682
15	lge2	Cheltenham	A L	0-2		2,706
16	lge2	Wycombe	A D	1-1	Asamoah 46	4,215
17	lge2	Bury	H D	0-0		4,147
18	lge2	Macclesfield	H L	0-1		3,816
19	facr1	Colchester	H D	1-1	Baptiste 28	3,202
20	lge2	Boston	A D	0-0		3,354
21	facr1r	Colchester	A L	1-4	Neil 87	2,492
22	lge2	Leyton Orient	H L	0-1		3,803
23	lge2	Darlington	A L	1-2	Barker 36	3,686
24	lge2	Rushden & D	H D	0-0		3,776
25	lge2	Shrewsbury	A W	2-0	Asamoah 22; Murray 74	3,469
26	lge2	Southend	A W	1-0	Warne 80	7,082
27	lge2	Northampton	A L	1-2	Rowson 45 og	6,122
28	lge2	Scunthorpe	H W	1-0	Murray 19	5,315
29	lge2	Cambridge	H D	0-0		3,557
30	lge2	Rochdale	A D	1-1	Barker 38	2,576
31	lge2	Southend	H D	1-1	Murray 53	3,894
32	lge2	Lincoln	A L	0-2		5,511
33	lge2	Notts County	A W	1-0	Barker 21	10,005
34	lge2	Swansea	H W	1-0	Barker 45	3,829
35	lge2	Cheltenham	H L	1-2	Larkin 73 pen	3,665
36	lge2	Bury	A W	2-0	Murray 38; Rundle 82	2,529
37	lge2	Wycombe	H L	1-4	Barker 54	2,497
38	lge2	Rushden & D	A D	0-0		3,096
39	lge2	Shrewsbury	H D	1-1	Neil 64	3,278
40	lge2	Oxford	H L	1-3	Larkin 90 pen	3,030
41	lge2	Bristol Rovers	A D	4-4	Barker 19,49; Larkin 46; Lloyd 68	5,294
42	lge2	Chester	H D	0-0		3,437
43	lge2	Kidderminster	A W	3-1	Barker 48,85; Brown 51	3,237
44	lge2	Grimsby	H W	2-0	Brown 36; Rundle 85	3,424
45	lge2	Yeovil	A L	2-5	Rundle 32; Day 51 pen	6,471
46	lge2	Darlington	H D	1-1	Day 90	3,569
47	lge2	Macclesfield	A L	1-3	Lloyd 54	2,456
48	lge2	Boston	H W	3-2	Barker 53; Lloyd 65; Rundle 70	3,223
49	lge2	Leyton Orient	A L	1-2	Lloyd 88	3,882

TEAM OF THE SEASON

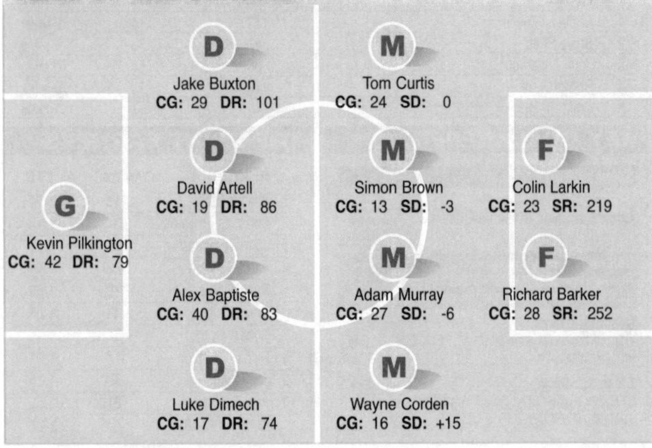

D
Jake Buxton
CG: 29 DR: 101
M
Tom Curtis
CG: 24 SD: 0
D
David Artell
CG: 19 DR: 86
M
Simon Brown
CG: 13 SD: -3
F
Colin Larkin
CG: 23 SR: 219
G
Kevin Pilkington
CG: 42 DR: 79
D
Alex Baptiste
CG: 40 DR: 83
M
Adam Murray
CG: 27 SD: -6
F
Richard Barker
CG: 28 SR: 252
D
Luke Dimech
CG: 17 DR: 74
M
Wayne Corden
CG: 16 SD: +15

KEY PLAYER APPEARANCES

	PLAYER	POS	AGE	APP	MINS ON	GOALS	CARDS(Y/R)	
1	Kevin Pilkington	GK	31	42	3780	0	2	0
2	Alex Baptiste	DEF	19	41	3635	1	5	0
3	Alex Neil	MID	24	41	3345	1	5	0
4	Jake Buxton	DEF	20	30	2632	1	2	0
5	Adam Murray	MID	23	32	2530	5	6	0
6	Richard Barker	ATT	30	28	2518	10	0	0
7	Colin Larkin	ATT	23	33	2413	11	0	0
8	Tom Curtis	MID	32	32	2394	0	1	0
9	Scott McNiven	DEF	27	25	2196	0	0	0
10	Derek Asamoah	ATT	24	30	2144	5	5	1
11	Luke Dimech	DEF	28	25	1773	0	2	1
12	David Artell	DEF	24	19	1710	2	3	0
13	Wayne Corden	MID	29	24	1677	3	2	0
14	Adam Rundle	MID	20	18	1538	4	0	0
15	Simon Brown	MID	21	21	1519	2	0	1
16	Fraser McLachlan	MID	22	21	1368	0	4	0
17	Gareth Jelleyman	DEF	24	14	1179	0	1	0
18	Rhys Day	DEF	22	18	1073	3	1	0

KEY PLAYERS - GOALSCORERS

Colin Larkin

Goals in the League 11

Contribution to Attacking Power 73
Average number of minutes between League team goals while on pitch

Player Strike Rate 219
Average number of minutes between League goals scored by player

Club Strike Rate 74
Average number of minutes between League goals scored by club

	PLAYER	LGE GOALS	POWER	STRIKE RATE
1	Colin Larkin	11	73	219 mins
2	Richard Barker	10	76	252 mins
3	Adam Rundle	4	64	385 mins
4	Derek Asamoah	5	71	429 mins
5	Adam Murray	5	90	506 mins

KEY PLAYERS - MIDFIELDERS

Wayne Corden

Goals in the League 3

Defensive Rating 99
Average number of mins between League goals conceded while on the pitch

Contribution to Attacking Power 84
Average number of minutes between League team goals while on pitch

Scoring Difference 15
Defensive Rating minus Contribution to Attacking Power

	PLAYER	LGE GOALS	DEF RATE	POWER	SCORE DIFF
1	Wayne Corden	3	99	84	15 mins
2	Tom Curtis	0	83	83	0 mins
3	Simon Brown	2	69	72	-3 mins
4	Adam Murray	5	84	90	-6 mins
5	Alex Neil	1	76	84	-8 mins

KEY PLAYERS - DEFENDERS

Jake Buxton

Goals Conceded while on the pitch 26

Defensive Rating 101
Ave number of mins between League goals conceded while on the pitch

Clean Sheets 14
In games when player was on pitch for at least 70 minutes

Club Defensive Rating 74
Average number of mins between League goals conceded by the club this season.

	PLAYER	CON LGE	CLN SHEETS	DEF RATE
1	Jake Buxton	26	14	101 mins
2	David Artell	20	4	86 mins
3	Alex Baptiste	44	15	83 mins
4	Luke Dimech	24	7	74 mins
5	Gareth Jelleyman	20	5	59 mins

KEY GOALKEEPER

Kevin Pilkington

Goals Conceded in the League 48

Defensive Rating 79
Ave number of mins between League goals conceded while on the pitch.

Counting Games 42
Games when player was on pitch for at least 70 minutes

Clean Sheets 15
In Games when player was on pitch for at least 70 minutes

TOP POINT EARNERS

	PLAYER	GAMES	AV PTS
1	Jake Buxton	29	1.69
2	Derek Asamoah	21	1.57
3	Adam Rundle	16	1.44
4	Wayne Corden	16	1.44
5	Tom Curtis	24	1.38
6	Alex Baptiste	40	1.38
7	Alex Neil	35	1.34
8	Kevin Pilkington	42	1.33
9	Simon Brown	13	1.31
10	Richard Barker	28	1.29
	CLUB AVERAGE:		1.30

CHELTENHAM

Final Position: **14th**

NICKNAME: THE ROBINS KEY: ☐Won ☐Drawn ☐Lost

								Attendance
1	lge2	Southend	A	W	2-0	Melligan 18; Odejayi 29		5,332
2	lge2	Scunthorpe	H	L	0-2			3,647
3	lge2	Leyton Orient	H	L	1-2	Cozic 75		3,346
4	lge2	Swansea	A	D	1-1	McCann 25		6,874
5	ccr1	Colchester	A	L	1-2	Devaney 70		2,144
6	lge2	Boston	H	W	1-0	Victory 57		3,596
7	lge2	Shrewsbury	A	L	0-2			3,862
8	lge2	Notts County	A	D	0-0			4,302
9	lge2	Yeovil	H	D	1-1	Guinan 25		3,966
10	lge2	Rushden & D	A	L	0-1			2,601
11	lge2	Wycombe	H	D	1-1	Victory 37		3,663
12	lge2	Grimsby	A	D	1-1	Spencer 85		6,133
13	lge2	Chester	H	D	0-0			3,670
14	lge2	Rochdale	A	W	2-1	Melligan 63; Wilson 84		2,778
15	lge2	Mansfield	H	W	2-0	Guinan 45; Devaney 87		2,706
16	lge2	Cambridge	H	W	2-1	Vincent 28; Spencer 90		3,315
17	lge2	Oxford	A	L	0-1			5,163
18	lge2	Bury	H	W	1-0	McCann 68 pen		3,061
19	facr1	Swansea	H	L	1-3	Spencer 71		4,551
20	lge2	Macclesfield	A	W	2-0	Guinan 60; McCann 71		1,796
21	lge2	Darlington	H	L	0-2			3,578
22	lge2	Northampton	A	D	1-1	Spencer 84		4,373
23	lge2	Lincoln	A	D	0-0			4,097
24	lge2	Kidderminster	H	W	2-0	Guinan 53; Bennett 90 og		3,718
25	lge2	Yeovil	A	L	1-4	Devaney 17		7,320
26	lge2	Bristol Rovers	H	D	1-1	Caines 37		5,511
27	lge2	Notts County	H	L	0-2			3,375
28	lge2	Wycombe	A	D	1-1	Caines 37		4,394
29	lge2	Rushden & D	H	W	4-1	Wilson 9; Gillespie 26; Devaney 58; McCann 69 pen		3,160
30	lge2	Bristol Rovers	A	D	1-1	Gillespie 38		6,954
31	lge2	Grimsby	H	L	2-3	Guinan 17; Devaney 76		3,327
32	lge2	Chester	A	W	3-0	Wilson 14; Gillespie 55,90 pen		1,643
33	lge2	Rochdale	H	W	2-0	Devaney 20,89 pen		2,951
34	lge2	Mansfield	A	W	2-1	Devaney 61; Finnigan 89		3,665
35	lge2	Oxford	H	L	0-1			5,044
36	lge2	Cambridge	A	L	0-1			2,021
37	lge2	Lincoln	H	W	1-0	Guinan 63		3,187
38	lge2	Kidderminster	A	L	0-1			2,879
39	lge2	Scunthorpe	A	L	1-4	Victory 48		4,659
40	lge2	Southend	H	L	0-3			3,689
41	lge2	Leyton Orient	A	W	3-2	Finnigan 17,53; Duff 19		3,261
42	lge2	Swansea	H	L	1-2	Devaney 26		4,669
43	lge2	Boston	A	L	1-2	Devaney 90 pen		2,192
44	lge2	Shrewsbury	H	D	1-1	Spencer 66		3,769
45	lge2	Northampton	H	W	1-0	Spencer 22		3,689
46	lge2	Bury	A	L	1-3	Gillespie 80 pen		2,490
47	lge2	Macclesfield	H	W	3-0	Morley 34 og; Spencer 64,77		3,622
48	lge2	Darlington	A	L	1-3	Spencer 29		5,575

TEAM OF THE SEASON

G Shane Higgs CG: 46 DR: 77

D Jamie Victory CG: 40 DR: 79
D Jeremy Gill CG: 41 DR: 77
D Shane Duff CG: 44 DR: 76
D Gavin Caines CG: 26 DR: 68

M Martin Devaney CG: 36 SD: 6
M David Bird CG: 23 SD: 4
M John Melligan CG: 20 SD: 3
M Brian Wilson CG: 32 SD: -6

F Stephen Guinan CG: 28 SR: 478
F Damian Spencer* CG: 11 SR: 202

KEY PLAYER APPEARANCES

	PLAYER	POS	AGE	APP	MINS ON	GOALS	CARDS(Y/R)	
1	Shane Higgs	GK	28	46	4140	0	0	0
2	Shane Duff	DEF	23	45	4008	1	5	0
3	Jeremy Gill	DEF	34	44	3771	0	5	0
4	Jamie Victory	DEF	29	42	3629	3	2	0
5	Grant McCann	MID	25	39	3470	4	6	2
6	Martin Devaney	MID	25	38	3244	9	4	0
7	Brian Wilson	MID	22	43	3196	3	2	0
8	Stephen Guinan	ATT	29	43	2870	6	1	0
9	John Finnigan	MID	29	32	2717	3	5	0
10	Gavin Caines	DEF	21	29	2396	2	4	0
11	David Bird	MID	20	34	2246	0	1	0
12	John Melligan	MID	24	29	2112	2	3	0
13	Damian Spencer	ATT	23	41	1612	8	4	0
14	Ashley Vincent	ATT	20	26	1256	1	2	0
15	Kayode Odejayi	ATT	23	32	1095	1	1	0
16	John Brough	DEF	32	13	987	0	0	0
17	Stephen Gillespie	ATT	21	12	821	5	1	0
18	Alan Morgan	DEF	21	8	666	0	0	0

KEY PLAYERS - GOALSCORERS

Martin Devaney

Goals in the League 9

Contribution to Attacking Power Average number of minutes between League team goals while on pitch 75

Player Strike Rate Average number of minutes between League goals scored by player 360

Club Strike Rate Average number of minutes between League goals scored by club 81

	PLAYER	LGE GOALS	POWER	STRIKE RATE
1	Martin Devaney	9	75	360 mins
2	Stephen Guinan	6	84	478 mins
3	Grant McCann	4	86	868 mins
4	John Finnigan	3	90	906 mins
5	John Melligan	2	78	1056 mins

KEY PLAYERS - MIDFIELDERS

Martin Devaney

Goals in the League 9

Defensive Rating Average number of mins between League goals conceded while on the pitch 81

Contribution to Attacking Power Average number of minutes between League team goals while on pitch 75

Scoring Difference Defensive Rating minus Contribution to Attacking Power 6

	PLAYER	LGE GOALS	DEF RATE	POWER	SCORE DIFF
1	Martin Devaney	9	81	75	6 mins
2	David Bird	0	70	66	4 mins
3	John Melligan	2	81	78	3 mins
4	Brian Wilson	3	74	80	-6 mins
5	Grant McCann	4	79	87	-8 mins

KEY PLAYERS - DEFENDERS

Jamie Victory

Goals Conceded while on the pitch 46

Defensive Rating Ave number of mins between League goals conceded while on the pitch 79

Clean Sheets In games when player was on pitch for at least 70 minutes 12

Club Defensive Rating Average number of mins between League goals conceded by the club this season. 77

	PLAYER	CON LGE	CLN SHEETS	DEF RATE
1	Jamie Victory	46	12	79 mins
2	Jeremy Gill	49	13	77 mins
3	Shane Duff	53	13	76 mins
4	Gavin Caines	35	8	68 mins

KEY GOALKEEPER

Shane Higgs

Goals Conceded in the League 54

Defensive Rating Ave number of mins between League goals conceded while on the pitch. 77

Counting Games Games when player was on pitch for at least 70 minutes 46

Clean Sheets In Games when player was on pitch for at least 70 minutes 14

TOP POINT EARNERS

	PLAYER	GAMES	AV PTS
1	Stephen Guinan	28	1.57
2	Martin Devaney	36	1.50
3	David Bird	23	1.43
4	Jeremy Gill	41	1.39
5	John Melligan	20	1.35
6	John Finnigan	30	1.33
7	Brian Wilson	32	1.31
8	Shane Duff	44	1.30
9	Shane Higgs	46	1.30
10	Grant McCann	39	1.28
	CLUB AVERAGE:		1.30

OXFORD UNITED

Final Position: **15th**

NICKNAME: THE U'S

KEY: ☐Won ☐Drawn ☐Lost

							Attendance
1	lge2	Boston	A	L	0-1		3,596
2	lge2	Mansfield	H	W	1-0	Mooney 36	5,029
3	lge2	Scunthorpe	H	D	1-1	Mooney 54	4,920
4	lge2	Leyton Orient	A	D	0-0		3,426
5	ccR1	Reading	H	L	0-2		5,919
6	lge2	Shrewsbury	H	W	2-0	Bradbury 3; Mooney 48	4,430
7	lge2	Notts County	A	W	1-0	Bradbury 16 pen	5,288
8	lge2	Wycombe	A	D	1-1	Roget 20	6,348
9	lge2	Rushden & D	H	D	0-0		4,756
10	lge2	Yeovil	A	L	1-6	E'Beyer 73	5,467
11	lge2	Bury	H	W	3-1	Basham 40; Scott 62 og; Mooney 72	4,308
12	lge2	Bristol Rovers	A	L	0-2		8,049
13	lge2	Darlington	H	L	1-2	Woozley 45	5,881
14	lge2	Lincoln	H	L	0-1		4,089
15	lge2	Northampton	A	L	0-1		5,455
16	lge2	Macclesfield	A	L	0-1		2,007
17	lge2	Cheltenham	H	W	1-0	Mooney 45	5,163
18	lge2	Southend	A	L	0-4		5,608
19	facr1	Rochdale	A	L	1-2	Bradbury 20	2,333
20	lge2	Rochdale	H	L	0-1		4,204
21	lge2	Chester	A	W	3-1	E'Beyer 16; Robinson 67; Basham 84	2,791
22	lge2	Swansea	H	L	0-1		4,767
23	lge2	Cambridge	H	W	2-1	Mooney 19; Davies 29	4,844
24	lge2	Grimsby	A	D	1-1	Mooney 52	4,777
25	lge2	Rushden & D	A	D	3-3	Hackett 14; Bradbury 43; Davies 77	4,140
26	lge2	Kidderminster	H	L	0-2		5,947
27	lge2	Wycombe	H	W	2-1	Brooks 23; Basham 87	7,195
28	lge2	Bury	A	D	0-0		2,783
29	lge2	Darlington	A	D	1-1	Brooks 31	3,735
30	lge2	Yeovil	H	W	2-1	Mooney 20; Davies 57	6,778
31	lge2	Kidderminster	A	W	3-1	Hackett 22; Davies 38; Basham 90	3,143
32	lge2	Bristol Rovers	H	W	3-2	Bradbury 15 pen; Roget 19; Davies 74	7,830
33	lge2	Lincoln	A	L	0-3		4,535
34	lge2	Northampton	H	L	1-2	Mooney 58	7,032
35	lge2	Cheltenham	A	W	1-0	Mooney 90	5,044
36	lge2	Cambridge	A	L	1-2	Basham 45	3,765
37	lge2	Grimsby	H	L	1-2	Cominelli 34	5,625
38	lge2	Mansfield	A	W	3-1	Basham 7; Hackett 33,52	3,030
39	lge2	Boston	H	W	2-0	Basham 39,63	5,176
40	lge2	Scunthorpe	A	D	1-1	Mooney 32	5,977
41	lge2	Leyton Orient	H	D	2-2	Basham 17; Mooney 54	5,320
42	lge2	Shrewsbury	A	L	0-3		3,974
43	lge2	Macclesfield	H	D	1-1	Wanless 3	4,273
44	lge2	Notts County	H	W	2-1	Mooney 75 pen,82 pen	4,436
45	lge2	Swansea	A	L	0-1		10,602
46	lge2	Southend	H	W	2-1	Davies 20; Mooney 40	5,916
47	lge2	Rochdale	A	L	1-5	Robinson 81	2,579
48	lge2	Chester	H	L	0-1		5,055

TEAM OF THE SEASON

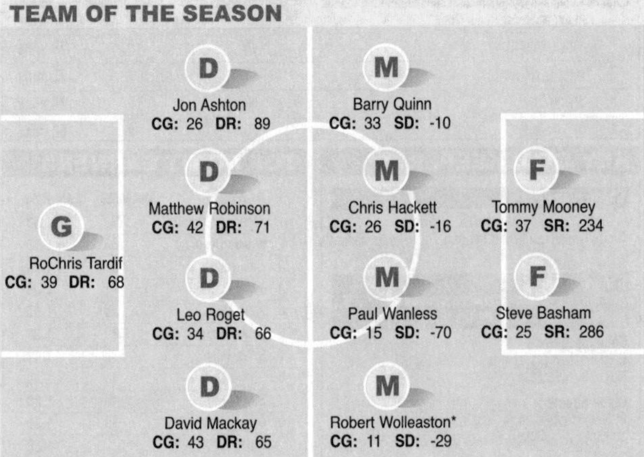
G
RoChris Tardif
CG: 39 DR: 68
D
Jon Ashton
CG: 26 DR: 89
D
Matthew Robinson
CG: 42 DR: 71
D
Leo Roget
CG: 34 DR: 66
D
David Mackay
CG: 43 DR: 65
M
Barry Quinn
CG: 33 SD: -10
M
Chris Hackett
CG: 26 SD: -16
M
Paul Wanless
CG: 15 SD: -70
M
Robert Wolleaston*
CG: 11 SD: -29
F
Tommy Mooney
CG: 37 SR: 234
F
Steve Basham
CG: 25 SR: 286

KEY PLAYER APPEARANCES

	PLAYER	POS	AGE	APP	MINS ON	GOALS	CARDS(Y/R)	
1	Matthew Robinson	DEF	30	45	3952	2	6	0
2	David Mackay	DEF	25	43	3818	0	5	0
3	Chris Tardif	GK	24	40	3552	0	1	0
4	Tommy Mooney	ATT	33	42	3510	15	5	0
5	Lee Bradbury	ATT	30	41	3360	4	5	0
6	Leo Roget	DEF	27	35	3099	2	6	1
7	Barry Quinn	MID	26	36	3060	0	10	0
8	Chris Hackett	MID	22	37	2701	4	5	1
9	Steve Basham	ATT	27	39	2570	9	1	0
10	Jon Ashton	DEF	22	30	2483	0	7	2
11	Paul Wanless	MID	31	27	1689	1	3	0
12	Craig Davies	ATT	19	28	1410	6	5	0
13	Robert Wolleaston	MID	25	20	1187	0	0	0
14	Mateo Corbo	DEF	29	13	1105	0	10	1
15	David Woozley	DEF	25	13	1059	1	2	0
16	Jamie Hand	MID	21	11	990	0	3	0
17	Lucas Cominelli	MID	28	16	948	1	5	0
18	Lee Molyneaux	DEF	22	16	797	0	3	0

KEY PLAYERS - GOALSCORERS

Tommy Mooney

Goals in the League 15

Player Strike Rate Average number of minutes between League goals scored by player 234

Contribution to Attacking Power Average number of minutes between League team goals while on pitch 79

Club Strike Rate Average number of minutes between League goals scored by club 83

	PLAYER	LGE GOALS	POWER	STRIKE RATE
1	Tommy Mooney	15	79	234 mins
2	Steve Basham	9	85	286 mins
3	Chris Hackett	4	81	675 mins
4	Lee Bradbury	4	81	840 mins
5	Leo Roget	2	75	1550 mins

KEY PLAYERS - MIDFIELDERS

Barry Quinn

Goals in the League 0

Contribution to Attacking Power Average number of minutes between League team goals while on pitch 78

Defensive Rating Average number of mins between League goals conceded while on the pitch 68

Scoring Difference Defensive Rating minus Contribution to Attacking Power -10

	PLAYER	LGE GOALS	DEF RATE	POWER	SCORE DIFF
1	Barry Quinn	0	68	78	-10 mins
2	Chris Hackett	4	66	82	-16 mins
3	Robert Wolleaston	0	79	108	-29 mins
4	Paul Wanless	1	60	130	-70 mins

KEY PLAYERS - DEFENDERS

Jon Ashton

Goals Conceded while on the pitch 28

Clean Sheets In games when player was on pitch for at least 70 minutes 9

Defensive Rating Ave number of mins between League goals conceded while on the pitch 89

Club Defensive Rating Average number of mins between League goals conceded by the club this season. 66

	PLAYER	CON LGE	CLN SHEETS	DEF RATE
1	Jon Ashton	28	9	89 mins
2	Matthew Robinson	56	8	71 mins
3	Leo Roget	47	6	66 mins
4	David Mackay	59	8	65 mins
5	Mateo Corbo	20	1	55 mins

KEY GOALKEEPER

Chris Tardif

Goals Conceded in the League 523

Defensive Rating Ave number of mins between League goals conceded while on the pitch. 68

Counting Games Games when player was on pitch for at least 70 minutes 39

Clean Sheets In Games when player was on pitch for at least 70 minutes 8

TOP POINT EARNERS

	PLAYER	GAMES	AV PTS
1	Jon Ashton	26	1.65
2	Mateo Corbo	12	1.58
3	Lee Bradbury	34	1.41
4	Barry Quinn	33	1.33
5	Tommy Mooney	37	1.32
6	Chris Tardif	39	1.31
7	Matthew Robinson	42	1.31
8	Leo Roget	34	1.29
9	David Mackay	43	1.28
10	Steve Basham	25	1.04
	CLUB AVERAGE:		1.28

BOSTON UNITED

Final Position: **16th**

NICKNAME: THE PILGRIMS

KEY: Won / Drawn / Lost

							Attendance
1	lge2	Oxford	H	W	1-0	Thompson 82	3,596
2	lge2	Grimsby	A	D	1-1	Melton 9	6,737
3	lge2	Yeovil	A	L	0-2		5,178
4	lge2	Macclesfield	H	D	1-1	Lee 81	2,736
5	lge2	Cheltenham	A	L	0-1		3,596
6	lge2	Chester	H	W	3-1	Thomas 3; Abbey 45; Pitt 73 pen	2,698
7	lge2	Cambridge	H	W	2-1	Lee 40; McCann 87	3,026
8	ccr1	Luton	H	W	4-3	Pitt 23; Lee 57; Thompson 90,94	2,631
9	lge2	Lincoln	A	D	2-2	Pitt 85 pen; Lee 88	7,142
10	lge2	Shrewsbury	H	D	2-2	Lee 31; Kirk 42	2,593
11	ccr2	Fulham	H	L	1-4	Beevers 56	5,373
12	lge2	Leyton Orient	A	D	0-0		4,753
13	lge2	Scunthorpe	H	W	2-1	Pitt 68; O'Halloran 90	3,640
14	lge2	Southend	A	L	1-2	Kirk 49	5,688
15	lge2	Wycombe	H	W	2-0	Kirk 14,51	2,635
16	lge2	Bury	A	D	1-1	Challinor 35 og	2,001
17	lge2	Notts County	A	L	1-2	Ellender 54	5,434
18	lge2	Bristol Rovers	H	D	2-2	Miller 68 og; Kirk 74	2,723
19	lge2	Kidderminster	A	W	4-0	Beevers 50; Kirk 56 pen,81 pen,90	2,208
20	facr1	Hornchurch	H	W	5-2	Thompson 48; McManus 49,67; Noble 81; Ellender 89	2,437
21	lge2	Mansfield	H	D	0-0		3,354
22	lge2	Rochdale	A	L	0-2		2,474
23	facr2	Hereford	A	W	3-2	Lee 30; Kirk 71,78	3,601
24	lge2	Rushden & D	H	W	1-0	Thomas 27	2,334
25	lge2	Northampton	A	L	1-2	Kirk 74	5,245
26	lge2	Darlington	H	W	3-1	Kirk 20 pen; Clare 41; Thomas 45	2,428
27	lge2	Swansea	A	L	1-3	Lee 86	10,162
28	lge2	Cambridge	A	W	1-0	Kirk 83	3,507
29	lge2	Leyton Orient	H	D	2-2	Kirk 50; Ellender 88	3,183
30	facr3	Hartlepool	A	D	0-0		5,342
31	lge2	Southend	H	W	2-0	Kirk 65,84	2,389
32	lge2	Shrewsbury	A	D	0-0		3,789
33	facr3r	Hartlepool	H	L	0-1		3,653
34	lge2	Swansea	H	L	2-3	Kirk 15; Rusk 72	2,545
35	lge2	Scunthorpe	A	D	1-1	Lee 57	5,056
36	lge2	Wycombe	A	W	2-1	Kirk 4,85	4,091
37	lge2	Bury	H	D	2-2	Kirk 9; Rusk 13	2,351
38	lge2	Lincoln	H	L	0-2		6,445
39	lge2	Bristol Rovers	A	D	1-1	Kirk 59	5,563
40	lge2	Northampton	H	L	0-1		2,749
41	lge2	Darlington	A	L	0-1		3,219
42	lge2	Grimsby	H	D	1-1	Clare 1	3,941
43	lge2	Notts County	H	W	4-0	Noble 76; Easter 84,90; Thompson 90	2,229
44	lge2	Oxford	A	L	0-2		5,176
45	lge2	Yeovil	H	L	1-2	Rusk 23	3,069
46	lge2	Macclesfield	A	D	1-1	Noble 15 pen	2,501
47	lge2	Cheltenham	H	W	2-1	Lee 15,88	2,192
48	lge2	Chester	A	L	1-2	Noble 9	2,040
49	lge2	Rushden & D	A	L	2-4	Clare 13 pen; Maylett 34	3,671
50	lge2	Kidderminster	H	W	3-0	Easter 15; Lee 28; Maylett 69	2,053
51	lge2	Mansfield	A	L	2-3	Maylett 49; Thompson 90	3,223
52	lge2	Rochdale	H	D	1-1	Pitt 71	2,528

TEAM OF THE SEASON

G — Nathan Abbey CG: 40 DR: 72

D — Mark Greaves CG: 20 DR: 89
D — Paul Ellender CG: 38 DR: 74
D — Austin McCann CG: 45 DR: 71
D — Lee Beevers CG: 30 DR: 78

M — David Noble CG: 25 SD: 6
M — Danny Thomas CG: 27 SD: 5
M — Chris Holland CG: 28 SD: 0
M — Courtney Pitt CG: 19 SD: 0

F — Jason Lee CG: 32 SR: 344
F — Andy Kirk CG: 25 SR: 113

KEY PLAYER APPEARANCES

	PLAYER	POS	AGE	APP	MINS ON	GOALS	CARDS(Y	/R)
1	Austin McCann	DEF	25	45	4050	1	7	0
2	Nathan Abbey	GK	26	40	3600	0	3	0
3	Paul Ellender	DEF	30	39	3465	2	9	0
4	Jason Lee	ATT	34	39	3094	9	12	0
5	Danny Thomas	MID	24	39	2751	3	4	0
6	Lee Beevers	DEF	21	31	2737	1	4	1
7	Chris Holland	MID	29	32	2623	0	8	0
8	David Noble	MID	23	32	2488	3	4	0
9	Andy Kirk	ATT	26	25	2148	19	2	0
10	Simon Rusk	MID	23	31	2108	3	4	0
11	Courtney Pitt	MID	23	32	1940	4	6	0
12	Mark Greaves	DEF	30	22	1872	0	9	1
13	Dean West	DEF	32	24	1749	0	1	0
14	Lee Thompson	MID	22	45	1389	3	2	0
15	Daryl Clare	ATT	26	19	1169	3	3	0
16	Tom Bennett	MID	35	11	944	0	5	0
17	Alan White	DEF	29	11	941	0	4	0
18	Brad Maylett	MID	24	9	745	3	3	0

KEY PLAYERS - GOALSCORERS

Andy Kirk

Goals in the League 19

Contribution to Attacking Power Average number of minutes between League team goals while on pitch 69

Player Strike Rate Average number of minutes between League goals scored by player 113

Club Strike Rate Average number of minutes between League goals scored by club 67

	PLAYER	LGE GOALS	POWER	STRIKE RATE
1	Andy Kirk	19	69	113 mins
2	Jason Lee	9	67	344 mins
3	Courtney Pitt	4	69	485 mins
4	Simon Rusk	3	68	703 mins
5	David Noble	3	67	829 mins

KEY PLAYERS - MIDFIELDERS

David Noble

Goals in the League 3

Defensive Rating Average number of mins between League goals conceded while on the pitch 73

Contribution to Attacking Power Average number of minutes between League team goals while on pitch 67

Scoring Difference Defensive Rating minus Contribution to Attacking Power 6

	PLAYER	LGE GOALS	DEF RATE	POWER	SCORE DIFF
1	David Noble	3	73	67	6 mins
2	Danny Thomas	3	69	64	5 mins
3	Courtney Pitt	4	69	69	0 mins
4	Chris Holland	0	69	69	0 mins
5	Simon Rusk	3	60	68	-8 mins

KEY PLAYERS - DEFENDERS

Mark Greaves

Goals Conceded while on the pitch 21

Defensive Rating Ave number of mins between League goals conceded while on the pitch 89

Clean Sheets In games when player was on pitch for at least 70 minutes 8

Club Defensive Rating Average number of mins between League goals conceded by the club this season. 71

	PLAYER	CON LGE	CLN SHEETS	DEF RATE
1	Mark Greaves	21	8	89 mins
2	Lee Beevers	35	8	78 mins
3	Paul Ellender	47	9	74 mins
4	Austin McCann	57	11	71 mins
5	Dean West	26	6	67 mins

KEY GOALKEEPER

Nathan Abbey

Goals Conceded in the League 50

Defensive Rating Ave number of mins between League goals conceded while on the pitch. 72

Counting Games Games when player was on pitch for at least 70 minutes 40

Clean Sheets In Games when player was on pitch for at least 70 minutes 10

TOP POINT EARNERS

	PLAYER	GAMES	AV PTS
1	Mark Greaves	20	1.60
2	Dean West	17	1.59
3	Lee Beevers	30	1.50
4	Danny Thomas	27	1.33
5	Chris Holland	28	1.32
6	Andy Kirk	25	1.32
7	Nathan Abbey	40	1.30
8	Austin McCann	45	1.27
9	Paul Ellender	38	1.21
10	David Noble	25	1.20
	CLUB AVERAGE:		1.26

BURY

Final Position: **17th**

NICKNAME: THE SHAKERS

KEY: ☐Won ☐Drawn ☐Lost

							Attendance
1	lge2	**Yeovil**	H	W	3-1	Nugent 66,77; Jones 81	3,171
2	lge2	**Bristol Rovers**	A	D	2-2	Mattis 7; Barry-Murphy 68	8,705
3	lge2	**Grimsby**	A	L	1-5	Barry-Murphy 2	4,277
4	lge2	**Chester**	H	D	1-1	Porter 60	2,870
5	ccr1	**Burnley**	H	L	2-3	Mattis 12; Challinor 18	3,648
6	lge2	**Rochdale**	A	W	3-0	Mattis 27; Swailes 52; Nugent 77	3,913
7	lge2	**Kidderminster**	H	W	4-0	Nugent 33; Porter 45,64; Flitcroft 60	2,504
8	lge2	**Lincoln**	H	L	0-1		3,188
9	lge2	**Shrewsbury**	A	D	2-2	Mattis 16; Nugent 54	3,801
10	lge2	**Scunthorpe**	H	L	0-1		2,846
11	lge2	**Oxford**	A	L	1-3	Nugent 70	4,308
12	lge2	**Macclesfield**	H	W	2-1	Newby 23; Nugent 72	2,859
13	lge2	**Leyton Orient**	A	D	1-1	Porter 75	3,398
14	lge2	**Darlington**	A	W	2-1	Porter 35; Dunfield 39	4,642
15	lge2	**Boston**	H	D	1-1	Challinor 10	2,001
16	lge2	**Rushden & D**	H	D	1-1	Mattis 65	2,672
17	lge2	**Mansfield**	A	D	0-0		4,147
18	lge2	**Cheltenham**	A	L	0-1		3,061
19	facr1	**Vaux Motors**	H	W	5-2	Mattis 8,26; Porter 19; Challinor 39; Nugent 74	2,566
20	lge2	**Notts County**	H	W	1-0	Porter 22	2,938
21	lge2	**Swansea**	A	W	3-1	Nugent 3; Mattis 7; Barry-Murphy 83	6,971
22	facr2	**Northampton**	A	L	0-1		4,415
23	lge2	**Wycombe**	H	D	2-2	Nugent 8,66	1,866
24	lge2	**Southend**	H	L	0-1		2,522
25	lge2	**Cambridge**	A	D	1-1	Nugent 49	2,875
26	lge2	**Northampton**	A	L	0-2		6,041
27	lge2	**Lincoln**	A	L	0-1		3,962
28	lge2	**Oxford**	H	D	0-0		2,783
29	lge2	**Leyton Orient**	H	D	0-0		2,192
30	lge2	**Scunthorpe**	A	L	2-3	Porter 31; Keogh 48	5,365
31	lge2	**Northampton**	H	W	2-0	Newby 42; Keogh 58	2,687
32	lge2	**Macclesfield**	A	L	1-2	Unsworth 14	2,513
33	lge2	**Darlington**	H	L	0-1		2,971
34	lge2	**Shrewsbury**	H	D	0-0		2,233
35	lge2	**Boston**	A	D	2-2	Kennedy 36 pen; Newby 51	2,351
36	lge2	**Mansfield**	H	L	0-2		2,529
37	lge2	**Rushden & D**	A	L	0-3		1,803
38	lge2	**Southend**	A	L	0-1		5,553
39	lge2	**Cambridge**	H	W	2-1	Newby 56; Flitcroft 90	2,437
40	lge2	**Bristol Rovers**	H	D	1-1	Whaley 78	2,132
41	lge2	**Yeovil**	A	W	1-0	Whaley 14	6,269
42	lge2	**Grimsby**	H	W	3-1	Porter 1; Barry-Murphy 12; Kazim-Richards 53	5,671
43	lge2	**Chester**	A	L	1-2	Kazim-Richards 12	3,107
44	lge2	**Rochdale**	H	D	0-0		4,606
45	lge2	**Kidderminster**	A	D	2-2	Porter 9; Shakes 90	2,474
46	lge2	**Wycombe**	A	W	2-1	Whaley 34; Flitcroft 81	4,703
47	lge2	**Cheltenham**	H	W	3-1	Barry-Murphy 3; Kazim-Richards 21; Shakes 38	2,490
48	lge2	**Notts County**	A	W	1-0	Barry-Murphy 47	6,424
49	lge2	**Swansea**	H	L	0-1		7,575

TEAM OF THE SEASON

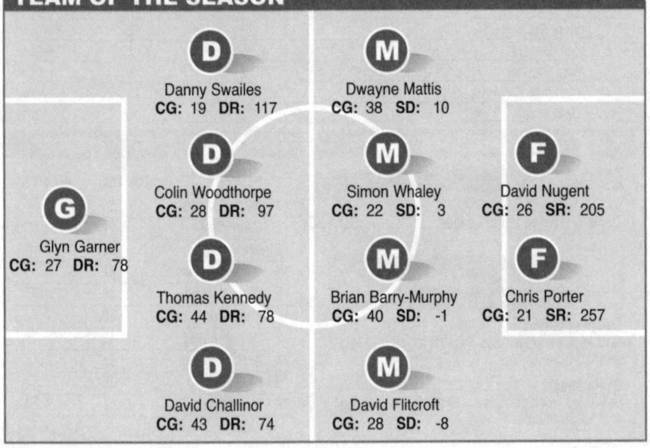
D
Danny Swailes
CG: 19 DR: 117
M
Dwayne Mattis
CG: 38 SD: 10
D
Colin Woodthorpe
CG: 28 DR: 97
M
Simon Whaley
CG: 22 SD: 3
F
David Nugent
CG: 26 SR: 205
G
Glyn Garner
CG: 27 DR: 78
D
Thomas Kennedy
CG: 44 DR: 78
M
Brian Barry-Murphy
CG: 40 SD: -1
F
Chris Porter
CG: 21 SR: 257
D
David Challinor
CG: 43 DR: 74
M
David Flitcroft
CG: 28 SD: -8

KEY PLAYER APPEARANCES

	PLAYER	POS	AGE	APP	MINS ON	GOALS	CARDS(Y/R)	
1	Thomas Kennedy	DEF	20	46	3995	1	2	0
2	David Challinor	DEF	29	43	3870	1	4	0
3	Brian Barry-Murphy	MID	26	45	3803	6	4	0
4	Dwayne Mattis	MID	23	39	3425	5	5	0
5	Lee Unsworth	DEF	32	36	3005	1	1	0
6	David Flitcroft	MID	31	36	2759	3	10	2
7	Colin Woodthorpe	DEF	36	30	2518	0	8	1
8	Glyn Garner	GK	28	27	2430	0	0	0
9	Simon Whaley	MID	20	38	2386	3	1	0
10	Chris Porter	ATT	21	32	2311	9	0	0
11	David Nugent	ATT	20	26	2255	11	3	0
12	Paul Scott	DEF	25	23	1756	0	2	0
13	Danny Swailes	DEF	26	20	1755	1	4	1
14	Andy Marriott	GK	34	19	1710	0	0	0
15	Jon Newby	ATT	26	36	1674	4	0	0
16	John Fitzgerald	DEF	21	14	1210	0	1	0
17	Colin Kazim-Richards	MID	18	30	1203	3	6	0
18	Matthew Barrass	MID	25	9	712	0	1	0

KEY PLAYERS - GOALSCORERS

David Nugent

Goals in the League	11
Contribution to Attacking Power: Average number of minutes between League team goals while on pitch	72
Player Strike Rate: Average number of minutes between League goals scored by player	205
Club Strike Rate: Average number of minutes between League goals scored by club	77

	PLAYER	LGE GOALS	POWER	STRIKE RATE
1	David Nugent	11	72	205 mins
2	Chris Porter	9	66	257 mins
3	Jon Newby	4	98	419 mins
4	Brian Barry-Murphy	6	76	634 mins
5	Dwayne Mattis	5	70	685 mins

KEY PLAYERS - MIDFIELDERS

Dwayne Mattis

Goals in the League	5
Defensive Rating: Average number of mins between League goals conceded while on the pitch	80
Contribution to Attacking Power: Average number of minutes between League team goals while on pitch	70
Scoring Difference: Defensive Rating minus Contribution to Attacking Power	10

	PLAYER	LGE GOALS	DEF RATE	POWER	SCORE DIFF
1	Dwayne Mattis	5	80	70	10 mins
2	Simon Whaley	3	85	82	3 mins
3	Brian Barry-Murphy	6	75	76	-1 mins
4	David Flitcroft	3	67	75	-8 mins

KEY PLAYERS - DEFENDERS

Danny Swailes

Goals Conceded while on the pitch	15
Defensive Rating: Ave number of mins between League goals conceded while on the pitch	117
Clean Sheets: In games when player was on pitch for at least 70 minutes	6
Club Defensive Rating: Average number of mins between League goals conceded by the club this season.	77

	PLAYER	CON LGE	CLN SHEETS	DEF RATE
1	Danny Swailes	15	6	117 mins
2	Colin Woodthorpe	26	8	97 mins
3	Thomas Kennedy	51	11	78 mins
4	David Challinor	52	10	74 mins
5	Paul Scott	24	4	73 mins

KEY GOALKEEPER

Glyn Garner

Goals Conceded in the League	31
Defensive Rating: Ave number of mins between League goals conceded while on the pitch.	78
Counting Games: Games when player was on pitch for at least 70 minutes	27
Clean Sheets: In Games when player was on pitch for at least 70 minutes	6

TOP POINT EARNERS

	PLAYER	GAMES	AV PTS
1	Glyn Garner	27	1.59
2	David Flitcroft	28	1.43
3	Dwayne Mattis	38	1.42
4	Colin Woodthorpe	28	1.39
5	Chris Porter	21	1.38
6	John Fitzgerald	13	1.38
7	Danny Swailes	19	1.37
8	Simon Whaley	22	1.32
9	Thomas Kennedy	44	1.32
10	Lee Unsworth	30	1.30
	CLUB AVERAGE:		1.26

GRIMSBY TOWN

Final Position: **18th**

NICKNAME: THE MARINERS

KEY: ☐ Won ☐ Drawn ☐ Lost

							Attendance
1	lge2	Darlington	A	L	0-1		4,807
2	lge2	Boston	H	D	1-1	Reddy 71	6,737
3	lge2	Bury	H	W	5-1	Mansaram 17; Sestanovich 49; Pinault 64,73; Reddy 78	4,277
4	lge2	Rushden & D	A	L	0-1		2,924
5	ccr1	Wigan	H	W	1-0	Parkinson 17	3,005
6	lge2	Mansfield	H	W	2-0	Pinault 5; Crowe 86	5,693
7	lge2	Wycombe	A	L	0-2		4,320
8	lge2	Rochdale	H	L	0-1		4,795
9	lge2	Macclesfield	A	L	1-3	Crowe 13	2,128
10	lge2	Leyton Orient	H	W	2-0	Crowe 57; Pinault 90 pen	5,082
11	ccr2	Charlton	H	L	0-2		5,735
12	lge2	Cambridge	A	W	2-0	Parkinson 65; McDermott 72	3,824
13	lge2	Cheltenham	H	D	1-1	Parkinson 16	6,133
14	lge2	Northampton	A	W	1-0	Gordon 86	5,805
15	lge2	Bristol Rovers	H	D	0-0		4,691
16	lge2	Shrewsbury	A	D	1-1	Fleming 5	2,956
17	lge2	Chester	A	L	1-2	Daly 45	3,233
18	lge2	Swansea	H	D	1-1	Cramb 56	4,618
19	lge2	Scunthorpe	A	L	0-2		8,054
20	facr1	Exeter	A	L	0-1		3,378
21	lge2	Kidderminster	H	W	2-1	Gordon 9; Pinault 24	3,605
22	lge2	Southend	A	D	1-1	McDermott 32	5,192
23	lge2	Notts County	H	W	3-2	Bull 7; Parkinson 49; Whittle 79	4,030
24	lge2	Yeovil	A	L	1-2	Sestanovich 86	5,733
25	lge2	Oxford	H	D	1-1	Cramb 18	4,777
26	lge2	Macclesfield	H	D	0-0		5,108
27	lge2	Lincoln	A	D	0-0		8,056
28	lge2	Cambridge	H	W	3-0	Pinault 34; Bull 38; Gritton 90	4,148
29	lge2	Northampton	H	L	1-2	Reddy 22	3,774
30	lge2	Leyton Orient	A	W	2-1	Parkinson 19; Gritton 71	3,816
31	lge2	Lincoln	H	L	2-4	Pinault 50; Coldicott 59	7,091
32	lge2	Cheltenham	A	W	3-2	Fleming 13; Reddy 56,85	3,327
33	lge2	Bristol Rovers	A	L	0-3		6,134
34	lge2	Shrewsbury	H	L	0-1		4,781
35	lge2	Swansea	A	D	0-0		7,760
36	lge2	Chester	H	W	1-0	Gritton 81	3,144
37	lge2	Yeovil	H	W	2-1	Gritton 60; Parkinson 87	4,414
38	lge2	Rochdale	A	L	0-2		2,312
39	lge2	Oxford	A	W	2-1	Harrold 46; Parkinson 71	5,625
40	lge2	Boston	A	D	1-1	Harrold 69	3,941
41	lge2	Darlington	H	L	0-1		4,578
42	lge2	Bury	A	L	1-3	Reddy 48	5,671
43	lge2	Rushden & D	H	D	0-0		4,566
44	lge2	Mansfield	A	L	0-2		3,424
45	lge2	Wycombe	H	D	0-0		3,452
46	lge2	Notts County	A	D	2-2	Parkinson 27; Crowe 50	5,478
47	lge2	Scunthorpe	H	D	0-0		7,941
48	lge2	Kidderminster	A	W	4-1	Jones 8; Reddy 13,78; Parkinson 48	2,340
49	lge2	Southend	H	D	1-1	Reddy 57	6,259

TEAM OF THE SEASON

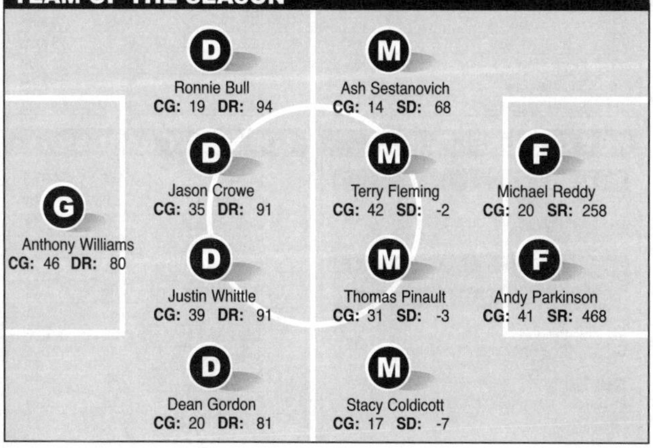

D
Ronnie Bull
CG: 19 DR: 94
M
Ash Sestanovich
CG: 14 SD: 68
D
Jason Crowe
CG: 35 DR: 91
M
Terry Fleming
CG: 42 SD: -2
F
Michael Reddy
CG: 20 SR: 258
G
Anthony Williams
CG: 46 DR: 80
D
Justin Whittle
CG: 39 DR: 91
M
Thomas Pinault
CG: 31 SD: -3
F
Andy Parkinson
CG: 41 SR: 468
D
Dean Gordon
CG: 20 DR: 81
M
Stacy Coldicott
CG: 17 SD: -7

KEY PLAYER APPEARANCES

	PLAYER	POS	AGE	APP	MINS ON	GOALS	CARDS(Y/R)	
1	Anthony Williams	GK	27	46	4140	0	2	0
2	Terry Fleming	MID	32	43	3760	2	9	1
3	Andy Parkinson	ATT	26	45	3743	8	2	0
4	Justin Whittle	DEF	34	40	3550	1	4	0
5	John McDermott	DEF	36	39	3426	2	2	0
6	Jason Crowe	DEF	26	37	3200	4	4	0
7	Thomas Pinault	MID	23	43	3114	7	2	0
8	Terrell Forbes	DEF	23	33	2970	0	1	0
9	Michael Reddy	ATT	25	40	2321	9	4	0
10	Simon Ramsden	DEF	23	25	1972	0	5	0
11	Martin Gritton	ATT	27	23	1886	4	1	0
12	Ronnie Bull	DEF	24	27	1878	2	5	1
13	Stacy Coldicott	MID	31	32	1877	1	5	0
14	Dean Gordon	DEF	32	20	1786	2	0	0
15	Robert Jones	DEF	25	20	1570	1	4	0
16	Ash Sestanovich	MID	23	22	1454	2	2	0
17	Colin Cramb	ATT	31	11	644	2	2	0
18	Matt Harrold	ATT	21	6	540	2	0	0

KEY PLAYERS - GOALSCORERS

Michael Reddy

Goals in the League	9
Contribution to Attacking Power Average number of minutes between League team goals while on pitch	72
Player Strike Rate Average number of minutes between League goals scored by player	258
Club Strike Rate Average number of minutes between League goals scored by club	81

	PLAYER	LGE GOALS	POWER	STRIKE RATE
1	Michael Reddy	9	72	258 mins
2	Thomas Pinault	7	72	445 mins
3	Andy Parkinson	8	79	468 mins
4	Martin Gritton	4	99	472 mins
5	Ash Sestanovich	2	77	727 mins

KEY PLAYERS - MIDFIELDERS

Ash Sestanovich

Goals in the League	2
Defensive Rating Average number of mins between League goals conceded while on the pitch	145
Contribution to Attacking Power Average number of minutes between League team goals while on pitch	77
Scoring Difference Defensive Rating minus Contribution to Attacking Power	68

	PLAYER	LGE GOALS	DEF RATE	POWER	SCORE DIFF
1	Ash Sestanovich	2	145	77	68 mins
2	Terry Fleming	2	82	84	-2 mins
3	Thomas Pinault	7	69	72	-3 mins
4	Stacy Coldicott	1	82	89	-7 mins

KEY PLAYERS - DEFENDERS

Ronnie Bull

Goals Conceded when he was on pitch	20
Defensive Rating Ave number of mins between League goals conceded while on the pitch	94
Clean Sheets In games when he played at least 70 minutes	6
Club Defensive Rating Average number of mins between League goals conceded by the club this season.	80

	PLAYER	CON LGE	CLN SHEETS	DEF RATE
1	Ronnie Bull	20	6	94 mins
2	Jason Crowe	35	12	91 mins
3	Justin Whittle	39	12	91 mins
4	Dean Gordon	22	5	81 mins
5	Terrell Forbes	37	11	80 mins

KEY GOALKEEPER

Anthony Williams

Goals Conceded in the League	52
Defensive Rating Ave number of mins between League goals conceded while on the pitch.	80
Counting Games Games when he played at least 70 mins	46
Clean Sheets In games when he played at least 70 mins	13

TOP POINT EARNERS

	PLAYER	GAMES	AV PTS
1	Ronnie Bull	19	1.68
2	Stacy Coldicott	17	1.53
3	Ash Sestanovich	14	1.43
4	Michael Reddy	20	1.40
5	Robert Jones	16	1.38
6	Dean Gordon	20	1.35
7	Terrell Forbes	33	1.30
8	Jason Crowe	35	1.29
9	Terry Fleming	42	1.29
10	Andy Parkinson	41	1.27
	CLUB AVERAGE:		1.26

NOTTS COUNTY

Final Position: **19th**

NICKNAME: THE MAGPIES

KEY: ☐Won ☐Drawn ☐Lost

							Attendance
1	lge2	Chester	H	D	1-1	Baudet 65 pen	6,432
2	lge2	Kidderminster	A	D	0-0		2,927
3	lge2	Bristol Rovers	A	L	1-2	Hurst 66	8,225
4	lge2	Yeovil	H	L	1-2	Gordon 56	5,024
5	ccr1	Bradford	A	W	2-1	Richardson 64; Ullathorne 105	3,517
6	lge2	Lincoln	A	W	2-1	Scully 27,63	5,173
7	lge2	Oxford	H	L	0-1		5,288
8	lge2	Cheltenham	H	D	0-0		4,302
9	lge2	Northampton	A	D	0-0		5,471
10	lge2	Southend	H	L	1-2	Hurst 86	4,487
11	ccr2	West Ham	A	L	2-3	Wilson 13; Richardson 57	11,111
12	lge2	Rochdale	A	W	3-0	Hurst 40,65,90	2,370
13	lge2	Leyton Orient	H	L	1-2	Baudet 7 pen	5,141
14	lge2	Macclesfield	A	W	2-1	Hurst 66,71	2,456
15	lge2	Mansfield	A	L	1-3	Gordon 90	7,682
16	lge2	Darlington	H	D	1-1	Hurst 28	3,620
17	lge2	Boston	H	W	2-1	Gordon 17; Palmer 51	5,434
18	lge2	Rushden & D	A	L	1-5	Pipe 55	3,504
19	lge2	Shrewsbury	H	W	3-0	Bolland 39; Hurst 70; Palmer 90	5,745
20	facr1	Woking	H	W	2-0	Baudet 35 pen; Gordon 90	4,700
21	lge2	Bury	A	L	0-1		2,938
22	lge2	Cambridge	H	W	2-1	Williams 39; Palmer 74	5,080
23	facr2	Swindon	A	D	1-1	Oakes 90	5,768
24	lge2	Grimsby	A	L	2-3	Oakes 18; Gordon 71	4,030
25	lge2	Wycombe	H	L	0-1		6,529
26	facr2r	Swindon	H	W	2-0	Gordon 31,47	3,770
27	lge2	Swansea	A	L	0-4		6,609
28	lge2	Scunthorpe	A	D	0-0		6,399
29	lge2	Cheltenham	A	W	2-0	Hurst 58; Palmer 69	3,375
30	lge2	Rochdale	H	D	0-0		5,258
31	facr3	Middlesbrough	H	L	1-2	Scully 2	13,671
32	lge2	Southend	A	D	0-0		5,304
33	lge2	Scunthorpe	H	W	2-0	Hurst 30; Gordon 57	6,429
34	lge2	Macclesfield	H	L	0-5		3,586
35	lge2	Leyton Orient	A	L	0-2		3,440
36	lge2	Mansfield	H	L	0-1		10,005
37	lge2	Darlington	A	W	2-1	Pipe 59; Wilson 67	4,213
38	lge2	Northampton	H	D	0-0		4,645
39	lge2	Rushden & D	H	D	1-1	Baudet 54 pen	4,556
40	lge2	Wycombe	A	W	2-1	Wilson 13; Oakes 71	4,199
41	lge2	Swansea	H	W	1-0	Stallard 50	4,644
42	lge2	Kidderminster	H	L	1-3	Stallard 88	4,358
43	lge2	Boston	A	L	0-4		2,229
44	lge2	Chester	A	L	2-3	Hurst 23; Zadkovich 82	2,324
45	lge2	Bristol Rovers	H	L	1-2	Hurst 9	4,258
46	lge2	Yeovil	A	W	3-1	Oakes 6; Hurst 25; Stallard 58	7,221
47	lge2	Lincoln	H	W	1-0	Baudet 41 pen	7,103
48	lge2	Oxford	A	L	1-2	Baudet 28	4,436
49	lge2	Grimsby	H	D	2-2	Oakes 76,88	5,478
50	lge2	Shrewsbury	A	D	1-1	Harrad 24	4,202
51	lge2	Bury	H	L	0-1		6,424
52	lge2	Cambridge	A	D	0-0		4,723

TEAM OF THE SEASON

D
Julien Baudet
CG: 35 DR: 76
M
Stefan Oakes
CG: 26 SD: -17
D
Michael Whitlow
CG: 18 DR: 73
M
Chris Palmer
CG: 20 SD: -17
F
Glynn Hurst
CG: 35 SR: 229
G
Saul Deeney
CG: 31 DR: 76
D
Kelvin Wilson
CG: 36 DR: 68
M
Paul Bolland
CG: 34 SD: -22
F
Gavin Gordon
CG: 21 SR: 399
D
Shane McFaul
CG: 13 DR: 65
M
Matthew Gill
CG: 36 SD: -27

KEY PLAYER APPEARANCES

	PLAYER	POS	AGE	APP	MINS ON	GOALS	CARDS(Y/R)	
1	Matthew Gill	MID	24	43	3450	0	5	0
2	Paul Bolland	MID	25	40	3366	1	4	1
3	David Pipe	MID	21	41	3355	2	5	0
4	Kelvin Wilson	DEF	19	41	3312	2	5	0
5	Julien Baudet	DEF	26	39	3262	5	7	0
6	Glynn Hurst	ATT	29	41	3207	14	2	1
7	Robert Ullathorne	DEF	33	36	2979	0	6	0
8	Saul Deeney	GK	22	32	2808	0	1	1
9	Stefan Oakes	MID	26	31	2501	5	4	1
10	Chris Palmer	MID	21	25	2018	4	2	0
11	Gavin Gordon	ATT	26	27	1994	5	5	0
12	Michael Whitlow	DEF	37	24	1900	0	4	0
13	Tony Scully	MID	29	31	1848	2	0	0
14	Shane McFaul	DEF	19	24	1506	0	1	0
15	Mark Stallard	ATT	30	16	1412	3	3	0
16	Wayne Henderson	GK	21	11	965	0	0	0
17	Ian Richardson	DEF	34	10	893	0	2	0
18	Matthew Williams	ATT	22	18	789	1	2	0

KEY PLAYERS - GOALSCORERS

Glynn Hurst

Goals in the League	14
Contribution to Attacking Power Average number of minutes between League team goals while on pitch	82
Player Strike Rate Average number of minutes between League goals scored by player	229
Club Strike Rate Average number of minutes between League goals scored by club	90

	PLAYER	LGE GOALS	POWER	STRIKE RATE
1	Glynn Hurst	14	82	229 mins
2	Gavin Gordon	5	104	399 mins
3	Mark Stallard	3	83	471 mins
4	Stefan Oakes	5	78	500 mins
5	Chris Palmer	4	92	505 mins

KEY PLAYERS - MIDFIELDERS

Stefan Oakes

Goals in the League	5
Defensive Rating Average number of mins between League goals conceded while on the pitch	61
Contribution to Attacking Power Average number of minutes between League team goals while on pitch	78
Scoring Difference Defensive Rating minus Contribution to Attacking Power	-17

	PLAYER	LGE GOALS	DEF RATE	POWER	SCORE DIFF
1	Stefan Oakes	5	61	78	-17 mins
2	Chris Palmer	4	75	92	-17 mins
3	Paul Bolland	1	64	86	-22 mins
4	Matthew Gill	0	64	91	-27 mins
5	David Pipe	2	66	96	-30 mins

KEY PLAYERS - DEFENDERS

Julien Baudet

Goals Conceded when he was on pitch	43
Defensive Rating Ave number of mins between League goals conceded while on the pitch	76
Clean Sheets In games when he played at least 70 minutes	11
Club Defensive Rating Average number of mins between League goals conceded by the club this season.	67

	PLAYER	CON LGE	CLN SHEETS	DEF RATE
1	Julien Baudet	43	11	76 mins
2	Michael Whitlow	26	6	73 mins
3	Kelvin Wilson	49	13	68 mins
4	Shane McFaul	23	3	65 mins
5	Robert Ullathorne	47	9	63 mins

KEY GOALKEEPER

Saul Deeney

Goals Conceded in the League	37
Defensive Rating Ave number of mins between League goals conceded while on the pitch.	76
Counting Games Games when he played at least 70 mins	31
Clean Sheets In games when he played at least 70 mins	11

TOP POINT EARNERS

	PLAYER	GAMES	AV PTS
1	Chris Palmer	20	1.40
2	Michael Whitlow	18	1.39
3	Shane McFaul	13	1.31
4	Saul Deeney	31	1.29
5	Kelvin Wilson	36	1.28
6	Glynn Hurst	35	1.26
7	Julien Baudet	35	1.26
8	Stefan Oakes	26	1.23
9	Mark Stallard	16	1.19
10	Paul Bolland	34	1.18
	CLUB AVERAGE:		1.13

CHESTER CITY

Final Position: **20th**

NICKNAME: THE BLUES

KEY: Won Drawn Lost

	Comp	Opponent	H/A	Res	Score	Scorers	Attendance
1	lge2	**Notts County**	A	D	1-1	Clare 87	6,432
2	lge2	**Wycombe**	H	L	0-2		2,881
3	lge2	**Mansfield**	H	L	0-3		2,648
4	lge2	**Bury**	A	D	1-1	Branch 21	2,870
5	ccr1	**Sunderland**	A	L	0-3		11,450
6	lge2	**Darlington**	H	L	0-3		2,392
7	lge2	**Boston**	A	L	1-3	Branch 84 pen	2,698
8	lge2	**Macclesfield**	H	W	1-0	Collins 90	2,913
9	lge2	**Scunthorpe**	A	W	2-1	Ellison 24; Bolland 31	4,203
10	lge2	**Cambridge**	H	D	0-0		2,771
11	lge2	**Lincoln**	A	D	1-1	Ellison 36	3,985
12	lge2	**Swansea**	H	D	1-1	Rapley 19	3,847
13	lge2	**Cheltenham**	A	D	0-0		3,670
14	lge2	**Rushden & D**	A	W	1-0	Drummond 77	2,735
15	lge2	**Grimsby**	H	W	2-1	Branch 39,42	3,233
16	lge2	**Kidderminster**	H	W	3-0	Branch 28; Ellison 52; Davies 64	2,968
17	lge2	**Yeovil**	A	L	1-4	Clare 73 pen	5,741
18	lge2	**Leyton Orient**	H	D	1-1	Belle 83	3,125
19	facr1	**Stafford**	A	W	2-0	Belle 32; Rapley 71	2,492
20	lge2	**Northampton**	A	D	1-1	Ellison 26	5,625
21	lge2	**Oxford**	H	L	1-3	Ellison 35	2,791
22	facr2	**Halifax**	A	W	3-1	Branch 41,50 pen; Rapley 74	4,497
23	lge2	**Bristol Rovers**	A	L	1-4	Ellison 27	5,524
24	lge2	**Shrewsbury**	H	D	1-1	Branch 90 pen	3,219
25	lge2	**Southend**	A	L	0-1		4,837
26	lge2	**Scunthorpe**	H	D	1-1	Ellison 19	3,216
27	lge2	**Rochdale**	A	D	2-2	Ellison 6; Branch 83	3,724
28	lge2	**Macclesfield**	A	W	2-1	Drummond 77; Ellison 81	3,076
29	lge2	**Lincoln**	H	L	0-1		2,839
30	facr3	**Bournemouth**	A	L	1-2	Ellison 69	7,653
31	lge2	**Cambridge**	A	D	0-0		3,185
32	lge2	**Rochdale**	H	D	0-0		2,985
33	lge2	**Swansea**	A	L	0-3		8,989
34	lge2	**Cheltenham**	H	L	0-3		1,643
35	lge2	**Rushden & D**	H	W	3-1	Atieno 15; Hessey 38; O'Neill 74	2,340
36	lge2	**Kidderminster**	A	W	1-0	Drummond 76	2,779
37	lge2	**Yeovil**	H	L	0-2		3,072
38	lge2	**Grimsby**	A	L	0-1		3,144
39	lge2	**Shrewsbury**	A	L	0-5		4,859
40	lge2	**Southend**	H	D	2-2	Walsh 9; Davies 49	2,396
41	lge2	**Wycombe**	A	L	2-4	Branch 26,88 pen	8,124
42	lge2	**Notts County**	H	W	3-2	Drummond 28; Branch 58,77	2,324
43	lge2	**Mansfield**	A	D	0-0		3,437
44	lge2	**Bury**	H	W	2-1	Lowe 59,70	3,107
45	lge2	**Darlington**	A	L	0-1		3,778
46	lge2	**Boston**	H	W	2-1	Booth 45; Lowe 77	2,040
47	lge2	**Bristol Rovers**	H	D	2-2	Drummond 60,72	2,475
48	lge2	**Leyton Orient**	A	L	0-2		3,192
49	lge2	**Northampton**	H	L	0-2		3,455
50	lge2	**Oxford**	A	W	1-0	Lowe 90	5,055

TEAM OF THE SEASON

- G — Chris MacKenzie — CG: 23 DR: 68
- D — Danny Collins — CG: 12 DR: 68
- D — Darren Edmondson — CG: 22 DR: 68
- D — Richard Hope — CG: 25 DR: 63
- D — Philip Bolland — CG: 40 DR: 60
- M — Paul Carden — CG: 36 SD: -24
- M — Ben Davies — CG: 36 SD: -25
- M — Stuart Drummond — CG: 42 SD: -31
- M — Kevin Ellison — CG: 22 SD: -31
- F — Michael Branch — CG: 27 SR: 238
- F — Cortez Belle — CG: 12 SR: 1522

KEY PLAYER APPEARANCES

	PLAYER	POS	AGE	APP	MINS ON	GOALS	CARDS(Y)	CARDS(R)
1	Stuart Drummond	MID	29	45	3905	6	9	0
2	Philip Bolland	DEF	28	42	3657	1	8	1
3	Ben Davies	MID	24	44	3418	2	10	0
4	Paul Carden	MID	26	39	3240	0	10	1
5	Sean Hessey	DEF	26	34	2701	1	8	1
6	Michael Branch	ATT	26	33	2621	11	8	0
7	Richard Hope	DEF	27	28	2383	0	3	0
8	Darren Edmondson	DEF	33	26	2120	0	6	0
9	Chris MacKenzie	GK	27	24	2101	0	1	0
10	Kevin Ellison	ATT	26	24	2064	9	11	1
11	Wayne Brown	GK	28	23	2039	0	1	0
12	Cortez Belle	ATT	33	22	1522	1	7	3
13	Stephen Vaughan	DEF	20	21	1355	0	1	0
14	Robbie Foy	ATT	19	13	1164	0	2	0
15	Kevin Rapley	ATT	27	21	1135	1	3	0
16	Danny Collins	DEF	24	12	1080	1	1	0
17	Michael Brown	MID	20	18	957	0	1	0
18	Andy Harris	DEF	28	19	925	0	4	0

KEY PLAYERS - GOALSCORERS

Kevin Ellison

- Goals in the League: 9
- Contribution to Attacking Power — Average number of minutes between League team goals while on pitch: 93
- Player Strike Rate — Average number of minutes between League goals scored by player: 229
- Club Strike Rate — Average number of minutes between League goals scored by club: 96

	PLAYER	LGE GOALS	POWER	STRIKE RATE
1	Kevin Ellison	9	94	229 mins
2	Michael Branch	11	100	238 mins
3	Stuart Drummond	6	93	651 mins
4	Danny Collins	1	135	1080 mins
5	Cortez Belle	1	95	1522 mins

KEY PLAYERS - MIDFIELDERS

Paul Carden

- Goals in the League: 0
- Defensive Rating — Average number of mins between League goals conceded while on the pitch: 74
- Contribution to Attacking Power — Average number of minutes between League team goals while on pitch: 98
- Scoring Difference — Defensive Rating minus Contribution to Attacking Power: -24

	PLAYER	LGE GOALS	DEF RATE	POWER	SCORE DIFF
1	Paul Carden	0	74	98	-24 mins
2	Ben Davies	2	63	88	-25 mins
3	Kevin Ellison	9	63	94	-31 mins
4	Stuart Drummond	6	62	93	-31 mins

KEY PLAYERS - DEFENDERS

Darren Edmondson

- Goals Conceded while on the pitch: 31
- Defensive Rating — Ave number of mins between League goals conceded while on the pitch: 68
- Clean Sheets — In games when player was on pitch for at least 70 minutes: 6
- Club Defensive Rating — Average number of mins between League goals conceded by the club this season: 60

	PLAYER	CON LGE	CLN SHEETS	DEF RATE
1	Darren Edmondson	31	6	68 mins
2	Danny Collins	16	3	68 mins
3	Richard Hope	38	7	63 mins
4	Philip Bolland	61	9	60 mins
5	Sean Hessey	47	5	57 mins

KEY GOALKEEPER

Chris MacKenzie

- Goals Conceded in the League: 31
- Defensive Rating — Ave number of mins between League goals conceded while on the pitch: 68
- Counting Games — Games when player was on pitch for at least 70 minutes: 23
- Clean Sheets — In Games when player was on pitch for at least 70 minutes: 6

TOP POINT EARNERS

	PLAYER	GAMES	AV PTS
1	Darren Edmondson	22	1.59
2	Cortez Belle	12	1.58
3	Richard Hope	25	1.36
4	Chris MacKenzie	23	1.35
5	Paul Carden	36	1.31
6	Ben Davies	36	1.25
7	Kevin Ellison	22	1.23
8	Sean Hessey	27	1.22
9	Michael Branch	27	1.22
10	Stuart Drummond	42	1.21
	CLUB AVERAGE:		1.13

SHREWSBURY TOWN

Final Position: **21st**

NICKNAME: THE SHREWS

KEY: ☐Won ☐Drawn ☐Lost

							Attendance
1	lge2	**Lincoln**	H	L	0-1		4,843
2	lge2	**Macclesfield**	A	L	1-2	Smith 66	2,641
3	lge2	**Cambridge**	A	L	0-1		3,135
4	lge2	**Northampton**	H	W	2-0	Grant 50; Smith 78	3,980
5	ccr1	**Tranmere**	A	L	1-2	Rodgers 67	4,489
6	lge2	**Oxford**	A	L	0-2		4,430
7	lge2	**Cheltenham**	H	W	2-0	Lowe 35; Rodgers 88	3,862
8	lge2	**Bristol Rovers**	A	D	0-0		8,381
9	lge2	**Bury**	H	D	2-2	Moss 70; Challinor 76 og	3,801
10	lge2	**Boston**	A	D	2-2	Logan 25; Smith 34	2,593
11	lge2	**Yeovil**	H	L	1-2	Rodgers 40	4,196
12	lge2	**Wycombe**	A	D	1-1	Moss 37	4,634
13	lge2	**Rushden & D**	H	L	0-1		3,882
14	lge2	**Leyton Orient**	A	L	1-4	Fox 90	3,718
15	lge2	**Grimsby**	H	D	1-1	Sedgemore 77	2,956
16	lge2	**Southend**	H	D	1-1	Street 14	3,719
17	lge2	**Kidderminster**	A	W	1-0	Lowe 82	3,830
18	lge2	**Notts County**	A	L	0-3		5,745
19	facr1	**Histon**	A	L	0-2		1,538
20	lge2	**Swansea**	H	W	2-0	Sedgemore 21; Walton 81	5,055
21	lge2	**Scunthorpe**	A	L	1-3	Tolley 70	4,418
22	lge2	**Rochdale**	H	L	0-2		3,677
23	lge2	**Chester**	A	D	1-1	Langmead 62	3,219
24	lge2	**Mansfield**	H	L	0-2		3,469
25	lge2	**Darlington**	H	W	4-0	Aiston 34; Tolley 38,44; Edwards 90	3,915
26	lge2	**Bristol Rovers**	H	W	2-0	Edwards 64; Grant 71	5,043
27	lge2	**Yeovil**	A	L	2-4	Sedgemore 64 pen; Edwards 74	7,250
28	lge2	**Rushden & D**	A	D	0-0		2,829
29	lge2	**Boston**	H	D	0-0		3,789
30	lge2	**Darlington**	A	L	0-3		3,934
31	lge2	**Wycombe**	H	L	0-1		3,884
32	lge2	**Leyton Orient**	H	W	4-1	Walton 43; Darby 52; Moss 68,75	3,496
33	lge2	**Bury**	A	D	0-0		2,233
34	lge2	**Grimsby**	A	W	1-0	Sedgemore 26	4,781
35	lge2	**Kidderminster**	H	W	4-2	Moss 33,40; Langmead 45; Rodgers 56	5,309
36	lge2	**Southend**	A	L	0-1		4,219
37	lge2	**Chester**	H	W	5-0	Tolley 28; Rodgers 41; Sedgemore 57 pen; Lowe 65; Langmead 78	4,859
38	lge2	**Mansfield**	A	D	1-1	Rodgers 75	3,278
39	lge2	**Macclesfield**	H	L	0-1		4,262
40	lge2	**Lincoln**	A	L	0-2		4,255
41	lge2	**Cambridge**	H	D	0-0		5,309
42	lge2	**Northampton**	A	L	0-2		6,514
43	lge2	**Oxford**	H	W	3-0	Edwards 47; Wanless 57 og; Rodgers 71	3,974
44	lge2	**Cheltenham**	A	D	1-1	Sheron 79	3,769
45	lge2	**Rochdale**	A	D	1-1	Sheron 6 pen	3,142
46	lge2	**Notts County**	H	D	1-1	Edwards 60	4,202
47	lge2	**Swansea**	A	L	0-1		11,469
48	lge2	**Scunthorpe**	H	D	0-0		6,285

TEAM OF THE SEASON

G — Scott Howie, CG: 40 DR: 73

D — Neil Ashton, CG: 19 DR: 139

D — David Walton, CG: 19 DR: 98

D — Trevor Challis, CG: 34 DR: 80

D — Stuart Whitehead, CG: 35 DR: 78

M — Jake Sedgemore, CG: 22 SD: 15

M — Sam Aiston, CG: 22 SD: 14

M — Ryan Lowe, CG: 16 SD: -16

M — Jamie Tolley, CG: 29 SD: -16

F — Luke Rodgers, CG: 31 SR: 500

F — Kelvin Langmead, CG: 22 SR: 732

KEY PLAYER APPEARANCES

	PLAYER	POS	AGE	APP	MINS ON	GOALS	CARDS(Y/R)	
1	Darren Tinson	DEF	35	43	3727	0	0	0
2	Scott Howie	GK	33	40	3600	0	1	0
3	Stuart Whitehead	DEF	28	40	3359	0	6	1
4	Trevor Challis	DEF	29	38	3219	0	6	0
5	Luke Rodgers	ATT	32	36	2998	6	9	1
6	Jamie Tolley	MID	22	35	2811	4	8	1
7	Sam Aiston	MID	28	37	2491	1	6	1
8	Darren Moss	DEF	24	26	2214	6	5	2
9	Kelvin Langmead	ATT	20	28	2196	3	2	0
10	Jake Sedgemore	MID	26	31	2175	5	2	0
11	Ryan Lowe	MID	26	30	1806	3	3	0
12	Neil Ashton	DEF	20	22	1803	0	4	0
13	David Walton	DEF	32	22	1771	2	1	1
14	David Edwards	MID	19	27	1572	5	0	0
15	Kevin Street	MID	27	21	1299	1	0	0
16	Martyn O'Connor	MID	37	21	1198	0	6	1
17	Ben Smith	MID	26	12	936	3	1	0
18	John Grant	ATT	23	19	849	2	0	0

KEY PLAYERS - GOALSCORERS

David Edwards

Goals in the League	5
Contribution to Attacking Power Average number of minutes between League team goals while on pitch	92
Player Strike Rate Average number of minutes between League goals scored by player	314
Club Strike Rate Average number of minutes between League goals scored by club	86

	PLAYER	LGE GOALS	POWER	STRIKE RATE
1	David Edwards	5	92	314 mins
2	Darren Moss	6	85	369 mins
3	Jake Sedgemore	5	65	435 mins
4	Luke Rodgers	6	81	500 mins
5	Ryan Lowe	3	95	602 mins

KEY PLAYERS - MIDFIELDERS

Jake Sedgemore

Goals in the League	5
Defensive Rating Average number of mins between League goals conceded while on the pitch	81
Contribution to Attacking Power Average number of minutes between League team goals while on pitch	66
Scoring Difference Defensive Rating minus Contribution to Attacking Power	15

	PLAYER	LGE GOALS	DEF RATE	POWER	SCORE DIFF
1	Jake Sedgemore	5	81	66	15 mins
2	Sam Aiston	1	100	86	14 mins
3	Ryan Lowe	3	79	95	-16 mins
4	Jamie Tolley	4	64	80	-16 mins
5	David Edwards	5	75	92	-17 mins

KEY PLAYERS - DEFENDERS

Neil Ashton

Goals Conceded while on the pitch	13
Defensive Rating Ave number of mins between League goals conceded while on the pitch	139
Clean Sheets In games when player was on pitch for at least 70 minutes	9
Club Defensive Rating Average number of mins between League goals conceded by the club this season.	78

	PLAYER	CON LGE	CLN SHEETS	DEF RATE
1	Neil Ashton	13	9	139 mins
2	David Walton	18	8	98 mins
3	Trevor Challis	40	11	80 mins
4	Stuart Whitehead	43	13	78 mins
5	Darren Tinson	49	12	76 mins

KEY GOALKEEPER

Scott Howie

Goals Conceded in the League	49
Defensive Rating Ave number of mins between League goals conceded while on the pitch.	73
Counting Games Games when player was on pitch for at least 70 minutes	40
Clean Sheets In Games when player was on pitch for at least 70 minutes	13

TOP POINT EARNERS

	PLAYER	GAMES	AV PTS
1	Neil Ashton	19	1.53
2	David Walton	19	1.42
3	Jake Sedgemore	22	1.36
4	Kelvin Langmead	22	1.18
5	Ryan Lowe	16	1.13
6	Darren Moss	24	1.13
7	Kevin Street	12	1.08
8	David Edwards	13	1.08
9	Stuart Whitehead	35	1.06
10	Sam Aiston	22	1.05
	CLUB AVERAGE:		1.07

RUSHDEN & DIAMONDS

Final Position: **22nd**

NICKNAME: THE DIAMONDS

KEY: Won Drawn Lost

		Opponent	H/A	Res	Score	Scorers	Attendance
1	lge2	Kidderminster	H	D	0-0		2,699
2	lge2	Northampton	A	L	0-1		7,107
3	lge2	Lincoln	A	W	3-1	Braniff 39; Hay 68; Dove 89	4,127
4	lge2	Grimsby	H	W	1-0	Braniff 72	2,924
5	ccr1	Swindon	H	L	0-1		1,672
6	lge2	Yeovil	A	L	1-3	Mills 83	5,088
7	lge2	Bristol Rovers	H	D	0-0		3,367
8	lge2	Southend	H	L	1-4	Burgess 50	2,804
9	lge2	Oxford	A	D	0-0		4,756
10	lge2	Cheltenham	H	W	1-0	Braniff 31	2,601
11	lge2	Swansea	A	L	0-1		7,410
12	lge2	Rochdale	H	D	0-0		2,619
13	lge2	Shrewsbury	A	W	1-0	Dove 45	3,882
14	lge2	Chester	H	L	0-1		2,735
15	lge2	Wycombe	A	D	1-1	Mulligan 18	3,844
16	lge2	Bury	A	D	1-1	Hay 58	2,672
17	lge2	Notts County	H	W	5-1	Broughton 1,11,68 pen; Dove 41,53	3,504
18	lge2	Darlington	H	L	1-2	Mulligan 85	3,036
19	facr1	Bradford	A	W	1-0	Robinson 87	4,171
20	lge2	Cambridge	A	L	1-3	Broughton 41	3,466
21	lge2	Macclesfield	H	L	0-2		2,643
22	facr2	Colchester	H	L	2-5	Broughton 82; Gray 86	3,077
23	lge2	Boston	A	L	0-1		2,334
24	lge2	Mansfield	A	D	0-0		3,776
25	lge2	Scunthorpe	H	L	1-3	Mulligan 4	3,198
26	lge2	Oxford	H	D	3-3	Dove 37; Bell 51; Taylor 62	4,140
27	lge2	Leyton Orient	A	D	2-2	Hay 28; Dove 63	3,777
28	lge2	Southend	A	L	0-3		5,930
29	lge2	Swansea	H	L	0-2		3,382
30	lge2	Shrewsbury	H	D	0-0		2,829
31	lge2	Cheltenham	A	L	1-4	Taylor 30	3,160
32	lge2	Leyton Orient	H	W	2-0	Gier 86; Bell 90	3,288
33	lge2	Rochdale	A	L	0-2		2,664
34	lge2	Chester	A	L	1-3	Sharp 86	2,340
35	lge2	Wycombe	H	L	1-2	Allen 50	3,490
36	lge2	Notts County	A	D	1-1	Sharp 52	4,556
37	lge2	Bury	H	W	3-0	Sharp 30; Gier 43; Bell 45	1,803
38	lge2	Mansfield	H	D	0-0		3,096
39	lge2	Scunthorpe	A	L	0-1		4,932
40	lge2	Northampton	H	W	3-2	Hawkins 7; Broughton 57 pen; Sharp 90	5,520
41	lge2	Kidderminster	A	D	0-0		3,860
42	lge2	Lincoln	H	L	1-4	Sharp 14	4,213
43	lge2	Grimsby	A	D	0-0		4,566
44	lge2	Yeovil	H	W	2-0	Gray 82; Sharp 88	3,726
45	lge2	Bristol Rovers	A	L	0-3		5,740
46	lge2	Boston	H	W	4-2	Broughton 27; Sharp 54,65,84	3,671
47	lge2	Darlington	A	L	0-2		4,579
48	lge2	Cambridge	H	L	0-1		5,104
49	lge2	Macclesfield	A	L	0-1		2,658

TEAM OF THE SEASON

G Billy Turley CG: 22 DR: 79

D Sean Connelly CG: 39 DR: 78

D Peter Hawkins CG: 41 DR: 67

D Graham Allen CG: 23 DR: 64

D Phil Gulliver CG: 28 DR: 64

M Stuart Gray CG: 35 SD: -18

M Neil McCafferty CG: 15 SD: -20

M Craig Dove CG: 25 SD: -28

M David Bell CG: 36 SD: -33

F Billy Sharp CG: 16 SR: 154

F Drewe Broughton CG: 21 SR: 296

KEY PLAYER APPEARANCES

	PLAYER	POS	AGE	APP	MINS ON	GOALS	CARDS(Y)	CARDS(R)
1	Peter Hawkins	DEF	26	41	3690	1	11	0
2	Andrew Burgess	MID	23	42	3683	1	1	0
3	Sean Connelly	DEF	35	42	3599	0	6	1
4	David Bell	MID	21	40	3416	3	3	0
5	Stuart Gray	MID	31	38	3275	1	2	0
6	Alex Hay	MID	23	42	2744	3	4	0
7	Robert Gier	DEF	24	32	2654	2	4	2
8	Craig Dove	MID	21	36	2637	6	3	0
9	Phil Gulliver	DEF	22	32	2609	0	2	0
10	Graham Allen	DEF	28	26	2170	1	3	1
11	Billy Turley	GK	31	22	1980	0	1	0
12	Drewe Broughton	ATT	26	21	1773	6	8	1
13	Billy Sharp	ATT	19	16	1384	9	2	0
14	Neil McCafferty	MID	20	16	1351	0	1	0
15	Scott Shearer	GK	24	13	1170	0	0	0
16	Gary Mulligan	ATT	20	13	1011	3	1	0
17	John Dempster	DEF	22	15	929	0	0	0
18	Kevin Braniff	ATT	22	12	915	3	1	0

KEY PLAYERS - GOALSCORERS

Billy Sharp

Goals in the League: **9**

Contribution to Attacking Power — Average number of minutes between League team goals while on pitch: **86**

Player Strike Rate — Average number of minutes between League goals scored by player: **154**

Club Strike Rate — Average number of minutes between League goals scored by club: **99**

	PLAYER	LGE GOALS	POWER	STRIKE RATE
1	Billy Sharp	9	86	154 mins
2	Drewe Broughton	6	84	296 mins
3	Craig Dove	6	90	440 mins
4	Alex Hay	3	109	915 mins
5	David Bell	3	100	1139 mins

KEY PLAYERS - MIDFIELDERS

Stuart Gray

Goals in the League: **1**

Defensive Rating — Average number of mins between League goals conceded while on the pitch: **68**

Contribution to Attacking Power — Average number of minutes between League team goals while on pitch: **86**

Scoring Difference — Defensive Rating minus Contribution to Attacking Power: **-18**

	PLAYER	LGE GOALS	DEF RATE	POWER	SCORE DIFF
1	Stuart Gray	1	68	86	-18 mins
2	Neil McCafferty	0	64	84	-20 mins
3	Craig Dove	6	63	91	-28 mins
4	David Bell	3	67	100	-33 mins
5	Andrew Burgess	1	64	115	-51 mins

KEY PLAYERS - DEFENDERS

Sean Connelly

Goals Conceded while on the pitch: **46**

Defensive Rating — Ave number of mins between League goals conceded while on the pitch: **78**

Clean Sheets — In games when player was on pitch for at least 70 minutes: **15**

Club Defensive Rating — Average number of mins between League goals conceded by the club this season: **66**

	PLAYER	CON LGE	CLN SHEETS	DEF RATE
1	Sean Connelly	46	15	78 mins
2	Peter Hawkins	55	14	67 mins
3	Graham Allen	34	7	64 mins
4	Phil Gulliver	41	8	64 mins
5	Robert Gier	42	11	63 mins

KEY GOALKEEPER

Billy Turley

Goals Conceded in the League: **25**

Defensive Rating — Ave number of mins between League goals conceded while on the pitch: **79**

Counting Games — Games when player was on pitch for at least 70 minutes: **22**

Clean Sheets — In Games when player was on pitch for at least 70 minutes: **8**

TOP POINT EARNERS

	PLAYER	GAMES	AV PTS
1	Scott Shearer	13	1.23
2	Billy Sharp	16	1.19
3	Robert Gier	28	1.11
4	Neil McCafferty	15	1.07
5	Peter Hawkins	41	1.05
6	Stuart Gray	35	1.03
7	Sean Connelly	39	1.03
8	Billy Turley	22	1.00
9	Graham Allen	23	1.00
10	David Bell	36	0.97
	CLUB AVERAGE:		0.96

KIDDERMINSTER

Final Position: **23rd**

NICKNAME: THE HARRIERS

KEY: ☐Won ☐Drawn ☐Lost

							Attendance
1	lge2	Rushden & D	A	D	0-0		2,699
2	lge2	Notts County	H	D	0-0		2,927
3	lge2	Darlington	H	W	1-0	Foster 51 pen	2,303
4	lge2	Mansfield	A	L	1-2	Roberts 1	3,859
5	ccr1	Cardiff	H	L	1-1*	Brown 32 (*aet, lost 5-4 on penalties)	1,897
6	lge2	Wycombe	H	L	0-2		2,444
7	lge2	Bury	A	L	0-4		2,504
8	lge2	Leyton Orient	H	L	1-2	Foster 89	2,367
9	lge2	Swansea	A	L	0-3		6,462
10	lge2	Macclesfield	H	W	1-0	Appleby 80 pen	2,290
11	lge2	Southend	A	L	0-1		4,087
12	lge2	Cambridge	H	D	1-1	Hatswell 67	2,356
13	lge2	Lincoln	A	L	0-3		3,605
14	lge2	Scunthorpe	H	W	3-2	Foster 26,69; Langmead 90	2,167
15	lge2	Bristol Rovers	A	L	0-2		7,020
16	lge2	Chester	A	L	0-3		2,968
17	lge2	Shrewsbury	H	L	0-1		3,830
18	lge2	Boston	H	L	0-4		2,208
19	facr1	Port Vale	A	L	1-3	Hatswell 4	4,141
20	lge2	Grimsby	A	L	1-2	Matias 71	3,605
21	lge2	Northampton	H	L	0-2		2,701
22	lge2	Yeovil	A	L	1-2	Stamp 33	5,639
23	lge2	Rochdale	H	W	2-1	Keates 5; Foster 69 pen	2,337
24	lge2	Cheltenham	A	L	0-2		3,718
25	lge2	Swansea	H	L	1-5	Birch 82	4,288
26	lge2	Oxford	A	W	2-0	Sturrock 37; Russell 68	5,947
27	lge2	Leyton Orient	A	L	1-2	Foster 11	3,573
28	lge2	Southend	H	L	1-3	Beardsley 79	2,755
29	lge2	Lincoln	H	W	2-1	Sturrock 16; Russell 51	2,283
30	lge2	Macclesfield	A	L	0-2		2,001
31	lge2	Oxford	H	L	1-3	Ashton 66 og	3,143
32	lge2	Cambridge	A	W	3-1	Beardsley 30; Mullins 61; Birch 86	3,948
33	lge2	Scunthorpe	A	L	1-2	Birch 59	5,023
34	lge2	Chester	H	L	0-1		2,779
35	lge2	Shrewsbury	A	L	2-4	Beardsley 13; Sturrock 27	5,309
36	lge2	Bristol Rovers	H	D	1-1	Sturrock 29	2,082
37	lge2	Rochdale	A	D	1-1	Beardsley 18	2,385
38	lge2	Cheltenham	H	W	1-0	Mullins 48	2,879
39	lge2	Notts County	A	W	3-1	Keates 76 pen,86 pen; Beardsley 90	4,358
40	lge2	Rushden & D	H	D	0-0		3,860
41	lge2	Darlington	A	W	2-0	Keates 81; Rawle 90	6,972
42	lge2	Mansfield	H	L	1-3	Rawle 41	3,237
43	lge2	Wycombe	A	L	0-3		4,608
44	lge2	Bury	H	D	2-2	Sturrock 12; Keates 81	2,474
45	lge2	Yeovil	H	D	1-1	Rawle 83	4,014
46	lge2	Boston	A	L	0-3		2,053
47	lge2	Grimsby	H	L	1-4	Birch 47	2,340
48	lge2	Northampton	A	L	0-3		6,786

TEAM OF THE SEASON

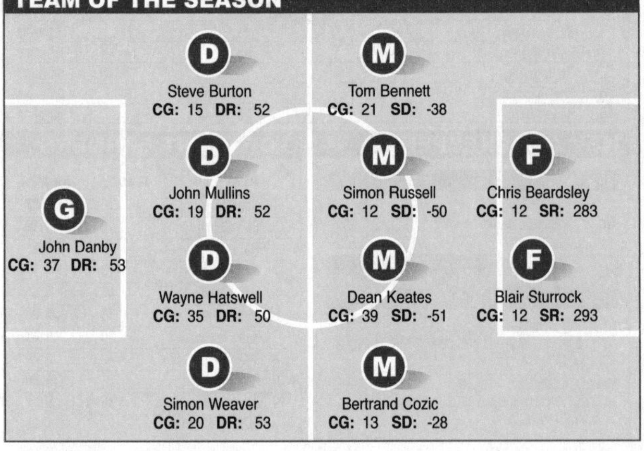

D
Steve Burton
CG: 15 DR: 52
M
Tom Bennett
CG: 21 SD: -38
D
John Mullins
CG: 19 DR: 52
M
Simon Russell
CG: 12 SD: -50
F
Chris Beardsley
CG: 12 SR: 283
G
John Danby
CG: 37 DR: 53
D
Wayne Hatswell
CG: 35 DR: 50
M
Dean Keates
CG: 39 SD: -51
F
Blair Sturrock
CG: 12 SR: 293
D
Simon Weaver
CG: 20 DR: 53
M
Bertrand Cozic
CG: 13 SD: -28

KEY PLAYER APPEARANCES

	PLAYER	POS	AGE	APP	MINS ON	GOALS	CARDS(Y/R)	
1	Dean Keates	MID	27	41	3559	5	7	0
2	John Danby	GK	21	37	3330	0	0	0
3	Wayne Hatswell	DEF	30	39	3299	1	6	2
4	Lee Jenkins	MID	26	32	2573	0	7	2
5	Tom Bennett	MID	35	24	1993	0	7	1
6	Simon Weaver	DEF	27	23	1899	0	4	0
7	John Mullins	DEF	19	21	1806	2	2	0
8	Simon Russell	MID	20	28	1622	2	0	0
9	John McGrath	MID	25	19	1603	0	3	1
10	Blair Sturrock	ATT	23	22	1465	5	1	0
11	Chris Beardsley	ATT	21	25	1414	5	4	0
12	Steve Burton	DEF	22	16	1395	0	0	0
13	Ian Foster	ATT	28	27	1350	6	2	0
14	Bertrand Cozic	MID	27	15	1180	0	1	0
15	Abdou Sall	DEF	24	14	1180	0	1	1
16	Mark Jackson	DEF	27	13	1170	0	1	0
17	Chris McHale	MID	20	14	1124	0	1	0
18	Jesper Christiansen	ATT	25	17	1046	0	2	0

KEY PLAYERS - GOALSCORERS

Chris Beardsley		Player Strike Rate Average number of minutes between League goals scored by player	283
Goals in the League	5		
Contribution to Attacking Power Average number of minutes between League team goals while on pitch	83	Club Strike Rate Average number of minutes between League goals scored by club	106

	PLAYER	LGE GOALS	POWER	STRIKE RATE
1	Chris Beardsley	5	83	283 mins
2	Blair Sturrock	5	91	293 mins
3	Dean Keates	5	101	712 mins
4	Simon Russell	2	101	811 mins
5	John Mullins	2	75	903 mins

KEY PLAYERS - MIDFIELDERS

Bertrand Cozic		Contribution to Attacking Power Average number of minutes between League team goals while on pitch	79
Goals in the League	0		
Defensive Rating Average number of mins between League goals conceded while on the pitch	51	Scoring Difference Defensive Rating minus Contribution to Attacking Power	-28

	PLAYER	LGE GOALS	DEF RATE	POWER	SCORE DIFF
1	Bertrand Cozic	0	51	79	-28 mins
2	John McGrath	0	53	89	-36 mins
3	Tom Bennett	0	45	83	-38 mins
4	Simon Russell	2	51	101	-50 mins
5	Dean Keates	5	51	102	-51 mins

KEY PLAYERS - DEFENDERS

Simon Weaver		Clean Sheets In games when player was on pitch for at least 70 minutes	3
Goals Conceded while on the pitch	36		
Defensive Rating Ave number of mins between League goals conceded while on the pitch	53	Club Defensive Rating Average number of mins between League goals conceded by the club this season.	49

	PLAYER	CON LGE	CLN SHEETS	DEF RATE
1	Simon Weaver	36	3	53 mins
2	John Mullins	35	4	52 mins
3	Steve Burton	27	4	52 mins
4	Mark Jackson	23	3	51 mins
5	Wayne Hatswell	66	6	50 mins

KEY GOALKEEPER

John Danby	
Goals Conceded in the League	63
Defensive Rating Ave number of mins between League goals conceded while on the pitch.	53
Counting Games Games when player was on pitch for at least 70 minutes	37
Clean Sheets In Games when player was on pitch for at least 70 minutes	8

TOP POINT EARNERS

	PLAYER	GAMES	AV PTS
1	Chris Beardsley	12	1.33
2	John Mullins	19	1.11
3	Blair Sturrock	12	1.08
4	Mark Jackson	13	1.08
5	Bertrand Cozic	13	1.00
6	Lee Jenkins	26	0.96
7	Simon Weaver	20	0.95
8	John Danby	37	0.95
9	Dean Keates	39	0.95
10	John McGrath	18	0.94
	CLUB AVERAGE:		0.83

CAMBRIDGE UNITED

Final Position: **24th**

NICKNAME: THE U'S

KEY: ☐Won ☐Drawn ☐Lost

								Attendance
1	lge2	Wycombe	A	L	1-2	Easter 70		4,726
2	lge2	Leyton Orient	H	D	1-1	Walker 53		4,114
3	lge2	Shrewsbury	H	W	1-0	Chillingworth 53		3,135
4	lge2	Southend	A	D	0-0			3,941
5	ccr1	Watford	A	L	0-1			6,558
6	lge2	Swansea	H	L	0-1			2,949
7	lge2	Darlington	A	D	1-1	Chillingworth 58		3,350
8	lge2	Boston	A	L	1-2	Easter 51		3,026
9	lge2	Mansfield	H	D	2-2	Oli 17; Easter 54		3,549
10	lge2	Chester	A	D	0-0			2,771
11	lge2	Grimsby	H	L	0-2			3,824
12	lge2	Kidderminster	A	D	1-1	Mbome 90		2,356
13	lge2	Bristol Rovers	H	W	1-0	Turner, J 46		2,748
14	lge2	Northampton	H	L	0-1			4,118
15	lge2	Macclesfield	A	D	1-1	Easter 39		1,436
16	lge2	Cheltenham	A	L	1-2	Tann 2		3,315
17	lge2	Lincoln	H	L	0-1			3,604
18	lge2	Rochdale	A	L	1-2	Konte 47		2,353
19	facr1	Halifax	A	L	1-3	Tudor 35		2,368
20	lge2	Rushden & D	H	W	3-1	Turner 5,10,52		3,466
21	lge2	Notts County	A	L	1-2	Tudor 53		5,080
22	lge2	Scunthorpe	H	L	1-2	Hodgson 35		2,666
23	lge2	Oxford	A	L	1-2	Easter 79		4,844
24	lge2	Bury	H	D	1-1	Konte 64		2,875
25	lge2	Yeovil	H	L	3-5	Hodgson 37; Konte 50; Easter 87		3,828
26	lge2	Boston	H	L	0-1			3,507
27	lge2	Grimsby	A	L	0-3			4,148
28	lge2	Bristol Rovers	A	D	1-1	Tudor 26		6,510
29	lge2	Mansfield	A	D	0-0			3,557
30	lge2	Chester	H	D	0-0			3,185
31	lge2	Yeovil	A	L	1-2	Tudor 77		6,204
32	lge2	Kidderminster	H	L	1-3	Tudor 16		3,948
33	lge2	Northampton	A	D	2-2	Chillingworth 48,60		6,615
34	lge2	Macclesfield	H	L	0-1			2,926
35	lge2	Lincoln	A	L	1-2	Webb 52		4,672
36	lge2	Cheltenham	H	W	1-0	Tudor 61		2,021
37	lge2	Oxford	H	W	2-1	Turner 69; Tudor 90		3,765
38	lge2	Bury	A	L	1-2	Roberts 28		2,437
39	lge2	Leyton Orient	A	D	1-1	Bramble 75		3,759
40	lge2	Wycombe	H	W	2-1	Bramble 13; Roberts 38		4,649
41	lge2	Shrewsbury	A	D	0-0			5,309
42	lge2	Southend	H	L	0-2			6,715
43	lge2	Swansea	A	L	0-3			8,664
44	lge2	Darlington	H	W	3-1	Roberts 24; Duncan 48; Turner 83		3,116
45	lge2	Scunthorpe	A	L	0-4			5,642
46	lge2	Rochdale	H	D	0-0			3,738
47	lge2	Rushden & D	A	W	1-0	Bramble 28 pen		5,104
48	lge2	Notts County	H	D	0-0			4,723

TEAM OF THE SEASON

G — John Ruddy CG: 38 DR: 76

D — Abdelhalim El Kholti CG: 13 DR: 104

D — Dan Gleeson CG: 16 DR: 78

D — Andrew Duncan CG: 39 DR: 72

D — Stevland Angus CG: 13 DR: 77

M — Darren Quinton CG: 13 SD: -20

M — Shane Tudor CG: 23 SD: -36

M — Justin Walker CG: 35 SD: -44

M — Luke Guttridge CG: 12 SD: -57

F — Jermaine Easter CG: 14 SR: 237

F — John Turner CG: 13 SR: 283

KEY PLAYER APPEARANCES

	PLAYER	POS	AGE	APP	MINS ON	GOALS	CARDS(Y/R)	
1	Andrew Duncan	DEF	27	42	3656	1	6	0
2	John Ruddy	GK	18	38	3420	0	1	0
3	Justin Walker	MID	29	36	3128	1	7	1
4	Adam Tann	DEF	23	36	3042	1	4	0
5	Warren Goodhind	DEF	27	26	2253	0	2	1
6	Ashley Nicholls	MID	23	28	2170	0	5	0
7	Shane Tudor	MID	23	27	2158	6	2	0
8	Matt Somner	DEF	22	24	2040	0	3	0
9	Dan Gleeson	DEF	20	30	1878	0	0	0
10	Daniel Chillingworth	ATT	23	28	1780	4	2	0
11	John Turner	ATT	19	38	1699	6	0	0
12	Darren Quinton	MID	19	31	1572	0	1	0
13	Stuart Bimson	DEF	35	19	1512	0	1	0
14	Jermaine Easter	ATT	23	23	1422	6	3	0
15	Daniel Webb	ATT	22	22	1255	1	5	0
16	Tom Newey	MID	22	16	1247	0	2	0
17	Luke Guttridge	MID	23	17	1229	0	1	0
18	Stevland Angus	DEF	24	14	1228	0	3	0

KEY PLAYERS - GOALSCORERS

Jermaine Easter

Goals in the League	6	Player Strike Rate Average number of minutes between League goals scored by player	237
Contribution to Attacking Power Average number of minutes between League team goals while on pitch	94	Club Strike Rate Average number of minutes between League goals scored by club	106

	PLAYER	LGE GOALS	POWER	STRIKE RATE
1	Jermaine Easter	6	94	237 mins
2	John Turner	6	99	283 mins
3	Shane Tudor	6	98	360 mins
4	Daniel Chillingworth	4	127	445 mins
5	Adam Tann	1	121	3042 mins

KEY PLAYERS - MIDFIELDERS

Luke Guttridge

Goals in the League	0	Contribution to Attacking Power Average number of minutes between League team goals while on pitch	72
Defensive Rating Average number of mins between League goals conceded while on the pitch	65	Scoring Difference Defensive Rating minus Contribution to Attacking Power	-7

	PLAYER	LGE GOALS	DEF RATE	POWER	SCORE DIFF
1	Luke Guttridge	0	65	72	-7 mins
2	Darren Quinton	0	63	83	-20 mins
3	Shane Tudor	6	62	98	-36 mins
4	Tom Newey	0	69	113	-44 mins
5	Justin Walker	1	68	112	-44 mins

KEY PLAYERS - DEFENDERS

Abdelhalim El Kholti

Goals Conceded while on the pitch	11	Clean Sheets In games when player was on pitch for at least 70 minutes	4
Defensive Rating Ave number of mins between League goals conceded while on the pitch	104	Club Defensive Rating Average number of mins between League goals conceded by the club this season.	67

	PLAYER	CON LGE	CLN SHEETS	DEF RATE
1	Abdelhalim El Kholti	11	4	104 mins
2	Dan Gleeson	24	5	78 mins
3	Stevland Angus	16	3	77 mins
4	Andrew Duncan	51	10	72 mins
5	Adam Tann	45	7	68 mins

KEY GOALKEEPER

John Ruddy

Goals Conceded in the League	45
Defensive Rating Ave number of mins between League goals conceded while on the pitch.	76
Counting Games Games when player was on pitch for at least 70 minutes	38
Clean Sheets In Games when player was on pitch for at least 70 minutes	11

TOP POINT EARNERS

	PLAYER	GAMES	AV PTS
1	Darren Quinton	13	1.08
2	Matt Somner	22	1.00
3	Ashley Nicholls	23	1.00
4	Stuart Bimson	15	0.93
5	Abdelhalim El Kholti	13	0.92
6	Tom Newey	12	0.92
7	Andrew Duncan	39	0.92
8	John Ruddy	38	0.92
9	Daniel Chillingworth	17	0.88
10	John Turner	13	0.85
	CLUB AVERAGE:		0.87

SCOTTISH PREMIERSHIP ROUND-UP

FINAL LEAGUE TABLE

	HOME						AWAY					TOTAL			
	P	W	D	L	F	A	W	D	L	F	A	F	A	DIF	PTS
Rangers	38	15	2	2	48	12	14	4	1	30	10	78	22	56	93
Celtic	38	15	0	4	41	15	15	2	2	44	20	85	35	50	92
Hibernian	38	9	4	6	32	26	9	3	7	32	31	64	57	7	61
Aberdeen	38	8	4	6	22	17	10	3	7	22	22	44	39	5	61
Hearts	38	9	4	6	25	15	4	7	8	18	26	43	41	2	50
Kilmarnock	38	10	2	7	32	20	5	2	12	17	35	49	55	-6	49
Motherwell	38	8	4	7	29	22	5	5	9	17	27	46	49	-3	48
Inverness CT	38	7	4	9	23	24	4	7	7	18	23	41	47	-6	44
Dundee Utd	38	4	7	8	22	28	4	5	10	19	31	41	59	-18	36
Livingston	38	5	4	10	22	34	4	4	11	12	27	34	61	-27	35
Dunfermline	38	5	9	5	23	19	3	1	15	11	41	34	60	-26	34
Dundee	38	7	4	8	21	24	1	5	13	16	47	37	71	-34	33

CLUB STRIKE FORCE

Boyd; striking for Killie

1 Celtic

Goals scored in the League	85
Club Strike Rate (CSR) Average number of minutes between League goals scored by club	40

	CLUB	LGE	CSR
1	Celtic	85	40
2	Rangers	78	44
3	Hibernian	64	53
4	Kilmarnock	49	70
5	Motherwell	46	74
6	Aberdeen	44	78
7	Hearts	43	80
8	Dundee Utd	41	83
9	Inverness CT	41	83
10	Dundee	37	92
11	Dunfermline	34	101
12	Livingston	34	101

CLUB DISCIPLINARY RECORDS

Pereira; five cards for Hearts

1 Hearts

League Yellow	74
League Red	4
League Total	78
Cards Average in League Average number of minutes between a card being shown of either colour	44

	CLUB	LEAGUE		TOTAL	AVE
1	Hearts	74 Y	4 R	78	44
2	Livingston	71	1	72	48
3	Aberdeen	60	4	64	53
4	Hibernian	57	4	61	56
5	Inverness CT	54	5	59	58
6	Dundee Utd	54	4	58	59
7	Motherwell	56	2	58	59
8	Rangers	53	3	56	61
9	Kilmarnock	53	2	55	62
10	Dunfermline	44	1	45	76
11	Celtic	42	2	44	78
12	Dundee	38	4	42	81

CLUB DEFENCES

	CLUB	LGE	CS	CDR
1	Rangers	22	19	155
2	Celtic	35	18	98
3	Aberdeen	39	15	88
4	Hearts	41	13	83
5	Inverness CT	47	9	73
6	Motherwell	49	10	70
7	Kilmarnock	55	10	62
8	Hibernian	57	6	60
9	Dundee Utd	59	5	58
10	Dunfermline	60	6	57
11	Livingston	61	10	56
12	Dundee	71	4	48

Vignal; Rangers' fullback

1 Rangers

Goals conceded in the League	22
Clean Sheets (CS) Number of league games where no goals were conceded	19
Club Defensive Rate (CDR) Average number of minutes between League goals conceded by club	155

STADIUM CAPACITY AND HOME CROWDS

	TEAM	CAPACITY	AVE	HIGH	LOW
1	Rangers	50444	96.50	50143	46278
2	Celtic	60832	95.25	59998	52500
3	Hibernian	17500	71.65	17450	9344
4	Hearts	18300	67.06	17676	9187
5	Inverness CT	6280	64.47	9530	1117
6	Aberdeen	22199	61.16	19028	9214
7	Dundee	11760	58.50	11263	4387
8	Dundee Utd	14223	57.73	12703	5097
9	Livingston	10024	51.46	8968	2536
10	Motherwell	13742	50.65	12944	4267
11	Dunfermline	12510	49.50	8678	3565
12	Kilmarnock	18128	32.71	11156	3770

Key: Average. The percentage of each stadium filled in League games over the season (AVE), the stadium capacity and the highest and lowest crowds recorded.

AWAY ATTENDANCE

	TEAM	AVE	HIGH	LOW
1	Celtic	84.50	50043	7000
2	Rangers	81.60	59041	6543
3	Aberdeen	73.15	59998	4569
4	Hibernian	68.04	58384	2011
5	Hearts	64.85	59562	2011
6	Dundee	59.34	56936	1254
7	Dundee Utd	58.69	56318	1125
8	Motherwell	54.61	58438	1117
9	Dunfermline	54.21	58908	1972
10	Inverness CT	53.13	57654	3310
11	Livingston	52.09	57593	1279
12	Kilmarnock	51.55	57348	1346

Key: Average. How close each club has come to filling grounds in its away league matches (AVE) and the highest and lowest crowds recorded.

CHART-TOPPING MIDFIELDERS

1 Ricksen - Rangers

Goals scored in the League	4
Defensive Rating Av number of mins between League goals conceded while on the pitch	155
Contribution to Attacking Power Average number of minutes between League team goals while on pitch	44
S… D… A…	

	PLAYER	CLUB
1	Ricksen	Rangers
2	Thompson	Celtic
3	Lennon	Celtic
4	Petrov	Celtic
5	McGeady	Celtic
6	Glass	Hibernian
7	Severin	Aberdeen
8	Heikkinen	Aberdeen
9	Leven	Kilmarnock
10	Murray, I	Hibernian
11	Whittaker	Hibernian
12	Hartley	Hearts
13	McBride	Motherwell
14	Hart	Inverness CT
15	Beuzelin	Hibernian

CHART-TOPPING GOALSCORERS

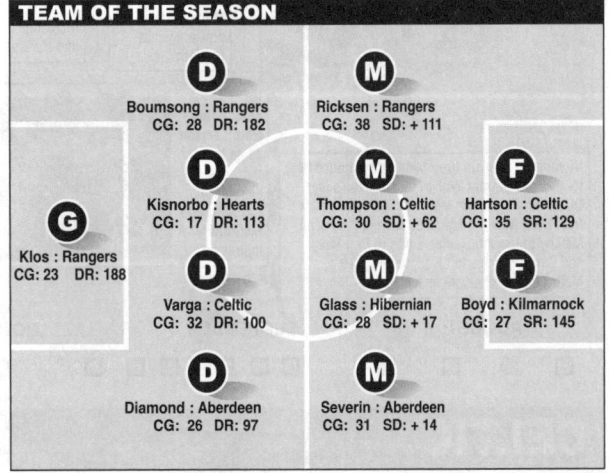

1 Hartson - Celtic

Goals scored in the League (GL)	25
Goals scored in all competitions (GA)	30
Contribution to Attacking Power (AP) Average number of minutes between League team goals while on pitch	40
Player Strike Rate **Average number of minutes between League goals scored by player**	**129**
Club Strike Rate (CSR) Average minutes between League goals scored by club	40

	GOALS: LGE	ALL	AP	CSR	S RATE
…c	25	30	40	40	129
…arnock	17	19	70	70	145
…herwell	15	15	68	74	145
…gers	18	21	46	44	151
…rnian	20	23	57	53	152
…gers	18	23	39	44	155
…ic	12	16	41	40	178
…ernian	14	18	53	53	193
…dee	12	15	97	92	234
…erdeen	12	15	74	78	241
…ndee	8	8	75	92	247
…arts	11	15	78	80	258
…erness CT	10	10	79	83	269
…ndee Utd	10	15	73	83	288
…ltic	11	12	39	40	292

CHART-TOPPING DEFE…

conceded by the …

	PLAYER	CLUB	CON: LGE	CS	CDR	DEF RATE
1	Boumsong	Rangers	9	11	155	182
2	Vignal	Rangers	15	12	155	167
3	Andrews	Rangers	17	15	155	158
4	Malcolm	Rangers	11	8	155	149
5	Kisnorbo	Hearts	13	9	83	115
6	Varga	Celtic	30	15	98	100
7	Diamond	Aberdeen	26	12	88	97
8	McNamara	Celtic	31	16	98	97
9	Balde	Celtic	32	16	98	95
10	Anderson	Aberdeen	29	12	88	94
11	Pressley	Hearts	30	13	83	94
12	Neilson	Hearts	34	13	83	90
13	Webster	Hearts	35	12	83	88
14	Dods	Inverness CT	29	8	73	87
15	McGuire	Aberdeen	24	7	88	86

…G GOALKEEPERS

1 Klos - Rangers

Counting Games League games when he played at least 70 minutes	23
Goals Conceded in the League The number of League goals conceded while he was on the pitch	11
Goals Conceded in all competitions The number of goals conceded while he was on the pitch in all competitions	18
Clean Sheets In games when he played at least 70 mins	13
Defensive Rating **Average number of minutes between League goals conceded while on pitch**	**188**

	PLAYER	CLUB	CG	CONC LGE	CS	DEF RATE
1	Klos	Rangers	23	11	13	188
2	Preece	Aberdeen	17	10	7	141
3	Gordon	Hearts	38	41	13	83
4	Marshall	Celtic	18	21	7	77
5	Brown	Inverness CT	37	47	9	72
6	Esson	Aberdeen	23	29	8	69
7	Marshall	Motherwell	33	42	9	69
8	Bullock	Dundee Utd	25	37	4	62
9	S. Brown	Hibernian	37	56	6	60
10	Combe	Kilmarnock	32	50	8	58
11	McKenzie	Livingston	33	51	9	58
12	Stillie	Dunfermline	38	60	6	57
13	Soutar	Dundee	37	67	4	49

PLAYER DISCIPLINARY RECORD

2 Kachloul - Livingston

Cards Average mins between cards	**195**
League Yellow	3
League Red	0
TOTAL	3

	PLAYER		LY	LR	TOT	AVE
1	Bahoken	Livingston	8	0	8	178
2	Kachloul	Livingston	3	0	3	195
3	Whelan	Aberdeen	7	0	7	196
4	Morrison	Aberdeen	3	0	3	204
5	Pereira	Hearts	5	0	5	204
6	Mikoliunas	Hearts	3	1	4	207
7	Craig	Aberdeen	2	1	3	222
8	Black	Inverness CT	3	0	3	225
9	Simmons	Hearts	2	0	2	226
10	Winter	Aberdeen	3	0	3	230
11	Ritchie	Dundee Utd	8	1	9	230
12	Murray, I	Hibernian	10	1	11	230
13	Maybury	Hearts	5	1	6	235
14	Greer	Kilmarnock	7	0	7	235
15	McInnes	Dundee Utd	8	0	8	242
16	McNamee	Livingston	9	1	10	258
17	Kyrgiakos	Rangers	5	0	5	266
18	Robson	Dundee Utd	10	1	11	277
19	Lovell	Dundee	9	1	10	281
20	Locke	Kilmarnock	7	0	7	281
21	Pressley	Hearts	9	1	10	283
22	Lilley	Kilmarnock	9	1	10	287
23	Hamilton	Livingston	5	0	5	292
24	Cesnauskis	Hearts	2	0	2	293

TEAM OF THE SEASON

G — Klos : Rangers — CG: 23 DR: 188

D — Boumsong : Rangers — CG: 28 DR: 182

D — Kisnorbo : Hearts — CG: 17 DR: 113

D — Varga : Celtic — CG: 32 DR: 100

D — Diamond : Aberdeen — CG: 26 DR: 97

M — Ricksen : Rangers — CG: 38 SD: + 111

M — Thompson : Celtic — CG: 30 SD: + 62

M — Glass : Hibernian — CG: 28 SD: + 17

M — Severin : Aberdeen — CG: 31 SD: + 14

F — Hartson : Celtic — CG: 35 SR: 129

F — Boyd : Kilmarnock — CG: 27 SR: 145

RANGERS

AUGUST | SEPTEMBER | OCTOBER | NOVEMBER | DECEMBER

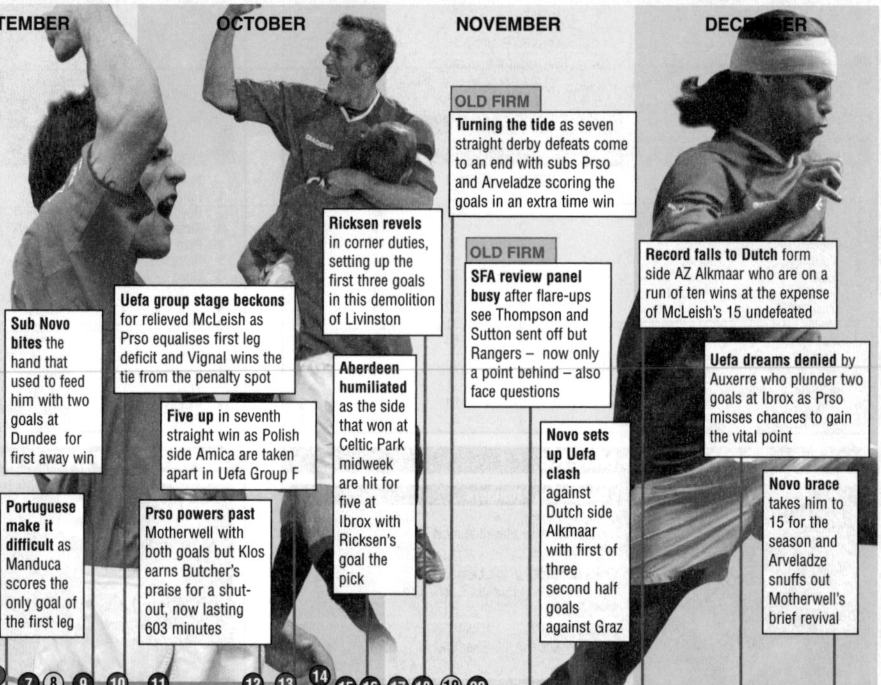

INS AND OUTS

IN Jean-Alain Boumsong from Auxerre, Alex Rae from Wolverhampton Wanderers, Dado Prso from Monaco, Marvin Andrews from Livingston all for free; Dragan Mladenovic from Crvena Zvezda for £1.1m; Nacho Novo from Dundee for £450K; Gregory Vignal from Liverpool on a season's loan **OUT** Mikel Arteta to Real Sociedad for £2.6m; Steven MacLean to Sheffield Wednesday for £100K; Christian Nerlinger to Kaiserslautern, Egil Ostenstad to Viking Stavanger (Norway), Emerson to Roma all for free; Ronald and Frank de Boer, Michael Mols, Henning Berg, Nuno Capucho all released

Novo nets away goal to give hope but Rae's boot connects with a Russian head to cause Uefa concern

From Russia its Love – as CSKA Moscow dump McLeish into the Uefa Cup

OLD FIRM

Six newcomers savour the Old Firm atmosphere but the result is the same as the last half dozen – a Celtic win and the gap is five points

"A couple of times a game of football threatened to break out." Hearts' manager Levein tries to calm the angry clashes at Tyneside

Sub Novo bites the hand that used to feed him with two goals at Dundee for first away win

Portuguese make it difficult as Manduca scores the only goal of the first leg

Uefa group stage beckons for relieved McLeish as Prso equalises first leg deficit and Vignal wins the tie from the penalty spot

Five up in seventh straight win as Polish side Amica are taken apart in Uefa Group F

Prso powers past Motherwell with both goals but Klos earns Butcher's praise for a shut-out, now lasting 603 minutes

Ricksen revels in corner duties, setting up the first three goals in this demolition of Livinston

Aberdeen humiliated as the side that won at Celtic Park midweek are hit for five at Ibrox with Ricksen's goal the pick

OLD FIRM

Turning the tide as seven straight derby defeats come to an end with subs Prso and Arveladze scoring the goals in an extra time win

OLD FIRM

SFA review panel busy after flare-ups see Thompson and Sutton sent off but Rangers – now only a point behind – also face questions

Novo sets up Uefa clash against Dutch side Alkmaar with first of three second half goals against Graz

Record falls to Dutch form side AZ Alkmaar who are on a run of ten wins at the expense of McLeish's 15 undefeated

Uefa dreams denied by Auxerre who plunder two goals at Ibrox as Prso misses chances to gain the vital point

Novo brace takes him to 15 for the season and Arveladze snuffs out Motherwell's brief revival

Sutton's 50th goal in the Scottish Premier League marks the start of the post-Larsson era with a win

OLD FIRM

Juninho debuts in seventh successive Old Firm victory as Thompson's volley breaks the deadlock

Hartson's sixth of the season denies Hibs after the Edinburgh side twice take the lead

Camara makes it five in five starts to earn O'Neill's praise against Dunfermline

Varga strikes with a late headed equaliser in Milan but sub Inzaghi and a deflected freekick steal the points in the final two minutes

Out of the running as Ukrainians take advantage of injuries to McNamara and Sutton to dash Champions League hopes

Four goal lead only just enough as injuries mount up for O'Neill with Camara, McManus and Varga all off and Hartson in stitches

No celebration from Larsson as he hits third goal to secure win for Barca and McNamara injures ankle

Thompson winner gets first points on the board as Shakhtar self-destruct finishing with nine men

Aberdeen good value handing out first league defeat with a last-minute winner after Hartson scores twice in comeback from early setbacks

First point to leave the Nou Camp this season as Hartson's goal helps O'Neill succeed where Madrid failed

Out of Europe as AC battle for a draw at Celtic Park to top the group and Barcelona capitulate against Shaktar

Sutton's header enough to down Dundee United but injuries to Thompson and Valgaeren are the price

Teen McGeady trumps Hearts with an early goal and Petrov scores his 12th away from home this season

INS AND OUTS

IN Juninho Paulista from Middlesbrough for free; Henri Camara from Wolves on a season's loan **OUT** Henrik Larrsson leaves for Barcelona on a free; Liam Miller to Manchester United, Johann Mjallby to Levante, Jamie Smith to Den Haag and Gary Arbuckle to Clyde for free; Kevin McBride to Motherwell on loan

AUGUST | SEPTEMBER | OCTOBER | NOVEMBER | DECEMBER

CELTIC

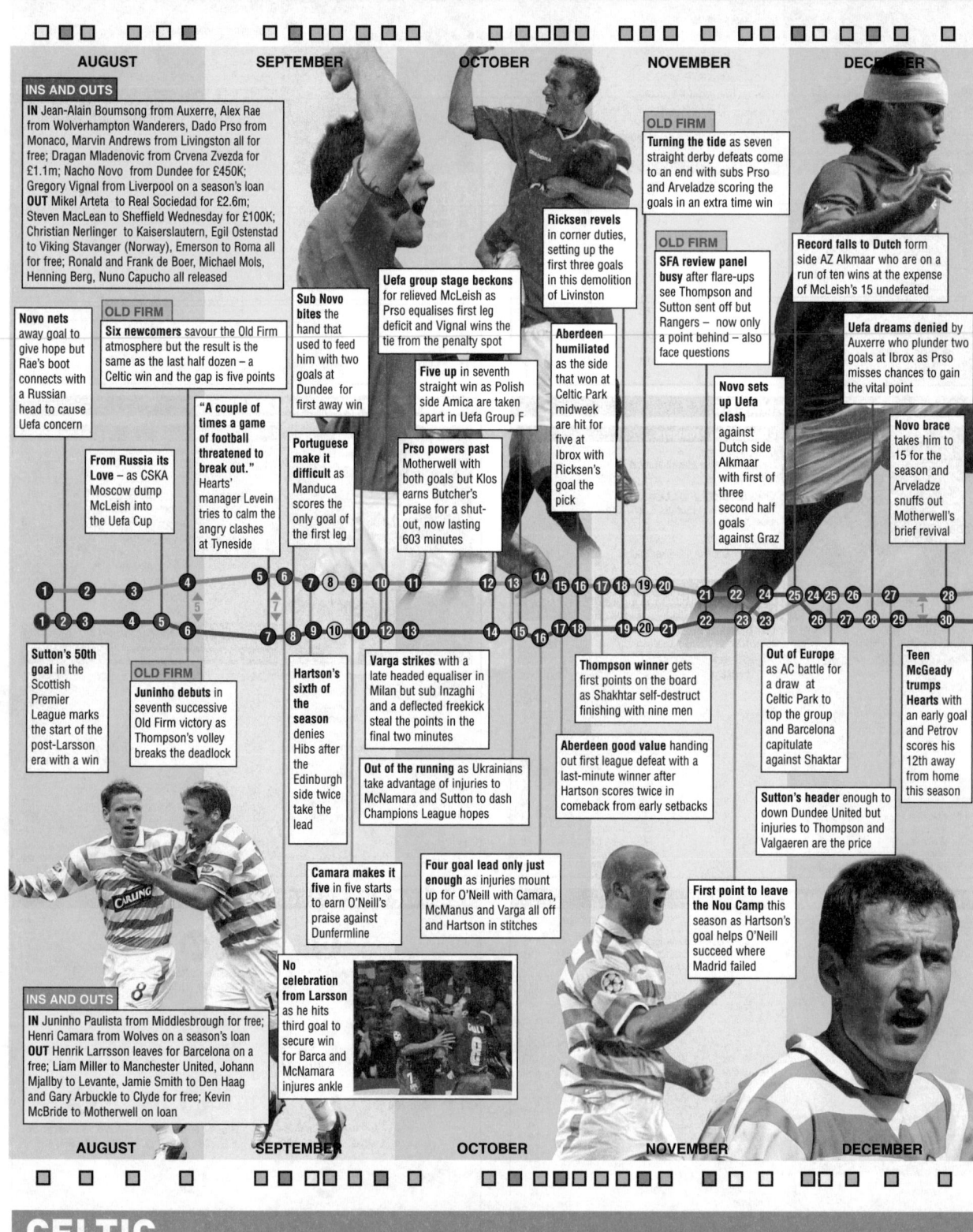

Wild Ibrox tunes in to title turnaround

Final Position: 1st

KEY: League, Champions Lge, UEFA Cup, Scottish FA Cup, Scottish League Cup, Other, Won, Drawn, Lost

JANUARY FEBRUARY MARCH APRIL MAY

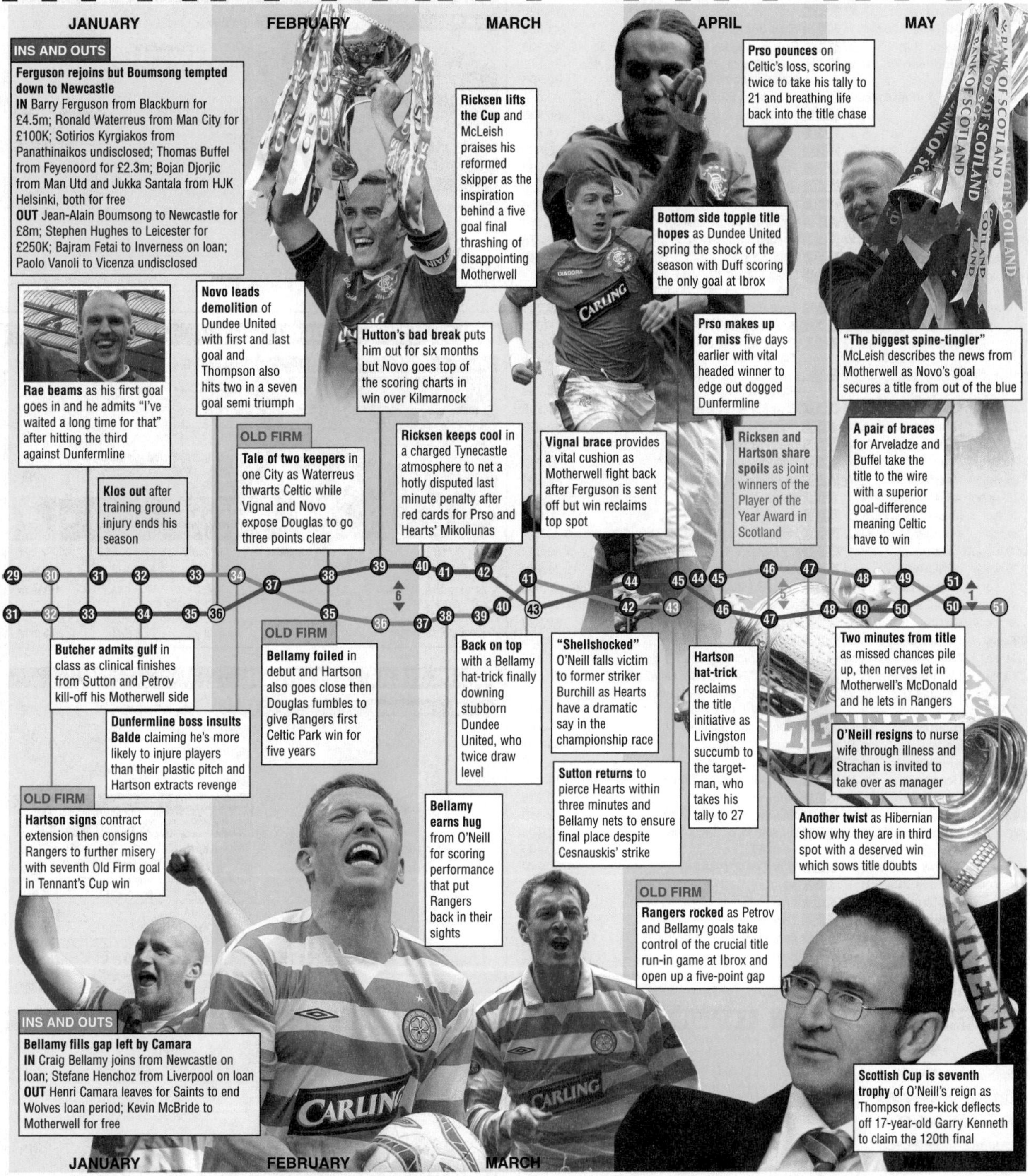

INS AND OUTS

Ferguson rejoins but Boumsong tempted down to Newcastle
IN Barry Ferguson from Blackburn for £4.5m; Ronald Waterreus from Man City for £100K; Sotirios Kyrgiakos from Panathinaikos undisclosed; Thomas Buffel from Feyenoord for £2.3m; Bojan Djorjic from Man Utd and Jukka Santala from HJK Helsinki, both for free
OUT Jean-Alain Boumsong to Newcastle for £8m; Stephen Hughes to Leicester for £250K; Bajram Fetai to Inverness on loan; Paolo Vanoli to Vicenza undisclosed

Rae beams as his first goal goes in and he admits "I've waited a long time for that" after hitting the third against Dunfermline

Klos out after training ground injury ends his season

Novo leads demolition of Dundee United with first and last goal and Thompson also hits two in a seven goal semi triumph

OLD FIRM

Tale of two keepers in one City as Waterreus thwarts Celtic while Vignal and Novo expose Douglas to go three points clear

Hutton's bad break puts him out for six months but Novo goes top of the scoring charts in win over Kilmarnock

Ricksen lifts the Cup and McLeish praises his reformed skipper as the inspiration behind a five goal final thrashing of disappointing Motherwell

Ricksen keeps cool in a charged Tynecastle atmosphere to net a hotly disputed last minute penalty after red cards for Prso and Hearts' Mikoliunas

Vignal brace provides a vital cushion as Motherwell fight back after Ferguson is sent off but win reclaims top spot

Bottom side topple title hopes as Dundee United spring the shock of the season with Duff scoring the only goal at Ibrox

Prso pounces on Celtic's loss, scoring twice to take his tally to 21 and breathing life back into the title chase

Prso makes up for miss five days earlier with vital headed winner to edge out dogged Dunfermline

Ricksen and Hartson share spoils as joint winners of the Player of the Year Award in Scotland

"The biggest spine-tingler" McLeish describes the news from Motherwell as Novo's goal secures a title from out of the blue

A pair of braces for Arveladze and Buffel take the title to the wire with a superior goal-difference meaning Celtic have to win

Butcher admits gulf in class as clinical finishes from Sutton and Petrov kill-off his Motherwell side

Dunfermline boss insults Balde claiming he's more likely to injure players than their plastic pitch and Hartson extracts revenge

OLD FIRM

Hartson signs contract extension then consigns Rangers to further misery with seventh Old Firm goal in Tennant's Cup win

OLD FIRM

Bellamy foiled in debut and Hartson also goes close then Douglas fumbles to give Rangers first Celtic Park win for five years

Back on top with a Bellamy hat-trick finally downing stubborn Dundee United, who twice draw level

Bellamy earns hug from O'Neill for scoring performance that put Rangers back in their sights

"Shellshocked" O'Neill falls victim to former striker Burchill as Hearts have a dramatic say in the championship race

Sutton returns to pierce Hearts within three minutes and Bellamy nets to ensure final place despite Cesnauskis' strike

Hartson hat-trick reclaims the title initiative as Livingston succumb to the target-man, who takes his tally to 27

OLD FIRM

Rangers rocked as Petrov and Bellamy goals take control of the crucial title run-in game at Ibrox and open up a five-point gap

Two minutes from title as missed chances pile up, then nerves let in Motherwell's McDonald and he lets in Rangers

O'Neill resigns to nurse wife through illness and Strachan is invited to take over as manager

Another twist as Hibernian show why they are in third spot with a deserved win which sows title doubts

INS AND OUTS

Bellamy fills gap left by Camara
IN Craig Bellamy joins from Newcastle on loan; Stefane Henchoz from Liverpool on loan
OUT Henri Camara leaves for Saints to end Wolves loan period; Kevin McBride to Motherwell for free

Scottish Cup is seventh trophy of O'Neill's reign as Thompson free-kick deflects off 17-year-old Garry Kenneth to claim the 120th final

JANUARY FEBRUARY MARCH

O'Neill bows out with Cup celebration

Final Position: 2nd

SCOTTISH PREMIER LEAGUE CHAMPIONS

RANGERS

Final Position: **1st**

NICKNAME: THE GERS

KEY: Won Drawn Lost

							Attendance
1	spl	Aberdeen	A	D	0-0		19,028
2	ecql1	CSKA Moscow	A	L	1-2	Novo 36	11,000
3	spl	Livingston	H	W	4-0	Prso 6; Hughes 32,78; Arveladze 88	48,102
4	spl	Hibernian	H	W	4-1	Arveladze 11; Prso 15; Boumsong 58; Lovenkrands 84	48,702
5	ecql2	CSKA Moscow	H	D	1-1	Thompson 88	49,010
6	spl	Celtic	A	L	0-1		58,935
7	spl	Hearts	A	D	0-0		14,601
8	uc1rl1	Maritimo	A	L	0-1		5,000
9	spl	Inverness CT	H	W	1-0	Prso 17	47,063
10	sccc3	Aberdeen	A	W	2-0	Ricksen 45; Thompson 89	14,876
11	spl	Dundee	A	W	2-0	Novo 78,80	9,404
12	uc1rl2	Maritimo	H	W	4-2*	Prso 71 (*on penalties)	47,360
13	spl	Kilmarnock	H	W	2-0	Andrews 10; Novo 82	46,278
14	spl	Motherwell	A	W	2-0	Prso 7,83	10,946
15	ucgpf	Amica Wronki	A	W	5-0	Lovenkrands 17; Novo 57; Ricksen 69; Arveladze 73 pen; Thompson 89	3,100
16	spl	Dundee Utd	H	D	1-1	Novo 69	46,796
17	spl	Dunfermline	A	W	2-1	Boumsong 47; Novo 58 pen	8,678
18	spl	Aberdeen	H	W	5-0	Thompson 39; Lovenkrands 68; Novo 75,90 pen; Ricksen 88	48,918
19	spl	Livingston	A	W	4-1	Lovenkrands 37; Novo 55; Thompson 67; Namouchi 84	8,780
20	sccqf	Celtic	H	W	2-1	Prso 85; Arveladze 100	47,298
21	spl	Hibernian	A	W	1-0	Prso 65 pen	13,829
22	spl	Celtic	H	W	2-0	Novo 15 pen; Prso 36	50,043
23	ucgpf	Grazer AK	H	W	3-0	Novo 58; Arveladze 86; Namouchi 90	46,453
24	spl	Hearts	H	W	3-2	McAllister 45 og; Novo 56,81	48,494
25	ucgpf	AZ Alkmaar	A	L	0-1		8,000
26	spl	Inverness CT	A	D	1-1	Prso 51	6,543
27	spl	Dundee	H	W	3-0	Novo 3 pen; Prso 4; Malcolm 50	48,114
28	ucgpf	Auxerre	H	L	0-2		48,847
29	spl	Kilmarnock	A	W	1-0	Arveladze 16	11,156
30	spl	Motherwell	H	W	4-1	Novo 3,15; Arveladze 53; Thompson 86	49,909
31	spl	Dundee Utd	A	D	1-1	Namouchi 90	10,461
32	scr3	Celtic	A	L	1-2	Ricksen 47	58,622
33	spl	Dunfermline	H	W	3-0	Thompson 6; Andrews 38; Rae, A 64	48,055
34	spl	Aberdeen	A	W	2-1	Prso 8; McNaughton 16 og	17,495
35	spl	Livingston	H	W	3-0	Prso 14; Ricksen 63; Novo 68	48,579
36	slc5	Dundee Utd	H	W	7-1	Novo 7,85; Prso 18; Buffel 67; Ricksen 77; Thompson 80,88	25,622
37	spl	Hibernian	H	W	3-0	Prso 35,50; Buffel 61	50,143
38	spl	Celtic	A	W	2-0	Vignal 71; Novo 82	59,041
39	spl	Kilmarnock	H	W	2-1	Prso 29; Novo 41	48,575
40	spl	Hearts	A	W	2-1	Novo 49; Ricksen 90 pen	13,842
41	spl	Inverness CT	H	D	1-1	Ferguson 57	49,345
42	spl	Dundee	A	W	2-0	Andrews 82; Ricksen 84	9,876
43	scccf	Motherwell	H	W	5-1	Ross 5; Kyrgiakos 9,86; Ricksen 33; Novo 48	50,182
44	spl	Motherwell	A	W	3-2	Vignal 4,32; Prso 51	10,210
45	spl	Dundee Utd	H	L	0-1		49,302
46	spl	Dunfermline	A	W	1-0	Prso 7	8,266
47	spl	Celtic	H	L	1-2	Thompson 88	49,593
48	spl	Aberdeen	A	W	3-1	Ferguson 10; Prso 43,58	17,198
49	spl	Hearts	H	W	2-1	Buffel 9; Andrews 42	49,342
50	spl	Motherwell	H	W	4-1	Buffel 12,57; Arveladze 17,54	49,495
51	spl	Hibernian	A	W	1-0	Novo 59	17,450

KEY PLAYERS - GOALSCORERS

Dado Prso

Goals in the League	18
Goals in all competitions	21
Contribution to Attacking Power Average number of minutes between League team goals while on pitch	46
Player Strike Rate Average number of minutes between League goals scored by player	151
Club Strike Rate Average number of minutes between League goals scored by club	44

	PLAYER	GOALS LGE	GOALS ALL	POWER	S RATE
1	Dado Prso	18	21	46	151 mins
2	Nacho Novo	18	24	39	155 mins
3	Thomas Buffel	4	5	38	291 mins
4	Barry Ferguson	2	2	43	576 mins
5	Marvin Andrews	4	4	39	673 mins

KEY PLAYERS - MIDFIELDERS

Thomas Buffel

Goals in the League	4
Counting Games	13
Defensive Rating Average number of mins between League goals conceded while on the pitch	233
Contribution to Attacking Power Average number of minutes between League team goals while on pitch	38
Scoring Difference Defensive Rating minus Contribution to Attacking Power	195

	PLAYER	GOALS LGE	DEF RATE	ATT POWER	SCORE DIFF
1	Thomas Buffel	4	233	38	195 mins
2	Fernando Ricksen	4	155	44	111 mins
3	Alex Rae	1	131	41	90 mins
4	Barry Ferguson	2	128	43	85 mins

KEY PLAYERS - DEFENDERS

Jean-Alain Boumsong

Goals Conceded in League	9
Counting Games	18
Clean Sheets In games when player was on pitch for at least 70 minutes	11
Defensive Rating Ave number of mins between League goals conceded while on the pitch	182
Club Defensive Rating Average number of mins between League goals conceded by the club this season	155

	PLAYER	CON LGE	CLN SHEETS	DEF RATE
1	Jean-Alain Boumsong	9	11	182 mins
2	Gregory Vignal	15	12	167 mins
3	Marvin Andrews	17	15	158 mins
4	Michael Ball	7	7	158 mins
5	Robert Malcolm	11	8	149 mins

MONTHLY POINTS TALLY

AUGUST	7	58%
SEPTEMBER	7	78%
OCTOBER	13	87%
NOVEMBER	12	100%
DECEMBER	10	83%
JANUARY	10	83%
FEBRUARY	9	100%
MARCH	7	78%
APRIL	6	50%
MAY	12	100%

LEAGUE GOALS

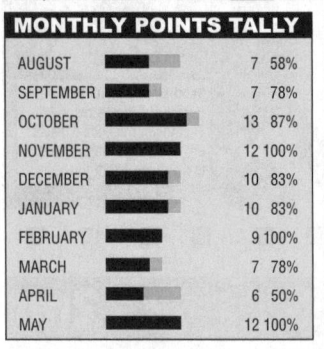

	PLAYER	MINS	GOALS			AVE
1	Prso	18	0	0	3	21
2	Novo	18	0	0	6	24
3	Arveladze	6	0	0	3	9
4	Thompson	5	0	0	5	10
5	Ricksen	4	0	0	5	9
6	Andrews	4	0	0	0	4
7	Buffel	4	0	0	1	5
8	Vignal	3	0	0	0	3
9	Lovenkrands	3	0	0	1	4
10	Boumsong	2	0	0	0	2
11	Namouchi	2	0	0	1	3
	Other	9	0	0	3	12
	TOTAL	78	0	0	28	106

KEY GOALKEEPER

Stefan Klos

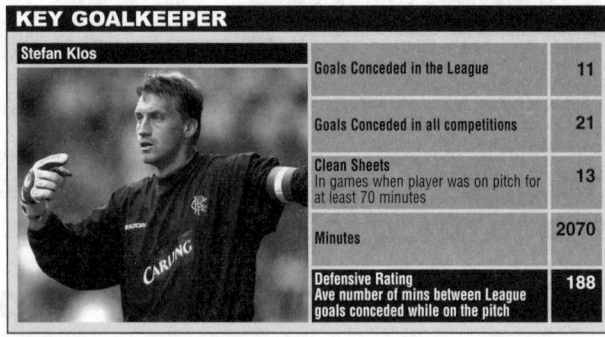

Goals Conceded in the League	11
Goals Conceded in all competitions	21
Clean Sheets In games when player was on pitch for at least 70 minutes	13
Minutes	2070
Defensive Rating Ave number of mins between League goals conceded while on the pitch	188

DISCIPLINARY RECORDS

	PLAYER	YELLOW	RED	AVE
1	Kyrgiakos	5	0	**266**
2	Thompson	3	0	**315**
3	Hutton	2	0	**343**
4	Ferguson	2	1	**383**
5	Khizanishvili	3	0	**402**
6	Vignal	6	0	**416**
7	Rae, A	4	0	**425**
8	Prso	5	1	**453**
9	Novo	5	1	**464**
10	Malcolm	3	0	**548**
11	Namouchi	2	0	**560**
12	Burke	1	0	**644**
13	Ricksen	3	0	**1134**
	Other	5	0	
	TOTAL	**49**	**3**	

TOP POINT EARNERS

	PLAYER	GAMES	AV PTS
1	Thomas Buffel	13	**2.85**
2	Marvin Andrews	30	**2.63**
3	Barry Ferguson	13	**2.62**
4	Alex Rae	16	**2.50**
5	Jean-Alain Boumsong	18	**2.50**
6	Michael Ball	12	**2.50**
7	Nacho Novo	29	**2.48**
8	Sotirios Kyrgiakos	15	**2.47**
9	Robert Malcolm	17	**2.47**
10	Fernando Ricksen	38	**2.45**
	CLUB AVERAGE:		**2.45**

LEAGUE APPEARANCES, BOOKINGS AND CAPS

	AGE (on 01/07/05)	IN NAMED 16	APPEARANCES	COUNTING GAMES	MINUTES ON PITCH	YELLOW CARDS	RED CARDS	THIS SEASON	HOME COUNTRY
Goalkeepers									
Stefan Klos	33	23	23	23	2070	0	0	-	Germany
Alan McGregor	23	16	2	2	180	0	0	-	Scotland
Graeme Smith	22	23	0	0	0	0	0	-	Scotland
Ronald Waterreus	34	13	13	13	1170	0	0	-	Holland
Defenders									
Marvin Andrews	29	33	30	30	2690	1	0	-	Trinidad & Tobago
Michael Ball	25	22	14	12	1106	0	0	-	England
Jean-Alain Boumsong	25	19	19	18	1637	1	0	8	France (4)
Alan Hutton	20	20	10	7	686	2	0	-	England
Zurab Khizanishvili	23	19	15	13	1206	3	0	-	Georgia
Sotirios Kyrgiakos	25	15	15	15	1330	5	0	-	Greece
Robert Malcolm	24	34	21	17	1644	3	0	-	Scotland
Brian McLean	20	8	0	0	0	0	0	-	Scotland
Craig Moore	29	3	3	3	270	2	0	-	Australia
Maurice Ross	24	17	14	12	1170	1	0	-	Scotland
Steven Smith	19	10	3	2	192	0	0	-	Scotland
Paolo Vanoli	32	7	5	1	241	1	0	-	Italy
Gregory Vignal	23	31	30	25	2500	6	0	-	France
Midfielders									
Thomas Buffel	24	15	15	13	1164	1	0	7	Belgium (42)
Chris Burke	21	28	12	6	644	1	0	-	Scotland
Bojan Djordjic	23	5	4	1	212	1	0	-	Sweden
Barry Ferguson	27	13	13	13	1151	2	1	-	Scotland
Stephen Hughes	22	21	11	4	601	0	0	-	Scotland
Dragan Mladenovic	29	10	7	4	476	0	0	4	Serbia & Mont (46)
Hamed Namouchi	21	25	20	8	1120	2	0	-	France
Alex Rae	35	28	24	16	1702	4	0	-	Scotland
Gavin Rae	27	1	1	1	90	0	0	-	Scotland
Fernando Ricksen	28	38	38	38	3403	3	0	-	Holland
Forwards									
Shota Arveladze	32	27	24	6	1217	0	0	-	Georgia
Robert Davidson	19	6	1	0	45	0	0	-	Scotland
Bajram Fetai	19	4	0	0	0	0	0	-	Denmark
Peter Lovenkrands	25	21	18	9	1171	1	0	1	Denmark (19)
Ross McCormack	18	18	1	0	1	0	0	-	Scotland
Nacho Novo	26	35	34	29	2785	5	1	-	Spain
Dado Prso	30	35	34	29	2721	5	1	-	France
Steven Thompson	26	32	24	6	946	3	0	3	Scotland (85)

TEAM OF THE SEASON

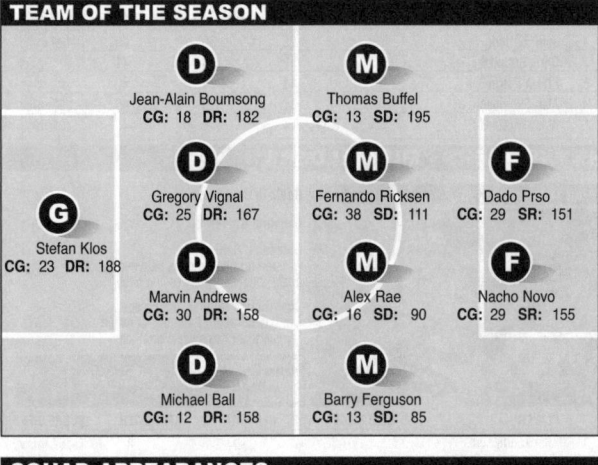

G Stefan Klos — **CG:** 23 **DR:** 188

D Jean-Alain Boumsong — **CG:** 18 **DR:** 182

D Gregory Vignal — **CG:** 25 **DR:** 167

D Marvin Andrews — **CG:** 30 **DR:** 158

D Michael Ball — **CG:** 12 **DR:** 158

M Thomas Buffel — **CG:** 13 **SD:** 195

M Fernando Ricksen — **CG:** 38 **SD:** 111

M Alex Rae — **CG:** 16 **SD:** 90

M Barry Ferguson — **CG:** 13 **SD:** 85

F Dado Prso — **CG:** 29 **SR:** 151

F Nacho Novo — **CG:** 29 **SR:** 155

SQUAD APPEARANCES

Match	1	2	3	4	5	6	7	8	9	10	11	12	13	14	15	16	17	18	19	20	21	22	23	24	25
Venue	A	A	H	H	H	A	A	A	H	A	A	H	H	A	A	H	A	H	A	H	A	H	H	H	A
Competition	L	C	L	L	C	L	L	E	L	W	L	E	L	L	E	L	L	L	L	W	L	L	E	L	E
Result	D	L	W	W	D	L	D	L	W	W	W	W	W	W	W	D	W	W	W	W	W	W	W	W	L

Match	26	27	28	29	30	31	32	33	34	35	36	37	38	39	40	41	42	43	44	45	46	47	48	49	50	51
Venue	A	H	H	A	H	A	A	H	A	H	H	H	A	H	A	H	A	H	A	H	A	H	A	H	H	A
Competition	L	L	E	L	L	L	F	L	L	L	W	L	L	L	L	L	L	W	L	L	L	L	L	L	L	L
Result	D	W	L	W	W	D	L	W	W	W	W	W	W	W	W	D	W	W	W	L	W	L	W	W	W	W

Goalkeepers
Stefan Klos
Alan McGregor
Graeme Smith
Ronald Waterreus

Defenders
Marvin Andrews
Michael Ball
Jean-Alain Boumsong
Alan Hutton
Zurab Khizanishvili
Sotirios Kyrgiakos
Robert Malcolm
Brian McLean
Craig Moore
Maurice Ross
Steven Smith
Paolo Vanoli
Gregory Vignal

Midfielders
Thomas Buffel
Chris Burke
Bojan Djordjic
Barry Ferguson
Stephen Hughes
Dragan Mladenovic
Hamed Namouchi
Alex Rae
Gavin Rae
Fernando Ricksen

Forwards
Shota Arveladze
Robert Davidson
Bajram Fetai
Peter Lovenkrands
Ross McCormack
Nacho Novo
Dado Prso
Steven Thompson

KEY: On all match · On bench · Subbed or sent off (Counting game) · Subbed or sent off (playing less than 70 minutes) · Subbed on from bench (Counting Game) · Subbed on (playing less than 70 minutes) · Subbed on and then subbed or sent off (Counting Game) · Subbed on and then subbed or sent off (playing less than 70 minutes) · Not in 16

CELTIC

Final Position: **2nd**

NICKNAME: THE BHOYS

KEY: ☐Won ☐Drawn ☐Lost

							Attendance
1	spl	Motherwell	H	W	2-0	McNamara 8; Sutton 55	57,245
2	spl	Kilmarnock	A	W	4-2	Hartson 15,70; Thompson 36,44	10,500
3	spl	Inverness CT	A	W	3-1	Hartson 25,76; Petrov 68	8,736
4	spl	Rangers	H	W	1-0	Thompson 85	58,935
5	spl	Dundee	H	W	3-0	Camara 22,86; Hartson 37	56,936
6	ecgpf	Barcelona	H	L	1-3	Sutton 59	60,000
7	spl	Hibernian	A	D	2-2	Camara 34; Hartson 45	13,500
8	sccc3	Falkirk	H	W	8-1	Sylla 2; Wallace 6,57,85; Balde 38; Lambert 45; McManus 48; McGeady 90	24,345
9	spl	Dunfermline	H	W	3-0	Varga 20; Camara 38,54	58,213
10	ecgpf	AC Milan	A	L	1-3	Varga 74	68,000
11	spl	Dundee Utd	A	W	3-0	Sutton 9,37 pen; Petrov 17	10,329
12	spl	Hearts	H	W	3-0	Camara 41; Juninho 57; Hartson 82	58,869
13	ecgpf	S Donetsk	A	L	0-3		30,000
14	spl	Livingston	A	W	4-2	Petrov 2; Camara 14; Hartson 19; Sutton 32	7,695
15	spl	Aberdeen	H	L	2-3	Hartson 45,69	57,151
16	spl	Motherwell	A	W	3-2	McGeady 41; Thompson 65 pen; Beattie 77	10,592
17	ecgpf	S Donetsk	H	W	1-0	Thompson 25	58,347
18	spl	Kilmarnock	H	W	2-1	McGeady 44; Thompson 64 pen	57,348
19	sccqf	Rangers	A	L	1-2	Hartson 66	47,298
20	spl	Inverness CT	H	W	3-0	Sutton 3; Hartson 53,77	57,654
21	spl	Rangers	A	L	0-2		50,043
22	ecgpf	Barcelona	A	D	1-1	Hartson 45	74,000
23	spl	Dundee	A	D	2-2	Camara 53; Hartson 62	9,539
24	spl	Hibernian	H	W	2-1	Hartson 18,83	58,384
25	ecgpf	AC Milan	H	D	0-0		59,228
26	spl	Dunfermline	A	W	2-0	Sutton 16; Petrov 31	7,650
27	spl	Dundee Utd	H	W	1-0	Sutton 18	56,318
28	spl	Hearts	A	W	2-0	McGeady 9; Petrov 68	16,163
29	spl	Livingston	H	W	2-1	Hartson 15; Sutton 57 pen	57,593
30	scr3	Rangers	H	W	2-1	Sutton 37; Hartson 77	58,622
31	spl	Aberdeen	A	W	1-0	Sutton 24	17,051
32	spl	Motherwell	H	W	2-0	Petrov 29; Sutton 57	58,438
33	spl	Kilmarnock	A	W	1-0	Sutton 38 pen	9,723
34	scr4	Dunfermline	A	W	3-0	Hartson 9,43; Sutton 10	8,014
35	spl	Rangers	H	L	0-2		59,041
36	scpqf	Clyde	A	W	5-0	Varga 40,68; Thompson 48 pen; Petrov 60; Bellamy 72	8,200
37	spl	Dundee	H	W	3-0	Petrov 49; Balde 60,87	52,500
38	spl	Hibernian	A	W	3-1	Petrov 5; Hartson 31; Bellamy 69	15,787
39	spl	Dunfermline	H	W	6-0	Hartson 9,69; McGeady 62; Petrov 72,75; Beattie 89	58,908
40	spl	Inverness CT	A	W	2-0	Bellamy 63; Thompson 84 pen	7,000
41	spl	Dundee Utd	A	W	3-2	Bellamy 5,34,80	10,828
42	spl	Hearts	H	L	0-2		59,562
43	scsf	Hearts	A	W	2-1	Sutton 3; Bellamy 49	38,505
44	spl	Livingston	A	W	4-0	Hartson 43,75,86 pen; Varga 90	8,750
45	spl	Aberdeen	H	W	3-2	Varga 27; Hartson 51; Bellamy 57	59,998
46	spl	Rangers	A	W	2-1	Petrov 21; Bellamy 34	49,593
47	spl	Hibernian	H	L	1-3	Beattie 59	58,322
48	spl	Aberdeen	H	W	2-0	Hartson 47,71	59,498
49	spl	Hearts	A	W	2-1	Thompson 25; Beattie 77	15,927
50	spl	Motherwell	A	L	1-2	Sutton 29	12,944
51	scfin	Dundee Utd	H	W	1-0	Thompson 11	50,635

KEY PLAYERS - GOALSCORERS

John Hartson

Goals in the League	25
Goals in all competitions	30
Contribution to Attacking Power Average number of minutes between League team goals while on pitch	40
Player Strike Rate Average number of minutes between League goals scored by player	129
Club Strike Rate Average number of minutes between League goals scored by club	40

	PLAYER	GOALS LGE	GOALS ALL	POWER	S RATE
1	John Hartson	25	30	40	129 mins
2	Chris Sutton	12	16	41	178 mins
3	Stilian Petrov	11	12	40	292 mins
4	Alan Thompson	7	9	40	395 mins
5	Aiden McGeady	4	5	40	437 mins

KEY PLAYERS - MIDFIELDERS

Alan Thompson

Goals in the League	7
Counting Games	30
Defensive Rating Average number of mins between League goals conceded while on the pitch	102
Contribution to Attacking Power Average number of minutes between League team goals while on pitch	40
Scoring Difference Defensive Rating minus Contribution to Attacking Power	62

	PLAYER	GOALS LGE	DEF RATE	ATT POWER	SCORE DIFF
1	Alan Thompson	7	102	40	62 mins
2	Neil Lennon	0	98	40	58 mins
3	Stilian Petrov	11	95	40	55 mins
4	Aiden McGeady	4	92	40	52 mins

KEY PLAYERS - DEFENDERS

Stanislav Varga

Goals Conceded in League	30
Counting Games	32
Clean Sheets In games when player was on pitch for at least 70 minutes	15
Defensive Rating Ave number of mins between League goals conceded while on the pitch	100
Club Defensive Rating Average number of mins between League goals conceded by the club this season	15

	PLAYER	CON LGE	CLN SHEETS	DEF RATE
1	Stanislav Varga	30	15	100 mins
2	Jackie McNamara	31	16	97 mins
3	Dianbobo Balde	32	16	95 mins
4	Didier Agathe	15	5	90 mins
5	Joos Valgaeren	18	6	83 mins

MONTHLY POINTS TALLY

AUGUST	12	100%
SEPTEMBER	7	78%
OCTOBER	12	80%
NOVEMBER	7	58%
DECEMBER	12	100%
JANUARY	12	100%
FEBRUARY	0	0%
MARCH	15	100%
APRIL	9	60%
MAY	6	67%

LEAGUE GOALS

	PLAYER	MINS	GOALS			AVE
1	Hartson	25	0	0	5	30
2	Sutton	12	0	0	4	16
3	Petrov	11	0	0	1	12
4	Camara	8	0	0	0	8
5	Bellamy	7	0	0	2	9
6	Thompson	7	0	0	2	9
7	McGeady	4	0	0	1	5
8	Beattie	4	0	0	0	4
9	Varga	3	0	0	3	6
10	Balde	2	0	0	1	3
11	Juninho	1	0	0	0	1
	Other	1	0	0	6	7
	TOTAL	85	0	0	25	110

KEY GOALKEEPER

Robert Douglas

Goals Conceded in the League	9
Goals Conceded in all competitions	14
Clean Sheets In games when player was on pitch for at least 70 minutes	8
Minutes played	1260
Defensive Rating Ave number of mins between League goals conceded while on the pitch	140

DISCIPLINARY RECORDS

	PLAYER	YELLOW	RED	AVE
1	Bellamy	3	0	345
2	Sutton	4	1	426
3	Thompson	5	1	460
4	Balde	6	0	508
5	Camara	2	0	527
6	Lennon	6	0	570
7	Hartson	4	0	804
8	McNamara	3	0	1006
9	Douglas	1	0	1260
10	Agathe	1	0	1346
11	Valgaeren	1	0	1487
12	Varga	2	0	1493
13	Petrov	2	0	1607
	Other	0	0	
	TOTAL	40	2	

TOP POINT EARNERS

	PLAYER	GAMES	AV PTS
1	Aiden McGeady	17	2.88
2	Chris Sutton	21	2.71
3	Robert Douglas	14	2.57
4	Alan Thompson	30	2.53
5	Didier Agathe	14	2.43
6	Neil Lennon	38	2.42
7	Jackie McNamara	34	2.41
8	David Marshall	18	2.39
9	Stanislav Varga	32	2.38
10	Stilian Petrov	35	2.37
	CLUB AVERAGE:		2.42

LEAGUE APPEARANCES, BOOKINGS AND CAPS

	AGE (on 01/07/05)	IN NAMED 16	APPEARANCES	COUNTING GAMES	MINUTES ON PITCH	YELLOW CARDS	RED CARDS	THIS SEASON	HOME COUNTRY
Goalkeepers									
Robert Douglas	33	23	14	14	1260	1	0	1	Scotland (85)
Magnus Hedman	32	15	6	6	540	0	0	7	Sweden (13)
David Marshall	20	38	18	18	1620	0	0	5	Scotland (85)
Defenders									
Didier Agathe	29	16	16	14	1346	1	0	-	France
Dianbobo Balde	29	34	34	34	3050	6	0	-	France
Scott Cuthbert	18	7	0	0	0	0	0	-	Scotland
Stephane Henchoz	30	10	6	1	168	0	0	7	Switzerland (45)
Ulrik Laursen	29	26	18	11	1164	0	0	-	Denmark
Stephen McManus	22	10	2	1	115	0	0	-	Scotland
Jackie McNamara	31	34	34	34	3020	3	0	3	Scotland (85)
Joos Valgaeren	29	26	19	15	1487	1	0	1	Belgium (42)
Stanislav Varga	32	34	34	32	2986	2	0	-	Slovakia
Midfielders									
Paulista Juninho	32	23	14	6	802	0	0	-	Brazil
Paul Lambert	35	28	4	0	79	1	0	-	Scotland
Paul Lawson	21	7	0	0	0	0	0	-	Scotland
Neil Lennon	34	38	38	38	3420	6	0	-	N Ireland
Aiden McGeady	19	38	27	17	1749	0	0	-	Rep or Ireland
Stephen Pearson	22	16	8	1	276	1	0	4	Scotland (85)
Stilian Petrov	26	37	37	35	3215	2	0	-	Bulgaria
Bobby Petta	30	1	0	0	0	0	0	-	Holland
Rocco Quinn	18	2	0	0	0	0	0	-	Scotland
Mohammed Sylla	28	16	6	1	157	0	0	-	Ivory coast
Alan Thompson	31	32	32	30	2765	5	1	-	England
Ross Wallace	20	33	16	4	531	0	0	-	Scotland
Forwards									
Craig Beattie	21	16	11	0	265	0	0	-	Scotland
Craig Bellamy	25	12	12	11	1037	3	0	8	Wales (74)
Henri Camara	28	20	18	9	1054	2	0	4	Senegal (33)
David Fernandez	29	6	1	0	10	0	0	-	Spain
John Hartson	30	38	38	35	3217	4	0	7	Wales (74)
Shaun Maloney	22	14	2	0	68	0	0	-	Scotland
Chris Sutton	32	27	27	21	2133	4	1	-	England

TEAM OF THE SEASON

D
Stanislav Varga
CG: 32 DR: 100
M
Alan Thompson
CG: 30 SD: 62
D
Jackie McNamara
CG: 34 DR: 97
M
Neil Lennon
CG: 38 SD: 58
F
John Hartson
CG: 35 SR: 129
G
Robert Douglas
CG: 14 DR: 140
D
Dianbobo Balde
CG: 34 DR: 95
M
Stilian Petrov
CG: 35 SD: 55
F
Chris Sutton
CG: 21 SR: 178
D
Didier Agathe
CG: 14 DR: 90
M
Aiden McGeady
CG: 17 SD: 52

SQUAD APPEARANCES

Match	1	2	3	4	5	6	7	8	9	10	11	12	13	14	15	16	17	18	19	20	21	22	23	24	25	26	27	28	29	30	31	32	33	34	35	36	37	38	39	40	41	42	43	44	45	46	47	48	49	50	51
Venue	H	A	A	H	H	H	A	H	H	A	A	H	A	A	H	A	H	H	A	H	A	A	A	H	H	A	H	A	H	H	A	H	A	A	H	A	H	A	H	A	A	H	A	A	H	A	H	H	A	A	H
Competition	L	L	L	L	L	C	L	W	L	C	L	L	C	L	L	L	C	L	W	L	L	C	L	L	C	L	L	L	L	F	L	L	L	F	L	F	L	L	L	L	L	L	F	L	L	L	L	L	L	L	F
Result	W	W	W	W	W	L	D	W	W	L	W	W	L	W	L	W	W	W	L	W	L	D	D	W	D	W	W	W	W	W	W	W	W	W	L	W	W	W	W	W	W	L	W	W	W	W	L	W	W	L	W

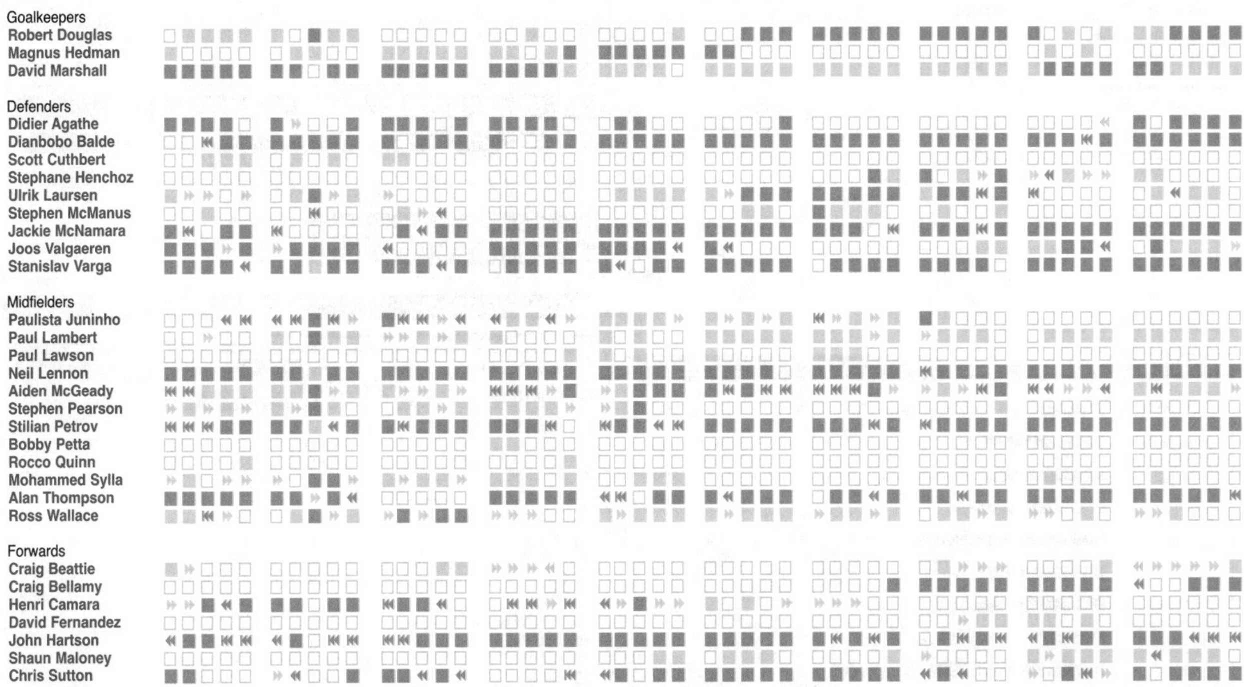
Goalkeepers
Robert Douglas
Magnus Hedman
David Marshall
Defenders
Didier Agathe
Dianbobo Balde
Scott Cuthbert
Stephane Henchoz
Ulrik Laursen
Stephen McManus
Jackie McNamara
Joos Valgaeren
Stanislav Varga
Midfielders
Paulista Juninho
Paul Lambert
Paul Lawson
Neil Lennon
Aiden McGeady
Stephen Pearson
Stilian Petrov
Bobby Petta
Rocco Quinn
Mohammed Sylla
Alan Thompson
Ross Wallace
Forwards
Craig Beattie
Craig Bellamy
Henri Camara
David Fernandez
John Hartson
Shaun Maloney
Chris Sutton

KEY: On all match | On bench | Subbed or sent off (Counting game) | Subbed or sent off (playing less than 70 minutes) | Subbed on from bench (Counting Game) | Subbed on (playing less than 70 minutes) | Subbed on and then subbed or sent off (Counting Game) | Subbed on and then subbed or sent off (playing less than 70 minutes) | Not in 16

HIBERNIAN

Final Position: **3rd**

NICKNAME: THE HIBEES

KEY: ☐ Won ☐ Drawn ☐ Lost

							Attendance
1	spl	Kilmarnock	H	L	0-1		10,933
2	spl	Motherwell	A	W	2-1	O'Connor 2,78	5,859
3	spl	Rangers	A	L	1-4	Caldwell 35	48,702
4	cisr2	Alloa	H	W	4-0	Glass 20; Orman 48; Murdock 51; Riordan 53	5,156
5	spl	Dundee	H	D	4-4	Shields 23; Riordan 41; O'Connor 46,50	9,344
6	spl	Inverness CT	A	W	2-1	Riordan 12,60	2,011
7	spl	Celtic	H	D	2-2	Balde 8 og; Murphy 35	13,500
8	cisr3	Albion	A	W	3-1	Dobbie 42; Shiels, D 43; O'Connor 71	1,454
9	spl	Aberdeen	A	W	1-0	Riordan 62	12,137
10	spl	Dunfermline	A	D	1-1	O'Connor 39	7,290
11	spl	Dundee Utd	H	W	2-0	O'Connor 11; Fletcher 55	9,927
12	spl	Hearts	A	L	1-2	Riordan 90	16,720
13	spl	Livingston	H	W	2-1	Beuzelin 9; Fletcher 23	9,534
14	spl	Kilmarnock	A	L	1-3	Shiels, D 69	5,959
15	spl	Motherwell	H	W	1-0	Murray 79	10,022
16	sccqf	Dundee Utd	A	L	1-2	Riordan 31	4,865
17	spl	Rangers	H	L	0-1		13,829
18	spl	Dundee	A	W	4-1	Beuzelin 17; Riordan 43; Orman 72; Shiels, D 88	5,274
19	spl	Inverness CT	H	W	2-1	Beuzelin 39; Riordan 47	9,728
20	spl	Celtic	A	L	1-2	Caldwell 75	58,384
21	spl	Aberdeen	H	W	2-1	Riordan 24; Glass 64	13,461
22	spl	Dunfermline	H	W	2-1	Glass 66; Riordan 90	9,859
23	spl	Dundee Utd	A	W	4-1	Riordan 13; O'Connor 22; Orman 58; Morrow 81	10,152
24	spl	Hearts	H	D	1-1	Riordan 24	17,259
25	scr3	Dundee	H	W	2-0	Whittaker 76; Morrow 87	9,706
26	spl	Livingston	A	W	2-0	O'Connor 53; Riordan 74	6,788
27	spl	Kilmarnock	H	W	3-0	Riordan 30,34,52	12,660
28	scr4	Brechin	H	W	4-0	Morrow 24; O'Connor 32,57; Caldwell 63	13,563
29	spl	Rangers	A	L	0-3		50,143
30	spl	Motherwell	A	D	1-1	Riordan 66 pen	7,453
31	spl	Dundee	H	W	4-0	O'Connor 27,77; Whittaker 47; Fletcher 76	10,938
32	scqf	St Mirren	H	W	2-0	Brown, Sc 45; O'Connor 72	15,195
33	spl	Inverness CT	A	L	0-3		4,443
34	spl	Celtic	H	L	1-3	Beuzelin 90	15,787
35	spl	Aberdeen	A	L	0-3		14,465
36	spl	Dunfermline	A	W	4-1	Riordan 66,81; Fletcher 69,75	7,204
37	spl	Dundee Utd	H	W	3-2	Shiels, D 35; O'Connor 69; Smith, G 90	11,058
38	scsf	Dundee Utd	A	L	1-2	Riordan 58 pen	27,271
39	spl	Hearts	A	W	2-1	O'Connor 68; Shiels, D 73	17,676
40	spl	Livingston	H	L	0-3		11,047
41	spl	Hearts	H	D	2-2	O'Connor 8; Riordan 63	16,620
42	spl	Celtic	A	W	3-1	O'Connor 7; Sproule 79; Brown, Sc 81	58,322
43	spl	Motherwell	A	D	2-2	Caldwell 81; Konte 90	8,903
44	spl	Aberdeen	H	L	1-2	Riordan 51	15,288
45	spl	Rangers	H	L	0-1		17,450

MONTHLY POINTS TALLY

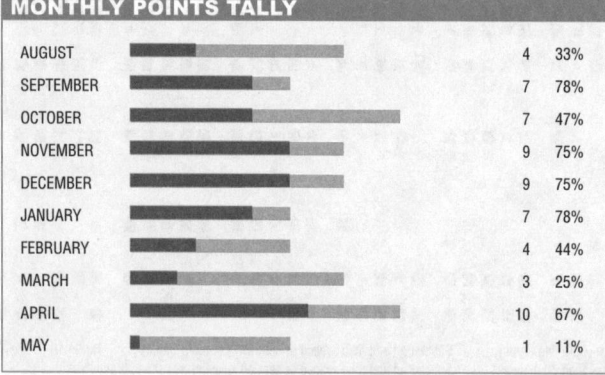

AUGUST	4	33%
SEPTEMBER	7	78%
OCTOBER	7	47%
NOVEMBER	9	75%
DECEMBER	9	75%
JANUARY	7	78%
FEBRUARY	4	44%
MARCH	3	25%
APRIL	10	67%
MAY	1	11%

KEY PLAYERS - GOALSCORERS

Derek Riordan

Goals in the League	20	**Player Strike Rate** Average number of minutes between League goals scored by player	152
Contribution to Attacking Power Average number of minutes between League team goals while on pitch	23	**Club Strike Rate** Average number of minutes between League goals scored by club	53

	PLAYER	LGE GOALS	GOALS ALL	POWER	STRIKE RATE
1	Derek Riordan	20	23	57	152 mins
2	Garry O'Connor	14	18	53	193 mins
3	Guillaume Beuzelin	4	4	59	483 mins
4	Dean Shiels	4	5	54	547 mins
5	Gary Caldwell	3	4	59	1076 mins

KEY PLAYERS - MIDFIELDERS

Stephen Glass

Goals in the League	2	**Contribution to Attacking Power** Average number of minutes between League team goals while on pitch	55
Defensive Rating Average number of mins between League goals conceded while on the pitch	72	**Scoring Difference** Defensive Rating minus Contribution to Attacking Power	17

	PLAYER	LGE GOALS	DEF RATE	POWER	SCORE DIFF
1	Stephen Glass	2	72	55	17 mins
2	Ian Murray	1	63	56	7 mins
3	Steven Whittaker	1	61	55	6 mins
4	Guillaume Beuzelin	4	60	59	1 mins

KEY PLAYERS - DEFENDERS

Gary Caldwell

Goals Conceded The number of League goals conceded while he was on the pitch	52	**Clean Sheets** In games when player was on pitch for at least 70 minutes	6
Defensive Rating Ave number of mins between League goals conceded while on the pitch	62	**Club Defensive Rating** Average number of mins between League goals conceded by the club this season	60

	PLAYER	CON LGE	CLEAN SHEETS	DEF RATE
1	Gary Caldwell	52	6	62 mins
2	David Murphy	47	2	51 mins
3	Gary Smith	33	3	51 mins

KEY GOALKEEPER

Simon Brown

Goals Conceded in the League	56	**Counting Games** League games when player was on pitch for at least 70 minutes	37
Defensive Rating Ave number of mins between League goals conceded while on the pitch	60	**Clean Sheets** In games when player was on pitch for at least 70 minutes	6

LEAGUE GOALS

Derek Riordan

Minutes on the pitch	3038	League average (mins between goals)	152
Goals in the League	20		

	PLAYER	MINS	GOALS	AVE
1	Riordan	3038	20	152
2	O'Connor	2706	14	193
3	Fletcher	942	5	188
4	Shiels, D	2187	4	547
5	Beuzelin	1933	4	483
6	Caldwell	3228	3	1076
7	Orman	756	2	378
8	Glass	2823	2	1412
9	Whittaker	3330	1	3330
10	Murphy	2374	1	2374
11	Morrow	720	1	720
12	Shields, J	441	1	441
	Other		6	
	TOTAL		64	

DISCIPLINARY RECORDS

	PLAYER	YELLOW	RED	AVE
1	Murray, I	10	1	230
2	Brown, Sc	5	0	310
3	Murray, A	2	0	429
4	Rocastle	2	0	507
5	Shiels, D	4	0	546
6	Whittaker	6	0	555
7	Glass	4	0	705
8	Morrow	1	0	720
9	Orman	1	0	756
10	Riordan	4	0	759
11	Caldwell	3	1	807
12	Smith, G	2	0	845
13	O'Connor	3	0	902
	Other	4	0	
	TOTAL	51	2	

TOP POINT EARNERS

	PLAYER	GAMES	AV PTS
1	Stephen Glass	28	1.71
2	Ian Murray	27	1.70
3	Dean Shiels	21	1.67
4	Derek Riordan	31	1.65
5	Garry O'Connor	26	1.65
6	Gary Caldwell	34	1.59
7	Guillaume Beuzelin	19	1.58
8	Simon Brown	37	1.57
9	Steven Whittaker	37	1.57
10	David Murphy	26	1.46
	CLUB AVERAGE:		1.61

TEAM OF THE SEASON

G
Simon Brown
CG: 37 DR: 60

D
Gary Caldwell
CG: 34 DR: 62

D
David Murphy
CG: 26 DR: 51

D
Gary Smith
CG: 18 DR: 51

D
CG: 0 DR: 0

M
Stephen Glass
CG: 28 SD: 17

M
Ian Murray
CG: 27 SD: 7

M
Steven Whittaker
CG: 37 SD: 6

M
Guillaume Beuzelin
CG: 19 SD: 1

F
Derek Riordan
CG: 31 SR: 152

F
Garry O'Connor
CG: 26 SR: 193

LEAGUE APPEARANCES AND BOOKINGS

	AGE (on 01/07/04)	IN NAMED 16	APPEARANCES	COUNTING GAMES	MINUTES ON PITCH	YELLOW CARDS	RED CARDS	THIS SEASON	HOME COUNTRY
Goalkeepers									
Alistair Brown	19	38	1	0	35	0	0	-	Scotland
Simon Brown	28	38	38	37	3385	1	0	-	England
Andy Reid	20	0	0	0	0	0	0	-	Scotland
Defenders									
Jonathan Baillie	19	3	1	0	45	0	0	-	Scotland
Gary Caldwell	24	37	37	34	3228	3	1	-	Scotland
Chris Hogg	20	7	0	0	0	0	0	-	England
Colin Murdock	30	11	5	5	425	1	1	-	N Ireland
David Murphy	21	32	27	26	2374	1	0	-	England
Gary Smith	34	27	20	18	1691	2	0	-	Scotland
Mark Venus	38	7	0	0	0	0	0	-	England
Midfielders									
Guillaume Beuzelin	26	27	26	19	1933	2	0	-	France
Grant Brebner	27	2	2	2	166	2	1	-	Scotland
Steven Fletcher	18	27	20	5	942	0	0	-	Scotland
Stephen Glass	29	36	36	28	2823	4	0	-	Scotland
Jamie McCluskey	17	26	10	0	178	0	0	-	Scotland
Kevin McDonald	20	16	2	0	47	0	0	-	Scotland
Antonio Murray	20	13	12	8	859	2	0	-	England
Ian Murray	24	29	29	27	2538	10	1	3	Scotland (85)
Kevin Nicol	23	4	1	1	72	0	0	-	Scotland
Steven Notman	18	1	0	0	0	0	0	-	Scotland
Alen Orman	27	23	12	6	756	1	0	-	Austria
Craig Rocastle	23	14	13	10	1015	2	0	-	England
Jay Shields	20	23	11	4	441	1	0	-	Scotland
Ivan Sproule	24	12	7	0	189	2	0	-	Scotland
Kevin Thomson	20	3	3	0	116	0	0	-	Scotland
Steven Whittaker	21	37	37	37	3330	6	0	-	Scotland
Forwards									
Scott Brown	20	20	20	16	1552	5	0	-	Scotland
Stephen Dobbie	22	16	7	0	187	0	0	-	Scotland
Amadou Konte	24	15	13	3	491	0	0	-	England
Tom McManus	24	4	2	0	112	0	0	-	Scotland
Sam Morrow	20	27	22	2	720	1	0	-	N Ireland
Garry O'Connor	22	36	36	26	2706	3	0	1	Scotland (85)
Derek Riordan	22	38	37	31	3038	4	0	-	Scotland
Dean Shiels	20	34	31	21	2187	4	0	-	Scotland

SQUAD APPEARANCES

Match	1	2	3	4	5	6	7	8	9	10	11	12	13	14	15	16	17	18	19	20	21	22	23	24	25	26	27	28	29	30	31	32	33	34	35	36	37	38	39	40	41	42	43	44	45
Venue	H	A	A	H	H	A	H	A	A	A	H	A	H	A	H	A	H	A	H	A	H	H	A	H	H	A	H	H	A	A	H	H	A	H	A	A	H	A	A	H	H	A	A	H	H
Competition	L	L	L	W	L	L	L	W	L	L	L	L	L	L	L	W	L	L	L	L	L	L	L	L	F	L	L	F	L	L	L	F	L	L	L	L	L	F	L	L	L	L	L	L	L
Result	L	W	L	W	D	W	D	W	W	D	W	L	W	L	W	L	L	W	W	L	W	W	W	D	W	W	W	W	L	D	W	W	L	L	L	W	W	L	W	L	D	W	D	L	L

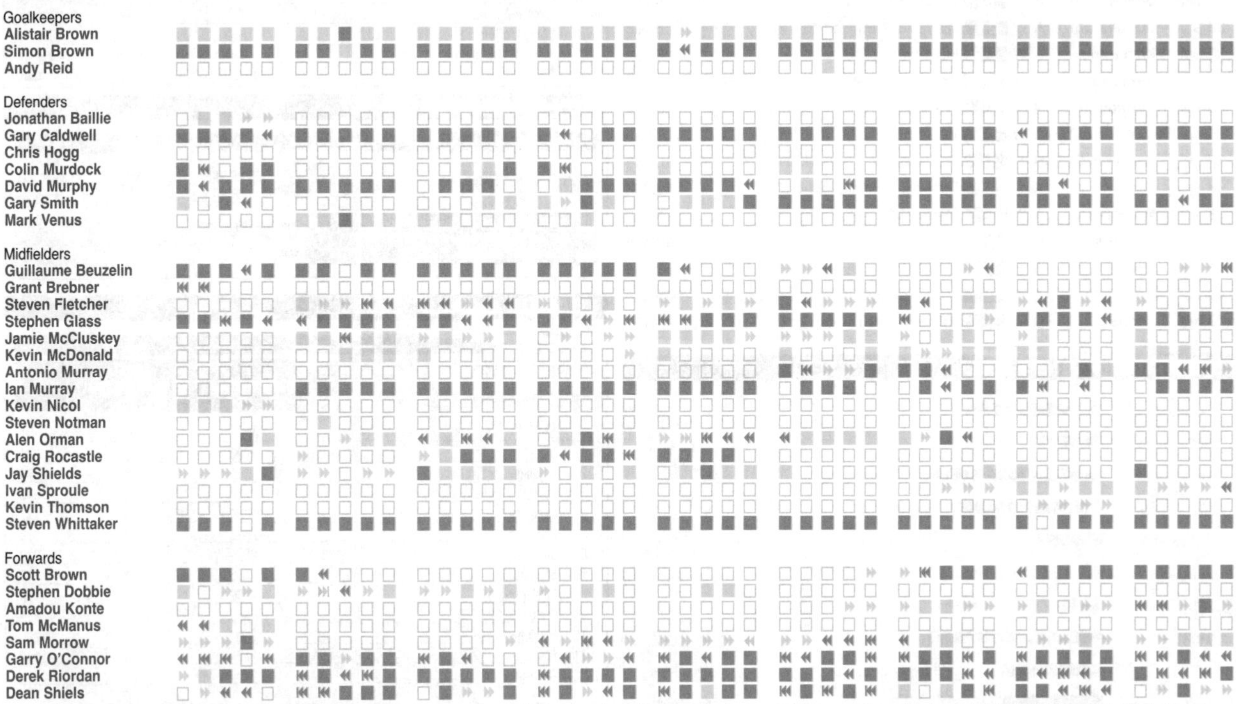
Goalkeepers
Alistair Brown
Simon Brown
Andy Reid
Defenders
Jonathan Baillie
Gary Caldwell
Chris Hogg
Colin Murdock
David Murphy
Gary Smith
Mark Venus
Midfielders
Guillaume Beuzelin
Grant Brebner
Steven Fletcher
Stephen Glass
Jamie McCluskey
Kevin McDonald
Antonio Murray
Ian Murray
Kevin Nicol
Steven Notman
Alen Orman
Craig Rocastle
Jay Shields
Ivan Sproule
Kevin Thomson
Steven Whittaker
Forwards
Scott Brown
Stephen Dobbie
Amadou Konte
Tom McManus
Sam Morrow
Garry O'Connor
Derek Riordan
Dean Shiels

KEY: On all match | On bench | Subbed or sent off (Counting game) | Subbed or sent off (playing less than 70 minutes) | Subbed on from bench (Counting Game) | Subbed on (playing less than 70 minutes) | Subbed on and then subbed or sent off (Counting Game) | Subbed on and then subbed or sent off (playing less than 70 minutes) | Not in 16

ABERDEEN

Final Position: **4th**

NICKNAME: THE DONS

KEY: Won / Drawn / Lost

							Attendance
1	spl	Rangers	H	D	0-0		19,028
2	spl	Hearts	A	D	0-0		13,864
3	spl	Dunfermline	A	W	1-0	Whelan 23	8,533
4	cisr2	Berwick	H	W	3-0	Diamond 5; Adams 36; Craig 46	4,549
5	spl	Livingston	H	W	2-0	Craig 65 pen,68	13,888
6	spl	Dundee Utd	A	D	1-1	Mackie 7	10,995
7	spl	Kilmarnock	A	W	1-0	Fowler 54 og	6,686
8	cisr3	Rangers	H	L	0-2		14,876
9	spl	Hibernian	H	L	0-1		12,137
10	spl	Dundee	H	D	1-1	Heikkinen 42	11,217
11	spl	Inverness CT	A	W	3-1	Adams 28,64 pen; Mackie 90 pen	9,530
12	spl	Motherwell	H	W	2-1	Adams 67; Severin 89	10,737
13	spl	Celtic	A	W	3-2	Mackie 5; Pasquinelli 6; Stewart 90	57,151
14	spl	Rangers	A	L	0-5		48,918
15	spl	Hearts	H	L	0-1		13,055
16	spl	Dunfermline	H	W	2-1	Tod 34 og; Mackie 50	10,398
17	spl	Livingston	A	W	2-0	Foster 1; Mackie 22	4,569
18	spl	Dundee Utd	H	W	1-0	Tosh 26	12,038
19	spl	Kilmarnock	H	W	3-2	Pasquinelli 9,31; Clark 72	11,139
20	spl	Hibernian	A	L	1-2	Mackie 37	13,461
21	spl	Dundee	A	L	0-1		7,310
22	spl	Inverness CT	H	D	0-0		18,250
23	spl	Motherwell	A	D	0-0		7,948
24	scr3	Arbroath	A	W	2-0	Heikkinen 12; Mackie 67	4,165
25	spl	Celtic	H	L	0-1		17,051
26	spl	Rangers	H	L	1-2	Mackie 19	17,495
27	spl	Hearts	A	L	0-1		12,269
28	scr4	Inverness CT	H	W	2-1	Mackie 15,34	10,595
29	spl	Dunfermline	A	L	1-2	Diamond 73	5,579
30	spl	Livingston	H	W	2-0	McNaughton 45; Whelan 59	9,214
31	scpqf	Dundee Utd	A	L	1-4	Byrne 33	8,661
32	spl	Dundee Utd	A	W	2-1	Diamond 9; Stewart 45	6,688
33	spl	Kilmarnock	A	W	1-0	McNaughton 80	5,181
34	spl	Hibernian	H	W	3-0	Anderson 12; Whelan 13; Mackie 85 pen	14,465
35	spl	Dundee	H	D	1-1	Whelan 63	10,474
36	spl	Inverness CT	A	W	1-0	Whelan 39	7,026
37	spl	Motherwell	H	L	1-3	Heikkinen 38	10,443
38	spl	Celtic	A	L	2-3	Diamond 11; Mackie 14	59,998
39	spl	Motherwell	A	W	1-0	Mackie 34	5,063
40	spl	Rangers	H	L	1-3	Clark 33	17,198
41	spl	Celtic	A	L	0-2		59,498
42	spl	Hibernian	A	W	2-1	Mackie 28,69	15,288
43	spl	Hearts	H	W	2-0	Byrne 45; Adams 49	16,155

MONTHLY POINTS TALLY

AUGUST	8	67%
SEPTEMBER	4	44%
OCTOBER	10	67%
NOVEMBER	9	75%
DECEMBER	4	33%
JANUARY	1	8%
FEBRUARY	3	50%
MARCH	10	83%
APRIL	6	50%
MAY	6	50%

KEY PLAYERS - GOALSCORERS

Darren Mackie

Goals in the League	12	Player Strike Rate Average number of minutes between League goals scored by player	241
Contribution to Attacking Power Average number of minutes between League team goals while on pitch	15	Club Strike Rate Average number of minutes between League goals scored by club	78

	PLAYER	LGE GOALS	GOALS ALL	POWER	STRIKE RATE
1	Darren Mackie	12	15	74	241 mins
2	Noel Whelan	5	5	72	275 mins
3	Derek Adams	4	5	73	346 mins
4	Alexander Diamond	3	4	78	838 mins
5	Markus Heikkinen	2	3	78	1290 mins

KEY PLAYERS - MIDFIELDERS

Derek Adams

Goals in the League	4	Contribution to Attacking Power Average number of minutes between League team goals while on pitch	73
Defensive Rating Average number of mins between League goals conceded while he was on the pitch	106	Scoring Difference Defensive Rating minus Contribution to Attacking Power	33

	PLAYER	LGE GOALS	DEF RATE	POWER	SCORE DIFF
1	Derek Adams	4	106	73	33 mins
2	Scott Severin	1	87	73	14 mins
3	Markus Heikkinen	2	92	78	14 mins
4	Christopher Clark	2	72	77	-5 mins

KEY PLAYERS - DEFENDERS

Alexander Diamond

Goals Conceded The number of League goals conceded while he was on the pitch	26	Clean Sheets In games when he played at least 70 minutes	12
Defensive Rating Ave number of mins between League goals conceded while on the pitch	97	Club Defensive Rating Average number of mins between League goals conceded by the club this season	88

	PLAYER	CON LGE	CLEAN SHEETS	DEF RATE
1	Alexander Diamond	26	12	97 mins
2	Russell Anderson	29	12	94 mins
3	Philip McGuire	24	7	86 mins
4	Kevin McNaughton	36	12	83 mins
5	Michael Hart	31	9	80 mins

KEY GOALKEEPER

David Preece

Goals Conceded in the League	10	Counting Games Games when he played at least 70 mins	17
Defensive Rating Ave number of mins between League goals conceded while on the pitch	141	Clean Sheets In games when he played at least 70 mins	7

LEAGUE GOALS

Darren Mackie

Minutes on the pitch	2896	League average (mins between goals)	241
Goals in the League	12		

	PLAYER	MINS	GOALS	AVE
1	Mackie	2896	12	241
2	Whelan	1374	5	275
3	Adams	1384	4	346
4	Pasquinelli	351	3	117
5	Diamond	2513	3	838
6	Clark	2604	2	1302
7	Stewart	835	2	418
8	McNaughton	2996	2	1498
9	Craig	668	2	334
10	Heikkinen	2580	2	1290
11	Foster	1184	1	1184
12	Anderson	2734	1	2734
	Other		5	
	TOTAL		44	

DISCIPLINARY RECORDS

	PLAYER	YELLOW	RED	AVE
1	Whelan	7	0	196
2	Morrison	3	0	204
3	Craig	2	1	222
4	Winter	3	0	230
5	Tosh	4	0	310
6	Adams	4	0	346
7	Diamond	6	1	359
8	Anderson	6	0	455
9	McNaughton	5	1	499
10	Mackie	5	0	579
11	Muirhead	1	0	620
12	Stewart	1	0	835
13	Clark	3	0	868
	Other	9	1	
	TOTAL	59	4	

TOP POINT EARNERS

	PLAYER	GAMES	AV PTS
1	David Preece	15	2.07
2	Derek Adams	13	2.00
3	Scott Severin	31	1.74
4	Noel Whelan	14	1.71
5	Darren Mackie	33	1.58
6	Markus Heikkinen	28	1.54
7	Russell Anderson	30	1.53
8	Kevin McNaughton	31	1.48
9	Alexander Diamond	26	1.46
10	Philip McGuire	18	1.44
	CLUB AVERAGE:		1.61

TEAM OF THE SEASON

D
Alexander Diamond
CG: 26 DR: 97
M
Derek Adams
CG: 13 SD: 33
D
Russell Anderson
CG: 30 DR: 94
M
Markus Heikkinen
CG: 28 SD: 14
F
Darren Mackie
CG: 33 SR: 241
G
David Preece
CG: 15 DR: 141
D
Philip McGuire
CG: 18 DR: 86
M
Scott Severin
CG: 31 SD: 14
F
Noel Whelan
CG: 14 SR: 275
D
Kevin McNaughton
CG: 31 DR: 83
M
Christopher Clark
CG: 28 SD: -5

LEAGUE APPEARANCES AND BOOKINGS

	AGE (on 01/07/04)	IN NAMED 16	APPEARANCES	COUNTING GAMES	MINUTES ON PITCH	YELLOW CARDS	RED CARDS	THIS SEASON	HOME COUNTRY
Goalkeepers									
James Blanchard	19	5	0	0	0	0	0	-	Scotland
Ryan Esson	25	38	23	22	2013	0	0	-	Scotland
Sasa Ilic	32	6	0	0	0	0	0	2	Serbia & Mont (46)
David Preece	28	26	17	15	1407	0	1	-	England
Defenders									
Russell Anderson	26	31	31	30	2734	6	0	-	Scotland
Richard Buckley	20	3	0	0	0	0	0	-	Scotland
Richie Byrne	23	13	13	9	924	1	0	-	Scotland
Andrew Considine	18	18	1	0	66	0	0	-	Scotland
Alexander Diamond	20	29	29	26	2513	6	1	-	Scotland
Michael Hart	25	32	32	27	2486	1	0	-	Scotland
Philip McGuire	25	31	30	18	2053	2	0	-	Scotland
Kevin McNaughton	22	35	35	31	2996	5	1	1	Scotland (85)
Scott Morrison	20	31	11	6	613	3	0	-	Scotland
Midfielders									
Derek Adams	30	26	20	13	1384	4	0	-	Scotland
Christopher Clark	24	31	31	28	2604	3	0	-	Scotland
Gary Dempsey	24	6	4	0	79	0	0	-	Rep of Ireland
Richard Foster	19	31	25	8	1184	1	0	-	Scotland
Markus Heikkinen	26	30	30	28	2580	1	0	-	Finland
Scott Muirhead	21	26	14	6	620	1	0	-	Scotland
Markus Paatelainen	22	2	0	0	0	0	0	-	Finland
Scott Severin	26	31	31	31	2782	3	0	3	Scotland (85)
Fergus Tiernan	23	10	0	0	0	0	0	-	Scotland
Steven Tosh	32	18	17	11	1243	4	0	-	Scotland
Jamie Winter	19	17	12	6	691	3	0	-	Scotland
Forwards									
Lubomir Blaha	27	8	8	0	297	1	0	-	Czech Republic
Steven Craig	24	19	14	6	668	2	1	-	Scotland
Thorarinn Kristjansson	24	5	3	0	95	0	0	-	Iceland
Darren Mackie	23	34	34	33	2896	5	0	-	Scotland
Fernando Pasquinelli	25	12	10	1	351	0	0	-	Argentina
John Stewart	19	34	25	5	835	1	0	-	Scotland
Noel Whelan	30	20	20	14	1374	7	0	-	England

SQUAD APPEARANCES

Match	1	2	3	4	5	6	7	8	9	10	11	12	13	14	15	16	17	18	19	20	21	22	23	24	25	26	27	28	29	30	31	32	33	34	35	36	37	38	39	40	41	42	43
Venue	H	A	A	H	H	A	A	H	H	H	A	H	A	A	H	H	A	H	H	A	A	H	A	A	H	H	A	H	A	H	A	A	A	H	H	A	H	A	A	H	A	A	H
Competition	L	L	L	W	L	L	L	W	L	L	L	L	L	L	L	L	L	L	L	L	L	L	L	F	L	L	L	F	L	L	F	L	L	L	L	L	L	L	L	L	L	L	L
Result	D	D	W	W	W	D	W	L	L	D	W	W	W	L	L	W	W	W	W	L	L	D	D	W	L	L	L	W	L	W	L	W	W	W	D	W	L	L	W	L	L	W	W

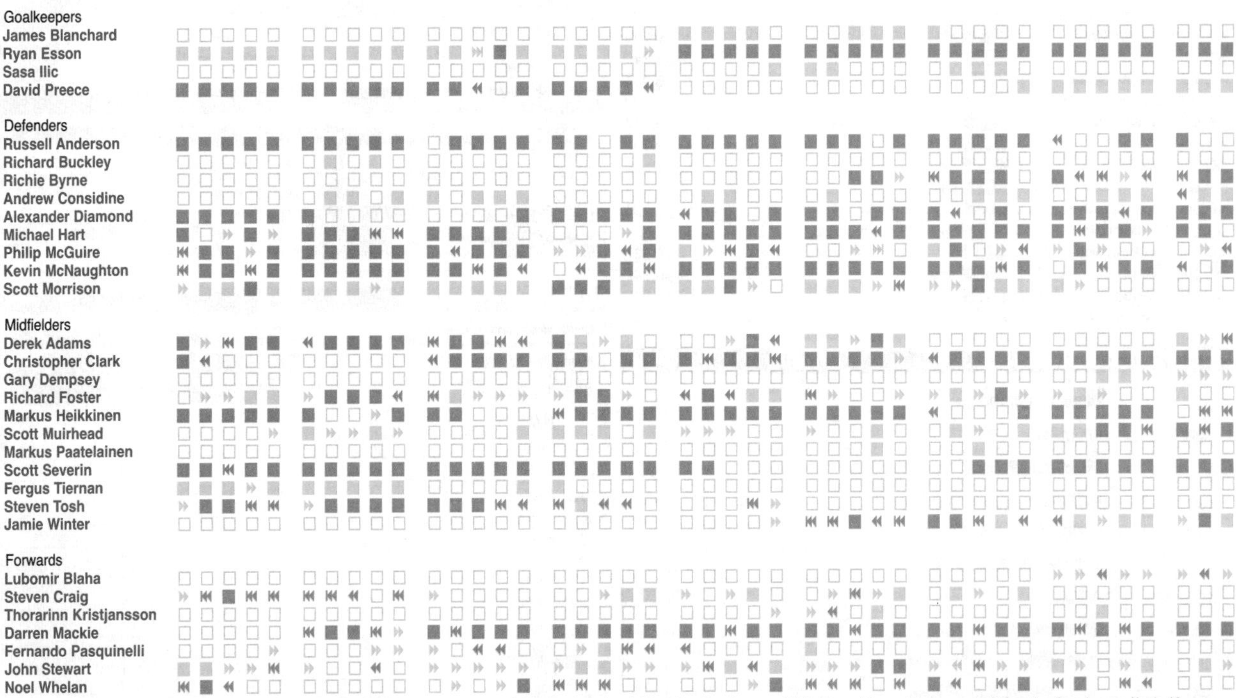

Goalkeepers
James Blanchard
Ryan Esson
Sasa Ilic
David Preece
Defenders
Russell Anderson
Richard Buckley
Richie Byrne
Andrew Considine
Alexander Diamond
Michael Hart
Philip McGuire
Kevin McNaughton
Scott Morrison
Midfielders
Derek Adams
Christopher Clark
Gary Dempsey
Richard Foster
Markus Heikkinen
Scott Muirhead
Markus Paatelainen
Scott Severin
Fergus Tiernan
Steven Tosh
Jamie Winter
Forwards
Lubomir Blaha
Steven Craig
Thorarinn Kristjansson
Darren Mackie
Fernando Pasquinelli
John Stewart
Noel Whelan

KEY: On all match | On bench | Subbed or sent off (Counting game) | Subbed or sent off (playing less than 70 minutes) | Subbed on from bench (Counting Game) | Subbed on (playing less than 70 minutes) | Subbed on and then subbed or sent off (Counting Game) | Subbed on and then subbed or sent off (playing less than 70 minutes) | Not in 16

HEART OF MIDLOTHIAN

Final Position: **5th**

NICKNAME: THE JAM TARTS

KEY: ☐Won ☐Drawn ☐Lost

							Attendance
1	spl	**Dundee**	A	W	1-0	Pressley 85 pen	7,770
2	spl	**Aberdeen**	H	D	0-0		13,864
3	spl	**Kilmarnock**	H	W	3-0	Weir 18; Pereira 57; Pressley 71 pen	11,403
4	spl	**Motherwell**	A	L	0-2		7,095
5	spl	**Rangers**	H	D	0-0		14,601
6	ur1L1	**Braga**	H	W	3-1	Webster 52; Hartley 62; Kisnorbo 90	18,203
7	spl	**Dunfermline**	A	L	0-1		5,883
8	cisr3	**Kilmarnock**	H	W	2-1	Hartley 15,52	5,924
9	spl	**Inverness CT**	H	W	1-0	Hartley 15	10,340
10	ur1L2	**Braga**	A	D	2-2	de Vries 27,47	13,007
11	spl	**Livingston**	H	D	0-0		10,646
12	spl	**Celtic**	A	L	0-3		58,869
13	ucgpa	**Feyenoord**	A	L	0-3		26,000
14	spl	**Hibernian**	H	W	2-1	Kisnorbo 15; Hamill 76	16,720
15	spl	**Dundee Utd**	A	D	1-1	McKenna 5	5,723
16	spl	**Dundee**	H	W	3-0	McKenna 34; Hartley 81; Wyness 90	10,172
17	ucgpa	**Schalke**	H	L	0-1		27,272
18	spl	**Aberdeen**	A	W	1-0	Hartley 60 pen	13,055
19	sccqf	**Dunfermline**	A	W	3-1	Webster 33; Hartley 66 pen; Hamill 84	4,405
20	spl	**Kilmarnock**	A	D	1-1	Wyness 69	6,129
21	spl	**Motherwell**	H	L	0-1		10,598
22	ucgpa	**Basel**	A	W	2-1	Wyness 31; Neilson 89	25,000
23	spl	**Rangers**	A	L	2-3	Hartley 15 pen; de Vries 66	48,494
24	spl	**Dunfermline**	H	W	3-0	Wyness 11; Pereira 46; Hartley 56 pen	10,084
25	spl	**Inverness CT**	A	D	1-1	Hartley 62 pen	2,011
26	ucgpa	**Ferencvaros**	H	L	0-1		26,182
27	spl	**Celtic**	H	L	0-2		16,163
28	spl	**Hibernian**	A	D	1-1	Hartley 55	17,259
29	scr3	**Partick**	A	D	0-0		5,666
30	spl	**Dundee Utd**	H	W	3-2	Pressley 44; Miller 49; Hartley 86	10,305
31	scr3r	**Partick**	H	W	2-1	MacFarlane 34; Wyness 89	7,340
32	spl	**Dundee**	A	D	1-1	Hamill 60	5,780
33	spl	**Livingston**	A	W	2-1	Hartley 85; Miller 86	4,318
34	spl	**Aberdeen**	H	W	1-0	Wyness 63 pen	12,269
35	slc5	**Motherwell**	A	L	2-3	Burchill 85; Thorarinsson 90	14,069
36	scr4	**Kilmarnock**	H	D	2-2	Wyness 16; Miller 45	10,308
37	spl	**Kilmarnock**	H	W	3-0	Mikoliunas 15; Fowler 25 og; Miller 67	9,220
38	scr4r	**Kilmarnock**	A	W	3-1	Wallace 6; Miller 13; Cesnauskis 57	6,366
39	spl	**Motherwell**	A	L	0-2		7,390
40	scqf	**Livingston**	H	W	2-1	Miller 1; McAllister 10	9,796
41	spl	**Rangers**	H	L	1-2	Burchill 87	13,842
42	spl	**Dunfermline**	A	D	1-1	Hartley 62 pen	5,934
43	spl	**Inverness CT**	H	L	0-2		9,822
44	spl	**Livingston**	H	W	3-1	Miller 22; Burchill 65; Neilson 68	9,187
45	spl	**Celtic**	A	W	2-0	Miller 8; Burchill 19	59,562
46	scsf	**Celtic**	H	L	1-2	Cesnauskis 60	38,505
47	spl	**Hibernian**	H	L	1-2	Miller 40	17,676
48	spl	**Dundee Utd**	A	L	1-2	Miller 39	7,704
49	spl	**Hibernian**	A	D	2-2	Miller 23; Webster 88	16,620
50	spl	**Motherwell**	H	D	0-0		10,337
51	spl	**Rangers**	A	L	1-2	Andrews 84 og	49,342
52	spl	**Celtic**	H	L	1-2	Hartley 71	15,927
53	spl	**Aberdeen**	A	L	0-2		16,155

MONTHLY POINTS TALLY

AUGUST	7	58%
SEPTEMBER	4	44%
OCTOBER	8	53%
NOVEMBER	4	33%
DECEMBER	4	44%
JANUARY	11	73%
FEBRUARY	3	50%
MARCH	4	33%
APRIL	5	33%
MAY	0	0%

KEY PLAYERS - GOALSCORERS

Lee Miller

Goals in the League	8	**Player Strike Rate** Average number of minutes between League goals scored by player	186
Contribution to Attacking Power Average number of minutes between League team goals while on the pitch	11	**Club Strike Rate** Average number of minutes between League goals scored by club	80

	PLAYER	LGE GOALS	GOALS ALL	POWER	STRIKE RATE
1	Lee Miller	8	11	70	**186 mins**
2	Paul Hartley	11	15	78	**258 mins**
3	Steven Pressley	3	3	72	**944 mins**
4	Joe Hamill	2	3	76	**1104 mins**
5	Patrick Kisnorbo	1	2	88	**1501 mins**

KEY PLAYERS - MIDFIELDERS

Phil Stamp

Goals in the League	0	**Contribution to Attacking Power** Average number of minutes between League team goals while on pitch	108
Defensive Rating Average number of mins between League goals conceded while on the pitch	132	**Scoring Difference** Defensive Rating minus Contribution to Attacking Power	24

	PLAYER	LGE GOALS	DEF RATE	POWER	SCORE DIFF
1	Phil Stamp	0	132	108	**24 mins**
2	Paul Hartley	11	84	79	**5 mins**
3	Neil MacFarlane	0	74	83	**-9 mins**

KEY PLAYERS - DEFENDERS

Alan Maybury

Goals Conceded Total number of goals conceded while the player was on the pitch	12	**Clean Sheets** In games when player was on pitch for at least 70 minutes	8
Defensive Rating Ave number of mins between League goals conceded while on the pitch	118	**Club Defensive Rating** Average number of mins between League goals conceded by the club this season	83

	PLAYER	CON LGE	CLEAN SHEETS	DEF RATE
1	Alan Maybury	12	8	**118 mins**
2	Patrick Kisnorbo	13	9	**115 mins**
3	Steven Pressley	30	13	**94 mins**
4	Robbie Neilson	34	13	**90 mins**
5	Andy Webster	35	12	**88 mins**

KEY GOALKEEPER

Craig Gordon

Goals Conceded in the League	41	**Counting Games** League games when player was on pitch for at least 70 minutes	38
Defensive Rating Ave number of mins between League goals conceded while on the pitch	83	**Clean Sheets** In games when player was on pitch for at least 70 minutes	13

LEAGUE GOALS

Paul Hartley

Minutes on the pitch	2839	League average (mins between goals)	258
Goals in the League	11		

	PLAYER	MINS	GOALS	AVE
1	Hartley	2839	**11**	258
2	Miller	1486	**8**	186
3	Wyness	1569	**4**	392
4	Pressley	2833	**3**	944
5	Burchill	535	**3**	178
6	McKenna	669	**2**	335
7	Hamill	2208	**2**	1104
8	Pereira	1023	**2**	512
9	Mikoliunas	830	**1**	830
11	Weir	1029	**1**	1029
13	de Vries	656	**1**	656
	Other		5	
	TOTAL		**43**	

DISCIPLINARY RECORDS

	PLAYER	YELLOW	RED	AVE
1	Pereira	5	0	204
2	Mikoliunas	3	1	207
3	Simmons	2	0	226
4	Maybury	5	1	235
5	Pressley	9	1	283
6	Cesnauskis	2	0	293
7	Stamp	4	0	296
8	Kisnorbo	5	0	300
9	Hartley	9	0	315
10	McAllister	6	0	352
11	Miller	3	0	495
12	MacFarlane	3	0	496
13	Neilson	6	0	512
	Other	11	1	
	TOTAL	73	4	

TOP POINT EARNERS

	PLAYER	GAMES	AV PTS
1	Phil Stamp	12	1.67
2	Alan Maybury	15	1.60
3	Patrick Kisnorbo	17	1.59
4	James McAllister	22	1.55
5	Steven Pressley	31	1.55
6	Robbie Neilson	33	1.48
7	Joe Hamill	21	1.48
8	Andy Webster	34	1.35
9	Craig Gordon	38	1.32
10	Paul Hartley	31	1.32
	CLUB AVERAGE:		1.32

LEAGUE APPEARANCES AND BOOKINGS

	AGE (on 01/07/04)	IN NAMED 16	APPEARANCES	COUNTING GAMES	MINUTES ON PITCH	YELLOW CARDS	RED CARDS	THIS SEASON	HOME COUNTRY
Goalkeepers									
Craig Gordon	22	38	38	38	3420	1	0	-	Scotland
Jamie MacDonald	19	1	0	0	0	0	0	-	Scotland
Defenders									
Christophe Berra	20	33	12	7	704	1	0	-	Scotland
Alan Maybury	26	17	17	15	1411	5	1	6	Rep of Ireland (15)
James McAllister	27	32	30	22	2114	6	0	-	Scotland
Kevin McKenna	24	20	13	5	669	0	0	-	Canada
Robbie Neilson	25	35	35	33	3076	6	0	-	Scotland
Marco Pelosi	19	3	0	0	0	0	0	-	Scotland
Steven Pressley	31	32	32	31	2833	9	1	3	Scotland (85)
Craig Sives	19	7	2	1	133	1	0	-	Scotland
Jason Thomson	17	5	4	4	346	0	0	-	Scotland
Gary Tierney	19	3	1	0	13	0	0	-	Scotland
Lee Wallace	17	13	12	12	1063	0	0	-	Scotland
Andy Webster	23	35	35	34	3074	2	1	-	Scotland
Midfielders									
Paul Hartley	28	33	33	31	2839	9	0	1	Scotland (85)
Neil Janczyk	22	15	6	1	235	0	0	-	Scotland
Patrick Kisnorbo	24	18	17	17	1501	5	0	-	Australia
Marius Kizys	23	8	7	1	229	0	0	-	Lithuania
Neil MacFarlane	27	36	20	17	1489	3	0	-	Scotland
David McGeown	21	2	2	0	45	0	0	-	Scotland
Stephen Simmons	23	15	11	3	453	2	0	-	Scotland
Phil Stamp	29	16	16	12	1187	4	0	-	England
Michael Stewart	24	28	17	2	573	1	0	-	Scotland
Forwards									
Mark Burchill	24	12	12	4	535	1	0	-	Scotland
Deividas Cesnauskis	24	9	8	5	586	2	0	-	Lithuania
Mark de Vries	29	9	9	6	656	1	0	-	Holland
Calum Elliot	18	8	4	0	90	0	0	-	Scotland
Joe Hamill	21	37	32	21	2208	0	0	-	Scotland
Saulius Mikoliunas	21	11	11	9	830	3	1	-	Lithuania
Lee Miller	22	18	18	15	1486	3	0	-	Scotland
Ramon Pereira	26	19	16	8	1023	5	0	-	Spain
Robert Sloan	21	7	2	0	13	0	0	-	Scotland
Hjalmar Thorarinsson	19	6	4	0	67	0	0	-	Iceland
Graham Weir	20	25	20	7	1029	2	0	-	Scotland
Dennis Wyness	28	38	29	8	1569	2	0	-	Scotland

TEAM OF THE SEASON

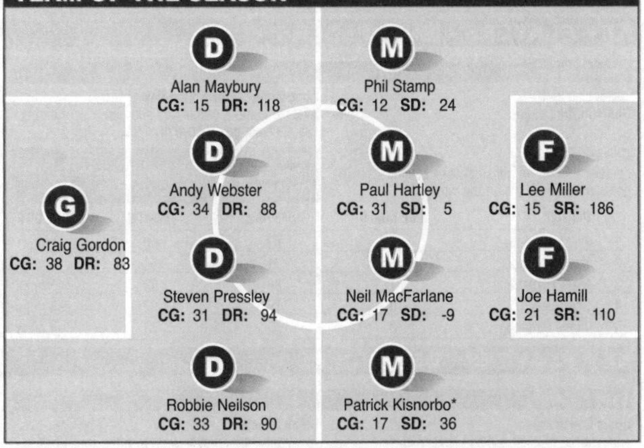

D
Alan Maybury
CG: 15 DR: 118
D
Andy Webster
CG: 34 DR: 88
D
Steven Pressley
CG: 31 DR: 94
D
Robbie Neilson
CG: 33 DR: 90
M
Phil Stamp
CG: 12 SD: 24
M
Paul Hartley
CG: 31 SD: 5
M
Neil MacFarlane
CG: 17 SD: -9
M
Patrick Kisnorbo*
CG: 17 SD: 36
F
Lee Miller
CG: 15 SR: 186
F
Joe Hamill
CG: 21 SR: 110
G
Craig Gordon
CG: 38 DR: 83

SQUAD APPEARANCES

Match	1	2	3	4	5	6	7	8	9	10	11	12	13	14	15	16	17	18	19	20	21	22	23	24	25	26	27	28	29	30	31	32	33	34	35	36	37	38	39	40	41	42	43	44	45	46	47	48	49	50	51	52	53
Venue	A	H	H	A	H	H	A	H	H	A	H	A	A	H	A	H	H	A	A	A	H	A	A	H	A	H	H	A	A	H	H	A	A	H	A	H	H	A	A	H	H	A	H	H	A	H	H	A	A	H	A	H	A
Competition	L	L	L	L	L	E	L	W	L	E	L	L	E	L	L	L	E	L	W	L	L	E	L	L	L	E	L	L	F	L	F	L	L	L	W	F	L	F	L	F	L	L	L	L	L	F	L	L	L	L	L	L	L
Result	W	D	W	L	D	W	L	W	W	D	D	L	L	W	D	W	L	W	W	D	L	W	L	W	D	L	L	D	D	W	W	D	W	W	L	D	W	W	L	W	L	D	L	W	W	L	L	L	D	D	L	L	L

Goalkeepers
Craig Gordon
Teuvo Moilanen

Defenders
Christophe Berra
Alan Maybury
James McAllister
Kevin McKenna
Robbie Neilson
Marco Pelosi
Steven Pressley
Craig Sives
Jason Thomson
Gary Tierney
Lee Wallace
Andy Webster

Midfielders
Paul Hartley
Neil Janczyk
Patrick Kisnorbo
Marius Kizys
Neil MacFarlane
David McGeown
Stephen Simmons
Phil Stamp
Michael Stewart

Forwards
Mark Burchill
Deividas Cesnauskis
Mark de Vries
Calum Elliot
Joe Hamill
Saulius Mikoliunas
Lee Miller
Ramon Pereira
Robert Sloan
Hjalmar Thorarinsson
Graham Weir
Dennis Wyness

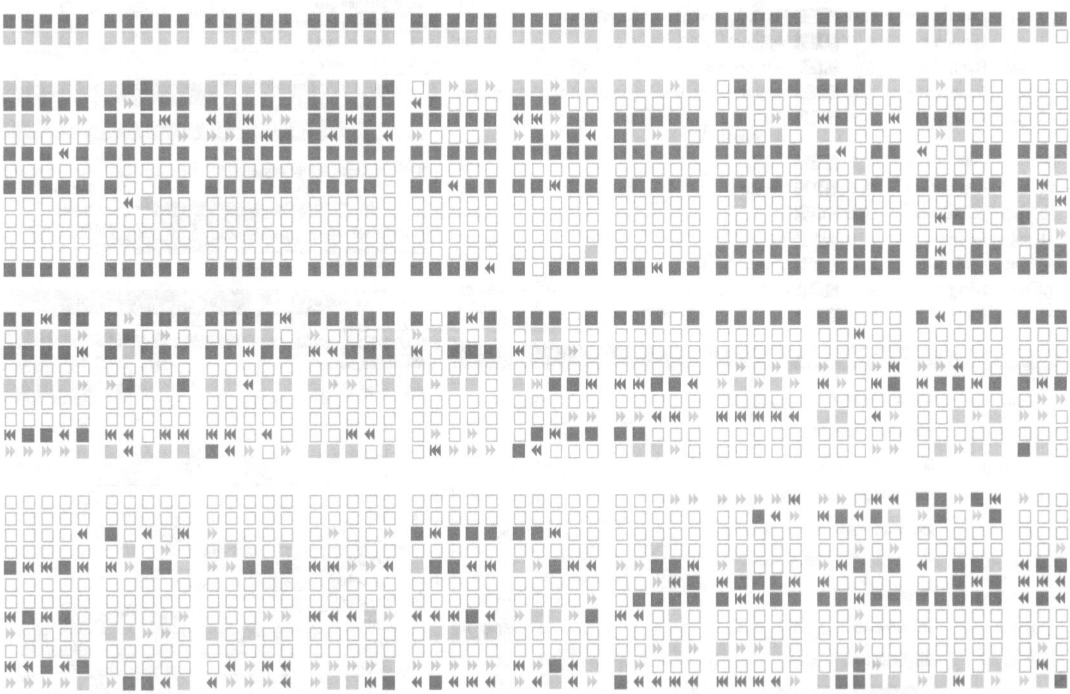

KEY: On all match | On bench | Subbed or sent off (Counting game) | Subbed or sent off (playing less than 70 minutes) | Subbed on from bench (Counting Game) | Subbed on (playing less than 70 minutes) | Subbed on and then subbed or sent off (Counting Game) | Subbed on and then subbed or sent off (playing less than 70 minutes) | Not in 16

MOTHERWELL

Final Position: **6th**

NICKNAME: THE WELL

KEY: Won Drawn Lost

	Comp	Opponent			Score	Scorers	Attendance
1	spl	**Celtic**	A	L	0-2		57,245
2	spl	**Hibernian**	H	L	1-2	O'Donnell 20	5,859
3	spl	**Dundee**	A	W	2-1	McDonald, S 28,62	4,849
4	cisr2	**G Morton**	A	W	3-0	Paterson 42; McBride 67 pen; Clarkson 75	3,767
5	spl	**Hearts**	H	W	2-0	McBride 59 pen; O'Donnell 67	7,095
6	spl	**Dunfermline**	A	D	1-1	McDonald, S 87	4,388
7	spl	**Dundee Utd**	H	W	4-2	McDonald, S 53,70; Clarkson 57; Burns 90	5,091
8	cisr3	**Inverness CT**	A	W	3-1	Foran 47; O'Donnell 52; McBride 85	1,464
9	spl	**Livingston**	A	W	3-2	McBride 11; McDonald, S 50; Foran 71	4,050
10	spl	**Inverness CT**	A	D	1-1	McDonald, S 38	1,117
11	spl	**Rangers**	H	L	0-2		10,946
12	spl	**Aberdeen**	A	L	1-2	McBride 29 pen	10,737
13	spl	**Kilmarnock**	H	L	0-1		4,521
14	spl	**Celtic**	H	L	2-3	Corrigan 67; Foran 71 pen	10,592
15	spl	**Hibernian**	A	L	0-1		10,022
16	sccqf	**Livingston**	A	W	5-0	Dorado 3 og; Foran 38,60 pen; O'Donnell 57; Wright 90	2,886
17	spl	**Dundee**	H	W	3-0	Clarkson 44; Paterson 53,64	4,406
18	spl	**Hearts**	A	W	1-0	Foran 28 pen	10,598
19	spl	**Dunfermline**	H	W	2-1	Tod 26 og; Foran 63	5,084
20	spl	**Dundee Utd**	A	W	1-0	Paterson 17	5,252
21	spl	**Livingston**	H	W	2-0	O'Donnell 17; Foran 47	4,363
22	spl	**Inverness CT**	H	L	1-2	Clarkson 65	4,267
23	spl	**Rangers**	A	L	1-4	McDonald, S 49	49,909
24	spl	**Aberdeen**	H	D	0-0		7,948
25	scr3	**Kilmarnock**	A	L	0-2		6,093
26	spl	**Kilmarnock**	A	L	0-2		5,225
27	spl	**Celtic**	A	L	0-2		58,438
28	slc5	**Hearts**	H	W	3-2	Craigan 20; Foran 78 pen; Fitzpatrick 120	14,069
29	spl	**Dundee**	A	L	1-2	McDonald, S 40	5,746
30	spl	**Hibernian**	H	D	1-1	Craigan 26	7,453
31	spl	**Hearts**	H	W	2-0	McDonald, S 25; Fitzpatrick 39	7,390
32	spl	**Dunfermline**	A	D	0-0		3,565
33	spl	**Dundee Utd**	H	W	2-0	Partridge 4; McDonald, S 47	5,110
34	spl	**Livingston**	A	D	1-1	McDonald, S 19	4,609
35	cisrf	**Rangers**	A	L	1-5	Partridge 15	50,182
36	spl	**Rangers**	H	L	2-3	McBride 71 pen; Corrigan 84	10,210
37	spl	**Aberdeen**	A	W	3-1	McBride 22 pen; Hamilton 32; McDonald, S 72	10,443
38	spl	**Inverness CT**	A	L	0-1		3,746
39	spl	**Kilmarnock**	H	D	1-1	Combe 86 og	4,999
40	spl	**Aberdeen**	H	L	0-1		5,063
41	spl	**Hearts**	A	D	0-0		10,337
42	spl	**Hibernian**	H	D	2-2	Craigan 16,49	8,903
43	spl	**Rangers**	A	L	1-4	Andrews 89 og	49,495
44	spl	**Celtic**	H	W	2-1	McDonald, S 88,90	12,944

MONTHLY POINTS TALLY

AUGUST	6	50%
SEPTEMBER	7	78%
OCTOBER	1	7%
NOVEMBER	9	75%
DECEMBER	6	50%
JANUARY	1	11%
FEBRUARY	4	44%
MARCH	5	56%
APRIL	5	28%
MAY	4	44%

KEY PLAYERS - GOALSCORERS

Scott McDonald

Goals in the League	15	**Player Strike Rate** Average number of minutes between League goals scored by player	145
Contribution to Attacking Power Average number of minutes between League team goals while on pitch	15	**Club Strike Rate** Average number of minutes between League goals scored by club	74

	PLAYER	LGE GOALS	GOALS ALL	POWER	STRIKE RATE
1	Scott McDonald	15	15	68	145 mins
2	Kevin McBride	5	7	66	410 mins
3	Ritchie Foran	5	9	78	471 mins
4	Philip O'Donnell	3	5	60	481 mins
5	David Clarkson	3	4	71	736 mins

KEY PLAYERS - MIDFIELDERS

Philip O'Donnell

Goals in the League	3	**Contribution to Attacking Power** Average number of minutes between League team goals while on pitch	60
Defensive Rating Average number of mins between League goals conceded while on the pitch	69	**Scoring Difference** Defensive Rating minus Contribution to Attacking Power	9

	PLAYER	LGE GOALS	DEF RATE	POWER	SCORE DIFF
1	Philip O'Donnell	3	69	60	9 mins
2	Kevin McBride	5	71	66	5 mins
3	Mark Fitzpatrick	1	88	83	5 mins
4	Scott Leitch	0	79	82	-3 mins
5	Jamie Paterson	3	65	73	-8 mins

KEY PLAYERS - DEFENDERS

David Partridge

Goals Conceded The number of League goals conceded while on the pitch	32	**Clean Sheets** In games when player was on pitch for at least 70 minutes	8
Defensive Rating Ave number of mins between League goals conceded while on the pitch	79	**Club Defensive Rating** Average number of mins between League goals conceded by the club this season	70

	PLAYER	CON LGE	CLEAN SHEETS	DEF RATE
1	David Partridge	32	8	79 mins
2	Stephen Craigan	45	10	74 mins
3	Steven Hammell	40	8	72 mins
4	Martyn Corrigan	44	8	65 mins
5	Paul Quinn	29	5	64 mins

KEY GOALKEEPER

Gordon Marshall

Goals Conceded in the League	42	**Counting Games** League games when player was on pitch for at least 70 minutes	33
Defensive Rating Ave number of mins between League goals conceded while on the pitch	69	**Clean Sheets** In games when player was on pitch for at least 70 minutes	9

LEAGUE GOALS

Scott McDonald

Minutes on the pitch	2176	League average (mins between goals)	145
Goals in the League	15		

	PLAYER	MINS	GOALS	AVE
1	McDonald, S	2176	15	145
2	Foran	2356	5	471
3	McBride	2051	5	410
4	Paterson	2267	3	756
5	Craigan	3320	3	1107
6	Clarkson	2209	3	736
7	O'Donnell	1443	3	481
8	Corrigan	2880	2	1440
9	Partridge	2522	1	2522
10	Fitzpatrick	1501	1	1501
11	Burns	387	1	387
	Other		4	
	TOTAL		46	

DISCIPLINARY RECORDS

	PLAYER	YELLOW	RED	AVE
1	Fagan	3	0	360
2	Partridge	7	0	360
3	Clarkson	5	1	368
4	Hamilton	3	0	390
5	Foran	6	0	392
6	Craigan	8	0	415
7	Leitch	5	0	443
8	Quinn	4	0	465
9	Hammell	4	0	720
10	McDonald, S	3	0	725
11	Kinniburgh	1	0	998
12	Paterson	2	0	1133
13	Corrigan	2	0	1440
	Other	3	1	
	TOTAL	56	2	

TOP POINT EARNERS

	PLAYER	GAMES	AV PTS
1	Mark Fitzpatrick	14	1.64
2	Jamie Paterson	21	1.52
3	Philip O'Donnell	14	1.50
4	Kevin McBride	21	1.43
5	Gordon Marshall	32	1.41
6	Jim Hamilton	13	1.38
7	Ritchie Foran	24	1.33
8	Stephen Craigan	37	1.30
9	David Clarkson	22	1.27
10	Scott Leitch	22	1.27
	CLUB AVERAGE:		1.26

TEAM OF THE SEASON

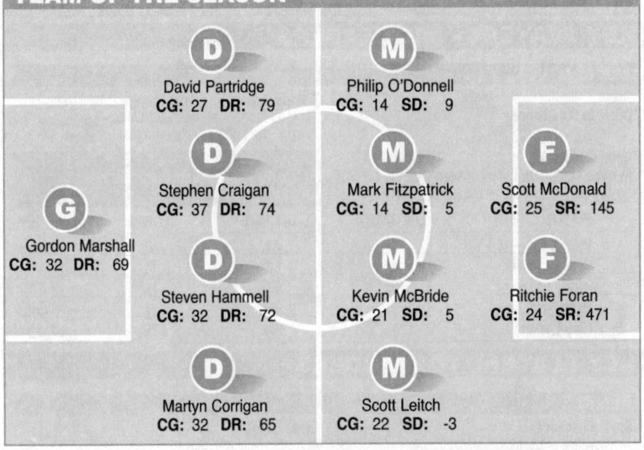
G
Gordon Marshall
CG: 32 DR: 69
D
David Partridge
CG: 27 DR: 79
D
Stephen Craigan
CG: 37 DR: 74
D
Steven Hammell
CG: 32 DR: 72
D
Martyn Corrigan
CG: 32 DR: 65
M
Philip O'Donnell
CG: 14 SD: 9
M
Mark Fitzpatrick
CG: 14 SD: 5
M
Kevin McBride
CG: 21 SD: 5
M
Scott Leitch
CG: 22 SD: -3
F
Scott McDonald
CG: 25 SR: 145
F
Ritchie Foran
CG: 24 SR: 471

LEAGUE APPEARANCES AND BOOKINGS

	AGE (on 01/07/04)	IN NAMED 16	APPEARANCES	COUNTING GAMES	MINUTES ON PITCH	YELLOW CARDS	RED CARDS	THIS SEASON	HOME COUNTRY
Goalkeepers									
Barry-John Corr	24	36	6	5	517	0	0	-	Scotland
Jamie Ewings	20	6	0	0	0	0	0	-	Scotland
Gordon Marshall	41	34	33	32	2903	0	1	-	Scotland
Defenders									
Martyn Corrigan	27	33	32	32	2880	2	0	-	Scotland
David Cowan	23	13	0	0	0	0	0	-	England
Stephen Craigan	28	37	37	37	3320	8	0	8	N Ireland (114)
Steven Hammell	23	32	32	32	2880	4	0	1	Scotland (85)
Chris Higgins	20	10	0	0	0	0	0	-	Scotland
David Keogh	18	11	3	0	54	0	0	-	Scotland
William Kinniburgh	20	35	13	10	998	1	0	-	Scotland
David Partridge	26	34	29	27	2522	7	0	-	Wales
Paul Quinn	20	32	23	19	1863	4	0	-	Scotland
Midfielders									
Kenneth Connolly	18	5	0	0	0	0	0	-	Scotland
Shaun Fagan	21	35	23	8	1080	3	0	-	Scotland
Mark Fitzpatrick	19	35	25	14	1501	1	0	-	Scotland
Brian Kerr	23	9	8	6	620	0	0	-	Scotland
Scott Leitch	35	28	28	22	2219	5	0	-	Scotland
Stephen Maguire	18	1	0	0	0	0	0	-	Scotland
Kevin McBride	24	25	25	21	2051	1	0	-	Scotland
Philip O'Donnell	33	18	18	14	1443	1	0	-	Scotland
Jamie Paterson	25	35	35	21	2267	2	0	-	Scotland
Forwards									
Gerry Britton	34	6	3	0	36	0	0	-	Scotland
Alex Burns	31	21	10	3	387	0	0	-	Scotland
David Clarkson	19	36	35	22	2209	5	1	-	Scotland
Adam Coakley	17	3	0	0	0	0	0	-	England
Ritchie Foran	25	37	35	24	2356	6	0	-	Rep of Ireland
Jim Hamilton	29	14	14	13	1172	3	0	-	Scotland
Scott McDonald	21	27	27	25	2176	3	0	-	Australia
Darren Smith	17	3	1	0	3	0	0	-	Scotland
Kenneth Wright	19	22	7	0	87	0	0	-	Scotland

SQUAD APPEARANCES

Match	1	2	3	4	5	6	7	8	9	10	11	12	13	14	15	16	17	18	19	20	21	22	23	24	25	26	27	28	29	30	31	32	33	34	35	36	37	38	39	40	41	42	43	44
Venue	A	H	A	A	H	A	H	A	A	A	H	A	H	H	A	A	H	A	H	A	H	H	A	H	A	A	A	H	A	H	H	A	H	A	A	H	A	A	H	H	A	H	A	H
Competition	L	L	L	W	L	L	L	W	L	L	L	L	L	L	L	W	L	L	L	L	L	L	L	L	F	L	L	W	L	L	L	L	L	L	W	L	L	L	L	L	L	L	L	L
Result	L	L	W	W	W	D	W	W	W	D	L	L	L	L	L	W	W	W	W	W	W	L	L	D	L	L	L	W	L	D	W	D	W	D	L	L	W	L	D	L	D	D	L	W

Goalkeepers
Barry-John Corr
Jamie Ewings
Gordon Marshall

Defenders
Martyn Corrigan
David Cowan
Stephen Craigan
Steven Hammell
Chris Higgins
David Keogh
William Kinniburgh
David Partridge
Paul Quinn

Midfielders
Kenneth Connolly
Shaun Fagan
Mark Fitzpatrick
Brian Kerr
Scott Leitch
Stephen Maguire
Kevin McBride
Philip O'Donnell
Jamie Paterson

Forwards
Gerry Britton
Alex Burns
David Clarkson
Adam Coakley
Ritchie Foran
Jim Hamilton
Scott McDonald
Darren Smith
Kenneth Wright

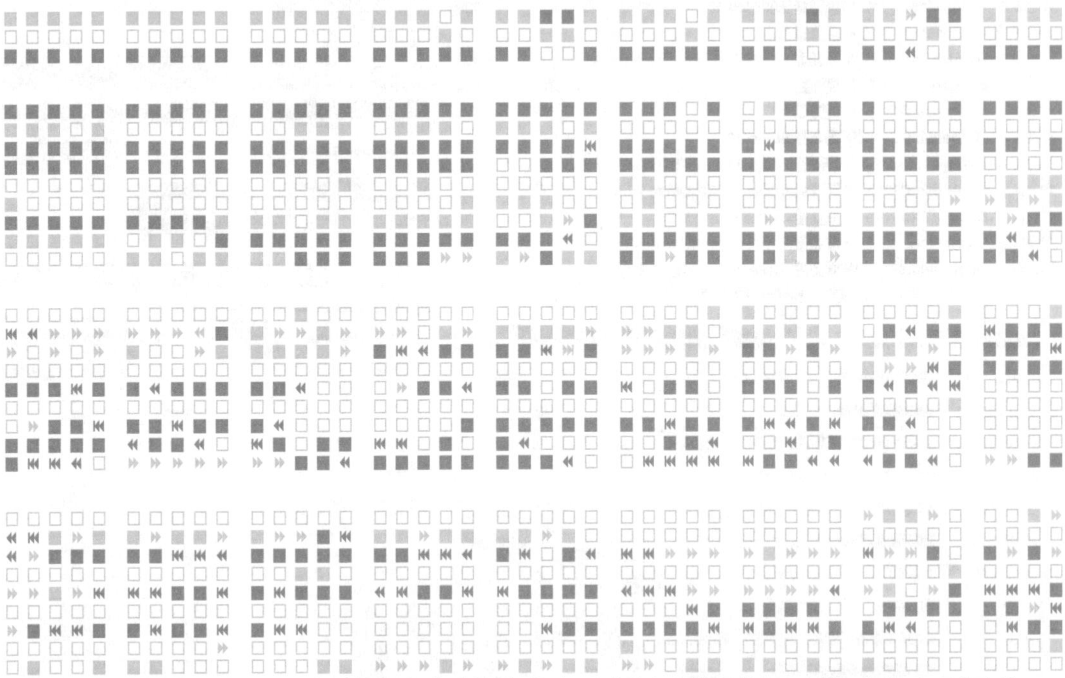

KEY: On all match | On bench | Subbed or sent off (Counting game) | Subbed or sent off (playing less than 70 minutes) | Subbed on from bench (Counting Game) | Subbed on (playing less than 70 minutes) | Subbed on and then subbed or sent off (Counting Game) | Subbed on and then subbed or sent off (playing less than 70 minutes) | Not in 16

KILMARNOCK

Final Position: **7th**

NICKNAME: KILLIE

KEY: Won / Drawn / Lost

							Attendance
1	spl	Hibernian	A	W	1-0	Boyd 73	10,933
2	spl	Celtic	H	L	2-4	McDonald 14; Wales 28	10,500
3	spl	Hearts	A	L	0-3		11,403
4	cisr2	Hamilton	H	W	3-0	Invincible 63,86; McDonald 70	3,375
5	spl	Dunfermline	H	W	1-0	Invincible 11	4,854
6	spl	Livingston	A	W	2-0	Lilley 60; Invincible 72	3,106
7	spl	Aberdeen	H	L	0-1		6,686
8	cisr3	Hearts	A	L	1-2	Leven 56	5,924
9	spl	Dundee Utd	H	W	5-2	Boyd 7,16,33,37 pen,84	4,711
10	spl	Rangers	A	L	0-2		46,278
11	spl	Dundee	A	L	1-3	Boyd 5	4,637
12	spl	Inverness CT	H	D	2-2	Murray 5; Greer 27	4,721
13	spl	Motherwell	A	W	1-0	Nish 57	4,521
14	spl	Hibernian	H	W	3-1	Nish 20,42; Dargo 40	5,959
15	spl	Celtic	A	L	1-2	Nish 89	57,348
16	spl	Hearts	H	D	1-1	Leven 31	6,129
17	spl	Dunfermline	A	L	1-4	Wales 80	4,344
18	spl	Livingston	H	L	1-3	Johnston 25	5,389
19	spl	Aberdeen	A	L	2-3	Invincible 7; Leven 18	11,139
20	spl	Dundee Utd	A	L	0-3		5,097
21	spl	Rangers	H	L	0-1		11,156
22	spl	Dundee	H	W	3-1	Invincible 18; Ford 38; Boyd 82	5,468
23	spl	Inverness CT	A	W	2-0	Invincible 79,90	1,346
24	scr3	Motherwell	H	W	2-0	McDonald 42; Boyd 45	6,093
25	spl	Motherwell	H	W	2-0	Boyd 1,44	5,225
26	spl	Hibernian	A	L	0-3		12,660
27	spl	Celtic	H	L	0-1		9,723
28	scr4	Hearts	A	D	2-2	Nish 25; Naismith 89	10,308
29	spl	Hearts	A	L	0-3		9,220
30	scr4r	Hearts	H	L	1-3	Boyd 90	6,366
31	spl	Dunfermline	H	W	2-1	Naismith 12; Boyd 43	4,701
32	spl	Rangers	A	L	1-2	Boyd 76	48,575
33	spl	Livingston	A	L	1-3	Johnston 13	2,536
34	spl	Aberdeen	H	L	0-1		5,181
35	spl	Dundee Utd	H	W	3-0	Boyd 27,78 pen; Invincible 88	4,353
36	spl	Dundee	A	L	0-1		5,494
37	spl	Inverness CT	H	L	0-1		4,862
38	spl	Motherwell	A	D	1-1	Leven 33	4,999
39	spl	Dundee	H	W	1-0	Dargo 84	3,770
40	spl	Inverness CT	A	W	2-1	McDonald 21; Leven 72 pen	3,108
41	spl	Dundee Utd	A	D	1-1	Boyd 53	6,576
42	spl	Livingston	H	W	2-0	Boyd 75; Johnston 85	4,184
43	spl	Dunfermline	H	W	4-0	Locke 26; Dodds 46; Boyd 54; McDonald 64	5,100

MONTHLY POINTS TALLY

AUGUST	6	50%
SEPTEMBER	6	67%
OCTOBER	7	47%
NOVEMBER	1	8%
DECEMBER	3	25%
JANUARY	6	50%
FEBRUARY	3	33%
MARCH	3	33%
APRIL	7	47%
MAY	7	78%

KEY PLAYERS - GOALSCORERS

Kris Boyd

Goals in the League	17	**Player Strike Rate** Average number of minutes between League goals scored by player	145
Contribution to Attacking Power Average number of minutes between League team goals while on pitch	19	**Club Strike Rate** Average number of minutes between League goals scored by club	70

	PLAYER	LGE GOALS	GOALS ALL	POWER	STRIKE RATE
1	Kris Boyd	17	19	70	145 mins
2	Danny Invincible	7	9	72	361 mins
3	Colin Nish	4	5	82	369 mins
4	Allan Johnston	3	3	78	548 mins
5	Peter Leven	4	5	61	624 mins

KEY PLAYERS - MIDFIELDERS

Peter Leven

Goals in the League	4	**Contribution to Attacking Power** Average number of minutes between League team goals while on pitch	61
Defensive Rating Average number of mins between League goals conceded while he was on the pitch	71	**Scoring Difference** Defensive Rating minus Contribution to Attacking Power	10

	PLAYER	LGE GOALS	DEF RATE	POWER	SCORE DIFF
1	Peter Leven	4	71	61	10 mins
2	Gary McDonald	3	60	71	-11 mins
3	James Fowler	0	63	76	-13 mins
4	Danny Invincible	7	59	72	-13 mins
5	Gary Locke	1	62	76	-14 mins

KEY PLAYERS - DEFENDERS

Garry Hay

Goals Conceded The number of League goals conceded while he was on the pitch	26	**Clean Sheets** In games when he played at least 70 minutes	7
Defensive Rating Ave number of mins between League goals conceded while on the pitch	76	**Club Defensive Rating** Average number of mins between League goals conceded by the club this season	62

	PLAYER	CON LGE	CLEAN SHEETS	DEF RATE
1	Garry Hay	26	7	76 mins
2	Frederic Dindeleux	39	7	63 mins
3	David Lilley	47	8	61 mins
4	Gordon Greer	28	4	59 mins
5	Simon Ford	29	3	54 mins

KEY GOALKEEPER

Alan Combe

Goals Conceded in the League	50	**Counting Games** Games when he played at least 70 mins	32
Defensive Rating Ave number of mins between League goals conceded while on the pitch	58	**Clean Sheets** In games when he played at least 70 mins	8

LEAGUE GOALS

Kris Boyd

Minutes on the pitch	2471	League average (mins between goals)	145
Goals in the League	17		

	PLAYER	MINS	GOALS	AVE
1	Boyd	2471	17	145
2	Invincible	2529	7	361
3	Nish	1476	4	369
4	Leven	2497	4	624
5	McDonald	3265	3	1088
6	Johnston	1643	3	548
7	Wales	1106	2	553
8	Dargo	900	2	450
9	Dodds	481	1	481
10	Naismith	1364	1	1364
11	Ford	1575	1	1575
12	Murray	909	1	909
	Other		3	
	TOTAL		49	

DISCIPLINARY RECORDS

	PLAYER	YELLOW	RED	AVE
1	Greer	7	0	235
2	Locke	7	0	281
3	Lilley	9	1	287
4	Nish	4	1	295
5	Fowler	5	0	439
6	Dargo	2	0	450
7	Hay	4	0	494
8	Naismith	2	0	682
9	Murray	1	0	909
10	Wales	1	0	1106
11	Boyd	2	0	1235
12	Leven	2	0	1248
13	Combe	2	0	1440
	Other	4	0	
	TOTAL	52	2	

TOP POINT EARNERS

	PLAYER	GAMES	AV PTS
1	Steven Naismith	12	1.75
2	Garry Hay	20	1.60
3	Gordon Greer	16	1.50
4	Frederic Dindeleux	26	1.38
5	Peter Leven	25	1.36
6	Danny Invincible	26	1.35
7	Colin Nish	12	1.33
8	Kris Boyd	27	1.30
9	David Lilley	31	1.29
10	Gary McDonald	36	1.28
	CLUB AVERAGE:		1.29

TEAM OF THE SEASON

D
Garry Hay
CG: 20 DR: 76
M
Peter Leven
CG: 25 SD: 10
D
Frederic Dindeleux
CG: 26 DR: 63
M
Gary McDonald
CG: 36 SD: -11
F
Kris Boyd
CG: 27 SR: 145
G
Alan Combe
CG: 32 DR: 58
D
David Lilley
CG: 31 DR: 61
M
James Fowler
CG: 23 SD: -13
F
Colin Nish
CG: 12 SR: 369
D
Gordon Greer
CG: 16 DR: 59
M
Danny Invincible
CG: 26 SD: -13

LEAGUE APPEARANCES AND BOOKINGS

	AGE (on 01/07/04)	IN NAMED 16	APPEARANCES	COUNTING GAMES	MINUTES ON PITCH	YELLOW CARDS	RED CARDS	THIS SEASON	HOME COUNTRY
Goalkeepers									
Cameron Bell	18	3	0	0	0	0	0	-	Scotland
Alan Combe	31	33	32	32	2880	2	0	1	Scotland (85)
Craig Samson	21	3	0	0	0	0	0	-	Scotland
Graeme Smith	22	37	6	6	540	0	0	-	Scotland
Defenders									
Shaun Dillon	20	9	6	4	436	1	0	-	Scotland
Frederic Dindeleux	31	31	29	26	2463	0	0	-	France
Liam Fontaine	19	7	3	1	162	0	0	-	England
Simon Ford	23	21	18	17	1575	1	0	-	England
Gordon Greer	24	28	22	16	1649	7	0	-	Scotland
Jamie Hamill	18	2	0	0	0	0	0	-	Scotland
Garry Hay	27	31	25	20	1978	4	0	-	Scotland
David Lilley	27	33	33	31	2872	9	1	-	Scotland
Neil McGregor	20	3	0	0	0	0	0	-	Scotland
Gary Wild	16	1	0	0	0	0	0	-	Scotland
Mickael Wolski	26	4	0	0	0	0	0	-	France
Midfielders									
Mark Canning	21	9	0	0	0	0	0	-	Scotland
Rhian Dodds	25	26	8	5	481	0	0	-	England
James Fowler	24	36	29	23	2198	5	0	-	Scotland
Danny Invincible	26	32	31	26	2529	0	0	-	Australia
Scott Johnstone	20	5	2	0	27	0	0	-	Scotland
Eric Joly	30	13	6	0	170	0	0	-	France
Peter Leven	21	34	32	25	2497	2	0	-	Scotland
Gary Locke	30	27	25	20	1970	7	0	-	Scotland
Gary McDonald	23	38	38	36	3265	2	0	-	Scotland
Stephen Murray	22	38	21	4	909	1	0	-	Scotland
Forwards									
Kris Boyd	21	30	30	27	2471	2	0	-	Scotland
Robert Campbell	18	1	0	0	0	0	0	-	Scotland
Craig Dargo	27	26	20	8	900	2	0	-	Scotland
Allan Johnston	31	32	27	14	1643	1	0	-	Scotland
Rory Loy	17	1	0	0	0	0	0	-	Scotland
Steven Naismith	18	29	24	12	1364	2	0	-	Scotland
Colin Nish	24	29	26	12	1476	4	1	-	Scotland
Gary Wales	26	28	24	8	1106	1	0	-	Scotland

SQUAD APPEARANCES

Match	1	2	3	4	5	6	7	8	9	10	11	12	13	14	15	16	17	18	19	20	21	22	23	24	25	26	27	28	29	30	31	32	33	34	35	36	37	38	39	40	41	42	43
Venue	A	H	A	H	H	A	H	A	H	A	A	H	A	H	A	H	A	H	A	A	H	H	A	H	H	A	H	A	A	H	H	A	A	H	H	A	H	A	H	A	A	H	H
Competition	L	L	L	W	L	L	L	W	L	L	L	L	L	L	L	L	L	L	L	L	L	L	L	F	L	L	L	F	L	F	L	L	L	L	L	L	L	L	L	L	L	L	L
Result	W	L	L	W	W	W	L	L	W	L	L	D	W	W	L	D	L	L	L	L	L	W	W	W	W	L	L	D	L	L	W	L	L	L	W	L	L	D	W	W	D	W	W

Goalkeepers
Cameron Bell
Alan Combe
Craig Samson
Graeme Smith

Defenders
Shaun Dillon
Frederic Dindeleux
Liam Fontaine
Simon Ford
Gordon Greer
Jamie Hamill
Garry Hay
David Lilley
Neil McGregor
Gary Wild
Mickael Wolski

Midfielders
Mark Canning
Rhian Dodds
James Fowler
Danny Invincible
Scott Johnstone
Eric Joly
Peter Leven
Gary Locke
Gary McDonald
Stephen Murray

Forwards
Kris Boyd
Robert Campbell
Craig Dargo
Allan Johnston
Rory Loy
Steven Naismith
Colin Nish
Gary Wales

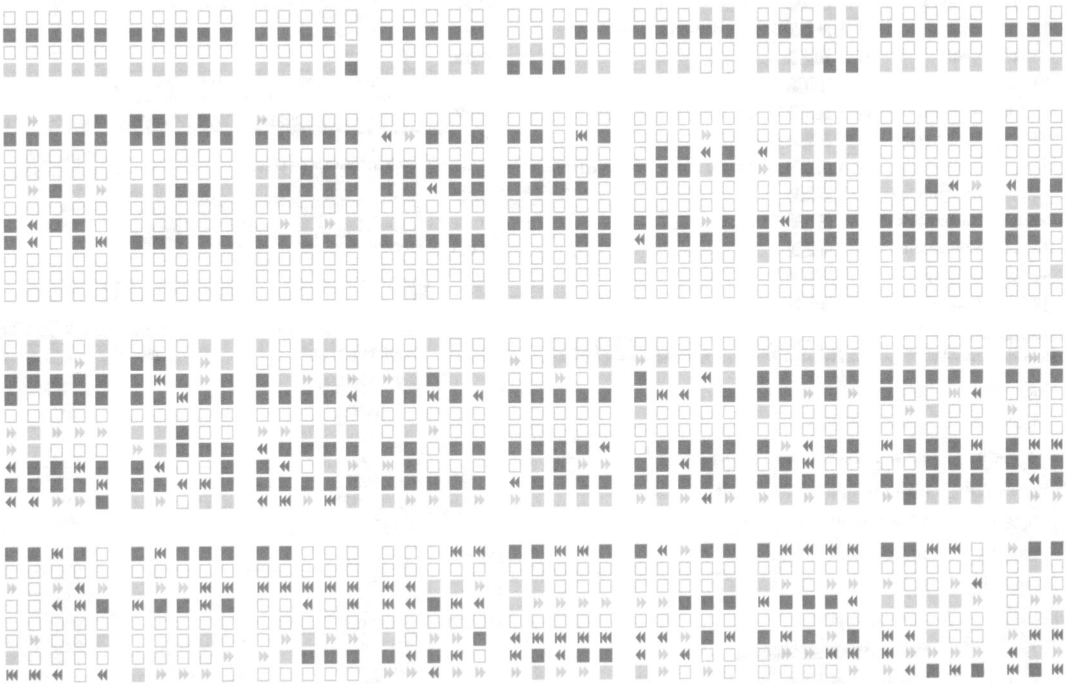

KEY: On all match | On bench | Subbed or sent off (Counting game) | Subbed or sent off (playing less than 70 minutes) | Subbed on from bench (Counting Game) | Subbed on (playing less than 70 minutes) | Subbed on and then subbed or sent off (Counting Game) | Subbed on and then subbed or sent off (playing less than 70 minutes) | Not in 16

INVERNESS CALEDONIAN THISTLE

Final Position: **8th**

NICKNAME: CALEY THISTLE

KEY: ☐Won ☐Drawn ☐Lost

							Attendance
1	spl	Livingston	A	L	0-3		3,310
2	spl	Dunfermline	H	W	2-0	Golabek 12; Juanjo 70	1,972
3	spl	Celtic	H	L	1-3	Wilson 44 pen	8,736
4	cisr2	Ross County	A	W	1-0	Tokely 64	3,315
5	spl	Dundee Utd	A	L	1-2	Wilson 60 pen	6,017
6	spl	Hibernian	H	L	1-2	Wilson 37 pen	2,011
7	spl	Rangers	A	L	0-1		47,063
8	cisr3	Motherwell	H	L	1-3	Tokely 58	1,464
9	spl	Hearts	A	L	0-1		10,340
10	spl	Motherwell	H	D	1-1	McCaffrey 90	1,117
11	spl	Aberdeen	H	L	1-3	McBain 36	9,530
12	spl	Kilmarnock	A	D	2-2	Wilson 16; Fox 83	4,721
13	spl	Dundee	H	W	2-1	Bayne 40; Juanjo 58	1,254
14	spl	Livingston	H	W	2-0	Bayne 39; Wilson 87	1,279
15	spl	Dunfermline	A	D	1-1	Duncan 79	4,921
16	spl	Celtic	A	L	0-3		57,654
17	spl	Dundee Utd	H	D	1-1	Juanjo 50	1,125
18	spl	Hibernian	A	L	1-2	Juanjo 34	9,728
19	spl	Rangers	H	D	1-1	Bayne 3	6,543
20	spl	Hearts	H	D	1-1	Juanjo 68 pen	2,011
21	spl	Motherwell	A	W	2-1	Hart 17; Bayne 45	4,267
22	spl	Aberdeen	A	D	0-0		18,250
23	spl	Kilmarnock	H	L	0-2		1,346
24	scr3	St Johnstone	H	W	1-0	Golabek 74	2,021
25	spl	Dundee	A	L	1-3	Brewster 90	5,567
26	spl	Livingston	A	W	4-1	Hart 8; Duncan 39; Bayne 50; Juanjo 73	4,106
27	spl	Dunfermline	H	W	2-0	Wilson 35; Brewster 74	5,449
28	scr4	Aberdeen	A	L	1-2	Brewster 24	10,595
29	spl	Dundee Utd	A	D	1-1	Wilson 37	6,110
30	spl	Hibernian	H	W	3-0	Juanjo 39; Brewster 50; Wilson 77	4,443
31	spl	Rangers	A	D	1-1	Prunty 90	49,345
32	spl	Hearts	A	W	2-0	Dods 55; Wilson 73 pen	9,822
33	spl	Celtic	H	L	0-2		7,000
34	spl	Aberdeen	H	L	0-1		7,026
35	spl	Kilmarnock	A	W	1-0	Wilson 32	4,862
36	spl	Motherwell	H	W	1-0	Bayne 20	3,746
37	spl	Dundee	H	W	3-2	McBain 17; Prunty 38; Brewster 65	4,786
38	spl	Dunfermline	A	D	0-0		4,481
39	spl	Kilmarnock	H	L	1-2	Tokely 28 pen	3,108
40	spl	Livingston	H	L	0-1		3,021
41	spl	Dundee	A	D	1-1	Fox 88	6,691
42	spl	Dundee Utd	H	L	0-1		5,479

MONTHLY POINTS TALLY

AUGUST	3	25%
SEPTEMBER	0	0%
OCTOBER	8	53%
NOVEMBER	2	17%
DECEMBER	6	50%
JANUARY	6	50%
FEBRUARY	1	33%
MARCH	7	58%
APRIL	10	56%
MAY	1	11%

KEY PLAYERS - GOALSCORERS

Barry Wilson

Goals in the League	10	Player Strike Rate Average number of minutes between League goals scored by player	269
Contribution to Attacking Power Average number of minutes between League team goals while on pitch	10	Club Strike Rate Average number of minutes between League goals scored by club	83

	PLAYER	LGE GOALS	GOALS ALL	POWER	STRIKE RATE
1	Barry Wilson	10	10	79	269 mins
2	Carricondo Juanjo	7	7	74	297 mins
3	Graham Bayne	6	6	91	459 mins
4	Stuart McCaffrey	1	1	80	1128 mins
5	Russell Duncan	2	2	83	1216 mins

KEY PLAYERS - MIDFIELDERS

Richard Hart

Goals in the League	2	Contribution to Attacking Power Average number of minutes between League team goals while on pitch	81
Defensive Rating Average number of mins between League goals conceded while he was on the pitch	84	Scoring Difference Defensive Rating minus Contribution to Attacking Power	3

	PLAYER	LGE GOALS	DEF RATE	POWER	SCORE DIFF
1	Richard Hart	2	84	81	3 mins
2	Russell Duncan	2	72	84	-12 mins
3	Barry Wilson	10	64	79	-15 mins
4	Roy McBain	2	70	88	-18 mins

KEY PLAYERS - DEFENDERS

Darren Dods

Goals Conceded The number of League goals conceded while he was on the pitch	29	Clean Sheets In games when he played at least 70 minutes	8
Defensive Rating Ave number of mins between League goals conceded while on the pitch	87	Club Defensive Rating Average number of mins between League goals conceded by the club this season	73

	PLAYER	CON LGE	CLEAN SHEETS	DEF RATE
1	Darren Dods	29	8	87 mins
2	Grant Munro	41	9	76 mins
3	Ross Tokely	41	9	76 mins
4	Stuart Golabek	45	9	74 mins
5	Stuart McCaffrey	23	1	49 mins

KEY GOALKEEPER

Mark Brown

Goals Conceded in the League	47	Counting Games Games when he played at least 70 mins	37
Defensive Rating Ave number of mins between League goals conceded while on the pitch	72	Clean Sheets In games when he played at least 70 mins	9

LEAGUE GOALS

Barry Wilson

Minutes on the pitch	2690	League average (mins between goals)	269
Goals in the League	10		

	PLAYER	MINS	GOALS	AVE
1	Wilson	2690	10	269
2	Juanjo	2077	7	297
3	Bayne	2756	6	459
4	Brewster	1035	4	259
5	Prunty	801	2	401
6	Fox	227	2	114
7	Duncan	2432	2	1216
8	Hart	2845	2	1423
9	McBain	2726	2	1363
10	Golabek	3330	1	3330
11	Dods	2520	1	2520
12	McCaffrey	1128	1	1128
	Other		1	
	TOTAL		41	

DISCIPLINARY RECORDS

	PLAYER	YELLOW	RED	AVE
1	Black	3	0	225
2	Tokely	7	2	347
3	McCaffrey	2	1	376
4	Munro	6	1	445
5	Duncan	5	0	486
6	Brewster	2	0	517
7	McBain	5	0	545
8	Golabek	6	0	555
9	Keogh	2	0	682
10	Bayne	4	0	689
11	Dods	3	0	840
12	Hart	3	0	948
13	Wilson	2	0	1345
	Other	2	1	
	TOTAL	52	5	

TOP POINT EARNERS

	PLAYER	GAMES	AV PTS
1	Carricondo Juanjo	21	1.43
2	Darren Dods	28	1.39
3	Richard Hart	29	1.38
4	Roy McBain	26	1.27
5	Grant Munro	34	1.26
6	Barry Wilson	28	1.21
7	Russell Duncan	26	1.19
8	Ross Tokely	34	1.18
9	Graham Bayne	29	1.17
10	Mark Brown	37	1.11
	CLUB AVERAGE:		1.16

TEAM OF THE SEASON

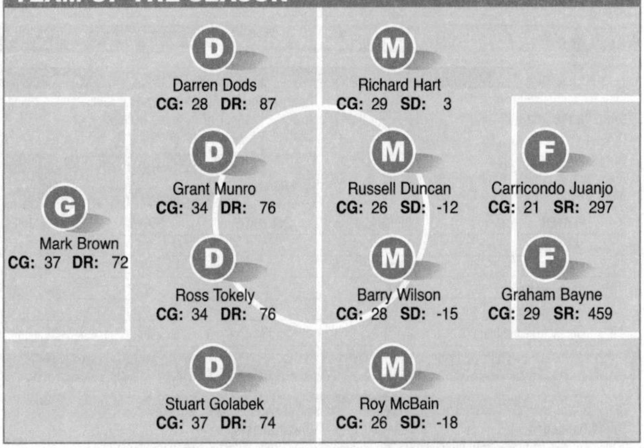

D
Darren Dods
CG: 28 DR: 87
M
Richard Hart
CG: 29 SD: 3
D
Grant Munro
CG: 34 DR: 76
M
Russell Duncan
CG: 26 SD: -12
F
Carricondo Juanjo
CG: 21 SR: 297
G
Mark Brown
CG: 37 DR: 72
D
Ross Tokely
CG: 34 DR: 76
M
Barry Wilson
CG: 28 SD: -15
F
Graham Bayne
CG: 29 SR: 459
D
Stuart Golabek
CG: 37 DR: 74
M
Roy McBain
CG: 26 SD: -18

LEAGUE APPEARANCES AND BOOKINGS

	AGE (on 01/07/04)	IN NAMED 16	APPEARANCES	COUNTING GAMES	MINUTES ON PITCH	YELLOW CARDS	RED CARDS	THIS SEASON	HOME COUNTRY
Goalkeepers									
Mark Brown	24	38	38	37	3371	2	0	-	Scotland
Mike Fraser	21	37	2	0	49	0	0	-	Scotland
Jonathon Smith	17	0	0	0	0	0	0	-	Scotland
Defenders									
Darren Dods	40	36	28	28	2520	3	0	-	Scotland
Stuart Golabek	30	37	37	37	3330	6	0	-	Scotland
Richard Hastings	28	27	11	6	660	0	0	-	Canada
Stuart McCaffrey	26	31	15	12	1128	2	1	-	Scotland
Grant Munro	24	36	36	34	3119	6	1	-	Scotland
Ross Tokely	26	35	35	34	3127	7	2	-	Scotland
Midfielders									
Ian Black	20	29	13	6	676	3	0	-	Scotland
Russell Duncan	24	38	30	26	2432	5	0	-	Scotland
Liam Fox	21	24	9	1	227	0	0	-	Scotland
Richard Hart	27	37	37	29	2845	3	0	-	Scotland
Roy McBain	30	37	35	26	2726	5	0	-	Scotland
David Proctor	21	25	5	0	126	0	0	-	Scotland
Darren Thomson	20	11	1	0	11	0	0	-	Scotland
Barry Wilson	33	37	36	28	2690	2	0	-	Scotland
Forwards									
Graham Bayne	25	38	38	29	2756	4	0	-	Scotland
Craig Brewster	38	13	13	11	1035	2	0	-	Scotland
Bajram Fetai	19	13	9	0	161	0	0	-	Denmark
Stephen Hislop	27	7	7	0	185	1	0	-	Scotland
Carricondo Juanjo	26	30	29	21	2077	0	1	-	Spain
Liam Keogh	23	22	21	13	1364	2	0	-	Scotland
Rory McAllister	-	5	4	0	71	1	0	-	Scotland
Bryan Prunty	22	37	27	5	801	0	0	-	Scotland

SQUAD APPEARANCES

Match	1	2	3	4	5	6	7	8	9	10	11	12	13	14	15	16	17	18	19	20	21	22	23	24	25	26	27	28	29	30	31	32	33	34	35	36	37	38	39	40	41	42
Venue	A	H	H	A	A	H	A	H	A	H	H	A	H	H	A	A	H	A	H	H	A	A	H	H	A	A	H	A	A	H	A	A	H	H	A	H	H	A	H	H	A	H
Competition	L	L	L	W	L	L	L	W	L	L	L	L	L	L	L	L	L	L	L	L	L	L	L	F	L	L	L	F	L	L	L	L	L	L	L	L	L	L	L	L	L	L
Result	L	W	L	W	L	L	L	L	L	D	L	D	W	W	D	L	D	L	D	D	W	D	L	W	L	W	W	L	D	W	D	W	L	L	W	W	W	D	L	L	D	L

Goalkeepers
Mark Brown
Mike Fraser
Jonathon Smith
Defenders
Darren Dods
Stuart Golabek
Richard Hastings
Stuart McCaffrey
Grant Munro
Ross Tokely
Midfielders
Ian Black
Russell Duncan
Liam Fox
Richard Hart
Roy McBain
David Proctor
Darren Thomson
Barry Wilson
Forwards
Graham Bayne
Craig Brewster
Bajram Fetai
Stephen Hislop
Carricondo Juanjo
Liam Keogh
Rory McAllister
Bryan Prunty

KEY: On all match · On bench · Subbed or sent off (Counting game) · Subbed or sent off (playing less than 70 minutes) · Subbed on from bench (Counting Game) · Subbed on (playing less than 70 minutes) · Subbed on and then subbed or sent off (Counting Game) · Subbed on and then subbed or sent off (playing less than 70 minutes) · Not in 16

DUNDEE UNITED

Final Position: **9th**

NICKNAME: THE TERRORS/ ARABS

KEY: Won / Drawn / Lost

							Attendance
1	spl	Dunfermline	A	D	1-1	McIntyre 75	6,512
2	spl	Dundee	H	L	1-2	Archibald 90	11,118
3	spl	Livingston	A	D	1-1	Dodds 61 pen	3,659
4	cisr2	Stranraer	H	W	3-1	Grady 43; Kerr 63; Innes 73	2,511
5	spl	Inverness CT	H	W	2-1	Innes 71; McIntyre 86	6,017
6	spl	Aberdeen	H	D	1-1	Wilson 83 pen	10,995
7	spl	Motherwell	A	L	2-4	Grady 45; McIntyre 69	5,091
8	cisr3	Clyde	H	W	4-0	McIntyre 35; Robson 45; Brebner 54; Wilson 64 pen	2,336
9	spl	Kilmarnock	A	L	2-5	Archibald 29; Dodds 73	4,711
10	spl	Celtic	H	L	0-3		10,329
11	spl	Hibernian	A	L	0-2		9,927
12	spl	Rangers	A	D	1-1	Robson 90	46,796
13	spl	Hearts	H	D	1-1	Wilson 62	5,723
14	spl	Dunfermline	H	L	1-2	Wilson 7 pen	6,297
15	spl	Dundee	A	L	0-1		9,845
16	scqf	Hibernian	H	W	2-1	McIntyre 87,107	4,865
17	spl	Livingston	H	W	1-0	McCracken 78	5,507
18	spl	Inverness CT	A	D	1-1	McIntyre 63	1,125
19	spl	Aberdeen	A	L	0-1		12,038
20	spl	Motherwell	H	L	0-1		5,252
21	spl	Kilmarnock	H	W	3-0	Brebner 17; Robson 22; McIntyre 46	5,097
22	spl	Celtic	A	L	0-1		56,318
23	spl	Hibernian	H	L	1-4	Scotland 8	10,152
24	spl	Rangers	H	D	1-1	McCracken 11	10,461
25	spl	Hearts	A	L	2-3	Robson 19; Archibald 53	10,305
26	scr3	Gretna	A	W	4-3	Robson 4; Kerr 7; Wilson 21 pen; Crawford 56	3,000
27	spl	Dunfermline	A	D	1-1	Crawford 72	6,589
28	spl	Dundee	H	D	2-2	Duff 12; McIntyre 79	12,703
29	slcr5	Rangers	A	L	1-7	Scotland 50	25,622
30	scr4	Queen of South	A	W	3-0	McIntyre 13; Wilson 24; Duff 39	5,532
31	spl	Livingston	A	W	2-0	Crawford 14; Grady 41	5,158
32	spl	Inverness CT	H	D	1-1	Munro 30 og	6,110
33	scqf	Aberdeen	H	W	4-1	Archibald 19; Grady 29,47; Crawford 41	8,661
34	spl	Aberdeen	H	L	1-2	Scotland 60	6,688
35	spl	Motherwell	A	L	0-2		5,110
36	spl	Kilmarnock	A	L	0-3		4,353
37	spl	Celtic	H	L	2-3	McIntyre 24; Robson 71	10,828
38	spl	Hibernian	A	L	2-3	McIntyre 63; Scotland 77	11,058
39	scsf	Hibernian	H	W	2-1	McIntyre 73; Scotland 76	27,271
40	spl	Rangers	A	W	1-0	Duff 8	49,302
41	spl	Hearts	H	W	2-1	Robson 37; Brebner 90	7,704
42	spl	Livingston	H	D	1-1	Crawford 37	7,687
43	spl	Dundee	A	W	2-1	Wilson 52; McIntyre 70	11,263
44	spl	Kilmarnock	H	D	1-1	McIntyre 16	6,576
45	spl	Dunfermline	H	L	0-1		10,763
46	spl	Inverness CT	A	W	1-0	Robson 82 pen	5,479
47	scfin	Celtic	N	L	0-1		50,635

MONTHLY POINTS TALLY

AUGUST	5	42%
SEPTEMBER	1	11%
OCTOBER	2	13%
NOVEMBER	4	33%
DECEMBER	3	25%
JANUARY	3	25%
FEBRUARY	4	67%
MARCH	0	0%
APRIL	10	67%
MAY	4	44%

KEY PLAYERS - GOALSCORERS

James McIntyre

Goals in the League	10	**Player Strike Rate** Average number of minutes between League goals scored by player	288
Contribution to Attacking Power Average number of minutes between League team goals while on pitch	15	**Club Strike Rate** Average number of minutes between League goals scored by club	83

	PLAYER	LGE GOALS	GOALS ALL	POWER	STRIKE RATE
1	James McIntyre	10	15	73	288 mins
2	Stevie Crawford	3	5	82	437 mins
3	Barry Robson	6	8	87	508 mins
4	James Grady	2	5	114	741 mins
5	Mark Wilson	4	7	83	817 mins

KEY PLAYERS - MIDFIELDERS

Mark Kerr

Goals in the League	0	**Contribution to Attacking Power** Average number of minutes between League team goals while on pitch	73
Defensive Rating Average number of mins between League goals conceded while on the pitch	60	**Scoring Difference** Defensive Rating minus Contribution to Attacking Power	-13

	PLAYER	LGE GOALS	DEF RATE	POWER	SCORE DIFF
1	Mark Kerr	0	60	73	-13 mins
2	Stuart Duff	2	57	85	-28 mins
3	Barry Robson	6	58	87	-29 mins
4	Grant Brebner	2	55	85	-30 mins
5	Derek McInnes	0	59	97	-38 mins

KEY PLAYERS - DEFENDERS

Paul Ritchie

Goals Conceded Total number of goals conceded while the player was on the pitch	32	**Clean Sheets** In games when player was on pitch for at least 70 minutes	3
Defensive Rating Ave number of mins between League goals conceded while on the pitch	65	**Club Defensive Rating** Average number of mins between League goals conceded by the club this season	58

	PLAYER	CON LGE	CLEAN SHEETS	DEF RATE
1	Paul Ritchie	32	3	65 mins
2	Alan Archibald	59	5	58 mins
3	Mark Wilson	57	4	57 mins
4	David McCracken	35	2	52 mins
5	Chris Innes	29	1	48 mins

KEY GOALKEEPER

Tony Bullock

Goals Conceded in the League	37	**Counting Games** In games when player was on pitch for at least 70 minutes	25
Defensive Rating Ave number of mins between League goals conceded while on the pitch	62	**Clean Sheets** In games when he played at least 70 mins	4

LEAGUE GOALS

James McIntyre

Minutes on the pitch	2881	League average (mins between goals)	288
Goals in the League	10		

	PLAYER	MINS	GOALS	AVE
1	McIntyre	2881	10	288
2	Robson	3048	6	508
3	Wilson	3267	4	817
4	Archibald	3420	3	1140
5	Crawford	1312	3	437
6	Scotland	1256	3	419
7	Brebner	2645	2	1323
8	McCracken	1803	2	902
9	Grady	1482	2	741
10	Dodds	970	2	485
11	Duff	1879	2	940
12	Innes	1405	1	1405
	Other		1	
	TOTAL		41	

DISCIPLINARY RECORDS

	PLAYER	YELLOW	RED	AVE
1	Ritchie	8	1	230
2	McInnes	8	0	242
3	Robson	10	1	277
4	Kenneth	3	0	326
5	Innes	2	1	468
6	Dodds	2	0	485
7	Brebner	5	0	529
8	Samuel	1	0	599
9	Grady	2	0	741
10	Wilson	3	1	816
11	Archibald	4	0	855
12	McIntyre	3	0	960
13	McCracken	1	0	1803
	Other	0	0	
	TOTAL	52	4	

TOP POINT EARNERS

	PLAYER	GAMES	AV PTS
1	Mark Kerr	20	1.25
2	Tony Bullock	25	1.16
3	James McIntyre	31	1.06
4	Grant Brebner	25	1.00
5	Paul Ritchie	23	0.96
6	Alan Archibald	38	0.95
7	Stuart Duff	20	0.95
8	Barry Robson	33	0.94
9	Mark Wilson	35	0.94
10	David McCracken	18	0.94
	CLUB AVERAGE:		0.95

LEAGUE APPEARANCES AND BOOKINGS

	AGE (on 01/07/04)	IN NAMED 16	APPEARANCES	COUNTING GAMES	MINUTES ON PITCH	YELLOW CARDS	RED CARDS	THIS SEASON	HOME COUNTRY
Goalkeepers									
Tony Bullock	33	27	26	25	2311	0	0	-	England
Nick Colgan	31	13	1	1	90	0	0	2	Rep of Ireland (15)
Lars Hirschfeld	26	18	2	1	119	0	0	-	Canada
Paul Jarvie	23	16	10	10	900	0	0	-	Scotland
Euan McLean	19	2	0	0	0	0	0	-	Scotland
Defenders									
Alan Archibald	27	38	38	38	3420	4	0	-	Scotland
Barry Callaghan	18	7	1	0	6	0	0	-	Scotland
Ross Gardiner	18	11	0	0	0	0	0	-	Scotland
Chris Innes	28	20	16	15	1405	2	1	-	Scotland
Gary Kenneth	18	21	11	11	980	3	0	-	Scotland
Lee Mair	24	4	4	3	296	1	0	-	Scotland
David McCracken	23	29	25	18	1803	1	0	-	Scotland
Paul Ritchie	29	29	24	23	2072	8	1	-	Scotland
Mark Wilson	21	37	37	35	3267	3	1	-	Scotland
Midfielders									
Steven Bell	20	4	0	0	0	0	0	-	Scotland
Grant Brebner	27	34	34	25	2645	5	0	-	Scotland
Greg Cameron	17	19	2	0	36	0	0	-	Scotland
Stuart Duff	23	29	25	20	1879	0	0	-	Scotland
Graeme Holmes	21	3	0	0	0	0	0	-	Scotland
Karim Kerkar	28	10	10	1	363	0	0	-	France
Mark Kerr	23	32	30	20	2333	0	0	-	Scotland
Derek McInnes	34	31	27	17	1937	8	0	-	Scotland
Andrew McLaren	32	7	6	0	142	1	0	-	Scotland
Stephen O'Donnell	21	3	0	0	0	0	0	-	Scotland
David Robertson	18	12	0	0	0	0	0	-	Scotland
Barry Robson	26	36	36	33	3048	10	1	-	Scotland
Forwards									
Aaron Conway	20	2	0	0	0	0	0	-	Scotland
Stevie Crawford	31	17	17	13	1312	0	0	-	Scotland
Billy Dodds	36	34	21	6	970	2	0	-	Scotland
James Grady	34	38	29	13	1482	2	0	-	Scotland
James McIntyre	33	36	35	31	2881	3	0	-	Scotland
Collin Samuel	23	27	18	1	599	1	0	-	Trinidad & Tobago
Jason Scotland	26	35	29	9	1256	0	0	-	Trinidad & Tobago

TEAM OF THE SEASON

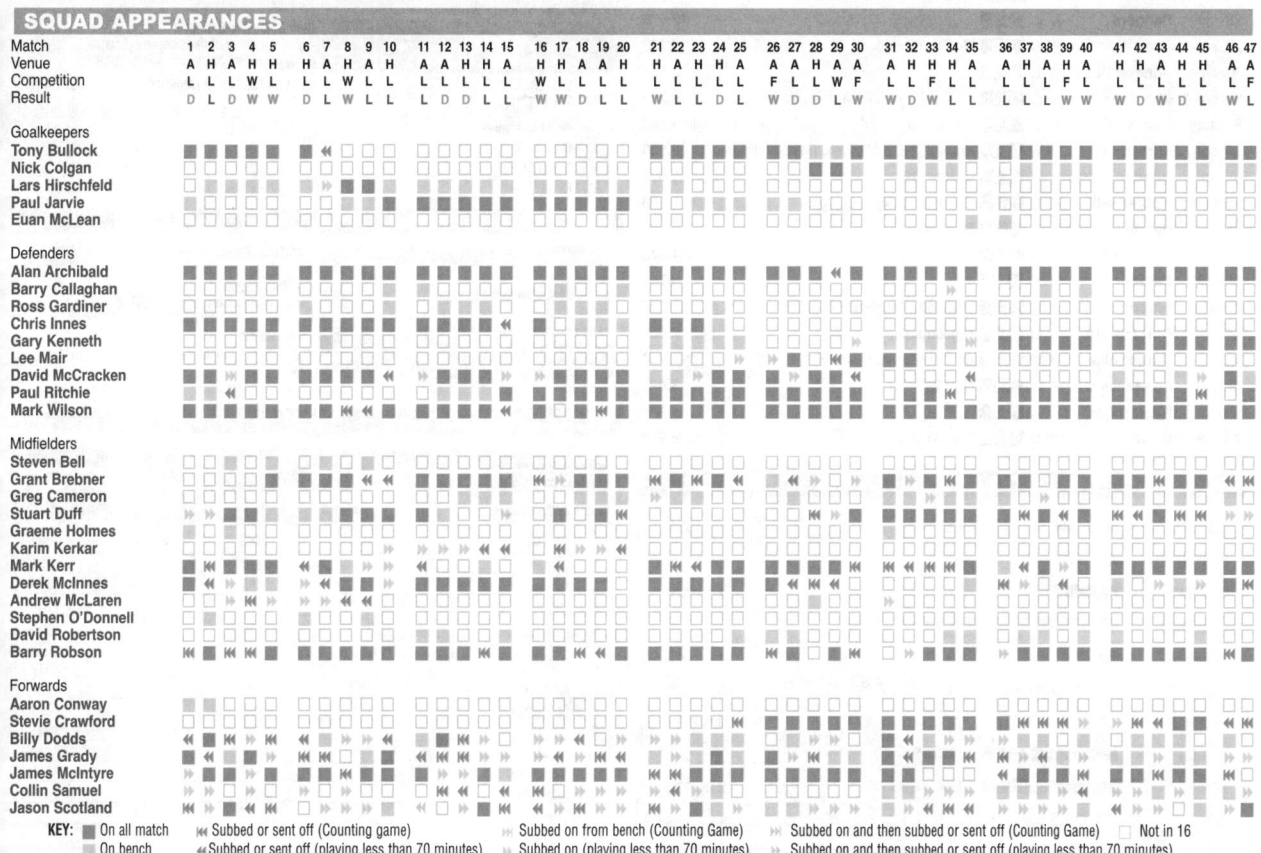

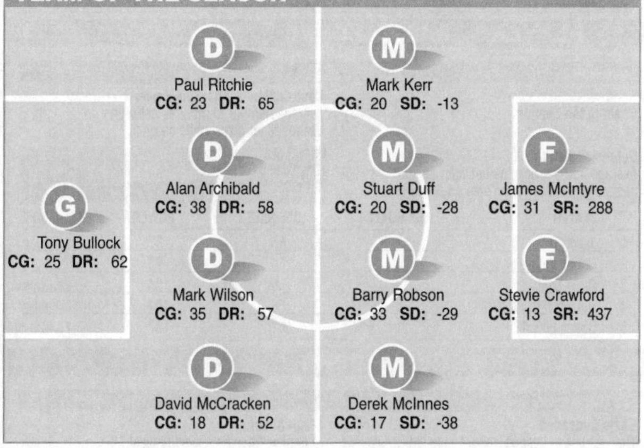
D
Paul Ritchie
CG: 23 DR: 65
M
Mark Kerr
CG: 20 SD: -13
D
Alan Archibald
CG: 38 DR: 58
M
Stuart Duff
CG: 20 SD: -28
F
James McIntyre
CG: 31 SR: 288
G
Tony Bullock
CG: 25 DR: 62
D
Mark Wilson
CG: 35 DR: 57
M
Barry Robson
CG: 33 SD: -29
F
Stevie Crawford
CG: 13 SR: 437
D
David McCracken
CG: 18 DR: 52
M
Derek McInnes
CG: 17 SD: -38

SQUAD APPEARANCES

Match	1	2	3	4	5	6	7	8	9	10	11	12	13	14	15	16	17	18	19	20	21	22	23	24	25	26	27	28	29	30	31	32	33	34	35	36	37	38	39	40	41	42	43	44	45	46	47
Venue	A	H	A	H	H	H	A	H	A	H	A	A	H	H	A	H	H	A	A	H	H	A	H	H	A	A	A	H	A	A	A	H	H	H	A	A	H	A	H	A	H	H	A	H	H	A	A
Competition	L	L	L	W	L	L	L	W	L	L	L	L	L	L	L	W	L	L	L	L	L	L	L	L	L	F	L	L	W	F	L	L	F	L	L	L	L	L	F	L	L	L	L	L	L	L	F
Result	D	L	D	W	W	D	L	W	L	L	L	D	D	L	L	W	W	D	L	L	W	L	L	D	L	W	D	D	L	W	W	D	W	L	L	L	L	L	W	W	W	D	W	D	L	W	L

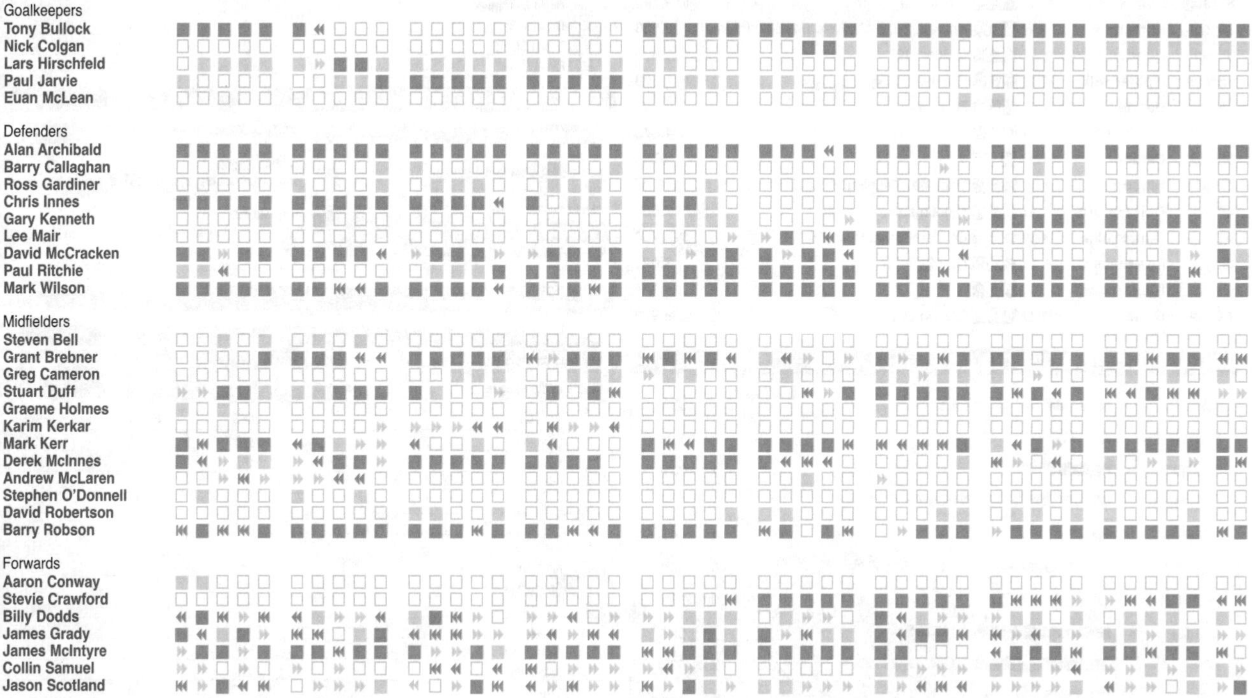
Goalkeepers
Tony Bullock
Nick Colgan
Lars Hirschfeld
Paul Jarvie
Euan McLean
Defenders
Alan Archibald
Barry Callaghan
Ross Gardiner
Chris Innes
Gary Kenneth
Lee Mair
David McCracken
Paul Ritchie
Mark Wilson
Midfielders
Steven Bell
Grant Brebner
Greg Cameron
Stuart Duff
Graeme Holmes
Karim Kerkar
Mark Kerr
Derek McInnes
Andrew McLaren
Stephen O'Donnell
David Robertson
Barry Robson
Forwards
Aaron Conway
Stevie Crawford
Billy Dodds
James Grady
James McIntyre
Collin Samuel
Jason Scotland

KEY: ■ On all match ■ On bench ⏮ Subbed or sent off (Counting game) « Subbed or sent off (playing less than 70 minutes) ⏭ Subbed on from bench (Counting Game) » Subbed on (playing less than 70 minutes) ⏭ Subbed on and then subbed or sent off (Counting Game) » Subbed on and then subbed or sent off (playing less than 70 minutes) □ Not in 16

LIVINGSTON

Final Position: **10th**

NICKNAME: THE LIVI' LIONS

KEY: ☐Won ☐Drawn ☐Lost

							Attendance
1	spl	Inverness CT	H	W	3-0	O'Brien 44; Easton 57; Lovell 66	3,310
2	spl	Rangers	A	L	0-4		48,102
3	spl	Dundee Utd	H	D	1-1	McMenimin 84	3,659
4	cisr2	Stirling	A	W	2-0	Easton 30; Hamilton 90	1,091
5	spl	Aberdeen	A	L	0-2		13,888
6	spl	Kilmarnock	H	L	0-2		3,106
7	spl	Dundee	A	D	0-0		4,387
8	cisr3	Dundee	H	W	2-1	Hamilton 90 pen,111	1,736
9	spl	Motherwell	H	L	2-3	O'Brien 37; Hamilton 45	4,050
10	spl	Hearts	A	D	0-0		10,646
11	spl	Dunfermline	H	W	2-0	Wilson, S 5 og; Snodgrass 41	2,815
12	spl	Celtic	H	L	2-4	O'Brien 45,53	7,695
13	spl	Hibernian	A	L	1-2	Lilley 65 pen	9,534
14	spl	Inverness CT	A	L	0-2		1,279
15	spl	Rangers	H	L	1-4	Easton 61	8,780
16	sccqf	Motherwell	H	L	0-5		2,886
17	spl	Dundee Utd	A	L	0-1		5,507
18	spl	Aberdeen	H	L	0-2		4,569
19	spl	Kilmarnock	A	W	3-1	Hamilton 7,40; O'Brien 60	5,389
20	spl	Dundee	H	W	1-0	McPake 24	4,509
21	spl	Motherwell	A	L	0-2		4,363
22	spl	Dunfermline	A	D	0-0		5,092
23	spl	Celtic	A	L	1-2	Hamilton 39	57,593
24	scr3	G Morton	H	W	2-1	Rubio 36; Snodgrass 77	2,761
25	spl	Hibernian	H	L	0-2		6,788
26	spl	Inverness CT	H	L	1-4	Horvath 43	4,106
27	spl	Hearts	H	L	1-2	Lilley 74	4,318
28	spl	Rangers	A	L	0-3		48,579
29	scr4	Alloa	A	W	1-0	McMenimin 88	2,103
30	spl	Dundee Utd	H	L	0-2		5,158
31	spl	Aberdeen	A	L	0-2		9,214
32	scqf	Hearts	A	L	1-2	Easton 60	9,796
33	spl	Kilmarnock	H	W	3-1	Horvath 36; McNamee 64; Snodgrass 83	2,536
34	spl	Dundee	A	W	1-0	O'Brien 49	5,830
35	spl	Motherwell	H	D	1-1	Craigan 81 og	4,609
36	spl	Hearts	A	L	1-3	Dair 45	9,187
37	spl	Dunfermline	H	D	1-1	Kachloul 78	4,573
38	spl	Celtic	H	L	0-4		8,750
39	spl	Hibernian	A	W	3-0	Lilley 49; Kachloul 61; O'Brien 87	11,047
40	spl	Dundee Utd	A	D	1-1	Deloumeaux 61	7,687
41	spl	Dunfermline	H	W	2-0	O'Brien 33; McPake 74	5,700
42	spl	Inverness CT	A	W	1-0	Dair 29	3,021
43	spl	Kilmarnock	A	L	0-2		4,184
44	spl	Dundee	H	D	1-1	Easton 26	8,968

MONTHLY POINTS TALLY

AUGUST	4	33%
SEPTEMBER	1	11%
OCTOBER	4	27%
NOVEMBER	3	25%
DECEMBER	4	44%
JANUARY	0	0%
FEBRUARY	0	0%
MARCH	7	58%
APRIL	8	53%
MAY	4	44%

KEY PLAYERS - GOALSCORERS

Jim Hamilton

Goals in the League	4	**Player Strike Rate** Average number of minutes between League goals scored by player	366
Contribution to Attacking Power Average number of minutes between League team goals while on pitch	7	**Club Strike Rate** Average number of minutes between League goals scored by club	101

	PLAYER	LGE GOALS	GOALS ALL	POWER	STRIKE RATE
1	Jim Hamilton	4	7	97	366 mins
2	Burton O'Brien	8	8	101	428 mins
3	Derek Lilley	3	3	119	716 mins
4	Craig Easton	3	5	84	732 mins
5	Jason Dair	2	2	87	919 mins

KEY PLAYERS - MIDFIELDERS

Jason Dair

Goals in the League	2	**Contribution to Attacking Power** Average number of minutes between League team goals while on pitch	87
Defensive Rating Average number of mins between League goals conceded while he was on the pitch	68	**Scoring Difference** Defensive Rating minus Contribution to Attacking Power	-19

	PLAYER	LGE GOALS	DEF RATE	POWER	SCORE DIFF
1	Jason Dair	2	68	87	-19 mins
2	Gabor Vincze	0	60	79	-19 mins
3	Craig Easton	3	56	84	-28 mins
4	Burton O'Brien	8	56	101	-45 mins
5	Stuart Lovell	1	51	137	-86 mins

KEY PLAYERS - DEFENDERS

Eric Deloumeaux

Goals Conceded The number of League goals conceded while he was on the pitch	17	**Clean Sheets** In games when he played at least 70 minutes	4
Defensive Rating Ave number of mins between League goals conceded while on the pitch	69	**Club Defensive Rating** Average number of mins between League goals conceded by the club this season	56

	PLAYER	CON LGE	CLEAN SHEETS	DEF RATE
1	Eric Deloumeaux	17	4	69 mins
2	David McNamee	40	9	65 mins
3	Gustave Bahoken	24	4	59 mins
4	Goran Stanic	29	5	55 mins
5	Oscar Rubio	41	6	55 mins

KEY GOALKEEPER

Roddy McKenzie

Goals Conceded in the League	51	**Counting Games** Games when he played at least 70 mins	33
Defensive Rating Ave number of mins between League goals conceded while on the pitch	58	**Clean Sheets** In games when he played at least 70 mins	9

LEAGUE GOALS

Burton O'Brien

Minutes on the pitch	3420	League average (mins between goals)	428
Goals in the League	8		

	PLAYER	MINS	GOALS	AVE
1	O'Brien	3420	8	428
2	Hamilton	1463	4	366
3	Easton	2195	3	732
4	Lilley	2149	3	716
5	McPake	637	2	319
6	Dair	1837	2	919
7	Kachloul	587	2	294
8	Snodgrass	765	2	383
9	Horvath	481	2	241
10	Lovell	1640	1	1640
11	McMenimin	1373	1	1373
12	McNamee	2586	1	2586
	Other		3	
	TOTAL		34	

DISCIPLINARY RECORDS

	PLAYER	YELLOW	RED	AVE
1	Bahoken	8	0	178
2	Kachloul	3	0	195
3	McNamee	9	1	258
4	Hamilton	5	0	292
5	McLaughlin, S	2	0	295
6	Dorado	9	0	299
7	Easton	7	0	313
8	Vincze	4	0	315
9	Rubio	7	0	320
10	Stanic	3	0	530
11	Strong	1	0	583
12	McPake	1	0	637
13	Brittain	1	0	659
	Other	9	0	
	TOTAL	69	1	

TOP POINT EARNERS

	PLAYER	GAMES	AV PTS
1	Eric Deloumeaux	13	1.38
2	Gabor Vincze	14	1.36
3	Jason Dair	17	1.12
4	Craig Easton	22	1.09
5	Colin McMenamin	12	1.08
6	David McNamee	29	1.07
7	Roddy McKenzie	33	1.03
8	Goran Stanic	16	1.00
9	Derek Lilley	23	0.96
10	Burton O'Brien	38	0.92
	CLUB AVERAGE:		0.92

TEAM OF THE SEASON

D
Eric Deloumeaux
CG: 13 DR: 69
M
Jason Dair
CG: 17 SD: -19
D
David McNamee
CG: 29 DR: 65
M
Gabor Vincze
CG: 14 SD: -19
F
Derek Lilley
CG: 23 SR: 716
G
Roddy McKenzie
CG: 33 DR: 58
D
Gustave Bahoken
CG: 13 DR: 59
M
Craig Easton
CG: 22 SD: -28
F
Jim Hamilton
CG: 14 SR: 366
D
Oscar Rubio
CG: 24 DR: 55
M
Burton O'Brien
CG: 38 SD: -45

LEAGUE APPEARANCES AND BOOKINGS

	AGE (on 01/07/04)	IN NAMED 16	APPEARANCES	COUNTING GAMES	MINUTES ON PITCH	YELLOW CARDS	RED CARDS	THIS SEASON	HOME COUNTRY
Goalkeepers									
Greg Fleming	18	2	0	0	0	0	0	-	Scotland
Roddy McKenzie	29	36	33	33	2970	0	0	-	Scotland
Colin Meldrum	29	38	6	5	484	0	0	-	Scotland
Defenders									
Gustave Bahoken	26	22	18	13	1427	8	0	-	Cameroon
Eric Deloumeaux	32	13	13	13	1170	1	0	-	France
Emmanuel Dorado	32	33	31	30	2694	9	0	-	Argentina
Alan Kernaghan	38	8	4	4	354	1	0	-	Rep of Ireland
David McNamee	24	29	29	29	2586	9	1	1	Scotland (85)
Oscar Rubio	29	33	27	24	2241	7	0	-	Portugal
William Snowdon	22	18	2	0	69	0	0	-	England
Goran Stanic	32	21	20	16	1592	3	0	-	Macedonia
Greg Strong	29	10	9	6	583	1	0	-	England
Midfielders									
Stephen Adam	18	8	7	3	406	0	0	-	Scotland
Steven Boyack	28	8	6	4	394	0	0	-	Scotland
Richard Brittain	21	34	13	5	659	1	0	-	Scotland
Jason Dair	31	31	24	17	1837	0	0	-	Scotland
Craig Easton	26	37	31	22	2195	7	0	-	Scotland
Jamie Hand	21	8	7	5	417	0	0	-	England
Ryan Harding	21	8	3	2	238	0	0	-	England
Hassan Kachloul	32	8	8	7	587	3	0	-	Morocco
Attila Kriston	30	6	5	2	307	0	0	-	Hungary
Stuart Lovell	33	20	20	18	1640	1	0	-	Australia
Scott McLaughlin	21	17	10	5	591	2	0	-	Scotland
Burton O'Brien	24	38	38	38	3420	2	0	-	Scotland
Gabor Vincze	28	17	14	14	1260	4	0	-	Hungary
Mark Wilson	26	8	5	3	317	0	0	-	England
Forwards									
Graeme Dorrans	-	3	1	0	3	0	0	-	Scotland
Jim Hamilton	29	22	21	14	1463	5	0	-	Scotland
Ferenc Horvath	32	14	8	3	481	0	0	-	Hungary
Marc Libbra	32	20	11	0	269	0	0	-	France
Derek Lilley	31	32	31	23	2149	3	0	-	Scotland
Colin McMenamin	24	30	22	12	1373	2	0	-	Scotland
James McPake	21	19	15	5	637	1	0	-	Scotland
Pascal Nouma	33	4	2	0	42	1	0	-	France
Robert Snodgrass	17	29	17	5	765	0	0	-	Scotland

SQUAD APPEARANCES

Match	1	2	3	4	5	6	7	8	9	10	11	12	13	14	15	16	17	18	19	20	21	22	23	24	25	26	27	28	29	30	31	32	33	34	35	36	37	38	39	40	41	42	43	44
Venue	H	A	H	A	A	H	A	H	H	A	H	H	A	A	H	H	A	H	A	H	A	A	A	H	H	H	H	A	A	H	A	A	H	A	H	A	H	H	A	A	H	A	A	H
Competition	L	L	L	W	L	L	L	W	L	L	L	L	L	L	L	W	L	L	L	L	L	L	L	F	L	L	L	L	F	L	L	F	L	L	L	L	L	L	L	L	L	L	L	L
Result	W	L	D	W	L	L	D	W	L	D	W	L	L	L	L	L	L	L	W	W	L	D	L	W	L	L	L	L	W	L	L	L	W	W	D	L	D	L	W	D	W	W	L	D

Goalkeepers
Greg Fleming
Roddy McKenzie
Colin Meldrum

Defenders
Gustave Bahoken
Eric Deloumeaux
Emmanuel Dorado
Alan Kernaghan
David McNamee
Oscar Rubio
William Snowdon
Goran Stanic
Greg Strong

Midfielders
Stephen Adam
Steven Boyack
Richard Brittain
Jason Dair
Craig Easton
Jamie Hand
Ryan Harding
Hassan Kachloul
Attila Kriston
Stuart Lovell
Scott McLaughlin
Burton O'Brien
Gabor Vincze
Mark Wilson

Forwards
Graeme Dorrans
Jim Hamilton
Ferenc Horvath
Marc Libbra
Derek Lilley
Colin McMenamin
James McPake
Pascal Nouma
Robert Snodgrass

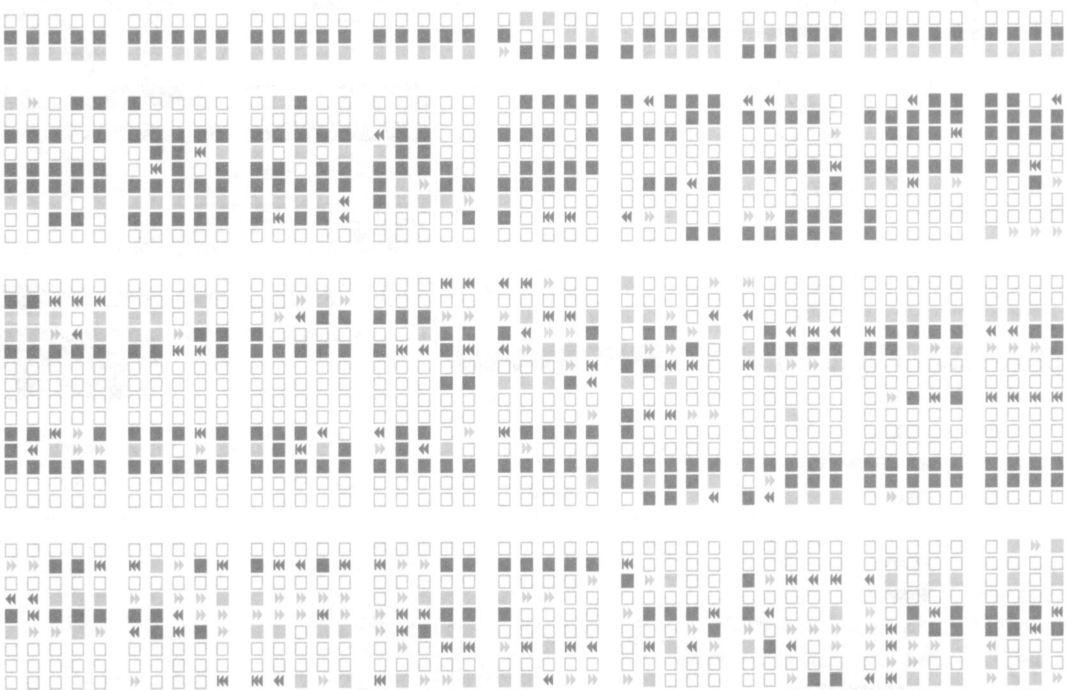

KEY: On all match | On bench | Subbed or sent off (Counting game) | Subbed or sent off (playing less than 70 minutes) | Subbed on from bench (Counting Game) | Subbed on (playing less than 70 minutes) | Subbed on and then subbed or sent off (Counting Game) | Subbed on and then subbed or sent off (playing less than 70 minutes) | Not in 16

DUNFERMLINE

Final Position: **11th**

NICKNAME: THE PARS

KEY: Won Drawn Lost

							Attendance
1	spl	Dundee Utd	H	D	1-1	Tod 48	6,512
2	spl	Inverness CT	A	L	0-2		1,972
3	spl	Aberdeen	H	L	0-1		8,533
4	spl	Kilmarnock	A	L	0-1		4,854
5	spl	Motherwell	H	D	1-1	Brewster 9	4,388
6	spl	Hearts	H	W	1-0	Nicholson 65	5,883
7	cisr3	Partick	H	W	3-1	Brewster 30; Thomson, S M 51; Hunt 76	2,301
8	spl	Celtic	A	L	0-3		58,213
9	spl	Hibernian	H	D	1-1	Donnelly 86	7,290
10	spl	Livingston	A	L	0-2		2,815
11	spl	Dundee	A	W	2-1	Thomson, S M 35; Young, Derek 48	5,456
12	spl	Rangers	H	L	1-2	Brewster 22	8,678
13	spl	Dundee Utd	A	W	2-1	Tod 8; Young, Darren 90	6,297
14	spl	Inverness CT	H	D	1-1	Young, Darren 28	4,921
15	sccqf	Hearts	H	L	1-3	Mehmet 60	4,405
16	spl	Aberdeen	A	L	1-2	Donnelly 70	10,398
17	spl	Kilmarnock	H	W	4-1	Nicholson 30; Mehmet 38; Wilson, S 57; Brewster 90	4,344
18	spl	Motherwell	A	L	1-2	Tod 65	5,084
19	spl	Hearts	A	L	0-3		10,084
20	spl	Celtic	H	L	0-2		7,650
21	spl	Hibernian	A	L	1-2	Tod 68	9,859
22	spl	Livingston	H	D	0-0		5,092
23	spl	Dundee	H	W	3-1	Tod 13,28,54	4,426
24	scr3	East Fife	A	D	0-0		1,722
25	spl	Rangers	A	L	0-3		48,055
26	scr3r	East Fife	H	W	3-1	Tod 1; Hunt 57; Dempsey 69	3,543
27	spl	Dundee Utd	H	D	1-1	Christiansen 44	6,589
28	spl	Inverness CT	A	L	0-2		5,449
29	scr4	Celtic	H	L	0-3		8,014
30	spl	Aberdeen	H	W	2-1	Mehmet 53; Donnelly 83	5,579
31	spl	Kilmarnock	A	L	1-2	Christiansen 20	4,701
32	spl	Motherwell	H	D	0-0		3,565
33	spl	Hearts	H	D	1-1	Wilson, S 32	5,934
34	spl	Celtic	A	L	0-6		58,908
35	spl	Hibernian	H	L	1-4	Nicholson 43	7,204
36	spl	Livingston	A	D	1-1	Hunt 79	4,573
37	spl	Dundee	A	L	1-2	Young, Darren 9	5,995
38	spl	Rangers	H	L	0-1		8,266
39	spl	Inverness CT	H	D	0-0		4,481
40	spl	Livingston	A	L	0-2		5,700
41	spl	Dundee	H	W	5-0	Young, Derek 2,29,64; MacDonald 33 og; Skerla 39	8,313
42	spl	Dundee Utd	A	W	1-0	Mason 89	10,763
43	spl	Kilmarnock	A	L	0-4		5,100

MONTHLY POINTS TALLY

AUGUST	1	8%
SEPTEMBER	4	44%
OCTOBER	7	47%
NOVEMBER	4	33%
DECEMBER	1	8%
JANUARY	4	33%
FEBRUARY	3	50%
MARCH	2	17%
APRIL	2	13%
MAY	6	67%

KEY PLAYERS - GOALSCORERS

Andy Tod

Goals in the League	7	Player Strike Rate: Average number of minutes between League goals scored by player	305
Contribution to Attacking Power: Average number of minutes between League team goals while on pitch	8	Club Strike Rate: Average number of minutes between League goals scored by club	101

	PLAYER	LGE GOALS	GOALS ALL	POWER	STRIKE RATE
1	Andy Tod	7	8	88	305 mins
2	Craig Brewster	3	4	87	379 mins
3	Simon Donnelly	3	3	92	519 mins
4	Barry Nicholson	3	3	96	771 mins
5	Billy Mehmet	2	3	97	831 mins

KEY PLAYERS - MIDFIELDERS

Gary Mason

Goals in the League	1	Contribution to Attacking Power: Average number of minutes between League team goals while on pitch	95
Defensive Rating: Average number of mins between League goals conceded while on the pitch	67	Scoring Difference: Defensive Rating minus Contribution to Attacking Power	-28

	PLAYER	LGE GOALS	DEF RATE	POWER	SCORE DIFF
1	Gary Mason	1	67	95	-28 mins
2	Simon Donnelly	3	50	92	-42 mins
3	Barry Nicholson	3	53	96	-43 mins
4	Darren Young	2	58	103	-45 mins
5	Gary Dempsey	0	56	226	-170 mins

KEY PLAYERS - DEFENDERS

Greg Shields

Goals Conceded: Total number of goals conceded while the player was on the pitch	18	Clean Sheets: In games when player was on pitch for at least 70 minutes	1
Defensive Rating: Ave number of mins between League goals conceded while on the pitch	65	Club Defensive Rating: Average number of mins between League goals conceded by the club this season	57

	PLAYER	CON LGE	CLEAN SHEETS	DEF RATE
1	Greg Shields	18	1	65 mins
2	Scott Wilson	46	6	61 mins
3	Scott Thomson	43	3	61 mins
4	Andrius Skerla	47	5	56 mins
5	Andy Tod	39	3	55 mins

KEY GOALKEEPER

Derek Stillie

Goals Conceded in the League	60	Counting Games: League games when player was on pitch for at least 70 minutes	38
Defensive Rating: Ave number of mins between League goals conceded while on the pitch	57	Clean Sheets: In games when player was on pitch for at least 70 minutes	6

LEAGUE GOALS

Andy Tod

Minutes on the pitch	2135	League average (mins between goals)	305
Goals in the League	7		

	PLAYER	MINS	GOALS	AVE
1	Tod	2135	7	305
2	Young, Derek	1265	4	316
3	Brewster	1136	3	379
4	Donnelly	1557	3	519
5	Nicholson	2314	3	771
6	Wilson, S	2790	2	1395
7	Christiansen	870	2	435
8	Young, Darren	2370	2	1185
9	Mehmet	1662	2	831
10	Thomson, S M	2642	1	2642
11	Skerla	2628	1	2628
12	Hunt	1148	1	1148
	Other		3	
	TOTAL		34	

DISCIPLINARY RECORDS

	PLAYER	YELLOW	RED	AVE
1	Campbell	3	0	353
2	Labonte	1	1	411
3	Young, Derek	3	0	421
4	Wilson, S	5	0	558
5	Hunt	2	0	574
6	Nicholson	4	0	578
7	Shields	2	0	585
8	Skerla	4	0	657
9	Mason	4	0	756
10	Donnelly	2	0	778
11	Young, Darren	3	0	790
12	Stillie	4	0	855
13	Makel	1	0	983
	Other	5	0	
	TOTAL	43	1	

TOP POINT EARNERS

	PLAYER	GAMES	AV PTS
1	Craig Wilson	4	1.50
2	Richie Byrne	4	1.25
3	Craig Brewster	13	1.15
4	Aaron Labonte	7	1.14
5	Greg Ross	11	1.09
6	Lee Makel	11	1.09
7	Ian Campbell	11	1.09
8	Scott Thomson	4	1.00
9	Derek Young	11	1.00
10	Gary Mason	33	1.00
	CLUB AVERAGE:		0.89

TEAM OF THE SEASON

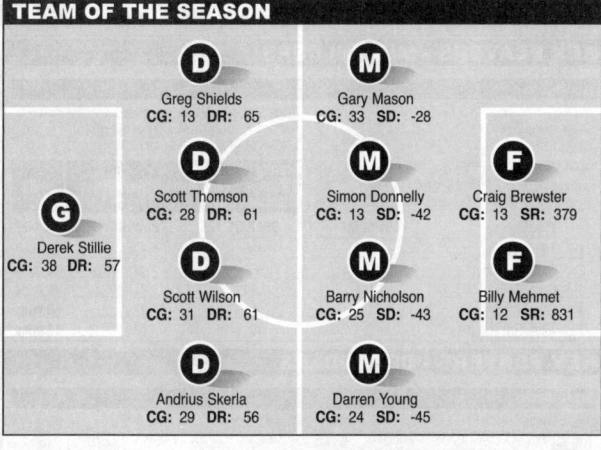

G Derek Stillie CG: 38 DR: 57

D Greg Shields CG: 13 DR: 65

D Scott Thomson CG: 28 DR: 61

D Scott Wilson CG: 31 DR: 61

D Andrius Skerla CG: 29 DR: 56

M Gary Mason CG: 33 SD: -28

M Simon Donnelly CG: 13 SD: -42

M Barry Nicholson CG: 25 SD: -43

M Darren Young CG: 24 SD: -45

F Craig Brewster CG: 13 SR: 379

F Billy Mehmet CG: 12 SR: 831

LEAGUE APPEARANCES AND BOOKINGS

	AGE (on 01/07/04)	IN NAMED 16	APPEARANCES	COUNTING GAMES	MINUTES ON PITCH	YELLOW CARDS	RED CARDS	THIS SEASON	HOME COUNTRY
Goalkeepers									
James Langfield	25	37	0	0	0	0	0	-	Scotland
Sean Murdoch	18	1	0	0	0	0	0	-	Scotland
Derek Stillie	31	38	38	38	3420	4	0	-	Scotland
Scott Thomson	38	4	4	4	360	0	0	-	Scotland
Defenders									
Richie Byrne	23	9	6	4	418	0	0	-	Scotland
Ian Campbell	24	26	13	11	1060	3	0	-	Scotland
Aaron Labonte	21	27	16	7	823	1	1	-	England
Craig McKeown	20	20	1	0	6	0	0	-	Scotland
Greg Ross	18	26	14	11	1104	1	0	-	Scotland
Patrick Sculion	19	14	1	0	38	0	0	-	Scotland
Greg Shields	28	13	13	13	1170	2	0	-	Scotland
Andrius Skerla	28	30	30	29	2628	4	0	-	Lithuania
Scott Thomson	33	31	31	28	2642	0	0	-	Scotland
Andy Tod	33	34	31	21	2135	2	0	-	Scotland
Scott Wilson	28	31	31	31	2790	5	0	-	Scotland
Midfielders									
Stephen Bradley	20	12	2	0	57	0	0	-	Rep or Ireland
Thomas Butler	24	16	12	5	573	0	0	-	England
Gary Dempsey	24	17	17	14	1354	1	0	-	Rep of Ireland
Simon Donnelly	30	30	26	13	1557	2	0	-	Scotland
Lee Makel	32	12	11	11	983	1	0	-	England
Gary Mason	25	35	35	33	3027	4	0	-	Scotland
Barry Nicholson	26	27	27	25	2314	4	0	1	Scotland (85)
Darren Young	26	34	32	24	2370	3	0	-	Scotland
Forwards									
Craig Brewster	38	14	14	13	1136	1	0	-	Scotland
Jesper Christiansen	25	14	13	8	870	0	0	4	Denmark (19)
John Dunn	18	8	0	0	0	0	0	-	Scotland
Gary Greenhill	20	2	0	0	0	0	0	-	Scotland
Georgi Hristov	29	9	8	1	300	1	0	-	Macedonia
Noel Hunt	22	26	23	7	1148	2	0	-	Rep of Ireland
Derek Lyle	24	3	0	0	0	0	0	-	Scotland
Stephen McGlichie	19	2	1	0	3	0	0	-	Scotland
Billy Mehmet	21	33	31	12	1662	0	0	-	England
Craig Wilson	19	21	4	4	346	0	0	-	Scotland
Derek Young	25	22	20	11	1265	3	0	-	Scotland

SQUAD APPEARANCES

Match	1	2	3	4	5	6	7	8	9	10	11	12	13	14	15	16	17	18	19	20	21	22	23	24	25	26	27	28	29	30	31	32	33	34	35	36	37	38	39	40	41	42	43
Venue	H	A	H	A	H	H	H	A	H	A	A	H	A	H	H	A	H	A	A	H	A	H	H	A	A	H	H	A	H	H	A	H	H	A	H	A	A	H	H	A	H	A	A
Competition	L	L	L	L	L	L	W	L	L	L	L	L	L	L	W	L	L	L	L	L	L	L	L	F	L	O	L	L	F	L	L	L	L	L	L	L	L	L	L	L	L	L	L
Result	D	L	L	L	D	W	W	L	D	L	W	L	W	D	L	L	W	L	L	L	L	D	W	D	L	W	D	L	L	W	L	D	D	L	L	D	L	L	D	L	W	W	L

Goalkeepers
James Langfield
Sean Murdoch
Derek Stillie
Scott Thomson

Defenders
Richie Byrne
Ian Campbell
Aaron Labonte
Craig McKeown
Greg Ross
Patrick Sculion
Greg Shields
Andrius Skerla
Scott Thomson
Andy Tod
Scott Wilson

Midfielders
Stephen Bradley
Thomas Butler
Gary Dempsey
Simon Donnelly
Lee Makel
Gary Mason
Barry Nicholson
Darren Young

Forwards
Craig Brewster
Jesper Christiansen
John Dunn
Gary Greenhill
Georgi Hristov
Noel Hunt
Derek Lyle
Stephen McGlichie
Billy Mehmet
Craig Wilson
Derek Young

KEY: On all match | On bench | Subbed or sent off (Counting game) | Subbed or sent off (playing less than 70 minutes) | Subbed on from bench (Counting Game) | Subbed on (playing less than 70 minutes) | Subbed on and then subbed or sent off (Counting Game) | Subbed on and then subbed or sent off (playing less than 70 minutes) | Not in 16

DUNDEE

Final Position: **12th**

NICKNAME: THE DARK BLUES

KEY: Won / Drawn / Lost

							Attendance
1	spl	**Hearts**	H	L	0-1		7,770
2	spl	**Dundee Utd**	A	W	2-1	Lovell 17 pen; Sutton 47	11,118
3	spl	**Motherwell**	H	L	1-2	Lovell 78	4,849
4	cisr2	**Forfar**	H	W	4-0	Lovell 66,82,90 pen; Anderson 87	3,047
5	spl	**Hibernian**	A	D	4-4	Sutton 7; Brady 65; Larsen 79; Hernandez Santos 90	9,344
6	spl	**Celtic**	A	L	0-3		56,936
7	spl	**Livingston**	H	D	0-0		4,387
8	cisr3	**Livingston**	A	L	1-2	Robb 67	1,736
9	spl	**Rangers**	H	L	0-2		9,404
10	spl	**Aberdeen**	A	D	1-1	Sutton 1	11,217
11	spl	**Kilmarnock**	H	W	3-1	Robb 30; Sutton 63; Anderson 87	4,637
12	spl	**Dunfermline**	H	L	1-2	Anderson 52	5,456
13	spl	**Inverness CT**	A	L	1-2	Lovell 72	1,254
14	spl	**Hearts**	A	L	0-3		10,172
15	spl	**Dundee Utd**	H	W	1-0	Sutton 86	9,845
16	spl	**Motherwell**	A	L	0-3		4,406
17	spl	**Hibernian**	H	L	1-4	Lovell 62	5,274
18	spl	**Celtic**	H	D	2-2	Lovell 35,76	9,539
19	spl	**Livingston**	A	L	0-1		4,509
20	spl	**Rangers**	A	L	0-3		48,114
21	spl	**Aberdeen**	H	W	1-0	Barrett 57	7,310
22	spl	**Kilmarnock**	A	L	1-3	Sutton 39	5,468
23	spl	**Dunfermline**	A	L	1-3	Barrett 40	4,426
24	scr3	**Hibernian**	A	L	0-2		9,706
25	spl	**Inverness CT**	H	W	3-1	Robb 28; McManus 48; Sutton 56 pen	5,567
26	spl	**Hearts**	H	D	1-1	Caballero 54	5,780
27	spl	**Dundee Utd**	A	D	2-2	McManus 71; Lovell 85	12,703
28	spl	**Motherwell**	H	W	2-1	Lovell 45,55	5,746
29	spl	**Hibernian**	A	L	0-4		10,938
30	spl	**Celtic**	A	L	0-3		52,500
31	spl	**Livingston**	H	L	0-1		5,830
32	spl	**Rangers**	H	L	0-2		9,876
33	spl	**Aberdeen**	A	D	1-1	McManus 75	10,474
34	spl	**Kilmarnock**	H	W	1-0	Lovell 62 pen	5,494
35	spl	**Dunfermline**	H	W	2-1	Lovell 56 pen; Sancho 62	5,995
36	spl	**Inverness CT**	A	L	2-3	McManus 74; Sutton 80	4,786
37	spl	**Kilmarnock**	A	L	0-1		3,770
38	spl	**Dundee Utd**	H	L	1-2	Lovell 64 pen	11,263
39	spl	**Dunfermline**	A	L	0-5		8,313
40	spl	**Inverness CT**	H	D	1-1	Sancho 49	6,691
41	spl	**Livingston**	A	D	1-1	MacDonald 18	8,968

MONTHLY POINTS TALLY

AUGUST	4	33%
SEPTEMBER	1	11%
OCTOBER	4	27%
NOVEMBER	4	33%
DECEMBER	3	25%
JANUARY	5	42%
FEBRUARY	3	50%
MARCH	1	8%
APRIL	6	40%
MAY	2	22%

KEY PLAYERS - GOALSCORERS

Steve Lovell

Goals in the League	12	Player Strike Rate Average number of minutes between League goals scored by player	234
Contribution to Attacking Power Average number of minutes between League team goals while on pitch	15	Club Strike Rate Average number of minutes between League goals scored by club	92

	PLAYER	LGE GOALS	GOALS ALL	POWER	STRIKE RATE
1	Steve Lovell	12	15	97	234 mins
2	John Sutton	8	8	75	247 mins
3	Tom McManus	4	4	72	291 mins
4	Iain Anderson	2	3	78	786 mins
5	Neil Barrett	2	2	103	1033 mins

KEY PLAYERS - MIDFIELDERS

Iain Anderson

Goals in the League	2	Contribution to Attacking Power Average number of minutes between League team goals while on pitch	79
Defensive Rating Average number of mins between League goals conceded while he was on the pitch	48	Scoring Difference Defensive Rating minus Contribution to Attacking Power	-31

	PLAYER	LGE GOALS	DEF RATE	POWER	SCORE DIFF
1	Iain Anderson	2	48	79	-31 mins
2	Stephen Robb	2	56	89	-33 mins
3	Barry Smith	0	49	95	-46 mins
4	Garry Brady	1	51	97	-46 mins
5	Mark Fotheringham	0	40	92	-52 mins

KEY PLAYERS - DEFENDERS

Brent Sancho

Goals Conceded The number of League goals conceded while he was on the pitch	39	Clean Sheets In games when he played at least 70 minutes	3
Defensive Rating Ave number of mins between League goals conceded while on the pitch	54	Club Defensive Rating Average number of mins between League goals conceded by the club this season	48

	PLAYER	CON LGE	CLEAN SHEETS	DEF RATE
1	Brent Sancho	39	3	54 mins
2	Calum MacDonald	58	4	49 mins
3	Robert Mann	55	2	47 mins
4	Steven McNally	38	2	45 mins
5	Jonay Hernandez Santos	29	0	39 mins

KEY GOALKEEPER

Derek Soutar

Goals Conceded in the League	67	Counting Games Games when he played at least 70 mins	37
Defensive Rating Ave number of mins between League goals conceded while on the pitch	49	Clean Sheets In games when he played at least 70 mins	4

LEAGUE GOALS

Steve Lovell

Minutes on the pitch	2813	League average (mins between goals)	234
Goals in the League	12		

	PLAYER	MINS	GOALS	AVE
1	Lovell	2813	12	234
2	Sutton	1972	8	247
3	McManus	1164	4	291
4	Anderson	1572	2	786
5	Robb	2679	2	1340
6	Sancho	2103	2	1052
7	Barrett	2065	2	1033
8	Larsen	315	1	315
9	MacDonald	2870	1	2870
10	Hernandez Santos	1143	1	1143
11	Caballero	1729	1	1729
	Other		1	
	TOTAL		37	

DISCIPLINARY RECORDS

	PLAYER	YELLOW	RED	AVE
1	Lovell	9	1	281
2	Fotheringham	3	1	461
3	Mann	5	0	514
4	Smith	6	0	553
5	Kitamirike	1	0	567
6	Hernandez Santos	1	1	571
7	McManus	1	1	582
8	Barrett	3	0	688
9	Robb	2	0	1339
10	Anderson	1	0	1572
11	McNally	1	0	1719
12	Caballero	1	0	1729
13	Sancho	1	0	2103
	Other	1	0	
	TOTAL	36	4	

TOP POINT EARNERS

	PLAYER	GAMES	AV PTS
1	Tom McManus	13	1.08
2	Neil Barrett	20	1.00
3	Stephen Robb	26	0.96
4	Brent Sancho	22	0.95
5	Fabian Caballero	16	0.94
6	Calum MacDonald	32	0.91
7	Mark Fotheringham	19	0.89
8	Garry Brady	19	0.89
9	Barry Smith	37	0.89
10	Steven McNally	18	0.89
	CLUB AVERAGE:		0.87

LEAGUE APPEARANCES AND BOOKINGS

	AGE (on 01/07/04)	IN NAMED 16	APPEARANCES	COUNTING GAMES	MINUTES ON PITCH	YELLOW CARDS	RED CARDS	THIS SEASON	HOME COUNTRY
Goalkeepers									
Francois Dubourdeau	24	10	0	0	0	0	0	-	France
Kelvin Jack	29	18	2	1	119	1	0	-	Trinidad & Tobago
Scott Murray	17	11	0	0	0	0	0	-	Scotland
Derek Soutar	24	37	37	36	3301	0	0	-	Scotland
Defenders									
Neil Clark	21	5	0	0	0	0	0	-	Scotland
Jonay Hernandez	26	17	14	12	1143	1	1	-	Spain
Tom Hutchinson	23	7	4	3	271	0	0	-	England
Joel Kitamirike	21	13	7	6	567	1	0	-	Uganda
Calum MacDonald	22	37	32	32	2870	1	0	-	Scotland
Robert Mann	31	38	30	28	2570	5	0	-	Scotland
Steven McNally	21	24	21	18	1719	1	0	-	Scotland
Brent Sancho	28	29	27	22	2103	1	0	-	Trinidad & Tobago
Lee Wilkie	25	14	12	10	985	0	0	-	Scotland
Midfielders									
Iain Anderson	27	21	20	16	1572	1	0	-	Scotland
Neil Barrett	23	33	30	20	2065	3	0	-	England
Garry Brady	28	33	26	19	1851	0	0	-	Scotland
Mark Fotheringham	21	35	27	19	1845	3	1	-	Scotland
Chris Hegarty	20	9	0	0	0	0	0	-	Scotland
Neil Jablonski	22	12	6	1	178	0	0	-	Scotland
Glen Atle Larsen	24	35	16	1	315	0	0	-	Norway
Andrew Reilly	19	2	2	0	26	0	0	-	Scotland
Stephen Robb	23	33	33	26	2679	2	0	-	Scotland
Scott Robertson	20	17	9	0	152	0	0	-	Scotland
Barry Smith	31	37	37	37	3323	6	0	-	Scotland
Forwards									
Fabian Caballero	27	30	28	16	1729	1	0	-	Argentina
Alex Cerdeira	-	12	6	1	191	1	0	-	Brazil
Aaron Conway	20	6	2	0	11	0	0	-	Scotland
Bobby Linn	19	5	0	0	0	0	0	-	Scotland
Steve Lovell	24	33	33	32	2813	9	1	-	England
Tom McManus	24	14	14	13	1164	1	1	-	Scotland
John Sutton	21	37	32	20	1972	0	0	-	England

TEAM OF THE SEASON

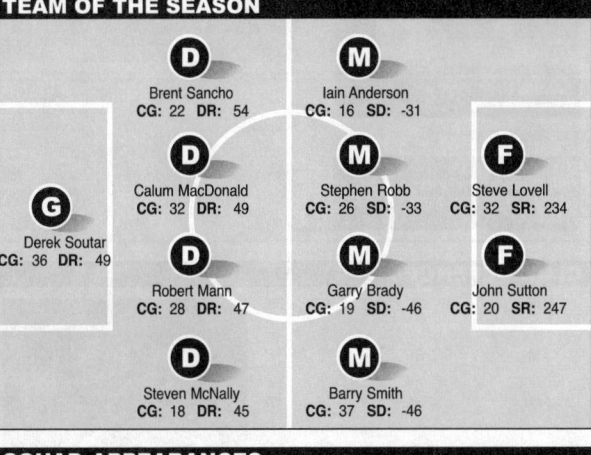

G
Derek Soutar
CG: 36 DR: 49

D
Brent Sancho
CG: 22 DR: 54

D
Calum MacDonald
CG: 32 DR: 49

D
Robert Mann
CG: 28 DR: 47

D
Steven McNally
CG: 18 DR: 45

M
Iain Anderson
CG: 16 SD: -31

M
Stephen Robb
CG: 26 SD: -33

M
Garry Brady
CG: 19 SD: -46

M
Barry Smith
CG: 37 SD: -46

F
Steve Lovell
CG: 32 SR: 234

F
John Sutton
CG: 20 SR: 247

SQUAD APPEARANCES

Match	1	2	3	4	5	6	7	8	9	10	11	12	13	14	15	16	17	18	19	20	21	22	23	24	25	26	27	28	29	30	31	32	33	34	35	36	37	38	39	40	41
Venue	H	A	H	H	A	A	H	A	H	A	H	H	A	A	H	A	H	H	A	A	H	A	A	A	H	H	A	H	A	A	H	H	A	H	H	A	A	H	A	H	A
Competition	L	L	L	W	L	L	L	W	L	L	L	L	L	L	L	L	L	L	L	L	L	L	L	F	L	L	L	L	L	L	L	L	L	L	L	L	L	L	L	L	L
Result	L	W	L	W	D	L	D	L	L	D	W	L	L	L	W	L	L	D	L	L	W	L	L	L	W	D	D	W	L	L	L	L	D	W	W	L	L	L	L	D	D

Goalkeepers
Francois Dubourdeau
Kelvin Jack
Scott Murray
Derek Soutar

Defenders
Neil Clark
Jonay Hernandez
Tom Hutchinson
Joel Kitamirike
Calum MacDonald
Robert Mann
Steven McNally
Brent Sancho
Lee Wilkie

Midfielders
Iain Anderson
Neil Barrett
Garry Brady
Mark Fotheringham
Chris Hegarty
Neil Jablonski
Glen Atle Larsen
Andrew Reilly
Stephen Robb
Scott Robertson
Barry Smith

Forwards
Fabian Caballero
Alex Cerdeira
Aaron Conway
Bobby Linn
Steve Lovell
Tom McManus
John Sutton

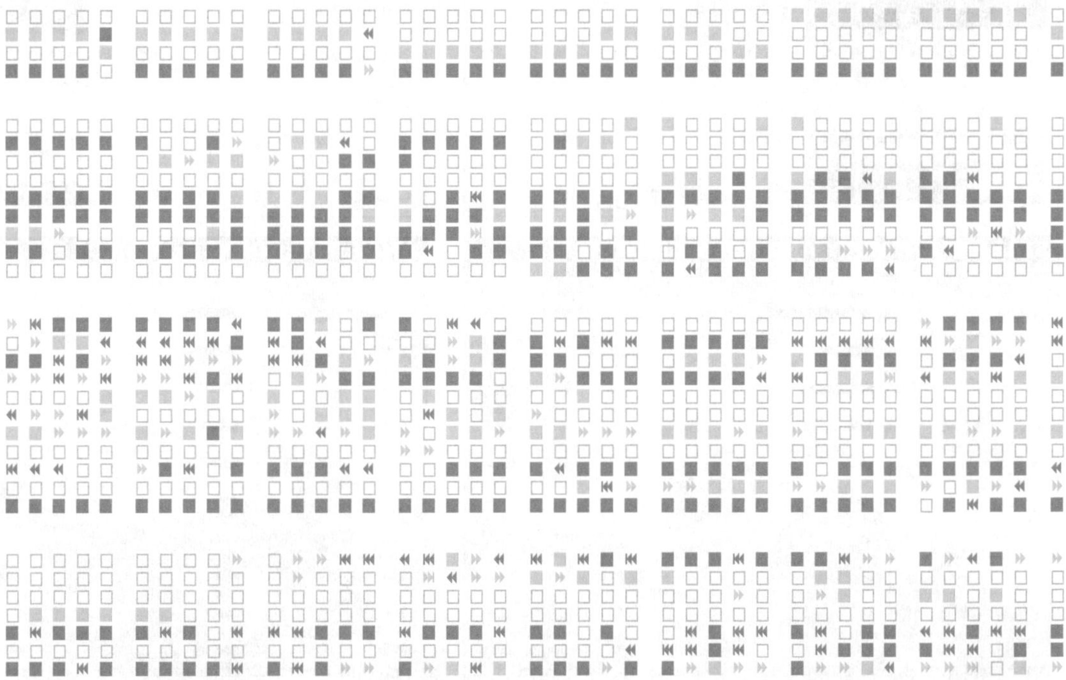

KEY: On all match | On bench | Subbed or sent off (Counting game) | Subbed or sent off (playing less than 70 minutes) | Subbed on from bench (Counting Game) | Subbed on (playing less than 70 minutes) | Subbed on and then subbed or sent off (Counting Game) | Subbed on and then subbed or sent off (playing less than 70 minutes) | Not in 16

SCOTTISH DIVISION ONE ROUND-UP

FINAL LEAGUE TABLE

	HOME						AWAY					TOTAL			
	P	W	D	L	F	A	W	D	L	F	A	F	A	DIF	PTS
Falkirk	36	10	6	2	35	15	12	3	3	31	15	66	30	36	74
St Mirren	36	10	6	2	24	11	5	9	4	17	12	41	23	18	60
Clyde	36	9	4	5	17	13	7	8	3	18	16	35	29	6	60
Queen of South	36	7	5	6	17	14	7	4	7	19	24	36	38	-2	51
Airdrie Utd	36	8	3	7	25	25	6	5	7	19	23	44	48	-4	50
Ross County	36	6	5	7	20	16	7	3	8	20	21	40	37	3	47
Hamilton	36	5	5	8	13	18	7	6	5	22	18	35	36	-1	47
St Johnstone	36	6	6	6	18	18	6	4	8	20	21	38	39	-1	46
Partick	36	7	5	6	23	25	3	4	11	15	27	38	52	-14	39
Raith	36	3	4	11	19	33	0	3	15	7	34	26	67	-41	16

CLUB STRIKE FORCE

Duffy of Falkirk

1 Airdrie Utd

Goals scored in the League	66
Club Strike Rate (CSR) Average number of minutes between League goals scored by club	49

	CLUB	LGE	ALL	CSR
1	Airdrie Utd	66	77	49
2	Clyde	44	48	74
3	Falkirk	41	48	79
4	Hamilton	40	48	81
5	Partick	38	45	85
6	Queen of South	38	40	85
7	Raith	36	39	90
8	Ross County	35	41	93
9	St Johnstone	35	39	93
10	St Mirren	26	27	125

CLUB DISCIPLINARY RECORDS

Referee Rowbotham; keeping order

1 Airdrie Utd

League Yellow	72
League Red	3
League Total	75
Cards Average in League Average number of minutes between a card being shown of either colour	43

	CLUB	LEAGUE		TOTAL		AVE
1	Airdrie Utd	72 Y	3 R	82 Y	3 R	43
2	Clyde	46	9	47	9	59
3	Falkirk	50	3	55	3	61
4	Hamilton	49	2	51	2	64
5	Partick	50	0	55	0	65
6	Queen of South	46	2	50	3	68
7	Raith	45	3	48	3	68
8	Ross County	41	0	43	0	79
9	St Johnstone	39	1	41	1	81
10	St Mirren	28	1	36	1	112

CLUB DEFENCES

	CLUB	LGE	ALL	CS	CDR
1	St Mirren	23	30	20	141
2	Clyde	29	39	19	112
3	Falkirk	30	43	16	108
4	Hamilton	36	43	11	90
5	Ross County	37	42	7	88
6	Queen of South	38	44	11	85
7	St Johnstone	39	43	14	83
8	Airdrie Utd	48	53	7	68
9	Partick	52	59	10	62
10	Raith	67	71	3	48

Dowie of Partick; second worst defence

1 St Mirren

Goals conceded in the League	23
Clean Sheets (CS) Number of league games where no goals were conceded	20
Club Defensive Rate (CDR) Average number of minutes between League goals conceded by club	141

STADIUM CAPACITY AND HOME CROWDS

	TEAM	CAPACITY	AVE	HIGH	LOW
1	Falkirk	7550	51.72	5209	3330
2	Ross County	5800	40.28	3151	1193
3	Hamilton	5300	39.68	3543	1371
4	Queen of South	6412	30.55	2734	1361
5	Partick	14538	23.77	5157	2334
6	St Johnstone	10673	22.62	3835	1770
7	St Mirren	15410	21.10	4711	2193
8	Clyde	8030	19.88	3800	1002
9	Airdrie Utd	10215	19.72	3245	1430
10	Raith	10104	17.36	3050	1127

Key: Average. The percentage of each stadium filled in League games over the season (AVE), the stadium capacity and the highest and lowest crowds recorded.

AWAY ATTENDANCE

	TEAM	AVE	HIGH	LOW
1	Partick	36.61	4711	1403
2	Falkirk	35.88	5157	1939
3	St Mirren	31.90	4949	1002
4	Airdrie Utd	29.26	4126	1296
5	St Johnstone	27.90	3720	1223
6	Clyde	26.84	4026	1394
7	Queen of South	25.54	5067	1060
8	Raith	25.09	3516	1122
9	Hamilton	24.02	3762	1200
10	Ross County	23.62	5209	1086

Key: Average. How close each club has come to filling grounds in its away league matches (AVE) and the highest and lowest crowds recorded.

CHART-TOPPING MIDFIELDERS

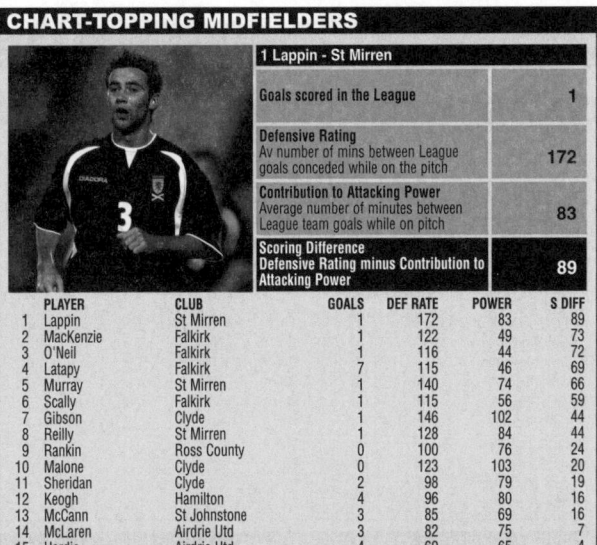

1 Lappin - St Mirren	
Goals scored in the League	1
Defensive Rating Av number of mins between League goals conceded while on the pitch	172
Contribution to Attacking Power Average number of minutes between League team goals while on pitch	83
Scoring Difference Defensive Rating minus Contribution to Attacking Power	89

	PLAYER	CLUB	GOALS	DEF RATE	POWER	S DIFF
1	Lappin	St Mirren	1	172	83	89
2	MacKenzie	Falkirk	1	122	49	73
3	O'Neil	Falkirk	1	116	44	72
4	Latapy	Falkirk	7	115	46	69
5	Murray	St Mirren	1	140	74	66
6	Scally	Falkirk	1	115	56	59
7	Gibson	Clyde	1	146	102	44
8	Reilly	St Mirren	1	128	84	44
9	Rankin	Ross County	0	100	76	24
10	Malone	Clyde	0	123	103	20
11	Sheridan	Clyde	2	98	79	19
12	Keogh	Hamilton	4	96	80	16
13	McCann	St Johnstone	3	85	69	16
14	McLaren	Airdrie Utd	3	82	75	7
15	Hardie	Airdrie Utd	4	69	65	4

CHART-TOPPING GOALSCORERS

2. McNiven; Queen of S'th

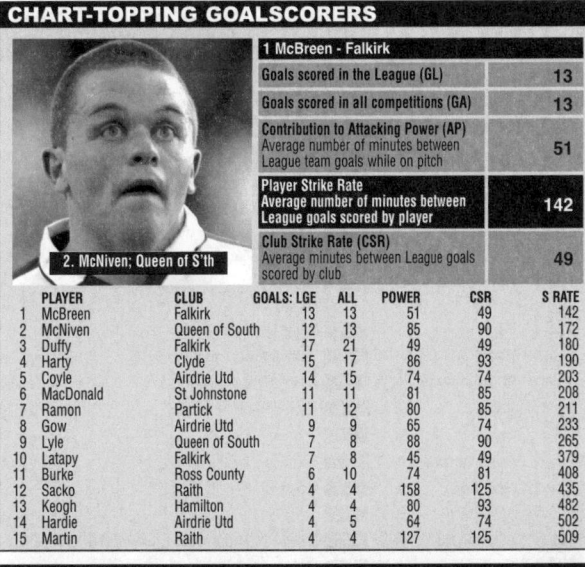

1 McBreen - Falkirk	
Goals scored in the League (GL)	13
Goals scored in all competitions (GA)	13
Contribution to Attacking Power (AP) Average number of minutes between League team goals while on pitch	51
Player Strike Rate Average number of minutes between League goals scored by player	142
Club Strike Rate (CSR) Average minutes between League goals scored by club	49

	PLAYER	CLUB	GOALS: LGE	ALL	POWER	CSR	S RATE
1	McBreen	Falkirk	13	13	51	49	142
2	McNiven	Queen of South	12	13	85	90	172
3	Duffy	Falkirk	17	21	49	49	180
4	Harty	Clyde	15	17	86	93	190
5	Coyle	Airdrie Utd	14	15	74	74	203
6	MacDonald	St Johnstone	11	11	81	85	208
7	Ramon	Partick	11	12	80	85	211
8	Gow	Airdrie Utd	9	9	65	74	233
9	Lyle	Queen of South	7	8	88	90	265
10	Latapy	Falkirk	7	8	45	49	379
11	Burke	Ross County	6	10	74	81	408
12	Sacko	Raith	4	4	158	125	435
13	Keogh	Hamilton	4	4	80	93	482
14	Hardie	Airdrie Utd	4	5	64	74	502
15	Martin	Raith	4	4	127	125	509

CHART-TOPPING DEFENDERS

3. McGowne; now at St Mirren

1 Millen - St Mirren	
Goals Conceded in the League The number of League goals conceded while he was on the pitch	23
Goals Conceded in all competitions The number of goals conceded while he was on the pitch in all competitions	30
Clean Sheets In games when he played at least 70 mins	20
Defensive Rating Average number of minutes between League goals conceded while on pitch	141
Club Defensive Rating Average mins between League goals conceded by the club this season	141

	PLAYER	CLUB	CON: LGE	ALL	CS	CDR	DEF RATE
1	Millen	St Mirren	23	30	20	141	141
2	Broadfoot	St Mirren	23	30	20	141	141
3	McGowne	St Mirren	20	27	17	141	138
4	van Zanten	St Mirren	22	27	15	141	125
5	Lawrie	Falkirk	21	33	12	108	119
6	Mensing	Clyde	23	33	17	112	117
7	Anderson	St Johnstone	14	14	9	83	114
8	James	Falkirk	23	34	14	108	113
9	Potter	Clyde	29	39	18	112	110
10	Bollan	Clyde	20	26	13	112	109
11	McPherson	Falkirk	27	40	13	108	105
12	Campbell	Falkirk	25	35	8	108	95
13	Reid	Queen of South	18	21	5	85	95
14	Hodge	Hamilton	30	35	10	90	91
15	Thomson	Queen of South	34	40	11	85	90

CHART-TOPPING GOALKEEPERS

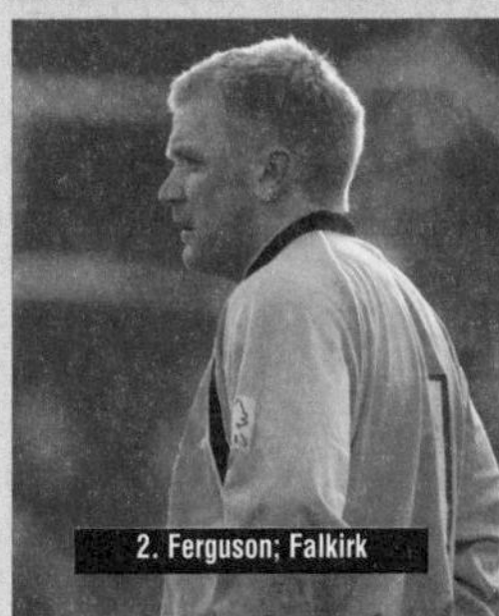
2. Ferguson; Falkirk

1 Hinchcliffe - St Mirren	
Counting Games League games when he played at least 70 minutes	34
Goals Conceded in the League The number of League goals conceded while he was on the pitch	23
Goals Conceded in all competitions The number of goals conceded while he was on the pitch in all competitions	30
Clean Sheets In games when he played at least 70 mins	18
Defensive Rating Average number of minutes between League goals conceded while on pitch	132

	PLAYER	CLUB	CG	CONC LGE	CONC ALL	CS	DEF RATE
1	Hinchcliffe	St Mirren	34	23	30	18	132
2	Ferguson	Falkirk	26	20	23	14	117
3	Halliwell	Clyde	36	28	38	19	114
4	McGregor	St Johnstone	20	16	19	10	113
5	Stewart	Ross County	21	18	21	5	101
6	McEwan	Hamilton	35	35	42	11	90
7	"Scott, Co"	Queen of South	24	26	32	7	79
8	McGeown	Airdrie Utd	30	42	47	6	64
9	Arthur	Partick	35	50	57	10	63
10	Berthelot	Raith	26	46	48	3	49

PLAYER DISCIPLINARY RECORD

5 Sheridan - Clyde - 13 cards

Cards Average mins between cards	188
League Yellow	11
League Red	2
TOTAL	13

	PLAYER		LY	LR	TOT	AVE
1	Stevenson	St Johnstone	3	1	4	141
2	Wilson	Clyde	9	0	9	158
3	Adam	Ross County	4	0	4	170
4	Aitken	Hamilton	5	0	5	183
5	Sheridan	Clyde	11	2	13	188
6	McConalogue	Partick	4	0	4	188
7	Blackadder	Hamilton	3	0	3	214
8	Bollan	Clyde	10	0	10	217
9	Mendy	Raith	3	0	3	222
10	Docherty	Airdrie Utd	8	1	9	231
11	Webb	St Johnstone	4	2	6	231
12	Scally	Falkirk	8	0	8	243
13	Wood	Queen of South	8	0	8	243
14	Wilkinson	Partick	2	1	3	248
15	Hardie	Airdrie Utd	8	0	8	250
16	Baird	St Mirren	1	1	2	252
17	Ross, I	Partick	2	0	2	253
18	Christie	Airdrie Utd	6	0	6	264
19	Hajovsky	Raith	2	0	2	266
20	Moore	St Johnstone	5	1	6	266
21	Malone	Clyde	9	0	9	273
22	McLaren	Partick	2	0	2	289
23	McBreen	Falkirk	6	0	6	307
24	Lovering	Airdrie Utd	7	1	8	309

TEAM OF THE SEASON

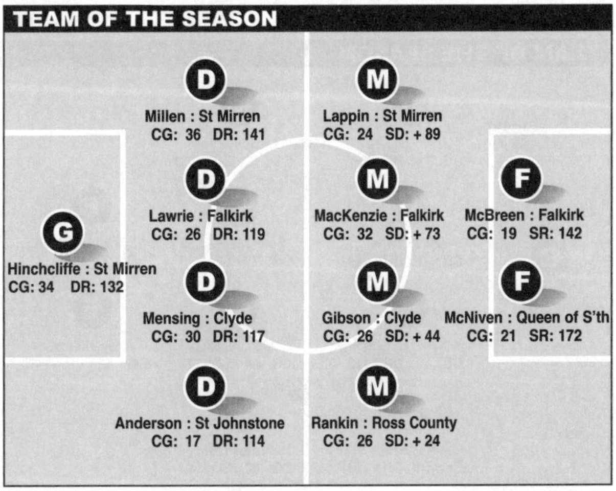
G
Hinchcliffe : St Mirren
CG: 34 DR: 132
D
Millen : St Mirren
CG: 36 DR: 141
D
Lawrie : Falkirk
CG: 26 DR: 119
D
Mensing : Clyde
CG: 30 DR: 117
D
Anderson : St Johnstone
CG: 17 DR: 114
M
Lappin : St Mirren
CG: 24 SD: + 89
M
MacKenzie : Falkirk
CG: 32 SD: + 73
M
Gibson : Clyde
CG: 26 SD: + 44
M
Rankin : Ross County
CG: 26 SD: + 24
F
McBreen : Falkirk
CG: 19 SR: 142
F
McNiven : Queen of S'th
CG: 21 SR: 172

FALKIRK

Final Position: **1st**

NICKNAME: THE BAIRNS

KEY: ☐Won ☐Drawn ☐Lost

	Comp	Opponent	H/A	Res	Score	Scorers	Attendance
1	div1	St Mirren	A	L	0-2		3,813
2	cisr1	Montrose	H	W	4-1	Duffy 15,31; Latapy 59; MacKenzie 88	1,372
3	div1	Hamilton	H	D	1-1	Duffy 71 pen	3,762
4	div1	Queen of South	A	W	3-1	Nicholls 9; Duffy 48; McAnespie 85	2,521
5	cisr2	Peterhead	A	W	6-1	O'Neil 4; Duffy 34,47; Thomson 58,83,89 pen	690
6	div1	Airdrie Utd	H	W	5-0	Thomson 9,78; Nicholls 24; Lawrie 54; Latapy 62	3,789
7	div1	Partick	A	W	4-1	Duffy 14,25; Campbell 51; Scally 87	5,157
8	div1	Raith	H	W	4-2	Duffy 54,59; Thomson 67,81	3,449
9	div1	St Johnstone	A	W	2-1	O'Neil 8; Nicholls 10	3,835
10	cisr3	Celtic	A	L	1-8	Thomson 66	24,345
11	div1	Clyde	H	D	1-1	Thomson 19	3,813
12	div1	Ross County	A	W	1-0	Thomson 39 pen	3,062
13	div1	Hamilton	A	W	1-0	Moutinho 51	2,870
14	div1	St Mirren	H	D	0-0		4,491
15	div1	Airdrie Utd	A	W	3-1	Latapy 7; Thomson 44; Lawrie 76	3,245
16	div1	Raith	A	W	2-0	McBreen 45; Duffy 59 pen	3,050
17	div1	St Johnstone	H	W	3-1	McBreen 33,76; Latapy 68	3,439
18	div1	Partick	H	W	3-0	Duffy 53; McBreen 73,86	3,335
19	div1	Ross County	H	D	2-2	McBreen 56; Thomson 67	3,330
20	div1	Clyde	A	W	2-0	Hughes 12; MacKenzie 19	2,864
21	div1	St Mirren	A	W	1-0	Moutinho 55	4,676
22	div1	Queen of South	H	W	4-2	Moutinho 17; McBreen 25,42,73	3,370
23	div1	Airdrie Utd	H	W	1-0	Duffy 34	4,126
24	div1	Partick	A	L	1-2	Duffy 6	4,120
25	div1	Raith	H	W	2-0	Latapy 6; Thomson 33	3,516
26	scr3	Clyde	A	L	0-3		4,011
27	div1	St Johnstone	A	W	3-0	Latapy 22; Moutinho 52; Duffy 76 pen	3,395
28	div1	Ross County	A	W	1-0	Duffy 45 pen	3,151
29	div1	Hamilton	H	D	1-1	Hughes 11	3,530
30	div1	Queen of South	A	D	1-1	Lawrie 55	2,551
31	div1	Partick	H	W	2-1	McBreen 17; Duffy 27	4,157
32	div1	Airdrie Utd	A	D	2-2	Duffy 3; James 84	3,111
33	div1	Clyde	H	D	0-0		3,842
34	div1	Raith	A	D	3-3	McBreen 16,69; Duffy 33	2,346
35	div1	St Johnstone	H	W	3-0	McBreen 36; Latapy 51; Duffy 65	3,720
36	div1	Ross County	H	W	1-0	McStay 67	5,209
37	div1	Clyde	A	W	1-0	Latapy 6 pen	1,939
38	div1	St Mirren	H	L	1-2	Duffy 41	4,342
39	div1	Hamilton	A	L	0-1		2,300
40	div1	Queen of South	H	L	1-2	Lawrie 17	5,067

TEAM OF THE SEASON

G Allan Ferguson CG: 26 DR: 117

D John Hughes CG: 14 DR: 131

D Andy Lawrie CG: 26 DR: 119

D Kevin James CG: 29 DR: 113

D Craig McPherson CG: 31 DR: 105

M David Nicholls CG: 13 SD: 100

M Scott MacKenzie CG: 32 SD: 73

M John O'Neil CG: 24 SD: 72

M Russell Latapy CG: 30 SD: 69

F Daniel McBreen CG: 20 SR: 142

F Andy Thomson CG: 13 SR: 147

KEY PLAYER APPEARANCES

	PLAYER	POS	AGE	APP	MINS ON	GOALS	CARDS(Y)	CARDS(R)
1	Darryl Duffy	ATT	21	35	3054	17	2	0
2	Scott MacKenzie	MID	35	34	2921	1	1	0
3	Craig McPherson	DEF	33	33	2837	0	0	0
4	Russell Latapy	MID	36	32	2651	7	2	0
5	Kevin James	DEF	29	29	2604	1	3	0
6	Andy Lawrie	DEF	26	31	2493	4	2	0
7	John O'Neil	MID	34	32	2445	1	0	1
8	Mark Campbell	DEF	27	32	2385	1	4	0
9	Allan Ferguson	GK	36	26	2340	0	1	0
10	Neil Scally	MID	26	32	1948	1	8	0
11	Daniel McBreen	ATT	28	23	1843	13	6	0
12	John Hughes	DEF	40	19	1436	2	3	0
13	Andy Thomson	ATT	34	24	1320	9	0	0
14	David Nicholls	MID	33	18	1162	3	3	0
15	Pedro Moutinho	ATT	25	19	950	4	1	0
16	Darren Hill	GK	23	10	900	0	0	0
17	Ryan McStay	ATT	19	15	892	1	1	0
18	Alan Kernaghan	DEF	38	9	779	0	0	0

KEY PLAYERS - GOALSCORERS

Daniel McBreen

Goals in the League	13
Contribution to Attacking Power Average number of minutes between League team goals while on pitch	51
Player Strike Rate Average number of minutes between League goals scored by player	142
Club Strike Rate Average number of minutes between League goals scored by club	49

	PLAYER	LGE GOALS	POWER	STRIKE RATE
1	Daniel McBreen	13	51	142 mins
2	Andy Thomson	9	48	147 mins
3	Darryl Duffy	17	49	180 mins
4	Russell Latapy	7	46	379 mins
5	David Nicholls	3	45	387 mins

KEY PLAYERS - MIDFIELDERS

David Nicholls

Goals in the League	3
Defensive Rating Average number of mins between League goals conceded while on the pitch	145
Contribution to Attacking Power Average number of minutes between League team goals while on pitch	45
Scoring Difference Defensive Rating minus Contribution to Attacking Power	100

	PLAYER	LGE GOALS	DEF RATE	POWER	SCORE DIFF
1	David Nicholls	3	145	45	100 mins
2	Scott MacKenzie	1	122	49	73 mins
3	John O'Neil	1	116	44	72 mins
4	Russell Latapy	7	115	46	69 mins
5	Neil Scally	1	115	56	59 mins

KEY PLAYERS - DEFENDERS

John Hughes

Goals Conceded while on the pitch	11
Defensive Rating Ave number of mins between League goals conceded while on the pitch	131
Clean Sheets In games when player was on pitch for at least 70 minutes	7
Club Defensive Rating Average number of mins between League goals conceded by the club this season.	108

	PLAYER	CON LGE	CLN SHEETS	DEF RATE
1	John Hughes	11	7	131 mins
2	Andy Lawrie	21	12	119 mins
3	Kevin James	23	14	113 mins
4	Craig McPherson	27	13	105 mins
5	Mark Campbell	25	8	95 mins

KEY GOALKEEPER

Allan Ferguson

Goals Conceded in the League	20
Defensive Rating Ave number of mins between League goals conceded while on the pitch.	117
Counting Games Games when player was on pitch for at least 70 minutes	26
Clean Sheets In Games when player was on pitch for at least 70 minutes	14

TOP POINT EARNERS

	PLAYER	GAMES	AV PTS
1	John O'Neil	24	2.42
2	David Nicholls	13	2.38
3	John Hughes	14	2.29
4	Andy Lawrie	26	2.27
5	Russell Latapy	30	2.20
6	Scott MacKenzie	32	2.19
7	Kevin James	29	2.17
8	Darryl Duffy	34	2.09
9	Andy Thomson	13	2.08
10	Allan Ferguson	26	2.08
	CLUB AVERAGE:		2.06

ST MIRREN

Final Position: **2nd**

NICKNAME: BUDDIES/SAINTS

KEY: ☐Won ☐Drawn ☐Lost

							Attendance
1	div1	Falkirk	H	W	2-0	Paatelainen 66; Russell 81	3,813
2	cisr1	Forfar	H	L	2-5	Paatelainen 5; O'Neill 78	1,100
3	div1	Ross County	A	D	1-1	O'Neill 89	2,666
4	div1	St Johnstone	H	W	2-1	O'Neill 47; Baird 86	3,079
5	div1	Hamilton	H	W	1-0	Paatelainen 36	2,978
6	div1	Clyde	A	D	0-0		2,484
7	div1	Partick	H	W	2-1	O'Neill 55; Paatelainen 70	4,711
8	div1	Raith	A	W	3-0	Lappin 25; Paatelainen 55; McGinty 58 pen	2,111
9	div1	Airdrie Utd	H	D	1-1	McGeown 16 og	3,500
10	div1	Queen of South	A	L	1-2	Baird 77	2,734
11	div1	Ross County	H	W	3-2	Ellis 19; Cowie 69; O'Neill 83	2,538
12	div1	Falkirk	A	D	0-0		4,491
13	div1	Hamilton	A	D	2-2	O'Neill 35 pen; Russell 75	2,529
14	div1	Clyde	H	D	0-0		3,788
15	div1	Partick	A	W	3-0	McGinty 50 pen; Russell 62; O'Neill 84	4,949
16	div1	Raith	H	W	1-0	McGinty 57 pen	3,010
17	div1	Queen of South	H	D	2-2	Broadfoot 57,74	2,850
18	div1	Airdrie Utd	A	L	2-3	Gillies 45; O'Neill 66	2,514
19	div1	Falkirk	H	L	0-1		4,676
20	div1	St Johnstone	A	L	0-1		2,233
21	div1	Hamilton	H	L	0-1		2,888
22	div1	Partick	H	D	1-1	Anis 51 og	3,779
23	scr3	Hamilton	H	W	3-0	Kean 24,80; Russell 77	2,700
24	div1	Raith	A	L	0-2		1,393
25	div1	Airdrie Utd	H	W	1-0	Kean 81	3,040
26	div1	Queen of South	A	D	0-0		2,016
27	scr4	Ayr	A	W	2-0	Kean 45; Murray 82	4,748
28	div1	St Johnstone	H	D	1-1	Broadfoot 50	2,716
29	Scpqf	Hibernian	A	L	0-2		15,195
30	div1	Ross County	A	W	1-0	Kean 28	1,302
31	div1	Clyde	H	D	0-0		2,736
32	div1	Clyde	A	D	0-0		1,002
33	div1	Hamilton	A	D	0-0		1,950
34	div1	Partick	A	D	0-0		3,730
35	div1	Raith	H	W	3-0	Ellis 14; Russell 16; Kean 20	2,193
36	div1	Queen of South	H	W	3-0	Baird 18; Murray 20; Reilly 90	2,327
37	div1	Airdrie Utd	A	W	2-0	Kean 65,76	1,989
38	div1	Falkirk	A	W	2-1	Broadfoot 30; Russell 68	4,342
39	div1	Ross County	H	W	1-0	van Zanten 32	3,906
40	div1	St Johnstone	A	D	0-0		2,920

TEAM OF THE SEASON

G — Craig Hinchcliffe CG: 33 DR: 132

D — Kirk Broadfoot CG: 36 DR: 141

D — Andy Millen CG: 36 DR: 141

D — Kevin McGowne CG: 30 DR: 138

D — David van Zanten CG: 28 DR: 125

M — Simon Lappin CG: 24 SD: 89

M — Hugh Murray CG: 28 SD: 66

M — Jon O'Neill CG: 13 SD: 52

M — Mark Reilly CG: 30 SD: 44

F — Stewart Kean CG: 13 SR: 240

F — Brian McGinty CG: 19 SR: 677

KEY PLAYER APPEARANCES

	PLAYER	POS	AGE	APP	MINS ON	GOALS	CARDS(Y/R)	
1	Kirk Broadfoot	DEF	20	36	3240	4	5	0
2	Andy Millen	DEF	40	36	3240	0	5	0
3	Craig Hinchcliffe	GK	33	34	3034	0	1	0
4	Mark Reilly	MID	36	35	2950	1	3	0
5	Kevin McGowne	DEF	35	31	2753	0	4	0
6	David van Zanten	DEF	23	33	2751	1	4	0
7	Hugh Murray	MID	26	32	2665	1	5	1
8	Simon Lappin	MID	22	34	2410	1	4	0
9	Brian McGinty	ATT	28	31	2031	3	3	0
10	Jon O'Neill	MID	31	30	1679	7	1	0
11	Laurence Ellis	DEF	25	22	1262	2	0	0
12	Allan Russell	ATT	24	25	1247	5	4	0
13	Ricky Gillies	MID	28	23	1202	1	1	0
14	Stewart Kean	ATT	22	15	1202	5	1	0
15	Mixu Paatelainen	ATT	38	15	1075	4	2	1
16	Ryan McCay	MID	2006	11	656	0	0	0
17	Alan Reid	MID	24	7	630	0	0	0
18	Mark Crilly	MID	25	9	529	0	1	0

KEY PLAYERS - GOALSCORERS

Jon O'Neill

Goals in the League: 7

Player Strike Rate — Average number of minutes between League goals scored by player: 240

Contribution to Attacking Power — Average number of minutes between League team goals while on pitch: 88

Club Strike Rate — Average number of minutes between League goals scored by club: 79

	PLAYER	LGE GOALS	POWER	STRIKE RATE
1	Jon O'Neill	7	88	240 mins
2	Stewart Kean	5	85	240 mins
3	Brian McGinty	3	78	677 mins
4	Kirk Broadfoot	4	79	810 mins
5	Simon Lappin	1	83	2410 mins

KEY PLAYERS - MIDFIELDERS

Simon Lappin

Goals in the League: 1

Contribution to Attacking Power — Average number of minutes between League team goals while on pitch: 83

Defensive Rating — Average number of mins between League goals conceded while on the pitch: 172

Scoring Difference — Defensive Rating minus Contribution to Attacking Power: 89

	PLAYER	LGE GOALS	DEF RATE	POWER	SCORE DIFF
1	Simon Lappin	1	172	83	89 mins
2	Hugh Murray	1	140	74	66 mins
3	Jon O'Neill	7	140	88	52 mins
4	Mark Reilly	1	128	84	44 mins

KEY PLAYERS - DEFENDERS

Andy Millen

Goals Conceded while on the pitch: 23

Clean Sheets — In games when player was on pitch for at least 70 minutes: 20

Defensive Rating — Ave number of mins between League goals conceded while on the pitch: 141

Club Defensive Rating — Average number of mins between League goals conceded by the club this season.: 141

	PLAYER	CON LGE	CLN SHEETS	DEF RATE
1	Andy Millen	23	20	141 mins
2	Kirk Broadfoot	23	20	141 mins
3	Kevin McGowne	20	17	138 mins
4	David van Zanten	22	15	125 mins

KEY GOALKEEPER

Craig Hinchcliffe

Goals Conceded in the League: 23

Defensive Rating — Ave number of mins between League goals conceded while on the pitch.: 132

Counting Games — Games when player was on pitch for at least 70 minutes: 34

Clean Sheets — In Games when player was on pitch for at least 70 minutes: 18

TOP POINT EARNERS

	PLAYER	GAMES	AV PTS
1	David van Zanten	28	1.96
2	Simon Lappin	24	1.92
3	Hugh Murray	28	1.82
4	Kevin McGowne	30	1.70
5	Stewart Kean	13	1.69
6	Jon O'Neill	13	1.69
7	Andy Millen	36	1.67
8	Kirk Broadfoot	36	1.67
9	Craig Hinchcliffe	33	1.61
10	Mark Reilly	30	1.60
	CLUB AVERAGE:		1.67

CLYDE

Final Position: **3rd**

NICKNAME: THE BULLY WEE

KEY: ☐Won ☐Drawn ☐Lost

							Attendance
1	div1	Partick	H	W	2-1	Harty 27; Gibson 45	3,800
2	div1	Raith	A	W	3-2	Bryson 4; Harty 42 pen; Potter 57	1,784
3	div1	Ross County	H	W	1-0	Wilford 55	1,101
4	cisr2	Airdrie Utd	A	W	1-0	Wilford 73	1,595
5	div1	Queen of South	A	W	1-0	Harty 20	1,639
6	div1	St Mirren	H	D	0-0		2,484
7	div1	Airdrie Utd	H	L	1-2	Wilford 16	1,367
8	div1	Hamilton	A	W	1-0	Harty 16	2,017
9	cisr3	Dundee Utd	A	L	0-4		2,336
10	div1	Falkirk	A	D	1-1	Harty 77	3,813
11	div1	St Johnstone	H	W	1-0	Sheridan, D 17	1,456
12	div1	Raith	H	W	2-0	Conway 11; Wilson 36	1,196
13	div1	Partick	A	D	0-0		4,026
14	div1	Queen of South	H	W	2-0	Harty 9,38	1,284
15	div1	St Mirren	A	D	0-0		3,788
16	div1	Airdrie Utd	A	L	1-3	Walker 81	1,862
17	div1	Hamilton	H	W	2-1	Sheridan 35; Potter 90	1,200
18	div1	St Johnstone	A	L	0-3		2,026
19	div1	Falkirk	H	L	0-2		2,864
20	div1	Partick	H	D	1-1	Bollan 20	1,800
21	div1	Ross County	A	W	1-0	Harty 70	1,953
22	div1	Airdrie Utd	H	W	1-0	Jones 78	1,513
23	scr3	Falkirk	H	W	3-0	Harty 35,72; Bollan 68	4,011
24	div1	Hamilton	A	W	1-0	Arbuckle 51	1,873
25	scr4	Ross County	A	D	0-0		1,629
26	div1	Raith	A	D	3-3	Harty 39,56 pen,73 pen	1,394
27	scr4r	Ross County	H	W	2-1	Bryson 35; Arbuckle 93	1,576
28	div1	Ross County	H	W	1-0	Harty 52	1,086
29	Scpqf	Celtic	H	L	0-5		8,200
30	div1	Queen of South	A	W	1-0	Bollan 23	1,448
31	div1	St Mirren	A	D	0-0		2,736
32	div1	St Mirren	H	D	0-0		1,002
33	div1	Queen of South	H	L	0-1		1,060
34	div1	Falkirk	A	D	0-0		3,842
35	div1	Airdrie Utd	A	W	4-2	Harty 2 pen,34,56; Jones 29	1,641
36	div1	St Johnstone	H	D	1-1	Burns 57	1,223
37	div1	Hamilton	H	L	1-3	Bryson 83	1,235
38	div1	St Johnstone	A	D	0-0		1,770
39	div1	Falkirk	H	L	0-1		1,939
40	div1	Partick	A	L	0-1		2,694
41	div1	Raith	H	W	1-0	Gilhaney 28	1,122
42	div1	Ross County	A	D	1-1	Bryson 23	2,130

TEAM OF THE SEASON

G — Bryn Halliwell — CG: 35 DR: 114

D — Simon Mensing — CG: 30 DR: 117
D — John-Paul Potter — CG: 35 DR: 110
D — Scott Wilson — CG: 14 DR: 110
D — Gary Bollan — CG: 24 DR: 109

M — Jim Gibson — CG: 23 SD: 44
M — Darren Sheridan — CG: 26 SD: 19
M — Craig Bryson — CG: 18 SD: -9
M — Edward Malone — CG: 0 SD: 20

F — Ian Harty — CG: 31 SR: 190
F — Alex Burns — CG: 14 SR: 1289

KEY PLAYER APPEARANCES

	PLAYER	POS	AGE	APP	MINS ON	GOALS	CARDS(Y	R)
1	Bryn Halliwell	GK	24	36	3195	0	0	0
2	John-Paul Potter	DEF	25	36	3179	2	4	0
3	Ian Harty	ATT	27	33	2846	15	5	0
4	Simon Mensing	DEF	23	30	2700	0	7	0
5	Edward Malone	MID	20	28	2463	0	9	0
6	Darren Sheridan	MID	37	29	2446	2	11	2
7	Jim Gibson	MID	25	29	2338	1	5	1
8	Gary Bollan	DEF	32	25	2178	2	10	0
9	Craig Bryson	MID	18	28	1980	3	0	0
10	Mark Gilhaney	ATT	20	33	1876	1	2	0
11	Scott Wilson	DEF	23	19	1430	1	9	0
12	Gary Arbuckle	ATT	20	26	1420	1	1	0
13	Alex Burns	ATT	31	15	1289	1	2	0
14	Stuart Balmer	DEF	35	13	1083	0	3	0
15	Aaron Wilford	DEF	23	18	1064	2	1	0
16	Graeme Jones	ATT	35	13	855	2	2	0
17	Alex Walker	DEF	21	14	798	1	1	0
18	Miguel Angel Espinola	DEF	31	6	540	0	0	0

KEY PLAYERS - GOALSCORERS

Ian Harty

Goals in the League	15	Player Strike Rate Average number of minutes between League goals scored by player	190
Contribution to Attacking Power Average number of minutes between League team goals while on pitch	86	Club Strike Rate Average number of minutes between League goals scored by club	93

	PLAYER	LGE GOALS	POWER	STRIKE RATE
1	Ian Harty	15	86	190 mins
2	Craig Bryson	3	99	660 mins
3	Gary Bollan	2	83	1089 mins
4	Darren Sheridan	2	79	1223 mins
5	Alex Burns	1	99	1289 mins

KEY PLAYERS - MIDFIELDERS

Jim Gibson

Goals in the League	1	Contribution to Attacking Power Average number of minutes between League team goals while on pitch	102
Defensive Rating Average number of mins between League goals conceded while on the pitch	146	Scoring Difference Defensive Rating minus Contribution to Attacking Power	44

	PLAYER	LGE GOALS	DEF RATE	POWER	SCORE DIFF
1	Jim Gibson	1	146	102	44 mins
2	Edward Malone	0	123	103	20 mins
3	Darren Sheridan	2	98	79	19 mins
4	Craig Bryson	3	90	99	-9 mins

KEY PLAYERS - DEFENDERS

Simon Mensing

Goals Conceded while on the pitch	23	Clean Sheets In games when player was on pitch for at least 70 minutes	17
Defensive Rating Ave number of mins between League goals conceded while on the pitch	117	Club Defensive Rating Average number of mins between League goals conceded by the club this season.	112

	PLAYER	CON LGE	CLN SHEETS	DEF RATE
1	Simon Mensing	23	17	117 mins
2	John-Paul Potter	29	18	110 mins
3	Scott Wilson	13	8	110 mins
4	Gary Bollan	20	13	109 mins

KEY GOALKEEPER

Bryn Halliwell

Goals Conceded in the League	28
Defensive Rating Ave number of mins between League goals conceded while on the pitch.	114
Counting Games Games when player was on pitch for at least 70 minutes	36
Clean Sheets In Games when player was on pitch for at least 70 minutes	19

TOP POINT EARNERS

	PLAYER	GAMES	AV PTS
1	Gary Arbuckle	12	2.17
2	Darren Sheridan	26	1.92
3	Gary Bollan	24	1.88
4	Simon Mensing	30	1.83
5	Jim Gibson	23	1.78
6	Ian Harty	31	1.74
7	John-Paul Potter	35	1.69
8	Bryn Halliwell	35	1.69
9	Edward Malone	26	1.58
10	Craig Bryson	18	1.56
	CLUB AVERAGE:		1.67

QUEEN OF THE SOUTH

Final Position: **4th**

NICKNAME: THE DOONHAMMER'S

KEY: ☐Won ☐Drawn ☐Lost

							Attendance
1	div1	Ross County	H	L	0-1		1,910
2	div1	St Johnstone	A	W	3-1	Wood 3; McNiven 33,73	2,384
3	cisr1	Albion	H	L	1-2	McNiven 28 pen	1,240
4	div1	Falkirk	H	L	1-3	McNiven 25 pen	2,521
5	div1	Clyde	H	L	0-1		1,639
6	div1	Airdrie Utd	A	W	1-0	McLaughlin 40	1,652
7	div1	Hamilton	H	D	1-1	McNiven 57	1,708
8	div1	Partick	A	W	2-1	McNiven 64; Payne 90	3,233
9	div1	Raith	A	W	2-1	English 45; Bowey 70	1,491
10	div1	St Mirren	H	W	2-1	Burns 5; McNiven 13	2,734
11	div1	St Johnstone	H	L	0-1		2,059
12	div1	Ross County	A	L	0-1		2,354
13	div1	Clyde	A	L	0-2		1,284
14	div1	Airdrie Utd	H	W	1-0	Bowey 53	2,022
15	div1	Hamilton	A	L	0-1		1,592
16	div1	Partick	H	W	1-0	Craig 80	2,221
17	div1	St Mirren	A	D	2-2	Lyle 52; Bowey 55	2,850
18	div1	Raith	H	W	2-0	Lyle 26; Paton 65	1,646
19	div1	Ross County	H	W	1-0	Lyle 20	1,588
20	div1	Falkirk	A	L	2-4	Lyle 12; McColligan 14	3,370
21	div1	Airdrie Utd	A	L	0-2		1,781
22	div1	Hamilton	H	L	1-2	Paton 54	1,790
23	scr3	Montrose	A	W	2-1	Lyle 42; Gibson 50	717
24	div1	Partick	A	L	1-3	Lyle 4	3,257
25	div1	Raith	A	W	1-0	Lyle 87	1,534
26	div1	St Mirren	H	D	0-0		2,016
27	scr4	Dundee Utd	H	L	0-3		5,532
28	div1	St Johnstone	A	D	0-0		1,882
29	div1	Falkirk	H	D	1-1	Lyle 35	2,551
30	div1	Clyde	H	L	0-1		1,448
31	div1	Airdrie Utd	H	D	0-0		1,683
32	div1	Clyde	A	W	1-0	McNiven 69	1,060
33	div1	Hamilton	A	D	1-1	McNiven 1	1,560
34	div1	Partick	H	W	3-1	McNiven 29,50; Paton 35	2,589
35	div1	St Mirren	A	L	0-3		2,327
36	div1	Raith	H	D	1-1	McNiven 25	1,361
37	div1	Ross County	A	D	1-1	Paton 21	2,147
38	div1	St Johnstone	H	W	2-0	Wood 27,29	1,784
39	div1	Falkirk	A	W	2-1	Kernaghan 79 og; McNiven 87	5,067

TEAM OF THE SEASON

G — Richard Barnard CG: 12 DR: 101

D — Brian Reid CG: 19 DR: 95
D — James Thomson CG: 34 DR: 90
D — Tommy English CG: 26 DR: 83
D — Brian McColligan CG: 23 DR: 83

M — Stuart Lovell CG: 12 SD: 18
M — Eric Paton CG: 25 SD: -6
M — Steve Bowey CG: 33 SD: -10
M — David Bagan CG: 12 SD: 0

F — David McNiven CG: 21 SR: 172
F — Derek Lyle CG: 20 SR: 265

KEY PLAYER APPEARANCES

	PLAYER	POS	AGE	APP	MINS ON	GOALS	CARDS(Y/R)	
1	James Thomson	DEF	34	34	3060	0	4	0
2	Steve Bowey	MID	30	34	2977	3	0	0
3	Tommy English	DEF	21	30	2483	1	0	0
4	Eric Paton	MID	26	30	2450	4	2	0
5	Brian McColligan	DEF	24	32	2398	1	7	0
6	David McNiven	ATT	27	29	2060	12	1	0
7	Colin Scott	GK	35	24	2043	0	1	0
8	Brian McLaughlin	MID	31	30	2039	1	0	0
9	Garry Wood	ATT	28	28	1947	3	8	0
10	Derek Lyle	ATT	24	23	1856	7	4	0
11	Brian Reid	DEF	35	19	1710	0	2	0
12	Paul Burns	MID	21	23	1706	1	1	0
13	David Craig	DEF	36	18	1592	1	1	0
14	David Bagan	MID	28	21	1462	0	2	0
15	William Gibson	MID	20	21	1303	0	4	0
16	Richard Barnard	GK	24	13	1108	0	0	0
17	Stuart Lovell	MID	33	12	1071	0	0	0
18	Stephen Payne	MID	21	17	977	1	1	0

KEY PLAYERS - GOALSCORERS

David McNiven

Goals in the League	12
Contribution to Attacking Power — Average number of minutes between League team goals while on pitch	85
Player Strike Rate — Average number of minutes between League goals scored by player	172
Club Strike Rate — Average number of minutes between League goals scored by club	90

	PLAYER	LGE GOALS	POWER	STRIKE RATE
1	David McNiven	12	85	172 mins
2	Derek Lyle	7	88	265 mins
3	Eric Paton	4	88	613 mins
4	Garry Wood	3	102	649 mins
5	Steve Bowey	3	93	992 mins

KEY PLAYERS - MIDFIELDERS

Stuart Lovell

Goals in the League	0
Defensive Rating — Average number of mins between League goals conceded while on the pitch	107
Contribution to Attacking Power — Average number of minutes between League team goals while on pitch	89
Scoring Difference — Defensive Rating minus Contribution to Attacking Power	18

	PLAYER	LGE GOALS	DEF RATE	POWER	SCORE DIFF
1	Stuart Lovell	0	107	89	18 mins
2	David Bagan	0	66	66	0 mins
3	Eric Paton	4	82	88	-6 mins
4	Steve Bowey	3	83	93	-10 mins
5	Paul Burns	1	81	95	-14 mins

KEY PLAYERS - DEFENDERS

Brian Reid

Goals Conceded while on the pitch	18
Defensive Rating — Ave number of mins between League goals conceded while on the pitch	95
Clean Sheets — In games when player was on pitch for at least 70 minutes	5
Club Defensive Rating — Average number of mins between League goals conceded by the club this season.	85

	PLAYER	CON LGE	CLN SHEETS	DEF RATE
1	Brian Reid	18	5	95 mins
2	James Thomson	34	11	90 mins
3	Brian McColligan	29	7	83 mins
4	Tommy English	30	9	83 mins
5	David Craig	22	6	72 mins

KEY GOALKEEPER

Richard Barnard

Goals Conceded in the League	11
Defensive Rating — Ave number of mins between League goals conceded while on the pitch.	101
Counting Games — Games when player was on pitch for at least 70 minutes	12
Clean Sheets — In Games when player was on pitch for at least 70 minutes	4

TOP POINT EARNERS

	PLAYER	GAMES	AV PTS
1	Tommy English	26	1.69
2	David Bagan	12	1.67
3	Brian McLaughlin	19	1.63
4	David McNiven	21	1.62
5	Stuart Lovell	12	1.50
6	Richard Barnard	12	1.50
7	Colin Scott	22	1.50
8	Derek Lyle	20	1.45
9	Brian McColligan	23	1.43
10	Brian Reid	19	1.42
	CLUB AVERAGE:		1.42

AIRDRIE UNITED

Final Position: **5th**

NICKNAME: THE DIAMONDS

KEY: ☐ Won ☐ Drawn ☐ Lost

							Attendance
1	div1	St Johnstone	H	W	1-0	Vareille 85	2,365
2	cisr1	East Fife	H	W	3-0	Vareille 10; Coyle 45; Roberts 61 pen	1,053
3	div1	Partick	A	L	2-3	Coyle 19,67	4,011
4	div1	Raith	H	D	1-1	McKeown 61	2,009
5	cisr2	Clyde	H	L	0-1		1,595
6	div1	Falkirk	A	L	0-5		3,789
7	div1	Queen of South	H	L	0-1		1,652
8	div1	Clyde	A	W	2-1	Barkey 39; Coyle 69	1,367
9	div1	Ross County	H	L	1-2	McKeown 41 pen	1,484
10	div1	St Mirren	A	D	1-1	Roberts 90	3,500
11	div1	Hamilton	H	L	0-2		1,900
12	div1	Partick	H	W	4-2	Wilson, M 20; Coyle 38,83; McLaren 58	2,548
13	div1	St Johnstone	A	D	1-1	Coyle 90	2,500
14	div1	Falkirk	H	L	1-3	Coyle 72	3,245
15	div1	Queen of South	A	L	0-1		2,022
16	div1	Clyde	H	W	3-1	Coyle 14; Roberts 16; Gow 75	1,862
17	div1	Ross County	A	W	2-1	Hardie 16; Lovering 86	2,345
18	div1	Hamilton	A	W	3-1	Coyle 24; Gow 43,78	2,295
19	div1	St Mirren	H	W	3-2	Coyle 32,83; Hardie 68	2,514
20	div1	St Johnstone	H	D	0-0		1,865
21	div1	Raith	A	W	2-0	Hardie 69; Wilson, M 89	1,795
22	div1	Falkirk	A	L	0-1		4,126
23	div1	Queen of South	H	W	2-0	Coyle 31; Gow 74	1,781
24	div1	Clyde	A	L	0-1		1,513
25	div1	Ross County	H	W	2-1	McLaren 42; Coyle 90	1,512
26	div1	St Mirren	A	L	0-1		3,040
27	scr3	Ross County	A	L	1-4	Hardie 40	1,302
28	div1	Partick	A	D	1-1	McManus 24	3,791
29	div1	Raith	H	W	2-1	Wilson, M 27; McKeown 86	1,599
30	div1	Queen of South	A	D	0-0		1,683
31	div1	Hamilton	H	W	1-0	Gow 90	1,430
32	div1	Falkirk	H	D	2-2	Gow 51 pen; McKeown 59	3,111
33	div1	Clyde	H	L	2-4	Hardie 8; Coyle 25	1,641
34	div1	Ross County	A	L	1-3	Gow 2	2,032
35	div1	Hamilton	A	D	1-1	Christie 44	2,030
36	div1	St Mirren	H	L	0-2		1,989
37	div1	St Johnstone	A	W	2-1	McLaren 21; Gow 90	2,239
38	div1	Partick	H	L	0-1		1,747
39	div1	Raith	A	W	1-0	Gow 39 pen	1,296

TEAM OF THE SEASON

- G — Mark McGeown, CG: 30 DR: 64
- D — Neil McGowan, CG: 25 DR: 75
- D — Paul Lovering, CG: 27 DR: 73
- D — Allan McManus, CG: 25 DR: 71
- D — Kevin Christie, CG: 17 DR: 51
- M — William McLaren, CG: 21 SD: 7
- M — Martin Hardie, CG: 22 SD: 4
- M — Marvyn Wilson, CG: 36 SD: -6
- M — Stevie Docherty, CG: 21 SD: -13
- F — Owen Coyle, CG: 33 SR: 203
- F — Alan Gow, CG: 23 SR: 233

KEY PLAYER APPEARANCES

	PLAYER	POS	AGE	APP	MINS ON	GOALS	CARDS(Y/R)	
1	Marvyn Wilson	MID	31	36	3219	3	3	0
2	Owen Coyle	ATT	38	33	2843	14	1	0
3	Mark McGeown	GK	35	30	2700	0	1	0
4	Neil McGowan	DEF	40	32	2563	0	1	0
5	Paul Lovering	DEF	29	29	2474	1	7	1
6	Allan McManus	DEF	30	30	2422	1	4	0
7	Alan Gow	ATT	22	25	2099	9	0	0
8	Stevie Docherty	MID	29	28	2082	0	8	1
9	Martin Hardie	MID	29	25	2006	4	8	0
10	William McLaren	MID	20	26	1959	3	3	0
11	Mark Roberts	ATT	29	31	1840	2	1	0
12	Kevin Christie	DEF	29	19	1586	1	6	0
13	Stephen McKeown	ATT	23	22	1531	4	1	0
14	Jerome Vareille	ATT	31	28	1179	1	1	0
15	David Dunn	MID	23	24	1134	0	0	0
16	Willie Wilson	MID	32	19	1065	0	1	0
17	Kevin Barkey	MID	20	18	993	1	0	0
18	Stephen McKenna	DEF	19	8	710	0	0	0

KEY PLAYERS - GOALSCORERS

Owen Coyle

Goals in the League	14
Contribution to Attacking Power — Average number of minutes between League team goals while on pitch	74
Player Strike Rate — Average number of minutes between League goals scored by player	203
Club Strike Rate — Average number of minutes between League goals scored by club	74

	PLAYER	LGE GOALS	POWER	STRIKE RATE
1	Owen Coyle	14	74	203 mins
2	Alan Gow	9	65	233 mins
3	Stephen McKeown	4	80	383 mins
4	Martin Hardie	4	65	502 mins
5	William McLaren	3	75	653 mins

KEY PLAYERS - MIDFIELDERS

William McLaren

Goals in the League	3
Defensive Rating — Average number of mins between League goals conceded while on the pitch	82
Contribution to Attacking Power — Average number of minutes between League team goals while on pitch	75
Scoring Difference — Defensive Rating minus Contribution to Attacking Power	7

	PLAYER	LGE GOALS	DEF RATE	POWER	SCORE DIFF
1	William McLaren	3	82	75	7 mins
2	Martin Hardie	4	69	65	4 mins
3	Marvyn Wilson	3	67	73	-6 mins
4	Stevie Docherty	0	67	80	-13 mins

KEY PLAYERS - DEFENDERS

Neil McGowan

Goals Conceded while on the pitch	34
Defensive Rating — Ave number of mins between League goals conceded while on the pitch	75
Clean Sheets — In games when player was on pitch for at least 70 minutes	5
Club Defensive Rating — Average number of mins between League goals conceded by the club this season.	68

	PLAYER	CON LGE	CLN SHEETS	DEF RATE
1	Neil McGowan	34	5	75 mins
2	Paul Lovering	34	7	73 mins
3	Allan McManus	34	5	71 mins
4	Kevin Christie	31	2	51 mins

KEY GOALKEEPER

Mark McGeown

Goals Conceded in the League	42
Defensive Rating — Ave number of mins between League goals conceded while on the pitch.	64
Counting Games — Games when player was on pitch for at least 70 minutes	30
Clean Sheets — In Games when player was on pitch for at least 70 minutes	6

TOP POINT EARNERS

	PLAYER	GAMES	AV PTS
1	Mark Roberts	15	1.93
2	Alan Gow	23	1.74
3	Paul Lovering	27	1.67
4	William McLaren	21	1.67
5	Stevie Docherty	21	1.48
6	Martin Hardie	22	1.45
7	Neil McGowan	25	1.40
8	Marvyn Wilson	36	1.39
9	Owen Coyle	33	1.33
10	Allan McManus	25	1.28
	CLUB AVERAGE:		1.39

ROSS COUNTY

Final Position: **6th**

NICKNAME: THE HIGHLANDERS — KEY: Won / Drawn / Lost

								Attendance
1	div1	Queen of South	A	W	1-0	Burke 40		1,910
2	cisr1	Dumbarton	A	W	3-1	Burke 26,40,85 pen		437
3	div1	St Mirren	H	D	1-1	Burke 3		2,666
4	div1	Clyde	A	L	0-1			1,101
5	cisr2	Inverness CT	H	L	0-1			3,315
6	div1	Partick	H	L	0-1			2,781
7	div1	Raith	A	W	2-1	Lauchlan 35; Adam 49		1,540
8	div1	St Johnstone	H	L	0-1			2,486
9	div1	Airdrie Utd	A	W	2-1	Canning 6; Winters 54		1,484
10	div1	Hamilton	A	W	2-1	Lauchlan 28; Higgins 74		1,522
11	div1	Falkirk	H	L	0-1			3,062
12	div1	St Mirren	A	L	2-3	Gillies 21 og; Adam 67		2,538
13	div1	Queen of South	H	W	1-0	Cowie 46		2,354
14	div1	Partick	A	L	0-4			2,898
15	div1	St Johnstone	A	D	1-1	Higgins 46		2,018
16	div1	Airdrie Utd	H	L	1-2	Docherty 40 og		2,345
17	div1	Raith	H	D	1-1	Burke 15		1,193
18	div1	Falkirk	A	D	2-2	McGarry 21; Malcolm 90		3,330
19	div1	Hamilton	H	D	1-1	McGarry 57		2,034
20	div1	Queen of South	A	L	0-1			1,588
21	div1	Clyde	H	L	0-1			1,953
22	div1	Partick	H	W	2-1	Cowie 10; Canning 52		3,112
23	div1	Raith	A	W	4-1	Cowie 53; Lauchlan 60; Winters 73; Burke 78		1,127
24	div1	St Johnstone	H	W	4-0	Winters 14,17; Canning 34; Lauchlan 81		3,105
25	div1	Airdrie Utd	A	L	1-2	Winters 60		1,512
26	div1	Hamilton	A	W	1-0	Winters 77		1,476
27	scr3	Airdrie Utd	H	W	4-1	Burke 23 pen; McGeown 32 og; Winters 51,55		1,302
28	div1	Falkirk	H	L	0-1			3,151
29	scr4	Clyde	H	D	0-0			1,629
30	scr4r	Clyde	A	L	1-2	Rankin 17		1,576
31	div1	Clyde	A	L	0-1			1,086
32	div1	St Mirren	H	L	0-1			1,302
33	div1	Raith	H	W	2-0	Burke 67; Higgins 86		2,083
34	div1	Partick	A	D	0-0			2,939
35	div1	St Johnstone	A	W	2-0	Canning 47; McGarry 55		1,828
36	div1	Airdrie Utd	H	W	3-1	Cowie 44; Higgins 57,78		2,032
37	div1	Falkirk	A	L	0-1			5,209
38	div1	Hamilton	H	W	2-1	Cowie 19; Kilgannon 59		2,107
39	div1	Queen of South	H	D	1-1	McGarry 12		2,147
40	div1	St Mirren	A	L	0-1			3,906
41	div1	Clyde	H	D	1-1	Burke 69		2,130

TEAM OF THE SEASON

G — Colin Stewart CG: 20 DR: 101

D — John Robertson CG: 23 DR: 90
D — Mark McCulloch CG: 36 DR: 88
D — Martin Canning CG: 33 DR: 87
D — Jim Lauchlan CG: 26 DR: 84

M — Fergus Tiernan CG: 14 SD: 29
M — John Rankin CG: 26 SD: 24
M — Sean Kilgannon CG: 14 SD: 5
M — Don Cowie CG: 33 SD: 2

F — David Winters CG: 12 SR: 290
F — Alex Burke CG: 25 SR: 408

KEY PLAYER APPEARANCES

	PLAYER	POS	AGE	APP	MINS ON	GOALS	CARDS(Y)	CARDS(R)
1	Mark McCulloch	DEF	30	36	3240	0	1	0
2	Don Cowie	MID	22	34	2970	5	1	0
3	Martin Canning	DEF	23	33	2970	4	0	0
4	John Rankin	MID	22	30	2492	0	3	0
5	Alex Burke	ATT	27	32	2447	6	2	0
6	Jim Lauchlan	DEF	28	28	2432	4	4	0
7	John Robertson	DEF	29	25	2169	0	1	0
8	Jamie McCunnie	MID	22	27	2168	0	3	0
9	Colin Stewart	GK	25	21	1826	0	0	0
10	Sean Kilgannon	MID	24	30	1810	1	1	0
11	David Winters	ATT	22	32	1742	6	0	0
12	Steven McGarry	ATT	25	33	1696	4	1	1
13	Stuart Garden	GK	33	16	1414	0	0	0
14	Fergus Tiernan	MID	23	16	1355	0	2	0
15	Sean Higgins	ATT	20	26	1210	5	1	0
16	Stuart Malcolm	DEF	25	13	952	1	3	0
17	Gary McSwegan	ATT	34	17	843	0	0	0
18	Charlie Adam	MID	19	10	681	2	4	0

KEY PLAYERS - GOALSCORERS

David Winters

Goals in the League	6	Player Strike Rate — Average number of minutes between League goals scored by player	290
Contribution to Attacking Power — Average number of minutes between League team goals while on pitch	79	Club Strike Rate — Average number of minutes between League goals scored by club	81

	PLAYER	LGE GOALS	POWER	STRIKE RATE
1	David Winters	6	79	290 mins
2	Alex Burke	6	74	408 mins
3	Steven McGarry	4	94	424 mins
4	Don Cowie	5	83	594 mins
5	Jim Lauchlan	4	81	608 mins

KEY PLAYERS - MIDFIELDERS

Fergus Tiernan

Goals in the League	0	Contribution to Attacking Power — Average number of minutes between League team goals while on pitch	68
Defensive Rating — Average number of mins between League goals conceded while on the pitch	97	Scoring Difference — Defensive Rating minus Contribution to Attacking Power	29

	PLAYER	LGE GOALS	DEF RATE	POWER	SCORE DIFF
1	Fergus Tiernan	0	97	68	29 mins
2	John Rankin	0	100	76	24 mins
3	Sean Kilgannon	1	75	70	5 mins
4	Don Cowie	5	85	83	2 mins
5	Jamie McCunnie	0	90	94	-4 mins

KEY PLAYERS - DEFENDERS

John Robertson

Goals Conceded while on the pitch	24	Clean Sheets — In games when player was on pitch for at least 70 minutes	3
Defensive Rating — Ave number of mins between League goals conceded while on the pitch	90	Club Defensive Rating — Average number of mins between League goals conceded by the club this season.	88

	PLAYER	CON LGE	CLN SHEETS	DEF RATE
1	John Robertson	24	3	90 mins
2	Mark McCulloch	37	7	88 mins
3	Martin Canning	34	7	87 mins
4	Jim Lauchlan	29	6	84 mins

KEY GOALKEEPER

Colin Stewart

Goals Conceded in the League	18
Defensive Rating — Ave number of mins between League goals conceded while on the pitch.	101
Counting Games — Games when player was on pitch for at least 70 minutes	20
Clean Sheets — In Games when player was on pitch for at least 70 minutes	5

TOP POINT EARNERS

	PLAYER	GAMES	AV PTS
1	Steven McGarry	13	1.69
2	Fergus Tiernan	14	1.57
3	Sean Kilgannon	14	1.50
4	Alex Burke	25	1.44
5	Jamie McCunnie	23	1.43
6	John Rankin	26	1.42
7	Colin Stewart	20	1.40
8	Jim Lauchlan	26	1.35
9	David Winters	12	1.33
10	Martin Canning	33	1.33
	CLUB AVERAGE:		1.31

HAMILTON ACADEMICAL

Final Position: **7th**

NICKNAME: THE ACCIES

KEY: ☐ Won ☐ Drawn ☐ Lost

	Comp	Opponent	H/A	Result	Score	Scorers	Attendance
1	div1	Raith	H	W	2-0	McLaughlin, M 77; Smart 80 og	2,176
2	div1	Falkirk	A	D	1-1	Carrigan 37 pen	3,762
3	cisr1	Ayr	H	W	4-1	Thomson 23; Convery 34,51,58	1,017
4	div1	Partick	H	L	0-1		3,543
5	cisr2	Kilmarnock	A	L	0-3		3,375
6	div1	St Mirren	A	L	0-1		2,978
7	div1	St Johnstone	H	D	1-1	Corcoran 46	1,904
8	div1	Queen of South	A	D	1-1	Lumsden 18	1,708
9	div1	Clyde	H	L	0-1		2,017
10	div1	Ross County	H	L	1-2	Tunbridge 9	1,522
11	div1	Airdrie Utd	A	W	2-0	McLaughlin, M 70; Tunbridge 90	1,900
12	div1	Falkirk	H	L	0-1		2,870
13	div1	Raith	A	D	2-2	Carrigan 7,51	1,943
14	div1	St Mirren	H	D	2-2	Carrigan 15; Tunbridge 58	2,529
15	div1	St Johnstone	A	L	0-3		1,869
16	div1	Queen of South	H	W	1-0	Thomson 88	1,592
17	div1	Clyde	A	L	1-2	Tunbridge 29	1,200
18	div1	Airdrie Utd	H	L	1-3	McPhee 11	2,295
19	div1	Ross County	A	D	1-1	Tunbridge 62	2,034
20	div1	Raith	H	W	1-0	McPhee 87	1,371
21	div1	Partick	A	W	1-0	McPhee 13	3,051
22	div1	St Mirren	A	W	1-0	van Zanten 69 og	2,888
23	div1	St Johnstone	H	L	0-3		1,718
24	div1	Queen of South	A	W	2-1	Corcoran 32; McLeod 48	1,790
25	scr3	St Mirren	A	L	0-3		2,700
26	div1	Clyde	H	L	0-1		1,873
27	div1	Ross County	H	L	0-1		1,476
28	div1	Falkirk	A	D	1-1	Javary 1	3,530
29	div1	Partick	H	W	1-0	Keogh 70	3,128
30	div1	St Johnstone	A	W	2-0	Corcoran 44; Cramb 73	1,832
31	div1	Airdrie Utd	A	L	0-1		1,430
32	div1	St Mirren	H	D	0-0		1,950
33	div1	Queen of South	H	D	1-1	Cramb 80 pen	1,560
34	div1	Clyde	A	W	3-1	Keogh 53,68; Hardy 55	1,235
35	div1	Airdrie Utd	H	D	1-1	Hardy 42	2,030
36	div1	Ross County	A	L	1-2	Convery 90	2,107
37	div1	Raith	A	W	2-0	Keogh 4; Hamilton 24	1,474
38	div1	Falkirk	H	W	1-0	Convery 31	2,300
39	div1	Partick	A	D	1-1	Hardy 60	2,806

TEAM OF THE SEASON

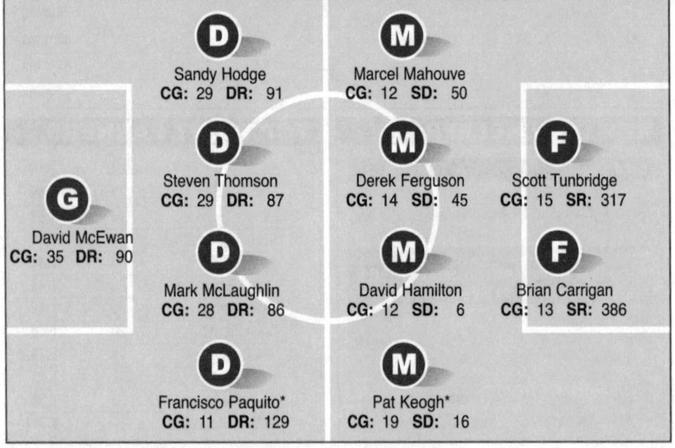
G
David McEwan
CG: 35 DR: 90
D
Sandy Hodge
CG: 29 DR: 91
D
Steven Thomson
CG: 29 DR: 87
D
Mark McLaughlin
CG: 28 DR: 86
D
Francisco Paquito*
CG: 11 DR: 129
M
Marcel Mahouve
CG: 12 SD: 50
M
Derek Ferguson
CG: 14 SD: 45
M
David Hamilton
CG: 12 SD: 6
M
Pat Keogh*
CG: 19 SD: 16
F
Scott Tunbridge
CG: 15 SR: 317
F
Brian Carrigan
CG: 13 SR: 386

KEY PLAYER APPEARANCES

	PLAYER	POS	AGE	APP	MINS ON	GOALS	CARDS (Y)	CARDS (R)
1	David McEwan	GK	23	35	3150	0	0	0
2	Sandy Hodge	DEF	24	32	2741	0	2	0
3	Steven Thomson	DEF	32	31	2707	1	1	0
4	Mark Corcoran	ATT	24	33	2668	3	3	0
5	Mark McLaughlin	DEF	29	28	2503	2	7	0
6	Pat Keogh	ATT	29	25	1928	4	3	0
7	Brian McPhee	ATT	34	27	1707	2	1	0
8	Scott Tunbridge	ATT	23	20	1586	5	4	0
9	Brian Carrigan	ATT	25	26	1542	4	3	1
10	Richard Waddell	ATT	24	19	1511	0	1	0
11	David Hamilton	MID	25	24	1361	1	3	0
12	Derek Ferguson	MID	37	18	1312	0	4	0
13	Iain Fyfe	DEF	23	17	1130	0	1	0
14	Lee Hardy	MID	33	13	1059	3	2	0
15	Marcel Mahouve	MID	32	12	1050	0	2	0
16	Francisco Paquito	DEF	35	12	1028	0	0	0
17	Chris Aitken	MID	24	18	919	0	5	0
18	Jean-Phillipe Javary	MID	27	13	864	1	1	0

KEY PLAYERS - GOALSCORERS

Scott Tunbridge

Goals in the League	5
Contribution to Attacking Power Average number of minutes between League team goals while on pitch	93
Player Strike Rate Average number of minutes between League goals scored by player	317
Club Strike Rate Average number of minutes between League goals scored by club	93

	PLAYER	LGE GOALS	POWER	STRIKE RATE
1	Scott Tunbridge	5	93	317 mins
2	Brian Carrigan	4	102	386 mins
3	Pat Keogh	4	80	482 mins
4	Brian McPhee	2	100	854 mins
5	Mark Corcoran	3	95	889 mins

KEY PLAYERS - MIDFIELDERS

Marcel Mahouve

Goals in the League	0
Defensive Rating Average number of mins between League goals conceded while on the pitch	131
Contribution to Attacking Power Average number of minutes between League team goals while on pitch	81
Scoring Difference Defensive Rating minus Contribution to Attacking Power	50

	PLAYER	LGE GOALS	DEF RATE	POWER	SCORE DIFF
1	Marcel Mahouve	0	131	81	50 mins
2	Pat Keogh	4	96	80	16 mins
3	Derek Ferguson	0	146	101	45 mins
4	David Hamilton	1	91	85	6 mins

KEY PLAYERS - DEFENDERS

Sandy Hodge

Goals Conceded while on the pitch	30
Defensive Rating Ave number of mins between League goals conceded while on the pitch	91
Clean Sheets In games when player was on pitch for at least 70 minutes	10
Club Defensive Rating Average number of mins between League goals conceded by the club this season.	90

	PLAYER	CON LGE	CLN SHEETS	DEF RATE
1	Sandy Hodge	30	10	91 mins
2	Steven Thomson	31	9	87 mins
3	Mark McLaughlin	29	9	86 mins
4	Francisco Paquito*	8	5	129 mins

KEY GOALKEEPER

David McEwan

Goals Conceded in the League	35
Defensive Rating Ave number of mins between League goals conceded while on the pitch.	90
Counting Games Games when player was on pitch for at least 70 minutes	35
Clean Sheets In Games when player was on pitch for at least 70 minutes	11

TOP POINT EARNERS

	PLAYER	GAMES	AV PTS
1	Marcel Mahouve	12	1.67
2	Derek Ferguson	14	1.64
3	Sandy Hodge	29	1.41
4	Scott Tunbridge	15	1.40
5	David Hamilton	12	1.33
6	Mark McLaughlin	28	1.32
7	David McEwan	35	1.31
8	Steven Thomson	29	1.21
9	Brian McPhee	17	1.18
10	Mark Corcoran	28	1.18
	CLUB AVERAGE:		1.31

ST JOHNSTONE

Final Position: **8th**

NICKNAME: THE SAINTS

KEY: ☐Won ☐Drawn ☐Lost

							Attendance
1	div1	Airdrie Utd	A	L	0-1		2,365
2	cisr1	Alloa	H	L	2-3	Hannah 84; Hay 85	1,500
3	div1	Queen of South	H	L	1-3	Fotheringham 79	2,384
4	div1	St Mirren	A	L	1-2	Moore 7	3,079
5	div1	Raith	H	W	1-0	Fotheringham 74	2,570
6	div1	Hamilton	A	D	1-1	Baxter 47	1,904
7	div1	Ross County	A	W	1-0	Hannah 31 pen	2,486
8	div1	Falkirk	H	L	1-2	Baxter 78	3,835
9	div1	Partick	H	W	2-1	MacDonald 84,90	2,763
10	div1	Clyde	A	L	0-1		1,456
11	div1	Queen of South	A	W	1-0	Hay 60	2,059
12	div1	Airdrie Utd	H	D	1-1	Christie 71 og	2,500
13	div1	Raith	A	L	0-1		2,089
14	div1	Hamilton	H	W	3-0	MacDonald 31; Moore 80; Hay 82	1,869
15	div1	Ross County	H	D	1-1	MacDonald 7	2,018
16	div1	Falkirk	A	L	1-3	Hannah 6 pen	3,439
17	div1	Clyde	H	W	3-0	Sheerin 51; Moore 80,85	2,026
18	div1	Partick	A	W	4-0	McCann 13; Anderson 32; MacDonald 73; Hay 82	2,945
19	div1	Airdrie Utd	A	D	0-0		1,865
20	div1	St Mirren	H	W	1-0	McCann 40	2,233
21	div1	Raith	H	W	2-0	Maxwell 12; MacDonald 45	2,579
22	div1	Hamilton	A	W	3-0	Hay 17; Sheerin 39; McCann 69	1,718
23	div1	Ross County	A	L	0-4		3,105
24	scr3	Inverness CT	A	L	0-1		2,021
25	div1	Falkirk	H	L	0-3		3,395
26	div1	Partick	H	D	1-1	MacDonald 65	2,814
27	div1	Queen of South	H	D	0-0		1,882
28	div1	St Mirren	A	D	1-1	MacDonald 13	2,716
29	div1	Hamilton	H	L	0-2		1,832
30	div1	Raith	A	W	2-1	Anderson 32; McAnespie 79	1,350
31	div1	Ross County	H	L	0-2		1,828
32	div1	Clyde	A	D	1-1	McManus 50	1,223
33	div1	Falkirk	A	L	0-3		3,720
34	div1	Clyde	H	D	0-0		1,770
35	div1	Partick	A	W	4-0	MacDonald 10,45,85; Dobbie 14	2,334
36	div1	Airdrie Utd	H	L	1-2	Dobbie 57	2,239
37	div1	Queen of South	A	L	0-2		1,784
38	div1	St Mirren	H	D	0-0		2,920

TEAM OF THE SEASON

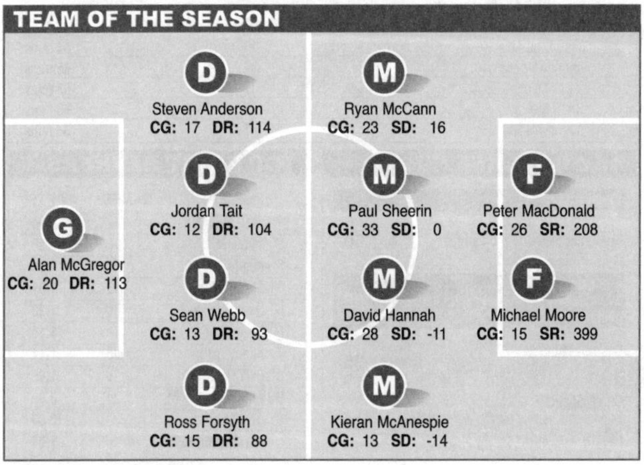

D
Steven Anderson
CG: 17 DR: 114
M
Ryan McCann
CG: 23 SD: 16
D
Jordan Tait
CG: 12 DR: 104
M
Paul Sheerin
CG: 33 SD: 0
F
Peter MacDonald
CG: 26 SR: 208
G
Alan McGregor
CG: 20 DR: 113
D
Sean Webb
CG: 13 DR: 93
M
David Hannah
CG: 28 SD: -11
F
Michael Moore
CG: 15 SR: 399
D
Ross Forsyth
CG: 15 DR: 88
M
Kieran McAnespie
CG: 13 SD: -14

KEY PLAYER APPEARANCES

	PLAYER	POS	AGE	APP	MINS ON	GOALS	CARDS(Y	/R)
1	Paul Sheerin	MID	30	34	2974	2	1	0
2	Ian Maxwell	DEF	30	33	2966	1	5	1
3	David Hannah	MID	31	29	2504	2	4	0
4	Peter MacDonald	ATT	24	27	2290	11	2	1
5	Ryan McCann	MID	23	26	2134	3	2	0
6	Alan McGregor	GK	23	20	1800	0	1	0
7	Michael Moore	ATT	24	23	1596	4	5	1
8	Steven Anderson	DEF	19	19	1589	2	4	1
9	Kevin Rutkiewicz	DEF	25	20	1457	0	3	1
10	Sean Webb	DEF	22	19	1391	0	4	2
11	Ross Forsyth	DEF	22	16	1322	0	4	0
12	Kieran McAnespie	MID	25	17	1212	1	0	0
13	Chris Hay	ATT	30	29	1193	4	1	0
14	Jordan Tait	DEF	25	14	1148	0	1	0
15	Mark Baxter	DEF	20	15	1076	2	0	0
16	Craig Samson	GK	21	12	1029	0	0	0
17	David Cowan	DEF	23	10	900	0	0	0
18	Lee Hardy	MID	33	13	852	0	0	0

KEY PLAYERS - GOALSCORERS

Peter MacDonald

Goals in the League	11	Player Strike Rate Average number of minutes between League goals scored by player	208
Contribution to Attacking Power Average number of minutes between League team goals while on pitch	81	Club Strike Rate Average number of minutes between League goals scored by club	85

	PLAYER	LGE GOALS	POWER	STRIKE RATE
1	Peter MacDonald	11	81	208 mins
2	Michael Moore	4	76	399 mins
3	Ryan McCann	3	69	711 mins
4	Steven Anderson	2	72	795 mins
5	Kieran McAnespie	1	101	1212 mins

KEY PLAYERS - MIDFIELDERS

Ryan McCann

Goals in the League	3	Contribution to Attacking Power Average number of minutes between League team goals while on pitch	69
Defensive Rating Average number of mins between League goals conceded while on the pitch	85	Scoring Difference Defensive Rating minus Contribution to Attacking Power	16

	PLAYER	LGE GOALS	DEF RATE	POWER	SCORE DIFF
1	Ryan McCann	3	85	69	16 mins
2	Paul Sheerin	2	87	87	0 mins
3	David Hannah	2	78	89	-11 mins
4	Kieran McAnespie	1	87	101	-14 mins

KEY PLAYERS - DEFENDERS

Steven Anderson

Goals Conceded while on the pitch	14	Clean Sheets In games when player was on pitch for at least 70 minutes	9
Defensive Rating Ave number of mins between League goals conceded while on the pitch	114	Club Defensive Rating Average number of mins between League goals conceded by the club this season.	83

	PLAYER	CON LGE	CLN SHEETS	DEF RATE
1	Steven Anderson	14	9	114 mins
2	Jordan Tait	11	7	104 mins
3	Sean Webb	15	8	93 mins
4	Ross Forsyth	15	5	88 mins
5	Ian Maxwell	35	14	85 mins

KEY GOALKEEPER

Alan McGregor

Goals Conceded in the League	16
Defensive Rating Ave number of mins between League goals conceded while on the pitch.	113
Counting Games Games when player was on pitch for at least 70 minutes	20
Clean Sheets In Games when player was on pitch for at least 70 minutes	10

TOP POINT EARNERS

	PLAYER	GAMES	AV PTS
1	Steven Anderson	17	1.82
2	Alan McGregor	20	1.70
3	Jordan Tait	12	1.67
4	Sean Webb	13	1.54
5	Ryan McCann	23	1.52
6	Paul Sheerin	33	1.36
7	Peter MacDonald	26	1.35
8	Ross Forsyth	15	1.33
9	David Hannah	28	1.29
10	Kevin Rutkiewicz	15	1.27
	CLUB AVERAGE:		1.28

PARTICK THISTLE

Final Position: **9th**

NICKNAME: THE JAGS

KEY: ☐Won ☐Drawn ☐Lost

							Attendance
1	div1	Clyde	A	L	1-2	Ramon 80	3,800
2	div1	Airdrie Utd	H	W	3-2	Ramon 34; Hinds 53; Mitchell 69	4,011
3	div1	Hamilton	A	W	1-0	Ramon 31	3,543
4	cisr2	Stenhousemuir	A	W	5-2	Gibson, B 13; Ramon 20; Fleming 38 pen; Hinds 84,86	1,562
5	div1	Ross County	A	W	1-0	Hinds 54	2,781
6	div1	Falkirk	H	L	1-4	Panther 65	5,157
7	div1	St Mirren	A	L	1-2	Ramon 16	4,711
8	div1	Queen of South	H	L	1-2	Ramon 9	3,233
9	cisr3	Dunfermline	A	L	1-3	Dowie 39	2,301
10	div1	St Johnstone	A	L	1-2	Milne 65	2,763
11	div1	Raith	H	W	2-0	Panther 2; One 21	3,059
12	div1	Airdrie Utd	A	L	2-4	Madaschi 44; Ramon 66	2,548
13	div1	Clyde	H	D	0-0		4,026
14	div1	Ross County	H	W	4-0	Ramon 13,17; Madaschi 53; One 88	2,898
15	div1	St Mirren	H	L	0-3		4,949
16	div1	Queen of South	A	L	0-1		2,221
17	div1	Falkirk	A	L	0-3		3,335
18	div1	Raith	A	D	0-0		2,452
19	div1	St Johnstone	H	L	0-4		2,945
20	div1	Clyde	A	D	1-1	Wilkinson 39	1,800
21	div1	Hamilton	H	L	0-1		3,051
22	div1	Ross County	A	L	1-2	Ramon 77	3,112
23	div1	Falkirk	H	W	2-1	One 9,61	4,120
24	div1	St Mirren	A	D	1-1	Fleming 41	3,779
25	scr3	Hearts	H	D	0-0		5,666
26	div1	Queen of South	H	W	3-1	One 20; Craig 37 og; Paton 69 og	3,257
27	scr3r	Hearts	A	L	1-2	One 8	7,340
28	div1	St Johnstone	A	D	1-1	Ramon 66	2,814
29	div1	Raith	H	W	4-1	Ross, A 41; One 58; McConalogue 80,85	3,181
30	div1	Airdrie Utd	H	D	1-1	Fleming 14	3,791
31	div1	Hamilton	A	L	0-1		3,128
32	div1	Falkirk	A	L	1-2	Murray 28 pen	4,157
33	div1	Ross County	H	D	0-0		2,939
34	div1	St Mirren	H	D	0-0		3,730
35	div1	Queen of South	A	L	1-3	McConalogue 57	2,589
36	div1	Raith	A	L	1-2	Ramon 87	1,403
37	div1	St Johnstone	H	L	0-4		2,334
38	div1	Clyde	H	W	1-0	McConalogue 43	2,694
39	div1	Airdrie Utd	A	W	1-0	Hinds 7	1,747
40	div1	Hamilton	H	D	1-1	Lumsden 21 og	2,806

TEAM OF THE SEASON

G Kenny Arthur CG: 35 DR: 63

D Jean Yves Anis CG: 12 DR: 84
D Andrew Dowie CG: 22 DR: 65
D Derek Fleming CG: 30 DR: 63
D Grant Murray CG: 30 DR: 58

M Jamie Mitchell CG: 12 SD: -14
M Steve Fulton CG: 13 SD: -15
M Ken Milne CG: 21 SD: -16
M Billy Gibson CG: 20 SD: -29

F Juan Ramon CG: 24 SR: 211
F Leigh Hinds CG: 19 SR: 731

KEY PLAYER APPEARANCES

	PLAYER	POS	AGE	APP	MINS ON	GOALS	CARDS(Y/R)	
1	Kenny Arthur	GK	26	35	3150	0	0	0
2	Derek Fleming	DEF	31	35	2825	2	5	0
3	Grant Murray	DEF	29	32	2774	1	2	1
4	Juan Ramon	ATT	28	30	2320	11	2	0
5	Adrian Madaschi	DEF	22	27	2314	2	2	0
6	Ken Milne	MID	25	30	2212	1	5	0
7	Andrew Dowie	DEF	22	27	2193	0	3	1
8	Leigh Hinds	ATT	26	35	2192	3	3	0
9	Billy Gibson	MID	23	26	1981	0	6	0
10	Jamie Mitchell	MID	29	20	1436	1	1	0
11	Steve Fulton	MID	34	19	1402	0	2	0
12	Jean Yves Anis	DEF	24	17	1263	0	0	0
13	Armand One	ATT	22	27	1226	6	3	0
14	Andy Ross	MID	22	15	1099	1	2	0
15	Andy Gibson	MID	23	14	1063	0	2	0
16	Darren Brady	MID	23	11	848	0	0	0
17	Stephen McConalogue	ATT	24	12	755	4	4	0
18	Andy Wilkinson	DEF	20	12	744	1	2	1

KEY PLAYERS - GOALSCORERS

Juan Ramon

Goals in the League	11	Player Strike Rate Average number of minutes between League goals scored by player	211
Contribution to Attacking Power Average number of minutes between League team goals while on pitch	80	Club Strike Rate Average number of minutes between League goals scored by club	85

	PLAYER	LGE GOALS	POWER	STRIKE RATE
1	Juan Ramon	11	80	211 mins
2	Leigh Hinds	3	95	731 mins
3	Adrian Madaschi	2	79	1157 mins
4	Derek Fleming	2	78	1413 mins
5	Jamie Mitchell	1	76	1436 mins

KEY PLAYERS - MIDFIELDERS

Jamie Mitchell

Goals in the League	1	Contribution to Attacking Power Average number of minutes between League team goals while on pitch	76
Defensive Rating Average number of mins between League goals conceded while on the pitch	62	Scoring Difference Defensive Rating minus Contribution to Attacking Power	-14

	PLAYER	LGE GOALS	DEF RATE	POWER	SCORE DIFF
1	Jamie Mitchell	1	62	76	-14 mins
2	Steve Fulton	0	67	82	-15 mins
3	Ken Milne	1	63	79	-16 mins
4	Billy Gibson	0	57	86	-29 mins

KEY PLAYERS - DEFENDERS

Jean Yves Anis

Goals Conceded while on the pitch	15	Clean Sheets In games when player was on pitch for at least 70 minutes	4
Defensive Rating Ave number of mins between League goals conceded while on the pitch	84	Club Defensive Rating Average number of mins between League goals conceded by the club this season.	62

	PLAYER	CON LGE	CLN SHEETS	DEF RATE
1	Jean Yves Anis	15	4	84 mins
2	Andrew Dowie	34	7	65 mins
3	Derek Fleming	45	9	63 mins
4	Grant Murray	48	7	58 mins
5	Adrian Madaschi	43	4	54 mins

KEY GOALKEEPER

Kenny Arthur

Goals Conceded in the League	50
Defensive Rating Ave number of mins between League goals conceded while on the pitch.	63
Counting Games Games when he played at least 70 mins	35
Clean Sheets In games when he played at least 70 mins	10

TOP POINT EARNERS

	PLAYER	GAMES	AV PTS
1	Jean Yves Anis	12	2.00
2	Jamie Mitchell	12	1.50
3	Ken Milne	21	1.33
4	Steve Fulton	13	1.31
5	Derek Fleming	30	1.23
6	Leigh Hinds	19	1.16
7	Kenny Arthur	35	1.11
8	Billy Gibson	20	1.05
9	Adrian Madaschi	24	0.96
10	Grant Murray	30	0.93
	CLUB AVERAGE:		1.08

RAITH ROVERS

Final Position: **10th**

NICKNAME: ROVERS

KEY: Won Drawn Lost

							Attendance
1	div1	Hamilton	A	L	0-2		2,176
2	cisr1	Stranraer	A	L	1-2	Paquito 52	420
3	div1	Clyde	H	L	2-3	Sacko 79; Potter 85 og	1,784
4	div1	Airdrie Utd	A	D	1-1	Sacko 6	2,009
5	div1	St Johnstone	A	L	0-1		2,570
6	div1	Ross County	H	L	1-2	Ebanda 58	1,540
7	div1	Falkirk	A	L	2-4	Sacko 12; Young 89	3,449
8	div1	St Mirren	H	L	0-3		2,111
9	div1	Queen of South	H	L	1-2	Ebanda 5	1,491
10	div1	Partick	A	L	0-2		3,059
11	div1	Clyde	A	L	0-2		1,196
12	div1	Hamilton	H	D	2-2	Sacko 4; Daly 64 pen	1,943
13	div1	St Johnstone	H	W	1-0	Martin 36	2,089
14	div1	Falkirk	H	L	0-2		3,050
15	div1	St Mirren	A	L	0-1		3,010
16	div1	Ross County	A	D	1-1	Ouattara 71	1,193
17	div1	Partick	H	D	0-0		2,452
18	div1	Queen of South	A	L	0-2		1,646
19	div1	Hamilton	A	L	0-1		1,371
20	div1	Airdrie Utd	H	L	0-2		1,795
21	div1	St Johnstone	A	L	0-2		2,579
22	div1	Ross County	H	L	1-4	Malcolm 14	1,127
23	div1	Falkirk	A	L	0-2		3,516
24	scr3	Alloa	H	L	0-2		1,545
25	div1	St Mirren	H	W	2-0	Brady 60; Martin 63	1,393
26	div1	Queen of South	H	L	0-1		1,534
27	div1	Partick	A	L	1-4	Murtagh 9	3,181
28	div1	Clyde	H	D	3-3	Tulloch 16; Clark 70,80	1,394
29	div1	Airdrie Utd	A	L	1-2	Tulloch 38	1,599
30	div1	Ross County	A	L	0-2		2,083
31	div1	St Johnstone	H	L	1-2	Clark 21	1,350
32	div1	Falkirk	H	D	3-3	Martin 45,58; McMullan 71	2,346
33	div1	St Mirren	A	L	0-3		2,193
34	div1	Partick	H	W	2-1	Jablonski 12; Clark 72	1,403
35	div1	Queen of South	A	D	1-1	Jablonski 35	1,361
36	div1	Hamilton	H	L	0-2		1,474
37	div1	Clyde	A	L	0-1		1,122
38	div1	Airdrie Utd	H	L	0-1		1,296

TEAM OF THE SEASON

G — David Berthelot, CG: 25 DR: 49

D — Shaun Dennis, CG: 12 DR: 57
D — Francisco Paquito, CG: 13 DR: 51
D — Jonathan Smart, CG: 26 DR: 49
D — Anthony Bartholome, CG: 23 DR: 48

M — Neil Jablonski, CG: 12 SD: -47
M — Darren Brady, CG: 18 SD: -99
M — Paul Millar, CG: 18 SD: -117
M — CG: 0 SD: 0

F — Hamed Sacko, CG: 18 SR: 435
F — John Martin, CG: 17 SR: 509

KEY PLAYER APPEARANCES

	PLAYER	POS	AGE	APP	MINS ON	GOALS	CARDS(Y	/R)
1	Moussa Ouattara	DEF	22	30	2524	1	4	0
2	Jonathan Smart	DEF	24	30	2492	0	4	0
3	David Berthelot	GK	27	26	2274	0	1	0
4	Iain Davidson	DEF	21	26	2168	0	6	0
5	Anthony Bartholome	DEF	22	25	2120	0	2	0
6	John Martin	ATT	20	33	2035	4	6	0
7	Hamed Sacko	ATT	24	22	1740	4	2	0
8	Paul Millar	MID	19	20	1701	0	2	0
9	Darren Brady	MID	23	19	1685	1	5	0
10	Francisco Paquito	DEF	35	14	1182	0	1	0
11	Herve Ebanda	ATT	26	16	1149	1	0	0
12	Neil Jablonski	MID	22	12	1080	2	0	0
13	Shaun Dennis	DEF	35	12	1080	0	0	0
14	Scott Crabbe	ATT	36	12	1057	0	2	0
15	Paul McMullan	MID	21	10	891	1	0	0
16	Rudy Pounoussamy	GK	26	11	876	0	1	0
17	Stephen Tulloch	MID	17	13	841	2	2	0
18	Conall Murtagh	MID	20	11	840	1	0	0

KEY PLAYERS - GOALSCORERS

Hamed Sacko

Goals in the League	4
Contribution to Attacking Power Average number of minutes between League team goals while on pitch	158
Player Strike Rate Average number of minutes between League goals scored by player	435
Club Strike Rate Average number of minutes between League goals scored by club	125

	PLAYER	LGE GOALS	POWER	STRIKE RATE
1	Hamed Sacko	4	158	435 mins
2	John Martin	4	127	509 mins
3	Neil Jablonski	2	90	540 mins
4	Darren Brady	1	153	1685 mins
5	Moussa Ouattara	1	126	2524 mins

KEY PLAYERS - MIDFIELDERS

Neil Jablonski

Goals in the League	2
Defensive Rating Average number of mins between League goals conceded while on the pitch	43
Contribution to Attacking Power Average number of minutes between League team goals while on pitch	90
Scoring Difference Defensive Rating minus Contribution to Attacking Power	-47

	PLAYER	LGE GOALS	DEF RATE	POWER	SCORE DIFF
1	Neil Jablonski	2	43	90	-47 mins
2	Darren Brady	1	54	153	-99 mins
3	Paul Millar	0	53	170	-117 mins

KEY PLAYERS - DEFENDERS

Shaun Dennis

Goals Conceded while on the pitch	19
Defensive Rating Ave number of mins between League goals conceded while on the pitch	57
Clean Sheets In games when player was on pitch for at least 70 minutes	2
Club Defensive Rating Average number of mins between League goals conceded by the club this season.	48

	PLAYER	CON LGE	CLN SHEETS	DEF RATE
1	Shaun Dennis	19	2	57 mins
2	Francisco Ortiz Rivas Paquito	23	2	51 mins
3	Jonathan Smart	51	2	49 mins
4	Anthony Bartholome	44	3	48 mins
5	Iain Davidson	45	1	48 mins

KEY GOALKEEPER

David Berthelot

Goals Conceded in the League	46
Defensive Rating Ave number of mins between League goals conceded while on the pitch.	49
Counting Games Games when player was on pitch for at least 70 minutes	25
Clean Sheets In Games when player was on pitch for at least 70 minutes	3

TOP POINT EARNERS

	PLAYER	GAMES	AV PTS
1	John Martin	17	0.59
2	Anthony Bartholome	23	0.57
3	David Berthelot	25	0.52
4	Shaun Dennis	12	0.50
5	Neil Jablonski	12	0.50
6	Scott Crabbe	12	0.50
7	Paul Millar	18	0.50
8	Moussa Ouattara	26	0.46
9	Francisco Rivas Paquito	13	0.46
10	Iain Davidson	22	0.45
	CLUB AVERAGE:		0.44

SPANISH LEAGUE ROUND-UP

FINAL LEAGUE TABLE

		HOME					AWAY					TOTAL			
	P	W	D	L	F	A	W	D	L	F	A	F	A	DIF	PTS
Barcelona	38	14	4	1	40	12	11	5	3	33	17	73	29	44	84
Real Madrid	38	15	1	3	43	12	10	4	5	28	20	71	32	39	80
Villarreal	38	14	4	1	41	10	4	7	8	28	27	69	37	32	65
Real Betis	38	12	5	2	36	22	4	9	6	26	28	62	50	12	62
Espanyol	38	12	5	2	34	18	5	5	9	20	28	54	46	8	61
Seville	38	10	5	4	25	19	7	4	8	19	22	44	41	3	60
Valencia	38	11	5	3	31	17	3	11	5	23	22	54	39	15	58
Athl Bilbao	38	11	4	4	39	24	3	5	11	20	30	59	54	5	51
Deportivo	38	6	7	6	25	29	6	8	5	21	21	46	50	-4	51
Malaga	38	8	4	7	19	24	7	2	10	21	24	40	48	-8	51
Atl Madrid	38	11	6	2	28	13	2	5	12	12	21	40	34	6	50
Real Zaragoza	38	11	3	5	35	25	3	5	11	17	32	52	57	-5	50
Getafe	38	11	4	4	23	12	1	7	11	15	34	38	46	-8	47
Real Sociedad	38	9	4	6	21	24	4	4	11	26	32	47	56	-9	47
Osasuna	38	9	6	4	28	24	3	4	12	18	41	46	65	-19	46
R Santander	38	8	6	5	25	23	4	2	13	16	35	41	58	-17	44
Mallorca	38	6	5	8	28	31	4	4	11	14	32	42	63	-21	39
Levante	38	6	6	7	19	20	3	4	12	20	38	39	58	-19	37
Numancia	38	4	9	6	19	23	2	2	15	11	38	30	61	-31	29
Albacete	38	4	7	8	17	22	2	3	14	16	34	33	56	-23	28

CLUB STRIKE FORCE

Eto'o; goals took Barca to the top

1. Barcelona

Goals scored in the League	73
Club Strike Rate (CSR) Average number of minutes between League goals scored by club	47

	CLUB	GOALS	CSR
1	Barcelona	73	47
2	Real Madrid	71	48
3	Villarreal	69	50
4	Real Betis	62	55
5	Athl Bilbao	59	58
6	Valencia	55	62
7	Espanyol	54	63
8	Real Zaragoza	52	66
9	Osasuna	47	73
10	Real Sociedad	47	73
11	Deportivo	46	74
12	Seville	44	78
13	Mallorca	42	81
14	R Santander	41	83
15	Atl Madrid	40	86
16	Malaga	40	86
17	Levante	39	88
18	Getafe	38	90
19	Albacete	33	104
20	Numancia	30	114

CLUB DISCIPLINARY RECORDS

Nafti; Racing to six cards

1. Racing Santander

League Yellow	125
League Red	7
League Total	132
Cards Average in League Average number of minutes between a card being shown of either colour	26

	CLUB	Y	R	TOTAL	AVE
1	R Santander	125	7	132	26
2	Osasuna	116	9	125	27
3	Malaga	108	9	117	29
4	Atl Madrid	105	6	111	31
5	Seville	104	6	110	31
6	Albacete	99	8	107	32
7	Real Betis	98	8	106	32
8	Valencia	101	5	106	32
9	Mallorca	97	6	103	33
10	Numancia	98	6	104	33
11	Real Madrid	99	5	104	33
12	Athl Bilbao	96	4	100	34
13	Getafe	98	2	100	34
14	Espanyol	90	8	98	35
15	Real Zaragoza	93	5	98	35
16	Levante	91	5	96	36
17	Deportivo	82	3	85	40
18	Villarreal	80	5	85	40
19	Barcelona	77	2	79	43
20	Real Sociedad	67	4	71	48

CLUB DEFENCES

	CLUB	LGE	CS	CDR
1	Barcelona	29	20	118
2	Real Madrid	32	15	107
3	Atl Madrid	34	15	101
4	Villarreal	37	14	92
5	Valencia	39	12	88
6	Seville	42	14	81
7	Espanyol	46	12	74
8	Getafe	46	13	74
9	Malaga	48	11	71
10	Deportivo	50	9	68
11	Real Betis	50	8	68
12	Athl Bilbao	54	9	63
13	Real Sociedad	56	8	61
14	Albacete	57	9	60
15	Real Zaragoza	57	11	60
16	Levante	58	9	59
17	R Santander	58	8	59
18	Numancia	61	5	56
19	Mallorca	63	5	54
20	Osasuna	65	7	53

Marquez; in Barca's defence

1. Barcelona

Goals conceded in the League	29
Clean Sheets (CS) Number of league games where no goals were conceded	20
Club Defensive Rate (CDR) Average number of minutes between League goals conceded by club	118

PLAYER NATIONALITIES

Overseas country with the most player appearances in the Spanish League - Argentina — 772 league appearances by Argentinian players

	COUNTRY	PLAYERS	IN SQUAD	LGE APP	% LGE ACT	CAPS	MOST APP	APP
1	Spain	442	9612	7042	66.6	75	Two Players	100.0
2	Argentina	38	907	772	7.6	67	Leonardo Franco	97.4
3	Brazil	29	787	706	7.1	54	Ricardo Oliveira	95.9
4	Uruguay	19	490	359	3.4	27	Diego Forlan	87.9
5	France	13	264	222	2.2	6	Stephane Pignol	84.9
6	Portugal	7	221	179	1.9	22	Jorge Andrade	94.7
7	Italy	9	209	152	1.4	9	Amadeo Carboni	63.9
8	Cameroon	4	134	120	1.2	10	Carlos Kameni	99.4
9	Israel	2	72	72	0.8		Dudu Aouate	97.4
10	Serbia & Montenegro	6	119	100	0.8	16	Darko Kovacevic	75.4
11	England	2	67	66	0.6	17	David Beckham	71.1
12	Mexico	2	56	54	0.5		Rafael Marquez	83.5
13	Colombia	2	64	59	0.5		Luis Perea	80.8
14	Holland	3	68	44	0.5	8	G Van Bronckhorst	72.4
15	Venezuela	1	35	34	0.4		Juan Arango	81.7
16	Switzerland	3	60	43	0.4		Fabio Celestini	58.5
17	Russia	1	35	33	0.4		Valeri Karpin	79.7
18	Denmark	2	33	33	0.4	13	Jesper Gronkjaer	39.8

CLUB MAKE-UP – HOME AND OVERSEAS PLAYERS

1 Barcelona — 58.8% of appearances by overseas players

	CLUB	OVERSEAS	HOME	% OVERSEAS	% LGE ACT	MOST APP	APP
1	Barcelona	14	19	42.4	58.8	Samuel Eto'o	91.2
2	Villarreal	11	22	33.3	53.1	Juan Riquelme	91.1
3	Real Madrid	9	22	29.0	52.8	Roberto Carlos	87.7
4	R Santander	14	22	38.9	45.5	Dudu Aouate	97.4
5	Real Zaragoza	7	21	25.0	44.0	Gabriel Milito	92.1
6	Valencia	14	17	45.2	42.7	Amadeo Carboni	63.9
7	Atl Madrid	10	22	31.3	40.4	Leonardo Franco	97.4
8	Espanyol	8	21	27.6	34.5	Carlos Kameni	99.4
9	Real Sociedad	7	24	22.6	34.0	Valeri Karpin	79.7
10	Deportivo	8	18	30.8	32.0	Jorge Andrade	94.7
11	Real Betis	7	23	23.3	30.0	Ricardo Oliveira	95.9
12	Malaga	8	19	29.6	29.2	Sergio Duda	80.9
13	Mallorca	13	21	38.2	28.5	Juan Arango	81.7
14	Osasuna	6	24	20.0	27.9	Pablo Garcia	71.5
15	Levante	8	17	32.0	27.8	Felix Dja Ettien	73.3
16	Seville	5	26	16.1	25.8	Julio Baptista	83.3
17	Albacete	8	30	21.1	23.7	Antonio Pacheco	84.3
18	Numancia	7	24	22.6	21.9	Stephane Pignol	84.9
19	Getafe	3	26	10.3	15.7	Mariano Pernia	94.5
20	Athl Bilbao	0	30	0.0	0.0	N/A	N/A

CHART-TOPPING MIDFIELDERS

1 Van Bronckhorst - Barcelona	
Goals scored in the League	4
Defensive Rating Av number of mins between League goals conceded while on the pitch	130
Contribution to Attacking Power Average number of minutes between League team goals while on pitch	46
Scoring Difference Defensive Rating minus Contribution to Attacking Power	84

	PLAYER	CLUB	GOALS	DEF RATE	POWER	S DIFF
1	Van Bronckhorst	Barcelona	4	130	46	84
2	Deco	Barcelona	7	127	44	83
3	Xavi	Barcelona	3	108	47	61
4	Beckham	Real Madrid	4	106	46	60
5	Giuly	Barcelona	11	102	47	55
6	Zidane	Real Madrid	6	98	46	52
7	Guti	Real Madrid	0	91	45	46
8	Figo	Real Madrid	3	95	51	44
9	Riquelme	Villarreal	15	94	51	43
10	Senna	Villarreal	1	91	49	42
11	Josico	Villarreal	1	89	48	41
12	Baraja	Valencia	7	93	57	36
13	Aimar	Valencia	4	94	66	28
14	Arzu	Real Betis	0	70	48	22
15	Marti	Seville	0	96	78	18

CHART-TOPPING GOALSCORERS

1 Forlan - Villarreal	
Goals scored in the League	24
Contribution to Attacking Power (AP) Average number of minutes between League team goals while on pitch	48
Club Strike Rate (CSR) Average minutes between League goals scored by club	50
Player Strike Rate Average number of minutes between League goals scored by player	125

	PLAYER	CLUB	GOALS: LGE	POWER	CSR	S RATE
1	Forlan	Villarreal	24	48	50	125
2	Eto'o	Barcelona	24	46	47	130
3	Ronaldo	Real Madrid	21	45	48	133
4	Nihat	Real Sociedad	13	69	71	144
5	Oliveira	Real Betis	22	53	55	149
6	Baptista	Seville	18	77	78	158
7	Villa	Real Zaragoza	15	57	65	187
8	Giuly	Barcelona	11	46	47	194
9	Maxi	Espanyol	15	60	63	199
10	Riquelme	Villarreal	15	51	50	208
11	Torres	Atl Madrid	16	84	86	212
12	Luque	Deportivo	11	75	74	218
13	Tamudo	Espanyol	11	61	63	229
14	Ezquerro	Athl Bilbao	11	55	57	235
15	Pacheco	Albacete	12	106	101	240

CHART-TOPPING DEFENDERS

1 Belletti - Barcelona	
Goals Conceded in the League The number of League goals conceded while he was on the pitch	19
Clean Sheets In games when he played at least 70 mins	16
Club Defensive Rating Average mins between League goals conceded by the club this season	118
Defensive Rating Average number of minutes between League goals conceded while on pitch	133

	PLAYER	CLUB	CON: LGE	CS	CDR	DEF RATE
1	Belletti	Barcelona	19	16	118	133
2	Marquez	Barcelona	22	15	118	130
3	Curro Torres	Valencia	14	7	88	127
4	Puyol	Barcelona	26	17	118	122
5	Sergi	Atl Madrid	19	11	101	119
6	Roberto Carlos	Real Madrid	26	14	104	115
7	Oleguer	Barcelona	25	15	118	114
8	Navarro	Valencia	19	8	88	109
9	Helguera	Real Madrid	27	12	104	106
10	Pablo Ibanez	Atl Madrid	30	15	101	105
11	Perea	Atl Madrid	27	12	101	102
12	Alvarez	Villarreal	21	10	92	102
13	Cesar Navas	Malaga	19	9	71	99
14	Salgado	Real Madrid	26	11	104	99
15	Pena	Villarreal	18	5	92	97

CHART-TOPPING GOALKEEPERS

1 Valdes - Barcelona	
Counting Games Games where he played at least 70 minutes	35
Goals Conceded The number of League goals conceded while he was on the pitch	25
Clean Sheets In games when he played at least 70 mins	19
Defensive Rating Average number of minutes between League goals conceded while on pitch	125

	PLAYER	CLUB	CG	Conc	CS	DEF RATE
1	Valdes	Barcelona	35	25	19	125
2	Casillas	Real Madrid	37	32	15	106
3	Franco	Atl Madrid	37	32	15	104
4	Arnau	Malaga	20	19	8	95
5	Reina	Villarreal	38	37	14	92
6	Canizares	Valencia	30	33	9	85
7	Broto	Getafe	20	22	9	82
8	Munua	Deportivo	17	20	5	77
9	Esteban	Seville	29	34	11	77
10	Doblas	Real Betis	29	35	8	75
11	Kameni	Espanyol	37	47	11	72
12	Gaspercic	Albacete	17	23	5	64
13	Aranzubia	Athl Bilbao	36	52	8	64
14	Luis Garcia	Real Zaragoza	37	52	11	64
15	Molina	Deportivo	20	29	4	62

PLAYER DISCIPLINARY RECORD

3. Cesar- Deportivo	
Cards Average mins between cards	113
League Yellow	9
League Red	1
TOTAL	10

	PLAYER		LY	LR	TOT	AVE
1	Jordi	Seville	8	0	8	105
2	Lembo	Real Betis	5	2	7	106
3	Cesar	Deportivo	9	1	10	113
4	Santi	Albacete	7	1	8	122
5	Pulido	Getafe	3	1	4	122
6	Garcia, P	Osasuna	18	2	20	122
7	Alexis	Malaga	7	1	8	123
8	Battaglia	Villarreal	6	1	7	131
9	Gaspar	Albacete	13	2	15	134
10	Reggi	Levante	4	1	5	134
11	Castellini	Real Betis	3	1	4	135
12	Sosa	Atl Madrid	11	1	12	140
13	Alkiza	Real Sociedad	5	0	5	141
14	Nafti	R Santander	6	0	6	144
15	Samuel	Real Madrid	16	2	18	148
16	Alex	Espanyol	7	1	8	150
17	G Calvo	Atl Madrid	7	1	8	154
18	Iuliano	Mallorca	6	2	8	154
19	Jonathan	R Santander	2	1	3	156
20	Juanma	R Santander	4	0	4	157
21	Perera	Mallorca	3	0	3	163
22	Torrado	R Santander	7	0	7	163
23	Gravesen	Real Madrid	8	0	8	164
24	Romero	Malaga	11	2	13	168

TEAM OF THE SEASON

D
Belletti : Barcelona
CG: 27 DR: 133
M
V Bronckhorst : Barcelona
CG: 27 SD: + 84
D
C Torres : Valencia
CG: 19 DR: 127
M
Beckham : Real Madrid
CG: 24 SD: + 60
F
Forlan : Villarreal
CG: 32 SR: 125
G
Valdes : Barcelona
CG: 35 DR: 125
D
Sergi Barjuan: Atl Madrid
CG: 22 DR: 119
M
Riquelme : Villarreal
CG: 35 SD: + 43
F
Eto'o : Barcelona
CG: 32 SR: 130
D
R Carlos : Real Madrid
CG: 33 DR: 115
M
Baraja : Valencia
CG: 22 SD: + 36

SPANISH PRIMEIRA LIGA CHAMPIONS

BARCELONA

Final Position: **1st**

KEY: Won, Drawn, Lost

							Attendance
1	sppr1	**R Santander**	A	W	2-0	Giuly 68; Eto'o 74 pen	21,000
2	sppr1	**Seville**	H	W	2-0	Giuly 35; Larsson 76	61,000
3	cl gf	**Celtic**	A	W	3-1	Deco 20; Giuly 78; Larsson 82	60,000
4	sppr1	**Atl Madrid**	A	D	1-1	Van Bronckhorst 22	55,000
5	sppr1	**Real Zaragoza**	H	W	4-1	Eto'o 26,46; Xavi 67; Van Bronckhorst 78	60,000
6	sppr1	**Mallorca**	A	W	3-1	Larsson 10; Eto'o 38 pen,40	20,000
7	cl gf	**S Donetsk**	H	W	3-0	Deco 15; Ronaldinho 64 pen; Eto'o 89	64,000
8	sppr1	**Numancia**	H	W	1-0	Larsson 70	79,000
9	sppr1	**Espanyol**	A	W	1-0	Deco 8	34,000
10	cl gf	**AC Milan**	A	L	0-1		77,000
11	sppr1	**Osasuna**	H	W	3-0	Eto'o 40,90; Ronaldinho 44 pen	67,000
12	sppr1	**Athl Bilbao**	A	D	1-1	Eto'o 12	39,000
13	cl gf	**AC Milan**	H	W	2-1	Eto'o 37; Ronaldinho 89	95,000
14	sppr1	**Deportivo**	H	W	2-1	Xavi 24; Eto'o 36	90,000
15	sppr1	**Real Betis**	A	L	1-2	Gerard 72	50,000
16	sppr1	**Real Madrid**	H	W	3-0	Eto'o 29; Van Bronckhorst 43; Ronaldinho 76 pen	98,000
17	cl gf	**Celtic**	H	D	1-1	Eto'o 24	74,000
18	sppr1	**Getafe**	A	W	2-1	Marquez 19; Deco 22	15,000
19	sppr1	**Malaga**	H	W	4-0	Eto'o 23,89; Deco 29; Iniesta 72	67,000
20	cl gf	**S Donetsk**	A	L	0-2		25,000
21	sppr1	**Albacete**	A	W	2-1	Iniesta 3; Xavi 86	17,000
22	sppr1	**Valencia**	H	D	1-1	Ronaldinho 79 pen	85,000
23	sppr1	**Levante**	H	W	2-1	Alexis 29 og; Eto'o 87	51,000
24	sppr1	**Villarreal**	A	L	0-3		22,000
25	sppr1	**Real Sociedad**	H	W	1-0	Eto'o 81	69,000
26	sppr1	**R Santander**	H	W	3-0	Eto'o 7; Ronaldinho 74; Deco 76	67,000
27	sppr1	**Seville**	A	W	4-0	Eto'o 49; Baptista 56 og; Ronaldinho 58; Giuly 74	45,000
28	sppr1	**Atl Madrid**	H	L	0-2		63,000
29	sppr1	**Real Zaragoza**	A	W	4-1	Toledo 1 og; Giuly 29; Eto'o 38; Marquez 74	35,000
30	sppr1	**Mallorca**	H	W	2-0	Deco 16,57	75,000
31	clr2l1	**Chelsea**	H	W	2-1	Lopez 67; Eto'o 73	78,000
32	sppr1	**Numancia**	A	D	1-1	Marquez 46	10,000
33	sppr1	**Espanyol**	H	D	0-0		85,000
34	sppr1	**Osasuna**	A	W	1-0	Eto'o 39	19,000
35	clr2l2	**Chelsea**	A	L	2-4	Ronaldinho 27 pen,38	41,515
36	sppr1	**Athl Bilbao**	H	W	2-0	Deco 20; Giuly 39	80,000
37	sppr1	**Deportivo**	A	W	1-0	Giuly 10	35,000
38	sppr1	**Real Betis**	H	D	3-3	Eto'o 16 pen,81 pen; Van Bronckhorst 90	90,000
39	sppr1	**Real Madrid**	A	L	2-4	Eto'o 29; Ronaldinho 73	78,000
40	sppr1	**Getafe**	H	W	2-0	Ronaldinho 30; Giuly 56	83,000
41	sppr1	**Malaga**	A	W	4-0	Oleguer 21; Giuly 33,68; Gerard 90	32,000
42	sppr1	**Albacete**	H	W	2-0	Eto'o 65; Messi 90	91,000
43	sppr1	**Valencia**	A	W	2-0	Ronaldinho 30; Eto'o 31	53,000
44	sppr1	**Levante**	A	D	1-1	Eto'o 60	20,000
45	sppr1	**Villarreal**	H	D	3-3	Ronaldinho 33; Giuly 37,47	98,000
46	sppr1	**Real Sociedad**	A	D	0-0		25,000

KEY PLAYERS - GOALSCORERS

Samuel Eto'o

Goals in the League	24
Contribution to Attacking Power Average number of minutes between League team goals while on pitch	46
Player Strike Rate Average number of minutes between League goals scored by player	130
Club Strike Rate Average number of minutes between League goals scored by club	47

	PLAYER	GOALS LGE	POWER	S RATE
1	Samuel Eto'o	24	46	130 mins
2	Ludovic Giuly	11	47	194 mins
3	Ronaldinho	9	45	341 mins
4	Anderson Deco	7	44	434 mins
5	Giovanni Van Bronckhorst	4	46	619 mins

KEY PLAYERS - MIDFIELDERS

Giovanni Van Bronckhorst

Goals in the League	4
Defensive Rating Average number of mins between League goals conceded while on the pitch	130
Contribution to Attacking Power Average number of minutes between League team goals while on pitch	46
Scoring Difference Defensive Rating minus Contribution to Attacking Power	84

	PLAYER	GOALS LGE	DEF RATE	ATT POWER	SCORE DIFF
1	Giovanni Van Bronckhorst	4	130	46	84 mins
2	Anderson Deco	7	127	44	83 mins
3	Xavi Hernandez	3	108	47	61 mins
4	Ludovic Giuly	11	102	47	55 mins

KEY PLAYERS - DEFENDERS

Juliano Belletti

Goals Conceded in League	19
Clean Sheets In games when player was on pitch for at least 70 minutes	16
Defensive Rating Ave number of mins between League goals conceded while on the pitch	133
Club Defensive Rating Average number of mins between League goals conceded by the club this season	118

	PLAYER	CON LGE	CLEAN SHEETS	DEF RATE
1	Juliano Belletti	19	16	133 mins
2	Rafael Marquez	22	15	130 mins
3	Carlos Puyol	26	17	122 mins
4	Presas Oleguer	25	15	114 mins

MONTHLY POINTS TALLY

AUGUST	3	100%
SEPTEMBER	10	83%
OCTOBER	10	83%
NOVEMBER	9	75%
DECEMBER	10	83%
JANUARY	9	75%
FEBRUARY	7	58%
MARCH	10	83%
APRIL	7	58%
MAY	9	60%

LEAGUE GOALS

	PLAYER	MINS	GOALS	AVE
1	Eto'o	3118	24	130
2	Giuly	2139	11	194
3	Ronaldinho	3068	9	341
4	Deco	3038	7	434
5	Van Bronckhorst	2477	4	619
6	Marquez	2855	3	952
7	Xavi	3139	3	1046
8	Larsson	662	3	221
9	Iniesta	1689	2	845
10	Gerard	390	2	195
11	Messi	77	1	77
12	Oleguer	2857	1	2857
	Other		3	
	TOTAL		73	

KEY GOALKEEPER

Victor Valdes

Goals Conceded in the League	25
Counting Games League games when player was on pitch for at least 70 minutes	35
Clean Sheets In games when player was on pitch for at least 70 minutes	17
League minutes played Number of minutes played in league matches	3133
Defensive Rating Ave number of mins between League goals conceded while on the pitch	125

DISCIPLINARY RECORDS

	PLAYER	YELLOW	RED	AVE
1	Deco	13	0	233
2	Belletti	10	0	253
3	Van Bronckhorst	8	0	309
4	Silvinho	3	0	320
5	Marquez	7	1	356
6	Puyol	6	0	529
7	Ronaldinho	5	0	613
8	Larsson	1	0	662
9	Eto'o	4	0	779
10	Xavi	4	0	784
11	Iniesta	2	0	844
12	Oleguer	3	0	952
13	Valdes	2	1	1044
	Other	1	0	
	TOTAL	69	2	

TOP POINT EARNERS

	PLAYER	GAMES	AV PTS
1	Juliano Belletti	27	2.48
2	Gio Van Bronckhorst	27	2.37
3	Ludovic Giuly	17	2.35
4	Anderson Deco	33	2.30
5	Victor Valdes	35	2.26
6	Rafael Marquez	28	2.25
7	Xavi Hernandez	35	2.20
8	Ronaldinho	34	2.18
9	Carlos Puyol	34	2.18
10	Presas Oleguer	29	2.14
	CLUB AVERAGE:		2.21

TEAM OF THE SEASON

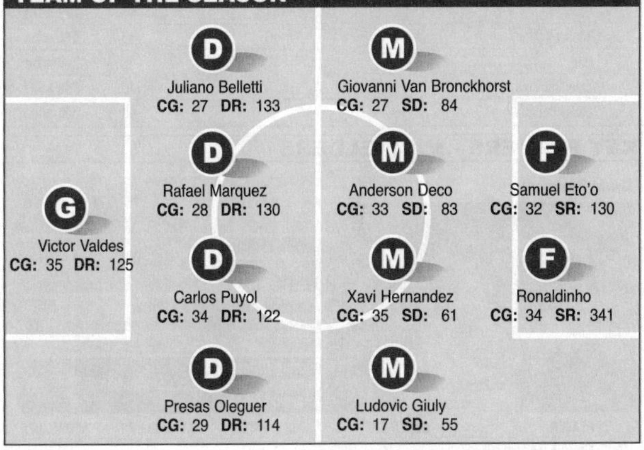

D
Juliano Belletti
CG: 27 DR: 133
M
Giovanni Van Bronckhorst
CG: 27 SD: 84
D
Rafael Marquez
CG: 28 DR: 130
M
Anderson Deco
CG: 33 SD: 83
F
Samuel Eto'o
CG: 32 SR: 130
G
Victor Valdes
CG: 35 DR: 125
D
Carlos Puyol
CG: 34 DR: 122
M
Xavi Hernandez
CG: 35 SD: 61
F
Ronaldinho
CG: 34 SR: 341
D
Presas Oleguer
CG: 29 DR: 114
M
Ludovic Giuly
CG: 17 SD: 55

LEAGUE APPEARANCES AND BOOKINGS

	AGE (on 01/07/05)	IN NAMED 18	APPEARANCES	COUNTING GAMES	MINUTES ON PITCH	YELLOW CARDS	RED CARDS	THIS SEASON	HOME COUNTRY
Goalkeepers									
Albert Jorquera	26	22	2	2	180	0	0	-	Spain
Ruben Martinez	21	17	2	1	107	0	0	-	Spain
Rafael Urko	22	1	0	0	0	0	0	-	Spain
Victor Valdes	23	37	35	35	3133	2	1	-	Spain
Defenders									
Juliano Belletti	29	32	31	27	2535	10	0	4	Brazil (1)
Abella Damia	23	20	8	2	364	3	0	-	Spain
Edmilson	28	7	6	3	362	1	0	-	Brazil
Rafael Marquez	26	36	35	28	2855	7	1	-	Mexico
Jose Mora	24	1	0	0	0	0	0	-	Spain
Fernando Navarro	23	35	6	3	308	0	0	-	Spain
Presas Oleguer	25	36	35	29	2857	3	0	-	Spain
Carlos Pena	21	0	0	0	0	0	0	-	Spain
Carlos Puyol	27	36	36	34	3176	6	0	7	Spain (8)
Sergio Rodri	20	4	1	0	2	0	0	-	Spain
Silvinho	31	29	20	8	962	3	0	-	Brazil
Midfielders									
Demetrio Albertini	33	12	5	1	260	1	0	-	Italy
Anderson Deco	27	35	35	33	3038	13	0	8	Portugal (9)
Garcia Gabri	26	7	4	1	146	0	0	-	Spain
Lopez Gerard	26	28	13	1	390	2	0	-	Spain
Ludovic Giuly	28	33	29	17	2139	1	0	6	France (4)
Andres Iniesta	21	38	37	11	1689	2	0	-	Spain
Lionel Messi	18	18	7	0	77	0	0	-	Argentina
Thiago Motta	22	9	8	1	276	1	0	-	Brazil
Gio Van Bronckhorst	30	36	30	27	2477	8	0	8	Holland (5)
Joan Verdu	22	6	0	0	0	0	0	-	Spain
Xavi Hernandez	25	36	36	35	3139	4	0	6	Spain (8)
Forwards									
Samuel Eto'o	24	37	37	32	3118	4	0	4	Cameroon (26)
Francisco Javito	21	2	0	0	0	0	0	-	Spain
Henrik Larsson	33	14	12	5	662	1	0	4	Sweden (13)
Manuel Lolo	22	4	0	0	0	0	0	-	Spain
Maxi Lopez	21	12	8	1	245	0	0	-	Argentina
Ronaldinho	25	35	35	34	3068	5	0	9	Brazil (1)

SQUAD APPEARANCES

Match	1	2	3	4	5	6	7	8	9	10	11	12	13	14	15	16	17	18	19	20	21	22	23	24	25	26	27	28	29	30	31	32	33	34	35	36	37	38	39	40	41	42	43	44	45	46
Venue	A	H	A	A	H	A	H	H	A	A	H	A	H	H	A	H	H	A	H	A	A	H	H	A	H	H	A	H	A	H	H	A	H	A	A	H	A	H	A	H	A	H	A	A	H	A
Competition	L	L	C	L	L	L	C	L	L	C	L	L	C	L	L	L	C	L	L	C	L	L	L	L	L	L	L	L	L	L	C	L	L	L	C	L	L	L	L	L	L	L	L	L	L	L
Result	W	W	W	D	W	W	W	W	W	L	W	D	W	W	L	W	D	W	W	L	W	D	W	L	W	W	W	L	W	W	W	D	D	W	L	W	W	D	L	W	W	W	W	D	D	D

Goalkeepers
Albert Jorquera
Ruben Martinez
Rafael Urko
Victor Valdes

Defenders
Juliano Belletti
Abella Damia
Edmilson
Rafael Marquez
Jose Mora
Fernando Navarro
Presas Oleguer
Carlos Pena
Carlos Puyol
Sergio Rodri
Silvinho

Midfielders
Demetrio Albertini
Anderson Deco
Garcia Gabri
Lopez Gerard
Ludovic Giuly
Andres Iniesta
Lionel Messi
Thiago Motta
Gio Van Bronckhorst
Joan Verdu
Xavi Hernandez

Forwards
Samuel Eto'o
Francisco Javito
Henrik Larsson
Manuel Lolo
Maxi Lopez
Ronaldinho

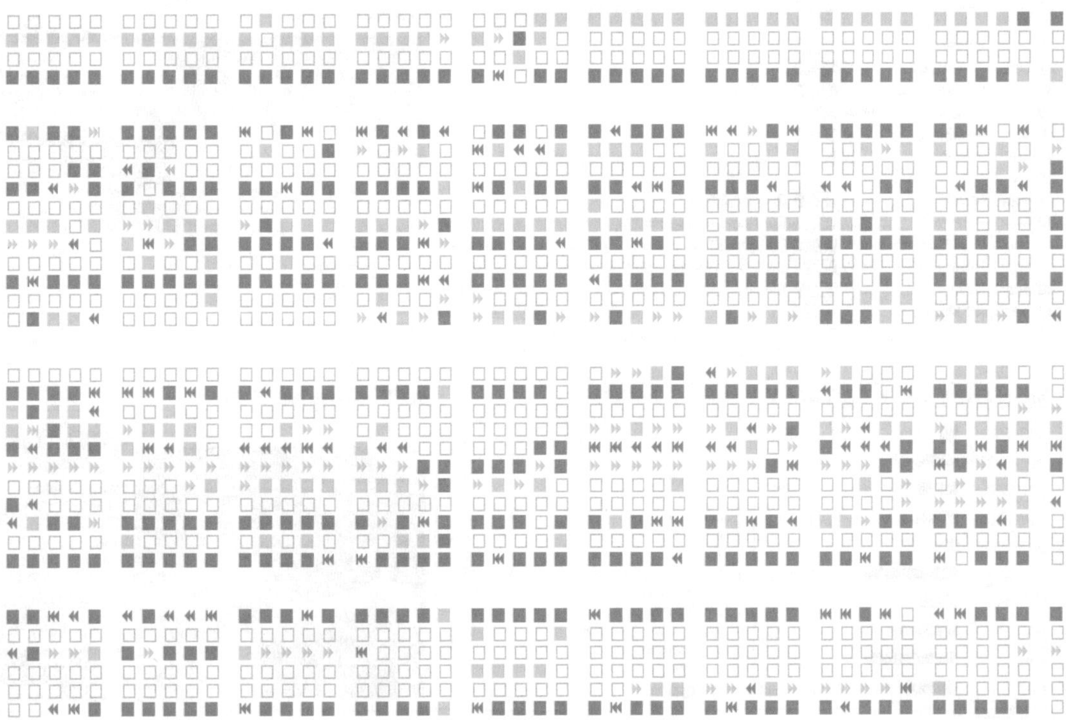

REAL MADRID

Final Position: **2nd**

KEY: ☐ Won ☐ Drawn ☐ Lost

							Attendance
1	clql1	**Wisla Krakow**	A	W	2-0	Morientes 72,90	10,000
2	clql2	**Wisla Krakow**	H	W	3-1	Ronaldo 3,30; Pavon 85	76,000
3	sppr1	**Mallorca**	A	W	1-0	Ronaldo 52	24,000
4	sppr1	**Numancia**	H	W	1-0	Beckham 18	66,000
5	cl gb	**B Leverkusen**	A	L	0-3		23,000
6	sppr1	**Espanyol**	A	L	0-1		40,000
7	sppr1	**Osasuna**	H	W	1-0	Beckham 62	50,000
8	sppr1	**Athl Bilbao**	A	L	1-2	Raul 51	38,000
9	cl gb	**Roma**	H	W	4-2	Raul 39,72; Figo 53 pen; Roberto Carlos 79	60,000
10	sppr1	**Deportivo**	H	L	0-1		67,000
11	sppr1	**Real Betis**	A	D	1-1	Ronaldo 66	42,000
12	cl gb	**Dinamo Kiev**	H	W	1-0	Owen 35	45,000
13	sppr1	**Valencia**	H	W	1-0	Owen 7	75,000
14	sppr1	**Getafe**	H	W	2-0	Owen 28; Ronaldo 79	70,000
15	cl gb	**Dinamo Kiev**	A	D	2-2	Raul 38; Figo 44 pen	80,000
16	sppr1	**Malaga**	A	W	2-0	Figo 24 pen; Owen 78	30,000
17	sppr1	**Albacete**	H	W	6-1	Ronaldo 3,90; Zidane 30; Raul 32; Samuel 49; Owen 89	79,000
18	sppr1	**Barcelona**	A	L	0-3		98,000
19	cl gb	**B Leverkusen**	H	D	1-1	Raul 70	72,000
20	sppr1	**Levante**	H	W	5-0	Ronaldo 42,51; Figo 50; Beckham 55; Owen 87	70,000
21	sppr1	**Villarreal**	A	D	0-0		20,000
22	cl gb	**Roma**	A	W	3-0	Ronaldo 9; Figo 60 pen,82	
23	sppr1	**R Santander**	A	W	3-2	Owen 34; Raul 61; Zidane 90	13,000
24	sppr1	**Seville**	H	L	0-1		57,000
25	sppr1	**Real Sociedad**	H	W	2-1	Ronaldo 41; Zidane 90 pen	70,000
26	sppr1	**Atl Madrid**	A	W	3-0	Ronaldo 15,84; Solari 81	56,000
27	sppr1	**Real Zaragoza**	H	W	3-1	Raul 41; Ronaldo 53; Owen 85	62,000
28	sppr1	**Mallorca**	H	W	3-1	Figo 36 pen; Samuel 80; Solari 90	60,000
29	sppr1	**Numancia**	A	W	2-1	Beckham 63; Salgado 83	10,000
30	sppr1	**Espanyol**	H	W	4-0	Zidane 13; Raul 29,75; Gravesen 84	63,000
31	sppr1	**Osasuna**	A	W	2-1	Owen 76; Helguera 79	15,000
32	sppr1	**Athl Bilbao**	H	L	0-2		75,000
33	clr2l1	**Juventus**	H	W	1-0	Helguera 31	78,000
34	sppr1	**Deportivo**	A	L	0-2		35,000
35	sppr1	**Real Betis**	H	W	3-1	Owen 10; Roberto Carlos 40; Helguera 61	67,000
36	sppr1	**Valencia**	A	D	1-1	Ronaldo 27	50,000
37	clr2l2	**Juventus**	A	L	0-2		59,000
38	sppr1	**Getafe**	A	L	1-2	Solari 90	14,000
39	sppr1	**Malaga**	H	W	1-0	Roberto Carlos 61	60,000
40	sppr1	**Albacete**	A	W	2-1	Helguera 15; Owen 45	15,000
41	sppr1	**Barcelona**	H	W	4-2	Zidane 7; Ronaldo 20; Raul 45; Owen 65	78,000
42	sppr1	**Levante**	A	W	2-0	Ronaldo 37,83	19,000
43	sppr1	**Villarreal**	H	W	2-1	Ronaldo 69; Salgado 74	80,000
44	sppr1	**Real Sociedad**	A	W	2-0	Ronaldo 82,90	26,000
45	sppr1	**R Santander**	H	W	5-0	Owen 28; Ronaldo 36,90; Raul 52,71	80,000
46	sppr1	**Seville**	A	D	2-2	Navarro 42 og; Zidane 74	45,000
47	sppr1	**Atl Madrid**	H	D	0-0		70,000
48	sppr1	**Real Zaragoza**	A	W	3-1	Owen 24; Roberto Carlos 54; Ronaldo 90	33,000

KEY PLAYERS - GOALSCORERS

Ronaldo

Goals in the League	21
Contribution to Attacking Power Average number of minutes between League team goals while on pitch	45
Player Strike Rate Average number of minutes between League goals scored by player	133
Club Strike Rate Average number of minutes between League goals scored by club	48

	PLAYER	GOALS LGE	POWER	S RATE
1	Ronaldo	21	45	**133 mins**
2	Michael Owen	13	48	**145 mins**
3	Raul	9	46	**285 mins**
4	Zinedine Zidane	6	46	**390 mins**
5	David Beckham	4	46	**608 mins**

KEY PLAYERS - MIDFIELDERS

David Beckham

Goals in the League	4
Defensive Rating Average number of mins between League goals conceded while on the pitch	106
Contribution to Attacking Power Average number of minutes between League team goals while on pitch	46
Scoring Difference Defensive Rating minus Contribution to Attacking Power	60

	PLAYER	GOALS LGE	DEF RATE	ATT POWER	SCORE DIFF
1	David Beckham	4	106	46	**60 mins**
2	Zinedine Zidane	6	98	46	**52 mins**
3	Jose Guti	0	91	45	**46 mins**
4	Luis Figo	3	95	51	**44 mins**
5	Thomas Gravesen	1	77	51	**26 mins**

KEY PLAYERS - DEFENDERS

Roberto Carlos

Goals Conceded in League	26
Clean Sheets In games when player was on pitch for at least 70 minutes	14
Defensive Rating Ave number of mins between League goals conceded while on the pitch	115
Club Defensive Rating Average number of mins between League goals conceded by the club this season	104

	PLAYER	CON LGE	CLEAN SHEETS	DEF RATE
1	Roberto Carlos	26	14	**115 mins**
2	Ivan Helguera	27	12	**106 mins**
3	Michel Salgado	26	11	**99 mins**
4	Walter Samuel	31	8	**86 mins**

MONTHLY POINTS TALLY

AUGUST	3	100%
SEPTEMBER	6	50%
OCTOBER	7	58%
NOVEMBER	9	75%
DECEMBER	4	44%
JANUARY	15	100%
FEBRUARY	6	50%
MARCH	7	58%
APRIL	15	100%
MAY	8	67%

LEAGUE GOALS

	PLAYER	MINS	GOALS	AVE
1	Ronaldo	2790	**21**	133
2	Owen	1884	**13**	145
3	Raul	2565	**9**	285
4	Zidane	2340	**6**	390
5	Beckham	2432	**4**	608
6	Helguera	2867	**3**	956
7	Solari	1128	**3**	376
8	Figo	2290	**3**	763
9	Roberto Carlos	3001	**3**	1000
10	Salgado	2571	**2**	1286
11	Samuel	2666	**2**	1333
12	Gravesen	1314	**1**	1314
	Other		1	
	TOTAL		**71**	

KEY GOALKEEPER

Iker Casillas

Goals Conceded in the League	32
Counting Games League games when player was on pitch for at least 70 minutes	37
Clean Sheets In games when player was on pitch for at least 70 minutes	15
League minutes played Number of minutes played in league matches	3383
Defensive Rating Ave number of mins between League goals conceded while on the pitch	106

DISCIPLINARY

	PLAYER	YELLOW	RED	AVE
1	Samuel	16	2	**148**
2	Gravesen	8	0	**164**
3	Guti	10	0	**191**
4	Salgado	11	1	**214**
5	Beckham	11	0	**221**
6	Figo	9	0	**254**
7	Raul Bravo	4	0	**265**
8	Celades	3	0	**310**
9	Helguera	7	1	**358**
10	Zidane	5	1	**390**
11	Roberto Carlos	6	0	**500**
12	Pavon	2	0	**590**
13	Casillas	2	0	**1691**
	Other	3	0	
	TOTAL	**97**	**5**	

TOP POINT EARNERS

	PLAYER	GAMES	AV PTS
1	Michael Owen	13	**2.46**
2	Zinedine Zidane	24	**2.38**
3	David Beckham	24	**2.38**
4	Ronaldo	30	**2.33**
5	Roberto Carlos	33	**2.30**
6	Raul	27	**2.22**
7	Ivan Helguera	31	**2.16**
8	Michel Salgado	28	**2.14**
9	Luis Figo	21	**2.10**
10	Iker Casillas	37	**2.08**
	CLUB AVERAGE:		**2.11**

TEAM OF THE SEASON

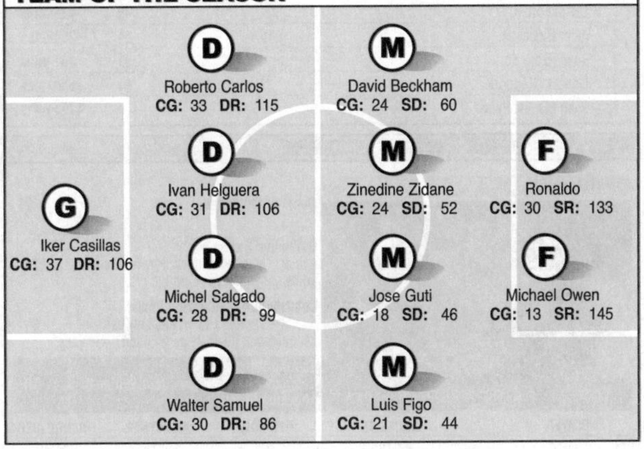
D
Roberto Carlos
CG: 33 DR: 115
M
David Beckham
CG: 24 SD: 60
D
Ivan Helguera
CG: 31 DR: 106
M
Zinedine Zidane
CG: 24 SD: 52
F
Ronaldo
CG: 30 SR: 133
G
Iker Casillas
CG: 37 DR: 106
D
Michel Salgado
CG: 28 DR: 99
M
Jose Guti
CG: 18 SD: 46
F
Michael Owen
CG: 13 SR: 145
D
Walter Samuel
CG: 30 DR: 86
M
Luis Figo
CG: 21 SD: 44

LEAGUE APPEARANCES, BOOKINGS AND CAPS

	AGE (on 01/07/04)	IN NAMED 18	APPEARANCES	COUNTING GAMES	MINUTES ON PITCH	YELLOW CARDS	RED CARDS	THIS SEASON	HOME COUNTRY
Goalkeepers									
Iker Casillas	24	38	38	37	3383	2	0	8	Spain (8)
Sanchez Cesar	33	31	1	0	37	0	0	-	Spain
Lopez Diego	23	7	0	0	0	0	0	-	Spain
Defenders									
Alvaro Arbeloa	22	7	2	1	123	0	0	-	Spain
Ivan Helguera	30	35	34	31	2867	7	1	2	Spain (8)
Alvaro Mejia	23	17	5	2	244	1	0	-	Spain
Miguel Palencia	21	3	2	0	63	0	0	-	Spain
Francisco Pavon	25	37	17	11	1181	2	0	-	Spain
Raul Bravo	24	37	14	9	1062	4	0	-	Spain
Roberto Carlos	32	37	34	33	3001	6	0	9	Brazil (1)
Michel Salgado	29	29	29	28	2571	11	1	-	Spain
Walter Samuel	27	30	30	30	2666	16	2	3	Argentina (3)
Midfielders									
David Beckham	30	31	30	24	2432	11	0	8	England (6)
Borja Fernandez	24	15	8	1	182	1	0	-	Spain
Albert Celades	29	32	22	9	932	3	0	-	Spain
Luis Figo	32	33	33	21	2290	9	0	-	Portugal
Thomas Gravesen	29	17	17	13	1314	8	0	7	Denmark (19)
Jose Guti	28	32	31	18	1917	10	0	-	Spain
Javi Garcia	18	5	3	1	117	0	0	-	Spain
Jotha	23	2	1	0	4	0	0	-	Spain
Juanfran	20	8	1	0	54	0	0	-	Spain
Jorge Solari	28	35	27	7	1128	0	0	-	Argentina
Roberto Soldado	20	1	1	1	90	0	0	-	Spain
Zinedine Zidane	33	29	29	24	2340	5	1	-	France
Forwards									
Fernando Morientes	29	16	13	1	256	0	0	-	Spain
Michael Owen	25	36	36	13	1884	1	0	9	England (6)
Javier Portillo	23	14	3	1	93	0	0	-	Spain
Raul	28	35	32	27	2565	1	0	7	Spain (8)
Ronaldo	28	35	34	30	2790	1	0	8	Brazil (1)

SQUAD APPEARANCES

Match	1	2	3	4	5	6	7	8	9	10	11	12	13	14	15	16	17	18	19	20	21	22	23	24
Venue	A	H	A	H	A	A	H	A	H	H	A	H	H	H	A	A	H	A	H	H	A	A	A	H
Competition	C	C	L	L	C	L	L	L	C	L	L	C	L	L	C	L	L	L	C	L	L	C	L	L
Result	W	W	W	W	L	L	W	L	W	L	D	W	W	W	D	W	W	L	D	W	D	W	W	L

Match	25	26	27	28	29	30	31	32	33	34	35	36	37	38	39	40	41	42	43	44	45	46	47	48
Venue	H	A	H	H	A	H	A	H	H	A	H	A	A	A	H	A	H	A	H	A	H	A	H	A
Competition	L	L	L	L	L	L	L	L	C	L	L	L	C	L	L	L	L	L	L	L	L	L	L	L
Result	W	W	W	W	W	W	W	L	W	L	W	D	L	L	W	W	W	W	W	W	W	D	D	W

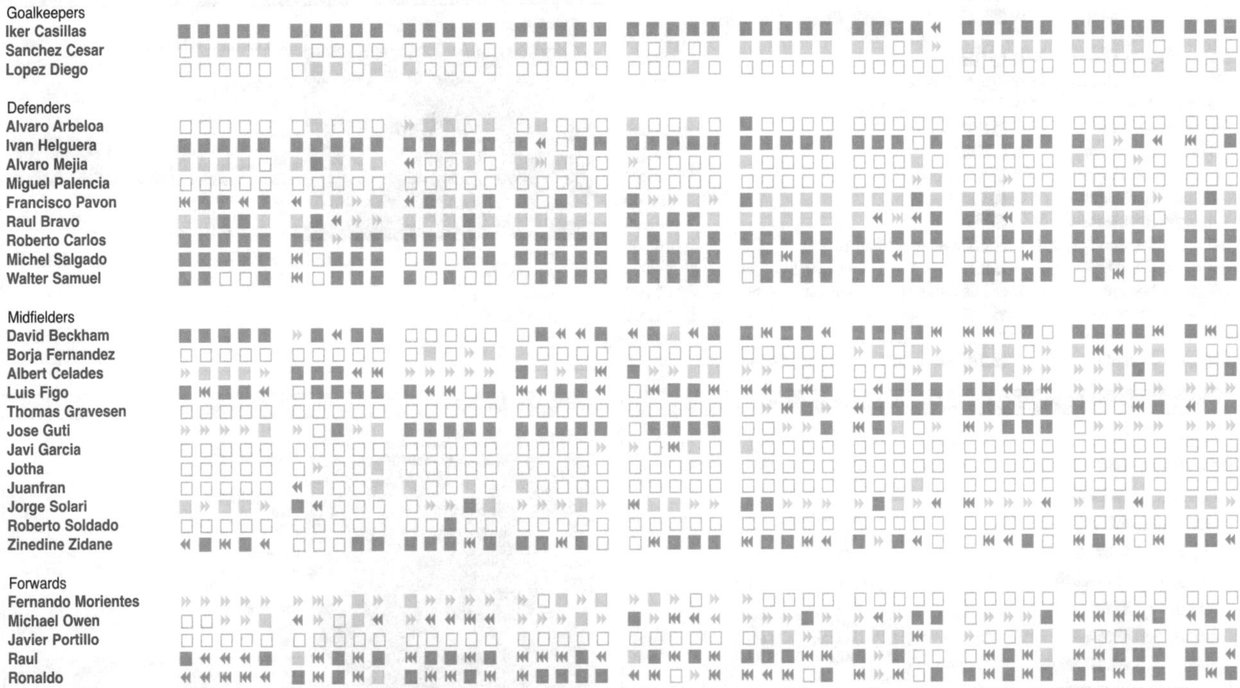
Goalkeepers
Iker Casillas
Sanchez Cesar
Lopez Diego
Defenders
Alvaro Arbeloa
Ivan Helguera
Alvaro Mejia
Miguel Palencia
Francisco Pavon
Raul Bravo
Roberto Carlos
Michel Salgado
Walter Samuel
Midfielders
David Beckham
Borja Fernandez
Albert Celades
Luis Figo
Thomas Gravesen
Jose Guti
Javi Garcia
Jotha
Juanfran
Jorge Solari
Roberto Soldado
Zinedine Zidane
Forwards
Fernando Morientes
Michael Owen
Javier Portillo
Raul
Ronaldo

KEY: On all match; On bench; Subbed or sent off (Counting game); Subbed or sent off (playing less than 70 minutes); Subbed on from bench (Counting Game); Subbed on (playing less than 70 minutes); Subbed on and then subbed or sent off (Counting Game); Subbed on and then subbed or sent off (playing less than 70 minutes); Not in 16

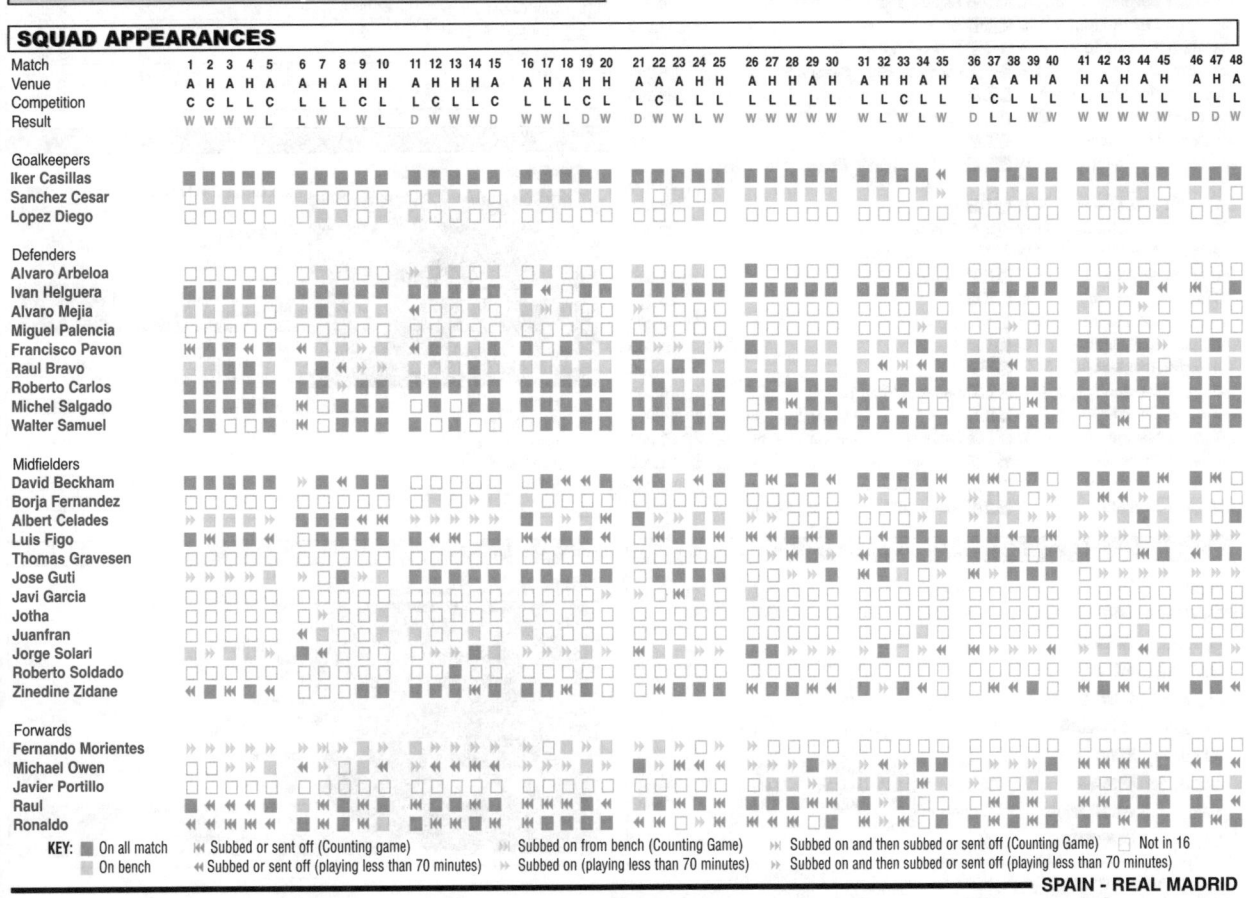

VILLARREAL

Final Position: **3rd**

KEY: ☐Won ☐Drawn ☐Lost

							Attendance
1	sppr1	**Valencia**	A	L	1-2	Forlan 78	42,000
2	sppr1	**Real Sociedad**	H	D	0-0		17,000
3	uc1rl1	**Hammarby**	A	W	2-1	Guayre 12; Rodriguez 23	11,122
4	sppr1	**R Santander**	A	D	1-1	Anderson 60	12,000
5	sppr1	**Seville**	H	D	0-0		17,000
6	sppr1	**Atl Madrid**	A	L	0-1		48,000
7	uc1rl2	**Hammarby**	H	W	3-0	Guayre 10; Font 57; Santi Cazorla 84	14,000
8	sppr1	**Real Zaragoza**	H	W	2-0	Alvaro 41 og; Forlan 49	14,000
9	sppr1	**Mallorca**	A	D	1-1	Forlan 22	14,000
10	ucge	**Lazio**	A	D	1-1	Jose Mari 4	8,000
11	sppr1	**Numancia**	H	W	4-0	Riquelme 19; Font 60,67; Forlan 86	16,000
12	sppr1	**Espanyol**	A	D	0-0		18,000
13	sppr1	**Osasuna**	H	W	3-0	Riquelme 38 pen,66; Rodriguez 40	16,000
14	sppr1	**Athl Bilbao**	A	L	1-2	Jose Mari 62	30,000
15	sppr1	**Deportivo**	H	L	0-2		16,000
16	ucge	**Middlesbrough**	H	W	2-0	Guayre 37; Javi Venta 74	14,250
17	sppr1	**Real Betis**	A	L	1-2	Guayre 54	35,000
18	ucge	**Partizan**	A	D	1-1	Santi Cazorla 17	26,000
19	sppr1	**Real Madrid**	H	D	0-0		20,000
20	sppr1	**Getafe**	A	W	2-1	Guayre 8; Forlan 59	12,000
21	ucge	**Aigaleo**	H	W	4-0	Font 13; Guayre 39; Javi Venta 53; Santi Cazorla 64	10,000
22	sppr1	**Malaga**	H	W	3-0	Pena 45; Riquelme 66; Forlan 84	14,000
23	sppr1	**Albacete**	A	D	2-2	Guayre 31,34	11,000
24	sppr1	**Barcelona**	H	W	3-0	Forlan 29,86; Rodriguez 48	22,000
25	sppr1	**Levante**	A	W	4-2	Guayre 2; Forlan 28,60; Marcos 87	16,000
26	sppr1	**Valencia**	H	W	3-1	Riquelme 19,45,90 pen	18,000
27	sppr1	**Real Sociedad**	A	W	4-0	Forlan 56,82; Riquelme 76; Jose Mari 90	20,000
28	sppr1	**R Santander**	H	W	2-1	Forlan 49; Riquelme 67 pen	20,000
29	sppr1	**Seville**	A	L	1-2	Riquelme 88 pen	40,000
30	uc3rl1	**Dinamo Kiev**	A	D	0-0		11,000
31	sppr1	**Atl Madrid**	H	W	3-2	Forlan 63; Perea 82 og; Sorin 90	15,000
32	uc3rl2	**Dinamo Kiev**	H	W	2-0	Lucho 19; Santi Cazorla 32	8,000
33	sppr1	**Real Zaragoza**	A	L	0-1		25,000
34	sppr1	**Mallorca**	H	W	2-1	Lucho 61; Forlan 83	17,000
35	sppr1	**Numancia**	A	D	1-1	Riquelme 28	7,000
36	sppr1	**Espanyol**	H	W	4-1	Forlan 24; Sorin 50; Riquelme 56; Lucho 82	20,000
37	uc4rl1	**S Bucharest**	A	D	0-0		30,000
38	uc4rl2	**S Bucharest**	H	W	2-0	Jose Mari 5; Riquelme 61 pen	22,000
39	sppr1	**Athl Bilbao**	H	W	3-1	Jose Mari 12,33; Forlan 56	13,000
40	ucqfl1	**AZ Alkmaar**	H	L	1-2	Riquelme 15	10,000
41	sppr1	**Deportivo**	A	D	1-1	Cesar Arzo 86	25,000
42	ucqfl2	**AZ Alkmaar**	A	D	1-1	Lucho 72	9,000
43	sppr1	**Real Betis**	H	D	0-0		21,000
44	sppr1	**Real Madrid**	A	L	1-2	Riquelme 39	80,000
45	sppr1	**Osasuna**	A	L	2-3	Senna 7; Sorin 76	16,000
46	sppr1	**Getafe**	H	W	4-0	Sorin 13; Forlan 17,50; Santi Cazorla 46	14,000
47	sppr1	**Malaga**	A	W	2-0	Riquelme 62; Santi Cazorla 65	20,000
48	sppr1	**Albacete**	H	W	1-0	Riquelme 68 pen	21,000
49	sppr1	**Barcelona**	A	D	3-3	Forlan 16,30 pen,70	98,000
50	sppr1	**Levante**	H	W	4-1	Josico 40; Forlan 45,89; Figueroa 90	23,000

MONTHLY POINTS TALLY

Month	Points	%
AUGUST	0	0%
SEPTEMBER	3	25%
OCTOBER	8	67%
NOVEMBER	3	25%
DECEMBER	8	67%
JANUARY	12	100%
FEBRUARY	6	50%
MARCH	7	78%
APRIL	5	33%
MAY	13	87%

LEAGUE GOALS

	PLAYER	MINS	GOALS	AVE
1	Forlan	3006	24	125
2	Riquelme	3117	15	208
3	Guayre	1174	5	235
4	Sorin	1588	4	397
5	Jose Mari	1493	4	373
6	Font	1552	2	776
7	Lucho	792	2	396
8	Rodriguez	3060	2	1530
9	Santi Cazorla	1335	2	668
10	Pena	1753	1	1753
11	Senna	1829	1	1829
12	Cesar Arzo	414	1	414
13	Josico	2314	1	2314
	Other		5	
	TOTAL		69	

KEY PLAYERS - GOALSCORERS

Diego Forlan

Goals in the League	24
Contribution to Attacking Power Average number of minutes between League team goals while on pitch	48
Player Strike Rate Average number of minutes between League goals scored by player	125
Club Strike Rate Average number of minutes between League goals scored by club	50

	PLAYER	GOALS LGE	POWER	S RATE
1	Diego Forlan	24	48	125 mins
2	Juan Riquelme	15	51	208 mins
3	Juan Pablo Sorin	4	51	397 mins
4	Gonzalo Rodriguez	2	51	1530 mins
5	Juan Manuel Pena	1	44	1753 mins

KEY PLAYERS - MIDFIELDERS

Santi Cazorla

Riqueime pictured

Goals in the League	2
Defensive Rating Average number of mins between League goals conceded while on the pitch	121
Contribution to Attacking Power Average number of minutes between League team goals while on pitch	51
Scoring Difference Defensive Rating minus Contribution to Attacking Power	70

	PLAYER	GOALS LGE	DEF RATE	ATT POWER	SCORE DIFF
1	Santi Cazorla	2	121	51	70 mins
2	Romero Hector Font	2	97	41	56 mins
3	Juan Riquelme	15	94	51	43 mins
4	Marcos Senna	1	91	49	42 mins
5	Josico	1	89	48	41 mins

KEY PLAYERS - DEFENDERS

Armando Sa

Alvarez pictured

Goals Conceded in League	12
Clean Sheets In games when player was on pitch for at least 70 minutes	9
Defensive Rating Ave number of mins between League goals conceded while on the pitch	118
Club Defensive Rating Average number of mins between League goals conceded by the club this season	92

	PLAYER	CON LGE	CLEAN SHEETS	DEF RATE
1	Armando Sa	12	9	118 mins
2	Quique Alvarez	21	10	102 mins
3	Juan Manuel Pena	18	5	97 mins
4	Gonzalo Rodriguez	34	13	90 mins
5	Javi Venta	33	11	86 mins

KEY GOALKEEPER

Jose Reina

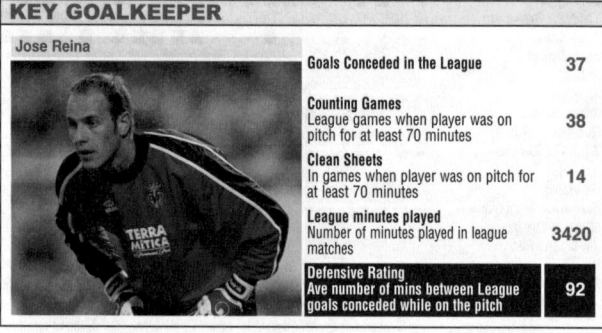

Goals Conceded in the League	37
Counting Games League games when player was on pitch for at least 70 minutes	38
Clean Sheets In games when player was on pitch for at least 70 minutes	14
League minutes played Number of minutes played in league matches	3420
Defensive Rating Ave number of mins between League goals conceded while on the pitch	92

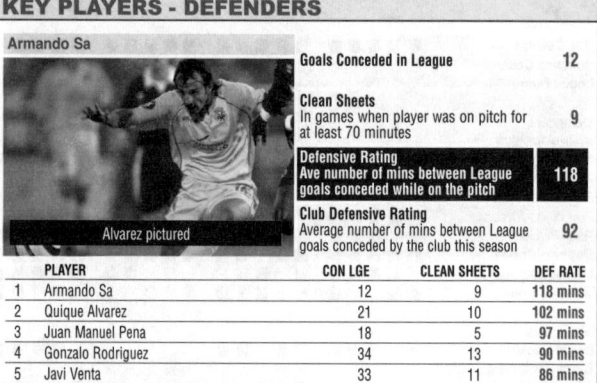

DISCIPLINARY RECORDS

	PLAYER	YELLOW	RED	AVE
1	Battaglia	6	1	131
2	Arruabarrena	11	2	174
3	Rodriguez	12	1	235
4	Sa	4	0	352
5	Alvarez	5	1	356
6	Senna	5	0	365
7	Sorin	4	0	397
8	Pena	4	0	438
9	Josico	5	0	462
10	Javi Venta	6	0	470
11	Jose Mari	3	0	497
12	Forlan	5	0	601
13	Riquelme	5	0	623
	Other	5	0	
	TOTAL	80	5	

TOP POINT EARNERS

	PLAYER	GAMES	AV PTS
1	Juan Manuel Pena	17	1.94
2	Rodolfo Arruabarrena	25	1.80
3	Diego Forlan	32	1.78
4	Marcos Senna	20	1.75
5	Juan Riquelme	35	1.74
6	Javi Venta	31	1.71
7	Jose Reina	38	1.71
8	Quique Alvarez	23	1.65
9	Gonzalo Rodriguez	34	1.62
10	Josico	24	1.54
	CLUB AVERAGE:		1.71

TEAM OF THE SEASON

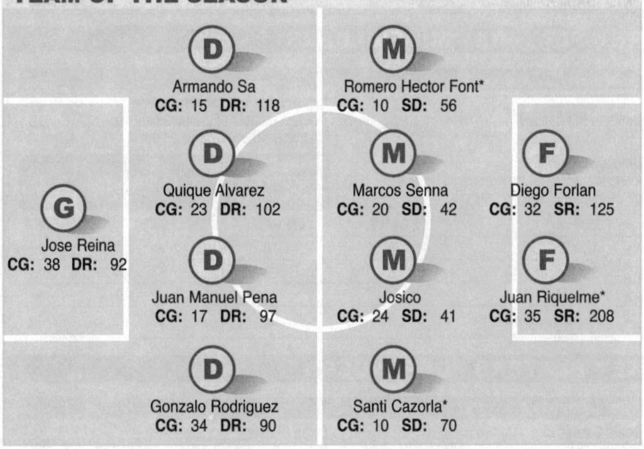

G
Jose Reina
CG: 38 DR: 92
D
Armando Sa
CG: 15 DR: 118
D
Quique Alvarez
CG: 23 DR: 102
D
Juan Manuel Pena
CG: 17 DR: 97
D
Gonzalo Rodriguez
CG: 34 DR: 90
M
Romero Hector Font*
CG: 10 SD: 56
M
Marcos Senna
CG: 20 SD: 42
M
Josico
CG: 24 SD: 41
M
Santi Cazorla*
CG: 10 SD: 70
F
Diego Forlan
CG: 32 SR: 125
F
Juan Riquelme*
CG: 35 SR: 208

LEAGUE APPEARANCES, BOOKINGS AND CAPS

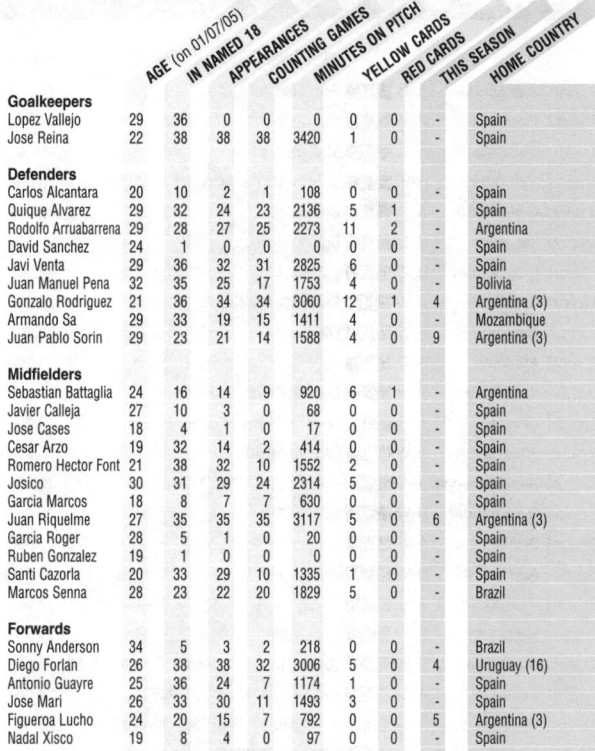

	AGE (on 01/07/05)	IN NAMED 18	APPEARANCES	COUNTING GAMES	MINUTES ON PITCH	YELLOW CARDS	RED CARDS	THIS SEASON	HOME COUNTRY
Goalkeepers									
Lopez Vallejo	29	36	0	0	0	0	0	-	Spain
Jose Reina	22	38	38	38	3420	1	0	-	Spain
Defenders									
Carlos Alcantara	20	10	2	1	108	0	0	-	Spain
Quique Alvarez	29	32	24	23	2136	5	1	-	Spain
Rodolfo Arruabarrena	29	28	27	25	2273	11	2	-	Argentina
David Sanchez	24	1	0	0	0	0	0	-	Spain
Javi Venta	29	36	32	31	2825	6	0	-	Spain
Juan Manuel Pena	32	35	25	17	1753	4	0	-	Bolivia
Gonzalo Rodriguez	21	36	34	34	3060	12	1	4	Argentina (3)
Armando Sa	29	33	19	15	1411	4	0	-	Mozambique
Juan Pablo Sorin	29	23	21	14	1588	4	0	9	Argentina (3)
Midfielders									
Sebastian Battaglia	24	16	14	9	920	6	1	-	Argentina
Javier Calleja	27	10	3	0	68	0	0	-	Spain
Jose Cases	18	4	1	0	17	0	0	-	Spain
Cesar Arzo	19	32	14	2	414	0	0	-	Spain
Romero Hector Font	21	38	32	10	1552	2	0	-	Spain
Josico	30	31	29	24	2314	5	0	-	Spain
Garcia Marcos	18	8	7	7	630	0	0	-	Spain
Juan Riquelme	27	35	35	35	3117	5	0	6	Argentina (3)
Garcia Roger	28	5	1	0	20	0	0	-	Spain
Ruben Gonzalez	19	1	0	0	0	0	0	-	Spain
Santi Cazorla	20	33	29	10	1335	1	0	-	Spain
Marcos Senna	28	23	22	20	1829	5	0	-	Brazil
Forwards									
Sonny Anderson	34	5	3	2	218	0	0	-	Brazil
Diego Forlan	26	38	38	32	3006	5	0	4	Uruguay (16)
Antonio Guayre	25	36	24	7	1174	1	0	-	Spain
Jose Mari	26	33	30	11	1493	3	0	-	Spain
Figueroa Lucho	24	20	15	7	792	0	0	5	Argentina (3)
Nadal Xisco	19	8	4	0	97	0	0	-	Spain

SQUAD APPEARANCES

Match	1 2 3 4 5	6 7 8 9 10	11 12 13 14 15	16 17 18 19 20	21 22 23 24 25	26 27 28 29 30	31 32 33 34 35	36 37 38 39 40	41 42 43 44 45	46 47 48 49 50
Venue	A H A A H	A H H A A	H A H A H	H A A H A	H H A H A	H A H A A	H H A H A	H A H H H	A A H A A	H A H A H
Competition	L L E L L	L E L L E	L L L L L	E L E L L	E L L L L	L L L L E	L E L L L	L E E L E	L E L L L	L L L L L
Result	L D W D D	L W W D D	W D W L L	W L D D W	W W D W W	W W W L D	W W L W D	W D W W L	D D D L L	W W W D W

Goalkeepers
Lopez Vallejo
Jose Reina

Defenders
Carlos Alcantara
Quique Alvarez
Rodolfo Arruabarrena
David Sanchez
Javi Venta
Juan Manuel Pena
Gonzalo Rodriguez
Armando Sa
Juan Pablo Sorin

Midfielders
Sebastian Battaglia
Javier Calleja
Jose Cases
Cesar Arzo
Romero Hector Font
Josico
Garcia Marcos
Juan Riquelme
Garcia Roger
Ruben Gonzalez
Santi Cazorla
Marcos Senna

Forwards
Sonny Anderson
Diego Forlan
Antonio Guayre
Jose Mari
Figueroa Lucho
Nadal Xisco

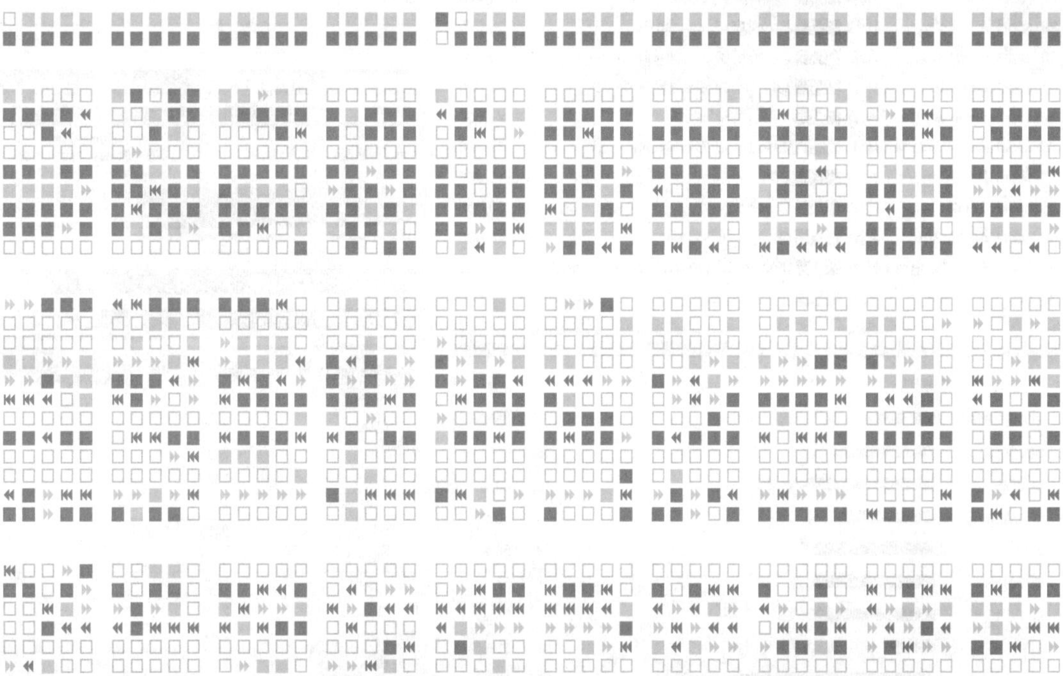

KEY: On all match / On bench / Subbed or sent off (Counting game) / Subbed or sent off (playing less than 70 minutes) / Subbed on from bench (Counting Game) / Subbed on (playing less than 70 minutes) / Subbed on and then subbed or sent off (Counting Game) / Subbed on and then subbed or sent off (playing less than 70 minutes) / Not in 16

REAL BETIS

Final Position: **4th**

KEY: Won / Drawn / Lost

							Attendance
1	sppr1	**Numancia**	A	D	1-1	Fernando 45	10,000
2	sppr1	**Espanyol**	H	L	1-4	Edu 49	24,000
3	sppr1	**Osasuna**	A	L	2-3	Melli 33; Edu 64	16,000
4	sppr1	**Athl Bilbao**	H	W	2-1	Juanito 37; Fernando 58	25,000
5	sppr1	**Deportivo**	A	D	1-1	Oliveira 68	30,000
6	sppr1	**Valencia**	H	D	1-1	Edu 30	28,000
7	sppr1	**Real Madrid**	H	D	1-1	Oliveira 32	42,000
8	sppr1	**Getafe**	A	W	2-0	Rivas 50; Oliveira 75	13,000
9	sppr1	**Malaga**	H	D	1-1	Oliveira 4	39,000
10	sppr1	**Albacete**	A	D	0-0		13,000
11	sppr1	**Barcelona**	H	W	2-1	Edu 49; Oliveira 69	50,000
12	sppr1	**Levante**	A	W	2-1	Oliveira 29 pen; Edu 82	19,000
13	sppr1	**Villarreal**	H	W	2-1	Oliveira 20,40	35,000
14	sppr1	**Real Sociedad**	A	L	0-1		18,000
15	sppr1	**R Santander**	H	W	2-1	Edu 28; Oliveira 71	35,000
16	sppr1	**Seville**	A	L	1-2	Fernando 44	45,000
17	sppr1	**Atl Madrid**	H	W	1-0	Joaquin 8	25,000
18	sppr1	**Real Zaragoza**	A	L	0-1		32,000
19	sppr1	**Mallorca**	H	W	2-0	Edu 27,86	35,000
20	sppr1	**Numancia**	H	W	4-0	Juanito 15; Assuncao 25; Oliveira 45,47	38,000
21	sppr1	**Espanyol**	A	D	2-2	Assuncao 49; Fernando 86	24,000
22	sppr1	**Osasuna**	H	W	3-1	Assuncao 10; Rivas 36; Oliveira 81	36,000
23	sppr1	**Athl Bilbao**	A	D	4-4	Oliveira 4,25,80; Joaquin 11	30,000
24	sppr1	**Deportivo**	H	W	2-0	Assuncao 38,56	38,000
25	sppr1	**Valencia**	A	L	1-2	Assuncao 14	46,000
26	sppr1	**Real Madrid**	A	L	1-3	Edu 59	67,000
27	sppr1	**Getafe**	H	D	2-2	Rivas 28; Assuncao 55	35,000
28	sppr1	**Malaga**	A	W	2-1	Juanito 4; Edu 17	25,000
29	sppr1	**Albacete**	H	W	2-1	Rivas 16; Assuncao 58	38,000
30	sppr1	**Barcelona**	A	D	3-3	Joaquin 12,63; Oliveira 40	90,000
31	sppr1	**Levante**	H	D	2-2	Edu 11; Oliveira 31	35,000
32	sppr1	**Villarreal**	A	D	0-0		21,000
33	sppr1	**Real Sociedad**	H	L	2-3	Joaquin 46; Oliveira 53	35,000
34	sppr1	**R Santander**	A	D	1-1	Dani 79	15,000
35	sppr1	**Seville**	H	W	1-0	Oliveira 7	50,000
36	sppr1	**Atl Madrid**	A	W	2-1	Oliveira 36,38 pen	45,000
37	sppr1	**Real Zaragoza**	H	W	3-2	Juanito 58; Oliveira 69; Fernando 82	42,000
38	sppr1	**Mallorca**	A	D	1-1	Assuncao 52	23,000

MONTHLY POINTS TALLY

AUGUST	1	33%
SEPTEMBER	4	33%
OCTOBER	6	50%
NOVEMBER	10	83%
DECEMBER	6	50%
JANUARY	7	58%
FEBRUARY	7	58%
MARCH	7	58%
APRIL	3	25%
MAY	11	73%

KEY PLAYERS - GOALSCORERS

Ricardo Oliveira

Goals in the League	22	Player Strike Rate Average number of minutes between League goals scored by player	149
Contribution to Attacking Power Average number of minutes between League team goals while on pitch	53	**Club Strike Rate** Average number of minutes between League goals scored by club	55

	PLAYER	LGE GOALS	POWER	STRIKE RATE
1	Ricardo Oliveira	22	53	149 mins
2	Edu	11	50	241 mins
3	Assuncao	9	53	298 mins
4	Fernandez Fernando	5	52	483 mins
5	Sanchez Joaquin	5	54	650 mins

KEY PLAYERS - MIDFIELDERS

Arzu

Goals in the League	0	**Contribution to Attacking Power** Average number of minutes between League team goals while on pitch	48
Defensive Rating Average number of mins between League goals conceded while on the pitch	70	Scoring Difference Defensive Rating minus Contribution to Attacking Power	22

	PLAYER	LGE GOALS	DEF RATE	POWER	SCORE DIFF
1	Arzu	0	70	48	22 mins
2	Sanchez Joaquin	5	69	54	15 mins
3	Juan Melli	1	72	57	15 mins
4	Fernando Varela	0	60	54	6 mins

KEY PLAYERS - DEFENDERS

Washington Tais

Goals Conceded Number of League goals conceded while the player was on the pitch	9	**Clean Sheets** In games when player was on pitch for at least 70 minutes	3
Defensive Rating Ave number of mins between League goals conceded while on the pitch	116	**Club Defensive Rating** Average number of mins between League goals conceded by the club this season	68

	PLAYER	CON LGE	CLEAN SHEETS	DEF RATE
1	Washington Tais	9	3	116 mins
2	David Rivas	32	8	86 mins
3	Juanito	44	6	67 mins
4	Luis Fernandez	29	3	59 mins

KEY GOALKEEPER

Antonio Doblas

Goals Conceded in the League	35	**Counting Games** Games when player was on pitch for at least 70 minutes	29
Defensive Rating Ave number of mins between League goals conceded while on the pitch	75	**Clean Sheets** In games when player was on pitch for at least 70 minutes	8

LEAGUE GOALS

Ricardo Oliveira

Minutes on the pitch	3279	Goals in the League	22
League average (mins between goals)	149		

	PLAYER	MINS	GOALS	AVE
1	Oliveira	3279	22	149
2	Edu	2651	11	241
3	Assuncao	2683	9	298
4	Joaquin	3249	5	650
5	Fernando	2416	5	483
6	Rivas	2759	4	690
7	Juanito	2937	4	734
8	Melli	2521	1	2521
9	Dani	86	1	86
	Other		0	
	TOTAL		62	

DISCIPLINARY RECORDS

	PLAYER	YELLOW	RED	AVE
1	Lembo	5	2	106
2	Castellini	3	1	135
3	Canas	8	0	189
4	Luis Fernandez	7	1	214
5	Varela	6	0	241
6	Juanito	11	1	244
7	Assuncao	8	1	298
8	Melli	8	0	315
9	Arzu	6	0	337
10	Rivas	6	1	394
11	Benjamin	2	0	484
12	Tais	2	0	524
13	Oliveira	5	1	546
	Other	15	0	
	TOTAL	92	8	

TOP POINT EARNERS

	PLAYER	GAMES	AV PTS
1	Arzu	20	1.95
2	David Rivas	30	1.77
3	Antonio Doblas	29	1.76
4	Juan Melli	28	1.71
5	Assuncao	28	1.68
6	Ricardo Oliveira	36	1.67
7	Juanito	33	1.67
8	Sanchez Joaquin	36	1.61
9	Luis Fernandez	18	1.50
10	Edu	26	1.50
	CLUB AVERAGE:		1.63

TEAM OF THE SEASON

D
David Rivas
CG: 30 DR: 86
D
Juanito
CG: 33 DR: 67
D
Luis Fernandez
CG: 18 DR: 59
D
Washington Tais*
CG: 11 DR: 116
M
Arzu
CG: 20 SD: 22
M
Sanchez Joaquin
CG: 36 SD: 15
M
Juan Melli
CG: 28 SD: 15
M
Fernando Varela
CG: 13 SD: 6
G
Antonio Doblas
CG: 29 DR: 75
F
Ricardo Oliveira
CG: 36 SR: 149
F
Edu
CG: 26 SR: 241

LEAGUE APPEARANCES, BOOKINGS AND CAPS

	AGE (on 01/07/05)	IN NAMED 18	APPEARANCES	COUNTING GAMES	MINUTES ON PITCH	YELLOW CARDS	RED CARDS	THIS SEASON	HOME COUNTRY
Goalkeepers									
Pedro Contreras	33	23	0	0	0	0	0	-	Spain
Antonio Doblas	25	33	29	29	2610	4	0	-	Spain
Antonio Prats	33	18	9	9	810	1	0	-	Spain
Defenders									
Paoli Castellini	26	8	6	6	540	3	1	-	Italy
David Llano	23	1	0	0	0	0	0	-	Spain
Juanito	28	34	33	33	2937	11	1	3	Spain (8)
Daniel Lembo	27	28	13	7	742	5	2	-	Uruguay
Luis Fernandez	32	26	22	18	1713	7	1	-	Spain
David Rivas	26	34	32	30	2759	6	1	-	Spain
Washington Tais	32	20	12	11	1048	2	0	-	Uruguay
Midfielders									
Arzu	24	36	30	20	2025	6	0	-	Spain
Zarandona Benjamin	29	32	26	7	969	2	0	-	Spain
Juan Jose Canas	33	35	24	11	1514	8	0	-	Spain
Jesus Capi	28	13	11	2	350	2	0	-	Spain
Denilson	27	17	10	0	287	0	0	-	Brazil
Bascon Israel	18	15	7	0	168	0	0	-	Spain
Sanchez Joaquin	24	38	38	36	3249	2	0	-	Spain
Juan Melli	21	33	29	28	2521	8	0	-	Spain
Pablo Nino	27	25	6	1	268	2	0	-	Spain
Fernando Varela	25	30	22	13	1451	6	0	-	Spain
Forwards									
Perez Alfonso	32	19	10	0	190	1	0	-	Spain
Assuncao	28	35	34	28	2683	8	1	-	Brazil
Dani	23	14	7	0	86	0	0	-	Spain
Edu	26	33	32	26	2651	4	0	8	Brazil (1)
Fernandez Fernando	31	34	34	20	2416	4	0	-	Spain
Gomez Isidoro	-	3	0	0	0	0	0	-	Spain
Lopez Ismael	27	13	5	1	123	1	0	-	Spain
Ricardo Oliveira	25	37	37	36	3279	5	1	4	Brazil (1)
Jorge Tote	26	6	1	1	90	0	0	-	Spain

SQUAD APPEARANCES

Match	1	2	3	4	5	6	7	8	9	10	11	12	13	14	15	16	17	18	19	20	21	22	23	24	25	26	27	28	29	30	31	32	33	34	35	36	37	38
Venue	A	H	A	H	A	H	H	A	H	A	H	A	H	A	H	A	H	A	H	H	A	H	A	H	A	A	H	A	H	A	H	A	H	A	H	A	H	A
Competition	L	L	L	L	L	L	L	L	L	L	L	L	L	L	L	L	L	L	L	L	L	L	L	L	L	L	L	L	L	L	L	L	L	L	L	L	L	L
Result	D	L	L	W	D	D	D	W	D	D	W	W	W	L	W	L	W	L	W	W	D	W	D	W	L	L	D	W	W	D	D	D	L	D	W	W	W	D

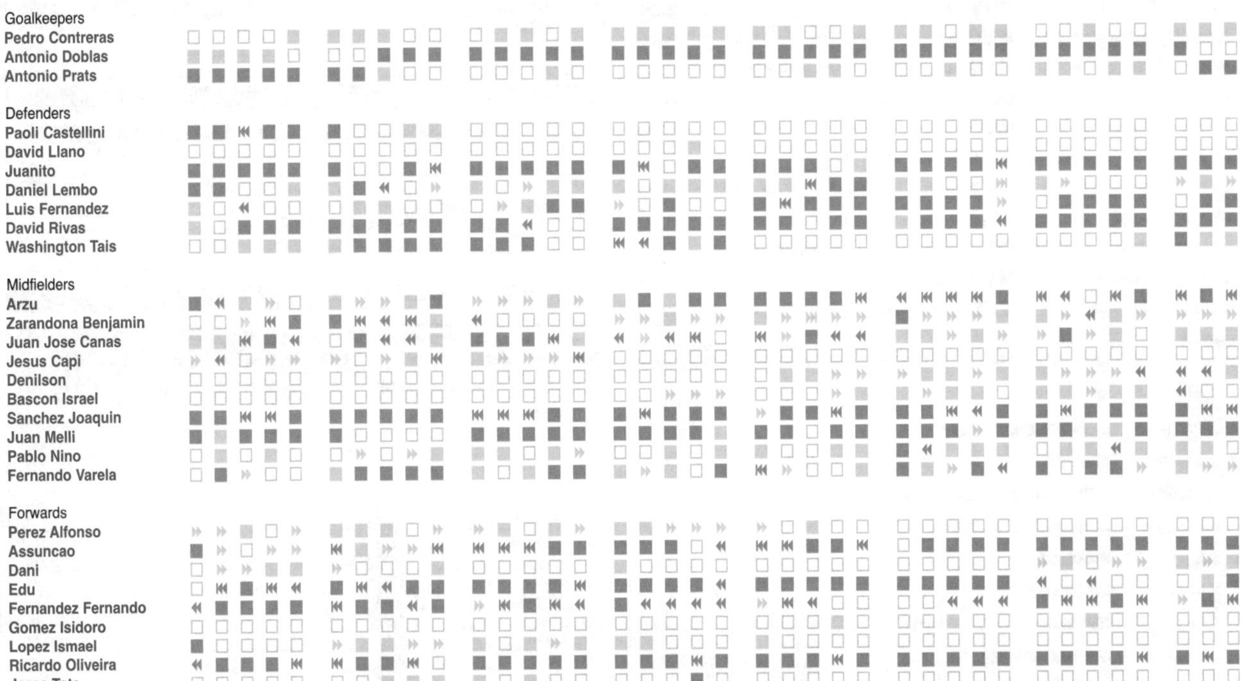

Goalkeepers
Pedro Contreras
Antonio Doblas
Antonio Prats
Defenders
Paoli Castellini
David Llano
Juanito
Daniel Lembo
Luis Fernandez
David Rivas
Washington Tais
Midfielders
Arzu
Zarandona Benjamin
Juan Jose Canas
Jesus Capi
Denilson
Bascon Israel
Sanchez Joaquin
Juan Melli
Pablo Nino
Fernando Varela
Forwards
Perez Alfonso
Assuncao
Dani
Edu
Fernandez Fernando
Gomez Isidoro
Lopez Ismael
Ricardo Oliveira
Jorge Tote

KEY: On all match
On bench
Subbed or sent off (Counting game)
Subbed or sent off (playing less than 70 minutes)
Subbed on from bench (Counting Game)
Subbed on (playing less than 70 minutes)
Subbed on and then subbed or sent off (Counting Game)
Subbed on and then subbed or sent off (playing less than 70 minutes)
Not in 16

ESPANYOL

Final Position: **5th**

KEY: Won Drawn Lost

						Attendance
1	sppr1 **Deportivo**	H	D	1-1	Tamudo 22	19,000
2	sppr1 **Real Betis**	A	W	4-1	Maxi 18,50,65; Dani 42	24,000
3	sppr1 **Real Madrid**	H	W	1-0	Maxi 41	40,000
4	sppr1 **Getafe**	A	L	0-1		16,000
5	sppr1 **Malaga**	H	W	1-0	De La Pena 51	23,000
6	sppr1 **Albacete**	A	L	0-1		15,000
7	sppr1 **Barcelona**	H	L	0-1		34,000
8	sppr1 **Levante**	A	W	2-0	Serrano 51; Lopo 72	18,000
9	sppr1 **Villarreal**	H	D	0-0		18,000
10	sppr1 **Real Sociedad**	A	W	2-0	Maxi 53,75	24,000
11	sppr1 **R Santander**	H	W	2-1	Dani 12; Maxi 80 pen	20,000
12	sppr1 **Seville**	A	L	0-1		40,000
13	sppr1 **Atl Madrid**	H	W	2-1	Dani 53,75	17,000
14	sppr1 **Real Zaragoza**	A	W	1-0	Tamudo 30	19,000
15	sppr1 **Mallorca**	H	W	2-1	Pocchettino 27; Serrano 35	15,000
16	sppr1 **Numancia**	A	D	0-0		10,000
17	sppr1 **Valencia**	A	L	0-3		40,000
18	sppr1 **Osasuna**	H	W	4-1	Maxi 31; Fredson 37,83; De La Pena 40	19,000
19	sppr1 **Athl Bilbao**	A	D	1-1	Maxi 32	38,000
20	sppr1 **Deportivo**	A	L	1-4	Fredson 17	24,000
21	sppr1 **Real Betis**	H	D	2-2	De La Pena 27; Tamudo 80	24,000
22	sppr1 **Real Madrid**	A	L	0-4		63,000
23	sppr1 **Getafe**	H	W	2-0	Soldevilla 90; Tamudo 90 pen	19,000
24	sppr1 **Malaga**	A	L	2-3	Dani 71; Sanz 87 og	21,000
25	sppr1 **Albacete**	H	W	2-1	Maxi 5; Tamudo 22	25,000
26	sppr1 **Barcelona**	A	D	0-0		85,000
27	sppr1 **Levante**	H	W	2-1	Amavisca 29; Maxi 64	20,000
28	sppr1 **Villarreal**	A	L	1-4	Lopo 30	20,000
29	sppr1 **Real Sociedad**	H	D	2-2	Tamudo 37 pen,56 pen	20,000
30	sppr1 **R Santander**	A	W	3-1	Tamudo 14 pen; Jarque 44; Maxi 49	12,000
31	sppr1 **Seville**	H	L	1-3	Jonathan 73	27,000
32	sppr1 **Atl Madrid**	A	D	0-0		47,000
33	sppr1 **Real Zaragoza**	H	W	3-1	Tamudo 33,90; Maxi 43	30,000
34	sppr1 **Mallorca**	A	L	2-3	Ibarra 9; Maxi 90	11,000
35	sppr1 **Numancia**	H	W	3-0	Amavisca 54; Coro 57; Antonio 83 og	20,000
36	sppr1 **Valencia**	H	D	2-2	Tamudo 33; Velamanzan 90	35,000
37	sppr1 **Osasuna**	A	D	1-1	Maxi 3	14,000
38	sppr1 **Athl Bilbao**	H	W	2-0	Velamanzan 32; Lopo 46	42,000

MONTHLY POINTS TALLY

AUGUST	1	33%
SEPTEMBER	9	75%
OCTOBER	4	33%
NOVEMBER	9	75%
DECEMBER	7	58%
JANUARY	5	42%
FEBRUARY	6	50%
MARCH	5	42%
APRIL	7	58%
MAY	8	53%

KEY PLAYERS - GOALSCORERS

Rodriguez Maxi

Goals in the League	15	Player Strike Rate Average number of minutes between League goals scored by player	199
Contribution to Attacking Power Average number of minutes between League team goals while on pitch	60	Club Strike Rate Average number of minutes between League goals scored by club	63

	PLAYER	LGE GOALS	POWER	STRIKE RATE
1	Rodriguez Maxi	15	60	199 mins
2	Raul Tamudo	11	61	229 mins
3	Garcia Dani	5	58	354 mins
4	Ivan De La Pena	3	66	745 mins
5	Oscar Serrano	2	71	971 mins

KEY PLAYERS - MIDFIELDERS

Antonio Ito

Goals in the League	0	Contribution to Attacking Power Average number of minutes between League team goals while on pitch	66
Defensive Rating Average number of mins between League goals conceded while on the pitch	82	Scoring Difference Defensive Rating minus Contribution to Attacking Power	16

	PLAYER	LGE GOALS	DEF RATE	POWER	SCORE DIFF
1	Antonio Ito	0	82	66	16 mins
2	David Garcia	0	76	63	13 mins
3	Ivan De La Pena	3	75	66	9 mins
4	Rodriguez Maxi	15	69	61	8 mins

KEY PLAYERS - DEFENDERS

Mauricio Pocchettino

Goals Conceded Number of League goals conceded while the player was on the pitch	26	Clean Sheets In games when player was on pitch for at least 70 minutes	8
Defensive Rating Ave number of mins between League goals conceded while on the pitch	86	Club Defensive Rating Average number of mins between League goals conceded by the club this season	71

	PLAYER	CON LGE	CLEAN SHEETS	DEF RATE
1	Mauricio Pocchettino	26	8	86 mins
2	Alberto Lopo	44	11	73 mins
3	Hugo Ibarra	39	8	69 mins
4	Antoni Soldevilla	27	4	55 mins
5	Daniel Jarque	33	2	53 mins

KEY GOALKEEPER

Carlos Kameni

Goals Conceded in the League	47	Counting Games Games when player was on pitch for at least 70 minutes	37
Defensive Rating Ave number of mins between League goals conceded while on the pitch	72	Clean Sheets In games when player was on pitch for at least 70 minutes	11

LEAGUE GOALS

Rodriguez Maxi

Minutes on the pitch	2985	Goals in the League	15
League average (mins between goals)	199		

	PLAYER	MINS	GOALS	AVE
1	Maxi	2985	15	199
2	Tamudo	2523	11	229
3	Dani	1768	5	354
4	Lopo	3194	3	1065
5	De La Pena	2235	3	745
6	Velamanzan	229	2	115
7	Amavisca	879	2	440
8	Serrano	1941	2	971
9	Jonathan	244	1	244
10	Jarque	1751	1	1751
11	Fredson	1137	1	1137
12	Ibarra	2691	1	2691
13	Coro	674	1	674
	Other		6	
	TOTAL		54	

DISCIPLINARY RECORDS

	PLAYER	YELLOW	RED	AVE
1	Alex	7	1	150
2	Soldevilla	7	0	211
3	Lopo	12	1	245
4	Ito	11	0	245
5	Pocchettino	8	1	248
6	Jarque	4	2	291
7	Tamudo	7	1	315
8	Ibarra	7	0	384
9	Serrano	4	1	388
10	De La Pena	5	0	447
11	Coro	1	0	674
12	Garcia	4	0	738
13	Maxi	3	1	746
	Other	6	0	
	TOTAL	86	8	

TOP POINT EARNERS

	PLAYER	GAMES	AV PTS
1	David Garcia	31	1.90
2	Garcia Dani	16	1.88
3	Antonio Ito	29	1.79
4	Oscar Serrano	17	1.76
5	Rodriguez Maxi	33	1.64
6	Mauricio Pocchettino	24	1.63
7	Carlos Kameni	37	1.62
8	Raul Tamudo	27	1.59
9	Alberto Lopo	35	1.57
10	Daniel Jarque	17	1.53
	CLUB AVERAGE:		1.61

TEAM OF THE SEASON

G
Carlos Kameni
CG: 37 DR: 72
D
Mauricio Pocchettino
CG: 24 DR: 86
D
Alberto Lopo
CG: 35 DR: 73
D
Hugo Ibarra
CG: 30 DR: 69
D
Antoni Soldevilla
CG: 15 DR: 55
M
Antonio Ito
CG: 29 SD: 16
M
David Garcia
CG: 31 SD: 13
M
Ivan De La Pena
CG: 24 SD: 9
M
Rodriguez Maxi
CG: 33 SD: 8
F
Raul Tamudo
CG: 27 SR: 229
F
Garcia Dani
CG: 16 SR: 354

LEAGUE APPEARANCES, BOOKINGS AND CAPS

	AGE (on 01/07/05)	IN NAMED 18	APPEARANCES	COUNTING GAMES	MINUTES ON PITCH	YELLOW CARDS	RED CARDS	THIS SEASON	HOME COUNTRY
Goalkeepers									
Gabriel Biel	19	2	1	0	22	0	0	-	Spain
Carlos Kameni	21	38	38	37	3398	3	0	5	Cameroon (26)
Erwin Lemmens	29	36	0	0	0	0	0	1	Belgium (42)
Defenders									
Marc Bertran	23	2	0	0	0	0	0	-	Spain
Didier Domi	27	11	4	2	222	0	0	-	France
Hugo Ibarra	31	35	31	30	2691	7	0	-	Argentina
Daniel Jarque	22	32	22	17	1751	4	2	-	Spain
Alberto Lopo	26	36	36	35	3194	12	1	-	Spain
Oscar Minambres	24	11	6	2	242	0	0	-	Spain
Mauricio Pocchettino	33	29	26	24	2238	8	1	-	Argentina
Sergio Sanchez	19	2	1	1	75	0	0	-	Spain
Antoni Soldevilla	26	34	21	15	1480	7	0	-	Spain
Midfielders									
Jose Amavisca	34	32	21	3	879	1	0	-	Spain
Ivan De La Pena	29	32	29	24	2235	5	0	3	Spain (8)
Fredson	24	35	27	7	1137	1	0	-	Brazil
David Garcia	24	37	34	31	2955	4	0	-	Spain
Simon Hector	21	1	0	0	0	0	0	-	Spain
Antonio Ito	30	33	31	29	2699	11	0	-	Spain
Rodriguez Maxi	24	37	37	33	2985	3	1	-	Argentina
Angel Morales	29	20	13	2	356	2	0	-	Spain
Antonio Velamanzan	28	13	6	1	229	1	0	-	Spain
Forwards									
Fernandez Alex	31	28	18	9	1207	7	1	-	Spain
Ferran Coro	22	32	23	2	674	1	0	-	Spain
Garcia Dani	30	31	26	16	1768	1	0	-	Spain
Soriano Jonathan	19	16	7	2	244	0	0	-	Spain
Garcia Junyent Oscar	32	1	0	0	0	0	0	-	Spain
Martin Posse	29	18	7	1	213	1	0	-	Argentina
Oscar Serrano	23	33	30	17	1941	4	1	-	Spain
Raul Tamudo	27	30	29	27	2523	7	1	2	Spain (8)

SQUAD APPEARANCES

Match	1	2	3	4	5	6	7	8	9	10	11	12	13	14	15	16	17	18	19	20	21	22	23	24	25	26	27	28	29	30	31	32	33	34	35	36	37	38
Venue	H	A	H	A	H	A	H	A	H	A	H	A	H	A	H	A	A	H	A	A	H	A	H	A	H	A	H	A	H	A	H	A	H	A	H	H	A	H
Competition	L	L	L	L	L	L	L	L	L	L	L	L	L	L	L	L	L	L	L	L	L	L	L	L	L	L	L	L	L	L	L	L	L	L	L	L	L	L
Result	D	W	W	L	W	L	L	W	D	W	W	L	W	W	W	D	L	W	D	L	D	L	W	L	W	D	W	L	D	W	L	D	W	L	W	D	D	W

Goalkeepers
Gabriel Biel
Carlos Kameni
Erwin Lemmens

Defenders
Marc Bertran
Didier Domi
Hugo Ibarra
Daniel Jarque
Alberto Lopo
Oscar Minambres
Mauricio Pocchettino
Sergio Sanchez
Antoni Soldevilla

Midfielders
Jose Amavisca
Ivan De La Pena
Fredson
David Garcia
Simon Hector
Antonio Ito
Rodriguez Maxi
Angel Morales
Antonio Velamanzan

Forwards
Fernandez Alex
Ferran Coro
Garcia Dani
Soriano Jonathan
Garcia Junyent Oscar
Martin Posse
Oscar Serrano
Raul Tamudo

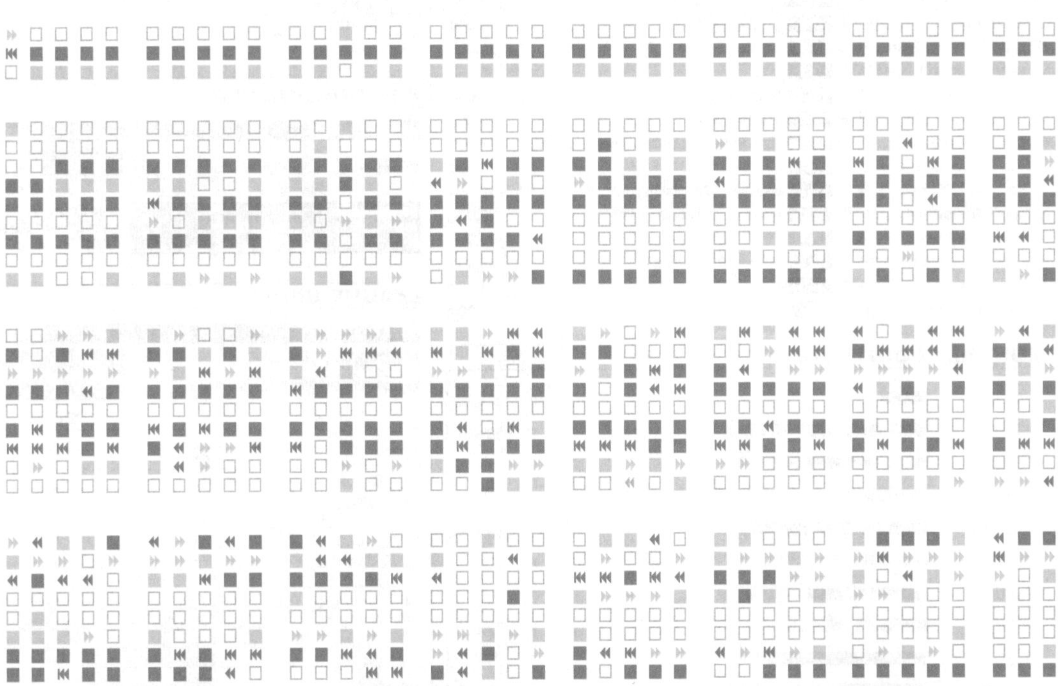

KEY: On all match | On bench | Subbed or sent off (Counting game) | Subbed or sent off (playing less than 70 minutes) | Subbed on from bench (Counting Game) | Subbed on (playing less than 70 minutes) | Subbed on and then subbed or sent off (Counting Game) | Subbed on and then subbed or sent off (playing less than 70 minutes) | Not in 16

FC SEVILLE

Final Position: **6th**

KEY: Won / Drawn / Lost

							Attendance
1	sppr1	**Albacete**	H	W	1-0	Renato 47	41,000
2	sppr1	**Barcelona**	A	L	0-2		61,000
3	uc1rl1	**Nacional**	H	W	2-0	Baptista 32; Sergio 79	35,000
4	sppr1	**Levante**	H	W	3-0	Dario Silva 22; Baptista 46,54	38,000
5	sppr1	**Villarreal**	A	D	0-0		17,000
6	sppr1	**Real Sociedad**	H	W	2-1	Sergio 44; Dario Silva 66	33,000
7	uc1rl2	**Nacional**	A	W	2-1	Jesuli 35; Renato 82	10,000
8	sppr1	**R Santander**	A	D	0-0		12,000
9	sppr1	**Valencia**	A	W	2-1	Baptista 65; Aranda 83	46,000
10	sppr1	**Atl Madrid**	H	W	2-1	Aitor Ocio 11; Baptista 52	45,000
11	sppr1	**Real Zaragoza**	A	L	0-3		31,000
12	ucgh	**Alem Aachen**	H	W	2-0	Aranda 7; Baptista 77 pen	40,000
13	sppr1	**Mallorca**	H	D	1-1	Antonio Lopez 71	40,000
14	sppr1	**Numancia**	A	L	1-2	Puerta 62	7,000
15	sppr1	**Espanyol**	H	W	1-0	Baptista 40	40,000
16	ucgh	**Z St Petersburg**	A	D	1-1	Baptista 72	20,000
17	sppr1	**Osasuna**	A	L	1-4	Carlitos 38	15,000
18	ucgh	**AEK Athens**	H	W	3-2	Baptista 18,89 pen; Antonito 28	29,000
19	sppr1	**Athl Bilbao**	H	W	2-0	Baptista 53; Carlitos 66	37,000
20	sppr1	**Deportivo**	A	D	2-2	Carlitos 42; Baptista 90	24,000
21	ucgh	**Lille**	A	L	0-1		9,000
22	sppr1	**Real Betis**	H	W	2-1	Daniel Alves 3; Navarro 47	45,000
23	sppr1	**Real Madrid**	A	W	1-0	Baptista 19	57,000
24	sppr1	**Getafe**	H	D	0-0		40,000
25	sppr1	**Malaga**	A	L	0-1		22,000
26	sppr1	**Albacete**	A	W	2-0	Renato 36; Antonito 45	13,000
27	sppr1	**Barcelona**	H	L	0-4		45,000
28	sppr1	**Levante**	A	W	3-0	Antonito 33; Makukula 55; Baptista 85	19,000
29	sppr1	**Villarreal**	H	W	2-1	Baptista 36,82 pen	40,000
30	uc3rl1	**Panathinaikos**	A	L	0-1		10,000
31	sppr1	**Real Sociedad**	A	L	0-1		24,000
32	uc3rl2	**Panathinaikos**	H	W	2-0	Makukula 82; Adriano 90	12,000
33	sppr1	**R Santander**	H	D	2-2	Baptista 14; Dario Silva 76	40,000
34	sppr1	**Valencia**	H	L	2-3	Jesuli 40; Baptista 67	32,000
35	sppr1	**Atl Madrid**	A	L	0-3		45,000
36	uc4rl1	**Parma**	H	D	0-0		40,000
37	sppr1	**Real Zaragoza**	H	L	0-1		32,000
38	uc4rl2	**Parma**	A	L	0-1		8,000
39	sppr1	**Mallorca**	A	W	1-0	Baptista 45 pen	17,000
40	sppr1	**Numancia**	H	W	1-0	Adriano 69	40,000
41	sppr1	**Espanyol**	A	W	3-1	Jordi 9; Baptista 19; Daniel Alves 90	27,000
42	sppr1	**Osasuna**	H	L	0-1		40,000
43	sppr1	**Athl Bilbao**	A	W	3-1	Baptista 7,77; Navas, J 21	32,000
44	sppr1	**Deportivo**	H	W	2-0	Adriano 13; Navas, J 19	40,000
45	sppr1	**Real Betis**	A	L	0-1		50,000
46	sppr1	**Real Madrid**	H	D	2-2	Sergio 19; Baptista 89	45,000
47	sppr1	**Getafe**	A	D	0-0		14,000
48	sppr1	**Malaga**	H	L	0-2		45,000

MONTHLY POINTS TALLY

AUGUST	3	100%
SEPTEMBER	7	58%
OCTOBER	7	58%
NOVEMBER	4	33%
DECEMBER	10	83%
JANUARY	4	33%
FEBRUARY	7	58%
MARCH	3	25%
APRIL	9	75%
MAY	5	33%

KEY PLAYERS - GOALSCORERS

Julio Baptista

Goals in the League	18	Player Strike Rate Average number of minutes between League goals scored by player	158
Contribution to Attacking Power Average number of minutes between League team goals while on pitch	77	Club Strike Rate Average number of minutes between League goals scored by club	78

	PLAYER	LGE GOALS	POWER	STRIKE RATE
1	Julio Baptista	18	77	158 mins
2	Jesus Navas	2	76	691 mins
3	Renato	2	76	1294 mins
4	Daniel Alves	2	84	1306 mins
5	Ramos Sergio	2	82	1353 mins

KEY PLAYERS - MIDFIELDERS

Jesus Navas

Goals in the League	2	Contribution to Attacking Power Average number of minutes between League team goals while on pitch	77
Defensive Rating Average number of mins between League goals conceded while on the pitch	126	Scoring Difference Defensive Rating minus Contribution to Attacking Power	49

	PLAYER	LGE GOALS	DEF RATE	POWER	SCORE DIFF
1	Jesus Navas	2	126	77	49 mins
2	Jose Luis Marti	0	96	78	18 mins
3	Renato	2	86	76	10 mins
4	Julio Baptista	18	69	77	-8 mins

KEY PLAYERS - DEFENDERS

Ramos Sergio

Goals Conceded Number of League goals conceded while the player was on the pitch	31	Clean Sheets In games when player was on pitch for at least 70 minutes	12
Defensive Rating Ave number of mins between League goals conceded while on the pitch	87	Club Defensive Rating Average number of mins between League goals conceded by the club this season	81

	PLAYER	CON LGE	CLEAN SHEETS	DEF RATE
1	Ramos Sergio	31	12	87 mins
2	Castedo David	39	13	83 mins
3	Aitor Ocio	18	4	83 mins
4	Javi Navarro	29	11	83 mins
5	Daniel Alves	32	10	82 mins

KEY GOALKEEPER

Andres Esteban

Goals Conceded in the League	34	Counting Games League games when player was on pitch for at least 70 minutes	29
Defensive Rating Ave number of mins between League goals conceded while on the pitch	77	Clean Sheets In games when player was on pitch for at least 70 minutes	11

LEAGUE GOALS

Julio Baptista

Minutes on the pitch	2849	Goals in the League	18
League average (mins between goals)	158		

	PLAYER	MINS	GOALS	AVE
1	Baptista	2849	18	158
2	Dario Silva	1030	3	343
3	Carlitos	645	3	215
4	Adriano	1173	2	587
5	Daniel Alves	2611	2	1306
6	Sergio	2706	2	1353
7	Antonito	1024	2	512
8	Renato	2588	2	1294
9	Navas, J	1382	2	691
10	Aranda	768	1	768
11	Makukula	634	1	634
12	Puerta	310	1	310
13	Jordi	845	1	845
	Other		4	
	TOTAL		44	

DISCIPLINARY

	PLAYER	YELLOW	RED	AVE
1	Jordi	8	0	105
2	Marti	14	0	199
3	Antonito	5	0	204
4	Antonio Lopez	4	0	204
5	Makukula	3	0	211
6	Carlitos	3	0	215
7	Navarro	9	1	241
8	Aitor Ocio	5	1	248
9	Dario Silva	4	0	257
10	Daniel Alves	9	1	261
11	Pablo Alfaro	5	1	262
12	Navas, J	4	0	345
13	Baptista	7	1	356
	Other	20	1	
	TOTAL	100	6	

TOP POINT EARNERS

	PLAYER	GAMES	AV PTS
1	Jesus Navas	13	1.77
2	Renato	24	1.75
3	Jose Luis Marti	30	1.73
4	Ramos Sergio	28	1.71
5	Aitor Ocio	17	1.65
6	Castedo David	35	1.60
7	Pablo Alfaro	17	1.59
8	Andres Esteban	29	1.55
9	Javi Navarro	27	1.48
10	Daniel Alves	27	1.41
	CLUB AVERAGE:		1.58

TEAM OF THE SEASON

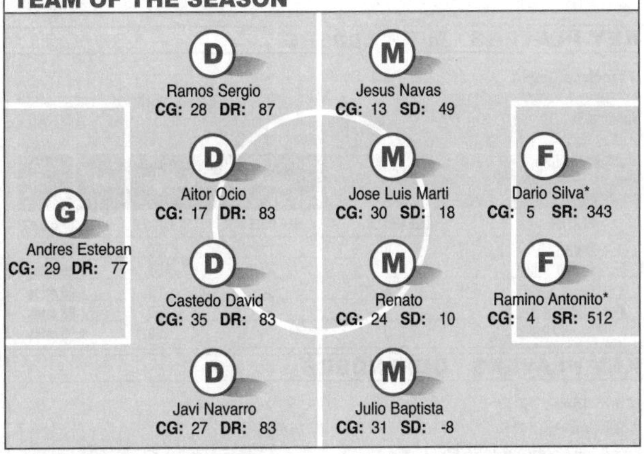
D
Ramos Sergio
CG: 28 DR: 87
M
Jesus Navas
CG: 13 SD: 49
D
Aitor Ocio
CG: 17 DR: 83
M
Jose Luis Marti
CG: 30 SD: 18
F
Dario Silva*
CG: 5 SR: 343
G
Andres Esteban
CG: 29 DR: 77
D
Castedo David
CG: 35 DR: 83
M
Renato
CG: 24 SD: 10
F
Ramino Antonito*
CG: 4 SR: 512
D
Javi Navarro
CG: 27 DR: 83
M
Julio Baptista
CG: 31 SD: -8

LEAGUE APPEARANCES, BOOKINGS AND CAPS

	AGE (on 01/07/05)	IN NAMED 18	APPEARANCES	COUNTING GAMES	MINUTES ON PITCH	YELLOW CARDS	RED CARDS	THIS SEASON	HOME COUNTRY
Goalkeepers									
Andres Esteban	30	38	29	29	2610	2	0	-	Spain
Antonio Notario Caro	32	38	9	9	810	0	0	-	Spain
Defenders									
Aitor Ocio	28	23	17	17	1493	5	1	-	Spain
Daniel Alves	22	36	34	27	2611	9	1	-	Brazil
Castedo David	31	37	37	35	3233	3	0	-	Spain
Javi Navarro	31	27	27	27	2410	9	1	-	Spain
Ruiz Pablo	24	10	6	4	370	0	0	-	Spain
Pablo Alfaro	36	32	18	17	1575	5	1	-	Spain
David Prieto	22	8	4	4	360	0	0	-	Spain
Ramos Sergio	24	32	31	28	2706	6	0	-	Spain
Midfielders									
Correia Adriano	20	16	16	9	1173	3	0	-	Spain
Jurado Alvaro	23	1	1	1	90	1	0	-	Spain
Antonio Lopez	25	21	13	6	819	4	0	-	Spain
Julio Baptista	23	34	33	31	2849	7	1	-	Brazil
Diego Capel	17	5	3	0	29	0	0	-	Spain
Francisco Casquero	28	20	9	3	411	2	0	-	Spain
Jesuli	27	19	16	7	871	1	0	-	Spain
Lopez Jordi	24	29	17	6	845	8	0	-	Spain
Jose Luis Marti	30	33	32	30	2795	14	0	-	Spain
Jesus Navas	19	26	23	13	1382	4	0	-	Spain
Antonio Puerta	20	9	7	3	310	0	0	-	Spain
Jean Redondo	28	15	6	1	164	1	0	-	Spain
Renato	26	36	34	24	2588	2	0	12	Brazil (1)
Forwards									
Ramiro Antonito	27	30	22	4	1024	5	0	-	Spain
Carlos Aranda	24	20	16	2	768	1	1	-	Spain
Kepa Blanco	21	2	2	0	81	0	0	-	Spain
Dominguez Carlitos	28	24	17	1	645	3	0	-	Spain
Dario Silva	32	24	21	5	1030	4	0	-	Uruguay
Ariza Makukula	24	16	13	3	634	3	0	-	Portugal
Fernando Sales	27	22	14	8	895	2	0	-	Spain

SQUAD APPEARANCES

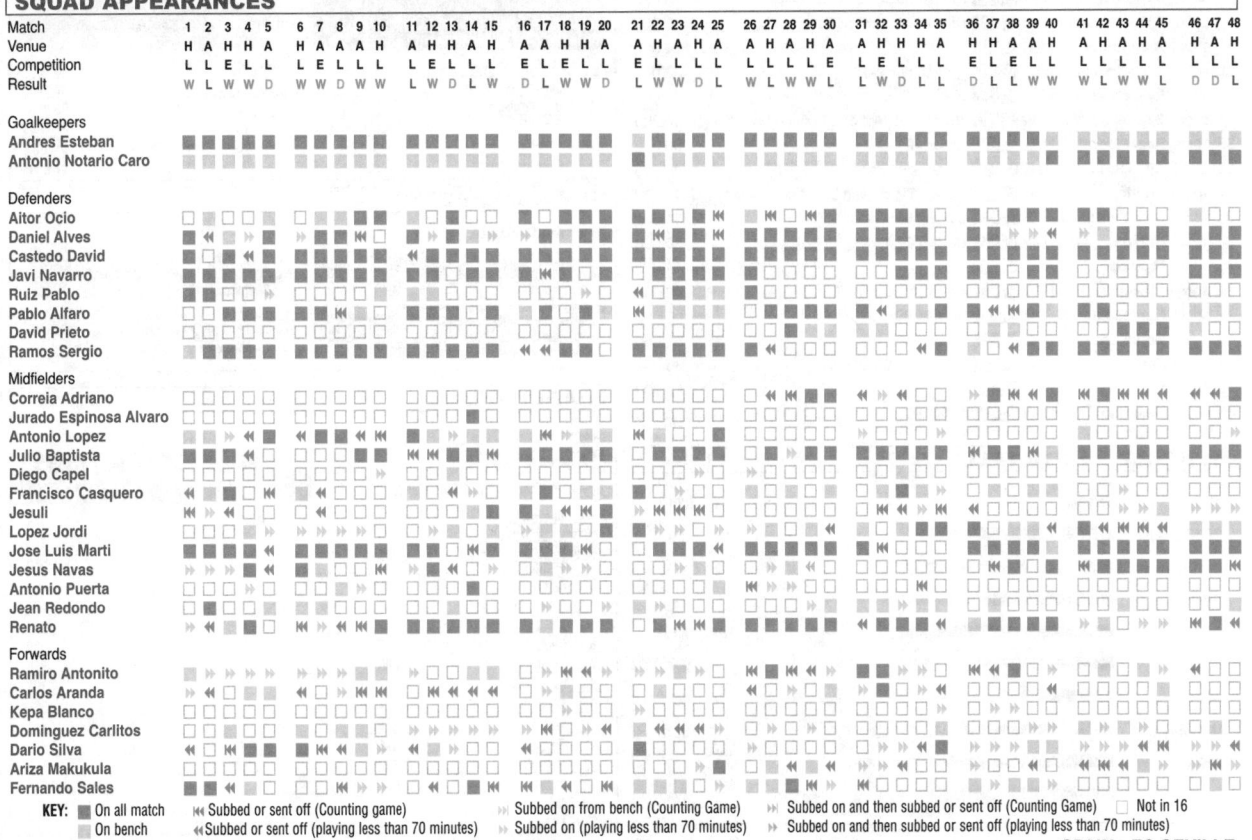

Match	1	2	3	4	5	6	7	8	9	10	11	12	13	14	15	16	17	18	19	20	21	22	23	24	25	26	27	28	29	30	31	32	33	34	35	36	37	38	39	40	41	42	43	44	45	46	47	48
Venue	H	A	H	H	A	H	A	A	A	H	A	H	H	A	H	A	A	H	H	A	A	H	A	H	A	A	H	A	H	A	A	H	H	H	A	H	H	A	A	H	A	H	A	H	A	H	A	H
Competition	L	L	E	L	L	L	E	L	L	L	L	E	L	L	L	E	L	E	L	L	E	L	L	L	L	L	L	L	L	E	L	E	L	L	L	E	L	E	L	L	L	L	L	L	L	L	L	L
Result	W	L	W	W	D	W	W	D	W	W	L	W	D	L	W	D	L	W	W	D	L	W	W	D	L	W	L	W	W	L	L	W	D	L	L	D	L	L	W	W	W	L	W	W	L	D	D	L

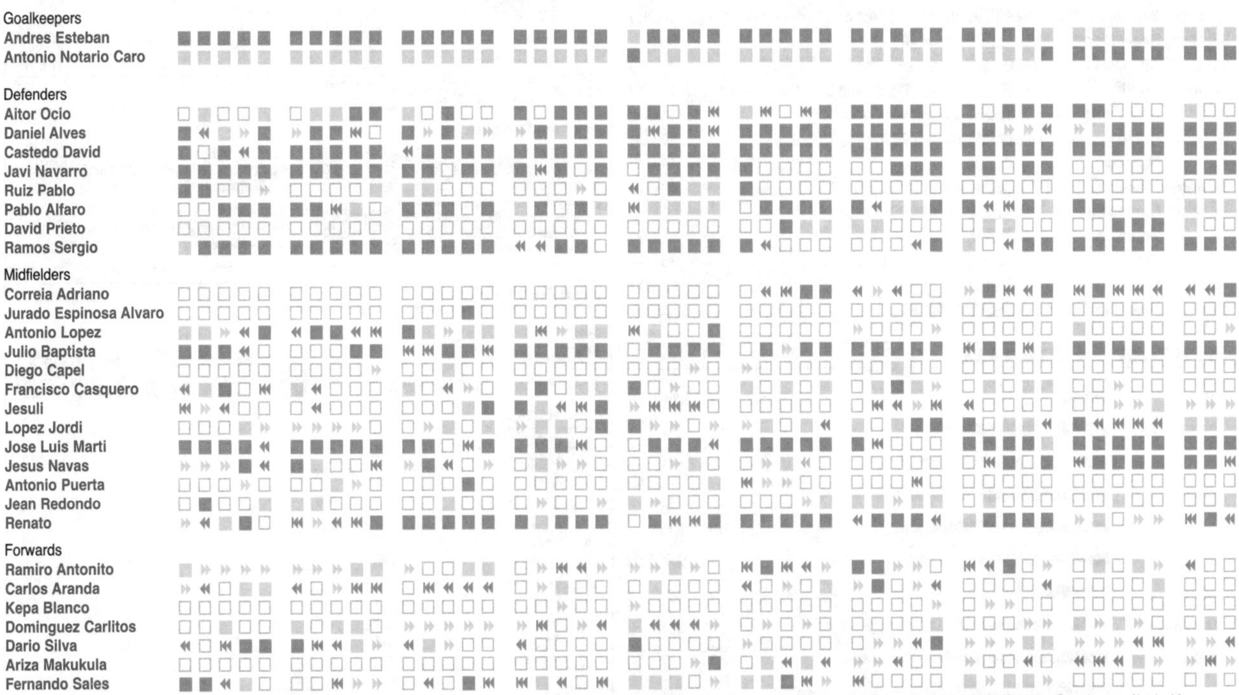
Goalkeepers
Andres Esteban
Antonio Notario Caro
Defenders
Aitor Ocio
Daniel Alves
Castedo David
Javi Navarro
Ruiz Pablo
Pablo Alfaro
David Prieto
Ramos Sergio
Midfielders
Correia Adriano
Jurado Espinosa Alvaro
Antonio Lopez
Julio Baptista
Diego Capel
Francisco Casquero
Jesuli
Lopez Jordi
Jose Luis Marti
Jesus Navas
Antonio Puerta
Jean Redondo
Renato
Forwards
Ramiro Antonito
Carlos Aranda
Kepa Blanco
Dominguez Carlitos
Dario Silva
Ariza Makukula
Fernando Sales

KEY: On all match | On bench | Subbed or sent off (Counting game) | Subbed or sent off (playing less than 70 minutes) | Subbed on from bench (Counting Game) | Subbed on (playing less than 70 minutes) | Subbed on and then subbed or sent off (Counting Game) | Subbed on and then subbed or sent off (playing less than 70 minutes) | Not in 16

VALENCIA

Final Position: **7th**

KEY: Won Drawn Lost

	Comp	Opponent	H/A	Res	Score	Scorers	Attendance
1	sppr1	**Villarreal**	H	W	2-1	Marchena 27; Baraja 39	42,000
2	sppr1	**Athl Bilbao**	A	D	2-2	Di Vaio 65; Angulo 77	37,000
3	cl gg	**Anderlecht**	H	W	2-0	Vicente 16; Baraja 45	34,000
4	sppr1	**Real Sociedad**	H	W	3-1	Di Vaio 37,50; Mista 74	35,000
5	sppr1	**Deportivo**	A	W	5-1	Corradi 18; Di Vaio 36; Vicente 43; Rufete 44; Baraja 51	18,000
6	sppr1	**R Santander**	H	W	2-0	Vicente 26; Fiore 45	45,000
7	cl gg	**W Bremen**	A	L	1-2	Vicente 2	36,000
8	sppr1	**Real Betis**	A	D	1-1	Di Vaio 10	28,000
9	sppr1	**Seville**	H	L	1-2	Aitor Ocio 59 og	46,000
10	cl gg	**Inter Milan**	H	L	1-5	Aimar 73	40,000
11	sppr1	**Real Madrid**	A	L	0-1		75,000
12	sppr1	**Atl Madrid**	H	D	1-1	Angulo 64	41,000
13	cl gg	**Inter Milan**	A	D	0-0		40,000
14	sppr1	**Getafe**	A	L	0-1		14,000
15	sppr1	**Real Zaragoza**	H	D	0-0		40,000
16	sppr1	**Malaga**	A	W	2-0	Corradi 45; Xisco 50	23,000
17	cl gg	**Anderlecht**	A	W	2-1	Corradi 19; Di Vaio 48	26,000
18	sppr1	**Mallorca**	H	W	2-0	Moretti 30; Baraja 64	48,000
19	sppr1	**Albacete**	A	W	1-0	Xisco 85	14,000
20	cl gg	**W Bremen**	H	L	0-2		40,000
21	sppr1	**Numancia**	H	W	1-0	Marchena 21	35,000
22	sppr1	**Barcelona**	A	D	1-1	Fiore 63	85,000
23	sppr1	**Espanyol**	H	W	3-0	Baraja 12; Mista 81,87	40,000
24	sppr1	**Levante**	H	W	2-1	Baraja 55; Mista 59	52,000
25	sppr1	**Osasuna**	A	D	0-0		16,000
26	sppr1	**Villarreal**	A	L	1-3	Aimar 90 pen	18,000
27	sppr1	**Athl Bilbao**	H	D	2-2	Mista 74; Di Vaio 81	38,000
28	sppr1	**Real Sociedad**	A	D	3-3	Di Vaio 9; Baraja 81; Xisco 87	16,000
29	sppr1	**Deportivo**	H	L	1-2	Di Vaio 50	45,000
30	uc3rl1	**S Bucharest**	H	W	2-0	Di Vaio 38; Aimar 55	30,000
31	sppr1	**R Santander**	A	L	0-1		18,000
32	uc3rl2	**S Bucharest**	A	L	3-4*	(*on penalties)	22,000
33	sppr1	**Real Betis**	H	W	2-1	Baraja 30; Mista 72	46,000
34	sppr1	**Seville**	A	W	3-2	Navarro 45; Aimar 60; Xisco 90	32,000
35	sppr1	**Real Madrid**	H	D	1-1	Aimar 12	50,000
36	sppr1	**Atl Madrid**	A	L	0-1		48,000
37	sppr1	**Getafe**	H	W	3-1	Rufete 31; Di Vaio 36; Mista 63 pen	42,000
38	sppr1	**Real Zaragoza**	A	D	2-2	Corradi 81; Caneira 84	31,000
39	sppr1	**Malaga**	H	D	2-2	Di Vaio 20,45	50,000
40	sppr1	**Mallorca**	A	D	0-0		14,000
41	sppr1	**Albacete**	H	W	2-0	Mista 70; Angulo 76	42,000
42	sppr1	**Numancia**	A	D	1-1	Vicente 83	8,000
43	sppr1	**Barcelona**	H	L	0-2		53,000
44	sppr1	**Espanyol**	A	D	2-2	Rufete 19; Garcia 67 og	35,000
45	sppr1	**Levante**	A	D	0-0		20,000
46	sppr1	**Osasuna**	H	W	1-0	Aimar 80	25,000

MONTHLY POINTS TALLY

AUGUST	3	100%
SEPTEMBER	10	83%
OCTOBER	2	17%
NOVEMBER	7	58%
DECEMBER	10	83%
JANUARY	5	42%
FEBRUARY	4	33%
MARCH	7	58%
APRIL	7	47%
MAY	5	42%

KEY PLAYERS - GOALSCORERS

Marco Di Vaio

Goals in the League	11	Player Strike Rate Average number of minutes between League goals scored by player	160
Contribution to Attacking Power Average number of minutes between League team goals while on pitch	60	Club Strike Rate Average number of minutes between League goals scored by club	62

	PLAYER	LGE GOALS	POWER	STRIKE RATE
1	Marco Di Vaio	11	60	**160 mins**
2	Mista	8	58	**219 mins**
3	Ruben Baraja	7	57	**291 mins**
4	Pablo Aimar	4	66	**494 mins**
5	Miguel Angulo	3	66	**507 mins**

KEY PLAYERS - MIDFIELDERS

Francisco Rufete

Goals in the League	3	Contribution to Attacking Power Average number of minutes between League team goals while on pitch	60
Defensive Rating Average number of mins between League goals conceded while on the pitch	111	Scoring Difference Defensive Rating minus Contribution to Attacking Power	51

	PLAYER	LGE GOALS	DEF RATE	POWER	SCORE DIFF
1	Francisco Rufete	3	111	60	**51 mins**
2	Ruben Baraja	7	93	57	**36 mins**
3	Pablo Aimar	4	94	66	**28 mins**
4	Stefano Fiore	2	76	53	**23 mins**
5	David Albelda	0	74	69	**5 mins**

KEY PLAYERS - DEFENDERS

Curro Torres

Goals Conceded Number of League goals conceded while the player was on the pitch	14	Clean Sheets In games when player was on pitch for at least 70 minutes	7
Defensive Rating Ave number of mins between League goals conceded while on the pitch	127	Club Defensive Rating Average number of mins between League goals conceded by the club this season	88

	PLAYER	CON LGE	CLEAN SHEETS	DEF RATE
1	Curro Torres	14	7	**127 mins**
2	David Navarro	19	8	**109 mins**
3	Fabio Aurelio	16	5	**87 mins**
4	Amadeo Carboni	26	4	**84 mins**
5	Emiliano Moretti	20	7	**81 mins**

KEY GOALKEEPER

Santiago Canizares

Goals Conceded in the League	33	Counting Games Games when player was on pitch for at least 70 minutes	30
Defensive Rating Ave number of mins between League goals conceded while on the pitch	85	Clean Sheets In games when player was on pitch for at least 70 minutes	9

LEAGUE GOALS

Marco Di Vaio

Minutes on the pitch	1765	Goals in the League	11
League average (mins between goals)	160		

	PLAYER	MINS	GOALS	AVE
1	Di Vaio	1765	**11**	160
2	Mista	1748	**8**	219
3	Baraja	2035	**7**	291
4	Aimar	1974	**4**	494
5	Xisco	702	**4**	176
6	Corradi	1077	**3**	359
7	Rufete	1669	**3**	556
8	Vicente	899	**3**	300
9	Angulo	1521	**3**	507
10	Marchena	2814	**2**	1407
11	Fiore	1375	**2**	688
12	Moretti	1622	**1**	1622
13	Caneira	1613	**1**	1613
	Other		3	
	TOTAL		**55**	

DISCIPLINARY RECORDS

	PLAYER	YELLOW	RED	AVE
1	Corradi	6	0	179
2	Marchena	13	1	201
3	Caneira	7	1	201
4	Albelda	11	0	220
5	Baraja	8	1	226
6	Xisco	2	1	234
7	Sissoko	6	0	237
8	Navarro	8	0	258
9	Curro Torres	5	0	355
10	Angulo	4	0	380
11	Mista	4	0	437
12	Aimar	4	0	493
13	Moretti	3	0	540
	Other	18	1	
	TOTAL	99	5	

TOP POINT EARNERS

	PLAYER	GAMES	AV PTS
1	David Navarro	23	2.00
2	Francisco Rufete	15	2.00
3	Curro Torres	19	1.89
4	Mista	15	1.87
5	Santiago Canizares	30	1.73
6	Emiliano Moretti	17	1.71
7	Ruben Baraja	22	1.68
8	Pablo Aimar	18	1.67
9	Marco Caneira	17	1.59
10	Fabio Aurelio	12	1.58
	CLUB AVERAGE:		1.53

LEAGUE APPEARANCES AND BOOKINGS

	AGE (on 01/07/05)	IN NAMED 18	APPEARANCES	COUNTING GAMES	MINUTES ON PITCH	YELLOW CARDS	RED CARDS	THIS SEASON	HOME COUNTRY
Goalkeepers									
Ludovic Butelle	22	2	0	0	0	0	0	-	France
Santiago Canizares	35	37	32	30	2820	4	0	-	Spain
Andres Palop	31	37	8	6	601	0	1	-	Spain
Defenders									
Fabio Aurelio	25	24	21	12	1386	2	0	-	Brazil
Roberto Ayala	32	21	16	14	1343	2	0	3	Argentina (3)
Marco Caneira	26	32	21	17	1613	7	1	6	Portugal (9)
Amadeo Carboni	40	35	28	22	2186	3	0	-	Italy
Curro Torres	28	20	20	19	1777	5	0	-	Spain
Carlos Marchena	26	34	32	31	2814	13	1	4	Spain (8)
Emiliano Moretti	24	33	23	17	1622	3	0	-	Italy
David Navarro	25	28	23	23	2070	8	0	-	Spain
Mauricio Pellegrino	33	8	2	2	180	0	0	-	Argentina
Manuel Ruz	19	3	3	3	265	1	0	-	Spain
Rafael Santa Cruz	22	3	1	1	90	1	0	-	Spain
Midfielders									
Pablo Aimar	25	33	31	18	1974	4	0	1	Argentina (3)
David Albelda	27	31	28	26	2428	11	0	-	Spain
Ruben Baraja	29	28	25	22	2035	8	1	4	Spain (8)
De Los Santos	28	5	1	0	45	0	0	2	Uruguay (16)
Stefano Fiore	30	29	20	13	1375	2	0	4	Italy (10)
Juanlu	21	2	1	0	38	0	0	-	Spain
Miguel Pallardo	19	3	1	0	10	0	0	-	Spain
Francisco Rufete	28	28	26	15	1669	2	0	-	Spain
Forwards									
Miguel Angulo	28	30	24	13	1521	4	0	-	Spain
Bernardo Corradi	29	33	20	9	1077	6	0	3	Italy (10)
Marco Di Vaio	28	34	30	14	1765	3	0	2	Italy (10)
Mista	26	35	28	15	1748	4	0	-	Spain
Momo Sissoko	20	27	24	12	1425	6	0	-	France
Rodriguez Vicente	23	14	12	9	899	0	0	-	Spain
Francisco Xisco	24	32	23	3	702	2	1	-	Spain

TEAM OF THE SEASON

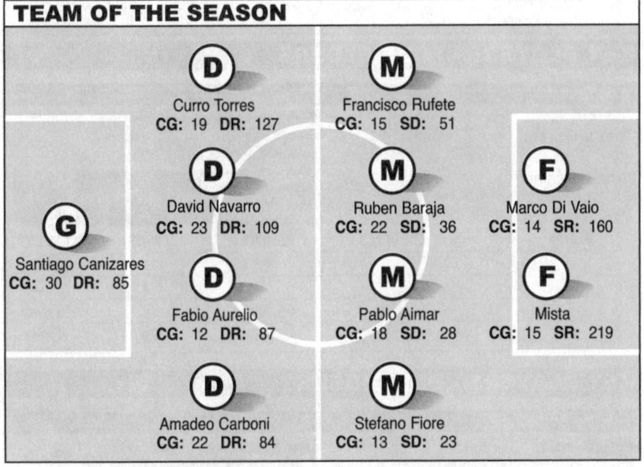
D
Curro Torres
CG: 19 DR: 127
D
David Navarro
CG: 23 DR: 109
G
Santiago Canizares
CG: 30 DR: 85
D
Fabio Aurelio
CG: 12 DR: 87
D
Amadeo Carboni
CG: 22 DR: 84
M
Francisco Rufete
CG: 15 SD: 51
M
Ruben Baraja
CG: 22 SD: 36
M
Pablo Aimar
CG: 18 SD: 28
M
Stefano Fiore
CG: 13 SD: 23
F
Marco Di Vaio
CG: 14 SR: 160
F
Mista
CG: 15 SR: 219

SQUAD APPEARANCES

Match	1	2	3	4	5	6	7	8	9	10	11	12	13	14	15	16	17	18	19	20	21	22	23	24	25	26	27	28	29	30	31	32	33	34	35	36	37	38	39	40	41	42	43	44	45	46
Venue	H	A	H	H	A	H	A	A	H	H	A	H	A	A	H	A	A	H	A	H	H	A	H	H	A	A	H	A	H	H	A	A	H	A	H	A	H	A	H	A	H	A	H	A	A	H
Competition	L	L	C	L	L	L	C	L	L	C	L	L	C	L	L	L	C	L	L	C	L	L	L	L	L	L	L	L	L	E	L	E	L	L	L	L	L	L	L	L	L	L	L	L	L	L
Result	W	D	W	W	W	W	L	D	L	L	L	D	D	L	D	W	W	W	W	L	W	D	W	W	D	L	D	D	L	W	L	L	W	W	D	L	W	D	D	D	W	D	L	D	D	W

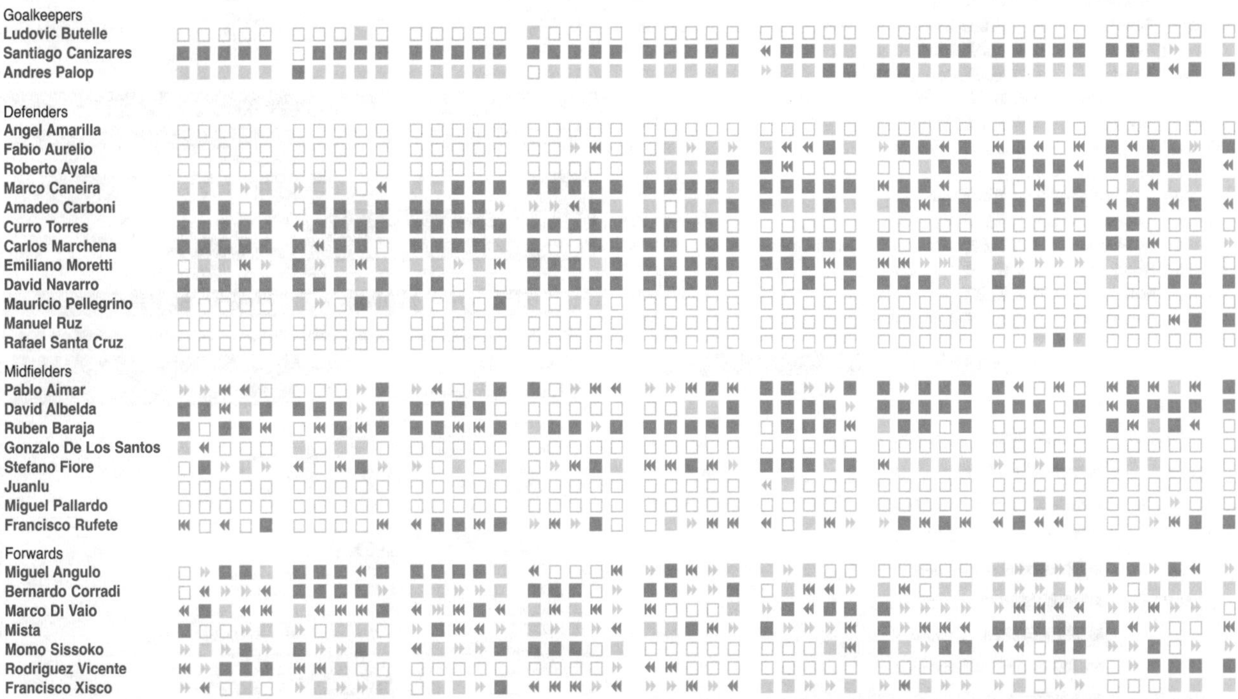
Goalkeepers
Ludovic Butelle
Santiago Canizares
Andres Palop
Defenders
Angel Amarilla
Fabio Aurelio
Roberto Ayala
Marco Caneira
Amadeo Carboni
Curro Torres
Carlos Marchena
Emiliano Moretti
David Navarro
Mauricio Pellegrino
Manuel Ruz
Rafael Santa Cruz
Midfielders
Pablo Aimar
David Albelda
Ruben Baraja
Gonzalo De Los Santos
Stefano Fiore
Juanlu
Miguel Pallardo
Francisco Rufete
Forwards
Miguel Angulo
Bernardo Corradi
Marco Di Vaio
Mista
Momo Sissoko
Rodriguez Vicente
Francisco Xisco

KEY: ■ On all match ■ On bench ⏮ Subbed or sent off (Counting game) « Subbed or sent off (playing less than 70 minutes) » Subbed on from bench (Counting Game) » Subbed on (playing less than 70 minutes) » Subbed on and then subbed or sent off (Counting Game) » Subbed on and then subbed or sent off (playing less than 70 minutes) □ Not in 16

DEPORTIVO LA CORUNA

Final Position: **8th**

KEY: Won Drawn Lost

							Attendance
1	clql1	**Shelbourne**	A	D	0-0		24,000
2	clql2	**Shelbourne**	H	W	3-0	Victor 60,66; Pandiani 88	27,000
3	sppr1	**Espanyol**	A	D	1-1	Pandiani 77	19,000
4	sppr1	**Osasuna**	H	L	1-3	Pandiani 19	23,000
5	cl ga	**Olympiakos**	H	D	0-0		22,000
6	sppr1	**Athl Bilbao**	A	W	2-1	Pandiani 56; Luque 90	30,000
7	sppr1	**Valencia**	H	L	1-5	Pandiani 64	18,000
8	sppr1	**Real Betis**	H	D	1-1	Victor 77	30,000
9	cl ga	**Monaco**	A	L	0-2		14,000
10	sppr1	**Real Madrid**	A	W	1-0	Luque 45	67,000
11	sppr1	**Getafe**	H	W	2-1	Sergio 17; Victor 72	26,000
12	cl ga	**Liverpool**	A	D	0-0		40,236
13	sppr1	**Malaga**	A	D	1-1	Tristan 85	26,000
14	sppr1	**Albacete**	H	D	0-0		20,000
15	cl ga	**Liverpool**	H	L	0-1		32,000
16	sppr1	**Barcelona**	A	L	1-2	Fran 8	90,000
17	sppr1	**Levante**	H	W	1-0	Tristan 55	24,000
18	sppr1	**Villarreal**	A	W	2-0	Tristan 32; Luque 60	16,000
19	cl ga	**Olympiakos**	A	L	0-1		33,000
20	sppr1	**Real Sociedad**	H	D	2-2	Luque 13; Munitis 28	24,000
21	sppr1	**R Santander**	A	D	2-2	Luque 50 pen; Pandiani 90	12,000
22	cl ga	**Monaco**	H	L	0-5		16,000
23	sppr1	**Seville**	H	D	2-2	Sergio 51; Scaloni 87	24,000
24	sppr1	**Atl Madrid**	A	L	0-1		45,000
25	sppr1	**Real Zaragoza**	H	L	2-3	Pablo Amo 49; Luque 51	15,000
26	sppr1	**Mallorca**	A	D	2-2	Luque 50,62	15,000
27	sppr1	**Numancia**	H	D	1-1	Pandiani 76	28,000
28	sppr1	**Espanyol**	H	W	4-1	Andrade 10; Tristan 22,62 pen; Valeron 81	24,000
29	sppr1	**Osasuna**	A	D	1-1	Sergio 86	14,000
30	sppr1	**Athl Bilbao**	H	D	1-1	Tristan 86 pen	23,000
31	sppr1	**Valencia**	A	W	2-1	Scaloni 44; Victor 71	45,000
32	sppr1	**Real Betis**	A	L	0-2		38,000
33	sppr1	**Real Madrid**	H	W	2-0	Luque 9; Pavon 13 og	35,000
34	sppr1	**Getafe**	A	D	1-1	Tristan 41	14,000
35	sppr1	**Malaga**	H	W	1-0	Tristan 45 pen	20,000
36	sppr1	**Albacete**	A	W	1-0	Coloccini 36	15,000
37	sppr1	**Barcelona**	H	L	0-1		35,000
38	sppr1	**Levante**	A	W	1-0	Tristan 40	14,000
39	sppr1	**Villarreal**	H	D	1-1	Luque 64	25,000
40	sppr1	**Real Sociedad**	A	L	0-1		16,000
41	sppr1	**R Santander**	H	L	1-4	Luque 23	23,000
42	sppr1	**Seville**	A	L	0-2		40,000
43	sppr1	**Atl Madrid**	H	W	2-0	Luccin 54 og; Capdevila 81	24,000
44	sppr1	**Real Zaragoza**	A	D	2-2	Xisco 27,38	32,000
45	sppr1	**Mallorca**	H	L	0-3		24,000
46	sppr1	**Numancia**	A	D	1-1	Juanpa 58 og	7,000

MONTHLY POINTS TALLY

AUGUST	1	33%
SEPTEMBER	4	33%
OCTOBER	8	67%
NOVEMBER	7	58%
DECEMBER	2	17%
JANUARY	6	50%
FEBRUARY	7	58%
MARCH	7	58%
APRIL	4	33%
MAY	5	33%

KEY PLAYERS - GOALSCORERS

Alberto Luque

Goals in the League	11	Player Strike Rate Average number of minutes between League goals scored by player	218
Contribution to Attacking Power Average number of minutes between League team goals while on pitch	75	Club Strike Rate Average number of minutes between League goals scored by club	74

	PLAYER	LGE GOALS	POWER	STRIKE RATE
1	Alberto Luque	11	75	218 mins
2	Sanchez Victor	3	78	573 mins
3	Gonzalez Sergio	3	79	946 mins
4	Lionel Scaloni	2	77	973 mins
5	Fabricio Coloccini	1	81	1308 mins

KEY PLAYERS - MIDFIELDERS

Aldo Duscher

Goals in the League	0	Contribution to Attacking Power Average number of minutes between League team goals while on pitch	72
Defensive Rating Average number of mins between League goals conceded while on the pitch	81	Scoring Difference Defensive Rating minus Contribution to Attacking Power	9

	PLAYER	LGE GOALS	DEF RATE	POWER	SCORE DIFF
1	Aldo Duscher	0	81	72	9 mins
2	Sanchez Victor	3	78	78	0 mins
3	Juan Valeron	1	68	78	-10 mins
4	Gonzalez Sergio	3	68	79	-11 mins

KEY PLAYERS - DEFENDERS

Fabricio Coloccini

Goals Conceded Number of League goals conceded while the player was on the pitch	14	Clean Sheets In games when player was on pitch for at least 70 minutes	5
Defensive Rating Ave number of mins between League goals conceded while on the pitch	93	Club Defensive Rating Average number of mins between League goals conceded by the club this season	68

	PLAYER	CON LGE	CLEAN SHEETS	DEF RATE
1	Fabricio Coloccini	14	5	93 mins
2	Enrique Romero	31	6	74 mins
3	Jorge Andrade	49	8	66 mins
4	Manuel Pablo	41	5	64 mins
5	Lionel Scaloni	31	4	63 mins

KEY GOALKEEPER

Gustavo Munua

Goals Conceded in the League	20	Counting Games Games when player was on pitch for at least 70 minutes	17
Defensive Rating Ave number of mins between League goals conceded while on the pitch	77	Clean Sheets In games when player was on pitch for at least 70 minutes	5

LEAGUE GOALS

Alberto Luque

Minutes on the pitch	2403	Goals in the League	11
League average (mins between goals)	218		

	PLAYER	MINS	GOALS	AVE
1	Luque	2403	11	218
2	Tristan	1504	9	167
3	Pandiani	922	6	154
4	Victor	1720	3	573
5	Sergio	2839	3	946
6	Scaloni	1945	2	973
7	Xisco	344	2	172
8	Fran	1152	1	1152
9	Munitis	1978	1	1978
10	Capdevila	1352	1	1352
11	Coloccini	1308	1	1308
12	Andrade	3240	1	3240
13	Valeron	3181	1	3181
	Other		4	
	TOTAL		46	

DISCIPLINARY RECORDS

	PLAYER	YELLOW	RED	AVE
1	Cesar	9	1	113
2	Scaloni	8	1	216
3	Duscher	8	0	234
4	Munitis	8	0	247
5	Coloccini	4	1	261
6	Pandiani	3	0	307
7	Capdevila	4	0	338
8	Victor	5	0	344
9	Romero	5	0	457
10	Andrade	7	0	462
11	Fran	2	0	576
12	Luque	4	0	600
13	Munua	2	0	765
	Other	12	0	
	TOTAL	81	3	

TOP POINT EARNERS

	PLAYER	GAMES	AV PTS
1	Sanchez Victor	13	1.69
2	Fabricio Coloccini	14	1.57
3	Aldo Duscher	18	1.56
4	Gonzalez Sergio	29	1.48
5	Enrique Romero	24	1.46
6	Juan Valeron	35	1.43
7	Manuel Pablo	27	1.41
8	Francisco Molina	20	1.35
9	Gustavo Munua	17	1.35
10	Jorge Andrade	36	1.31
	CLUB AVERAGE:		1.34

TEAM OF THE SEASON

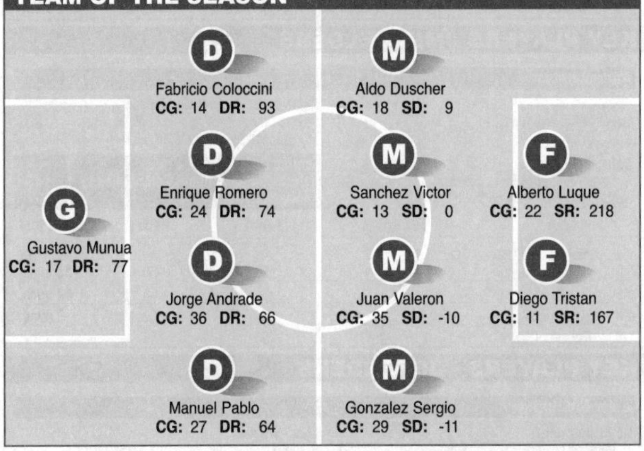

G
Gustavo Munua
CG: 17 DR: 77
D
Fabricio Coloccini
CG: 14 DR: 93
D
Enrique Romero
CG: 24 DR: 74
D
Jorge Andrade
CG: 36 DR: 66
D
Manuel Pablo
CG: 27 DR: 64
M
Aldo Duscher
CG: 18 SD: 9
M
Sanchez Victor
CG: 13 SD: 0
M
Juan Valeron
CG: 35 SD: -10
M
Gonzalez Sergio
CG: 29 SD: -11
F
Alberto Luque
CG: 22 SR: 218
F
Diego Tristan
CG: 11 SR: 167

LEAGUE APPEARANCES AND BOOKINGS

	AGE (on 01/07/05)	IN NAMED 18	APPEARANCES	COUNTING GAMES	MINUTES ON PITCH	YELLOW CARDS	RED CARDS	THIS SEASON	HOME COUNTRY
Goalkeepers									
Castro Dani Mallo	26	13	1	1	90	0	0	-	Spain
Francisco Molina	34	25	20	20	1800	1	0	-	Spain
Gustavo Munua	27	37	17	17	1530	2	0	-	Uruguay
Defenders									
Jorge Andrade	27	36	36	36	3240	7	0	8	Portugal (9)
Joan Capdevila	27	33	21	13	1352	4	0	-	Spain
Martin Cesar	28	26	14	11	1136	9	1	-	Spain
Fabricio Coloccini	23	15	15	14	1308	4	1	9	Argentina (3)
Del Pino Hector	30	29	6	2	260	0	0	-	Spain
Manuel Pablo	29	34	31	27	2631	3	0	-	Spain
Pablo Amo	27	29	13	9	853	0	0	-	Spain
Enrique Romero	34	37	28	24	2285	5	0	4	Spain (8)
Lionel Scaloni	27	31	26	19	1945	8	1	6	Argentina (3)
Midfielders									
Roberto Acuna	33	11	1	0	36	0	0	-	Paraguay
Ruben Castro	24	0	0	0	0	0	0	-	Spain
Marcos Changui	28	10	2	0	14	0	0	-	Spain
Aldo Duscher	26	32	29	18	1872	8	0	2	Argentina (3)
Javier Fran	35	31	29	4	1152	2	0	-	Spain
Mauro Silva	37	21	20	11	1163	1	0	-	Brazil
Carlos Pita	20	8	1	0	12	0	0	-	Spain
Gonzalez Sergio	28	36	34	29	2839	3	0	2	Spain (8)
Juan Valeron	30	38	38	35	3181	3	0	-	Spain
Sanchez Victor	29	32	30	13	1720	5	0	-	Spain
Forwards									
Alberto Luque	27	37	37	22	2403	4	0	6	Spain (8)
Pedro Munitis	30	37	36	18	1978	8	0	-	Spain
Walter Pandiani	29	18	15	8	922	3	0	-	Uruguay
Diego Tristan	29	24	23	11	1504	1	0	-	Spain
Nadal Xisco	19	7	7	2	344	1	0	-	Spain

SQUAD APPEARANCES

1	2	3	4	5	6	7	8	9	10	11	12	13	14	15	16	17	18	19	20	21	22	23	24	25	26	27	28	29	30	31	32	33	34	35	36	37	38	39	40	41	42	43	44	45	46	Match
Venue	A	H	A	H	H	A	H	H	A	A	H	A	A	H	H	A	H	A	A	H	A	H	H	A	H	A	H	H	A	H	A	A	H	A	H	A	H	A	H	A	H	A	H	A	H	A
Competition	C	C	L	L	C	L	L	L	C	L	L	C	L	L	C	L	L	L	C	L	L	C	L	L	L	L	L	L	L	L	L	L	L	L	L	L	L	L	L	L	L	L	L	L	L	L
Result	D	W	D	L	D	W	L	D	L	W	W	D	D	D	L	L	W	W	L	D	D	L	D	L	L	D	D	W	D	D	W	L	W	D	W	W	L	W	D	L	L	L	W	D	L	D

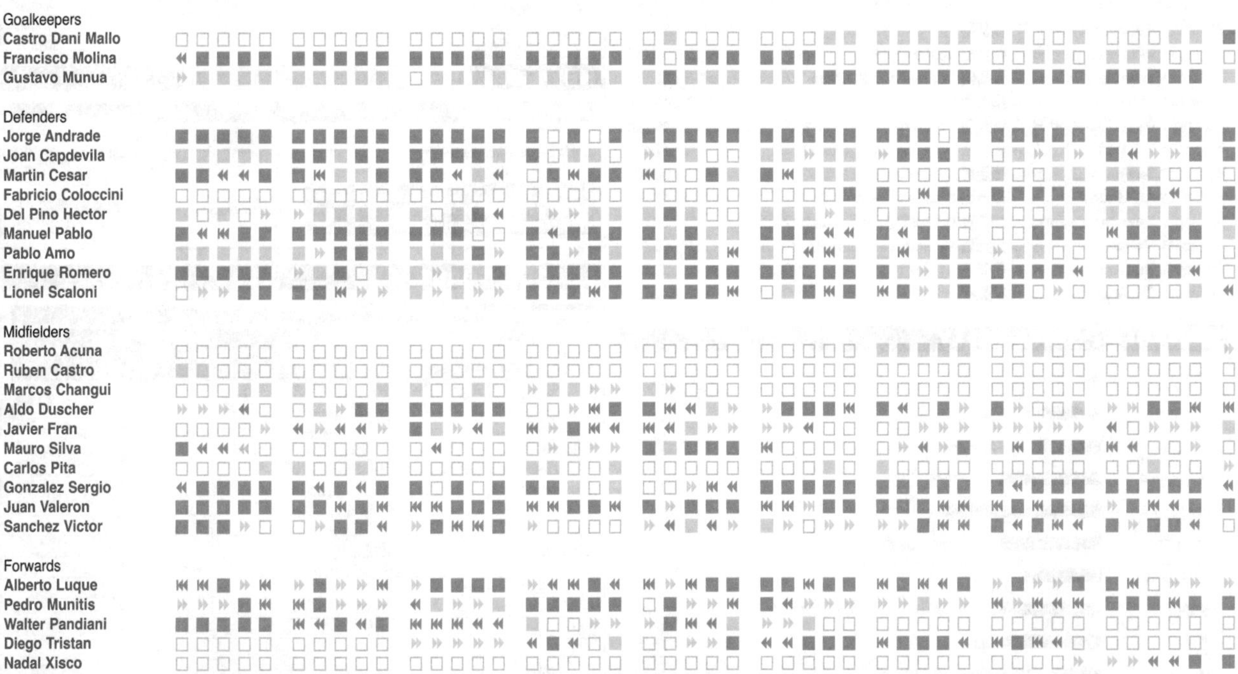

Goalkeepers
Castro Dani Mallo
Francisco Molina
Gustavo Munua
Defenders
Jorge Andrade
Joan Capdevila
Martin Cesar
Fabricio Coloccini
Del Pino Hector
Manuel Pablo
Pablo Amo
Enrique Romero
Lionel Scaloni
Midfielders
Roberto Acuna
Ruben Castro
Marcos Changui
Aldo Duscher
Javier Fran
Mauro Silva
Carlos Pita
Gonzalez Sergio
Juan Valeron
Sanchez Victor
Forwards
Alberto Luque
Pedro Munitis
Walter Pandiani
Diego Tristan
Nadal Xisco

KEY: On all match | On bench | Subbed or sent off (Counting game) | Subbed or sent off (playing less than 70 minutes) | Subbed on from bench (Counting Game) | Subbed on (playing less than 70 minutes) | Subbed on and then subbed or sent off (Counting Game) | Subbed on and then subbed or sent off (playing less than 70 minutes) | Not in 16

ATHLETIC BILBAO

Final Position: **9th**

KEY: Won / Drawn / Lost

	Comp	Opponent			Score	Scorers	Attendance
1	sppr1	**Osasuna**	A	D	1-1	Joseba Etxeberria 16	19,000
2	sppr1	**Valencia**	H	D	2-2	Urzaiz 15; Iraola 21 pen	37,000
3	uc1rl1	**Trabzonspor**	A	L	2-3	Gurpegui 74,80	20,000
4	sppr1	**Deportivo**	H	L	1-2	Iraola 55	30,000
5	sppr1	**Real Betis**	A	L	1-2	Urzaiz 38	25,000
6	sppr1	**Real Madrid**	H	W	2-1	Del Horno 13; Ezquerro 45	38,000
7	uc1rl2	**Trabzonspor**	H	W	2-0	Ezquerro 5; Yeste 61	30,000
8	sppr1	**Getafe**	A	L	1-3	Joseba Etxeberria 52	15,000
9	sppr1	**Malaga**	H	W	1-0	Urzaiz 33	30,000
10	ucgb	**Parma**	H	W	2-0	Gurpegui 5; Del Horno 48	32,000
11	sppr1	**Albacete**	A	L	0-1		14,000
12	sppr1	**Barcelona**	H	D	1-1	Yeste 13	39,000
13	ucgb	**Besiktas**	A	L	1-3	Ezquerro 49	30,000
14	sppr1	**Levante**	A	L	0-1		19,000
15	sppr1	**Villarreal**	H	W	2-1	Urzaiz 49,53	30,000
16	sppr1	**Real Sociedad**	A	L	2-3	Ezquerro 40; Urzaiz 43	26,000
17	sppr1	**R Santander**	H	W	3-0	Ezquerro 7; Gurpegui 26; Urzaiz 64	32,000
18	ucgb	**S Bucharest**	H	W	1-0	Joseba Etxeberria 45	35,000
19	sppr1	**Seville**	A	L	0-2		37,000
20	sppr1	**Atl Madrid**	H	W	1-0	Del Horno 45	35,000
21	ucgb	**Standard Liege**	A	W	7-1	Ezquerro 5,8,54; Yeste 34; Iraola 57 pen; Del Horno 63; Joseba Etxeberria 70	27,000
22	sppr1	**Real Zaragoza**	A	W	2-0	Ezquerro 54,79	33,000
23	sppr1	**Mallorca**	H	W	4-0	Yeste 6,90; Ezquerro 11; Gurpegui 77	30,000
24	sppr1	**Numancia**	A	D	1-1	Del Horno 45	10,000
25	sppr1	**Espanyol**	H	D	1-1	Yeste 3	38,000
26	sppr1	**Osasuna**	H	W	4-3	Yeste 60,65; Tiko 83; Guerrero 89	32,000
27	sppr1	**Valencia**	A	D	2-2	Iraola 31 pen; Ezquerro 60	38,000
28	sppr1	**Deportivo**	A	D	1-1	Orbaiz 51	23,000
29	sppr1	**Real Betis**	H	D	4-4	Urzaiz 32,34; Gurpegui 47; Yeste 70	30,000
30	sppr1	**Real Madrid**	A	W	2-0	Del Horno 58; Iraola 73	75,000
31	uc3l1	**Austria Vienna**	A	D	0-0		17,000
32	uc3rl2	**Austria Vienna**	H	L	1-2	Yeste 20 pen	39,000
33	sppr1	**Malaga**	A	L	0-1		19,000
34	sppr1	**Albacete**	H	W	3-1	Ezquerro 41; Lacruz Gomez 71; Guerrero 90	28,000
35	sppr1	**Barcelona**	A	L	0-2		80,000
36	sppr1	**Getafe**	H	L	1-2	Ezquerro 36	30,000
37	sppr1	**Levante**	H	W	3-1	Llorente 12,52; Urzaiz 87	30,000
38	sppr1	**Villarreal**	A	L	1-3	Ezquerro 22	13,000
39	sppr1	**Real Sociedad**	H	W	3-0	Ezquerro 35; Yeste 74; Tiko 90	40,000
40	sppr1	**R Santander**	A	W	2-0	Orbaiz 90 pen; Tiko 90	17,000
41	sppr1	**Seville**	H	L	1-3	Guerrero 87	32,000
42	sppr1	**Atl Madrid**	A	D	1-1	Joseba Etxeberria 65	45,000
43	sppr1	**Real Zaragoza**	H	W	2-0	Urzaiz 54; Lacruz Gomez 84	32,000
44	sppr1	**Mallorca**	A	L	3-4	Llorente 27; Gurpegui 30; Orbaiz 58,58	18,000
45	sppr1	**Numancia**	H	L	0-2		35,000
46	sppr1	**Espanyol**	A	L	0-2		42,000

MONTHLY POINTS TALLY

Month	Points	%
AUGUST	1	33%
SEPTEMBER	4	33%
OCTOBER	4	33%
NOVEMBER	6	50%
DECEMBER	9	75%
JANUARY	6	50%
FEBRUARY	5	56%
MARCH	6	40%
APRIL	7	47%
MAY	3	25%

KEY PLAYERS - GOALSCORERS

Ismael Urzaiz

Goals in the League	9	Player Strike Rate Average number of minutes between League goals scored by player	194
Contribution to Attacking Power Average number of minutes between League team goals while on pitch	58	Club Strike Rate Average number of minutes between League goals scored by club	57

	PLAYER	LGE GOALS	POWER	STRIKE RATE
1	Ismael Urzaiz	9	58	194 mins
2	Santiago Ezquerro	11	55	235 mins
3	Francisco Yeste	8	53	261 mins
4	Asier Del Horno	4	56	539 mins
5	Roberto Tiko	3	55	678 mins

KEY PLAYERS - MIDFIELDERS

Andoni Iraola

Goals in the League	4	Contribution to Attacking Power Average number of minutes between League team goals while on pitch	53
Defensive Rating Average number of mins between League goals conceded while on the pitch	69	Scoring Difference Defensive Rating minus Contribution to Attacking Power	16

	PLAYER	LGE GOALS	DEF RATE	POWER	SCORE DIFF
1	Andoni Iraola	4	69	53	16 mins
2	Carlos Gurpegui	4	65	50	15 mins
3	Francisco Yeste	8	65	53	12 mins
4	Luis Prieto	0	59	50	9 mins
5	Roberto Tiko	3	60	55	5 mins

KEY PLAYERS - DEFENDERS

Asier Del Horno

Goals Conceded Number of League goals conceded while the player was on the pitch	31	Clean Sheets In games when player was on pitch for at least 70 minutes	6
Defensive Rating Ave number of mins between League goals conceded while on the pitch	69	Club Defensive Rating Average number of mins between League goals conceded by the club this season	62

	PLAYER	CON LGE	CLEAN SHEETS	DEF RATE
1	Asier Del Horno	31	6	69 mins
2	Pablo Orbaiz	48	7	67 mins
3	Ander Murillo	41	6	63 mins
4	Javier Casas	19	1	59 mins
5	Lacruz Gomez	20	2	56 mins

KEY GOALKEEPER

Daniel Aranzubia

Goals Conceded in the League	52	Counting Games Games when player was on pitch for at least 70 minutes	36
Defensive Rating Ave number of mins between League goals conceded while on the pitch	64	Clean Sheets In games when player was on pitch for at least 70 minutes	8

LEAGUE GOALS

Santiago Ezquerro

Minutes on the pitch	2588	Goals in the League	11
League average (mins between goals)	235		

	PLAYER	MINS	GOALS	AVE
1	Ezquerro	2588	11	235
2	Urzaiz	1744	9	194
3	Yeste	2085	8	261
4	Orbaiz	3203	4	801
5	Del Horno	2154	4	539
6	Gurpegui	2911	4	728
7	Iraola	2753	4	688
8	Tiko	2034	3	678
9	Joseba Etxeberria	2705	3	902
10	Guerrero	234	3	78
11	Llorente	819	3	273
12	Lacruz Gomez	1114	2	557
	Other		2	
	TOTAL		60	

DISCIPLINARY RECORDS

	PLAYER	YELLOW	RED	AVE
1	Yeste	9	1	208
2	Del Horno	10	0	215
3	Orbaiz	13	0	246
4	Prieto	9	1	249
5	Casas	4	0	281
6	Tiko	7	0	290
7	Javi Gonzalez	2	0	331
8	Gurpegui	7	1	363
9	Joseba Etxeberria	7	0	386
10	Murillo	6	0	429
11	Urzaiz	4	0	436
12	Lacruz Gomez	2	0	557
13	Iraola	4	0	688
	Other	5	1	
	TOTAL	89	4	

TOP POINT EARNERS

	PLAYER	GAMES	AV PTS
1	Luis Prieto	26	1.65
2	Francisco Yeste	21	1.62
3	Carlos Gurpegui	32	1.59
4	Andoni Iraola	29	1.59
5	Joseba Etxeberria	29	1.59
6	Asier Del Horno	22	1.50
7	Ismael Urzaiz	14	1.50
8	Santiago Ezquerro	25	1.44
9	Pablo Orbaiz	35	1.34
10	Roberto Tiko	18	1.33
	CLUB AVERAGE:		1.34

TEAM OF THE SEASON

D
Asier Del Horno
CG: 22 DR: 69
M
Andoni Iraola
CG: 29 SD: 16
D
Pablo Orbaiz
CG: 35 DR: 67
M
Carlos Gurpegui
CG: 32 SD: 15
F
Ismael Urzaiz
CG: 14 SR: 194
G
Daniel Aranzubia
CG: 36 DR: 64
D
Ander Murillo
CG: 28 DR: 63
M
Francisco Yeste
CG: 21 SD: 12
F
Santiago Ezquerro
CG: 25 SR: 235
D
Lacruz Gomez
CG: 10 DR: 56
M
Luis Prieto
CG: 26 SD: 9

LEAGUE APPEARANCES, BOOKINGS AND CAPS

	AGE (on 01/07/05)	IN NAMED 18	APPEARANCES	COUNTING GAMES	MINUTES ON PITCH	YELLOW CARDS	RED CARDS	THIS SEASON	HOME COUNTRY
Goalkeepers									
Daniel Aranzubia	25	38	37	36	3302	3	1	-	Spain
Inaki Lafuente	29	31	0	0	0	0	0	-	Spain
Roberto Pampin	21	6	2	1	118	0	0	-	Spain
Defenders									
Gorka Azkorra	22	11	5	0	140	0	0	-	Spain
Javier Casas	23	29	19	10	1126	4	0	-	Spain
Fernandez Cesar	27	18	7	4	389	1	0	-	Spain
Asier Del Horno	24	31	29	22	2154	10	0	-	Spain
Aitor Karanka	31	20	5	4	375	3	0	-	Spain
Lacruz Gomez	27	17	16	10	1114	2	0	-	Spain
Jon Moya	22	2	2	1	91	1	0	-	Spain
Ander Murillo	21	34	31	28	2579	6	0	-	Spain
Pablo Orbaiz	26	36	36	35	3203	13	0	-	Spain
Oscar Vales	30	1	1	1	90	0	0	-	Spain
Midfielders									
Igor Angulo	21	5	2	1	151	0	0	-	Spain
Endika Bordas	23	11	3	0	105	0	0	-	Spain
Gurendez Felipe	29	11	4	1	146	0	0	-	Spain
Julen Guerrero	31	23	12	0	234	1	0	-	Spain
Carlos Gurpegui	24	36	33	32	2911	7	1	-	Spain
Andoni Iraola	23	34	34	29	2753	4	0	-	Spain
Luis Prieto	26	31	30	26	2492	9	1	-	Spain
Aritz Solabarrieta	21	24	11	2	330	1	0	-	Spain
Roberto Tiko	28	33	31	18	2034	7	0	-	Spain
Francisco Yeste	25	30	27	21	2085	9	1	1	Spain (8)
Forwards									
Joseba Arriaga	22	26	14	3	626	0	0	-	Spain
Santiago Ezquerro	28	34	32	25	2588	1	0	-	Spain
Javi Gonzalez	31	15	10	5	662	2	0	-	Spain
Garcia Jonan	22	23	13	1	473	0	0	-	Spain
Joseba Etxeberria	27	34	33	29	2705	7	0	-	Spain
Fernando Llorente	20	20	15	5	819	1	0	-	Spain
Ismael Urzaiz	33	35	30	14	1744	4	0	-	Spain

SQUAD APPEARANCES

Match	1	2	3	4	5	6	7	8	9	10	11	12	13	14	15	16	17	18	19	20	21	22	23	24	25	26	27	28	29	30	31	32	33	34	35	36	37	38	39	40	41	42	43	44	45	46
Venue	A	H	A	H	A	H	H	A	H	H	A	H	A	A	H	A	H	H	A	H	A	A	H	A	H	H	A	A	H	A	A	H	A	H	A	H	H	A	H	A	H	A	H	A	H	A
Competition	L	L	E	L	L	L	E	L	L	E	L	L	E	L	L	L	L	E	L	L	E	L	L	L	L	L	L	L	L	L	E	E	L	L	L	L	L	L	L	L	L	L	L	L	L	L
Result	D	D	L	L	L	W	W	L	W	W	L	D	L	L	W	L	W	W	L	W	W	W	W	D	D	W	D	D	D	W	D	L	L	W	L	L	W	L	W	W	L	D	W	L	L	L

Goalkeepers
Daniel Aranzubia
Inaki Lafuente
Roberto Pampin

Defenders
Gorka Azkorra
Javier Casas
Fernandez Cesar
Asier Del Horno
Aitor Karanka
Lacruz Gomez
Jon Moya
Ander Murillo
Pablo Orbaiz
Oscar Vales

Midfielders
Igor Angulo
Endika Bordas
Gurendez Felipe
Julen Guerrero
Carlos Gurpegui
Andoni Iraola
Luis Prieto
Aritz Solabarrieta
Roberto Tiko
Francisco Yeste

Forwards
Joseba Arriaga
Santiago Ezquerro
Javi Gonzalez
Garcia Jonan
Joseba Etxeberria
Fernando Llorente
Ismael Urzaiz

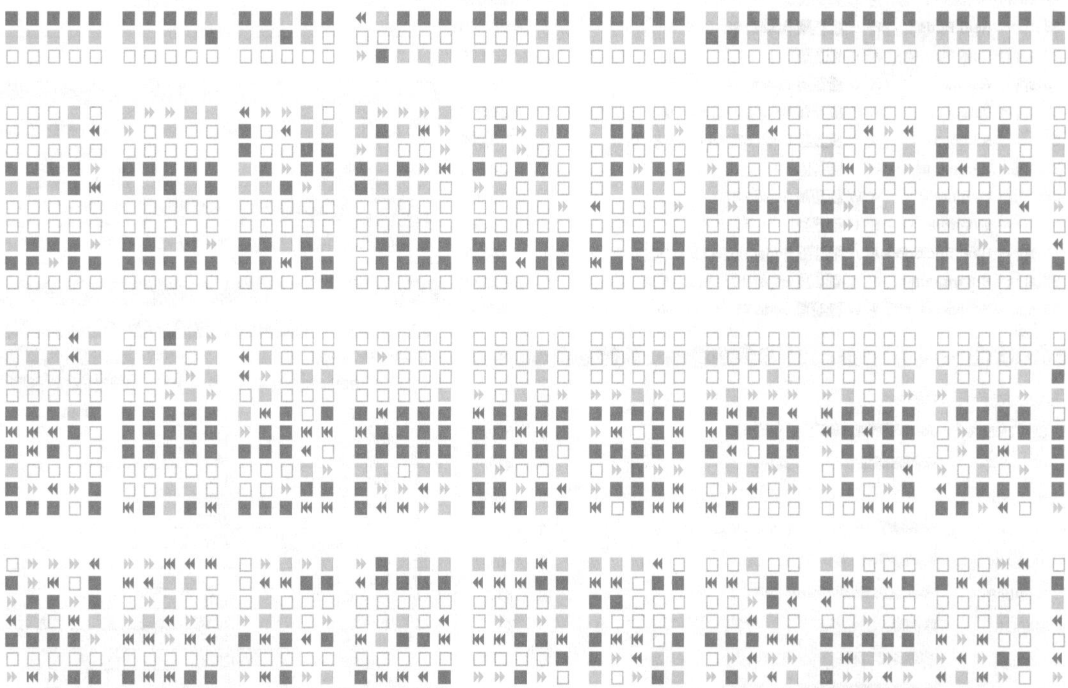

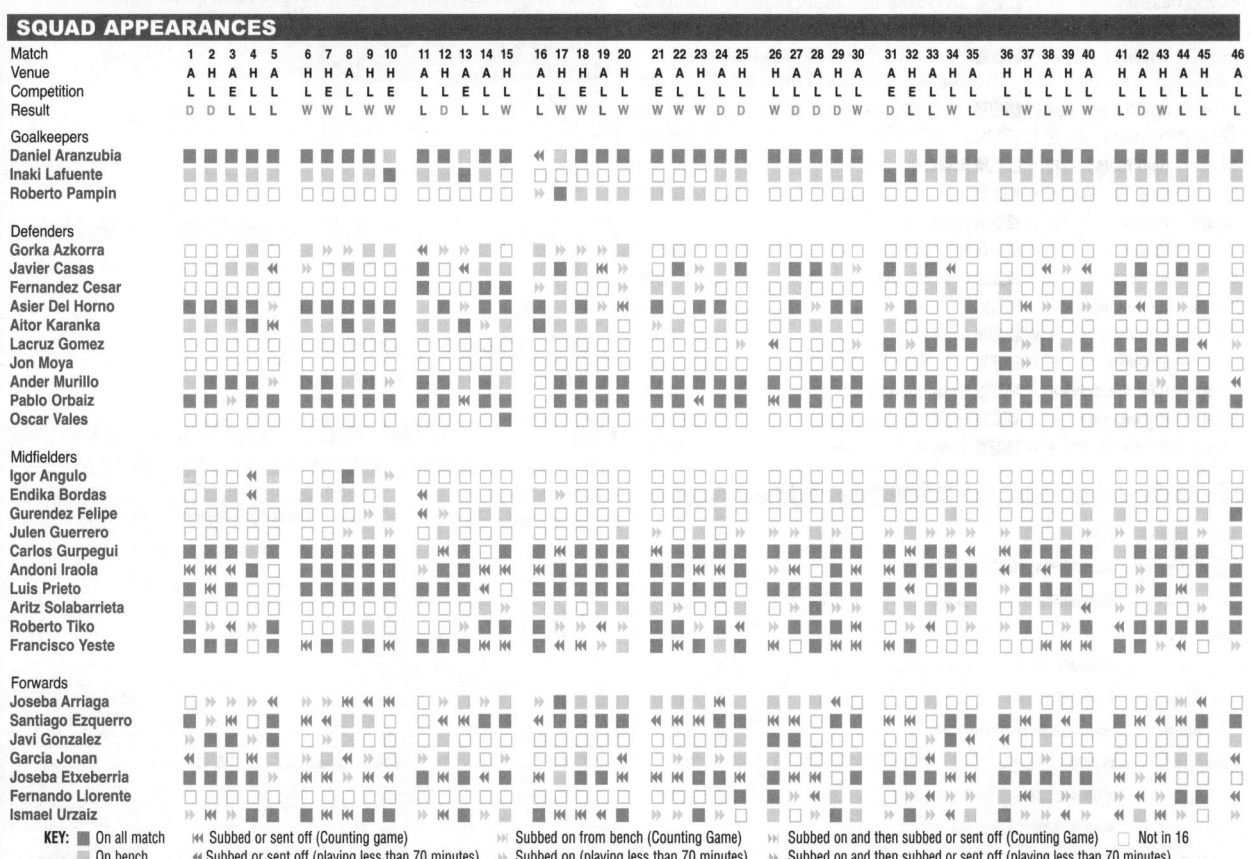

KEY: On all match | On bench | Subbed or sent off (Counting game) | Subbed or sent off (playing less than 70 minutes) | Subbed on from bench (Counting Game) | Subbed on (playing less than 70 minutes) | Subbed on and then subbed or sent off (Counting Game) | Subbed on and then subbed or sent off (playing less than 70 minutes) | Not in 16

MALAGA

Final Position: **10th**

KEY: Won Drawn Lost

							Attendance
1	sppr1	**Atl Madrid**	A	L	0-2		40,000
2	sppr1	**Real Zaragoza**	H	D	0-0		24,000
3	sppr1	**Mallorca**	A	W	2-1	Edgar 24; Wanchope 81	14,000
4	sppr1	**Numancia**	H	W	4-1	Miguel Angel 5; Wanchope 8; Amoroso 20; Luque 90	25,000
5	sppr1	**Espanyol**	A	L	0-1		23,000
6	sppr1	**Osasuna**	H	W	2-0	Amoroso 23; Wanchope 61	25,000
7	sppr1	**Athl Bilbao**	A	L	0-1		30,000
8	sppr1	**Deportivo**	H	D	1-1	Wanchope 6	26,000
9	sppr1	**Real Betis**	A	D	1-1	Gerardo 43	39,000
10	sppr1	**Real Madrid**	H	L	0-2		30,000
11	sppr1	**Getafe**	A	L	0-1		13,000
12	sppr1	**Valencia**	H	L	0-2		23,000
13	sppr1	**Albacete**	H	L	0-2		20,000
14	sppr1	**Barcelona**	A	L	0-4		67,000
15	sppr1	**Levante**	H	W	1-0	Amoroso 47	20,000
16	sppr1	**Villarreal**	A	L	0-3		14,000
17	sppr1	**Real Sociedad**	H	L	1-5	Valcarce 42	16,000
18	sppr1	**R Santander**	A	L	1-2	Cesar Navas 86	11,000
19	sppr1	**Seville**	H	W	1-0	Wanchope 66	22,000
20	sppr1	**Atl Madrid**	H	W	1-0	Juan Rodriguez 83	22,000
21	sppr1	**Real Zaragoza**	A	L	0-1		29,000
22	sppr1	**Mallorca**	H	D	0-0		20,000
23	sppr1	**Numancia**	A	W	1-0	Juan Rodriguez 43	8,000
24	sppr1	**Espanyol**	H	W	3-2	Juan Rodriguez 7; Miguel Angel 14; Juanito 52	21,000
25	sppr1	**Osasuna**	A	W	6-1	Miguel Angel 3; Duda 12; Baiano 38,51; Juan Rodriguez 79; Wanchope 83	15,000
26	sppr1	**Athl Bilbao**	H	W	1-0	Juan Rodriguez 1	19,000
27	sppr1	**Deportivo**	A	L	0-1		20,000
28	sppr1	**Real Betis**	H	L	1-2	Baiano 26	25,000
29	sppr1	**Real Madrid**	A	L	0-1		60,000
30	sppr1	**Getafe**	H	D	1-1	Baiano 14	18,000
31	sppr1	**Valencia**	A	D	2-2	Baiano 33; Duda 90	50,000
32	sppr1	**Albacete**	A	W	2-1	Duda 52; Amoroso 84 pen	8,000
33	sppr1	**Barcelona**	H	L	0-4		32,000
34	sppr1	**Levante**	A	W	1-0	Baiano 37	15,000
35	sppr1	**Villarreal**	H	L	0-2		20,000
36	sppr1	**Real Sociedad**	A	W	3-1	Edgar 45; Baiano 57,68	16,000
37	sppr1	**R Santander**	H	W	2-0	Edgar 18; Amoroso 90	12,000
38	sppr1	**Seville**	A	W	2-0	Duda 74; Baiano 90	45,000

MONTHLY POINTS TALLY

AUGUST	0	0%
SEPTEMBER	7	58%
OCTOBER	5	42%
NOVEMBER	0	0%
DECEMBER	3	25%
JANUARY	6	50%
FEBRUARY	10	83%
MARCH	3	25%
APRIL	5	42%
MAY	12	80%

KEY PLAYERS - GOALSCORERS

Paulo Wanchope

Goals in the League	6	Player Strike Rate Average number of minutes between League goals scored by player	241
Contribution to Attacking Power Average number of minutes between League team goals while on pitch	96	Club Strike Rate Average number of minutes between League goals scored by club	86

	PLAYER	LGE GOALS	POWER	STRIKE RATE
1	Paulo Wanchope	6	96	241 mins
2	Juan Rodriguez	5	71	329 mins
3	Patricio Edgar	3	101	537 mins
4	Sergio Duda	4	75	692 mins
5	Miguel Angel	3	85	994 mins

KEY PLAYERS - MIDFIELDERS

Marcelo Romero

Goals in the League	0	Contribution to Attacking Power Average number of minutes between League team goals while on pitch	81
Defensive Rating Average number of mins between League goals conceded while on the pitch	84	Scoring Difference Defensive Rating minus Contribution to Attacking Power	3

	PLAYER	LGE GOALS	DEF RATE	POWER	SCORE DIFF
1	Marcelo Romero	0	84	81	3 mins
2	Sergio Duda	4	69	75	-6 mins
3	Juan Rodriguez	5	61	71	-10 mins
4	Patricio Edgar	3	85	101	-16 mins
5	Miguel Angel	3	66	85	-19 mins

KEY PLAYERS - DEFENDERS

Cesar Navas

Goals Conceded Number of League goals conceded while the player was on the pitch	19	Clean Sheets In games when player was on pitch for at least 70 minutes	9
Defensive Rating Ave number of mins between League goals conceded while on the pitch	99	Club Defensive Rating Average number of mins between League goals conceded by the club this season	71

	PLAYER	CON LGE	CLEAN SHEETS	DEF RATE
1	Cesar Navas	19	9	99 mins
2	Vicente Valcarce	40	11	80 mins
3	Garcia Gerardo	36	10	79 mins
4	Fernando Sanz	43	11	72 mins

KEY GOALKEEPER

Francesco Arnau

Goals Conceded in the League	19	Counting Games Games when player was on pitch for at least 70 minutes	20
Defensive Rating Ave number of mins between League goals conceded while on the pitch	95	Clean Sheets In games when player was on pitch for at least 70 minutes	8

LEAGUE GOALS

Fernando Baiano

Minutes on the pitch	1269	Goals in the League	9
League average (mins between goals)	141		

	PLAYER	MINS	GOALS	AVE
1	Baiano	1269	9	141
2	Wanchope	1447	6	241
3	Juan Rodriguez	1644	5	329
4	Amoroso	1558	5	312
5	Duda	2766	4	692
6	Miguel Angel	2983	3	994
7	Edgar	1612	3	537
8	Luque	216	1	216
9	Cesar Navas	1889	1	1889
10	Juanito	3000	1	3000
11	Valcarce	3212	1	3212
12	Gerardo	2828	1	2828
	Other		0	
	TOTAL		40	

DISCIPLINARY RECORDS

	PLAYER	YELLOW	RED	AVE
1	Alexis	7	1	123
2	Romero	11	2	168
3	Juanito	12	0	250
4	Gerardo	10	1	257
5	Leko	4	0	263
6	Cesar Navas	6	1	269
7	Miguel Angel	10	1	271
8	Juan Rodriguez	6	0	274
9	Duda	8	1	307
10	Amoroso	4	1	311
11	Wanchope	4	0	361
12	Fernando Sanz	7	0	440
13	Valcarce	6	0	535
	Other	7	1	
	TOTAL	102	9	

TOP POINT EARNERS

	PLAYER	GAMES	AV PTS
1	Patricio Edgar	12	2.08
2	Cesar Navas	21	1.86
3	Francesco Arnau	20	1.80
4	Garcia Gerardo	30	1.57
5	Juanito	31	1.52
6	Juan Rodriguez	16	1.50
7	Vicente Valcarce	36	1.42
8	Sergio Duda	27	1.41
9	Marcelo Romero	22	1.36
10	Fernando Sanz	33	1.36
	CLUB AVERAGE:		1.34

TEAM OF THE SEASON

D
Cesar Navas
CG: 21 DR: 99
M
Marcelo Romero
CG: 22 SD: 3
D
Vicente Valcarce
CG: 36 DR: 80
M
Sergio Duda
CG: 27 SD: -6
F
Paulo Wanchope
CG: 13 SR: 241
G
Francesco Arnau
CG: 20 DR: 95
D
Garcia Gerardo
CG: 30 DR: 79
M
Juan Rodriguez
CG: 16 SD: -10
F
Fernando Baiano*
CG: 11 SR: 141
D
Fernando Sanz
CG: 33 DR: 72
M
Patricio Edgar
CG: 12 SD: -16

LEAGUE APPEARANCES, BOOKINGS AND CAPS

	AGE (on 01/07/05)	IN NAMED 18	APPEARANCES	COUNTING GAMES	MINUTES ON PITCH	YELLOW CARDS	RED CARDS	THIS SEASON	HOME COUNTRY
Goalkeepers									
Francesco Arnau	30	32	20	20	1800	1	0	-	Spain
Juan Calatayud	26	38	18	18	1620	2	0	-	Spain
Inaki Goitia	23	1	0	0	0	0	0	-	Spain
Defenders									
Ruano Alexis	19	22	13	10	988	7	1	-	Spain
Cesar Navas	25	23	21	21	1889	6	1	-	Spain
Fernando Sanz	31	37	35	33	3081	7	0	-	Spain
Garcia Gerardo	30	35	33	30	2828	10	1	-	Spain
Raul Iznata	27	25	6	2	234	2	0	-	Spain
Carlos Litos	31	33	5	4	362	1	0	-	Portugal
Vicente Valcarce	30	37	36	36	3212	6	0	-	Spain
Midfielders									
Sergio Duda	25	36	36	27	2766	8	1	-	Portugal
Patricio Edgar	27	33	28	12	1612	2	1	-	Spain
Paco Esteban	23	8	7	1	233	0	0	-	Spain
Juan Rodriguez	23	30	26	16	1644	6	0	-	Spain
Ivan Leko	27	20	17	9	1053	4	0	-	Croatia
Jose Luque	27	15	8	1	216	0	0	-	Spain
Sanchez Manu	26	26	15	4	594	1	0	-	Spain
Michel	29	12	9	1	300	1	0	-	Spain
Miguel Angel	26	36	35	32	2983	10	1	-	Spain
Marcelo Romero	29	33	29	22	2193	11	2	-	Uruguay
Fernando Usero	21	2	2	1	94	0	0	-	Spain
Forwards									
Marcio Amoroso	31	34	29	11	1558	4	1	-	Brazil
Fernando Baiano	26	17	17	11	1269	1	0	-	Brazil
Alexandre Geijo	23	16	12	1	318	1	0	-	Switzerland
Juanito	25	36	35	31	3000	12	0	3	Spain (8)
Jorge Tote	26	16	9	0	203	1	0	-	Spain
Paulo Wanchope	29	30	25	13	1447	4	0	-	Costa Rica

SQUAD APPEARANCES

Match	1	2	3	4	5	6	7	8	9	10	11	12	13	14	15	16	17	18	19	20	21	22	23	24	25	26	27	28	29	30	31	32	33	34	35	36	37	38
Venue	A	H	A	H	A	H	A	H	A	H	A	H	H	A	H	A	H	A	H	H	A	H	A	H	A	H	A	H	A	H	A	A	H	A	H	A	H	A
Competition	L	L	L	L	L	L	L	L	L	L	L	L	L	L	L	L	L	L	L	L	L	L	L	L	L	L	L	L	L	L	L	L	L	L	L	L	L	L
Result	L	D	W	W	L	W	L	D	D	L	L	L	L	L	W	L	L	L	W	W	L	D	W	W	W	W	L	L	L	D	D	W	L	W	L	W	W	W

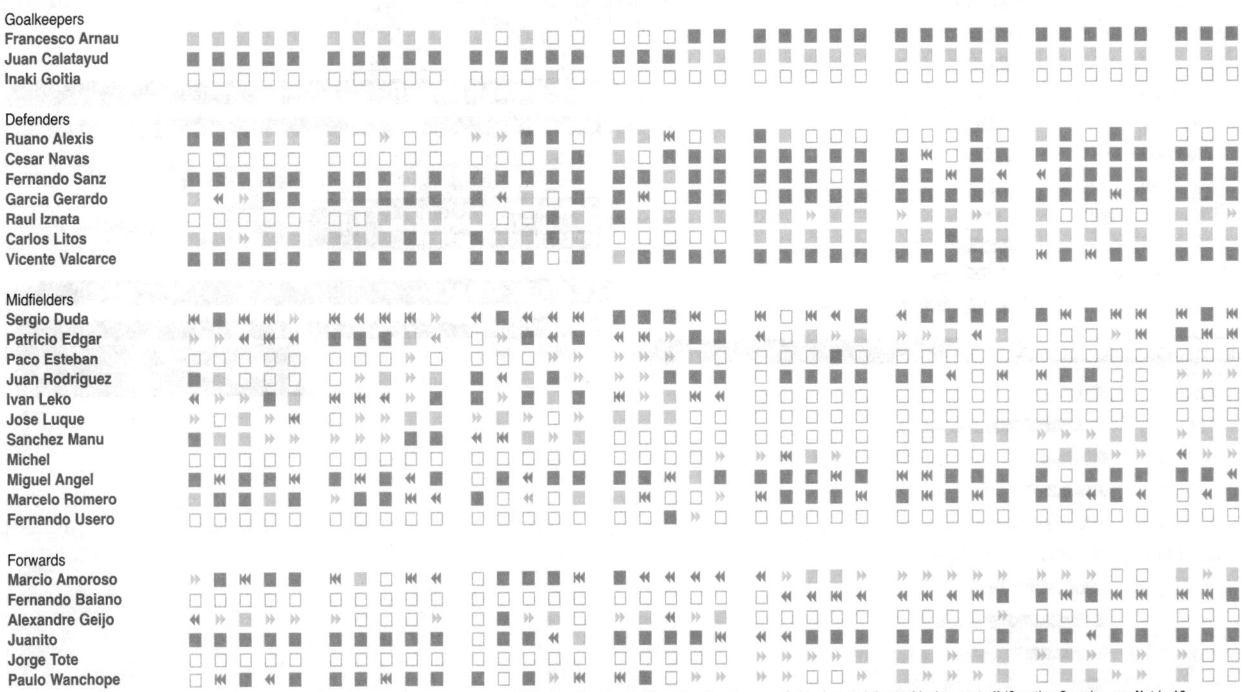

Goalkeepers
Francesco Arnau
Juan Calatayud
Inaki Goitia
Defenders
Ruano Alexis
Cesar Navas
Fernando Sanz
Garcia Gerardo
Raul Iznata
Carlos Litos
Vicente Valcarce
Midfielders
Sergio Duda
Patricio Edgar
Paco Esteban
Juan Rodriguez
Ivan Leko
Jose Luque
Sanchez Manu
Michel
Miguel Angel
Marcelo Romero
Fernando Usero
Forwards
Marcio Amoroso
Fernando Baiano
Alexandre Geijo
Juanito
Jorge Tote
Paulo Wanchope

KEY: On all match | On bench | Subbed or sent off (Counting game) | Subbed or sent off (playing less than 70 minutes) | Subbed on from bench (Counting Game) | Subbed on (playing less than 70 minutes) | Subbed on and then subbed or sent off (Counting Game) | Subbed on and then subbed or sent off (playing less than 70 minutes) | Not in 16

ATLETICO MADRID

Final Position: **11th**

KEY: Won Drawn Lost

							Attendance
1	sppr1	**Malaga**	H	W	2-0	Calatayud 45 og; Torres 48	40,000
2	sppr1	**Albacete**	A	W	2-0	Torres 86; Ibagaza 90	14,000
3	sppr1	**Barcelona**	H	D	1-1	Torres 49	55,000
4	sppr1	**Levante**	A	L	0-1		15,000
5	sppr1	**Villarreal**	H	W	1-0	Salva 43	48,000
6	sppr1	**Real Sociedad**	A	L	0-1		21,000
7	sppr1	**R Santander**	H	W	1-0	Torres 8	45,000
8	sppr1	**Seville**	A	L	1-2	Pablo Ibanez 90	45,000
9	sppr1	**Valencia**	A	D	1-1	Torres 79	41,000
10	sppr1	**Real Zaragoza**	H	D	1-1	Salva 82	50,000
11	sppr1	**Mallorca**	A	D	1-1	Colsa 84	15,000
12	sppr1	**Numancia**	H	W	2-0	Pablo Ibanez 51; Torres 78	45,000
13	sppr1	**Espanyol**	A	L	1-2	Nano 56	17,000
14	sppr1	**Osasuna**	H	W	3-2	Torres 16; Salva 30; Colsa 55	45,000
15	sppr1	**Athl Bilbao**	A	L	0-1		35,000
16	sppr1	**Deportivo**	H	W	1-0	Antonio Lopez 27	45,000
17	sppr1	**Real Betis**	A	L	0-1		25,000
18	sppr1	**Real Madrid**	H	L	0-3		56,000
19	sppr1	**Getafe**	A	D	1-1	Jorge 35	14,000
20	sppr1	**Malaga**	A	L	0-1		22,000
21	sppr1	**Albacete**	H	W	3-1	Torres 20; Ibagaza 29; Pablo Ibanez 45	50,000
22	sppr1	**Barcelona**	A	W	2-0	Torres 1,90 pen	63,000
23	sppr1	**Levante**	H	D	0-0		45,000
24	sppr1	**Villarreal**	A	L	2-3	Torres 26,38	15,000
25	sppr1	**Real Sociedad**	H	W	1-0	Antonio Lopez 25	45,000
26	sppr1	**R Santander**	A	L	1-2	Torres 11	19,000
27	sppr1	**Seville**	H	W	3-0	Salva 15; Torres 36; Antonio Lopez 41	45,000
28	sppr1	**Valencia**	H	W	1-0	Torres 12	48,000
29	sppr1	**Real Zaragoza**	A	D	0-0		30,000
30	sppr1	**Mallorca**	H	W	4-0	Colsa 26; Torres 60 pen; Salva 85,88	45,000
31	sppr1	**Numancia**	A	L	0-1		9,000
32	sppr1	**Espanyol**	H	D	0-0		47,000
33	sppr1	**Osasuna**	A	L	0-1		16,000
34	sppr1	**Athl Bilbao**	H	D	1-1	Colsa 77	45,000
35	sppr1	**Deportivo**	A	L	0-2		24,000
36	sppr1	**Real Betis**	H	L	1-2	Melli 53 og	45,000
37	sppr1	**Real Madrid**	A	D	0-0		70,000
38	sppr1	**Getafe**	H	D	2-2	Richard Nunez 46,90	15,000

MONTHLY POINTS TALLY

AUGUST	3	100%
SEPTEMBER	7	58%
OCTOBER	4	33%
NOVEMBER	5	42%
DECEMBER	6	50%
JANUARY	4	33%
FEBRUARY	7	58%
MARCH	7	58%
APRIL	5	33%
MAY	2	17%

KEY PLAYERS - GOALSCORERS

Fernando Torres

Goals in the League	16	Player Strike Rate Average number of minutes between League goals scored by player	212
Contribution to Attacking Power Average number of minutes between League team goals while on pitch	84	Club Strike Rate Average number of minutes between League goals scored by club	86

	PLAYER	LGE GOALS	POWER	STRIKE RATE
1	Fernando Torres	16	84	212 mins
2	Ballesta Salva	6	71	286 mins
3	Gonzalo Colsa	4	76	476 mins
4	Antonio Lopez	3	96	901 mins
5	Pablo Ibanez	3	85	1050 mins

KEY PLAYERS - MIDFIELDERS

Gonzalo Colsa

Goals in the League	4	Contribution to Attacking Power Average number of minutes between League team goals while on pitch	76
Defensive Rating Average number of mins between League goals conceded while on the pitch	119	Scoring Difference Defensive Rating minus Contribution to Attacking Power	43

	PLAYER	LGE GOALS	DEF RATE	POWER	SCORE DIFF
1	Gonzalo Colsa	4	119	76	43 mins
2	Jesper Gronkjaer	0	113	80	33 mins
3	Marcelo Sosa	0	84	76	8 mins
4	Peter Luccin	0	105	105	0 mins

KEY PLAYERS - DEFENDERS

Sergi Barjuan

Goals Conceded Number of League goals conceded while the player was on the pitch	19	Clean Sheets In games when player was on pitch for at least 70 minutes	11
Defensive Rating Ave number of mins between League goals conceded while on the pitch	119	Club Defensive Rating Average number of mins between League goals conceded by the club this season	101

	PLAYER	CON LGE	CLEAN SHEETS	DEF RATE
1	Sergi Barjuan	19	11	119 mins
2	Juan Velasco	15	7	115 mins
3	Pablo Ibanez	30	15	105 mins
4	Jose Garcia Calvo	12	4	103 mins
5	Luis Perea	27	12	102 mins

KEY GOALKEEPER

Leonardo Franco

Goals Conceded in the League	32	Counting Games League games when player was on pitch for at least 70 minutes	37
Defensive Rating Ave number of mins between League goals conceded while on the pitch	104	Clean Sheets In games when player was on pitch for at least 70 minutes	15

LEAGUE GOALS

Fernando Torres

Minutes on the pitch	3390	Goals in the League	16
League average (mins between goals)	212		

	PLAYER	MINS	GOALS	AVE
1	Torres	3390	16	212
2	Salva	1716	6	286
3	Colsa	1905	4	476
4	Pablo Ibanez	3150	3	1050
5	Antonio Lopez	2703	3	901
6	Richard Nunez	409	2	205
7	Ibagaza	2195	2	1098
8	Nano	380	1	380
9	Jorge	1436	1	1436
	Other		2	
	TOTAL		40	

DISCIPLINARY RECORDS

	PLAYER	YELLOW	RED	AVE
1	Sosa	11	1	140
2	Garcia Calvo	7	1	154
3	Gronkjaer	6	0	226
4	Luccin	9	0	245
5	Salva	6	1	245
6	Perea	10	1	251
7	Molinero	4	0	266
8	Pablo Ibanez	11	0	286
9	Colsa	6	0	317
10	Sergi	7	0	324
11	Ibagaza	6	0	365
12	Antonio Lopez	6	1	386
13	Aguilera	2	0	391
	Other	8	0	
	TOTAL	99	5	

TOP POINT EARNERS

	PLAYER	GAMES	AV PTS
1	Gonzalo Colsa	15	1.87
2	Sergi Barjuan	22	1.55
3	Juan Velasco	16	1.44
4	Ballesta Salva	12	1.42
5	Jose Garcia Calvo	12	1.42
6	Jesper Gronkjaer	15	1.40
7	Pablo Ibanez	35	1.37
8	Fernando Torres	37	1.35
9	Leonardo Franco	37	1.32
10	Luis Perea	30	1.30
	CLUB AVERAGE:		1.32

TEAM OF THE SEASON

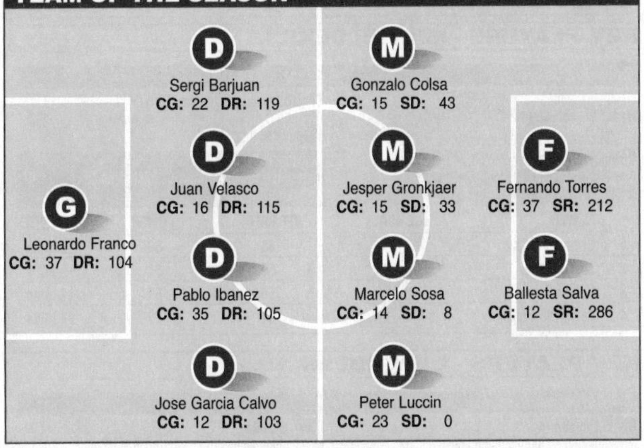
G
Leonardo Franco
CG: 37 DR: 104
D
Sergi Barjuan
CG: 22 DR: 119
D
Juan Velasco
CG: 16 DR: 115
D
Pablo Ibanez
CG: 35 DR: 105
D
Jose Garcia Calvo
CG: 12 DR: 103
M
Gonzalo Colsa
CG: 15 SD: 43
M
Jesper Gronkjaer
CG: 15 SD: 33
M
Marcelo Sosa
CG: 14 SD: 8
M
Peter Luccin
CG: 23 SD: 0
F
Fernando Torres
CG: 37 SR: 212
F
Ballesta Salva
CG: 12 SR: 286

LEAGUE APPEARANCES, BOOKINGS AND CAPS

	AGE (on 01/07/05)	IN NAMED 18	APPEARANCES	COUNTING GAMES	MINUTES ON PITCH	YELLOW CARDS	RED CARDS	THIS SEASON	HOME COUNTRY
Goalkeepers									
Sergio Aragoneses	28	5	0	0	0	0	0	-	Spain
Ivan Cuellar	21	28	1	1	90	0	0	-	Spain
Leonardo Franco	28	38	37	37	3330	1	0	6	Argentina (3)
Defenders									
Antonio Lopez	23	34	32	30	2703	6	1	-	Spain
Jose Garcia Calvo	30	31	16	12	1237	7	1	-	Spain
Ariel Ibagaza	28	30	30	20	2195	6	0	1	Argentina (3)
Francisco Molinero	19	22	14	10	1066	4	0	-	Spain
Pablo Ibanez	23	35	35	35	3150	11	0	6	Spain (8)
Luis Perea	26	33	33	30	2763	10	1	-	Colombia
Sergi Barjuan	33	30	28	22	2268	7	0	-	Spain
Pablo Sicillia	23	7	0	0	0	0	0	-	Spain
Juan Velasco	28	30	21	16	1731	0	0	-	Spain
Jose Zahinos	27	3	1	0	20	0	0	-	Spain
Midfielders									
Carlos Aguilera	36	22	14	5	782	2	0	-	Spain
Gonzalo Colsa	26	34	30	15	1905	6	0	-	Spain
Jesper Gronkjaer	27	16	16	15	1361	6	0	6	Denmark (19)
Larena Jorge	23	35	26	5	1436	1	0	-	Spain
Peter Luccin	26	30	29	23	2206	9	0	-	France
Raul Medina	22	8	6	0	122	1	0	-	Spain
Kiki Musampa	27	10	8	4	494	1	0	-	Holland
Alvaro Novo	27	6	5	1	204	0	0	-	Spain
Diego Simeone	35	12	8	1	326	0	0	-	Argentina
Marcelo Sosa	27	32	28	14	1680	11	1	5	Uruguay (16)
Forwards									
Nobrega Braulio	19	17	10	1	208	1	0	-	Spain
Fernando Nano	23	30	10	2	380	2	0	-	Spain
Veljko Paunovic	27	11	10	2	407	2	1	-	Serbia & Montenegro
Richard Nunez	29	16	10	3	409	0	0	-	Uruguay
Ballesta Salva	30	29	28	12	1716	6	1	-	Spain
Fernando Torres	21	38	38	37	3390	5	0	6	Spain (8)

SQUAD APPEARANCES

Match	1	2	3	4	5	6	7	8	9	10	11	12	13	14	15	16	17	18	19	20	21	22	23	24	25	26	27	28	29	30	31	32	33	34	35	36	37	38
Venue	H	H	A	A	H	A	H	A	A	H	A	H	A	H	A	H	A	H	A	A	H	A	H	A	H	A	H	H	A	H	A	H	A	H	A	H	A	H
Competition	L	L	L	L	L	L	L	L	L	L	L	L	L	L	L	L	L	L	L	L	L	L	L	L	L	L	L	L	L	L	L	L	L	L	L	L	L	L
Result	W	W	D	L	W	L	W	L	D	D	D	W	L	W	L	W	L	L	D	L	W	W	D	L	W	L	W	W	D	W	L	D	L	D	L	L	D	D

Goalkeepers
Sergio Aragoneses
Ivan Cuellar
Leonardo Franco

Defenders
Antonio Lopez
Jose Garcia Calvo
Ariel Ibagaza
Francisco Molinero
Pablo Ibanez
Luis Perea
Sergi Barjuan
Pablo Sicillia
Juan Velasco
Jose Zahinos

Midfielders
Carlos Aguilera
Gonzalo Colsa
Jesper Gronkjaer
Larena Jorge
Peter Luccin
Raul Medina
Kiki Musampa
Alvaro Novo
Diego Simeone
Marcelo Sosa

Forwards
Nobrega Braulio
Fernando Nano
Veljko Paunovic
Richard Nunez
Ballesta Salva
Fernando Torres

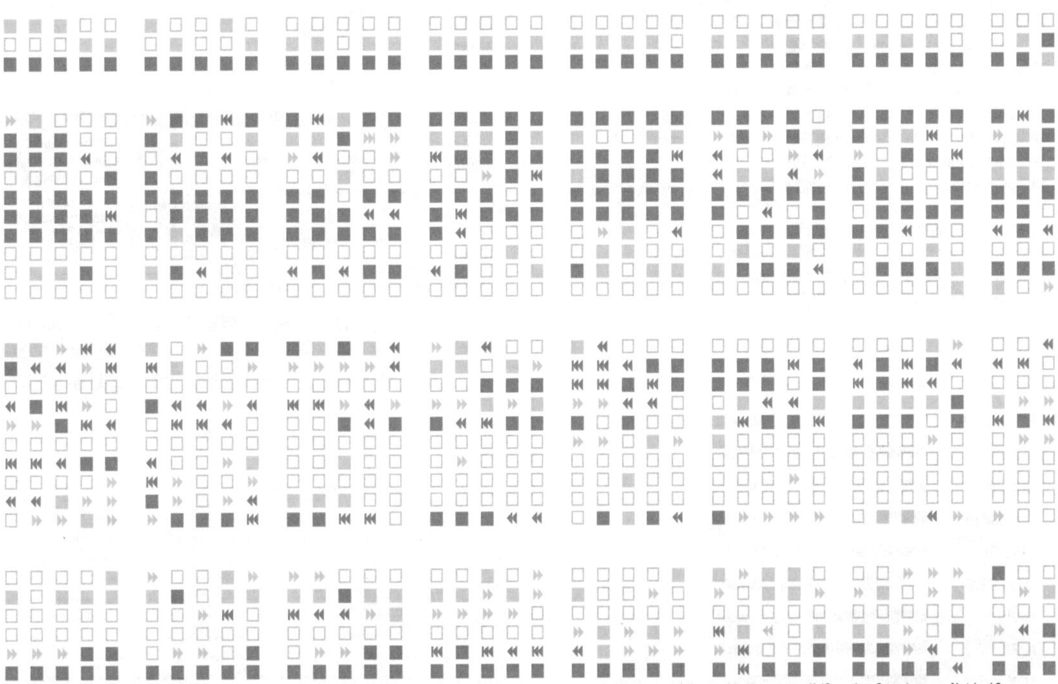

KEY: On all match; On bench; Subbed or sent off (Counting game); Subbed or sent off (playing less than 70 minutes); Subbed on from bench (Counting Game); Subbed on (playing less than 70 minutes); Subbed on and then subbed or sent off (Counting Game); Subbed on and then subbed or sent off (playing less than 70 minutes); Not in 16

REAL ZARAGOZA

Final Position: **12th**

KEY: ☐ Won ☐ Drawn ☐ Lost

							Attendance
1	sppr1	**Getafe**	H	W	3-1	Alvaro 23,80; Savio 63	33,000
2	sppr1	**Malaga**	A	D	0-0		24,000
3	uc1rl1	**Sigma Olomouc**	H	W	1-0	Generelo 83	32,000
4	sppr1	**Albacete**	H	W	4-3	Javi Moreno 3,54; Savio 58; Villa 69	32,000
5	sppr1	**Barcelona**	A	L	1-4	Villa 14	60,000
6	sppr1	**Levante**	H	W	4-3	Villa 36 pen; Javi Moreno 47,75; Savio 52	32,000
7	uc1rl2	**Sigma Olomouc**	A	W	3-2	Soriano 77; Hudec 80 og; Javi Moreno 86	8,764
8	sppr1	**Villarreal**	A	L	0-2		14,000
9	sppr1	**Real Sociedad**	H	W	2-1	Villa 30 pen; Savio 66	29,000
10	ucgc	**Utrecht**	H	W	2-0	Villa 76,82	27,000
11	sppr1	**R Santander**	A	L	0-1		12,000
12	sppr1	**Seville**	H	W	3-0	Galletti 13; Villa 28 pen,59	31,000
13	ucgc	**Austria Vienna**	A	L	0-1		19,000
14	sppr1	**Atl Madrid**	A	D	1-1	Savio 3	50,000
15	sppr1	**Valencia**	A	D	0-0		40,000
16	sppr1	**Mallorca**	H	L	0-1		32,000
17	sppr1	**Numancia**	A	L	1-2	Milito 37	10,000
18	ucgc	**Dnipro**	H	W	2-1	Savio 9; Generelo 73	10,000
19	sppr1	**Espanyol**	H	L	0-1		19,000
20	sppr1	**Osasuna**	A	D	2-2	Oscar 14,64	13,000
21	ucgc	**Club Brugge**	A	D	1-1	Savio 39	23,000
22	sppr1	**Athl Bilbao**	H	L	0-2		33,000
23	sppr1	**Deportivo**	A	W	3-2	Cani 35; Milito 56; Villa 67	15,000
24	sppr1	**Real Betis**	H	W	1-0	Savio 44	32,000
25	sppr1	**Real Madrid**	A	L	1-3	Villa 21	62,000
26	sppr1	**Getafe**	A	L	0-3		13,000
27	sppr1	**Malaga**	H	W	1-0	Cani 15	29,000
28	sppr1	**Albacete**	A	L	1-2	Oscar 15	15,000
29	sppr1	**Barcelona**	H	L	1-4	Galletti 62	35,000
30	uc3rl1	**Fenerbahce**	A	W	1-0	Alvaro 72	49,000
31	sppr1	**Levante**	A	D	0-0		15,000
32	uc3rl2	**Fenerbahce**	H	W	2-1	Galletti 11; Savio 70	25,000
33	sppr1	**Villarreal**	H	W	1-0	Villa 38	25,000
34	sppr1	**Real Sociedad**	A	L	1-2	Zapater 31	25,000
35	sppr1	**R Santander**	H	W	1-0	Capi 58	32,000
36	uc4rl1	**Austria Vienna**	A	D	1-1	Savio 74	21,000
37	sppr1	**Seville**	A	W	1-0	Milito 32	32,000
38	uc4rl2	**Austria Vienna**	H	D	2-2	Villa 58; Galletti 62	27,000
39	sppr1	**Atl Madrid**	H	D	0-0		30,000
40	sppr1	**Valencia**	H	D	2-2	Generelo 44; Albelda 49 og	31,000
41	sppr1	**Mallorca**	A	W	2-0	Savio 55; Villa 85	9,000
42	sppr1	**Numancia**	H	W	4-1	Villa 64,70; Ponzio 79; Savio 82	33,000
43	sppr1	**Espanyol**	A	L	1-3	Villa 60	30,000
44	sppr1	**Osasuna**	H	W	5-1	Villa 10,85; Savio 38; Oscar 59; Generelo 63	29,000
45	sppr1	**Athl Bilbao**	A	L	0-2		32,000
46	sppr1	**Deportivo**	H	D	2-2	Generelo 58,65	32,000
47	sppr1	**Real Betis**	A	L	2-3	Savio 36; Oscar 90	42,000
48	sppr1	**Real Madrid**	H	L	1-3	Oscar 43; Camacho 72	33,000

MONTHLY POINTS TALLY

AUGUST	3	100%
SEPTEMBER	7	58%
OCTOBER	6	50%
NOVEMBER	2	17%
DECEMBER	4	33%
JANUARY	6	50%
FEBRUARY	4	33%
MARCH	7	58%
APRIL	7	58%
MAY	4	27%

KEY PLAYERS - GOALSCORERS

David Villa

Goals in the League	15	Player Strike Rate Average number of minutes between League goals scored by player	187
Contribution to Attacking Power Average number of minutes between League team goals while on pitch	57	Club Strike Rate Average number of minutes between League goals scored by club	65

	PLAYER	LGE GOALS	POWER	STRIKE RATE
1	David Villa	15	57	187 mins
2	Gonzalez Oscar	6	59	283 mins
3	Savio	10	62	312 mins
4	Ruben Cani	2	67	904 mins
5	Gabriel Milito	3	61	1050 mins

KEY PLAYERS - MIDFIELDERS

Gonzalez Oscar

Goals in the League	6	Contribution to Attacking Power Average number of minutes between League team goals while on pitch	59
Defensive Rating Average number of mins between League goals conceded while on the pitch	68	Scoring Difference Defensive Rating minus Contribution to Attacking Power	9

	PLAYER	LGE GOALS	DEF RATE	POWER	SCORE DIFF
1	Gonzalez Oscar	6	68	59	9 mins
2	Jose Movilla	0	59	61	-2 mins
3	Ruben Cani	2	56	67	-11 mins
4	Leonardo Ponzio	1	61	84	-23 mins

KEY PLAYERS - DEFENDERS

Gabriel Milito

Goals Conceded Number of League goals conceded while the player was on the pitch	49	Clean Sheets In games when player was on pitch for at least 70 minutes	11
Defensive Rating Ave number of mins between League goals conceded while on the pitch	64	Club Defensive Rating Average number of mins between League goals conceded by the club this season	60

	PLAYER	CON LGE	CLEAN SHEETS	DEF RATE
1	Gabriel Milito	49	11	64 mins
2	Agustin Aranzabal	31	6	62 mins
3	Alvaro	51	10	61 mins
4	Alberto Zapater	37	6	60 mins
5	Delio Toledo	34	4	52 mins

KEY GOALKEEPER

Luis Garcia

Goals Conceded in the League	52	Counting Games Games when player was on pitch for at least 70 minutes	37
Defensive Rating Ave number of mins between League goals conceded while on the pitch	64	Clean Sheets In games when player was on pitch for at least 70 minutes	11

LEAGUE GOALS

David Villa

Minutes on the pitch	2806	Goals in the League	15
League average (mins between goals)	187		

	PLAYER	MINS	GOALS	AVE
1	Villa	2806	15	187
2	Savio	3116	10	312
3	Oscar	1700	6	283
4	Javi Moreno	954	4	239
5	Generelo	1092	4	273
6	Milito	3150	3	1050
7	Alvaro	3104	2	1552
8	Galletti	2564	2	1282
9	Cani	1807	2	904
10	Zapater	2212	1	2212
11	Ponzio	2514	1	2514
12	Camacho	59	1	59
13	Capi	247	1	247
	Other		1	
	TOTAL		53	

DISCIPLINARY

	PLAYER	YELLOW	RED	AVE
1	Javi Moreno	5	0	190
2	Toledo	9	0	196
3	Cani	9	0	200
4	Generelo	5	0	218
5	Zapater	7	1	276
6	Alvaro	9	2	282
7	Galletti	7	0	366
8	Milito	8	0	393
9	Villa	7	0	400
10	Ponzio	6	0	419
11	Soriano	1	0	466
12	Cuartero	2	0	492
13	Oscar	2	1	566
	Other	14	1	
	TOTAL	91	5	

TOP POINT EARNERS

	PLAYER	GAMES	AV PTS
1	Gonzalez Oscar	15	1.87
2	Agustin Aranzabal	20	1.80
3	David Villa	27	1.48
4	Gabriel Milito	35	1.43
5	Alberto Zapater	21	1.43
6	Ruben Cani	13	1.38
7	Luis Garcia	37	1.35
8	Savio	35	1.34
9	Jose Movilla	35	1.31
10	Luciano Galletti	23	1.30
	CLUB AVERAGE:		1.32

LEAGUE APPEARANCES, BOOKINGS AND CAPS

	AGE (on 01/07/05)	IN NAMED 18	APPEARANCES	COUNTING GAMES	MINUTES ON PITCH	YELLOW CARDS	RED CARDS	THIS SEASON	HOME COUNTRY
Goalkeepers									
Ruben Falcon	27	6	2	1	97	0	0	-	Spain
Cesar Lainez	28	13	0	0	0	0	0	-	Spain
Luis Garcia	26	37	37	37	3322	4	1	1	Spain (8)
Martinez Miguel	23	5	0	0	0	0	0	-	Spain
Jorge Zapa	21	8	0	0	0	0	0	-	Spain
Defenders									
Alvaro	28	35	35	34	3104	9	2	-	Brazil
Agustin Aranzabal	32	32	23	20	1924	2	0	-	Spain
Manuel Capi	24	8	3	3	247	1	0	-	Spain
Jimenez Cesar	27	14	1	0	22	0	0	-	Spain
Luis Cuartero	30	28	19	8	985	2	0	-	Spain
Gabriel Milito	24	36	35	35	3150	8	0	4	Argentina (3)
Delio Toledo	28	31	22	19	1764	9	0	-	Paraguay
Alberto Zapater	20	34	31	21	2212	7	1	-	Spain
Midfielders									
Juan Camacho	24	15	5	0	59	0	0	-	Spain
Ruben Cani	23	37	35	13	1807	9	0	-	Spain
David Generelo	22	32	21	7	1092	5	0	-	Spain
Juan Granero	24	12	3	0	65	1	0	-	Spain
Jose Movilla	30	37	37	35	3186	4	0	-	Spain
Gonzalez Oscar	22	31	30	15	1700	2	1	-	Spain
David Pirri	31	8	2	0	14	0	0	-	Spain
Leonardo Ponzio	23	36	33	27	2514	6	0	2	Argentina (3)
Fernando Soriano	25	35	19	2	466	1	0	-	Spain
Forwards									
Goran Drulic	28	18	8	1	283	0	0	-	Serbia & Montenegro
Luciano Galletti	24	37	37	23	2564	7	0	5	Argentina (3)
Javi Moreno	30	22	17	7	954	5	0	-	Spain
Miguel Piti	24	7	3	0	32	0	0	-	Spain
Savio	31	37	36	35	3116	4	0	-	Brazil
David Villa	23	35	35	27	2806	7	0	-	Spain

TEAM OF THE SEASON

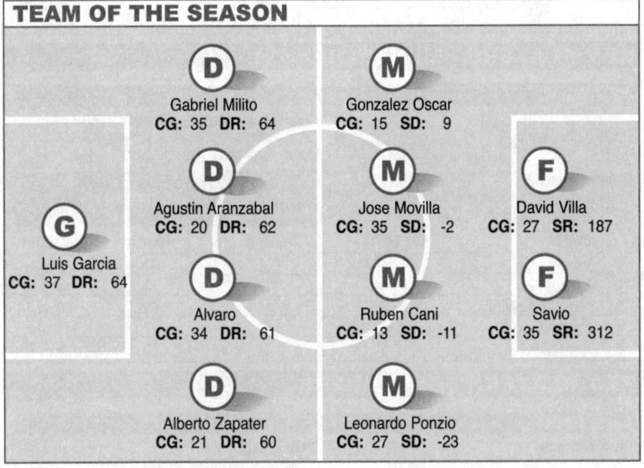

G
Luis Garcia
CG: 37 DR: 64
D
Gabriel Milito
CG: 35 DR: 64
D
Agustin Aranzabal
CG: 20 DR: 62
D
Alvaro
CG: 34 DR: 61
D
Alberto Zapater
CG: 21 DR: 60
M
Gonzalez Oscar
CG: 15 SD: 9
M
Jose Movilla
CG: 35 SD: -2
M
Ruben Cani
CG: 13 SD: -11
M
Leonardo Ponzio
CG: 27 SD: -23
F
David Villa
CG: 27 SR: 187
F
Savio
CG: 35 SR: 312

SQUAD APPEARANCES

Match	1	2	3	4	5	6	7	8	9	10	11	12	13	14	15	16	17	18	19	20	21	22	23	24	25	26	27	28	29	30	31	32	33	34	35	36	37	38	39	40	41	42	43	44	45	46	47	48
Venue	H	A	H	H	A	H	A	A	H	H	A	H	A	A	A	H	A	H	H	A	A	H	A	H	A	A	H	A	H	A	A	H	H	A	H	A	A	H	H	H	A	H	A	H	A	H	A	H
Competition	L	L	E	L	L	L	E	L	L	E	L	L	E	L	L	L	L	E	L	L	E	L	L	L	L	L	L	L	L	E	L	E	L	L	L	E	L	E	L	L	L	L	L	L	L	L	L	L
Result	W	D	W	W	L	W	W	L	W	W	L	W	L	D	D	L	L	W	L	D	D	L	W	W	L	L	W	L	L	W	D	W	W	L	W	D	W	D	D	D	W	W	L	W	L	D	L	L

Goalkeepers
Ruben Falcon
Cesar Lainez
Luis Garcia
Martinez Miguel
Jorge Zapa

Defenders
Alvaro
Agustin Aranzabal
Manuel Capi
Jimenez Cesar
Luis Cuartero
Gabriel Milito
Delio Toledo
Alberto Zapater

Midfielders
Juan Camacho
Ruben Cani
David Generelo
Juan Granero
Jose Movilla
Gonzalez Oscar
David Pirri
Leonardo Ponzio
Fernando Soriano

Forwards
Goran Drulic
Luciano Galletti
Javi Moreno
Miguel Piti
Savio
David Villa

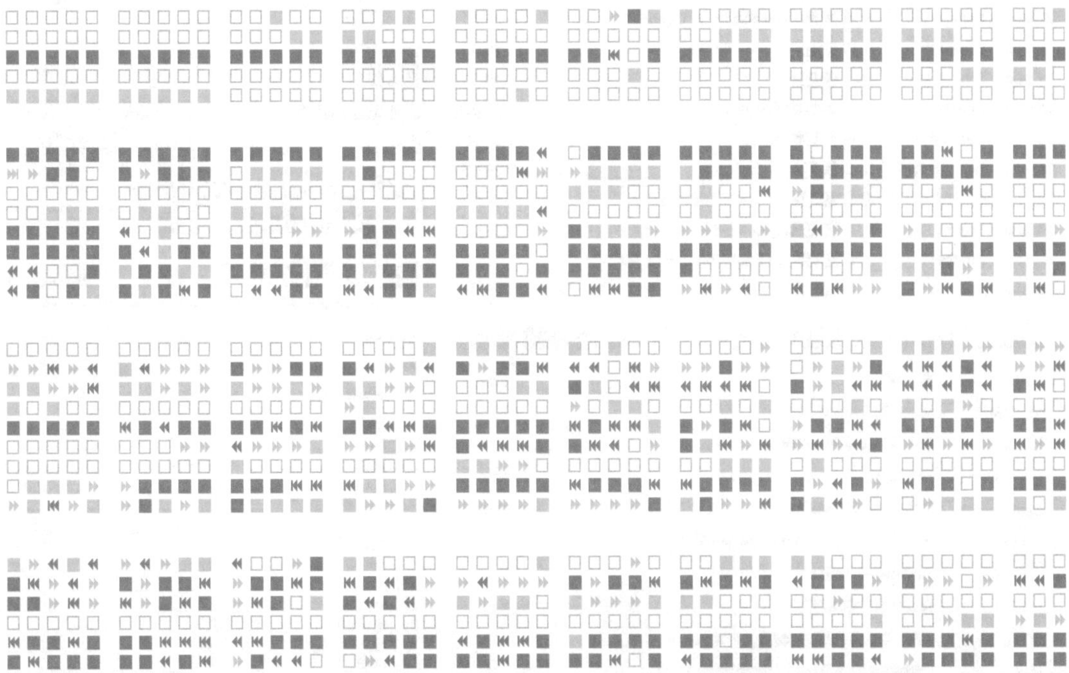

KEY: On all match | On bench | Subbed or sent off (Counting game) | Subbed or sent off (playing less than 70 minutes) | Subbed on from bench (Counting Game) | Subbed on (playing less than 70 minutes) | Subbed on and then subbed or sent off (Counting Game) | Subbed on and then subbed or sent off (playing less than 70 minutes) | Not in 16

REAL SOCIEDAD

Final Position: **13th**

KEY: Won / Drawn / Lost

							Attendance
1	sppr1	**Levante**	H	D	1-1	Nihat 47	32,000
2	sppr1	**Villarreal**	A	D	0-0		17,000
3	sppr1	**Valencia**	A	L	1-3	Arteta 81 pen	35,000
4	sppr1	**R Santander**	H	L	0-1		22,000
5	sppr1	**Seville**	A	L	1-2	Rossato 33	33,000
6	sppr1	**Atl Madrid**	H	W	1-0	Kovacevic 41	21,000
7	sppr1	**Real Zaragoza**	A	L	1-2	Karpin 36 pen	29,000
8	sppr1	**Mallorca**	H	W	2-1	Karpin 13 pen; De Paula 85	23,000
9	sppr1	**Numancia**	A	W	2-0	Labaka 69; Karpin 80	10,000
10	sppr1	**Espanyol**	H	L	0-2		24,000
11	sppr1	**Osasuna**	A	L	0-1		15,000
12	sppr1	**Athl Bilbao**	H	W	3-2	Nihat 57,66; Gabilondo 74	26,000
13	sppr1	**Deportivo**	A	D	2-2	Nihat 33; Kovacevic 51	24,000
14	sppr1	**Real Betis**	H	W	1-0	Kovacevic 36	18,000
15	sppr1	**Getafe**	H	D	1-1	Nihat 70	22,000
16	sppr1	**Malaga**	A	W	5-1	Kovacevic 11,52; Labaka 60; Nihat 70,81	16,000
17	sppr1	**Real Madrid**	A	L	1-2	Nihat 72	70,000
18	sppr1	**Albacete**	H	L	0-2		21,000
19	sppr1	**Barcelona**	A	L	0-1		69,000
20	sppr1	**Levante**	A	L	1-2	Nihat 54	14,000
21	sppr1	**Villarreal**	H	L	0-4		20,000
22	sppr1	**Valencia**	H	D	3-3	Nihat 45,90; Aramburu 79	16,000
23	sppr1	**R Santander**	A	W	3-1	Aramburu 8; Nihat 10,35	14,000
24	sppr1	**Seville**	H	W	1-0	Kovacevic 86	24,000
25	sppr1	**Atl Madrid**	A	L	0-1		45,000
26	sppr1	**Real Zaragoza**	H	W	2-1	Karpin 45 pen; Barkero 74	25,000
27	sppr1	**Mallorca**	A	L	2-3	Aramburu 7; Uranga 16	10,000
28	sppr1	**Numancia**	H	W	2-1	Kovacevic 7; Barkero 85	22,000
29	sppr1	**Espanyol**	A	D	2-2	Kovacevic 23; De Paula 76,78	20,000
30	sppr1	**Osasuna**	H	W	2-0	Uranga 42; Karpin 45	25,000
31	sppr1	**Athl Bilbao**	A	L	0-3		40,000
32	sppr1	**Deportivo**	H	W	1-0	Uranga 17	16,000
33	sppr1	**Real Betis**	A	W	3-2	Labaka 4; Barkero 66; Uranga 90	35,000
34	sppr1	**Real Madrid**	H	L	0-2		26,000
35	sppr1	**Getafe**	A	L	0-2		14,000
36	sppr1	**Malaga**	H	L	1-3	Agirretxe 82	16,000
37	sppr1	**Albacete**	A	D	2-2	De Paula 82; Uranga 90	6,000
38	sppr1	**Barcelona**	H	D	0-0		25,000

MONTHLY POINTS TALLY

AUGUST	1	33%
SEPTEMBER	1	8%
OCTOBER	9	75%
NOVEMBER	4	33%
DECEMBER	7	78%
JANUARY	0	0%
FEBRUARY	7	58%
MARCH	7	58%
APRIL	9	60%
MAY	2	17%

KEY PLAYERS - GOALSCORERS

Kahveci Nihat

Goals in the League	13	Player Strike Rate Average number of minutes between League goals scored by player	144
Contribution to Attacking Power Average number of minutes between League team goals while on pitch	69	Club Strike Rate Average number of minutes between League goals scored by club	71

	PLAYER	LGE GOALS	POWER	STRIKE RATE
1	Kahveci Nihat	13	69	144 mins
2	Garikoitz Uranga	5	76	290 mins
3	Darko Kovacevic	8	71	322 mins
4	Valeri Karpin	5	61	545 mins
5	Mikel Labaka	3	62	900 mins

KEY PLAYERS - MIDFIELDERS

Valeri Karpin

Goals in the League	5	Contribution to Attacking Power Average number of minutes between League team goals while on pitch	61
Defensive Rating Average number of mins between League goals conceded while on the pitch	62	Scoring Difference Defensive Rating minus Contribution to Attacking Power	1

	PLAYER	LGE GOALS	DEF RATE	POWER	SCORE DIFF
1	Valeri Karpin	5	62	61	1 mins
2	Xavier Prieto	0	70	74	-4 mins
3	Miguel Aramburu	3	61	69	-8 mins
4	Mikel Alonso	0	67	77	-10 mins
5	Igor Gabilondo	1	54	78	-24 mins

KEY PLAYERS - DEFENDERS

Lopez Rekarte

Goals Conceded Number of League goals conceded while the player was on the pitch	33	Clean Sheets In games when player was on pitch for at least 70 minutes	5
Defensive Rating Ave number of mins between League goals conceded while on the pitch	65	Club Defensive Rating Average number of mins between League goals conceded by the club this season	61

	PLAYER	CON LGE	CLEAN SHEETS	DEF RATE
1	Lopez Rekarte	33	5	65 mins
2	Javier Garrido	36	6	65 mins
3	Adriano Rossato	23	3	61 mins
4	Luiz Alberto	39	5	60 mins
5	Mikel Labaka	45	6	60 mins

KEY GOALKEEPER

Asier Riesgo

Goals Conceded in the League	52	Counting Games Games when player was on pitch for at least 70 minutes	36
Defensive Rating Ave number of mins between League goals conceded while on the pitch	61	Clean Sheets In games when player was on pitch for at least 70 minutes	8

LEAGUE GOALS

Kahveci Nihat

Minutes on the pitch	1877	Goals in the League	13
League average (mins between goals)	144		

	PLAYER	MINS	GOALS	AVE
1	Nihat	1877	13	144
2	Kovacevic	2578	8	322
3	Karpin	2727	5	545
4	Uranga	1451	5	290
5	De Paula	837	4	209
6	Barkero	701	3	234
7	Aramburu	2913	3	971
8	Labaka	2700	3	900
9	Rossato	1404	1	1404
10	Arteta	487	1	487
11	Gabilondo	1407	1	1407
12	Agirretxe	60	1	60
	Other		0	
	TOTAL		48	

DISCIPLINARY RECORDS

	PLAYER	YELLOW	RED	AVE
1	Alkiza	5	0	141
2	Mladenovic	2	0	237
3	Arteta	2	0	243
4	Prieto	3	1	313
5	Barkero	2	0	350
6	Rossato	3	1	351
7	Nihat	5	0	375
8	Karpin	6	1	389
9	Aramburu	7	0	416
10	Lopez Rekarte	5	0	432
11	Kovacevic	5	0	515
12	Alonso	4	0	555
13	Riesgo	4	1	632
	Other	12	0	
	TOTAL	65	4	

TOP POINT EARNERS

	PLAYER	GAMES	AV PTS
1	Darko Kovacevic	27	1.48
2	Iban Zubiaurre	14	1.43
3	Mikel Labaka	30	1.40
4	Valeri Karpin	29	1.38
5	Javier Garrido	24	1.38
6	Miguel Aramburu	32	1.31
7	Adriano Rossato	14	1.29
8	Garikoitz Uranga	12	1.25
9	Kahveci Nihat	21	1.24
10	Mikel Alonso	21	1.24
	CLUB AVERAGE:		1.24

TEAM OF THE SEASON

G
Asier Riesgo
CG: 35 DR: 61
D
Javier Garrido
CG: 24 DR: 65
D
Lopez Rekarte
CG: 24 DR: 65
D
Adriano Rossato
CG: 14 DR: 61
D
Mikel Labaka
CG: 30 DR: 60
M
Valeri Karpin
CG: 29 SD: 1
M
Miguel Aramburu
CG: 32 SD: -8
M
Mikel Alonso
CG: 21 SD: -10
M
Xavier Prieto
CG: 11 SD: -4
F
Kahveci Nihat
CG: 21 SR: 144
F
Garikoitz Uranga
CG: 12 SR: 290

LEAGUE APPEARANCES, BOOKINGS AND CAPS

	AGE (on 01/07/05)	IN NAMED 18	APPEARANCES	COUNTING GAMES	MINUTES ON PITCH	YELLOW CARDS	RED CARDS	THIS SEASON	HOME COUNTRY
Goalkeepers									
Lopez Alberto	36	38	4	2	259	0	0	-	Spain
Asier Riesgo	21	36	36	35	3161	4	1	-	Spain
Defenders									
Ignacio Azpilicueta	23	8	0	0	0	0	0	-	Spain
Jeremie Brechet	25	20	18	15	1356	1	0	-	France
Javier Garrido	20	33	29	24	2356	2	0	-	Spain
Mikel Labaka	24	37	30	30	2700	3	0	-	Spain
Lopez Rekarte	29	36	24	24	2160	5	0	-	Spain
Luiz Alberto	27	35	27	26	2350	2	0	-	Brazil
Adriano Rossato	27	31	21	14	1404	3	1	-	Brazil
Iban Zubiaurre	22	21	14	14	1260	1	0	-	Spain
Midfielders									
Bittor Alkiza	34	16	10	5	709	5	0	-	Spain
Mikel Alonso	25	33	30	21	2220	4	0	-	Spain
Miguel Aramburu	26	37	36	32	2913	7	0	-	Spain
Mikel Arteta	23	16	15	2	487	2	0	-	Spain
Jose Barkero	26	18	13	6	701	2	0	-	Spain
Igor Gabilondo	26	35	26	11	1407	0	0	-	Spain
Igor Jauregui	31	5	5	5	450	2	0	-	Spain
Valeri Karpin	36	35	33	29	2727	6	1	-	Russia
Gorka Larrea	21	6	3	0	20	0	0	-	Spain
Gonzalez Mikel	-	5	4	3	318	0	0	-	Spain
Dragan Mladenovic	29	15	12	3	475	2	0	4	Serbia & Mont (46)
Xavier Prieto	21	27	23	11	1255	3	1	-	Spain
Forwards									
Imanol Agirretxe	18	4	3	0	60	0	0	-	Spain
Oscar De Paula	30	24	18	7	837	1	0	-	Spain
Juan Dominguez	21	6	2	0	23	0	0	-	Spain
Darko Kovacevic	31	31	30	27	2578	5	0	5	Serbia & Mont (46)
Kahveci Nihat	25	23	23	21	1877	5	0	-	Turkey
Estefania Oskitz	18	13	3	0	64	0	0	-	Spain
Garikoitz Uranga	25	34	28	12	1451	2	0	-	Spain

SQUAD APPEARANCES

Match	1	2	3	4	5	6	7	8	9	10	11	12	13	14	15	16	17	18	19	20	21	22	23	24	25	26	27	28	29	30	31	32	33	34	35	36	37	38
Venue	H	A	A	H	A	H	A	H	A	H	A	H	A	H	H	A	A	H	A	A	H	H	A	H	A	H	A	H	A	H	A	H	A	H	A	H	A	H
Competition	L	L	L	L	L	L	L	L	L	L	L	L	L	L	L	L	L	L	L	L	L	L	L	L	L	L	L	L	L	L	L	L	L	L	L	L	L	L
Result	D	D	L	L	L	W	L	W	W	L	L	W	D	W	D	W	L	L	L	L	L	D	W	W	L	W	L	W	D	W	L	W	W	L	L	L	D	D

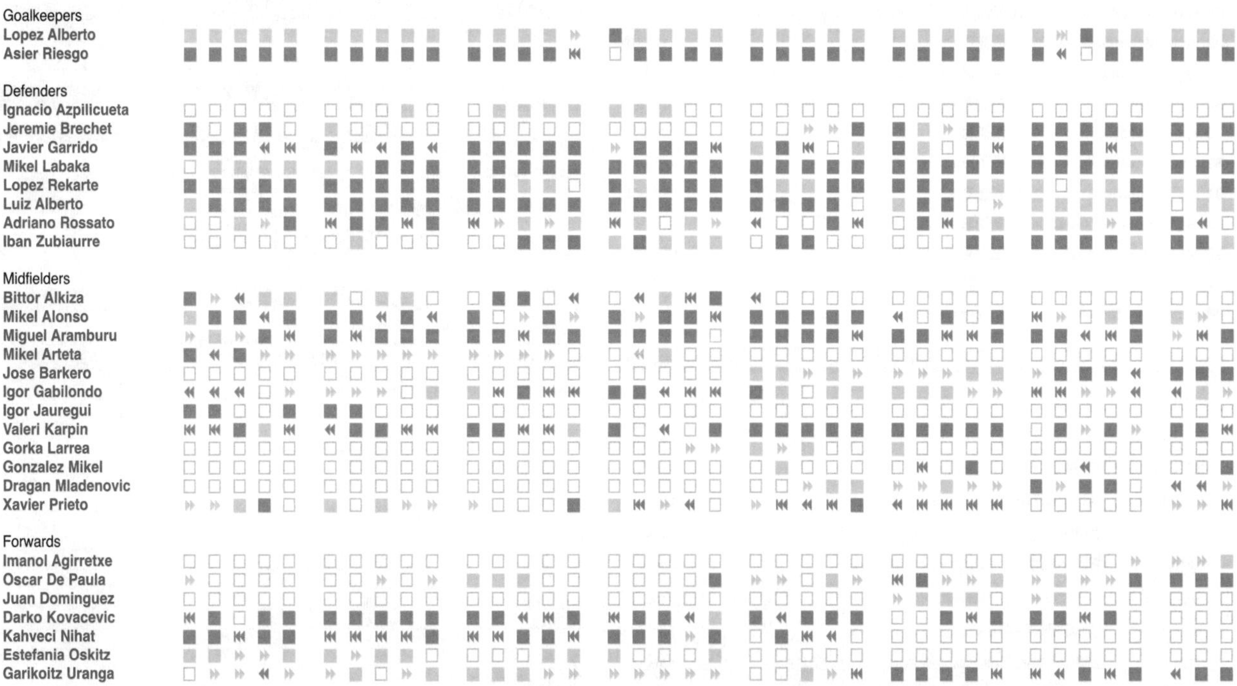

Goalkeepers
Lopez Alberto
Asier Riesgo
Defenders
Ignacio Azpilicueta
Jeremie Brechet
Javier Garrido
Mikel Labaka
Lopez Rekarte
Luiz Alberto
Adriano Rossato
Iban Zubiaurre
Midfielders
Bittor Alkiza
Mikel Alonso
Miguel Aramburu
Mikel Arteta
Jose Barkero
Igor Gabilondo
Igor Jauregui
Valeri Karpin
Gorka Larrea
Gonzalez Mikel
Dragan Mladenovic
Xavier Prieto
Forwards
Imanol Agirretxe
Oscar De Paula
Juan Dominguez
Darko Kovacevic
Kahveci Nihat
Estefania Oskitz
Garikoitz Uranga

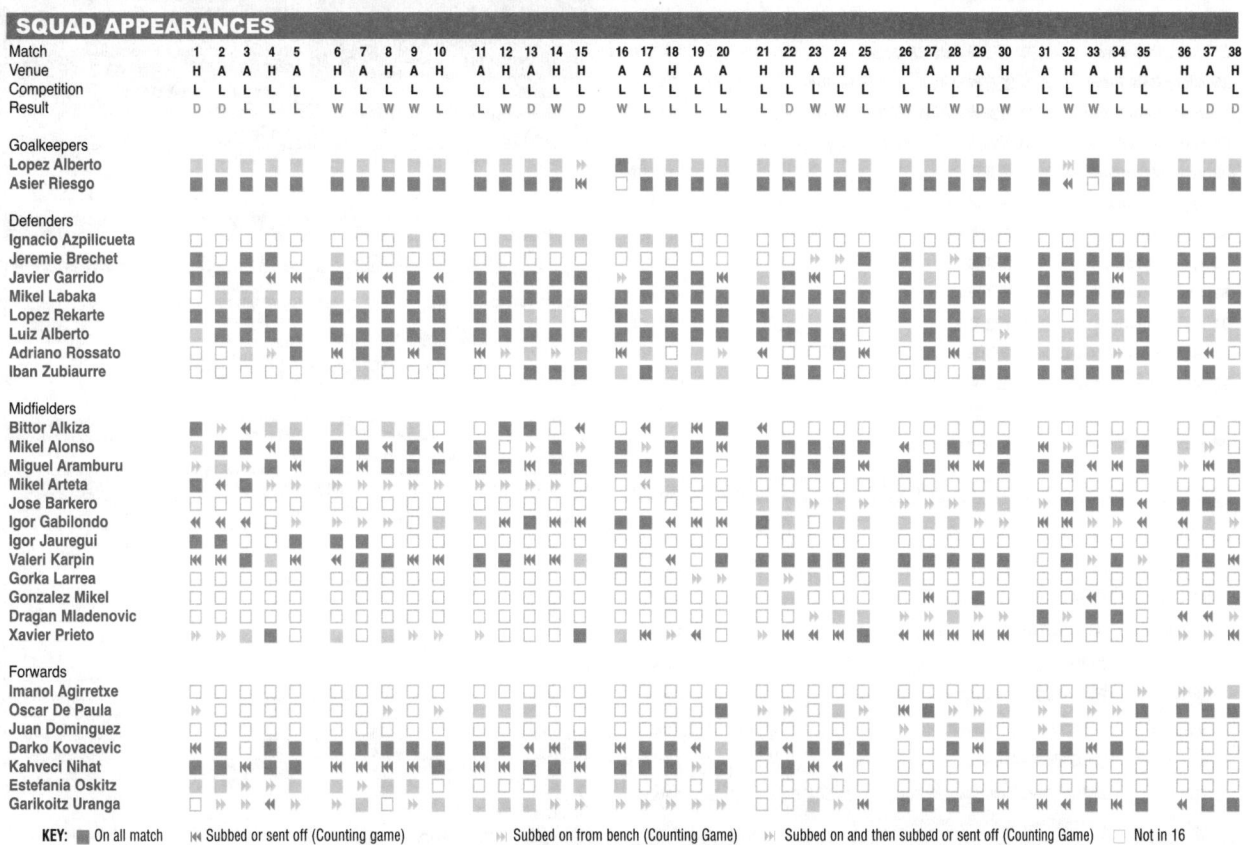

KEY: On all match · On bench · Subbed or sent off (Counting game) · Subbed or sent off (playing less than 70 minutes) · Subbed on from bench (Counting Game) · Subbed on (playing less than 70 minutes) · Subbed on and then subbed or sent off (Counting Game) · Subbed on and then subbed or sent off (playing less than 70 minutes) · Not in 16

GETAFE

Final Position: **14th**

KEY: Won Drawn Lost

							Attendance
1	sppr1	**Real Zaragoza**	A	L	1-3	Jose Antonio 17	33,000
2	sppr1	**Mallorca**	H	L	1-2	Nano 85	13,000
3	sppr1	**Numancia**	A	L	0-1		9,000
4	sppr1	**Espanyol**	H	W	1-0	Ibarra 11 og	16,000
5	sppr1	**Osasuna**	A	L	1-2	Pachon 45	14,000
6	sppr1	**Athl Bilbao**	H	W	3-1	Pachon 2,61,65	15,000
7	sppr1	**Deportivo**	A	L	1-2	Cotelo 90	26,000
8	sppr1	**Real Betis**	H	L	0-2		13,000
9	sppr1	**Real Madrid**	A	L	0-2		70,000
10	sppr1	**Valencia**	H	W	1-0	Michel 18	14,000
11	sppr1	**Malaga**	H	W	1-0	Gallardo 47	13,000
12	sppr1	**Albacete**	A	D	1-1	Gabi 85	15,000
13	sppr1	**Barcelona**	H	L	1-2	Craioveanu 68	15,000
14	sppr1	**Levante**	A	D	0-0		10,000
15	sppr1	**Villarreal**	H	L	1-2	Nano 81	12,000
16	sppr1	**Real Sociedad**	A	D	1-1	Pernia 80 pen	22,000
17	sppr1	**R Santander**	H	W	2-0	Riki 5,32	12,000
18	sppr1	**Seville**	A	D	0-0		40,000
19	sppr1	**Atl Madrid**	H	D	1-1	Pachon 64	14,000
20	sppr1	**Real Zaragoza**	H	W	3-0	Yordi 13; Nano 15; Cotelo 35	13,000
21	sppr1	**Mallorca**	A	L	1-3	Yordi 25	17,000
22	sppr1	**Numancia**	H	W	1-0	Kome 28	10,000
23	sppr1	**Espanyol**	A	L	0-2		19,000
24	sppr1	**Osasuna**	H	D	0-0		12,000
25	sppr1	**Deportivo**	H	D	1-1	Gabi 72	14,000
26	sppr1	**Real Betis**	A	D	2-2	Dorado 16; Pernia 48	35,000
27	sppr1	**Real Madrid**	H	W	2-1	Raul Albiol 36; Riki 47	14,000
28	sppr1	**Athl Bilbao**	A	W	2-1	Kome 64; Michel 80	30,000
29	sppr1	**Valencia**	A	L	1-3	Pernia 75	42,000
30	sppr1	**Malaga**	A	D	1-1	Nano 32	18,000
31	sppr1	**Albacete**	H	W	1-0	Dorado 65	5,000
32	sppr1	**Barcelona**	A	L	0-2		83,000
33	sppr1	**Levante**	H	W	1-0	Michel 20	16,000
34	sppr1	**Villarreal**	A	L	0-4		14,000
35	sppr1	**Real Sociedad**	H	W	2-0	Michel 31,42	14,000
36	sppr1	**R Santander**	A	L	1-2	Dorado 52	13,000
37	sppr1	**Seville**	H	D	0-0		14,000
38	sppr1	**Atl Madrid**	A	D	2-2	Cubillo 21 pen; Craioveanu 54	15,000

MONTHY POINTS TALLY

AUGUST	0	0%
SEPTEMBER	3	25%
OCTOBER	3	25%
NOVEMBER	7	58%
DECEMBER	5	42%
JANUARY	5	42%
FEBRUARY	4	44%
MARCH	8	53%
APRIL	7	58%
MAY	5	33%

KEY PLAYERS - GOALSCORERS

Valentin Pachon

Goals in the League	5	**Player Strike Rate** Average number of minutes between League goals scored by player	267
Contribution to Attacking Power Average number of minutes between League team goals while on pitch	102	**Club Strike Rate** Average number of minutes between League goals scored by club	90

	PLAYER	LGE GOALS	POWER	STRIKE RATE
1	Valentin Pachon	5	102	267 mins
2	Ivan Riki	3	89	624 mins
3	Victoriano Nano	4	92	833 mins
4	Angel Dorado	3	92	1044 mins
5	Mariano Pernia	3	89	1077 mins

KEY PLAYERS - MIDFIELDERS

Raul Albiol

Goals in the League	1	**Contribution to Attacking Power** Average number of minutes between League team goals while on pitch	85
Defensive Rating Average number of mins between League goals conceded while on the pitch	97	**Scoring Difference** Defensive Rating minus Contribution to Attacking Power	12

	PLAYER	LGE GOALS	DEF RATE	POWER	SCORE DIFF
1	Raul Albiol	1	97	85	12 mins
2	Fernandez Gabi	2	87	93	-6 mins
3	Mario Cotelo	2	69	84	-15 mins
4	Angel Dorado	3	75	92	-17 mins
5	Diego Rivas	0	71	93	-22 mins

KEY PLAYERS - DEFENDERS

David Belenguer

Goals Conceded Number of League goals conceded while the player was on the pitch	30	**Clean Sheets** In games when player was on pitch for at least 70 minutes	12
Defensive Rating Ave number of mins between League goals conceded while on the pitch	87	**Club Defensive Rating** Average number of mins between League goals conceded by the club this season	74

	PLAYER	CON LGE	CLEAN SHEETS	DEF RATE
1	David Belenguer	30	12	87 mins
2	Jose Yanguas	22	6	79 mins
3	Victoriano Nano	45	13	74 mins
4	Mariano Pernia	44	12	73 mins

KEY GOALKEEPER

Javier Broto

Goals Conceded in the League	22	**Counting Games** Games when player was on pitch for at least 70 minutes	20
Defensive Rating Ave number of mins between League goals conceded while on the pitch	82	**Clean Sheets** In games when player was on pitch for at least 70 minutes	9

LEAGUE GOALS

Valentin Pachon

Minutes on the pitch	1333	**Goals in the League**	5
League average (mins between goals)	267		

	PLAYER	MINS	GOALS	AVE
1	Pachon	1333	5	267
2	Michel	540	4	135
3	Nano	3330	4	833
4	Riki	1872	3	624
5	Pernia	3232	3	1077
6	Dorado	3133	3	1044
7	Gabi	2686	2	1343
8	Cotelo	2424	2	1212
9	Craioveanu	1634	2	817
10	Yordi	1244	2	622
11	Kome	1022	2	511
12	Cubillo	307	1	307
13	Jose Antonio	79	1	79
	Other		4	
	TOTAL		38	

DISCIPLINARY RECORDS

	PLAYER	YELLOW	RED	AVE
1	Pulido	3	1	122
2	Diego Rivas	14	0	193
3	Cotelo	10	0	242
4	Michel	2	0	270
5	Gallardo	3	0	308
6	Belenguer	8	0	325
7	Gabi	8	0	335
8	Raul Albiol	4	0	340
9	Kome	3	0	340
10	Pernia	9	0	359
11	Dorado	8	0	391
12	Yordi	3	0	414
13	Nano	8	0	416
	Other	11	1	
	TOTAL	94	2	

TOP POINT EARNERS

	PLAYER	GAMES	AV PTS
1	Raul Albiol	14	1.57
2	Jose Yanguas	19	1.42
3	David Belenguer	29	1.41
4	Javier Broto	20	1.30
5	Diego Rivas	28	1.29
6	Angel Dorado	34	1.26
7	Fernandez Gabi	28	1.25
8	Mario Cotelo	23	1.22
9	Mariano Pernia	36	1.22
10	Victoriano Nano	37	1.19
	CLUB AVERAGE:		1.24

TEAM OF THE SEASON

G
Javier Broto
CG: 20 DR: 82
D
David Belenguer
CG: 29 DR: 87
D
Jose Yanguas
CG: 19 DR: 79
D
Victoriano Nano
CG: 37 DR: 74
D
Mariano Pernia
CG: 36 DR: 73
M
Raul Albiol
CG: 14 SD: 12
M
Fernandez Gabi
CG: 28 SD: -6
M
Mario Cotelo
CG: 23 SD: -15
M
Angel Dorado
CG: 34 SD: -17
F
Valentin Pachon
CG: 14 SR: 267
F
Ivan Riki
CG: 18 SR: 624

LEAGUE APPEARANCES, BOOKINGS AND CAPS

	AGE (on 01/07/05)	IN NAMED 18	APPEARANCES	COUNTING GAMES	MINUTES ON PITCH	YELLOW CARDS	RED CARDS	THIS SEASON	HOME COUNTRY
Goalkeepers									
Sergio Aragoneses	28	16	11	10	901	1	0	-	Spain
Javier Broto	33	30	20	20	1800	1	1	-	Spain
Sanchez Sergio	28	27	8	8	720	1	0	-	Spain
Defenders									
Ivan Amaya	26	12	5	5	450	1	0	-	Spain
David Belenguer	32	37	30	29	2605	8	0	-	Spain
Jose Antonio	20	2	1	1	79	0	0	-	Spain
Victoriano Nano	25	37	37	37	3330	8	0	-	Spain
Mariano Pernia	31	37	36	36	3232	9	0	-	Argentina
Martin Pulido	26	16	8	5	490	3	1	-	Spain
Quique Medina	30	3	1	0	8	0	0	-	Spain
Manuel Tena	28	20	4	2	308	0	0	-	Spain
Jose Yanguas	33	34	20	19	1741	2	0	-	Spain
Midfielders									
Ruiz Alberto	27	6	2	0	107	0	0	-	Spain
Mario Cotelo	30	34	32	23	2424	10	0	-	Spain
David Cubillo	27	29	6	2	307	2	0	-	Spain
Diego Rivas	25	35	33	28	2707	14	0	-	Spain
Angel Dorado	28	37	36	34	3133	8	0	-	Spain
Fernandez Gabi	21	32	32	28	2686	8	0	-	Spain
Daniel Kome	25	26	21	8	1022	3	0	1	Cameroon (26)
Michel	29	15	10	0	265	0	0	-	Spain
Raul Albiol	19	23	17	14	1360	4	0	-	Spain
Martin Vitali	29	7	2	1	136	1	0	-	Spain
Forwards									
Jaime Asen	26	12	6	0	217	0	0	-	Spain
Gheorghe Craioveanu	37	35	35	10	1634	3	0	-	Romania
Francisco Gallardo	25	34	22	5	924	3	0	-	Spain
Gonzalez Michel	27	13	11	5	540	2	0	-	Spain
Valentin Pachon	28	18	18	14	1333	2	0	-	Spain
Ivan Riki	24	31	29	18	1872	1	0	-	Spain
Jorge Yordi	30	32	26	9	1244	3	0	-	Spain

SQUAD APPEARANCES

Match	1	2	3	4	5	6	7	8	9	10	11	12	13	14	15	16	17	18	19	20	21	22	23	24	25	26	27	28	29	30	31	32	33	34	35	36	37	38
Venue	A	H	A	H	A	H	A	H	A	H	H	A	H	A	H	A	H	A	H	H	A	H	A	H	H	A	H	A	A	A	H	A	H	A	H	A	H	A
Competition	L	L	L	L	L	L	L	L	L	L	L	L	L	L	L	L	L	L	L	L	L	L	L	L	L	L	L	L	L	L	L	L	L	L	L	L	L	L
Result	L	L	L	W	L	W	L	L	L	W	W	D	L	D	L	D	W	D	D	W	L	W	L	D	D	D	W	W	L	D	W	L	W	L	W	L	D	D

Goalkeepers
Sergio Aragoneses
Javier Broto
Sanchez Sergio

Defenders
Ivan Amaya
David Belenguer
Jose Antonio
Victoriano Nano
Mariano Pernia
Martin Pulido
Quique Medina
Manuel Tena
Jose Yanguas

Midfielders
Ruiz Alberto
Mario Cotelo
David Cubillo
Diego Rivas
Angel Dorado
Fernandez Gabi
Daniel Kome
Michel
Raul Albiol
Martin Vitali

Forwards
Jaime Asen
Gheorghe Craioveanu
Francisco Gallardo
Gonzalez Michel
Valentin Pachon
Ivan Riki
Jorge Yordi

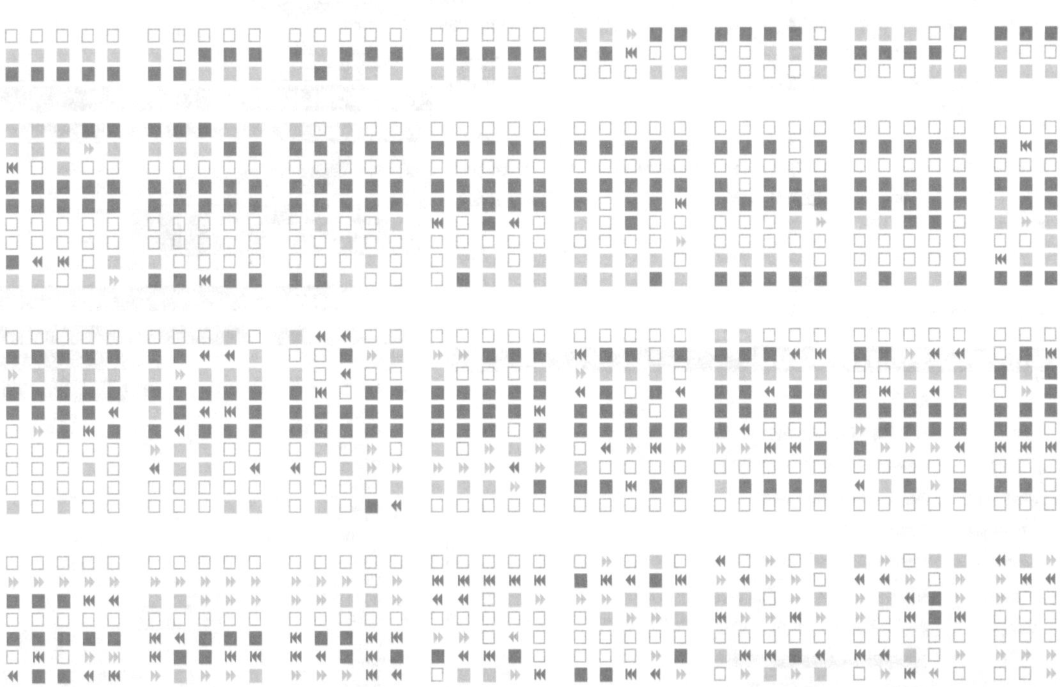

KEY: On all match | On bench | Subbed or sent off (Counting game) | Subbed or sent off (playing less than 70 minutes) | Subbed on from bench (Counting Game) | Subbed on (playing less than 70 minutes) | Subbed on and then subbed or sent off (Counting Game) | Subbed on and then subbed or sent off (playing less than 70 minutes) | Not in 16

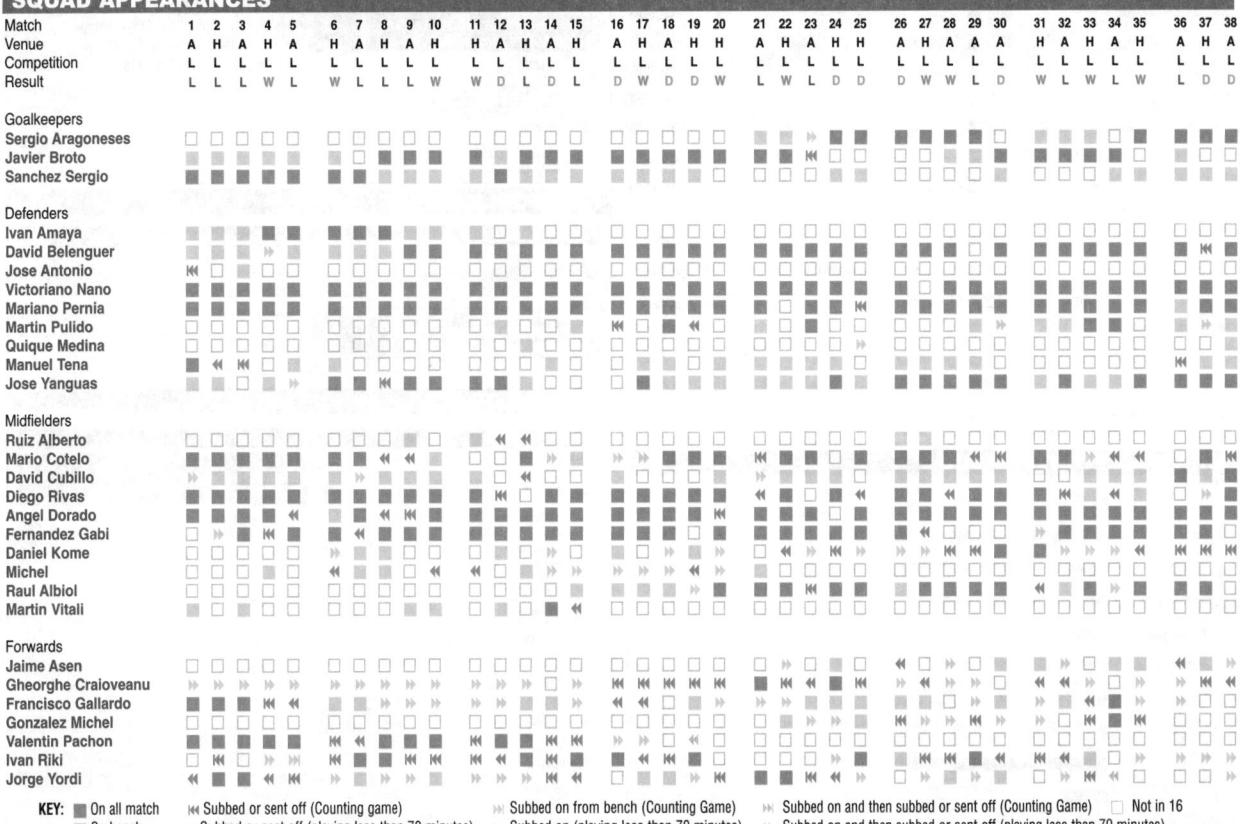

OSASUNA

Final Position: **15th**

KEY: Won Drawn Lost

							Attendance
1	sppr1	**Athl Bilbao**	H	D	1-1	Milosevic 40	19,000
2	sppr1	**Deportivo**	A	W	3-1	Aloisi 57 pen; Milosevic 62,81	23,000
3	sppr1	**Real Betis**	H	W	3-2	Aloisi 54; Melli 72 og; Milosevic 81	16,000
4	sppr1	**Real Madrid**	A	L	0-1		50,000
5	sppr1	**Getafe**	H	W	2-1	Moha 21; Milosevic 45	14,000
6	sppr1	**Malaga**	A	L	0-2		25,000
7	sppr1	**Albacete**	H	W	4-2	Punal 20; Valdo 40; Lopez 66; Francisco 90 og	13,000
8	sppr1	**Barcelona**	A	L	0-3		67,000
9	sppr1	**Levante**	H	L	0-1		14,000
10	sppr1	**Villarreal**	A	L	0-3		16,000
11	sppr1	**Real Sociedad**	H	W	1-0	Morales 69	15,000
12	sppr1	**R Santander**	A	D	1-1	Morales 20	13,000
13	sppr1	**Seville**	H	W	4-1	Munoz 21; Webo 57; Morales 86; Moha 90	15,000
14	sppr1	**Atl Madrid**	A	L	2-3	Valdo 45; Morales 74	45,000
15	sppr1	**Real Zaragoza**	H	D	2-2	Morales 4; Punal 75 pen	13,000
16	sppr1	**Mallorca**	A	W	2-1	Valdo 33,41	14,000
17	sppr1	**Numancia**	H	W	2-0	Morales 49,68	14,000
18	sppr1	**Espanyol**	A	L	1-4	Webo 16	19,000
19	sppr1	**Valencia**	H	D	0-0		16,000
20	sppr1	**Athl Bilbao**	A	L	3-4	Garcia, P 14; Webo 48; Punal 56	32,000
21	sppr1	**Deportivo**	H	D	1-1	Pablo Amo 65 og	14,000
22	sppr1	**Real Betis**	A	L	1-3	Valdo 17	36,000
23	sppr1	**Real Madrid**	H	L	1-2	Webo 36	15,000
24	sppr1	**Getafe**	A	D	0-0		12,000
25	sppr1	**Malaga**	H	L	1-6	Aloisi 52	15,000
26	sppr1	**Albacete**	A	D	1-1	Morales 67	15,000
27	sppr1	**Barcelona**	H	L	0-1		19,000
28	sppr1	**Levante**	A	L	0-4		16,000
29	sppr1	**Real Sociedad**	A	L	0-2		25,000
30	sppr1	**R Santander**	H	W	1-0	Webo 49	18,000
31	sppr1	**Seville**	A	W	1-0	Morales 25	40,000
32	sppr1	**Atl Madrid**	H	W	1-0	Aloisi 4	16,000
33	sppr1	**Villarreal**	H	W	3-2	Webo 39; Ortiz 67; Aloisi 88	16,000
34	sppr1	**Real Zaragoza**	A	L	1-5	Moha 65	29,000
35	sppr1	**Mallorca**	H	D	1-1	Milosevic 83	10,000
36	sppr1	**Numancia**	A	D	2-2	Ortiz 12; Aloisi 16	7,000
37	sppr1	**Espanyol**	H	D	1-1	Lopo 22 og	14,000
38	sppr1	**Valencia**	A	L	0-1		25,000

MONTHLY POINTS TALLY

AUGUST	1	33%
SEPTEMBER	9	75%
OCTOBER	3	25%
NOVEMBER	7	58%
DECEMBER	7	58%
JANUARY	2	17%
FEBRUARY	1	8%
MARCH	1	11%
APRIL	12	80%
MAY	3	20%

KEY PLAYERS - GOALSCORERS

Richard Morales

Goals in the League	9	Player Strike Rate Average number of minutes between League goals scored by player	180
Contribution to Attacking Power Average number of minutes between League team goals while on pitch	64	Club Strike Rate Average number of minutes between League goals scored by club	73

	PLAYER	LGE GOALS	POWER	STRIKE RATE
1	Richard Morales	9	64	180 mins
2	Savo Milosevic	6	89	269 mins
3	Pierre Webo	6	66	278 mins
4	Valmiro Valdo	5	60	345 mins
5	El Yaagoubi Moha	3	92	734 mins

KEY PLAYERS - MIDFIELDERS

Valmiro Valdo

Goals in the League	5	Contribution to Attacking Power Average number of minutes between League team goals while on pitch	60
Defensive Rating Average number of mins between League goals conceded while on the pitch	69	Scoring Difference Defensive Rating minus Contribution to Attacking Power	9

	PLAYER	LGE GOALS	DEF RATE	POWER	SCORE DIFF
1	Valmiro Valdo	5	69	60	9 mins
2	Pablo Garcia	1	57	68	-11 mins
3	Francisco Punal	3	50	73	-23 mins
4	El Yaagoubi Moha	3	55	92	-37 mins
5	Inaki Munoz	1	47	88	-41 mins

KEY PLAYERS - DEFENDERS

Unai Exposito

Goals Conceded Number of League goals conceded while the player was on the pitch	31	Clean Sheets In games when player was on pitch for at least 70 minutes	3
Defensive Rating Ave number of mins between League goals conceded while on the pitch	56	Club Defensive Rating Average number of mins between League goals conceded by the club this season	53

	PLAYER	CON LGE	CLEAN SHEETS	DEF RATE
1	Unai Exposito	31	3	56 mins
2	Jose Romero Josetxo	48	6	55 mins
3	Enrique Corrales	45	3	54 mins
4	Cesar Cruchaga	54	5	50 mins
5	Jose Izquierdo	33	3	49 mins

KEY GOALKEEPER

Ricardo Sanzol

Goals Conceded in the League	28	Counting Games League games when player was on pitch for at least 70 minutes	17
Defensive Rating Ave number of mins between League goals conceded while on the pitch	55	Clean Sheets In games when player was on pitch for at least 70 minutes	2

LEAGUE GOALS

Richard Morales

Minutes on the pitch	1620	Goals in the League	9
League average (mins between goals)	180		

	PLAYER	MINS	GOALS	AVE
1	Morales	1620	9	180
2	Milosevic	1613	6	269
3	Webo	1665	6	278
4	Aloisi	1353	6	226
5	Valdo	1726	5	345
6	Moha	2203	3	734
7	Punal	2776	3	925
8	Ortiz	1223	2	612
9	Garcia, P	2447	1	2447
10	Antonio Lopez	129	1	129
11	Munoz	1501	1	1501
	Other		4	
	TOTAL		47	

DISCIPLINARY RECORDS

	PLAYER	YELLOW	RED	AVE
1	Garcia, P	18	2	122
2	Delporte	8	0	168
3	Clavero	5	0	198
4	Izquierdo	5	3	201
5	Punal	12	0	231
6	Moha	8	1	244
7	Cuellar	3	1	247
8	Josetxo	9	1	265
9	Morales	6	0	270
10	Exposito	6	0	289
11	Munoz	5	0	300
12	Ortiz	4	0	305
13	Corrales	7	0	347
	Other	18	1	
	TOTAL	114	9	

TOP POINT EARNERS

	PLAYER	GAMES	AV PTS
1	Pierre Webo	15	1.53
2	Savo Milosevic	14	1.50
3	Pablo Garcia	25	1.44
4	Unai Exposito	19	1.42
5	Enrique Corrales	27	1.33
6	Valmiro Valdo	14	1.29
7	Jose Romero Josetxo	29	1.28
8	Francisco Punal	28	1.25
9	Ricardo Sanzol	17	1.24
10	Juantxo Elia	21	1.19
	CLUB AVERAGE:		1.21

LEAGUE APPEARANCES, BOOKINGS AND CAPS

	AGE (on 01/07/05)	IN NAMED 18	APPEARANCES	COUNTING GAMES	MINUTES ON PITCH	YELLOW CARDS	RED CARDS	THIS SEASON	HOME COUNTRY
Goalkeepers									
Juantxo Elia	35	38	21	21	1890	1	0	-	Spain
Eraso Gonzalo	24	6	0	0	0	0	0	-	Spain
Ricardo Sanzol	29	32	17	17	1530	0	0	-	Spain
Defenders									
Antonio Lopez	23	5	3	1	129	0	0	-	Spain
Rafael Clavero	28	22	11	11	990	5	0	-	Spain
Enrique Corrales	23	27	27	27	2430	7	0	-	Spain
Cesar Cruchaga	31	32	31	30	2703	6	1	-	Spain
Carlos Cuellar	33	37	12	11	991	3	1	-	Spain
Unai Exposito	25	26	20	19	1738	6	0	-	Spain
Miguel Flano	20	13	6	4	423	1	0	-	Spain
Jose Izquierdo	24	25	20	16	1608	5	3	-	Spain
Jose Romero Josetxo	30	32	30	29	2657	9	1	-	Spain
Antonio Lopez	23	3	1	0	30	0	0	-	Spain
Juan Ortiz	23	31	23	6	1223	4	0	-	Spain
Midfielders									
David Lopez	22	19	9	3	442	1	0	-	Spain
Ludovic Delporte	25	35	27	9	1348	8	0	-	Spain
Pablo Garcia	28	33	30	25	2447	18	2	5	Uruguay (16)
Raul Garcia	18	2	1	0	1	0	0	-	Spain
Francisco Jusue	25	1	1	1	90	0	0	-	Spain
El Yaagoubi Moha	27	37	36	17	2203	8	1	-	Spain
Inaki Munoz	27	37	26	13	1501	5	0	-	Spain
Francisco Punal	29	36	35	28	2776	12	0	-	Spain
Luis Sota	23	1	1	0	31	0	0	-	Spain
Valmiro Valdo	24	31	26	14	1726	2	0	-	Brazil
Forwards									
John Aloisi	29	32	26	9	1353	3	0	-	Australia
Ivan Rosado	31	10	7	1	211	0	0	-	Spain
Savo Milosevic	31	30	28	14	1613	4	0	7	Serbia & Mont (46)
Richard Morales	30	26	23	15	1620	6	0	5	Uruguay (16)
Pierre Webo	23	33	24	15	1665	2	0	-	Cameroon

TEAM OF THE SEASON

G Ricardo Sanzol CG: 17 DR: 55

D Unai Exposito CG: 19 DR: 56
D Jose Romero Josetxo CG: 29 DR: 55
D Enrique Corrales CG: 27 DR: 54
D Cesar Cruchaga CG: 30 DR: 50

M Valmiro Valdo CG: 14 SD: 9
M Pablo Garcia CG: 25 SD: -11
M Francisco Punal CG: 28 SD: -23
M El Yaagoubi Moha CG: 17 SD: -37

F Richard Morales CG: 15 SR: 180
F Savo Milosevic CG: 14 SR: 269

SQUAD APPEARANCES

Match	1	2	3	4	5	6	7	8	9	10	11	12	13	14	15	16	17	18	19	20	21	22	23	24	25	26	27	28	29	30	31	32	33	34	35	36	37	38
Venue	H	A	H	A	H	A	H	A	H	A	H	A	H	A	H	A	H	A	H	A	H	A	H	A	H	A	H	A	A	H	A	H	H	A	H	A	H	A
Competition	L	L	L	L	L	L	L	L	L	L	L	L	L	L	L	L	L	L	L	L	L	L	L	L	L	L	L	L	L	L	L	L	L	L	L	L	L	L
Result	D	W	W	L	W	L	W	L	L	L	W	D	W	L	D	W	W	L	D	L	D	L	L	D	L	D	L	L	L	W	W	W	W	L	D	D	D	L

Goalkeepers
Juantxo Elia
Eraso Gonzalo
Ricardo Sanzol

Defenders
Antonio Lopez
Rafael Clavero
Enrique Corrales
Cesar Cruchaga
Carlos Cuellar
Unai Exposito
Miguel Flano
Jose Izquierdo
Jose Romero Josetxo
Antonio Lopez
Juan Ortiz

Midfielders
David Lopez
Ludovic Delporte
Pablo Garcia
Raul Garcia
Francisco Jusue
El Yaagoubi Moha
Inaki Munoz
Francisco Punal
Luis Sota
Valmiro Valdo

Forwards
John Aloisi
Ivan Rosado
Savo Milosevic
Richard Morales
Pierre Webo

KEY: On all match / On bench / Subbed or sent off (Counting game) / Subbed or sent off (playing less than 70 minutes) / Subbed on from bench (Counting Game) / Subbed on (playing less than 70 minutes) / Subbed on and then subbed or sent off (Counting Game) / Subbed on and then subbed or sent off (playing less than 70 minutes) / Not in 16

RACING SANTANDER

Final Position: **16th**

KEY: ☐ Won ☐ Drawn ☐ Lost

							Attendance
1	sppr1	**Barcelona**	H	L	0-2		21,000
2	sppr1	**Levante**	A	L	1-3	Aganzo 19	13,000
3	sppr1	**Villarreal**	H	D	1-1	Juanma 90	12,000
4	sppr1	**Real Sociedad**	A	W	1-0	Regueiro 43	22,000
5	sppr1	**Valencia**	A	L	0-2		45,000
6	sppr1	**Seville**	H	D	0-0		12,000
7	sppr1	**Atl Madrid**	A	L	0-1		45,000
8	sppr1	**Real Zaragoza**	H	W	1-0	Regueiro 3	12,000
9	sppr1	**Mallorca**	A	W	2-1	Pedro Lopez 3; Benayoun 90	10,000
10	sppr1	**Numancia**	H	W	2-0	Mora 67; Guerrero 87	13,000
11	sppr1	**Espanyol**	A	L	1-2	Guerrero 56	20,000
12	sppr1	**Osasuna**	H	D	1-1	Corrales 47 og	13,000
13	sppr1	**Athl Bilbao**	A	L	0-3		32,000
14	sppr1	**Deportivo**	H	D	2-2	Benayoun 22; Guerrero 85	12,000
15	sppr1	**Real Betis**	A	L	1-2	Arizmendi 90	35,000
16	sppr1	**Real Madrid**	H	L	2-3	Benayoun 24; Guerrero 50	13,000
17	sppr1	**Getafe**	A	L	0-2		12,000
18	sppr1	**Malaga**	H	W	2-1	Guerrero 26; Regueiro 41	11,000
19	sppr1	**Albacete**	A	D	0-0		15,000
20	sppr1	**Barcelona**	A	L	0-3		67,000
21	sppr1	**Levante**	H	D	2-2	Guerrero 44; Aganzo 75 pen	13,000
22	sppr1	**Villarreal**	A	L	1-2	Regueiro 25	20,000
23	sppr1	**Real Sociedad**	H	L	1-3	Anderson Silva 58	14,000
24	sppr1	**Valencia**	H	W	1-0	Regueiro 52	18,000
25	sppr1	**Seville**	A	D	2-2	Aganzo 41; Regueiro 84	40,000
26	sppr1	**Atl Madrid**	H	W	2-1	Regueiro 38; Aganzo 50	19,000
27	sppr1	**Real Zaragoza**	A	L	0-1		32,000
28	sppr1	**Mallorca**	H	W	3-0	Anderson Silva 1; Aganzo 3; Benayoun 51	13,000
29	sppr1	**Numancia**	A	W	3-2	Regueiro 24; Aganzo 45; Arizmendi 54	9,000
30	sppr1	**Espanyol**	H	L	1-3	Aganzo 35	12,000
31	sppr1	**Osasuna**	A	L	0-1		18,000
32	sppr1	**Athl Bilbao**	H	L	0-2		17,000
33	sppr1	**Deportivo**	A	W	4-1	Benayoun 57,64,84; Guerrero 71	23,000
34	sppr1	**Real Betis**	H	D	1-1	Benayoun 61	15,000
35	sppr1	**Real Madrid**	A	L	0-5		80,000
36	sppr1	**Getafe**	H	W	2-1	Ayoze 12; Arizmendi 36	13,000
37	sppr1	**Malaga**	A	L	0-2		12,000
38	sppr1	**Albacete**	H	W	1-0	Aganzo 32	11,000

MONTHLY POINTS TALLY

AUGUST	0	0%
SEPTEMBER	4	33%
OCTOBER	7	58%
NOVEMBER	4	33%
DECEMBER	1	8%
JANUARY	5	42%
FEBRUARY	4	33%
MARCH	9	75%
APRIL	3	25%
MAY	7	47%

KEY PLAYERS - GOALSCORERS

David Aganzo

Goals in the League	8	Player Strike Rate Average number of minutes between League goals scored by player	178
Contribution to Attacking Power Average number of minutes between League team goals while on pitch	74	Club Strike Rate Average number of minutes between League goals scored by club	81

	PLAYER	LGE GOALS	POWER	STRIKE RATE
1	David Aganzo	8	74	178 mins
2	Javier Guerrero	8	72	325 mins
3	Mario Regueiro	8	75	349 mins
4	Yossi Benayoun	8	77	373 mins
5	Anderson Silva	2	79	1151 mins

KEY PLAYERS - MIDFIELDERS

Fernando Moran

Goals in the League	0	Contribution to Attacking Power Average number of minutes between League team goals while on pitch	66
Defensive Rating Average number of mins between League goals conceded while on the pitch	62	Scoring Difference Defensive Rating minus Contribution to Attacking Power	-4

	PLAYER	LGE GOALS	DEF RATE	POWER	SCORE DIFF
1	Fernando Moran	0	62	66	-4 mins
2	Mario Regueiro	8	61	75	-14 mins
3	Yossi Benayoun	8	59	77	-18 mins
4	Anderson Silva	2	55	79	-24 mins

KEY PLAYERS - DEFENDERS

Pedro Lopez

Goals Conceded Number of League goals conceded while the player was on the pitch	21	Clean Sheets In games when player was on pitch for at least 70 minutes	6
Defensive Rating Ave number of mins between League goals conceded while on the pitch	80	Club Defensive Rating Average number of mins between League goals conceded by the club this season	59

	PLAYER	CON LGE	CLEAN SHEETS	DEF RATE
1	Pedro Lopez	21	6	80 mins
2	Jose Mora	53	7	57 mins
3	Lozano Oriol	37	4	57 mins
4	Pablo Casar	21	3	56 mins
5	Juanma	23	3	55 mins

KEY GOALKEEPER

Dudu Aouate

Goals Conceded in the League	56	Counting Games Games when player was on pitch for at least 70 minutes	37
Defensive Rating Ave number of mins between League goals conceded while on the pitch	59	Clean Sheets In games when player was on pitch for at least 70 minutes	8

LEAGUE GOALS

David Aganzo

Minutes on the pitch	1423	Goals in the League	8
League average (mins between goals)	178		

	PLAYER	MINS	GOALS	AVE
1	Aganzo	1423	8	178
2	Guerrero	2599	8	325
3	Regueiro	2789	8	349
4	Benayoun	2987	8	373
5	Arizmendi	842	3	281
6	Anderson Silva	2301	2	1151
7	Juanma	631	1	631
8	Pedro Lopez	1671	1	1671
9	Ayoze	971	1	971
10	Mora	3031	1	3031
	Other		1	
	TOTAL		42	

DISCIPLINARY

	PLAYER	YELLOW	RED	AVE
1	Nafti	6	0	**144**
2	Jonathan	2	1	**156**
3	Juanma	4	0	**157**
4	Torrado	7	0	**163**
5	Regragui	7	1	**172**
6	Anderson Silva	12	0	**191**
7	Oriol	9	1	**209**
8	Regueiro	12	0	**232**
9	Parri	5	0	**234**
10	Casar	5	0	**235**
11	Aganzo	6	0	**237**
12	Pedro Lopez	6	1	**238**
13	Mora	12	0	**252**
	Other	24	2	
	TOTAL	**117**	**6**	

TOP POINT EARNERS

	PLAYER	GAMES	AV PTS
1	Fernando Moran	22	**1.59**
2	Pablo Casar	12	**1.58**
3	David Aganzo	13	**1.54**
4	Pedro Lopez	18	**1.44**
5	Juanma	13	**1.38**
6	Hoalid Regragui	14	**1.29**
7	Yossi Benayoun	33	**1.24**
8	Mario Regueiro	29	**1.21**
9	Anderson Silva	24	**1.21**
10	Dudu Aouate	37	**1.19**
	CLUB AVERAGE:		**1.16**

TEAM OF THE SEASON

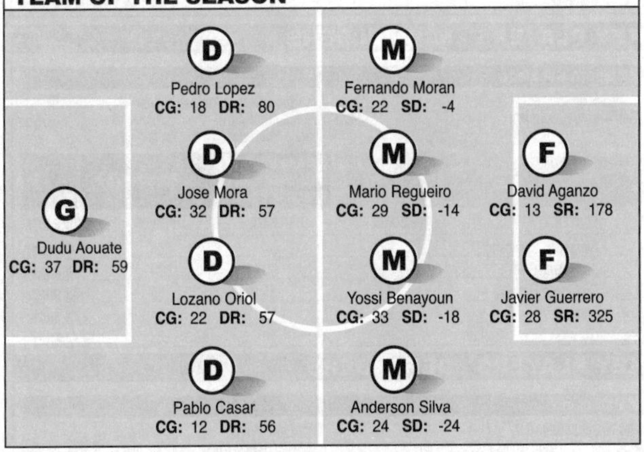

D
Pedro Lopez
CG: 18 DR: 80
M
Fernando Moran
CG: 22 SD: -4
D
Jose Mora
CG: 32 DR: 57
M
Mario Regueiro
CG: 29 SD: -14
F
David Aganzo
CG: 13 SR: 178
G
Dudu Aouate
CG: 37 DR: 59
D
Lozano Oriol
CG: 22 DR: 57
M
Yossi Benayoun
CG: 33 SD: -18
F
Javier Guerrero
CG: 28 SR: 325
D
Pablo Casar
CG: 12 DR: 56
M
Anderson Silva
CG: 24 SD: -24

LEAGUE APPEARANCES, BOOKINGS AND CAPS

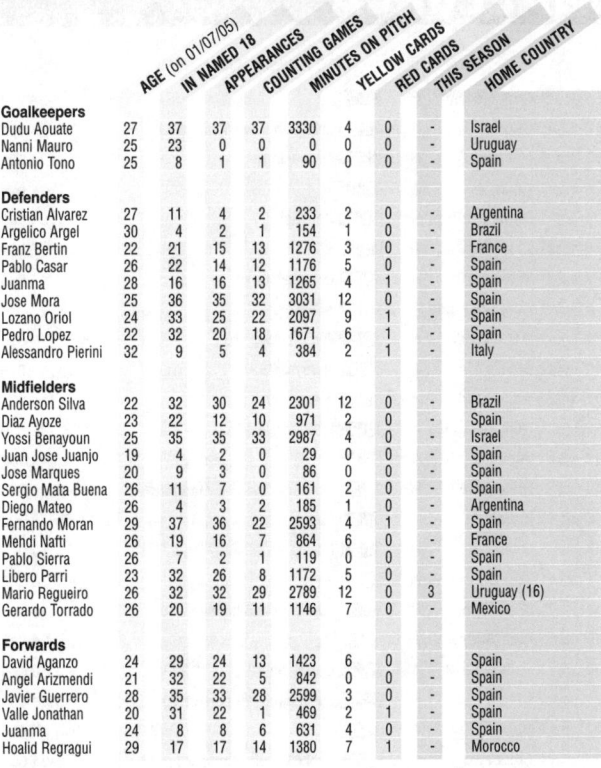

	AGE (on 01/07/05)	IN NAMED 18	APPEARANCES	COUNTING GAMES	MINUTES ON PITCH	YELLOW CARDS	RED CARDS	THIS SEASON	HOME COUNTRY
Goalkeepers									
Dudu Aouate	27	37	37	37	3330	4	0	-	Israel
Nanni Mauro	25	23	0	0	0	0	0	-	Uruguay
Antonio Tono	25	8	1	1	90	0	0	-	Spain
Defenders									
Cristian Alvarez	27	11	4	2	233	2	0	-	Argentina
Argelico Argel	30	4	2	1	154	1	0	-	Brazil
Franz Bertin	22	21	15	13	1276	3	0	-	France
Pablo Casar	26	22	14	12	1176	5	0	-	Spain
Juanma	28	16	16	13	1265	4	1	-	Spain
Jose Mora	25	36	35	32	3031	12	0	-	Spain
Lozano Oriol	24	33	25	22	2097	9	1	-	Spain
Pedro Lopez	22	32	20	18	1671	6	1	-	Spain
Alessandro Pierini	32	9	5	4	384	2	1	-	Italy
Midfielders									
Anderson Silva	22	32	30	24	2301	12	0	-	Brazil
Diaz Ayoze	23	22	12	10	971	2	0	-	Spain
Yossi Benayoun	25	35	35	33	2987	4	0	-	Israel
Juan Jose Juanjo	19	4	2	0	29	0	0	-	Spain
Jose Marques	20	9	3	0	86	0	0	-	Spain
Sergio Mata Buena	26	11	7	0	161	2	0	-	Spain
Diego Mateo	26	4	3	2	185	1	0	-	Argentina
Fernando Moran	29	37	36	22	2593	4	1	-	Spain
Mehdi Nafti	26	19	16	7	864	6	0	-	France
Pablo Sierra	26	7	2	1	119	0	0	-	Spain
Libero Parri	23	32	26	8	1172	5	0	-	Spain
Mario Regueiro	26	32	32	29	2789	12	0	3	Uruguay (16)
Gerardo Torrado	26	20	19	11	1146	7	0	-	Mexico
Forwards									
David Aganzo	24	29	24	13	1423	6	0	-	Spain
Angel Arizmendi	21	32	22	5	842	0	0	-	Spain
Javier Guerrero	28	35	33	28	2599	3	0	-	Spain
Valle Jonathan	20	31	22	1	469	2	1	-	Spain
Juanma	24	8	8	6	631	4	0	-	Spain
Hoalid Regragui	29	17	17	14	1380	7	1	-	Morocco

SQUAD APPEARANCES

Match	1	2	3	4	5	6	7	8	9	10	11	12	13	14	15	16	17	18	19	20	21	22	23	24	25	26	27	28	29	30	31	32	33	34	35	36	37	38
Venue	H	A	H	A	A	H	A	H	A	H	A	H	A	H	A	H	A	H	A	A	H	A	H	H	A	H	A	H	A	H	A	H	A	H	A	H	A	H
Competition	L	L	L	L	L	L	L	L	L	L	L	L	L	L	L	L	L	L	L	L	L	L	L	L	L	L	L	L	L	L	L	L	L	L	L	L	L	L
Result	L	L	D	W	L	D	L	W	W	W	L	D	L	D	L	L	L	W	D	L	D	L	L	W	D	W	L	W	W	L	L	L	W	D	L	W	L	W

Goalkeepers
Dudu Aouate
Nanni Mauro
Antonio Tono

Defenders
Cristian Alvarez
Argelico Argel
Franz Bertin
Pablo Casar
Juanma
Jose Mora
Lozano Oriol
Pedro Lopez
Alessandro Pierini

Midfielders
Anderson Silva
Diaz Ayoze
Yossi Benayoun
Juan Jose Juanjo
Jose Marques
Sergio Mata Buena
Diego Mateo
Fernando Moran
Mehdi Nafti
Pablo Sierra
Libero Parri
Mario Regueiro
Gerardo Torrado

Forwards
David Aganzo
Angel Arizmendi
Javier Guerrero
Valle Jonathan
Juanma
Hoalid Regragui

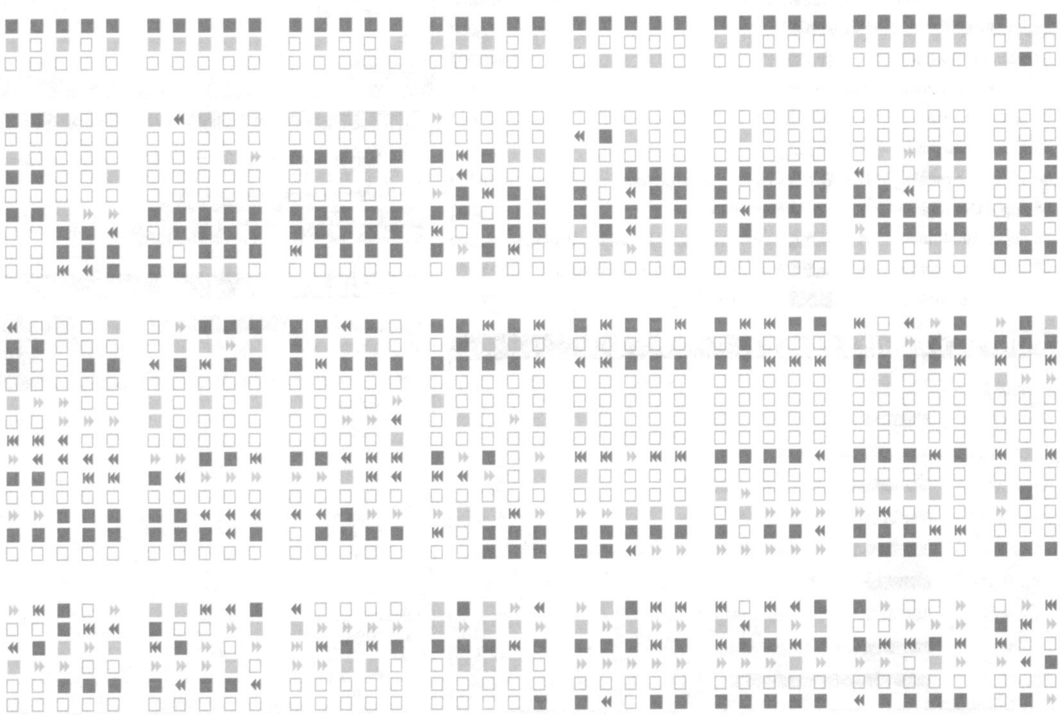

MALLORCA

Final Position: **17th**

KEY: ☐Won ☐Drawn ☐Lost

								Attendance
1	sppr1	**Real Madrid**	H	L	0-1			24,000
2	sppr1	**Getafe**	A	W	2-1	Luis Garcia 40; Arango 52		13,000
3	sppr1	**Malaga**	H	L	1-2	Delibasic 71		14,000
4	sppr1	**Albacete**	A	D	0-0			14,000
5	sppr1	**Barcelona**	H	L	1-3	Delibasic 77		20,000
6	sppr1	**Levante**	A	L	0-2			15,000
7	sppr1	**Villarreal**	H	D	1-1	Luis Garcia 19		14,000
8	sppr1	**Real Sociedad**	A	L	1-2	Arango 52		23,000
9	sppr1	**R Santander**	H	L	1-2	Jorge Lopez 80		10,000
10	sppr1	**Seville**	A	D	1-1	Pereyra 79		40,000
11	sppr1	**Atl Madrid**	H	D	1-1	Arango 27		15,000
12	sppr1	**Real Zaragoza**	A	W	1-0	Luis Garcia 19		32,000
13	sppr1	**Valencia**	A	L	0-2			48,000
14	sppr1	**Numancia**	H	W	3-2	Delibasic 79; Luis Garcia 81,86		20,000
15	sppr1	**Espanyol**	A	L	1-2	Pereyra 60		15,000
16	sppr1	**Osasuna**	H	L	1-2	Perera 80		14,000
17	sppr1	**Athl Bilbao**	A	L	0-4			30,000
18	sppr1	**Deportivo**	H	D	2-2	Luis Garcia 57; Okubo 66		15,000
19	sppr1	**Real Betis**	A	L	0-2			35,000
20	sppr1	**Real Madrid**	A	L	1-3	Campano 42		60,000
21	sppr1	**Getafe**	H	W	3-1	Luis Garcia 10 pen,52; Arango 36		17,000
22	sppr1	**Malaga**	A	D	0-0			20,000
23	sppr1	**Albacete**	H	W	2-1	Tuni 53; Luis Garcia 72 pen		21,000
24	sppr1	**Barcelona**	A	L	0-2			75,000
25	sppr1	**Levante**	H	L	1-2	Luis Garcia 54		18,000
26	sppr1	**Villarreal**	A	L	1-2	Venta 15 og		17,000
27	sppr1	**Real Sociedad**	H	W	3-2	Romeo 15,54; Luis Garcia 20		10,000
28	sppr1	**R Santander**	A	L	0-3			13,000
29	sppr1	**Seville**	H	L	0-1			17,000
30	sppr1	**Atl Madrid**	A	L	0-4			45,000
31	sppr1	**Real Zaragoza**	H	L	0-2			9,000
32	sppr1	**Valencia**	H	D	0-0			14,000
33	sppr1	**Numancia**	A	W	2-1	Victor 54; Iuliano 59		6,000
34	sppr1	**Espanyol**	H	W	3-2	Campano 50,81; Arango 70		11,000
35	sppr1	**Osasuna**	A	D	1-1	Farinos 33		10,000
36	sppr1	**Athl Bilbao**	H	W	4-3	Farinos 11 pen; Victor 48,62; Okubo 51		18,000
37	sppr1	**Deportivo**	A	W	3-0	Farinos 10; Arango 37; Okubo 63		24,000
38	sppr1	**Real Betis**	H	D	1-1	Pereyra 87		23,000

MONTHLY POINTS TALLY

AUGUST	0	0%
SEPTEMBER	4	33%
OCTOBER	1	8%
NOVEMBER	5	42%
DECEMBER	3	25%
JANUARY	4	33%
FEBRUARY	4	33%
MARCH	3	25%
APRIL	4	33%
MAY	11	73%

KEY PLAYERS - GOALSCORERS

Fernandez Luis Garcia

Goals in the League	11	Player Strike Rate Average number of minutes between League goals scored by player	271
Contribution to Attacking Power Average number of minutes between League team goals while on pitch	87	Club Strike Rate Average number of minutes between League goals scored by club	81

	PLAYER	LGE GOALS	POWER	STRIKE RATE
1	Fernandez Luis Garcia	11	87	271 mins
2	Juan Arango	6	74	466 mins
3	Alejandro Campano	3	56	638 mins
4	Guillermo Pereyra	3	88	674 mins
5	Francisco Farinos	3	84	729 mins

KEY PLAYERS - MIDFIELDERS

Alejandro Campano

Goals in the League	3	Contribution to Attacking Power Average number of minutes between League team goals while on pitch	56
Defensive Rating Average number of mins between League goals conceded while on the pitch	50	Scoring Difference Defensive Rating minus Contribution to Attacking Power	-6

	PLAYER	LGE GOALS	DEF RATE	POWER	SCORE DIFF
1	Alejandro Campano	3	50	56	-6 mins
2	Juan Arango	6	50	74	-24 mins
3	Guillermo Pereyra	3	55	88	-33 mins
4	Francisco Farinos	3	51	84	-33 mins
5	Gonzalo De Los Santos	0	50	92	-42 mins

KEY PLAYERS - DEFENDERS

Mark Iuliano

Goals Conceded (GC) Number of League goals conceded while the player was on the pitch	19	Clean Sheets In games when player was on pitch for at least 70 minutes	3
Defensive Rating Ave number of mins between League goals conceded while on the pitch	65	Club Defensive Rating Average number of mins between League goals conceded by the club this season	53

	PLAYER	CON LGE	CLEAN SHEETS	DEF RATE
1	Mark Iuliano	19	3	65 mins
2	Sergio Ballesteros	50	4	55 mins
3	Fernandez Poli	57	5	53 mins
4	David Cortez	54	4	52 mins
5	Ivan Ramis	39	2	48 mins

KEY GOALKEEPER

Miguel Moya

Goals Conceded in the League	57	Counting Games Games when player was on pitch for at least 70 minutes	32
Defensive Rating Ave number of mins between League goals conceded while on the pitch	51	Clean Sheets In games when player was on pitch for at least 70 minutes	4

LEAGUE GOALS

Fernandez Luis Garcia

Minutes on the pitch	2980	Goals in the League	11
League average (mins between goals)	271		

	PLAYER	MINS	GOALS	AVE
1	Luis Garcia	2980	11	271
2	Arango	2794	6	466
3	Farinos	2186	3	729
4	Campano	1914	3	638
5	Delibasic	642	3	214
6	Pereyra	2023	3	674
7	Okubo	649	3	216
8	Victor	549	3	183
9	Romeo	552	2	276
10	Tuni	1727	1	1727
11	Perera	489	1	489
12	Iuliano	1239	1	1239
	Other		2	
	TOTAL		42	

DISCIPLINARY RECORDS

	PLAYER	YELLOW	RED	AVE
1	Iuliano	6	2	154
2	Perera	3	0	163
3	Poli	15	1	188
4	De Los Santos	5	1	200
5	Nino	3	1	201
6	Ballesteros	10	1	248
7	Pereyra	8	0	252
8	Victor	2	0	274
9	Delibasic	2	0	321
10	Okubo	2	0	324
11	Farinos	6	0	364
12	Cortez	6	0	465
13	Campano	4	0	478
	Other	21	0	
	TOTAL	93	6	

TOP POINT EARNERS

	PLAYER	GAMES	AV PTS
1	Mark Iuliano	13	1.46
2	Alejandro Campano	19	1.37
3	Antoni Tuni	15	1.27
4	Fernandez Poli	33	1.15
5	Sergio Ballesteros	29	1.14
6	David Cortez	28	1.11
7	Francisco Farinos	23	1.04
8	Fernandez Luis Garcia	32	0.97
9	Guillermo Pereyra	19	0.95
10	Miguel Moya	32	0.94
	CLUB AVERAGE:		1.03

LEAGUE APPEARANCES, BOOKINGS AND CAPS

	AGE (on 01/07/05)	IN NAMED 18	APPEARANCES	COUNTING GAMES	MINUTES ON PITCH	YELLOW CARDS	RED CARDS	THIS SEASON	HOME COUNTRY
Goalkeepers									
Miguel Moya	21	32	32	32	2880	2	0	-	Spain
Sander Westerveld	30	22	6	6	540	1	0	-	Holland
Defenders									
Sergio Ballesteros	29	36	32	29	2732	10	1	-	Spain
Fracisco Campos	23	5	2	0	39	0	0	-	Spain
David Cortez	25	37	34	28	2795	6	0	-	Spain
Mark Iuliano	31	16	15	13	1239	6	2	-	Italy
Marcos Vales	30	11	6	3	374	1	0	-	Spain
Miguel Nadal	38	14	6	2	255	0	0	-	Spain
Fernando Nino	30	12	10	9	805	3	1	-	Spain
Fernandez Poli	28	35	35	33	3015	15	1	-	Spain
Ivan Ramis	20	34	22	20	1875	3	0	-	Spain
Midfielders									
Juan Arango	25	35	34	28	2794	5	0	-	Venezuela
Alejandro Campano	26	38	29	19	1914	4	0	-	Spain
Carlos Carmona	18	10	1	0	12	0	0	-	Spain
De Los Santos	28	18	16	12	1202	5	1	2	Uruguay (16)
Francisco Farinos	27	35	28	23	2186	6	0	-	Spain
Jorge Lopez	26	36	29	16	1753	2	0	-	Spain
Martin Marcos	36	23	10	1	411	2	0	-	Spain
Felipe Melo	21	11	8	2	353	1	0	-	Brazil
Patrick Muller	28	12	6	4	422	0	0	-	Switzerland
Guillermo Pereyra	25	35	30	19	2023	8	0	-	Argentina
Castano Victor	20	7	7	5	549	2	0	-	Spain
Forwards									
Fernando Correa	31	15	9	1	263	0	0	-	Uruguay
Andrija Delibasic	24	14	12	4	642	2	0	-	Serbia & Montenegro
Luis Garcia	24	38	37	32	2980	5	0	-	Spain
Yoshito Okubo	23	16	13	6	649	2	0	-	Japan
Jose Perera	25	18	13	3	489	3	0	-	Spain
Bernardo Romeo	27	12	10	5	552	0	0	-	Argentina
Antoni Tuni	23	36	32	15	1727	3	0	-	Spain

TEAM OF THE SEASON

D
Mark Iuliano
CG: 13 DR: 65
M
Alejandro Campano
CG: 19 SD: -6
D
Sergio Ballesteros
CG: 29 DR: 55
M
Juan Arango
CG: 28 SD: -24
F
Fernandez Luis Garcia
CG: 32 SR: 271
G
Miguel Moya
CG: 32 DR: 51
D
Fernandez Poli
CG: 33 DR: 53
M
Francisco Farinos
CG: 23 SD: -33
F
Antoni Tuni
CG: 15 SR: 1727
D
David Cortez
CG: 28 DR: 52
M
Guillermo Pereyra
CG: 19 SD: -33

SQUAD APPEARANCES

Match	1	2	3	4	5	6	7	8	9	10	11	12	13	14	15	16	17	18	19	20	21	22	23	24	25	26	27	28	29	30	31	32	33	34	35	36	37	38
Venue	H	A	H	A	H	A	H	A	H	A	H	A	A	H	A	H	A	H	A	A	H	A	H	A	H	A	H	A	H	A	H	H	A	H	A	H	A	H
Competition	L	L	L	L	L	L	L	L	L	L	L	L	L	L	L	L	L	L	L	L	L	L	L	L	L	L	L	L	L	L	L	L	L	L	L	L	L	L
Result	L	W	L	D	L	L	D	L	L	D	D	W	L	W	L	L	L	D	L	L	W	D	W	L	L	L	W	L	L	L	L	D	W	W	D	W	W	D

Goalkeepers
Miguel Moya
Sander Westerveld

Defenders
Sergio Ballesteros
Fracisco Campos
David Cortez
Mark Iuliano
Marcos Vales
Miguel Nadal
Fernando Nino
Fernandez Poli
Ivan Ramis

Midfielders
Juan Arango
Alejandro Campano
Carlos Carmona
Gonzalo De Los Santos
Francisco Farinos
Jorge Lopez
Martin Marcos
Felipe Melo
Patrick Muller
Guillermo Pereyra
Castano Victor

Forwards
Fernando Correa
Andrija Delibasic
Fernandez Luis Garcia
Yoshito Okubo
Jose Perera
Bernardo Romeo
Antoni Tuni

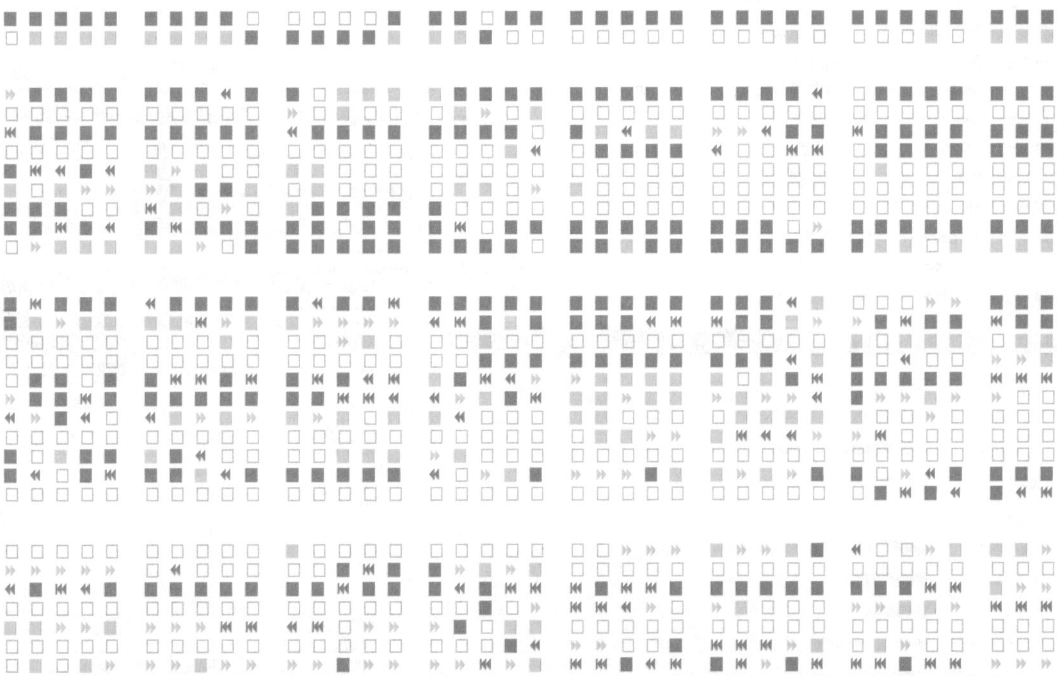

KEY: On all match · On bench · Subbed or sent off (Counting game) · Subbed or sent off (playing less than 70 minutes) · Subbed on from bench (Counting Game) · Subbed on (playing less than 70 minutes) · Subbed on and then subbed or sent off (Counting Game) · Subbed on and then subbed or sent off (playing less than 70 minutes) · Not in 16

LEVANTE

Final Position: **18th**

KEY: Won Drawn Lost

							Attendance
1	sppr1	**Real Sociedad**	A	D	1-1	Harte 42	32,000
2	sppr1	**R Santander**	H	W	3-1	Manchev 48; Nacho 68; Ettien 89	13,000
3	sppr1	**Seville**	A	L	0-3		38,000
4	sppr1	**Atl Madrid**	H	W	1-0	Rivera 21 pen	15,000
5	sppr1	**Real Zaragoza**	A	L	3-4	Manchev 26,45; Celestini 76	32,000
6	sppr1	**Mallorca**	H	W	2-0	Manchev 27; Sergio Garcia 34	15,000
7	sppr1	**Numancia**	A	W	3-1	Manchev 30; Sergio Garcia 59; Nacho 64	7,000
8	sppr1	**Espanyol**	H	L	0-2		18,000
9	sppr1	**Osasuna**	A	W	1-0	Sergio Garcia 23	14,000
10	sppr1	**Athl Bilbao**	H	W	1-0	Jesule 68	19,000
11	sppr1	**Deportivo**	A	L	0-1		24,000
12	sppr1	**Real Betis**	H	L	1-2	Rivera 7 pen	19,000
13	sppr1	**Real Madrid**	A	L	0-5		70,000
14	sppr1	**Getafe**	H	D	0-0		10,000
15	sppr1	**Malaga**	A	L	0-1		20,000
16	sppr1	**Albacete**	H	D	1-1	Culebras 41	15,000
17	sppr1	**Barcelona**	A	L	1-2	Jofre 61	51,000
18	sppr1	**Valencia**	A	L	1-2	Congo 73	52,000
19	sppr1	**Villarreal**	H	L	2-4	Rivera 46; Reggi 71	16,000
20	sppr1	**Real Sociedad**	H	W	2-1	Nacho 4; Congo 47	14,000
21	sppr1	**R Santander**	A	D	2-2	Nacho 51; Juanma 60	13,000
22	sppr1	**Seville**	H	L	0-3		19,000
23	sppr1	**Atl Madrid**	A	D	0-0		45,000
24	sppr1	**Real Zaragoza**	H	D	0-0		15,000
25	sppr1	**Mallorca**	A	W	2-1	Sergio Garcia 63; Jofre 82	18,000
26	sppr1	**Numancia**	H	D	1-1	Ettien 40	15,000
27	sppr1	**Espanyol**	A	L	1-2	Sergio Garcia 24	20,000
28	sppr1	**Osasuna**	H	W	4-0	Juanma 6,21; Manchev 35; Sergio Garcia 63	16,000
29	sppr1	**Athl Bilbao**	A	L	1-3	Juanma 73	30,000
30	sppr1	**Deportivo**	H	L	0-1		14,000
31	sppr1	**Real Betis**	A	D	2-2	Rivera 25; Juanma 66	35,000
32	sppr1	**Real Madrid**	H	L	0-2		19,000
33	sppr1	**Getafe**	A	L	0-1		16,000
34	sppr1	**Malaga**	H	L	0-1		15,000
35	sppr1	**Albacete**	A	L	1-3	Sergio Garcia 60	9,000
36	sppr1	**Barcelona**	H	D	1-1	Rivera 35	20,000
37	sppr1	**Valencia**	H	D	0-0		20,000
38	sppr1	**Villarreal**	A	L	1-4	Reggi 22	23,000

MONTHLY POINTS TALLY

AUGUST	1	33%
SEPTEMBER	6	50%
OCTOBER	9	75%
NOVEMBER	3	25%
DECEMBER	2	17%
JANUARY	4	33%
FEBRUARY	5	42%
MARCH	4	33%
APRIL	1	8%
MAY	2	13%

KEY PLAYERS - GOALSCORERS

Sergio Garcia

Goals in the League	7	Player Strike Rate Average number of minutes between League goals scored by player	316
Contribution to Attacking Power Average number of minutes between League team goals while on pitch	85	Club Strike Rate Average number of minutes between League goals scored by club	88

	PLAYER	LGE GOALS	POWER	STRIKE RATE
1	Sergio Garcia	7	85	**316 mins**
2	Vladimir Manchev	6	68	**353 mins**
3	Nacho	4	88	**461 mins**
4	Alberto Rivera	5	87	**662 mins**
5	Mateu Jofre	2	94	**806 mins**

KEY PLAYERS - MIDFIELDERS

Felix Dja Ettien

Goals in the League	2	Contribution to Attacking Power Average number of minutes between League team goals while on pitch	84
Defensive Rating Average number of mins between League goals conceded while on the pitch	68	Scoring Difference Defensive Rating minus Contribution to Attacking Power	-16

	PLAYER	LGE GOALS	DEF RATE	POWER	SCORE DIFF
1	Felix Dja Ettien	2	68	84	**-16 mins**
2	Sergio Garcia	7	65	85	**-20 mins**
3	Nacho	4	62	88	**-26 mins**
4	Alberto Rivera	5	58	87	**-29 mins**
5	Fabio Celestini	1	51	83	**-32 mins**

KEY PLAYERS - DEFENDERS

Pablo Pinillos

Goals Conceded Number of League goals conceded while the player was on the pitch	48	Clean Sheets In games when player was on pitch for at least 70 minutes	9
Defensive Rating Ave number of mins between League goals conceded while on the pitch	63	Club Defensive Rating Average number of mins between League goals conceded by the club this season	59

	PLAYER	CON LGE	CLEAN SHEETS	DEF RATE
1	Pablo Pinillos	48	9	**63 mins**
2	Barbadilla Jesule	50	9	**61 mins**
3	Jose Culebras	36	6	**59 mins**
4	Ian Harte	35	5	**58 mins**
5	Suarez Alexis	36	4	**53 mins**

KEY GOALKEEPER

Jose Luis Mora

Goals Conceded in the League	58	Counting Games Games when player was on pitch for at least 70 minutes	38
Defensive Rating Ave number of mins between League goals conceded while on the pitch	59	Clean Sheets In games when player was on pitch for at least 70 minutes	9

LEAGUE GOALS

Sergio Garcia

Minutes on the pitch	2211	Goals in the League	7
League average (mins between goals)	316		

	PLAYER	MINS	GOALS	AVE
1	Sergio Garcia	2211	**7**	316
2	Manchev	2117	**6**	353
3	Rivera	3311	**5**	662
4	Juanma	1122	**5**	224
5	Nacho	1845	**4**	461
6	Reggi	670	**2**	335
7	Ettien	2506	**2**	1253
8	Jofre	1612	**2**	806
9	Congo	828	**2**	414
10	Harte	2043	**1**	2043
11	Celestini	2002	**1**	2002
12	Culebras	2130	**1**	2130
13	Jesule	3039	**1**	3039
	Other		0	
	TOTAL		**39**	

DISCIPLINARY RECORDS

	PLAYER	YELLOW	RED	AVE
1	Reggi	4	1	134
2	Pinillos	12	1	234
3	Harte	8	0	255
4	Alexis	7	0	274
5	Congo	3	0	276
6	Nacho	6	0	307
7	Celestini	6	0	333
8	Camacho	5	0	336
9	Jesule	9	0	337
10	Rivera	9	0	367
11	Descarga	2	0	385
12	Manchev	5	0	423
13	Culebras	4	1	426
	Other	10	2	
	TOTAL	90	5	

TOP POINT EARNERS

	PLAYER	GAMES	AV PTS
1	Vladimir Manchev	17	1.29
2	Nacho	19	1.26
3	Jose Culebras	23	1.22
4	Sergio Garcia	20	1.20
5	Felix Dja Ettien	26	1.19
6	Pablo Pinillos	34	1.09
7	Ian Harte	22	1.00
8	Fabio Celestini	22	1.00
9	Alberto Rivera	37	0.97
10	Jose Luis Mora	38	0.97
	CLUB AVERAGE:		0.97

TEAM OF THE SEASON

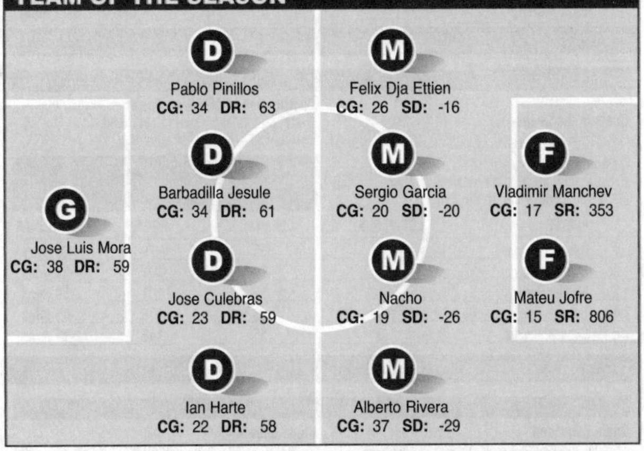
D
Pablo Pinillos
CG: 34 DR: 63
M
Felix Dja Ettien
CG: 26 SD: -16
D
Barbadilla Jesule
CG: 34 DR: 61
M
Sergio Garcia
CG: 20 SD: -20
F
Vladimir Manchev
CG: 17 SR: 353
G
Jose Luis Mora
CG: 38 DR: 59
D
Jose Culebras
CG: 23 DR: 59
M
Nacho
CG: 19 SD: -26
F
Mateu Jofre
CG: 15 SR: 806
D
Ian Harte
CG: 22 DR: 58
M
Alberto Rivera
CG: 37 SD: -29

LEAGUE APPEARANCES, BOOKINGS AND CAPS

	AGE (on 01/07/05)	IN NAMED 18	APPEARANCES	COUNTING GAMES	MINUTES ON PITCH	YELLOW CARDS	RED CARDS	THIS SEASON	HOME COUNTRY
Goalkeepers									
Jose Aizpurua	35	27	0	0	0	0	0	-	Spain
Pablo Cavallero	31	10	0	0	0	0	0	1	Argentina (3)
Jose Luis Mora	31	38	38	38	3420	1	0	-	Spain
Defenders									
Suarez Alexis	31	28	22	21	1921	7	0	-	Spain
Jose Culebras	26	37	25	23	2130	4	1	-	Spain
Inaki Descarga	28	27	10	7	770	2	0	-	Spain
Ian Harte	27	24	24	22	2043	8	0	-	Rep of Ireland
Barbadilla Jesule	32	37	34	34	3039	9	0	-	Spain
Johan Mjallby	34	3	3	3	270	0	0	1	Sweden (13)
Pablo Pinillos	31	34	34	34	3043	12	1	-	Spain
Luis Rubiales	27	10	3	1	183	1	0	-	Spain
Midfielders									
Diego Camacho	28	36	27	16	1680	5	0	-	Spain
Fabio Celestini	29	32	25	22	2002	6	0	-	Switzerland
Felix Dja Ettien	25	35	34	26	2506	4	0	-	Ivory Coast
Nacho	25	30	27	19	1845	6	0	-	Spain
Alberto Rivera	27	37	37	37	3311	9	0	-	Spain
Carlos Sandro	30	13	3	1	89	0	0	-	Spain
Sergio Garcia	22	36	31	20	2211	3	1	-	Spain
Vicente Tito	33	15	9	3	468	0	0	-	Spain
Forwards									
Edwin Congo	28	31	26	6	828	3	0	-	Colombia
Angel Cuellar	32	15	7	1	194	0	0	-	Spain
Mateu Jofre	25	33	27	15	1612	1	0	-	Spain
Juanma	24	36	26	7	1122	1	1	-	Spain
Vladimir Manchev	27	34	33	17	2117	5	0	-	Bulgaria
Gustavo Reggi	32	32	22	4	670	4	1	-	Argentina

SQUAD APPEARANCES

Match	1	2	3	4	5	6	7	8	9	10	11	12	13	14	15	16	17	18	19	20	21	22	23	24	25	26	27	28	29	30	31	32	33	34	35	36	37	38
Venue	A	H	A	H	A	H	A	H	A	H	A	H	A	H	A	H	A	A	H	H	A	H	A	H	A	H	A	H	A	H	A	H	A	H	A	H	H	A
Competition	L	L	L	L	L	L	L	L	L	L	L	L	L	L	L	L	L	L	L	L	L	L	L	L	L	L	L	L	L	L	L	L	L	L	L	L	L	L
Result	D	W	L	W	L	W	W	L	W	W	L	L	L	D	L	D	L	L	L	W	D	L	D	D	W	D	L	W	L	L	D	L	L	L	L	D	D	L

Goalkeepers
Jose Aizpurua
Pablo Cavallero
Jose Luis Mora

Defenders
Suarez Alexis
Jose Culebras
Inaki Descarga
Ian Harte
Barbadilla Jesule
Johan Mjallby
Pablo Pinillos
Luis Rubiales

Midfielders
Diego Camacho
Fabio Celestini
Felix Dja Ettien
Nacho
Alberto Rivera
Carlos Sandro
Sergio Garcia
Vicente Tito

Forwards
Edwin Congo
Angel Cuellar
Mateu Jofre
Juanma
Vladimir Manchev
Gustavo Reggi

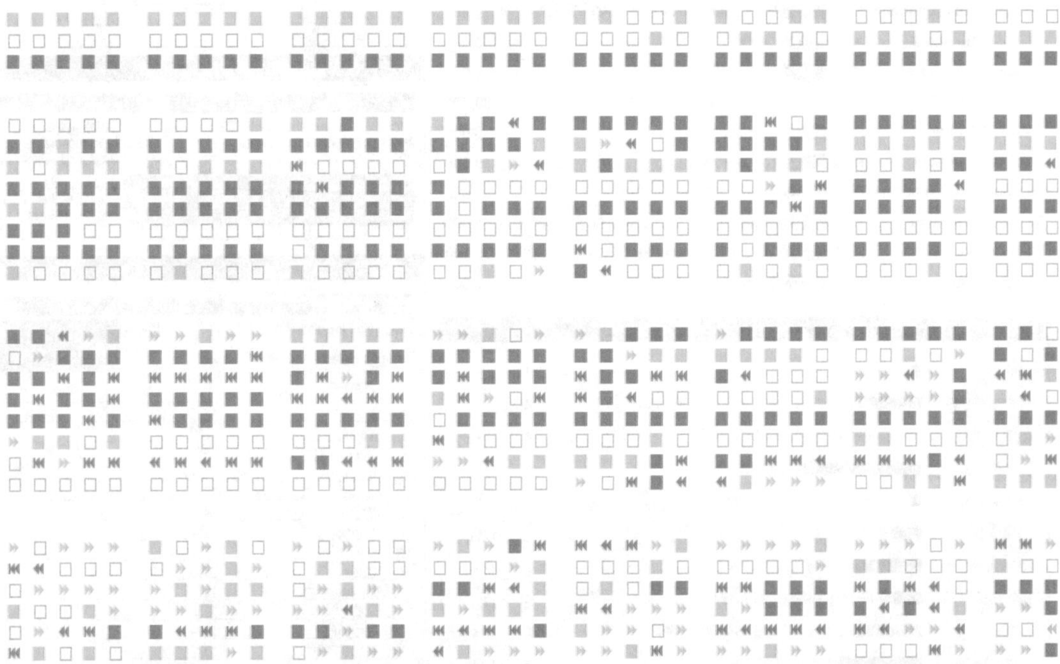

KEY: On all match | On bench | Subbed or sent off (Counting game) | Subbed or sent off (playing less than 70 minutes) | Subbed on from bench (Counting Game) | Subbed on (playing less than 70 minutes) | Subbed on and then subbed or sent off (Counting Game) | Subbed on and then subbed or sent off (playing less than 70 minutes) | Not in 16

NUMANCIA

Final Position: **19th**

KEY: ☐Won ☐Drawn ☐Lost

							Attendance
1	sppr1	**Real Betis**	H	D	1-1	Juanlu 20	10,000
2	sppr1	**Real Madrid**	A	L	0-1		66,000
3	sppr1	**Getafe**	H	W	1-0	Pineda 6	9,000
4	sppr1	**Malaga**	A	L	1-4	Otxoa 68	25,000
5	sppr1	**Albacete**	H	D	0-0		7,000
6	sppr1	**Barcelona**	A	L	0-1		79,000
7	sppr1	**Levante**	H	L	1-3	Pineda 85	7,000
8	sppr1	**Villarreal**	A	L	0-4		16,000
9	sppr1	**Real Sociedad**	H	L	0-2		10,000
10	sppr1	**R Santander**	A	L	0-2		13,000
11	sppr1	**Seville**	H	W	2-1	Osorio 84; Antonio 90	7,000
12	sppr1	**Atl Madrid**	A	L	0-2		45,000
13	sppr1	**Real Zaragoza**	H	W	2-1	Osorio 9,33	10,000
14	sppr1	**Mallorca**	A	L	2-3	Tevenet 21; Moreno 57	20,000
15	sppr1	**Valencia**	A	L	0-1		35,000
16	sppr1	**Espanyol**	H	D	0-0		10,000
17	sppr1	**Osasuna**	A	L	0-2		14,000
18	sppr1	**Athl Bilbao**	H	D	1-1	Tevenet 65	10,000
19	sppr1	**Deportivo**	A	D	1-1	Merino 80	28,000
20	sppr1	**Real Betis**	A	L	0-4		38,000
21	sppr1	**Real Madrid**	H	L	1-2	Miguel 88	10,000
22	sppr1	**Getafe**	A	L	0-1		10,000
23	sppr1	**Malaga**	H	L	0-1		8,000
24	sppr1	**Albacete**	A	W	2-1	Merino 50 pen; Miguel 85	14,000
25	sppr1	**Barcelona**	H	D	1-1	Juanlu 44	10,000
26	sppr1	**Levante**	A	D	1-1	Graff 20	15,000
27	sppr1	**Villarreal**	H	D	1-1	Merino 59	7,000
28	sppr1	**Real Sociedad**	A	L	1-2	Tevenet 48	22,000
29	sppr1	**R Santander**	H	L	2-3	Pablo Sanz 5; Tarantino 40	9,000
30	sppr1	**Seville**	A	L	0-1		40,000
31	sppr1	**Atl Madrid**	H	W	1-0	Miguel 85	9,000
32	sppr1	**Real Zaragoza**	A	L	1-4	Cani 67 og	33,000
33	sppr1	**Mallorca**	H	L	1-2	Merino 81	6,000
34	sppr1	**Valencia**	H	D	1-1	Tevenet 74	8,000
35	sppr1	**Espanyol**	A	L	0-3		20,000
36	sppr1	**Osasuna**	H	D	2-2	Miguel Perez 18; Miguel 71	7,000
37	sppr1	**Athl Bilbao**	A	W	2-0	Merino 9; Tevenet 89 pen	35,000
38	sppr1	**Deportivo**	H	D	1-1	Tevenet 49	7,000

MONTHLY POINTS TALLY

AUGUST	1	33%
SEPTEMBER	4	33%
OCTOBER	0	0%
NOVEMBER	6	50%
DECEMBER	1	8%
JANUARY	2	17%
FEBRUARY	4	33%
MARCH	2	17%
APRIL	4	27%
MAY	5	42%

KEY PLAYERS - GOALSCORERS

Luis Tevenet

Goals in the League	6	**Player Strike Rate** Average number of minutes between League goals scored by player	316
Contribution to Attacking Power Average number of minutes between League team goals while on pitch	105	**Club Strike Rate** Average number of minutes between League goals scored by club	110

	PLAYER	LGE GOALS	POWER	STRIKE RATE
1	Luis Tevenet	6	105	316 mins
2	Jose Antonio	2	111	726 mins
3	Julio Pineda	2	149	745 mins
4	Juanlu	2	88	972 mins
5	Juan Moreno	1	141	1271 mins

KEY PLAYERS - MIDFIELDERS

Carlos Merino

Goals in the League	5	**Contribution to Attacking Power** Average number of minutes between League team goals while on pitch	79
Defensive Rating Average number of mins between League goals conceded while on the pitch	56	**Scoring Difference** Defensive Rating minus Contribution to Attacking Power	-23

	PLAYER	LGE GOALS	DEF RATE	POWER	SCORE DIFF
1	Carlos Merino	5	56	79	-23 mins
2	Pablo Sanz	1	64	101	-37 mins
3	Miguel Perez	1	51	101	-50 mins
4	Ramon Ros	0	55	138	-83 mins
5	Cesar Palacios	0	55	146	-91 mins

KEY PLAYERS - DEFENDERS

Juan Velasco

Goals Conceded Number of League goals conceded while the player was on the pitch	20	**Clean Sheets** In games when player was on pitch for at least 70 minutes	2
Defensive Rating Ave number of mins between League goals conceded while on the pitch	67	**Club Defensive Rating** Average number of mins between League goals conceded by the club this season	56

	PLAYER	CON LGE	CLEAN SHEETS	DEF RATE
1	Juan Velasco	20	2	67 mins
2	Francisco Tarantino	22	2	59 mins
3	Juan Cruz Otxoa	48	4	58 mins
4	Patricio Graff	34	3	57 mins
5	Stephane Pignol	52	4	56 mins

KEY GOALKEEPER

Barrero Juanma

Goals Conceded in the League	37	**Counting Games** League games when player was on pitch for at least 70 minutes	25
Defensive Rating Ave number of mins between League goals conceded while on the pitch	61	**Clean Sheets** In games when player was on pitch for at least 70 minutes	3

LEAGUE GOALS

Luis Tevenet

Minutes on the pitch	1893	**Goals in the League**	6
League average (mins between goals)	316		

	PLAYER	MINS	GOALS	AVE
1	Tevenet	1893	6	316
2	Merino	1350	5	270
3	Miguel	967	4	242
4	Osorio	827	3	276
5	Juanlu	1944	2	972
6	Pineda	1490	2	745
7	Antonio	1452	2	726
8	Pablo Sanz	1410	1	1410
9	Otxoa	2790	1	2790
10	Moreno	1271	1	1271
11	Graff	1938	1	1938
12	Tarantino	1294	1	1294
13	Miguel Perez	1317	1	1317
	Other		1	
	TOTAL		**31**	

DISCIPLINARY RECORDS

	PLAYER	YELLOW	RED	AVE
1	Antonio	8	0	181
2	Miguel	4	1	193
3	Moreno	6	0	211
4	Ros	5	0	220
5	Pignol	11	1	242
6	Jaime Molina	7	0	269
7	Tevenet	6	1	270
8	Graff	6	1	276
9	Otxoa	9	1	279
10	Lee	3	0	280
11	Tarantino	4	0	323
12	Juanlu	6	0	324
13	Pablo Sanz	4	0	352
	Other	17	1	
	TOTAL	96	6	

TOP POINT EARNERS

	PLAYER	GAMES	AV PTS
1	Juan Velasco	12	1.08
2	De Miguel Juanpa	17	1.00
3	Juanlu	20	0.95
4	Juan Moreno	12	0.92
5	Luis Tevenet	13	0.92
6	Juan Cruz Otxoa	29	0.90
7	Francisco Tarantino	14	0.86
8	Barrero Juanma	25	0.84
9	Pablo Sanz	12	0.83
10	Jose Antonio	16	0.69
	CLUB AVERAGE:		0.76

TEAM OF THE SEASON

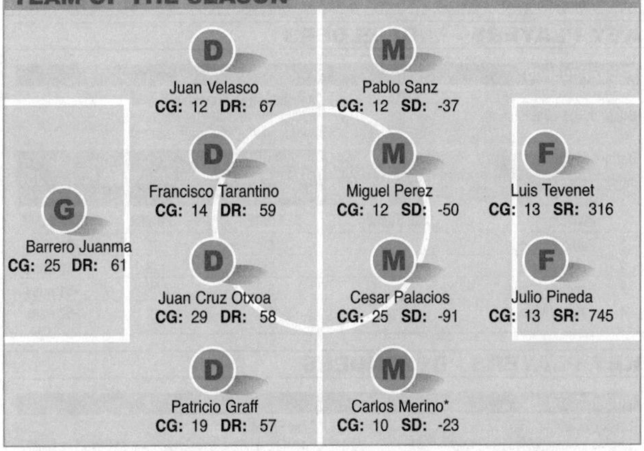
D
Juan Velasco
CG: 12 DR: 67
M
Pablo Sanz
CG: 12 SD: -37
D
Francisco Tarantino
CG: 14 DR: 59
M
Miguel Perez
CG: 12 SD: -50
F
Luis Tevenet
CG: 13 SR: 316
G
Barrero Juanma
CG: 25 DR: 61
D
Juan Cruz Otxoa
CG: 29 DR: 58
M
Cesar Palacios
CG: 25 SD: -91
F
Julio Pineda
CG: 13 SR: 745
D
Patricio Graff
CG: 19 DR: 57
M
Carlos Merino*
CG: 10 SD: -23

LEAGUE APPEARANCES, BOOKINGS AND CAPS

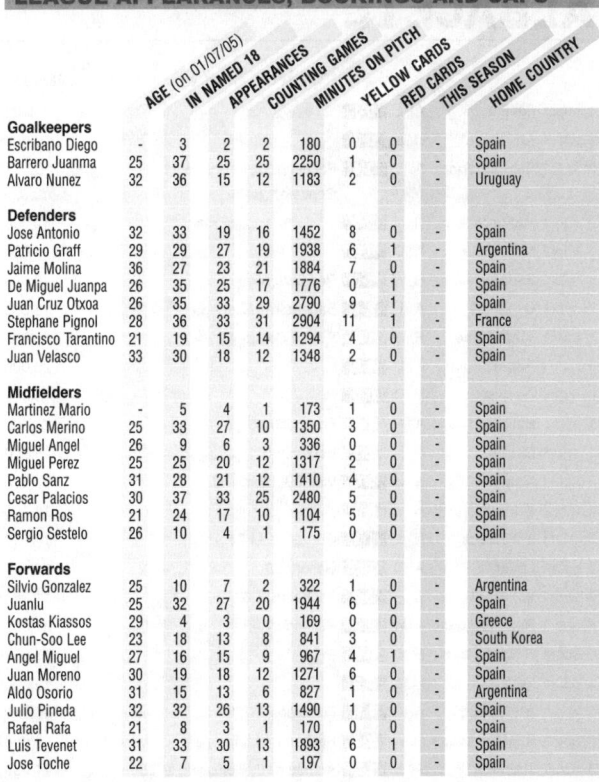

	AGE (on 01/07/05)	IN NAMED 18	APPEARANCES	COUNTING GAMES	MINUTES ON PITCH	YELLOW CARDS	RED CARDS	THIS SEASON	HOME COUNTRY
Goalkeepers									
Escribano Diego	-	3	2	2	180	0	0	-	Spain
Barrero Juanma	25	37	25	25	2250	1	0	-	Spain
Alvaro Nunez	32	36	15	12	1183	2	0	-	Uruguay
Defenders									
Jose Antonio	32	33	19	16	1452	8	0	-	Spain
Patricio Graff	29	29	27	19	1938	6	1	-	Argentina
Jaime Molina	36	27	23	21	1884	7	0	-	Spain
De Miguel Juanpa	26	35	25	17	1776	0	1	-	Spain
Juan Cruz Otxoa	26	35	33	29	2790	9	1	-	Spain
Stephane Pignol	28	36	33	31	2904	11	1	-	France
Francisco Tarantino	21	19	15	14	1294	4	0	-	Spain
Juan Velasco	33	30	18	12	1348	2	0	-	Spain
Midfielders									
Martinez Mario	-	5	4	1	173	1	0	-	Spain
Carlos Merino	25	33	27	10	1350	3	0	-	Spain
Miguel Angel	26	9	6	3	336	0	0	-	Spain
Miguel Perez	25	25	20	12	1317	2	0	-	Spain
Pablo Sanz	31	28	21	12	1410	4	0	-	Spain
Cesar Palacios	30	37	33	25	2480	5	0	-	Spain
Ramon Ros	21	24	17	10	1104	5	0	-	Spain
Sergio Sestelo	26	10	4	1	175	0	0	-	Spain
Forwards									
Silvio Gonzalez	25	10	7	2	322	1	0	-	Argentina
Juanlu	25	32	27	20	1944	6	0	-	Spain
Kostas Kiassos	29	4	3	0	169	0	0	-	Greece
Chun-Soo Lee	23	18	13	8	841	3	0	-	South Korea
Angel Miguel	27	16	15	9	967	4	1	-	Spain
Juan Moreno	30	19	18	12	1271	6	0	-	Spain
Aldo Osorio	31	15	13	6	827	1	0	-	Argentina
Julio Pineda	32	32	26	13	1490	1	0	-	Spain
Rafael Rafa	21	8	3	1	170	0	0	-	Spain
Luis Tevenet	31	33	30	13	1893	6	1	-	Spain
Jose Toche	22	7	5	1	197	0	0	-	Spain

SQUAD APPEARANCES

Match	1	2	3	4	5	6	7	8	9	10	11	12	13	14	15	16	17	18	19	20	21	22	23	24	25	26	27	28	29	30	31	32	33	34	35	36	37	38
Venue	H	A	H	A	H	A	H	A	H	A	H	A	H	A	A	H	A	H	A	A	H	A	H	A	H	A	H	A	H	A	H	A	H	H	A	H	A	H
Competition	L	L	L	L	L	L	L	L	L	L	L	L	L	L	L	L	L	L	L	L	L	L	L	L	L	L	L	L	L	L	L	L	L	L	L	L	L	L
Result	D	L	W	L	D	L	L	L	L	L	W	L	W	L	L	D	L	D	D	L	L	L	L	W	D	D	D	L	L	L	W	L	L	D	L	D	W	D

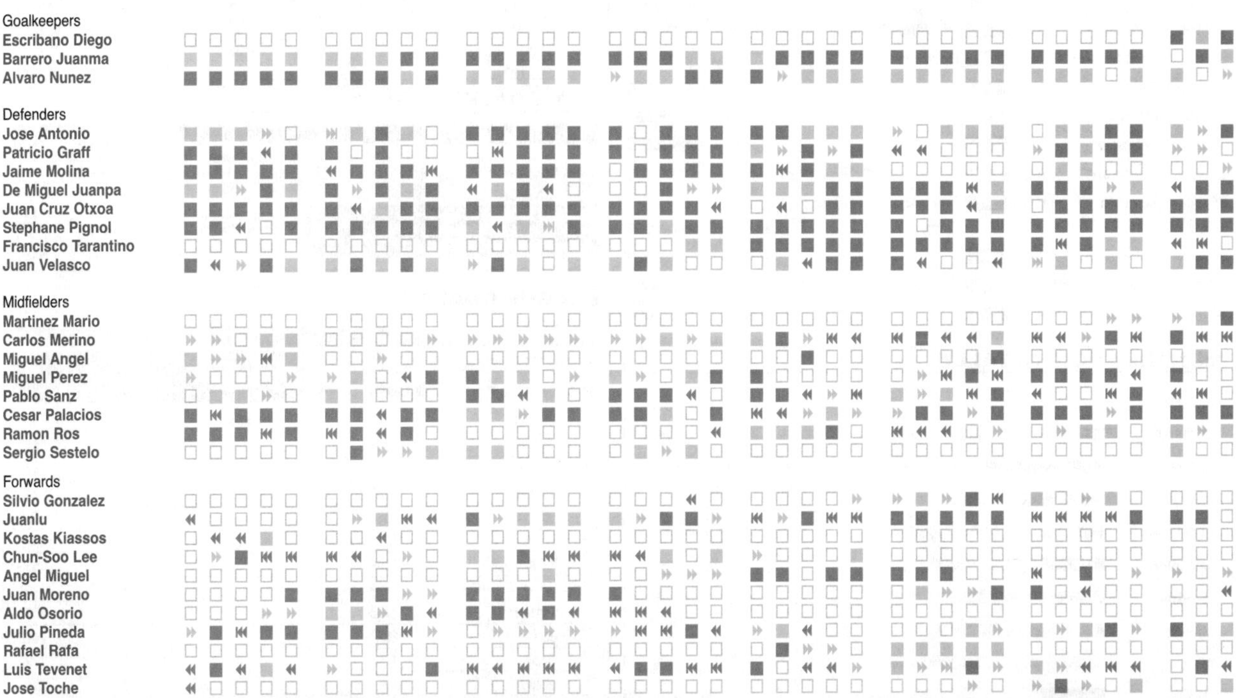
Goalkeepers
Escribano Diego
Barrero Juanma
Alvaro Nunez
Defenders
Jose Antonio
Patricio Graff
Jaime Molina
De Miguel Juanpa
Juan Cruz Otxoa
Stephane Pignol
Francisco Tarantino
Juan Velasco
Midfielders
Martinez Mario
Carlos Merino
Miguel Angel
Miguel Perez
Pablo Sanz
Cesar Palacios
Ramon Ros
Sergio Sestelo
Forwards
Silvio Gonzalez
Juanlu
Kostas Kiassos
Chun-Soo Lee
Angel Miguel
Juan Moreno
Aldo Osorio
Julio Pineda
Rafael Rafa
Luis Tevenet
Jose Toche

KEY: ■ On all match ■ On bench ⏮ Subbed or sent off (Counting game) « Subbed or sent off (playing less than 70 minutes) ⏭ Subbed on from bench (Counting Game) » Subbed on (playing less than 70 minutes) ⏭ Subbed on and then subbed or sent off (Counting Game) » Subbed on and then subbed or sent off (playing less than 70 minutes) □ Not in 16

ALBACETE

Final Position: **20th**

KEY: Won Drawn Lost

							Attendance
1	sppr1	**Seville**	A	L	0-1		41,000
2	sppr1	**Atl Madrid**	H	L	0-2		14,000
3	sppr1	**Real Zaragoza**	A	L	3-4	Pacheco 32; Redondo 41; Gonzalez, R 89	32,000
4	sppr1	**Mallorca**	H	D	0-0		14,000
5	sppr1	**Numancia**	A	D	0-0		7,000
6	sppr1	**Espanyol**	H	W	1-0	Redondo 65	15,000
7	sppr1	**Osasuna**	A	L	2-4	Baudes 41; Redondo 51	13,000
8	sppr1	**Athl Bilbao**	H	W	1-0	Ruben Castro 44	14,000
9	sppr1	**Deportivo**	A	D	0-0		20,000
10	sppr1	**Real Betis**	H	D	0-0		13,000
11	sppr1	**Real Madrid**	A	L	1-6	Francisco 15	79,000
12	sppr1	**Getafe**	H	D	1-1	Baudes 50	15,000
13	sppr1	**Malaga**	A	W	2-0	Viaud 9; Momo 48	20,000
14	sppr1	**Valencia**	H	L	0-1		14,000
15	sppr1	**Barcelona**	H	L	1-2	Gonzalez, M 74	17,000
16	sppr1	**Levante**	A	D	1-1	Gaspar 29	15,000
17	sppr1	**Villarreal**	H	D	2-2	Pacheco 15,87	11,000
18	sppr1	**Real Sociedad**	A	W	2-0	Pacheco 7,49	21,000
19	sppr1	**R Santander**	H	D	0-0		15,000
20	sppr1	**Seville**	H	L	0-2		13,000
21	sppr1	**Atl Madrid**	A	L	1-3	Francisco 11	50,000
22	sppr1	**Real Zaragoza**	H	W	2-1	Pacheco 48,84	15,000
23	sppr1	**Mallorca**	A	L	1-2	Aramburu 8; Gonzalez, M 28	21,000
24	sppr1	**Numancia**	H	L	1-2	Gonzalez, M 37	14,000
25	sppr1	**Espanyol**	A	L	1-2	Pacheco 57	25,000
26	sppr1	**Osasuna**	H	D	1-1	Pacheco 82 pen	15,000
27	sppr1	**Athl Bilbao**	A	L	1-3	Ruben Castro 11	28,000
28	sppr1	**Deportivo**	H	L	0-1		15,000
29	sppr1	**Real Betis**	A	L	1-2	Gonzalez, M 74	38,000
30	sppr1	**Real Madrid**	H	L	1-2	Redondo 9	15,000
31	sppr1	**Getafe**	A	L	0-1		5,000
32	sppr1	**Malaga**	H	L	1-2	Pacheco 67	8,000
33	sppr1	**Valencia**	A	L	0-2		42,000
34	sppr1	**Barcelona**	A	L	0-2		91,000
35	sppr1	**Levante**	H	W	3-1	Francisco 38; Redondo 51; Gonzalez, M 53	9,000
36	sppr1	**Villarreal**	A	L	0-1		21,000
37	sppr1	**Real Sociedad**	H	D	2-2	Pacheco 9,32	6,000
38	sppr1	**R Santander**	A	L	0-1		11,000

MONTHLY POINTS TALLY

AUGUST	0	0%
SEPTEMBER	2	17%
OCTOBER	7	58%
NOVEMBER	5	42%
DECEMBER	2	17%
JANUARY	4	33%
FEBRUARY	3	25%
MARCH	1	8%
APRIL	0	0%
MAY	4	27%

KEY PLAYERS - GOALSCORERS

Antonio Pacheco

Goals in the League	12	Player Strike Rate Average number of minutes between League goals scored by player	240
Contribution to Attacking Power Average number of minutes between League team goals while on pitch	106	Club Strike Rate Average number of minutes between League goals scored by club	101

	PLAYER	LGE GOALS	POWER	STRIKE RATE
1	Antonio Pacheco	12	106	**240 mins**
2	Mark Gonzalez	5	94	**342 mins**
3	Pablo Redondo	5	95	**477 mins**
4	Miguel Baudes	2	97	**1359 mins**
5	Ruben Gonzalez	1	91	**1738 mins**

KEY PLAYERS - MIDFIELDERS

Pablo Redondo

Goals in the League	5	Contribution to Attacking Power Average number of minutes between League team goals while on pitch	95
Defensive Rating Average number of mins between League goals conceded while on the pitch	60	Scoring Difference Defensive Rating minus Contribution to Attacking Power	-35

	PLAYER	LGE GOALS	DEF RATE	POWER	SCORE DIFF
1	Pablo Redondo	5	60	95	**-35 mins**
2	Rubio Alvaro	0	65	113	**-48 mins**
3	Sanchez Jaime	0	54	105	**-51 mins**
4	Laurent Viaud	1	60	112	**-52 mins**

KEY PLAYERS - DEFENDERS

Ruben Gonzalez

Goals Conceded Number of League goals conceded while the player was on the pitch	24	Clean Sheets In games when player was on pitch for at least 70 minutes	6
Defensive Rating Ave number of mins between League goals conceded while on the pitch	72	Club Defensive Rating Average number of mins between League goals conceded by the club this season	60

	PLAYER	CON LGE	CLEAN SHEETS	DEF RATE
1	Ruben Gonzalez	24	6	**72 mins**
2	Carles Mingo	19	3	**69 mins**
3	Miguel Baudes	42	8	**65 mins**
4	Burgos Gaspar	33	8	**61 mins**
5	Paco Pena	53	6	**54 mins**

KEY GOALKEEPER

Ronny Gaspercic

Goals Conceded in the League	23	Counting Games Games when player was on pitch for at least 70 minutes	16
Defensive Rating Ave number of mins between League goals conceded while on the pitch	64	Clean Sheets In games when player was on pitch for at least 70 minutes	5

LEAGUE GOALS

Antonio Pacheco

Minutes on the pitch	2884	Goals in the League	12
League average (mins between goals)	240		

	PLAYER	MINS	GOALS	AVE
1	Pacheco	2884	**12**	240
2	Redondo	2383	**5**	477
3	Gonzalez, M	1708	**5**	342
4	Francisco	1527	**3**	509
5	Baudes	2718	**2**	1359
6	Ruben Castro	1109	**2**	555
7	Momo	1404	**1**	1404
8	Gonzalez, R	1738	**1**	1738
9	Gaspar	2023	**1**	2023
10	Viaud	1798	**1**	1798
	Other		1	
	TOTAL		**34**	

DISCIPLINARY

	PLAYER	YELLOW	RED	AVE
1	Santi	7	1	**122**
2	Gaspar	13	2	**134**
3	Viaud	9	1	**179**
4	David Sanchez	3	1	**189**
5	Jaime	6	1	**224**
6	Mingo	5	0	**263**
7	Oscar Montiel	5	0	**294**
8	Baudes	8	1	**302**
9	Agus	2	0	**315**
10	Peralta	2	0	**322**
11	Gonzalez, M	5	0	**341**
12	Paco Pena	8	0	**360**
13	Pacheco	6	1	**412**
	Other	17	0	
	TOTAL	**96**	**8**	

TOP POINT EARNERS

	PLAYER	GAMES	AV PTS
1	Ronny Gaspercic	16	**1.13**
2	Ruben Gonzalez	19	**0.95**
3	Rubio Alvaro	20	**0.95**
4	Burgos Gaspar	22	**0.86**
5	Pablo Redondo	25	**0.84**
6	Miguel Baudes	29	**0.83**
7	Mark Gonzalez	14	**0.79**
8	Paco Pena	32	**0.72**
9	Antonio Pacheco	30	**0.67**
10	Carles Mingo	14	**0.64**
	CLUB AVERAGE:		**0.74**

LEAGUE APPEARANCES, BOOKINGS AND CAPS

	AGE (on 01/07/05)	IN NAMED 18	APPEARANCES	COUNTING GAMES	MINUTES ON PITCH	YELLOW CARDS	RED CARDS	THIS SEASON	HOME COUNTRY
Goalkeepers									
Espinosa Casto	23	2	1	0	62	0	0	-	Spain
Ronny Gaspercic	36	36	17	16	1482	0	0	-	Belgium
Javier Pindado	29	13	1	1	90	0	0	-	Spain
Raul Valbuena	30	23	20	19	1758	1	0	-	Spain
Defenders									
Garcia Agus	20	7	7	7	630	2	0	-	Spain
Miguel Baudes	25	33	31	29	2718	8	1	-	Spain
Martin Camano	-	1	1	0	11	0	0	-	Spain
Jordi Ferron	26	6	1	0	5	1	0	-	Spain
Burgos Gaspar	26	29	25	22	2023	13	2	-	Spain
Ruben Gonzalez	23	23	20	19	1738	2	0	-	Spain
Carles Mingo	28	17	15	14	1316	5	0	-	Spain
Oscar Montiel	35	33	22	13	1474	5	0	-	Spain
Paco Pena	26	33	33	33	2970	8	0	-	Spain
Denia Santi	31	16	12	9	979	7	1	-	Spain
Gustavo Siviero	35	10	2	2	180	0	0	-	Argentina
Midfielders									
Rubio Alvaro	26	29	29	20	2156	5	0	-	Spain
Alberto Cano	21	2	2	1	119	0	0	-	Spain
David Sanchez	22	27	18	4	759	3	1	-	Spain
Ruiz Ivan Diaz	26	17	8	0	295	1	0	-	Spain
Sanchez Jaime	32	28	22	13	1572	6	1	-	Spain
Abass Lawal	24	3	1	0	56	1	0	-	Nigeria
Jeronimo Momo	22	30	24	9	1404	1	0	-	Spain
Pablo Garcia	20	4	2	1	87	0	0	-	Spain
Pablo Redondo	23	33	30	25	2383	5	0	-	Spain
Laurent Viaud	35	33	25	18	1798	9	1	-	France
Forwards									
Molina Elias	23	3	1	0	52	0	0	-	Spain
Rodriguez Francisco	26	38	28	10	1527	2	0	-	Spain
Manuel Gato	21	2	2	0	53	0	0	-	Spain
Mark Gonzalez	20	31	28	14	1708	5	0	-	Chile
Nicolas Olivera	27	8	4	0	124	0	0	1	Uruguay (16)
Antonio Pacheco	29	36	34	30	2884	6	1	-	Uruguay
Horacio Peralta	23	12	12	6	645	2	0	-	Uruguay
Ruben Castro	24	31	21	8	1109	0	0	-	Spain

TEAM OF THE SEASON

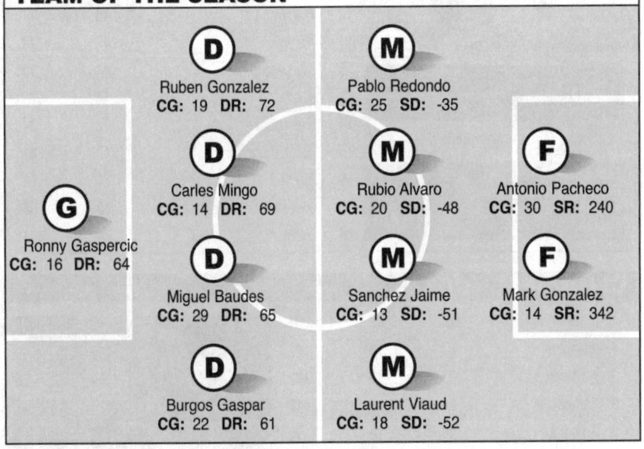

D
Ruben Gonzalez
CG: 19 DR: 72
M
Pablo Redondo
CG: 25 SD: -35
D
Carles Mingo
CG: 14 DR: 69
M
Rubio Alvaro
CG: 20 SD: -48
F
Antonio Pacheco
CG: 30 SR: 240
G
Ronny Gaspercic
CG: 16 DR: 64
D
Miguel Baudes
CG: 29 DR: 65
M
Sanchez Jaime
CG: 13 SD: -51
F
Mark Gonzalez
CG: 14 SR: 342
D
Burgos Gaspar
CG: 22 DR: 61
M
Laurent Viaud
CG: 18 SD: -52

SQUAD APPEARANCES

Match	1	2	3	4	5	6	7	8	9	10	11	12	13	14	15	16	17	18	19	20	21	22	23	24	25	26	27	28	29	30	31	32	33	34	35	36	37	38
Venue	A	H	A	H	A	H	A	H	A	H	A	H	A	H	H	A	H	A	H	H	A	H	A	H	A	H	A	H	A	H	A	H	A	A	H	A	H	A
Competition	L	L	L	L	L	L	L	L	L	L	L	L	L	L	L	L	L	L	L	L	L	L	L	L	L	L	L	L	L	L	L	L	L	L	L	L	L	L
Result	L	L	L	D	D	W	L	W	D	D	L	D	W	L	L	D	D	W	D	L	L	W	L	L	L	D	L	L	L	L	L	L	L	L	W	L	D	L

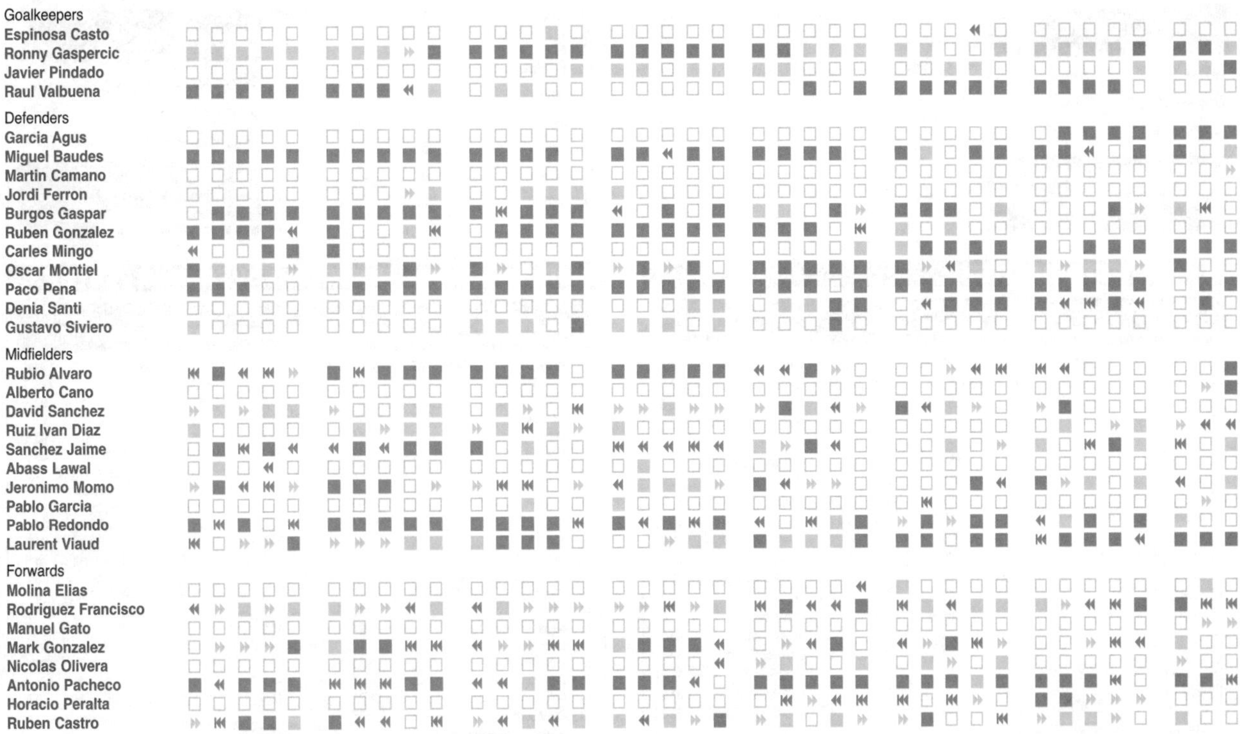

Goalkeepers
Espinosa Casto
Ronny Gaspercic
Javier Pindado
Raul Valbuena
Defenders
Garcia Agus
Miguel Baudes
Martin Camano
Jordi Ferron
Burgos Gaspar
Ruben Gonzalez
Carles Mingo
Oscar Montiel
Paco Pena
Denia Santi
Gustavo Siviero
Midfielders
Rubio Alvaro
Alberto Cano
David Sanchez
Ruiz Ivan Diaz
Sanchez Jaime
Abass Lawal
Jeronimo Momo
Pablo Garcia
Pablo Redondo
Laurent Viaud
Forwards
Molina Elias
Rodriguez Francisco
Manuel Gato
Mark Gonzalez
Nicolas Olivera
Antonio Pacheco
Horacio Peralta
Ruben Castro

ITALIAN LEAGUE ROUND-UP

FINAL LEAGUE TABLE

	HOME						AWAY					TOTAL			
	P	W	D	L	F	A	W	D	L	F	A	F	A	DIF	PTS
Juventus	38	15	2	2	38	13	11	6	2	29	14	67	27	40	86
AC Milan	38	11	5	3	38	17	12	5	2	25	11	63	28	35	79
Inter Milan	38	11	7	1	34	16	7	11	1	31	21	65	37	28	72
Udinese	38	8	7	4	29	18	9	4	6	27	22	56	40	16	62
Sampdoria	38	10	3	6	21	13	7	7	5	21	16	42	29	13	61
Palermo	38	9	7	3	28	22	3	10	6	20	22	48	44	4	53
Messina	38	10	7	2	26	19	2	5	12	18	33	44	52	-8	48
Roma	38	6	8	5	31	26	5	4	10	24	32	55	58	-3	45
Livorno	38	9	5	5	28	25	2	7	10	21	35	49	60	-11	45
Lazio	38	6	6	7	26	24	5	5	9	22	29	48	53	-5	44
Lecce	38	8	8	3	40	30	2	6	11	26	43	66	73	-7	44
Cagliari	38	9	9	1	30	17	1	5	13	21	43	51	60	-9	44
Reggina	38	7	6	6	21	23	3	8	8	15	22	36	45	-9	44
Siena	38	5	8	6	21	27	4	8	7	23	28	44	55	-11	43
Chievo	38	8	5	6	19	18	3	5	11	12	31	31	49	-18	43
Bologna	38	6	7	6	20	17	3	8	8	13	19	33	36	-3	42
Fiorentina	38	7	7	5	29	22	2	8	9	13	27	42	49	-7	42
Parma	38	8	9	2	33	25	2	3	14	15	40	48	65	-17	42
Brescia	38	6	3	10	15	22	5	5	9	22	32	37	54	-17	41
Atalanta	38	7	6	6	21	17	1	5	13	13	28	34	45	-11	35

CLUB STRIKE FORCE

Ibrahimovic striking for Juvé

1 Juventus

Goals scored in the League	67
Club Strike Rate (CSR) Average number of minutes between League goals scored by club	51

	CLUB	GOALS	CSR
1	Juventus	67	51
2	Lecce	66	52
3	Inter Milan	65	53
4	AC Milan	63	54
5	Udinese	56	61
6	Roma	55	62
7	Cagliari	51	67
8	Livorno	49	70
9	Lazio	48	71
10	Palermo	48	71
11	Parma	47	73
12	Messina	44	78
13	Siena	44	78
14	Fiorentina	42	81
15	Sampdoria	42	81
16	Brescia	37	92
17	Reggina	36	95
18	Atalanta	34	101

CLUB DISCIPLINARY RECORDS

Jorge Bolano, Parma

1 Parma

League Yellow	95
League Red	11
League Total	106
Cards Average in League Average number of minutes between a card being shown of either colour	32

	CLUB	Y	R	TOTAL	AVE
1	Parma	95	11	106	32
2	Roma	98	7	105	33
3	Bologna	96	5	101	34
4	Brescia	90	12	102	34
5	Palermo	93	6	99	35
6	Cagliari	87	9	96	36
7	Lazio	84	10	94	36
8	Messina	88	6	94	36
9	Reggina	90	5	95	36
10	Chievo	83	8	91	38
11	Lecce	82	6	88	39
12	Livorno	83	5	88	39
13	Sampdoria	80	4	84	41
14	Atalanta	75	5	80	43
15	Fiorentina	72	6	78	44
16	Inter Milan	74	3	77	44
17	Siena	70	8	78	44
18	Udinese	68	3	71	48

CLUB DEFENCES

	CLUB	LGE	CS	CDR
1	Juventus	27	19	127
2	AC Milan	28	17	122
3	Sampdoria	29	18	118
4	Bologna	36	10	95
5	Inter Milan	37	16	92
6	Udinese	40	13	86
7	Palermo	44	13	78
8	Atalanta	45	10	76
9	Reggina	45	11	76
10	Fiorentina	48	11	71
11	Chievo	49	11	70
12	Messina	52	11	66
13	Lazio	53	7	65
14	Brescia	54	8	63
15	Siena	55	8	62
16	Roma	58	8	59
17	Cagliari	60	8	57
18	Livorno	60	9	57

Nesta, No 2 spot for Milan

1 Juventus

Goals conceded in the League	27
Clean Sheets (CS) Number of league games where no goals were conceded	19
Club Defensive Rate (CDR) Average number of minutes between League goals conceded by club	127

PLAYER NATIONALITIES

Overseas country with the most player appearances in the Italian League - Brazil

591 league appearances by Brazilian players

	COUNTRY	PLAYERS	IN SQUAD	LGE APP	% LGE ACT	CAPS	MOST APP	APP
1	Italy	430	9500	7166	70.1	134	Gianluca Pagliuca	100.0
2	Brazil	30	717	591	5.5	45	Nelson Dida	92.3
3	Argentina	23	507	383	3.8	33	Mauro Camoranesi	89.0
4	France	14	319	272	2.6	11	Lilian Thuram	97.4
5	Uruguay	10	235	167	1.5	17	Guillermo Giacomazzi	79.7
6	Croatia	6	149	119	1.1	14	Igor Budan	52.7
7	Czech Republic	4	98	91	1.0	14	Marek Jankulovski	81.3
8	Serbia & Montenegro	5	123	108	1.0	7	Dejan Stankovic	66.1
9	Greece	7	140	93	1.0		Theodoros Zagorakis	79.0
10	Portugal	6	134	98	0.9		Jose Luis Vidigal	65.2
11	Chile	4	95	82	0.8		David Marcelo Pizarro	83.5
12	Denmark	4	115	96	0.8	22	Per Kroldrup	60.8
13	Nigeria	4	90	81	0.8		Christian Obodo	73.0
14	Ghana	5	134	88	0.8		Sulley Muntari	73.5
15	Holland	5	97	82	0.7	5	Clarence Seedorf	69.1
16	Australia	2	63	58	0.6		Mark Bresciano	81.3
17	Colombia	2	61	53	0.6		Ivan Cordoba	81.6
18	Japan	3	102	75	0.6		Shunsuke Nakamura	62.8

CLUB MAKE-UP – HOME AND OVERSEAS PLAYERS

1 Inter Milan

69.2% of appearances by overseas players

	CLUB	OVERSEAS	HOME	% OVERSEAS	% LGE ACT	MOST APP	APP
1	Inter Milan	21	16	56.8	69.2	Javier Zanetti	88.0
2	AC Milan	17	15	53.1	61.7	Nelson Dida	92.3
3	Juventus	15	14	51.7	57.1	Lilian Thuram	97.4
4	Lecce	13	17	43.3	46.3	S Diamoutene	83.8
5	Udinese	12	13	48.0	41.0	David Pizarro	83.5
6	Roma	10	27	27.0	33.1	Vincenzo Montella	87.5
7	Parma	7	28	20.0	32.3	Sebastian Frey	94.0
8	Brescia	10	22	31.3	28.4	Gilberto Martinez	81.7
9	Lazio	11	23	32.4	27.8	Ousmane Dabo	67.4
10	Messina	8	24	25.0	27.7	Rahman Rezaei	94.6
11	Fiorentina	10	21	32.3	25.9	Christian Obodo	73.0
12	Bologna	6	27	18.2	23.8	T Zagorakis	79.0
13	Cagliari	6	22	21.4	21.9	Diego Luis Lopez	78.0
14	Reggina	7	23	23.3	21.2	Mozart	89.7
15	Siena	6	27	18.2	20.2	Alex Manninger	50.0
16	Livorno	8	19	29.6	19.4	Jose Luis Vidigal	65.2
17	Atalanta	6	30	16.7	14.6	Igor Budan	52.7
18	Palermo	5	23	17.9	10.2	Mario Santana	56.2
19	Chievo	5	27	15.6	8.7	Oliveira Amauri	36.9
20	Sampdoria	2	28	6.7	5.3	Vitaly Kutuzov	39.6

CHART-TOPPING MIDFIELDERS

1 Seedorf - AC Milan	
Goals scored in the League	5
Defensive Rating Av number of mins between League goals conceded while on the pitch	169
Contribution to Attacking Power Average number of minutes between League team goals while on pitch	61
Scoring Difference Defensive Rating minus Contribution to Attacking Power	108

	PLAYER	CLUB	GOALS	DEF RATE	POWER	S DIFF
1	Seedorf	AC Milan	5	169	61	108
2	Blasi	Juventus	0	161	59	102
3	Pirlo	AC Milan	4	144	55	89
4	Kaka	AC Milan	7	139	55	84
5	Emerson	Juventus	1	139	55	84
6	Camoranesi	Juventus	4	132	49	83
7	Zambrotta	Juventus	0	124	51	73
8	Gattuso	AC Milan	0	129	57	72
9	Nedved	Juventus	8	113	45	68
10	Tonetto	Sampdoria	5	146	82	64
11	Diana	Sampdoria	5	159	96	63
12	Cambiasso	Inter Milan	2	112	54	58
13	Volpi	Sampdoria	2	127	79	48
14	Pizarro	Udinese	2	102	58	44
15	Veron	Inter Milan	3	94	53	41

CHART-TOPPING GOALSCORERS

1 Shevchenko - AC Milan	
Goals scored in the League	17
Contribution to Attacking Power (AP) Average number of minutes between League team goals while on pitch	47
Club Strike Rate (CSR) Average minutes between League goals scored by club	54
Player Strike Rate Average number of minutes between League goals scored by player	132

	PLAYER	CLUB	GOALS: LGE	POWER	CSR	S RATE
1	Shevchenko	AC Milan	17	47	54	132
2	Adriano	Inter Milan	16	50	53	142
3	Montella	Roma	21	62	62	142
4	Gilardino	Parma	22	70	73	151
5	Toni	Palermo	20	67	71	156
6	C Lucarelli	Livorno	19	65	68	162
7	Ibrahimovic	Juventus	16	49	50	172
8	Esposito	Cagliari	16	66	67	182
9	Di Michele	Udinese	15	57	61	187
10	Zampagna	Messina	12	71	78	192
11	Crespo	AC Milan	10	69	54	201
12	Iaquinta	Udinese	13	57	61	205
13	Totti	Roma	12	59	62	214
14	Flachi	Sampdoria	14	82	81	217
15	Miccoli	Fiorentina	12	87	80	220

CHART-TOPPING DEFENDERS

1 Zebina - Juventus	
Goals Conceded in the League The number of League goals conceded while he was on the pitch	12
Clean Sheets In games when he played at least 70 mins	11
Club Defensive Rating Average mins between League goals conceded by the club this season	127
Defensive Rating Average number of minutes between League goals conceded while on pitch	173

	PLAYER	CLUB	CON: LGE	CS	CDR	DEF RATE
1	Zebina	Juventus	12	11	127	173
2	Nesta	AC Milan	16	12	122	159
3	Falcone	Sampdoria	16	12	118	146
4	Cannavaro	Juventus	24	19	127	139
5	Maldini	AC Milan	22	16	122	137
6	Cafu	AC Milan	22	13	122	129
7	Thuram	Juventus	26	19	127	128
8	Zenoni	Sampdoria	27	17	118	114
9	Pisano	Sampdoria	21	10	118	114
10	Castellini	Sampdoria	19	10	118	109
11	Gamberini	Bologna	22	8	95	108
12	Torrisi	Bologna	19	7	95	108
13	Juarez	Bologna	22	8	95	104
14	Sussi	Bologna	23	8	95	102
15	Favalli	Inter Milan	20	10	92	102

CHART-TOPPING GOALKEEPERS

1 Buffon - Juventus	
Counting Games Games in which he played at least 70 minutes	37
Goals Conceded in the League The number of League goals conceded while he was on the pitch	23
Clean Sheets In games when he played at least 70 mins	19
Defensive Rating Average number of minutes between League goals conceded while on pitch	143

	PLAYER	CLUB	CG	CONC	CS	DEF RATE
1	Buffon	Juventus	37	23	19	143
2	Dida	AC Milan	35	23	16	137
3	Antonioli	Sampdoria	36	26	18	126
4	Pagliuca	Bologna	38	36	10	95
5	Toldo	Inter Milan	29	28	14	95
6	De Sanctis	Udinese	35	38	13	84
7	Pavarini	Reggina	21	23	7	83
8	Guardalben	Palermo	37	41	13	81
9	Lupatelli	Fiorentina	28	32	8	80
10	Sereni	Lazio	16*	21	4	78
11	Marchegiani	Chievo	36	44	11	75
12	Storari	Messina	29	37	10	71
13	Fortin	Siena	19	26	3	66
14	Taibi	Atalanta	23	31	3	65
15	Soviero	Reggina	16*	23	4	65

PLAYER DISCIPLINARY RECORD

1 Olivera - Juventus	
Cards Average mins between cards	85
League Yellow	7
League Red	1
TOTAL	8

	PLAYER		LY	LR	TOT	AVE
1	Olivera	Juventus	7	1	8	85
2	Scurto	Roma	4	0	4	118
3	Pasquale	Siena	5	2	7	122
4	Conti	Cagliari	13	0	13	137
5	Maggio	Fiorentina	5	2	7	148
6	Del Nero	Brescia	6	0	6	153
7	Pazienza	Udinese	8	0	8	154
8	Pinzi	Udinese	12	2	14	158
9	Ambrosini	AC Milan	5	1	6	159
10	Cipriani	Bologna	7	1	8	160
11	Borriello	Reggina	6	0	6	163
12	Bazzani	Lazio	5	0	5	167
13	Colucci	Bologna	12	0	12	168
14	Contini	Parma	12	2	14	170
15	Piangarelli	Fiorentina	6	0	6	173
16	Eremenko	Lecce	4	0	4	176
17	Bolano	Parma	8	0	8	178
18	Muntari	Udinese	14	0	14	179
19	Abeijon	Cagliari	12	1	13	180
20	Zoro	Messina	12	1	13	188
21	Cardone	Parma	6	0	6	188
22	Sculli	Brescia	8	1	9	189
23	D'moutene	Lecce	13	2	15	191
24	Balleri	Livorno	9	1	10	191

TEAM OF THE SEASON

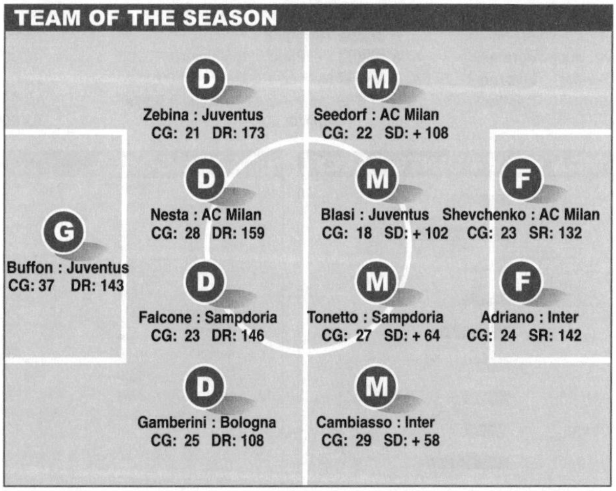
G
Buffon : Juventus
CG: 37 DR: 143
D
Zebina : Juventus
CG: 21 DR: 173
D
Nesta : AC Milan
CG: 28 DR: 159
D
Falcone : Sampdoria
CG: 23 DR: 146
D
Gamberini : Bologna
CG: 25 DR: 108
M
Seedorf : AC Milan
CG: 22 SD: + 108
M
Blasi : Juventus
CG: 18 SD: + 102
M
Tonetto : Sampdoria
CG: 27 SD: + 64
M
Cambiasso : Inter
CG: 29 SD: + 58
F
Shevchenko : AC Milan
CG: 23 SR: 132
F
Adriano : Inter
CG: 24 SR: 142

ITALIAN SERIE A CHAMPIONS

JUVENTUS

Final Position: **1st**

KEY: Won / Drawn / Lost

		Opponent			Score	Scorers	Attendance
1	clql1	Djurgarden	H	D	2-2	Trezeguet 50; Emerson 59	26,000
2	clql2	Djurgarden	A	W	4-1	Del Piero 10; Trezeguet 34,86; Nedved 54	32,000
3	itpr1	Brescia	A	W	3-0	Nedved 34; Trezeguet 38; Ibrahimovic 69	18,000
4	cl gc	Ajax	A	W	1-0	Nedved 42	49,000
5	itpr1	Atalanta	H	W	2-0	Trezeguet 14,58	22,000
6	itpr1	Sampdoria	A	W	3-0	Del Piero 18 pen; Ibrahimovic 69; Trezeguet 86	36,000
7	itpr1	Palermo	H	D	1-1	Ibrahimovic 54	27,000
8	cl gc	M Tel-Aviv	H	W	1-0	Camoranesi 37	6,000
9	itpr1	Udinese	A	W	1-0	Zalayeta 61	28,000
10	itpr1	Messina	H	W	2-1	Zalayeta 27; Nedved 56	30,000
11	cl gc	Bayern Munich	H	W	1-0	Nedved 75	18,000
12	itpr1	Siena	A	W	3-0	Del Piero 53,60; Camoranesi 63	15,000
13	itpr1	Roma	H	W	2-0	Del Piero 31; Zalayeta 74	28,000
14	itpr1	Chievo	H	W	3-0	Zalayeta 25; Nedved 65; Ibrahimovic 79	22,000
15	cl gc	Bayern Munich	A	W	1-0	Del Piero 90	59,000
16	itpr1	Reggina	A	L	1-2	Ibrahimovic 14; Kapo Obou 49	25,000
17	itpr1	Fiorentina	H	W	1-0	Olivera 73	24,000
18	itpr1	Lecce	A	W	1-0	Del Piero 14	30,000
19	cl gc	Ajax	H	W	1-0	Zalayeta 14	7,000
20	itpr1	Inter Milan	A	D	2-2	Nedved 53; Ibrahimovic 66 pen	78,000
21	itpr1	Lazio	H	W	2-1	Olivera 40; Ibrahimovic 75	21,000
22	cl gc	M Tel-Aviv	A	D	1-1	Del Piero 71	19,000
23	itpr1	Bologna	A	W	1-0	Nedved 86	12,000
24	itpr1	AC Milan	H	D	0-0		54,000
25	itpr1	Parma	A	D	1-1	Ibrahimovic 63	25,000
26	itpr1	Livorno	H	W	4-2	Del Piero 17; Camoranesi 25,90 pen; Ibrahimovic 75	21,000
27	itpr1	Cagliari	A	D	1-1	Del Piero 54	22,000
28	itpr1	Brescia	H	W	2-0	Trezeguet 12; Domizzi 43 og	19,000
29	itpr1	Atalanta	A	W	2-1	Olivera 23; Del Piero 80 pen	15,000
30	itpr1	Sampdoria	H	L	0-1		20,000
31	itpr1	Palermo	A	L	0-1		34,000
32	itpr1	Udinese	H	W	2-1	Ibrahimovic 1; Camoranesi 49	21,000
33	itpr1	Messina	A	D	0-0		40,000
34	clr2l1	Real Madrid	A	L	0-1		78,000
35	itpr1	Siena	H	W	3-0	Del Piero 35,63 pen; Emerson 49	20,000
36	itpr1	Roma	A	W	2-1	Cannavaro 11; Del Piero 44	35,000
37	clr2l2	Real Madrid	H	W	2-0	Trezeguet 75; Zalayeta 116	59,000
38	itpr1	Chievo	A	W	1-0	Olivera 87	25,000
39	itpr1	Reggina	H	W	1-0	Del Piero 65	21,000
40	clqfl1	Liverpool	A	L	1-2	Cannavaro 63	41,216
41	itpr1	Fiorentina	A	D	3-3	Del Piero 22; Ibrahimovic 59,82	46,000
42	clqfl2	Liverpool	H	D	0-0		50,000
43	itpr1	Lecce	H	W	5-2	Appiah 16; Ibrahimovic 34,43,84; Nedved 56	21,000
44	itpr1	Inter Milan	H	L	0-1		25,000
45	itpr1	Lazio	A	W	1-0	Nedved 85	45,000
46	itpr1	Bologna	H	W	2-1	Cannavaro 18; Zalayeta 24	21,000
47	itpr1	AC Milan	A	W	1-0	Trezeguet 27	68,000
48	itpr1	Parma	H	W	2-0	Del Piero 6; Ibrahimovic 23	40,000
49	itpr1	Livorno	A	D	2-2	Nedved 10; Trezeguet 66	22,000
50	itpr1	Cagliari	H	W	4-2	Del Piero 43; Trezeguet 52,74; Appiah 60	53,000

KEY PLAYERS - GOALSCORERS

Alessandro Del Piero

Goals in the League	15
Contribution to Attacking Power Average number of minutes between League team goals while on pitch	55
Player Strike Rate Average number of minutes between League goals scored by player	129
Club Strike Rate Average number of minutes between League goals scored by club	50

	PLAYER	GOALS LGE	POWER	S RATE
1	Alessandro Del Piero	15	55	129 mins
2	Zlatan Ibrahimovic	16	49	172 mins
3	Pavel Nedved	8	44	297 mins
4	Stephen Appiah	2	45	635 mins
5	Mauro Camoranesi	4	49	761 mins

KEY PLAYERS - MIDFIELDERS

Manuele Blasi

Goals in the League	0
Defensive Rating Average number of mins between League goals conceded while on the pitch	161
Contribution to Attacking Power Average number of minutes between League team goals while on pitch	59
Scoring Difference Defensive Rating minus Contribution to Attacking Power	102

	PLAYER	GOALS LGE	DEF RATE	ATT POWER	SCORE DIFF
1	Manuele Blasi	0	161	59	102 mins
2	Emerson	1	139	55	84 mins
3	Mauro Camoranesi	4	132	49	83 mins
4	Gianluca Zambrotta	0	124	51	73 mins
5	Stephen Appiah	2	115	45	70 mins

KEY PLAYERS - DEFENDERS

Jonathan Zebina

Goals Conceded in League	12
Clean Sheets In games when player was on pitch for at least 70 minutes	11
Defensive Rating Ave number of mins between League goals conceded while on the pitch	173
Club Defensive Rating Average number of mins between League goals conceded by the club this season	127

	PLAYER	CON LGE	CLEAN SHEETS	DEF RATE
1	Jonathan Zebina	12	11	173 mins
2	Fabio Cannavaro	24	19	139 mins
3	Lilian Thuram	26	19	128 mins
4	Gianluca Pessotto	12	6	96 mins

MONTHLY POINTS TALLY

SEPTEMBER	10	83%
OCTOBER	15	100%
NOVEMBER	7	58%
DECEMBER	7	78%
JANUARY	11	73%
FEBRUARY	7	47%
MARCH	9	100%
APRIL	7	58%
MAY	13	87%

LEAGUE GOALS

	PLAYER	MINS	GOALS	AVE
1	Ibrahimovic	2757	16	172
2	Del Piero	1941	15	129
3	Trezeguet	1168	9	130
4	Nedved	2379	8	297
5	Zalayeta	1334	5	267
6	Camoranesi	3045	4	761
7	Olivera	682	4	171
8	Appiah	1270	2	635
9	Cannavaro	3333	2	1667
10	Emerson	2785	1	2785
11	Kapo Obou	281	1	281
	Other		1	
	TOTAL		68	

KEY GOALKEEPER

Gianluigi Buffon

Goals Conceded in the League	23
Counting Games League games when player was on pitch for at least 70 minutes	36
Clean Sheets In games when player was on pitch for at least 70 minutes	19
League minutes played Number of minutes played in league matches	3285
Defensive Rating Ave number of mins between League goals conceded while on the pitch	143

DISCIPLINARY RECORDS

	PLAYER	YELLOW	RED	AVE
1	Olivera	7	1	85
2	Blasi	6	0	295
3	Appiah	4	0	317
4	Nedved	7	0	339
5	Zebina	6	0	345
6	Tacchinardi	2	0	376
7	Birindelli	1	0	483
8	Camoranesi	6	0	507
9	Emerson	4	1	557
10	Thuram	5	0	666
11	Ibrahimovic	4	0	689
12	Del Piero	2	0	970
13	Zambrotta	3	0	1078
	Other	4	0	
	TOTAL	61	2	

TOP POINT EARNERS

	PLAYER	GAMES	AV PTS
1	Stephen Appiah	13	2.62
2	Jonathan Zebina	21	2.38
3	Alessandro Del Piero	15	2.33
4	Lilian Thuram	37	2.30
5	Mauro Camoranesi	33	2.30
6	Gianluigi Buffon	36	2.28
7	Pavel Nedved	26	2.23
8	Fabio Cannavaro	36	2.22
9	Gianluca Zambrotta	36	2.22
10	Emerson	28	2.18
	CLUB AVERAGE:		2.26

TEAM OF THE SEASON

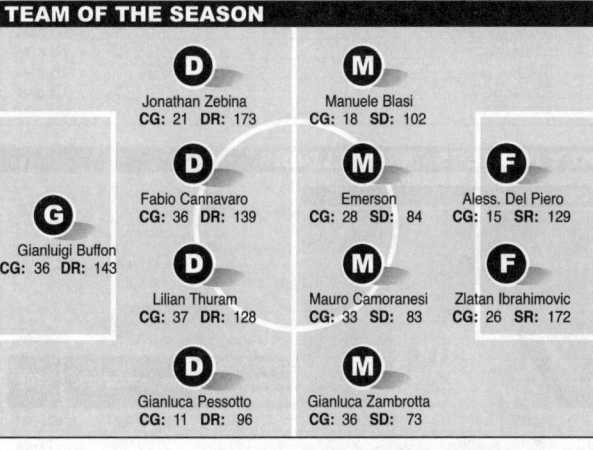

G — Gianluigi Buffon CG: 36 DR: 143

D — Jonathan Zebina CG: 21 DR: 173
D — Fabio Cannavaro CG: 36 DR: 139
D — Lilian Thuram CG: 37 DR: 128
D — Gianluca Pessotto CG: 11 DR: 96

M — Manuele Blasi CG: 18 SD: 102
M — Emerson CG: 28 SD: 84
M — Mauro Camoranesi CG: 33 SD: 83
M — Gianluca Zambrotta CG: 36 SD: 73

F — Aless. Del Piero CG: 15 SR: 129
F — Zlatan Ibrahimovic CG: 26 SR: 172

LEAGUE APPEARANCES AND BOOKINGS

	AGE (on 01/07/05)	IN NAMED 18	APPEARANCES	COUNTING GAMES	MINUTES ON PITCH	YELLOW CARDS	RED CARDS	THIS SEASON	HOME COUNTRY
Goalkeepers									
Landry Bonnefoi	21	9	0	0	0	0	0	-	France
Gianluigi Buffon	27	37	37	36	3285	0	0	7	Italy (10)
Antonio Chimenti	35	30	2	1	135	0	0	-	Italy
Defenders									
Alessandro Birindelli	30	23	12	2	483	1	0	1	Italy (10)
Fabio Cannavaro	31	38	38	36	3333	2	0	4	Italy (10)
Ciro Ferrara	38	18	4	0	27	0	0	-	Italy
Nicola Legrottaglie	28	2	0	0	0	0	0	1	Italy (10)
Andrea Masiello	19	5	1	0	34	0	0	-	Italy
Paolo Montero	33	17	5	3	315	2	0	4	Uruguay (16)
Gianluca Pessotto	34	31	19	11	1152	1	0	-	Italy
Lilian Thuram	33	37	37	37	3330	5	0	-	France
Igor Tudor	27	8	2	0	16	1	0	6	Croatia (21)
Jonathan Zebina	26	26	24	21	2070	6	0	5	France (4)
Midfielders									
Stephen Appiah	24	33	18	13	1270	4	0	-	Ghana
Manuele Blasi	24	33	26	18	1772	6	0	-	Italy
Mauro Camoranesi	28	36	36	33	3045	6	0	-	Argentina
Emerson	29	33	33	28	2785	4	1	3	Brazil (1)
Pavel Nedved	32	27	27	26	2379	7	0	-	Czech Republic
Ruben Olivera	22	27	18	3	682	7	1	1	Uruguay (16)
Alessio Tacchinardi	29	29	17	4	753	2	0	-	Italy
Gianluca Zambrotta	28	36	36	36	3236	3	0	5	Italy (10)
Forwards									
Alessandro Del Piero	30	35	30	15	1941	2	0	1	Italy (10)
Zlatan Ibrahimovic	23	35	35	26	2757	4	0	6	Sweden (13)
Olivier Kapo Obou	24	23	14	1	281	0	0	-	France
Fabrizio Miccoli	26	0	0	0	0	0	0	4	Italy (10)
Adrian Mutu	26	1	1	0	34	0	0	-	Romania
David Trezeguet	27	18	18	10	1168	0	0	3	France (4)
Marcelo Zalayeta	26	37	28	9	1334	1	0	2	Uruguay (16)

SQUAD APPEARANCES

Match	1	2	3	4	5	6	7	8	9	10	11	12	13	14	15	16	17	18	19	20	21	22	23	24	25
Venue	H	A	A	A	H	A	H	H	A	H	H	A	H	H	A	A	H	A	H	A	H	A	A	H	A
Competition	C	C	O	C	O	O	O	C	O	O	C	O	O	O	C	O	O	O	C	O	O	C	O	O	O
Result	D	W	W	W	W	W	D	W	W	W	W	W	W	W	W	L	W	W	W	D	W	D	W	D	D

Match	26	27	28	29	30	31	32	33	34	35	36	37	38	39	40	41	42	43	44	45	46	47	48	49	50
Venue	H	A	H	A	H	A	H	A	A	H	A	H	A	H	A	A	H	H	H	A	H	A	H	A	H
Competition	O	O	O	O	O	O	O	O	C	O	O	C	O	O	C	O	C	O	O	O	O	O	O	O	O
Result	W	D	W	W	L	L	W	D	L	W	W	W	W	W	L	D	D	W	L	W	W	W	W	D	W

Goalkeepers
Landry Bonnefoi
Gianluigi Buffon
Antonio Chimenti

Defenders
Alessandro Birindelli
Fabio Cannavaro
Ciro Ferrara
Nicola Legrottaglie
Andrea Masiello
Paolo Montero
Gianluca Pessotto
Lilian Thuram
Igor Tudor
Jonathan Zebina

Midfielders
Stephen Appiah
Manuele Blasi
Mauro German Camoranesi
Paolo De Ceglie
Emerson
Pavel Nedved
Ruben Olivera
Alessio Tacchinardi
Gianluca Zambrotta

Forwards
Alessandro Del Piero
Zlatan Ibrahimovic
Narcisse Olivier Kapo Obou
Fabrizio Miccoli
Adrian Mutu
Michele Paolucci
David Trezeguet
Marcelo Zalayeta

KEY: On all match | On bench | Subbed or sent off (Counting game) | Subbed or sent off (playing less than 70 minutes) | Subbed on from bench (Counting Game) | Subbed on (playing less than 70 minutes) | Subbed on and then subbed or sent off (Counting Game) | Subbed on and then subbed or sent off (playing less than 70 minutes) | Not in 16

AC MILAN

Final Position: **2nd**

KEY: Won / Drawn / Lost

							Attendance
1	itpr1	Livorno	H	D	2-2	Seedorf 4,47	69,000
2	cl gf	S Donetsk	A	W	1-0	Seedorf 84	30,000
3	itpr1	Bologna	A	W	2-0	Shevchenko 83; Kaka 90	35,000
4	itpr1	Messina	H	L	1-2	Pancaro 54	60,000
5	itpr1	Lazio	A	W	2-1	Shevchenko 70,74	50,000
6	cl gf	Celtic	H	W	3-1	Shevchenko 8; Inzaghi 89; Pirlo 90	68,000
7	itpr1	Reggina	H	W	3-1	Shevchenko 12,88; Kaka 66	59,000
8	itpr1	Cagliari	A	W	1-0	Pirlo 21	20,000
9	cl gf	Barcelona	H	W	1-0	Shevchenko 31	77,000
10	itpr1	Inter Milan	H	D	0-0		80,000
11	itpr1	Atalanta	H	W	3-0	Tomasson 54; Kaladze 72; Serginho 90	40,000
12	itpr1	Sampdoria	A	W	1-0	Shevchenko 76	29,000
13	cl gf	Barcelona	A	L	1-2	Shevchenko 17	95,000
14	itpr1	Roma	H	D	1-1	Shevchenko 6	64,000
15	itpr1	Brescia	A	D	0-0		16,000
16	itpr1	Siena	H	W	2-1	Shevchenko 26,37	58,000
17	cl gf	S Donetsk	H	W	4-0	Kaka 52,90; Crespo 53,85	39,000
18	itpr1	Chievo	A	W	1-0	Crespo 51	25,000
19	itpr1	Parma	A	W	2-1	Kaka 82; Pirlo 89	21,000
20	cl gf	Celtic	A	D	0-0		59,228
21	itpr1	Fiorentina	H	W	6-0	Seedorf 16,83; Chiellini 23 og; Shevchenko 53,74; Crespo 62	69,000
22	itpr1	Juventus	A	D	0-0		54,000
23	itpr1	Lecce	H	W	5-2	Crespo 23,36,57; Shevchenko 51; Tomasson 89	70,000
24	itpr1	Palermo	A	D	0-0		34,000
25	itpr1	Udinese	H	W	3-1	Shevchenko 31; Jankulovski 53 og; Kaka 90	67,000
26	itpr1	Livorno	A	L	0-1		19,000
27	itpr1	Bologna	H	L	0-1		57,000
28	itpr1	Messina	A	W	4-1	Crespo 9,64; Tomasson 18,90	35,000
29	itpr1	Lazio	H	W	2-1	Shevchenko 72; Crespo 90	57,000
30	itpr1	Reggina	A	W	1-0	Zamboni 39 og	24,000
31	itpr1	Cagliari	H	W	1-0	Serginho 90	60,000
32	cl r2l1	Man Utd	A	W	1-0	Crespo 78	67,162
33	itpr1	Inter Milan	A	W	1-0	Kaka 74	78,000
34	itpr1	Atalanta	A	W	2-1	Ambrosini 71; Pirlo 89	23,000
35	clr212	Man Utd	H	W	1-0	Crespo 61	79,000
36	itpr1	Sampdoria	H	W	1-0	Kaka 65	69,000
37	itpr1	Roma	A	W	2-0	Crespo 63; Pirlo 71 pen	59,000
38	clqfl1	Inter Milan	H	W	2-0	Stam 45; Shevchenko 74	80,000
39	itpr1	Brescia	H	D	1-1	Rui Costa 14	65,000
40	clqfl2	Inter Milan	A	W	3-0		
41	itpr1	Siena	A	L	1-2	Crespo 63	15,000
42	itpr1	Chievo	H	W	1-0	Seedorf 66	55,000
43	itpr1	Parma	H	W	3-0	Kaka 34; Tomasson 62; Cafu 70	61,000
44	clsfl1	PSV Eindhoven	H	W	2-0	Shevchenko 42; Tomasson 89	75,000
45	itpr1	Fiorentina	A	W	2-1	Shevchenko 46,55	46,000
46	clsfl2	PSV Eindhoven	A	L	1-3	Ambrosini 90	35,000
47	itpr1	Juventus	H	L	0-1		68,000
48	itpr1	Lecce	A	D	2-2	Kaladze 12; Shevchenko 53	22,000
49	itpr1	Palermo	H	D	3-3	Serginho 8,16; Tomasson 32	61,000
50	ecfin	Liverpool	H	L	2-4*	Maldini 1; Crespo 39,44 (*on penalties)	65,000
51	itpr1	Udinese	A	D	1-1	Serginho 85	23,000

KEY PLAYERS - GOALSCORERS

Andriy Shevchenko

Goals in the League	17
Contribution to Attacking Power Average number of minutes between League team goals while on pitch	47
Player Strike Rate Average number of minutes between League goals scored by player	132
Club Strike Rate Average number of minutes between League goals scored by club	54

	PLAYER	GOALS LGE	POWER	S RATE
1	Andriy Shevchenko	17	47	132 mins
2	Hernan Crespo	10	69	201 mins
3	Ricardo Kaka	7	55	417 mins
4	Clarence Seedorf	5	61	472 mins
5	Andrea Pirlo	4	55	574 mins

KEY PLAYERS - MIDFIELDERS

Clarence Seedorf

Goals in the League	5
Defensive Rating Average number of mins between League goals conceded while on the pitch	169
Contribution to Attacking Power Average number of minutes between League team goals while on pitch	61
Scoring Difference Defensive Rating minus Contribution to Attacking Power	108

	PLAYER	GOALS LGE	DEF RATE	ATT POWER	SCORE DIFF
1	Clarence Seedorf	5	169	61	108 mins
2	Andrea Pirlo	4	144	55	89 mins
3	Ricardo Kaka	7	139	55	84 mins
4	Gennaro Gattuso	0	129	57	72 mins
5	Manuel Rui Costa	1	107	53	54 mins

KEY PLAYERS - DEFENDERS

Kakha Kaladze

Goals Conceded in League	9
Clean Sheets In games when player was on pitch for at least 70 minutes	8
Defensive Rating Ave number of mins between League goals conceded while on the pitch	162
Club Defensive Rating Average number of mins between League goals conceded by the club this season	122

	PLAYER	CON LGE	CLEAN SHEETS	DEF RATE
1	Kakha Kaladze	9	8	162 mins
2	Alessandro Nesta	16	12	159 mins
3	Paolo Maldini	22	16	137 mins
4	Cafu	22	13	129 mins
5	Jaap Stam	13	4	103 mins

MONTHLY POINTS TALLY

SEPTEMBER	7	58%
OCTOBER	13	87%
NOVEMBER	8	67%
DECEMBER	7	78%
JANUARY	7	47%
FEBRUARY	15	100%
MARCH	9	100%
APRIL	10	67%
MAY	3	25%

LEAGUE GOALS

	PLAYER	MINS	GOALS	AVE
1	Shevchenko	2251	17	132
2	Crespo	2008	10	201
3	Kaka	2917	7	417
4	Tomasson	1484	6	247
5	Serginho	952	5	190
6	Seedorf	2362	5	472
7	Pirlo	2296	4	574
8	Kaladze	1457	2	729
9	Ambrosini	955	1	955
10	Cafu	2828	1	2828
11	Rui Costa	1387	1	1387
12	Pancaro	1136	1	1136
	Other		3	
	TOTAL		63	

KEY GOALKEEPER

Nelson Dida

Goals Conceded in the League	23
Counting Games League games when player was on pitch for at least 70 minutes	35
Clean Sheets In games when player was on pitch for at least 70 minutes	16
League minutes played Number of minutes played in league matches	3157
Defensive Rating Ave number of mins between League goals conceded while on the pitch	137

DISCIPLINARY RECORDS

	PLAYER	YELLOW	RED	AVE
1	Ambrosini	5	1	159
2	Costacurta	3	0	223
3	Pancaro	4	1	227
4	Stam	5	0	267
5	Nesta	6	2	318
6	Kaladze	4	0	364
7	Dhorasoo	2	0	375
8	Rui Costa	3	0	462
9	Gattuso	5	0	465
10	Cafu	6	0	471
11	Pirlo	4	0	574
12	Kaka	5	0	583
13	Tomasson	2	0	742
	Other	10	1	
	TOTAL	64	5	

TOP POINT EARNERS

	PLAYER	GAMES	AV PTS
1	Clarence Seedorf	22	2.50
2	Andrea Pirlo	22	2.32
3	Kakha Kaladze	13	2.31
4	Gennaro Gattuso	22	2.27
5	Hernan Crespo	19	2.26
6	Alessandro Nesta	28	2.25
7	Paolo Maldini	33	2.12
8	Nelson Dida	35	2.11
9	Ricardo Kaka	31	2.06
10	Andriy Shevchenko	23	2.04
	CLUB AVERAGE:		2.08

LEAGUE APPEARANCES AND BOOKINGS

	AGE (on 01/07/05)	IN NAMED 18	APPEARANCES	COUNTING GAMES	MINUTES ON PITCH	YELLOW CARDS	RED CARDS	THIS SEASON	HOME COUNTRY
Goalkeepers									
Christian Abbiati	28	34	3	3	263	0	0	1	Italy (10)
Nelson Dida	31	36	36	35	3157	0	1	5	Brazil (1)
Valerio Fiori	36	5	0	0	0	0	0	-	Italy
Defenders									
Cafu	35	34	33	30	2828	6	0	6	Brazil (1)
Fabricio Coloccini	23	5	1	0	64	0	0	9	Argentina (3)
Aless. Costacurta	39	27	12	6	669	3	0	-	Italy
Kakha Kaladze	27	27	19	13	1457	4	0	-	Georgia
Paolo Maldini	37	34	34	33	3003	4	0	-	Italy
Lino Marzoratti	18	1	1	1	72	0	0	-	Italy
Alessandro Nesta	29	32	29	28	2547	6	2	5	Italy (10)
Guiseppe Pancaro	33	32	18	11	1136	4	1	3	Italy (10)
Romano Perticone	18	1	1	0	18	0	0	-	Italy
Dario Simic	29	6	2	2	180	0	0	-	Croatia
Jaap Stam	32	17	17	14	1338	5	0	-	Holland
Midfielders									
Ignazio Abate	18	1	0	0	0	0	0	-	Italy
Massimo Ambrosini	28	32	22	7	955	5	1	1	Italy (10)
Christian Brocchi	29	20	11	5	599	0	0	-	Italy
Vikash Dhorasoo	31	23	12	6	750	2	0	-	France
Gennaro Gattuso	27	34	32	22	2326	5	0	7	Italy (10)
Ricardo Kaka	23	36	36	31	2917	5	0	4	Brazil (1)
Andrea Pirlo	26	30	30	22	2296	4	0	4	Italy (10)
Manuel Rui Costa	33	35	24	12	1387	3	0	-	Portugal
Clarence Seedorf	29	35	33	22	2362	3	0	-	Holland
Serginho	34	29	22	6	952	0	0	-	Brazil
Forwards									
Hernan Crespo	30	33	28	19	2008	1	0	2	Argentina (3)
Filippo Inzaghi	31	14	11	2	451	0	0	-	Italy
Andriy Shevchenko	28	29	29	23	2251	2	0	-	Ukraine
Jon Dahl Tomasson	28	33	30	9	1484	2	0	8	Denmark (19)

TEAM OF THE SEASON

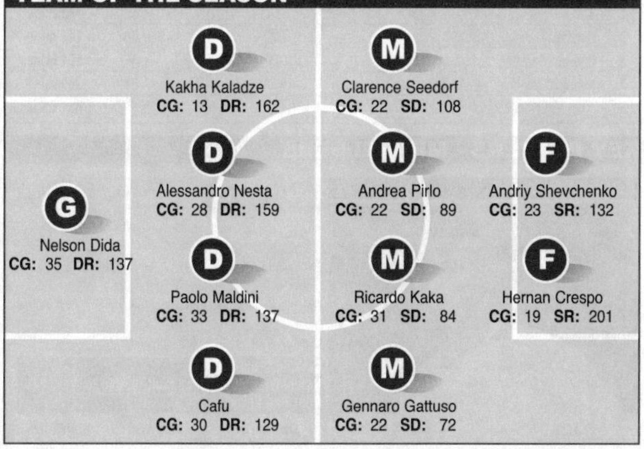

D
Kakha Kaladze
CG: 13 DR: 162
M
Clarence Seedorf
CG: 22 SD: 108
D
Alessandro Nesta
CG: 28 DR: 159
M
Andrea Pirlo
CG: 22 SD: 89
F
Andriy Shevchenko
CG: 23 SR: 132
G
Nelson Dida
CG: 35 DR: 137
D
Paolo Maldini
CG: 33 DR: 137
M
Ricardo Kaka
CG: 31 SD: 84
F
Hernan Crespo
CG: 19 SR: 201
D
Cafu
CG: 30 DR: 129
M
Gennaro Gattuso
CG: 22 SD: 72

SQUAD APPEARANCES

Match	1	2	3	4	5	6	7	8	9	10	11	12	13	14	15	16	17	18	19	20	21	22	23	24	25	26	27	28	29	30	31	32	33	34	35	36	37	38	39	40	41	42	43	44	45	46	47	48	49	50	51
Venue	H	A	A	H	A	H	H	A	H	H	H	A	A	H	A	H	H	A	A	A	H	A	H	A	H	A	H	A	H	A	H	A	A	A	H	H	A	H	H	A	A	H	H	H	A	A	H	A	H	H	A
Competition	L	C	L	L	L	L	L	L	C	L	L	L	C	L	L	L	L	L	L	C	L	L	L	L	L	L	L	L	L	L	L	L	L	L	L	L	L	L	L	L	L	L	L	L	L	L	L	L	L	C	L
Result	D	W	W	L	W	W	W	W	W	D	W	W	L	D	D	W	W	W	W	D	W	D	W	D	W	L	L	W	W	W	W	W	W	W	W	W	W	W	D	W	L	W	W	W	W	L	L	D	D	L	D

Goalkeepers
Christian Abbiati
Nelson Dida
Valerio Fiori

Defenders
Cafu
Fabricio Coloccini
Alessandro Costacurta
Kakha Kaladze
Paolo Maldini
Lino Marzoratti
Alessandro Nesta
Guiseppe Pancaro
Romano Perticone
Dario Simic
Jaap Stam

Midfielders
Ignazio Abate
Massimo Ambrosini
Christian Brocchi
Vikash Dhorasoo
Gennaro Gattuso
Ricardo Kaka
Andrea Pirlo
Manuel Rui Costa
Clarence Seedorf
Serginho

Forwards
Hernan Crespo
Filippo Inzaghi
Andriy Shevchenko
Jon Dahl Tomasson

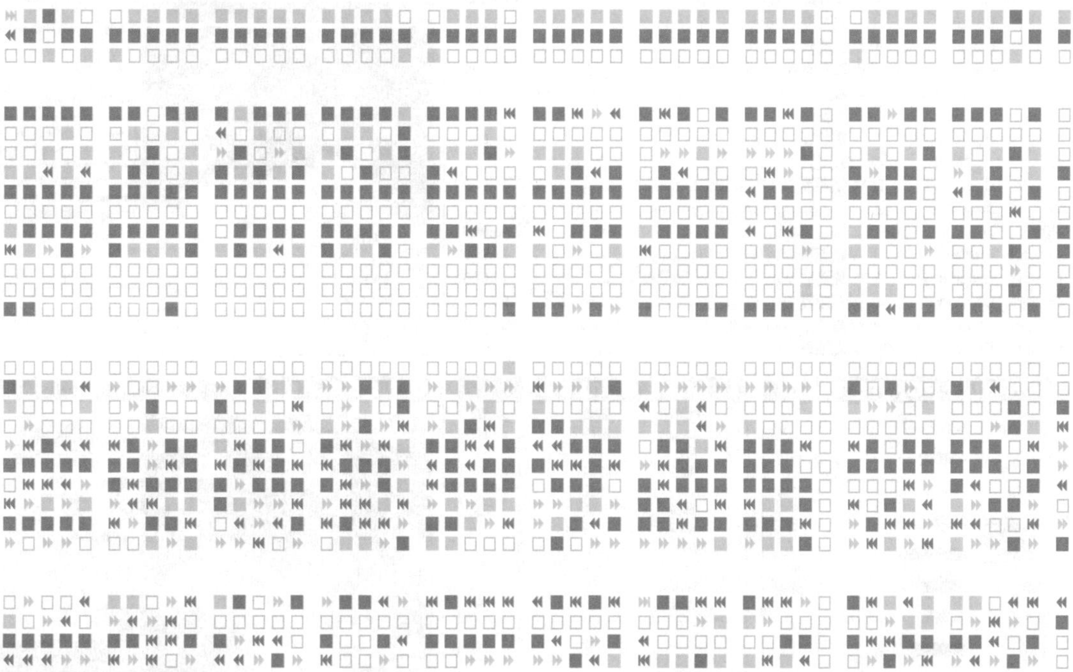

KEY: On all match · On bench · Subbed or sent off (Counting game) · Subbed or sent off (playing less than 70 minutes) · Subbed on from bench (Counting Game) · Subbed on (playing less than 70 minutes) · Subbed on and then subbed or sent off (Counting Game) · Subbed on and then subbed or sent off (playing less than 70 minutes) · Not in 16

INTER MILAN

Final Position: **3rd**

KEY: ☐Won ☐Drawn ☐Lost

							Attendance
1	clql1	**Basel**	A	D	1-1	Adriano 19	30,000
2	clql2	**Basel**	H	W	4-1	Adriano 2,54; Stankovic 13; Recoba 61	4,000
3	itpr1	**Chievo**	A	D	2-2	Stankovic 15; Adriano 48	33,000
4	cl gg	**W Bremen**	H	W	2-0	Adriano 34 pen,89	45,000
5	itpr1	**Palermo**	H	D	1-1	Adriano 46	68,000
6	itpr1	**Atalanta**	A	W	3-2	Stankovic 54; Recoba 79; Adriano 87	22,000
7	itpr1	**Parma**	H	D	2-2	Martins 72,82	60,000
8	cl gg	**Anderlecht**	A	W	3-1	Martins 9; Adriano 51; Stankovic 55	22,000
9	itpr1	**Roma**	A	D	3-3	Cambiasso 45; Veron 51; Recoba 54	58,000
10	itpr1	**Udinese**	H	W	3-1	Adriano 8,12; Vieri 57	62,000
11	cl gg	**Valencia**	A	W	5-1	Stankovic 47; Vieri 49; van der Meyde 76; Adriano 81; Cruz 90	40,000
12	itpr1	**AC Milan**	A	D	0-0		80,000
13	itpr1	**Lecce**	A	D	2-2	Adriano 4; Martins 33	18,000
14	itpr1	**Lazio**	H	D	1-1	Adriano 47	50,000
15	cl gg	**Valencia**	H	D	0-0		40,000
16	itpr1	**Fiorentina**	A	D	1-1	Adriano 81	44,000
17	itpr1	**Bologna**	H	D	2-2	Mihajlovic 39; Adriano 72	49,000
18	itpr1	**Cagliari**	A	D	3-3	Stankovic 35; Martins 77,89	20,000
19	cl gg	**W Bremen**	A	D	1-1	Martins 55	37,000
20	itpr1	**Juventus**	H	D	2-2	Vieri 79; Adriano 85	78,000
21	itpr1	**Messina**	H	W	5-0	Adriano 3,13,36; Eleftheropoulos 55 og; Vieri 84	45,000
22	cl gg	**Anderlecht**	H	W	3-0	Cruz 33; Martins 60,63	30,000
23	itpr1	**Siena**	A	D	2-2	Adriano 36 pen; Vieri 90	15,000
24	itpr1	**Brescia**	H	W	1-0	Mihajlovic 25	50,000
25	itpr1	**Livorno**	A	W	2-0	Materazzi 42; Vieri 73 pen	18,000
26	itpr1	**Sampdoria**	H	W	3-2	Martins 88; Vieri 90; Recoba 90	55,000
27	itpr1	**Reggina**	A	D	0-0		22,000
28	itpr1	**Chievo**	H	D	1-1	Martins 83	51,000
29	itpr1	**Palermo**	A	W	2-0	Vieri 5,58	34,000
30	itpr1	**Atalanta**	H	W	1-0	Martins 33	49,000
31	itpr1	**Parma**	A	D	2-2	Cordoba 76; Vieri 82	19,000
32	itpr1	**Roma**	H	W	2-0	Mihajlovic 23,87	61,000
33	itpr1	**Udinese**	A	D	1-1	Veron 58	19,000
34	clr2l1	**Porto**	A	D	1-1	Martins 24	50,000
35	itpr1	**AC Milan**	H	L	0-1		78,000
36	itpr1	**Lecce**	H	W	2-1	Cordoba 26; Adriano 89 pen	50,000
37	itpr1	**Lazio**	A	D	1-1	Cruz 70	52,000
38	clr2l2	**Porto**	H	W	3-1	Adriano 6,63,86	71,000
39	itpr1	**Fiorentina**	H	W	3-2	Cambiasso 27; Veron 53; Cordoba 65	55,000
40	clqf1	**AC Milan**	A	L	0-2		80,000
41	itpr1	**Bologna**	A	W	1-0	Cruz 3	25,000
42	clqf2	**AC Milan**	H	L	0-3		
43	itpr1	**Cagliari**	H	W	2-0	Ze Maria 40; Martins 65	40,000
44	itpr1	**Juventus**	A	W	1-0	Cruz 24	25,000
45	itpr1	**Messina**	A	L	1-2	Cruz 46	40,000
46	itpr1	**Siena**	H	W	2-0	Cruz 2 pen; Vieri 31	45,000
47	itpr1	**Brescia**	A	W	3-0	Martins 54,66; Vieri 90	11,000
48	itpr1	**Livorno**	H	W	1-0	Vieri 13	53,000
49	itpr1	**Sampdoria**	A	W	1-0	Adriano 36	36,000
50	itpr1	**Reggina**	H	D	0-0		50,000

KEY PLAYERS - GOALSCORERS

Adriano

Goals in the League	16
Contribution to Attacking Power Average number of minutes between League team goals while on pitch	50
Player Strike Rate Average number of minutes between League goals scored by player	142
Club Strike Rate Average number of minutes between League goals scored by club	53

	PLAYER	GOALS LGE	POWER	S RATE
1	Adriano	16	50	142 mins
2	Christian Vieri	12	53	144 mins
3	Obafemi Martins	11	45	161 mins
4	Sinisa Mihajlovic	4	51	363 mins
5	Juan Sebastian Veron	3	53	657 mins

KEY PLAYERS - MIDFIELDERS

Esteban Cambiasso

Goals in the League	2
Defensive Rating Average number of mins between League goals conceded while on the pitch	112
Contribution to Attacking Power Average number of minutes between League team goals while on pitch	54
Scoring Difference Defensive Rating minus Contribution to Attacking Power	58

	PLAYER	GOALS LGE	DEF RATE	ATT POWER	SCORE DIFF
1	Esteban Cambiasso	2	112	54	58 mins
2	Juan Sebastian Veron	3	94	53	41 mins
3	Cristiano Zanetti	0	108	67	41 mins
4	Javier Zanetti	0	91	52	39 mins
5	Dejan Stankovic	3	78	47	31 mins

KEY PLAYERS - DEFENDERS

Sinisa Mihajlovic

Goals Conceded in League	14
Clean Sheets In games when player was on pitch for at least 70 minutes	6
Defensive Rating Ave number of mins between League goals conceded while on the pitch	104
Club Defensive Rating Average number of mins between League goals conceded by the club this season	92

	PLAYER	CON LGE	CLEAN SHEETS	DEF RATE
1	Sinisa Mihajlovic	14	6	104 mins
2	Giuseppe Favalli	20	10	102 mins
3	Marco Materazzi	23	10	99 mins
4	Ivan Cordoba	32	12	87 mins
5	Ze Maria	16	6	87 mins

MONTHLY POINTS TALLY

SEPTEMBER	6	50%
OCTOBER	7	47%
NOVEMBER	4	33%
DECEMBER	7	78%
JANUARY	11	73%
FEBRUARY	8	53%
MARCH	7	78%
APRIL	9	75%
MAY	13	87%

LEAGUE GOALS

	PLAYER	MINS	GOALS	AVE
1	Adriano	2278	**16**	142
2	Vieri	1724	**12**	144
3	Martins	1774	**11**	161
4	Cruz	942	**5**	188
5	Mihajlovic	1451	**4**	363
6	Stankovic	2259	**3**	753
7	Veron	1971	**3**	657
8	Cordoba	2790	**3**	930
9	Recoba	492	**3**	164
10	Cambiasso	2580	**2**	1290
11	Materazzi	2272	**1**	2272
12	Ze Maria	1389	**1**	1389
	Other		1	
	TOTAL		**65**	

KEY GOALKEEPER

Francesco Toldo

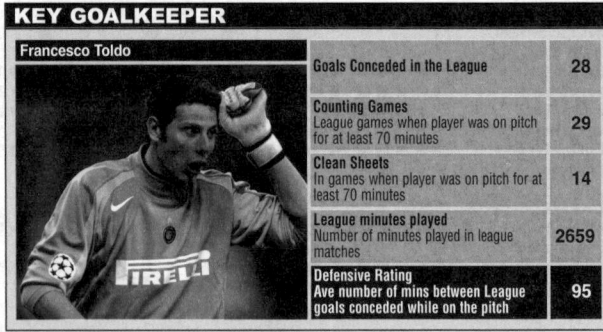

Goals Conceded in the League	28
Counting Games League games when player was on pitch for at least 70 minutes	29
Clean Sheets In games when player was on pitch for at least 70 minutes	14
League minutes played Number of minutes played in league matches	2659
Defensive Rating Ave number of mins between League goals conceded while on the pitch	95

DISCIPLINARY RECORDS

	PLAYER	YELLOW	RED	AVE
1	Zanetti, C	8	0	216
2	van der Meyde	4	0	243
3	Recoba	2	0	246
4	Emre Belozoglu	4	0	257
5	Cordoba	10	0	279
6	Veron	7	0	281
7	Stankovic	7	1	282
8	Materazzi	6	1	324
9	Favalli	6	0	341
10	Mihajlovic	4	0	362
11	Cambiasso	7	0	368
12	Burdisso	1	0	549
13	Davids	1	0	699
	Other	7	1	
	TOTAL	74	3	

TOP POINT EARNERS

	PLAYER	GAMES	AV PTS
1	Cristiano Zanetti	16	2.19
2	Esteban Cambiasso	29	2.14
3	Giuseppe Favalli	21	2.10
4	Obafemi Martins	15	2.00
5	Christian Vieri	16	1.94
6	Francesco Toldo	29	1.90
7	Marco Materazzi	24	1.88
8	Javier Zanetti	32	1.88
9	Sinisa Mihajlovic	14	1.86
10	Ivan Cordoba	31	1.84
	CLUB AVERAGE:		1.89

TEAM OF THE SEASON

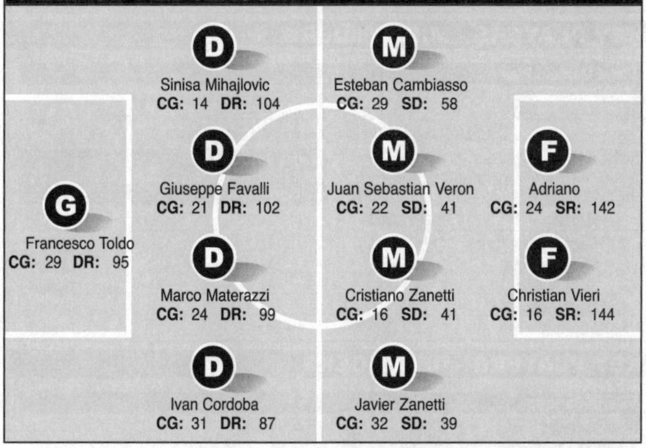

D
Sinisa Mihajlovic
CG: 14 DR: 104
M
Esteban Cambiasso
CG: 29 SD: 58
D
Giuseppe Favalli
CG: 21 DR: 102
M
Juan Sebastian Veron
CG: 22 SD: 41
F
Adriano
CG: 24 SR: 142
G
Francesco Toldo
CG: 29 DR: 95
D
Marco Materazzi
CG: 24 DR: 99
M
Cristiano Zanetti
CG: 16 SD: 41
F
Christian Vieri
CG: 16 SR: 144
D
Ivan Cordoba
CG: 31 DR: 87
M
Javier Zanetti
CG: 32 SD: 39

LEAGUE APPEARANCES AND BOOKINGS

	AGE (on 01/07/05)	IN NAMED 18	APPEARANCES	COUNTING GAMES	MINUTES ON PITCH	YELLOW CARDS	RED CARDS	THIS SEASON	HOME COUNTRY
Goalkeepers									
Fabian Carini	25	18	4	3	312	0	0	5	Uruguay (16)
Alberto Fontana	38	20	5	5	450	0	0	-	Italy
Francesco Toldo	33	36	30	29	2659	2	1	-	Italy
Defenders									
Marco Andreolli	19	3	1	0	55	0	0	-	Italy
Nicolas Burdisso	24	21	8	5	549	1	0	-	Argentina
Ivan Cordoba	28	34	31	31	2790	10	0	-	Colombia
Giuseppe Favalli	33	29	26	21	2048	6	0	2	Italy (10)
Carlos Alberto	34	10	3	1	115	0	0	-	Paraguay
Marco Materazzi	31	34	27	24	2272	6	1	9	Italy (10)
Sinisa Mihajlovic	36	25	19	14	1451	4	0	-	Serbia & Mont
Giovanni Pasquale	23	10	4	3	331	0	0	-	Italy
Ze Maria	31	31	22	13	1389	1	0	-	Brazil
Midfielders									
Esteban Cambiasso	24	35	30	29	2580	7	0	6	Argentina (3)
Francesco Coco	28	7	3	1	167	0	0	-	Italy
Edgar Davids	32	21	14	4	699	1	0	5	Holland (5)
Emre Belozoglu	24	28	19	10	1028	4	0	-	Turkey
Georgios Karagounis	28	17	12	5	485	0	0	-	Greece
Kily Gonzalez	30	16	14	6	871	0	0	3	Argentina (3)
Dino Marino	20	3	2	1	98	0	0	-	Italy
Dejan Stankovic	26	31	30	24	2259	7	1	7	Serbia & Mont (46)
Andy van der Meyde	25	21	18	7	973	4	0	-	Holland
Juan Sebastian Veron	30	24	24	22	1971	7	0	-	Argentina
Cristiano Zanetti	28	26	24	16	1733	8	0	-	Italy
Javier Zanetti	31	36	35	32	3010	1	0	9	Argentina (3)
Forwards									
Adriano	23	30	30	24	2278	1	0	9	Brazil (1)
Julio Cruz	30	26	18	9	942	0	0	-	Argentina
Obafemi Martins	20	34	31	15	1774	0	0	-	Nigeria
Riccardo Meggiorini	19	1	1	0	3	0	0	-	Italy
Alvaro Recoba	29	15	13	3	492	2	0	2	Uruguay (16)
Christian Vieri	31	30	27	16	1724	2	0	1	Italy (10)

SQUAD APPEARANCES

Match	1	2	3	4	5	6	7	8	9	10	11	12	13	14	15	16	17	18	19	20	21	22	23	24	25
Venue	A	H	A	H	H	A	H	A	A	H	A	A	A	H	H	A	H	A	A	H	H	H	A	H	A
Competition	C	L	L	L	L	L	L	L	L	L	C	L	L	L	C	L	L	L	L	L	L	C	L	L	L
Result	D	W	D	W	D	W	D	W	D	W	W	D	D	D	D	D	D	D	D	D	W	W	D	W	W

Match	26	27	28	29	30	31	32	33	34	35	36	37	38	39	40	41	42	43	44	45	46	47	48	49	50
Venue	H	A	H	A	H	A	H	A	A	H	H	A	H	H	A	A	H	H	A	A	H	A	H	A	H
Competition	L	L	L	L	L	L	L	L	C	L	L	L	L	L	L	L	C	L	L	L	L	L	L	L	L
Result	W	D	D	W	W	D	W	D	D	L	W	D	W	W	L	W	L	W	W	L	W	W	W	W	D

Goalkeepers
Fabian Carini
Alberto Fontana
Francesco Toldo

Defenders
Marco Andreolli
Nicolas Burdisso
Ivan Cordoba
Giuseppe Favalli
Carlos Alberto Gamarra
Marco Materazzi
Sinisa Mihajlovic
Giovanni Pasquale
Ze Maria

Midfielders
Esteban Cambiasso
Francesco Coco
Edgar Davids
Emre Belozoglu
Georgios Karagounis
Cristian Alberto Kily Gonzalez
Dino Marino
Dejan Stankovic
Andy van der Meyde
Juan Sebastian Veron
Cristiano Zanetti
Javier Zanetti

Forwards
Adriano
Julio Cruz
Obafemi Martins
Riccardo Meggiorini
Alvaro Recoba
Christian Vieri

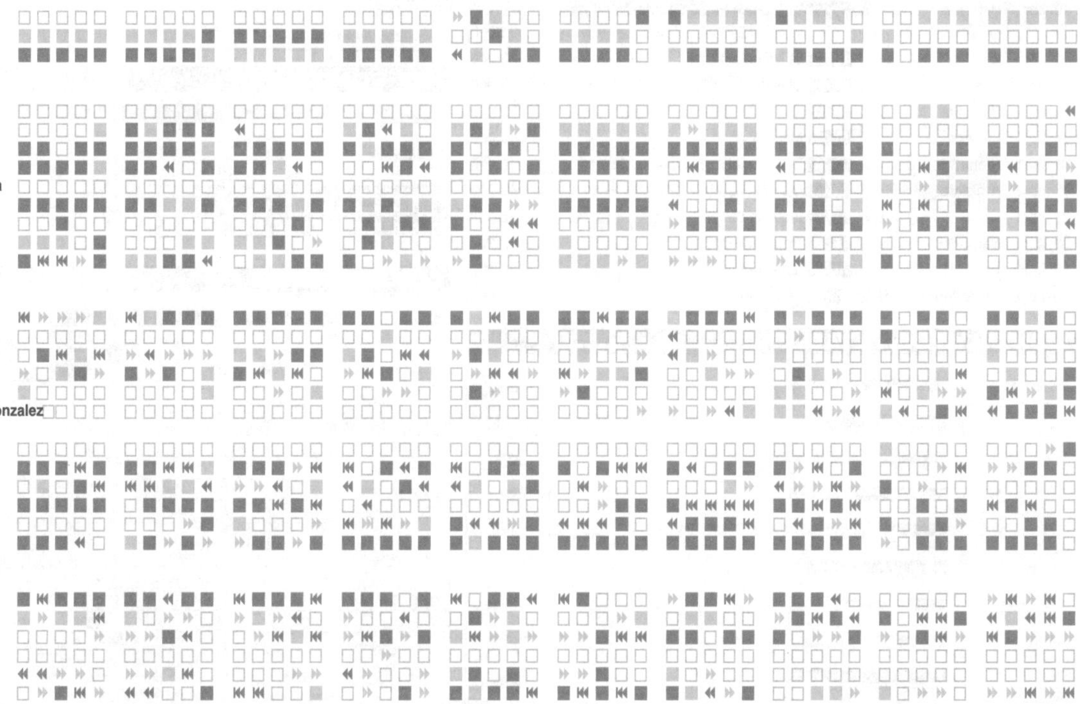

UDINESE

Final Position: **4th**

KEY: Won Drawn Lost

							Attendance
1	itpr1	Reggina	A	D	0-0		20,000
2	uc1rl1	Panionios	A	L	1-3	Pinzi 28	7,500
3	itpr1	Parma	H	W	4-0	Di Natale 16; Jankulovski 75 pen; Di Michele 77; Fava 90	21,000
4	itpr1	Chievo	A	D	0-0		10,000
5	itpr1	Brescia	H	L	1-2	Di Michele 57	14,000
6	uc1rl2	Panionios	H	W	1-0	Mauri 82	21,000
7	itpr1	Juventus	H	L	0-1		28,000
8	itpr1	Inter Milan	A	L	1-3	Mauri 50	62,000
9	itpr1	Fiorentina	H	D	2-2	Mauri 17; Sensini 52	15,000
10	itpr1	Bologna	A	W	1-0	Fava 56	15,000
11	itpr1	Palermo	H	W	1-0	Mauri 59	18,000
12	itpr1	Lecce	A	W	4-3	Jankulovski 44,90 pen; Di Natale 72; Iaquinta 79	13,000
13	itpr1	Roma	A	W	3-0	Iaquinta 45,84; Pizarro 61 pen	40,000
14	itpr1	Messina	H	D	1-1	Di Michele 55	14,000
15	itpr1	Livorno	A	W	2-1	Iaquinta 13; Di Michele 53	12,000
16	itpr1	Siena	H	W	1-0	Di Natale 17	21,000
17	itpr1	Atalanta	A	W	1-0	Iaquinta 8	12,000
18	itpr1	Lazio	H	W	3-0	Pizarro 13 pen; Di Michele 17; Iaquinta 36	15,000
19	itpr1	Sampdoria	A	L	0-2		33,000
20	itpr1	Cagliari	H	W	2-0	Di Natale 23,59	18,000
21	itpr1	AC Milan	A	L	1-3	Di Natale 9	67,000
22	itpr1	Reggina	H	L	0-2		19,000
23	itpr1	Parma	A	L	0-1		13,000
24	itpr1	Chievo	H	W	3-0	Jankulovski 47; Moro 52 og; Iaquinta 82	15,000
25	itpr1	Brescia	A	W	1-0	Iaquinta 85	8,000
26	itpr1	Juventus	A	L	1-2	Di Michele 90	21,000
27	itpr1	Inter Milan	H	D	1-1	Goitom 90	19,000
28	itpr1	Fiorentina	A	D	2-2	Muntari 41; Di Natale 56	28,000
29	itpr1	Bologna	H	L	0-1		15,000
30	itpr1	Palermo	A	W	5-1	Di Michele 29,36,54; Muntari 45; Iaquinta 82	32,000
31	itpr1	Lecce	H	W	2-1	Di Michele 42,89	18,000
32	itpr1	Roma	H	D	3-3	Di Natale 27; Pinzi 32; Di Michele 75	15,000
33	itpr1	Messina	A	L	0-1		30,000
34	itpr1	Livorno	H	D	1-1	Mauri 8	13,000
35	itpr1	Siena	A	W	3-2	Di Michele 6,53; Iaquinta 66	10,000
36	itpr1	Atalanta	H	W	2-1	Mauri 2; Iaquinta 37	17,000
37	itpr1	Lazio	A	W	1-0	Iaquinta 65	35,000
38	itpr1	Sampdoria	H	D	1-1	Pisano 36 og	22,000
39	itpr1	Cagliari	A	D	1-1	Iaquinta 48	15,000
40	itpr1	AC Milan	H	D	1-1	Di Michele 56	23,000

MONTHLY POINTS TALLY

SEPTEMBER	5	42%
OCTOBER	7	47%
NOVEMBER	10	83%
DECEMBER	9	100%
JANUARY	3	20%
FEBRUARY	8	53%
MARCH	6	67%
APRIL	5	42%
MAY	9	60%

KEY PLAYERS - GOALSCORERS

David Di Michele

Goals in the League	15	Player Strike Rate Average number of minutes between League goals scored by player	187
Contribution to Attacking Power Average number of minutes between League team goals while on pitch	57	Club Strike Rate Average number of minutes between League goals scored by club	61

	PLAYER	LGE GOALS	POWER	STRIKE RATE
1	David Di Michele	15	57	**187 mins**
2	Vincenzo Iaquinta	13	57	**205 mins**
3	Antonio Di Natale	8	66	**251 mins**
4	Stefano Mauri	5	62	**335 mins**
5	Marek Jankulovski	4	59	**695 mins**

KEY PLAYERS - MIDFIELDERS

David Marcelo Pizarro

Goals in the League	2	Contribution to Attacking Power Average number of minutes between League team goals while on pitch	58
Defensive Rating Average number of mins between League goals conceded while on the pitch	102	Scoring Difference Defensive Rating minus Contribution to Attacking Power	44

	PLAYER	LGE GOALS	DEF RATE	POWER	SCORE DIFF
1	David Marcelo Pizarro	2	102	58	**44 mins**
2	Giampiero Pinzi	1	82	58	**24 mins**
3	Sulley Muntari	2	87	64	**23 mins**
4	Marek Jankulovski	4	82	59	**23 mins**
5	Stefano Mauri	5	80	62	**18 mins**

KEY PLAYERS - DEFENDERS

Valerio Bertotto

Goals Conceded Number of League goals conceded while the player was on the pitch	33	Clean Sheets In League games when player was on pitch for at least 70 minutes	12
Defensive Rating Ave number of mins between League goals conceded while on the pitch	94	Club Defensive Rating Average number of mins between League goals conceded by the club this season	86

	PLAYER	CON LGE	CLEAN SHEETS	DEF RATE
1	Valerio Bertotto	33	12	**94 mins**
2	Per Kroldrup	24	6	**87 mins**
3	Felipe Dal Belo	28	6	**86 mins**
4	Roberto Nester Sensini	23	8	**77 mins**

KEY GOALKEEPER

Morgan De Sanctis

Goals Conceded in the League	38	Counting Games League games when player was on pitch for at least 70 minutes	35
Defensive Rating Ave number of mins between League goals conceded while on the pitch	84	Clean Sheets In games when player was on pitch for at least 70 minutes	13

LEAGUE GOALS

David Di Michele

Minutes on the pitch	2800	Goals in the League	15
League average (mins between goals)	187		

	PLAYER	MINS	GOALS	AVE
1	Di Michele	2800	**15**	187
2	Iaquinta	2661	**13**	205
3	Di Natale	2009	**8**	251
4	Mauri	1675	**5**	335
5	Jankulovski	2781	**4**	695
6	Muntari	2513	**2**	1257
7	Fava	843	**2**	422
8	Pizarro	2854	**2**	1427
9	Sensini	1774	**1**	1774
10	Pinzi	2220	**1**	2220
11	Goitom	9	**1**	9
	Other		2	
	TOTAL		**56**	

DISCIPLINARY RECORDS

	PLAYER	YELLOW	RED	AVE
1	Pazienza	8	0	154
2	Pinzi	12	2	158
3	Muntari	14	0	179
4	Cribari	2	0	291
5	Zenoni	3	0	375
6	Jankulovski	6	1	397
7	Mauri	3	0	558
8	Di Michele	4	0	700
9	Pieri	1	0	767
10	Felipe Dal Belo	3	0	806
11	Pizarro	3	0	951
12	Iaquinta	2	0	1330
13	Bertotto	2	0	1548
	Other	3	0	
	TOTAL	66	3	

TOP POINT EARNERS

	PLAYER	GAMES	AV PTS
1	Stefano Mauri	12	1.83
2	David Marcelo Pizarro	31	1.81
3	Roberto Nester Sensini	19	1.79
4	Vincenzo Iaquinta	30	1.77
5	Sulley Muntari	24	1.75
6	Valerio Bertotto	33	1.73
7	David Di Michele	25	1.72
8	Marek Jankulovski	32	1.72
9	Giampiero Pinzi	20	1.70
10	Morgan De Sanctis	35	1.69
	CLUB AVERAGE:		1.63

TEAM OF THE SEASON

- G: Morgan De Sanctis — CG: 35 DR: 84
- D: Valerio Bertotto — CG: 33 DR: 94
- D: Per Kroldrup — CG: 22 DR: 87
- D: Felipe Dal Belo — CG: 24 DR: 86
- D: Roberto Nester Sensini — CG: 19 DR: 77
- M: David Marcelo Pizarro — CG: 31 SD: 44
- M: Giampiero Pinzi — CG: 20 SD: 24
- M: Marek Jankulovski — CG: 32 SD: 23
- M: Sulley Muntari — CG: 24 SD: 23
- F: David Di Michele — CG: 25 SR: 187
- F: Vincenzo Iaquinta — CG: 30 SR: 205

LEAGUE APPEARANCES, BOOKINGS AND CAPS

	AGE (on 01/07/05)	IN NAMED 18	APPEARANCES	COUNTING GAMES	MINUTES ON PITCH	YELLOW CARDS	RED CARDS	THIS SEASON	HOME COUNTRY
Goalkeepers									
Adriano Bonaiuti	38	2	0	0	0	0	0	-	Italy
Morgan De Sanctis	28	36	36	35	3177	2	0	2	Italy (10)
Samir Handanovic	20	38	3	2	243	0	0	-	Slovenia
Defenders									
Alberto	30	11	2	1	117	1	0	-	Brazil
Manuel Belleri	27	37	19	4	582	0	0	-	Italy
Valerio Bertotto	32	35	35	33	3096	2	0	-	Italy
Cribari	25	18	8	6	582	2	0	-	Brazil
Felipe Dal Belo	20	38	30	24	2418	3	0	-	Brazil
Gustavo	21	9	1	0	26	0	0	-	Brazil
Per Kroldrup	25	29	26	22	2081	0	0	6	Denmark (19)
Mirko Pieri	26	30	16	7	767	1	0	-	Italy
Roberto Sensini	38	28	21	19	1774	1	0	-	Argentina
Midfielders									
Henok Goitom	21	7	1	0	9	0	0	-	Sierra Leone
Marek Jankulovski	28	32	32	32	2781	6	1	8	Czech Republic (2)
Stefano Mauri	25	36	32	12	1675	3	0	-	Italy
Sulley Muntari	20	33	33	24	2513	14	0	-	Ghana
Michele Pazienza	22	36	26	9	1237	8	0	-	Italy
Giampiero Pinzi	24	30	30	20	2220	12	2	1	Italy (10)
David Pizarro	25	35	34	31	2854	3	0	-	Chile
Fernando Tissone	18	8	2	0	14	1	0	-	Argentina
Robson Toledo	23	0	0	0	0	0	0	-	Brazil
Damiano Zenoni	28	16	16	10	1127	3	0	-	Italy
Forwards									
David Di Michele	29	37	37	25	2800	4	0	-	Italy
Antonio Di Natale	27	34	32	18	2009	0	0	-	Italy
Dino Passaro Fava	28	38	24	8	843	0	0	-	Italy
Vincenzo Iaquinta	25	33	31	30	2661	2	0	1	Italy (10)

SQUAD APPEARANCES

Match	1	2	3	4	5	6	7	8	9	10	11	12	13	14	15	16	17	18	19	20	21	22	23	24	25	26	27	28	29	30	31	32	33	34	35	36	37	38	39	40
Venue	A	A	H	A	H	H	H	A	H	A	H	A	A	H	A	H	A	H	A	H	A	H	A	H	A	A	H	A	H	A	H	H	A	H	A	H	A	H	A	H
Competition	L	E	L	L	L	E	L	L	L	L	L	L	L	L	L	L	L	L	L	L	L	L	L	L	L	L	L	L	L	L	L	L	L	L	L	L	L	L	L	L
Result	D	L	W	D	L	W	L	L	D	W	W	W	W	D	W	W	W	W	L	W	L	L	L	W	W	L	D	D	L	W	W	D	L	D	W	W	W	D	D	D

Goalkeepers
- Adriano Bonaiuti
- Morgan De Sanctis
- Samir Handanovic

Defenders
- Alberto
- Manuel Belleri
- Valerio Bertotto
- Cribari
- Felipe Dal Belo
- Gustavo
- Per Kroldrup
- Mirko Pieri
- Roberto Sensini

Midfielders
- Henok Goitom
- Marek Jankulovski
- Stefano Mauri
- Sulley Muntari
- Michele Pazienza
- Giampiero Pinzi
- David Pizarro
- Fernando Tissone
- Robson Toledo
- Damiano Zenoni

Forwards
- David Di Michele
- Antonio Di Natale
- Dino Passaro Fava
- Vincenzo Iaquinta

KEY: On all match · On bench · Subbed or sent off (Counting game) · Subbed or sent off (playing less than 70 minutes) · Subbed on from bench (Counting Game) · Subbed on (playing less than 70 minutes) · Subbed on and then subbed or sent off (Counting Game) · Subbed on and then subbed or sent off (playing less than 70 minutes) · Not in 16

SAMPDORIA

Final Position: **5th**

KEY: Won Drawn Lost

							Attendance
1	itpr1	**Lazio**	H	L	0-1		24,000
2	itpr1	**Siena**	A	L	1-2	Flachi 5	10,000
3	itpr1	**Juventus**	H	L	0-3		36,000
4	itpr1	**Fiorentina**	A	W	2-0	Bazzani 11; Sacchetti 65	32,000
5	itpr1	**Livorno**	H	W	2-0	Rossini 78; Diana 88	25,000
6	itpr1	**Reggina**	A	W	1-0	Bazzani 36	18,000
7	itpr1	**Brescia**	H	L	0-1		23,000
8	itpr1	**Chievo**	A	W	2-0	Volpi 32; Diana 36	8,000
9	itpr1	**AC Milan**	H	L	0-1		29,000
10	itpr1	**Atalanta**	A	D	0-0		14,000
11	itpr1	**Cagliari**	H	D	0-0		22,000
12	itpr1	**Palermo**	A	L	0-2		35,000
13	itpr1	**Parma**	H	W	1-0	Flachi 90 pen	22,000
14	itpr1	**Roma**	A	D	1-1	Pagano 81	45,000
15	itpr1	**Messina**	H	W	1-0	Flachi 16	21,000
16	itpr1	**Lecce**	A	W	4-1	Flachi 38 pen,50; Tonetto 61; Kutuzov 90	13,000
17	itpr1	**Udinese**	H	W	2-0	Flachi 68; Castellini 76	33,000
18	itpr1	**Inter Milan**	A	L	2-3	Tonetto 44; Kutuzov 83	55,000
19	itpr1	**Bologna**	H	D	0-0		22,000
20	itpr1	**Lazio**	A	W	2-1	Kutuzov 1; Flachi 4 pen	35,000
21	itpr1	**Siena**	H	D	1-1	Rossini 81	21,000
22	itpr1	**Juventus**	A	W	1-0	Diana 33	20,000
23	itpr1	**Fiorentina**	H	W	3-0	Flachi 15; Tonetto 33; Diana 74	23,000
24	itpr1	**Livorno**	A	L	0-1		16,000
25	itpr1	**Reggina**	H	W	3-2	Flachi 8,45,70 pen	20,000
26	itpr1	**Brescia**	A	W	1-0	Tonetto 76	8,000
27	itpr1	**Chievo**	H	W	1-0	Gasbarroni 82	23,000
28	itpr1	**AC Milan**	A	L	0-1		69,000
29	itpr1	**Atalanta**	H	L	1-2	Doni 30	23,000
30	itpr1	**Cagliari**	A	D	0-0		15,000
31	itpr1	**Palermo**	H	W	1-0	Flachi 90 pen	24,000
32	itpr1	**Parma**	A	D	1-1	Gasbarroni 35	14,000
33	itpr1	**Roma**	H	W	2-1	Tonetto 33; Flachi 79 pen	24,000
34	itpr1	**Messina**	A	D	2-2	Flachi 27; Volpi 75	32,000
35	itpr1	**Lecce**	H	W	3-0	Diana 23; Kutuzov 32; Edusei 87	23,000
36	itpr1	**Udinese**	A	D	1-1	Castellini 25	22,000
37	itpr1	**Inter Milan**	H	L	0-1		36,000
38	itpr1	**Bologna**	A	D	0-0		38,000

MONTHLY POINTS TALLY

SEPTEMBER	3	25%
OCTOBER	9	60%
NOVEMBER	5	42%
DECEMBER	7	78%
JANUARY	8	53%
FEBRUARY	12	80%
MARCH	3	33%
APRIL	8	67%
MAY	6	40%

KEY PLAYERS - GOALSCORERS

Francesco Flachi

Goals in the League	14	Player Strike Rate Average number of minutes between League goals scored by player	217
Contribution to Attacking Power Average number of minutes between League team goals while on pitch	82	Club Strike Rate Average number of minutes between League goals scored by club	81

	PLAYER	LGE GOALS	POWER	STRIKE RATE
1	Francesco Flachi	14	82	217 mins
2	Stefano Aimo Diana	5	96	478 mins
3	Max Tonetto	5	82	527 mins
4	Fabio Bazzani	2	127	573 mins
5	Fausto Rossini	2	71	782 mins

KEY PLAYERS - MIDFIELDERS

Max Tonetto

Goals in the League	5	Contribution to Attacking Power Average number of minutes between League team goals while on pitch	82
Defensive Rating Average number of mins between League goals conceded while on the pitch	146	Scoring Difference Defensive Rating minus Contribution to Attacking Power	64

	PLAYER	LGE GOALS	DEF RATE	POWER	SCORE DIFF
1	Max Tonetto	5	146	82	64 mins
2	Stefano Aimo Diana	5	159	96	63 mins
3	Sergio Volpi	2	127	79	48 mins
4	Angelo Palombo	0	114	79	35 mins

KEY PLAYERS - DEFENDERS

Guilio Falcone

Goals Conceded Number of League goals conceded while the player was on the pitch	16	Clean Sheets In League games when player was on pitch for at least 70 minutes	12
Defensive Rating Ave number of mins between League goals conceded while on the pitch	146	Club Defensive Rating Average number of mins between League goals conceded by the club this season	118

	PLAYER	CON LGE	CLEAN SHEETS	DEF RATE
1	Guilio Falcone	16	12	146 mins
2	Cristiano Zenoni	27	17	114 mins
3	Marco Pisano	21	10	114 mins
4	Marcello Castellini	19	10	109 mins
5	Simone Pavan	22	10	102 mins

KEY GOALKEEPER

Francesco Antonioli

Goals Conceded in the League	26	Counting Games League games when player was on pitch for at least 70 minutes	36
Defensive Rating Ave number of mins between League goals conceded while on the pitch	126	Clean Sheets In games when player was on pitch for at least 70 minutes	18

LEAGUE GOALS

Francesco Flachi

Minutes on the pitch	3037	Goals in the League	14
League average (mins between goals)	217		

	PLAYER	MINS	GOALS	AVE
1	Flachi	3037	14	217
2	Tonetto	2635	5	527
3	Diana	2389	5	478
4	Kutuzov	1353	4	338
5	Castellini	2079	2	1040
6	Rossini	1564	2	782
7	Volpi	2926	2	1463
8	Bazzani	1146	2	573
9	Gasbarroni	390	2	195
10	Pagano	26	1	26
11	Doni	1196	1	1196
12	Edusei	640	1	640
13	Sacchetti	881	1	881
	Other		0	
	TOTAL		42	

DISCIPLINARY RECORDS

	PLAYER	YELLOW	RED	AVE
1	Volpi	13	1	209
2	Bazzani	4	0	286
3	Doni	4	0	299
4	Pavan	7	0	321
5	Zenoni	8	1	343
6	Rossini	4	0	391
7	Castellini	5	0	415
8	Sacchetti	2	0	440
9	Flachi	6	0	506
10	Edusei	1	0	640
11	Tonetto	4	0	658
12	Kutuzov	2	0	676
13	Palombo	4	0	771
	Other	9	1	
	TOTAL	73	3	

TOP POINT EARNERS

	PLAYER	GAMES	AV PTS
1	Fausto Rossini	13	1.77
2	Cristiano Zenoni	33	1.73
3	Francesco Flachi	34	1.71
4	Marco Pisano	24	1.71
5	Angelo Palombo	33	1.70
6	Max Tonetto	27	1.70
7	Francesco Antonioli	36	1.69
8	Fabio Bazzani	12	1.67
9	Sergio Volpi	32	1.66
10	Stefano Aimo Diana	23	1.65
	CLUB AVERAGE:		1.61

LEAGUE APPEARANCES, BOOKINGS AND CAPS

	AGE (on 01/07/05)	IN NAMED 18	APPEARANCES	COUNTING GAMES	MINUTES ON PITCH	YELLOW CARDS	RED CARDS	THIS SEASON	HOME COUNTRY
Goalkeepers									
Francesco Antonioli	35	37	37	36	3267	0	1	-	Italy
Daniele Padelli	19	4	0	0	0	0	0	-	Italy
Luigi Turci	35	35	2	1	153	0	0	-	Italy
Defenders									
Ivan Artipoli	19	1	0	0	0	0	0	-	Italy
Morris Carrozzieri	24	36	3	0	95	1	1	-	Italy
Marcello Castellini	32	27	24	23	2079	5	0	-	Italy
Guilio Falcone	31	28	28	23	2333	3	0	-	Italy
Simone Pavan	31	35	28	23	2249	7	0	-	Italy
Marco Pisano	23	33	29	24	2397	3	0	-	Italy
Stefano Sacchetti	32	20	13	8	881	2	0	-	Italy
Cristiano Zenoni	28	36	35	33	3087	8	1	-	Italy
Midfielders									
Andrea Cittadino	18	2	0	0	0	0	0	-	Italy
Stefano Aimo Diana	27	34	32	23	2389	3	0	5	Italy (10)
Marco Donadel	22	18	8	4	412	2	0	-	Italy
Cristiano Doni	32	23	22	7	1196	4	0	-	Italy
Mark Edusei	28	36	20	4	640	1	0	-	Ghana
Andrea Gasbarroni	23	11	10	2	390	2	0	-	Italy
Vincenzo Iacopino	28	9	1	0	9	0	0	-	Italy
Biagio Pagano	22	8	2	0	26	1	0	-	Italy
Angelo Palombo	23	37	37	33	3086	4	0	-	Italy
Mattia Roselli	18	7	1	0	1	0	0	-	Italy
Max Tonetto	30	32	32	27	2635	4	0	-	Italy
Sergio Volpi	31	34	34	32	2926	13	1	1	Italy (10)
Forwards									
Fabio Bazzani	28	15	14	12	1146	4	0	1	Italy (10)
Francesco Flachi	30	35	35	34	3037	6	0	-	Italy
Simone Inzaghi	29	14	5	0	146	1	0	-	Italy
Vitaly Kutuzov	25	38	32	8	1353	2	0	-	Belarus
Fausto Rossini	27	36	31	13	1564	4	0	-	Italy

TEAM OF THE SEASON

D
Guilio Falcone
CG: 23 DR: 146
M
Max Tonetto
CG: 27 SD: 64
D
Marco Pisano
CG: 24 DR: 114
M
Stefano Aimo Diana
CG: 23 SD: 63
F
Francesco Flachi
CG: 34 SR: 217
G
Francesco Antonioli
CG: 36 DR: 126
D
Cristiano Zenoni
CG: 33 DR: 114
M
Sergio Volpi
CG: 32 SD: 48
F
Fabio Bazzani
CG: 12 SR: 573
D
Marcello Castellini
CG: 23 DR: 109
M
Angelo Palombo
CG: 33 SD: 35

SQUAD APPEARANCES

Match	1	2	3	4	5	6	7	8	9	10	11	12	13	14	15	16	17	18	19	20	21	22	23	24	25	26	27	28	29	30	31	32	33	34	35	36	37	38
Venue	H	A	H	A	H	A	H	A	H	A	H	A	H	A	H	A	H	A	H	A	H	A	H	A	H	A	H	A	H	A	H	A	H	A	H	A	H	A
Competition	L	L	L	L	L	L	L	L	L	L	L	L	L	L	L	L	L	L	L	L	L	L	L	L	L	L	L	L	L	L	L	L	L	L	L	L	L	L
Result	L	L	L	W	W	W	L	W	L	D	D	L	W	D	W	W	W	L	D	W	D	W	W	L	W	W	W	L	L	D	W	D	W	D	W	D	L	D

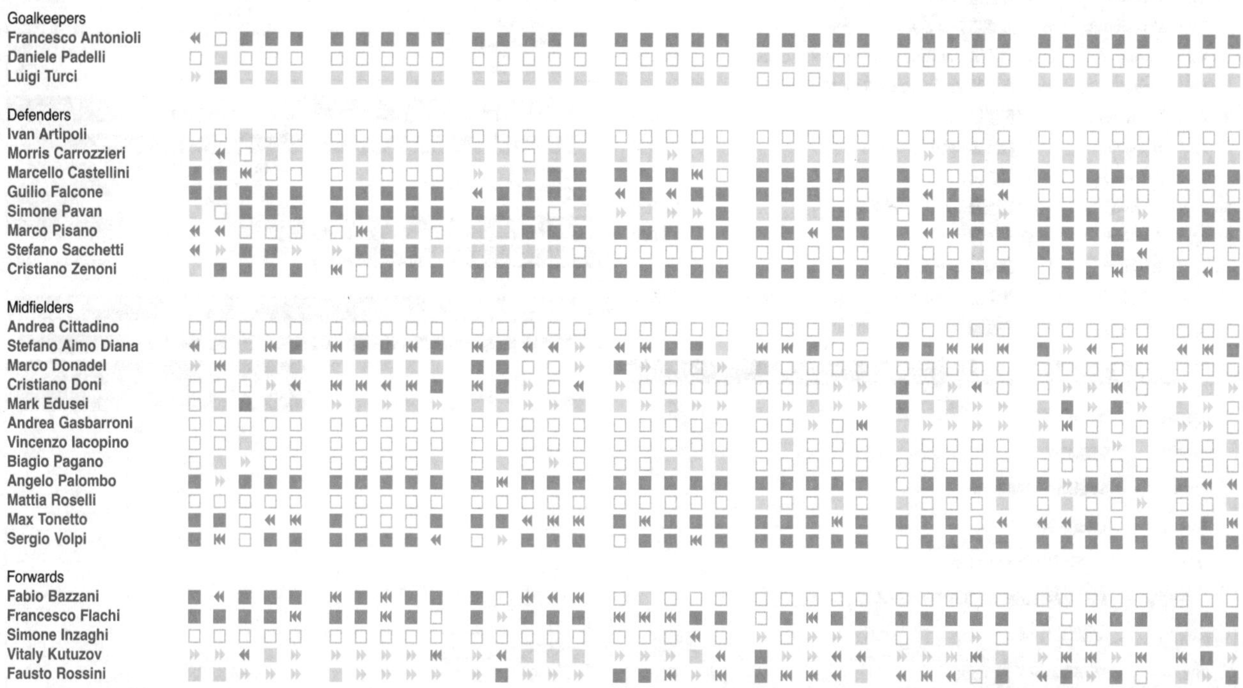
Goalkeepers
Francesco Antonioli
Daniele Padelli
Luigi Turci
Defenders
Ivan Artipoli
Morris Carrozzieri
Marcello Castellini
Guilio Falcone
Simone Pavan
Marco Pisano
Stefano Sacchetti
Cristiano Zenoni
Midfielders
Andrea Cittadino
Stefano Aimo Diana
Marco Donadel
Cristiano Doni
Mark Edusei
Andrea Gasbarroni
Vincenzo Iacopino
Biagio Pagano
Angelo Palombo
Mattia Roselli
Max Tonetto
Sergio Volpi
Forwards
Fabio Bazzani
Francesco Flachi
Simone Inzaghi
Vitaly Kutuzov
Fausto Rossini

KEY: ■ On all match · On bench · ⏮ Subbed or sent off (Counting game) · « Subbed or sent off (playing less than 70 minutes) · Subbed on from bench (Counting Game) · » Subbed on (playing less than 70 minutes) · Subbed on and then subbed or sent off (Counting Game) · » Subbed on and then subbed or sent off (playing less than 70 minutes) · □ Not in 16

PALERMO

Final Position: **6th**

KEY: Won Drawn Lost

							Attendance
1	itpr1	**Siena**	H	W	1-0	Toni 22	33,000
2	itpr1	**Inter Milan**	A	D	1-1	Toni 69	68,000
3	itpr1	**Fiorentina**	H	D	0-0		25,000
4	itpr1	**Juventus**	A	D	1-1	Zaccardo 17	27,000
5	itpr1	**Bologna**	H	W	1-0	Brienza 40	32,000
6	itpr1	**Lecce**	A	L	0-2		18,000
7	itpr1	**Roma**	A	D	1-1	Grosso 32	55,000
8	itpr1	**Livorno**	H	L	1-2	Mutarelli 5	30,000
9	itpr1	**Udinese**	A	L	0-1		18,000
10	itpr1	**Parma**	H	D	1-1	Gonzalez 74	33,000
11	itpr1	**Messina**	A	D	0-0		32,000
12	itpr1	**Sampdoria**	H	W	2-0	Toni 18; Brienza 48	35,000
13	itpr1	**Brescia**	A	W	2-0	Zauli 10; Brienza 24	10,000
14	itpr1	**Atalanta**	H	W	1-0	Brienza 44	33,000
15	itpr1	**Chievo**	A	L	1-2	Toni 89	9,000
16	itpr1	**Cagliari**	H	W	3-0	Zauli 33; Brienza 38; Toni 40	33,000
17	itpr1	**Reggina**	A	L	0-1		18,000
18	itpr1	**AC Milan**	H	D	0-0		34,000
19	itpr1	**Lazio**	A	W	3-1	Toni 42,90; Zauli 67	35,000
20	itpr1	**Siena**	A	D	0-0		8,000
21	itpr1	**Inter Milan**	H	L	0-2		34,000
22	itpr1	**Fiorentina**	A	W	2-1	Lupatelli 58 og; Gonzalez 69	29,000
23	itpr1	**Juventus**	H	W	1-0	Brienza 12	34,000
24	itpr1	**Bologna**	A	D	1-1	Toni 35	21,000
25	itpr1	**Lecce**	H	W	3-2	Santana 42,45; Toni 76	34,000
26	itpr1	**Roma**	H	W	2-0	Brienza 54; Toni 90	33,000
27	itpr1	**Livorno**	A	D	2-2	Toni 26,64	12,000
28	itpr1	**Udinese**	H	L	1-5	Santana 70	32,000
29	itpr1	**Parma**	A	D	3-3	Cannavaro 13 og; Toni 34; Brienza 48	15,000
30	itpr1	**Messina**	H	W	2-1	Zaccardo 52; Toni 76	34,000
31	itpr1	**Sampdoria**	A	L	0-1		24,000
32	itpr1	**Brescia**	H	D	3-3	Terlizzi 13; Toni 39 pen,79	33,000
33	itpr1	**Atalanta**	A	L	0-1		11,000
34	itpr1	**Chievo**	H	D	2-2	Toni 18; Zauli 28	33,000
35	itpr1	**Cagliari**	A	D	0-0		15,000
36	itpr1	**Reggina**	H	D	1-1	Barone 90	36,000
37	itpr1	**AC Milan**	A	D	3-3	Costacurta 9 og; Toni 77; Barone 79	61,000
38	itpr1	**Lazio**	H	D	3-3	Toni 2,65; Brienza 61	33,000

MONTHLY POINTS TALLY

SEPTEMBER	6	50%
OCTOBER	4	27%
NOVEMBER	8	67%
DECEMBER	6	67%
JANUARY	5	33%
FEBRUARY	13	87%
MARCH	2	22%
APRIL	4	33%
MAY	5	33%

KEY PLAYERS - GOALSCORERS

Luca Toni

Goals in the League	20	Player Strike Rate Average number of minutes between League goals scored by player	156
Contribution to Attacking Power Average number of minutes between League team goals while on pitch	67	Club Strike Rate Average number of minutes between League goals scored by club	71

	PLAYER	LGE GOALS	POWER	STRIKE RATE
1	Luca Toni	20	67	**156 mins**
2	Franco Brienza	9	66	**258 mins**
3	Lamberto Zauli	4	59	**518 mins**
4	Mario Santana	3	69	**640 mins**
5	Simone Barone	2	71	**1430 mins**

KEY PLAYERS - MIDFIELDERS

Massimo Mutarelli

Goals in the League	1	Contribution to Attacking Power Average number of minutes between League team goals while on pitch	70
Defensive Rating Average number of mins between League goals conceded while on the pitch	86	Scoring Difference Defensive Rating minus Contribution to Attacking Power	16

	PLAYER	LGE GOALS	DEF RATE	POWER	SCORE DIFF
1	Massimo Mutarelli	1	86	70	**16 mins**
2	Lamberto Zauli	4	74	59	**15 mins**
3	Mario Santana	3	84	69	**15 mins**
4	Franco Brienza	9	80	66	**14 mins**
5	Eugenio Corini	0	79	68	**11 mins**

KEY PLAYERS - DEFENDERS

Cristian Zaccardo

Goals Conceded Number of League goals conceded while the player was on the pitch	37	Clean Sheets In League games when player was on pitch for at least 70 minutes	10
Defensive Rating Ave number of mins between League goals conceded while on the pitch	82	Club Defensive Rating Average number of mins between League goals conceded by the club this season	78

	PLAYER	CON LGE	CLEAN SHEETS	DEF RATE
1	Cristian Zaccardo	37	10	**82 mins**
2	Guiseppe Biava	33	10	**79 mins**
3	Andrea Barzagli	43	13	**77 mins**
4	Christian Terlizzi	13	4	**75 mins**

KEY GOALKEEPER

Matteo Guardalben

Goals Conceded in the League	41	Counting Games League games when player was on pitch for at least 70 minutes	37
Defensive Rating Ave number of mins between League goals conceded while on the pitch	81	Clean Sheets In games when player was on pitch for at least 70 minutes	13

LEAGUE GOALS

Luca Toni

Minutes on the pitch	3125	Goals in the League	20
League average (mins between goals)	156		

	PLAYER	MINS	GOALS	AVE
1	Toni	3125	**20**	156
2	Brienza	2319	**9**	258
3	Zauli	2072	**4**	518
4	Santana	1921	**3**	640
5	Zaccardo	3017	**2**	1509
6	Gonzalez	988	**2**	494
7	Barone	2860	**2**	1430
8	Terlizzi	977	**1**	977
9	Grosso	3164	**1**	3164
10	Mutarelli	1462	**1**	1462
	Other		**3**	
	TOTAL		**48**	

DISCIPLINARY RECORDS

	PLAYER	YELLOW	RED	AVE
1	Mutarelli	7	0	208
2	Morrone	4	1	228
3	Barone	11	1	238
4	Terlizzi	3	1	244
5	Corini	11	1	248
6	Zauli	8	0	259
7	Zaccardo	9	1	301
8	Biava	7	1	325
9	Grosso	9	0	351
10	Toni	8	0	390
11	Gonzalez	2	0	494
12	Conteh	1	0	584
13	Barzagli	4	0	830
	Other	1	0	
	TOTAL	85	6	

TOP POINT EARNERS

	PLAYER	GAMES	AV PTS
1	Franco Brienza	20	1.65
2	Lamberto Zauli	20	1.65
3	Mario Santana	17	1.59
4	Guiseppe Biava	29	1.48
5	Eugenio Corini	32	1.47
6	Fabio Grosso	35	1.46
7	Luca Toni	35	1.46
8	Simone Barone	30	1.43
9	Matteo Guardalben	37	1.41
10	Cristian Zaccardo	33	1.36
	CLUB AVERAGE:		1.39

TEAM OF THE SEASON

G
Matteo Guardalben
CG: 37 DR: 81
D
Cristian Zaccardo
CG: 33 DR: 82
D
Guiseppe Biava
CG: 29 DR: 79
D
Andrea Barzagli
CG: 37 DR: 77
D
Christian Terlizzi
CG: 10 DR: 75
M
Massimo Mutarelli
CG: 14 SD: 16
M
Mario Santana
CG: 17 SD: 15
M
Lamberto Zauli
CG: 20 SD: 15
M
Eugenio Corini
CG: 32 SD: 11
F
Luca Toni
CG: 35 SR: 156
F
Franco Brienza
CG: 20 SR: 258

LEAGUE APPEARANCES, BOOKINGS AND CAPS

	AGE (on 01/07/05)	IN NAMED 18	APPEARANCES	COUNTING GAMES	MINUTES ON PITCH	YELLOW CARDS	RED CARDS	THIS SEASON	HOME COUNTRY
Goalkeepers									
Matteo Guardalben	31	38	37	37	3330	0	0	-	Italy
Nicola Santoni	26	38	1	1	90	0	0	-	Italy
Defenders									
Pietro Accardi	22	8	1	1	90	1	0	-	Italy
Adriano	23	5	1	0	45	1	0	9	Brazil (1)
Andrea Barzagli	24	37	37	37	3322	4	0	3	Italy (10)
Guiseppe Biava	28	31	29	29	2602	7	1	-	Italy
Kewullay Conteh	27	19	14	6	584	1	0	-	Sierra Leone
Rocca D'Aiello	19	2	0	0	0	0	0	-	Italy
Michele Ferri	24	20	6	1	153	1	0	-	Italy
Christian Terlizzi	25	33	16	10	977	3	1	-	Italy
Cristian Zaccardo	23	35	35	33	3017	9	1	4	Italy (10)
Midfielders									
Simone Barone	27	35	35	30	2860	11	1	4	Italy (10)
Franco Brienza	26	35	33	20	2319	1	0	-	Italy
Eugenio Corini	34	35	35	32	2986	11	1	-	Italy
Antonino Di Franco	18	2	0	0	0	0	0	-	Italy
Andrea Gasbarroni	23	16	9	0	343	2	0	-	Italy
Mariano Gonzalez	24	32	22	4	988	2	0	1	Argentina (3)
Fabio Grosso	27	36	36	35	3164	9	0	2	Italy (10)
Nicola Milano	22	1	0	0	0	0	0	-	Italy
Stefano Morrone	26	36	23	9	1143	4	1	-	Italy
Massimo Mutarelli	27	28	22	14	1462	7	0	-	Italy
Cristian Raimondi	24	33	14	0	439	3	0	-	Italy
Mario Santana	23	33	30	17	1921	0	0	1	Argentina (3)
Lamberto Zauli	33	27	27	20	2072	8	0	-	Italy
Forwards									
Pietro Balistreri	19	11	2	0	54	0	0	-	Italy
Ernesto Farias	25	18	13	1	302	0	0	-	Argentina
Davide Possanzini	29	3	2	1	123	0	0	-	Italy
Luca Toni	28	35	35	35	3125	8	0	8	Italy (10)

SQUAD APPEARANCES

Match	1	2	3	4	5	6	7	8	9	10	11	12	13	14	15	16	17	18	19	20	21	22	23	24	25	26	27	28	29	30	31	32	33	34	35	36	37	38
Venue	H	A	H	A	H	A	A	H	A	H	A	H	A	H	A	H	A	H	A	A	H	A	H	A	H	H	A	H	A	H	A	H	A	H	A	H	A	H
Competition	L	L	L	L	L	L	L	L	L	L	L	L	L	L	L	L	L	L	L	L	L	L	L	L	L	L	L	L	L	L	L	L	L	L	L	L	L	L
Result	W	D	D	D	W	L	D	L	L	D	D	W	W	W	L	W	L	D	W	D	L	W	W	D	W	W	D	L	D	W	L	D	L	D	D	D	D	D

Goalkeepers
Matteo Guardalben
Nicola Santoni

Defenders
Pietro Accardi
Adriano
Andrea Barzagli
Guiseppe Biava
Kewullay Conteh
Rocca D'Aiello
Michele Ferri
Christian Terlizzi
Cristian Zaccardo

Midfielders
Simone Barone
Franco Brienza
Eugenio Corini
Antonino Di Franco
Andrea Gasbarroni
Mariano Gonzalez
Fabio Grosso
Nicola Milano
Stefano Morrone
Massimo Mutarelli
Cristian Raimondi
Mario Santana
Lamberto Zauli

Forwards
Pietro Balistreri
Ernesto Farias
Davide Possanzini
Luca Toni

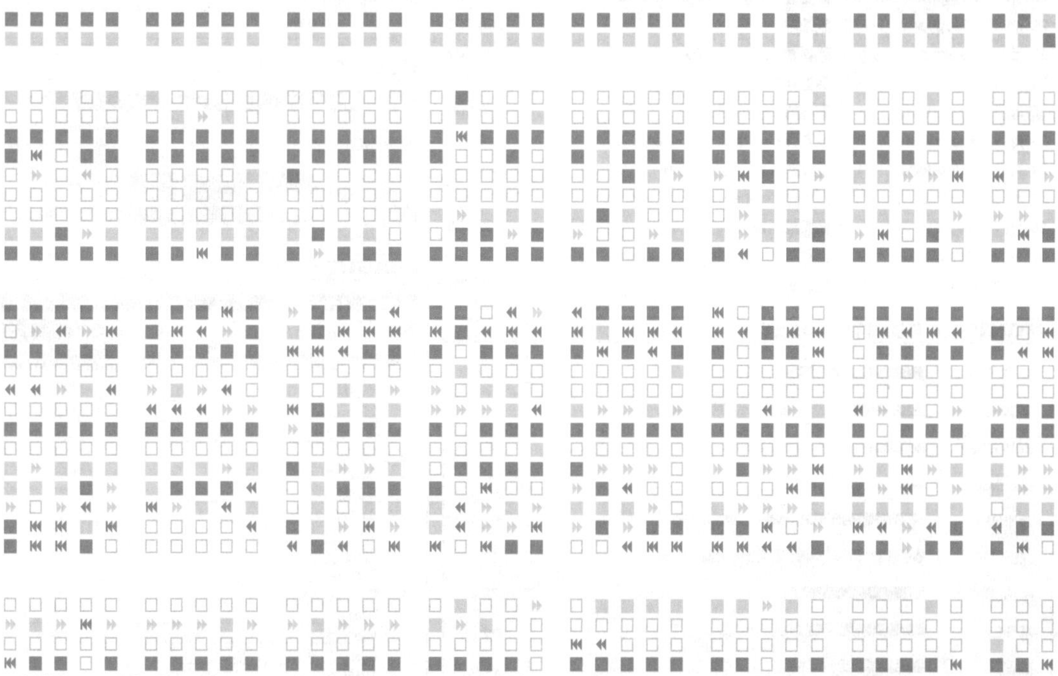

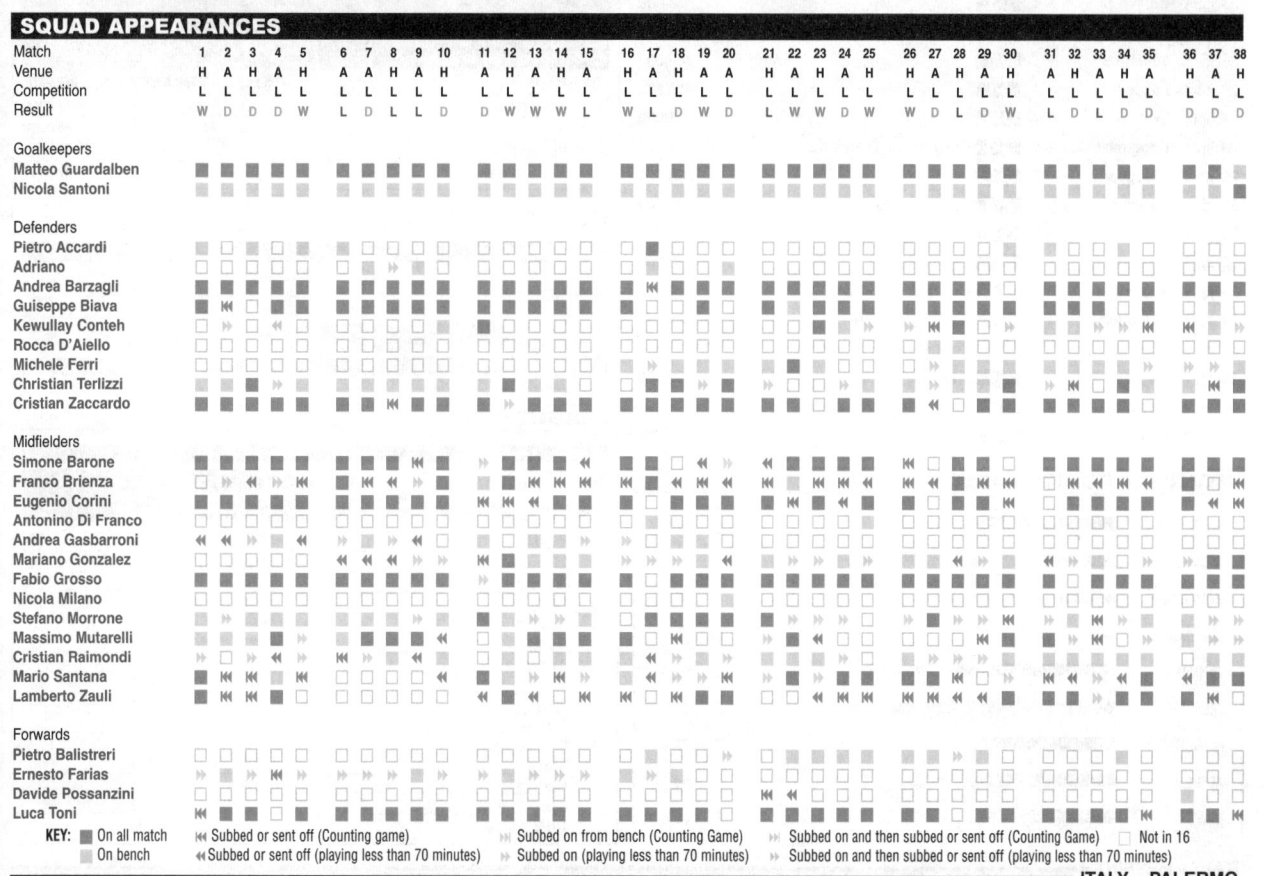

KEY: On all match / On bench / Subbed or sent off (Counting game) / Subbed or sent off (playing less than 70 minutes) / Subbed on from bench (Counting Game) / Subbed on (playing less than 70 minutes) / Subbed on and then subbed or sent off (Counting Game) / Subbed on and then subbed or sent off (playing less than 70 minutes) / Not in 16

MESSINA

Final Position: **7th**

KEY: Won, Drawn, Lost

							Attendance
1	itpr1	**Parma**	A	D	0-0		18,000
2	itpr1	**Roma**	H	W	4-3	Parisi 21 pen; Sullo 46; Giampa 74; Zampagna 77	15,000
3	itpr1	**AC Milan**	A	W	2-1	Giampa 55; Zampagna 59	60,000
4	itpr1	**Chievo**	H	D	0-0		29,000
5	itpr1	**Siena**	H	W	4-1	Parisi 33; Di Napoli 36,54; Amoruso 83 pen	21,000
6	itpr1	**Juventus**	A	L	1-2	Zampagna 65	30,000
7	itpr1	**Lecce**	H	L	1-4	Di Napoli 43	32,000
8	itpr1	**Lazio**	A	L	0-2		25,000
9	itpr1	**Reggina**	H	W	2-1	Zampagna 65; Di Napoli 74	28,000
10	itpr1	**Bologna**	A	D	2-2	Di Napoli 4; Amoruso 33	17,000
11	itpr1	**Palermo**	H	D	0-0		32,000
12	itpr1	**Udinese**	A	D	1-1	Amoruso 12	14,000
13	itpr1	**Fiorentina**	H	D	1-1	Parisi 70 pen	34,000
14	itpr1	**Inter Milan**	A	L	0-5		45,000
15	itpr1	**Sampdoria**	A	L	0-1		21,000
16	itpr1	**Cagliari**	A	L	1-2	Zampagna 21	16,000
17	itpr1	**Brescia**	H	W	2-0	Donati 6; Parisi 70 pen	29,000
18	itpr1	**Livorno**	A	L	1-3	Giampa 78	13,000
19	itpr1	**Atalanta**	H	W	1-0	Sullo 54	25,000
20	itpr1	**Parma**	H	W	1-0	Di Napoli 80	25,000
21	itpr1	**Roma**	A	L	2-3	Zampagna 12; Parisi 32	46,000
22	itpr1	**AC Milan**	H	L	1-4	Zampagna 30	35,000
23	itpr1	**Chievo**	A	L	0-1		7,000
24	itpr1	**Siena**	A	D	2-2	Di Napoli 5; Parisi 68 pen	7,000
25	itpr1	**Juventus**	H	D	0-0		40,000
26	itpr1	**Lecce**	A	L	0-1		12,000
27	itpr1	**Lazio**	H	W	1-0	Coppola 44	35,000
28	itpr1	**Reggina**	A	W	2-0	Cristante 13; D'Agostino 40	20,000
29	itpr1	**Bologna**	H	D	0-0		38,000
30	itpr1	**Palermo**	A	L	1-2	Zampagna 68	34,000
31	itpr1	**Udinese**	H	W	1-0	Iliev 60	30,000
32	itpr1	**Fiorentina**	A	D	1-1	Di Napoli 90	28,000
33	itpr1	**Inter Milan**	H	W	2-1	Di Napoli 59; Rafael 90	40,000
34	itpr1	**Sampdoria**	H	D	2-2	Zampagna 31,60	32,000
35	itpr1	**Atalanta**	A	L	1-2	Zampagna 37	12,000
36	itpr1	**Cagliari**	H	W	2-1	D'Agostino 45; Amoruso 87	33,000
37	itpr1	**Brescia**	A	L	1-2	Amoruso 90	15,000
38	itpr1	**Livorno**	H	D	1-1	Zampagna 71	30,000

MONTHLY POINTS TALLY

SEPTEMBER	8	67%
OCTOBER	6	40%
NOVEMBER	4	33%
DECEMBER	0	0%
JANUARY	9	50%
FEBRUARY	2	13%
MARCH	7	78%
APRIL	7	58%
MAY	5	33%

KEY PLAYERS - GOALSCORERS

Riccardo Zampagna

Goals in the League	12	Player Strike Rate Average number of minutes between League goals scored by player	192
Contribution to Attacking Power Average number of minutes between League team goals while on pitch	71	Club Strike Rate Average number of minutes between League goals scored by club	78

	PLAYER	LGE GOALS	POWER	STRIKE RATE
1	Riccardo Zampagna	12	71	**192 mins**
2	Arturo Di Napoli	9	66	**207 mins**
3	Alessandro Parisi	6	70	**363 mins**
4	Domenico Giampa	3	65	**582 mins**
5	Gaetano D'Agostino	2	86	**599 mins**

KEY PLAYERS - MIDFIELDERS

Gaetano D'Agostino

Goals in the League	2	Contribution to Attacking Power Average number of minutes between League team goals while on pitch	86
Defensive Rating Average number of mins between League goals conceded while on the pitch	92	Scoring Difference Defensive Rating minus Contribution to Attacking Power	6

	PLAYER	LGE GOALS	DEF RATE	POWER	SCORE DIFF
1	Gaetano D'Agostino	2	92	86	**6 mins**
2	Domenico Giampa	3	60	65	**-5 mins**
3	Massimo Donati	1	69	75	**-6 mins**
4	Carmine Coppola	1	66	72	**-6 mins**
5	Marc Zoro	0	58	85	**-27 mins**

KEY PLAYERS - DEFENDERS

Marco Zanchi

Goals Conceded Number of League goals conceded while the player was on the pitch	31	Clean Sheets In games when player was on pitch for at least 70 minutes	6
Defensive Rating Ave number of mins between League goals conceded while on the pitch	72	Club Defensive Rating Average number of mins between League goals conceded by the club this season	66

	PLAYER	CON LGE	CLEAN SHEETS	DEF RATE
1	Marco Zanchi	31	6	**72 mins**
2	Salvatore Aronica	39	7	**66 mins**
3	Rahman Rezaei	50	11	**65 mins**
4	Alessandro Parisi	35	9	**62 mins**

KEY GOALKEEPER

Marco Storari

Goals Conceded in the League	37	Counting Games Games when player was on pitch for at least 70 minutes	29
Defensive Rating Ave number of mins between League goals conceded while on the pitch	71	Clean Sheets In games when player was on pitch for at least 70 minutes	10

LEAGUE GOALS

Riccardo Zampagna

Minutes on the pitch	2299	Goals in the League	12
League average (mins between goals)	192		

	PLAYER	MINS	GOALS	AVE
1	Zampagna	2299	**12**	192
2	Di Napoli	1866	**9**	207
3	Parisi	2180	**6**	363
4	Amoruso	1025	**5**	205
5	Giampa	1745	**3**	582
6	D'Agostino	1197	**2**	599
7	Sullo	1274	**2**	637
8	Rafael	789	**1**	789
9	Coppola	2721	**1**	2721
10	Cristante	1027	**1**	1027
11	Donati	2691	**1**	2691
12	Iliev	2053	**1**	2053
	Other		0	
	TOTAL		**44**	

DISCIPLINARY

	PLAYER	YELLOW	RED	AVE
1	Zoro	12	1	**188**
2	Parisi	9	1	**218**
3	Coppola	11	0	**247**
4	Aronica	8	1	**286**
5	D'Agostino	3	1	**299**
6	Zanchi	7	0	**319**
7	Zampagna	7	0	**328**
8	Iliev	5	1	**342**
9	Yanagisawa	2	0	**398**
10	Giampa	4	0	**436**
11	Donati	5	1	**448**
12	Cristante	2	0	**513**
13	Rezaei	5	0	**647**
	Other	5	0	
	TOTAL	**85**	**6**	

TOP POINT EARNERS

	PLAYER	GAMES	AV PTS
1	Alessandro Parisi	20	**1.55**
2	Gaetano D'Agostino	13	**1.54**
3	Domenico Giampa	16	**1.50**
4	Carmine Coppola	30	**1.47**
5	Massimo Donati	29	**1.38**
6	Arturo Di Napoli	16	**1.38**
7	Marco Storari	29	**1.38**
8	Rahman Rezaei	36	**1.31**
9	Ivica Iliev	16	**1.19**
10	Riccardo Zampagna	26	**1.19**
	CLUB AVERAGE:		**1.26**

TEAM OF THE SEASON

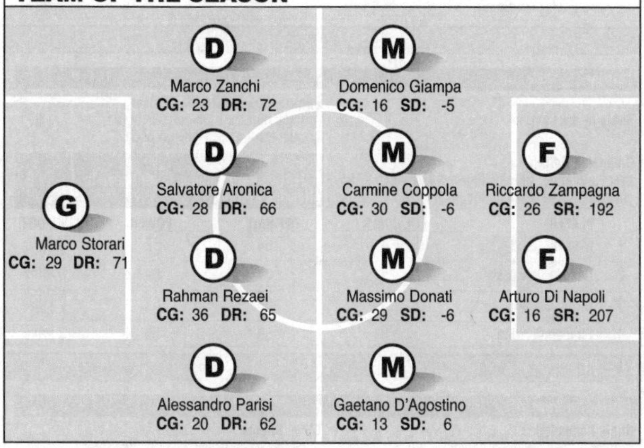

D
Marco Zanchi
CG: 23 DR: 72
M
Domenico Giampa
CG: 16 SD: -5
D
Salvatore Aronica
CG: 28 DR: 66
M
Carmine Coppola
CG: 30 SD: -6
F
Riccardo Zampagna
CG: 26 SR: 192
G
Marco Storari
CG: 29 DR: 71
D
Rahman Rezaei
CG: 36 DR: 65
M
Massimo Donati
CG: 29 SD: -6
F
Arturo Di Napoli
CG: 16 SR: 207
D
Alessandro Parisi
CG: 20 DR: 62
M
Gaetano D'Agostino
CG: 13 SD: 6

LEAGUE APPEARANCES, BOOKINGS AND CAPS

	AGE (on 01/07/05)	IN NAMED 18	APPEARANCES	COUNTING GAMES	MINUTES ON PITCH	YELLOW CARDS	RED CARDS	THIS SEASON	HOME COUNTRY
Goalkeepers									
D Eleftheropoulos	28	36	9	8	765	0	0	-	Greece
Giuseppe Santoro	17	8	1	0	45	0	0	-	Italy
Marco Storari	28	29	29	29	2610	3	0	-	Italy
Defenders									
Salvatore Aronica	27	34	30	28	2578	8	1	-	Italy
Mirko Conte	30	7	5	4	405	0	0	-	Italy
Filippo Cristante	28	15	13	11	1027	2	0	-	Italy
Simone Eramo	19	5	2	0	3	0	0	-	Italy
Luca Fusco	27	10	5	5	431	0	0	-	Italy
Alessandro Parisi	28	30	27	20	2180	9	1	1	Italy (10)
Rafael	25	32	26	4	789	1	0	-	Brazil
Rahman Rezaei	30	36	36	36	3236	5	0	-	Iran
Marco Zanchi	28	31	29	23	2234	7	0	-	Italy
Midfielders									
Raffaele Ametrano	32	7	3	2	187	1	0	-	Italy
Carmine Coppola	26	34	32	30	2721	11	0	-	Italy
Alessandro Cucciari	35	27	10	3	391	2	0	-	Italy
Gaetano D'Agostino	23	15	15	13	1197	3	1	-	Italy
Salvatore D'Alterio	25	17	5	1	145	0	0	-	Italy
Massimo Donati	24	37	34	29	2691	5	1	-	Italy
Domenico Giampa	28	29	24	16	1745	4	0	-	Italy
Panayotis Gonias	33	11	3	0	117	0	0	-	Greece
Jose Mamede	21	3	2	2	180	0	0	-	Portugal
Giuseppe Oliva	18	2	0	0	0	0	0	-	Italy
Salvatore Sullo	33	19	19	8	1274	0	0	-	Italy
Marc Zoro	21	32	29	26	2452	12	1	2	Ivory Coast (44)
Forwards									
Nicola Amoruso	30	31	22	7	1025	1	0	-	Italy
Vittorio Bernardo	19	7	2	0	48	0	0	-	Italy
Arturo Di Napoli	31	34	29	16	1866	0	0	-	Italy
Ivica Iliev	25	36	31	16	2053	5	1	-	Serbia & Montenegro
Atsushi Yanagisawa	28	34	22	5	796	2	0	-	Japan
Riccardo Zampagna	30	28	28	26	2299	7	0	-	Italy

SQUAD APPEARANCES

Match	1	2	3	4	5	6	7	8	9	10	11	12	13	14	15	16	17	18	19	20	21	22	23	24	25	26	27	28	29	30	31	32	33	34	35	36	37	38
Venue	A	H	A	H	H	A	H	A	H	A	H	A	H	A	A	A	H	A	H	H	A	H	A	A	H	A	H	A	H	A	H	A	H	H	A	H	A	H
Competition	L	L	L	L	L	L	L	L	L	L	L	L	L	L	L	L	L	L	L	L	L	L	L	L	L	L	L	L	L	L	L	L	L	L	L	L	L	L
Result	D	W	W	D	W	L	L	L	W	D	D	D	D	L	L	L	W	L	W	W	L	L	L	D	D	L	W	W	D	L	W	D	W	D	L	W	L	D

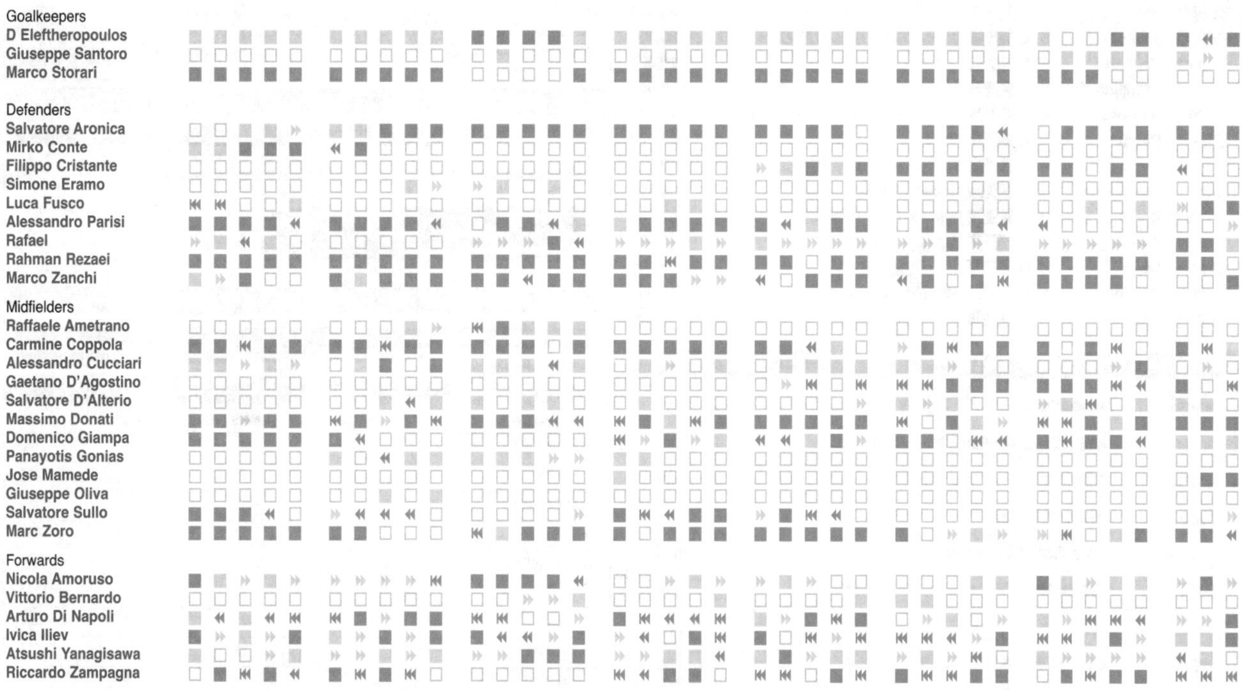

Goalkeepers
D Eleftheropoulos
Giuseppe Santoro
Marco Storari
Defenders
Salvatore Aronica
Mirko Conte
Filippo Cristante
Simone Eramo
Luca Fusco
Alessandro Parisi
Rafael
Rahman Rezaei
Marco Zanchi
Midfielders
Raffaele Ametrano
Carmine Coppola
Alessandro Cucciari
Gaetano D'Agostino
Salvatore D'Alterio
Massimo Donati
Domenico Giampa
Panayotis Gonias
Jose Mamede
Giuseppe Oliva
Salvatore Sullo
Marc Zoro
Forwards
Nicola Amoruso
Vittorio Bernardo
Arturo Di Napoli
Ivica Iliev
Atsushi Yanagisawa
Riccardo Zampagna

KEY: ■ On all match — ■ On bench — ⏮ Subbed or sent off (Counting game) — « Subbed or sent off (playing less than 70 minutes) — ⏭ Subbed on from bench (Counting Game) — » Subbed on (playing less than 70 minutes) — Subbed on and then subbed or sent off (Counting Game) — Subbed on and then subbed or sent off (playing less than 70 minutes) — □ Not in 16

ROMA

Final Position: **8th**

KEY: Won Drawn Lost

						Attendance
1	itpr1	Fiorentina	H W	1-0	Montella 53	58,000
2	cl gb	Dinamo Kiev	H L	0-3		
3	itpr1	Messina	A L	3-4	Montella 35,64,68	15,000
4	itpr1	Lecce	H D	2-2	Cassano 54; Mancini 72	36,000
5	itpr1	Bologna	A L	1-3	Totti 59	22,000
6	cl gb	Real Madrid	A L	2-4	De Rossi 3; Cassano 21	60,000
7	itpr1	Inter Milan	H D	3-3	Montella 9; Totti 57; De Rossi 74	58,000
8	itpr1	Livorno	A W	2-0	Totti 30; Montella 69	19,000
9	cl gb	B Leverkusen	A L	1-3	Jones 26 og	23,000
10	itpr1	Palermo	H D	1-1	Totti 58 pen	55,000
11	itpr1	Juventus	A L	0-2		28,000
12	itpr1	Cagliari	H W	5-1	Dellas 2; Totti 6 pen; Perrotta 64; Montella 90,90	55,000
13	cl gb	B Leverkusen	H D	1-1	Montella 90	
14	itpr1	AC Milan	A D	1-1	Montella 48	64,000
15	itpr1	Udinese	H L	0-3		40,000
16	itpr1	Reggina	A L	0-1		15,000
17	cl gb	Dinamo Kiev	A L	0-2		55,000
18	itpr1	Siena	A W	4-0	Montella 59,68; Totti 71,90	10,000
19	itpr1	Sampdoria	H D	1-1	Totti 84 pen	45,000
20	cl gb	Real Madrid	H L	0-3		
21	itpr1	Brescia	A W	1-0	Mancini 90 pen	9,000
22	itpr1	Parma	H W	5-1	Cassano 10,50; Totti 29,58; Montella 52	45,000
23	itpr1	Lazio	A L	1-3	Cassano 69	65,000
24	itpr1	Atalanta	H W	2-1	Montella 40,53	43,000
25	itpr1	Chievo	A D	2-2	Montella 34,52	10,000
26	itpr1	Fiorentina	A W	2-1	Cassano 23; Montella 67	23,000
27	itpr1	Messina	H W	3-2	Totti 57; Cassano 61; Mancini 82	46,000
28	itpr1	Lecce	A D	1-1	Giacomazzi 49 og	13,000
29	itpr1	Bologna	H D	1-1	Montella 9	43,000
30	itpr1	Inter Milan	A L	0-2		61,000
31	itpr1	Livorno	H W	3-0	Montella 8; Perrotta 69; Totti 81	42,000
32	itpr1	Palermo	A L	0-2		33,000
33	itpr1	Juventus	H L	1-2	Cassano 39	35,000
34	itpr1	Cagliari	A L	0-3		20,000
35	itpr1	AC Milan	H L	0-2		59,000
36	itpr1	Udinese	A D	3-3	Chivu 14; Montella 23; Mancini 44	15,000
37	itpr1	Reggina	H L	1-2	Chivu 24	44,000
38	itpr1	Siena	H L	0-2		40,000
39	itpr1	Sampdoria	A L	1-2	Montella 90 pen	24,000
40	itpr1	Brescia	H D	2-2	Perrotta 1; De Rossi 76	47,000
41	itpr1	Parma	A L	1-2	Cassano 4	15,000
42	itpr1	Lazio	H D	0-0		68,000
43	itpr1	Atalanta	A W	1-0	Cassano 50	15,000
44	itpr1	Chievo	H D	0-0		55,000

MONTHLY POINTS TALLY

SEPTEMBER	4	33%
OCTOBER	8	53%
NOVEMBER	4	33%
DECEMBER	7	78%
JANUARY	10	67%
FEBRUARY	5	33%
MARCH	0	0%
APRIL	1	8%
MAY	6	40%

KEY PLAYERS - GOALSCORERS

Vincenzo Montella

Goals in the League	21	**Player Strike Rate** Average number of minutes between League goals scored by player	142
Contribution to Attacking Power Average number of minutes between League team goals while on pitch	62	**Club Strike Rate** Average number of minutes between League goals scored by club	62

	PLAYER	LGE GOALS	POWER	STRIKE RATE
1	Vincenzo Montella	21	62	142 mins
2	Francesco Totti	12	59	214 mins
3	Antonio Cassano	9	63	284 mins
4	Mancini	4	57	638 mins
5	Simone Perrotta	3	76	789 mins

KEY PLAYERS - MIDFIELDERS

Mancini

Goals in the League	4	**Contribution to Attacking Power** Average number of minutes between League team goals while on pitch	57
Defensive Rating Average number of mins between League goals conceded while on the pitch	62	**Scoring Difference** Defensive Rating minus Contribution to Attacking Power	5

	PLAYER	LGE GOALS	DEF RATE	POWER	SCORE DIFF
1	Mancini	4	62	57	5 mins
2	Daniele De Rossi	2	64	61	3 mins
3	Olivier Dacourt	0	54	61	-7 mins
4	Simone Perrotta	3	59	76	-17 mins

KEY PLAYERS - DEFENDERS

Christian Panucci

Goals Conceded Number of League goals conceded while the player was on the pitch	31	**Clean Sheets** In games when player was on pitch for at least 70 minutes	7
Defensive Rating Ave number of mins between League goals conceded while on the pitch	71	**Club Defensive Rating** Average number of mins between League goals conceded by the club this season	59

	PLAYER	CON LGE	CLEAN SHEETS	DEF RATE
1	Christian Panucci	31	7	71 mins
2	Leandro Cufre	48	8	60 mins
3	Traianos Dellas	29	3	59 mins
4	Philippe Mexes	37	3	57 mins
5	Matteo Ferrari	53	5	55 mins

KEY GOALKEEPER

Ivan Pellizzoli

Goals Conceded in the League	33	**Counting Games** League games when player was on pitch for at least 70 minutes	20
Defensive Rating Ave number of mins between League goals conceded while on the pitch	55	**Clean Sheets** In games when player was on pitch for at least 70 minutes	4

LEAGUE GOALS

Vincenzo Montella

Minutes on the pitch	2991	Goals in the League	21
League average (mins between goals)	142		

	PLAYER	MINS	GOALS	AVE
1	Montella	2991	21	142
2	Totti	2565	12	214
3	Cassano	2552	9	284
4	Mancini	2552	4	638
5	Perrotta	2366	3	789
6	De Rossi	2493	2	1247
7	Chivu	732	2	366
8	Dellas	1723	1	1723
	Other		1	
	TOTAL		55	

DISCIPLINARY RECORDS

	PLAYER	YELLOW	RED	AVE
1	Scurto	4	0	118
2	Totti	11	2	197
3	Dacourt	8	0	207
4	De Rossi	11	1	207
5	Perrotta	9	0	262
6	Cassano	7	1	319
7	Aquilani	4	0	348
8	Mexes	5	1	350
9	Ferrari	8	0	366
10	Cufre	7	0	413
11	Dellas	4	0	430
12	Panucci	4	1	437
13	Montella	6	0	498
	Other	6	0	
	TOTAL	94	6	

TOP POINT EARNERS

	PLAYER	GAMES	AV PTS
1	Traianos Dellas	17	1.65
2	Daniele De Rossi	27	1.48
3	Mancini	24	1.38
4	Ivan Pellizzoli	20	1.30
5	Francesco Totti	28	1.29
6	Leandro Cufre	32	1.28
7	Matteo Ferrari	29	1.24
8	Philippe Mexes	21	1.19
9	Christian Panucci	23	1.17
10	Vincenzo Montella	31	1.13
	CLUB AVERAGE:		1.18

LEAGUE APPEARANCES, BOOKINGS AND CAPS

	AGE (on 01/07/05)	IN NAMED 18	APPEARANCES	COUNTING GAMES	MINUTES ON PITCH	YELLOW CARDS	RED CARDS	THIS SEASON	HOME COUNTRY
Goalkeepers									
Gianluca Curci	19	25	11	11	990	0	0	-	Italy
Ivan Pellizzoli	24	23	20	20	1800	0	0	4	Italy (10)
Carlo Zotti	22	20	7	7	630	0	0	-	Italy
Defenders									
Andrea Briotti	19	10	1	0	3	0	0	-	Italy
Vincent Candela	31	9	8	1	279	1	0	-	France
Christian Chivu	24	10	10	7	732	1	0	-	Romania
Leandro Cufre	27	33	33	32	2892	7	0	2	Argentina (3)
Traianos Dellas	29	23	21	17	1723	4	0	-	Greece
Matteo Ferrari	25	35	35	29	2933	8	0	-	Italy
Philippe Mexes	23	27	27	21	2100	5	1	-	France
Christian Panucci	32	26	26	23	2188	4	1	-	Italy
Luigi Sartor	30	14	7	3	443	0	1	-	Italy
Giuseppe Scurto	21	34	9	4	473	4	0	-	Italy
Abel Xavier	32	11	3	2	199	0	0	-	Portugal
Midfielders									
Alberto Aquilani	20	34	29	9	1393	4	0	-	Italy
Gaetano D'Agostino	23	15	6	1	252	1	0	-	Italy
Olivier Dacourt	30	23	23	15	1660	8	0	3	France (4)
Raffaele De Martino	19	11	5	1	132	0	0	-	Italy
Daniele De Rossi	20	31	30	27	2493	11	1	7	Italy (10)
Leandro Greco	18	5	1	0	15	0	0	-	Italy
Mancini	24	34	34	24	2552	5	0	-	Brazil
Massimiliano Marsili	17	7	1	0	35	0	0	-	Italy
Simone Perrotta	27	30	30	24	2366	9	0	2	Italy (10)
Alesandro Rosi	18	5	1	0	3	0	0	-	Italy
Forwards									
Antonio Cassano	22	31	31	26	2552	7	1	1	Italy (10)
Alessio Cerci	17	11	2	0	24	0	0	-	Italy
Daniele Corvia	20	34	13	1	344	0	0	-	Italy
Marco Delvecchio	32	8	4	0	98	0	0	-	Italy
Hossam Mido	22	13	8	0	251	1	0	-	Egypt
Vincenzo Montella	31	37	37	31	2991	6	0	2	Italy (10)
Francesco Totti	28	29	29	28	2565	11	2	4	Italy (10)
Valerio Virga	19	11	6	3	352	1	0	-	Italy

TEAM OF THE SEASON

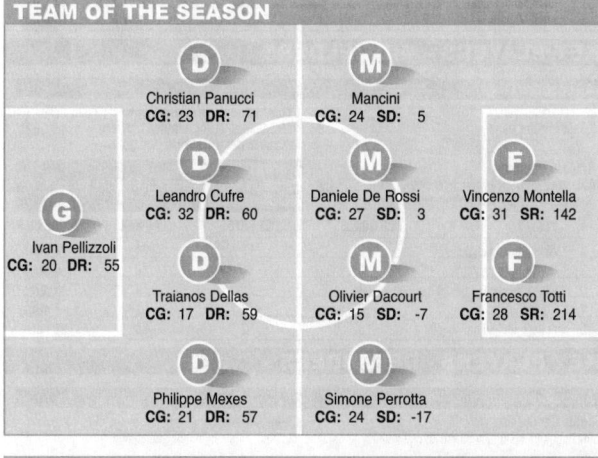

G
Ivan Pellizzoli
CG: 20 DR: 55

D
Christian Panucci
CG: 23 DR: 71

D
Leandro Cufre
CG: 32 DR: 60

D
Traianos Dellas
CG: 17 DR: 59

D
Philippe Mexes
CG: 21 DR: 57

M
Mancini
CG: 24 SD: 5

M
Daniele De Rossi
CG: 27 SD: 3

M
Olivier Dacourt
CG: 15 SD: -7

M
Simone Perrotta
CG: 24 SD: -17

F
Vincenzo Montella
CG: 31 SR: 142

F
Francesco Totti
CG: 28 SR: 214

SQUAD APPEARANCES

Match	1	2	3	4	5	6	7	8	9	10	11	12	13	14	15	16	17	18	19	20	21	22	23	24	25	26	27	28	29	30	31	32	33	34	35	36	37	38	39	40	41	42	43	44
Venue	H	H	A	H	A	A	H	A	A	H	A	H	H	A	H	A	A	A	H	H	A	H	A	H	A	A	H	A	H	A	H	A	H	A	H	A	H	H	A	H	A	H	A	H
Competition	O	C	O	O	O	C	O	O	C	O	O	O	C	O	O	O	C	O	O	C	O	O	O	O	O	O	O	O	O	O	O	O	O	O	O	O	O	O	O	O	O	O	O	O
Result	W	L	L	D	L	L	D	W	L	D	L	W	D	D	L	L	L	W	D	L	W	W	L	W	D	W	W	D	D	L	W	L	L	L	L	D	L	L	L	D	L	D	W	D

Goalkeepers
Gianluca Curci
Ivan Pellizzoli
Carlo Zotti

Defenders
Andrea Briotti
Vincent Candela
Christian Chivu
Leandro Cufre
Traianos Dellas
Matteo Ferrari
Philippe Mexes
Christian Panucci
Luigi Sartor
Giuseppe Scurto
Abel Xavier

Midfielders
Alberto Aquilani
Gaetano D'Agostino
Olivier Dacourt
Raffaele De Martino
Daniele De Rossi
Leandro Greco
Mancini
Massimiliano Marsili
Simone Perrotta
Alesandro Rosi

Forwards
Antonio Cassano
Alessio Cerci
Daniele Corvia
Marco Delvecchio
Hossam Mido
Vincenzo Montella
Francesco Totti
Valerio Virga

LIVORNO

Final Position: **9th**

KEY: Won Drawn Lost

							Attendance
1	itpr1	**AC Milan**	A	D	2-2	Lucarelli 10 pen,68	69,000
2	itpr1	**Chievo**	H	L	1-2	Protti 15	20,000
3	itpr1	**Reggina**	A	L	1-2	Lucarelli 31	14,000
4	itpr1	**Atalanta**	H	D	1-1	Vigiani 74	16,000
5	itpr1	**Sampdoria**	A	L	0-2		25,000
6	itpr1	**Roma**	H	L	0-2		19,000
7	itpr1	**Bologna**	H	W	1-0	Lucarelli, A 72	17,000
8	itpr1	**Palermo**	A	W	2-1	Vidigal 37; Lucarelli, C 62	30,000
9	itpr1	**Brescia**	H	W	2-1	Lucarelli, A 45; Doga 72	15,000
10	itpr1	**Cagliari**	A	D	0-0		12,000
11	itpr1	**Lazio**	H	W	1-0	Lucarelli, C 42	16,000
12	itpr1	**Fiorentina**	A	D	1-1	Lucarelli, C 78	33,000
13	itpr1	**Udinese**	H	L	1-2	Lucarelli, A 65	12,000
14	itpr1	**Lecce**	A	L	2-3	Vigiani 30; Danilevicus 40	11,000
15	itpr1	**Parma**	H	W	2-0	Lucarelli, C 40,89	15,000
16	itpr1	**Siena**	A	D	1-1	Lucarelli, A 56	10,000
17	itpr1	**Inter Milan**	H	L	0-2		18,000
18	itpr1	**Juventus**	A	L	2-4	Vidigal 42; Melara 80	21,000
19	itpr1	**Messina**	H	W	3-1	Vigiani 54; Colombo 58; Protti 75	13,000
20	itpr1	**AC Milan**	H	W	1-0	Colombo 28	19,000
21	itpr1	**Chievo**	A	L	0-1		7,000
22	itpr1	**Reggina**	H	D	1-1	Vidigal 84	13,000
23	itpr1	**Atalanta**	A	L	0-1		10,000
24	itpr1	**Sampdoria**	H	W	1-0	Lucarelli, A 82	16,000
25	itpr1	**Roma**	A	L	0-3		42,000
26	itpr1	**Bologna**	A	D	0-0		15,000
27	itpr1	**Palermo**	H	D	2-2	Lucarelli, A 60; Passoni 73	12,000
28	itpr1	**Brescia**	A	W	3-2	Doga 51; Protti 71 pen; Danilevicus 85	9,000
29	itpr1	**Cagliari**	H	D	3-3	Lucarelli, C 37,63; Protti 39	14,000
30	itpr1	**Lazio**	A	L	1-3	Protti 62	37,000
31	itpr1	**Fiorentina**	H	W	2-0	Lucarelli, C 12 pen,42	18,000
32	itpr1	**Udinese**	A	D	1-1	Lucarelli, C 85	13,000
33	itpr1	**Lecce**	H	W	1-0	Lucarelli, C 90	14,000
34	itpr1	**Parma**	A	L	4-6	Lucarelli, C 22,25,58,74	15,000
35	itpr1	**Siena**	H	L	3-6	Lucarelli, C 35,55; Colombo 72	17,000
36	itpr1	**Inter Milan**	A	L	0-1		53,000
37	itpr1	**Juventus**	H	D	2-2	Protti 47; Lucarelli, C 55	22,000
38	itpr1	**Messina**	A	D	1-1	Lucarelli, C 83	30,000

MONTHLY POINTS TALLY

SEPTEMBER	2	17%
OCTOBER	9	60%
NOVEMBER	5	42%
DECEMBER	4	44%
JANUARY	6	40%
FEBRUARY	5	33%
MARCH	5	56%
APRIL	7	58%
MAY	2	13%

KEY PLAYERS - GOALSCORERS

Cristiano Lucarelli

Goals in the League	19	Player Strike Rate Average number of minutes between League goals scored by player	162
Contribution to Attacking Power Average number of minutes between League team goals while on pitch	65	Club Strike Rate Average number of minutes between League goals scored by club	68

	PLAYER	LGE GOALS	POWER	STRIKE RATE
1	Cristiano Lucarelli	19	65	162 mins
2	Igor Protti	6	66	309 mins
3	Alessandro Lucarelli	6	66	408 mins
4	Jose Luis Vidigal	3	68	743 mins
5	Luca Vigiani	3	61	776 mins

KEY PLAYERS - MIDFIELDERS

Alessandro Doga

Goals in the League	2	Contribution to Attacking Power Average number of minutes between League team goals while on pitch	61
Defensive Rating Average number of mins between League goals conceded while on the pitch	63	Scoring Difference Defensive Rating minus Contribution to Attacking Power	2

	PLAYER	LGE GOALS	DEF RATE	POWER	SCORE DIFF
1	Alessandro Doga	2	63	61	2 mins
2	Jorge Vargas	0	80	86	-6 mins
3	Dario Passoni	1	68	74	-6 mins
4	Luca Vigiani	3	54	61	-7 mins
5	Jose Luis Vidigal	3	57	68	-11 mins

KEY PLAYERS - DEFENDERS

Alessandro Lucarelli

Goals Conceded Number of League goals conceded while the player was on the pitch	40	Clean Sheets In League games when player was on pitch for at least 70 minutes	7
Defensive Rating Ave number of mins between League goals conceded while on the pitch	61	Club Defensive Rating Average number of mins between League goals conceded by the club this season	57

	PLAYER	CON LGE	CLEAN SHEETS	DEF RATE
1	Alessandro Lucarelli	40	7	61 mins
2	Fabio Galante	31	5	59 mins
3	David Balleri	33	4	58 mins
4	Andrea Giallombardo	25	2	57 mins
5	Alessandro Grandoni	33	4	55 mins

KEY GOALKEEPER

Marco Amelia

Goals Conceded in the League	44	Counting Games League games when player was on pitch for at least 70 minutes	28
Defensive Rating Ave number of mins between League goals conceded while on the pitch	58	Clean Sheets In games when player was on pitch for at least 70 minutes	7

LEAGUE GOALS

Cristiano Lucarelli

Minutes on the pitch	3078	Goals in the League	19
League average (mins between goals)	162		

	PLAYER	MINS	GOALS	AVE
1	Lucarelli, C	3078	19	162
2	Protti	1856	6	309
3	Lucarelli, A	2446	6	408
4	Colombo	809	3	270
5	Vidigal	2230	3	743
6	Vigiani	2329	3	776
7	Doga	1897	2	949
8	Melara	2048	1	2048
9	Passoni	2500	1	2500
10	Danilevicus	796	1	796
	Other		5	
	TOTAL		50	

DISCIPLINARY RECORDS

	PLAYER	YELLOW	RED	AVE
1	Balleri	9	1	191
2	Giallombardo	6	1	203
3	Melara	8	0	256
4	Vargas	7	0	284
5	Lucarelli, A	7	0	349
6	Ruotolo	3	0	364
7	Galante	3	2	365
8	Grauso	4	0	390
9	Danilevicus	2	0	398
10	Colombo	2	0	404
11	Lucarelli, C	7	0	439
12	Vidigal	5	0	446
13	Protti	3	1	464
	Other	15	0	
	TOTAL	81	5	

TOP POINT EARNERS

	PLAYER	GAMES	AV PTS
1	Alessandro Doga	18	1.56
2	Fabio Galante	18	1.39
3	Igor Protti	16	1.38
4	Alessandro Lucarelli	25	1.36
5	Jorge Vargas	20	1.35
6	Marco Amelia	28	1.29
7	Dario Passoni	28	1.29
8	David Balleri	19	1.26
9	Cristiano Lucarelli	34	1.26
10	Claudio Grauso	16	1.25
	CLUB AVERAGE:		1.18

TEAM OF THE SEASON

G Marco Amelia CG: 28 DR: 58

D Alessandro Lucarelli CG: 25 DR: 61

D Fabio Galante CG: 18 DR: 59

D David Balleri CG: 19 DR: 58

D Andrea Giallombardo CG: 14 DR: 57

M Alessandro Doga CG: 18 SD: 2

M Dario Passoni CG: 28 SD: -6

M Jorge Vargas CG: 20 SD: -6

M Luca Vigiani CG: 21 SD: -7

F Cristiano Lucarelli CG: 34 SR: 162

F Igor Protti CG: 16 SR: 309

LEAGUE APPEARANCES, BOOKINGS AND CAPS

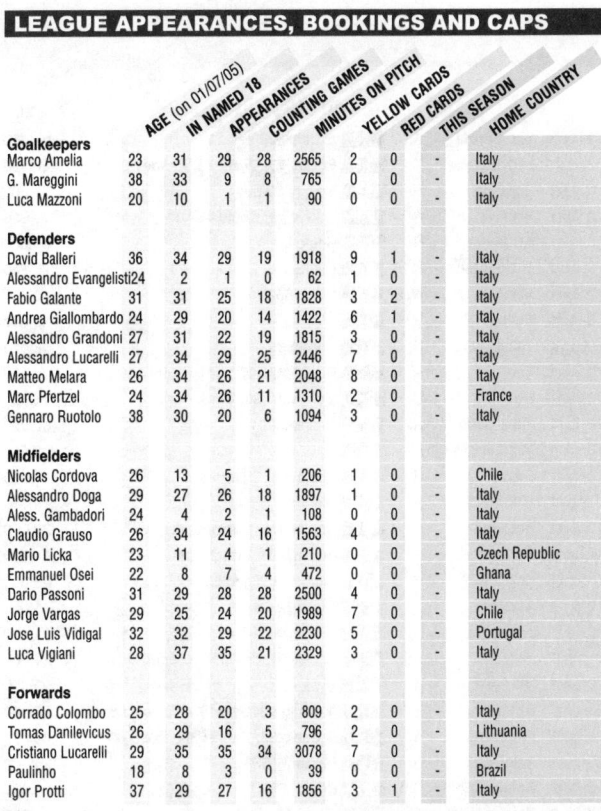

	AGE (on 01/07/05)	IN NAMED 18	APPEARANCES	COUNTING GAMES	MINUTES ON PITCH	YELLOW CARDS	RED CARDS	THIS SEASON	HOME COUNTRY
Goalkeepers									
Marco Amelia	23	31	29	28	2565	2	0	-	Italy
G. Mareggini	38	33	9	8	765	0	0	-	Italy
Luca Mazzoni	20	10	1	1	90	0	0	-	Italy
Defenders									
David Balleri	36	34	29	19	1918	9	1	-	Italy
Alessandro Evangelisti	24	2	1	0	62	1	0	-	Italy
Fabio Galante	31	31	25	18	1828	3	2	-	Italy
Andrea Giallombardo	24	29	20	14	1422	6	1	-	Italy
Alessandro Grandoni	27	31	22	19	1815	3	0	-	Italy
Alessandro Lucarelli	27	34	29	25	2446	7	0	-	Italy
Matteo Melara	26	34	26	21	2048	8	0	-	Italy
Marc Pfertzel	24	34	26	11	1310	2	0	-	France
Gennaro Ruotolo	38	30	20	6	1094	3	0	-	Italy
Midfielders									
Nicolas Cordova	26	13	5	1	206	1	0	-	Chile
Alessandro Doga	29	27	26	18	1897	1	0	-	Italy
Aless. Gambadori	24	4	2	1	108	0	0	-	Italy
Claudio Grauso	26	34	24	16	1563	4	0	-	Italy
Mario Licka	23	11	4	1	210	0	0	-	Czech Republic
Emmanuel Osei	22	8	7	4	472	0	0	-	Ghana
Dario Passoni	31	29	28	28	2500	4	0	-	Italy
Jorge Vargas	29	25	24	20	1989	7	0	-	Chile
Jose Luis Vidigal	32	32	29	22	2230	5	0	-	Portugal
Luca Vigiani	28	37	35	21	2329	3	0	-	Italy
Forwards									
Corrado Colombo	25	28	20	3	809	2	0	-	Italy
Tomas Danilevicus	26	29	16	5	796	2	0	-	Lithuania
Cristiano Lucarelli	29	35	35	34	3078	7	0	-	Italy
Paulinho	18	8	3	0	39	0	0	-	Brazil
Igor Protti	37	29	27	16	1856	3	1	-	Italy

SQUAD APPEARANCES

Match	1	2	3	4	5	6	7	8	9	10	11	12	13	14	15	16	17	18	19	20	21	22	23	24	25	26	27	28	29	30	31	32	33	34	35	36	37	38
Venue	A	H	A	H	A	H	H	A	H	A	H	A	H	A	H	A	H	A	H	H	A	H	A	H	A	A	H	A	H	A	H	A	H	A	H	A	H	A
Competition	L	L	L	L	L	L	L	L	L	L	L	L	L	L	L	L	L	L	L	L	L	L	L	L	L	L	L	L	L	L	L	L	L	L	L	L	L	L
Result	D	L	L	D	L	L	W	W	W	D	W	D	L	L	W	D	L	L	W	W	L	D	L	W	L	D	D	W	D	L	W	D	W	L	L	L	D	D

Goalkeepers
Marco Amelia
Gianmatteo Mareggini
Luca Mazzoni

Defenders
David Balleri
Alessandro Evangelisti
Fabio Galante
Andrea Giallombardo
Alessandro Grandoni
Alessandro Lucarelli
Matteo Melara
Marc Pfertzel
Gennaro Ruotolo

Midfielders
Nicolas Andrea Cordova
Alessandro Doga
Alessandro Gambadori
Claudio Grauso
Mario Licka
Emmanuel Osei
Dario Passoni
Jorge Vargas
Jose Luis Vidigal
Luca Vigiani

Forwards
Corrado Colombo
Tomas Danilevicus
Cristiano Lucarelli
Paulinho
Igor Protti

KEY: On all match | On bench | Subbed or sent off (Counting game) | Subbed or sent off (playing less than 70 minutes) | Subbed on from bench (Counting Game) | Subbed on (playing less than 70 minutes) | Subbed on and then subbed or sent off (Counting Game) | Subbed on and then subbed or sent off (playing less than 70 minutes) | Not in 16

LAZIO

Final Position: **10th**

KEY: Won Drawn Lost

							Attendance
1	itpr1	**Sampdoria**	A	W	1-0	di Canio 29 pen	24,000
2	uc1rl1	**M Donetsk**	A	W	3-0	Rocchi 73; Cesar 75; Pandev 85	20,000
3	itpr1	**Reggina**	H	D	1-1	Inzaghi 32 pen	35,000
4	itpr1	**Brescia**	A	W	2-0	Rocchi 29; Couto 45	12,000
5	itpr1	**AC Milan**	H	L	1-2	Couto 37	50,000
6	uc1rl2	**M Donetsk**	H	W	3-0	Liverani 10,27; Muzzi 23	5,000
7	itpr1	**Atalanta**	A	D	1-1	Muzzi 85	12,000
8	itpr1	**Chievo**	H	L	0-1		35,000
9	uc ge	**Villarreal**	H	D	1-1	Rocchi 83	8,000
10	itpr1	**Parma**	A	L	1-3	Rocchi 37	12,000
11	itpr1	**Messina**	H	W	2-0	Manfredini 36; De Sousa 66	25,000
12	itpr1	**Inter Milan**	A	D	1-1	Talamonti 84	50,000
13	uc ge	**Middlesbrough**	A	L	0-2		33,991
14	itpr1	**Siena**	H	D	1-1	Couto 47	32,000
15	itpr1	**Livorno**	A	L	0-1		16,000
16	itpr1	**Bologna**	H	W	2-1	Rocchi 6; di Canio 85 pen	32,000
17	uc ge	**Partizan**	H	D	2-2	di Canio 51; Inzaghi 73	12,000
18	itpr1	**Cagliari**	H	L	2-3	Pandev 9; Oddo 85	35,000
19	uc ge	**Aigaleo**	A	D	2-2	Muzzi 12,36	1,000
20	itpr1	**Juventus**	A	L	1-2	Pandev 10	21,000
21	itpr1	**Lecce**	H	D	3-3	Rocchi 51; di Canio 69 pen,78	35,000
22	itpr1	**Udinese**	A	L	0-3		15,000
23	itpr1	**Roma**	H	W	3-1	di Canio 29; Cesar 74; Rocchi 85	65,000
24	itpr1	**Fiorentina**	A	W	3-2	di Canio 33; Pandev 64; Dabo 82	30,000
25	itpr1	**Palermo**	H	L	1-3	Bazzani 16	35,000
26	itpr1	**Sampdoria**	H	L	1-2	Rocchi 63	35,000
27	itpr1	**Reggina**	A	L	1-2	Cesar 10	19,000
28	itpr1	**Brescia**	H	D	0-0		30,000
29	itpr1	**AC Milan**	A	L	1-2	Oddo 56 pen	57,000
30	itpr1	**Atalanta**	H	W	2-1	Bazzani 45; Liverani 89	30,000
31	itpr1	**Chievo**	A	W	1-0	Rocchi 76	10,000
32	itpr1	**Parma**	H	W	2-0	Oddo 19 pen; Filippini, A 89	30,000
33	itpr1	**Messina**	A	L	0-1		35,000
34	itpr1	**Inter Milan**	H	D	1-1	Filippini, A 45	52,000
35	itpr1	**Siena**	A	L	0-1		11,000
36	itpr1	**Livorno**	H	W	3-1	Muzzi 16; Cesar 45 pen; Rocchi 55	37,000
37	itpr1	**Bologna**	A	W	2-1	Oddo 54 pen; Rocchi 74	18,000
38	itpr1	**Cagliari**	A	D	1-1	Siviglia 90	15,000
39	itpr1	**Juventus**	H	L	0-1		45,000
40	itpr1	**Lecce**	A	L	3-5	Rocchi 30,52,58	21,000
41	itpr1	**Udinese**	H	L	0-1		35,000
42	itpr1	**Roma**	A	D	0-0		68,000
43	itpr1	**Fiorentina**	H	D	1-1	Siviglia 18	40,000
44	itpr1	**Palermo**	A	D	3-3	Rocchi 43; Bazzani 71; Muzzi 88	33,000

MONTHLY POINTS TALLY

SEPTEMBER	7	58%
OCTOBER	5	33%
NOVEMBER	4	33%
DECEMBER	1	11%
JANUARY	6	40%
FEBRUARY	10	67%
MARCH	1	11%
APRIL	7	58%
MAY	3	20%

KEY PLAYERS - GOALSCORERS

Tommaso Rocchi

Goals in the League	13	Player Strike Rate Average number of minutes between League goals scored by player	218
Contribution to Attacking Power Average number of minutes between League team goals while on pitch	74	**Club Strike Rate** Average number of minutes between League goals scored by club	71

	PLAYER	LGE GOALS	POWER	STRIKE RATE
1	Tommaso Rocchi	13	74	218 mins
2	Fernando Couto	3	83	693 mins
3	Massimo Oddo	4	77	738 mins
4	Leonardo Talamonti	1	61	1170 mins
5	Sebastiano Siviglia	2	81	1184 mins

KEY PLAYERS - MIDFIELDERS

Emanuele Filippini

Goals in the League	0	**Contribution to Attacking Power** Average number of minutes between League team goals while on pitch	73
Defensive Rating Average number of mins between League goals conceded while on the pitch	75	Scoring Difference Defensive Rating minus Contribution to Attacking Power	2

	PLAYER	LGE GOALS	DEF RATE	POWER	SCORE DIFF
1	Emanuele Filippini	0	75	73	2 mins
2	Ousmane Dabo	0	72	77	-5 mins
3	Luciano Zauri	0	74	80	-6 mins
4	Fabio Liverani	1	62	69	-7 mins
5	Guiliano Giannichedda	0	58	67	-9 mins

KEY PLAYERS - DEFENDERS

Fernando Couto

Goals Conceded Number of League goals conceded while the player was on the pitch	28	**Clean Sheets** In League games when player was on pitch for at least 70 minutes	4
Defensive Rating Ave number of mins between League goals conceded while on the pitch	74	**Club Defensive Rating** Average number of mins between League goals conceded by the club this season	65

	PLAYER	CON LGE	CLEAN SHEETS	DEF RATE
1	Fernando Couto	28	4	74 mins
2	Sebastiano Siviglia	32	5	74 mins
3	Massimo Oddo	42	7	70 mins
4	Leonardo Talamonti	19	2	62 mins

KEY GOALKEEPER

Matteo Sereni

Goals Conceded in the League	21	**Counting Games** League games when player was on pitch for at least 70 minutes	16
Defensive Rating Ave number of mins between League goals conceded while on the pitch	78	**Clean Sheets** In games when player was on pitch for at least 70 minutes	4

LEAGUE GOALS

Tommaso Rocchi

Minutes on the pitch	2834	Goals in the League	13
League average (mins between goals)	218		

	PLAYER	MINS	GOALS	AVE
1	Rocchi	2834	13	218
2	di Canio	1091	6	182
3	Oddo	2953	4	738
4	Bazzani	839	3	280
5	Muzzi	744	3	248
6	Couto	2079	3	693
7	Pandev	1134	3	378
8	Cesar	1168	3	389
9	Filippini, A	2825	2	1413
10	Siviglia	2368	2	1184
11	Liverani	1667	1	1667
12	Talamonti	1170	1	1170
13	De Sousa	82	1	82
	Other		3	
	TOTAL		48	

DISCIPLINARY RECORDS

	PLAYER	YELLOW	RED	AVE
1	Bazzani	5	0	167
2	Dabo	10	1	209
3	Cesar	3	2	233
4	Filippini, E	8	0	264
5	Seric	3	0	290
6	Giannichedda	8	1	291
7	Couto	5	2	297
8	Inzaghi	2	0	329
9	di Canio	2	1	363
10	Talamonti	3	0	390
11	Siviglia	5	1	394
12	Filippini, A	7	0	403
13	Oddo	6	0	492
	Other	15	2	
	TOTAL	82	10	

TOP POINT EARNERS

	PLAYER	GAMES	AV PTS
1	Leonardo Talamonti	13	1.46
2	Emanuele Filippini	23	1.35
3	Fabio Liverani	16	1.31
4	Luciano Zauri	20	1.25
5	Matteo Sereni	16	1.19
6	Massimo Oddo	32	1.19
7	Ousmane Dabo	23	1.17
8	Guiliano Giannichedda	27	1.15
9	Tommaso Rocchi	29	1.14
10	Angelo Peruzzi	15	1.13
	CLUB AVERAGE:		1.16

LEAGUE APPEARANCES, BOOKINGS AND CAPS

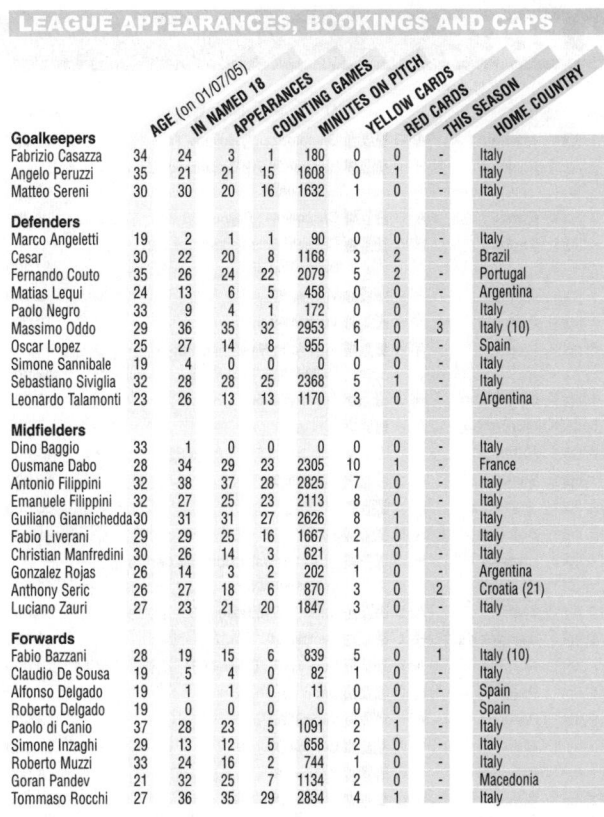

	AGE (on 01/07/05)	IN NAMED 18	APPEARANCES	COUNTING GAMES	MINUTES ON PITCH	YELLOW CARDS	RED CARDS	THIS SEASON	HOME COUNTRY
Goalkeepers									
Fabrizio Casazza	34	24	3	1	180	0	0	-	Italy
Angelo Peruzzi	35	21	21	15	1608	0	1	-	Italy
Matteo Sereni	30	30	20	16	1632	1	0	-	Italy
Defenders									
Marco Angeletti	19	2	1	1	90	0	0	-	Italy
Cesar	30	22	20	8	1168	3	2	-	Brazil
Fernando Couto	35	26	24	22	2079	5	2	-	Portugal
Matias Lequi	24	13	6	5	458	0	0	-	Argentina
Paolo Negro	33	9	4	1	172	0	0	-	Italy
Massimo Oddo	29	36	35	32	2953	6	0	3	Italy (10)
Oscar Lopez	25	27	14	8	955	1	0	-	Spain
Simone Sannibale	19	4	0	0	0	0	0	-	Italy
Sebastiano Siviglia	32	28	28	25	2368	5	1	-	Italy
Leonardo Talamonti	23	26	13	13	1170	3	0	-	Argentina
Midfielders									
Dino Baggio	33	1	0	0	0	0	0	-	Italy
Ousmane Dabo	28	34	29	23	2305	10	1	-	France
Antonio Filippini	32	38	37	28	2825	7	0	-	Italy
Emanuele Filippini	32	27	25	23	2113	8	0	-	Italy
Guiliano Giannichedda	30	31	31	27	2626	8	1	-	Italy
Fabio Liverani	29	29	25	16	1667	2	0	-	Italy
Christian Manfredini	30	26	14	3	621	1	0	-	Italy
Gonzalez Rojas	26	14	3	2	202	1	0	-	Argentina
Anthony Seric	26	27	18	6	870	3	0	2	Croatia (21)
Luciano Zauri	27	23	21	20	1847	3	0	-	Italy
Forwards									
Fabio Bazzani	28	19	15	6	839	5	0	1	Italy (10)
Claudio De Sousa	19	5	4	0	82	1	0	-	Italy
Alfonso Delgado	19	1	1	0	11	0	0	-	Spain
Roberto Delgado	19	0	0	0	0	0	0	-	Spain
Paolo di Canio	37	28	23	5	1091	2	1	-	Italy
Simone Inzaghi	29	13	12	5	658	2	0	-	Italy
Roberto Muzzi	33	24	16	2	744	1	0	-	Italy
Goran Pandev	21	32	25	7	1134	2	0	-	Macedonia
Tommaso Rocchi	27	36	35	29	2834	4	1	-	Italy

TEAM OF THE SEASON

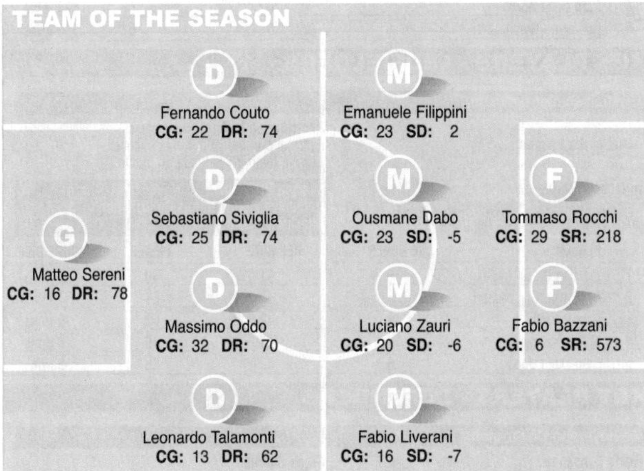

D
Fernando Couto
CG: 22 DR: 74
M
Emanuele Filippini
CG: 23 SD: 2
D
Sebastiano Siviglia
CG: 25 DR: 74
M
Ousmane Dabo
CG: 23 SD: -5
F
Tommaso Rocchi
CG: 29 SR: 218
G
Matteo Sereni
CG: 16 DR: 78
D
Massimo Oddo
CG: 32 DR: 70
M
Luciano Zauri
CG: 20 SD: -6
F
Fabio Bazzani
CG: 6 SR: 573
D
Leonardo Talamonti
CG: 13 DR: 62
M
Fabio Liverani
CG: 16 SD: -7

SQUAD APPEARANCES

Match	1	2	3	4	5	6	7	8	9	10	11	12	13	14	15	16	17	18	19	20	21	22	23	24	25	26	27	28	29	30	31	32	33	34	35	36	37	38	39	40	41	42	43	44
Venue	A	A	H	A	H	H	A	H	H	A	H	A	A	H	A	H	H	H	A	A	H	A	H	A	H	H	A	H	A	H	A	H	A	H	A	H	A	A	H	A	H	A	H	A
Competition	L	E	L	L	L	E	L	L	E	L	L	L	E	L	L	L	E	O	E	L	L	L	L	L	L	L	L	L	L	L	L	L	L	L	L	L	L	L	L	L	L	L	L	L
Result	W	W	D	W	L	W	D	L	D	L	W	D	L	D	L	W	D	L	D	L	D	L	W	W	L	L	L	D	L	W	W	W	L	D	L	W	W	D	L	L	L	D	D	D

Goalkeepers
Fabrizio Casazza
Angelo Peruzzi
Matteo Sereni

Defenders
Marco Angeletti
Cesar
Fernando Couto
Matias Lequi
Paolo Negro
Massimo Oddo
Oscar Lopez
Simone Sannibale
Sebastiano Siviglia
Leonardo Talamonti

Midfielders
Dino Baggio
Ousmane Dabo
Antonio Filippini
Emanuele Filippini
Guiliano Giannichedda
Fabio Liverani
Christian Manfredini
Esteban Rojas
Anthony Seric
Luciano Zauri

Forwards
Fabio Bazzani
Claudio De Sousa
Alfonso Delgado
Paolo di Canio
Simone Inzaghi
Roberto Muzzi
Goran Pandev
Tommaso Rocchi

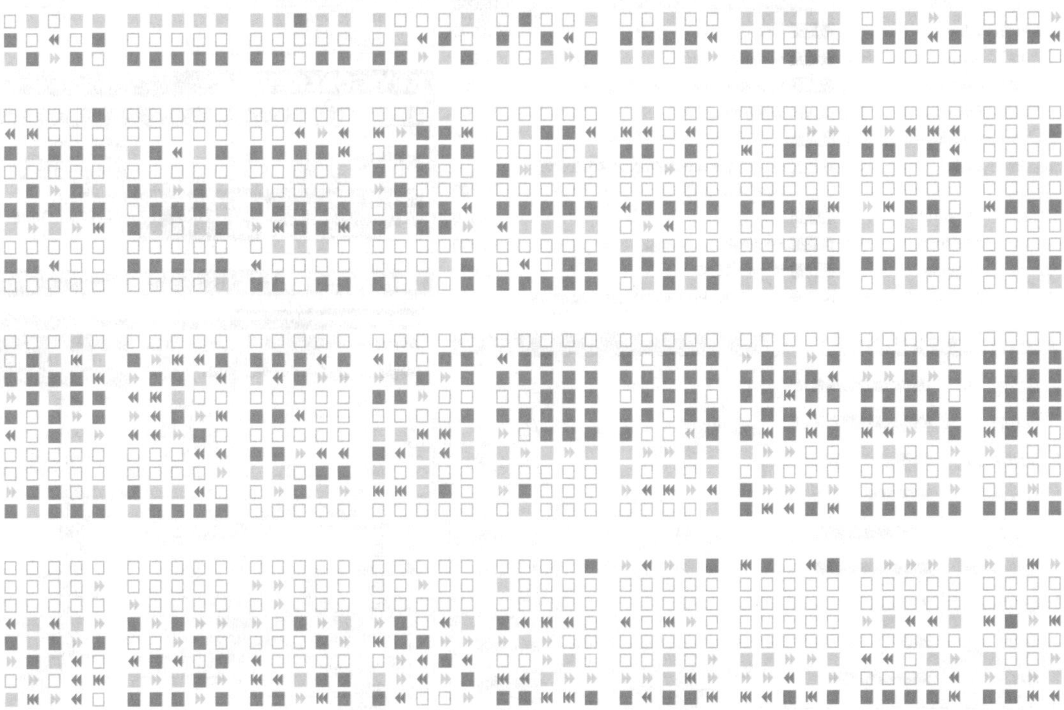

LECCE

Final Position: **11th**

KEY: Won Drawn Lost

							Attendance
1	itpr1	**Atalanta**	A	D	2-2	Giacomazzi 7; Bojinov 76	15,000
2	itpr1	**Brescia**	H	W	4-1	Bojinov 38,73; Bjelanovic 52; Giacomazzi 83	14,000
3	itpr1	**Roma**	A	D	2-2	Cassetti 41; Bojinov 58	36,000
4	itpr1	**Cagliari**	H	W	3-1	Cassetti 58; Giacomazzi 74; Bjelanovic 85	15,000
5	itpr1	**Chievo**	A	L	1-2	Vucinic 90	8,000
6	itpr1	**Palermo**	H	W	2-0	Vucinic 49,80	18,000
7	itpr1	**Messina**	A	W	4-1	Vucinic 5; Bjelanovic 38,44; Dalla Bona 90	32,000
8	itpr1	**Inter Milan**	H	D	2-2	Bojinov 36,50	18,000
9	itpr1	**Fiorentina**	A	L	0-4		31,000
10	itpr1	**Udinese**	H	L	3-4	Bojinov 35,57; Vucinic 89	13,000
11	itpr1	**Siena**	A	D	1-1	Cassetti 71	10,000
12	itpr1	**Juventus**	H	L	0-1		30,000
13	itpr1	**Bologna**	A	D	0-0		21,000
14	itpr1	**Livorno**	H	W	3-2	Rullo 39; Dalla Bona 56 pen; Giacomazzi 59	11,000
15	itpr1	**Lazio**	A	D	3-3	Babu 10,76; Bojinov 33	35,000
16	itpr1	**Sampdoria**	H	L	1-4	Vucinic 54	13,000
17	itpr1	**AC Milan**	A	L	2-5	Bojinov 75; Cassetti 84	70,000
18	itpr1	**Reggina**	H	D	1-1	Babu 43	13,000
19	itpr1	**Parma**	A	L	1-2	Vucinic 82	13,000
20	itpr1	**Atalanta**	H	W	1-0	Bojinov 33	15,000
21	itpr1	**Brescia**	A	W	1-0	Konan 16	8,000
22	itpr1	**Roma**	H	D	1-1	Vucinic 79	13,000
23	itpr1	**Cagliari**	A	L	1-3	Vucinic 39	15,000
24	itpr1	**Chievo**	H	W	3-0	Konan 27; Valdes 74; Vucinic 77	11,000
25	itpr1	**Palermo**	A	L	2-3	Konan 6,68	34,000
26	itpr1	**Messina**	H	W	1-0	Bjelanovic 86	12,000
27	itpr1	**Inter Milan**	A	L	1-2	Pinardi 21	50,000
28	itpr1	**Fiorentina**	H	D	2-2	Dalla Bona 28; Vucinic 31	15,000
29	itpr1	**Udinese**	A	L	1-2	Pinardi 31	18,000
30	itpr1	**Siena**	H	D	2-2	Konan 10; Paci 55	11,000
31	itpr1	**Juventus**	A	L	2-5	Vucinic 7; Dalla Bona 89	21,000
32	itpr1	**Bologna**	H	D	1-1	Giacomazzi 20	11,000
33	itpr1	**Livorno**	A	L	0-1		14,000
34	itpr1	**Lazio**	H	W	5-3	Dalla Bona 6 pen; Vucinic 45,78,82; Diamoutene 71	21,000
35	itpr1	**Sampdoria**	A	L	0-3		23,000
36	itpr1	**AC Milan**	H	D	2-2	Konan 46; Vucinic 82	22,000
37	itpr1	**Reggina**	A	D	2-2	Vucinic 15,43	20,000
38	itpr1	**Parma**	H	D	3-3	Pinardi 30; Vucinic 41; Dalla Bona 48	15,000

MONTHLY POINTS TALLY

SEPTEMBER	8	67%
OCTOBER	7	47%
NOVEMBER	2	17%
DECEMBER	4	44%
JANUARY	7	47%
FEBRUARY	7	47%
MARCH	1	11%
APRIL	2	17%
MAY	6	40%

KEY PLAYERS - GOALSCORERS

Mirko Vucinic

Goals in the League	19	**Player Strike Rate** Average number of minutes between League goals scored by player	96
Contribution to Attacking Power Average number of minutes between League team goals while on pitch	49	**Club Strike Rate** Average number of minutes between League goals scored by club	52

	PLAYER	LGE GOALS	POWER	STRIKE RATE
1	Mirko Vucinic	19	49	96 mins
2	Emilov Valeri Bojinov	11	50	133 mins
3	Sasa Bjelanovic	5	52	265 mins
4	Sam Dalla Bona	6	56	494 mins
5	Guillermo Giacomazzi	5	51	545 mins

KEY PLAYERS - MIDFIELDERS

Cristian Daniel Ledesma

Goals in the League	0	**Contribution to Attacking Power** Average number of minutes between League team goals while on pitch	49
Defensive Rating Average number of mins between League goals conceded while on the pitch	51	**Scoring Difference** Defensive Rating minus Contribution to Attacking Power	2

	PLAYER	LGE GOALS	DEF RATE	POWER	SCORE DIFF
1	Cristian Daniel Ledesma	0	51	49	2 mins
2	Guillermo Giacomazzi	5	47	51	-4 mins
3	Alex Pinardi	3	48	53	-5 mins
4	Mirko Vucinic	19	43	49	-6 mins
5	Sam Dalla Bona	6	48	56	-8 mins

KEY PLAYERS - DEFENDERS

Souleymane Diamoutene

Goals Conceded Number of League goals conceded while the player was on the pitch	58	**Clean Sheets** In League games when player was on pitch for at least 70 minutes	5
Defensive Rating Ave number of mins between League goals conceded while on the pitch	49	**Club Defensive Rating** Average number of mins between League goals conceded by the club this season	47

	PLAYER	CON LGE	CLEAN SHEETS	DEF RATE
1	Souleymane Diamoutene	58	5	49 mins
2	Marco Cassetti	64	6	49 mins
3	Lorenzo Stovini	72	6	46 mins
4	Erminio Rullo	68	4	45 mins

KEY GOALKEEPER

Vincenzo Sicignano

Goals Conceded in the League	71	**Counting Games** League games when player was on pitch for at least 70 minutes	34
Defensive Rating Ave number of mins between League goals conceded while on the pitch	45	**Clean Sheets** In games when player was on pitch for at least 70 minutes	4

LEAGUE GOALS

Mirko Vucinic

Minutes on the pitch	1818	**Goals in the League**	19
League average (mins between goals)	96		

	PLAYER	MINS	GOALS	AVE
1	Vucinic	1818	19	96
2	Bojinov	1463	11	133
3	Konan	1217	6	203
4	Dalla Bona	2961	6	494
5	Giacomazzi	2727	5	545
6	Bjelanovic	1324	5	265
7	Cassetti	3161	4	790
8	Pinardi	2311	3	770
9	Babu	779	3	260
10	Paci	746	1	746
11	Valdes	775	1	775
12	Rullo	3073	1	3073
13	Diamoutene	2867	1	2867
	Other		0	
	TOTAL		66	

DISCIPLINARY RECORDS

	PLAYER	YELLOW	RED	AVE
1	Eremenko Jr	4	0	176
2	Diamoutene	13	2	191
3	Giacomazzi	8	0	340
4	Vucinic	5	0	363
5	Dalla Bona	7	1	370
6	Paci	2	0	373
7	Rullo	8	0	384
8	Cassetti	8	0	395
9	Ledesma	5	1	469
10	Bojinov	3	0	487
11	Pinardi	4	0	577
12	Konan	1	1	608
13	Bjelanovic	2	0	662
	Other	9	1	
	TOTAL	79	6	

TOP POINT EARNERS

	PLAYER	GAMES	AV PTS
1	Sasa Bjelanovic	12	1.75
2	Emilov Valeri Bojinov	14	1.43
3	Cristian Ledesma	31	1.35
4	Soul Diamoutene	31	1.32
5	Marco Cassetti	35	1.26
6	Guillermo Giacomazzi	29	1.24
7	Lorenzo Stovini	37	1.19
8	Mirko Vucinic	17	1.12
9	Sam Dalla Bona	30	1.10
10	Vincenzo Sicignano	34	1.09
	CLUB AVERAGE:		1.16

TEAM OF THE SEASON

D
Marco Cassetti
CG: 35 DR: 49
M
Cristian Ledesma
CG: 31 SD: 2
D
Soul Diamoutene
CG: 31 DR: 49
M
Guillermo Giacomazzi
CG: 29 SD: -4
F
Emilov Bojinov
CG: 14 SR: 133
G
Vincenzo Sicignano
CG: 34 DR: 45
D
Lorenzo Stovini
CG: 37 DR: 46
M
Alex Pinardi
CG: 23 SD: -5
F
Sasa Bjelanovic
CG: 12 SR: 265
D
Erminio Rullo
CG: 34 DR: 45
M
Mirko Vucinic
CG: 17 SD: -6

LEAGUE APPEARANCES, BOOKINGS AND CAPS

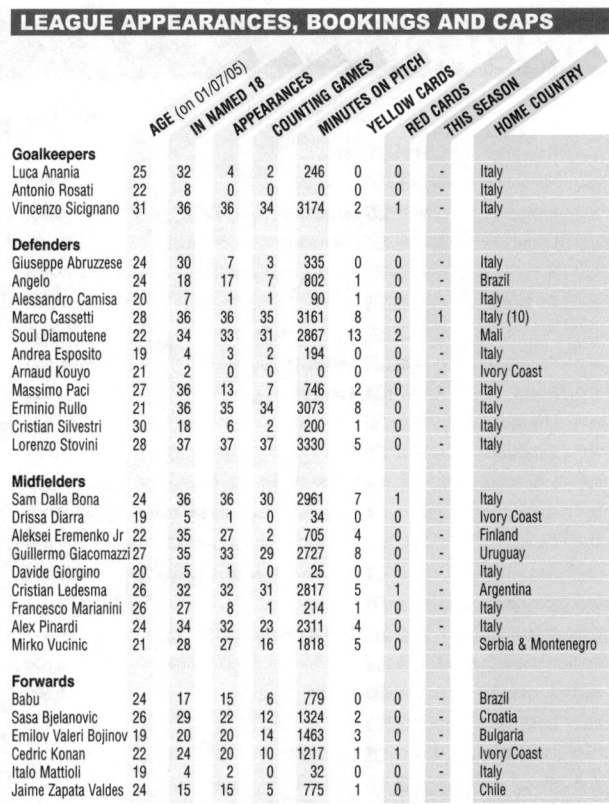

	AGE (on 01/07/05)	IN NAMED 18	APPEARANCES	COUNTING GAMES	MINUTES ON PITCH	YELLOW CARDS	RED CARDS	THIS SEASON	HOME COUNTRY
Goalkeepers									
Luca Anania	25	32	4	2	246	0	0	-	Italy
Antonio Rosati	22	8	0	0	0	0	0	-	Italy
Vincenzo Sicignano	31	36	36	34	3174	2	1	-	Italy
Defenders									
Giuseppe Abruzzese	24	30	7	3	335	0	0	-	Italy
Angelo	24	18	17	7	802	1	0	-	Brazil
Alessandro Camisa	20	7	1	1	90	1	0	-	Italy
Marco Cassetti	28	36	36	35	3161	8	0	1	Italy (10)
Soul Diamoutene	22	34	33	31	2867	13	2	-	Mali
Andrea Esposito	19	4	3	2	194	0	0	-	Italy
Arnaud Kouyo	21	2	0	0	0	0	0	-	Ivory Coast
Massimo Paci	27	36	13	7	746	2	0	-	Italy
Erminio Rullo	21	36	35	34	3073	8	0	-	Italy
Cristian Silvestri	30	18	6	2	200	1	0	-	Italy
Lorenzo Stovini	28	37	37	37	3330	5	0	-	Italy
Midfielders									
Sam Dalla Bona	24	36	36	30	2961	7	1	-	Italy
Drissa Diarra	19	5	1	0	34	0	0	-	Ivory Coast
Aleksei Eremenko Jr	22	35	27	2	705	4	0	-	Finland
Guillermo Giacomazzi	27	35	33	29	2727	8	0	-	Uruguay
Davide Giorgino	20	5	1	0	25	0	0	-	Italy
Cristian Ledesma	26	32	32	31	2817	5	1	-	Argentina
Francesco Marianini	26	27	8	1	214	1	0	-	Italy
Alex Pinardi	24	34	32	23	2311	4	0	-	Italy
Mirko Vucinic	21	28	27	16	1818	5	0	-	Serbia & Montenegro
Forwards									
Babu	24	17	15	6	779	0	0	-	Brazil
Sasa Bjelanovic	26	29	22	12	1324	2	0	-	Croatia
Emilov Valeri Bojinov	19	20	20	14	1463	3	0	-	Bulgaria
Cedric Konan	22	24	20	10	1217	1	1	-	Ivory Coast
Italo Mattioli	19	4	2	0	32	0	0	-	Italy
Jaime Zapata Valdes	24	15	15	5	775	1	0	-	Chile

SQUAD APPEARANCES

Match	1	2	3	4	5	6	7	8	9	10	11	12	13	14	15	16	17	18	19	20	21	22	23	24	25	26	27	28	29	30	31	32	33	34	35	36	37	38
Venue	A	H	A	H	A	H	A	H	A	H	A	H	A	H	A	H	A	H	A	H	A	H	A	H	A	H	A	H	A	H	A	H	A	H	A	H	A	H
Competition	L	L	L	L	L	L	L	L	L	L	L	L	L	L	L	L	L	L	L	L	L	L	L	L	L	L	L	L	L	L	L	L	L	L	L	L	L	L
Result	D	W	D	W	L	W	W	D	L	L	D	L	D	W	D	L	L	D	L	W	W	D	L	W	L	W	L	D	L	D	L	D	L	W	L	D	D	D

Goalkeepers
Luca Anania
Antonio Rosati
Vincenzo Sicignano

Defenders
Giuseppe Abruzzese
Angelo
Alessandro Camisa
Marco Cassetti
Soul Diamoutene
Andrea Esposito
Arnaud Kouyo
Massimo Paci
Erminio Rullo
Cristian Silvestri
Lorenzo Stovini

Midfielders
Sam Dalla Bona
Drissa Diarra
Aleksei Eremenko Jr
Guillermo Giacomazzi
Davide Giorgino
Cristian Ledesma
Francesco Marianini
Alex Pinardi
Mirko Vucinic

Forwards
Babu
Sasa Bjelanovic
Emilov Valeri Bojinov
Cedric Konan
Italo Mattioli
Jaime Zapata Valdes

KEY: On all match | On bench | Subbed or sent off (Counting game) | Subbed or sent off (playing less than 70 minutes) | Subbed on from bench (Counting Game) | Subbed on (playing less than 70 minutes) | Subbed on and then subbed or sent off (Counting Game) | Subbed on and then subbed or sent off (playing less than 70 minutes) | Not in 16

CAGLIARI

Final Position: **12th**

KEY: ☐Won ☐Drawn ☐Lost

							Attendance
1	itpr1	**Bologna**	H	W	1-0	Esposito 19	15,000
2	itpr1	**Fiorentina**	A	L	1-2	Suazo 90	28,000
3	itpr1	**Siena**	H	W	2-0	Esposito 19; Suazo 79	12,000
4	itpr1	**Lecce**	A	L	1-3	Esposito 49	15,000
5	itpr1	**Brescia**	H	W	2-1	Zola 13 pen; Langella 83	12,000
6	itpr1	**AC Milan**	H	L	0-1		20,000
7	itpr1	**Atalanta**	A	D	2-2	Esposito 12; Loria 29	12,000
8	itpr1	**Parma**	H	W	2-1	Abeijon 45; Esposito 86	15,000
9	itpr1	**Roma**	A	L	1-5	Suazo 31	55,000
10	itpr1	**Livorno**	H	D	0-0		12,000
11	itpr1	**Sampdoria**	A	D	0-0		22,000
12	itpr1	**Inter Milan**	H	D	3-3	Zola 6; Langella 33; Esposito 62	20,000
13	itpr1	**Lazio**	A	W	3-2	Langella 35; Esposito 66; Zola 71	35,000
14	itpr1	**Chievo**	H	W	4-2	Zola 33,39 pen; Langella 45; Abeijon 59	14,000
15	itpr1	**Reggina**	A	L	2-3	Langella 6; Esposito 73	16,000
16	itpr1	**Palermo**	A	L	0-3		33,000
17	itpr1	**Messina**	H	W	2-1	Esposito 48; Gobbi 55	16,000
18	itpr1	**Udinese**	A	L	0-2		18,000
19	itpr1	**Juventus**	H	D	1-1	Zola 89	22,000
20	itpr1	**Bologna**	A	L	0-1		18,000
21	itpr1	**Fiorentina**	H	W	1-0	Esposito 11	14,000
22	itpr1	**Siena**	A	D	2-2	Lopez 58; Langella 84	7,000
23	itpr1	**Lecce**	H	W	3-1	Gobbi 11; Esposito 74,76	15,000
24	itpr1	**Brescia**	A	L	0-2		9,000
25	itpr1	**AC Milan**	A	L	0-1		60,000
26	itpr1	**Atalanta**	H	D	3-3	Langella 10; Esposito 43; Abeijon 68	15,000
27	itpr1	**Parma**	A	L	2-3	Bonera 4 og; Suazo 90	13,000
28	itpr1	**Roma**	H	W	3-0	Zola 24; Esposito 41; Suazo 48	20,000
29	itpr1	**Livorno**	A	D	3-3	Suazo 42,45 pen; Abeijon 90	14,000
30	itpr1	**Sampdoria**	H	D	0-0		15,000
31	itpr1	**Inter Milan**	A	L	0-2		40,000
32	itpr1	**Lazio**	H	D	1-1	Esposito 70	15,000
33	itpr1	**Chievo**	A	D	1-1	Gobbi 72	7,000
34	itpr1	**Reggina**	H	D	1-1	Bianchi 90	15,000
35	itpr1	**Palermo**	H	D	0-0		15,000
36	itpr1	**Messina**	A	L	1-2	Alvarez 52	33,000
37	itpr1	**Udinese**	H	D	1-1	Esposito 67	15,000
38	itpr1	**Juventus**	A	L	2-4	Zola 61,87	53,000

MONTHLY POINTS TALLY

SEPTEMBER	6	50%
OCTOBER	7	47%
NOVEMBER	6	50%
DECEMBER	3	33%
JANUARY	7	47%
FEBRUARY	5	33%
MARCH	4	44%
APRIL	4	27%
MAY	2	17%

KEY PLAYERS - GOALSCORERS

Mauro Esposito

Goals in the League	16	Player Strike Rate Average number of minutes between League goals scored by player	182
Contribution to Attacking Power Average number of minutes between League team goals while on pitch	66	Club Strike Rate Average number of minutes between League goals scored by club	67

	PLAYER	LGE GOALS	POWER	STRIKE RATE
1	Mauro Esposito	16	66	182 mins
2	Gianfranco Zola	8	69	270 mins
3	Antonio Langella	7	58	309 mins
4	Nelson Abeijon	4	78	587 mins
5	Massimo Gobbi	3	67	1054 mins

KEY PLAYERS - MIDFIELDERS

Mauro Esposito

Goals in the League	16	Contribution to Attacking Power Average number of minutes between League team goals while on pitch	66
Defensive Rating Average number of mins between League goals conceded while on the pitch	59	Scoring Difference Defensive Rating minus Contribution to Attacking Power	-7

	PLAYER	LGE GOALS	DEF RATE	POWER	SCORE DIFF
1	Mauro Esposito	16	59	66	-7 mins
2	Massimo Gobbi	3	58	67	-9 mins
3	Daniele Conti	0	58	75	-17 mins
4	Nelson Abeijon	4	59	78	-19 mins

KEY PLAYERS - DEFENDERS

Diego Luis Lopez

Goals Conceded Number of League goals conceded while the player was on the pitch	44	Clean Sheets In League games when player was on pitch for at least 70 minutes	8
Defensive Rating Ave number of mins between League goals conceded while on the pitch	61	Club Defensive Rating Average number of mins between League goals conceded by the club this season	57

	PLAYER	CON LGE	CLEAN SHEETS	DEF RATE
1	Diego Luis Lopez	44	8	61 mins
2	Roberto Maltagliati	46	8	60 mins
3	Alessandro Agostini	53	7	59 mins
4	Francesco Bega	48	7	59 mins
5	Simone Loria	23	1	53 mins

KEY GOALKEEPER

Gennaro Iezzo

Goals Conceded in the League	35	Counting Games League games when player was on pitch for at least 70 minutes	23
Defensive Rating Ave number of mins between League goals conceded while on the pitch	59	Clean Sheets In games when player was on pitch for at least 70 minutes	4

LEAGUE GOALS

Mauro Esposito

Minutes on the pitch	2915	Goals in the League	16
League average (mins between goals)	182		

	PLAYER	MINS	GOALS	AVE
1	Esposito	2915	16	182
2	Zola	2163	8	270
3	Langella	2166	7	309
4	Suazo	1249	7	178
5	Abeijon	2346	4	587
6	Gobbi	3163	3	1054
7	Lopez	2667	1	2667
8	Loria	1228	1	1228
9	Alvarez	573	1	573
10	Bianchi	993	1	993
	Other		2	
	TOTAL		51	

DISCIPLINARY RECORDS

	PLAYER	YELLOW	RED	AVE
1	Conti	13	0	137
2	Abeijon	12	1	180
3	Bega	12	1	218
4	Lopez	9	2	242
5	Del Nevo	2	0	249
6	Pisano	3	0	251
7	Langella	7	1	270
8	Brambilla	3	1	285
9	Budel	2	1	305
10	Gobbi	8	0	395
11	Esposito	6	1	416
12	Alvarez	1	0	573
13	Loria	2	0	614
	Other	6	1	
	TOTAL	86	9	

TOP POINT EARNERS

	PLAYER	GAMES	AV PTS
1	Theofanis Kateryannakis	15	1.47
2	Mauro Esposito	32	1.31
3	Gianfranco Zola	17	1.29
4	Roberto Maltagliati	31	1.23
5	Francesco Bega	31	1.23
6	Nelson Abeijon	26	1.23
7	Alessandro Agostini	34	1.21
8	Diego Luis Lopez	27	1.19
9	Simone Loria	13	1.15
10	Massimo Gobbi	35	1.14
	CLUB AVERAGE:		1.16

TEAM OF THE SEASON

G — Gennaro Iezzo CG: 23 DR: 59

D — Diego Luis Lopez CG: 27 DR: 61

D — Roberto Maltagliati CG: 31 DR: 60

D — Alessandro Agostini CG: 34 DR: 59

D — Francesco Bega CG: 31 DR: 59

M — Mauro Esposito CG: 32 SD: -7

M — Massimo Gobbi CG: 35 SD: -9

M — Daniele Conti CG: 16 SD: -17

M — Nelson Abeijon CG: 26 SD: -19

F — Gianfranco Zola CG: 17 SR: 270

F — Antonio Langella CG: 20 SR: 309

LEAGUE APPEARANCES, BOOKINGS AND CAPS

	AGE (on 01/07/05)	IN NAMED 18	APPEARANCES	COUNTING GAMES	MINUTES ON PITCH	YELLOW CARDS	RED CARDS	THIS SEASON	HOME COUNTRY
Goalkeepers									
Alex Brunner	31	16	0	0	0	0	0	-	Italy
Gennaro Iezzo	32	37	23	23	2070	0	0	-	Italy
Fanis Kateryannakis	31	20	15	15	1350	0	0	-	Greece
Luca Tomasig	21	1	0	0	0	0	0	-	Italy
Defenders									
Alessandro Agostini	25	35	35	34	3128	4	1	-	Italy
Francesco Bega	30	34	32	31	2835	12	1	-	Italy
Diego Luis Lopez	30	34	33	27	2667	9	2	3	Uruguay (16)
Simone Loria	28	32	19	13	1228	2	0	-	Italy
Roberto Maltagliati	36	37	31	31	2782	0	0	-	Italy
Francesco Pisano	19	35	13	6	755	3	0	-	Italy
Rocco Sabato	23	9	3	2	222	0	0	-	Italy
Fabio Vignati	21	3	1	0	3	0	0	-	Italy
Midfielders									
Nelson Abeijon	31	31	30	26	2346	12	1	-	Uruguay
Marcello Albino	33	27	14	3	436	1	0	-	Italy
Edgar Alvarez	25	21	15	3	573	1	0	-	Honduras
Massimo Brambilla	28	25	16	8	1140	3	1	-	Italy
Alessandro Budel	24	16	14	8	915	2	1	-	Italy
Daniele Conti	26	32	29	16	1788	13	0	-	Italy
Loris Del Nevo	30	25	12	4	498	2	0	-	Italy
Mauro Esposito	26	34	34	32	2915	6	1	6	Italy (10)
Massimo Gobbi	24	37	37	35	3163	8	0	-	Italy
Claudio Pani	19	2	1	0	29	0	0	-	Italy
Forwards									
Rolando Bianchi	22	34	24	6	993	0	0	-	Italy
Andrea Cocco	19	2	0	0	0	0	0	-	Italy
Antonio Langella	28	33	33	20	2166	7	1	2	Italy (10)
Horacio Peralta	23	6	1	0	11	0	0	-	Uruguay
David Suazo	25	24	23	8	1249	2	0	-	Honduras
Gianfranco Zola	39	32	30	17	2163	0	0	-	Italy

SQUAD APPEARANCES

Match	1	2	3	4	5	6	7	8	9	10	11	12	13	14	15	16	17	18	19	20	21	22	23	24	25	26	27	28	29	30	31	32	33	34	35	36	37	38
Venue	H	A	H	A	H	H	A	H	A	H	A	H	A	H	A	A	H	A	H	A	H	A	H	A	A	H	A	H	A	H	A	H	A	H	H	A	H	A
Competition	L	L	L	L	L	L	L	L	L	L	L	L	L	L	L	L	L	L	L	L	L	L	L	L	L	L	L	L	L	L	L	L	L	L	L	L	L	L
Result	W	L	W	L	W	L	D	W	L	D	D	D	W	W	L	L	W	L	D	L	W	D	W	L	L	D	L	W	D	D	L	D	D	D	D	L	D	L

Goalkeepers: Alex Brunner, Gennaro Iezzo, Fanis Kateryannakis, Luca Tomasig

Defenders: Alessandro Agostini, Francesco Bega, Diego Luis Lopez, Simone Loria, Roberto Maltagliati, Francesco Pisano, Rocco Sabato, Fabio Vignati

Midfielders: Nelson Abeijon, Marcello Albino, Edgar Alvarez, Massimo Brambilla, Alessandro Budel, Daniele Conti, Loris Del Nevo, Mauro Esposito, Massimo Gobbi, Claudio Pani

Forwards: Rolando Bianchi, Andrea Cocco, Antonio Langella, Horacio Peralta, David Suazo, Gianfranco Zola

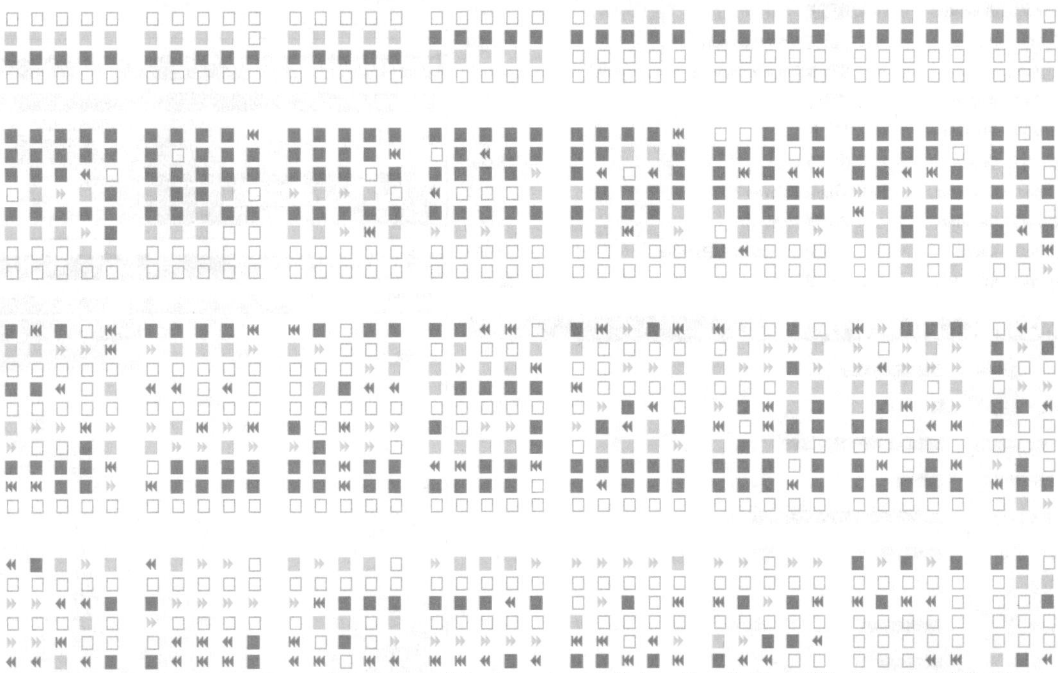

KEY: On all match · On bench · Subbed or sent off (Counting game) · Subbed or sent off (playing less than 70 minutes) · Subbed on from bench (Counting Game) · Subbed on (playing less than 70 minutes) · Subbed on and then subbed or sent off (Counting Game) · Subbed on and then subbed or sent off (playing less than 70 minutes) · Not in 16

REGGINA

Final Position: **13th**

KEY: Won Drawn Lost

							Attendance
1	itpr1	Udinese	H	D	0-0		20,000
2	itpr1	Lazio	A	D	1-1	Bonazzoli 35	35,000
3	itpr1	Livorno	H	W	2-1	Bonazzoli 8; Colucci 61	14,000
4	itpr1	Siena	A	D	0-0		8,000
5	itpr1	AC Milan	A	L	1-3	Franceschini 59	59,000
6	itpr1	Sampdoria	H	L	0-1		18,000
7	itpr1	Chievo	A	D	0-0		8,000
8	itpr1	Fiorentina	H	L	1-2	Paredes 60	18,000
9	itpr1	Messina	A	L	1-2	Bonazzoli 32	28,000
10	itpr1	Juventus	H	W	2-1	Colucci 12; Zamboni 29	25,000
11	itpr1	Parma	A	L	0-1		15,000
12	itpr1	Roma	H	W	1-0	Bonazzoli 15	15,000
13	itpr1	Atalanta	A	W	1-0	Paredes 12	10,000
14	itpr1	Brescia	H	L	1-3	Zamboni 75	20,000
15	itpr1	Cagliari	H	W	3-2	Paredes 8; De Rosa 53,77	16,000
16	itpr1	Bologna	A	L	0-2		18,000
17	itpr1	Palermo	H	W	1-0	Nakamura 7	18,000
18	itpr1	Lecce	A	D	1-1	Mozart 45 pen	13,000
19	itpr1	Inter Milan	H	D	0-0		22,000
20	itpr1	Udinese	A	W	2-0	Bonazzoli 39; Borriello 90	19,000
21	itpr1	Lazio	H	W	2-1	Bonazzoli 73,90	19,000
22	itpr1	Livorno	A	D	1-1	Paredes 14	13,000
23	itpr1	Siena	H	D	3-3	Franceschini 45; Borriello 81; Paredes 84	18,000
24	itpr1	AC Milan	H	L	0-1		24,000
25	itpr1	Sampdoria	A	L	2-3	Cannarsa 50; Tedesco 88	20,000
26	itpr1	Chievo	H	W	1-0	Nakamura 40	15,000
27	itpr1	Fiorentina	A	L	1-2	Colucci 79	30,000
28	itpr1	Messina	H	L	0-2		20,000
29	itpr1	Juventus	A	L	0-1		21,000
30	itpr1	Parma	H	L	1-3	Mozart 53 pen	15,000
31	itpr1	Roma	A	W	2-1	Franceschini 72; Bonazzoli 82	44,000
32	itpr1	Atalanta	H	D	0-0		15,000
33	itpr1	Brescia	A	L	0-2		7,000
34	itpr1	Cagliari	A	D	1-1	Colucci 36	15,000
35	itpr1	Bologna	H	D	1-1	Esteves 32	15,000
36	itpr1	Palermo	A	D	1-1	Mesto 37	36,000
37	itpr1	Lecce	H	D	2-2	Bonazzoli 9; Paredes 31	20,000
38	itpr1	Inter Milan	A	D	0-0		50,000

MONTHLY POINTS TALLY

SEPTEMBER	6	50%
OCTOBER	1	7%
NOVEMBER	9	75%
DECEMBER	3	33%
JANUARY	11	73%
FEBRUARY	5	33%
MARCH	0	0%
APRIL	5	33%
MAY	4	33%

KEY PLAYERS - GOALSCORERS

Emiliano Bonazzoli

Goals in the League	9	Player Strike Rate Average number of minutes between League goals scored by player	324
Contribution to Attacking Power Average number of minutes between League team goals while on pitch	88	Club Strike Rate Average number of minutes between League goals scored by club	95

	PLAYER	LGE GOALS	POWER	STRIKE RATE
1	Emiliano Bonazzoli	9	88	324 mins
2	Carlos Humberto Paredes	6	85	342 mins
3	Giuseppe Colucci	4	98	567 mins
4	Ivan Franceschini	3	92	955 mins
5	Shunsuke Nakamura	2	98	1074 mins

KEY PLAYERS - MIDFIELDERS

Mozart

Goals in the League	2	Contribution to Attacking Power Average number of minutes between League team goals while on pitch	93
Defensive Rating Average number of mins between League goals conceded while on the pitch	77	Scoring Difference Defensive Rating minus Contribution to Attacking Power	-16

	PLAYER	LGE GOALS	DEF RATE	POWER	SCORE DIFF
1	Mozart	2	77	93	-16 mins
2	Giandomenico Mesto	1	76	93	-17 mins
3	Carlos Humberto Paredes	6	68	86	-18 mins
4	Jacopo Balestri	0	75	94	-19 mins
5	Shunsuke Nakamura	2	74	98	-24 mins

KEY PLAYERS - DEFENDERS

Marco Zamboni

Goals Conceded Number of League goals conceded while the player was on the pitch	27	Clean Sheets In League games when player was on pitch for at least 70 minutes	7
Defensive Rating Ave number of mins between League goals conceded while on the pitch	81	Club Defensive Rating Average number of mins between League goals conceded by the club this season	74

	PLAYER	CON LGE	CLEAN SHEETS	DEF RATE
1	Marco Zamboni	27	7	81 mins
2	Gaetano De Rosa	37	10	77 mins
3	Juriy Cannarsa	36	9	73 mins
4	Ivan Franceschini	41	8	70 mins

KEY GOALKEEPER

Nicola Pavarini

Goals Conceded in the League	23	Counting Games League games when player was on pitch for at least 70 minutes	21
Defensive Rating Ave number of mins between League goals conceded while on the pitch	83	Clean Sheets In games when player was on pitch for at least 70 minutes	7

LEAGUE GOALS

Emiliano Bonazzoli

Minutes on the pitch	2915	Goals in the League	9
League average (mins between goals)	324		

	PLAYER	MINS	GOALS	AVE
1	Bonazzoli	2915	9	324
2	Paredes	2054	6	342
3	Colucci	2267	4	567
4	Franceschini	2866	3	955
5	Zamboni	2187	2	1094
6	Mozart	3069	2	1535
7	Borriello	983	2	492
8	Nakamura	2148	2	1074
9	De Rosa	2865	2	1433
10	Cannarsa	2644	1	2644
11	Esteves	496	1	496
12	Tedesco	2533	1	2533
13	Mesto	2972	1	2972
	Other		0	
	TOTAL		36	

DISCIPLINARY RECORDS

	PLAYER	YELLOW	RED	AVE
1	Borriello	6	0	163
2	Colucci	8	2	226
3	Mesto	13	0	228
4	Esteves	2	0	248
5	Franceschini	9	1	286
6	Bonazzoli	9	0	323
7	De Rosa	7	0	409
8	Tedesco	5	1	422
9	Zamboni	5	0	437
10	Soviero	2	1	501
11	Mozart	6	0	511
12	Nakamura	4	0	537
13	Pavarini	3	0	639
	Other	9	0	
	TOTAL	88	5	

TOP POINT EARNERS

	PLAYER	GAMES	AV PTS
1	Shunsuke Nakamura	19	1.63
2	Salvatore Soviero	16	1.38
3	Gaetano De Rosa	32	1.31
4	Jacopo Balestri	36	1.22
5	Mozart	34	1.21
6	Giacomo Tedesco	24	1.21
7	Emiliano Bonazzoli	33	1.21
8	Giandomenico Mesto	31	1.19
9	Marco Zamboni	23	1.17
10	Juriy Cannarsa	24	1.17
	CLUB AVERAGE:		1.16

LEAGUE APPEARANCES, BOOKINGS AND CAPS

	AGE (on 01/07/05)	IN NAMED 18	APPEARANCES	COUNTING GAMES	MINUTES ON PITCH	YELLOW CARDS	RED CARDS	THIS SEASON	HOME COUNTRY
Goalkeepers									
Giacomo Mazzi	26	4	0	0	0	0	0	-	Italy
Nicola Pavarini	31	34	23	21	1917	3	0	-	Italy
Salvatore Soviero	31	36	18	16	1503	2	1	-	Italy
Agostino Spicuzza	18	2	0	0	0	0	0	-	Italy
Defenders									
Juriy Cannarsa	29	37	33	24	2644	3	0	-	Italy
Francesco Cosenza	19	7	0	0	0	0	0	-	Italy
Gaetano De Rosa	31	33	32	32	2865	7	0	-	Italy
Ricardo Esteves	25	27	16	3	496	2	0	-	Portugal
Ivan Franceschini	28	33	33	32	2866	9	1	-	Italy
Giovanni Morabito	26	12	1	0	22	0	0	-	Italy
Felice Piccolo	21	34	8	2	265	0	0	-	Italy
Marco Zamboni	27	33	29	23	2187	5	0	-	Italy
Midfielders									
Alberto Baggio	18	1	0	0	0	0	0	-	Italy
Jacopo Balestri	30	37	37	36	3289	3	0	-	Italy
Viktor Boudianski	21	9	2	0	50	0	0	-	Ukraine
Giuseppe Colucci	24	30	30	20	2267	8	2	-	Italy
Giandomenico Mesto	23	35	35	31	2972	13	0	-	Italy
Mozart	25	35	35	34	3069	6	0	-	Brazil
Shunsuke Nakamura	27	35	33	19	2148	4	0	-	Japan
Carlos Paredes	28	33	28	21	2054	3	0	-	Paraguay
Giacomo Tedesco	29	34	33	24	2533	5	1	-	Italy
Ricardo Matias Veron	24	13	2	1	92	0	0	-	Argentina
Forwards									
Emiliano Bonazzoli	26	35	35	33	2915	9	0	-	Italy
Marco Borriello	23	37	29	3	983	6	0	-	Italy
Fabio Ceravolo	18	6	0	0	0	0	0	-	Italy
Davide Dionigi	31	15	10	0	147	1	0	-	Italy
Masimo Ganci	23	17	10	1	192	1	0	-	Italy
Simone Missiroli	19	8	4	0	51	0	0	-	Italy
Ilyas Zeytulaev	20	7	2	0	39	0	0	-	Uzbekistan

TEAM OF THE SEASON

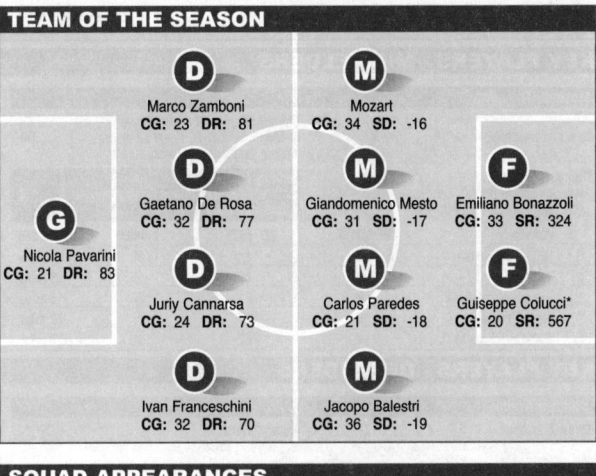

D Marco Zamboni — CG: 23 DR: 81

D Gaetano De Rosa — CG: 32 DR: 77

D Juriy Cannarsa — CG: 24 DR: 73

D Ivan Franceschini — CG: 32 DR: 70

G Nicola Pavarini — CG: 21 DR: 83

M Mozart — CG: 34 SD: -16

M Giandomenico Mesto — CG: 31 SD: -17

M Carlos Paredes — CG: 21 SD: -18

M Jacopo Balestri — CG: 36 SD: -19

F Emiliano Bonazzoli — CG: 33 SR: 324

F Guiseppe Colucci* — CG: 20 SR: 567

SQUAD APPEARANCES

Match	1	2	3	4	5	6	7	8	9	10	11	12	13	14	15	16	17	18	19	20	21	22	23	24	25	26	27	28	29	30	31	32	33	34	35	36	37	38
Venue	H	A	H	A	A	H	A	H	A	H	A	H	A	H	H	A	H	A	H	A	H	A	H	H	A	H	A	H	A	H	A	H	A	A	H	A	H	A
Competition	L	L	L	L	L	L	L	L	L	L	L	L	L	L	L	L	L	L	L	L	L	L	L	L	L	L	L	L	L	L	L	L	L	L	L	L	L	L
Result	D	D	W	D	L	L	D	L	L	W	L	W	W	L	W	L	W	D	D	W	W	D	D	L	L	W	L	L	L	L	W	D	L	D	D	D	D	D

Goalkeepers
Giacomo Mazzi
Nicola Pavarini
Salvatore Soviero
Agostino Spicuzza

Defenders
Juriy Cannarsa
Francesco Cosenza
Gaetano De Rosa
Ricardo Esteves
Ivan Franceschini
Giovanni Morabito
Felice Piccolo
Marco Zamboni

Midfielders
Alberto Baggio
Jacopo Balestri
Viktor Boudianski
Giuseppe Colucci
Giandomenico Mesto
Mozart
Shunsuke Nakamura
Carlos Paredes
Giacomo Tedesco
Ricardo Matias Veron

Forwards
Emiliano Bonazzoli
Marco Borriello
Fabio Ceravolo
Davide Dionigi
Masimo Ganci
Simone Missiroli
Ilyas Zeytulaev

KEY: ■ On all match ■ On bench
⏮ Subbed or sent off (Counting game)
« Subbed or sent off (playing less than 70 minutes)
⏭ Subbed on from bench (Counting Game)
» Subbed on (playing less than 70 minutes)
⏭ Subbed on and then subbed or sent off (Counting Game)
» Subbed on and then subbed or sent off (playing less than 70 minutes)
□ Not in 16

SIENA

Final Position: **14th**

KEY: Won Drawn Lost

						Attendance
1 itpr1	**Palermo**	A	L	0-1		33,000
2 itpr1	**Sampdoria**	H	W	2-1	Vergassola 9; Portanova 71	10,000
3 itpr1	**Cagliari**	A	L	0-2		12,000
4 itpr1	**Reggina**	H	D	0-0		8,000
5 itpr1	**Messina**	A	L	1-4	Portanova 39	21,000
6 itpr1	**Fiorentina**	A	D	0-0		34,000
7 itpr1	**Juventus**	H	L	0-3		15,000
8 itpr1	**Brescia**	A	W	1-0	Pecchia 18	9,000
9 itpr1	**Bologna**	H	D	1-1	Chiesa 53	8,000
10 itpr1	**Lazio**	A	D	1-1	Portanova 67	32,000
11 itpr1	**Lecce**	H	D	1-1	Pecchia 29	10,000
12 itpr1	**AC Milan**	A	L	1-2	Argilli 32	58,000
13 itpr1	**Roma**	H	L	0-4		10,000
14 itpr1	**Udinese**	A	L	0-1		21,000
15 itpr1	**Inter Milan**	H	D	2-2	Portanova 41; Flo 88	15,000
16 itpr1	**Livorno**	H	D	1-1	Vergassola 43	10,000
17 itpr1	**Chievo**	A	W	3-1	Taddei 44; Flo 54,66	7,000
18 itpr1	**Parma**	H	L	0-1		8,000
19 itpr1	**Atalanta**	A	D	1-1	Chiesa 45	15,000
20 itpr1	**Palermo**	H	D	0-0		8,000
21 itpr1	**Sampdoria**	A	D	1-1	Vergassola 67	21,000
22 itpr1	**Cagliari**	H	D	2-2	Chiesa 4; Flo 37	7,000
23 itpr1	**Reggina**	A	D	3-3	Vergassola 6; Chiesa 26,57	18,000
24 itpr1	**Messina**	H	D	2-2	Chiesa 48; Chiumiento 83	7,000
25 itpr1	**Fiorentina**	H	W	1-0	Flo 6	12,000
26 itpr1	**Juventus**	A	L	0-3		20,000
27 itpr1	**Brescia**	H	L	2-3	Chiesa 53; Maccarone 89	8,000
28 itpr1	**Bologna**	A	D	1-1	Maccarone 65	15,000
29 itpr1	**Lazio**	H	W	1-0	Tudor 60	11,000
30 itpr1	**Lecce**	A	D	2-2	Maccarone 17; Taddei 81	11,000
31 itpr1	**AC Milan**	H	W	2-1	Chiesa 71; Cozza 86	15,000
32 itpr1	**Roma**	A	W	2-0	Maccarone 61; Chiesa 88	40,000
33 itpr1	**Udinese**	H	L	2-3	Maccarone 9; Taddei 57	10,000
34 itpr1	**Inter Milan**	A	L	0-2		45,000
35 itpr1	**Livorno**	A	W	6-3	Argilli 15; Chiesa 38; Vergassola 52,60; Maccarone 62,81	17,000
36 itpr1	**Chievo**	H	L	0-1		9,000
37 itpr1	**Parma**	A	D	0-0		22,000
38 itpr1	**Atalanta**	H	W	2-1	Chiesa 8; Argilli 80	11,000

MONTHLY POINTS TALLY

SEPTEMBER	4	33%
OCTOBER	5	33%
NOVEMBER	2	17%
DECEMBER	2	22%
JANUARY	6	40%
FEBRUARY	6	40%
MARCH	4	44%
APRIL	7	58%
MAY	7	47%

KEY PLAYERS - GOALSCORERS

Enrico Chiesa

Goals in the League	11	Player Strike Rate Average number of minutes between League goals scored by player	259
Contribution to Attacking Power Average number of minutes between League team goals while on pitch	74	Club Strike Rate Average number of minutes between League goals scored by club	78

	PLAYER	LGE GOALS	POWER	STRIKE RATE
1	Enrico Chiesa	11	74	259 mins
2	Tore Andre Flo	5	77	340 mins
3	Daniele Portanova	4	74	501 mins
4	Taddei	3	65	518 mins
5	Simone Vergassola	6	76	541 mins

KEY PLAYERS - MIDFIELDERS

Roberto D'aversa

Goals in the League	0	Contribution to Attacking Power Average number of minutes between League team goals while on pitch	50
Defensive Rating Average number of mins between League goals conceded while on the pitch	64	Scoring Difference Defensive Rating minus Contribution to Attacking Power	14

	PLAYER	LGE GOALS	DEF RATE	POWER	SCORE DIFF
1	Roberto D'aversa	0	64	50	14 mins
2	Taddei	3	62	65	-3 mins
3	Simone Vergassola	6	61	76	-15 mins
4	Fabio Pecchia	2	67	97	-30 mins
5	Daniele di Donato	0	62	112	-50 mins

KEY PLAYERS - DEFENDERS

Stefano Argilli

Goals Conceded Number of League goals conceded while the player was on the pitch	24	Clean Sheets In League games when player was on pitch for at least 70 minutes	4
Defensive Rating Ave number of mins between League goals conceded while on the pitch	71	Club Defensive Rating Average number of mins between League goals conceded by the club this season	62

	PLAYER	CON LGE	CLEAN SHEETS	DEF RATE
1	Stefano Argilli	24	4	71 mins
2	Gianluca Falsini	28	5	67 mins
3	Igor Tudor	21	4	64 mins
4	Francesco Colonnese	23	3	63 mins
5	Davide Nicola	20	1	60 mins

KEY GOALKEEPER

Marco Fortin

Goals Conceded in the League	26	Counting Games League games when player was on pitch for at least 70 minutes	19
Defensive Rating Ave number of mins between League goals conceded while on the pitch	66	Clean Sheets In games when player was on pitch for at least 70 minutes	3

LEAGUE GOALS

Enrico Chiesa

Minutes on the pitch	2848	Goals in the League	11
League average (mins between goals)	259		

	PLAYER	MINS	GOALS	AVE
1	Chiesa	2848	11	259
2	Maccarone	846	7	121
3	Vergassola	3248	6	541
4	Flo	1701	5	340
5	Portanova	2002	4	501
6	Taddei	1555	3	518
7	Argilli	1710	2	855
8	Pecchia	1751	2	876
9	Chiumiento	694	1	694
10	Cozza	608	1	608
11	Tudor	1350	1	1350
	Other		1	
	TOTAL		44	

DISCIPLINARY RECORDS

	PLAYER	YELLOW	RED	AVE
1	Pasquale	5	2	122
2	Alberto	5	0	212
3	Tudor	5	1	225
4	Cirillo	8	1	279
5	D'aversa	5	0	282
6	Colonnese	5	0	288
7	di Donato	6	0	297
8	Portanova	5	1	333
9	Taddei	4	0	388
10	Maccarone	2	0	423
11	Graffiedi	1	0	557
12	Cozza	1	0	608
13	Falsini	3	0	627
	Other	13	3	
	TOTAL	68	8	

TOP POINT EARNERS

	PLAYER	GAMES	AV PTS
1	Roberto D'aversa	14	1.64
2	Igor Tudor	15	1.53
3	Alex Manninger	19	1.37
4	Gianluca Falsini	19	1.32
5	Taddei	14	1.21
6	Daniele Portanova	21	1.14
7	Tore Andre Flo	15	1.13
8	Francesco Colonnese	15	1.13
9	Simone Vergassola	34	1.09
10	Bruno Cirillo	27	1.00
	CLUB AVERAGE:		1.13

TEAM OF THE SEASON

G
Marco Fortin
CG: 19 DR: 66
D
Stefano Argilli
CG: 17 DR: 71
D
Gianluca Falsini
CG: 19 DR: 67
D
Igor Tudor
CG: 15 DR: 64
D
Francesco Colonnese
CG: 15 DR: 63
M
Roberto D'aversa
CG: 14 SD: 14
M
Taddei
CG: 14 SD: -3
M
Simone Vergassola
CG: 34 SD: -15
M
Fabio Pecchia
CG: 16 SD: -30
F
Enrico Chiesa
CG: 29 SR: 259
F
Tore Andre Flo
CG: 15 SR: 340

LEAGUE APPEARANCES, BOOKINGS AND CAPS

	AGE (on 01/07/05)	IN NAMED 18	APPEARANCES	COUNTING GAMES	MINUTES ON PITCH	YELLOW CARDS	RED CARDS	THIS SEASON	HOME COUNTRY
Goalkeepers									
Marco Fortin	31	36	19	19	1710	0	0	-	Italy
Alex Manninger	28	26	19	19	1710	2	0	-	Austria
Adriano Zancope	33	13	0	0	0	0	0	-	Italy
Defenders									
Alberto	30	15	15	10	1063	5	0	-	Brazil
Stefano Argilli	32	32	22	17	1710	0	1	-	Italy
Bruno Cirillo	28	34	32	27	2517	8	1	-	Italy
Francesco Colonnese	33	23	19	15	1443	5	0	-	Italy
Gianluca Falsini	29	31	24	19	1881	3	0	-	Italy
Paolo Foglio	29	24	12	3	368	0	0	-	Italy
Michele Mignani	33	13	13	11	1058	0	0	-	Italy
Davide Nicola	32	17	15	13	1195	1	0	-	Italy
Giovanni Pasquale	23	17	14	7	860	5	2	-	Italy
Jacopo Piazzi	18	1	0	0	0	0	0	-	Italy
Daniele Portanova	26	27	25	21	2002	5	1	-	Italy
Igor Tudor	27	15	15	15	1350	5	1	6	Croatia (21)
Midfielders									
Andrea Ardito	28	15	5	0	148	1	0	-	Italy
Alfonso Camorani	27	15	12	5	738	1	0	-	Italy
Davide Chiumiento	20	21	15	5	694	0	0	-	Italy
Francesco Cozza	31	11	10	5	608	1	0	-	Italy
Roberto D'aversa	29	18	18	14	1411	5	0	-	Italy
Daniele di Donato	28	34	23	19	1784	6	0	-	Italy
Menegazzo	24	19	7	0	173	0	0	-	Brazil
Fabio Pecchia	31	31	24	16	1751	1	1	-	Italy
Taddei	25	21	21	14	1555	4	0	-	Brazil
Simone Vergassola	29	37	37	34	3248	4	1	-	Italy
Forwards									
Marco Carparelli	29	14	7	1	338	1	0	-	Italy
Enrico Chiesa	34	38	36	29	2848	2	0	-	Italy
Tore Andre Flo	32	33	30	15	1701	2	0	-	Norway
Mattia Graffiedi	25	14	12	2	557	1	0	-	Italy
Massimo Maccarone	25	19	16	7	846	2	0	-	Italy
Manuel Mugnai	18	1	0	0	0	0	0	-	Italy
Matteo Serafini	27	13	7	0	124	0	0	-	Italy

SQUAD APPEARANCES

Match	1	2	3	4	5	6	7	8	9	10	11	12	13	14	15	16	17	18	19	20	21	22	23	24	25	26	27	28	29	30	31	32	33	34	35	36	37	38
Venue	A	H	A	H	A	A	H	A	H	A	H	A	H	A	H	H	A	H	A	H	A	H	A	H	H	A	H	A	H	A	H	A	H	A	A	H	A	H
Competition	L	L	L	L	L	L	L	L	L	L	L	L	L	L	L	L	L	L	L	L	L	L	L	L	L	L	L	L	L	L	L	L	L	L	L	L	L	L
Result	L	W	L	D	L	D	L	W	D	D	D	L	L	L	D	D	W	L	D	D	D	D	D	D	W	L	L	D	W	D	W	W	L	L	W	L	D	W

Goalkeepers
Marco Fortin
Alex Manninger
Adriano Zancope

Defenders
Alberto
Stefano Argilli
Bruno Cirillo
Francesco Colonnese
Gianluca Falsini
Paolo Foglio
Michele Mignani
Davide Nicola
Giovanni Pasquale
Jacopo Piazzi
Daniele Portanova
Igor Tudor

Midfielders
Andrea Ardito
Alfonso Camorani
Davide Chiumiento
Francesco Cozza
Roberto D'aversa
Daniele di Donato
Menegazzo
Fabio Pecchia
Taddei
Simone Vergassola

Forwards
Marco Carparelli
Enrico Chiesa
Tore Andre Flo
Mattia Graffiedi
Massimo Maccarone
Manuel Mugnai
Matteo Serafini

CHIEVO VERONA

Final Position: **15th**

KEY: ☐ Won ☐ Drawn ☐ Lost

							Attendance
1	itpr1	**Inter Milan**	H	D	2-2	Semioli 28; Pellissier 36	33,000
2	itpr1	**Livorno**	A	W	2-1	Cossato 50; Semioli 58	20,000
3	itpr1	**Udinese**	H	D	0-0		10,000
4	itpr1	**Messina**	A	D	0-0		29,000
5	itpr1	**Lecce**	H	W	2-1	Baronio 48; Tiribocchi 79	8,000
6	itpr1	**Lazio**	A	W	1-0	Brighi 72	35,000
7	itpr1	**Reggina**	H	D	0-0		8,000
8	itpr1	**Sampdoria**	H	L	0-2		8,000
9	itpr1	**Juventus**	A	L	0-3		22,000
10	itpr1	**Brescia**	A	L	0-1		7,000
11	itpr1	**Atalanta**	H	W	1-0	Tiribocchi 75	7,000
12	itpr1	**Parma**	A	D	2-2	Amauri 63; Cesar 68	12,000
13	itpr1	**AC Milan**	H	L	0-1		25,000
14	itpr1	**Cagliari**	A	L	2-4	Pellissier 58; Amauri 87	14,000
15	itpr1	**Palermo**	H	W	2-1	Cossato 8,38	9,000
16	itpr1	**Fiorentina**	A	L	0-2		28,000
17	itpr1	**Siena**	H	L	1-3	Semioli 74	7,000
18	itpr1	**Bologna**	A	L	1-3	Zanchetta 77	18,000
19	itpr1	**Roma**	H	D	2-2	Pellissier 15; Tiribocchi 20	10,000
20	itpr1	**Inter Milan**	A	D	1-1	Mandelli 73	51,000
21	itpr1	**Livorno**	H	W	1-0	Tiribocchi 31	7,000
22	itpr1	**Udinese**	A	L	0-3		15,000
23	itpr1	**Messina**	H	W	1-0	Tiribocchi 15	7,000
24	itpr1	**Lecce**	A	L	0-3		11,000
25	itpr1	**Lazio**	H	L	0-1		10,000
26	itpr1	**Reggina**	A	L	0-1		15,000
27	itpr1	**Sampdoria**	A	L	0-1		23,000
28	itpr1	**Juventus**	H	L	0-1		25,000
29	itpr1	**Brescia**	H	W	3-1	D'Anna 60 pen; Pellissier 80,87	9,000
30	itpr1	**Atalanta**	A	L	0-3		22,000
31	itpr1	**Parma**	H	W	2-0	Marchesetti 66; Cossato 78	12,000
32	itpr1	**AC Milan**	A	L	0-1		55,000
33	itpr1	**Cagliari**	H	D	1-1	Pellissier 32	7,000
34	itpr1	**Palermo**	A	D	2-2	Pellissier 10; Semioli 56	33,000
35	itpr1	**Fiorentina**	H	L	0-2		15,000
36	itpr1	**Siena**	A	W	1-0	Semioli 80	9,000
37	itpr1	**Bologna**	H	W	1-0	Mandelli 81	18,000
38	itpr1	**Roma**	A	D	0-0		55,000

MONTHLY POINTS TALLY

SEPTEMBER	6	50%
OCTOBER	7	47%
NOVEMBER	4	33%
DECEMBER	3	33%
JANUARY	5	33%
FEBRUARY	3	20%
MARCH	3	33%
APRIL	4	33%
MAY	8	53%

KEY PLAYERS - GOALSCORERS

Sergio Pellissier

Goals in the League	7	Player Strike Rate Average number of minutes between League goals scored by player	310
Contribution to Attacking Power Average number of minutes between League team goals while on pitch	103	**Club Strike Rate** Average number of minutes between League goals scored by club	110

	PLAYER	LGE GOALS	POWER	STRIKE RATE
1	Sergio Pellissier	7	103	310 mins
2	Federico Cossato	4	100	427 mins
3	Franco Semioli	5	112	559 mins
4	Davide Mandelli	2	112	1575 mins
5	Roberto Baronio	1	103	2057 mins

KEY PLAYERS - MIDFIELDERS

Roberto Baronio

Goals in the League	1	**Contribution to Attacking Power** Average number of minutes between League team goals while on pitch	103
Defensive Rating Average number of mins between League goals conceded while on the pitch	71	Scoring Difference Defensive Rating minus Contribution to Attacking Power	-32

	PLAYER	LGE GOALS	DEF RATE	POWER	SCORE DIFF
1	Roberto Baronio	1	71	103	-32 mins
2	Franco Semioli	5	74	112	-38 mins
3	Matteo Brighi	1	65	112	-47 mins
4	Daniele Franceschini	0	72	130	-58 mins

KEY PLAYERS - DEFENDERS

Salvatore Lanna

Goals Conceded Number of League goals conceded while the player was on the pitch	42	**Clean Sheets** In League games when player was on pitch for at least 70 minutes	10
Defensive Rating Ave number of mins between League goals conceded while on the pitch	74	**Club Defensive Rating** Average number of mins between League goals conceded by the club this season	70

	PLAYER	CON LGE	CLEAN SHEETS	DEF RATE
1	Salvatore Lanna	42	10	74 mins
2	Lorenzo D'Anna	43	10	71 mins
3	Marco Malago	21	6	70 mins
4	Davide Mandelli	46	10	68 mins
5	Fabio Moro	36	7	67 mins

KEY GOALKEEPER

Luca Marchegiani

Goals Conceded in the League	44	**Counting Games** League games when player was on pitch for at least 70 minutes	36
Defensive Rating Ave number of mins between League goals conceded while on the pitch	75	**Clean Sheets** In games when player was on pitch for at least 70 minutes	11

LEAGUE GOALS

Sergio Pellissier

Minutes on the pitch	2172	Goals in the League	7
League average (mins between goals)	310		

	PLAYER	MINS	GOALS	AVE
1	Pellissier	2172	7	310
2	Semioli	2795	5	559
3	Tiribocchi	1221	5	244
4	Cossato	1709	4	427
5	Amauri	1262	2	631
6	Mandelli	3150	2	1575
7	Cesar	316	1	316
8	Baronio	2057	1	2057
9	D'Anna	3060	1	3060
10	Zanchetta	1129	1	1129
11	Marchesetti	356	1	356
12	Brighi	2803	1	2803
	Other		0	
	TOTAL		31	

DISCIPLINARY RECORDS

	PLAYER	YELLOW	RED	AVE
1	Tiribocchi	5	1	203
2	Malago	6	0	245
3	Mensah	2	1	252
4	D'Anna	12	0	255
5	Moro	8	0	302
6	Lanna	8	2	310
7	Brighi	8	1	311
8	Cossato	4	1	341
9	Zanchetta	3	0	376
10	Baronio	4	1	411
11	Amauri	2	1	420
12	Mandelli	7	0	450
13	Sammarco	2	0	463
	Other	11	0	
	TOTAL	82	8	

TOP POINT EARNERS

	PLAYER	GAMES	AV PTS
1	Roberto Baronio	17	1.41
2	Daniele Franceschini	17	1.29
3	Federico Cossato	16	1.25
4	Salvatore Lanna	34	1.21
5	Luca Marchegiani	36	1.19
6	Franco Semioli	29	1.17
7	Sergio Pellissier	18	1.17
8	Lorenzo D'Anna	34	1.15
9	Fabio Moro	26	1.12
10	Davide Mandelli	35	1.11
	CLUB AVERAGE:		1.13

TEAM OF THE SEASON

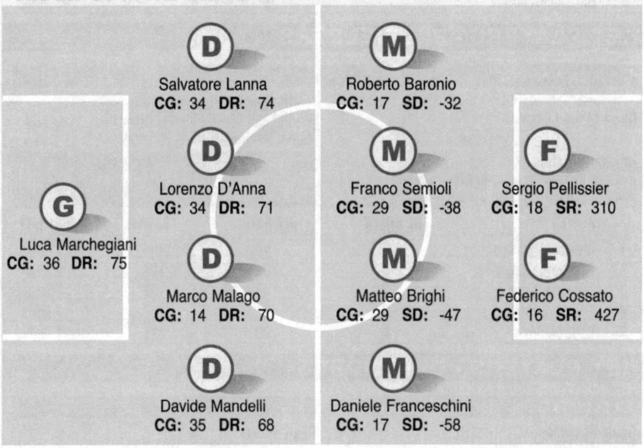
G
Luca Marchegiani
CG: 36 DR: 75
D
Salvatore Lanna
CG: 34 DR: 74
D
Lorenzo D'Anna
CG: 34 DR: 71
D
Marco Malago
CG: 14 DR: 70
D
Davide Mandelli
CG: 35 DR: 68
M
Roberto Baronio
CG: 17 SD: -32
M
Franco Semioli
CG: 29 SD: -38
M
Matteo Brighi
CG: 29 SD: -47
M
Daniele Franceschini
CG: 17 SD: -58
F
Sergio Pellissier
CG: 18 SR: 310
F
Federico Cossato
CG: 16 SR: 427

LEAGUE APPEARANCES, BOOKINGS AND CAPS

	AGE (on 01/07/05)	IN NAMED 18	APPEARANCES	COUNTING GAMES	MINUTES ON PITCH	YELLOW CARDS	RED CARDS	THIS SEASON	HOME COUNTRY
Goalkeepers									
Enrico Alfonso	17	1	0	0	0	0	0	-	Italy
Paolo Codognola	24	7	0	0	0	0	0	-	Italy
Luca Marchegiani	39	37	37	36	3285	2	0	-	Italy
Sergio Marcon	34	27	2	1	135	0	0	-	Italy
Defenders									
Cesar	26	15	5	3	316	0	0	-	Brazil
Lorenzo D'Anna	33	34	34	34	3060	12	0	-	Italy
Salvatore Lanna	28	35	35	34	3104	8	2	-	Italy
Marco Malago	26	30	23	14	1470	6	0	-	Italy
Davide Mandelli	28	35	35	35	3150	7	0	-	Italy
John Mensah	22	24	10	8	757	2	1	-	Ghana
Fabio Moro	29	29	28	26	2423	8	0	-	Italy
Emanuele Pesaresi	28	6	1	0	1	0	0	-	Italy
Alessandro Potenza	21	9	2	1	141	0	0	-	Italy
Midfielders									
Riccardo Allegretti	27	15	7	0	88	0	0	-	Italy
Roberto Baronio	27	35	30	17	2057	4	1	-	Italy
Matteo Brighi	24	35	35	29	2803	8	1	-	Italy
Ivone De Franceschi	31	9	2	0	17	0	0	-	Italy
Daniele Franceschini	29	36	30	17	1944	0	0	-	Italy
Massimilano Fusani	25	11	6	1	227	1	0	-	Italy
Luciano	29	26	20	5	931	2	0	-	Brazil
Mattia Marchesetti	21	18	10	1	356	0	0	-	Italy
Paolo Sammarco	22	21	13	9	927	2	0	-	Italy
Franco Semioli	25	36	35	29	2795	6	0	-	Italy
Andrea Zanchetta	30	28	21	8	1129	3	0	-	Italy
Forwards									
Carvalho Amauri	25	32	23	10	1262	2	1	-	Brazil
Federico Cossato	32	26	24	16	1709	4	1	-	Italy
Sergio Pellissier	26	36	34	18	2172	1	0	-	Italy
Davide Succi	23	1	1	0	3	0	0	-	Italy
Simone Tiribocchi	27	24	21	9	1221	5	1	-	Italy

SQUAD APPEARANCES

Match	1	2	3	4	5	6	7	8	9	10	11	12	13	14	15	16	17	18	19	20	21	22	23	24	25	26	27	28	29	30	31	32	33	34	35	36	37	38
Venue	H	A	H	A	H	A	H	H	A	A	H	A	H	A	H	A	H	A	H	A	H	A	H	A	H	A	A	H	H	A	H	A	H	A	H	A	H	A
Competition	L	L	L	L	L	L	L	L	L	L	L	L	L	L	L	L	L	L	L	L	L	L	L	L	L	L	L	L	L	L	L	L	L	L	L	L	L	L
Result	D	W	D	D	W	W	D	L	L	L	W	D	L	L	W	L	L	L	D	D	W	L	W	L	L	L	L	L	W	L	W	L	D	D	L	W	W	D

Goalkeepers
Enrico Alfonso
Paolo Codognola
Luca Marchegiani
Sergio Marcon

Defenders
Cesar
Lorenzo D'Anna
Salvatore Lanna
Marco Malago
Davide Mandelli
John Mensah
Fabio Moro
Emanuele Pesaresi
Alessandro Potenza

Midfielders
Riccardo Allegretti
Roberto Baronio
Matteo Brighi
Ivone De Franceschi
Daniele Franceschini
Massimilano Fusani
Luciano
Mattia Marchesetti
Paolo Sammarco
Franco Semioli
Andrea Zanchetta

Forwards
Carvalho Amauri
Federico Cossato
Sergio Pellissier
Davide Succi
Simone Tiribocchi

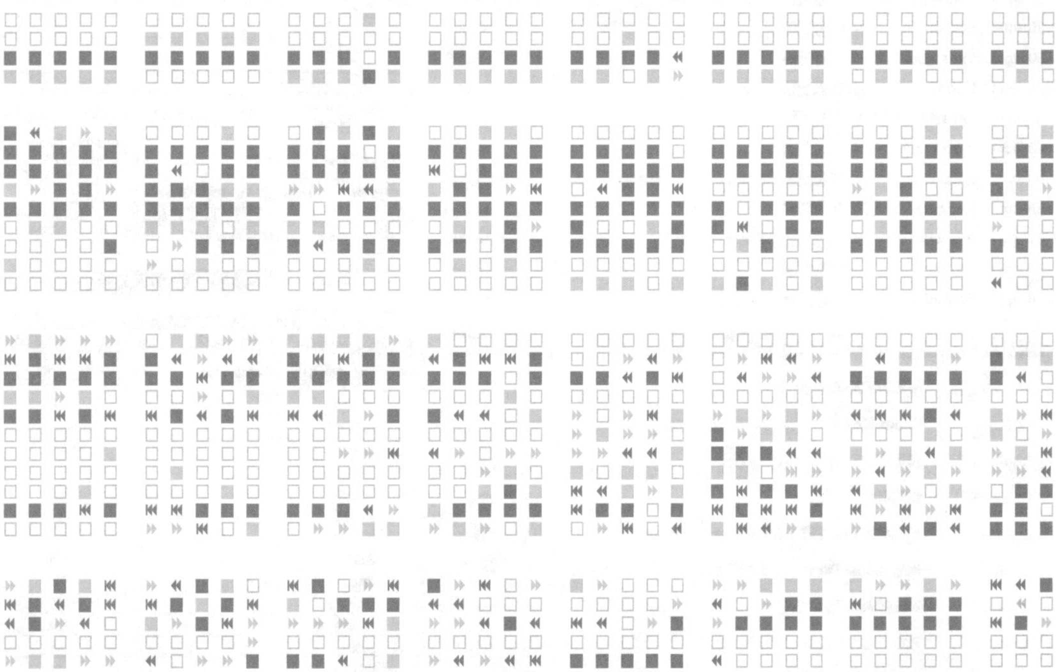

KEY: On all match | On bench | Subbed or sent off (Counting game) | Subbed or sent off (playing less than 70 minutes) | Subbed on from bench (Counting Game) | Subbed on (playing less than 70 minutes) | Subbed on and then subbed or sent off (Counting Game) | Subbed on and then subbed or sent off (playing less than 70 minutes) | Not in 16

BOLOGNA

Final Position: **16th**

KEY: Won Drawn Lost

							Attendance
1	itpr1	**Cagliari**	A	L	0-1		15,000
2	itpr1	**AC Milan**	H	L	0-2		35,000
3	itpr1	**Parma**	A	W	2-1	Locatelli 12; Petruzzi 20	13,000
4	itpr1	**Roma**	H	W	3-1	Meghni 5,37; Cipriani 34	22,000
5	itpr1	**Palermo**	A	L	0-1		32,000
6	itpr1	**Atalanta**	H	W	2-1	Bellucci 38 pen; Amoroso 60	17,000
7	itpr1	**Livorno**	A	L	0-1		17,000
8	itpr1	**Udinese**	H	L	0-1		15,000
9	itpr1	**Siena**	A	D	1-1	Cipriani 37	8,000
10	itpr1	**Messina**	H	D	2-2	Loviso 31; Cipriani 54	17,000
11	itpr1	**Inter Milan**	A	D	2-2	Petruzzi 50; Bellucci 88	49,000
12	itpr1	**Lazio**	A	L	1-2	Tare 54	32,000
13	itpr1	**Lecce**	H	D	0-0		21,000
14	itpr1	**Fiorentina**	A	L	0-1		28,000
15	itpr1	**Juventus**	H	L	0-1		12,000
16	itpr1	**Reggina**	H	W	2-0	Bellucci 5 pen; Meghni 63	18,000
17	itpr1	**Brescia**	A	D	1-1	Tare 17	8,000
18	itpr1	**Chievo**	H	W	3-1	Locatelli 27; Tare 60; Bellucci 87 pen	18,000
19	itpr1	**Sampdoria**	A	D	0-0		22,000
20	itpr1	**Cagliari**	H	W	1-0	Bellucci 70	18,000
21	itpr1	**AC Milan**	A	W	1-0	Locatelli 27	57,000
22	itpr1	**Parma**	H	W	3-1	Sussi 55; Amoroso 72; Bellucci 90	16,000
23	itpr1	**Roma**	A	D	1-1	Della Rocca 62	43,000
24	itpr1	**Palermo**	H	D	1-1	Tare 76	21,000
25	itpr1	**Atalanta**	A	L	0-2		10,000
26	itpr1	**Livorno**	H	D	0-0		15,000
27	itpr1	**Udinese**	A	W	1-0	Tare 4	15,000
28	itpr1	**Siena**	H	D	1-1	Bellucci 56 pen	15,000
29	itpr1	**Messina**	A	D	0-0		38,000
30	itpr1	**Inter Milan**	H	L	0-1		25,000
31	itpr1	**Lazio**	H	L	1-2	Giunti 15	18,000
32	itpr1	**Lecce**	A	D	1-1	Bellucci 42	11,000
33	itpr1	**Fiorentina**	H	D	0-0		15,000
34	itpr1	**Juventus**	A	L	1-2	Giunti 27	21,000
35	itpr1	**Reggina**	A	D	1-1	Bellucci 16	15,000
36	itpr1	**Brescia**	H	L	1-2	Bellucci 90	18,000
37	itpr1	**Chievo**	A	L	0-1		18,000
38	itpr1	**Sampdoria**	H	D	0-0		38,000

MONTHLY POINTS TALLY

SEPTEMBER	6	50%
OCTOBER	4	27%
NOVEMBER	3	25%
DECEMBER	3	33%
JANUARY	11	73%
FEBRUARY	6	40%
MARCH	5	56%
APRIL	2	17%
MAY	2	13%

KEY PLAYERS - GOALSCORERS

Claudio Bellucci

Goals in the League	10	Player Strike Rate Average number of minutes between League goals scored by player	264
Contribution to Attacking Power Average number of minutes between League team goals while on pitch	94	Club Strike Rate Average number of minutes between League goals scored by club	104

	PLAYER	LGE GOALS	POWER	STRIKE RATE
1	Claudio Bellucci	10	94	264 mins
2	Igli Tare	5	165	364 mins
3	Tomas Locatelli	3	109	688 mins
4	Fabio Petruzzi	2	96	723 mins
5	Christian Amoroso	2	106	793 mins

KEY PLAYERS - MIDFIELDERS

Christian Amoroso

Goals in the League	2	Contribution to Attacking Power Average number of minutes between League team goals while on pitch	106
Defensive Rating Average number of mins between League goals conceded while on the pitch	144	Scoring Difference Defensive Rating minus Contribution to Attacking Power	38

	PLAYER	LGE GOALS	DEF RATE	POWER	SCORE DIFF
1	Christian Amoroso	2	144	106	38 mins
2	Theodoros Zagorakis	0	104	104	0 mins
3	Federico Giunti	2	100	107	-7 mins
4	Tomas Locatelli	3	98	109	-11 mins
5	Carlo Nervo	0	80	111	-31 mins

KEY PLAYERS - DEFENDERS

Alessandro Gamberini

Goals Conceded Number of League goals conceded while the player was on the pitch	22	Clean Sheets In League games when player was on pitch for at least 70 minutes	8
Defensive Rating Ave number of mins between League goals conceded while on the pitch	108	Club Defensive Rating Average number of mins between League goals conceded by the club this season	95

	PLAYER	CON LGE	CLEAN SHEETS	DEF RATE
1	Alessandro Gamberini	22	8	108 mins
2	Stefano Torrisi	19	7	108 mins
3	Juarez	22	8	104 mins
4	Andrea Sussi	23	8	102 mins
5	Fabio Petruzzi	20	1	72 mins

KEY GOALKEEPER

Gianluca Pagliuca

Goals Conceded in the League	36	Counting Games League games when player was on pitch for at least 70 minutes	38
Defensive Rating Ave number of mins between League goals conceded while on the pitch	95	Clean Sheets In games when player was on pitch for at least 70 minutes	10

LEAGUE GOALS

Claudio Bellucci

Minutes on the pitch	2638	Goals in the League	10
League average (mins between goals)	264		

	PLAYER	MINS	GOALS	AVE
1	Bellucci	2638	10	264
2	Tare	1819	5	364
3	Locatelli	2064	3	688
4	Meghni	877	3	292
5	Cipriani	1287	3	429
6	Petruzzi	1446	2	723
7	Giunti	1605	2	803
8	Amoroso	1585	2	793
9	Loviso	1030	1	1030
10	Della Rocca	129	1	129
11	Sussi	2345	1	2345
	Other		0	
	TOTAL		33	

DISCIPLINARY RECORDS

	PLAYER	YELLOW	RED	AVE
1	Cipriani	7	1	160
2	Colucci	12	0	168
3	Giunti	8	0	200
4	Meghni	4	0	219
5	Nastase	5	0	224
6	Loviso	4	0	257
7	Sussi	8	1	260
8	Juarez	7	1	286
9	Zagorakis	8	1	300
10	Torrisi	6	0	342
11	Nervo	4	0	360
12	Petruzzi	4	0	361
13	Amoroso	4	0	396
	Other	14	1	
	TOTAL	95	5	

TOP POINT EARNERS

	PLAYER	GAMES	AV PTS
1	Stefano Torrisi	21	1.57
2	Tomas Locatelli	18	1.44
3	Christian Amoroso	16	1.44
4	Andrea Sussi	25	1.36
5	Claudio Bellucci	26	1.23
6	Juarez	22	1.23
7	Theodoros Zagorakis	29	1.14
8	Federico Giunti	15	1.13
9	Gianluca Pagliuca	38	1.11
10	Carlo Nervo	14	1.07
	CLUB AVERAGE:		1.11

LEAGUE APPEARANCES, BOOKINGS AND CAPS

	AGE (on 01/07/05)	IN NAMED 18	APPEARANCES	COUNTING GAMES	MINUTES ON PITCH	YELLOW CARDS	RED CARDS	THIS SEASON	HOME COUNTRY
Goalkeepers									
Fabrizio Ferron	39	21	0	0	0	0	0	-	Italy
Gianluca Pagliuca	38	38	38	38	3420	3	0	-	Italy
Andrea Pansera	25	17	0	0	0	0	0	-	Italy
Defenders									
Ciro Capuano	23	28	18	10	1078	1	0	-	Italy
Daniele Daino	25	25	13	7	794	1	0	-	Italy
Aless Gamberini	23	35	29	25	2376	5	0	-	Italy
Juarez	30	31	29	22	2294	7	1	-	Brazil
Nicola Legrottaglie	28	11	9	7	729	0	0	1	Italy (10)
Vasile Nastase	30	29	16	10	1123	5	0	-	Romania
Fabio Petruzzi	34	17	17	15	1446	4	0	-	Italy
Vlado Smit	25	3	1	1	90	0	0	-	Serbia & Montenegro
Andrea Sussi	31	34	29	25	2345	8	1	-	Italy
Luca Tedeschi	18	3	1	0	1	0	0	-	Italy
Stefano Torrisi	34	25	25	21	2054	6	0	-	Italy
Midfielders									
Christian Amoroso	28	25	23	16	1585	4	0	-	Italy
Jonatan Binotto	30	26	8	1	261	1	0	-	Italy
Leonardo Colucci	32	31	29	21	2022	12	0	-	Italy
Francesco Rocca	17	11	4	1	129	0	0	-	Italy
Federico Giunti	33	25	23	15	1605	8	0	-	Italy
Tomas Locatelli	29	32	32	18	2064	2	0	-	Italy
Massimo Loviso	21	36	28	7	1030	4	0	-	Italy
Mourad Meghni	21	17	17	5	877	4	0	-	France
Carlo Nervo	33	23	21	14	1441	4	0	-	Italy
Theodoros Zagorakis	33	32	32	29	2703	8	1	-	Greece
Forwards									
Claudio Bellucci	30	35	33	26	2638	2	0	-	Italy
Giacomo Cipriani	24	24	22	11	1287	7	1	-	Italy
Marco Ferrante	34	6	6	1	216	0	0	-	Italy
Gennaro Fragiello	21	2	1	0	15	0	0	-	Italy
Igli Tare	31	30	26	17	1819	0	1	-	Albania

TEAM OF THE SEASON

D
Alessandro Gamberini
CG: 25 DR: 108
M
Christian Amoroso
CG: 16 SD: 38
D
Stefano Torrisi
CG: 21 DR: 108
M
Theodoros Zagorakis
CG: 29 SD: 0
F
Claudio Bellucci
CG: 26 SR: 264
G
Gianluca Pagliuca
CG: 38 DR: 95
D
Juarez
CG: 22 DR: 104
M
Federico Giunti
CG: 15 SD: -7
F
Igli Tare
CG: 17 SR: 364
D
Andrea Sussi
CG: 25 DR: 102
M
Tomas Locatelli
CG: 18 SD: -11

SQUAD APPEARANCES

Match	1	2	3	4	5	6	7	8	9	10	11	12	13	14	15	16	17	18	19	20	21	22	23	24	25	26	27	28	29	30	31	32	33	34	35	36	37	38
Venue	A	H	A	H	A	H	A	H	A	H	A	A	H	A	H	H	A	H	A	H	A	H	A	H	A	H	A	H	A	H	H	A	H	A	A	H	A	H
Competition	L	L	L	L	L	L	L	L	L	L	L	L	L	L	L	L	L	L	L	L	L	L	L	L	L	L	L	L	L	L	L	L	L	L	L	L	L	L
Result	L	L	W	W	L	W	L	L	D	D	D	L	D	L	L	W	D	W	D	W	W	W	D	D	L	D	W	D	D	L	L	D	D	L	D	L	L	D

Goalkeepers
Fabrizio Ferron
Gianluca Pagliuca
Andrea Pansera

Defenders
Ciro Capuano
Daniele Daino
Alessandro Gamberini
Juarez
Nicola Legrottaglie
Vasile Nastase
Fabio Petruzzi
Vlado Smit
Andrea Sussi
Luca Tedeschi
Stefano Torrisi

Midfielders
Christian Amoroso
Jonatan Binotto
Leonardo Colucci
Francesco Rocca
Federico Giunti
Tomas Locatelli
Massimo Loviso
Mourad Meghni
Carlo Nervo
Theodoros Zagorakis

Forwards
Claudio Bellucci
Giacomo Cipriani
Marco Ferrante
Gennaro Fragiello
Igli Tare

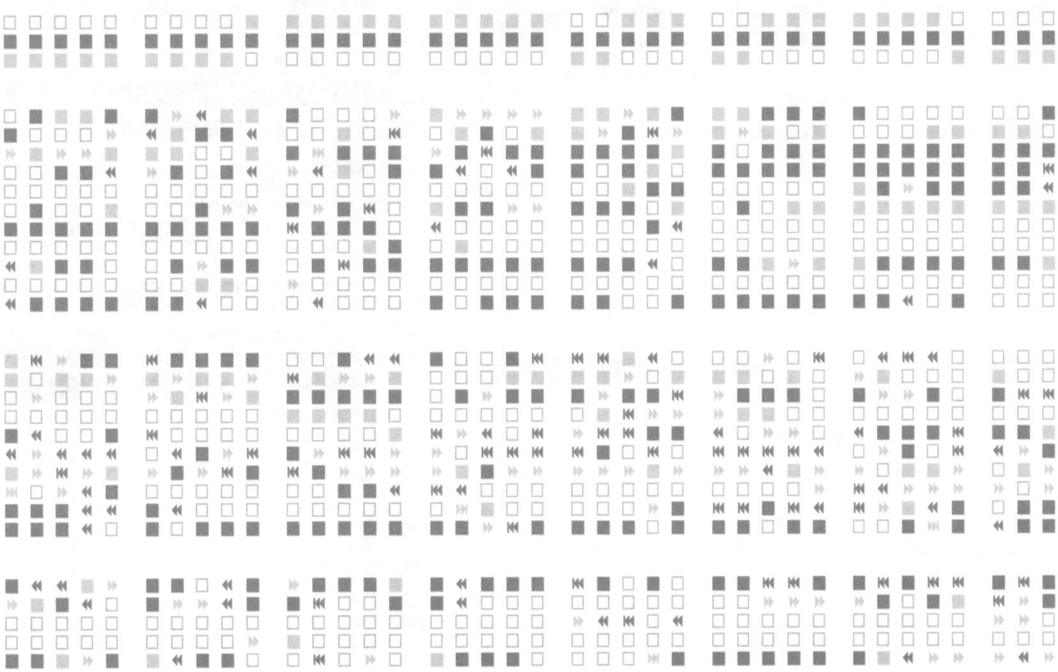

KEY: On all match | On bench | Subbed or sent off (Counting game) | Subbed or sent off (playing less than 70 minutes) | Subbed on from bench (Counting Game) | Subbed on (playing less than 70 minutes) | Subbed on and then subbed or sent off (Counting Game) | Subbed on and then subbed or sent off (playing less than 70 minutes) | Not in 16

FIORENTINA

Final Position: **17th**

KEY: ☐ Won ☐ Drawn ☐ Lost

							Attendance
1	itpr1	**Roma**	A	L	0-1		58,000
2	itpr1	**Cagliari**	H	W	2-1	Miccoli 16; Dainelli 89	28,000
3	itpr1	**Palermo**	A	D	0-0		25,000
4	itpr1	**Sampdoria**	H	L	0-2		32,000
5	itpr1	**Parma**	A	D	0-0		14,000
6	itpr1	**Siena**	H	D	0-0		34,000
7	itpr1	**Udinese**	A	D	2-2	Miccoli 15,66	15,000
8	itpr1	**Reggina**	A	W	2-1	Maresca 73; Miccoli 89	18,000
9	itpr1	**Lecce**	H	W	4-0	Jorgensen 45; Obodo 62,71; Chiellini 90	31,000
10	itpr1	**Inter Milan**	H	D	1-1	Dainelli 26	44,000
11	itpr1	**Juventus**	A	L	0-1		24,000
12	itpr1	**Livorno**	H	D	1-1	Rigano 71	33,000
13	itpr1	**Messina**	A	D	1-1	Ariatti 55	34,000
14	itpr1	**Bologna**	H	W	1-0	Maresca 62	28,000
15	itpr1	**AC Milan**	A	L	0-6		69,000
16	itpr1	**Chievo**	H	W	2-0	Rigano 45; Portillo 70	28,000
17	itpr1	**Atalanta**	A	L	0-1		15,000
18	itpr1	**Lazio**	H	L	2-3	Miccoli 21,85	30,000
19	itpr1	**Brescia**	A	D	1-1	Miccoli 49	10,000
20	itpr1	**Roma**	H	L	1-2	Maresca 19	23,000
21	itpr1	**Cagliari**	A	L	0-1		14,000
22	itpr1	**Palermo**	H	L	1-2	Miccoli 72	29,000
23	itpr1	**Sampdoria**	A	L	0-3		23,000
24	itpr1	**Parma**	H	W	2-0	Chiellini 48; Miccoli 81	30,000
25	itpr1	**Siena**	A	L	0-1		12,000
26	itpr1	**Udinese**	H	D	2-2	Bojinov 22; Ariatti 32	28,000
27	itpr1	**Reggina**	H	W	2-1	Pazzini 48; Miccoli 69 pen	30,000
28	itpr1	**Lecce**	A	D	2-2	Jorgensen 47; Maggio 86	15,000
29	itpr1	**Inter Milan**	A	L	2-3	Pazzini 40; Cordoba 87 og	55,000
30	itpr1	**Juventus**	H	D	3-3	Pazzini 14; Chiellini 36; Dainelli 75	46,000
31	itpr1	**Livorno**	A	L	0-2		18,000
32	itpr1	**Messina**	H	D	1-1	Dainelli 61	28,000
33	itpr1	**Bologna**	A	D	0-0		15,000
34	itpr1	**AC Milan**	H	L	1-2	Maresca 25	46,000
35	itpr1	**Chievo**	A	W	2-0	Miccoli 43; Bojinov 79	15,000
36	itpr1	**Atalanta**	H	D	0-0		43,000
37	itpr1	**Lazio**	A	D	1-1	Maresca 2	40,000
38	itpr1	**Brescia**	H	W	3-0	Miccoli 43 pen; Jorgensen 59; Rigano 66; Viali 74	45,000

MONTHLY POINTS TALLY

SEPTEMBER	4	33%
OCTOBER	9	60%
NOVEMBER	3	25%
DECEMBER	6	67%
JANUARY	1	7%
FEBRUARY	4	27%
MARCH	4	44%
APRIL	3	20%
MAY	8	67%

KEY PLAYERS - GOALSCORERS

Fabrizio Miccoli

Goals in the League	12	Player Strike Rate Average number of minutes between League goals scored by player	220
Contribution to Attacking Power Average number of minutes between League team goals while on pitch	87	Club Strike Rate Average number of minutes between League goals scored by club	80

	PLAYER	LGE GOALS	POWER	STRIKE RATE
1	Fabrizio Miccoli	12	87	220 mins
2	Enzo Maresca	5	70	418 mins
3	Martin Jorgensen	3	65	649 mins
4	Dario Dainelli	4	73	662 mins
5	Giorgio Chiellini	3	77	1085 mins

KEY PLAYERS - MIDFIELDERS

Martin Jorgensen

Goals in the League	3	Contribution to Attacking Power Average number of minutes between League team goals while on pitch	65
Defensive Rating Average number of mins between League goals conceded while on the pitch	97	Scoring Difference Defensive Rating minus Contribution to Attacking Power	32

	PLAYER	LGE GOALS	DEF RATE	POWER	SCORE DIFF
1	Martin Jorgensen	3	97	65	32 mins
2	Luca Ariatti	2	82	85	-3 mins
3	Enzo Maresca	5	65	70	-5 mins
4	Christian Obodo	2	71	78	-7 mins

KEY PLAYERS - DEFENDERS

Tomas Ujfalusi

Goals Conceded Number of League goals conceded while the player was on the pitch	32	Clean Sheets In League games when player was on pitch for at least 70 minutes	9
Defensive Rating Ave number of mins between League goals conceded while on the pitch	76	Club Defensive Rating Average number of mins between League goals conceded by the club this season	71

	PLAYER	CON LGE	CLEAN SHEETS	DEF RATE
1	Tomas Ujfalusi	32	9	76 mins
2	Giorgio Chiellini	45	11	72 mins
3	William Viali	40	11	71 mins
4	Dario Dainelli	38	7	70 mins
5	Daniele Delli Carri	23	3	64 mins

KEY GOALKEEPER

Cristiano Lupatelli

Goals Conceded in the League	32	Counting Games League games when player was on pitch for at least 70 minutes	28
Defensive Rating Ave number of mins between League goals conceded while on the pitch	80	Clean Sheets In games when player was on pitch for at least 70 minutes	8

LEAGUE GOALS

Fabrizio Miccoli

Minutes on the pitch	2634	Goals in the League	12
League average (mins between goals)	220		

	PLAYER	MINS	GOALS	AVE
1	Miccoli	2634	12	220
2	Maresca	2091	5	418
3	Dainelli	2646	4	662
4	Chiellini	3255	3	1085
5	Pazzini	1090	3	363
6	Rigano	864	3	288
7	Jorgensen	1948	3	649
8	Obodo	2498	2	1249
9	Bojinov	341	2	171
10	Ariatti	2303	2	1152
11	Maggio	1040	1	1040
12	Portillo	459	1	459
13	Viali	2828	1	2828
	Other		1	
	TOTAL		43	

DISCIPLINARY RECORDS

	PLAYER	YELLOW	RED	AVE
1	Maggio	5	2	148
2	Piangarelli	6	0	173
3	Viali	10	1	257
4	Donadel	4	0	281
5	Savini	2	0	293
6	Delli Carri	4	1	294
7	Ariatti	7	0	329
8	Miccoli	7	0	376
9	Maresca	5	0	418
10	Rigano	2	0	432
11	Di Livio	1	0	496
12	Obodo	4	0	624
13	Dainelli	4	0	661
	Other	7	0	
	TOTAL	68	4	

TOP POINT EARNERS

	PLAYER	GAMES	AV PTS
1	Martin Jorgensen	17	1.65
2	Christian Obodo	26	1.27
3	Cristiano Lupatelli	28	1.18
4	Enzo Maresca	22	1.18
5	Dario Dainelli	29	1.14
6	Giorgio Chiellini	36	1.14
7	William Viali	31	1.13
8	Luca Ariatti	24	1.08
9	Tomas Ujfalusi	26	1.08
10	Fabrizio Miccoli	24	0.92
	CLUB AVERAGE:		1.11

LEAGUE APPEARANCES AND BOOKINGS

	AGE (on 01/07/05)	IN NAMED 16	APPEARANCES	COUNTING GAMES	MINUTES ON PITCH	YELLOW CARDS	RED CARDS	THIS SEASON	HOME COUNTRY
Goalkeepers									
Sebastian Cejas	30	19	7	7	630	0	0	-	Argentina
Cristiano Lupatelli	27	37	29	28	2565	0	0	-	Italy
Marco Roccati	30	20	3	2	225	0	0	-	Italy
Defenders									
Giorgio Chiellini	20	37	37	36	3255	2	0	4	Italy (10)
Dario Dainelli	26	31	30	29	2646	4	0	-	Italy
Daniele Delli Carri	33	31	21	15	1473	4	1	-	Italy
Gianni Guigou	30	15	2	0	80	0	0	-	Uruguay
Mirko Savini	26	26	11	6	586	2	0	-	Italy
Tomas Ujfalusi	27	28	28	26	2425	3	0	6	Czech Republic (2)
William Viali	30	35	34	31	2828	10	1	-	Italy
Midfielders									
Luca Ariatti	26	31	29	24	2303	7	0	-	Italy
Angelo Di Livio	38	33	12	4	496	1	0	-	Italy
Marco Donadel	22	16	14	11	1127	4	0	-	Italy
Gaetano Fontana	35	6	3	1	116	2	1	-	Italy
Martin Jorgensen	29	30	30	17	1948	0	0	8	Denmark (19)
Cristian Maggio	23	23	13	10	1040	5	2	-	Italy
Enzo Maresca	25	25	25	22	2091	5	0	-	Italy
Hidetoshi Nakata	28	33	20	9	1175	1	0	-	Japan
Christian Obodo	21	37	33	26	2498	4	0	-	Nigeria
Luigi Piangarelli	31	27	15	10	1041	6	0	-	Italy
Forwards									
Emilov Valeri Bojinov	19	10	9	1	341	1	1	-	Bulgaria
Enrico Fantini	29	31	25	11	1311	0	0	-	Italy
Fabrizio Miccoli	26	35	35	24	2634	7	0	4	Italy (10)
Francesco Palmieri	37	1	0	0	0	0	0	-	Italy
Gianpaolo Pazzini	20	15	15	10	1090	1	0	-	Italy
Javier Portillo	23	18	11	3	459	0	0	-	Spain
Christian Rigano	31	23	18	5	864	2	0	-	Italy
Jaime Zapata Valdes	24	7	4	1	121	1	0	-	Chile

TEAM OF THE SEASON

G — Cristiano Lupatelli, CG: 28 DR: 80

D — Tomas Ujfalusi, CG: 26 DR: 76

D — Giorgio Chiellini, CG: 36 DR: 72

D — William Viali, CG: 31 DR: 71

D — Dario Dainelli, CG: 29 DR: 70

M — Martin Jorgensen, CG: 17 SD: 32

M — Luca Ariatti, CG: 24 SD: -3

M — Enzo Maresca, CG: 22 SD: -5

M — Christian Obodo, CG: 26 SD: -7

F — Fabrizio Miccoli, CG: 24 SR: 220

F — Gianpaolo Pazzini*, CG: 10 SR: 363

SQUAD APPEARANCES

Match	1	2	3	4	5	6	7	8	9	10	11	12	13	14	15	16	17	18	19	20	21	22	23	24	25	26	27	28	29	30	31	32	33	34	35	36	37	38
Venue	A	H	A	H	A	H	A	A	H	H	A	H	A	H	A	H	A	H	A	H	A	H	A	H	A	H	H	A	A	H	A	H	A	H	A	H	A	H
Competition	L	L	L	L	L	L	L	L	L	L	L	L	L	L	L	L	L	L	L	L	L	L	L	L	L	L	L	L	L	L	L	L	L	L	L	L	L	L
Result	L	W	D	L	D	D	D	W	W	D	L	D	D	W	L	W	L	L	D	L	L	L	L	W	L	D	W	D	L	D	L	D	D	L	W	D	D	W

Goalkeepers
Sebastian Cejas
Cristiano Lupatelli
Marco Roccati

Defenders
Giorgio Chiellini
Dario Dainelli
Daniele Delli Carri
Gianni Guigou
Mirko Savini
Tomas Ujfalusi
William Viali

Midfielders
Luca Ariatti
Angelo Di Livio
Marco Donadel
Gaetano Fontana
Martin Jorgensen
Cristian Maggio
Enzo Maresca
Hidetoshi Nakata
Christian Obodo
Luigi Piangarelli

Forwards
Emilov Valeri Bojinov
Enrico Fantini
Fabrizio Miccoli
Francesco Palmieri
Gianpaolo Pazzini
Javier Portillo
Christian Rigano
Jaime Zapata Valdes

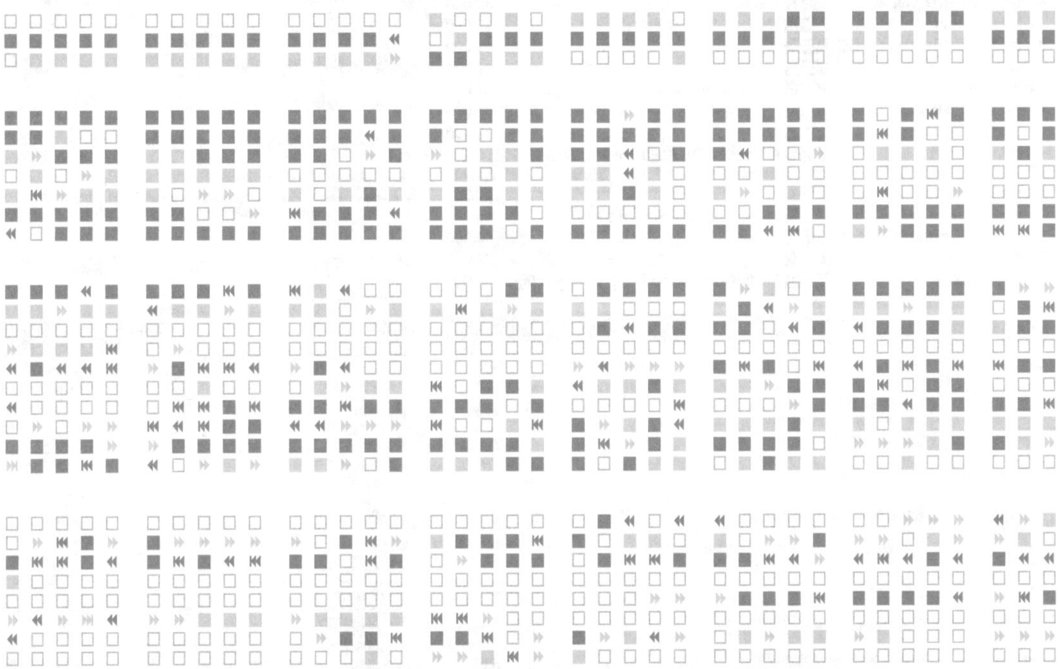

KEY: On all match · On bench · Subbed or sent off (Counting game) · Subbed or sent off (playing less than 70 minutes) · Subbed on from bench (Counting Game) · Subbed on (playing less than 70 minutes) · Subbed on and then subbed or sent off (Counting Game) · Subbed on and then subbed or sent off (playing less than 70 minutes) · Not in 16

PARMA

Final Position: **18th**

KEY: Won Drawn Lost

							Attendance
1	itpr1	**Messina**	H	D	0-0		18,000
2	uc1rl1	**Maribor**	H	W	3-2	Maccarone 8,25,67	5,148
3	itpr1	**Udinese**	A	L	0-4		21,000
4	itpr1	**Bologna**	H	L	1-2	Cannavaro 58	13,000
5	itpr1	**Inter Milan**	A	D	2-2	Gilardino 17; Marchionni 74	60,000
6	uc1rl2	**Maribor**	A	D	0-0		5,500
7	itpr1	**Fiorentina**	H	D	0-0		14,000
8	itpr1	**Brescia**	A	L	1-3	Gilardino 11	7,000
9	uc gb	**Athl Bilbao**	A	L	0-2		32,000
10	itpr1	**Lazio**	H	W	3-1	Marchionni 16; Bresciano 27; Gilardino 65	12,000
11	itpr1	**Cagliari**	A	L	1-2	Marchionni 64	15,000
12	itpr1	**Atalanta**	H	D	2-2	Gilardino 41,55 pen	12,000
13	uc gb	**S Bucharest**	H	W	1-0	Budel 79	3,949
14	itpr1	**Palermo**	A	D	1-1	Gilardino 37	33,000
15	itpr1	**Reggina**	H	W	1-0	Morfeo 80	15,000
16	itpr1	**Chievo**	H	D	2-2	Amauri 55 og; Morfeo 76	12,000
17	uc gb	**Standard Liege**	A	L	1-2	Pisanu 44	21,000
18	itpr1	**Sampdoria**	A	L	0-1		22,000
19	itpr1	**AC Milan**	H	L	1-2	Gilardino 67	21,000
20	itpr1	**Livorno**	A	L	0-2		15,000
21	uc gb	**Besiktas**	H	W	3-2	Gilardino 16; Cardone 35; Degano 59	15,000
22	itpr1	**Roma**	A	L	1-5	Bovo 45	45,000
23	itpr1	**Juventus**	H	D	1-1	Marchionni 85	25,000
24	itpr1	**Siena**	A	W	1-0	Gilardino 21	8,000
25	itpr1	**Lecce**	H	W	2-1	Bresciano 53; Gilardino 90	13,000
26	itpr1	**Messina**	A	L	0-1		25,000
27	itpr1	**Udinese**	H	W	1-0	Gilardino 34	13,000
28	itpr1	**Bologna**	A	L	1-3	Sorrentino 87	16,000
29	itpr1	**Inter Milan**	H	D	2-2	Simplicio 36; Gilardino 60	19,000
30	itpr1	**Fiorentina**	A	L	0-2		30,000
31	uc3rl1	**Stuttgart**	H	D	0-0		5,486
32	itpr1	**Brescia**	H	W	2-1	Gilardino 22; Morfeo 50	13,000
33	uc3rl2	**Stuttgart**	A	W	2-0	Marchionni 98; Pisanu 116	38,000
34	itpr1	**Lazio**	A	L	0-2		30,000
35	itpr1	**Cagliari**	H	W	3-2	Gilardino 10; Bovo 17; Simplicio 90	13,000
36	uc4rl1	**Seville**	A	D	0-0		40,000
37	itpr1	**Atalanta**	A	L	0-1		15,000
38	uc4rl2	**Seville**	H	W	1-0	Cardone 9	8,000
39	itpr1	**Palermo**	H	D	3-3	Morfeo 20; Gilardino 51,90	15,000
40	ucqf1	**Austria Vienna**	A	D	1-1	Pisanu 34	39,000
41	itpr1	**Reggina**	A	W	3-1	Morfeo 21,49; Simplicio 62	15,000
42	ucqf2	**Austria Vienna**	H	D	0-0		11,000
43	itpr1	**Chievo**	A	L	0-2		12,000
44	itpr1	**Sampdoria**	H	D	1-1	Gilardino 39	14,000
45	itpr1	**AC Milan**	A	L	0-3		61,000
46	ucsf1	**CSKA Moscow**	H	D	0-0		15,000
47	itpr1	**Livorno**	H	W	6-4	Gilardino 3,37,72,85; Pisanu 27; Simplicio 47	15,000
48	ucsf2	**CSKA Moscow**	A	L	0-3		26,000
49	itpr1	**Roma**	H	W	2-1	Morfeo 62; Gilardino 79 pen	15,000
50	itpr1	**Juventus**	A	L	0-2		40,000
51	itpr1	**Siena**	H	D	0-0		22,000
52	itpr1	**Lecce**	A	D	3-3	Morfeo 22; Bresciano 43; Gilardino 56	15,000

MONTHLY POINTS TALLY

SEPTEMBER	2	17%
OCTOBER	5	33%
NOVEMBER	5	42%
DECEMBER	0	0%
JANUARY	10	67%
FEBRUARY	4	27%
MARCH	4	44%
APRIL	4	33%
MAY	8	53%

KEY PLAYERS - GOALSCORERS

Alberto Gilardino

Goals in the League 22

Player Strike Rate Average number of minutes between League goals scored by player 151

Contribution to Attacking Power Average number of minutes between League team goals while on pitch 70

Club Strike Rate Average number of minutes between League goals scored by club 73

	PLAYER	LGE GOALS	POWER	STRIKE RATE
1	Alberto Gilardino	22	70	151 mins
2	Domenico Morfeo	8	54	291 mins
3	Marco Marchionni	4	75	474 mins
4	Simplicio	4	63	674 mins
5	Mark Bresciano	3	71	926 mins

KEY PLAYERS - MIDFIELDERS

Domenico Morfeo

Goals in the League 8

Contribution to Attacking Power Average number of minutes between League team goals while on pitch 54

Defensive Rating Average number of mins between League goals conceded while on the pitch 51

Scoring Difference Defensive Rating minus Contribution to Attacking Power -3

	PLAYER	LGE GOALS	DEF RATE	POWER	SCORE DIFF
1	Domenico Morfeo	8	51	54	-3 mins
2	Jorge Bolano	0	53	60	-7 mins
3	Simplicio	4	52	63	-11 mins
4	Vincenzo Grella	0	53	114	-61 mins

KEY PLAYERS - DEFENDERS

Daniele Bonera

Goals Conceded Number of League goals conceded while the player was on the pitch 53

Clean Sheets In League games when player was on pitch for at least 70 minutes 6

Defensive Rating Ave number of mins between League goals conceded while on the pitch 57

Club Defensive Rating Average number of mins between League goals conceded by the club this season 53

	PLAYER	CON LGE	CLEAN SHEETS	DEF RATE
1	Daniele Bonera	53	6	57 mins
2	Matteo Contini	43	4	55 mins
3	Paolo Cannavaro	42	4	53 mins
4	Cesare Bovo	51	5	50 mins
5	Giuseppe Cardone	27	1	42 mins

KEY GOALKEEPER

Sebastian Frey

Goals Conceded in the League 62

Counting Games League games when player was on pitch for at least 70 minutes 35

Defensive Rating Ave number of mins between League goals conceded while on the pitch 52

Clean Sheets In games when player was on pitch for at least 70 minutes 6

LEAGUE GOALS

Alberto Gilardino

Minutes on the pitch 3325

League average (mins between goals) 151

Goals in the League 22

	PLAYER	MINS	GOALS	AVE
1	Gilardino	3325	22	151
2	Morfeo	2327	8	291
3	Simplicio	2694	4	674
4	Marchionni	1895	4	474
5	Bresciano	2779	3	926
6	Bovo	2531	2	1266
7	Cannavaro	2212	1	2212
8	Pisanu	1149	1	1149
9	Sorrentino	191	1	191
	Other		1	
	TOTAL		47	

DISCIPLINARY RECORDS

	PLAYER	YELLOW	RED	AVE
1	Contini	12	2	170
2	Bolano	8	0	178
3	Cardone	6	0	188
4	Pisanu	5	1	191
5	Potenza	3	1	259
6	Bonera	10	1	272
7	Bettarini	2	0	279
8	Bovo	7	2	281
9	Morfeo	6	1	332
10	Simplicio	7	0	384
11	Grella	4	0	398
12	Cannavaro	4	1	442
13	Vignaroli	1	0	554
	Other	12	2	
	TOTAL	87	11	

TOP POINT EARNERS

	PLAYER	GAMES	AV PTS
1	Domenico Morfeo	21	1.57
2	Giuseppe Cardone	12	1.33
3	Daniele Bonera	32	1.22
4	Matteo Contini	24	1.21
5	Alberto Gilardino	36	1.17
6	Cesare Bovo	26	1.15
7	Simplicio	28	1.14
8	Mark Bresciano	30	1.13
9	Marco Marchionni	19	1.11
10	Sebastian Frey	35	1.09
	CLUB AVERAGE:		1.11

LEAGUE APPEARANCES, BOOKINGS AND CAPS

	AGE (on 01/07/05)	IN NAMED 18	APPEARANCES	COUNTING GAMES	MINUTES ON PITCH	YELLOW CARDS	RED CARDS	THIS SEASON	HOME COUNTRY
Goalkeepers									
Gianluca Berti	38	18	1	1	90	1	0	-	Italy
Luca Bucci	36	17	2	1	109	0	0	-	Italy
Alfonso De Lucia	21	3	0	0	0	0	0	-	Italy
Sebastian Frey	25	37	36	35	3216	0	1	-	France
Defenders									
Stefano Bettarini	33	9	8	6	558	2	0	-	Italy
Daniele Bonera	24	35	35	32	3000	10	1	7	Italy (10)
Cesare Bovo	22	34	31	26	2531	7	2	-	Italy
Paolo Cannavaro	24	36	28	24	2212	4	1	-	Italy
Giuseppe Cardone	31	20	15	12	1128	6	0	-	Italy
Matteo Contini	25	35	29	24	2383	12	2	-	Italy
Damiano Ferronetti	21	16	10	4	541	0	0	-	Italy
Alessandro Potenza	21	17	16	9	1038	3	1	-	Italy
Midfielders									
Jorge Bolano	28	27	22	11	1430	8	0	-	Colombia
Alessandro Budel	24	19	10	4	560	1	0	-	Italy
Ibrahima Camara	20	19	8	2	274	1	0	-	Guinea
Daniele Dessena	18	5	2	0	90	0	0	-	Italy
Alberto Galuppo	19	5	0	0	0	0	0	-	Italy
Vincenzo Grella	25	29	24	14	1593	4	0	-	Australia
Domenico Morfeo	29	31	31	21	2327	6	1	-	Italy
Renato Olive	34	14	7	2	304	3	0	-	Italy
Alessandro Rosina	20	18	12	3	548	0	0	-	Italy
Filippo Savi	18	5	3	1	205	1	0	-	Italy
Simplicio	25	34	33	28	2694	7	0	-	Brazil
Tonino Sorrentino	20	12	6	0	191	0	0	-	Italy
Forwards									
Mark Bresciano	25	34	34	30	2779	4	1	-	Australia
Daniele Degano	22	2	2	1	112	0	0	-	Italy
Alberto Gilardino	23	38	38	36	3325	4	0	-	Italy
Gaetano Grieco	22	3	0	0	0	0	0	-	Italy
Massimo Maccarone	25	11	7	1	298	0	0	-	Italy
Marco Marchionni	24	24	24	19	1895	3	0	-	Italy
Andrea Pisanu	23	29	18	11	1149	5	1	-	Italy
Francesco Ruopolo	22	21	9	0	114	1	0	-	Italy
Fabio Vignaroli	29	18	16	1	554	1	0	-	Italy
Ianis Zicu	21	5	2	0	74	1	0	-	Romania

TEAM OF THE SEASON

D
Daniele Bonera
CG: 32 DR: 57
M
Domenico Morfeo
CG: 21 SD: -3
D
Matteo Contini
CG: 24 DR: 55
M
Simplicio
CG: 28 SD: -11
F
Alberto Gilardino
CG: 36 SR: 151
G
Sebastian Frey
CG: 35 DR: 52
D
Paolo Cannavaro
CG: 24 DR: 53
M
Vincenzo Grella
CG: 14 SD: -61
F
Marco Marchionni
CG: 19 SR: 474
D
Cesare Bovo
CG: 26 DR: 50
M
Jorge Bolano*
CG: 11 SD: -7

SQUAD APPEARANCES

Match	1	2	3	4	5	6	7	8	9	10	11	12	13	14	15	16	17	18	19	20	21	22	23	24	25	26
Venue	H	H	A	H	A	A	H	A	A	H	A	H	H	A	H	H	A	A	H	A	H	A	H	A	H	A
Competition	L	E	L	L	L	E	L	L	E	L	L	L	E	L	L	L	E	L	L	L	E	L	L	L	L	L
Result	D	W	L	L	D	D	D	L	L	W	L	D	W	D	W	D	L	L	L	L	W	L	D	W	W	L

Match	27	28	29	30	31	32	33	34	35	36	37	38	39	40	41	42	43	44	45	46	47	48	49	50	51	52
Venue	H	A	H	A	H	H	A	A	H	A	A	H	H	A	A	H	A	H	A	H	H	A	H	A	H	A
Competition	L	L	L	L	E	O	E	O	O	E	L	E	L	E	L	E	L	L	L	E	L	E	L	L	L	L
Result	W	L	D	L	D	W	W	L	W	D	L	W	D	D	W	D	L	D	L	D	W	L	W	L	D	D

Goalkeepers
Gianluca Berti
Luca Bucci
Alfonso De Lucia
Sebastian Frey

Defenders
Stefano Bettarini
Daniele Bonera
Cesare Bovo
Paolo Cannavaro
Giuseppe Cardone
Matteo Contini
Damiano Ferronetti
Alessandro Potenza

Midfielders
Jorge Bolano
Alessandro Budel
Ibrahima Camara
Daniele Dessena
Alberto Galuppo
Vincenzo Grella
Domenico Morfeo
Renato Olive
Alessandro Rosina
Filippo Savi
Simplicio
Tonino Sorrentino

Forwards
Mark Bresciano
Daniele Degano
Alberto Gilardino
Gaetano Grieco
Massimo Maccarone
Marco Marchionni
Andrea Pisanu
Francesco Ruopolo
Fabio Vignaroli
Ianis Zicu

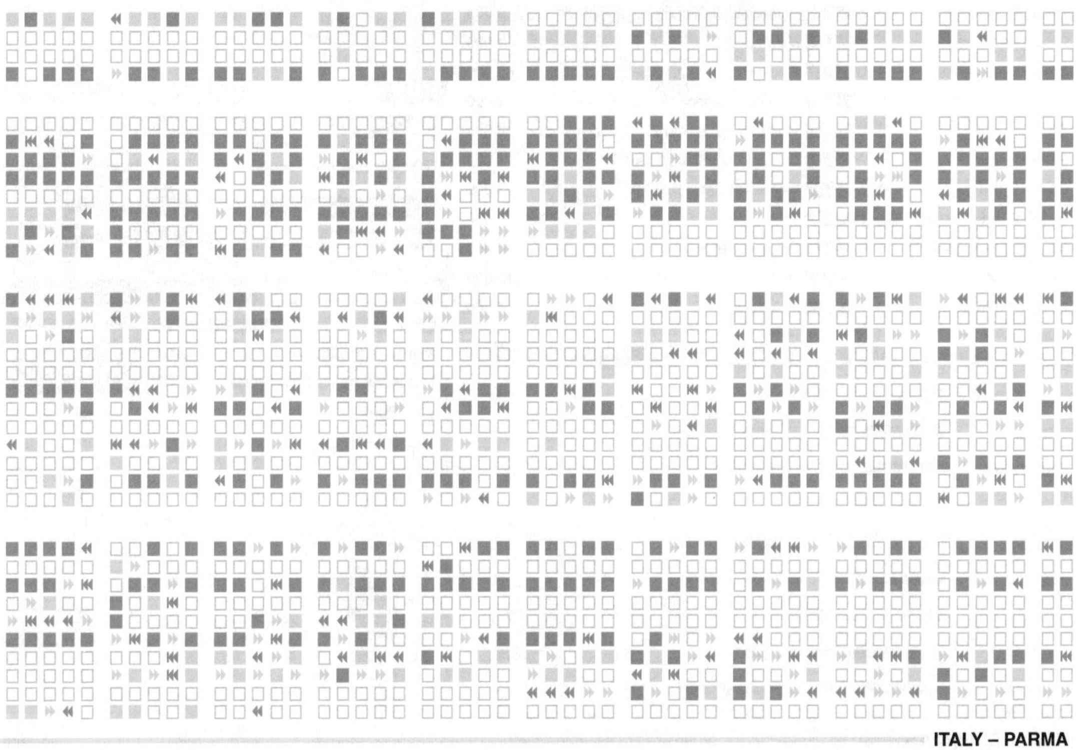

BRESCIA

Final Position: **19th**

KEY: Won Drawn Lost

							Attendance
1	itpr1	**Juventus**	H	L	0-3		18,000
2	itpr1	**Lecce**	A	L	1-4	Caracciolo 27	14,000
3	itpr1	**Lazio**	H	L	0-2		12,000
4	itpr1	**Udinese**	A	W	2-1	Caracciolo 7; Mannini 76	14,000
5	itpr1	**Cagliari**	A	L	1-2	Caracciolo 38	12,000
6	itpr1	**Parma**	H	W	3-1	Di Biagio 25; Caracciolo 27; Mannini 47	7,000
7	itpr1	**Sampdoria**	A	W	1-0	Di Biagio 58 pen	23,000
8	itpr1	**Siena**	H	L	0-1		9,000
9	itpr1	**Livorno**	A	L	1-2	Caracciolo 25	15,000
10	itpr1	**Chievo**	H	W	1-0	Schopp 86	7,000
11	itpr1	**AC Milan**	H	D	0-0		16,000
12	itpr1	**Atalanta**	A	D	0-0		18,000
13	itpr1	**Palermo**	H	L	0-2		10,000
14	itpr1	**Reggina**	A	W	3-1	Stankevicius 18; Martinez 40; Caracciolo 80	20,000
15	itpr1	**Roma**	H	L	0-1		9,000
16	itpr1	**Inter Milan**	A	L	0-1		50,000
17	itpr1	**Bologna**	H	D	1-1	Di Biagio 66 pen	8,000
18	itpr1	**Messina**	A	L	0-2		29,000
19	itpr1	**Fiorentina**	H	D	1-1	Di Biagio 62	10,000
20	itpr1	**Juventus**	A	L	0-2		19,000
21	itpr1	**Lecce**	H	L	0-1		8,000
22	itpr1	**Lazio**	A	D	0-0		30,000
23	itpr1	**Udinese**	H	L	0-1		8,000
24	itpr1	**Cagliari**	H	W	2-0	Zoboli 6; Caracciolo 90	9,000
25	itpr1	**Parma**	A	L	1-2	Di Biagio 51	13,000
26	itpr1	**Sampdoria**	H	L	0-1		8,000
27	itpr1	**Siena**	A	W	3-2	Di Biagio 40; Caracciolo 45; Mannini 73	8,000
28	itpr1	**Livorno**	H	L	2-3	Caracciolo 16 pen,89	9,000
29	itpr1	**Chievo**	A	L	1-3	Mareco 18	9,000
30	itpr1	**AC Milan**	A	D	1-1	Wome 87	65,000
31	itpr1	**Atalanta**	H	W	1-0	Di Biagio 90 pen	12,000
32	itpr1	**Palermo**	A	D	3-3	Wome 17; Di Biagio 22; Caracciolo 85	33,000
33	itpr1	**Reggina**	H	W	2-0	Di Biagio 48; Stankevicius 77	7,000
34	itpr1	**Roma**	A	D	2-2	Wome 48; Caracciolo 79	47,000
35	itpr1	**Inter Milan**	H	L	0-3		11,000
36	itpr1	**Bologna**	A	W	2-1	Del Nero 50; Stankevicius 77	18,000
37	itpr1	**Messina**	H	W	2-1	Di Biagio 62; Milanetto 72	15,000
38	itpr1	**Fiorentina**	A	L	0-3		45,000

MONTHLY POINTS TALLY

SEPTEMBER	3	25%
OCTOBER	6	40%
NOVEMBER	5	42%
DECEMBER	3	33%
JANUARY	2	13%
FEBRUARY	4	27%
MARCH	3	33%
APRIL	8	67%
MAY	7	47%

KEY PLAYERS - GOALSCORERS

Andrea Caracciolo

Goals in the League	12	**Player Strike Rate** Average number of minutes between League goals scored by player	241
Contribution to Attacking Power Average number of minutes between League team goals while on pitch	90	**Club Strike Rate** Average number of minutes between League goals scored by club	92

	PLAYER	LGE GOALS	POWER	STRIKE RATE
1	Andrea Caracciolo	12	90	241 mins
2	Luigi Di Biagio	10	95	293 mins
3	Pierre Nlend Wome	3	65	480 mins
4	Daniele Mannini	3	88	501 mins
5	Marius Stankevicius	3	95	860 mins

KEY PLAYERS - MIDFIELDERS

Omar Milanetto

Goals in the League	1	**Contribution to Attacking Power** Average number of minutes between League team goals while on pitch	87
Defensive Rating Average number of mins between League goals conceded while on the pitch	57	**Scoring Difference** Defensive Rating minus Contribution to Attacking Power	-30

	PLAYER	LGE GOALS	DEF RATE	POWER	SCORE DIFF
1	Omar Milanetto	1	57	87	-30 mins
2	Daniele Mannini	3	54	88	-34 mins
3	Luigi Di Biagio	10	61	95	-34 mins
4	Roberto Guana	0	82	126	-44 mins

KEY PLAYERS - DEFENDERS

Simone Dallamano

Goals Conceded Number of League goals conceded while the player was on the pitch	24	**Clean Sheets** In League games when player was on pitch for at least 70 minutes	5
Defensive Rating Ave number of mins between League goals conceded while on the pitch	78	**Club Defensive Rating** Average number of mins between League goals conceded by the club this season	62

	PLAYER	CON LGE	CLEAN SHEETS	DEF RATE
1	Simone Dallamano	24	5	78 mins
2	Marius Stankevicius	38	7	68 mins
3	Davide Zoboli	34	4	64 mins
4	Gilberto Martinez	44	7	64 mins
5	Victor Hugo Mareco	26	5	63 mins

KEY GOALKEEPER

Luca Castellazzi

Goals Conceded in the League	55	**Counting Games** League games when player was on pitch for at least 70 minutes	37
Defensive Rating Ave number of mins between League goals conceded while on the pitch	61	**Clean Sheets** In games when player was on pitch for at least 70 minutes	8

LEAGUE GOALS

Andrea Caracciolo

Minutes on the pitch	2886	**Goals in the League**	12
League average (mins between goals)	241		

	PLAYER	MINS	GOALS	AVE
1	Caracciolo	2886	12	241
2	Di Biagio	2933	10	293
3	Wome	1440	3	480
4	Mannini	1504	3	501
5	Stankevicius	2579	3	860
6	Zoboli	2183	1	2183
7	Del Nero	920	1	920
8	Schopp	938	1	938
9	Milanetto	2436	1	2436
10	Mareco	1649	1	1649
11	Martinez	2795	1	2795
	Other		0	
	TOTAL		37	

DISCIPLINARY RECORDS

	PLAYER	YELLOW	RED	AVE
1	Del Nero	6	0	153
2	Sculli	8	1	189
3	Schopp	4	0	234
4	Mareco	7	0	235
5	Milanetto	9	1	243
6	Di Biagio	9	3	244
7	Domizzi	7	1	269
8	Caracciolo	9	1	288
9	Zambrella	2	0	310
10	Zoboli	4	2	363
11	Mannini	4	0	376
12	Guana	5	0	378
13	Stankevicius	5	0	515
	Other	5	1	
	TOTAL	84	10	

TOP POINT EARNERS

	PLAYER	GAMES	AV PTS
1	Victor Hugo Mareco	15	1.40
2	Maurizio Domizzi	22	1.36
3	Pierre Nlend Wome	16	1.31
4	Marius Stankevicius	26	1.31
5	Giuseppe Sculli	15	1.20
6	Davide Zoboli	22	1.14
7	Gilberto Martinez	31	1.13
8	Luca Castellazzi	37	1.08
9	Daniele Mannini	12	1.08
10	Roberto Guana	19	1.05
	CLUB AVERAGE:		1.08

TEAM OF THE SEASON

G
Luca Castellazzi
CG: 37 DR: 61

D
Simone Dallamano
CG: 19 DR: 78

D
Marius Stankevicius
CG: 26 DR: 68

D
Gilberto Martinez
CG: 31 DR: 64

D
Davide Zoboli
CG: 22 DR: 64

M
Omar Milanetto
CG: 25 SD: -30

M
Luigi Di Biagio
CG: 31 SD: -34

M
Daniele Mannini
CG: 12 SD: -34

M
Roberto Guana
CG: 19 SD: -44

F
Andrea Caracciolo
CG: 31 SR: 241

F
Guiseppi Sculli
CG: 15 SR: 0

LEAGUE APPEARANCES, BOOKINGS AND CAPS

	AGE (on 01/07/05)	IN NAMED 18	APPEARANCES	COUNTING GAMES	MINUTES ON PITCH	YELLOW CARDS	RED CARDS	THIS SEASON	HOME COUNTRY
Goalkeepers									
Federico Agliardi	22	38	1	0	45	0	0	-	Italy
Luca Castellazzi	29	38	38	37	3375	0	0	-	Italy
Defenders									
Daniele Adani	30	16	13	9	947	1	0	-	Italy
Simone Dallamano	21	31	26	19	1871	2	1	-	Italy
Maurizio Domizzi	25	34	29	22	2153	7	1	-	Italy
Victor Hugo Mareco	21	34	24	15	1649	7	0	-	Paraguay
Gilberto Martinez	26	34	32	31	2795	1	0	-	Costa Rica
Marius Stankevicius	23	37	33	26	2579	5	0	-	Lithuania
Pierre Nlend Wome	26	16	16	16	1440	1	0	-	Cameroon
Marco Zambelli	19	13	5	0	130	0	0	-	Italy
Davide Zoboli	23	35	28	22	2183	4	2	-	Italy
Midfielders									
Matias Almeyda	31	5	5	5	435	0	1	-	Argentina
Jonathan Bachini	30	5	3	3	270	1	0	-	Italy
Daniele Berretta	33	10	7	2	276	0	0	-	Italy
Luigi Di Biagio	34	34	34	31	2933	9	3	-	Italy
Roberto Guana	24	24	24	19	1890	5	0	-	Italy
Marek Hamsik	17	6	1	1	71	0	0	-	Slovakia
Daniele Mannini	21	35	30	12	1504	4	0	-	Italy
Omar Milanetto	29	34	31	25	2436	9	1	-	Italy
Marc Nygaard	28	23	10	3	386	0	1	-	Denmark
Markus Schopp	31	19	17	7	938	4	0	-	Austria
Johan Vonlanthen	19	14	9	0	240	0	0	7	Switzerland (45)
Fabrizio Zambrella	19	22	14	1	620	2	0	-	Italy
Forwards									
Andrea Caracciolo	23	34	34	31	2886	9	1	-	Italy
Simone Del Nero	23	30	21	5	920	6	0	-	Italy
Marco Delvecchio	32	5	4	3	305	3	0	-	Italy
Luigi Di Pasquale	22	16	8	2	315	1	0	-	Italy
Abderrazak Jadid	22	7	3	0	61	1	0	-	Morocco
Giuseppe Sculli	24	32	28	15	1706	8	1	-	Italy

SQUAD APPEARANCES

Match	1	2	3	4	5	6	7	8	9	10	11	12	13	14	15	16	17	18	19	20	21	22	23	24	25	26	27	28	29	30	31	32	33	34	35	36	37	38
Venue	H	A	H	A	A	H	A	H	A	H	H	A	H	A	H	A	H	A	H	A	H	A	H	H	A	H	A	H	A	A	H	A	H	A	H	A	H	A
Competition	L	L	L	L	L	L	L	L	L	L	L	L	L	L	L	L	L	L	L	L	L	L	L	L	L	L	L	L	L	L	L	L	L	L	L	L	L	L
Result	L	L	L	W	L	W	W	L	L	W	D	D	L	W	L	L	D	L	D	L	L	D	L	W	L	L	W	L	L	D	W	D	W	D	L	W	W	L

Goalkeepers
Federico Agliardi
Luca Castellazzi

Defenders
Daniele Adani
Simone Dallamano
Maurizio Domizzi
Victor Hugo Mareco
Gilberto Martinez
Marius Stankevicius
Pierre Nlend Wome
Marco Zambelli
Davide Zoboli

Midfielders
Matias Almeyda
Jonathan Bachini
Daniele Berretta
Luigi Di Biagio
Roberto Guana
Marek Hamsik
Daniele Mannini
Omar Milanetto
Marc Nygaard
Markus Schopp
Johan Vonlanthen
Fabrizio Zambrella

Forwards
Andrea Caracciolo
Simone Del Nero
Marco Delvecchio
Luigi Di Pasquale
Abderrazak Jadid
Giuseppe Sculli

KEY: On all match · On bench · Subbed or sent off (Counting game) · Subbed or sent off (playing less than 70 minutes) · Subbed on from bench (Counting Game) · Subbed on (playing less than 70 minutes) · Subbed on and then subbed or sent off (Counting Game) · Subbed on and then subbed or sent off (playing less than 70 minutes) · Not in 16

ATALANTA

Final Position: **20th**

KEY: ☐ Won ☐ Drawn ☐ Lost

							Attendance
1	itpr1	**Lecce**	H	D	2-2	Pazzini 3; Albertini 51	15,000
2	itpr1	**Juventus**	A	L	0-2		22,000
3	itpr1	**Inter Milan**	H	L	2-3	Budan 25; Pazzini 85	22,000
4	itpr1	**Livorno**	A	D	1-1	Gautieri 73	16,000
5	itpr1	**Lazio**	H	D	1-1	Gautieri 12	12,000
6	itpr1	**Bologna**	A	L	1-2	Budan 12	17,000
7	itpr1	**Cagliari**	H	D	2-2	Pazzini 2; Montolivo 40	12,000
8	itpr1	**AC Milan**	A	L	0-3		40,000
9	itpr1	**Parma**	A	D	2-2	Budan 45; Montolivo 76	12,000
10	itpr1	**Sampdoria**	H	D	0-0		14,000
11	itpr1	**Chievo**	A	L	0-1		7,000
12	itpr1	**Brescia**	H	D	0-0		18,000
13	itpr1	**Reggina**	H	L	0-1		10,000
14	itpr1	**Palermo**	A	L	0-1		33,000
15	itpr1	**Udinese**	H	L	0-1		12,000
16	itpr1	**Fiorentina**	H	W	1-0	Budan 80	15,000
17	itpr1	**Roma**	A	L	1-2	Marcolini 85	43,000
18	itpr1	**Siena**	H	D	1-1	Sinigaglia 20	15,000
19	itpr1	**Messina**	A	L	0-1		25,000
20	itpr1	**Lecce**	A	L	0-1		15,000
21	itpr1	**Juventus**	H	L	1-2	Thuram 90 og	15,000
22	itpr1	**Inter Milan**	A	L	0-1		49,000
23	itpr1	**Livorno**	H	W	1-0	Sala 23	10,000
24	itpr1	**Lazio**	A	L	1-2	Makinwa 45	30,000
25	itpr1	**Bologna**	H	W	2-0	Marcolini 24; Makinwa 62	10,000
26	itpr1	**Cagliari**	A	D	3-3	Sala 17; Makinwa 61; Marcolini 90 pen	15,000
27	itpr1	**AC Milan**	H	L	1-2	Makinwa 73	23,000
28	itpr1	**Parma**	H	W	1-0	Adriano 79	15,000
29	itpr1	**Sampdoria**	A	W	2-1	Makinwa 3; Natali 68	23,000
30	itpr1	**Chievo**	H	W	3-0	Marcolini 6 pen; Makinwa 15; Montolivo 54	22,000
31	itpr1	**Brescia**	A	L	0-1		12,000
32	itpr1	**Reggina**	A	D	0-0		15,000
33	itpr1	**Palermo**	H	W	1-0	Sala 89	11,000
34	itpr1	**Udinese**	A	L	1-2	Lazzari 4	17,000
35	itpr1	**Messina**	H	W	2-1	Adriano 49; Bernardini 54	12,000
36	itpr1	**Fiorentina**	A	D	0-0		43,000
37	itpr1	**Roma**	H	L	0-1		15,000
38	itpr1	**Siena**	A	L	1-2	Budan 62	11,000

MONTHLY POINTS TALLY

SEPTEMBER	2	17%
OCTOBER	3	20%
NOVEMBER	2	17%
DECEMBER	0	0%
JANUARY	4	22%
FEBRUARY	7	47%
MARCH	6	67%
APRIL	7	58%
MAY	4	27%

KEY PLAYERS - GOALSCORERS

Stephen Ayodele Makinwa

Goals in the League	6	**Player Strike Rate** Average number of minutes between League goals scored by player	237
Contribution to Attacking Power Average number of minutes between League team goals while on pitch	78	**Club Strike Rate** Average number of minutes between League goals scored by club	101

	PLAYER	LGE GOALS	POWER	STRIKE RATE
1	Stephen Ayodele Makinwa	6	78	237 mins
2	Igor Budan	5	138	360 mins
3	Michele Marcolini	4	89	709 mins
4	Riccardo Montolivo	3	114	723 mins
5	Luigi Sala	3	108	798 mins

KEY PLAYERS - MIDFIELDERS

Thiago Motta

Goals in the League	0	**Contribution to Attacking Power** Average number of minutes between League team goals while on pitch	81
Defensive Rating Average number of mins between League goals conceded while on the pitch	93	**Scoring Difference** Defensive Rating minus Contribution to Attacking Power	12

	PLAYER	LGE GOALS	DEF RATE	POWER	SCORE DIFF
1	Thiago Motta	0	93	81	12 mins
2	Antonio Bernardini	1	92	92	0 mins
3	Michele Marcolini	4	71	89	-18 mins
4	Andrea Lazzari	1	71	89	-18 mins
5	Demetrio Albertini	1	61	96	-35 mins

KEY PLAYERS - DEFENDERS

Luigi Sala

Goals Conceded Number of League goals conceded while the player was on the pitch	24	**Clean Sheets** In League games when player was on pitch for at least 70 minutes	9
Defensive Rating Ave number of mins between League goals conceded while on the pitch	100	**Club Defensive Rating** Average number of mins between League goals conceded by the club this season	74

	PLAYER	CON LGE	CLEAN SHEETS	DEF RATE
1	Luigi Sala	24	9	100 mins
2	Cesare Natali	42	8	74 mins
3	Claudio Rivalta	38	8	73 mins
4	Giampaolo Bellini	35	5	73 mins

KEY GOALKEEPER

Alex Calderoni

Goals Conceded in the League	15	**Counting Games** League games when player was on pitch for at least 70 minutes	15
Defensive Rating Ave number of mins between League goals conceded while on the pitch	93	**Clean Sheets** In games when player was on pitch for at least 70 minutes	6

LEAGUE GOALS

Stephen Ayodele Makinwa

Minutes on the pitch	1419	Goals in the League	6
League average (mins between goals)	237		

	PLAYER	MINS	GOALS	AVE
1	Makinwa	1419	6	237
2	Budan	1802	5	360
3	Marcolini	2837	4	709
4	Sala	2393	3	798
5	Montolivo	2168	3	723
6	Pazzini	706	3	235
7	Gautieri	485	2	243
8	Adriano	664	2	332
9	Lazzari	1777	1	1777
10	Natali	3101	1	3101
11	Bernardini	1924	1	1924
12	Albertini	1154	1	1154
13	Sinigaglia	391	1	391
	Other		1	
	TOTAL		34	

DISCIPLINARY RECORDS

	PLAYER	YELLOW	RED	AVE
1	Capelli	3	0	210
2	Gautieri	2	0	242
3	Montolivo	7	1	271
4	Migliaccio	3	0	279
5	Mingazzini	6	0	281
6	Albertini	4	0	288
7	Rivalta	8	1	310
8	Marcolini	7	1	354
9	Makinwa	4	0	354
10	Bellini	7	0	364
11	Sala	5	0	478
12	Lazzari	2	1	592
13	Motta	2	0	607
	Other	11	1	
	TOTAL	71	5	

TOP POINT EARNERS

	PLAYER	GAMES	AV PTS
1	Thiago Motta	13	1.54
2	Alex Calderoni	15	1.40
3	Antonio Bernardini	18	1.33
4	Ayodele Makinwa	16	1.31
5	Luigi Sala	26	1.19
6	Andrea Lazzari	14	1.14
7	Claudio Rivalta	31	1.06
8	Cesare Natali	34	0.91
9	Michele Marcolini	29	0.90
10	Nicola Mingazzini	16	0.88
	CLUB AVERAGE:		0.92

TEAM OF THE SEASON

D
Luigi Sala
CG: 26 DR: 100
M
Thiago Motta
CG: 13 SD: 12
D
Cesare Natali
CG: 34 DR: 74
M
Antonio Bernardini
CG: 18 SD: 0
F
Ayodele Makinwa
CG: 16 SR: 237
G
Alex Calderoni
CG: 15 DR: 93
D
Giampaolo Bellini
CG: 28 DR: 73
M
Andrea Lazzari
CG: 14 SD: -18
F
Igor Budan
CG: 17 SR: 360
D
Claudio Rivalta
CG: 31 DR: 73
M
Michele Marcolini
CG: 29 SD: -18

LEAGUE APPEARANCES, BOOKINGS AND CAPS

	AGE (on 01/07/05)	IN NAMED 18	APPEARANCES	COUNTING GAMES	MINUTES ON PITCH	YELLOW CARDS	RED CARDS	THIS SEASON	HOME COUNTRY
Goalkeepers									
Nicholas Caglioni	22	1	0	0	0	0	0	-	Italy
Alex Calderoni	29	36	16	15	1395	0	0	-	Italy
Massimo Taibi	35	35	23	22	2025	0	0	-	Italy
Defenders									
Adriano	23	16	10	7	664	1	0	9	Brazil (1)
Giampaolo Bellini	25	30	29	28	2552	7	0	-	Italy
Daniele Capelli	19	20	8	7	632	3	0	-	Italy
Natale Gonnella	29	18	11	11	990	1	0	-	Italy
Duccio Innocenti	29	24	7	2	325	2	0	-	Italy
Stefano Lorenzi	28	4	1	0	2	0	0	-	Italy
Marco Motta	19	4	4	4	344	1	0	-	Italy
Cesare Natali	26	36	35	34	3101	4	0	-	Italy
Claudio Rivalta	27	32	31	31	2790	8	1	-	Italy
Luigi Sala	31	36	28	26	2393	5	0	-	Italy
Midfielders									
Demetrio Albertini	33	14	14	13	1154	4	0	-	Italy
Antonio Bernardini	31	36	29	18	1924	1	0	-	Italy
Carmine Gautieri	34	13	13	4	485	2	0	-	Italy
Andrea Lazzari	20	35	31	14	1777	2	1	-	Italy
Michele Marcolini	29	35	35	29	2837	7	1	-	Italy
Giulio Migliaccio	24	18	13	8	838	3	0	-	Italy
Nicola Mingazzini	24	37	27	16	1687	6	0	-	Italy
Riccardo Montolivo	20	34	32	19	2168	7	1	-	Italy
Thiago Motta	22	17	15	13	1215	2	0	-	Brazil
Biagio Pagano	22	16	6	0	138	0	0	-	Italy
Damiano Zenoni	28	19	17	13	1255	2	0	-	Italy
Forwards									
Igor Budan	25	30	28	17	1802	2	0	-	Croatia
Lampros Choutos	25	1	1	0	13	0	0	-	Greece
Gianni Comandini	28	5	2	0	7	0	0	-	Italy
Mario Defendi	19	3	1	0	1	0	0	-	Italy
Inacio Pia	23	12	9	2	361	1	0	-	Brazil
Ayodele Makinwa	21	17	17	16	1419	4	0	-	Nigeria
Gianpaolo Pazzini	20	13	12	5	706	0	1	-	Italy
Luca Saudati	27	7	5	0	152	0	0	-	Italy
Davide Sinigaglia	23	16	12	2	391	0	0	-	Italy

SQUAD APPEARANCES

Match	1	2	3	4	5	6	7	8	9	10	11	12	13	14	15	16	17	18	19	20	21	22	23	24	25	26	27	28	29	30	31	32	33	34	35	36	37	38
Venue	H	A	H	A	H	A	H	A	A	H	A	H	H	A	H	H	A	H	A	A	H	A	H	A	H	A	H	H	A	H	A	A	H	A	H	A	H	A
Competition	L	L	L	L	L	L	L	L	L	L	L	L	L	L	L	L	L	L	L	L	L	L	L	L	L	L	L	L	L	L	L	L	L	L	L	L	L	L
Result	D	L	L	D	D	L	D	L	D	D	L	D	L	L	L	W	L	D	L	L	L	L	W	L	W	D	L	W	W	W	L	D	W	L	W	D	L	L

Goalkeepers
Alex Calderoni
Andrea Consigli
Massimo Taibi

Defenders
Adriano
Giampaolo Bellini
Daniele Capelli
Natale Gonnella
Duccio Innocenti
Stefano Lorenzi
Marco Motta
Cesare Natali
Claudio Rivalta
Luigi Sala

Midfielders
Demetrio Albertini
Antonio Bernardini
Carmine Gautieri
Andrea Lazzari
Michele Marcolini
Giulio Migliaccio
Nicola Mingazzini
Riccardo Montolivo
Thiago Motta
Biagio Pagano
Damiano Zenoni

Forwards
Igor Budan
Lampros Choutos
Gianni Comandini
Mario Defendi
Inacio Pia
Stephen Ayodele Makinwa
Gianpaolo Pazzini
Luca Saudati
Davide Sinigaglia

DUTCH LEAGUE ROUND-UP

FINAL LEAGUE TABLE

		HOME					AWAY					TOTAL			
	P	W	D	L	F	A	W	D	L	F	A	F	A	DIF	PTS
PSV Eindhoven	34	16	0	1	50	8	11	6	0	39	10	89	18	71	87
Ajax	34	11	3	3	32	17	13	2	2	42	16	74	33	41	77
AZ Alkmaar	34	10	6	1	39	12	9	1	7	32	29	71	41	30	64
Feyenoord	34	11	1	5	55	27	8	4	5	35	24	90	51	39	62
Heerenveen	34	9	2	6	32	26	9	4	4	32	26	64	52	12	60
Twente	34	7	5	5	29	19	8	4	5	19	19	48	38	10	54
Vitesse Arnhem	34	7	3	7	23	24	9	3	5	30	25	53	49	4	54
Roda JC Kerk	34	8	4	5	34	21	5	4	8	26	34	60	55	5	47
RKC Waalwijk	34	8	5	4	26	22	5	3	9	18	29	44	51	-7	47
Willem II Tilb	34	9	2	6	30	25	4	4	9	14	31	44	56	-12	45
Utrecht	34	8	3	6	23	20	4	5	8	17	23	40	43	-3	44
Groningen	34	5	5	7	23	24	6	2	9	27	34	50	58	-8	40
NEC Nijmegen	34	7	6	4	27	21	2	4	11	14	26	41	47	-6	37
Den Haag	34	7	2	8	25	26	3	4	10	19	33	44	59	-15	36
NAC Breda	34	4	4	9	24	32	5	4	8	19	35	43	67	-24	35
Roosendaal	34	6	2	9	22	27	4	0	13	16	50	38	77	-39	32
De Graafschap	34	3	5	9	19	38	1	2	14	13	40	32	78	-46	19
Den Bosch	34	4	1	12	13	33	1	3	13	10	42	23	75	-52	19

CLUB STRIKE FORCE

Salomon Kalou; Feyenoord

1 Feyenoord

Goals scored in the League	90
Club Strike Rate (CSR) Average number of minutes between League goals scored by club	34

	CLUB	LGE	CSR
1	Feyenoord	90	34
2	PSV Eindhoven	89	34
3	Ajax	74	41
4	AZ Alkmaar	71	43
5	Heerenveen	64	48
6	Roda JC Kerk	60	51
7	Vitesse Arnhem	53	58
8	Groningen	50	61
9	Twente	48	64
10	Den Haag	44	70
11	RKC Waalwijk	44	70
12	Willem II Tilb	44	70
13	NAC Breda	43	71
14	NEC Nijmegen	41	75
15	Utrecht	40	77
16	Roosendaal	38	81
17	De Graafschap	32	96
18	Den Bosch	23	133

CLUB DISCIPLINARY RECORDS

Willem's Raymond Victoria

1 Willem II Tilb

League Yellow	61
League Red	4
League Total	65
Cards Average in League Average number of minutes between a card being shown of either colour	47

	CLUB	LEAGUE		TOTAL	AVE
1	Willem II Tilb	61Y	4R	65	47
2	Twente	60	3	63	49
3	Vitesse Arnhem	60	2	62	49
4	De Graafschap	58	2	60	51
5	NAC Breda	54	4	58	53
6	NEC Nijmegen	57	1	58	53
7	Roda JC Kerk	53	3	56	55
8	Groningen	53	2	55	56
9	Roosendaal	52	3	55	56
10	RKC Waalwijk	50	1	51	60
11	Utrecht	49	2	51	60
12	Den Bosch	48	1	49	62
13	Den Haag	46	2	48	64
14	Heerenveen	45	3	48	64
15	Ajax	41	0	41	75
16	AZ Alkmaar	37	2	39	78
17	PSV Eindhoven	37	2	39	78
18	Feyenoord	34	4	38	81

CLUB DEFENCES

	CLUB	LGE	CS	CDR
1	PSV Eindhoven	18	23	170
2	Ajax	33	15	93
3	Twente	38	13	81
4	AZ Alkmaar	41	12	75
5	Utrecht	43	13	71
6	NEC Nijmegen	47	8	65
7	Vitesse Arnhem	49	8	62
8	Feyenoord	51	11	60
9	RKC Waalwijk	51	13	60
10	Heerenveen	52	7	59
11	Roda JC Kerk	55	6	56
12	Willem II Tilb	56	7	55
13	Groningen	58	7	53
14	Den Haag	59	6	52
15	NAC Breda	67	7	46
16	Den Bosch	75	4	41
17	Roosendaal	77	6	40
18	De Graafschap	78	5	39

Young Pyo-Lee; part of PSV's rearguard

1 PSV Eindhoven

Goals conceded in the League	18
Clean Sheets (CS) Number of league games where no goals were conceded	23
Club Defensive Rate (CDR) Average number of minutes between League goals conceded by club	170

PLAYER NATIONALITIES

Overseas country with the most player appearances in the Dutch League - Belgium

636 league appearances by Belgian players

	COUNTRY	PLAYERS	IN SQUAD	LGE APP	% LGE ACT	CAPS	MOST APP	APP
1	Holland	318	6370	4622	58.5	97	Dennis Gentenaar	99.5
2	Belgium	35	774	636	8.2	15	Gill Swerts	96.7
3	Brazil	16	293	248	3.3		Sergio	95.8
4	Serbia & Montenegro	8	224	200	2.6	8	Predrag Filipovic	98.7
5	Sweden	9	174	164	2.3	22	Petter Hansson	97.1
6	Morocco	9	245	198	2.2		Khalid Sinouh	100.0
7	Denmark	7	154	136	1.7	9	Michael Krohn-Dehli	83.9
8	Ghana	5	117	101	1.4	0	Matthew Amoah	98.9
9	Hungary	5	120	95	1.3		Boldizar Bodor	72.1
10	France	5	114	93	1.3		David Di Tommaso	89.0
11	Poland	6	120	84	1.2		Arek Radomski	75.7
12	Ivory Coast	3	92	89	1.2		Arouna Kone	94.5
13	Australia	5	87	76	1.1	8	Jason Culina	90.9
14	South Korea	3	71	69	1.1		Young-Pyo Lee	91.2
15	Switzerland	4	93	76	0.9	14	Blaise N'Kufo	91.7
16	South Africa	3	73	64	0.9		Steven Pienaar	59.2
17	Portugal	4	76	62	0.8		Virgilio Teixeira	53.2
18	Tunisia	2	55	54	0.8		Karim Saidi	80.0

CLUB MAKE-UP – HOME AND OVERSEAS PLAYERS

1 Roda JC Kerk

78.3% of appearances by overseas players

	CLUB	OVERSEAS	HOME	% OVERSEAS	% LGE ACT	MOST APP	APP
1	Roda JC Kerk	18	9	66.7	78.3	Predrag Filipovic	98.7
2	Feyenoord	21	14	60.0	65.2	Bart Goor	95.2
3	Ajax	22	10	68.8	63.8	Maxwell	82.4
4	PSV Eindhoven	16	15	51.6	51.2	Young-Pyo Lee	91.2
5	Heerenveen	11	18	37.9	49.9	Petter Hansson	97.1
6	Twente	12	18	40.0	46.3	Blaise N'Kufo	91.7
7	Roosendaal	11	21	34.4	44.8	Azubuike Oliseh	86.5
8	RKC Waalwijk	8	23	25.8	38.2	Khalid Sinouh	100.0
9	Vitesse Arnhem	8	18	30.8	37.9	Matthew Amoah	98.9
10	Groningen	10	19	34.5	37.8	Kurt Elshot	87.3
11	De Graafschap	10	23	30.3	35.1	Garry de Graef	82.6
12	NAC Breda	6	23	20.7	34.8	Davy Schollen	92.7
13	Den Haag	6	21	22.2	26.6	Gill Swerts	96.7
14	AZ Alkmaar	7	19	26.9	24.4	Kenneth Perez	73.8
15	NEC Nijmegen	7	23	23.3	23.9	Tininho	77.1
16	Utrecht	4	26	13.3	21.4	David Di Tommaso	89.0
17	Den Bosch	5	25	16.7	20.1	Kris Mampaey	67.3
18	Willem	9	23	28.1	14.1	Tom Caluwe	72.5

CHART-TOPPING MIDFIELDERS

1 Vogel - PSV Eindhoven	
Goals scored in the League	1
Defensive Rating Av number of mins between League goals conceded while on the pitch	245
Contribution to Attacking Power Average number of minutes between League team goals while on pitch	36
Scoring Difference Defensive Rating minus Contribution to Attacking Power	209

	PLAYER	CLUB	GOALS	DEF RATE	POWER	S DIFF
1	Vogel	PSV Eindhoven	1	245	36	209
2	Cocu	PSV Eindhoven	6	188	38	150
3	van Bommel	PSV Eindhoven	14	175	33	142
4	Park	PSV Eindhoven	7	158	32	126
5	Sneijder	Ajax	7	97	40	57
6	Pienaar	Ajax	4	91	40	51
7	Bosschaart	Feyenoord	0	79	38	41
8	Maxwell	Ajax	3	81	42	39
9	van der Vaart	Ajax	6	88	49	39
10	Touma	Twente	4	95	56	39
11	Landzaat	AZ Alkmaar	10	75	42	33
12	Buskermolen	AZ Alkmaar	2	81	49	32
13	Goor	Feyenoord	7	61	33	28
14	Castelen	Feyenoord	10	60	32	28
15	Culina	Twente	11	87	60	27

CHART-TOPPING GOALSCORERS

1 Kuijt - Feyenoord	
Goals scored in the League	29
Contribution to Attacking Power Average number of minutes between League team goals while on pitch	34
Club Strike Rate (CSR) Average minutes between League goals scored by club	34
Player Strike Rate Average number of minutes between League goals scored by player	102

	PLAYER	CLUB	GOALS: LGE	POWER	CSR	S RATE
1	Kuijt	Feyenoord	29	34	34	102
2	Nevland	Groningen	16	54	61	106
3	Vennegoor	PSV Eindhoven	19	32	34	115
4	Kalou	Feyenoord	20	36	34	116
5	Huntelaar	Heerenveen	17	51	48	146
6	Perez	AZ Alkmaar	13	40	43	174
7	N'Kufo	Twente	16	63	64	175
8	Boussaboun	NAC Breda	13	66	71	183
9	van Bommel	PSV Eindhoven	14	32	34	188
10	Cristiano	Roda JC Kerk	9	52	51	200
11	van de Haar	Utrecht	9	70	77	202
12	Reuser	Willem II Tilb	10	58	67	205
13	Hoogendorp	RKC Waalwijk	12	69	70	213
14	Kone	Roda JC Kerk	13	49	51	223
15	Amoah	Vitesse Arnhem	13	60	58	233

CHART-TOPPING DEFENDERS

1 Bouma - PSV Eindhoven	
Goals Conceded in the League The number of League goals conceded while he was on the pitch	13
Clean Sheets In games when he played at least 70 mins	20
Club Defensive Rating Average mins between League goals conceded by the club this season	170
Defensive Rating Average number of minutes between League goals conceded while on pitch	190

	PLAYER	CLUB	CON: LGE	CS	CDR	DEF RATE
1	Bouma	PSV Eindhoven	13	20	170	190
2	Lee	PSV Eindhoven	16	22	170	174
3	Alex	PSV Eindhoven	14	14	170	157
4	Ooijer	PSV Eindhoven	14	13	170	141
5	Grygera	Ajax	13	9	93	125
6	Mathijsen	AZ Alkmaar	19	11	75	107
7	de Jong	Ajax	22	12	93	105
8	Trabelsi	Ajax	23	10	93	93
9	Heubach	Twente	29	11	81	91
10	Schut	Utrecht	19	8	71	91
11	Escude	Ajax	26	10	93	89
12	Heitinga	Ajax	24	11	93	89
13	Zomer	Twente	22	7	81	89
14	Kromkamp	AZ Alkmaar	27	10	75	88
15	Majstorovic	Twente	31	13	81	86

CHART-TOPPING GOALKEEPERS

1 Gomes - PSV Eindhoven	
Counting Games (CG) Games where he played at least 70 minutes	29
Goals Conceded in the League The number of League goals conceded while he was on the pitch	14
Clean Sheets (CS) In games when he played at least 70 mins	21
Defensive Rating Average number of minutes between League goals conceded while on pitch	189

	PLAYER	CLUB	CG	CONC	CS	DEF RATE
1	Gomes	PSV Eindhoven	29	14	21	189
2	Vonk	Ajax	17	13	8	124
3	Ponk	Utrecht	18	20	9	81
4	Timmer	AZ Alkmaar	33	40	12	75
5	Boschker	Twente	29	34	11	75
6	Jevric	Vitesse Arnhem	17	23	5	67
7	Gentenaar	NEC Nijmegen	34	47	8	65
8	Vandenbussche	Heerenveen	29	42	6	62
9	Sinouh	RKC Waalwijk	34	51	13	60
10	Wapenaar	Vitesse Arnhem	17	26	3	59
11	de Vries	Den Haag	31	47	6	57
12	Kujovic	Roda JC Kerk	33	52	6	57
13	Babos	Feyenoord	23	37	7	56
14	Roorda	Groningen	33	54	7	55
15	Moens	Willem II Tilb	34	56	7	55

PLAYER DISCIPLINARY RECORD

3. Haarala- Heerenveen	
Cards Average mins between cards	172
League Yellow	5
League Red	1
TOTAL	6

	PLAYER		LY	LR	TOT	AVE
1	Brouwers	Roda JC Kerk	8	1	9	109
2	Quinn	Willem II Tilb	4	1	5	122
3	Haarala	Heerenveen	5	1	6	172
4	Fleur	Roosendaal	3	1	4	173
5	Bouchiba	Twente	3	1	4	198
6	Ebbinge	NEC Nijmegen	6	1	7	208
7	Zonneveld	NAC Breda	7	1	8	215
8	Loovens	De Graafschap	4	0	4	218
9	Touzani	Twente	6	0	6	219
10	Hofs	Feyenoord	4	0	4	223
11	Ikedia	Roosendaal	3	1	4	224
12	Drent	Groningen	3	0	3	226
13	Molhoek	RKC Waalwijk	6	0	6	226
14	Ouedraogo	Twente	4	0	4	226
15	Bakkati	Heerenveen	5	1	6	230
16	Van den Eede	NAC Breda	2	0	2	233
17	Pothuizen	NEC Nijmegen	5	0	5	236
18	Snoyl	Den Bosch	9	0	9	238
19	van Galen	AZ Alkmaar	6	0	6	240
20	Roelofsen	De Graafschap	2	0	2	253
21	Sankoh	Groningen	2	0	2	254
22	Tiendalli	Utrecht	2	0	2	260
23	Stam	NAC Breda	3	0	3	263
24	Agustien	Willem II Tilb	4	0	4	263

TEAM OF THE SEASON

G
Gomes : PSV
CG: 30 DR: 189

D
Bouma : PSV
CG: 27 DR: 190

D
Grygera : Ajax
CG: 18 DR: 125

D
Mathijsen : AZ Alkmaar
CG: 22 DR: 107

D
Heubach : Twente
CG: 28 DR: 91

M
Vogel : PSV
CG: 19 SD: + 209

M
Sneijder : Ajax
CG: 19 SD: + 57

M
Bosschaart : F'eyen'd
CG: 17 SD: + 41

M
Touma : Twente
CG: 18 SD: + 39

F
Kuijt : Feyen'd
CG: 33 SR: 102

F
Nevland : Groningen
CG: 19 SR: 106

PSV EINDHOVEN

Final Position: **1st**

KEY: ☐Won ☐Drawn ☐Lost

No	Comp	Opponent	Venue	Result	Score	Scorers	Attendance
1	cl ql1	Crvena Zvezda	A	L	2-3	Park 9; de Jong 66	50,000
2	hopr1	Roosendaal	A	W	5-2	Vennegoor 31,62,74; Sibon 59; Beasley 75	5,000
3	hopr1	AZ Alkmaar	H	W	5-1	van Bommel 21; Ooijer 59; de Jong 70,88; Park 75	33,000
4	cl ql2	Crvena Zvezda	H	W	5-0	van Bommel 9 pen,56; Beasley 32; de Jong 58; Vennegoor 80	32,000
5	hopr1	NAC Breda	A	D	2-2	van Bommel 1; Sibon 62	13,000
6	hopr1	RKC Waalwijk	H	W	1-0	Vennegoor 46	33,000
7	cl ge	Arsenal	A	L	0-1		34,068
8	hopr1	NEC Nijmegen	A	W	3-0	van Bommel 29 pen; Lamey 72; Vonlanthen 89	12,000
9	hopr1	Heerenveen	H	W	4-0	Lucius 49; Farfan 57; Vennegoor 63,74	31,000
10	cl ge	Panathinaikos	H	W	1-0	Vennegoor 80	27,000
11	hopr1	Groningen	H	W	3-0	Elshot 5 og; Beasley 32; de Jong 65	30,000
12	hopr1	Den Haag	A	W	2-0	Vonlanthen 1,53	7,000
13	cl ge	Rosenborg BK	A	W	2-1	Farfan 26; de Jong 86	21,000
14	hopr1	Ajax	H	W	2-0	Lee 39; de Jong 49	35,000
15	hopr1	Utrecht	A	D	0-0		22,000
16	cl ge	Rosenborg BK	H	W	1-0	Beasley 10	26,000
17	hopr1	Den Bosch	A	W	3-0	Farfan 41; Alex 68; Cocu 73	6,000
18	hopr1	Willem II Tilb	H	W	1-0	Vennegoor 16	31,000
19	hopr1	Vitesse Arnhem	A	W	2-0	Sibon 56; Beasley 90	17,000
20	cl ge	Arsenal	H	D	1-1	Ooijer 9	35,000
21	hopr1	Twente	H	W	2-0	Sibon 15; Cocu 66	30,000
22	hopr1	De Graafschap	A	W	4-0	Alex 20; van Bommel 66 pen; Farfan 77,82	11,000
23	cl ge	Panathinaikos	A	L	1-4	Beasley 37	10,000
24	hopr1	Feyenoord	A	D	3-3	Cocu 6; Farfan 24; Beasley 70	45,000
25	hopr1	Roda JC Kerk	H	L	0-2		31,000
26	hopr1	NAC Breda	H	W	4-0	Vennegoor 28,38; Penders 71 og; van Bommel 76	31,000
27	hopr1	RKC Waalwijk	A	W	4-1	Beasley 35; Vennegoor 38,69,82	7,000
28	hopr1	Roosendaal	H	W	4-1	van Bommel 52 pen,58; Vennegoor 76 pen; de Jong 83	30,000
29	hopr1	AZ Alkmaar	A	D	0-0		9,000
30	hopr1	NEC Nijmegen	H	W	4-1	Park 21; Beasley 45; Vennegoor 71; Ooijer 77	30,000
31	clr2l1	Monaco	H	W	1-0	Alex 8	42,000
32	hopr1	Heerenveen	A	W	3-0	Park 39; Farfan 82,90	19,000
33	clr2l2	Monaco	A	W	2-0	Vennegoor 27; Beasley 69	16,000
34	hopr1	Den Haag	H	W	4-0	Park 6,42; van Bommel 29; Alex 88	31,000
35	hopr1	Groningen	A	W	1-0	Farfan 45	13,000
36	hopr1	Ajax	A	W	4-0	Cocu 24; van Bommel 45,54 pen,59	51,000
37	hopr1	Utrecht	H	W	2-0	Vennegoor 37; Park 42	31,000
38	clqfl1	Lyon	A	D	1-1	Cocu 79	35,000
39	hopr1	Den Bosch	H	W	3-0	Cocu 30; Bouma 61; van Bommel 89	31,000
40	clqfl2	Lyon	H	W	4-2*	Alex 50 (*on penalties)	35,000
41	hopr1	Willem II Tilb	A	W	1-0	Robert 62	13,000
42	hopr1	Vitesse Arnhem	H	W	3-0	Park 23; van Bommel 43; Sibon 87	34,000
43	clsfl1	AC Milan	A	L	0-2		75,000
44	hopr1	Twente	A	D	2-2	Sibon 67; Vennegoor 77	13,000
45	clsfl2	AC Milan	H	W	3-1	Park 9; Cocu 65,90	35,000
46	hopr1	De Graafschap	H	W	4-1	Vennegoor 2,10; Cocu 12; Vogel 55	32,000
47	hopr1	Feyenoord	H	W	4-2	Afellay 13,71; Vennegoor 40; van Bommel 52	33,000
48	hopr1	Roda JC Kerk	A	D	0-0		16,000

KEY PLAYERS - GOALSCORERS

Jan Vennegoor of Hesselink

Goals in the League	19
Contribution to Attacking Power Average number of minutes between League team goals while on pitch	32
Player Strike Rate Average number of minutes between League goals scored by player	115
Club Strike Rate Average number of minutes between League goals scored by club	34

	PLAYER	GOALS LGE	POWER	S RATE
1	Jan Vennegoor of Hesselink	19	32	115 mins
2	Mark van Bommel	14	33	188 mins
3	Jefferson Farfan	8	38	242 mins
4	DaMarcus Beasley	6	34	272 mins
5	Ji-Sung Park	7	32	339 mins

KEY PLAYERS - MIDFIELDERS

Johann Vogel

Goals in the League	1
Defensive Rating Average number of mins between League goals conceded while on the pitch	245
Contribution to Attacking Power Average number of minutes between League team goals while on pitch	36
Scoring Difference Defensive Rating minus Contribution to Attacking Power	209

	PLAYER	GOALS LGE	DEF RATE	ATT POWER	SCORE DIFF
1	Johann Vogel	1	245	36	209 mins
2	Theo Lucius	1	229	34	195 mins
3	Phillip Cocu	6	188	38	150 mins
4	Mark van Bommel	14	175	33	142 mins
5	Ji-Sung Park	7	158	32	126 mins

KEY PLAYERS - DEFENDERS

Wilfred Bouma

Alex (pictured)

Goals Conceded in League	13
Clean Sheets In games when player was on pitch for at least 70 minutes	20
Defensive Rating Ave number of mins between League goals conceded while on the pitch	190
Club Defensive Rating Average number of mins between League goals conceded by the club this season	170

	PLAYER	CON LGE	CLEAN SHEETS	DEF RATE
1	Wilfred Bouma	13	20	190 mins
2	Young-Pyo Lee	16	22	174 mins
3	Alex	14	14	157 mins
4	Andre Ooijer	14	13	141 mins

MONTHLY POINTS TALLY

Month	Points	%
AUGUST	7	78%
SEPTEMBER	9	100%
OCTOBER	10	83%
NOVEMBER	12	100%
DECEMBER	4	44%
JANUARY	6	100%
FEBRUARY	10	83%
MARCH	9	100%
APRIL	13	87%
MAY	7	78%

LEAGUE GOALS

	PLAYER	MINS	GOALS	AVE
1	Vennegoor	2186	19	115
2	van Bommel	2631	14	188
3	Farfan	1936	8	242
4	Park	2375	7	339
5	Beasley	1630	6	272
6	Cocu	2448	6	408
7	Sibon	828	6	138
8	de Jong	939	5	188
9	Alex	2199	3	733
10	Vonlanthen	232	3	77
11	Ooijer	1972	2	986
12	Afellay	507	2	254
13	Lee	2790	1	2790
	Other		7	
	TOTAL		89	

KEY GOALKEEPER

Heurelho Gomes

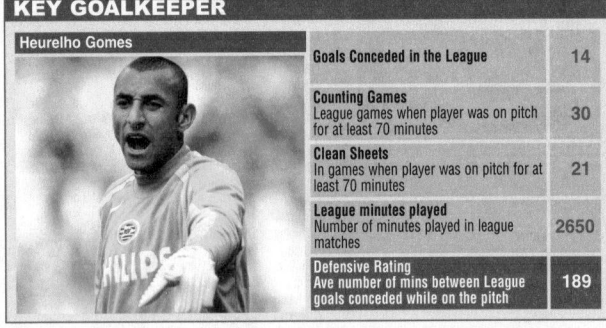

Goals Conceded in the League	14
Counting Games League games when player was on pitch for at least 70 minutes	30
Clean Sheets In games when player was on pitch for at least 70 minutes	21
League minutes played Number of minutes played in league matches	2650
Defensive Rating Ave number of mins between League goals conceded while on the pitch	189

DISCIPLINARY RECORDS

	PLAYER	YELLOW	RED	AVE
1	van Bommel	7	0	375
2	Sibon	2	0	414
3	Lucius	3	0	458
4	Bogelund	2	0	472
5	Cocu	4	1	489
6	Afellay	1	0	507
7	Alex	3	1	549
8	Vogel	3	0	654
9	Ooijer	3	0	657
10	Bouma	3	0	825
11	Farfan	2	0	968
12	Vennegoor	2	0	1093
13	Lee	1	0	2790
	Other	0	0	
	TOTAL	36	2	

TOP POINT EARNERS

	PLAYER	GAMES	AV PTS
1	Alex	22	2.73
2	Mark van Bommel	29	2.69
3	Jan Vennegoor	21	2.62
4	Heurelho Gomes	29	2.62
5	Wilfred Bouma	27	2.59
6	Johann Vogel	19	2.58
7	Theo Lucius	13	2.54
8	Young-Pyo Lee	31	2.52
9	Phillip Cocu	26	2.50
10	Ji-Sung Park	26	2.50
	CLUB AVERAGE:		2.56

TEAM OF THE SEASON

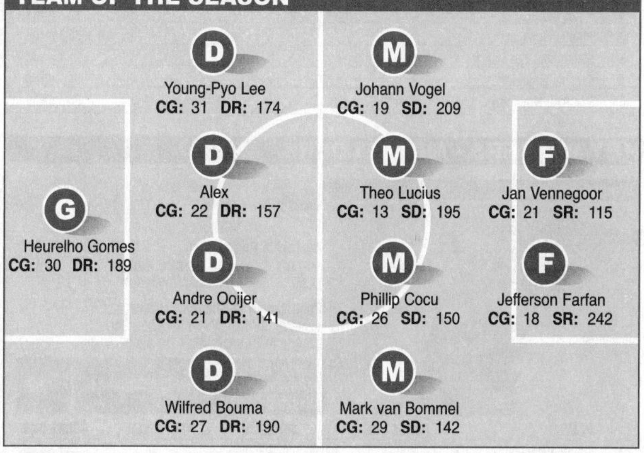
D
Young-Pyo Lee
CG: 31 DR: 174
M
Johann Vogel
CG: 19 SD: 209
D
Alex
CG: 22 DR: 157
M
Theo Lucius
CG: 13 SD: 195
F
Jan Vennegoor
CG: 21 SR: 115
G
Heurelho Gomes
CG: 30 DR: 189
D
Andre Ooijer
CG: 21 DR: 141
M
Phillip Cocu
CG: 26 SD: 150
F
Jefferson Farfan
CG: 18 SR: 242
D
Wilfred Bouma
CG: 27 DR: 190
M
Mark van Bommel
CG: 29 SD: 142

LEAGUE APPEARANCES, BOOKINGS AND CAPS

	AGE (on 01/07/05)	IN NAMED 18	APPEARANCES	COUNTING GAMES	MINUTES ON PITCH	YELLOW CARDS	RED CARDS	THIS SEASON	HOME COUNTRY
Goalkeepers									
Nathan Coe	21	1	0	0	0	0	0	-	Australia
Heurelho Gomes	24	33	30	29	2650	0	0	-	Brazil
Edwin Zoetebier	35	33	6	4	410	0	0	2	Holland (5)
Defenders									
Erik Addo	26	24	2	2	180	0	0	-	Ghana
Alex	23	30	27	22	2199	3	1	-	Brazil
Kasper Bogelund	24	22	14	10	945	2	0	3	Denmark (19)
Wilfred Bouma	27	30	28	27	2475	3	0	6	Holland (5)
Csaba Feher	29	16	4	2	210	0	0	-	Hungary
Michael Lamey	25	13	5	4	355	1	0	-	Holland
Young-Pyo Lee	28	32	31	31	2790	1	0	-	South Korea
Andre Ooijer	30	25	24	21	1972	3	0	3	Holland (5)
Midfielders									
Ibrahim Afellay	19	10	7	5	507	1	0	-	Holland
Ismael Aissati	16	3	0	0	0	0	0	-	Morocco
Phillip Cocu	34	29	29	26	2448	4	1	5	Holland (5)
John de Jong	28	17	15	8	939	0	0	-	Holland
Leandro	21	4	3	0	120	0	0	-	Brazil
Theo Lucius	28	29	22	13	1375	3	0	-	Holland
Ji-Sung Park	24	28	28	26	2375	0	0	-	South Korea
Mark van Bommel	28	30	30	29	2631	7	0	9	Holland (5)
R. van der Schaaf	26	13	4	0	88	0	0	-	Holland
Johann Vogel	28	29	27	19	1963	3	0	7	Switzerland (45)
Johan Vonlanthen	19	17	10	1	232	0	0	7	Switzerland (45)
Forwards									
DaMarcus Beasley	23	31	29	12	1630	0	0	-	United States
Jefferson Farfan	20	29	28	18	1936	2	0	-	Peru
Robert	24	9	6	0	164	0	0	-	Brazil
Gerald Sibon	31	32	19	5	828	2	0	-	Holland
Jan Vennegoor	26	28	28	21	2186	2	0	1	Holland (5)

SQUAD APPEARANCES

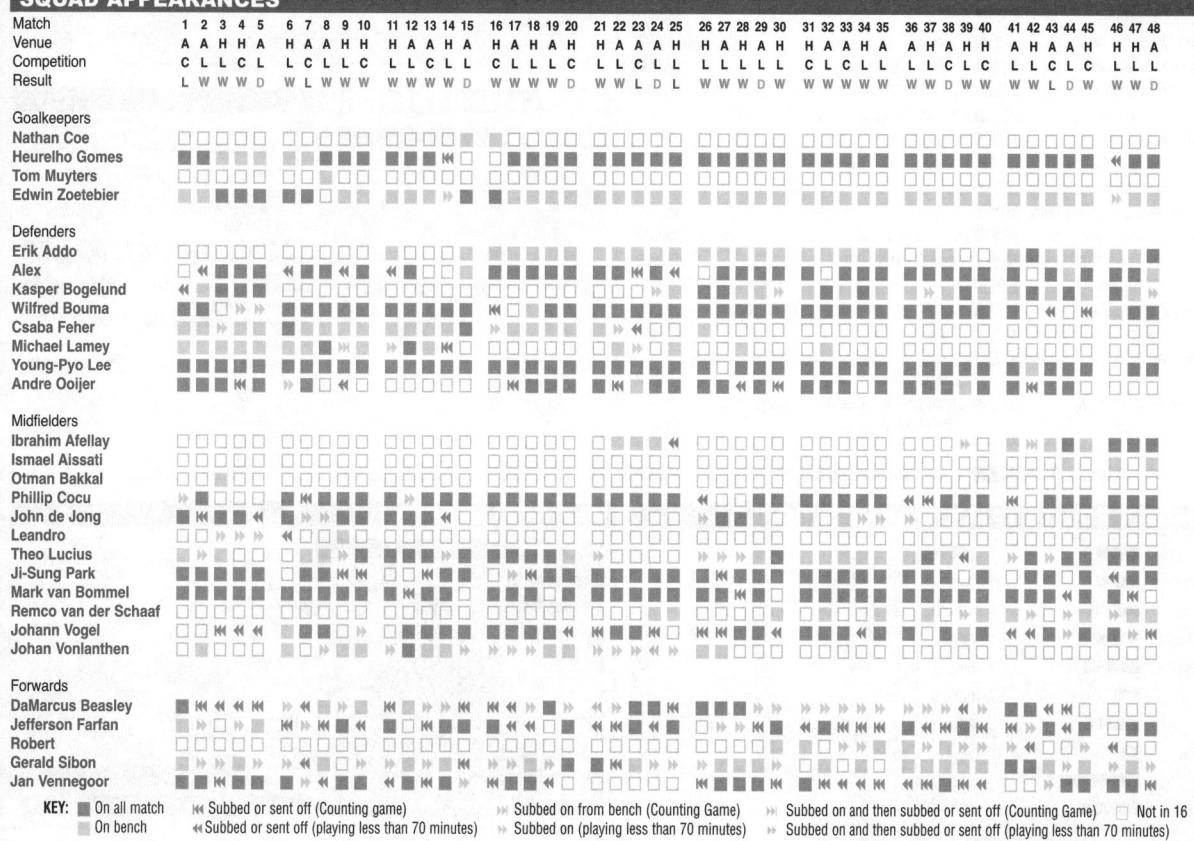

Match	1	2	3	4	5	6	7	8	9	10	11	12	13	14	15	16	17	18	19	20	21	22	23	24	25	26	27	28	29	30	31	32	33	34	35	36	37	38	39	40	41	42	43	44	45	46	47	48
Venue	A	A	H	H	A	H	A	A	H	H	H	A	A	H	A	H	A	H	A	H	H	A	A	A	H	H	A	H	A	H	H	A	A	H	A	A	H	A	H	H	A	H	A	A	H	H	H	A
Competition	C	L	L	C	L	L	C	L	L	C	L	L	C	L	L	C	L	L	L	C	L	L	C	L	L	L	L	L	L	L	C	L	C	L	L	L	L	C	L	C	L	L	C	L	C	L	L	L
Result	L	W	W	W	D	W	L	W	W	W	W	W	W	W	D	W	W	W	W	D	W	W	L	D	L	W	W	W	D	W	W	W	W	W	W	W	W	D	W	W	W	W	L	D	W	W	W	D

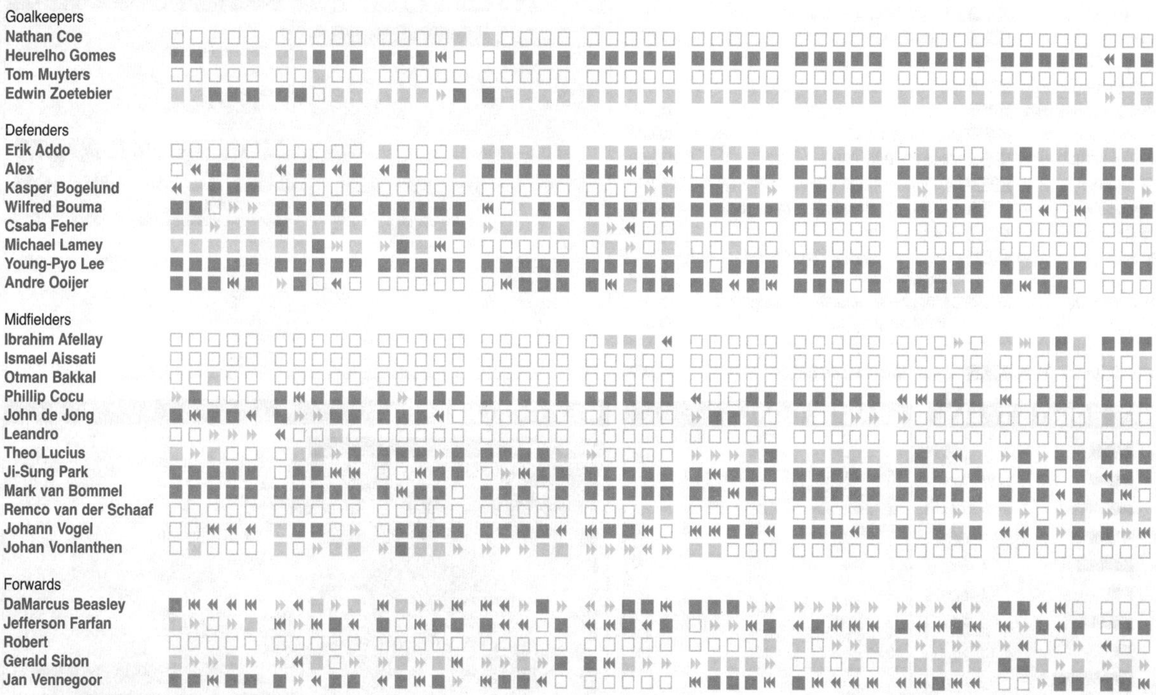
Goalkeepers
Nathan Coe
Heurelho Gomes
Tom Muyters
Edwin Zoetebier
Defenders
Erik Addo
Alex
Kasper Bogelund
Wilfred Bouma
Csaba Feher
Michael Lamey
Young-Pyo Lee
Andre Ooijer
Midfielders
Ibrahim Afellay
Ismael Aissati
Otman Bakkal
Phillip Cocu
John de Jong
Leandro
Theo Lucius
Ji-Sung Park
Mark van Bommel
Remco van der Schaaf
Johann Vogel
Johan Vonlanthen
Forwards
DaMarcus Beasley
Jefferson Farfan
Robert
Gerald Sibon
Jan Vennegoor

KEY: On all match / On bench / Subbed or sent off (Counting game) / Subbed or sent off (playing less than 70 minutes) / Subbed on from bench (Counting Game) / Subbed on (playing less than 70 minutes) / Subbed on and then subbed or sent off (Counting Game) / Subbed on and then subbed or sent off (playing less than 70 minutes) / Not in 16

AJAX

Final Position: **2nd**

KEY: Won / Drawn / Lost

No	Comp	Opponent	H/A	Res	Score	Scorers	Attendance
1	hosc	**Utrecht**	H	L	2-4	Pienaar 51; Sneijder 80	
2	hopr1	**Twente**	A	W	3-2	De Mul 30; van der Vaart 40; Ibrahimovic 46	13,000
3	hopr1	**NAC Breda**	H	W	6-2	Ibrahimovic 12,76; Zonneveld 41 og; Heitinga 51; Sneijder 70; Maxwell 86	46,000
4	hopr1	**Utrecht**	H	D	1-1	Pienaar 62	45,000
5	hopr1	**Den Haag**	A	D	3-3	Sonck 7; Pienaar 14; Boukhari 31	9,000
6	cl gc	**Juventus**	H	L	0-1		49,000
7	hopr1	**Den Bosch**	A	W	5-0	Sneijder 13; van der Vaart 41,90; Grygera 58; de Jong 73	7,000
8	hopr1	**Roda JC Kerk**	H	W	1-0	Anastasiou 88	48,000
9	cl gc	**Bayern Munich**	A	L	0-4		50,000
10	hopr1	**AZ Alkmaar**	A	D	0-0		8,000
11	hopr1	**Heerenveen**	H	L	1-3	Anastasiou 33	49,000
12	cl gc	**M. Tel-Aviv**	H	W	3-0	Sonck 3; de Jong 21; van der Vaart 33	48,000
13	hopr1	**PSV Eindhoven**	A	L	0-2		35,000
14	hopr1	**NEC Nijmegen**	H	W	1-0	van der Vaart 24	46,000
15	cl gc	**M. Tel-Aviv**	A	L	1-2	de Ridder 87	32,000
16	hopr1	**Willem II Tilb**	A	W	3-1	Rosales 36,43; Maxwell 62	13,000
17	hopr1	**Feyenoord**	H	D	1-1	Rosales 27	50,000
18	hopr1	**De Graafschap**	A	W	5-0	Escude 47,65; Rosales 53; Babel 66; Galasek 71	11,000
19	cl gc	**Juventus**	A	L	0-1		7,000
20	hopr1	**Roosendaal**	H	W	4-1	Anastasiou 13; Maxwell 33; Escude 51; Rosales 84	48,000
21	hopr1	**RKC Waalwijk**	A	W	2-1	Sneijder 11; Rosales 36	7,000
22	cl gc	**Bayern Munich**	H	D	2-2	Galasek 39; Mitea 63	50,000
23	hopr1	**Vitesse Arnhem**	H	W	1-0	Babel 87	48,000
24	hopr1	**Groningen**	A	W	4-0	Sneijder 58; Mitea 64; Babel 74,78	13,000
25	hopr1	**Utrecht**	A	W	2-0	Sneijder 66; Babel 90	23,000
26	hopr1	**Den Haag**	H	D	0-0		45,000
27	hopr1	**Twente**	H	L	1-2	Escude 6	47,000
28	hopr1	**NAC Breda**	A	W	2-1	Boukhari 3,88	15,000
29	uc3rl1	**Auxerre**	H	W	1-0	Maxwell 36	42,319
30	hopr1	**Den Bosch**	H	W	2-0	de Ridder 90; Boukhari 90	46,000
31	uc3rl2	**Auxerre**	A	L	1-3	Babel 37	12,000
32	hopr1	**Roda JC Kerk**	A	W	2-1	Charisteas 33; Escude 42	18,000
33	hopr1	**NEC Nijmegen**	A	W	1-0	Maduro 51	12,000
34	hopr1	**PSV Eindhoven**	H	L	0-4		51,000
35	hopr1	**Heerenveen**	A	L	1-2	Charisteas 34	20,000
36	hopr1	**Willem II Tilb**	H	W	2-0	Mitea 20; Babel 90	45,000
37	hopr1	**AZ Alkmaar**	H	W	4-2	de Jong 19,42; Sneijder 51; Pienaar 62	50,000
38	hopr1	**Feyenoord**	A	W	3-2	de Jong 57; Grygera 86; Maduro 90	49,000
39	hopr1	**De Graafschap**	H	W	1-0	Anastasiou 86	49,000
40	hopr1	**Roosendaal**	A	W	4-1	Pienaar 23; Sneijder 38; Charisteas 39; Galasek 62 pen	5,000
41	hopr1	**RKC Waalwijk**	H	W	4-0	Babel 34; Grygera 36; de Jong 77; Charisteas 90	49,000
42	hopr1	**Vitesse Arnhem**	A	W	2-0	Grygera 56; van der Vaart 80	23,000
43	hopr1	**Groningen**	H	W	2-1	van der Vaart 64; de Ridder 77	49,000

KEY PLAYERS - GOALSCORERS

Ryan Babel

Goals in the League	7
Contribution to Attacking Power Average number of minutes between League team goals while on pitch	36
Player Strike Rate Average number of minutes between League goals scored by player	182
Club Strike Rate Average number of minutes between League goals scored by club	41

	PLAYER	GOALS LGE	POWER	S RATE
1	Ryan Babel	7	36	182 mins
2	Mauro Rosales	6	55	288 mins
3	Rafael van der Vaart	6	49	293 mins
4	Wesley Sneijder	7	40	305 mins
5	Nourdin Boukhari	4	33	346 mins

KEY PLAYERS - MIDFIELDERS

Wesley Sneijder

Goals in the League	7
Defensive Rating Average number of mins between League goals conceded while on the pitch	97
Contribution to Attacking Power Average number of minutes between League team goals while on pitch	40
Scoring Difference Defensive Rating minus Contribution to Attacking Power	57

	PLAYER	GOALS LGE	DEF RATE	ATT POWER	SCORE DIFF
1	Wesley Sneijder	7	97	40	57 mins
2	Steven Pienaar	4	91	40	51 mins
3	Maxwell	3	81	42	39 mins
4	Rafael van der Vaart	6	88	49	39 mins

KEY PLAYERS - DEFENDERS

Zdenek Grygera

Goals Conceded in League	13
Clean Sheets In games when player was on pitch for at least 70 minutes	9
Defensive Rating Ave number of mins between League goals conceded while on the pitch	125
Club Defensive Rating Average number of mins between League goals conceded by the club this season	93

	PLAYER	CON LGE	CLEAN SHEETS	DEF RATE
1	Zdenek Grygera	13	9	125 mins
2	Nigel de Jong	22	12	105 mins
3	Hatem Trabelsi	23	10	93 mins
4	John Heitinga	24	11	89 mins
5	Julien Escude	26	10	89 mins

MONTHLY POINTS TALLY

AUGUST	7	78%
SEPTEMBER	7	78%
OCTOBER	4	33%
NOVEMBER	10	83%
DECEMBER	9	100%
JANUARY	4	67%
FEBRUARY	9	75%
MARCH	3	50%
APRIL	15	83%
MAY	9	100%

LEAGUE GOALS

	PLAYER	MINS	GOALS	AVE
1	Babel	1274	7	182
2	Sneijder	2135	7	305
3	van der Vaart	1760	6	293
4	Rosales	1725	6	288
5	de Jong	2305	5	461
6	Escude	2320	5	464
7	Charisteas	967	4	242
8	Boukhari	1385	4	346
9	Anastasiou	638	4	160
10	Pienaar	1813	4	453
11	Grygera	1620	4	405
12	Maxwell	2521	3	840
13	Ibrahimovic	251	3	84
	Other		12	
	TOTAL		74	

KEY GOALKEEPER

Hans Vonk

Goals Conceded in the League	13
Counting Games League games when player was on pitch for at least 70 minutes	17
Clean Sheets In games when player was on pitch for at least 70 minutes	8
League minutes played Number of minutes played in league matches	1610
Defensive Rating Ave number of mins between League goals conceded while on the pitch	124

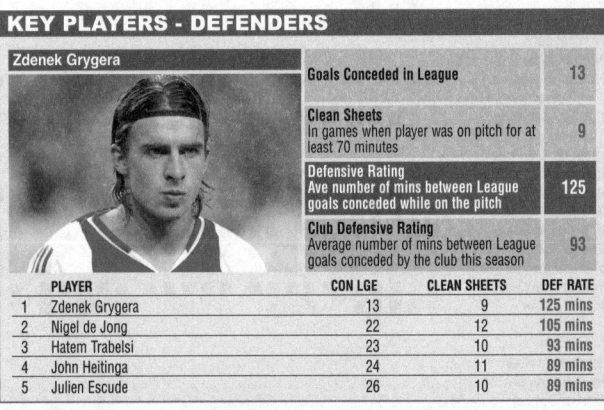

DISCIPLINARY RECORDS

	PLAYER	YELLOW	RED	AVE
1	Escude	6	0	386
2	Sneijder	5	0	427
3	van der Vaart	4	0	440
4	Pienaar	4	0	453
5	Boukhari	3	0	461
6	de Jong	4	0	576
7	Obodai	1	0	616
8	Heitinga	3	0	708
9	Trabelsi	3	0	715
10	Grygera	2	0	810
11	Galasek	1	0	991
12	Maxwell	2	0	1260
13	Rosales	1	0	1725
	Other	0	0	
	TOTAL	39	0	

TOP POINT EARNERS

	PLAYER	GAMES	AV PTS
1	Zdenek Grygera	18	2.56
2	Hedwiges Maduro	12	2.50
3	Ryan Babel	12	2.50
4	Julien Escude	24	2.46
5	Nordin Boukhari	12	2.42
6	Hans Vonk	17	2.41
7	Nigel de Jong	24	2.38
8	Steven Pienaar	20	2.25
9	Hatem Trabelsi	24	2.21
10	Rafael van der Vaart	19	2.21
	CLUB AVERAGE:		2.44

LEAGUE APPEARANCES, BOOKINGS AND CAPS

	AGE (on 01/07/05)	IN NAMED 18	APPEARANCES	COUNTING GAMES	MINUTES ON PITCH	YELLOW CARDS	RED CARDS	THIS SEASON	HOME COUNTRY
Goalkeepers									
Bogdan L. Lobont	27	13	7	5	527	0	0	-	Romania
M. Stekelenburg	22	28	11	9	923	0	0	4	Holland (5)
Hans Vonk	35	27	19	17	1610	0	0	-	South Africa
Defenders									
Nigel de Jong	20	33	31	24	2305	4	0	5	Holland (5)
Urby Emanuelson	19	10	3	1	147	0	0	-	Holland
Julien Escude	25	32	28	24	2320	6	0	-	France
Zdenek Grygera	25	27	18	18	1620	2	0	4	Czech Republic (2)
John Heitinga	21	28	26	22	2125	3	0	5	Holland (5)
Hedwiges Maduro	20	15	12	12	1080	0	0	-	Holland
John O'Brien	27	3	1	1	78	0	0	-	United States
Hatem Trabelsi	26	24	24	24	2146	3	0	-	Tunisia
Midfielders									
Stanley Aborah	18	4	4	0	96	0	0	-	Belgium
Tomas Galasek	32	15	13	11	991	1	0	4	Czech Republic (2)
Rasmus Lindgren	20	9	4	3	271	1	0	-	Sweden
Maxwell	23	29	29	28	2521	2	0	-	Brazil
Anthony Obodai	22	24	13	4	616	1	0	-	Ghana
Steven Pienaar	23	24	24	20	1813	4	0	-	South Africa
Wesley Sneijder	21	30	30	19	2135	5	0	6	Holland (5)
Rafael van der Vaart	22	24	22	19	1760	4	0	8	Holland (5)
Forwards									
Ioannis Anastasiou	32	31	14	3	638	0	0	-	Greece
Ryan Babel	19	23	20	12	1274	0	0	-	Holland
Nourdin Boukhari	25	30	23	12	1385	3	0	-	Morocco
Angelos Charisteas	25	14	13	8	967	0	0	-	Greece
Tom De Mul	19	7	6	4	411	0	0	1	Belgium (42)
Daniel de Ridder	21	31	15	2	430	0	0	-	Holland
Zlatan Ibrahimovic	23	3	3	3	251	1	0	6	Sweden (13)
Nicolae Mitea	20	32	21	7	1029	0	0	-	Romania
Mauro Rosales	24	22	22	18	1725	1	0	4	Argentina (3)
Wesley Sonck	26	10	9	3	466	0	0	4	Belgium (42)

TEAM OF THE SEASON

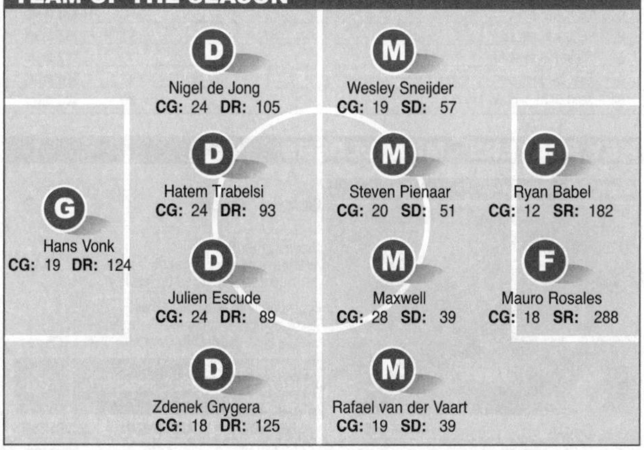

D
Nigel de Jong
CG: 24 DR: 105
D
Hatem Trabelsi
CG: 24 DR: 93
D
Julien Escude
CG: 24 DR: 89
D
Zdenek Grygera
CG: 18 DR: 125
G
Hans Vonk
CG: 19 DR: 124
M
Wesley Sneijder
CG: 19 SD: 57
M
Steven Pienaar
CG: 20 SD: 51
M
Maxwell
CG: 28 SD: 39
M
Rafael van der Vaart
CG: 19 SD: 39
F
Ryan Babel
CG: 12 SR: 182
F
Mauro Rosales
CG: 18 SR: 288

SQUAD APPEARANCES

Match	1	2	3	4	5	6	7	8	9	10	11	12	13	14	15	16	17	18	19	20	21	22	23	24	25	26	27	28	29	30	31	32	33	34	35	36	37	38	39	40	41	42	43
Venue	H	A	H	H	A	H	A	H	A	A	H	H	A	H	A	A	H	A	A	H	A	H	H	A	A	H	H	A	H	H	A	A	A	H	A	H	H	A	H	A	H	A	H
Competition	O	L	L	L	L	C	L	L	C	L	L	C	L	L	C	L	L	L	C	L	L	C	L	L	L	L	L	L	E	L	E	L	L	L	L	L	L	L	L	L	L	L	L
Result	L	W	W	D	D	L	W	W	L	D	L	W	L	W	L	W	D	W	L	W	W	D	W	W	W	D	L	W	W	W	L	W	W	L	L	W	W	W	W	W	W	W	W

Goalkeepers
- Bogdan Lonut Lobont
- Maarten Stekelenburg
- Hans Vonk

Defenders
- Nigel de Jong
- Urby Emanuelson
- Julien Escude
- Zdenek Grygera
- John Heitinga
- Hedwiges Maduro
- John O'Brien
- Hatem Trabelsi

Midfielders
- Stanley Aborah
- Tomas Galasek
- Rasmus Lindgren
- Maxwell
- Anthony Obodai
- Steven Pienaar
- Wesley Sneijder
- Rafael van der Vaart

Forwards
- Ioannis Anastasiou
- Ryan Babel
- Nourdin Boukhari
- Angelos Charisteas
- Tom De Mul
- Daniel de Ridder
- Zlatan Ibrahimovic
- Nicolae Mitea
- Mauro Rosales
- Wesley Sonck

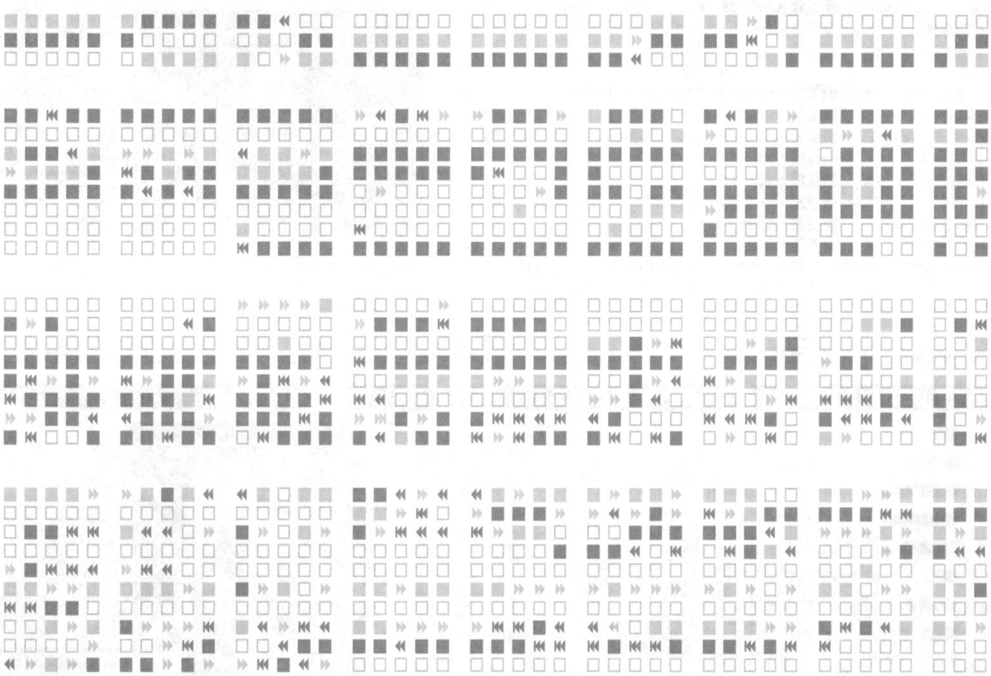

KEY: On all match | On bench | Subbed or sent off (Counting game) | Subbed or sent off (playing less than 70 minutes) | Subbed on from bench (Counting Game) | Subbed on (playing less than 70 minutes) | Subbed on and then subbed or sent off (Counting Game) | Subbed on and then subbed or sent off (playing less than 70 minutes) | Not in 16

AZ ALKMAAR

Final Position: **3rd**

KEY: ☐Won ☐Drawn ☐Lost

							Attendance
1	hopr1	**Heerenveen**	H	D	1-1	Huysegems 12	8,000
2	hopr1	**PSV Eindhoven**	A	L	1-5	Ramzi 85	33,000
3	hopr1	**NEC Nijmegen**	A	W	2-1	Landzaat 14; Perez 77	12,000
4	hopr1	**Den Bosch**	H	W	5-0	Elkhattabi 19; Perez 23,31; Landzaat 57; Huysegems 83	8,000
5	uc1rl1	**PAOK Salonika**	A	W	3-2	van Galen 15; Landzaat 36; Meerdink 50	9,000
6	hopr1	**Roda JC Kerk**	A	D	1-1	Landzaat 1	13,000
7	hopr1	**Willem II Tilb**	H	W	3-1	Perez 2; van Galen 10; Landzaat 81	8,000
8	uc1rl2	**PAOK Salonika**	H	W	2-1	Buskermolen 10; Mathijsen 72	7,923
9	hopr1	**Ajax**	H	D	0-0		8,000
10	hopr1	**De Graafschap**	A	W	3-1	Landzaat 43 pen; Huysegems 58; Nelisse 86	11,000
11	hopr1	**Vitesse Arnhem**	A	W	3-0	Buskermolen 31; van Galen 48; Perez 51	17,000
12	hopr1	**Feyenoord**	H	W	4-1	Mathijsen 4; Perez 62,76; Nelisse 88	8,000
13	ucgpf	**Auxerre**	H	W	2-0	Huysegems 4,19	8,123
14	hopr1	**Utrecht**	H	W	4-0	Meerdink 3; Perez 50; Nelisse 85; Lindenbergh 89	8,000
15	hopr1	**NAC Breda**	A	W	3-0	Meerdink 34; Sektioui 88,90	15,000
16	hopr1	**RKC Waalwijk**	H	W	3-0	Landzaat 16; van Galen 51; Huysegems 90	8,000
17	ucgpf	**Amica Wronki**	A	W	3-1	van Galen 13; Meerdink 37; Huysegems 39	2,500
18	hopr1	**Groningen**	A	W	2-1	van Galen 17; Opdam 73	13,000
19	ucgpf	**Rangers**	H	W	1-0	Landzaat 7	8,000
20	hopr1	**Den Haag**	H	W	2-0	Meerdink 17; Elkhattabi 73	8,000
21	hopr1	**Twente**	H	W	5-0	Touzani 6 og,38 og; Perez 59,87; Landzaat 67 pen	8,000
22	ucgpf	**Grazer AK**	A	L	0-2		13,000
23	hopr1	**Roosendaal**	A	W	2-0	Nelisse 24; Landzaat 62	5,000
24	hopr1	**NEC Nijmegen**	H	D	1-1	Perez 45	8,000
25	hopr1	**Den Bosch**	A	W	1-0	Huysegems 18	6,000
26	hopr1	**Heerenveen**	A	W	3-1	Huysegems 40; Sektioui 87; Lindenbergh 90	18,000
27	hopr1	**PSV Eindhoven**	H	D	0-0		9,000
28	uc3rl1	**Alem Aachen**	A	D	0-0		38,000
29	hopr1	**Roda JC Kerk**	H	D	1-1	de Cler 26	8,000
30	uc3rl2	**Alem Aachen**	H	W	2-1	van Galen 62; Mathijsen 81	8,000
31	hopr1	**Willem II Tilb**	A	W	3-1	van Galen 45,68; Lindenbergh 55	12,000
32	uc4rl1	**S Donetsk**	A	W	3-1	Nelisse 28; Mathijsen 52; Perez 90 pen	20,000
33	hopr1	**De Graafschap**	H	W	3-2	Kromkamp 40; Landzaat 45; Elkhattabi 70	8,000
34	uc4rl2	**S Donetsk**	H	W	2-1	van Galen 9; Meerdink 65	8,000
35	hopr1	**Vitesse Arnhem**	H	W	3-0	Jaliens 44; Landzaat 80 pen; Lindenbergh 88	9,000
36	hopr1	**Feyenoord**	A	L	2-4	Nelisse 49; Buskermolen 88	47,000
37	ucqfl1	**Villarreal**	A	W	2-1	Landzaat 12; Nelisse 74	10,000
38	hopr1	**Ajax**	A	L	2-4	Nelisse 38; Sektioui 86	50,000
39	ucqfl2	**Villarreal**	H	D	1-1	Perez 8	9,000
40	hopr1	**NAC Breda**	H	D	1-1	Sektioui 6	8,000
41	hopr1	**Utrecht**	A	L	2-3	van Galen 35; Perez 61	20,000
42	hopr1	**RKC Waalwijk**	A	L	1-2	Opdam 24	7,000
43	ucsfl1	**Sp Lisbon**	A	L	1-2	Landzaat 35	35,000
44	hopr1	**Groningen**	H	W	2-1	Lindenbergh 16; Ramzi 75	8,000
45	ucsfl2	**Sp Lisbon**	H	W	3-2	Perez 6; Huysegems 79; Jaliens 109	9,000
46	hopr1	**Den Haag**	A	L	1-2	Perez 57	6,000
47	hopr1	**Twente**	A	L	0-3		13,000
48	hopr1	**Roosendaal**	H	L	1-3	Huysegems 89	8,000

KEY PLAYERS - GOALSCORERS

Kenneth Perez

DSB BANK

Goals in the League	13
Contribution to Attacking Power Average number of minutes between League team goals while on pitch	40
Player Strike Rate Average number of minutes between League goals scored by player	174
Club Strike Rate Average number of minutes between League goals scored by club	43

	PLAYER	GOALS LGE	POWER	S RATE
1	Kenneth Perez	13	40	174 mins
2	Denny Landzaat	10	41	292 mins
3	Stein Huysegems	7	43	312 mins
4	Olaf Lindenbergh	5	44	360 mins
5	Martijn Meerdink	3	39	473 mins

KEY PLAYERS - MIDFIELDERS

Martijn Meerdink

DSB BAN

Goals in the League	3
Defensive Rating Average number of mins between League goals conceded while on the pitch	142
Contribution to Attacking Power Average number of minutes between League team goals while on pitch	39
Scoring Difference Defensive Rating minus Contribution to Attacking Power	103

	PLAYER	GOALS LGE	DEF RATE	ATT POWER	SCORE DIFF
1	Martijn Meerdink	3	142	39	103 mins
2	Denny Landzaat	10	75	42	33 mins
3	Michael Buskermolen	2	81	49	32 mins
4	Olaf Lindenbergh	5	55	44	11 mins

KEY PLAYERS - DEFENDERS

Joris Mathijsen

Goals Conceded in League	19
Clean Sheets In games when player was on pitch for at least 70 minutes	11
Defensive Rating Ave number of mins between League goals conceded while on the pitch	107
Club Defensive Rating Average number of mins between League goals conceded by the club this season	75

	PLAYER	CON LGE	CLEAN SHEETS	DEF RATE
1	Joris Mathijsen	19	11	107 mins
2	Jan Kromkamp	27	10	88 mins
3	Tim de Cler	34	12	83 mins
4	Barry Opdam	34	11	83 mins
5	Kew Jaliens	29	3	49 mins

MONTHLY POINTS TALLY

AUGUST	4	44%
SEPTEMBER	7	78%
OCTOBER	10	83%
NOVEMBER	12	100%
DECEMBER	9	100%
JANUARY	4	67%
FEBRUARY	8	67%
MARCH	6	100%
APRIL	1	7%
MAY	3	25%

LEAGUE GOALS

	PLAYER	MINS	GOALS	AVE
1	Perez	2257	13	174
2	Landzaat	2916	10	292
3	Huysegems	2183	7	312
4	van Galen	1444	7	206
5	Nelisse	1062	6	177
6	Lindenbergh	1801	5	360
7	Sektioui	1516	5	303
8	Elkhattabi	1116	3	372
9	Meerdink	1420	3	473
10	Buskermolen	1777	2	889
11	Ramzi	1149	2	575
12	Opdam	2805	2	1403
13	Jaliens	1413	1	1413
	Other		5	
	TOTAL		71	

KEY GOALKEEPER

Henk Timmer

Goals Conceded in the League	40
Counting Games League games when player was on pitch for at least 70 minutes	33
Clean Sheets In games when player was on pitch for at least 70 minutes	12
League minutes played Number of minutes played in league matches	2980
Defensive Rating Ave number of mins between League goals conceded while on the pitch	75

DISCIPLINARY RECORDS

	PLAYER	YELLOW	RED	AVE
1	van Galen	6	0	240
2	Jaliens	2	1	471
3	Meerdink	3	0	473
4	Opdam	5	0	561
5	de Cler	4	1	563
6	Kromkamp	4	0	594
7	Lindenbergh	3	0	600
8	Perez	3	0	752
9	Nelisse	1	0	1062
10	Huysegems	2	0	1091
11	Sektioui	1	0	1516
12	Buskermolen	1	0	1777
13	Landzaat	1	0	2916
	Other	1	0	
	TOTAL	37	2	

TOP POINT EARNERS

	PLAYER	GAMES	AV PTS
1	Martijn Meerdink	14	2.57
2	Joris Mathijsen	22	2.41
3	Kenneth Perez	21	2.14
4	Jan Kromkamp	26	2.12
5	Stein Huysegems	19	2.11
6	Tim de Cler	31	2.03
7	Denny Landzaat	32	1.97
8	Barry Opdam	29	1.97
9	Michael Buskermolen	17	1.94
10	Henk Timmer	33	1.85
	CLUB AVERAGE:		1.88

TEAM OF THE SEASON

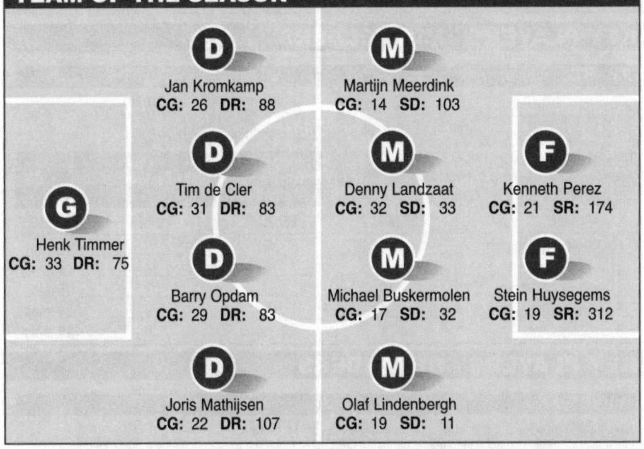
D
Jan Kromkamp
CG: 26 DR: 88
M
Martijn Meerdink
CG: 14 SD: 103
D
Tim de Cler
CG: 31 DR: 83
M
Denny Landzaat
CG: 32 SD: 33
F
Kenneth Perez
CG: 21 SR: 174
G
Henk Timmer
CG: 33 DR: 75
D
Barry Opdam
CG: 29 DR: 83
M
Michael Buskermolen
CG: 17 SD: 32
F
Stein Huysegems
CG: 19 SR: 312
D
Joris Mathijsen
CG: 22 DR: 107
M
Olaf Lindenbergh
CG: 19 SD: 11

LEAGUE APPEARANCES, BOOKINGS AND CAPS

	AGE (on 01/07/05)	IN NAMED 18	APPEARANCES	COUNTING GAMES	MINUTES ON PITCH	YELLOW CARDS	RED CARDS	THIS SEASON	HOME COUNTRY
Goalkeepers									
Henk Timmer	33	34	34	33	2980	1	0	3	Holland (5)
Theo Zwarthoed	22	34	1	1	80	0	0	-	Holland
Defenders									
Tim de Cler	26	33	32	31	2818	4	1	-	Holland
J. Fortes Rodriguez	33	11	0	0	0	0	0	-	Spain
Kew Jaliens	26	33	22	13	1413	2	1	-	Holland
Jan Kromkamp	24	28	27	26	2376	4	0	5	Holland (5)
Joris Mathijsen	25	26	25	22	2035	0	0	4	Holland (5)
Barry Opdam	29	33	33	29	2805	5	0	-	Holland
Juha Reini	30	2	0	0	0	0	0	-	Finland
Ron Vlaar	20	14	3	3	270	0	0	-	Holland
Tom Zoontjes	20	6	1	1	90	0	0	-	Holland
Midfielders									
Michael Buskermolen	33	29	23	17	1777	1	0	-	Holland
Christy Janga	19	1	0	0	0	0	0	-	Holland
Denny Landzaat	29	34	33	32	2916	1	0	9	Holland (5)
Olaf Lindenbergh	31	29	23	19	1801	3	0	-	Holland
Miel Mans	27	4	0	0	0	0	0	-	Holland
Haris Medunjanin	20	10	3	1	101	0	0	-	Holland
Martijn Meerdink	28	23	21	14	1420	3	0	-	Holland
Tarik Sektioui	28	32	30	10	1516	1	0	-	Morocco
Barry van Galen	35	28	22	7	1444	6	0	1	Holland (5)
Forwards									
Ali Elkhattabi	28	30	22	9	1116	0	0	-	Morocco
Stein Huysegems	23	34	33	19	2183	2	0	-	Belgium
Robin Nelisse	27	32	26	7	1062	1	0	-	Holland
Kenneth Perez	30	32	30	21	2257	3	0	6	Denmark (19)
Adil Ramzi	27	33	24	8	1149	0	0	-	Morocco
Arjan Wisse	20	6	1	0	27	0	0	-	Holland

SQUAD APPEARANCES

Match	1	2	3	4	5	6	7	8	9	10	11	12	13	14	15	16	17	18	19	20	21	22	23	24	25	26	27	28	29	30	31	32	33	34	35	36	37	38	39	40	41	42	43	44	45	46	47	48
Venue	H	A	A	H	A	A	H	H	H	A	A	H	H	H	A	H	A	A	H	H	H	A	A	H	A	A	H	A	H	H	A	A	H	H	H	A	A	A	H	H	A	A	A	H	H	A	A	H
Competition	L	L	L	L	E	L	L	E	L	L	L	L	E	L	L	L	E	L	E	L	L	E	L	L	L	L	L	E	L	E	L	E	L	E	L	L	E	L	E	L	L	L	E	L	E	L	L	L
Result	D	L	W	W	W	D	W	W	D	W	W	W	W	W	W	W	W	W	W	W	W	L	W	D	W	W	D	D	D	W	W	W	W	W	W	L	W	L	D	D	L	L	L	W	W	L	L	L

Goalkeepers
Henk Timmer
Theo Zwarthoed

Defenders
Tim de Cler
Jose Fortes Rodriguez
Kew Jaliens
Jan Kromkamp
Joris Mathijsen
Barry Opdam
Juha Reini
Ron Vlaar
Tom Zoontjes

Midfielders
Michael Buskermolen
Christy Janga
Denny Landzaat
Olaf Lindenbergh
Miel Mans
Haris Medunjanin
Martijn Meerdink
Tarik Sektioui
Barry van Galen

Forwards
Ali Elkhattabi
Stein Huysegems
Robin Nelisse
Kenneth Perez
Adil Ramzi
Arjan Wisse

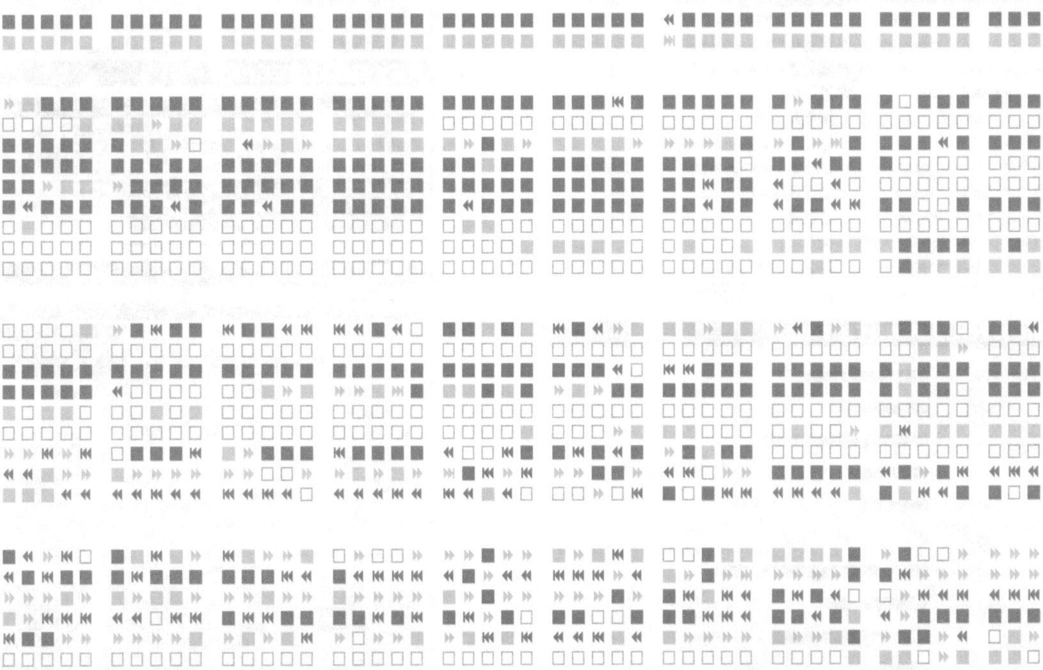

KEY: On all match | On bench | Subbed or sent off (Counting game) | Subbed or sent off (playing less than 70 minutes) | Subbed on from bench (Counting Game) | Subbed on (playing less than 70 minutes) | Subbed on and then subbed or sent off (Counting Game) | Subbed on and then subbed or sent off (playing less than 70 minutes) | Not in 16

FEYENOORD

Final Position: **4th**

KEY: Won Drawn Lost

							Attendance
1	hopr1	**De Graafschap**	H	W	6-1	Kuijt 10,37,51; Castelen 54,57; Kalou 72	42,000
2	hopr1	**Willem II Tilb**	A	W	4-0	Kalou 39; Ono 54; Ghali 74; Kuijt 90	14,000
3	hopr1	**Vitesse Arnhem**	A	D	1-1	Saidi 25	17,000
4	hopr1	**Twente**	H	W	3-1	Ono 44; Kalou 52,77	42,000
5	uc1rl1	**Odd Grenland**	A	W	1-0	Ono 74	4,125
6	hopr1	**Utrecht**	H	L	0-3		38,000
7	hopr1	**Roosendaal**	A	W	4-0	Kalou 6,61; Goor 33; Kuijt 66	5,000
8	uc1rl2	**Odd Grenland**	H	W	4-1	Bosschaart 2; Kuijt 45; Goor 74; Kalou 90	18,500
9	hopr1	**Den Bosch**	H	W	4-2	Kalou 23,59; Kuijt 35 pen; Castelen 68	36,000
10	hopr1	**Roda JC Kerk**	A	W	2-0	Kuijt 60; Kalou 90	17,000
11	ucgpa	**Hearts**	H	W	3-0	Kuijt 21,83; Goor 58	26,000
12	hopr1	**RKC Waalwijk**	H	W	4-0	Castelen 10; Goor 65,85; Kuijt 69	41,000
13	hopr1	**AZ Alkmaar**	A	L	1-4	Kromkamp 42 og	8,000
14	ucgpa	**Ferencvaros**	A	D	1-1	Kalou 62	28,000
15	hopr1	**NAC Breda**	H	W	4-0	Kuijt 14; Goor 46,90; Buffel 86	37,000
16	hopr1	**Ajax**	A	D	1-1	Kuijt 44	50,000
17	hopr1	**Groningen**	H	L	1-2	Kuijt 38	40,000
18	hopr1	**Heerenveen**	A	D	2-2	Buffel 40; Kuijt 71	18,000
19	ucgpa	**Schalke**	H	W	2-1	Kalou 32,41	48,000
20	hopr1	**NEC Nijmegen**	H	W	2-1	Kuijt 19; Kalou 85	36,000
21	hopr1	**PSV Eindhoven**	H	D	3-3	Kalou 49; Ono 82; Goor 90	45,000
22	ucgpa	**Basel**	A	L	0-1		25,660
23	hopr1	**Den Haag**	A	L	0-2		8,000
24	hopr1	**Vitesse Arnhem**	H	L	1-2	Kuijt 49	40,000
25	hopr1	**Twente**	A	D	0-0		13,000
26	hopr1	**De Graafschap**	A	W	7-2	Kuijt 4,32,67; Castelen 25; Lazovic 47,52; Hofs 61	12,000
27	hopr1	**Willem II Tilb**	H	W	7-0	Gibbs 23; Hofs 28,43,61; Kuijt 40 pen,52; Basto 88	37,000
28	uc3rl1	**Sp Lisbon**	A	L	1-2	Goor 9	19,000
29	hopr1	**Utrecht**	A	W	2-0	Castelen 10; Kuijt 57	23,000
30	uc3rl2	**Sp Lisbon**	H	L	1-2	Hofs 88	30,000
31	hopr1	**Roosendaal**	H	W	3-0	Kuijt 25; Kalou 80; Ono 83	35,000
32	hopr1	**Roda JC Kerk**	H	W	4-1	Ono 6; Castelen 23; Kuijt 70 pen; Kalou 85	39,000
33	hopr1	**RKC Waalwijk**	A	W	4-2	Castelen 24,90; Kalou 32; Lazovic 89	7,000
34	hopr1	**AZ Alkmaar**	H	W	4-2	Kalou 19,47,64; Castelen 43	47,000
35	hopr1	**NAC Breda**	A	W	2-0	Kalou 43; Ono 82	15,000
36	hopr1	**Den Bosch**	A	L	1-4	Bahia 63	7,000
37	hopr1	**Ajax**	H	L	2-3	Kalou 48; Kuijt 80	49,000
38	hopr1	**Groningen**	A	W	2-0	Bahia 35; Hofs 89	13,000
39	hopr1	**Heerenveen**	H	L	1-3	Kuijt 37	41,000
40	hopr1	**NEC Nijmegen**	A	L	0-2		12,000
41	hopr1	**PSV Eindhoven**	A	L	2-4	Kuijt 22,51	33,000
42	hopr1	**Den Haag**	H	W	6-3	Goor 14; Ono 23; Kalou 38; Kuijt 46,78,86	35,000

MONTHLY POINTS TALLY

AUGUST	7	78%
SEPTEMBER	6	67%
OCTOBER	9	75%
NOVEMBER	5	42%
DECEMBER	4	44%
JANUARY	1	17%
FEBRUARY	12	100%
MARCH	6	100%
APRIL	9	60%
MAY	3	25%

KEY PLAYERS - GOALSCORERS

Dirk Kuijt

Goals in the League	29	**Player Strike Rate** Average number of minutes between League goals scored by player	102
Contribution to Attacking Power Average number of minutes between League team goals while on pitch	34	**Club Strike Rate** Average number of minutes between League goals scored by club	34

	PLAYER	LGE GOALS	POWER	STRIKE RATE
1	Dirk Kuijt	29	34	102 mins
2	Salomon Kalou	20	36	116 mins
3	Romeo Castelen	10	31	244 mins
4	Shinji Ono	7	35	247 mins
5	Bart Goor	7	33	416 mins

KEY PLAYERS - MIDFIELDERS

Pascal Bosschaart

Goals in the League	0	**Contribution to Attacking Power** Average number of minutes between League team goals while on pitch	38
Defensive Rating Average number of mins between League goals conceded while on the pitch	79	**Scoring Difference** Defensive Rating minus Contribution to Attacking Power	41

	PLAYER	LGE GOALS	DEF RATE	POWER	SCORE DIFF
1	Pascal Bosschaart	0	79	38	41 mins
2	Bart Goor	7	61	33	28 mins
3	Romeo Castelen	10	60	32	28 mins
4	Corey Gibbs	1	53	29	24 mins
5	Shinji Ono	7	54	36	18 mins

KEY PLAYERS - DEFENDERS

Patrick Paauwe

Goals Conceded Number of League goals conceded while the player was on the pitch	25	**Clean Sheets** In games when player was on pitch for at least 70 minutes	6
Defensive Rating Ave number of mins between League goals conceded while on the pitch	69	**Club Defensive Rating** Average number of mins between League goals conceded by the club this season	59

	PLAYER	CON LGE	CLEAN SHEETS	DEF RATE
1	Patrick Paauwe	25	6	69 mins
2	Patrick Mtiliga	16	3	68 mins
3	Karim Saidi	42	8	58 mins
4	Bruno Basto	30	5	51 mins
5	Alexander Ostlund	28	4	49 mins

KEY GOALKEEPER

Gabor Babos

Goals Conceded in the League	37	**Counting Games** League games when player was on pitch for at least 70 minutes	23
Defensive Rating Ave number of mins between League goals conceded while on the pitch	56	**Clean Sheets** In games when player was on pitch for at least 70 minutes	7

LEAGUE GOALS

Dirk Kuijt

Minutes on the pitch	2955	**Goals in the League**	29
League average (mins between goals)	102		

	PLAYER	MINS	GOALS	AVE
1	Kuijt	2955	29	102
2	Kalou	2318	20	116
3	Castelen	2442	10	244
4	Ono	1726	7	247
5	Goor	2912	7	416
6	Hofs	895	5	179
7	Lazovic	637	3	212
8	Buffel	578	2	289
9	Bahia	384	2	192
10	Gibbs	1281	1	1281
11	Basto	1531	1	1531
12	Saidi	2448	1	2448
	Other		2	
	TOTAL		90	

DISCIPLINARY RECORDS

	PLAYER	YELLOW	RED	AVE
1	Hofs	4	0	223
2	Lazovic	1	1	318
3	Bosschaart	2	2	432
4	Ono	3	0	575
5	Buffel	1	0	578
6	Saidi	4	0	612
7	Song	0	1	874
8	Mtiliga	1	0	1080
9	Kalou	2	0	1159
10	Ghali	1	0	1269
11	Gibbs	1	0	1281
12	Basto	1	0	1531
13	Paauwe	1	0	1733
	Other	3	0	
	TOTAL	25	4	

TOP POINT EARNERS

	PLAYER	GAMES	AV PTS
1	Romeo Castelen	24	2.13
2	Patrick Paauwe	19	1.95
3	Pascal Bosschaart	17	1.94
4	Corey Gibbs	13	1.92
5	Bruno Basto	17	1.88
6	Shinji Ono	16	1.88
7	Bart Goor	31	1.87
8	Karim Saidi	25	1.84
9	Dirk Kuijt	33	1.79
10	Patrick Mtiliga	12	1.75
	CLUB AVERAGE:		1.82

TEAM OF THE SEASON

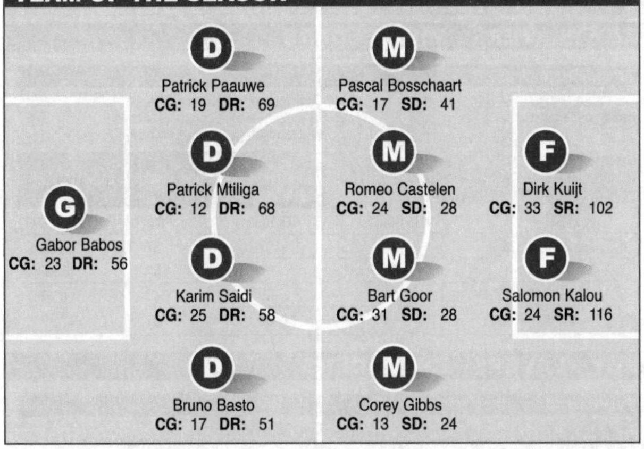

G
Gabor Babos
CG: 23 DR: 56
D
Patrick Paauwe
CG: 19 DR: 69
D
Patrick Mtiliga
CG: 12 DR: 68
D
Karim Saidi
CG: 25 DR: 58
D
Bruno Basto
CG: 17 DR: 51
M
Pascal Bosschaart
CG: 17 SD: 41
M
Romeo Castelen
CG: 24 SD: 28
M
Bart Goor
CG: 31 SD: 28
M
Corey Gibbs
CG: 13 SD: 24
F
Dirk Kuijt
CG: 33 SR: 102
F
Salomon Kalou
CG: 24 SR: 116

LEAGUE APPEARANCES, BOOKINGS AND CAPS

	AGE (on 01/07/05)	IN NAMED 18	APPEARANCES	COUNTING GAMES	MINUTES ON PITCH	YELLOW CARDS	RED CARDS	THIS SEASON	HOME COUNTRY
Goalkeepers									
Gabor Babos	30	31	23	23	2070	1	0	-	Hungary
Patrick Lodewijks	38	25	10	10	900	0	0	-	Holland
Zbigniew Malkowski	27	11	1	1	90	0	0	-	Poland
Defenders									
Bahia	21	15	5	4	384	1	0	-	Brazil
Bruno Basto	27	30	18	17	1531	1	0	-	Portugal
Christian Gyan	26	13	8	5	563	0	0	-	Ghana
Glenn Loovens	21	16	6	1	238	2	0	-	Holland
Patrick Mtiliga	24	17	12	12	1080	1	0	-	Denmark
Alexander Ostlund	26	16	16	15	1375	0	0	8	Sweden (13)
Patrick Paauwe	29	24	20	19	1733	1	0	-	Holland
Karim Saidi	21	31	30	25	2448	4	0	-	Tunisia
Chong-Gug Song	26	11	10	10	874	0	1	-	South Korea
Gianni Zuiverloon	18	26	10	3	428	2	0	-	Holland
Midfielders									
Pascal Bosschaart	25	28	23	17	1729	2	2	-	Holland
Thomas Buffel	24	17	15	4	578	1	0	7	Belgium (42)
Romeo Castelen	22	30	30	24	2442	1	0	8	Holland (5)
Edwin de Graaf	25	10	4	0	145	1	0	-	Holland
Hossam Ghali	23	22	20	11	1269	1	0	-	Egypt
Corey Gibbs	25	15	15	13	1281	1	0	-	United States
Bart Goor	32	34	34	31	2912	1	0	3	Belgium (42)
Nick Hofs	22	12	12	8	895	4	0	-	Holland
Shinji Ono	25	24	24	16	1726	3	0	-	Japan
Sebastien Pardo	23	15	7	2	344	0	0	-	Chile
Tim Vincken	18	3	3	1	184	0	0	-	Holland
Forwards									
Gerson Magrao	20	3	2	0	42	0	0	-	Brazil
Salomon Kalou	19	31	31	24	2318	2	0	-	Ivory Coast
Dirk Kuijt	24	34	34	33	2955	0	0	8	Holland (5)
Danko Lazovic	22	25	18	4	637	1	1	1	Serbia & Mont. (46)
Leonardo	22	7	4	1	135	1	0	-	Brazil
Magrao	20	13	4	0	122	1	0	-	Brazil
Ebi Smolarek	24	15	3	1	108	1	0	-	Poland

SQUAD APPEARANCES

Match	1	2	3	4	5	6	7	8	9	10	11	12	13	14	15	16	17	18	19	20	21	22	23	24	25	26	27	28	29	30	31	32	33	34	35	36	37	38	39	40	41	42
Venue	H	A	A	H	A	H	A	H	H	A	H	H	A	A	H	A	H	A	H	H	H	A	A	H	A	A	H	A	A	H	H	H	A	H	A	A	H	A	H	A	A	H
Competition	L	L	L	L	E	L	L	E	L	L	E	L	L	E	L	L	L	L	E	L	L	E	L	L	L	L	L	E	L	E	L	L	L	L	L	L	L	L	L	L	L	L
Result	W	W	D	W	W	L	W	W	W	W	W	W	L	D	W	D	L	D	W	W	D	L	L	L	D	W	W	L	W	L	W	W	W	W	W	L	L	W	L	L	L	W

Goalkeepers
Gabor Babos
Patrick Lodewijks
Zbigniew Malkowski

Defenders
Bahia
Bruno Basto
Christian Gyan
Glenn Loovens
Patrick Mtiliga
Alexander Ostlund
Patrick Paauwe
Karim Saidi
Chong-Gug Song
Gianni Zuiverloon

Midfielders
Pascal Bosschaart
Thomas Buffel
Romeo Castelen
Edwin de Graaf
Hossam Ghali
Corey Gibbs
Bart Goor
Nick Hofs
Shinji Ono
Sebastien Pardo
Tim Vincken

Forwards
Gerson Magrao
Salomon Kalou
Dirk Kuijt
Danko Lazovic
Leonardo
Magrao
Ebi Smolarek

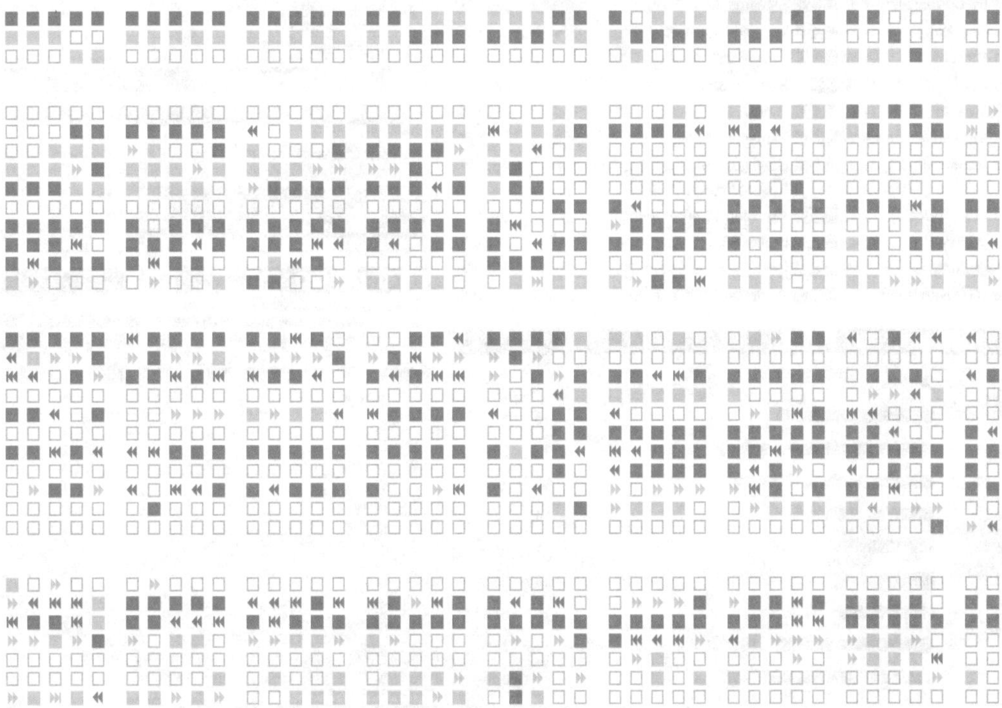

HEERENVEEN

Final Position: **5th**

KEY: Won Drawn Lost

							Attendance
1	hopr1	**AZ Alkmaar**	A	D	1-1	Huntelaar 78	8,000
2	hopr1	**Roda JC Kerk**	H	L	3-4	Huntelaar 30; Seip 73; Rose 86	17,000
3	hopr1	**Twente**	A	L	1-4	Yildirim 45	13,000
4	hopr1	**De Graafschap**	H	W	2-0	Samaras 85; Yildirim 89	17,000
5	hopr1	**NAC Breda**	H	W	3-0	Huntelaar 30,57; Selakovic 63	17,000
6	hopr1	**PSV Eindhoven**	A	L	0-4		31,000
7	uc1rl2	**M Petach-Tikva**	H	W	5-0	Bruggink 15; Vayrynen 19; Hansson 56; Sikora 71; Selakovic 80	17,500
8	hopr1	**Den Haag**	H	W	1-0	Samaras 90	17,000
9	hopr1	**Ajax**	A	W	3-1	Yildirim 52; Vayrynen 60; Selakovic 87	49,000
10	ucgpg	**Benfica**	A	L	2-4	Yildirim 49; Huntelaar 53 pen	15,000
11	hopr1	**Utrecht**	H	W	2-1	Huntelaar 80,83	18,000
12	hopr1	**Den Bosch**	A	W	4-2	Huntelaar 44,79; Rose 87; Samaras 90	6,000
13	hopr1	**RKC Waalwijk**	A	D	0-0		6,000
14	hopr1	**Vitesse Arnhem**	H	L	0-3		17,000
15	hopr1	**Roosendaal**	A	W	3-1	Hestad 28,49; Huntelaar 55	5,000
16	ucgpg	**Stuttgart**	H	W	1-0	Yildirim 65	17,500
17	hopr1	**Feyenoord**	H	D	2-2	Samaras 74; Yildirim 86	18,000
18	ucgpg	**Dinamo Zagreb**	A	D	2-2	Yildirim 84; Huntelaar 89 pen	12,000
19	hopr1	**Willem II Tilb**	A	D	2-2	Sikora 6; Huntelaar 67	11,000
20	hopr1	**Groningen**	H	W	1-0	Vayrynen 66	18,000
21	ucgpg	**Beveren**	H	W	1-0	Bruggink 26	18,000
22	hopr1	**NEC Nijmegen**	A	L	2-3	Hestad 17; Vayrynen 90	12,000
23	hopr1	**Den Bosch**	H	W	2-1	Huntelaar 29; Samaras 60	17,000
24	hopr1	**NAC Breda**	A	D	1-1	Huntelaar 90	11,000
25	hopr1	**AZ Alkmaar**	H	L	1-3	Hansson 77	18,000
26	hopr1	**Roda JC Kerk**	A	W	3-2	Vayrynen 15,55; Nilsson 78	13,000
27	uc3rl1	**Newcastle**	H	L	1-2	Huntelaar 24	19,500
28	hopr1	**De Graafschap**	A	L	1-2	Rose 73	11,000
29	uc3rl2	**Newcastle**	A	L	1-2	Bruggink 80 pen	26,000
30	hopr1	**PSV Eindhoven**	H	L	0-3		19,000
31	hopr1	**RKC Waalwijk**	H	L	1-2	Samaras 82	20,000
32	hopr1	**Den Haag**	A	W	2-0	Vayrynen 4; Bruggink 74 pen	7,000
33	hopr1	**Utrecht**	A	W	1-0	Yildirim 25	21,000
34	hopr1	**Ajax**	H	W	2-1	Seip 62; Samaras 86	20,000
35	hopr1	**Twente**	H	L	1-2	Yildirim 61	21,000
36	hopr1	**Vitesse Arnhem**	A	W	3-1	Samaras 67; Yildirim 72; Nilsson 86	23,000
37	hopr1	**Roosendaal**	H	W	7-1	Huntelaar 19 pen,29,34; Samaras 43,64,76; Nilsson 86	20,000
38	hopr1	**Feyenoord**	A	W	3-1	Vayrynen 15,40; Hansson 78	41,000
39	hopr1	**Willem II Tilb**	H	D	2-2	Breuer 55,57	21,000
40	hopr1	**Groningen**	A	W	2-1	Hestad 27; Huntelaar 60	13,000
41	hopr1	**NEC Nijmegen**	H	W	2-1	Huntelaar 61; Breuer 82	21,000

MONTHLY POINTS TALLY

AUGUST	1	11%
SEPTEMBER	6	67%
OCTOBER	12	100%
NOVEMBER	5	42%
DECEMBER	4	44%
JANUARY	4	67%
FEBRUARY	3	25%
MARCH	6	67%
APRIL	9	75%
MAY	10	83%

KEY PLAYERS - GOALSCORERS

Klaas Jan Huntelaar

Goals in the League	17	Player Strike Rate Average number of minutes between League goals scored by player	146
Contribution to Attacking Power Average number of minutes between League team goals while on pitch	51	Club Strike Rate Average number of minutes between League goals scored by club	48

	PLAYER	LGE GOALS	POWER	STRIKE RATE
1	Klaas Jan Huntelaar	17	51	146 mins
2	Mika Vayrynen	8	52	305 mins
3	Ugur Yildirim	7	48	406 mins
4	Michel Breuer	3	43	445 mins
5	Daniel Berg Hestad	4	51	449 mins

KEY PLAYERS - MIDFIELDERS

Arnold Bruggink

Goals in the League	1	Contribution to Attacking Power Average number of minutes between League team goals while on pitch	67
Defensive Rating Average number of mins between League goals conceded while on the pitch	103	Scoring Difference Defensive Rating minus Contribution to Attacking Power	36

	PLAYER	LGE GOALS	DEF RATE	POWER	SCORE DIFF
1	Arnold Bruggink	1	103	67	36 mins
2	Mika Vayrynen	8	68	52	16 mins
3	Arek Radomski	0	55	47	8 mins
4	Daniel Berg Hestad	4	58	51	7 mins

KEY PLAYERS - DEFENDERS

Said Bakkati

Goals Conceded Number of League goals conceded while the player was on the pitch	21	Clean Sheets In games when player was on pitch for at least 70 minutes	3
Defensive Rating Ave number of mins between League goals conceded while on the pitch	66	Club Defensive Rating Average number of mins between League goals conceded by the club this season	59

	PLAYER	CON LGE	CLEAN SHEETS	DEF RATE
1	Said Bakkati	21	3	66 mins
2	Michel Breuer	21	1	64 mins
3	Marcel Seip	42	6	62 mins
4	Petter Hansson	50	7	59 mins
5	Tomasz Rzasa	35	6	56 mins

KEY GOALKEEPER

Brian Vandenbussche

Goals Conceded in the League	42	Counting Games League games when player was on pitch for at least 70 minutes	29
Defensive Rating Ave number of mins between League goals conceded while on the pitch	62	Clean Sheets In games when player was on pitch for at least 70 minutes	6

LEAGUE GOALS

Klaas-Jan Huntelaar

Minutes on the pitch	2480	Goals in the League	17
League average (mins between goals)	146		

	PLAYER	MINS	GOALS	AVE
1	Huntelaar	2480	17	146
2	Samaras	1215	11	110
3	Vayrynen	2438	8	305
4	Yildirim	2841	7	406
5	Hestad	1794	4	449
6	Nilsson	884	3	295
7	Breuer	1335	3	445
8	Rose	463	3	154
9	Hansson	2970	2	1485
10	Seip	2593	2	1297
11	Selakovic	576	2	288
12	Sikora	871	1	871
	Other		9	
	TOTAL		64	

DISCIPLINARY RECORDS

	PLAYER	YELLOW	RED	AVE
1	Haarala	5	1	172
2	Bakkati	5	1	230
3	Rzasa	5	1	324
4	Sikora	2	0	435
5	Rose	1	0	463
6	Selakovic	1	0	576
7	Samaras	2	0	607
8	Vayrynen	4	0	609
9	Seip	4	0	648
10	Breuer	2	0	667
11	Hansson	4	0	742
12	Bruggink	2	0	775
13	Nilsson	1	0	884
	Other	7	0	
	TOTAL	45	3	

TOP POINT EARNERS

	PLAYER	GAMES	AV PTS
1	Michel Breuer	13	2.00
2	Marcel Seip	28	1.89
3	Ugur Yildirim	27	1.85
4	Arek Radomski	25	1.84
5	Brian Vandenbussche	29	1.83
6	Petter Hansson	33	1.79
7	Mika Vayrynen	26	1.77
8	Tomasz Rzasa	21	1.71
9	Daniel Berg Hestad	16	1.69
10	Arnold Bruggink	15	1.67
	CLUB AVERAGE:		1.76

TEAM OF THE SEASON

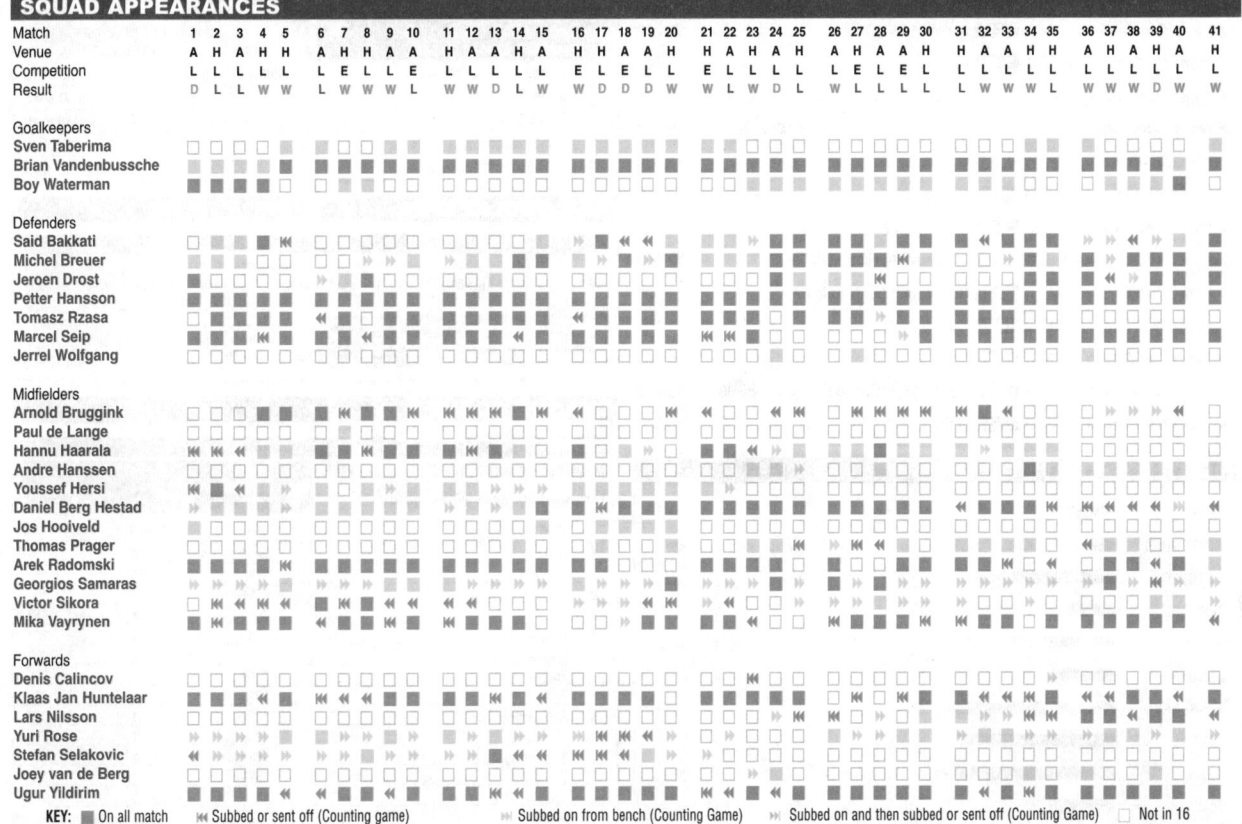

G
Brian Vandenbussche
CG: 29 DR: 62
D
Michel Breuer
CG: 13 DR: 64
D
Marcel Seip
CG: 28 DR: 62
D
Petter Hansson
CG: 33 DR: 59
D
Said Bakkati
CG: 12 DR: 66
M
Arnold Bruggink
CG: 15 SD: 36
M
Mika Vayrynen
CG: 26 SD: 16
M
Arek Radomski
CG: 25 SD: 8
M
Daniel Berg Hestad
CG: 16 SD: 7
F
Klaas Jan Huntelaar
CG: 22 SR: 146
F
Ugur Yildirim
CG: 27 SR: 406

LEAGUE APPEARANCES, BOOKINGS AND CAPS

	AGE (on 01/07/05)	IN NAMED 18	APPEARANCES	COUNTING GAMES	MINUTES ON PITCH	YELLOW CARDS	RED CARDS	THIS SEASON	HOME COUNTRY
Goalkeepers									
Sven Taberima	19	16	0	0	0	0	0	-	Holland
Brian Vandenbussche	23	34	29	29	2610	0	0	-	Belgium
Boy Waterman	21	18	5	5	450	0	0	-	Holland
Defenders									
Said Bakkati	23	26	19	12	1383	5	1	-	Holland
Michel Breuer	25	29	20	13	1335	2	0	-	Holland
Jeroen Drost	18	16	13	10	1002	0	0	-	Holland
Petter Hansson	28	33	33	33	2970	4	0	7	Sweden (13)
Tomasz Rzasa	32	23	23	21	1949	5	1	-	Poland
Marcel Seip	23	30	30	28	2593	4	0	-	Holland
Jerrel Wolfgang	20	2	0	0	0	0	0	-	Holland
Midfielders									
Arnold Bruggink	27	22	22	15	1550	2	0	-	Holland
Paul de Lange	24	0	0	0	0	0	0	-	Holland
Hannu Haarala	23	25	15	9	1036	5	1	-	Finland
Andre Hanssen	24	12	2	1	106	0	0	-	Norway
Youssef Hersi	22	17	9	2	420	0	0	-	Holland
Daniel Berg Hestad	29	34	26	16	1794	2	0	-	Norway
Jos Hooiveld	22	5	0	0	0	0	0	-	Holland
Thomas Prager	19	16	4	1	213	0	0	-	Holland
Arek Radomski	28	28	27	25	2317	2	0	-	Poland
Georgios Samaras	20	34	31	6	1215	2	0	-	Holland
Victor Sikora	27	22	19	3	871	2	0	-	Holland
Mika Vayrynen	23	29	29	26	2438	4	0	-	Finland
Forwards									
Denis Calincov	20	2	2	1	101	0	0	-	Moldova
Klaas Jan Huntelaar	21	31	31	22	2480	1	0	-	Holland
Lars Nilsson	23	16	14	7	884	1	0	-	Sweden
Yuri Rose	26	31	19	1	463	1	0	-	Holland
Stefan Selakovic	28	16	14	2	576	1	0	-	Sweden
Joey van de Berg	19	5	1	0	10	0	0	-	Holland
Ugur Yildirim	23	34	34	27	2841	2	0	-	Holland

SQUAD APPEARANCES

Match	1	2	3	4	5	6	7	8	9	10	11	12	13	14	15	16	17	18	19	20	21	22	23	24	25	26	27	28	29	30	31	32	33	34	35	36	37	38	39	40	41
Venue	A	H	A	H	H	A	H	H	A	A	H	A	A	H	A	H	H	A	A	H	H	A	H	A	H	A	H	A	A	H	H	A	A	H	H	A	H	A	H	A	H
Competition	L	L	L	L	L	L	E	L	L	E	L	L	L	L	L	E	L	E	L	L	E	L	L	L	L	L	E	L	E	L	L	L	L	L	L	L	L	L	L	L	L
Result	D	L	L	W	W	L	W	W	W	L	W	W	D	L	W	W	D	D	D	W	W	L	W	D	L	W	L	L	L	L	L	W	W	W	L	W	W	W	D	W	W

Goalkeepers
Sven Taberima
Brian Vandenbussche
Boy Waterman

Defenders
Said Bakkati
Michel Breuer
Jeroen Drost
Petter Hansson
Tomasz Rzasa
Marcel Seip
Jerrel Wolfgang

Midfielders
Arnold Bruggink
Paul de Lange
Hannu Haarala
Andre Hanssen
Youssef Hersi
Daniel Berg Hestad
Jos Hooiveld
Thomas Prager
Arek Radomski
Georgios Samaras
Victor Sikora
Mika Vayrynen

Forwards
Denis Calincov
Klaas Jan Huntelaar
Lars Nilsson
Yuri Rose
Stefan Selakovic
Joey van de Berg
Ugur Yildirim

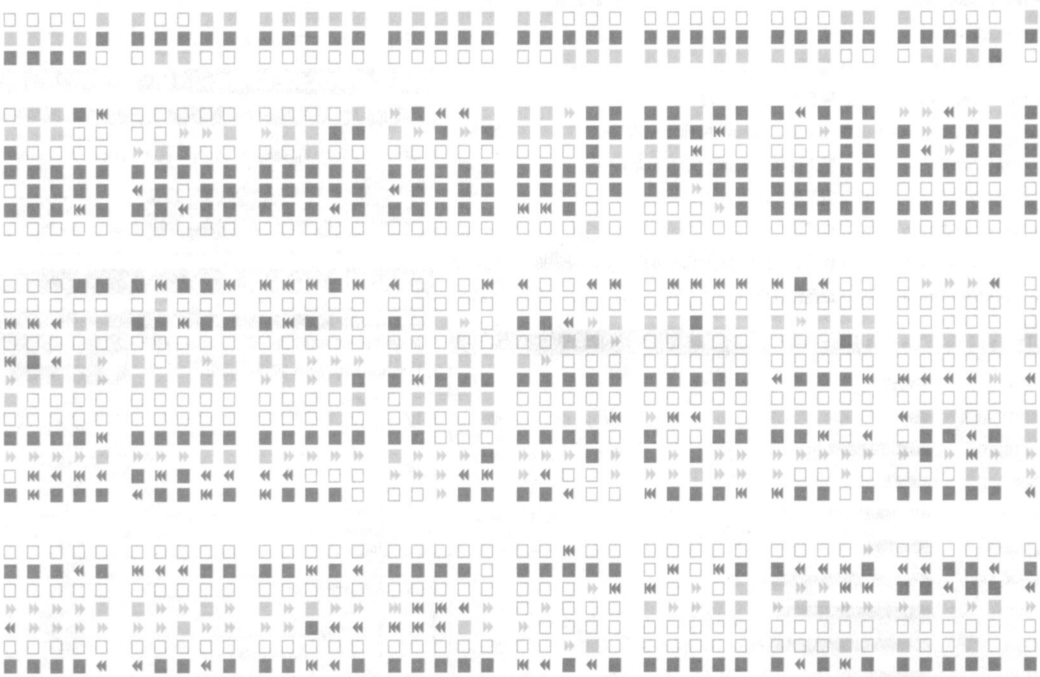

KEY: On all match · On bench · Subbed or sent off (Counting game) · Subbed or sent off (playing less than 70 minutes) · Subbed on from bench (Counting Game) · Subbed on (playing less than 70 minutes) · Subbed on and then subbed or sent off (Counting Game) · Subbed on and then subbed or sent off (playing less than 70 minutes) · Not in 16

TWENTE ENSCHEDE

Final Position: **6th**

KEY: ☐Won ☐Drawn ☐Lost

							Attendance
1	hopr1	**Ajax**	H	L	2-3	Touzani 48; N'Kufo 66	13,000
2	hopr1	**RKC Waalwijk**	A	L	0-1		5,000
3	hopr1	**Heerenveen**	H	W	4-1	N'Kufo 17; Culina 22,70; Zomer 37	13,000
4	hopr1	**Feyenoord**	A	L	1-3	Zomer 38	42,000
5	hopr1	**Willem II Tilb**	H	D	0-0		13,000
6	hopr1	**De Graafschap**	A	D	0-0		11,000
7	hopr1	**Roda JC Kerk**	H	L	2-3	N'Kufo 8,75	13,000
8	hopr1	**Roosendaal**	A	W	1-0	Christensen 61	5,000
9	hopr1	**Den Haag**	A	W	1-0	Christensen 83	5,000
10	hopr1	**Vitesse Arnhem**	H	L	1-4	Christensen 90	13,000
11	hopr1	**Groningen**	H	L	1-2	Culina 10	13,000
12	hopr1	**NEC Nijmegen**	A	W	2-0	Culina 17; El Ahmadi 87	10,000
13	hopr1	**Utrecht**	H	L	0-1		13,000
14	hopr1	**PSV Eindhoven**	A	L	0-2		30,000
15	hopr1	**Den Bosch**	H	W	4-0	Culina 15; N'Kufo 28; Shoukov 59; Touzani 61	13,000
16	hopr1	**AZ Alkmaar**	A	L	0-5		8,000
17	hopr1	**NAC Breda**	H	D	0-0		13,000
18	hopr1	**Willem II Tilb**	A	W	3-0	N'Kufo 7,88; Culina 80	13,000
19	hopr1	**Feyenoord**	H	D	0-0		13,000
20	hopr1	**Ajax**	A	W	2-1	N'Kufo 36; Touma 68	47,000
21	hopr1	**RKC Waalwijk**	H	W	3-1	Touma 8; N'Kufo 39; Majstorovic 69	13,000
22	hopr1	**Groningen**	A	W	1-0	N'Kufo 14	12,000
23	hopr1	**De Graafschap**	H	D	0-0		13,000
24	hopr1	**Roda JC Kerk**	A	W	2-1	Shoukov 51; N'Kufo 58	12,000
25	hopr1	**Roosendaal**	H	W	3-0	Shoukov 12; Touma 39; Culina 88	13,000
26	hopr1	**Den Haag**	H	W	2-1	Cziommer 5; N'Kufo 90 pen	13,000
27	hopr1	**Vitesse Arnhem**	A	D	1-1	N'Kufo 53 pen	20,000
28	hopr1	**Heerenveen**	A	W	2-1	Culina 38,59	21,000
29	hopr1	**NEC Nijmegen**	H	W	2-1	Shoukov 19; Niemeyer 59	13,000
30	hopr1	**Utrecht**	A	D	2-2	Schuurman 60; N'Kufo 89	20,000
31	hopr1	**PSV Eindhoven**	H	D	2-2	Culina 62; Touma 69	13,000
32	hopr1	**Den Bosch**	A	L	0-1		5,000
33	hopr1	**AZ Alkmaar**	H	W	3-0	Culina 55; N'Kufo 62; Majstorovic 89	13,000
34	hopr1	**NAC Breda**	A	D	1-1	N'Kufo 55	10,000

MONTHLY POINTS TALLY

AUGUST	3	33%
SEPTEMBER	2	22%
OCTOBER	6	50%
NOVEMBER	3	25%
DECEMBER	4	44%
JANUARY	4	67%
FEBRUARY	10	83%
MARCH	9	100%
APRIL	9	60%
MAY	4	44%

KEY PLAYERS - GOALSCORERS

Blaise N'Kufo

Goals in the League	16	Player Strike Rate Average number of minutes between League goals scored by player	175
Contribution to Attacking Power Average number of minutes between League team goals while on pitch	63	Club Strike Rate Average number of minutes between League goals scored by club	64

	PLAYER	LGE GOALS	POWER	STRIKE RATE
1	Blaise N'Kufo	16	63	175 mins
2	Jason Culina	11	60	253 mins
3	Sharbel Touma	4	56	403 mins
4	Dmitri Shoukov	4	76	513 mins
5	Ramon Zomer	2	54	980 mins

KEY PLAYERS - MIDFIELDERS

Sharbel Touma

Goals in the League	4	Contribution to Attacking Power Average number of minutes between League team goals while on pitch	56
Defensive Rating Average number of mins between League goals conceded while on the pitch	95	Scoring Difference Defensive Rating minus Contribution to Attacking Power	39

	PLAYER	LGE GOALS	DEF RATE	POWER	SCORE DIFF
1	Sharbel Touma	4	95	56	39 mins
2	Jason Culina	11	87	60	27 mins
3	Peter Niemeyer	1	79	59	20 mins
4	Niels Wellenberg	0	91	79	12 mins
5	Dmitri Shoukov	4	86	76	10 mins

KEY PLAYERS - DEFENDERS

Jeroen Heubach

Goals Conceded Number of League goals conceded while the player was on the pitch	29	Clean Sheets In games when player was on pitch for at least 70 minutes	11
Defensive Rating Ave number of mins between League goals conceded while on the pitch	91	Club Defensive Rating Average number of mins between League goals conceded by the club this season	81

	PLAYER	CON LGE	CLEAN SHEETS	DEF RATE
1	Jeroen Heubach	29	11	91 mins
2	Ramon Zomer	22	7	89 mins
3	Daniel Majstorovic	31	13	86 mins
4	Resit Schuurman	37	11	76 mins

KEY GOALKEEPER

Sander Boschker

Goals Conceded in the League	34	Counting Games League games when player was on pitch for at least 70 minutes	28
Defensive Rating Ave number of mins between League goals conceded while on the pitch	75	Clean Sheets In games when player was on pitch for at least 70 minutes	11

LEAGUE GOALS

Blaise N'Kufo

Minutes on the pitch	2807	Goals in the League	16
League average (mins between goals)	175		

	PLAYER	MINS	GOALS	AVE
1	N'Kufo	2807	16	175
2	Culina	2782	11	253
3	Touma	1611	4	403
4	Shoukov	2052	4	513
5	Christensen	782	3	261
6	Majstorovic	2658	2	1329
7	Zomer	1959	2	980
8	Touzani	1315	2	658
9	El Ahmadi	1052	1	1052
10	Niemeyer	2056	1	2056
11	Schuurman	2821	1	2821
12	Cziommer	898	1	898
	Other		0	
	TOTAL		48	

DISCIPLINARY RECORDS

	PLAYER	YELLOW	RED	AVE
1	Bouchiba	3	1	198
2	Touzani	6	0	219
3	Ouedraogo	4	0	226
4	Zomer	6	1	279
5	Cziommer	3	0	299
6	Touma	4	1	322
7	Sibum	2	0	454
8	Shoukov	4	0	513
9	Niemeyer	4	0	514
10	Wellenberg	2	0	635
11	Heubach	4	0	656
12	Majstorovic	4	0	664
13	Culina	4	0	695
	Other	10	0	
	TOTAL	60	3	

TOP POINT EARNERS

	PLAYER	GAMES	AV PTS
1	Peter Niemeyer	20	1.95
2	Sharbel Touma	18	1.89
3	Blaise N'Kufo	31	1.71
4	Resit Schuurman	30	1.67
5	Dmitri Shoukov	21	1.67
6	Daniel Majstorovic	29	1.66
7	Jason Culina	31	1.65
8	Jeroen Heubach	28	1.64
9	Ramon Zomer	21	1.57
10	Sander Boschker	28	1.57
	CLUB AVERAGE:		1.59

LEAGUE APPEARANCES, BOOKINGS AND CAPS

	AGE (on 01/07/05)	IN NAMED 18	APPEARANCES	COUNTING GAMES	MINUTES ON PITCH	YELLOW CARDS	RED CARDS	THIS SEASON	HOME COUNTRY
Goalkeepers									
Sander Boschker	34	31	30	28	2562	1	0	-	Holland
Cees Paauwe	27	17	4	4	353	0	0	-	Holland
Remco Pasveer	21	20	2	1	145	0	0	-	Holland
Defenders									
Jeroen Heubach	30	31	31	28	2627	4	0	-	Holland
Patrick Jurgens	21	1	0	0	0	0	0	-	Holland
Jordi Koster	21	3	0	0	0	0	0	-	Holland
Daniel Majstorovic	28	30	30	29	2658	4	0	-	Sweden
Resit Schuurman	26	33	32	30	2821	4	0	-	Holland
Ramon Zomer	22	32	24	21	1959	6	1	-	Holland
Midfielders									
Elbekay Bouchiba	26	27	14	6	793	3	1	-	Morocco
Wout Brama	18	2	0	0	0	0	0	-	Holland
Jason Culina	24	32	32	31	2782	4	0	-	Australia
Simon Cziommer	24	13	13	8	898	3	0	-	Germany
Karim El Ahmadi	20	25	19	6	1052	1	0	-	Holland
Peter Niemeyer	21	27	27	20	2056	4	0	-	Germany
Rahim Ouedraogo	24	33	20	7	907	4	0	-	Burkino Faso
Dmitri Shoukov	29	27	25	21	2052	4	0	-	Russia
Bas Sibum	22	32	22	6	908	2	0	-	Holland
Sharbel Touma	26	19	19	18	1611	4	1	1	Sweden (13)
Karim Touzani	24	30	19	11	1315	6	0	-	Holland
Niels Wellenberg	22	26	20	12	1271	2	0	-	Holland
Forwards									
Guilherme Afonso	19	15	7	0	137	0	0	-	Switzerland
Ruud Bruns	20	1	1	0	7	0	0	-	Holland
Timothy Cathalina	20	1	0	0	0	0	0	-	Holland
Kim Christensen	25	26	23	4	782	1	0	-	Denmark
Raymond Fafiani	21	33	21	5	975	1	0	-	Holland
Georgi Gakhokidze	29	2	2	1	118	0	0	-	Georgia
Blaise N'Kufo	30	32	32	31	2807	2	0	-	Switzerland
Tim Velten	19	7	1	0	8	0	0	-	Holland

TEAM OF THE SEASON

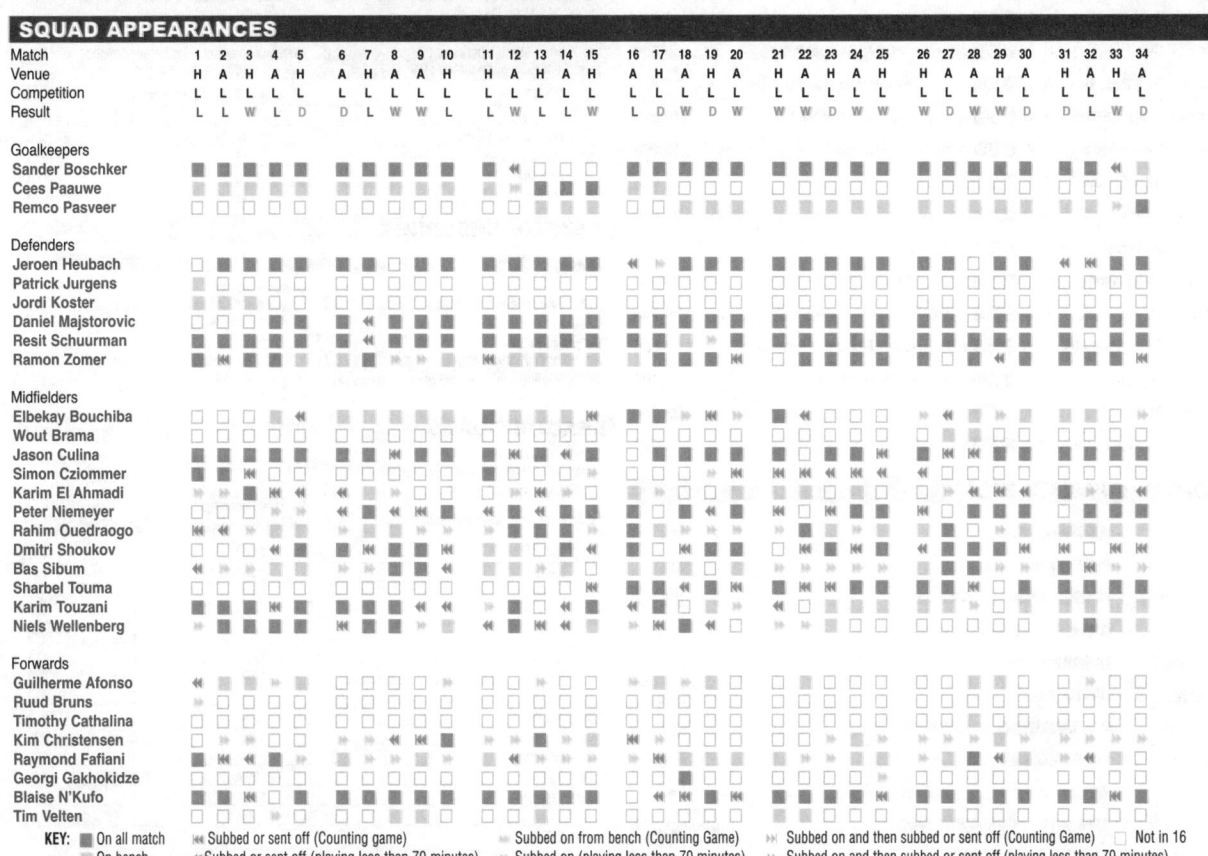

D
Jeroen Heubach
CG: 28 DR: 91
D
Ramon Zomer
CG: 21 DR: 89
D
Daniel Majstorovic
CG: 29 DR: 86
D
Resit Schuurman
CG: 30 DR: 76
G
Sander Boschker
CG: 28 DR: 75
M
Sharbel Touma
CG: 18 SD: 39
M
Dimitri Shoukov
CG: 21 SD: 10
M
Peter Niemeyer
CG: 20 SD: 20
M
Niels Wellenberg
CG: 12 SD: 12
F
Blaise N'Kufo
CG: 31 SR: 175
F
Jason Culina*
CG: 31 SR: 253

SQUAD APPEARANCES

Match	1	2	3	4	5	6	7	8	9	10	11	12	13	14	15	16	17	18	19	20	21	22	23	24	25	26	27	28	29	30	31	32	33	34
Venue	H	A	H	A	H	A	H	A	A	H	H	A	H	A	H	A	H	A	H	A	H	A	H	A	H	H	A	A	H	A	H	A	H	A
Competition	L	L	L	L	L	L	L	L	L	L	L	L	L	L	L	L	L	L	L	L	L	L	L	L	L	L	L	L	L	L	L	L	L	L
Result	L	L	W	L	D	D	L	W	W	L	L	W	L	L	W	L	D	W	D	W	W	W	D	W	W	W	D	W	W	D	D	L	W	D

Goalkeepers
Sander Boschker
Cees Paauwe
Remco Pasveer

Defenders
Jeroen Heubach
Patrick Jurgens
Jordi Koster
Daniel Majstorovic
Resit Schuurman
Ramon Zomer

Midfielders
Elbekay Bouchiba
Wout Brama
Jason Culina
Simon Cziommer
Karim El Ahmadi
Peter Niemeyer
Rahim Ouedraogo
Dmitri Shoukov
Bas Sibum
Sharbel Touma
Karim Touzani
Niels Wellenberg

Forwards
Guilherme Afonso
Ruud Bruns
Timothy Cathalina
Kim Christensen
Raymond Fafiani
Georgi Gakhokidze
Blaise N'Kufo
Tim Velten

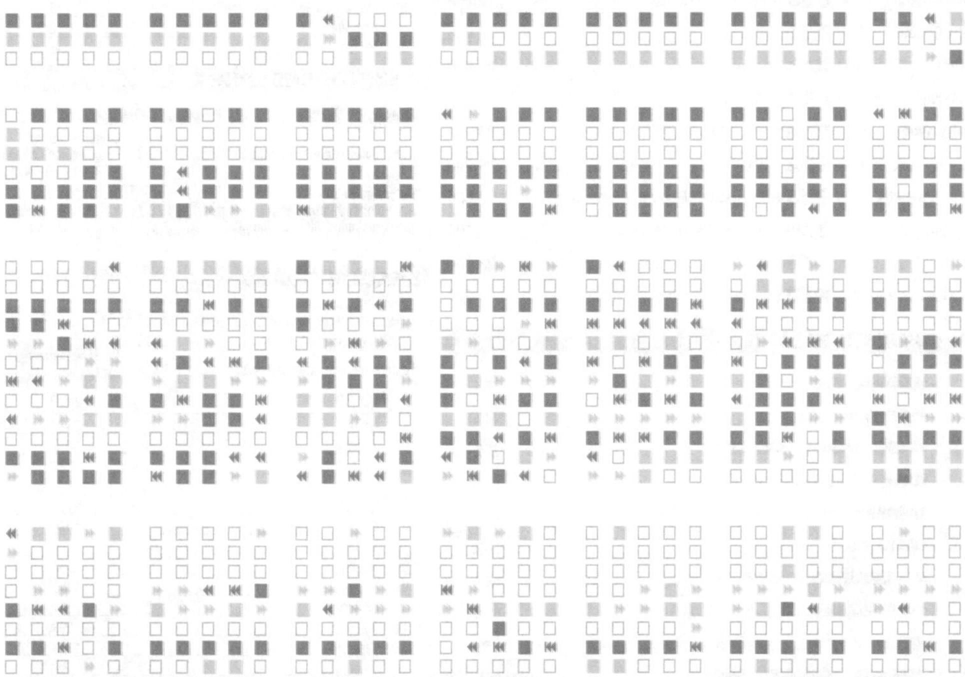

KEY: On all match | On bench | Subbed or sent off (Counting game) | Subbed or sent off (playing less than 70 minutes) | Subbed on from bench (Counting Game) | Subbed on (playing less than 70 minutes) | Subbed on and then subbed or sent off (Counting Game) | Subbed on and then subbed or sent off (playing less than 70 minutes) | Not in 16

VITESSE ARNHEM

Final Position: **7th**

KEY: ☐Won ☐Drawn ☐Lost

							Attendance
1	hopr1	**Roda JC Kerk**	A	W	3-2	Hofs 32,73; Janssen 85	11,000
2	hopr1	**Groningen**	H	W	1-0	Janssen 32	16,000
3	hopr1	**Feyenoord**	H	D	1-1	Dingsdag 83	17,000
4	hopr1	**Roosendaal**	A	L	1-4	Amoah 17	5,000
5	hopr1	**Den Haag**	A	W	4-0	Janssen 42,59; Gluscevic 81; Amoah 88	6,000
6	hopr1	**Den Bosch**	H	D	0-0		19,000
7	hopr1	**Willem II Tilb**	A	L	2-3	Hofs 83; Gluscevic 90	12,000
8	hopr1	**NAC Breda**	H	L	1-2	Janssen 44	16,000
9	hopr1	**AZ Alkmaar**	H	L	0-3		17,000
10	hopr1	**Twente**	A	W	4-1	Frankel 35; Hofs 69; Knopper 81; Janssen 84	13,000
11	hopr1	**NEC Nijmegen**	H	W	1-0	Amoah 67	18,000
12	hopr1	**Heerenveen**	A	W	3-0	Hofs 57; Amoah 80,88	17,000
13	hopr1	**PSV Eindhoven**	H	L	0-2		17,000
14	hopr1	**RKC Waalwijk**	A	D	2-2	Schaars 36; Amoah 88	6,000
15	hopr1	**Utrecht**	H	W	2-1	Hofs 18; Jansen, M 90	16,000
16	hopr1	**Ajax**	A	L	0-1		48,000
17	hopr1	**De Graafschap**	H	W	3-1	Schaars 55,58; Amoah 79	20,000
18	hopr1	**Feyenoord**	A	W	2-1	Gluscevic 81,83	40,000
19	hopr1	**Roosendaal**	H	L	1-3	Frankel 6	20,000
20	hopr1	**Roda JC Kerk**	H	W	3-0	Hersi 25; Jansen, M 36; Amoah 84	17,000
21	hopr1	**Groningen**	A	D	0-0		12,000
22	hopr1	**Den Haag**	H	L	3-4	Janssen 21,57; Gluscevic 90	18,000
23	hopr1	**Den Bosch**	A	W	2-1	Jansen, M 42; Knopper 83	5,000
24	hopr1	**Willem II Tilb**	H	W	2-0	Knopper 28; Gluscevic 83	19,000
25	hopr1	**NAC Breda**	A	W	2-1	Amoah 23; Knopper 80	12,000
26	hopr1	**AZ Alkmaar**	A	L	0-3		9,000
27	hopr1	**Twente**	H	D	1-1	Knopper 23	20,000
28	hopr1	**NEC Nijmegen**	A	D	1-1	Amoah 6	12,000
29	hopr1	**Heerenveen**	H	L	1-3	Amoah 20	23,000
30	hopr1	**PSV Eindhoven**	A	L	0-3		34,000
31	hopr1	**RKC Waalwijk**	H	W	3-1	Rankovic 36; Rojer 57; Amoah 82 pen	21,000
32	hopr1	**Utrecht**	A	W	2-1	Rankovic 16; Schaars 90	19,000
33	hopr1	**Ajax**	H	L	0-2		23,000
34	hopr1	**De Graafschap**	A	W	2-1	Benson 82; Amoah 90	11,000

MONTHLY POINTS TALLY

AUGUST	7	78%
SEPTEMBER	4	44%
OCTOBER	3	25%
NOVEMBER	7	58%
DECEMBER	6	67%
JANUARY	3	50%
FEBRUARY	7	58%
MARCH	6	67%
APRIL	2	17%
MAY	9	75%

KEY PLAYERS - GOALSCORERS

Nick Hofs

Goals in the League 6

Player Strike Rate
Average number of minutes between League goals scored by player 229

Contribution to Attacking Power
Average number of minutes between League team goals while on pitch 62

Club Strike Rate
Average number of minutes between League goals scored by club 58

	PLAYER	LGE GOALS	POWER	STRIKE RATE
1	Nick Hofs	6	62	229 mins
2	Matthew Amoah	13	60	233 mins
3	Theo Janssen	8	51	322 mins
4	Richard Knopper	5	57	425 mins
5	Aleksandar Rankovic	2	59	623 mins

KEY PLAYERS - MIDFIELDERS

Theo Janssen

Goals in the League 8

Contribution to Attacking Power
Average number of minutes between League team goals while on pitch 51

Defensive Rating
Average number of mins between League goals conceded while on the pitch 66

Scoring Difference
Defensive Rating minus Contribution to Attacking Power 15

	PLAYER	LGE GOALS	DEF RATE	POWER	SCORE DIFF
1	Theo Janssen	8	66	51	15 mins
2	Abubakari Yakubu	0	63	57	6 mins
3	Aleksandar Rankovic	2	59	59	0 mins
4	Nick Hofs	6	60	63	-3 mins
5	Youssef Hersi	1	59	64	-5 mins

KEY PLAYERS - DEFENDERS

Purrel Frankel

Goals Conceded
Number of League goals conceded while the player was on the pitch 40

Clean Sheets
In games when player was on pitch for at least 70 minutes 8

Defensive Rating
Ave number of mins between League goals conceded while on the pitch 68

Club Defensive Rating
Average number of mins between League goals conceded by the club this season 62

	PLAYER	CON LGE	CLEAN SHEETS	DEF RATE
1	Purrel Frankel	40	8	68 mins
2	Peter van den Berg	32	7	67 mins
3	Michael Jansen	33	5	65 mins
4	Stijn Vreven	42	6	62 mins
5	Michael Dingsdag	42	8	61 mins

KEY GOALKEEPER

Dragoslav Jevric

Goals Conceded in the League 23

Counting Games
League games when player was on pitch for at least 70 minutes 17

Defensive Rating
Ave number of mins between League goals conceded while on the pitch 67

Clean Sheets
In games when player was on pitch for at least 70 minutes 5

LEAGUE GOALS

Matthew Amoah

Minutes on the pitch 3026

League average (mins between goals) 233

Goals in the League 13

	PLAYER	MINS	GOALS	AVE
1	Amoah	3026	13	233
2	Janssen	2573	8	322
3	Gluscevic	1529	6	255
4	Hofs	1376	6	229
5	Knopper	2126	5	425
6	Schaars	1078	4	270
7	Jansen	2129	3	710
8	Frankel	2706	2	1353
9	Rankovic	1245	2	623
10	Dingsdag	2569	1	2569
11	Rojer	863	1	863
12	Hersi	1352	1	1352
	Other		1	
	TOTAL		53	

DISCIPLINARY RECORDS

	PLAYER	YELLOW	RED	AVE
1	Hofs	5	0	**275**
2	Janssen	9	0	**285**
3	Schaars	3	0	**359**
4	Vreven	7	0	**369**
5	Yakubu	7	0	**398**
6	Knopper	5	0	**425**
7	Frankel	6	0	**451**
8	Dingsdag	4	1	**513**
9	van den Berg	4	0	**539**
10	Hersi	2	0	**676**
11	Gluscevic	1	1	**764**
12	Amoah	3	0	**1008**
13	Jansen	2	0	**1064**
	Other	1	0	
	TOTAL	**59**	**2**	

TOP POINT EARNERS

	PLAYER	GAMES	AV PTS
1	Theo Janssen	28	**1.86**
2	Michael Dingsdag	26	**1.81**
3	Youssef Hersi	12	**1.67**
4	Michael Jansen	21	**1.62**
5	Abubakarl Yakubu	31	**1.61**
6	Purrel Frankel	28	**1.61**
7	Richard Knopper	23	**1.61**
8	Peter van den Berg	23	**1.61**
9	Dragoslav Jevric	17	**1.59**
10	Matthew Amoah	34	**1.59**
	CLUB AVERAGE:		**1.59**

LEAGUE APPEARANCES, BOOKINGS AND CAPS

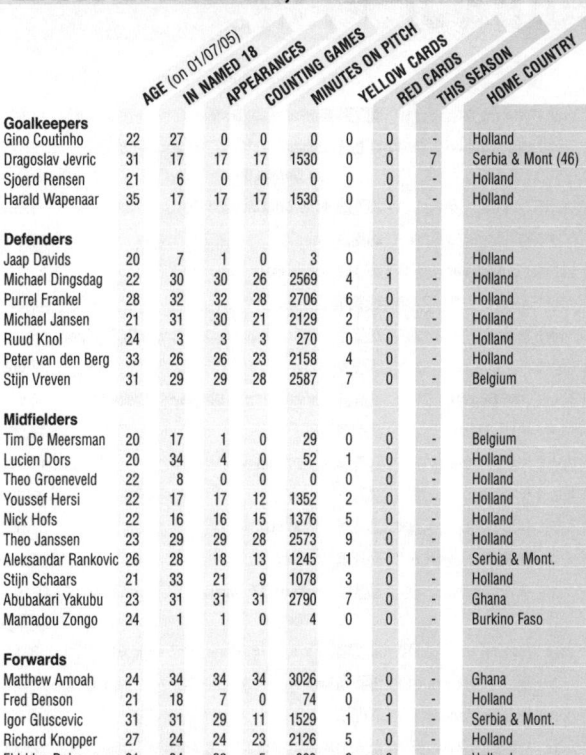

	AGE (on 01/07/05)	IN NAMED 18	APPEARANCES	COUNTING GAMES	MINUTES ON PITCH	YELLOW CARDS	RED CARDS	THIS SEASON	HOME COUNTRY
Goalkeepers									
Gino Coutinho	22	27	0	0	0	0	0	-	Holland
Dragoslav Jevric	31	17	17	17	1530	0	0	7	Serbia & Mont (46)
Sjoerd Rensen	21	6	0	0	0	0	0	-	Holland
Harald Wapenaar	35	17	17	17	1530	0	0	-	Holland
Defenders									
Jaap Davids	20	7	1	0	3	0	0	-	Holland
Michael Dingsdag	22	30	30	26	2569	4	1	-	Holland
Purrel Frankel	28	32	32	28	2706	6	0	-	Holland
Michael Jansen	21	31	30	21	2129	2	0	-	Holland
Ruud Knol	24	3	3	3	270	0	0	-	Holland
Peter van den Berg	33	26	26	23	2158	4	0	-	Holland
Stijn Vreven	31	29	29	28	2587	7	0	-	Belgium
Midfielders									
Tim De Meersman	20	17	1	0	29	0	0	-	Belgium
Lucien Dors	20	34	4	0	52	1	0	-	Holland
Theo Groeneveld	22	8	0	0	0	0	0	-	Holland
Youssef Hersi	22	17	17	12	1352	2	0	-	Holland
Nick Hofs	22	16	16	15	1376	5	0	-	Holland
Theo Janssen	23	29	29	28	2573	9	0	-	Holland
Aleksandar Rankovic	26	28	18	13	1245	1	0	-	Serbia & Mont.
Stijn Schaars	21	33	21	9	1078	3	0	-	Holland
Abubakari Yakubu	23	31	31	31	2790	7	0	-	Ghana
Mamadou Zongo	24	1	1	0	4	0	0	-	Burkino Faso
Forwards									
Matthew Amoah	24	34	34	34	3026	3	0	-	Ghana
Fred Benson	21	18	7	0	74	0	0	-	Holland
Igor Gluscevic	31	31	29	11	1529	1	1	-	Serbia & Mont.
Richard Knopper	27	24	24	23	2126	5	0	-	Holland
Eldridge Rojer	21	34	26	5	863	0	0	-	Holland

TEAM OF THE SEASON

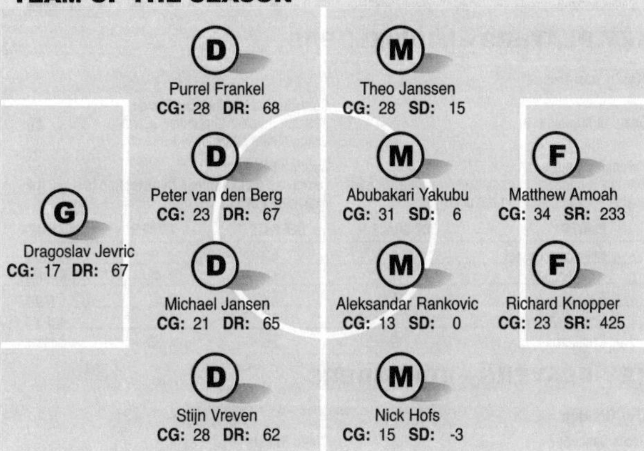

D
Purrel Frankel
CG: 28 DR: 68
D
Peter van den Berg
CG: 23 DR: 67
D
Michael Jansen
CG: 21 DR: 65
D
Stijn Vreven
CG: 28 DR: 62
G
Dragoslav Jevric
CG: 17 DR: 67
M
Theo Janssen
CG: 28 SD: 15
M
Abubakari Yakubu
CG: 31 SD: 6
M
Aleksandar Rankovic
CG: 13 SD: 0
M
Nick Hofs
CG: 15 SD: -3
F
Matthew Amoah
CG: 34 SR: 233
F
Richard Knopper
CG: 23 SR: 425

SQUAD APPEARANCES

Match	1	2	3	4	5	6	7	8	9	10	11	12	13	14	15	16	17	18	19	20	21	22	23	24	25	26	27	28	29	30	31	32	33	34
Venue	A	H	H	A	A	H	A	H	H	A	H	A	H	A	H	A	H	A	H	H	A	H	A	H	A	A	H	A	H	A	H	A	H	A
Competition	L	L	L	L	L	L	L	L	L	L	L	L	L	L	L	L	L	L	L	L	L	L	L	L	L	L	L	L	L	L	L	L	L	L
Result	W	W	D	L	W	D	L	L	L	W	W	W	L	D	W	L	W	W	L	W	D	L	W	W	W	L	D	D	L	L	W	W	L	W

Goalkeepers
Gino Coutinho
Dragoslav Jevric
Sjoerd Rensen
Harald Wapenaar

Defenders
Jaap Davids
Michael Dingsdag
Purrel Frankel
Michael Jansen
Ruud Knol
Peter van den Berg
Stijn Vreven

Midfielders
Tim De Meersman
Lucien Dors
Theo Groeneveld
Youssef Hersi
Nick Hofs
Theo Janssen
Aleksandar Rankovic
Stijn Schaars
Abubakari Yakubu
Mamadou Zongo

Forwards
Matthew Amoah
Fred Benson
Igor Gluscevic
Richard Knopper
Eldridge Rojer

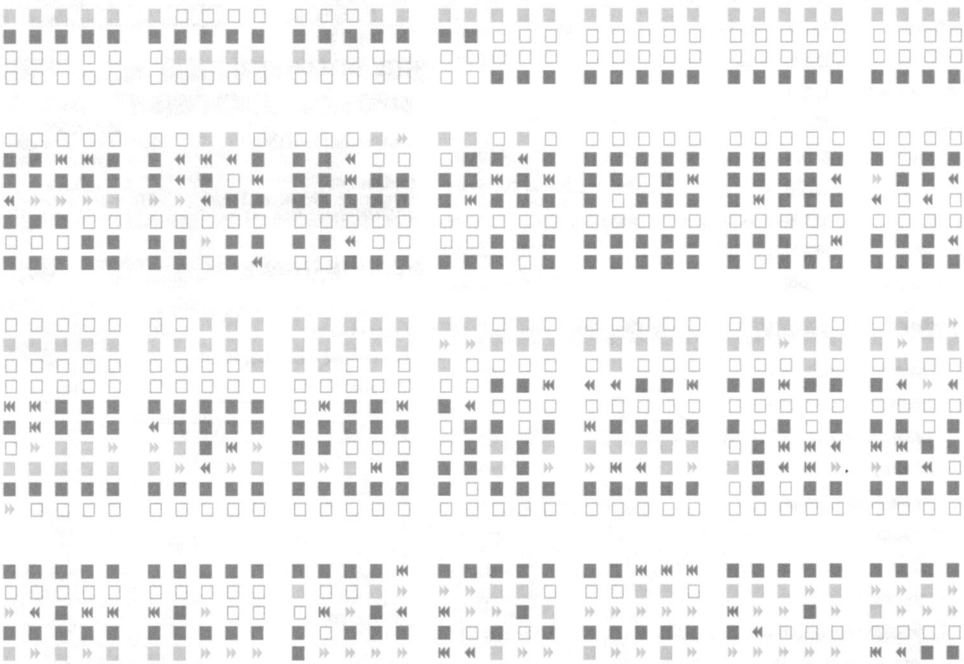

KEY: On all match · On bench · Subbed or sent off (Counting game) · Subbed or sent off (playing less than 70 minutes) · Subbed on from bench (Counting Game) · Subbed on (playing less than 70 minutes) · Subbed on and then subbed or sent off (Counting Game) · Subbed on and then subbed or sent off (playing less than 70 minutes) · Not in 16

RODA JC KERK

Final Position: **8th**

KEY: ☐ Won ☐ Drawn ☐ Lost

							Attendance
1	hopr1	**Vitesse Arnhem**	H	L	2-3	Cristiano 29; Bodnar 40	11,000
2	hopr1	**Heerenveen**	A	W	4-3	Cristiano 7; Kone 33; Sonko 78; van Dessel 90	17,000
3	hopr1	**De Graafschap**	H	W	2-1	Kone 69; Cristiano 78	13,000
4	hopr1	**Willem II Tilb**	A	L	1-3	Cisse 54	12,000
5	hopr1	**AZ Alkmaar**	H	D	1-1	Sergio 80	13,000
6	hopr1	**Ajax**	A	L	0-1		48,000
7	hopr1	**Twente**	A	W	3-2	Sergio 15; Cristiano 39; van Dijk 62 pen	13,000
8	hopr1	**Feyenoord**	H	L	0-2		17,000
9	hopr1	**Den Bosch**	H	W	5-0	Kone 41,47,64; Sergio 69; Cisse 88	12,000
10	hopr1	**NAC Breda**	A	L	0-4		12,000
11	hopr1	**RKC Waalwijk**	H	D	1-1	van Dijk 86 pen	12,000
12	hopr1	**Utrecht**	A	D	1-1	Sergio 44	20,000
13	hopr1	**Den Haag**	H	D	1-1	Sergio 86	11,000
14	hopr1	**NEC Nijmegen**	A	D	1-1	Cristiano 9	12,000
15	hopr1	**Groningen**	H	W	5-1	Cristiano 17; van Dijk 24 pen; Bodnar 37,52; Collinet 60	12,000
16	hopr1	**Roosendaal**	H	W	3-1	Cristiano 18; Kone 25; Sergio 81	13,000
17	hopr1	**PSV Eindhoven**	A	W	2-0	Bodnar 45; Sergio 80	31,000
18	hopr1	**De Graafschap**	A	L	0-2		11,000
19	hopr1	**Willem II Tilb**	H	W	4-0	Kah 7; Vicelich 41; Kone 89; Cristiano 90	12,000
20	hopr1	**Vitesse Arnhem**	A	L	0-3		17,000
21	hopr1	**Heerenveen**	H	L	2-3	Cisse 62; Kah 87	13,000
22	hopr1	**AZ Alkmaar**	A	D	1-1	Kah 32	8,000
23	hopr1	**Ajax**	H	L	1-2	Cristiano 64	18,000
24	hopr1	**Twente**	H	L	1-2	Kone 15	12,000
25	hopr1	**Feyenoord**	A	L	1-4	Ostlund 53 og	39,000
26	hopr1	**Den Bosch**	A	W	3-0	Cisse 26; Bodnar 45; Jongen 89	6,000
27	hopr1	**NAC Breda**	H	W	2-1	Sergio 50; Kah 79	12,000
28	hopr1	**RKC Waalwijk**	A	L	0-1		6,000
29	hopr1	**Utrecht**	H	W	3-2	Collinet 31,57; Sergio 42	14,000
30	hopr1	**Den Haag**	A	W	4-1	Kone 23,44,81; Bodnar 36	7,000
31	hopr1	**NEC Nijmegen**	H	W	1-0	Sergio 77	12,000
32	hopr1	**Groningen**	A	D	4-4	Cisse 37; Sergio 40; Kone 64,82	11,000
33	hopr1	**Roosendaal**	A	L	1-3	Cisse 36	5,000
34	hopr1	**PSV Eindhoven**	H	D	0-0		16,000

MONTHLY POINTS TALLY

AUGUST	6	67%
SEPTEMBER	1	11%
OCTOBER	7	47%
NOVEMBER	3	33%
DECEMBER	9	100%
JANUARY	3	50%
FEBRUARY	1	8%
MARCH	3	33%
APRIL	12	80%
MAY	2	22%

KEY PLAYERS - GOALSCORERS

Cristiano

Goals in the League	9	**Player Strike Rate** Average number of minutes between League goals scored by player	200
Contribution to Attacking Power Average number of minutes between League team goals while on pitch	52	**Club Strike Rate** Average number of minutes between League goals scored by club	51

	PLAYER	LGE GOALS	POWER	STRIKE RATE
1	Cristiano	9	53	200 mins
2	Arouna Kone	13	49	223 mins
3	Sekou Cisse	6	50	235 mins
4	Sergio	11	51	266 mins
5	Laszlo Bodnar	6	43	337 mins

KEY PLAYERS - MIDFIELDERS

Kevin van Dessel

Goals in the League	1	**Contribution to Attacking Power** Average number of minutes between League team goals while on pitch	48
Defensive Rating Average number of mins between League goals conceded while on the pitch	62	**Scoring Difference** Defensive Rating minus Contribution to Attacking Power	14

	PLAYER	LGE GOALS	DEF RATE	POWER	SCORE DIFF
1	Kevin van Dessel	1	62	48	14 mins
2	Ivan Vicelich	1	58	49	9 mins
3	Sergio	11	59	51	8 mins
4	Gregoor van Dijk	3	55	51	4 mins
5	Cristiano	9	56	53	3 mins

KEY PLAYERS - DEFENDERS

Ger Senden

Goals Conceded Number of League goals conceded while the player was on the pitch	24	**Clean Sheets** In games when player was on pitch for at least 70 minutes	2
Defensive Rating Ave number of mins between League goals conceded while on the pitch	59	**Club Defensive Rating** Average number of mins between League goals conceded by the club this season	56

	PLAYER	CON LGE	CLEAN SHEETS	DEF RATE
1	Ger Senden	24	2	59 mins
2	Boldizar Bodor	39	4	57 mins
3	Pa Modou Kah	25	4	57 mins
4	Predrag Filipovic	54	6	56 mins
5	Laszlo Bodnar	37	6	55 mins

KEY GOALKEEPER

Vladan Kujovic

Goals Conceded in the League	52	**Counting Games** League games when player was on pitch for at least 70 minutes	33
Defensive Rating Ave number of mins between League goals conceded while on the pitch	57	**Clean Sheets** In games when player was on pitch for at least 70 minutes	6

LEAGUE GOALS

Arouna Kone

Minutes on the pitch	2893	**Goals in the League**	13
League average (mins between goals)	223		

	PLAYER	MINS	GOALS	AVE
1	Kone	2893	13	223
2	Sergio	2931	11	266
3	Cristiano	1801	9	200
4	Bodnar	2021	6	337
5	Cisse	1411	6	235
6	Kah	1430	4	358
7	Collinet	980	3	327
8	van Dijk	2933	3	978
9	Jongen	154	1	154
10	Vicelich	2105	1	2105
11	van Dessel	1486	1	1486
12	Sonko	931	1	931
	Other		1	
	TOTAL		60	

DISCIPLINARY RECORDS

	PLAYER	YELLOW	RED	AVE
1	Brouwers	8	1	**109**
2	Bodnar	6	0	**336**
3	Cisse	3	1	**352**
4	Senden	4	0	**354**
5	Kah	4	0	**357**
6	Luijpers	4	0	**422**
7	Bodor	5	0	**441**
8	Sonko	2	0	**465**
9	Vicelich	4	0	**526**
10	Sergio	4	0	**732**
11	van Dijk	3	1	**733**
12	Kone	3	0	**964**
13	Filipovic	3	0	**1007**
	Other	0	0	
	TOTAL	53	3	

TOP POINT EARNERS

	PLAYER	GAMES	AV PTS
1	Ger Senden	15	**1.67**
2	Ivan Vicelich	20	**1.65**
3	Cristiano	18	**1.56**
4	Kevin van Dessel	17	**1.53**
5	Laszlo Bodnar	22	**1.50**
6	Boldizar Bodor	20	**1.45**
7	Vladan Kujovic	33	**1.42**
8	Sergio	33	**1.42**
9	Arouna Kone	31	**1.39**
10	Predrag Filipovic	34	**1.38**
	CLUB AVERAGE:		**1.38**

TEAM OF THE SEASON

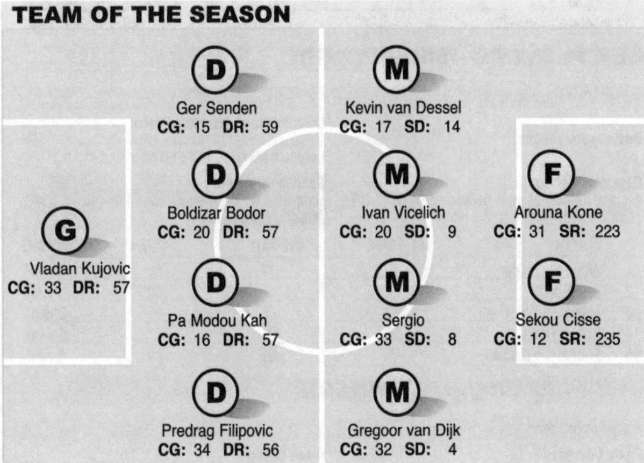

G
Vladan Kujovic
CG: 33 DR: 57
D
Ger Senden
CG: 15 DR: 59
D
Boldizar Bodor
CG: 20 DR: 57
D
Pa Modou Kah
CG: 16 DR: 57
D
Predrag Filipovic
CG: 34 DR: 56
M
Kevin van Dessel
CG: 17 SD: 14
M
Ivan Vicelich
CG: 20 SD: 9
M
Sergio
CG: 33 SD: 8
M
Gregoor van Dijk
CG: 32 SD: 4
F
Arouna Kone
CG: 31 SR: 223
F
Sekou Cisse
CG: 12 SR: 235

LEAGUE APPEARANCES, BOOKINGS AND CAPS

	AGE (on 01/07/05)	IN NAMED 18	APPEARANCES	COUNTING GAMES	MINUTES ON PITCH	YELLOW CARDS	RED CARDS	THIS SEASON	HOME COUNTRY
Goalkeepers									
Guido Budziak	22	34	1	1	90	0	0	-	Holland
Vladan Kujovic	26	34	33	33	2970	0	0	-	Serbia & Montenegro
Pascal Muller	20	3	0	0	0	0	0	-	Holland
Defenders									
Laszlo Bodnar	26	25	23	22	2021	6	0	-	Hungary
Boldizar Bodor	23	32	31	20	2206	5	0	-	Hungary
Roel Brouwers	23	30	14	10	986	8	1	-	Holland
Predrag Filipovic	30	34	34	34	3021	3	0	-	Serbia & Montenegro
Pa Modou Kah	24	16	16	16	1430	4	0	-	Norway
Vincent Lachambre	24	8	0	0	0	0	0	-	Belgium
Ken Leemans	22	13	0	0	0	0	0	-	Belgium
Mark Luijpers	34	33	27	15	1690	4	0	-	Holland
Dave Roemgens	22	5	1	0	4	0	0	-	Belgium
Ger Senden	34	29	19	15	1418	4	0	-	Holland
Midfielders									
Jerome Collinet	22	33	15	9	980	0	0	-	Belgium
Cristiano	24	24	24	18	1801	0	0	-	Brazil
Olaf Rompelberg	18	3	0	0	0	0	0	-	Holland
Sergio	24	33	33	33	2931	4	0	-	Brazil
Edrissa Sonko	25	32	25	5	931	2	0	-	Gambia
Kevin van Dessel	26	17	17	17	1486	0	0	-	Belgium
Gregoor van Dijk	23	33	33	32	2933	3	1	-	Holland
Sven Vandenbroeck	25	13	1	0	24	0	0	-	Belgium
Ivan Vicelich	29	32	28	20	2105	4	0	-	New Zealand
Forwards									
Sekou Cisse	20	28	25	12	1411	3	1	-	Ivory Coast
Mohammed Elberkani	22	8	1	0	16	0	0	-	Holland
Diego Jongen	22	11	8	0	154	0	0	-	Holland
Arouna Kone	21	33	33	31	2893	3	0	-	Ivory Coast
Youssef Sofiane	20	8	3	0	88	0	0	-	France

SQUAD APPEARANCES

Match	1	2	3	4	5	6	7	8	9	10	11	12	13	14	15	16	17	18	19	20	21	22	23	24	25	26	27	28	29	30	31	32	33	34	35	36	37
Venue	A	H	A	H	A	H	H	A	A	H	H	A	H	A	A	H	A	H	H	A	A	H	A	H	A	H	H	A	A	H	A	H	A	H	A	A	H
Competition	L	L	L	L	L	L	L	L	L	L	L	L	L	L	L	L	L	L	L	L	L	L	L	L	L	L	L	L	L	L	L	L	L	L	L	O	O
Result	D	L	W	W	L	D	W	L	W	L	W	L	D	L	D	D	D	W	W	W	L	W	L	L	D	L	L	L	W	W	L	W	W	W	D	L	D

Goalkeepers
Guido Budziak
Vladan Kujovic
Pascal Muller

Defenders
Laszlo Bodnar
Boldizar Bodor
Roel Brouwers
Predrag Filipovic
Pa Modou Kah
Vincent Lachambre
Ken Leemans
Mark Luijpers
Dave Roemgens
Ger Senden

Midfielders
Jerome Collinet
Cristiano
Olaf Rompelberg
Sergio
Edrissa Sonko
Kevin van Dessel
Gregoor van Dijk
Sven Vandenbroeck
Ivan Vicelich

Forwards
Sekou Cisse
Mohammed Elberkani
Diego Jongen
Arouna Kone
Youssef Sofiane

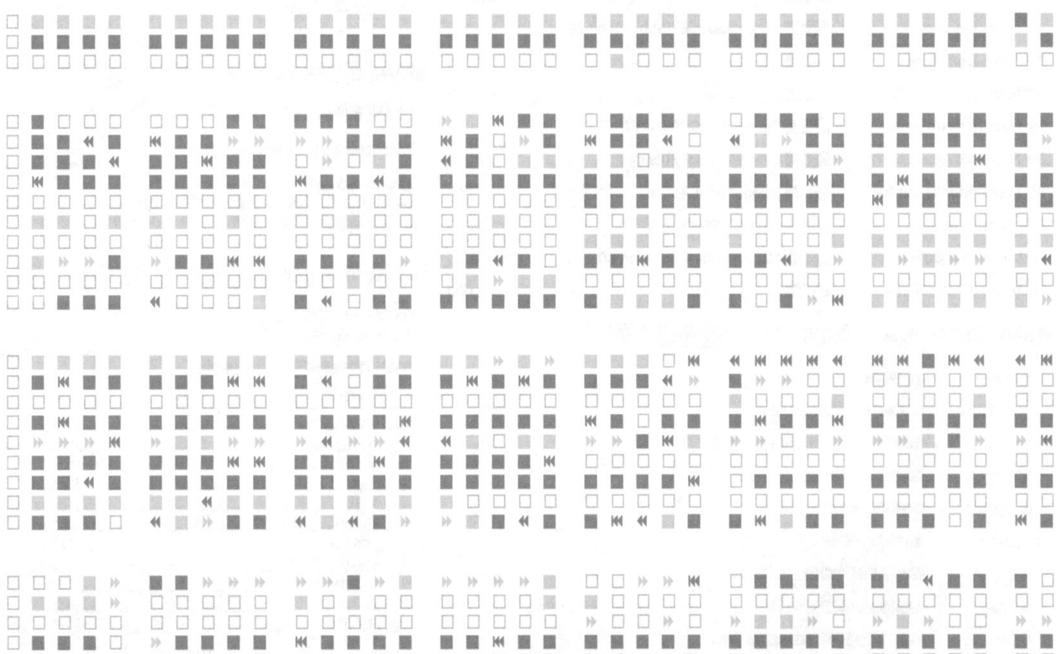

KEY: On all match / On bench / Subbed or sent off (Counting game) / Subbed or sent off (playing less than 70 minutes) / Subbed on from bench (Counting Game) / Subbed on (playing less than 70 minutes) / Subbed on and then subbed or sent off (Counting Game) / Subbed on and then subbed or sent off (playing less than 70 minutes) / Not in 16

RKC WAALWIJK

Final Position: **9th**

KEY: ☐Won ☐Drawn ☐Lost

							Attendance
1	hopr1	Groningen	A	D	0-0		12,000
2	hopr1	Twente	H	W	1-0	Martens 53	5,000
3	hopr1	Den Haag	H	L	1-3	Hoogendorp 6	5,000
4	hopr1	PSV Eindhoven	A	L	0-1		33,000
5	hopr1	Roosendaal	H	W	2-0	Fuchs 43; Hoogendorp 70	6,000
6	hopr1	NAC Breda	A	W	4-0	Fuchs 7; Putter 10; Hoogendorp 20; Krohn-Dehli 65	12,000
7	hopr1	Utrecht	A	L	2-3	Putter 26,56	19,000
8	hopr1	NEC Nijmegen	H	D	2-2	Hoogendorp 22 pen; Takak 36	5,000
9	hopr1	Feyenoord	A	L	0-4		41,000
10	hopr1	Roda JC Kerk	A	D	1-1	Fuchs 7	12,000
11	hopr1	Heerenveen	H	D	0-0		6,000
12	hopr1	De Graafschap	H	D	2-2	Janssen 10; Takak 58	4,000
13	hopr1	AZ Alkmaar	A	L	0-3		8,000
14	hopr1	Vitesse Arnhem	H	D	2-2	Oost 68; Takak 90	6,000
15	hopr1	Ajax	H	L	1-2	Fuchs 7	7,000
16	hopr1	Den Bosch	A	W	2-0	Hoogendorp 31; Janssen 85	6,000
17	hopr1	Willem II Tilb	H	W	1-0	Hoogendorp 76	6,000
18	hopr1	Roosendaal	A	W	1-0	Hoogendorp 74	5,000
19	hopr1	PSV Eindhoven	H	L	1-4	Hoogendorp 20	7,000
20	hopr1	Groningen	H	W	3-0	Hoogendorp 9; Molhoek 22; Oost 23	5,000
21	hopr1	Twente	A	L	1-3	Fuchs 7	13,000
22	hopr1	NAC Breda	H	W	1-0	Hoogendorp 12	5,000
23	hopr1	NEC Nijmegen	A	L	0-1		11,000
24	hopr1	Utrecht	H	D	2-2	Hoogendorp 15 pen; Vermaelen 68	6,000
25	hopr1	Heerenveen	A	W	2-1	Oost 77; Putter 85	20,000
26	hopr1	Feyenoord	H	L	2-4	Vasconcelos 6; Krohn-Dehli 26	7,000
27	hopr1	Den Haag	A	D	0-0		7,000
28	hopr1	Roda JC Kerk	H	W	1-0	Oost 67	6,000
29	hopr1	De Graafschap	A	W	4-2	Oost 1,40,90; Takak 60	11,000
30	hopr1	AZ Alkmaar	H	W	2-1	Jaliens 32 og; Fuchs 87	7,000
31	hopr1	Vitesse Arnhem	A	L	1-3	Hoogendorp 24	21,000
32	hopr1	Ajax	A	L	0-4		49,000
33	hopr1	Den Bosch	H	W	2-0	Martens 60; Vermaelen 80	6,000
34	hopr1	Willem II Tilb	A	L	0-3		13,000

MONTHLY POINTS TALLY

AUGUST	4	44%
SEPTEMBER	6	67%
OCTOBER	2	17%
NOVEMBER	3	25%
DECEMBER	6	67%
JANUARY	3	50%
FEBRUARY	6	50%
MARCH	4	44%
APRIL	10	83%
MAY	3	25%

KEY PLAYERS - GOALSCORERS

Rick Hoogendorp

Goals in the League 12

Player Strike Rate Average number of minutes between League goals scored by player 213

Contribution to Attacking Power Average number of minutes between League team goals while on pitch 69

Club Strike Rate Average number of minutes between League goals scored by club 70

	PLAYER	LGE GOALS	POWER	STRIKE RATE
1	Rick Hoogendorp	12	69	213 mins
2	Jason Oost	7	63	236 mins
3	Jasar Takak	4	62	432 mins
4	Robert Fuchs	6	67	481 mins
5	Thomas Vermaelen	2	68	581 mins

KEY PLAYERS - MIDFIELDERS

Alfred Schreuder

Goals in the League 0

Contribution to Attacking Power Average number of minutes between League team goals while on pitch 59

Defensive Rating Average number of mins between League goals conceded while on the pitch 72

Scoring Difference Defensive Rating minus Contribution to Attacking Power 13

	PLAYER	LGE GOALS	DEF RATE	POWER	SCORE DIFF
1	Alfred Schreuder	0	72	59	13 mins
2	Jasar Takak	4	67	62	5 mins
3	Michael Krohn-Dehli	2	66	69	-3 mins
4	Robert Fuchs	6	61	67	-6 mins
5	Patrick van Diemen	0	61	69	-8 mins

KEY PLAYERS - DEFENDERS

Virgilio Teixeira

Goals Conceded Number of League goals conceded while the player was on the pitch 22

Clean Sheets In games when player was on pitch for at least 70 minutes 8

Defensive Rating Ave number of mins between League goals conceded while on the pitch 74

Club Defensive Rating Average number of mins between League goals conceded by the club this season 60

	PLAYER	CON LGE	CLEAN SHEETS	DEF RATE
1	Virgilio Teixeira	22	8	74 mins
2	Marc van Hintum	35	7	60 mins
3	Serginho Greene	46	11	60 mins
4	Thomas Vermaelen	23	4	51 mins

KEY GOALKEEPER

Khalid Sinouh

Goals Conceded in the League 51

Counting Games League games when player was on pitch for at least 70 minutes 34

Defensive Rating Ave number of mins between League goals conceded while on the pitch 60

Clean Sheets In games when player was on pitch for at least 70 minutes 13

LEAGUE GOALS

Rick Hoogendorp

Minutes on the pitch 2553

League average (mins between goals) 213

Goals in the League 12

	PLAYER	MINS	GOALS	AVE
1	Hoogendorp	2553	12	213
2	Oost	1655	7	236
3	Fuchs	2887	6	481
4	Putter	1079	4	270
5	Takak	1729	4	432
6	Martens	1085	2	543
7	Vermaelen	1162	2	581
8	Krohn-Dehli	2566	2	1283
9	Janssen	755	2	378
10	Vasconcelos	871	1	871
11	Molhoek	1360	1	1360
	Other		1	
	TOTAL		44	

DISCIPLINARY RECORDS

	PLAYER	YELLOW	RED	AVE
1	Molhoek	6	0	226
2	Teixeira	5	0	325
3	Putter	3	0	359
4	Schreuder	4	0	412
5	Vasconcelos	2	0	435
6	Hoogendorp	4	0	638
7	Greene	3	1	689
8	van Hintum	3	0	701
9	van Diemen	4	0	720
10	Fuchs	3	0	962
11	Vermaelen	1	0	1162
12	Krohn-Dehli	2	0	1283
13	Sinouh	2	0	1530
	Other	2	0	
	TOTAL	44	1	

TOP POINT EARNERS

	PLAYER	GAMES	AV PTS
1	Alfred Schreuder	17	1.76
2	Jason Oost	14	1.64
3	Jasar Takak	18	1.61
4	Michael Krohn-Dehli	27	1.48
5	Thomas Vermaelen	13	1.46
6	Robert Fuchs	32	1.44
7	Serginho Greene	30	1.43
8	Khalid Sinouh	34	1.38
9	Patrick van Diemen	32	1.38
10	Marc van Hintum	22	1.36
	CLUB AVERAGE:		1.38

TEAM OF THE SEASON

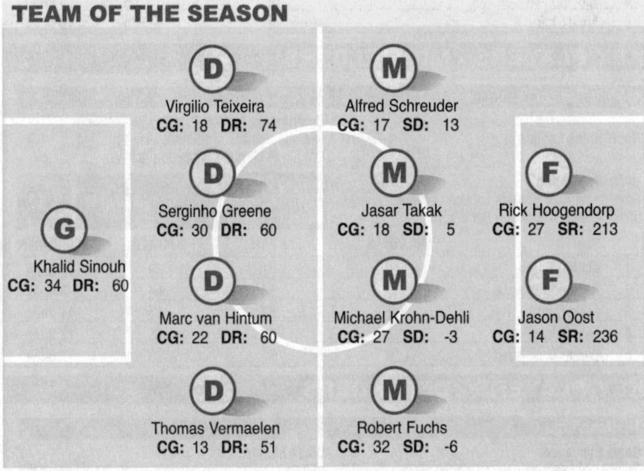
G
Khalid Sinouh
CG: 34 DR: 60
D
Virgilio Teixeira
CG: 18 DR: 74
D
Serginho Greene
CG: 30 DR: 60
D
Marc van Hintum
CG: 22 DR: 60
D
Thomas Vermaelen
CG: 13 DR: 51
M
Alfred Schreuder
CG: 17 SD: 13
M
Jasar Takak
CG: 18 SD: 5
M
Michael Krohn-Dehli
CG: 27 SD: -3
M
Robert Fuchs
CG: 32 SD: -6
F
Rick Hoogendorp
CG: 27 SR: 213
F
Jason Oost
CG: 14 SR: 236

LEAGUE APPEARANCES, BOOKINGS AND CAPS

	AGE (on 01/07/05)	IN NAMED 18	APPEARANCES	COUNTING GAMES	MINUTES ON PITCH	YELLOW CARDS	RED CARDS	THIS SEASON	HOME COUNTRY
Goalkeepers									
Khalid Sinouh	30	34	34	34	3060	2	0	-	Morocco
Jurgen Wevers	26	34	0	0	0	0	0	-	Holland
Defenders									
Khalid Boulahrouz	23	3	3	3	270	3	0	7	Holland (5)
Serginho Greene	23	31	31	30	2759	3	1	-	Holland
Tieme Klompe	29	11	2	1	79	1	0	-	Holland
Jerold Promes	21	18	7	4	374	1	0	-	Holland
Randy Rustenberg	21	24	11	4	459	0	0	-	Holland
Sjoerd Schrier	21	7	1	1	90	1	0	-	Holland
Virgilio Teixeira	31	19	19	18	1628	5	0	-	Portugal
Marc van Hintum	38	25	25	22	2103	3	0	-	Holland
Sjack van Rijsbergen	20	2	0	0	0	0	0	-	Holland
Thomas Vermaelen	19	13	13	13	1162	1	0	-	Belgium
Midfielders									
Robert Fuchs	30	33	33	32	2887	3	0	-	Holland
Michael Krohn-Dehli	22	31	31	27	2566	2	0	-	Denmark
Didi Longuet	23	16	3	1	136	0	0	-	Holland
Maarten Martens	21	30	23	9	1085	0	0	-	Belgium
Rogier Molhoek	23	22	21	11	1360	6	0	-	Holland
Alfred Schreuder	32	20	20	17	1651	4	0	-	Holland
Jasar Takak	23	23	22	18	1729	1	0	-	Turkey
M. Van der Heijden	23	6	0	0	0	0	0	-	Holland
Patrick van Diemen	33	32	32	32	2880	4	0	-	Holland
Forwards									
Ferdi Elmas	20	15	9	0	183	0	0	-	Holland
Cerezo Fung-A-Wing	21	6	4	1	162	0	0	-	Holland
Rick Hoogendorp	30	33	33	27	2553	4	0	-	Holland
Jochen Janssen	29	16	15	5	755	0	0	-	Belgium
Jason Oost	22	32	28	14	1655	1	0	-	Holland
Eddy Putter	23	25	22	7	1079	3	0	-	Holland
Nick van der Velden	20	20	8	0	93	0	0	-	Holland
Bernardo Vasconcelos	26	16	15	7	871	2	0	-	Portugal

SQUAD APPEARANCES

Match	1	2	3	4	5	6	7	8	9	10	11	12	13	14	15	16	17	18	19	20	21	22	23	24	25	26	27	28	29	30	31	32	33	34
Venue	A	H	H	A	H	A	A	H	A	A	H	H	A	H	H	A	H	A	H	H	A	H	A	H	A	H	A	H	A	H	A	A	H	A
Competition	L	L	L	L	L	L	L	L	L	L	L	L	L	L	L	L	L	L	L	L	L	L	L	L	L	L	L	L	L	L	L	L	L	L
Result	D	W	L	L	W	W	L	D	L	D	D	D	L	D	L	W	W	W	L	W	L	W	L	D	W	L	D	W	W	W	L	L	W	L

Goalkeepers
Khalid Sinouh
Jurgen Wevers

Defenders
Khalid Boulahrouz
Serginho Greene
Tieme Klompe
Jerold Promes
Randy Rustenberg
Sjoerd Schrier
Virgilio Teixeira
Marc van Hintum
Sjack van Rijsbergen
Thomas Vermaelen

Midfielders
Robert Fuchs
Michael Krohn-Dehli
Didi Longuet
Maarten Martens
Rogier Molhoek
Alfred Schreuder
Jasar Takak
Michael Van der Heijden
Patrick van Diemen

Forwards
Ferdi Elmas
Cerezo Fung-A-Wing
Rick Hoogendorp
Jochen Janssen
Jason Oost
Eddy Putter
Nick van der Velden
Bernardo Vasconcelos

KEY: ■ On all match ■ On bench ⏮ Subbed or sent off (Counting game) « Subbed or sent off (playing less than 70 minutes) ⏭ Subbed on from bench (Counting Game) » Subbed on (playing less than 70 minutes) ⏭ Subbed on and then subbed or sent off (Counting Game) » Subbed on and then subbed or sent off (playing less than 70 minutes) □ Not in 16

WILLEM II TILB

Final Position: **10th**

KEY: ☐Won ☐Drawn ☐Lost

		Opponent	H/A	Res	Score	Scorers	Attendance
1	hopr1	**NEC Nijmegen**	A	L	0-2		12,000
2	hopr1	**Feyenoord**	H	L	0-4		14,000
3	hopr1	**Den Bosch**	A	W	2-1	Mathijssen 27; Bobson 44	6,000
4	hopr1	**Roda JC Kerk**	H	W	3-1	Bobson 5,25; Redan 63	12,000
5	hopr1	**Twente**	A	D	0-0		13,000
6	hopr1	**AZ Alkmaar**	A	L	1-3	Reuser 8	8,000
7	hopr1	**Vitesse Arnhem**	H	W	3-2	Reuser 13,33 pen,45 pen	12,000
8	hopr1	**Groningen**	H	W	4-2	Redan 3; Matthijs 53 og; Victoria 77; Reuser 90	11,000
9	hopr1	**De Graafschap**	A	D	2-2	Hadouir 12; Reuser 58	11,000
10	hopr1	**Roosendaal**	H	W	3-0	Redan 68; Hadouir 72; Caluwe 77	12,000
11	hopr1	**Ajax**	H	L	1-3	van Nieuwstadt 13	13,000
12	hopr1	**PSV Eindhoven**	A	L	0-1		31,000
13	hopr1	**NAC Breda**	H	L	0-1		13,000
14	hopr1	**Den Haag**	A	W	1-0	Bobson 36; Reuser 89	6,000
15	hopr1	**Heerenveen**	H	D	2-2	Caluwe 30; van Nieuwstadt 90	11,000
16	hopr1	**Utrecht**	H	D	0-0		13,000
17	hopr1	**RKC Waalwijk**	A	L	0-1		6,000
18	hopr1	**Twente**	H	L	0-3		13,000
19	hopr1	**Roda JC Kerk**	A	L	0-4		12,000
20	hopr1	**NEC Nijmegen**	H	W	3-1	Ceesay 22; Smit 27; Redan 48	12,000
21	hopr1	**Feyenoord**	A	L	0-7		37,000
22	hopr1	**Roosendaal**	A	L	0-2		5,000
23	hopr1	**AZ Alkmaar**	H	L	1-3	Ceesay 26	12,000
24	hopr1	**Vitesse Arnhem**	A	L	0-2		19,000
25	hopr1	**Den Bosch**	H	W	2-1	Denissen 74; Caluwe 86	12,000
26	hopr1	**Groningen**	A	D	1-1	Bobson 21	12,000
27	hopr1	**De Graafschap**	H	W	4-1	Ceesay 42; Bobson 48; Augustien 56; Denissen 90	13,000
28	hopr1	**Ajax**	A	L	0-2		45,000
29	hopr1	**PSV Eindhoven**	H	L	0-1		13,000
30	hopr1	**NAC Breda**	A	W	2-1	Caluwe 2; Redan 57	13,000
31	hopr1	**Den Haag**	H	W	1-0	Reuser 20	12,000
32	hopr1	**Heerenveen**	A	D	2-2	Bobson 22; Redan 33	21,000
33	hopr1	**Utrecht**	A	W	3-0	Caluwe 53; Reuser 63,83	19,000
34	hopr1	**RKC Waalwijk**	H	W	3-0	Ceesay 16; Bobson 23; Caluwe 50	13,000

MONTHLY POINTS TALLY

AUGUST	3	33%
SEPTEMBER	4	44%
OCTOBER	10	83%
NOVEMBER	3	25%
DECEMBER	2	22%
JANUARY	0	0%
FEBRUARY	3	25%
MARCH	4	44%
APRIL	6	50%
MAY	10	83%

KEY PLAYERS - GOALSCORERS

Martijn Reuser

Goals in the League	10	**Player Strike Rate** Average number of minutes between League goals scored by player	205
Contribution to Attacking Power Average number of minutes between League team goals while on pitch	58	**Club Strike Rate** Average number of minutes between League goals scored by club	67

	PLAYER	LGE GOALS	POWER	STRIKE RATE
1	Martijn Reuser	10	59	205 mins
2	Iwan Redan	6	62	272 mins
3	Kevin Bobson	8	71	348 mins
4	Tom Caluwe	6	65	370 mins
5	Arvid Smit	2	65	618 mins

KEY PLAYERS - MIDFIELDERS

Martijn Reuser

Goals in the League	10	**Contribution to Attacking Power** Average number of minutes between League team goals while on pitch	59
Defensive Rating Average number of mins between League goals conceded while on the pitch	71	**Scoring Difference** Defensive Rating minus Contribution to Attacking Power	12

	PLAYER	LGE GOALS	DEF RATE	POWER	SCORE DIFF
1	Martijn Reuser	10	71	59	12 mins
2	Raymond Victoria	1	56	64	-8 mins
3	Arvid Smit	2	54	65	-11 mins
4	Tom Caluwe	6	53	65	-12 mins
5	Danny Mathijssen	1	56	73	-17 mins

KEY PLAYERS - DEFENDERS

Nuelson Wau

Goals Conceded Number of League goals conceded while the player was on the pitch	27	**Clean Sheets** In games when player was on pitch for at least 70 minutes	6
Defensive Rating Ave number of mins between League goals conceded while on the pitch	65	**Club Defensive Rating** Average number of mins between League goals conceded by the club this season	55

	PLAYER	CON LGE	CLEAN SHEETS	DEF RATE
1	Nuelson Wau	27	6	65 mins
2	Frank van Mosselveld	29	4	56 mins
3	Albert van der Haar	52	7	55 mins
4	Frank Van der Struijk	32	3	50 mins
5	Michel Kreek	32	2	47 mins

KEY GOALKEEPER

Oscar Moens

Goals Conceded in the League	56	**Counting Games** League games when player was on pitch for at least 70 minutes	34
Defensive Rating Ave number of mins between League goals conceded while on the pitch	55	**Clean Sheets** In games when player was on pitch for at least 70 minutes	7

LEAGUE GOALS

Martijn Reuser

Minutes on the pitch	2052	**Goals in the League**	10
League average (mins between goals)	205		

	PLAYER	MINS	GOALS	AVE
1	Reuser	2052	10	205
2	Bobson	2781	8	348
3	Caluwe	2218	6	370
4	Redan	1631	6	272
5	Ceesay	1090	4	273
6	van Nieuwstadt	1688	2	844
7	Hadouir	952	2	476
8	Denissen	459	2	230
9	Smit	1235	2	618
10	Augustien	1052	1	1052
11	Mathijssen	1465	1	1465
12	Victoria	2415	1	2415
	Other		1	
	TOTAL		46	

DISCIPLINARY RECORDS

	PLAYER	YELLOW	RED	AVE
1	Quinn	4	1	122
2	Augustien	4	0	263
3	van Nieuwstadt	6	0	281
4	Smit	4	0	308
5	Van der Struijk	4	1	319
6	Wau	5	0	352
7	Caluwe	6	0	369
8	van Mosselveld	3	1	402
9	Kreek	2	1	497
10	Reuser	4	0	513
11	Ceesay	2	0	545
12	Kolsi	1	0	551
13	Victoria	4	0	603
	Other	11	0	
	TOTAL	60	4	

TOP POINT EARNERS

	PLAYER	GAMES	AV PTS
1	Frank van Mosselveld	15	1.73
2	Nuelson Wau	18	1.72
3	Frank Van der Struijk	17	1.47
4	Martijn Reuser	22	1.45
5	Arvid Smit	14	1.43
6	Iwan Redan	17	1.35
7	Oscar Moens	34	1.32
8	Albert van der Haar	32	1.31
9	Raymond Victoria	24	1.29
10	Danny Mathijssen	14	1.29
	CLUB AVERAGE:		1.32

TEAM OF THE SEASON

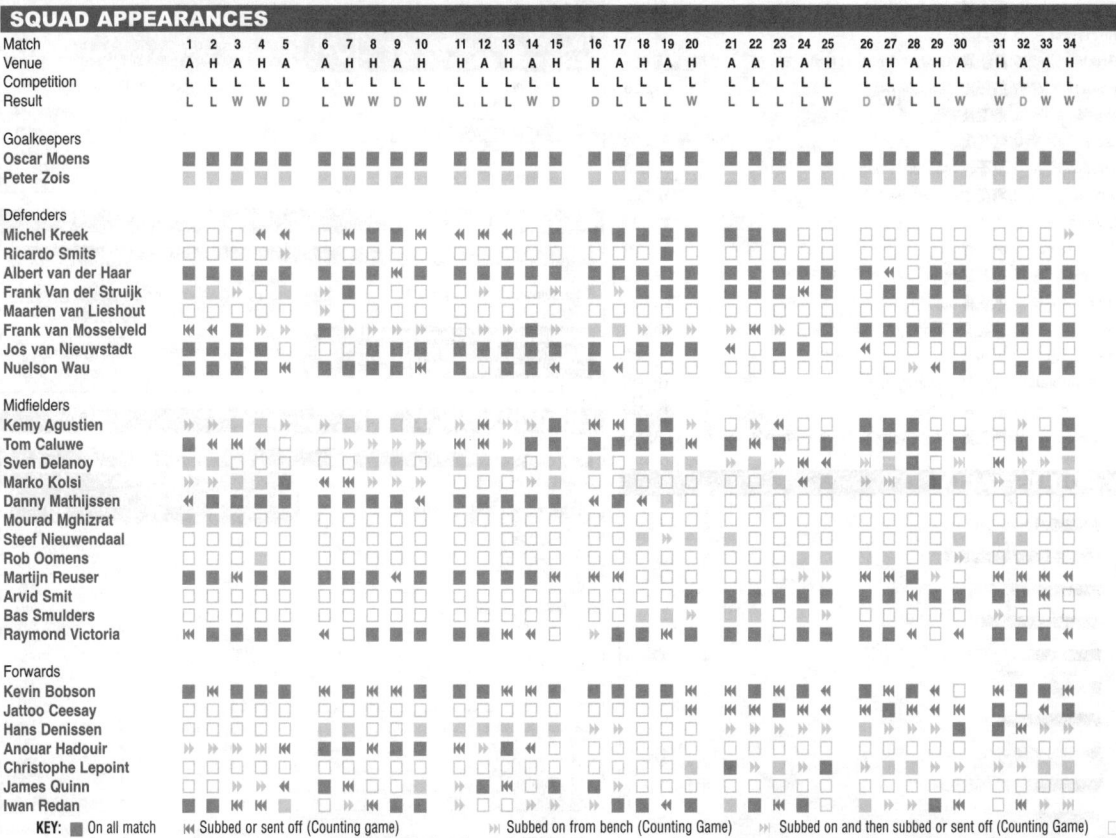

G Oscar Moens CG: 34 DR: 55

D Nuelson Wau CG: 18 DR: 65

D Frank van Mosselveld CG: 15 DR: 56

D Albert van der Haar CG: 32 DR: 55

D Frank Van der Struijk CG: 17 DR: 50

M Martijn Reuser CG: 22 SD: 12

M Raymond Victoria CG: 24 SD: -8

M Arvid Smit CG: 14 SD: -11

M Tom Caluwe CG: 23 SD: -12

F Iwan Redan CG: 17 SR: 272

F Kevin Bobson CG: 30 SR: 348

LEAGUE APPEARANCES, BOOKINGS AND CAPS

	AGE (on 01/07/05)	IN NAMED 18	APPEARANCES	COUNTING GAMES	MINUTES ON PITCH	YELLOW CARDS	RED CARDS	THIS SEASON	HOME COUNTRY
Goalkeepers									
Oscar Moens	32	34	34	34	3060	2	0	-	Holland
Peter Zois	27	34	0	0	0	0	0	-	Australia
Defenders									
Michel Kreek	34	19	19	14	1492	2	1	-	Holland
Ricardo Smits	23	2	2	1	91	0	0	-	Holland
Albert van der Haar	29	33	33	32	2875	2	0	-	Holland
Frank Van der Struijk	20	25	21	17	1596	4	1	-	Holland
Maarten van Lieshout	19	5	1	0	4	0	0	-	Belgium
Frank van Mosselveld	21	32	30	15	1610	3	1	-	Holland
Jos van Nieuwstadt	25	20	20	18	1688	6	0	-	Holland
Nuelson Wau	24	22	22	18	1764	5	0	-	Holland
Midfielders									
Kemy Agustien	18	27	21	10	1052	4	0	-	Holland
Tom Caluwe	30	30	30	23	2218	6	0	-	Belgium
Sven Delanoy	21	25	10	5	510	0	0	-	Belgium
Marko Kolsi	20	24	14	4	551	1	0	-	Holland
Danny Mathijssen	22	19	18	14	1465	2	0	-	Holland
Mourad Mghizrat	30	3	0	0	0	0	0	-	Morocco
Steef Nieuwendaal	19	7	1	0	33	0	0	-	Holland
Rob Oomens	24	7	1	0	2	0	0	-	Holland
Martijn Reuser	30	27	27	22	2052	4	0	-	Holland
Arvid Smit	24	14	14	14	1235	4	0	-	Holland
Bas Smulders	19	8	3	0	41	0	0	-	Holland
Raymond Victoria	32	30	30	24	2415	4	0	-	Holland
Forwards									
Kevin Bobson	24	33	33	30	2781	2	0	1	Holland (5)
Jattoo Ceesay	30	14	14	10	1090	2	0	-	Gambia
Hans Denissen	21	24	15	3	459	0	0	-	Holland
Anouar Hadouir	22	14	14	9	952	1	0	-	Holland
Christophe Lepoint	23	15	9	2	314	1	0	-	Belgium
James Quinn	30	12	11	6	611	4	1	5	N Ireland (114)
Iwan Redan	24	29	26	17	1631	2	0	-	Holland

SQUAD APPEARANCES

Match	1	2	3	4	5	6	7	8	9	10	11	12	13	14	15	16	17	18	19	20	21	22	23	24	25	26	27	28	29	30	31	32	33	34
Venue	A	H	A	H	A	A	H	H	A	H	H	A	H	A	H	H	A	H	A	H	A	A	H	A	H	A	H	A	H	A	H	A	A	H
Competition	L	L	L	L	L	L	L	L	L	L	L	L	L	L	L	L	L	L	L	L	L	L	L	L	L	L	L	L	L	L	L	L	L	L
Result	L	L	W	W	D	L	W	W	D	W	L	L	L	W	D	D	L	L	L	W	L	L	L	L	W	D	W	L	L	W	W	D	W	W

Goalkeepers
Oscar Moens
Peter Zois

Defenders
Michel Kreek
Ricardo Smits
Albert van der Haar
Frank Van der Struijk
Maarten van Lieshout
Frank van Mosselveld
Jos van Nieuwstadt
Nuelson Wau

Midfielders
Kemy Agustien
Tom Caluwe
Sven Delanoy
Marko Kolsi
Danny Mathijssen
Mourad Mghizrat
Steef Nieuwendaal
Rob Oomens
Martijn Reuser
Arvid Smit
Bas Smulders
Raymond Victoria

Forwards
Kevin Bobson
Jattoo Ceesay
Hans Denissen
Anouar Hadouir
Christophe Lepoint
James Quinn
Iwan Redan

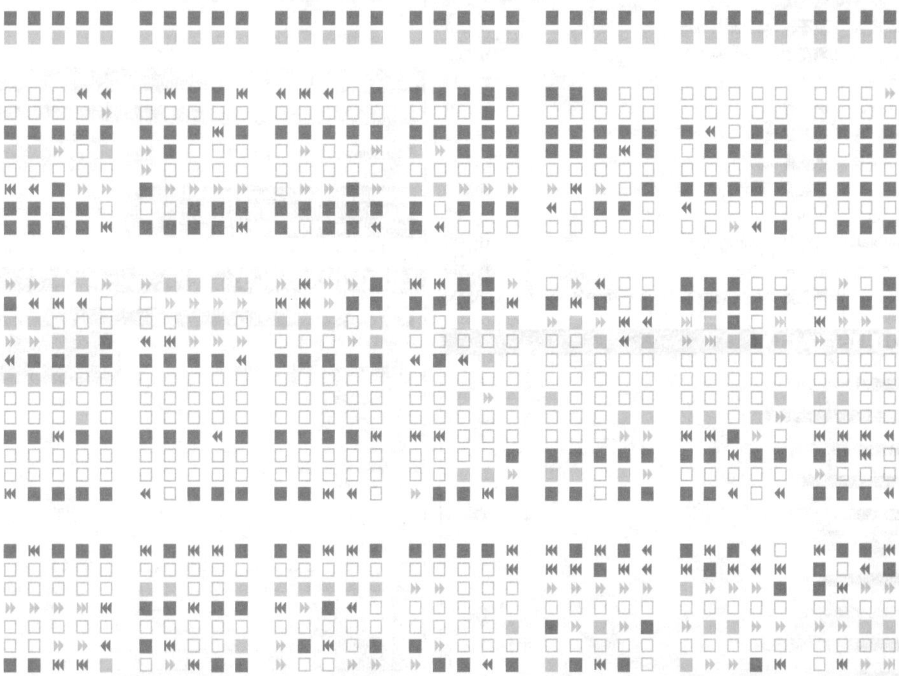

KEY: On all match · On bench · Subbed or sent off (Counting game) · Subbed or sent off (playing less than 70 minutes) · Subbed on from bench (Counting Game) · Subbed on (playing less than 70 minutes) · Subbed on and then subbed or sent off (Counting Game) · Subbed on and then subbed or sent off (playing less than 70 minutes) · Not in 16

UTRECHT

Final Position: **11th**

KEY: ☐Won ☐Drawn ☐Lost

							Attendance
1	hosc	**Ajax**	A	W	4-2	Schut 72; Somers 87,90; Maxwell 90 og	
2	hopr1	**NAC Breda**	A	L	2-3	Calabro 5; van den Bergh 41	11,000
3	hopr1	**Roosendaal**	H	W	5-1	van de Haar 35,54 pen,62; Cornelisse 75; Tanghe 90	17,000
4	hopr1	**Ajax**	A	D	1-1	Douglas 21	45,000
5	hopr1	**NEC Nijmegen**	H	W	1-0	van de Haar 53	18,000
6	uc1rl1	**Djurgarden**	H	W	4-0	van de Haar 2; Tanghe 27,87; van den Bergh 73	18,000
7	hopr1	**Feyenoord**	A	W	3-0	Schut 31; Somers 88; Broerse 90	38,000
8	hopr1	**Den Haag**	H	W	2-0	Schut 41; Tanghe 50	18,000
9	uc1rl2	**Djurgarden**	A	L	0-3		4,449
10	hopr1	**RKC Waalwijk**	H	W	3-2	van de Haar 60,83; Somers 69	19,000
11	hopr1	**Groningen**	A	L	0-3		12,000
12	ucgpc	**Real Zaragoza**	A	L	0-2		27,000
13	hopr1	**Heerenveen**	A	L	1-2	Leitoe 90	18,000
14	hopr1	**PSV Eindhoven**	H	D	0-0		22,000
15	ucgpc	**Dnipro**	H	L	1-2	Douglas 88	14,150
16	hopr1	**AZ Alkmaar**	A	L	0-4		8,000
17	hopr1	**Roda JC Kerk**	H	D	1-1	van den Bergh 66	20,000
18	hopr1	**Twente**	A	W	1-0	Tanghe 37	13,000
19	ucgpc	**Club Brugge**	A	L	0-1		21,561
20	hopr1	**De Graafschap**	H	W	1-0	Kruys 81	18,000
21	hopr1	**Vitesse Arnhem**	A	L	1-2	Douglas 85	16,000
22	hopr1	**Willem II Tilb**	A	D	0-0		13,000
23	ucgpc	**Austria Vienna**	H	L	1-2	Douglas 55	13,500
24	hopr1	**Den Bosch**	H	W	1-0	van de Haar 55	19,000
25	hopr1	**Ajax**	H	L	0-2		23,000
26	hopr1	**NEC Nijmegen**	A	D	0-0		12,000
27	hopr1	**NAC Breda**	H	W	2-0	van den Bergh 1; Keller 60	18,000
28	hopr1	**Roosendaal**	A	W	1-0	Tiendalli 74	5,000
29	hopr1	**Feyenoord**	H	L	0-2		23,000
30	hopr1	**Den Haag**	A	L	0-1		5,000
31	hopr1	**RKC Waalwijk**	A	D	2-2	Mols 39; Douglas 42	6,000
32	hopr1	**Groningen**	H	L	1-2	Cornelisse 17	18,000
33	hopr1	**Heerenveen**	H	L	0-1		21,000
34	hopr1	**PSV Eindhoven**	A	L	0-2		31,000
35	hopr1	**Roda JC Kerk**	A	L	2-3	Kruys 37; van de Haar 79	14,000
36	hopr1	**AZ Alkmaar**	H	W	3-2	de Jong 37; Tanghe 54,65	20,000
37	hopr1	**Twente**	H	D	2-2	Tanghe 27; van de Haar 63	20,000
38	hopr1	**De Graafschap**	A	D	0-0		11,000
39	hopr1	**Vitesse Arnhem**	H	L	1-2	Keller 30	19,000
40	hopr1	**Willem II Tilb**	H	L	0-3		19,000
41	hopr1	**Den Bosch**	A	W	3-0	van den Bergh 9,88; Verhaegh 45 og	6,000

MONTHLY POINTS TALLY

AUGUST	4	44%
SEPTEMBER	9	100%
OCTOBER	4	33%
NOVEMBER	7	58%
DECEMBER	4	44%
JANUARY	1	17%
FEBRUARY	6	50%
MARCH	1	11%
APRIL	4	33%
MAY	4	33%

KEY PLAYERS - GOALSCORERS

Hans van de Haar

Goals in the League	9	**Player Strike Rate** Average number of minutes between League goals scored by player	202
Contribution to Attacking Power Average number of minutes between League team goals while on pitch	70	**Club Strike Rate** Average number of minutes between League goals scored by club	77

	PLAYER	LGE GOALS	POWER	STRIKE RATE
1	Hans van de Haar	9	70	202 mins
2	Stefaan Tanghe	6	70	421 mins
3	Dave van den Bergh	5	79	476 mins
4	Rick Kruys	2	85	773 mins
5	Sander Keller	2	84	849 mins

KEY PLAYERS - MIDFIELDERS

Tim Cornelisse

Goals in the League	2	**Contribution to Attacking Power** Average number of minutes between League team goals while on pitch	71
Defensive Rating Average number of mins between League goals conceded while on the pitch	77	**Scoring Difference** Defensive Rating minus Contribution to Attacking Power	6

	PLAYER	LGE GOALS	DEF RATE	POWER	SCORE DIFF
1	Tim Cornelisse	2	77	71	6 mins
2	Jean-Paul de Jong	1	65	60	5 mins
3	Stefaan Tanghe	6	72	70	2 mins
4	Darl Douglas	3	72	70	2 mins
5	David Di Tommaso	0	68	74	-6 mins

KEY PLAYERS - DEFENDERS

Alje Schut

Goals Conceded Number of League goals conceded while the player was on the pitch	19	**Clean Sheets** In games when player was on pitch for at least 70 minutes	8
Defensive Rating Ave number of mins between League goals conceded while on the pitch	91	**Club Defensive Rating** Average number of mins between League goals conceded by the club this season	71

	PLAYER	CON LGE	CLEAN SHEETS	DEF RATE
1	Alje Schut	19	8	91 mins
2	Etienne Shew-Atjon	23	7	76 mins
3	Edson Braafheid	21	4	67 mins
4	Sander Keller	27	7	63 mins

KEY GOALKEEPER

Rene Ponk

Goals Conceded in the League	20	**Counting Games** League games when player was on pitch for at least 70 minutes	18
Defensive Rating Ave number of mins between League goals conceded while on the pitch	81	**Clean Sheets** In games when player was on pitch for at least 70 minutes	9

LEAGUE GOALS

Hans van de Haar

Minutes on the pitch	1821	**Goals in the League**	9
League average (mins between goals)	202		

	PLAYER	MINS	GOALS	AVE
1	van de Haar	1821	9	202
2	Tanghe	2527	6	421
3	van den Bergh	2379	5	476
4	Douglas	2793	3	931
5	Schut	1722	2	861
6	Keller	1698	2	849
7	Kruys	1546	2	773
8	Somers	1406	2	703
9	Cornelisse	2550	2	1275
10	Leitoe	284	1	284
11	Tiendalli	520	1	520
12	Calabro	95	1	95
13	Mols	802	1	802
	Other		3	
	TOTAL		40	

DISCIPLINARY RECORDS

	PLAYER	YELLOW	RED	AVE
1	Tiendalli	2	0	260
2	Kruys	5	0	309
3	de Jong	4	0	405
4	Schut	4	0	430
5	Shew-Atjon	4	0	439
6	Tanghe	4	1	505
7	Cornelisse	5	0	510
8	Keller	3	0	566
9	Braafheid	2	0	699
10	Somers	2	0	703
11	van den Bergh	3	0	793
12	Broerse	2	0	803
13	Di Tommaso	2	0	1361
	Other	3	0	
	TOTAL	45	1	

TOP POINT EARNERS

	PLAYER	GAMES	AV PTS
1	Rene Ponk	18	1.61
2	Jean-Paul de Jong	15	1.60
3	Hans van de Haar	17	1.47
4	Alje Schut	18	1.44
5	Tim Cornelisse	28	1.43
6	Stefaan Tanghe	27	1.41
7	Darl Douglas	31	1.39
8	Joost Broerse	14	1.36
9	Edson Braafheid	12	1.33
10	David Di Tommaso	30	1.27
	CLUB AVERAGE:		1.29

LEAGUE APPEARANCES, BOOKINGS AND CAPS

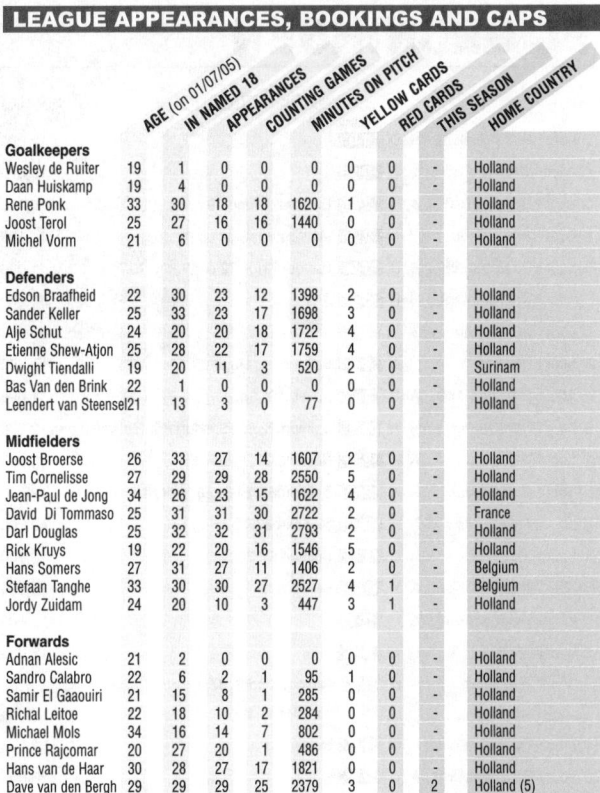

	AGE (on 01/07/05)	IN NAMED 18	APPEARANCES	COUNTING GAMES	MINUTES ON PITCH	YELLOW CARDS	RED CARDS	THIS SEASON	HOME COUNTRY
Goalkeepers									
Wesley de Ruiter	19	1	0	0	0	0	0	-	Holland
Daan Huiskamp	19	4	0	0	0	0	0	-	Holland
Rene Ponk	33	30	18	18	1620	1	0	-	Holland
Joost Terol	25	27	16	16	1440	0	0	-	Holland
Michel Vorm	21	6	0	0	0	0	0	-	Holland
Defenders									
Edson Braafheid	22	30	23	12	1398	2	0	-	Holland
Sander Keller	25	33	23	17	1698	3	0	-	Holland
Alje Schut	24	20	20	18	1722	4	0	-	Holland
Etienne Shew-Atjon	25	28	22	17	1759	4	0	-	Holland
Dwight Tiendalli	19	20	11	3	520	2	0	-	Surinam
Bas Van den Brink	22	1	0	0	0	0	0	-	Holland
Leendert van Steensel	21	13	3	0	77	0	0	-	Holland
Midfielders									
Joost Broerse	26	33	27	14	1607	2	0	-	Holland
Tim Cornelisse	27	29	29	28	2550	5	0	-	Holland
Jean-Paul de Jong	34	26	23	15	1622	4	0	-	Holland
David Di Tommaso	25	31	31	30	2722	2	0	-	France
Darl Douglas	25	32	32	31	2793	2	0	-	Holland
Rick Kruys	19	22	20	16	1546	5	0	-	Holland
Hans Somers	27	31	27	11	1406	2	0	-	Belgium
Stefaan Tanghe	33	30	30	27	2527	4	1	-	Belgium
Jordy Zuidam	24	20	10	3	447	3	1	-	Holland
Forwards									
Adnan Alesic	21	2	0	0	0	0	0	-	Holland
Sandro Calabro	22	6	2	1	95	1	0	-	Holland
Samir El Gaaouiri	21	15	8	1	285	0	0	-	Holland
Richal Leitoe	22	18	10	2	284	0	0	-	Holland
Michael Mols	34	16	14	7	802	0	0	-	Holland
Prince Rajcomar	20	27	20	1	486	0	0	-	Holland
Hans van de Haar	30	28	27	17	1821	0	0	-	Holland
Dave van den Bergh	29	29	29	25	2379	3	0	2	Holland (5)

TEAM OF THE SEASON

D
Alje Schut
CG: 18 DR: 91
M
Tim Cornelisse
CG: 28 SD: 6
D
Etienne Shew-Atjon
CG: 17 DR: 76
M
Jean-Paul de Jong
CG: 15 SD: 5
F
Hans van de Haar
CG: 17 SR: 202
G
Rene Ponk
CG: 18 DR: 81
D
Edson Braafheid
CG: 12 DR: 67
M
Darl Douglas
CG: 31 SD: 2
F
Dave van den Bergh
CG: 25 SR: 476
D
Sander Keller
CG: 17 DR: 63
M
Stefaan Tanghe
CG: 27 SD: 2

SQUAD APPEARANCES

Match	1	2	3	4	5	6	7	8	9	10	11	12	13	14	15	16	17	18	19	20	21	22	23	24	25	26	27	28	29	30	31	32	33	34	35	36	37	38	39	40	41
Venue	A	A	H	A	H	H	A	H	A	H	A	A	A	H	H	A	H	A	A	H	A	A	H	H	H	A	H	A	H	A	A	H	H	A	A	H	H	A	H	H	A
Competition	O	L	L	L	L	E	L	L	E	L	L	E	L	L	E	L	L	L	E	L	L	L	E	L	L	L	L	L	L	L	L	L	L	L	L	L	L	L	L	L	L
Result	W	L	W	D	W	W	W	W	L	W	L	L	L	D	L	L	D	W	L	W	L	D	L	W	L	D	W	W	L	L	D	L	L	L	L	W	D	D	L	L	W

Goalkeepers
Wesley de Ruiter
Daan Huiskamp
Rene Ponk
Joost Terol
Michel Vorm

Defenders
Edson Braafheid
Sander Keller
Alje Schut
Etienne Shew-Atjon
Dwight Tiendalli
Bas Van den Brink
L. van Steensel

Midfielders
Joost Broerse
Tim Cornelisse
Jean-Paul de Jong
David Di Tommaso
Darl Douglas
Rick Kruys
Hans Somers
Stefaan Tanghe
Jordy Zuidam

Forwards
Adnan Alesic
Sandro Calabro
Samir El Gaaouiri
Richal Leitoe
Michael Mols
Prince Rajcomar
Hans van de Haar
Dave van den Bergh

KEY: On all match · On bench · Subbed or sent off (Counting game) · Subbed or sent off (playing less than 70 minutes) · Subbed on from bench (Counting Game) · Subbed on (playing less than 70 minutes) · Subbed on and then subbed or sent off (Counting Game) · Subbed on and then subbed or sent off (playing less than 70 minutes) · Not in 16

FC GRONINGEN

Final Position: **12th**

KEY: ☐Won ☐Drawn ☐Lost

#		Opponent	H/A	Res	Score	Scorers	Attendance
1	hopr1	**RKC Waalwijk**	H	D	0-0		12,000
2	hopr1	**Vitesse Arnhem**	A	L	0-1		16,000
3	hopr1	**Roosendaal**	A	D	2-2	Drent 43; Hugo 79	5,000
4	hopr1	**NAC Breda**	H	L	2-3	Matthijs 20; Salmon 81	11,000
5	hopr1	**De Graafschap**	A	D	2-2	van der Kruis 72 og; Pinas 75	11,000
6	hopr1	**NEC Nijmegen**	H	D	0-0		11,000
7	hopr1	**PSV Eindhoven**	A	L	0-3		30,000
8	hopr1	**Utrecht**	H	W	3-0	Seedorf 11; Hugo 62; Elshot 73	12,000
9	hopr1	**Willem II Tilb**	A	L	2-4	Krstev 10; Seedorf 54	11,000
10	hopr1	**Den Haag**	H	W	4-3	Salmon 22,60; Seedorf 45; Elshot 49 pen	12,000
11	hopr1	**Twente**	A	W	2-1	Nevland 29; Krstev 53	13,000
12	hopr1	**Den Bosch**	H	W	3-1	Salmon 55; Buijs 58; Floren 75	12,000
13	hopr1	**Feyenoord**	A	W	2-1	Nevland 23,71	40,000
14	hopr1	**AZ Alkmaar**	H	L	1-2	Salmon 57	13,000
15	hopr1	**Roda JC Kerk**	A	L	1-5	van Gessel 78	12,000
16	hopr1	**Heerenveen**	A	L	0-1		18,000
17	hopr1	**Ajax**	H	L	0-4		13,000
18	hopr1	**Den Haag**	A	W	3-0	van der Linden 37; Nevland 42; van Gessel 83	6,000
19	hopr1	**De Graafschap**	H	W	1-0	Nevland 35	12,000
20	hopr1	**RKC Waalwijk**	A	L	0-3		5,000
21	hopr1	**Vitesse Arnhem**	H	D	0-0		12,000
22	hopr1	**Twente**	H	L	0-1		12,000
23	hopr1	**NAC Breda**	A	W	4-1	Nevland 15; van Gessel 62; Seedorf 71; Krstev 84	12,000
24	hopr1	**Utrecht**	A	W	2-1	Nevland 8,41	18,000
25	hopr1	**PSV Eindhoven**	H	L	0-1		13,000
26	hopr1	**Willem II Tilb**	H	D	1-1	Nevland 85	12,000
27	hopr1	**NEC Nijmegen**	A	L	3-4	Hugo 33; Seedorf 45; van Gessel 61	12,000
28	hopr1	**Roosendaal**	H	W	3-0	Seedorf 17,82; Fledderus 74	12,000
29	hopr1	**Den Bosch**	A	W	2-1	Nevland 48,50	6,000
30	hopr1	**Feyenoord**	H	L	0-2		13,000
31	hopr1	**AZ Alkmaar**	A	L	1-2	Nevland 84	8,000
32	hopr1	**Roda JC Kerk**	H	D	4-4	Nevland 6,65,70; Drent 67	11,000
33	hopr1	**Heerenveen**	H	L	1-2	Buijs 75	13,000
34	hopr1	**Ajax**	A	L	1-2	Nevland 44	49,000

MONTHLY POINTS TALLY

Month	Points	%
AUGUST	2	22%
SEPTEMBER	2	22%
OCTOBER	6	50%
NOVEMBER	9	75%
DECEMBER	0	0%
JANUARY	6	100%
FEBRUARY	4	33%
MARCH	4	44%
APRIL	6	50%
MAY	1	8%

KEY PLAYERS - GOALSCORERS

Erik Nevland

Goals in the League	16	Player Strike Rate Average number of minutes between League goals scored by player	106
Contribution to Attacking Power Average number of minutes between League team goals while on pitch	54	**Club Strike Rate** Average number of minutes between League goals scored by club	61

	PLAYER	LGE GOALS	POWER	STRIKE RATE
1	Erik Nevland	16	54	106 mins
2	Stefano Seedorf	7	63	317 mins
3	Glen Salmon	5	58	325 mins
4	Hugo	3	50	551 mins
5	Mile Krstev	3	57	560 mins

KEY PLAYERS - MIDFIELDERS

Hugo

Goals in the League	3	**Contribution to Attacking Power** Average number of minutes between League team goals while on pitch	50
Defensive Rating Average number of mins between League goals conceded while on the pitch	55	Scoring Difference Defensive Rating minus Contribution to Attacking Power	5

	PLAYER	LGE GOALS	DEF RATE	POWER	SCORE DIFF
1	Hugo	3	55	50	5 mins
2	Paul Matthijs	1	55	57	-2 mins
3	Stefano Seedorf	7	56	63	-7 mins
4	Sander van Gessel	4	50	58	-8 mins

KEY PLAYERS - DEFENDERS

Mathias Floren

Goals Conceded Number of League goals conceded while the player was on the pitch	46	**Clean Sheets** In games when player was on pitch for at least 70 minutes	6
Defensive Rating Ave number of mins between League goals conceded while on the pitch	57	**Club Defensive Rating** Average number of mins between League goals conceded by the club this season	53

	PLAYER	CON LGE	CLEAN SHEETS	DEF RATE
1	Mathias Floren	46	6	57 mins
2	Kurt Elshot	50	6	53 mins
3	Danny Buijs	53	6	52 mins
4	Arnold Kruiswijk	42	4	51 mins
5	Mile Krstev	34	2	49 mins

KEY GOALKEEPER

Bas Roorda

Goals Conceded in the League	54	**Counting Games** League games when player was on pitch for at least 70 minutes	33
Defensive Rating Ave number of mins between League goals conceded while on the pitch	55	**Clean Sheets** In games when player was on pitch for at least 70 minutes	7

LEAGUE GOALS

Erik Nevland

Minutes on the pitch	1702	Goals in the League	16
League average (mins between goals)	106		

	PLAYER	MINS	GOALS	AVE
1	Nevland	1702	16	106
2	Seedorf	2221	7	317
3	Salmon	1627	5	325
4	van Gessel	2825	4	706
5	Krstev	1681	3	560
6	Hugo	1653	3	551
7	Elshot	2670	2	1335
8	Buijs	2743	2	1372
9	Drent	679	2	340
10	Floren	2615	1	2615
12	Pinas	850	1	850
13	Matthijs	2790	1	2790
	Other		3	
	TOTAL		50	

DISCIPLINARY

	PLAYER	YELLOW	RED	AVE
1	Drent	3	0	226
2	Sankoh	2	0	254
3	Krstev	6	0	280
4	Buijs	7	0	391
5	Elshot	6	0	445
6	Floren	5	0	523
7	Salmon	3	0	542
8	Matthijs	5	0	558
9	Fledderus	1	0	618
10	van der Linden	3	0	655
11	Bechan	1	0	676
12	Seedorf	3	0	740
13	Pinas	1	0	850
	Other	6	1	
	TOTAL	52	1	

TOP POINT EARNERS

	PLAYER	GAMES	AV PTS
1	Mile Krstev	14	1.71
2	Erik Nevland	19	1.58
3	Glen Salmon	17	1.47
4	Hugo	15	1.33
5	Stefano Seedorf	22	1.32
6	Arnold Kruiswijk	24	1.29
7	Paul Matthijs	31	1.29
8	Bas Roorda	33	1.21
9	Kurt Elshot	30	1.20
10	Sander van Gessel	31	1.19
	CLUB AVERAGE:		1.18

TEAM OF THE SEASON

G — Bas Roorda, CG: 33 DR: 55

D — Mathias Floren, CG: 28 DR: 57

D — Kurt Elshot, CG: 30 DR: 53

D — Danny Buijs, CG: 31 DR: 52

D — Arnold Kruiswijk, CG: 24 DR: 51

M — Hugo, CG: 15 SD: 5

M — Paul Matthijs, CG: 31 SD: -2

M — Stefano Seedorf, CG: 22 SD: -7

M — Sander van Gessel, CG: 31 SD: -8

F — Erik Nevland, CG: 19 SR: 106

F — Glen Salmon, CG: 17 SR: 325

LEAGUE APPEARANCES, BOOKINGS AND CAPS

	AGE (on 01/07/05)	IN NAMED 18	APPEARANCES	COUNTING GAMES	MINUTES ON PITCH	YELLOW CARDS	RED CARDS	THIS SEASON	HOME COUNTRY
Goalkeepers									
Jeroen Lambers	24	33	1	0	67	0	0	-	Holland
Mike Romer	19	1	0	0	0	0	0	-	Holland
Bas Roorda	32	34	34	33	2993	0	1	-	Holland
Defenders									
Danny Buijs	23	31	31	31	2743	7	0	-	Holland
Kurt Elshot	28	30	30	30	2670	6	0	-	Surinam
Mathias Floren	28	32	31	28	2615	5	0	-	Sweden
Ray Frankel	22	3	0	0	0	0	0	-	Holland
Mile Krstev	26	28	25	14	1681	6	0	-	Macedonia
Arnold Kruiswijk	20	27	25	24	2144	1	0	-	Holland
Gibril Sankoh	22	17	8	5	508	2	0	-	Sierra Leone
Antoine van der Linden	29	29	25	20	1966	3	0	-	Holland
Midfielders									
Mark Jan Fledderus	20	27	18	5	618	1	0	-	Holland
Hugo	30	30	26	15	1653	0	0	-	Brazil
Gijs Luirink	21	1	1	0	26	0	0	-	Holland
Paul Matthijs	28	31	31	31	2790	5	0	-	Holland
Stefano Seedorf	23	29	28	22	2221	3	0	-	Holland
Jack Tuyp	21	29	11	0	212	0	0	-	Holland
Sander van Gessel	28	32	32	31	2825	3	0	-	Holland
Mark Veldmate	20	12	2	0	56	0	0	-	Holland
Kristian Westerveld	21	6	0	0	0	0	0	-	Holland
Forwards									
Kiran Bechan	22	17	14	5	676	1	0	-	Holland
Kassim Bizimana	19	9	4	1	118	1	1	-	Burundi
Chris de Witte	27	2	2	1	107	0	0	-	Belgium
Martin Drent	35	25	18	4	679	3	0	-	Holland
Erik Nevland	27	20	20	19	1702	2	0	-	Norway
Brian Pinas	26	25	20	7	850	1	0	-	Holland
Ribeiro	22	6	0	0	0	0	0	-	Brazil
Glen Salmon	27	22	21	17	1627	3	0	-	South Africa
Valery Sedoc	19	16	2	0	39	0	0	-	Holland

SQUAD APPEARANCES

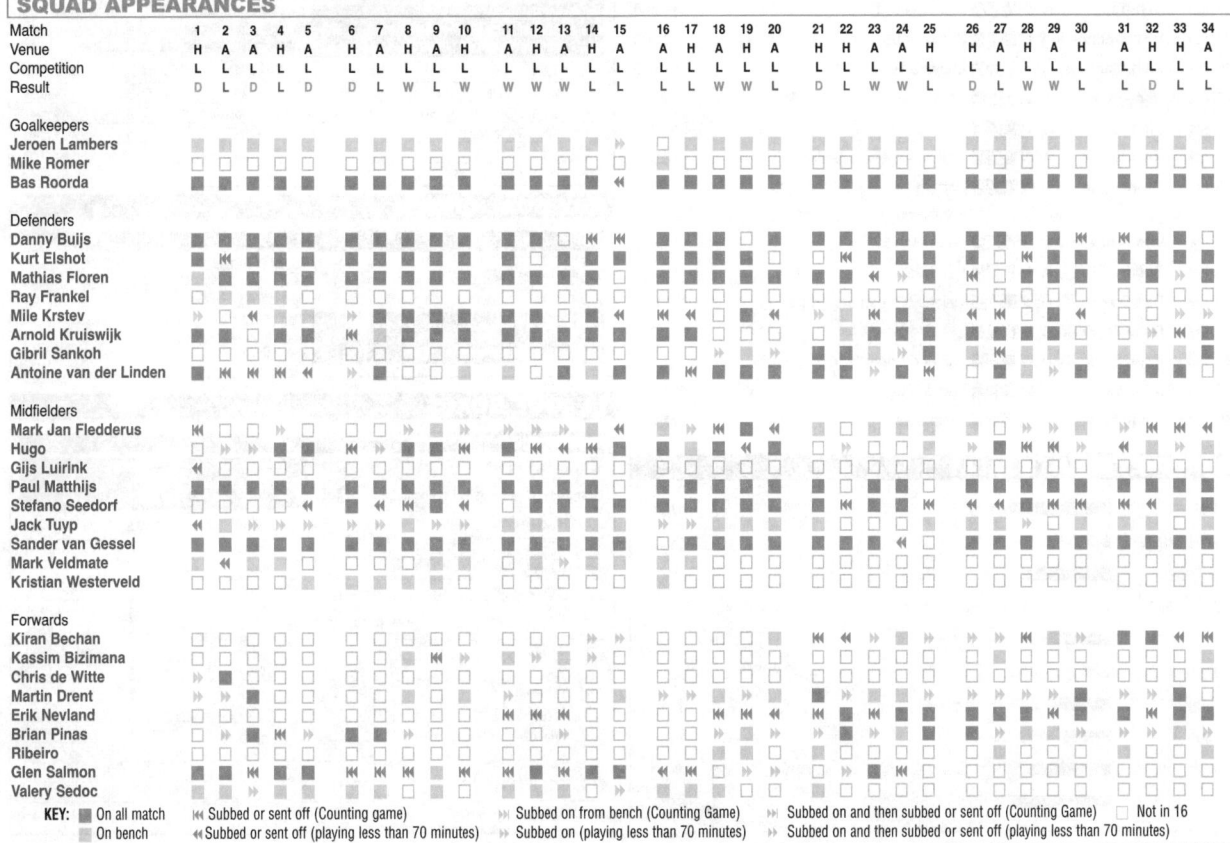

Match	1	2	3	4	5	6	7	8	9	10	11	12	13	14	15	16	17	18	19	20	21	22	23	24	25	26	27	28	29	30	31	32	33	34
Venue	H	A	A	H	A	H	A	H	A	H	A	H	A	H	A	A	H	A	H	A	H	H	A	A	H	H	A	H	A	H	A	H	H	A
Competition	L	L	L	L	L	L	L	L	L	L	L	L	L	L	L	L	L	L	L	L	L	L	L	L	L	L	L	L	L	L	L	L	L	L
Result	D	L	D	L	D	D	L	W	L	W	W	W	W	L	L	L	L	W	W	L	D	L	W	W	L	D	L	W	W	L	L	D	L	L

Goalkeepers
Jeroen Lambers
Mike Romer
Bas Roorda

Defenders
Danny Buijs
Kurt Elshot
Mathias Floren
Ray Frankel
Mile Krstev
Arnold Kruiswijk
Gibril Sankoh
Antoine van der Linden

Midfielders
Mark Jan Fledderus
Hugo
Gijs Luirink
Paul Matthijs
Stefano Seedorf
Jack Tuyp
Sander van Gessel
Mark Veldmate
Kristian Westerveld

Forwards
Kiran Bechan
Kassim Bizimana
Chris de Witte
Martin Drent
Erik Nevland
Brian Pinas
Ribeiro
Glen Salmon
Valery Sedoc

KEY: On all match | On bench | Subbed or sent off (Counting game) | Subbed or sent off (playing less than 70 minutes) | Subbed on from bench (Counting Game) | Subbed on (playing less than 70 minutes) | Subbed on and then subbed or sent off (Counting Game) | Subbed on and then subbed or sent off (playing less than 70 minutes) | Not in 16

NEC NIJMEGEN

Final Position: **13th**

KEY: ☐ Won ☐ Drawn ☐ Lost

							Attendance
1	lge	Willem II Tilb	H	W	2-0	Boutahar 7; Denneboom 20	12,000
2	lge	Den Haag	A	W	2-1	Denneboom 79; Boutahar 90	7,000
3	lge	AZ Alkmaar	H	L	1-2	Denneboom 90	12,000
4	lge	Utrecht	A	L	0-1		18,000
5	lge	PSV Eindhoven	H	L	0-3		12,000
6	hocr1	Roosendaal	H	W	4-0	Pothuizen 12; Wielaert 15 pen; Denneboom 34,66	
7	lge	Groningen	A	D	0-0		11,000
8	lge	Roosendaal	H	W	3-0	Barreto 15,20; Boutahar 29	11,000
9	lge	RKC Waalwijk	A	D	2-2	Boutahar 45; Wielaert 66 pen	5,000
10	lge	NAC Breda	H	D	3-3	Barreto 14; Boutahar 43; Denneboom 59	12,000
11	lge	Ajax	A	L	0-1		46,000
12	lge	Vitesse Arnhem	A	L	0-1		18,000
13	hocr3	Twente	H	L	0-2		8,100
14	lge	Twente	H	L	0-2		10,000
15	lge	Den Bosch	A	D	0-0		5,000
16	lge	Roda JC Kerk	H	D	1-1	Wisgerhof 69	12,000
17	lge	Feyenoord	A	L	1-2	Barreto 43	36,000
18	lge	De Graafschap	A	L	2-3	Tininho 12; Denneboom 57	11,000
19	lge	Heerenveen	H	W	3-2	Wielaert 4 pen; Denneboom 48; Seip 74 og	12,000
20	lge	AZ Alkmaar	A	D	1-1	Niedzielan 23	8,000
21	lge	Utrecht	H	D	0-0		12,000
22	lge	Willem II Tilb	A	L	1-3	Denneboom 78	12,000
23	lge	Den Haag	H	D	1-1	Niedzielan 21	11,000
24	lge	PSV Eindhoven	A	L	1-4	Boutahar 55	30,000
25	lge	RKC Waalwijk	H	W	1-0	Ebbinge 10	11,000
26	lge	Roosendaal	A	L	0-1		5,000
27	lge	Ajax	H	L	0-1		12,000
28	lge	NAC Breda	A	W	2-1	Tininho 78; Ebbinge 86	12,000
29	lge	Groningen	H	W	4-3	Barreto 14; Van den Eede 24,69; Niedzielan 80	12,000
30	lge	Vitesse Arnhem	H	D	1-1	Niedzielan 32	12,000
31	lge	Twente	A	L	1-2	Hendriks, T 66	13,000
32	lge	Den Bosch	H	D	2-2	Tininho 58; Van den Eede 81	12,000
33	lge	Roda JC Kerk	A	L	0-1		12,000
34	lge	Feyenoord	H	W	2-0	Van den Eede 71 pen; Niedzielan 86	12,000
35	lge	De Graafschap	H	W	3-0	Van den Eede 9; Boutahar 43,63	12,000
36	lge	Heerenveen	A	L	1-2	Tininho 22	21,000

MONTHLY POINTS TALLY

AUGUST	6	67%
SEPTEMBER	1	11%
OCTOBER	5	42%
NOVEMBER	2	17%
DECEMBER	3	33%
JANUARY	2	33%
FEBRUARY	4	33%
MARCH	3	33%
APRIL	5	33%
MAY	6	67%

KEY PLAYERS - GOALSCORERS

Said Boutahar

Goals in the League	8	Player Strike Rate Average number of minutes between League goals scored by player	319
Contribution to Attacking Power Average number of minutes between League team goals while on pitch	75	Club Strike Rate Average number of minutes between League goals scored by club	75

	PLAYER	LGE GOALS	POWER	STRIKE RATE
1	Said Boutahar	8	75	319 mins
2	Romano Denneboom	7	71	378 mins
3	Edgar Barreto	5	69	428 mins
4	Andrzej Niedzielan	5	78	442 mins
5	Tininho	4	69	590 mins

KEY PLAYERS - MIDFIELDERS

Tininho

Goals in the League	4	Contribution to Attacking Power Average number of minutes between League team goals while on pitch	69
Defensive Rating Average number of mins between League goals conceded while on the pitch	67	Scoring Difference Defensive Rating minus Contribution to Attacking Power	-2

	PLAYER	LGE GOALS	DEF RATE	POWER	SCORE DIFF
1	Tininho	4	67	69	-2 mins
2	Said Boutahar	8	67	75	-8 mins
3	Edgar Barreto	5	59	69	-10 mins
4	Bjorn van der Doelen	0	63	81	-18 mins

KEY PLAYERS - DEFENDERS

Arjan Ebbinge

Goals Conceded (GC) Number of League goals conceded while the player was on the pitch	20	Clean Sheets In games when player was on pitch for at least 70 minutes	3
Defensive Rating Ave number of mins between League goals conceded while on the pitch	73	Club Defensive Rating Average number of mins between League goals conceded by the club this season	65

	PLAYER	CON LGE	CLEAN SHEETS	DEF RATE
1	Arjan Ebbinge	20	3	73 mins
2	Rob Wielaert	35	6	65 mins
3	Muslu Nalbantoglu	33	5	63 mins
4	Peter Wisgerhof	36	5	63 mins
5	Jeffrey Leiwakabessy	33	5	61 mins

KEY GOALKEEPER

Dennis Gentenaar

Goals Conceded in the League	47	Counting Games League games when player was on pitch for at least 70 minutes	34
Defensive Rating Ave number of mins between League goals conceded while on the pitch	65	Clean Sheets In games when player was on pitch for at least 70 minutes	8

LEAGUE GOALS

Said Boutahar

Minutes on the pitch	2554	Goals in the League	8
League average (mins between goals)	319		

	PLAYER	MINS	GOALS	AVE
1	Boutahar	2554	8	319
2	Denneboom	2644	7	378
3	Van den Eede	923	5	185
4	Niedzielan	2208	5	442
5	Barreto	2141	5	428
6	Tininho	2358	4	590
7	Wielaert	2277	2	1139
8	Ebbinge	1457	2	729
9	Hendriks, T	67	1	67
10	Wisgerhof	2277	1	2277
	Other		1	
	TOTAL		41	

DISCIPLINARY RECORDS

	PLAYER	YELLOW	RED	AVE
1	Ebbinge	6	1	208
2	Pothuizen	5	0	236
3	Valencia	6	0	298
4	Wisgerhof	6	0	379
5	van der Doelen	5	0	390
6	Heije	3	0	421
7	Denneboom	5	0	528
8	Barreto	4	0	535
9	Niedzielan	4	0	552
10	Boutahar	3	0	851
11	Van den Eede	1	0	923
12	Nalbantoglu	2	0	1040
13	Wielaert	2	0	1138
	Other	3	0	
	TOTAL	55	1	

TOP POINT EARNERS

	PLAYER	GAMES	AV PTS
1	Jeffrey Leiwakabessy	21	1.29
2	Bjorn van der Doelen	17	1.24
3	Andrzej Niedzielan	24	1.17
4	Romano Denneboom	29	1.14
5	Arjan Ebbinge	14	1.14
6	Muslu Nalbantoglu	22	1.14
7	Dennis Gentenaar	34	1.09
8	Tininho	23	1.09
9	Edgar Barreto	22	1.09
10	Peter Wisgerhof	25	1.08
	CLUB AVERAGE:		1.09

LEAGUE APPEARANCES, BOOKINGS AND CAPS

	AGE (on 01/07/05)	IN NAMED 18	APPEARANCES	COUNTING GAMES	MINUTES ON PITCH	YELLOW CARDS	RED CARDS	THIS SEASON	HOME COUNTRY
Goalkeepers									
Dennis Gentenaar	29	34	34	34	3044	0	0	-	Holland
Albert Van der Sleen	42	30	1	0	16	0	0	-	Holland
R. van Emmerik	25	7	0	0	0	0	0	-	Holland
Defenders									
Bas Bakker	19	5	1	0	54	0	0	-	Holland
Arjan Ebbinge	30	20	19	14	1457	6	1	-	Holland
Pascal Heije	25	25	17	11	1265	3	0	-	Holland
Charles Kazlauskas	22	26	11	0	152	1	0	-	United States
Jeffrey Leiwakabessy	24	30	25	21	2016	1	0	-	Holland
Chaimil Mormon	22	8	0	0	0	0	0	-	Surinam
Muslu Nalbantoglu	21	31	25	22	2081	2	0	-	Holland
Patrick Pothuizen	33	30	19	8	1184	5	0	-	Holland
Jose Valencia	23	31	27	17	1789	6	0	-	Holland
Rob Wielaert	26	28	27	25	2277	2	0	-	Holland
Peter Wisgerhof	25	28	27	25	2277	6	0	-	Holland
Midfielders									
Edgar Barreto	20	26	25	22	2141	4	0	-	Paraguay
Said Boutahar	22	31	30	28	2554	3	0	-	Holland
Ralf de Haan	21	1	0	0	0	0	0	-	Holland
Thijs Hendriks	20	13	3	0	67	0	0	-	Holland
Alexander Prent	22	9	9	2	362	0	0	-	Holland
Jarda Simr	26	18	7	2	263	0	0	-	Czech Republic
Tininho	27	33	33	23	2358	2	0	-	Brazil
Jim van Alst	20	3	0	0	0	0	0	-	Holland
Bjorn van der Doelen	28	31	27	17	1950	5	0	-	Holland
Sven Werkhoven	21	1	1	0	11	0	0	-	Holland
Forwards									
Frank Demouge	23	5	5	3	279	1	0	-	Holland
Romano Denneboom	24	32	32	29	2644	5	0	1	Holland (5)
Andrzej Niedzielan	26	27	27	24	2208	4	0	-	Poland
Bart Van den Eede	31	12	12	10	923	1	0	-	Belgium
Rutger Worm	19	18	10	1	267	0	0	-	Holland

TEAM OF THE SEASON

G
Dennis Gentenaar
CG: 34 DR: 65
D
Arjan Ebbinge
CG: 14 DR: 73
D
Rob Wielaert
CG: 25 DR: 65
D
Muslu Nalbantoglu
CG: 22 DR: 63
D
Peter Wisgerhof
CG: 25 DR: 63
M
Tininho
CG: 23 SD: -2
M
Said Boutahar
CG: 28 SD: -8
M
Edgar Barreto
CG: 22 SD: -10
M
Bjorn van der Doelen
CG: 17 SD: -18
F
Romano Denneboom
CG: 29 SR: 378
F
Andrzej Niedzielan
CG: 24 SR: 442

SQUAD APPEARANCES

Match	1	2	3	4	5	6	7	8	9	10	11	12	13	14	15	16	17	18	19	20	21	22	23	24	25	26	27	28	29	30	31	32	33	34
Venue	H	A	H	A	H	A	H	A	H	A	A	H	A	H	A	A	H	A	H	A	H	A	H	A	H	A	H	H	A	H	A	H	H	A
Competition	L	L	L	L	L	L	L	L	L	L	L	L	L	L	L	L	L	L	L	L	L	L	L	L	L	L	L	L	L	L	L	L	L	L
Result	W	W	L	L	L	D	W	D	D	L	L	L	D	D	L	L	W	D	D	L	D	L	W	L	L	W	W	D	L	D	L	W	W	L

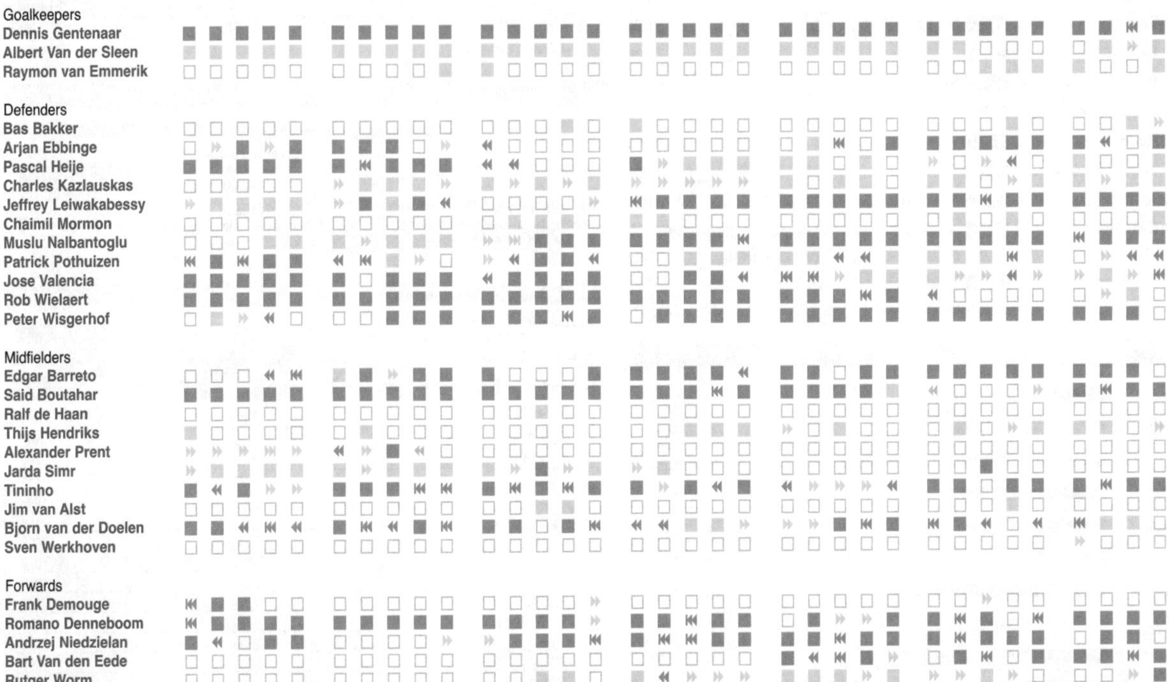

Goalkeepers
Dennis Gentenaar
Albert Van der Sleen
Raymon van Emmerik
Defenders
Bas Bakker
Arjan Ebbinge
Pascal Heije
Charles Kazlauskas
Jeffrey Leiwakabessy
Chaimil Mormon
Muslu Nalbantoglu
Patrick Pothuizen
Jose Valencia
Rob Wielaert
Peter Wisgerhof
Midfielders
Edgar Barreto
Said Boutahar
Ralf de Haan
Thijs Hendriks
Alexander Prent
Jarda Simr
Tininho
Jim van Alst
Bjorn van der Doelen
Sven Werkhoven
Forwards
Frank Demouge
Romano Denneboom
Andrzej Niedzielan
Bart Van den Eede
Rutger Worm

KEY: ■ On all match / On bench / ⏮ Subbed or sent off (Counting game) / « Subbed or sent off (playing less than 70 minutes) / ⏭ Subbed on from bench (Counting Game) / » Subbed on (playing less than 70 minutes) / Subbed on and then subbed or sent off (Counting Game) / Subbed on and then subbed or sent off (playing less than 70 minutes) / □ Not in 16

ADO DEN HAAG

Final Position: **14th**

KEY: ☐Won ☐Drawn ☐Lost

							Attendance
1	hopr1	**Den Bosch**	A	L	0-1		5,000
2	hopr1	**NEC Nijmegen**	H	L	1-2	Platvoet 37	7,000
3	hopr1	**RKC Waalwijk**	A	W	3-1	van der Gun 29; van der Leegte 88; den Ouden 90	5,000
4	hopr1	**Ajax**	H	D	3-3	van der Gun 44; den Ouden 68 pen; Stroeve 83	9,000
5	hopr1	**Vitesse Arnhem**	H	L	0-4		6,000
6	hopr1	**Utrecht**	A	L	0-2		18,000
7	hopr1	**Heerenveen**	A	L	0-1		17,000
8	hopr1	**PSV Eindhoven**	H	L	0-2		7,000
9	hopr1	**De Graafschap**	A	W	2-1	Bodde 16; El-Akchaoui 74	11,000
10	hopr1	**Twente**	H	L	0-1		5,000
11	hopr1	**Groningen**	A	L	3-4	den Ouden 18; van der Gun 87; Polak 90	12,000
12	hopr1	**Roosendaal**	H	W	5-1	den Ouden 10,21; van der Gun 31; Polak 52; Platvoet 88	5,000
13	hopr1	**Roda JC Kerk**	A	D	1-1	den Ouden 40	11,000
14	hopr1	**Willem II Tilb**	H	L	0-1		6,000
15	hopr1	**AZ Alkmaar**	A	L	0-2		8,000
16	hopr1	**NAC Breda**	A	D	1-1	Swerts 85	12,000
17	hopr1	**Feyenoord**	H	W	2-0	den Ouden 2; Polak 64	8,000
18	hopr1	**Groningen**	H	L	0-3		6,000
19	hopr1	**Ajax**	A	D	0-0		45,000
20	hopr1	**Den Bosch**	H	W	2-0	Bodde 41; Edson Silva 69	6,000
21	hopr1	**NEC Nijmegen**	A	D	1-1	Stroeve 66	11,000
22	hopr1	**Vitesse Arnhem**	A	W	4-3	den Ouden 43,63; Stroeve 70; van der Gun 77	18,000
23	hopr1	**Utrecht**	H	W	1-0	Edson Silva 85	5,000
24	hopr1	**PSV Eindhoven**	A	L	0-4		31,000
25	hopr1	**Heerenveen**	H	L	0-2		7,000
26	hopr1	**Twente**	A	L	1-2	Niemeyer 47 og	13,000
27	hopr1	**RKC Waalwijk**	H	D	0-0		7,000
28	hopr1	**De Graafschap**	H	W	2-0	Stroeve 18; Edson Silva 69	6,000
29	hopr1	**Roosendaal**	A	L	0-2		5,000
30	hopr1	**Roda JC Kerk**	H	L	1-4	Verhoek 84	7,000
31	hopr1	**Willem II Tilb**	A	L	0-1		12,000
32	hopr1	**AZ Alkmaar**	H	W	2-1	den Ouden 87; Elia 89	6,000
33	hopr1	**NAC Breda**	H	W	6-2	Smith, J 24; van der Leegte 26; Stroeve 28; Polak 42; Saeijs 68; den Ouden 82	5,000
34	hopr1	**Feyenoord**	A	L	3-6	Polak 52; van der Gun 55; den Ouden 62	35,000

MONTHLY POINTS TALLY

AUGUST	3	33%
SEPTEMBER	1	11%
OCTOBER	3	20%
NOVEMBER	4	44%
DECEMBER	4	44%
JANUARY	1	17%
FEBRUARY	10	83%
MARCH	0	0%
APRIL	4	33%
MAY	6	50%

KEY PLAYERS - GOALSCORERS

Geert den Ouden

Goals in the League 12

Player Strike Rate Average number of minutes between League goals scored by player 167

Contribution to Attacking Power Average number of minutes between League team goals while on pitch 69

Club Strike Rate Average number of minutes between League goals scored by club 70

	PLAYER	LGE GOALS	POWER	STRIKE RATE
1	Geert den Ouden	12	69	167 mins
2	Roy Stroeve	5	71	415 mins
3	Cedric van der Gun	6	70	457 mins
4	Sjaak Polak	5	71	499 mins
5	Ferrie Bodde	2	53	1022 mins

KEY PLAYERS - MIDFIELDERS

Ferrie Bodde

Goals in the League 2

Contribution to Attacking Power Average number of minutes between League team goals while on pitch 54

Defensive Rating Average number of mins between League goals conceded while on the pitch 48

Scoring Difference Defensive Rating minus Contribution to Attacking Power -6

	PLAYER	LGE GOALS	DEF RATE	POWER	SCORE DIFF
1	Ferrie Bodde	2	48	54	-6 mins
2	Sjaak Polak	5	57	71	-14 mins
3	Gill Swerts	1	54	70	-16 mins
4	Tom van der Leegte	2	51	68	-17 mins
5	Jamie Smith	1	54	71	-17 mins

KEY PLAYERS - DEFENDERS

Spira Grujic

Goals Conceded Number of League goals conceded while the player was on the pitch 31

Clean Sheets In games when player was on pitch for at least 70 minutes 6

Defensive Rating Ave number of mins between League goals conceded while on the pitch 57

Club Defensive Rating Average number of mins between League goals conceded by the club this season 51

	PLAYER	CON LGE	CLEAN SHEETS	DEF RATE
1	Spira Grujic	31	6	57 mins
2	Jan-Paul Saeijs	56	6	51 mins
3	Youssef El-Akchaoui	54	6	50 mins
4	Alberto Saavedra	35	0	44 mins

KEY GOALKEEPER

Dorus de Vries

Goals Conceded in the League 47

Counting Games League games when player was on pitch for at least 70 minutes 29

Defensive Rating Ave number of mins between League goals conceded while on the pitch 57

Clean Sheets In games when player was on pitch for at least 70 minutes 6

LEAGUE GOALS

Geert den Ouden

Minutes on the pitch 2002

League average (mins between goals) 167

Goals in the League 12

	PLAYER	MINS	GOALS	AVE
1	den Ouden	2002	12	167
2	van der Gun	2739	6	457
3	Stroeve	2073	5	415
4	Polak	2496	5	499
5	Edson Silva	331	3	110
6	Bodde	2043	2	1022
7	Platvoet	543	2	272
8	van der Leegte	2636	2	1318
9	Smith, J	2329	1	2329
10	El-Akchaoui	2709	1	2709
11	Saeijs	2835	1	2835
13	Swerts	2959	1	2959
	Other		3	
	TOTAL		44	

DISCIPLINARY RECORDS

	PLAYER	YELLOW	RED	AVE
1	Bodde	6	0	340
2	Saavedra	4	0	388
3	Saeijs	7	0	405
4	van der Leegte	5	1	439
5	Rijaard	2	0	502
6	van der Gun	5	0	547
7	den Ouden	3	0	667
8	Swerts	4	0	739
9	Polak	3	0	832
10	El-Akchaoui	3	0	903
11	Grujic	1	0	1774
12	Smith, J	1	0	2329
13	de Vries	0	1	2664
	Other	0	0	
	TOTAL	44	2	

TOP POINT EARNERS

	PLAYER	GAMES	AV PTS
1	Ferrie Bodde	20	1.55
2	Jamie Smith	23	1.30
3	Geert den Ouden	16	1.19
4	Spira Grujic	17	1.12
5	Gill Swerts	33	1.09
6	Youssef El-Akchaoui	29	1.07
7	Tom van der Leegte	29	1.07
8	Jean Paul Saeijs	31	1.06
9	Dorus de Vries	29	1.03
10	Roy Stroeve	17	1.00
	CLUB AVERAGE:		1.06

TEAM OF THE SEASON

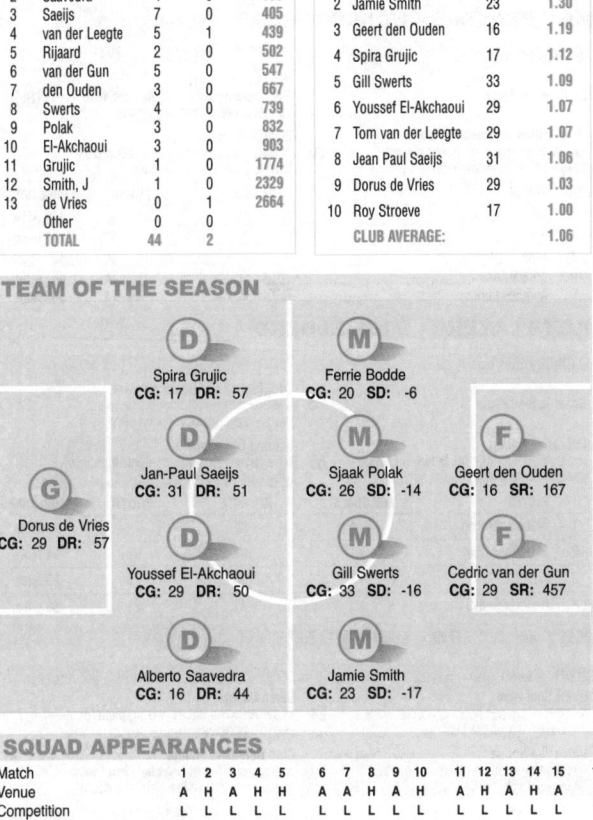

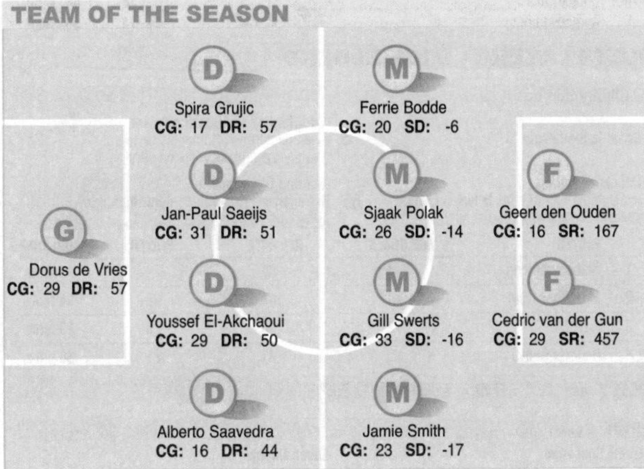
G
Dorus de Vries
CG: 29 DR: 57
D
Spira Grujic
CG: 17 DR: 57
D
Jan-Paul Saeijs
CG: 31 DR: 51
D
Youssef El-Akchaoui
CG: 29 DR: 50
D
Alberto Saavedra
CG: 16 DR: 44
M
Ferrie Bodde
CG: 20 SD: -6
M
Sjaak Polak
CG: 26 SD: -14
M
Gill Swerts
CG: 33 SD: -16
M
Jamie Smith
CG: 23 SD: -17
F
Geert den Ouden
CG: 16 SR: 167
F
Cedric van der Gun
CG: 29 SR: 457

LEAGUE APPEARANCES, BOOKINGS AND CAPS

	AGE (on 01/07/05)	IN NAMED 18	APPEARANCES	COUNTING GAMES	MINUTES ON PITCH	YELLOW CARDS	RED CARDS	THIS SEASON	HOME COUNTRY
Goalkeepers									
Dorus de Vries	24	31	31	29	2664	0	1	-	Holland
Raymond Jansz	22	0	0	0	0	0	0	-	Holland
Cees Paauwe	27	15	4	4	346	0	0	-	Holland
Arjan van der Kaay	22	18	1	0	43	0	0	-	Holland
Jimmy van Fessem	29	3	1	0	8	0	0	-	Holland
Defenders									
Jamie Coyne	24	10	0	0	0	0	0	-	Australia
Youssef El-Akchaoui	24	34	33	29	2709	3	0	-	Holland
Spira Grujic	33	25	23	17	1774	1	0	-	Serbia & Montenegro
Daniel Rijaard	28	30	20	7	1004	2	0	-	Holland
Alberto Saavedra	23	33	20	16	1552	4	0	-	Spain
Jan-Paul Saeijs	27	32	32	31	2835	7	0	-	Holland
Midfielders									
Ferrie Bodde	23	31	29	20	2043	6	0	-	Holland
Stefan Huisman	21	11	0	0	0	0	0	-	Holland
Sjaak Polak	29	34	34	26	2496	3	0	-	Holland
Marcel Pronk	21	19	0	0	0	0	0	-	Holland
Jamie Smith	24	32	30	23	2329	1	0	-	Scotland
Roy Stroeve	28	33	32	17	2073	0	0	-	Holland
Gill Swerts	22	33	33	33	2959	4	0	-	Belgium
Tom van der Leegte	28	32	32	29	2636	5	1	-	Holland
Forwards									
Geert den Ouden	28	34	34	16	2002	3	0	-	Holland
Edson Silva	21	9	7	2	331	0	0	-	Cape Verde
Eljero Elia	18	17	4	0	72	1	0	-	Holland
Peter Jungschlager	21	8	0	0	0	0	0	-	Holland
Geoffrey Knijnenburg	22	5	0	0	0	0	0	-	Holland
Daniel Koegler	23	2	0	0	0	0	0	-	Holland
Rik Platvoet	29	14	12	4	543	0	0	-	Holland
Cedric van der Gun	26	32	32	29	2739	5	0	-	Holland
Wesley Verhoek	18	14	9	2	415	1	0	-	Holland

SQUAD APPEARANCES

Match	1	2	3	4	5	6	7	8	9	10	11	12	13	14	15	16	17	18	19	20	21	22	23	24	25	26	27	28	29	30	31	32	33	34
Venue	A	H	A	H	H	A	A	H	A	H	A	H	A	H	A	A	H	H	A	H	A	A	H	A	H	A	H	H	A	H	A	H	H	A
Competition	L	L	L	L	L	L	L	L	L	L	L	L	L	L	L	L	L	L	L	L	L	L	L	L	L	L	L	L	L	L	L	L	L	L
Result	L	L	W	D	L	L	L	L	W	L	L	W	D	L	L	D	W	L	D	W	D	W	W	L	L	L	D	W	L	L	L	W	W	L

Goalkeepers
Dorus de Vries
Raymond Jansz
Cees Paauwe
Arjan van der Kaay
Jimmy van Fessem

Defenders
Jamie Coyne
Youssef El-Akchaoui
Spira Grujic
Daniel Rijaard
Alberto Saavedra
Jan-Paul Saeijs

Midfielders
Ferrie Bodde
Stefan Huisman
Sjaak Polak
Marcel Pronk
Jamie Smith
Roy Stroeve
Gill Swerts
Tom van der Leegte

Forwards
Geert den Ouden
Edson Silva
Eljero Elia
Peter Jungschlager
Geoffrey Knijnenburg
Daniel Koegler
Rik Platvoet
Cedric van der Gun
Wesley Verhoek

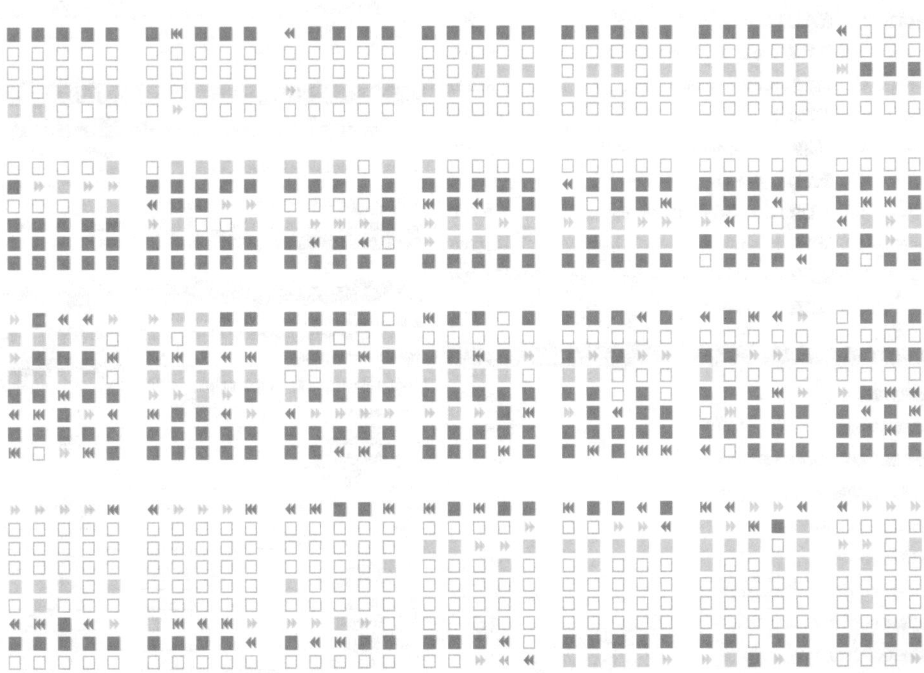

KEY: On all match | On bench | Subbed or sent off (Counting game) | Subbed or sent off (playing less than 70 minutes) | Subbed on from bench (Counting Game) | Subbed on (playing less than 70 minutes) | Subbed on and then subbed or sent off (Counting Game) | Subbed on and then subbed or sent off (playing less than 70 minutes) | Not in 16

NAC BREDA

Final Position: **15th**

KEY: Won Drawn Lost

	Competition	Opponent	Venue	Result	Score	Scorers	Attendance
1	hopr1	**Utrecht**	H	W	3-2	Engelaar 7; Boussaboun 63; Diba 66	11,000
2	hopr1	**Ajax**	A	L	2-6	Cornelisse 11; Slot 81	46,000
3	hopr1	**PSV Eindhoven**	H	D	2-2	Slot 43; Zonneveld 50	13,000
4	hopr1	**Groningen**	A	W	3-2	Zonneveld 23; Slot 44; Boussaboun 87	11,000
5	hopr1	**Heerenveen**	A	L	0-3		17,000
6	hopr1	**RKC Waalwijk**	H	L	0-4		12,000
7	hopr1	**De Graafschap**	H	W	3-2	Cornelisse 10; Boussaboun 22; Penders 45	13,000
8	hopr1	**Vitesse Arnhem**	A	W	2-1	Boussaboun 35; Cornelisse 38	16,000
9	hopr1	**NEC Nijmegen**	A	D	3-3	Zonneveld 5; Lurling 48; Cornelisse 63	12,000
10	hopr1	**Roda JC Kerk**	H	W	4-0	Boussaboun 2,23 pen,58; Lurling 17	12,000
11	hopr1	**Feyenoord**	A	L	0-4		37,000
12	hopr1	**AZ Alkmaar**	H	L	0-3		15,000
13	hopr1	**Willem II Tilb**	A	W	1-0	Mendes Da Silva 27	13,000
14	hopr1	**Den Bosch**	H	W	3-0	Boussaboun 58; Zonneveld 84; Cornelisse 90	11,000
15	hopr1	**Roosendaal**	A	D	0-0		5,000
16	hopr1	**Den Haag**	H	D	1-1	Boussaboun 70	12,000
17	hopr1	**Twente**	A	D	0-0		13,000
18	hopr1	**PSV Eindhoven**	A	L	0-4		31,000
19	hopr1	**Heerenveen**	H	D	1-1	Lurling 85	11,000
20	hopr1	**Utrecht**	A	L	0-2		18,000
21	hopr1	**Ajax**	H	L	1-2	Cornelisse 54	15,000
22	hopr1	**RKC Waalwijk**	A	L	0-1		5,000
23	hopr1	**Groningen**	H	L	1-4	Peto 7	12,000
24	hopr1	**De Graafschap**	A	W	2-0	Diba 27,57	11,000
25	hopr1	**Vitesse Arnhem**	H	L	1-2	Boussaboun 84	12,000
26	hopr1	**NEC Nijmegen**	H	L	1-2	Mendes Da Silva 68	12,000
27	hopr1	**Roda JC Kerk**	A	L	1-2	Mendes Da Silva 43	12,000
28	hopr1	**Feyenoord**	H	L	0-2		15,000
29	hopr1	**AZ Alkmaar**	A	D	1-1	Boussaboun 70	8,000
30	hopr1	**Willem II Tilb**	H	L	1-2	Lurling 44	13,000
31	hopr1	**Den Bosch**	A	W	2-0	Boussaboun 64; Colin 68	6,000
32	hopr1	**Roosendaal**	H	L	1-2	Boussaboun 15	12,000
33	hopr1	**Den Haag**	A	L	2-6	Cornelisse 8; Jenner 88	5,000
34	hopr1	**Twente**	H	D	1-1	Cornelisse 90	10,000

MONTHLY POINTS TALLY

Month	Points	%
AUGUST	4	44%
SEPTEMBER	3	33%
OCTOBER	10	83%
NOVEMBER	6	50%
DECEMBER	3	33%
JANUARY	1	17%
FEBRUARY	0	0%
MARCH	3	33%
APRIL	1	8%
MAY	4	33%

KEY PLAYERS - GOALSCORERS

Ali Boussaboun

Goals in the League 13

Player Strike Rate Average number of minutes between League goals scored by player 183

Contribution to Attacking Power Average number of minutes between League team goals while on pitch 66

Club Strike Rate Average number of minutes between League goals scored by club 71

	PLAYER	LGE GOALS	POWER	STRIKE RATE
1	Ali Boussaboun	13	66	**183 mins**
2	Yuri Cornelisse	8	63	**285 mins**
3	Mike Zonneveld	4	66	**431 mins**
4	Anouar Diba	3	76	**487 mins**
5	Anthony Lurling	4	74	**592 mins**

KEY PLAYERS - MIDFIELDERS

Anthony Lurling

Goals in the League 4

Contribution to Attacking Power Average number of minutes between League team goals while on pitch 74

Defensive Rating Average number of mins between League goals conceded while on the pitch 55

Scoring Difference Defensive Rating minus Contribution to Attacking Power -19

	PLAYER	LGE GOALS	DEF RATE	POWER	SCORE DIFF
1	Anthony Lurling	4	55	74	**-19 mins**
2	Mike Zonneveld	4	42	66	**-24 mins**
3	Arne Slot	3	46	75	**-29 mins**
4	Nebosja Gudelj	0	41	71	**-30 mins**

KEY PLAYERS - DEFENDERS

Pieter Collen

Goals Conceded Number of League goals conceded while the player was on the pitch 54

Clean Sheets In games when player was on pitch for at least 70 minutes 7

Defensive Rating Ave number of mins between League goals conceded while on the pitch 51

Club Defensive Rating Average number of mins between League goals conceded by the club this season 46

	PLAYER	CON LGE	CLEAN SHEETS	DEF RATE
1	Pieter Collen	54	7	**51 mins**
2	Jurgen Colin	48	7	**51 mins**
3	Rob Penders	48	7	**49 mins**
4	David Mendes Da Silva	59	6	**46 mins**

KEY GOALKEEPER

Davy Schollen

Goals Conceded in the League 61

Counting Games League games when player was on pitch for at least 70 minutes 31

Defensive Rating Ave number of mins between League goals conceded while on the pitch 47

Clean Sheets In games when player was on pitch for at least 70 minutes 7

LEAGUE GOALS

Ali Boussaboun

Minutes on the pitch 2382

League average (mins between goals) 183

Goals in the League 13

	PLAYER	MINS	GOALS	AVE
1	Boussaboun	2382	**13**	183
2	Cornelisse	2276	**8**	285
3	Lurling	2368	**4**	592
4	Zonneveld	1725	**4**	431
5	Diba	1461	**3**	487
6	Mendes Da Silva	2692	**3**	897
7	Slot	2258	**3**	753
8	Penders	2340	**1**	2340
9	Colin	2438	**1**	2438
10	Engelaar	90	**1**	90
11	Jenner	132	**1**	132
12	Peto	935	**1**	935
	Other		0	
	TOTAL		**43**	

DISCIPLINARY RECORDS

	PLAYER	YELLOW	RED	AVE
1	Zonneveld	7	1	**215**
2	Van den Eede	2	0	**233**
3	Stam	3	0	**263**
4	Kerstens	3	0	**307**
5	Peto	3	0	**311**
6	Slot	6	1	**322**
7	Collen	6	1	**394**
8	Gudelj	4	1	**456**
9	Diba	3	0	**487**
10	Penders	3	0	**780**
11	Lurling	3	0	**789**
12	Boussaboun	3	0	**794**
13	Cornelisse	2	0	**1138**
	Other	4	0	
	TOTAL	**52**	**4**	

TOP POINT EARNERS

	PLAYER	GAMES	AV PTS
1	Arne Slot	23	**1.17**
2	Mike Zonneveld	18	**1.17**
3	Pieter Collen	30	**1.17**
4	Ali Boussaboun	26	**1.15**
5	Davy Schollen	31	**1.13**
6	Nebosja Gudelj	23	**1.13**
7	Yuri Cornelisse	23	**1.09**
8	David Mendes Da Silva	30	**1.07**
9	Jurgen Colin	26	**1.04**
10	Anthony Lurling	24	**1.04**
	CLUB AVERAGE:		**1.03**

TEAM OF THE SEASON

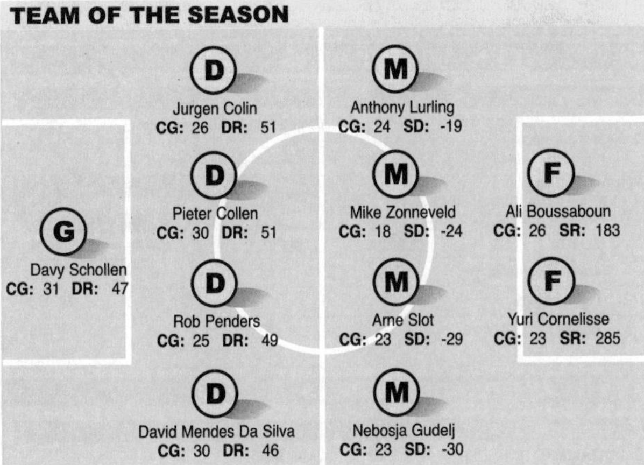
G
Davy Schollen
CG: 31 DR: 47
D
Jurgen Colin
CG: 26 DR: 51
D
Pieter Collen
CG: 30 DR: 51
D
Rob Penders
CG: 25 DR: 49
D
David Mendes Da Silva
CG: 30 DR: 46
M
Anthony Lurling
CG: 24 SD: -19
M
Mike Zonneveld
CG: 18 SD: -24
M
Arne Slot
CG: 23 SD: -29
M
Nebosja Gudelj
CG: 23 SD: -30
F
Ali Boussaboun
CG: 26 SR: 183
F
Yuri Cornelisse
CG: 23 SR: 285

LEAGUE APPEARANCES, BOOKINGS AND CAPS

	AGE (on 01/07/05)	IN NAMED 18	APPEARANCES	COUNTING GAMES	MINUTES ON PITCH	YELLOW CARDS	RED CARDS	THIS SEASON	HOME COUNTRY
Goalkeepers									
Arjan Cristianen	22	3	0	0	0	0	0	-	Holland
Davy Schollen	29	32	32	31	2838	1	0	-	Belgium
Arno van Zwam	35	32	3	2	222	0	0	-	Holland
Defenders									
Eric Atuahene	2006	1	0	0	0	0	0	-	Holland
Adnan Barakat	22	30	8	3	320	2	0	-	Holland
Jurgen Colin	24	28	28	26	2438	2	0	-	Holland
Pieter Collen	25	32	32	30	2759	6	1	-	Belgium
Benny Kerstens	22	29	11	10	923	3	0	-	Holland
Wilmer Kousemaker	19	15	2	1	135	0	0	-	Holland
D. Mendes Da Silva	22	30	30	30	2692	1	0	-	Holland
Rob Penders	29	27	27	25	2340	3	0	-	Holland
Niek Ripson	21	2	0	0	0	0	0	-	Holland
Levi Risamasu	22	10	7	7	617	0	0	-	Holland
Mark Schenning	34	19	16	6	756	0	0	-	Holland
Midfielders									
Orlando Engelaar	25	1	1	1	90	0	0	-	Holland
Nebosja Gudelj	35	30	28	23	2281	4	1	-	Serbia & Montenegro
Marcel Koning	30	9	5	1	144	0	0	-	Holland
Anthony Lurling	28	29	29	24	2368	3	0	-	Holland
Tamas Peto	31	16	14	8	935	3	0	-	Hungary
Arne Slot	26	28	28	23	2258	6	1	-	Holland
Ronnie Stam	21	21	14	7	789	3	0	-	Holland
Mike Zonneveld	24	20	20	18	1725	7	1	-	Holland
Forwards									
Ali Boussaboun	26	29	29	26	2382	3	0	-	Morocco
Robert Braber	22	8	0	0	0	0	0	-	Holland
Yuri Cornelisse	30	34	33	23	2276	2	0	-	Holland
Anouar Diba	22	21	20	15	1461	3	0	-	Holland
Julian Jenner	21	31	5	1	132	0	0	-	Holland
Maceo Rigters	21	6	5	2	197	0	0	-	Holland
Bart Van den Eede	31	18	13	2	467	2	0	-	Belgium

SQUAD APPEARANCES

Match	1	2	3	4	5	6	7	8	9	10	11	12	13	14	15	16	17	18	19	20	21	22	23	24	25	26	27	28	29	30	31	32	33	34
Venue	H	A	H	A	A	H	H	A	A	H	A	H	A	H	A	H	A	A	H	A	H	A	H	A	H	H	A	H	A	H	A	H	A	H
Competition	L	L	L	L	L	L	L	L	L	L	L	L	L	L	L	L	L	L	L	L	L	L	L	L	L	L	L	L	L	L	L	L	L	L
Result	W	L	D	W	L	L	W	W	D	W	L	L	W	W	D	D	D	L	D	L	L	L	L	W	L	L	L	L	D	L	W	L	L	D

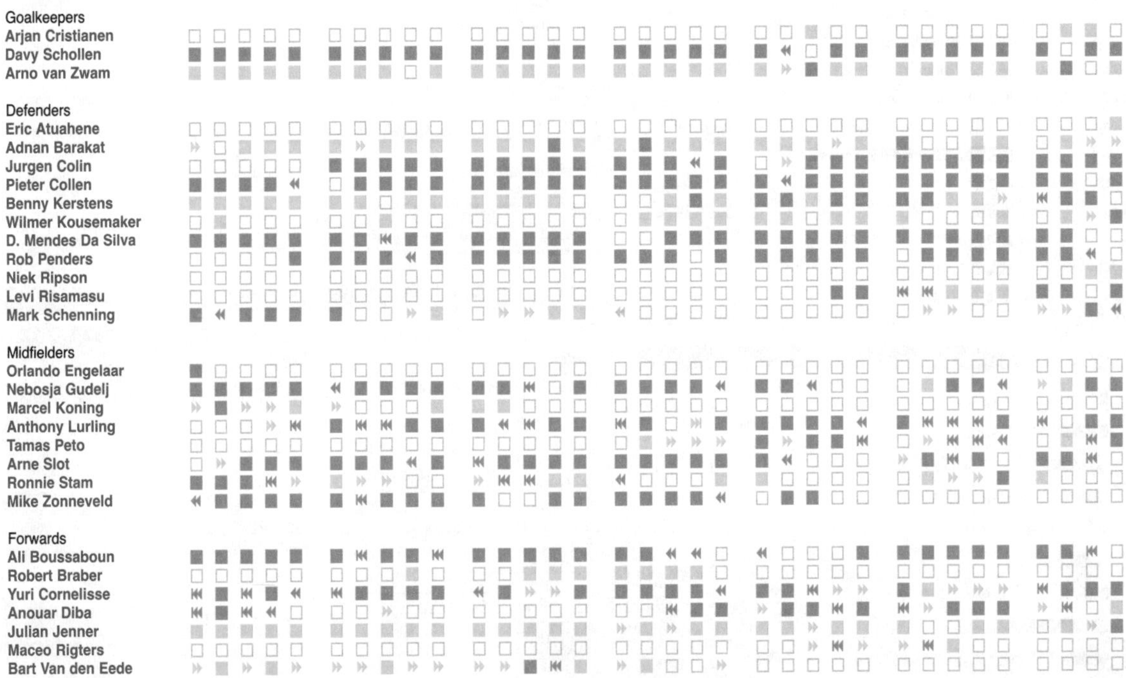
Goalkeepers
Arjan Cristianen
Davy Schollen
Arno van Zwam
Defenders
Eric Atuahene
Adnan Barakat
Jurgen Colin
Pieter Collen
Benny Kerstens
Wilmer Kousemaker
D. Mendes Da Silva
Rob Penders
Niek Ripson
Levi Risamasu
Mark Schenning
Midfielders
Orlando Engelaar
Nebosja Gudelj
Marcel Koning
Anthony Lurling
Tamas Peto
Arne Slot
Ronnie Stam
Mike Zonneveld
Forwards
Ali Boussaboun
Robert Braber
Yuri Cornelisse
Anouar Diba
Julian Jenner
Maceo Rigters
Bart Van den Eede

KEY: On all match | On bench | Subbed or sent off (Counting game) | Subbed or sent off (playing less than 70 minutes) | Subbed on from bench (Counting Game) | Subbed on (playing less than 70 minutes) | Subbed on and then subbed or sent off (Counting Game) | Subbed on and then subbed or sent off (playing less than 70 minutes) | Not in 16

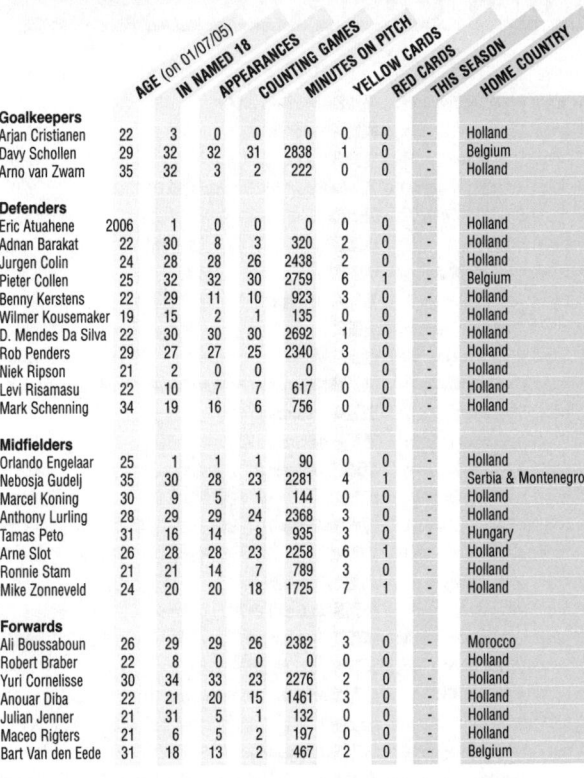

RBC ROOSENDAAL

Final Position: **16th**

KEY: ☐Won ☐Drawn ☐Lost

							Attendance
1	hopr1	PSV Eindhoven	H	L	2-5	Smolders 22,40	5,000
2	hopr1	Utrecht	A	L	1-5	Molenaar 37	17,000
3	hopr1	Groningen	H	D	2-2	Ikedia 23,54	5,000
4	hopr1	Vitesse Arnhem	H	W	4-1	Ikedia 55; Smolders 56,65,72	5,000
5	hopr1	RKC Waalwijk	A	L	0-2		6,000
6	hopr1	Feyenoord	H	L	0-4		5,000
7	hopr1	NEC Nijmegen	A	L	0-3		11,000
8	hopr1	Den Bosch	A	L	1-2	Hertog 82	5,000
9	hopr1	Twente	H	L	0-1		5,000
10	hopr1	Willem II Tilb	A	L	0-3		12,000
11	hopr1	De Graafschap	H	W	3-0	Hakansson 3; Molenaar 45; Ikedia 58	5,000
12	hopr1	Den Haag	A	L	1-5	Hakansson 35	5,000
13	hopr1	Heerenveen	H	L	1-3	de Graaf 17	5,000
14	hopr1	Ajax	A	L	1-4	de Graaf 23	48,000
15	hopr1	NAC Breda	H	D	0-0		5,000
16	hopr1	Roda JC Kerk	A	L	1-3	Hertog 31	13,000
17	hopr1	AZ Alkmaar	H	L	0-2		5,000
18	hopr1	RKC Waalwijk	H	L	0-1		5,000
19	hopr1	Vitesse Arnhem	A	W	3-1	de Groot 21,90; Luijten 63	20,000
20	hopr1	PSV Eindhoven	A	L	1-4	Guijt 73	30,000
21	hopr1	Utrecht	H	L	0-1		5,000
22	hopr1	Willem II Tilb	H	W	2-0	de Groot 59; Hammond 90	5,000
23	hopr1	Feyenoord	A	L	0-3		35,000
24	hopr1	NEC Nijmegen	H	W	1-0	Smolders 52	5,000
25	hopr1	Twente	A	L	0-3		13,000
26	hopr1	De Graafschap	A	W	1-0	de Groot 68	11,000
27	hopr1	Den Bosch	H	L	1-2	de Groot 4	5,000
28	hopr1	Groningen	A	L	0-3		12,000
29	hopr1	Den Haag	H	W	2-0	Guijt 3; Loran 21	5,000
30	hopr1	Heerenveen	A	L	1-7	de Groot 52	20,000
31	hopr1	Ajax	H	L	1-4	Smolders 80	5,000
32	hopr1	NAC Breda	A	W	2-1	Hakansson 29; Hammond 88	12,000
33	hopr1	Roda JC Kerk	H	W	3-1	Hakansson 24,77; Guijt 90	5,000
34	hopr1	AZ Alkmaar	A	W	3-1	Molenaar 36; de Groot 39; Hakansson 82	8,000
35	relpo*	VVV	H	W	2-0	Hammond 45; Youssouf 74	
36	relpo*	Volendam	A	D	0-0		
37	relpo*	Telstar	A	D	0-0		
38	relpo*	Telstar	H	W	2-1	Hammond 65; 70	
39	relpo*	Volendam	H	W	4-0	Guijt 3; Ikedia 32; Hammond 74, 80	
40	relpo*	VVV	A	L	1-2	Youssoof 9	

relpo* refers to relegation play-offs

MONTHLY POINTS TALLY

AUGUST	1	11%
SEPTEMBER	3	33%
OCTOBER	0	0%
NOVEMBER	3	25%
DECEMBER	1	11%
JANUARY	3	50%
FEBRUARY	3	25%
MARCH	6	67%
APRIL	3	20%
MAY	9	100%

KEY PLAYERS - GOALSCORERS

Donny de Groot

Goals in the League	7	Player Strike Rate Average number of minutes between League goals scored by player	191
Contribution to Attacking Power Average number of minutes between League team goals while on pitch	88	Club Strike Rate Average number of minutes between League goals scored by club	81

	PLAYER	LGE GOALS	POWER	STRIKE RATE
1	Donny de Groot	7	88	191 mins
2	Tim Smolders	7	86	346 mins
3	Jesper Hakansson	6	66	352 mins
4	Elvis Hammond	2	79	635 mins
5	Robert Molenaar	3	65	695 mins

KEY PLAYERS - MIDFIELDERS

Jesper Hakansson

Goals in the League	6	Contribution to Attacking Power Average number of minutes between League team goals while on pitch	66
Defensive Rating Average number of mins between League goals conceded while on the pitch	45	Scoring Difference Defensive Rating minus Contribution to Attacking Power	-21

	PLAYER	LGE GOALS	DEF RATE	POWER	SCORE DIFF
1	Jesper Hakansson	6	45	66	-21 mins
2	Paul de Lange	0	44	76	-32 mins
3	Azubuike Oliseh	0	40	95	-55 mins

KEY PLAYERS - DEFENDERS

Tyrone Loran

Goals Conceded Number of League goals conceded while the player was on the pitch	32	Clean Sheets In games when player was on pitch for at least 70 minutes	4
Defensive Rating Ave number of mins between League goals conceded while on the pitch	48	Club Defensive Rating Average number of mins between League goals conceded by the club this season	40

	PLAYER	CON LGE	CLEAN SHEETS	DEF RATE
1	Tyrone Loran	32	4	48 mins
2	Adam Farouk	24	2	45 mins
3	Danny Hesp	56	4	43 mins
4	Robert Molenaar	52	3	40 mins
5	Sidney Lammens	62	5	36 mins

KEY GOALKEEPER

Erwin Friebel

Goals Conceded in the League	25	Counting Games League games when player was on pitch for at least 70 minutes	13
Defensive Rating Ave number of mins between League goals conceded while on the pitch	47	Clean Sheets In games when player was on pitch for at least 70 minutes	4

LEAGUE GOALS

Tim Smolders

Minutes on the pitch	2419	Goals in the League	7
League average (mins between goals)	346		

	PLAYER	MINS	GOALS	AVE
1	Smolders	2419	7	346
2	de Groot	1334	7	191
3	Hakansson	2110	6	352
4	Ikedia	898	4	225
5	Molenaar	2086	3	695
6	Guijt	1331	3	444
7	Hertog	971	2	486
8	Hammond	1270	2	635
9	de Graaf	792	2	396
10	Luijten	608	1	608
11	Loran	1530	1	1530
	Other		0	
	TOTAL		38	

DISCIPLINARY RECORDS

	PLAYER	YELLOW	RED	AVE
1	Fleur	3	1	173
2	Ikedia	3	1	224
3	Viedma	3	0	271
4	Fortes Rodriguez	3	1	291
5	Hesp	6	0	398
6	Hertog	2	0	485
7	Loran	3	0	510
8	Oliseh	5	0	529
9	Lammens	4	0	563
10	Luijten	1	0	608
11	Hammond	2	0	635
12	Van De Ven	1	0	641
13	de Groot	2	0	667
	Other	11	0	
	TOTAL	49	3	

TOP POINT EARNERS

	PLAYER	GAMES	AV PTS
1	Tyrone Loran	17	1.41
2	Donny de Groot	13	1.38
3	Elvis Hammond	14	1.29
4	Jesper Hakansson	23	1.22
5	Paul de Lange	25	1.12
6	Robert Molenaar	23	1.09
7	Danny Hesp	24	0.96
8	Maikel Aerts	21	0.95
9	Erwin Friebel	13	0.92
10	Tim Smolders	26	0.88
	CLUB AVERAGE:		0.94

TEAM OF THE SEASON

D
Tyrone Loran
CG: 17 DR: 48
M
Jesper Hakansson
CG: 23 SD: -21
D
Adam Farouk
CG: 12 DR: 45
M
Paul de Lange
CG: 25 SD: -32
F
Donny de Groot
CG: 13 SR: 191
G
Erwin Friebel
CG: 13 DR: 47
D
Danny Hesp
CG: 24 DR: 43
M
Azubuike Oliseh
CG: 30 SD: -55
F
Tim Smolders
CG: 26 SR: 346
D
Robert Molenaar
CG: 23 DR: 40
M
Elvis Hammond
CG: 14 SD: -

LEAGUE APPEARANCES, BOOKINGS AND CAPS

	AGE (on 01/07/05)	IN NAMED 18	APPEARANCES	COUNTING GAMES	MINUTES ON PITCH	YELLOW CARDS	RED CARDS	THIS SEASON	HOME COUNTRY
Goalkeepers									
Maikel Aerts	28	22	21	21	1890	0	0	-	Holland
Erwin Friebel	22	34	13	13	1170	0	0	-	Holland
Jordy Schoute	19	8	0	0	0	0	0	-	Holland
Defenders									
Adam Farouk	19	21	13	12	1070	1	0	-	France
Melvin Fleur	23	11	10	6	694	3	1	-	Holland
J. Fortes Rodriguez	33	14	14	11	1164	3	1	-	Spain
Eric Hellemons	34	12	6	2	304	1	0	-	Holland
Danny Hesp	35	30	29	24	2388	6	0	-	Holland
Sidney Lammens	28	30	28	24	2255	4	0	-	Belgium
Tyrone Loran	24	17	17	17	1530	3	0	-	Holland
Robert Molenaar	36	24	24	23	2086	2	0	-	Holland
Midfielders									
Edwin de Graaf	25	10	10	8	792	1	0	-	Holland
Paul de Lange	24	26	25	25	2213	3	0	-	Holland
Niels Dominicus	21	4	1	0	9	0	0	-	Holland
Danny Guijt	24	34	29	9	1331	0	0	-	Holland
Jesper Hakansson	24	24	24	23	2110	3	0	-	Denmark
Damien Hertog	30	16	14	10	971	2	0	-	Holland
Ramon Luijten	23	19	13	5	608	1	0	-	Holland
Fouad Makhout	20	20	10	2	326	0	0	-	Holland
Azubuike Oliseh	26	31	30	30	2647	5	0	-	Nigeria
Robert Stols	19	12	1	0	2	0	0	-	Holland
Juan Jose Viedma	30	32	14	8	815	3	0	-	Holland
Forwards									
Bjorn Daelemans	27	13	13	3	482	0	0	-	Belgium
Donny de Groot	25	17	17	13	1334	2	0	-	Holland
Elvis Hammond	24	15	15	14	1270	2	0	-	Ghana
Pius Ikedia	24	12	12	9	898	3	1	-	Nigeria
Tim Smolders	24	33	32	26	2419	1	0	-	Belgium
Birger Van De Ven	23	18	11	4	641	1	0	-	Belgium
Mohammed Yeral	21	8	1	0	16	0	0	-	Holland
Sammy Youssouf	28	2	2	0	73	2	0	-	Denmark

SQUAD APPEARANCES

Match	1	2	3	4	5	6	7	8	9	10	11	12	13	14	15	16	17	18	19	20	21	22	23	24	25	26	27	28	29	30	31	32	33	34
Venue	H	H	A	H	H	A	A	H	A	A	H	A	H	A	H	A	H	A	H	H	A	A	H	H	A	H	A	A	H	A	H	A	H	A
Competition	L	L	L	L	L	L	L	L	L	L	L	L	L	L	L	L	L	L	L	L	L	L	L	L	L	L	L	L	L	L	L	L	L	L
Result	D	L	L	D	W	L	L	L	L	L	L	L	W	L	L	L	D	L	L	L	W	L	L	W	L	W	L	W	L	L	W	L	L	W

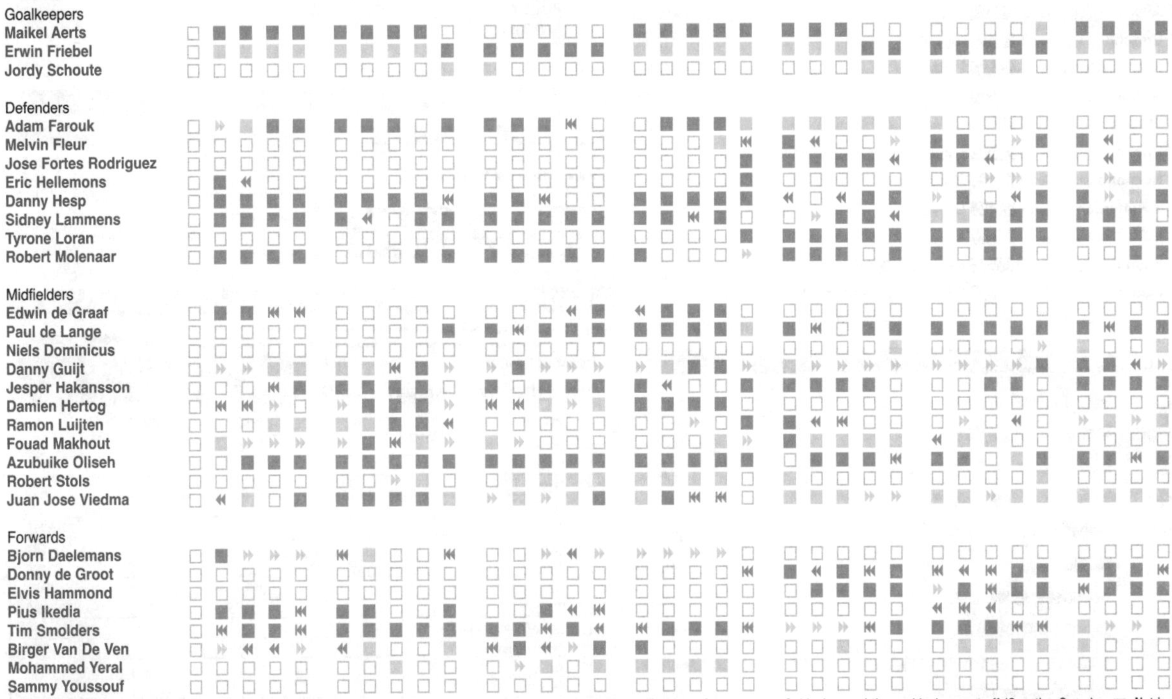

Goalkeepers
Maikel Aerts
Erwin Friebel
Jordy Schoute
Defenders
Adam Farouk
Melvin Fleur
Jose Fortes Rodriguez
Eric Hellemons
Danny Hesp
Sidney Lammens
Tyrone Loran
Robert Molenaar
Midfielders
Edwin de Graaf
Paul de Lange
Niels Dominicus
Danny Guijt
Jesper Hakansson
Damien Hertog
Ramon Luijten
Fouad Makhout
Azubuike Oliseh
Robert Stols
Juan Jose Viedma
Forwards
Bjorn Daelemans
Donny de Groot
Elvis Hammond
Pius Ikedia
Tim Smolders
Birger Van De Ven
Mohammed Yeral
Sammy Youssouf

KEY: On all match | On bench | Subbed or sent off (Counting game) | Subbed or sent off (playing less than 70 minutes) | Subbed on from bench (Counting Game) | Subbed on (playing less than 70 minutes) | Subbed on and then subbed or sent off (Counting Game) | Subbed on and then subbed or sent off (playing less than 70 minutes) | Not in 16

DE GRAAFSCHAP

Final Position: **17th**

KEY: ☐Won ☐Drawn ☐Lost

							Attendance
1	hopr1	**Feyenoord**	A	L	1-6	van Beukering 45	42,000
2	hopr1	**Den Bosch**	H	D	1-1	van Beukering 34	11,000
3	hopr1	**Roda JC Kerk**	A	L	1-2	Zongo 24	13,000
4	hopr1	**Heerenveen**	A	L	0-2		17,000
5	hopr1	**Groningen**	H	D	2-2	Duits 52; Zongo 59	11,000
6	hopr1	**Twente**	H	D	0-0		11,000
7	hopr1	**NAC Breda**	A	L	2-3	Loval 38,89	13,000
8	hopr1	**AZ Alkmaar**	H	L	1-3	Van Leerdam 59	11,000
9	hopr1	**Den Haag**	H	L	1-2	Kalezic 59	11,000
10	hopr1	**Willem II Tilb**	H	D	2-2	Valeev 49; de Graef 90	11,000
11	hopr1	**Roosendaal**	A	L	0-3		5,000
12	hopr1	**RKC Waalwijk**	A	D	2-2	van Beukering 26; Loval 81	4,000
13	hopr1	**Ajax**	H	L	0-5		11,000
14	hopr1	**Utrecht**	A	L	0-1		18,000
15	hopr1	**PSV Eindhoven**	H	L	0-4		11,000
16	hopr1	**NEC Nijmegen**	H	W	3-2	Magno 14; Van Leerdam 41; de Graef 65	11,000
17	hopr1	**Vitesse Arnhem**	A	L	1-3	Magno 1	20,000
18	hopr1	**Roda JC Kerk**	H	W	2-0	Van Leerdam 80; van Beukering 90	11,000
19	hopr1	**Groningen**	A	L	0-1		12,000
20	hopr1	**Feyenoord**	H	L	2-7	Bot 9; van Beukering 85	12,000
21	hopr1	**Den Bosch**	A	W	2-0	van Beukering 70; Berck-Beelenkamp 90	6,000
22	hopr1	**Heerenveen**	H	W	2-1	van Beukering 48,79	11,000
23	hopr1	**Twente**	A	D	0-0		13,000
24	hopr1	**NAC Breda**	H	L	0-2		11,000
25	hopr1	**AZ Alkmaar**	A	L	2-3	Magno 25,90	8,000
26	hopr1	**Roosendaal**	H	L	0-1		11,000
27	hopr1	**Willem II Tilb**	A	L	1-4	Ax 33	13,000
28	hopr1	**Den Haag**	A	L	0-2		6,000
29	hopr1	**RKC Waalwijk**	H	L	2-4	van Beukering 25 pen; Robbemond 57	11,000
30	hopr1	**Ajax**	A	L	0-1		49,000
31	hopr1	**Utrecht**	H	D	0-0		11,000
32	hopr1	**PSV Eindhoven**	A	L	1-4	Loval 85	32,000
33	hopr1	**NEC Nijmegen**	A	L	0-3		12,000
34	hopr1	**Vitesse Arnhem**	H	L	1-2	Loval 33	11,000
35	relpo*	**Zwolle**	H	W	3-2	van Beukering 79; Zongo 88; Valeev 90	
36	relpo*	**Helmond Sport**	A	D	1-1	Zongo 60	
37	relpo*	**S Rotterdam**	H	D	1-3	Bot 78	
38	relpo*	**S Rotterdam**	A	L	0-1		
39	relpo*	**Helmond Sport**	H	D	2-2	Haklander 24; Valeev 31	
40	relpo*	**Zwolle**	A	W	4-1	Loval 1; Robbemond 14; Duits 27,43	

relpo* refers to relegation play-offs

MONTHLY POINTS TALLY

AUGUST	1	11%
SEPTEMBER	2	22%
OCTOBER	1	8%
NOVEMBER	1	8%
DECEMBER	3	33%
JANUARY	3	50%
FEBRUARY	7	58%
MARCH	0	0%
APRIL	0	0%
MAY	1	8%

KEY PLAYERS - GOALSCORERS

Jhonny van Beukering

Goals in the League	9	Player Strike Rate Average number of minutes between League goals scored by player	289
Contribution to Attacking Power Average number of minutes between League team goals while on pitch	96	Club Strike Rate Average number of minutes between League goals scored by club	96

	PLAYER	LGE GOALS	POWER	STRIKE RATE
1	Jhonny van Beukering	9	96	289 mins
2	Magno	4	106	400 mins
3	Ilja Van Leerdam	3	90	602 mins
4	Mamadou Zongo	2	110	772 mins
5	Reinier Robbemond	1	86	1112 mins

KEY PLAYERS - MIDFIELDERS

Reinier Robbemond

Goals in the League	1	Contribution to Attacking Power Average number of minutes between League team goals while on pitch	86
Defensive Rating Average number of mins between League goals conceded while on the pitch	40	Scoring Difference Defensive Rating minus Contribution to Attacking Power	-46

	PLAYER	LGE GOALS	DEF RATE	POWER	SCORE DIFF
1	Reinier Robbemond	1	40	86	-46 mins
2	Sven Vandenbroeck	0	42	92	-50 mins
3	Ilja Van Leerdam	3	37	90	-53 mins
4	Garry de Graef	2	39	94	-55 mins
5	Mamadou Zongo	2	43	110	-67 mins

KEY PLAYERS - DEFENDERS

Milan Berck-Beelenkamp

Goals Conceded Number of League goals conceded while the player was on the pitch	53	Clean Sheets In games when player was on pitch for at least 70 minutes	4
Defensive Rating Ave number of mins between League goals conceded while on the pitch	45	Club Defensive Rating Average number of mins between League goals conceded by the club this season	39

	PLAYER	CON LGE	CLEAN SHEETS	DEF RATE
1	Milan Berck-Beelenkamp	53	4	45 mins
2	Rene Bot	72	5	40 mins
3	Dave Bus	63	3	39 mins
4	Darije Kalezic	43	3	37 mins

KEY GOALKEEPER

Jimmy van Fessem

Goals Conceded in the League	35	Counting Games League games when player was on pitch for at least 70 minutes	17
Defensive Rating Ave number of mins between League goals conceded while on the pitch	44	Clean Sheets In games when player was on pitch for at least 70 minutes	4

LEAGUE GOALS

Jhonny van Beukering

Minutes on the pitch	2604	Goals in the League	9
League average (mins between goals)	289		

	PLAYER	MINS	GOALS	AVE
1	van Beukering	2604	9	289
2	Loval	1011	5	202
3	Magno	1600	4	400
4	Van Leerdam	1806	3	602
5	Zongo	1543	2	772
6	de Graef	2527	2	1264
7	Duits	266	1	266
8	Bot	2857	1	2857
9	Valeev	902	1	902
10	Berck-Beelenkamp	2399	1	2399
11	Robbemond	1112	1	1112
12	Kalezic	1604	1	1604
	Other		1	
	TOTAL		32	

DISCIPLINARY RECORDS

	PLAYER	YELLOW	RED	AVE
1	Loovens	4	0	218
2	Roelofsen	2	0	253
3	Carrilho	2	0	295
4	Bus	8	0	304
5	de Graef	8	0	315
6	Kooijman	3	0	335
7	Ax	2	0	391
8	Van Leerdam	4	0	451
9	Zongo	2	1	514
10	Kalezic	2	1	534
11	Vandenbroeck	3	0	554
12	Robbemond	2	0	556
13	Berck-Beelenkamp	4	0	599
	Other	10	0	
	TOTAL	56	2	

TOP POINT EARNERS

	PLAYER	GAMES	AV PTS
1	Magno	13	1.08
2	Reinier Robbemond	12	0.83
3	Sven Vandenbroeck	18	0.78
4	M Berck-Beelenkamp	24	0.67
5	Jhonny van Beukering	29	0.66
6	Jimmy van Fessem	17	0.65
7	Rene Bot	31	0.61
8	Ilja Van Leerdam	15	0.60
9	Garry de Graef	27	0.59
10	Dave Bus	25	0.56
	CLUB AVERAGE:		0.56

LEAGUE APPEARANCES, BOOKINGS AND CAPS

	AGE (on 01/07/05)	IN NAMED 18	APPEARANCES	COUNTING GAMES	MINUTES ON PITCH	YELLOW CARDS	RED CARDS	THIS SEASON	HOME COUNTRY
Goalkeepers									
Aleksander Klak	34	16	3	3	270	0	0	-	Poland
Raymond Lenting	21	16	0	0	0	0	0	-	Holland
Rob van Dijk	36	15	14	14	1260	0	0	-	Holland
Jimmy van Fessem	29	17	17	17	1530	0	0	-	Holland
Defenders									
M. Berck-Beelenkamp	27	33	32	24	2399	4	0	-	Holland
Rene Bot	27	32	32	31	2857	3	0	-	Holland
Dave Bus	27	30	29	25	2433	8	0	-	Holland
Mirano Carrilho	29	15	8	6	590	2	0	-	Holland
Darije Kalezic	35	29	23	14	1604	2	1	-	Bosnia
Andre Karnebeek	34	5	0	0	0	0	0	-	Holland
Glenn Loovens	21	11	11	9	873	4	0	-	Holland
Michael van der Kruis	26	24	19	11	1300	2	0	-	Holland
Cihan Yalcin	20	6	0	0	0	0	0	-	Turkey
Midfielders									
Patrick Ax	25	22	18	4	783	2	0	-	Holland
Garry de Graef	30	29	29	27	2527	8	0	-	Belgium
Sander Duits	21	17	6	2	266	1	0	-	Holland
Richard Haklander	21	28	18	2	429	1	0	-	Holland
Dick Kooijman	32	15	13	10	1006	3	0	-	Holland
Reinier Robbemond	33	13	13	12	1112	2	0	-	Holland
Richard Roelofsen	35	10	10	3	507	2	0	-	Holland
Ricardo Sousa	26	11	10	6	677	0	0	-	Portugal
Jory Ten Brinke	20	26	3	0	25	0	0	-	Holland
Ilja Van Leerdam	26	32	28	15	1806	4	0	-	Holland
Sven Vandenbroeck	25	19	19	18	1664	3	0	-	Belgium
Mamadou Zongo	24	32	24	12	1543	2	1	-	Burkino Faso
Forwards									
Loic Loval	23	22	18	9	1011	1	0	-	France
Magno	31	23	22	13	1600	2	0	-	Brazil
Ruslan Valeev	23	24	18	6	902	0	0	-	Ukraine
J. van Beukering	21	31	31	29	2604	2	0	-	Holland

TEAM OF THE SEASON

D
M. Berck-Beelenkamp
CG: 24 DR: 45
M
Reinier Robbemond
CG: 12 SD: -46
D
Rene Bot
CG: 31 DR: 40
M
Ilja Van Leerdam
CG: 15 SD: -53
F
J. van Beukering
CG: 29 SR: 289
G
Rob van Dijk
CG: 14 DR: 37
D
Dave Bus
CG: 25 DR: 39
M
Garry de Graef
CG: 27 SD: -55
F
Magno
CG: 13 SR: 400
D
Darije Kalezic
CG: 14 DR: 37
M
Sven Vandenbroek
CG: 18 SD: -50

SQUAD APPEARANCES

Match	1	2	3	4	5	6	7	8	9	10	11	12	13	14	15	16	17	18	19	20	21	22	23	24	25	26	27	28	29	30	31	32	33	34	35
Venue	A	H	A	A	H	H	H	A	H	H	H	A	A	H	A	H	H	A	H	A	H	A	H	A	H	A	H	A	A	H	A	H	A	A	H
Competition	L	L	L	L	L	L	L	L	L	L	L	L	L	L	L	L	L	L	L	L	L	L	L	L	L	L	L	L	L	L	L	L	L	L	L
Result	L	D	L	L	D	D	D	L	L	L	D	L	D	L	L	L	W	L	W	L	L	W	W	D	L	L	L	L	L	L	L	D	L	L	L

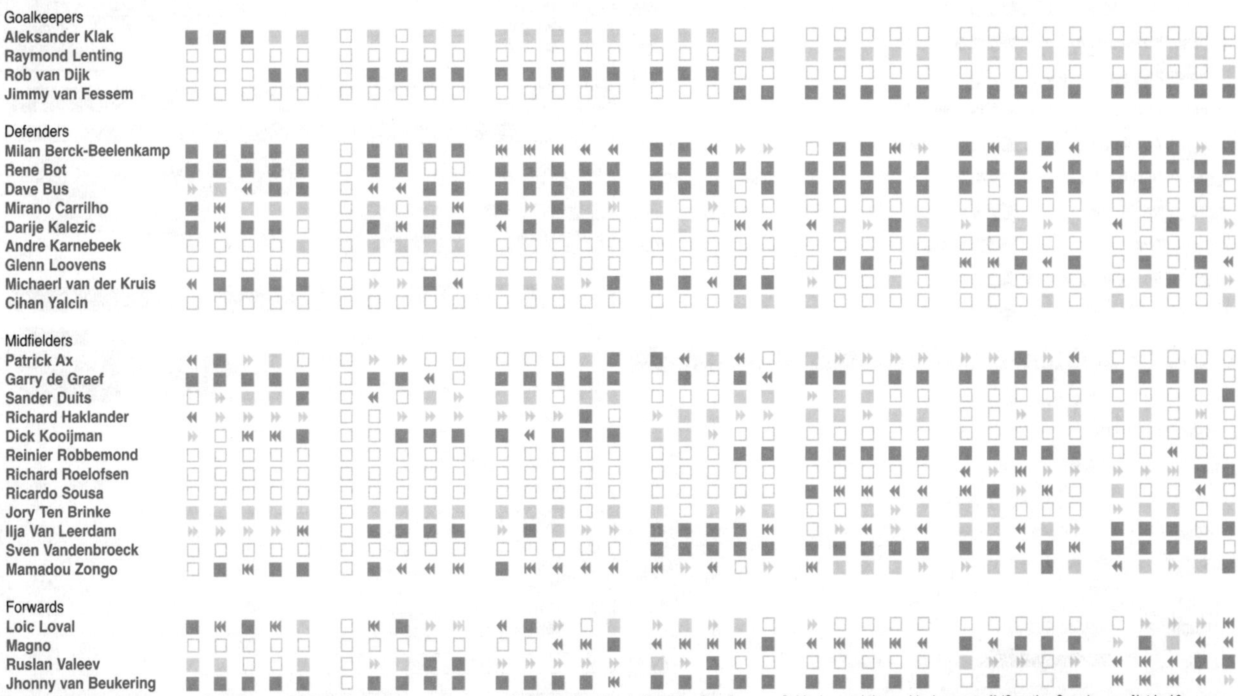

Goalkeepers
Aleksander Klak
Raymond Lenting
Rob van Dijk
Jimmy van Fessem
Defenders
Milan Berck-Beelenkamp
Rene Bot
Dave Bus
Mirano Carrilho
Darije Kalezic
Andre Karnebeek
Glenn Loovens
Michaerl van der Kruis
Cihan Yalcin
Midfielders
Patrick Ax
Garry de Graef
Sander Duits
Richard Haklander
Dick Kooijman
Reinier Robbemond
Richard Roelofsen
Ricardo Sousa
Jory Ten Brinke
Ilja Van Leerdam
Sven Vandenbroeck
Mamadou Zongo
Forwards
Loic Loval
Magno
Ruslan Valeev
Jhonny van Beukering

KEY: On all match — On bench — Subbed or sent off (Counting game) — Subbed or sent off (playing less than 70 minutes) — Subbed on from bench (Counting Game) — Subbed on (playing less than 70 minutes) — Subbed on and then subbed or sent off (Counting Game) — Subbed on and then subbed or sent off (playing less than 70 minutes) — Not in 16

DEN BOSCH

Final Position: **18th**

KEY: ☐Won ☐Drawn ☐Lost

		Opponent	H/A	Res	Score	Scorers	Attendance
1	hopr1	**Den Haag**	H	W	1-0	van der Laak 81	5,000
2	hopr1	**De Graafschap**	A	D	1-1	Schulp 16	11,000
3	hopr1	**Willem II Tilb**	H	L	1-2	van den Ouweland 59	6,000
4	hopr1	**AZ Alkmaar**	A	L	0-5		8,000
5	hopr1	**Ajax**	H	L	0-5		7,000
6	hopr1	**Vitesse Arnhem**	A	D	0-0		19,000
7	hopr1	**Feyenoord**	A	L	2-4	Biekman 2; van de Laak 83 pen	36,000
8	hopr1	**Roosendaal**	H	W	2-1	van den Ouweland 5; Powel 74	5,000
9	hopr1	**Roda JC Kerk**	A	L	0-5		12,000
10	hopr1	**Heerenveen**	H	L	2-4	van de Laak 27; Schulp 64	6,000
11	hopr1	**PSV Eindhoven**	H	L	0-3		6,000
12	hopr1	**Groningen**	A	L	1-3	van den Ouweland 22	12,000
13	hopr1	**NEC Nijmegen**	H	D	0-0		5,000
14	hopr1	**NAC Breda**	A	L	0-3		11,000
15	hopr1	**Twente**	A	L	0-4		13,000
16	hopr1	**RKC Waalwijk**	H	L	0-2		6,000
17	hopr1	**Utrecht**	A	L	0-1		19,000
18	hopr1	**Heerenveen**	A	L	1-2	Cas 71	17,000
19	hopr1	**AZ Alkmaar**	H	L	0-1		6,000
20	hopr1	**Den Haag**	A	L	0-2		6,000
21	hopr1	**De Graafschap**	H	L	0-2		6,000
22	hopr1	**Ajax**	A	L	0-2		46,000
23	hopr1	**Vitesse Arnhem**	H	L	1-2	Schulp 47	5,000
24	hopr1	**Willem II Tilb**	A	L	1-2	van de Laak 36	12,000
25	hopr1	**Roda JC Kerk**	H	L	0-3		6,000
26	hopr1	**Roosendaal**	A	W	2-1	Janssen 5,50	5,000
27	hopr1	**PSV Eindhoven**	A	L	0-3		31,000
28	hopr1	**Feyenoord**	H	W	4-1	Cales 17; van de Laak 75,78; Olfers 88	7,000
29	hopr1	**Groningen**	H	L	1-2	Mghzirat 80	6,000
30	hopr1	**NEC Nijmegen**	A	D	2-2	Powel 48; van den Ouweland 90	12,000
31	hopr1	**NAC Breda**	H	L	0-2		6,000
32	hopr1	**Twente**	H	W	1-0	Volmer 25	5,000
33	hopr1	**RKC Waalwijk**	A	L	0-2		6,000
34	hopr1	**Utrecht**	H	L	0-3		6,000

MONTHLY POINTS TALLY

AUGUST	4	44%
SEPTEMBER	1	11%
OCTOBER	3	25%
NOVEMBER	1	8%
DECEMBER	0	0%
JANUARY	0	0%
FEBRUARY	0	0%
MARCH	0	0%
APRIL	7	47%
MAY	3	25%

KEY PLAYERS - GOALSCORERS

Dennis Schulp

Goals in the League	3	**Player Strike Rate** Average number of minutes between League goals scored by player	524
Contribution to Attacking Power Average number of minutes between League team goals while on pitch	143	**Club Strike Rate** Average number of minutes between League goals scored by club	133

	PLAYER	LGE GOALS	POWER	STRIKE RATE
1	Dennis Schulp	3	143	524 mins
2	Koen van de Laak	5	119	549 mins
3	Charlie van den Ouweland	4	138	655 mins
4	Jochen Janssen	2	120	664 mins
5	Steve Olfers	1	111	1343 mins

KEY PLAYERS - MIDFIELDERS

Paul Beekmans

Goals in the League	0	**Contribution to Attacking Power** Average number of minutes between League team goals while on pitch	117
Defensive Rating Average number of mins between League goals conceded while on the pitch	38	**Scoring Difference** Defensive Rating minus Contribution to Attacking Power	-79

	PLAYER	LGE GOALS	DEF RATE	POWER	SCORE DIFF
1	Paul Beekmans	0	38	117	-79 mins
2	Rob Haemhouts	0	38	117	-79 mins
3	Marcel Cas	1	46	132	-86 mins
4	Charlie van den Ouweland	4	40	138	-98 mins
5	Mounir Biyadat	0	39	140	-101 mins

KEY PLAYERS - DEFENDERS

Steve Olfers

Goals Conceded Number of League goals conceded while the player was on the pitch	28	**Clean Sheets** In games when player was on pitch for at least 70 minutes	1
Defensive Rating Ave number of mins between League goals conceded while on the pitch	48	**Club Defensive Rating** Average number of mins between League goals conceded by the club this season	41

	PLAYER	CON LGE	CLEAN SHEETS	DEF RATE
1	Steve Olfers	28	1	48 mins
2	Ferne Snoyl	46	4	47 mins
3	Paul Verhaegh	70	4	41 mins
4	Peter Uneken	61	3	40 mins

KEY GOALKEEPER

Kris Mampaey

Goals Conceded in the League	51	**Counting Games** League games when player was on pitch for at least 70 minutes	23
Defensive Rating Ave number of mins between League goals conceded while on the pitch	40	**Clean Sheets** In games when player was on pitch for at least 70 minutes	3

LEAGUE GOALS

Koen van de Laak

Minutes on the pitch	2747	**Goals in the League**	5
League average (mins between goals)	549		

	PLAYER	MINS	GOALS	AVE
1	van de Laak	2747	5	549
2	van den Ouweland	2620	4	655
3	Schulp	1573	3	524
4	Janssen	1327	2	664
5	Powel	1175	2	588
6	Mghzirat	1133	1	1133
7	Biekman	575	1	575
8	Volmer	1028	1	1028
9	Olfers	1343	1	1343
10	Cales	471	1	471
11	Cas	2109	1	2109
	Other		1	
	TOTAL		23	

DISCIPLINARY RECORDS

	PLAYER	YELLOW	RED	AVE
1	Loovens	4	0	218
2	Roelofsen	2	0	253
3	Carrilho	2	0	295
4	Bus	8	0	304
5	de Graef	8	0	315
6	Kooijman	3	0	335
7	Ax	2	0	391
8	Van Leerdam	4	0	451
9	Zongo	2	1	514
10	Kalezic	2	1	534
11	Vandenbroeck	3	0	554
12	Robbemond	2	0	556
13	Berck-Beelenkamp	4	0	599
	Other	10	0	
	TOTAL	56	2	

TOP POINT EARNERS

	PLAYER	GAMES	AV PTS
1	Marcel Cas	20	0.70
2	Kris Mampaey	23	0.65
3	Ferne Snoyl	23	0.65
4	Rob Haemhouts	19	0.63
5	Koen van de Laak	30	0.60
6	Dennis Schulp	15	0.60
7	Paul Verhaegh	32	0.59
8	Jochen Janssen	12	0.58
9	Paul Beekmans	22	0.55
10	Steve Olfers	14	0.50
	CLUB AVERAGE:		0.56

LEAGUE APPEARANCES, BOOKINGS AND CAPS

	AGE (on 01/07/05)	IN NAMED 18	APPEARANCES	COUNTING GAMES	MINUTES ON PITCH	YELLOW CARDS	RED CARDS	THIS SEASON	HOME COUNTRY
Goalkeepers									
Kris Mampaey	34	28	23	23	2060	3	0	-	Belgium
Martijn van Strien	26	32	12	11	1000	0	0	-	Holland
Danilo Verus	22	8	0	0	0	0	0	-	Holland
Defenders									
Pieter Kuypers	19	1	0	0	0	0	0	-	Holland
Geoffrey Meye	22	5	0	0	0	0	0	-	Holland
Steve Olfers	23	16	16	14	1343	0	0	-	Holland
Tom Rietberg	22	6	1	0	13	0	0	-	Holland
Ferne Snoyl	20	26	25	23	2149	9	0	-	Holland
Peter Uneken	33	29	29	26	2413	5	1	-	Holland
Thijs van der Meulen	24	30	1	0	19	0	0	-	Holland
Erwin van Iersel	21	12	0	0	0	0	0	-	Holland
Paul Verhaegh	21	32	32	32	2860	3	0	-	Holland
Joost Volmer	31	16	13	10	1028	1	0	-	Holland
Midfielders									
Otman Bakkal	20	9	6	2	275	0	0	-	Holland
Paul Beekmans	23	33	29	22	2214	2	0	-	Holland
Mounir Biyadat	21	33	27	25	2245	4	0	-	Holland
Marcel Cas	33	30	28	20	2109	3	0	-	Holland
Vincent Euvrard	23	22	11	1	221	0	0	-	Belgium
Rob Haemhouts	21	31	27	19	1997	3	0	-	Belgium
C. van den Ouweland	23	34	33	27	2620	2	0	-	Holland
E. van der Meerakker	24	3	0	0	0	0	0	-	Holland
Forwards									
Brayton Biekman	26	19	14	3	575	0	0	-	Holland
Gijs Cales	28	17	14	3	471	0	0	-	Holland
Jochen Janssen	29	17	17	12	1327	3	0	-	Belgium
Mourad Mghzirat	30	27	22	9	1133	2	0	-	Morocco
Berry Powel	25	31	29	4	1175	2	0	-	Holland
Dennis Schulp	27	22	22	15	1573	1	0	-	Holland
Derk Schut	20	3	1	0	15	0	0	-	Holland
Koen van de Laak	22	31	31	30	2747	5	0	-	Holland

TEAM OF THE SEASON

G — Kris Mampaey — CG: 23 DR: 40

D — Steve Olfers — CG: 14 DR: 48

D — Ferne Snoyl — CG: 23 DR: 47

D — Paul Verhaegh — CG: 32 DR: 41

D — Peter Uneken — CG: 26 DR: 40

M — Paul Beekmans — CG: 22 SD: -79

M — Rob Haemhouts — CG: 19 SD: -79

M — Marcel Cas — CG: 20 SD: -86

M — Charlie van den Ouweland — CG: 27 SD: -98

F — Dennis Schulp — CG: 15 SR: 524

F — Koen van de Laak — CG: 30 SR: 549

SQUAD APPEARANCES

Match	1	2	3	4	5	6	7	8	9	10	11	12	13	14	15	16	17	18	19	20	21	22	23	24	25	26	27	28	29	30	31	32	33	34
Venue	H	A	H	A	H	A	A	H	A	H	H	A	H	A	A	H	A	A	H	A	H	A	H	A	H	A	A	H	H	A	H	H	A	H
Competition	L	L	L	L	L	L	L	L	L	L	L	L	L	L	L	L	L	L	L	L	L	L	L	L	L	L	L	L	L	L	L	L	L	L
Result	W	D	L	L	L	D	L	W	L	L	L	L	D	L	L	L	L	L	L	L	L	L	L	L	L	W	L	W	L	D	L	W	L	L

Goalkeepers
Kris Mampaey
Martijn van Strien
Danilo Verus

Defenders
Pieter Kuypers
Geoffrey Meye
Steve Olfers
Tom Rietberg
Ferne Snoyl
Peter Uneken
Thijs van der Meulen
Erwin van Iersel
Paul Verhaegh
Joost Volmer

Midfielders
Otman Bakkal
Paul Beekmans
Mounir Biyadat
Marcel Cas
Vincent Euvrard
Rob Haemhouts
Charlie van den Ouweland
Emile van der Meerakker

Forwards
Brayton Biekman
Gijs Cales
Jochen Janssen
Mourad Mghzirat
Berry Powel
Dennis Schulp
Derk Schut
Koen van de Laak

KEY: On all match | On bench | Subbed or sent off (Counting game) | Subbed or sent off (playing less than 70 minutes) | Subbed on from bench (Counting Game) | Subbed on (playing less than 70 minutes) | Subbed on and then subbed or sent off (Counting Game) | Subbed on and then subbed or sent off (playing less than 70 minutes) | Not in 16

GERMAN LEAGUE ROUND-UP

FINAL LEAGUE TABLE

		HOME					AWAY					TOTAL			
	P	W	D	L	F	A	W	D	L	F	A	F	A	DIF	PTS
Bayern Munich	34	14	2	1	44	14	10	3	4	31	19	75	33	42	77
Schalke	34	11	2	4	33	24	9	1	7	23	22	56	46	10	63
W Bremen	34	9	4	4	33	15	9	1	7	35	22	68	37	31	59
Hertha Berlin	34	8	8	1	34	13	7	5	5	25	18	59	31	28	58
Stuttgart	34	12	2	3	34	15	5	5	7	20	25	54	40	14	58
B Leverkusen	34	12	3	2	42	18	4	6	7	23	26	65	44	21	57
B Dortmund	34	8	5	4	24	18	7	5	5	23	26	47	44	3	55
Hamburg	34	9	1	7	27	22	7	2	8	28	28	55	50	5	51
Wolfsburg	34	10	1	6	35	20	5	2	10	14	31	49	51	-2	48
Hannover 96	34	8	2	7	21	19	5	4	8	13	17	34	36	-2	45
Mainz	34	9	3	5	28	21	3	4	10	22	34	50	55	-5	43
Kaiserslautern	34	8	2	7	20	21	4	4	9	23	31	43	52	-9	42
Arminia B	34	7	3	7	21	21	4	4	9	16	28	37	49	-12	40
Nuremberg	34	4	6	7	25	25	6	2	9	30	38	55	63	-8	38
B M'gladbach	34	8	5	4	26	21	0	7	10	9	30	35	51	-16	36
Bochum	34	6	5	6	30	29	3	3	11	17	39	47	68	-21	35
Hansa Rostock	34	4	5	8	17	31	3	4	10	14	34	31	65	-34	30
Freiburg	34	2	6	9	18	31	1	3	13	12	44	30	75	-45	18

CLUB STRIKE FORCE

Pizarro; celebrating for Bayern

1 Bayern Munich

Goals scored in the League	75
Club Strike Rate (CSR) Average number of minutes between League goals scored by club	41

	CLUB	GOALS	CSR
1	Bayern Munich	75	41
2	W Bremen	68	45
3	B Leverkusen	65	47
4	Hertha Berlin	59	52
5	Schalke	56	55
6	Hamburg	55	56
7	Nuremberg	55	56
8	Stuttgart	54	57
9	Mainz	50	61
10	Wolfsburg	49	62
11	B Dortmund	47	65
12	Bochum	47	65
13	Kaiserslautern	43	71
14	Arminia B	37	83
15	B M'gladbach	35	87
16	Hannover 96	34	90
17	Hansa Rostock	31	99
18	Freiburg	30	102

CLUB DISCIPLINARY RECORDS

Gorlitz of Bayern; tangles with Alan Smith

1. Hamburg

League Yellow	88
League Red	4
League Total	92
Cards Average in League Average number of minutes between a card being shown of either colour	33

	CLUB	Y	R	TOTAL	AVE
1	Hamburg	88	4	92	33
2	B M'gladbach	86	4	90	34
3	Hansa Rostock	81	4	85	36
4	Nuremberg	80	4	84	36
5	Stuttgart	80	4	84	36
6	Kaiserslautern	77	3	80	38
7	Bochum	72	4	76	40
8	Schalke	73	4	77	40
9	Hertha Berlin	70	4	74	41
10	Wolfsburg	64	5	69	44
11	Bayern Munich	63	3	66	46
12	Freiburg	62	4	66	46
13	B Leverkusen	63	2	65	48
14	B Dortmund	61	2	63	49
15	W Bremen	56	4	60	51
16	Mainz	49	2	51	60
17	Arminia B	48	0	48	64
18	Hannover 96	34	1	35	87

CLUB DEFENCES

	CLUB	LGE	CS	CDR
1	Hertha Berlin	31	11	99
2	Bayern Munich	33	14	93
3	Hannover 96	36	12	85
4	W Bremen	37	9	83
5	Stuttgart	40	14	77
6	B Dortmund	44	7	70
7	B Leverkusen	44	8	70
8	Schalke	46	9	67
9	Arminia B	49	7	62
10	Hamburg	50	6	61
11	B M'gladbach	51	10	60
12	Wolfsburg	51	10	60
13	Kaiserslautern	52	8	59
14	Mainz	55	6	56
15	Nuremberg	63	8	49
16	Hansa Rostock	65	7	47
17	Bochum	68	4	45
18	Freiburg	75	6	41

Hertha Berlin's Frank Baumann

1 Hertha Berlin

Goals conceded in the League	31
Clean Sheets (CS) Number of league games where no goals were conceded	11
Club Defensive Rate (CDR) Average number of minutes between League goals conceded by club	99

PLAYER NATIONALITIES

Overseas country with the most player appearances in the German League - Brazil

531 league appearances by Brazilian players

	COUNTRY	PLAYERS	IN SQUAD	LGE APP	% LGE ACT	CAPS	MOST APP	APP
1	Germany	272	5120	3678	45.0	132	Christian Fiedler	100.0
2	Brazil	25	586	531	6.8	39	Gilberto	94.4
3	Czech Republic	13	361	329	4.1	27	Vratislav Lokvenc	91.0
4	Denmark	12	315	257	3.2	28	Soren Colding	81.7
5	Holland	8	223	209	2.9	16	Roy Makaay	92.7
6	Croatia	14	363	262	2.9	45	Zvonimir Soldo	92.0
7	Poland	13	273	205	2.5		Dariusz Zuraw	91.8
8	Belgium	9	217	170	1.9	15	Daniel Van Buyten	100.0
9	France	8	192	142	1.8	3	Johan Micoud	94.5
10	Argentina	10	187	149	1.7	19	Diego Placente	77.6
11	Sweden	6	149	132	1.6	19	Marcus Lantz	85.5
12	Switzerland	10	163	128	1.5	13	Mario Cantaluppi	72.7
13	Slovakia	5	129	111	1.4		Marek Mintal	97.8
14	Albania	4	119	111	1.3		Altin Lala	89.4
15	Serbia & Montenegro	8	138	122	1.3	6	Mladen Krstajic	82.4
16	Georgia	4	92	89	1.2		Levan Kobiashvili	93.3
17	Turkey	12	182	126	1.2		Halil Altintop	72.1
18	Bosnia	6	132	108	1.1		Sergei Barbarez	84.3

CLUB MAKE-UP – HOME AND OVERSEAS PLAYERS

1 Schalke

73.1% of appearances by overseas players

	CLUB	OVERSEAS	HOME	% OVERSEAS	% LGE ACT	MOST APP	APP
1	Schalke	14	14	50.0	73.1	Levan Kobiashvili	93.3
2	Freiburg	18	12	60.0	67.5	Ismael Coulibaly	88.6
3	Bochum	21	12	63.6	65.8	Vratislav Lokvenc	91.0
4	Hamburg	14	15	48.3	63.1	D Van Buyten	100.0
5	Hannover 96	20	11	64.5	62.5	Steve Cherundolo	92.5
6	Wolfsburg	16	12	57.1	61.0	Pablo Thiam	94.7
7	Bayern Munich	14	14	50.0	60.8	Roy Makaay	92.7
8	Hansa Rostock	15	15	50.0	59.2	Marcus Lantz	85.5
9	B Leverkusen	15	16	48.4	57.7	Dimitar Berbatov	98.5
10	Hertha Berlin	12	18	40.0	56.2	Gilberto	94.4
11	B M'gladbach	17	15	53.1	55.2	Jeff Strasser	79.1
12	W Bremen	14	15	48.3	52.9	Johan Micoud	94.5
13	B Dortmund	18	17	51.4	52.4	Leonardo Dede	89.5
14	Nuremberg	12	17	41.4	47.9	Marek Mintal	97.8
15	Arminia B	16	16	50.0	46.0	Petr Gabriel	90.8
16	Stuttgart	15	15	50.0	45.5	Alexander Hleb	98.5
17	Kaiserslautern	12	19	38.7	41.1	Hervi Nzelo Lembi	89.1
18	Mainz	5	24	17.2	22.8	Antonio da Silva	88.2

CHART-TOPPING MIDFIELDERS

1 Basturk - Hertha Berlin	
Goals scored in the League	7
Defensive Rating Av number of mins between League goals conceded while on the pitch	115
Contribution to Attacking Power Average number of minutes between League team goals while on pitch	49
Scoring Difference Defensive Rating minus Contribution to Attacking Power	66

	PLAYER	CLUB	GOALS	DEF RATE	POWER	S DIFF
1	Basturk	Hertha Berlin	7	115	49	66
2	Frings	Bayern Munich	3	102	48	54
3	Kovac	Hertha Berlin	4	102	54	48
4	Gilberto	Hertha Berlin	6	100	54	46
5	Salihamidzic	Bayern Munich	2	88	46	42
6	Ballack	Bayern Munich	13	83	41	42
7	Marx	Hertha Berlin	3	90	49	41
8	Stalteri	W Bremen	0	84	44	40
9	Ernst	W Bremen	2	81	46	35
10	Micoud	W Bremen	8	78	44	34
11	Freier	B Leverkusen	6	67	42	25
12	Soldo	Stuttgart	2	85	60	25
13	Krzynowek	B Leverkusen	6	68	44	24
14	Meissner	Stuttgart	9	75	52	23
15	Ramelow	B Leverkusen	1	66	46	20

CHART-TOPPING GOALSCORERS

1 Makaay - Bayern Munich	
Goals scored in the League	22
Contribution to Attacking Power Average number of minutes between League team goals while on pitch	39
Club Strike Rate (CSR) Average minutes between League goals scored by club	41
Player Strike Rate Average number of minutes between League goals scored by player	129

	PLAYER	CLUB	GOALS: LGE	POWER	CSR	S RATE
1	Makaay	Bayern Munich	22	39	41	129
2	Mintal	Nuremberg	23	55	56	130
3	Voronin	B Leverkusen	15	43	48	143
4	Berbatov	B Leverkusen	20	48	48	151
5	Marcelinho	Hertha Berlin	18	52	52	157
6	Ailton	Schalke	14	55	55	159
7	Klose	W Bremen	15	46	44	161
8	Buckley	Arminia B	15	80	83	171
9	Koller	B Dortmund	15	69	65	175
10	Kuranyi	Stuttgart	13	56	57	175
11	Ballack	Bayern Munich	13	41	41	184
12	Lincoln	Schalke	13	49	55	191
13	Klasnic	W Bremen	10	55	44	206
14	Petrov	Wolfsburg	12	60	62	206
15	Brdaric	Wolfsburg	12	59	62	213

CHART-TOPPING DEFENDERS

1 Kovac - Bayern Munich	
Goals Conceded in the League The number of League goals conceded while he was on the pitch	15
Clean Sheets In games when he played at least 70 mins	12
Club Defensive Rating Average mins between League goals conceded by the club this season	93
Defensive Rating Average number of minutes between League goals conceded while on pitch	134

	PLAYER	CLUB	CON: LGE	CS	CDR	DEF RATE
1	Kovac	Bayern Munich	15	12	93	134
2	Van Burik	Hertha Berlin	19	9	99	114
3	Sagnol	Bayern Munich	16	8	93	112
4	Friedrich	Hertha Berlin	22	9	99	102
5	Pasanen	W Bremen	19	7	81	100
6	Simunic	Hertha Berlin	27	10	99	97
7	Stranzl	Stuttgart	27	13	77	96
8	Pander	Schalke	22	8	67	94
9	Mertesacker	Hannover 96	31	11	81	90
10	Lucio	Bayern Munich	32	11	93	87
11	Zuraw	Hannover 96	33	10	81	85
12	Fathi	Hertha Berlin	24	8	99	85
13	Hinkel	Stuttgart	30	12	77	83
14	Baumann	W Bremen	23	7	81	83
15	Ismael	W Bremen	34	9	81	83

CHART-TOPPING GOALKEEPERS

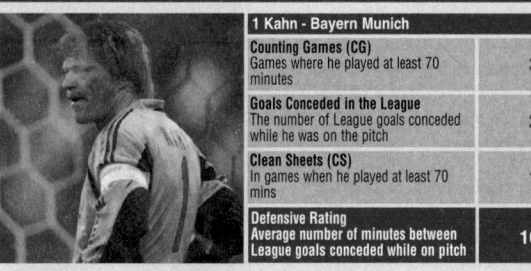

1 Kahn - Bayern Munich	
Counting Games (CG) Games where he played at least 70 minutes	32
Goals Conceded in the League The number of League goals conceded while he was on the pitch	28
Clean Sheets (CS) In games when he played at least 70 mins	13
Defensive Rating Average number of minutes between League goals conceded while on pitch	100

	PLAYER	CLUB	CG	CONC	CS	DEF RATE
1	Kahn	Bayern Munich	30	28	13	100
2	Fiedler	Hertha Berlin	34	31	11	99
3	Enke	Hannover 96	34	38	11	81
4	Reinke	W Bremen	34	38	9	81
5	Weidenfeller	B Dortmund	26	30	7	78
6	Hildebrand	Stuttgart	34	40	14	77
7	Keller	B M'gladbach	17	21	7	73
8	Butt	B Leverkusen	34	46	8	68
9	Rost	Schalke	31	41	8	68
10	Ernst	Kaiserslautern	20	29	6	63
11	Hain	Arminia B	34	49	7	62
12	Jentzsch	Wolfsburg	33	50	10	59
13	Pieckenhagen	Hamburg	23	36	3	58
14	Wache	Mainz	29	47	6	56
15	Schafer	Nuremberg	25	43	7	52

PLAYER DISCIPLINARY RECORD

1. Lagerblom - Nuremberg	
Cards Average mins between cards	114
League Yellow	5
League Red	0
TOTAL	5

	PLAYER		LY	LR	TOT	AVE
1	Lagerblom	Nuremberg	5	0	5	114
2	Gorlitz	Bayern Munich	3	1	4	121
3	Neuendorf	Hertha Berlin	6	1	7	127
4	Varela	Schalke	4	0	4	129
5	Olajengbesi	Freiburg	4	1	5	130
6	Moore	B M'gladbach	7	1	8	132
7	Zivkovic	Stuttgart	4	1	5	132
8	Bajramovic	Freiburg	8	0	8	137
9	Prica	Hansa Rostock	12	1	13	147
10	Sonck	B M'gladbach	3	0	3	151
11	Weiland	Mainz	4	0	4	151
12	Grammozis	Kaiserslautern	3	2	5	159
13	Linke	Bayern Munich	5	0	5	169
14	Cantaluppi	Nuremberg	12	1	13	171
15	Teber	Kaiserslautern	3	0	3	172
16	Wolf	Nuremberg	6	1	7	172
17	Balitsch	Mainz	6	0	6	175
18	Hofland	Wolfsburg	12	1	13	175
19	Bohme	B M'gladbach	6	0	6	176
20	Meichelbeck	Bochum	8	1	9	176
21	Gerber	Stuttgart	3	0	3	177
22	Hajto	Nuremberg	6	1	7	181
23	Boulahrouz	Hamburg	10	1	11	193
24	Willi	Freiburg	3	0	3	201

TEAM OF THE SEASON

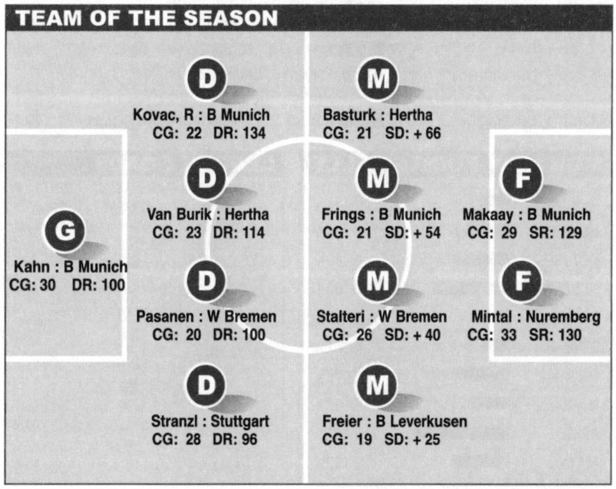
D
Kovac, R : B Munich
CG: 22 DR: 134
M
Basturk : Hertha
CG: 21 SD: + 66
G
Kahn : B Munich
CG: 30 DR: 100
D
Van Burik : Hertha
CG: 23 DR: 114
M
Frings : B Munich
CG: 21 SD: + 54
F
Makaay : B Munich
CG: 29 SR: 129
D
Pasanen : W Bremen
CG: 20 DR: 100
M
Stalteri : W Bremen
CG: 26 SD: + 40
F
Mintal : Nuremberg
CG: 33 SR: 130
D
Stranzl : Stuttgart
CG: 28 DR: 96
M
Freier : B Leverkusen
CG: 19 SD: + 25

BAYERN MUNICH

Final Position: **1st**

KEY: Won Drawn Lost

							Attendance
1	grpr1	**Hamburg**	A	W	2-0	Ballack 22; Deisler 71	55,000
2	grpr1	**Hertha Berlin**	H	D	1-1	Makaay 47	50,000
3	grpr1	**B Leverkusen**	A	L	1-4	Ballack 84	22,000
4	grpr1	**Arminia B**	H	W	1-0	Makaay 26	45,000
5	cl gc	**M Tel-Aviv**	A	W	1-0	Makaay 64 pen	20,000
6	grpr1	**B Dortmund**	A	D	2-2	Lucio 88; Makaay 90	83,000
7	grpr1	**Freiburg**	H	W	3-1	Makaay 19; Frings 45; Ballack 72	27,000
8	cl gc	**Ajax**	H	W	4-0	Makaay 28,44,52 pen; Ze Roberto 55	50,000
9	grpr1	**W Bremen**	A	W	2-1	Ballack 20; Schweinsteiger 75	43,000
10	grpr1	**Schalke**	H	L	0-1		63,000
11	cl gc	**Juventus**	A	L	0-1		18,000
12	grpr1	**Hansa Rostock**	A	W	2-0	Sagnol 83; Scholl 85	29,000
13	grpr1	**Wolfsburg**	H	W	2-0	Pizarro 24,45	35,000
14	grpr1	**B M'gladbach**	A	L	0-2		53,000
15	cl gc	**Juventus**	H	L	0-1		59,000
16	grpr1	**Hannover 96**	H	W	3-0	Pizarro 3; Makaay 80; Guerrero 90	52,000
17	grpr1	**Bochum**	A	W	3-1	Guerrero 77,81; Colding 82 og	33,000
18	grpr1	**Kaiserslautern**	H	W	3-1	Pizarro 12; Frings 26; Guerrero 64	35,000
19	cl gc	**M Tel-Aviv**	H	W	5-1	Pizarro 12; Salihamidzic 37; Frings 44; Makaay 71,80	25,000
20	grpr1	**Mainz**	H	W	4-2	Pizarro 14; Scholl 35; Makaay 45; Ballack 88	50,000
21	grpr1	**Nuremburg**	A	D	2-2	Makaay 26 pen; Ze Roberto 60	42,000
22	cl gc	**Ajax**	A	D	2-2	Makaay 8; Ballack 78	50,000
23	grpr1	**Stuttgart**	H	D	2-2	Pizarro 67; Guerrero 89	63,000
24	grpr1	**Hamburg**	H	W	3-0	Pizarro 22; Schweinsteiger 48; Makaay 55	39,000
25	grpr1	**Hertha Berlin**	A	D	0-0		74,000
26	grpr1	**B Leverkusen**	H	W	2-0	Makaay 45 pen; Guerrero 68	45,000
27	grpr1	**Arminia B**	A	L	1-3	Lucio 80	26,000
28	grpr1	**B Dortmund**	H	W	5-0	Salihamidzic 5; Makaay 6,34,54; Pizarro 28	48,000
29	clr2l1	**Arsenal**	H	W	3-1	Pizarro 3,58; Salihamidzic 65	59,000
30	grpr1	**Freiburg**	A	W	1-0	Deisler 52	25,000
31	grpr1	**W Bremen**	H	W	1-0	Ballack 7	53,000
32	clr2l2	**Arsenal**	A	L	0-1		35,463
33	grpr1	**Schalke**	A	L	0-1		62,000
34	grpr1	**Hansa Rostock**	H	W	3-1	Lucio 41; Pizarro 65; Ballack 89 pen	45,000
35	grpr1	**Wolfsburg**	A	W	3-0	Schweinsteiger 29; Hofland 45 og; Frings 55	30,000
36	clqf1	**Chelsea**	A	L	2-4	Schweinsteiger 52; Ballack 90 pen	40,253
37	grpr1	**B M'gladbach**	H	W	2-1	Scholl 66; Ballack 84	60,000
38	clqf2	**Chelsea**	H	W	3-2	Pizarro 65; Guerrero 90; Scholl 90	59,000
39	grpr1	**Hannover 96**	A	W	1-0	Hargreaves 90	49,000
40	grpr1	**Bochum**	H	W	3-1	Pizarro 9; Ballack 27; Makaay 63	60,000
41	grpr1	**Kaiserslautern**	A	W	4-0	Ballack 19; Makaay 35,48,67	40,000
42	grpr1	**Mainz**	A	W	4-2	Makaay 17,83,89; Ballack 42	20,000
43	grpr1	**Nuremburg**	H	W	6-3	Pizarro 8; Ballack 24; Makaay 31,41 pen; Deisler 44,78	63,000
44	grpr1	**Stuttgart**	A	W	3-1	Ballack 27; Salihamidzic 30; Makaay 71	49,000

KEY PLAYERS - GOALSCORERS

Roy Makaay

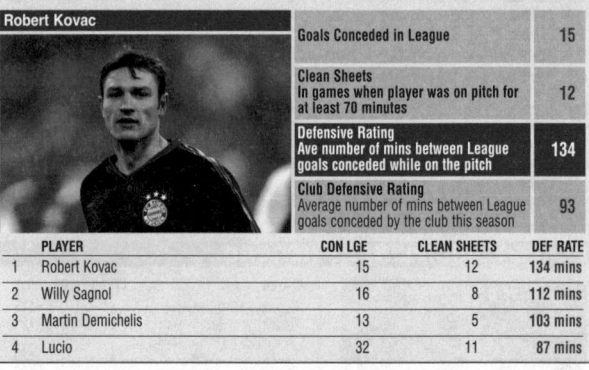

Goals in the League	22
Contribution to Attacking Power Average number of minutes between League team goals while on pitch	39
Player Strike Rate Average number of minutes between League goals scored by player	129
Club Strike Rate Average number of minutes between League goals scored by club	41

	PLAYER	GOALS LGE	POWER	S RATE
1	Roy Makaay	22	39	129 mins
2	Claudio Pizarro	11	36	155 mins
3	Michael Ballack	13	41	184 mins
4	Bastian Schweinsteiger	3	46	548 mins
5	Torsten Frings	3	48	717 mins

KEY PLAYERS - MIDFIELDERS

Bastian Schweinsteiger

Goals in the League	3
Defensive Rating Average number of mins between League goals conceded while on the pitch	118
Contribution to Attacking Power Average number of minutes between League team goals while on pitch	46
Scoring Difference Defensive Rating minus Contribution to Attacking Power	72

	PLAYER	GOALS LGE	DEF RATE	ATT POWER	SCORE DIFF
1	Bastian Schweinsteiger	3	118	46	72 mins
2	Torsten Frings	3	102	48	54 mins
3	Owen Hargreaves	1	96	46	50 mins
4	Michael Ballack	13	83	41	42 mins
5	Hazan Salihamidzic	2	88	46	42 mins

KEY PLAYERS - DEFENDERS

Robert Kovac

Goals Conceded in League	15
Clean Sheets In games when player was on pitch for at least 70 minutes	12
Defensive Rating Ave number of mins between League goals conceded while on the pitch	134
Club Defensive Rating Average number of mins between League goals conceded by the club this season	93

	PLAYER	CON LGE	CLEAN SHEETS	DEF RATE
1	Robert Kovac	15	12	134 mins
2	Willy Sagnol	16	8	112 mins
3	Martin Demichelis	13	5	103 mins
4	Lucio	32	11	87 mins

MONTHLY POINTS TALLY

AUGUST	4	44%
SEPTEMBER	7	78%
OCTOBER	9	60%
NOVEMBER	12	100%
DECEMBER	2	33%
JANUARY	4	67%
FEBRUARY	9	75%
MARCH	6	67%
APRIL	15	100%
MAY	9	100%

LEAGUE GOALS

	PLAYER	MINS	GOALS	AVE
1	Makaay	2836	22	129
2	Ballack	2395	13	184
3	Pizarro	1708	11	155
4	Guerrero	699	6	117
5	Deisler	1043	4	261
6	Scholl	937	3	312
7	Frings	2150	3	717
8	Schweinsteiger	1645	3	548
9	Lucio	2791	3	930
10	Salihamidzic	2210	2	1105
11	Ze Roberto	1437	1	1437
12	Sagnol	1799	1	1799
13	Hargreaves	1640	1	1640
	Other		2	
	TOTAL		75	

KEY GOALKEEPER

Oliver Kahn

Goals Conceded in the League	28
Counting Games League games when player was on pitch for at least 70 minutes	30
Clean Sheets In games when player was on pitch for at least 70 minutes	13
League minutes played Number of minutes played in league matches	2790
Defensive Rating Ave number of mins between League goals conceded while on the pitch	100

DISCIPLINARY RECORDS

	PLAYER	YELLOW	RED	AVE
1	Gorlitz	3	1	121
2	Linke	5	0	169
3	Kuffour	2	0	243
4	Schweinsteiger	6	0	274
5	Demichelis	4	0	334
6	Ballack	7	0	342
7	Frings	6	0	358
8	Hargreaves	4	0	410
9	Ze Roberto	3	0	479
10	Lizarazu	2	0	495
11	Kovac, R	4	0	502
12	Deisler	2	0	521
13	Sagnol	3	0	599
	Other	8	2	
	TOTAL	59	3	

TOP POINT EARNERS

	PLAYER	GAMES	AV PTS
1	Martin Demichelis	12	2.83
2	Bastian Schweinsteiger	13	2.46
3	Willy Sagnol	19	2.42
4	Robert Kovac	22	2.41
5	Claudio Pizarro	16	2.38
6	Lucio	29	2.34
7	Roy Makaay	29	2.24
8	Hazan Salihamidzic	21	2.19
9	Oliver Kahn	30	2.17
10	Michael Ballack	26	2.12
	CLUB AVERAGE:		2.26

TEAM OF THE SEASON

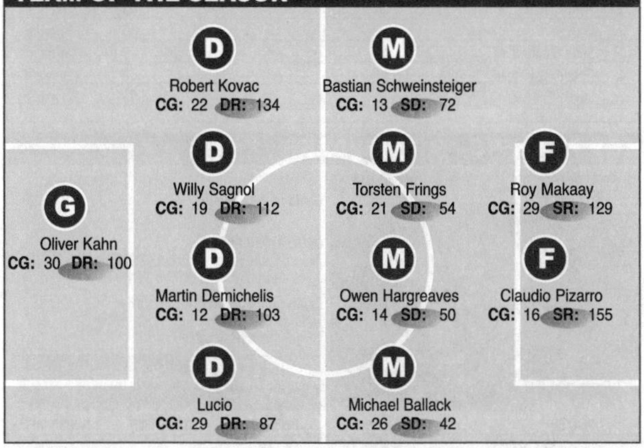
D
Robert Kovac
CG: 22 DR: 134
M
Bastian Schweinsteiger
CG: 13 SD: 72
D
Willy Sagnol
CG: 19 DR: 112
M
Torsten Frings
CG: 21 SD: 54
F
Roy Makaay
CG: 29 SR: 129
G
Oliver Kahn
CG: 30 DR: 100
D
Martin Demichelis
CG: 12 DR: 103
M
Owen Hargreaves
CG: 14 SD: 50
F
Claudio Pizarro
CG: 16 SR: 155
D
Lucio
CG: 29 DR: 87
M
Michael Ballack
CG: 26 SD: 42

LEAGUE APPEARANCES, BOOKINGS AND CAPS

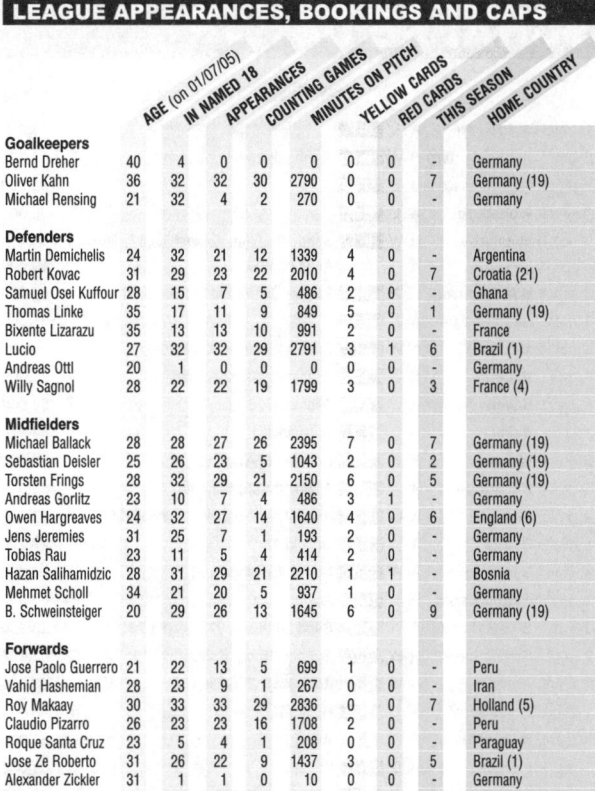

	AGE (on 01/07/05)	IN NAMED 18	APPEARANCES	COUNTING GAMES	MINUTES ON PITCH	YELLOW CARDS	RED CARDS	THIS SEASON	HOME COUNTRY
Goalkeepers									
Bernd Dreher	40	4	0	0	0	0	0	-	Germany
Oliver Kahn	36	32	32	30	2790	0	0	7	Germany (19)
Michael Rensing	21	32	4	2	270	0	0	-	Germany
Defenders									
Martin Demichelis	24	32	21	12	1339	4	0	-	Argentina
Robert Kovac	31	29	23	22	2010	4	0	7	Croatia (21)
Samuel Osei Kuffour	28	15	7	5	486	2	0	-	Ghana
Thomas Linke	35	17	11	9	849	5	0	1	Germany (19)
Bixente Lizarazu	35	13	13	10	991	2	0	-	France
Lucio	27	32	32	29	2791	3	1	6	Brazil (1)
Andreas Ottl	20	1	0	0	0	0	0	-	Germany
Willy Sagnol	28	22	22	19	1799	3	0	3	France (4)
Midfielders									
Michael Ballack	28	28	27	26	2395	7	0	7	Germany (19)
Sebastian Deisler	25	26	23	5	1043	2	0	2	Germany (19)
Torsten Frings	28	32	29	21	2150	6	0	5	Germany (19)
Andreas Gorlitz	23	10	7	4	486	3	1	-	Germany
Owen Hargreaves	24	32	27	14	1640	4	0	6	England (6)
Jens Jeremies	31	25	7	1	193	2	0	-	Germany
Tobias Rau	23	11	5	4	414	2	0	-	Germany
Hazan Salihamidzic	28	31	29	21	2210	1	1	-	Bosnia
Mehmet Scholl	34	21	20	5	937	1	0	-	Germany
B. Schweinsteiger	20	29	26	13	1645	6	0	9	Germany (19)
Forwards									
Jose Paolo Guerrero	21	22	13	5	699	1	0	-	Peru
Vahid Hashemian	28	23	9	1	267	0	0	-	Iran
Roy Makaay	30	33	33	29	2836	0	0	7	Holland (5)
Claudio Pizarro	26	23	23	16	1708	2	0	-	Peru
Roque Santa Cruz	23	5	4	1	208	0	0	-	Paraguay
Jose Ze Roberto	31	26	22	9	1437	3	0	5	Brazil (1)
Alexander Zickler	31	1	1	0	10	0	0	-	Germany

SQUAD APPEARANCES

Match	1	2	3	4	5	6	7	8	9	10	11	12	13	14	15	16	17	18	19	20	21	22	23	24	25	26	27	28	29	30	31	32	33	34	35	36	37	38	39	40	41	42	43	44
Venue	A	H	A	H	A	A	H	H	A	H	A	A	H	A	H	H	A	H	H	H	A	A	H	H	A	H	A	H	H	A	H	A	A	H	A	A	H	H	A	H	A	A	H	A
Competition	L	L	L	L	C	L	L	C	L	L	C	L	L	L	C	L	L	L	C	L	L	C	L	L	L	L	L	L	C	L	L	C	L	L	L	C	L	C	L	L	L	L	L	L
Result	W	D	L	W	W	D	W	W	W	L	L	W	W	L	L	W	W	W	W	W	D	D	D	W	D	W	L	W	W	W	W	L	L	W	W	L	W	W	W	W	W	W	W	W

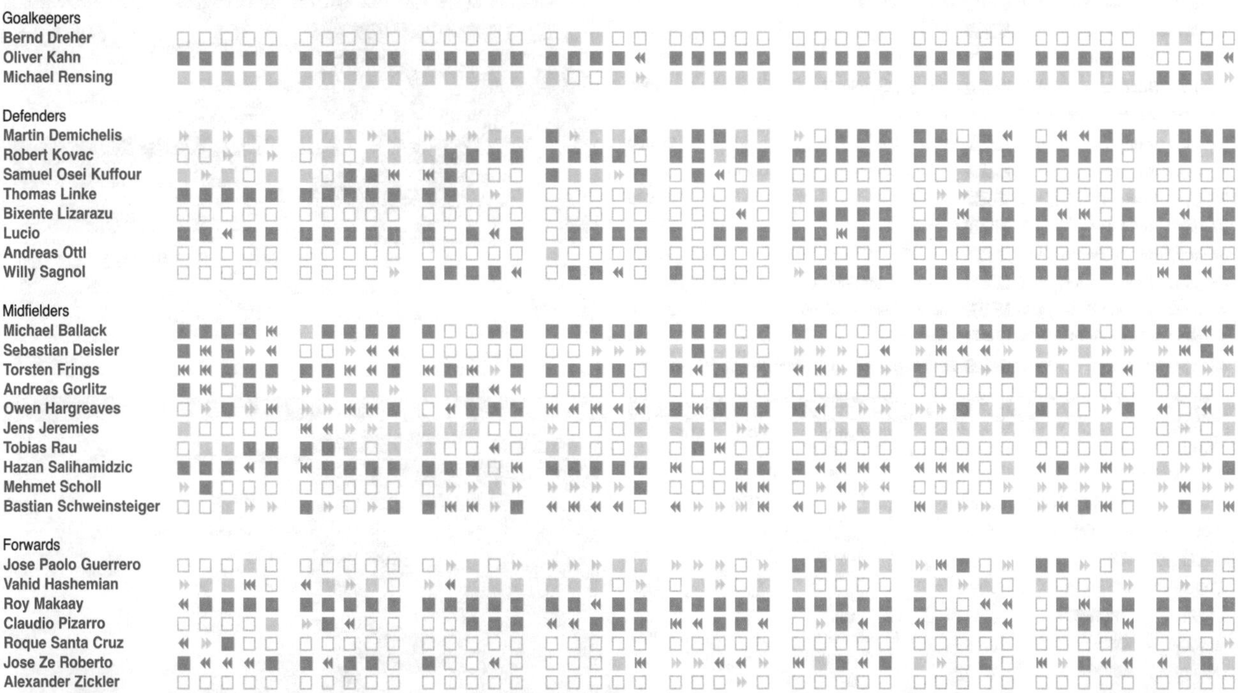
Goalkeepers
Bernd Dreher
Oliver Kahn
Michael Rensing
Defenders
Martin Demichelis
Robert Kovac
Samuel Osei Kuffour
Thomas Linke
Bixente Lizarazu
Lucio
Andreas Ottl
Willy Sagnol
Midfielders
Michael Ballack
Sebastian Deisler
Torsten Frings
Andreas Gorlitz
Owen Hargreaves
Jens Jeremies
Tobias Rau
Hazan Salihamidzic
Mehmet Scholl
Bastian Schweinsteiger
Forwards
Jose Paolo Guerrero
Vahid Hashemian
Roy Makaay
Claudio Pizarro
Roque Santa Cruz
Jose Ze Roberto
Alexander Zickler

KEY: On all match | On bench | Subbed or sent off (Counting game) | Subbed or sent off (playing less than 70 minutes) | Subbed on from bench (Counting Game) | Subbed on (playing less than 70 minutes) | Subbed on and then subbed or sent off (Counting Game) | Subbed on and then subbed or sent off (playing less than 70 minutes) | Not in 16

SCHALKE 04

Final Position: **2nd**

KEY: Won / Drawn / Lost

							Attendance
1	grpr1	**W Bremen**	A	L	0-1		43,000
2	grpr1	**Kaiserslautern**	H	W	2-1	Asamoah 25,65	62,000
3	grpr1	**Hansa Rostock**	H	L	0-2		62,000
4	grpr1	**Wolfsburg**	A	L	0-3		25,000
5	uc1rl1	**Metalurgs**	H	W	5-1	Sand 20,52,60; Kobiashvili 67; Asamoah 90	50,000
6	grpr1	**B M'gladbach**	H	W	3-2	Pander 35; Varela 59; Sand 66	61,000
7	grpr1	**Hannover 96**	A	L	0-1		35,000
8	uc1rl2	**Metalurgs**	A	W	4-0	Sand 44; Hanke 63,78,90	2,000
9	grpr1	**Bochum**	H	W	3-2	Asamoah 10; Kobiashvili 14; Lincoln 44	61,000
10	grpr1	**Bayern Munich**	A	W	1-0	Asamoah 76	63,000
11	cl ga	**Basel**	H	D	1-1	Kobiashvili 8	52,870
12	grpr1	**Mainz**	H	W	2-1	Lincoln 25; Ailton 69	62,000
13	grpr1	**Nuremburg**	A	W	2-0	Ailton 10 pen; Sand 45	32,000
14	grpr1	**Stuttgart**	H	W	3-2	Ailton 1; Kobiashvili 2; Lincoln 25	62,000
15	cl ga	**Hearts**	A	W	1-0	Lincoln 73	27,272
16	grpr1	**Hamburg**	A	W	2-1	Hanke 79; Lincoln 81	53,000
17	grpr1	**Hertha Berlin**	H	L	1-3	Asamoah 50	62,000
18	grpr1	**B Leverkusen**	A	W	3-0	Sand 26; Ailton 37; Lincoln 73	23,000
19	cl ga	**Ferencvaros**	H	W	2-0	Gyepes 15 og; Kobiashvili 40	21,127
20	grpr1	**Arminia B**	H	W	2-1	Kobiashvili 29; Ailton 39	62,000
21	cl ga	**Feyenoord**	A	L	1-2	Hanke 7	48,000
22	grpr1	**B Dortmund**	A	W	1-0	Ailton 17	83,000
23	grpr1	**Freiburg**	H	D	1-1	Krstajic 24	61,000
24	grpr1	**W Bremen**	H	W	2-1	Asamoah 47; Ailton 67	62,000
25	grpr1	**Kaiserslautern**	A	L	0-2		38,000
26	grpr1	**Hansa Rostock**	A	D	2-2	Sand 25; Ailton 90	24,000
27	grpr1	**Wolfsburg**	H	W	3-0	Asamoah 13; Sand 35; Hanke 85	62,000
28	uc3rl1	**S Donetsk**	A	D	1-1	Ailton 7	28,000
29	grpr1	**B M'gladbach**	A	W	3-1	Ailton 44,65,79	53,000
30	uc3rl2	**SDonetsk**	H	L	0-1		51,000
31	grpr1	**Hannover 96**	H	W	1-0	Hanke 66	60,000
32	grpr1	**Bochum**	A	W	2-0	Ailton 30; Lincoln 77	33,000
33	grpr1	**Bayern Munich**	H	W	1-0	Lincoln 69	62,000
34	grpr1	**Mainz**	A	L	1-2	Lincoln 70 pen	20,000
35	grpr1	**Nuremburg**	H	W	4-1	Hanke 24,36; Ailton 40; Lincoln 74	62,000
36	grpr1	**Stuttgart**	A	L	0-3		49,000
37	grpr1	**Hamburg**	H	L	1-2	Asamoah 3	61,000
38	grpr1	**Hertha Berlin**	A	L	1-4	Sand 28	75,000
39	grpr1	**B Leverkusen**	H	D	3-3	Lincoln 30,38; Sand 41	62,000
40	grpr1	**Arminia B**	A	W	2-0	Lincoln 9 pen; Ailton 90	27,000
41	grpr1	**B Dortmund**	H	L	1-2	Waldoch 19	62,000
42	grpr1	**Freiburg**	A	W	3-2	Sand 6; Bordon 55; Lincoln 89	24,000

MONTHLY POINTS TALLY

AUGUST	3	33%
SEPTEMBER	3	33%
OCTOBER	15	100%
NOVEMBER	9	75%
DECEMBER	4	67%
JANUARY	3	50%
FEBRUARY	10	83%
MARCH	6	67%
APRIL	4	27%
MAY	6	67%

LEAGUE GOALS

	PLAYER	MINS	GOALS	AVE
1	Ailton	2229	14	159
2	Lincoln	2486	13	191
3	Asamoah	2381	8	298
4	Sand	2354	8	294
5	Hanke	815	5	163
6	Kobiashvili	2854	3	951
7	Bordon	2362	1	2362
8	Pander	2069	1	2069
9	Varela	518	1	518
10	Krstajic	2520	1	2520
11	Waldoch	1208	1	1208
	Other		0	
	TOTAL		**56**	

KEY PLAYERS - GOALSCORERS

Ailton

Goals in the League	14
Contribution to Attacking Power Average number of minutes between League team goals while on pitch	55
Player Strike Rate Average number of minutes between League goals scored by player	159
Club Strike Rate Average number of minutes between League goals scored by club	55

	PLAYER	GOALS LGE	POWER	S RATE
1	Ailton	14	55	159 mins
2	Lincoln	13	50	191 mins
3	Ebbe Sand	8	50	294 mins
4	Gerald Asamoah	8	50	298 mins
5	Levan Kobiashvili	3	53	951 mins

KEY PLAYERS - MIDFIELDERS

Levan Kobiashvili

Goals in the League	3
Defensive Rating Average number of mins between League goals conceded while on the pitch	68
Contribution to Attacking Power Average number of minutes between League team goals while on pitch	53
Scoring Difference Defensive Rating minus Contribution to Attacking Power	15

	PLAYER	GOALS LGE	DEF RATE	ATT POWER	SCORE DIFF
1	Levan Kobiashvili	3	68	53	15 mins
2	Lincoln	13	64	50	14 mins
3	Christian Poulsen	0	67	58	9 mins
4	Sven Vermant	0	62	57	5 mins
5	Niels Oude Kamphuis	0	57	53	4 mins

KEY PLAYERS - DEFENDERS

Christian Pander

Goals Conceded in League	22
Clean Sheets In games when player was on pitch for at least 70 minutes	8
Defensive Rating Ave number of mins between League goals conceded while on the pitch	94
Club Defensive Rating Average number of mins between League goals conceded by the club this season	67

	PLAYER	CON LGE	CLEAN SHEETS	DEF RATE
1	Christian Pander	22	8	94 mins
2	Bordon	32	7	74 mins
3	Mladen Krstajic	37	7	68 mins
4	Tomasz Waldoch	22	3	55 mins

KEY GOALKEEPER

Frank Rost

Goals Conceded in the League	41
Counting Games League games when player was on pitch for at least 70 minutes	31
Clean Sheets In games when player was on pitch for at least 70 minutes	8
League minutes played Number of minutes played in league matches	2790
Defensive Rating Ave number of mins between League goals conceded while on the pitch	68

DISCIPLINARY RECORDS

	PLAYER	YELLOW	RED	AVE
1	Varela	4	0	129
2	Poulsen	10	1	207
3	Lincoln	7	2	276
4	Kobiashvili	9	0	317
5	Rodriguez	2	0	325
6	Altintop	5	0	329
7	Krstajic	7	0	360
8	Bordon	6	0	393
9	Hanke	2	0	407
10	Asamoah	5	0	476
11	Oude Kamphuis	4	0	480
12	Vermant	3	0	492
13	Sand	3	0	784
	Other	5	1	
	TOTAL	72	4	

TOP POINT EARNERS

	PLAYER	GAMES	AV PTS
1	Christian Pander	22	2.23
2	Lincoln	27	2.11
3	Gerald Asamoah	24	2.08
4	Bordon	25	2.00
5	Ebbe Sand	26	1.96
6	Christian Poulsen	21	1.95
7	Levan Kobiashvili	32	1.94
8	Mladen Krstajic	28	1.93
9	Frank Rost	31	1.90
10	Ailton	20	1.90
	CLUB AVERAGE:		1.85

LEAGUE APPEARANCES, BOOKINGS AND CAPS

	AGE (on 01/07/05)	IN NAMED 18	APPEARANCES	COUNTING GAMES	MINUTES ON PITCH	YELLOW CARDS	RED CARDS	THIS SEASON	HOME COUNTRY
Goalkeepers									
Christofer Heimeroth	23	32	3	3	270	0	0	-	Germany
Frank Rost	32	31	31	31	2790	1	0	-	Germany
Volkan Unlu	21	4	0	0	0	0	0	-	Turkey
Defenders									
Bordon	29	27	27	25	2362	6	0	-	Brazil
Tim Hoogland	20	8	2	1	106	0	0	-	Germany
Thomas Klasener	28	12	3	2	209	0	0	-	Germany
Mladen Krstajic	31	29	28	28	2520	7	0	6	Serbia & Mont (46)
Fabian Lamotte	22	18	3	2	177	1	0	-	Germany
Christian Pander	21	27	25	22	2069	2	0	-	Germany
Dario Rodriguez	30	19	15	6	651	2	0	5	Uruguay (16)
Tomasz Waldoch	34	34	14	13	1208	1	0	-	Poland
Midfielders									
Hamit Altintop	22	32	30	14	1647	5	0	-	Turkey
Alexander Baumjohann	18	2	0	0	0	0	0	-	Germany
Jorg Bohme	31	8	2	0	57	0	0	-	Germany
Niko Bungert	18	1	0	0	0	0	0	-	Germany
Levan Kobiashvili	27	32	32	32	2854	9	0	-	Georgia
Lincoln	26	31	31	27	2486	7	2	-	Brazil
Niels Oude Kamphuis	27	26	25	20	1923	4	0	-	Holland
Christian Poulsen	25	32	32	21	2281	10	1	8	Denmark (19)
Gustavo Varela	27	12	11	4	518	4	0	2	Uruguay (16)
Sven Vermant	32	31	22	14	1476	3	0	2	Belgium (42)
Forwards									
Ailton	31	30	29	20	2229	1	1	-	Brazil
Gerald Asamoah	26	32	31	24	2381	5	0	8	Germany (19)
Ahmet Cebe	22	4	0	0	0	0	0	-	Germany
Michael Delura	20	30	8	0	129	0	0	-	Germany
Michael Hanke	21	31	25	5	815	2	0	-	Germany
Kai Hesse	20	3	0	0	0	0	0	-	Germany
Ebbe Sand	32	28	28	26	2354	3	0	-	Denmark

TEAM OF THE SEASON

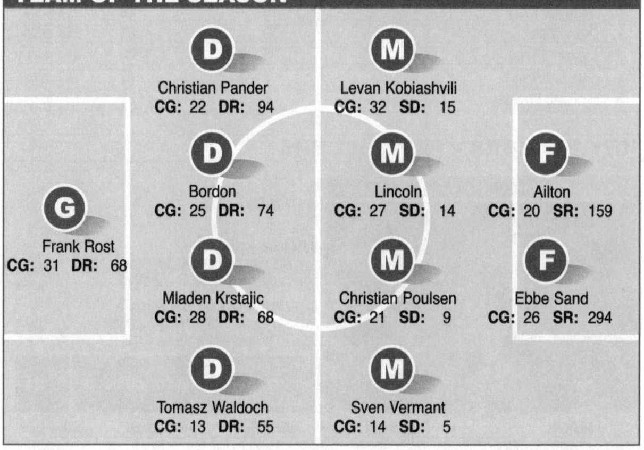
D
Christian Pander
CG: 22 DR: 94
M
Levan Kobiashvili
CG: 32 SD: 15
D
Bordon
CG: 25 DR: 74
M
Lincoln
CG: 27 SD: 14
F
Ailton
CG: 20 SR: 159
G
Frank Rost
CG: 31 DR: 68
D
Mladen Krstajic
CG: 28 DR: 68
M
Christian Poulsen
CG: 21 SD: 9
F
Ebbe Sand
CG: 26 SR: 294
D
Tomasz Waldoch
CG: 13 DR: 55
M
Sven Vermant
CG: 14 SD: 5

SQUAD APPEARANCES

Match	1	2	3	4	5	6	7	8	9	10	11	12	13	14	15	16	17	18	19	20	21	22	23	24	25	26	27	28	29	30	31	32	33	34	35	36	37	38	39	40	41	42
Venue	A	H	H	A	H	H	A	A	H	A	H	H	A	H	A	A	H	A	H	H	A	A	H	H	A	A	H	A	A	H	H	A	H	A	H	A	H	A	H	A	H	A
Competition	L	L	L	L	E	L	L	E	L	L	E	L	L	L	E	L	L	L	E	L	E	L	L	L	L	L	L	E	L	E	L	L	L	L	L	L	L	L	L	L	L	L
Result	L	W	L	L	W	W	L	W	W	W	D	W	W	W	W	W	L	W	W	W	L	W	D	W	L	D	W	D	W	L	W	W	W	L	W	L	L	L	D	W	L	W

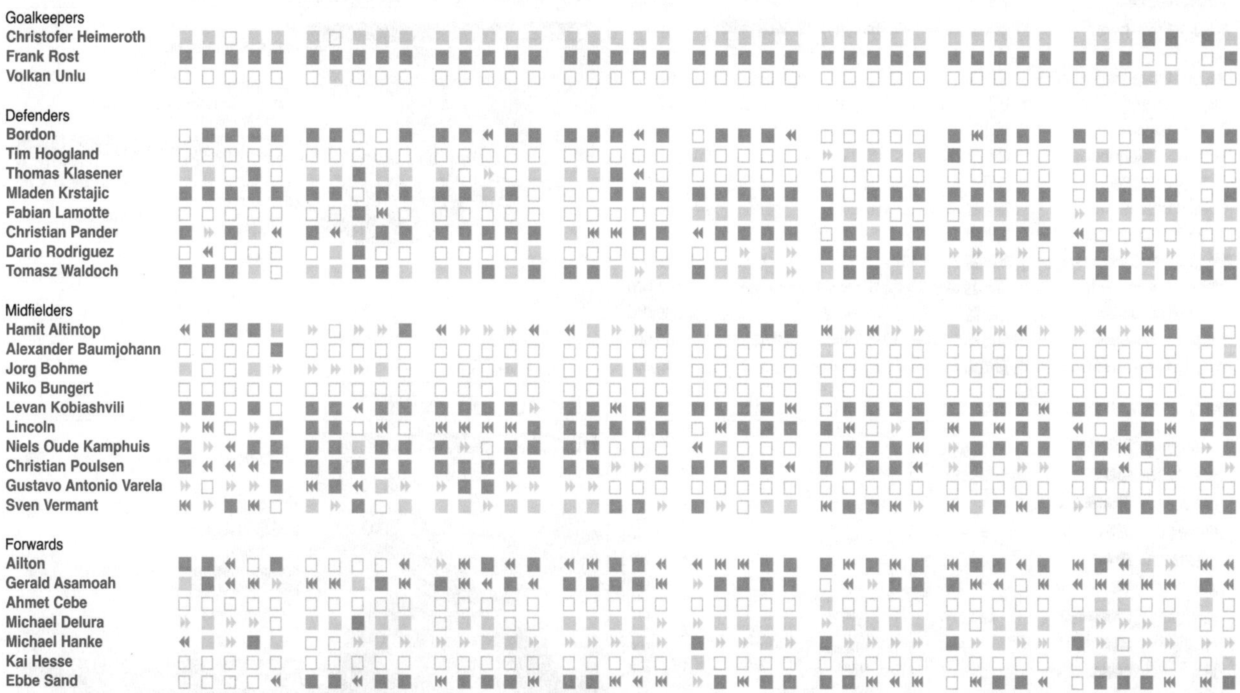
Goalkeepers
Christofer Heimeroth
Frank Rost
Volkan Unlu
Defenders
Bordon
Tim Hoogland
Thomas Klasener
Mladen Krstajic
Fabian Lamotte
Christian Pander
Dario Rodriguez
Tomasz Waldoch
Midfielders
Hamit Altintop
Alexander Baumjohann
Jorg Bohme
Niko Bungert
Levan Kobiashvili
Lincoln
Niels Oude Kamphuis
Christian Poulsen
Gustavo Antonio Varela
Sven Vermant
Forwards
Ailton
Gerald Asamoah
Ahmet Cebe
Michael Delura
Michael Hanke
Kai Hesse
Ebbe Sand

KEY: On all match | On bench | Subbed or sent off (Counting game) | Subbed or sent off (playing less than 70 minutes) | Subbed on from bench (Counting Game) | Subbed on (playing less than 70 minutes) | Subbed on and then subbed or sent off (Counting Game) | Subbed on and then subbed or sent off (playing less than 70 minutes) | Not in 16

WERDER BREMEN

Final Position: **3rd**

KEY: ☐Won ☐Drawn ☐Lost

							Attendance
1	grpr1	Schalke	H	W	1-0	Valdez 84	43,000
2	grpr1	Hansa Rostock	A	W	4-0	Klasnic 54,64; Micoud 58; Pasanen 89	25,000
3	grpr1	Wolfsburg	H	L	1-2	Klose 71	40,000
4	grpr1	B M'gladbach	A	L	1-3	Valdez 69	52,000
5	cl gg	Inter Milan	A	L	0-2		45,000
6	grpr1	Hannover 96	H	W	3-0	Ismael 20 pen; Micoud 78; Klose 88	43,000
7	grpr1	Bochum	A	W	4-1	Borowski 54; Klose 70,88,89	25,000
8	cl gg	Valencia	H	W	2-1	Klose 60; Charisteas 84	36,000
9	grpr1	Bayern Munich	H	L	1-2	Klose 81	43,000
10	grpr1	Mainz	A	L	1-2	Charisteas 56	20,000
11	cl gg	Anderlecht	A	W	2-1	Klasnic 36,59	22,000
12	grpr1	Nuremburg	H	W	4-1	Klasnic 14; Micoud 18; Schulz 76; Ernst 89	43,000
13	grpr1	Stuttgart	A	W	2-1	Klose 78; Valdez 80	41,000
14	grpr1	Hamburg	H	D	1-1	Schulz 74	43,000
15	cl gg	Anderlecht	H	W	5-1	Klasnic 2,16,79; Klose 33; Jensen 90	37,000
16	grpr1	Hertha Berlin	A	D	1-1	Charisteas 80	40,000
17	grpr1	B Leverkusen	H	D	2-2	Klose 19; Valdez 72	38,000
18	grpr1	Arminia B	A	L	1-2	Klasnic 83	22,000
19	cl gg	Inter Milan	H	D	1-1	Ismael 49 pen	37,000
20	grpr1	B Dortmund	H	W	2-0	Micoud 31; Ismael 57	37,000
21	grpr1	Freiburg	A	W	6-0	Klose 20,24; Charisteas 29,58,88; Micoud 64	24,000
22	cl gg	Valencia	A	W	2-0	Valdez 83,90	40,000
23	grpr1	Kaiserslautern	H	D	1-1	Borowski 59	39,000
24	grpr1	Schalke	A	L	1-2	Ismael 51 pen	62,000
25	grpr1	Hansa Rostock	H	W	3-2	Klasnic 5,62; Klose 31	38,000
26	grpr1	Wolfsburg	A	W	3-2	Klose 51; Magnin 59; Valdez 90	24,000
27	grpr1	B M'gladbach	H	W	2-0	Hunt 28; Zidan 88	40,000
28	grpr1	Hannover 96	A	W	4-1	Magnin 6; Borowski 8; Ernst 62; Zidan 85,85	45,000
29	cl r2l1	Lyon	H	L	0-3		37,000
30	grpr1	Bochum	H	W	4-0	Ismael 45; Baumann 49; Valdez 53; Micoud 73	32,000
31	grpr1	Bayern Munich	A	L	0-1		53,000
32	cl r2l2	Lyon	A	L	2-7	Micoud 32; Ismael 57 pen	37,000
33	grpr1	Mainz	H	D	0-0		35,000
34	grpr1	Nuremburg	A	W	2-1	Klasnic 22,45	22,000
35	grpr1	Stuttgart	H	L	1-2	Klasnic 52	42,000
36	grpr1	Hamburg	A	W	2-1	Klose 9; Klasnic 70	56,000
37	grpr1	Hertha Berlin	H	L	0-1		43,000
38	grpr1	B Leverkusen	A	L	1-2	Klose 38	23,000
39	grpr1	Arminia B	H	W	3-0	Magnin 43; Borowski 53; Klose 78	40,000
40	grpr1	B Dortmund	A	L	0-1		80,000
41	grpr1	Freiburg	H	W	4-1	Micoud 48,90; Borowski 49,53	35,000
42	grpr1	Kaiserslautern	A	W	2-1	Borowski 13; Valdez 42	40,000

KEY PLAYERS - GOALSCORERS

Miroslav Klose

Goals in the League	15
Contribution to Attacking Power Average number of minutes between League team goals while on pitch	46
Player Strike Rate Average number of minutes between League goals scored by player	161
Club Strike Rate Average number of minutes between League goals scored by club	44

	PLAYER	GOALS LGE	POWER	S RATE
1	Miroslav Klose	15	46	161 mins
2	Ivan Klasnic	10	55	206 mins
3	Johan Micoud	8	44	361 mins
4	Tim Borowski	7	45	367 mins
5	Ludovic Magnin	3	39	528 mins

KEY PLAYERS - MIDFIELDERS

Ludovic Magnin

Goals in the League	3
Defensive Rating Average number of mins between League goals conceded while on the pitch	83
Contribution to Attacking Power Average number of minutes between League team goals while on pitch	39
Scoring Difference Defensive Rating minus Contribution to Attacking Power	44

	PLAYER	GOALS LGE	DEF RATE	ATT POWER	SCORE DIFF
1	Ludovic Magnin	3	83	39	44 mins
2	Paul Stalteri	0	84	44	40 mins
3	Fabian Ernst	2	81	46	35 mins
4	Johan Micoud	8	78	44	34 mins
5	Christian Schulz	2	68	57	11 mins

KEY PLAYERS - DEFENDERS

Petri Pasanen

Goals Conceded in League	19
Clean Sheets In games when player was on pitch for at least 70 minutes	7
Defensive Rating Ave number of mins between League goals conceded while on the pitch	100
Club Defensive Rating Average number of mins between League goals conceded by the club this season	81

	PLAYER	CON LGE	CLEAN SHEETS	DEF RATE
1	Petri Pasanen	19	7	100 mins
2	Frank Baumann	23	7	83 mins
3	Valerien Ismael	34	9	83 mins
4	Tim Borowski	33	8	78 mins
5	Frank Fahrenhorst	17	3	73 mins

MONTHLY POINTS TALLY

AUGUST	6	67%
SEPTEMBER	6	67%
OCTOBER	7	47%
NOVEMBER	5	42%
DECEMBER	4	67%
JANUARY	3	50%
FEBRUARY	12	100%
MARCH	4	44%
APRIL	6	40%
MAY	6	67%

LEAGUE GOALS

	PLAYER	MINS	GOALS	AVE
1	Klose	2410	15	161
2	Klasnic	2064	10	206
3	Micoud	2891	8	361
4	Valdez	1224	7	175
5	Borowski	2572	7	367
6	Charisteas	403	5	81
7	Ismael	2806	4	702
8	Zidan	211	3	70
9	Magnin	1585	3	528
10	Schulz	1356	2	678
11	Ernst	2900	2	1450
12	Pasanen	1908	1	1908
13	Hunt	328	1	328
	Other		1	
	TOTAL		69	

KEY GOALKEEPER

Andreas Reinke

Goals Conceded in the League	38
Counting Games League games when player was on pitch for at least 70 minutes	34
Clean Sheets In games when player was on pitch for at least 70 minutes	9
League minutes played Number of minutes played in league matches	3060
Defensive Rating Ave number of mins between League goals conceded while on the pitch	81

DISCIPLINARY RECORDS

	PLAYER	YELLOW	RED	AVE
1	Valdez	5	1	204
2	Umit Davala	2	0	225
3	Magnin	5	1	264
4	Jensen	4	0	339
5	Ismael	7	1	350
6	Ernst	6	0	483
7	Fahrenhorst	2	0	617
8	Stalteri	3	1	632
9	Baumann	3	0	637
10	Micoud	4	0	722
11	Klose	3	0	803
12	Borowski	3	0	857
13	Pasanen	2	0	954
	Other	4	0	
	TOTAL	53	4	

TOP POINT EARNERS

	PLAYER	GAMES	AV PTS
1	Ludovic Magnin	14	2.21
2	Frank Baumann	20	2.00
3	Petri Pasanen	20	2.00
4	Tim Borowski	26	1.85
5	Paul Stalteri	26	1.77
6	Frank Fahrenhorst	12	1.75
7	Andreas Reinke	34	1.74
8	Fabian Ernst	31	1.71
9	Ivan Klasnic	22	1.68
10	Johan Micoud	31	1.68
	CLUB AVERAGE:		1.74

LEAGUE APPEARANCES, BOOKINGS AND CAPS

	AGE (on 01/07/05)	IN NAMED 18	APPEARANCES	COUNTING GAMES	MINUTES ON PITCH	YELLOW CARDS	RED CARDS	THIS SEASON	HOME COUNTRY
Goalkeepers									
Pascal Borel	25	23	0	0	0	0	0	-	Germany
Michael Jurgen	31	1	0	0	0	0	0	-	Germany
Andreas Reinke	44	34	34	34	3060	1	0	-	Germany
Alexander Walke	22	10	0	0	0	0	0	-	Germany
Defenders									
Francis Banecki	19	12	2	1	72	0	0	-	Germany
Frank Baumann	29	22	22	20	1913	3	0	4	Germany (19)
Tim Borowski	25	31	31	26	2572	3	0	6	Germany (19)
Frank Fahrenhorst	27	26	16	12	1235	2	0	3	Germany (19)
Valerien Ismael	29	32	32	31	2806	7	1	-	France
Florian Mohr	20	4	0	0	0	0	0	-	Germany
Petri Pasanen	24	26	23	20	1908	2	0	-	Finland
Robert Paul	20	2	0	0	0	0	0	-	Germany
Midfielders									
Fabian Ernst	26	33	33	31	2900	6	0	7	Germany (19)
Daniel Jensen	26	23	21	11	1358	4	0	4	Denmark (19)
Pekka Lagerblom	23	12	4	0	156	0	0	-	Finland
Krisztian Lisztes	29	4	2	0	59	0	0	-	Hungary
Ludovic Magnin	26	29	25	14	1585	5	1	7	Switzerland (45)
Johan Micoud	31	33	33	31	2891	4	0	-	France
Gustavo Nery	27	5	3	1	133	1	0	4	Brazil (1)
Christian Schulz	22	33	22	12	1356	1	0	4	Germany (19)
Paul Stalteri	27	33	32	26	2531	3	1	-	Canada
Umit Davala	31	21	10	3	451	2	0	-	Turkey
Forwards									
Angelos Charisteas	25	12	11	2	403	2	0	-	Greece
Aaron Hunt	18	21	10	2	328	0	0	-	Germany
Ivan Klasnic	25	29	28	22	2064	2	0	8	Croatia (21)
Miroslav Klose	27	32	32	24	2410	3	0	7	Germany (19)
Marco Stier	21	2	0	0	0	0	0	-	Germany
Nelson Haedo Valdez	21	30	27	7	1224	5	1	-	Paraguay
Mohamed Zidan	23	14	10	0	211	0	0	-	Egypt

TEAM OF THE SEASON

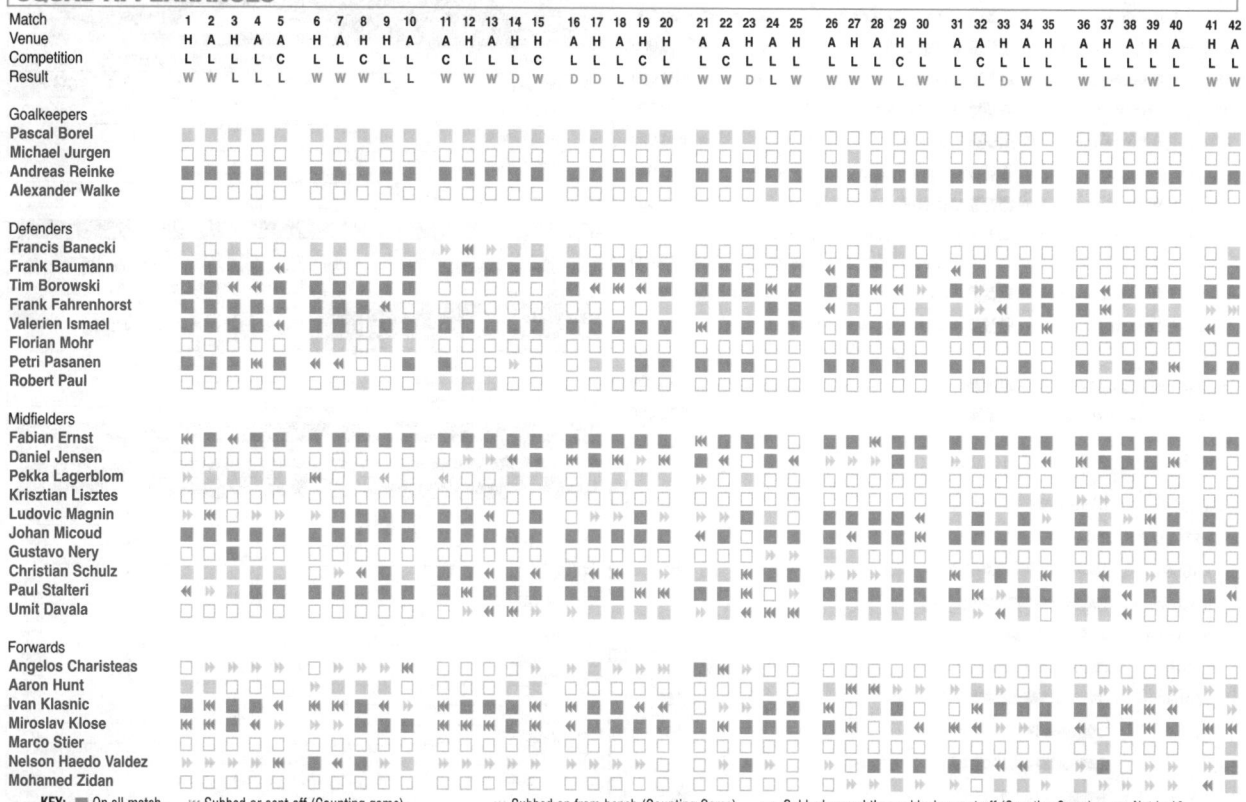

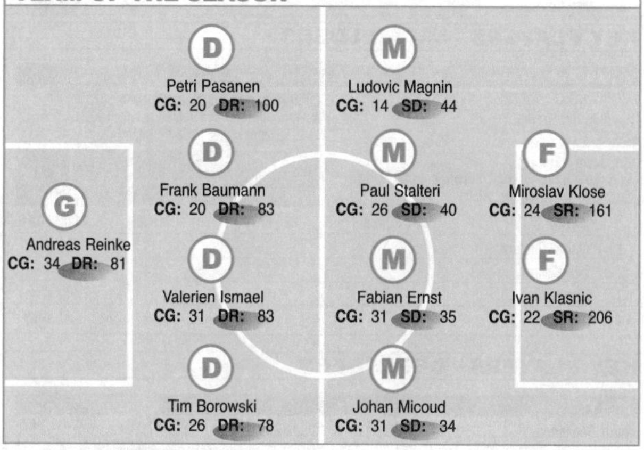
D
Petri Pasanen
CG: 20 DR: 100
M
Ludovic Magnin
CG: 14 SD: 44
D
Frank Baumann
CG: 20 DR: 83
M
Paul Stalteri
CG: 26 SD: 40
F
Miroslav Klose
CG: 24 SR: 161
G
Andreas Reinke
CG: 34 DR: 81
D
Valerien Ismael
CG: 31 DR: 83
M
Fabian Ernst
CG: 31 SD: 35
F
Ivan Klasnic
CG: 22 SR: 206
D
Tim Borowski
CG: 26 DR: 78
M
Johan Micoud
CG: 31 SD: 34

SQUAD APPEARANCES

Match	1	2	3	4	5	6	7	8	9	10	11	12	13	14	15	16	17	18	19	20	21	22	23	24	25	26	27	28	29	30	31	32	33	34	35	36	37	38	39	40	41	42
Venue	H	A	H	A	A	H	A	H	H	A	A	H	A	H	H	A	H	A	H	H	A	A	H	A	H	A	H	A	H	H	A	A	H	A	H	A	H	A	H	A	H	A
Competition	L	L	L	L	C	L	L	C	L	L	C	L	L	L	C	L	L	L	C	L	L	C	L	L	L	L	L	L	C	L	L	C	L	L	L	L	L	L	L	L	L	L
Result	W	W	L	L	L	W	W	W	L	L	W	W	W	D	W	D	D	L	D	W	W	W	D	L	W	W	W	W	L	W	L	L	D	W	L	W	L	L	W	L	W	W

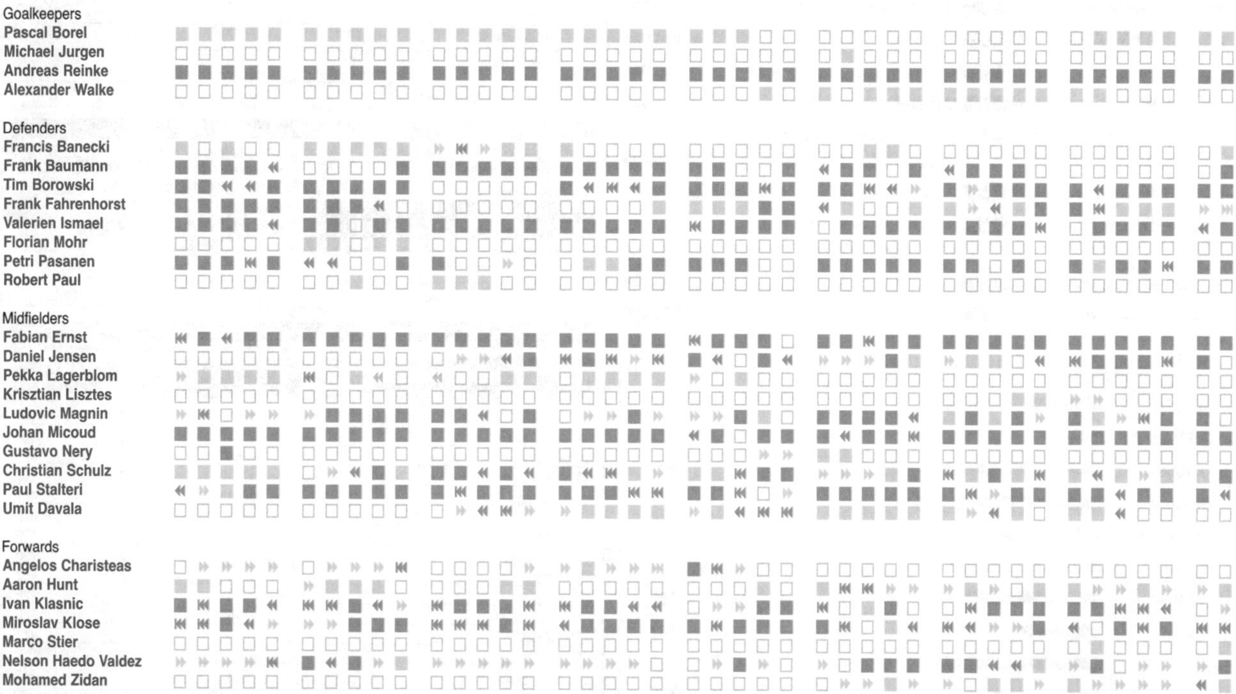
Goalkeepers
Pascal Borel
Michael Jurgen
Andreas Reinke
Alexander Walke
Defenders
Francis Banecki
Frank Baumann
Tim Borowski
Frank Fahrenhorst
Valerien Ismael
Florian Mohr
Petri Pasanen
Robert Paul
Midfielders
Fabian Ernst
Daniel Jensen
Pekka Lagerblom
Krisztian Lisztes
Ludovic Magnin
Johan Micoud
Gustavo Nery
Christian Schulz
Paul Stalteri
Umit Davala
Forwards
Angelos Charisteas
Aaron Hunt
Ivan Klasnic
Miroslav Klose
Marco Stier
Nelson Haedo Valdez
Mohamed Zidan

KEY: On all match | On bench | Subbed or sent off (Counting game) | Subbed or sent off (playing less than 70 minutes) | Subbed on from bench (Counting Game) | Subbed on (playing less than 70 minutes) | Subbed on and then subbed or sent off (Counting Game) | Subbed on and then subbed or sent off (playing less than 70 minutes) | Not in 16

HERTHA BERLIN

Final Position: **4th**

KEY: Won Drawn Lost

							Attendance
1	grpr1	**Bochum**	H	D	2-2	Gilberto 6; Marcelinho 44	40,000
2	grpr1	**Bayern Munich**	A	D	1-1	Marcelinho 15	50,000
3	grpr1	**Mainz**	H	D	1-1	Bobic 68	28,000
4	grpr1	**Nuremburg**	A	D	0-0		31,000
5	grpr1	**Stuttgart**	H	D	0-0		45,000
6	grpr1	**Hamburg**	A	L	1-2	Muller 12	43,000
7	grpr1	**Kaiserslautern**	A	W	2-0	Kovac 18; Muller 46	30,000
8	grpr1	**B Leverkusen**	H	W	3-1	Gilberto 39; Marx 52; Marcelinho 78	47,000
9	grpr1	**Arminia B**	A	L	0-1		22,000
10	grpr1	**B Dortmund**	H	L	0-1		40,000
11	grpr1	**Freiburg**	A	W	3-1	Rafael 36; Gilberto 50; Friedrich 63	23,000
12	grpr1	**W Bremen**	H	D	1-1	Madlung 90	40,000
13	grpr1	**Schalke**	A	W	3-1	Marcelinho 42; Rafael 71; Kovac 83	62,000
14	grpr1	**Hansa Rostock**	H	D	1-1	Marcelinho 90	40,000
15	grpr1	**Wolfsburg**	A	W	3-2	Marcelinho 16,47,74	25,000
16	grpr1	**B M'gladbach**	H	W	6-0	Reina 38; Rafael 54; Madlung 63; Basturk 71,78; Marcelinho 81 pen	40,000
17	grpr1	**Hannover 96**	A	W	1-0	Rafael 54	42,000
18	grpr1	**Bochum**	A	D	2-2	Rafael 3; Gilberto 18	23,000
19	grpr1	**Bayern Munich**	H	D	0-0		74,000
20	grpr1	**Mainz**	A	W	3-0	Basturk 26,76; Neuendorf 69	20,000
21	grpr1	**Nuremburg**	H	W	2-1	Kovac 30; Wichinarek 90	38,000
22	grpr1	**Stuttgart**	A	L	0-1		29,000
23	grpr1	**Hamburg**	H	W	4-1	Reina 4; Gilberto 16,81; Marcelinho 31	30,000
24	grpr1	**Kaiserslautern**	H	D	1-1	Madlung 85	35,000
25	grpr1	**B Leverkusen**	A	D	3-3	Marcelinho 24,29; Neuendorf 62	23,000
26	grpr1	**Arminia B**	H	W	3-0	Marx 29,56; Basturk 90	33,000
27	grpr1	**B Dortmund**	A	L	1-2	Friedrich 62	74,000
28	grpr1	**Freiburg**	H	W	3-1	Marcelinho 6,21 pen; Kovac 89	30,000
29	grpr1	**W Bremen**	A	W	1-0	Marcelinho 32	43,000
30	grpr1	**Schalke**	H	W	4-1	Basturk 14; Marcelinho 35 pen,57; Rafael 51	75,000
31	grpr1	**Hansa Rostock**	A	L	1-2	Basturk 74	25,000
32	grpr1	**Wolfsburg**	H	W	3-1	Friedrich 63; Marcelinho 81 pen; Madlung 87	58,000
33	grpr1	**B M'gladbach**	A	D	0-0		53,000
34	grpr1	**Hannover 96**	H	D	0-0		75,000

MONTHLY POINTS TALLY

AUGUST	3	33%
SEPTEMBER	2	22%
OCTOBER	9	60%
NOVEMBER	8	67%
DECEMBER	6	100%
JANUARY	2	33%
FEBRUARY	9	75%
MARCH	5	56%
APRIL	9	60%
MAY	5	56%

KEY PLAYERS - GOALSCORERS

Marcelinho

Goals in the League	18	Player Strike Rate Average number of minutes between League goals scored by player	157
Contribution to Attacking Power Average number of minutes between League team goals while on pitch	52	Club Strike Rate Average number of minutes between League goals scored by club	52

	PLAYER	LGE GOALS	POWER	STRIKE RATE
1	Marcelinho	18	52	157 mins
2	Nando Rafael	6	63	287 mins
3	Yildiray Basturk	7	49	295 mins
4	Gilberto	6	54	481 mins
5	Nico Kovac	4	54	638 mins

KEY PLAYERS - MIDFIELDERS

Yildiray Basturk

Goals in the League	7	Contribution to Attacking Power Average number of minutes between League team goals while on pitch	49
Defensive Rating Average number of mins between goals conceded while on the pitch	115	Scoring Difference Defensive Rating minus Contribution to Attacking Power	66

	PLAYER	LGE GOALS	DEF RATE	POWER	SCORE DIFF
1	Yildiray Basturk	7	115	49	66 mins
2	Nico Kovac	4	102	54	48 mins
3	Gilberto	6	100	54	46 mins
4	Thorben Marx	3	90	49	41 mins

KEY PLAYERS - DEFENDERS

Dick Van Burik

Goals Conceded Number of League goals conceded while the player was on the pitch	19	Clean Sheets In games when player was on pitch for at least 70 minutes	9
Defensive Rating Ave number of mins between League goals conceded while on the pitch	114	Club Defensive Rating Average number of mins between League goals conceded by the club this season	99

	PLAYER	CON LGE	CLEAN SHEETS	DEF RATE
1	Dick Van Burik	19	9	114 mins
2	Arne Friedrich	22	9	102 mins
3	Josip Simunic	27	10	97 mins
4	Malik Fathi	24	8	85 mins

KEY GOALKEEPER

Christian Fiedler

Goals Conceded in the League	31	Counting Games League games when player was on pitch for at least 70 minutes	34
Defensive Rating Ave number of mins between League goals conceded while on the pitch	99	Clean Sheets In games when player was on pitch for at least 70 minutes	11

LEAGUE GOALS

Marcelinho

Minutes on the pitch	2821	Goals in the League	18
League average (mins between goals)	157		

	PLAYER	MINS	GOALS	AVE
1	Marcelinho	2821	**18**	157
2	Basturk	2064	**7**	295
3	Rafael	1720	**6**	287
4	Gilberto	2888	**6**	481
5	Kovac	2553	**4**	638
6	Madlung	1247	**4**	312
7	Friedrich	2250	**3**	750
8	Marx	1971	**3**	657
9	Muller	456	**2**	228
10	Reina	575	**2**	288
11	Neuendorf	894	**2**	447
12	Bobic	1022	**1**	1022
13	Wichinarek	943	**1**	943
	Other		0	
	TOTAL		**59**	

DISCIPLINARY

	PLAYER	YELLOW	RED	AVE
1	Neuendorf	6	1	127
2	Kovac	11	0	232
3	Friedrich	8	0	281
4	Simunic	9	0	290
5	Schroder	3	0	321
6	Marx	6	0	328
7	Dardai	2	0	396
8	Marcelinho	7	0	403
9	Madlung	2	1	415
10	Rafael	4	0	430
11	Muller	1	0	456
12	Basturk	3	1	516
13	Fathi	3	0	678
	Other	4	1	
	TOTAL	69	4	

TOP POINT EARNERS

	PLAYER	GAMES	AV PTS
1	Nando Rafael	16	2.06
2	Malik Fathi	19	1.89
3	Arne Friedrich	25	1.88
4	Yildiray Basturk	21	1.86
5	Nico Kovac	26	1.81
6	Dick Van Burik	23	1.78
7	Gilberto	32	1.72
8	Christian Fiedler	34	1.71
9	Thorben Marx	21	1.67
10	Marcelinho	31	1.65
	CLUB AVERAGE:		1.71

TEAM OF THE SEASON

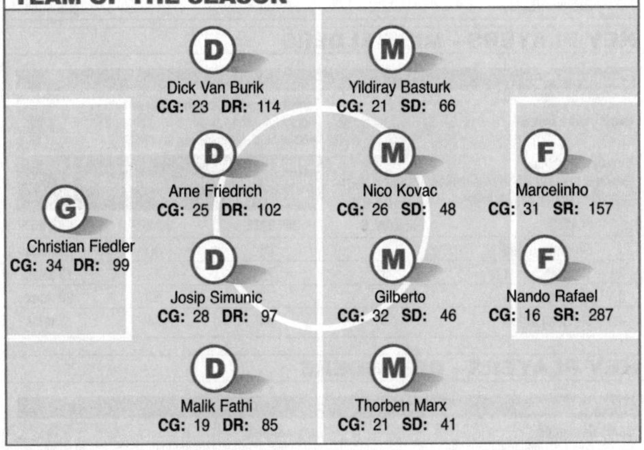

D
Dick Van Burik
CG: 23 DR: 114
M
Yildiray Basturk
CG: 21 SD: 66
G
Christian Fiedler
CG: 34 DR: 99
D
Arne Friedrich
CG: 25 DR: 102
M
Nico Kovac
CG: 26 SD: 48
F
Marcelinho
CG: 31 SR: 157
D
Josip Simunic
CG: 28 DR: 97
M
Gilberto
CG: 32 SD: 46
F
Nando Rafael
CG: 16 SR: 287
D
Malik Fathi
CG: 19 DR: 85
M
Thorben Marx
CG: 21 SD: 41

LEAGUE APPEARANCES, BOOKINGS AND CAPS

	AGE (on 01/07/05)	IN NAMED 18	APPEARANCES	COUNTING GAMES	MINUTES ON PITCH	YELLOW CARDS	RED CARDS	THIS SEASON	HOME COUNTRY
Goalkeepers									
Christian Fiedler	30	34	34	34	3060	1	0	-	Germany
Gerhard Tremmel	26	34	0	0	0	0	0	-	Germany
Defenders									
Pascal Bieler	19	1	0	0	0	0	0	-	Germany
Dennis Cagara	20	4	0	0	0	0	0	-	Germany
Sofian Chahed	22	2	0	0	0	0	0	-	Germany
Malik Fathi	21	31	29	19	2036	3	0	-	Germany
Arne Friedrich	26	25	25	25	2250	8	0	4	Germany (19)
Alexander Madlung	22	29	24	11	1247	2	1	-	Germany
Marko Rehmer	33	1	0	0	0	0	0	-	Germany
Josip Simunic	27	31	30	28	2616	9	0	7	Croatia (21)
Dick Van Burik	31	29	26	23	2173	2	1	-	Holland
Midfielders									
Yildiray Basturk	26	25	25	21	2064	3	1	-	Turkey
Pal Dardai	29	34	17	7	793	2	0	-	Hungary
Gilberto	28	33	33	32	2888	1	0	-	Brazil
Michael Hartmann	30	6	3	2	225	1	0	-	Germany
Nico Kovac	33	31	30	26	2553	11	0	8	Croatia (21)
Alexander Ludwig	21	1	0	0	0	0	0	-	Germany
Thorben Marx	24	31	26	21	1971	6	0	-	Germany
Alexander Mladenov	23	1	0	0	0	0	0	-	Bulgaria
Christian Muller	21	10	8	4	456	1	0	-	Germany
Andreas Neuendorf	30	31	23	7	894	6	1	-	Germany
Andreas Schmidt	31	5	0	0	0	0	0	-	Germany
Oliver Schroder	25	27	13	10	964	3	0	-	Germany
Forwards									
Fredi Bobic	33	32	21	9	1022	0	0	-	Germany
Ashkan Dejagah	19	1	1	0	6	0	0	-	Iran
Marcelinho	30	32	32	31	2821	7	0	-	Brazil
Nando Rafael	21	30	28	16	1720	4	0	-	Angola
Giuseppe Reina	33	21	16	2	575	0	0	-	Germany
Sejad Salihovic	20	10	6	2	256	0	0	-	Bosnia
Artur Wichinarek	28	31	22	5	943	0	0	-	Poland

SQUAD APPEARANCES

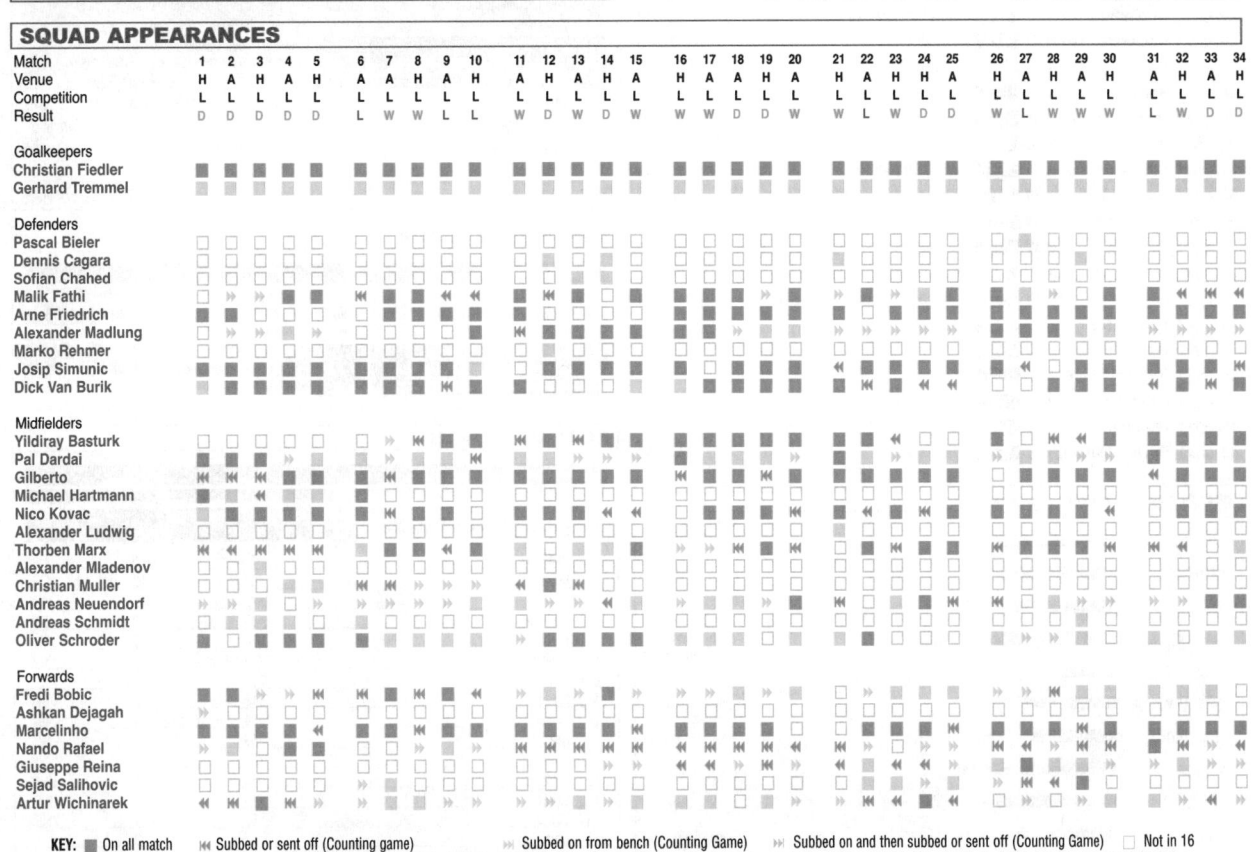

Match	1	2	3	4	5	6	7	8	9	10	11	12	13	14	15	16	17	18	19	20	21	22	23	24	25	26	27	28	29	30	31	32	33	34
Venue	H	A	H	A	H	A	A	H	A	H	A	H	A	H	A	H	A	A	H	A	H	A	H	H	A	H	A	H	A	H	A	H	A	H
Competition	L	L	L	L	L	L	L	L	L	L	L	L	L	L	L	L	L	L	L	L	L	L	L	L	L	L	L	L	L	L	L	L	L	L
Result	D	D	D	D	D	L	W	W	L	L	W	D	W	D	W	W	W	D	D	W	W	L	W	D	D	W	L	W	W	W	L	W	D	D

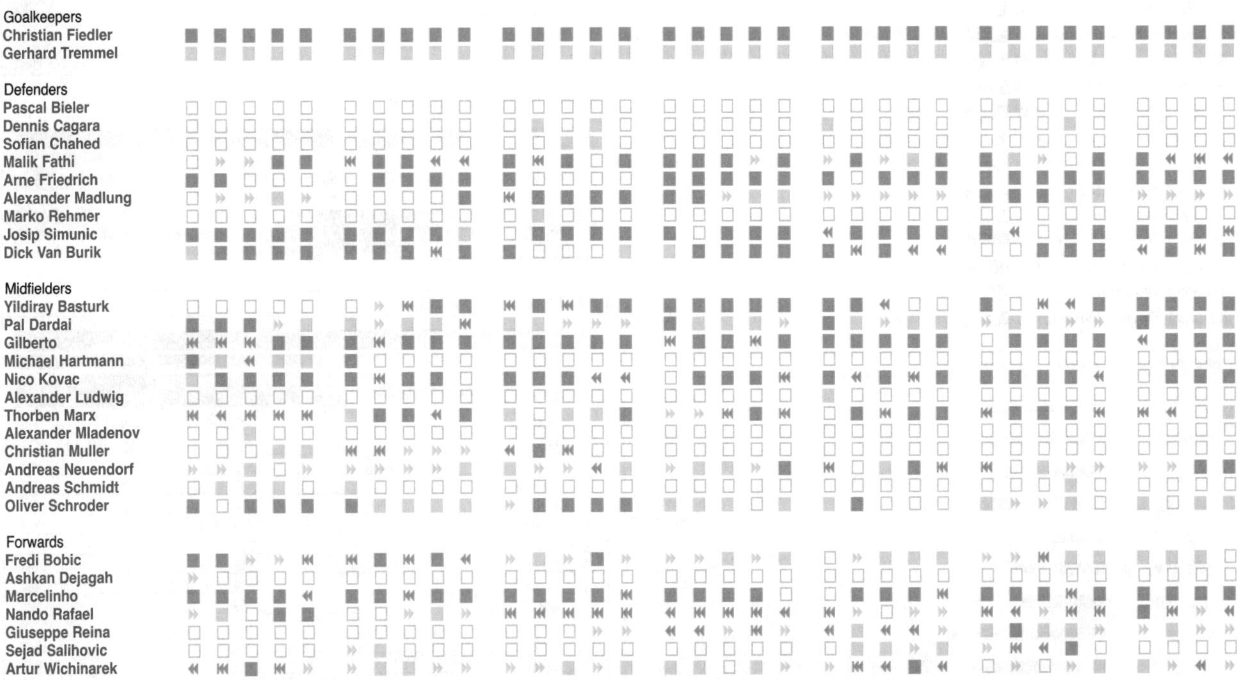

Goalkeepers
Christian Fiedler
Gerhard Tremmel
Defenders
Pascal Bieler
Dennis Cagara
Sofian Chahed
Malik Fathi
Arne Friedrich
Alexander Madlung
Marko Rehmer
Josip Simunic
Dick Van Burik
Midfielders
Yildiray Basturk
Pal Dardai
Gilberto
Michael Hartmann
Nico Kovac
Alexander Ludwig
Thorben Marx
Alexander Mladenov
Christian Muller
Andreas Neuendorf
Andreas Schmidt
Oliver Schroder
Forwards
Fredi Bobic
Ashkan Dejagah
Marcelinho
Nando Rafael
Giuseppe Reina
Sejad Salihovic
Artur Wichinarek

KEY: On all match | On bench | Subbed or sent off (Counting game) | Subbed or sent off (playing less than 70 minutes) | Subbed on from bench (Counting Game) | Subbed on (playing less than 70 minutes) | Subbed on and then subbed or sent off (Counting Game) | Subbed on and then subbed or sent off (playing less than 70 minutes) | Not in 16

VFB STUTTGART

Final Position: **5th**

KEY: Won / Drawn / Lost

							Attendance
1	grpr1	**Mainz**	H	W	4-2	Cacau 20,30,78; Meissner 51	44,000
2	grpr1	**Nuremburg**	A	D	1-1	Cacau 8	40,000
3	grpr1	**Kaiserslautern**	A	W	3-2	Kuranyi 31,53,81	38,000
4	grpr1	**Hamburg**	H	W	2-0	Meissner 16; Szabics 90	44,000
5	uc1rl1	**Ujpesti**	A	W	3-1	Cacau 25,90; Kuranyi 30	11,420
6	grpr1	**Hertha Berlin**	A	D	0-0		45,000
7	grpr1	**B Leverkusen**	H	W	3-0	Lahm 12; Stranzl 42; Meissner 90 pen	35,000
8	uc1r12	**Ujpesti**	H	W	4-0	Hinkel 14; Cacau 55,61; Heldt 57 pen	23,000
9	grpr1	**Arminia B**	A	W	2-0	Babbel 43; Cacau 90	23,000
10	grpr1	**B Dortmund**	H	W	2-0	Hinkel 52; Cacau 67	48,000
11	ucgpg	**Beveren**	A	W	5-1	Cacau 9,52; Kuranyi 40; Lahm 76; Szabics 90	7,000
12	grpr1	**Freiburg**	A	L	0-2		25,000
13	grpr1	**W Bremen**	H	L	1-2	Delpierre 45	41,000
14	grpr1	**Schalke**	A	L	2-3	Soldo 30; Szabics 32	62,000
15	ucgpg	**Benfica**	H	W	3-0	Cacau 32; Meissner 52; Kuranyi 73	47,000
16	grpr1	**Hansa Rostock**	H	W	4-0	Meissner 7; Kuranyi 38; Cacau 56; Heldt 80	43,000
17	grpr1	**Wolfsburg**	A	L	0-3		29,000
18	grpr1	**B M'gladbach**	H	W	1-0	Kuranyi 56	38,000
19	ucgpg	**Heerenveen**	A	L	0-1		17,500
20	grpr1	**Hannover 96**	A	D	0-0		34,000
21	grpr1	**Bochum**	H	W	5-2	Kalla 5 og; Kuranyi 24,81; Hleb 68; Meissner 75	36,000
22	grpr1	**Bayern Munich**	A	D	2-2	Meissner 29; Kuranyi 65	63,000
23	ucgpg	**Dinamo Zagreb**	H	W	2-1	Tiffert 15; Meira 75	41,000
24	grpr1	**Mainz**	A	W	3-2	Wache 51 og; Hleb 54; Cacau 66	20,000
25	grpr1	**Nuremburg**	H	L	2-4	Meira 52; Szabics 70	46,000
26	grpr1	**Kaiserslautern**	H	D	1-1	Kuranyi 15	37,000
27	grpr1	**Hamburg**	A	L	1-2	Szabics 15	49,000
28	uc3rl1	**Parma**	A	D	0-0		5,486
29	grpr1	**Hertha Berlin**	H	W	1-0	Cacau 10	29,000
30	uc3rl2	**Parma**	H	L	0-2		38,000
31	grpr1	**B Leverkusen**	A	D	1-1	Cacau 89 pen	23,000
32	grpr1	**Arminia B**	H	W	2-1	Soldo 48; Cacau 75	28,000
33	grpr1	**B Dortmund**	A	W	2-0	Meissner 43,90 pen	75,000
34	grpr1	**Freiburg**	H	W	1-0	Babbel 20	40,000
35	grpr1	**W Bremen**	A	W	2-1	Meissner 48; Tiffert 87	42,000
36	grpr1	**Schalke**	H	W	3-0	Kuranyi 15,47,63	49,000
37	grpr1	**Hansa Rostock**	A	L	1-2	Cacau 46	23,000
38	grpr1	**Wolfsburg**	H	D	0-0		48,000
39	grpr1	**B M'gladbach**	A	L	0-2		53,000
40	grpr1	**Hannover 96**	H	W	1-0	Kuranyi 88	40,000
41	grpr1	**Bochum**	A	L	0-2		27,000
42	grpr1	**Bayern Munich**	H	L	1-3	Szabics 88	49,000

MONTHLY POINTS TALLY

AUGUST	7	78%
SEPTEMBER	7	78%
OCTOBER	6	40%
NOVEMBER	7	58%
DECEMBER	4	67%
JANUARY	3	50%
FEBRUARY	5	42%
MARCH	9	100%
APRIL	7	47%
MAY	3	33%

KEY PLAYERS - GOALSCORERS

Kevin Kuranyi

Goals in the League	13	Player Strike Rate Average number of minutes between League goals scored by player	175
Contribution to Attacking Power Average number of minutes between League team goals while on pitch	56	Club Strike Rate Average number of minutes between League goals scored by club	57

	PLAYER	LGE GOALS	POWER	STRIKE RATE
1	Kevin Kuranyi	13	56	175 mins
2	Cacau	12	58	214 mins
3	Silvio Meissner	9	52	276 mins
4	Markus Babbel	2	59	1378 mins
5	Zvonimir Soldo	2	60	1408 mins

KEY PLAYERS - MIDFIELDERS

Zvonimir Soldo

Goals in the League	2	Contribution to Attacking Power Average number of minutes between League team goals while on pitch	60
Defensive Rating Average number of mins between goals conceded while on the pitch	85	Scoring Difference Defensive Rating minus Contribution to Attacking Power	25

	PLAYER	LGE GOALS	DEF RATE	POWER	SCORE DIFF
1	Zvonimir Soldo	2	85	60	25 mins
2	Silvio Meissner	9	75	52	23 mins
3	Alexander Hleb	2	77	57	20 mins
4	Christian Tiffert	1	64	61	3 mins

KEY PLAYERS - DEFENDERS

Martin Stranzl

Goals Conceded Number of League goals conceded while the player was on the pitch	27	Clean Sheets In games when player was on pitch for at least 70 minutes	13
Defensive Rating Ave number of mins between League goals conceded while on the pitch	96	Club Defensive Rating Average number of mins between League goals conceded by the club this season	77

	PLAYER	CON LGE	CLEAN SHEETS	DEF RATE
1	Martin Stranzl	27	13	96 mins
2	Andreas Hinkel	30	12	83 mins
3	Philip Lahm	21	9	82 mins
4	Markus Babbel	35	12	79 mins

KEY GOALKEEPER

Timo Hildebrand

Goals Conceded in the League	40	Counting Games League games when player was on pitch for at least 70 minutes	34
Defensive Rating Ave number of mins between League goals conceded while on the pitch	77	Clean Sheets In games when player was on pitch for at least 70 minutes	14

LEAGUE GOALS

Kevin Kuranyi

Minutes on the pitch	2269	Goals in the League	13
League average (mins between goals)	175		

	PLAYER	MINS	GOALS	AVE
1	Kuranyi	2269	13	175
2	Cacau	2572	12	214
3	Meissner	2480	9	276
4	Szabics	976	5	195
5	Babbel	2755	2	1378
6	Hleb	3013	2	1507
7	Soldo	2815	2	1408
8	Hinkel	2484	1	2484
9	Delpierre	565	1	565
10	Lahm	1720	1	1720
11	Heldt	1032	1	1032
12	Tiffert	1843	1	1843
13	Stranzl	2588	1	2588
	Other		3	
	TOTAL		54	

DISCIPLINARY

	PLAYER	YELLOW	RED	AVE
1	Zivkovic	4	1	132
2	Gerber	3	0	177
3	Meissner	10	0	248
4	Cacau	9	1	257
5	Kuranyi	8	0	283
6	Vranjes	2	0	287
7	Meira	2	2	296
8	Soldo	9	0	312
9	Tiffert	5	0	368
10	Babbel	7	0	393
11	Stranzl	6	0	431
12	Hinkel	5	0	496
13	Delpierre	1	0	565
	Other	8	0	
	TOTAL	79	4	

TOP POINT EARNERS

	PLAYER	GAMES	AV PTS
1	Martin Stranzl	28	1.86
2	Andreas Hinkel	27	1.78
3	Silvio Meissner	28	1.75
4	Zvonimir Soldo	31	1.74
5	Kevin Kuranyi	23	1.74
6	Timo Hildebrand	34	1.71
7	Alexander Hleb	34	1.71
8	Cacau	27	1.67
9	Philip Lahm	18	1.67
10	Christian Tiffert	17	1.65
	CLUB AVERAGE:		1.71

LEAGUE APPEARANCES, BOOKINGS AND CAPS

	AGE (on 01/07/05)	IN NAMED 18	APPEARANCES	COUNTING GAMES	MINUTES ON PITCH	YELLOW CARDS	RED CARDS	THIS SEASON	HOME COUNTRY
Goalkeepers									
Diego Benaglio	21	7	0	0	0	0	0	-	Switzerland
Dirk Heinen	34	27	0	0	0	0	0	-	Germany
Timo Hildebrand	26	34	34	34	3060	0	0	3	Germany (19)
Defenders									
Markus Babbel	32	33	32	29	2755	7	0	-	Germany
Heiko Butscher	24	2	0	0	0	0	0	-	Germany
Steffen Dangelmayr	26	1	0	0	0	0	0	-	Germany
Mathieu Delpierre	24	24	10	4	565	1	0	-	France
Andreas Hinkel	23	31	29	27	2484	5	0	7	Germany (19)
Philip Lahm	21	23	22	18	1720	2	0	6	Germany (19)
Fernando Meira	27	17	16	11	1187	2	2	3	Portugal (9)
Martin Stranzl	25	30	29	28	2588	6	0	-	Austria
Boris Zivkovic	29	18	11	6	662	4	1	-	Croatia
Midfielders									
Marco Caligiuri	21	6	0	0	0	0	0	-	Germany
Elson	23	4	3	0	100	0	0	-	Brazil
Christian Gentner	19	3	1	0	10	0	0	-	Germany
Heiko Gerber	32	29	11	5	532	3	0	-	Germany
Horst Heldt	35	30	19	8	1032	1	0	-	Germany
Alexander Hleb	24	34	34	34	3013	4	0	-	Belarus
Silvio Meissner	32	30	28	28	2480	10	0	-	Germany
Zvonimir Soldo	37	32	32	31	2815	9	0	-	Croatia
Ivan Stojanov	21	2	0	0	0	0	0	-	Bulgaria
Christian Tiffert	23	33	30	17	1843	5	0	-	Germany
Jurica Vranjes	25	31	17	3	574	2	0	8	Croatia (21)
Forwards									
Cacau	24	32	32	27	2572	9	1	-	Brazil
Emanuel Centurion	22	3	1	0	10	0	0	-	Argentina
Mario Gomez	19	22	8	0	65	1	0	-	Germany
Kevin Kuranyi	23	29	29	23	2269	8	0	7	Germany (19)
Marco Streller	24	8	8	0	178	0	0	-	Switzerland
Imre Szabics	24	31	22	6	976	1	0	-	Hungary
Hakan Yakin	28	3	1	0	20	0	0	-	Switzerland

TEAM OF THE SEASON

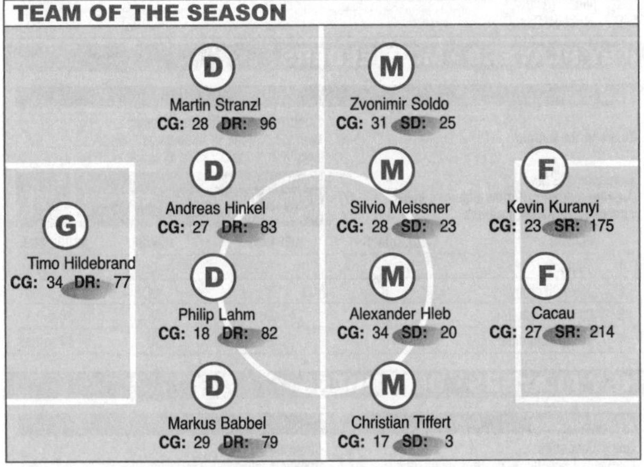
D
Martin Stranzl
CG: 28 DR: 96
M
Zvonimir Soldo
CG: 31 SD: 25
D
Andreas Hinkel
CG: 27 DR: 83
M
Silvio Meissner
CG: 28 SD: 23
F
Kevin Kuranyi
CG: 23 SR: 175
G
Timo Hildebrand
CG: 34 DR: 77
D
Philip Lahm
CG: 18 DR: 82
M
Alexander Hleb
CG: 34 SD: 20
F
Cacau
CG: 27 SR: 214
D
Markus Babbel
CG: 29 DR: 79
M
Christian Tiffert
CG: 17 SD: 3

SQUAD APPEARANCES

Match	1	2	3	4	5	6	7	8	9	10	11	12	13	14	15	16	17	18	19	20	21	22	23	24	25	26	27	28	29	30	31	32	33	34	35	36	37	38	39	40	41	42
Venue	H	A	A	H	A	A	H	H	A	H	A	A	H	A	H	H	A	H	A	A	H	A	H	A	H	H	A	A	H	H	A	H	A	H	A	H	A	H	A	H	A	H
Competition	L	L	L	L	E	L	L	E	L	L	E	L	L	L	E	L	L	L	E	L	L	L	E	L	L	L	L	E	L	E	L	L	L	L	L	L	L	L	L	L	L	L
Result	W	D	W	W	W	D	W	W	W	W	W	L	L	L	W	W	L	W	L	D	W	D	W	W	L	D	L	D	W	L	D	W	W	W	W	W	L	D	L	W	L	L

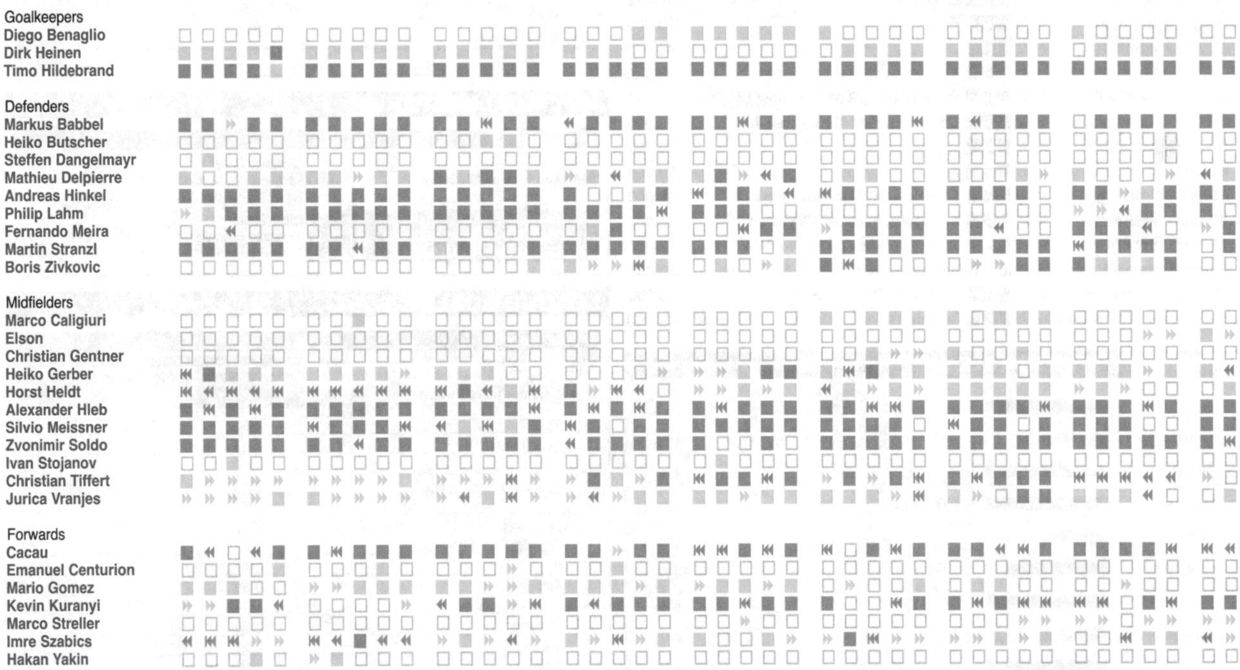
Goalkeepers
Diego Benaglio
Dirk Heinen
Timo Hildebrand
Defenders
Markus Babbel
Heiko Butscher
Steffen Dangelmayr
Mathieu Delpierre
Andreas Hinkel
Philip Lahm
Fernando Meira
Martin Stranzl
Boris Zivkovic
Midfielders
Marco Caligiuri
Elson
Christian Gentner
Heiko Gerber
Horst Heldt
Alexander Hleb
Silvio Meissner
Zvonimir Soldo
Ivan Stojanov
Christian Tiffert
Jurica Vranjes
Forwards
Cacau
Emanuel Centurion
Mario Gomez
Kevin Kuranyi
Marco Streller
Imre Szabics
Hakan Yakin

KEY: On all match / On bench / Subbed or sent off (Counting game) / Subbed or sent off (playing less than 70 minutes) / Subbed on from bench (Counting Game) / Subbed on (playing less than 70 minutes) / Subbed on and then subbed or sent off (Counting Game) / Subbed on and then subbed or sent off (playing less than 70 minutes) / Not in 16

BAYER LEVERKUSEN

Final Position: **6th**

KEY: Won / Drawn / Lost

							Attendance
1	grpr1	Hannover 96	H	W	2-1	Schneider 49; Franca 90	20,000
2	ecql1	Banik Ostrava	H	W	5-0	Franca 10,67; Juan 74; Berbatov 82,89	20,000
3	grpr1	Bochum	A	D	2-2	Berbatov 66; Voronin 87	25,000
4	cl3ql2	Banik Ostrava	A	L	1-2	Berbatov 77	5,000
5	grpr1	Bayern Munich	H	W	4-1	Berbatov 20,59; Franca 52,56	22,000
6	grpr1	Mainz	A	L	0-2		20,000
7	cl gb	Real Madrid	H	W	3-0	Krzynowek 39; Franca 50; Berbatov 55	23,000
8	grpr1	Nuremburg	H	D	2-2	Butt 76 pen; Berbatov 80	23,000
9	grpr1	Stuttgart	A	L	0-3		35,000
10	cl gb	Dinamo Kiev	A	L	2-4	Voronin 59; Nowotny 68	83,000
11	grpr1	Hamburg	H	W	3-0	Krzynowek 10; Juan 74; Berbatov 87	22,000
12	grpr1	Hertha Berlin	A	L	1-3	Schneider 54	47,000
13	cl gb	Roma	H	W	3-1	Roque Junior 48; Krzynowek 59; Franca 94	23,000
14	grpr1	Kaiserslautern	A	D	0-0		32,000
15	grpr1	Arminia B	H	W	3-2	Voronin 50,54,78	22,000
16	grpr1	B Dortmund	A	L	0-1		78,000
17	cl gb	Roma	A	D	1-1	Berbatov 82	
18	grpr1	Freiburg	H	W	4-1	Freier 48,88; Krzynowek 53; Voronin 90	22,000
19	grpr1	W Bremen	A	D	2-2	Voronin 51; Berbatov 53	38,000
20	grpr1	Schalke	H	L	0-3		23,000
21	cl gb	Real Madrid	A	D	1-1	Berbatov 36	72,000
22	grpr1	Hansa Rostock	A	W	2-0	Berbatov 36; Voronin 64	17,000
23	grpr1	Wolfsburg	H	W	2-1	Voronin 46; Franca 89	23,000
24	cl gb	Dinamo Kiev	H	W	3-0	Juan 51; Voronin 77; Babic 86	23,000
25	grpr1	B M'gladbach	A	D	1-1	Berbatov 58	52,000
26	grpr1	Hannover 96	A	W	3-0	Voronin 18; Berbatov 36; Freier 58	38,000
27	grpr1	Bochum	H	W	4-0	Krzynowek 28; Voronin 31; Ponte 70; Freier 78	23,000
28	grpr1	Bayern Munich	A	L	0-2		45,000
29	grpr1	Mainz	H	W	2-0	Freier 64; Krzynowek 69	22,000
30	grpr1	Nuremburg	A	W	4-2	Berbatov 3,60; Ramelow 33; Krzynowek 79	18,000
31	clr2l1	Liverpool	A	L	1-3	Franca 90	40,942
32	grpr1	Stuttgart	H	D	1-1	Berbatov 80	23,000
33	grpr1	Hamburg	A	L	0-1		48,000
34	clr2l2	Liverpool	H	L	1-3	Krzynowek 88	23,000
35	grpr1	Hertha Berlin	H	D	3-3	Ponte 5; Butt 13 pen; Voronin 84	23,000
36	grpr1	Kaiserslautern	H	W	2-0	Callsen-Bracker 13; Voronin 46	23,000
37	grpr1	Arminia B	A	L	0-1		24,000
38	grpr1	B Dortmund	H	L	0-1		23,000
39	grpr1	Freiburg	A	W	3-1	Schneider 26; Berbatov 66,83	22,000
40	grpr1	W Bremen	H	W	2-1	Krzynowek 3; Babic 37; Castro 86	23,000
41	grpr1	Schalke	A	D	3-3	Freier 23; Berbatov 56; Voronin 64	62,000
42	grpr1	Hansa Rostock	H	W	3-0	Berbatov 28,89; Voronin 59	23,000
43	grpr1	Wolfsburg	A	D	2-2	Franca 61; Bierofka 87	25,000
44	grpr1	B M'gladbach	H	W	5-1	Berbatov 41,58,61; Voronin 59; Franca 69	23,000

MONTHLY POINTS TALLY

AUGUST	7	78%
SEPTEMBER	1	11%
OCTOBER	7	47%
NOVEMBER	7	58%
DECEMBER	4	67%
JANUARY	6	100%
FEBRUARY	7	58%
MARCH	4	44%
APRIL	7	47%
MAY	7	78%

KEY PLAYERS - GOALSCORERS

Andriy Voronin

Goals in the League	15	Player Strike Rate Average number of minutes between League goals scored by player	143
Contribution to Attacking Power Average number of minutes between League team goals while on pitch	43	Club Strike Rate Average number of minutes between League goals scored by club	48

	PLAYER	LGE GOALS	POWER	STRIKE RATE
1	Andriy Voronin	15	43	143 mins
2	Dimitar Berbatov	20	48	151 mins
3	Paul Freier	6	42	392 mins
4	Jacek Krzynowek	6	44	455 mins
5	Robson Ponte	2	59	924 mins

KEY PLAYERS - MIDFIELDERS

Paul Freier

Goals in the League	6	Contribution to Attacking Power Average number of minutes between League team goals while on pitch	42
Defensive Rating Average number of mins between goals conceded while on the pitch	67	Scoring Difference Defensive Rating minus Contribution to Attacking Power	25

	PLAYER	LGE GOALS	DEF RATE	POWER	SCORE DIFF
1	Paul Freier	6	67	42	25 mins
2	Jacek Krzynowek	6	68	44	24 mins
3	Carsten Ramelow	1	66	46	20 mins
4	Bernd Schneider	3	67	50	17 mins

KEY PLAYERS - DEFENDERS

Jens Nowotny

Goals Conceded Number of League goals conceded while the player was on the pitch	17	Clean Sheets In games when player was on pitch for at least 70 minutes	5
Defensive Rating Ave number of mins between League goals conceded while on the pitch	81	Club Defensive Rating Average number of mins between League goals conceded by the club this season	68

	PLAYER	CON LGE	CLEAN SHEETS	DEF RATE
1	Jens Nowotny	17	5	81 mins
2	Juan	34	7	74 mins
3	Diego Placente	34	6	70 mins
4	Roque Junior	31	2	55 mins

KEY GOALKEEPER

Hans-Jorg Butt

Goals Conceded in the League	46	Counting Games League games when player was on pitch for at least 70 minutes	35
Defensive Rating Ave number of mins between League goals conceded while on the pitch	68	Clean Sheets In games when player was on pitch for at least 70 minutes	8

LEAGUE GOALS

Dimitar Berbatov

Minutes on the pitch	3013	Goals in the League	20
League average (mins between goals)	151		

	PLAYER	MINS	GOALS	AVE
1	Berbatov	3013	20	151
2	Voronin	2148	15	143
3	Freier	2353	6	392
4	Franca	975	6	163
5	Krzynowek	2727	6	455
6	Schneider	3036	3	1012
7	Ponte	1847	2	924
8	Butt	3150	2	1575
9	Callsen-Bracker	823	1	823
10	Ramelow	2790	1	2790
11	Juan	2521	1	2521
12	Bierofka	303	1	303
13	Babic	1315	1	1315
	Other		1	
	TOTAL		66	

DISCIPLINARY RECORDS

	PLAYER	YELLOW	RED	AVE
1	Ramelow	12	0	232
2	Balitsch	2	0	234
3	Ponte	7	0	263
4	Nowotny	4	1	276
5	Castro	3	0	326
6	Callsen-Bracker	2	0	411
7	Juan	6	0	420
8	Roque Junior	3	1	428
9	Babic	3	0	438
10	Placente	5	0	475
11	Schneider	5	0	607
12	Berbatov	3	0	1004
13	Voronin	2	0	1074
	Other	3	0	
	TOTAL	60	2	

TOP POINT EARNERS

	PLAYER	GAMES	AV PTS
1	Jens Nowotny	15	1.87
2	Andriy Voronin	19	1.74
3	Paul Freier	19	1.74
4	Dimitar Berbatov	33	1.67
5	Roque Junior	18	1.67
6	Jacek Krzynowek	30	1.67
7	Juan	28	1.64
8	Diego Placente	24	1.63
9	Hans-Jorg Butt	35	1.63
10	Carsten Ramelow	31	1.61
	CLUB AVERAGE:		1.68

TEAM OF THE SEASON

D Jens Nowotny CG: 15 DR: 81
D Juan CG: 28 DR: 74
D Diego Placente CG: 24 DR: 70
D Roque Junior CG: 18 DR: 55
G Hans-Jorg Butt CG: 35 DR: 68
M Paul Freier CG: 19 SD: 25
M Jacek Krzynowek CG: 30 SD: 24
M Carsten Ramelow CG: 31 SD: 20
M Bernd Schneider CG: 33 SD: 17
F Andriy Voronin CG: 19 SR: 143
F Dimitar Berbatov CG: 33 SR: 151

LEAGUE APPEARANCES, BOOKINGS AND CAPS

	AGE (on 01/07/05)	IN NAMED 18	APPEARANCES	COUNTING GAMES	MINUTES ON PITCH	YELLOW CARDS	RED CARDS	THIS SEASON	HOME COUNTRY
Goalkeepers									
Rene Adler	20	2	0	0	0	0	0	-	Germany
Hans-Jorg Butt	31	35	35	35	3150	0	0	-	Germany
Tom Starke	24	31	0	0	0	0	0	-	Germany
Defenders									
Jl Callsen-Bracker	20	33	10	9	823	2	0	-	Germany
Sascha Dum	19	13	5	1	213	1	0	-	Germany
Juan	26	29	29	28	2521	6	0	10	Brazil (1)
Teddy Lucic	32	4	0	0	0	0	0	10	Sweden (13)
Jens Nowotny	31	17	16	15	1381	4	1	-	Germany
Diego Placente	28	30	29	24	2376	5	0	8	Argentina (3)
Roque Junior	28	21	20	18	1712	3	1	6	Brazil (1)
Marius Schultens	18	1	0	0	0	0	0	-	Germany
Midfielders									
Marko Babic	24	32	28	8	1315	3	0	7	Croatia (21)
Hanno Balitsch	24	14	8	4	469	2	0	-	Germany
Daniel Bierofka	26	22	16	0	303	0	0	-	Germany
Gonzalo Castro	18	19	14	10	978	3	0	-	Spain
Domenico Cozza	22	1	0	0	0	0	0	-	Germany
Paul Freier	25	35	34	19	2353	2	0	1	Germany (19)
Radoslaw Kaluzny	31	5	2	1	104	1	0	-	Poland
Jacek Krzynowek	29	32	32	30	2727	1	0	-	Poland
Sezer Ozturk	19	19	6	0	48	0	0	-	Turkey
Carsten Ramelow	31	31	31	31	2790	12	0	-	Germany
Timo Rottger	19	1	0	0	0	0	0	-	Germany
Bernd Schneider	31	34	34	33	3036	5	0	8	Germany (19)
Forwards									
Dimitar Berbatov	24	34	34	33	3013	3	0	-	Bulgaria
Landon Donovan	23	9	7	1	149	0	0	-	United States
Franca	29	30	22	4	975	0	0	-	Brazil
Clemens Fritz	24	4	0	0	0	0	0	-	Germany
Jermaine Jones	23	11	5	1	187	1	0	-	Germany
Robson Ponte	28	25	24	20	1847	7	0	-	Brazil
Kenan Sahin	20	2	1	0	8	0	0	-	Turkey
Andriy Voronin	25	34	33	19	2148	2	0	-	Ukraine

SQUAD APPEARANCES

Match	1	2	3	4	5	6	7	8	9	10	11	12	13	14	15	16	17	18	19	20	21	22
Venue	H	H	A	A	H	A	H	H	A	A	H	A	H	A	H	A	A	H	A	H	A	A
Competition	L	C	L	C	L	L	C	L	L	C	L	L	C	L	L	L	C	L	L	L	C	L
Result	W	W	D	L	W	L	W	D	L	L	W	L	W	D	W	L	D	W	D	L	D	W

Match	23	24	25	26	27	28	29	30	31	32	33	34	35	36	37	38	39	40	41	42	43	44
Venue	H	H	A	A	H	A	H	A	A	H	A	H	H	H	A	H	A	H	A	H	A	H
Competition	L	C	L	L	L	L	L	L	C	L	L	C	L	L	L	L	L	L	L	L	L	L
Result	W	W	D	W	W	L	W	W	L	D	L	L	D	W	L	L	W	W	D	W	D	W

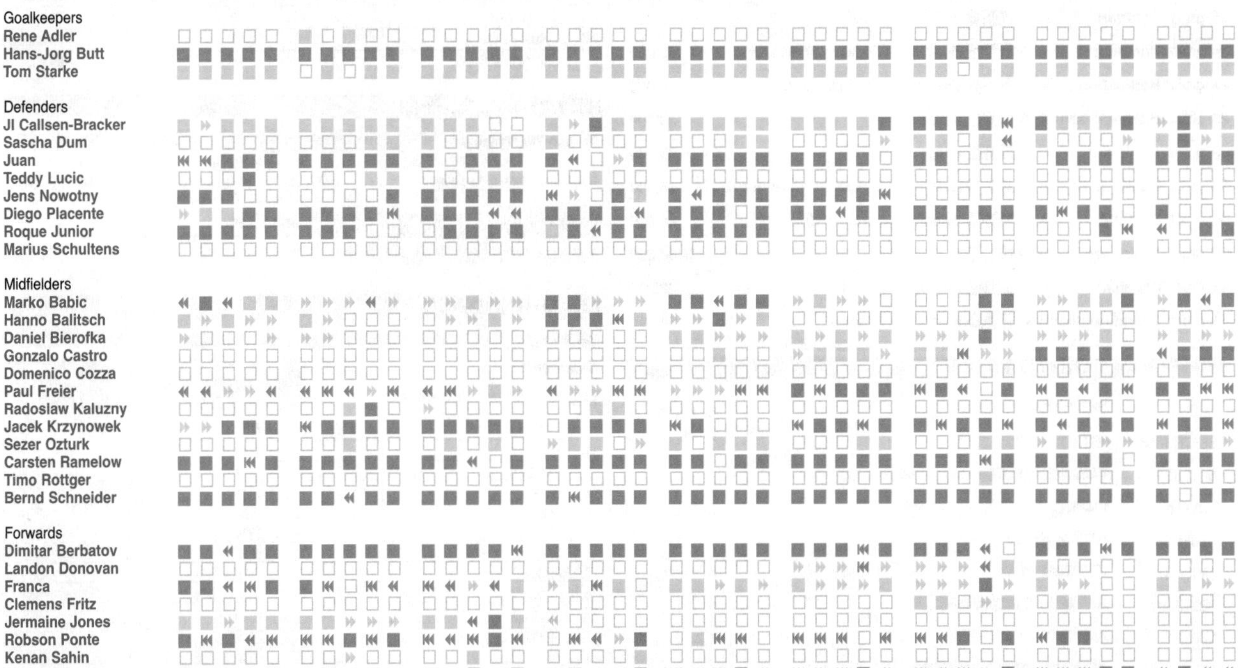

Goalkeepers
Rene Adler
Hans-Jorg Butt
Tom Starke
Defenders
Jl Callsen-Bracker
Sascha Dum
Juan
Teddy Lucic
Jens Nowotny
Diego Placente
Roque Junior
Marius Schultens
Midfielders
Marko Babic
Hanno Balitsch
Daniel Bierofka
Gonzalo Castro
Domenico Cozza
Paul Freier
Radoslaw Kaluzny
Jacek Krzynowek
Sezer Ozturk
Carsten Ramelow
Timo Rottger
Bernd Schneider
Forwards
Dimitar Berbatov
Landon Donovan
Franca
Clemens Fritz
Jermaine Jones
Robson Ponte
Kenan Sahin
Andriy Voronin

KEY: On all match | On bench | Subbed or sent off (Counting game) | Subbed or sent off (playing less than 70 minutes) | Subbed on from bench (Counting Game) | Subbed on (playing less than 70 minutes) | Subbed on and then subbed or sent off (Counting Game) | Subbed on and then subbed or sent off (playing less than 70 minutes) | Not in 16

BORUSSIA DORTMUND

Final Position: **7th**

KEY: ☐Won ☐Drawn ☐Lost

							Attendance
1	grpr1	Wolfsburg	H	L	1-2	Ewerthon 30	73,000
2	grpr1	B M'gladbach	A	W	3-2	Jensen 13; Koller 35; Ewerthon 37	53,000
3	grpr1	Hannover 96	H	D	1-1	Rosicky 29	74,000
4	grpr1	Bochum	A	D	2-2	Koller 48; Ewerthon 59	33,000
5	grpr1	Bayern Munich	H	D	2-2	Ewerthon 45,69 pen	83,000
6	grpr1	Mainz	A	D	1-1	Koller 9	20,000
7	grpr1	Nuremburg	H	D	2-2	Koller 29,45	75,000
8	grpr1	Stuttgart	A	L	0-2		48,000
9	grpr1	Hamburg	H	L	0-2		80,000
10	grpr1	Hertha Berlin	A	W	1-0	Koller 44	40,000
11	grpr1	B Leverkusen	H	W	1-0	Ewerthon 41	78,000
12	grpr1	Arminia B	A	L	0-1		27,000
13	grpr1	Kaiserslautern	A	L	0-1		37,000
14	grpr1	Freiburg	H	W	2-0	Brzenska 4; Madouni 81	76,000
15	grpr1	W Bremen	A	L	0-2		37,000
16	grpr1	Schalke	H	L	0-1		83,000
17	grpr1	Hansa Rostock	A	D	1-1	Kehl 41	13,000
18	grpr1	Wolfsburg	A	W	2-1	Smolarek 54; Koller 60	30,000
19	grpr1	B M'gladbach	H	D	1-1	Koller 29	80,000
20	grpr1	Hannover 96	A	W	3-1	Koller 6; Ricken 30,56	35,000
21	grpr1	Bochum	H	W	1-0	Koller 21	78,000
22	grpr1	Bayern Munich	A	L	0-5		48,000
23	grpr1	Mainz	H	W	3-0	Smolarek 28; Koller 54; Ricken 74	75,000
24	grpr1	Nuremburg	A	D	2-2	Worns 62; Rosicky 85 pen	24,000
25	grpr1	Stuttgart	H	L	0-2		75,000
26	grpr1	Hamburg	A	W	3-2	Rosicky 10; Ricken 61; Ewerthon 87	55,000
27	grpr1	Hertha Berlin	H	W	2-1	Ewerthon 27; Smolarek 36	74,000
28	grpr1	B Leverkusen	A	W	1-0	Kehl 88	23,000
29	grpr1	Arminia B	H	D	1-1	Kringe 16	78,000
30	grpr1	Kaiserslautern	H	W	4-2	Ewerthon 10; Kehl 28; Koller 64,75	76,000
31	grpr1	Freiburg	A	D	2-2	Ewerthon 37; Koller 40	25,000
32	grpr1	W Bremen	H	W	1-0	Rosicky 32	80,000
33	grpr1	Schalke	A	W	2-1	Kehl 17; Ricken 43	62,000
34	grpr1	Hansa Rostock	H	W	2-1	Kruska 52; Koller 67	80,000

MONTHLY POINTS TALLY

AUGUST	4	44%
SEPTEMBER	3	33%
OCTOBER	7	47%
NOVEMBER	3	25%
DECEMBER	1	17%
JANUARY	4	67%
FEBRUARY	9	75%
MARCH	4	44%
APRIL	11	73%
MAY	9	100%

KEY PLAYERS - GOALSCORERS

Jan Koller

Goals in the League: 15

Player Strike Rate — Average number of minutes between League goals scored by player: 175

Contribution to Attacking Power — Average number of minutes between League team goals while on pitch: 69

Club Strike Rate — Average number of minutes between League goals scored by club: 65

	PLAYER	LGE GOALS	POWER	STRIKE RATE
1	Jan Koller	15	69	175 mins
2	Ewerthon	10	64	218 mins
3	Ebi Smolarek	3	49	427 mins
4	Tomas Rosicky	4	67	576 mins
5	Sebastian Kehl	4	64	720 mins

KEY PLAYERS - MIDFIELDERS

Florian Kringe

Goals in the League: 1

Contribution to Attacking Power — Average number of minutes between League team goals while on pitch: 66

Defensive Rating — Average number of mins between goals conceded while on the pitch: 81

Scoring Difference — Defensive Rating minus Contribution to Attacking Power: 15

	PLAYER	LGE GOALS	DEF RATE	POWER	SCORE DIFF
1	Florian Kringe	1	81	66	15 mins
2	Tomas Rosicky	4	72	68	4 mins
3	Leonardo Dede	0	70	68	2 mins
4	Niclas Jensen	1	62	69	-7 mins

KEY PLAYERS - DEFENDERS

Markus Brzenska

Goals Conceded — Number of League goals conceded while the player was on the pitch: 26

Clean Sheets — In games when player was on pitch for at least 70 minutes: 6

Defensive Rating — Ave number of mins between League goals conceded while on the pitch: 76

Club Defensive Rating — Average number of mins between League goals conceded by the club this season: 70

	PLAYER	CON LGE	CLEAN SHEETS	DEF RATE
1	Markus Brzenska	26	6	76 mins
2	Christian Worns	34	7	74 mins
3	Sebastian Kehl	40	7	72 mins
4	Christoph Metzelder	18	3	69 mins

KEY GOALKEEPER

Roman Weidenfeller

Goals Conceded in the League: 30

Counting Games — League games when player was on pitch for at least 70 minutes: 26

Defensive Rating — Ave number of mins between League goals conceded while on the pitch: 78

Clean Sheets — In games when player was on pitch for at least 70 minutes: 7

LEAGUE GOALS

Jan Koller

Minutes on the pitch: 2622

League average (mins between goals): 175

Goals in the League: 15

	PLAYER	MINS	GOALS	AVE
1	Koller	2622	15	175
2	Ewerthon	2177	10	218
3	Ricken	1041	5	208
4	Kehl	2880	4	720
5	Rosicky	2304	4	576
6	Smolarek	1280	3	427
7	Madouni	559	1	559
8	Kruska	962	1	962
9	Brzenska	1979	1	1979
10	Kringe	2429	1	2429
11	Worns	2526	1	2526
12	Jensen	1238	1	1238
	Other		0	
	TOTAL		47	

DISCIPLINARY RECORDS

	PLAYER	YELLOW	RED	AVE
1	Demel	5	0	**207**
2	Kruska	4	0	**240**
3	Oliseh	3	0	**265**
4	Jensen	3	1	**309**
5	Worns	5	1	**421**
6	Koller	6	0	**437**
7	Kringe	5	0	**485**
8	Brzenska	4	0	**494**
9	Dede	5	0	**547**
10	Madouni	1	0	**559**
11	Metzelder, C	2	0	**618**
12	Smolarek	2	0	**640**
13	Warmuz	1	0	**720**
	Other	12	0	
	TOTAL	**58**	**2**	

TOP POINT EARNERS

	PLAYER	GAMES	AV PTS
1	Christoph Metzelder	13	**2.31**
2	Ebi Smolarek	14	**2.00**
3	Markus Brzenska	22	**1.82**
4	Roman Weidenfeller	26	**1.81**
5	Florian Kringe	26	**1.77**
6	Leonardo Dede	29	**1.76**
7	Sebastian Kehl	32	**1.69**
8	Ewerthon	25	**1.68**
9	Christian Worns	28	**1.57**
10	Niclas Jensen	12	**1.50**
	CLUB AVERAGE:		**1.62**

LEAGUE APPEARANCES, BOOKINGS AND CAPS

	AGE (on 01/07/05)	IN NAMED 18	APPEARANCES	COUNTING GAMES	MINUTES ON PITCH	YELLOW CARDS	RED CARDS	THIS SEASON	HOME COUNTRY
Goalkeepers									
Matthias Kleinsteiber	27	6	0	0	0	0	0	-	Germany
Soren Pirson	19	1	0	0	0	0	0	-	Germany
Guillaume Warmuz	34	27	8	8	720	1	0	-	France
Roman Weidenfeller	24	34	26	26	2340	3	0	-	Germany
Defenders									
Andre Bergdolmo	33	30	12	8	805	1	0	-	Norway
Markus Brzenska	21	26	23	22	1979	4	0	-	Germany
Marc Heitmeier	20	3	0	0	0	0	0	-	Germany
Uwe Hunemeier	19	2	0	0	0	0	0	-	Germany
Sebastian Kehl	25	32	32	32	2880	4	0	-	Germany
Patrick Kohlmann	22	1	1	0	42	0	0	-	Germany
Ahmed Madouni	24	19	8	4	559	1	0	-	France
Christoph Metzelder	24	16	15	13	1237	2	0	-	Germany
Malte Metzelder	23	1	1	1	79	0	0	-	Germany
Sascha Rammel	20	7	0	0	0	0	0	-	Germany
Christian Worns	33	29	29	28	2526	5	1	6	Germany (19)
Midfielders									
Otto Addo	30	11	3	0	34	0	0	-	Ghana
Leonardo Dede	27	33	33	29	2738	5	0	-	Brazil
Guy Demel	24	24	16	10	1038	5	0	1	Ivory Coast (44)
Evanilson	29	9	9	9	810	0	0	-	Brazil
Niclas Jensen	30	33	16	12	1238	3	1	8	Denmark (19)
Florian Kringe	22	33	30	26	2429	5	0	-	Germany
Marc-Andre Kruska	18	24	18	8	962	4	0	-	Germany
Sunday Oliseh	30	13	11	8	796	3	0	-	Nigeria
Lars Ricken	28	31	17	8	1041	0	0	-	Germany
Tomas Rosicky	24	27	27	25	2304	3	0	7	Czech Republic (2)
Sahr Senesie	20	19	10	1	197	0	0	-	Sierra Leone
Forwards									
Ewerthon	24	28	28	25	2177	1	0	-	Brazil
Salvatore Gambino	21	15	10	1	263	1	0	-	Italy
Jan Koller	32	30	30	29	2622	6	0	6	Czech Republic (2)
Akgun Mehmet	18	4	1	0	24	0	0	-	Turkey
David Odonkor	21	12	7	3	435	2	0	-	Germany
Mahir Saglik	22	6	0	0	0	0	0	-	Turkey
Ebi Smolarek	24	15	15	14	1280	2	0	-	Poland
Marcus Steegmann	24	3	3	0	73	0	0	-	Germany

TEAM OF THE SEASON

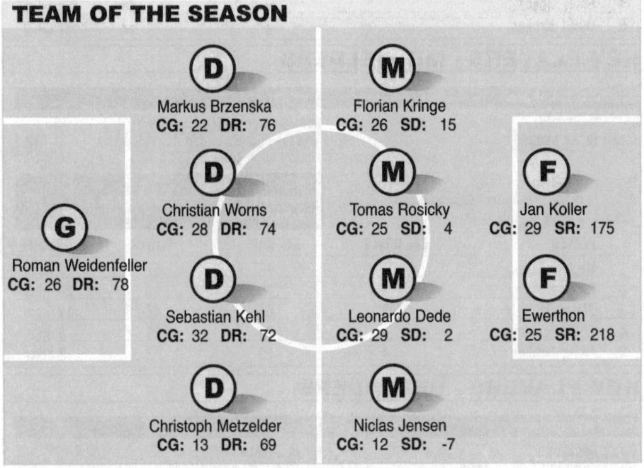
D
Markus Brzenska
CG: 22 DR: 76
M
Florian Kringe
CG: 26 SD: 15
D
Christian Worns
CG: 28 DR: 74
M
Tomas Rosicky
CG: 25 SD: 4
F
Jan Koller
CG: 29 SR: 175
G
Roman Weidenfeller
CG: 26 DR: 78
D
Sebastian Kehl
CG: 32 DR: 72
M
Leonardo Dede
CG: 29 SD: 2
F
Ewerthon
CG: 25 SR: 218
D
Christoph Metzelder
CG: 13 DR: 69
M
Niclas Jensen
CG: 12 SD: -7

SQUAD APPEARANCES

Match	1	2	3	4	5	6	7	8	9	10	11	12	13	14	15	16	17	18	19	20	21	22	23	24	25	26	27	28	29	30	31	32	33	34
Venue	H	A	H	A	H	A	H	A	H	A	H	A	A	H	A	H	A	A	H	A	H	A	H	A	H	A	H	A	H	H	A	H	A	H
Competition	L	L	L	L	L	L	L	L	L	L	L	L	L	L	L	L	L	L	L	L	L	L	L	L	L	L	L	L	L	L	L	L	L	L
Result	L	W	D	D	D	D	D	L	L	W	W	L	L	W	L	L	D	W	D	W	W	L	W	D	L	W	W	W	D	W	D	W	W	W

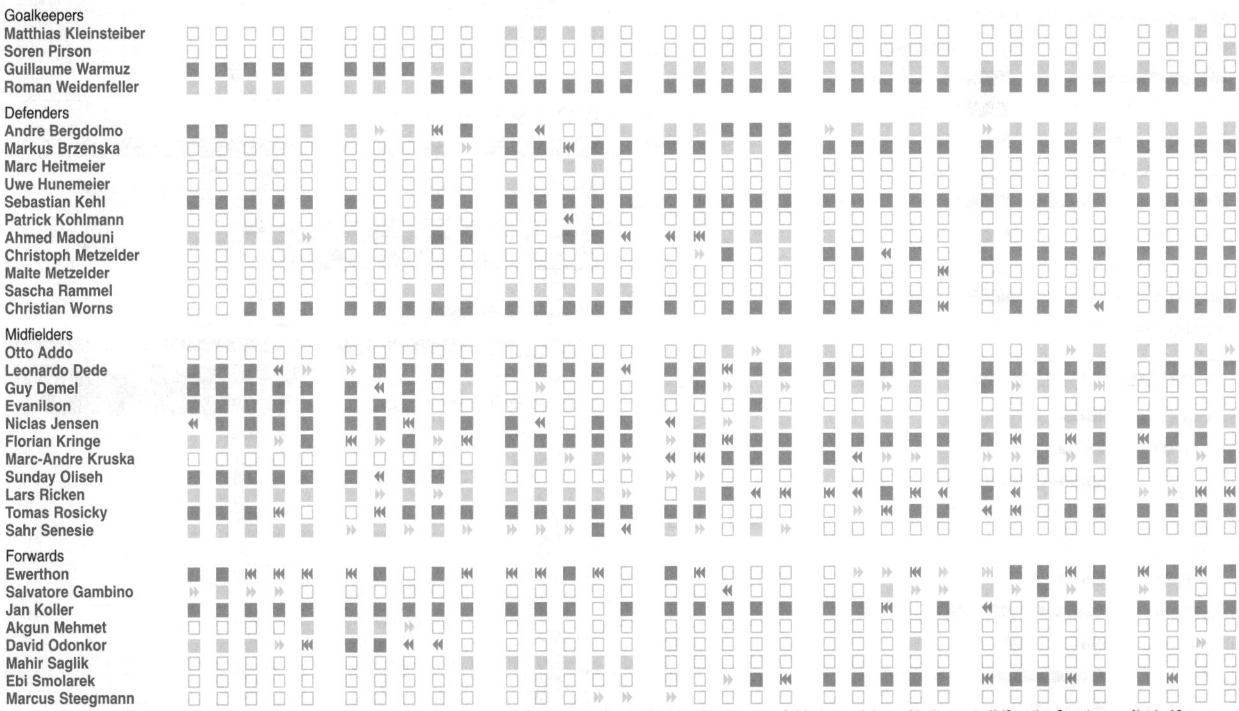
Goalkeepers
Matthias Kleinsteiber
Soren Pirson
Guillaume Warmuz
Roman Weidenfeller
Defenders
Andre Bergdolmo
Markus Brzenska
Marc Heitmeier
Uwe Hunemeier
Sebastian Kehl
Patrick Kohlmann
Ahmed Madouni
Christoph Metzelder
Malte Metzelder
Sascha Rammel
Christian Worns
Midfielders
Otto Addo
Leonardo Dede
Guy Demel
Evanilson
Niclas Jensen
Florian Kringe
Marc-Andre Kruska
Sunday Oliseh
Lars Ricken
Tomas Rosicky
Sahr Senesie
Forwards
Ewerthon
Salvatore Gambino
Jan Koller
Akgun Mehmet
David Odonkor
Mahir Saglik
Ebi Smolarek
Marcus Steegmann

KEY: On all match | On bench | Subbed or sent off (Counting game) | Subbed or sent off (playing less than 70 minutes) | Subbed on from bench (Counting Game) | Subbed on (playing less than 70 minutes) | Subbed on and then subbed or sent off (Counting Game) | Subbed on and then subbed or sent off (playing less than 70 minutes) | Not in 16

HAMBURG SV

Final Position: **8th**

KEY: Won / Drawn / Lost

						Attendance
1	grpr1	**Bayern Munich**	H	L	0-2		55,000
2	grpr1	**Mainz**	A	L	1-2	Van Buyten 28	19,000
3	grpr1	**Nuremburg**	H	W	4-3	Van Buyten 12; Schlicke 40; Mpenza 51; Lauth 86	40,000
4	grpr1	**Stuttgart**	A	L	0-2		44,000
5	grpr1	**Kaiserslautern**	A	L	1-2	Wicky 64	36,000
6	grpr1	**Hertha Berlin**	H	W	2-1	Takahara 3,80	43,000
7	grpr1	**B Leverkusen**	A	L	0-3		22,000
8	grpr1	**Arminia B**	H	L	0-2		43,000
9	grpr1	**B Dortmund**	A	W	2-0	Mpenza 9; Jarolim 70	80,000
10	grpr1	**Freiburg**	H	W	4-0	Mpenza 5; Barbarez 28,51,58	42,000
11	grpr1	**W Bremen**	A	D	1-1	Jarolim 22	43,000
12	grpr1	**Schalke**	H	L	1-2	Beinlich 47	53,000
13	grpr1	**Hansa Rostock**	A	W	6-0	Benjamin 21; Jarolim 36,63; Takahara 43; Moreira 48; Romeo 82	18,000
14	grpr1	**Wolfsburg**	H	W	3-1	Van Buyten 39; Barbarez 45; Romeo 90	48,000
15	grpr1	**B M'gladbach**	A	W	3-1	Barbarez 41,81 pen; Beinlich 44	50,000
16	grpr1	**Hannover 96**	H	L	0-2		50,000
17	grpr1	**Bochum**	A	W	2-1	Barbarez 26; Benjamin 34	28,000
18	grpr1	**Bayern Munich**	A	L	0-3		39,000
19	grpr1	**Mainz**	H	W	2-1	Barbarez 31; Lauth 80	43,000
20	grpr1	**Nuremburg**	A	W	3-1	Takahara 31,53; Lauth 90	30,000
21	grpr1	**Stuttgart**	H	W	2-1	Barbarez 17; Van Buyten 54	49,000
22	grpr1	**Kaiserslautern**	H	W	2-1	Takahara 29; Moreira 40	52,000
23	grpr1	**Hertha Berlin**	A	L	1-4	Barbarez 78	30,000
24	grpr1	**B Leverkusen**	H	W	1-0	Van Buyten 21	48,000
25	grpr1	**Arminia B**	A	W	4-3	Lauth 2; Barbarez 38; Boulahrouz 43; Mahdavikia 71	27,000
26	grpr1	**B Dortmund**	H	L	2-3	Benjamin 29; Beinlich 57	55,000
27	grpr1	**Freiburg**	A	D	1-1	Moreira 41	20,000
28	grpr1	**W Bremen**	H	L	1-2	Mahdavikia 58	56,000
29	grpr1	**Schalke**	A	W	2-1	Wicky 62; Mpenza 87	61,000
30	grpr1	**Hansa Rostock**	H	W	3-0	Mpenza 53; Benjamin 61; Takahara 64	56,000
31	grpr1	**Wolfsburg**	A	L	0-1		27,000
32	grpr1	**B M'gladbach**	H	D	0-0		45,000
33	grpr1	**Hannover 96**	A	L	1-2	Benjamin 12	49,000
34	grpr1	**Bochum**	H	L	0-1		55,000

MONTHLY POINTS TALLY

AUGUST	3	33%
SEPTEMBER	3	33%
OCTOBER	7	47%
NOVEMBER	9	75%
DECEMBER	3	50%
JANUARY	3	50%
FEBRUARY	9	75%
MARCH	6	67%
APRIL	7	58%
MAY	1	8%

KEY PLAYERS - GOALSCORERS

Sergei Barbarez

Goals in the League	11	Player Strike Rate Average number of minutes between League goals scored by player	235
Contribution to Attacking Power Average number of minutes between League team goals while on pitch	54	Club Strike Rate Average number of minutes between League goals scored by club	56

	PLAYER	LGE GOALS	POWER	STRIKE RATE
1	Sergei Barbarez	11	54	235 mins
2	Naohiro Takahara	7	52	288 mins
3	Collin Benjamin	5	54	339 mins
4	Emile Mpenza	5	75	407 mins
5	David Jarolim	4	52	597 mins

KEY PLAYERS - MIDFIELDERS

Naohiro Takahara

Goals in the League	7	Contribution to Attacking Power Average number of minutes between League team goals while on pitch	52
Defensive Rating Average number of mins between goals conceded while on the pitch	72	Scoring Difference Defensive Rating minus Contribution to Attacking Power	20

	PLAYER	LGE GOALS	DEF RATE	POWER	SCORE DIFF
1	Naohiro Takahara	7	72	52	20 mins
2	Raphael Wicky	2	70	50	20 mins
3	Stefan Beinlich	3	64	47	17 mins
4	Collin Benjamin	5	63	55	8 mins
5	David Jarolim	4	60	52	8 mins

KEY PLAYERS - DEFENDERS

Rene Klingbeil

Goals Conceded Number of League goals conceded while the player was on the pitch	27	Clean Sheets In games when player was on pitch for at least 70 minutes	5
Defensive Rating Ave number of mins between League goals conceded while on the pitch	74	Club Defensive Rating Average number of mins between League goals conceded by the club this season	61

	PLAYER	CON LGE	CLEAN SHEETS	DEF RATE
1	Rene Klingbeil	27	5	74 mins
2	Khalid Boulahrouz	33	5	64 mins
3	Bjorn Schlicke	34	3	61 mins
4	Daniel Van Buyten	50	6	61 mins
5	Bastian Reinhardt	24	1	49 mins

KEY GOALKEEPER

Martin Pieckenhagen

Goals Conceded in the League	36	Counting Games League games when player was on pitch for at least 70 minutes	23
Defensive Rating Ave number of mins between League goals conceded while on the pitch	58	Clean Sheets In games when player was on pitch for at least 70 minutes	3

LEAGUE GOALS

Sergei Barbarez

Minutes on the pitch	2581	Goals in the League	11
League average (mins between goals)	235		

	PLAYER	MINS	GOALS	AVE
1	Barbarez	2581	11	235
2	Takahara	2015	7	288
3	Mpenza	2035	5	407
4	Van Buyten	3060	5	612
5	Benjamin	1697	5	339
6	Lauth	391	4	98
7	Jarolim	2389	4	597
8	Beinlich	2416	3	805
9	Mahdavikia	1264	2	632
10	Wicky	2088	2	1044
11	Romeo	248	2	124
12	Moreira	1265	2	633
13	Boulahrouz	2124	1	2124
	Other		2	
	TOTAL		55	

DISCIPLINARY

	PLAYER	YELLOW	RED	AVE
1	Boulahrouz	10	1	193
2	Beinlich	9	0	268
3	Rahn	2	0	268
4	Barbarez	8	1	286
5	Klingbeil	7	0	287
6	Schlicke	7	0	294
7	Wicky	7	0	298
8	Mahdavikia	3	1	316
9	Moreira	4	0	316
10	Benjamin	5	0	339
11	Jarolim	7	0	341
12	Reinhardt	3	0	393
13	Mpenza	5	0	407
	Other	3	0	
	TOTAL	80	3	

TOP POINT EARNERS

	PLAYER	GAMES	AV PTS
1	Naohiro Takahara	16	1.94
2	Rene Klingbeil	20	1.90
3	Stefan Beinlich	26	1.73
4	Bjorn Schlicke	21	1.67
5	David Jarolim	23	1.65
6	Martin Pieckenhagen	23	1.61
7	Raphael Wicky	22	1.59
8	Sergei Barbarez	29	1.55
9	Khalid Boulahrouz	23	1.52
10	Daniel Van Buyten	34	1.50
	CLUB AVERAGE:		1.50

LEAGUE APPEARANCES, BOOKINGS AND CAPS

	AGE (on 01/07/05)	IN NAMED 18	APPEARANCES	COUNTING GAMES	MINUTES ON PITCH	YELLOW CARDS	RED CARDS	THIS SEASON	HOME COUNTRY
Goalkeepers									
Martin Pieckenhagen	33	32	23	23	2070	0	0	-	Germany
Stefan Wachter	27	34	11	11	990	0	0	-	Germany
Defenders									
Khalid Boulahrouz	23	24	24	23	2124	10	1	7	Holland (5)
Carlos Donde Jean	21	4	1	0	27	0	0	-	Brazil
Stephan Kling	24	7	5	2	340	1	0	-	Germany
Rene Klingbeil	24	27	25	20	2010	7	0	-	Germany
Bastian Reinhardt	29	27	19	13	1180	3	0	-	Germany
Bjorn Schlicke	24	31	26	21	2058	7	0	-	Germany
Daniel Van Buyten	27	34	34	34	3060	3	0	6	Belgium (42)
Midfielders									
Sergei Barbarez	33	30	30	29	2581	8	1	-	Bosnia
Stefan Beinlich	33	32	29	26	2416	9	0	-	Germany
Collin Benjamin	26	30	26	16	1697	5	0	-	Namibia
Miso Brecko	21	27	7	4	369	2	1	-	Slovenia
Oliver Hampel	20	5	0	0	0	0	0	-	Germany
Vjatscheslaw Hleb	22	13	3	0	43	1	0	-	Belarus
David Jarolim	26	33	31	23	2389	7	0	-	Czech Republic
Alexander Laas	21	9	1	0	9	0	0	-	Germany
Christian Rahn	26	16	14	3	536	2	0	-	Germany
Naohiro Takahara	26	32	31	16	2015	0	0	-	Japan
Charles Takyi	20	1	0	0	0	0	0	-	Germany
Piotr Trochowski	21	3	3	0	90	0	0	-	Germany
Raphael Wicky	28	26	25	22	2088	7	0	2	Switzerland (45)
Forwards									
Mustafa Kucukovic	18	16	9	1	287	2	0	-	Germany
Benjamin Lauth	23	10	10	3	391	2	0	-	Germany
Mehdi Mahdavikia	27	32	25	8	1264	3	1	-	Iran
Almani Moreira	27	27	21	9	1265	4	0	-	Portugal
Emile Mpenza	27	26	26	21	2035	5	0	3	Belgium (42)
Bernardo Romeo	27	11	6	2	248	0	0	-	Argentina
Eren Sen	20	5	0	0	0	0	0	-	Germany

TEAM OF THE SEASON

G – Martin Pieckenhagen – CG: 23 DR: 58

D – Rene Klingbeil – CG: 20 DR: 74

D – Khalid Boulahrouz – CG: 23 DR: 64

D – Bjorn Schlicke – CG: 21 DR: 61

D – Daniel Van Buyten – CG: 34 DR: 61

M – Naohiro Takahara – CG: 16 SD: 20

M – Raphael Wicky – CG: 22 SD: 20

M – Stefan Beinlich – CG: 26 SD: 17

M – Collin Benjamin – CG: 16 SD: 8

F – Emile Mpenza – CG: 21 SR: 407

F – Sergei Barbarez* – CG: 29 SR: 235

SQUAD APPEARANCES

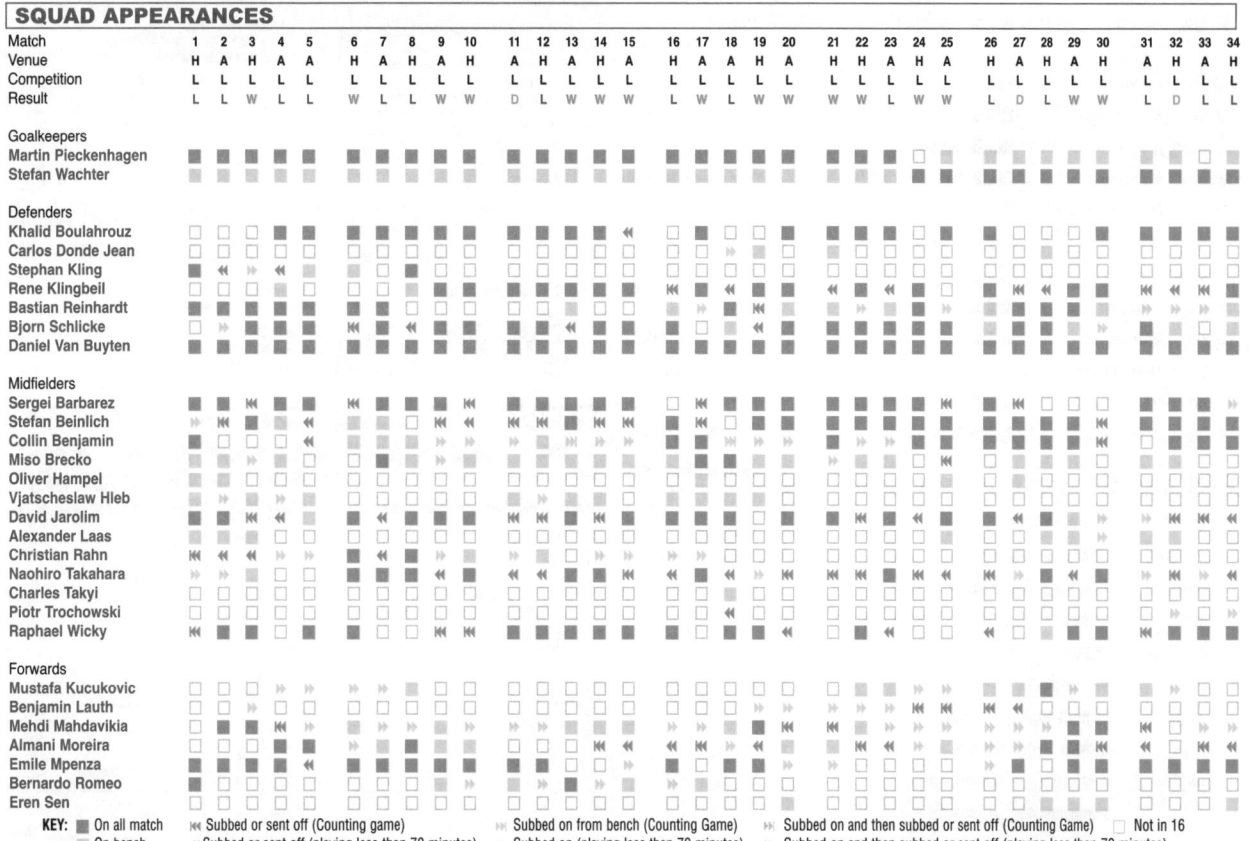

Match	1	2	3	4	5	6	7	8	9	10	11	12	13	14	15	16	17	18	19	20	21	22	23	24	25	26	27	28	29	30	31	32	33	34
Venue	H	A	H	A	A	H	A	H	A	H	A	H	A	H	A	H	A	A	H	A	H	H	A	H	A	H	A	H	A	H	A	H	A	H
Competition	L	L	L	L	L	L	L	L	L	L	L	L	L	L	L	L	L	L	L	L	L	L	L	L	L	L	L	L	L	L	L	L	L	L
Result	L	L	W	L	L	W	L	L	W	W	D	L	W	W	W	L	W	L	W	W	W	W	L	W	W	L	D	L	W	W	L	D	L	L

Goalkeepers
Martin Pieckenhagen
Stefan Wachter

Defenders
Khalid Boulahrouz
Carlos Donde Jean
Stephan Kling
Rene Klingbeil
Bastian Reinhardt
Bjorn Schlicke
Daniel Van Buyten

Midfielders
Sergei Barbarez
Stefan Beinlich
Collin Benjamin
Miso Brecko
Oliver Hampel
Vjatscheslaw Hleb
David Jarolim
Alexander Laas
Christian Rahn
Naohiro Takahara
Charles Takyi
Piotr Trochowski
Raphael Wicky

Forwards
Mustafa Kucukovic
Benjamin Lauth
Mehdi Mahdavikia
Almani Moreira
Emile Mpenza
Bernardo Romeo
Eren Sen

KEY: On all match; On bench; Subbed or sent off (Counting game); Subbed or sent off (playing less than 70 minutes); Subbed on from bench (Counting Game); Subbed on (playing less than 70 minutes); Subbed on and then subbed or sent off (Counting Game); Subbed on and then subbed or sent off (playing less than 70 minutes); Not in 16

VFL WOLFSBURG

Final Position: **9th**

KEY: Won / Drawn / Lost

							Attendance
1	grpr1	**B Dortmund**	A	W	2-1	Brdaric 43,64	73,000
2	grpr1	**Freiburg**	H	L	0-1		23,000
3	grpr1	**W Bremen**	A	W	2-1	Brdaric 46; Thiam 53	40,000
4	grpr1	**Schalke**	H	W	3-0	Hristov 31,41; Klimowicz 90	25,000
5	grpr1	**Hansa Rostock**	A	W	2-1	Klimowicz 16; Thiam 78	15,000
6	grpr1	**Kaiserslautern**	H	W	2-1	Petrov 13; Klimowicz 90	20,000
7	grpr1	**B M'gladbach**	H	W	2-1	D'Alessandro 13; Schnoor 43	24,000
8	grpr1	**Hannover 96**	A	L	0-3		34,000
9	grpr1	**Bochum**	H	W	3-0	Thiam 28; Klimowicz 41; D'Alessandro 43	22,000
10	grpr1	**Bayern Munich**	A	L	0-2		35,000
11	grpr1	**Mainz**	H	W	4-3	Petrov 45 pen,45,57,62	22,000
12	grpr1	**Nuremburg**	A	L	0-4		25,000
13	grpr1	**Stuttgart**	H	W	3-0	Brdaric 42; Petrov 69,76	29,000
14	grpr1	**Hamburg**	A	L	1-3	Brdaric 1	48,000
15	grpr1	**Hertha Berlin**	H	L	2-3	Thiam 50; Brdaric 68	25,000
16	grpr1	**B Leverkusen**	A	L	1-2	Klimowicz 5	23,000
17	grpr1	**Arminia B**	H	W	5-0	Rytter 14; Klimowicz 26; Brdaric 38,40; Petrov 67 pen	22,000
18	grpr1	**B Dortmund**	H	L	1-2	Quiroga 82	30,000
19	grpr1	**Freiburg**	A	L	0-1		21,000
20	grpr1	**W Bremen**	H	L	2-3	Brdaric 26; Thiam 49	24,000
21	grpr1	**Schalke**	A	L	0-3		62,000
22	grpr1	**Hansa Rostock**	H	W	4-0	D'Alessandro 3; Klimowicz 7; Thiam 63; Maric 83	23,000
23	grpr1	**Kaiserslautern**	A	D	0-0		35,000
24	grpr1	**B M'gladbach**	A	L	0-1		45,000
25	grpr1	**Hannover 96**	H	W	1-0	Menseguez 6	25,000
26	grpr1	**Bochum**	A	L	1-5	Petrov 53	19,000
27	grpr1	**Bayern Munich**	H	L	0-3		30,000
28	grpr1	**Mainz**	A	W	2-0	Brdaric 64; Schnoor 78	20,000
29	grpr1	**Nuremburg**	H	L	0-1		19,000
30	grpr1	**Stuttgart**	A	D	0-0		48,000
31	grpr1	**Hamburg**	H	W	1-0	Petrov 41	27,000
32	grpr1	**Hertha Berlin**	A	L	1-3	Petrov 17	58,000
33	grpr1	**B Leverkusen**	H	D	2-2	Karhan 24; Brdaric 30	25,000
34	grpr1	**Arminia B**	A	W	2-1	Petrov 41 pen; Brdaric 56	20,000

MONTHLY POINTS TALLY

AUGUST	6	67%
SEPTEMBER	9	100%
OCTOBER	9	60%
NOVEMBER	3	25%
DECEMBER	3	50%
JANUARY	0	0%
FEBRUARY	4	33%
MARCH	3	33%
APRIL	4	33%
MAY	7	58%

KEY PLAYERS - GOALSCORERS

Martin Petrov

Goals in the League	12	Player Strike Rate Average number of minutes between League goals scored by player	206
Contribution to Attacking Power Average number of minutes between League team goals while on pitch	60	**Club Strike Rate** Average number of minutes between League goals scored by club	62

	PLAYER	LGE GOALS	POWER	STRIKE RATE
1	Martin Petrov	12	60	206 mins
2	Thomas Brdaric	12	59	213 mins
3	Diego Fernando Klimowicz	7	55	296 mins
4	Andres D'Alessandro	3	46	448 mins
5	Pablo Thiam	6	63	483 mins

KEY PLAYERS - MIDFIELDERS

Andres D'Alessandro

Goals in the League	3	**Contribution to Attacking Power** Average number of minutes between League team goals while on pitch	46
Defensive Rating **Average number of mins between goals conceded while on the pitch**	67	Scoring Difference Defensive Rating minus Contribution to Attacking Power	21

	PLAYER	LGE GOALS	DEF RATE	POWER	SCORE DIFF
1	Andres D'Alessandro	3	67	46	21 mins
2	Patrick Weiser	0	57	55	2 mins
3	Hans Sarpei	0	68	68	0 mins
4	Pablo Thiam	6	59	63	-4 mins

KEY PLAYERS - DEFENDERS

Kevin Hofland

Goals Conceded Number of League goals conceded while the player was on the pitch	32	**Clean Sheets** In games when player was on pitch for at least 70 minutes	9
Defensive Rating Ave number of mins between League goals conceded while on the pitch	71	**Club Defensive Rating** Average number of mins between League goals conceded by the club this season	60

	PLAYER	CON LGE	CLEAN SHEETS	DEF RATE
1	Kevin Hofland	32	9	71 mins
2	Thomas Rytter	30	8	69 mins
3	Miroslav Karhan	48	10	60 mins
4	Facundo Quiroga	35	6	58 mins
5	Stefan Schnoor	36	6	57 mins

KEY GOALKEEPER

Simon Jentzsch

Goals Conceded in the League	50	**Counting Games** League games when player was on pitch for at least 70 minutes	33
Defensive Rating Ave number of mins between League goals conceded while on the pitch	59	**Clean Sheets** **In games when player was on pitch for at least 70 minutes**	10

LEAGUE GOALS

Thomas Brdaric

Minutes on the pitch	2561	Goals in the League	12
League average (mins between goals)	213		

	PLAYER	MINS	GOALS	AVE
1	Brdaric	2561	12	213
2	Petrov	2469	12	206
3	Klimowicz	2070	7	296
4	Thiam	2899	6	483
5	D'Alessandro	1343	3	448
6	Schnoor	2061	2	1031
7	Hristov	375	2	188
8	Quiroga	2039	1	2039
9	Maric	167	1	167
10	Menseguez	736	1	736
11	Karhan	2875	1	2875
	Other		1	
	TOTAL		49	

DISCIPLINARY RECORDS

	PLAYER	YELLOW	RED	AVE
1	Hofland	12	1	175
2	Schnoor	10	0	206
3	Franz	5	0	223
4	Quiroga	6	2	254
5	Petrov	6	0	411
6	Weiser	4	0	482
7	Klimowicz	4	0	517
8	Sarpei	1	1	608
9	D'Alessandro	1	1	671
10	Rytter	3	0	688
11	Karhan	4	0	718
12	Thiam	3	0	966
13	Fischer	1	0	974
	Other	2	0	
	TOTAL	62	5	

TOP POINT EARNERS

	PLAYER	GAMES	AV PTS
1	Andres D'Alessandro	13	1.77
2	Fernando Klimowicz	22	1.68
3	Kevin Hofland	25	1.64
4	Facundo Quiroga	22	1.64
5	Hans Sarpei	12	1.58
6	Thomas Rytter	22	1.50
7	Miroslav Karhan	32	1.50
8	Stefan Schnoor	22	1.50
9	Patrick Weiser	21	1.48
10	Thomas Brdaric	28	1.46
	CLUB AVERAGE:		1.41

LEAGUE APPEARANCES, BOOKINGS AND CAPS

	AGE (on 01/07/05)	IN NAMED 18	APPEARANCES	COUNTING GAMES	MINUTES ON PITCH	YELLOW CARDS	RED CARDS	THIS SEASON	HOME COUNTRY
Goalkeepers									
Simon Jentzsch	29	33	33	33	2970	0	0	-	Germany
Andre Lenz	31	33	1	1	90	0	0	-	Germany
Patrick Platins	22	1	0	0	0	0	0	-	Germany
Defenders									
Marino Biliskov	29	22	8	1	223	0	0	-	Croatia
Karsten Fischer	21	16	14	10	974	1	0	-	Germany
Maik Franz	23	31	16	11	1119	5	0	-	Germany
Kevin Hofland	26	27	27	25	2284	12	1	2	Holland (5)
Mirko Hrgovic	26	18	7	0	48	1	0	-	Bosnia
Miroslav Karhan	29	34	34	32	2875	4	0	-	Slovakia
Stefan Lorenz	23	3	0	0	0	0	0	-	Germany
Facundo Quiroga	27	24	24	22	2039	6	2	6	Argentina (3)
Thomas Rytter	31	27	25	22	2065	3	0	-	Denmark
Stefan Schnoor	34	32	26	22	2061	10	0	-	Germany
Midfielders									
Oscar Ahumada	22	13	4	0	73	0	0	-	Argentina
Andres D'Alessandro	24	19	19	13	1343	1	1	5	Argentina (3)
Marian Hristov	31	6	6	3	375	1	0	-	Bulgaria
Cedric Makiadi	21	10	8	1	201	0	0	-	Congo DR
Hans Sarpei	29	32	21	12	1217	1	1	-	Germany
Pablo Thiam	31	33	33	32	2899	3	0	-	Guinea
Patrick Weiser	33	22	22	21	1931	4	0	-	Germany
Forwards									
Thomas Brdaric	30	32	32	28	2561	2	0	6	Germany (19)
Fernando Klimowicz	31	27	27	22	2070	4	0	-	Argentina
Tomislav Maric	32	17	11	0	167	0	0	-	Croatia
J-Carlos Menseguez	21	25	18	4	736	0	0	-	Argentina
Martin Petrov	26	31	30	27	2469	6	0	-	Bulgaria
Roy Prager	33	5	0	0	0	0	0	-	Germany
Christian Ritter	20	2	2	1	135	0	0	-	Germany
Marko Topic	29	28	21	4	571	0	0	-	Bosnia

TEAM OF THE SEASON

D
Kevin Hofland
CG: 25 DR: 71
M
Andres D'Alessandro
CG: 13 SD: 21
D
Thomas Rytter
CG: 22 DR: 69
M
Patrick Weiser
CG: 21 SD: 2
F
Martin Petrov
CG: 27 SR: 206
G
Simon Jentzsch
CG: 33 DR: 59
D
Miroslav Karhan
CG: 32 DR: 60
M
Hans Sarpei
CG: 12 SD: 0
F
Thomas Brdaric
CG: 28 SR: 213
D
Facundo Quiroga
CG: 22 DR: 58
M
Pablo Thiam
CG: 32 SD: -4

SQUAD APPEARANCES

Match	1	2	3	4	5	6	7	8	9	10	11	12	13	14	15	16	17	18	19	20	21	22	23	24	25	26	27	28	29	30	31	32	33	34
Venue	A	H	A	H	A	H	H	A	H	A	H	A	H	A	H	A	H	H	A	H	A	H	A	A	H	A	H	A	H	A	H	A	H	A
Competition	L	L	L	L	L	L	L	L	L	L	L	L	L	L	L	L	L	L	L	L	L	L	L	L	L	L	L	L	L	L	L	L	L	L
Result	W	L	W	W	W	W	W	L	W	L	W	L	W	L	L	L	W	L	L	L	L	W	D	L	W	L	L	W	L	D	W	L	D	W

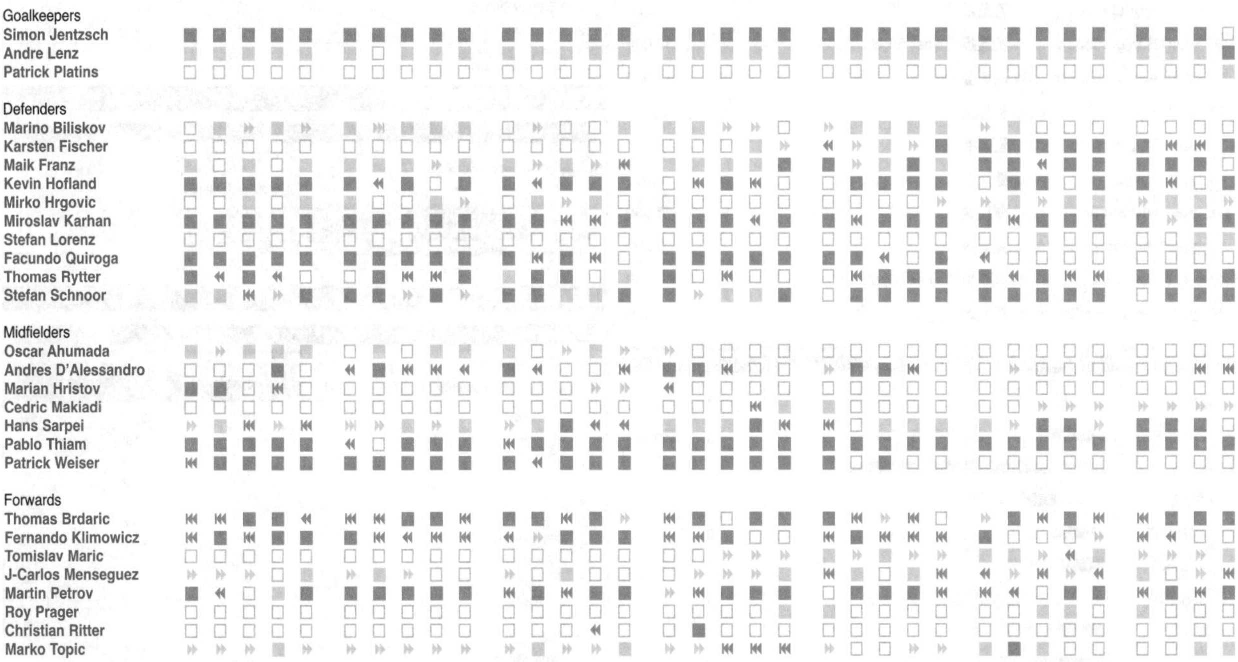
Goalkeepers
Simon Jentzsch
Andre Lenz
Patrick Platins
Defenders
Marino Biliskov
Karsten Fischer
Maik Franz
Kevin Hofland
Mirko Hrgovic
Miroslav Karhan
Stefan Lorenz
Facundo Quiroga
Thomas Rytter
Stefan Schnoor
Midfielders
Oscar Ahumada
Andres D'Alessandro
Marian Hristov
Cedric Makiadi
Hans Sarpei
Pablo Thiam
Patrick Weiser
Forwards
Thomas Brdaric
Fernando Klimowicz
Tomislav Maric
J-Carlos Menseguez
Martin Petrov
Roy Prager
Christian Ritter
Marko Topic

KEY: ■ On all match
■ On bench
⏮ Subbed or sent off (Counting game)
« Subbed or sent off (playing less than 70 minutes)
⏭ Subbed on from bench (Counting Game)
» Subbed on (playing less than 70 minutes)
⏭ Subbed on and then subbed or sent off (Counting Game)
» Subbed on and then subbed or sent off (playing less than 70 minutes)
□ Not in 16

HANNOVER 96

Final Position: **10th**

KEY: Won Drawn Lost

							Attendance
1	grpr1	B Leverkusen	A	L	1-2	Tarnat 14	20,000
2	grpr1	B Dortmund	A	D	1-1	Mertesacker 90	74,000
3	grpr1	Freiburg	H	D	2-2	Stajner 2,8	32,000
4	grpr1	W Bremen	A	L	0-3		43,000
5	grpr1	Schalke	H	W	1-0	Mathis 83	35,000
6	grpr1	Arminia B	H	L	0-1		31,000
7	grpr1	Hansa Rostock	A	W	3-1	Leandro 14; Barnetta 23; Stendel 85	16,000
8	grpr1	Wolfsburg	H	W	3-0	Schroter 7,64; Stendel 90	34,000
9	grpr1	B M'gladbach	A	W	2-0	Mertesacker 17; Cherundolo 33	43,000
10	grpr1	Kaiserslautern	H	W	3-1	Tarnat 33; Stajner 65,86	25,000
11	grpr1	Bochum	H	W	3-0	Christiansen 16; Stendel 64; Leandro 88	26,000
12	grpr1	Bayern Munich	A	L	0-3		52,000
13	grpr1	Mainz	H	W	2-0	Christiansen 34; Schroter 51	31,000
14	grpr1	Nuremburg	A	D	1-1	Stendel 56	22,000
15	grpr1	Stuttgart	H	D	0-0		34,000
16	grpr1	Hamburg	A	W	2-0	Cherundolo 19; Stendel 59	50,000
17	grpr1	Hertha Berlin	H	L	0-1		42,000
18	grpr1	B Leverkusen	H	L	0-3		38,000
19	grpr1	Arminia B	A	W	1-0	Stendel 30	20,000
20	grpr1	B Dortmund	H	L	1-3	Krupnikovic 72 pen	35,000
21	grpr1	Freiburg	A	D	0-0		21,000
22	grpr1	W Bremen	H	L	1-4	Zuraw 38	45,000
23	grpr1	Schalke	A	L	0-1		60,000
24	grpr1	Hansa Rostock	H	L	0-1		25,000
25	grpr1	Wolfsburg	A	L	0-1		25,000
26	grpr1	B M'gladbach	H	W	2-1	Stajner 59; Vinicius 74	37,000
27	grpr1	Kaiserslautern	A	W	2-0	Kaufman 72,90	31,000
28	grpr1	Bochum	A	L	0-1		23,000
39	grpr1	Bayern Munich	H	L	0-1		49,000
40	grpr1	Mainz	A	L	0-2		20,000
41	grpr1	Nuremburg	H	W	1-0	Kaufman 87	28,000
42	grpr1	Stuttgart	A	L	0-1		40,000
43	grpr1	Hamburg	H	W	2-1	Stajner 43; Barnetta 87	49,000
44	grpr1	Hertha Berlin	A	D	0-0		75,000

MONTHLY POINTS TALLY

AUGUST	1	17%
SEPTEMBER	4	33%
OCTOBER	15	100%
NOVEMBER	5	42%
DECEMBER	3	50%
JANUARY	3	50%
FEBRUARY	1	8%
MARCH	3	33%
APRIL	3	25%
MAY	7	58%

KEY PLAYERS - GOALSCORERS

Daniel Stendel

Goals in the League	6	Player Strike Rate Average number of minutes between League goals scored by player	240
Contribution to Attacking Power Average number of minutes between League team goals while on pitch	89	Club Strike Rate Average number of minutes between League goals scored by club	90

	PLAYER	LGE GOALS	POWER	STRIKE RATE
1	Daniel Stendel	6	89	240 mins
2	Jiri Stajner	6	110	312 mins
3	Silvio Schroter	3	84	587 mins
4	Thomas Christiansen	2	73	739 mins
5	Michael Tarnat	2	77	964 mins

KEY PLAYERS - MIDFIELDERS

Michael Tarnat

Goals in the League	2	Contribution to Attacking Power Average number of minutes between League team goals while on pitch	77
Defensive Rating Average number of mins between goals conceded while on the pitc h	92	Scoring Difference Defensive Rating minus Contribution to Attacking Power	15

	PLAYER	LGE GOALS	DEF RATE	POWER	SCORE DIFF
1	Michael Tarnat	2	92	77	15 mins
2	Silvio Schroter	3	93	84	9 mins
3	Nebosja Krupnikovic	1	89	83	6 mins
4	Julian De Guzman	0	79	93	-14 mins
5	Altin Lala	0	88	105	-17 mins

KEY PLAYERS - DEFENDERS

Per Mertesacker

Goals Conceded Number of League goals conceded while the player was on the pitch	31	Clean Sheets In games when player was on pitch for at least 70 minutes	11
Defensive Rating Ave number of mins between League goals conceded while on the pitch	90	Club Defensive Rating Average number of mins between League goals conceded by the club this season	81

	PLAYER	CON LGE	CLEAN SHEETS	DEF RATE
1	Per Mertesacker	31	11	90 mins
2	Dariusz Zuraw	33	10	85 mins
3	Vinicius	11	3	83 mins
4	Steve Cherundolo	36	10	79 mins

KEY GOALKEEPER

Robert Enke

Goals Conceded in the League	38	Counting Games League games when player was on pitch for at least 70 minutes	34
Defensive Rating Ave number of mins between League goals conceded while on the pitch	81	Clean Sheets In games when player was on pitch for at least 70 minutes	11

LEAGUE GOALS

Jiri Stajner

Minutes on the pitch	1870	Goals in the League	6
League average (mins between goals)	312		

	PLAYER	MINS	GOALS	AVE
1	Stajner	1870	6	312
2	Stendel	1438	6	240
3	Kaufman	544	3	181
4	Schroter	1760	3	587
5	Leandro	857	2	429
6	Cherundolo	2832	2	1416
7	Mertesacker	2782	2	1391
8	Tarnat	1927	2	964
9	Christiansen	1477	2	739
10	Barnetta	393	2	197
11	Vinicius	911	1	911
12	Krupnikovic	2497	1	2497
13	Zuraw	2809	1	2809
	Other		1	
	TOTAL		34	

DISCIPLINARY RECORDS

	PLAYER	YELLOW	RED	AVE
1	Lala	7	0	391
2	De Guzman	5	0	520
3	Dabrowski	2	0	535
4	Cherundolo	4	0	708
5	Leandro	1	0	857
6	Vinicius	1	0	911
7	Enke	3	0	1020
8	Krupnikovic	2	0	1248
9	Zuraw	1	1	1404
10	Stendel	1	0	1438
11	Stajner	1	0	1870
12	Tarnat	1	0	1927
13	Mertesacker	1	0	2782
	Other	0	0	
	TOTAL	30	1	

TOP POINT EARNERS

	PLAYER	GAMES	AV PTS
1	Thomas Christiansen	14	1.86
2	Silvio Schroter	15	1.73
3	Michael Tarnat	21	1.48
4	Nebosja Krupnikovic	28	1.43
5	Per Mertesacker	31	1.42
6	Jiri Stajner	15	1.40
7	Daniel Stendel	13	1.38
8	Dariusz Zuraw	31	1.32
9	Robert Enke	34	1.32
10	Steve Cherundolo	31	1.26
	CLUB AVERAGE:		1.32

TEAM OF THE SEASON

D
Per Mertesacker
CG: 31 DR: 90
M
Michael Tarnat
CG: 21 SD: 15
D
Dariusz Zuraw
CG: 31 DR: 85
M
Silvio Schroter
CG: 15 SD: 9
F
Daniel Stendel
CG: 13 SR: 240
G
Robert Enke
CG: 34 DR: 81
D
Steve Cherundolo
CG: 31 DR: 79
M
Nebosja Krupnikovic
CG: 28 SD: 6
F
Jiri Stajner
CG: 15 SR: 312
D
Vinicius*
CG: 10 DR: 183
M
Julian De Guzman
CG: 29 SD: -14

LEAGUE APPEARANCES, BOOKINGS AND CAPS

	AGE (on 01/07/05)	IN NAMED 18	APPEARANCES	COUNTING GAMES	MINUTES ON PITCH	YELLOW CARDS	RED CARDS	THIS SEASON	HOME COUNTRY
Goalkeepers									
Robert Enke	27	34	34	34	3060	3	0	-	Germany
Frank Juric	31	34	0	0	0	0	0	-	Australia
Defenders									
Gurman Agac	22	1	0	0	0	0	0	-	Germany
Steve Cherundolo	26	32	32	31	2832	4	0	-	United States
Dame Diouf	27	1	0	0	0	0	0	-	Senegal
Moritz Marheineke	20	1	0	0	0	0	0	-	Germany
Per Mertesacker	20	32	31	31	2782	1	0	6	Germany (19)
Thomas Schneider	32	26	5	0	35	0	0	-	Germany
Vinicius	24	23	12	10	911	1	0	-	Brazil
Dariusz Zuraw	32	32	32	31	2809	1	1	-	Poland
Midfielders									
Tranquillo Barnetta	20	7	7	4	393	0	0	3	Switzerland (45)
Vladimir But	27	9	1	0	1	0	0	-	Russia
Christophe Dabrowski	27	27	19	9	1071	2	0	-	Germany
Julian De Guzman	24	30	30	29	2602	5	0	-	Canada
Soren Halfar	18	12	7	4	432	1	0	-	Germany
Nebosja Krupnikovic	31	29	29	28	2497	2	0	-	Serbia & Montenegro
Altin Lala	29	32	32	29	2737	7	0	-	Albania
Silvio Schroter	26	28	24	15	1760	0	0	-	Germany
Ricardo Sousa	26	9	5	1	254	1	0	-	Portugal
Danijel Stefulj	32	20	4	0	148	0	0	-	Croatia
Michael Tarnat	35	22	22	21	1927	1	0	-	Germany
Forwards									
Thomas Christiansen	32	28	25	14	1477	0	0	-	Spain
Mohamadou Idrissou	25	5	4	2	214	0	0	-	Cameroon
Jiri Kaufman	25	18	13	3	544	0	0	-	Czech Republic
Leandro	30	23	20	5	857	1	0	-	Brazil
Clint Mathis	28	6	5	2	292	0	0	-	United States
Veljko Paunovic	27	6	6	3	368	2	0	-	Serbia & Montenegro
Jiri Stajner	29	34	31	15	1870	1	0	-	Czech Republic
Daniel Stendel	31	25	23	13	1438	1	0	-	Germany
Roman Wallner	23	23	10	0	188	0	0	-	Austria
Denis Wolf	22	1	1	1	90	0	0	-	Germany

SQUAD APPEARANCES

Match	1	2	3	4	5	6	7	8	9	10	11	12	13	14	15	16	17	18	19	20	21	22	23	24	25	26	27	28	29	30	31	32	33	34
Venue	A	A	H	A	H	H	A	H	A	H	H	A	H	A	H	A	H	H	A	H	A	H	A	H	A	H	A	A	H	A	H	A	H	A
Competition	L	L	L	L	L	L	L	L	L	L	L	L	L	L	L	L	L	L	L	L	L	L	L	L	L	L	L	L	L	L	L	L	L	L
Result	L	D	D	L	W	L	W	W	W	W	W	L	W	D	D	W	L	L	W	L	D	L	L	L	L	W	W	L	L	L	W	L	W	D

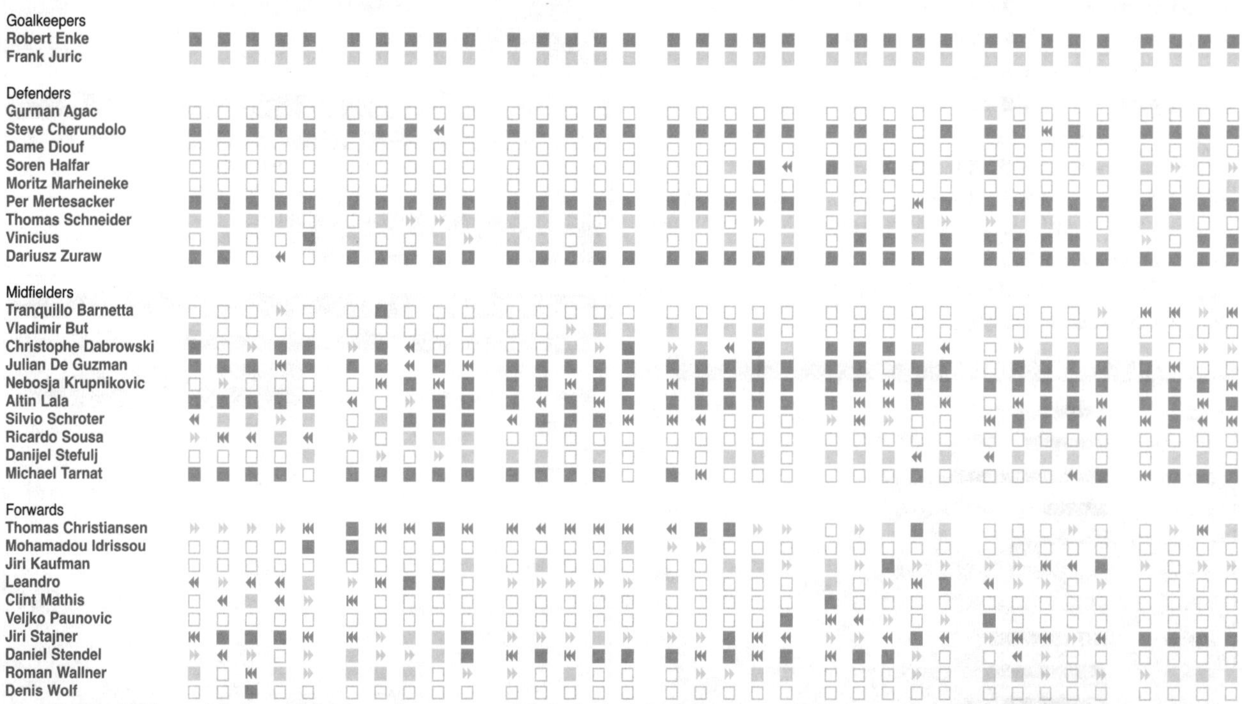
Goalkeepers
Robert Enke
Frank Juric
Defenders
Gurman Agac
Steve Cherundolo
Dame Diouf
Soren Halfar
Moritz Marheineke
Per Mertesacker
Thomas Schneider
Vinicius
Dariusz Zuraw
Midfielders
Tranquillo Barnetta
Vladimir But
Christophe Dabrowski
Julian De Guzman
Nebosja Krupnikovic
Altin Lala
Silvio Schroter
Ricardo Sousa
Danijel Stefulj
Michael Tarnat
Forwards
Thomas Christiansen
Mohamadou Idrissou
Jiri Kaufman
Leandro
Clint Mathis
Veljko Paunovic
Jiri Stajner
Daniel Stendel
Roman Wallner
Denis Wolf

KEY: On all match | On bench | Subbed or sent off (Counting game) | Subbed or sent off (playing less than 70 minutes) | Subbed on from bench (Counting Game) | Subbed on (playing less than 70 minutes) | Subbed on and then subbed or sent off (Counting Game) | Subbed on and then subbed or sent off (playing less than 70 minutes) | Not in 16

MAINZ

Final Position: **11th**

KEY: □ Won □ Drawn □ Lost

							Attendance
1	grpr1	**Stuttgart**	A	L	2-4	Babatz 48; Bodog 75	44,000
2	grpr1	**Hamburg**	H	W	2-1	da Silva 51,53	19,000
3	grpr1	**Hertha Berlin**	A	D	1-1	Kramny 78	28,000
4	grpr1	**B Leverkusen**	H	W	2-0	Weiland, D 65; Auer 68	20,000
5	grpr1	**Arminia B**	A	D	1-1	Azaouagh 82	20,000
6	grpr1	**B Dortmund**	H	D	1-1	Auer 56	20,000
7	grpr1	**Freiburg**	A	W	2-1	Gerber 22; Rose 90	22,000
8	grpr1	**W Bremen**	H	W	2-1	Weiland, D 83; Auer 90	20,000
9	grpr1	**Schalke**	A	L	1-2	Weiland, D 60	62,000
10	grpr1	**Hansa Rostock**	H	W	3-1	Gerber 54; Weiland, N 70; Kramny 90	20,000
11	grpr1	**Wolfsburg**	A	L	3-4	Abel 15; Casey 17; Babatz 75	22,000
12	grpr1	**B M'gladbach**	H	D	1-1	Noveski 58	20,000
13	grpr1	**Hannover 96**	A	L	0-2		31,000
14	grpr1	**Bochum**	H	W	1-0	da Silva 19	20,000
15	grpr1	**Bayern Munich**	A	L	2-4	Babatz 84; Weber 90	50,000
16	grpr1	**Kaiserslautern**	A	L	0-2		40,000
17	grpr1	**Nuremburg**	H	L	0-1		20,000
18	grpr1	**Stuttgart**	H	L	2-3	Gerber 13; Weiland, N 90	20,000
19	grpr1	**Hamburg**	A	L	1-2	Auer 40	43,000
20	grpr1	**Hertha Berlin**	H	L	0-3		20,000
21	grpr1	**B Leverkusen**	A	L	0-2		22,000
22	grpr1	**Arminia B**	H	D	0-0		20,000
23	grpr1	**B Dortmund**	A	L	0-3		75,000
24	grpr1	**Freiburg**	H	W	5-0	Gerber 23; Friedrich 26; Babatz 43 pen; da Silva 71; Thurk 81	20,000
25	grpr1	**W Bremen**	A	D	0-0		35,000
26	grpr1	**Schalke**	H	W	2-1	Gerber 1; Thurk 80	20,000
27	grpr1	**Hansa Rostock**	A	L	0-2		22,000
28	grpr1	**Wolfsburg**	H	L	0-2		20,000
29	grpr1	**B M'gladbach**	A	D	1-1	Thurk 90	53,000
30	grpr1	**Hannover 96**	H	W	2-0	Abel 23; Gerber 79	20,000
31	grpr1	**Bochum**	A	W	6-2	Auer 6; Thurk 60; Gerber 65; da Silva 68; Weigelt 78; Casey 84	30,000
32	grpr1	**Bayern Munich**	H	L	2-4	Auer 31; Thurk 59	20,000
33	grpr1	**Kaiserslautern**	H	W	3-2	Abel 29,47; Noveski 57	20,000
34	grpr1	**Nuremburg**	A	W	2-1	Weiland, N 15; Thurk 87	35,000

MONTHLY POINTS TALLY

AUGUST	4	44%
SEPTEMBER	5	56%
OCTOBER	9	60%
NOVEMBER	4	33%
DECEMBER	0	0%
JANUARY	0	0%
FEBRUARY	1	8%
MARCH	7	78%
APRIL	7	47%
MAY	6	67%

KEY PLAYERS - GOALSCORERS

Fabian Gerber

Goals in the League	7	Player Strike Rate Average number of minutes between League goals scored by player	360
Contribution to Attacking Power Average number of minutes between League team goals while on pitch	61	Club Strike Rate Average number of minutes between League goals scored by club	61

	PLAYER	LGE GOALS	POWER	STRIKE RATE
1	Fabian Gerber	7	61	360 mins
2	Benjamin Auer	6	56	398 mins
3	Mathias Abel	4	57	462 mins
4	Antonio da Silva	5	59	540 mins
5	Niclas Weiland	3	76	584 mins

KEY PLAYERS - MIDFIELDERS

Antonio da Silva

Goals in the League	5	Contribution to Attacking Power Average number of minutes between League team goals while on pitch	60
Defensive Rating Average number of mins between League goals conceded while on the pitch	60	Scoring Difference Defensive Rating minus Contribution to Attacking Power	0

	PLAYER	LGE GOALS	DEF RATE	POWER	SCORE DIFF
1	Antonio da Silva	5	60	60	0 mins
2	Manuel Friedrich	1	57	66	-9 mins
3	Christof Babatz	4	57	69	-12 mins
4	Niclas Weiland	3	60	76	-16 mins

KEY PLAYERS - DEFENDERS

Benjamin Weigelt

Goals Conceded Number of League goals conceded while the player was on the pitch	26	Clean Sheets In games when player was on pitch for at least 70 minutes	4
Defensive Rating Ave number of mins between League goals conceded while on the pitch	63	Club Defensive Rating Average number of mins between League goals conceded by the club this season	56

	PLAYER	CON LGE	CLEAN SHEETS	DEF RATE
1	Benjamin Weigelt	26	4	63 mins
2	Mathias Abel	31	5	60 mins
3	Nikolce Noveski	46	5	53 mins
4	Marko Rose	29	2	51 mins

KEY GOALKEEPER

Dimo Wache

Goals Conceded in the League	47	Counting Games League games when player was on pitch for at least 70 minutes	29
Defensive Rating Ave number of mins between League goals conceded while on the pitch	56	Clean Sheets In games when player was on pitch for at least 70 minutes	6

LEAGUE GOALS

Fabian Gerber

Minutes on the pitch	2517	Goals in the League	7
League average (mins between goals)	360		

	PLAYER	MINS	GOALS	AVE
1	Gerber	2517	7	360
2	Thurk	921	6	154
3	Auer	2389	6	398
4	da Silva	2699	5	540
5	Babatz	2611	4	653
6	Abel	1849	4	462
7	Weiland, N	1752	3	584
8	Noveski	2430	2	1215
9	Kramny	733	2	367
10	Casey	1420	2	710
11	Weiland, D	605	2	303
12	Azaouagh	517	1	517
13	Weigelt	1629	1	1629
	Other		5	
	TOTAL		50	

DISCIPLINARY RECORDS

	PLAYER	YELLOW	RED	AVE
1	Weiland, D	4	0	151
2	Balitsch	6	0	175
3	Kramny	2	1	244
4	Azaouagh	2	0	258
5	Rose	4	1	294
6	Casey	4	0	355
7	Weigelt	3	0	543
8	Nikolic	2	0	559
9	Babatz	4	0	652
10	Bodog	1	0	736
11	Weiland, N	2	0	876
12	Thurk	1	0	921
13	Abel	2	0	924
	Other	9	0	
	TOTAL	46	2	

TOP POINT EARNERS

	PLAYER	GAMES	AV PTS
1	Benjamin Weigelt	17	1.59
2	Niclas Weiland	16	1.56
3	Mathias Abel	19	1.47
4	Benjamin Auer	25	1.44
5	Fabian Gerber	27	1.37
6	Christof Babatz	25	1.32
7	Antonio da Silva	29	1.28
8	Dimo Wache	29	1.21
9	Manuel Friedrich	33	1.21
10	Nikolce Noveski	27	1.15
	CLUB AVERAGE:		1.26

TEAM OF THE SEASON

G
Dimo Wache
CG: 29 DR: 56
D
Benjamin Weigelt
CG: 17 DR: 63
D
Mathias Abel
CG: 19 DR: 60
D
Nikolce Noveski
CG: 27 DR: 53
D
Marko Rose
CG: 15 DR: 51
M
Antonio da Silva
CG: 29 SD: 0
M
Manuel Friedrich
CG: 33 SD: -9
M
Christof Babatz
CG: 25 SD: -12
M
Niclas Weiland
CG: 16 SD: -16
F
Fabian Gerber
CG: 27 SR: 360
F
Benjamin Auer
CG: 25 SR: 398

LEAGUE APPEARANCES, BOOKINGS AND CAPS

	AGE (on 01/07/05)	IN NAMED 18	APPEARANCES	COUNTING GAMES	MINUTES ON PITCH	YELLOW CARDS	RED CARDS	THIS SEASON	HOME COUNTRY
Goalkeepers									
Sven Hoffmeister	34	10	0	0	0	0	0	-	Germany
Dimo Wache	31	30	30	29	2655	2	0	-	Germany
Christian Wetklo	25	26	5	4	405	1	0	-	Germany
Defenders									
Mathias Abel	24	29	23	19	1849	2	0	-	Germany
Tamas Bodog	34	21	12	8	736	1	0	-	Hungary
Christian Demirtas	21	5	3	0	31	0	0	-	Germany
Murat Doymus	19	1	0	0	0	0	0	-	Germany
Christopher Ihm	22	2	0	0	0	0	0	-	Germany
Robert Nikolic	36	22	15	11	1118	2	0	-	Germany
Nikolce Noveski	26	28	27	27	2430	2	0	-	Macedonia
Dennis Probst	26	3	0	0	0	0	0	-	Germany
Marko Rose	28	29	17	15	1471	4	1	-	Germany
Benjamin Weigelt	22	33	21	17	1629	3	0	-	Germany
Midfielders									
Mimoun Azaouagh	22	8	8	4	517	2	0	-	Germany
Christof Babatz	30	34	34	25	2611	4	0	-	Germany
Hanno Balitsch	24	14	14	10	1054	6	0	-	Germany
Antonio da Silva	27	32	32	29	2699	0	0	-	Brazil
Manuel Friedrich	25	33	33	33	2955	3	0	-	Germany
Jimmy Kramny	33	30	19	5	733	2	1	-	Germany
Dennis Weiland	30	22	13	5	605	4	0	-	Germany
Niclas Weiland	32	28	27	16	1752	2	0	-	Germany
Forwards									
Benjamin Auer	24	31	31	25	2389	0	0	-	Germany
Connor Casey	23	33	28	12	1420	4	0	-	United States
Markus Dworrak	27	4	3	1	144	0	0	-	Germany
Fabian Gerber	25	30	30	27	2517	2	0	-	Germany
Ranisav Jovanovic	24	20	16	1	387	1	0	-	Serbia & Montenegro
Christoph Teinert	25	19	9	2	332	1	0	-	Germany
Michael Thurk	29	15	13	8	921	1	0	-	Germany
Claudius Weber	27	12	7	1	239	0	0	-	Germany

SQUAD APPEARANCES

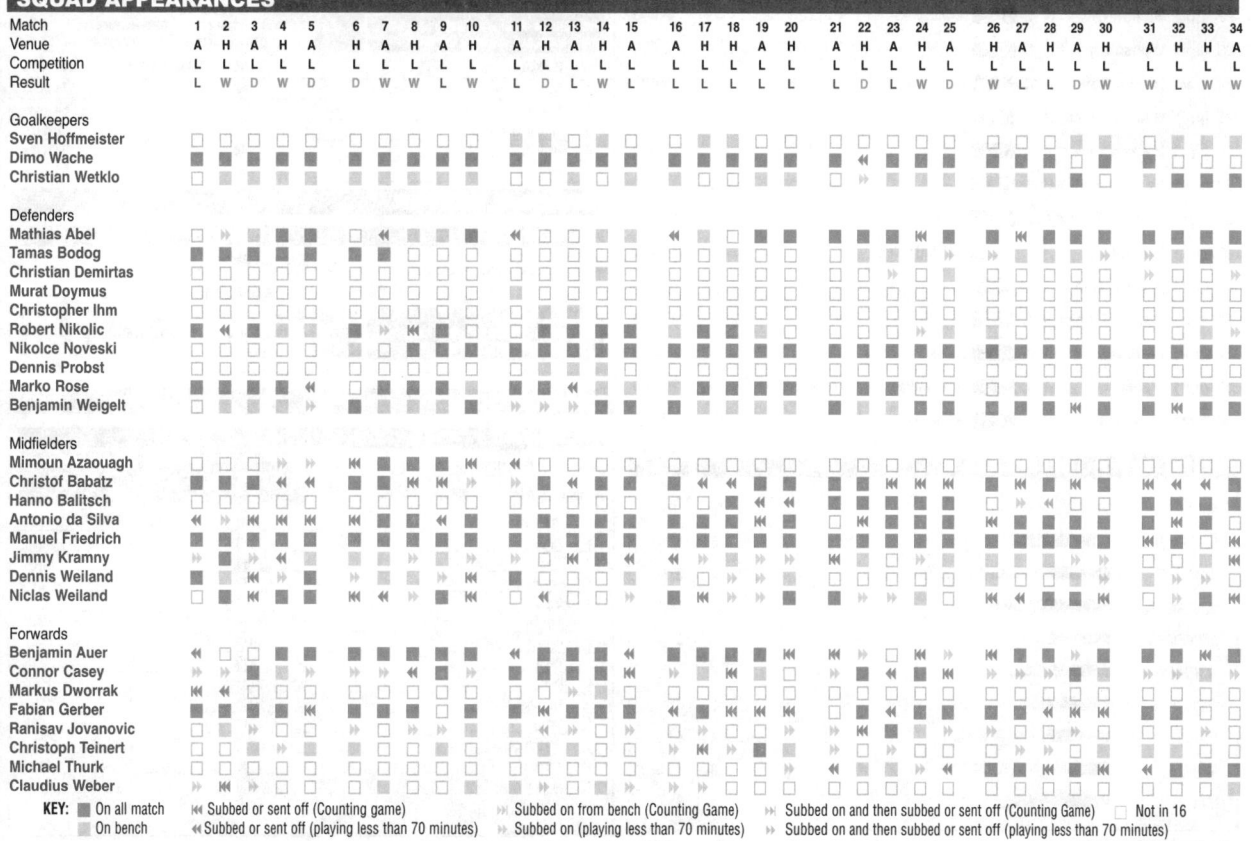

Match	1	2	3	4	5	6	7	8	9	10	11	12	13	14	15	16	17	18	19	20	21	22	23	24	25	26	27	28	29	30	31	32	33	34
Venue	A	H	A	H	A	H	A	H	A	H	A	H	A	H	A	A	H	H	A	H	A	H	A	H	A	H	A	H	A	H	A	H	H	A
Competition	L	L	L	L	L	L	L	L	L	L	L	L	L	L	L	L	L	L	L	L	L	L	L	L	L	L	L	L	L	L	L	L	L	L
Result	L	W	D	W	D	D	W	W	L	W	L	D	L	W	L	L	L	L	L	L	L	D	L	W	D	W	L	L	D	W	W	L	W	W

Goalkeepers
Sven Hoffmeister
Dimo Wache
Christian Wetklo

Defenders
Mathias Abel
Tamas Bodog
Christian Demirtas
Murat Doymus
Christopher Ihm
Robert Nikolic
Nikolce Noveski
Dennis Probst
Marko Rose
Benjamin Weigelt

Midfielders
Mimoun Azaouagh
Christof Babatz
Hanno Balitsch
Antonio da Silva
Manuel Friedrich
Jimmy Kramny
Dennis Weiland
Niclas Weiland

Forwards
Benjamin Auer
Connor Casey
Markus Dworrak
Fabian Gerber
Ranisav Jovanovic
Christoph Teinert
Michael Thurk
Claudius Weber

KEY: On all match · On bench · Subbed or sent off (Counting game) · Subbed or sent off (playing less than 70 minutes) · Subbed on from bench (Counting Game) · Subbed on (playing less than 70 minutes) · Subbed on and then subbed or sent off (Counting Game) · Subbed on and then subbed or sent off (playing less than 70 minutes) · Not in 16

KAISERSLAUTERN

Final Position: **12th**

KEY: ☐Won ☐Drawn ☐Lost

								Attendance
1	grpr1	**Nuremburg**	H	L	1-3	Zandi 58 pen		37,000
2	grpr1	**Schalke**	A	L	1-2	Seitz 18		62,000
3	grpr1	**Stuttgart**	H	L	2-3	Seitz 35; Jancker 38		38,000
4	grpr1	**Hansa Rostock**	A	W	3-2	Drescher 42; Riedl 44; Altintop 56		19,000
5	grpr1	**Hamburg**	H	W	2-1	Zandi 17 pen; Engelhardt 55		36,000
6	grpr1	**Wolfsburg**	A	L	1-2	Jancker 82		20,000
7	grpr1	**Hertha Berlin**	H	L	0-2			30,000
8	grpr1	**B M'gladbach**	A	L	0-2			53,000
9	grpr1	**B Leverkusen**	H	D	0-0			32,000
10	grpr1	**Hannover 96**	A	L	1-3	Amanatidis 26		25,000
11	grpr1	**Arminia B**	H	W	2-1	Teber 81,89		32,000
12	grpr1	**Bochum**	A	D	1-1	Lembi 26		23,000
13	grpr1	**B Dortmund**	H	W	1-0	Zandi 71		37,000
14	grpr1	**Bayern Munich**	A	L	1-3	Riedl 7		35,000
15	grpr1	**Freiburg**	H	W	3-0	Amanatidis 44,70; Zandi 87		30,000
16	grpr1	**Mainz**	H	W	2-0	Abel 20 og; Kosowski 59		40,000
17	grpr1	**W Bremen**	A	D	1-1	Jancker 49		39,000
18	grpr1	**Nuremburg**	A	W	3-1	Lembi 51; Blank 60; Grammozis 84		20,000
19	grpr1	**Schalke**	H	W	2-0	Amanatidis 56; Blank 73		38,000
20	grpr1	**Stuttgart**	A	D	1-1	Engelhardt 61		37,000
21	grpr1	**Hansa Rostock**	H	W	2-1	Seitz 5; Zandi 52		28,000
22	grpr1	**Hamburg**	A	L	1-2	Altintop 53		52,000
23	grpr1	**Wolfsburg**	H	D	0-0			35,000
24	grpr1	**Hertha Berlin**	A	D	1-1	Mettomo 50		35,000
25	grpr1	**B M'gladbach**	H	W	1-0	Altintop 45		39,000
26	grpr1	**B Leverkusen**	A	L	0-2			23,000
27	grpr1	**Hannover 96**	H	L	0-2			31,000
28	grpr1	**Arminia B**	A	W	2-0	Jancker 6; Altintop 24		18,000
29	grpr1	**Bochum**	H	L	1-2	Blank 61 pen		34,000
30	grpr1	**B Dortmund**	A	L	2-4	Altintop 4; Amanatidis 42		76,000
31	grpr1	**Bayern Munich**	H	L	0-4			40,000
32	grpr1	**Freiburg**	A	W	2-1	Blank 24; Zandi 40 pen		18,000
33	grpr1	**Mainz**	A	L	2-3	Amanatidis 35; Noveski 86 og		20,000
34	grpr1	**W Bremen**	H	L	1-2	Altintop 45		40,000

MONTHLY POINTS TALLY

AUGUST	0	0%
SEPTEMBER	6	67%
OCTOBER	4	27%
NOVEMBER	7	58%
DECEMBER	4	67%
JANUARY	6	100%
FEBRUARY	5	42%
MARCH	4	44%
APRIL	3	20%
MAY	3	33%

KEY PLAYERS - GOALSCORERS

Ioannis Amanatidis

Goals in the League	6	Player Strike Rate Average number of minutes between League goals scored by player	279
Contribution to Attacking Power Average number of minutes between League team goals while on pitch	72	Club Strike Rate Average number of minutes between League goals scored by club	71

	PLAYER	LGE GOALS	POWER	STRIKE RATE
1	Ioannis Amanatidis	6	72	279 mins
2	Stefan Blank	4	78	315 mins
3	Ferydoon Zandi	6	68	318 mins
4	Halil Altintop	6	66	368 mins
5	Carsten Jancker	4	71	410 mins

KEY PLAYERS - MIDFIELDERS

Kamil Kosowski

Goals in the League	1	Contribution to Attacking Power Average number of minutes between League team goals while on pitch	67
Defensive Rating Average number of mins between goals conceded while on the pitch	76	Scoring Difference Defensive Rating minus Contribution to Attacking Power	9

	PLAYER	LGE GOALS	DEF RATE	POWER	SCORE DIFF
1	Kamil Kosowski	1	76	67	9 mins
2	Ciriaco Sforza	0	72	66	6 mins
3	Ferydoon Zandi	6	58	68	-10 mins
4	Thomas Riedl	2	60	73	-13 mins

KEY PLAYERS - DEFENDERS

Stefan Blank

Goals Conceded Number of League goals conceded while the player was on the pitch	17	Clean Sheets In games when player was on pitch for at least 70 minutes	4
Defensive Rating Ave number of mins between League goals conceded while on the pitch	74	Club Defensive Rating Average number of mins between League goals conceded by the club this season	59

	PLAYER	CON LGE	CLEAN SHEETS	DEF RATE
1	Stefan Blank	17	4	74 mins
2	Marco Engelhardt	42	8	64 mins
3	Lucien Mettomo	23	4	62 mins
4	Hervi Nzelo Lembi	44	6	62 mins
5	Ingo Hertzsch	48	8	60 mins

KEY GOALKEEPER

Thomas Ernst

Goals Conceded in the League	29	Counting Games League games when player was on pitch for at least 70 minutes	21
Defensive Rating Ave number of mins between League goals conceded while on the pitch	63	Clean Sheets In games when player was on pitch for at least 70 minutes	6

LEAGUE GOALS

Ferydoon Zandi

Minutes on the pitch	1910	Goals in the League	6
League average (mins between goals)	318		

	PLAYER	MINS	GOALS	AVE
1	Zandi	1910	6	318
2	Altintop	2206	6	368
3	Amanatidis	1673	6	279
4	Blank	1260	4	315
5	Jancker	1638	4	410
6	Seitz	1042	3	347
7	Riedl	2629	2	1315
8	Lembi	2727	2	1364
9	Engelhardt	2669	2	1335
10	Teber	516	2	258
11	Drescher	370	1	370
12	Kosowski	1138	1	1138
13	Mettomo	1416	1	1416
	Other		3	
	TOTAL		43	

DISCIPLINARY RECORDS

	PLAYER	YELLOW	RED	AVE
1	Grammozis	3	2	159
2	Teber	3	0	172
3	Nurmela	2	0	227
4	Riedl	9	0	292
5	Blank	4	0	315
6	Engelhardt	8	0	333
7	Seitz	3	0	347
8	Hertzsch	8	0	357
9	Sforza	4	0	361
10	Zandi	5	0	382
11	Tchato	3	0	383
12	Wenzel	4	0	383
13	Lembi	6	0	454
	Other	11	1	
	TOTAL	73	3	

TOP POINT EARNERS

	PLAYER	GAMES	AV PTS
1	Ioannis Amanatidis	15	1.60
2	Stefan Blank	14	1.50
3	Lucien Mettomo	14	1.43
4	Ferydoon Zandi	17	1.41
5	Ciriaco Sforza	13	1.38
6	Marco Engelhardt	30	1.37
7	Ingo Hertzsch	32	1.28
8	Thomas Ernst	20	1.25
9	Hervi Nzelo Lembi	27	1.22
10	Tim Wiese	13	1.08
	CLUB AVERAGE:		1.24

TEAM OF THE SEASON

G
Thomas Ernst
CG: 20 DR: 63
D
Stefan Blank
CG: 14 DR: 74
D
Marco Engelhardt
CG: 30 DR: 64
D
Hervi Nzelo Lembi
CG: 27 DR: 62
D
Lucien Mettomo
CG: 14 DR: 62
M
Ciriaco Sforza
CG: 13 SD: 6
M
Ferydoon Zandi
CG: 17 SD: -10
M
Thomas Riedl
CG: 27 SD: -13
M
Kamil Kosowski*
CG: 11 SD: 9
F
Ioannis Amanatidis
CG: 15 SR: 279
F
Halil Altintop
CG: 21 SR: 368

LEAGUE APPEARANCES, BOOKINGS AND CAPS

	AGE (on 01/07/05)	IN NAMED 18	APPEARANCES	COUNTING GAMES	MINUTES ON PITCH	YELLOW CARDS	RED CARDS	THIS SEASON	HOME COUNTRY
Goalkeepers									
Thomas Ernst	37	34	21	20	1829	0	0	-	Germany
Florian Fromlowitz	19	3	0	0	0	0	0	-	Germany
Jurgen Macho	27	17	0	0	0	0	0	-	Austria
Tim Wiese	23	14	14	13	1231	2	0	-	Germany
Defenders									
Stefan Blank	28	14	14	14	1260	4	0	-	Germany
Marco Engelhardt	24	30	30	30	2669	8	0	2	Germany (19)
Matthias Henn	20	1	1	0	36	0	0	-	Germany
Ingo Hertzsch	27	32	32	32	2861	8	0	-	Germany
Hervi Nzelo Lembi	29	33	33	27	2727	6	0	-	Congo DR
Lucien Mettomo	33	29	17	14	1416	1	1	5	Cameroon (26)
Bill Tchato	30	26	16	10	1149	3	0	4	Cameroon (26)
Timo Wenzel	27	27	19	17	1534	4	0	-	Germany
Midfielders									
Daniel Damm	23	1	0	0	0	0	0	-	Germany
Thomas Drecher	26	1	1	1	90	0	0	-	Germany
Thomas Drescher	26	11	5	3	370	0	0	-	Germany
Jurgen Gjasula	19	20	7	1	166	1	0	-	Germany
Dimitrios Grammozis	27	19	13	7	797	3	2	-	Greece
Kamil Kosowski	27	25	20	11	1138	0	0	-	Poland
Mathias Lehmann	22	2	1	1	72	0	0	-	Germany
Mihael Mikic	25	19	6	1	263	0	0	-	Croatia
Christian Nerlinger	32	9	5	4	383	3	0	-	Germany
Thomas Riedl	29	31	31	27	2629	9	0	-	Germany
Ciriaco Sforza	35	19	19	13	1444	4	0	-	Switzerland
Ferydoon Zandi	26	29	26	17	1910	5	0	-	Germany
Forwards									
Halil Altintop	22	34	30	21	2206	3	0	-	Turkey
Ioannis Amanatidis	23	23	23	15	1673	2	0	-	Greece
Carsten Jancker	30	27	25	15	1638	3	0	-	Germany
Mike Nurmela	33	20	7	5	454	2	0	-	Finland
Jochen Seitz	28	25	19	8	1042	3	0	-	Germany
Selim Teber	24	29	22	1	516	3	0	-	Turkey
Christian Timm	26	4	2	0	72	0	0	-	Germany

SQUAD APPEARANCES

Match	1	2	3	4	5	6	7	8	9	10	11	12	13	14	15	16	17	18	19	20	21	22	23	24	25	26	27	28	29	30	31	32	33	34
Venue	H	A	H	A	H	A	H	A	H	A	H	A	H	A	H	H	A	A	H	A	H	A	H	A	H	A	H	A	H	A	H	A	A	H
Competition	L	L	L	L	L	L	L	L	L	L	L	L	L	L	L	L	L	L	L	L	L	L	L	L	L	L	L	L	L	L	L	L	L	L
Result	L	L	L	W	W	L	L	L	D	L	W	D	W	L	W	W	D	W	W	D	W	L	D	D	W	L	L	W	L	L	L	W	L	L

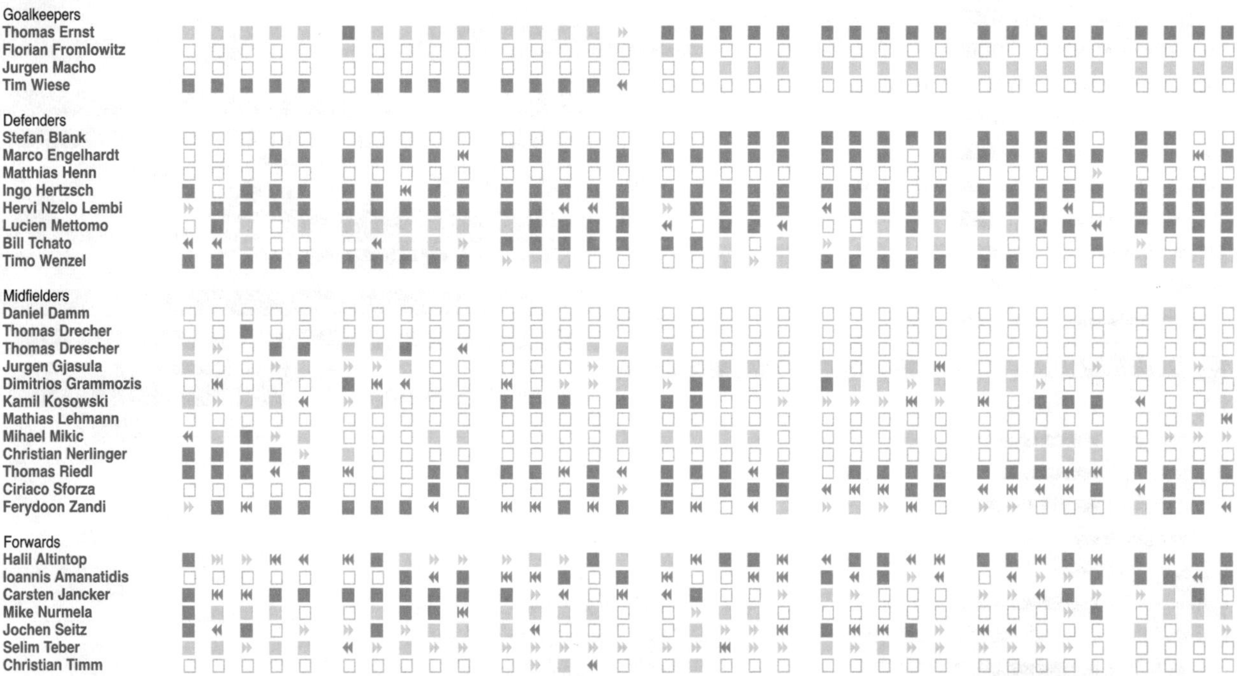

KEY: On all match · On bench · Subbed or sent off (Counting game) · Subbed or sent off (playing less than 70 minutes) · Subbed on from bench (Counting Game) · Subbed on (playing less than 70 minutes) · Subbed on and then subbed or sent off (Counting Game) · Subbed on and then subbed or sent off (playing less than 70 minutes) · Not in 16

ARMINIA BIELEFELD

Final Position: **13th**

KEY: ☐Won ☐Drawn ☐Lost

							Attendance
1	grpr1	**B M'gladbach**	H	D	0-0		27,000
2	grpr1	**Bochum**	H	L	1-2	Buckley 87	18,000
3	grpr1	**Bayern Munich**	A	L	0-1		45,000
4	grpr1	**Mainz**	H	D	1-1	Buckley 64	20,000
5	grpr1	**Nuremburg**	A	W	2-1	Vata 18; Owomoyela 64	18,000
6	grpr1	**Hannover 96**	A	W	1-0	Buckley 79	31,000
7	grpr1	**Stuttgart**	H	L	0-2		23,000
8	grpr1	**Hamburg**	A	W	2-0	Owomoyela 58; Buckley 66	43,000
9	grpr1	**Hertha Berlin**	H	W	1-0	Buckley 41	22,000
10	grpr1	**B Leverkusen**	A	L	2-3	Buckley 20; Vata 71	22,000
11	grpr1	**Kaiserslautern**	A	L	1-2	Buckley 80	32,000
12	grpr1	**B Dortmund**	H	W	1-0	Buckley 8	27,000
13	grpr1	**Freiburg**	A	W	3-2	Buckley 16,87; Owomoyela 20	21,000
14	grpr1	**W Bremen**	H	W	2-1	Vata 45; Kuntzel 77	22,000
15	grpr1	**Schalke**	A	L	1-2	Kauf 20	62,000
16	grpr1	**Hansa Rostock**	H	D	1-1	Owomoyela 64	23,000
17	grpr1	**Wolfsburg**	A	L	0-5		22,000
18	grpr1	**B M'gladbach**	A	L	0-1		45,000
19	grpr1	**Hannover 96**	H	L	0-1		20,000
20	grpr1	**Bochum**	A	D	1-1	Buckley 29	20,000
21	grpr1	**Bayern Munich**	H	W	3-1	Porcello 23; Buckley 61,83	26,000
22	grpr1	**Mainz**	A	D	0-0		20,000
23	grpr1	**Nuremburg**	H	W	3-1	Buckley 6; Owomoyela 19; Pinto 72	18,000
24	grpr1	**Stuttgart**	A	L	1-2	Boakye 77 pen	28,000
25	grpr1	**Hamburg**	H	L	3-4	Porcello 21; Vata 27; Buckley 87	27,000
26	grpr1	**Hertha Berlin**	A	L	0-3		33,000
27	grpr1	**B Leverkusen**	H	W	1-0	Djalovic 66	24,000
28	grpr1	**Kaiserslautern**	H	L	0-2		18,000
29	grpr1	**B Dortmund**	A	D	1-1	Boakye 87	78,000
30	grpr1	**Freiburg**	H	W	3-1	Porcello 5,58,69	18,000
31	grpr1	**W Bremen**	A	L	0-3		40,000
32	grpr1	**Schalke**	H	L	0-2		27,000
33	grpr1	**Hansa Rostock**	A	D	1-1	Kuntzel 21	15,000
34	grpr1	**Wolfsburg**	H	L	1-2	Vata 35	20,000

MONTHLY POINTS TALLY

AUGUST	1	17%
SEPTEMBER	7	58%
OCTOBER	6	40%
NOVEMBER	9	75%
DECEMBER	1	17%
JANUARY	0	0%
FEBRUARY	8	67%
MARCH	0	0%
APRIL	7	47%
MAY	1	11%

KEY PLAYERS - GOALSCORERS

Delron Buckley

Goals in the League	15	Player Strike Rate Average number of minutes between League goals scored by player	171
Contribution to Attacking Power Average number of minutes between League team goals while on pitch	80	Club Strike Rate Average number of minutes between League goals scored by club	83

	PLAYER	LGE GOALS	POWER	STRIKE RATE
1	Delron Buckley	15	80	171 mins
2	Fatmir Vata	5	81	454 mins
3	Patrick Owomoyela	5	83	536 mins
4	Ruediger Kauf	1	78	2790 mins

KEY PLAYERS - MIDFIELDERS

Ruediger Kauf

Goals in the League	1	Contribution to Attacking Power Average number of minutes between League team goals while on pitch	78
Defensive Rating Average number of mins between League goals conceded while on the pitch	72	Scoring Difference Defensive Rating minus Contribution to Attacking Power	-6

	PLAYER	LGE GOALS	DEF RATE	POWER	SCORE DIFF
1	Ruediger Kauf	1	72	78	-6 mins
2	Fatmir Vata	5	60	81	-21 mins
3	Detlev Dammeier	0	67	89	-22 mins
4	Ervin Skela	0	68	91	-23 mins
5	Patrick Owomoyela	5	60	84	-24 mins

KEY PLAYERS - DEFENDERS

Petr Gabriel

Goals Conceded Number of League goals conceded while the player was on the pitch	43	Clean Sheets In games when player was on pitch for at least 70 minutes	7
Defensive Rating Ave number of mins between League goals conceded while on the pitch	65	Club Defensive Rating Average number of mins between League goals conceded by the club this season	62

	PLAYER	CON LGE	CLEAN SHEETS	DEF RATE
1	Petr Gabriel	43	7	65 mins
2	Markus Schuler	36	6	62 mins
3	Matthias Langkamp	31	4	61 mins
4	Borges	27	3	60 mins
5	Benjamin Lenze	32	4	60 mins

KEY GOALKEEPER

Mathias Hain

Goals Conceded in the League	49	Counting Games League games when player was on pitch for at least 70 minutes	34
Defensive Rating Ave number of mins between League goals conceded while on the pitch	62	Clean Sheets In games when player was on pitch for at least 70 minutes	7

LEAGUE GOALS

Delron Buckley

Minutes on the pitch	2565	Goals in the League	15
League average (mins between goals)	171		

	PLAYER	MINS	GOALS	AVE
1	Buckley	2565	15	171
2	Owomoyela	2682	5	536
3	Vata	2271	5	454
4	Porcello	932	5	186
5	Kuntzel	604	2	302
6	Boakye	472	2	236
7	Kauf	2790	1	2790
8	Djalovic	249	1	249
9	Pinto	494	1	494
	Other		0	
	TOTAL		37	

DISCIPLINARY RECORDS

	PLAYER	YELLOW	RED	AVE
1	Vata	7	0	324
2	Kauf	7	0	398
3	Boakye	1	0	472
4	Lenze	4	0	476
5	Duro	1	0	535
6	Borges	3	0	536
7	Hain	5	0	612
8	Langkamp	3	0	626
9	Schuler	3	0	745
10	Skela	3	0	815
11	Gabriel	3	0	926
12	Porcello	1	0	932
13	Dammeier	2	0	1240
	Other	4	0	
	TOTAL	47	0	

TOP POINT EARNERS

	PLAYER	GAMES	AV PTS
1	Benjamin Lenze	18	1.56
2	Detlev Dammeier	23	1.52
3	Markus Schuler	25	1.36
4	Ruediger Kauf	31	1.29
5	Fatmir Vata	23	1.26
6	Petr Gabriel	31	1.26
7	Delron Buckley	29	1.24
8	Mathias Hain	34	1.18
9	Ervin Skela	24	1.13
10	Patrick Owomoyela	30	1.10
	CLUB AVERAGE:		1.18

LEAGUE APPEARANCES, BOOKINGS AND CAPS

	AGE (on 01/07/05)	IN NAMED 18	APPEARANCES	COUNTING GAMES	MINUTES ON PITCH	YELLOW CARDS	RED CARDS	THIS SEASON	HOME COUNTRY
Goalkeepers									
Dennis Eilhoff	22	32	0	0	0	0	0	-	Germany
Mathias Hain	32	34	34	34	3060	5	0	-	Germany
Ronny Kockel	29	2	0	0	0	0	0	-	Germany
Defenders									
Daniel Bogusz	30	22	8	4	426	1	0	-	Poland
Borges	32	18	18	18	1609	3	0	-	Brazil
Martin Fink	23	24	11	2	289	0	0	-	Germany
Petr Gabriel	32	31	31	31	2778	3	0	-	Czech Republic
Matthias Langkamp	21	28	22	21	1880	3	0	-	Germany
Benjamin Lenze	26	25	24	18	1904	4	0	-	Germany
Markus Schuler	27	26	26	25	2235	3	0	-	Germany
Tomasz Wisio	23	1	1	0	45	0	0	-	Poland
Midfielders									
Detlev Dammeier	36	34	33	23	2480	2	0	-	Germany
Radomir Djalovic	22	13	8	1	249	0	0	-	Serbia & Montenegro
Klodian Duro	27	26	19	0	535	1	0	-	Albania
Henning Grieneisen	20	4	1	0	1	0	0	-	Germany
Finn Holsing	21	7	3	1	151	0	0	-	Germany
Ruediger Kauf	30	31	31	31	2790	7	0	-	Germany
Diego Leon	21	15	10	0	232	0	0	-	Spain
Patrick Owomoyela	25	30	30	30	2682	2	0	5	Germany (19)
Roberto Pinto	26	14	12	2	494	0	0	-	Portugal
Massimiliano Porcello	25	24	15	8	932	1	0	-	Italy
Bernd Gerd Rauw	25	24	8	1	308	0	0	-	Belgium
Ervin Skela	28	33	32	24	2447	3	0	-	Albania
Vanco Trajanov	26	6	1	0	19	0	0	-	Macedonia
Fatmir Vata	33	28	28	23	2271	7	0	-	Albania
Forwards									
Isaac Boakye	23	12	10	2	472	1	0	-	Ghana
Delron Buckley	27	29	29	29	2565	2	0	-	South Africa
Ferhat Cerci	23	1	1	0	10	0	0	-	Germany
Marco Kuntzel	29	17	15	4	604	0	0	-	Germany
Marijo Maric	28	9	5	0	82	0	0	-	Germany/Croatia
Claudiu Raducanu	28	9	5	0	110	0	0	-	Romania
Engin Yildiz	19	1	0	0	0	0	0	-	Germany

TEAM OF THE SEASON

D
Petr Gabriel
CG: 31 DR: 65
M
Ruediger Kauf
CG: 31 SD: -6
D
Markus Schuler
CG: 25 DR: 62
M
Fatmir Vata
CG: 23 SD: -21
F
Delron Buckley
CG: 29 SR: 171
G
Mathias Hain
CG: 34 DR: 62
D
Matthias Langkamp
CG: 21 DR: 61
M
Detlev Dammeier
CG: 23 SD: -22
F
Patrick Owomoyela*
CG: 30 SR: 536
D
Borges
CG: 18 DR: 60
M
Ervin Skela
CG: 24 SD: -23

SQUAD APPEARANCES

Match	1	2	3	4	5	6	7	8	9	10	11	12	13	14	15	16	17	18	19	20	21	22	23	24	25	26	27	28	29	30	31	32	33	34
Venue	H	H	A	H	A	A	H	A	H	A	A	H	A	H	A	H	A	A	H	A	H	A	H	A	H	A	H	H	A	H	A	H	A	H
Competition	L	L	L	L	L	L	L	L	L	L	L	L	L	L	L	L	L	L	L	L	L	L	L	L	L	L	L	L	L	L	L	L	L	L
Result	D	L	L	D	W	W	L	W	W	L	L	W	W	W	L	D	L	L	L	D	W	D	W	L	L	L	W	L	D	W	L	L	D	L

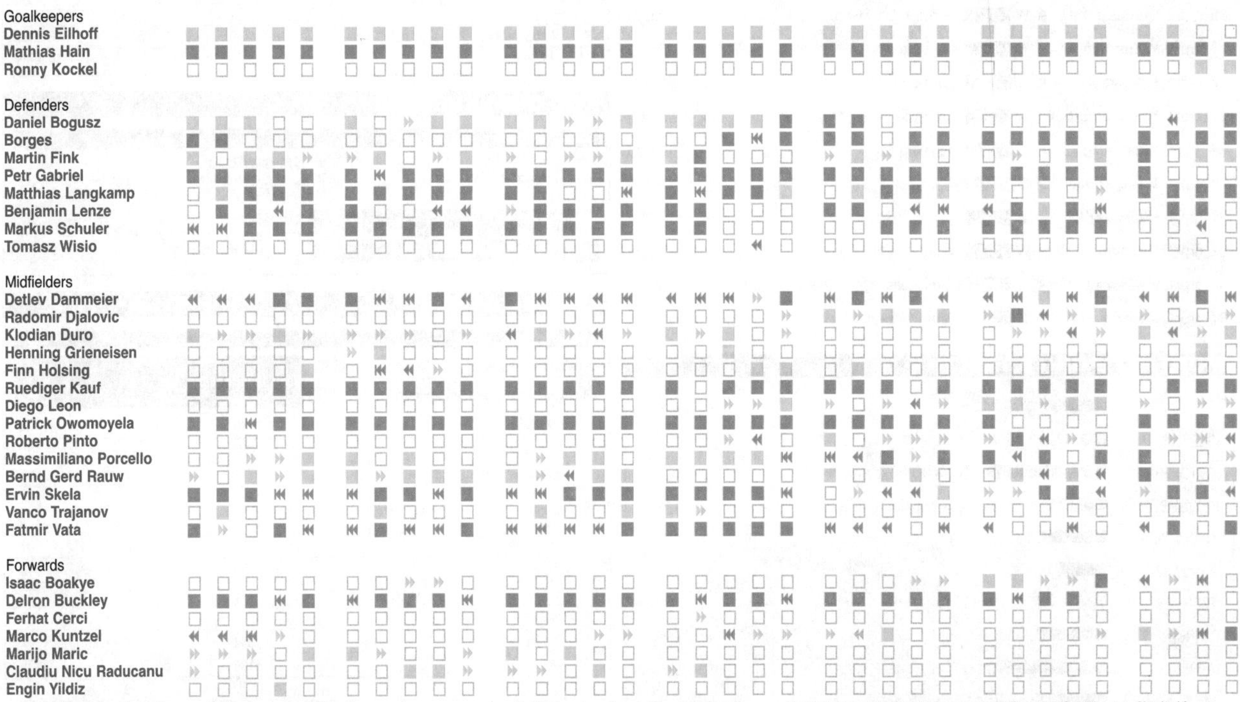

Goalkeepers
Dennis Eilhoff
Mathias Hain
Ronny Kockel
Defenders
Daniel Bogusz
Borges
Martin Fink
Petr Gabriel
Matthias Langkamp
Benjamin Lenze
Markus Schuler
Tomasz Wisio
Midfielders
Detlev Dammeier
Radomir Djalovic
Klodian Duro
Henning Grieneisen
Finn Holsing
Ruediger Kauf
Diego Leon
Patrick Owomoyela
Roberto Pinto
Massimiliano Porcello
Bernd Gerd Rauw
Ervin Skela
Vanco Trajanov
Fatmir Vata
Forwards
Isaac Boakye
Delron Buckley
Ferhat Cerci
Marco Kuntzel
Marijo Maric
Claudiu Nicu Raducanu
Engin Yildiz

KEY: On all match | On bench | Subbed or sent off (Counting game) | Subbed or sent off (playing less than 70 minutes) | Subbed on from bench (Counting Game) | Subbed on (playing less than 70 minutes) | Subbed on and then subbed or sent off (Counting Game) | Subbed on and then subbed or sent off (playing less than 70 minutes) | Not in 16

NUREMBURG

Final Position: **14th**

KEY: Won Drawn Lost

								Attendance
1	grpr1	**Kaiserslautern**	A	W	3-1	Banovic 12 pen; Vittek 61; Muller, L 84		37,000
2	grpr1	**Stuttgart**	H	D	1-1	Banovic 15		40,000
3	grpr1	**Hamburg**	A	L	3-4	Mintal 37,76; Vittek 83		40,000
4	grpr1	**Hertha Berlin**	H	D	0-0			31,000
5	grpr1	**B Leverkusen**	A	D	2-2	Muller, S 23; Placente 69 og		23,000
6	grpr1	**Arminia B**	H	L	1-2	Kiessling 76		18,000
7	grpr1	**B Dortmund**	A	D	2-2	Mintal 23; Vittek 25		75,000
8	grpr1	**Freiburg**	H	W	3-0	Mintal 26; Vittek 49; Schroth 56		21,000
9	grpr1	**W Bremen**	A	L	1-4	Mintal 65 pen		43,000
10	grpr1	**Schalke**	H	L	0-2			32,000
11	grpr1	**Hansa Rostock**	A	W	2-0	Schroth 57,60		16,000
12	grpr1	**Wolfsburg**	H	W	4-0	Mintal 2,28,49; Schroth 45		25,000
13	grpr1	**B M'gladbach**	A	L	1-2	Mintal 90 pen		44,000
14	grpr1	**Hannover 96**	H	D	1-1	Mintal 81		22,000
15	grpr1	**Bochum**	A	L	1-3	Mintal 65		16,000
16	grpr1	**Bayern Munich**	H	D	2-2	Mintal 24; Banovic 74 pen		42,000
17	grpr1	**Mainz**	A	W	1-0	Schroth 10		20,000
18	grpr1	**Kaiserslautern**	H	L	1-3	Muller, S 67		20,000
19	grpr1	**Stuttgart**	A	W	4-2	Muller, S 6; Schroth 11,85; Mintal 83		46,000
20	grpr1	**Hamburg**	H	L	1-3	Vittek 82		30,000
21	grpr1	**Hertha Berlin**	A	L	1-2	Mintal 79		38,000
22	grpr1	**B Leverkusen**	H	L	2-4	Mintal 30,54		18,000
23	grpr1	**Arminia B**	A	L	1-3	Mintal 31		18,000
24	grpr1	**B Dortmund**	H	D	2-2	Mintal 76; Vittek 89 pen		24,000
25	grpr1	**Freiburg**	A	W	3-2	Muller, L 24; Mintal 85,90		17,000
26	grpr1	**W Bremen**	H	L	1-2	Kiessling 69		22,000
27	grpr1	**Schalke**	A	L	1-4	Slovak 55		62,000
28	grpr1	**Hansa Rostock**	H	W	3-0	Wagefeld 59,88; Mintal 68		28,000
29	grpr1	**Wolfsburg**	A	W	1-0	Kiessling 63		19,000
30	grpr1	**B M'gladbach**	H	D	0-0			43,000
31	grpr1	**Hannover 96**	A	L	0-1			28,000
32	grpr1	**Bochum**	H	W	2-1	Daun 21; Mintal 84		44,000
33	grpr1	**Bayern Munich**	A	L	3-6	Demichelis 52 og; Slovak 80,83		63,000
34	grpr1	**Mainz**	H	L	1-2	Mintal 18 pen		35,000

MONTHLY POINTS TALLY

AUGUST	4	44%
SEPTEMBER	2	22%
OCTOBER	7	47%
NOVEMBER	4	33%
DECEMBER	4	67%
JANUARY	3	50%
FEBRUARY	0	0%
MARCH	4	44%
APRIL	7	58%
MAY	3	25%

KEY PLAYERS - GOALSCORERS

Marek Mintal

Goals in the League	23	Player Strike Rate Average number of minutes between League goals scored by player	130
Contribution to Attacking Power Average number of minutes between League team goals while on pitch	55	Club Strike Rate Average number of minutes between League goals scored by club	56

	PLAYER	LGE GOALS	POWER	STRIKE RATE
1	Marek Mintal	23	55	130 mins
2	Markus Schroth	7	52	253 mins
3	Robert Vittek	5	52	364 mins
4	Maik Wagefeld	2	53	692 mins
5	Sven Muller	3	55	907 mins

KEY PLAYERS - MIDFIELDERS

Tommy Svindal Larsen

Goals in the League	0	Contribution to Attacking Power Average number of minutes between League team goals while on pitch	54
Defensive Rating Average number of mins between goals conceded while on the pitc h	51	Scoring Difference Defensive Rating minus Contribution to Attacking Power	-3

	PLAYER	LGE GOALS	DEF RATE	POWER	SCORE DIFF
1	Tommy Svindal Larsen	0	51	54	-3 mins
2	Maik Wagefeld	2	48	53	-5 mins
3	Marek Mintal	23	49	55	-6 mins
4	Lars Muller	2	49	56	-7 mins
5	Mario Cantaluppi	0	54	64	-10 mins

KEY PLAYERS - DEFENDERS

Marek Nikl

Goals Conceded Number of League goals conceded while the player was on the pitch	36	Clean Sheets In games when player was on pitch for at least 70 minutes	6
Defensive Rating Ave number of mins between League goals conceded while on the pitch	54	Club Defensive Rating Average number of mins between League goals conceded by the club this season	49

	PLAYER	CON LGE	CLEAN SHEETS	DEF RATE
1	Marek Nikl	36	6	54 mins
2	Sven Muller	54	6	50 mins
3	Tomasz Hajto	30	2	42 mins
4	Andreas Wolf	30	1	40 mins

KEY GOALKEEPER

Raphael Schafer

Goals Conceded in the League	43	Counting Games League games when player was on pitch for at least 70 minutes	25
Defensive Rating Ave number of mins between League goals conceded while on the pitch	52	Clean Sheets In games when player was on pitch for at least 70 minutes	7

LEAGUE GOALS

Marek Mintal

Minutes on the pitch	2992	Goals in the League	23
League average (mins between goals)	130		

	PLAYER	MINS	GOALS	AVE
1	Mintal	2992	23	130
2	Schroth	1772	7	253
3	Vittek	1822	5	364
4	Banovic	1226	3	409
5	Muller, S	2721	3	907
6	Kiessling	929	3	310
7	Slovak	398	3	133
8	Wagefeld	1383	2	692
9	Muller, L	2834	2	1417
10	Daun	1138	1	1138
	Other		3	
	TOTAL		55	

DISCIPLINARY RECORDS

	PLAYER	YELLOW	RED	AVE
1	Lagerblom	5	0	114
2	Cantaluppi	12	1	171
3	Wolf	6	1	172
4	Hajto	6	1	181
5	Paulus	2	1	208
6	Banovic	5	0	245
7	Larsen	9	0	270
8	Muller, S	7	0	388
9	Kiessling	2	0	464
10	Nikl	4	0	483
11	Daun	2	0	569
12	Schroth	3	0	590
13	Wagefeld	2	0	691
	Other	10	0	
	TOTAL	75	4	

TOP POINT EARNERS

	PLAYER	GAMES	AV PTS
1	Maik Wagefeld	12	1.42
2	Markus Schroth	17	1.35
3	Tommy Svindal Larsen	24	1.33
4	Marek Nikl	20	1.25
5	Robert Vittek	19	1.21
6	Raphael Schafer	25	1.20
7	Mario Cantaluppi	23	1.13
8	Marek Mintal	33	1.12
9	Lars Muller	31	1.10
10	Tomasz Hajto	13	1.08
	CLUB AVERAGE:		1.12

TEAM OF THE SEASON

G
Raphael Schafer
CG: 25 DR: 52
D
Marek Nikl
CG: 20 DR: 54
D
Sven Muller
CG: 29 DR: 50
D
Tomasz Hajto
CG: 13 DR: 42
D
Andreas Wolf
CG: 11 DR: 40
M
Tommy Svindal Larsen
CG: 24 SD: -3
M
Maik Wagefeld
CG: 12 SD: -5
M
Mario Cantaluppi
CG: 23 SD: -10
M
Lars Muller
CG: 31 SD: -7
F
Marek Mintal*
CG: 33 SR: 130
F
Markus Schroth
CG: 17 SR: 253

LEAGUE APPEARANCES, BOOKINGS AND CAPS

	AGE (on 01/07/05)	IN NAMED 18	APPEARANCES	COUNTING GAMES	MINUTES ON PITCH	YELLOW CARDS	RED CARDS	THIS SEASON	HOME COUNTRY
Goalkeepers									
Daniel Klewer	28	28	6	6	540	0	0	-	Germany
Dirk Langerbein	33	8	3	3	270	0	0	-	Germany
Raphael Schafer	26	26	25	25	2250	0	0	-	Germany
Phillip Tschauner	19	4	0	0	0	0	0	-	Germany
Defenders									
Bartosz Bosacki	29	19	13	10	929	1	0	-	Poland
Tomasz Hajto	32	20	17	13	1271	6	1	-	Poland
Sven Muller	25	33	33	29	2721	7	0	-	Germany
Marek Nikl	29	26	24	20	1934	4	0	-	Czech Republic
Thomas Paulus	23	25	9	4	624	2	1	-	Germany
Dominik Reinhardt	20	14	13	9	960	1	0	-	Germany
Leandro Tigrao	23	8	3	0	49	1	0	-	Brazil
Frank Wiblishauser	27	31	13	6	699	0	0	-	Germany
Andreas Wolf	23	18	16	11	1204	6	1	-	Germany
Midfielders									
Ivica Banovic	24	30	22	7	1226	5	0	-	Croatia
Mario Cantaluppi	31	26	26	23	2225	12	1	-	Switzerland
Pekka Lagerblom	23	12	11	3	573	5	0	-	Finland
Tommy Larsen	31	29	29	24	2438	9	0	-	Norway
Alexander Ludwig	21	1	0	0	0	0	0	-	Germany
Marek Mintal	27	34	34	33	2992	3	0	-	Slovakia
Lars Muller	29	34	33	31	2834	4	0	-	Germany
Samuel Slovak	29	19	13	0	398	0	0	-	Slovakia
Sebastian Szikal	18	1	0	0	0	0	0	-	Germany
Maik Wagefeld	24	31	21	12	1383	2	0	-	Germany
Forwards									
Lawrence Aidoo	23	11	7	0	165	4	0	-	Ghana
Markus Daun	24	26	20	8	1138	2	0	-	Germany
Marcel Ketelaer	27	10	4	0	116	0	0	-	Germany
Stefan Kiessling	21	32	27	6	929	2	0	-	Germany
Markus Schroth	30	24	23	17	1772	3	0	-	Germany
Robert Vittek	23	24	23	19	1822	1	0	-	Slovakia

SQUAD APPEARANCES

Match	1	2	3	4	5	6	7	8	9	10	11	12	13	14	15	16	17	18	19	20	21	22	23	24	25	26	27	28	29	30	31	32	33	34
Venue	A	H	A	H	A	H	A	H	A	H	A	H	A	H	A	H	A	H	A	H	A	H	A	H	A	H	A	H	A	H	A	H	A	H
Competition	L	L	L	L	L	L	L	L	L	L	L	L	L	L	L	L	L	L	L	L	L	L	L	L	L	L	L	L	L	L	L	L	L	L
Result	W	D	L	D	D	L	D	W	L	L	W	W	L	D	L	D	W	L	W	L	L	L	L	D	W	L	L	W	W	D	L	W	L	L

Goalkeepers
Daniel Klewer
Dirk Langerbein
Raphael Schafer
Phillip Tschauner

Defenders
Bartosz Bosacki
Tomasz Hajto
Sven Muller
Marek Nikl
Thomas Paulus
Dominik Reinhardt
Leandro Tigrao
Frank Wiblishauser
Andreas Wolf

Midfielders
Ivica Banovic
Mario Cantaluppi
Pekka Lagerblom
Tommy Svindal Larsen
Alexander Ludwig
Marek Mintal
Lars Muller
Samuel Slovak
Sebastian Szikal
Maik Wagefeld

Forwards
Lawrence Aidoo
Markus Daun
Marcel Ketelaer
Stefan Kiessling
Markus Schroth
Robert Vittek

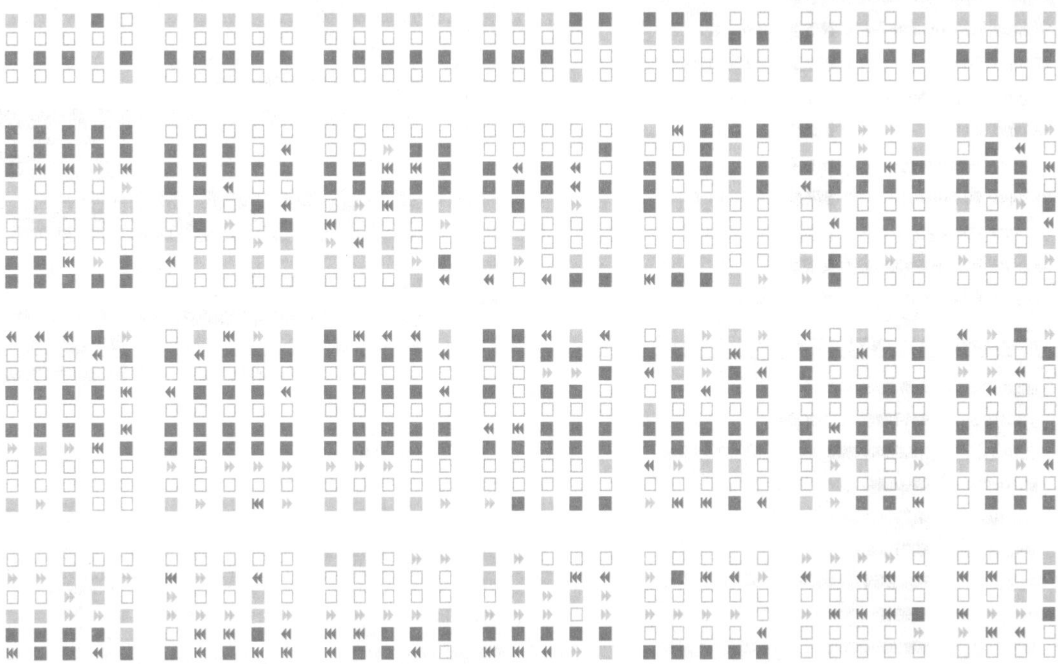

KEY: On all match | On bench | Subbed or sent off (Counting game) | Subbed or sent off (playing less than 70 minutes) | Subbed on from bench (Counting Game) | Subbed on (playing less than 70 minutes) | Subbed on and then subbed or sent off (Counting Game) | Subbed on and then subbed or sent off (playing less than 70 minutes) | Not in 16

BORUSSIA MONCHENGLADBACH

Final Position: **15th**

KEY: Won Drawn Lost

							Attendance
1	grpr1	**Arminia B**	A	D	0-0		27,000
2	grpr1	**B Dortmund**	H	L	2-3	Ulich 7; Hausweiler 34	53,000
3	grpr1	**Freiburg**	A	D	1-1	Neuville 78	21,000
4	grpr1	**W Bremen**	H	W	3-1	Heinz 12; Neuville 53; Ivic 90	52,000
5	grpr1	**Schalke**	A	L	2-3	Korzynietz 5; Neuville 47	61,000
6	grpr1	**Hansa Rostock**	H	D	2-2	Neuville 19,30 pen	40,000
7	grpr1	**Wolfsburg**	A	L	1-2	Neuville 15	24,000
8	grpr1	**Kaiserslautern**	H	W	2-0	Neuville 53,78	53,000
9	grpr1	**Hannover 96**	H	L	0-2		43,000
10	grpr1	**Bochum**	A	L	0-3		31,000
11	grpr1	**Bayern Munich**	H	W	2-0	Pletsch 49; Van Hout 83	53,000
12	grpr1	**Mainz**	A	D	1-1	Sverkos 13	20,000
13	grpr1	**Nuremburg**	H	W	2-1	Neuville 20 pen; Sverkos 73	44,000
14	grpr1	**Stuttgart**	A	L	0-1		38,000
15	grpr1	**Hamburg**	H	L	1-3	Van Hout 46	50,000
16	grpr1	**Hertha Berlin**	A	L	0-6		40,000
17	grpr1	**B Leverkusen**	H	D	1-1	Sverkos 67 pen	52,000
18	grpr1	**Arminia B**	H	W	1-0	Moore 53	45,000
19	grpr1	**B Dortmund**	A	D	1-1	Kluge 48	80,000
20	grpr1	**Freiburg**	H	W	3-2	Sverkos 25; Sonck 30,49	40,000
21	grpr1	**W Bremen**	A	L	0-2		40,000
22	grpr1	**Schalke**	H	L	1-3	Bohme 38 pen	53,000
23	grpr1	**Hansa Rostock**	A	D	0-0		12,000
24	grpr1	**Wolfsburg**	H	W	1-0	Sverkos 87	45,000
25	grpr1	**Kaiserslautern**	A	L	0-1		39,000
26	grpr1	**Hannover 96**	A	L	1-2	Sverkos 31	37,000
27	grpr1	**Bochum**	H	D	2-2	Kluge 30; Jansen 53	45,000
28	grpr1	**Bayern Munich**	A	L	1-2	Ulich 65	60,000
29	grpr1	**Mainz**	H	D	1-1	Neuville 51	53,000
30	grpr1	**Nuremburg**	A	D	0-0		43,000
31	grpr1	**Stuttgart**	H	W	2-0	Neuville 16; Sverkos 24	53,000
32	grpr1	**Hamburg**	A	D	0-0		45,000
33	grpr1	**Hertha Berlin**	H	D	0-0		53,000
34	grpr1	**B Leverkusen**	A	L	1-5	Neuville 2	23,000

MONTHLY POINTS TALLY

AUGUST	2	22%
SEPTEMBER	4	44%
OCTOBER	6	40%
NOVEMBER	4	33%
DECEMBER	1	17%
JANUARY	4	67%
FEBRUARY	4	33%
MARCH	3	33%
APRIL	6	40%
MAY	2	22%

KEY PLAYERS - GOALSCORERS

Oliver Neuville

Goals in the League	12	Player Strike Rate Average number of minutes between League goals scored by player	233
Contribution to Attacking Power Average number of minutes between League team goals while on pitch	82	**Club Strike Rate** Average number of minutes between League goals scored by club	87

	PLAYER	LGE GOALS	POWER	STRIKE RATE
1	Oliver Neuville	12	82	233 mins
2	Vaclav Sverkos	7	87	262 mins
3	Ivo Ulich	2	99	939 mins
4	Jorg Bohme	1	81	1057 mins
5	Craig Moore	1	96	1061 mins

KEY PLAYERS - MIDFIELDERS

Jorg Bohme

Goals in the League	1	**Contribution to Attacking Power** Average number of minutes between League team goals while on pitch	81
Defensive Rating **Average number of mins between goals conceded while on the pitch**	76	Scoring Difference Defensive Rating minus Contribution to Attacking Power	-5

	PLAYER	LGE GOALS	DEF RATE	POWER	SCORE DIFF
1	Jorg Bohme	1	76	81	-5 mins
2	Peer Kluge	2	65	86	-21 mins
3	Bernd Korzynietz	1	55	77	-22 mins
4	Bernd Thijs	0	78	103	-25 mins
5	Ivo Ulich	2	70	99	-29 mins

KEY PLAYERS - DEFENDERS

Milan Fukal

Goals Conceded Number of League goals conceded while the player was on the pitch	16	**Clean Sheets** In games when player was on pitch for at least 70 minutes	6
Defensive Rating Ave number of mins between League goals conceded while on the pitch	83	**Club Defensive Rating** Average number of mins between League goals conceded by the club this season	60

	PLAYER	CON LGE	CLEAN SHEETS	DEF RATE
1	Milan Fukal	16	6	83 mins
2	Nico van Kerckhoven	17	6	81 mins
3	Craig Moore	14	4	76 mins
4	Jeff Strasser	42	8	58 mins
5	Marcelo Pletsch	30	2	51 mins

KEY GOALKEEPER

Kasey Keller

Goals Conceded in the League	21	**Counting Games** League games when player was on pitch for at least 70 minutes	17
Defensive Rating Ave number of mins between League goals conceded while on the pitch	73	**Clean Sheets** **In games when player was on pitch for at least 70 minutes**	7

LEAGUE GOALS

Oliver Neuville

Minutes on the pitch	2795	Goals in the League	12
League average (mins between goals)	233		

	PLAYER	MINS	GOALS	AVE
1	Neuville	2795	12	233
2	Sverkos	1831	7	262
3	Ulich	1878	2	939
4	Van Hout	1119	2	560
5	Kluge	2582	2	1291
6	Sonck	453	2	227
7	Ivic	134	1	134
8	Heinz	1249	1	1249
9	Moore	1061	1	1061
10	Korzynietz	1536	1	1536
11	Pletsch	1518	1	1518
12	Jansen	1443	1	1443
13	Hausweiler	620	1	620
	Other		1	
	TOTAL		35	

DISCIPLINARY

	PLAYER	YELLOW	RED	AVE
1	Moore	7	1	132
2	Sonck	3	0	151
3	Bohme	6	0	176
4	Strasser	10	1	220
5	Ziege	4	0	255
6	Korzynietz	5	1	256
7	Thijs	5	0	266
8	Pletsch	4	1	303
9	Sverkos	6	0	305
10	Hausweiler	2	0	310
11	van Kerckhoven	4	0	345
12	Kluge	7	0	368
13	Fukal	3	0	441
	Other	15	0	
	TOTAL	81	4	

TOP POINT EARNERS

	PLAYER	GAMES	AV PTS
1	Milan Fukal	12	1.42
2	Jorg Bohme	12	1.25
3	Nico van Kerckhoven	13	1.23
4	Bernd Thijs	15	1.20
5	Peer Kluge	28	1.18
6	Vaclav Sverkos	19	1.16
7	Oliver Neuville	31	1.13
8	Kasey Keller	17	1.12
9	Jeff Strasser	26	1.08
10	Craig Moore	12	1.08
	CLUB AVERAGE:		1.06

LEAGUE APPEARANCES, BOOKINGS AND CAPS

	AGE (on 01/07/05)	IN NAMED 18	APPEARANCES	COUNTING GAMES	MINUTES ON PITCH	YELLOW CARDS	RED CARDS	THIS SEASON	HOME COUNTRY
Goalkeepers									
Darius Kampa	28	26	16	16	1440	0	0	-	Germany
Kasey Keller	35	17	17	17	1530	1	0	-	United States
Michael Melka	26	24	1	1	90	0	0	-	Germany
Defenders									
Filip Daems	26	16	11	4	578	1	0	-	Belgium
Milan Fukal	30	22	17	12	1324	3	0	-	Czech Republic
Enrico Gaede	23	16	9	7	676	1	0	-	Germany
Markus Hausweiler	29	11	8	6	620	2	0	-	Germany
Steffan Korell	33	9	2	0	43	0	0	-	Germany
Craig Moore	29	14	13	12	1061	7	1	-	Australia
Marcelo Pletsch	29	21	19	16	1518	4	1	-	Brazil
Jeff Strasser	30	31	28	26	2420	10	1	-	Luxembourg
Nico van Kerckhoven	34	29	18	13	1380	4	0	-	Belgium
Christian Ziege	33	14	13	10	1020	4	0	-	Germany
Midfielders									
Jorg Bohme	31	13	13	12	1057	6	0	-	Germany
Thomas Broich	24	30	27	14	1489	2	0	-	Germany
Bradley Carnell	28	13	6	1	256	2	0	-	South Africa
Igor Demo	29	18	7	4	419	0	0	-	Slovakia
Vladimir Ivic	28	7	4	0	134	1	0	-	Serbia & Montenegro
Marcel Jansen	19	19	18	14	1443	1	0	-	Germany
Oliver Kirch	22	2	0	0	0	0	0	-	Germany
Peer Kluge	24	33	32	28	2582	7	0	-	Germany
Bernd Korzynietz	25	25	20	15	1536	5	1	-	Germany
Sebastian Plate	25	3	1	0	45	0	0	-	Germany
Eugen Polanski	19	8	1	0	10	1	0	-	Poland
Jan Schlaudraff	21	11	6	1	191	1	0	-	Germany
Bernd Thijs	27	17	15	15	1334	5	0	-	Belgium
Ivo Ulich	30	29	28	17	1878	4	0	-	Czech Republic
Forwards									
Marek Heinz	27	23	20	9	1249	1	0	6	Czech Republic (2)
Oliver Neuville	32	32	32	31	2795	3	0	1	Germany (19)
Wesley Sonck	26	9	7	4	453	3	0	4	Belgium (42)
Vaclav Sverkos	21	32	26	19	1831	6	0	-	Czech Republic
Joris Van Hout	28	31	29	8	1119	1	0	-	Belgium

TEAM OF THE SEASON

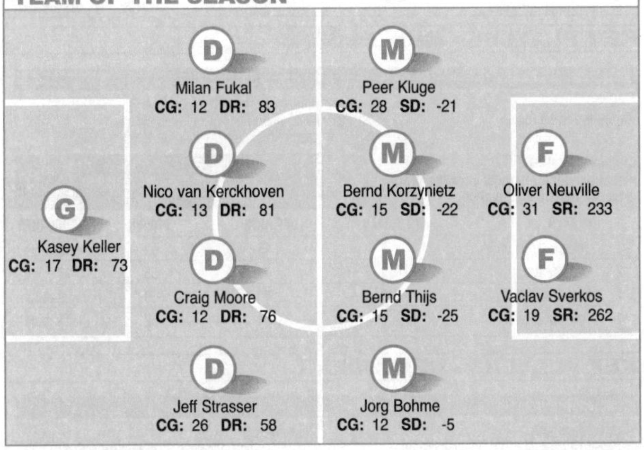
D
Milan Fukal
CG: 12 DR: 83
D
Nico van Kerckhoven
CG: 13 DR: 81
D
Craig Moore
CG: 12 DR: 76
D
Jeff Strasser
CG: 26 DR: 58
G
Kasey Keller
CG: 17 DR: 73
M
Peer Kluge
CG: 28 SD: -21
M
Bernd Korzynietz
CG: 15 SD: -22
M
Bernd Thijs
CG: 15 SD: -25
M
Jorg Bohme
CG: 12 SD: -5
F
Oliver Neuville
CG: 31 SR: 233
F
Vaclav Sverkos
CG: 19 SR: 262

SQUAD APPEARANCES

Match	1	2	3	4	5	6	7	8	9	10	11	12	13	14	15	16	17	18	19	20	21	22	23	24	25	26	27	28	29	30	31	32	33	34
Venue	A	H	A	H	A	H	A	H	H	A	H	A	H	A	H	A	H	H	A	H	A	H	A	H	A	A	H	A	H	A	H	A	H	A
Competition	L	L	L	L	L	L	L	L	L	L	L	L	L	L	L	L	L	L	L	L	L	L	L	L	L	L	L	L	L	L	L	L	L	L
Result	D	L	D	W	L	D	L	W	L	L	W	D	W	L	L	L	D	W	D	W	L	L	D	W	L	L	D	L	D	D	W	D	D	L

Goalkeepers
Darius Kampa
Kasey Keller
Michael Melka

Defenders
Filip Daems
Milan Fukal
Enrico Gaede
Markus Hausweiler
Steffan Korell
Craig Moore
Marcelo Pletsch
Jeff Strasser
Nico van Kerckhoven
Christian Ziege

Midfielders
Jorg Bohme
Thomas Broich
Bradley Carnell
Igor Demo
Vladimir Ivic
Marcel Jansen
Oliver Kirch
Peer Kluge
Bernd Korzynietz
Sebastian Plate
Eugen Polanski
Jan Schlaudraff
Bernd Thijs
Ivo Ulich

Forwards
Marek Heinz
Oliver Neuville
Wesley Sonck
Vaclav Sverkos
Joris Van Hout

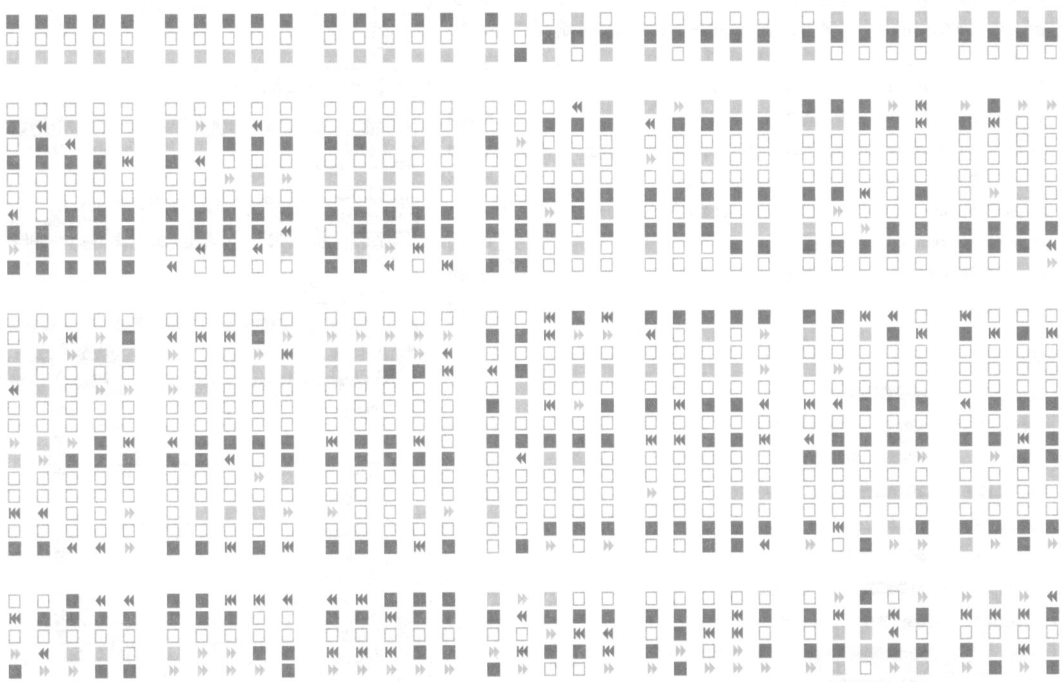

KEY: On all match — On bench — Subbed or sent off (Counting game) — Subbed or sent off (playing less than 70 minutes) — Subbed on from bench (Counting Game) — Subbed on (playing less than 70 minutes) — Subbed on and then subbed or sent off (Counting Game) — Subbed on and then subbed or sent off (playing less than 70 minutes) — Not in 16

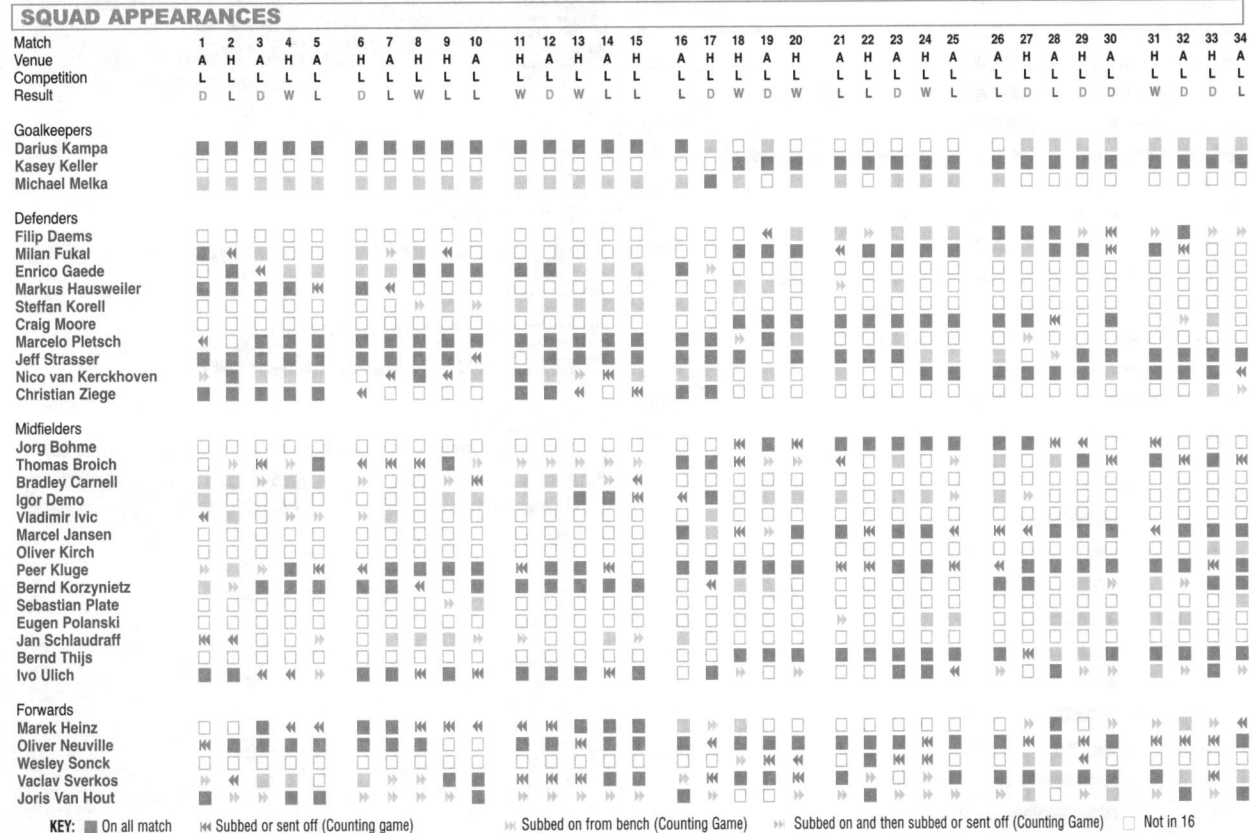

VFL BOCHUM

Final Position: **16th**

KEY: Won / Drawn / Lost

							Attendance
1	grpr1	**Hertha Berlin**	A	D	2-2	Kalla 66; Madsen 70 pen	40,000
2	grpr1	**B Leverkusen**	H	D	2-2	Lokvenc 29; Preuss 70	25,000
3	grpr1	**Arminia B**	A	W	2-1	Zdebel 31; Diabang 90	18,000
4	grpr1	**B Dortmund**	H	D	2-2	Kalla 15; Demel 75 og	33,000
5	uc1rl1	**Standard Liege**	A	D	0-0		12,000
6	grpr1	**Freiburg**	A	D	1-1	Bechmann 55	22,000
7	grpr1	**W Bremen**	H	L	1-4	Knavs 68	25,000
8	uc1rl2	**Standard Liege**	H	D	1-1	Maltritz 45	24,000
9	grpr1	**Schalke**	A	L	2-3	Misimovic 50; Kalla 65	61,000
10	grpr1	**Hansa Rostock**	H	L	0-1		21,000
11	grpr1	**Wolfsburg**	A	L	0-3		22,000
12	grpr1	**B M'gladbach**	H	W	3-0	Preuss 54; Wosz 85; Madsen 90	31,000
13	grpr1	**Hannover 96**	A	L	0-3		26,000
14	grpr1	**Kaiserslautern**	H	D	1-1	Lokvenc 62	23,000
15	grpr1	**Bayern Munich**	H	L	1-3	Lokvenc 66	33,000
16	grpr1	**Mainz**	A	L	0-1		20,000
17	grpr1	**Nuremburg**	H	W	3-1	Lokvenc 21,50; Kalla 41	16,000
18	grpr1	**Stuttgart**	A	L	2-5	Edu 33; Maltritz 59	36,000
19	grpr1	**Hamburg**	H	L	1-2	Bechmann 83	28,000
20	grpr1	**Hertha Berlin**	H	D	2-2	Madsen 39 pen; Lokvenc 80	23,000
21	grpr1	**B Leverkusen**	A	L	0-4		23,000
22	grpr1	**Arminia B**	H	D	1-1	Madsen 19 pen	20,000
23	grpr1	**B Dortmund**	A	L	0-1		78,000
24	grpr1	**Freiburg**	H	W	3-1	Misimovic 35 pen; Kalla 56; Bechmann 84	18,000
25	grpr1	**W Bremen**	A	L	0-4		32,000
26	grpr1	**Schalke**	H	L	0-2		33,000
27	grpr1	**Hansa Rostock**	A	L	1-3	Edu 70	20,000
28	grpr1	**Wolfsburg**	H	W	5-1	Edu 15,38; Wosz 24; Lokvenc 39; Madsen 57	19,000
29	grpr1	**B M'gladbach**	A	D	2-2	Lokvenc 70; Pletsch 90 og	45,000
30	grpr1	**Hannover 96**	H	W	1-0	Cherundolo 56 og	23,000
31	grpr1	**Kaiserslautern**	A	W	2-1	Meichelbeck 39; Diabang 75	34,000
32	grpr1	**Bayern Munich**	A	L	1-3	Tapalovic, F 54	60,000
33	grpr1	**Mainz**	H	L	2-6	Lokvenc 26; Bechmann 87	30,000
34	grpr1	**Nuremburg**	A	L	1-2	Meichelbeck 89	44,000
35	grpr1	**Stuttgart**	H	W	2-0	Misimovic 60; Lokvenc 72	27,000
36	grpr1	**Hamburg**	A	W	1-0	Diabang 3	55,000

MONTHLY POINTS TALLY

AUGUST	5	56%
SEPTEMBER	2	22%
OCTOBER	3	20%
NOVEMBER	4	33%
DECEMBER	0	0%
JANUARY	1	17%
FEBRUARY	4	33%
MARCH	3	33%
APRIL	7	47%
MAY	6	67%

KEY PLAYERS - GOALSCORERS

Vratislav Lokvenc

Goals in the League	10	Player Strike Rate Average number of minutes between League goals scored by player	279
Contribution to Attacking Power Average number of minutes between League team goals while on pitch	63	Club Strike Rate Average number of minutes between League goals scored by club	65

	PLAYER	LGE GOALS	POWER	STRIKE RATE
1	Vratislav Lokvenc	10	63	279 mins
2	Peter Madsen	5	68	329 mins
3	Raymond Kalla	5	75	395 mins
4	Martin Meichelbeck	2	58	793 mins
5	Christoph Preuss	2	72	1013 mins

KEY PLAYERS - MIDFIELDERS

Zvjezdan Misimovic

Goals in the League	3	Contribution to Attacking Power Average number of minutes between League team goals while on pitch	58
Defensive Rating Average number of mins between goals conceded while on the pitch	45	Scoring Difference Defensive Rating minus Contribution to Attacking Power	-13

	PLAYER	LGE GOALS	DEF RATE	POWER	SCORE DIFF
1	Zvjezdan Misimovic	3	45	58	-13 mins
2	Dariusz Wosz	2	49	65	-16 mins
3	Filip Trojan	0	40	69	-29 mins
4	Tomasz Zdebel	1	44	82	-38 mins

KEY PLAYERS - DEFENDERS

Christoph Preuss

Goals Conceded Number of League goals conceded while the player was on the pitch	41	Clean Sheets In games when player was on pitch for at least 70 minutes	3
Defensive Rating Ave number of mins between League goals conceded while on the pitch	49	Club Defensive Rating Average number of mins between League goals conceded by the club this season	45

	PLAYER	CON LGE	CLEAN SHEETS	DEF RATE
1	Christoph Preuss	41	3	49 mins
2	Phillip Bonig	49	2	46 mins
3	Marcel Maltritz	50	4	46 mins
4	Martin Meichelbeck	35	3	45 mins
5	Soren Colding	55	2	45 mins

KEY GOALKEEPER

Rein Van Duijnhoven

Goals Conceded in the League	39	Counting Games League games when player was on pitch for at least 70 minutes	22
Defensive Rating Ave number of mins between League goals conceded while on the pitch	51	Clean Sheets In games when player was on pitch for at least 70 minutes	15

LEAGUE GOALS

Vratislav Lokvenc

Minutes on the pitch	2785	Goals in the League	10
League average (mins between goals)	279		

	PLAYER	MINS	GOALS	AVE
1	Lokvenc	2785	10	279
2	Kalla	1973	5	395
3	Madsen	1643	5	329
4	Bechmann	1478	4	370
5	Edu	1091	4	273
6	Misimovic	1627	3	542
7	Diabang	399	3	133
8	Meichelbeck	1585	2	793
9	Preuss	2025	2	1013
10	Wosz	2157	2	1079
11	Maltritz	2305	1	2305
12	Knavs	2115	1	2115
13	Tapalovic, F	642	1	642
	Other		4	
	TOTAL		47	

DISCIPLINARY

	PLAYER	YELLOW	RED	AVE
1	Meichelbeck	8	1	176
2	Maltritz	10	0	230
3	Zdebel	8	0	278
4	Preuss	5	1	337
5	Edu	3	0	363
6	Bechmann	4	0	369
7	Lokvenc	7	0	397
8	Madsen	4	0	410
9	Colding	5	0	500
10	Wosz	4	0	539
11	Bonig	4	0	560
12	Kalla	3	0	657
13	Knavs	3	0	705
	Other	3	1	
	TOTAL	71	3	

TOP POINT EARNERS

	PLAYER	GAMES	AV PTS
1	Dariusz Wosz	20	1.20
2	Rein Van Duijnhoven	22	1.18
3	Phillip Bonig	23	1.17
4	Marcel Maltritz	24	1.17
5	Aleksander Knavs	23	1.09
6	Vratislav Lokvenc	30	1.07
7	Martin Meichelbeck	16	1.06
8	Christoph Preuss	17	1.06
9	Soren Colding	23	0.91
10	Tomasz Zdebel	23	0.87
	CLUB AVERAGE:		1.03

LEAGUE APPEARANCES, BOOKINGS AND CAPS

	AGE (on 01/07/05)	IN NAMED 18	APPEARANCES	COUNTING GAMES	MINUTES ON PITCH	YELLOW CARDS	RED CARDS	THIS SEASON	HOME COUNTRY
Goalkeepers									
Polat Keser	19	2	0	0	0	0	0	-	Turkey
Peter Skov-Jensen	34	9	2	2	180	0	0	4	Denmark (19)
Rein Van Duijnhoven	37	25	24	22	2032	0	1	-	Holland
Christian Vander	24	32	10	9	848	0	0	-	Germany
Defenders									
Fatih Akyel	27	4	1	0	45	0	0	-	Turkey
Phillip Bonig	25	33	29	23	2241	4	0	-	Germany
Soren Colding	32	32	31	23	2501	5	0	1	Denmark (19)
Raymond Kalla	30	30	23	21	1973	3	0	-	Cameroon
Aleksander Knavs	29	26	25	23	2115	3	0	-	Slovenia
Marcel Maltritz	26	28	27	24	2305	10	0	-	Germany
Marvin-Job Matip	19	2	1	0	45	0	0	-	Germany
Martin Meichelbeck	28	28	21	16	1585	8	1	-	Germany
Christoph Preuss	24	32	30	17	2025	5	1	-	Germany
Filip Tapalovic	28	22	12	4	642	0	0	-	Croatia
Midfielders									
Michael Bemben	29	27	6	1	213	0	0	-	Germany
Claus Costa	21	2	0	0	0	0	0	-	Germany
Dennis Grote	18	9	4	0	67	0	0	-	Germany
Thordur Gudjonsson	31	10	3	0	53	0	0	-	Iceland
Zvjezdan Misimovic	23	33	31	11	1627	2	0	-	Serbia & Montenegro
Moharram Navidkia	22	5	0	0	0	0	0	-	Iran
Miroslav Stevic	35	1	0	0	0	0	0	-	Serbia & Montenegro
Ersan Tekkan	20	1	0	0	0	0	0	-	Germany
Alexander Thamm	22	2	1	0	1	0	0	-	Germany
Filip Trojan	22	24	19	10	1239	1	0	-	Czech Republic
Luciano Velardi	23	1	0	0	0	0	0	-	Italy
Dariusz Wosz	36	33	30	20	2157	4	0	-	Germany
Tomasz Zdebel	31	29	28	23	2224	8	0	-	Poland
Forwards									
Tommy Bechmann	23	32	25	11	1478	4	0	-	Denmark
Mamadou Diabang	26	14	11	2	399	0	1	-	Senegal
Edu	23	30	17	11	1091	3	0	8	Brazil (1)
Vratislav Lokvenc	31	32	32	30	2785	7	0	8	Czech Republic (2)
Peter Madsen	27	20	19	17	1643	4	0	3	Denmark (19)
Gaetano Manno	22	2	2	0	29	1	0	-	Italy

TEAM OF THE SEASON

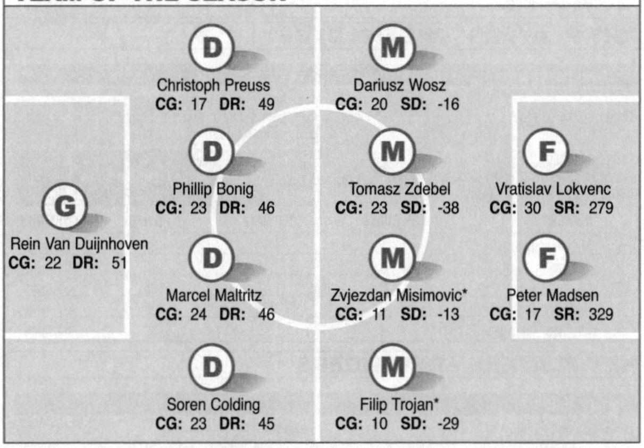
D
Christoph Preuss
CG: 17 DR: 49
M
Dariusz Wosz
CG: 20 SD: -16
D
Phillip Bonig
CG: 23 DR: 46
M
Tomasz Zdebel
CG: 23 SD: -38
F
Vratislav Lokvenc
CG: 30 SR: 279
G
Rein Van Duijnhoven
CG: 22 DR: 51
D
Marcel Maltritz
CG: 24 DR: 46
M
Zvjezdan Misimovic*
CG: 11 SD: -13
F
Peter Madsen
CG: 17 SR: 329
D
Soren Colding
CG: 23 DR: 45
M
Filip Trojan*
CG: 10 SD: -29

SQUAD APPEARANCES

Match	1	2	3	4	5	6	7	8	9	10	11	12	13	14	15	16	17	18	19	20	21	22	23	24	25	26	27	28	29	30	31	32	33	34	35	36
Venue	A	H	A	H	A	A	H	H	A	H	A	H	A	H	H	A	H	A	H	H	A	H	A	H	A	H	A	H	A	H	A	A	H	A	H	A
Competition	L	L	L	L	E	L	L	E	L	L	L	L	L	L	L	L	L	L	L	L	L	L	L	L	L	L	L	L	L	L	L	L	L	L	L	L
Result	D	D	W	D	D	D	L	D	L	L	L	W	L	D	L	L	W	L	L	D	L	D	L	W	L	L	L	W	D	W	W	L	L	L	W	W

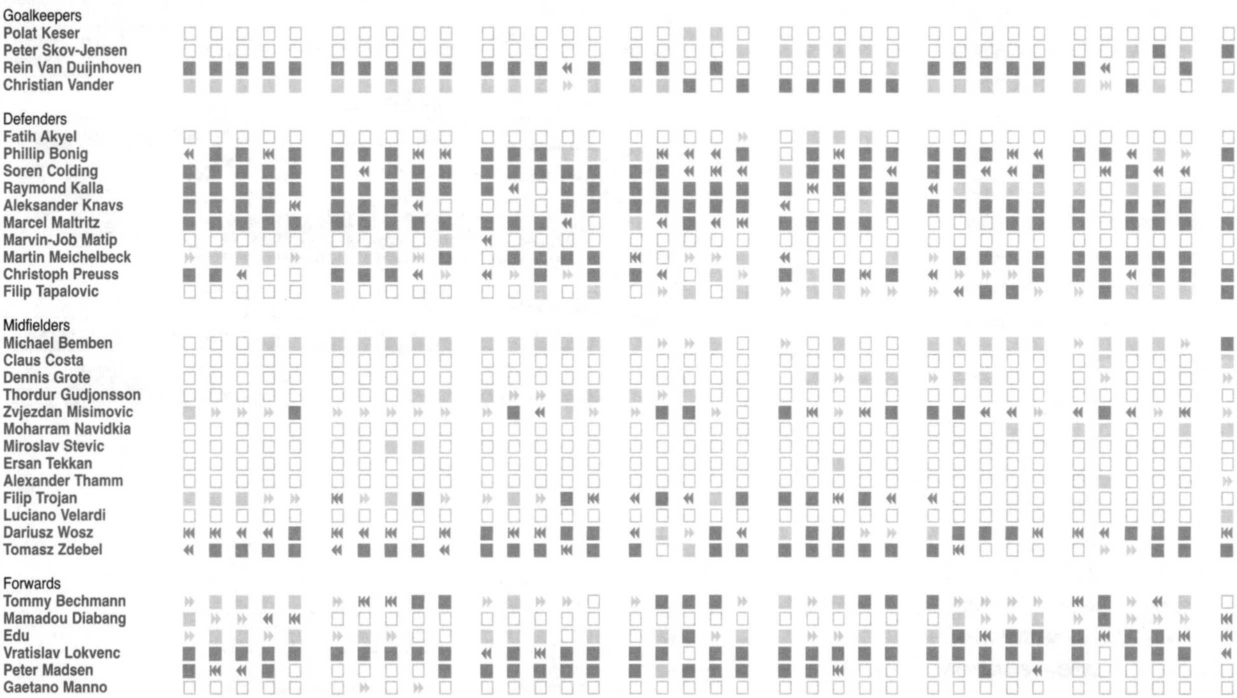
Goalkeepers
Polat Keser
Peter Skov-Jensen
Rein Van Duijnhoven
Christian Vander
Defenders
Fatih Akyel
Phillip Bonig
Soren Colding
Raymond Kalla
Aleksander Knavs
Marcel Maltritz
Marvin-Job Matip
Martin Meichelbeck
Christoph Preuss
Filip Tapalovic
Midfielders
Michael Bemben
Claus Costa
Dennis Grote
Thordur Gudjonsson
Zvjezdan Misimovic
Moharram Navidkia
Miroslav Stevic
Ersan Tekkan
Alexander Thamm
Filip Trojan
Luciano Velardi
Dariusz Wosz
Tomasz Zdebel
Forwards
Tommy Bechmann
Mamadou Diabang
Edu
Vratislav Lokvenc
Peter Madsen
Gaetano Manno

KEY: On all match · On bench · Subbed or sent off (Counting game) · Subbed or sent off (playing less than 70 minutes) · Subbed on from bench (Counting Game) · Subbed on (playing less than 70 minutes) · Subbed on and then subbed or sent off (Counting Game) · Subbed on and then subbed or sent off (playing less than 70 minutes) · Not in 16

HANSA ROSTOCK

Final Position: **17th**

KEY: Won / Drawn / Lost

							Attendance
1	grpr1	**Freiburg**	A	D	0-0		20,000
2	grpr1	**W Bremen**	H	L	0-4		25,000
3	grpr1	**Schalke**	A	W	2-0	Di Salvo 33,77	62,000
4	grpr1	**Kaiserslautern**	H	L	2-3	Allback 71,90	19,000
5	grpr1	**Wolfsburg**	H	L	1-2	Madsen 33	15,000
6	grpr1	**B M'gladbach**	A	D	2-2	Di Salvo 53,59	40,000
7	grpr1	**Hannover 96**	H	L	1-3	Tjikuzu 88	16,000
8	grpr1	**Bochum**	A	W	1-0	Prica 75	21,000
9	grpr1	**Bayern Munich**	H	L	0-2		29,000
10	grpr1	**Mainz**	A	L	1-3	Arvidsson 81	20,000
11	grpr1	**Nuremburg**	H	L	0-2		16,000
12	grpr1	**Stuttgart**	A	L	0-4		43,000
13	grpr1	**Hamburg**	H	L	0-6		18,000
14	grpr1	**Hertha Berlin**	A	D	1-1	Rasmussen, T 36	40,000
15	grpr1	**B Leverkusen**	H	L	0-2		17,000
16	grpr1	**Arminia B**	A	D	1-1	Di Salvo 52	23,000
17	grpr1	**B Dortmund**	H	D	1-1	Allback 33	13,000
18	grpr1	**Freiburg**	H	D	0-0		22,000
19	grpr1	**W Bremen**	A	L	2-3	Rasmussen, D 45; Rasmussen, T 64	38,000
20	grpr1	**Schalke**	H	D	2-2	Prica 66; Arvidsson 73	24,000
21	grpr1	**Kaiserslautern**	A	L	1-2	Prica 83	28,000
22	grpr1	**Wolfsburg**	A	L	0-4		23,000
23	grpr1	**B M'gladbach**	H	D	0-0		12,000
24	grpr1	**Hannover 96**	A	W	1-0	Prica 28	25,000
25	grpr1	**Bochum**	H	W	3-1	Di Salvo 36,49; Prica 52	20,000
26	grpr1	**Bayern Munich**	A	L	1-3	Mohrle 16	45,000
27	grpr1	**Mainz**	H	W	2-0	Rasmussen, T 41; Hartmann 58	22,000
28	grpr1	**Nuremburg**	A	L	0-3		28,000
29	grpr1	**Stuttgart**	H	W	2-1	Allback 39; Prica 74	23,000
30	grpr1	**Hamburg**	A	L	0-3		56,000
31	grpr1	**Hertha Berlin**	H	W	2-1	Sebastian 45; Litmanen 70	25,000
32	grpr1	**B Leverkusen**	A	L	0-3		23,000
33	grpr1	**Arminia B**	H	D	1-1	Rasmussen, T 27 pen	15,000
34	grpr1	**B Dortmund**	A	L	1-2	Vorbeck 15	80,000

MONTHLY POINTS TALLY

AUGUST	4	44%
SEPTEMBER	1	11%
OCTOBER	3	20%
NOVEMBER	1	8%
DECEMBER	2	33%
JANUARY	1	17%
FEBRUARY	2	17%
MARCH	6	67%
APRIL	9	60%
MAY	1	11%

KEY PLAYERS - GOALSCORERS

Antonio Di Salvo

Goals in the League	7	Player Strike Rate Average number of minutes between League goals scored by player	319
Contribution to Attacking Power Average number of minutes between League team goals while on pitch	106	Club Strike Rate Average number of minutes between League goals scored by club	99

	PLAYER	LGE GOALS	POWER	STRIKE RATE
1	Antonio Di Salvo	7	106	319 mins
2	Rade Prica	6	79	320 mins
3	Marcus Allback	4	92	395 mins
4	Thomas Rasmussen	4	132	596 mins
5	Michael Hartmann	1	81	1211 mins

KEY PLAYERS - MIDFIELDERS

Michael Hartmann

Goals in the League	1	Contribution to Attacking Power Average number of minutes between League team goals while on pitch	81
Defensive Rating Average number of mins between goals conceded while on the pitch	53	Scoring Difference Defensive Rating minus Contribution to Attacking Power	-28

	PLAYER	LGE GOALS	DEF RATE	POWER	SCORE DIFF
1	Michael Hartmann	1	53	81	-28 mins
2	Joakim Persson	0	49	100	-51 mins
3	Marcus Lantz	0	48	105	-57 mins
4	Rene Rydlewicz	0	38	105	-67 mins
5	Thomas Rasmussen	4	48	132	-84 mins

KEY PLAYERS - DEFENDERS

Ronald Maul

Goals Conceded Number of League goals conceded while the player was on the pitch	35	Clean Sheets In games when player was on pitch for at least 70 minutes	5
Defensive Rating Ave number of mins between League goals conceded while on the pitch	55	Club Defensive Rating Average number of mins between League goals conceded by the club this season	47

	PLAYER	CON LGE	CLEAN SHEETS	DEF RATE
1	Ronald Maul	35	5	55 mins
2	Razundara Tjikuzu	26	3	50 mins
3	Uwe Mohrle	64	6	45 mins
4	Delano Hill	34	4	44 mins

KEY GOALKEEPER

Matthias Schober

Goals Conceded in the League	65	Counting Games League games when player was on pitch for at least 70 minutes	34
Defensive Rating Ave number of mins between League goals conceded while on the pitch	47	Clean Sheets In games when player was on pitch for at least 70 minutes	7

LEAGUE GOALS

Antonio Di Salvo

Minutes on the pitch	2232	Goals in the League	7
League average (mins between goals)	319		

	PLAYER	MINS	GOALS	AVE
1	Di Salvo	2232	7	319
2	Prica	1918	6	320
3	Rasmussen, T	2384	4	596
4	Allback	1579	4	395
5	Arvidsson	933	2	467
6	Mohrle	2910	1	2910
7	Vorbeck	516	1	516
8	Rasmussen, D	733	1	733
9	Sebastian	720	1	720
10	Tjikuzu	1294	1	1294
11	Hartmann	1211	1	1211
12	Litmanen	1075	1	1075
13	Madsen	933	1	933
	Other		0	
	TOTAL		31	

DISCIPLINARY

	PLAYER	YELLOW	RED	AVE
1	Prica	12	1	147
2	Hartmann	5	0	242
3	Rasmussen, D	2	1	244
4	Lantz	10	0	261
5	Lapaczinski	3	0	310
6	Rydlewicz	5	1	332
7	Persson	7	0	372
8	Maul	5	0	385
9	Allback	3	1	394
10	Mohrle	6	0	485
11	Hill	3	0	500
12	Vorbeck	1	0	516
13	Di Salvo	4	0	558
	Other	11	0	
	TOTAL	77	4	

TOP POINT EARNERS

	PLAYER	GAMES	AV PTS
1	Michael Hartmann	14	1.21
2	Ronald Maul	18	1.11
3	Rade Prica	16	1.06
4	Antonio Di Salvo	20	1.00
5	Marcus Lantz	28	1.00
6	Joakim Persson	28	0.96
7	Marcus Allback	16	0.94
8	Uwe Mohrle	32	0.91
9	Matthias Schober	34	0.88
10	Thomas Rasmussen	22	0.82
	CLUB AVERAGE:		0.88

TEAM OF THE SEASON

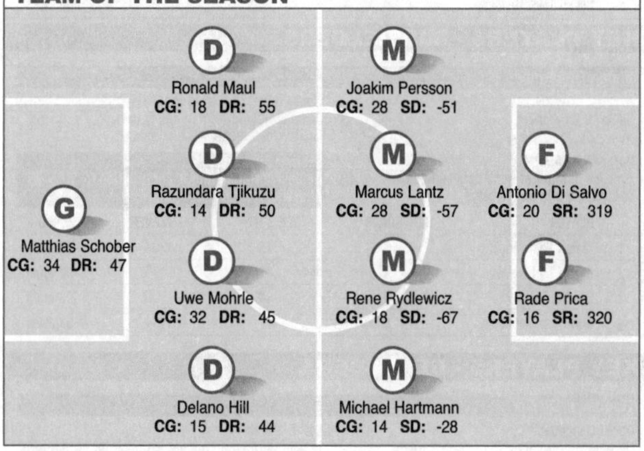

D
Ronald Maul
CG: 18 DR: 55
M
Joakim Persson
CG: 28 SD: -51
D
Razundara Tjikuzu
CG: 14 DR: 50
M
Marcus Lantz
CG: 28 SD: -57
F
Antonio Di Salvo
CG: 20 SR: 319
G
Matthias Schober
CG: 34 DR: 47
D
Uwe Mohrle
CG: 32 DR: 45
M
Rene Rydlewicz
CG: 18 SD: -67
F
Rade Prica
CG: 16 SR: 320
D
Delano Hill
CG: 15 DR: 44
M
Michael Hartmann
CG: 14 SD: -28

LEAGUE APPEARANCES, BOOKINGS AND CAPS

	AGE (on 01/07/05)	IN NAMED 18	APPEARANCES	COUNTING GAMES	MINUTES ON PITCH	YELLOW CARDS	RED CARDS	THIS SEASON	HOME COUNTRY
Goalkeepers									
Carsten Busch	24	1	0	0	0	0	0	-	Germany
Alex Keller	28	30	0	0	0	0	0	-	Germany
Matthias Schober	29	34	34	34	3060	3	0	-	Germany
Defenders									
Delano Hill	30	31	22	15	1500	3	0	-	Holland
Denis Lapaczinski	23	24	13	10	931	3	0	-	Germany
Kim Madsen	31	19	11	10	933	1	0	-	Denmark
Ronald Maul	32	31	26	18	1925	5	0	-	Germany
Uwe Mohrle	25	33	33	32	2910	6	0	-	Germany
Martin Pohl	24	2	0	0	0	0	0	-	Germany
Tim Sebastian	21	15	8	8	720	0	0	-	Germany
Razundara Tjikuzu	25	17	15	14	1294	2	0	-	Namibia
Midfielders									
Godfried Aduobe	29	9	4	0	64	0	0	-	Ghana
Kevin Hansen	25	1	0	0	0	0	0	-	Germany
Michael Hartmann	30	14	14	14	1211	5	0	-	Germany
Marcus Lantz	29	31	30	28	2617	10	0	-	Sweden
Thomas Meggle	30	26	14	3	404	4	0	-	Germany
Gabriel Melkam	25	3	1	0	29	0	0	-	Nigeria
Joakim Persson	30	31	30	28	2604	7	0	-	Sweden
David Rasmussen	28	28	15	5	733	2	1	-	Denmark
Thomas Rasmussen	28	32	32	22	2384	4	0	-	Denmark
Rene Rydlewicz	31	31	31	18	1995	5	1	-	Germany
Marc Stein	19	1	0	0	0	0	0	-	Germany
Forwards									
Marcus Allback	32	25	23	16	1579	3	1	8	Sweden (13)
Magnus Arvidsson	31	29	20	6	933	0	0	-	Sweden
Shergo Biran	26	4	2	0	27	0	0	-	Germany
Antonio Di Salvo	26	34	33	20	2232	4	0	-	Italy
Jari Litmanen	34	13	13	11	1075	1	0	-	Finland
Rade Prica	25	29	29	16	1918	12	1	1	Sweden (13)
Amir Shapourzadeh	22	2	0	0	0	0	0	-	Iran
Marco Vorbeck	24	16	11	2	516	1	0	-	Germany

SQUAD APPEARANCES

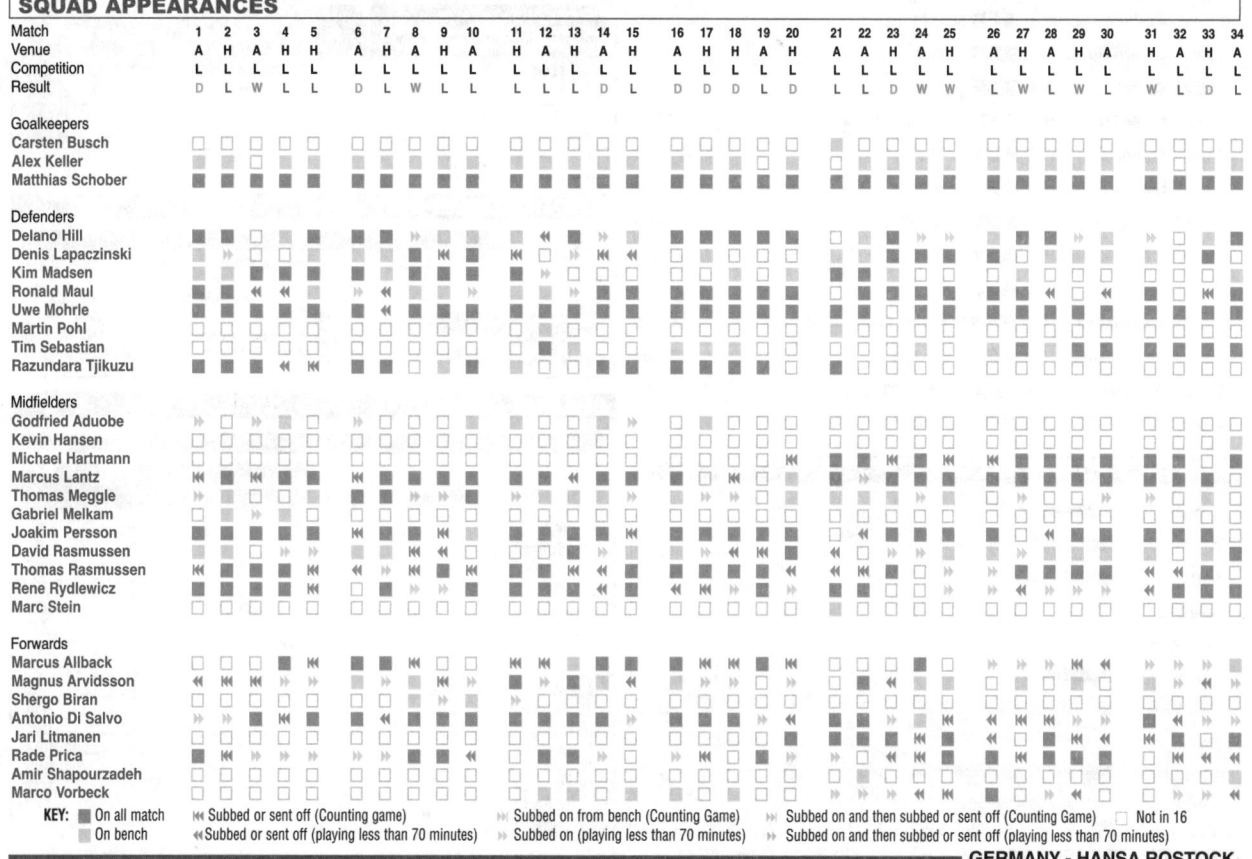

Match	1	2	3	4	5	6	7	8	9	10	11	12	13	14	15	16	17	18	19	20	21	22	23	24	25	26	27	28	29	30	31	32	33	34
Venue	A	H	A	H	H	A	H	A	H	A	H	A	H	A	H	A	H	H	A	H	A	A	H	A	H	A	H	A	H	A	H	A	H	A
Competition	L	L	L	L	L	L	L	L	L	L	L	L	L	L	L	L	L	L	L	L	L	L	L	L	L	L	L	L	L	L	L	L	L	L
Result	D	L	W	L	L	D	L	W	L	L	L	L	L	D	L	D	D	D	L	D	L	L	D	W	W	L	W	L	W	L	W	L	D	L

Goalkeepers
Carsten Busch
Alex Keller
Matthias Schober

Defenders
Delano Hill
Denis Lapaczinski
Kim Madsen
Ronald Maul
Uwe Mohrle
Martin Pohl
Tim Sebastian
Razundara Tjikuzu

Midfielders
Godfried Aduobe
Kevin Hansen
Michael Hartmann
Marcus Lantz
Thomas Meggle
Gabriel Melkam
Joakim Persson
David Rasmussen
Thomas Rasmussen
Rene Rydlewicz
Marc Stein

Forwards
Marcus Allback
Magnus Arvidsson
Shergo Biran
Antonio Di Salvo
Jari Litmanen
Rade Prica
Amir Shapourzadeh
Marco Vorbeck

KEY: On all match / On bench
Subbed or sent off (Counting game) / Subbed or sent off (playing less than 70 minutes)
Subbed on from bench (Counting Game) / Subbed on (playing less than 70 minutes)
Subbed on and then subbed or sent off (Counting Game) / Subbed on and then subbed or sent off (playing less than 70 minutes)
Not in 16

FC FREIBURG

Final Position: **18th**

KEY: Won Drawn Lost

								Attendance
1	grpr1	**Hansa Rostock**	H	D	0-0			20,000
2	grpr1	**Wolfsburg**	A	W	1-0	Dorn 85		23,000
3	grpr1	**B M'gladbach**	H	D	1-1	Antar 28		21,000
4	grpr1	**Hannover 96**	A	D	2-2	Dorn 59; Cairo 73		32,000
5	grpr1	**Bochum**	H	D	1-1	Schumann 58		22,000
6	grpr1	**Bayern Munich**	A	L	1-3	Sanou 3		27,000
7	grpr1	**Mainz**	H	L	1-2	Tskitishvilli 70		22,000
8	grpr1	**Nuremburg**	A	L	0-3			21,000
9	grpr1	**Stuttgart**	H	W	2-0	Iaschvili 35; Coulibaly 90		25,000
10	grpr1	**Hamburg**	A	L	0-4			42,000
11	grpr1	**Hertha Berlin**	H	L	1-3	Cairo 25		23,000
12	grpr1	**B Leverkusen**	A	L	1-4	Coulibaly 29		22,000
13	grpr1	**Arminia B**	H	L	2-3	Coulibaly 15; Iaschvili 39		21,000
14	grpr1	**B Dortmund**	A	L	0-2			76,000
15	grpr1	**Kaiserslautern**	A	L	0-3			30,000
16	grpr1	**W Bremen**	H	L	0-6			24,000
17	grpr1	**Schalke**	A	D	1-1	Antar 86		61,000
18	grpr1	**Hansa Rostock**	A	D	0-0			22,000
19	grpr1	**Wolfsburg**	H	W	1-0	Bajramovic 57		21,000
20	grpr1	**B M'gladbach**	A	L	2-3	Coulibaly 13; Riether 61		40,000
21	grpr1	**Hannover 96**	H	D	0-0			21,000
22	grpr1	**Bochum**	A	L	1-3	Aogo 81		18,000
23	grpr1	**Bayern Munich**	H	L	0-1			25,000
24	grpr1	**Mainz**	A	L	0-5			20,000
25	grpr1	**Nuremburg**	H	L	2-3	Koejoe 8; Bajramovic 60		17,000
26	grpr1	**Stuttgart**	A	L	0-1			40,000
27	grpr1	**Hamburg**	H	D	1-1	Kruppke 19		20,000
28	grpr1	**Hertha Berlin**	A	L	1-3	Koejoe 73		30,000
29	grpr1	**B Leverkusen**	H	L	1-3	Iaschvili 37		22,000
30	grpr1	**Arminia B**	A	L	1-3	Cairo 15		18,000
31	grpr1	**B Dortmund**	H	D	2-2	Sanou 11; Coulibaly 84		25,000
32	grpr1	**Kaiserslautern**	H	L	1-2	Bajramovic 73		18,000
33	grpr1	**W Bremen**	A	L	1-4	Coulibaly 23		35,000
34	grpr1	**Schalke**	H	L	2-3	Iaschvili 11; Antar 78		24,000

MONTHLY POINTS TALLY

AUGUST	5	56%
SEPTEMBER	2	22%
OCTOBER	3	20%
NOVEMBER	0	0%
DECEMBER	1	17%
JANUARY	4	67%
FEBRUARY	1	8%
MARCH	0	0%
APRIL	2	13%
MAY	0	0%

KEY PLAYERS - GOALSCORERS

Soumaila Coulibaly

Goals in the League	6	Player Strike Rate Average number of minutes between League goals scored by player	452
Contribution to Attacking Power Average number of minutes between League team goals while on pitch	104	Club Strike Rate Average number of minutes between League goals scored by club	99

	PLAYER	LGE GOALS	POWER	STRIKE RATE
1	Soumaila Coulibaly	6	104	452 mins
2	Alexander Iaschvili	4	88	598 mins
3	Ellery Cairo	3	106	813 mins
4	Daniel Schumann	1	103	1442 mins
5	Levan Tskitishvilli	1	93	1588 mins

KEY PLAYERS - MIDFIELDERS

Zlatan Bajramovic

Goals in the League	3	Contribution to Attacking Power Average number of minutes between League team goals while on pitch	91
Defensive Rating Average number of mins between goals conceded while on the pitch	46	Scoring Difference Defensive Rating minus Contribution to Attacking Power	-45

	PLAYER	LGE GOALS	DEF RATE	POWER	SCORE DIFF
1	Zlatan Bajramovic	3	46	91	-45 mins
2	Levan Tskitishvilli	1	41	93	-52 mins
3	Sascha Riether	1	44	106	-62 mins
4	Soumaila Coulibaly	6	41	104	-63 mins

KEY PLAYERS - DEFENDERS

Boubacar Diarra

Goals Conceded Number of League goals conceded while the player was on the pitch	32	Clean Sheets In games when player was on pitch for at least 70 minutes	3
Defensive Rating Ave number of mins between League goals conceded while on the pitch	46	Club Defensive Rating Average number of mins between League goals conceded by the club this season	41

	PLAYER	CON LGE	CLEAN SHEETS	DEF RATE
1	Boubacar Diarra	32	3	46 mins
2	Youssef Wasef Mohamad	54	6	45 mins
3	Andreas Ibertsberger	26	3	43 mins
4	Daniel Schumann	42	2	34 mins

KEY GOALKEEPER

Richard Golz

Goals Conceded in the League	71	Counting Games League games when player was on pitch for at least 70 minutes	32
Defensive Rating Ave number of mins between League goals conceded while on the pitch	40	Clean Sheets In games when player was on pitch for at least 70 minutes	6

LEAGUE GOALS

Soumaila Coulibaly

Minutes on the pitch	2712	Goals in the League	6
League average (mins between goals)	452		

	PLAYER	MINS	GOALS	AVE
1	Coulibaly	2712	6	452
2	Iaschvili	2393	4	598
3	Koejoe	961	3	320
4	Cairo	2439	3	813
5	Antar	1322	3	441
6	Bajramovic	1096	3	365
7	Sanou	1287	2	644
8	Dorn	601	2	301
9	Riether	2016	1	2016
10	Tskitishvilli	1588	1	1588
11	Kruppke	1632	1	1632
12	Aogo	1010	1	1010
13	Schumann	1442	1	1442
	Other		0	
	TOTAL		31	

DISCIPLINARY RECORDS

	PLAYER	YELLOW	RED	AVE
1	Olajengbesi	4	1	130
2	Bajramovic	8	0	137
3	Willi	3	0	201
4	Berner	2	0	302
5	Mohamad	7	1	306
6	Antar	4	0	330
7	Cairo	6	0	406
8	Kruppke	4	0	408
9	Tanko	2	0	423
10	Sanou	3	0	429
11	Schumann	3	0	480
12	Aogo	2	0	505
13	Riether	3	0	672
	Other	9	2	
	TOTAL	60	4	

TOP POINT EARNERS

	PLAYER	GAMES	AV PTS
1	Boubacar Diarra	14	0.79
2	Levan Tskitishvilli	16	0.69
3	Youssef Wasef Mohamad	26	0.69
4	Alexander Iaschvili	24	0.67
5	Sascha Riether	21	0.62
6	Andreas Ibertsberger	12	0.58
7	Richard Golz	32	0.53
8	Ellery Cairo	27	0.52
9	Ismael Soumaila Coulibaly	29	0.52
10	Daniel Schumann	13	0.38
	CLUB AVERAGE:		0.53

LEAGUE APPEARANCES, BOOKINGS AND CAPS

	AGE (on 01/07/05)	IN NAMED 18	APPEARANCES	COUNTING GAMES	MINUTES ON PITCH	YELLOW CARDS	RED CARDS	THIS SEASON	HOME COUNTRY
Goalkeepers									
Richard Golz	37	32	32	32	2860	0	1	-	Germany
Julian Reinard	22	21	2	1	110	0	0	-	Germany
Timo Reus	31	15	1	1	90	0	0	-	Germany
Defenders									
Bruno Berner	27	23	12	3	605	2	0	1	Switzerland (45)
Boubacar Diarra	25	27	20	14	1468	1	1	-	Mali
Lars Hermel	34	13	12	9	888	1	0	-	Germany
Andreas Ibertsberger	22	13	13	12	1125	0	0	-	Austria
Otar Khizaneishvili	23	8	8	7	673	0	0	-	Georgia
Oumar Konde	25	15	5	2	308	1	0	-	Switzerland
Youssef Mohamad	25	29	29	26	2455	7	1	-	Lebanon
Stefan Muller	31	17	6	1	231	1	0	-	Germany
Seyi Olajengbesi	24	10	9	6	654	4	1	-	Nigeria
Daniel Schumann	28	27	19	13	1442	3	0	-	Germany
Midfielders									
Roda Antar	24	29	27	9	1322	4	0	-	Lebanon
Dennis Aogo	18	20	15	9	1010	2	0	-	Germany
Zlatan Bajramovic	25	15	15	10	1096	8	0	-	Bosnia
Dennis Buhrer	22	1	0	0	0	0	0	-	Germany
Soumaila Coulibaly	27	32	32	29	2712	4	0	-	Mali
Torge Hollmann	23	4	1	0	7	0	0	-	Germany
Jonathan Pitroipa	19	9	4	0	112	0	0	-	Burkino Faso
Sascha Riether	22	25	25	21	2016	3	0	-	Germany
Levan Tskitishvilli	28	21	20	16	1588	1	0	-	Georgia
Iobias Willi	25	16	11	4	604	3	0	-	Germany
Forwards									
Ellery Cairo	26	28	28	27	2439	6	0	-	Holland
Regis Dorn	25	22	16	3	601	0	0	-	France
Alexander Iaschvili	27	31	29	24	2393	1	0	-	Georgia
Sam Koejoe	30	13	12	10	961	1	0	-	Surinam
Dennis Kruppke	25	30	26	14	1632	4	0	-	Germany
Wilfried Sanou	21	32	22	10	1287	3	0	-	Burkino Faso
Ibrahim Tanko	27	27	20	4	847	2	0	-	Ghana

TEAM OF THE SEASON

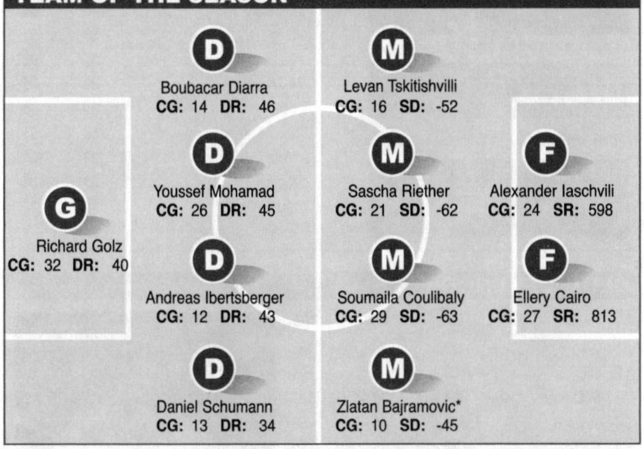
D
Boubacar Diarra
CG: 14 DR: 46
D
Youssef Mohamad
CG: 26 DR: 45
D
Andreas Ibertsberger
CG: 12 DR: 43
D
Daniel Schumann
CG: 13 DR: 34
G
Richard Golz
CG: 32 DR: 40
M
Levan Tskitishvilli
CG: 16 SD: -52
M
Sascha Riether
CG: 21 SD: -62
M
Soumaila Coulibaly
CG: 29 SD: -63
M
Zlatan Bajramovic*
CG: 10 SD: -45
F
Alexander Iaschvili
CG: 24 SR: 598
F
Ellery Cairo
CG: 27 SR: 813

SQUAD APPEARANCES

Match	1	2	3	4	5	6	7	8	9	10	11	12	13	14	15	16	17	18	19	20	21	22	23	24	25	26	27	28	29	30	31	32	33	34
Venue	H	A	H	A	H	A	H	A	H	A	H	A	H	A	A	H	A	A	H	A	H	A	H	A	H	A	H	A	H	A	H	H	A	H
Competition	L	L	L	L	L	L	L	L	L	L	L	L	L	L	L	L	L	L	L	L	L	L	L	L	L	L	L	L	L	L	L	L	L	L
Result	D	W	D	D	D	L	L	L	W	L	L	L	L	L	L	L	D	D	W	L	D	L	L	L	L	L	D	L	L	L	D	L	L	L

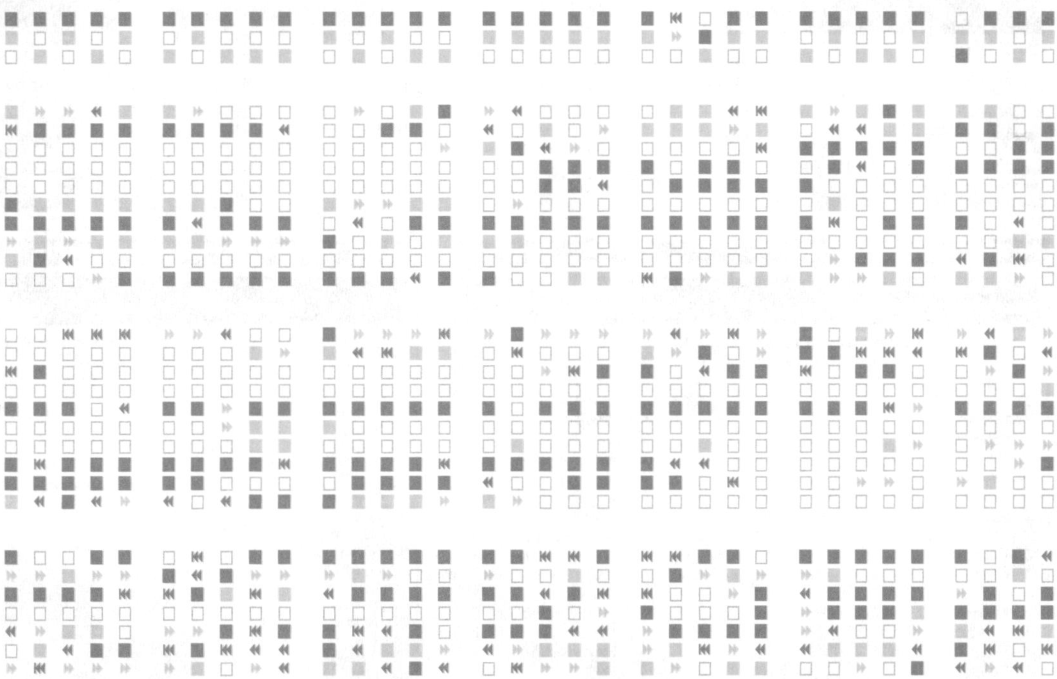

Goalkeepers
Richard Golz
Julian Reinard
Timo Reus

Defenders
Bruno Berner
Boubacar Diarra
Lars Hermel
Andreas Ibertsberger
Otar Khizaneishvili
Oumar Konde
Youssef Wasef Mohamad
Stefan Muller
Seyi Olajengbesi
Daniel Schumann

Midfielders
Roda Antar
Dennis Aogo
Zlatan Bajramovic
Dennis Buhrer
Ismael Soumaila Coulibaly
Torge Hollmann
Jonathan Pitroipa
Sascha Riether
Levan Tskitishvilli
Iobias Willi

Forwards
Ellery Cairo
Regis Dorn
Alexander Iaschvili
Sam Koejoe
Dennis Kruppke
Wilfried Sanou
Ibrahim Tanko

KEY: On all match | On bench | Subbed or sent off (Counting game) | Subbed or sent off (playing less than 70 minutes) | Subbed on from bench (Counting Game) | Subbed on (playing less than 70 minutes) | Subbed on and then subbed or sent off (Counting Game) | Subbed on and then subbed or sent off (playing less than 70 minutes) | Not in 16

FRENCH LEAGUE ROUND-UP

FINAL LEAGUE TABLE

	HOME						AWAY					TOTAL			
	P	W	D	L	F	A	W	D	L	F	A	F	A	DIF	PTS
Lyon	38	13	5	1	33	10	9	8	2	23	12	56	22	34	79
Lille	38	11	6	2	30	11	7	7	5	21	18	51	29	22	67
Monaco	38	11	6	2	38	21	4	12	3	14	14	52	35	17	63
Rennes	38	13	4	2	35	12	2	6	11	14	30	49	42	7	55
Marseille	38	9	4	6	26	19	6	6	7	21	23	47	42	5	55
St Etienne	38	9	8	2	25	7	3	9	7	22	27	47	34	13	53
Lens	38	10	6	3	30	15	3	7	9	15	24	45	39	6	52
Auxerre	38	10	7	2	33	19	4	3	12	15	28	48	47	1	52
Paris SG	38	9	8	2	24	15	3	7	9	16	26	40	41	-1	51
Sochaux	38	10	3	6	25	16	3	8	8	17	25	42	41	1	50
Strasbourg	38	10	5	4	29	17	2	7	10	13	26	42	43	-1	48
Nice	38	7	10	2	22	13	3	6	10	16	32	38	45	-7	46
Toulouse	38	9	4	6	20	19	3	6	10	16	24	36	43	-7	46
AC Ajaccio	38	7	10	2	24	15	3	5	11	12	25	36	40	-4	45
Bordeaux	38	5	11	3	24	18	3	9	7	13	23	37	41	-4	44
Metz	38	7	9	3	22	15	3	5	11	11	30	33	45	-12	44
Nantes	38	7	9	3	21	16	3	4	12	12	22	33	38	-5	43
Caen	38	5	8	6	15	18	5	4	10	21	42	36	60	-24	42
Bastia	38	10	4	5	24	19	1	4	14	8	29	32	48	-16	41
Istres	38	5	5	9	11	19	1	9	9	14	32	25	51	-26	32

CLUB STRIKE FORCE

Juninho; on target for Lyon

1 Lyon

Goals scored in the League	56
Club Strike Rate (CSR) Average number of minutes between League goals scored by club	61

	CLUB	GOALS	CSR
1	Lyon	56	61
2	Monaco	52	66
3	Lille	51	67
4	Auxerre	48	71
5	Rennes	48	71
6	Marseille	47	73
7	St Etienne	47	73
8	Lens	45	76
9	Sochaux	42	81
10	Strasbourg	42	81
11	Paris SG	40	86
12	Nice	38	90
13	Bordeaux	37	92
14	AC Ajaccio	36	95
15	Caen	36	95
16	Toulouse	36	95
17	Metz	33	104
18	Nantes	33	104
19	Bastia	32	107
20	Istres	25	137

CLUB DISCIPLINARY RECORDS

Omar Daf; nine cards for Sochaux

1 Istres

League Yellow	99
League Red	8
League Total	107
Cards Average in League Average number of minutes between a card being shown of either colour	32

	CLUB	Y	R	TOTAL	AVE
1	Istres	99	8	107	32
2	Nice	98	6	104	33
3	Monaco	86	4	90	38
4	Paris SG	83	7	90	38
5	AC Ajaccio	83	5	88	39
6	Marseille	84	2	86	40
7	Caen	81	2	83	41
8	Lille	74	7	81	42
9	Toulouse	77	4	81	42
10	Bastia	71	6	77	44
11	Bordeaux	70	8	78	44
12	Rennes	73	5	78	44
13	Strasbourg	70	7	77	44
14	Lens	70	3	73	47
15	St Etienne	68	3	71	48
16	Sochaux	66	4	70	49
17	Nantes	63	6	69	50
18	Metz	65	2	67	51
19	Lyon	53	1	54	63
20	Auxerre	53	0	53	65

CLUB DEFENCES

	CLUB	LGE	CS	CDR
1	Lyon	22	20	155
2	Lille	29	16	118
3	St Etienne	34	18	101
4	Monaco	35	15	98
5	Nantes	38	15	90
6	AC Ajaccio	39	13	88
7	Lens	39	12	88
8	Bordeaux	41	16	83
9	Paris SG	41	12	83
10	Sochaux	41	15	83
11	Marseille	42	11	81
12	Rennes	42	13	81
13	Strasbourg	43	12	80
14	Toulouse	43	12	80
15	Metz	45	11	76
16	Nice	45	14	76
17	Auxerre	47	13	73
18	Bastia	48	10	71
19	Istres	50	10	68
20	Caen	60	10	57

Cris defending for Lyon

1 Lyon

Goals conceded in the League	22
Clean Sheets (CS) Number of league games where no goals were conceded	20
Club Defensive Rate (CDR) Average number of minutes between League goals conceded by club	155

PLAYER NATIONALITIES

Overseas country with the most player appearances in the French League - Brazil

540 league appearances by Brazilian players

	COUNTRY	PLAYERS	IN SQUAD	LGE APP	% LGE ACT	CAPS	MOST APP	APP
1	France	383	7843	6450	63.4	88	Rio Mavuba	100.0
2	Brazil	25	585	540	5.3	16	Rodrigo	93.9
3	Senegal	24	511	437	4.3	51	Tony Mario Sylva	98.7
4	Ivory Coast	13	361	302	3.2	20	Didier Zokora	91.9
5	Cameroon	19	313	275	2.7	18	Achille Emana	90.3
6	Mali	8	204	181	1.8		Mahamadou Diarra	85.7
7	Serbia & Montenegro	12	214	183	1.7	5	Nisa Saveljic	80.6
8	Morocco	7	191	177	1.6		Abdeslam Ouaddou	86.8
9	Nigeria	7	166	153	1.4		John Utaka	86.8
10	Sweden	4	134	124	1.2	9	Andreas Isaksson	99.2
11	Argentina	5	127	116	1.2	7	Juan-Pablo Francia	70.3
12	Greece	3	92	91	1.1		Vassilis Zikos	81.5
13	Switzerland	5	105	94	1.0	15	Alexander Frei	88.1
14	Algeria	6	109	94	0.9		Yacine Abdessadki	87.5
15	Colombia	3	94	90	0.9		Mario Yepes	82.3
16	Belgium	5	113	100	0.8	15	Roberto Bisconti	50.2
17	Portugal	4	86	67	0.6	8	Pauleta	78.0
18	Czech Republic	2	53	52	0.6	10	Rene Bolf	73.7

CLUB MAKE-UP – HOME AND OVERSEAS PLAYERS

1 Lyon

90.0% of appearances by overseas players

	CLUB	OVERSEAS	HOME	% OVERSEAS	% LGE ACT	MOST APP	APP
1	Lyon	15	13	53.6	90.0	Michael Essien	93.4
2	Monaco	18	8	69.2	89.3	Flavio Roma	86.8
3	Marseille	15	16	48.4	67.9	Habib Beye	95.7
4	Paris SG	17	14	54.8	62.1	Mario Yepes	82.3
5	Nantes	14	21	40.0	50.3	Gilles Yapi Yapo	84.6
6	Rennes	10	16	38.5	46.6	Andreas Isaksson	99.2
7	Sochaux	15	16	48.4	45.2	S Diawara	73.2
8	Lille	11	15	42.3	45.1	Tony Mario Sylva	98.7
9	Lens	12	14	46.2	44.8	John Utaka	86.8
10	Istres	10	23	30.3	41.6	Nisa Saveljic	80.6
11	AC Ajaccio	10	18	35.7	40.7	Rodrigo	93.9
12	Auxerre	9	21	30.0	37.9	Rene Bolf	73.7
13	St Etienne	8	18	30.8	37.0	Herita Ilunga	96.2
14	Strasbourg	10	16	38.5	36.9	Yacine Abdessadki	87.5
15	Bordeaux	9	17	34.6	35.1	Michalis Kapsis	75.6
16	Bastia	10	21	32.3	29.4	Youssouf Hadji	75.5
17	Nice	8	24	25.0	26.9	Sammy Traore	75.1
18	Toulouse	5	25	16.7	21.0	Achille Emana	90.3
19	Caen	7	25	21.9	19.5	Ibrahima Faye	68.9
20	Metz	9	22	29.0	19.3	Herve Tum	75.1

CHART-TOPPING MIDFIELDERS

1 Essien - Lyon	
Goals scored in the League	4
Defensive Rating Av number of mins between League goals conceded while on the pitch	177
Contribution to Attacking Power Average number of minutes between League team goals while on pitch	64
Scoring Difference Defensive Rating minus Contribution to Attacking Power	113

	PLAYER	CLUB	GOALS	DEF RATE	POWER	S DIFF
1	Essien	Lyon	4	177	64	113
2	Malouda	Lyon	5	166	58	108
3	Diarra	Lyon	2	163	62	101
4	Juninho	Lyon	13	153	61	92
5	Chalme	Lille	0	120	60	60
6	Zikos	Monaco	0	112	61	51
7	Bodmer	Lille	4	124	75	49
8	Zokora	St Etienne	0	112	73	39
9	Dumont	Lille	3	102	66	36
10	Andre Luiz	AC Ajaccio	5	117	82	35
11	Evra	Monaco	0	102	67	35
12	Bernardi	Monaco	1	107	74	33
13	Mathieu	Sochaux	3	109	76	33
14	Sable	St Etienne	5	104	72	32
15	Rool	Bordeaux	2	133	103	30

CHART-TOPPING GOALSCORERS

1 Frei - Rennes	
Goals scored in the League	20
Contribution to Attacking Power (AP) Average number of minutes between League team goals while on pitch	71
Club Strike Rate (CSR) Average minutes between League goals scored by club	71
Player Strike Rate Average number of minutes between League goals scored by player	151

	PLAYER	CLUB	GOALS: LGE	POWER	CSR	S RATE
1	Frei	Rennes	20	71	71	151
2	Moussilou	Lille	13	63	67	170
3	Pagis	Strasbourg	14	77	81	177
4	Mazure	Caen	13	87	95	194
5	Lucas Pereira	AC Ajaccio	11	84	95	199
6	Chevanton	Monaco	10	60	66	200
7	Kallon	Monaco	11	65	66	204
8	Pauleta	Paris SG	13	86	86	205
9	Juninho	Lyon	13	61	61	212
10	Niang	Strasbourg	12	81	81	219
11	Feindouno	St Etienne	13	68	73	232
12	Moreira	Toulouse	11	99	95	235
13	Watier	Caen	9	107	95	239
14	Utaka	Lens	12	74	76	248
15	Vahirua	Nice	10	73	90	248

CHART-TOPPING DEFENDERS

1 Abidal - Lyon	
Goals Conceded in the League The number of League goals conceded while he was on the pitch	13
Clean Sheets In games when he played at least 70 mins	14
Club Defensive Rating Average mins between League goals conceded by the club this season	155
Defensive Rating Average number of minutes between League goals conceded while on pitch	188

	PLAYER	CLUB	CON: LGE	CS	CDR	DEF RATE
1	Abidal	Lyon	13	14	155	188
2	Reveillere	Lyon	16	20	155	185
3	Cris	Lyon	17	18	155	175
4	Cacapa	Lyon	10	10	155	166
5	Angbwa	Lille	10	9	118	165
6	Schmitz	Lille	19	10	118	121
7	Tafforeau	Lille	17	11	118	121
8	Diawara	St Etienne	17	14	101	119
9	Jemmali	Bordeaux	18	11	81	115
10	Tavlaridis	Lille	23	11	118	115
11	Ilunga	St Etienne	30	18	101	110
12	Vitakic	Lille	20	9	118	109
13	Squillaci	Monaco	23	12	98	107
14	Dzodic	AC Ajaccio	21	11	88	105
15	Modesto	Monaco	17	10	98	105

CHART-TOPPING GOALKEEPERS

1 Coupet - Lyon	
Counting Games Games in which he played at least 70 minutes	31
Goals Conceded in the League The number of League goals conceded while he was on the pitch	18
Clean Sheets In games when he played at least 70 mins	16
Defensive Rating Average number of minutes between League goals conceded while on pitch	155

	PLAYER	CLUB	GG	CONC	CS	DEF RATE
1	Coupet	Lyon	31	18	16	155
2	Sylva	Lille	38	29	16	116
3	Janot	St Etienne	38	32	18	107
4	Barthez	Marseille	30	28	10	96
5	Roma	Monaco	33	31	12	96
6	Porato	AC Ajaccio	35	35	13	90
7	Landreau	Nantes	37	37	15	90
8	Cassard	Strasbourg	33	33	12	90
9	Letizi	Paris SG	32	33	11	89
10	Rame	Bordeaux	37	38	16	88
11	Itandje	Lens	38	39	12	88
12	Richert	Sochaux	37	38	14	88
13	Isaksson	Rennes	37	42	13	81
14	Revault	Toulouse	38	43	12	80
15	Gregorini	Nice	38	44	14	78

PLAYER DISCIPLINARY RECORD

Bruno Cheyrou; a card every 147 minutes

4. Cheyrou - Marseille	
Cards Average mins between cards	147
League Yellow	5
League Red	0
TOTAL	5

	PLAYER		LY	LR	TOT	AVE
1	Bakour	Caen	5	1	6	91
2	Sirieix	Toulouse	8	1	9	140
3	Ilic	Istres	10	1	11	146
4	Cheyrou	Marseille	5	0	5	147
5	Die	Nice	10	1	11	149
6	Jankauskas	Nice	7	0	7	153
7	Leugueun	Istres	5	1	6	155
8	Faye	Istres	11	2	13	159
9	Daf	Sochaux	8	1	9	167
10	Nsame	Toulouse	4	0	4	168
11	Cherrad	Bastia	3	0	3	172
12	Rool	Bordeaux	10	3	13	173
13	Compan	St Etienne	3	0	3	176
14	Delaye	Istres	5	0	5	178
15	Keita	Strasbourg	5	1	6	183
16	Matingou	Bastia	9	0	9	188
17	Bisconti	Nice	9	0	9	190
18	Cardy	Toulouse	7	0	7	190
19	Jarjat	Nice	8	1	9	194
20	Robin	AC Ajaccio	12	1	13	198
21	Tavlaridis	Lille	11	2	13	203
22	Dieuze	Toulouse	9	0	9	204
23	Jemmali	Bordeaux	9	1	10	206
24	Mendy	Paris SG	10	1	11	206

TEAM OF THE SEASON

G
Coupet : Lyon
CG: 31 DR: 155

D
Abidal : Lyon
CG: 26 DR: 188

D
Angbwa : Lille
CG: 18 DR: 165

D
Diawara : St Etienne
CG: 22 DR: 119

D
Jemmali : Bordeaux
CG: 21 DR: 115

M
Essien : Lyon
CG: 34 SD: + 113

M
Chalme : Lille
CG: 25 SD: + 60

M
Zikos : Monaco
CG: 31 SD: + 51

M
Zokora : St Etienne
CG: 35 SD: + 39

F
Frei : Rennes
CG: 32 SR: 151

F
Moussilou : Lille
CG: 22 SR: 170

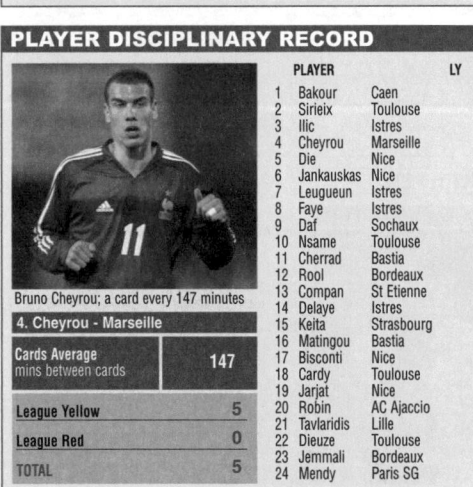

LYON

Final Position: **1st**

KEY: ☐Won ☐Drawn ☐Lost

							Attendance
1	frpr1	Nice	A	W	1-0	Elber 76	14,000
2	frpr1	Sochaux	H	D	1-1	Juninho 71	40,000
3	frpr1	Metz	A	D	1-1	Balmont 65	24,000
4	frpr1	Lille	H	W	1-0	Frau 8	20,000
5	frpr1	Rennes	A	W	2-1	Nilmar 80,87	23,000
6	ecgpd	Man Utd	H	D	2-2	Cris 35; Frau 44	35,000
7	frpr1	Bastia	H	D	0-0		32,000
8	frpr1	Toulouse	A	W	2-0	Essien 53; Malouda 90	31,000
9	frpr1	Monaco	H	D	0-0		40,000
10	ecgpd	Sparta Prague	A	W	2-1	Essien 25; Wiltord 58	12,000
11	frpr1	St Etienne	A	W	3-2	Juninho 34,89 pen; Govou 90	35,000
12	frpr1	Caen	H	W	4-0	Diarra 11; Malouda 15; Essien 33; Frau 70 pen	34,000
13	ecgpd	Fenerbahce	A	W	3-1	Juninho 55; Cris 66; Frau 87	49,000
14	frpr1	Istres	A	D	0-0		7,000
15	frpr1	Strasbourg	H	W	1-0	Frau 66	39,000
16	ecgpd	Fenerbahce	H	W	4-2	Essien 22; Malouda 53; Nilmar 90,90	36,000
17	frpr1	Lens	A	W	1-0	Itandje 35 og	40,000
18	frpr1	Nantes	H	W	2-0	Frau 46; Govou 60	36,000
19	frpr1	Paris SG	A	D	0-0		45,000
20	ecgpd	Man Utd	A	L	1-2	Diarra 40	66,398
21	frpr1	Auxerre	H	W	2-1	Wiltord 7; Juninho 30	39,000
22	frpr1	AC Ajaccio	A	D	1-1	Juninho 87	7,000
23	ecgpd	Sparta Prague	H	W	5-0	Essien 7; Nilmar 19,51; Idangar 83; Bergougnoux 90	39,000
24	frpr1	Bordeaux	A	D	0-0		33,000
25	frpr1	Marseille	H	D	1-1	Govou 39	37,000
26	frpr1	Sochaux	A	W	2-0	Bergougnoux 5; Diarra 41	18,000
27	frpr1	Metz	H	W	2-0	Juninho 82; Bergougnoux 86	38,000
28	frpr1	Lille	A	L	1-2	Juninho 77	21,000
29	frpr1	Rennes	H	W	2-1	Bergougnoux 44; Govou 45	37,000
30	frpr1	Bastia	A	D	1-1	Essien 18	5,000
31	frpr1	Toulouse	H	W	4-0	Juninho 1,51; Malouda 45; Bergougnoux 56	30,000
32	frpr1	Monaco	A	D	1-1	Clement 90	18,000
33	eckol1	W Bremen	A	W	3-0	Wiltord 9; Diarra 77; Juninho 80	37,000
34	frpr1	St Etienne	H	W	3-2	Wiltord 45; Malouda 46; Frau 48	39,000
35	frpr1	Caen	A	L	0-1		21,000
36	eckol2	W Bremen	H	W	7-2	Wiltord 8,55,64; Essien 17,30; Malouda 60; Berthod 80 pen	37,000
37	frpr1	Istres	H	W	2-1	Juninho 19; Govou 77	35,000
38	frpr1	Strasbourg	A	W	1-0	Wiltord 58	23,000
39	frpr1	Lens	H	W	1-0	Juninho 64	36,000
40	ecqfl1	PSV Eindhoven	H	D	1-1	Malouda 12	35,000
41	frpr1	Nantes	A	D	2-2	Frau 36,83	32,000
42	ecqfl2	PSV Eindhoven	A	L	1-1*	Wiltord 10 (*drew 2-2 on agg aet, lost 4-2 on penalties)	35,000
43	frpr1	Paris SG	H	L	0-1		40,000
44	frpr1	Auxerre	A	W	3-0	Juninho 27; Essien 45; Cris 55	14,000
45	frpr1	AC Ajaccio	H	W	2-1	Govou 35; Cacapa 64	39,000
46	frpr1	Bordeaux	H	W	5-1	Malouda 24; Cris 34,45; Govou 67,84	38,000
47	frpr1	Marseille	A	W	1-0	Juninho 54	58,000
48	frpr1	Nice	H	D	0-0		38,000

MONTHLY POINTS TALLY

AUGUST	4	33%
SEPTEMBER	12	100%
OCTOBER	9	75%
NOVEMBER	6	50%
DECEMBER	5	56%
JANUARY	8	53%
FEBRUARY	3	33%
MARCH	2	22%
APRIL	9	100%
MAY	9	60%

LEAGUE GOALS

	PLAYER	MINS	GOALS	AVE
1	Juninho	2672	13	212
2	Govou	2660	8	344
3	Frau	1863	7	266
4	Malouda	2916	5	599
5	Bergougnoux	635	4	159
6	Wiltord	1726	3	599
7	Essien	3104	3	1035
8	Cris	2880	2	1440
9	Nilmar	1056	2	528
10	Diarra	2840	2	1420
11	Balmont	57	1	57
12	Clement	522	1	522
13	Cacapa	1569	1	1569
	Other		2	
	TOTAL		53	

KEY PLAYERS - GOALSCORERS

Pernambucano Juninho

Goals in the League	13
Contribution to Attacking Power Average number of minutes between League team goals while on pitch	61
Player Strike Rate Average number of minutes between League goals scored by player	212
Club Strike Rate Average number of minutes between League goals scored by club	61

	PLAYER	GOALS LGE	POWER	S RATE
1	Pernambucano Juninho	13	61	212 mins
2	Pierre-Alain Frau	7	66	266 mins
3	Sydney Govou	8	58	344 mins
4	Florent Malouda	5	57	599 mins
5	Sylvain Wiltord	3	66	599 mins

KEY PLAYERS - MIDFIELDERS

Michael Essien

Goals in the League	4
Defensive Rating Average number of mins between League goals conceded while on the pitch	177
Contribution to Attacking Power Average number of minutes between League team goals while on pitch	64
Scoring Difference Defensive Rating minus Contribution to Attacking Power	113

	PLAYER	GOALS LGE	DEF RATE	ATT POWER	SCORE DIFF
1	Michael Essien	4	177	64	113 mins
2	Florent Malouda	5	166	58	108 mins
3	Mahamadou Diarra	2	163	62	101 mins
4	Pernambucano Juninho	13	153	61	92 mins

KEY PLAYERS - DEFENDERS

Eric Abidal

Goals Conceded in League	13
Clean Sheets In games when player was on pitch for at least 70 minutes	14
Defensive Rating Ave number of mins between League goals conceded while on the pitch	188
Club Defensive Rating Average number of mins between League goals conceded by the club this season	155

	PLAYER	CON LGE	CLEAN SHEETS	DEF RATE
1	Eric Abidal	13	14	188 mins
2	Anthony Reveillere	16	20	185 mins
3	Cris	17	18	175 mins
4	Cacapa	10	10	166 mins
5	Lamine Diatta	11	7	131 mins

KEY GOALKEEPER

Gregory Coupet

Goals Conceded in the League	18
Counting Games League games when player was on pitch for at least 70 minutes	31
Clean Sheets In games when player was on pitch for at least 70 minutes	16
League minutes played Number of minutes played in league matches	2790
Defensive Rating Ave number of mins between League goals conceded while on the pitch	155

DISCIPLINARY RECORDS

	PLAYER	YELLOW	RED	AVE
1	Essien	12	1	245
2	Reveillere	9	0	329
3	Berthod	4	0	331
4	Juninho	8	0	344
5	Diatta	3	0	481
6	Diarra	5	0	586
7	Cris	4	0	742
8	Cacapa	2	0	829
9	Frau	2	0	931
10	Nilmar	1	0	1074
11	Abidal	2	0	1221
12	Govou	1	0	2750
	Other	0	0	
	TOTAL	53	1	

TOP POINT EARNERS

	PLAYER	GAMES	AV PTS
1	Sydney Govou	27	2.37
2	Cacapa	17	2.29
3	Eric Abidal	26	2.23
4	Anthony Reveillere	33	2.15
5	Pernambucano Juninho	31	2.13
6	Gregory Coupet	31	2.13
7	Cris	33	2.12
8	Michael Essien	34	2.09
9	Sylvain Wiltord	18	2.06
10	Florent Malouda	33	2.06
	CLUB AVERAGE:		2.08

TEAM OF THE SEASON

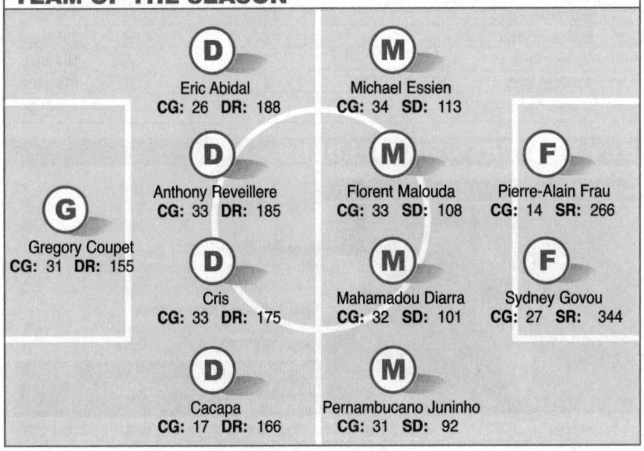
D
Eric Abidal
CG: 26 DR: 188
M
Michael Essien
CG: 34 SD: 113
D
Anthony Reveillere
CG: 33 DR: 185
M
Florent Malouda
CG: 33 SD: 108
F
Pierre-Alain Frau
CG: 14 SR: 266
G
Gregory Coupet
CG: 31 DR: 155
D
Cris
CG: 33 DR: 175
M
Mahamadou Diarra
CG: 32 SD: 101
F
Sydney Govou
CG: 27 SR: 344
D
Cacapa
CG: 17 DR: 166
M
Pernambucano Juninho
CG: 31 SD: 92

LEAGUE APPEARANCES AND BOOKINGS

	AGE (on 01/07/05)	IN NAMED 16	APPEARANCES	COUNTING GAMES	MINUTES ON PITCH	YELLOW CARDS	RED CARDS	THIS SEASON	HOME COUNTRY
Goalkeepers									
Gregory Coupet	32	31	31	31	2790	0	0	8	France (4)
Johan Harlock	18	9	0	0	0	0	0	-	France
Daniel Jaccard	20	0	0	0	0	0	0	-	France
Nicolas Puydebois	24	35	7	7	630	0	0	-	France
Defenders									
Eric Abidal	25	28	28	26	2442	2	0	6	France (4)
Jeremie Berthod	21	30	23	11	1324	4	0	-	France
Cacapa	29	20	20	17	1659	2	0	-	Brazil
Cris	28	34	33	33	2970	4	0	-	Brazil
Lamine Diatta	30	27	19	15	1443	3	0	5	Senegal (33)
Yohann Gomez	23	7	0	0	0	0	0	-	France
Anthony Reveillere	25	33	33	33	2962	9	0	1	France (4)
Johann Truchet	21	5	1	1	90	0	0	-	France
Midfielders									
Florent Balmont	25	3	2	0	57	0	0	-	France
Jeremie Clement	20	30	18	3	522	0	0	-	France
Mahamadou Diarra	24	34	34	32	2930	5	0	-	Mali
Michael Essien	22	37	37	34	3194	12	1	-	Ghana
Yacine Hima	21	2	2	0	53	0	0	-	France
Sylvain Idangar	21	1	0	0	0	0	0	-	France
Juninho	30	33	32	31	2755	8	0	8	Brazil (1)
Florent Malouda	25	37	37	33	2996	0	0	3	France (4)
Forwards									
Hatem Benarfa	18	11	9	0	272	0	0	-	France
Karim Benzema	17	6	6	0	114	0	0	-	France
Bryan Bergougnoux	22	23	22	3	635	0	0	-	France
Elber	32	3	3	2	225	0	0	-	Brazil
Pierre-Alain Frau	25	32	32	14	1863	2	0	1	France (4)
Sydney Govou	25	36	35	27	2750	1	0	4	France (4)
Nilmar	20	33	32	6	1074	1	0	-	Brazil
Julien Viale	23	3	2	0	47	0	0	-	France
Sylvain Wiltord	31	25	25	18	1798	0	0	4	France (4)

SQUAD APPEARANCES

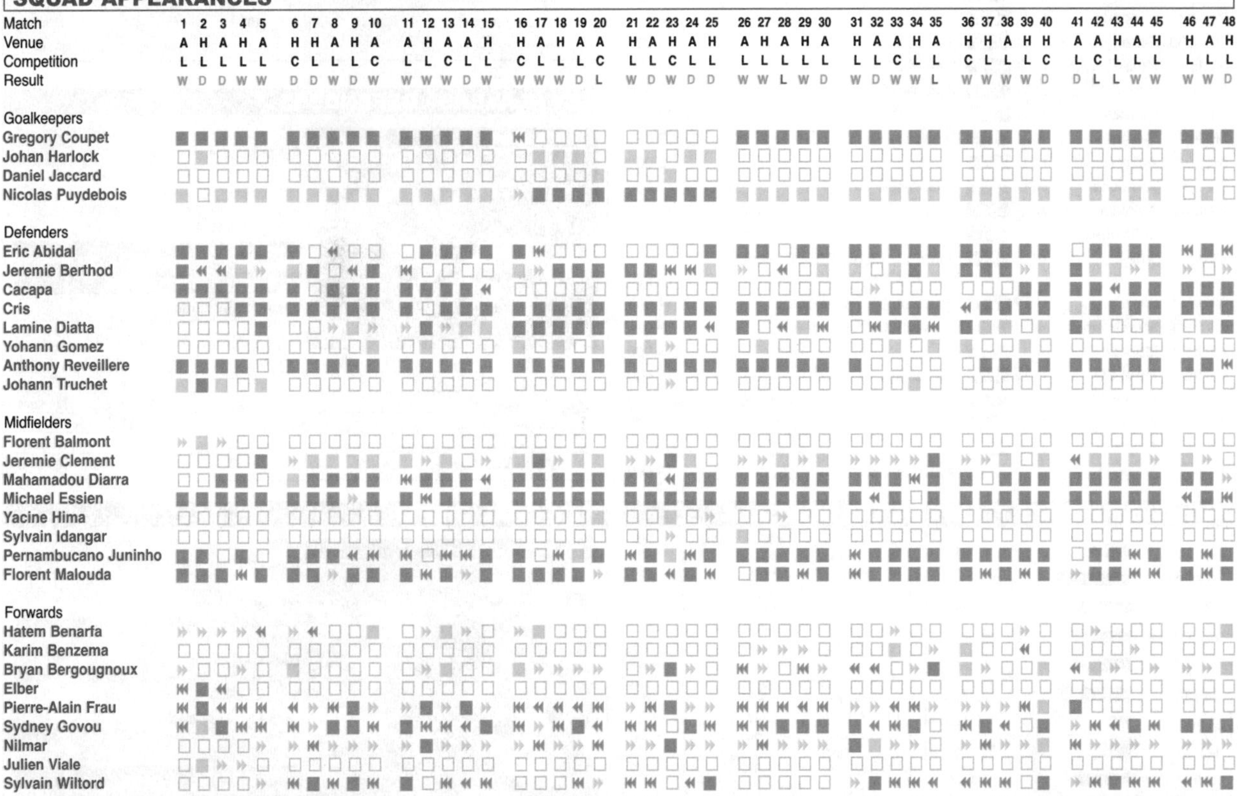
Match 1 2 3 4 5 6 7 8 9 10 11 12 13 14 15 16 17 18 19 20 21 22 23 24 25 26 27 28 29 30 31 32 33 34 35 36 37 38 39 40 41 42 43 44 45 46 47 48
Venue A H A H A H H A H A A H A A H H A H A A H A H A H A H A H A H A A H A H H A H H A A H A H H A H
Competition L L L L L C L L L C L L C L L C L L L C L L C L L L L L L L L L C L L C L L L C L C L L L L L L
Result W D D W W D D W D W W W W D W W W W D L W D W D D W W L W D W D W W L W W W W D D L L W W W W D
Goalkeepers
Gregory Coupet
Johan Harlock
Daniel Jaccard
Nicolas Puydebois
Defenders
Eric Abidal
Jeremie Berthod
Cacapa
Cris
Lamine Diatta
Yohann Gomez
Anthony Reveillere
Johann Truchet
Midfielders
Florent Balmont
Jeremie Clement
Mahamadou Diarra
Michael Essien
Yacine Hima
Sylvain Idangar
Pernambucano Juninho
Florent Malouda
Forwards
Hatem Benarfa
Karim Benzema
Bryan Bergougnoux
Elber
Pierre-Alain Frau
Sydney Govou
Nilmar
Julien Viale
Sylvain Wiltord

KEY: On all match · On bench · Subbed or sent off (Counting game) · Subbed or sent off (playing less than 70 minutes) · Subbed on from bench (Counting Game) · Subbed on (playing less than 70 minutes) · Subbed on and then subbed or sent off (Counting Game) · Subbed on and then subbed or sent off (playing less than 70 minutes) · Not in 16

LILLE

Final Position: **2nd**

KEY: Won Drawn Lost

							Attendance
1	frpr1	**Auxerre**	H	W	2-0	Brunel 44; Dernis 46	14,000
2	frpr1	**Marseille**	A	L	0-3		60,000
3	frpr1	**Bordeaux**	H	D	0-0		11,000
4	frpr1	**Lyon**	A	L	0-1		20,000
5	frpr1	**Nice**	H	W	1-0	Brunel 92	9,000
6	uc1rl1	**Shelbourne**	A	D	2-2	Bodmer 20; Landrin 45	7,463
7	frpr1	**Caen**	H	W	2-0	Acimovic 23; Brunel 90	10,000
8	frpr1	**Sochaux**	A	W	2-0	Potillon 52 og; Brunel 92	12,000
9	frpr1	**Metz**	H	W	4-0	Acimovic 17; Moussilou 50,70; Audel 80	12,000
10	uc1rl2	**Shelbourne**	H	W	2-0	Acimovic 17; Moussilou 27	11,000
11	frpr1	**Rennes**	A	W	1-0	Moussilou 64	10,000
12	frpr1	**Bastia**	H	W	2-1	Bodmer 4; Dernis 82	13,000
13	ucgph	**Alem Aachen**	A	L	0-1		20,352
14	frpr1	**Toulouse**	A	L	0-1		30,000
15	frpr1	**St Etienne**	H	W	1-0	Dumont 9	9,000
16	ucgph	**Z St Petersburg**	H	W	2-1	Tafforeau 35; Moussilou 42	9,109
17	frpr1	**Istres**	A	W	2-0	Odemwingie 37; Brunel 54 pen	5,000
18	frpr1	**Monaco**	H	D	1-1	Landrin 44	14,000
19	frpr1	**Lens**	A	D	1-1	Landrin 59	40,000
20	ucgph	**AEK Athens**	A	W	2-1	Vitakic 26; Debuchy 63	15,000
21	frpr1	**Strasbourg**	H	D	1-1	Odemwingie 87	11,000
22	frpr1	**Paris SG**	A	D	1-1	Bodmer 16	30,000
23	frpr1	**Nantes**	H	W	2-1	Dernis 49; Moussilou 52	10,000
24	ucgph	**Seville**	H	W	1-0	Moussilou 77	9,000
25	frpr1	**AC Ajaccio**	A	D	0-0		4,000
26	frpr1	**Marseille**	H	L	1-2	Brunel 53	16,000
27	frpr1	**Bordeaux**	A	W	3-1	Debuchy 1; Brunel 43; Audel 79	20,000
28	frpr1	**Lyon**	H	W	2-1	Moussilou 3,69	21,000
29	frpr1	**Nice**	A	D	1-1	Acimovic 38 pen	10,000
30	frpr1	**Caen**	A	D	0-0		17,000
31	frpr1	**Sochaux**	H	D	0-0		12,000
32	uc3rl1	**Basel**	A	D	0-0		19,000
33	frpr1	**Metz**	A	D	1-1	Acimovic 7	15,000
34	uc3rl2	**Basel**	H	W	2-0	Moussilou 37; Acimovic 78 pen	13,000
35	frpr1	**Rennes**	H	D	0-0		12,000
36	frpr1	**Bastia**	A	L	1-3	Debuchy 18	3,000
37	uc4rl1	**Auxerre**	H	L	0-1		8,000
38	frpr1	**Toulouse**	H	D	1-1	Odemwingie 60	10,000
39	uc4rl2	**Auxerre**	A	D	0-0		12,000
40	frpr1	**St Etienne**	A	D	0-0		30,000
41	frpr1	**Istres**	H	W	7-0	Moussilou 12,16,17,55; Bodmer 21; Brunel 27,59	13,000
42	frpr1	**Lens**	H	W	2-1	Moussilou 39; Fauverge 89	14,000
43	frpr1	**Strasbourg**	A	W	2-1	Moussilou 33; Dumont 62	19,000
44	frpr1	**Monaco**	A	L	0-2		12,000
45	frpr1	**Paris SG**	H	W	1-0	Mirallas 84	17,000
46	frpr1	**Nantes**	A	W	3-1	Dumont 9; Schmitz 51; Debuchy 73	31,000
47	frpr1	**AC Ajaccio**	H	L	0-2		17,000
48	frpr1	**Auxerre**	A	W	3-1	Odemwingie 26; Bodmer 48; Moussilou 86	15,000

KEY PLAYERS - GOALSCORERS

Matt Moussilou

Goals in the League	13
Contribution to Attacking Power Average number of minutes between League team goals while on pitch	63
Player Strike Rate Average number of minutes between League goals scored by player	170
Club Strike Rate Average number of minutes between League goals scored by club	67

	PLAYER	GOALS LGE	POWER	S RATE
1	Matt Moussilou	13	63	170 mins
2	Phillipe Brunel	9	66	282 mins
3	Mathieu Bodmer	4	75	654 mins
4	Stephane Dumont	3	66	816 mins
5	Christophe Landrin	2	83	1125 mins

KEY PLAYERS - MIDFIELDERS

Mathieu Chalme

Goals in the League	0
Defensive Rating Average number of mins between League goals conceded while on the pitch	120
Contribution to Attacking Power Average number of minutes between League team goals while on pitch	60
Scoring Difference Defensive Rating minus Contribution to Attacking Power	60

	PLAYER	GOALS LGE	DEF RATE	ATT POWER	SCORE DIFF
1	Mathieu Chalme	0	120	60	60 mins
2	Mathieu Bodmer	4	124	75	49 mins
3	Stephane Dumont	3	102	66	36 mins
4	Christophe Landrin	2	98	83	15 mins

KEY PLAYERS - DEFENDERS

Benoit Angbwa

Rafael Schmitz (pictured)

Goals Conceded in League	10
Clean Sheets In games when player was on pitch for at least 70 minutes	9
Defensive Rating Ave number of mins between League goals conceded while on the pitch	165
Club Defensive Rating Average number of mins between League goals conceded by the club this season	118

	PLAYER	CON LGE	CLEAN SHEETS	DEF RATE
1	Benoit Angbwa	10	9	165 mins
2	Rafael Schmitz	19	10	121 mins
3	Gregory Tafforeau	17	11	121 mins
4	Efstathios Tavlaridis	23	11	115 mins
5	Milivoje Vitakic	20	9	109 mins

MONTHLY POINTS TALLY

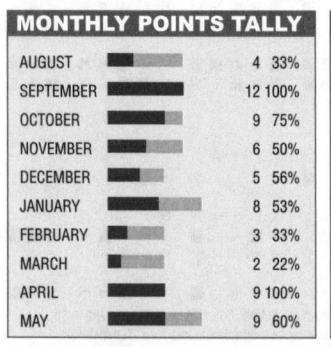

AUGUST	4	33%
SEPTEMBER	12	100%
OCTOBER	9	75%
NOVEMBER	6	50%
DECEMBER	5	56%
JANUARY	8	53%
FEBRUARY	3	33%
MARCH	2	22%
APRIL	9	100%
MAY	9	60%

LEAGUE GOALS

	PLAYER	MINS	GOALS	AVE
1	Moussilou	2211	13	170
2	Brunel	2538	9	282
3	Acimovic	1107	4	277
4	Bodmer	2614	4	654
5	Debuchy	822	3	274
6	Dernis	1251	3	417
7	Dumont	2449	3	816
8	Odemwingie	930	3	310
9	Audel	584	2	292
10	Landrin	2249	2	1125
11	Fauverge	150	1	150
12	Schmitz	2308	1	2308
13	Mirallas	33	1	33
	Other		2	
	TOTAL		51	

KEY GOALKEEPER

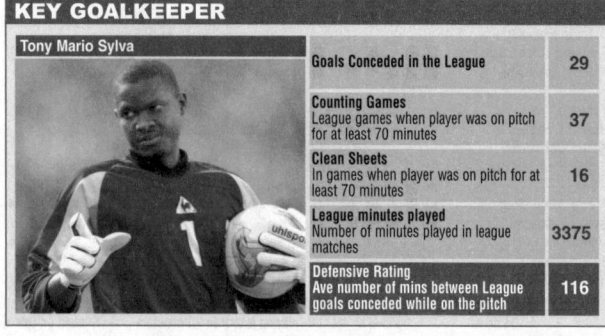

Tony Mario Sylva

Goals Conceded in the League	29
Counting Games League games when player was on pitch for at least 70 minutes	37
Clean Sheets In games when player was on pitch for at least 70 minutes	16
League minutes played Number of minutes played in league matches	3375
Defensive Rating Ave number of mins between League goals conceded while on the pitch	116

DISCIPLINARY RECORDS

	PLAYER	YELLOW	RED	AVE
1	Tavlaridis	11	2	203
2	Debuchy	3	0	274
3	Schmitz	7	1	288
4	Dernis	4	0	312
5	Makoun	7	0	362
6	Vitakic	5	1	362
7	Acimovic	3	0	369
8	Bodmer	7	0	373
9	Chalme	4	1	455
10	Plestan	2	0	463
11	Odemwingie	2	0	465
12	Tafforeau	4	0	513
13	Angbwa	2	1	550
	Other	10	0	
	TOTAL	71	6	

TOP POINT EARNERS

	PLAYER	GAMES	AV PTS
1	Mathieu Chalme	25	1.96
2	Jean Makoun	27	1.89
3	Milivoje Vitakic	23	1.87
4	Matt Moussilou	22	1.82
5	Gregory Tafforeau	22	1.82
6	Phillipe Brunel	26	1.81
7	Rafael Schmitz	25	1.76
8	Efstathios Tavlaridis	29	1.76
9	Stephane Dumont	24	1.75
10	Tony Mario Sylva	37	1.73
	CLUB AVERAGE:		1.76

TEAM OF THE SEASON

D
Benoit Angbwa
CG: 18 DR: 165
M
Mathieu Chalme
CG: 25 SD: 60
D
Efstathios Tavalaridis
CG: 29 DR: 115
M
Stephane Dumont
CG: 24 SD: 36
F
Matt Moussilou
CG: 22 SR: 170
G
Tony Mario Sylva
CG: 37 DR: 116
D
Rafael Schmitz
CG: 25 DR: 121
M
Christophe Landrin
CG: 24 SD: 15
F
Phillipe Brunel
CG: 26 SR: 282
D
Gregory Tafforeau
CG: 22 DR: 121
M
Mathieu Bodmer
CG: 28 SD: 49

LEAGUE APPEARANCES AND BOOKINGS

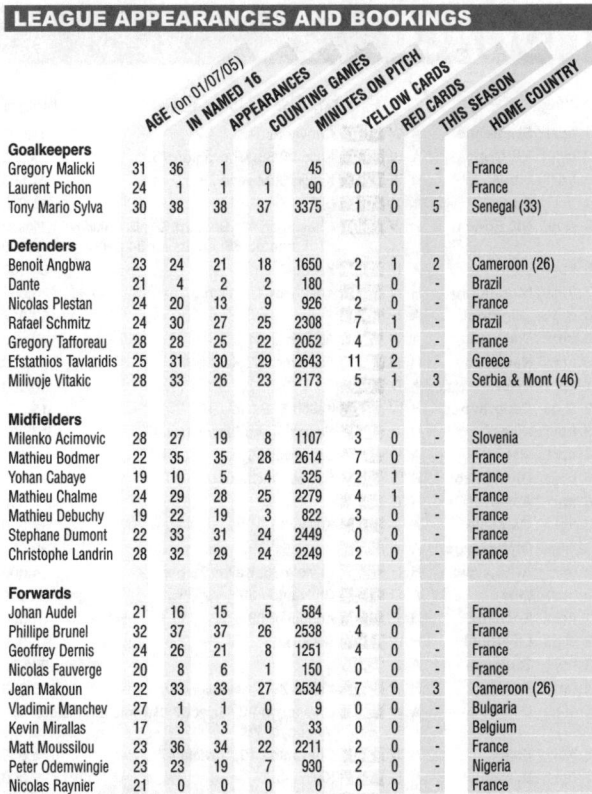

Player	AGE (on 01/07/05)	IN NAMED 16	APPEARANCES	COUNTING GAMES	MINUTES ON PITCH	YELLOW CARDS	RED CARDS	THIS SEASON	HOME COUNTRY
Goalkeepers									
Gregory Malicki	31	36	1	0	45	0	0	-	France
Laurent Pichon	24	1	1	1	90	0	0	-	France
Tony Mario Sylva	30	38	38	37	3375	1	0	5	Senegal (33)
Defenders									
Benoit Angbwa	23	24	21	18	1650	2	1	2	Cameroon (26)
Dante	21	4	2	2	180	1	0	-	Brazil
Nicolas Plestan	24	20	13	9	926	2	0	-	France
Rafael Schmitz	24	30	27	25	2308	7	1	-	Brazil
Gregory Tafforeau	28	28	25	22	2052	4	0	-	France
Efstathios Tavlaridis	25	31	30	29	2643	11	2	-	Greece
Milivoje Vitakic	28	33	26	23	2173	5	1	3	Serbia & Mont (46)
Midfielders									
Milenko Acimovic	28	27	19	8	1107	3	0	-	Slovenia
Mathieu Bodmer	22	35	35	28	2614	7	0	-	France
Yohan Cabaye	19	10	5	4	325	2	1	-	France
Mathieu Chalme	24	29	28	25	2279	4	1	-	France
Mathieu Debuchy	19	22	19	3	822	3	0	-	France
Stephane Dumont	22	33	31	24	2449	0	0	-	France
Christophe Landrin	28	32	29	24	2249	2	0	-	France
Forwards									
Johan Audel	21	16	15	5	584	1	0	-	France
Phillipe Brunel	32	37	37	26	2538	4	0	-	France
Geoffrey Dernis	24	26	21	8	1251	4	0	-	France
Nicolas Fauverge	20	8	6	1	150	0	0	-	France
Jean Makoun	22	33	33	27	2534	7	0	3	Cameroon (26)
Vladimir Manchev	27	1	1	0	9	0	0	-	Bulgaria
Kevin Mirallas	17	3	3	0	33	0	0	-	Belgium
Matt Moussilou	23	36	34	22	2211	2	0	-	France
Peter Odemwingie	23	23	19	7	930	2	0	-	Nigeria
Nicolas Raynier	21	0	0	0	0	0	0	-	France

SQUAD APPEARANCES

Match	1	2	3	4	5	6	7	8	9	10	11	12	13	14	15	16	17	18	19	20	21	22	23	24	25	26	27	28	29	30	31	32	33	34	35	36	37	38	39	40	41	42	43	44	45	46	47	48
Venue	H	A	H	A	H	A	H	A	H	H	A	H	A	A	H	H	A	H	A	A	H	A	H	H	A	H	A	H	A	A	H	A	A	H	H	A	H	H	A	A	H	H	A	A	H	A	H	A
Competition	L	L	L	L	L	E	L	L	L	E	L	L	E	L	L	E	L	L	L	E	L	L	L	E	L	L	L	L	L	L	L	E	L	E	L	L	E	L	E	L	L	L	L	L	L	L	L	L
Result	W	L	D	L	W	D	W	W	W	W	W	W	L	L	W	W	W	D	D	W	D	D	W	W	D	L	W	W	D	D	D	D	D	W	D	L	L	D	D	D	W	W	W	L	W	W	L	W

Goalkeepers
Gregory Malicki
Laurent Pichon
Tony Mario Sylva

Defenders
Benoit Angbwa
Dante
Nicolas Plestan
Rafael Schmitz
Gregory Tafforeau
Efstathios Tavlaridis
Milivoje Vitakic

Midfielders
Milenko Acimovic
Mathieu Bodmer
Yohan Cabaye
Mathieu Chalme
Mathieu Debuchy
Stephane Dumont
Christophe Landrin

Forwards
Johan Audel
Phillipe Brunel
Geoffrey Dernis
Nicolas Fauverge
Jean Makoun
Vladimir Manchev
Kevin Mirallas
Matt Moussilou
Peter Odemwingie
Nicolas Raynier

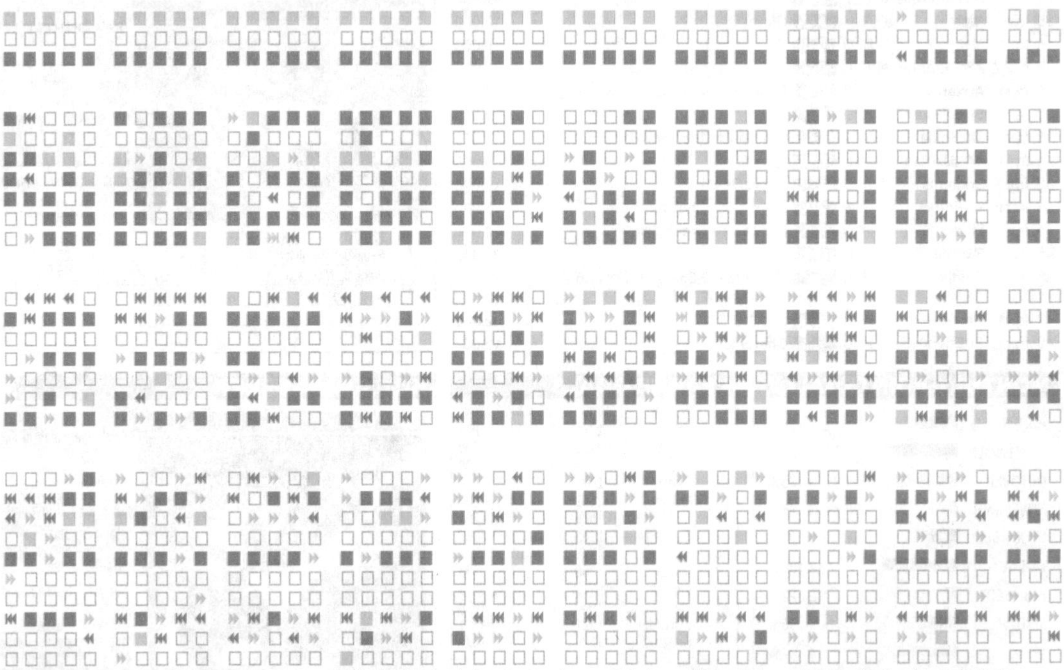

KEY: On all match | On bench | Subbed or sent off (Counting game) | Subbed or sent off (playing less than 70 minutes) | Subbed on from bench (Counting Game) | Subbed on (playing less than 70 minutes) | Subbed on and then subbed or sent off (Counting Game) | Subbed on and then subbed or sent off (playing less than 70 minutes) | Not in 16

MONACO

Final Position: **3rd**

KEY: Won / Drawn / Lost

							Attendance
1	frpr1	**St Etienne**	A	W	1-0	Chevanton 1	34,000
2	cl ql1	**NK Gorica**	A	W	3-0	Kallon 9,88; Chevanton 75	3,000
3	frpr1	**Istres**	H	W	2-1	Kallon 5; Maicon 28	11,000
4	frpr1	**Caen**	A	L	0-1		21,000
5	cl ql2	**NK Gorica**	H	W	6-0	Chevanton 17; Bernardi 31; El Fakiri 41; Kallon 47; Farnerud 66; Adebayor 84 pen	7,000
6	frpr1	**Lens**	A	D	1-1	Kallon 7	39,000
7	frpr1	**Strasbourg**	H	W	3-1	Adebayor 4; Kallon 57 pen; Saviola 85	15,000
8	cl ga	**Liverpool**	A	L	0-2		33,517
9	frpr1	**Paris SG**	A	W	1-0	Adebayor 84	42,000
10	frpr1	**Nantes**	H	W	2-1	Farnerud 47; Kallon 89	5,000
11	frpr1	**Lyon**	A	D	0-0		40,000
12	cl ga	**Deportivo**	H	W	2-0	Kallon 5; Saviola 10	14,000
13	frpr1	**Nice**	H	L	3-4	Saviola 4; Adebayor 19,59	17,000
14	frpr1	**Metz**	A	D	1-1	Adebayor 55	24,000
15	cl ga	**Olympiakos**	H	W	2-1	Saviola 3; Chevanton 10	17,000
16	frpr1	**Auxerre**	H	D	0-0		8,000
17	frpr1	**Marseille**	A	D	1-1	Kallon 33	57,000
18	cl ga	**Olympiakos**	A	L	0-1		33,000
19	frpr1	**AC Ajaccio**	H	D	2-2	Saviola 36; Kallon 79 pen	4,000
20	frpr1	**Lille**	A	D	1-1	Chevanton 30	14,000
21	frpr1	**Sochaux**	H	L	1-3	Adebayor 68	4,000
22	cl ga	**Liverpool**	H	W	1-0	Saviola 55	15,000
23	frpr1	**Toulouse**	A	D	0-0		30,000
24	frpr1	**Rennes**	H	W	2-0	Kallon 29; Chevanton 30	8,000
25	cl ga	**Deportivo**	A	W	5-0	Chevanton 22; Givet 37; Saviola 39; Maicon 55; Adebayor 76	16,000
26	frpr1	**Bastia**	A	W	2-0	Chevanton 19; Saviola 47	5,000
27	frpr1	**Bordeaux**	H	D	1-1	Kallon 42	9,000
28	frpr1	**Istres**	A	W	1-0	Camara 15	10,000
29	frpr1	**Caen**	H	W	5-2	Kallon 7,49 pen; Maicon 36; Saviola 42; Plasil 80	5,000
30	frpr1	**Lens**	H	W	2-0	Saviola 20; Maicon 39	8,000
31	frpr1	**Paris SG**	H	W	2-0	Kallon 35; Bernardi 55	14,000
32	frpr1	**Nantes**	A	D	0-0		33,000
33	frpr1	**Lyon**	H	D	1-1	Rodriguez 83	18,000
34	clr2l1	**PSV Eindhoven**	A	L	0-1		42,000
35	frpr1	**Nice**	A	L	1-2	Gigliotti 58	13,000
36	frpr1	**Metz**	H	D	0-0		8,000
37	clr2l2	**PSV Eindhoven**	H	L	0-2		16,000
38	frpr1	**Auxerre**	A	D	2-2	Rodriguez 45; Modesto 56	8,000
39	frpr1	**Strasbourg**	A	D	0-0		22,000
40	frpr1	**Marseille**	H	W	2-1	Maicon 24; Adebayor 41	17,000
41	frpr1	**AC Ajaccio**	A	L	0-3		3,000
42	frpr1	**Sochaux**	A	D	1-1	Chevanton 9	19,000
43	frpr1	**Toulouse**	H	W	2-1	Saviola 55; Chevanton 65	10,000
44	frpr1	**Lille**	H	W	2-0	Squillaci 64; Adebayor 90	12,000
45	frpr1	**Rennes**	A	D	0-0		29,000
46	frpr1	**Bastia**	H	W	5-2	Chevanton 9,35,45; Saviola 46; Adebayor 87	10,000
47	frpr1	**Bordeaux**	A	D	1-1	Squillaci 90	22,000
48	frpr1	**St Etienne**	H	D	1-1	Chevanton 1	18,000

KEY PLAYERS - GOALSCORERS

Ernesto Chevanton

Goals in the League	10
Contribution to Attacking Power Average number of minutes between League team goals while on pitch	60
Player Strike Rate Average number of minutes between League goals scored by player	200
Club Strike Rate Average number of minutes between League goals scored by club	66

	PLAYER	GOALS LGE	POWER	S RATE
1	Ernesto Chevanton	10	60	200 mins
2	Mohammed Kallon	11	65	204 mins
3	Emmanuel Adebayor	9	59	283 mins
4	Javier Saviola	7	64	314 mins
5	Maicon	4	64	666 mins

KEY PLAYERS - MIDFIELDERS

Vassilis Zikos

Goals in the League	0
Defensive Rating Average number of mins between League goals conceded while on the pitch	112
Contribution to Attacking Power Average number of minutes between League team goals while on pitch	61
Scoring Difference Defensive Rating minus Contribution to Attacking Power	51

	PLAYER	GOALS LGE	DEF RATE	ATT POWER	SCORE DIFF
1	Vassilis Zikos	0	112	61	51 mins
2	Patrice Evra	0	102	67	35 mins
3	Lucas Bernardi	1	107	74	33 mins
4	Jaroslav Plasil	1	80	62	18 mins
5	Diego Fernando Perez	0	91	76	15 mins

KEY PLAYERS - DEFENDERS

Sebastien Squillaci

Goals Conceded in League	23
Clean Sheets In games when player was on pitch for at least 70 minutes	12
Defensive Rating Ave number of mins between League goals conceded while on the pitch	107
Club Defensive Rating Average number of mins between League goals conceded by the club this season	98

	PLAYER	CON LGE	CLEAN SHEETS	DEF RATE
1	Sebastien Squillaci	23	12	107 mins
2	Francois Modesto	17	10	105 mins
3	Gael Givet	29	12	98 mins
4	Maicon	28	11	95 mins
5	Julien Rodriguez	21	5	73 mins

MONTHLY POINTS TALLY

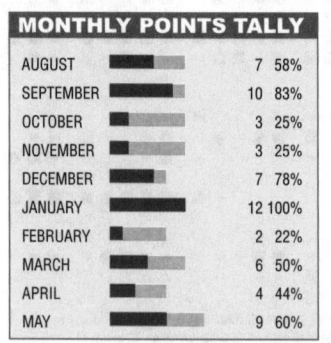

AUGUST	7	58%
SEPTEMBER	10	83%
OCTOBER	3	25%
NOVEMBER	3	25%
DECEMBER	7	78%
JANUARY	12	100%
FEBRUARY	2	22%
MARCH	6	50%
APRIL	4	44%
MAY	9	60%

LEAGUE GOALS

	PLAYER	MINS	GOALS	AVE
1	Kallon	2242	11	204
2	Chevanton	1998	10	200
3	Adebayor	2545	9	283
4	Saviola	2197	7	314
5	Maicon	2662	4	666
6	Rodriguez	1528	2	764
7	Squillaci	2463	2	1232
8	Modesto	1778	1	1778
9	Camara	258	1	258
10	Gigliotti	218	1	218
11	Plasil	1680	1	1680
12	Bernardi	1921	1	1921
13	Farnerud	1328	1	1328
	Other		1	
	TOTAL		52	

KEY GOALKEEPER

Flavio Roma

Goals Conceded in the League	31
Counting Games League games when player was on pitch for at least 70 minutes	33
Clean Sheets In games when player was on pitch for at least 70 minutes	12
League minutes played Number of minutes played in league matches	2970
Defensive Rating Ave number of mins between League goals conceded while on the pitch	96

DISCIPLINARY RECORDS

	PLAYER	YELLOW	RED	AVE
1	Perez	8	1	211
2	Zikos	12	0	232
3	Chevanton	8	0	249
4	Evra	10	1	279
5	Modesto	5	0	355
6	Kallon	6	0	373
7	Maicon	7	0	380
8	Rodriguez	3	1	382
9	Bernardi	5	0	384
10	Givet	5	0	567
11	Squillaci	4	0	615
12	Farnerud	2	0	664
13	Plasil	2	0	840
	Other	5	1	
	TOTAL	82	4	

TOP POINT EARNERS

	PLAYER	GAMES	AV PTS
1	Vassilis Zikos	31	1.87
2	Mohammed Kallon	21	1.86
3	Emmanuel Adebayor	25	1.84
4	Sebastien Squillaci	27	1.78
5	Lucas Bernardi	21	1.76
6	Jaroslav Plasil	16	1.75
7	Maicon	30	1.73
8	Javier Saviola	22	1.73
9	Julien Rodriguez	16	1.69
10	Flavio Roma	33	1.67
	CLUB AVERAGE:		1.66

TEAM OF THE SEASON

G
Flavio Roma
CG: 33 DR: 96
D
Sebastien Squillaci
CG: 27 DR: 107
D
Francois Modesto
CG: 18 DR: 105
D
Gael Givet
CG: 31 DR: 98
D
Maicon
CG: 30 DR: 95
M
Vassilis Zikos
CG: 31 SD: 51
M
Patrice Evra
CG: 32 SD: 35
M
Lucas Bernardi
CG: 21 SD: 33
M
Jaroslav Plasil
CG: 16 SD: 18
F
Ernesto Chevanton
CG: 18 SR: 200
F
Mohammed Kallon
CG: 21 SR: 204

LEAGUE APPEARANCES AND BOOKINGS

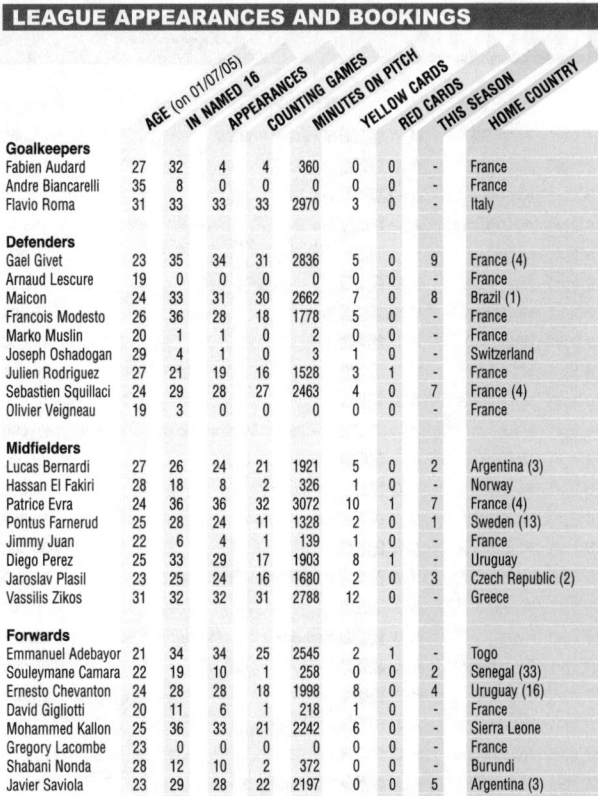

	AGE (on 01/07/05)	IN NAMED 16	APPEARANCES	COUNTING GAMES	MINUTES ON PITCH	YELLOW CARDS	RED CARDS	THIS SEASON	HOME COUNTRY
Goalkeepers									
Fabien Audard	27	32	4	4	360	0	0	-	France
Andre Biancarelli	35	8	0	0	0	0	0	-	France
Flavio Roma	31	33	33	33	2970	3	0	-	Italy
Defenders									
Gael Givet	23	35	34	31	2836	5	0	9	France (4)
Arnaud Lescure	19	0	0	0	0	0	0	-	France
Maicon	24	33	31	30	2662	7	0	8	Brazil (1)
Francois Modesto	26	36	28	18	1778	5	0	-	France
Marko Muslin	20	1	1	0	2	0	0	-	France
Joseph Oshadogan	29	4	1	0	3	1	0	-	Switzerland
Julien Rodriguez	27	21	19	16	1528	3	1	-	France
Sebastien Squillaci	24	29	28	27	2463	4	0	7	France (4)
Olivier Veigneau	19	3	0	0	0	0	0	-	France
Midfielders									
Lucas Bernardi	27	26	24	21	1921	5	0	2	Argentina (3)
Hassan El Fakiri	28	18	8	2	326	1	0	-	Norway
Patrice Evra	24	36	36	32	3072	10	1	7	France (4)
Pontus Farnerud	25	28	24	11	1328	2	0	1	Sweden (13)
Jimmy Juan	22	6	4	1	139	1	0	-	France
Diego Perez	25	33	29	17	1903	8	1	-	Uruguay
Jaroslav Plasil	23	25	24	16	1680	2	0	3	Czech Republic (2)
Vassilis Zikos	31	32	32	31	2788	12	0	-	Greece
Forwards									
Emmanuel Adebayor	21	34	34	25	2545	2	1	-	Togo
Souleymane Camara	22	19	10	1	258	0	0	2	Senegal (33)
Ernesto Chevanton	24	28	28	18	1998	8	0	4	Uruguay (16)
David Gigliotti	20	11	6	1	218	1	0	-	France
Mohammed Kallon	25	36	33	21	2242	6	0	-	Sierra Leone
Gregory Lacombe	23	0	0	0	0	0	0	-	France
Shabani Nonda	28	12	10	2	372	0	0	-	Burundi
Javier Saviola	23	29	28	22	2197	0	0	5	Argentina (3)

SQUAD APPEARANCES

Match	1	2	3	4	5	6	7	8	9	10	11	12	13	14	15	16	17	18	19	20	21	22	23	24	25	26	27	28	29	30	31	32	33	34	35	36	37	38	39	40	41	42	43	44	45	46	47	48
Venue	A	A	H	A	H	A	H	A	A	H	A	H	H	A	H	H	A	A	H	A	H	H	A	H	A	A	H	A	H	H	H	A	H	A	A	H	H	A	A	H	A	A	H	H	A	H	A	H
Competition	L	C	L	L	C	L	L	C	L	L	L	C	L	L	C	L	L	C	L	L	L	C	L	L	C	L	L	L	L	L	L	L	L	C	L	L	C	L	L	L	L	L	L	L	L	L	L	L
Result	W	W	W	L	W	D	W	L	W	W	D	W	L	D	W	D	D	L	D	D	L	W	D	W	W	W	D	W	W	W	W	D	D	L	L	D	L	D	D	W	L	D	W	W	D	W	D	D

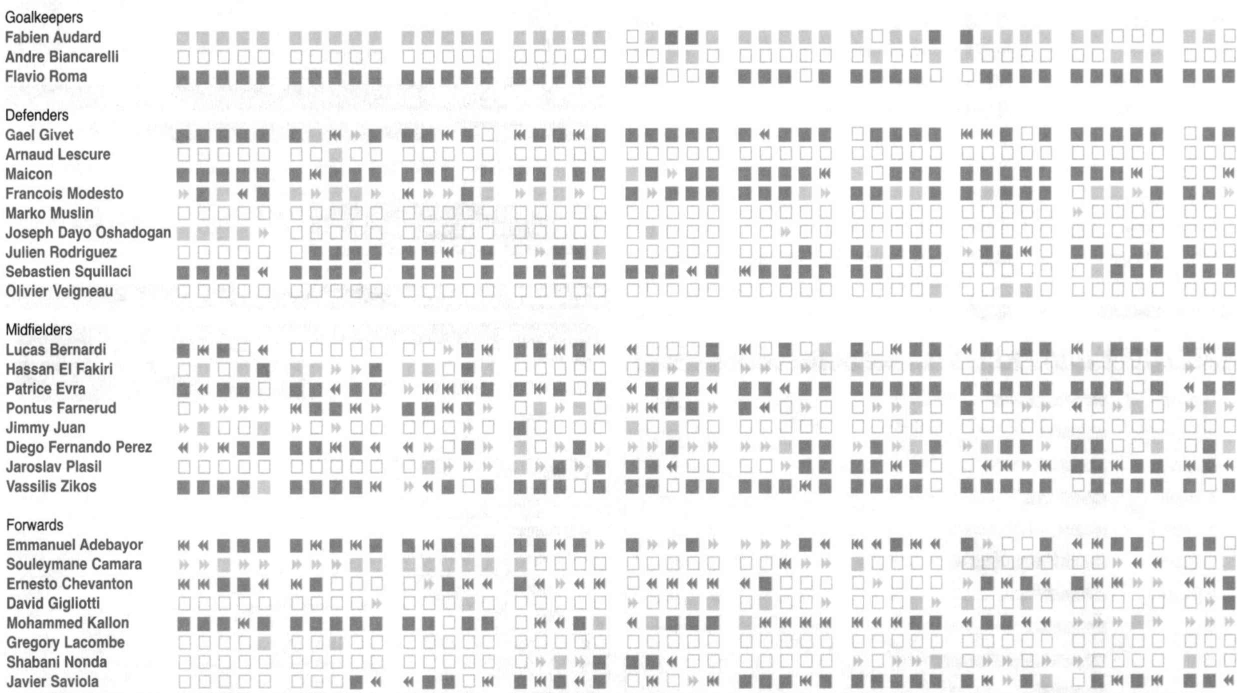
Goalkeepers
Fabien Audard
Andre Biancarelli
Flavio Roma
Defenders
Gael Givet
Arnaud Lescure
Maicon
Francois Modesto
Marko Muslin
Joseph Dayo Oshadogan
Julien Rodriguez
Sebastien Squillaci
Olivier Veigneau
Midfielders
Lucas Bernardi
Hassan El Fakiri
Patrice Evra
Pontus Farnerud
Jimmy Juan
Diego Fernando Perez
Jaroslav Plasil
Vassilis Zikos
Forwards
Emmanuel Adebayor
Souleymane Camara
Ernesto Chevanton
David Gigliotti
Mohammed Kallon
Gregory Lacombe
Shabani Nonda
Javier Saviola

KEY: On all match | On bench | Subbed or sent off (Counting game) | Subbed or sent off (playing less than 70 minutes) | Subbed on from bench (Counting Game) | Subbed on (playing less than 70 minutes) | Subbed on and then subbed or sent off (Counting Game) | Subbed on and then subbed or sent off (playing less than 70 minutes) | Not in 16

RENNES

Final Position: **4th**

KEY: Won Drawn Lost

							Attendance
1	frpr1	**Paris SG**	H	W	2-1	Sorlin 21; Frei 23	25,000
2	frpr1	**Auxerre**	A	L	1-3	Frei 83	12,000
3	frpr1	**Nantes**	H	W	1-0	Frei 32	24,000
4	frpr1	**AC Ajaccio**	A	D	1-1	Frei 3	4,000
5	frpr1	**Lyon**	H	L	1-2	Cearense 91	23,000
6	frpr1	**Bordeaux**	A	D	0-0		28,000
7	frpr1	**Marseille**	H	W	1-0	Frei 57	26,000
8	frpr1	**Nice**	A	L	0-2		12,000
9	frpr1	**Lille**	H	L	0-1		10,000
10	frpr1	**Sochaux**	A	L	0-3		14,000
11	frpr1	**Metz**	H	W	3-1	Frei 29,41; Monterrubio 65	29,000
12	frpr1	**Caen**	H	D	1-1	Monterrubio 84	22,000
13	frpr1	**Bastia**	A	D	1-1	Kallstrom 77	5,000
14	frpr1	**Toulouse**	H	D	1-1	Monterrubio 70	18,000
15	frpr1	**St Etienne**	A	L	0-1		30,000
16	frpr1	**Istres**	H	W	3-1	Sorlin 8,90; Monterrubio 57	18,000
17	frpr1	**Monaco**	A	L	0-2		8,000
18	frpr1	**Lens**	H	W	3-1	Maoulida 17,75; Monterrubio 60	20,000
19	frpr1	**Strasbourg**	A	L	0-1		25,000
20	frpr1	**Auxerre**	H	W	1-0	Frei 61	18,000
21	frpr1	**Nantes**	A	L	0-2		29,000
22	frpr1	**AC Ajaccio**	H	W	1-0	Frei 28	21,000
23	frpr1	**Lyon**	A	L	1-2	Monterrubio 90	37,000
24	frpr1	**Bordeaux**	H	W	2-0	Ouaddou 15; Monterrubio 66 pen	15,000
25	frpr1	**Marseille**	A	L	1-3	Maoulida 80	50,000
26	frpr1	**Nice**	H	W	4-1	Maoulida 47,77; Frei 62; Monterrubio 74	17,000
27	frpr1	**Lille**	A	D	0-0		12,000
28	frpr1	**Sochaux**	H	W	3-0	Frei 4,90; Kallstrom 12	23,000
29	frpr1	**Metz**	A	D	1-1	Frei 45	14,000
30	frpr1	**Caen**	A	D	2-2	Frei 59; Ouaddou 74	21,000
31	frpr1	**Bastia**	H	W	1-0	Kallstrom 28	20,000
32	frpr1	**Toulouse**	A	W	2-0	Frei 25; Kallstrom 86	14,000
33	frpr1	**St Etienne**	H	D	2-2	Frei 32; Monterrubio 75	30,000
34	frpr1	**Istres**	A	W	2-0	Maoulida 13; Frei 88	5,000
35	frpr1	**Monaco**	H	D	0-0		29,000
36	frpr1	**Lens**	A	L	2-5	Frei 15,61	39,000
37	frpr1	**Strasbourg**	H	W	4-0	Maoulida 43; Didot 58; Frei 60; Kallstrom 84	28,000
38	frpr1	**Paris SG**	A	L	0-1		45,000

MONTHLY POINTS TALLY

AUGUST	7	58%
SEPTEMBER	4	33%
OCTOBER	4	33%
NOVEMBER	5	42%
DECEMBER	3	33%
JANUARY	9	60%
FEBRUARY	4	44%
MARCH	5	56%
APRIL	10	83%
MAY	4	33%

KEY PLAYERS - GOALSCORERS

Alexander Frei

Goals in the League	20	Player Strike Rate Average number of minutes between League goals scored by player	151
Contribution to Attacking Power Average number of minutes between League team goals while on pitch	71	Club Strike Rate Average number of minutes between League goals scored by club	71

	PLAYER	LGE GOALS	POWER	STRIKE RATE
1	Alexander Frei	20	71	151 mins
2	Toifilou Maoulida	7	79	284 mins
3	Olivier Monterrubio	9	74	314 mins
4	Kim Kallstrom	5	77	524 mins
5	Oliver Sorlin	3	70	957 mins

KEY PLAYERS - MIDFIELDERS

Etienne Didot

Goals in the League	1	Contribution to Attacking Power Average number of minutes between League team goals while on pitch	74
Defensive Rating Average number of mins between League goals conceded while on the pitch	88	Scoring Difference Defensive Rating minus Contribution to Attacking Power	14

	PLAYER	LGE GOALS	DEF RATE	POWER	SCORE DIFF
1	Etienne Didot	1	88	74	14 mins
2	Cyril Jeunechamp	0	79	68	11 mins
3	Oliver Sorlin	3	80	70	10 mins
4	Kim Kallstrom	5	82	77	5 mins

KEY PLAYERS - DEFENDERS

Gregory Bourillon

Goals Conceded Number of League goals conceded while the player was on the pitch	14	Clean Sheets In League games when player was on pitch for at least 70 minutes	5
Defensive Rating Ave number of mins between League goals conceded while on the pitch	87	Club Defensive Rating Average number of mins between League goals conceded by the club this season	81

	PLAYER	CON LGE	CLEAN SHEETS	DEF RATE
1	Gregory Bourillon	14	5	87 mins
2	Jacques Faty	33	9	82 mins
3	Adailton	23	7	82 mins
4	Abdeslam Ouaddou	37	12	80 mins
5	Arnaud le Lan	16	3	74 mins

KEY GOALKEEPER

Andreas Isaksson

Goals Conceded in the League	42	Counting Games League games when player was on pitch for at least 70 minutes	37
Defensive Rating Ave number of mins between League goals conceded while on the pitch	81	Clean Sheets In games when player was on pitch for at least 70 minutes	13

LEAGUE GOALS

Alexander Frei

Minutes on the pitch	3014	Goals in the League	20
League average (mins between goals)	151		

	PLAYER	MINS	GOALS	AVE
1	Frei	3014	20	151
2	Monterrubio	2823	9	314
3	Maoulida	1986	7	284
4	Kallstrom	2618	5	524
5	Sorlin	2871	3	957
6	Ouaddou	2970	2	1485
7	Didot	2726	1	2726
8	Cearense	852	1	852
	Other		0	
	TOTAL		48	

DISCIPLINARY RECORDS

	PLAYER	YELLOW	RED	AVE
1	Cearense	4	0	213
2	Perrier Doumbe	7	1	249
3	Mornar	2	0	295
4	Gourcuff	2	0	319
5	Kallstrom	7	1	327
6	Ouaddou	8	0	371
7	Didot	6	1	389
8	Bourillon	3	0	404
9	Adailton	4	0	470
10	Monterrubio	6	0	470
11	Frei	6	0	502
12	Jeunechamp	5	1	512
13	Faty	5	0	541
	Other	7	1	
	TOTAL	72	5	

TOP POINT EARNERS

	PLAYER	GAMES	AV PTS
1	Cyril Jeunechamp	33	1.64
2	Alexander Frei	32	1.63
3	Adailton	19	1.63
4	Etienne Didot	29	1.62
5	Olivier Monterrubio	29	1.59
6	Oliver Sorlin	32	1.53
7	Toifilou Maoulida	21	1.52
8	Gregory Bourillon	12	1.50
9	Arnaud le Lan	13	1.46
10	Jacques Faty	28	1.46
	CLUB AVERAGE:		1.45

TEAM OF THE SEASON

D
Gregory Bourillon
CG: 12 DR: 87
M
Etienne Didot
CG: 29 SD: 14
D
Adailton
CG: 19 DR: 82
M
Cyril Jeunechamp
CG: 33 SD: 11
F
Alexander Frei
CG: 32 SR: 151
G
Andreas Isaksson
CG: 37 DR: 81
D
Jacques Faty
CG: 28 DR: 82
M
Oliver Sorlin
CG: 32 SD: 10
F
Toifilou Maoulida
CG: 21 SR: 284
D
Abdeslam Ouaddou
CG: 31 DR: 80
M
Kim Kallstrom
CG: 28 SD: 5

LEAGUE APPEARANCES, BOOKINGS AND CAPS

	AGE (on 01/07/05)	IN NAMED 16	APPEARANCES	COUNTING GAMES	MINUTES ON PITCH	YELLOW CARDS	RED CARDS	THIS SEASON	HOME COUNTRY
Goalkeepers									
Florent Chaigneau	21	5	0	0	0	0	0	-	France
Gardien Douard	20	1	0	0	0	0	0	-	France
Andreas Isaksson	23	38	38	37	3394	1	1	8	Sweden (13)
Simon Pouplin	20	31	0	0	0	0	0	-	France
Defenders									
Adailton	21	32	24	19	1880	4	0	-	Brazil
Gregory Bourillon	21	26	20	12	1214	3	0	-	France
Jacques Faty	21	38	36	28	2705	5	0	-	France
Arnaud le Lan	27	19	15	13	1185	1	0	-	France
Abdeslam Ouaddou	26	35	34	31	2970	8	0	-	Morocco
J-N Perrier Doumbe	26	31	26	21	1999	7	1	3	Cameroon (26)
Midfielders									
Cedric Barbosa	29	7	6	1	180	0	0	-	France
Jimmy Briand	20	13	10	1	263	0	0	-	France
Cearense	22	15	15	9	852	4	0	-	Brazil
Etienne Didot	21	36	34	29	2726	6	1	-	France
Yoann Gourcuff	18	27	21	5	639	2	0	-	France
Cyril Jeunechamp	29	35	35	33	3074	5	1	-	France
Kim Kallstrom	22	31	31	28	2618	7	1	-	Sweden
Stephane M'Bia	19	2	1	0	9	0	0	-	Cameroon
Arnold Mvuemba	20	9	8	3	307	0	0	-	France
Stephane N'Guema	20	14	13	1	153	1	0	-	Gabon
Oliver Sorlin	26	35	34	32	2871	3	0	-	France
Forwards									
Alexander Frei	25	36	36	32	3014	6	0	-	Switzerland
Toifilou Maoulida	26	34	31	21	1986	2	0	-	France
Olivier Monterrubio	28	37	37	29	2823	6	0	-	France
Ivica Mornar	31	16	15	5	590	2	0	4	Croatia (21)
Moussa Sow	19	4	3	0	46	0	0	-	France

SQUAD APPEARANCES

Match	1	2	3	4	5	6	7	8	9	10	11	12	13	14	15	16	17	18	19	20	21	22	23	24	25	26	27	28	29	30	31	32	33	34	35	36	37	38
Venue	H	A	H	A	H	A	H	A	H	A	H	H	A	H	A	H	A	H	A	H	A	H	A	H	A	H	A	H	A	A	H	A	H	A	H	A	H	A
Competition	L	L	L	L	L	L	L	L	L	L	L	L	L	L	L	L	L	L	L	L	L	L	L	L	L	L	L	L	L	L	L	L	L	L	L	L	L	L
Result	W	L	W	D	L	D	W	L	L	L	W	D	D	D	L	W	L	W	L	W	L	W	L	W	L	W	D	W	D	D	W	W	D	W	D	L	W	L

Goalkeepers
Florent Chaigneau
Gardien Douard
Andreas Isaksson
Simon Pouplin

Defenders
Adailton
Gregory Bourillon
Jacques Faty
Arnaud le Lan
Abdeslam Ouaddou
Jean-Noel Perrier Doumbe

Midfielders
Cedric Barbosa
Jimmy Briand
Cearense
Etienne Didot
Yoann Gourcuff
Cyril Jeunechamp
Kim Kallstrom
Stephane M'Bia
Arnold Mvuemba
Stephane N'Guema
Oliver Sorlin

Forwards
Alexander Frei
Toifilou Maoulida
Olivier Monterrubio
Ivica Mornar
Moussa Sow

KEY: On all match · On bench · Subbed or sent off (Counting game) · Subbed or sent off (playing less than 70 minutes) · Subbed on from bench (Counting Game) · Subbed on (playing less than 70 minutes) · Subbed on and then subbed or sent off (Counting Game) · Subbed on and then subbed or sent off (playing less than 70 minutes) · Not in 16

MARSEILLE

Final Position: **5th**

NICKNAME:

KEY: ☐Won ☐Drawn ☐Lost

							Attendance
1	frpr1	**Bordeaux**	H	W	1-0	Battles 90	60,000
2	frpr1	**Lille**	H	W	3-0	Bamogo 38; Marlet 89; Costa 90	60,000
3	frpr1	**Nice**	A	D	1-1	Pedretti 46	15,000
4	frpr1	**Metz**	H	L	1-3	Luyindula 27	60,000
5	frpr1	**Sochaux**	A	L	0-2		20,000
6	frpr1	**Toulouse**	H	W	1-0	Luyindula 34	56,000
7	frpr1	**Rennes**	A	L	0-1		26,000
8	frpr1	**Bastia**	H	W	1-0	Battles 77	5,000
9	frpr1	**Istres**	A	W	2-0	Bamogo 16; N'Diaye, S 49	11,000
10	frpr1	**St Etienne**	H	D	1-1	Koke 90	50,000
11	frpr1	**Lens**	A	D	0-0		41,000
12	frpr1	**Monaco**	H	D	1-1	Koke 20	57,000
13	frpr1	**Paris SG**	A	L	1-2	Battles 42	43,000
14	frpr1	**Strasbourg**	H	W	2-0	Bamogo 53; Koke 68	35,000
15	frpr1	**AC Ajaccio**	A	L	0-2		7,000
16	frpr1	**Nantes**	H	W	3-1	Meite 15; Fiorese 21; Marlet 90	50,000
17	frpr1	**Caen**	A	W	3-2	Bamogo 25,49 pen; Koke 67	21,000
18	frpr1	**Auxerre**	H	L	0-1		54,000
19	frpr1	**Lyon**	A	D	1-1	Luyindula 3	37,000
20	frpr1	**Lille**	A	W	2-1	Marlet 3; Nasri 22	16,000
21	frpr1	**Nice**	H	W	2-0	Luyindula 3,14	48,000
22	frpr1	**Metz**	A	W	1-0	Luyindula 25	26,000
23	frpr1	**Sochaux**	H	L	0-2		52,000
24	frpr1	**Toulouse**	A	W	3-1	Battles 11; Marlet 43; Luyindula 80	35,000
25	frpr1	**Rennes**	H	W	3-1	Cheyrou 34; Battles 41; Marlet 51	50,000
26	frpr1	**Bastia**	A	W	1-0	Pedretti 62	10,000
27	frpr1	**Istres**	H	D	1-1	Battles 55	50,000
28	frpr1	**St Etienne**	A	L	0-2		35,000
29	frpr1	**Lens**	H	W	2-1	Marlet 30,72	57,000
30	frpr1	**Monaco**	A	L	1-2	Bernardi 55 og	17,000
31	frpr1	**Paris SG**	H	D	1-1	Battles 74	58,000
32	frpr1	**Strasbourg**	A	L	0-1		26,000
33	frpr1	**AC Ajaccio**	H	L	1-2	Beye 58	50,000
34	frpr1	**Nantes**	A	D	2-2	Pedretti 68; Koke 82	37,000
35	frpr1	**Caen**	H	L	2-3	Battles 38; Luyindula 66	53,000
36	frpr1	**Auxerre**	A	D	0-0		21,000
37	frpr1	**Lyon**	H	L	0-1		58,000
38	frpr1	**Bordeaux**	A	D	3-3	Luyindula 21,90; Fiorese 26	34,000

MONTHLY POINTS TALLY

AUGUST	7	58%
SEPTEMBER	6	50%
OCTOBER	6	50%
NOVEMBER	6	50%
DECEMBER	4	44%
JANUARY	12	80%
FEBRUARY	7	78%
MARCH	3	33%
APRIL	2	17%
MAY	2	17%

KEY PLAYERS - GOALSCORERS

Laurent Battles

Goals in the League	8	**Player Strike Rate** Average number of minutes between League goals scored by player	224
Contribution to Attacking Power Average number of minutes between League team goals while on pitch	59	**Club Strike Rate** Average number of minutes between League goals scored by club	73

	PLAYER	LGE GOALS	POWER	STRIKE RATE
1	Laurent Battles	8	60	224 mins
2	Pegguy Luyindula	10	75	249 mins
3	Steve Marlet	7	71	295 mins
4	Habib Bamogo	5	79	364 mins
5	Benoit Pedretti	3	71	824 mins

KEY PLAYERS - MIDFIELDERS

Salomon Olembe

Goals in the League	0	**Contribution to Attacking Power** Average number of minutes between League team goals while on pitch	54
Defensive Rating Average number of mins between League goals conceded while on the pitch	85	**Scoring Difference** Defensive Rating minus Contribution to Attacking Power	31

	PLAYER	LGE GOALS	DEF RATE	POWER	SCORE DIFF
1	Salomon Olembe	0	85	54	31 mins
2	Eduardo Costa	1	98	77	21 mins
3	Laurent Battles	8	78	60	18 mins
4	Benoit Pedretti	3	85	71	14 mins
5	Frederic Dehu	0	82	69	13 mins

KEY PLAYERS - DEFENDERS

Bixente Lizarazu

Goals Conceded Number of League goals conceded while the player was on the pitch	13	**Clean Sheets** In League games when player was on pitch for at least 70 minutes	6
Defensive Rating Ave number of mins between League goals conceded while on the pitch	96	**Club Defensive Rating** Average number of mins between League goals conceded by the club this season	81

	PLAYER	CON LGE	CLEAN SHEETS	DEF RATE
1	Bixente Lizarazu	13	6	96 mins
2	Abdoulaye Meite	34	10	89 mins
3	Habib Beye	38	11	86 mins
4	Ferreira	20	3	84 mins

KEY GOALKEEPER

Fabien Barthez

Goals Conceded in the League	28	**Counting Games** League games when player was on pitch for at least 70 minutes	30
Defensive Rating Ave number of mins between League goals conceded while on the pitch	96	**Clean Sheets** In games when player was on pitch for at least 70 minutes	10

LEAGUE GOALS

Pegguy Luyindula

Minutes on the pitch	2485	Goals in the League	10
League average (mins between goals)	249		

	PLAYER	MINS	GOALS	AVE
1	Luyindula	2485	10	249
2	Battles	1791	8	224
3	Marlet	2064	7	295
4	Koke	1259	5	252
5	Bamogo	1818	5	364
6	Pedretti	2473	3	824
7	Fiorese	1034	2	517
8	N'Diaye, S	1500	1	1500
9	Meite	3021	1	3021
10	Cheyrou	735	1	735
11	Costa	2452	1	2452
12	Nasri	1420	1	1420
13	Beye	3273	1	3273
	Other		1	
	TOTAL		47	

DISCIPLINARY

	PLAYER	YELLOW	RED	AVE
1	Cheyrou	5	0	147
2	Costa	10	0	245
3	Pedretti	9	1	247
4	Ferreira	6	0	281
5	Lizarazu	4	0	313
6	Koke	4	0	314
7	Battles	5	0	358
8	Meite	8	0	377
9	Olembe	4	0	402
10	Marlet	5	0	412
11	Bamogo	4	0	454
12	N'Diaye, S	3	0	500
13	Fiorese	2	0	517
	Other	13	0	
	TOTAL	82	1	

TOP POINT EARNERS

	PLAYER	GAMES	AV PTS
1	Salomon Olembe	16	1.88
2	Eduardo Costa	25	1.64
3	Fabien Barthez	30	1.63
4	Benoit Pedretti	26	1.62
5	Steve Marlet	20	1.55
6	Laurent Battles	14	1.50
7	Frederic Dehu	25	1.48
8	Abdoulaye Meite	34	1.47
9	Pegguy Luyindula	23	1.43
10	Habib Beye	37	1.41
	CLUB AVERAGE:		1.45

LEAGUE APPEARANCES, BOOKINGS AND CAPS

	AGE (on 01/07/05)	IN NAMED 16	APPEARANCES	COUNTING GAMES	MINUTES ON PITCH	YELLOW CARDS	RED CARDS	THIS SEASON	HOME COUNTRY
Goalkeepers									
Pegguy Arphexad	32	8	0	0	0	0	0	-	France
Fabien Barthez	34	30	30	30	2700	3	0	5	France (4)
Cedric Carasso	23	1	0	0	0	0	0	-	France
Jeremy Gavanon	21	36	8	8	720	1	0	-	France
Rais M'Bolhi	19	1	0	0	0	0	0	-	France
Defenders									
Habib Beye	28	38	37	37	3273	3	0	3	Senegal (33)
Johnny Ecker	32	6	3	1	189	1	1	-	France
Ferreira	31	30	23	17	1686	6	0	-	Brazil
Bixente Lizarazu	35	14	14	14	1253	4	0	-	France
Abdoulaye Meite	24	34	34	34	3021	8	0	3	Ivory Coast (44)
Leyti N'Diaye	19	6	3	2	203	0	0	-	Senegal
Koji Nakata	25	10	5	3	361	0	0	-	Japan
Taye Ismaila Taiwo	20	4	4	3	330	0	0	-	Nigeria
Midfielders									
Laurent Battles	29	33	30	14	1791	5	0	-	France
Fabien Camus	20	1	0	0	0	0	0	-	France
Bruno Cheyrou	27	22	19	4	735	5	0	-	France
Eduardo Costa	22	29	29	25	2452	10	0	-	Brazil
Frederic Dehu	32	27	27	25	2293	4	0	-	France
Ibrahim Hemdani	27	21	11	6	693	1	0	-	France
Sylvain N'Diaye	29	28	23	13	1500	3	0	3	Senegal (33)
Samir Nasri	18	24	24	11	1420	1	0	-	France
Salomon Olembe	24	25	24	16	1609	4	0	3	Cameroon (26)
Benoit Pedretti	24	30	30	26	2473	9	1	7	France (4)
Ahmed Yahiaoui	18	5	5	0	63	1	0	-	France
Forwards									
Habib Bamogo	23	30	30	17	1818	4	0	-	France
Rakhmane Barry	18	3	1	0	45	0	0	-	France
Fabrice Fiorese	29	20	18	9	1034	2	0	-	France
Sergio Pardo Koke	22	27	24	10	1259	4	0	-	Spain
Pegguy Luyindula	26	35	35	23	2485	0	0	5	France (4)
Steve Marlet	31	32	31	20	2064	5	0	1	France (4)
Hossam Mido	22	1	1	1	90	0	0	-	Egypt

TEAM OF THE SEASON

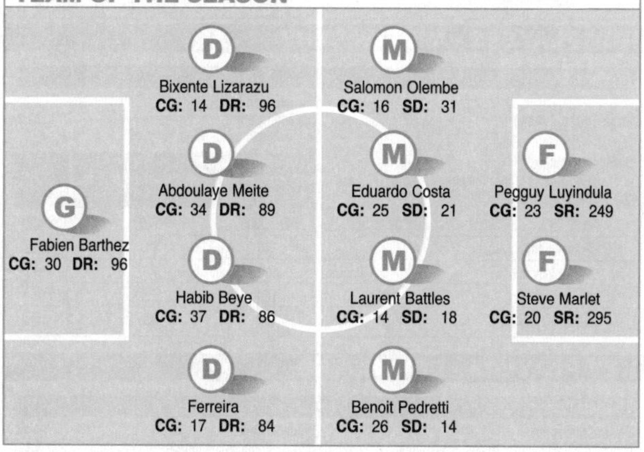
D
Bixente Lizarazu
CG: 14 DR: 96
M
Salomon Olembe
CG: 16 SD: 31
D
Abdoulaye Meite
CG: 34 DR: 89
M
Eduardo Costa
CG: 25 SD: 21
F
Pegguy Luyindula
CG: 23 SR: 249
G
Fabien Barthez
CG: 30 DR: 96
D
Habib Beye
CG: 37 DR: 86
M
Laurent Battles
CG: 14 SD: 18
F
Steve Marlet
CG: 20 SR: 295
D
Ferreira
CG: 17 DR: 84
M
Benoit Pedretti
CG: 26 SD: 14

SQUAD APPEARANCES

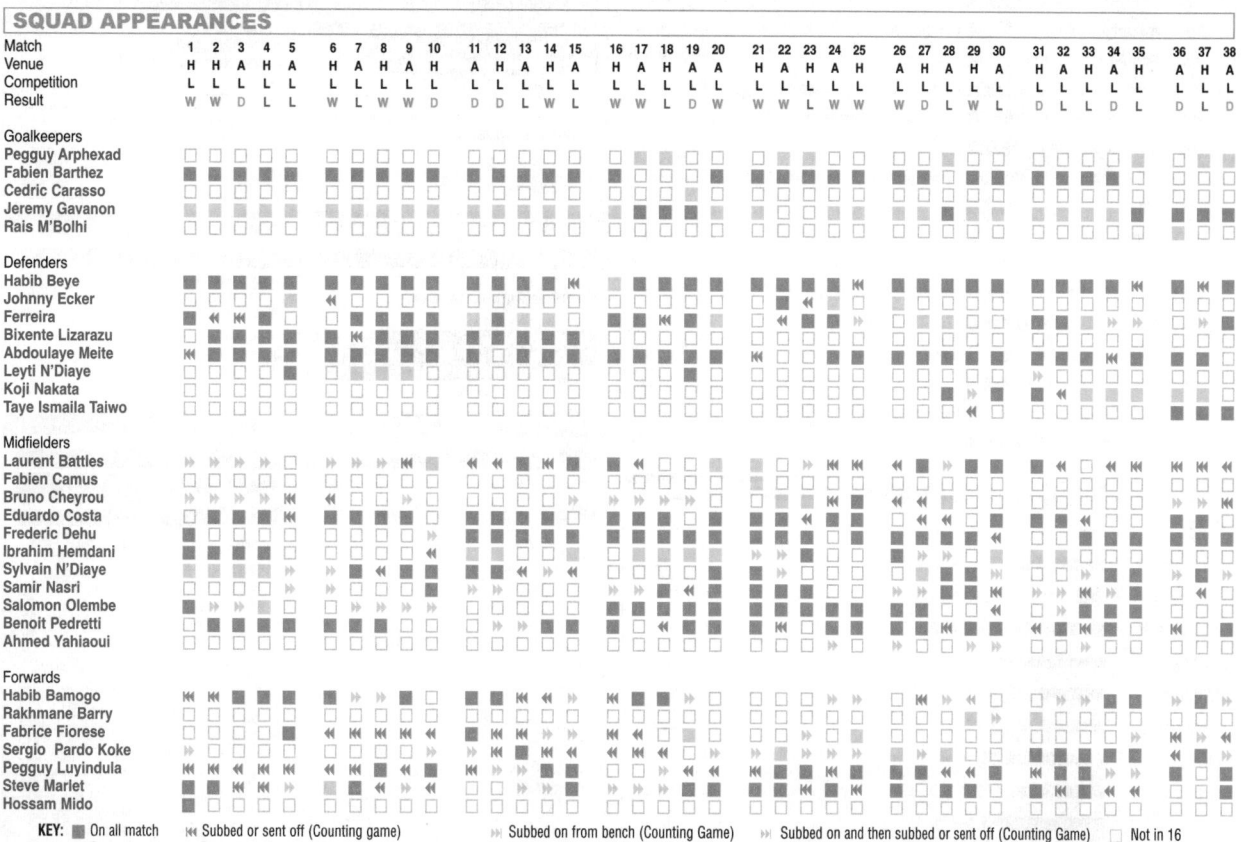

Match	1	2	3	4	5	6	7	8	9	10	11	12	13	14	15	16	17	18	19	20	21	22	23	24	25	26	27	28	29	30	31	32	33	34	35	36	37	38
Venue	H	H	A	H	A	H	A	H	A	H	A	H	A	H	A	H	A	H	A	A	H	A	H	A	H	A	H	A	H	A	H	A	H	A	H	A	H	A
Competition	L	L	L	L	L	L	L	L	L	L	L	L	L	L	L	L	L	L	L	L	L	L	L	L	L	L	L	L	L	L	L	L	L	L	L	L	L	L
Result	W	W	D	L	L	W	L	W	W	D	D	D	L	W	L	W	W	L	D	W	W	W	L	W	W	W	D	L	W	L	D	L	L	D	L	D	L	D

Goalkeepers
Pegguy Arphexad
Fabien Barthez
Cedric Carasso
Jeremy Gavanon
Rais M'Bolhi

Defenders
Habib Beye
Johnny Ecker
Ferreira
Bixente Lizarazu
Abdoulaye Meite
Leyti N'Diaye
Koji Nakata
Taye Ismaila Taiwo

Midfielders
Laurent Battles
Fabien Camus
Bruno Cheyrou
Eduardo Costa
Frederic Dehu
Ibrahim Hemdani
Sylvain N'Diaye
Samir Nasri
Salomon Olembe
Benoit Pedretti
Ahmed Yahiaoui

Forwards
Habib Bamogo
Rakhmane Barry
Fabrice Fiorese
Sergio Pardo Koke
Pegguy Luyindula
Steve Marlet
Hossam Mido

KEY: ■ On all match · ■ On bench · ⏮ Subbed or sent off (Counting game) · « Subbed or sent off (playing less than 70 minutes) · ⏭ Subbed on from bench (Counting Game) · » Subbed on (playing less than 70 minutes) · ⏭ Subbed on and then subbed or sent off (Counting Game) · » Subbed on and then subbed or sent off (playing less than 70 minutes) · □ Not in 16

ST ETIENNE

Final Position: **6th**

KEY: ☐Won ☐Drawn ☐Lost

							Attendance
1	frpr1	**Monaco**	H	L	0-1		34,000
2	frpr1	**Lens**	A	L	0-3		39,000
3	frpr1	**Strasbourg**	H	D	1-1	Le Tallec 35	27,000
4	frpr1	**Paris SG**	A	D	2-2	Piquionne 65,88	38,000
5	frpr1	**Nantes**	H	D	0-0		30,000
6	frpr1	**AC Ajaccio**	A	D	1-1	Feindouno 41	4,000
7	frpr1	**Auxerre**	H	W	3-1	Ilunga 2; Marin 14,37	30,000
8	frpr1	**Sochaux**	A	L	1-2	Piquionne 33	19,000
9	frpr1	**Lyon**	H	L	2-3	Ilunga 48; Feindouno 61	35,000
10	frpr1	**Marseille**	A	D	1-1	Feindouno 16	50,000
11	frpr1	**Bordeaux**	H	D	0-0		35,000
12	frpr1	**Lille**	A	L	0-1		9,000
13	frpr1	**Nice**	H	W	2-1	Feindouno 25 pen,90	30,000
14	frpr1	**Bastia**	A	W	3-0	Hellebuyck 62,69; Piquionne 89	8,000
15	frpr1	**Rennes**	H	W	1-0	Compan 83	30,000
16	frpr1	**Metz**	A	D	2-2	Sable 12; Hognon 73	12,000
17	frpr1	**Toulouse**	H	D	0-0		30,000
18	frpr1	**Caen**	H	W	5-0	Piquionne 2,44; Hellebuyck 30; Mendy 33; Compan 83	25,000
19	frpr1	**Istres**	A	W	2-0	Sable 30; Mendy 45	10,000
20	frpr1	**Lens**	H	D	0-0		30,000
21	frpr1	**Strasbourg**	A	D	1-1	Hognon 32	10,000
22	frpr1	**Paris SG**	H	D	0-0		32,000
23	frpr1	**Nantes**	A	D	0-0		30,000
24	frpr1	**Auxerre**	A	D	2-2	Compan 13; Feindouno 80	15,000
25	frpr1	**Sochaux**	H	W	1-0	Feindouno 60 pen	28,000
26	frpr1	**Lyon**	A	L	2-3	Feindouno 55; Compan 89	39,000
27	frpr1	**Marseille**	H	W	2-0	Feindouno 35 pen; Hellebuyck 82	35,000
28	frpr1	**Bordeaux**	A	L	0-2		32,000
29	frpr1	**AC Ajaccio**	H	W	3-0	Feindouno 52; Piquionne 63,65	29,000
30	frpr1	**Lille**	H	D	0-0		30,000
31	frpr1	**Nice**	A	L	0-2		12,000
32	frpr1	**Bastia**	H	W	3-0	Sable 7; Feindouno 85; Piquionne 92	31,000
33	frpr1	**Rennes**	A	D	2-2	Piquionne 7; Sable 62	30,000
34	frpr1	**Metz**	H	D	0-0		33,000
35	frpr1	**Toulouse**	A	W	2-0	Sakho 36; Feindouno 61	26,000
36	frpr1	**Caen**	A	L	0-2		21,000
37	frpr1	**Istres**	H	W	2-0	Piquionne 68; Feindouno 74	35,000
38	frpr1	**Monaco**	A	D	1-1	Sable 9	18,000

MONTHLY POINTS TALLY

AUGUST	2	17%
SEPTEMBER	5	42%
OCTOBER	2	17%
NOVEMBER	10	83%
DECEMBER	7	78%
JANUARY	4	33%
FEBRUARY	4	44%
MARCH	7	58%
APRIL	5	42%
MAY	7	58%

KEY PLAYERS - GOALSCORERS

Pascal Feindouno

Goals in the League	13	**Player Strike Rate** Average number of minutes between League goals scored by player	232
Contribution to Attacking Power Average number of minutes between League team goals while on pitch	68	**Club Strike Rate** Average number of minutes between League goals scored by club	73

	PLAYER	LGE GOALS	POWER	STRIKE RATE
1	Pascal Feindouno	13	68	232 mins
2	Frederic Piquionne	11	73	282 mins
3	Julien Sable	5	72	665 mins
4	David Hellebuyck	4	80	797 mins
5	Frederic Mendy	2	71	819 mins

KEY PLAYERS - MIDFIELDERS

Frederic Mendy

Goals in the League	2	**Contribution to Attacking Power** Average number of minutes between League team goals while on pitch	71
Defensive Rating Average number of mins between League goals conceded while on the pitch	149	**Scoring Difference** Defensive Rating minus Contribution to Attacking Power	78

	PLAYER	LGE GOALS	DEF RATE	POWER	SCORE DIFF
1	Frederic Mendy	2	149	71	78 mins
2	Didier Zokora	0	112	73	39 mins
3	Julien Sable	5	104	72	32 mins
4	David Hellebuyck	4	103	80	23 mins

KEY PLAYERS - DEFENDERS

Fousseni Diawara

Goals Conceded Number of League goals conceded while the player was on the pitch	17	**Clean Sheets** In League games when player was on pitch for at least 70 minutes	14
Defensive Rating Ave number of mins between League goals conceded while on the pitch	119	**Club Defensive Rating** Average number of mins between League goals conceded by the club this season	101

	PLAYER	CON LGE	CLEAN SHEETS	DEF RATE
1	Fousseni Diawara	17	14	119 mins
2	Herita Nkolongo Ilunga	30	18	110 mins
3	Vincent Hognon	28	15	105 mins
4	Zoumana Camara	31	15	101 mins

KEY GOALKEEPER

Jeremie Janot

Goals Conceded in the League	32	**Counting Games** League games when player was on pitch for at least 70 minutes	38
Defensive Rating Ave number of mins between League goals conceded while on the pitch	107	**Clean Sheets** In games when player was on pitch for at least 70 minutes	18

LEAGUE GOALS

Pascal Feindouno

Minutes on the pitch	3011	Goals in the League	13
League average (mins between goals)	232		

	PLAYER	MINS	GOALS	AVE
1	Feindouno	3011	13	232
2	Piquionne	3102	11	282
3	Sable	3325	5	665
4	Hellebuyck	3188	4	797
5	Compan	528	4	132
6	Marin	1144	2	572
7	Ilunga	3290	2	1645
8	Hognon	2950	2	1475
9	Mendy	1637	2	819
10	Le Tallec	294	1	294
11	Sakho	363	1	363
	Other		0	
	TOTAL		47	

DISCIPLINARY RECORDS

	PLAYER	YELLOW	RED	AVE
1	Compan	3	0	176
2	Zokora	9	1	314
3	Ilunga	9	0	365
4	Hernandez	2	0	396
5	Diawara	5	0	403
6	Garrido	2	0	427
7	Feindouno	7	0	430
8	Piquionne	6	0	517
9	Sable	5	1	554
10	Marin	2	0	572
11	Camara	4	1	623
12	Janot	4	0	855
13	Hognon	3	0	983
	Other	3	0	
	TOTAL	64	3	

TOP POINT EARNERS

	PLAYER	GAMES	AV PTS
1	Frederic Mendy	16	1.81
2	Fousseni Diawara	22	1.77
3	Herita Nkolongo Ilunga	36	1.47
4	Frederic Piquionne	34	1.47
5	Pascal Feindouno	33	1.45
6	Julien Sable	37	1.41
7	Didier Zokora	35	1.40
8	Jeremie Janot	38	1.39
9	Zoumana Camara	33	1.33
10	David Hellebuyck	35	1.31
	CLUB AVERAGE:		1.39

TEAM OF THE SEASON

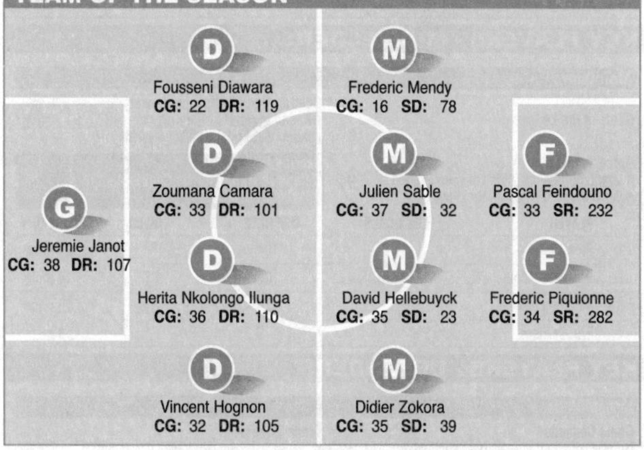

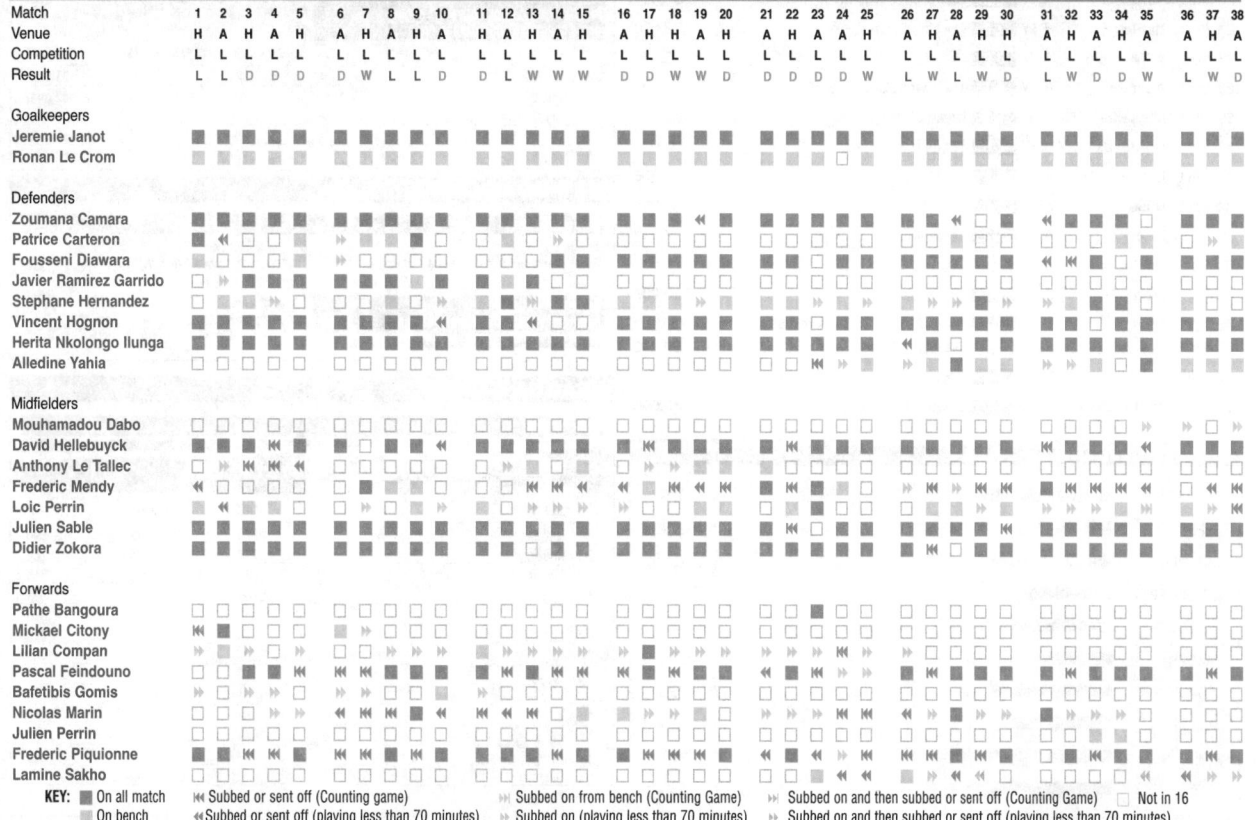

D
Fousseni Diawara
CG: 22 DR: 119
M
Frederic Mendy
CG: 16 SD: 78
D
Zoumana Camara
CG: 33 DR: 101
M
Julien Sable
CG: 37 SD: 32
F
Pascal Feindouno
CG: 33 SR: 232
G
Jeremie Janot
CG: 38 DR: 107
D
Herita Nkolongo Ilunga
CG: 36 DR: 110
M
David Hellebuyck
CG: 35 SD: 23
F
Frederic Piquionne
CG: 34 SR: 282
D
Vincent Hognon
CG: 32 DR: 105
M
Didier Zokora
CG: 35 SD: 39

LEAGUE APPEARANCES, BOOKINGS AND CAPS

	AGE (on 01/07/05)	IN NAMED 16	APPEARANCES	COUNTING GAMES	MINUTES ON PITCH	YELLOW CARDS	RED CARDS	THIS SEASON	HOME COUNTRY
Goalkeepers									
Jeremie Janot	27	38	38	38	3420	4	0	-	France
Ronan Le Crom	30	37	0	0	0	0	0	-	France
Defenders									
Zoumana Camara	26	36	36	33	3119	4	1	-	France
Patrice Carteron	34	14	6	2	257	1	0	-	France
Fousseni Diawara	24	26	24	22	2019	5	0	-	France
Javier Garrido	26	12	10	9	855	2	0	-	Spain
Stephane Hernandez	25	30	16	7	793	2	0	-	France
Vincent Hognon	30	34	34	32	2950	3	0	-	France
Herita Ilunga	23	37	37	36	3290	9	0	-	Congo
Alledine Yahia	23	15	7	3	353	1	0	-	France
Midfielders									
Mouhamadou Dabo	18	3	3	0	51	0	0	-	Senegal
David Hellebuyck	26	37	37	35	3188	3	0	-	France
Anthony Le Tallec	20	12	7	2	294	0	0	-	France
Frederic Mendy	31	28	24	16	1637	0	0	-	France
Loic Perrin	19	28	15	3	372	1	0	-	France
Julien Sable	24	37	37	37	3325	5	1	-	France
Didier Zokora	24	35	35	35	3144	9	1	2	Ivory Coast (44)
Forwards									
Pathe Bangoura	21	1	1	1	90	0	0	-	Guinea
Mickael Citony	24	4	3	2	184	0	0	-	France
Lilian Compan	28	23	21	2	528	3	0	-	France
Pascal Feindouno	24	36	36	33	3011	7	0	-	Guinea
Bafetibis Gomis	19	7	6	0	94	0	0	-	France
Nicolas Marin	24	29	26	9	1144	2	0	-	France
Julien Perrin	-	2	0	0	0	0	0	-	France
Frederic Piquionne	26	37	37	34	3102	6	0	-	France
Lamine Sakho	27	11	9	0	363	1	0	-	Senegal

SQUAD APPEARANCES

Match	1	2	3	4	5	6	7	8	9	10	11	12	13	14	15	16	17	18	19	20	21	22	23	24	25	26	27	28	29	30	31	32	33	34	35	36	37	38
Venue	H	A	H	A	H	A	H	A	H	A	H	A	H	A	H	A	H	H	A	H	A	H	A	A	H	A	H	A	H	H	A	H	A	H	A	A	H	A
Competition	L	L	L	L	L	L	L	L	L	L	L	L	L	L	L	L	L	L	L	L	L	L	L	L	L	L	L	L	L	L	L	L	L	L	L	L	L	L
Result	L	L	D	D	D	D	W	L	L	D	D	L	W	W	W	D	D	W	W	D	D	D	D	D	W	L	W	L	W	D	L	W	D	D	W	L	W	D

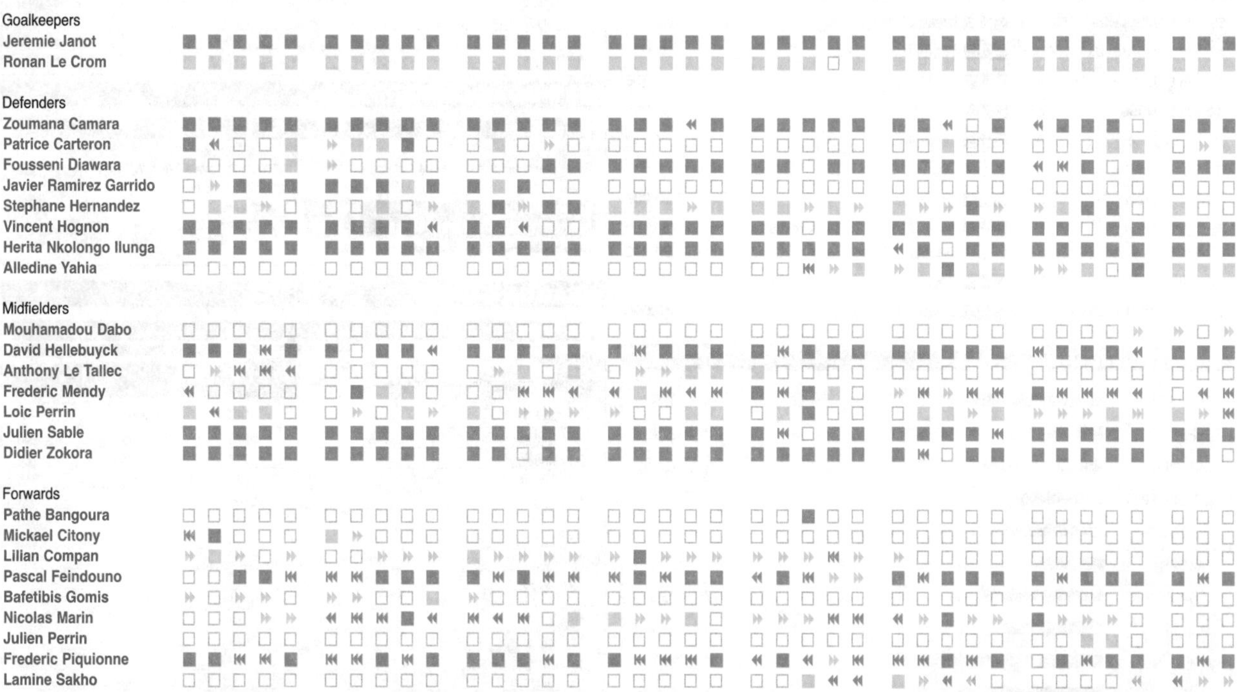

Goalkeepers
Jeremie Janot
Ronan Le Crom
Defenders
Zoumana Camara
Patrice Carteron
Fousseni Diawara
Javier Ramirez Garrido
Stephane Hernandez
Vincent Hognon
Herita Nkolongo Ilunga
Alledine Yahia
Midfielders
Mouhamadou Dabo
David Hellebuyck
Anthony Le Tallec
Frederic Mendy
Loic Perrin
Julien Sable
Didier Zokora
Forwards
Pathe Bangoura
Mickael Citony
Lilian Compan
Pascal Feindouno
Bafetibis Gomis
Nicolas Marin
Julien Perrin
Frederic Piquionne
Lamine Sakho

KEY: ■ On all match ■ On bench | ⏮ Subbed or sent off (Counting game) « Subbed or sent off (playing less than 70 minutes) | ⏭ Subbed on from bench (Counting Game) » Subbed on (playing less than 70 minutes) | ⏭ Subbed on and then subbed or sent off (Counting Game) » Subbed on and then subbed or sent off (playing less than 70 minutes) | □ Not in 16

LENS

Final Position: **7th**

KEY: Won Drawn Lost

							Attendance
1	frpr1	**Toulouse**	A	D	0-0		25,000
2	frpr1	**St Etienne**	H	W	3-0	Keita 26,39; Cousin 72	39,000
3	frpr1	**Istres**	A	W	2-0	Hilton 30; Utaka 87	8,000
4	frpr1	**Monaco**	H	D	1-1	Gillet 41	39,000
5	frpr1	**Caen**	A	L	0-1		20,000
6	frpr1	**Strasbourg**	A	D	2-2	Cousin 32; Carriere 86	10,000
7	frpr1	**Paris SG**	H	D	2-2	Bak 81; Hilton 85	37,000
8	frpr1	**Nantes**	A	L	0-1		15,000
9	frpr1	**AC Ajaccio**	H	D	1-1	Diarra 1	32,000
10	frpr1	**Auxerre**	A	L	0-3		15,000
11	frpr1	**Marseille**	H	D	0-0		41,000
12	frpr1	**Bordeaux**	A	D	1-1	Utaka 59	23,000
13	frpr1	**Lyon**	H	L	0-1		40,000
14	frpr1	**Nice**	A	D	1-1	Utaka 33	11,000
15	frpr1	**Lille**	H	D	1-1	Thomert 45	40,000
16	frpr1	**Sochaux**	A	W	2-1	Cousin 77; Sarr 90	14,000
17	frpr1	**Metz**	H	W	2-0	Utaka 35; Keita 67	32,000
18	frpr1	**Rennes**	A	L	1-3	Leroy 40	20,000
19	frpr1	**Bastia**	H	W	2-1	Cousin 35,69	31,000
20	frpr1	**St Etienne**	A	D	0-0		30,000
21	frpr1	**Istres**	H	L	0-1		31,000
22	frpr1	**Monaco**	A	L	0-2		8,000
23	frpr1	**Caen**	H	L	0-1		28,000
24	frpr1	**Strasbourg**	H	W	2-1	Thomert 29,59	32,000
25	frpr1	**Paris SG**	A	W	2-0	Diarra 42; Leroy 50	37,000
26	frpr1	**Nantes**	H	W	2-0	Cousin 23; Carriere 74	32,000
27	frpr1	**AC Ajaccio**	A	D	0-0		3,000
28	frpr1	**Auxerre**	H	W	3-1	Thomert 1; Utaka 75,81	30,000
29	frpr1	**Marseille**	A	L	1-2	Utaka 28	57,000
30	frpr1	**Bordeaux**	H	W	2-0	Thomert 32; Utaka 49	32,000
31	frpr1	**Lyon**	A	L	0-1		36,000
32	frpr1	**Nice**	H	D	0-0		33,000
33	frpr1	**Lille**	A	L	1-2	Leroy 43	14,000
34	frpr1	**Sochaux**	H	W	3-2	Cousin 10 pen; Utaka 14; Thomert 81	32,000
35	frpr1	**Metz**	A	D	1-1	Jussie 49	20,000
36	frpr1	**Rennes**	H	W	5-2	Utaka 28,41,58; Carriere 56; Ouaddou 84 og	39,000
37	frpr1	**Bastia**	A	L	1-3	Cousin 20 pen	5,000
38	frpr1	**Toulouse**	H	W	1-0	Cousin 32	40,000

MONTHLY POINTS TALLY

AUGUST	8	67%
SEPTEMBER	2	17%
OCTOBER	3	25%
NOVEMBER	5	42%
DECEMBER	6	67%
JANUARY	4	27%
FEBRUARY	7	78%
MARCH	6	67%
APRIL	4	33%
MAY	7	58%

KEY PLAYERS - GOALSCORERS

John Utaka

Goals in the League	12	Player Strike Rate Average number of minutes between League goals scored by player	248
Contribution to Attacking Power Average number of minutes between League team goals while on pitch	74	Club Strike Rate Average number of minutes between League goals scored by club	76

	PLAYER	LGE GOALS	POWER	STRIKE RATE
1	John Utaka	12	74	248 mins
2	Daniel Cousin	9	68	266 mins
3	Olivier Thomert	6	90	316 mins
4	Jerome Leroy	3	67	823 mins
5	Eric Carriere	3	71	870 mins

KEY PLAYERS - MIDFIELDERS

Alou Diarra

Goals in the League	2	Contribution to Attacking Power Average number of minutes between League team goals while on pitch	73
Defensive Rating Average number of mins between League goals conceded while on the pitch	94	Scoring Difference Defensive Rating minus Contribution to Attacking Power	21

	PLAYER	LGE GOALS	DEF RATE	POWER	SCORE DIFF
1	Alou Diarra	2	94	73	21 mins
2	Seyadou Keita	3	103	89	14 mins
3	Jerome Leroy	3	77	67	10 mins
4	Eric Carriere	3	79	71	8 mins

KEY PLAYERS - DEFENDERS

Nicholas Gillet

Goals Conceded Number of League goals conceded while the player was on the pitch	32	Clean Sheets In League games when player was on pitch for at least 70 minutes	11
Defensive Rating Ave number of mins between League goals conceded while on the pitch	93	Club Defensive Rating Average number of mins between League goals conceded by the club this season	88

	PLAYER	CON LGE	CLEAN SHEETS	DEF RATE
1	Nicholas Gillet	32	11	93 mins
2	Eric Cubilier	28	9	87 mins
3	Benoit Assou-Ekotto	31	9	83 mins
4	Hilton	29	9	82 mins
5	Jacek Bak	17	1	68 mins

KEY GOALKEEPER

Charles-Hubert Itandje

Goals Conceded in the League	39	Counting Games League games when player was on pitch for at least 70 minutes	38
Defensive Rating Ave number of mins between League goals conceded while on the pitch	88	Clean Sheets In games when player was on pitch for at least 70 minutes	12

LEAGUE GOALS

John Utaka

Minutes on the pitch	2970	Goals in the League	12
League average (mins between goals)	248		

	PLAYER	MINS	GOALS	AVE
1	Utaka	2970	12	248
2	Cousin	2394	9	266
3	Thomert	1897	6	316
4	Keita	2769	3	923
5	Leroy	2468	3	823
6	Carriere	2610	3	870
7	Hilton	2371	2	1186
8	Diarra	2917	2	1459
9	Sarr	4	1	4
10	Bak	1163	1	1163
11	Gillet	2969	1	2969
12	Jussie	965	1	965
	Other		1	
	TOTAL		45	

DISCIPLINARY RECORDS

	PLAYER	YELLOW	RED	AVE
1	Diarra	11	0	265
2	Leroy	8	1	274
3	Assou-Ekotto	7	0	368
4	Bak	3	0	387
5	Hilton	5	1	395
6	Barul	3	0	397
7	Cubilier	6	0	406
8	Jussie	2	0	482
9	Keita	5	0	553
10	Gillet	5	0	593
11	Lachor	1	0	595
12	Utaka	4	0	742
13	Cousin	3	0	798
	Other	5	0	
	TOTAL	68	2	

TOP POINT EARNERS

	PLAYER	GAMES	AV PTS
1	Jerome Leroy	25	1.56
2	Alou Diarra	32	1.56
3	Benoit Assou-Ekotto	28	1.46
4	Daniel Cousin	25	1.44
5	Hilton	26	1.42
6	Eric Carriere	28	1.39
7	Nicholas Gillet	33	1.39
8	Charles-Hubert Itandje	38	1.37
9	Seyadou Keita	30	1.37
10	Eric Cubilier	27	1.33
	CLUB AVERAGE:		1.37

TEAM OF THE SEASON

G Charles-Hubert Itandje CG: 38 DR: 88

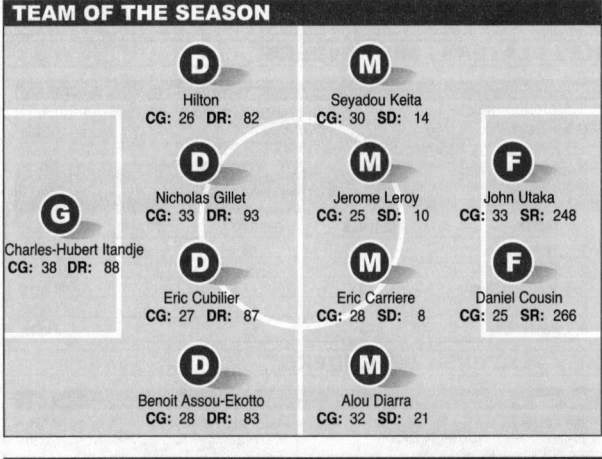

D Hilton CG: 26 DR: 82

D Nicholas Gillet CG: 33 DR: 93

D Eric Cubilier CG: 27 DR: 87

D Benoit Assou-Ekotto CG: 28 DR: 83

M Seyadou Keita CG: 30 SD: 14

M Jerome Leroy CG: 25 SD: 10

M Eric Carriere CG: 28 SD: 8

M Alou Diarra CG: 32 SD: 21

F John Utaka CG: 33 SR: 248

F Daniel Cousin CG: 25 SR: 266

LEAGUE APPEARANCES, BOOKINGS AND CAPS

	AGE (on 01/07/05)	IN NAMED 16	APPEARANCES	COUNTING GAMES	MINUTES ON PITCH	YELLOW CARDS	RED CARDS	THIS SEASON	HOME COUNTRY
Goalkeepers									
Sebastien Chabbert	26	36	0	0	0	0	0	-	France
Charles-H Itandje	22	38	38	38	3420	1	0	-	France
Niki Maenpaa	20	2	0	0	0	0	0	-	Finland
Defenders									
Benoit Assou-Ekotto	21	33	29	28	2581	7	0	-	France
Jacek Bak	32	23	20	12	1163	3	0	-	Poland
Patrick Barul	27	35	29	9	1191	3	0	-	France
Adama Coulibaly	24	29	17	8	849	0	0	-	Mali
Eric Cubilier	26	33	31	27	2438	6	0	-	France
Nicholas Gillet	28	36	33	33	2969	5	0	-	France
Hilton	27	27	27	26	2371	5	1	-	Brazil
Daouda Jabi	23	7	3	0	157	1	0	-	France
Yoan Lachor	29	8	8	7	595	1	0	-	France
Midfielders									
Eric Carriere	32	36	33	28	2610	2	0	-	France
Mounir Diane	23	24	22	1	399	1	1	-	Morocco
Alou Diarra	23	34	34	32	2917	11	0	5	France (4)
Seyadou Keita	25	34	34	30	2769	5	0	-	Mali
Seid Khiter	20	2	0	0	0	0	0	-	France
Jerome Leroy	30	31	31	25	2468	8	1	-	France
Lesly Malouda	21	10	7	1	190	0	0	-	France
Pape Sarr	27	3	1	0	4	0	0	-	Senegal
Forwards									
Dagui Bakari	30	13	8	1	209	0	0	-	France
Daniel Cousin	28	38	37	25	2394	3	0	-	Gabon
Jussie	21	12	12	10	965	2	0	-	Brazil
Emelson Rosario	19	1	1	0	16	0	0	-	Cape Verde
Olivier Thomert	25	29	28	20	1897	2	0	-	France
John Utaka	23	34	34	33	2970	4	0	-	Nigeria

SQUAD APPEARANCES

Match	1	2	3	4	5	6	7	8	9	10	11	12	13	14	15	16	17	18	19	20	21	22	23	24	25	26	27	28	29	30	31	32	33	34	35	36	37	38
Venue	A	H	A	H	A	A	H	A	H	A	H	A	H	A	H	A	H	A	H	A	H	A	H	H	A	H	A	H	A	H	A	H	A	H	A	H	A	H
Competition	L	L	L	L	L	L	L	L	L	L	L	L	L	L	L	L	L	L	L	L	L	L	L	L	L	L	L	L	L	L	L	L	L	L	L	L	L	L
Result	D	W	W	D	L	D	D	L	D	L	D	D	L	D	D	W	W	L	W	D	L	L	L	W	W	W	D	W	L	W	L	D	L	W	D	W	L	W

Goalkeepers
Sebastien Chabbert
Charles-Hubert Itandje
Niki Maenpaa

Defenders
Benoit Assou-Ekotto
Jacek Bak
Patrick Barul
Adama Coulibaly
Eric Cubilier
Nicholas Gillet
Hilton
Daouda Jabi
Yoan Lachor

Midfielders
Eric Carriere
Mounir Diane
Alou Diarra
Seyadou Keita
Seid Khiter
Jerome Leroy
Lesly Malouda
Pape Sarr

Forwards
Dagui Bakari
Daniel Cousin
Jussie
Emelson Rosario
Olivier Thomert
John Utaka

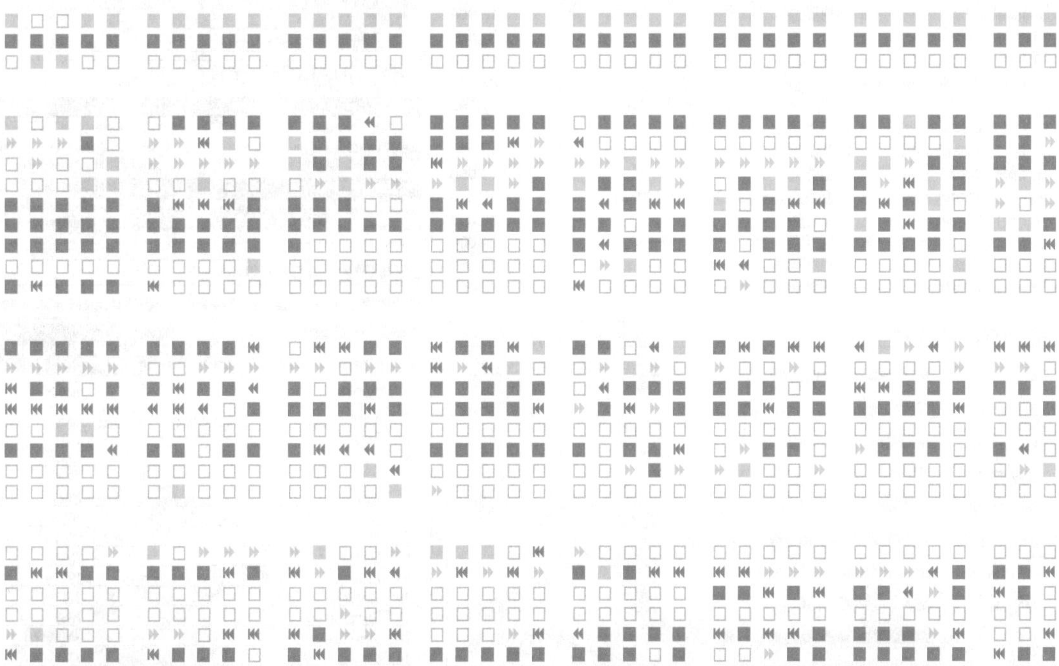

KEY: On all match / On bench / Subbed or sent off (Counting game) / Subbed or sent off (playing less than 70 minutes) / Subbed on from bench (Counting Game) / Subbed on (playing less than 70 minutes) / Subbed on and then subbed or sent off (Counting Game) / Subbed on and then subbed or sent off (playing less than 70 minutes) / Not in 16

AUXERRE

Final Position: **8th**

KEY: ☐Won ☐Drawn ☐Lost

							Attendance
1	frpr1	**Lille**	A	L	0-2		14,000
2	frpr1	**Rennes**	H	W	3-1	Bolf 49,53; Kalou 67	12,000
3	frpr1	**Sochaux**	A	W	2-1	Kalou 13; Mignot 83	16,000
4	frpr1	**Caen**	H	W	1-0	Lachuer 90	10,000
5	frpr1	**Bastia**	A	L	0-1		8,000
6	uc1rl1	**Odense**	A	D	1-1	Mwaruwari 38	6,084
7	frpr1	**Metz**	H	W	4-0	Mwaruwari 6,21; Kalou 25; Mathis 68	10,000
8	frpr1	**St Etienne**	A	L	1-3	Mathis 91	30,000
9	frpr1	**Istres**	H	D	0-0		7,000
10	uc1rl2	**Odense**	H	W	2-0	Kalou 4; Mwaruwari 72	10,000
11	frpr1	**Toulouse**	A	W	2-1	Pieroni 60,71	26,000
12	frpr1	**Lens**	H	W	3-0	Grichting 23; Benjani 41; Violeau 83	15,000
13	ucgpf	**Grazer AK**	H	D	0-0		5,000
14	frpr1	**Monaco**	A	D	0-0		8,000
15	frpr1	**Paris SG**	H	D	1-1	Kalou 57	22,000
16	ucgpf	**AZ Alkmaar**	A	L	0-2		8,123
17	frpr1	**Nantes**	A	D	1-1	Tainio 77	27,000
18	frpr1	**AC Ajaccio**	H	W	1-0	Lachuer 57	13,000
19	frpr1	**Strasbourg**	A	L	1-3	Pieroni 65	15,000
20	frpr1	**Lyon**	A	L	1-2	Cheyrou 68	39,000
21	ucgpf	**Amica Wronki**	H	W	5-1	Mignot 1; Pieroni 5,23,26; Kalou 56	7,000
22	frpr1	**Bordeaux**	H	D	0-0		14,000
23	frpr1	**Marseille**	A	W	1-0	Benjani 62	54,000
24	ucgpf	**Rangers**	A	W	2-0	Kalou 10,47	48,847
25	frpr1	**Nice**	H	W	4-3	Bolf 45; Benjani 55,62; Kalou 58	11,000
26	frpr1	**Rennes**	A	L	0-1		18,000
27	frpr1	**Sochaux**	H	W	2-0	Akale 67; Pieroni 84	15,000
28	frpr1	**Caen**	A	W	2-0	Bolf 66; Mignot 79	21,000
29	frpr1	**Bastia**	H	W	4-1	Benjani 11,61; Akale 75; Kalou 90	10,000
30	frpr1	**Metz**	A	L	0-3		8,000
31	frpr1	**St Etienne**	H	D	2-2	Benjani 32; Kalou 85	15,000
32	uc3rl1	**Ajax**	A	L	0-1		42,319
33	frpr1	**Istres**	A	L	0-1		5,000
34	uc3rl2	**Ajax**	H	W	3-1	Kalou 30; Cheyrou 55; Mathis 86	12,000
35	frpr1	**Lens**	A	L	1-3	Gonzalez 87	30,000
36	uc4rl1	**Lille**	A	W	1-0	Akale 45	8,000
37	frpr1	**Monaco**	H	D	2-2	Pieroni 53; Jaures 76	8,000
38	uc4rl2	**Lille**	H	D	0-0		12,000
39	frpr1	**Paris SG**	A	L	0-1		35,000
40	frpr1	**Nantes**	H	W	2-1	Kaboul 81; Pieroni 90	10,000
41	ucqfl1	**CSKA Moscow**	A	L	0-4		26,000
42	frpr1	**AC Ajaccio**	A	L	3-4	Kalou 3; Tainio 85; Akale 90	7,000
43	ucqfl2	**CSKA Moscow**	H	W	2-0	Lachuer 9; Kalou 80 pen	13,000
44	frpr1	**Strasbourg**	H	D	0-0		12,000
45	frpr1	**Lyon**	H	L	0-3		14,000
46	frpr1	**Toulouse**	H	W	3-2	Jaures 25; Benjani 51,73	10,000
47	frpr1	**Bordeaux**	A	D	0-0		30,000
48	frpr1	**Marseille**	H	D	0-0		21,000
49	frpr1	**Nice**	A	L	0-1		15,000
50	frpr1	**Lille**	H	L	1-3	Kalou 28	15,000

MONTHLY POINTS TALLY

AUGUST	9	75%
SEPTEMBER	4	33%
OCTOBER	8	67%
NOVEMBER	4	33%
DECEMBER	7	78%
JANUARY	9	60%
FEBRUARY	1	17%
MARCH	1	11%
APRIL	7	47%
MAY	2	17%

KEY PLAYERS - GOALSCORERS

Mwaruwari Benjani

Goals in the League	7	Player Strike Rate — Average number of minutes between League goals scored by player	172
Contribution to Attacking Power — Average number of minutes between League team goals while on pitch	57	Club Strike Rate — Average number of minutes between League goals scored by club	71

	PLAYER	LGE GOALS	POWER	STRIKE RATE
1	Mwaruwari Benjani	7	57	172 mins
2	Bonaventure Kalou	8	66	299 mins
3	Rene Bolf	4	74	630 mins
4	Kanga Akale	3	70	797 mins
5	Teemu Tainio	2	66	828 mins

KEY PLAYERS - MIDFIELDERS

Teemu Tainio

Goals in the League	2	Contribution to Attacking Power — Average number of minutes between League team goals while on pitch	66
Defensive Rating — Average number of mins between League goals conceded while on the pitch	83	Scoring Difference — Defensive Rating minus Contribution to Attacking Power	17

	PLAYER	LGE GOALS	DEF RATE	POWER	SCORE DIFF
1	Teemu Tainio	2	83	66	17 mins
2	Benoit Cheyrou	1	86	73	13 mins
3	Mwaruwari Benjani	7	67	57	10 mins
4	Philippe Violeau	1	68	67	1 mins
5	Kanga Akale	3	63	70	-7 mins

KEY PLAYERS - DEFENDERS

Stephane Grichting

Goals Conceded — Number of League goals conceded while the player was on the pitch	21	Clean Sheets — In League games when player was on pitch for at least 70 minutes	10
Defensive Rating — Ave number of mins between League goals conceded while on the pitch	89	Club Defensive Rating — Average number of mins between League goals conceded by the club this season	73

	PLAYER	CON LGE	CLEAN SHEETS	DEF RATE
1	Stephane Grichting	21	10	89 mins
2	Rene Bolf	32	10	79 mins
3	Bacary Sagna	30	9	78 mins
4	Younes Kaboul	17	5	77 mins
5	Jean-Sebastien Jaures	33	7	67 mins

KEY GOALKEEPER

Fabien Cool

Goals Conceded in the League	44	Counting Games — League games when player was on pitch for at least 70 minutes	37
Defensive Rating — Ave number of mins between League goals conceded while on the pitch	77	Clean Sheets — In games when player was on pitch for at least 70 minutes	13

LEAGUE GOALS

Bonaventure Kalou

Minutes on the pitch	2388	Goals in the League	8
League average (mins between goals)	299		

	PLAYER	MINS	GOALS	AVE
1	Kalou	2388	8	299
2	Benjani	1204	7	172
3	Pieroni	1251	6	209
4	Bolf	2520	4	630
5	Akale	2390	3	797
6	Tainio	1655	2	828
7	Mwaruwari	955	2	478
8	Mignot	2094	2	1047
9	Lachuer	1917	2	959
10	Jaures	2210	2	1105
11	Grichting	1866	1	1866
12	Cheyrou	2416	1	2416
13	Violeau	3146	1	3146
	Other		7	
	TOTAL		48	

DISCIPLINARY

	PLAYER	YELLOW	RED	AVE
1	Recorbet	2	0	230
2	Cheyrou	7	0	345
3	Kalou	6	0	398
4	Mignot	5	0	418
5	Mathis	5	0	459
6	Grichting	4	0	466
7	Violeau	6	0	524
8	Radet	2	0	540
9	Jaures	4	0	552
10	Bolf	4	0	630
11	Akale	3	0	796
12	Benjani	1	0	1204
13	Tainio	1	0	1655
	Other	2	0	
	TOTAL	52	0	

TOP POINT EARNERS

	PLAYER	GAMES	AV PTS
1	Mwaruwari Benjani	12	2.08
2	Bonaventure Kalou	25	1.64
3	Stephane Grichting	20	1.55
4	Younes Kaboul	14	1.50
5	Teemu Tainio	15	1.47
6	Philippe Violeau	35	1.43
7	Rene Bolf	28	1.43
8	Benoit Cheyrou	26	1.42
9	Bacary Sagna	26	1.42
10	Fabien Cool	37	1.41
	CLUB AVERAGE:		1.37

LEAGUE APPEARANCES, BOOKINGS AND CAPS

	AGE (on 01/07/05)	IN NAMED 16	APPEARANCES	COUNTING GAMES	MINUTES ON PITCH	YELLOW CARDS	RED CARDS	THIS SEASON	HOME COUNTRY
Goalkeepers									
Baptiste Chabert	22	12	0	0	0	0	0	-	France
Fabien Cool	32	38	38	37	3375	0	0	-	France
Sebastien Hamel	29	25	1	0	45	0	0	-	France
Defenders									
Rene Bolf	31	28	28	28	2520	4	0	7	Czech Republic (2)
Mickael Ciani	21	1	0	0	0	0	0	-	France
Mamoutou Coulibaly	21	6	1	0	11	1	0	-	Mali
Stephane Grichting	26	27	22	20	1866	4	0	3	Switzerland (45)
J-S Jaures	27	30	27	24	2210	4	0	-	France
Younes Kaboul	19	17	15	14	1304	0	0	-	France
Baptiste Martin	20	0	0	0	0	0	0	-	France
Jean Pascal Mignot	24	28	24	23	2094	5	0	-	France
Johan Radet	28	12	12	12	1080	2	0	-	France
David Recorbet	28	26	6	5	460	2	0	-	France
Bacary Sagna	22	28	26	26	2329	1	0	-	France
Pierre Vignaud	22	1	0	0	0	0	0	-	France
Midfielders									
Kanga Akale	24	33	30	25	2390	3	0	2	Ivory Coast (44)
Mwaruwari Benjani	21	18	17	12	1204	1	0	-	Cameroon
Benoit Cheyrou	24	29	28	26	2416	7	0	-	France
Vassiriki Diaby	19	9	5	2	193	0	0	-	France
Damien Dufour	23	1	1	0	8	0	0	-	France
Nicolas Gourio	19	0	0	0	0	0	0	-	France
Yann Lachuer	33	24	24	19	1917	1	0	-	France
Lionel Mathis	23	32	29	25	2298	5	0	-	France
Teemu Tainio	25	30	27	15	1655	1	0	-	Finland
Philippe Violeau	34	36	36	35	3146	6	0	-	France
Hassan Yebda	21	1	0	0	0	0	0	-	France
Forwards									
Garra Dembele	19	1	0	0	0	0	0	-	France
Arnaud Gonzalez	27	14	10	3	400	0	0	-	France
Bonaventure Kalou	27	29	29	25	2388	6	0	3	Ivory Coast (44)
Kevin Lejeune	20	0	0	0	0	0	0	-	France
Benjamin Mwaruwari	26	15	14	8	955	0	0	-	Zimbabwe
Luigi Pieroni	24	38	30	11	1251	0	0	6	Belgium (42)
D Vandenbossche	24	17	6	0	105	0	0	-	France

TEAM OF THE SEASON

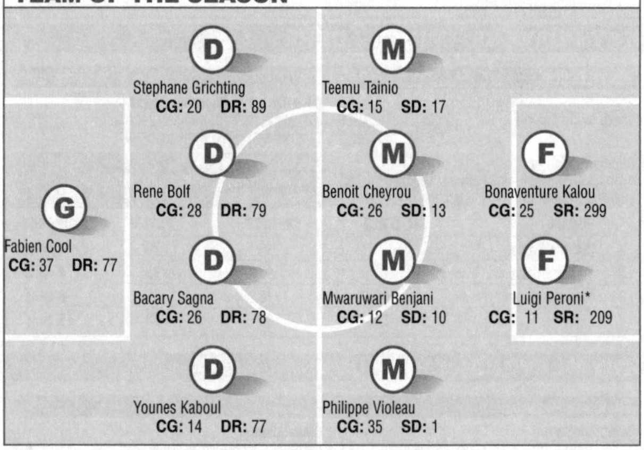

D
Stephane Grichting
CG: 20 DR: 89
D
Rene Bolf
CG: 28 DR: 79
D
Bacary Sagna
CG: 26 DR: 78
D
Younes Kaboul
CG: 14 DR: 77
M
Teemu Tainio
CG: 15 SD: 17
M
Benoit Cheyrou
CG: 26 SD: 13
M
Mwaruwari Benjani
CG: 12 SD: 10
M
Philippe Violeau
CG: 35 SD: 1
F
Bonaventure Kalou
CG: 25 SR: 299
F
Luigi Peroni*
CG: 11 SR: 209
G
Fabien Cool
CG: 37 DR: 77

SQUAD APPEARANCES

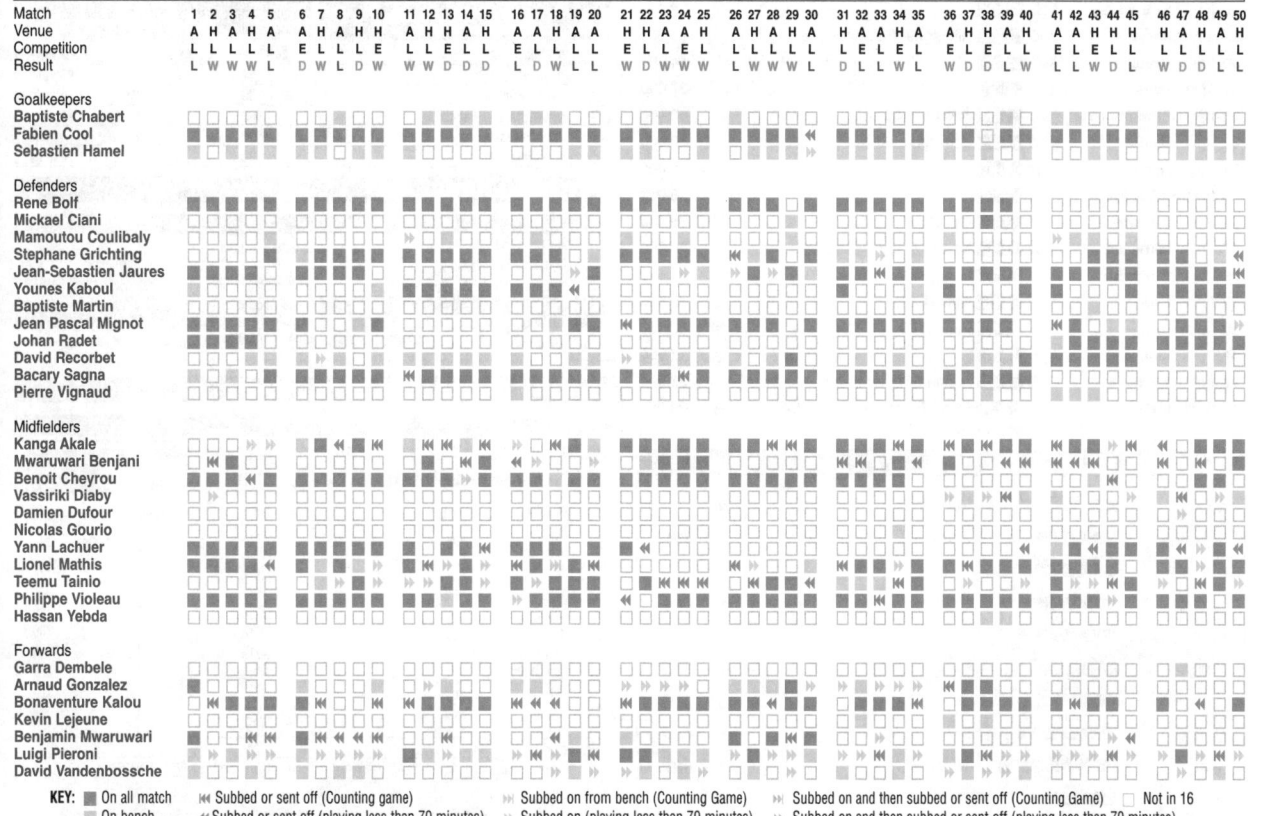

Match	1	2	3	4	5	6	7	8	9	10	11	12	13	14	15	16	17	18	19	20	21	22	23	24	25	26	27	28	29	30	31	32	33	34	35	36	37	38	39	40	41	42	43	44	45	46	47	48	49	50
Venue	A	H	A	H	A	A	H	A	H	H	A	H	H	A	H	A	A	H	A	A	H	H	A	A	H	A	H	A	H	A	H	A	A	H	A	A	H	H	A	H	A	A	H	H	H	H	A	H	A	H
Competition	L	L	L	L	L	E	L	L	L	E	L	L	E	L	L	E	L	L	L	L	E	L	L	E	L	L	L	L	L	L	L	E	L	E	L	E	L	E	L	L	E	L	E	L	L	L	L	L	L	L
Result	L	W	W	W	L	D	W	L	D	W	W	W	D	D	D	L	D	W	L	L	W	D	W	W	W	L	W	W	W	L	D	L	L	W	L	W	D	D	L	W	L	L	W	D	L	W	D	D	L	L

Goalkeepers
Baptiste Chabert
Fabien Cool
Sebastien Hamel

Defenders
Rene Bolf
Mickael Ciani
Mamoutou Coulibaly
Stephane Grichting
Jean-Sebastien Jaures
Younes Kaboul
Baptiste Martin
Jean Pascal Mignot
Johan Radet
David Recorbet
Bacary Sagna
Pierre Vignaud

Midfielders
Kanga Akale
Mwaruwari Benjani
Benoit Cheyrou
Vassiriki Diaby
Damien Dufour
Nicolas Gourio
Yann Lachuer
Lionel Mathis
Teemu Tainio
Philippe Violeau
Hassan Yebda

Forwards
Garra Dembele
Arnaud Gonzalez
Bonaventure Kalou
Kevin Lejeune
Benjamin Mwaruwari
Luigi Pieroni
David Vandenbossche

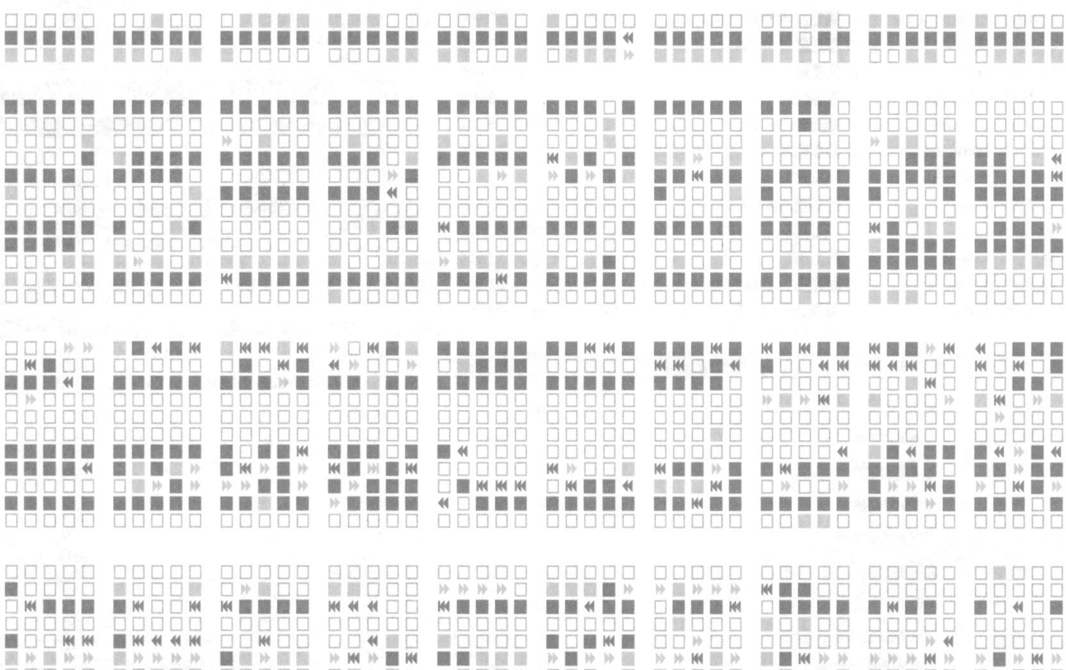

KEY: ■ On all match · ■ On bench · ⏮ Subbed or sent off (Counting game) · « Subbed or sent off (playing less than 70 minutes) · ⏭ Subbed on from bench (Counting Game) · » Subbed on (playing less than 70 minutes) · ⏭ Subbed on and then subbed or sent off (Counting Game) · » Subbed on and then subbed or sent off (playing less than 70 minutes) · □ Not in 16

PARIS St GERMAIN

Final Position: **9th**

KEY: ☐Won ☐Drawn ☐Lost

							Attendance
1	frpr1	Rennes	A	L	1-2	Pauleta 39 pen	25,000
2	frpr1	Caen	H	D	2-2	Fiorese 11; Yepes 56	35,000
3	frpr1	Toulouse	A	L	1-2	Reinaldo 75	35,000
4	frpr1	St Etienne	H	D	2-2	Pauleta 71 pen; Ogbeche 74	38,000
5	frpr1	Istres	A	D	1-1	Pauleta 60 pen	11,000
6	cl gh	Chelsea	H	L	0-3		45,000
7	frpr1	Monaco	H	L	0-1		42,000
8	frpr1	Lens	A	D	2-2	Cana 47; Pancrate 76	37,000
9	frpr1	Strasbourg	H	W	1-0	Pauleta 79	33,000
10	cl gh	CSKA Moscow	A	L	0-2		10,000
11	frpr1	Bastia	A	W	2-1	Pancrate 26; Reinaldo 28	10,000
12	frpr1	Nantes	A	L	0-1		32,000
13	cl gh	Porto	H	W	2-0	Coridon 30; Pauleta 31	48,000
14	frpr1	AC Ajaccio	H	W	1-0	Pancrate 9	35,000
15	frpr1	Auxerre	A	D	1-1	Pauleta 34	22,000
16	cl gh	Porto	A	D	0-0		30,000
17	frpr1	Marseille	H	W	2-1	Pauleta 31; Cisse 68	43,000
18	frpr1	Bordeaux	A	L	0-3		32,000
19	frpr1	Lyon	H	D	0-0		45,000
20	cl gh	Chelsea	A	D	0-0		39,626
21	frpr1	Nice	A	D	1-1	Pancrate 35	15,000
22	frpr1	Lille	H	D	1-1	Reinaldo 33	30,000
23	cl gh	CSKA Moscow	H	L	1-3	Pancrate 37	40,000
24	frpr1	Sochaux	A	W	2-1	Pauleta 24,42	15,000
25	frpr1	Metz	H	W	3-0	Meniri 39 og; Pauleta 60; Pancrate 75	35,000
26	frpr1	Caen	A	D	0-0		21,000
27	frpr1	Toulouse	H	D	0-0		35,000
28	frpr1	St Etienne	A	D	0-0		32,000
29	frpr1	Istres	H	D	2-2	Helder 29; Pauleta 51	23,000
30	frpr1	Monaco	A	L	0-2		14,000
31	frpr1	Lens	H	L	0-2		37,000
32	frpr1	Strasbourg	A	L	1-3	Johansen 86 og	18,000
33	frpr1	Bastia	H	W	1-0	Benachour 66 pen	40,000
34	frpr1	Nantes	H	W	1-0	Pauleta 87	35,000
35	frpr1	AC Ajaccio	A	L	0-1		5,000
36	frpr1	Auxerre	H	W	1-0	Pauleta 7	35,000
37	frpr1	Marseille	A	D	1-1	Nakata 47 og	58,000
38	frpr1	Bordeaux	H	D	1-1	Ljuboja 31	41,000
39	frpr1	Lyon	A	W	1-0	Ljuboja 45	40,000
40	frpr1	Nice	H	W	3-1	Pauleta 39 pen; Rothen 42; Semak 84	30,000
41	frpr1	Lille	A	L	0-1		17,000
42	frpr1	Sochaux	H	D	2-2	Armand 91; Yepes 93	32,000
43	frpr1	Metz	A	L	2-3	Pierre-Fanfan 50; Yepes 57	24,000
44	frpr1	Rennes	H	W	1-0	Pauleta 52	45,000

MONTHLY POINTS TALLY

AUGUST	2	17%
SEPTEMBER	5	42%
OCTOBER	7	58%
NOVEMBER	5	42%
DECEMBER	7	78%
JANUARY	4	27%
FEBRUARY	3	33%
MARCH	6	67%
APRIL	8	67%
MAY	4	33%

KEY PLAYERS - GOALSCORERS

Pauleta

Goals in the League	13	Player Strike Rate Average number of minutes between League goals scored by player	205
Contribution to Attacking Power Average number of minutes between League team goals while on pitch	86	Club Strike Rate Average number of minutes between League goals scored by club	86

	PLAYER	LGE GOALS	POWER	STRIKE RATE
1	Pauleta	13	86	205 mins
2	Fabrice Pancrate	5	91	331 mins
3	Reinaldo	3	94	722 mins
4	Mario Yepes	3	104	938 mins
5	Jerome Rothen	1	76	1529 mins

KEY PLAYERS - MIDFIELDERS

Jerome Rothen

Goals in the League	1	Contribution to Attacking Power Average number of minutes between League team goals while on pitch	76
Defensive Rating Average number of mins between League goals conceded while on the pitch	80	Scoring Difference Defensive Rating minus Contribution to Attacking Power	4

	PLAYER	LGE GOALS	DEF RATE	POWER	SCORE DIFF
1	Jerome Rothen	1	80	76	4 mins
2	Edouard Cisse	1	97	93	4 mins
3	Modeste Mbami	0	73	81	-8 mins
4	Lorik Cana	1	83	98	-15 mins

KEY PLAYERS - DEFENDERS

Stephane Pichot

Goals Conceded Number of League goals conceded while the player was on the pitch	21	Clean Sheets In League games when player was on pitch for at least 70 minutes	7
Defensive Rating Ave number of mins between League goals conceded while on the pitch	93	Club Defensive Rating Average number of mins between League goals conceded by the club this season	83

	PLAYER	CON LGE	CLEAN SHEETS	DEF RATE
1	Stephane Pichot	21	7	93 mins
2	Sylvain Armand	39	12	84 min
3	Jose Karl Pierre-Fanfan	38	9	78 mins
4	Mario Yepes	36	9	78 mins
5	Bernard Mendy	29	8	78 mins

KEY GOALKEEPER

Lionel Letizi

Goals Conceded in the League	33	Counting Games League games when player was on pitch for at least 70 minutes	32
Defensive Rating Ave number of mins between League goals conceded while on the pitch	89	Clean Sheets In games when player was on pitch for at least 70 minutes	11

LEAGUE GOALS

Pauleta

Minutes on the pitch	2668	Goals in the League	205
League average (mins between goals)	13		

	PLAYER	MINS	GOALS	AVE
1	Pauleta	2668	13	205
2	Pancrate	1653	5	331
3	Reinaldo	2166	3	722
4	Yepes	2814	3	938
5	Ljuboja	1219	2	610
6	Armand	3259	1	3259
7	Rothen	1529	1	1529
8	Benachour	256	1	256
9	Ogbeche	173	1	173
10	Cana	2644	1	2644
11	Semak	769	1	769
12	Helder	1031	1	1031
13	Pierre-Fanfan	2970	1	2970
	Other		6	
	TOTAL		40	

DISCIPLINARY RECORDS

	PLAYER	YELLOW	RED	AVE
1	Mendy	10	1	**206**
2	Cana	11	1	**220**
3	Cisse	9	1	**233**
4	Helder	4	0	**257**
5	Yepes	8	2	**281**
6	Mbami	4	0	**382**
7	Pierre-Fanfan	7	0	**424**
8	Pauleta	6	0	**444**
9	Pichot	4	0	**489**
10	Ljuboja	2	0	**609**
11	Reinaldo	3	0	**722**
12	Rothen	2	0	**764**
13	Semak	1	0	**769**
	Other	7	1	
	TOTAL	**78**	**6**	

TOP POINT EARNERS

	PLAYER	GAMES	AV PTS
1	Stephane Pichot	19	**1.68**
2	Fabrice Pancrate	16	**1.56**
3	Jerome Rothen	17	**1.53**
4	Pauleta	29	**1.52**
5	Edouard Cisse	23	**1.48**
6	Bernard Mendy	24	**1.38**
7	Lionel Letizi	32	**1.34**
8	Lorik Cana	28	**1.32**
9	Modeste Mbami	14	**1.29**
10	Sylvain Armand	36	**1.25**
	CLUB AVERAGE:		**1.34**

LEAGUE APPEARANCES AND BOOKINGS

	AGE (on 01/07/05)	IN NAMED 16	APPEARANCES	COUNTING GAMES	MINUTES ON PITCH	YELLOW CARDS	RED CARDS	THIS SEASON	HOME COUNTRY
Goalkeepers									
Jerome Alonzo	32	34	6	5	485	0	0	-	France
Mohamed Benhamou	25	4	0	0	0	0	0	-	France
Nicolas Cousin	19	2	0	0	0	0	0	-	France
Lionel Letizi	32	36	33	32	2935	2	0	-	France
Defenders									
Sylvain Armand	24	37	37	36	3259	3	1	1	France (4)
Jean Bilayi Ateba	23	17	8	3	351	1	0	-	Cameroon
Jean-Michel Badiane	22	10	7	2	263	2	0	-	France
Souleymane Bamba	20	2	1	0	2	0	0	-	Ivory Coast
Boukari Drame	-	1	0	0	0	0	0	-	France
Rodriques Helder	34	24	16	10	1031	4	0	-	Portugal
Bernard Mendy	23	30	29	24	2275	10	1	2	France (4)
Stephane Pichot	28	31	25	19	1959	4	0	-	France
Jose Pierre-Fanfan	29	33	33	33	2970	7	0	-	France
Mario Yepes	29	32	32	31	2814	8	2	-	Colombia
Midfielders									
Lorik Cana	21	32	32	28	2644	11	1	-	Bosnia
Edouard Cisse	27	32	31	23	2337	9	1	-	France
Charles Coridon	32	20	18	10	1164	1	0	-	France
Rudy Haddad	20	4	4	0	27	0	0	-	France
Danijel Ljuboja	27	26	25	11	1219	2	0	2	Serbia & Mont (46)
Modeste Mbami	22	20	19	14	1530	4	0	2	Cameroon (26)
Jerome Rothen	27	18	18	17	1529	2	0	3	France (4)
Sergei Semak	29	14	13	7	769	1	0	-	Russia
Felipe Teixeira	24	12	10	0	138	0	0	-	France
Forwards									
Selim Benachour	23	14	9	1	256	1	0	-	Tunisia
Branco Boskovic	25	14	12	2	335	0	0	-	Serbia & Mont
Fabrice Fiorese	29	3	3	3	270	0	0	-	France
Vedad Ibisevic	20	5	5	1	203	0	1	-	Bosnia
B Ogbeche	20	6	5	1	173	1	0	-	Nigeria
Fabrice Pancrate	25	30	29	16	1653	1	0	-	France
Pauleta	32	36	34	29	2668	6	0	8	Portugal (9)
Reinaldo	26	33	32	21	2166	3	0	-	Brazil

TEAM OF THE SEASON

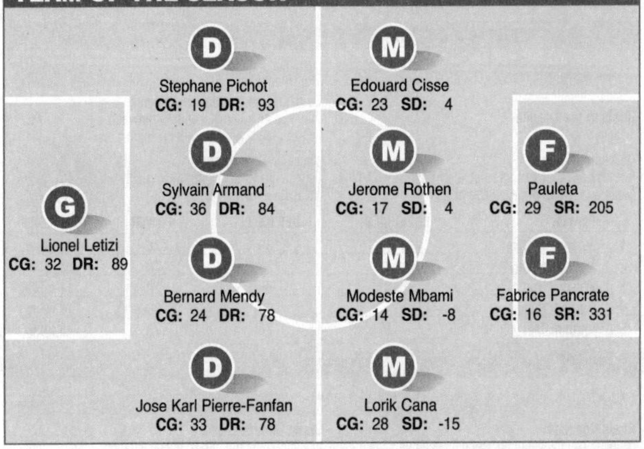
D
Stephane Pichot
CG: 19 DR: 93
D
Sylvain Armand
CG: 36 DR: 84
D
Bernard Mendy
CG: 24 DR: 78
D
Jose Karl Pierre-Fanfan
CG: 33 DR: 78
M
Edouard Cisse
CG: 23 SD: 4
M
Jerome Rothen
CG: 17 SD: 4
M
Modeste Mbami
CG: 14 SD: -8
M
Lorik Cana
CG: 28 SD: -15
G
Lionel Letizi
CG: 32 DR: 89
F
Pauleta
CG: 29 SR: 205
F
Fabrice Pancrate
CG: 16 SR: 331

SQUAD APPEARANCES

Match	1	2	3	4	5	6	7	8	9	10	11	12	13	14	15	16	17	18	19	20	21	22	23	24	25	26	27	28	29	30	31	32	33	34	35	36	37	38	39	40	41	42	43	44
Venue	A	H	A	H	A	H	H	A	H	A	A	A	H	H	A	A	H	A	H	A	A	H	H	A	H	A	H	A	H	A	H	A	H	H	A	H	A	H	A	H	A	H	A	H
Competition	L	L	L	L	L	C	L	L	L	C	L	L	C	L	L	C	L	L	L	C	L	L	C	L	L	L	L	L	L	L	L	L	L	L	L	L	L	L	L	L	L	L	L	L
Result	L	D	L	D	D	L	L	D	W	L	W	L	W	W	D	D	W	L	D	D	D	D	L	W	W	D	D	D	D	L	L	L	W	W	L	W	D	D	W	W	L	D	L	W

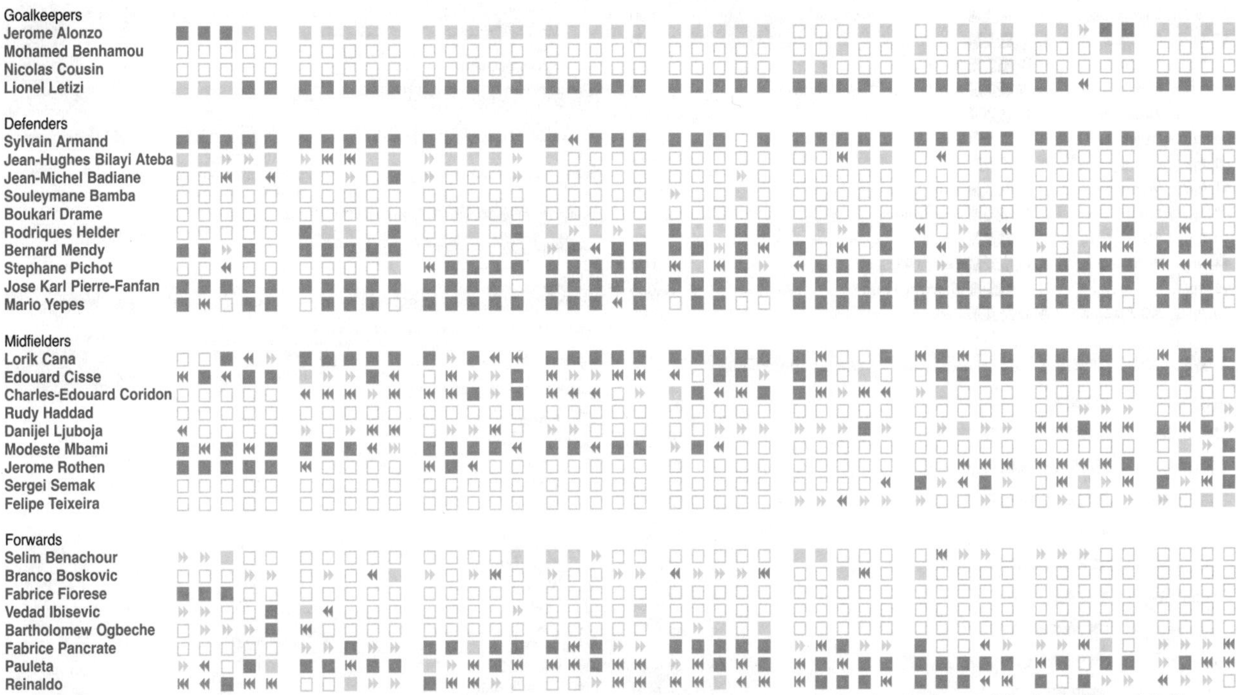
Goalkeepers
Jerome Alonzo
Mohamed Benhamou
Nicolas Cousin
Lionel Letizi
Defenders
Sylvain Armand
Jean-Hughes Bilayi Ateba
Jean-Michel Badiane
Souleymane Bamba
Boukari Drame
Rodriques Helder
Bernard Mendy
Stephane Pichot
Jose Karl Pierre-Fanfan
Mario Yepes
Midfielders
Lorik Cana
Edouard Cisse
Charles-Edouard Coridon
Rudy Haddad
Danijel Ljuboja
Modeste Mbami
Jerome Rothen
Sergei Semak
Felipe Teixeira
Forwards
Selim Benachour
Branco Boskovic
Fabrice Fiorese
Vedad Ibisevic
Bartholomew Ogbeche
Fabrice Pancrate
Pauleta
Reinaldo

KEY: On all match | On bench | Subbed or sent off (Counting game) | Subbed or sent off (playing less than 70 minutes) | Subbed on from bench (Counting Game) | Subbed on (playing less than 70 minutes) | Subbed on and then subbed or sent off (Counting Game) | Subbed on and then subbed or sent off (playing less than 70 minutes) | Not in 16

SOCHAUX

Final Position: **10th**

KEY: Won Drawn Lost

							Attendance
1	frpr1	**AC Ajaccio**	H	W	1-0	Monsoreau 29	19,000
2	frpr1	**Lyon**	A	D	1-1	Potillon 38	40,000
3	frpr1	**Auxerre**	H	L	1-2	Santos 42	16,000
4	frpr1	**Bordeaux**	A	L	0-2		22,000
5	frpr1	**Marseille**	H	W	2-0	Mathieu 38; Santos 63	20,000
6	uc1rl1	**Stabaek**	H	W	4-0	Oruma 25; Zairi 60; Ilan 69; Isabey 84	10,677
7	frpr1	**Nice**	A	L	1-2	Boudarene 12	10,000
8	frpr1	**Lille**	H	L	0-2		12,000
9	frpr1	**St Etienne**	H	W	2-1	Isabey 4; Oruma 76	19,000
10	uc1rl2	**Stabaek**	A	W	5-0	Santos 25; Zairi 35; Ilan 76,90; Mathieu 81	500
11	frpr1	**Metz**	A	D	0-0		15,000
12	frpr1	**Rennes**	H	W	3-0	Ilan 20,58,75	14,000
13	ucgpd	**Dinamo Tbilisi**	A	W	2-0	Ilan 18; Paisley 38	30,000
14	frpr1	**Bastia**	A	D	1-1	Santos 9	6,000
15	frpr1	**Toulouse**	H	W	2-0	Mathieu 45; Ilan 85	15,000
16	frpr1	**Caen**	A	W	2-0	Ilan 17; Zairi 66	20,000
17	frpr1	**Istres**	H	D	1-1	Mathieu 82	15,000
18	frpr1	**Monaco**	A	W	3-1	Menez 30; Oruma 62; Ilan 79	4,000
19	ucgpd	**Newcastle**	H	L	0-4		15,173
20	frpr1	**Lens**	H	L	1-2	Diawara 72	14,000
21	ucgpd	**Sp Lisbon**	A	W	1-0	Lonfat 2	21,349
22	frpr1	**Strasbourg**	A	D	0-0		20,000
23	frpr1	**Paris SG**	H	L	1-2	Santos 75	15,000
24	ucgpd	**Panionios**	H	W	1-0	Isabey 86	10,479
25	frpr1	**Nantes**	A	D	2-2	Ilan 27,45	20,000
26	frpr1	**Lyon**	H	L	0-2		18,000
27	frpr1	**Auxerre**	A	L	0-2		15,000
28	frpr1	**Bordeaux**	H	W	4-0	Monsoreau 76; Menez 78,82,84	15,000
29	frpr1	**Marseille**	A	W	2-0	Santos 53; Pitau 69	52,000
30	frpr1	**Nice**	H	D	0-0		9,000
31	frpr1	**Lille**	A	D	0-0		12,000
32	uc3rl1	**Olympiakos**	A	L	0-1		33,000
33	frpr1	**St Etienne**	A	L	0-1		28,000
34	uc3rl2	**Olympiakos**	H	L	0-1		11,000
35	frpr1	**Rennes**	A	L	0-3		23,000
36	frpr1	**Bastia**	H	W	1-0	Ilan 1	13,000
37	frpr1	**Metz**	H	W	2-1	Ilan 11 pen; Caillet 61 og	13,000
38	frpr1	**Toulouse**	A	D	0-0		25,000
39	frpr1	**Caen**	H	W	1-0	Ilan 64	14,000
40	frpr1	**Istres**	A	L	0-2		5,000
41	frpr1	**Monaco**	H	D	1-1	Ilan 37	19,000
42	frpr1	**Lens**	A	L	2-3	Santos 60,87	32,000
43	frpr1	**Strasbourg**	H	L	1-2	Zairi 63	19,000
44	frpr1	**Paris SG**	A	D	2-2	Santos 48,57	32,000
45	frpr1	**Nantes**	H	W	1-0	Thebaux 11 og	19,000
46	frpr1	**AC Ajaccio**	A	L	1-3	Kader 6	8,000

MONTHLY POINTS TALLY

AUGUST	4	33%
SEPTEMBER	6	50%
OCTOBER	8	67%
NOVEMBER	7	58%
DECEMBER	2	22%
JANUARY	7	47%
FEBRUARY	1	17%
MARCH	7	58%
APRIL	4	33%
MAY	4	33%

KEY PLAYERS - GOALSCORERS

Ilan

Goals in the League 12

Player Strike Rate Average number of minutes between League goals scored by player 153

Contribution to Attacking Power Average number of minutes between League team goals while on pitch 73

Club Strike Rate Average number of minutes between League goals scored by club 80

	PLAYER	LGE GOALS	POWER	STRIKE RATE
1	Ilan	12	73	153 mins
2	Francileudo Santos	9	81	262 mins
3	Wilson Oruma	2	72	896 mins
4	Sylvain Monsoreau	2	90	945 mins
5	Jeremy Mathieu	3	76	1014 mins

KEY PLAYERS - MIDFIELDERS

Jeremy Mathieu

Goals in the League 3

Contribution to Attacking Power Average number of minutes between League team goals while on pitch 76

Defensive Rating Average number of mins between League goals conceded while on the pitch 109

Scoring Difference Defensive Rating minus Contribution to Attacking Power 33

	PLAYER	LGE GOALS	DEF RATE	POWER	SCORE DIFF
1	Jeremy Mathieu	3	109	76	33 mins
2	Mickael Isabey	1	106	78	28 mins
3	Wilson Oruma	2	85	72	13 mins
4	Romain Pitau	1	94	86	8 mins
5	Ibrahim Tall	0	70	73	-3 mins

KEY PLAYERS - DEFENDERS

Omar Daf

Goals Conceded Number of League goals conceded while the player was on the pitch 15

Clean Sheets In League games when player was on pitch for at least 70 minutes 6

Defensive Rating Ave number of mins between League goals conceded while on the pitch 101

Club Defensive Rating Average number of mins between League goals conceded by the club this season 83

	PLAYER	CON LGE	CLEAN SHEETS	DEF RATE
1	Omar Daf	15	6	101 mins
2	Souleymane Diawara	25	12	100 mins
3	Lionel Potillon	16	6	97 mins
4	Johan Lonfat	26	10	95 mins
5	Sylvain Monsoreau	21	9	90 mins

KEY GOALKEEPER

Teddy Richert

Goals Conceded in the League 38

Counting Games League games when player was on pitch for at least 70 minutes 37

Defensive Rating Ave number of mins between League goals conceded while on the pitch 88

Clean Sheets In games when player was on pitch for at least 70 minutes 14

LEAGUE GOALS

Ilan

Minutes on the pitch 1840

League average (mins between goals) 153

Goals in the League 12

	PLAYER	MINS	GOALS	AVE
1	Ilan	1840	12	153
2	Santos	2356	9	262
3	Menez	1161	4	290
4	Mathieu	3043	3	1014
5	Zairi	1400	2	700
6	Oruma	1791	2	896
7	Monsoreau	1890	2	945
8	Isabey	2981	1	2981
9	Diawara	2503	1	2503
10	Pitau	2907	1	2907
11	Potillon	1551	1	1551
12	Daf	1511	1	1511
13	Boudarene	916	1	916
	Other		3	
	TOTAL		43	

DISCIPLINARY RECORDS

	PLAYER	YELLOW	RED	AVE
1	Daf	8	1	167
2	Menez	4	1	232
3	Isabey	10	0	298
4	Paisley	6	0	334
5	Tall	4	0	439
6	Ilan	4	0	460
7	Pitau	6	0	484
8	Oruma	2	1	597
9	Mathieu	5	0	608
10	Lonfat	4	0	617
11	Diawara	3	1	625
12	Potillon	2	0	775
13	Boudarene	1	0	916
	Other	2	0	
	TOTAL	61	4	

TOP POINT EARNERS

	PLAYER	GAMES	AV PTS
1	Mickael Isabey	30	1.57
2	Jeremy Mathieu	33	1.48
3	Johan Lonfat	26	1.46
4	Romain Pitau	31	1.45
5	Wilson Oruma	16	1.44
6	Souleymane Diawara	28	1.39
7	Ilan	15	1.33
8	Teddy Richert	37	1.32
9	Sylvain Monsoreau	21	1.29
10	Ibrahim Tall	17	1.24
	CLUB AVERAGE:		1.32

TEAM OF THE SEASON

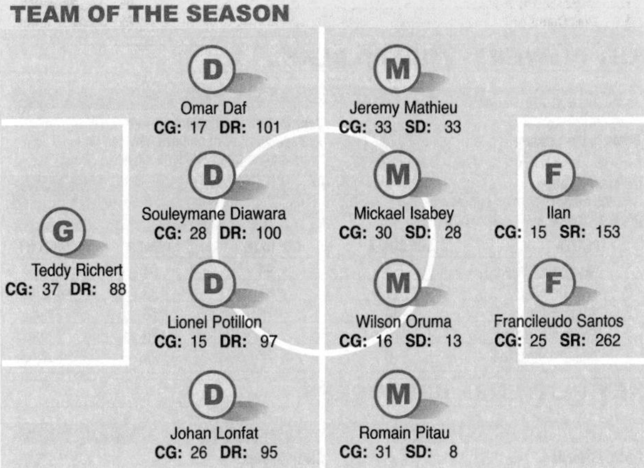

G
Teddy Richert
CG: 37 DR: 88
D
Omar Daf
CG: 17 DR: 101
D
Souleymane Diawara
CG: 28 DR: 100
D
Lionel Potillon
CG: 15 DR: 97
D
Johan Lonfat
CG: 26 DR: 95
M
Jeremy Mathieu
CG: 33 SD: 33
M
Mickael Isabey
CG: 30 SD: 28
M
Wilson Oruma
CG: 16 SD: 13
M
Romain Pitau
CG: 31 SD: 8
F
Ilan
CG: 15 SR: 153
F
Francileudo Santos
CG: 25 SR: 262

LEAGUE APPEARANCES, BOOKINGS AND CAPS

	AGE (on 01/07/05)	IN NAMED 16	APPEARANCES	COUNTING GAMES	MINUTES ON PITCH	YELLOW CARDS	RED CARDS	THIS SEASON	HOME COUNTRY
Goalkeepers									
Gerard Gnanhouan	26	35	1	1	90	0	0	3	Ivory Coast (44)
Alexandre Martinovic	30	2	0	0	0	0	0	-	France
Teddy Richert	30	37	37	37	3330	0	0	-	France
Defenders									
Jean Calve	21	0	0	0	0	0	0	-	France
Omar Daf	28	21	18	17	1511	8	1	4	Senegal (33)
Souleymane Diawara	26	28	28	28	2503	3	1	5	Senegal (33)
Maxence Flachez	32	1	1	1	73	0	0	-	France
Maxime Josse	18	3	3	2	248	0	0	-	France
Aime Lavie	20	5	3	1	111	1	0	-	France
Johan Lonfat	31	34	31	26	2468	4	0	7	Switzerland (45)
Sylvain Monsoreau	24	21	21	21	1890	0	0	-	France
Gregory Paisley	28	29	25	21	2005	6	0	-	France
Lionel Potillon	31	19	19	15	1551	2	0	-	France
Cedric Rey	20	2	1	0	68	0	0	-	France
Midfielders									
Fabien Boudarene	26	25	18	8	916	1	0	-	France
Mickael Isabey	30	37	36	30	2981	10	0	-	France
Jeremy Mathieu	21	35	35	33	3043	5	0	-	France
Guirane N'Daw	21	22	15	4	561	0	0	1	Senegal (33)
Wilson Oruma	28	26	25	16	1791	2	1	-	Nigeria
Romain Pitau	27	36	36	31	2907	6	0	-	France
Badara Sene	20	1	0	0	0	0	0	-	Senegal
Ibrahim Tall	29	32	26	17	1759	4	0	-	Senegal
Forwards									
Basile De Carvalho	24	10	5	1	238	0	0	-	Senegal
Sigamary Diarra	21	13	7	2	234	1	0	-	France
Ilan	24	27	27	15	1840	4	0	-	Brazil
Mohamed Kader	26	6	4	0	130	1	0	-	Togo
Jeremy Menez	18	28	23	8	1161	4	1	-	France
Thomas Regnier	21	1	1	0	34	0	0	-	France
Francileudo Santos	26	31	31	25	2356	1	0	-	Tunisia
Abdel Kader Toure	26	4	4	2	252	2	0	-	Togo
Marcelo Trapasso	29	4	3	0	75	0	0	-	Argentina
Jaouad Zairi	23	30	30	8	1400	1	0	-	Morocco

SQUAD APPEARANCES

Match	1	2	3	4	5	6	7	8	9	10	11	12	13	14	15	16	17	18	19	20	21	22	23	24	25	26	27	28	29	30	31	32	33	34	35	36	37	38	39	40	41	42	43	44	45	46
Venue	H	A	H	A	H	H	A	H	H	A	A	H	A	A	H	H	A	H	H	H	A	A	H	H	A	H	A	H	A	H	A	A	A	H	A	H	H	A	H	A	H	A	H	A	H	A
Competition	L	L	L	L	L	E	L	L	L	E	L	L	E	L	L	L	L	L	E	L	E	L	L	E	L	L	L	L	L	L	L	E	L	E	L	L	L	L	L	L	L	L	L	L	L	L
Result	W	D	L	L	W	W	L	L	W	W	D	W	W	D	W	W	D	W	L	L	W	D	L	W	D	L	L	W	W	D	D	L	L	L	L	W	W	D	W	L	D	L	L	D	W	L

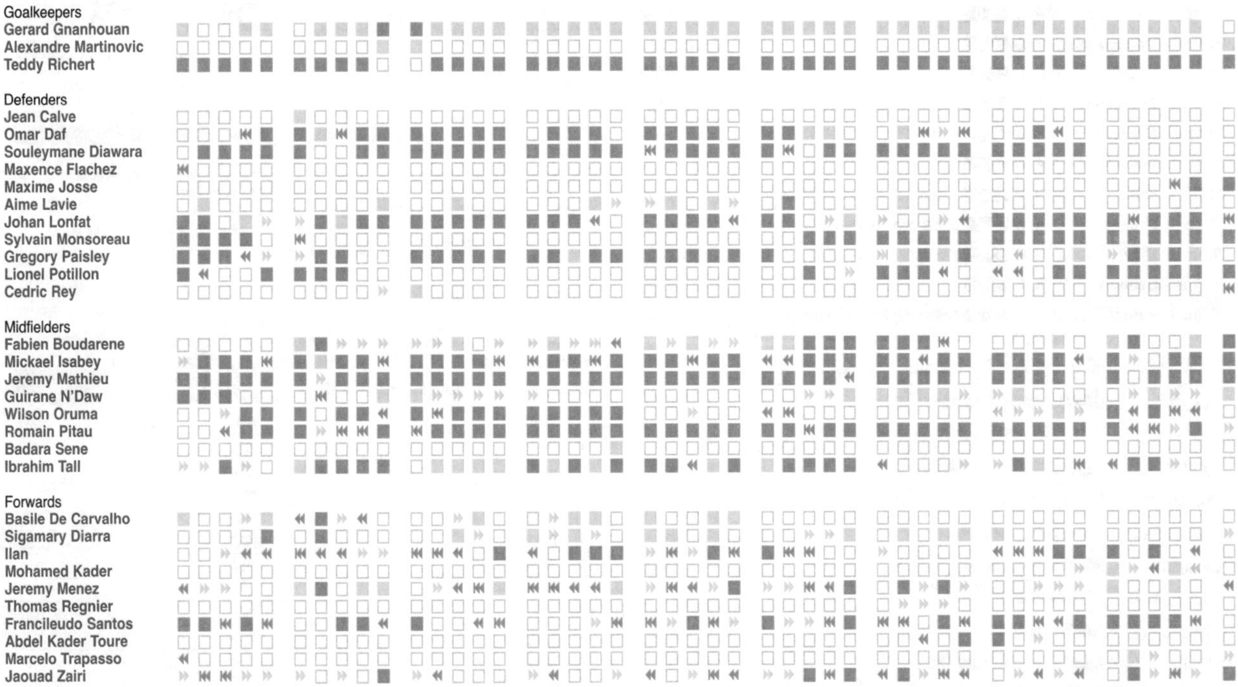

Goalkeepers
Gerard Gnanhouan
Alexandre Martinovic
Teddy Richert
Defenders
Jean Calve
Omar Daf
Souleymane Diawara
Maxence Flachez
Maxime Josse
Aime Lavie
Johan Lonfat
Sylvain Monsoreau
Gregory Paisley
Lionel Potillon
Cedric Rey
Midfielders
Fabien Boudarene
Mickael Isabey
Jeremy Mathieu
Guirane N'Daw
Wilson Oruma
Romain Pitau
Badara Sene
Ibrahim Tall
Forwards
Basile De Carvalho
Sigamary Diarra
Ilan
Mohamed Kader
Jeremy Menez
Thomas Regnier
Francileudo Santos
Abdel Kader Toure
Marcelo Trapasso
Jaouad Zairi

KEY: On all match; On bench; Subbed or sent off (Counting game); Subbed or sent off (playing less than 70 minutes); Subbed on from bench (Counting Game); Subbed on (playing less than 70 minutes); Subbed on and then subbed or sent off (Counting Game); Subbed on and then subbed or sent off (playing less than 70 minutes); Not in 16

STRASBOURG

Final Position: **11th**

KEY: ☐ Won ☐ Drawn ☐ Lost

							Attendance
1	frpr1	**Bastia**	A	L	1-2	Pagis 46	5,000
2	frpr1	**Toulouse**	H	L	1-4	Niang 90	13,000
3	frpr1	**St Etienne**	A	D	1-1	Farnerud 83	27,000
4	frpr1	**Istres**	H	D	1-1	Pagis 16	11,000
5	frpr1	**Monaco**	A	L	1-3	Pagis 40	15,000
6	frpr1	**Lens**	H	D	2-2	Abdessadki 11; Le Pen 71	10,000
7	frpr1	**Caen**	A	D	0-0		15,000
8	frpr1	**Paris SG**	A	L	0-1		33,000
9	frpr1	**Nantes**	H	L	0-2		15,000
10	frpr1	**AC Ajaccio**	A	D	2-2	Pagis 27; Niang 64	4,000
11	frpr1	**Nice**	H	W	3-1	Deroff 36; Pagis 82; Arrache 85	12,000
12	frpr1	**Lyon**	A	L	0-1		39,000
13	frpr1	**Bordeaux**	H	W	1-0	Pagis 90	8,000
14	frpr1	**Marseille**	A	L	0-2		35,000
15	frpr1	**Auxerre**	H	W	3-1	Abdessadki 20,56; Niang 34	15,000
16	frpr1	**Lille**	A	D	1-1	Niang 58	11,000
17	frpr1	**Sochaux**	H	D	0-0		20,000
18	frpr1	**Metz**	A	L	0-1		24,000
19	frpr1	**Rennes**	H	W	1-0	Kante 15	25,000
20	frpr1	**Toulouse**	A	L	0-2		17,000
21	frpr1	**St Etienne**	H	D	1-1	Niang 9	10,000
22	frpr1	**Istres**	A	D	1-1	Pagis 45	4,000
23	frpr1	**Lens**	A	L	1-2	Farnerud 66	32,000
24	frpr1	**Caen**	H	W	5-0	Pagis 9,55,81; Abdessadki 27; Niang 38	11,000
25	frpr1	**Paris SG**	H	W	3-1	Niang 20; Pagis 37 pen; Abdessadki 63	18,000
26	frpr1	**Nantes**	A	L	1-2	Niang 48	25,000
27	frpr1	**AC Ajaccio**	H	W	1-0	Devaux 35	20,000
28	frpr1	**Nice**	A	D	0-0		10,000
29	frpr1	**Monaco**	H	D	0-0		22,000
30	frpr1	**Lyon**	H	L	0-1		23,000
31	frpr1	**Bordeaux**	A	W	2-0	Abdessadki 73; Niang 76	21,000
32	frpr1	**Marseille**	H	W	1-0	Niang 91	26,000
33	frpr1	**Auxerre**	A	D	0-0		12,000
34	frpr1	**Lille**	H	L	1-2	Niang 69	19,000
35	frpr1	**Sochaux**	A	W	2-1	Johansen 70; Pagis 87	19,000
36	frpr1	**Metz**	H	W	3-1	Niang 23; Pagis 75,91	24,000
37	frpr1	**Rennes**	A	L	0-4		28,000
38	frpr1	**Bastia**	H	W	2-0	Niang 84; Farnerud 90	20,000

MONTHLY POINTS TALLY

AUGUST	2	17%
SEPTEMBER	2	17%
OCTOBER	4	33%
NOVEMBER	7	58%
DECEMBER	4	44%
JANUARY	2	17%
FEBRUARY	6	67%
MARCH	5	42%
APRIL	7	58%
MAY	9	75%

KEY PLAYERS - GOALSCORERS

Michael Pagis

Goals in the League	14	**Player Strike Rate** Average number of minutes between League goals scored by player	177
Contribution to Attacking Power Average number of minutes between League team goals while on pitch	77	**Club Strike Rate** Average number of minutes between League goals scored by club	81

	PLAYER	LGE GOALS	POWER	STRIKE RATE
1	Michael Pagis	14	77	177 mins
2	Mamadou Niang	12	81	219 mins
3	Yacine Abdessadki	6	85	499 mins
4	Alexander Farnerud	3	84	562 mins
5	Yves Deroff	1	82	1652 mins

KEY PLAYERS - MIDFIELDERS

Alexander Farnerud

Goals in the League	3	**Contribution to Attacking Power** Average number of minutes between League team goals while on pitch	84
Defensive Rating Average number of mins between League goals conceded while on the pitch	94	**Scoring Difference** Defensive Rating minus Contribution to Attacking Power	10

	PLAYER	LGE GOALS	DEF RATE	POWER	SCORE DIFF
1	Alexander Farnerud	3	94	84	10 mins
2	Yves Deroff	1	87	83	4 mins
3	Arthur Boka	0	78	76	2 mins
4	Guillaume Lacour	0	78	76	2 mins
5	Yacine Abdessadki	6	77	85	-8 mins

KEY PLAYERS - DEFENDERS

Karim Haggui

Goals Conceded Number of League goals conceded while the player was on the pitch	12	**Clean Sheets** In League games when player was on pitch for at least 70 minutes	7
Defensive Rating Ave number of mins between League goals conceded while on the pitch	126	**Club Defensive Rating** Average number of mins between League goals conceded by the club this season	80

	PLAYER	CON LGE	CLEAN SHEETS	DEF RATE
1	Karim Haggui	12	7	126 mins
2	Christian Bassila	24	7	82 mins
3	Cedric Kante	40	11	79 mins
4	Jean-Christophe Devaux	28	9	77 mins

KEY GOALKEEPER

Stephane Cassard

Goals Conceded in the League	33	**Counting Games** League games when player was on pitch for at least 70 minutes	33
Defensive Rating Ave number of mins between League goals conceded while on the pitch	90	**Clean Sheets** In games when player was on pitch for at least 70 minutes	12

LEAGUE GOALS

Michael Pagis

Minutes on the pitch	2474	Goals in the League	14
League average (mins between goals)	177		

	PLAYER	MINS	GOALS	AVE
1	Pagis	2474	14	177
2	Niang	2622	12	219
3	Abdessadki	2992	6	499
4	Farnerud	1686	3	562
5	Deroff	1652	1	1652
6	Devaux	2154	1	2154
7	Kante	3150	1	3150
8	Le Pen	1081	1	1081
9	Johansen	2620	1	2620
10	Arrache	2064	1	2064
	Other		1	
	TOTAL		42	

DISCIPLINARY

	PLAYER	YELLOW	RED	AVE
1	Keita	5	1	183
2	Bassila	8	1	217
3	Deroff	5	1	275
4	Haggui	5	0	302
5	Fahmi	1	1	303
6	Pagis	5	2	353
7	Devaux	6	0	359
8	Johansen	7	0	374
9	Niang	6	0	437
10	Arrache	4	0	516
11	Boka	5	0	560
12	Abdessadki	4	0	748
13	Camadini	0	1	801
	Other	9	0	
	TOTAL	70	7	

TOP POINT EARNERS

	PLAYER	GAMES	AV PTS
1	Jean-Christophe Devaux	23	1.61
2	Alexander Farnerud	15	1.60
3	Guillaume Lacour	22	1.50
4	Pascal Johansen	29	1.48
5	Mamadou Niang	29	1.48
6	Yves Deroff	17	1.41
7	Stephane Cassard	33	1.39
8	Salim Arrache	19	1.37
9	Karim Haggui	15	1.33
10	Yacine Abdessadki	32	1.25
	CLUB AVERAGE:		1.26

LEAGUE APPEARANCES, BOOKINGS AND CAPS

	AGE (on 01/07/05)	IN NAMED 16	APPEARANCES	COUNTING GAMES	MINUTES ON PITCH	YELLOW CARDS	RED CARDS	THIS SEASON	HOME COUNTRY
Goalkeepers									
Nicolas Bonis	23	9	1	0	3	0	0	-	France
Stephane Cassard	32	38	33	33	2970	2	0	-	France
Remi Vercoutre	25	28	5	5	450	0	0	-	France
Defenders									
Christian Bassila	27	27	23	21	1960	8	1	-	France
Habib Bellaid	19	9	0	0	0	0	0	-	France
Jean-C Devaux	30	30	27	23	2154	6	0	-	France
Abdelilah Fahmi	31	12	9	6	606	1	1	-	Morocco
Karim Haggui	21	20	20	15	1510	5	0	-	Tunisia
Cedric Kante	25	37	35	35	3150	3	0	-	France
Jacques Momha	22	5	2	0	97	0	0	-	Cameroon
Midfielders									
Yacine Abdessadki	24	36	35	32	2992	4	0	-	Algeria
Arthur Boka	22	35	34	29	2801	5	0	2	Ivory Coast (44)
Pascal Camadini	33	22	18	7	801	0	1	-	France
Yves Deroff	26	31	22	17	1652	5	1	-	France
Alexander Farnerud	21	37	31	15	1686	2	0	-	Sweden
Sidi Yaya Keita	20	20	15	11	1102	5	1	-	Mali
Guillaume Lacour	24	38	35	22	2195	2	0	-	France
Ulrich Le Pen	31	18	17	9	1081	0	0	-	France
Forwards									
Salim Arrache	22	35	33	19	2064	4	0	-	France
Rudy Carlier	19	5	2	0	38	0	0	-	France
Kevin Gameiro	18	2	0	0	0	0	0	-	France
Pascal Johansen	26	31	31	29	2620	7	0	-	France
Katlego Abel M'Phela	20	16	11	1	312	0	0	-	South Africa
Eric Mouloungui	21	5	3	0	105	0	0	-	Gabon
Mamadou Niang	25	31	31	29	2622	6	0	3	Senegal (33)
Michael Pagis	31	30	30	27	2474	5	2	-	France

TEAM OF THE SEASON

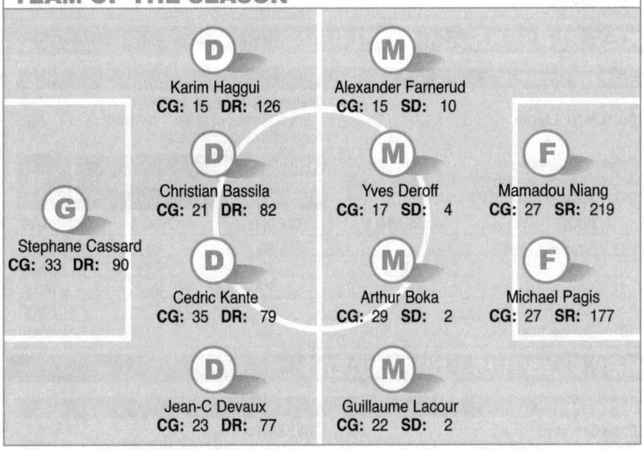
D
Karim Haggui
CG: 15 DR: 126
M
Alexander Farnerud
CG: 15 SD: 10
D
Christian Bassila
CG: 21 DR: 82
M
Yves Deroff
CG: 17 SD: 4
F
Mamadou Niang
CG: 27 SR: 219
G
Stephane Cassard
CG: 33 DR: 90
D
Cedric Kante
CG: 35 DR: 79
M
Arthur Boka
CG: 29 SD: 2
F
Michael Pagis
CG: 27 SR: 177
D
Jean-C Devaux
CG: 23 DR: 77
M
Guillaume Lacour
CG: 22 SD: 2

SQUAD APPEARANCES

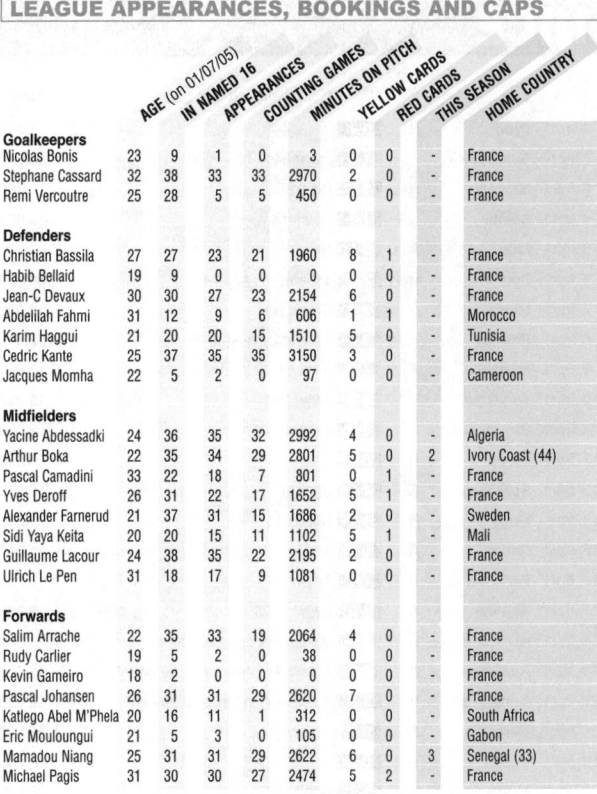

Match	1	2	3	4	5	6	7	8	9	10	11	12	13	14	15	16	17	18	19	20	21	22	23	24	25	26	27	28	29	30	31	32	33	34	35	36	37	38
Venue	A	H	A	H	A	H	A	A	H	A	H	A	H	A	H	A	H	A	H	A	H	A	A	H	H	A	H	A	H	H	A	H	A	H	A	H	A	H
Competition	L	L	L	L	L	L	L	L	L	L	L	L	L	L	L	L	L	L	L	L	L	L	L	L	L	L	L	L	L	L	L	L	L	L	L	L	L	L
Result	L	L	D	D	L	D	D	L	L	D	W	L	W	L	W	D	D	L	W	L	D	D	L	W	W	L	W	D	D	L	W	W	D	L	W	W	L	W

Goalkeepers
Nicolas Bonis
Stephane Cassard
Remi Vercoutre

Defenders
Christian Bassila
Habib Bellaid
Jean-Christophe Devaux
Abdelilah Fahmi
Karim Haggui
Cedric Kante
Jacques Momha

Midfielders
Yacine Abdessadki
Arthur Boka
Pascal Camadini
Yves Deroff
Alexander Farnerud
Sidi Yaya Keita
Guillaume Lacour
Ulrich Le Pen

Forwards
Salim Arrache
Rudy Carlier
Kevin Gameiro
Pascal Johansen
Katlego Abel M'Phela
Eric Mouloungui
Mamadou Niang
Michael Pagis

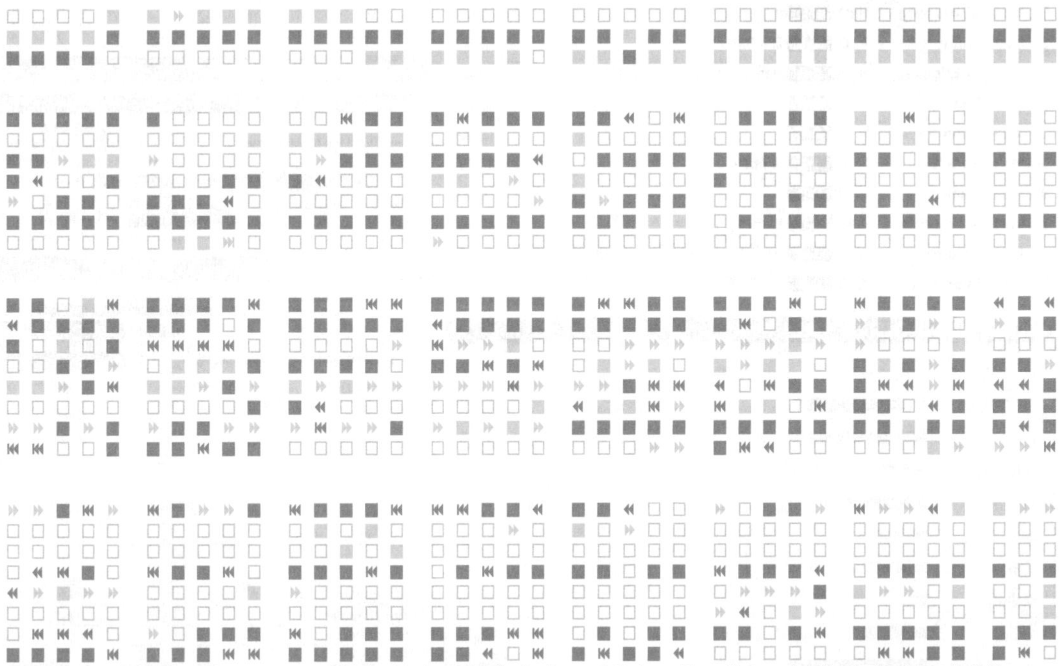

KEY: On all match | On bench | Subbed or sent off (Counting game) | Subbed or sent off (playing less than 70 minutes) | Subbed on from bench (Counting Game) | Subbed on (playing less than 70 minutes) | Subbed on and then subbed or sent off (Counting Game) | Subbed on and then subbed or sent off (playing less than 70 minutes) | Not in 16

NICE

Final Position: **12th**

KEY: Won / Drawn / Lost

							Attendance
1	frpr1	**Lyon**	H	L	0-1		14,000
2	frpr1	**Bordeaux**	A	L	1-5	Jarjat 64	29,000
3	frpr1	**Marseille**	H	D	1-1	Die 61	15,000
4	frpr1	**Bastia**	H	D	1-1	Roudet 4	10,000
5	frpr1	**Lille**	A	L	0-1		9,000
6	frpr1	**Sochaux**	H	W	2-1	Vahirua 27; Agali 49	10,000
7	frpr1	**Metz**	A	D	1-1	Cobos 90	16,000
8	frpr1	**Rennes**	H	W	2-0	Roudet 2; Vahirua 25	12,000
9	frpr1	**Monaco**	A	W	4-3	Agali 67,72,74; Vahirua 83	17,000
10	frpr1	**Toulouse**	H	W	1-0	Jarjat 26	12,000
11	frpr1	**Strasbourg**	A	L	1-3	Balmont 78	12,000
12	frpr1	**Istres**	H	D	0-0		8,000
13	frpr1	**St Etienne**	A	L	1-2	Agali 30	30,000
14	frpr1	**Lens**	H	D	1-1	Cobos 16	11,000
15	frpr1	**Caen**	A	D	0-0		21,000
16	frpr1	**Paris SG**	H	D	1-1	Traore 67	15,000
17	frpr1	**Nantes**	A	W	1-0	Balmont 29	29,000
18	frpr1	**AC Ajaccio**	H	W	3-0	Vahirua 44 pen,90; Grenet 82	10,000
19	frpr1	**Auxerre**	A	L	3-4	Traore 47; Vahirua 57; Echouafni 61	11,000
20	frpr1	**Bordeaux**	H	D	3-3	Traore 33; Vahirua 45,90 pen	12,000
21	frpr1	**Marseille**	A	L	0-2		48,000
22	frpr1	**Bastia**	A	L	0-2		4,000
23	frpr1	**Lille**	H	D	1-1	Cobos 90	10,000
24	frpr1	**Sochaux**	A	D	0-0		9,000
25	frpr1	**Metz**	H	D	1-1	Vahirua 76	7,000
26	frpr1	**Rennes**	A	L	1-4	Balmont 60	17,000
27	frpr1	**Monaco**	H	W	2-1	Balmont 13; Ederson 66	13,000
28	frpr1	**Toulouse**	A	L	0-1		15,000
29	frpr1	**Strasbourg**	H	D	0-0		10,000
30	frpr1	**Istres**	A	D	1-1	Die 33	3,000
31	frpr1	**St Etienne**	H	W	2-0	Vahirua 9; Larbi 33	12,000
32	frpr1	**Lens**	A	D	0-0		33,000
33	frpr1	**Caen**	H	L	0-1		12,000
34	frpr1	**Paris SG**	A	L	1-3	Armand 90	30,000
35	frpr1	**Nantes**	H	D	0-0		15,000
36	frpr1	**AC Ajaccio**	A	W	1-0	Larbi 52	6,000
37	frpr1	**Auxerre**	H	W	1-0	Agali 28	15,000
38	frpr1	**Lyon**	A	D	0-0		38,000

MONTHLY POINTS TALLY

AUGUST	2	17%
SEPTEMBER	7	58%
OCTOBER	7	58%
NOVEMBER	3	25%
DECEMBER	6	67%
JANUARY	3	20%
FEBRUARY	4	44%
MARCH	2	22%
APRIL	4	33%
MAY	8	67%

KEY PLAYERS - GOALSCORERS

Marama Vahirua

Goals in the League	10	**Player Strike Rate** Average number of minutes between League goals scored by player	248
Contribution to Attacking Power Average number of minutes between League team goals while on pitch	73	**Club Strike Rate** Average number of minutes between League goals scored by club	90

	PLAYER	LGE GOALS	POWER	STRIKE RATE
1	Marama Vahirua	10	73	248 mins
2	Victor Agali	6	84	367 mins
3	Florent Balmont	4	85	764 mins
4	Serge Die	2	126	821 mins
5	Sammy Traore	3	80	856 mins

KEY PLAYERS - MIDFIELDERS

Francois Grenet

Goals in the League	1	**Contribution to Attacking Power** Average number of minutes between League team goals while on pitch	80
Defensive Rating Average number of mins between League goals conceded while on the pitch	90	**Scoring Difference** Defensive Rating minus Contribution to Attacking Power	10

	PLAYER	LGE GOALS	DEF RATE	POWER	SCORE DIFF
1	Francois Grenet	1	90	80	10 mins
2	Florent Balmont	4	83	85	-2 mins
3	Sebastien Roudet	2	77	83	-6 mins
4	Olivier Echouafni	1	57	67	-10 mins
5	Sammy Traore	3	68	80	-12 mins

KEY PLAYERS - DEFENDERS

Serge Die

Goals Conceded Number of League goals conceded while the player was on the pitch	20	**Clean Sheets** In League games when player was on pitch for at least 70 minutes	5
Defensive Rating Ave number of mins between League goals conceded while on the pitch	82	**Club Defensive Rating** Average number of mins between League goals conceded by the club this season	76

	PLAYER	CON LGE	CLEAN SHEETS	DEF RATE
1	Serge Die	20	5	82 mins
2	Jose Cobos	37	12	81 mins
3	Florian Jarjat	22	8	80 mins
4	Cedric Varrault	30	7	78 mins
5	Jacques Abardonado	36	11	77 mins

KEY GOALKEEPER

Damien Gregorini

Goals Conceded in the League	44	**Counting Games** League games when player was on pitch for at least 70 minutes	38
Defensive Rating Ave number of mins between League goals conceded while on the pitch	78	**Clean Sheets** In games when player was on pitch for at least 70 minutes	14

LEAGUE GOALS

Marama Vahirua

Minutes on the pitch	2484	**Goals in the League**	10
League average (mins between goals)	248		

	PLAYER	MINS	GOALS	AVE
1	Vahirua	2484	10	248
2	Agali	2201	6	367
3	Balmont	3056	4	764
4	Traore	2568	3	856
5	Jarjat	1753	2	877
6	Roudet	2068	2	1034
7	Larbi	742	2	371
8	Die	1642	2	821
9	Cobos	2991	2	1496
10	Grenet	1445	1	1445
11	Echouafni	1132	1	1132
12	Ederson	184	1	184
	Other		2	
	TOTAL		38	

DISCIPLINARY RECORDS

	PLAYER	YELLOW	RED	AVE
1	Die	10	1	149
2	Jankauskas	7	0	153
3	Bisconti	9	0	190
4	Jarjat	8	1	194
5	Agali	9	1	220
6	Cobos	9	1	299
7	Linz	2	0	300
8	Grenet	4	0	361
9	Balmont	8	0	382
10	Varrault	5	1	389
11	Traore	5	1	428
12	Roudet	4	0	517
13	Bigne	2	0	527
	Other	11	0	
	TOTAL	93	6	

TOP POINT EARNERS

	PLAYER	GAMES	AV PTS
1	Marama Vahirua	19	1.47
2	Francois Grenet	15	1.40
3	Roberto Bisconti	17	1.35
4	Olivier Echouafni	12	1.33
5	Florent Balmont	34	1.29
6	Victor Agali	19	1.26
7	Jose Cobos	32	1.22
8	Damien Gregorini	38	1.21
9	Sammy Traore	28	1.21
10	Jacques Abardonado	31	1.19
	CLUB AVERAGE:		1.21

LEAGUE APPEARANCES, BOOKINGS AND CAPS

	AGE (on 01/07/05)	IN NAMED 16	APPEARANCES	COUNTING GAMES	MINUTES ON PITCH	YELLOW CARDS	RED CARDS	THIS SEASON	HOME COUNTRY
Goalkeepers									
Damien Gregorini	26	38	38	38	3420	3	0	-	France
Hugo Lloris	18	10	0	0	0	0	0	-	France
Hilaire Munoz	22	5	0	0	0	0	0	-	France
Bruno Valencony	37	23	3	0	28	0	0	-	France
Defenders									
Jacques Abardonado	27	34	31	31	2786	5	0	-	France
Jose Cobos	37	34	34	32	2991	9	1	-	France
Serge Die	27	30	29	16	1642	10	1	1	Ivory Coast (44)
Florian Jarjat	25	27	22	18	1753	8	1	-	France
Noe Pamarot	26	2	2	2	180	1	0	-	France
Cedric Varrault	25	32	30	24	2336	5	1	-	France
Midfielders									
Florent Balmont	25	34	34	34	3056	8	0	-	France
Yohann Bigne	27	25	17	10	1054	2	0	-	France
Roberto Bisconti	31	25	24	17	1718	9	0	7	Belgium (42)
Martin Djetou	30	6	5	5	432	2	0	-	France
Olivier Echouafni	32	18	17	12	1132	1	0	-	France
Ederson	19	5	5	0	184	0	0	-	Brazil
Francois Grenet	30	24	22	15	1445	4	0	-	France
Franck Padovani	20	1	1	1	90	0	0	-	France
Romain Pitau	27	2	2	2	180	0	0	-	France
Sebastien Roudet	24	26	25	21	2068	4	0	-	France
A Scaramozzino	20	2	2	1	102	0	0	-	France
T Scotto Di Porfirio	26	18	14	6	682	0	0	-	France
Sammy Traore	23	34	30	28	2568	5	1	-	Ivory Coast
Forwards									
Victor Agali	26	30	30	19	2201	9	1	-	Nigeria
Bakary Diakite	24	1	1	1	90	0	0	-	Germany
Pablo Franco Dolci	21	9	4	1	135	1	0	-	France
Olivier Fauconnier	29	2	2	0	43	1	0	-	France
Edgaras Jankauskas	30	24	21	6	1071	7	0	-	Lithuania
Kamel Larbi	20	15	12	7	742	1	0	-	France
Roland Linz	23	17	15	5	601	2	0	-	Austria
Christophe Meslin	27	15	9	0	296	0	0	-	France
Marama Vahirua	25	36	34	19	2484	1	0	-	France

TEAM OF THE SEASON

D
Serge Die
CG: 16 DR: 82
M
Francois Grenet
CG: 15 SD: 10
D
Jose Cobos
CG: 32 DR: 81
M
Florent Balmont
CG: 34 SD: -2
F
Marama Vahirua
CG: 19 SR: 248
G
Damien Gregorini
CG: 38 DR: 78
D
Florian Jarjat
CG: 18 DR: 80
M
Sebastien Roudet
CG: 21 SD: -6
F
Victor Agali
CG: 19 SR: 367
D
Cedric Varrault
CG: 24 DR: 78
M
Olivier Echouafni
CG: 12 SD: -10

SQUAD APPEARANCES

Match	1	2	3	4	5	6	7	8	9	10	11	12	13	14	15	16	17	18	19	20	21	22	23	24	25	26	27	28	29	30	31	32	33	34	35	36	37	38
Venue	H	A	H	H	A	H	A	H	A	H	A	H	A	H	A	H	A	H	A	H	A	A	H	A	H	A	H	A	H	A	H	A	H	A	H	A	H	A
Competition	L	L	L	L	L	L	L	L	L	L	L	L	L	L	L	L	L	L	L	L	L	L	L	L	L	L	L	L	L	L	L	L	L	L	L	L	L	L
Result	L	L	D	D	L	W	D	W	W	W	L	D	L	D	D	D	W	W	L	D	L	L	D	D	D	L	W	L	D	D	W	D	L	L	D	W	W	D

Goalkeepers
Damien Gregorini
Hugo Lloris
Hilaire Munoz
Bruno Valencony

Defenders
Jacques Abardonado
Jose Cobos
Serge Die
Florian Jarjat
Noe Pamarot
Cedric Varrault

Midfielders
Florent Balmont
Yohann Bigne
Roberto Bisconti
Martin Djetou
Olivier Echouafni
Ederson
Francois Grenet
Franck Padovani
Romain Pitau
Sebastien Roudet
Anthony Scaramozzino
Thibault Scotto Di Porfirio
Sammy Traore

Forwards
Victor Agali
Bakary Diakite
Pablo Franco Dolci
Olivier Fauconnier
Edgaras Jankauskas
Kamel Larbi
Roland Linz
Christophe Meslin
Marama Vahirua

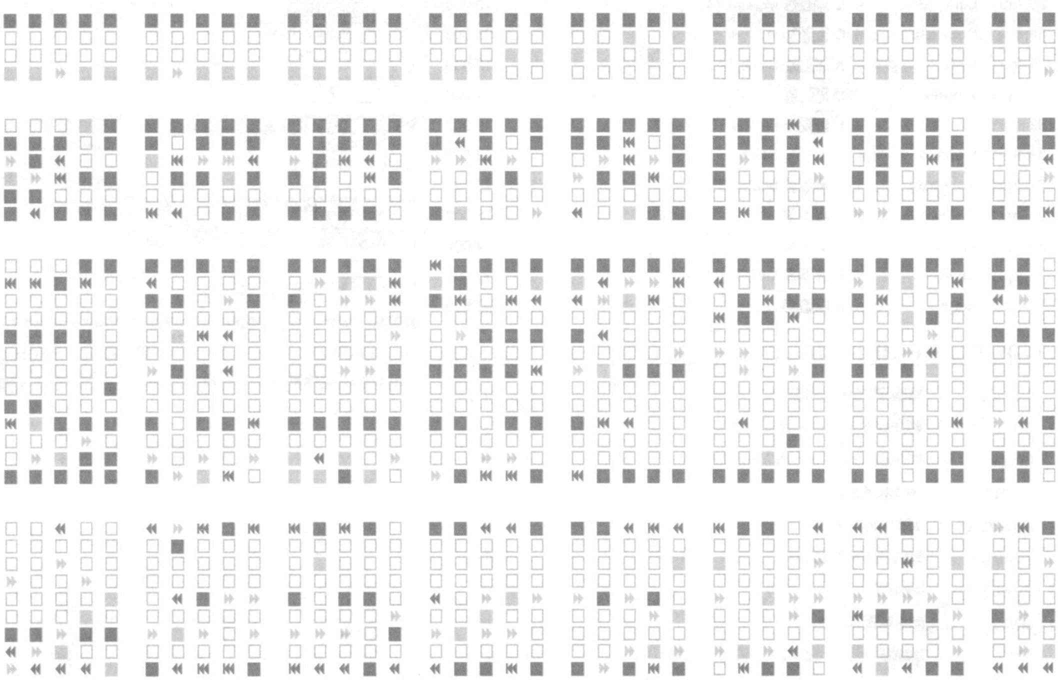

KEY: On all match; On bench; Subbed or sent off (Counting game); Subbed or sent off (playing less than 70 minutes); Subbed on from bench (Counting Game); Subbed on (playing less than 70 minutes); Subbed on and then subbed or sent off (Counting Game); Subbed on and then subbed or sent off (playing less than 70 minutes); Not in 16

TOULOUSE

Final Position: **13th**

KEY: Won Drawn Lost

							Attendance
1	frpr1	Lens	H	D	0-0		25,000
2	frpr1	Strasbourg	A	W	4-1	Dalmat 5; Suarez 8,76; Moreira 26	13,000
3	frpr1	Paris SG	H	W	2-1	Moreira 55; Eduardo 70	35,000
4	frpr1	Nantes	A	D	2-2	Caceres 2 og; Sirieix 39	30,000
5	frpr1	AC Ajaccio	H	W	3-1	Taider 9; Eduardo 84; Arribage 88	18,000
6	frpr1	Marseille	A	L	0-1		56,000
7	frpr1	Lyon	H	L	0-2		31,000
8	frpr1	Bordeaux	A	D	1-1	Moreira 87	20,000
9	frpr1	Auxerre	H	L	1-2	Moreira 31	26,000
10	frpr1	Nice	A	L	0-1		12,000
11	frpr1	Lille	H	W	1-0	Eduardo 89	30,000
12	frpr1	Sochaux	A	L	0-2		15,000
13	frpr1	Metz	H	D	1-1	Giresse 34	15,000
14	frpr1	Rennes	A	D	1-1	Moreira 75	18,000
15	frpr1	Bastia	H	W	1-0	Dieuze 67	15,000
16	frpr1	Monaco	H	D	0-0		30,000
17	frpr1	St Etienne	A	D	0-0		30,000
18	frpr1	Istres	H	W	2-1	Emana 25; Giresse 60	21,000
19	frpr1	Caen	A	W	2-0	Psaume 27; Moreira 57	19,000
20	frpr1	Strasbourg	H	W	2-0	Psaume 21; Eduardo 90	17,000
21	frpr1	Paris SG	A	D	0-0		35,000
22	frpr1	Nantes	H	W	2-1	Emana 30; Psaume 73	23,000
23	frpr1	AC Ajaccio	A	L	0-1		3,000
24	frpr1	Marseille	H	L	1-3	Taider 25	35,000
25	frpr1	Lyon	A	L	0-4		30,000
26	frpr1	Bordeaux	H	W	1-0	Moreira 78	23,000
27	frpr1	Nice	H	W	1-0	Moreira 36	15,000
28	frpr1	Lille	A	D	1-1	Moreira 74	10,000
29	frpr1	Sochaux	H	D	0-0		25,000
30	frpr1	Metz	A	W	1-0	Sirieix 35	16,000
31	frpr1	Rennes	H	L	0-2		14,000
32	frpr1	Bastia	A	L	1-2	Emana 77	6,000
33	frpr1	Monaco	A	L	1-2	Suarez 72	10,000
34	frpr1	Auxerre	A	L	2-3	Suarez 57,62	10,000
35	frpr1	St Etienne	H	L	0-2		26,000
36	frpr1	Istres	A	L	0-1		4,000
37	frpr1	Caen	H	L	2-3	Moreira 36,57	19,000
38	frpr1	Lens	A	L	0-1		40,000

MONTHLY POINTS TALLY

AUGUST	8	67%
SEPTEMBER	4	33%
OCTOBER	3	25%
NOVEMBER	6	50%
DECEMBER	7	78%
JANUARY	7	47%
FEBRUARY	3	50%
MARCH	5	56%
APRIL	3	20%
MAY	0	0%

KEY PLAYERS - GOALSCORERS

Daniel Moreira

Goals in the League	11	Player Strike Rate Average number of minutes between League goals scored by player	235
Contribution to Attacking Power Average number of minutes between League team goals while on pitch	99	Club Strike Rate Average number of minutes between League goals scored by club	95

	PLAYER	LGE GOALS	POWER	STRIKE RATE
1	Daniel Moreira	11	100	235 mins
2	Thibault Giresse	2	91	861 mins
3	Achille Emana	3	93	1030 mins
4	Nabil Taider	2	93	1351 mins
5	Stephane Dalmat	1	91	1643 mins

KEY PLAYERS - MIDFIELDERS

Julien Cardy

Goals in the League	0	Contribution to Attacking Power Average number of minutes between League team goals while on pitch	89
Defensive Rating Average number of mins between League goals conceded while on the pitch	89	Scoring Difference Defensive Rating minus Contribution to Attacking Power	0

	PLAYER	LGE GOALS	DEF RATE	POWER	SCORE DIFF
1	Julien Cardy	0	89	89	0 mins
2	Thibault Giresse	2	86	91	-5 mins
3	Daniel Moreira	11	86	100	-14 mins
4	Nabil Taider	2	71	93	-22 mins
5	Stephane Dalmat	1	61	91	-30 mins

KEY PLAYERS - DEFENDERS

Albin Ebondo

Goals Conceded Number of League goals conceded while the player was on the pitch	33	Clean Sheets In League games when player was on pitch for at least 70 minutes	11
Defensive Rating Ave number of mins between League goals conceded while on the pitch	85	Club Defensive Rating Average number of mins between League goals conceded by the club this season	80

	PLAYER	CON LGE	CLEAN SHEETS	DEF RATE
1	Albin Ebondo	33	11	85 mins
2	Ludovic Clement	16	5	84 mins
3	Lucien Aubey	36	10	80 mins
4	Dominique Arribage	38	10	78 mins
5	Daniel Congre	22	7	74 mins

KEY GOALKEEPER

Christophe Revault

Goals Conceded in the League	43	Counting Games League games when player was on pitch for at least 70 minutes	38
Defensive Rating Ave number of mins between League goals conceded while on the pitch	80	Clean Sheets In games when player was on pitch for at least 70 minutes	12

LEAGUE GOALS

Daniel Moreira

Minutes on the pitch	2589	Goals in the League	11
League average (mins between goals)	235		

	PLAYER	MINS	GOALS	AVE
1	Moreira	2589	11	235
2	Suarez	987	5	197
3	Eduardo	1475	4	369
4	Emana	3089	3	1030
5	Psaume	863	3	288
6	Giresse	1722	2	861
7	Taider	2702	2	1351
8	Sirieix	1268	2	634
9	Arribage	2970	1	2970
10	Dalmat	1643	1	1643
11	Dieuze	1839	1	1839
	Other		1	
	TOTAL		36	

DISCIPLINARY

	PLAYER	YELLOW	RED	AVE
1	Sirieix	8	1	140
2	Nsame	4	0	168
3	Cardy	7	0	190
4	Dieuze	9	0	204
5	Clement	4	1	268
6	Dalmat	5	0	328
7	Suarez	3	0	329
8	Emana	7	0	441
9	Lievre	2	0	481
10	Moreira	5	0	517
11	Aubey	3	1	720
12	Eduardo	1	1	737
13	Arribage	4	0	742
	Other	12	0	
	TOTAL	74	4	

TOP POINT EARNERS

	PLAYER	GAMES	AV PTS
1	Thibault Giresse	16	1.56
2	Nicolas Dieuze	18	1.39
3	Ludovic Clement	13	1.38
4	Julien Cardy	12	1.33
5	Achille Emana	31	1.32
6	Daniel Moreira	28	1.25
7	Albin Ebondo	29	1.24
8	Christophe Revault	38	1.21
9	Lucien Aubey	31	1.19
10	Nabil Taider	27	1.19
	CLUB AVERAGE:		1.21

TEAM OF THE SEASON

G Christophe Revault CG: 38 DR: 80

D Albin Ebondo CG: 29 DR: 85
D Ludovic Clement CG: 13 DR: 84
D Lucien Aubey CG: 31 DR: 80
D Dominique Arribage CG: 33 DR: 78

M Julien Cardy CG: 12 SD: 0
M Thibault Giresse CG: 16 SD: -5
M Daniel Moreira CG: 28 SD: -14
M Nabil Taider CG: 27 SD: -22

F Achille Emana CG: 31 SR: 1030
F Nicolas Dieuze CG: 18 SR: 1839

LEAGUE APPEARANCES, BOOKINGS AND CAPS

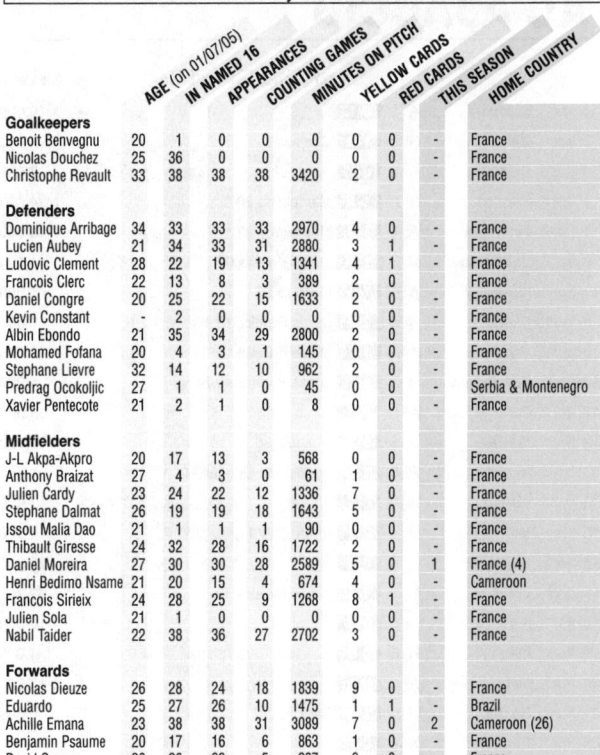

	AGE (on 01/07/05)	IN NAMED 16	APPEARANCES	COUNTING GAMES	MINUTES ON PITCH	YELLOW CARDS	RED CARDS	THIS SEASON	HOME COUNTRY
Goalkeepers									
Benoit Benvegnu	20	1	0	0	0	0	0	-	France
Nicolas Douchez	25	36	0	0	0	0	0	-	France
Christophe Revault	33	38	38	38	3420	2	0	-	France
Defenders									
Dominique Arribage	34	33	33	33	2970	4	0	-	France
Lucien Aubey	21	34	33	31	2880	3	1	-	France
Ludovic Clement	28	22	19	13	1341	4	1	-	France
Francois Clerc	22	13	8	3	389	2	0	-	France
Daniel Congre	20	25	22	15	1633	2	0	-	France
Kevin Constant	-	2	0	0	0	0	0	-	France
Albin Ebondo	21	35	34	29	2800	2	0	-	France
Mohamed Fofana	20	4	3	1	145	0	0	-	France
Stephane Lievre	32	14	12	10	962	2	0	-	France
Predrag Ocokoljic	27	1	1	0	45	0	0	-	Serbia & Montenegro
Xavier Pentecote	21	2	1	0	8	0	0	-	France
Midfielders									
J-L Akpa-Akpro	20	17	13	3	568	0	0	-	France
Anthony Braizat	27	4	3	0	61	1	0	-	France
Julien Cardy	23	24	22	12	1336	7	0	-	France
Stephane Dalmat	26	19	19	18	1643	5	0	-	France
Issou Malia Dao	21	1	1	1	90	0	0	-	France
Thibault Giresse	24	32	28	16	1722	2	0	-	France
Daniel Moreira	27	30	30	28	2589	5	0	1	France (4)
Henri Bedimo Nsame	21	20	15	4	674	4	0	-	Cameroon
Francois Sirieix	24	28	25	9	1268	8	1	-	France
Julien Sola	21	1	0	0	0	0	0	-	France
Nabil Taider	22	38	36	27	2702	3	0	-	France
Forwards									
Nicolas Dieuze	26	28	24	18	1839	9	0	-	France
Eduardo	25	27	26	10	1475	1	1	-	Brazil
Achille Emana	23	38	38	31	3089	7	0	2	Cameroon (26)
Benjamin Psaume	20	17	16	6	863	1	0	-	France
David Suarez	26	26	22	5	987	3	0	-	France

SQUAD APPEARANCES

Match	1	2	3	4	5	6	7	8	9	10	11	12	13	14	15	16	17	18	19	20	21	22	23	24	25	26	27	28	29	30	31	32	33	34	35	36	37	38
Venue	H	A	H	A	H	A	H	A	H	A	H	A	H	A	H	H	A	H	A	H	A	H	A	H	A	H	H	A	H	A	H	A	A	A	H	A	H	A
Competition	L	L	L	L	L	L	L	L	L	L	L	L	L	L	L	L	L	L	L	L	L	L	L	L	L	L	L	L	L	L	L	L	L	L	L	L	L	L
Result	D	W	W	D	W	L	L	D	L	L	W	L	D	D	W	D	D	W	W	W	D	W	L	L	L	W	W	D	D	W	L	L	L	L	L	L	L	L

Goalkeepers
Benoit Benvegnu
Nicolas Douchez
Christophe Revault

Defenders
Dominique Arribage
Lucien Aubey
Ludovic Clement
Francois Clerc
Daniel Congre
Kevin Constant
Albin Ebondo
Mohamed Fofana
Stephane Lievre
Predrag Ocokoljic
Xavier Pentecote

Midfielders
Jean-Louis Akpa-Akpro
Anthony Braizat
Julien Cardy
Stephane Dalmat
Issou Malia Dao
Thibault Giresse
Daniel Moreira
Henri Bedimo Nsame
Francois Sirieix
Julien Sola
Nabil Taider

Forwards
Nicolas Dieuze
Eduardo
Achille Emana
Benjamin Psaume
David Suarez

KEY: ■ On all match ■ On bench
⏮ Subbed or sent off (Counting game)
« Subbed or sent off (playing less than 70 minutes)
⏭ Subbed on from bench (Counting Game)
» Subbed on (playing less than 70 minutes)
Subbed on and then subbed or sent off (Counting Game)
Subbed on and then subbed or sent off (playing less than 70 minutes)
□ Not in 16

AC AJACCIO

Final Position: **14th**

KEY: ☐Won ☐Drawn ☐Lost

							Attendance
1	frpr1	Sochaux	A	L	0-1		19,000
2	frpr1	Metz	H	L	1-2	Chapuis 61	7,000
3	frpr1	Bastia	A	L	0-1		7,000
4	frpr1	Rennes	H	D	1-1	Marcelinho 20	4,000
5	frpr1	Toulouse	A	L	1-3	Marcelinho 22	18,000
6	frpr1	St Etienne	H	D	1-1	Lucas Pereira 90	4,000
7	frpr1	Istres	A	W	1-0	Chapuis 23	6,000
8	frpr1	Caen	H	D	2-2	Lucas Pereira 13,46	5,000
9	frpr1	Lens	A	D	1-1	Lucas Pereira 15	32,000
10	frpr1	Strasbourg	H	D	2-2	Lucas Pereira 49,74	4,000
11	frpr1	Paris SG	A	L	0-1		35,000
12	frpr1	Nantes	H	D	1-1	Chapuis 36	4,000
13	frpr1	Monaco	A	D	2-2	Dzodic 16; Ouadah 90	4,000
14	frpr1	Auxerre	A	L	0-1		13,000
15	frpr1	Marseille	H	W	2-0	Andre Luiz 11,45	7,000
16	frpr1	Bordeaux	A	D	0-0		20,000
17	frpr1	Lyon	H	D	1-1	Lucas Pereira 90	7,000
18	frpr1	Nice	A	L	0-3		10,000
19	frpr1	Lille	H	D	0-0		4,000
20	frpr1	Metz	A	L	0-1		13,000
21	frpr1	Bastia	H	W	1-0	Seck 43	8,000
22	frpr1	Rennes	A	L	0-1		21,000
23	frpr1	Toulouse	H	W	1-0	Lucas Pereira 27	3,000
24	frpr1	Istres	H	D	0-0		4,000
25	frpr1	Caen	A	D	2-2	Andre Luiz 10; Lucas Pereira 30	18,000
26	frpr1	Lens	H	D	0-0		3,000
27	frpr1	Strasbourg	A	L	0-1		20,000
28	frpr1	Paris SG	H	W	1-0	Andre Luiz 16 pen	5,000
29	frpr1	St Etienne	A	L	0-3		29,000
30	frpr1	Nantes	A	D	0-0		25,000
31	frpr1	Monaco	H	W	3-0	Edson 32,41; Andre Luiz 45	3,000
32	frpr1	Auxerre	H	W	4-3	Lucas Pereira 1; Ouadah 39,68; Edson 57	7,000
33	frpr1	Marseille	A	W	2-1	Demont 24; Edson 52	50,000
34	frpr1	Bordeaux	H	D	0-0		10,000
35	frpr1	Lyon	A	L	1-2	Demont 51	39,000
36	frpr1	Nice	H	L	0-1		6,000
37	frpr1	Lille	A	W	2-0	Ouadah 10; Robin 70	17,000
38	frpr1	Sochaux	H	W	3-1	Lucas Pereira 12; Ouadah 52; Merlin 87	8,000

MONTHLY POINTS TALLY

AUGUST	1	8%
SEPTEMBER	5	42%
OCTOBER	3	25%
NOVEMBER	5	42%
DECEMBER	2	22%
JANUARY	6	50%
FEBRUARY	3	33%
MARCH	4	33%
APRIL	10	83%
MAY	6	50%

KEY PLAYERS - GOALSCORERS

Lucas Pereira

Goals in the League	11	Player Strike Rate Average number of minutes between League goals scored by player	199
Contribution to Attacking Power Average number of minutes between League team goals while on pitch	84	Club Strike Rate Average number of minutes between League goals scored by club	95

	PLAYER	LGE GOALS	POWER	STRIKE RATE
1	Lucas Pereira	11	84	199 mins
2	Andre Luiz	5	82	444 mins
3	Cyril Chapuis	3	120	482 mins
4	Abdelnasser Ouadah	5	96	612 mins
5	Yohan Demont	2	86	1331 mins

KEY PLAYERS - MIDFIELDERS

Andre Luiz

Goals in the League	5	Contribution to Attacking Power Average number of minutes between League team goals while on pitch	82
Defensive Rating Average number of mins between League goals conceded while on the pitch	117	Scoring Difference Defensive Rating minus Contribution to Attacking Power	35

	PLAYER	LGE GOALS	DEF RATE	POWER	SCORE DIFF
1	Andre Luiz	5	117	82	35 mins
2	Yohan Demont	2	95	86	9 mins
3	Rodrigo	0	87	94	-7 mins
4	Abdelnasser Ouadah	5	87	96	-9 mins
5	Martial Robin	1	92	112	-20 mins

KEY PLAYERS - DEFENDERS

Nenad Dzodic

Goals Conceded Number of League goals conceded while the player was on the pitch	21	Clean Sheets In League games when player was on pitch for at least 70 minutes	11
Defensive Rating Ave number of mins between League goals conceded while on the pitch	105	Club Defensive Rating Average number of mins between League goals conceded by the club this season	88

	PLAYER	CON LGE	CLEAN SHEETS	DEF RATE
1	Nenad Dzodic	21	11	105 mins
2	Xavier Collin	30	9	88 mins
3	Fabien Laurenti	34	11	83 mins
4	Mamadou Seck	28	6	75 mins

KEY GOALKEEPER

Stephane Porato

Goals Conceded in the League	35	Counting Games League games when player was on pitch for at least 70 minutes	35
Defensive Rating Ave number of mins between League goals conceded while on the pitch	90	Clean Sheets In games when player was on pitch for at least 70 minutes	13

LEAGUE GOALS

Lucas Pereira

Minutes on the pitch	2193	Goals in the League	11
League average (mins between goals)	199		

	PLAYER	MINS	GOALS	AVE
1	Lucas Pereira	2193	11	199
2	Andre Luiz	2222	5	444
3	Ouadah	3061	5	612
4	Edson	1239	4	310
5	Chapuis	1446	3	482
6	Marcelinho	769	2	385
7	Demont	2662	2	1331
8	Seck	2110	1	2110
9	Merlin	310	1	310
10	Dzodic	2201	1	2201
11	Robin	2577	1	2577
	Other		0	
	TOTAL		36	

DISCIPLINARY

	PLAYER	YELLOW	RED	AVE
1	Robin	12	1	198
2	Dzodic	9	1	220
3	Gaspar	5	0	227
4	Rodrigo	9	1	321
5	Terrier	3	0	351
6	Seck	4	2	351
7	Chapuis	4	0	361
8	Marcelinho	2	0	384
9	Ouadah	7	0	437
10	Connen	2	0	445
11	Laurenti	6	0	472
12	Collin	5	0	526
13	Andre Luiz	4	0	555
	Other	8	0	
	TOTAL	80	5	

TOP POINT EARNERS

	PLAYER	GAMES	AV PTS
1	Andre Luiz	23	1.48
2	Yohan Demont	29	1.41
3	Nenad Dzodic	24	1.29
4	Stephane Porato	35	1.29
5	Mamadou Seck	22	1.27
6	Abdelnasser Ouadah	34	1.26
7	Xavier Collin	28	1.21
8	Rodrigo	35	1.17
9	Fabien Laurenti	31	1.16
10	Martial Robin	26	1.15
	CLUB AVERAGE:		1.18

LEAGUE APPEARANCES, BOOKINGS AND CAPS

	AGE (on 01/07/05)	IN NAMED 16	APPEARANCES	COUNTING GAMES	MINUTES ON PITCH	YELLOW CARDS	RED CARDS	THIS SEASON	HOME COUNTRY
Goalkeepers									
Florian Lucchini	24	24	0	0	0	0	0	-	France
Stephane Porato	31	35	35	35	3150	1	0	-	France
Stephane Trevisan	31	16	4	4	360	0	0	-	France
Defenders									
Xavier Collin	30	32	31	28	2631	5	0	-	France
C Destruhaut	32	6	3	0	77	0	0	-	France
Nenad Dzodic	28	26	26	24	2201	9	1	-	Serbia & Montenegro
Jose Gaspar	30	25	16	11	1138	5	0	-	Portugal
Fabien Laurenti	22	35	34	31	2836	6	0	-	France
Mamadou Seck	25	30	27	22	2110	4	2	4	Senegal (33)
David Terrier	31	23	17	8	1053	3	0	-	France
Abderaouf Zarabi	26	2	1	0	20	0	0	-	Algeria
Midfielders									
Djamel Abnoun	19	5	2	0	32	0	0	-	France
Andre Luiz	31	28	28	23	2222	4	0	-	Brazil
Yacine Bezzaz	23	19	10	0	148	1	0	-	Algeria
Renaud Connen	25	22	19	6	891	2	0	-	France
Yohan Demont	27	35	32	29	2662	3	0	-	France
Edson	25	29	24	8	1239	1	0	-	Brazil
Azite Franklin	19	1	0	0	0	0	0	-	France
Marcelinho	34	12	11	7	769	2	0	-	Brazil
Laurent Merlin	20	17	11	0	310	1	0	-	France
Abdelnasser Ouadah	29	36	36	34	3061	7	0	-	France
Martial Robin	27	36	33	26	2577	12	1	-	France
Rodrigo	24	36	36	35	3212	9	1	-	Brazil
Forwards									
Nicolas Bonnal	28	17	16	6	845	1	0	-	France
Cyril Chapuis	26	23	22	13	1446	4	0	-	France
Olivier Fauconnier	29	4	4	3	288	1	0	-	France
Lucas Pereira	23	34	33	17	2193	2	0	-	Brazil
Mickael Marquet	23	1	0	0	0	0	0	-	France

TEAM OF THE SEASON

G – Stephane Porato CG: 35 DR: 90

D – Nenad Dzodic CG: 24 DR: 105
D – Xavier Collin CG: 28 DR: 88
D – Fabien Laurenti CG: 31 DR: 83
D – Mamadou Seck CG: 22 DR: 75

M – Andre Luiz CG: 23 SD: 35
M – Yohan Demont CG: 29 SD: 9
M – Rodrigo CG: 35 SD: -7
M – Abdelnasser Ouadah CG: 34 SD: -9

F – Lucas Pereira CG: 17 SR: 199
F – Cyril Chapuis CG: 13 SR: 482

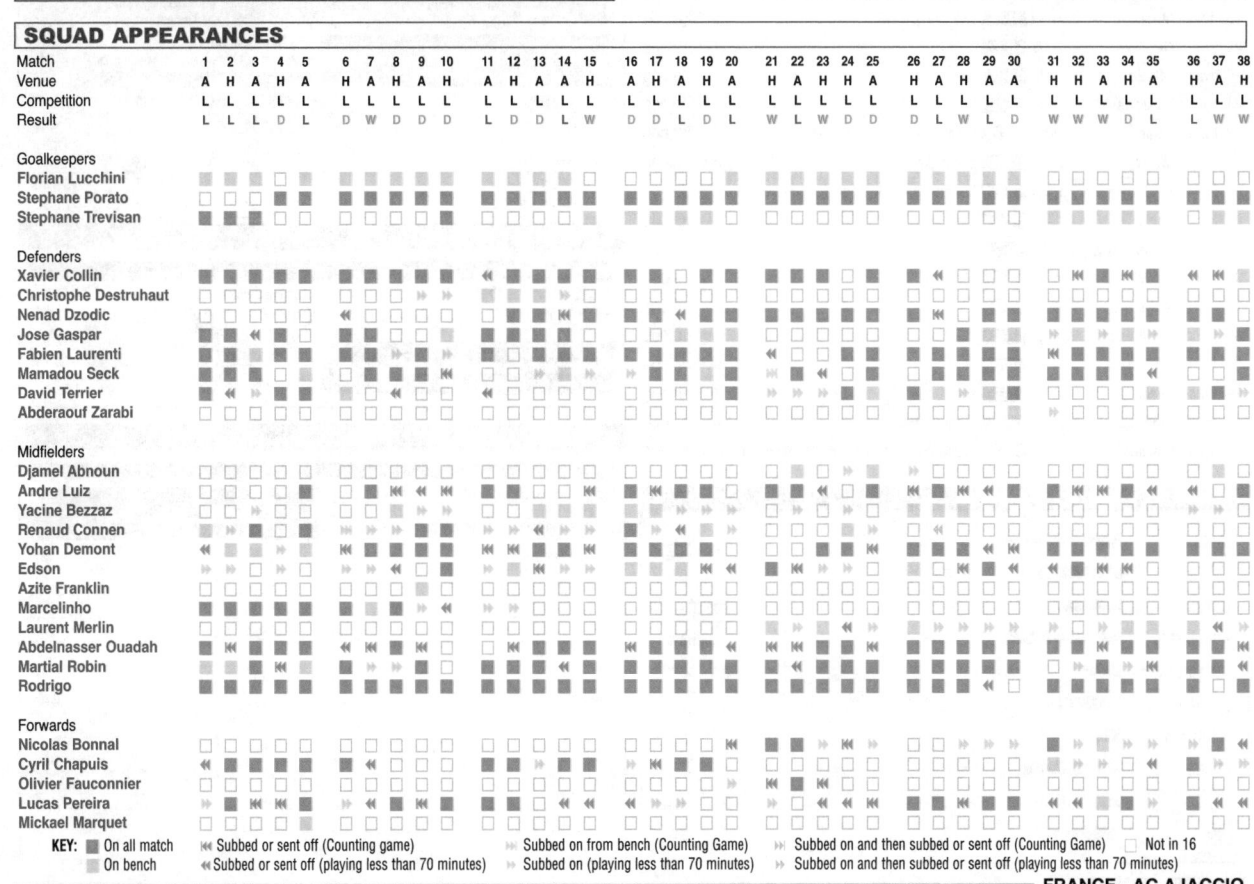

SQUAD APPEARANCES

Match	1	2	3	4	5	6	7	8	9	10	11	12	13	14	15	16	17	18	19	20	21	22	23	24	25	26	27	28	29	30	31	32	33	34	35	36	37	38
Venue	A	H	A	H	A	H	A	H	A	H	A	H	A	A	H	A	H	A	H	A	H	A	H	H	A	H	A	H	A	A	H	H	A	H	A	H	A	H
Competition	L	L	L	L	L	L	L	L	L	L	L	L	L	L	L	L	L	L	L	L	L	L	L	L	L	L	L	L	L	L	L	L	L	L	L	L	L	L
Result	L	L	L	D	L	D	W	D	D	D	L	D	D	L	W	D	D	L	D	L	W	L	W	D	D	D	L	W	L	D	W	W	W	D	L	L	W	W

Goalkeepers
Florian Lucchini
Stephane Porato
Stephane Trevisan

Defenders
Xavier Collin
Christophe Destruhaut
Nenad Dzodic
Jose Gaspar
Fabien Laurenti
Mamadou Seck
David Terrier
Abderaouf Zarabi

Midfielders
Djamel Abnoun
Andre Luiz
Yacine Bezzaz
Renaud Connen
Yohan Demont
Edson
Azite Franklin
Marcelinho
Laurent Merlin
Abdelnasser Ouadah
Martial Robin
Rodrigo

Forwards
Nicolas Bonnal
Cyril Chapuis
Olivier Fauconnier
Lucas Pereira
Mickael Marquet

KEY: On all match / On bench
Subbed or sent off (Counting game)
Subbed or sent off (playing less than 70 minutes)
Subbed on from bench (Counting Game)
Subbed on (playing less than 70 minutes)
Subbed on and then subbed or sent off (Counting Game)
Subbed on and then subbed or sent off (playing less than 70 minutes)
Not in 16

BORDEAUX

Final Position: **15th**

KEY: Won Drawn Lost

							Attendance
1	frpr1	**Marseille**	A	L	0-1		60,000
2	frpr1	**Nice**	H	W	5-1	Gregorini 15 og; Chamakh 23,55,71; Laslandes 88	29,000
3	frpr1	**Lille**	A	D	0-0		11,000
4	frpr1	**Sochaux**	H	W	2-0	Rool 38; Laslandes 86	22,000
5	frpr1	**Metz**	A	D	0-0		25,000
6	frpr1	**Rennes**	H	D	0-0		28,000
7	frpr1	**Bastia**	A	W	4-1	Laslandes 32,38; Faubert 39; Chamakh 82	10,000
8	frpr1	**Toulouse**	H	D	1-1	Chamakh 60	20,000
9	frpr1	**Caen**	A	D	1-1	Meriem 59	20,000
10	frpr1	**Istres**	H	D	2-2	Riera 38; Meriem 54	18,000
11	frpr1	**St Etienne**	A	D	0-0		35,000
12	frpr1	**Lens**	H	D	1-1	Meriem 67	23,000
13	frpr1	**Strasbourg**	A	L	0-1		8,000
14	frpr1	**Paris SG**	H	W	3-0	Pichot 6 og; Laslandes 47; Rool 75	32,000
15	frpr1	**Nantes**	A	W	1-0	Meriem 25	34,000
16	frpr1	**AC Ajaccio**	H	D	0-0		20,000
17	frpr1	**Auxerre**	A	D	0-0		14,000
18	frpr1	**Lyon**	H	D	0-0		33,000
19	frpr1	**Monaco**	A	D	1-1	Darcheville 8	9,000
20	frpr1	**Nice**	A	D	3-3	Cid 45; Francia 55; Chamakh 63	12,000
21	frpr1	**Lille**	H	L	1-3	Chamakh 84	20,000
22	frpr1	**Sochaux**	A	L	0-4		15,000
23	frpr1	**Metz**	H	W	1-0	Darcheville 68	10,000
24	frpr1	**Rennes**	A	L	0-2		15,000
25	frpr1	**Bastia**	H	D	0-0		15,000
26	frpr1	**Toulouse**	A	L	0-1		23,000
27	frpr1	**Caen**	H	D	2-2	Chamakh 22; Darcheville 57	17,000
28	frpr1	**Istres**	A	W	1-0	Uche 78	5,000
29	frpr1	**St Etienne**	H	W	2-0	Darcheville 15; Chamakh 89	32,000
30	frpr1	**Lens**	A	L	0-2		32,000
31	frpr1	**Strasbourg**	H	L	0-2		21,000
32	frpr1	**Paris SG**	A	D	1-1	Meriem 71 pen	41,000
33	frpr1	**Nantes**	H	L	0-2		20,000
34	frpr1	**AC Ajaccio**	A	D	0-0		10,000
35	frpr1	**Auxerre**	H	D	0-0		30,000
36	frpr1	**Lyon**	A	L	1-5	Riera 10	38,000
37	frpr1	**Monaco**	H	D	1-1	Chamakh 79	22,000
38	frpr1	**Marseille**	H	D	3-3	Laslandes 16; Meriem 65; Francia 85	34,000

MONTHLY POINTS TALLY

AUGUST	7	58%
SEPTEMBER	6	50%
OCTOBER	4	33%
NOVEMBER	7	58%
DECEMBER	3	33%
JANUARY	4	27%
FEBRUARY	2	22%
MARCH	6	67%
APRIL	2	17%
MAY	3	25%

KEY PLAYERS - GOALSCORERS

Lilian Laslandes

Goals in the League	6	Player Strike Rate Average number of minutes between League goals scored by player	241
Contribution to Attacking Power Average number of minutes between League team goals while on pitch	53	Club Strike Rate Average number of minutes between League goals scored by club	92

	PLAYER	LGE GOALS	POWER	STRIKE RATE
1	Lilian Laslandes	6	53	241 mins
2	Maromane Chamakh	9	90	262 mins
3	Jean-Claude Darcheville	4	190	334 mins
4	Camel Meriem	6	100	451 mins
5	Albert Riera	2	100	701 mins

KEY PLAYERS - MIDFIELDERS

Cyril Rool

Goals in the League	2	Contribution to Attacking Power Average number of minutes between League team goals while on pitch	103
Defensive Rating Average number of mins between League goals conceded while on the pitch	133	Scoring Difference Defensive Rating minus Contribution to Attacking Power	30

	PLAYER	LGE GOALS	DEF RATE	POWER	SCORE DIFF
1	Cyril Rool	2	133	103	30 mins
2	Juan-Pablo Francia	2	92	80	12 mins
3	Rio Mavuba	0	83	92	-9 mins
4	Camel Meriem	6	87	100	-13 mins
5	Albert Riera	2	67	100	-33 mins

KEY PLAYERS - DEFENDERS

David Jemmali

Goals Conceded Number of League goals conceded while the player was on the pitch	18	Clean Sheets In League games when player was on pitch for at least 70 minutes	11
Defensive Rating Ave number of mins between League goals conceded while on the pitch	115	Club Defensive Rating Average number of mins between League goals conceded by the club this season	81

	PLAYER	CON LGE	CLEAN SHEETS	DEF RATE
1	David Jemmali	18	11	115 mins
2	Franck Jurietti	27	14	100 mins
3	Marc Planus	31	15	99 mins
4	Michalis Kapsis	33	12	78 mins
5	Julien Faubert	32	8	72 mins

KEY GOALKEEPER

Ulrich Rame

Goals Conceded in the League	38	Counting Games League games when player was on pitch for at least 70 minutes	37
Defensive Rating Ave number of mins between League goals conceded while on the pitch	88	Clean Sheets In games when player was on pitch for at least 70 minutes	16

LEAGUE GOALS

Maromane Chamakh

Minutes on the pitch	2360	Goals in the League	9
League average (mins between goals)	262		

	PLAYER	MINS	GOALS	AVE
1	Chamakh	2360	9	262
2	Meriem	2704	6	451
3	Laslandes	1443	6	241
4	Darcheville	1335	4	334
5	Riera	1401	2	701
6	Francia	2403	2	1202
7	Rool	2261	2	1131
8	Cid	581	1	581
9	Faubert	2318	1	2318
10	Uche	853	1	853
	Other		3	
	TOTAL		37	

DISCIPLINARY RECORDS

	PLAYER	YELLOW	RED	AVE
1	Rool	10	3	173
2	Jemmali	9	1	206
3	Cid	2	0	290
4	Jurietti	8	0	337
5	Chamakh	6	1	337
6	Cohade	3	0	341
7	Laslandes	3	1	360
8	Faubert	5	0	463
9	Riera	3	0	467
10	Planus	5	0	612
11	Darcheville	2	0	667
12	Meriem	4	0	676
13	Uche	0	1	853
	Other	8	0	
	TOTAL	68	7	

TOP POINT EARNERS

	PLAYER	GAMES	AV PTS
1	Juan-Pablo Francia	22	1.41
2	Maromane Chamakh	23	1.39
3	Franck Jurietti	30	1.30
4	Cyril Rool	24	1.29
5	Lilian Laslandes	16	1.25
6	Marc Planus	34	1.24
7	David Jemmali	21	1.24
8	Michalis Kapsis	28	1.21
9	Julien Faubert	21	1.19
10	Ulrich Rame	37	1.16
	CLUB AVERAGE:		1.16

LEAGUE APPEARANCES, BOOKINGS AND CAPS

	AGE (on 01/07/05)	IN NAMED 16	APPEARANCES	COUNTING GAMES	MINUTES ON PITCH	YELLOW CARDS	RED CARDS	THIS SEASON	HOME COUNTRY
Goalkeepers									
Ulrich Rame	32	37	37	37	3330	2	0	-	France
Frederick Roux	32	30	1	1	90	1	1	-	France
Mathieu Valverde	22	9	1	0	1	0	0	-	France
Defenders									
Kodjo Afanou	27	17	11	8	813	0	0	-	France
Bruno Basto	27	1	1	0	19	0	0	-	Portugal
Gerald Cid	22	20	8	6	581	2	0	-	France
Julien Faubert	21	36	36	21	2318	5	0	-	France
David Jemmali	30	26	26	21	2062	9	1	-	France
Franck Jurietti	30	30	30	30	2700	8	0	-	France
Michalis Kapsis	31	29	29	28	2587	2	0	-	Greece
Florian Marange	19	8	5	5	450	1	0	-	France
Marc Planus	23	34	34	34	3060	5	0	-	France
Midfielders									
Renaud Cohade	20	30	20	9	1023	3	0	-	France
Juan-Pablo Francia	20	37	35	22	2403	1	0	-	Argentina
Ted Lavie	19	2	0	0	0	0	0	-	France
Rio Mavuba	21	38	38	38	3420	3	0	4	France (4)
Camel Meriem	25	32	32	29	2704	4	0	-	France
Albert Riera	23	21	21	15	1401	3	0	-	Spain
Cyril Rool	30	30	28	24	2261	10	3	-	France
Forwards									
Herve Bugnet	23	16	6	0	100	0	0	-	France
Maromane Chamakh	21	33	32	23	2360	6	1	-	Morocco
Jean Darcheville	29	23	21	13	1335	2	0	-	France
Alexei Kossonogov	23	2	0	0	0	0	0	-	Russia
Lilian Laslandes	33	22	21	16	1443	3	1	-	France
Thiago	19	16	7	0	73	0	0	-	Brazil
Kalu Uche	22	31	24	6	853	0	1	-	Nigeria

TEAM OF THE SEASON

D
David Jemmali
CG: 21 DR: 115
M
Cyril Rool
CG: 24 SD: 30
D
Franck Jurietti
CG: 30 DR: 100
M
Juan-Pablo Francia
CG: 22 SD: 12
F
Lilian Laslandes
CG: 16 SR: 241
G
Ulrich Rame
CG: 37 DR: 88
D
Marc Planus
CG: 34 DR: 99
M
Rio Mavuba
CG: 38 SD: -9
F
M Chamakh
CG: 23 SR: 262
D
Michalis Kapsis
CG: 28 DR: 78
M
Camel Meriem
CG: 29 SD: -13

SQUAD APPEARANCES

Match	1	2	3	4	5	6	7	8	9	10	11	12	13	14	15	16	17	18	19	20	21	22	23	24	25	26	27	28	29	30	31	32	33	34	35	36	37	38
Venue	A	H	A	H	A	H	A	H	A	H	A	H	A	H	A	H	A	H	A	A	H	A	H	A	H	A	H	A	H	A	H	A	H	A	H	A	H	H
Competition	L	L	L	L	L	L	L	L	L	L	L	L	L	L	L	L	L	L	L	L	L	L	L	L	L	L	L	L	L	L	L	L	L	L	L	L	L	L
Result	L	W	D	W	D	D	W	D	D	D	D	D	L	W	W	D	D	D	D	D	L	L	W	L	D	L	D	W	W	L	L	D	L	D	D	L	D	D

Goalkeepers
Ulrich Rame
Frederick Roux
Mathieu Valverde

Defenders
Kodjo Afanou
Bruno Basto
Gerald Cid
Julien Faubert
David Jemmali
Franck Jurietti
Michalis Kapsis
Florian Marange
Marc Planus

Midfielders
Renaud Cohade
Juan-Pablo Francia
Ted Lavie
Rio Mavuba
Camel Meriem
Albert Riera
Cyril Rool

Forwards
Herve Bugnet
Maromane Chamakh
Jean-Claude Darcheville
Alexei Kossonogov
Lilian Laslandes
Thiago
Kalu Uche

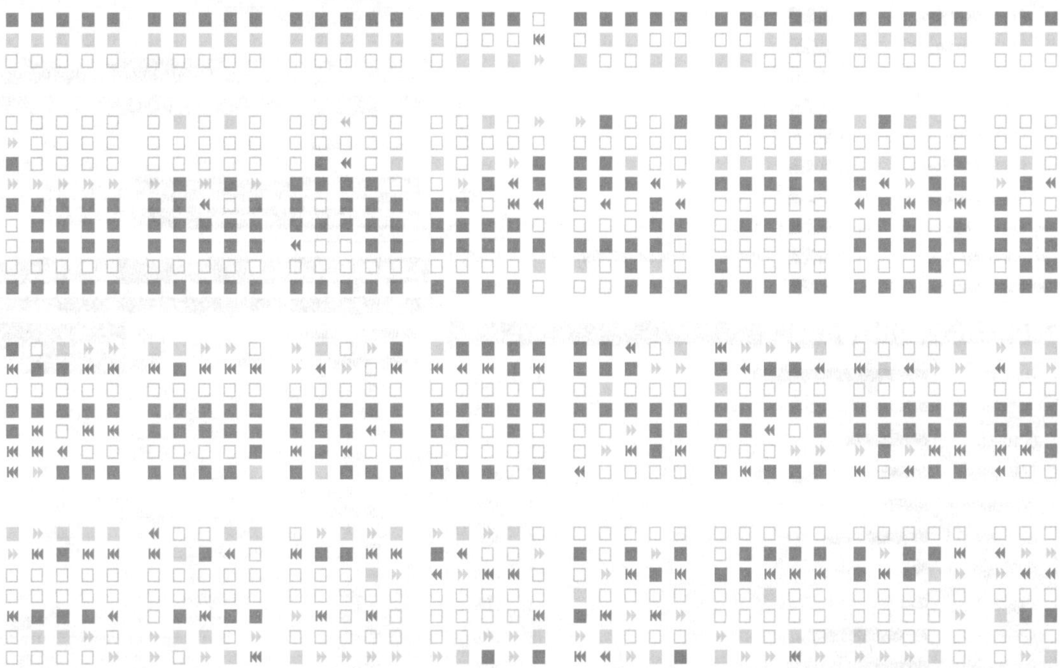

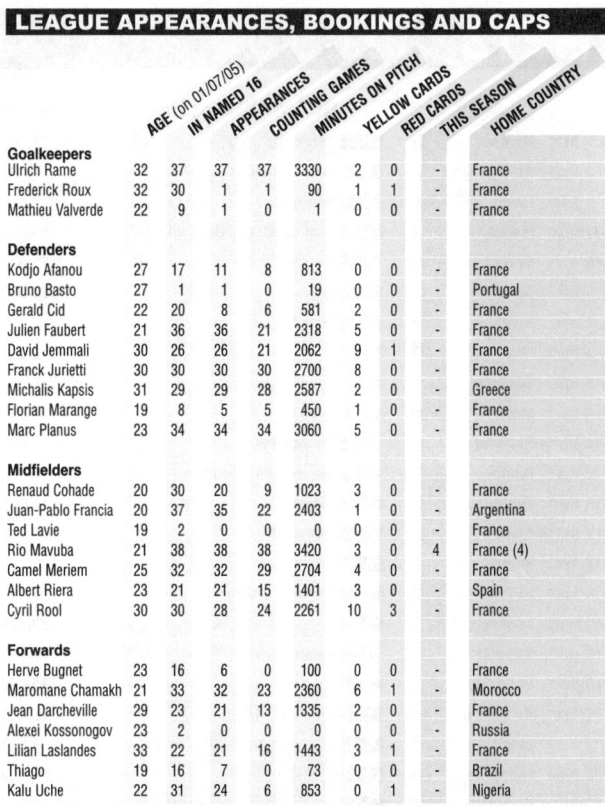

KEY: On all match · On bench · Subbed or sent off (Counting game) · Subbed or sent off (playing less than 70 minutes) · Subbed on from bench (Counting Game) · Subbed on (playing less than 70 minutes) · Subbed on and then subbed or sent off (Counting Game) · Subbed on and then subbed or sent off (playing less than 70 minutes) · Not in 16

METZ

Final Position: **16th**

KEY: Won Drawn Lost

							Attendance
1	frpr1	**Nantes**	H	W	1-0	Socrier 86	21,000
2	frpr1	**AC Ajaccio**	A	W	2-1	Tum 6; Gueye 50	7,000
3	frpr1	**Lyon**	H	D	1-1	Ribery 30	24,000
4	frpr1	**Marseille**	A	W	3-1	Tum 12,90; Signorino 89	60,000
5	frpr1	**Bordeaux**	H	D	0-0		25,000
6	frpr1	**Auxerre**	A	L	0-4		10,000
7	frpr1	**Nice**	H	D	1-1	Tum 78	16,000
8	frpr1	**Lille**	A	L	0-4		12,000
9	frpr1	**Sochaux**	H	D	0-0		15,000
10	frpr1	**Monaco**	H	D	1-1	Djiba 83	24,000
11	frpr1	**Rennes**	A	L	1-3	Borbiconi 20	29,000
12	frpr1	**Bastia**	H	W	2-0	Renouard 4; Leca 6	12,000
13	frpr1	**Toulouse**	A	D	1-1	Ribery 82	15,000
14	frpr1	**Caen**	H	L	1-2	Gueye 39	14,000
15	frpr1	**Istres**	A	D	0-0		5,000
16	frpr1	**St Etienne**	H	D	2-2	Meniri 6; Proment 21	12,000
17	frpr1	**Lens**	A	L	0-2		32,000
18	frpr1	**Strasbourg**	H	W	1-0	Renouard 41	24,000
19	frpr1	**Paris SG**	A	L	0-3		35,000
20	frpr1	**AC Ajaccio**	H	W	1-0	Proment 85	13,000
21	frpr1	**Lyon**	A	L	0-2		38,000
22	frpr1	**Marseille**	H	L	0-1		26,000
23	frpr1	**Bordeaux**	A	L	0-1		10,000
24	frpr1	**Auxerre**	H	W	3-0	Gueye 51; Tum 59,62	8,000
25	frpr1	**Nice**	A	D	1-1	Proment 68	7,000
26	frpr1	**Lille**	H	D	1-1	Obraniak 50 pen	15,000
27	frpr1	**Monaco**	A	D	0-0		8,000
28	frpr1	**Rennes**	H	D	1-1	Borbiconi 22	14,000
29	frpr1	**Sochaux**	A	L	1-2	Proment 16 pen	13,000
30	frpr1	**Bastia**	A	L	0-1		5,000
31	frpr1	**Toulouse**	H	L	0-1		16,000
32	frpr1	**Caen**	A	W	1-0	Ogbeche 53	20,000
33	frpr1	**Istres**	H	W	2-1	Tum 6,90	18,000
34	frpr1	**St Etienne**	A	D	0-0		33,000
35	frpr1	**Lens**	H	D	1-1	Socrier 10	20,000
36	frpr1	**Strasbourg**	A	L	1-3	Leca 35	24,000
37	frpr1	**Paris SG**	H	W	3-2	Signorino 7; Obraniak 26; Tum 72	24,000
38	frpr1	**Nantes**	A	L	0-1		36,000

MONTHLY POINTS TALLY

AUGUST	10	83%
SEPTEMBER	2	17%
OCTOBER	5	42%
NOVEMBER	3	25%
DECEMBER	3	33%
JANUARY	6	40%
FEBRUARY	2	33%
MARCH	2	17%
APRIL	7	58%
MAY	4	33%

KEY PLAYERS - GOALSCORERS

Herve Tum

Goals in the League	9	Player Strike Rate Average number of minutes between League goals scored by player	285
Contribution to Attacking Power Average number of minutes between League team goals while on pitch	102	Club Strike Rate Average number of minutes between League goals scored by club	104

	PLAYER	LGE GOALS	POWER	STRIKE RATE
1	Herve Tum	9	102	285 mins
2	Gregory Proment	4	105	500 mins
3	Babacar Gueye	3	94	723 mins
4	Franck Ribery	2	95	853 mins
5	Sebastien Renouard	2	99	943 mins

KEY PLAYERS - MIDFIELDERS

Ludovic Obraniak

Goals in the League	2	Contribution to Attacking Power Average number of minutes between League team goals while on pitch	91
Defensive Rating Average number of mins between League goals conceded while on the pitch	84	Scoring Difference Defensive Rating minus Contribution to Attacking Power	-7

	PLAYER	LGE GOALS	DEF RATE	POWER	SCORE DIFF
1	Ludovic Obraniak	2	84	91	-7 mins
2	Sebastien Renouard	2	79	99	-20 mins
3	Gregory Proment	4	80	105	-25 mins
4	Franck Ribery	2	66	95	-29 mins
5	Gregory Leca	2	74	120	-46 mins

KEY PLAYERS - DEFENDERS

Mehdi Meniri

Goals Conceded Number of League goals conceded while the player was on the pitch	33	Clean Sheets In League games when player was on pitch for at least 70 minutes	8
Defensive Rating Ave number of mins between League goals conceded while on the pitch	81	Club Defensive Rating Average number of mins between League goals conceded by the club this season	74

	PLAYER	CON LGE	CLEAN SHEETS	DEF RATE
1	Mehdi Meniri	33	8	81 mins
2	Stephane Borbiconi	37	8	80 mins
3	Franck Signorino	42	9	76 mins
4	Jean-Philippe Caillet	25	5	75 mins
5	Bruno Pompiere	25	5	69 mins

KEY GOALKEEPER

Gregory Wimbee

Goals Conceded in the League	43	Counting Games League games when player was on pitch for at least 70 minutes	37
Defensive Rating Ave number of mins between League goals conceded while on the pitch	77	Clean Sheets In games when player was on pitch for at least 70 minutes	10

LEAGUE GOALS

Herve Tum

Minutes on the pitch	2569	Goals in the League	9
League average (mins between goals)	285		

	PLAYER	MINS	GOALS	AVE
1	Tum	2569	9	285
2	Proment	2000	4	500
3	Gueye	2170	3	723
4	Renouard	1886	2	943
5	Signorino	3199	2	1600
6	Obraniak	2004	2	1002
7	Socrier	759	2	380
8	Ribery	1705	2	853
9	Leca	2753	2	1377
10	Borbiconi	2970	2	1485
11	Meniri	2685	1	2685
12	Djiba	761	1	761
13	Ogbeche	898	1	898
	Other		0	
	TOTAL		33	

DISCIPLINARY RECORDS

	PLAYER	YELLOW	RED	AVE
1	Gvozdenovic	2	0	240
2	Avezac	4	0	241
3	Djiba	3	0	253
4	Renouard	5	0	377
5	Signorino	7	1	399
6	Pompiere	4	0	430
7	Caillet	4	0	469
8	Contout	1	0	473
9	Proment	4	0	500
10	Obraniak	4	0	501
11	Tum	5	0	513
12	Leca	5	0	550
13	Beria	1	0	630
	Other	10	0	
	TOTAL	59	1	

TOP POINT EARNERS

	PLAYER	GAMES	AV PTS
1	Ludovic Obraniak	19	1.42
2	Franck Ribery	19	1.37
3	Babacar Gueye	21	1.24
4	Bruno Pompiere	19	1.21
5	Mehdi Meniri	30	1.20
6	Franck Signorino	35	1.20
7	Herve Tum	28	1.18
8	Gregory Leca	29	1.17
9	Gregory Wimbee	37	1.16
10	Jean-Philippe Caillet	20	1.15
	CLUB AVERAGE:		1.16

TEAM OF THE SEASON

D
Mehdi Meniri
CG: 30 DR: 81
M
Ludovic Obraniak
CG: 19 SD: -7
D
Stephane Borbiconi
CG: 33 DR: 80
M
Sebastien Renouard
CG: 15 SD: -20
F
Herve Tum
CG: 28 SR: 285
G
Gregory Wimbee
CG: 37 DR: 77
D
Franck Signorino
CG: 35 DR: 76
M
Gregory Proment
CG: 21 SD: -25
F
Babacar Gueye
CG: 21 SR: 723
D
Jean-Philippe Caillet
CG: 20 DR: 75
M
Franck Ribery
CG: 19 SD: -29

LEAGUE APPEARANCES, BOOKINGS AND CAPS

	AGE (on 01/07/05)	IN NAMED 16	APPEARANCES	COUNTING GAMES	MINUTES ON PITCH	YELLOW CARDS	RED CARDS	THIS SEASON	HOME COUNTRY
Goalkeepers									
Kossi Agassa	27	34	1	1	90	0	0	-	Togo
Ludovic Butelle	22	1	1	1	90	0	0	-	France
Guillaume Cherreau	22	2	0	0	0	0	0	-	France
Joslain Mayebi	18	2	0	0	0	0	0	-	Cameroon
Gregory Wimbee	33	38	37	37	3330	0	0	-	France
Defenders									
Samuel Allegro	27	20	9	5	634	0	0	-	France
Frank Beria	22	7	7	7	630	1	0	-	France
Stephane Borbiconi	26	34	33	33	2970	1	0	-	France
Jean-Philippe Caillet	28	24	22	20	1878	4	0	-	France
Ivan Gvozdenovic	26	6	6	5	480	2	0	-	Serbia & Montenegro
Mehdi Meniri	28	30	30	30	2685	4	0	-	France
Bruno Pompiere	25	24	21	19	1720	4	0	-	France
Franck Signorino	23	36	36	35	3199	7	1	-	France
Midfielders									
Dino Djiba	19	14	10	7	761	3	0	-	Senegal
Julien Gorius	20	1	1	0	21	0	0	-	France
Gregory Leca	24	35	34	29	2753	5	0	-	France
Hemza Mihoubi	19	3	2	1	127	0	0	-	France
Benjamin Nicaise	24	21	13	3	439	2	0	-	France
Ludovic Obraniak	20	36	30	19	2004	4	0	-	France
Gregory Proment	26	24	24	21	2000	4	0	-	France
Sebastien Renouard	21	27	27	15	1886	5	0	-	France
Franck Ribery	22	20	20	19	1705	1	0	-	France
Venn Toure	21	2	1	0	65	2	1	-	France
Forwards									
Christophe Avezac	28	28	24	4	967	4	0	-	France
Roy Contout	20	23	19	1	473	1	0	-	France
Babacar Gueye	19	33	32	21	2170	3	0	5	Senegal (33)
Momar N'Diaye	17	9	3	0	64	0	0	-	Senegal
B Ogbeche	20	12	12	8	898	1	0	-	Nigeria
Rouslan Pimenov	23	5	3	2	228	2	0	-	Russia
Richard Socrier	26	28	22	6	759	0	0	-	France
Herve Tum	26	31	31	28	2569	5	0	2	Cameroon (26)

SQUAD APPEARANCES

Match	1	2	3	4	5	6	7	8	9	10	11	12	13	14	15	16	17	18	19	20	21	22	23	24	25	26	27	28	29	30	31	32	33	34	35	36	37	38
Venue	H	A	H	A	H	A	H	A	H	H	A	H	A	H	A	H	A	H	A	H	A	H	A	H	A	H	A	H	A	A	H	A	H	A	H	A	H	A
Competition	L	L	L	L	L	L	L	L	L	L	L	L	L	L	L	L	L	L	L	L	L	L	L	L	L	L	L	L	L	L	L	L	L	L	L	L	L	L
Result	W	W	D	W	D	L	D	L	D	D	L	W	D	L	D	D	L	W	L	W	L	L	L	W	D	D	D	D	L	L	L	W	W	D	D	L	W	L

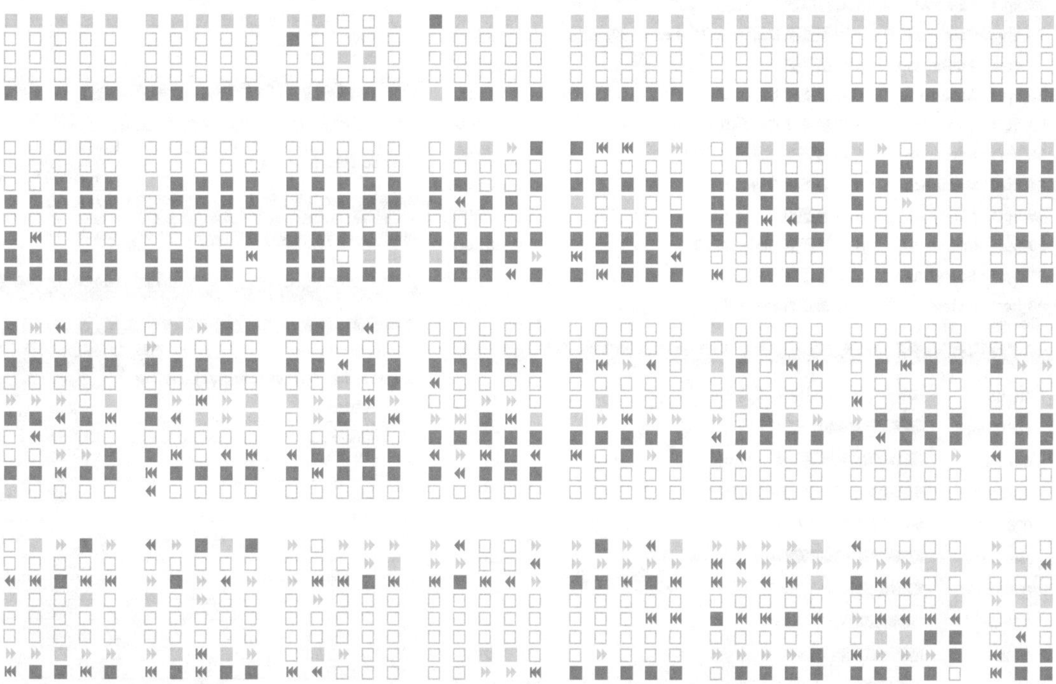

Goalkeepers
Kossi Agassa
Ludovic Butelle
Guillaume Cherreau
Joslain Mayebi
Gregory Wimbee
Defenders
Samuel Allegro
Frank Beria
Stephane Borbiconi
Jean-Philippe Caillet
Ivan Gvozdenovic
Mehdi Meniri
Bruno Pompiere
Franck Signorino
Midfielders
Dino Djiba
Julien Gorius
Gregory Leca
Hemza Mihoubi
Benjamin Nicaise
Ludovic Obraniak
Gregory Proment
Sebastien Renouard
Franck Ribery
Venn Toure
Forwards
Christophe Avezac
Roy Contout
Babacar Gueye
Momar N'Diaye
Bartholomew Ogbeche
Rouslan Pimenov
Richard Socrier
Herve Tum

KEY: On all match | On bench | Subbed or sent off (Counting game) | Subbed or sent off (playing less than 70 minutes) | Subbed on from bench (Counting Game) | Subbed on (playing less than 70 minutes) | Subbed on and then subbed or sent off (Counting Game) | Subbed on and then subbed or sent off (playing less than 70 minutes) | Not in 16

NANTES

Final Position: **17th**

KEY: ☐ Won ☐ Drawn ☐ Lost

							Attendance
1	frpr1	**Metz**	A	L	0-1		21,000
2	frpr1	**Bastia**	H	D	1-1	Ahamada 48	30,000
3	frpr1	**Rennes**	A	L	0-1		24,000
4	frpr1	**Toulouse**	H	D	2-2	Bagayoko 33; Savinaud 83	30,000
5	frpr1	**St Etienne**	A	D	0-0		30,000
6	frpr1	**Istres**	H	W	1-0	Savinaud 54	25,000
7	frpr1	**Monaco**	A	L	1-2	Bratu 44	5,000
8	frpr1	**Lens**	H	W	1-0	Pujol 59	15,000
9	frpr1	**Strasbourg**	A	W	2-0	Bagayoko 34; Toulalan 90	15,000
10	frpr1	**Paris SG**	H	W	1-0	Savinaud 85	32,000
11	frpr1	**Caen**	A	L	1-2	Bratu 6	21,000
12	frpr1	**AC Ajaccio**	A	D	1-1	Bagayoko 30	4,000
13	frpr1	**Auxerre**	H	D	1-1	Bagayoko 44	27,000
14	frpr1	**Lyon**	A	L	0-2		36,000
15	frpr1	**Bordeaux**	H	L	0-1		34,000
16	frpr1	**Marseille**	A	L	1-3	Yapi Yapo 58	50,000
17	frpr1	**Nice**	H	L	0-1		29,000
18	frpr1	**Lille**	A	L	1-2	N'Zigou 32	10,000
19	frpr1	**Sochaux**	H	D	2-2	Savinaud 19; Fae 86	20,000
20	frpr1	**Bastia**	A	D	0-0		3,000
21	frpr1	**Rennes**	H	W	2-0	Keseru 30; Savinaud 62 pen	29,000
22	frpr1	**Toulouse**	A	L	1-2	Diallo 15	23,000
23	frpr1	**St Etienne**	H	D	0-0		30,000
24	frpr1	**Istres**	A	W	1-0	Ca 83	8,000
25	frpr1	**Monaco**	H	D	0-0		33,000
26	frpr1	**Lens**	A	L	0-2		32,000
27	frpr1	**Strasbourg**	H	W	2-1	Keseru 45; Quint 54	25,000
28	frpr1	**Paris SG**	A	L	0-1		35,000
29	frpr1	**Caen**	H	W	2-0	Bagayoko 12; Keseru 90	28,000
30	frpr1	**AC Ajaccio**	H	D	0-0		25,000
31	frpr1	**Auxerre**	A	L	1-2	Diallo 50	10,000
32	frpr1	**Lyon**	H	D	2-2	Cetto 45; Bagayoko 64	32,000
33	frpr1	**Bordeaux**	A	W	2-0	Diallo 17; Bagayoko 90	20,000
34	frpr1	**Marseille**	H	D	2-2	Quint 28,46	37,000
35	frpr1	**Nice**	A	D	0-0		15,000
36	frpr1	**Lille**	H	L	1-3	Savinaud 20	31,000
37	frpr1	**Sochaux**	A	L	0-1		19,000
38	frpr1	**Metz**	H	W	1-0	Diallo 40	36,000

MONTHLY POINTS TALLY

AUGUST	2	17%
SEPTEMBER	7	58%
OCTOBER	7	58%
NOVEMBER	1	8%
DECEMBER	1	11%
JANUARY	8	53%
FEBRUARY	4	44%
MARCH	4	44%
APRIL	5	42%
MAY	4	33%

KEY PLAYERS - GOALSCORERS

Mamadou Bagayoko

Goals in the League 7

Player Strike Rate Average number of minutes between League goals scored by player 309

Contribution to Attacking Power Average number of minutes between League team goals while on pitch 98

Club Strike Rate Average number of minutes between League goals scored by club 104

	PLAYER	LGE GOALS	POWER	STRIKE RATE
1	Mamadou Bagayoko	7	98	309 mins
2	Mohamed Diallo	4	94	331 mins
3	Nicolas Savinaud	6	105	526 mins
4	Olivier Quint	3	108	539 mins
5	Emerse Fae	1	114	1832 mins

KEY PLAYERS - MIDFIELDERS

Olivier Quint

Goals in the League 3

Contribution to Attacking Power Average number of minutes between League team goals while on pitch 108

Defensive Rating Average number of mins between League goals conceded while on the pitch 124

Scoring Difference Defensive Rating minus Contribution to Attacking Power 16

	PLAYER	LGE GOALS	DEF RATE	POWER	SCORE DIFF
1	Olivier Quint	3	124	108	16 mins
2	Mohamed Diallo	4	102	94	8 mins
3	Loic Guillon	0	87	87	0 mins
4	Jeremy Toulalan	1	87	104	-17 mins

KEY PLAYERS - DEFENDERS

Pascal Delhommeau

Goals Conceded Number of League goals conceded while the player was on the pitch 21

Clean Sheets In League games when player was on pitch for at least 70 minutes 10

Defensive Rating Ave number of mins between League goals conceded while on the pitch 99

Club Defensive Rating Average number of mins between League goals conceded by the club this season 90

	PLAYER	CON LGE	CLEAN SHEETS	DEF RATE
1	Pascal Delhommeau	21	10	99 mins
2	Nicolas Savinaud	33	14	96 mins
3	Alexander Viveros	24	13	95 mins
4	Mauro Cetto	26	11	87 mins
5	Emerse Fae	23	6	80 mins

KEY GOALKEEPER

Mickael Landreau

Goals Conceded in the League 37

Counting Games League games when player was on pitch for at least 70 minutes 37

Defensive Rating Ave number of mins between League goals conceded while on the pitch 90

Clean Sheets In games when player was on pitch for at least 70 minutes 15

LEAGUE GOALS

Mamadou Bagayoko

Minutes on the pitch 2160

League average (mins between goals) 309

Goals in the League 7

	PLAYER	MINS	GOALS	AVE
1	Bagayoko	2160	7	309
2	Savinaud	3158	6	526
3	Diallo	1322	4	331
4	Quint	1618	3	539
5	Keseru	545	3	182
6	Bratu	559	2	280
7	Cetto	2265	1	2265
8	Yapi Yapo	2892	1	2892
9	Toulalan	2704	1	2704
10	Fae	1832	1	1832
11	N'Zigou	352	1	352
12	Pujol	1041	1	1041
13	Ahamada	565	1	565
	Other		1	
	TOTAL		33	

DISCIPLINARY RECORDS

	PLAYER	YELLOW	RED	AVE
1	Capoue	3	0	221
2	Fae	5	2	261
3	Yapi Yapo	9	1	289
4	Caceres	3	0	315
5	Toulalan	8	0	338
6	Viveros	5	1	379
7	Bagayoko	5	0	432
8	Stinat	1	0	535
9	Ahamada	1	0	565
10	Cetto	4	0	566
11	Da Rocha	4	0	569
12	Guillon	3	0	727
13	Quint	2	0	809
	Other	4	1	
	TOTAL	57	5	

TOP POINT EARNERS

	PLAYER	GAMES	AV PTS
1	Mohamed Diallo	14	1.57
2	Frederic Da Rocha	24	1.42
3	Alexander Viveros	25	1.40
4	Loic Guillon	23	1.22
5	Gilles Yapi Yapo	30	1.17
6	Pascal Delhommeau	23	1.17
7	Mickael Landreau	37	1.16
8	Mauro Cetto	25	1.16
9	Mamadou Bagayoko	21	1.14
10	Emerse Fae	16	1.13
	CLUB AVERAGE:		1.13

LEAGUE APPEARANCES, BOOKINGS AND CAPS

	AGE (on 01/07/05)	IN NAMED 16	APPEARANCES	COUNTING GAMES	MINUTES ON PITCH	YELLOW CARDS	RED CARDS	THIS SEASON	HOME COUNTRY
Goalkeepers									
Willy Grondin	30	15	0	0	0	0	0	-	France
Mickael Landreau	26	37	37	37	3330	0	0	4	France (4)
Alexis Thebaux	20	15	1	1	90	0	0	-	France
Defenders									
Julio Cesar Caceres	25	14	11	10	945	3	0	-	Paraguay
Mauro Cetto	23	31	26	25	2265	4	0	-	Argentina
Pascal Delhommeau	26	23	23	23	2070	2	0	-	France
Stephen Drouin	21	7	6	4	417	3	0	-	France
Emerse Fae	21	28	28	16	1832	5	2	1	Ivory Coast (44)
David Leray	21	11	5	3	298	1	0	-	France
Guillaume Norbert	24	2	2	1	156	0	0	-	France
Nicolas Savinaud	29	36	36	34	3158	2	1	-	France
Denis Stinat	21	12	7	5	535	1	0	-	France
Alexander Viveros	27	27	26	25	2279	5	1	-	Colombia
Midfielders									
Bocundji Ca	18	10	8	1	193	2	0	-	France
Aurelien Capoue	23	19	18	6	663	3	0	-	France
Mohamed Diallo	23	19	19	14	1322	0	0	-	Mali
Milos Dimitrijevic	21	14	10	3	433	0	1	-	France
Luigi Glombard	20	4	3	1	104	0	0	-	France
Loic Guillon	23	38	29	23	2183	3	0	-	France
Fodil Hadjadj	22	9	5	3	376	0	0	-	Algeria
Loic Pailleres	25	1	1	1	71	0	0	-	France
Olivier Quint	33	26	24	15	1618	2	0	-	France
Goran Rubil	24	2	1	0	30	0	0	-	Croatia
Jeremy Toulalan	21	31	31	29	2704	8	0	-	France
Forwards									
Hassan Ahamada	24	12	11	5	565	1	0	-	France
Mamadou Bagayoko	26	30	30	21	2160	5	0	-	Mali
Fouad Bouguerra	24	5	5	0	74	0	0	-	France
Florin Bratu	25	14	13	3	559	0	0	-	Romania
Frederic Da Rocha	30	28	28	24	2279	4	0	-	France
Claudiu A Keseru	18	18	15	4	545	0	0	-	Romania
Shiva N'Zigou	21	7	6	4	352	0	0	-	Gambia
Gregory Pujol	25	18	17	10	1041	0	0	-	France
Gilles Yapi Yapo	23	36	36	30	2892	9	1	3	Ivory Coast (44)

TEAM OF THE SEASON

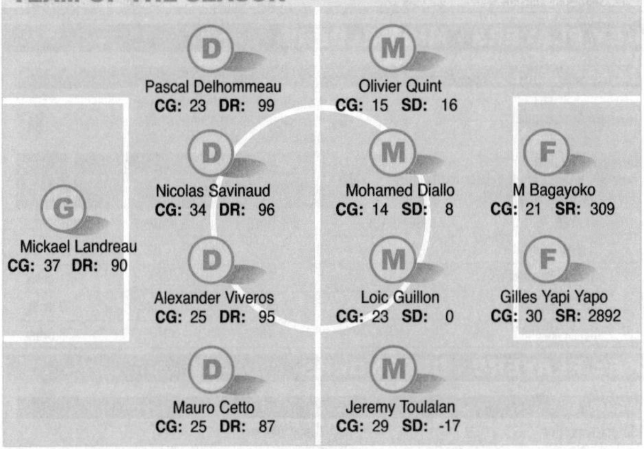

D
Pascal Delhommeau
CG: 23 DR: 99
D
Nicolas Savinaud
CG: 34 DR: 96
D
Alexander Viveros
CG: 25 DR: 95
D
Mauro Cetto
CG: 25 DR: 87
G
Mickael Landreau
CG: 37 DR: 90
M
Olivier Quint
CG: 15 SD: 16
M
Mohamed Diallo
CG: 14 SD: 8
M
Loic Guillon
CG: 23 SD: 0
M
Jeremy Toulalan
CG: 29 SD: -17
F
M Bagayoko
CG: 21 SR: 309
F
Gilles Yapi Yapo
CG: 30 SR: 2892

SQUAD APPEARANCES

Match	1	2	3	4	5	6	7	8	9	10	11	12	13	14	15	16	17	18	19	20	21	22	23	24	25	26	27	28	29	30	31	32	33	34	35	36	37	38
Venue	A	H	A	H	A	H	A	H	A	H	A	A	H	A	H	A	H	A	H	A	H	A	A	A	H	A	H	A	H	H	A	H	A	H	A	H	A	H
Competition	L	L	L	L	L	L	L	L	L	L	L	L	L	L	L	L	L	L	L	L	L	L	L	L	L	L	L	L	L	L	L	L	L	L	L	L	L	L
Result	L	D	L	D	D	W	L	W	W	W	L	D	D	L	L	L	L	L	D	D	W	L	D	W	D	L	W	L	W	D	L	D	W	D	D	L	L	W

Goalkeepers
Willy Grondin
Mickael Landreau
Alexis Thebaux

Defenders
Julio Cesar Caceres
Mauro Cetto
Pascal Delhommeau
Stephen Drouin
Emerse Fae
David Leray
Guillaume Norbert
Nicolas Savinaud
Denis Stinat
Alexander Viveros

Midfielders
Bocundji Ca
Aurelien Capoue
Mohamed Diallo
Milos Dimitrijevic
Luigi Glombard
Loic Guillon
Fodil Hadjadj
Loic Pailleres
Olivier Quint
Goran Rubil
Jeremy Toulalan

Forwards
Hassan Ahamada
Mamadou Bagayoko
Fouad Bouguerra
Florin Bratu
Frederic Da Rocha
Claudiu Andrei Keseru
Shiva N'Zigou
Gregory Pujol
Gilles Yapi Yapo

KEY: On all match | On bench | Subbed or sent off (Counting game) | Subbed or sent off (playing less than 70 minutes) | Subbed on from bench (Counting Game) | Subbed on (playing less than 70 minutes) | Subbed on and then subbed or sent off (Counting Game) | Subbed on and then subbed or sent off (playing less than 70 minutes) | Not in 16

CAEN

Final Position: **18th**

KEY: Won / Drawn / Lost

							Attendance
1	frpr1	**Istres**	H	D	1-1	Watier 16	16,000
2	frpr1	**Paris SG**	A	D	2-2	Hengbart 43; Sarr 72 pen	35,000
3	frpr1	**Monaco**	H	W	1-0	Watier 21	21,000
4	frpr1	**Auxerre**	A	L	0-1		10,000
5	frpr1	**Lens**	H	W	1-0	Mazure 57	20,000
6	frpr1	**Lille**	A	L	0-2		10,000
7	frpr1	**Strasbourg**	H	D	0-0		15,000
8	frpr1	**AC Ajaccio**	A	D	2-2	Watier 29; Lemaitre 85	5,000
9	frpr1	**Bordeaux**	H	D	1-1	Mazure 21	20,000
10	frpr1	**Lyon**	A	L	0-4		34,000
11	frpr1	**Nantes**	H	W	2-1	Lemaitre 42; Watier 62	21,000
12	frpr1	**Rennes**	A	D	1-1	Bakour 72	22,000
13	frpr1	**Sochaux**	H	L	0-2		20,000
14	frpr1	**Metz**	A	W	2-1	Mazure 45,81	14,000
15	frpr1	**Nice**	H	D	0-0		21,000
16	frpr1	**Bastia**	A	L	0-2		1,000
17	frpr1	**Marseille**	H	L	2-3	Dufer 43; Watier 81 pen	21,000
18	frpr1	**St Etienne**	A	L	0-5		25,000
19	frpr1	**Toulouse**	H	L	0-2		19,000
20	frpr1	**Paris SG**	H	D	0-0		21,000
21	frpr1	**Monaco**	A	L	2-5	Watier 33; Lemaitre 87	5,000
22	frpr1	**Auxerre**	H	L	0-2		21,000
23	frpr1	**Lens**	A	W	1-0	Mazure 47	28,000
24	frpr1	**Lille**	H	D	0-0		17,000
25	frpr1	**Strasbourg**	A	L	0-5		11,000
26	frpr1	**AC Ajaccio**	H	D	2-2	Mazure 12,28	18,000
27	frpr1	**Bordeaux**	A	D	2-2	Mazure 68; Deroin 78	17,000
28	frpr1	**Lyon**	H	W	1-0	Mazure 71	21,000
29	frpr1	**Nantes**	A	L	0-2		28,000
30	frpr1	**Rennes**	H	D	2-2	Eudeline 53; Watier 73 pen	21,000
31	frpr1	**Sochaux**	A	L	0-1		14,000
32	frpr1	**Metz**	H	L	0-1		20,000
33	frpr1	**Nice**	A	W	1-0	Mazure 67	12,000
34	frpr1	**Bastia**	H	L	0-1		20,000
35	frpr1	**Marseille**	A	W	3-2	Mazure 27; Valero 42; Watier 92	53,000
36	frpr1	**St Etienne**	H	W	2-0	Watier 41; Zubar 92	21,000
37	frpr1	**Toulouse**	A	W	3-2	Mazure 70; Ben Askar 78; Hengbart 81	19,000
38	frpr1	**Istres**	A	L	2-3	Mazure 28; Deroin 73	6,000

MONTHLY POINTS TALLY

AUGUST	5	42%
SEPTEMBER	5	42%
OCTOBER	5	42%
NOVEMBER	4	33%
DECEMBER	0	0%
JANUARY	5	33%
FEBRUARY	2	22%
MARCH	4	44%
APRIL	3	25%
MAY	9	75%

KEY PLAYERS - GOALSCORERS

Sebastien Mazure

Goals in the League	13	Player Strike Rate Average number of minutes between League goals scored by player	194
Contribution to Attacking Power Average number of minutes between League team goals while on pitch	87	Club Strike Rate Average number of minutes between League goals scored by club	95

	PLAYER	LGE GOALS	POWER	STRIKE RATE
1	Sebastien Mazure	13	87	194 mins
2	Cyrille Watier	9	107	239 mins
3	Reynald Lemaitre	3	91	668 mins
4	Cedric Hengbart	2	88	1197 mins
5	Anthony Deroin	2	99	1527 mins

KEY PLAYERS - MIDFIELDERS

Reynald Lemaitre

Goals in the League	3	Contribution to Attacking Power Average number of minutes between League team goals while on pitch	91
Defensive Rating Average number of mins between League goals conceded while on the pitch	72	Scoring Difference Defensive Rating minus Contribution to Attacking Power	-19

	PLAYER	LGE GOALS	DEF RATE	POWER	SCORE DIFF
1	Reynald Lemaitre	3	72	91	-19 mins
2	Steve Dugardein	0	73	104	-31 mins
3	Anthony Deroin	2	59	99	-40 mins
4	Cyrille Watier	9	49	107	-58 mins

KEY PLAYERS - DEFENDERS

Ibrahima Faye

Goals Conceded Number of League goals conceded while the player was on the pitch	38	Clean Sheets In League games when player was on pitch for at least 70 minutes	7
Defensive Rating Ave number of mins between League goals conceded while on the pitch	62	Club Defensive Rating Average number of mins between League goals conceded by the club this season	57

	PLAYER	CON LGE	CLEAN SHEETS	DEF RATE
1	Ibrahima Faye	38	7	62 mins
2	Aziz Ben Askar	45	7	56 mins
3	Cedric Hengbart	43	6	56 mins
4	Frederic Danjou	49	9	56 mins
5	Ronald Zubar	47	6	55 mins

KEY GOALKEEPER

Vincent Plante

Goals Conceded in the League	38	Counting Games League games when player was on pitch for at least 70 minutes	25
Defensive Rating Ave number of mins between League goals conceded while on the pitch	59	Clean Sheets In games when player was on pitch for at least 70 minutes	6

LEAGUE GOALS

Sebastien Mazure

Minutes on the pitch	2527	Goals in the League	13
League average (mins between goals)	194		

	PLAYER	MINS	GOALS	AVE
1	Mazure	2527	13	194
2	Watier	2147	9	239
3	Lemaitre	2005	3	668
4	Deroin	3054	2	1527
5	Hengbart	2393	2	1197
6	Valero	191	1	191
7	Zubar	2578	1	2578
8	Bakour	551	1	551
9	Eudeline	1553	1	1553
10	Dufer	1293	1	1293
11	Sarr	569	1	569
12	Ben Askar	2520	1	2520
	Other		0	
	TOTAL		36	

DISCIPLINARY RECORDS

	PLAYER	YELLOW	RED	AVE
1	Bakour	5	1	91
2	Lemaitre	9	0	222
3	Dugardein	6	0	242
4	Rankovic	3	0	253
5	Hengbart	6	1	341
6	Danjou	8	0	345
7	Watier	6	0	357
8	Faye	6	0	392
9	Zubar	6	0	429
10	Deroin	7	0	436
11	Seube	4	0	504
12	Ben Askar	5	0	504
13	Eudeline	3	0	517
	Other	6	0	
	TOTAL	80	2	

TOP POINT EARNERS

	PLAYER	GAMES	AV PTS
1	Steve Dugardein	12	1.58
2	Reynald Lemaitre	20	1.35
3	Sebastien Mazure	26	1.35
4	Yohann Eudeline	17	1.24
5	Vincent Plante	25	1.24
6	Ibrahima Faye	24	1.17
7	Cedric Hengbart	25	1.16
8	Ronald Zubar	27	1.07
9	Aziz Ben Askar	28	1.07
10	Anthony Deroin	32	1.06
	CLUB AVERAGE:		1.11

TEAM OF THE SEASON

G
Vincent Plante
CG: 25 DR: 59
D
Ibrahima Faye
CG: 24 DR: 62
D
Aziz Ben Askar
CG: 28 DR: 56
D
Frederic Danjou
CG: 30 DR: 56
D
Cedric Hengbart
CG: 25 DR: 56
M
Reynald Lemaitre
CG: 20 SD: -19
M
Steve Dugardein
CG: 12 SD: -31
M
Anthony Deroin
CG: 32 SD: -40
M
Cyrille Watier
CG: 17 SD: -58
F
Sebastien Mazure
CG: 26 SR: 194
F
Yohann Eudeline
CG: 17 SR: 1553

LEAGUE APPEARANCES, BOOKINGS AND CAPS

	AGE (on 01/07/05)	IN NAMED 16	APPEARANCES	COUNTING GAMES	MINUTES ON PITCH	YELLOW CARDS	RED CARDS	THIS SEASON	HOME COUNTRY
Goalkeepers									
Benoit Costil	18	3	0	0	0	0	0	-	France
Steeve Elana	24	18	13	13	1170	0	0	-	France
Vincent Plante	24	26	25	25	2250	2	0	-	France
Defenders									
Aziz Ben Askar	26	30	28	28	2520	5	0	-	France
Alexandre Clement	30	2	1	0	5	0	0	-	France
Frederic Danjou	30	31	31	30	2763	8	0	-	France
Ibrahima Faye	25	35	30	24	2357	6	0	3	Senegal (33)
Cedric Hengbart	24	34	30	25	2393	6	1	-	France
Nicolas Seube	25	35	27	21	2019	4	0	-	France
Gael Suares	24	3	2	2	180	0	0	-	France
Ronald Zubar	19	37	34	27	2578	6	0	-	France
Midfielders									
Salah Bakour	23	19	14	3	551	5	1	-	France
Anthony Deroin	26	37	37	32	3054	7	0	-	France
Gregory Dufer	23	23	22	10	1293	1	0	2	Belgium (42)
Steve Dugardein	31	24	21	12	1452	6	0	-	Belgium
Jimmy Hebert	33	28	20	11	1248	2	0	-	France
Matthias Jouan	21	1	1	0	16	0	0	-	France
Reynald Lemaitre	22	30	29	20	2005	9	0	-	France
Benoit Lesoimier	22	7	3	1	142	0	0	-	France
Igor Matic	23	12	11	2	516	0	0	-	Serbia & Montenegro
Samy Mawene	20	1	1	0	8	0	0	-	France
Ljubisa Rankovic	31	19	13	4	761	3	0	-	Serbia & Montenegro
Cyrille Watier	33	36	32	17	2147	6	0	-	France
Forwards									
Franck Berrier	21	5	1	0	49	0	0	-	France
Yohann Eudeline	23	24	24	17	1553	3	0	-	France
Yoan Gouffran	19	10	8	3	344	0	0	-	France
Elliot Grandin	17	1	1	0	33	0	0	-	France
Zoran Jovicic	32	16	11	3	382	0	0	-	Serbia & Montenegro
Sebastien Mazure	26	34	32	26	2527	1	0	-	France
Kordaba Sarr	29	12	11	3	569	0	0	-	Senegal
Jeremy Sorbon	21	12	5	5	450	1	0	-	France
Julien Valero	2006	6	5	0	191	0	0	-	France

SQUAD APPEARANCES

Match	1	2	3	4	5	6	7	8	9	10	11	12	13	14	15	16	17	18	19	20	21	22	23	24	25	26	27	28	29	30	31	32	33	34	35	36	37	38
Venue	H	A	H	A	H	A	H	A	H	A	H	A	H	A	H	A	H	A	H	H	A	H	A	H	A	H	A	H	A	H	A	H	A	H	A	H	A	A
Competition	L	L	L	L	L	L	L	L	L	L	L	L	L	L	L	L	L	L	L	L	L	L	L	L	L	L	L	L	L	L	L	L	L	L	L	L	L	L
Result	D	D	W	L	W	L	D	D	D	L	W	D	L	W	D	L	L	L	L	D	L	L	W	D	L	D	D	W	L	D	L	L	W	L	W	W	W	L

Goalkeepers
Benoit Costil
Steeve Elana
Vincent Plante

Defenders
Aziz Ben Askar
Alexandre Clement
Frederic Danjou
Ibrahima Faye
Cedric Hengbart
Nicolas Seube
Gael Suares
Ronald Zubar

Midfielders
Salah Bakour
Anthony Deroin
Gregory Dufer
Steve Dugardein
Jimmy Hebert
Matthias Jouan
Reynald Lemaitre
Benoit Lesoimier
Igor Matic
Samy Mawene
Ljubisa Rankovic
Cyrille Watier

Forwards
Franck Berrier
Yohann Eudeline
Yoan Gouffran
Elliot Grandin
Zoran Jovicic
Sebastien Mazure
Kordaba Sarr
Jeremy Sorbon
Julien Valero

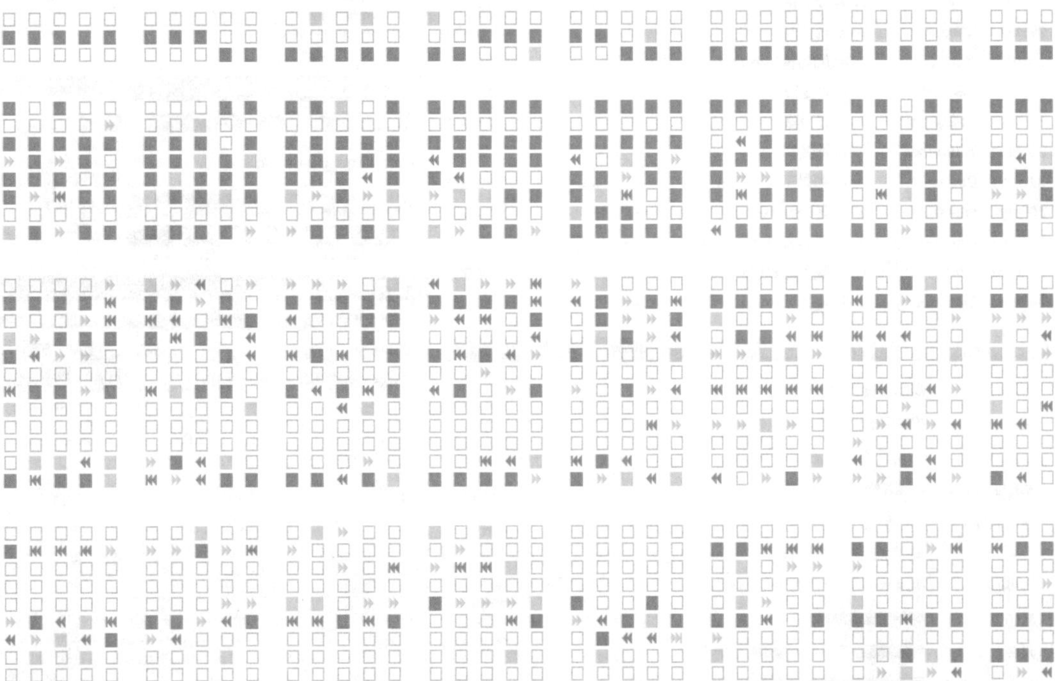

KEY: On all match | On bench | Subbed or sent off (Counting game) | Subbed or sent off (playing less than 70 minutes) | Subbed on from bench (Counting Game) | Subbed on (playing less than 70 minutes) | Subbed on and then subbed or sent off (Counting Game) | Subbed on and then subbed or sent off (playing less than 70 minutes) | Not in 16

BASTIA

Final Position: **19th**

KEY: ☐ Won ☐ Drawn ☐ Lost

						Attendance
1 frpr1	**Strasbourg**	H	W	2-1	Jau 43; Vairelles 74	5,000
2 frpr1	**Nantes**	A	D	1-1	Andre 74	30,000
3 frpr1	**AC Ajaccio**	H	W	1-0	Jau 69	7,000
4 frpr1	**Nice**	A	D	1-1	Vairelles 80	10,000
5 frpr1	**Auxerre**	H	W	1-0	Yahia 32	8,000
6 frpr1	**Lyon**	A	D	0-0		32,000
7 frpr1	**Bordeaux**	H	L	1-4	Nee 31	10,000
8 frpr1	**Marseille**	A	L	0-1		5,000
9 frpr1	**Paris SG**	H	L	1-2	Hadji 17	10,000
10 frpr1	**Lille**	A	L	1-2	Ben Saada 21	13,000
11 frpr1	**Sochaux**	H	D	1-1	Sidibe 40	6,000
12 frpr1	**Metz**	A	L	0-2		12,000
13 frpr1	**Rennes**	H	D	1-1	Jau 39	5,000
14 frpr1	**St Etienne**	H	L	0-3		8,000
15 frpr1	**Toulouse**	A	L	0-1		15,000
16 frpr1	**Caen**	H	W	2-0	Sidibe 6; Vairelles 57	1,000
17 frpr1	**Istres**	A	L	0-1		4,000
18 frpr1	**Monaco**	H	L	0-2		5,000
19 frpr1	**Lens**	A	L	1-2	Vairelles 82	31,000
20 frpr1	**Nantes**	H	D	0-0		3,000
21 frpr1	**AC Ajaccio**	A	L	0-1		8,000
22 frpr1	**Nice**	H	W	2-0	Nee 18; Hadji 85	4,000
23 frpr1	**Auxerre**	A	L	1-4	Nee 8	10,000
24 frpr1	**Lyon**	H	D	1-1	Chimbonda 49	5,000
25 frpr1	**Bordeaux**	A	D	0-0		15,000
26 frpr1	**Marseille**	H	L	0-1		10,000
27 frpr1	**Paris SG**	A	L	0-1		40,000
28 frpr1	**Lille**	H	W	3-1	Hadji 21; Ziani 27; Rocchi 39	3,000
29 frpr1	**Sochaux**	A	L	0-1		13,000
30 frpr1	**Metz**	H	W	1-0	Yahia 90	5,000
31 frpr1	**Rennes**	A	L	0-1		20,000
32 frpr1	**St Etienne**	A	L	0-3		31,000
33 frpr1	**Toulouse**	H	W	2-1	Andre 20,51	6,000
34 frpr1	**Caen**	A	W	1-0	Andre 56	20,000
35 frpr1	**Istres**	H	W	2-0	Jau 51; Hadji 87	5,000
36 frpr1	**Monaco**	A	L	2-5	Hadji 1; Chimbonda 56	10,000
37 frpr1	**Lens**	H	W	3-1	Hadji 15,35; Chimbonda 56	5,000
38 frpr1	**Strasbourg**	A	L	0-2		20,000

MONTHLY POINTS TALLY

AUGUST	8	67%
SEPTEMBER	4	33%
OCTOBER	1	8%
NOVEMBER	4	33%
DECEMBER	0	0%
JANUARY	4	33%
FEBRUARY	2	17%
MARCH	6	67%
APRIL	6	50%
MAY	6	50%

KEY PLAYERS - GOALSCORERS

Youssouf Hadji

Goals in the League	7	**Player Strike Rate** Average number of minutes between League goals scored by player	369
Contribution to Attacking Power Average number of minutes between League team goals while on pitch	107	**Club Strike Rate** Average number of minutes between League goals scored by club	107

	PLAYER	LGE GOALS	POWER	STRIKE RATE
1	Youssouf Hadji	7	107	369 mins
2	Pierre-Yves Andre	4	92	371 mins
3	Frederic Nee	3	105	494 mins
4	Fabrice Jau	4	92	550 mins
5	Pascal Chimbonda	3	100	1071 mins

KEY PLAYERS - MIDFIELDERS

Romain Rocchi

Goals in the League	1	**Contribution to Attacking Power** Average number of minutes between League team goals while on pitch	82
Defensive Rating Average number of mins between League goals conceded while on the pitch	76	**Scoring Difference** Defensive Rating minus Contribution to Attacking Power	-6

	PLAYER	LGE GOALS	DEF RATE	POWER	SCORE DIFF
1	Romain Rocchi	1	76	82	-6 mins
2	Fabrice Jau	4	65	92	-27 mins
3	Djibril Sidibe	1	70	108	-38 mins
4	Alexandre Song Billong	0	73	123	-50 mins

KEY PLAYERS - DEFENDERS

Greg Vanney

Goals Conceded Number of League goals conceded while the player was on the pitch	17	**Clean Sheets** In League games when player was on pitch for at least 70 minutes	4
Defensive Rating Ave number of mins between League goals conceded while on the pitch	86	**Club Defensive Rating** Average number of mins between League goals conceded by the club this season	71

	PLAYER	CON LGE	CLEAN SHEETS	DEF RATE
1	Greg Vanney	17	4	86 mins
2	Franck Matingou	20	3	85 mins
3	Anthar Yahia	35	9	77 mins
4	Pascal Chimbonda	44	10	73 mins
5	David Sauget	20	5	69 mins

KEY GOALKEEPER

Nicolas Penneteau

Goals Conceded in the League	46	**Counting Games** League games when player was on pitch for at least 70 minutes	37
Defensive Rating Ave number of mins between League goals conceded while on the pitch	72	**Clean Sheets** In games when player was on pitch for at least 70 minutes	10

LEAGUE GOALS

Youssouf Hadji

Minutes on the pitch	2583	**Goals in the League**	369
League average (mins between goals)	7		

	PLAYER	MINS	GOALS	AVE
1	Hadji	2583	7	369
2	Vairelles	1374	4	344
3	Andre	1482	4	371
4	Jau	2199	4	550
5	Chimbonda	3212	3	1071
6	Nee	1481	3	494
7	Yahia	2700	2	1350
8	Rocchi	1977	1	1977
9	Sidibe	2386	1	2386
10	Ben Saada	1035	1	1035
11	Ziani	1144	1	1144
	Other		1	
	TOTAL		32	

DISCIPLINARY RECORDS

	PLAYER	YELLOW	RED	AVE
1	Cherrad	3	0	172
2	Matingou	9	0	188
3	Karembeu	3	0	210
4	Rocchi	6	1	282
5	Vanney	5	0	292
6	Yahia	8	1	300
7	Song Billong	7	0	333
8	Andre	3	1	370
9	Kvarme	2	0	447
10	Sauget	3	0	457
11	Chimbonda	6	0	535
12	Jau	4	0	549
13	Ziani	2	0	572
	Other	9	3	
	TOTAL	70	6	

TOP POINT EARNERS

	PLAYER	GAMES	AV PTS
1	Pierre-Yves Andre	16	1.75
2	Romain Rocchi	20	1.40
3	David Sauget	15	1.27
4	Anthar Yahia	30	1.23
5	Stephane Ziani	13	1.23
6	Fabrice Jau	24	1.21
7	Pascal Chimbonda	36	1.14
8	Djibril Sidibe	24	1.13
9	Cedric Uras	17	1.12
10	Franck Matingou	15	1.07
	CLUB AVERAGE:		1.08

LEAGUE APPEARANCES, BOOKINGS AND CAPS

	AGE (on 01/07/05)	IN NAMED 16	APPEARANCES	COUNTING GAMES	MINUTES ON PITCH	YELLOW CARDS	RED CARDS	THIS SEASON	HOME COUNTRY
Goalkeepers									
Jean-Louis Leca	19	23	2	1	91	0	0	-	France
Nicolas Penneteau	24	37	37	37	3328	1	1	-	France
Daniel Yeboah	20	15	0	0	0	0	0	-	Ivory Coast
Defenders									
Yannick Cahuzac	-	1	0	0	0	0	0	-	France
Pascal Chimbonda	26	36	36	36	3212	6	0	-	France
Bernt Haas	27	4	4	4	346	0	0	5	Switzerland (45)
Bjorn Tore Kvarme	33	11	10	10	894	2	0	-	Norway
Benjamin Longue	24	8	1	0	13	0	0	-	France
Franck Matingou	25	25	22	15	1700	9	0	-	France
David Sauget	25	23	17	15	1372	3	0	-	France
A Song Billong	18	36	32	24	2336	7	0	1	Cameroon (26)
Cedric Uras	27	27	22	17	1646	1	1	-	France
Greg Vanney	30	21	17	16	1461	5	0	-	United States
Anthar Yahia	23	33	31	30	2700	8	1	-	France
Midfielders									
Henoch Conombo	19	13	10	1	281	0	0	-	Burkino Faso
Gary Coulibaly	-	1	1	0	17	0	0	-	France
Paul Essola	23	11	8	1	244	1	0	-	Cameroon
Florent Ghisolfi	20	3	0	0	0	0	0	-	France
Fabrice Jau	26	25	25	24	2199	4	0	-	France
Christian Karembeu	34	7	7	7	630	3	0	-	France
Sebastien Piocelle	26	26	15	10	1070	1	0	-	France
Romain Rocchi	23	25	25	20	1977	6	1	-	France
Djibril Sidibe	23	32	31	24	2386	3	1	-	Mali
Forwards									
Pierre-Yves Andre	31	22	21	16	1482	3	1	-	France
Chaouki Ben Saada	21	29	20	8	1035	1	0	-	France
Abdelmalek Cherrad	24	8	8	4	517	3	0	-	Algeria
Bertin D'Avesnes	19	1	0	0	0	0	0	-	France
Youssouf Hadji	25	33	33	27	2583	1	0	-	Morocco
Frederic Nee	30	29	26	13	1481	0	0	-	France
Tony Vairelles	32	30	27	10	1374	1	0	-	France
Stephane Ziani	32	15	15	13	1144	2	0	-	France

TEAM OF THE SEASON

D
Greg Vanney
CG: 16 DR: 86
M
Romain Rocchi
CG: 20 SD: -6
D
Franck Matingou
CG: 15 DR: 85
M
Fabrice Jau
CG: 24 SD: -27
F
Youssouf Hadji
CG: 27 SR: 369
G
Nicolas Penneteau
CG: 37 DR: 72
D
Anthar Yahia
CG: 30 DR: 77
M
Djibril Sidibe
CG: 24 SD: -38
F
Pierre-Yves Andre
CG: 16 SR: 371
D
Pascal Chimbonda
CG: 36 DR: 73
M
Alexandre Song Billong
CG: 24 SD: -50

SQUAD APPEARANCES

Match	1	2	3	4	5	6	7	8	9	10	11	12	13	14	15	16	17	18	19	20	21	22	23	24	25	26	27	28	29	30	31	32	33	34	35	36	37	38
Venue	H	A	H	A	H	A	H	A	H	A	H	A	H	H	A	H	A	H	A	H	A	H	A	H	A	H	A	H	A	H	A	A	H	A	H	A	H	A
Competition	L	L	L	L	L	L	L	L	L	L	L	L	L	L	L	L	L	L	L	L	L	L	L	L	L	L	L	L	L	L	L	L	L	L	L	L	L	L
Result	W	D	W	D	W	D	L	L	L	L	D	L	D	L	L	W	L	L	L	D	L	W	L	D	D	L	L	W	L	W	L	L	W	W	W	L	W	L

Goalkeepers
Jean-Louis Leca
Nicolas Penneteau
Daniel Yeboah

Defenders
Yannick Cahuzac
Pascal Chimbonda
Bernt Haas
Bjorn Tore Kvarme
Benjamin Longue
Franck Matingou
David Sauget
Cedric Uras
Greg Vanney
Anthar Yahia

Midfielders
Henoch Conombo
Gary Coulibaly
Paul Essola
Florent Ghisolfi
Fabrice Jau
Christian Karembeu
Sebastien Piocelle
Romain Rocchi
Djibril Sidibe
Alexandre Song Billong

Forwards
Pierre-Yves Andre
Chaouki Ben Saada
Abdelmalek Cherrad
Samir Bertin D'Avesnes
Youssouf Hadji
Frederic Nee
Tony Vairelles
Stephane Ziani

KEY: On all match · On bench · Subbed or sent off (Counting game) · Subbed or sent off (playing less than 70 minutes) · Subbed on from bench (Counting Game) · Subbed on (playing less than 70 minutes) · Subbed on and then subbed or sent off (Counting Game) · Subbed on and then subbed or sent off (playing less than 70 minutes) · Not in 16

ISTRES

Final Position: **20th**

KEY: Won Drawn Lost

							Attendance
1	frpr1	**Caen**	A	D	1-1	N'Diaye 3	16,000
2	frpr1	**Monaco**	A	L	1-2	Montano 80	11,000
3	frpr1	**Lens**	H	L	0-2		8,000
4	frpr1	**Strasbourg**	A	D	1-1	N'Diaye 47	11,000
5	frpr1	**Paris SG**	H	D	1-1	Saifi 1	11,000
6	frpr1	**Nantes**	A	L	0-1		25,000
7	frpr1	**AC Ajaccio**	H	L	0-1		6,000
8	frpr1	**Auxerre**	A	D	0-0		7,000
9	frpr1	**Marseille**	H	L	0-2		11,000
10	frpr1	**Bordeaux**	A	D	2-2	Montano 8; Saifi 60; Courtois 94	18,000
11	frpr1	**Lyon**	H	D	0-0		7,000
12	frpr1	**Nice**	A	D	0-0		8,000
13	frpr1	**Lille**	H	L	0-2		5,000
14	frpr1	**Sochaux**	A	D	1-1	Courtois 53	15,000
15	frpr1	**Metz**	H	D	0-0		5,000
16	frpr1	**Rennes**	A	L	1-3	Pele 82	18,000
17	frpr1	**Bastia**	H	W	1-0	N'Diaye 75	4,000
18	frpr1	**Toulouse**	A	L	1-2	Courtois 33	21,000
19	frpr1	**St Etienne**	H	L	0-2		10,000
20	frpr1	**Monaco**	H	L	0-1		10,000
21	frpr1	**Lens**	A	W	1-0	Saifi 20	31,000
22	frpr1	**Strasbourg**	H	D	1-1	Chaussidiere 52	4,000
23	frpr1	**Paris SG**	A	D	2-2	Bakayoko 60; Pele 81	23,000
24	frpr1	**Nantes**	H	L	0-1		8,000
25	frpr1	**AC Ajaccio**	A	D	0-0		4,000
26	frpr1	**Auxerre**	H	W	1-0	Bakayoko 26 pen	5,000
27	frpr1	**Marseille**	A	D	1-1	N'Diaye 48	50,000
28	frpr1	**Bordeaux**	H	L	0-1		5,000
29	frpr1	**Lyon**	A	L	1-2	N'Diaye 30	35,000
30	frpr1	**Nice**	H	D	1-1	Delaye 81	3,000
31	frpr1	**Lille**	A	L	0-7		13,000
32	frpr1	**Sochaux**	H	W	2-0	Bakayoko 49; Saveljic 81	5,000
33	frpr1	**Metz**	A	L	1-2	N'Diaye 86	18,000
34	frpr1	**Rennes**	H	L	0-2		5,000
35	frpr1	**Bastia**	A	L	0-2		5,000
36	frpr1	**Toulouse**	H	W	1-0	Ourahou 79	4,000
37	frpr1	**St Etienne**	A	L	0-2		35,000
38	frpr1	**Caen**	H	W	3-2	Saifi 4; Chaussidiere 32; Ourahou 59	6,000

MONTHLY POINTS TALLY

AUGUST	2	17%
SEPTEMBER	2	17%
OCTOBER	3	25%
NOVEMBER	2	17%
DECEMBER	3	33%
JANUARY	5	33%
FEBRUARY	5	56%
MARCH	1	11%
APRIL	3	25%
MAY	6	50%

KEY PLAYERS - GOALSCORERS

Ibrahim Bakayoko

Goals in the League	3	**Player Strike Rate** Average number of minutes between League goals scored by player	392
Contribution to Attacking Power Average number of minutes between League team goals while on pitch	130	**Club Strike Rate** Average number of minutes between League goals scored by club	132

	PLAYER	LGE GOALS	POWER	STRIKE RATE
1	Ibrahim Bakayoko	3	130	**392 mins**
2	Moussa N'Diaye	6	134	**405 mins**
3	Rafik Saifi	4	143	**681 mins**
4	Laurent Courtois	3	109	**730 mins**
5	Steven Pele	2	136	**886 mins**

KEY PLAYERS - MIDFIELDERS

Laurent Courtois

Goals in the League	3	**Contribution to Attacking Power** Average number of minutes between League team goals while on pitch	109
Defensive Rating Average number of mins between League goals conceded while on the pitch	78	**Scoring Difference** Defensive Rating minus Contribution to Attacking Power	-31

	PLAYER	LGE GOALS	DEF RATE	POWER	SCORE DIFF
1	Laurent Courtois	3	78	109	**-31 mins**
2	Dejan Ilic	0	77	124	**-47 mins**
3	Adel Chedli	0	68	159	**-91 mins**
4	Abdoulaye Faye	0	77	207	**-130 mins**

KEY PLAYERS - DEFENDERS

Nisa Saveljic

Goals Conceded Number of League goals conceded while the player was on the pitch	34	**Clean Sheets** In League games when player was on pitch for at least 70 minutes	8
Defensive Rating Ave number of mins between League goals conceded while on the pitch	81	**Club Defensive Rating** Average number of mins between League goals conceded by the club this season	68

	PLAYER	CON LGE	CLEAN SHEETS	DEF RATE
1	Nisa Saveljic	34	8	**81 mins**
2	Christophe Dumolin	37	8	**66 mins**
3	Noureddine Kacemi	21	4	**65 mins**
4	Ibrahim Thiam	41	7	**62 mins**
5	Steven Pele	29	4	**61 mins**

KEY GOALKEEPER

Rudy Riou

Goals Conceded in the League	35	**Counting Games** League games when player was on pitch for at least 70 minutes	27
Defensive Rating Ave number of mins between League goals conceded while on the pitch	69	**Clean Sheets** In games when player was on pitch for at least 70 minutes	10

LEAGUE GOALS

Moussa N'Diaye

Minutes on the pitch	2428	**Goals in the League**	6
League average (mins between goals)	405		

	PLAYER	MINS	GOALS	AVE
1	N'Diaye	2428	**6**	405
2	Saifi	2724	**4**	681
3	Courtois	2189	**3**	730
4	Bakayoko	1175	**3**	392
5	Chaussidiere	941	**2**	471
6	Ourahou	573	**2**	287
7	Montano	1438	**2**	719
8	Pele	1772	**2**	886
9	Delaye	892	**1**	892
10	Saveljic	2758	**1**	2758
	Other		0	
	TOTAL		**26**	

DISCIPLINARY RECORDS

	PLAYER	YELLOW	RED	AVE
1	Ilic	10	1	**146**
2	Leugueun	5	1	**155**
3	Faye	11	2	**159**
4	Delaye	5	0	**178**
5	Chedli	8	1	**212**
6	Saveljic	13	0	**212**
7	Saifi	10	1	**247**
8	Perez	3	0	**249**
9	Kehiha	2	0	**327**
10	Montano	4	0	**359**
11	Thiam	6	1	**365**
12	Courtois	4	1	**437**
13	Pele	4	0	**443**
	Other	14	0	
	TOTAL	**99**	**8**	

TOP POINT EARNERS

	PLAYER	GAMES	AV PTS
1	Rudy Riou	27	**1.04**
2	Noureddine Kacemi	14	**1.00**
3	Adel Chedli	19	**0.95**
4	Laurent Courtois	16	**0.94**
5	Moussa N'Diaye	22	**0.91**
6	Dejan Ilic	18	**0.89**
7	Christophe Dumolin	27	**0.85**
8	Rafik Saifi	27	**0.85**
9	Steven Pele	18	**0.83**
10	Ibrahim Thiam	28	**0.82**
	CLUB AVERAGE:		**0.84**

LEAGUE APPEARANCES AND BOOKINGS

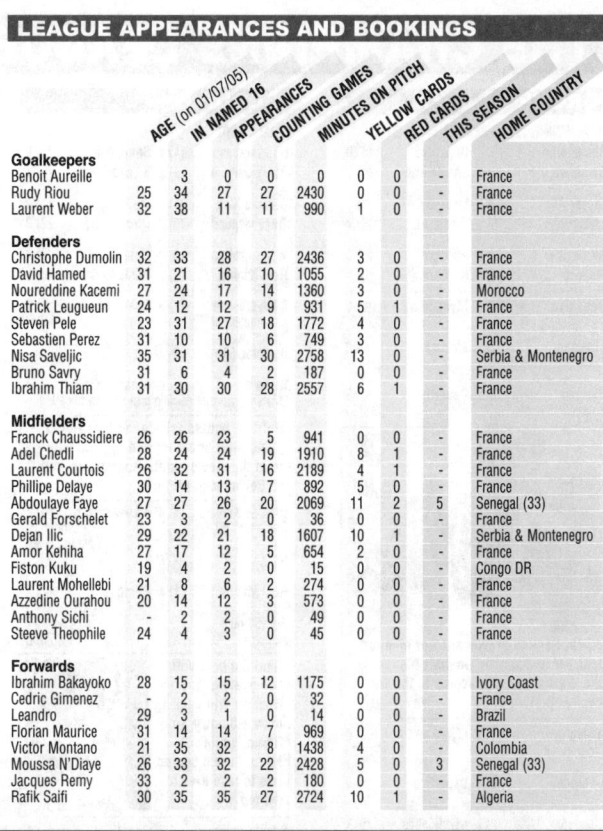

	AGE (on 01/07/05)	IN NAMED 16	APPEARANCES	COUNTING GAMES	MINUTES ON PITCH	YELLOW CARDS	RED CARDS	THIS SEASON	HOME COUNTRY
Goalkeepers									
Benoit Aureille		3	0	0	0	0	0	-	France
Rudy Riou	25	34	27	27	2430	0	0	-	France
Laurent Weber	32	38	11	11	990	1	0	-	France
Defenders									
Christophe Dumolin	32	33	28	27	2436	3	0	-	France
David Hamed	31	21	16	10	1055	2	0	-	France
Noureddine Kacemi	27	24	17	14	1360	3	0	-	Morocco
Patrick Leugueun	24	12	12	9	931	5	1	-	France
Steven Pele	23	31	27	18	1772	4	0	-	France
Sebastien Perez	31	10	10	6	749	3	0	-	France
Nisa Saveljic	35	31	31	30	2758	13	0	-	Serbia & Montenegro
Bruno Savry	31	6	4	2	187	0	0	-	France
Ibrahim Thiam	31	30	30	28	2557	6	1	-	France
Midfielders									
Franck Chaussidiere	26	26	23	5	941	0	0	-	France
Adel Chedli	28	24	24	19	1910	8	1	-	France
Laurent Courtois	26	32	31	16	2189	4	1	-	France
Phillipe Delaye	30	14	13	7	892	5	0	-	France
Abdoulaye Faye	27	27	26	20	2069	11	2	5	Senegal (33)
Gerald Forschelet	23	3	2	0	36	0	0	-	France
Dejan Ilic	29	22	21	18	1607	10	1	-	Serbia & Montenegro
Amor Kehiha	27	17	12	5	654	2	0	-	France
Fiston Kuku	19	4	2	0	15	0	0	-	Congo DR
Laurent Mohellebi	21	8	6	2	274	0	0	-	France
Azzedine Ourahou	20	14	12	3	573	0	0	-	France
Anthony Sichi	-	2	2	0	49	0	0	-	France
Steeve Theophile	24	4	3	0	45	0	0	-	France
Forwards									
Ibrahim Bakayoko	28	15	15	12	1175	0	0	-	Ivory Coast
Cedric Gimenez	-	2	2	0	32	0	0	-	France
Leandro	29	3	1	0	14	0	0	-	Brazil
Florian Maurice	31	14	14	7	969	0	0	-	France
Victor Montano	21	35	32	8	1438	4	0	-	Colombia
Moussa N'Diaye	26	33	32	22	2428	5	0	3	Senegal (33)
Jacques Remy	33	2	2	2	180	0	0	-	France
Rafik Saifi	30	35	35	27	2724	10	1	-	Algeria

TEAM OF THE SEASON

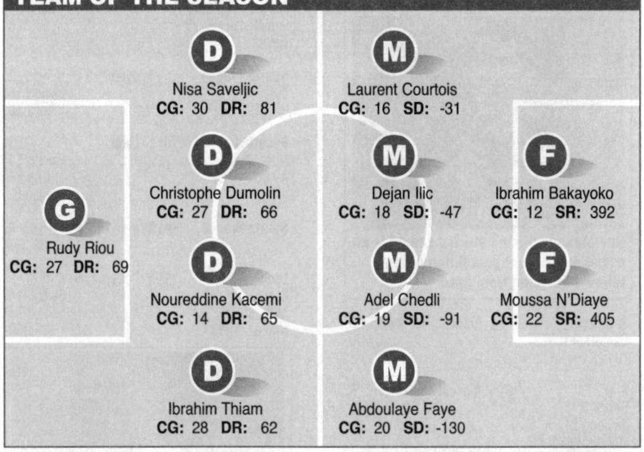
D
Nisa Saveljic
CG: 30 DR: 81
M
Laurent Courtois
CG: 16 SD: -31
D
Christophe Dumolin
CG: 27 DR: 66
M
Dejan Ilic
CG: 18 SD: -47
F
Ibrahim Bakayoko
CG: 12 SR: 392
G
Rudy Riou
CG: 27 DR: 69
D
Noureddine Kacemi
CG: 14 DR: 65
M
Adel Chedli
CG: 19 SD: -91
F
Moussa N'Diaye
CG: 22 SR: 405
D
Ibrahim Thiam
CG: 28 DR: 62
M
Abdoulaye Faye
CG: 20 SD: -130

SQUAD APPEARANCES

Match	1	2	3	4	5	6	7	8	9	10	11	12	13	14	15	16	17	18	19	20	21	22	23	24	25	26	27	28	29	30	31	32	33	34	35	36	37	38
Venue	A	A	H	A	H	A	H	A	H	A	H	A	H	A	H	A	H	A	H	H	A	H	A	H	A	H	A	H	A	H	A	H	A	H	A	H	A	H
Competition	L	L	L	L	L	L	L	L	L	L	L	L	L	L	L	L	L	L	L	L	L	L	L	L	L	L	L	L	L	L	L	L	L	L	L	L	L	L
Result	D	L	L	D	D	L	L	D	L	D	D	D	L	D	D	L	W	L	L	L	W	D	D	L	D	W	D	L	L	D	L	W	L	L	L	W	L	W

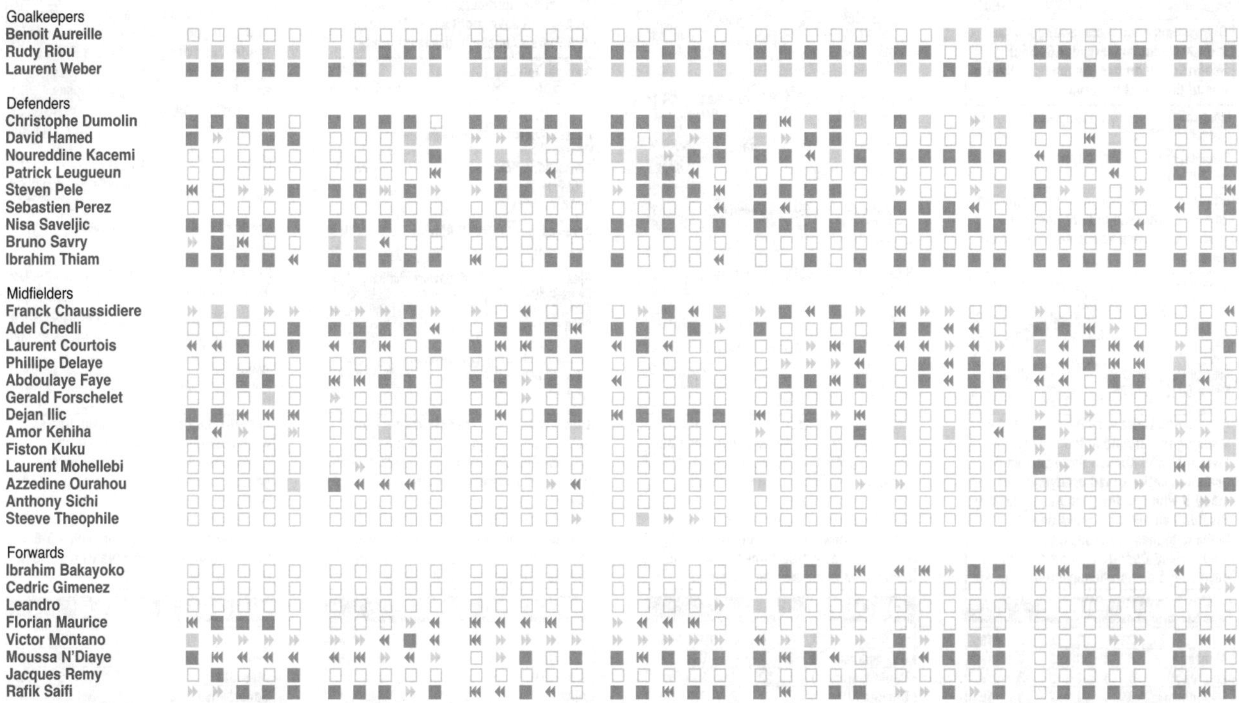
Goalkeepers
Benoit Aureille
Rudy Riou
Laurent Weber
Defenders
Christophe Dumolin
David Hamed
Noureddine Kacemi
Patrick Leugueun
Steven Pele
Sebastien Perez
Nisa Saveljic
Bruno Savry
Ibrahim Thiam
Midfielders
Franck Chaussidiere
Adel Chedli
Laurent Courtois
Phillipe Delaye
Abdoulaye Faye
Gerald Forschelet
Dejan Ilic
Amor Kehiha
Fiston Kuku
Laurent Mohellebi
Azzedine Ourahou
Anthony Sichi
Steeve Theophile
Forwards
Ibrahim Bakayoko
Cedric Gimenez
Leandro
Florian Maurice
Victor Montano
Moussa N'Diaye
Jacques Remy
Rafik Saifi

KEY: On all match | Subbed or sent off (Counting game) | Subbed on from bench (Counting Game) | Subbed on and then subbed or sent off (Counting Game) | Not in 16
On bench | Subbed or sent off (playing less than 70 minutes) | Subbed on (playing less than 70 minutes) | Subbed on and then subbed or sent off (playing less than 70 minutes)

THE CHAMPIONS LEAGUE

GROUP A

QUALIFYING

Shelbourne (0) 0 Deportivo (0) 0
Deportivo (0) 3 Shelbourne (0) 0

Grazer AK (0) 0 Liverpool (1) 2
Liverpool (0) 0 Grazer AK (0) 1

NK Gorica (0) 0 Monaco (1) 3
Monaco (3) 6 NK Gorica (0) 0

Deportivo (0) 0 Olympiakos (0) 0
22,000

Liverpool (1) 2 Monaco (0) 0
Cisse 22, Baros 84 33,517

Monaco (2) 2 Deportivo (0) 0
Kallon 5, Saviola 10 14,000

Javier Saviola proves another inspired loan for last-season finalists Monaco as the Barca loan-star scores in the win over Deportivo

Olympiakos (1) 1 Liverpool (0) 0
Stoltidis 17 33,000

Liverpool (0) 0 Deportivo (0) 0
40,236

Monaco (2) 2 Olympiakos (0) 1
Saviola 3 Okkas 60
Chevanton 10 17,000

Deportivo (0) 0 Liverpool (1) 1
32,000 Andrade 14 og

Olympiakos (0) 1 Monaco (0) 0
Schurrer 84 33,000

Olympiakos need a close-range strike from Argentinean defender Gabriel Schurrer to leap over opponents Monaco and to the top of the group

Monaco (0) 1 Liverpool (0) 0
Saviola 55 15,000

Olympiakos (0) 1 Deportivo (0) 0
Djordjevic 68 33,000

Predrag Djordjevic condemns Deportivo to a first failure to qualify from the group stages and keeps his Olympiakos side top

Deportivo (0) 0 Monaco (3) 5
Chevanton 22
Givet 37, Saviola 39
16,000 Maicon 55, Adebayor 76

Liverpool (0) 3 Olympiakos (1) 1
Sinama-Pongolle 47 Rivaldo 27
Mellor 80, Gerrard 86 42,045

A fearsome Gerrard strike completed a stunning turnaround in the fortunes of Liverpool who needed three second half goals to qualify ahead of Olympiakos and made it with just four minutes to go after Rivaldo had put the Greeks ahead. Monaco topped the group and emphasised Deportivo's role as whipping boys with a comprehensive 5-0 away win

GROUP A TABLE

	P	W	D	L	DIF	PTS
Monaco	6	4	0	2	6	12
Liverpool	6	3	1	2	3	10
Olympiakos	6	3	1	2	0	10
Deportivo	6	0	2	4	-9	2

GROUP B

QUALIFYING

B Leverkusen (1) 5 Banik Ostrava (0) 0
Banik Ostrava (1) 2 B Leverkusen (0) 1

Dinamo Kiev (1) 1 Trabzonspor (1) 2
Trabzonspor (0) 0 Dinamo Kiev (2) 2

Wisla Krakow (0) 0 Real Madrid (0) 2
Real Madrid (2) 3 Wisla Krakow (0) 1

B Leverkusen (1) 3 Real Madrid (0) 0
Krzynowek 39 23,000
Franca 50
Berbatov 55

Roma 0 Dinamo Kiev 3
Match abandonded. Dinamo Kiev awarded win

Referee Anders Frisk abandons Roma game after being injured by a missile from the crowd, while Real are rocked as Leverkusen hit three

Dinamo Kiev (1) 4 B Leverkusen (0) 2
Rincon 30,69 Voronin 59
Cernat 74,90 Nowotny 68
83,000

Real Madrid (1) 4 Roma (2) 2
Raul 39,72 De Rossi 3
Figo 53 pen Cassano 21
Roberto Carlos 79 60,000

Raul the hero with two goals to haul Real Madrid back from 2-0 down to Roma, while sub Florin Cernat scores late to take Kiev to the top

B Leverkusen (0) 3 Roma (1) 1
Roque Junior 48 Jones 26 og
Krzynowek 59 22,000
Franca 94

Real Madrid (1) 1 Dinamo Kiev (0) 0
Owen 35 45,000

Dinamo Kiev (2) 2 Real Madrid (2) 2
Yussuf 13 Raul 38
Verpakovskis 23 Figo 44 pen
80,000

Roma (0) 1 B Leverkusen (0) 1
Montella 90 Berbatov 82

Dinamo Kiev (0) 2 Roma (0) 0
Dellas 73 og 55,000
Shatskikh 82

Real Madrid (0) 1 B Leverkusen (1) 1
Raul 70 Berbatov 36
72,000

B Leverkusen (0) 3 Dinamo Kiev (0) 0
Juan 51 23,000
Voronin 77
Babic 86

Roma (0) 0 Real Madrid (1) 3
Ronaldo 9
Figo 60 pen,82

Dinamo Kiev needed only a point from their final game at Bayer Leverkusen but failed to get it as Juan scored the first of three for the Germans to take them through in top place.
Real Madrid made sure of a place in the last 16 by beating disappointing Roma, who never recovered from a disastrous abandoned game start to the group

GROUP B TABLE

	P	W	D	L	DIF	PTS
B Leverkusen	6	3	2	1	6	11
Real Madrid	6	3	2	1	3	11
Dinamo Kiev	6	3	1	2	3	10
Roma	6	0	1	5	-12	1

GROUP C

QUALIFYING

Juventus (0) 2 Djurgarden (1) 2
Djurgarden (1) 1 Juventus (2) 4

PAOK Salonika (0) 0 Maccabi Tel-Aviv (2) 3
Maccabi Tel-Aviv (1) 1 PAOK Salonika (0) 0

Ajax (0) 0 Juventus (1) 1
49,000 Nedved 42

Maccabi Tel-Aviv (0) 0 Bayern Munich (0) 1
20,000 Makaay 64 pen

Bayern Munich (2) 4 Ajax (0) 0
Makaay 28,44,52 pen 50,000
Ze Roberto 55

Roy MaKaay hits a hat-trick and adds an assist in a Bayern demolition of his fellow Dutchmen from Ajax

Juventus (1) 1 Maccabi Tel-Aviv (0) 0
Camoranesi 37 6,000

Ajax (3) 3 Maccabi Tel-Aviv (0) 0
Sonck 3 48,000
de Jong 21
van der Vaart 33

Juventus (0) 1 Bayern Munich (0) 0
Nedved 75 18,000

Bayern Munich (0) 0 Juventus (0) 1
59,000 Del Piero 90

Gianluigi Buffon's brilliance keeps Bayern and particularly striker Makaay at bay and Juve profit when Alessandro Del Piero pounces in the last minute

Maccabi Tel-Aviv (0) 2 Ajax (0) 1
Dego 49,56 de Ridder 87
32,000

Bayern Munich (3) 5 Maccabi Tel-Aviv (0) 1
Pizarro 12 Dego 55 pen
Salihamidzic 37 25,000
Frings 44
Makaay 71,80

Juventus (1) 1 Ajax (0) 0
Zalayeta 14 7,000

Ajax (1) 2 Bayern Munich (1) 2
Galasek 39 Makaay 8
Mitea 63 Ballack 78
50,000

Maccabi Tel-Aviv (1) 1 Juventus (0) 1
Dego 29 pen Del Piero 71
19,000

Dutch champions Ajax claimed a Uefa spot in the final game with a 2-2 draw against Bayern Munich who were already assured of second spot going into the game.
Italian form side Juventus dropped their only points of an impressive campaign when they drew with Tel Aviv but still finished six points ahead of Bayern

GROUP C TABLE

	P	W	D	L	DIF	PTS
Juventus	6	5	1	0	5	16
B Munich	6	3	1	2	7	10
Ajax	6	1	1	4	-4	4
Macc Tel-Aviv	6	1	1	4	-8	4

GROUP D

QUALIFYING

D Bucharest (1) 1 Man Utd (1) 2
Man Utd (0) 3 D Bucharest (0) 0

Ferencvaros (1) 1 Sparta Prague (0) 0
Sparta Prague (1) 2 Ferencvaros (0) 0

Fenerbahce (1) 1 Sparta Prague (0) 0
van Hooijdonk 16 52,000

Lyon (2) 2 Man Utd (0) 2
Cris 35 van Nistelrooy 56,61
Frau 44 35,000

Man Utd (3) 6 Fenerbahce (0) 2
Giggs 7 Nobre 46
Rooney 17,28,54 Sanli 60
van Nistelrooy 78 67,128
Bellion 81

Sparta Prague (1) 1 Lyon (1) 2
Jun 7 Essien 25
12,000 Wiltord 58

Fenerbahce (0) 1 Lyon (0) 3
Nobre 68 Juninho 55
49,000 Cris 66
Frau 87

Sparta Prague (0) 0 Man Utd (0) 0
20,654

Lyon (1) 4 Fenerbahce (1) 2
Essien 22 Selcuk 14
Malouda 53 Sanli 73
Nilmar 90,90 36,000

Lyon sub Nilmar hits two in injury time to secure a late win against Fenerbahce and then goes on to get another brace in the last match against Sparta Prague

Man Utd (2) 4 Sparta Prague (0) 1
van Nistelrooy 14, Zelenka 53
25 pen,60,90 66,706

Man Utd (1) 2 Lyon (1) 1
Neville, G 19 Diarra 40
van Nistelrooy 53 66,398

Sparta Prague (0) 0 Fenerbahce (1) 1
11,000 Kovac 20 og

Fenerbahce (0) 3 Man Utd (0) 0
Sanli 46,62,90 35,000

Lyon (2) 5 Sparta Prague (0) 0
Essien 7 39,000
Nilmar 19,51
Idangar 83
Bergougnoux 90

Fenerbache finished the group games with a comprehensive win over the Manchester United second string and gained revenge for a hammering at Old Trafford. It will give the Turks confidence for their Uefa Cup campaign. Lyon took advantage to top the group with a 5-0 thrashing of Sparta Prague who finished with just one group point

GROUP D TABLE

	P	W	D	L	DIF	PTS
Lyon	6	4	1	1	9	13
Man Utd	6	3	2	1	5	11
Fenerbahce	6	3	0	3	-3	9
Sparta Prague	6	0	1	5	-11	1

QUALIFYING AND GROUP STAGES

GROUP E

QUALIFYING

Crvena Zvezda (2) 3 PSV Eindhoven (1) 2
PSV Eindhoven (2) 5 Crvena Zvezda (0) 0

Rosenborg BK (2) 2 Maccabi Haifa (1) 1
Maccabi Haifa (2) 2 Rosenborg BK (0) 3

Arsenal (1) 1 PSV (0) 0
Alex 42 og — 34,068

Panathinaikos (1) 2 Rosenborg BK (0) 1
Gonzalez 43,79 — Johnsen, F 90
13,000

PSV Eindhoven (0) 1 Panathinaikos (0) 0
Vennegoor 80 — 27,000

Rosenborg BK (0) 1 Arsenal (1) 1
Strand 52 — Ljungberg 6
21,000

Norwegian international Roar Strand's well-placed strike equalises Freddie Ljungberg's sixth minute goal to earn Rosenborg an unlikely home draw against the English champions

Panathinaikos (0) 2 Arsenal (1) 2
Gonzalez 65 — Ljungberg 18
Olisadebe 82 — Henry 74
12,000

Rosenborg BK (1) 1 PSV Eindhoven (1) 2
Storflor 42 — Farfan 26
21,000 — de Jong 86

Arsenal (1) 1 Panathinaikos (0) 1
Henry 16 pen — Cygan 75 og
35,137

PSV Eindhoven (1) 1 Rosenborg BK (0) 0
Beasley 10 — 26,000

PSV Eindhoven (1) 1 Arsenal (1) 1
Ooijer 9 — Henry 31
35,000

Rosenborg BK (0) 2 Panathinaikos (1) 2
Helstad 68,76 — Konstantinou 16
19,000 — Skacel 71

Arsenal (4) 5 Rosenborg BK (1) 1
Reyes 3 — Hoftun 38
Henry 24 — 35,421
Fabregas 29
Pires 41 pen
van Persie 84

Panathinaikos (2) 4 PSV Eindhoven (1) 1
Papadopoulos 30 — Beasley 37
Munch 45 pen,57 — 10,000
Sanmartean 81

Panathinaikos went out of the competition in style with two goals by German Markus Munch helping them to a 4-1 win over already qualified PSV, who qualified for the first time in nine attempts. However, the win only earned the Greeks a Uefa Cup spot as Arsenal swept to the top of the group with a 5-1 thrashing of Rosenborg

GROUP E TABLE

	P	W	D	L	DIF	PTS
Arsenal	6	2	4	0	5	10
PSV Eindhoven	6	3	1	2	-1	10
Panathinaikos	6	2	3	1	3	9
Rosenborg	6	0	2	4	-7	2

GROUP F

QUALIFYING

Shakhtar Donetsk (1) 4 Club Brugge (0) 1
Club Brugge (2) 2 Shakhtar Donetsk (1) 2

Celtic (0) 1 Barcelona (1) 3
Sutton 59 — Deco 20
60,000 — Giuly 78
Larsson 82

Former Hoops' favourite Henrik Larsson scores from the bench on his return to Celtic Park as Barcelona claim revenge for last season's 4th round UEFA exit

Shakhtar Donetsk (0) 0 AC Milan (0) 1
30,000 — Seedorf 84

AC Milan (1) 3 Celtic (0) 1
Shevchenko 8 — Varga 74
Inzaghi 89 — 68,000
Pirlo 90

Barcelona (1) 3 Shakhtar Donetsk (0) 0
Deco 15 — 64,000
Ronaldinho 64 pen
Eto'o 89

AC Milan (1) 1 Barcelona (0) 0
Shevchenko 31 — 77,000

A header from Andriy Shevchenko is enough to put AC Milan clear at the top of the group spoiling the 100% record of Barca coach Frank Rijkaard

Shakhtar Donetsk (0) 3 Celtic (0) 0
Matuzalem 57,62 — 30,000
Brandao 78

Barcelona (1) 2 AC Milan (1) 1
Eto'o 37 — Shevchenko 17
Ronaldinho 89 — 95,000

Celtic (1) 1 Shakhtar Donetsk (0) 0
Thompson 25 — 58,347

AC Milan (0) 4 Shakhtar Donetsk (0) 0
Kaka 52,90 — 39,000
Crespo 53,85

Barcelona (1) 1 Celtic (1) 1
Eto'o 24 — Hartson 45
74,000

Celtic (0) 0 AC Milan (0) 0
59,228

Shakhtar Donetsk (2) 2 Barcelona (0) 0
Aghahowa 14,22 — 25,000

Two favourites for this season's competition sorted out the qualifying places early. So, on the final night Barcelona and AC Milan were only battling for top spot in the group. It went to Milan after Ukrainian side Shakhtar Donetsk won the scrap for the Uefa spot by beating a weakened Barcelona, while Celtic could only draw against AC Milan

GROUP F TABLE

	P	W	D	L	DIF	PTS
AC Milan	6	4	1	1	7	13
Barcelona	6	3	1	2	3	10
Shakhtar	6	2	0	4	-4	6
Celtic	6	1	2	3	-6	5

GROUP G

QUALIFYING

Benfica (1) 1 Anderlecht (0) 0
Anderlecht (1) 3 Benfica (0) 0

Basel (1) 1 Inter milan (1) 1
Inter Milan (2) 4 Basel (0) 1

Inter Milan (1) 2 W Bremen (0) 0
Adriano 34 pen,89 — 45,000

Valencia (2) 2 Anderlecht (0) 0
Vicente 16 — 34,000
Baraja 45

Anderlecht (0) 1 Inter Milan (1) 3
Baseggio 90 — Martins 9
22,000 — Adriano 51
Stankovic 55

W Bremen (0) 2 Valencia (1) 1
Klose 60 — Vicente 2
Charisteas 84 — 36,000

Anderlecht (1) 1 W Bremen (1) 2
Wilhelmsson 26 — Klasnic 36,59
22,000

Valencia (0) 1 Inter Milan (0) 5
Aimar 73 — Stankovic 47
40,000 — Vieri 49
van der Meyde 76
Adriano 81
Cruz 90

Dejan Stankovic and Christian Vieri do the damage in Spain as a rampant Inter Milan put injury-hit Valencia to the sword with a 5-1 thrashing

Inter Milan (0) 0 Valencia (0) 0
40,000

W Bremen (3) 5 Anderlecht (1) 1
Klasnic 2,16,79 — Iachtchouk 30
Klose 33 — 37,000
Jensen 90

Anderlecht (1) 1 Valencia (1) 2
Wilhelmsson 24 — Corradi 19
26,000 — Di Vaio 48

W Bremen (0) 1 Inter Milan (0) 1
Ismael 49 pen — Martins 55
37,000

Inter Milan (1) 3 Anderlecht (0) 0
Cruz 33 — 30,000
Martins 60,63

Valencia (0) 0 W Bremen (0) 2
40,000 — Valdez 83,90

Spanish champions Valencia were condemned to a defence of their Uefa Cup crown. They needed to beat Werder Bremen in the final game to match the Germans on points in the tussle for the second qualifying spot. Bremen won a tense match through substitute Nelson Valdez who scored twice. Inter Milan won the group only dropping four points

GROUP G TABLE

	P	W	D	L	DIF	PTS
Inter Milan	6	4	2	0	11	14
W Bremen	6	4	1	1	6	13
Valencia	6	2	1	3	-4	7
Anderlecht	6	0	0	6	-13	0

GROUP H

QUALIFYING

CSKA Moscow (1) 2 Rangers (1) 1
Rangers (0) 1 CSKA Moscow (0) 1

Porto (0) 0 CSKA Moscow (0) 0
39,000

Paris SG (0) 0 Chelsea (2) 3
45,000 — Terry 29, Drogba 45,76

CSKA Moscow (0) 2 Paris SG (0) 0
Semak 64 — 10,000
Vagner Love 77 pen

Chelsea (1) 3 Porto (0) 1
Smertin 7 — McCarthy 68
Drogba 50 — 39,237
Terry 70

Chelsea (2) 2 CSKA Moscow (0) 0
Terry 9 — 33,945
Gudjohnsen 45

Paris SG (2) 2 Porto (0) 0
Coridon 30 — 48,000
Pauleta 31

Portuguese striker Pauleta is recalled by Paris St-Germain and scores to get the French's side's campaign started with a win over his fellow countrymen

CSKA Moscow (0) 0 Chelsea (1) 1
28,000 — Robben 24

Porto (0) 0 Paris SG (0) 0
30,000

CSKA Moscow (0) 0 Porto (1) 1
21,000 — McCarthy 28

Chelsea (0) 0 Paris SG (0) 0
39,626

Porto (0) 2 Chelsea (1) 1
Diego 60 — Duff 33
McCarthy 85 — 42,000

A trademark leap and header from Benny McCarthy saves Porto from being the first holders not to survive the group stages as his late goal beats Chelsea

Paris SG (1) 1 CSKA Moscow (1) 3
Pancrate 37 — Semak 28,64,70
40,000

Chelsea were the first side to qualify for the competition with four straight wins. José Mourinho could afford to relax in his defence of the title and field weaker teams. That gave cup holders Porto the chance to hand a rare defeat to their former manager and slip through at the expense of CSKA Moscow who had to settle for the Uefa spot

GROUP H TABLE

	P	W	D	L	DIF	PTS
Chelsea	6	4	1	1	7	13
Porto	6	2	2	2	-2	8
CSKA Moscow	6	2	1	3	0	7
Paris SG	6	1	2	3	-5	5

LAST 16

Barcelona (0) 2 **Chelsea** (1) 1
Lopez 67 — Belletti 33 og
Eto'o 73 — 78,000

Chelsea (3) 4 **Barcelona** (2) 2
Gudjohnsen 8 — Ronaldinho 27 pen,38
Lampard 17 — 41,515
Duff 19
Terry 76

A spat between José Mourinho and Barca's Frank Rijkaard leaves a sour taste at the Nou Camp. Back at Stamford Bridge both sides let the football do the talking in a pulsating match finally won by John Terry's header

Bayern Munich (1) 3 **Arsenal** (0) 1
Pizarro 3,58 — Toure 88
Salihamidzic 65 — 59,000

Arsenal (0) 1 **Bayern Munich** (0) 0
Henry 66 — 35,463

Liverpool (2) 3 **B Leverkusen** (0) 1
Luis Garcia 15 — Franca 90
Riise 35 — 40,942
Hamann 90

B Leverkusen (0) 1 **Liverpool** (2) 3
Krzynowek 88 — Luis Garcia 28,32
23,000 — Baros 67

Man Utd (0) 0 **AC Milan** (0) 1
67,162 — Crespo 78

AC Milan (0) 1 **Man Utd** (0) 0
Crespo 61 — 79,000

Hernan Crespo makes light of the absence of strike partner Shevchenko with a crucial away goal at Old Trafford And repeats the dose in Milan with a well-directed far-post header to beat Howard in a poor night for United

Porto (0) 1 **Inter Milan** (1) 1
Ricardo Costa 61 — Martins 24
50,000

Inter Milan (1) 3 **Porto** (0) 1
Adriano 6,63,86 — Jorge Costa 68
71,000

Ricardo Costa keeps Porto's defence of their trophy alive against unbeaten Inter who start with a Obafemi Martins's goal. Adriano's hat-trick back in Milan denies holders Porto a place in the quarter finals to send Inter through

PSV Eindhoven (1) 1 **Monaco** (0) 0
Alex 8 — 42,000

Monaco (0) 0 **PSV Eindhoven** (1) 2
16,000 — Vennegoor 27
Beasley 69

Real Madrid (1) 1 **Juventus** (0) 0
Helguera 31 — 78,000

Juventus (0) 2 **Real Madrid** (0) 0
Trezeguet 75 — 59,000
Zalayeta 116
After extra time

W Bremen (0) 0 **Lyon** (1) 3
37,000 — Wiltord 9
Diarra 77
Juninho 80

Lyon (3) 7 **W Bremen** (1) 2
Wiltord 8,55,64 — Micoud 32
Essien 17,30 — Ismael 57 pen
Malouda 60
Berthod 80 pen — 37,000

QUARTER-FINALS

AC Milan (1) 2 **Inter Milan** (0) 0
Stam 45 — 80,000
Shevchenko 74

Inter Milan 0 **AC Milan** 3
Match abandoned. AC Milan awarded win

Two goals and a clean sheet put AC in the driving seat in the battle of the Milanese. Stam and Shevchenko are the scorers – both from Andrea Pirlo free-kicks - and this tie looks like confirming Inter as the lesser of the two Milans. Inter 'Ultras' cause the abandonment of the quarter-final as a rocket strikes AC keeper Dida and the players leave the flare-covered pitch in the 73rd minute with Uefa later ruling that AC go through

Chelsea (1) 4 **Bayern Munich** (0) 2
Cole 4 — Schweinsteiger 52
Lampard 59,70 — Ballack 90 pen
Drogba 81 — 40,253

Bayern Munich (0) 3 **Chelsea** (1) 2
Pizarro 65 — Lampard 30
Guerrero 90 — Drogba 80
Scholl 90 — 59,000

Frank Lampard fires Chelsea into a commanding position at Stamford Bridge while an injury-time German rally in Munich is too late to unseat the Blues

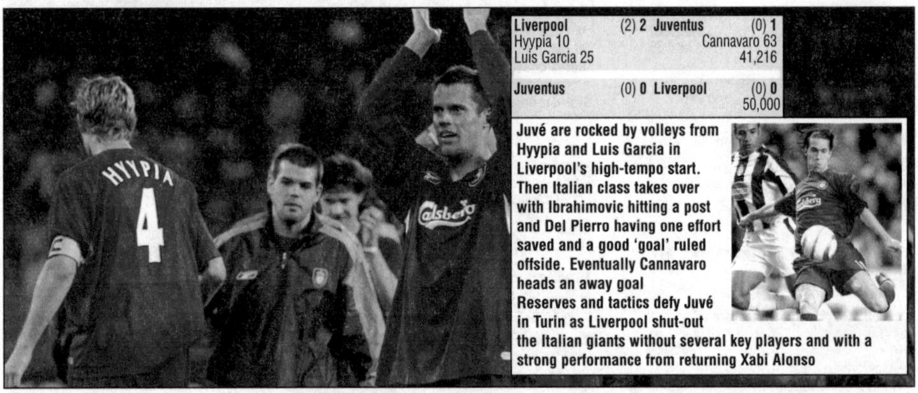

Liverpool (2) 2 **Juventus** (0) 1
Hyypia 10 — Cannavaro 63
Luis Garcia 25 — 41,216

Juventus (0) 0 **Liverpool** (0) 0
50,000

Juvé are rocked by volleys from Hyypia and Luis Garcia in Liverpool's high-tempo start. Then Italian class takes over with Ibrahimovic hitting a post and Del Pierro having one effort saved and a good 'goal' ruled offside. Eventually Cannavaro heads an away goal Reserves and tactics defy Juvé in Turin as Liverpool shut-out the Italian giants without several key players and with a strong performance from returning Xabi Alonso

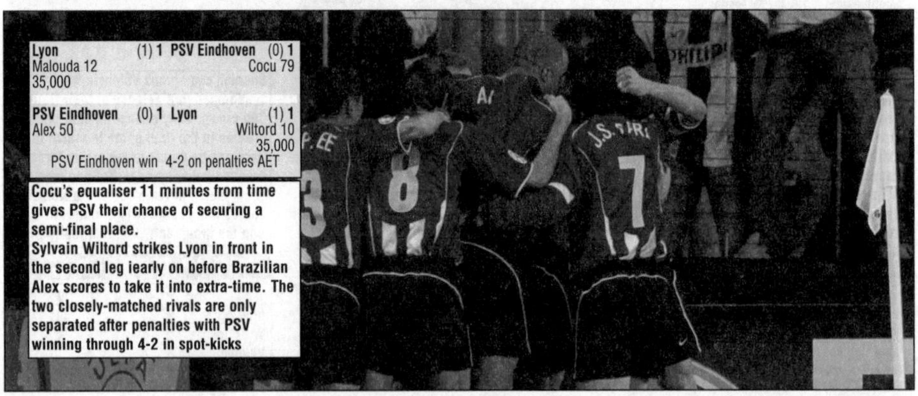

Lyon (1) 1 **PSV Eindhoven** (0) 1
Malouda 12 — Cocu 79
35,000

PSV Eindhoven (0) 1 **Lyon** (1) 1
Alex 50 — Wiltord 10
35,000
PSV Eindhoven win 4-2 on penalties AET

Cocu's equaliser 11 minutes from time gives PSV their chance of securing a semi-final place. Sylvain Wiltord strikes Lyon in front in the second leg iearly on before Brazilian Alex scores to take it into extra-time. The two closely-matched rivals are only separated after penalties with PSV winning through 4-2 in spot-kicks

SEMI-FINALS

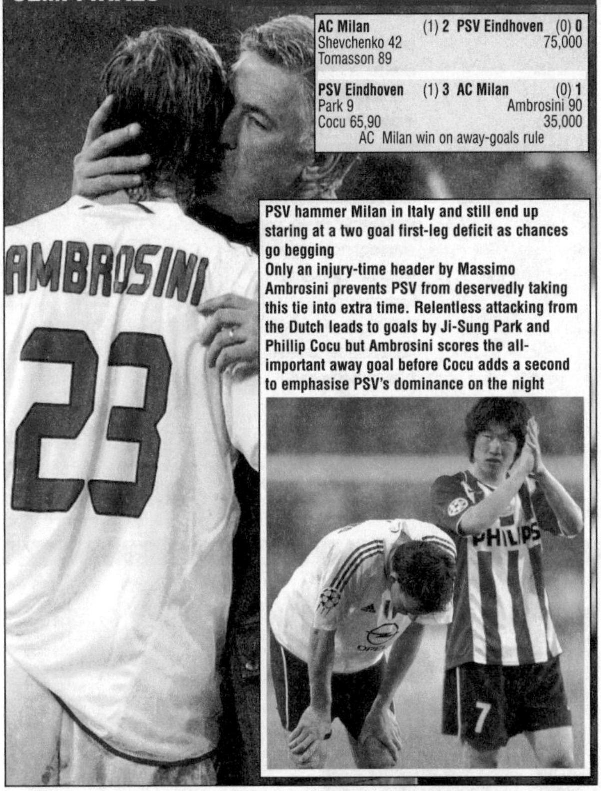
AMBROSINI
23

AC Milan	(1) 2	PSV Eindhoven	(0) 0
Shevchenko 42			75,000
Tomasson 89			

PSV Eindhoven	(1) 3	AC Milan	(0) 1
Park 9			Ambrosini 90
Cocu 65,90			35,000

AC Milan win on away-goals rule

PSV hammer Milan in Italy and still end up staring at a two goal first-leg deficit as chances go begging

Only an injury-time header by Massimo Ambrosini prevents PSV from deservedly taking this tie into extra time. Relentless attacking from the Dutch leads to goals by Ji-Sung Park and Phillip Cocu but Ambrosini scores the all-important away goal before Cocu adds a second to emphasise PSV's dominance on the night

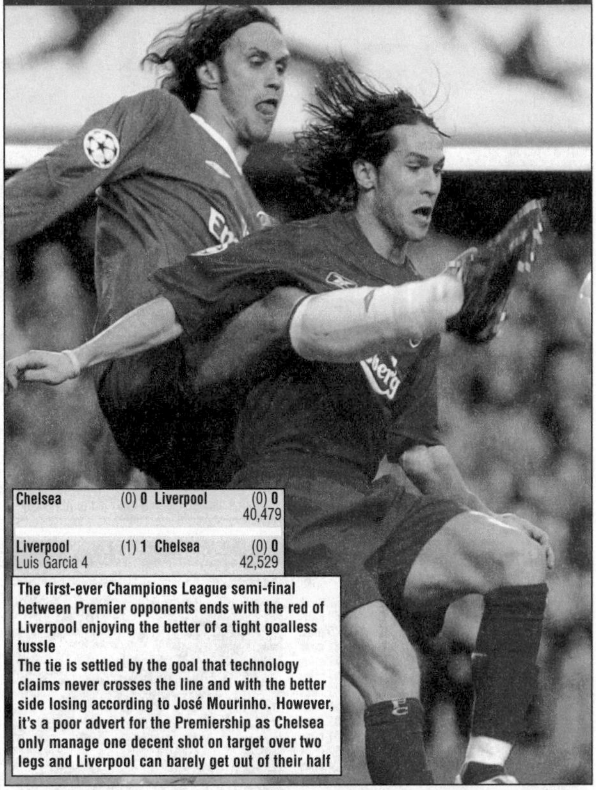

Chelsea	(0) 0	Liverpool	(0) 0
			40,479

Liverpool	(1) 1	Chelsea	(0) 0
Luis Garcia 4			42,529

The first-ever Champions League semi-final between Premier opponents ends with the red of Liverpool enjoying the better of a tight goalless tussle

The tie is settled by the goal that technology claims never crosses the line and with the better side losing according to José Mourinho. However, it's a poor advert for the Premiership as Chelsea only manage one decent shot on target over two legs and Liverpool can barely get out of their half

FINAL

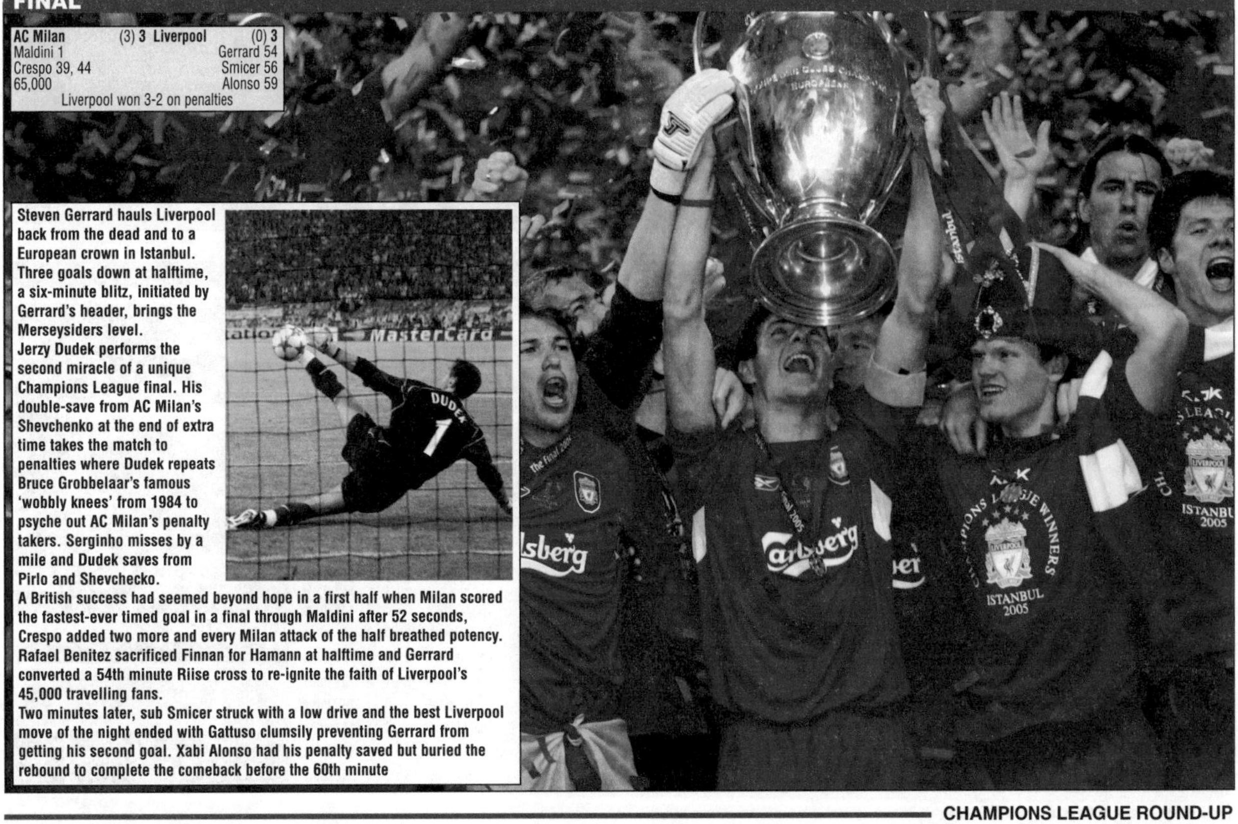
Carlsberg
ISTANBUL
2005

AC Milan	(3) 3	Liverpool	(0) 3
Maldini 1			Gerrard 54
Crespo 39, 44			Smicer 56
65,000			Alonso 59

Liverpool won 3-2 on penalties

Steven Gerrard hauls Liverpool back from the dead and to a European crown in Istanbul. Three goals down at halftime, a six-minute blitz, initiated by Gerrard's header, brings the Merseysiders level.

Jerzy Dudek performs the second miracle of a unique Champions League final. His double-save from AC Milan's Shevchenko at the end of extra time takes the match to penalties where Dudek repeats Bruce Grobbelaar's famous 'wobbly knees' from 1984 to psyche out AC Milan's penalty takers. Serginho misses by a mile and Dudek saves from Pirlo and Shevchecko.

A British success had seemed beyond hope in a first half when Milan scored the fastest-ever timed goal in a final through Maldini after 52 seconds, Crespo added two more and every Milan attack of the half breathed potency. Rafael Benitez sacrificed Finnan for Hamann at halftime and Gerrard converted a 54th minute Riise cross to re-ignite the faith of Liverpool's 45,000 travelling fans.

Two minutes later, sub Smicer struck with a low drive and the best Liverpool move of the night ended with Gattuso clumsily preventing Gerrard from getting his second goal. Xabi Alonso had his penalty saved but buried the rebound to complete the comeback before the 60th minute

STADIUM CAPACITY AND HOME CROWDS

	CLUB	CAPACITY	AVGE (%)	HIGH	LOW
1	B Leverkusen	23000	100	23000	23000
2	Man Utd	68190	97.88	67128	66398
3	Chelsea	42449	91.19	40479	33945
4	Arsenal	38500	90.58	35421	34068
5	Liverpool	45362	87.98	42529	33517
6	PSV Eindhoven	36500	86.58	35000	26000
7	Lyon	42000	86.31	39000	35000
8	W Bremen	43000	85.27	37000	36000
9	Monaco	18521	82.79	17000	14000
10	AC Milan	85700	79.11	80000	39000
11	Barcelona	98800	78.61	95000	64000
12	Porto	50106	73.84	42000	30000
13	Bayern Munich	69060	69.87	59000	25000
14	Real Madrid	87000	67.82	72000	45000
15	Inter Milan	85700	33.55	45000	0*
16	Juventus	69041	29.33	50000	6000

Key: Average. The percentage of each stadium filled in Champions League games over the season (AVE), the stadium capacity and the highest and lowest crowds recorded.

*match abandoned and awarded to AC Milan

AWAY ATTENDANCE

	CLUB	AVGE (%)	HIGH	LOW
1	Lyon	89.4	66398	12000
2	Chelsea	89.22	59000	28000
3	Liverpool	87.63	50000	15000
4	Porto	87.45	48000	22000
5	Man Utd	86.24	35000	20500
6	Barcelona	84.92	77000	25000
7	Inter Milan	84.58	80000	22000
8	Arsenal	81.03	35000	12000
9	Juventus	79.36	59000	19000
10	PSV Eindhoven	78.9	75000	10000
11	AC Milan	73.79	95000	0*
12	Monaco	72.86	33517	16000
13	W Bremen	70.48	45000	22000
14	Bayern Munich	66.61	50000	18000
15	Real Madrid	65.4	80000	0**
16	B Leverkusen	60.86	83000	0**

Key: Average. How close each club has come to filling grounds in its away Champions League matches (AVE) and the highest and lowest crowds recorded.

** played behind closed doors

CLUB STRIKE FORCE

	CLUB	GOALS	CSR
1	Lyon	29	32 mins
2	B Leverkusen	21	43 mins
3	Bayern Munich	20	45 mins
4	Inter Milan	23	47 mins
5	Man Utd	19	47 mins
6	Monaco	19	47 mins
7	Panathinaikos	11	49 mins
8	Chelsea	21	51 mins
9	Dinamo Kiev	14	51 mins
10	W Bremen	14	51 mins
11	AC Milan	23	52 mins
12	Fenerbahce	10	54 mins
13	Arsenal	13	55 mins
14	Barcelona	13	55 mins
15	Real Madrid	17	55 mins
16	PSV Eindhoven	21	61 mins
17	Shakhtar Donetsk	11	65 mins
18	Rosenborg BK	11	68 mins
19	Liverpool	20	69 mins
20	Juventus	15	74 mins
21	Ajax	6	90 mins
22	CSKA Moscow	8	90 mins
23	Maccabi Tel-Aviv	8	90 mins
24	Valencia	6	90 mins
25	Anderlecht	7	103 mins
26	Olympiakos	5	108 mins
27	Porto	6	120 mins
28	Celtic	4	135 mins
29	Roma	4	135 mins
30	Paris SG	3	180 mins
31	Sparta Prague	4	188 mins
32	Deportivo	3	240 mins

Lyon's Cris and Frau celebrate a goal

1 Lyon

Goals in the Champions League	29
Club Strike Rate (CSR) Average number of minutes between League goals scored by club	32

CLUB DEFENCE

Thuram; keeping it tight at Juventus

1 Juventus

Goals conceded in the Champions League	7
Club Defensive Rate (CSR) Average number of minutes between goals conceded by club	159

	CLUB	CONCEDED	CS	CDR
1	Juventus	7	7	159 mins
2	Liverpool	10	7	138 mins
3	AC Milan	9	9	133 mins
4	Monaco	7	5	129 mins
5	Olympiakos	5	4	108 mins
6	CSKA Moscow	7	2	103 mins
7	Inter Milan	12	3	90 mins
8	PSV Eindhoven	15	5	86 mins
9	Real Madrid	11	4	85 mins
10	Chelsea	13	5	83 mins
11	Arsenal	9	2	80 mins
12	Deportivo	9	4	80 mins
13	Lyon	12	2	78 mins
14	Man Utd	12	2	75 mins
15	Dinamo Kiev	10	3	72 mins
16	Porto	10	3	72 mins
17	Bayern Munich	13	2	69 mins
18	Panathinaikos	8	0	68 mins
19	Paris SG	8	3	68 mins
20	Barcelona	11	1	65 mins
21	B Leverkusen	15	3	60 mins
22	Maccabi Tel-Aviv	12	2	60 mins
23	Shakhtar Donetsk	12	2	60 mins
24	Ajax	10	1	54 mins
25	Celtic	10	2	54 mins
26	Sparta Prague	14	2	54 mins
27	Valencia	10	2	54 mins
28	Rosenborg BK	16	0	47 mins
29	W Bremen	16	1	45 mins
30	Fenerbahce	13	3	42 mins
31	Anderlecht	18	1	40 mins
32	Roma	16	0	34 mins

CLUB DISCIPLINARY RECORD

TOTTI
10

Bad discipline on and off the field at Roma

1 Roma

Yellow	14
Red	3
Cards Average Average number of minutes between a card being shown of either colour	26

	CLUB	Y	R	TOT	CA
1	Roma	14	3	17	26 mins
2	Valencia	18	2	20	27 mins
3	Olympiakos	17	1	18	30 mins
4	Dinamo Kiev	17	1	18	35 mins
5	B Leverkusen	24	1	25	36 mins
6	Porto	20	0	20	36 mins
7	Shakhtar Donetsk	15	4	19	38 mins
8	W Bremen	18	1	19	38 mins
9	Fenerbahce	12	2	14	39 mins
10	Juventus	27	1	28	40 mins
11	Panathinaikos	13	0	13	42 mins
12	Celtic	12	0	12	45 mins
13	CSKA Moscow	15	1	16	45 mins
14	Deportivo	16	0	16	45 mins
15	Paris SG	11	1	12	45 mins
16	Chelsea	21	1	22	49 mins
17	Monaco	16	2	18	50 mins
18	Arsenal	12	2	14	51 mins
19	Inter Milan	18	1	19	52 mins
20	Real Madrid	16	1	17	55 mins
21	Bayern Munich	16	0	16	56 mins
22	Liverpool	24	0	24	58 mins
23	Ajax	9	0	9	60 mins
24	Anderlecht	12	0	12	60 mins
25	Man Utd	15	0	15	60 mins
26	PSV Eindhoven	20	1	21	61 mins
27	Sparta Prague	11	1	12	63 mins
28	Maccabi Tel-Aviv	9	0	9	70 mins
29	AC Milan	14	0	14	79 mins
30	Lyon	10	0	10	93 mins
31	Barcelona	7	0	7	103 mins
32	Rosenborg BK	7	0	7	107 mins

PLAYER DISCIPLINARY RECORD

	PLAYER	CLUB	Y	R	TOT	Avge
1	Ponte	B Leverkusen	5	0	5	125 mins
2	Hasi	Anderlecht	4	0	4	127 mins
3	Barcauan	Shakhtar	3	1	4	127 mins
4	Vieira	Arsenal	3	1	4	132 mins
5	Semberas	CSKA	4	1	5	136 mins
6	Evra	Monaco	4	1	5	138 mins
7	Lauren	Arsenal	3	1	4	151 mins
8	Freier	B Leverkusen	3	0	3	153 mins
9	Jorge Costa	Porto	4	0	4	153 mins
10	Baumann	W Bremen	3	0	3	161 mins
11	Cesar	Deportivo	3	0	3	165 mins
12	Drogba	Chelsea	3	1	4	174 mins
13	Aurelio	Fenerbahce	3	0	3	180 mins
14	Anatolakis	Olympiakos	3	0	3	180 mins
15	Schurrer	Olympiakos	3	0	3	180 mins
16	Ismael	W Bremen	2	1	3	181 mins
17	Hamann	Liverpool	4	0	4	185 mins
18	Samuel	Real Madrid	4	0	4	187 mins
19	Poborsky	Sparta Prague	2	1	3	189 mins
20	Blasi	Juventus	3	0	3	202 mins

RWE

Leverkusen's Ponte; five cards

1 Ponte

Yellow	5
Red	0
Cards Average Average number of minutes between a card being shown of either colour	125

CHART-TOPPING GOALSCORERS

1 van Nistelrooy

Goals in Chapions League	8
Contribution to Attacking Power (AP) Average number of minutes between League team goals while on pitch	40
Player Strike Rate (SR) Average number of minutes between League goals scored by player	66

	PLAYER	TEAM	G	AP	SR
1	van Nistelrooy	Man Utd	8	40	66
2	Adriano	Inter Milan	10	37	67
3	Dego	Maccabi Tel-Aviv	4	67	68
4	Nilmar	Lyon	4	26	73
5	Franca	B Leverkusen	5	36	88
6	Crespo	AC Milan	6	41	91
7	Trezeguet	Juventus	4	36	91
8	Martins	Inter Milan	5	52	94
9	Vicente	Valencia	2	66	99
10	Makaay	Bayern Munich	7	43	100

CHART-TOPPING MIDFIELDERS

1 Hamann

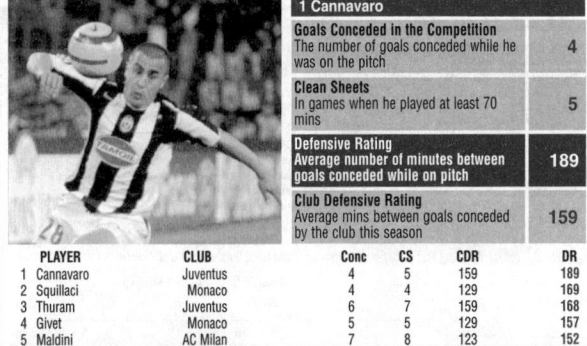

Goals scored in the Champions League	1
Defensive Rating Av number of mins between goals conceded while on the pitch	247
Contribution to Attacking Power Average number of minutes between team goals while on pitch	62
Scoring Difference Defensive Rating minus Contribution to Attacking Power	185

	PLAYER	CLUB	G	DR	AP	SD
1	Hamann	Liverpool	1	247	62	185
2	Camoranesi	Juventus	1	263	99	164
3	Zambrotta	Juventus	0	174	69	105
4	Emerson	Juventus	1	170	73	97
5	Nedved	Juventus	3	168	77	91

CHART-TOPPING DEFENDERS

1 Cannavaro

Goals Conceded in the Competition The number of goals conceded while he was on the pitch	4
Clean Sheets In games when he played at least 70 mins	5
Defensive Rating Average number of minutes between goals conceded while on pitch	189
Club Defensive Rating Average mins between goals conceded by the club this season	159

	PLAYER	CLUB	Conc	CS	CDR	DR
1	Cannavaro	Juventus	4	5	159	189
2	Squillaci	Monaco	4	4	129	169
3	Thuram	Juventus	6	7	159	168
4	Givet	Monaco	5	5	129	157
5	Maldini	AC Milan	7	8	123	152

CHART-TOPPING GOALKEEPERS

1 Buffon

Goals conceded in the Champions League	6
Counting Games Competition games when he played at least 70 minutes	11
Clean Sheets In games when he played at least 70 mins	7
Defensive Rating Average number of minutes between League goals conceded while on pitch	170

	PLAYER	CLUB	CG	Conc	CS	DR
1	Buffon	Juventus	11	6	7	170
2	Dudek	Liverpool	10	7	5	133
3	Roma	Monaco	10	7	5	129
4	Dida	AC Milan	12	9	8	123
5	Akinfeev	CSKA Moscow	8	7	2	103

TEAM OF THE SEASON

BUFFON
JUVENTUS
M 1020 DR 170
CARRAGHER
LIVERPOOL
M 1359 DR 151
SQUILLACI
MONACO
M 675 DR 169
CANNAVARO
JUVENTUS
M 756 DR 189
MALDINI
AC MILAN
M 1065 DR 152
CAMORANESI
JUVENTUS
M 788 SD 164
SALIHAMIDZIC
BAYERN MUNICH
M 670 SD 89
KAKA
AC MILAN
M 1001 SD 75
HAMANN
LIVERPOOL
M 740 SD 185
ADRIANO
INTER
M 671 AP 37
VAN NISTELROOY
MAN UTD
M 527 SR 66

KEY: DR = Defensive Rating, SD = Scoring Difference AP = Attacking Power SR = Strike Rate, M = Minutes played in Champions League proper.

The Champions League Team of the Season shows a 4-4-2 of the best players in the competition based upon the selection criteria used for the chart-toppers. The players selected are taken from the lists for each 'last 16' club except that to get into the Team of the Season you must have played at least 500 minutes in the competition. The other restriction is that we are only allowing one player from each club in each position. So the maximum number of players one club can have in the divisional team is four.

- **The Champions League team's goalkeeper** is the player with the highest *Defensive Rating*
- **The Champions League team's defenders** are also tested by *Defensive Rating*, i.e. the average number of minutes between league goals conceded while on the pitch.
- **The Champions League team's midfield** are selected on their *Scoring Difference*, i.e.their *Defensive Rating* minus their *Contribution to Attacking Power* (average number of minutes between league goals scored while on the pitch. It takes no account of assists.
- **The Champions League team strikeforce** is made up of the striker with the highest *Strike Rate* (his average number of minutes between league goals scored while on the pitch) together with the striker with the highest *Contribution to Attacking Power.*

CHART-TOPPING POINT EARNERS

	PLAYER	TEAM	GAMES	PNTS	AVE	C.AV.
1	Maldini	AC Milan	11	26	2.36	2.08
2	Pirlo	AC Milan	11	25	2.27	2.08
3	Kaka	AC Milan	11	25	2.27	2.08
4	Gattuso	AC Milan	11	25	2.27	2.08
5	Cafu	AC Milan	11	25	2.27	2.08
6	Dida	AC Milan	12	26	2.17	2.08
7	Essien	Lyon	10	21	2.10	2.10
8	Nesta	AC Milan	11	23	2.09	2.08
9	Zambrotta	Juventus	11	23	2.09	2.26
10	Emerson	Juventus	11	23	2.09	2.26
11	Thuram	Juventus	11	23	2.09	2.26
12	Buffon	Juventus	11	23	2.09	2.26
13	Finnan	Liverpool	11	23	2.09	2.00
14	Luis Garcia	Liverpool	11	22	2.00	2.00
15	Gerrard	Liverpool	10	20	2.00	2.00
16	Helguera	Real Madrid	10	20	2.00	2.11
17	Casillas	Real Madrid	10	20	2.00	2.11
18	Roberto Carlos	Real Madrid	10	20	2.00	2.11
19	Riise	Liverpool	14	27	1.93	2.00
20	Makelele	Chelsea	10	19	1.90	1.67

(Playing a minimum of ten games over the competition)

1 Maldini - AC Milan

Counting Games Competition games where he played at least 70 minutes	11
Total Competition Points Taken in Counting Games with a win equal to 3 points	26
Average Competition Points Taken in Counting Games	2.36

LIVERPOOL

ENGLAND
Champions

1	clql1	Grazer AK	A	W	2-0	Gerrard 23,79	15,000
2	clql2	Grazer AK	H	L	0-1		42,950
3	cl ga	Monaco	H	W	2-0	Cisse 22; Baros 84	33,517
4	cl ga	Olympiakos	A	L	0-1		33,000
5	cl ga	Deportivo	H	D	0-0		40,236
6	cl ga	Deportivo	A	W	1-0	Andrade 14 og	32,000
7	cl ga	Monaco	A	L	0-1		15,000
8	cl ga	Olympiakos	H	W	3-1	Sinama-Pongolle 47; Mellor 80; Gerrard 86	42,045
9	clr2l1	B Leverkusen	H	W	3-1	Luis Garcia 15; Riise 35; Hamann 90	40,942
10	clr2l2	B Leverkusen	A	W	3-1	Luis Garcia 28,32; Baros 67	23,000
11	clqfl1	Juventus	H	W	2-1	Hyypia 10; Luis Garcia 25	41,216
12	clqfl2	Juventus	A	D	0-0		50,000
13	clsfl1	Chelsea	A	D	0-0		40,479
14	clsfl2	Chelsea	H	W	1-0	Luis Garcia 4	42,529
15	clfin	AC Milan	A	W	3-3*	Gerrard 54; Smicer 56; Xabi Alonso 60 (* won 4-2 on penalties)	65,000

SECOND GROUP A

	P	W	D	L	F	A	DIF	PTS
Monaco	6	4	0	2	10	4	6	12
Liverpool	6	3	1	2	6	3	3	10
Olympiakos	6	3	1	2	5	5	0	10
Deportivo	6	0	2	4	0	9	-9	2

PLAYER APPEARANCES

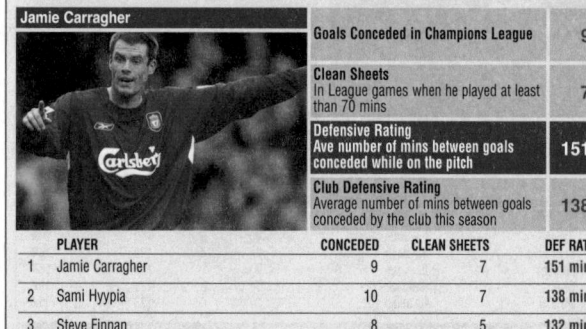

Sami Hyypia

Carlsberg

Age (on 01/07/05)	31
Appearances in Champions league	15
Total minutes on the pitch	1380
Goals	1
Yellow cards	1
Red cards	0
Home Country	Finland

	PLAYER	POS	AGE	APP	MINS ON	GOALS	CARDS(Y/R)		HOME COUNTRY
1	Sami Hyypia	DEF	31	15	1380	1	1	0	Finland
2	Jamie Carragher	DEF	27	15	1359	0	3	0	England
3	John Arne Riise	MID	24	15	1353	1	0	0	Norway
4	Steve Finnan	DEF	29	14	1053	0	2	0	England
5	Milan Baros	ATT	23	14	1044	2	3	0	Czech Republic
6	Javier Luis Garcia	ATT	27	12	999	5	0	0	Spain
7	Jerzy Dudek	GK	32	10	930	0	1	0	Poland
8	Steven Gerrard	MID	25	10	918	4	3	0	England
9	Djimi Traore	DEF	25	10	854	0	1	0	France
10	Dietmar Hamann	MID	31	10	740	1	4	0	Germany
11	Igor Biscan	MID	27	9	720	0	1	0	Croatia
12	Xabi Alonso	MID	23	8	661	1	2	0	Spain
13	Harry Kewell	MID	26	12	592	0	0	0	Australia
14	Miguel Josemi	DEF	25	7	498	0	0	0	Spain
15	Djibril Cisse	ATT	23	9	436	1	0	0	France
16	Chris Kirkland	GK	24	4	360	0	0	0	England
17	Stephen Warnock	DEF	23	6	220	0	2	0	England
18	Antonio Nunez	MID	26	5	196	0	0	0	Spain

KEY PLAYERS - GOALSCORERS

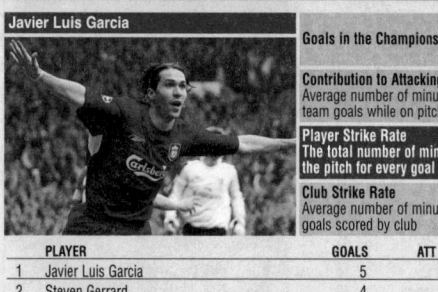

Javier Luis Garcia

Goals in the Champions League	5
Contribution to Attacking Power Average number of minutes between team goals while on pitch	66
Player Strike Rate The total number of minutes he was on the pitch for every goal scored	200
Club Strike Rate Average number of minutes between goals scored by club	69

	PLAYER	GOALS	ATT POWER	STRIKE RATE
1	Javier Luis Garcia	5	66	200 mins
2	Steven Gerrard	4	61	230 mins
3	Milan Baros	2	69	522 mins
4	Xabi Alonso	1	82	661 mins
5	Dietmar Hamann	1	61	740 mins

KEY PLAYERS - MIDFIELDERS

Dietmar Hamann

Carlsberg

Goals in the Champions League	1
Defensive Rating Average number of mins between goals conceded while on the pitch	247
Contribution to Attacking Power Average number of minutes between team goals while on pitch	62
Scoring Difference Defensive Rating minus Contribution to attacking power	185

	PLAYER	GOALS	DEF RATE	ATT POWER	SCORE DIFF
1	Dietmar Hamann	1	247	62	185 mins
2	John Arne Riise	1	150	71	79 mins
3	Steven Gerrard	4	115	61	54 mins
4	Xabi Alonso	1	132	83	49 mins

KEY PLAYERS - DEFENDERS

Jamie Carragher

Carlsberg

Goals Conceded in Champions League	9
Clean Sheets In League games when he played at least than 70 mins	7
Defensive Rating Ave number of mins between goals conceded while on the pitch	151
Club Defensive Rating Average number of mins between goals conceded by the club this season	138

	PLAYER	CONCEDED	CLEAN SHEETS	DEF RATE
1	Jamie Carragher	9	7	151 mins
2	Sami Hyypia	10	7	138 mins
3	Steve Finnan	8	5	132 mins
4	Djimi Traore	7	5	122 mins

KEY GOALKEEPER

Jerzy Dudek

Goals Conceded	7
Clean Sheets	6
Counting Games (at least 70mins)	10
Defensive Rating Ave number of mins between goals conceded while on the pitch	133

TOP POINT EARNERS

	PLAYER	GAMES	AV PTS
1	Harry Kewell	2	3.00
2	Djimi Traore	2	2.00
3	Steven Gerrard	3	2.00
4	John Arne Riise	5	1.80
5	Chris Kirkland	4	1.75
6	Javier Luis Garcia	4	1.75
7	Milan Baros	4	1.75
8	Miguel Josemi	4	1.75
9	Xabi Alonso	4	1.75
10	Jamie Carragher	6	1.67
	CLUB AVERAGE:		1.67

Note: No points awarded for knock-out section

AC MILAN

ITALY
Final

1	cl gf	Shakhtar	A	W	1-0	Seedorf 84	30,000
2	cl gf	Celtic	H	W	3-1	Shevchenko 8; Inzaghi 89; Pirlo 90	68,000
3	cl gf	Barcelona	H	W	1-0	Shevchenko 31	77,000
4	cl gf	Barcelona	A	L	1-2	Shevchenko 17	95,000
5	cl gf	Shakhtar	H	W	4-0	Kaka 52,90; Crespo 53,85	39,000
6	cl gf	Celtic	A	D	0-0		59,228
7	clr2l1	Man Utd	A	W	1-0	Crespo 78	67,162
8	clr2l2	Man Utd	H	W	1-0	Crespo 61	79,000
9	clqfl1	Inter Milan	H	W	2-0	Stam 45; Shevchenko 74	80,000
10	clqfl2	Inter Milan	A	W	3-0	Match abandoned. AC awarded 3-0 victory	
11	clsfl1	PSV Eindhoven	H	W	2-0	Shevchenko 42; Tomasson 89	75,000
12	clsfl2	PSV Eindhoven	A	L	1-3	Ambrosini 90	35,000
13	clfin	Liverpool	H	L	3-3*	Maldini 1; Crespo 39,44 (lost 2-4 on penalties)	65,000

FIRST GROUP F

	P	W	D	L	F	A	DIF	PTS
AC Milan	6	4	1	1	10	3	7	13
Barcelona	6	3	1	2	9	6	3	10
Shakhtar	6	2	0	4	5	9	-4	6
Celtic	6	1	2	3	4	10	-6	5

PLAYER APPEARANCES

3. Cafu

OPEL

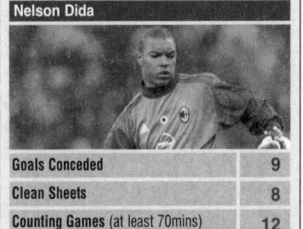

Age (on 01/07/05)	35
Appearances in Champions league	11
Total minutes on the pitch	1015
Goals	0
Yellow cards	1
Red cards	0
Home Country	Brazil

	PLAYER	POS	AGE	APP	MINS ON	GOALS	CARDS(Y/R)		HOME COUNTRY
1	Nelson Dida	GK	31	12	1110	0	0	0	Brazil
2	Paolo Maldini	DEF	37	12	1065	1	0	0	Italy
3	Cafu	DEF	35	11	1015	0	1	0	Brazil
4	Ricardo Kaka	MID	23	12	1001	2	1	0	Brazil
5	Alessandro Nesta	DEF	29	11	1000	0	2	0	Italy
6	Gennaro Gattuso	MID	27	11	977	0	3	0	Italy
7	Andrea Pirlo	MID	26	11	959	1	0	0	Italy
8	Clarence Seedorf	MID	29	12	877	1	1	0	Holland
9	Andriy Shevchenko	ATT	28	9	806	5	1	0	Ukraine
10	Jaap Stam	DEF	32	7	660	1	1	0	Holland
11	Hernan Crespo	ATT	30	9	544	6	0	0	Argentina
12	Manuel Rui Costa	MID	33	8	374	0	0	0	Portugal
13	Massimo Ambrosini	MID	28	10	366	1	1	0	Italy
14	Kakha Kaladze	DEF	27	5	335	0	0	0	Georgia
15	Jon Dahl Tomasson	ATT	28	6	227	1	1	0	Denmark
16	Serginho	MID	34	6	217	0	0	0	Brazil
17	Alessandro Costacurta	DEF	39	5	188	0	0	0	Italy
18	Vikash Dhorasoo	MID	31	4	123	0	1	0	France

KEY PLAYERS - GOALSCORERS

Andriy Shevchenko

OPEL

Goals in the Champions League	5
Contribution to Attacking Power Average number of minutes between team goals while on pitch	57
Player Strike Rate The total number of minutes he was on the pitch for every goal scored	161
Club Strike Rate Average number of minutes between goals scored by club	56

	PLAYER	GOALS	ATT POWER	STRIKE RATE
1	Andriy Shevchenko	5	57	161 mins
2	Ricardo Kaka	2	50	501 mins
3	Jaap Stam	1	60	660 mins
4	Clarence Seedorf	1	58	877 mins
5	Andrea Pirlo	1	59	959 mins

KEY PLAYERS - MIDFIELDERS

Ricardo Kaka

Goals in the Champions League	2
Defensive Rating Average number of mins between goals conceded while on the pitch	125
Contribution to Attacking Power Average number of minutes between team goals while on pitch	50
Scoring Difference Defensive Rating minus Contribution to attacking power	75

	PLAYER	GOALS	DEF RATE	ATT POWER	SCORE DIFF
1	Ricardo Kaka	2	125	50	75 mins
2	Clarence Seedorf	1	125	58	67 mins
3	Andrea Pirlo	1	107	60	47 mins
4	Gennaro Gattuso	0	109	65	44 mins

KEY PLAYERS - DEFENDERS

Paolo Maldini

Goals Conceded in Champions League	7
Clean Sheets In League games when he played at least than 70 mins	8
Defensive Rating Ave number of mins between goals conceded while on the pitch	152
Club Defensive Rating Average number of mins between goals conceded by the club this season	123

	PLAYER	CONCEDED	CLEAN SHEETS	DEF RATE
1	Paolo Maldini	7	8	152 mins
2	Cafu	9	7	113 mins
3	Alessandro Nesta	9	7	111 mins
4	Jaap Stam	6	5	110 mins

KEY GOALKEEPER

Nelson Dida

Goals Conceded	9
Clean Sheets	8
Counting Games (at least 70mins)	12
Defensive Rating Ave number of mins between goals conceded while on the pitch	123

TOP POINT EARNERS

	PLAYER	GAMES	AV PTS
1	Clarence Seedorf	4	3.00
2	Jaap Stam	2	3.00
3	Cafu	5	2.40
4	Andrea Pirlo	5	2.40
5	Ricardo Kaka	5	2.40
6	Gennaro Gattuso	5	2.40
7	Andriy Shevchenko	4	2.25
8	Paolo Maldini	6	2.17
9	Nelson Dida	6	2.17
10	Alessandro Nesta	6	2.17
	CLUB AVERAGE:		2.17

Note: No points awarded for knock-out section

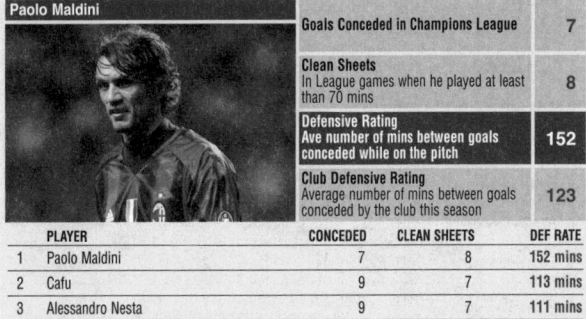

CHELSEA

ENGLAND
Semi-Final

1	cl gh	Paris SG	A	W	3-0	Terry 29; Drogba 45,76	45,000
2	cl gh	Porto	H	W	3-1	Smertin 7; Drogba 50; Terry 70	39,237
3	cl gh	CSKA Moscow	H	W	2-0	Terry 9; Gudjohnsen 45	33,945
4	cl gh	CSKA Moscow	A	W	1-0	Robben 24	28,000
5	cl gh	Paris SG	H	D	0-0		39,626
6	cl gh	Porto	A	L	1-2	Duff 33	42,000
7	clr2l1	Barcelona	A	L	1-2	Belletti 33 og	78,000
8	clr2l2	Barcelona	H	W	4-2	Gudjohnsen 8; Lampard 17; Duff 19; Terry 76	41,515
9	clqfl1	Bayern Munich	H	W	4-2	Cole 4; Lampard 59,70; Drogba 81	40,253
10	clqfl2	Bayern Munich	A	L	2-3	Lampard 30; Drogba 80	59,000
11	clsfl1	Liverpool	H	D	0-0		40,479
12	clsf2	Liverpool	A	L	0-1		42,529

FIRST GROUP H

	P	W	D	L	F	A	DIF	PTS
Chelsea	6	4	1	1	9	3	6	13
Sparta	6	2	2	2	5	5	0	8
Besiktas	6	2	1	3	5	7	-2	7
Lazio	6	1	2	3	6	10	-4	5

PLAYER APPEARANCES

2. Frank Lampard

Age (on 01/07/05)	27
Appearances in Champions league	12
Total minutes on the pitch	1041
Goals	4
Yellow cards	1
Red cards	0
Home Country	England

	PLAYER	POS	AGE	APP	MINS ON	GOALS	CARDS(Y/R)		HOME COUNTRY
1	William Gallas	DEF	27	12	1043	0	2	0	France
2	Frank Lampard	MID	27	12	1041	4	1	0	England
3	John Terry	DEF	24	11	990	4	0	0	England
4	Petr Cech	GK	23	11	990	0	0	0	Czech Republic
5	Claude Makelele	MID	32	10	900	0	1	0	France
6	Ricardo Carvalho	DEF	27	10	900	0	2	0	Portugal
7	Eidur Gudjohnsen	ATT	26	11	735	2	1	0	Iceland
8	Didier Drogba	ATT	27	9	698	5	3	1	Ivory Coast
9	Damien Duff	MID	26	10	661	2	0	0	Rep of Ireland
10	Joe Cole	MID	23	9	646	1	1	0	England
11	Paulo Ferreira	DEF	26	7	537	0	1	0	Portugal
12	Cardoso Tiago	MID	24	11	448	0	1	0	Portugal
13	Glen Johnson	DEF	20	6	395	0	2	0	England
14	Mateja Kezman	ATT	26	9	365	0	4	0	Serbia & M'gro
15	Wayne Bridge	DEF	24	4	360	0	0	0	England
16	Alexei Smertin	MID	30	5	329	1	2	0	Russia
17	Scott Parker	MID	24	4	251	0	0	0	England
18	Arjen Robben	MID	21	5	226	1	0	0	Holland

KEY PLAYERS - GOALSCORERS

Didier Drogba

Goals in the Champions League	5
Contribution to Attacking Power Average number of minutes between team goals while on pitch	49
Player Strike Rate The total number of minutes he was on the pitch for every goal scored	140
Club Strike Rate Average number of minutes between goals scored by club	51

	PLAYER	GOALS	ATT POWER	STRIKE RATE
1	Didier Drogba	5	49	140 mins
2	John Terry	4	47	248 mins
3	Frank Lampard	4	49	260 mins
4	Damien Duff	2	41	331 mins
5	Eidur Gudjohnsen	2	45	368 mins

KEY PLAYERS - MIDFIELDERS

Joe Cole

Goals in the Champions League	1
Defensive Rating Average number of mins between goals conceded while on the pitch	108
Contribution to Attacking Power Average number of minutes between team goals while on pitch	50
Scoring Difference Defensive Rating minus Contribution to attacking power	58

	PLAYER	GOALS	DEF RATE	ATT POWER	SCORE DIFF
1	Joe Cole	1	108	50	58 mins
2	Damien Duff	2	94	41	53 mins
3	Claude Makelele	0	82	45	37 mins
4	Frank Lampard	4	80	50	30 mins

KEY PLAYERS - DEFENDERS

William Gallas

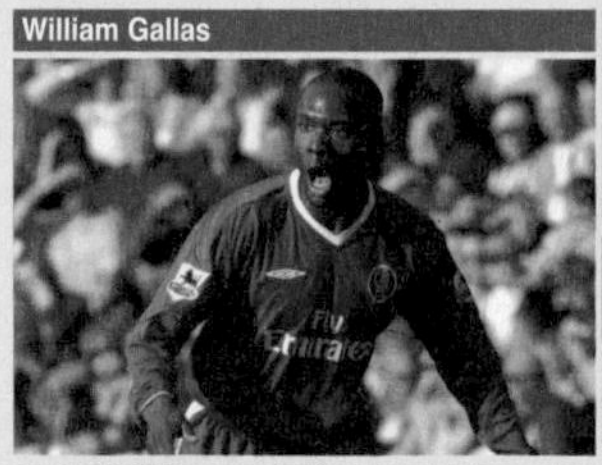

Goals Conceded in Champions League	13
Clean Sheets In League games when he played at least than 70 mins	4
Defensive Rating Ave number of mins between goals conceded while on the pitch	80
Club Defensive Rating Average number of mins between goals conceded by the club this season	83

	PLAYER	CONCEDED	CLEAN SHEETS	DEF RATE
1	William Gallas	13	4	80 mins
2	Paulo Ferreira	7	2	77 mins
3	John Terry	13	4	76 mins
4	Ricardo Carvalho	13	3	69 mins

KEY GOALKEEPER

Petr Cech

Goals Conceded	13
Clean Sheets	4
Counting Games (at least 70mins)	11
Defensive Rating Ave number of mins between goals conceded while on the pitch	76

TOP POINT EARNERS

	PLAYER	GAMES	AV PTS
1	Eidur Gudjohnsen	2	3.00
2	Claude Makelele	4	3.00
3	Damien Duff	2	3.00
4	Frank Lampard	5	2.40
5	John Terry	5	2.40
6	Petr Cech	5	2.40
7	Alexei Smertin	3	2.33
8	Paulo Ferreira	4	2.25
9	Joe Cole	2	2.00
10	Glen Johnson	2	2.00
	CLUB AVERAGE:		2.17

Note: No points awarded for knock-out section

PSV EINDHOVEN

HOLLAND
Semi-Final

1	clql1	Crvena Zvezda	A	L	2-3	Park 9; de Jong 66	50,000
2	clql2	Crvena Zvezda	H	W	5-0	van Bommel 9 pen,56; Beasley 32; de Jong 58; Vennegoor 80	32,000
3	cl ge	Arsenal	A	L	0-1		34,068
4	cl ge	Panathinaikos	H	W	1-0	Vennegoor 80	27,000
5	cl ge	Rosenborg BK	A	W	2-1	Farfan 26; de Jong 86	21,000
6	cl ge	Rosenborg BK	H	W	1-0	Beasley 10	26,000
7	cl ge	Arsenal	H	D	1-1	Ooijer 9	35,000
8	cl ge	Panathinaikos	A	L	1-4	Beasley 37	10,000
9	clr2l1	Monaco	H	W	1-0	Alex 8	42,000
10	clr2l2	Monaco	A	W	2-0	Vennegoor 27; Beasley 69	16,000
11	clqfl1	Lyon	A	D	1-1	Cocu 79	35,000
12	clqfl2	Lyon	H	W	1-1*	Alex 50 (*won 4-2 on penalties)	35,000
13	clsfl1	AC Milan	A	L	0-2		75,000
14	clsfl2	AC Milan	H	W	3-1	Park 9; Cocu 65,90	35,000

SECOND GROUP E

	P	W	D	L	F	A	DIF	PTS
Arsenal	6	2	4	0	11	6	5	10
PSV	6	3	1	2	6	7	-1	10
Panathinaikos	6	2	3	1	11	8	3	9
Rosenborg BK	6	0	2	4	6	13	-7	2

PLAYER APPEARANCES

Mark van Bommel

Age (on 01/07/05)	28
Appearances in Champions league	14
Total minutes on the pitch	1290
Goals	2
Yellow cards	2
Red cards	0
Home Country	Holland

	PLAYER	POS	AGE	APP	MINS ON	GOALS	CARDS(Y)	CARDS(R)	HOME COUNTRY
1	Mark van Bommel	MID	28	14	1290	2	2	0	Holland
2	Young-Pyo Lee	DEF	28	14	1290	0	1	0	South Korea
3	Ji-Sung Park	MID	24	13	1198	2	3	1	South Korea
4	Wilfred Bouma	DEF	27	14	1158	0	0	0	Holland
5	Phillip Cocu	MID	34	13	1147	3	2	0	Holland
6	Alex	DEF	23	12	1095	2	1	0	Brazil
7	Johann Vogel	MID	28	13	1061	0	2	0	Switzerland
8	Heurelho Gomes	GK	24	11	1020	0	2	0	Brazil
9	Jefferson Farfan	ATT	20	13	928	1	0	0	Peru
10	Jan Vennegoor	ATT	26	12	881	3	2	0	Holland
11	Andre Ooijer	DEF	30	9	822	1	3	0	Holland
12	DaMarcus Beasley	ATT	23	13	708	4	1	0	United States
13	Theo Lucius	MID	28	5	405	0	0	0	Holland
14	John de Jong	MID	28	5	368	3	1	0	Holland
15	Edwin Zoetebier	GK	35	3	270	0	0	0	Holland
16	Gerald Sibon	ATT	31	5	198	0	0	0	Holland
17	Kasper Bogelund	DEF	24	2	135	0	0	0	Denmark
18	Robert	ATT	24	3	69	0	0	0	Brazil

KEY PLAYERS - GOALSCORERS

DaMarcus Beasley

PHILIP

Goals in the Champions League	4
Contribution to Attacking Power Average number of minutes between team goals while on pitch	54
Player Strike Rate The total number of minutes he was on the pitch for every goal scored	177
Club Strike Rate Average number of minutes between goals scored by club	61

	PLAYER	GOALS	ATT POWER	STRIKE RATE
1	DaMarcus Beasley	4	54	177 mins
2	Jan Vennegoor of Hesselink	3	48	294 mins
3	Phillip Cocu	3	76	382 mins
4	Alex	2	64	548 mins
5	Ji-Sung Park	2	59	599 mins

KEY PLAYERS - MIDFIELDERS

Johann Vogel

PHILIPS

Goals in the Champions League	0
Defensive Rating Average number of mins between goals conceded while on the pitch	88
Contribution to Attacking Power Average number of minutes between team goals while on pitch	62
Scoring Difference Defensive Rating minus Contribution to attacking power	26

	PLAYER	GOALS	DEF RATE	ATT POWER	SCORE DIFF
1	Johann Vogel	0	88	62	26 mins
2	Mark van Bommel	2	86	61	25 mins
3	Ji-Sung Park	2	80	60	20 mins
4	Phillip Cocu	3	88	76	12 mins

KEY PLAYERS - DEFENDERS

Alex

Goals Conceded in Champions League	10
Clean Sheets In League games when he played at least than 70 mins	5
Defensive Rating Ave number of mins between goals conceded while on the pitch	110
Club Defensive Rating Average number of mins between goals conceded by the club this season	86

	PLAYER	CONCEDED	CLEAN SHEETS	DEF RATE
1	Alex	10	5	110 mins
2	Andre Ooijer	9	3	91 mins
3	Wilfred Bouma	13	4	89 mins
4	Young-Pyo Lee	15	5	86 mins

KEY GOALKEEPER

Heurelho Gomes

Goals Conceded	14
Clean Sheets	3
Counting Games (at least 70mins)	11
Defensive Rating Ave number of mins between goals conceded while on the pitch	73

TOP POINT EARNERS

	PLAYER	GAMES	AV PTS
1	John de Jong	2	3.00
2	Jan Vennegoor	3	3.00
3	Theo Lucius	3	3.00
4	Jefferson Farfan	4	1.75
5	Heurelho Gomes	4	1.75
6	Mark van Bommel	6	1.67
7	Phillip Cocu	6	1.67
8	Young-Pyo Lee	6	1.67
9	Wilfred Bouma	6	1.67
10	DaMarcus Beasley	2	1.50
	CLUB AVERAGE:		1.67

Note: No points awarded for knock-out section

JUVENTUS

ITALY
Quarter-Final

1	clql1	Djurgarden	H	D	2-2	Trezeguet 50; Emerson 59	26,000
2	clql2	Djurgarden	A	W	4-1	Del Piero 10; Trezeguet 34,86; Nedved 54	32,000
3	cl gc	Ajax	A	W	1-0	Nedved 42	49,000
4	cl gc	M Tel-Aviv	H	W	1-0	Camoranesi 37	6,000
5	cl gc	Bayern Munich	H	W	1-0	Nedved 75	18,000
6	cl gc	Bayern Munich	A	W	1-0	Del Piero 90	59,000
7	cl gc	Ajax	H	W	1-0	Zalayeta 14	7,000
8	cl gc	M Tel-Aviv	A	D	1-1	Del Piero 71	19,000
9	clr2l1	Real Madrid	A	L	0-1		78,000
10	clr2l2	Real Madrid	H	W	2-0	Trezeguet 75; Zalayeta 116	59,000
11	clqfl1	Liverpool	A	L	1-2	Cannavaro 63	41,216
12	clqfl2	Liverpool	H	D	0-0		50,000

FIRST GROUP C

	P	W	D	L	F	A	DIF	PTS
Juventus	6	5	1	0	6	1	5	16
Bayern	6	3	1	2	12	5	7	10
Ajax	6	1	1	4	6	10	-4	4
M. Tel-Aviv	6	1	1	4	4	12	-8	4

PLAYER APPEARANCES

Gianluca Zambrotta

Age (on 01/07/05)	28
Appearances in Champions league	12
Total minutes on the pitch	1042
Goals	0
Yellow cards	2
Red cards	0
Home Country	Italy

	PLAYER	POS	AGE	APP	MINS ON	GOALS	CARDS(Y/R)		HOME COUNTRY
1	Gianluca Zambrotta	MID	28	12	1042	0	2	0	Italy
2	Gianluigi Buffon	GK	27	11	1020	0	0	0	Italy
3	Emerson	MID	29	11	1020	1	3	0	Brazil
4	Lilian Thuram	DEF	33	11	1010	0	2	0	France
5	Pavel Nedved	MID	32	10	842	3	1	0	Czech Republic
6	Zlatan Ibrahimovic	ATT	23	10	831	0	2	0	Sweden
7	Mauro Camoranesi	MID	28	9	788	1	3	0	Argentina
8	Fabio Cannavaro	DEF	31	9	756	1	2	0	Italy
9	Alessandro Del Piero	ATT	30	10	742	3	1	0	Italy
10	Manuele Blasi	MID	24	8	608	0	3	0	Italy
11	Jonathan Zebina	DEF	26	6	560	0	1	0	France
12	Paolo Montero	DEF	33	6	452	0	2	0	Uruguay
13	Marcelo Zalayeta	ATT	26	8	407	2	0	0	Uruguay
14	Alessio Tacchinardi	MID	29	6	390	0	2	1	Italy
15	David Trezeguet	ATT	27	5	364	4	0	0	France
16	Gianluca Pessotto	DEF	34	6	300	0	0	0	Italy
17	Ruben Olivera	MID	22	8	288	0	1	0	Uruguay
18	Alessandro Birindelli	DEF	30	4	250	0	1	0	Italy

KEY PLAYERS - GOALSCORERS

Alessandro Del Piero

Goals in the Champions League	3
Contribution to Attacking Power Average number of minutes between team goals while on pitch	92
Player Strike Rate The total number of minutes he was on the pitch for every goal scored	247
Club Strike Rate Average number of minutes between goals scored by club	74

	PLAYER	GOALS	ATT POWER	STRIKE RATE
1	Alessandro Del Piero	3	92	247 mins
2	Pavel Nedved	3	76	281 mins
3	Fabio Cannavaro	1	108	756 mins
4	Mauro German Camoranesi	1	98	788 mins
5	Emerson	1	72	1020 mins

KEY PLAYERS - MIDFIELDERS

Mauro German Camoranesi

Goals in the Champions League	1
Defensive Rating Average number of mins between goals conceded while on the pitch	263
Contribution to Attacking Power Average number of minutes between team goals while on pitch	99
Scoring Difference Defensive Rating minus Contribution to attacking power	164

	PLAYER	GOALS	DEF RATE	ATT POWER	SCORE DIFF
1	Mauro German Camoranesi	1	263	99	164 mins
2	Gianluca Zambrotta	0	174	69	105 mins
3	Emerson	1	170	73	97 mins
4	Pavel Nedved	3	168	77	91 mins

KEY PLAYERS - DEFENDERS

Fabio Cannavaro

Goals Conceded in Champions League	4
Clean Sheets In League games when he played at least than 70 mins	5
Defensive Rating Ave number of mins between goals conceded while on the pitch	189
Club Defensive Rating Average number of mins between goals conceded by the club this season	159

	PLAYER	CONCEDED	CLEAN SHEETS	DEF RATE
1	Fabio Cannavaro	4	5	189 mins
2	Lilian Thuram	6	7	168 mins
3	Jonathan Zebina	4	3	140 mins

KEY GOALKEEPER

Gianluigi Buffon

Goals Conceded	6
Clean Sheets	7
Counting Games (at least 70mins)	11
Defensive Rating Ave number of mins between goals conceded while on the pitch	170

TOP POINT EARNERS

	PLAYER	GAMES	AV PTS
1	Emerson	5	3.00
2	Lilian Thuram	5	3.00
3	Gianluigi Buffon	5	3.00
4	Gianluca Zambrotta	5	3.00
5	Manuele Blasi	3	3.00
6	Zlatan Ibrahimovic	5	3.00
7	Mauro Camoranesi	4	3.00
8	Pavel Nedved	6	2.67
9	Fabio Cannavaro	4	2.50
10	Alessandro Del Piero	3	2.33
	CLUB AVERAGE:		2.67

Note: No points awarded for knock-out section

BAYERN MUNICH

GERMANY
Quarter-Final

1	cl gc	M Tel-Aviv	A W	1-0	Makaay 64 pen	20,000
2	cl gc	Ajax	H W	4-0	Makaay 28,44,52 pen; Ze Roberto 55	50,000
3	cl gc	Juventus	A L	0-1		18,000
4	cl gc	Juventus	H L	0-1		59,000
5	cl gc	M Tel-Aviv	H W	5-1	Pizarro 12; Salihamidzic 37; Frings 44; Makaay 71,80	25,000
6	cl gc	Ajax	A D	2-2	Makaay 8; Ballack 78	50,000
7	clr2l1	Arsenal	H W	3-1	Pizarro 3,58; Salihamidzic 65	59,000
8	clr2l2	Arsenal	A L	0-1		35,463
9	clqfl1	Chelsea	A L	2-4	Schweinsteiger 52; Ballack 90 pen	40,253
10	clqfl2	Chelsea	H W	3-2	Pizarro 65; Guerrero 90; Scholl 90	59,000

SECOND GROUP C

	P	W	D	L	F	A	DIF	PTS
Juventus	6	5	1	0	6	1	5	16
Bayern	6	3	1	2	12	5	7	10
Ajax	6	1	1	4	6	10	-4	4
M. Tel-Aviv	6	1	1	4	4	12	-8	4

PLAYER APPEARANCES

3. Michael Ballack

Age (on 01/07/05)	28
Appearances in Champions league	9
Total minutes on the pitch	809
Goals	2
Yellow cards	2
Red cards	0
Home Country	Germany

	PLAYER	POS	AGE	APP	MINS ON	GOALS	CARDS(Y/R)		HOME COUNTRY
1	Oliver Kahn	GK	36	10	900	0	0	0	Germany
2	Lucio	DEF	27	9	810	0	1	0	Brazil
3	Michael Ballack	MID	28	9	809	2	2	0	Germany
4	Roy Makaay	ATT	30	8	702	7	0	0	Holland
5	Hazan Salihamidzic	MID	28	9	670	2	2	0	Bosnia
6	Torsten Frings	MID	28	8	659	1	1	0	Germany
7	Robert Kovac	DEF	31	8	631	0	3	0	Croatia
8	Jose Ze Roberto	ATT	31	8	551	1	1	0	Brazil
9	Willy Sagnol	DEF	28	7	540	0	0	0	France
10	Claudio Pizarro	ATT	26	7	530	4	0	0	Peru
11	Owen Hargreaves	MID	24	8	465	0	0	0	England
12	Bastian Schweinsteiger	MID	20	7	404	1	1	0	Germany
13	Bixente Lizarazu	DEF	35	4	347	0	1	0	France
14	Martin Demichelis	DEF	24	5	326	0	3	0	Argentina
15	Samuel Osei Kuffour	DEF	28	4	314	0	0	0	Ghana
16	Sebastian Deisler	MID	25	5	284	0	1	0	Germany
17	Thomas Linke	DEF	35	4	276	0	0	0	Germany
18	Jose Paolo Guerrero	ATT	21	6	261	1	0	0	Peru

KEY PLAYERS - GOALSCORERS

Roy Makaay

Goals in the Champions League	7
Contribution to Attacking Power Average number of minutes between team goals while on pitch	43
Player Strike Rate The total number of minutes he was on the pitch for every goal scored	100
Club Strike Rate Average number of minutes between goals scored by club	45

	PLAYER	GOALS	ATT POWER	STRIKE RATE
1	Roy Makaay	7	43	100 mins
2	Claudio Pizarro	4	33	133 mins
3	Hazan Salihamidzic	2	44	335 mins
4	Michael Ballack	2	47	405 mins
5	Jose Ze Roberto	1	50	551 mins

KEY PLAYERS - MIDFIELDERS

Hazan Salihamidzic

Goals in the Champions League	2
Defensive Rating Average number of mins between goals conceded while on the pitch	134
Contribution to Attacking Power Average number of minutes between team goals while on pitch	45
Scoring Difference Defensive Rating minus Contribution to attacking power	89

	PLAYER	GOALS	DEF RATE	ATT POWER	SCORE DIFF
1	Hazan Salihamidzic	2	134	45	89 mins
2	Torsten Frings	1	73	41	32 mins
3	Michael Ballack	2	67	48	19 mins

KEY PLAYERS - DEFENDERS

Lucio

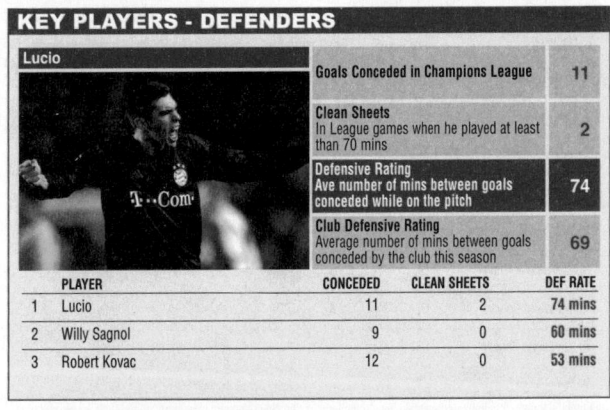

Goals Conceded in Champions League	11
Clean Sheets In League games when he played at least than 70 mins	2
Defensive Rating Ave number of mins between goals conceded while on the pitch	74
Club Defensive Rating Average number of mins between goals conceded by the club this season	69

	PLAYER	CONCEDED	CLEAN SHEETS	DEF RATE
1	Lucio	11	2	74 mins
2	Willy Sagnol	9	0	60 mins
3	Robert Kovac	12	0	53 mins

KEY GOALKEEPER

Oliver Kahn

Goals Conceded	13
Clean Sheets	2
Counting Games (at least 70mins)	10
Defensive Rating Ave number of mins between goals conceded while on the pitch	69

TOP POINT EARNERS

	PLAYER	GAMES	AV PTS
1	Jose Ze Roberto	3	2.00
2	Thomas Linke	3	2.00
3	Tobias Rau	2	2.00
4	Lucio	5	1.80
5	Torsten Frings	5	1.80
6	Hazan Salihamidzic	5	1.80
7	Owen Hargreaves	4	1.75
8	Michael Ballack	6	1.67
9	Oliver Kahn	6	1.67
10	Roy Makaay	6	1.67
	CLUB AVERAGE:		1.67

Note: No points awarded for knock-out section

INTER MILAN

ITALY
Quarter-Final

1	clql1	Basel	A	D	1-1	Adriano 19	30,000
2	clql2	Basel	H	W	4-1	Adriano 2,54; Stankovic 13; Recoba 61	4,000
3	cl gg	W Bremen	H	W	2-0	Adriano 34 pen,89	45,000
4	cl gg	Anderlecht	A	W	3-1	Martins 9; Adriano 51; Stankovic 55	22,000
5	cl gg	Valencia	A	W	5-1	Stankovic 47; Vieri 49; van der Meyde 76; Adriano 81; Cruz 90	40,000
6	cl gg	Valencia	H	D	0-0		40,000
7	cl gg	W Bremen	A	D	1-1	Martins 55	37,000
8	cl gg	Anderlecht	H	W	3-0	Cruz 33; Martins 60,63	30,000
9	clr2l1	Porto	A	D	1-1	Martins 24	50,000
10	clr3l2	Porto	H	W	3-1	Adriano 6,63,86	71,000
11	clqfl1	AC Milan	A	L	0-2		80,000
12	clqfl2	AC Milan	H	L	0-3	Match abandoned. AC awarded 3-0 victory	

FIRST GROUP G

	P	W	D	L	F	A	DIF	PTS
Internazionale	6	4	2	0	14	3	11	14
Bremen	6	4	1	1	12	6	6	13
Valencia	6	2	1	3	6	10	-4	7
Anderlecht	6	0	0	6	4	17	-13	0

PLAYER APPEARANCES

Dejan Stankovic

Age (on 01/07/05)	26
Appearances in Champions league	10
Total minutes on the pitch	832
Goals	3
Yellow cards	1
Red cards	0
Home Country	Serbia & M'gro

	PLAYER	POS	AGE	APP	MINS ON	GOALS	CARDS(Y/R)		HOME COUNTRY
1	Dejan Stankovic	MID	26	10	832	3	1	0	Serbia & M'gro
2	Ivan Cordoba	DEF	28	9	810	0	3	0	Colombia
3	Javier Zanetti	MID	31	10	765	0	0	0	Argentina
4	Juan Sebastian Veron	MID	30	9	756	0	2	0	Argentina
5	Esteban Cambiasso	MID	24	10	721	0	1	0	Argentina
6	Francesco Toldo	GK	33	8	720	0	0	0	Italy
7	Marco Materazzi	DEF	31	8	720	0	1	0	Italy
8	Giuseppe Favalli	DEF	33	8	681	0	3	0	Italy
9	Adriano	ATT	23	8	671	10	0	1	Brazil
10	Ze Maria	DEF	31	7	572	0	0	0	Brazil
11	Obafemi Martins	ATT	20	7	470	5	1	0	Nigeria
12	Edgar Davids	MID	32	5	372	0	1	0	Holland
13	Cristiano Zanetti	MID	28	6	340	0	2	0	Italy
14	Emre Belozoglu	MID	24	6	337	0	0	0	Turkey
15	Julio Cruz	ATT	30	7	326	2	1	0	Argentina
16	Christian Vieri	ATT	31	6	292	1	0	0	Italy
17	Sinisa Mihajlovic	DEF	36	3	270	0	1	0	Serbia & M'gro
18	Alvaro Recoba	ATT	29	5	245	1	1	0	Uruguay

KEY PLAYERS - GOALSCORERS

Adriano

Goals in the Champions League	10
Contribution to Attacking Power Average number of minutes between team goals while on pitch	37
Player Strike Rate The total number of minutes he was on the pitch for every goal scored	67
Club Strike Rate Average number of minutes between goals scored by club	43

	PLAYER	GOALS	ATT POWER	STRIKE RATE
1	Adriano	10	37	67 mins
2	Dejan Stankovic	3	46	277 mins

*500 minutes required to qualify for table

KEY PLAYERS - MIDFIELDERS

Juan Sebastian Veron

Goals in the Champions League	0
Defensive Rating Average number of mins between goals conceded while on the pitch	108
Contribution to Attacking Power Average number of minutes between team goals while on pitch	40
Scoring Difference Defensive Rating minus Contribution to attacking power	68

	PLAYER	GOALS	DEF RATE	ATT POWER	SCORE DIFF
1	Juan Sebastian Veron	0	108	40	68 mins
2	Dejan Stankovic	3	104	46	58 mins
3	Esteban Cambiasso	0	90	48	42 mins
4	Javier Zanetti	0	85	45	40 mins

KEY PLAYERS - DEFENDERS

Marco Materazzi

Goals Conceded in Champions League	5
Clean Sheets In League games when he played at least than 70 mins	3
Defensive Rating Ave number of mins between goals conceded while on the pitch	144
Club Defensive Rating Average number of mins between goals conceded by the club this season	110

	PLAYER	CONCEDED	CLEAN SHEETS	DEF RATE
1	Marco Materazzi	5	3	144 mins
2	Ze Maria	4	2	143 mins
3	Ivan Cordoba	8	2	101 mins
4	Giuseppe Favalli	7	1	97 mins

KEY GOALKEEPER

Francesco Toldo

Goals Conceded	8
Clean Sheets	1
Counting Games (at least 70mins)	8
Defensive Rating Ave number of mins between goals conceded while on the pitch	90

TOP POINT EARNERS

	PLAYER	GAMES	AV PTS
1	Emre Belozoglu	3	3.00
2	Nicolas Burdisso	2	3.00
3	Juan Sebastian Veron	4	2.50
4	Marco Materazzi	4	2.50
5	Obafemi Martins	3	2.33
6	Francesco Toldo	3	2.33
7	Dejan Stankovic	3	2.33
8	Ze Maria	3	2.33
9	Adriano	3	2.33
10	Christian Vieri	3	2.33
	CLUB AVERAGE:		2.33

Note: No points awarded for knock-out section

LYON

FRANCE
Quarter-Final

1	cl gd	Man Utd	H	D	2-2	Cris 35; Frau 44	35,000
2	cl gd	Sparta Prague	A	W	2-1	Essien 25; Wiltord 58	12,000
3	cl gd	Fenerbahce	A	W	3-1	Juninho 55; Cris 66; Frau 87	49,000
4	cl gd	Fenerbahce	H	W	4-2	Essien 22; Malouda 53; Nilmar 90,90	36,000
5	cl gd	Man Utd	A	L	1-2	Diarra 40	66,398
6	cl gd	Sparta Prague	H	W	5-0	Essien 7; Nilmar 19,51; Idangar 83; Bergougnoux 90	39,000
7	clr2rl1	W Bremen	A	W	3-0	Wiltord 9; Diarra 77; Juninho 80	37,000
8	clr3l2	W Bremen	H	W	7-2	Wiltord 8,55,64; Essien 17,30; Malouda 60; Berthod 80 pen	37,000
9	clqfl1	PSV Eindhoven	H	D	1-1	Malouda 12	35,000
10	clqfl2	PSV Eindhoven	A	L	1-1*	Wiltord 10 (*lost 2-4 on penalties)	35,000

FIRST GROUP D

	P	W	D	L	F	A	DIF	PTS
Lyon	6	4	1	1	17	8	9	13
Man. United	6	3	2	1	14	9	5	11
Fenerbahce	6	3	0	3	10	13	-3	9
Sparta	6	0	1	5	2	13	-11	1

PLAYER APPEARANCES

3. Juninho

RENAULT
TRUCKS

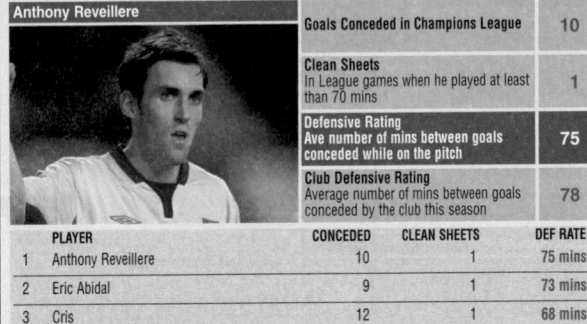

Age (on 01/07/05)	30
Appearances in Champions league	9
Total minutes on the pitch	820
Goals	2
Yellow cards	0
Red cards	0
Home Country	Brazil

	PLAYER	POS	AGE	APP	MINS ON	GOALS	CARDS(Y)	CARDS(R)	HOME COUNTRY
1	Michael Essien	MID	22	10	930	5	0	0	Ghana
2	Florent Malouda	MID	25	10	836	3	1	0	France
3	Pernambucano Juninho	MID	30	9	820	2	0	0	Brazil
4	Cris	DEF	28	9	812	2	2	0	Brazil
5	Mahamadou Diarra	MID	24	9	805	2	2	0	Mali
6	Anthony Reveillere	DEF	25	8	750	0	0	0	France
7	Gregory Coupet	GK	32	8	732	0	0	0	France
8	Sydney Govou	ATT	25	9	707	0	1	0	France
9	Eric Abidal	DEF	25	7	660	0	1	0	France
10	Sylvain Wiltord	ATT	31	8	606	6	1	0	France
11	Cacapa	DEF	29	5	480	0	0	0	Brazil
12	Lamine Diatta	DEF	30	7	470	0	0	0	Senegal
13	Pierre-Alain Frau	ATT	25	8	409	2	0	0	France
14	Jeremie Berthod	DEF	21	4	350	1	1	0	France
15	Nilmar	ATT	20	9	291	4	0	0	Brazil
16	Nicolas Puydebois	GK	24	3	198	0	0	0	France
17	Jeremie Clement	MID	20	4	135	0	0	0	France
18	Bryan Bergougnoux	ATT	22	2	110	1	1	0	France

KEY PLAYERS - GOALSCORERS

Michael Essien

Goals in the Champions League	5
Contribution to Attacking Power Average number of minutes between team goals while on pitch	32
Player Strike Rate The total number of minutes he was on the pitch for every goal scored	186
Club Strike Rate Average number of minutes between goals scored by club	32

	PLAYER	GOALS	ATT POWER	STRIKE RATE
1	Michael Essien	5	32	186 mins
2	Florent Malouda	3	32	279 mins
3	Mahamadou Diarra	2	32	403 mins
4	Cris	2	36	406 mins
5	Pernambucano Juninho	2	35	410 mins

KEY PLAYERS - MIDFIELDERS

Florent Malouda

Goals in the Champions League	3
Defensive Rating Average number of mins between goals conceded while on the pitch	84
Contribution to Attacking Power Average number of minutes between team goals while on pitch	32
Scoring Difference Defensive Rating minus Contribution to attacking power	52

	PLAYER	GOALS	DEF RATE	ATT POWER	SCORE DIFF
1	Florent Malouda	3	84	32	52 mins
2	Mahamadou Diarra	2	81	32	49 mins
3	Michael Essien	5	78	32	46 mins
4	Pernambucano Juninho	2	68	36	32 mins

KEY PLAYERS - DEFENDERS

Anthony Reveillere

Goals Conceded in Champions League	10
Clean Sheets In League games when he played at least than 70 mins	1
Defensive Rating Ave number of mins between goals conceded while on the pitch	75
Club Defensive Rating Average number of mins between goals conceded by the club this season	78

	PLAYER	CONCEDED	CLEAN SHEETS	DEF RATE
1	Anthony Reveillere	10	1	75 mins
2	Eric Abidal	9	1	73 mins
3	Cris	12	1	68 mins

KEY GOALKEEPER

Gregory Coupet

Goals Conceded	9
Clean Sheets	1
Counting Games (at least 70mins)	8
Defensive Rating Ave number of mins between goals conceded while on the pitch	81

TOP POINT EARNERS

	PLAYER	GAMES	AV PTS
1	Florent Malouda	4	2.50
2	Sydney Govou	4	2.50
3	Gregory Coupet	4	2.50
4	Cacapa	3	2.33
5	Eric Abidal	3	2.33
6	Sylvain Wiltord	3	2.33
7	Mahamadou Diarra	4	2.25
8	Michael Essien	6	2.17
9	Anthony Reveillere	6	2.17
10	Cris	5	2.00
	CLUB AVERAGE:		2.17

Note: No points awarded for knock-out section

BAYER LEVERKUSEN

GERMANY
Last 16

1	clql1	Banik Ostrava	H	W	5-0	Franca 10,67; Juan 74; Berbatov 82,89	20,000
2	clql2	Banik Ostrava	A	L	1-2	Berbatov 77	5,000
3	cl gb	Real Madrid	H	W	3-0	Krzynowek 39; Franca 50; Berbatov 55	23,000
4	cl gb	Dinamo Kiev	A	L	2-4	Voronin 59; Nowotny 68	83,000
5	cl gb	Roma	H	W	3-1	Roque Junior 48; Krzynowek 59; Franca 94	23,000
6	cl gb	Roma	A	D	1-1	Berbatov 82	
7	cl gb	Real Madrid	A	D	1-1	Berbatov 36	72,000
8	cl gb	Dinamo Kiev	H	W	3-0	Juan 51; Voronin 77; Babic 86	23,000
9	clr2l1	Liverpool	A	L	1-3	Franca 90	40,942
10	clr2l2	Liverpool	H	L	1-3	Krzynowek 88	23,000

KEY PLAYERS - GOALSCORERS

Dimitar Berbatov

RWE

Goals in the Champions League	6
Contribution to Attacking Power Average number of minutes between team goals while on pitch	44
Player Strike Rate The total number of minutes he was on the pitch for every goal scored	140
Club Strike Rate Average number of minutes between goals scored by club	43

	PLAYER	GOALS	ATT POWER	STRIKE RATE
1	Dimitar Berbatov	6	44	140 mins
2	Jacek Krzynowek	3	45	244 mins
3	Juan	2	44	382 mins
4	Roque Junior	1	39	630 mins

FIRST GROUP E

	P	W	D	L	F	A	DIF	PTS
Leverkusen	6	3	2	1	13	7	6	11
Real Madrid	6	3	2	1	11	8	3	11
Dinamo Kiev	6	3	1	2	11	8	3	10
Roma	6	0	1	5	4	16	-12	1

PLAYER APPEARANCES

2. Bernd Schneider

Age (on 01/07/05)	31
Appearances in Champions league	10
Total minutes on the pitch	895
Goals	0
Yellow cards	2
Red cards	0
Home Country	Germany

	PLAYER	POS	AGE	APP	MINS ON	GOALS	CARDS(Y/R)		HOME COUNTRY
1	Hans-Jorg Butt	GK	31	10	900	0	0	0	Germany
2	Bernd Schneider	MID	31	10	895	0	2	0	Germany
3	Dimitar Berbatov	ATT	24	10	841	6	0	0	Bulgaria
4	Carsten Ramelow	MID	31	10	820	0	2	0	Germany
5	Juan	DEF	26	9	763	2	1	0	Brazil
6	Jacek Krzynowek	MID	29	9	732	3	0	0	Poland
7	Diego Placente	DEF	28	8	708	0	3	0	Argentina
8	Roque Junior	DEF	28	7	630	1	1	0	Brazil
9	Robson Ponte	ATT	28	8	628	0	5	0	Brazil
10	Jens Nowotny	DEF	31	6	492	1	1	0	Germany
11	Marko Babic	MID	24	7	484	1	1	0	Croatia
12	Paul Freier	MID	25	9	459	0	3	0	Germany
13	Franca	ATT	29	7	438	5	0	0	Brazil
14	Andriy Voronin	ATT	25	6	348	2	2	1	Ukraine
15	J-I Callsen-Bracker	DEF	20	4	186	0	0	0	Germany
16	Hanno Balitsch	MID	24	7	150	0	2	0	Germany
17	Daniel Bierofka	MID	26	4	115	0	1	0	Germany
18	Teddy Lucic	DEF	32	1	90	0	0	0	Sweden

REAL MADRID

SPAIN
Last 16

1	clql1	Wisla Krakow	A	W	2-0	Morientes 72,90	10,000
2	clql2	Wisla Krakow	H	W	3-1	Ronaldo 3,30; Pavon 85	76,000
3	cl gb	B Leverkusen	A	L	0-3		23,000
4	cl gb	Roma	H	W	4-2	Raul 39,72; Figo 53 pen; Roberto Carlos 79	60,000
5	cl gb	Dinamo Kiev	H	W	1-0	Owen 35	45,000
6	cl gb	Dinamo Kiev	A	D	2-2	Raul 38; Figo 44 pen	80,000
7	cl gb	B Leverkusen	H	D	1-1	Raul 70	72,000
8	cl gb	Roma	A	W	3-0	Ronaldo 9; Figo 60 pen,82	-
9	clr2l1	Juventus	H	W	1-0	Helguera 31	78,000
10	clr2l2	Juventus	A	L	0-2		59,000

KEY PLAYERS - GOALSCORERS

Luis Figo

SIEMENS
mobile

Goals in the Champions League	4
Contribution to Attacking Power Average number of minutes between team goals while on pitch	54
Player Strike Rate The total number of minutes he was on the pitch for every goal scored	204
Club Strike Rate Average number of minutes between goals scored by club	55

	PLAYER	GOALS	ATT POWER	STRIKE RATE
1	Luis Figo	4	54	204 mins
2	Raul	4	54	217 mins
3	Ronaldo	3	57	266 mins
4	Ivan Helguera	1	54	930 mins
5	Roberto Carlos	1	54	930 mins

SECOND GROUP B

	P	W	D	L	F	A	DIF	PTS
Leverkusen	6	3	2	1	13	7	6	11
Real Madrid	6	3	2	1	11	8	3	11
Dinamo Kiev	6	3	1	2	11	8	3	10
Roma	6	0	1	5	4	16	-12	1

PLAYER APPEARANCES

Iker Casillas

SIEMENS

Age (on 01/07/05)	24
Appearances in Champions league	10
Total minutes on the pitch	930
Goals	0
Yellow cards	0
Red cards	0
Home Country	Spain

	PLAYER	POS	AGE	APP	MINS ON	GOALS	CARDS(Y/R)		HOME COUNTRY
1	Iker Casillas	GK	24	10	930	0	0	0	Spain
2	Roberto Carlos	DEF	32	10	930	1	1	0	Brazil
3	Ivan Helguera	DEF	30	10	930	1	1	0	Spain
4	Raul	ATT	28	10	868	4	0	0	Spain
5	Luis Figo	MID	32	10	816	4	2	0	Portugal
6	Zinedine Zidane	MID	33	10	810	0	1	0	France
7	Ronaldo	ATT	28	10	799	3	0	1	Brazil
8	Walter Samuel	DEF	27	8	750	0	4	0	Argentina
9	Michel Salgado	DEF	29	9	728	0	0	0	Spain
10	David Beckham	MID	30	8	669	0	0	0	England
11	Jose Guti	MID	28	8	485	0	1	0	Spain
12	Francisco Pavon	DEF	25	7	461	1	2	0	Spain
13	Thomas Gravesen	MID	29	2	210	0	1	0	Denmark
14	Raul Bravo	DEF	24	3	208	0	0	0	Spain
15	Michael Owen	ATT	25	5	170	1	0	0	England
16	Albert Celades	MID	29	6	164	0	1	0	Spain
17	Jorge Solari	MID	28	4	150	0	1	0	Argentina
18	Fernando Morientes	ATT	29	6	145	2	1	0	Spain

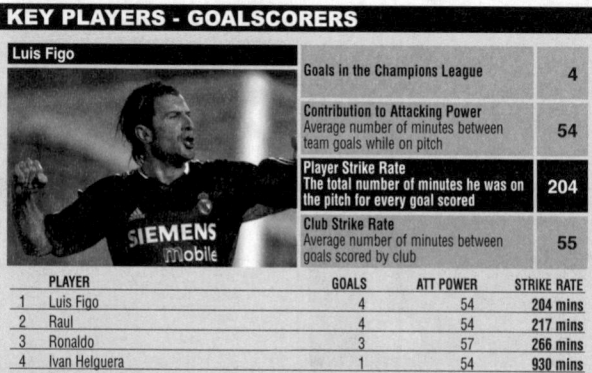

MANCHESTER UNITED

ENGLAND
Last 16

1	clql1	D Bucharest	A	W	2-1	Giggs 38; Alistar 71 og	58,000
2	clql2	D Bucharest	H	W	3-0	Smith 47,50; Bellion 70	61,041
3	cl gd	Lyon	A	D	2-2	van Nistelrooy 56,61	35,000
4	cl gd	Fenerbahce	H	W	6-2	Giggs 7; Rooney 17,28,54; van Nistelrooy 78; Bellion 81	67,128
5	cl gd	Sparta Prague	A	D	0-0		20,500
6	cl gd	Sparta Prague	H	W	4-1	van Nistelrooy 14,25 pen,60,90	66,706
7	cl gd	Lyon	H	W	2-1	Neville, G 19; van Nistelrooy 53	66,398
8	cl gd	Fenerbahce	A	L	0-3		35,000
9	clr2l1	AC Milan	H	L	0-1		67,162
10	clr2l2	AC Milan	A	L	0-1		79,000

KEY PLAYERS - GOALSCORERS

Ruud van Nistelrooy

Goals in the Champions League	8
Contribution to Attacking Power Average number of minutes between team goals while on pitch	40
Player Strike Rate The total number of minutes he was on the pitch for every goal scored	66
Club Strike Rate Average number of minutes between goals scored by club	47

	PLAYER	GOALS	ATT POWER	STRIKE RATE
1	Ruud van Nistelrooy	8	40	**66 mins**
2	Wayne Rooney	3	44	**176 mins**
3	Gary Neville	1	35	**538 mins**

SECOND GROUP D

	P	W	D	L	F	A	DIF	PTS
Lyon	6	4	1	1	17	8	9	13
Man. United	6	3	2	1	14	9	5	11
Fenerbahce	6	3	0	3	10	13	-3	9
Sparta	6	0	1	5	2	13	-11	1

PLAYER APPEARANCES

Mikael Silvestre

Age (on 01/07/05)	27
Appearances in Champions league	8
Total minutes on the pitch	641
Goals	0
Yellow cards	1
Red cards	0
Home Country	France

	PLAYER	POS	AGE	APP	MINS ON	GOALS	CARDS(Y/R)		HOME COUNTRY
1	Mikael Silvestre	DEF	27	8	641	0	1	0	France
2	Gabriel Ivan Heinze	DEF	27	7	620	0	2	0	Argentina
3	Paul Scholes	MID	30	7	606	0	2	0	England
4	Christiano Ronaldo	MID	20	8	564	0	0	0	Portugal
5	Wes Brown	DEF	25	7	551	0	1	0	England
6	Roy Keane	MID	33	6	539	0	1	0	Rep of Ireland
7	Gary Neville	DEF	30	7	538	1	1	0	England
8	Wayne Rooney	ATT	19	6	528	3	0	0	England
9	Ruud van Nistelrooy	ATT	29	7	527	8	0	0	Holland
10	Tim Howard	GK	26	5	450	0	0	0	United States
11	Eric Djemba-Djemba	MID	24	5	450	0	1	0	Cameroon
12	Rio Ferdinand	DEF	26	5	450	0	0	0	England
13	Roy Carroll	GK	27	5	450	0	0	0	N Ireland
14	John O'Shea	DEF	24	5	442	0	0	0	Rep of Ireland
15	Ryan Giggs	MID	31	6	437	2	0	0	Wales
16	Quinton Fortune	MID	28	5	294	0	2	0	South Africa
17	Darren Fletcher	MID	21	5	293	0	0	0	Scotland
18	Liam Miller	MID	24	5	290	0	2	0	Rep of Ireland

PORTO

PORTUGAL
Last 16

1	cl gh	CSKA Moscow	H	D	0-0		39,000
2	cl gh	Chelsea	A	L	1-3	McCarthy 68	39,237
3	cl gh	Paris SG	A	L	0-2		48,000
4	cl gh	Paris SG	H	D	0-0		30,000
5	cl gh	CSKA Moscow	A	W	1-0	McCarthy 28	22,000
6	cl gh	Chelsea	H	W	2-1	Diego 60; McCarthy 85	42,000
7	clr2l1	Inter Milan	H	D	1-1	Ricardo Costa 61	50,000
8	clr2l2	Inter Milan	A	L	1-3	Jorge Costa 68	71,000

KEY PLAYERS - GOALSCORERS

4. Jorge Costa

Goals in the Champions League	1
Contribution to Attacking Power Average number of minutes between team goals while on pitch	123
Player Strike Rate The total number of minutes he was on the pitch for every goal scored	615
Club Strike Rate Average number of minutes between goals scored by club	120

	PLAYER	GOALS	ATT POWER	STRIKE RATE
1	Benni McCarthy	3	90	**181 mins**
2	Ribas da Cunha Santos Diego	1	167	**502 mins**
3	Ricardo Costa	1	171	**515 mins**
4	Jorge Costa	1	123	**615 mins**

SECOND GROUP H

	P	W	D	L	F	A	DIF	PTS
Chelsea	6	4	1	1	10	3	7	13
Porto	6	2	2	2	4	6	-2	8
CSKA Moscow	6	2	1	3	5	5	0	7
PSG	6	1	2	3	3	8	-5	5

PLAYER APPEARANCES

Maniche

Age (on 01/07/05)	27
Appearances in Champions league	8
Total minutes on the pitch	720
Goals	0
Yellow cards	2
Red cards	0
Home Country	Portugal

	PLAYER	POS	AGE	APP	MINS ON	GOALS	CARDS(Y/R)		HOME COUNTRY
1	Maniche	MID	27	8	720	0	2	0	Portugal
2	Georgios Seitaridis	DEF	24	7	630	0	1	0	Greece
3	Jorge Costa	DEF	33	7	615	1	4	0	Portugal
4	Francisco Costinha	MID	30	7	591	0	2	0	Portugal
5	Benni McCarthy	ATT	27	8	544	3	0	0	South Africa
6	Vitor Manuel Baia	GK	35	6	540	0	0	0	Portugal
7	Ricardo Costa	DEF	24	6	515	1	0	0	Portugal
8	Diego	MID	20	6	502	1	1	0	Brazil
9	Ricardo Quaresma	ATT	21	8	461	0	1	0	Portugal
10	Pedro Emanuel	DEF	30	5	439	0	1	0	Portugal
11	Derlei	ATT	29	5	385	0	2	0	Brazil
12	Bosingwa	MID	22	5	312	0	1	0	Portugal
13	Pepe	DEF	22	5	282	0	2	0	Brazil
14	Luis Fabiano	ATT	24	4	221	0	1	0	Brazil
15	Carlos Alberto	ATT	20	4	213	0	0	0	Brazil
16	Nuno Valente	DEF	30	2	180	0	1	0	Portugal
17	Simoes Nuno	GK	31	2	180	0	0	0	Portugal
18	Miguel Alexandre Areias	DEF	28	2	180	0	0	0	Portugal

BARCELONA

SPAIN
Last 16

1	cl gf	Celtic	A	W	3-1	Deco 20; Giuly 78; Larsson 82	60,000
2	cl gf	Shakhtar	H	W	3-0	Deco 15; Ronaldinho 64 pen; Eto'o 89	64,000
3	cl gf	AC Milan	A	L	0-1		77,000
4	cl gf	AC Milan	H	W	2-1	Eto'o 37; Ronaldinho 89	95,000
5	cl gf	Celtic	H	D	1-1	Eto'o 24	74,000
6	cl gf	Shakhtar	A	L	0-2		25,000
7	clr2l1	Chelsea	H	W	2-1	Lopez 67; Eto'o 73	78,000
8	clr2l2	Chelsea	A	L	2-4	Ronaldinho 27 pen,38	41,515

KEY PLAYERS - GOALSCORERS

Samuel Eto'o

Goals in the Champions League	4
Contribution to Attacking Power Average number of minutes between team goals while on pitch	53
Player Strike Rate The total number of minutes he was on the pitch for every goal scored	148
Club Strike Rate Average number of minutes between goals scored by club	55

	PLAYER	GOALS	ATT POWER	STRIKE RATE
1	Samuel Eto'o	4	53	148 mins
2	Ronaldinho	4	54	151 mins
3	Anderson Deco	2	51	311 mins

SECOND GROUP F

	P	W	D	L	F	A	DIF	PTS
Milan	6	4	1	1	10	3	7	13
Barcelona	6	3	1	2	9	6	3	10
Shakhtar	6	2	0	4	5	9	-4	6
Celtic	6	1	2	3	4	10	-6	5

PLAYER APPEARANCES

Victor Valdes

Age (on 01/07/05)	23
Appearances in Champions league	8
Total minutes on the pitch	720
Goals	0
Yellow cards	0
Red cards	0
Home Country	Spain

	PLAYER	POS	AGE	APP	MINS ON	GOALS	CARDS(Y/R)		HOME COUNTRY
1	Victor Valdes	GK	23	8	720	0	0	0	Spain
2	Xavi Hernandez	MID	25	8	720	0	1	0	Spain
3	Carlos Puyol	DEF	27	8	676	0	1	0	Spain
4	Juliano Belletti	DEF	29	8	675	0	0	0	Brazil
5	Gio Van Bronckhorst	MID	30	8	630	0	2	0	Holland
6	Anderson Deco	MID	27	7	622	2	0	0	Portugal
7	Ronaldinho	ATT	25	7	602	4	1	0	Brazil
8	Samuel Eto'o	ATT	24	7	591	4	0	0	Cameroon
9	Presas Oleguer	DEF	25	7	521	0	0	0	Spain
10	Rafael Marquez	DEF	26	5	411	0	2	0	Mexico
11	Ludovic Giuly	MID	28	6	360	1	0	0	France
12	Andres Iniesta	MID	21	8	310	0	0	0	Spain
13	Lopez Gerard	MID	26	3	186	0	0	0	Spain
14	Silvinho	DEF	31	3	180	0	0	0	Brazil
15	Henrik Larsson	ATT	33	4	144	1	0	0	Sweden
16	Fernando Navarro	DEF	23	2	91	0	0	0	Spain
17	Edmilson	DEF	28	1	90	0	0	0	Brazil
18	Joan Verdu	MID	22	1	90	0	0	0	Spain

ARSENAL

ENGLAND
Last 16

1	cl ge	PSV Eindhoven	H	W	1-0	Alex 42 og	34,068
2	cl ge	Rosenborg BK	A	D	1-1	Ljungberg 6	21,000
3	cl ge	Panathinaikos	A	D	2-2	Ljungberg 18; Henry 74	12,000
4	cl ge	Panathinaikos	H	D	1-1	Henry 16 pen	35,137
5	cl ge	PSV Eindhoven	A	D	1-1	Henry 31	35,000
6	cl ge	Rosenborg BK	H	W	5-1	Reyes 3; Henry 24; Fabregas 29; Pires 41 pen; van Persie 84	35,421
7	clr2l1	Bayern Munich	A	L	1-3	Toure 88	59,000
8	clr2l2	Bayern Munich	H	W	1-0	Henry 66	35,463

KEY PLAYERS - GOALSCORERS

Thierry Henry

Goals in the Champions League	5
Contribution to Attacking Power Average number of minutes between team goals while on pitch	55
Player Strike Rate The total number of minutes he was on the pitch for every goal scored	144
Club Strike Rate Average number of minutes between goals scored by club	55

	PLAYER	GOALS	ATT POWER	STRIKE RATE
1	Thierry Henry	5	55	144 mins
2	Robert Pires	1	48	624 mins
3	Habib Kolo Toure	1	55	720 mins

FIRST GROUP E

	P	W	D	L	F	A	DIF	PTS
Arsenal	6	2	4	0	11	6	5	10
PSV	6	3	1	2	6	7	-1	10
Panathinaikos	6	2	3	1	11	8	3	9
Rosenborg BK	6	0	2	4	6	13	-7	2

PLAYER APPEARANCES

2. Kolo Toure

Age (on 01/07/05)	24
Appearances in Champions league	8
Total minutes on the pitch	720
Goals	1
Yellow cards	1
Red cards	0
Home Country	Ivory Coast

	PLAYER	POS	AGE	APP	MINS ON	GOALS	CARDS(Y/R)		HOME COUNTRY
1	Thierry Henry	ATT	27	8	720	5	1	0	France
2	Habib Kolo Toure	DEF	24	8	720	1	1	0	Ivory Coast
3	Jens Lehmann	GK	35	7	630	0	0	0	Germany
4	Robert Pires	MID	31	8	624	1	0	0	France
5	Ashley Cole	DEF	24	8	622	0	0	0	England
6	Etame Mayer Lauren	DEF	28	7	605	0	3	1	Cameroon
7	Jose Antonio Reyes	ATT	21	8	579	1	0	0	Spain
8	Patrick Vieira	MID	29	6	528	0	3	1	France
9	Fredrik Ljungberg	MID	28	6	505	2	1	0	Sweden
10	Cesc Fabregas	MID	18	5	388	1	1	0	Spain
11	Sol Campbell	DEF	30	4	360	0	0	0	England
12	Dennis Bergkamp	ATT	36	4	322	0	1	0	Holland
13	Pascal Cygan	DEF	31	3	270	0	0	0	France
14	Edu	MID	27	4	229	0	0	0	Brazil
15	Mathieu Flamini	MID	21	4	217	0	1	0	France
16	Justin Hoyte	DEF	20	2	112	0	0	0	England
17	Gael Clichy	DEF	19	2	101	0	0	0	France
18	Gilberto Silva	MID	28	1	90	0	0	0	Brazil

WERDER BREMEN

GERMANY
Last 16

1	cl gg	Inter Milan	A	L	0-2		45,000
2	cl gg	Valencia	H	W	2-1	Klose 60; Charisteas 84	36,000
3	cl gg	Anderlecht	A	W	2-1	Klasnic 36,59	22,000
4	cl gg	Anderlecht	H	W	5-1	Klasnic 2,16,79; Klose 33; Jensen 90	37,000
5	cl gg	Inter Milan	H	D	1-1	Ismael 49 pen	37,000
6	cl gg	Valencia	A	W	2-0	Valdez 83,90	40,000
7	clr2l1	Lyon	H	L	0-3		37,000
8	clr2l2	Lyon	A	L	2-7	Micoud 32; Ismael 57 pen	37,000

KEY PLAYERS - GOALSCORERS

Ivan Klasnic

Goals in the Champions League	5
Contribution to Attacking Power Average number of minutes between team goals while on pitch	47
Player Strike Rate The total number of minutes he was on the pitch for every goal scored	104
Club Strike Rate Average number of minutes between goals scored by club	51

	PLAYER	GOALS	ATT POWER	STRIKE RATE
1	Ivan Klasnic	5	47	104 mins
2	Valerien Ismael	2	45	273 mins
3	Johan Micoud	1	51	720 mins

SECOND GROUP G

	P	W	D	L	F	A	DIF	PTS
Inter Milan	6	4	2	0	14	3	11	14
Bremen	6	4	1	1	12	6	6	13
Valencia	6	2	1	3	6	10	-4	7
Anderlecht	6	0	0	6	4	17	-13	0

PLAYER APPEARANCES

Andreas Reinke

Age (on 01/07/05)	44
Appearances in Champions league	8
Total minutes on the pitch	720
Goals	0
Yellow cards	0
Red cards	0
Home Country	Germany

	PLAYER	POS	AGE	APP	MINS ON	GOALS	CARDS(Y/R)		HOME COUNTRY
1	Andreas Reinke	GK	44	8	720	0	0	0	Germany
2	Fabian Ernst	MID	26	8	720	0	1	0	Germany
3	Johan Micoud	MID	31	8	720	1	2	0	France
4	Paul Stalteri	MID	27	8	697	0	2	0	Canada
5	Ludovic Magnin	MID	26	8	641	0	0	0	Switzerland
6	Valerien Ismael	DEF	29	7	545	2	2	1	France
7	Petri Pasanen	DEF	24	6	540	0	0	0	Finland
8	Ivan Klasnic	ATT	25	8	521	5	2	0	Croatia
9	Frank Baumann	DEF	29	6	485	0	3	0	Germany
10	Miroslav Klose	ATT	27	7	470	2	1	0	Germany
11	Tim Borowski	DEF	25	6	441	0	2	0	Germany
12	Nelson Haedo Valdez	ATT	21	8	439	2	1	0	Paraguay
13	Daniel Jensen	MID	26	4	248	1	0	0	Denmark
14	Christian Schulz	MID	22	3	215	0	2	0	Germany
15	Frank Fahrenhorst	DEF	27	3	202	0	0	0	Germany
16	Angelos Charisteas	ATT	25	5	156	1	0	0	Greece
17	Umit Davala	MID	31	2	40	0	0	0	Turkey
18	Aaron Hunt	ATT	18	1	30	0	0	0	Germany

MONACO

FRANCE
Last 16

1	clql1	NK Gorica	A	W	3-0	Kallon 9,88; Chevanton 75	3,000
2	clql2	NK Gorica	H	W	6-0	Chevanton 17; Bernardi 31; El Fakiri 41; Kallon 47; Farnerud 66; Adebayor 84 pen	7,000
3	cl ga	Liverpool	A	L	0-2		33,517
4	cl ga	Deportivo	H	W	2-0	Kallon 5; Saviola 10	14,000
5	cl ga	Olympiakos	H	W	2-1	Saviola 3; Chevanton 10	17,000
6	cl ga	Olympiakos	A	L	0-1		33,000
7	cl ga	Liverpool	H	W	1-0	Saviola 55	15,000
8	cl ga	Deportivo	A	W	5-0	Chevanton 22; Givet 37; Saviola 39; Maicon 55; Adebayor 76	16,000
9	clr2l1	PSV Eindhoven	A	L	0-1		42,000
10	clr2l2	PSV Eindhoven	H	L	0-2		16,000

KEY PLAYERS - GOALSCORERS

Mohammed Kallon

FEDCOM

Goals in the Champions League	4
Contribution to Attacking Power Average number of minutes between team goals while on pitch	43
Player Strike Rate The total number of minutes he was on the pitch for every goal scored	195
Club Strike Rate Average number of minutes between goals scored by club	47

	PLAYER	GOALS	ATT POWER	STRIKE RATE
1	Mohammed Kallon	4	43	195 mins
2	Emmanuel Adebayor	2	51	311 mins
3	Gael Givet	1	46	786 mins
4	Maicon	1	42	810 mins

FIRST GROUP A

	P	W	D	L	F	A	DIF	PTS
Monaco	6	4	0	2	10	4	6	12
Liverpool	6	3	1	2	6	3	3	10
Olympiakos	6	3	1	2	5	5	0	10
Deportivo	6	0	2	4	0	9	-9	2

PLAYER APPEARANCES

Flavio Roma

Age (on 01/07/05)	31
Appearances in Champions league	10
Total minutes on the pitch	900
Goals	0
Yellow cards	0
Red cards	0
Home Country	Italy

	PLAYER	POS	AGE	APP	MINS ON	GOALS	CARDS(Y/R)		HOME COUNTRY
1	Flavio Roma	GK	31	10	900	0	0	0	Italy
2	Maicon	DEF	24	9	810	1	1	0	Brazil
3	Gael Givet	DEF	23	9	786	1	2	1	France
4	Mohammed Kallon	ATT	25	9	780	4	0	0	Sierra Leone
5	Vassilis Zikos	MID	31	9	777	0	2	0	Greece
6	Patrice Evra	MID	24	9	692	0	4	1	France
7	Sebastien Squillaci	DEF	24	8	675	0	1	0	France
8	Emmanuel Adebayor	ATT	21	10	622	2	0	0	Togo
9	Lucas Bernardi	MID	27	7	562	1	1	0	Argentina
10	Javier Saviola	ATT	23	7	557	4	0	0	Argentina
11	Julien Rodriguez	DEF	27	6	540	0	1	0	France
12	Ernesto Chevanton	ATT	24	8	467	4	1	0	Uruguay
13	Pontus Farnerud	MID	25	8	365	0	0	0	Sweden
14	Jaroslav Plasil	MID	23	5	347	0	1	0	Czech Republic
15	Diego Fernando Perez	MID	25	8	347	0	1	0	Uruguay
16	Francois Modesto	DEF	26	5	288	0	0	0	France
17	Shabani Nonda	ATT	28	3	118	0	0	0	Burundi
18	Hassan El Fakiri	MID	28	2	101	1	1	0	Norway

OLYMPIAKOS
GREECE
3rd in Group A

1	cl ga	Deportivo	A	D	0-0		22,000
2	cl ga	Liverpool	H	W	1-0	Stoltidis 17	33,000
3	cl ga	Monaco	A	L	1-2	Okkas 60	17,000
4	cl ga	Monaco	H	W	1-0	Schurrer 84	33,000
5	cl ga	Deportivo	H	W	1-0	Djordjevic 68	33,000
6	cl ga	Liverpool	A	L	1-3	Rivaldo 27	42,045

PLAYER APPEARANCES

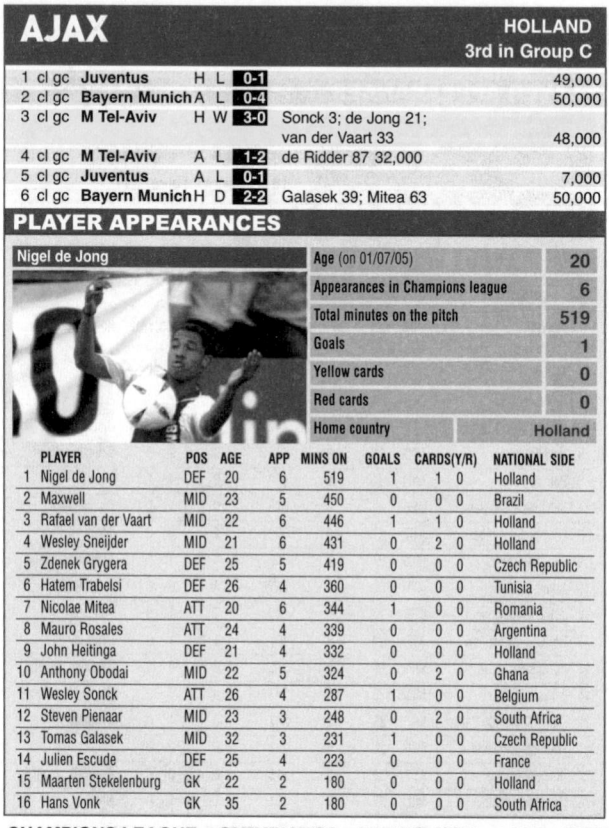

Gabriel Schurrer

Age (on 01/07/05)	33
Appearances in Champions league	6
Total minutes on the pitch	540
Goals	1
Yellow cards	3
Red cards	0
Home country	Argentina

	PLAYER	POS	AGE	APP	MINS ON	GOALS	CARDS(Y)	CARDS(R)	NATIONAL SIDE
1	Gabriel Peralta Schurrer	DEF	33	6	540	1	3	0	Argentina
2	Antonios Nikopolidis	GK	34	6	540	0	0	0	Greece
3	Ieroklis Stoltidis	MID	30	6	540	1	1	0	Greece
4	Georgios Anatolakis	DEF	31	6	540	0	3	0	Greece
5	Rivaldo Ferreira	ATT	33	6	535	1	0	0	Brazil
6	Pantelis Kafes	MID	27	6	521	0	1	0	Greece
7	Silva Giovanni	MID	32	6	443	0	0	0	Brazil
8	Anastasios Pantos	DEF	29	5	440	0	4	1	Greece
9	Yiannis Okkas	ATT	28	6	420	1	1	0	Cyprus
10	Stelios Venetidis	DEF	28	5	373	0	1	0	Greece
11	Predrag Djordjevic	MID	32	3	244	1	0	0	Serbia & M'gro
12	Dimitrios Mavrogenidis	DEF	28	4	243	0	1	0	Greece
13	Grigorios Georgatos	MID	32	5	239	0	1	0	Greece
14	Georgios Georgiadis	MID	33	5	161	0	0	0	Greece
15	Milos Maric	MID	23	4	83	0	0	0	Serbia & Mont.
16	Nery Castillo	MID	21	2	40	0	1	0	Uruguay

DINAMO KIEV
UKRAINE
3rd in Group B

1	clql1	Trabzonspor	H	L	1-2	Verpakovskis 21	35,000
2	clql2	Trabzonspor	A	W	2-0	Gavrancic 7; Rincon 29	20,000
3	cl gb	Roma	A	W	3-0		
4	cl gb	B Leverkusen	H	W	4-2	Rincon 30,69; Cernat 74,90	83,000
5	cl gb	Real Madrid	A	L	0-1		45,000
6	cl gb	Real Madrid	H	D	2-2	Yussuf 13; Verpakeovskis 23	80,000
7	cl gb	Roma	H	W	2-0	Dellas 73 og; Shatskikh 82	55,000
8	cl gb	B Leverkusen	A	L	0-3		23,000

PLAYER APPEARANCES

Goran Gavrancic

Age (on 01/07/05)	26
Appearances in Champions league	7
Total minutes on the pitch	630
Goals	1
Yellow cards	0
Red cards	0
Home country	Serbia & M'gro

	PLAYER	POS	AGE	APP	MINS ON	GOALS	CARDS(Y)	CARDS(R)	NATIONAL SIDE
1	Goran Gavrancic	DEF	26	7	630	1	0	0	Serbia & M'gro
2	Olexandr Shovkovskiy	GK	30	7	630	0	0	0	Ukraine
3	Diogo Rincon	ATT	25	7	590	3	2	0	Brazil
4	Goran Sablic	DEF	25	6	540	0	0	0	Ukraine
5	Badr El Kaddouri	MID	24	6	514	0	2	0	Morocco
6	Tiberiu Ghioane	MID	24	6	502	0	1	0	Romania
7	Kleber	ATT	22	5	450	0	0	0	Brazil
8	Dantas Bispo Rodolfo	DEF	22	6	444	0	4	1	Brazil
9	Maris Verpakovskis	ATT	25	6	428	2	3	0	Latvia
10	Oleg Gusev	MID	22	6	371	0	2	0	Ukraine
11	Atanda Yussuf	DEF	20	4	360	1	1	0	Ukraine
12	Jerko Leko	MID	25	5	282	0	2	0	Croatia
13	Maksim Shatskikh	ATT	26	6	273	1	0	0	Uzbekistan
14	Andriy Husin	MID	32	4	244	0	0	0	Ukraine
15	Sergeiy Fedorov	DEF	30	2	119	0	0	0	Ukraine
16	Andrii Nesmachnyi	DEF	26	2	116	0	0	0	Ukraine

AJAX
HOLLAND
3rd in Group C

1	cl gc	Juventus	H	L	0-1		49,000
2	cl gc	Bayern Munich	A	L	0-4		50,000
3	cl gc	M Tel-Aviv	H	W	3-0	Sonck 3; de Jong 21; van der Vaart 33	48,000
4	cl gc	M Tel-Aviv	A	L	1-2	de Ridder 87 32,000	
5	cl gc	Juventus	A	L	0-1		7,000
6	cl gc	Bayern Munich	H	D	2-2	Galasek 39; Mitea 63	50,000

PLAYER APPEARANCES

Nigel de Jong

Age (on 01/07/05)	20
Appearances in Champions league	6
Total minutes on the pitch	519
Goals	1
Yellow cards	0
Red cards	0
Home country	Holland

	PLAYER	POS	AGE	APP	MINS ON	GOALS	CARDS(Y)	CARDS(R)	NATIONAL SIDE
1	Nigel de Jong	DEF	20	6	519	1	1	0	Holland
2	Maxwell	MID	23	5	450	0	0	0	Brazil
3	Rafael van der Vaart	MID	22	6	446	1	1	0	Holland
4	Wesley Sneijder	MID	21	6	431	0	2	0	Holland
5	Zdenek Grygera	DEF	25	5	419	0	0	0	Czech Republic
6	Hatem Trabelsi	DEF	26	4	360	0	0	0	Tunisia
7	Nicolae Mitea	ATT	20	6	344	1	0	0	Romania
8	Mauro Rosales	ATT	24	4	339	0	0	0	Argentina
9	John Heitinga	DEF	21	4	332	0	0	0	Holland
10	Anthony Obodai	MID	22	5	324	0	2	0	Ghana
11	Wesley Sonck	ATT	26	4	287	1	0	0	Belgium
12	Steven Pienaar	MID	23	3	248	0	2	0	South Africa
13	Tomas Galasek	MID	32	3	231	1	0	0	Czech Republic
14	Julien Escude	DEF	25	4	223	0	0	0	France
15	Maarten Stekelenburg	GK	22	2	180	0	0	0	Holland
16	Hans Vonk	GK	35	2	180	0	0	0	South Africa

FENERBAHCE
TURKEY
3rd in Group D

1	cl gd	Sparta Prague	H	W	1-0	van Hooijdonk 16	52,000
2	cl gd	Man Utd	A	L	2-6	Nobre 46; Sanli 60	67,128
3	cl gd	Lyon	H	L	1-3	Nobre 68	49,000
4	cl gd	Lyon	A	L	2-4	Selcuk 14; Sanli 73	36,000
5	cl gd	Sparta Prague	A	W	1-0	Kovac 20 og	12,000
6	cl gd	Man Utd	H	W	3-0	Sanli 46,62,90	35,000

PLAYER APPEARANCES

2. Marco Aurelio

Age (on 01/07/05)	28
Appearances in Champions league	6
Total minutes on the pitch	540
Goals	
Yellow cards	3
Red cards	0
Home country	Brazil

	PLAYER	POS	AGE	APP	MINS ON	GOALS	CARDS(Y)	CARDS(R)	NATIONAL SIDE
1	Luciano	DEF	30	6	540	0	1	0	Brazil
2	Marco Aurelio	MID	28	6	540	0	3	0	Brazil
3	Alex	MID	27	6	537	0	0	0	Brazil
4	Umit Ozat	DEF	28	6	534	0	0	0	Turkey
5	Sanli	ATT	23	6	524	5	2	0	Turkey
6	Recber Rustu	GK	32	6	495	0	1	0	Turkey
7	Nobre	ATT	24	5	368	2	0	0	Brazil
8	Servet Cetin	DEF	24	4	329	0	4	2	Turkey
9	Pierre van Hooijdonk	ATT	35	4	272	1	0	0	Holland
10	Selcuk	MID	24	3	270	1	0	0	Turkey
11	Balci	MID	21	3	251	0	1	0	Turkey
12	Deniz	DEF	28	3	225	0	0	0	Turkey
13	Serhat Akin	ATT	24	4	197	0	0	0	Turkey
14	Onder	DEF	23	3	194	0	0	0	Turkey
15	Mehmet Yozgatli	MID	26	4	159	0	0	0	Turkey
16	Fabiano	DEF	26	4	98	0	0	0	Brazil

PANATHINAIKOS

GREECE
3rd in Group E

1	cl ge	Rosenborg BK	H	W	2-1	Gonzalez 43,79	13,000
2	cl ge	PSV Eindhoven	A	L	0-1		27,000
3	cl ge	Arsenal	H	D	2-2	Gonzalez 65; Olisadebe 82	12,000
4	cl ge	Arsenal	A	D	1-1	Cygan 75 og	35,137
5	cl ge	Rosenborg BK	A	D	2-2	Konstantinou 16; Skacel 71	19,000
6	cl ge	PSV Eindhoven	H	W	4-1	Papadopoulos 30; Munch 45 pen,57; Sanmartean 81	10,000

PLAYER APPEARANCES

Angelis Basinas

Age (on 01/07/05)	29
Appearances in Champions league	6
Total minutes on the pitch	540
Goals	0
Yellow cards	2
Red cards	0
Home country	Spain

	PLAYER	POS	AGE	APP	MINS ON	GOALS	CARDS(Y/R)		NATIONAL SIDE
1	Angelis Basinas	MID	29	6	540	0	2	0	Greece
2	Sotirios Kyrgiakos	DEF	25	6	531	0	0	0	Greece
3	Ezequiel Gonzalez	MID	24	6	495	3	1	0	Argentina
4	Loukas Vintra	DEF	24	5	443	0	2	0	Greece
5	Rudolf Skacel	MID	25	5	415	1	2	0	Czech Republic
6	Konstantinos Chalkias	GK	31	4	360	0	0	0	Greece
7	Pantelis Konstanindis	MID	29	5	359	0	1	0	Greece
8	Michael Konstantinou	ATT	27	5	331	1	1	0	Cyprus
9	Dimitrios Papadopoulos	ATT	23	4	311	1	0	0	Greece
10	Nasief Morris	DEF	24	5	292	0	0	0	South Africa
11	Yannis Goumas	DEF	30	4	282	0	1	0	Greece
12	Markus Munch	DEF	32	3	270	2	0	0	Germany
13	Silvio Maric	MID	30	4	265	0	2	0	Croatia
14	Mitu	MID	-	5	198	0	0	0	
15	Mario Galinovic	GK	28	2	180	0	1	0	Croatia
16	Rene Henriksen	DEF	35	2	180	0	0	0	Denmark

SHAKHTAR DONETSK

UKRAINE
3rd in Group F

1	clql1	Club Brugge	H	W	4-1	Aghahowa 14; Marica 70; Vorobiei 79; Brandao 90	30,000
2	clql2	Club Brugge	A	D	2-2	Vukic 5,53	17,000
3	cl gf	AC Milan	H	L	0-1		30,000
4	cl gf	Barcelona	A	L	0-3		64,000
5	cl gf	Celtic	H	W	3-0	Matuzalem 57,62; Brandao 78	30,000
6	cl gf	Celtic	A	L	0-1		58,347
7	cl gf	AC Milan	A	L	0-4		39,000
8	cl gf	Barcelona	H	W	2-0	Aghahowa 14,22	25,000

PLAYER APPEARANCES

Lewandowski

Age (on 01/07/05)	26
Appearances in Champions league	8
Total minutes on the pitch	720
Goals	2
Yellow cards	0
Red cards	0
Home country	Poland

	PLAYER	POS	AGE	APP	MINS ON	GOALS	CARDS(Y/R)		NATIONAL SIDE
1	Lewandowski	MID	26	8	720	0	2	0	Poland
2	Jan Lastuvka	GK	22	8	720	0	1	0	Czech Republic
3	Francelin Matuzalem	MID	24	8	692	2	1	0	Brazil
4	Zvonimir Vukic	MID	25	8	651	2	1	0	Serbia & M'gro
5	Flavius Stoican	DEF	28	7	612	0	2	1	Romania
6	Igor Duljaj	MID	25	8	548	0	1	0	Serbia & M'gro
7	Andriy Vorobiei	ATT	26	8	518	1	0	0	Ukraine
8	Barcauan	DEF	26	6	509	0	3	1	Romania
9	Anatoliy Tymoschuk	DEF	26	6	493	0	1	1	Ukraine
10	Rat	DEF	24	5	450	0	0	0	Romania
11	Ciprian Marica	ATT	19	7	431	1	0	0	Romania
12	Julius Aghahowa	ATT	23	7	426	3	0	0	Nigeria
13	Darijo Srna	MID	23	6	337	0	3	1	Croatia
14	Tomas Hubschmann	DEF	23	4	301	0	0	0	Czech Republic
15	Brandao	ATT	25	6	222	2	0	0	Brazil
16	Joao Batista	MID	30	5	125	0	0	0	Brazil

VALENCIA

SPAIN
3rd in Group G

1	cl gg	Anderlecht	H	W	2-0	Vicente 16; Baraja 45	34,000
2	cl gg	W Bremen	A	L	1-2	Vicente 2	36,000
3	cl gg	Inter Milan	H	L	1-5	Aimar 73	40,000
4	cl gg	Inter Milan	A	D	0-0		40,000
5	cl gg	Anderlecht	A	W	2-1	Corradi 19; Di Vaio 48	26,000
6	cl gg	W Bremen	H	L	0-2		40,000

PLAYER APPEARANCES

Curro Torres

Age (on 01/07/05)	28
Appearances in Champions league	6
Total minutes on the pitch	540
Goals	0
Yellow cards	1
Red cards	0
Home country	Spain

	PLAYER	POS	AGE	APP	MINS ON	GOALS	CARDS(Y/R)		NATIONAL SIDE
1	Curro Torres	DEF	28	6	540	0	1	0	Spain
2	Santiago Canizares	GK	35	6	540	0	1	0	Spain
3	Ruben Baraja	MID	29	6	506	1	2	0	Spain
4	David Navarro	DEF	25	5	450	0	1	0	Spain
5	Miguel Angulo	ATT	28	5	450	0	2	1	Spain
6	Amadeo Carboni	DEF	40	5	369	0	1	0	Italy
7	David Albelda	MID	27	4	341	0	1	0	Spain
8	Marco Caneira	DEF	26	4	334	0	1	0	Portugal
9	Marco Di Vaio	ATT	28	5	332	1	0	0	Italy
10	Carlos Marchena	DEF	26	4	325	0	4	1	Spain
11	Francisco Rufete	MID	28	4	297	0	1	0	Spain
12	Bernardo Corradi	ATT	29	6	290	1	2	0	Italy
13	Pablo Aimar	MID	25	3	225	1	0	0	Argentina
14	Emiliano Moretti	DEF	24	4	199	0	0	0	Italy
15	Rodriguez Vicente	ATT	23	3	198	2	1	0	Spain
16	Mista	ATT	26	3	147	0	0	0	Spain

CSKA MOSCOW

RUSSIA
3rd in Group H

1	clql1	Rangers	H	W	2-1	Vagner Love 4; Jarosik 46	11,000
2	clql2	Rangers	A	D	1-1	Vagner Love 61	49,010
3	cl gh	Porto	A	D	0-0		39,000
4	cl gh	Paris SG	H	W	2-0	Semak 64; Vagner Love 77 pen	10,000
5	cl gh	Chelsea	A	L	0-2		33,945
6	cl gh	Chelsea	H	L	0-1		28,000
7	cl gh	Porto	H	L	0-1		22,000
8	cl gh	Paris SG	A	W	3-1	Semak 28,64,70	40,000

PLAYER APPEARANCES

Alexei Berezoutski

sibneft

Age (on 01/07/05)	23
Appearances in Champions league	8
Total minutes on the pitch	720
Goals	0
Yellow cards	0
Red cards	0
Home country	Russia

	PLAYER	POS	AGE	APP	MINS ON	GOALS	CARDS(Y/R)		NATIONAL SIDE
1	Alexei Berezoutski	DEF	23	8	720	0	0	0	Russia
2	Elvir Rahimic	MID	29	8	720	0	1	0	Bosnia
3	Yuri Zhirkov	MID	26	8	720	0	3	0	Russia
4	Igor Akinfeev	GK	19	8	720	0	1	0	Russia
5	Deividas Semberas	DEF	26	8	684	0	4	1	Lithuania
6	Vagner Love	ATT	21	8	656	3	1	0	Brazil
7	Sergei Ignashevitch	DEF	25	7	630	0	0	0	Russia
8	Jiri Jarosik	MID	27	7	605	1	0	0	Czech Republic
9	Yevgeny Aldonin	MID	25	8	564	0	1	0	Russia
10	Sergei Semak	MID	29	8	413	4	1	0	Russia
11	Chidi Odiah	DEF	21	4	360	0	2	0	Nigeria
12	Rolan Gusev	MID	27	5	346	0	0	0	Russia
13	Ivica Olic	ATT	25	5	335	0	1	0	Croatia
14	Milos Krasic	MID	20	3	133	0	0	0	Serbia & M'gro
15	Vassili Berezoutski	DEF	23	4	82	0	0	0	Russia
16	Jurijs Laizans	DEF	26	2	67	0	0	0	Latvia

DEPORTIVO

SPAIN
4th in Group A

1	clql1	Shelbourne	A	D	0-0		24,000
2	clql2	Shelbourne	H	W	3-0	Victor 60,66; Pandiani 88	27,000
3	cl ga	Olympiakos	H	D	0-0		22,000
4	cl ga	Monaco	A	L	0-2		14,000
5	cl ga	Liverpool	A	D	0-0		40,236
6	cl ga	Liverpool	H	L	0-1		32,000
7	cl ga	Olympiakos	A	L	0-1		33,000
8	cl ga	Monaco	H	L	0-5		16,000

PLAYER APPEARANCES

Juan Valeron

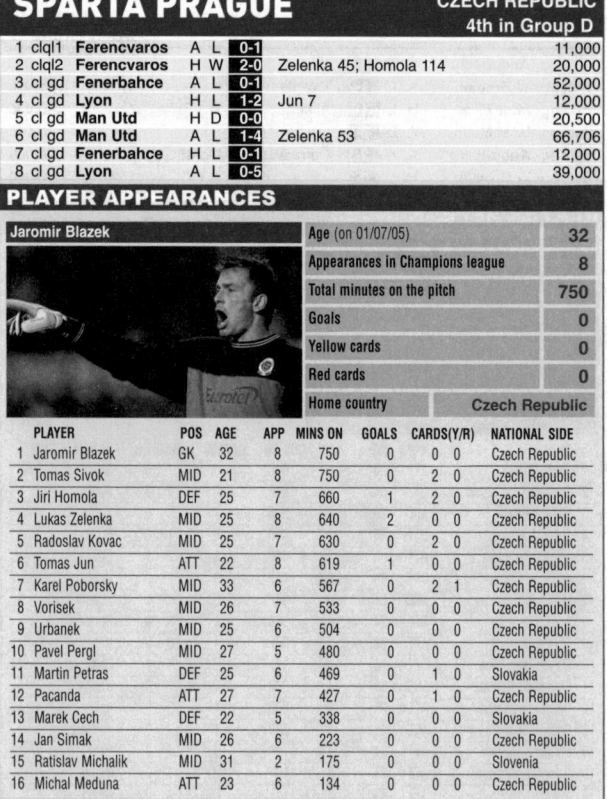

Age (on 01/07/05)	30
Appearances in Champions league	8
Total minutes on the pitch	654
Goals	0
Yellow cards	0
Red cards	0
Home country	Spain

	PLAYER	POS	AGE	APP	MINS ON	GOALS	CARDS(Y/R)		NATIONAL SIDE
1	Juan Valeron	MID	30	8	654	0	0	0	Spain
2	Jorge Andrade	DEF	27	7	630	0	3	0	Portugal
3	Francisco Molina	GK	34	7	580	0	0	0	Spain
4	Walter Pandiani	ATT	29	8	574	1	2	0	Uruguay
5	Alberto Luque	ATT	27	8	558	0	1	0	Spain
6	Manuel Pablo	DEF	29	6	517	0	0	0	Spain
7	Sanchez Victor	MID	29	6	512	2	1	0	Spain
8	Martin Cesar	DEF	28	6	495	0	3	0	Spain
9	Aldo Duscher	MID	26	7	488	0	2	0	Argentina
10	Enrique Romero	DEF	34	6	459	0	0	0	Spain
11	Lionel Scaloni	DEF	27	7	383	0	0	0	Argentina
12	Gonzalez Sergio	MID	28	5	381	0	3	0	Spain
13	Pedro Munitis	ATT	30	6	321	0	0	0	Spain
14	Pablo Amo	DEF	27	4	315	0	0	0	Spain
15	Joan Capdevila	DEF	27	3	270	0	0	0	Spain
16	Javier Fran	MID	35	4	230	0	0	0	Spain

ROMA

ITALY
4th in Group B

1	cl gb	Dinamo Kiev	H	L	0-3		
2	cl gb	Real Madrid	A	L	2-4	De Rossi 3; Cassano 21	60,000
3	cl gb	B Leverkusen	A	L	1-3	Jones 26 og	23,000
4	cl gb	B Leverkusen	H	D	1-1	Montella 90	
5	cl gb	Dinamo Kiev	A	L	0-2		

PLAYER APPEARANCES

Leandro Cufre

Age (on 01/07/05)	27
Appearances in Champions league	5
Total minutes on the pitch	374
Goals	0
Yellow cards	0
Red cards	0
Home country	Argentina

	PLAYER	POS	AGE	APP	MINS ON	GOALS	CARDS(Y/R)		NATIONAL SIDE
1	Leandro Cufre	DEF	27	5	374	0	0	0	Argentina
2	Traianos Dellas	DEF	29	4	360	0	1	0	Greece
3	Mancini	MID	24	4	336	0	1	0	Brazil
4	Simone Perrotta	MID	27	4	334	0	3	0	Italy
5	Alberto Aquilani	MID	20	4	311	0	1	0	Italy
6	Matteo Ferrari	DEF	25	3	270	0	1	0	Italy
7	Ivan Pellizzoli	GK	24	3	270	0	0	0	Italy
8	Antonio Cassano	ATT	22	3	270	1	0	0	Italy
9	Francesco Totti	ATT	28	3	270	0	1	0	Italy
10	Vincent Candela	DEF	31	3	240	0	0	0	France
11	Luigi Sartor	DEF	30	4	192	0	0	0	Italy
12	Daniele Corvia	ATT	20	3	181	0	0	0	Italy
13	Carlo Zotti	GK	22	2	180	0	1	0	Italy
14	Philippe Mexes	DEF	23	2	180	0	1	0	France
15	Giuseppe Scurto	DEF	21	2	166	0	2	1	Italy
16	Daniele De Rossi	MID	20	2	162	1	0	1	Italy

MACCABI TEL-AVIV

ISRAEL
4th in Group C

1	clql1	PAOK Salonika	A	W	3-0	Addo 13; Mesika 43	20,000
2	clql2	PAOK Salonika	H	W	1-0	Cohen, L 8	20,000
3	cl gc	Bayern Munich	H	L	0-1		20,000
4	cl gc	Juventus	A	L	0-1		6,000
5	cl gc	Ajax	A	L	0-3		48,000
6	cl gc	Ajax	H	W	2-1	Dego 49,56	32,000
7	cl gc	Bayern Munich	A	L	1-5	Dego 55 pen	25,000
8	cl gc	Juventus	H	D	1-1	Dego 29 pen	19,000

PLAYER APPEARANCES

Giovanni

Age (on 01/07/05)	26
Appearances in Champions league	7
Total minutes on the pitch	630
Goals	0
Yellow cards	1
Red cards	0
Home country	Brazil

	PLAYER	POS	AGE	APP	MINS ON	GOALS	CARDS(Y/R)		NATIONAL SIDE
1	Marcio Giovanni	DEF	26	7	630	0	1	0	Brazil
2	Avi Strool	DEF	24	7	611	0	1	0	Israel
3	Liran Strauber	GK	30	6	540	0	0	0	Israel
4	Addo	ATT	23	7	526	0	0	0	Ghana
5	Moshe Mishaelof	DEF	21	7	510	0	1	0	Israel
6	Pantsil	DEF	24	6	464	0	1	0	Ghana
7	Mesika	MID	25	7	458	0	0	0	Israel
8	Tamir Cohen,	MID	23	5	450	0	0	0	Israel
9	Liran Cohen,	MID	22	5	404	1	0	0	Israel
10	Salem Abo-siam	DEF	22	4	360	0	0	0	Israel
11	Bruno Reis Lino	MID	27	6	341	0	0	0	Brazil
12	Barukh Dego	ATT	24	3	270	4	0	0	Israel
13	Nagar	DEF	27	3	270	0	1	0	Israel
14	Koby Moosa	DEF	23	3	195	0	0	0	Israel
16	Mbamba	ATT	22	5	166	0	0	0	Cameroon

SPARTA PRAGUE

CZECH REPUBLIC
4th in Group D

1	clql1	Ferencvaros	A	L	0-1		11,000
2	clql2	Ferencvaros	H	W	2-0	Zelenka 45; Homola 114	20,000
3	cl gd	Fenerbahce	A	L	0-1		52,000
4	cl gd	Lyon	H	L	1-2	Jun 7	12,000
5	cl gd	Man Utd	H	D	0-0		20,500
6	cl gd	Man Utd	A	L	1-4	Zelenka 53	66,706
7	cl gd	Fenerbahce	H	L	0-1		12,000
8	cl gd	Lyon	A	L	0-5		39,000

PLAYER APPEARANCES

Jaromir Blazek

Age (on 01/07/05)	32
Appearances in Champions league	8
Total minutes on the pitch	750
Goals	0
Yellow cards	0
Red cards	0
Home country	Czech Republic

	PLAYER	POS	AGE	APP	MINS ON	GOALS	CARDS(Y/R)		NATIONAL SIDE
1	Jaromir Blazek	GK	32	8	750	0	0	0	Czech Republic
2	Tomas Sivok	MID	21	8	750	0	2	0	Czech Republic
3	Jiri Homola	DEF	25	7	660	1	2	0	Czech Republic
4	Lukas Zelenka	MID	25	8	640	2	0	0	Czech Republic
5	Radoslav Kovac	MID	25	7	630	0	2	0	Czech Republic
6	Tomas Jun	ATT	22	8	619	1	0	0	Czech Republic
7	Karel Poborsky	MID	33	6	567	0	2	1	Czech Republic
8	Vorisek	MID	26	7	533	0	0	0	Czech Republic
9	Urbanek	MID	25	6	504	0	0	0	Czech Republic
10	Pavel Pergl	MID	27	5	480	0	0	0	Czech Republic
11	Martin Petras	DEF	25	6	469	0	1	0	Slovakia
12	Pacanda	ATT	27	7	427	0	1	0	Czech Republic
13	Marek Cech	DEF	22	5	338	0	0	0	Slovakia
14	Jan Simak	MID	26	6	223	0	0	0	Czech Republic
15	Ratislav Michalik	MID	31	2	175	0	0	0	Slovenia
16	Michal Meduna	ATT	23	6	134	0	0	0	Czech Republic

ROSENBORG BK

Norway
4th in Group E

1	clql1	Maccabi Haifa	H	W	2-1	Brattbakk 1; Solli 8	20,000
2	clql2	Maccabi Haifa	A	W	3-2	Brattbakk 90; Braathen 94; Berg 120	10,000
3	cl ge	Panathinaikos	A	L	1-2	Johnsen, F 90	13,000
4	cl ge	Arsenal	H	D	1-1	Strand 52	21,000
5	cl ge	PSV Eindhoven	H	L	1-2	Storflor 42	21,000
6	cl ge	PSV Eindhoven	A	L	0-1		26,000
7	cl ge	Panathinaikos	H	D	2-2	Helstad 68,76	19,000
8	cl ge	Arsenal	A	L	1-5	Hoftun 38	35,421

PLAYER APPEARANCES

Espen Johnsen

Age (on 01/07/05)	25
Appearances in Champions league	8
Total minutes on the pitch	750
Goals	0
Yellow cards	1
Red cards	0
Home country	Norway

	PLAYER	POS	AGE	APP	MINS ON	GOALS	CARDS(Y/R)		NATIONAL SIDE
1	Espen Johnsen	GK	25	8	750	0	1	0	Norway
2	Erik Hoftun	DEF	36	8	750	1	1	0	Norway
3	Frode Johnsen	ATT	31	8	742	1	0	0	Norway
4	Jan Gunnar Solli	MID	24	8	740	1	0	0	Norway
5	Roar Strand	MID	35	8	594	1	0	0	Norway
6	Frederik Winsnes	MID	29	7	583	0	0	0	Norway
7	Mikael Dorsin	MID	23	6	512	0	0	0	Sweden
8	Oyvind Storflor	ATT	24	8	484	1	0	0	Norway
9	Vidar Riseth	MID	33	5	480	0	1	0	Norway
10	Harald Brattbakk	ATT	34	7	474	2	1	0	Norway
11	Stale Stensaas	DEF	34	5	393	0	0	0	Norway
12	Daniel Braathen	ATT	28	8	341	1	1	0	Norway
13	Orjan Berg	MID	36	3	300	1	1	0	Norway
14	Torjus Hansen	DEF	31	3	270	0	0	0	Norway
15	Christer Basma	DEF	32	4	266	0	1	0	Norway
16	Robble Russell	DEF	25	4	264	0	0	0	USA

CELTIC

SCOTLAND
4th in Group F

1	cl gf	Barcelona	H	L	1-3	Sutton 59	60,000
2	cl gf	AC Milan	A	L	1-3	Varga 74	68,000
3	cl gf	Shakhtar	A	L	0-3		30,000
4	cl gf	Shakhtar	H	W	1-0	Thompson 25	58,347
5	cl gf	Barcelona	A	D	1-1	Hartson 45	74,000
6	cl gf	AC Milan	H	D	0-0		59,228

PLAYER APPEARANCES

Neil Lennon

Age (on 01/07/05)	34
Appearances in Champions league	6
Total minutes on the pitch	540
Goals	0
Yellow cards	2
Red cards	0
Home country	N Ireland

	PLAYER	POS	AGE	APP	MINS ON	GOALS	CARDS(Y/R)		NATIONAL SIDE
1	Neil Lennon	MID	34	6	540	0	2	0	N Ireland
2	Stilian Petrov	MID	26	6	526	0	0	0	Bulgaria
3	Stanislav Varga	DEF	32	6	515	1	1	0	Slovakia
4	John Hartson	ATT	30	6	507	1	2	0	Wales
5	Dianbobo Balde	DEF	29	5	450	0	1	0	France
6	Didier Agathe	DEF	29	5	450	0	0	0	France
7	Alan Thompson	MID	31	5	414	1	0	0	England
8	Henri Camara	ATT	28	6	400	0	1	0	Senegal
9	Jackie McNamara	DEF	31	5	379	0	1	0	Scotland
10	Joos Valgaeren	DEF	29	5	363	0	1	0	Belgium
11	David Marshall	GK	20	4	360	0	0	0	Scotland
12	Chris Sutton	ATT	32	5	360	1	1	0	England
13	Aiden McGeady	MID	19	3	188	0	0	0	Rep or Ireland
14	Magnus Hedman	GK	32	2	180	0	0	0	Sweden
15	Paulista Juninho	MID	32	4	161	0	2	0	Brazil
16	Ross Wallace	MID	20	3	61	0	0	0	Scotland

PARIS St GERMAIN

FRANCE
4th in Group H

1	cl gh	Chelsea	H	L	0-3		45,000
2	cl gh	CSKA Moscow	A	L	0-2		10,000
3	cl gh	Porto	H	W	2-0	Coridon 30; Pauleta 31	48,000
4	cl gh	Porto	A	D	0-0		30,000
5	cl gh	Chelsea	A	D	0-0		39,626
6	cl gh	CSKA Moscow	H	L	1-3	Pancrate 37	40,000

PLAYER APPEARANCES

Sylvain Armand

Age (on 01/07/05)	24
Appearances in Champions league	6
Total minutes on the pitch	540
Goals	0
Yellow cards	1
Red cards	0
Home country	France

	PLAYER	POS	AGE	APP	MINS ON	GOALS	CARDS(Y/R)		NATIONAL SIDE
1	Sylvain Armand	DEF	24	6	540	0	1	0	France
2	Lorik Cana	MID	21	6	540	0	1	0	Bosnia
3	Jose Karl Pierre-Fanfan	DEF	29	6	540	0	1	0	France
4	Lionel Letizi	GK	32	6	540	0	0	0	France
5	Pauleta	ATT	32	6	528	1	0	0	Portugal
6	Modeste Mbami	MID	22	6	433	0	1	0	Cameroon
7	Charles-Edouard Coridon	MID	32	6	378	1	0	0	France
8	Bernard Mendy	DEF	23	5	372	0	3	1	France
9	Mario Yepes	DEF	29	4	360	0	0	0	Colombia
10	Stephane Pichot	DEF	28	4	342	0	2	0	France
11	Edouard Cisse	MID	27	5	297	0	0	0	France
12	Fabrice Pancrate	ATT	25	5	216	1	0	0	France
13	Rodriques Helder	DEF	34	2	180	0	1	0	Portugal
14	Reinaldo	ATT	26	3	158	0	0	0	Brazil
15	Danijel Ljuboja	MID	27	5	134	0	0	0	Serbia & M'gro
16	Jerome Rothen	MID	27	2	131	0	0	0	France

ANDERLECHT

BELGIUM
4th in Group G

1	clql1	Benfica	A	L	0-1		65,000
2	clql2	Benfica	H	W	3-0	Dindane 33,61; Jestrovic 73 pen	25,000
3	cl gg	Valencia	A	L	0-2		34,000
4	cl gg	Inter Milan	H	L	1-3	Baseggio 90	22,000
5	cl gg	W Bremen	H	L	1-2	Wilhelmsson 26	22,000
6	cl gg	W Bremen	A	L	1-5	Iachtchouk 30	37,000
7	cl gg	Valencia	H	L	1-2	Wilhelmsson 24	26,000
8	cl gg	Inter Milan	A	L	0-3		30,000

PLAYER APPEARANCES

Aruna Dindane

Age (on 01/07/05)	24
Appearances in Champions league	8
Total minutes on the pitch	719
Goals	2
Yellow cards	0
Red cards	0
Home country	Ivory Coast

	PLAYER	POS	AGE	APP	MINS ON	GOALS	CARDS(Y/R)		NATIONAL SIDE
1	Aruna Dindane	MID	24	8	719	2	0	0	Ivory Coast
2	Christian Wilhelmsson	MID	25	8	704	2	1	0	Sweden
3	Oliver Deschacht	DEF	24	8	660	0	0	0	Belgium
4	Walter Baseggio	MID	26	8	657	1	2	0	Belgium
5	Vincent Kompany	DEF	19	7	630	0	1	0	Belgium
6	Mbo Mpenza	ATT	28	7	545	0	0	0	Belgium
7	Lamine Traore	DEF	23	6	540	0	2	0	Burkina Faso
8	Michal Zewlakow	DEF	29	6	518	0	1	0	Poland
9	Besnik Hasi	MID	33	7	509	0	4	0	Albania
10	Daniel Zitka	GK	30	5	450	0	0	0	Czech Republic
11	Par Zetterberg	MID	34	5	330	0	0	0	Sweden
12	Anthony Vanden Borre	DEF	17	6	279	0	0	0	Belgium
13	Glen De Boeck	DEF	33	3	251	0	0	0	Belgium
14	Oleg Iachtchouk	MID	27	6	248	1	0	0	Ukraine
15	Tristan Peersman	GK	25	2	180	0	0	0	Belgium
16	Yves Vanderhaeghe	MID	35	2	180	0	0	0	Belgium

THE UEFA CUP

1ST ROUND

	AGG		LEG1	LEG2
Aigaleo	2-1	Genclerbirligi	1-0	1-1
Austria Vienna	4-1	Legia Warsaw	1-0	3-1
Bodo	1-2	Besiktas	1-1	0-1
Club Brugge	6-1	Chateauroux	4-0	2-1
DB Bystrica	0-5	Benfica	0-3	0-2
Dinamo Zagreb	2-0	Elfsborg	2-0	0-0
FK Ventspils	1-2	Amica Wronki	1-1	0-1
Grazer AK	5-1	Liteks Lovetch	5-0	0-1
Hafnarfjordur	1-5	Alem Aachen	1-5	0-0
Hammarby	1-5	Villarreal	1-2	0-3
Hearts	5-3	Braga	3-1	2-2
Levski Sofia	1-2	Beveren	1-1	0-1
M Petach-Tikva	0-5	Heerenveen	-	0-5
Result decided over one match				
Maccabi Haifa	1-2	Dnipro	1-0	0-2
Maritimo	1-1	Rangers	1-0	0-1
Rangers win 4-2 on penalties				
Metalurh D	0-6	Lazio	0-3	0-3
Middlesbrough	4-1	Banik Ostrava	3-0	1-1
Millwall	2-4	Ferencvaros	1-1	1-3

Mark de Vries defies injury to play with painkilling injections and score twice to take Hearts through against Portuguese side Braga

Dado Prso scores the vital goal to pull Rangers level on aggregate with Portuguese side Maritimo at Ibrox and they win through on penalties

A Dennis Wise freekick is Millwall's first European goal but Hungarian champions Ferencvaros grab a point at the New Den and progress despite violence and racist taunts in the second leg

GROUP A

Feyenoord	(1) **3**	**Hearts**	(0) **0**
Kuijt 21,83			26,000
Goor 58			
Schalke	(1) **1**	**Basel**	(0) **1**
Kobiashvili 8			Delgado 82
53,000			
Ferencvaros	(1) **1**	**Feyenoord**	(0) **1**
Tozser 26 fk			Kalou 62
28,000			
Hearts	(0) **0**	**Schalke**	(0) **1**
27,272			Lincoln 73

Schalke's Brazilian Lincoln strikes from midfield to clinch a win over ten-man Hearts. Debut manager John Robertson suffers defeat after Jason Kisnorbo is dismissed

Basel	(0) **1**	**Hearts**	(1) **2**
Carignano 76			Wyness 31
25,000			Neilson 89
Schalke	(2) **2**	**Ferencvaros**	(0) **0**
Gyepes 15 og			21,000
Kobiashvili 40			
Ferencvaros	(1) **1**	**Basel**	(0) **2**
Denes Rosa 22			Rossi 59
17,000			Huggel 79
Feyenoord	(2) **2**	**Schalke**	(1) **1**
Kalou 32,41			Hanke 7
48,000			
Basel	(0) **1**	**Feyenoord**	(0) **0**
Carignano 53			26,000
Hearts	(0) **0**	**Ferencvaros**	(1) **1**
26,182			Denes Rosa 30

Last Scottish representatives fall as Hearts go out to a goal by Ferencvaros' Denes Rosa at Tynecastle. However, neither side progress as Christian Gross' Swiss side FC Basel gain the final Group A qualification spot with a win over leaders Feyenoord thanks to Carignano's only goal of the game. FC Schalke had already qualified

GROUP A TABLE

	P	W	D	L	DIF	PTS
Feyenoord	4	2	1	1	3	7
Schalke	4	2	1	1	2	7
Basel	4	2	1	1	1	7
Ferencváros	4	1	1	2	-2	4
Hearts	4	1	0	3	-4	3

GROUP B

Athl Bilbao	(1) **2**	**Parma**	(0) **0**
Gurpegui 5			32,000
Del Horno 48			
Steaua Bucharest	(0) **2**	**Standard Liege**	(0) **0**
Dragutinovic 68 og			20,000
Neaga 81			
Besiktas	(1) **3**	**Athl Bilbao**	(0) **1**
Gunes 26			Ezquerro 49
Carew 63			30,000
Akin 89			
Parma	(0) **1**	**Steaua Bucharest**	(0) **0**
Budel 79			4,000
Standard Liege	(0) **2**	**Parma**	(1) **1**
Geraerts 54			Pisanu 44
Garbini 90			21,000
Steaua Bucharest	(2) **2**	**Besiktas**	(0) **1**
Neaga 3			Ibrahim 87
Ciocoiu 18			20,000
Athl Bilbao	(1) **1**	**Steaua Bucharest**	(0) **0**
Joseba Etxeberria 45			35,000

Steaua Bucharest celebrate qualification for the next phase despite losing to a goal from Spanish international Etxeberria in Bilbao

Besiktas	(1) **1**	**Standard Liege**	(0) **1**
Okan 30			Bangoura 81
14,000			
Parma	(2) **3**	**Besiktas**	(1) **2**
Gilardino 16			Okan 5
Cardone 35			Tumer 88
Degano 59			15,000
Standard Liege	(1) **1**	**Athl Bilbao**	(3) **7**
Onyewu 14			Ezquerro 5,8,54
27,000			Yeste 34, Iraola 57
			Del Horno 63
			Joseba Etxeberria 70

Parma sneak through to gain the final Group B qualification spot with a tough win over Besiktas with Gilardino scoring the first goal and missing from the spot but Degano nets the eventual winner. Their rivals Standard Liege ship seven, including a Ezquerro hat-trick, against group winners Athletic Bilbao. Steaua Bucharest already through

GROUP B TABLE

	P	W	D	L	DIF	PTS
Athl Bilbao	4	3	0	1	7	9
S Bucharest	4	2	0	2	1	6
Parma	4	2	0	2	-1	6
Besiktas	4	1	1	2	0	4
S Liege	4	1	1	2	-7	4

GROUP C

Dnipro	(2) **3**	**Club Brugge**	(2) **2**
Venhlynsky 14,63			Ceh 37
Rykun 45			Balaban 41
22,000			
Real Zaragoza	(0) **2**	**Utrecht**	(0) **0**
Villa 76,82			27,000
Austria Vienna	(0) **1**	**Real Zaragoza**	(0) **0**
Gilewicz 71			19,000

Polish striker Gilewicz gives Austria Vienna a winning start against Group C favourites Zaragoza, for whom former Bolton squad player Moreno comes closest

Utrecht	(0) **1**	**Dnipro**	(1) **2**
Douglas 88			Rotan 12
14,000			Semochko 83
Club Brugge	(0) **1**	**Utrecht**	(0) **0**
Lange 63			22,000

Norwegian striker Lange scores the only goal to give Belgian side Club Brugge a narrow win over Dutch rivals Utrecht

Dnipro	(1) **1**	**Austria Vienna**	(0) **0**
Nazarenko 19			18,000
Austria Vienna	(0) **1**	**Club Brugge**	(0) **1**
Gilewicz 50			Lange 90
20,000			
Real Zaragoza	(1) **2**	**Dnipro**	(1) **1**
Savio 9			Yezerskyy 2
Generelo 73			10,000
Club Brugge	(0) **1**	**Real Zaragoza**	(1) **1**
Ceh 67			Savio 39
23,000			
Utrecht	(0) **1**	**Austria Vienna**	(1) **2**
Douglas 55			Sionko 14
14,000			Rushfeldt 78

Austria Vienna qualify with Rushfeldt scoring the decisive goal in a win over pointless Utrecht on the final night. They are behind Real Zaragoza who can only draw with Club Brugge, leaving Ukrainian side Dnipro as the surprise Group C table toppers with only one defeat, away to Zaragoza – and that after they had already qualified

GROUP C TABLE

	P	W	D	L	DIF	PTS
Dnipro	4	3	0	1	2	9
R Zaragoza	4	2	1	1	2	7
Austria Vienna	4	2	1	1	1	7
Club Brugge	4	1	2	1	0	5
Utrecht	4	0	0	4	-5	0

GROUP D

Dinamo Tbilisi	(0) **0**	**Sochaux**	(2) **2**
30,000			Ilan 18
			Paisley 38
Panionios	(0) **0**	**Newcastle**	(0) **1**
8,000			Shearer 87 pen
Newcastle	(1) **2**	**Dinamo Tbilisi**	(0) **0**
Shearer 38			27,218
Bellamy 56			
Sp Lisbon	(0) **4**	**Panionios**	(0) **1**
Custodio 5			Marcora 35
Douala 38			19,000
Liedson 79			
Viana 80			
Dinamo Tbilisi	(0) **0**	**Sp Lisbon**	(2) **4**
28,000			Liedson 5,28,59
			Chichveishvili 89
Sochaux	(0) **0**	**Newcastle**	(1) **4**
15,000			Bowyer 29, Ameobi 46
			Bellamy 75
			Robert 90
Panionios	(0) **5**	**Dinamo Tbilisi**	(1) **2**
Mantzios 58,67,78			Kakaladze 38
Breska 90			Akhalaia 60
Marcora 90			3,000
Sp Lisbon	(0) **0**	**Sochaux**	(1) **1**
21,000			Lonfat 2

Sporting Lisbon lose at home to a goal from Lonfat and only Portuguese keeper Ricardo prevents a worse defeat

Newcastle	(1) **1**	**Sp Lisbon**	(1) **1**
Bellamy 5			Custodio 40
28,017			
Sochaux	(0) **1**	**Panionios**	(0) **0**
Isabey 86			10,000

Custódio makes sure of qualification for third place Sporting Lisbon with an equalising goal before the break to take an away point after Bellamy's strike for top-of-the-table Newcastle. In the final night's other tie, Sochaux show why they're through with captain Isabey scoring the only goal past Drobny in a 1-0 defeat of Panionios

GROUP D TABLE

	P	W	D	L	DIF	PTS
Newcastle	4	3	1	0	7	10
Sochaux	4	3	0	1	0	9
Sp Lisbon	4	2	1	1	6	7
Panionios	4	1	0	3	-2	3
Dinamo Tbilisi	4	0	0	4	-11	0

FIRST ROUND AND GROUP STAGE

Newcastle 7-1 Bnei Sachnin 2-0 5-1

Patrick Kluivert and Alan Shearer bring all their class to bear, scoring all five goals as Israeli side Bnei Sachnin are humiliated at home

NK Gorica 1-2 AEK Athens 1-1 0-1

Odd Grenland 1-5 Feyenoord 0-1 1-4

Odense 1-3 Auxerre 1-1 0-2

Panionios 3-2 Udinese 3-1 0-1

PAOK Salonika 3-5 AZ Alkmaar 2-3 1-2

Parma 3-2 Maribor 3-2 0-0

Partizan 3-1 Dinamo Bucuresti 3-1 0-0

Real Zaragoza 4-2 Sigma Olomouc 1-0 3-2

Schalke 9-1 Metalurgs 5-1 4-0

Seville 4-1 Nacional 2-0 2-1

Shelbourne 2-4 Lille 2-2 0-2

Dubliners Shelbourne cause Lille some flutters, coming back from 2-0 down to draw at home in their first leg with two late Glen Fitzpatrick goals but Lille progress into the Group stage after holding onto another two-goal lead in France

Sochaux 9-0 Stabaek 4-0 5-0

Sp Lisbon 2-0 Rapid Vienna 2-0 0-0

Standard Liege 1-1 Bochum 0-0 1-1
Standard Liege win on away goals

Steaua 4-3 CSKA Sofia 2-1 2-2

Terek Grozny 1-3 Basel 1-1 0-2

Trabzonspor 3-4 Athletic 3-2 0-2

Ujpesti 1-7 Stuttgart 1-3 0-4

Utrecht 4-3 Djurgarden 4-0 0-3

Wisla Krakow 5-5 Dinamo Tbilisi 4-3 1-2

Z St Petersburg 6-1 Crvena Zvezda 4-0 2-1

40 clubs go through to the Group Stage into eight groups of five teams, each playing two home and two away games. The top three clubs in each group go through to the Round of 32, joined by the eight third-placed clubs from the Champions League Group Stage.

GROUP E

Aigaleo (0) **0** **Middlesbro** (0) **1**
4,000 — Downing 78

Lazio (0) **1** **Villarreal** (1) **1**
Rocchi 83 — Jose Mari 4
8,000

Middlesbro (1) **2** **Lazio** (0) **0**
Zenden 16,71 — 33,991

Partizan (1) **4** **Aigaleo** (0) **0**
Christou 23 og — 20,000
Ilic 55,60, Vukcevic 68

Lazio (0) **2** **Partizan** (2) **2**
di Canio 51 — Boya 6,24
Inzaghi 73 — 12,000

A Di Canio goal gives Lazio a lifeline and Inzaghi grasps it to claw back from 2-0 down at home against Partizan Belgrade and keep their hopes alive

Villarreal (1) **2** **Middlesbro** (0) **0**
Guayre 37, Javi Venta 74 — 14,000

Aigaleo (1) **2** **Lazio** (2) **2**
Chloros 8 — Muzzi 12,36
Agritis 55 — 1,000

Partizan (0) **1** **Villarreal** (1) **1**
Tomic 65 pen — Santi Cazorla 17
26,000

Middlesbro (2) **3** **Partizan** (0) **0**
Nemeth 10 — 20,856
Job 22, Morrison 90

Villarreal (2) **4** **Aigaleo** (0) **0**
Font 13, Guayre 39 — 10,000
Javi Venta 53
Santi Cazorla 64

Villarreal's Uefa confidence, following a semi-final appearance last year, is in evidence as they hit four past Greek side Egaleo to leapfrog Partizan. The Serbian side also qualify despite being well beaten by group winners, Middlesbrough who score three at the Riverside Stadium. Italy's former giants Lazio can only finish in fourth spot

GROUP E TABLE

	P	W	D	L	DIF	PTS
Middlesbrough	4	3	0	1	4	9
Villarreal	4	2	2	0	6	8
Partizan	4	1	2	1	1	5
Lazio	4	0	3	1	-2	3
Aigaleo	4	0	1	3	-9	1

GROUP F

Amica Wronki (0) **0** **Rangers** (1) **5**
3,000 — Lovenkrands 17
Novo 57, Ricksen 69
Arveladze 73 pen
Thompson 89

Auxerre (0) **0** **Grazer AK** (0) **0**
5,000

AZ Alkmaar (2) **2** **Auxerre** (0) **0**
Huysegems 4,19 — 8,000

Grazer AK (1) **3** **Amica Wronki** (1) **1**
Kollmann 32,61 pen,71 — Dembinski 27
6,000

Amica Wronki (0) **1** **AZ Alkmaar** (3) **3**
Dembinski 58 pen — van Galen 13
3,000 — Meerdink 37
Huysegems 39

Rangers (0) **3** **Grazer AK** (0) **0**
Novo 58 — 46,453
Arveladze 86
Namouchi 90

AZ Alkmaar (1) **1** **Rangers** (0) **0**
Landzaat 7 — 8,000

Auxerre (4) **5** **Amica Wronki** (1) **1**
Mignot 1 — Kryszalowicz 17
Pieroni 5,23,26 — 7,000
Kalou 56

Grazer AK (1) **2** **AZ Alkmaar** (0) **0**
Aufhauser 41 — 13,000
Kollmann 54 pen

Rangers (0) **0** **Auxerre** (1) **2**
48,847 — Kalou 10,47

A brace from Kalou ends Rangers' European adventure for the season at Ibrox after a bright start in the group

Alex McLeish sees results go against him as Austrian title-holders Grazer AK beat Dutch form team AZ Alkmaar on the final night. Alkmaar have already qualified at the top of the group. Rangers could still go through by beating Auxerre but that never looks likely in a 2-0 defeat at Ibrox, so Grazer qualify at the Scottish side's expense

GROUP F TABLE

	P	W	D	L	DIF	PTS
AZ Alkmaar	4	3	0	1	3	9
Auxerre	4	2	1	1	4	7
Grazer AK	4	2	1	1	1	7
Rangers	4	2	0	2	5	6
Amica Wronki	4	0	0	4	-13	0

GROUP G

Benfica (2) **4** **Heerenveen** (0) **2**
Manuel dos Santos 14 — Yildirim 49
Nuno Gomes 31,78 — Huntelaar 53 pen
Karadas 74 — 15,000

Beveren (0) **1** **Stuttgart** (2) **5**
Romaric 86 — Cacau 9,52
7,000 — Kuranyi 40, Lahm 76
Szabics 90

Dinamo Zagreb (4) **6** **Beveren** (0) **1**
Eduardo 16 — Vleminckx 82
Mijatovic 21 — 10,000
Zahora 35,41
Kranjcar 55, Mujcin 87

Stuttgart (1) **3** **Benfica** (0) **0**
Cacau 32, — 47,000
Meissner 52, Kuranyi 73

Cacau, Meissner and Kuranyi hit the goals that gives Stuttgart the Group G ascendancy over rivals Benfica

Benfica (2) **2** **Dinamo Zagreb** (0) **0**
Sokota 11 — 12,000
Simao Sabrosa 29 pen

Heerenveen (0) **1** **Stuttgart** (0) **0**
Yildirim 65 — 18,000

Beveren (0) **0** **Benfica** (2) **3**
8,000 — Simao Sabrosa 4 pen
Zahovic 19,59

Dinamo Zagreb (1) **2** **Heerenveen** (0) **2**
Bosnjak 15 — Yildirim 84
Pranjic 57 — Huntelaar 89 pen
12,000

Heerenveen (1) **1** **Beveren** (0) **0**
Bruggink 26 — 18,000

Stuttgart (1) **2** **Dinamo Zagreb** (0) **1**
Tiffert 15 — Bosnjak 66
Meira 75 — 41,000

Bruggink scores the only goal as Heerenveen beat ten-man Beveren to qualify third from the group. The Dutch side's job is made easier as rivals Dinamo Zagreb are beaten by the group's eventual winners Stuttgart thanks to goals by Tiffert and Meira. No final night game for Benfica who are already through

GROUP G TABLE

	P	W	D	L	DIF	PTS
Stuttgart	4	3	0	1	7	9
Benfica	4	3	0	1	4	9
Heerenveen	4	2	1	1	0	7
Dinamo Zagreb	4	1	1	2	2	4
Beveren	4	0	0	4	-13	0

GROUP H

Alem Aachen (0) **1** **Lille** (0) **0**
Meijer 67 — 20,000

Z St Petersburg (1) **5** **AEK Athens** (1) **1**
Arshavin 44 — Krassas 3
Kherzhakov 48,54,68 — 22,000
Denisov 81

Lille (2) **2** **Z St Petersburg** (1) **1**
Tafforeau 35 — Kherzhakov 39
Moussilou 42 — 9,109

Seville (1) **2** **Alem Aachen** (0) **0**
Aranda 7 — 40,000
Baptista 77 pen

AEK Athens (0) **1** **Lille** (1) **2**
Amponsah 72 — Vitakic 26
15,000 — Debuchy 63

Z St Petersburg (1) **1** **Seville** (0) **1**
Arshavin 35 — Baptista 72
20,000

Alem Aachen (1) **2** **Z St Petersburg** (1) **2**
Meijer 25 — Radimov 38 pen
Blank 89 pen — Gorshkov 76
25,000

Seville (2) **3** **AEK Athens** (1) **2**
Baptista 18,89 pen — Liberopoulos 9
Antonito 28 — Tziortziopoulos 47
29,000

Brazilian striker Baptista's 89th minute penalty gives Seville a hard-fought win over AEK to eliminate the Greeks early

AEK Athens (0) **0** **Alem Aachen** (0) **2**
5,000 — Meijer 56
Gomez 84

Lille (0) **1** **Seville** (0) **0**
Moussilou 77 — 9,000

Lille win tussle for Group H bragging rights over second-placed Seville with a 77th minute goal from substitute Moussilou settling the tie to put the French side top. German minnows Aachen gain third spot after a win in Athens over AEK, who finish without a point and Russian side Zenit from St Petersburg also miss out

GROUP H TABLE

	P	W	D	L	DIF	PTS
Lille	4	3	0	1	2	9
Seville	4	2	1	1	2	7
Alem Aachen	4	2	1	1	1	7
Z St Petersburg	4	1	2	1	3	5
AEK Athens	4	0	0	4	-8	0

ROUND OF 32

Eight third placed clubs from Champions League Groups join the 24 through from the Group Stage:
Olympiakos, Dinamo Kiev, Ajax, Fenerbahce, Panathinaikos, Shakhtar Donetsk, Valencia, CSKA Moscow

Ajax (1) **1** **Auxerre** (0) **0**
Maxwell 36
42,000

Auxerre (1) **3** **Ajax** (1) **1**
Kalou 30 — Babel 37
Cheyrou 55 — 12,000
Mathis 86

PlayStation

Dutch champions Ajax are dumped out of the Uefa Cup by Auxerre after their narrow one goal first leg lead is overtaken by goals from Bonaventure Kalou, Benoit Cheyrou and finally Lionel Mathis

Alem Aachen (0) **0** **AZ Alkmaar** (0) **0**
38,000

AZ Alkmaar (0) **2** **Alem Aachen** (1) **1**
van Galen 62 — Meijer 31
Mathijsen 81 — 8,000

Austria Vienna (0) **0** **Athl Bilbao** (0) **0**
17,000

Athl Bilbao (1) **1** **Austria Vienna** (1) **2**
Yeste 20 pen — Sionko 35,70
39,000

Basel (0) **0** **Lille** (0) **0**
19,000

Lille (1) **2** **Basel** (0) **0**
Moussilou 37 — 13,000
Acimovic 78 pen

CSKA Moscow (1) **2** **Benfica** (0) **0**
Berezoutski, V 12 — 28,000
Vagner Love 61

Benfica (0) **1** **CSKA Moscow** (0) **1**
Karadas 64 — Ignashevitch 49
25,000

Dinamo Kiev (0) **0** **Villarreal** (0) **0**
11,000

Villarreal (2) **2** **Dinamo Kiev** (0) **0**
Lucho 19 — 8,000
Santi Cazorla 32

First-half goals from Figueroa (formerly with Birmingham) and Cazorla relax the tension at El Madrigal to put the InterToto Cup winners into the next round without their leading scorer, cup-tied Forlan

Fenerbahce (0) **0** **Real Zaragoza** (0) **1**
49,000 — Alvaro 72

Real Zaragoza (1) **2** **Fenerbahce** (0) **1**
Galletti 11 — Sanli 87
Savio 70 — 25,000

Heerenveen (1) **1** **Newcastle** (0) **2**
Huntelaar 24 — Shearer 69
20,000 — Bowyer 82

Newcastle (2) **2** **Heerenveen** (0) **1**
Breuer 10 og — Bruggink 80 pen
Shearer 25 — 26,000

Grazer AK (0) **2** **Middlesbro** (0) **2**
13,000 — Zenden 52
Hasselbaink 66

Middlesbro (1) **2** **Grazer AK** (1) **1**
Morrison 19 — Bazina 9
Hasselbaink 61 — 20,000

Olympiakos (1) **1** **Sochaux** (0) **0**
Okkas 29 — 33,000

Sochaux (0) **0** **Olympiakos** (0) **1**
11,000 — Stoltidis 66

Panathinaikos (0) **1** **Seville** (0) **0**
Vintra 76 — 10,000

Seville (0) **2** **Panathinaikos** (0) **0**
Makukula 82 — 12,000
Adriano 90

Parma (0) **0** **Stuttgart** (0) **0**
5,000

Stuttgart (0) **0** **Parma** (0) **2**
38,000 — Marchionni 98
Pisanu 116

Partizan (2) **2** **Dnipro** (1) **2**
Odita 12,45 — Nazarenko 28
15,000 — Ruzol 56

Dnipro (0) **0** **Partizan** (0) **1**
14,000 — Djordjevic 87

Shakhtar Donetsk (0) **1** **Schalke** (1) **1**
Brandao 86 — Ailton 7
28,000

Schalke (0) **0** **Shakhtar Donetsk** (1) **1**
51,000 — Aghahowa 21

Sp Lisbon (2) **2** **Feyenoord** (1) **1**
Custodio 22 — Goor 9
Liedson 37 — 19,000

Feyenoord (0) **1** **Sp Lisbon** (0) **2**
Hofs 88 — Liedson 62
30,000 — Rochemback 82

Sporting's on-loan Viana leads the way back against Ruud Gullit's Feyenoord in a home tie with an unlikely Newcastle connection. Viana hits the bar and crosses for Custódio's equalising goal before Liedson strikes the winner

Valencia (1) **2** **Steaua Bucharest** (0) **0**
Di Vaio 38 — 30,000
Aimar 55

Steaua Bucharest (0) **2** **Valencia** (0) **0**
Cristea 50,70 — 22,000
Steaua Bucharest win 4-3 on penalties

A brace from Cristea takes Steaua into a penalty shoot-out with cup holders Valencia and the Romanians emerge victorious, eventually leading to the dismissal of Claudio Ranieri as Valencia manager

LAST 16

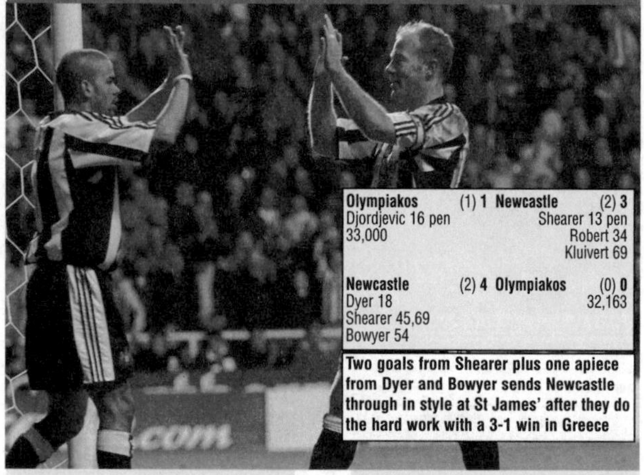

Olympiakos (1) **1** **Newcastle** (2) **3**
Djordjevic 16 pen — Shearer 13 pen
33,000 — Robert 34
Kluivert 69

Newcastle (2) **4** **Olympiakos** (0) **0**
Dyer 18 — 32,163
Shearer 45,69
Bowyer 54

Two goals from Shearer plus one apiece from Dyer and Bowyer sends Newcastle through in style at St James' after they do the hard work with a 3-1 win in Greece

Austria Vienna (1) **1** **Real Zaragoza** (0) **1**
Rushfeldt 32 — Savio 74
21,000

Real Zaragoza (0) **2** **Austria Vienna** (2) **2**
Villa 58 — Papac 5
Galletti 62 — Dosunmu 12
27,000
Austra Vienna win on away goals

Austria Vienna take a surprise lead at Real Zaragoza's La Romareda stadium with goals from Papac and Dosunmu on six and 12 minutes. The Spanish battle back to draw in the second half but go out on the away goals rule

Lille (0) **0** **Auxerre** (1) **1**
8,000 — Akale 45

Auxerre (0) **0** **Lille** (0) **0**
12,000

Kanga Akalé's goal is the only one in two legs of French struggle and the Ivory Coast striker provides a route through for Auxerre

Partizan (0) **1** **CSKA Moscow** (1) **1**
Tomic 83 pen — Aldonin 18
18,000

CSKA Moscow (0) **2** **Partizan** (0) **0**
Carvalho 69 — 29,000
Vagner Love 85 pen

Partizan lose out to Love – CSKA's Brazilian striker Vagner Love who is a thorn in their side all night in the second leg in Moscow. Love's penalty makes sure after Carvalho scores the first goal of the game

Seville (0) **0** **Parma** (0) **0**
40,000

Parma (1) **1** **Seville** (0) **0**
Cardone 9 — 8,000

After a goalless draw in the first leg in Spain, Italian Serie A side Parma despatch Seville thanks to a close-range shot from captain Cardone inside the first ten minutes, which proves the only goal of the tie

Shakhtar Donetsk (1) **1** **AZ Alkmaar** (1) **3**
Matuzalem 45 — Nelisse 28
20,000 — Mathijsen 52
Perez 90 pen

AZ Alkmaar (1) **2** **Shakhtar Donetsk** (0) **1**
van Galen 9 — Elano 67
Meerdink 65 — 8,000

Van Galen strikes early to put this tie well beyond Shakhtar Donetsk who already have a mountain to climb after a 3-1 home defeat in the first game. Meerdink scores to put the form Dutch side further ahead

Steaua Bucharest (0) **0** **Villarreal** (0) **0**
30,000

Villarreal (1) **2** **Steaua Bucharest** (0) **0**
Jose Mari 5 — 22,000
Riquelme 61 pen

A sixth-minute goal by José Mari Romero puts Spanish side Villarreal in the driving seat against Steaua Bucharest from Romania. Juan Román Riquelme adds a 62nd minute penalty to close the tie out

Middlesbro (0) **2** **Sp Lisbon** (0) **3**
Job 79 — Barbosa 48
Riggott 86 — Liedson 53
23,739 — Douala 65

Sp Lisbon (0) **1** **Middlesbro** (0) **0**
Barbosa 90 — 21,000

A topsy-turvy game at the Riverside sees Barbosa, Liedson and Douala fire Sporting Lisbon into a 3-0 lead before Job and Riggott score for the home side. A good performance in Portugal can't save Boro

QUARTER-FINALS

Austria Vienna	(0) 1	Parma	(1) 1
Mila 61			Pisanu 34
39,000			
Parma	(0) 0	Austria Vienna	(0) 0
			11,000

Parma win on away goals

Newcastle	(1) 1	Sp Lisbon	(0) 0
Shearer 37			36,753
Sp Lisbon	(1) 4	Newcastle	(1) 1
Niculae 40			Dyer 20
Sa Pinto 71, Beto 77			45,000
Rochemback 90			

A stunning game in the José Alvalade stadium that would have graced the final to be played there this year. Newcastle's Dyer puts the visitors 2-0 ahead on aggregate before an unstoppable onslaught led by the brilliant Sa Pinto sweeps Sporting into the semi-final

CSKA Moscow	(1) 4	Auxerre	(0) 0
Odiah 21			26,000
Ignashevitch 63 pen			
Vagner Love 71, Gusev 77			
Auxerre	(1) 2	CSKA Moscow	(0) 0
Lachuer 9, Kalou 80 pen			13,000

CSKA Moscow virtually ensure their place in the Uefa Cup semi-final with a comprehensive defeat of Auxerre 4-0 in the first leg. Odiah opens the scoring against overwhelmed Auxerre who only manage two goals in the home tie

Villarreal	(1) 1	AZ Alkmaar	(1) 2
Riquelme 15			Landzaat 12
10,000			Nelisse 74
AZ Alkmaar	(1) 1	Villarreal	(0) 1
Perez 8			Lucho 72
9,000			

AZ Alkmaar's class is underlined when Robin Nelisse gives the Dutch side a crucial away first-leg victory at Villarreal - the Spanish side's first-ever home Uefa Cup defeat. Kenneth Perez scores early in the home leg to make sure

SEMI-FINALS

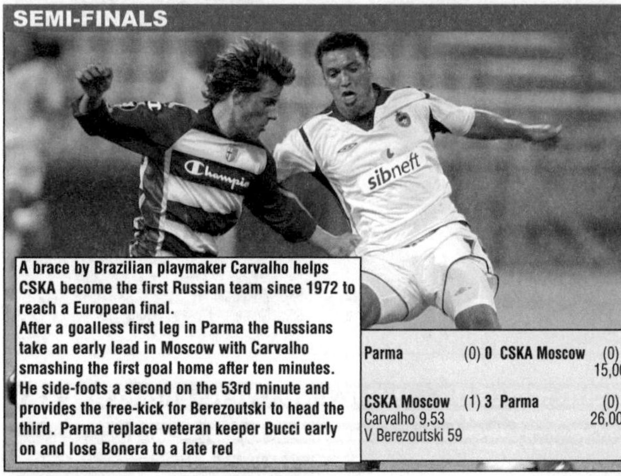

A brace by Brazilian playmaker Carvalho helps CSKA become the first Russian team since 1972 to reach a European final.
After a goalless first leg in Parma the Russians take an early lead in Moscow with Carvalho smashing the first goal home after ten minutes. He side-foots a second on the 53rd minute and provides the free-kick for Berezoutski to head the third. Parma replace veteran keeper Bucci early on and lose Bonera to a late red

Parma	(0) 0	CSKA Moscow	(0) 0
			15,000
CSKA Moscow	(1) 3	Parma	(0) 0
Carvalho 9,53			26,000
V Berezoutski 59			

Sp Lisbon	(1) 2	AZ Alkmaar	(1) 1
Douala 36			Landzaat 35
Pinilla 80			35,000
AZ Alkmaar	(1) 3	Sp Lisbon	(1) 2
Perez 6			Liedson 45
Huysegems 79			Miguel Garcia 120
Jaliens 109			8,603

SP Lisbon win on away goals

Sporting Lisbon reach the final in their home stadium as Garcia strikes two minutes into injury time at the end of extra time.
Both legs end in 2-1 home wins, leaving the tie all square and requiring extra time in Holland.
AZ Alkmaar take the lead in extra time with Jaliens scoring to give the Dutch the lead but Garcia shatters their dreams with his late strike

THE FINAL

Roman Abramovic's stunning season ends in European glory after all. It isn't the millions lavished on Chelsea but his second side CSKA Moscow - sponsored by the Russian's oil company – who triumph in the Uefa Cup.

Sporting Lisbon thought they had done the hard work in battling through to a final in their own stadium and had the home fans were in ecstasy after Rogerio gave them a deserved half-time lead. Moscow were a different proposition in the second half and dominated after Berezoutski got on the end of a 56th minute Carvalho freekick. Then Zhirkov and Love both profited from Carvalho assists for Russia to claim its first ever club success in European football

Sporting Lisbon	(1) 1	CSKA Moscow	(0) 3
Rogerio 29			Berezoutski 56
			Zhirkov 65
			Love 75
			46,679

EUROPEAN LEAGUES ROUND-UP

FINAL PREMIERSHIP LEAGUE TABLE - TOP THREE

		HOME					AWAY					TOTAL			
	P	W	D	L	F	A	W	D	L	F	A	F	A	DIF	PTS
Chelsea	38	14	5	0	35	6	15	3	1	37	9	72	15	57	95
Arsenal	38	13	5	1	54	19	12	3	4	33	17	87	36	51	83
Man Utd	38	12	6	1	31	12	10	5	4	27	14	58	26	32	77

FINAL DUTCH LEAGUE TABLE - TOP THREE

		HOME					AWAY					TOTAL			
	P	W	D	L	F	A	W	D	L	F	A	F	A	DIF	PTS
PSV Eindhoven	34	16	0	1	50	8	11	6	0	39	10	89	18	71	87
Ajax	34	11	3	3	32	17	13	2	2	42	16	74	33	41	77
AZ Alkmaar	34	10	6	1	39	12	9	1	7	32	29	71	41	30	64

FINAL FRENCH LEAGUE TABLE - TOP THREE

		HOME					AWAY					TOTAL			
	P	W	D	L	F	A	W	D	L	F	A	F	A	DIF	PTS
Lyon	38	13	5	1	33	10	9	8	2	23	12	56	22	34	79
Lille	38	11	6	2	30	11	7	7	5	21	18	51	29	22	67
Monaco	38	11	6	2	38	21	4	12	3	14	14	52	35	17	63

FINAL GERMAN LEAGUE TABLE - TOP THREE

		HOME					AWAY					TOTAL			
	P	W	D	L	F	A	W	D	L	F	A	F	A	DIF	PTS
Bayern Munich	34	14	2	1	44	14	10	3	4	31	19	75	33	42	77
Schalke	34	11	2	4	33	24	9	1	7	23	22	56	46	10	63
W Bremen	34	9	4	4	33	15	9	1	7	35	22	68	37	31	59

FINAL ITALIAN LEAGUE TABLE - TOP THREE

		HOME					AWAY					TOTAL			
	P	W	D	L	F	A	W	D	L	F	A	F	A	DIF	PTS
Juventus	38	15	2	2	38	13	11	6	2	29	14	67	27	40	86
AC Milan	38	11	5	3	38	17	12	5	2	25	11	63	28	35	79
Inter Milan	38	11	7	1	34	16	7	11	1	31	21	65	37	28	72

FINAL SPANISH LEAGUE TABLE - TOP THREE

		HOME					AWAY					TOTAL			
	P	W	D	L	F	A	W	D	L	F	A	F	A	DIF	PTS
Barcelona	38	14	4	1	40	12	11	5	3	33	17	73	29	44	84
Real Madrid	38	15	1	3	43	12	10	4	5	28	20	71	32	39	80
Villarreal	38	14	4	1	41	10	4	7	8	28	27	69	37	32	65

CLUB STRIKE FORCE

TIS
21

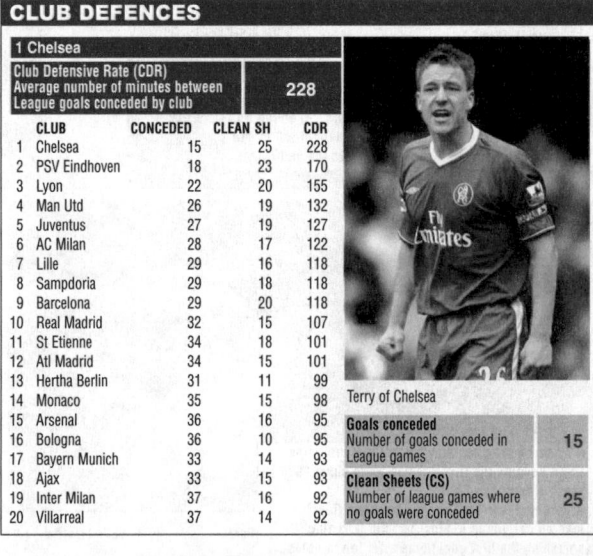

Kalou of Feyenoord

Goals scored in the League	90

1 Feyenoord

Club Strike Rate (CSR) Average number of minutes between League goals scored by club	34

	CLUB	LEAGUE GOALS	CSR
1	Feyenoord	90	34
2	PSV Eindhoven	89	34
3	Arsenal	87	39
4	Bayern Munich	75	41
5	Ajax	74	41
6	AZ Alkmaar	71	43
7	W Bremen	68	45
8	B Leverkusen	65	47
9	Barcelona	73	47
10	Chelsea	72	48
11	Heerenveen	64	48
12	Real Madrid	71	48
13	Villarreal	69	50
14	Roda JC Kerk	60	51
15	Juventus	67	51
16	Hertha Berlin	59	52
17	Lecce	66	52
18	Inter Milan	65	53
19	AC Milan	63	54
20	Schalke	56	55

CLUB DEFENCES

1 Chelsea

Club Defensive Rate (CDR) Average number of minutes between League goals conceded by club	228

	CLUB	CONCEDED	CLEAN SH	CDR
1	Chelsea	15	25	228
2	PSV Eindhoven	18	23	170
3	Lyon	22	20	155
4	Man Utd	26	19	132
5	Juventus	27	19	127
6	AC Milan	28	17	122
7	Lille	29	16	118
8	Sampdoria	29	18	118
9	Barcelona	29	20	118
10	Real Madrid	32	15	107
11	St Etienne	34	18	101
12	Atl Madrid	34	15	101
13	Hertha Berlin	31	11	99
14	Monaco	35	15	98
15	Arsenal	36	16	95
16	Bologna	36	10	95
17	Bayern Munich	33	14	93
18	Ajax	33	15	93
19	Inter Milan	37	16	92
20	Villarreal	37	14	92

Terry of Chelsea

Goals conceded Number of goals conceded in League games	15
Clean Sheets (CS) Number of league games where no goals were conceded	25

PLAYER NATIONALITIES

1 Country with the most player representation across major European leagues - France

Number of players	458	International appearances 04-05	157
Number of occasions in squad	9563	Total minutes played	583728
Actual League appearances	7907	% of European League action	14.23

COUNTRY	NO OF PLAYERS	CAPS	IN SQUAD	LGE APP	MINS PLAYED	% LGE ACT
1 France	458	157	9563	7907	583728	14.23
2 Italy	450	147	9930	7480	546437	13.32
3 Spain	464	81	10137	7455	526555	12.83
4 Holland	350	149	7243	5359	392493	9.57
5 Germany	281	148	5287	3820	282630	6.89
6 England	221	148	4571	3784	280854	6.84
7 Brazil	128	181	3014	2655	196180	4.78
8 Argentina	77	138	1829	1486	110148	2.68
9 Belgium	52	67	1262	984	70749	1.72
10 Serbia & Montenegro	40	51	892	777	53025	1.29
11 Sweden	30	94	734	671	49527	1.21
12 Denmark	34	107	834	673	48230	1.18
13 Czech Republic	28	78	695	627	47889	1.17
14 Portugal	31	68	756	622	45058	1.10
15 Uruguay	33	59	853	644	44205	1.08
16 Ivory Coast	26	27	665	568	43354	1.06
17 Senegal	33	74	686	580	42058	1.02
18 Cameroon	29	50	662	562	40838	1.00
19 Rep of Ireland	22	89	558	504	40055	0.98
20 Morocco	20		519	445	29235	0.71
Others (71 countries)	495		10958	8907	630161	15.35

CLUB MAKE-UP – HOME AND OVERSEAS PLAYERS

1 Club which used the most overseas players in league action - Lyon

Overseas players in named 16s	15	Home country players in named 16s	13
Percent of overseas players	53.6	Percent of League action	90.0
Most appearances	Michael Essien	% of match time played	93.4

	CLUB	OVERSEAS	HOME	% OVERSEAS	% LGE ACT	MOST APP	% APP
1	Lyon	15	13	53.6	90.0	Michael Essien	93.4
2	Monaco	18	8	69.2	89.3	Flavio Roma	86.8
3	Arsenal	22	5	81.5	86.3	Habib Kolo Toure	91.6
4	Roda JC Kerk	18	9	66.7	78.3	Predrag Filipovic	98.7
5	Schalke	14	14	50.0	73.1	Levan Kobiashvili	93.3
6	Liverpool	21	11	65.6	70.1	John Arne Riise	87
7	Inter Milan	21	16	56.8	69.2	Javier Zanetti	88.0
8	Bolton	16	9	64	68	Bruno N'Gotty	95.2
9	Marseille	15	16	48.4	67.9	Habib Beye	95.7
10	Freiburg	18	12	60.0	67.5	Ismael Coulibaly	88.6
11	Bochum	21	12	63.6	65.8	Vratislav Lokvenc	91.0
12	Feyenoord	21	14	60.0	65.2	Bart Goor	95.2
13	Chelsea	20	10	66.7	65.1	Claude Makelele	94.7
14	Ajax	22	10	68.8	63.8	Maxwell	82.4
15	Hamburg	14	15	48.3	63.1	Daniel Van Buyten	100.0
16	Hannover 96	20	11	64.5	62.5	Steve Cherundolo	92.5
17	Fulham	14	13	51.9	62.5	Edwin Van der Sar	86
18	Paris SG	17	14	54.8	62.1	Mario Yepes	82.3
19	AC Milan	17	15	53.1	61.7	Nelson Dida	92.3
20	Wolfsburg	16	12	57.1	61.0	Pablo Thiam	94.7

CLUB DISCIPLINARY RECORDS

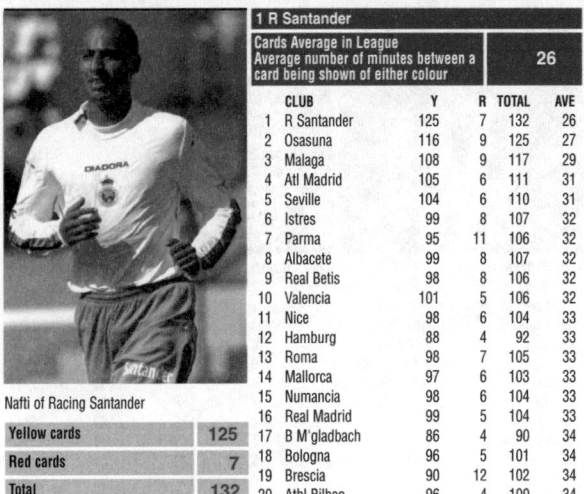

Nafti of Racing Santander

Yellow cards	125
Red cards	7
Total	132

1 R Santander

Cards Average in League Average number of minutes between a card being shown of either colour	26

	CLUB	Y	R	TOTAL	AVE
1	R Santander	125	7	132	26
2	Osasuna	116	9	125	27
3	Malaga	108	9	117	29
4	Atl Madrid	105	6	111	31
5	Seville	104	6	110	31
6	Istres	99	8	107	32
7	Parma	95	11	106	32
8	Albacete	99	8	107	32
9	Real Betis	98	8	106	32
10	Valencia	101	5	106	32
11	Nice	98	6	104	33
12	Hamburg	88	4	92	33
13	Roma	98	7	105	33
14	Mallorca	97	6	103	33
15	Numancia	98	6	104	33
16	Real Madrid	99	5	104	33
17	B M'gladbach	86	4	90	34
18	Bologna	96	5	101	34
19	Brescia	90	12	102	34
20	Athl Bilbao	96	4	100	34

PLAYER DISCIPLINARY RECORD

1 Olivera - Juventus

Cards Average mins between cards	85

League Yellow	7
League Red	1
TOTAL	8

	PLAYER	LEAGUE	Y	R	TOTAL	AVE
1	Olivera	Juventus	7	1	8	85
2	Bakour	Caen	5	1	6	91
3	Jordi	Seville	8	0	8	105
4	Lembo	Real Betis	5	2	7	106
5	Brouwers	Roda JC Kerk	8	1	9	109
6	Cesar	Deportivo	9	1	10	113
7	Lagerblom	Nuremberg	5	0	5	114
8	Scurto	Roma	4	0	4	118
9	Gorlitz	Bayern Munich	3	1	4	121
10	Quinn	Willem II Tilb	4	1	5	122
11	Pasquale	Siena	5	2	7	122
12	Santi	Albacete	7	1	8	122
13	Pulido	Getafe	3	1	4	122
14	"Garcia, P"	Osasuna	18	2	20	122
15	Alexis	Malaga	7	1	8	123
16	Neuendorf	Hertha Berlin	6	1	7	127
17	Varela	Schalke	4	0	4	129
18	Olajengbesi	Freiburg	4	1	5	130
19	Battaglia	Villarreal	6	1	7	131
20	Moore	B M'gladbach	7	1	8	132

TEAM OF THE SEASON

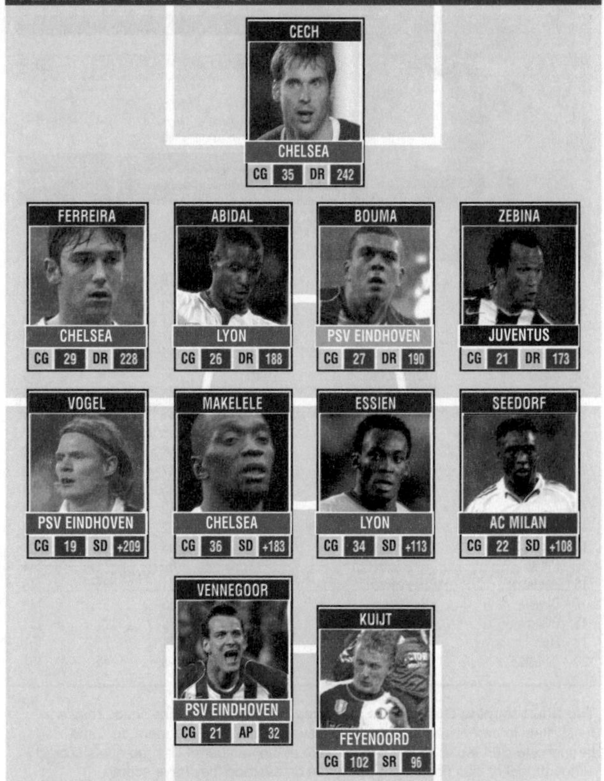
CECH
CHELSEA
CG 35 DR 242
FERREIRA
CHELSEA
CG 29 DR 228
ABIDAL
LYON
CG 26 DR 188
BOUMA
PSV EINDHOVEN
CG 27 DR 190
ZEBINA
JUVENTUS
CG 21 DR 173
VOGEL
PSV EINDHOVEN
CG 19 SD +209
MAKELELE
CHELSEA
CG 36 SD +183
ESSIEN
LYON
CG 34 SD +113
SEEDORF
AC MILAN
CG 22 SD +108
VENNEGOOR
PSV EINDHOVEN
CG 21 AP 32
KUIJT
FEYENOORD
CG 102 SR 96

The European Team of the Season shows a 4-4-2 of the best players in the major European Leagues based upon the selection criteria used for the chart-toppers. The players selected are taken from the lists for each club except that to get into this Team of the Season you must have played at least 17 Counting Games in league matches (roughly half the league season) and not 12 as is the case in the club lists. The other restriction is that we are only allowing one player from each club in each position.

- **The Top team's goalkeeper** is the player with the highest *Defensive Rating*
- **The Top team's defenders** are also tested by *Defensive Rating*, i.e. the average number of minutes between league goals conceded while on the pitch.
- **The Top team's midfield** are selected on their *Scoring Difference*, i.e.their *Defensive Rating* minus their *Contribution to Attacking Power* (average number of minutes between league goals scored while on the pitch. It takes no account of assists.
- **The Top team strikeforce** is made up of the striker with the highest *Strike Rate* (his average number of minutes between league goals scored while on the pitch) together with the striker with the highest *Contribution to Attacking Power.*

CHART-TOPPING POINT EARNERS

	PLAYER	TEAM	GAMES	POINTS	AVE
1	Alex	PSV Eindhoven	22	60	2.73
2	Gallas	Chelsea	26	68	2.62
3	Grygera	Ajax	18	46	2.56
4	Seedorf	AC Milan	22	55	2.50
5	Belletti	Barcelona	27	67	2.48
6	Sagnol	Bayern Munich	19	46	2.42
7	Mathijsen	AZ Alkmaar	22	53	2.41
8	Reyes	Arsenal	18	43	2.39
9	Beckham	Real Madrid	24	57	2.38
10	Zebina	Juventus	21	50	2.38
11	Govou	Lyon	27	64	2.37
12	Rooney	Man Utd	22	51	2.32
13	Pander	Schalke	22	49	2.23
14	Castelen	Feyenoord	24	51	2.13
15	Favalli	Inter Milan	21	44	2.10
16	Navarro	Valencia	23	46	2.00
17	Baumann	W Bremen	20	40	2.00
18	Chalme	Lille	25	49	1.96
19	Arzu	Real Betis	20	39	1.95
20	Niemeyer	Twente	20	39	1.95

(Selection limited to top player per club)

PHILIPS

1 Alex - PSV Eindhoven

Counting Games Played at least 70mins.	22
Total Points Taken in Counting Games	60
Average points per game Taken in Counting Games	2.73

MOST MISSED PLAYERS

	PLAYER	TEAM	AVERAGE	CLUB	DIFF
1	Jorgensen	Fiorentina	1.65	1.11	0.54
2	Mathijsen	AZ Alkmaar	2.41	1.88	0.53
3	Cesar Navas	Malaga	1.86	1.34	0.52
4	Kishishev	Charlton	1.72	1.21	0.51
5	Albrechtsen	West Brom	1.39	0.89	0.50
6	Bodde	Den Haag	1.55	1.06	0.49
7	Aranzabal	Real Zaragoza	1.80	1.32	0.48
8	Navarro	Valencia	2.00	1.53	0.47
9	Dellas	Roma	1.65	1.18	0.47
10	Nakamura	Reggina	1.63	1.16	0.47
11	Loran	Roosendaal	1.41	0.94	0.47
12	Arnau	Malaga	1.80	1.34	0.46
13	Torrisi	Bologna	1.57	1.11	0.46
14	Morfeo	Parma	1.57	1.11	0.46
15	Moran	R Santander	1.59	1.16	0.43
16	Seedorf	AC Milan	2.50	2.08	0.42
17	Bernardini	Atalanta	1.33	0.92	0.41
18	Klingbeil	Hamburg	1.90	1.50	0.40
19	Wau	Willem II Tilb	1.72	1.32	0.40
20	Nevland	Groningen	1.58	1.18	0.40

(No limit on the number of players per club selected)

DSB BAN

2 Mathijsen - AZ Alkmaar

Average points	2.41
Club average	1.88
Difference	0.53

CHART-TOPPING GOALSCORERS

1 Kuijt - Feyenoord	
Goals scored in the League	29
Contribution to Attacking Power Average number of minutes between League team goals while on pitch	34
Player Strike Rate Average number of minutes between League goals scored by player	102
Club Strike Rate (CSR) Average minutes between League goals scored by club	34

	PLAYER	CLUB	GOALS	POWER	CSR	S RATE
1	Kuijt	Feyenoord	29	34	34	102
2	Nevland	Groningen	16	54	61	106
3	Henry	Arsenal	25	37	39	113
4	Vennegoor	PSV Eindhoven	19	32	34	115
5	Kalou	Feyenoord	20	36	34	116
6	Forlan	Villarreal	24	48	50	125
7	Makaay	Bayern Munich	22	39	41	129
8	Mintal	Nuremberg	23	55	56	130
9	Eto'o	Barcelona	24	46	47	130
10	Shevchenko	AC Milan	17	47	54	132
11	Ronaldo	Real Madrid	21	45	48	133
12	Adriano	Inter Milan	16	50	53	142
13	Montella	Roma	21	62	62	142
14	Voronin	B Leverkusen	15	43	48	143
15	Nihat	Real Sociedad	13	69	71	144
16	Huntelaar	Heerenveen	17	51	48	146
17	Oliveira	Real Betis	22	53	55	149
18	Gilardino	Parma	22	70	73	151
19	Frei	Rennes	20	71	71	151
20	Berbatov	B Leverkusen	20	48	48	151

The Chart-topping Goalscorers measures the players by Strike Rate. They are most likely to be Forwards but Midfield players and even Defenders do come through the club tables. It is not a measure of the number of League goals scored - although that is also noted - but how often on average they have scored.

CHART-TOPPING MIDFIELDERS

1 Vogel - PSV Eindhoven	
Goals scored in the League	1
Defensive Rating Av number of mins between League goals conceded while on the pitch	245
Contribution to Attacking Power Average number of minutes between League team goals while on pitch	36
Scoring Difference Defensive Rating minus Contribution to Attacking Power	209

	PLAYER	CLUB	GOALS	DEF R	POWER	SCORE DIFF
1	Vogel	PSV Eindhoven	1	245	36	209
2	Makelele	Chelsea	1	231	48	183
3	Lampard	Chelsea	13	227	47	180
4	Duff	Chelsea	6	218	46	172
5	Cocu	PSV Eindhoven	6	188	38	150
6	van Bommel	PSV Eindhoven	14	175	33	142
7	Park	PSV Eindhoven	7	158	32	126
8	Essien	Lyon	4	177	64	113
9	Malouda	Lyon	5	166	58	108
10	Seedorf	AC Milan	5	169	61	108
11	Blasi	Juventus	0	161	59	102
12	Diarra	Lyon	2	163	62	101
13	Juninho	Lyon	13	153	61	92
14	Giggs	Man Utd	6	137	48	89
15	Pirlo	AC Milan	4	144	55	89
16	Kaka	AC Milan	7	139	55	84
17	Emerson	Juventus	1	139	55	84
18	Van Bronckhorst	Barcelona	4	130	46	84
19	Keane	Man Utd	1	137	54	83
20	Camoranesi	Juventus	4	132	49	83

The Divisional Round-up charts combine the records of chart-topping keepers, defenders, midfield players and forwards, from every club in the division.. The one above is for **the Chart-topping Midfielders**. The players are ranked by their Scoring Difference although other attributes are shown for you to compare.

TOP LEAGUES IN EUROPE

	UEFA Cup Group Phase	Pts	Champions League Group Phase	Pts	UEFA Cup Round of 32	Pts	Champions League last 16	Pts
England	**Newcastle Middlesbrough**	2	**Liverpool Chelsea Arsenal Man Utd**	8	**Newcastle Middlesbrough**	2	**Liverpool Chelsea** Arsenal Man Utd	8
Italy	**Parma** Lazio	2	**Juventus AC Milan Inter** Roma	8	**Parma**	1	**Juventus AC Milan Inter**	6
Spain	**Villarreal Seville R Zaragosa Ath Bilbao**	4	**Barcelona R Madrid** Valencia (U) Deportivo	8	**Villarreal Seville R Zaragosa** Valencia (U) A Bilbao	5	Barcelona R Madrid	4
Holland	**AZ Alkmaar Heerenveen Feyenoord** Utrecht	4	**PSV** Ajax (U)	4	**AZ Alkmaar** Heerenveen Feyenoord Ajax (U)	4	**PSV**	2
France	**Auxerre Lille Sochaux**	3	**Monaco Lyon** Paris SG	6	**Auxerre Lille** Sochaux	3	**Lyon** AS Monaco	4
Germany	**Stuttgart Schalke Aachen**	3	**Bayern B Leverk'n W Bremen**	6	Stuttgart Schalke Aachen	3	**Bayern** B Leverk'n W Bremen	6
Portugal	**Sp Lisbon Benfica**	2	**FC Porto**	2	**Sp Lisbon** Benfica	2	Porto	2
Greece	Panionios Egaleo AEK Athens	3	Olympiacos(U) Panathinaikos (U)	4	**Olympiakos (U)** Panathinaikos (U)	2		
Ukraine	**Dnipro**	1	Shakhtar (U) Dynamo Kiev (U)	4	**Shakhtar (U)** Dynamo Kiev (U) Dnipro	3		
Russia	Zenit	1	CSKA (U)	2	**CSKA (U)**	1		
Austria	**A Vienna Grazer AK**	2			**A Vienna** Grazer AK	2		
Belgium	S Liege C Brugge Beveren	3	Anderlecht	2				
Scotland	Hearts Rangers	2	Celtic	2				
Turkey	Besiktas	1	Fenerbache (U)	2	Fenerbache (U)	1		
Serbia & Mont	**Partizan Belgrade**	1			**Partizan Belgrade**	1		
Romania	**Steaua Bucharest**	1			**Steaua Bucharest**	1		
Switzerland	**Basel**	1			Basel	1		
Norway			Rosenborg	2				
Israel			Maccabi Tel-Aviv	2				
Czech Rep.			Sparta Prague	2				
Croatia	Dinamo Zagreb	1						
Poland	Amica	1						
Hungary	Ferencvaros	1						
Georgia	Dinamo Tbilisi	1						

(U) shows clubs qualifying for Uefa Cup round of 32 from Champions League Group phase

CHART-TOPPING DEFENDERS

1 Ferreira - Chelsea	
Goals conceded in the League	10
Clean Sheets In games when he played at least 70 mins	21
Defensive Rating Average number of minutes between League goals conceded while on pitch	228
Club Defensive Rating Average mins between League goals conceded by the club this season	261

	PLAYER	CLUB	CON: LGE	CS	CDR	DEF RATE
1	Ferreira	Chelsea	10	21	228	261
2	Terry	Chelsea	13	25	228	249
3	Gallas	Chelsea	10	19	228	245
4	Bouma	PSV Eindhoven	13	20	170	190
5	Abidal	Lyon	13	14	155	188
6	Reveillere	Lyon	16	20	155	185
7	Cris	Lyon	17	18	155	175
8	Lee	PSV Eindhoven	16	22	170	174
9	Zebina	Juventus	12	11	127	173
10	Cacapa	Lyon	10	10	155	166
11	Angbwa	Lille	10	9	118	165
12	Nesta	AC Milan	16	12	122	159
13	Alex	PSV Eindhoven	14	14	170	157
14	Carvalho	Chelsea	13	12	228	152
15	Falcone	Sampdoria	16	12	118	146
16	Todd	Blackburn	16	14	80	143
17	Heinze	Man Utd	16	14	132	143
18	Ooijer	PSV Eindhoven	14	13	170	141
19	Ferdinand	Man Utd	20	17	132	140
20	Cannavaro	Juventus	24	19	127	139

The Chart-topping Defenders are resolved by their Defensive Rating, how often their team concedes a goal while they are playing. All these rightly favour players at the best performing clubs because good players win matches. However, good players in lower-table clubs will chart where they have lifted the team's performance.

CHART-TOPPING GOALKEEPERS

1 Cech - Chelsea	
Counting Games Games where he played at least 70 minutes	35
Goals Conceded in the League The number of League goals conceded while he was on the pitch	13
Clean Sheets In games when he played at least 70 mins	24
Defensive Rating Average number of minutes between League goals conceded while on pitch	242

	PLAYER	CLUB	CG	CONC	CS	DEF RATE
1	Cech	Chelsea	35	13	24	242
2	Gomes	PSV Eindhoven	30	14	21	189
3	Coupet	Lyon	31	18	16	155
4	Carroll	Man Utd	26	16	15	146
5	Buffon	Juventus	37	23	19	143
6	Dida	AC Milan	35	23	16	137
7	Antonioli	Sampdoria	37	26	18	126
8	Valdes	Barcelona	35	25	19	125
9	Vonk	Ajax	19	13	8	124
10	Sylva	Lille	38	29	16	116
11	Martyn	Everton	32	26	13	109
12	Janot	St Etienne	38	32	18	107
13	Casillas	Real Madrid	38	32	15	106
14	Franco	Atl Madrid	37	32	15	104
15	Kahn	Bayern Munich	32	28	13	100
16	Fiedler	Hertha Berlin	34	31	11	99
17	Barthez	Marseille	30	28	10	96
18	Roma	Monaco	33	31	12	96
19	Pagliuca	Bologna	38	36	10	95
20	Toldo	Inter Milan	30	28	14	95

The Chart-topping Goalkeepers are positioned by their Defensive Rating. We also show Clean Sheets where the team has not conceded and the Keeper has played all or most (at least 70 minutes) of the game. Only one keeper is selected from each club.

UEFA last 16	Pts	Champ's L. Q-finals	Pts	UEFA Q. finals	Pts	Champ's L.S-finals	Pts	UEFA Semi-finals	Pts	Champ's L.Final Winners	Pts	UEFA Final Winners	Pts	TOTAL
Newcastle Middlesbrough	2	**Chelsea Liverpool**	4	Newcastle	1	**Liverpool** Chelsea	4			**Liverpool**	4			**35 England**
Parma	1	**AC Milan** Inter Juventus	6	**Parma**	1	**AC Milan**	2	Parma	1	AC Milan	2			**30 Italy**
Villarreal Seville R Zaragosa	3			Villarreal	1									**25 Spain**
AZ Alkmaar	1	**PSV**	2	**AZ Alkmaar**	1	PSV	ˆ2	AZ Alkmaar	1					**21 Holland**
Auxerre Lille	2	Lyon	2	Auxerre	1									**21 France**
		Bayern	2											**20 Germany**
Sp Lisbon	1			**Sp Lisbon**	1			**S Lisbon**	1			S Lisbon	1	**12 Portugal**
Olympiakos	1													**10 Greece**
Shakhtar	1													**9 Ukraine**
CSKA	1			**CSKA**	1			**CSKA**	1			**CSKA**	2	**9 Russia**
A Vienna	1			A Vienna	1									**6 Austria**
														5 Belgium
														4 Scotland
														4 Turkey
Partizan Belgrade	1													**3 Serbia & Mont**
Steaua Bucharest	1													**3 Romania**
														2 Switzerland
														2 Norway
														2 Israel
														2 Czech Rep.
														1 Croatia
														1 Poland
														1 Hungary
														1 Georgia

Top Leagues in Europe
This chart sees how different country's leagues fared in cross-border rivalries. Picking up from the Champions League and UEFA Cup Group Phases we've noted every surviving club. 24 leagues feature initially and it's gradually whittled down to two winners.
Each league wins one point for every survivor in the UEFA Cup each round and two points in the Champions League.

International Football

Where tournament stars play

Portugal and Greece have followed their Euro 2004 final exploits by being two of the highest climbers in the Fifa World Rankings over the past 12 months.

Portugal broke into the top ten and lead their qualifying group for the forthcoming World Cup.

Their stars have also made a huge impact on the Premiership with Paulo Ferreira, Ricardo Carvalho and Tiago prominent in Chelsea's first Championship for 50 years. Manchester United's Cristiano Ronaldo joins them in the Portuguese International squad and is currently top scorer in the Eurozone World Cup qualifiers, and Fulham's Luis Boa Morte has also been hitting the net for Portugal.

Pauleta has topped the scoring charts for PSG in France, while Deco knits the movements together in Barca's championship-winning midfield. Portugal's confident keeper Ricardo helped Sporting Lisbon to the Uefa Cup finals and so it goes on.

Watching where an international team's stars are playing is the role of this section of the book.

We have run a chart of the international registrations of all the players in the top six leagues in Europe. The top 20 makes fascinating reading on page 498 (the European Leagues Round-up), and it extends to over 90 nationalities in the six divisions. This year we've followed the 20 countries with the most players plying their trade in the six major European leagues we follow and added the home countries. These are the international teams whose caps we note on our club pages. They are shown in the table below with their Fifa ranking changes over the year.

The top 16 countries based on player registrations (plus home nations) feature on our international pages, showing which club sides they are drawing their international squads from.

HOW OUR 24 COUNTRY TEAMS HAVE FARED

	RANKING 2004	RANKING 2005	DIFFERENCE
Ivory Coast	69	44	25
Portugal	22	9	13
Uruguay	29	16	13
Czech Republic	11	2	9
England	13	6	7
Sweden	18	13	5
Argentina	5	3	2
Switzerland	47	45	2
Italy	10	10	no change
Brazil	1	1	no change
Holland	5	5	no change
Croatia	20	21	-1
Rep of Ireland	14	15	-1
Serbia & Montenegro	44	46	-2
France	2	4	-2
N Ireland	110	114	-4
Denmark	15	19	-4
Spain	3	8	-5
Senegal	26	33	-7
Germany	8	19	-11
Wales	60	74	-14
Cameroon	12	26	-14
Belgium	17	42	-25
Scotland	55	85	-30

FIFA Rankings

Here are the top 80 teams from the 205 countries ranked in the Coca-Cola-sponsored FIFA World Rankings.

The table shows how teams have fared over the 12 months to May 31st. The vagaries of world football don't make the rankings a definitive guide to team performance or quality, but they give a rough guide to how football power ebbs and flows within each individual continent.

Mexico may be flying high in the chart, but they rarely play far afield, and few of their players are plying their trade in Europe. The small chart above focuses on the teams whose players dominate European club football and shows how their rankings have risen or fallen over the year.

FIFA RANKINGS

RANK MAY 05	COUNTRY	POINTS MAY 05	RANK JUNE 04	RANK DIFF	POINTS JUNE 04	POINTS DIFF
1	Brazil	831	1	0	842	-11
2	Czech Republic	784	11	9	719	65
3	Argentina	778	5	2	733	45
4	France	769	2	-2	812	-43
5	Holland	759	5	0	733	26
6	England	754	13	7	711	43
7	Mexico	753	4	-3	735	18
8	Spain	752	3	-5	785	-33
9	Portugal	740	22	13	661	79
=10	Italy	734	10	0	723	11
=10	USA	734	9	-1	724	10
12	Greece	727	35	23	627	100
13	Sweden	722	18	5	667	55
14	Turkey	712	5	-9	733	-21
15	Republic of Ireland	709	14	-1	705	4
16	Uruguay	706	29	13	649	57
17	Japan	703	23	6	658	45
18	Iran	699	19	1	663	36
=19	Denmark	697	15	-4	696	1
=19	Germany	697	8	-11	726	-29
=21	Costa Rica	686	26	5	652	34
=21	Croatia	686	20	-1	662	24
=21	Korea Republic	686	20	-1	662	24
=24	Poland	675	26	2	652	23
25	Nigeria	671	16	-9	691	-20
26	Cameroon	666	12	-14	717	-51
27	Egypt	660	29	2	649	11
28	Colombia	657	37	9	615	42
29	Paraguay	656	25	-4	654	2
30	Russia	653	31	1	645	8
31	Saudi Arabia	652	24	-7	657	-5
32	Romania	647	31	-1	645	2
33	Senegal	646	26	-7	652	-6
34	Ecuador	642	37	3	615	27
35	Morocco	633	33	-2	639	-6
36	Norway	627	36	0	616	11
37	Finland	626	42	5	586	40
38	South Africa	624	39	1	613	11
39	Ukraine	617	71	32	523	94
40	Tunisia	616	33	-7	639	-23
41	Jamaica	614	51	10	553	61
42	Belgium	611	17	-25	670	-59
43	Bulgaria	608	40	-3	609	-1
44	Ivory Coast	607	69	25	525	82
45	Switzerland	603	47	2	576	27
=46	Serbia and Mont	601	44	-2	581	20
=46	Slovenia	601	41	-5	608	-7
48	Slovakia	598	61	13	542	56
49	Bahrain	596	57	8	546	50
=50	Honduras	595	55	5	547	48
=50	Israel	595	57	7	546	49
=50	Jordan	595	42	-8	586	9
53	Iraq	591	45	-8	580	11
54	Uzbekistan	586	83	29	504	82
55	Kuwait	584	59	4	544	40
56	Australia	578	49	-7	558	20
57	Zimbabwe	576	48	-9	560	16
58	China PR	575	65	7	527	48
59	Oman	573	63	4	538	35
60	Guatemala	572	87	27	493	79
61	Mali	571	46	-15	579	-8
62	Trinidad and Tobago	567	77	15	515	52
63	Belarus	565	86	23	502	63
64	Cuba	563	80	16	510	53
65	Latvia	559	53	-12	551	8
66	Peru	558	72	6	522	36
67	Qatar	555	54	-13	550	5
68	Zambia	554	77	9	560	-6
69	Hungary	552	74	5	519	33
=70	Libya	551	82	12	508	43
=70	Venezuela	551	50	-20	554	-3
72	Austria	547	70	-2	524	23
73	Angola	545	85	12	503	42
74	Wales	541	60	-14	543	-2
75	Ghana	531	89	14	486	45
76	Chile	530	65	-11	527	3
=77	Algeria	529	52	-25	552	-23
=77	Congo DR	529	65	-12	527	2
=79	Kenya	527	79	0	513	14
=79	Togo	527	94	15	471	56

FRANCE

FIFA/COCA COLA WORLD RANKING: **4th** EURO LEAGUE CLUB RANKING: **1st***

MANAGER: RAYMOND DOMENECH (FRA)

1	intnls	**Bosnia**	H	D	1-1	Luyindula 6	26,527
2	wc e4	**Israel**	H	D	0-0		43,527
3	wc e4	**Faroe Islands**	A	W	2-0	Giuly 31; Cisse 72	5,917
4	wc e4	**Rep of Ireland**	H	D	0-0		78,863
5	wc e4	**Cyprus**	A	W	2-0	Wiltord 38; Henry 72	3,319
6	intnls	**Poland**	H	D	0-0		41,251
7	intnls	**Sweden**	H	D	1-1	Trezeguet 35	58,923
8	wc e4	**Switzerland**	H	D	0-0		79,373
9	wc e4	**Israel**	A	D	1-1	Trezeguet 50	32,150
10	intnls	**Hungary**	H	W	2-1	Cisse 11; Malouda 35	26,200

KEY PLAYERS - GOALSCORERS

David Trezeguet

Goals in Internationals	2
Contribution to Attacking Power Average number of minutes between team goals while on pitch	135
Player Strike Rate The total number of minutes he was on the pitch for every goal scored	135
Team Strike Rate Average number of minutes between goals scored by club	100

	PLAYER	GOALS	ATT POWER	STRIKE RATE
1	David Trezeguet	2	135	135 mins
2	Djibril Cisse	2	70	141 mins
3	Pegguy Luyindula	1	77	155 mins
4	Florent Malouda	1	75	226 mins
5	Ludovic Giuly	1	106	319 mins

TOP PLAYER APPEARANCES

William Gallas

Age (on 01/07/05)	27
Caps this season	10
Total minutes on the pitch	891
Goals	0
Yellow Cards	0
Red Cards	0
Club Side	Chelsea

	PLAYER	POS	AGE	CAPS	MINS	GOALS	CARDS(Y)	CARDS(R)	CLUB SIDE
1	William Gallas	DEF	27	10	891	0	0	0	Chelsea
2	Gael Givet	DEF	23	9	720	0	0	0	Monaco
3	Benoit Pedretti	MID	24	7	630	0	0	0	Marseille
4	Patrick Vieira	MID	29	7	596	0	4	1	Arsenal
5	Thierry Henry	ATT	27	7	557	1	0	0	Arsenal
6	Sebastien Squillaci	DEF	24	8	549	0	0	0	Monaco
7	Fabien Barthez	GK	34	5	450	0	0	0	Marseille
8	Sylvain Wiltord	ATT	31	5	408	1	0	0	Arsenal
9	Jean-Alain Boumsong	DEF	25	4	360	0	0	0	Newcastle
10	Gregory Coupet	GK	32	4	360	0	0	0	Lyon
11	Ludovic Giuly	MID	28	6	319	1	0	0	Barcelona
12	Robert Pires	MID	31	5	295	0	0	0	Arsenal
13	Patrice Evra	MID	24	5	294	0	0	0	Monaco
14	Djibril Cisse	ATT	23	4	281	2	0	0	Auxerre
15	David Trezeguet	ATT	27	3	270	2	1	0	Juventus
16	Willy Sagnol	DEF	28	3	270	0	1	0	Bayern Munich
17	Jerome Rothen	MID	27	3	245	0	1	0	Paris SG
18	Vikash Dhorasoo	MID	31	5	241	0	0	0	AC Milan

*EURO LEAGUE RANKING based on number of players of that nationality playing in the top six European Leagues

SPAIN

FIFA/COCA COLA WORLD RANKING: **8th** EURO LEAGUE CLUB RANKING: **2nd**

MANAGER: LUIS ARAGONES (SPA)

1	intnls	**Venezuela**	H	W	3-2	Morientes 41; Tamudo 57,67	30,000
2	wc e7	**Bosnia**	A	D	1-1	Vicente 66	14,380
3	wc e7	**Belgium**	H	W	2-0	Luque 59; Raul 65	22,500
4	wc e7	**Lithuania**	A	D	0-0		9,114
5	intnls	**England**	H	W	1-0	Del Horno 9	48,000
6	wc e7	**San Marino**	H	W	5-0	Joaquin 15; Torres 33; Raul 43; Guti 64; Del Horno 79	12,580
7	intnls	**China PR**	H	W	3-0	Torres 3 pen; Xavi 32; Joaquin 52	17,000
8	wc e7	**Serbia & M**	A	D	0-0		48,910

KEY PLAYERS - GOALSCORERS

Alberto Luque

Goals in Internationals	2
Contribution to Attacking Power Average number of minutes between team goals while on pitch	37
Player Strike Rate The total number of minutes he was on the pitch for every goal scored	150
Team Strike Rate Average number of minutes between goals scored by club	51

	PLAYER	GOALS	ATT POWER	STRIKE RATE
1	Alberto Luque	2	37	150 mins
2	Rodriguez Guillen Vicente	1	75	225 mins
3	Fernando Torres	2	42	232 mins
4	Asier Del Horno	2	46	255 mins
5	Sanchez Joaquin	2	42	257 mins

TOP PLAYER APPEARANCES

Iker Casillas

Age (on 01/07/05)	24
Caps this season	8
Total minutes on the pitch	720
Goals	0
Yellow Cards	0
Red Cards	0
Club Side	Real Madrid

	PLAYER	POS	AGE	CAPS	MINS	GOALS	CARDS(Y)	CARDS(R)	CLUB SIDE
1	Iker Casillas	GK	24	8	720	0	0	0	Real Madrid
2	Carlos Puyol	DEF	27	8	630	0	1	0	Barcelona
3	Xavi Hernandez	MID	25	7	612	1	1	0	Barcelona
4	Michel Salgado	DEF	29	6	540	0	2	0	Real Madrid
5	Raul	ATT	28	8	528	2	0	0	Real Madrid
6	Sanchez Joaquin	MID	24	7	514	2	1	0	Real Madrid
7	Asier Del Horno	DEF	24	6	510	2	0	0	Athl Bilbao
8	David Albelda	MID	27	7	503	0	4	0	Valencia
9	Fernando Torres	ATT	21	7	464	2	0	0	Atl Madrid
10	Carlos Marchena	DEF	26	5	405	0	0	0	Valencia
11	Jose Antonio Reyes	ATT	21	6	372	0	0	0	Arsenal
12	Alberto Luque	ATT	27	6	299	2	0	0	Deportivo
13	Rodriguez Guillen Vicente	ATT	23	3	225	1	0	0	Valencia
14	Juanito	DEF	28	3	225	0	0	0	Real Betis
15	Pablo Ibanez	DEF	23	3	225	0	0	0	Atl Madrid
16	Ivan De La Pena	MID	29	3	207	0	0	0	Espanyol
17	Enrique Romero	DEF	34	3	191	0	1	0	Deportivo
18	Ruben Baraja	MID	29	4	182	0	0	0	Valencia

ITALY

FIFA/COCA COLA WORLD RANKING: **10th** EURO LEAGUE CLUB RANKING: **3rd**

MANAGER: MARCELLO LIPPI (ITA)

1	intnls	**Iceland**	A	L	0-2		20,000
2	wc e5	**Norway**	H	W	2-1	de Rossi 4; Toni 80	21,463
3	wc e5	**Moldova**	A	W	1-0	Del Piero 32	5,200
4	wc e5	**Slovenia**	A	L	0-1		9,262
5	wc e5	**Belarus**	H	W	4-3	Totti 27 pen,75; De Rossi 33; Gilardino 86	19,833
6	intnls	**Finland**	H	W	1-0	Miccoli 33	7,043
7	intnls	**Russia**	H	W	2-0	Gilardino 56; Barone 62	20,000
8	wc e5	**Scotland**	H	W	2-0	Pirlo 35,85	40,745
9	intnls	**Iceland**	H	D	0-0		23,000

KEY PLAYERS - GOALSCORERS

Francesco Totti

Goals in Internationals	2
Contribution to Attacking Power Average number of minutes between team goals while on pitch	59
Player Strike Rate The total number of minutes he was on the pitch for every goal scored	149
Team Strike Rate Average number of minutes between goals scored by club	75

	PLAYER	GOALS	ATT POWER	STRIKE RATE
1	Francesco Totti	2	59	149 mins
2	Andrea Pirlo	2	106	160 mins
3	Fabrizio Miccoli	1	81	162 mins
4	Alberto Gilardino	2	43	216 mins
5	Daniele De Rossi	1	92	557 mins

TOP PLAYER APPEARANCES

3 Gennaro Gattuso

Age (on 01/07/05)	27
Caps this season	7
Total minutes on the pitch	630
Goals	0
Yellow Cards	2
Red Cards	0
Club Side	AC Milan

	PLAYER	POS	AGE	CAPS	MINS	GOALS	CARDS(Y)	CARDS(R)	CLUB SIDE
1	Marco Materazzi	DEF	31	9	752	0	2	0	Inter Milan
2	Gianluigi Buffon	GK	27	8	720	0	0	0	Juventus
3	Gennaro Gattuso	MID	27	7	630	0	2	0	AC Milan
4	Daniele De Rossi	DEF	20	8	557	1	1	0	Roma
5	Gianluca Zambrotta	MID	28	6	540	0	3	0	Juventus
6	Daniele Bonera	DEF	24	6	533	0	3	0	Parma
7	Alessandro Nesta	DEF	29	5	450	0	1	0	AC Milan
8	Alberto Gilardino	ATT	23	6	432	2	0	0	Parma
9	Fabio Cannavaro	DEF	31	5	383	0	1	0	Juventus
10	Andrea Pirlo	MID	26	4	319	2	0	0	AC Milan
11	Francesco Totti	ATT	28	4	297	2	0	0	Roma
12	Manuele Blasi	MID	24	6	288	0	2	0	Juventus
13	Stefano Aimo Diana	DEF	27	6	277	0	0	0	Sampdoria
14	Mauro Camoranesi	MID	28	3	263	0	1	0	Juventus
15	Mauro Esposito	ATT	26	4	248	0	0	0	Cagliari
16	Luca Toni	ATT	28	8	239	0	0	0	Palermo
17	Giorgio Chiellini	DEF	20	4	203	0	0	0	Fiorentina
18	Stefano Fiore	MID	30	3	201	0	0	0	Valencia

HOLLAND

FIFA/COCA COLA WORLD RANKING: **5th** EURO LEAGUE CLUB RANKING: **4th**

MANAGER: MARCO VAN BASTEN (NED)

1	intnls	**Sweden**	A	D	2-2	Sneijder 17; van Bommel 43	20,377
2	intnls	**Liechtenstein**	H	W	3-0	van Bommel 23; Ooijer 56; Landzaat 78	15,000
3	wc e1	**Czech Rep**	H	W	2-0	van Hooijdonk 33,84	49,000
4	wc e1	**Macedonia**	A	D	2-2	Bouma 43; Kuijt 66	15,000
5	wc e1	**Finland**	H	W	3-1	Sneijder 39; van Nistelrooy 41,63	50,000
6	wc e1	**Andorra**	A	W	3-0	Cocu 21; Robben 31; Sneijder 78	2,000
7	intnls	**England**	A	D	0-0		40,705
8	wc e1	**Romania**	A	W	2-0	Cocu 1; Babel 84	19,000
9	wc e1	**Armenia**	H	W	2-0	Castelen 3; van Nistelrooy 34	35,000

KEY PLAYERS - GOALSCORERS

Arjen Robben

Goals in Internationals	2
Contribution to Attacking Power Average number of minutes between team goals while on pitch	33
Player Strike Rate The total number of minutes he was on the pitch for every goal scored	101
Team Strike Rate Average number of minutes between goals scored by club	43

	PLAYER	GOALS	ATT POWER	STRIKE RATE
1	Arjen Robben	2	33	101 mins
2	Pierre van Hooijdonk	2	35	106 mins
3	Ruud van Nistelrooy	3	33	122 mins
4	Wesley Sneijder	3	35	175 mins
5	Phillip Cocu	2	37	206 mins

TOP PLAYER APPEARANCES

Edwin Van der Sar

Age (on 01/07/05)	34
Caps this season	10
Total minutes on the pitch	855
Goals	0
Yellow Cards	0
Red Cards	0
Club Side	Fulham

	PLAYER	POS	AGE	CAPS	MINS	GOALS	CARDS(Y)	CARDS(R)	CLUB SIDE
1	Edwin Van der Sar	GK	34	10	855	0	0	0	Fulham
2	Dirk Kuijt	ATT	24	9	753	2	1	0	Feyenoord
3	Gio Van Bronckhorst	MID	30	8	563	0	0	0	Barcelona
4	Denny Landzaat	MID	29	8	554	1	1	0	AZ Alkmaar
5	Mark van Bommel	MID	28	9	553	2	1	0	PSV Eindhoven
6	Wesley Sneijder	MID	21	6	525	3	0	0	Ajax
7	Romeo Castelen	MID	22	7	427	1	0	0	Feyenoord
8	Rafael van der Vaart	MID	22	8	426	0	2	0	Ajax
9	John Heitinga	DEF	21	5	421	0	0	0	Ajax
10	Phillip Cocu	MID	34	5	411	2	0	0	PSV Eindhoven
11	Edgar Davids	MID	32	5	405	0	0	0	Inter Milan
12	Khalid Boulahrouz	DEF	23	5	388	0	1	0	Hamburg
13	Nigel de Jong	DEF	20	5	380	0	0	0	Ajax
14	Ruud van Nistelrooy	ATT	29	5	367	3	0	0	Man Utd
15	Roy Makaay	ATT	30	7	342	0	0	0	Bayern Munich
16	Jan Kromkamp	DEF	24	4	291	0	0	0	AZ Alkmaar
17	Joris Mathijsen	DEF	25	4	278	0	0	0	AZ Alkmaar
18	Andre Ooijer	DEF	30	3	270	1	0	0	PSV Eindhoven

GERMANY

FIFA/COCA COLA WORLD RANKING: **19th** EURO LEAGUE CLUB RANKING: **5th**

MANAGER: JUERGEN KLINSMANN (GER)

1	intnls	**Austria**	A	W	3-1	Kuranyi 2,61,73	37,900
2	intnls	**Brazil**	H	D	1-1	Kuranyi 17	74,315
3	intnls	**Iran**	A	W	2-0	Ernst 5; Brdaric 53	110,000
4	intnls	**Cameroon**	H	W	3-0	Kuranyi 71; Klose 78,88	44,200
5	intnls	**Japan**	A	W	3-0	Klose 54,90; Ballack 69	72,000
6	intnls	**South Korea**	A	L	1-3	Ballack 26	30,000
7	intnls	**Thailand**	A	W	5-1	Kuranyi 34,38; Podolski 73,89; Asamoah 84	25,000
8	intnls	**Argentina**	H	D	2-2	Frings 28 pen; Kuranyi 45	52,000
9	intnls	**Slovenia**	A	W	1-0	Podolski 27	9,500

KEY PLAYERS - GOALSCORERS

Kevin Kuranyi

Goals in Internationals	8
Contribution to Attacking Power Average number of minutes between team goals while on pitch	32
Player Strike Rate The total number of minutes he was on the pitch for every goal scored	77
Club Strike Rate Average number of minutes between goals scored by club	36

	PLAYER	GOALS	ATT POWER	STRIKE RATE
1	Kevin Kuranyi	8	32	77 mins
2	Lukas Podolski	3	49	82 mins
3	Miroslav Klose	4	35	89 mins
4	Michael Ballack	4	40	180 mins
5	Gerald Asamoah	2	32	279 mins

TOP PLAYER APPEARANCES

Michael Ballack

Age (on 01/07/05)	28
Caps this season	8
Total minutes on the pitch	720
Goals	4
Yellow Cards	1
Red Cards	0
Club Side	Bayern Munich

	PLAYER	POS	AGE	CAPS	MINS	GOALS	CARDS(Y)	CARDS(R)	CLUB SIDE
1	Michael Ballack	MID	28	8	720	4	1	0	Bayern Munich
2	Kevin Kuranyi	ATT	23	8	619	8	0	0	Stuttgart
3	Bernd Schneider	MID	31	7	588	0	0	0	B Leverkusen
4	Gerald Asamoah	ATT	26	9	557	2	0	0	Schalke
5	Fabian Ernst	MID	26	7	539	1	0	0	W Bremen
6	Torsten Frings	MID	28	6	535	1	0	0	Bayern Munich
7	Philip Lahm	DEF	21	6	484	0	0	0	Stuttgart
8	Per Mertesacker	DEF	20	6	460	0	0	0	Hannover 96
9	Bastian Schweinsteiger	MID	20	8	442	0	0	0	Bayern Munich
10	Oliver Kahn	GK	36	5	405	0	0	0	Bayern Munich
11	Jens Lehmann	GK	35	5	405	0	0	0	Arsenal
12	Patrick Owomoyela	MID	25	6	392	0	1	0	Arminia B
13	Robert Huth	DEF	20	6	380	0	1	1	Chelsea
14	Christian Worns	DEF	33	5	372	0	0	0	B Dortmund
15	Miroslav Klose	ATT	27	6	357	4	0	0	W Bremen
16	Andreas Hinkel	DEF	23	5	319	0	0	0	Stuttgart
17	Tomas Hitzlsperger	MID	23	5	318	0	0	0	Aston Villa
18	Arne Friedrich	DEF	26	3	246	0	0	0	Hertha Berlin

ENGLAND

FIFA/COCA COLA WORLD RANKING: **6th** EURO LEAGUE CLUB RANKING: **6th**

MANAGER: SVEN GORAN ERIKSSON (SWE)

1	intnls	**Ukraine**	H	W	3-0	Beckham 28; Owen 50; Wright-Phillips 72	35,387
2	wc e6	**Austria**	A	D	2-2	Lampard 24; Gerrard 65	48,000
3	wc e6	**Poland**	A	W	2-1	Defoe 37; Glowacki 58 og	38,000
4	wc e6	**Wales**	H	W	2-0	Lampard 4; Beckham 76	65,224
5	wc e6	**Azerbaijan**	A	W	1-0	Owen 22	17,000
6	intnls	**Spain**	A	L	0-1		48,000
7	intnls	**Holland**	H	D	0-0		40,705
8	wc e6	**N Ireland**	H	W	4-0	Cole, J 47; Owen 52; Baird 54 og; Lampard 62	65,239
9	wc e6	**Azerbaijan**	H	W	2-0	Gerrard 51; Beckham 62	49,046
10	intnls	**United States**	A	W	2-1	Richardson 4,44	45,000
11	intnls	**Colombia**	A	W	3-2	Owen 36,43,58	58,000

KEY PLAYERS - GOALSCORERS

Michael Owen

Goals in Internationals	6
Contribution to Attacking Power Average number of minutes between team goals while on pitch	46
Player Strike Rate The total number of minutes he was on the pitch for every goal scored	147
Team Strike Rate Average number of minutes between goals scored by club	47

	PLAYER	GOALS	ATT POWER	STRIKE RATE
1	Michael Owen	6	46	147 mins
2	Steven Gerrard	2	41	229 mins
3	Frank Lampard	3	44	239 mins
4	David Beckham	3	40	240 mins
5	Jermain Defoe	1	57	347 mins

TOP PLAYER APPEARANCES

Ashley Cole

Age (on 01/07/05)	24
Caps this season	11
Total minutes on the pitch	918
Goals	0
Yellow Cards	3
Red Cards	0
Club Side	Arsenal

	PLAYER	POS	AGE	CAPS	MINS	GOALS	CARDS(Y)	CARDS(R)	CLUB SIDE
1	Ashley Cole	DEF	24	11	918	0	3	0	Arsenal
2	Michael Owen	ATT	25	10	882	6	2	0	Real Madrid
3	David Beckham	MID	30	9	720	3	3	0	Real Madrid
4	Frank Lampard	MID	27	9	717	3	0	0	Chelsea
5	Gary Neville	DEF	30	9	706	0	0	0	Man Utd
6	Paul Robinson	GK	26	7	630	0	0	0	Tottenham
7	John Terry	DEF	24	6	514	0	0	0	Chelsea
8	Steven Gerrard	MID	25	6	458	2	0	0	Liverpool
9	Wayne Rooney	ATT	19	6	425	0	2	0	Man Utd
10	Rio Ferdinand	DEF	26	5	407	0	0	0	Man Utd
11	Joe Cole	MID	23	6	368	1	0	0	Chelsea
12	Jermain Defoe	ATT	24	10	347	1	0	0	Tottenham
13	Alan Smith	ATT	24	7	334	0	0	0	Man Utd
14	Nicky Butt	MID	30	4	321	0	1	0	Newcastle
15	David James	GK	34	4	315	0	0	0	Man City
16	Jermaine Jenas	MID	22	6	307	0	0	0	Newcastle
17	Ledley King	DEF	24	5	288	0	0	0	Tottenham
18	Wayne Bridge	DEF	24	3	263	0	0	0	Chelsea

BRAZIL

FIFA/COCA COLA WORLD RANKING: **1st** EURO LEAGUE CLUB RANKING: **7th**

MANAGER: CARLOS ALBERTO PARREIRA (BRA)

1	copa	**Mexico**	A	W	4-0	Alex 28 pen; Adriano 66,79; Oliveira 87	22,000
2	copa	**Uruguay**	A	W	1-1*	Adriano 47 (*won 5-3 on penalties)	
3	copa	**Argentina**	A	W	2-2*	Luisao 45; Adriano 90 (*won 4-2 on pens)	43,000
4	intnls	**Haiti**	A	W	6-0	Roger 19,41; Ronaldinho 32,67,81; Nilmar 85	15,000
5	wcq1	**Bolivia**	H	W	3-1	Ronaldo 1; Ronaldinho 12 pen; Adriano 44	60,000
6	intnls	**Germany**	A	D	1-1	Ronaldinho 9	74,315
7	wcq1	**Venezuela**	A	W	5-2	Kaka 5,34; Ronaldo 48,50; Adriano 75	26,133
8	wcq1	**Colombia**	H	D	0-0		20,000
9	wcq1	**Ecuador**	A	L	0-1		38,308
10	intnls	**Hong Kong**	A	W	7-1	Lucio 20; Roberto Carlos 30; Oliveira 45,57; Ronaldinho 49; Robinho 77; Alex 79	25,400
11	wcq1	**Peru**	H	W	1-0	Kaka 74	49,163
12	wcq1	**Uruguay**	A	D	1-1	Emerson 67	60,000
13	intnls	**Guatemala**	H	W	3-0	A Polga 5; Romario 17; Grafite 65	36,325

KEY PLAYERS - GOALSCORERS

Adriano

Goals in Internationals	6
Contribution to Attacking Power Average number of minutes between team goals while on pitch	36
Player Strike Rate The total number of minutes he was on the pitch for every goal scored	92
Team Strike Rate Average number of minutes between goals scored by club	35

	PLAYER	GOALS	ATT POWER	STRIKE RATE
1	Adriano	6	36	92 mins
2	Ricardo Kaka	3	53	106 mins
3	Ronaldinho	6	32	120 mins
4	Pinho Alex	2	45	206 mins
5	Ronaldo	3	50	218 mins

TOP PLAYER APPEARANCES

4 Ronaldinho

Age (on 01/07/05)	25
Caps this season	9
Total minutes on the pitch	717
Goals	6
Yellow Cards	1
Red Cards	0
Club Side	Barcelona

	PLAYER	POS	AGE	CAPS	MINS	GOALS	CARDS(Y)	CARDS(R)	CLUB SIDE
1	Juan	DEF	26	10	885	0	2	0	B Leverkusen
2	Roberto Carlos	DEF	32	9	748	1	0	0	Real Madrid
3	Renato	MID	26	12	722	0	0	0	Seville
4	Ronaldinho	ATT	25	9	717	6	1	0	Barcelona
5	Julio Cesar	GK	25	7	660	0	0	0	Flamengo
6	Ronaldo	ATT	28	8	655	3	1	0	Real Madrid
7	Adriano	ATT	23	9	550	6	1	0	Inter Milan
8	Roque Junior	DEF	28	6	540	0	0	0	B Leverkusen
9	Edu	MID	27	8	529	0	1	0	Arsenal
10	Cafu	DEF	35	6	508	0	1	0	AC Milan
11	Pernambucano Juninho	MID	30	7	454	0	0	0	Lyon
12	Nelson Dida	GK	31	5	450	0	0	0	AC Milan
13	Pinho Alex	MID	33	8	412	2	0	0	Vasco da Gama
14	Jose Ze Roberto	MID	31	5	404	0	0	0	Bayern Munich
15	Luis Fabiano	ATT	24	4	365	0	0	0	Porto
16	Anderson Luisao	MID	24	4	350	1	1	0	Benfica
17	Maicon	DEF	24	4	330	0	0	0	Monaco
18	Ricardo Kaka	MID	23	4	319	3	1	0	AC Milan

ARGENTINA

FIFA/COCA COLA WORLD RANKING: **3rd** EURO LEAGUE CLUB RANKING: **8th**

MANAGER: JOSE PEKERMAN (ARG)

1	copa	**Peru**	A	W	1-0	Tevez 61	
2	copa	**Colombia**	H	W	3-0	Tevez 33; Gonzalez, L 50; Sorin 80	
3	copa	**Brazil**	H	L	2-2*	Kily Gonzalez 20 pen; Cesar Delgado 87 (* lost 4-2 on penalties)	43,000
4	intnls	**Japan**	A	W	2-1	Galletti 4; Santana 39	45,000
5	wcq1	**Peru**	A	W	3-1	Rosales 14; Coloccini 66; Sorin 90	28,000
6	wcq1	**Uruguay**	H	W	4-2	Gonzalez, L 6; Lucho 31,54; Zanetti 44	50,000
7	wcq1	**Chile**	A	D	0-0		57,671
8	wcq1	**Venezuela**	H	W	3-2	Rey 3 og; Riquelme 46; Saviola 65	30,000
9	intnls	**Germany**	A	D	2-2	Crespo 40,81	52,000
10	intnls	**Mexico**	H	D	1-1	Zarate 67	51,345
11	wcq1	**Bolivia**	A	W	2-1	Lucho 57; Galletti 63	25,000
12	wcq1	**Colombia**	H	W	1-0	Crespo 65	40,000

KEY PLAYERS - GOALSCORERS

Hernan Crespo

Goals in Internationals	3
Contribution to Attacking Power Average number of minutes between team goals while on pitch	60
Player Strike Rate The total number of minutes he was on the pitch for every goal scored	60
Team Strike Rate Average number of minutes between goals scored by club	46

	PLAYER	GOALS	ATT POWER	STRIKE RATE
1	Hernan Crespo	3	60	60 mins
2	Luciano Galletti	2	32	98 mins
3	Figueroa Lucho	3	37	151 mins
4	Carlos Tevez	2	40	161 mins
5	Mauro Rosales	1	39	198 mins

TOP PLAYER APPEARANCES

4 Gabriel Ivan Heinze

Age (on 01/07/04)	27
Caps this season	8
Total minutes on the pitch	750
Goals	0
Yellow Cards	3
Red Cards	0
Club Side	Manchester United

	PLAYER	POS	AGE	CAPS	MINS	GOALS	CARDS(Y)	CARDS(R)	CLUB SIDE
1	Roberto Abbondancieri	GK	32	10	930	0	0	0	Boca Juniors
2	Javier Zanetti	MID	31	9	840	1	1	0	Inter Milan
3	Juan Pablo Sorin	MID	29	9	772	2	1	0	Villarreal
4	Gabriel Ivan Heinze	DEF	27	8	750	0	3	0	Man Utd
5	Javier Mascherano	MID	21	7	578	0	3	0	River Plate
6	Fabricio Coloccini	DEF	23	6	570	1	2	0	Deportivo
7	Juan Riquelme	MID	27	6	540	1	0	0	Villarreal
8	Esteban Cambiasso	MID	24	6	483	0	1	0	Inter Milan
9	Luis Gonzalez	MID	24	7	472	2	2	0	River Plate
10	Figueroa Lucho	ATT	24	6	453	3	1	0	Villarreal
11	Javier Saviola	ATT	23	5	366	1	1	0	Monaco
12	Gabriel Milito	DEF	24	4	360	0	0	0	Real Zaragoza
13	Carlos Tevez	ATT	21	5	322	2	1	0	Corinthians
14	Cesar Delgado	ATT	23	5	317	1	1	0	Cruz Azul
15	Cristian Kily Gonzalez	MID	30	3	294	1	1	0	Inter Milan
16	Roberto Ayala	DEF	32	3	292	0	1	1	Valencia
17	Walter Samuel	DEF	27	3	270	0	1	0	Real Madrid
18	Lionel Scaloni	DEF	27	3	225	0	0	0	Deportivo

BELGIUM

FIFA/COCA COLA WORLD RANKING: **42nd** EURO LEAGUE CLUB RANKING: **9th**

MANAGER: AIME ANTHUENIS (BEL)

1	intnls **Norway**	A	D	2-2	Buffel 25,34	15,000
2	wc e7 **Lithuania**	H	D	1-1	Sonck 61	18,000
3	wc e7 **Spain**	A	L	0-2		22,500
4	wc e7 **Serbia & Mont**	H	L	0-2		35,000
5	intnls **Egypt**	A	L	0-4		5,000
6	wc e7 **Bosnia**	H	W	4-1	Mpenza, E 15,64; Daerden 44; Buffel 76	36,700
7	wc e7 **San Marino**	A	W	2-1	Simons 19 pen; Van Buyten 65	871

KEY PLAYERS - GOALSCORERS

2 Thomas Buffel

Goals in Internationals	3
Contribution to Attacking Power Average number of minutes between team goals while on pitch	76
Player Strike Rate The total number of minutes he was on the pitch for every goal scored	203
Team Strike Rate Average number of minutes between goals scored by club	80

	PLAYER	GOALS	ATT POWER	STRIKE RATE
1	Emile Mpenza	2	85	171 mins
2	Thomas Buffel	3	76	203 mins
3	Wesley Sonck	1	275	275 mins
4	Koen Daerden	1	59	354 mins
5	Daniel Van Buyten	1	68	476 mins

TOP PLAYER APPEARANCES

2 Philippe Clement

Age (on 01/07/05)	31
Caps this season	7
Total minutes on the pitch	541
Goals	0
Yellow Cards	0
Red Cards	0
Club Side	Club Brugge

	PLAYER	POS	AGE	CAPS	MINS	GOALS	CARDS(Y)	CARDS(R)	CLUB SIDE
1	Thomas Buffel	MID	24	8	610	3	2	0	Rangers
2	Philippe Clement	DEF	31	7	541	0	0	0	Club Brugge
3	Timmy Simons	MID	29	6	540	1	0	0	Club Brugge
4	Vincent Kompany	DEF	19	7	527	0	2	0	Anderlecht
5	Daniel Van Buyten	DEF	27	6	476	1	0	0	Hamburg
6	Sylvio Proto	GK	22	5	450	0	0	0	La Louviere
7	Yves Vanderhaeghe	MID	35	4	360	0	1	0	Anderlecht
8	Peter Van der Heyden	DEF	28	4	360	0	2	0	Club Brugge
9	Koen Daerden	MID	23	5	354	1	0	0	Genk
10	Emile Mpenza	ATT	27	4	341	2	0	0	Hamburg
11	Roberto Bisconti	MID	31	7	337	0	1	0	Nice
12	Mbo Mpenza	ATT	28	5	315	0	1	0	Anderlecht
13	Wesley Sonck	ATT	26	4	275	1	0	0	B M'gladbach
14	Luigi Pieroni	ATT	24	7	272	0	0	0	Auxerre
15	Tristan Peersman	GK	25	3	270	0	0	0	Anderlecht
16	Bart Goor	MID	32	3	247	0	2	1	Feyenoord
17	Oliver Deschacht	DEF	24	4	229	0	1	0	Anderlecht
18	Olivier Doll	DEF	32	4	209	0	0	0	Lokeren

SERBIA & MONTENEGRO

FIFA/COCA COLA WORLD RANKING: **45th** EURO LEAGUE CLUB RANKING: **10th**

MANAGER: ILIJA PETKOVIC (SCG)

1	intnls **Slovenia**	A	D	1-1	Jestrovic 50	8,000
2	wc e7 **San Marino**	A	W	3-0	Vukic 4; Jestrovic 15,83	1,000
3	wc e7 **Bosnia**	A	D	0-0		22,440
4	wc e7 **San Marino**	H	W	5-0	Milosevic 35; Stankovic, D 45,50; Koroman 52; Vukic 69	4,000
5	wc e7 **Belgium**	A	W	2-0	Vukic 10; Kezman 59	35,000
6	intnls **Bulgaria**	A	D	0-0		2,957
7	wc e7 **Spain**	H	D	0-0		48,910

KEY PLAYERS - GOALSCORERS

Nenad Jestrovic

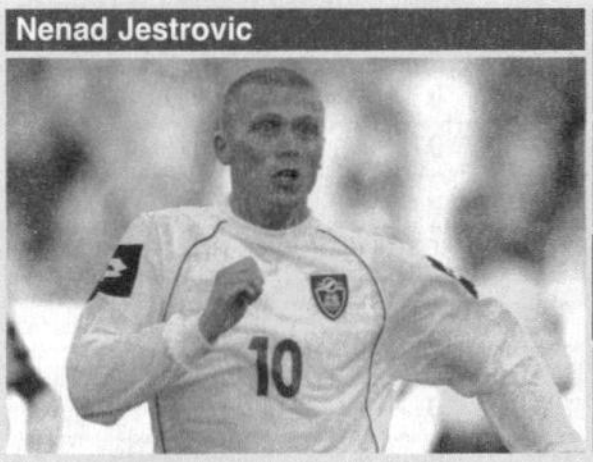

Goals in Internationals	3
Contribution to Attacking Power Average number of minutes between team goals while on pitch	49
Player Strike Rate The total number of minutes he was on the pitch for every goal scored	66
Team Strike Rate Average number of minutes between goals scored by club	65

	PLAYER	GOALS	ATT POWER	STRIKE RATE
1	Nenad Jestrovic	3	49	66 mins
2	Zvonimir Vukic	3	50	186 mins
3	Mateja Kezman	1	99	299 mins
4	Dejan Stankovic	2	58	323 mins

TOP PLAYER APPEARANCES

4 Dejan Stankovic

Age (on 01/07/05)	26
Caps this season	8
Total minutes on the pitch	646
Goals	2
Yellow Cards	0
Red Cards	0
Club Side	Inter Milan

	PLAYER	POS	AGE	CAPS	MINS	GOALS	CARDS(Y)	CARDS(R)	CLUB SIDE
1	Dragoslav Jevric	GK	31	8	720	0	0	0	Vitesse Arnhem
2	Goran Gavrancic	DEF	26	8	720	0	0	0	Dinamo Kiev
3	Ivica Dragutinovic	DEF	29	8	682	0	0	0	Standard Liege
4	Dejan Stankovic	MID	26	8	646	2	0	0	Inter Milan
5	Mladen Krstajic	DEF	31	7	630	0	0	0	Schalke
6	Ognjen Koroman	MID	26	7	570	1	1	0	Dinamo Minsk
7	Zvonimir Vukic	MID	25	7	557	3	2	0	Shakhtar Donetsk
8	Nemanja Vidic	DEF	23	6	540	0	1	0	Crvena Zvezda
9	Igor Duljaj	MID	25	8	495	0	0	0	Partizan
10	Savo Milosevic	ATT	31	7	446	1	0	0	Osasuna
11	Mateja Kezman	ATT	26	5	299	1	0	0	Chelsea
12	Danijel Ljuboja	MID	27	3	251	0	0	0	Paris SG
13	Predrag Djordjevic	MID	32	3	249	0	2	0	Olympiakos
14	Marjan Markovic	DEF	23	3	214	0	0	0	Genoa
15	Dragan Mladenovic	MID	29	4	211	0	0	0	Real Sociedad
16	Nenad Jestrovic	ATT	29	4	198	3	0	0	Anderlecht
17	Simon Vukcevic	MID	19	2	100	0	0	0	Partizan
18	Milwoje Cirkovic	DEF	28	1	86	0	0	0	Partizan

DENMARK

FIFA/COCA COLA WORLD RANKING: **19th** EURO LEAGUE CLUB RANKING: **11th**

MANAGER: MORTEN OLSEN (DEN)

1	intnls	Poland	A	W	5-1	Madsen 23,30,90; Gaardsoe 51; Jensen, C 86	4,500
2	wc e2	Ukraine	H	D	1-1	Jorgensen 9	36,335
3	wc e2	Albania	A	W	2-0	Jorgensen 52; Tomasson 71	18,000
4	wc e2	Turkey	H	D	1-1	Tomasson 27 pen	41,331
5	wc e2	Georgia	A	D	2-2	Tomasson 7,64	20,000
6	wc e2	Greece	A	L	1-2	Rommedahl 46	32,430
7	wc e2	Kazakhstan	H	W	3-0	Moller 8,47; Poulsen 34	20,980
8	wc e2	Ukraine	A	L	0-1		60,000

KEY PLAYERS - GOALSCORERS

Peter Madsen

Goals in Internationals	3
Contribution to Attacking Power Average number of minutes between team goals while on pitch	31
Player Strike Rate The total number of minutes he was on the pitch for every goal scored	63
Team Strike Rate Average number of minutes between goals scored by club	48

	PLAYER	GOALS	ATT POWER	STRIKE RATE
1	Peter Madsen	3	31	63 mins
2	Jon Dahl Tomasson	4	57	158 mins
3	Dennis Rommedahl	1	50	305 mins
4	Martin Jorgensen	2	47	307 mins
5	Christian Poulsen	1	46	694 mins

TOP PLAYER APPEARANCES

Christian Poulsen

Age (on 01/07/05)	25
Caps this season	8
Total minutes on the pitch	694
Goals	1
Yellow Cards	0
Red Cards	0
Club Side	Schalke

	PLAYER	POS	AGE	CAPS	MINS	GOALS	CARDS(Y)	CARDS(R)	CLUB SIDE
1	Christian Poulsen	MID	25	8	694	1	0	0	Schalke
2	Niclas Jensen	DEF	30	8	675	0	0	0	B Dortmund
3	Brian Priske	DEF	28	8	666	0	1	0	Genk
4	Thomas Gravesen	MID	29	7	630	0	3	0	Real Madrid
5	Jon Dahl Tomasson	ATT	28	8	630	4	0	0	AC Milan
6	Martin Jorgensen	MID	29	8	614	2	0	0	Fiorentina
7	Thomas Helveg	DEF	34	6	540	0	3	0	Norwich
8	Thomas Sorensen	GK	29	6	540	0	1	0	Aston Villa
9	Per Kroldrup	DEF	25	6	540	0	3	0	Udinese
10	Jesper Gronkjaer	MID	28	6	428	0	0	1	Atl Madrid
11	Dennis Rommedahl	ATT	26	6	305	1	0	0	Charlton
12	Kenneth Perez	ATT	30	5	228	0	0	0	AZ Alkmaar
13	Daniel Jensen	MID	26	3	223	0	0	0	W Bremen
14	Peter Madsen	ATT	27	3	189	3	0	0	Bochum
15	Peter Skov-Jensen	GK	34	2	180	0	0	0	Bochum
16	Steven Lustu	DEF	34	2	154	0	2	0	FC Copenhagen
17	Martin Laursen	DEF	33	2	135	0	0	0	Aston Villa
18	Claus Jensen	MID	27	4	123	1	0	0	Fulham

URUGUAY

FIFA/COCA COLA WORLD RANKING: **16th** EURO LEAGUE CLUB RANKING: **12th**

MANAGER: JORGE FOSSATI (URU)

1	copa	Brazil	H	L	1-1*	Sosa 22 (*lost 5-3 on penalties)	
2	wcq1	Ecuador	H	W	1-0	Bueno 57	28,000
3	wcq1	Argentina	A	L	2-4	Rodriguez, C 62; Chevanton 85 pen	50,000
4	wcq1	Bolivia	A	D	0-0		24,349
5	wcq1	Paraguay	H	W	1-0	Montero 78	35,000
6	wcq1	Chile	A	D	1-1	Regueiro 4	55,000
7	wcq1	Brazil	H	D	1-1	Forlan 48	60,000

KEY PLAYERS - GOALSCORERS

Mario Regueiro

Goals in Internationals	1
Contribution to Attacking Power Average number of minutes between team goals while on pitch	104
Player Strike Rate The total number of minutes he was on the pitch for every goal scored	209
Team Strike Rate Average number of minutes between goals scored by club	90

	PLAYER	GOALS	ATT POWER	STRIKE RATE
1	Mario Regueiro	1	104	209 mins
2	Ernesto Chevanton	1	71	214 mins
3	Diego Forlan	1	54	216 mins
4	Paolo Montero	1	90	360 mins

TOP PLAYER APPEARANCES

2 Dario Rodriguez

Age (on 01/07/05)	30
Caps this season	5
Total minutes on the pitch	450
Goals	0
Yellow Cards	1
Red Cards	0
Club Side	Schalke

	PLAYER	POS	AGE	CAPS	MINS	GOALS	CARDS(Y)	CARDS(R)	CLUB SIDE
1	Sebastian Viera	GK	22	6	540	0	1	0	Nacional
2	Dario Rodriguez	DEF	30	5	450	0	1	0	Schalke
3	Carlos Diogo	DEF	21	5	446	0	1	0	River Plate
4	Pablo Garcia	MID	28	5	396	0	2	0	Osasuna
5	Paolo Montero	DEF	33	4	360	1	1	0	Juventus
6	Javier Delgado	MID	30	4	303	0	1	0	Saturn Ramenskoe
7	Diego Lugano	DEF	24	3	270	0	1	0	Sao Paulo
8	Diego Luis Lopez	DEF	30	3	270	0	1	0	Cagliari
9	Marcelo Sosa	MID	27	4	229	0	1	0	Atl Madrid
10	Diego Forlan	ATT	26	3	216	1	0	0	Villarreal
11	Ernesto Chevanton	ATT	24	4	214	1	1	0	Monaco
12	Mario Regueiro	MID	26	3	209	1	1	0	R Santander
13	Guillermo Rodriguez, G	DEF	21	2	180	0	0	0	Atlas
14	Vicente Sanchez	ATT	25	4	171	0	0	0	Toluca
15	Marcelo Zalayeta	ATT	26	2	158	0	0	0	Juventus
16	Gustavo Antonio Varela	MID	27	2	156	0	0	0	Schalke
17	Cristian Rodriguez	DEF	28	2	150	1	0	0	Cruz Azul
18	Alvaro Recoba	ATT	29	2	146	0	1	0	Inter Milan

PORTUGAL

FIFA/COCA COLA WORLD RANKING: **9th** EURO LEAGUE CLUB RANKING: **13th**

MANAGER: LUIZ FELIPE SCOLARI (BRA)

1	wc e3	**Latvia**	A W	2-0	Ronaldo 57; Pauleta 58	9,500
2	wc e3	**Estonia**	H W	4-0	Ronaldo 75; Postiga 83,90; Pauleta 86	27,214
3	wc e3	**Liechtenstein**	A D	2-2	Pauleta 23; Hasler, D 39 og	3,548
4	wc e3	**Russia**	H W	7-1	Pauleta 26; Ronaldo 39,69; Deco 45; Sabrosa 83; Petit 90,90	27,258
5	wc e3	**Luxembourg**	A W	5-0	Federspiel 11 og; Ronaldo 28; Maniche 52; Pauleta 67,82	8,045
6	intnls	**Rep of Ireland**	A L	0-1		44,100
7	intnls	**Canada**	H W	4-1	Manuel Fernandes 8; Pauleta 12; Postiga 82; Nuno Gomes 90	13,000
8	wc e3	**Slovakia**	A D	1-1	Postiga 62	21,000

KEY PLAYERS - GOALSCORERS

2 Pauleta

Goals in Internationals	7
Contribution to Attacking Power Average number of minutes between team goals while on pitch	93
Player Strike Rate The total number of minutes he was on the pitch for every goal scored	93
Team Strike Rate Average number of minutes between goals scored by club	30

	PLAYER	GOALS	ATT POWER	STRIKE RATE
1	Manuel Marques Helder Postiga	4	22	50 mins
2	Pauleta	7	32	93 mins
3	Christiano Ronaldo	6	31	109 mins
4	Armando Teixeira Petit	2	32	148 mins
5	Fernando Meira	1	50	203 mins

TOP PLAYER APPEARANCES

2 Anderson Deco

Age (on 01/07/05)	27
Caps this season	9
Total minutes on the pitch	741
Goals	1
Yellow Cards	0
Red Cards	0
Club Side	Barcelona

	PLAYER	POS	AGE	CAPS	MINS	GOALS	CARDS(Y)	CARDS(R)	CLUB SIDE
1	Jorge Andrade	DEF	27	9	810	0	1	0	Deportivo
2	Anderson Deco	MID	27	9	741	1	0	0	Barcelona
3	Pereira Ricardo	GK	29	8	720	0	0	0	Boavista
4	Christiano Ronaldo	MID	20	9	653	6	0	0	Man Utd
5	Paulo Ferreira	DEF	26	8	648	0	0	0	Chelsea
6	Pauleta	ATT	32	9	648	7	0	0	Paris SG
7	Maniche	MID	27	8	611	1	1	0	Porto
8	Ricardo Carvalho	DEF	27	6	540	0	0	0	Chelsea
9	Francisco Costinha	MID	30	6	462	0	2	0	Porto
10	Simao Sabrosa	MID	25	7	456	1	0	0	Benfica
11	Armando Teixeira Petit	MID	28	6	296	2	0	0	Benfica
12	Nuno Valente	DEF	30	3	207	0	0	0	Porto
13	Fernando Meira	DEF	27	3	203	1	0	0	Stuttgart
14	Manuel Helder Postiga	ATT	22	5	199	4	0	0	Porto
15	Luis Garcia Miguel	DEF	25	4	198	0	1	0	Benfica
16	Marco Caneira	DEF	26	3	198	0	0	0	Valencia
17	Miguel Jorge Ribeiro	DEF	23	2	180	0	0	0	Varzim
18	Cardoso Tiago	MID	24	4	160	0	1	0	Chelsea

SWEDEN

FIFA/COCA COLA WORLD RANKING: **13th** EURO LEAGUE CLUB RANKING: **14th**

MANAGER: LARS LAGERBACK (SWE)

1	intnls	**Holland**	H D	2-2	Jonson 3; Ibrahimovic 69	20,377
2	wc e8	**Malta**	A W	7-0	Ibrahimovic 4,11,14,71; Ljungberg 46,74; Larsson 76	4,200
3	wc e8	**Croatia**	H L	0-1		40,023
4	wc e8	**Hungary**	H W	3-0	Ljungberg 26; Larsson 50; Svensson, A 67	32,288
5	wc e8	**Iceland**	A W	4-1	Larsson 23,38; Allback 27; Wilhelmsson 44	7,037
6	intnls	**Scotland**	A W	4-1	Allback 27,49; Elmander 72; Berglund 73	15,071
7	intnls	**South Korea**	H D	1-1	Rosenberg 86	9,941
8	intnls	**Mexico**	A D	0-0		35,521
9	intnls	**France**	A D	1-1	Ljungberg 12	58,923
10	wc e8	**Bulgaria**	A W	3-0	Ljungberg 17,90 pen; Edman 73	42,530

KEY PLAYERS - GOALSCORERS

Zlatan Ibrahimovic

Goals in Internationals	6
Contribution to Attacking Power Average number of minutes between team goals while on pitch	27
Player Strike Rate The total number of minutes he was on the pitch for every goal scored	81
Team Strike Rate Average number of minutes between goals scored by club	32

	PLAYER	GOALS	ATT POWER	STRIKE RATE
1	Zlatan Ibrahimovic	6	27	81 mins
2	Henrik Larsson	4	23	81 mins
3	Fredrik Ljungberg	7	23	85 mins
4	Mattias Jonson	2	29	116 mins

TOP PLAYER APPEARANCES

Teddy Lucic

Age (on 01/07/05)	32
Caps this season	11
Total minutes on the pitch	955
Goals	0
Yellow Cards	0
Red Cards	0
Club Side	Bayern Leverkusen

	PLAYER	POS	AGE	CAPS	MINS	GOALS	CARDS(Y)	CARDS(R)	CLUB SIDE
1	Teddy Lucic	DEF	32	11	955	0	0	0	B Leverkusen
2	Tobias Linderoth	MID	26	9	729	0	0	0	FC Copenhagen
3	Olof Mellberg	DEF	27	9	691	0	0	0	Aston Villa
4	Christian Wilhelmsson	MID	25	9	686	2	0	0	Anderlecht
5	Andreas Isaksson	GK	23	8	659	0	0	0	Rennes
6	Fredrik Ljungberg	MID	28	8	595	7	1	0	Arsenal
7	Alexander Ostlund	DEF	26	8	565	0	2	0	Feyenoord
8	Niclas Alexandersson	MID	33	9	538	0	0	0	IFK Gothenburg
9	Anders Svensson	MID	28	7	527	2	0	0	Southampton
10	Zlatan Ibrahimovic	ATT	23	6	488	6	1	0	Juventus
11	Erik Edman	DEF	26	6	478	1	0	0	Tottenham
12	Marcus Allback	ATT	32	8	386	3	0	0	Hansa Rostock
13	Henrik Larsson	ATT	33	4	322	4	0	0	Barcelona
14	Mikael Nilsson	MID	27	5	286	0	0	0	Southampton
15	Mattias Jonson	MID	31	5	232	2	1	0	Norwich
16	Petter Hansson	DEF	28	3	225	0	1	0	Heerenveen
17	Mikael Dorsin	MID	23	3	200	0	1	0	Mikael Dorsin
18	Daniel Andersson	MID	27	3	195	0	0	0	Ancona

CAMEROON

FIFA/COCA COLA WORLD RANKING: **26th** EURO LEAGUE CLUB RANKING: **15th**

MANAGER: ARTUR JORGE (POR)

1	wcqa	**Egypt**	A	L	2-3	Tchato 88; Eto'o 89	25,000
2	wcqa	**Sudan**	A	D	1-1	Job 90	30,000
3	intnls	**Germany**	A	L	0-3		44,200
4	intnls	**Senegal**	H	W	1-0	Geremi 87	10,000
5	wcqa	**Sudan**	H	W	2-1	Geremi 34; Webo 90	30,000

KEY PLAYERS - GOALSCORERS

Nijtap Geremi

Goals in Internationals	2
Contribution to Attacking Power Average number of minutes between team goals while on pitch	75
Player Strike Rate The total number of minutes he was on the pitch for every goal scored	225
TeamStrike Rate Average number of minutes between goals scored by club	75

	PLAYER	GOALS	ATT POWER	STRIKE RATE
1	Nijtap Geremi	2	75	225 mins
2	Bill Tchato	1	83	249 mins
3	Samuel Eto'o	1	72	360 mins
4	Joseph-Desire Job	1	130	392 mins

TOP PLAYER APPEARANCES

5 Samuel Eto'o

Age (on 01/07/05)	24
Caps this season	4
Total minutes on the pitch	360
Goals	1
Yellow Cards	1
Red Cards	0
Club Side	Barcelona

	PLAYER	POS	AGE	CAPS	MINS	GOALS	CARDS(Y)	CARDS(R)	CLUB SIDE
1	Nijtap Geremi	MID	26	5	450	2	0	0	Chelsea
2	Rigobert Song	DEF	29	5	450	0	2	0	Galatasaray
3	Timothee Atouba	MID	23	5	431	0	0	0	Tottenham
4	Joseph-Desire Job	ATT	27	5	392	1	0	0	Middlesbrough
5	Samuel Eto'o	ATT	24	4	360	1	1	0	Barcelona
6	Carlos Kameni	GK	21	4	360	0	0	0	Espanyol
7	Eric Djemba-Djemba	MID	24	3	261	0	2	1	Aston Villa
8	Lucien Mettomo	DEF	28	4	259	0	0	0	Kaiserslautern
9	Bill Tchato	DEF	30	4	249	1	0	0	Kaiserslautern
10	Jean-Noel Doumbe	DEF	26	3	236	0	0	0	Rennes
11	Jean Makoun	ATT	22	3	191	0	0	0	Lille
12	Benoit Angbwa	DEF	23	2	180	0	0	0	Lille
13	Salomon Olembe	MID	31	2	171	0	0	0	Marseille
14	Modeste Mbami	MID	22	2	124	0	1	0	Paris SG
15	Rudolph Douala	ATT	26	2	111	0	0	0	Sp Lisbon
16	Herve Tum	ATT	26	2	109	0	1	0	Metz
17	Guy Feutchine	ATT	28	3	107	0	0	0	PAOK Salonika
18	Alioum Saidou	MID	27	1	90	0	0	0	Malatyaspor

CZECH REPUBLIC

FIFA/COCA COLA WORLD RANKING: **2nd** EURO LEAGUE CLUB RANKING: **16th**

MANAGER: KAREL BRUCKNER (CZE)

1	intnls	**Greece**	H	D	0-0		15,050
2	wc e1	**Holland**	A	L	0-2		49,000
3	wc e1	**Romania**	H	W	1-0	Koller 36	16,028
4	wc e1	**Armenia**	A	W	3-0	Koller 3,76; Rosicky 30	3,205
5	wc e1	**Macedonia**	A	W	2-0	Lokvenc 88; Koller 90	7,000
6	intnls	**Slovenia**	A	W	3-0	Koller 10; Jun 47; Polak 79	4,000
7	wc e1	**Finland**	H	W	4-3	Baros 7; Rosicky 34; Polak 58; Lokvenc 87	16,200
8	wc e1	**Andorra**	A	W	4-0	Jankulovski 31 pen; Baros 40; Lokvenc 53; Rosicky 90 pen	900

KEY PLAYERS - GOALSCORERS

Vratislav Lokvenc

Goals in Internationals	5
Contribution to Attacking Power Average number of minutes between team goals while on pitch	19
Player Strike Rate The total number of minutes he was on the pitch for every goal scored	79
Team Strike Rate Average number of minutes between goals scored by club	32

	PLAYER	GOALS	ATT POWER	STRIKE RATE
1	Vratislav Lokvenc	5	19	79 mins
2	Jan Koller	6	46	84 mins
3	Jan Polak	3	20	87 mins
4	Milan Baros	3	31	160 mins
5	Tomas Rosicky	4	32	180 mins

TOP PLAYER APPEARANCES

Petr Cech

Age (on 01/07/05)	23
Caps this season	8
Total minutes on the pitch	720
Goals	0
Yellow Cards	0
Red Cards	0
Club Side	Chelsea

	PLAYER	POS	AGE	CAPS	MINS	GOALS	CARDS(Y)	CARDS(R)	CLUB SIDE
1	Petr Cech	GK	23	8	720	0	0	0	Chelsea
2	Tomas Rosicky	MID	24	8	719	4	0	0	B Dortmund
3	Marek Jankulovski	DEF	28	8	691	1	0	0	Udinese
4	Tomas Ujfalusi	DEF	27	7	630	0	1	0	Fiorentina
5	Rene Bolf	DEF	31	7	585	0	0	0	Auxerre
6	Jan Koller	ATT	32	7	506	6	0	0	B Dortmund
7	Milan Baros	ATT	23	8	479	3	2	0	Liverpool
8	Marek Heinz	ATT	27	6	458	0	1	0	B M'gladbach
9	Stepan Vachousek	ATT	25	7	413	0	0	0	Marseille
10	Karel Poborsky	MID	33	5	402	0	0	0	Sparta Prague
11	Vratislav Lokvenc	ATT	31	8	396	5	0	0	Bochum
12	Martin Jiranek	DEF	26	5	388	0	0	0	Spartak Moscow
13	Zdenek Grygera	DEF	25	5	379	0	0	0	Ajax
14	Tomas Galasek	DEF	32	5	369	1	0	0	Ajax
15	David Rozehnal	DEF	25	4	313	0	1	0	Club Brugge
16	Libor Sionko	MID	28	5	294	0	1	0	Austria Vienna
17	Jan Polak	MID	24	4	261	3	0	0	Slovan Liberec
18	Roman Tyce	DEF	28	3	192	0	1	0	1860 Munich

REPUBLIC OF IRELAND

FIFA/COCA COLA WORLD RANKING: **15th**

EURO LEAGUE CLUB RANKING: **19th**

MANAGER: BRIAN KERR (IRL)

1	intnls	**Bulgaria**	H	D	1-1	Reid, A 15	31,887
2	wc e4	**Cyprus**	H	W	3-0	Morrison 33; Reid, A 38; Keane, Rob 55	36,000
3	wc e4	**Switzerland**	A	D	1-1	Morrison 8	28,000
4	wc e4	**France**	A	D	0-0		78,863
5	wc e4	**Faroe Islands**	H	W	2-0	Keane, Robbie 14 pen,33	36,000
6	intnls	**Croatia**	H	W	1-0	Keane, Robbie 24	30,000
7	intnls	**Portugal**	H	W	1-0	O'Brien 21	44,100
8	wc e4	**Israel**	A	D	1-1	Morrison 43	32,150
9	intnls	**China PR**	H	W	1-0	Morrison 82	35,222

KEY PLAYERS - GOALSCORERS

Clinton Morrison

Goals in Internationals	4
Contribution to Attacking Power Average number of minutes between team goals while on pitch	56
Player Strike Rate The total number of minutes he was on the pitch for every goal scored	140
Team Strike Rate Average number of minutes between goals scored by club	69

	PLAYER	GOALS	ATT POWER	STRIKE RATE
1	Clinton Morrison	4	56	140 mins
2	Robbie Keane	5	64	142 mins
3	Andrew Reid	2	53	265 mins
4	Andy O'Brien	1	60	669 mins

TOP PLAYER APPEARANCES

Damien Duff

Age (on 01/07/05)	26
Caps this season	10
Total minutes on the pitch	833
Goals	0
Yellow Cards	2
Red Cards	0
Club Side	Chelsea

	PLAYER	POS	AGE	CAPS	MINS	GOALS	CARDS(Y/R)		CLUB SIDE
1	Damien Duff	MID	26	10	833	0	2	0	Chelsea
2	Kevin Kilbane	MID	28	10	820	0	1	0	Everton
3	Kenny Cunningham	DEF	34	10	772	0	1	0	Birmingham
4	John O'Shea	DEF	24	9	768	0	1	0	Man Utd
5	Shay Given	GK	29	9	711	0	0	0	Newcastle
6	Robbie Keane	ATT	24	9	708	5	0	0	Tottenham
7	Andy O'Brien	DEF	26	8	669	1	1	1	Newcastle
8	Steve Finnan	DEF	29	8	630	0	0	0	Liverpool
9	Clinton Morrison	ATT	26	8	560	4	1	0	Birmingham
10	Andrew Reid	MID	22	7	530	2	1	0	Tottenham
11	Stephen Carr	DEF	28	6	469	0	2	0	Newcastle
12	Roy Keane	MID	33	6	448	0	2	0	Man Utd
13	Graham Kavanagh	MID	31	7	423	0	0	0	Wigan
14	Liam Miller	MID	24	5	242	0	0	0	Man Utd
15	Richard Dunne	DEF	25	3	211	0	0	0	Man City
16	Patrick Kenny	GK	26	3	189	0	0	0	Sheff Utd
17	Matt Holland	MID	31	3	186	0	0	0	Charlton
18	Stephen Elliott	ATT	21	2	156	0	0	0	Sunderland

SCOTLAND

FIFA/COCA COLA WORLD RANKING: **85th**

EURO LEAGUE CLUB RANKING: **22nd**

MANAGER: WALTER SMITH (SCO)

1	intnls	**Hungary**	H	L	0-3		15,933
2	wc e5	**Slovenia**	H	D	0-0		38,278
3	wc e5	**Norway**	H	L	0-1		51,000
4	wc e5	**Moldova**	A	D	1-1	*Thompson 31	7,000
5	intnls	**Sweden**	H	L	1-4	McFadden 78 pen	15,071
6	wc e5	**Italy**	A	L	0-2		40,745

KEY PLAYERS - GOALSCORERS

James McFadden

Goals in Internationals	2
Contribution to Attacking Power Average number of minutes between team goals while on pitch	171
Player Strike Rate The total number of minutes he was on the pitch for every goal scored	171
Team Strike Rate Average number of minutes between goals scored by club	158

	PLAYER	GOALS	ATT POWER	STRIKE RATE
1	James McFadden	2	171	171 mins

***Thompson did not play sufficient minutes to rank**

TOP PLAYER APPEARANCES

Barry Ferguson

Age (on 01/07/05)	27
Caps this season	6
Total minutes on the pitch	520
Goals	0
Yellow Cards	0
Red Cards	0
Club Side	Rangers

	PLAYER	POS	AGE	CAPS	MINS	GOALS	CARDS(Y/R)		CLUB SIDE
1	Barry Ferguson	MID	27	6	520	0	0	0	Rangers
2	Andy Webster	DEF	23	6	503	0	1	0	Hearts
3	Craig Gordon	GK	22	5	412	0	0	0	Hearts
4	Darren Fletcher	MID	21	5	408	0	0	0	Scotland
5	Gary Caldwell	DEF	24	5	405	0	2	0	Hibernian
6	Gary Naysmith	DEF	26	5	373	0	0	0	Everton
7	Nigel Quashie	MID	26	4	358	0	1	0	Southampton
8	Kenny Miller	ATT	25	6	342	0	0	0	Wolverhampton
9	James McFadden	ATT	22	5	342	2	1	1	Everton
10	Gary Holt	MID	32	4	291	0	0	0	Norwich
11	Steven Pressley	DEF	31	3	270	0	1	0	Hearts
12	Jackie McNamara	DEF	31	4	268	0	1	0	Celtic
13	David Weir	DEF	35	2	180	0	0	0	Everton
14	David Marshall	GK	20	2	180	0	0	0	Celtic
15	Russell Anderson	DEF	26	2	180	0	0	0	Aberdeen
16	Stevie Crawford	ATT	31	5	169	0	0	0	Dundee Utd
17	Lee McCulloch	MID	27	3	168	0	0	0	Wigan
18	Paul Hartley	MID	28	2	165	0	2	0	Hearts

NORTHERN IRELAND

FIFA/COCA COLA WORLD RANKING: **114th** EURO LEAGUE CLUB RANKING: **33rd**

MANAGER: LAWRIE SANCHEZ (NIR)

1	intnls	**Switzerland**	A	D	0-0		4,000
2	wc e6	**Poland**	H	L	0-3		14,000
3	wc e6	**Wales**	A	D	2-2	Whitley 11; Healy, D 21	63,500
4	wc e6	**Azerbaijan**	A	D	0-0		6,460
5	wc e6	**Austria**	H	D	3-3	Healy, D 35; Murdock 60; Elliott 90	20,000
6	intnls	**Canada**	H	L	0-1		11,156
7	wc e6	**England**	A	L	0-4		65,239
8	wc e6	**Poland**	A	L	0-1		13,515

KEY PLAYERS - GOALSCORERS

David Healy

Goals in Internationals	3
Contribution to Attacking Power Average number of minutes between team goals while on pitch	101
Player Strike Rate The total number of minutes he was on the pitch for every goal scored	203
Club Strike Rate Average number of minutes between goals scored by club	135

	PLAYER	GOALS	ATT POWER	STRIKE RATE
1	David Healy	3	101	203 mins
2	Stuart Elliott	1	213	426 mins
3	Colin Murdock	1	126	507 mins
4	Jeff Whitley	1	109	546 mins

TOP PLAYER APPEARANCES

Aaron Hughes

Age (on 01/07/05)	25
Caps this season	8
Total minutes on the pitch	720
Goals	0
Yellow Cards	0
Red Cards	0
Club Side	Newcastle

	PLAYER	POS	AGE	CAPS	MINS	GOALS	CARDS(Y	/R)	CLUB SIDE
1	Aaron Hughes	DEF	25	8	720	0	0	0	Newcastle
2	Damien Johnson	MID	26	7	630	0	2	0	Birmingham
3	David Healy	ATT	25	8	608	3	3	1	Leeds
4	Maik Taylor	GK	33	7	585	0	1	0	Birmingham
5	Keith Gillespie	MID	30	7	566	0	0	0	Leicester
6	Jeff Whitley	MID	26	7	546	1	1	0	Sunderland
7	Anthony Capaldi	MID	23	6	526	0	2	0	Plymouth
8	Mark Williams	DEF	34	6	514	0	2	0	MK Dons
9	Colin Murdock	DEF	30	7	507	1	1	0	Crewe
10	Chris Baird	DEF	23	5	450	0	1	0	Southampton
11	Stuart Elliott	ATT	26	7	426	1	0	0	Hull City
12	James Quinn	ATT	30	5	328	0	3	0	Sheff Wed
13	Steven Davis	MID	20	4	301	0	0	0	Aston Villa
14	Tommy Doherty	MID	26	4	284	0	1	0	Bristol City
15	George McCartney	DEF	24	4	271	0	0	0	Sunderland
16	Mark Clyde	DEF	22	3	270	0	0	0	Wolverhampton
17	Stephen Craigan	DEF	28	4	270	0	0	0	Motherwell
18	Roy Carroll	GK	27	3	225	0	0	0	Man Utd

WALES

FIFA/COCA COLA WORLD RANKING: **74th** EURO LEAGUE CLUB RANKING: **36th**

MANAGER: John Toshack (WAL)

1	intnls	**Latvia**	A	W	2-0	Hartson 81; Bellamy 89	10,000
2	wc e6	**Azerbaijan**	A	D	1-1	Speed 48	8,000
3	wc e6	**N Ireland**	H	D	2-2	Hartson 32; Earnshaw 75	63,500
4	wc e6	**England**	A	L	0-2		65,224
5	wc e6	**Poland**	H	L	2-3	Earnshaw 56; Hartson 90	56,685
6	intnls	**Hungary**	H	W	2-0	Bellamy 63,80	16,672
7	wc e6	**Austria**	H	L	0-2		47,760
8	wc e6	**Austria**	A	L	0-1		29,500

KEY PLAYERS - GOALSCORERS

Robert Earnshaw

Goals in Internationals	2
Contribution to Attacking Power Average number of minutes between team goals while on pitch	52
Player Strike Rate The total number of minutes he was on the pitch for every goal scored	132
Club Strike Rate Average number of minutes between goals scored by club	80

	PLAYER	GOALS	ATT POWER	STRIKE RATE
1	Robert Earnshaw	2	52	132 mins
2	John Hartson	3	89	149 mins
3	Craig Bellamy	3	80	240 mins
4	Gary Speed	1	74	447 mins

TOP PLAYER APPEARANCES

Craig Bellamy

Nationwide

Age (on 01/07/05)	25
Caps this season	8
Total minutes on the pitch	720
Goals	3
Yellow Cards	1
Red Cards	0
Club Side	Celtic

	PLAYER	POS	AGE	CAPS	MINS	GOALS	CARDS(Y	/R)	CLUB SIDE
1	Craig Bellamy	ATT	25	8	720	3	1	0	Celtic
2	Daniel Gabbidon	DEF	25	7	630	0	1	0	Cardiff
3	Mark Delaney	DEF	29	7	566	0	1	0	Aston Villa
4	Gary Speed	MID	35	5	447	1	0	0	Bolton
5	John Hartson	ATT	30	6	446	3	1	0	Celtic
6	Simon Davies	MID	25	5	434	0	0	0	Tottenham
7	Jason Koumas	MID	25	5	424	0	1	0	West Brom
8	Paul Jones	GK	38	5	405	0	0	0	Wolverhampton
9	Robert Page	DEF	30	5	393	0	1	0	Coventry
10	James Collins	DEF	21	5	331	0	0	0	Cardiff
11	Ben Thatcher	DEF	29	4	331	0	0	0	Man City
12	Carl Robinson	MID	28	4	300	0	0	0	Sunderland
13	Ryan Giggs	MID	31	3	270	0	0	0	Man Utd
14	Samuel Ricketts	DEF	23	3	270	0	0	0	Swansea
15	Carl Fletcher	MID	25	3	270	0	1	0	West Ham
16	Danny Coyne	GK	26	3	270	0	0	0	Burnley
17	Robert Earnshaw	ATT	24	6	264	2	0	0	West Brom
18	Robbie Savage	MID	30	4	234	0	1	1	Blackburn